2009 Standard Catalog of® WORLD COINS 2001-Date

Colin R. Bruce II
Senior Editor &
New Issues Editor

Thomas Michael
Market Analyst

George Cuhaj
Editor

Merna Dudley
Coordinating Editor

Deborah McCue
Database Specialist

Harry Miller
U.S. Market Analyst

Randy Thern
Numismatic
Cataloging Supervisor

Special Contributors
Paul Baker
Albert Beck
Melvyn Kassenoff

Bullion Value (VB) Market Valuations

Valuations for all platinum, gold, palladium and silver coins of the more common, basically bullion types, or those possessing only modest numismatic premiums are presented in this edition based on the market ranges of:

$1,450 - $2,000 per ounce for **platinum**

$800 - $950 per ounce for **gold**

$350 - $470 per ounce for **palladium**

$14.50 - $18.50 per ounce for **silver**

Published by

krause publications
An Imprint of F+W Publications

700 East State Street • Iola, WI 54990-0001
715-445-2214 • 888-457-2873
www.krausebooks.com

Our toll-free number to place an order or obtain
a free catalog is (800) 258-0929.

ISSN 1935-4339

ISBN-13: 978-0-89689-631-4
ISBN-10: 0-89689-631-5

Designed by Sally Olson
Edited by Randy Thern

Printed in the United States of America

TABLE OF CONTENTS

INTRODUCTION

Welcome to the 3rd edition of the 21st Century Standard Catalog of World Coins. This most recent annual version, of our ever changing and evolving series of comprehensive reference catalogs, is designed to meet the needs of those whose interest in coins exceeds the casual jingle in your pants pocket. Perhaps you've traveled overseas and still have some coins that came home with you, maybe you read in the news about the newest Euro coins, or it could be that you are a long term collector who wants to wade out into the most current of numismatic trends. In all cases, this book is for you.

Arranged in a basic alphabetic fashion by country and with groupings for political structure, coinage type and denomination to help better organize the data, this volume is as easy to use as the phone book. You will find photographs of many 21st Century coins, plenty of information on metal content, descriptions of types and varieties, date listings and of course values presented in multiple grades of preservation. In short, just about all the information you could want on the most modern coins of our world.

Marvel at the ingenuity of today's most inventive world mints, which are striking coins in a variety of shapes and sizes, colors and textures. Enjoy the practicality of coins designed for serious circulation in durable metals. Celebrate the advent of coins made of acrylic materials and those, which house precious stones or display gold overlays. All are here in our 21st Century edition.

The accuracy of the data offered in this volume is assured through the assistance of over one hundred contributing coin dealers, collectors and researchers who have lent their knowledge to the compiling of this new reference, providing our staff with information on new coinage types, new dates and accurate mintage figures. To them we offer a heartfelt "Thank you!" for their generosity and dedication to the advancement of our shared field of coin collecting.

Finally to you, the reader, we extend our wishes that you may enjoy using this catalog as much as we enjoyed its' production. Look it over, put it to good use and please let us know if you have any comments or questions.

Best Wishes,

The Editorial Staff of the
Standard Catalog of World Coins

STANDARD INTERNATIONAL NUMERAL SYSTEMS

Prepared especially for the ***Standard Catalog of World Coins***© 2007 by Krause Publications

Western	0	½	1	2	3	4	5	6	7	8	9	10	50	100	500	1000
Roman			I	II	III	IV	V	VI	VII	VIII	IX	X	L	C	D	M
Arabic-Turkish	٠	١/٢	١	٢	٣	٤	٥	٦	٧	٨	٩	١٠	٥٠	١٠٠	٥٠٠	١٠٠٠
Malay-Persian	٠	١/٢	١	٢	٣	۴	۵	٦ or ۶	٧	٨	٩	١٠	۵٠	١٠٠	۵٠٠	١٠٠٠
Eastern Arabic	۰	۱/۲	۱	۲	۳	۴	۵	۶	۷	۸	۹	۱۰	۵۰	۱۰۰	۵۰۰	۱۰۰۰
Hyderabad Arabic	٠	١/٢	١	٢	٣	۴	۵	۶	٧	٨	٩	١٠	۵٠	١٠٠	۵٠٠	١٠٠٠
Indian (Sanskrit)	०	१/२	१	२	३	४	५	६	७	८	९	१०	५०	१००	५००	१०००
Assamese	০	১/২	১	২	৩	৪	৫	৬	৭	৮	৯	১০	৫০	১০০	৫০০	১০০০
Bengali	০	১/২	১	২	৩	৪	৫	৬	৭	৮	৯	১০	৫০	১০০	৫০০	১০০০
Gujarati	૦	૧/૨	૧	૨	૩	૪	૫	૬	૭	૮	૯	૧૦	૫૦	૧૦૦	૫૦૦	૧૦૦૦
Kutch	०	१/२	१	२	३	४	५	६	७	८	९	१०	५०	१००	५००	१०००
Devavnagri	०	९/२	९	२	३	४	५	६ or ६	७	८	९ or ९	९०	५०	९००	५००	९०००
Nepalese	०	१/२	१	२	३	४	५	६	७	८	९	१०	५०	१००	५००	१०००
Tibetan	༠	༡/༢	༡	༢	༣	༤	༥	༦	༧	༨	༩	༡༠	༥༠	༡༠༠	༥༠༠	༡༠༠༠
Mongolian	᠐	᠑/᠒	᠑	᠒	᠓	᠔	᠕	᠖	᠗	᠘	᠙	᠑᠐	᠕᠐	᠑᠐᠐	᠕᠐᠐	᠑᠐᠐᠐
Burmese	၀	၁/၂	၁	၂	၃	၄	၅	၆	၇	၈	၉	၁၀	၅၀	၁၀၀	၅၀၀	၁၀၀၀
Thai-Lao	๐	๑/๒	๑	๒	๓	๔	๕	๖	๗	๘	๙	๑๐	๕๐	๑๐๐	๕๐๐	๑๐๐๐
Lao-Laotian	໐		໑	໒	໓	໔	໕	໖	໗	໘	໙	໑໐				
Javanese	꧐		꧑	꧒	꧓	꧔	꧕	꧖	꧗	꧘	꧙	꧑꧐	꧕꧐	꧑꧐꧐	꧕꧐꧐	꧑꧐꧐꧐
Ordinary Chinese Japanese-Korean	零	半	一	二	三	四	五	六	七	八	九	十	十五	百	百五	千
Official Chinese			壹	貳	叁	肆	伍	陸	柒	捌	玖	拾	拾伍	佰	佰伍	仟
Commercial Chinese			〡	〢	〣	〤	〥	〦	〧	〨	〩	十	〥十	〡百	〥百	〡千
Korean		반	일	이	삼	사	오	육	칠	팔	구	십	오십	백	오백	천
Georgian			ა	ბ	გ	დ	ე	ვ	ზ	ჱ	თ	ი	ნ	რ	ფ	ჩ
			11 [illegible]	20 კ	30 ლ	40 მ	60 ჲ	70 ო	80 პ	90 ჟ	200 ს	300 ტ	400 უ	600 ქ	700 ღ	800 ყ
Ethiopian	◆		፩	፪	፫	፬	፭	፮	፯	፰	፱	፲	፶	፻	፭፻	፲፻
				20 ፳	30 ፴	40 ፵	60 ፷	70 ፸	80 ፹	90 ፺						
Hebrew			א	ב	ג	ד	ה	ו	ז	ח	ט	י	נ	ק	תק	
				20 כ	30 ל	40 מ	60 ס	70 ע	80 פ	90 צ	200 ר	300 ש	400 ת	600 תר	700 תש	800 תת
Greek			Α	Β	Γ	Δ	Ε	Τ	Ζ	Η	Θ	Ι	Ν	Ρ	Φ	Α
				20 Κ	30 Λ	40 Μ	60 Ξ	70 Ο	80 Π		200 Σ	300 Τ	400 Υ	600 Χ	700 Ψ	800 Ω

ACKNOWLEDGMENTS

Many individuals have contributed countless changes, which have been incorporated into this third edition. While all may not be acknowledged, special appreciation is extended to the following who have exhibited a special enthusiasm for this edition.

David Addey
Esko Ahlroth
Raul Aries
Adrian Ataman
Antonio Alessandrini
Don Bailey
Paul Baker
Oksana Bandrivska
Yuri Barshay
Albert Beck
Richard Benson
Allen G. Berman
Joseph Boling
Al Boulanger
Mahdi Bseiso
Chris Budesa
John T. Bucek
Doru Calin
Luis V. Costa
Raymond E. Czahor
Howard A. Daniel III
Joe Dettling
Yossi Dotan
James R. Douglas
Dr. Jan M. Dyroff
Stephen Eccles
Dr. Iorio Fabio
Daniil Fishteyn
Thomas Fitzgerald
Eugene Freeman
Arthur Friedburg
Tom Galway
David R. Gotkin
Marcel Haberling
Edward Hackney
J. Halfpenny
Liliana N. Hanganu
Brian Hannon
Flemming Lyngbeck Hansen
David Harrison
Martin Rodney Hayter
Istvan Hegedus
F. Hellendall
Serge Huard
Armen Hovsepian
Nelva G. Icaza
Ton Jacobs
A.K. Jain
Hector Carlos Janson
Børge R. Juul
Alex Kaglyan
Melvyn Kassenoff
George Katsikis
Craig Keplinger
E. James Kindrake
Rob Kooy
Peter Kraneveld
Matti Kuronen
Samson Kin Chiu Lai
Alex Lazarovici
Lee Shin Song
Richard Lobel
Rudi Lotter
Ma Tak Wo
Ranko Mandic
Miguel Angel Pratt Mayans
Juozas Minikevicius
Robert Mish
Dr. Richard Montrey
Paul Montz
Edward Moschetti
Arkady Nakhimovsky
Richard Nelson
Michael G. Nielsen
Gus Pappas
Dick Parker
Frank Passic
Marc Pelletier
Kirsten F. Petersen
Jens Pilegaard
Gastone Polacco
Elena Pop
Michel Prier
Martin Purdy
Luis R. Ponte Puigbo
Frank Putrow
Yahya Qureshi
Mircea Raicopol
Dr. Dennis G. Rainey
Tony Raymond
Dr. Kerry A. Rodgers
William M. Rosenblum
Egon Conti Rossini
Pabrita K. Saha
Remy Said
Leon Saryan
Erwin Schaffer
Gerhard Schön
George Schumacher
Dr. Wolfgang Schuster
Alexander Shapiro
Ladislav Sin
Ole Sjoelund
Benjamin Swagerty
Steven Tan
Mehmet Tolga Taner
Tonin Thaci
Anthony Tumonis
J. J. Van Grover
Erik J. Van Loon
Carmen Viciedo
R.W. Walter
Paul Welz
Stewart Westdal
J. Brix Westergaard
J. Hugh Witherow
Joseph Zaffern

AUCTION HOUSES

Dix-Noonan-Webb
Heritage World Coin Auctions
Hess-Divo Ltd.
Gerhard Hirsch
Thomas Høiland Møntauktion
Fritz Rudolf Künker
Leu Numismatik AG
Münzenhandlung Harald Möller, GmbH
Noble Numismatics, Pty. Ltd.
Ponterio & Associates
Stack's
UBS, AG
World Wide Coins of California

INTERNATIONAL SOCIETIES AND INSTITUTIONS

American Numismatic Association
American Numismatic Society
British Museum
Numismatics International
Smithsonian Institution

WORLD MINTS, CENTRAL BANKS AND DISTRIBUTORS

Austrian Mint
Banco de Mexico
Banque Centrale Du Luxembourg
Casa de la Moneda de Cuba
Central Bank of D.P.R. Korea - Kumbyol Trading Corp.
Central Bank of the Russian Federation
Educational Coin Company
Global Coins & Medals Ltd. - Official Sales Company of the Bulgarian Mint
Imprensa Nacional - Casa da Moeda, S.A.
Israel Government Coins & Medals Corp. Ltd.
Istituto Poligrafico e Zecca dello Stato I.p.A.
Jablonex Group - Division of Czech Mint
Japan Mint
Kazakhstan Mint
KOMSCO - South Korea
Latvijas Banka
Lithuanian Mint
Magyar Penzvero Zrt.
Mennica Polska
Mincovna Kremnica
Mint of Finland, Ltd.
Monnaie de Paris
New Zealand Mint
Numiscom
Numistrade Gmbh & Co. kg.
Omni Trading B.V.
Perth Mint
Pobjoy Mint
Real Casa de la Moneda - Spain
Royal Australian Mint
Royal Belgian Mint
Royal Canadian Mint
Royal Dutch Mint
Royal Mint
Servei D'Emissions Principat D'Andorra
Singapore Mint
South African Mint
Staatliche Munze Berlin
Staatliche Munze Baden-Wurttemberg
Talisman Coins
Ufficio Filatelico e Numismatico - Vatican
United States Mint

COUNTRY INDEX

HOW TO USE THIS CATALOG

This catalog is designed to serve the needs of both the novice and advanced collectors. It is generally arranged so that persons with no more than a basic knowledge of world history and a casual acquaintance with coin collecting can consult it with confidence and ease. The following explanations summarize the general practices used in preparing this catalog's listings.

ARRANGEMENT

Countries are arranged alphabetically. Political changes within a country are arranged chronologically. In countries where Rulers are the single most significant political entity, a chronological arrangement by Ruler has been employed. Distinctive sub-geographic regions are listed alphabetically following the country's main listings.

Diverse coinage types relating to fabrication methods, revaluations, denomination systems, non-circulating categories and such have been identified, separated and arranged in logical fashion. Chronological arrangement is employed for most circulating coinage. Monetary reforms will flow in order of their institution. Non-circulating types such as Essais, Pieforts, Patterns, Trial Strikes, Mint and Proof sets will follow the main listings.

Within a coinage type coins will be listed by denomination, from smallest to largest. Numbered types within a denomination will be ordered by their first date of issue.

IDENTIFICATION

The most important step in the identification of a coin is the determination of the nation of origin. This is generally easily accomplished where English-speaking lands are concerned, however, use of the country index is sometimes required.

The coins of many countries beyond the English-language realm, such as those of French, Italian or Spanish heritage, are also quite easy to identify through reference to their legends, which appear in the national languages based on Western alphabets. In many instances the name is spelled exactly the same in English as in the national language, such as France; while in other cases it varies only slightly, like Italia for Italy, Belgique or Belgie for Belgium, Brasil for Brazil and Danmark for Denmark.

This is not always the case, however, as in Norge for Norway, Espana for Spain, Sverige for Sweden and Helvetia for Switzerland. Coins bearing Cyrillic lettering are attributable to Bulgaria, Russia, the Slavic states and Mongolia; the Greek script peculiar to Greece, Crete and the Ionian Islands; the Amharic characters of Ethiopia; or Hebrew in the case of Israel.

The toughra monogram, occurs on some of the coins of Afghanistan, Egypt, Sudan, Pakistan, and Turkey. A predominant design feature on the coins of Nepal is the trident; while neighboring Tibet features a lotus blossom or lion on many of their issues.

DATING

Coin dating is the final basic attribution consideration. Here, the problem can be more difficult because the reading of a coin date is subject not only to the vagaries of numeric styling, but to calendar variations caused by the observance of various religious eras or regal periods from country to country, or even within a country. Here again, with the exception of the sphere from North Africa through the Orient, it will be found that most countries rely on Western date numerals and Christian (AD) era reckoning, although in a few instances, coin dating has been tied to the year of a reign or government. The Vatican, for example dates its coinage according to the year of reign of the current pope, in addition to the Christian-era date.

Countries in the Arabic sphere generally date their coins to the Muslim era (AH).

The following table indicates the year dating for the various eras, which correspond to 2008 in Christian calendar reckoning, but it must be remembered that there are overlaps between the eras in some instances.

Christian era (AD)	-2008
Muslim era (AH)	-AH1429
Solar year (SH)	-SH1386
Monarchic Solar era (MS)	-MS2567
Vikrama Samvat (VS)	-VS2065
Saka era (SE)	-SE1930
Buddhist era (BE)	-BE2551
Bangkok era (RS)	-RS227
Chula-Sakarat era (CS)	-CS1370
Ethiopian era (EE)	-EE2001
Korean era	-4341
Javanese Aji Saka era (AS)	-AS1941
Fasli era (FE)	-FE1418
Jewish era (JE)	-JE5768

More detailed guides to less prevalent coin dating systems, which are strictly local in nature, are presented with the appropriate listings.

Some coins carry dates according to both locally observed and Christian eras. This is particularly true in the Arabic world, where the Hejira date may be indicated in Arabic numerals and the Christian date in Western numerals, or both dates in either form.

HEJIRA DATE CONVERSION CHART

HEJIRA (Hijira, Hegira), the name of the Muslim era (A.H. = Anno Hegirae) dates back to the Christian year 622 when Mohammed "fled" from Mecca, escaping to Medina to avoid persecution from the Koreish tribemen. Based on a lunar year the Muslim year is 11 days shorter.

*=Leap Year (Christian Calendar)

AH Hejira	AD Christian Date
1420	1999, April 17
1421	2000, April 6*
1422	2001, March 26
1423	2002, March 15
1424	2003, March 5
1425	2004, February 22*
1426	2005, February 10
1427	2006, January 31
1428	2007, January 20
1429	2008, January 10*
1430	2008, December 29
1431	2009, December 18
1432	2010, December 8
1433	2011, November 27*
1434	2012, November 15
1435	2013, November 5
1436	2014, October 25
1437	2015, October 15*
1438	2016, October 3
1439	2017, September 22
1440	2018, September 12
1441	2019, September 11*
1442	2020, August 20
1443	2021, August 10
1444	2022, July 30
1445	2023, July 19*
1446	2024, July 8
1447	2025, June 27
1448	2026, June 17
1449	2027, June 6*
1450	2028, May25

The date actually carried on a given coin is generally cataloged here in the first column (Date) to the right of the catalog number. If this date is by a non-Christian dating system, such as 'AH' (Muslim), the Christian equivalent date will appear in parentheses(), for example AH1336(1917). Dates listed alone in the date column which do not actually appear on a given coin, or dates which are known, but do not appear on the coin, are generally enclosed by parentheses with 'ND' at the left, for example ND(2001).

Timing differentials between some era of reckoning, particularly the 354-day Mohammedan and 365-day Christian years, cause situations whereby coins which carry dates for both eras exist bearing two year dates from one calendar combined with a single date from another.

Countermarked Coinage is presented with both 'Countermark Date' and 'Host Coin' date for each type. Actual date representation follows the rules outlined above.

DENOMINATIONS

The second basic consideration to be met in the attribution of a coin is the determination of denomination. Since denominations are usually expressed in numeric rather than word form on a coin, this is usually quite easily accomplished on coins from nations which use Western numerals, except in those instances where issues are devoid of any mention of face value, and denomination must be attributed by size, metallic composition or weight. Coins listed in this volume are generally illustrated in actual size.

The sphere of countries stretching from North Africa through the Orient, on which numeric symbols generally unfamiliar to Westerners are employed, often provide the collector with a much greater challenge. This is particularly true on nearly all pre-20th Century issues. On some of the more modern issues and increasingly so as the years progress, Western-style numerals usually presented in combination with the local numeric system are becoming more commonplace on these coins.

The included table of Standard International Numeral Systems presents charts of the basic numeric designations found on coins of non-Western origin. Although denomination numerals are generally prominently displayed on coins, it must be remembered that these are general representations of characters, which individual coin engravers may have rendered in widely varying styles. Where numeric or script denominations designation forms peculiar to a given coin or country apply, such as the script used on some Persian (Iranian) issues. They are so indicated or illustrated in conjunction with the appropriate listings.

MINTAGES

Quantities minted of each date are indicated where that information is available, generally stated in millions or rounded off to the nearest 10,000 pieces when more exact figures are not available. On quantities of a few thousand or less, actual mintages are generally indicated. For combined mintage figures the abbreviation "Inc. Above" means Included Above, while "Inc. Below" means Included Below. "Est." beside a mintage figure indicates the number given is an estimate or mintage limit.

METALS

Each numbered type listing will contain a description of the coins metallic content. The traditional coinage metals and their symbolic chemical abbreviations sometimes used in this catalog are:

Platinum - (PT)	Copper - (Cu)
Gold - (Au)	Brass -
Silver - (Ag)	Copper-nickel- (CN)
Billion -	Lead - (Pb)
Nickel - (Ni)	Steel -
Zinc - (Zn)	Tin - (Sn)
Bronze - (Ae)	Aluminum - (Al)

Modern commemorative coins have employed still more unusual methods such as bimetallic coins, color applications and precious metal or gem inlays.

PRECIOUS METAL WEIGHTS

Listings of weight, fineness and actual silver (ASW), gold (AGW), platinum or palladium (APW) content of most machine-struck silver, gold, platinum and palladium coins are provided in this edition. This information will be found incorporated in each separate type listing, along with other data related to the coin.

The ASW, AGW or APW figure can be multiplied by the spot price of each precious metal to determine the current intrinsic value of any coin accompanied by these designations.

As the silver and gold bullion markets have advanced and declined sharply over the years, the fineness and total precious metal content of coins has become especially significant where bullion coins - issues which trade on the basis of their intrinsic metallic content rather than numismatic value - are concerned. In many instances, such issues have become worth more in bullion form than their nominal collector values or denominations indicate.

BULLION VALUE

The simplest method for determining the bullion value of a precious metal coin is to multiply the actual precious metal weight by the current spot price for that metal. A silver coin with a .6822 actual silver weight (ASW) would have an intrinsic value of $9.55 when the spot price of silver is $14.00. If the spot price of silver rose to $17.95 that same coins intrinsic value would rise to $12.25.

PHOTOGRAPHS

To assist the reader in coin identification, every effort has been made to present actual size photographs of every coinage type listed. Obverse and reverse are illustrated, except when a change in design is restricted to one side, and the coin has a diameter of 39mm or larger, in which case only the side required for identification of the type is generally illustrated. All coins up to 60mm are illustrated actual size, to the nearest 1/2mm up to 25mm, and to the nearest 1mm thereafter. Coins larger than 60mm diameter are illustrated in reduced size, with the actual size noted in the descriptive text block. Where slight change in size is important to coin type identification, actual millimeter measurements are stated.

VALUATIONS

Values quoted in this catalog represent the current market and are compiled from recommendations provided and verified through various source documents and specialized consultants. It should be stressed, however, that this book is intended to serve only as an aid for evaluating coins, actual market conditions are constantly changing and additional influences, such as particularly strong local demand for certain coin series, fluctuation of international exchange rates, changes in spot price of precious metals and worldwide collection patterns must also be considered. Publication of this catalog is not intended as a solicitation by the publisher, editors or contributors to buy or sell the coins listed at the prices indicated.

All valuations are stated in U.S. dollars, based on careful assessment of the varied international collector market. Valuations for coins priced below $100.00 are generally stated in full amounts - i.e. 37.50 or 95.00 - while valuations at or above that figure are rounded off in even dollars - i.e. $125.00 is expressed 125. A comma is added to indicate thousands of dollars in value.

For the convenience of overseas collectors and for U.S. collectors doing business with overseas dealers, the base exchange rate for the national currencies of approximately 180 countries are presented in the Foreign Exchange Table.

It should be noted that when particularly select uncirculated or proof-like examples of uncirculated coins become available they can be expected to command proportionately high premiums. Such examples in reference to choice Germanic Thalers are referred to as "erst schlage" or first strikes.

NEW ISSUES

All newly released coins dated up to the year 2006 that have been physically observed by our staff or identified by reliable sources and have been confirmed by press time have been incorporated in this edition. Exceptions exist in some countries where current date coin production lags far behind or information on current issues is less accessible.

SETS

Listings in this catalog for specimen, proof and mint sets are for official, government-produced sets. In many instances privately packaged sets also exist.

Mint Sets/Fleur de Coin Sets: Specially prepared by worldwide mints to provide banks, collectors and government dignitaries with examples of current coinage. Usually subjected to rigorous inspection to insure that top quality specimens of selected business strikes are provided.

Specimen Sets: Forerunners of today's proof sets. In most cases the coins were specially struck, perhaps even double struck, to produce a very soft or matte finish on the effigies and fields, along with high, sharp, "wire" rims. The finish is rather dull to the naked eye.

The original purpose of these sets was to provide VIPs, monarchs and mintmasters around the world with samples of the highest quality workmanship of a particular mint. These were usually housed in elaborate velvet-lined leather and metal cases.

Proof-like Sets are relatively new to the field of numismatics. During the mid 1950s the Royal Canadian Mint furnished the hobby with specially selected early business strike coins that exhibited some qualities similar to proof coinage. However, the "proof-like" fields are generally flawed and the edges are rounded. These pieces are not double struck. These are commonly encountered in cardboard holders, later in soft plastic or pliofilm packaging. Of late, the Royal Canadian Mint packages such sets in rigid plastic cases.

Many worldwide officially issued proof sets would in reality fall into this category upon careful examination of the quality of the coin's finish.

Another term encountered in this category is "Special Select," used to describe the crowns of the Union of South Africa and 100-schilling coins produced for collectors in the late 1970s by the Austrian Mint.

Proof Sets: This is undoubtedly among the most misused terms in the hobby, not only by collectors and dealers, but also by many of the world mints.

A true proof set must be at least double-struck on specially prepared polished planchets and struck using dies (often themselves polished) of the highest quality.

Modern-day proof quality consists of frosted effigies surrounded by absolute mirror-like fields.

Listings for proof sets in this catalog are for officially issued proof sets so designated by the issuing authority, and may or may not possess what are considered modern proof quality standards.

It is necessary for collectors to acquire the knowledge to allow them to differentiate true proof sets from would-be proof sets and proof-like sets which may be encountered.

CONDITIONS/GRADING

Wherever possible, coin valuations are given in four or five grades of preservation. For modern commemoratives, which do not circulate, only uncirculated values are usually sufficient. Proof issues are indicated by the word "Proof" next to the date, with valuation proceeded by the word "value" following the mintage. For very recent circulating coins and coins of limited value, one, two or three grade values are presented.

There are almost no grading guides for world coins. What follows is an attempt to help bridge that gap until a detailed, illustrated guide becomes available.

In grading world coins, there are two elements to look for: 1) Overall wear, and 2) loss of design details, such as strands of hair, feathers on eagles, designs on coats of arms, etc.

The age, rarity or type of a coin should not be a consideration in grading.

Grade each coin by the weaker of the two sides. This method appears to give results most nearly consistent with conservative

Coin Alignment

Medal Alignment

COIN vs MEDAL ALIGNMENT

Some coins are struck with obverse and reverse aligned at a rotation of 180 degrees from each other. When a coin is held for vertical viewing with the obverse design aligned upright and the index finger and thumb at the top and bottom, upon rotation from left to right for viewing the reverse, the latter will be upside down. Such alignment is called "coin rotation." Other coins are struck with the obverse and reverse designs mated on an alignment of zero or 360 degrees. If such an example is held and rotated as described, the reverse will appear upright. This is the alignment, which is generally observed in the striking of medals, and for that reason coins produced in this manner are considered struck in "medal rotation". In some instances, often through error, certain coin issues have been struck to both alignment standards, creating interesting collectible varieties, which will be found noted in some listings. In addition, some countries are now producing coins with other designated obverse to reverse alignments which are considered standard for this type.

American Numismatic Association standards for U.S. coins. Split grades, i.e., F/VF for obverse and reverse, respectively, are normally no more than one grade apart. If the two sides are more than one grade apart, the series of coins probably wears differently on each side and should then be graded by the weaker side alone.

Grade by the amount of overall wear and loss of design detail evident on each side of the coin. On coins with a moderately small design element, which is prone to early wear, grade by that design alone. For example, the 5-ore (KM#554) of Sweden has a crown above the monogram on which the beads on the arches show wear most clearly. So, grade by the crown alone.

For **Brilliant Uncirculated** (BU) grades there will be no visible signs of wear or handling, even under a 30-power microscope. Full mint luster will be present. Ideally no bags marks will be evident.

For **Uncirculated** (Unc.) grades there will be no visible signs of wear or handling, even under a 30-power microscope. Bag marks may be present.

For **Almost Uncirculated** (AU), all detail will be visible. There will be wear only on the highest point of the coin. There will often be half or more of the original mint luster present.

On the **Extremely Fine** (XF or EF) coin, there will be about 95% of the original detail visible. Or, on a coin with a design with no inner detail to wear down, there will be a light wear over nearly all the coin. If a small design is used as the grading area, about 90% of the original detail will be visible. This latter rule stems from the logic that a smaller amount of detail needs to be present because a small area is being used to grade the whole coin.

The **Very Fine** (VF) coin will have about 75% of the original detail visible. Or, on a coin with no inner detail, there will be moderate wear over the entire coin. Corners of letters and numbers may be weak. A small grading area will have about 66% of the original detail.

For **Fine** (F), there will be about 50% of the original detail visible. Or, on a coin with no inner detail, there will be fairly heavy wear over all of the coin. Sides of letters will be weak. A typically uncleaned coin will often appear as dirty or dull. A small grading area will have just under 50% of the original detail.

On the **Very Good** (VG) coin, there will be about 25% of the original detail visible. There will be heavy wear on all of the coin.

The **Good** (G) coin's design will be clearly outlined but with substantial wear. Some of the larger detail may be visible. The rim may have a few weak spots of wear.

On the **About Good** (AG) coin, there will typically be only a silhouette of a large design. The rim will be worn down into the letters if any.

Strong or weak strikes, partially weak strikes, damage, corrosion, attractive or unattractive toning, dipping or cleaning should be described along with the above grades. These factors affect the quality of the coin just as do wear and loss of detail, but are easier to describe.

STANDARD INTERNATIONAL GRADING TERMINOLOGY AND ABBREVIATIONS

	PROOF	UNCIRCULATED	EXTREMELY FINE	VERY FINE	FINE	VERY GOOD	GOOD	POOR
U.S. and ENGLISH SPEAKING LANDS	PRF	UNC	EF or XF	VF	F	VG	G	PR
BRAZIL	—	(1)FDC or FC	(3) S	(5) MBC	(7) BC	(8) BC/R	(9) R	UT GeG
DENMARK	M	0	01	1+	1	1÷	2	3
FINLAND	00	0	01	1+	1	1?	2	3
FRANCE	FB Flan Bruni	FDC Fleur de Coin	SUP Superbe	TTB Très très beau	TB Très beau	B Beau	TBC Très Bien Conservée	BC Bien Conservée
GERMANY	PP Polierte Platte	STG Stempelglanz	VZ Vorzüglich	SS Sehr schön	S Schön	S.G.E. Sehr gut erhalten	G.E. Gut erhalten	Gering erhalten
ITALY	FS Fondo Specchio	FDC Fior di Conio	SPL Splendido	BB Bellissimo	MB Molto Bello	B Bello	M	—
JAPAN	—	未 使 用	極 美 品	美 品	並 品	—	—	—
NETHERLANDS	— Proef	FDC Fleur de Coin	Pr. Prachtig	Z.f. Zeer fraai	Fr. Fraai	Z.g. Zeer goed	G	—
NORWAY	M	0	01	1+	1	1÷	2	3
PORTUGAL	—	Soberba	Bela	MBC	BC	MREG	REG	MC
SPAIN	Prueba	SC	EBC	MBC	BC+	BC	RC	MC
SWEDEN	Polerad	0	01	1+	1	1?	2	—

Sending Scanned Images by Email

Over the past 2 years or so, we have been receiving an ever-increasing flow of scanned images from sources worldwide. Unfortunately, many of these scans could not be used due to the type of scan, or simple incompatability with our systems. We appreciate the effort it takes to produce these images and accuracy they add to the catalog listings.

Here are a few simple instructions to follow when producing these scans. We encourage you to continue sending new images or upgrades to those currently illustrated and please do not hesitate to ask questions about this process.

— Scan all images within a resolution range of 200 dpi to 300 dpi
— Size setting should be at 100%
— Scan in true 4-color
— Save images as 'jpeg' or 'tiff' and name in such a way, which clearly identifies the country of origin and diameter size of coin in millimeters (mm)
— Please email with a request to confirm receipt of the attachment
— Please send images to Randy.Thern@fwpubs.com

HOW TO USE THE DVD

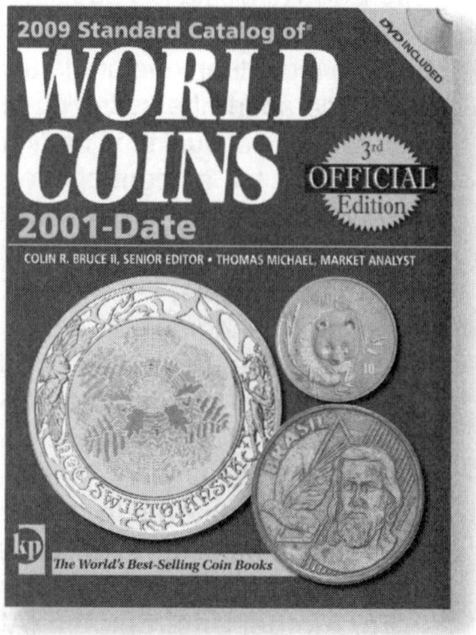

This DVD is PC and Macintosh® compatible when used with Adobe Acrobat Reader® version 6.0 or later. A step-by-step free download of Adobe Acrobat Reader® 8 is available at www.adobe.com. Adobe Reader® 8 was used in creating the instructions that follow.

To help you successfully navigate through the PDF document, several types of searches are available.

USING BOOKMARKS

Click on the Bookmarks icon to open the Bookmarks window. Use these links to go to specific points of interest. To scroll through pages in each section, use the arrows at the top of the screen (see next page for instructions to find page navigators).

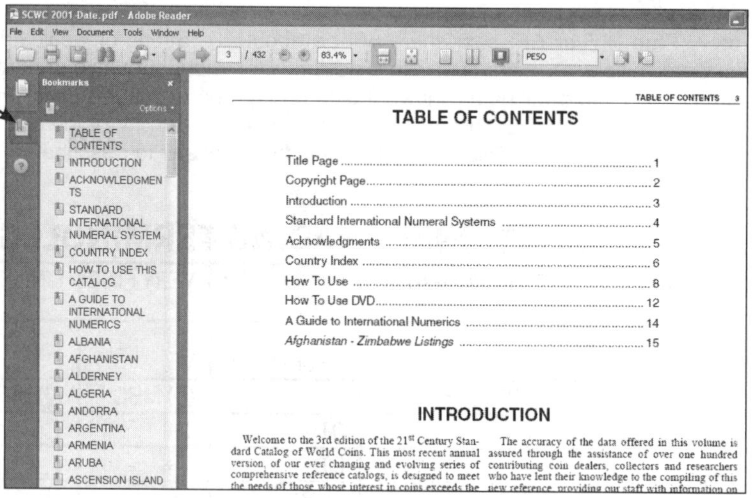

USING THE FIND BOX

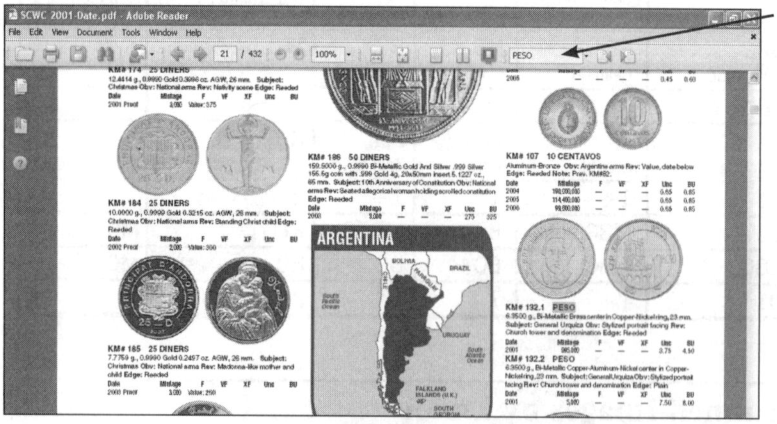

Locate the find box in the tool bar and enter the word(s) you are searching for.

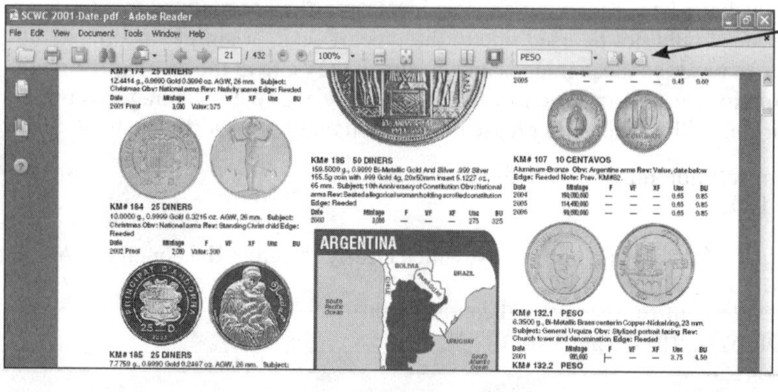

To navigate through the results of your search, use the Find Next icon.

USING THE SEARCH OPTION

Locate the Search button by choosing Customize Toolbars in the Tools pull-down menu. Check Search (binocular icon) to have the Search option available in the toolbar.

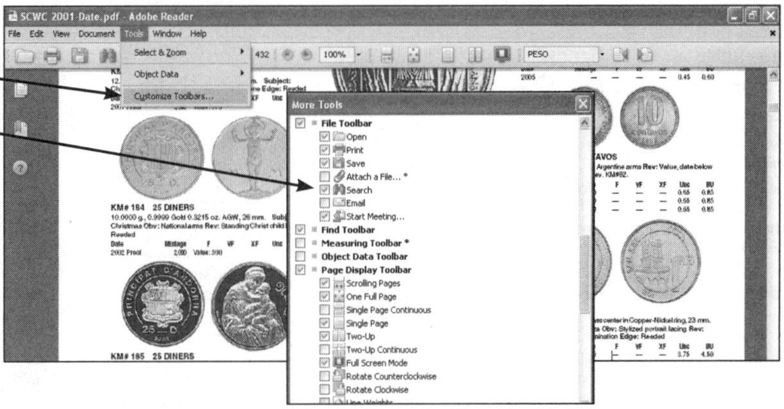

Click on the Search icon to open the Search dialog box.

In the Search dialog box, enter the word(s) you are searching for and click on the Search button.

The list of results will appear in the dialog box. Click on the listings to view each page that contains your searched word(s).

To begin a new word search, click on the New Search button.

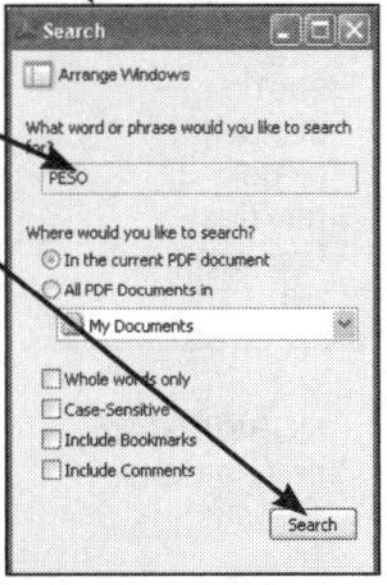

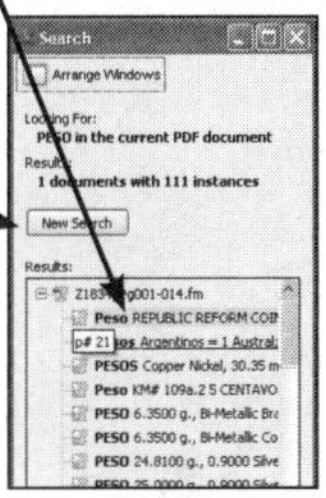

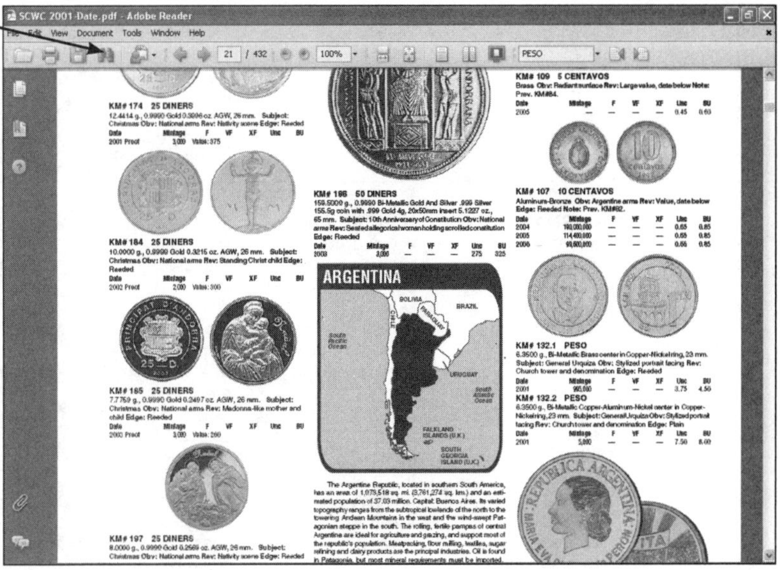

USING PAGE NAVIGATORS

Activate the Page Navigator Toolbar by choosing Customize Toolbars in the Tools pull-down menu. Check each tool as shown at right. You are now able to page through the PDF document by using the arrows at the top of the screen or by entering a page number you wish to view.

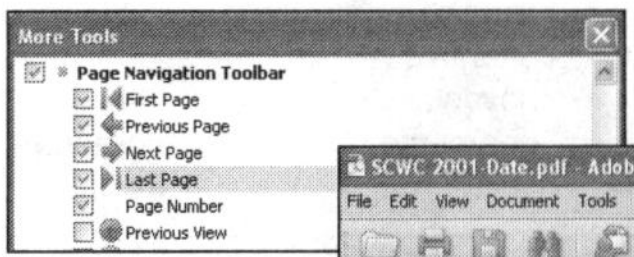

The Table of Contents is on page 3, the Country Index is on page 6.

You may also enlarge the images of the coins up to 400% for easy viewing

A GUIDE TO INTERNATIONAL NUMERICS

	ENGLISH	CZECH	DANISH	DUTCH	ESPERANTO	FRENCH
1/4	one-quarter	jeden-ctvrt	én kvart	een-kwart	unu-kvar'ono	un-quart
1/2	one-half	jeden-polovieni or pul	én halv	een-half	unu-du'one	un-demi
1	one	jeden	én	een	unu	un
2	two	dve	to	twee	du	deux
3	three	tri	tre	drie	tri	trois
4	four	ctyri	fire	vier	kvar	quatre
5	five	pet	fem	vijf	kvin	cinq
6	six	sest	seks	zes	ses	six
7	seven	sedm	syv	zeven	sep	sept
8	eight	osm	otte	acht	ok	huit
9	nine	devet	ni	negen	nau	neuf
10	ten	deset	ti	tien	dek	dix
12	twelve	dvanáct	tolv	twaalf	dek du	douze
15	fifteen	patnáct	femten	vijftien	dek kvin	quinze
20	twenty	dvacet	tyve	twintig	du'dek	vingt
24	twenty-four	dvacet-ctyri	fire og tyve	vierentwinting	du'dek kvar	vingt-quatre
25	twenty-five	dvacet-pet	fem og tyve	vifentwintig	du'dek kvin	vingt-cinq
30	thirty	tricet	tredive	dertig	tri'dek	trente
40	forty	ctyricet	fyrre	veertig	kvar'dek	quarante
50	fifty	padesát	halvtreds	vijftig	kvin'dek	cinquante
60	sixty	sedesát	tres	zestig	ses'dek	soixante
70	seventy	sedmdesát	halvfjerds	zeventig	sep'dek	soixante dix
80	eighty	osemdesát	firs	tachtig	ok'dek	quatre-vingt
90	ninety	devadesát	halvfems	negentig	nau'dek	quatre-vingt-dix
100	one hundred	jedno sto	et hundrede	een-honderd	unu-cento	un-cent
1000	thousand	tisíc	tusind	duizend	mil	mille

	GERMAN	HUNGARIAN	INDONESIAN	ITALIAN	NORWEGIAN	POLISH
1/4	ein viertel	egy-negyed	satu-suku	uno-guarto	en-fjeerdedel	jeden-c weirc
1/2	einhalb	egy-fél	satu-setengah	uno-mezzo	en-halv	jeden-polowa
1	ein	egy	satu	uno	en	jeden
2	zwei	kettö	dud	due	to	dwa
3	drei	három	tiga	tre	tre	trzy
4	vier	négy	empot	quattro	fire	cztery
5	fünf	öt	lima	cinque	fem	piec'
6	sechs	hat	enam	sei	seks	szes'c'
7	sieben	hét	tudjuh	sette	sju	siedem
8	acht	nyolc	delapan	otto	atte	osiem
9	neun	kilenc	sembilan	nove	ni	dziewiec'
10	zehn	tí z	sepuluh	dieci	ti	dziesiec'
12	zwölf	tizenketto	duabelas	dodici	tolv	dwanas' cie
15	fünfzehn	tizenöt	lima belas	quindici	femten	pietnas'cie
20	zwanzig	húsz	dua pulah	venti	tjue or tyve	dwadzies'cia
24	vierundzwanzig	húsz-négy	dua pulah-empot	venti-quattro	tjue-fire or tyve-fire	dwadzies'cia-cztery
25	fünfundzwanzig	húsz-öt	dua-pulah-lima	venti-cinque	tjue-fem or tyve-fem	dwadzies'cia-piec
30	dreissig	harminc	tigapulah	trenta	tredve	trydzies'ci
40	vierzig	negyven	empat pulah	quaranta	forti	czterdries'ci
50	fünfzig	otven	lima pulah	cinquanta	femti	piec'dziesiat
60	sechzig	hatvan	enam pulah	sessanta	seksti	szes'c'dziesiat
70	siebzig	hetven	tudjuh pulu	settanta	sytti	siedemdziesiat
80	achtzig	nyolvan	delapan puluh	ottanta	atti	osiemdziesiat
90	neunzig	kilencven	sembilan puluh	novanta	nitty	dziewiec'dziesiat
100	ein hundert	egy-száz	satu-seratus	uno-cento	en-hundre	jeden-sto
1000	tausend	ezer	seribu	mille	tusen	tysiac

	PORTUGUESE	ROMANIAN	SERBO-CROATIAN	SPANISH	SWEDISH	TURKISH
1/4	um-quarto	un-sfert	jedan-ceturtina	un-cuarto	en-fjärdedel	bir-ceyrek
1/2	un-meio	o-jumatate	jedan-polovina	un-medio	en-hälft	bir-yarim
1	um	un	jedan	uno	en	bir
2	dois	doi	dva	dos	tva	iki
3	trés	trei	tri	tres	tre	üc
4	quatro	patru	cetiri	cuatro	fyra	dört
5	cinco	cinci	pet	cinco	fem	bes
6	seis	sase	sest	seis	sex	alti
7	sete	sapte	sedam	siete	sju	yedi
8	oito	opt	osam	ocho	atta	sekiz
9	nove	noua	devet	nueve	nio	dokuz
10	dez	zece	deset	diez	tio	on
12	doze	doisprezece	dvanaest	doce	tolv	on iki
15	quinze	cincisprezece	petnaest	quince	femton	on bes
20	vinte	douazeci	dvadset	veinte	tjugu	yirmi
24	vinte-quatro	douazeci-patru	dvadesel-citiri	veinticuatro	tjugu-fyra	yirmi-dört
25	vinte-cinco	douazeci-cinci	dvadeset-pet	veinticinco	tjugu-fem	yirmi-bes
30	trinta	treizeci	trideset	treinta	trettio	otuz
40	quarenta	patruzeci	cetrdeset	cuarenta	fyrtio	kirk
50	cinqüenta	cincizeci	padeset	cincuenta	femtio	elli
60	sessenta	saizeci	sezdeset	sesenta	sextio	altmis
70	setenta	saptezeci	sedamdeset	setenta	sjuttio	yetmis
80	oitenta	optzeci	osamdeset	ochenta	attio	seksen
90	noventa	novazeci	devedeset	noventa	nittio	doksan
100	un-cem	o-suta	jedan-sto	cien	en-hundra	bir-yüz
1000	mil	mie	hiljada	mil	tusen	bin

AFGHANISTAN

The Islamic State of Afghanistan, which occupies a mountainous region of Southwest Asia, has an area of 251,825 sq. mi. (652,090 sq. km.) and a population of 25.59 million. Presently, about a fifth of the total population lives in exile as refugees, (mostly in Pakistan). Capital: Kabul. It is bordered by Iran, Pakistan, Turkmenistan, Uzbekistan, Tajikistan, and China's Sinkiang Province. Agriculture and herding are the principal industries; textile mills and cement factories add to the industrial sector. Cotton, wool, fruits, nuts, oil, sheepskin coats and hand-woven carpets are normally exported but foreign trade has been interrupted since 1979.

ISLAMIC STATE

SH1373-1381 / 1994-2002AD

STANDARD COINAGE

KM# 1043 500 AFGHANIS
19.8700 g., 0.9990 Silver 0.6382 oz. ASW, 37.9 mm. **Subject:** World Championship of Soccer - 2006 - Germany **Obv:** State Emblem **Rev:** Soccer ball on German map **Edge:** Reeded

Date	Mintage	F	VF	XF	Unc	BU
2001 Proof	—	Value: 40.00				

REPUBLIC

SH1381- / 2002- AD

DECIMAL COINAGE

100 Pul = 1 Afghani; 20 Afghani = 1 Amani

KM# 1044 AFGHANI
3.2500 g., Copper-Plated-Steel, 19.5 mm. **Obv:** Value **Rev:** Mosque in wreath

Date	Mintage	F	VF	XF	Unc	BU
SH1383(2004)	—	—	—	—	—	2.00
SH1384(2005)	—	—	—	—	—	2.00

KM# 1045 2 AFGHANIS
4.2500 g., Stainless Steel, 21 mm. **Obv:** Value **Rev:** Mosque in wreath

Date	Mintage	F	VF	XF	Unc	BU
SH1383(2004)	—	—	—	—	—	3.00
SH1384(2005)	—	—	—	—	—	3.00

KM# 1046 5 AFGHANIS
5.2600 g., Brass, 23.5 mm. **Obv:** Value **Rev:** Mosque in wreath

Date	Mintage	F	VF	XF	Unc	BU
SH1383(2004)	—	—	—	—	—	4.00
SE1384(2005)	—	—	—	—	—	4.00

ALBANIA

The Republic of Albania, a Balkan republic bounded by Macedonia, Greece, Montenegro, and the Adriatic Sea, has an area of 11,100 sq. mi. (28,748 sq. km.) and a population of 3.49 million. Capital: Tirane. The country is predominantly agricultural, although recent progress has been made in the manufacturing and mining sectors. Petroleum, chrome, iron, copper, cotton textiles, tobacco and wood products are exported.

MINT MARKS
L - London
R - Rome
V - Vienna

MONETARY SYSTEM
100 Qindar Leku = 1 Lek
100 Qindar Ari = 1 Frang Ar = 5 Lek

REPUBLIC

STANDARD COINAGE

KM# 87 20 LEKE
8.5400 g., Brass, 26.1 mm. **Subject:** Prehistoric art **Obv:** Horseman **Rev:** Ancient coin design with Apollo portrait **Edge:** Reeded

Date	Mintage	F	VF	XF	Unc	BU
2002	—	—	—	—	3.00	4.00

KM# 81 50 LEKE
7.5000 g., Copper-Nickel, 28 mm. **Subject:** Michaelangelo's "David" **Obv:** Towered building **Rev:** Statue's head and denomination **Edge:** Plain

Date	Mintage	F	VF	XF	Unc	BU
2001	1,000	—	—	—	6.50	8.00

KM# 88 50 LEKE
11.9200 g., Brass, 28.1 mm. **Obv:** Value within circle **Rev:** Bust facing, dates below **Edge:** Reeded

Date	Mintage	F	VF	XF	Unc	BU
2002	—	—	—	—	3.00	4.00

KM# 89 50 LEKE
11.8400 g., Brass, 28 mm. **Obv:** Bust 3/4 facing, dates below, circle surrounds **Rev:** Value within box within circle **Edge:** Plain

Date	Mintage	F	VF	XF	Unc	BU
2003	—	—	—	—	3.00	4.00

KM# 86 50 LEKE
5.4600 g., Copper-Nickel, 24.2 mm. **Obv:** Value and legend **Rev:** Ancient Illyrian helmet **Edge:** Reeded

Date	Mintage	F	VF	XF	Unc	BU
2003 (2004)	200,000	—	—	—	6.00	7.50

KM# 90 50 LEKE
5.5000 g., Copper-Nickel, 24.2 mm. **Obv:** Wheel design **Rev:** Ancient bust above value within circle **Edge:** Reeded

Date	Mintage	F	VF	XF	Unc	BU
2004	—	—	—	—	3.00	4.00

KM# 91 50 LEKE
5.5000 g., Copper-Nickel, 24.2 mm. **Obv:** Soldier within circle **Rev:** Value within circle **Edge:** Reeded

Date	Mintage	F	VF	XF	Unc	BU
2004	—	—	—	—	3.00	4.00

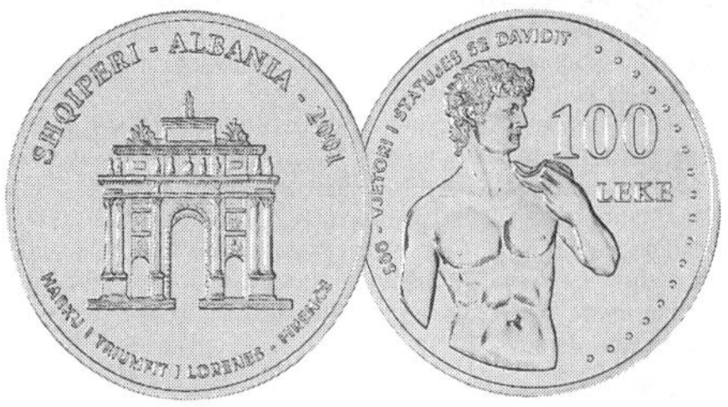

KM# 82 100 LEKE
15.7000 g., 0.9250 Silver 0.4669 oz. ASW, 32.65 mm. **Subject:** Michaelangelo's "David" **Obv:** Arch of Triumph **Rev:** Statue's upper half and denomination **Edge:** Plain

Date	Mintage	F	VF	XF	Unc	BU
2001	1,000	—	—	—	32.00	35.00

KM# 84 100 LEKE
15.0000 g., 0.9250 Silver 0.4461 oz. ASW, 32 mm. **Subject:** Albanian-European Integration **Obv:** Dove in flight, stars encircle **Rev:** European and Albanian maps, stars encircle **Edge:** Plain

Date	Mintage	F	VF	XF	Unc	BU
2001	1,000	—	—	—	26.00	29.00

KM# 83 200 LEKE
7.6500 g., 0.9000 Gold 0.2213 oz. AGW, 25.45 mm. **Subject:** Michaelangelo's "David" **Obv:** City plaza **Rev:** Statue of "David" and denomination **Edge:** Plain

Date	Mintage	F	VF	XF	Unc	BU
2001	500	—	—	—	200	240

KM# 85 200 LEKE
15.0000 g., 0.9250 Silver 0.4461 oz. ASW, 32 mm. **Subject:** Albanian-European Integration **Obv:** Dove in flight within inner circle, stars encircle **Rev:** Adult and infant hand within inner circle, stars encircle **Edge:** Plain

Date	Mintage	F	VF	XF	Unc	BU
2001	1,000	—	—	—	36.00	39.00

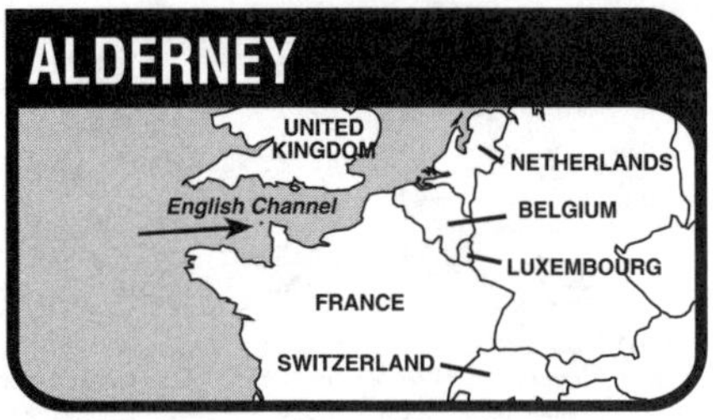

Alderney, the northernmost and third largest of the Channel Islands, separated from the coast of France by the dangerous 8-mile-wide tidal channel, has an area of 3 sq. mi. (8 km.) and a population of 1,686. It is a dependency of the British island of Guernsey, to the southwest. Capital: St. Anne. Principal industries are agriculture and raising cattle.

The Channel Islands have never been subject to the British Parliament and are self-governing units under the direct rule of the Crown acting through the Privy Council. Alderney is one of the nine Channel Islands, the only part of the Duchy of Normandy still belonging to the British Crown, and has been a British possession since the Norman Conquest of 1066. Legislation was only recently introduced for the issue of its own coinage, a right it now shares with Jersey and Guernsey.

RULER
British

MONETARY SYSTEM
100 Pence = 1 Pound Sterling

DEPENDENCY

STANDARD COINAGE

KM# 59 5 POUNDS

28.2800 g., 0.9250 Silver 0.8410 oz. ASW, 38.6 mm. **Ruler:** Elizabeth II **Subject:** Queen's 75th Birthday **Obv:** Queens portrait right **Obv. Designer:** Raphael Maklouf **Rev:** Queen in casual dress surrounded by rose, thistle, daffodil and pimper nickel **Rev. Designer:** David Cornell

Date	Mintage	F	VF	XF	Unc	BU
2001 Proof	—	Value: 50.00				

KM# 60 5 POUNDS

28.2800 g., Copper-Nickel, 38.6 mm. **Ruler:** Elizabeth II **Subject:** Queen's 75th Birrthday **Obv:** Queens portrait right **Obv. Designer:** Raphael Maklouf **Rev:** Queen in casual dress surrounded by rose, thistle, daffodil and primper nickel **Rev. Designer:** David Cornell

Date	Mintage	F	VF	XF	Unc	BU
2001	—	—	—	—	13.50	15.00

KM# 24 5 POUNDS

28.2800 g., 0.9250 Copper-Nickel 0.8410 oz., 38.6 mm. **Ruler:** Elizabeth II **Subject:** Queen Elizabeth II - 50 Years of Reigh **Obv:** Queen's head right **Rev:** Sword hilt and denomination with royal arms background **Rev. Designer:** Marcel Canioni **Edge:** Reeded

Date	Mintage	F	VF	XF	Unc	BU
2002 Proof	15,000	Value: 50.00				

KM# 24a 5 POUNDS

28.2800 g., 0.9250 Silver 0.8410 oz. ASW, 38.6 mm. **Ruler:** Elizabeth II **Subject:** Queen Elizabeth II - 50 Years of Reign **Obv:** Queen's head right **Rev:** Sword hilt and denomination with royal arms background **Rev. Designer:** Marcel Canioni **Edge:** Reeded

Date	Mintage	F	VF	XF	Unc	BU
2002 Proof	15,000	Value: 40.00				

KM# 25 5 POUNDS

28.2800 g., 0.9250 Silver 0.8410 oz. ASW, 38.6 mm. **Ruler:** Elizabeth II **Subject:** Queen's Golden Jubilee **Obv:** Queens portrait **Rev:** Honor guard and trumpets **Rev. Designer:** Robert Lowe **Edge:** Reeded

Date	Mintage	F	VF	XF	Unc	BU
2002 Proof	15,000	Value: 45.00				

KM# 27 5 POUNDS

28.2800 g., Copper-Nickel, 38.6 mm. **Ruler:** Elizabeth II **Obv:** Queens portrait **Rev:** Diana accepting flowers from girl **Edge:** Reeded

Date	Mintage	F	VF	XF	Unc	BU
2002	—	—	—	—	13.50	15.00

KM# 27a 5 POUNDS

28.2800 g., 0.9250 Silver 0.8410 oz. ASW, 38.6 mm. **Ruler:** Elizabeth II **Subject:** Princess Diana **Obv:** Queens portrait **Rev:** Diana accepting flowers from girl **Edge:** Reeded

Date	Mintage	F	VF	XF	Unc	BU
2002 Proof	20,000	Value: 45.00				

KM# 27b 5 POUNDS

39.9400 g., 0.9167 Gold 1.1771 oz. AGW, 38.6 mm. **Ruler:** Elizabeth II **Subject:** Princess Diana **Obv:** Queens portrait **Rev:** Diana accepting flowers from girl **Edge:** Reeded

Date	Mintage	F	VF	XF	Unc	BU
2002 Proof	100	Value: 1,150				

KM# 29 5 POUNDS

28.2800 g., Copper-Nickel, 38.6 mm. **Ruler:** Elizabeth II **Subject:** The Duke of Wellington **Obv:** Queens portrait **Rev:** Coat of arms, castle and portrait **Rev. Designer:** Willem Vis **Edge:** Reeded

Date	Mintage	F	VF	XF	Unc	BU
2002	—	—	—	—	13.50	15.00

KM# 29a 5 POUNDS

28.2800 g., 0.9250 Silver 0.8410 oz. ASW, 38.6 mm. **Ruler:** Elizabeth II **Subject:** The Duke of Wellington **Obv:** Queens portrait **Rev:** Multicolor coat of arms, portrait and castle **Rev. Designer:** Willem Vis **Edge:** Reeded

Date	Mintage	VG	F	VF	XF	Unc
2002 Proof	15,000	Value: 55.00				

KM# 29b 5 POUNDS

39.9400 g., 0.9167 Gold 1.1771 oz. AGW, 38.6 mm. **Ruler:** Elizabeth II **Subject:** The Duke of Wellington **Obv:** Queens portrait **Rev:** Coat of arms, castle and portrait **Rev. Designer:** Willem Vis **Edge:** Reeded

Date	Mintage	VG	F	VF	XF	Unc
2002 Proof	200	Value: 1,100				

KM# 31 5 POUNDS

28.2800 g., Copper-Nickel, 38.6 mm. **Ruler:** Elizabeth II **Subject:** Prince William **Obv:** Queens portrait **Obv. Designer:** Raphael Maklouf **Rev:** Portrait with open shirt collar **Edge:** Reeded

Date	Mintage	F	VF	XF	Unc	BU
2003	—	—	—	—	16.50	18.00

KM# 44 5 POUNDS

28.2800 g., Copper-Nickel, 38.6 mm. **Ruler:** Elizabeth II **Obv:** Queens portrait **Rev:** HMS Mary Rose **Rev. Designer:** Willem Vis **Edge:** Reeded

Date	Mintage	F	VF	XF	Unc	BU
2003	—	—	—	—	12.00	13.50

KM# 44a 5 POUNDS

28.2800 g., 0.9250 Silver 0.8410 oz. ASW, 38.6 mm. **Ruler:** Elizabeth II **Obv:** Queens portrait **Rev:** HMS Mary Rose below multicolor flag **Rev. Designer:** Willem Vis **Edge:** Reeded

Date	Mintage	F	VF	XF	Unc	BU
2003 Proof	15,000	Value: 60.00				

KM# 45 5 POUNDS

28.2800 g., Copper-Nickel, 38.6 mm. **Ruler:** Elizabeth II **Obv:** Queens portrait **Rev:** Alfred the Great on ship **Rev. Designer:** Willem Vis **Edge:** Reeded

Date	Mintage	F	VF	XF	Unc	BU
2003	—	—	—	—	12.00	13.50

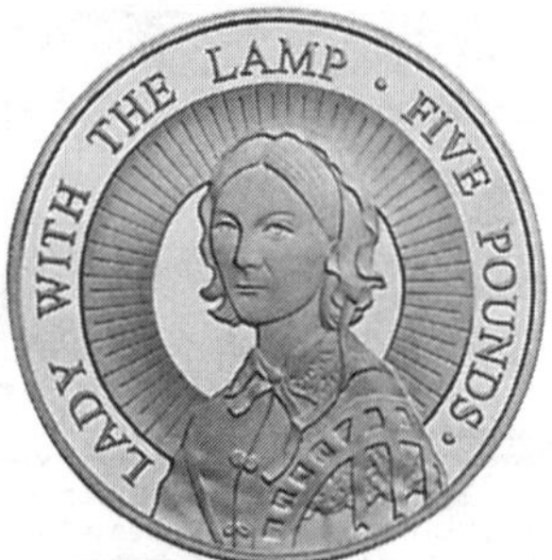

KM# 45a 5 POUNDS

28.2800 g., 0.9250 Silver 0.8410 oz. ASW, 38.6 mm. **Ruler:** Elizabeth II **Obv:** Queens portrait **Rev:** Alfred the Great on ship below multicolor flag **Rev. Designer:** Willem Vis **Edge:** Reeded

Date	Mintage	F	VF	XF	Unc	BU
2003 Proof	15,000	Value: 60.00				

KM# 45b 5 POUNDS

39.9400 g., 0.9167 Gold 1.1771 oz. AGW, 38.6 mm. **Ruler:** Elizabeth II **Obv:** Queens portrait **Rev:** Alfred the Great on ship **Rev. Designer:** Willem Vis **Edge:** Reeded

Date	Mintage	F	VF	XF	Unc	BU
2003 Proof	500	Value: 1,100				

KM# 31a 5 POUNDS

28.2800 g., 0.9250 Silver 0.8410 oz. ASW, 38.6 mm. **Ruler:** Elizabeth II **Subject:** Prince William **Obv:** Queens portrait **Obv. Designer:** Raphael Maklouf **Rev:** Portrait with open shirt collar **Edge:** Reeded

Date	Mintage	F	VF	XF	Unc	BU
2003 Proof	—	Value: 47.50				

KM# 31b 5 POUNDS

39.9400 g., 0.9166 Gold 1.1770 oz. AGW, 38.6 mm. **Ruler:** Elizabeth II **Subject:** Prince Willliam **Obv:** Queens portrait **Obv. Designer:** Raphael Maklouf **Rev:** Portrait with open shirt collar **Edge:** Reeded

Date	Mintage	F	VF	XF	Unc	BU
2003 Proof	200	Value: 1,100				

KM# 35a 5 POUNDS

28.2800 g., 0.9250 Silver 0.8410 oz. ASW, 38.6 mm. **Ruler:** Elizabeth II **Subject:** Last Flight of the Concorde, October 24, 2003 **Obv:** Portrait right **Rev:** Concorde in flight **Rev. Designer:** Emma Noble **Edge:** Reeded

Date	Mintage	F	VF	XF	Unc	BU
2003 Proof	5,000	Value: 70.00				

KM# 35 5 POUNDS

Copper-Nickel **Ruler:** Elizabeth II **Subject:** Last Flight of the Concorde, Octboer 24, 2003 **Obv:** Portrait right **Rev:** Concorde in flight **Rev. Designer:** Emma Noble **Edge:** Reeded

Date	Mintage	F	VF	XF	Unc	BU
2003	5,000	—	—	—	12.00	15.50

KM# 35b 5 POUNDS

39.9400 g., 0.9166 Gold 1.1770 oz. AGW, 38.6 mm. **Ruler:** Elizabeth II **Obv:** Queens portrait **Rev:** Concorde in flight, October 24, 2003 **Rev. Designer:** Emma Noble **Edge:** Reeded

Date	Mintage	F	VF	XF	Unc	BU
2003 Proof	500	Value: 1,100				

KM# 38 5 POUNDS

28.2800 g., Copper-Nickel, 38.6 mm. **Ruler:** Elizabeth II **Obv:** Queens portrait **Rev:** Battleship and transports, HMS Belfast **Rev. Designer:** Mike Guilfoyle **Edge:** Reeded **Note:** D-Day

Date	Mintage	F	VF	XF	Unc	BU
2004	—	—	—	—	15.00	17.50

KM# 38a 5 POUNDS

28.2800 g., 0.9250 Silver 0.8410 oz. ASW, 38.6 mm. **Ruler:** Elizabeth II **Obv:** Queens portrait **Rev:** Battleship and transports **Rev. Designer:** Mike Guilfoyle

Date	Mintage	F	VF	XF	Unc	BU
2004 Proof	10,000	Value: 85.00				

KM# 38b 5 POUNDS

39.9400 g., 0.9167 Gold 1.1771 oz. AGW, 38.6 mm. **Ruler:** Elizabeth II **Obv:** Queens portrait **Rev:** Battleship and transports **Rev. Designer:** Mike Guilfoyle

Date	Mintage	F	VF	XF	Unc	BU
2004 Proof	500	Value: 1,100				

KM# 42 5 POUNDS

28.2800 g., Copper-Nickel, 38.6 mm. **Ruler:** Elizabeth II **Obv:** Queens portrait **Rev:** Florence Nightingale **Edge:** Reeded

Date	Mintage	F	VF	XF	Unc	BU
2004	—	—	—	—	18.00	20.00

KM# 42a 5 POUNDS

28.2800 g., 0.9250 Silver 0.8410 oz. ASW, 38.6 mm. **Ruler:** Elizabeth II **Obv:** Queens portrait **Rev:** Florence Nightingale **Edge:** Reeded

Date	Mintage	F	VF	XF	Unc	BU
2004 Proof	25,000	Value: 70.00				

KM# 43 5 POUNDS

28.2800 g., Copper-Nickel, 38.6 mm. **Ruler:** Elizabeth II **Obv:** Queens portrait **Rev:** Florence Nightingale head above the Battle of Inkerman scene with one multicolor soldier **Edge:** Reeded

Date	Mintage	F	VF	XF	Unc	BU
2004	—	—	—	—	22.50	25.00

KM# 43a 5 POUNDS

28.2800 g., 0.9250 Silver 0.8410 oz. ASW, 38.6 mm. **Ruler:** Elizabeth II **Obv:** Queens portrait **Rev:** Florence Nightingale head above Battle of Inkerman scene with one multicolor soldier **Edge:** Reeded

Date	Mintage	F	VF	XF	Unc	BU
2004 Proof	10,000	Value: 85.00				

KM# 43b 5 POUNDS

39.9400 g., 0.9166 Gold 1.1770 oz. AGW, 38.6 mm. **Ruler:** Elizabeth II **Obv:** Queens portrait **Rev:** Florence Nightingale head above Battle of Inkerman scene with one multicolor soldier **Edge:** Reeded

Date	Mintage	F	VF	XF	Unc	BU
2004 Proof	500	Value: 1,100				

KM# 47 5 POUNDS

28.2800 g., Copper-Nickel, 38.6 mm. **Ruler:** Elizabeth II **Obv:** Queens portrait **Rev:** Locomotive, The Rocket **Rev. Designer:** Robert Lowe **Edge:** Reeded

Date	Mintage	F	VF	XF	Unc	BU
2004	—	—	—	—	16.00	18.50

KM# 47a 5 POUNDS

28.2800 g., 0.9250 Silver 0.8410 oz. ASW, 38.6 mm. **Ruler:** Elizabeth II **Obv:** Queens portrait **Rev:** Locomotive, The Rocket **Rev. Designer:** Robert Lowe **Edge:** Reeded

Date	Mintage	F	VF	XF	Unc	BU
2004 Proof	20,000	Value: 60.00				

KM# 47b 5 POUNDS

39.9400 g., 0.9167 Gold 1.1771 oz. AGW, 38.6 mm. **Ruler:** Elizabeth II **Obv:** Queens portrait **Rev:** Locomotive, The Rocket **Rev. Designer:** Robert Lowe **Edge:** Reeded

Date	Mintage	F	VF	XF	Unc	BU
2004 Proof	500	Value: 1,100				

KM# 48 5 POUNDS

28.2800 g., Copper-Nickel, 38.6 mm. **Ruler:** Elizabeth II **Obv:** Queens portrait **Rev:** Locomotive, The Royal Scot **Rev. Designer:** Robert Lowe **Edge:** Reeded

Date	Mintage	F	VF	XF	Unc	BU
2004	—	—	—	—	16.00	18.50

KM# 48a 5 POUNDS

28.2800 g., 0.9250 Silver 0.8410 oz. ASW, 38.6 mm. **Ruler:** Elizabeth II **Obv:** Queens portrait **Rev:** Locomotive, The Royal Scot **Rev. Designer:** Robert Lowe **Edge:** Reeded

Date	Mintage	F	VF	XF	Unc	BU
2004 Proof	10,000	Value: 60.00				

KM# 49 5 POUNDS

28.2800 g., Copper-Nickel, 38.6 mm. **Ruler:** Elizabeth II **Obv:** Queens portrait **Rev:** Locomotive, The Merchant Navy 21C1 **Edge:** Reeded

Date	Mintage	F	VF	XF	Unc	BU
2004	—	—	—	—	16.00	18.50

KM# 49a 5 POUNDS

28.2800 g., 0.9250 Silver 0.8410 oz. ASW, 38.6 mm. **Ruler:** Elizabeth II **Obv:** Queens portrait **Rev:** Locomotive, The Merchant Navy 21C1 **Rev. Designer:** Robert Lowe **Edge:** Reeded

Date	Mintage	F	VF	XF	Unc	BU
2004 Proof	10,000	Value: 60.00				

KM# 53a 5 POUNDS

28.2800 g., 0.9250 Silver 0.8410 oz. ASW, 38.6 mm. **Ruler:** Elizabeth II **Subject:** End of WWII **Obv:** Elizabeth II by Maklouf **Rev:** Flag waving crowd **Edge:** Reeded

Date	Mintage	F	VF	XF	Unc	BU
2005 Proof	5,000	Value: 85.00				

KM# 53b 5 POUNDS

39.9400 g., 0.9167 Gold 1.1771 oz. AGW, 38.6 mm. **Ruler:** Elizabeth II **Subject:** End of WWII **Obv:** Elizabeth II by Maklouf **Rev:** Flag waving crowd **Edge:** Reeded

Date	Mintage	F	VF	XF	Unc	BU
2005 Proof	150	Value: 1,150				

KM# 54a 5 POUNDS

39.9400 g., 0.9167 Gold 1.1771 oz. AGW, 38.6 mm. **Ruler:** Elizabeth II **Subject:** WWII Liberation **Obv:** Elizabeth II by Maklouf **Rev:** Churchill flashing the "V" sign **Edge:** Reeded

Date	Mintage	F	VF	XF	Unc	BU
2005 Proof	150	Value: 1,150				

KM# 66 5 POUNDS

28.2800 g., Copper-Nickel, 38.6 mm. **Ruler:** Elizabeth II **Subject:** Viscount Samuel Hood on his flagship after the Battle of Saints Passage in 1782 **Obv:** Queens portrait **Rev. Designer:** Willem Vis

Date	Mintage	F	VF	XF	Unc	BU
2005	—	—	—	—	13.50	15.00

KM# 66a 5 POUNDS

28.2800 g., 0.9250 Silver 0.8410 oz. ASW, 38.6 mm. **Ruler:** Elizabeth II **Subject:** Viscount Samuel Hood on his flagship after the Battle of Saints Passage in 1782 **Obv:** Queens portrait **Rev. Designer:** Willem Vis **Note:** Ensign is colored.

Date	Mintage	F	VF	XF	Unc	BU
2005 Proof	—	Value: 50.00				

KM# 68 5 POUNDS

28.2800 g., Copper-Nickel, 38.6 mm. **Ruler:** Elizabeth II **Obv:** Crowned head right **Rev:** HMS Revenge fighting at Azores, 1591 **Rev. Designer:** Willem Vis

Date	Mintage	F	VF	XF	Unc	BU
2005	—	—	—	—	12.00	14.00

KM# 68a 5 POUNDS

28.2800 g., 0.9250 Silver 0.8410 oz. ASW, 38.6 mm. **Ruler:** Elizabeth II **Obv:** Crowned head right **Rev:** HMS Revenge fighting at Azores, 1591 **Rev. Designer:** Willem Vis **Note:** Ensign is colorized.

Date	Mintage	F	VF	XF	Unc	BU
2005 Proof	—	Value: 60.00				

KM# 70 5 POUNDS

28.2800 g., 0.9250 Silver 0.8410 oz. ASW, 38.6 mm. **Ruler:** Elizabeth II **Subject:** Queen's 80th Birthday **Obv:** Crowned bust right - gilt **Obv. Legend:** ELIZABETH II - ALDERNARY **Rev:** 1/2 length figures of Queen mother and daughter hugging, facing

Date	Mintage	F	VF	XF	Unc	BU
2006 Proof	—	Value: 40.00				

KM# 36 10 POUNDS

155.5170 g., 0.9250 Silver 4.6248 oz. ASW, 65 mm. **Ruler:** Elizabeth II **Subject:** Last Flight of the Concorde **Obv:** Queens portrait **Rev:** Gold-plated Concorde in flight **Edge:** Reeded

Date	Mintage	F	VF	XF	Unc	BU
2003 Proof	1,969	Value: 320				

KM# 55 10 POUNDS

155.5100 g., 0.9250 Silver 4.6246 oz. ASW, 65 mm. **Ruler:** Elizabeth II **Subject:** WWII Liberation **Obv:** Elizabeth II by Maklouf sign **Rev:** Churchill flashing the "V" **Edge:** Reeded

Date	Mintage	F	VF	XF	Unc	BU
2005 Proof	1,945	Value: 350				

KM# 61 25 POUNDS

7.9800 g., 0.9167 Gold 0.2352 oz. AGW, 22 mm. **Ruler:** Elizabeth II **Subject:** Queen's 75th Birthday **Obv:** Queens portrait right **Obv. Designer:** Raphael Maklouf **Rev:** Queen in casual dress surrounded by rose, thistle, daffodil and pimper nickel **Rev. Designer:** David Cornell

Date	Mintage	F	VF	XF	Unc	BU
2001 Proof	—	Value: 325				

KM# 28 25 POUNDS

7.9800 g., 0.9167 Gold 0.2352 oz. AGW, 22.05 mm. **Ruler:** Elizabeth II **Subject:** Princess Diana **Obv:** Queens portrait **Rev:** Diana's cameo portrait above denomination **Rev. Designer:** Avril Vaughan **Edge:** Reeded

Date	Mintage	VG	F	VF	XF	Unc
2002 Proof	2,500	Value: 275				

KM# 30 25 POUNDS

7.9800 g., 0.9166 Gold 0.2352 oz. AGW, 22 mm. **Ruler:** Elizabeth II **Subject:** The Duke of Wellington **Obv:** Queens portrait **Rev:** Coat of arms, castle and portrait **Rev. Designer:** Willem Vis **Edge:** Reeded

Date	Mintage	VG	F	VF	XF	Unc
2002 Proof	2,500	Value: 300				

KM# 58 25 POUNDS

7.9800 g., 0.9166 Gold 0.2352 oz. AGW, 22 mm. **Ruler:** Elizabeth II **Obv:** Queen's portrait right

Date	Mintage	F	VF	XF	Unc	BU
2002 Proof	2,500	Value: 300				

KM# 32 25 POUNDS

7.9800 g., 0.9166 Gold 0.2352 oz. AGW, 22 mm. **Ruler:** Elizabeth II **Subject:** Prince William **Obv:** Queens portrait **Rev:** Portrait with open shirt collar **Edge:** Reeded

Date	Mintage	F	VF	XF	Unc	BU
2003 Proof	1,500	Value: 325				

KM# 46 25 POUNDS

7.9800 g., 0.9167 Gold 0.2352 oz. AGW, 22 mm. **Ruler:** Elizabeth II **Obv:** Queens portrait **Rev:** HMS Mary Rose **Rev. Designer:** Willem Vis **Edge:** Reeded

Date	Mintage	F	VF	XF	Unc	BU
2003 Proof	2,500	Value: 365				

KM# 39 25 POUNDS

7.9800 g., 0.9167 Gold 0.2352 oz. AGW, 22 mm. **Ruler:** Elizabeth II **Subject:** D-Day **Obv:** Queens portrait **Rev:** Battleship and transports **Edge:** Reeded

Date	Mintage	F	VF	XF	Unc	BU
2004 Proof	500	Value: 325				

KM# 50 25 POUNDS

7.9800 g., 0.9167 Gold 0.2352 oz. AGW, 22 mm. **Ruler:** Elizabeth II **Obv:** Queens portrait **Rev:** Locomotive, The Rocket **Rev. Designer:** Robert Lowe **Edge:** Reeded

Date	Mintage	F	VF	XF	Unc	BU
2004 Proof	2,500	Value: 365				

KM# 51 25 POUNDS

7.9800 g., 0.9167 Gold 0.2352 oz. AGW, 22 mm. **Ruler:** Elizabeth II **Obv:** Queens portrait **Rev:** Locomotive, The Merchant Navy 21C1 **Rev. Designer:** Robert Lowe **Edge:** Reeded

Date	Mintage	F	VF	XF	Unc	BU
2004 Proof	1,500	Value: 365				

KM# 67 25 POUNDS
7.9800 g., 0.9167 Gold 0.2352 oz. AGW, 22 mm. **Ruler:** Elizabeth II **Subject:** Viscount Samuel Hood on his flagship after the Battle of Saints Passage in 1782 **Obv:** Queens portrait **Rev. Designer:** Willem Vis

Date	Mintage	F	VF	XF	Unc	BU
2005 Proof	—	Value: 300				

KM# 69 25 POUNDS
7.9800 g., 0.9167 Gold 0.2352 oz. AGW, 22 mm. **Ruler:** Elizabeth II **Obv:** Queens portrait right **Rev:** HMS Revenge fighting at Azores, 1591 **Rev. Designer:** Willem Vis

Date	Mintage	F	VF	XF	Unc	BU
2005 Proof	—	Value: 365				

KM# 62 50 POUNDS
1000.0000 g., 0.9250 Silver 29.738 oz. ASW, 100 mm. **Ruler:** Elizabeth II **Subject:** 50th Anniversary of Coronation **Obv:** Queens portrait right **Rev:** State coach in whicht he Queen travelled to and from her coronation

Date	Mintage	F	VF	XF	Unc	BU
2003 Proof	—	Value: 1,000				

KM# 33 50 POUNDS
1000.0000 g., 0.9250 Silver 29.738 oz. ASW, 100 mm. **Ruler:** Elizabeth II **Subject:** Prince William **Obv:** Queens portrait **Rev:** Portrait with open shirt collar **Edge:** Reeded

Date	Mintage	F	VF	XF	Unc	BU
2003 Proof	500	Value: 995				

KM# 63 50 POUNDS
1000.0000 g., 0.9250 Silver 29.738 oz. ASW, 100 mm. **Ruler:** Elizabeth II **Subject:** 50th Anniversary of Coronation **Obv:** Queens portrait right **Rev:** St. Edward's crown, royal scepter, orb of England

Date	Mintage	F	VF	XF	Unc	BU
2003 Proof	—	Value: 1,000				

KM# 64 50 POUNDS
1000.0000 g., 0.9250 Silver 29.738 oz. ASW, 100 mm. **Ruler:** Elizabeth II **Subject:** 50th Anniversary of Coronation **Obv:** Queens portrait right **Rev:** Queen on horseback dressed in the ceremonial uniform of the Colonel in Chief of the Household Brigade

Date	Mintage	F	VF	XF	Unc	BU
2003 Proof	—	Value: 1,000				

KM# 65 50 POUNDS
1000.0000 g., 0.9250 Silver 29.738 oz. ASW, 100 mm. **Ruler:** Elizabeth II **Subject:** 50th Anniversary of Coronation **Obv:** Queens portrait right **Rev:** The Queen crowned, seated, holding the orb and scepter

Date	Mintage	F	VF	XF	Unc	BU
2003 Proof	—	Value: 1,000				

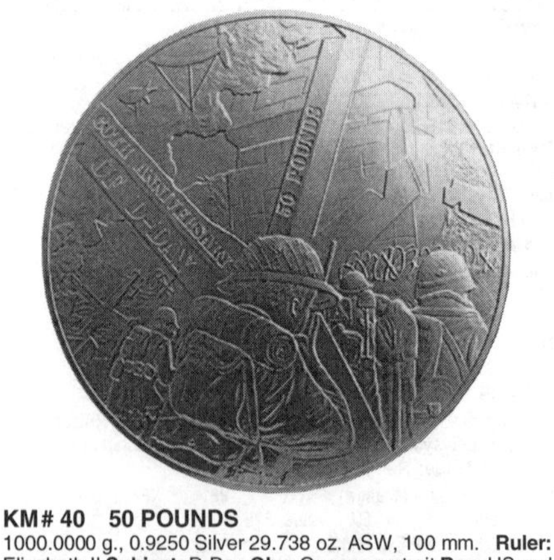

KM# 40 50 POUNDS
1000.0000 g., 0.9250 Silver 29.738 oz. ASW, 100 mm. **Ruler:** Elizabeth II **Subject:** D-Day **Obv:** Queens portrait **Rev:** US and British troops wading ashore **Rev. Designer:** Matthew Bonaccorsi **Edge:** Reeded

Date	Mintage	F	VF	XF	Unc	BU
2004 Proof	600	Value: 1,200				

KM# 34 100 POUNDS
1000.0000 g., 0.9166 Gold 29.468 oz. AGW, 100 mm. **Ruler:** Elizabeth II **Subject:** Prince William **Obv:** Queens portrait **Rev:** Portrait with open shirt collar **Edge:** Reeded

Date	Mintage	F	VF	XF	Unc	BU
2003 Proof	—	Value: 26,500				

KM# 37 1000 POUNDS
1090.8600 g., 0.9166 Gold 32.145 oz. AGW, 100 mm. **Ruler:** Elizabeth II **Subject:** Last Flight of the Concorde **Obv:** Queens portrait **Rev:** Concorde in flight **Edge:** Reeded

Date	Mintage	F	VF	XF	Unc	BU
2003 Proof	34	Value: 28,000				

KM# 41 1000 POUNDS
1000.0000 g., 0.9167 Gold 29.471 oz. AGW, 100 mm. **Ruler:** Elizabeth II **Subject:** D-Day **Obv:** Queens portrait **Rev:** US and British troops wading ashore **Rev. Designer:** Matthew Bonaccorsi **Edge:** Reeded

Date	Mintage	F	VF	XF	Unc	BU
2004 Proof	60	Value: 26,000				

ALGERIA

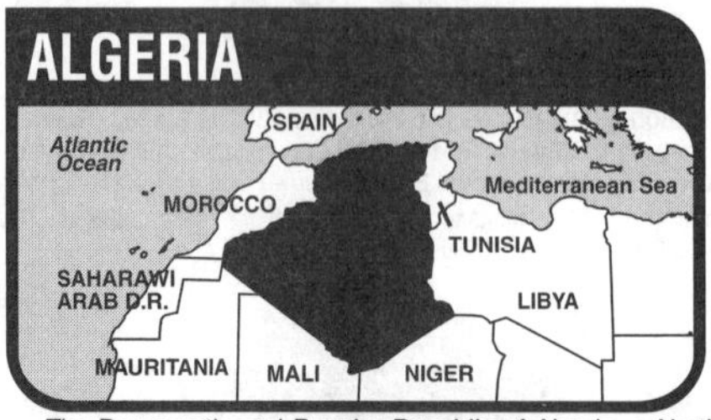

The Democratic and Popular Republic of Algeria, a North African country fronting on the Mediterranean Sea between Tunisia and Morocco, has an area of 919,595 sq. mi. (2,381,740 sq. km.) and a population of 31.6 million. Capital: Algiers (Alger). Most of the country's working population is engaged in agriculture although a recent industrial diversification, financed by oil revenues, is making steady progress. Wines, fruits, iron and zinc ores, phosphates, tobacco products, liquified natural gas, and petroleum are exported.

MINT MARK
(a) – Paris, privy marks only

MONETARY SYSTEMS
100 Centimes = 1 Franc

REPUBLIC

MONETARY SYSTEM
100 Centimes = 1 Dinar

STANDARD COINAGE

KM# 127 1/4 DINAR
1.1500 g., Aluminum **Subject:** Fennec Fox **Obv:** Value in small circle **Rev:** Head facing

Date	Mintage	F	VF	XF	Unc	BU
2003-AH1423	—	—	1.50	3.00	4.50	5.50

KM# 129 DINAR
4.2400 g., Steel **Subject:** Buffalo **Obv:** Value on silhouette of country, within circle **Rev:** Prehistoric head 3/4 facing, ancient drawings back of horns

Date	Mintage	F	VF	XF	Unc	BU
AH1422-2002	—	—	1.00	2.00	3.50	5.50
AH1423-2003	—	—	1.00	2.00	3.50	5.50
AH1424-2004	—	—	1.00	2.00	3.50	5.50

KM# 130 2 DINARS
5.1300 g., Steel, 22.5 mm. **Subject:** Camel **Obv:** Value on silhouette of country **Rev:** Head right

Date	Mintage	F	VF	XF	Unc	BU
AH1422-2002	—	—	1.00	2.00	4.00	6.00
AH1423-2002	—	—	1.00	2.00	4.00	6.00
AH1424-2003	—	—	1.00	2.00	4.00	6.00

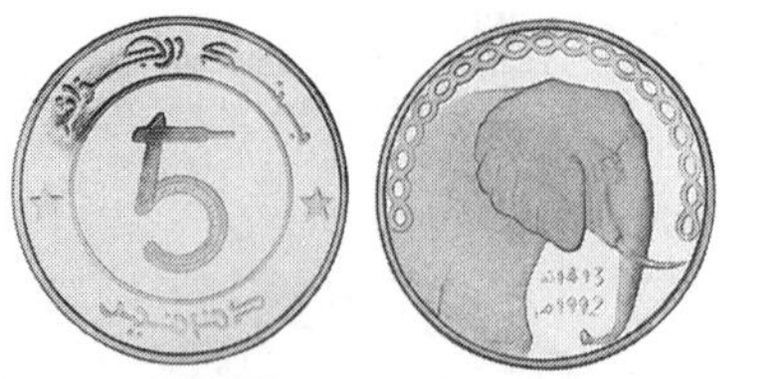

KM# 123 5 DINARS
6.2000 g., Steel **Subject:** Elephant **Obv:** Denomination within circle **Rev:** Head right

Date	Mintage	F	VF	XF	Unc	BU
AH1422-2003	—	—	1.50	3.50	6.50	9.50
AH1423-2003	—	—	1.50	3.50	6.50	9.50
AH1424-2004	—	—	1.50	3.50	6.50	9.50
AH1426-2006	—	—	1.00	3.50	6.50	9.50

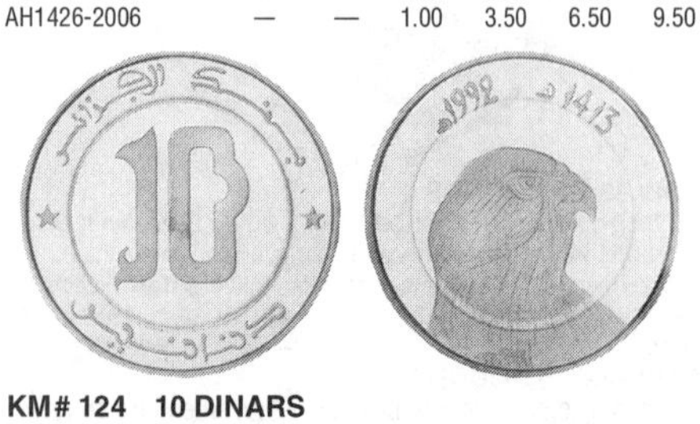

KM# 124 10 DINARS
4.9500 g., Bi-Metallic Aluminum center in Steel ring, 26.5 mm. **Subject:** Falcon **Obv:** Denomination **Rev:** Head right

Date	Mintage	F	VF	XF	Unc	BU
AH1423-2002	—	—	2.00	4.00	8.00	—
AH1425-2004	—	—	2.00	4.00	8.00	—

KM# 125 20 DINARS
8.6200 g., Bi-Metallic Brass center in Steel ring, 27.5 mm. **Subject:** Lion **Obv:** Denomination **Rev:** Head left

Date	Mintage	F	VF	XF	Unc	BU
AH1424-2004	—	—	3.00	6.00	12.00	—

KM# 126 50 DINARS
9.2700 g., Bi-Metallic Steel center in Brass ring, 28.5 mm. **Subject:** Gazelle **Obv:** Denomination **Rev:** Head left

Date	Mintage	F	VF	XF	Unc	BU
AH1424-2003	—	—	4.00	8.00	16.50	—
AH1425-2004	—	—	4.00	8.00	16.50	—

KM# 138 50 DINARS
Bi-Metallic **Rev:** Two men with guns

Date	Mintage	F	VF	XF	Unc	BU
AH1425-2004	—	—	—	—	12.50	15.00

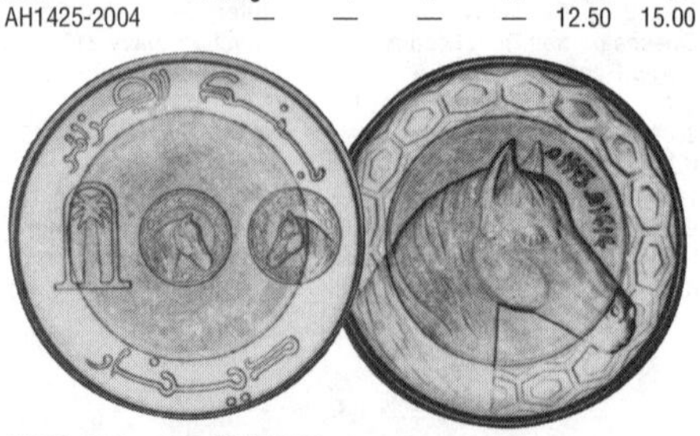

KM# 132 100 DINARS
11.0000 g., Bi-Metallic Aluminum-Bronze center in Stainless Steel ring, 29.5 mm. **Obv:** Denomination stylized with reverse design **Rev:** Horse head right

Date	Mintage	F	VF	XF	Unc	BU
AH1422-2002	—	—	6.00	12.00	20.00	24.00
AH1423-2002	—	—	6.00	12.00	20.00	24.00
AH1425-2004	—	—	6.00	12.00	20.00	24.00

KM# 137 100 DINARS
11.0000 g., Bi-Metallic Brass center in Stainless Steel ring, 29.5 mm. **Subject:** 40th Anniversary of Independence **Obv:** Stylized value **Rev:** Number 40 and stylized face **Edge:** Reeded

Date	Mintage	F	VF	XF	Unc	BU
AH1422-2002	—	—	—	—	25.00	27.50

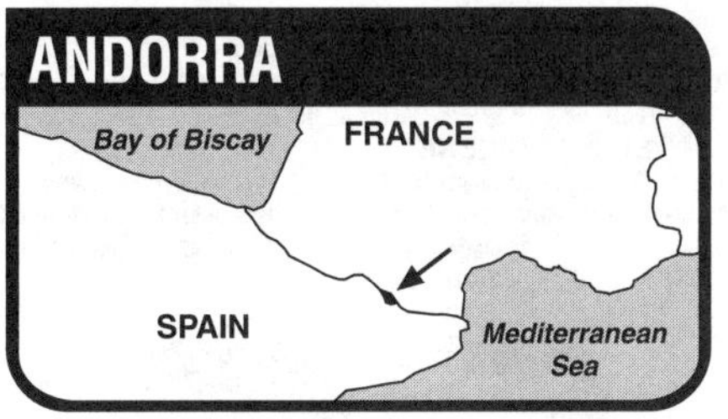

Principality of Andorra (Principat d'Andorra), situated on the southern slopes of the Pyrenees Mountains between France and Spain, has an area of 181 sq. mi. (453 sq. km.) and a population of 80,000. Capital: Andorra la Vella. Tourism is the chief source of income. Timber, cattle and derivatives, and furniture are exported.

RULER
Joan D.M. Bisbe D'Urgell I

MONETARY SYSTEM
100 Centims = 1 Diner

NOTE: The Diners have been struck for collectors while the Euro is used in everyday commerce.

MINT MARK
Crowned M = Madrid

PRINCIPALITY
DECIMAL COINAGE

KM# 176 CENTIM
2.1000 g., Aluminum, 27 mm. **Subject:** Charlemagne **Obv:** National arms, date below **Rev:** Crowned head facing, denomination below **Edge:** Plain

Date	Mintage	F	VF	XF	Unc	BU
2002	—	—	—	—	1.50	2.00

KM# 177 CENTIM
2.1300 g., Aluminum, 27 mm. **Subject:** Isard **Obv:** National arms, date below **Rev:** Mountain goat left facing, denomination at right **Edge:** Plain

Date	Mintage	F	VF	XF	Unc	BU
2002	—	—	—	—	1.50	2.00

KM# 178 CENTIM
2.1400 g., Aluminum, 27 mm. **Subject:** Agnus Dei **Obv:** National arms **Rev:** Lamb of God **Edge:** Plain

Date	Mintage	F	VF	XF	Unc	BU
2002	—	—	—	—	1.00	1.50

KM# 198 CENTIM
Aluminum-Magnesium, 27 mm. **Obv:** National arms **Rev:** A piece of the wall paintings belonging to the 12th century Romanesque church of St. Marti de la Cortinado

Date	Mintage	F	VF	XF	Unc	BU
2003	—	—	—	—	1.25	1.75

KM# 200 CENTIM
Aluminum-Magnesium, 27 mm. **Obv:** National arms **Rev:** Image of the 12th century Romanesque church of St. Miquel d'Engolasters with its bell tower, the Romanesque apse, the small portico and the large Lombard windows

Date	Mintage	F	VF	XF	Unc	BU
2003	—	—	—	—	1.25	1.75

KM# 199 CENTIM
Aluminum-Magnesium, 27 mm. **Obv:** National arms **Rev:** Pont de la Margineda, reproduction of the bridge

Date	Mintage	F	VF	XF	Unc	BU
2003	—	—	—	—	1.25	1.75

KM# 179 2 CENTIMS
Brass, 18 mm. **Subject:** Grandalla **Obv:** National arms **Rev:** Edelweiss flower **Edge:** Plain

Date	Mintage	F	VF	XF	Unc	BU
2002	—	—	—	—	1.50	2.00

KM# 201 2 CENTIMS
Copper-Zinc-Nickel, 18.15 mm. **Obv:** National arms **Rev:** Clavell Deltoide, a flower found in Andorra

Date	Mintage	F	VF	XF	Unc	BU
2003	—	—	—	—	1.75	2.50

KM# 180 5 CENTIMS
Brass, 21.8 mm. **Subject:** Squirrel **Obv:** National arms **Rev:** Squirrel on tree stump **Edge:** Plain

Date	Mintage	F	VF	XF	Unc	BU
2002	—	—	—	—	2.00	2.50

KM# 181 5 CENTIMS
Brass, 21.8 mm. **Subject:** Gall Fer **Obv:** National arms **Rev:** Male capercaillie (grouse) displaying plumage **Edge:** Plain

Date	Mintage	F	VF	XF	Unc	BU
2002	—	—	—	—	2.00	2.50

KM# 203 5 CENTIMS
Copper-Zinc, 21.8 mm. **Obv:** National arms **Rev:** Wall painting from the 11th century church of Sant Serni de Nagol showing an eagle

Date	Mintage	F	VF	XF	Unc	BU
2003	—	—	—	—	2.25	2.75

KM# 202 5 CENTIMS
Copper-Zinc, 21.8 mm. **Obv:** National arms **Rev:** The cross of Seven Arms, traditional Gothic cross

Date	Mintage	F	VF	XF	Unc	BU
2003	—	—	—	—	2.25	2.75

KM# 182 10 CENTIMS
Brass **Subject:** St. Joan de Caselles **Obv:** National arms **Rev:** Tower and building **Edge:** Plain

Date	Mintage	F	VF	XF	Unc	BU
2002	—	—	—	—	3.00	4.00

KM# 204 10 CENTIMS
Copper-Nickel, 27.8 mm. **Obv:** National arms **Rev:** 12th century wood carving image from Our Lady of Meritxell

Date	Mintage	F	VF	XF	Unc	BU
2003	—	—	—	—	3.50	4.50

KM# 193 5 DINERS
1.2400 g., 0.9990 Gold 0.0398 oz. AGW, 13.92 mm. **Obv:** National arms **Rev:** The Escorial Palace in Madrid **Edge:** Reeded

Date	Mintage	F	VF	XF	Unc	BU
2004 Proof	3,000	Value: 65.00				

KM# 194 5 DINERS
1.2400 g., 0.9990 Gold 0.0398 oz. AGW, 13.92 mm. **Obv:** National arms **Rev:** Eiffel Tower **Edge:** Reeded

Date	Mintage	F	VF	XF	Unc	BU
2004 Proof	3,000	Value: 65.00				

KM# 195 5 DINERS
1.2400 g., 0.9990 Gold 0.0398 oz. AGW, 13.92 mm. **Obv:** National arms **Rev:** Atomic model monument **Edge:** Reeded

Date	Mintage	F	VF	XF	Unc	BU
2004 Proof	3,000	Value: 65.00				

KM# 196 5 DINERS
1.2400 g., 0.9990 Gold 0.0398 oz. AGW, 13.92 mm. **Subject:** Andorran membership in the United Nations **Obv:** National arms **Rev:** Seated woman, world globe and UN logo **Edge:** Reeded

Date	Mintage	F	VF	XF	Unc	BU
2004 Proof	3,000	Value: 75.00				

KM# 172 10 DINERS
31.4700 g., 0.9250 Silver 0.9359 oz. ASW, 38.6 mm. **Subject:** Europa **Obv:** National arms **Rev:** Europa in chariot **Edge:** Reeded

Date	Mintage	F	VF	XF	Unc	BU
2001 Proof	15,000	Value: 40.00				

KM# 173 10 DINERS
31.4700 g., 0.9250 Silver 0.9359 oz. ASW, 38.6 mm. **Subject:** Concordia Europea **Obv:** National arms **Rev:** Two crowned women holding hands **Edge:** Reeded

Date	Mintage	F	VF	XF	Unc	BU
2001 Proof	15,000	Value: 40.00				

KM# 175 10 DINERS
31.4700 g., 0.9250 Silver 0.9359 oz. ASW, 38.6 mm. **Subject:** Olympics **Obv:** National arms **Rev:** Snowboarder **Edge:** Reeded

Date	Mintage	F	VF	XF	Unc	BU
2002 Proof	15,000	Value: 40.00				

KM# 183 10 DINERS
31.4700 g., 0.9250 Silver 0.9359 oz. ASW, 38.6 mm. **Subject:** Mouflon **Obv:** National arms **Rev:** Big Horn sheep **Edge:** Reeded

Date	Mintage	F	VF	XF	Unc	BU
2002 Proof	15,000	Value: 50.00				

KM# 188 10 DINERS
31.1035 g., 0.9250 Silver 0.9250 oz. ASW, 38.6 mm. **Obv:** National arms **Rev:** Pope with doves **Edge:** Reeded

Date	Mintage	F	VF	XF	Unc	BU
2004 Proof	9,999	Value: 40.00				

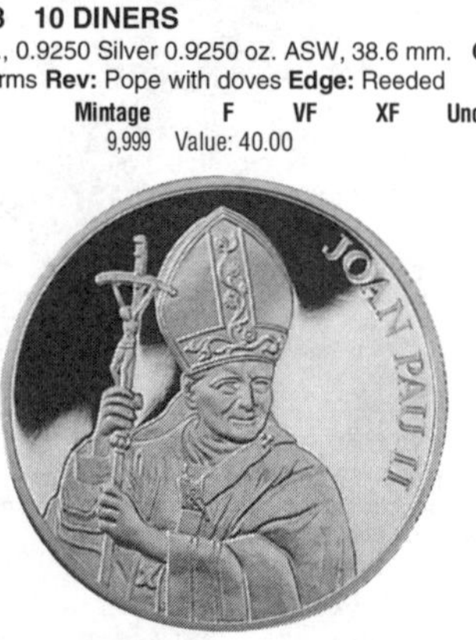

KM# 189 10 DINERS
31.1035 g., 0.9250 Silver 0.9250 oz. ASW, 38.6 mm. **Obv:** National arms **Rev:** Pope holding staff with 2 hands **Edge:** Reeded

Date	Mintage	F	VF	XF	Unc	BU
2004 Proof	9,999	Value: 40.00				

KM# 190 10 DINERS
31.1035 g., 0.9250 Silver 0.9250 oz. ASW, 38.6 mm. **Obv:** National arms **Rev:** Pope raising a chalice **Edge:** Reeded

Date	Mintage	F	VF	XF	Unc	BU
2004 Proof	9,999	Value: 40.00				

KM# 191 10 DINERS
31.1035 g., 0.9250 Silver 0.9250 oz. ASW, 38.6 mm. **Obv:** National arms **Rev:** Pope with hammer **Edge:** Reeded

Date	Mintage	F	VF	XF	Unc	BU
2004 Proof	9,999	Value: 40.00				

KM# 192 10 DINERS
31.1035 g., 0.9250 Silver 0.9250 oz. ASW, 38.6 mm. **Obv:** National arms **Rev:** Gold-plated Pope writing **Edge:** Reeded

Date	Mintage	F	VF	XF	Unc	BU
2004 Proof	9,999	Value: 40.00				

KM# 205 10 DINERS
31.1000 g., 0.9250 Silver 0.9249 oz. ASW, 38.6 mm. **Obv. Designer:** National arms **Rev:** Gold plated Pope John Paul II wearing mitre and holding crucifix staff **Edge:** Reeded

Date	Mintage	F	VF	XF	Unc	BU
2005 Proof	9,999	Value: 40.00				

KM# 206 10 DINERS
31.1000 g., 0.9250 Silver 0.9249 oz. ASW, 38.6 mm. **Obv:** National arms **Rev:** Pope John Paul II with the Holy Virgin in background **Edge:** Reeded

Date	Mintage	F	VF	XF	Unc	BU
2005 Proof	9,999	Value: 40.00				

KM# 207 10 DINERS
31.1000 g., 0.9250 Silver 0.9249 oz. ASW, 38.6 mm. **Obv:** National arms **Rev:** Pope John Paul II in prayer with crucifix at right **Edge:** Reeded

Date	Mintage	F	VF	XF	Unc	BU
2005 Proof	9,999	Value: 40.00				

KM# 208 10 DINERS
31.1000 g., 0.9250 Silver 0.9249 oz. ASW, 38.6 mm. **Obv:** National arms **Rev:** Pope John Paul II blessing Vatican crowd **Edge:** Reeded

Date	Mintage	F	VF	XF	Unc	BU
2005 Proof	9,999	Value: 40.00				

KM# 209 10 DINERS
31.1000 g., 0.9250 Silver 0.9249 oz. ASW, 38.6 mm. **Obv:** National arms **Rev:** Pope John Paul II and Mother Teresa **Edge:** Reeded

Date	Mintage	F	VF	XF	Unc	BU
2005 Proof	9,999	Value: 40.00				

KM# 210 10 DINERS
31.1000 g., 0.9250 Silver 0.9249 oz. ASW, 38.6 mm. **Obv:** National arms **Rev:** Bearded man above Vatican City **Edge:** Reeded

Date	Mintage	F	VF	XF	Unc	BU
2005 Proof	9,999	Value: 40.00				

KM# 211 10 DINERS
31.1000 g., 0.9250 Silver 0.9249 oz. ASW, 38.6 mm. **Obv:** National arms **Rev:** Sad woman above Fatima **Edge:** Reeded

Date	Mintage	F	VF	XF	Unc	BU
2005 Proof	9,999	Value: 40.00				

KM# 212 10 DINERS
31.1000 g., 0.9250 Silver 0.9249 oz. ASW, 38.6 mm. **Obv:** National arms **Rev:** Radiant woman above Guadalupe Cathedral **Edge:** Reeded

Date	Mintage	F	VF	XF	Unc	BU
2005 Proof	9,999	Value: 40.00				

KM# 213 10 DINERS
31.1000 g., 0.9250 Silver 0.9249 oz. ASW, 38.6 mm. **Obv:** National arms **Rev:** Sea shell above Santiago De Compostel-la Cathedral **Edge:** Reeded

Date	Mintage	F	VF	XF	Unc	BU
2005 Proof	9,999	Value: 40.00				

KM# 214 10 DINERS
31.1000 g., 0.9250 Silver 0.9249 oz. ASW, 38.6 mm. **Obv:** National arms **Rev:** Dead man's face with Church of the Holy Sepulchure in the background **Edge:** Reeded

Date	Mintage	F	VF	XF	Unc	BU
2005 Proof	9,999	Value: 40.00				

KM# 215 10 DINERS
28.8000 g., 0.9250 Silver 0.8565 oz. ASW, 38.6 mm. **Obv:** National arms **Rev:** 2006 Olympics freestyle skier **Edge:** Reeded

Date	Mintage	F	VF	XF	Unc	BU
2005 Proof	15,000	Value: 35.00				

KM# 217 10 DINERS
3.1100 g., 0.9999 Gold 0.1000 oz. AGW, 20 mm. **Obv:** National arms **Rev:** Jesus carrying the cross **Edge:** Reeded

Date	Mintage	F	VF	XF	Unc	BU
2006 Proof	9,999	Value: 110				

KM# 218 10 DINERS
31.1035 g., 0.9250 Silver 0.9250 oz. ASW, 38.6 mm. **Obv:** National arms **Rev:** Birth of Jesus **Edge:** Reeded

Date	Mintage	F	VF	XF	Unc	BU
2006 Proof	9,999	Value: 40.00				

KM# 219 10 DINERS
31.1035 g., 0.9250 Silver 0.9250 oz. ASW, 38.6 mm. **Obv:** National arms **Rev:** The Last Supper **Edge:** Reeded

Date	Mintage	F	VF	XF	Unc	BU
2006 Proof	9,999	Value: 40.00				

KM# 174 25 DINERS

12.4414 g., 0.9990 Gold 0.3996 oz. AGW, 26 mm. **Subject:** Christmas **Obv:** National arms **Rev:** Nativity scene **Edge:** Reeded

Date	Mintage	F	VF	XF	Unc	BU
2001 Proof	3,000	Value: 375				

KM# 184 25 DINERS

10.0000 g., 0.9999 Gold 0.3215 oz. AGW, 26 mm. **Subject:** Christmas **Obv:** National arms **Rev:** Standing Christ child **Edge:** Reeded

Date	Mintage	F	VF	XF	Unc	BU
2002 Proof	2,000	Value: 300				

KM# 185 25 DINERS

7.7759 g., 0.9990 Gold 0.2497 oz. AGW, 26 mm. **Subject:** Christmas **Obv:** National arms **Rev:** Madonna-like mother and child **Edge:** Reeded

Date	Mintage	F	VF	XF	Unc	BU
2003 Proof	3,000	Value: 260				

KM# 197 25 DINERS

8.0000 g., 0.9990 Gold 0.2569 oz. AGW, 26 mm. **Subject:** Christmas **Obv:** National arms **Rev:** Nativity scene **Edge:** Reeded

Date	Mintage	F	VF	XF	Unc	BU
2004 Proof	5,000	Value: 245				

KM# 216 25 DINERS

6.0000 g., 0.9999 Gold 0.1929 oz. AGW, 26 mm. **Obv:** National arms **Rev:** St. Joseph holding infant Jesus **Edge:** Reeded

Date	Mintage	F	VF	XF	Unc	BU
2005 Proof	9,999	Value: 200				

KM# 186 50 DINERS

159.5000 g., 0.9990 Bi-Metallic Gold And Silver .999 Silver 155.5g coin with .999 Gold 4g, 20x50mm insert 5.1227 oz., 65 mm. **Subject:** 10th Anniversary of Constitution **Obv:** National arms **Rev:** Seated allegorical woman holding scrolled constitution **Edge:** Reeded

Date	Mintage	F	VF	XF	Unc	BU
2003	3,000	—	—	—	275	325

The Argentine Republic, located in southern South America, has an area of 1,073,518 sq. mi. (3,761,274 sq. km.) and an estimated population of 37.03 million. Capital: Buenos Aires. Its varied topography ranges from the subtropical lowlands of the north to the towering Andean Mountains in the west and the wind-swept Patagonian steppe in the south. The rolling, fertile pampas of central Argentina are ideal for agriculture and grazing, and support most of the republic's population. Meatpacking, flour milling, textiles, sugar refining and dairy products are the principal industries. Oil is found in Patagonia, but most mineral requirements must be imported.

Internal conflict through the first half century of Argentine independence resulted in a provisional national coinage, chiefly of crown-sized silver. Provincial issues mainly of minor denominations supplemented this.

MONETARY SYSTEM

(Commencing 1992)

100 Centavos = 1 Peso

REPUBLIC

REFORM COINAGE

1985-1992; 1,000 Pesos Argentinos = 1 Austral;
100 Centavos = 1 Austral

KM# 145 2 PESOS

Copper Nickel, 30.35 mm. **Subject:** !00th Anniversary First Oil Well **Obv:** First oil well **Obv. Legend:** REPÚBLICA ARGENTINA - DESCUBRIMIENTO DEL PETRÓLEO **Rev:** Modern pump **Rev. Inscription:** CHUBUT **Edge:** Reeded

Date	Mintage	F	VF	XF	Unc	BU
2007	—	—	—	—	—	—

REFORM COINAGE

1992; 100 Centavos = 1 Peso

KM# 109a.2 5 CENTAVOS

Copper-Nickel **Obv:** Radiant sunface. Bold lettering **Note:** Prev. KM#84a.2.

Date	Mintage	F	VF	XF	Unc	BU
2004	30,000,000	—	—	—	0.45	0.60
2005	76,000,000	—	—	—	0.45	0.60

KM# 109 5 CENTAVOS

Brass **Obv:** Radiant sunface **Rev:** Large value, date below **Note:** Prev. KM#84.

Date	Mintage	F	VF	XF	Unc	BU
2005	—	—	—	—	0.45	0.60

KM# 107 10 CENTAVOS

Aluminum-Bronze **Obv:** Argentine arms **Rev:** Value, date below **Edge:** Reeded **Note:** Prev. KM#82.

Date	Mintage	F	VF	XF	Unc	BU
2004	190,000,000	—	—	—	0.65	0.85
2005	114,400,000	—	—	—	0.65	0.85
2006	99,600,000	—	—	—	0.65	0.85

KM# 132.1 PESO

6.3500 g., Bi-Metallic Brass center in Copper-Nickel ring, 23 mm. **Subject:** General Urquiza **Obv:** Stylized portrait facing **Rev:** Church tower and denomination **Edge:** Reeded

Date	Mintage	F	VF	XF	Unc	BU
2001	995,000	—	—	—	3.75	4.50

KM# 132.2 PESO

6.3500 g., Bi-Metallic Copper-Aluminum-Nickel center in Copper-Nickel ring, 23 mm. **Subject:** General Urquiza **Obv:** Stylized portrait facing **Rev:** Church tower and denomination **Edge:** Plain

Date	Mintage	F	VF	XF	Unc	BU
2001	5,000	—	—	—	7.50	8.00

KM# 141 PESO

24.8100 g., 0.9000 Silver 0.7179 oz. ASW, 36.9 mm. **Obv:** Maria Eva Duarte de Peron **Rev:** "EVITA" audience **Edge:** Reeded

Date	Mintage	F	VF	XF	Unc	BU
ND (2004) Proof	5,000	Value: 40.00				

KM# 140 PESO

25.0000 g., 0.9000 Silver 0.7234 oz. ASW, 37 mm. **Subject:** 70th Anniversary of Central Bank **Obv:** Bank building **Rev:** Liberty head in wreath **Edge:** Reeded

Date	Mintage	F	VF	XF	Unc	BU
2005 Proof	2,000	Value: 50.00				

KM# 112.1 PESO

Bi-Metallic Brass center in Copper-Nickel ring **Obv:** Argentine arms in outer ring, design of first Argetine coin in center **Note:** Prev. KM#87.1.

Date	Mintage	F	VF	XF	Unc	BU
2006	—	—	—	—	—	—
2007	—	—	—	—	—	—

KM# 112.4 PESO
Bi-Metallic Brass center in Copper-Nickel ring **Obv:** Argentine arms in outer ring, design of first Argetine coin in center **Rev:** Radiant sun, legend in circle, value at top, date at bottom

Date	Mintage	F	VF	XF	Unc	BU
2006	30,000,000	—	—	—	4.50	5.00

KM# 135 2 PESOS
10.4400 g., Copper-Nickel, 30.2 mm. **Subject:** Eva Peron **Obv:** Head left **Rev:** Stylized crowd scene and value **Edge:** Reeded

Date	Mintage	F	VF	XF	Unc	BU
2002	—	—	—	—	7.50	9.00

KM# 144 2 PESOS
10.4700 g., Copper Nickel, 30.35 mm. **Subject:** 25th Anniversary Mavinas Islands Occupation **Obv:** Soldier's bust facing **Obv. Legend:** REPUBLICA ARGENTINA - 1982 - 2007 - LA NACION A SUS HÉROES **Rev:** Outlined map of islands **Rev. Legend:** MALVINAS ARGENTINAS **Rev. Inscription:** 2 DE APRIL / 1982 **Edge:** Reeded

Date	Mintage	F	VF	XF	Unc	BU
2007	—	—	—	—	7.50	9.00

KM# 133 5 PESOS
8.0640 g., 0.9000 Gold 0.2333 oz. AGW, 22 mm. **Subject:** Gral. Justo Jose de Urquiza **Obv:** Stylized portrait facing **Rev:** Church tower and denomination **Edge:** Reeded

Date	Mintage	F	VF	XF	Unc	BU
2001	1,000	—	—	—	210	225

KM# 142 5 PESOS
8.0640 g., 0.9000 Gold 0.2333 oz. AGW, 22 mm. **Obv:** Maria Eva Duarte de Peron **Rev:** "EVITA" and audience

Date	Mintage	F	VF	XF	Unc	BU
ND (2004) Proof	1,000	Value: 225				

KM# 138 25 PESOS
27.0000 g., 0.9250 Silver 0.8029 oz. ASW, 40 mm. **Subject:** IBERO-AMERICA Series **Obv:** Coats of arms **Rev:** Tall ship "Presidente Sarmiento" **Edge:** Reeded

Date	Mintage	F	VF	XF	Unc	BU
2002 Proof	—	Value: 55.00				

KM# 139 25 PESOS
27.0000 g., 0.9250 Silver 0.8029 oz. ASW, 40 mm. **Subject:** Ibero-America **Obv:** National arms in circle of arms **Rev:** Colon Theater building **Edge:** Reeded

Date	Mintage	F	VF	XF	Unc	BU
2005 Proof	15,500	Value: 50.00				

The Republic of Armenia, formerly Armenian S.S.R., is bordered to the north by Georgia, the east by Azerbaijan and the south and west by Turkey and Iran. It has an area of 11,506 sq. mi. (29,800 sq. km) and an estimated population of 3.66 million. Capital: Yerevan. Agriculture including cotton, vineyards and orchards, hydroelectricity, chemicals - primarily synthetic rubber and fertilizers, vast mineral deposits of copper, zinc and aluminum, and production of steel and paper are major industries.

Fighting between Christians in Armenia and Muslim forces of Azerbaijan escalated in 1992 and continued through early 1994. Each country claimed the Nagorno-Karabakh, an Armenian ethnic enclave, in Azerbaijan. A temporary cease-fire was announced in May 1994.

MONETARY SYSTEM
100 Luma = 1 Dram

MINT NAME
Revan, (Erevan, now Yerevan)

REPUBLIC

STANDARD COINAGE

KM# 112 10 DRAM
1.3000 g., Aluminum, 20 mm. **Obv:** National arms **Rev:** Value **Edge:** Reeded

Date	Mintage	F	VF	XF	Unc	BU
2004	—	—	—	—	1.00	1.50

KM# 93 20 DRAM
2.8000 g., Copper Plated Steel, 20.5 mm. **Obv:** National arms **Rev:** Denomination **Edge:** Plain

Date	Mintage	F	VF	XF	Unc	BU
2003	—	—	—	—	1.00	1.50

KM# 94 50 DRAM
3.4500 g., Brass Plated Steel, 21.5 mm. **Obv:** National arms **Rev:** Value **Edge:** Reeded

Date	Mintage	F	VF	XF	Unc	BU
2003	—	—	—	—	1.25	1.50

KM# 86 100 DRAM
31.1000 g., 0.9990 Silver 0.9988 oz. ASW, 38 mm. **Obv:** National arms **Rev:** Bust of General Garegin Nzhdeh facing at right **Edge:** Plain **Edge Lettering:** Serial number

Date	Mintage	F	VF	XF	Unc	BU
2001 Proof	170	Value: 300				

KM# 86a 100 DRAM
31.1000 g., 0.9990 Gold Plated Silver 0.9988 oz. ASW AGW, 38 mm. **Obv:** National arms **Obv. Inscription:** Bust of General Garegin Nzhdeh facing at right **Edge:** Plain **Edge Lettering:** Serial number

Date	Mintage	F	VF	XF	Unc	BU
2001 Proof	30	Value: 850				

KM# 87 100 DRAM
31.0400 g., 0.9990 Silver 0.9969 oz. ASW, 38 mm. **Subject:** Armenian Membership in the Council of Europe joined January 1, 2001 **Obv:** National arms **Rev:** Spiral design with star circle **Edge:** Plain **Edge Lettering:** Serial number

Date	Mintage	F	VF	XF	Unc	BU
2001 Proof	200	Value: 100				

KM# 98 100 DRAM
31.1000 g., 0.9250 Silver 0.9249 oz. ASW, 40 mm. **Obv:** National arms **Rev:** Aram Khachatryan, Birth Centennial **Edge:** Reeded

Date	Mintage	F	VF	XF	Unc	BU
2002	300	—	—	—	65.00	75.00

KM# 99 100 DRAM
31.1000 g., 0.9250 Silver 0.9249 oz. ASW, 40 mm. **Obv:** The Book of Sadness **Rev:** Saint Grigor Narekatsi with book and quill millenium of this poem "The Book of Sadness" **Edge:** Reeded

Date	Mintage	F	VF	XF	Unc	BU
2002 Proof	500	Value: 65.00				

KM# 110 100 DRAM
33.9200 g., 0.9250 Silver 1.0087 oz. ASW, 39 mm. **Subject:** 110th Anniversary of State Banking in Armenia and 10th Year of National Currency October 7 1893 - November 22, 1993 **Obv:** Building above value **Rev:** State Bank emblem **Edge:** Reeded

Date	Mintage	F	VF	XF	Unc	BU
2003 Proof	300	Value: 110				

KM# 95 100 DRAM
4.0000 g., Nickel Plated Steel, 22.5 mm. **Obv:** National arms **Rev:** Value **Edge:** Reeded

Date	Mintage	F	VF	XF	Unc	BU
2003	—	—	—	—	1.50	2.00

KM# 111 100 DRAM
28.2800 g., 0.9250 Silver 0.8410 oz. ASW, 38.6 mm. **Subject:** FIFA World Cup Soccer Games - Germany **Obv:** National arms **Rev:** Three soccer players

Date	Mintage	F	VF	XF	Unc	BU
2004 Proof	300	Value: 110				

KM# 113 100 DRAM

31.1000 g., 0.9990 Silver 0.9988 oz. ASW, 38 mm. **Subject:** Gandzasar Monastery **Obv:** Monastery **Rev:** Folk art crucifix and denomination

Date	Mintage	F	VF	XF	Unc	BU
2004 Proof	500	Value: 65.00				

KM# 115 100 DRAM

31.1000 g., 0.9250 Silver 0.9249 oz. ASW, 40 mm. **Subject:** Anania Shirakatsi 1400 Anniversary, Scientist **Obv:** Profile of Shirakatsi, deep in thought **Rev:** Planets and stars, denomination

Date	Mintage	F	VF	XF	Unc	BU
2005 Proof	500	Value: 65.00				

KM# 123 100 DRAM

31.1000 g., 0.9250 Silver 0.9249 oz. ASW, 40.00 mm. **Subject:** Creation of the Armenian alphabet **Obv:** National arms **Rev:** King Vramshapuh standing at left, alphabet at right

Date	Mintage	F	VF	XF	Unc	BU
2005	500	—	—	—	—	—

KM# 124 100 DRAM

31.1000 g., 0.9250 Silver 0.9249 oz. ASW, 40.00 mm. **Subject:** Creation of the Armenian alphabet **Obv:** National arms **Rev:** Sahak Partev standing at left, alphabet at right

Date	Mintage	F	VF	XF	Unc	BU
2005	500	—	—	—	—	—

KM# 125 100 DRAM

31.1000 g., 0.9250 Silver 0.9249 oz. ASW, 40.00 mm. **Subject:** 100th Anniversary Birth of Inventor of MIG Jet Artem Mikoyan **Obv:** Three jet airplanes **Rev:** Bust of Mikoyan 3/4 left

Date	Mintage	F	VF	XF	Unc	BU
2005	500	—	—	—	—	—

KM# 127 100 DRAM

28.2800 g., 0.9250 Silver 0.8410 oz. ASW, 38.61 mm. **Subject:** International Polar Year **Obv:** National arms **Obv. Legend:** REPUBLIC OF ARMENIA **Rev:** Bust of Fridtjof Nansen right at left, ship stuck in ice at lower right, multicolor emblem above

Date	Mintage	F	VF	XF	Unc	BU
2006	10,000	—	—	—	—	—

KM# 129 100 DRAM

28.2800 g., 0.9250 Silver 0.8410 oz. ASW **Subject:** Hovhannes Aivazovsky **Obv:** National arms at lower left, sailing ship listing at center right multicolor **Rev:** Bast of Aivazovsky 3/4 left at lower left, sailing ships at center right **Shape:** Rectangular, 40 x 28 mm

Date	Mintage	F	VF	XF	Unc	BU
2006	5,000	—	—	—	—	—

KM# 119 100 DRAM

28.3500 g., 0.9250 Silver 0.8431 oz. ASW, 38.5 mm. **Obv:** National arms **Rev:** Brown bear and two red lines **Edge:** Plain

Date	Mintage	F	VF	XF	Unc	BU
2006 Proof	3,000	Value: 50.00				

KM# 120 100 DRAM

28.3500 g., 0.9250 Silver 0.8431 oz. ASW, 38.5 mm. **Obv:** National arms **Rev:** Wide-eared Hedgehog and two red lines **Edge:** Plain

Date	Mintage	F	VF	XF	Unc	BU
2006 Proof	3,000	Value: 50.00				

KM# 121 100 DRAM

28.2800 g., 0.9250 Silver 0.8410 oz. ASW, 38.6 mm. **Obv:** National arms, date and value **Rev:** Caucasian Forest Cat **Edge:** Plain

Date	Mintage	F	VF	XF	Unc	BU
2006 Proof	3,000	Value: 50.00				

KM# 122 100 DRAM

28.2800 g., 0.9250 Silver 0.8410 oz. ASW, 38.6 mm. **Obv:** National arms, date and value **Rev:** Armenian Tortoise **Edge:** Plain

Date	Mintage	F	VF	XF	Unc	BU
2006 Proof	3,000	Value: 50.00				

KM# 136 100 DRAM

28.2400 g., 0.9250 Silver 0.8398 oz. ASW, 38.55 mm. **Subject:** Northern Shoveler duck **Obv:** National arms **Obv. Legend:** REPUBLIC OF ARMENIA **Rev:** Duck standing left **Edge:** Plain

Date	Mintage	F	VF	XF	Unc	BU
2007 Proof	3,000	Value: 65.00				

KM# 141 100 DRAM

28.2800 g., 0.9250 Silver 0.8410 oz. ASW, 38.61 mm. **Series:** Signs of the Zodiac **Obv:** National arms within ring of signs of the Zodiac **Obv. Legend:** REPUBLIC OF ARMENIA **Obv. Designer:** Ursula Valenazh **Rev:** Capricorn multicolor **Edge:** Plain

Date	Mintage	F	VF	XF	Unc	BU
2007 Proof	12,000	Value: 75.00				

KM# 153 100 DRAM

Silver **Obv:** National arms **Obv. Legend:** REPUBLIC OF ARMENIA **Rev:** Trout

Date	Mintage	F	VF	XF	Unc	BU
2007	3,000	—	—	—	—	65.00

KM# 154 100 DRAM

Silver **Obv:** National arms **Obv. Legend:** REPUBLIC OF ARMENIA **Rev:** Armenian viper

Date	Mintage	F	VF	XF	Unc	BU
2007	3,000	—	—	—	—	65.00

KM# 96 200 DRAM

4.5000 g., Brass, 24 mm. **Obv:** National arms **Rev:** Value **Edge:** Reeded

Date	Mintage	F	VF	XF	Unc	BU
2003	—	—	—	—	3.00	4.00

KM# 106 500 DRAM

155.5000 g., 0.9250 Silver 4.6243 oz. ASW, 63 mm. **Subject:** 10th Anniversary of Independence **Obv:** National arms **Rev:** Tower with flag, logo at right 9-21-91

Date	Mintage	F	VF	XF	Unc	BU
2001 Proof	200	Value: 380				

KM# 97 500 DRAM

5.0000 g., Bi-Metallic Copper-Nickel center in a Brass ring, 22 mm. **Obv:** National arms **Rev:** Value **Edge:** Segmented reeding

Date	Mintage	F	VF	XF	Unc	BU
2003	—	—	—	—	6.00	8.00

KM# 109 1000 DRAM

15.5550 g., 0.5850 Gold 0.2925 oz. AGW, 26 mm. **Obv:** National arms on ancient coin design **Rev:** Tigran the Great ancient coin portrait

Date	Mintage	F	VF	XF	Unc	BU
2003	500	—	—	—	785	1,200

KM# 128 1000 DRAM

33.6000 g., 0.9250 Silver 0.9992 oz. ASW, 38.00 mm. **Subject:** 100th Anniversary Birth of Marshal Babajanian **Obv:** National arms **Rev:** Bust of Babajanian 3/4 right

Date	Mintage	F	VF	XF	Unc	BU
2006	500	—	—	—	—	—

KM# 133 1000 DRAM

33.6000 g., 0.9250 Silver 0.9992 oz. ASW, 40.00 mm. **Series:** Armenian grapes **Obv:** National arms **Rev:** Large bunch of grapes at left

Date	Mintage	F	VF	XF	Unc	BU
2007	5,000	—	—	—	—	—

KM# 134 1957 DRAM

33.6000 g., 0.9250 Silver 0.9992 oz. ASW, 40.00 mm. **Subject:** 50th Anniversay of Matenadaran **Obv:** Small national arms at center surrounded by intricate pattern **Rev:** Building at left center

Date	Mintage	F	VF	XF	Unc	BU
2007	—	500	—	—	—	135

KM# 117 5000 DRAM

31.1000 g., 0.9250 Silver 0.9249 oz. ASW, 38 mm. **Subject:** Armenian Armed Forces **Obv:** Order of the Combat Cross of the Second Degree and the Emblem of the Ministry of Defense of the Republic of Armenia **Obv. Designer:** H. Samuelian **Rev:** Arms, date and denomination **Shape:** Octagonal

Date	Mintage	F	VF	XF	Unc	BU
2005 Proof	500	Value: 130				

KM# 126 5000 DRAM

168.1000 g., 0.9250 Silver 4.9990 oz. ASW, 63.00 mm. **Subject:** 15th Anniversary of Independence **Obv:** National arms **Rev:** Building at center left, multicolor emblem above, mountains in background

Date	Mintage	F	VF	XF	Unc	BU
2006	300	—	—	—	—	—

KM# 139 5000 DRAM

4.3000 g., 0.9000 Gold 0.1244 oz. AGW, 18.00 mm. **Subject:** Haik Nahapet **Obv:** Small national arms at upper left, Orion constellation at right **Rev:** 3/4 length classical Archer right

Date	Mintage	F	VF	XF	Unc	BU
2007	3,000	—	—	—	—	195

KM# 107 10000 DRAM

8.6000 g., 0.9990 Gold 0.2762 oz. AGW, 22 mm. **Obv:** Mesrop Mashtots, creater of the Armenian Alphabet **Rev:** Armenian Alphabet

Date	Mintage	F	VF	XF	Unc	BU
2002 Proof	1,000	Value: 300				

KM# 108 10000 DRAM

8.6000 g., 0.9990 Gold 0.2762 oz. AGW, 22 mm. **Obv:** Building above value **Rev:** Aram Khachatryan left birth centennial

Date	Mintage	F	VF	XF	Unc	BU
2002 Proof	500	Value: 300				

KM# 114 10000 DRAM

8.6000 g., 0.9990 Gold 0.2762 oz. AGW, 22 mm. **Subject:** Arshile Gorky birth April 15, 1904 **Obv:** Bust of Gorky **Rev:** Denomination

Date	Mintage	F	VF	XF	Unc	BU
2004 Proof	1,000	Value: 300				

KM# 116 10000 DRAM

8.6000 g., 0.9990 Gold 0.2762 oz. AGW, 22 mm. **Subject:** Martiros Sarian 125th Anniversary of Birth **Obv:** Bust of Sarian **Rev:** Landscape, denomination

Date	Mintage	F	VF	XF	Unc	BU
2005 Proof	1,000	Value: 300				

KM# 130 10000 DRAM

8.6000 g., 0.9990 Gold 0.2762 oz. AGW, 22.00 mm. **Subject:** Komitas Vardapet **Obv:** Musical notations and score **Rev:** Bust of Vardapet 3/4 right

Date	Mintage	F	VF	XF	Unc	BU
2006	1,000	—	—	—	—	—

KM# 131 10000 DRAM

8.6000 g., 0.9000 Gold 0.2488 oz. AGW, 22.00 mm. **Subject:** 37th Chess Olympiad **Obv:** Chess piece at right **Rev:** National arms within 6 chess pieces in circle

Date	Mintage	F	VF	XF	Unc	BU
2006	1,000	—	—	—	—	—

KM# 132 10000 DRAM

8.6000 g., 0.9000 Gold 0.2488 oz. AGW, 22.00 mm. **Subject:** Hakob Gurjian **Obv:** Seated female sculpture **Rev:** Head 3/4 right

Date	Mintage	F	VF	XF	Unc	BU
2006	1,000	—	—	—	—	—

KM# 137 10000 DRAM

8.6000 g., 0.9000 Gold 0.2488 oz. AGW, 22.00 mm. **Subject:** Jean Garzou **Obv:** National arms with stylized view of shopping bourse **Rev:** Bust of Garzou 3/4 right at laft center

Date	Mintage	F	VF	XF	Unc	BU
2007	1,000	—	—	—	—	385

KM# 138 10000 DRAM

8.6000 g., 0.9000 Gold 0.2488 oz. AGW, 22.00 mm. **Subject:** 15th Anniversary of Armenian Army **Obv:** National arms **Rev:** Military badge

Date	Mintage	F	VF	XF	Unc	BU
2007	1,000	—	—	—	—	385

KM# 140 10000 DRAM

8.6000 g., 0.9000 Gold 0.2488 oz. AGW, 22.00 mm. **Subject:** 15th Anniversary Liberation of Shusi **Obv:** Bird with wings outspread above two shields **Rev:** Swirl in bachground

Date	Mintage	F	VF	XF	Unc	BU
2007	1,000	—	—	—	—	385

KM# 118 50000 DRAM

8.6000 g., 0.9990 Gold 0.2762 oz. AGW, 22 mm. **Subject:** Armenian Armed Forces **Obv:** Order of the Combat Cross of the Second Degree and the Emblem of the Ministry of Defense of the Republic of Armenia **Obv. Designer:** H. Samuelian **Rev:** Arms, date and denomination

Date	Mintage	F	VF	XF	Unc	BU
2005 Proof	1,000	Value: 300				

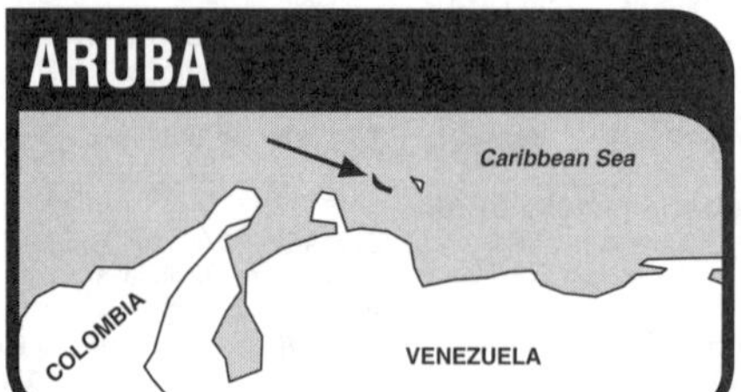

The second largest island of the Netherlands Antilles, Aruba is situated near the Venezuelan coast. The island has an area of 74-1/2 sq. mi. (193 sq. km.) and a population of 65,974. Capital: Oranjestad, named after the Dutch royal family. Aruba was important in the processing and transportation of petroleum products in the first part of the twentieth century, but today the chief industry is tourism.

For earlier issues see Curacao and the Netherlands Antilles.

RULER

Dutch

MINT MARKS

(u) Utrecht - Privy marks only
Winetendril with grapes, 2001-
Winetendril with grapes plus star, 2002-
Sails of a clipper, 2003-

MONETARY SYSTEM

100 Cents = 1 Florin

DUTCH STATE

"Status Aparte"

REGULAR COINAGE

KM# 1 5 CENTS

2.0000 g., Nickel Bonded Steel, 16 mm. **Ruler:** Beatrix 1980- **Obv:** National arms **Rev:** Geometric design with value **Edge:** Plain

Date	Mintage	F	VF	XF	Unc	BU
2001(u)	946,900	—	—	—	0.30	0.60
2002(u)	1,006,000	—	—	—	0.20	0.50
2003(u)	1,104,100	—	—	—	0.20	0.50
2004(u)	502,500	—	—	0.20	0.50	1.00
2005(u)	602,500	—	—	—	0.20	0.50
2006(u)	602,000	—	—	—	0.20	0.50
2007(u)	1,152,000	—	—	—	0.20	0.50
2008(u)	—	—	—	—	0.20	0.50

KM# 2 10 CENTS

3.0000 g., Nickel Bonded Steel, 18 mm. **Ruler:** Beatrix 1980- **Obv:** National arms **Rev:** Geometric design with value **Edge:** Reeded

Date	Mintage	F	VF	XF	Unc	BU
2001(u)	1,006,900	—	—	—	0.30	0.50
2002(u)	1,006,000	—	—	—	0.30	0.50
2003(u)	1,004,000	—	—	—	0.30	0.50
2004(u)	402,500	—	0.20	0.35	0.60	0.75
2005(u)	602,500	—	—	—	0.30	0.50
2006(u)	602,000	—	—	—	0.30	0.50
2007(u)	1,152,000	—	—	—	0.30	0.50
2008(u)	—	—	—	—	0.30	0.50

KM# 3 25 CENTS

3.5000 g., Nickel Bonded Steel, 20 mm. **Ruler:** Beatrix 1980- **Obv:** National arms **Rev:** Geometric design with value **Edge:** Plain

Date	Mintage	F	VF	XF	Unc	BU
2001(u)	716,900	—	—	—	0.35	0.80
2002(u)	806,000	—	—	—	0.35	0.80
2003(u)	804,000	—	—	—	0.35	0.80
2004(u)	362,500	—	—	—	0.40	0.80
2005(u)	302,500	—	—	—	0.40	0.80
2006(u)	302,000	—	—	—	0.40	0.80
2007(u)	202,000	—	—	—	0.50	1.00
2008(u)	—	—	—	—	0.50	1.00

KM# 4 50 CENTS

5.0000 g., Nickel Bonded Steel, 20 mm. **Ruler:** Beatrix 1980- **Obv:** National arms **Rev:** Geometric design with value **Edge:** Plain **Shape:** 4-sided

Date	Mintage	F	VF	XF	Unc	BU
2001(u)	506,900	—	—	0.30	0.65	0.80
2002(u)	306,000	—	—	0.30	0.65	0.80
2003(u)	279,000	—	—	0.40	0.80	1.00
2004(u)	402,500	—	—	0.50	0.85	1.10
2005(u)	102,500	—	—	0.35	0.65	0.85
2006(u)	102,000	—	—	0.35	0.65	0.85
2007(u)	32,000	—	—	0.60	1.20	1.50

KM# 5 FLORIN

8.5000 g., Nickel Bonded Steel, 26 mm. **Ruler:** Beatrix 1980- **Obv:** Head left **Rev:** National arms **Edge:** Lettered **Edge Lettering:** GOD * ZiJ * MET * ONS

Date	Mintage	F	VF	XF	Unc	BU
2001(u)	406,900	—	—	0.65	1.25	2.25
2002(u)	206,000	—	—	0.75	1.30	2.50
2003(u)	179,000	—	—	0.80	1.50	3.00
2004(u)	410,000	—	—	0.70	1.35	2.35
2005(u)	352,500	—	—	0.70	1.35	2.35
2006(u)	402,000	—	—	0.70	1.35	2.35
2007(u)	502,000	—	—	0.70	1.35	2.35
2008(u)	—	—	—	0.70	1.35	2.35

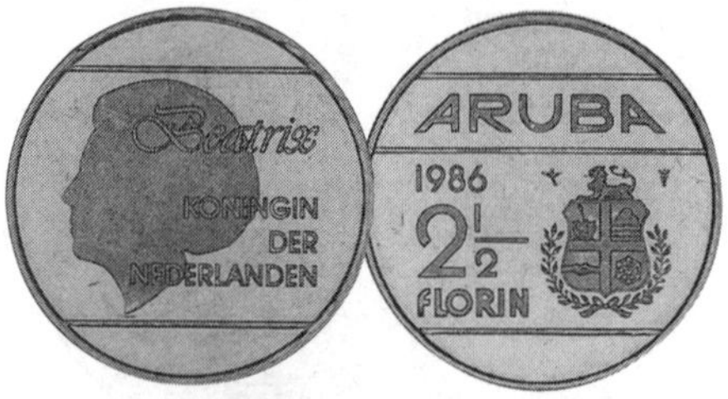

KM# 6 2-1/2 FLORIN

10.3000 g., Nickel Bonded Steel, 30 mm. **Ruler:** Beatrix 1980- **Obv:** Head left **Rev:** National arms **Edge:** Lettered **Edge Lettering:** GOD * ZiJ * MET * ONS

Date	Mintage	F	VF	XF	Unc	BU
2001(u)	6,900	—	—	—	3.50	5.00
Note: In sets only						
2002(u)	6,000	—	—	—	3.50	5.00
Note: In sets only						
2003(u)	4,000	—	—	—	3.50	5.00
Note: In sets only						
2004(u)	2,500	—	—	—	3.50	5.00
Note: In sets only						
2005(u)	2,500	—	—	—	3.50	5.00
Note: In sets only						
2006(u)	2,000	—	—	—	3.50	5.00
Note: In sets only						
2007(u)	2,000	—	—	—	3.50	5.00
2008(u)	—	—	—	—	3.50	5.00

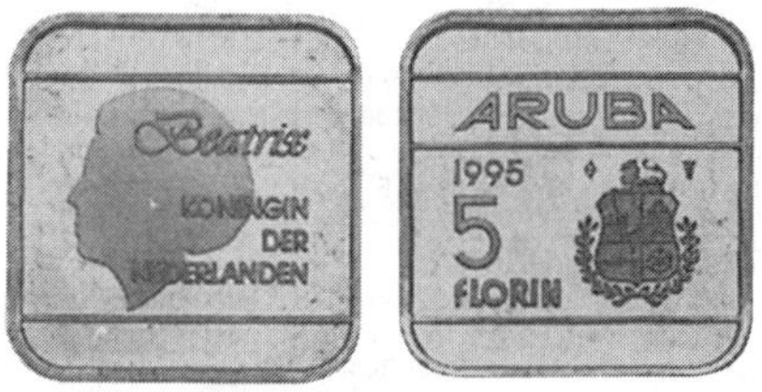

KM# 12 5 FLORIN

8.6400 g., Nickel Bonded Steel, 26 mm. **Ruler:** Beatrix 1980- **Obv:** Head left **Rev:** National arms **Edge:** Plain **Shape:** Square

Date	Mintage	F	VF	XF	Unc	BU
2001(u)	6,900	—	—	—	6.00	7.50
Note: In sets only						
2002(u)	6,000	—	—	—	6.00	7.50
Note: In sets only						
2003(u)	4,000	—	—	—	6.00	7.50
Note: In sets only						
2004(u)	2,500	—	—	—	7.00	8.50
Note: In sets only						
2005(u)	2,500	—	—	—	7.00	8.50
Note: In sets only						

KM# 25 5 FLORIN

11.9000 g., 0.9250 Silver 0.3539 oz. ASW, 29 mm. **Ruler:** Beatrix 1980- **Subject:** 50th Anniversary of Autonomy **Obv:** Head left **Rev:** Royal seal **Rev. Designer:** E. Fingal **Edge:** lettered **Edge Lettering:** GOD Z'J MET ONS

Date	Mintage	F	VF	XF	Unc	BU
2004 Proof	4,000	Value: 38.00				

KM# 34 5 FLORIN

11.9000 g., 0.9250 Silver 0.3539 oz. ASW, 29 mm. **Ruler:** Beatrix 1980- **Subject:** Queen's Silver Jubilee **Obv:** Head left **Rev:** Flag **Rev. Designer:** F.L. Croes **Edge:** lettered **Edge Lettering:** GOD Z'J MET ONS

Date	Mintage	F	VF	XF	Unc	BU
2005(u) Proof	4,000	Value: 32.50				

KM# 38 5 FLORIN

8.4000 g., Nickel Bonded Steel, 22.5 mm. **Ruler:** Beatrix 1980- **Obv:** Queen **Rev:** Value and arms **Edge:** Reeded and lettered **Edge Lettering:** GOD Z'J MET ONS **Shape:** Round

Date	Mintage	F	VF	XF	Unc	BU
2005(u)	827,500	—	—	—	5.50	7.00
2006(u)	102,000	—	—	—	5.50	8.00
2007(u)	52,000	—	—	—	5.50	8.00
2008(u)	—	—	—	—	5.50	7.00

KM# 20 10 FLORIN
25.0000 g., 0.9250 Silver 0.7435 oz. ASW, 38 mm. **Ruler:** Beatrix 1980- **Subject:** Green Sea Turtles **Obv:** Head left **Rev:** Seven sea turtles **Edge:** Plain **Designer:** E. Fingal

Date	Mintage	F	VF	XF	Unc	BU
2001(u) Prooflike	2,000	—	—	—	—	65.00

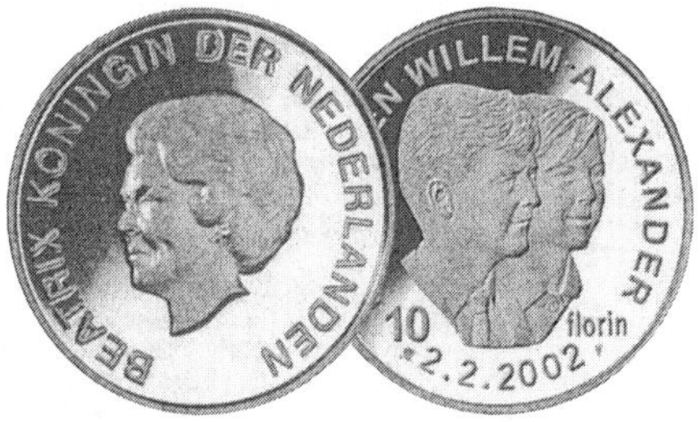

KM# 24 10 FLORIN
17.8000 g., 0.9250 Silver 0.5293 oz. ASW, 33 mm. **Ruler:** Beatrix 1980- **Subject:** Crown Prince's Wedding **Obv:** Head left **Rev:** Conjoined busts of prince and princess Maxima, right **Edge Lettering:** GOD ZIJ MET ONS **Designer:** G. Colley

Date	Mintage	F	VF	XF	Unc	BU
ND(2002)(u) Prooflike	5,000	—	—	—	—	40.00

KM# 27 10 FLORIN
25.0000 g., 0.9250 Silver 0.7435 oz. ASW **Ruler:** Beatrix 1980- **Obv:** Head left **Obv. Designer:** E. Fingal **Rev:** Sea Shells **Rev. Designer:** Royal Dutch Mint

Date	Mintage	F	VF	XF	Unc	BU
2003 Prooflike	2,000	—	—	—	—	60.00

KM# 28 10 FLORIN
25.0000 g., 0.9250 Silver 0.7435 oz. ASW **Ruler:** Beatrix 1980- **Obv:** Head left **Obv. Designer:** E. Fingal **Rev:** Snake **Rev. Designer:** Royal Dutch Mint

Date	Mintage	F	VF	XF	Unc	BU
2003 Prooflike	2,000	—	—	—	—	60.00

KM# 29 10 FLORIN
25.0000 g., 0.9250 Silver 0.7435 oz. ASW **Ruler:** Beatrix 1980- **Obv:** Head left **Obv. Designer:** E. Fingal **Rev:** Owl **Rev. Designer:** Royal Dutch Mint

Date	Mintage	F	VF	XF	Unc	BU
2003 Prooflike	1,000	—	—	—	—	75.00

KM# 30 10 FLORIN
25.0000 g., 0.9250 Silver 0.7435 oz. ASW **Ruler:** Beatrix 1980- **Obv:** Head left **Obv. Designer:** E. Fingal **Rev:** Frog **Rev. Designer:** Royal Dutch Mint

Date	Mintage	F	VF	XF	Unc	BU
2004 Prooflike	1,000	—	—	—	—	75.00

KM# 31 10 FLORIN
25.0000 g., 0.9250 Silver 0.7435 oz. ASW **Ruler:** Beatrix 1980- **Obv:** Head left **Obv. Designer:** E. Fingal **Rev:** Fish **Rev. Designer:** Royal Dutch Mint

Date	Mintage	F	VF	XF	Unc	BU
2004	1,000	—	—	—	—	75.00

KM# 33 10 FLORIN
1.2442 g., 0.9990 Gold 0.0400 oz. AGW, 13.9 mm. **Ruler:** Beatrix 1980- **Subject:** Death of Juliana **Obv:** Head left **Obv. Designer:** E. Fingal **Rev:** Juliana in center **Edge:** Reeded

Date	Mintage	F	VF	XF	Unc	BU
ND (2004)(u) Proof	10,000	Value: 60.00				

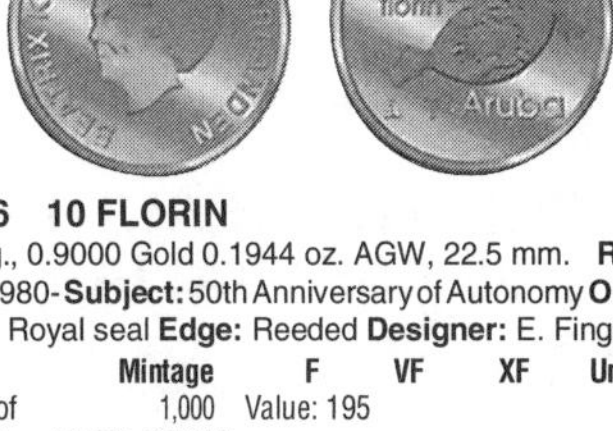

KM# 26 10 FLORIN
6.7200 g., 0.9000 Gold 0.1944 oz. AGW, 22.5 mm. **Ruler:** Beatrix 1980- **Subject:** 50th Anniversary of Autonomy **Obv:** Head left **Rev:** Royal seal **Edge:** Reeded **Designer:** E. Fingal

Date	Mintage	F	VF	XF	Unc	BU
2004 Proof	1,000	Value: 195				

KM# 35 10 FLORIN
6.7200 g., 0.9000 Gold 0.1944 oz. AGW, 22.5 mm. **Ruler:** Beatrix 1980- **Subject:** Queen's Silver Jubilee **Obv:** Head left **Rev:** Flag **Edge:** Reeded **Designer:** F.L. Croes

Date	Mintage	F	VF	XF	Unc	BU
2005(u) Proof	1,500	Value: 185				

KM# 36 10 FLORIN
25.0000 g., 0.9250 Silver 0.7435 oz. ASW, 38 mm. **Ruler:** Beatrix 1980- **Subject:** Status Aparte **Obv:** Queen's portrait **Rev:** Queen standing next to value and country name **Edge Lettering:** DIOS TA CU NOS

Date	Mintage	F	VF	XF	Unc	BU
2006(u) Proof	2,000	Value: 35.00				

KM# 22 25 FLORIN
25.0000 g., 0.9250 Silver 0.7435 oz. ASW, 38 mm. **Ruler:** Beatrix 1980- **Subject:** 15th Anniversary of Autonomy **Obv:** Head left **Rev:** National arms and inscription **Edge:** Plain

Date	Mintage	F	VF	XF	Unc	BU
2001(u) Proof	3,000	Value: 45.00				

KM# 37 25 FLORIN
6.7200 g., 0.9000 Gold 0.1944 oz. AGW, 22.5 mm. **Ruler:** Beatrix 1980- **Obv:** Queen's portrait **Rev:** Queen standing next to value and country name **Edge:** Reeded **Note:** Status Aparte

Date	Mintage	F	VF	XF	Unc	BU
2006(u) Proof	1,500	Value: 200				

KM# 23 100 FLORIN
6.7200 g., Gold, 22.5 mm. **Ruler:** Beatrix 1980- **Subject:** Independence **Obv:** Arms, treaty name, dates **Rev:** Head left **Edge:** Grained

Date	Mintage	F	VF	XF	Unc	BU
2001 Proof	1,000	Value: 275				

MINT SETS

KM#	Date	Mintage	Identification	Issue Price	Mkt Val
MS18	2001	—	KM#1-6, 12, with medal	15.00	14.50
MS19	2001 (7)	6,900	KM#1-6, 12	13.25	12.50
MS20	2002 (7)	6,000	KM# 1-6, 12	15.00	16.50
MS21	2003 (7)	4,000	KM# 1-6, 12	15.00	16.50
MS22	2004 (7)	2,500	KM# 1-6, 12	15.00	16.50
MS23	2005	2,500	KM# 1-6, 12	15.00	16.50
MS24	2006 (6)	2,000	KM# 1-6	15.00	16.50
MS25	2007 (5)	2,500	KM#1-2, 4-6	20.00	20.00

ASCENSION ISLAND

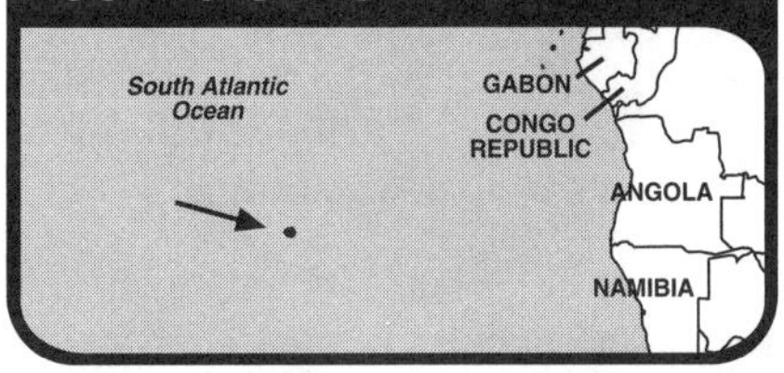

An island of volcanic origin, Ascension Island lies in the South Atlantic, 700 miles (1,100 km.) northwest of St. Helena. It has an area of 34 sq. mi. (88 sq. km.) on an island 9 miles (14 km.) long and 6 miles (10 km.) wide. Approximate population: 1,146. Although having little vegetation and scant rainfall, the island has a very healthy climate. The island is the nesting place for a large number of sea turtles and sooty terns. Phosphates and guano are the chief natural sources of income. Ascension is a dependency of the British Colony of St. Helena.

RULER
British

MINT MARKS
PM - Pobjoy Mint

BRITISH ADMINISTRATION

STANDARD COINAGE

KM# 13 50 PENCE
28.6300 g., Copper-Nickel, 38.6 mm. **Subject:** 75th Birthday of Queen Elizabeth **Obv:** Crowned bust right, denomination below **Obv. Designer:** Raphael Maklouf **Rev:** Crowned monogram above flowers within circle, date below **Edge:** Reeded

Date	Mintage	F	VF	XF	Unc	BU
2001	—	—	—	—	8.00	9.50

KM# 13a 50 PENCE
28.2800 g., 0.9250 Silver 0.8410 oz. ASW, 38.6 mm. **Subject:** Queen Elizabeth II's 75th Birthday **Obv:** Crowned bust right, denomination below **Obv. Designer:** Raphael Maklouf **Rev:** Crowned monogram above roses within circle, date below **Edge:** Reeded

Date	Mintage	F	VF	XF	Unc	BU
2001 Proof	10,000	Value: 40.00				

KM# 13b 50 PENCE
47.5400 g., 0.9166 Gold 1.4009 oz. AGW, 38.6 mm. **Subject:** Queen Elizabeth II's 75th Birthday **Obv:** Crowned bust right, denomination below **Obv. Designer:** Raphael Maklouf **Rev:** Crowned monogram above roses within circle, date below **Edge:** Reeded

Date	Mintage	F	VF	XF	Unc	BU
2001 Proof	75	Value: 1,250				

KM# 14 50 PENCE
28.6300 g., Copper-Nickel, 38.6 mm. **Subject:** Centennial - Queen Victoria's Death **Obv:** Crowned bust right, denomination below **Obv. Designer:** Raphael Maklouf **Rev:** Crowned bust left, three dates **Edge:** Reeded

Date	Mintage	F	VF	XF	Unc	BU
2001	—	—	—	—	8.00	9.50

KM# 14a 50 PENCE
28.2800 g., 0.9250 Silver 0.8410 oz. ASW, 38.6 mm. **Subject:** Centennial of Queen Victoria's Death **Obv:** Crowned bust right, denomination below **Obv. Designer:** Raphael Maklouf **Rev:** Crowned bust left, three dates **Edge:** Reeded

Date	Mintage	F	VF	XF	Unc	BU
2001 Proof	10,000	Value: 40.00				

KM# 14b 50 PENCE
47.5400 g., 0.9166 Gold 1.4009 oz. AGW, 38.6 mm. **Subject:** Centennial of Queen Victoria's Death **Obv:** Crowned bust right, denomination below **Obv. Designer:** Raphael Maklouf **Rev:** Crowned bust left, three dates **Edge:** Reeded

Date	Mintage	F	VF	XF	Unc	BU
2001 Proof	100	Value: 1,250				

KM# 15 50 PENCE
28.3500 g., Copper-Nickel, 38.6 mm. **Subject:** Queen's Golden Jubilee **Obv:** Crowned bust right, denomination below **Obv. Designer:** Raphael Maklouf **Rev:** Westminster Abby, monogram at left, circle surrounds, two dates below **Edge:** Reeded

Date	Mintage	F	VF	XF	Unc	BU
ND(2002)	—	—	—	—	8.00	9.50

KM# 15a 50 PENCE
28.2800 g., 0.9250 Silver 0.8410 oz. ASW, 38.6 mm. **Subject:** Queen Elizabeth II's Golden Jubilee **Obv:** Gold plated crowned bust right, denomination below **Obv. Designer:** Raphael Maklouf **Rev:** Monogram and Westminster Abbey within circle, dates below **Edge:** Reeded

Date	Mintage	F	VF	XF	Unc	BU
ND(2002) Proof	10,000	Value: 40.00				

KM# 18 50 PENCE
28.2800 g., Copper-Nickel, 38.6 mm. **Subject:** Death of Queen Mother **Obv:** Crowned bust right, denomination below **Obv. Designer:** Raphael Maklouf **Rev:** Queen Mother bust right, between her life dates **Edge:** Reeded

Date	Mintage	F	VF	XF	Unc	BU
ND(2002)	—	—	—	—	10.00	12.00

KM# 18a 50 PENCE
28.2800 g., 0.9250 Silver 0.8410 oz. ASW, 38.6 mm. **Subject:** Death of Queen Mother **Obv:** Crowned bust right, denomination below **Rev:** Queen Mother bust right, between her life dates **Edge:** Reeded

Date	Mintage	F	VF	XF	Unc	BU
ND(2002) Proof	10,000	Value: 35.00				

KM# 16 50 PENCE
28.3600 g., Copper-Nickel, 38.6 mm. **Subject:** Coronation Jubilee **Obv:** Crowned bust right, denomination below **Obv. Designer:** Raphael Maklouf **Rev:** Crown, two sceptres and the ampula **Edge:** Reeded

Date	Mintage	F	VF	XF	Unc	BU
ND (2003) Prooflike	—	—	—	—	10.00	12.00

KM# 16a 50 PENCE
28.2800 g., 0.9250 Silver 0.8410 oz. ASW, 38.6 mm. **Subject:** Queen Elizabeth II's - 50th Anniversary of Coronation **Obv:** Crowned bust right, denomination below **Obv. Designer:** Raphael Maklouf **Rev:** Crown, two sceptres and the ampula **Edge:** Reeded

Date	Mintage	F	VF	XF	Unc	BU
ND(2003) Proof	5,000	Value: 50.00				

KM# 16b 50 PENCE
39.9400 g., 0.9166 Gold 1.1770 oz. AGW, 38.6 mm. **Subject:** Queen Elizabeth II's - 50th Anniversary of Coronation **Obv:** Crowned bust right, denomination below **Obv. Designer:** Raphael Maklouf **Rev:** Crown, two sceptres and the ampula **Edge:** Reeded

Date	Mintage	F	VF	XF	Unc	BU
ND(2003) Proof	50	Value: 1,150				

KM# 17 50 PENCE
28.2800 g., Copper-Nickel, 38.6 mm. **Subject:** Queen Elizabeth II's- 50th Anniversary of Coronation **Obv:** Crowned head right, denomination below **Obv. Designer:** Raphael Maklouf **Rev:** Crowned monogram **Edge:** Reeded

Date	Mintage	F	VF	XF	Unc	BU
ND(2003)	—	—	—	—	10.00	12.00

KM# 17a 50 PENCE
28.2800 g., 0.9250 Silver 0.8410 oz. ASW, 38.6 mm. **Subject:** Queen Elizabeth II's- 50th Anniversary of Coronation **Obv:** Crowned head right, denomination below **Obv. Designer:** Raphael Maklouf **Rev:** Crowned monogram **Edge:** Reeded

Date	Mintage	F	VF	XF	Unc	BU
ND(2003) Proof	5,000	Value: 50.00				

KM# 17b 50 PENCE
39.9400 g., 0.9166 Gold 1.1770 oz. AGW, 38.6 mm. **Subject:** Queen Elizabeth II's - 50th Anniversary of Coronation **Obv:** Crowned bust right, denomination below **Obv. Designer:** Raphael Maklouf **Rev:** Crowned monogram **Edge:** Reeded

Date	Mintage	F	VF	XF	Unc	BU
ND(2003) Proof	50	Value: 1,150				

AUSTRALIA

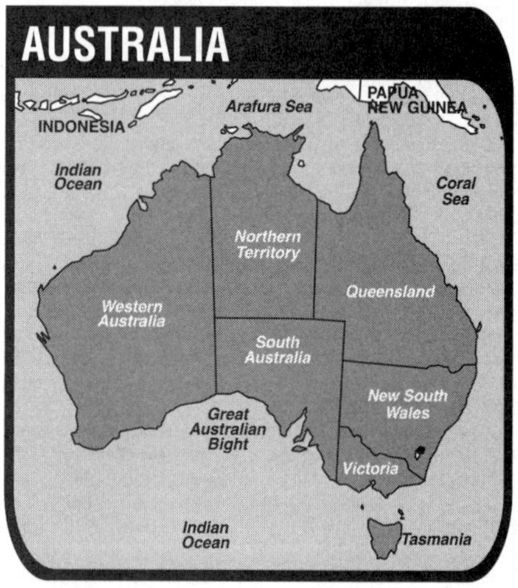

The Commonwealth of Australia, the smallest continent in the world, is located south of Indonesia between the Indian and Pacific oceans. It has an area of 2,967,893 sq. mi. (7,686,850 sq. km.) and an estimated population of 18.84 million. Capital: Canberra. Due to its early and sustained isolation, Australia is the habitat of such curious and unique fauna as the kangaroo, koala, platypus, wombat, echidna and frilled-necked lizard. The continent possesses extensive mineral deposits, the most important of which are iron ore, coal, gold, silver, nickel, uranium, lead and zinc. Raising livestock, mining and manufacturing are the principal industries. Chief exports are wool, meat, wheat, iron ore, coal and nonferrous metals.

Australia is a founding member of the Commonwealth of Nations. Elizabeth II is the Head of State as Queen of Australia; the Prime Minister is Head of Government.

NOTE: Home market grading of Australian coinage is generally stricter than USA practiced standards. The pricing in this catalog reflects strict home market grading standard.

RULER
British until 1942

MONETARY SYSTEM

Decimal Coinage (Commencing 1966)
100 Cents = 1 Dollar

COMMONWEALTH OF AUSTRALIA

MINT MARKS
M – Melbourne
P – Perth
S – Sydney
(sy) - Sydney

DECIMAL COINAGE

KM# 767 CENT

2.5900 g., Bronze, 17.53 mm. **Ruler:** Elizabeth II **Obv:** Head with tiara right **Obv. Designer:** Ian Rank-Broadley **Rev:** Feather-tailed glider **Rev. Designer:** Stuart Devlin **Edge:** Plain

Date	Mintage	F	VF	XF	Unc	BU
2006	—	—	—	—	2.25	3.00
Note: In sets only						
2006 Proof	—	Value: 5.00				

KM# 62a CENT

2.5900 g., 0.9990 Silver 0.0832 oz. ASW, 17.53 mm. **Ruler:** Elizabeth II **Obv:** Young bust right **Obv. Designer:** Arnold Machin **Rev:** Feather-tailed glider **Rev. Designer:** Stuart Devlin **Edge:** Plain

Date	Mintage	F	VF	XF	Unc	BU
2006 Proof	6,500	Value: 15.00				

KM# 767b CENT

5.6100 g., 0.9990 Gold 0.1802 oz. AGW, 17.53 mm. **Ruler:** Elizabeth II **Obv:** Head with tiara right **Obv. Designer:** Ian Rank-Broadley **Rev:** Feather-tailed glider **Rev. Designer:** Stuart Devlin **Edge:** Plain

Date	Mintage	F	VF	XF	Unc	BU
2006 Proof	300	Value: 600				

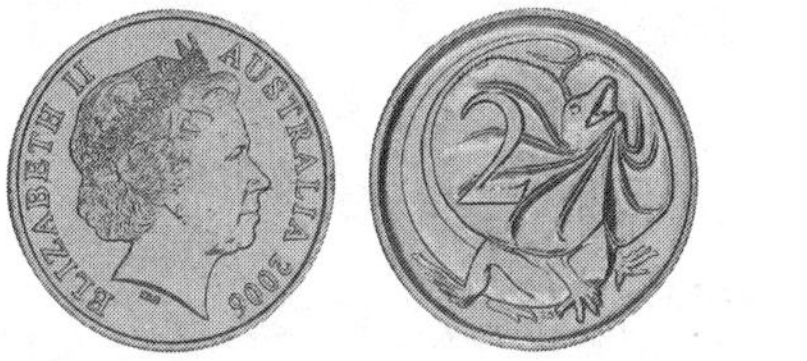

KM# 768 2 CENTS

5.1800 g., Bronze, 21.59 mm. **Ruler:** Elizabeth II **Obv:** Head with tiara right **Obv. Designer:** Ian Rank-Broadley **Rev:** Frilled-necked lizard

Date	Mintage	F	VF	XF	Unc	BU
2006	—	—	—	—	2.25	3.00
2006 Proof	—	Value: 5.00				

KM# 63a 2 CENTS

5.1800 g., 0.9990 Silver 0.1664 oz. ASW, 21.59 mm. **Ruler:** Elizabeth II **Obv:** Young bust right **Obv. Designer:** Arnold Machin **Rev:** Frilled-necked lizard **Rev. Designer:** Stuart Devlin **Edge:** Plain

Date	Mintage	F	VF	XF	Unc	BU
2006 Proof	6,500	Value: 15.00				

KM# 768b 2 CENTS

11.3100 g., 0.9990 Gold 0.3632 oz. AGW, 21.59 mm. **Ruler:** Elizabeth II **Obv:** Head with tiara right **Obv. Designer:** Ian Rank-Broadley **Rev:** Frilled-necked lizard **Rev. Designer:** Stuart Devlin **Edge:** Plain

Date	Mintage	F	VF	XF	Unc	BU
2006 Proof	300	Value: 600				

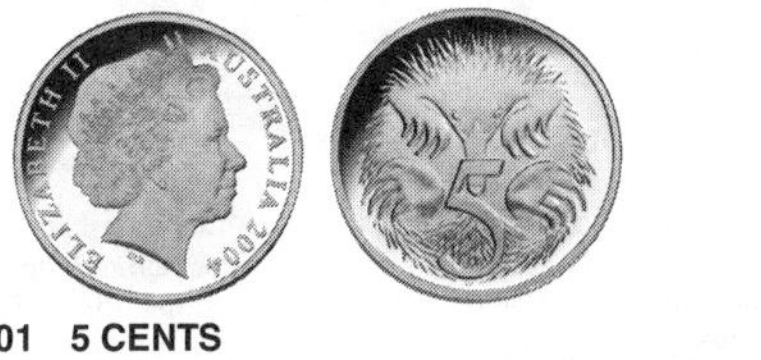

KM# 401 5 CENTS

2.8300 g., Copper-Nickel, 19.4 mm. **Ruler:** Elizabeth II **Obv:** Head with tiara right **Obv. Designer:** Ian Rank-Broadley **Rev:** Short-beaked Spiny Anteater **Rev. Designer:** Stuart Devlin **Edge:** Reeded

Date	Mintage	F	VF	XF	Unc	BU
2001	174,579,000	—	—	—	0.75	0.20
Note: Large obverse head, IRB spaced						
2001	Inc. above	—	—	—	0.75	0.20
Note: Smaller obverse head, RB joined						
2001 Proof	59,569	Value: 3.00				
2002	148,812,000	—	—	—	0.75	0.20
2002 Proof	39,514	Value: 2.50				
2003	113,470,000	—	—	—	0.75	0.20
2003 Proof	39,090	Value: 2.00				
2004	147,658,000	—	—	—	0.75	0.20
Note: Normal sized SD						
2004	Inc. above	—	—	—	—	0.20
Note: Smaller SD						
2004 Proof	50,000	Value: 2.50				
2005	194,300,000	—	—	—	0.75	0.20
Note: Normal sized SD						
2005	Inc. above	—	—	—	0.75	0.20
Note: Smaller SD						
2005 Proof	33,520	Value: 2.50				
2006	—	—	—	—	0.50	0.20
2006 Proof	—	Value: 2.50				
2007	—	—	—	—	0.50	0.20
2007 Proof	—	Value: 2.00				

KM# 401a 5 CENTS

6.0300 g., 0.9990 Gold 0.1937 oz. AGW, 19.41 mm. **Ruler:** Elizabeth II **Subject:** Federation Centennial **Obv:** Head with tiara right **Obv. Designer:** Ian Rank-Broadley **Rev:** Short-beaked Spiny Anteater **Rev. Designer:** Stuart Devlin

Date	Mintage	F	VF	XF	Unc	BU
2001 Proof	650	Value: 600				
2005 Proof	650	Value: 350				
2006 Proof	300	Value: 600				

KM# 401b 5 CENTS

3.2400 g., 0.9999 Silver 0.1042 oz. ASW, 19.41 mm. **Ruler:** Elizabeth II **Obv:** Head with tiara right **Obv. Designer:** Ian Rank-Broadley **Rev:** Short-beaked Spiny Anteater **Rev. Designer:** Stuart Devlin **Edge:** Reeded

Date	Mintage	F	VF	XF	Unc	BU
2003 Proof	6,500	Value: 20.00				
2004 Proof	6,500	Value: 15.00				
2005 Proof	6,500	Value: 15.00				

KM# 64a 5 CENTS

3.2400 g., 0.9990 Silver 0.1041 oz. ASW, 19.41 mm. **Ruler:** Elizabeth II **Obv:** Young bust right **Obv. Designer:** Arnold Machin **Rev:** Short-beaked Spiny Anteater **Rev. Designer:** Stuart Devlin **Edge:** Reeded

Date	Mintage	F	VF	XF	Unc	BU
2006 Proof	6,500	Value: 15.00				

KM# 402 10 CENTS

5.6600 g., Copper-Nickel, 23.6 mm. **Ruler:** Elizabeth II **Obv:** Head with tiara right **Obv. Designer:** Ian Rank-Broadley **Rev:** Superb Lyre-bird **Rev. Designer:** Stuart Devlin **Edge:** Reeded

Date	Mintage	F	VF	XF	Unc	BU
2001	109,357,000	—	—	—	1.00	0.50
Note: Large obverse head, IRB spaced						
2001	Inc. above	—	—	—	1.00	0.50
Note: Smaller obverse head, RB joined						
2001 Proof	59,569	Value: 3.00				
2002	70,329,000	—	—	—	1.00	0.50
2002 Proof	39,514	Value: 3.00				
2003	53,635,000	—	—	—	1.00	0.50
2003 Proof	39,090	Value: 3.00				
2004	147,658,000	—	—	—	1.00	0.50
2004 Proof	50,000	Value: 3.00				
2005	—	—	—	—	0.75	0.50
2005 Proof	33,520	Value: 3.00				
2006	—	—	—	—	0.75	0.50
2006 Proof	—	Value: 3.00				
2007	—	—	—	—	0.75	0.50
2007 Proof	—	Value: 3.00				

KM# 402a 10 CENTS

12.1400 g., 0.9999 Gold 0.3903 oz. AGW, 23.6 mm. **Ruler:** Elizabeth II **Subject:** Federation Centennial **Obv:** Head with tiara right **Obv. Designer:** Ian Rank-Broadley **Rev:** Super Lyrebird **Rev. Designer:** Stuart Devlin **Edge:** Reeded

Date	Mintage	F	VF	XF	Unc	BU
2001 Proof	650	Value: 650				
2005 Proof	650	Value: 350				
2006 Proof	300	Value: 650				

KM# 402b 10 CENTS

6.5700 g., 0.9999 Silver 0.2112 oz. ASW, 23.6 mm. **Ruler:** Elizabeth II **Obv:** Head with tiara right **Obv. Designer:** Ian Rank-Broadley **Rev:** Superb Lyrebird **Rev. Designer:** Stuart Devlin **Edge:** Reeded

Date	Mintage	F	VF	XF	Unc	BU
2003 Proof	6,500	Value: 20.00				
2004 Proof	6,500	Value: 15.00				
2005 Proof	6,500	Value: 15.00				

KM# 65a 10 CENTS

6.5700 g., 0.9990 Silver 0.2110 oz. ASW, 23.6 mm. **Ruler:** Elizabeth II **Obv:** Young bust right **Obv. Designer:** Arnold Machin **Rev:** Superb Lyrebird **Rev. Designer:** Stuart Devlin **Edge:** Reeded

Date	Mintage	F	VF	XF	Unc	BU
2006 Proof	6,500	Value: 15.00				

KM# 403 20 CENTS

11.3000 g., Copper-Nickel, 26.87 mm. **Ruler:** Elizabeth II **Obv:** Head with tiara right **Obv. Designer:** Ian Rank-Broadley **Rev:** Duckbill Platypus **Rev. Designer:** Stuart Devlin **Edge:** Reeded

Date	Mintage	F	VF	XF	Unc	BU
2001	81,967,000	—	—	—	1.75	0.80
Note: IRB spaced						
2001	Inc. above	—	—	—	1.75	0.80
Note: RB joined						
2001	Inc. above	—	—	—	1.50	0.80
Note: IRB joined						
2001 Proof	59,569	Value: 10.00				
2002	27,244,000	—	—	—	1.50	0.80
2002 Proof	39,514	Value: 6.00				
2004	74,609,000	—	—	—	1.50	0.80
Note: Small obverse head, flat top A						
2004	Est. 400,000	—	—	—	4.00	7.00
Note: Large obverse head, pointed A						
2004 Proof	50,000	Value: 6.00				
2005	1,600,000	—	—	—	5.00	7.50
2006	—	—	—	—	0.60	0.80
2006 Proof	—	Value: 6.00				
2007	—	—	—	—	1.25	0.80
2007 Proof	—	Value: 6.00				

KM# 819 20 CENTS

24.3600 g., 0.9990 Gold 0.7824 oz. AGW, 28.52 mm. **Ruler:** Elizabeth II **Obv:** Head with tiara right **Obv. Designer:** Ian Rank-Broadley **Rev:** Platypus with federation star **Rev. Designer:** Stuart Devlin **Edge:** Reeded

Date	Mintage	F	VF	XF	Unc	BU
2001 Proof	650	Value: 675				

KM# 532 20 CENTS

11.3100 g., Copper-Nickel, 28.52 mm. **Ruler:** Elizabeth II **Subject:** Centenary of Federation - Norfolk Island **Obv:** Head with tiara right **Obv. Designer:** Ian Rank-Broadley **Rev:** Norfolk Pine over map of island **Rev. Designer:** Megan Cummings **Edge:** Reeded

Date	Mintage	F	VF	XF	Unc	BU
2001	2,000,000	—	—	—	3.50	5.00
2001 Proof	—	Value: 10.00				

KM# 550 20 CENTS

11.3000 g., Copper-Nickel, 28.5 mm. **Ruler:** Elizabeth II **Series:** Centenary of Federation - New South Wales **Obv:** Head with tiara right **Obv. Designer:** Ian Rank-Broadley **Rev:** Flower on state map **Rev. Designer:** Joseph Neve **Edge:** Reeded

Date	Mintage	F	VF	XF	Unc	BU
2001	2,000,000	—	—	—	3.50	5.00
2001 Proof	—	Value: 10.00				

KM# 552 20 CENTS

11.3000 g., Copper-Nickel, 28.5 mm. **Ruler:** Elizabeth II **Series:** Centenary of Federation - Australian Capital Territory **Obv:** Head with tiara right **Obv. Designer:** Ian Rank-Broadley **Rev:** Parliament house, map, flowers **Rev. Designer:** Stacy Jo-Ann Paine **Edge:** Reeded **Note:** Prev. KM#551.

Date	Mintage	F	VF	XF	Unc	BU
2001	2,000,000	—	—	—	3.50	5.00
2001 Proof	—	Value: 5.00				

KM# 554 20 CENTS

11.3000 g., Copper-Nickel, 28.5 mm. **Ruler:** Elizabeth II **Series:** Centenary of Federation - Queensland **Obv:** Head with tiara right **Obv. Designer:** Ian Rank-Broadley **Rev:** Jennifer Gray **Edge:** Reeded

Date	Mintage	F	VF	XF	Unc	BU
2001	2,320,000	—	—	—	3.50	5.00
2001 Proof	—	Value: 10.00				

KM# 556 20 CENTS

11.3000 g., Copper-Nickel, 28.5 mm. **Ruler:** Elizabeth II **Series:** Centenary of Federation - Victoria **Obv:** Head with tiara right **Obv. Designer:** Ian Rank-Broadley **Rev:** Capital building **Rev. Designer:** Ryan Ladd & Mark Kennedy **Edge:** Reeded

Date	Mintage	F	VF	XF	Unc	BU
2001	2,000,000	—	—	—	3.50	5.00
2001 Proof	—	Value: 10.00				

KM# 558 20 CENTS

11.3000 g., Copper-Nickel, 28.5 mm. **Ruler:** Elizabeth II **Series:** Centenary of Federation - Northern Territory **Obv:** Head with tiara right **Obv. Designer:** Ian Rank-Broadley **Rev:** Two brolga cranes in ritual dance **Rev. Designer:** Lisa Brett **Edge:** Reeded

Date	Mintage	F	VF	XF	Unc	BU
2001	2,100,000	—	—	—	3.50	5.00
2001 Proof	—	Value: 10.00				

KM# 560 20 CENTS

11.3000 g., Copper-Nickel, 28.5 mm. **Ruler:** Elizabeth II **Series:** Centenary of Federation - South Australia **Obv:** Head with tiara right **Obv. Designer:** Ian Rank-Broadley **Rev:** Flower, landscape and stars **Rev. Designer:** Lisa Murphy **Edge:** Reeded

Date	Mintage	F	VF	XF	Unc	BU
2001	2,320,000	—	—	—	3.50	5.00
2001 Proof	—	Value: 10.00				

KM# 562 20 CENTS

11.3000 g., Copper-Nickel, 28.5 mm. **Ruler:** Elizabeth II **Series:** Centenary of Federation - Western Australia **Obv:** Head with tiara right **Obv. Designer:** Ian Rank-Broadley **Rev:** Rabbit-eared Bandicoot (bilby), plant and map **Rev. Designer:** Janice Ng **Edge:** Reeded

Date	Mintage	F	VF	XF	Unc	BU
2001	2,000,000	—	—	—	3.50	5.00
2001 Proof	—	Value: 10.00				

KM# 564 20 CENTS

11.3000 g., Copper-Nickel, 28.5 mm. **Ruler:** Elizabeth II **Series:** Centenary of Federation - Tasmania **Obv:** Head with tiara right **Obv. Designer:** Ian Rank-Broadley **Rev:** Tasmanian Devil on map **Rev. Designer:** Abbey MacDonald **Edge:** Reeded

Date	Mintage	F	VF	XF	Unc	BU
2001	2,000,000	—	—	—	3.50	5.00
2001 Proof	—	Value: 10.00				

KM# 589 20 CENTS

11.3000 g., Copper-Nickel, 28.5 mm. **Ruler:** Elizabeth II **Subject:** Sir Donald Bradman **Obv:** Head with tiara right **Obv. Designer:** Ian Rank-Broadley **Rev:** Cricket batsman **Edge:** Reeded

Date	Mintage	F	VF	XF	Unc	BU
2001	10,000,000	—	—	—	1.50	3.00

KM# 688 20 CENTS

11.3000 g., Copper-Nickel, 28.52 mm. **Ruler:** Elizabeth II **Obv:** Head with tiara right **Obv. Designer:** Ian Rank-Broadley **Rev:** Group of Australian Volunteers **Edge:** Reeded

Date	Mintage	F	VF	XF	Unc	BU
2003	7,600,000	—	—	—	1.50	2.50

KM# 688a 20 CENTS

11.3000 g., 0.9990 Silver 0.3629 oz. ASW, 28.52 mm. **Ruler:** Elizabeth II **Obv:** Head right **Rev:** Group of Australian Volunteers **Edge:** Reeded

Date	Mintage	F	VF	XF	Unc	BU
2003 Proof	6,500	Value: 25.00				

KM# 403a 20 CENTS

13.3600 g., 0.9999 Silver 0.4295 oz. ASW, 28.52 mm. **Ruler:** Elizabeth II **Obv:** Head with tiara right **Obv. Designer:** Ian Rank-Broadley **Rev:** Platypus **Rev. Designer:** Stuart Devlin **Edge:** Reeded

Date	Mintage	F	VF	XF	Unc	BU
2003 Proof	6,500	Value: 20.00				
2004 Proof	6,500	Value: 15.00				
2006 Proof	6,500	Value: 15.00				

KM# 688b 20 CENTS

24.3600 g., 0.9990 Gold 0.7824 oz. AGW, 28.52 mm. **Ruler:** Elizabeth II **Obv:** Head with tiara right **Obv. Designer:** Ian Rank-Broadley **Rev:** Group of Australian Volunteers **Rev. Designer:** Vladimir Gottwald **Edge:** Reeded

Date	Mintage	F	VF	XF	Unc	BU
2003 Proof	650	Value: 675				

KM# 745 20 CENTS

11.3000 g., Copper-Nickel, 28.52 mm. **Ruler:** Elizabeth II **Obv:** Head right **Rev:** Soldier with wife and child **Edge:** Reeded

Date	Mintage	F	VF	XF	Unc	BU
2005 Proof	—	Value: 6.00				
2005	33,500,000	—	—	—	1.50	2.00

KM# 745a 20 CENTS

13.3600 g., 0.9990 Silver 0.4291 oz. ASW, 28.52 mm. **Ruler:** Elizabeth II **Obv:** Head right **Rev:** Soldier with wife and child **Edge:** Reeded

Date	Mintage	F	VF	XF	Unc	BU
2005 Proof	6,500	Value: 15.00				

KM# 745b 20 CENTS

24.3600 g., 0.9999 Gold 0.7831 oz. AGW, 28.52 mm. **Ruler:** Elizabeth II **Obv:** Head right **Rev:** Soldier with wife and child **Edge:** Reeded

Date	Mintage	F	VF	XF	Unc	BU
2005 Proof	650	Value: 675				

KM# 403b 20 CENTS

24.5600 g., 0.9999 Gold 0.7895 oz. AGW, 28.52 mm. **Ruler:** Elizabeth II **Subject:** Federation Centennial **Obv:** Head with tiara right **Obv. Designer:** Ian Rank-Broadley **Rev:** Duckbill Platyus **Rev. Designer:** Stuart Devlin **Edge:** Reeded

Date	Mintage	F	VF	XF	Unc	BU
2006 Proof	300	Value: 675				

KM# 66a 20 CENTS

13.3600 g., 0.9990 Silver 0.4291 oz. ASW, 28.52 mm. **Ruler:** Elizabeth II **Obv:** Young bust right **Obv. Designer:** Arnold Machin **Rev:** Platypus **Rev. Designer:** Stuart Devlin **Edge:** Reeded

Date	Mintage	F	VF	XF	Unc	BU
2006 Proof	6,500	Value: 15.00				

KM# 820 20 CENTS

11.3100 g., Copper-Nickel, 28.52 mm. **Ruler:** Elizabeth II **Subject:** Year of the Surf Lifesaver **Obv:** Head with tiara right **Obv. Designer:** Ian Rank-Broadley **Rev:** Lifesaver working line **Rev. Designer:** Vladimir Gottwald **Edge:** Reeded

Date	Mintage	F	VF	XF	Unc	BU
2007	—	—	—	—	3.50	6.00
2007 Proof	—	Value: 10.00				

KM# 599 25 CENTS (The Dump)

7.7750 g., 0.9990 Silver 0.2497 oz. ASW, 24.8 mm. **Ruler:** Elizabeth II **Obv:** Head with tiara right **Obv. Designer:** Ian Rank-Broadley **Rev:** Parliament House **Edge:** Plain **Shape:** 7-pointed star **Note:** "The Dump" portion of the "Holey Dollar" KM#598.

Date	Mintage	F	VF	XF	Unc	BU
2001 Prooflike	30,000	—	—	—	15.00	17.50

KM# 1010 25 CENTS (The Dump)

0.9990 Silver Gilt, 17.80 mm. **Ruler:** Elizabeth II **Obv:** Bust with tiara right **Obv. Legend:** ELIZABETH II - AUSTRALIA **Obv. Designer:** Ian Rank-Broadley **Rev:** 4 Chinese characters **Rev. Legend:** LUNAR NEW YEAR - GOOD FORTUNE & PROSPERITY

Date	Mintage	F	VF	XF	Unc	BU
2007 Proof	8,888	Value: 35.00				

KM# 533 50 CENTS

15.6000 g., Copper-Nickel, 31.51 mm. **Ruler:** Elizabeth II **Subject:** Centennial - Norfolk Island Federation **Obv:** Head with tiara right **Obv. Designer:** Ian Rank-Broadley **Rev:** Norfolk Island coat of arms **Edge:** Plain **Shape:** 12-sided

Date	Mintage	F	VF	XF	Unc	BU
2001	2,000,000	—	—	—	3.50	5.00
2001 Proof	—	Value: 12.50				

KM# 535 50 CENTS

16.8860 g., 0.9990 Silver 0.5423 oz. ASW, 32.1 mm. **Ruler:** Elizabeth II **Subject:** Year of the Snake **Obv:** Head right **Rev:** Snake with eggs **Edge:** Plain

Date	Mintage	F	VF	XF	Unc	BU
2001P Proof	5,000	Value: 30.00				
2001	500,000	—	—	—	12.50	10.00

KM# 551 50 CENTS

15.5500 g., Copper-Nickel, 31.5 mm. **Ruler:** Elizabeth II **Series:** Centenary of Federation - New South Wales **Obv:** Head with tiara right **Rev:** New South Wales state arms **Edge:** Plain **Shape:** 12-sided

Date	Mintage	F	VF	XF	Unc	BU
2001	3,000,000	—	—	—	3.50	5.00
2001 Proof	—	Value: 12.50				

KM# 553 50 CENTS

15.5500 g., Copper-Nickel, 31.5 mm. **Ruler:** Elizabeth II **Series:** Centenary of Federation - Australian Capital Territory **Obv:** Head right **Rev:** Austrian Capital Territory arms **Edge:** Plain **Shape:** 12-sided

Date	Mintage	F	VF	XF	Unc	BU
2001 Proof	—	Value: 12.50				
2001	2,000,000	—	—	—	3.50	5.00

KM# 555 50 CENTS

15.5500 g., Copper-Nickel, 31.5 mm. **Ruler:** Elizabeth II **Series:** Centenary of Federation - Queensland **Obv:** Head with tiara right **Rev:** Queensland state arms **Edge:** Plain **Shape:** 12-sided

Date	Mintage	F	VF	XF	Unc	BU
2001 Proof	—	Value: 12.50				
2001	2,300,000	—	—	—	3.50	5.00

KM# 557 50 CENTS

15.5500 g., Copper-Nickel, 31.5 mm. **Ruler:** Elizabeth II **Series:** Centenary of Federation - Victoria **Obv:** Head with tiara right **Rev:** Victoria state arms **Edge:** Plain **Shape:** 12-sided

Date	Mintage	F	VF	XF	Unc	BU
2001 Proof	—	Value: 12.50				
2001	2,800,000	—	—	—	3.50	5.00

KM# 559 50 CENTS

15.5500 g., Copper-Nickel, 31.5 mm. **Ruler:** Elizabeth II **Series:** Centenary of Federation - Northern Territory **Obv:** Head with tiara right **Rev:** Northern Territory state arms **Edge:** Plain **Shape:** 12-sided

Date	Mintage	F	VF	XF	Unc	BU
2001 Proof	—	Value: 12.50				
2001	2,100,000	—	—	—	3.50	5.00

KM# 561 50 CENTS

15.5500 g., Copper-Nickel, 31.5 mm. **Ruler:** Elizabeth II **Series:** Centenary of Federation - South Australia **Obv:** Head with tiara right **Rev:** South Australia state arms **Edge:** Plain **Shape:** 12-sided

Date	Mintage	F	VF	XF	Unc	BU
2001 Proof	—	Value: 12.50				
2001	2,400,000	—	—	—	3.50	5.00

KM# 563 50 CENTS

15.5500 g., Copper-Nickel, 31.5 mm. **Ruler:** Elizabeth II **Series:** Centenary of Federation - Western Australia **Obv:** Head with tiara right **Rev:** Western Australia state arms **Edge:** Plain **Shape:** 12-sided

Date	Mintage	F	VF	XF	Unc	BU
2001 Proof	—	Value: 12.50				
2001	2,400,000	—	—	—	3.50	5.00

KM# 565 50 CENTS

15.5500 g., Copper-Nickel, 31.5 mm. **Ruler:** Elizabeth II **Series:** Centenary of Federation - Tasmania **Obv:** Head with tiara right **Rev:** Tasmania state arms **Edge:** Plain **Shape:** 12-sided

Date	Mintage	F	VF	XF	Unc	BU
2001 Proof	—	Value: 12.50				
2001	2,200,000	—	—	—	3.50	5.00

KM# 491.2 50 CENTS

15.5500 g., Copper-Nickel, 31.51 mm. **Ruler:** Elizabeth II **Subject:** Federation Centennial **Obv:** Elizabeth II right **Rev:** Multicolor arms above value **Edge:** Plain **Shape:** 12-sided

Date	Mintage	F	VF	XF	Unc	BU
2001 Proof	60,000	Value: 20.00				

KM# 491.1a 50 CENTS

33.8800 g., 0.9999 Gold 1.0891 oz. AGW, 31.51 mm. **Ruler:** Elizabeth II **Subject:** Federation Centennial **Obv:** Elizabeth II **Rev:** Commonwealth arms above value

Date	Mintage	F	VF	XF	Unc	BU
2001 Proof	650	Value: 950				

KM# 491.1 50 CENTS

Copper-Nickel, 31.5 mm. **Ruler:** Elizabeth II **Subject:** Centenary of Federation, 1901-2001 **Obv:** Head with tiara right **Rev:** Commonwealth coat of arms **Edge:** Plain **Shape:** 12-sided **Note:** Prev. KM#491.

Date	Mintage	F	VF	XF	Unc	BU
2001	43,149,600	—	—	—	2.00	3.00

KM# 491.2a 50 CENTS

Copper-Nickel, 31.5 mm. **Ruler:** Elizabeth II **Subject:** Centenary of Federation, 1901-2001 **Obv:** Head with tiara right **Rev:** Multicolored Commonwealth coat of arms **Edge:** Plain **Shape:** 12-sided **Note:** Prev. KM#491a.

Date	Mintage	F	VF	XF	Unc	BU
2001 Proof	—	Value: 27.50				

KM# 602 50 CENTS

15.5500 g., Copper-Nickel, 31.5 mm. **Ruler:** Elizabeth II **Subject:** The Outback Region **Obv:** Head right **Rev:** Windmill **Rev. Designer:** Wojciech Pietronik **Edge:** Plain **Shape:** 12-sided

Date	Mintage	F	VF	XF	Unc	BU
2002	11,507,000	—	—	—	3.00	4.50
2002 Proof	39,000	Value: 10.00				

KM# 645 50 CENTS

15.5500 g., Copper-Nickel, 31.51 mm. **Ruler:** Elizabeth II **Subject:** Queen's 50th Anniversary of Succession **Obv:** Head right **Rev:** Crown and star **Rev. Designer:** Peter Soobik **Shape:** 12-sided

Date	Mintage	F	VF	XF	Unc	BU
2002	32,102	—	—	—	40.00	60.00

Note: Issued only in PNC cover

KM# 645a 50 CENTS

18.2400 g., 0.9990 Silver 0.5858 oz. ASW, 31.51 mm. **Ruler:** Elizabeth II **Subject:** Queen's 50th Anniversary of Accession **Obv:** Head right **Rev:** Crown and star **Rev. Designer:** Peter Soobik **Shape:** 12-sided

Date	Mintage	F	VF	XF	Unc	BU
2002 Proof	13,500	Value: 45.00				

KM# 689 50 CENTS

15.5500 g., Copper-Nickel, 31.5 mm. **Ruler:** Elizabeth II **Obv:** Head right **Rev:** Value within circle of volunteer activities **Rev. Designer:** Wojciech Pietronik **Edge:** Plain **Shape:** 12-sided

Date	Mintage	F	VF	XF	Unc	BU
2003	13,927,000	—	—	—	3.00	4.50

KM# 689a 50 CENTS

15.5500 g., 0.9990 Silver 0.4994 oz. ASW, 31.5 mm. **Ruler:** Elizabeth II **Obv:** Head right **Rev:** Value within circle of volunteer activities

Date	Mintage	F	VF	XF	Unc	BU
2003 Proof	6,500	Value: 35.00				

KM# 799 50 CENTS

14.0900 g., Aluminum-Bronze, 31.51 mm. **Ruler:** Elizabeth II **Subject:** 50th Anniversary of the Coronation of Elizabeth II **Obv:** Head with tiara right **Obv. Designer:** Ian Rank-Broadley **Rev:** Crown, Federation star, dates **Rev. Designer:** Peter Soobik **Edge:** Plain **Shape:** 12-sided

Date	Mintage	F	VF	XF	Unc	BU
2006	65,003	—	—	—	15.00	—

KM# 799a 50 CENTS

18.2400 g., 0.9990 Silver 0.5858 oz. ASW, 31.51 mm. **Ruler:** Elizabeth II **Subject:** 50th Anniversary of the Coronation of Elizabeth II **Obv:** Head with tiara right **Obv. Designer:** Ian Rank-Broadley **Rev:** Crown, Federation star, dates **Rev. Designer:** Peter Soobik **Edge:** Plain **Shape:** 12-sided

Date	Mintage	F	VF	XF	Unc	BU
2003 Proof	6,967	Value: 35.00				

KM# 404 50 CENTS

15.5500 g., Copper-Nickel, 31.51 mm. **Ruler:** Elizabeth II **Obv:** Head with tiara right **Obv. Designer:** Ian Rank-Broadley **Rev:** Australian coat of arms with kangaroo and emu supporters **Rev. Designer:** Stuart Devlin **Edge:** Plain **Shape:** 12-sided

Date	Mintage	F	VF	XF	Unc	BU
2004 Proof	—	Value: 10.00				
2004	17,918,000	—	—	—	2.00	3.00
2005	30,000	—	—	—	25.00	40.00

Note: Issued as part of a PNC only

Date	Mintage	F	VF	XF	Unc	BU
2006	—	—	—	—	1.00	1.50
2007	—	—	—	—	1.00	1.50

KM# 404a 50 CENTS
18.2400 g., 0.9999 Silver 0.5863 oz. ASW, 31.51 mm. **Ruler:** Elizabeth II **Obv:** Head with tiara right **Obv. Designer:** Ian Rank-Broadley **Rev:** Arms **Rev. Designer:** Stuart Devlin **Edge:** Plain **Shape:** 12-sided

Date	Mintage	F	VF	XF	Unc	BU
2004 Proof	6,500	Value: 15.00				

KM# 694 50 CENTS
15.5500 g., Copper-Nickel, 31.5 mm. **Ruler:** Elizabeth II **Obv:** Head with tiara right **Obv. Designer:** Ian Rank-Broadley **Rev:** Koala, Lorikeet (bird) and a Wombat **Rev. Designer:** John Serrano **Edge:** Plain **Shape:** 12-sided

Date	Mintage	F	VF	XF	Unc	BU
2004	10,577,000	—	—	—	3.00	4.50

KM# 694a 50 CENTS
18.2400 g., 0.9990 Silver 0.5858 oz. ASW, 31.5 mm. **Ruler:** Elizabeth II **Obv:** Head with tiara right **Rev:** Wombat, lorikeet and koala **Rev. Designer:** John Serrano **Edge:** Plain **Shape:** 12-sided

Date	Mintage	F	VF	XF	Unc	BU
2004 Proof	8,203	Value: 45.00				

KM# 746 50 CENTS
15.5500 g., Copper-Nickel, 31.51 mm. **Ruler:** Elizabeth II **Obv:** Head with tiara right **Rev:** Military cemetery scene **Edge:** Plain **Shape:** 12-sided

Date	Mintage	F	VF	XF	Unc	BU
2005 Proof	—	Value: 10.00				
2005	11,033,000	—	—	—	2.50	3.50

KM# 746a 50 CENTS
18.2400 g., 0.9990 Silver 0.5858 oz. ASW, 31.51 mm. **Ruler:** Elizabeth II **Obv:** Head with tiara right **Rev:** Military cemetery scene **Edge:** Plain **Shape:** 12-sided

Date	Mintage	F	VF	XF	Unc	BU
2005 Proof	6,500	Value: 28.00				

KM# 746b 50 CENTS
33.6300 g., 0.9999 Gold 1.0811 oz. AGW, 31.51 mm. **Ruler:** Elizabeth II **Obv:** Head with tiara right **Rev:** Military cemetery scene **Edge:** Plain **Shape:** 12-sided

Date	Mintage	F	VF	XF	Unc	BU
2005 Proof	650	Value: 950				

KM# 769 50 CENTS
Copper-Nickel **Ruler:** Elizabeth II **Subject:** Commonweath Games, Secondary School Design Competition **Obv:** Head with tiara right **Rev:** Athletes **Rev. Designer:** Kelly Jost

Date	Mintage	F	VF	XF	Unc	BU
2005	20,500,000	—	—	—	2.50	3.50
2005 Proof	5,402	Value: 35.00				

KM# 814 50 CENTS
Silver **Ruler:** Elizabeth II **Subject:** Bullion Lunar Year - Rooster **Obv:** Head with tiara right

Date	Mintage	F	VF	XF	Unc	BU
2005	—	—	—	—	—	10.00

KM# 1001 50 CENTS
15.5500 g., Copper Nickel, 31.50 mm. **Ruler:** Elizabeth II **Subject:** Squash **Obv:** Head with tiarra right **Obv. Legend:** ELIZABETH II - AUSTRALIA **Obv. Designer:** Ian Rank-Broadley **Rev:** Player, Melbourne 2006 logo **Rev. Legend:** XVIII COMMONWEALTH GAMES **Rev. Designer:** Wojciech Pietranik **Edge:** Plain **Shape:** 12-sided

Date	Mintage	F	VF	XF	Unc	BU
2006	—	—	—	—	—	—

KM# 1002 50 CENTS
15.5500 g., Copper Nickel, 31.50 mm. **Ruler:** Elizabeth II **Subject:** Lawn bowling **Obv:** Head with tiarre right **Obv. Legend:** ELIZABETH II - AUSTRALIA **Obv. Designer:** Ian Rank-Broadlet **Rev:** Bowler, Melbourne 2006 **Rev. Legend:** XVIII COMMONWEALTH GAMES **Rev. Designer:** Wojciech Pietranik **Edge:** Plain **Shape:** 12-sided

Date	Mintage	F	VF	XF	Unc	BU
2006	—	—	—	—	—	—

KM# 1003 50 CENTS
15.5500 g., Copper Nickel, 31.50 mm. **Ruler:** Elizabeth II **Subject:** Boxing **Obv:** Head with tiarra right **Obv. Legend:** ELIZABETH II - AUSTRALIA **Obv. Designer:** Ian Rank-Broadley **Rev:** Boxer, Melbourne 2006 logo **Rev. Legend:** XVIII COMMONWEALTH GAMES **Rev. Designer:** Wojciech Pietranik **Edge:** Plain **Shape:** 12-sided

Date	Mintage	F	VF	XF	Unc	BU
2006	—	—	—	—	—	—

KM# 1004 50 CENTS
Aluminum-Bronze, 30.00 mm. **Ruler:** Elizabeth II **Obv:** Head with tiara right **Obv. Legend:** ELIZABETH II - AUSTRALIA **Obv. Designer:** Ian Rank-Broadley **Rev:** Everage head facing, multicolor **Rev. Legend:** DAME EDNA EVERAGE - 50TH ANNIVERSARY

Date	Mintage	F	VF	XF	Unc	BU
ND(2006)P	—	—	—	—	—	—

KM# 801a 50 CENTS
18.2400 g., 0.9990 Silver 0.5858 oz. ASW, 31.51 mm. **Ruler:** Elizabeth II **Subject:** 80th Birthday of Queen Elizabeth II **Obv:** Head with tiara right **Obv. Designer:** Ian Rank-Broadley **Rev:** Royal Cipher **Rev. Designer:** Stuart Devlin **Edge:** Plain **Shape:** 12-sided **Note:** Partially Gold-plated.

Date	Mintage	F	VF	XF	Unc	BU
2006 Proof	7,500	Value: 50.00				

KM# 802a 50 CENTS
18.2400 g., 0.9990 Silver 0.5858 oz. ASW, 31.51 mm. **Ruler:** Elizabeth II **Subject:** Visit of Queen Elizabeth II **Obv:** Head with tiara right **Obv. Designer:** Ian Rank-Broadley **Rev:** Australian map and world globe **Rev. Designer:** Stuart Devlin **Edge:** Plain **Shape:** 12-sided **Note:** Partially Gold-plated.

Date	Mintage	F	VF	XF	Unc	BU
2006 Proof	7,500	Value: 50.00				

KM# 67a 50 CENTS
18.2400 g., 0.9990 Silver 0.5858 oz. ASW, 31.51 mm. **Ruler:** Elizabeth II **Obv:** Young bust right **Obv. Designer:** Arnold Machin **Rev:** Australian coat of arms **Rev. Designer:** Stuart Devlin **Edge:** Reeded **Shape:** Round

Date	Mintage	F	VF	XF	Unc	BU
2006 Proof	6,500	Value: 50.00				

KM# 801 50 CENTS
15.5500 g., Copper-Nickel, 31.51 mm. **Ruler:** Elizabeth II **Subject:** 80th Birthday of Queen Elizabeth II **Obv:** Head with tiara right **Obv. Designer:** Ian Rank-Broadley **Rev:** Royal Cipher **Rev. Designer:** Stuart Devlin **Edge:** Plain **Shape:** 12-sided

Date	Mintage	F	VF	XF	Unc	BU
2006	—	—	—	—	5.00	8.50

KM# 802 50 CENTS
15.5500 g., Copper-Nickel, 31.51 mm. **Ruler:** Elizabeth II **Subject:** Visit of Queen Elizabeth II **Obv:** Head with tiara right **Obv. Designer:** Ian Rank-Broadley **Rev:** Australian map and world globe **Rev. Designer:** Stuart Devlin **Edge:** Plain **Shape:** 12-sided

Date	Mintage	F	VF	XF	Unc	BU
2006	—	—	—	—	5.00	8.50

KM# 821 50 CENTS
13.2800 g., 0.8000 Silver 0.3416 oz. ASW, 31.51 mm. **Ruler:** Elizabeth II **Obv:** Head with tiara right **Obv. Designer:** Ian Rank-Broadley **Rev:** Australian coat of arms **Rev. Designer:** Stuart Devlin **Edge:** Reeded **Shape:** Round

Date	Mintage	F	VF	XF	Unc	BU
2006 Proof	—	Value: 50.00				

KM# 770 50 CENTS
15.5500 g., Copper-Nickel, 31.50 mm. **Ruler:** Elizabeth II **Subject:** Basketball **Obv:** Head with tiara right **Obv. Legend:** ELIZABETH II - AUSTRALIA **Obv. Designer:** Ian Rank-Broadley **Rev:** Basketball player shooting basket, Melbourne 2006 logo at left **Rev. Legend:** XVIII COMMONWEALTH GAMES **Rev. Designer:** Wojciech Pietranik **Edge:** Plain **Shape:** 12-sided

Date	Mintage	F	VF	XF	Unc	BU
2006	5,002	—	—	—	8.50	10.00

KM# 771 50 CENTS
15.5500 g., Copper-Nickel, 31.50 mm. **Ruler:** Elizabeth II **Subject:** Hockey **Obv:** Head with tiara right **Obv. Legend:** ELIZABETH II - AUSTRALIA **Obv. Designer:** Ian Rank-Broadley **Rev:** Hockey player hitting puck, Melboune 2006 logo at upper left **Rev. Legend:** XVIII COMMONWEALTH GAMES **Rev. Designer:** Wojciech Pietranik **Edge:** Plain **Shape:** 12-sided

Date	Mintage	F	VF	XF	Unc	BU
2006	4,082	—	—	—	8.50	10.00

KM# 821a 50 CENTS
25.3000 g., 0.9990 Gold 0.8126 oz. AGW, 31.51 mm. **Ruler:** Elizabeth II **Obv:** Head with tiara right **Obv. Designer:** Ian Rank-Broadley **Rev:** Australian coat of arms **Rev. Designer:** Stuart Devlin **Edge:** Reeded **Shape:** Round

Date	Mintage	F	VF	XF	Unc	BU
2006 Proof	300	Value: 850				

KM# 772 50 CENTS
15.5500 g., Copper-Nickel, 31.50 mm. **Ruler:** Elizabeth II **Subject:** Shooting **Obv:** Head with tiara right **Obv. Legend:** ELIZABETH II - AUSTRALIA **Obv. Designer:** Ian Rank-Broadley **Rev:** Shooter, Melbourne 2006 logo at upper right **Rev. Legend:** XVIII COMMONWEALTH GAMES **Rev. Designer:** Wojciech Pietranik **Edge:** Plain **Shape:** 12-sided

Date	Mintage	F	VF	XF	Unc	BU
2006	4,302	—	—	—	8.50	10.00

KM# 773 50 CENTS
15.5500 g., Copper-Nickel, 31.50 mm. **Ruler:** Elizabeth II **Subject:** Weightlifting **Obv:** Head with tiara right **Obv. Legend:** ELIZABETH II - AUSTRALIA **Obv. Designer:** Ian Rank-Broadley **Rev:** Weightlifter holding barbells above head, Melbourne 2006 logo at left **Rev. Legend:** XVIII COMMONWEALTH GAMES **Rev. Designer:** Wojciech Pietranik **Edge:** Plain **Shape:** 12-sided

Date	Mintage	F	VF	XF	Unc	BU
2006	4,402	—	—	—	8.50	10.00

KM# 774 50 CENTS
15.5500 g., Copper-Nickel, 31.50 mm. **Ruler:** Elizabeth II **Subject:** Gymnastics **Obv:** Head with tiara right **Obv. Legend:** ELIZABETH II - AUSTRALIA **Obv. Designer:** Ian Rank-Broadley **Rev:** Gymnast standing with right leg up, Melbourne 2006 logo at left **Rev. Legend:** XVIII COMMONWEALTH GAMES **Rev. Designer:** Wojciech Pietranik **Edge:** Plain **Shape:** 12-sided

Date	Mintage	F	VF	XF	Unc	BU
2006	3,000	—	—	—	8.50	10.00

KM# 775 50 CENTS
15.5500 g., Copper-Nickel, 31.50 mm. **Ruler:** Elizabeth II **Subject:** Rugby 7's **Obv:** Head with tiara right **Obv. Legend:** ELIZABETH II - AUSTRALIA **Obv. Designer:** Ian Rank-Broadley **Rev:** Rugby player running right, Melbourne 2006 logo at upper left **Rev. Legend:** XVIII COMMONWEALTH GAMES **Rev. Designer:** Wojciech Pietranik **Edge:** Plain **Shape:** 12-sided

Date	Mintage	F	VF	XF	Unc	BU
2006	2,992	—	—	—	8.50	10.00

KM# 776 50 CENTS
15.5500 g., Copper-Nickel, 31.50 mm. **Ruler:** Elizabeth II **Subject:** Cucling **Obv:** Head with tiara right **Obv. Legend:** ELIZABETH II - AUSTRALIA **Obv. Designer:** Ian Rank-Broadley **Rev:** Cyclist heading right, Melbourne 2006 logo at upper right **Rev. Legend:** XVIII COMMONWEALTH GAMES **Rev. Designer:** Wojciech Pietranik **Edge:** Plain **Shape:** 12-sided

Date	Mintage	F	VF	XF	Unc	BU
2006	—	—	—	—	8.50	10.00

KM# 777 50 CENTS
15.5500 g., Copper-Nickel, 31.50 mm. **Ruler:** Elizabeth II **Subject:** Athletics **Obv:** Head with tiara right **Obv. Legend:** ELIZABETH II - AUSTRALIA **Obv. Designer:** Ian Rank-Broadley **Rev:** Runner right, Melbourne 2006 logo at lower right **Rev. Legend:** XVIII COMMONWEALTH GAMES **Rev. Designer:** Wojciech Pietranik **Edge:** Plain **Shape:** 12-sided

Date	Mintage	F	VF	XF	Unc	BU
2006	—	—	—	—	8.50	10.00

KM# 778 50 CENTS
15.5500 g., Copper-Nickel, 31.50 mm. **Ruler:** Elizabeth II **Subject:** Triathlon **Obv:** Head with tiara right **Obv. Legend:** ELIZABETH II - AUSRALIA **Obv. Designer:** Ian Rank-Broadley **Rev:** Bicycle, runner, Melbourne 2006 logo below **Rev. Legend:** XVIII COMMONWEALTH GAMES **Rev. Designer:** Wojciech Pietranik **Edge:** Plain **Shape:** 12-sided

Date	Mintage	F	VF	XF	Unc	BU
2006	—	—	—	—	8.50	10.00

KM# 779 50 CENTS
15.5500 g., Copper-Nickel, 31.50 mm. **Ruler:** Elizabeth II **Subject:** Netball **Obv:** Head with tiara right **Obv. Legend:** ELIZABETH II - AUSTRALIA **Obv. Designer:** Ian Rank-Broadley **Rev:** Player shooting basket, Melbourne 2006 logo at upper left **Rev. Legend:** XVIII COMMONWEALTH GAMES **Rev. Designer:** Wojciech Pietranik **Edge:** Plain **Shape:** 12-sided

Date	Mintage	F	VF	XF	Unc	BU
2006	—	—	—	—	8.50	10.00

KM# 780 50 CENTS
15.5500 g., Copper-Nickel, 31.50 mm. **Ruler:** Elizabeth II **Subject:** Table tennis **Obv:** Head with tiara right **Obv. Legend:** ELIZABETH II - AUSTRALIA **Obv. Designer:** Ian Rank-Broadley **Rev:** Player hitting ball, Melbourne 2006 logo below **Rev. Legend:** XVIII COMMONWEALTH GAMES **Rev. Designer:** Wojciech Pietranik **Edge:** Plain **Shape:** 12-sided

Date	Mintage	F	VF	XF	Unc	BU
2006	—	—	—	—	8.50	10.00

KM# 781 50 CENTS
15.5500 g., Copper-Nickel, 31.50 mm. **Ruler:** Elizabeth II **Subject:** Aquatics **Obv:** Head with tiara right **Obv. Legend:** ELIZABETH II - AUSTRALIA **Obv. Designer:** Ian Rank-Broadley **Rev:** Swimmer, Melbourne 2006 logo **Rev. Legend:** XVIII COMMONWEALTH GAMES **Rev. Designer:** Wojciech Pietranik **Edge:** Plain **Shape:** 12-sided

Date	Mintage	F	VF	XF	Unc	BU
2006	—	—	—	—	8.50	10.00

KM# 1011 DOLLAR (Holey Dollar)
0.9990 Silver, 40.00 mm. **Ruler:** Elizabeth II **Obv:** Crowned bust right at top **Obv. Legend:** ELIZABETH II - AUSTRALIA **Rev:** 12 Lunar figures

Date	Mintage	F	VF	XF	Unc	BU
2007 Proof	8,888	Value: 50.00				

KM# 489 DOLLAR
9.0000 g., Aluminum-Bronze, 25 mm. **Ruler:** Elizabeth II **Subject:** Kangaroos **Obv:** Head with tiara right **Obv. Designer:** Ian Rank-Broadley **Rev:** Circle of 5 kangaroos **Rev. Designer:** Stuart Devlin **Edge:** Reeded and plain sections

Date	Mintage	F	VF	XF	Unc	BU
2001 Proof	1,001,000	Value: 45.00				
2004	9,565,000	—	—	—	3.50	5.00
2004 Proof	50,000	Value: 65.00				
2005	5,792,000	—	—	—	3.50	5.00
2005 Proof	33,520	Value: 75.00				
2006	—	—	—	—	—	5.00
2007	—	—	—	—	—	5.00

KM# 530 DOLLAR
9.0000 g., Aluminum-Bronze, 25 mm. **Ruler:** Elizabeth II **Subject:** Army Centennial **Obv:** Head with tiara right **Obv. Designer:** Ian Rank-Broadley **Rev:** Army crest **Rev. Designer:** Vladimir Gottwald **Edge:** Reeded and plain sections

Date	Mintage	F	VF	XF	Unc	BU
2001C	125,186	—	—	—	6.00	10.00
Note: IRB spaced						
2001C	Inc. above	—	—	—	6.00	10.00
Note: IRB joined						
2001S	38,095	—	—	—	10.00	15.00
Note: IRB joined only						

KM# 531 DOLLAR
9.0000 g., Aluminum-Bronze, 25 mm. **Ruler:** Elizabeth II **Subject:** 80th Anniversary Royal Australian Air Force **Obv:** Head with tiara right **Obv. Designer:** Ian Rank-Broadley **Rev:** Air Force crest **Rev. Designer:** Vladimir Gottwald **Edge:** Reeded and plain sections

Date	Mintage	F	VF	XF	Unc	BU
2001	99,281	—	—	—	6.00	10.00
Note: IRB spaced						
2001	Inc. above	—	—	—	6.00	10.00
Note: IRB joined						

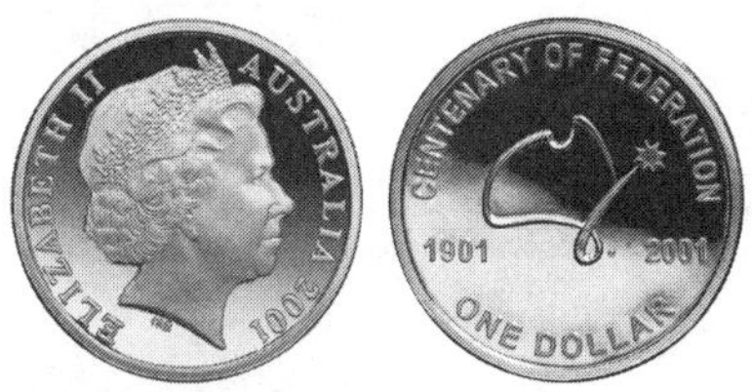

KM# 534.1 DOLLAR
9.0000 g., Aluminum-Bronze, 25 mm. **Ruler:** Elizabeth II **Subject:** Centenary - Norfolk Island Federation **Obv:** Head with tiara right **Obv. Designer:** Ian Rank-Broadley **Rev:** Stylized ribbon map of Australia with star **Rev. Designer:** Wojciech Pietranik **Edge:** Plain and reeded sections **Note:** Reverse design raised above field. Prev. KM#534.

Date	Mintage	F	VF	XF	Unc	BU
2001	6,781,200	—	—	—	2.50	3.50
Note: IRB joined						
2001	Inc. above	—	—	—	5.00	10.00
Note: IRB spaced						

KM# 530a DOLLAR
11.6600 g., 0.9990 Silver 0.3745 oz. ASW, 24.9 mm. **Ruler:** Elizabeth II **Subject:** Army Centennial **Obv:** Head with tiara right **Rev:** Army crest **Edge:** Reeded and plain sections

Date	Mintage	F	VF	XF	Unc	BU
2001 Proof	17,839	Value: 40.00				

KM# 534.1a DOLLAR
21.7000 g., 0.9999 Gold 0.6976 oz. AGW, 25 mm. **Ruler:** Elizabeth II **Subject:** Federation Centennial **Obv:** Elizabeth II **Rev:** Federation logo

Date	Mintage	F	VF	XF	Unc	BU
2001 Proof	650	Value: 1,130				

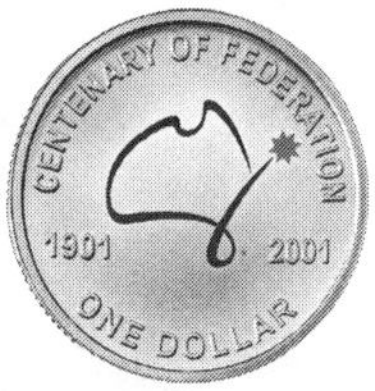

KM# 534.2 DOLLAR
9.0000 g., Aluminum-Bronze, 25 mm. **Ruler:** Elizabeth II **Subject:** Centenary of Norfolk Island Federation **Obv:** Head with tiara right **Obv. Designer:** Ian Rank-Broadley **Rev:** Colorized ribbon design of Australia with star **Rev. Designer:** Wojciech Pietranik **Edge:** Plain and reeded sections **Note:** Reverse design printed on surface.

Date	Mintage	F	VF	XF	Unc	BU
2001 Proof	—	Value: 12.50				

KM# 588 DOLLAR
9.0000 g., Aluminum-Bronze, 25 mm. **Ruler:** Elizabeth II **Subject:** 90th Anniversary Royal Australian Navy **Obv:** Head with tiara right **Obv. Designer:** Ian Rank-Broadley **Rev:** Navy crest **Rev. Designer:** Vladimir Gottwald **Edge:** Reeded and plain sections

Date	Mintage	F	VF	XF	Unc	BU
2001	62,429	—	—	—	15.00	20.00

KM# 594 DOLLAR
31.1035 g., 0.9990 Silver 0.9990 oz. ASW, 40 mm. **Ruler:** Elizabeth II **Subject:** Millennium **Obv:** Head with tiara right **Obv. Designer:** Ian Rank-Broadley **Rev:** Gold inset Sun on multicolor Earth above Egyptian obelisk **Edge:** Reeded

Date	Mintage	F	VF	XF	Unc	BU
2001 Prooflike	30,000	—	—	—	15.00	20.00

KM# 598 DOLLAR
31.1000 g., 0.9990 Silver 0.9988 oz. ASW, 40.4 mm. **Ruler:** Elizabeth II **Subject:** Centenary of Federation "Holey Dollar" **Obv:** Legend around star-shaped center hole **Rev:** Seven coats of arms around star-shaped hole **Edge:** Reeded

Date	Mintage	F	VF	XF	Unc	BU
ND(2001) Prooflike	30,000	—	—	—	25.00	30.00

KM# 682 DOLLAR
9.0000 g., Aluminum-Nickel-Bronze, 25 mm. **Ruler:** Elizabeth II **Subject:** International Year of Volunteers **Rev:** Volunteers in wreath **Designer:** Wojciech Pietranik

Date	Mintage	F	VF	XF	Unc	BU
2001	6,000,000	—	—	—	3.00	4.50

KM# 600.1a DOLLAR
11.6600 g., 0.9900 Silver 0.3711 oz. ASW, 25 mm. **Ruler:** Elizabeth II **Subject:** Year of the Outback **Obv:** Head with tiara right **Obv. Designer:** Ian Rank-Broadley **Rev:** Stylized map of Australia **Rev. Designer:** Wojciech Pietranik **Edge:** Segmented reeding

Date	Mintage	F	VF	XF	Unc	BU
2002 Proof	12,500	Value: 40.00				

KM# 600.1 DOLLAR
9.0000 g., Aluminum-Bronze, 25 mm. **Ruler:** Elizabeth II **Subject:** Year of the Outback **Obv:** Head with tiara right **Obv. Designer:** Ian Rank-Broadley **Rev:** Stylized Australian map **Rev. Designer:** Wojciech Pietranik **Edge:** Reeded and plain sections **Note:** Prev. KM#600.

Date	Mintage	F	VF	XF	Unc	BU
2002	34,074,000	—	—	—	2.50	3.50
2002 Proof	—	Value: 4.00				
2002B	32,698	—	—	—	4.50	6.50
2002C	68,447	—	—	—	3.50	5.00
2002M	—	—	—	—	2.50	3.00
2002S	36,931	—	—	—	4.00	6.00

KM# 600.2 DOLLAR
9.0000 g., Aluminum-Bronze, 25 mm. **Ruler:** Elizabeth II **Subject:** Year Of The Outback **Obv:** Head with tiara right **Obv. Designer:** Ian Rank-Broadley **Rev:** Multicolor stylized Australian map **Rev. Designer:** Wojciech Pietranik **Edge:** Reeded and plain sections

Date	Mintage	F	VF	XF	Unc	BU
2002(c) Proof	39,514	—	—	—	—	—

KM# 632 DOLLAR
31.1035 g., 0.9990 Silver 0.9990 oz. ASW, 40 mm. **Ruler:** Elizabeth II **Subject:** Queen's Golden Jubilee **Obv:** Head right **Rev:** Queen on horse with multicolor flag background **Edge:** Reeded

Date	Mintage	F	VF	XF	Unc	BU
2002P Proof	40,000	Value: 30.00				

KM# 660 DOLLAR
31.1035 g., 0.9990 Silver 0.9990 oz. ASW, 40 mm. **Ruler:** Elizabeth II **Subject:** Melbourne Mint **Obv:** Head with tiara right **Obv. Designer:** Ian Rank-Broadley **Rev:** Mint entrance between two gold foil inserts replicating gold sovereign reverse designs **Edge:** Reeded

Date	Mintage	F	VF	XF	Unc	BU
2002 Proof	13,328	Value: 35.00				

KM# 690.1 DOLLAR
9.0000 g., Aluminum-Bronze, 25 mm. **Ruler:** Elizabeth II **Subject:** Volunteers **Obv:** Elizabeth II **Rev:** Multicolor Australian Volunteers logo **Edge:** Segmented reeding

Date	Mintage	F	VF	XF	Unc	BU
2003 Proof	39,090	Value: 15.00				

KM# 822 DOLLAR
54.3000 g., 0.9990 Silver 1.7440 oz. ASW, 50 mm. **Ruler:** Elizabeth II **Obv:** Superimposed head above replica of Holey Dollar **Obv. Designer:** Ian Rank-Broadley **Rev:** Replica of Holey Dollar **Edge:** Reeded **Note:** Holey Dollar replica is embedded in silver collar and comes with replica Dump also in 0.999 silver.

Date	Mintage	F	VF	XF	Unc	BU
2003 Proof	14,204	Value: 85.00				

KM# 803 DOLLAR
Aluminum-Bronze, 25 mm. **Ruler:** Elizabeth II **Subject:** Vietnam War 1962-1997 **Obv:** Head with tiara right

Date	Mintage	F	VF	XF	Unc	BU
2003	—	—	—	—	—	—

KM# 823 DOLLAR
31.1035 g., 0.9990 Silver 0.9990 oz. ASW, 40 mm. **Ruler:** Elizabeth II **Subject:** 50th Anniversary Coronation Elizabeth II **Obv:** Head with tiara right **Obv. Designer:** Ian Rank-Broadley **Rev:** Crown in lettered garland **Note:** Colored design.

Date	Mintage	F	VF	XF	Unc	BU
2003P Proof	40,400	Value: 35.00				

KM# 824 DOLLAR

31.1035 g., 0.9990 Silver 0.9990 oz. ASW, 40 mm. **Ruler:** Elizabeth II **Subject:** Golden Pipeline **Obv:** Head with tiara right **Obv. Designer:** Ian Rank-Broadley **Rev:** Charles Yelverton O'Conner, innovative engineer **Note:** Colored design.

Date	Mintage	F	VF	XF	Unc	BU
2003P Proof	5,000	Value: 90.00				

KM# 663 DOLLAR

9.0000 g., Aluminum-Bronze, 25 mm. **Ruler:** Elizabeth II **Subject:** 50th Anniversary of the end of Korean War **Obv:** Head with tiara right **Obv. Designer:** Ian Rank-Broadley **Rev:** Dove of Peace **Rev. Designer:** Vladimir Gottwald **Edge:** Segmented reeding

Date	Mintage	F	VF	XF	Unc	BU
2003C	93,572	—	—	—	2.50	3.50
2003B	34,949	—	—	—	3.50	5.00
2003M	36,142	—	—	—	3.50	5.00
2003S	36,091	—	—	—	3.50	5.00

KM# 663a DOLLAR

11.6600 g., 0.9990 Silver 0.3745 oz. ASW, 25 mm. **Ruler:** Elizabeth II **Subject:** Korean War **Obv:** Queens head right **Obv. Designer:** Ian Rank-Broadley **Rev:** Dove of Peace **Rev. Designer:** Vladimir Gottwald **Edge:** Segmented reeding

Date	Mintage	F	VF	XF	Unc	BU
2003	15,000	Value: 20.00				

KM# 685 DOLLAR

31.1035 g., 0.9990 Silver 0.9990 oz. ASW, 40.6 mm. **Ruler:** Elizabeth II **Subject:** 21st Birthday of William **Obv:** Head right **Rev:** Multicolor Crown Prince William **Edge:** Segmented reeding

Date	Mintage	F	VF	XF	Unc	BU
ND(2003)P Proof	12,500	Value: 25.00				

KM# 690 DOLLAR

9.0000 g., Aluminum-Bronze, 25 mm. **Ruler:** Elizabeth II **Obv:** Queens head right **Rev:** Australia Volunteers logo **Edge:** Segmented reeding

Date	Mintage	F	VF	XF	Unc	BU
2003	4,149,000	—	—	—	3.50	4.50

KM# 690a DOLLAR

9.0000 g., 0.9990 Silver 0.2891 oz. ASW, 25 mm. **Ruler:** Elizabeth II **Obv:** Queens head right **Rev:** Australia Volunteers logo

Date	Mintage	F	VF	XF	Unc	BU
2003 Proof	6,500	Value: 20.00				

KM# 754 DOLLAR

9.0000 g., Aluminum-Bronze, 25 mm. **Ruler:** Elizabeth II **Subject:** Womens Suffrage **Obv:** Queens head right **Rev:** Suffragette talking to Britannia **Edge:** Segmented reeding

Date	Mintage	F	VF	XF	Unc	BU
2003	10,007,000	—	—	—	3.00	4.00

KM# 763 DOLLAR

13.3600 g., 0.9990 Silver 0.4291 oz. ASW, 28.5 mm. **Ruler:** Elizabeth II **Series:** Masterpieces in Silver - Port Phillip Patterns **Obv:** 1/4 Ounce design **Rev:** Kangaroo design **Edge:** Reeded

Date	Mintage	F	VF	XF	Unc	BU
2003 Proof	10,000	Value: 7.50				

KM# 726 DOLLAR

9.0000 g., Aluminum-Bronze, 25 mm. **Ruler:** Elizabeth II **Subject:** Eureka Stockade 1854-2004 **Obv:** Head with tiara right **Obv. Designer:** Ian Rank-Broadley **Rev:** Stockade and stylized soldiers **Rev. Designer:** Wojciech Pietranik **Edge:** Reeded and plain sections

Date	Mintage	F	VF	XF	Unc	BU
2004	—	—	—	—	20.00	50.00

Note: no mintmark

Date	Mintage	F	VF	XF	Unc	BU
2004 B	32,142	—	—	—	3.50	5.00
2004 C	70,913	—	—	—	2.50	3.50
2004 E	89,276	—	—	—	2.50	3.50
2004 S	35,483	—	—	—	3.50	5.00
2004 M	37,526	—	—	—	3.50	5.00

KM# 489a DOLLAR

11.6600 g., 0.9990 Silver 0.3745 oz. ASW, 25 mm. **Ruler:** Elizabeth II **Obv:** Head with tiara right **Obv. Designer:** Ian Rank-Broadley **Rev:** Kangaroos **Rev. Designer:** Stuart Devlin **Edge:** Segmented reeding

Date	Mintage	F	VF	XF	Unc	BU
2004 Proof	6,500	Value: 30.00				

KM# 725 DOLLAR

56.2300 g., 0.9990 Bi-Metallic Copper center in Silver ring 1.8060 oz., 50 mm. **Ruler:** Elizabeth II **Subject:** The Last Penny **Obv:** 1964 dated penny obverse **Rev:** 1964 date penny reverse **Edge:** Reeded

Date	Mintage	F	VF	XF	Unc	BU
2004 Proof	16,437	Value: 50.00				

KM# 726a DOLLAR

11.6600 g., 0.9990 Silver 0.3745 oz. ASW, 25 mm. **Ruler:** Elizabeth II **Subject:** Eureka Stockade **Obv:** Head with tiara right **Rev:** Stockade and stylized soldiers **Edge:** Reeded and Plain sections

Date	Mintage	F	VF	XF	Unc	BU
2004 Proof	16,447	Value: 15.00				

KM# 733 DOLLAR

9.0000 g., Aluminum-Bronze, 25 mm. **Ruler:** Elizabeth II **Obv:** Head with tiara right **Rev:** Multicolor holographic five kangaroos design **Edge:** Reeded and plain sections

Date	Mintage	F	VF	XF	Unc	BU
2004 Proof	—	Value: 15.00				

KM# 733.1 DOLLAR

9.0000 g., Aluminum-Bronze, 25 mm. **Ruler:** Elizabeth II **Obv:** Elizabeth II **Rev:** Five kangaroos, not colored or holographic **Edge:** Segmented reeding

Date	Mintage	F	VF	XF	Unc	BU
2004	—	—	—	—	—	4.50

KM# 733.1a DOLLAR

11.6600 g., 0.9999 Silver 0.3748 oz. ASW, 25 mm. **Ruler:** Elizabeth II

Date	Mintage	F	VF	XF	Unc	BU
2004 Proof	6,500	Value: 25.00				

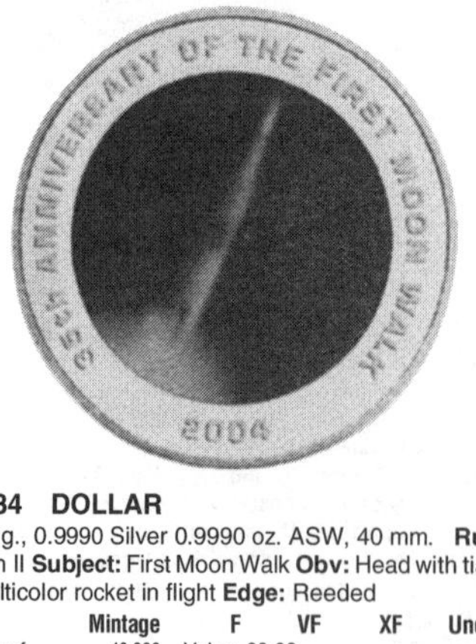

KM# 734 DOLLAR

31.1035 g., 0.9990 Silver 0.9990 oz. ASW, 40 mm. **Ruler:** Elizabeth II **Subject:** First Moon Walk **Obv:** Head with tiara right **Rev:** Multicolor rocket in flight **Edge:** Reeded

Date	Mintage	F	VF	XF	Unc	BU
2004P Proof	40,000	Value: 28.00				

KM# 735 DOLLAR

31.1035 g., 0.9990 Silver 0.9990 oz. ASW, 40 mm. **Ruler:** Elizabeth II **Subject:** First Moon Walk **Obv:** Head with tiara right **Rev:** Multicolor scene of astronauts planting flag on moon **Edge:** Reeded

Date	Mintage	F	VF	XF	Unc	BU
2004P Proof	40,000	Value: 28.00				

KM# 736 DOLLAR

31.1035 g., 0.9990 Silver 0.9990 oz. ASW, 40 mm. **Ruler:** Elizabeth II **Subject:** First Moon Walk **Obv:** Head with tiara right **Rev:** Multicolor close up of astronaut on moon **Edge:** Reeded

Date	Mintage	F	VF	XF	Unc	BU
2004P Proof	40,000	Value: 25.00				

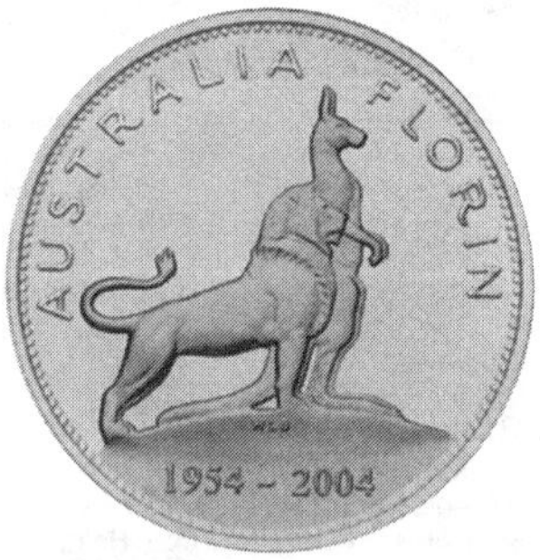

KM# 738 DOLLAR

31.1035 g., 0.9990 Silver 0.9990 oz. ASW, 40 mm. **Ruler:** Elizabeth II **Subject:** 50th Anniversary of Royal Visit **Obv:** Queens head right **Rev:** Gold-plated lion and kangaroo **Rev. Designer:** Leslie Bowles **Edge:** Reeded

Date	Mintage	F	VF	XF	Unc	BU
ND (2004) Proof	12,500	Value: 30.00				

KM# 740 DOLLAR

24.3750 g., 0.9990 Silver Encapsulated gold nuggets center in Silver ring 0.7829 oz. ASW, 40.6 mm. **Ruler:** Elizabeth II **Obv:** Crowned head right **Rev:** Eureka Stockade leader, miners and flag **Edge:** Reeded

Date	Mintage	F	VF	XF	Unc	BU
2004 Proof	12,500	Value: 50.00				

KM# 748 DOLLAR

9.0000 g., Aluminum-Bronze, 38.74 mm. **Ruler:** Elizabeth II **Subject:** 90th Anniversary Gallipoli Landing 1915-2005 **Obv:** Head with tiara right **Obv. Designer:** Ian Rank-Broadley **Rev:** Bugler silhouette **Rev. Designer:** Vladimir Gottwald **Edge:** Segmented reeding

Date	Mintage	F	VF	XF	Unc	BU
2005	15,000	—	—	—	25.00	30.00
2005B	36,108	—	—	—	3.50	5.00
2005C	76,173	—	—	—	2.50	3.50
2005G	35,452	—	—	—	20.00	30.00
2005M	—	—	—	—	2.50	3.50
2005S	39,569	—	—	—	3.50	5.00

KM# 825 DOLLAR

56.4500 g., 0.9990 Silver 1.8130 oz. ASW, 50 mm. **Ruler:** Elizabeth II **Obv:** Small head with tiara right superimposed above replica of Sydney Mint Sovereign **Obv. Designer:** Ian Rank-Broadley **Rev:** Replica of Sydney Mint Sovereign **Edge:** Reeded **Note:** Sydney Mint Sovereign replica is embedded in silver collar and overlaid with 24 carat gold.

Date	Mintage	F	VF	XF	Unc	BU
2005 Proof	11,845	Value: 80.00				

KM# 831 DOLLAR

31.6000 g., 0.9990 Silver 1.0149 oz. ASW, 40 mm. **Ruler:** Elizabeth II **Subject:** Centenary Australian PGA Gold Open 1905-2005 **Obv:** Head with tiara right **Obv. Designer:** Ian Rank-Broadley **Rev:** Golfer **Note:** Colorized image.

Date	Mintage	F	VF	XF	Unc	BU
2005P Proof	7,500	Value: 40.00				

KM# 835 DOLLAR

Aluminum-Bronze, 38.74 mm. **Ruler:** Elizabeth II **Subject:** Living Icons of Australia and New Zealand **Obv:** Head with tiara right **Obv. Designer:** Ian Rank-Broadley **Rev:** Indigenous image of kangaroo **Rev. Designer:** Charmaine Cole

Date	Mintage	F	VF	XF	Unc	BU
2005	20,000	—	—	—	15.00	20.00

KM# 747 DOLLAR

9.0000 g., Aluminum-Bronze, 25 mm. **Ruler:** Elizabeth II **Subject:** 60th Anniversary World War II **Obv:** Head with tiara right **Obv. Designer:** Ian Rank-Broadley **Rev:** Rejoicing serviceman **Rev. Designer:** Wojciech Pietranik **Edge:** Segmented reeding

Date	Mintage	F	VF	XF	Unc	BU
2005	10,607,000	—	—	—	2.00	3.00
2005 Proof	—	Value: 35.00				

KM# 747a DOLLAR

11.6600 g., 0.9990 Silver 0.3745 oz. ASW, 25 mm. **Ruler:** Elizabeth II **Obv:** Queens head right **Rev:** Rejoicing servicemen **Edge:** Segmented reeding

Date	Mintage	F	VF	XF	Unc	BU
2005 Proof	6,500	Value: 42.00				

KM# 747b DOLLAR

21.5200 g., 0.9999 Gold 0.6918 oz. AGW, 25 mm. **Ruler:** Elizabeth II **Obv:** Queens head right **Rev:** Rejoicing servicemen **Edge:** Segmented reeding

Date	Mintage	F	VF	XF	Unc	BU
2005 Proof	650	Value: 650				

KM# 748a DOLLAR

11.6600 g., 0.9990 Silver 0.3745 oz. ASW, 25 mm. **Ruler:** Elizabeth II **Subject:** Gallipoli **Obv:** Queens head right **Rev:** Bugler silhouette **Edge:** Segmented reeding

Date	Mintage	F	VF	XF	Unc	BU
2005 Proof	14,900	Value: 18.00				

KM# 749 DOLLAR

31.6000 g., 0.9990 Silver 1.0149 oz. ASW, 40 mm. **Ruler:** Elizabeth II **Obv:** Head with tiara right **Obv. Designer:** Ian Rank-Broadley **Rev:** Kangaroo bounding under Southern Cross and above Federation Star **Rev. Designer:** Wojcieck Pietranik **Edge:** Reeded

Date	Mintage	F	VF	XF	Unc	BU
2005	—	—	—	—	16.50	18.50
2005 Proof	12,500	Value: 30.00				

KM# 749a DOLLAR

31.1035 g., 0.9990 Silver Partially Gold Plated 0.9990 oz. ASW, 40 mm. **Ruler:** Elizabeth II **Obv:** Head with tiara right **Obv. Designer:** Ian Rank-Broadley **Rev:** Kangaroo bounding under Southern Cross and above Federation Star **Rev. Designer:** Wojcieck Pietranik **Edge:** Reeded

Date	Mintage	F	VF	XF	Unc	BU
2005 Proof	12,500	Value: 35.00				

KM# 804 DOLLAR

Aluminum-Bronze, 25 mm. **Ruler:** Elizabeth II **Subject:** XXIII Commonwealth Games **Obv:** Head with tiara right

Date	Mintage	F	VF	XF	Unc	BU
2006	—	—	—	—	—	—

KM# 1005 DOLLAR

0.9990 Silver, 40 mm. **Ruler:** Elizabeth II **Obv:** Head with tiarra right **Obv. Legend:** ELIZABETH II - AUSTRALIA **Obv. Designer:** Ian Rank-Broadley **Rev:** Everage head facing, multicolor **Rev. Legend:** DAME EDNA EVERAGE - 50TH ANNIVERSARY

Date	Mintage	F	VF	XF	Unc	BU
ND(2006)P Proof	6,500	—	—	—	—	—

KM# 489b DOLLAR

21.5200 g., 0.9990 Gold 0.6912 oz. AGW, 25 mm. **Ruler:** Elizabeth II **Obv:** Head with tiara right **Obv. Designer:** Ian Rank-Broadley **Rev:** Kangaroos **Rev. Designer:** Stuart Devlin **Edge:** Segmented reeding

Date	Mintage	F	VF	XF	Unc	BU
2006 Proof	300	Value: 700				

KM# 77a DOLLAR

11.6600 g., 0.9990 Silver 0.3745 oz. ASW, 25 mm. **Ruler:** Elizabeth II **Obv:** Young bust right **Obv. Designer:** Arnold Machin **Rev:** Kangaroos **Rev. Designer:** Stuart Devlin **Edge:** Segmented reeding

Date	Mintage	F	VF	XF	Unc	BU
2006 Proof	6,500	Value: 30.00				

KM# 805 DOLLAR

9.0000 g., Aluminum-Bronze, 25 mm. **Ruler:** Elizabeth II **Subject:** 50 Years of Television **Obv:** Head with tiara right **Obv. Designer:** Ian Rank-Broadley **Rev:** TV mast and camera **Rev. Designer:** Vladimir Gottwald **Edge:** Segmented reeding

Date	Mintage	F	VF	XF	Unc	BU
2006C	—	—	—	—	2.50	3.50
2006 TV	—	—	—	—	7.50	10.00
2006S	—	—	—	—	2.50	3.50
2006B	—	—	—	—	3.50	5.50
2006M	—	—	—	—	3.50	5.50

KM# 805a DOLLAR

11.6600 g., 0.9990 Silver 0.3745 oz. ASW, 25 mm. **Ruler:** Elizabeth II **Subject:** 50 Years of Television **Obv:** Head with tiara right **Obv. Designer:** Ian Rank-Broadley **Rev:** TV mast and camera **Rev. Designer:** Vladimir Gottwald **Edge:** Segmented reeding

Date	Mintage	F	VF	XF	Unc	BU
2006 Proof	12,500	Value: 25.00				
2006A Proof	6,000	Value: 35.00				

KM# 807 DOLLAR

9.0000 g., Aluminum-Bronze, 25 mm. **Ruler:** Elizabeth II **Subject:** Colored Oceans **Obv:** Head with tiara right **Obv. Designer:** Ian Rank-Broadley **Rev:** Multicolor clown fish **Rev. Designer:** Vladimir Gottwald **Edge:** Segmented reeding

Date	Mintage	F	VF	XF	Unc	BU
2006	—	—	—	—	3.00	4.00

KM# 806 DOLLAR

9.0000 g., Aluminum-Bronze, 25 mm. **Ruler:** Elizabeth II **Subject:** Colored Oceans **Obv:** Head with tiara right **Obv. Designer:** Ian Rank-Broadley **Rev:** Multicolor jumping dolphins **Rev. Designer:** Vladimir Gottwald **Edge:** Segmented reeding

Date	Mintage	F	VF	XF	Unc	BU
2006	—	—	—	—	3.00	4.00

KM# 826 DOLLAR

60.5000 g., 0.9990 Silver 1.9431 oz. ASW, 50 mm. **Ruler:** Elizabeth II **Obv:** Replica of obverse of 1758 Mexico City Mint 8 Reales **Obv. Legend:** ELIZABETH II (small head right) AUSTRALIA **Rev:** Replica of reverse of 1758 Mexico City Mint 8 Reales **Rev. Legend:** PILLAR DOLLAR **Edge:** Reeded **Note:** Pillar 8 Reales replica is embedded, antique finish

Date	Mintage	F	VF	XF	Unc	BU
2006	9,846	Value: 80.00				

KM# 809 DOLLAR

9.0000 g., Aluminum-Bronze, 25 mm. **Ruler:** Elizabeth II **Subject:** Year of the Pig **Obv:** Head with tiara right **Obv. Designer:** Ian Rank-Broadley **Rev:** Pig **Rev. Designer:** Vladimir Gottwald **Edge:** Segmented reeding

Date	Mintage	F	VF	XF	Unc	BU
2007	—	—	—	—	3.00	4.00

KM# 809a DOLLAR

11.6600 g., 0.9990 Silver 0.3745 oz. ASW, 25 mm. **Ruler:** Elizabeth II **Subject:** Year of the Pig **Obv:** Head with tiara right **Obv. Designer:** Ian Rank-Broadley **Rev:** Pig **Rev. Designer:** Vladimir Gottwald **Edge:** Segmented reeding

Date	Mintage	F	VF	XF	Unc	BU
2007 Proof	—	Value: 25.00				

KM# 808 DOLLAR

9.0000 g., Aluminum-Bronze, 25 mm. **Ruler:** Elizabeth II **Subject:** Ashes Cricket Series 1882-2007 **Obv:** Head with tiara right **Obv. Designer:** Ian Rank-Broadley **Rev:** Urn with supporters **Rev. Designer:** Vladimir Gottwald **Edge:** Segmented reeding

Date	Mintage	F	VF	XF	Unc	BU
2007	—	—	—	—	3.00	4.00

KM# 828 DOLLAR

9.0000 g., Aluminum-Bronze, 25 mm. **Ruler:** Elizabeth II **Subject:** Year of the Surf Lifesaver **Obv:** Head with tiara right **Obv. Designer:** Ian Rank-Broadley **Rev:** Lifesavers with rescued person **Rev. Designer:** Vladimir Gottwald **Edge:** Segmented reeding

Date	Mintage	F	VF	XF	Unc	BU
2007 Proof	—	—	—	—	—	—

Note: Only available in proof sets

KM# 829 DOLLAR

9.0000 g., Aluminum-Bronze, 25 mm. **Ruler:** Elizabeth II **Subject:** Norman Lindsay and his Magic Pudding **Obv:** Head with tiara right **Obv. Designer:** Ian Rank-Broadley **Rev:** Lindsay and Pudding characters **Rev. Designer:** Vladimir Gottwald **Edge:** Segmented reeding

Date	Mintage	F	VF	XF	Unc	BU
2007	—	—	—	—	—	—

Note: Only available in Baby Sets

KM# 1009 DOLLAR

31.1030 g., 0.9990 Silver 0.9989 oz. ASW, 40.00 mm. **Ruler:** Elizabeth II **Subject:** 75th Anniversary Death of Phar Lap **Obv:** Head with tiara right **Obv. Legend:** ELIZABETH II - AUSRALIA **Rev:** Horse and rider racing right

Date	Mintage	F	VF	XF	Unc	BU
ND(2007)P Proof	7,500	Value: 67.50				

KM# 1012 DOLLAR

31.1030 g., 0.9990 Silver 0.9989 oz. ASW, 40.00 mm. **Ruler:** Elizabeth II **Obv:** Bust with tiara right **Obv. Legend:** ELIZABETH II - AUSTRALIA **Obv. Designer:** Ian Rank-Broadley **Rev:** Bridge, multicolor fireworks above **Rev. Legend:** 75th ANNIVERSARY - SYDNEY HARBOUR BRIDGE

Date	Mintage	F	VF	XF	Unc	BU
ND(2007)P Proof	10,000	Value: 67.50				

KM# 1016 DOLLAR

11.6600 g., 0.9990 Silver 0.3745 oz. ASW, 25.00 mm. **Ruler:** Elizabeth II **Subject:** 75th Anniversary **Obv:** Head with tiara right **Obv. Legend:** ELIZABETH II _ AUSTRALIA **Obv. Designer:** Ian Rank-Broadley **Rev:** Three men standing at bridge joint **Rev. Legend:** SYDNEY HARBOUR BRIDGE **Edge:** Segmented reeding

Date	Mintage	F	VF	XF	Unc	BU
2007 Proof	12,500	Value: 30.00				

KM# 850 DOLLAR

27.2200 g., Copper-Nickel, 38.74 mm. **Ruler:** Elizabeth II **Obv:** Head with tiara right **Obv. Designer:** Ian Rank-Broadley **Rev:** Kangaroo mother and joey **Rev. Designer:** Rolf Harris **Edge:** Reeded

Date	Mintage	F	VF	XF	Unc	BU
2007	—	—	—	—	12.50	15.00

KM# 406 2 DOLLARS

6.6000 g., Aluminum-Bronze, 20.62 mm. **Ruler:** Elizabeth II **Obv:** Head right **Obv. Designer:** Ian Rank-Broadley **Rev:** Aboriginal man at left, stars above at right **Rev. Designer:** Horst Hahn **Edge:** Reeded, smooth alternating edge

Date	Mintage	F	VF	XF	Unc	BU
2001	3,565,000	—	—	—	4.00	6.00
Note: Large obverse head, IRB spaced						
2001	Inc. above	—	—	—	—	—
Note: Smaller obverse head, IRB joined						
2001 Proof	59,569	Value: 8.00				
2002	29,689,000	—	—	—	4.00	6.00
2002 Proof	39,514	Value: 8.00				
2003	13,656,000	—	—	—	4.00	6.00
2003 Proof	39,090	Value: 8.00				
2004	20,084,000	—	—	—	3.50	5.00
2004 Proof	50,000	Value: 7.00				
2005	—	—	—	—	3.50	5.00
2005 Proof	33,520	Value: 7.00				
2006	—	—	—	—	3.50	5.00
2006 Proof	—	Value: 7.00				
2007	—	—	—	—	3.00	4.50
2007 Proof	—	Value: 6.00				

KM# 406a 2 DOLLARS

15.8800 g., 0.9999 Gold 0.5105 oz. AGW, 20.5 mm. **Ruler:** Elizabeth II **Subject:** Federation Centennial **Obv:** Head with tiara right **Obv. Designer:** Ian Rank-Broadley **Rev:** Aboriginal elder **Rev. Designer:** Horst Hahn **Edge:** Segmented reeding

Date	Mintage	F	VF	XF	Unc	BU
2001 Proof	350	Value: 550				
2005 Proof	650	Value: 550				
2006 Proof	300	Value: 550				

KM# 406b 2 DOLLARS

8.5500 g., 0.9999 Silver 0.2748 oz. ASW, 20.5 mm. **Ruler:** Elizabeth II **Obv:** Head with tiara right **Obv. Designer:** Ian Rank-Broadley **Rev:** Aboriginal elder **Rev. Designer:** Horst Hahn **Edge:** Segmented reeding

Date	Mintage	F	VF	XF	Unc	BU
2003 Proof	6,500	Value: 20.00				
2004 Proof	6,500	Value: 20.00				
2005 Proof	6,500	Value: 20.00				

KM# 764 2 DOLLARS

18.2200 g., 0.9990 Silver 0.5852 oz. ASW, 32.5 mm. **Ruler:** Elizabeth II **Series:** Masterpieces in Silver - Port Phillip Patterns **Obv:** 1/2 Ounce design **Rev:** Kangaroo design **Edge:** Reeded

Date	Mintage	F	VF	XF	Unc	BU
2003 Proof	10,000	Value: 15.00				

KM# 755 2 DOLLARS

62.2700 g., 0.9990 Silver 1.9999 oz. ASW, 50.3 mm. **Ruler:** Elizabeth II **Series:** Australian Peacekeepers **Obv:** Queens head right **Rev:** Australian army and color insignia **Edge:** Reeded

Date	Mintage	F	VF	XF	Unc	BU
2005P Proof	2,500	Value: 65.00				

KM# 756 2 DOLLARS
62.2700 g., 0.9990 Silver 1.9999 oz. ASW, 50.3 mm. **Ruler:** Elizabeth II **Series:** Australian Peacekeepers **Obv:** Queens head right **Rev:** Australian Navy and color insignia **Edge:** Reeded

Date	Mintage	F	VF	XF	Unc	BU
2005P Proof	2,500	Value: 65.00				

KM# 757 2 DOLLARS
62.2700 g., 0.9990 Silver 1.9999 oz. ASW, 50.3 mm. **Ruler:** Elizabeth II **Subject:** Australian Peacekeepers Set **Obv:** Queens head right **Rev:** Australian Airforce and color insignia **Edge:** Reeded

Date	Mintage	F	VF	XF	Unc	BU
2005P Proof	2,500	Value: 65.00				

KM# 758 2 DOLLARS
62.2700 g., 0.9990 Silver 1.9999 oz. ASW, 50.3 mm. **Ruler:** Elizabeth II **Series:** Australian Peacekeepers **Obv:** Queens head right **Rev:** Australian Federal Police and color insignia **Edge:** Reeded

Date	Mintage	F	VF	XF	Unc	BU
2005P Proof	2,500	Value: 65.00				

KM# 759 2 DOLLARS
62.2700 g., 0.9990 Silver 1.9999 oz. ASW, 50.3 mm. **Ruler:** Elizabeth II **Series:** Australian Peacekeepers **Obv:** Queens head right **Rev:** Australian Agency for International Development and color insignia **Edge:** Reeded

Date	Mintage	F	VF	XF	Unc	BU
2005P Proof	2,500	Value: 65.00				

KM# 852 2 DOLLARS
8.8500 g., 0.9990 Silver 0.2842 oz. ASW, 20.5 mm. **Ruler:** Elizabeth II **Obv:** Young bust right **Obv. Designer:** Arnold Machin **Rev:** Aboriginal elder **Rev. Designer:** Horst Hahn **Edge:** Segmented reeding

Date	Mintage	F	VF	XF	Unc	BU
2006 Proof	6,500	Value: 20.00				

KM# 853 2 DOLLARS
1.2441 g., 0.9990 Gold 0.0400 oz. AGW **Ruler:** Elizabeth II **Subject:** FIFA World Cup **Obv:** Head with tiara right **Obv. Designer:** Ian Rank-Broadley **Rev:** FIFA World Cup

Date	Mintage	F	VF	XF	Unc	BU
2006P Proof	50,000	Value: 37.50				

KM# 591 5 DOLLARS
36.3100 g., 0.9990 Silver 1.1662 oz. ASW, 38.74 mm. **Ruler:** Elizabeth II **Subject:** Centennial of Federation Series Finale **Obv:** Queens head right **Rev:** Multicolor dual hologram: map and rotunda **Edge:** Reeded

Date	Mintage	F	VF	XF	Unc	BU
2001 Proof	—	Value: 30.00				

KM# 592 5 DOLLARS
36.3100 g., 0.9990 Silver 1.1662 oz. ASW, 38.74 mm. **Ruler:** Elizabeth II **Subject:** Barton and Reid **Obv:** Queens head right **Rev:** Portraits of Dame Flora Reid and Lady Jean Barton **Edge:** Reeded

Date	Mintage	F	VF	XF	Unc	BU
2001 Proof	5,000	Value: 50.00				

Note: In sets only

KM# 637 5 DOLLARS
36.3100 g., 0.9990 Silver 1.1662 oz. ASW, 38.74 mm. **Ruler:** Elizabeth II **Subject:** Kingston, Barton and Deakin **Obv:** Queens head right **Rev:** Three rectangular portraits and value **Edge:** Reeded

Date	Mintage	F	VF	XF	Unc	BU
2001 Proof	5,000	Value: 50.00				

Note: In sets only

KM# 638 5 DOLLARS
36.3100 g., 0.9990 Silver 1.1662 oz. ASW, 38.74 mm. **Ruler:** Elizabeth II **Subject:** Clark, Parkes and Griffith **Obv:** Queens head right **Rev:** Three rectangular portraits and value **Edge:** Reeded

Date	Mintage	F	VF	XF	Unc	BU
2001 Proof	5,000	Value: 50.00				

Note: In sets only

KM# 639 5 DOLLARS
36.3100 g., 0.9990 Silver 1.1662 oz. ASW, 38.74 mm. **Ruler:** Elizabeth II **Subject:** Spence, Nicholls and Anderson **Obv:** Queens head right **Rev:** Three circular portraits and value **Edge:** Reeded

Date	Mintage	F	VF	XF	Unc	BU
2001 Proof	5,000	Value: 50.00				

Note: In sets only

KM# 640 5 DOLLARS
36.3100 g., 0.9990 Silver 1.1662 oz. ASW, 38.74 mm. **Ruler:** Elizabeth II **Subject:** Reid, Forrest and Quick **Obv:** Queens head right **Rev:** Three rectangular portraits and value **Edge:** Reeded

Date	Mintage	F	VF	XF	Unc	BU
2001 Proof	5,000	Value: 50.00				

Note: In sets only

KM# 641 5 DOLLARS
36.3100 g., 0.9990 Silver 1.1662 oz. ASW, 38.74 mm. **Ruler:** Elizabeth II **Subject:** Bathurst Ladies Organizing Committee **Obv:** Queens head right **Rev:** Circular design with names above value **Edge:** Reeded

Date	Mintage	F	VF	XF	Unc	BU
2001 Proof	5,000	Value: 50.00				

Note: In sets only

KM# 662 5 DOLLARS
36.3100 g., 0.9990 Silver 1.1662 oz. ASW, 38.74 mm. **Ruler:** Elizabeth II **Subject:** Year of the Outback **Obv:** Queens head right **Rev:** Multicolor holographic landscape **Edge:** Reeded

Date	Mintage	F	VF	XF	Unc	BU
2002 Proof	15,000	Value: 100				

KM# 761 5 DOLLARS
36.3100 g., 0.9990 Silver 1.1662 oz. ASW **Ruler:** Elizabeth II **Obv:** Queens head right **Rev:** Sir Donald Bradman

Date	Mintage	F	VF	XF	Unc	BU
2001 Proof	—	Value: 35.00				

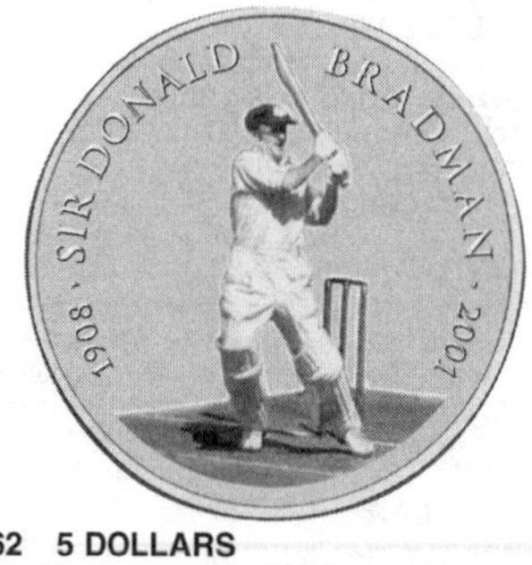

KM# 762 5 DOLLARS
20.0000 g., Aluminum-Bronze, 38.74 mm. **Ruler:** Elizabeth II **Obv:** Queens head right **Rev:** Sir Donald Bradman

Date	Mintage	F	VF	XF	Unc	BU
2001	—	—	—	—	8.50	9.50

KM# 601 5 DOLLARS
10.5200 g., Bi-Metallic Aluminumn-Bronze center in Stainless Steel ring, 27.8 mm. **Ruler:** Elizabeth II **Subject:** Battle of Sunda Strait **Obv:** Head with tiara right within circle **Obv. Designer:** Ian Rank-Broadley **Rev:** Ships bell from the "USS Houston", denomination below, circle surrounds **Rev. Designer:** Vladimir Gottwald **Edge:** Plain **Shape:** 24-sided **Note:** Demagnetized.

Date	Mintage	F	VF	XF	Unc	BU
2002	—	—	—	—	7.50	9.50

KM# 647 5 DOLLARS
28.0000 g., Aluminum-Bronze, 38.74 mm. **Ruler:** Elizabeth II **Subject:** Battle of Sunda Strait **Obv:** Queens head right **Rev:** Two ships; USS Houston and HMS Perth **Edge:** Reeded

Date	Mintage	F	VF	XF	Unc	BU
2002 Proof	15,000	Value: 25.00				

KM# 649 5 DOLLARS
20.0000 g., Aluminum-Bronze, 38.74 mm. **Ruler:** Elizabeth II **Subject:** Commonwealth Games **Obv:** Head with tiara right, denomination below **Obv. Designer:** Ian Rank-Broadley **Rev:** Eight arms, each represents an event of the games **Edge:** Reeded

Date	Mintage	F	VF	XF	Unc	BU
2002	11,145	—	—	—	8.50	9.50

KM# 650 5 DOLLARS
20.0000 g., Aluminum-Bronze, 38.74 mm. **Ruler:** Elizabeth II **Subject:** Commonwealth Games **Obv:** Head with tiara right, denomination below **Obv. Designer:** Ian Rank-Broadley **Rev:** Eight arms, each represents an event at the games **Edge:** Reeded

Date	Mintage	F	VF	XF	Unc	BU
2002	11,145	—	—	—	8.50	9.50

KM# 651 5 DOLLARS
20.0000 g., Aluminum-Bronze, 38.74 mm. **Ruler:** Elizabeth II **Subject:** Commonwealth Games **Obv:** Head with tiara right, denomination below **Rev:** Blue games logo; star above stylized kangaroo and torch **Edge:** Reeded

Date	Mintage	F	VF	XF	Unc	BU
2002	11,145	—	—	—	8.50	9.50

KM# 652 5 DOLLARS
36.3100 g., 0.9990 Silver 1.1662 oz. ASW, 38.74 mm. **Ruler:** Elizabeth II **Subject:** Commonwealth Games **Obv:** Head with tiara right, denomination below **Obv. Designer:** Ian Rank-Broadley **Rev:** Victorious athletes **Edge:** Reeded

Date	Mintage	F	VF	XF	Unc	BU
2002 Proof	7,581	Value: 37.50				

KM# 653 5 DOLLARS
36.3100 g., 0.9990 Silver 1.1662 oz. ASW, 38.74 mm. **Ruler:** Elizabeth II **Obv:** Queens head right **Rev:** Dutch sailing ship, The Duyfken **Edge:** Reeded

Date	Mintage	F	VF	XF	Unc	BU
2002 Proof	9,096	Value: 35.00				

KM# 654 5 DOLLARS
36.3100 g., 0.9990 Silver 1.1662 oz. ASW, 38.74 mm. **Ruler:** Elizabeth II **Obv:** Queens head right **Rev:** HMS Endeavour sailing ship **Edge:** Reeded

Date	Mintage	F	VF	XF	Unc	BU
2002 Proof	9,096	Value: 35.00				

KM# 655 5 DOLLARS
36.3100 g., 0.9990 Silver 1.1662 oz. ASW, 38.74 mm. **Ruler:** Elizabeth II **Obv:** Queens head right **Rev:** HMS Sirius sailing ship **Edge:** Reeded

Date	Mintage	F	VF	XF	Unc	BU
2002 Proof	9,096	Value: 35.00				

KM# 656 5 DOLLARS
36.3100 g., 0.9990 Silver 1.1662 oz. ASW, 38.74 mm. **Ruler:** Elizabeth II **Obv:** Queens head right **Rev:** HMS Investigator sailing ship **Edge:** Reeded

Date	Mintage	F	VF	XF	Unc	BU
2002 Proof	9,096	Value: 35.00				

KM# 659 5 DOLLARS
31.1035 g., 0.9990 Silver 0.9990 oz. ASW, 40 mm. **Ruler:** Elizabeth II **Subject:** Queen Mother **Obv:** Queens head right **Rev:** Queen Mother circa 1927 within wreath of roses **Rev. Designer:** Stuart Devlin **Edge:** Reeded

Date	Mintage	F	VF	XF	Unc	BU
2002 Proof	30,000	Value: 25.00				

KM# 765 5 DOLLARS
36.3100 g., 0.9990 Silver 1.1662 oz. ASW, 38.7 mm. **Ruler:** Elizabeth II **Series:** Masterpieces in Silver - Port Phillip Patterns **Obv:** 1 Ounce design **Rev:** Kangaroo design **Edge:** Reeded

Date	Mintage	F	VF	XF	Unc	BU
2003 Proof	10,000	Value: 35.00				

KM# 854 5 DOLLARS
20.0000 g., Aluminum-Bronze, 38.74 mm. **Ruler:** Elizabeth II **Subject:** Rugby World Cup **Obv:** Head with tiara right **Obv. Designer:** Ian Rank-Broadley **Rev:** Player kicking ball at posts, Official logo **Edge:** Reeded

Date	Mintage	F	VF	XF	Unc	BU
2003	43,802	—	—	—	15.00	16.50

KM# 1017 5 DOLLARS
36.2100 g., 0.9990 Silver 1.1630 oz. ASW, 38.69 mm. **Ruler:** Elizabeth II **Obv:** Head with tiara right **Obv. Legend:** ELIZABETH II - AUSTRALIA **Rev:** Faces in oval hologram in ornate frame **Rev. Legend:** AUSTRALIA'S VOLUNTEERS - MAKING A DIFFERENCE **Edge:** Reeded

Date	Mintage	F	VF	XF	Unc	BU
2003 Proof	15,000	Value: 40.00				

KM# 810 5 DOLLARS
36.3100 g., 0.9950 Silver 1.1615 oz. ASW, 40 mm. **Ruler:** Elizabeth II **Subject:** Rugby World Cup **Obv:** Head with tiara right **Obv. Designer:** Ian Rank-Broadley **Rev:** Rugby World Cup and official logos **Edge:** Reeded **Note:** Partially plated in gold.

Date	Mintage	F	VF	XF	Unc	BU
2003 Proof	20,501	Value: 85.00				

KM# 855 5 DOLLARS
27.2500 g., Copper-Nickel, 38.74 mm. **Ruler:** Elizabeth II **Subject:** Australia's Own Game **Obv:** Head with tiara right **Obv. Designer:** Ian Rank-Broadley **Rev:** Cup and logos **Edge:** Reeded **Note:** Partially gilded.

Date	Mintage	F	VF	XF	Unc	BU
2004	16,163	—	—	—	12.00	14.00

KM# 811 5 DOLLARS
Aluminum-Bronze, 38.74 mm. **Ruler:** Elizabeth II **Subject:** Bicentenary of Tasmania **Obv:** Head with tiara right

Date	Mintage	F	VF	XF	Unc	BU
2004	—	—	—	—	12.00	14.00

KM# 812 5 DOLLARS
Aluminum-Bronze, 38.74 mm. **Ruler:** Elizabeth II **Subject:** Olympic Games 2000-2004 **Obv:** Head with tiara right

Date	Mintage	F	VF	XF	Unc	BU
2004	—	—	—	—	15.00	16.50

KM# 728a 5 DOLLARS
20.0000 g., Aluminum-Bronze, 38.74 mm. **Ruler:** Elizabeth II **Subject:** Tasmanian Bicentennial **Obv:** Head with tiara right **Obv. Designer:** Ian Rank-Broadley **Rev:** Ship, map, state flower **Edge:** Reeded

Date	Mintage	F	VF	XF	Unc	BU
2004	18,561	—	—	—	12.00	14.00
2004H	2,841	—	—	—	17.50	20.00

KM# 856 5 DOLLARS
20.0000 g., Aluminum-Bronze, 38.74 mm. **Ruler:** Elizabeth II **Subject:** Olympic Games - Sydney To Athens **Obv:** Head with tiara right **Obv. Designer:** Ian Rank-Broadley **Rev:** Silhouettes ancient Greek athlete and Aboriginal **Edge:** Reeded

Date	Mintage	F	VF	XF	Unc	BU
2004	24,376	—	—	—	15.00	16.50

KM# 727 5 DOLLARS
36.3100 g., 0.9990 Silver 1.1662 oz. ASW, 38.74 mm. **Ruler:** Elizabeth II **Subject:** Olympics **Obv:** Queens head right **Rev:** Parthenon, Sydney Opera House and shield with multicolor flag and rings **Edge:** Reeded

Date	Mintage	F	VF	XF	Unc	BU
2004 Proof	17,500	Value: 35.00				

KM# 728 5 DOLLARS
36.3100 g., 0.9990 Silver 1.1662 oz. ASW, 38.74 mm. **Ruler:** Elizabeth II **Subject:** Tasmania **Obv:** Queens head right **Rev:** Ship on island map **Edge:** Reeded

Date	Mintage	F	VF	XF	Unc	BU
2004 Proof	7,500	Value: 35.00				

KM# 729 5 DOLLARS
31.1035 g., 0.9990 Silver 0.9990 oz. ASW, 40 mm. **Ruler:** Elizabeth II **Subject:** Adelaide to Darwin Railroad **Obv:** Queens head right **Rev:** Train, tracks and outline map **Edge:** Reeded

Date	Mintage	F	VF	XF	Unc	BU
2004 Proof	12,500	Value: 30.00				

KM# 730 5 DOLLARS
31.1035 g., 0.9990 Silver 0.9990 oz. ASW, 40 mm. **Ruler:** Elizabeth II **Subject:** 150 Years of Australian Steam Railways **Obv:** Queens head right **Rev:** Old steam train **Edge:** Reeded

Date	Mintage	F	VF	XF	Unc	BU
2004 Proof	15,000	Value: 30.00				

KM# 750 5 DOLLARS
20.0000 g., Aluminum-Brass, 38.74 mm. **Ruler:** Elizabeth II **Obv:** Queens head right **Rev:** Tennis player **Edge:** Reeded

Date	Mintage	F	VF	XF	Unc	BU
2005	—	—	—	—	7.50	8.50

KM# 1014 5 DOLLARS
1.2441 g., 0.9999 Gold 0.0400 oz. AGW, 19.00 mm. **Ruler:** Elizabeth II **Obv:** Bust with tiara right **Obv. Legend:** ELIZABETH II - AUSTRALIA **Obv. Designer:** Ian Rank-Broadley **Rev:** Sydney Opera House **Rev. Inscription:** SYDNEY / OPERA / HOUSE

Date	Mintage	F	VF	XF	Unc	BU
2006P Proof	100,000	Value: 50.00				

KM# 813 5 DOLLARS
20.0000 g., Aluminum-Bronze, 38.74 mm. **Ruler:** Elizabeth II **Subject:** Voyage of Discovery 1606 **Obv:** Head with tiara right **Obv. Designer:** Ian Rank-Broadley **Rev:** Dutch yacht Duyfken **Rev. Designer:** Wojciech Pietranik **Edge:** Reeded **Note:** Mintmark: G.

Date	Mintage	F	VF	XF	Unc	BU
2006	—	—	—	—	15.00	16.50

KM# 813a 5 DOLLARS
36.3100 g., 0.9990 Silver 1.1662 oz. ASW, 38.74 mm. **Ruler:** Elizabeth II **Subject:** Voyage of Discovery 1606 **Obv:** Head with tiara right **Obv. Designer:** Ian Rank-Broadley **Rev:** Dutch yacht Duyfken **Rev. Designer:** Wojciech Pietranik **Edge:** Reeded **Note:** Mintmark: Tulip.

Date	Mintage	F	VF	XF	Unc	BU
2006P Proof	8,500	Value: 125				

KM# 857 5 DOLLARS
36.3100 g., 0.9999 Silver 1.1672 oz. ASW, 38.74 mm. **Ruler:** Elizabeth II **Subject:** 150 Year of State Government **Obv:** Head with tiara right **Obv. Designer:** Ian Rank-Broadley **Rev:** Outline map of State of New South Wales **Rev. Designer:** Wojciech Pietranik **Edge:** Reeded

Date	Mintage	F	VF	XF	Unc	BU
2006 Proof	12,500	Value: 85.00				

KM# 858 5 DOLLARS
36.3100 g., 0.9990 Silver 1.1662 oz. ASW, 38.74 mm. **Ruler:** Elizabeth II **Subject:** 150 Year of State Government **Obv:** Head with tiara right **Obv. Designer:** Ian Rank-Broadley **Rev:** Outline map of State of Tasmania **Rev. Designer:** Wojciech Pietranik **Edge:** Reeded

Date	Mintage	F	VF	XF	Unc	BU
2006 Proof	12,500	Value: 85.00				

KM# 859 5 DOLLARS
36.3100 g., 0.9990 Silver 1.1662 oz. ASW, 38.74 mm. **Ruler:** Elizabeth II **Subject:** 150 Year of State Government **Obv:** Head with tiara right **Obv. Designer:** Ian Rank-Broadley **Rev:** Outline map of State of Victoria **Rev. Designer:** Wojciech Pietranik **Edge:** Reeded

Date	Mintage	F	VF	XF	Unc	BU
2006 Proof	12,500	Value: 85.00				

KM# 860 5 DOLLARS
36.3100 g., 0.9990 Silver 1.1662 oz. ASW, 38.74 mm. **Ruler:** Elizabeth II **Subject:** Masterpieces in Silver: Australia's Artists **Obv:** Ian Rank-Broadley **Rev:** Jeffrey Smart: Keswick Siding **Rev. Designer:** Vladimir Gottwald

Date	Mintage	F	VF	XF	Unc	BU
2006 Proof	10,000	Value: 60.00				

Note: In sets only

KM# 815a 5 DOLLARS
1.2441 g., 0.9990 Gold 0.0400 oz. AGW **Ruler:** Elizabeth II **Obv:** Head with tiara right **Obv. Designer:** Ian Rank-Broadley **Rev:** Sydney Opera House

Date	Mintage	F	VF	XF	Unc	BU
2006P Proof	—	Value: 82.50				

KM# 782 5 DOLLARS
36.3100 g., 0.9999 Silver 1.1672 oz. ASW, 38.74 mm. **Ruler:** Elizabeth II **Subject:** XVIII Commonwealth Games City of Sport **Obv:** Head with tiara right, denomination below **Obv. Designer:** Ian Rank-Broadley **Rev:** City skyline alongside river

Date	Mintage	F	VF	XF	Unc	BU
2006 Proof	10,000	Value: 50.00				

KM# 783 5 DOLLARS
20.0000 g., Aluminum-Bronze, 38.74 mm. **Ruler:** Elizabeth II **Subject:** XVIII Commonwealth Games, Commonwealth of Nations **Obv:** Head with tiara right, denomination below **Obv. Designer:** Ian Rank-Broadley **Rev:** Games logo and crown surrounded by stylized athletes **Rev. Designer:** Wojciech Pietranik **Edge:** Reeded

Date	Mintage	F	VF	XF	Unc	BU
2006	—	—	—	—	15.00	16.50

KM# 786 5 DOLLARS
20.0000 g., Aluminum-Bronze, 38.74 mm. **Ruler:** Elizabeth II **Subject:** XVIII Commonwealth Games Queen's Baton Relay **Obv:** Head with tiara right **Obv. Designer:** Ian Rank-Broadley **Rev:** Stylized baton running **Rev. Designer:** Peter Soobik **Edge:** Reeded

Date	Mintage	F	VF	XF	Unc	BU
2006	20,488	—	—	—	15.00	16.50

KM# 786a 5 DOLLARS
36.3100 g., 0.9990 Silver 1.1662 oz. ASW, 38.74 mm. **Ruler:** Elizabeth II **Subject:** XVIII Commonwealth Games Queen's Baton Relay **Obv:** Head with tiara right **Obv. Designer:** Ian Rank-Broadley **Rev:** Stylized baton running **Rev. Designer:** Peter Soobik **Edge:** Reeded

Date	Mintage	F	VF	XF	Unc	BU
2006 Proof	9,100	Value: 75.00				

KM# 787 5 DOLLARS
36.3100 g., 0.9990 Silver 1.1662 oz. ASW, 38.74 mm. **Ruler:** Elizabeth II **Subject:** Masterpieces in Silver: Australia's Artists **Obv:** Head with tiara right **Obv. Designer:** Ian Rank-Broadley **Rev:** Sidney Nolan: Burke & Wills **Rev. Designer:** Vladimir Gottwald

Date	Mintage	F	VF	XF	Unc	BU
2006 Proof	10,000	Value: 60.00				

Note: In sets only

KM# 788 5 DOLLARS
Silver **Ruler:** Elizabeth II **Subject:** Masters in Art - Siding

Date	Mintage	F	VF	XF	Unc	BU
2006 Proof	10,000	Value: 35.00				

KM# 789 5 DOLLARS
36.3100 g., 0.9990 Silver 1.1662 oz. ASW, 38.74 mm. **Ruler:** Elizabeth II **Subject:** Masterpieces in Silver: Australia's Artists **Obv:** Head with tiara right **Obv. Designer:** Ian Rank-Broadley **Rev:** Brett Whitley: Self Portrait in the Studio **Rev. Designer:** Vladimir Gottwald

Date	Mintage	F	VF	XF	Unc	BU
2006 Proof	10,000	Value: 60.00				

Note: In sets only

KM# 790 5 DOLLARS
36.3100 g., 0.9990 Silver 1.1662 oz. ASW, 38.74 mm. **Ruler:** Elizabeth II **Subject:** Masterpieces in Silver: Australia's Artists **Obv:** Head with tiara right **Obv. Designer:** Ian Rank-Broadley **Rev:** Russell Drysdale: The Drover's Wife **Rev. Designer:** Vladimir Gottwald

Date	Mintage	F	VF	XF	Unc	BU
2006 Proof	10,000	Value: 60.00				

Note: In sets only

KM# 861 5 DOLLARS
36.3100 g., 0.9990 Silver 1.1662 oz. ASW, 8.74 mm. **Ruler:** Elizabeth II **Subject:** Masterpieces in Silver: Australia's Artists **Obv:** Head with tiara right **Obv. Designer:** Ian Rank-Broadley **Rev:** Grace Cossington-Smith: Curve of the Bridge **Rev. Designer:** Vladimir Gottwald

Date	Mintage	F	VF	XF	Unc	BU
2007 Proof	10,000	Value: 50.00				

Note: In sets only

KM# 862 5 DOLLARS
36.3100 g., 0.9990 Silver 1.1662 oz. ASW, 38.74 mm. **Ruler:** Elizabeth II **Subject:** Masterpieces in Silver: Australia's Artists **Obv:** Head with tiara right **Obv. Designer:** Ian Rank-Broadley **Rev:** Clifford Possum Tjpaltjarri: Yuelamu Honey Ant Dreaming **Rev. Designer:** Vladimir Gottwald

Date	Mintage	F	VF	XF	Unc	BU
2007 Proof	10,000	Value: 50.00				

Note: In sets only

KM# 864 5 DOLLARS
36.3100 g., 0.9990 Silver 1.1662 oz. ASW, 38.74 mm. **Ruler:** Elizabeth II **Subject:** Masterpieces in Silver: Australia's Artists **Obv:** Ian Rank-Broadley **Rev:** Margaret Preston: Implement Blue **Rev. Designer:** Vladimir Gottwald

Date	Mintage	F	VF	XF	Unc	BU
2007 Proof	10,000	Value: 50.00				

Note: In sets only

KM# 865 5 DOLLARS
36.3100 g., 0.9990 Silver 1.1662 oz. ASW, 38.74 mm. **Ruler:** Elizabeth II **Subject:** Ashes Cricket Series 1882-2007 **Obv:** Head with tiara right **Obv. Designer:** Ian Rank-Broadley **Rev:** Urn with supporters **Rev. Designer:** Vladimir Gottwald **Edge:** Reeded

Date	Mintage	F	VF	XF	Unc	BU
2007 Proof	12,500	Value: 35.00				

Note: In sets only

KM# 863 5 DOLLARS
36.3100 g., 0.9990 Silver 1.1662 oz. ASW, 38.74 mm. **Ruler:** Elizabeth II **Subject:** Masterpieces in Silver: Australia's Artists **Obv:** Head with tiara right **Obv. Designer:** Ian Rank-Broadley **Rev:** William Dobell: Margaret Olley **Rev. Designer:** Vladimir Gottwald

Date	Mintage	F	VF	XF	Unc	BU
2007 Proof	10,000	Value: 50.00				

Note: In sets only

KM# 1013 5 DOLLARS
1.2441 g., 0.9999 Gold 0.0400 oz. AGW, 19.00 mm. **Ruler:** Elizabeth II **Subject:** 75th Anniversary Sydney Harbour Bridge **Obv:** Bust with tiara right **Obv. Legend:** ELIZABETH II - AUSTRALIA **Obv. Designer:** Ian Rank-Broadley **Rev:** Bridge **Rev. Inscription:** SYDNEY / HARBOUR / BRIDGE

Date	Mintage	F	VF	XF	Unc	BU
2007P Proof	100,000	Value: 50.00				

KM# 593 10 DOLLARS
33.1500 g., Bi-Metallic Gold plated .999 Silver center in Copper ring, 38.74 mm. **Ruler:** Elizabeth II **Subject:** "The Future" **Obv:** Queens portrait **Rev:** Tree, map and denomination **Rev. Designer:** Peter Soobik and Wojciech Pietraink **Edge:** Reeded

Date	Mintage	F	VF	XF	Unc	BU
2001 Proof	20,000	Value: 40.00				

KM# 661 10 DOLLARS
60.5000 g., 0.9990 Silver 1.9431 oz. ASW, 50 mm. **Ruler:** Elizabeth II **Subject:** The Adelaide Pound **Obv:** Queens portrait above gold plated coin design **Rev:** Legend around gold plated coin design **Edge:** Reeded

Date	Mintage	F	VF	XF	Unc	BU
2002 Proof	10,000	Value: 55.00				

KM# 751 10 DOLLARS
60.5000 g., 0.9990 Silver Partially Gold Plated 1.9431 oz. ASW, 50 mm. **Ruler:** Elizabeth II **Subject:** 150th Anniversary - Sydney Mint **Obv:** Head with tiara right above gold plated replica of obverse of 1853 original Sovereign Pattern showing Queen Victoria facing left **Obv. Designer:** Ian Rank-Broadley **Rev:** Gold plated replica of reverse of original 1853 Sovereign Pattern surrounded by silver ring **Rev. Designer:** Vladimir Gottwald **Edge:** Reeded

Date	Mintage	F	VF	XF	Unc	BU
2003 Proof	10,000	Value: 85.00				
ND(2005) Proof	10,000	Value: 55.00				

KM# 766 10 DOLLARS
36.3100 g., 0.9990 Silver 1.1662 oz. ASW, 38.7 mm. **Ruler:** Elizabeth II **Series:** Masterpieces in Silver - Port Phillip Patterns **Obv:** Queens head right **Rev:** Kangaroo design **Edge:** Reeded

Date	Mintage	F	VF	XF	Unc	BU
2003 Proof	10,000	Value: 70.00				

KM# 866 10 DOLLARS
7.7508 g., 0.9990 Gold 0.2489 oz. AGW **Ruler:** Elizabeth II **Subject:** 90th Anniversary Gallipoli Landings **Obv:** Head with tiara right **Obv. Designer:** Ian Rank-Broadley **Rev:** Australian slouch hat on inverted rifle before memorial

Date	Mintage	F	VF	XF	Unc	BU
2005 Proof	1,000	Value: 750				

KM# 869 10 DOLLARS
7.7759 g., 0.9990 Gold 0.2497 oz. AGW, 17.53 mm. **Ruler:** Elizabeth II **Subject:** FIFA World Cup **Obv:** Head with tiara right **Obv. Designer:** Ian Rank-Broadley **Rev:** Kangaroo and players on football

Date	Mintage	F	VF	XF	Unc	BU
2006P Proof	25,000	Value: 300				

KM# 867 10 DOLLARS
3.1103 g., 0.9990 Gold 0.0999 oz. AGW **Ruler:** Elizabeth II **Subject:** Ashes Cricket Series 1882-2007 **Obv:** Head with tiara right **Obv. Designer:** Ian Rank-Broadley **Rev:** Urn and supporters **Rev. Designer:** Vladimir Gottwald **Edge:** Reeded

Date	Mintage	F	VF	XF	Unc	BU
2007 Proof	—	Value: 95.00				

KM# 1000 10 DOLLARS
3.1103 g., 0.9990 Gold 0.0999 oz. AGW, 17.53 mm. **Ruler:** Elizabeth II **Subject:** Year of the Pig **Obv:** Head with tiara right **Obv. Designer:** Ian Rank-Broadley **Rev:** Mother kangaroo with joey **Rev. Designer:** Rolf Harris **Edge:** Reeded

Date	Mintage	F	VF	XF	Unc	BU
2007 Proof	—	Value: 125				

KM# 595 20 DOLLARS
Bi-Metallic .999 4.5287 Silver center in .9999 9.499 Gold ring, 32.1 mm. **Ruler:** Elizabeth II **Subject:** Gregorian Millennium **Obv:** Head with tiara right, beaded circle surrounds, denomination below **Obv. Designer:** Ian Rank-Broadley **Rev:** Chronograph watch face with observatory in center and three depictions of the Earth's rotation **Edge:** Reeded **Note:** 14.03 grams total weight.

Date	Mintage	F	VF	XF	Unc	BU
2001 Prooflike	7,500	—	—	—	—	350

KM# 597 20 DOLLARS
Bi-Metallic .9999 8.8645 Gold center in .9999 10.7618 Silver ring, 32.1 mm. **Ruler:** Elizabeth II **Subject:** Centenary of Federation **Obv:** Head with tiara right within star design, denomination below **Obv. Designer:** Ian Rank-Broadley **Rev:** National arms on a flowery background **Edge:** Reeded **Note:** 19.63 grams total weight.

Date	Mintage	F	VF	XF	Unc	BU
ND(2001) Prooflike	7,500	—	—	—	—	425

KM# 760 20 DOLLARS
Bi-Metallic Gold center in Silver ring **Ruler:** Elizabeth II **Rev:** Sir Donald Bradman portrait

Date	Mintage	F	VF	XF	Unc	BU
2001 Proof	—	Value: 375				

KM# 634 20 DOLLARS
18.3510 g., Bi-Metallic .999 Silver, 4.6655g, breast star shaped center in a .9999 Gold ,13.6855g outer ring, 32.1 mm. **Ruler:** Elizabeth II **Subject:** Queen's Golden Jubilee **Obv:** Queens head right **Rev:** Queen before Buckingham Palace **Edge:** Reeded

Date	Mintage	F	VF	XF	Unc	BU
2002P Proof	7,500	Value: 450				

KM# 687 20 DOLLARS
13.4056 g., 0.9990 Bi-Metallic .999 Gold 8.3979g Center in a .999 Silver 5.0077g Ring 0.4306 oz., 32 mm. **Ruler:** Elizabeth II **Subject:** Golden Jubilee of Coronation **Obv:** Head with tiara right within circle, denomination below **Obv. Designer:** Ian Rank-Broadley **Rev:** Four different coinage portraits of Queen Elizabeth II **Rev. Designer:** Mary Gillick, Arnold Machin, Raphael Maklouf and Ian Rank-Broadley **Edge:** Reeded

Date	Mintage	F	VF	XF	Unc	BU
2003P Proof	7,500	Value: 600				

KM# 868 25 DOLLARS
7.9881 g., 0.9167 Gold 0.2354 oz. AGW **Ruler:** Elizabeth II **Subject:** 150th Anniversary First Australian Sovereign **Obv:** Head with tiara right **Obv. Designer:** Ian Rank-Broadley

Date	Mintage	F	VF	XF	Unc	BU
2005 Proof	7,500	Value: 225				

KM# 784 30 DOLLARS
1000.0000 g., 0.9990 Silver 32.117 oz. ASW **Ruler:** Elizabeth II **Subject:** Commonwealth Games **Obv:** Head with tiara right, denomination below **Rev:** Two figures within circle of all the sports

Date	Mintage	F	VF	XF	Unc	BU
2006 Proof	500	Value: 540				

KM# 648 50 DOLLARS
36.5100 g., Tri-Metallic .9999 Gold 7.8g, 13.1 mm center in .999 Silver 13.39g, 26.85mm inner ring within a copper 15.32g, 3, 38.74 mm. **Ruler:** Elizabeth II **Subject:** Commonwealth Games **Obv:** Head with tiara right, denomination below **Obv. Designer:** Ian Rank-Broadley **Rev:** Victorious athletes within inscriptions and runners **Edge:** Reeded

Date	Mintage	F	VF	XF	Unc	BU
2002 Proof	5,000	Value: 450				

KM# 724 50 DOLLARS
36.5100 g., 0.9990 Tri-Metallic .999 Gold 7.8g center in .999 Silver 13.39g ring within .999 Copper 15.32g outer ring 1.1726 oz., 38.74 mm. **Ruler:** Elizabeth II **Subject:** Olympics - Sydney to Athens **Obv:** Head with tiara right, denomination below **Obv. Designer:** Ian Rank-Broadley **Rev:** Crossed olive and wattle branches about Australian flag and Olympic ring logo **Rev. Designer:** Wojciech Pietranik **Edge:** Reeded

Date	Mintage	F	VF	XF	Unc	BU
2004 Proof	2,500	Value: 475				

Note: In three coin set only

KM# 785 50 DOLLARS
Tri-Metallic Gold center within Silver ring within Copper outer ring, 38.74 mm. **Ruler:** Elizabeth II **Subject:** Melbourne Commonwealth Games **Obv:** Head with tiara right, denomination below **Obv. Designer:** Ian Rank-Broadley **Rev:** Two stylized athletes on central plug surrounded by Games legend and circle of athletes **Rev. Designer:** Wojciech Pietranik

Date	Mintage	F	VF	XF	Unc	BU
2006 Proof	5,000	Value: 400				

Note: In three coin set only

KM# 643 100 DOLLARS
10.3678 g., 0.9999 Gold 0.3333 oz. AGW, 25 mm. **Ruler:** Elizabeth II **Subject:** Golden Wattle Flower **Obv:** Queens head right **Rev:** Flower and denomination **Edge:** Reeded

Date	Mintage	F	VF	XF	Unc	BU
2001 Proof	2,500	Value: 320				
2001	3,000	—	—	—	285	300

KM# 635 100 DOLLARS
31.1035 g., 0.9999 Gold 0.9999 oz. AGW, 32.1 mm. **Ruler:** Elizabeth II **Subject:** Gold Panning **Obv:** Queens head right **Rev:** Two prospectors dry panning for gold with color highlighted pans and dust **Edge:** Reeded

Date	Mintage	F	VF	XF	Unc	BU
2002P Proof	1,500	Value: 875				

KM# 636 100 DOLLARS
31.1035 g., 0.9995 Platinum 0.9995 oz. APW, 32.1 mm. **Ruler:** Elizabeth II **Subject:** Multiculturalism **Obv:** Head with tiara right **Obv. Designer:** Ian Rank-Broadley **Rev:** Six racially diverse portraits against a blue background **Edge:** Reeded

Date	Mintage	F	VF	XF	Unc	BU
2002 Proof	1,000	Value: 1,550				

KM# 646 100 DOLLARS
31.4000 g., 0.9999 Gold 1.0094 oz. AGW, 34.1 mm. **Ruler:** Elizabeth II **Subject:** Queen's 50th Anniversary of Accession **Obv:** Queens head right **Rev:** Silhouette of George-VI, Queen's portrait and denomination **Rev. Designer:** Peter Soobik **Edge:** Reeded

Date	Mintage	F	VF	XF	Unc	BU
2002 Proof	2,002	Value: 875				

KM# 657 100 DOLLARS
10.3678 g., 0.9999 Gold 0.3333 oz. AGW, 25 mm. **Ruler:** Elizabeth II **Obv:** Queens head right **Rev:** Sturt's Desert Rose **Rev. Designer:** Horst Hahne **Edge:** Reeded

Date	Mintage	F	VF	XF	Unc	BU
2002	3,000	—	—	—	285	300
2002 Proof	2,500	Value: 325				

KM# 800 100 DOLLARS
31.1036 g., 0.9990 Gold 0.9990 oz. AGW, 34 mm. **Ruler:** Elizabeth II **Subject:** 50th Anniversary of the Coronation of Elizabeth II **Obv:** Head with tiara right **Rev:** Young portrait of Queen Elizabeth facing left, royal cipher, crown **Rev. Designer:** Peter Soobik **Edge:** Plain

Date	Mintage	F	VF	XF	Unc	BU
2003 Proof	660	Value: 925				

KM# 870 100 DOLLARS
10.3670 g., 0.9990 Gold 0.3330 oz. AGW, 25 mm. **Ruler:** Elizabeth II **Subject:** State Floral Emblems **Obv:** Head with tiara right **Obv. Designer:** Ian Rank-Broadley **Rev:** Royal Blue Bell flowers **Rev. Designer:** Horst Hahne **Edge:** Reeded

Date	Mintage	F	VF	XF	Unc	BU
2003 Proof	1,383	Value: 300				

KM# 741 100 DOLLARS
31.1035 g., 0.9999 Gold 0.9999 oz. AGW, 32 mm. **Ruler:** Elizabeth II **Subject:** Eureka Stockade **Obv:** Head with tiara right, denomination below **Obv. Designer:** Ian Rank-Broadley **Rev:** Eureka Stockade leader Peter Lalor and blue flag, colored image **Edge:** Reeded

Date	Mintage	F	VF	XF	Unc	BU
2004	1,500	—	—	—	900	—
2004P Proof	1,500	Value: 900				

KM# 742 100 DOLLARS
31.1035 g., 0.9995 Platinum 0.9995 oz. APW, 32.1 mm. **Ruler:** Elizabeth II **Obv:** Head with tiara right, denomination below **Obv. Designer:** Ian Rank-Broadley **Rev:** Sports: Australian sportsmen and women, colored image **Edge:** Reeded

Date	Mintage	F	VF	XF	Unc	BU
2004P Proof	1,000	Value: 1,600				

KM# 797 100 DOLLARS
31.1070 g., 0.9990 Gold 0.9991 oz. AGW, 25.1 mm. **Ruler:** Elizabeth II **Subject:** 60th Anniversary of end of World War II **Obv:** Head with tiara right **Obv. Designer:** Ian Rank-Broadley **Rev:** Latent news real photographic images of a dancing man celebrating the end of WWII

Date	Mintage	F	VF	XF	Unc	BU
2005P Proof	750	Value: 900				

KM# 644 150 DOLLARS
15.5517 g., 0.9999 Gold 0.4999 oz. AGW, 30 mm. **Ruler:** Elizabeth II **Obv:** Queens head right **Rev:** Golden Wattle Flower, value **Edge:** Reeded

Date	Mintage	F	VF	XF	Unc	BU
2001 Proof	1,500	Value: 450				

KM# 658 150 DOLLARS
15.5517 g., 0.9999 Gold 0.4999 oz. AGW, 30 mm. **Ruler:** Elizabeth II **Subject:** Sturt's Desert Rose Flower **Obv:** Queens head right **Rev:** Flowers **Rev. Designer:** Horst Hahne **Edge:** Reeded

Date	Mintage	F	VF	XF	Unc	BU
2002 Proof	1,500	Value: 450				

KM# 872 150 DOLLARS
15.5510 g., 0.9990 Gold 0.4995 oz. AGW, 30 mm. **Ruler:** Elizabeth II **Subject:** State Floral Emblems **Obv:** Head with tiara right **Obv. Designer:** Ian Rank-Broadley **Rev:** Royal Blue Bell flowers **Rev. Designer:** Horst Hahne **Edge:** Reeded

Date	Mintage	F	VF	XF	Unc	BU
2003	1,105	Value: 450				

KM# 874 150 DOLLARS
15.5510 g., 0.9990 Gold 0.4995 oz. AGW, 30 mm. **Ruler:** Elizabeth II **Subject:** Rare Australian Birds **Obv:** Head with tiara right **Obv. Designer:** Ian Rank-Broadley **Rev:** Red-tailed Cockatoo **Rev. Designer:** Wojciech Pietranik **Edge:** Reeded

Date	Mintage	F	VF	XF	Unc	BU
2003 Proof	2,500	Value: 465				

KM# 731 150 DOLLARS
10.3678 g., 0.9990 Gold 0.3330 oz. AGW, 25 mm. **Ruler:** Elizabeth II **Obv:** Queens head right **Rev:** Cassowary bird **Edge:** Reeded

Date	Mintage	F	VF	XF	Unc	BU
2004 Proof	2,500	Value: 300				

KM# 752 150 DOLLARS
10.3678 g., 0.9999 Gold 0.3333 oz. AGW, 25 mm. **Ruler:** Elizabeth II **Obv:** Queens head right **Rev:** Malleefowl bird **Edge:** Reeded

Date	Mintage	F	VF	XF	Unc	BU
2005 Proof	2,500	Value: 335				

KM# 873 150 DOLLARS
10.3670 g., 0.9990 Gold 0.3330 oz. AGW, 25 mm. **Ruler:** Elizabeth II **Subject:** Rare Australian Birds **Obv:** Head with tiara right **Obv. Designer:** Ian Rank-Broadley **Rev:** Red-tailed Cockatoo **Rev. Designer:** Wojciech Pietranik **Edge:** Reeded

Date	Mintage	F	VF	XF	Unc	BU
2006	2,500	Value: 385				

KM# 732 200 DOLLARS
15.5518 g., 0.9990 Gold 0.4995 oz. AGW, 30 mm. **Ruler:** Elizabeth II **Obv:** Queens head right **Rev:** Cassowary bird **Edge:** Reeded

Date	Mintage	F	VF	XF	Unc	BU
2004 Proof	2,500	Value: 440				

KM# 753 200 DOLLARS
15.5518 g., 0.9999 Gold 0.4999 oz. AGW, 30 mm. **Ruler:** Elizabeth II **Obv:** Queens head right **Rev:** Malleefowl bird **Edge:** Reeded

Date	Mintage	F	VF	XF	Unc	BU
2005 Proof	2,500	Value: 450				

SILVER BULLION - KANGAROO

KM# 590 DOLLAR
31.1035 g., 0.9990 Silver 0.9990 oz. ASW, 40 mm. **Ruler:** Elizabeth II **Obv:** Queens portrait **Rev:** Aboriginal kangaroo design with dots **Rev. Designer:** Jeanette Timbery **Edge:** Reeded

Date	Mintage	F	VF	XF	Unc	BU
2001 Frosted Unc	—	—	—	—	16.50	—
2001 Proof	—	Value: 25.00				

KM# 642 DOLLAR

31.1035 g., 0.9990 Silver 0.9990 oz. ASW, 40 mm. **Ruler:** Elizabeth II **Obv:** Head with tiara right, denomination below **Rev:** Aboriginal style kangaroo with wavy line background **Edge:** Reeded

Date	Mintage	F	VF	XF	Unc	BU
2002	—	—	—	—	24.00	26.00
2002 Proof	—	Value: 35.00				

KM# 798a DOLLAR

31.1035 g., 0.9990 Silver 0.9990 oz. ASW, 40 mm. **Ruler:** Elizabeth II **Obv:** Head with tiara right **Obv. Designer:** Ian Rank-Broadley **Rev:** Aboriginal style kangaroo design **Rev. Designer:** Wojcieck Pietanik **Edge:** Reeded **Note:** Partially gold plated.

Date	Mintage	F	VF	XF	Unc	BU
2003	7,450	—	—	—	—	125

KM# 798 DOLLAR

31.1035 g., 0.9990 Silver 0.9990 oz. ASW, 40 mm. **Ruler:** Elizabeth II **Obv:** Head with tiara right **Obv. Designer:** Ian Rank-Broadley **Rev:** Aboriginal style kangaroo design **Rev. Designer:** Wojcieck Pietranik **Edge:** Reeded

Date	Mintage	F	VF	XF	Unc	BU
2003	35,230	—	—	—	—	30.00
2003 Proof	20,400	Value: 35.00				

KM# 723 DOLLAR

31.1035 g., 0.9990 Silver 0.9990 oz. ASW, 40 mm. **Ruler:** Elizabeth II **Obv:** Head with tiara right, denomination below **Rev:** Kangaroo with semi-circle background **Edge:** Reeded

Date	Mintage	F	VF	XF	Unc	BU
2004 Frosted finish	—	—	—	—	18.50	20.00
2004 Proof	12,500	Value: 40.00				

KM# 723a DOLLAR

31.1035 g., 0.9990 Silver 0.9990 oz. ASW, 40 mm. **Ruler:** Elizabeth II **Obv:** Head with tiara right, denomination below **Rev:** Kangaroo with semi-circle background **Edge:** Reeded **Note:** Partially gold plated.

Date	Mintage	F	VF	XF	Unc	BU
2004 Frosted finish	—	—	—	—	55.00	60.00

KM# 830 DOLLAR

31.6000 g., 0.9990 Silver 1.0149 oz. ASW, 40 mm. **Ruler:** Elizabeth II **Subject:** Centenary Australian Tennis Open 1905-2005 **Obv:** Head with tiara right **Obv. Designer:** Ian Rank-Broadley **Rev:** Tennis players **Note:** Colorized image.

Date	Mintage	F	VF	XF	Unc	BU
2005P Proof	10,000	—	—	—	—	40.00

KM# 832 DOLLAR

31.6000 g., 0.9990 Silver 1.0149 oz. ASW, 40 mm. **Ruler:** Elizabeth II **Subject:** Centenary Rotaroy 1905-2005 **Obv:** Head with tiara right **Obv. Designer:** Ian Rank-Broadley **Rev:** Rotary International Logo **Note:** Colorized image.

Date	Mintage	F	VF	XF	Unc	BU
2005P Proof	10,000	Value: 40.00				

KM# 833 DOLLAR

31.1035 g., 0.9990 Silver 0.9990 oz. ASW, 40 mm. **Ruler:** Elizabeth II **Subject:** 90th Anniversary Gallipoli Landings **Obv:** Head with tiara right **Obv. Designer:** Ian Rank-Broadley **Rev:** Australian and New Zealand soldiers beneath Australian flag **Note:** Colorized image.

Date	Mintage	F	VF	XF	Unc	BU
2005 Proof	15,000	Value: 85.00				

KM# 834 DOLLAR

31.1035 g., 0.9990 Silver 0.9990 oz. ASW, 40 mm. **Ruler:** Elizabeth II **Subject:** 50th Anniversary Cocos Keeling Islands **Obv:** Head with tiara right **Obv. Designer:** Ian Rank-Broadley **Rev:** Booby on island **Note:** Colorized image.

Date	Mintage	F	VF	XF	Unc	BU
2005P Proof	7,500	Value: 20.00				

KM# 836 DOLLAR

31.1035 g., 0.9990 Silver 0.9990 oz. ASW, 40 mm. **Ruler:** Elizabeth II **Subject:** 21st Birthday Prince Harry of Wales **Obv:** Head with tiara right **Obv. Designer:** Ian Rank-Broadley **Rev:** Prince Henry **Note:** Colorized image.

Date	Mintage	F	VF	XF	Unc	BU
2005P Proof	12,500	Value: 20.00				

KM# 838 DOLLAR

31.1035 g., 0.9990 Silver 0.9990 oz. ASW, 40 mm. **Ruler:** Elizabeth II **Subject:** Australain-Japan Year of Exchange **Obv:** Head with tiara right **Obv. Designer:** Ian Rank-Broadley **Rev:** Kangaroo leaping with kangaroo rim decoration **Note:** Colorized image.

Date	Mintage	F	VF	XF	Unc	BU
2006P Proof	5,000	Value: 20.00				

KM# 839 DOLLAR

31.1035 g., 0.9990 Silver 0.9990 oz. ASW **Ruler:** Elizabeth II **Subject:** Tercentenary of first European Landing on Australian Mainland **Obv:** Head with tiara right **Obv. Designer:** Ian Rank-Broadley **Rev:** Dutch yacht Duyfken in sail, Janzoons map of Cape York **Note:** Colorized image.

Date	Mintage	F	VF	XF	Unc	BU
2006P Proof	10,000	Value: 40.00				

KM# 840 DOLLAR

31.1035 g., 0.9990 Silver 0.9990 oz. ASW, 40 mm. **Ruler:** Elizabeth II **Subject:** Antarctic Territory **Obv:** Head with tiara right **Obv. Designer:** Ian Rank-Broadley **Rev:** Edgeworth David Base **Note:** Colorized image.

Date	Mintage	F	VF	XF	Unc	BU
2006P Proof	7,500	Value: 25.00				

KM# 843 DOLLAR

31.1035 g., 0.9990 Silver 0.9990 oz. ASW, 40 mm. **Ruler:** Elizabeth II **Subject:** 80th Birthday of Queen Elizabeth II **Obv:** Head with tiara right **Obv. Designer:** Ian Rank-Broadley **Rev:** Queen Elizabeth II **Note:** Colorized image.

Date	Mintage	F	VF	XF	Unc	BU
2006P Proof	12,500	Value: 25.00				

KM# 844 DOLLAR

31.1035 g., 0.9990 Silver 0.9990 oz. ASW, 40 mm. **Ruler:** Elizabeth II **Subject:** Figures of Note **Obv:** Head with tiara right **Obv. Designer:** Ian Rank-Broadley **Rev:** Queen Elizabeth as portrayed on Australia 1 dollar banknote **Note:** Colorized image.

Date	Mintage	F	VF	XF	Unc	BU
2006P Proof	1,000	Value: 40.00				

KM# 845 DOLLAR

31.1035 g., 0.9990 Silver 0.9990 oz. ASW, 40 mm. **Ruler:** Elizabeth II **Subject:** Figures of Note **Obv:** Head with tiara right **Obv. Designer:** Ian Rank-Broadley **Rev:** MacArthur and Farrer as portrayed on Australia 2 dollar banknote **Note:** Colorized image.

Date	Mintage	F	VF	XF	Unc	BU
2006P Proof	1,000	Value: 40.00				

KM# 846 DOLLAR

31.1035 g., 0.9990 Silver 0.9990 oz. ASW, 40 mm. **Ruler:** Elizabeth II **Subject:** Figures of Note **Obv:** Head with tiara right **Obv. Designer:** Ian Rank-Broadley **Rev:** Banks and Chisholm as portrayed on Australia 5 dollar banknote **Note:** Colorized image.

Date	Mintage	F	VF	XF	Unc	BU
2006P Proof	1,000	Value: 40.00				

KM# 847 DOLLAR

31.1035 g., 0.9990 Silver 0.9990 oz. ASW, 40 mm. **Ruler:** Elizabeth II **Subject:** Figures of Note **Obv:** Head with tiara right **Obv. Designer:** Ian Rank-Broadley **Rev:** Greenway and Lawson as portrayed on Australia 10 dollar banknote **Note:** Colorized image.

Date	Mintage	F	VF	XF	Unc	BU
2006P Proof	1,000	Value: 40.00				

KM# 848 DOLLAR

31.1035 g., 0.9990 Silver 0.9990 oz. ASW, 40 mm. **Ruler:** Elizabeth II **Subject:** Figures of Note **Obv:** Head with tiara right **Obv. Designer:** Ian Rank-Broadley **Rev:** Kingsford-Smith and Hargrave as portrayed on Australia 20 dollar banknote **Note:** Colorized image.

Date	Mintage	F	VF	XF	Unc	BU
2006P Proof	1,000	Value: 40.00				

KM# 849 DOLLAR

31.1035 g., 0.9990 Silver 0.9990 oz. ASW, 40 mm. **Ruler:** Elizabeth II **Subject:** 50th Anniversary of Dame Edna Everage **Obv:** Head with tiara right **Obv. Designer:** Ian Rank-Broadley **Rev:** Dame Edna **Note:** Colorized image.

Date	Mintage	F	VF	XF	Unc	BU
2006P Proof	6,500	Value: 20.00				

KM# 841 DOLLAR

31.1035 g., 0.9990 Silver 0.9990 oz. ASW **Ruler:** Elizabeth II **Subject:** 50 Years of Television in Australia 1956-2006 **Obv:** Head with tiara right **Obv. Designer:** Ian Rank-Broadley **Rev:** Historic TV images **Shape:** Square with rounded corners **Note:** Colorized lenticular display.

Date	Mintage	F	VF	XF	Unc	BU
2006P Proof	12,500	Value: 45.00				

KM# 842 DOLLAR

31.1035 g., 0.9990 Silver 0.9990 oz. ASW, 40 mm. **Ruler:** Elizabeth II **Subject:** 40th Anniversary of Demise of Pre-Decimal Coins **Obv:** Head with tiara right above transparent locket containing small replicas of pre-decimal currency **Obv. Designer:** Ian Rank-Broadley **Rev:** Rim legend about locket

Date	Mintage	F	VF	XF	Unc	BU
2006P Proof	7,500	Value: 100				

KM# 837 DOLLAR

31.6000 g., 0.9990 Silver 1.0149 oz. ASW, 40 mm. **Ruler:** Elizabeth II **Obv:** Head with tiara right **Obv. Designer:** Ian Rank-Broadley **Rev:** Kangaroo bounding under Australian sun **Rev. Designer:** Wojcieck Pietranik **Edge:** Reeded

Date	Mintage	F	VF	XF	Unc	BU
2006	—	—	—	—	—	30.00
2006 Proof	12,500	Value: 35.00				

KM# 837a DOLLAR

31.6000 g., 0.9990 Silver partially Gold-Plated 1.0149 oz. ASW, 40 mm. **Ruler:** Elizabeth II **Obv:** Head with tiara right **Obv. Designer:** Ian Rank-Broadley **Rev:** Kangaroo bounding under Australian sun **Rev. Designer:** Wojcieck Pietranik **Edge:** Reeded

Date	Mintage	F	VF	XF	Unc	BU
2006	7,500	—	—	—	—	50.00

KM# 851 DOLLAR

31.6000 g., 0.9990 Silver 1.0149 oz. ASW, 40 mm. **Ruler:** Elizabeth II **Obv:** Head with tiara right **Obv. Designer:** Ian Rank-Broadley **Rev:** Kangaroo mother and joey **Rev. Designer:** Rolf Harris **Edge:** Reeded

Date	Mintage	F	VF	XF	Unc	BU
2007	15,000	—	—	—	—	40.00
2007 Proof	12,500	Value: 35.00				

BULLION - FAUNA

KM# 950 5 DOLLARS

1.2441 g., 0.9990 Gold 0.0400 oz. AGW **Ruler:** Elizabeth II **Subject:** Australian Fauna **Obv:** Head with tiara right **Obv. Designer:** Ian Rank-Broadley **Rev:** Saltwater Crocodile

Date	Mintage	F	VF	XF	Unc	BU
2006 Proof	25,000	Value: 45.00				

KM# 953 5 DOLLARS

1.2441 g., 0.9990 Gold 0.0400 oz. AGW **Ruler:** Elizabeth II **Subject:** Australian Fauna **Obv:** Head with tiara right **Obv. Designer:** Ian Rank-Broadley **Rev:** Grey kangaroo

Date	Mintage	F	VF	XF	Unc	BU
2006 Proof	25,000	Value: 45.00				

KM# 956 5 DOLLARS

1.2441 g., 0.9990 Gold 0.0400 oz. AGW **Ruler:** Elizabeth II **Subject:** Australian Fauna **Obv:** Head with tiara right **Obv. Designer:** Ian Rank-Broadley **Rev:** Emu

Date	Mintage	F	VF	XF	Unc	BU
2006 Proof	25,000	Value: 45.00				

KM# 959 5 DOLLARS

1.2441 g., 0.9990 Gold 0.0400 oz. AGW **Ruler:** Elizabeth II **Subject:** Australian Fauna **Obv:** Head with tiara right **Obv. Designer:** Ian Rank-Broadley **Rev:** Koala

Date	Mintage	F	VF	XF	Unc	BU
2006 Proof	25,000	Value: 45.00				

KM# 962 5 DOLLARS

1.2441 g., 0.9990 Gold 0.0400 oz. AGW **Ruler:** Elizabeth II **Subject:** Australian Fauna **Obv:** Head with tiara right **Obv. Designer:** Ian Rank-Broadley **Rev:** Kookaburra

Date	Mintage	F	VF	XF	Unc	BU
2006 Proof	25,000	Value: 45.00				

KM# 965 5 DOLLARS

1.2441 g., 0.9990 Gold 0.0400 oz. AGW **Ruler:** Elizabeth II **Subject:** Australian Fauna **Obv:** Head with tiara right **Obv. Designer:** Ian Rank-Broadley **Rev:** Echidna

Date	Mintage	F	VF	XF	Unc	BU
2007 Proof	25,000	Value: 45.00				

KM# 968 5 DOLLARS

1.2441 g., 0.9990 Gold 0.0400 oz. AGW **Ruler:** Elizabeth II **Subject:** Australian Fauna **Obv:** Head with tiara right **Obv. Designer:** Ian Rank-Broadley **Rev:** Common Wombat

Date	Mintage	F	VF	XF	Unc	BU
2007 Proof	25,000	Value: 45.00				

KM# 971 5 DOLLARS

1.2441 g., 0.9990 Gold 0.0400 oz. AGW **Ruler:** Elizabeth II **Subject:** Australian Fauna **Obv:** Head with tiara right **Obv. Designer:** Ian Rank-Broadley **Rev:** Tasmanian Devil

Date	Mintage	F	VF	XF	Unc	BU
2007 Proof	25,000	Value: 45.00				

KM# 974 5 DOLLARS

1.2441 g., 0.9990 Gold 0.0400 oz. AGW **Ruler:** Elizabeth II **Subject:** Australian Fauna **Obv:** Head with tiara right **Obv. Designer:** Ian Rank-Broadley **Rev:** Great White Shark

Date	Mintage	F	VF	XF	Unc	BU
2007 Proof	25,000	Value: 45.00				

KM# 977 5 DOLLARS

1.2441 g., 0.9990 Gold 0.0400 oz. AGW **Ruler:** Elizabeth II **Subject:** Australian Fauna **Obv:** Head with tiara right **Obv. Designer:** Ian Rank-Broadley **Rev:** Platypus

Date	Mintage	F	VF	XF	Unc	BU
2007 Proof	25,000	Value: 45.00				

KM# 951 15 DOLLARS
3.1101 g., 0.9990 Gold 0.0999 oz. AGW **Ruler:** Elizabeth II **Subject:** Australian Fauna **Obv:** Head with tiara right **Obv. Designer:** Ian Rank-Broadley **Rev:** Saltwater Crocodile

Date	Mintage	F	VF	XF	Unc	BU
2006 Proof	2,500	Value: 90.00				

KM# 954 15 DOLLARS
3.1101 g., 0.9990 Gold 0.0999 oz. AGW **Ruler:** Elizabeth II **Subject:** Australian Fauna **Obv:** Head with tiara right **Obv. Designer:** Ian Rank-Broadley **Rev:** Grey kangaroo

Date	Mintage	F	VF	XF	Unc	BU
2006 Proof	2,500	Value: 90.00				

KM# 957 15 DOLLARS
3.1101 g., 0.9990 Gold 0.0999 oz. AGW **Ruler:** Elizabeth II **Subject:** Australian Fauna **Obv:** Head with tiara right **Obv. Designer:** Ian Rank-Broadley **Rev:** Emu

Date	Mintage	F	VF	XF	Unc	BU
2006 Proof	2,500	Value: 90.00				

KM# 960 15 DOLLARS
3.1101 g., 0.9990 Gold 0.0999 oz. AGW **Ruler:** Elizabeth II **Subject:** Australian Fauna **Obv:** Head with tiara right **Obv. Designer:** Ian Rank-Broadley **Rev:** Koala

Date	Mintage	F	VF	XF	Unc	BU
2006 Proof	2,500	Value: 90.00				

KM# 963 15 DOLLARS
3.1101 g., 0.9990 Gold 0.0999 oz. AGW **Ruler:** Elizabeth II **Subject:** Australian Fauna **Obv:** Head with tiara right **Obv. Designer:** Ian Rank-Broadley **Rev:** Kookaburra

Date	Mintage	F	VF	XF	Unc	BU
2006 Proof	2,500	Value: 90.00				

KM# 966 15 DOLLARS
3.1101 g., 0.9990 Gold 0.0999 oz. AGW **Ruler:** Elizabeth II **Subject:** Australian Fauna **Obv:** Head with tiara right **Obv. Designer:** Ian Rank-Broadley **Rev:** Echidna

Date	Mintage	F	VF	XF	Unc	BU
2007 Proof	2,500	Value: 90.00				

KM# 969 15 DOLLARS
3.1101 g., 0.9990 Gold 0.0999 oz. AGW **Ruler:** Elizabeth II **Subject:** Australian Fauna **Obv:** Head with tiara right **Obv. Designer:** Ian Rank-Broadley **Rev:** Common Wombat

Date	Mintage	F	VF	XF	Unc	BU
2007 Proof	2,500	Value: 90.00				

KM# 972 15 DOLLARS
3.1101 g., 0.9990 Gold 0.0999 oz. AGW **Ruler:** Elizabeth II **Subject:** Australian Fauna **Obv:** Head with tiara right **Obv. Designer:** Ian Rank-Broadley **Rev:** Tasmanian Devil

Date	Mintage	F	VF	XF	Unc	BU
2007 Proof	2,500	Value: 90.00				

KM# 975 15 DOLLARS
3.1101 g., 0.9990 Gold 0.0999 oz. AGW **Ruler:** Elizabeth II **Subject:** Australian Fauna **Obv:** Head with tiara right **Obv. Designer:** Ian Rank-Broadley **Rev:** Great White Shark

Date	Mintage	F	VF	XF	Unc	BU
2007 Proof	2,500	Value: 90.00				

KM# 978 15 DOLLARS
3.1101 g., 0.9990 Gold 0.0999 oz. AGW **Ruler:** Elizabeth II **Subject:** Australian Fauna **Obv:** Head with tiara right **Obv. Designer:** Ian Rank-Broadley **Rev:** Platypus

Date	Mintage	F	VF	XF	Unc	BU
2007 Proof	2,500	Value: 90.00				

KM# 952 50 DOLLARS
15.5017 g., 0.9990 Gold 0.4979 oz. AGW **Ruler:** Elizabeth II **Subject:** Australian Fauna **Obv:** Head with tiara right **Obv. Designer:** Ian Rank-Broadley **Rev:** Saltwater Crocodile

Date	Mintage	F	VF	XF	Unc	BU
2006 Proof	1,000	Value: 450				

KM# 955 50 DOLLARS
15.5017 g., 0.9990 Gold 0.4979 oz. AGW **Ruler:** Elizabeth II **Subject:** Australian Fauna **Obv:** Head with tiara right **Obv. Designer:** Ian Rank-Broadley **Rev:** Grey kangaroo

Date	Mintage	F	VF	XF	Unc	BU
2006 Proof	1,000	Value: 450				

KM# 958 50 DOLLARS
15.5017 g., 0.9990 Gold 0.4979 oz. AGW **Ruler:** Elizabeth II **Subject:** Australian Fauna **Obv:** Head with tiara right **Obv. Designer:** Ian Rank-Broadley **Rev:** Emu

Date	Mintage	F	VF	XF	Unc	BU
2006 Proof	1,000	Value: 450				

KM# 961 50 DOLLARS
15.5017 g., 0.9990 Gold 0.4979 oz. AGW **Ruler:** Elizabeth II **Subject:** Australian Fauna **Obv:** Head with tiara right **Obv. Designer:** Ian Rank-Broadley **Rev:** Koala

Date	Mintage	F	VF	XF	Unc	BU
2006 Proof	1,000	Value: 450				

KM# 964 50 DOLLARS
15.5017 g., 0.9990 Gold 0.4979 oz. AGW **Ruler:** Elizabeth II **Subject:** Australian Fauna **Obv:** Head with tiara right **Obv. Designer:** Ian Rank-Broadley **Rev:** Kookaburra

Date	Mintage	F	VF	XF	Unc	BU
2006 Proof	1,000	Value: 450				

KM# 967 50 DOLLARS
15.5017 g., 0.9990 Gold 0.4979 oz. AGW **Ruler:** Elizabeth II **Subject:** Australian Fauna **Obv:** Head with tiara right **Obv. Designer:** Ian Rank-Broadley **Rev:** Echidna

Date	Mintage	F	VF	XF	Unc	BU
2007 Proof	1,000	Value: 450				

KM# 970 50 DOLLARS
15.5017 g., 0.9990 Gold 0.4979 oz. AGW **Ruler:** Elizabeth II **Subject:** Australian Fauna **Obv:** Head with tiara right **Obv. Designer:** Ian Rank-Broadley **Rev:** Common Wombat

Date	Mintage	F	VF	XF	Unc	BU
2007 Proof	1,000	Value: 450				

KM# 973 50 DOLLARS
15.5017 g., 0.9990 Gold 0.4979 oz. AGW **Ruler:** Elizabeth II **Subject:** Australian Fauna **Obv:** Head with tiara right **Obv. Designer:** Ian Rank-Broadley **Rev:** Tasmanian Devil

Date	Mintage	F	VF	XF	Unc	BU
2007 Proof	1,000	Value: 450				

KM# 976 50 DOLLARS
15.5017 g., 0.9990 Gold 0.4979 oz. AGW **Ruler:** Elizabeth II **Subject:** Australian Fauna **Obv:** Head with tiara right **Obv. Designer:** Ian Rank-Broadley **Rev:** Great White Shark

Date	Mintage	F	VF	XF	Unc	BU
2007 Proof	1,000	Value: 450				

KM# 979 50 DOLLARS
15.5017 g., 0.9990 Gold 0.4979 oz. AGW **Ruler:** Elizabeth II **Subject:** Australian Fauna **Obv:** Head with tiara right **Obv. Designer:** Ian Rank-Broadley **Rev:** Platypus

Date	Mintage	F	VF	XF	Unc	BU
2007 Proof	1,000	Value: 450				

BULLION - FLORA

KM# 980 15 DOLLARS
3.1101 g., 0.9990 Platinum 0.0999 oz. APW **Ruler:** Elizabeth II **Subject:** Australian Flora **Obv:** Head with tiara right **Obv. Designer:** Ian Rank-Broadley **Rev:** Cooktown Orchid

Date	Mintage	F	VF	XF	Unc	BU
2006 Proof	2,500	Value: 165				

KM# 982 15 DOLLARS
3.1101 g., 0.9990 Platinum 0.0999 oz. APW **Ruler:** Elizabeth II **Subject:** Australian Flora **Obv:** Head with tiara right **Obv. Designer:** Ian Rank-Broadley **Rev:** Sturt's Desert Rose

Date	Mintage	F	VF	XF	Unc	BU
2006 Proof	2,500	Value: 165				

KM# 984 15 DOLLARS
3.1101 g., 0.9990 Platinum 0.0999 oz. APW **Ruler:** Elizabeth II **Subject:** Australian Flora **Obv:** Head with tiara right **Obv. Designer:** Ian Rank-Broadley **Rev:** Royal Bluebell

Date	Mintage	F	VF	XF	Unc	BU
2006 Proof	2,500	Value: 165				

KM# 986 15 DOLLARS
3.1101 g., 0.9990 Platinum 0.0999 oz. APW **Ruler:** Elizabeth II **Subject:** Australian Flora **Obv:** Head with tiara right **Obv. Designer:** Ian Rank-Broadley **Rev:** Kangaroo Paw

Date	Mintage	F	VF	XF	Unc	BU
2006 Proof	2,500	Value: 165				

KM# 988 15 DOLLARS
3.1101 g., 0.9990 Platinum 0.0999 oz. APW **Ruler:** Elizabeth II **Subject:** Australian Flora **Obv:** Head with tiara right **Obv. Designer:** Ian Rank-Broadley **Rev:** Common Pink Heath

Date	Mintage	F	VF	XF	Unc	BU
2006 Proof	2,500	Value: 165				

KM# 990 15 DOLLARS
3.1101 g., 0.9990 Platinum 0.0999 oz. APW **Ruler:** Elizabeth II **Subject:** Australian Flora **Obv:** Head with tiara right **Obv. Designer:** Ian Rank-Broadley **Rev:** Anemone Buttercup

Date	Mintage	F	VF	XF	Unc	BU
2007 Proof	2,500	Value: 165				

KM# 992 15 DOLLARS
3.1101 g., 0.9990 Platinum 0.0999 oz. APW **Ruler:** Elizabeth II **Subject:** Australian Flora **Obv:** Head with tiara right **Obv. Designer:** Ian Rank-Broadley **Rev:** Sturt's Desert Pea

Date	Mintage	F	VF	XF	Unc	BU
2007 Proof	2,500	Value: 165				

KM# 994 15 DOLLARS
3.1101 g., 0.9990 Platinum 0.0999 oz. APW **Ruler:** Elizabeth II **Subject:** Australian Flora **Obv:** Head with tiara right **Obv. Designer:** Ian Rank-Broadley **Rev:** Tasmanian Bluegum

Date	Mintage	F	VF	XF	Unc	BU
2007 Proof	2,500	Value: 165				

KM# 996 15 DOLLARS
3.1101 g., 0.9990 Platinum 0.0999 oz. APW **Ruler:** Elizabeth II **Subject:** Australian Flora **Obv:** Head with tiara right **Obv. Designer:** Ian Rank-Broadley **Rev:** Waratah

Date	Mintage	F	VF	XF	Unc	BU
2007 Proof	2,500	Value: 165				

KM# 998 15 DOLLARS
3.1101 g., 0.9990 Platinum 0.0999 oz. APW **Ruler:** Elizabeth II **Subject:** Australian Flora **Obv:** Head with tiara right **Obv. Designer:** Ian Rank-Broadley **Rev:** Golden Wattle

Date	Mintage	F	VF	XF	Unc	BU
2007 Proof	2,500	Value: 165				

KM# 981 50 DOLLARS
15.5017 g., 0.9990 Platinum 0.4979 oz. APW **Ruler:** Elizabeth II **Subject:** Australian Flora **Obv:** Head with tiara right **Obv. Designer:** Ian Rank-Broadley **Rev:** Cooktown Orchid

Date	Mintage	F	VF	XF	Unc	BU
2006 Proof	1,000	Value: 825				

KM# 983 50 DOLLARS
15.5017 g., 0.9990 Gold 0.4979 oz. AGW **Ruler:** Elizabeth II **Subject:** Australian Flora **Obv:** Head with tiara right **Obv. Designer:** Ian Rank-Broadley **Rev:** Sturt's Desert Rose

Date	Mintage	F	VF	XF	Unc	BU
2006 Proof	1,000	Value: 825				

KM# 985 50 DOLLARS
15.5017 g., 0.9990 Platinum 0.4979 oz. APW **Ruler:** Elizabeth II **Subject:** Australian Flora **Obv:** Head with tiara right **Obv. Designer:** Ian Rank-Broadley **Rev:** Royal Bluebell

Date	Mintage	F	VF	XF	Unc	BU
2006 Proof	1,000	Value: 825				

KM# 987 50 DOLLARS
15.5017 g., 0.9990 Platinum 0.4979 oz. APW **Ruler:** Elizabeth II **Subject:** Australian Flora **Obv:** Head with tiara right **Obv. Designer:** Ian Rank-Broadley **Rev:** Kangaroo Paw

Date	Mintage	F	VF	XF	Unc	BU
2006 Proof	1,000	Value: 825				

KM# 989 50 DOLLARS
15.5017 g., 0.9990 Platinum 0.4979 oz. APW **Ruler:** Elizabeth II **Subject:** Australian Flora **Obv:** Head with tiara right **Obv. Designer:** Ian Rank-Broadley **Rev:** Common Pink Heath

Date	Mintage	F	VF	XF	Unc	BU
2006 Proof	1,000	Value: 825				

KM# 991 50 DOLLARS
15.5017 g., 0.9990 Platinum 0.4979 oz. APW **Ruler:** Elizabeth II **Subject:** Australian Flora **Obv:** Head with tiara right **Obv. Designer:** Ian Rank-Broadley **Rev:** Anemone Buttercup

Date	Mintage	F	VF	XF	Unc	BU
2007 Proof	1,000	Value: 825				

KM# 993 50 DOLLARS
15.5017 g., 0.9990 Platinum 0.4979 oz. APW **Ruler:** Elizabeth II **Subject:** Australian Flora **Obv:** Head with tiara right **Obv. Designer:** Ian Rank-Broadley **Rev:** Sturt's Desert Pea

Date	Mintage	F	VF	XF	Unc	BU
2007 Proof	1,000	Value: 825				

KM# 995 50 DOLLARS
15.5017 g., 0.9990 Platinum 0.4979 oz. APW **Ruler:** Elizabeth II **Subject:** Australian Flora **Obv:** Head with tiara right **Obv. Designer:** Ian Rank-Broadley **Rev:** Tasmanian Bluegum

Date	Mintage	F	VF	XF	Unc	BU
2007 Proof	1,000	Value: 825				

KM# 997 50 DOLLARS
15.5017 g., 0.9990 Platinum 0.4979 oz. APW **Ruler:** Elizabeth II **Subject:** Australian Flora **Obv:** Head with tiara right **Obv. Designer:** Ian Rank-Broadley **Rev:** Waratah

Date	Mintage	F	VF	XF	Unc	BU
2007 Proof	1,000	Value: 825				

KM# 999 50 DOLLARS
15.5017 g., 0.9990 Platinum 0.4979 oz. APW **Ruler:** Elizabeth II **Subject:** Australian Flora **Obv:** Head with tiara right **Obv. Designer:** Ian Rank-Broadley **Rev:** Golden Wattle

Date	Mintage	F	VF	XF	Unc	BU
2007 Proof	1,000	Value: 825				

BULLION - LANDMARKS

KM# 737 DOLLAR
31.1035 g., 0.9990 Silver 0.9990 oz. ASW, 40 mm. **Ruler:** Elizabeth II **Obv:** Head with tiara right **Rev:** Multicolor Antarctic view of Mawson Station and penguins **Edge:** Reeded

Date	Mintage	F	VF	XF	Unc	BU
2004P Proof	7,500	Value: 35.00				

KM# 1015 DOLLAR
31.6000 g., 0.9990 Silver 1.0149 oz. ASW, 40.48 mm. **Ruler:** Elizabeth II **Subject:** 50th Anniversary Australian Territory **Obv:** Head with tiara right **Obv. Legend:** ELIZABETH II • AUSTRALIA **Obv. Designer:** Ian Rank-Broadley **Rev:** Red-footed Booby perched on a branch, multicolor **Rev. Legend:** COCOS (KEELING) ISLANDS **Edge:** Reeded

Date	Mintage	F	VF	XF	Unc	BU
2005P Proof	7,500	Value: 60.00				

KM# 1018 DOLLAR
31.7500 g., 0.9990 Silver 1.0197 oz. ASW, 40.45 mm. **Ruler:** Elizabeth II **Obv:** Head with tiara right **Obv. Legend:** ELIZABETH II - AUSTRALIA **Obv. Designer:** Ian Rank-Broadley **Rev:** Leopard seal with pup on ice, multicolor **Rev. Legend:** Australian Antarctic Territory **Edge:** Reeded

Date	Mintage	F	VF	XF	Unc	BU
2005P Proof	7,500	Value: 50.00				

KM# 1019 DOLLAR
31.3000 g., 0.9990 Silver 1.0053 oz. ASW, 40.53 mm. **Ruler:** Elizabeth II **Subject:** 20th Anniversary of base **Obv:** Head with tiara right **Obv. Legend:** ELIZABETH II - AUSTRALIA **Obv. Designer:** Ian Rank-Broadley **Rev:** Plane above Albatross and chick on ice, multicolor **Rev. Legend:** Australian Antarctic Territory - EDGEWORTH DAVID BASE **Edge:** Reeded

Date	Mintage	F	VF	XF	Unc	BU
ND(2006)P Proof	7,500	Value: 50.00				

KM# 1008 DOLLAR
31.1030 g., 0.9990 Silver 0.9989 oz. ASW **Ruler:** Elizabeth II **Subject:** Quadricentennial **Obv:** Head with tiarra right **Obv. Legend:** ELIZABETH II - AUSTRALIA **Obv. Designer:** Ian Rank-Broadley **Rev:** Sailing ship at left, early map at right **Rev. Legend:** *Australia on the Map*

Date	Mintage	F	VF	XF	Unc	BU
ND(2006)	—	—	—	—	—	25.00

KM# 940 DOLLAR
31.1035 g., 0.9990 Silver 0.9990 oz. ASW **Ruler:** Elizabeth II **Subject:** Australian Landmarks **Obv:** Head with tiara right **Obv. Designer:** Ian Rank-Broadley **Rev:** Melbourne

Date	Mintage	F	VF	XF	Unc	BU
2006 Proof	7,500	Value: 30.00				

KM# 941 DOLLAR
31.1035 g., 0.9990 Silver 0.9990 oz. ASW **Ruler:** Elizabeth II **Subject:** Australian Landmarks **Obv:** Head with tiara right **Obv. Designer:** Ian Rank-Broadley **Rev:** Uluru

Date	Mintage	F	VF	XF	Unc	BU
2006 Proof	7,500	Value: 30.00				

KM# 942 DOLLAR
31.1035 g., 0.9990 Silver 0.9990 oz. ASW **Ruler:** Elizabeth II **Subject:** Australian Landmarks **Obv:** Head with tiara right **Obv. Designer:** Ian Rank-Broadley **Rev:** Canberra

Date	Mintage	F	VF	XF	Unc	BU
2006 Proof	7,500	Value: 30.00				

KM# 943 DOLLAR
31.1035 g., 0.9990 Silver 0.9990 oz. ASW **Ruler:** Elizabeth II **Subject:** Australian Landmarks **Obv:** Head with tiara right **Obv. Designer:** Ian Rank-Broadley **Rev:** Perth

Date	Mintage	F	VF	XF	Unc	BU
2006 Proof	7,500	Value: 30.00				

KM# 944 DOLLAR
31.1035 g., 0.9990 Silver 0.9990 oz. ASW **Ruler:** Elizabeth II **Subject:** Australian Landmarks **Obv:** Head with tiara right **Obv. Designer:** Ian Rank-Broadley **Rev:** Great Barrier Reef

Date	Mintage	F	VF	XF	Unc	BU
2006 Proof	7,500	Value: 30.00				

KM# 945 DOLLAR
31.1035 g., 0.9990 Silver 0.9990 oz. ASW **Ruler:** Elizabeth II **Subject:** Australian Landmarks **Obv:** Head with tiara right **Obv. Designer:** Ian Rank-Broadley **Rev:** Gold Coast

Date	Mintage	F	VF	XF	Unc	BU
2007 Proof	7,500	Value: 30.00				

KM# 946 DOLLAR
31.1035 g., 0.9990 Silver 0.9990 oz. ASW **Ruler:** Elizabeth II **Subject:** Australian Landmarks **Obv:** Head with tiara right **Obv. Designer:** Ian Rank-Broadley **Rev:** Phillip Island

Date	Mintage	F	VF	XF	Unc	BU
2007 Proof	7,500	Value: 30.00				

KM# 947 DOLLAR
31.1035 g., 0.9990 Silver 0.9990 oz. ASW **Ruler:** Elizabeth II **Subject:** Australian Landmarks **Obv:** Head with tiara right **Obv. Designer:** Ian Rank-Broadley **Rev:** Port Arthur

Date	Mintage	F	VF	XF	Unc	BU
2007 Proof	7,500	Value: 30.00				

KM# 948 DOLLAR
31.1035 g., 0.9990 Silver 0.9990 oz. ASW **Ruler:** Elizabeth II **Subject:** Australian Landmarks **Obv:** Head with tiara right **Obv. Designer:** Ian Rank-Broadley **Rev:** Adelaide

Date	Mintage	F	VF	XF	Unc	BU
2007 Proof	7,500	Value: 30.00				

KM# 949 DOLLAR
31.1035 g., 0.9990 Silver 0.9990 oz. ASW **Ruler:** Elizabeth II **Subject:** Australian Landmarks **Obv:** Head with tiara right **Obv. Designer:** Ian Rank-Broadley **Rev:** Sydney

Date	Mintage	F	VF	XF	Unc	BU
2007	7,500	Value: 30.00				

KM# 1020 DOLLAR
31.4800 g., 0.9990 Silver 1.0111 oz. ASW, 40.51 mm. **Ruler:** Elizabeth II **Subject:** 50th Anniversary of Station **Obv:** Head with tiara right **Obv. Legend:** ELIZABETH II - AUSTRALIA **Obv. Designer:** Ian Rank-Broadley **Rev:** Ship "Kista Dan", multicolor **Rev. Legend:** Australian Antarctic Territory - DAVIS STATION **Edge:** Reeded

Date	Mintage	F	VF	XF	Unc	BU
ND(2007)P Proof	7,500	Value: 50.00				

SILVER BULLION - KOOKABURRA

KM# 875 50 CENTS
15.5500 g., 0.9990 Silver 0.4994 oz. ASW, 38.74 mm. **Ruler:** Elizabeth II **Obv:** Head with tiara right **Obv. Designer:** Ian Rank-Broadley **Rev:** Kookaburra on branch, tail above, two leaves **Edge:** Reeded **Shape:** Square with rounded corners **Note:** Lenticular technology makes kookaburra appear to move.

Date	Mintage	F	VF	XF	Unc	BU
2002P Proof	75,350	Value: 30.00				

KM# 684 50 CENTS
15.5500 g., 0.9990 Silver 0.4994 oz. ASW, 32.1 mm. **Ruler:** Elizabeth II **Obv:** Head with tiara right, denomination below **Obv. Designer:** Ian Rank-Broadley **Rev:** Two Kookaburras, one in flight **Edge:** Reeded **Shape:** Square with rounded corners

Date	Mintage	F	VF	XF	Unc	BU
2003P Proof	75,350	Value: 25.00				

KM# 876 50 CENTS
15.5500 g., 0.9990 Silver 0.4994 oz. ASW, 38.74 mm. **Ruler:** Elizabeth II **Obv:** Head with tiara right **Obv. Designer:** Ian Rank-Broadley **Rev:** Kookaburra perched on branch, tail below, four leaves **Edge:** Reeded **Shape:** Square with rounded corners

Date	Mintage	F	VF	XF	Unc	BU
2004P Proof	30,350	Value: 25.00				

KM# 877 50 CENTS
15.5500 g., 0.9990 Silver 0.4994 oz. ASW, 38.74 mm. **Ruler:** Elizabeth II **Obv:** Head with tiara right **Obv. Designer:** Ian Rank-Broadley **Rev:** Two kookaburras on branch, one laughing **Edge:** Reeded **Shape:** Squar with rounded corners

Date	Mintage	F	VF	XF	Unc	BU
2005P Proof	30,350	Value: 25.00				

KM# 479 DOLLAR
31.9700 g., 0.9990 Silver 1.0268 oz. ASW **Ruler:** Elizabeth II **Obv:** Head with tiara right, denomination below **Obv. Designer:** Ian Rank-Broadley **Rev:** Two Kookaburras back to back on branch

Date	Mintage	F	VF	XF	Unc	BU
2001	—	—	—	—	17.50	—
2001	10,000	—	—	—	35.00	—
Note: Federation star privy mark						
2001	50,000	—	—	—	25.00	—
Note: Santa Claus privy mark						
2001	1,000	—	—	—	120	—
Note: Love token personal message						
2001	75,000	—	—	—	30.00	—
Note: New York State Quarter privy mark						
2001	75,000	—	—	—	30.00	—
Note: North Carolina State Quarter privy mark						
2001	75,000	—	—	—	30.00	—
Note: Rhode Island State Quarter privy mark						
2001	75,000	—	—	—	30.00	—
Note: Vermont State Quarter privy mark						
2001	75,000	—	—	—	30.00	—
Note: Kentucky State Quarter privy mark						

KM# 691.1 DOLLAR
31.1035 g., 0.9990 Silver 0.9990 oz. ASW, 40 mm. **Ruler:** Elizabeth II **Obv:** Head with tiara right, denomination below **Obv. Designer:** Ian Rank-Broadley **Rev:** Kookaburra flying over map of Australia **Edge:** Reeded

Date	Mintage	F	VF	XF	Unc	BU
2001P Proof	5,000	Value: 25.00				
2002	—	—	—	—	20.00	22.50

KM# 625 DOLLAR
31.1035 g., 0.9990 Silver 0.9990 oz. ASW, 40.4 mm. **Ruler:** Elizabeth II **Subject:** U.S. State Quarter

Date	Mintage	F	VF	XF	Unc	BU
2002	75,000	—	—	—	30.00	—
Note: Tennessee State Quarter privy mark						
2002	75,000	—	—	—	30.00	—
Note: Ohio State Quarter privy mark						
2002	75,000	—	—	—	30.00	—
Note: Louisiana State Quarter privy mark						
2002	75,000	—	—	—	30.00	—
Note: Indiana State Quarter privy mark						
2002	75,000	—	—	—	30.00	—
Note: Mississippi State Quarter privy mark						

KM# 666 DOLLAR
31.6200 g., 0.9990 Silver 1.0155 oz. ASW, 40.3 mm. **Ruler:** Elizabeth II **Obv:** Head with tiara right, denomination below **Obv. Designer:** Ian Rank-Broadley **Rev:** Kookaburra perched on branch **Edge:** Reeded

Date	Mintage	F	VF	XF	Unc	BU
2002	5,000	Value: 25.00				

KM# 691.2 DOLLAR
31.6200 g., 0.9990 Silver 1.0155 oz. ASW, 40.5 mm. **Ruler:** Elizabeth II **Obv:** Head with tiara right, denomination below **Obv. Designer:** Ian Rank-Broadley **Rev:** Multicolor US flag above a kookaburra flying over Australia **Edge:** Reeded

Date	Mintage	F	VF	XF	Unc	BU
2002	18,500	—	—	—	25.00	30.00

KM# 683 DOLLAR
31.1035 g., 0.9990 Silver 0.9990 oz. ASW, 40 mm. **Ruler:** Elizabeth II **Obv:** Head with tiara right, denomination below **Obv. Designer:** Ian Rank-Broadley **Rev:** Two kookaburras, one in flight **Edge:** Reeded **Note:** Gilded.

Date	Mintage	F	VF	XF	Unc	BU
2003P Proof	5,000	Value: 25.00				
2004	10,000	—	—	—	—	25.00
2004 Proof	15,000	Value: 35.00				

KM# 883a DOLLAR
31.1035 g., 0.9990 Silver 0.9990 oz. ASW, 40 mm. **Ruler:** Elizabeth II **Obv:** Head with tiara right **Obv. Designer:** Ian Rank-Broadley **Rev:** Kookaburra purched on branch with four leaves **Note:** Gilded.

Date	Mintage	F	VF	XF	Unc	BU
2004	10,000	—	—	—	50.00	—

KM# 883 DOLLAR
31.5600 g., 0.9990 Silver 1.0136 oz. ASW, 40.5 mm. **Ruler:** Elizabeth II **Obv:** Head with tiara right **Obv. Designer:** Ian Rank-Broadley **Rev:** Kookaburra perched on branch with four leaves **Edge:** Reeded

Date	Mintage	F	VF	XF	Unc	BU
2004P Proof	5,000	Value: 25.00				
2005	5,000	—	—	—	30.00	—
Note: Gemini privy mark						
2005	5,000	—	—	—	30.00	—
Note: Aquarius privy mark						
2005	5,000	—	—	—	30.00	—

Date	Mintage	F	VF	XF	Unc	BU
Note: Pisces privy mark						
2005	5,000	—	—	—	30.00	—
Note: Aries privy mark						
2005	5,000	—	—	—	30.00	—
Note: Taurus privy mark						
2005	5,000	—	—	—	30.00	—
Note: Cancer privy mark						
2005	5,000	—	—	—	30.00	—
Note: Leo privy mark						
2005	5,000	—	—	—	30.00	—
Note: Virgo privy mark						
2005	5,000	—	—	—	30.00	—
Note: Libra privy mark						
2005	5,000	—	—	—	30.00	—
Note: Scorpio privy mark						
2005	5,000	—	—	—	30.00	—
Note: Sagittarius privy mark						
2005	5,000	—	—	—	30.00	—
Note: Capricorn privy mark						

KM# 886 DOLLAR

31.5600 g., 0.9990 Silver 1.0136 oz. ASW, 40.5 mm. **Ruler:** Elizabeth II **Obv:** Head with tiara right **Obv. Designer:** Ian Rank-Broadley **Rev:** Two kookaburras on branch, one laughing **Edge:** Reeded

Date	Mintage	F	VF	XF	Unc	BU
2005P Proof	5,000	Value: 25.00				

KM# 720 DOLLAR

1.0350 g., 0.9990 Silver 0.0332 oz. ASW **Ruler:** Elizabeth II **Obv:** Head with tiara right, denomination below **Rev:** Kookabarra

Date	Mintage	F	VF	XF	Unc	BU
2005	—	—	—	—	20.00	22.50

KM# 889 DOLLAR

31.5600 g., 0.9990 Silver 1.0136 oz. ASW, 40.5 mm. **Ruler:** Elizabeth II **Obv:** Head with tiara right **Obv. Designer:** Ian Rank-Broadley **Rev:** Kookaburras on branch, no leaves

Date	Mintage	F	VF	XF	Unc	BU
2007	300,000	—	—	—	25.00	—

KM# 678 2 DOLLARS

62.2070 g., 0.9990 Silver 1.9979 oz. ASW, 40 mm. **Ruler:** Elizabeth II **Obv:** Head with tiara right, denomination below **Obv. Designer:** Ian Rank-Broadley **Rev:** Kookaburra flying over Australian map **Edge:** Reeded

Date	Mintage	F	VF	XF	Unc	BU
2001P Proof	5,000	Value: 55.00				
2002	1,500	—	—	—	35.00	—
Note: 1661 Spanish cob privy mark						
2002	1,500	—	—	—	35.00	—
Note: 1771 Spanish pillar dllar privy mark						
2002	1,500	—	—	—	35.00	—
Note: 1881 Gold sovereign privy mark						
2002	1,500	—	—	—	35.00	—
Note: 1991 Gld Australian nugget privy mark						

KM# 623.1 2 DOLLARS

62.8500 g., 0.9990 Silver 2.0186 oz. ASW, 50 mm. **Ruler:** Elizabeth II **Obv:** Head with tiara right, denomination below **Rev:** Two Kookaburras back to back **Edge:** Reeded

Date	Mintage	F	VF	XF	Unc	BU
2001	—	—	—	—	40.00	45.00

KM# 623.2 2 DOLLARS

62.2070 g., 0.9990 Silver 1.9979 oz. ASW **Ruler:** Elizabeth II **Subject:** USA State Quarters - 2001 **Obv:** Head with tiara right, denomination below **Rev:** Two kookaburras on branch with five state quarter designs added **Edge:** Reeded and plain sections **Note:** Prev. KM#623

Date	Mintage	F	VF	XF	Unc	BU
2001	10,000	—	—	—	150	165

KM# 879 2 DOLLARS

62.8500 g., 0.9990 Silver 2.0186 oz. ASW, 40 mm. **Ruler:** Elizabeth II **Obv:** Head with tiara right **Obv. Designer:** Ian Rank-Broadley **Rev:** Kookaburra on branch plus two leaves **Edge:** Reeded

Date	Mintage	F	VF	XF	Unc	BU
2002P Proof	5,000	Value: 55.00				
2003	1,000	—	—	—	100	—
Note: Boer War privy mark						
2003	1,000	—	—	—	100	—
Note: World War I privy mark						
2003	1,000	—	—	—	100	—
Note: World War II privy mark						
2003	1,000	—	—	—	100	—
Note: Korean War privy mark						
2003	1,000	—	—	—	100	—
Note: Vietnam War privy mark						

KM# 881 2 DOLLARS

62.2070 g., 0.9990 Silver 1.9979 oz. ASW, 50 mm. **Ruler:** Elizabeth II **Obv:** Head with tiara right **Obv. Designer:** Ian Rank-Broadley **Rev:** Two kookaburras, one in flight **Edge:** Reeded

Date	Mintage	F	VF	XF	Unc	BU
2003P Proof	800	Value: 55.00				

KM# 884 2 DOLLARS

62.2070 g., 0.9990 Silver 1.9979 oz. ASW, 50 mm. **Ruler:** Elizabeth II **Obv:** Head with tiara right **Obv. Designer:** Ian Rank-Broadley **Rev:** Kookaburra perched on branch with four leaves **Edge:** Reeded

Date	Mintage	F	VF	XF	Unc	BU
2004P Proof	800	Value: 55.00				

KM# 887 2 DOLLARS

62.2070 g., 0.9990 Silver 1.9979 oz. ASW, 50 mm. **Ruler:** Elizabeth II **Obv:** Head with tiara right **Obv. Designer:** Ian Rank-Broadley **Rev:** Two kookaburras on branch, one laughing **Edge:** Reeded

Date	Mintage	F	VF	XF	Unc	BU
2005P Proof	800	Value: 55.00				
Note: In sets only						

KM# 890 2 DOLLARS

62.2070 g., 0.9990 Silver 1.9979 oz. ASW, 50 mm. **Ruler:** Elizabeth II **Obv:** Head with tiara right **Obv. Designer:** Ian Rank-Broadley **Rev:** Kookaburra on branch, no leaves

Date	Mintage	F	VF	XF	Unc	BU
2007	—	—	—	—	45.00	—

KM# 596 10 DOLLARS

311.0350 g., 0.9990 Silver 9.9896 oz. ASW, 75.5 mm. **Ruler:** Elizabeth II **Subject:** Calendar Evolution **Obv:** Head with tiara right, denomination below **Obv. Designer:** Ian Rank-Broadley **Rev:** Multicolor solar system in center, zodiac symbols in outer circle **Edge:** Segmented reeding **Note:** Illustration reduced.

Date	Mintage	F	VF	XF	Unc	BU
ND(2001) Proof	15,000	Value: 225				

KM# 603 10 DOLLARS

311.0350 g., 0.9990 Silver 9.9896 oz. ASW, 74.9 mm. **Ruler:** Elizabeth II **Subject:** Kookaburra **Obv:** Head with tiara right, denomination below **Obv. Designer:** Ian Rank-Broadley **Rev:** Flying bird over map **Edge:** Reeded

Date	Mintage	F	VF	XF	Unc	BU
2002 Proof	—	Value: 175				

KM# 633 10 DOLLARS

311.0350 g., 0.9990 Silver 9.9896 oz. ASW, 75.5 mm. **Ruler:** Elizabeth II **Subject:** Evolution of Time **Obv:** Queens portrait right **Rev:** Various time keeping devices **Edge:** Segmented reeding

Date	Mintage	F	VF	XF	Unc	BU
2002P Proof	1,500	Value: 250				

KM# 686 10 DOLLARS

311.0000 g., 0.9990 Silver 9.9885 oz. ASW, 75.5 mm. **Ruler:** Elizabeth II **Obv:** Queens head right **Rev:** Alphabet Evolution design **Edge:** Reeded

Date	Mintage	F	VF	XF	Unc	BU
2003P Proof	1,500	Value: 275				

KM# 739 10 DOLLARS

311.0350 g., 0.9990 Silver 9.9896 oz. ASW, 75.5 mm. **Ruler:** Elizabeth II **Subject:** Evolution of Numbers **Obv:** Queens head right **Rev:** Numbers, symbols, abacus and calculator **Edge:** Reeded

Date	Mintage	F	VF	XF	Unc	BU
2004 Proof	1,500	Value: 250				

KM# 744 10 DOLLARS

311.3460 g., 0.9990 Silver 9.9996 oz. ASW, 75.5 mm. **Ruler:** Elizabeth II **Obv:** Queens head right **Rev:** Multicolor symbolic design **Edge:** Reeded

Date	Mintage	F	VF	XF	Unc	BU
2005 Proof	1,500	Value: 250				

KM# 891 10 DOLLARS

311.0350 g., 0.9990 Silver 9.9896 oz. ASW, 74.9 mm. **Ruler:** Elizabeth II **Obv:** Head with tiara right **Obv. Designer:** Ian Rank-Broadley **Rev:** Kookaburra on branch, no leaves

Date	Mintage	F	VF	XF	Unc	BU
2007	—	—	—	—	175	—

KM# 630 20 DOLLARS

62.2070 g., 0.9990 Silver 1.9979 oz. ASW **Ruler:** Elizabeth II **Subject:** USA State Quarters - 2002 **Obv:** Head with tiara right, denomination below **Rev:** Kookaburra on branch with five state quarter designs added below **Edge:** Reeded and plain sections

Date	Mintage	F	VF	XF	Unc	BU
2002	10,000	—	—	—	42.00	45.00

KM# 680 30 DOLLARS
1002.5020 g., 0.9990 Silver 32.197 oz. ASW, 101 mm. **Ruler:** Elizabeth II **Obv:** Head with tiara right, denomination below **Obv. Designer:** Ian Rank-Broadley **Rev:** Kookaburra in flight above Australian map **Edge:** Segmented reeding

Date	Mintage	F	VF	XF	Unc	BU
2001P Proof	350	Value: 525				
Note: In sets only						
2002	—	—	—	—	—	550

KM# 624 30 DOLLARS
1002.5020 g., 0.9990 Silver 32.197 oz. ASW **Ruler:** Elizabeth II **Subject:** USA State Quarters - 2001 **Obv:** Head with tiara right, denomination below **Rev:** Two kookaburras on branch with five state quarter designs added below **Edge:** Reeded and plain sections

Date	Mintage	F	VF	XF	Unc	BU
2001	1,000	—	—	—	—	525

KM# 880 30 DOLLARS
1002.5020 g., 0.9990 Silver 32.197 oz. ASW, 101 mm. **Ruler:** Elizabeth II **Obv:** Head with tiara right **Obv. Designer:** Ian Rank-Broadley **Rev:** Kookaburra standing on branch **Edge:** Reeded

Date	Mintage	F	VF	XF	Unc	BU
2002P Proof	350	Value: 525				
Note: In sets only						

KM# 631 30 DOLLARS
1002.5020 g., 0.9990 Silver 32.197 oz. ASW **Ruler:** Elizabeth II **Subject:** USA State Quarters - 2002 **Obv:** Head with tiara right, denomination below **Rev:** Kookaburra on branch with five state quarter designs added in gold **Edge:** Reeded and plain sections

Date	Mintage	F	VF	XF	Unc	BU
2002	1,000	—	—	—	—	525

KM# 882 30 DOLLARS
1002.5020 g., 0.9990 Silver 32.197 oz. ASW, 101 mm. **Ruler:** Elizabeth II **Obv:** Head with tiara right **Obv. Designer:** Ian Rank-Broadley **Rev:** Two kookaburras, one in flight **Edge:** Reeded

Date	Mintage	F	VF	XF	Unc	BU
2003P Proof	350	Value: 525				
Note: In sets only						

KM# 885 30 DOLLARS
1002.5020 g., 0.9990 Silver 32.197 oz. ASW, 101 mm. **Ruler:** Elizabeth II **Obv:** Head with tiara right **Obv. Designer:** Ian Rank-Broadley **Rev:** Kookaburra perched on branch with four leaves **Edge:** Reeded

Date	Mintage	F	VF	XF	Unc	BU
2004P Proof	350	Value: 525				
Note: In sets only						

KM# 888 30 DOLLARS
1002.5020 g., 0.9990 Silver 32.197 oz. ASW, 101 mm. **Ruler:** Elizabeth II **Obv:** Head with tiara right **Obv. Designer:** Ian Rank-Broadley **Rev:** Two kookaburras on branch, one laughing **Edge:** Reeded

Date	Mintage	F	VF	XF	Unc	BU
2005P Proof	800	Value: 525				
Note: In sets only						

KM# 892 30 DOLLARS
1002.5020 g., 0.9990 Silver 32.197 oz. ASW, 101 mm. **Ruler:** Elizabeth II **Obv:** Head with tiara right **Obv. Designer:** Ian Rank-Broadley **Rev:** Kookaburras on branch, no leaves

Date	Mintage	F	VF	XF	Unc	BU
2007	—	—	—	—	525	—

KM# 878 200 DOLLARS
31.6000 g., 0.9990 Silver 1.0149 oz. ASW, 40 mm. **Ruler:** Elizabeth II **Obv:** Head with tiara right with denomination **Obv. Designer:** Ian Rank-Broadley **Rev:** Kookaburra in flight over map of Australia **Note:** Mule.

Date	Mintage	F	VF	XF	Unc	BU
ND(2001) Proof	Est. 20	Value: 2,500				

BULLION - LUNAR YEAR

KM# 579 50 CENTS
15.5518 g., 0.9990 Silver 0.4995 oz. ASW, 32.1 mm. **Ruler:** Elizabeth II **Subject:** Year of the Horse **Obv:** Head with tiara right, denomination below **Obv. Designer:** Ian Rank-Broadley **Rev:** Horse running left **Edge:** Reeded

Date	Mintage	F	VF	XF	Unc	BU
2002P Proof	5,000	Value: 36.00				

KM# 664 50 CENTS
16.4000 g., 0.9990 Silver 0.5267 oz. ASW, 31.9 mm. **Ruler:** Elizabeth II **Subject:** Year of the Goat **Obv:** Head with tiara right, denomination below **Obv. Designer:** Ian Rank-Broadley **Rev:** Two goats **Edge:** Reeded

Date	Mintage	F	VF	XF	Unc	BU
2003	—	—	—	—	12.00	20.00
2003 Proof	—	Value: 36.00				

KM# 673 50 CENTS
15.5518 g., 0.9990 Silver 0.4995 oz. ASW, 32.1 mm. **Ruler:** Elizabeth II **Subject:** Year of the Monkey **Obv:** Head with tiara right, denomination below **Rev:** Monkey sitting on branch **Edge:** Reeded

Date	Mintage	F	VF	XF	Unc	BU
2004(2003) Proof	11,000	Value: 25.00				

KM# 791 50 CENTS
15.5680 g., 0.9990 Silver 0.5000 oz. ASW, 32.1 mm. **Ruler:** Elizabeth II **Subject:** Year of the Rooster **Obv:** Elizabeth II **Rev:** Standing Rooster looking backwards **Edge:** Reeded

Date	Mintage	F	VF	XF	Unc	BU
2005P Proof	6,000	Value: 36.00				

KM# 536 DOLLAR
31.1035 g., 0.9990 Silver 0.9990 oz. ASW, 40.6 mm. **Ruler:** Elizabeth II **Subject:** Year of the Snake **Obv:** Head with tiara right, denomination below **Obv. Designer:** Ian Rank-Broadley **Rev:** Snake with eggs **Edge:** Reeded

Date	Mintage	F	VF	XF	Unc	BU
2001	300,000	—	—	—	25.00	28.00
2001P Proof	2,500	Value: 42.00				

KM# 536a DOLLAR
31.6350 g., 0.9990 Silver 1.0160 oz. ASW, 40.6 mm. **Ruler:** Elizabeth II **Subject:** Year of the Snake **Obv:** Head with tiara right, denomination below **Rev:** Gold-plated snake **Edge:** Reeded

Date	Mintage	F	VF	XF	Unc	BU
2001	50,000	—	—	—	45.00	50.00

KM# 580 DOLLAR
31.1035 g., 0.9990 Silver 0.9990 oz. ASW, 40.6 mm. **Ruler:** Elizabeth II **Subject:** Year of the Horse **Obv:** Head with tiara right, denomination below **Obv. Designer:** Ian Rank-Broadley **Rev:** Horse running left **Edge:** Reeded

Date	Mintage	F	VF	XF	Unc	BU
2002P	—	—	—	—	25.00	28.00
2002P Proof	2,500	Value: 42.00				

KM# 580a DOLLAR
31.6350 g., 0.9990 Silver 1.0160 oz. ASW, 40.6 mm. **Ruler:** Elizabeth II **Obv:** Head with tiara right **Rev:** Gold-plated horse **Edge:** Reeded

Date	Mintage	F	VF	XF	Unc	BU
2002	50,000	—	—	—	25.00	30.00

KM# 665 DOLLAR
31.6200 g., 0.9990 Silver 1.0155 oz. ASW, 40.3 mm. **Ruler:** Elizabeth II **Subject:** Year of the Goat **Obv:** Head with tiara right, denomination below **Obv. Designer:** Ian Rank-Broadley **Rev:** Two goats **Edge:** Reeded

Date	Mintage	F	VF	XF	Unc	BU
2003	—	—	—	—	22.50	25.00
Proof	—	Value: 35.00				

KM# 665a DOLLAR
31.6350 g., 0.9990 Silver 1.0160 oz. ASW, 40.6 mm. **Ruler:** Elizabeth II **Subject:** Year of the Goat **Obv:** Head with tiara right, denomination below **Rev:** Gold-plated goat **Edge:** Reeded

Date	Mintage	F	VF	XF	Unc	BU
2003	50,000	—	—	—	50.00	55.00

KM# 674 DOLLAR
31.1035 g., 0.9990 Silver 0.9990 oz. ASW, 40.6 mm. **Ruler:** Elizabeth II **Subject:** Year of the Monkey **Obv:** Head with tiara right, denomination below **Rev:** Monkey sitting on branch **Edge:** Reeded

Date	Mintage	F	VF	XF	Unc	BU
2004(2003)	—	—	—	—	22.50	25.00
2004(2003) Proof	8,500	Value: 35.00				

KM# 674a DOLLAR
31.6350 g., 0.9990 Silver 1.0160 oz. ASW, 40.6 mm. **Ruler:** Elizabeth II **Subject:** Year of the Monkey **Obv:** Head with tiara right, denomination below **Rev:** Gold-plated Monkey **Edge:** Reeded

Date	Mintage	F	VF	XF	Unc	BU
2004	50,000	—	—	—	50.00	55.00

KM# 695 DOLLAR
31.6350 g., 0.9990 Silver 1.0160 oz. ASW, 40.5 mm. **Ruler:** Elizabeth II **Subject:** Year of the Rooster **Obv:** Head with tiara right, denomination below **Rev:** Rooster **Edge:** Reeded

Date	Mintage	F	VF	XF	Unc	BU
2005	—	—	—	—	22.50	25.00

KM# 695a.1 DOLLAR

31.6350 g., 0.9990 Silver 1.0160 oz. ASW, 40.5 mm. **Ruler:** Elizabeth II **Subject:** Year of the Rooster **Obv:** Head with tiara right, denomination below **Rev:** Gold-plated Rooster on polished surface **Edge:** Reeded

Date	Mintage	F	VF	XF	Unc	BU
2005	47,200	—	—	—	45.00	50.00

KM# 695a.2 DOLLAR

31.6350 g., 0.9990 Silver 1.0160 oz. ASW, 40.5 mm. **Ruler:** Elizabeth II **Subject:** Year of the Rooster **Obv:** Head with tiara right, denomination below **Rev:** Gold-plated Rooster on matte surface **Edge:** Reeded

Date	Mintage	F	VF	XF	Unc	BU
2005	2,800	—	—	—	175	185

KM# 792 DOLLAR

31.1035 g., 0.9990 Silver 0.9990 oz. ASW, 40.6 mm. **Ruler:** Elizabeth II **Subject:** Year of the Rooster **Obv:** Elizabeth II **Rev:** Standing Rooster looking backwards **Edge:** Reeded

Date	Mintage	F	VF	XF	Unc	BU
2005P Proof	3,500	Value: 37.50				

KM# 537 2 DOLLARS

62.2070 g., 0.9990 Silver 1.9979 oz. ASW, 50.3 mm. **Ruler:** Elizabeth II **Subject:** Year of the Snake **Obv:** Head with tiara right, denomination below **Rev:** Snake with eggs **Edge:** Segmented reeding

Date	Mintage	F	VF	XF	Unc	BU
2001P Proof	1,000	Value: 100				
2001	—	—	—	—	45.00	50.00

KM# 581 2 DOLLARS

62.2070 g., 0.9990 Silver 1.9979 oz. ASW, 50 mm. **Ruler:** Elizabeth II **Subject:** Year of the Horse **Obv:** Head with tiara right, denomination below **Rev:** Horse running left **Edge:** Reeded

Date	Mintage	F	VF	XF	Unc	BU
2002	—	—	—	—	45.00	50.00
2002P Proof	1,000	Value: 100				

KM# 675 2 DOLLARS

62.2070 g., 0.9990 Silver 1.9979 oz. ASW, 50 mm. **Ruler:** Elizabeth II **Subject:** Year of the Monkey **Obv:** Head with tiara right, denomination below **Rev:** Monkey sitting on branch **Edge:** Reeded

Date	Mintage	F	VF	XF	Unc	BU
2004(2003)	—	—	—	—	42.50	47.50
2004(2003) Proof	7,000	Value: 90.00				

KM# 679 2 DOLLARS

62.8500 g., 0.9990 Silver 2.0186 oz. ASW, 50 mm. **Ruler:** Elizabeth II **Subject:** Year of the Goat **Obv:** Head with tiara right, denomination below **Rev:** Two goats **Edge:** Reeded

Date	Mintage	F	VF	XF	Unc	BU
2003	—	—	—	—	45.00	50.00

KM# 793 2 DOLLARS

62.2700 g., 0.9990 Silver 1.9999 oz. ASW, 50.3 mm. **Ruler:** Elizabeth II **Subject:** Year of the Rooster **Obv:** Elizabeth II **Rev:** Standing Rooster looking backwards **Edge:** Reeded

Date	Mintage	F	VF	XF	Unc	BU
2005P Proof	2,000	Value: 70.00				

KM# 538 5 DOLLARS

1.5710 g., 0.9990 Gold 0.0505 oz. AGW, 14.1 mm. **Ruler:** Elizabeth II **Subject:** Year of the Snake **Obv:** Head with tiara right, denomination below **Rev:** Snake in tree **Edge:** Reeded

Date	Mintage	F	VF	XF	Unc	BU
2001P Proof	100,000	Value: 50.00				
2001	100,000	—	—	—	—	50.00

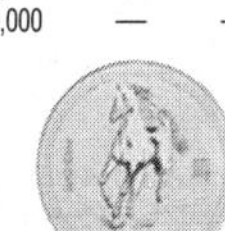

KM# 582 5 DOLLARS

1.5552 g., 0.9990 Gold 0.0499 oz. AGW, 14.1 mm. **Ruler:** Elizabeth II **Subject:** Year of the Horse **Obv:** Head with tiara right, denomination below **Rev:** Horse galloping towards us **Edge:** Reeded

Date	Mintage	F	VF	XF	Unc	BU
2002P	100,000	—	—	—	—	55.00

KM# 668 5 DOLLARS

1.5710 g., 0.9999 Gold 0.0505 oz. AGW, 14.1 mm. **Ruler:** Elizabeth II **Subject:** Year of the Monkey **Obv:** Head with tiara right, denomination below **Obv. Designer:** Ian Rank-Broadley **Rev:** Monkey **Edge:** Reeded

Date	Mintage	F	VF	XF	Unc	BU
2004(2003)P Proof	100,000	Value: 55.00				

KM# 743 8 DOLLARS

155.5175 g., 0.9990 Silver 4.9948 oz. ASW, 65 mm. **Ruler:** Elizabeth II **Subject:** Year of the Monkey **Obv:** Head with tiara right, denomination below **Rev:** Gold-plated seated monkey and multicolored ornamentation **Edge:** Reeded

Date	Mintage	F	VF	XF	Unc	BU
2004	6,000	—	—	—	—	200

KM# 539 10 DOLLARS

311.0350 g., 0.9990 Silver 9.9896 oz. ASW, 75.5 mm. **Ruler:** Elizabeth II **Subject:** Year of the Snake **Obv:** Head with tiara right, denomination below **Rev:** Snake with eggs **Edge:** Segmented reeding

Date	Mintage	F	VF	XF	Unc	BU
2001P Proof	250	Value: 300				
2001	—	—	—	—	175	190

KM# 583 10 DOLLARS

311.0350 g., 0.9990 Silver 9.9896 oz. ASW, 75.5 mm. **Ruler:** Elizabeth II **Subject:** Year of the Horse **Obv:** Head with tiara right, denomination below **Rev:** Horse running left **Edge:** Segmented reeding

Date	Mintage	F	VF	XF	Unc	BU
2002	—	—	—	—	170	185
2002P Proof	500	Value: 285				

KM# 676 10 DOLLARS

311.0350 g., 0.9990 Silver 9.9896 oz. ASW, 75.5 mm. **Ruler:** Elizabeth II **Subject:** Year of the Monkey **Obv:** Head with tiara right, denomination below **Rev:** Monkey sitting on branch **Edge:** Segmented reeding

Date	Mintage	F	VF	XF	Unc	BU
2004(2003)	—	—	—	—	165	180
2004(2003) Proof	5,000	Value: 275				

KM# 710 10 DOLLARS

311.0350 g., 0.9990 Silver 9.9896 oz. ASW **Ruler:** Elizabeth II **Subject:** Year of the Goat **Obv:** Head with tiara right, denomination below **Rev:** Goat

Date	Mintage	F	VF	XF	Unc	BU
2003	—	—	—	—	165	180
2003 Proof	—	Value: 285				

KM# 696 10 DOLLARS

311.0350 g., 0.9990 Silver 9.9896 oz. ASW **Ruler:** Elizabeth II **Subject:** Year of the Rooster **Obv:** Head with tiara right, denomination below **Rev:** Rooster

Date	Mintage	F	VF	XF	Unc	BU
2005	—	—	—	—	165	180
2005 Proof	—	Value: 285				

KM# 540 15 DOLLARS

3.1103 g., 0.9990 Gold 0.0999 oz. AGW, 16.1 mm. **Ruler:** Elizabeth II **Subject:** Year of the Snake **Obv:** Head with tiara right, denomination below **Rev:** Snake in tree **Edge:** Reeded

Date	Mintage	F	VF	XF	Unc	BU
2001P Proof	7,000	Value: 115				
2001	80,000	—	—	—	—	95.00

KM# 584 15 DOLLARS

3.1103 g., 0.9990 Gold 0.0999 oz. AGW, 16.1 mm. **Ruler:** Elizabeth II **Subject:** Year of the Horse **Obv:** Head with tiara right, denomination below **Rev:** Horse galloping left **Edge:** Reeded

Date	Mintage	F	VF	XF	Unc	BU
2002P	—	—	—	—	—	95.00
2002P Proof	7,000	Value: 115				

KM# 711 15 DOLLARS

3.1100 g., 0.9999 Gold 0.1000 oz. AGW **Ruler:** Elizabeth II **Subject:** Year of the Goat **Obv:** Head with tiara right, denomination below **Rev:** Goat

Date	Mintage	F	VF	XF	Unc	BU
2003	—	—	—	—	—	95.00
2003 Proof	—	Value: 110				

KM# 669 15 DOLLARS

3.1103 g., 0.9999 Gold 0.1000 oz. AGW, 16.1 mm. **Ruler:** Elizabeth II **Subject:** Year of the Monkey **Obv:** Head with tiara right, denomination below **Rev:** Monkey **Edge:** Reeded

Date	Mintage	F	VF	XF	Unc	BU
2004P	—	—	—	—	—	95.00
2004(2003)P Proof	80,000	Value: 110				

KM# 794 15 DOLLARS

3.1103 g., 0.9999 Gold 0.1000 oz. AGW, 16.1 mm. **Ruler:** Elizabeth II **Subject:** Year of the Rooster **Obv:** Elizabeth II **Rev:** Standing Rooster right **Edge:** Reeded

Date	Mintage	F	VF	XF	Unc	BU
2005P Proof	7,000	Value: 95.00				

KM# 541 25 DOLLARS

7.7508 g., 0.9990 Gold 0.2489 oz. AGW, 20.1 mm. **Ruler:** Elizabeth II **Subject:** Year of the Snake **Obv:** Head with tiara right, denomination below **Rev:** Snake in tree **Edge:** Reeded

Date	Mintage	F	VF	XF	Unc	BU
2001P Proof	7,000	Value: 245				
2001	60,000	—	—	—	—	225

KM# 585 25 DOLLARS

7.7759 g., 0.9990 Gold 0.2497 oz. AGW, 20.1 mm. **Ruler:** Elizabeth II **Subject:** Year of the Horse **Obv:** Head with tiara right, denomination below **Rev:** Horse galloping half left **Edge:** Reeded

Date	Mintage	F	VF	XF	Unc	BU
2002P	—	—	—	—	—	225
2002P Proof	7,000	Value: 300				

KM# 670 25 DOLLARS

7.7508 g., 0.9999 Gold 0.2492 oz. AGW, 20.1 mm. **Ruler:** Elizabeth II **Subject:** Year of the Monkey **Obv:** Head with tiara right, denomination below **Rev:** Monkey **Edge:** Reeded

Date	Mintage	F	VF	XF	Unc	BU
2004P	—	—	—	—	—	235
2004(2003)P Proof	60,000	Value: 250				

KM# 712 25 DOLLARS

7.7500 g., 0.9999 Gold 0.2491 oz. AGW **Ruler:** Elizabeth II **Subject:** Year of the Goat **Obv:** Head with tiara right, denomination below **Rev:** Goat

Date	Mintage	F	VF	XF	Unc	BU
2003	—	—	—	—	—	225
2003 Proof	—	Value: 250				

KM# 795 25 DOLLARS

7.7759 g., 0.9999 Gold 0.2500 oz. AGW, 20.1 mm. **Ruler:** Elizabeth II **Subject:** Year of the Rooster **Obv:** Elizabeth II **Rev:** Standing Rooster right **Edge:** Reeded

Date	Mintage	F	VF	XF	Unc	BU
2005P Proof	7,000	Value: 240				

KM# 542 30 DOLLARS

1002.5020 g., 0.9990 Silver 32.197 oz. ASW, 101 mm. **Ruler:** Elizabeth II **Subject:** Year of the Snake **Obv:** Head with tiara right, denomination below **Rev:** Snake with eggs **Edge:** Segmented reeding

Date	Mintage	F	VF	XF	Unc	BU
2001P Proof	250	Value: 575				
2001	—	—	—	—	—	525

KM# 586 30 DOLLARS
1002.5020 g., 0.9990 Silver 32.197 oz. ASW, 101 mm. **Ruler:** Elizabeth II **Subject:** Year of the Horse **Obv:** Head with tiara right, denomination below **Rev:** Horse running left **Edge:** Segmented reeding **Note:** Illustration reduced.

Date	Mintage	F	VF	XF	Unc	BU
2002	—	—	—	—	—	525
2002P Proof	250	Value: 575				

KM# 677.1 30 DOLLARS
1000.0000 g., 0.9990 Silver 32.117 oz. ASW, 101 mm. **Ruler:** Elizabeth II **Subject:** Year of the Monkey **Obv:** Head with tiara right, denomination below **Rev:** Monkey sitting on branch **Edge:** Segmented reeding

Date	Mintage	F	VF	XF	Unc	BU
2004(2003)	—	—	—	—	—	525
2004(2003) Proof	5,250	Value: 585				

KM# 677.2 30 DOLLARS
1000.0000 g., 0.9990 Silver 32.117 oz. ASW, 101 mm. **Ruler:** Elizabeth II **Subject:** Year of the Monkey **Obv:** Head with tiara right, denomination below **Obv. Designer:** Ian Rank-Broadley **Rev:** Multicolor ornamentation and Monkey with diamond chip eyes sitting on branch **Edge:** Segmented reeding **Note:** Illustration reduced.

Date	Mintage	F	VF	XF	Unc	BU
2004(2003) Proof	5,000	Value: 600				

KM# 681 30 DOLLARS
1000.0000 g., 0.9990 Silver 32.117 oz. ASW, 101 mm. **Ruler:** Elizabeth II **Subject:** Year of the Goat **Obv:** Head with tiara right, denomination below **Rev:** Nanny goat and kid **Edge:** Segmented reeding

Date	Mintage	F	VF	XF	Unc	BU
2003	—	—	—	—	—	525
2003P Proof	—	Value: 575				

KM# 697 30 DOLLARS
1000.0000 g., 0.9990 Silver 32.117 oz. ASW **Ruler:** Elizabeth II **Subject:** Year of the Rooster **Obv:** Head with tiara right, denomination below **Rev:** Rooster

Date	Mintage	F	VF	XF	Unc	BU
2005	—	—	—	—	—	525
2005 Proof	—	Value: 600				

KM# 671 50 DOLLARS
15.5940 g., 0.9999 Gold 0.5013 oz. AGW, 25.1 mm. **Ruler:** Elizabeth II **Subject:** Year of the Monkey **Obv:** Head with tiara right, denomination below **Rev:** Monkey **Edge:** Reeded

Date	Mintage	F	VF	XF	Unc	BU
2004(2003)P Proof	40,000	Value: 450				

KM# 543 100 DOLLARS
31.1035 g., 0.9990 Gold 0.9990 oz. AGW, 32.1 mm. **Ruler:** Elizabeth II **Subject:** Year of the Snake **Obv:** Head with tiara right, denomination below **Obv. Designer:** Ian Rank-Broadley **Rev:** Snake in tree **Edge:** Reeded

Date	Mintage	F	VF	XF	Unc	BU
2001	30,000	—	—	—	—	875
2001P Proof	—	Value: 920				

KM# 587 100 DOLLARS
31.1035 g., 0.9990 Gold 0.9990 oz. AGW, 32.1 mm. **Ruler:** Elizabeth II **Subject:** Year of the Horse **Obv:** Head with tiara right, denomination below **Rev:** Horse running left **Edge:** Reeded

Date	Mintage	F	VF	XF	Unc	BU
2002	—	—	—	—	—	875
2002P Proof	—	Value: 900				

KM# 713 100 DOLLARS
31.1035 g., 0.9999 Gold 0.9999 oz. AGW **Ruler:** Elizabeth II **Subject:** Year of the Goat **Obv:** Head with tiara right, denomination below **Rev:** Goat

Date	Mintage	F	VF	XF	Unc	BU
2003	—	—	—	—	—	875
2003 Proof	—	Value: 900				

KM# 672 100 DOLLARS
31.1035 g., 0.9999 Gold 0.9999 oz. AGW, 32.1 mm. **Ruler:** Elizabeth II **Subject:** Year of the Monkey **Obv:** Head with tiara right, denomination below **Rev:** Monkey **Edge:** Reeded

Date	Mintage	F	VF	XF	Unc	BU
2004	30,000	—	—	—	—	875
2004(2003)P Proof	—	Value: 900				

KM# 796 100 DOLLARS
31.1035 g., 0.9999 Gold 0.9999 oz. AGW, 32.1 mm. **Ruler:** Elizabeth II **Subject:** Year of the Rooster **Obv:** Elizabeth II **Rev:** Standing Rooster right **Edge:** Reeded

Date	Mintage	F	VF	XF	Unc	BU
2005P Proof	3,000	Value: 875				

KM# 704 200 DOLLARS
62.2140 g., 0.9999 Gold 1.9999 oz. AGW **Ruler:** Elizabeth II **Subject:** Year of the Snake **Obv:** Head with tiara right, denomination below **Rev:** Snake

Date	Mintage	F	VF	XF	Unc	BU
2001 Proof	—	Value: 1,750				

KM# 707 200 DOLLARS
62.2140 g., 0.9999 Gold 1.9999 oz. AGW **Ruler:** Elizabeth II **Subject:** Year of the Horse **Rev:** Horse

Date	Mintage	F	VF	XF	Unc	BU
2002 Proof	—	Value: 1,750				

KM# 714 200 DOLLARS
62.2140 g., 0.9999 Gold 1.9999 oz. AGW **Ruler:** Elizabeth II **Subject:** Year of the Goat **Obv:** Head with tiara right, denomination below **Rev:** Goat

Date	Mintage	F	VF	XF	Unc	BU
2003 Proof	—	Value: 1,750				

KM# 717 200 DOLLARS
62.2100 g., 0.9999 Gold 1.9998 oz. AGW **Ruler:** Elizabeth II **Subject:** Year of the Monkey **Obv:** Head with tiara right, denomination below **Rev:** Monkey

Date	Mintage	F	VF	XF	Unc	BU
2004 Proof	—	Value: 1,750				

KM# 698 200 DOLLARS
62.2100 g., 0.9999 Gold 1.9998 oz. AGW **Ruler:** Elizabeth II **Subject:** Year of the Rooster **Obv:** Head with tiara right, denomination below **Rev:** Rooster

Date	Mintage	F	VF	XF	Unc	BU
2005 Proof	—	Value: 1,750				

KM# 1006 300 DOLLARS
10000.0000 g., 0.9990 Silver 321.17 oz. ASW **Ruler:** Elizabeth II **Series:** Lunar year **Subject:** Year of the Dog **Obv:** Head with tiarra right **Obv. Legend:** ELIZABETH II - AUSTRALIA **Obv. Designer:** Ian Rank-Broadlet **Rev:** Dog sitting, facing right

Date	Mintage	F	VF	XF	Unc	BU
2006	—	—	—	—	—	—

KM# 705 1000 DOLLARS
311.0480 g., 0.9999 Gold 9.9990 oz. AGW **Ruler:** Elizabeth II **Subject:** Year of the Snake **Obv:** Head with tiara right, denomination below **Rev:** Snake

Date	Mintage	F	VF	XF	Unc	BU
2001	—	—	—	—	—	9,500

KM# 708 1000 DOLLARS
311.0480 g., 0.9999 Gold 9.9990 oz. AGW **Ruler:** Elizabeth II **Subject:** Year of the Horse **Obv:** Head with tiara right, denomination below **Rev:** Horse

Date	Mintage	F	VF	XF	Unc	BU
2002	—	—	—	—	—	9,500

KM# 715 1000 DOLLARS
311.0480 g., 0.9999 Gold 9.9990 oz. AGW **Ruler:** Elizabeth II **Subject:** Year of the Goat **Obv:** Head with tiara right, denomination below **Rev:** Goat

Date	Mintage	F	VF	XF	Unc	BU
2003	—	—	—	—	—	9,500

KM# 718 1000 DOLLARS
311.0480 g., 0.9999 Gold 9.9990 oz. AGW **Ruler:** Elizabeth II **Subject:** Year of the Monkey **Obv:** Head with tiara right, denomination below **Rev:** Monkey

Date	Mintage	F	VF	XF	Unc	BU
2004	—	—	—	—	—	9,500

KM# 699 1000 DOLLARS
311.0480 g., 0.9999 Gold 9.9990 oz. AGW **Ruler:** Elizabeth II **Subject:** Year of the Rooster **Obv:** Head with tiara right, denomination below **Rev:** Rooster

Date	Mintage	F	VF	XF	Unc	BU
2005	—	—	—	—	—	9,500

KM# 706 3000 DOLLARS
1000.0000 g., 0.9999 Gold 32.146 oz. AGW **Ruler:** Elizabeth II **Subject:** Year of the Snake **Obv:** Head with tiara right, denomination below **Rev:** Snake

Date	Mintage	F	VF	XF	Unc	BU
2001	—	—	—	—	BV+3%	—

KM# 709 3000 DOLLARS
1000.0000 g., 0.9999 Gold 32.146 oz. AGW **Ruler:** Elizabeth II **Subject:** Year of the Horse **Obv:** Head with tiara right, denomination below **Rev:** Horse

Date	Mintage	F	VF	XF	Unc	BU
2002	—	—	—	—	BV+3%	—

KM# 716 3000 DOLLARS
1000.0000 g., 0.9999 Gold 32.146 oz. AGW **Ruler:** Elizabeth II **Subject:** Year of the Goat **Obv:** Head with tiara right, denomination below **Rev:** Goat

Date	Mintage	F	VF	XF	Unc	BU
2003	—	—	—	—	BV+3%	—

KM# 719 3000 DOLLARS
1000.0000 g., 0.9999 Gold 32.146 oz. AGW **Ruler:** Elizabeth II **Subject:** Year of the Monkey **Obv:** Head with tiara right, denomination below **Rev:** Monkey

Date	Mintage	F	VF	XF	Unc	BU
2004	—	—	—	—	BV+3%	—

KM# 700 3000 DOLLARS
1000.0000 g., 0.9999 Gold 32.146 oz. AGW **Ruler:** Elizabeth II **Subject:** Year of the Rooster **Obv:** Head with tiara right, denomination below **Rev:** Rooster

Date	Mintage	F	VF	XF	Unc	BU
2005	—	—	—	—	BV+3%	—

KM# 1007 30000 DOLLARS
10000.0000 g., 0.9999 Gold 321.46 oz. AGW **Ruler:** Elizabeth II **Series:** Lunar year **Subject:** Year of the Dog **Obv:** Head with tiarra right **Obv. Legend:** ELIZABETH II - AUSTRALIA **Obv. Designer:** Ian Rank-Broadley **Rev:** Dog standing left

Date	Mintage	F	VF	XF	Unc	BU
2006	—	—	—	—	BV+3%	—

GOLD BULLION - KANGAROO

KM# 893 5 DOLLARS
1.5710 g., 0.9990 Gold 0.0505 oz. AGW **Ruler:** Elizabeth II **Obv:** Head with tiara right **Obv. Designer:** Ian Rank-Broadley **Rev:** Two kangaroos on map of Australia

Date	Mintage	F	VF	XF	Unc	BU
2001	10,000	—	—	—	50.00	60.00

KM# 894 15 DOLLARS
3.1101 g., 0.9990 Gold 0.0999 oz. AGW **Ruler:** Elizabeth II **Obv:** Head with tiara right **Obv. Designer:** Ian Rank-Broadley **Rev:** Two kangaroos on map of Australia

Date	Mintage	F	VF	XF	Unc	BU
2001	800	—	—	—	95.00	—

KM# 897 15 DOLLARS
3.1101 g., 0.9990 Gold 0.0999 oz. AGW **Ruler:** Elizabeth II **Obv:** Head with tiara right **Obv. Designer:** Ian Rank-Broadley **Rev:** Kangaroo browsing

Date	Mintage	F	VF	XF	Unc	BU
2002	800	—	—	—	95.00	—

KM# 902 15 DOLLARS
3.1101 g., 0.9990 Gold 0.0999 oz. AGW **Ruler:** Elizabeth II **Obv:** Head with tiara right **Obv. Designer:** Ian Rank-Broadley **Rev:** Two kangaroos hopping

Date	Mintage	F	VF	XF	Unc	BU
2003	500	—	—	—	95.00	—

KM# 907 15 DOLLARS
3.1101 g., 0.9990 Gold 0.0999 oz. AGW **Ruler:** Elizabeth II **Obv:** Head with tiara right **Obv. Designer:** Ian Rank-Broadley **Rev:** Crouching kangaroos facing left, Grass tree plant at right

Date	Mintage	F	VF	XF	Unc	BU
2004	500	—	—	—	95.00	—

KM# 911 15 DOLLARS
3.1101 g., 0.9990 Gold 0.0999 oz. AGW **Ruler:** Elizabeth II **Obv:** Head with tiara right **Obv. Designer:** Ian Rank-Broadley **Rev:** Kangaroo in bush

Date	Mintage	F	VF	XF	Unc	BU
2005	500	—	—	—	95.00	—

KM# 895 25 DOLLARS
7.7508 g., 0.9990 Gold 0.2489 oz. AGW **Ruler:** Elizabeth II **Obv:** Head with tiara right **Obv. Designer:** Ian Rank-Broadley **Rev:** Two kangaroos on map of Australia

Date	Mintage	F	VF	XF	Unc	BU
2001	500	—	—	—	—	225

KM# 898 25 DOLLARS
7.7508 g., 0.9990 Gold 0.2489 oz. AGW **Ruler:** Elizabeth II **Obv:** Head with tiara right **Obv. Designer:** Ian Rank-Broadley **Rev:** Kangaroo browsing

Date	Mintage	F	VF	XF	Unc	BU
2002	500	—	—	—	225	—

KM# 903 25 DOLLARS
7.7508 g., 0.9990 Gold 0.2489 oz. AGW **Ruler:** Elizabeth II **Obv:** Head with tiara right **Obv. Designer:** Ian Rank-Broadley **Rev:** Two kangaroos hopping

Date	Mintage	F	VF	XF	Unc	BU
2003	250	—	—	—	—	225

KM# 908 25 DOLLARS
7.7508 g., 0.9990 Gold 0.2489 oz. AGW **Ruler:** Elizabeth II **Obv:** Head with tiara right **Obv. Designer:** Ian Rank-Broadley **Rev:** Crouching kangaroos facing left, Grass tree plant at right

Date	Mintage	F	VF	XF	Unc	BU
2004	250	—	—	—	—	225

KM# 912 25 DOLLARS
7.7508 g., 0.9990 Gold 0.2489 oz. AGW **Ruler:** Elizabeth II **Obv:** Head with tiara right **Obv. Designer:** Ian Rank-Broadley **Rev:** Kangaroo in bush

Date	Mintage	F	VF	XF	Unc	BU
2005	250	—	—	—	—	225

KM# 692 50 DOLLARS
15.5017 g., 0.9999 Gold 0.4983 oz. AGW, 25.1 mm. **Ruler:** Elizabeth II **Subject:** Tribute to Liberty **Obv:** Head with tiara right, denomination below **Obv. Designer:** Ian Rank-Broadley **Rev:** Two kangaroos on map above silver Liberty Bell insert **Edge:** Reeded

Date	Mintage	F	VF	XF	Unc	BU
2001	650	—	—	—	475	500
Note: In sets only						
2002	1,498	—	—	—	475	500
Note: In sets only						
2002	—	—	—	—	—	500

KM# 899 50 DOLLARS
15.5017 g., 0.9990 Gold 0.4979 oz. AGW **Ruler:** Elizabeth II **Obv:** Head with tiara right **Obv. Designer:** Ian Rank-Broadley **Rev:** Kangaroo browsing

Date	Mintage	F	VF	XF	Unc	BU
2002	650	—	—	—	475	500
Note: In sets only						

KM# 904 50 DOLLARS
15.5017 g., 0.9990 Gold 0.4979 oz. AGW **Ruler:** Elizabeth II **Obv:** Head with tiara right **Obv. Designer:** Ian Rank-Broadley **Rev:** Two kangaroos hopping

Date	Mintage	F	VF	XF	Unc	BU
2003	500	—	—	—	475	500
Note: In sets only						

KM# 909 50 DOLLARS
15.5017 g., 0.9990 Gold 0.4979 oz. AGW **Ruler:** Elizabeth II **Obv:** Head with tiara right **Obv. Designer:** Ian Rank-Broadley **Rev:** Crouching kangaroos facing left, Grass tree plant at right

Date	Mintage	F	VF	XF	Unc	BU
2004	500	—	—	—	475	500
Note: In sets only						

KM# 913 50 DOLLARS
15.5017 g., 0.9990 Gold 0.4979 oz. AGW **Ruler:** Elizabeth II **Obv:** Head with tiara right **Obv. Designer:** Ian Rank-Broadley **Rev:** Kangaroo in bush

Date	Mintage	F	VF	XF	Unc	BU
2005	500	—	—	—	475	500
Note: In sets only						

KM# 693 100 DOLLARS
31.1035 g., 0.9999 Gold 0.9999 oz. AGW, 32.1 mm. **Ruler:** Elizabeth II **Subject:** Tribute to Liberty **Obv:** Head with tiara right, denomination below **Obv. Designer:** Ian Rank-Broadley **Rev:** Two kangaroos on map above silver Liberty Bell insert, colored image **Edge:** Reeded

Date	Mintage	F	VF	XF	Unc	BU
2001	1,498	—	—	—	900	860
Note: In sets only						
2002	—	—	—	—	—	875

KM# 900 100 DOLLARS
31.1035 g., 0.9999 Gold 0.9999 oz. AGW **Ruler:** Elizabeth II **Obv:** Head with tiara right **Obv. Designer:** Ian Rank-Broadley **Rev:** Prospectors dry-blowing gold dust, colored image

Date	Mintage	F	VF	XF	Unc	BU
2002	1,500	—	—	—	900	—

KM# 906 100 DOLLARS
31.1035 g., 0.9990 Gold 0.9990 oz. AGW **Ruler:** Elizabeth II **Obv:** Head with tiara right **Obv. Designer:** Ian Rank-Broadley **Rev:** Prospectors camp, colored image

Date	Mintage	F	VF	XF	Unc	BU
2003	1,500	—	—	—	900	—

KM# 896 200 DOLLARS
62.2140 g., 0.9990 Gold 1.9981 oz. AGW **Ruler:** Elizabeth II **Obv:** Head with tiara right **Obv. Designer:** Ian Rank-Broadley **Rev:** Two kangaroos on map of Australia

Date	Mintage	F	VF	XF	Unc	BU
2001	300	—	—	—	1,750	—

KM# 901 200 DOLLARS
62.2140 g., 0.9990 Gold 1.9981 oz. AGW **Ruler:** Elizabeth II **Obv:** Head with tiara right **Obv. Designer:** Ian Rank-Broadley **Rev:** Kangaroo browsing

Date	Mintage	F	VF	XF	Unc	BU
2002	300	—	—	—	1,750	—

KM# 905 200 DOLLARS
62.2140 g., 0.9990 Gold 1.9981 oz. AGW **Ruler:** Elizabeth II **Obv:** Head with tiara right **Obv. Designer:** Ian Rank-Broadley **Rev:** Two kangaroos hopping

Date	Mintage	F	VF	XF	Unc	BU
2003	200	—	—	—	1,750	—

KM# 910 200 DOLLARS
62.2140 g., 0.9990 Gold 1.9981 oz. AGW **Ruler:** Elizabeth II **Obv:** Head with tiara right **Obv. Designer:** Ian Rank-Broadley **Rev:** Crouching kangaroos facing left, Grass tree plant at right

Date	Mintage	F	VF	XF	Unc	BU
2004	200	—	—	—	1,750	—

KM# 914 200 DOLLARS
62.2140 g., 0.9990 Gold 1.9981 oz. AGW **Ruler:** Elizabeth II **Obv:** Head with tiara right **Obv. Designer:** Ian Rank-Broadley **Rev:** Kangaroo in bush

Date	Mintage	F	VF	XF	Unc	BU
2005	200	—	—	—	1,750	—

GOLD BULLION - NUGGET

KM# 915 100 DOLLARS
31.1035 g., 0.9990 Gold 0.9990 oz. AGW **Ruler:** Elizabeth II **Subject:** Welcome Stranger Nugget **Obv:** Head with tiara right **Obv. Designer:** Ian Rank-Broadley **Rev:** Welcome Stranger Nugget surrounded by Outback setting, colored image

Date	Mintage	F	VF	XF	Unc	BU
2005	1,500	—	—	—	900	860

PLATINUM BULLION - KOALA

KM# 916 5 DOLLARS
1.5710 g., 0.9990 Platinum 0.0505 oz. APW **Ruler:** Elizabeth II **Obv:** Head with tiara right **Obv. Designer:** Ian Rank-Broadley **Rev:** Two koalas on branch

Date	Mintage	F	VF	XF	Unc	BU
2001 Proof	5,000	Value: 85.00				

KM# 917 15 DOLLARS
3.1101 g., 0.9990 Platinum 0.0999 oz. APW **Ruler:** Elizabeth II **Obv:** Head with tiara right **Obv. Designer:** Ian Rank-Broadley **Rev:** Two koalas on a branch

Date	Mintage	F	VF	XF	Unc	BU
2001 Proof	650	Value: 165				

KM# 922 15 DOLLARS
3.1101 g., 0.9990 Platinum 0.0999 oz. APW **Ruler:** Elizabeth II **Obv:** Head with tiara right **Obv. Designer:** Ian Rank-Broadley **Rev:** Koala up a gum tree

Date	Mintage	F	VF	XF	Unc	BU
2002 Proof	650	Value: 165				

KM# 926 15 DOLLARS
3.1101 g., 0.9990 Platinum 0.0999 oz. APW **Ruler:** Elizabeth II **Obv:** Head with tiara right **Obv. Designer:** Ian Rank-Broadley **Rev:** Mother and baby koala

Date	Mintage	F	VF	XF	Unc	BU
2003 Proof	500	Value: 165				

KM# 931 15 DOLLARS
3.1101 g., 0.9990 Platinum 0.0999 oz. APW **Ruler:** Elizabeth II **Obv:** Head with tiara right **Obv. Designer:** Ian Rank-Broadley **Rev:** Single koala on branch

Date	Mintage	F	VF	XF	Unc	BU
2004 Proof	500	Value: 165				

KM# 935 15 DOLLARS
3.1101 g., 0.9990 Platinum 0.0999 oz. APW **Ruler:** Elizabeth II **Obv:** Head with tiara right **Obv. Designer:** Ian Rank-Broadley **Rev:** Single koala with gum leaves

Date	Mintage	F	VF	XF	Unc	BU
2005 Proof	500	Value: 165				

KM# 918 25 DOLLARS
7.7508 g., 0.9990 Platinum 0.2489 oz. APW **Ruler:** Elizabeth II **Obv:** Head with tiara right **Obv. Designer:** Ian Rank-Broadley **Rev:** Two koalas on a branch

Date	Mintage	F	VF	XF	Unc	BU
2001 Proof	275	Value: 420				
Note: In sets only						

KM# 923 25 DOLLARS
7.7508 g., 0.9990 Platinum 0.2489 oz. APW **Ruler:** Elizabeth II **Obv:** Head with tiara right **Obv. Designer:** Ian Rank-Broadley **Rev:** Koala up a gum tree

Date	Mintage	F	VF	XF	Unc	BU
2002 Proof	275	Value: 420				
Note: In sets only						

KM# 927 25 DOLLARS
7.7508 g., 0.9990 Platinum 0.2489 oz. APW **Ruler:** Elizabeth II **Obv:** Head with tiara right **Obv. Designer:** Ian Rank-Broadley **Rev:** Mother and baby koala

Date	Mintage	F	VF	XF	Unc	BU
2003 Proof	200	Value: 420				
Note: In sets only						

KM# 932 25 DOLLARS
7.7508 g., 0.9990 Platinum 0.2489 oz. APW **Ruler:** Elizabeth II **Obv:** Head with tiara right **Obv. Designer:** Ian Rank-Broadley **Rev:** Single koala on branch

Date	Mintage	F	VF	XF	Unc	BU
2004 Proof	200	Value: 420				
Note: In sets only						

KM# 936 25 DOLLARS
7.7508 g., 0.9990 Platinum 0.2489 oz. APW **Ruler:** Elizabeth II **Obv:** Head with tiara right **Obv. Designer:** Ian Rank-Broadley **Rev:** Single koala with gum leaves

Date	Mintage	F	VF	XF	Unc	BU
2005 Proof	200	Value: 420				
Note: In sets only						

KM# 919 50 DOLLARS
15.5017 g., 0.9990 Platinum 0.4979 oz. APW **Ruler:** Elizabeth II **Obv:** Head with tiara right **Obv. Designer:** Ian Rank-Broadley **Rev:** Two koalas on a branch

Date	Mintage	F	VF	XF	Unc	BU
2001 Proof	350	Value: 800				

KM# 924 50 DOLLARS
15.5017 g., 0.9990 Platinum 0.4979 oz. APW **Ruler:** Elizabeth II **Obv:** Head with tiara right **Obv. Designer:** Ian Rank-Broadley **Rev:** Koala up a gum tree

Date	Mintage	F	VF	XF	Unc	BU
2002 Proof	350	Value: 800				

KM# 928 50 DOLLARS
15.5017 g., 0.9990 Platinum 0.4979 oz. APW **Ruler:** Elizabeth II **Obv:** Head with tiara right **Obv. Designer:** Ian Rank-Broadley **Rev:** Mother and baby koala

Date	Mintage	F	VF	XF	Unc	BU
2003 Proof	350	Value: 800				

KM# 933 50 DOLLARS
15.5017 g., 0.9990 Platinum 0.4979 oz. APW **Ruler:** Elizabeth II **Obv:** Head with tiara right **Obv. Designer:** Ian Rank-Broadley **Rev:** Single koala on branch

Date	Mintage	F	VF	XF	Unc	BU
2004 Proof	350	Value: 800				

KM# 937 50 DOLLARS
15.5017 g., 0.9990 Platinum 0.4979 oz. APW **Ruler:** Elizabeth II **Obv:** Head with tiara right **Obv. Designer:** Ian Rank-Broadley **Rev:** Single koala with gum leaves

Date	Mintage	F	VF	XF	Unc	BU
2005 Proof	350	Value: 800				

KM# 921 100 DOLLARS
31.1035 g., 0.9990 Platinum 0.9990 oz. APW **Ruler:** Elizabeth II **Obv:** Head with tiara right **Obv. Designer:** Ian Rank-Broadley **Rev:** Federation: Sir Henry Parkes, flag, parliament house, colored image **Note:** Colored image.

Date	Mintage	F	VF	XF	Unc	BU
2001 Proof	1,000	Value: 1,600				

KM# 930 100 DOLLARS
31.1035 g., 0.9990 Platinum 0.9990 oz. APW **Ruler:** Elizabeth II **Obv:** Head with tiara right **Obv. Designer:** Ian Rank-Broadley **Rev:** The Arts: Dancers, paint brushes, opera house, colored image

Date	Mintage	F	VF	XF	Unc	BU
2003 Proof	1,000	Value: 1,600				

KM# 939 100 DOLLARS
31.1035 g., 0.9990 Platinum 0.9990 oz. APW **Ruler:** Elizabeth II **Obv:** Head with tiara right **Obv. Designer:** Ian Rank-Broadley **Rev:** Two workers and machine, colored image

Date	Mintage	F	VF	XF	Unc	BU
2005 Proof	1,000	Value: 1,600				

KM# 920 200 DOLLARS
62.2140 g., 0.9990 Platinum 1.9981 oz. APW **Ruler:** Elizabeth II **Obv:** Head with tiara right **Obv. Designer:** Ian Rank-Broadley **Rev:** Two koalas sitting on branch

Date	Mintage	F	VF	XF	Unc	BU
2001	250	Value: 3,200				

KM# 925 200 DOLLARS
62.2140 g., 0.9990 Platinum 1.9981 oz. APW **Ruler:** Elizabeth II **Obv:** Head with tiara right **Obv. Designer:** Ian Rank-Broadley **Rev:** Koala up a gum tree

Date	Mintage	F	VF	XF	Unc	BU
2002 Proof	250	Value: 3,200				

KM# 929 200 DOLLARS
62.2140 g., 0.9990 Platinum 1.9981 oz. APW **Ruler:** Elizabeth II **Obv:** Head with tiara right **Obv. Designer:** Ian Rank-Broadley **Rev:** Mother and baby koala

Date	Mintage	F	VF	XF	Unc	BU
2003 Proof	200	Value: 3,200				

KM# 934 200 DOLLARS
62.2140 g., 0.9990 Platinum 1.9981 oz. APW **Ruler:** Elizabeth II **Obv:** Head with tiara right **Obv. Designer:** Ian Rank-Broadley **Rev:** Single koala on branch

Date	Mintage	F	VF	XF	Unc	BU
2004 Proof	200	Value: 3,200				

KM# 938 200 DOLLARS
62.2140 g., 0.9990 Platinum 1.9981 oz. APW **Ruler:** Elizabeth II **Obv:** Head with tiara right **Obv. Designer:** Ian Rank-Broadley **Rev:** Single koala with gum leaves

Date	Mintage	F	VF	XF	Unc	BU
2005 Proof	200	Value: 3,200				

BABY MINT SETS

KM#	Date	Mintage	Identification	Issue Price	Mkt Val
BMS9	2001 (6)	32,494	KM#401-403, 406, 491.1, 534.1 plus bronze medal	—	110
BMS10	2002 (6)	32,479	KM#401-403, 406, 600.1, 602 plus bronze medal	—	47.50
BMS11	2003 (6)	37,748	KM#401-402, 406, 688-690 plus bronze medal	—	40.00
BMS12	2004 (6)	31,000	KM#401-404, 406, 733.1 plus bronze medal	—	40.00
BMS13	2005 (6)	34,748	KM#401-402, 406, 745-747 plus bronze medal	24.00	25.00
BMS14	2006 (6)	—	KM#401-404, 406, 489 plus bronze medal	24.00	25.00

BABY PROOF SETS

KM#	Date	Mintage	Identification	Issue Price	Mkt Val
BPS7	2001 (6)	15,011	KM#401-403, 406, 491.1, 534.1 plus silver medal	—	165
BPS8	2002 (6)	13,996	KM#401, 403, 406, 600.2, 602 plus silver medal	—	153
BPS9	2003 (6)	14,799	KM#401-402, 406, 688-689, 690.1 plus silver medal	—	125
BPS10	2004 (6)	13,996	KM#401-404, 406, 733 plus silver medal	—	110
BPS11	2005 (6)	—	KM#401-402, 406, 745-747 plus silver medal	—	95.00
BPS12	2006 (6)	—	KM#401-404, 406, 489 plus silver medal	—	95.00

MINT SETS

KM#	Date	Mintage	Identification	Issue Price	Mkt Val
MS39	2001 (3)	—	KM532-533, 534.1	7.80	7.50
MS40	2001 (3)	—	KM534.1, 550-551	7.80	7.50
MS41	2001 (3)	—	KM534.1, 552-553	7.80	7.50
MS42	2001 (3)	—	KM534.1, 554-555	7.80	7.50
MS43	2001 (3)	—	KM534.1, 556-557	7.80	7.50
MS44	2001 (3)	—	KM534.1, 558-559	7.80	7.50
MS45	2001 (3)	—	KM534.1, 560-561	7.80	7.50
MS46	2001 (3)	—	KM534.1, 562-563	7.80	7.50
MS47	2001 (3)	—	KM534.1, 564-565	7.80	7.50
MS48	2001 (20)	—	KM532-533, 534.1, 491.1, 550-565	43.68	70.00
MS49	2001 (6)	—	KM#401-403,406,491.1,534.1	—	—
MS51	2002 (3)	—	KM#691, 692, 693	—	1,000
MS50	2002 (6)	—	KM#401-403, 406, 600.1, 602	—	15.00
MS52	2003 (5)	—	KM401-402, 406, 689-690	—	15.00
MS53	2004 (6)	—	KM401-404, 406, 733.1	—	15.00
MS54	2005 (6)	—	KM#401-402, 406, 745-747	—	—
MS55	2006 (8)	—	KM#401-404, 406, 489, 767-768 40 Years of Decimal Currency	18.50	—
MS56	2006 (15)	—	KM#770-781, 1001-1003	80.00	—

PROOF SETS

KM#	Date	Mintage	Identification	Issue Price	Mkt Val
PS118	2001 (6)	650	Federation Centennial Set	—	6,000
PS107	2001 (3)	—	KM532-533, 534.2	21.00	22.50
PS109	2001 (3)	—	KM534.2, 552-553	21.00	22.50
PS110	2001 (3)	—	KM534.2, 554-555	21.00	22.50
PS111	2001 (3)	—	KM534.2, 556-557	21.00	22.50
PS112	2001 (3)	—	KM534.2, 558-559	21.00	22.50
PS113	2001 (3)	—	KM534.2, 560-561	21.00	22.50
PS114	2001 (3)	—	KM534.2, 562-563	21.00	22.50
PS115	2001 (3)	—	KM534.2, 564-565	21.00	22.50
PS116	2001 (20)	—	KM491.2, 532-533, 534.2, 549.2, 550-565	120	200
PS117	2001 (6)	—	KM#401-403, 406, 491.1, 534.1	—	145
PS108	2001 (3)	—	KM534.2, 550-551	21.00	22.50
PS119	2002 (6)	39,513	KM#401-403, 406, 600.2, 602	—	95.00
PS120	2006 (6)	39,090	KM#401-402, 406, 688-689, 690.1	—	70.00
PS121	2003 (6)	6,500	KM#401b, 402b, 406b, 688a, 689a, 690a	—	275
PS122	2003 (4)	10,000	KM763-766	118	128
PS123	2004 (6)	50,000	KM#401-404, 406, 733	—	78.00
PS124	2004 (6)	6,500	KM#401b, 402b, 403b, 404a, 406b, 733.1a	—	200
PS125	2005 (6)	—	KM#401-402, 406, 745-747	—	70.00
PS126	2005 (6)	6,500	KM#401b, 402b, 406b, 745a, 746a, 747a	—	200
PS127	2005 (6)	650	KM#401a, 402a, 406a, 745b, 746b, 747b	—	5,850
PS128	2006 (8)	—	KM#401-404, 406, 489, 767-768	62.50	65.00
PS129	2006 (8)	6,500	KM#62a, 63a, 64a, 65a, 66a, 77a, 852	180	185

WEDDING SPECIMEN SETS

KM#	Date	Mintage	Identification	Issue Price	Mkt Val
WSS1	2002 (6)	3,322	KM#401-403, 406, 600.1, 602 Plaque	—	97.50
WSS2	2003 (6)	3,249	KM#401-402, 406, 688-690 Plaque	—	55.00
WSS3	2004 (6)	4,000	KM#401-404, 406, 733.1 Plaque	—	58.50
WSS4	2005 (6)	—	KM#401-402, 406, 745-747 Plaque	60.00	60.00
WSS5	2006 (8)	—	KM#401-404, 406, 489, 767-768 Plaque	60.00	60.00

AUSTRIA

The Republic of Austria, a parliamentary democracy located in mountainous central Europe, has an area of 32,374 sq. mi. (83,850 sq. km.) and a population of 8.08 million. Capital: Wien (Vienna). Austria is primarily an industrial country. Machinery, iron, steel, textiles, yarns and timber are exported.

REPUBLIC

POST WWII DECIMAL COINAGE

100 Groschen - 1 Schilling

KM# 2878 10 GROSCHEN
1.1000 g., Aluminum, 20 mm. **Obv:** Small Imperial Eagle with Austrian shield on breast, at top between numbers, scalloped rim, stylized inscription below **Rev:** Large value above date, scalloped rim **Edge:** Plain **Designer:** Hans Köttenstorfer

Date	Mintage	F	VF	XF	Unc	BU
2001 Proof	75,000	Value: 1.50				
2001	—	—	—	—	0.45	—

KM# 2885 50 GROSCHEN
2.9700 g., Aluminum-Bronze, 19.44 mm. **Obv:** Austrian shield **Obv. Designer:** Hans Köttenstorfer **Rev:** Large value above date **Rev. Designer:** Ferdinand Welz **Edge:** Reeded

Date	Mintage	F	VF	XF	Unc	BU
2001 Proof	75,000	Value: 2.00				
Note: In sets only						
2001	—	—	—	—	0.45	—

KM# 2886 SCHILLING
4.2000 g., Aluminum-Bronze, 22.5 mm. **Obv:** Large value above date **Obv. Designer:** Edwin Grienauer **Rev:** Edelweiss flower **Rev. Designer:** Ferdinand Welz **Edge:** Plain

Date	Mintage	F	VF	XF	Unc	BU
2001 Proof	75,000	Value: 2.00				
Note: In sets only						
2001	—	—	—	—	1.25	—

KM# 2889a 5 SCHILLING
4.8000 g., Copper-Nickel, 23.5 mm. **Obv:** Lippizaner stallion with rider, rearing left **Obv. Designer:** Hans Köttenstorfer **Rev:** Austrian shield divides date, value above, sprays below **Rev. Designer:** Josef Köblinger **Edge:** Plain

Date	Mintage	F	VF	XF	Unc	BU
2001 Proof	75,000	Value: 2.50				
Note: In sets only						
2001	—	—	—	—	2.00	—

KM# 2918 10 SCHILLING
6.2000 g., Copper-Nickel Plated Nickel, 26 mm. **Obv:** Imperial Eagle with Austrian shield on breast, holding hammer and sickle **Obv. Designer:** Kurt Bodlak **Rev:** Woman of Wachau left, value and date right of hat **Rev. Designer:** Ferdinand Welz

Date	Mintage	F	VF	XF	Unc	BU
2001 Proof	75,000	Value: 2.50				
Note: In sets only						
2001	—	—	—	—	2.00	—

KM# 3075 20 SCHILLING
8.1300 g., Brass, 27.8 mm. **Subject:** Johann Nepomuk Nestroy **Obv:** Denomination within square **Rev:** Bust half left **Edge:** Plain **Designer:** Herbert Wähner

Date	Mintage	F	VF	XF	Unc	BU
2001 Proof	75,000	Value: 10.00				
2001	300,000	—	—	—	4.50	—

KM# 3076 50 SCHILLING
8.1100 g., Bi-Metallic Copper-Nickel clad Nickel center in Aluminumn-Bronze ring, 26.5 mm. **Subject:** The Schilling Era **Obv:** Denomination and shields **Rev:** Four old coin designs **Edge:** Plain

Date	Mintage	F	VF	XF	Unc	BU
2001	600,000	—	—	—	7.50	—
2001 Special Unc.	100,000	—	—	—	9.50	—

KM# 3073 100 SCHILLING
Ring Weight: 7.0000 g. **Ring Composition:** 0.9000 Silver 0.2025 oz. ASW **Center Weight:** 3.7500 g. **Center Composition:** Titanium, 34 mm. **Subject:** Transportation **Obv:** Automobile engine **Obv. Designer:** Thomas Pesendorfer **Rev:** Car, train, truck, and plane **Rev. Designer:** Andreas Zanaschka **Edge:** Plain

Date	Mintage	F	VF	XF	Unc	BU
2001 Proof	50,000	Value: 40.00				

KM# 3077 100 SCHILLING
20.0000 g., 0.9000 Silver 0.5787 oz. ASW, 34 mm. **Subject:** Charlemagne **Obv:** Holy Roman Emperor's crown above denomination **Obv. Designer:** Thomas Pesendorfer **Rev:** Bust 3/4 facing with scepter, two shields at right **Rev. Designer:** Herbert Wähner **Edge:** Reeded

Date	Mintage	F	VF	XF	Unc	BU
2001 Proof	30,000	Value: 40.00				

KM# 3079 100 SCHILLING
20.0000 g., 0.9000 Silver 0.5787 oz. ASW, 34 mm. **Subject:** Duke Rudolf IV **Obv:** University teaching scene **Obv. Designer:** Thomas Pesendorfer **Rev:** Bust on right looking left, St. Stephen's Cathedral at left **Rev. Designer:** Herbert Wähner **Edge:** Reeded

Date	Mintage	F	VF	XF	Unc	BU
2001 Proof	30,000	Value: 40.00				

KM# 3074 500 SCHILLING
10.1400 g., 0.9860 Gold 0.3214 oz. AGW, 22 mm. **Subject:** 2000 Years of Christianity - Bible **Obv:** Bible and symbols of the saints: Matthew, Luke, Mark, and John **Rev:** St. Paul reading from a scroll to two listeners **Edge:** Reeded **Designer:** Thomas Pesendorfer

Date	Mintage	F	VF	XF	Unc	BU
2001	50,000	—	—	—	—	285

KM# 3078 500 SCHILLING
24.0000 g., 0.9250 Silver 0.7137 oz. ASW, 37 mm. **Subject:** Kufstein Castle **Obv:** Castle view above denomination **Rev:** Emperor Maximilian being shown one of his new cannons **Edge:** Lettered **Designer:** Thomas Pesendorfer

Date	Mintage	F	VF	XF	Unc	BU
2001	95,000	—	—	—	45.00	—
2001 Special Unc.	25,000	—	—	—	50.00	—
2001 Proof	50,000	Value: 60.00				

KM# 3080 500 SCHILLING
24.0000 g., 0.9250 Silver 0.7137 oz. ASW, 37 mm. **Subject:** Schattenburg Castle **Obv:** Castle view **Obv. Designer:** Thomas Pesendorfer **Rev:** Two medieval armourers at work **Rev. Designer:** Helmut Andexlinger **Edge:** Lettered

Date	Mintage	F	VF	XF	Unc	BU
2001 Special Unc	15,000	—	—	—	50.00	—
2001 Proof	43,000	Value: 60.00				
2001	95,000	—	—	—	42.00	—

KM# 3081 1000 SCHILLING
16.2200 g., 0.9860 Gold 0.5142 oz. AGW, 30 mm. **Subject:** Austrian National Library **Obv:** Archduke Maximilian as a student **Obv. Designer:** Thomas Pesendorfer **Rev:** Library interior view **Rev. Designer:** Herbert Wähner **Edge:** Reeded

Date	Mintage	F	VF	XF	Unc	BU
2001	30,000	—	—	—	—	450

BULLION COINAGE

Philharmonic Issues

KM# 3004 200 SCHILLING
3.1100 g., 0.9999 Gold 0.1000 oz. AGW **Series:** Vienna Philharmonic Orchestra **Obv:** The Golden Hall organ **Rev:** Wind and string instruments **Designer:** Thomas Pesendorfer

Date	Mintage	F	VF	XF	Unc	BU
2001	26,400	—	—	—BV+13%		—

KM# 2989 500 SCHILLING
7.7760 g., 0.9999 Gold 0.2500 oz. AGW **Series:** Vienna Philharmonic Orchestra **Obv:** The Golden Hall organ **Rev:** Wind and string instruments **Designer:** Thomas Pesendorfer

Date	Mintage	F	VF	XF	Unc	BU
2001	25,800	—	—	—BV+10%		—

KM# 3031 1000 SCHILLING
15.5500 g., 0.9999 Gold 0.4999 oz. AGW **Series:** Vienna Philharmonic Orchestra **Obv:** The Golden Hall organ **Rev:** Wind and string instruments **Designer:** Thomas Pesendorfer

Date	Mintage	F	VF	XF	Unc	BU
2001	26,800	—	—	—	BV+8%	—

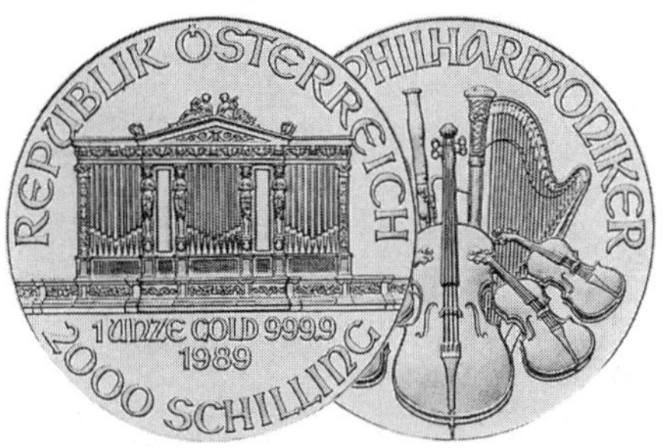

KM# 2990 2000 SCHILLING
31.1035 g., 0.9999 Gold 0.9999 oz. AGW **Series:** Vienna Philharmonic Orchestra **Obv:** The Golden Hall organ **Rev:** Wind and string instruments **Designer:** Thomas Pesendorfer

Date	Mintage	F	VF	XF	Unc	BU
2001	51,700	—	—	—	BV+4%	—

EURO COINAGE

European Union Issues

KM# 3082 EURO CENT
2.3500 g., Copper Plated Steel, 16.18 mm. **Obv:** Gentian flower **Obv. Legend:** EIN EURO CENT **Obv. Designer:** Josef Kaiser **Rev:** Denomination and globe **Rev. Designer:** Luc Luycx **Edge:** Plain

Date	Mintage	F	VF	XF	Unc	BU
2002	378,500,000	—	—	—	0.35	0.50
2002 Proof	10,000	Value: 15.00				
2003	10,925,000	—	—	—	0.35	0.50
2003 Proof	25,000	Value: 3.00				
2004	115,100,000	—	—	—	—	0.35
2004 Proof	20,000	Value: 3.00				
2005	123,000,000	—	—	—	—	0.35
2005 Proof	20,000	Value: 4.00				
2006	—	—	—	—	—	0.35
2006 Proof	20,000	Value: 4.00				
2007	—	—	—	—	—	0.35

KM# 3083 2 EURO CENT
3.0700 g., Copper Plated Steel, 18.69 mm. **Obv:** Edelweiss flower in inner circle, stars in outer circle **Obv. Legend:** ZWEI EURO CENT **Obv. Designer:** Josef Kaiser **Rev:** Denomination and globe **Rev. Designer:** Luc Luycx **Edge:** Plain

Date	Mintage	F	VF	XF	Unc	BU
2002	326,500,000	—	—	—	0.50	0.65
2002 Proof	10,000	Value: 20.00				
2003	118,625,000	—	—	—	0.50	0.65
2003 Proof	25,000	Value: 5.00				
2004	156,500,000	—	—	—	—	0.50
2004 Proof	20,000	Value: 5.00				
2005	113,000,000	—	—	—	—	0.50
2005 Proof	20,000	Value: 6.00				
2006	—	—	—	—	—	0.50
2006 Proof	20,000	Value: 6.00				
2007	—	—	—	—	—	0.35

KM# 3084 5 EURO CENT
3.8600 g., Copper Plated Steel, 21.25 mm. **Obv:** Alpine prim rose flower in inner ring, stars in outer ring **Obv. Legend:** FUNF EURO CENT **Obv. Designer:** Josef Kaiser **Rev:** Denomination and globe **Rev. Designer:** Luc Luycx **Edge:** Plain

Date	Mintage	F	VF	XF	Unc	BU
2002	217,100,000	—	—	—	0.75	1.00
2002 Proof	10,000	Value: 30.00				
2003	108,625,000	—	—	—	0.75	1.00
2003 Proof	25,000	Value: 8.50				
2004	89,400,000	—	—	—	—	0.75
2004 Proof	20,000	Value: 9.00				
2005	66,300,000	—	—	—	—	0.75
2005 Proof	20,000	Value: 10.00				
2006	—	—	—	—	—	0.75
2006 Proof	20,000	Value: 10.00				
2007	—	—	—	—	—	0.75

KM# 3085 10 EURO CENT
4.0700 g., Brass, 19.75 mm. **Obv:** St. Stephen's Cathedral spires **Obv. Designer:** Josef Kaiser **Rev:** Relief map of European Union at left, denomination at center right **Rev. Designer:** Luc Luycx **Edge:** Reeded

Date	Mintage	F	VF	XF	Unc	BU
2002	441,700,000	—	—	—	0.75	1.00
2002 Proof	10,000	Value: 45.00				
2003	125,000	—	—	—	0.75	1.00
2003 Proof	25,000	Value: 8.50				
2004	5,300,000	—	—	—	—	0.75
2004 Proof	20,000	Value: 9.00				
2005	5,300,000	—	—	—	—	0.75
2005 Proof	20,000	Value: 10.00				
2006	—	—	—	—	—	0.75
2006 Proof	20,000	Value: 10.00				
2007	—	—	—	—	—	0.75

KM# 3139 10 EURO CENT
4.0700 g., Brass, 19.7 mm. **Obv:** St. Stephen's Cathedral spires **Obv. Designer:** Josef Kaiser **Rev:** Relief Map of Western Europe, stars, lines and value **Rev. Designer:** Luc Luycx **Edge:** Reeded

Date	Mintage	F	VF	XF	Unc	BU
2008	—	—	—	—	—	0.75
2008 Proof	—	Value: 10.00				

KM# 3086 20 EURO CENT
5.7300 g., Brass, 22.25 mm. **Obv:** Belvedere Palace gate **Obv. Designer:** Josef Kaiser **Rev:** Relief map of European Union at left, denomination at center right **Rev. Designer:** Luc Luycx **Edge:** Notched

Date	Mintage	F	VF	XF	Unc	BU
2002	203,500,000	—	—	—	1.00	1.25
2002 Proof	10,000	Value: 60.00				
2003	51,038,200	—	—	—	1.00	1.25
2003 Proof	25,000	Value: 10.00				
2004	54,900,000	—	—	—	—	1.00
2004 Proof	20,000	Value: 11.50				
2005	4,200,000	—	—	—	—	1.00
2005 Proof	20,000	Value: 12.50				
2006	—	—	—	—	—	1.00
2006 Proof	20,000	Value: 12.50				
2007	—	—	—	—	—	1.00

KM# 3140 20 EURO CENT
5.7300 g., Brass, 22.25 mm. **Obv:** Belvedere Palace gate **Obv. Designer:** Josef Kaiser **Rev:** Expanded relief map of European Union at left, denomination at center right **Rev. Designer:** Luc Luycx **Edge:** Notched

Date	Mintage	F	VF	XF	Unc	BU
2008	—	—	—	—	—	1.00

KM# 3087 50 EURO CENT
7.8100 g., Brass, 24.25 mm. **Obv:** Secession building in Vienna **Obv. Designer:** Josef Kaiser **Rev:** Relief map of European Union at left, denomination at center right **Rev. Designer:** Luc Luycx **Edge:** Reeded

Date	Mintage	F	VF	XF	Unc	BU
2002	169,200,000	—	—	—	1.25	1.50
2002 Proof	10,000	Value: 75.00				
2003	9,199,000	—	—	—	1.25	1.50
2003 Proof	25,000	Value: 12.50				
2004	3,200,000	—	—	—	—	1.25
2004 Proof	20,000	Value: 13.50				
2005	3,200,000	—	—	—	—	1.25
2005 Proof	20,000	Value: 15.00				
2006	—	—	—	—	—	1.25
2006 Proof	20,000	Value: 15.00				
2007	—	—	—	—	—	1.25

KM# 3141 50 EURO CENT
7.8100 g., Brass, 24.25 mm. **Obv:** Secession building in Vienna **Obv. Designer:** Josef Kaiser **Rev:** Expanded relief map of European Union at left, denomination at right **Rev. Designer:** Luc Luycx **Edge:** Reeded

Date	Mintage	F	VF	XF	Unc	BU
2008	—	—	—	—	—	1.25

KM# 3088 EURO
7.5000 g., Bi-Metallic Copper-Nickel center in Brass ring, 23.25 mm. **Obv:** Bust of Mozart right within inner circle, stars in outer circle **Obv. Designer:** Josef Kaiser **Rev:** Value at left, relief map of European Union at right **Rev. Designer:** Luc Luycx **Edge:** Reeded and plain sections

Date	Mintage	F	VF	XF	Unc	BU
2002	223,600,000	—	—	—	2.50	2.75
2002 Proof	10,000	Value: 100				
2003	125,000	—	—	—	2.50	2.75
2003 Proof	25,000	Value: 16.50				
2004	2,700,000	—	—	—	—	2.50
2004 Proof	20,000	Value: 17.50				
2005	2,700,000	—	—	—	—	2.50
2005 Proof	20,000	Value: 18.50				
2006	—	—	—	—	—	2.50
2006 Proof	20,000	Value: 18.50				
2007	—	—	—	—	—	2.50

KM# 3142 EURO
7.5000 g., Bi-Metallic Copper-Nickel center in Brass ring, 23.25 mm. **Obv:** Bust of Mozart right within inner circle, stars in outer circle **Obv. Designer:** Josef Kaiser **Rev:** Value at left, expanded relief map ofEuropean Union at right **Rev. Designer:** Luc Luycx **Edge:** Reeded and plain sections

Date	Mintage	F	VF	XF	Unc	BU
2008	—	—	—	—	—	1.50

KM# 3089 2 EURO
8.5200 g., Bi-Metallic Brass center in Copper-Nickel ring, 25.75 mm. **Obv:** Bust of Bertha von Suttner, Novelist and winner of 1905 Peace Prize, facing left within inner circle, stars in outer circle **Obv. Designer:** Joaef Kaiser **Rev:** Value at left, relief map of European Union at right **Rev. Designer:** Luc Luycx **Edge:** Reeded and lettered: 2 EURO (star) (star) (star) (star)

Date	Mintage	F	VF	XF	Unc	BU
2002	196,500,000	—	—	—	3.75	4.00
2002 Proof	10,000	Value: 125				
2003	4,804,500	—	—	—	3.75	4.00
2003 Proof	25,000	Value: 25.00				
2004	2,600,000	—	—	—	—	3.75
2004 Proof	20,000	Value: 27.50				
2006	—	—	—	—	—	3.75
2006 Proof	20,000	Value: 27.50				

KM# 3124 2 EURO
8.5200 g., Bi-Metallic Brass center in Copper-Nickel ring, 25.7 mm. **Subject:** 50th Anniversary of the State Treaty **Obv:** Treaty seals and signatures **Rev:** Denomination and map **Edge:** Reeding over lettering **Edge Lettering:** "2 EURO" and 3 stars repeated four times **Note:** No country name on this coin!

Date	Mintage	F	VF	XF	Unc	BU
2005	6,880,000	—	—	—	5.00	6.00
2005 Proof	20,000	Value: 27.50				

KM# 3150 2 EURO
Center Composition: Bi-Metallic Brass center in Copper-Nickel Ring **Subject:** 50th Anniversary - Treaty of Rome

Date	Mintage	F	VF	XF	Unc	BU
2007	8,900,000	—	—	—	4.00	5.00
2007 Proof	20,000	Value: 27.50				

KM# 3152 2 EURO
8.5200 g., Bi-Metallic **Ring Composition:** Copper Nickel **Center Composition:** Brass, 25.75 mm. **Subject:** 50th Anniversary Treaty of Rome **Obv:** Open Treaty book on Michelangelo's star or rose shaped background **Rev:** Value at left, expanded relief map of European Union at right **Rev. Designer:** Luc Luycx **Edge:** Reeded and lettered: 2 EURO (star) (star) (star) (star)

Date	Mintage	F	VF	XF	Unc	BU
2007	—	—	—	—	4.00	5.00

KM# 3143 2 EURO
8.5200 g., Bi-Metallic Brass center in Copper-Nickel ring, 25.75 mm. **Obv:** Bust of Bertha von Suttner, Novelist and winner of 1905 Peace Prize, at right facing left in inner circle, stars in outer circle **Obv. Designer:** Josef Kaiser **Rev:** Value at left, expanded relief map of European Union at right **Rev. Designer:** Luc Luycx **Edge:** Reeded and lettered: 2 EURO ★ ★ ★

Date	Mintage	F	VF	XF	Unc	BU
2008	—	—	—	—	5.00	6.00

KM# 3091 5 EURO
8.0000 g., 0.8000 Silver 0.2058 oz. ASW, 29 mm. **Subject:** Schoenbrunn Zoo **Obv:** Denomination within sun design at center, provincial arms surround **Rev:** Building and animals **Edge:** Plain **Shape:** 9-sided

Date	Mintage	F	VF	XF	Unc	BU
ND(2002)	500,000	—	—	—	12.50	—
ND(2002) Special Unc	100,000	—	—	—	22.50	—

KM# 3105 5 EURO
10.0500 g., 0.8000 Silver 0.2585 oz. ASW, 28.1 mm. **Subject:** Water Power **Obv:** Denomination within sun design at center, provincial arms surround **Rev:** Dam with turbine, electric power plant and fish **Edge:** Plain **Shape:** 9-sided

Date	Mintage	F	VF	XF	Unc	BU
2003 Special Unc	100,000	—	—	—	15.00	—
2003	500,000	—	—	—	10.00	—

KM# 3122 5 EURO
10.0000 g., 0.8000 Silver 0.2572 oz. ASW, 28.5 mm. **Subject:** Enlargement of the European Union **Obv:** Denomination within sun design at center, provincial arms surround **Rev:** Map of Europe above country names **Edge:** Plain **Shape:** 9-sided

Date	Mintage	F	VF	XF	Unc	BU
2004 Special select	125,000	—	—	—	12.50	—
2004	275,000	—	—	—	9.50	—

KM# 3113 5 EURO
8.0000 g., 0.8000 Silver 0.2058 oz. ASW, 28.5 mm. **Obv:** Denomination within sun design at center, provincial arms surround **Rev:** Soccer player scoring a goal **Edge:** Plain **Shape:** 9-sided **Note:** Centennial of Austrian Soccer

Date	Mintage	F	VF	XF	Unc	BU
2004	500,000	—	—	—	9.50	—
2004 Special select	100,000	—	—	—	12.50	—

KM# 3117 5 EURO
10.0000 g., 0.8000 Silver 0.2572 oz. ASW, 28.5 mm. **Subject:** Centennial of sport Skiing **Obv:** Denomination within sun design at center, provincial arms surround **Rev:** Skier within snowflake design **Edge:** Plain **Shape:** 9-sided

Date	Mintage	F	VF	XF	Unc	BU
2005	100,000	—	—	—	12.50	14.50

KM# 3120 5 EURO
10.0000 g., 0.8000 Silver 0.2572 oz. ASW, 28.5 mm. **Subject:** 10th Anniversary of Austrian E U Membership **Obv:** Denomination within sun design at center, provincial arms surround **Rev:** Carinthian Gate Theater and Beethoven cameo portrait **Edge:** Plain **Shape:** 9-sided

Date	Mintage	F	VF	XF	Unc	BU
2005	100,000	—	—	—	12.50	14.50

KM# 3131 5 EURO
10.0800 g., 0.8000 Silver 0.2593 oz. ASW, 28.5 mm. **Subject:** Mozart **Obv:** Denomination within sun design at center, provincial arms surround **Rev:** Mozart and the Salzburg Cathedral **Edge:** Plain **Shape:** Nine sided

Date	Mintage	F	VF	XF	Unc	BU
2006	125,000	—	—	—	15.00	17.50

KM# 3132 5 EURO
10.0000 g., 0.8000 Silver 0.2572 oz. ASW, 28.5 mm. **Subject:** Austrian Presidency of the EU **Obv:** Value in circle of arms **Rev:** Vienna Hofburg and Josefsplatz view **Edge:** Plain **Shape:** Nine sided

Date	Mintage	F	VF	XF	Unc	BU
2006	100,000	—	—	—	12.50	14.50

KM# 3144 5 EURO
10.0000 g., 0.8000 Silver 0.2572 oz. ASW, 28.5 mm. **Subject:** Universal Male Suffrage Centennial **Obv:** Value in circle of shields **Rev:** Cameo portraits of Franz Joseph and von Beck on Reichsrat scene **Edge:** Plain **Shape:** 9-sided

Date	Mintage	F	VF	XF	Unc	BU
2007	100,000	—	—	—	—	15.00

KM# 3145 5 EURO
10.0000 g., 0.8000 Silver 0.2572 oz. ASW, 28.5 mm. **Obv:** Value in circle of shields **Rev:** Mariazell church **Edge:** Plain **Shape:** 9-sided

Date	Mintage	F	VF	XF	Unc	BU
2007	100,000	—	—	—	—	15.00

KM# 3096 10 EURO
16.0000 g., 0.9250 Silver 0.4758 oz. ASW, 32 mm. **Subject:** Ambras Palace **Obv:** Palace, denomination below **Rev:** Three strolling musicians **Edge:** Reeded

Date	Mintage	F	VF	XF	Unc	BU
2002 Special Select	20,000	—	—	—	—	30.00
2002 Proof	50,000	Value: 40.00				
2002	130,000	—	—	—	15.00	18.00

KM# 3099 10 EURO
16.0000 g., 0.9250 Silver 0.4758 oz. ASW, 32 mm. **Subject:** Eggenberg Palace and Johannes Kepler **Obv:** Palace, denomination below **Rev:** Half figure seated with tools **Edge:** Reeded

Date	Mintage	F	VF	XF	Unc	BU
2002	130,000	—	—	—	17.50	20.00
2002 Proof	50,000	Value: 32.50				
2002 Special Select	20,000	—	—	—	—	30.00

KM# 3103 10 EURO
16.0000 g., 0.9250 Silver 0.4758 oz. ASW, 32 mm. **Subject:** Schloss Hof **Obv:** Baroque fountain and palace, denomination below **Rev:** Two gardeners at work **Edge:** Reeded

Date	Mintage	F	VF	XF	Unc	BU
2003	130,000	—	—	—	17.50	20.00
2003 Special Select	20,000	—	—	—	—	30.00
2003 Proof	50,000	Value: 32.50				

KM# 3106 10 EURO
16.0000 g., 0.9250 Silver 0.4758 oz. ASW, 32 mm. **Subject:** Schoenbrunn Palace **Obv:** Fountain with palace background, denomination below **Rev:** Palmenhaus greenhouse **Edge:** Reeded

Date	Mintage	F	VF	XF	Unc	BU
2003	100,000	—	—	—	17.50	20.00
2003 Special Select	40,000	—	—	—	—	27.50
2003 Proof	60,000	Value: 30.00				

KM# 3111 10 EURO
17.2973 g., 0.9250 Silver 0.5144 oz. ASW, 32 mm. **Obv:** Hellbrunn Palace, denomination below **Rev:** Archbishop Marcus Sitticus and Hellbrunn's "Roman Theatre" **Edge:** Reeded

Date	Mintage	F	VF	XF	Unc	BU
2004 Special Select	40,000	—	—	—	—	25.00
2004 Proof	60,000	Value: 30.00				
2004	130,000	—	—	—	15.00	18.00

KM# 3115 10 EURO
17.2973 g., 0.9250 Silver 0.5144 oz. ASW, 32 mm. **Obv:** Artstetten Palace, denomination below **Rev:** Crypt entrance behind portraits of Franz Ferdinand and Sophie **Edge:** Reeded

Date	Mintage	F	VF	XF	Unc	BU
2004 Special Select	40,000	—	—	—	—	25.00
2004 Proof	60,000	Value: 30.00				
2004	130,000	—	—	—	15.00	18.00

KM# 3121 10 EURO
17.3000 g., 0.9250 Silver 0.5145 oz. ASW, 32 mm. **Subject:** 60th Anniversary of the Republic **Obv:** Statue of Athena, nine provincial shields and denomination at right **Rev:** Parliament building above broken chain, crowd below **Edge:** Reeded

Date	Mintage	F	VF	XF	Unc	BU
2005 Special Select	40,000	—	—	—	—	25.00
2005 Proof	60,000	Value: 35.00				

KM# 3125 10 EURO
17.3000 g., 0.9250 Silver 0.5145 oz. ASW, 32 mm. **Subject:** Reopening of the Burg Theater and Opera **Obv:** Two large buildings, denomination at left **Rev:** Comedy and Tragedy Masks **Edge:** Reeded

Date	Mintage	F	VF	XF	Unc	BU
2005 Special Select	40,000	—	—	—	—	25.00
2005 Proof	60,000	Value: 35.00				

KM# 3129 10 EURO
17.2973 g., 0.9250 Silver 0.5144 oz. ASW, 32 mm. **Subject:** Nonnenberg Abbey **Obv:** Abbey view, denomination below **Rev:** Statue of St. Erentrudis **Edge:** Reeded

Date	Mintage	F	VF	XF	Unc	BU
2006 Special Select	40,000	—	—	—	—	25.00
2006 Proof	60,000	Value: 35.00				

KM# 3137 10 EURO
16.0000 g., 0.9250 Silver 0.4758 oz. ASW, 32 mm. **Obv:** Gottweig Abby above value **Rev:** Charles VI and staircase **Edge:** Reeded

Date	Mintage	F	VF	XF	Unc	BU
2006 Proof	60,000	Value: 40.00				
2006	40,000	—	—	—	—	30.00

KM# 3146 10 EURO
17.3000 g., 0.9250 Silver 0.5145 oz. ASW, 32 mm. **Obv:** Melk Abbey view **Rev:** Inner view of the Melk Abbey dome **Edge:** Reeded

Date	Mintage	F	VF	XF	Unc	BU
2007 Proof	60,000	Value: 35.00				
2007	40,000	—	—	—	—	25.00

KM# 3148 10 EURO
17.3000 g., 0.9250 Silver 0.5145 oz. ASW, 32 mm. **Obv:** St. Paul's Abbey complex **Obv. Legend:** ST. PAUL IM LAVANTTAL **Obv. Inscription:** REPUBLIK / ÖSTERREICH **Rev:** Entrance facade

Date	Mintage	F	VF	XF	Unc	BU
2007 Proof	—	Value: 35.00				

KM# 3097 20 EURO
18.0000 g., 0.9000 Silver 0.5208 oz. ASW, 34 mm. **Subject:** Ferdinand I - Renaissance **Obv:** Hofburg Palace "Swiss Gate" with two guards, denomination below **Rev:** Bust looking left, coat of arms at left, dates at right **Edge:** Reeded

Date	Mintage	F	VF	XF	Unc	BU
2002 Proof	50,000	Value: 37.50				

KM# 3098 20 EURO
18.0000 g., 0.9000 Silver 0.5208 oz. ASW, 34 mm. **Subject:** Prince Eugen - Baroque Period **Obv:** Baroque staircase with statues, denomination below **Rev:** Uniformed bust 1/4 left and dates at right, flags above cannons at left **Edge:** Reeded

Date	Mintage	F	VF	XF	Unc	BU
2002 Proof	50,000	Value: 42.00				

KM# 3104 20 EURO
18.0000 g., 0.9000 Silver 0.5208 oz. ASW, 34 mm. **Subject:** Prince Metternich **Obv:** Early steam locomotive, denomination below **Rev:** Portrait with map background **Edge:** Reeded

Date	Mintage	F	VF	XF	Unc	BU
2003 Proof	50,000	Value: 45.00				

KM# 3107 20 EURO
18.0000 g., 0.9000 Silver 0.5208 oz. ASW, 34 mm. **Obv:** Republic of Austria arms, denomination below **Rev:** Four men in a jeep **Edge:** Reeded **Note:** Post War Austrian Reconstruction

Date	Mintage	F	VF	XF	Unc	BU
2003 Proof	50,000	Value: 50.00				

KM# 3112 20 EURO
20.0000 g., 0.9000 Silver 0.5787 oz. ASW, 34 mm. **Obv:** S.M.S Novara under sail in Chinese waters, denomination below **Rev:** Standing figures behind table with globe and microscope **Edge:** Reeded **Note:** First Global Circumnavigation by an Austrian ship.

Date	Mintage	F	VF	XF	Unc	BU
2004 Proof	50,000	Value: 50.00				

KM# 3114 20 EURO
20.0000 g., 0.9000 Silver 0.5787 oz. ASW, 34 mm. **Obv:** SMS Erzherzog Ferdinand Max sailing to the Battle of Lissa, denomination below **Rev:** Sailors at the wheel with Admiral Tegetthof in background **Edge:** Reeded

Date	Mintage	F	VF	XF	Unc	BU
2004 Proof	50,000	Value: 52.50				

KM# 3126 20 EURO
20.0000 g., 0.9000 Silver 0.5787 oz. ASW, 34 mm. **Obv:** Ship, "Admiral Tegetthoff" in arctic waters, denomination below **Rev:** Expedition leaders, von Payer and Weyprecht with their icebound ship behind them **Edge:** Reeded

Date	Mintage	F	VF	XF	Unc	BU
2005 Proof	50,000	Value: 50.00				

KM# 3127 20 EURO
20.0000 g., 0.9000 Silver 0.5787 oz. ASW, 34 mm. **Obv:** SMS St. George sailing past the Statue of Liberty, denomination below **Rev:** Shipyard at Pola, boat on water **Edge:** Reeded

Date	Mintage	F	VF	XF	Unc	BU
2005 Proof	50,000	Value: 50.00				

KM# 3133 20 EURO
20.0000 g., 0.9000 Silver 0.5787 oz. ASW, 34 mm. **Subject:** Austrian Merchant Marine **Obv:** Two passing steam ships **Rev:** 19th Century Triest harbor view **Edge:** Reeded

Date	Mintage	F	VF	XF	Unc	BU
2006 Proof	50,000	Value: 50.00				

KM# 3134 20 EURO
20.0000 g., 0.9000 Silver 0.5787 oz. ASW, 34 mm. **Obv:** SMS Viribus Unitis, flag ship of the Austrian fleet, and other ships steaming left **Rev:** SMS Viribus Unitis, submarine conning tower and seaplane **Edge:** Reeded

Date	Mintage	F	VF	XF	Unc	BU
2006 Proof	50,000	Value: 50.00				

KM# 3149 20 EURO
0.9000 Silver, 34 mm. **Obv:** Steam locomotive 1837 with passenger wagons **Obv. Legend:** REPUBLIK ÖSTERREICH **Obv. Inscription:** DAMPFLOKOMOTIVE / AUSTRIA / 1837 **Rev:** People waving at passenger train crossing a trestle **Rev. Legend:** KAISER - FERDINANDS - NORDBAHN

Date	Mintage	F	VF	XF	Unc	BU
2007 Proof	—	Value: 50.00				

KM# 3151 20 EURO
0.9000 Silver, 34 mm. **Obv:** Steam locomotive 1848 standing still, viaduct in background **Obv. Legend:** REPUBLIK ÖSRERREICH **Obv. Inscription:** DAMPF-/ LOKOMOTIVE / STEINBRÜCK / 1848 **Rev:** Steam train traveling right through city **Rev. Legend:** K.K. SÜDBAHN WIEN - TRIEST

Date	Mintage	F	VF	XF	Unc	BU
2007 Proof	—	Value: 50.00				

KM# 3101 25 EURO

16.1500 g., Bi-Metallic 7.15g pure Niobium (Columbium) blue color center in a 9 g., .900 Silver ring, 34 mm. **Subject:** City of Hall in Tyrol **Obv:** Satellite mapping the city from outer space **Rev:** Depiction of the die face used to strike the 1486 guldiner coin **Edge:** Plain

Date	Mintage	F	VF	XF	Unc	BU
2003 Proof	50,000	Value: 125				

KM# 3109 25 EURO

16.1500 g., Bi-Metallic Niobium center (7.15) in .900 SILVER 9g, ring, 34 mm. **Subject:** Semmering Alpine Railway **Obv:** Modern and antique locomotives **Rev:** Steam train **Edge:** Plain

Date	Mintage	F	VF	XF	Unc	BU
2004 Proof	50,000	Value: 100				

KM# 3119 25 EURO

16.1500 g., Bi-Metallic Purple color pure Niobium 7.15g center in .900 Silver 9g, ring, 34 mm. **Subject:** 50 Years Austrian Television **Obv:** The original test pattern of the 1950's **Rev:** World globe behind "rabbit ear" antenna. Television developmental milestones from 7-1 oclock **Edge:** Plain

Date	Mintage	F	VF	XF	Unc	BU
2005 Proof	65,000	Value: 60.00				

KM# 3135 25 EURO

16.1500 g., Bi-Metallic Niobium 7.15g center in .900 Silver 9g ring, 34 mm. **Subject:** European Satellite Navigation **Obv:** Austrian Mint's global location inscribed on a compass face **Rev:** Satellites in orbit around the world globe **Edge:** Plain

Date	Mintage	F	VF	XF	Unc	BU
2006	65,000	—	—	—	—	60.00

KM# 3147 25 EURO

17.1500 g., Bi-Metallic 7.15g Niobium center in .900 Silver 10g ring, 34 mm. **Subject:** Austrian Aviation **Obv:** Interior view of modern cockpit **Rev:** Taube airplane flying above glider and pilot **Edge:** Plain

Date	Mintage	F	VF	XF	Unc	BU
2007	65,000	—	—	—	—	60.00

KM# 3090 50 EURO

10.0000 g., 0.9860 Gold 0.3170 oz. AGW, 22 mm. **Subject:** Saints Benedict and Scholastica **Obv:** St. Benedict and his sister St. Scholastica **Rev:** Monk copying a manuscript **Edge:** Reeded

Date	Mintage	F	VF	XF	Unc	BU
2002	50,000	—	—	—	—	285

KM# 3102 50 EURO

10.1420 g., 0.9860 Gold 0.3215 oz. AGW, 22 mm. **Subject:** Christian Charity **Obv:** Nursing Sister with hospital patient **Rev:** The Good Samaritan **Edge:** Reeded

Date	Mintage	F	VF	XF	Unc	BU
2003	50,000	—	—	—	—	285

KM# 3110 50 EURO

10.1420 g., 0.9860 Gold 0.3215 oz. AGW, 22 mm. **Subject:** Great Composers - Joseph Hayden (1732-1809) **Obv:** Esterhazy Palace **Rev:** Bust 3/4 right **Edge:** Reeded

Date	Mintage	F	VF	XF	Unc	BU
2004 Proof	50,000	Value: 285				

KM# 3118 50 EURO

10.1420 g., 0.9860 Gold 0.3215 oz. AGW, 22 mm. **Subject:** Great Composers - Ludwig Van Beethoven (1770-1827) **Obv:** Lobkowitz Palace above value and document **Rev:** Bust 3/4 facing, dates at left **Edge:** Reeded

Date	Mintage	F	VF	XF	Unc	BU
2005 Proof	50,000	Value: 285				

KM# 3130 50 EURO

10.1420 g., 0.9860 Gold 0.3215 oz. AGW, 22 mm. **Subject:** Great Composers - Mozart **Obv:** Mozart's birthplace, denomination below **Rev:** Leopold and Wolfgang Mozart **Edge:** Reeded

Date	Mintage	F	VF	XF	Unc	BU
2006 Proof	50,000	Value: 275				

KM# 3138 50 EURO

10.0000 g., 0.9860 Gold 0.3170 oz. AGW, 22 mm. **Obv:** Gerard Van Swieten holding book and facing left **Rev:** Akademie der Wissenschaften building **Edge:** Reeded

Date	Mintage	F	VF	XF	Unc	BU
2007	50,000	Value: 275				

KM# 3153 50 EURO

10.0000 g., 0.9860 Gold 0.3170 oz. AGW, 22.00 mm. **Subject:** Ignaz Philipp Sammelweis - Personal Hygiene **Obv:** Bust of Sammelweis 3/4 right, medical symbol at lower right **Obv. Legend:** REPUBLIK ÖSTERREICH **Rev:** Vienna Clinic complex, Sammelweis helping patient wash at lower right **Rev. Legend:** ALLGEMEINES KRANKENHAUS WEIN

Date	Mintage	F	VF	XF	Unc	BU
2008 Proof	50,000	Value: 365				

KM# 3100 100 EURO

16.2272 g., 0.9860 Gold 0.5144 oz. AGW, 30 mm. **Subject:** Raphael Donner **Obv:** Portrait in front of building **Rev:** Providentia Fountain **Edge:** Reeded

Date	Mintage	F	VF	XF	Unc	BU
2002	30,000	—	—	—	—	450

KM# 3108 100 EURO

16.2272 g., 0.9860 Gold 0.5144 oz. AGW, 30 mm. **Obv:** Gustav Klimt standing **Rev:** Klimt's painting "The Kiss" **Edge:** Reeded

Date	Mintage	F	VF	XF	Unc	BU
2003	30,000	—	—	—	—	450

KM# 3116 100 EURO

16.2272 g., 0.9860 Gold 0.5144 oz. AGW, 30 mm. **Obv:** Secession Exhibit Hall in Vienna **Rev:** Knight in armor, "strength" with two women, "ambition and sympathy" **Edge:** Reeded

Date	Mintage	F	VF	XF	Unc	BU
2004 Proof	30,000	Value: 450				

KM# 3128 100 EURO

16.2272 g., 0.9860 Gold 0.5144 oz. AGW, 30 mm. **Subject:** St. Leopold's Church at Steinhof **Obv:** Domed church building, denomination below **Rev:** Two angels flank stained glass portrait **Edge:** Reeded

Date	Mintage	F	VF	XF	Unc	BU
2005 Proof	30,000	Value: 450				

KM# 3136 100 EURO

16.2272 g., 0.9860 Gold 0.5144 oz. AGW, 30 mm. **Subject:** Vienna's River Gate Park **Obv:** Bridge over river scene **Rev:** One of two "sculpted ladies" flanking the park entrance **Edge:** Reeded

Date	Mintage	F	VF	XF	Unc	BU
2006 Proof	30,000	Value: 450				

EURO BULLION COINAGE

Philharmonic Issues

KM# 3092 10 EURO

3.1210 g., 0.9999 Gold 0.1003 oz. AGW, 16 mm. **Subject:** Vienna Philharmonic **Obv:** The Golden Hall organ **Rev:** Musical instruments **Edge:** Segmented reeding

Date	Mintage	F	VF	XF	Unc	BU
2002	75,800	—	—	—	—	BV+13%
2003	59,700	—	—	—	—	BV+13%
2004	68,100	—	—	—	—	BV+13%
2005	—	—	—	—	—	BV+13%
2006	—	—	—	—	—	BV+13%

KM# 3093 25 EURO

7.7760 g., 0.9999 Gold 0.2500 oz. AGW, 22 mm. **Subject:** Vienna Philharmonic **Obv:** The Golden Hall organ **Rev:** Musical instruments **Edge:** Segmented reeding

Date	Mintage	F	VF	XF	Unc	BU
2002	40,800	—	—	—	—	BV+10%
2003	34,000	—	—	—	—	BV+10%
2004	26,600	—	—	—	—	BV+10%
2005	—	—	—	—	—	BV+10%
2006	—	—	—	—	—	BV+10%
2007	—	—	—	—	—	BV+10%

KM# 3094 50 EURO

15.5520 g., 0.9999 Gold 0.4999 oz. AGW, 28 mm. **Subject:** Vienna Philharmonic **Obv:** The Golden Hall organ **Rev:** Musical instruments **Edge:** Segmented reeding

Date	Mintage	F	VF	XF	Unc	BU
2002	40,900	—	—	—	—	BV+8%
2003	26,800	—	—	—	—	BV+8%
2004	21,800	—	—	—	—	BV+8%
2005	—	—	—	—	—	BV+8%
2006	—	—	—	—	—	BV+8%

KM# 3095 100 EURO

31.1035 g., 0.9999 Gold 0.9999 oz. AGW, 37 mm. **Subject:** Vienna Philharmonic **Obv:** The Golden Hall organ **Rev:** Musical instruments **Edge:** Segmented reeding

Date	Mintage	F	VF	XF	Unc	BU
2002	164,100	—	—	—	—	BV+4%
2003	179,900	—	—	—	—	BV+4%
2004	169,800	—	—	—	—	BV+4%
2005	—	—	—	—	—	BV+4%
2006	—	—	—	—	—	BV+4%

KM# 3123 100000 EURO

31103.5000 g., 0.9999 Gold 999.85 oz. AGW **Obv:** The Golden Hall organ **Rev:** Musical instruments **Edge:** Reeded

Date	Mintage	F	VF	XF	Unc	BU
2004 Proof	—	BV+3%				

MINT SETS

KM#	Date	Mintage	Identification	Issue Price	Mkt Val
MS15	2006 (8)	—	KM#3082-3089	—	35.00
MS10	2001 (6)	75,000	KM#2878, 2885, 2886, 2889a, 2918, 3075	25.00	25.00
MS11	2002 (8)	100,000	KM#3082-3089	22.50	45.00
MS12	2003 (8)	125,000	KM#3082-3089	22.50	35.00
MS13	2004 (8)	100,000	KM#3082-3089	—	35.00
MS14	2005 (8)	—	KM#3082-3088, 3124	—	35.00
MS16	2007 (7)	—	KM#3082-3087, 3152	—	—

PROOF SETS

KM#	Date	Mintage	Identification	Issue Price	Mkt Val
PS63	2002 (8)	10,000	KM#3082-3089	85.00	470
PS64	2003 (8)	25,000	KM#3082-3089	85.00	90.00
PS65	2004 (8)	20,000	KM#3082-3089	—	95.00
PS66	2005 (8)	20,000	KM#3082-3089	—	100

AZERBAIJAN

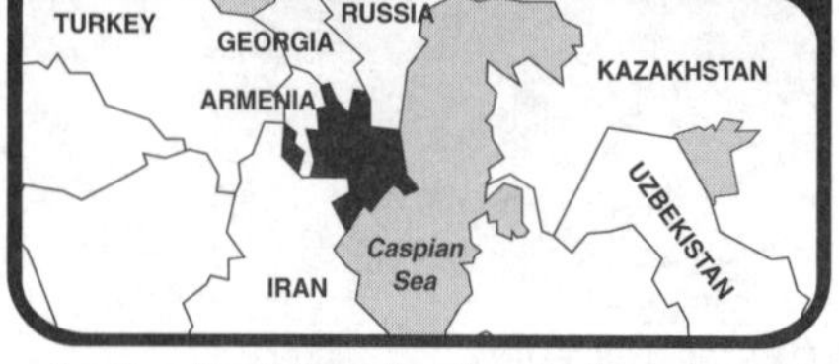

The Republic of Azerbaijan (formerly Azerbaijan S.S.R.) includes the Nakhichevan Autonomous Republic. Situated in the eastern area of Transcaucasia, it is bordered in the west by Armenia, in the north by Georgia and Dagestan, to the east by the Caspian Sea and to the south by Iran. It has an area of 33,430 sq. mi. (86,600 sq. km.) and a population of 7.8 million. Capital: Baku. The area is rich in mineral deposits of aluminum, copper, iron, lead, salt and zinc, with oil as its leading industry. Agriculture and livestock follow in importance.

MONETARY SYSTEM

100 Qapik = 1 Manat

REPUBLIC

DECIMAL COINAGE

KM# 39 QAPIK

2.7300 g., Copper Plated Steel, 16.2 mm. **Obv:** Map above value **Rev:** Value and musical instruments **Edge:** Plain

Date	Mintage	F	VF	XF	Unc	BU
ND (2006)	—	—	—	—	—	2.00

KM# 40 3 QAPIK

3.3600 g., Copper-Plated-Steel, 17.9 mm. **Obv:** Map above value **Rev:** Value above books **Edge:** Grooved

Date	Mintage	F	VF	XF	Unc	BU
ND (2006)	—	—	—	—	—	2.50

KM# 41 5 QAPIK

4.7200 g., Copper-Plated-Steel, 29.75 mm. **Obv:** Map above value **Rev:** Building above value **Edge:** Reeded

Date	Mintage	F	VF	XF	Unc	BU
ND (2006)	—	—	—	—	—	2.75

KM# 42 10 QAPIK

5.1000 g., Brass-Plated Steel, 22.2 mm. **Obv:** Map above value **Rev:** Dome shaped object to right of value **Edge:** Notched

Date	Mintage	F	VF	XF	Unc	BU
ND (2006)	—	—	—	—	—	3.00

KM# 43 20 QAPIK

6.3500 g., Brass Plated Steel, 24.2 mm. **Obv:** Map above value **Rev:** Value and spiral staircase **Edge:** Segmented reeding

Date	Mintage	F	VF	XF	Unc	BU
ND (2006)	—	—	—	—	—	4.00

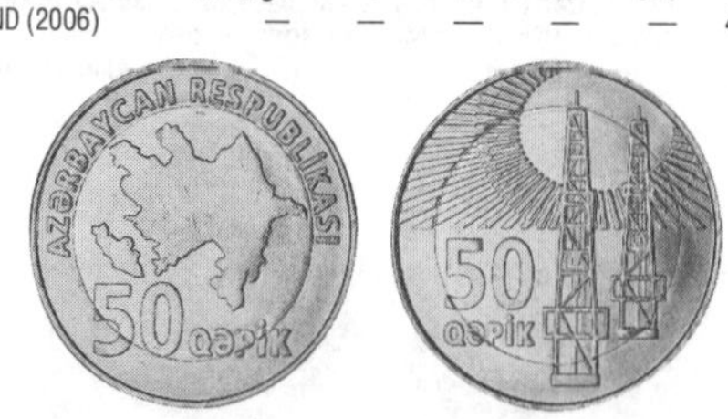

KM# 44 50 QAPIK

7.4200 g., Bi-Metallic Brass plated Steel center in Stainless Steel ring, 25.4 mm. **Obv:** Map above value **Rev:** Two oil wells **Edge:** Reeding over lettering

Date	Mintage	F	VF	XF	Unc	BU
ND (2006)	—	—	—	—	—	5.00

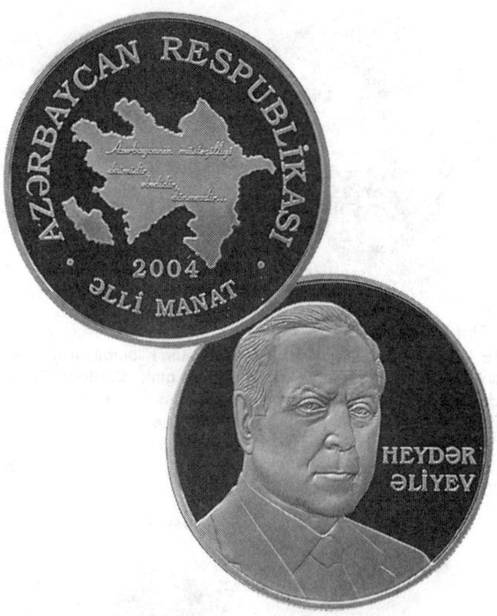

KM# 37 50 MANAT

28.3400 g., 0.9250 Silver 0.8428 oz. ASW, 38.6 mm. **Obv:** National map **Rev:** Bust 3/4 facing **Edge:** Reeded

Date	Mintage	F	VF	XF	Unc	BU
2004 Proof	2,000	Value: 70.00				

BAHAMAS

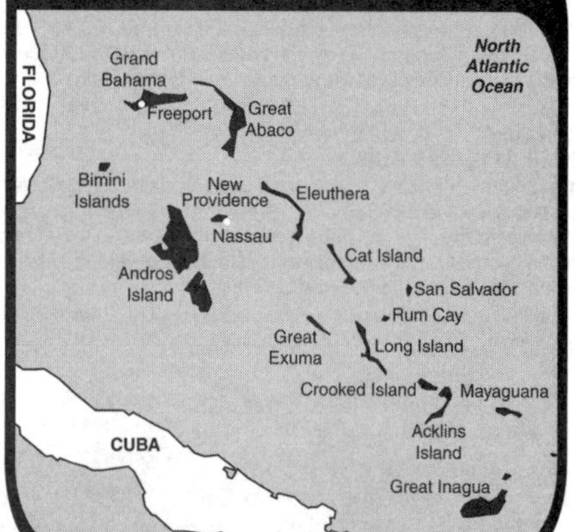

The Commonwealth of the Bahamas is an archipelago of about 3,000 islands, cays and rocks located in the Atlantic Ocean east of Florida and north of Cuba. The total land area of the 800 mile (1,287 km.) long chain of islands is 5,382 sq. mi. (13,935 sq. km.). They have a population of 302,000. Capital: Nassau. The Bahamas import most of their food and manufactured products and export cement, refined oil, pulpwood and lobsters. Tourism is the principal industry. The Bahamas is a member of the Commonwealth of Nations. Elizabeth II is Head of State as Queen of The Bahamas.

The coinage of Great Britain was legal tender in the Bahamas from 1825 to the issuing of a definitive coinage in 1966.

RULER

British

MONETARY SYSTEM

12 Pence = 1 Shilling

COMMONWEALTH

DECIMAL COINAGE

100 Cents = 1 Dollar

KM# 59a CENT

2.5800 g., Copper Plated Zinc, 19 mm. **Ruler:** Elizabeth II **Obv:** National arms above date **Rev:** Starfish, value at top **Edge:** Plain

Date	Mintage	F	VF	XF	Unc	BU
2000	—	—	—	0.10	0.25	0.75
2001	—	—	—	0.10	0.25	0.75

BAHRAIN

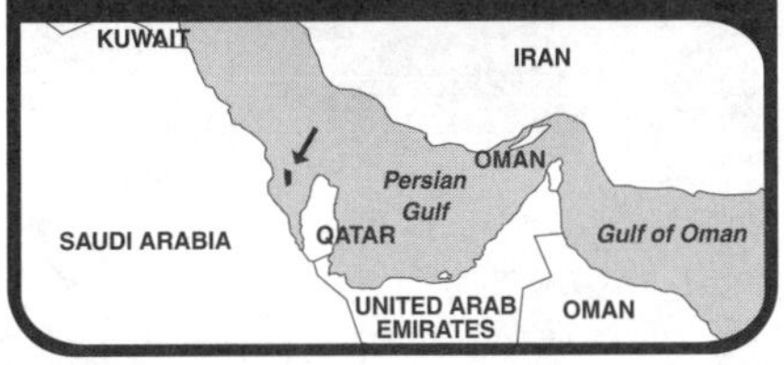

The Kingdom of Bahrain, a group of islands in the Persian Gulf off Saudi Arabia, has an area of 268 sq. mi. (622 sq. km.) and a population of 618,000. Capital: Manama. Prior to the depression of the 1930's, the economy was based on pearl fishing. Petroleum and aluminum industries and transit trade are the vital factors in the economy today.

The coinage of the Kingdom of Bahrain was struck at the Royal Mint, London, England.

RULERS

Al Khalifa Dynasty

Hamed Bin Isa, 1999-

TITLES

دولة البحرين

State of Bahrain

مملكة البحرين

Kingdom of Bahrain

MINT MARKS

بحرين

Bahrain

البحرين

al-Bahrain = of the two seas

MONETARY SYSTEM

فلساً فلس فلوس

Falus, Fulus **Fals, Fils** **Falsan**

1000 Fils = 1 Dinar

KINGDOM

STANDARD COINAGE

KM# 30 5 FILS

2.5000 g., Brass, 18.98 mm. **Ruler:** Hamad Bin Isa **Obv:** Palm tree **Obv. Legend:** KINGDOM OF BAHRAIN **Rev:** Numeric value behind boxed denomination within circle, chainlink border

Date	Mintage	F	VF	XF	Unc	BU
AH1426-2005	—	—	—	—	—	—

KM# 28 10 FILS

3.3500 g., Brass, 21 mm. **Ruler:** Hamed Bin Isa **Obv:** Palm Tree, "Kingdom Of Bahrain" **Rev:** Value **Edge:** Plain

Date	Mintage	F	VF	XF	Unc	BU
AH 1423- 2002	—	—	—	—	0.75	1.00
AH1424-2004	—	—	—	—	0.75	1.00

KM# 24 25 FILS

3.5300 g., Copper-Nickel, 19.8 mm. **Obv:** Ancient painting within circle, dates at either side **Obv. Legend:** KINGDOM OF BAHRAIN **Rev:** Numeric denomination back of boxed denomination within circle, chain surrounds **Edge:** Reeded

Date	Mintage	F	VF	XF	Unc	BU
AH1423-2002	—	—	—	—	1.25	1.50

KM# 25 50 FILS

4.4700 g., Copper-Nickel, 21.8 mm. **Subject:** Kingdom **Obv:** Stylized sailboats within circle, dates at either side **Obv. Legend:** KINGDOM OF BAHRAIN **Rev:** Numeric denomination back of boxed denomination within circle, chain surrounds **Edge:** Reeded

Date	Mintage	F	VF	XF	Unc	BU
AH1423-2002	—	—	—	—	1.50	1.75

KM# 20 100 FILS

5.9600 g., Bi-Metallic Copper-Nickel center in Brass ring, 24 mm. **Obv:** Coat of arms within circle **Obv. Legend:** STATE OF BAHRAIN **Rev:** Numeric denomination back of boxed denomination within circle, chain surrounds **Edge:** Reeded

Date	Mintage	F	VF	XF	Unc	BU
AH1420-2001	—	—	—	—	3.50	4.00
AH1422-2001	—	—	—	—	3.50	4.00

KM# 26 100 FILS

5.9500 g., Bi-Metallic Copper-Nickel center in Brass ring, 23.9 mm. **Subject:** Kingdom **Obv:** Coat of arms within circle, dates at either side **Obv. Legend:** KINGDOM OF BAHRAIN **Rev:** Numeric denomination back of boxed denomination within circle, chain surrounds **Edge:** Reeded

Date	Mintage	F	VF	XF	Unc	BU
AH1423-2002	—	—	—	—	3.50	5.00
AH1426-2005	—	—	—	—	3.50	5.00

KM# 29 100 FILS

5.9500 g., Bi-Metallic Copper-Nickel center in Brass ring, 23.9 mm. **Subject:** 1st Bahrain Grand Prix **Obv:** Maze design within circle **Rev:** Numeric denomination back of boxed denomination within circle, chain surrounds **Edge:** Reeded

Date	Mintage	F	VF	XF	Unc	BU
AH1425-2004	30,000	—	—	—	12.50	15.00

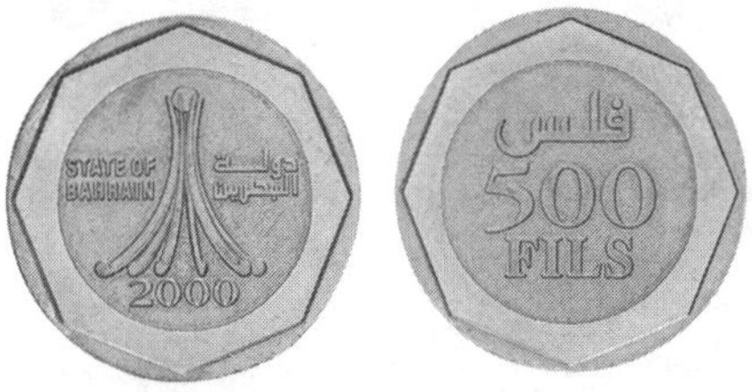

KM# 22 500 FILS

Bi-Metallic Brass center in Copper-Nickel ring, 27 mm. **Ruler:** Hamed Bin Isa **Obv:** Monument and inscription **Obv. Inscription:** STATE OF BAHRAIN **Rev:** Denomination **Edge:** Reeded **Note:** Total weight: 9.05 grams.

Date	Mintage	F	VF	XF	Unc	BU
2001	—	—	—	—	6.00	7.50

KM# 27 500 FILS

9.0500 g., Bi-Metallic Brass center Copper-Nickel ring, 27 mm. **Subject:** Kingdom **Obv:** Monument and inscription **Obv. Legend:** KINGDOM OF BAHRAIN **Rev:** Denomination **Edge:** Reeded

Date	Mintage	F	VF	XF	Unc	BU
2002	—	—	—	—	6.50	8.00

BANGLADESH

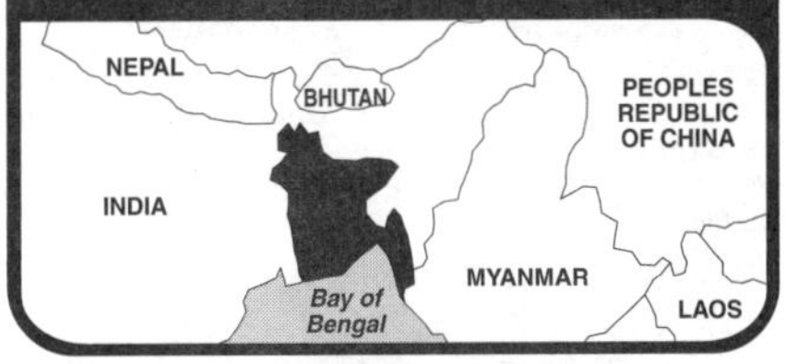

The Peoples Republic of Bangladesh (formerly East Pakistan), a parliamentary democracy located on the Bay of Bengal bordered by India and Burma, has an area of 55,598 sq. mi. (143,998 sq. km.) and a population of 128.1 million. Capital: Dhaka. The economy is predominantly agricultural. Jute products, jute and tea are exported.

Bangladesh is a member of the Commonwealth of Nations. The president is the Head of State and the Government.

MONETARY SYSTEM

100 Poisha = 1 Taka

DATING

Christian era using Bengali numerals.

PEOPLES REPUBLIC

STANDARD COINAGE

KM# 24 50 POISHA

2.6000 g., Stainless Steel, 19.3 mm. **Obv:** National emblem, Shapla (water lily) within wreath above water **Rev:** Fish, chicken and produce within inner circle **Edge:** Plain **Shape:** Octagonal

Date	Mintage	F	VF	XF	Unc	BU
2001	—	—	—	—	1.50	—

KM# 9.5 TAKA

Stainless Steel **Obv:** National emblem, Shapla (water lily) within wreath above water **Rev:** Stylized family, value at right

Date	Mintage	F	VF	XF	Unc	BU
2002	—	—	0.20	0.65	1.75	—

KM# 9.3 TAKA

3.9800 g., Brass **Obv:** National emblem, Shapla (water lily) **Rev:** Stylized family, value at right **Edge:** Reeded

Date	Mintage	F	VF	XF	Unc	BU
2003	—	—	0.20	0.65	1.85	—

KM# 25 2 TAKA

7.0000 g., Stainless Steel, 26 mm. **Obv:** State emblem and "TWO 2 TAKA" within beaded border **Rev:** Two children reading and legend within beaded border **Edge:** Plain

Date	Mintage	F	VF	XF	Unc	BU
2004	—	—	—	—	3.00	5.00

KM# 19 2 TAKA

7.0100 g., Stainless Steel, 26.04 mm. **Obv:** National emblem, Shapla (water lily) within wreath above water **Rev:** 2 children reading books, value below **Edge:** Plain

Date	Mintage	F	VF	XF	Unc	BU
2004	—	—	—	—	2.00	—

KM# 18.3 5 TAKA

8.1700 g., Steel **Obv:** National emblem, Shapla (water lily) within wreath above water **Rev:** Bridge, date and denomination below

Date	Mintage	F	VF	XF	Unc	BU
2006	—	—	—	—	2.50	3.50

BARBADOS

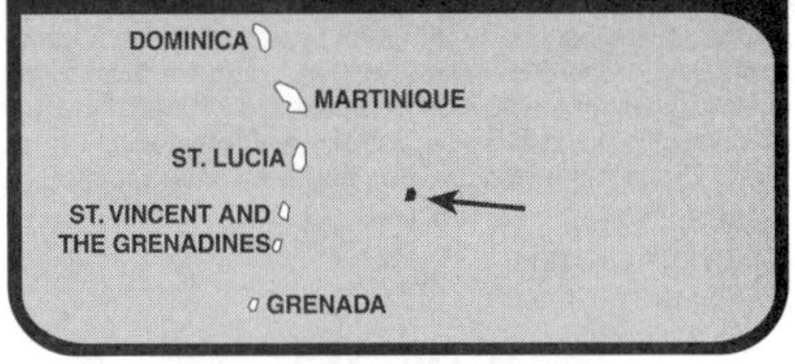

Barbados, an independent state within the Commonwealth of Nations, is located in the Windward Islands of the West Indies east of St. Vincent. The coral island has an area of 166 sq. mi. (430 sq. km.) and a population of 269,000. Capital: Bridgetown. The economy is based on sugar and tourism. Sugar, petroleum products, molasses, and rum are exported.

MONETARY SYSTEM

100 Cents = 1 Dollar

COMMONWEALTH

DECIMAL COINAGE

KM# 10a CENT

2.5000 g., Copper Plated Zinc, 19 mm. **Obv:** National arms **Rev:** Broken trident above value **Rev. Designer:** Philip Nathan **Edge:** Plain

Date	Mintage	F	VF	XF	Unc	BU
2001	—	—	—	0.10	0.25	0.75
2004	—	—	—	0.10	0.25	0.75

KM# 11 5 CENTS

3.8100 g., Brass, 19.21 mm. **Obv:** National arms **Rev:** South Point Lighthouse **Rev. Designer:** Philip Nathan **Edge:** Plain

Date	Mintage	F	VF	XF	Unc	BU
2001	—	—	—	0.10	0.25	0.75

KM# 12 10 CENTS

2.2900 g., Copper-Nickel, 17.5 mm. **Obv:** National arms **Rev:** Laughing Gull left **Rev. Designer:** Philip Nathan **Edge:** Reeded

Date	Mintage	F	VF	XF	Unc	BU
2001	—	—	0.10	0.15	0.50	1.50

KM# 69 5 DOLLARS

28.2700 g., 0.9250 Silver 0.8407 oz. ASW, 38.6 mm. **Subject:** UNICEF **Obv:** National arms divide date, denomination below **Rev:** Three boys playing cricket **Edge:** Reeded

Date	Mintage	F	VF	XF	Unc	BU
2001 Proof	—	Value: 42.50				

BELARUS

Belarus (Byelorussia, Belorussia, or White Russia- formerly the Belorussian S.S.R.) is situated along the western Dvina and Dnieper Rivers, bounded in the west by Poland, to the north by Latvia and Lithuania, to the east by Russia and the south by the Ukraine. It has an area of 80,154 sq. mi. (207,600 sq. km.) and a population of 4.8 million. Capital: Minsk. Chief products: peat, salt, and agricultural products including flax, fodder and grasses for cattle breeding and dairy products.

MONETARY SYSTEM

100 Kapeek = 1 Rouble

REPUBLIC

STANDARD COINAGE

KM# 110 ROUBLE

Copper-Nickel, 32 mm. **Subject:** 900th Anniversary of Euphrasinta **Obv:** National arms **Rev:** Euphrasinta of Polatsk **Designer:** S.P. Zaskevitch

Date	Mintage	F	VF	XF	Unc	BU
2001	Est. 2,000	—	—	—	50.00	—

KM# 112 ROUBLE

Copper-Nickel, 32 mm. **Subject:** Tower of Kamyantes **Obv:** National arms **Rev:** Kamyanets Tower, seal **Designer:** S.P. Zaskevich

Date	Mintage	F	VF	XF	Unc	BU
2001	2,000	—	—	—	40.00	—

KM# 47 ROUBLE

13.1400 g., Copper-Nickel, 31.9 mm. **Obv:** National arms **Rev:** Bison **Edge:** Reeded **Designer:** S.P. Zaskevich

Date	Mintage	F	VF	XF	Unc	BU
2001 Proof	5,000	Value: 40.00				

KM# 50 ROUBLE

12.8000 g., Copper-Nickel, 28.6 mm. **Subject:** 2002 Winter Olympics **Obv:** National arms **Rev:** Two freestyle skiers **Edge:** Reeded **Designer:** S.P. Zaskevich

Date	Mintage	F	VF	XF	Unc	BU
2001 Proof	2,000	Value: 35.00				

KM# 69 ROUBLE

Copper-Nickel, 33 mm. **Subject:** 80th Anniversary of the Savings Bank **Obv:** Folk art design **Obv. Designer:** S.P. Zaskevich **Rev. Designer:** V. Titor

Date	Mintage	F	VF	XF	Unc	BU
2002 Prooflike	10,000	—	—	—	15.00	—

KM# 105 ROUBLE

Copper-Nickel, 31.9 mm. **Subject:** Pointer Yanka Kupala 1881-1942

Date	Mintage	F	VF	XF	Unc	BU
2002 Proof	—	Value: 35.00				

KM# 106 ROUBLE

Copper-Nickel, 31.9 mm. **Subject:** Jakub Kalas 1881-1956

Date	Mintage	F	VF	XF	Unc	BU
2002 Proof	—	Value: 35.00				

KM# 44 ROUBLE

13.1400 g., Copper-Nickel, 31.9 mm. **Obv:** National arms **Rev:** Beaver and young **Edge:** Reeded **Designer:** S.P. Zaskevich

Date	Mintage	F	VF	XF	Unc	BU
2002 Proof	5,000	Value: 20.00				

KM# 114 ROUBLE

Copper-Nickel, 32 mm. **Subject:** 200th Birthday of Ignatius Dameika **Obv:** National arms **Rev:** Ignatius Dameika, hammer **Rev. Designer:** S.P. Zaskevich

Date	Mintage	F	VF	XF	Unc	BU
2002 Prooflike	—	—	—	—	—	40.00

KM# 116 ROUBLE

33.0000 Copper-Nickel **Subject:** 120th Birthday of Yanka Kupala **Obv:** National arms **Rev:** Yanka Kupala, 1882-1942 **Rev. Designer:** S.P. Zaskevich

Date	Mintage	F	VF	XF	Unc	BU
2002	2,000	—	—	—	40.00	—

KM# 118 ROUBLE

Copper-Nickel, 33 mm. **Subject:** 120th Birthday of Yakub Kolas **Obv:** National arms **Rev:** Yukab Kolas, 1882-1956 **Rev. Designer:** S.P. Zaskevich

Date	Mintage	F	VF	XF	Unc	BU
2002	2,000	—	—	—	40.00	—

KM# 61 ROUBLE

12.5000 g., Copper-Nickel, 32 mm. **Obv:** National arms **Rev:** Wrestlers **Edge:** Reeded **Designer:** S.P. Zaskevich

Date	Mintage	F	VF	XF	Unc	BU
2003 Proof	5,000	Value: 10.00				

KM# 54 ROUBLE

13.1200 g., Copper-Nickel, 31.9 mm. **Obv:** National arms **Rev:** Mute swans on water with reflections **Edge:** Reeded **Designer:** S.P. Zaskevich

Date	Mintage	F	VF	XF	Unc	BU
2003 Proof	5,000	Value: 22.00				

KM# 55 ROUBLE

13.1000 g., Copper-Nickel, 31.9 mm. **Obv:** State arms **Rev:** Herring Gull in flight **Edge:** Reeded **Designer:** S.P. Zaskevich

Date	Mintage	F	VF	XF	Unc	BU
2003 Proof	5,000	Value: 25.00				

KM# 56 ROUBLE

13.1000 g., Copper-Nickel, 32 mm. **Obv:** National arms **Rev:** Church of the Savior and Transfiguration **Edge:** Reeded **Designer:** S.P. Zaskevich

Date	Mintage	F	VF	XF	Unc	BU
2003	2,000	—	—	—	35.00	—

KM# 60 ROUBLE

13.1000 g., Copper-Nickel, 31.9 mm. **Obv:** National arms **Rev:** Two Common Cranes **Edge:** Reeded **Designer:** S.P. Zaskevich

Date	Mintage	F	VF	XF	Unc	BU
2004 Proof	5,000	Value: 25.00				

KM# 75 ROUBLE

15.9200 g., Copper-Nickel Antiqued Finish, 33 mm. **Subject:** "Kupalle" **Obv:** Folk art cross design **Rev:** Flower above ferns **Edge:** Reeded **Designer:** S.P. Zaskevich

Date	Mintage	F	VF	XF	Unc	BU
2004	5,000	—	—	—	30.00	—

KM# 76 ROUBLE

15.9200 g., Copper-Nickel, 33 mm. **Subject:** "Kalyady" **Obv:** Folk art cross design **Rev:** Stylized sun flower **Edge:** Reeded **Designer:** S.P. Zaskevich

Date	Mintage	F	VF	XF	Unc	BU
2004	5,000	—	—	—	25.00	—

KM# 78 ROUBLE

15.9000 g., Copper-Nickel, 33 mm. **Obv:** National arms **Rev:** Radziwill's Castle in Neswizh **Edge:** Reeded **Designer:** S.P. Zaskevich

Date	Mintage	F	VF	XF	Unc	BU
2004 Proof-like	2,000	—	—	—	—	35.00

KM# 80 ROUBLE

15.9000 g., Copper-Nickel, 33 mm. **Subject:** Defenders of Brest **Obv:** Soviet Patriotic War Order **Rev:** "Courage" monument **Edge:** Reeded **Designer:** S.P. Zaskevich

Date	Mintage	F	VF	XF	Unc	BU
2004	5,000	—	—	—	15.00	—

KM# 85 ROUBLE

Copper-Nickel, 33 mm. **Subject:** Soviet Warriors - Liberators **Obv:** Order of the Patriotric War **Obv. Designer:** S.P. Zaskevich **Rev:** Partisans with blown up railway track **Rev. Designer:** E.N. Vishnyakova

Date	Mintage	F	VF	XF	Unc	BU
2004	3,000	—	—	—	15.00	—

KM# 83 ROUBLE

Copper-Nickel, 33 mm. **Subject:** Memory of Facist Victims **Obv:** National arms **Obv. Designer:** S.P. Zaskevich **Rev:** Man holding dead **Rev. Designer:** E.N. Vishnyakova

Date	Mintage	F	VF	XF	Unc	BU
2004	3,000	—	—	—	15.00	—

KM# 62 ROUBLE

Copper-Nickel, 31.9 mm. **Subject:** Sculling **Obv:** National arms **Obv. Designer:** S.P. Zaskevich **Rev:** Two rowers against a background of stylized oars **Rev. Designer:** S.V. Nekrasova

Date	Mintage	F	VF	XF	Unc	BU
2004	3,000	—	—	—	15.00	—

KM# 81 ROUBLE
Copper-Nickel, 33 mm. **Subject:** 60th Anniversary of Victory **Obv:** Order of the Victory **Rev:** Star and arrows **Rev. Designer:** S.V. Necrasova

Date	Mintage	F	VF	XF	Unc	BU
2005	2,000	—	—	—	15.00	—

KM# 127 ROUBLE
Copper-Nickel, 32 mm. **Subject:** 100th Anniversary of Vaukavysk **Obv:** National arms **Rev:** National arms of Vaukavysk **Rev. Designer:** S.P. Zaskevitch

Date	Mintage	F	VF	XF	Unc	BU
2005	2,000	—	—	—	30.00	—

KM# 130 ROUBLE
Copper-Nickel, 32 mm. **Subject:** Jesnit Roman Catholic Church **Obv:** National arms **Rev:** Jesnit Roman Catholic Church in Neswizh **Designer:** S.P. Zaskevich

Date	Mintage	F	VF	XF	Unc	BU
2005	2,000	—	—	—	30.00	—

KM# 104 ROUBLE
Copper-Nickel, 33 mm. **Subject:** Easter Egg **Obv:** National arms and solar symbol **Rev:** Easter egg with an inserted lilac colored crystal **Designer:** S.P. Zaskevich

Date	Mintage	F	VF	XF	Unc	BU
2005	5,000	—	—	—	25.00	—

KM# 107 ROUBLE
Copper-Nickel, 31.9 mm. **Subject:** Bagach - Candle in Basket **Obv:** National arms and solar symbol **Rev:** Basket of grain, candle, ear, table, tablecloth

Date	Mintage	F	VF	XF	Unc	BU
2005	5,000	—	—	—	25.00	—

KM# 132 ROUBLE
Copper-Nickel, 33 mm. **Subject:** Usyaslau of Polatsk **Obv:** Cathedral of St. Sophia **Rev:** Usyaslav of Polatsk, wolf on a solar disk

Date	Mintage	F	VF	XF	Unc	BU
2005	5,000	—	—	—	12.00	—

KM# 134 ROUBLE
Copper-Nickel, 33 mm. **Subject:** Tennis **Obv:** National arms **Rev:** Tennis player against racket background **Rev. Designer:** S.V. Nekrasova

Date	Mintage	F	VF	XF	Unc	BU
2005	5,000	—	—	—	12.00	—

KM# 97 ROUBLE
14.5000 g., Copper-Nickel, 33 mm. **Subject:** Almany Bogs **Obv:** Blooming plant on frosted design **Rev:** Great Grey Owl **Edge:** Lettered **Designer:** S.V. Nekrasova

Date	Mintage	F	VF	XF	Unc	BU
2005 Proof	5,000	Value: 25.00				

KM# 135 ROUBLE
Copper-Nickel, 32 mm. **Subject:** Vtaselle Wedding **Obv:** National arms, birds, shamrock **Rev:** Loaf of bread, wedding rings, diadem of flowers, background of honeycomb

Date	Mintage	F	VF	XF	Unc	BU
2006	5,000	—	—	—	12.00	—

KM# 138 ROUBLE
Copper-Nickel, 33 mm. **Subject:** Sophia of Galshany 600th Anniversary **Obv:** Castle of Galshany **Rev:** National arms and Sophia of Galshany **Designer:** S.P. Zaskevich

Date	Mintage	F	VF	XF	Unc	BU
2006	5,000	—	—	—	12.00	—

KM# 140 ROUBLE
Copper-Nickel, 33 mm. **Subject:** Syomukha **Obv:** National arms, solar symbol **Rev:** Chalice, Chaplet of birch, maple, rowan sweet flag leaves **Designer:** S.P. Zaskevich

Date	Mintage	F	VF	XF	Unc	BU
2006	5,000	—	—	—	25.00	—

KM# 146 ROUBLE
Copper-Nickel, 33 mm. **Subject:** Chyrvomy Bar **Obv:** National arms, blooming plant **Rev:** European Mink **Designer:** S.V. Nekrasova

Date	Mintage	F	VF	XF	Unc	BU
2006 Proof	5,000	Value: 15.00				

KM# 150 ROUBLE
16.0000 g., Copper-Nickel, 33 mm. **Subject:** Holidays and Ceremonies **Obv:** Small arms above quilted star design **Rev:** Food, bowl with spoon - Maslenica

Date	Mintage	F	VF	XF	Unc	BU
2007 Antique finish	—	—	—	—	—	—

KM# 64 10 ROUBLES
16.8200 g., 0.9250 Silver 0.5002 oz. ASW, 32.9 mm. **Obv:** National arms **Rev:** Jakub Kolas (1882-1956) **Edge:** Reeded **Designer:** S.P. Zaskevich

Date	Mintage	F	VF	XF	Unc	BU
2002 Proof	1,000	Value: 150				

KM# 117 10 ROUBLES
15.5500 g., 0.9250 Silver 0.4624 oz. ASW, 33 mm. **Subject:** 120th Birthday of Yanka Kupala **Obv:** National arms **Rev:** Yanka Kupala, 1882-1942 **Rev. Designer:** S.P. Zaskevich

Date	Mintage	F	VF	XF	Unc	BU
2002 Proof	1,000	Value: 150				

KM# 129 10 ROUBLES
1.2400 g., 0.9990 Gold 0.0398 oz. AGW, 13.92 mm. **Subject:** Belarussian Ballet **Obv:** National arms **Obv. Designer:** S.P. Zaskevich **Rev:** Dancing ballerina **Rev. Designer:** Michael Schulze

Date	Mintage	F	VF	XF	Unc	BU
2005	25,000	—	—	—	50.00	—

KM# 111 20 ROUBLES
31.1000 g., 0.9250 Silver 0.9249 oz. ASW, 38.61 mm. **Subject:** 900th Anniversary of Euphrasinta **Obv:** National arms **Rev:** Euphrasinta of Polatsk, gold cross **Designer:** S.P. Zaskevitch

Date	Mintage	F	VF	XF	Unc	BU
2001 Proof	Est. 2,000	Value: 350				

KM# 113 20 ROUBLES
31.1000 g., 0.9250 Silver 0.9249 oz. ASW, 38.61 mm. **Subject:** Tower of Kamyantes **Obv:** National arms **Rev:** Kamyanets Tower, seal **Designer:** S.P. Zaskevich

Date	Mintage	F	VF	XF	Unc	BU
2001 Proof	2,000	Value: 100				

KM# 46 20 ROUBLES
33.7300 g., 0.9250 Silver 1.0031 oz. ASW, 38.6 mm. **Subject:** Wildlife **Obv:** National arms **Rev:** Bison **Edge:** Reeded **Designer:** S.P. Zaskevich

Date	Mintage	F	VF	XF	Unc	BU
2001 Proof	2,000	Value: 250				

KM# 49 20 ROUBLES
28.3200 g., 0.9250 Silver 0.8422 oz. ASW, 38.6 mm. **Subject:** 2002 Winter Olympics **Obv:** National arms **Rev:** Marksman aiming at bullseye **Edge:** Reeded **Designer:** S.P. Zaskevich

Date	Mintage	F	VF	XF	Unc	BU
2001 Proof	15,000	Value: 45.00				

KM# 51 20 ROUBLES
33.6500 g., 0.9250 Silver 1.0007 oz. ASW, 38.6 mm. **Subject:** 2002 Winter Olympics **Obv:** National arms **Rev:** Two freestyle skiers **Edge:** Reeded **Designer:** S.P. Zaskevich

Date	Mintage	F	VF	XF	Unc	BU
2001 Proof	2,000	Value: 60.00				

KM# 45 20 ROUBLES
33.7300 g., 0.9250 Silver 1.0031 oz. ASW, 38.8 mm. **Obv:** National arms **Rev:** Beaver and young **Edge:** Reeded **Designer:** S.P. Zaskevich

Date	Mintage	F	VF	XF	Unc	BU
2002 Proof	2,000	Value: 190				

KM# 115 20 ROUBLES
31.1000 g., 0.9250 Silver 0.9249 oz. ASW, 38.61 mm. **Subject:** 200th Birthday of Ignatius Dameika **Obv:** National arms **Rev:** Ignatius Dameika, hammer and inset with a dameikit stone **Rev. Designer:** S.P. Zaskevich

Date	Mintage	F	VF	XF	Unc	BU
2002 Proof	1,000	Value: 350				

KM# 119 20 ROUBLES
31.1000 g., 0.9250 Silver 0.9249 oz. ASW, 38.61 mm. **Subject:** 2006 World Cup Football **Obv:** National arms **Rev:** Stylized 2006, football **Designer:** S.P. Zaskevich

Date	Mintage	F	VF	XF	Unc	BU
2002 Proof	Est. 25,000	Value: 45.00				

KM# 59 20 ROUBLES
28.6300 g., 0.9250 Silver 0.8514 oz. ASW, 38.6 mm. **Obv:** National arms **Obv. Designer:** S.P. Zaskevich **Rev:** Bear with two cubs **Rev. Designer:** Waldemar Vronski **Edge:** Reeded

Date	Mintage	F	VF	XF	Unc	BU
2002 Proof	5,000	Value: 100				

KM# 70 20 ROUBLES
33.8500 g., 0.9250 Silver 1.0066 oz. ASW, 38.61 mm. **Obv:** National arms **Obv. Designer:** S.P. Zaskevich **Rev:** 80th Anniversary - National Savings Bank **Rev. Designer:** V. Titov **Edge:** Reeded

Date	Mintage	F	VF	XF	Unc	BU
2002 Proof	1,000	Value: 225				

KM# 120 20 ROUBLES
31.1000 g., 0.9250 Silver 0.9249 oz. ASW, 38.61 mm. **Subject:** Freestyle Wrestling **Obv:** National arms **Rev:** Two wrestlers **Designer:** S.P. Zaskevich

Date	Mintage	F	VF	XF	Unc	BU
2003 Proof	3,000	Value: 30.00				

KM# 122 20 ROUBLES
31.1000 g., 0.9250 Silver 0.9249 oz. ASW, 38.61 mm. **Subject:** Herring Gull **Obv:** National arms **Rev:** Herring gull in flight **Designer:** S.P. Zaskevitch

Date	Mintage	F	VF	XF	Unc	BU
2003 Proof	2,000	Value: 150				

KM# 53 20 ROUBLES
33.8400 g., 0.9250 Silver 1.0063 oz. ASW, 38.5 mm. **Obv:** State arms **Rev:** Two Mute swans on water with reflections **Edge:** Reeded **Designer:** S.P. Zaskevich

Date	Mintage	F	VF	XF	Unc	BU
2003 Proof	2,000	Value: 200				

KM# 57 20 ROUBLES

31.1000 g., 0.9250 Silver 0.9249 oz. ASW, 38.6 mm. **Obv:** National arms **Rev:** Church of the Savior and Transfiguration **Edge:** Reeded **Designer:** S.P. Zaskevich

Date	Mintage	F	VF	XF	Unc	BU
2003 Proof	2,000	Value: 100				

KM# 149 20 ROUBLES

26.1600 g., 0.9250 Silver 0.7780 oz. ASW, 38.61 mm. **Subject:** 2004 Olympic Games **Obv:** National arms **Rev:** Female shot-putter **Designer:** S.P. Zaskevich

Date	Mintage	F	VF	XF	Unc	BU
2003 Proof	25,000	Value: 25.00				

KM# 91 20 ROUBLES

31.1000 g., 0.9250 Silver 0.9249 oz. ASW, 38.61 mm. **Subject:** Trade Union Movement Centennial **Obv:** National arms **Obv. Designer:** S.P. Zaskevich **Rev. Designer:** G.A. Maximor

Date	Mintage	F	VF	XF	Unc	BU
2004 Proof	1,500	Value: 200				

KM# 86 20 ROUBLES

31.1000 g., 0.9250 Silver 0.9249 oz. ASW, 38.61 mm. **Subject:** Soviet Warriors - Liberators **Obv:** Multicolored Order of the Patriotic War **Obv. Designer:** S.P. Zaskevich **Rev:** Partisans with blown up railway track **Rev. Designer:** E.N. Vishnyakova

Date	Mintage	F	VF	XF	Unc	BU
2004	2,000	—	—	—	60.00	—

KM# 84 20 ROUBLES

31.1000 g., 0.9250 Silver 0.9249 oz. ASW, 38.61 mm. **Subject:** Memory of Facist Victims **Obv:** Multicolored Order of the Patriotic War **Obv. Designer:** S.P. Zaskevich **Rev:** Man holding dead **Rev. Designer:** E.N. Vishnyakova

Date	Mintage	F	VF	XF	Unc	BU
2004	2,000	—	—	—	60.00	—

KM# 124 20 ROUBLES

31.1000 g., 0.9250 Silver 0.9249 oz. ASW, 38.61 mm. **Subject:** Sculling **Obv:** National arms **Obv. Designer:** S.P. Zaskevich **Rev:** Two rowers against a background of stylized oars **Rev. Designer:** S.V. Nekrasova

Date	Mintage	F	VF	XF	Unc	BU
2004	3,000	—	—	—	25.00	—

KM# 71 20 ROUBLES

31.1000 g., 0.9250 Silver 0.9249 oz. ASW, 38.6 mm. **Subject:** "Kupalle" **Obv:** Folk art design **Rev:** Fern flower with inset red synthetic crystal **Edge:** Reeded **Designer:** S.P. Zaskevich

Date	Mintage	F	VF	XF	Unc	BU
2004 Antique finish	3,000	—	—	—	400	—

KM# 72 20 ROUBLES

31.1000 g., 0.9250 Silver 0.9249 oz. ASW, 38.6 mm. **Subject:** Defense of Brest **Obv:** Multicolor Soviet Order of the Patriotic War **Rev:** "Courage" monument **Edge:** Reeded **Designer:** S.P. Zaskevich

Date	Mintage	F	VF	XF	Unc	BU
2004 Proof	3,000	Value: 60.00				

KM# 73 20 ROUBLES

31.1000 g., 0.9250 Silver 0.9249 oz. ASW, 38.6 mm. **Obv:** National arms **Rev:** 2 common cranes **Edge:** Reeded

Date	Mintage	F	VF	XF	Unc	BU
2004 Proof	2,000	Value: 200				

KM# 77 20 ROUBLES

31.1000 g., 0.9250 Silver 0.9249 oz. ASW, 38.6 mm. **Subject:** "Kalyady" **Obv:** Folk art cross design **Rev:** Stylized sunflower with inset blue synthetic crystal **Edge:** Reeded **Designer:** S.P. Zaskevich

Date	Mintage	F	VF	XF	Unc	BU
2004 Antique finish	5,000	—	—	—	300	—

KM# 79 20 ROUBLES

31.1000 g., 0.9250 Silver 0.9249 oz. ASW, 38.6 mm. **Obv:** National arms **Rev:** Radziwill's Castle in Neswizh **Edge:** Reeded **Designer:** S.P. Zaskevich

Date	Mintage	F	VF	XF	Unc	BU
2004 Proof	2,000	Value: 100				

KM# 82 20 ROUBLES

28.7200 g., 0.9250 Silver 0.8541 oz. ASW, 38.6 mm. **Subject:** WW II Victory **Obv:** Multicolor Soviet Order of Victory **Rev:** Soviet soldiers raising their flag in the Reichstag in Berlin **Rev. Designer:** S.V. Necrasova **Edge:** Reeded

Date	Mintage	F	VF	XF	Unc	BU
2005 Proof	12,000	Value: 50.00				

KM# 92 20 ROUBLES

28.6300 g., 0.9250 Silver 0.8514 oz. ASW, 38.6 mm. **Obv:** Two children sitting on crescent moon **Rev:** Symon the Musician and inset orange color glass crystal **Edge:** Plain **Designer:** S.V. Necrasova

Date	Mintage	F	VF	XF	Unc	BU
2005 Antique finish	20,000	—	—	—	50.00	—

KM# 93 20 ROUBLES

28.6300 g., 0.9250 Silver 0.8514 oz. ASW, 38.6 mm. **Subject:** Kalyady's star **Obv:** Two children sitting on a crescent moon **Rev:** Snow Queen; Blue glass crystal inset on forehead, flower **Edge:** Plain **Designer:** S.V. Necrasova

Date	Mintage	F	VF	XF	Unc	BU
2005 Antique finish	20,000	—	—	—	50.00	—

KM# 94 20 ROUBLES
28.6300 g., 0.9250 Silver 0.8514 oz. ASW, 38.6 mm. **Obv:** Two children sitting on a crescent moon **Rev:** White glass crystal inset above landscape with fox, the Little Prince **Edge:** Plain **Designer:** S.V. Necrasova

Date	Mintage	F	VF	XF	Unc	BU
2005 Antique finish	20,000	—	—	—	50.00	—

KM# 95 20 ROUBLES
28.6300 g., 0.9250 Silver 0.8514 oz. ASW, 38.61 mm. **Obv:** Two children sitting on a crescent moon **Rev:** The Stone Flower, Yellow glass crystal inset in flower design, heads flank **Edge:** Plain **Designer:** S.V. Necrasova

Date	Mintage	F	VF	XF	Unc	BU
2005 Antique finish	20,000	—	—	—	50.00	—

KM# 96 20 ROUBLES
33.6600 g., 0.9250 Silver 1.0010 oz. ASW, 38.6 mm. **Obv:** Small national arms above quilted star design **Rev:** Yellow glass crystal inset in candle flame above basket **Edge:** Reeded **Designer:** S.P. Zaskevich

Date	Mintage	F	VF	XF	Unc	BU
2005 Antique finish	5,000	—	—	—	50.00	—

KM# 98 20 ROUBLES
33.6300 g., 0.9250 Silver 1.0000 oz. ASW, 38.6 mm. **Subject:** Almany Bogs **Obv:** Blooming plant on frosted design **Rev:** Great Grey Owl in flight **Edge:** Reeded **Designer:** S.V. Nekrasova

Date	Mintage	F	VF	XF	Unc	BU
2005 Proof	5,000	Value: 50.00				

KM# 99 20 ROUBLES
31.1000 g., 0.9250 Silver 0.9249 oz. ASW, 38.6 mm. **Series:** Easter Egg **Obv:** Quilted cross design **Rev:** Decorated Easter egg with inset pink glass crystal

Date	Mintage	F	VF	XF	Unc	BU
2005 Oxidized finish	5,000	—	—	—	250	—

KM# 100 20 ROUBLES
33.6200 g., 0.9250 Silver 0.9998 oz. ASW, 38.6 mm. **Obv:** Large church **Rev:** Usyaslau of Polatsk

Date	Mintage	F	VF	XF	Unc	BU
2005 Proof	5,000	Value: 50.00				

KM# 102 20 ROUBLES
33.9400 g., 0.9250 Silver 1.0093 oz. ASW, 39 mm. **Obv:** National arms **Rev:** Female tennis player

Date	Mintage	F	VF	XF	Unc	BU
2005 Proof	7,000	Value: 50.00				

KM# 128 20 ROUBLES
31.1000 g., 0.9250 Silver 0.9249 oz. ASW, 38.61 mm. **Subject:** 1000th Anniversary of Vaukavysk **Obv:** National arms **Rev:** National arms of Vaukavysk **Rev. Designer:** S.P. Zaskevitch

Date	Mintage	F	VF	XF	Unc	BU
2005 Proof	2,000	Value: 100				

KM# 131 20 ROUBLES
31.1000 g., 0.9250 Silver 0.9249 oz. ASW, 38.61 mm. **Subject:** Jesnit Roman Catholic Church **Obv:** National arms **Rev:** Jesnit Roman Catholic Church in Niasvizh **Designer:** S.P. Zaskevich

Date	Mintage	F	VF	XF	Unc	BU
2005 Proof	2,000	Value: 100				

KM# 133 20 ROUBLES
26.1600 g., 0.9250 Silver 0.7780 oz. ASW, 38.61 mm. **Subject:** 2006 Olympic Games **Obv:** National arms **Obv. Designer:** S.P. Zaskevich **Rev:** Two hockey players **Rev. Designer:** S.V. Necrasova and Ruth Oswald Koppers

Date	Mintage	F	VF	XF	Unc	BU
2005	15,000	—	—	—	20.00	—

KM# 101 20 ROUBLES
25.0000 g., 0.9250 Silver 0.7435 oz. ASW, 38.6 mm. **Subject:** 2006 FIFA World Cup Germany **Obv:** National arms **Rev:** Multicolor Europe, Asia and African maps on soccer ball **Rev. Designer:** S.V. Nekrasova **Note:** 2006 World Cup Soccer

Date	Mintage	F	VF	XF	Unc	BU
2005 Proof	50,000	Value: 50.00				

KM# 148 20 ROUBLES
28.2800 g., 0.9250 Silver 0.8410 oz. ASW, 38.5 mm. **Obv:** Two children sitting on a crescent moon **Rev:** Campfire with inset stone in a circle of produce **Edge:** Plain **Note:** Antiqued finish.

Date	Mintage	F	VF	XF	Unc	BU
2006	20,000	—	—	—	50.00	—

KM# 137 20 ROUBLES
28.6300 g., 0.9250 Silver 0.8514 oz. ASW, 38.6 mm. **Subject:** The Twelve Months **Obv:** Two children sitting on a crescent moon **Rev:** Raindrops, snowflakes, campfire with an inserted round piece of amber

Date	Mintage	Good	VG	F	VF	XF
2006	20,000	—	—	—	40.00	—

KM# 136 20 ROUBLES
33.6300 g., 0.9250 Silver 1.0000 oz. ASW, 38.61 mm. **Subject:** Vtaselle Wedding **Obv:** National arms, birds, shamrock **Rev:** Loaf of bread, golden wedding rings, diadem of flowers, background of honeycomb

Date	Mintage	F	VF	XF	Unc	BU
2006	25,000	—	—	—	70.00	—

KM# 139 20 ROUBLES
33.6200 g., 0.9250 Silver 0.9998 oz. ASW, 38.61 mm. **Subject:** Sophia of Galshany 600th Anniversary **Obv:** Castle of Galshany **Rev:** National arms and Sophia of Galshany **Designer:** S.P. Zaskevich

Date	Mintage	F	VF	XF	Unc	BU
2006 Proof	5,000	Value: 40.00				

KM# 141 20 ROUBLES
33.6200 g., 0.9250 Silver 0.9998 oz. ASW, 38.61 mm. **Subject:** Syomukha **Obv:** National arms, solar symbol **Rev:** Chalice, Chaplet of birch, maple, rowan, sweet flag leaves inserted in green crystal **Designer:** S.P. Zaskevich

Date	Mintage	F	VF	XF	Unc	BU
2006	5,000	—	—	—	150	—

KM# 147 20 ROUBLES
33.6300 g., 0.9250 Silver 1.0000 oz. ASW, 38.61 mm. **Subject:** Chyrvomy Bar **Obv:** National arms, blooming plant **Rev:** European Mink **Designer:** S.V. Nekrasova

Date	Mintage	F	VF	XF	Unc	BU
2006 Proof	5,000	Value: 50.00				

KM# 121 50 ROUBLES
4.4500 g., 0.9990 Gold 0.1429 oz. AGW, 25 mm. **Subject:** Fox **Obv:** National arms **Obv. Designer:** S.P. Zaskevich **Rev:** Fox with inset diamond eyes **Rev. Designer:** Waldemar Wronski

Date	Mintage	F	VF	XF	Unc	BU
2002	Est. 2,000	—	—	—	1,000	—

KM# 126 50 ROUBLES
62.2000 g., 0.9250 Silver 1.8497 oz. ASW, 50 mm. **Subject:** 60th Anniversary of Victory **Obv:** Order of the Victory, multicolored **Rev:** Stars and arrows **Rev. Designer:** S.V. Necrasova

Date	Mintage	F	VF	XF	Unc	BU
2005	2,000	—	—	—	80.00	—

KM# 142 50 ROUBLES
7.7800 g., 0.9990 Gold 0.2499 oz. AGW, 25 mm. **Subject:** Peregrine Falcon **Obv:** National arms **Obv. Designer:** S.P. Zaskevich **Rev:** Peregrine falcon with inset diamond eye **Rev. Designer:** S.V. Nekrasova

Date	Mintage	F	VF	XF	Unc	BU
2006	2,000	—	—	750	1,000	—

KM# 143 50 ROUBLES
7.2000 g., 0.9000 Gold 0.2083 oz. AGW, 21 mm. **Subject:** Bison **Obv:** National arms **Rev:** Bison **Designer:** S.P. Zaskevich

Date	Mintage	F	VF	XF	Unc	BU
2006	3,000	—	—	—	300	—

KM# 144 50 ROUBLES
7.2000 g., 0.9000 Gold 0.2083 oz. AGW, 21 mm. **Subject:** Beaver **Obv:** National arms **Rev:** Family of beavers **Designer:** S.P. Zaskovich

Date	Mintage	F	VF	XF	Unc	BU
2006	3,000	—	—	—	350	—

KM# 145 50 ROUBLES
7.2000 g., 0.9000 Gold 0.2083 oz. AGW, 21 mm. **Subject:** Mute Swan **Obv:** National arms **Rev:** Pair of mute swans **Designer:** S.P. Zaskevich

Date	Mintage	F	VF	XF	Unc	BU
2006	3,000	—	—	—	350	—

KM# 123 50 ROUBLES
7.2000 g., 0.9000 Silver 0.2083 oz. ASW, 21 mm. **Subject:** Herring Gull **Obv:** National arms **Rev:** Herring gull in flight **Designer:** S.P. Zaskevitch

Date	Mintage	F	VF	XF	Unc	BU
2006	3,000	—	—	—	325	—

KM# 125 50 ROUBLES
7.2000 g., 0.9000 Gold 0.2083 oz. AGW, 21 mm. **Obv:** National arms **Rev:** Pair of common cranes **Designer:** S.P. Zaskevich

Date	Mintage	F	VF	XF	Unc	BU
2006	3,000	—	—	—	325	—

KM# 58 100 ROUBLES
155.5000 g., 0.9250 Silver 4.6243 oz. ASW, 64 mm. **Obv:** Theater building **Rev:** Two ballet dancers **Edge:** Reeded **Designer:** S.P. Zaskevich **Note:** Illustration reduced.

Date	Mintage	F	VF	XF	Unc	BU
2003 Proof	1,000	Value: 600				

KM# 103 200 ROUBLES
31.1000 g., 0.9990 Gold 0.9988 oz. AGW, 40 mm. **Obv:** National arms **Obv. Designer:** S.P. Zaskevich **Rev:** Belarussian ballerina **Rev. Designer:** Michael Schulze

Date	Mintage	F	VF	XF	Unc	BU
2005 Proof	1,500	Value: 1,650				

KM# 74 1000 ROUBLES
1000.0000 g., 0.9990 Silver 32.117 oz. ASW, 100 mm. **Subject:** 2004 Olympics **Obv:** National arms **Rev:** Ancient charioteer **Rev. Designer:** Waldemar Wronski **Note:** Illustration reduced.

Date	Mintage	F	VF	XF	Unc	BU
2004 Proof	650	Value: 1,500				

BELGIUM

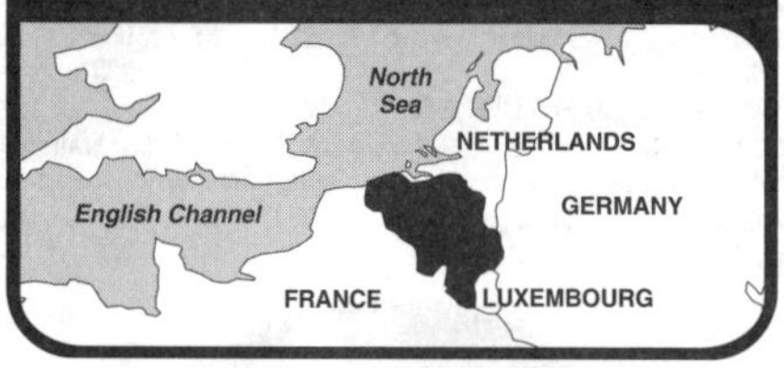

The Kingdom of Belgium, a constitutional monarchy in northwest Europe, has an area of 11,780 sq. mi. (30,519 sq. km.) and a population of 10.1 million, chiefly Dutch-speaking Flemish and French-speaking Walloons. Capital: Brussels. Agriculture, dairy farming, and the processing of raw materials for re-export are the principal industries. Beurs voor Diamant in Antwerp is the world's largest diamond trading center. Iron and steel, machinery motor vehicles, chemicals, textile yarns and fabrics comprise the principal exports.

RULER
Albert II, 1993-

MINT MARK
Angel head - Brussels

MINTMASTERS' INITIALS & PRIVY MARKS
(b) - bird - Vogelier
Lamb head – Lambret

NOTE: Beginning in 1987, the letters "qp" appear on the coins - (quality proof)

MONETARY SYSTEM
100 Centimes = 1 Franc
1 Euro = 100 Cents

LEGENDS
Belgian coins are usually inscribed either in Dutch, French or both. However some modern coins are being inscribed in Latin or German. The language used is best told by noting the spelling of the name of the country.
(Fr) French: BELGIQUE or BELGES
(Du) Dutch: BELGIE or BELGEN
(La) Latin: BELGICA
(Ge) German: BELGIEN

KINGDOM

DECIMAL COINAGE

KM# 148.1 50 CENTIMES
2.7500 g., Bronze, 19 mm. **Ruler:** Baudouin I **Obv:** Crowned denomination divides date, legend in French **Obv. Legend:** BELGIQUE **Rev:** Helmeted miner left, miners lamp at right, smaller head, tip of neck 1mm from rim **Edge:** Plain **Designer:** Rau

Date	Mintage	F	VF	XF	Unc	BU
2001	60,000	—	—	—	2.00	—

Note: In sets only

Date	Mintage	F	VF	XF	Unc	BU
2001 Proof	5,000	Value: 25.00				

Note: Medal alignment

KM# 148.2 50 CENTIMES
2.7500 g., Bronze, 19 mm. **Edge:** Plain **Note:** Medal alignment.

Date	Mintage	F	VF	XF	Unc	BU
2001 Proof	—	Value: 30.00				

Note: In sets only

KM# 149.1 50 CENTIMES
2.7500 g., Bronze, 19 mm. **Ruler:** Baudouin I **Obv:** Crowned denomination divides date **Obv. Legend:** BELGIE **Rev:** Helmeted miner left, miners lamp at right, smaller head, legend in Dutch **Edge:** Plain **Designer:** Rau

Date	Mintage	F	VF	XF	Unc	BU
2001	60,000	—	—	—	3.00	—

Note: In sets only

Date	Mintage	F	VF	XF	Unc	BU
2001 Proof	5,000	Value: 25.00				

Note: Medal alignment

Date	Mintage	F	VF	XF	Unc	BU
2007	60,000	—	—	—	2.00	—

Note: In sets only

KM# 149.2 50 CENTIMES
2.7500 g., Bronze, 19 mm. **Edge:** Plain **Note:** Medal alignment.

Date	Mintage	F	VF	XF	Unc	BU
2001 Proof	—	Value: 30.00				

Note: In sets only

KM# 187 FRANC
Nickel Plated Iron, 18 mm. **Ruler:** Albert II **Obv:** Head left, outline around back of head **Rev:** Vertical line divides date and large denomination, legend in French **Rev. Legend:** BELGIQUE **Note:** Mint mark - Angel Head. Unknown mintmaster's privy mark - scales.

Date	Mintage	F	VF	XF	Unc	BU
2001	60,000	—	—	—	3.00	—

Note: In sets only

Date	Mintage	F	VF	XF	Unc	BU
2001 Proof	5,000	Value: 25.00				

Note: Medal alignment; in sets only

KM# 188 FRANC
2.7700 g., Nickel Plated Iron, 18 mm. **Ruler:** Albert II **Obv:** Head left, outline around back of head **Rev:** Vertical line divides date and large denomination, legend in Dutch **Rev. Legend:** BELGIE **Edge:** Plain

Date	Mintage	F	VF	XF	Unc	BU
2001	60,000	—	—	—	3.00	—

Note: In sets only

Date	Mintage	F	VF	XF	Unc	BU
2001 Proof	5,000	Value: 25.00				

Note: Medal alignment; in sets only

KM# 189 5 FRANCS (5 Frank)
5.5000 g., Aluminum-Bronze, 24 mm. **Ruler:** Albert II **Obv:** Head left, outline around back of head **Rev:** Vertical line divides date and denomination, legend in French **Rev. Legend:** BELGIQUE **Note:** Mint mark - Angel head. Mintmaster R. Coenen's privy mark - Scale.

Date	Mintage	F	VF	XF	Unc	BU
2001	60,000	—	—	—	4.00	—

Note: In sets only

Date	Mintage	F	VF	XF	Unc	BU
2001 Proof	5,000	Value: 25.00				

Note: Medal alignment; in sets only

KM# 190 5 FRANCS (5 Frank)
Aluminum-Bronze, 24 mm. **Ruler:** Albert II **Obv:** Head left, outline around back of head **Rev:** Vertical line divides date and large denomination, legend in Dutch **Rev. Legend:** BELGIE **Note:** Mint mark - Angel head. Mintmaster R. Coenen's privy mark - Scale.

Date	Mintage	F	VF	XF	Unc	BU
2001	60,000	—	—	—	4.00	—

Note: In sets only

Date	Mintage	F	VF	XF	Unc	BU
2001 Proof	5,000	Value: 25.00				

Note: Medal alignment, in sets only

KM# 191 20 FRANCS (20 Frank)
8.5000 g., Nickel-Bronze, 25.65 mm. **Ruler:** Albert II **Obv:** Head left, outline around back of head **Rev:** Vertical line divides date and large denomination, legend in French **Rev. Legend:** BELGIQUE **Note:** Mint mark - Angel head. Mintmaster R. Coenen's privy mark - Scale.

Date	Mintage	F	VF	XF	Unc	BU
2001	60,000	—	—	—	4.00	—

Note: In sets only

Date	Mintage	F	VF	XF	Unc	BU
2001 Proof	5,000	Value: 25.00				

Note: Medal alignment; in sets only

KM# 192 20 FRANCS (20 Frank)
8.5000 g., Nickel-Bronze, 25.65 mm. **Ruler:** Albert II **Obv:** Head left, outline around back of head **Rev:** Vertical line divides date and large denomination, legend in Dutch **Rev. Legend:** BELGIE **Note:** Mint mark - Angel head. Mintmaster R. Coenen's privy mark - Scale.

Date	Mintage	F	VF	XF	Unc	BU
2001	60,000	—	—	—	5.00	—

Note: In sets only

Date	Mintage	F	VF	XF	Unc	BU
2001 Proof	5,000	Value: 25.00				

Note: Medal alignment; in sets only

KM# 193 50 FRANCS (50 Frank)
7.0500 g., Nickel, 22.5 mm. **Ruler:** Albert II **Obv:** Head left, outline around back of head **Rev:** Vertical line divides large denomination and date, legend in French **Rev. Legend:** BELGIQUE **Note:** Mint mark - Angel head. Mintmaster R. Coenen's privy mark - Scale.

Date	Mintage	F	VF	XF	Unc	BU
2001	60,000	—	—	—	8.00	—

Note: In sets only

Date	Mintage	F	VF	XF	Unc	BU
2001 Proof	5,000	Value: 25.00				

Note: Medal alignment; in sets only

KM# 194 50 FRANCS (50 Frank)
Nickel, 22.5 mm. **Ruler:** Albert II **Obv:** Head left, outline around back of head **Rev:** Vertical line divides large denomination and date, legend in Dutch **Rev. Legend:** BELGIE **Note:** Mint mark - Angel head. Mintmaster R. Coenen's privy mark - Scale.

Date	Mintage	F	VF	XF	Unc	BU
2001	60,000	—	—	—	8.00	—

Note: In sets only

Date	Mintage	F	VF	XF	Unc	BU
2001 Proof	5,000	Value: 25.00				

Note: Medal alignment; in sets only

KM# 222 500 FRANCS (500 Frank)
22.8500 g., 0.9250 Silver 0.6795 oz. ASW, 37 mm. **Ruler:** Albert II **Subject:** Europe: Europa and the Bull **Obv:** Map and denomination **Rev:** Europa sitting on a bull **Edge:** Plain

Date	Mintage	F	VF	XF	Unc	BU
2001 (qp) Proof	40,000	Value: 55.00				

KM# 223 5000 FRANCS
15.5500 g., 0.9990 Gold 0.4994 oz. AGW, 29 mm. **Ruler:** Albert II **Subject:** Europe: Europa and the Bull **Obv:** Map and denomination **Rev:** Europa sitting on a bull **Edge:** Plain

Date	Mintage	F	VF	XF	Unc	BU
2001 (qp) Proof	2,000	Value: 550				

EURO COINAGE

European Union Issues

KM# 224 EURO CENT
2.2700 g., Copper Plated Steel, 16.2 mm. **Ruler:** Albert II **Obv:** Head left within inner circle, stars 3/4 surround, date below **Obv. Designer:** Jan Alfons Keustermans **Rev:** Denomination and globe **Rev. Designer:** Luc Luycx **Edge:** Plain

Date	Mintage	F	VF	XF	Unc	BU
2001	99,840,000	—	—	—	0.60	1.00
2001 Proof	15,000	Value: 12.00				

Date	Mintage	F	VF	XF	Unc	BU
2002	140,000	—	—	—	18.50	22.50
2002 Proof	15,000	Value: 15.00				
2003	10,135,000	—	—	—	0.35	0.75
2003 Proof	15,000	Value: 12.00				
2004	180,000,000	—	—	—	0.35	0.75
2004 Proof	—	Value: 12.00				
2005	—	—	—	—	0.35	0.75
2005 Proof	3,000	Value: 12.00				
2006	—	—	—	—	0.35	0.75
2006 Proof	—	Value: 12.00				

KM# 225 2 EURO CENT

3.0300 g., Copper Plated Steel, 18.7 mm. **Ruler:** Albert II **Obv:** Head left within circle, stars 3/4 surround, date below **Obv. Designer:** Jan Alfons Keustermans **Rev:** Denomination and globe **Rev. Designer:** Luc Luycx **Edge:** Grooved

Date	Mintage	F	VF	XF	Unc	BU
2001	40,000	—	—	—	7.00	9.00

Note: Only available in sets at present, circulation strikes not yet released

Date	Mintage	F	VF	XF	Unc	BU
2001 Proof	15,000	Value: 15.00				
2002	140,000	—	—	—	3.50	6.50
2002 Proof	15,000	Value: 12.00				
2003	40,135,000	—	—	—	0.50	1.00
2003 Proof	15,000	Value: 12.00				
2004	140,000,000	—	—	—	0.50	1.00
2004 Proof	15,000	Value: 12.00				
2005	—	—	—	—	0.50	1.00
2005 Proof	—	Value: 12.00				
2006	—	—	—	—	0.50	1.00
2006 Proof	—	Value: 12.00				

KM# 226 5 EURO CENT

3.8600 g., Copper Plated Steel, 21.2 mm. **Ruler:** Albert II **Obv:** Head left within circle, stars 3/4 surround, date below **Obv. Designer:** Jan Alfons Keustermans **Rev:** Denomination and globe **Rev. Designer:** Luc Luycx **Edge:** Plain

Date	Mintage	F	VF	XF	Unc	BU
2001	40,000	—	—	—	10.00	12.50
2001 Proof	15,000	Value: 15.00				
2002	140,000	—	—	—	6.00	8.00
2002 Proof	15,000	Value: 15.00				
2003	30,135,000	—	—	—	1.00	1.50
2003 Proof	15,000	Value: 12.00				
2004	97,000,000	—	—	—	1.00	1.50
2004 Proof	—	Value: 12.00				
2005	—	—	—	—	1.00	1.50
2005 Proof	3,000	Value: 12.00				
2006	—	—	—	—	1.00	1.50

KM# 227 10 EURO CENT

4.0700 g., Brass, 19.7 mm. **Ruler:** Albert II **Obv:** Head left within inner circle, stars 3/4 surround, date below **Obv. Designer:** Jan Alfons Keustermans **Rev:** Denomination and map **Rev. Designer:** Luc Luycx **Edge:** Reeded

Date	Mintage	F	VF	XF	Unc	BU
2001	145,790,000	—	—	—	0.75	1.25
2001 Proof	15,000	Value: 12.00				
2002	140,000	—	—	—	6.00	8.00
2002 Proof	15,000	Value: 15.00				
2003	135,000	—	—	—	6.00	8.00
2003 Proof	15,000	Value: 15.00				
2004	20,000,000	—	—	—	1.00	1.50
2004 Proof	—	Value: 12.00				
2005	—	—	—	—	1.00	1.50
2005 Proof	3,000	Value: 12.00				
2006	—	—	—	—	1.00	1.50

KM# 242 10 EURO CENT

4.0700 g., Brass, 19.7 mm. **Ruler:** Albert II **Obv:** King's portrait **Obv. Designer:** Jan Alfons Keustermans **Rev:** Relief Map of Western Europe, stars, lines and value **Rev. Designer:** Luc Luycx **Edge:** Reeded

Date	Mintage	F	VF	XF	Unc	BU
2007	—	—	—	—	1.00	1.50

KM# 228 20 EURO CENT

5.7300 g., Brass, 22.1 mm. **Ruler:** Albert II **Obv:** Head left within circle, stars 3/4 surround, date below **Obv. Designer:** Jan Alfons Keustermans **Rev:** Denomination and map **Rev. Designer:** Luc Luycx **Edge:** Notched

Date	Mintage	F	VF	XF	Unc	BU
2001	40,000	—	—	—	10.00	12.50

Note: Only available in sets at present, circulation strikes not yet released

Date	Mintage	F	VF	XF	Unc	BU
2001 Proof	15,000	Value: 15.00				
2002	104,140,000	—	—	—	1.00	1.50

Date	Mintage	F	VF	XF	Unc	BU
2002 Proof	15,000	Value: 12.00				
2003	30,135,000	—	—	—	1.25	1.75
2003 Proof	15,000	Value: 12.00				
2004	109,550,000	—	—	—	1.25	1.75
2004 Proof	—	Value: 12.00				
2005	—	—	—	—	1.25	1.75
2005 Proof	3,000	Value: 12.00				
2006	—	—	—	—	1.25	1.75

KM# 243 20 EURO CENT

5.7300 g., Brass, 22.1 mm. **Ruler:** Albert II **Obv:** King's portrait **Obv. Designer:** Jan Alfons Keustermans **Rev:** Relief Map of Western Europe, stars, lines and value **Rev. Designer:** Luc Luycx **Edge:** Notched

Date	Mintage	F	VF	XF	Unc	BU
2007	—	—	—	—	1.25	1.75

KM# 229 50 EURO CENT

7.8100 g., Brass, 24.2 mm. **Ruler:** Albert II **Obv:** Head left within circle, stars 3/4 surround, date below **Obv. Designer:** Jan Alfons Keustermans **Rev:** Denomination and map **Rev. Designer:** Luc Luycx **Edge:** Reeded

Date	Mintage	F	VF	XF	Unc	BU
2001	40,000	—	—	—	10.00	12.50
2001 Proof	15,000	Value: 15.00				
2002	50,040,000	—	—	—	1.00	1.50
2002 Proof	15,000	Value: 12.00				
2003	135,000	—	—	—	1.25	1.75
2003 Proof	15,000	Value: 12.00				
2004	15,000,000	—	—	—	1.25	1.75
2004 Proof	—	Value: 12.00				
2005	—	—	—	—	1.25	1.75
2005 Proof	3,000	Value: 12.00				
2006	—	—	—	—	1.25	1.75

KM# 244 50 EURO CENT

7.8100 g., Brass, 24.2 mm. **Ruler:** Albert II **Obv:** King's portrait **Obv. Designer:** Jan Alfons Keustermans **Rev:** Relief Map of Western Europe, stars, lines and value **Rev. Designer:** Luc Luycx **Edge:** Reeded

Date	Mintage	F	VF	XF	Unc	BU
2007	—	—	—	—	1.25	1.75

KM# 230 EURO

7.5700 g., Bi-Metallic Copper-Nickel center in Brass ring, 23.2 mm. **Ruler:** Albert II **Obv:** Head left within circle, stars 3/4 surround, date below **Obv. Designer:** Jan Alfons Keustermans **Rev:** Denomination and map **Rev. Designer:** Luc Luycx **Edge:** Reeded and plain sections

Date	Mintage	F	VF	XF	Unc	BU
2001	40,000	—	—	—	12.50	15.00

Note: Only available in sets at present, circulation strikes not yet released

Date	Mintage	F	VF	XF	Unc	BU
2001 Proof	15,000	Value: 18.00				
2002	90,640,000	—	—	—	3.00	5.00

Note: Only a fraction of the mintage released at present

Date	Mintage	F	VF	XF	Unc	BU
2002 Proof	15,000	Value: 15.00				
2003	135,000	—	—	—	3.00	5.00
2003 Proof	15,000	Value: 15.00				
2004	15,000,000	—	—	—	3.00	5.00
2004 Proof	—	Value: 15.00				
2005	—	—	—	—	3.00	5.00
2005 Proof	3,000	Value: 15.00				
2006	—	—	—	—	3.00	5.00

KM# 245 EURO

7.5000 g., Bi-Metallic Copper-Nickel center in Brass ring, 23.2 mm. **Ruler:** Albert II **Obv:** King's portrait **Obv. Designer:** Jan Alfons Keustermans **Rev:** Relief Map of Western Europe, stars, lines and value **Rev. Designer:** Luc Luycx **Edge:** Reeded and plain sections

Date	Mintage	F	VF	XF	Unc	BU
2007	—	—	—	—	3.00	5.00

KM# 231 2 EURO

8.5200 g., Bi-Metallic **Ring Composition:** Copper-Nickel **Center Composition:** Brass, 25.7 mm. **Ruler:** Albert II **Obv:** Head left within circle, stars 3/4 surround, date below **Obv. Designer:** Jan Alfons Keustermans **Rev:** Denomination and map **Rev. Designer:** Luc Luycx **Edge:** Reeded with 2's and stars

Date	Mintage	F	VF	XF	Unc	BU
2001	40,000	—	—	—	12.50	15.00

Note: Only available in sets at present, circulation strikes not yet released

Date	Mintage	F	VF	XF	Unc	BU
2001 Proof	15,000	Value: 20.00				
2002	50,140,000	—	—	—	3.75	6.00
2002 Proof	15,000	Value: 18.00				
2003	30,135,000	—	—	—	3.75	6.00
2003 Proof	15,000	Value: 18.00				
2004	65,500,000	—	—	—	3.75	6.00
2004 Proof	—	Value: 18.00				
2005	—	—	—	—	3.75	6.00
2005 Proof	3,000	Value: 18.00				
2006	—	—	—	—	3.75	6.00

KM# 240 2 EURO

8.5200 g., Bi-Metallic **Ring Composition:** Copper-Nickel **Center Composition:** Brass, 25.7 mm. **Ruler:** Albert II **Subject:** Schengen Agreement **Obv:** Albert II of Belgium and Henri of Luxembourg **Rev:** Value and map **Edge:** Reeding over stars

Date	Mintage	F	VF	XF	Unc	BU
2005	6,020,000	—	—	—	5.00	7.50
2005 Proof	3,000	Value: 25.00				

KM# 241 2 EURO

8.5200 g., Bi-Metallic Brass center in Copper-Nickel ring, 25.7 mm. **Ruler:** Albert II **Obv:** Atomic model **Rev:** Value and map **Edge:** Reeding over stars and 2's

Date	Mintage	F	VF	XF	Unc	BU
2006	—	—	—	—	—	3.50

KM# 246 2 EURO

8.5200 g., Bi-Metallic Brass center in Copper-Nickel ring, 25.7 mm. **Ruler:** Albert II **Obv:** King's portrait **Obv. Designer:** Jan Alfons Keustermans **Rev:** Relief Map of Western Europe, stars, lines and value **Rev. Designer:** Luc Luycx **Edge:** Reeded with 2's and stars

Date	Mintage	F	VF	XF	Unc	BU
2007	—	—	—	—	3.75	6.00

KM# 247 2 EURO

8.4500 g., Bi-Metallic **Ring Composition:** Copper Nickel **Center Composition:** Brass, 25.70 mm. **Ruler:** Albert II **Subject:** 50th Anniversary Treaty of Rome **Obv:** Open treaty book **Rev:** Large value at left, modified outline of Europe at right **Edge:** Reeded with stars and 2's

Date	Mintage	F	VF	XF	Unc	BU
2007	—	—	—	—	—	9.00

KM# 233 10 EURO

18.9300 g., 0.9250 Silver 0.5629 oz. ASW, 32.9 mm. **Ruler:** Albert II **Subject:** Belgian Railway System **Obv:** Value, head at right transposed on map **Rev:** Train exiting tunnel **Edge:** Reeded

Date	Mintage	F	VF	XF	Unc	BU
ND (2002) Proof	50,000	Value: 50.00				

KM# 235 10 EURO

18.9300 g., 0.9250 Silver 0.5629 oz. ASW, 32.9 mm. **Ruler:** Albert II **Subject:** "Simenon" **Edge:** Reeded

Date	Mintage	F	VF	XF	Unc	BU
2003 Proof	50,000	Value: 40.00				

KM# 236 10 EURO

18.9300 g., 0.9250 Silver 0.5629 oz. ASW, 32.9 mm. **Ruler:** Albert II **Subject:** "Tintin" **Edge:** Reeded

Date	Mintage	F	VF	XF	Unc	BU
2004 Proof	50,000	Value: 85.00				

KM# 234 10 EURO

18.7500 g., 0.9250 Silver 0.5576 oz. ASW, 33 mm. **Ruler:** Albert II **Obv:** Value **Rev:** Western Europe map and Goddess Europa riding a bull **Edge:** Reeded

Date	Mintage	F	VF	XF	Unc	BU
2004 Proof	50,000	Value: 40.00				

KM# 237 100 EURO

15.5500 g., 0.9990 Gold 0.4994 oz. AGW, 29 mm. **Ruler:** Albert II **Subject:** Founding Fathers

Date	Mintage	F	VF	XF	Unc	BU
2002 Proof	5,000	Value: 575				

KM# 238 100 EURO

15.5500 g., 0.9990 Gold 0.4994 oz. AGW, 29 mm. **Ruler:** Albert II **Subject:** 10th Anniversary of Reign

Date	Mintage	F	VF	XF	Unc	BU
2003 Proof	5,000	Value: 500				

KM# 239 100 EURO
15.5500 g., 0.9990 Gold 0.4994 oz. AGW, 29 mm. **Ruler:** Albert II **Subject:** Franc Germinal

Date	Mintage	F	VF	XF	Unc	BU
2004 Proof	5,000	Value: 500				

MINT SETS

KM#	Date	Mintage	Identification	Issue Price	Mkt Val
MS14	2001 (10)	60,000	KM#148.1, 149.1, 187-194	15.00	45.00

PROOF SETS

KM#	Date	Mintage	Identification	Issue Price	Mkt Val
PS10	2001 (8)	15,000	KM#224-231	80.00	125
PS11	2002 (8)	15,000	KM#224-231	80.00	85.00
PS12	2003 (8)	15,000	KM#224-231	80.00	85.00
PS13	2004 (8)	15,000	KM#224-231	80.00	85.00

BELIZE

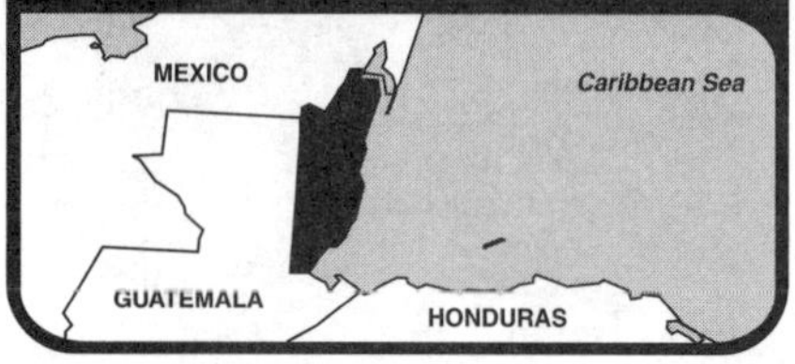

Belize, formerly British Honduras, but now an independent member of the Commonwealth of Nations, is situated in Central America south of Mexico and east and north of Guatemala, with an area of 8,867 sq. mi. (22,960 sq. km.) and a population of *242,000. Capital: Belmopan. Tourism now augments Belize's economy, in addition to sugar, citrus fruits, chicle and hardwoods which are exported.

MONETARY SYSTEM

Commencing 1864
100 Cents = 1 Dollar

COMMONWEALTH

DECIMAL COINAGE

KM# 33a CENT
0.8000 g., Aluminum, 19.5 mm. **Obv:** Bust of Queen Elizabeth right **Rev:** Denomination within circle **Edge:** Smooth, scalloped

Date	Mintage	F	VF	XF	Unc	BU
2002	—	—	—	0.10	0.15	0.45

KM# 34a 5 CENTS
1.0700 g., Aluminum, 20.15 mm. **Obv:** Bust of Queen Elizabeth II right **Obv. Designer:** Cecil Thomas **Rev:** Denomination within circle **Edge:** Plain

Date	Mintage	F	VF	XF	Unc	BU
2002	—	—	—	0.10	0.20	0.45

KM# 36 25 CENTS
5.6500 g., Copper-Nickel, 23.6 mm. **Obv:** Crowned bust of Queen Elizabeth II right **Obv. Designer:** Cecil Thomas **Rev:** Denomination within circle, date below **Edge:** Reeded

Date	Mintage	F	VF	XF	Unc	BU
2003	—	—	0.20	0.35	0.75	1.50

KM# 134 DOLLAR
30.9400 g., 0.9990 Silver 0.9937 oz. ASW, 39.9 mm. **Subject:** Mayan King **Obv:** National arms **Rev:** Mayan portrait in ornate headdress **Edge:** Reeded

Date	Mintage	F	VF	XF	Unc	BU
2002	—	—	—	—	35.00	37.50

BENIN

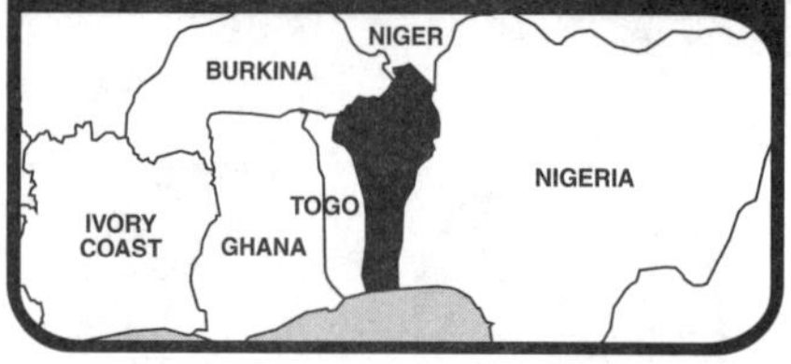

The Republic of Benin (formerly the Republic of Dahomey), located on the south side of the African bulge between Togo and Nigeria, has an area of 43,500 sq. mi. (112,620 sq. km.) and a population of 5.5 million. Capital: Porto-Novo. The principal industry of Benin, one of the poorest countries of West Africa, is the processing of palm oil products. Palm kernel oil, peanuts, cotton, and coffee are exported.

PEOPLES REPUBLIC

STANDARD COINAGE

KM# 37 1000 CFA FRANCS
14.9500 g., 0.9990 Silver 0.4802 oz. ASW, 35 mm. **Subject:** Leif Ericksson **Obv:** National arms, denomination below **Rev:** Viking ship to right of head **Edge:** Plain

Date	Mintage	F	VF	XF	Unc	BU
2001 Proof	—	Value: 30.00				

KM# 38 1000 CFA FRANCS
20.0000 g., 0.9990 Silver 0.6423 oz. ASW, 37.9 mm. **Subject:** Endangered Species **Obv:** National arms **Rev:** Two zebras grazing **Edge:** Reeded

Date	Mintage	F	VF	XF	Unc	BU
2001 Proof	—	Value: 40.00				

KM# 49 1000 CFA FRANCS
20.1100 g., 0.9990 Silver 0.6459 oz. ASW, 40 mm. **Obv:** National arms, denomination below **Rev:** Soccer player and wall of flags **Edge:** Reeded

Date	Mintage	F	VF	XF	Unc	BU
2002 Proof	—	Value: 40.00				

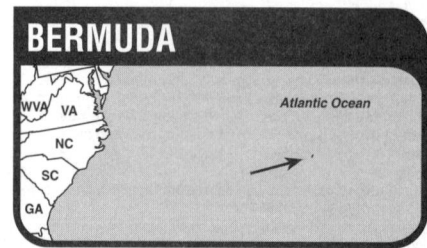

BERMUDA

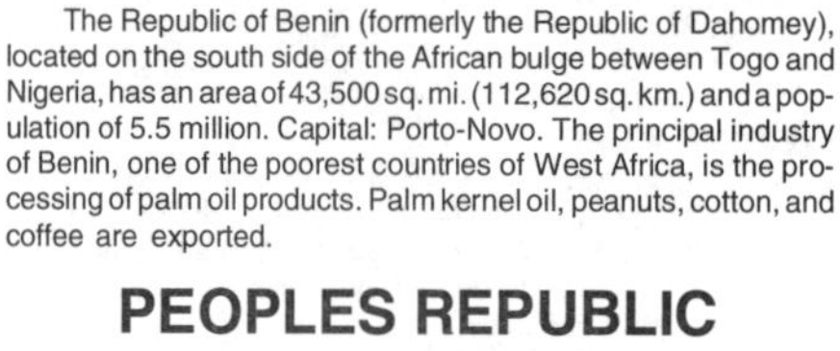

The Parliamentary British Colony of Bermuda, situated in the western Atlantic Ocean 660 miles (1,062 km.) east of North Carolina, has an area of 20.6 sq. mi. (53 sq. km.) and a population of 61,600. Capital: Hamilton. Concentrated essences, beauty preparations, and cut flowers are exported. Most Bermudians derive their livelihood from tourism. The British monarch is the head of state and is represented by a governor. U.S. Currency circulates in common with the Eastern Caribbean Dollar.

RULER
British

BRITISH COLONY

DECIMAL COINAGE

100 Cents = 1 Dollar

KM# 107 CENT
Copper Plated Zinc, 19 mm. **Ruler:** Elizabeth II **Obv:** Head with tiara right **Obv. Designer:** Ian Rank-Broadley **Rev:** Wild boar left **Rev. Designer:** Michael Rizzello **Edge:** Smooth

Date	Mintage	F	VF	XF	Unc	BU
2001	1,600,000	—	—	—	0.50	0.75
2002	1,120,000	—	—	—	0.50	0.75
2003	800,000	—	—	—	0.50	0.75
2004	1,600,000	—	—	—	0.50	0.75
2005	3,200,000	—	—	—	0.50	0.75

KM# 108 5 CENTS
5.0600 g., Copper-Nickel, 21 mm. **Ruler:** Elizabeth II **Obv:** Head with tiara right **Obv. Designer:** Ian Rank-Broadley **Rev:** Queen angel fish left **Rev. Designer:** Michael Rizzello **Edge:** Smooth

Date	Mintage	F	VF	XF	Unc	BU
2001	1,000,000	—	—	—	0.75	1.00
2002	700,000	—	—	—	0.75	1.00
2003	700,000	—	—	—	0.75	1.00
2004	700,000	—	—	—	0.75	1.00
2005	600,000	—	—	—	0.75	1.00

KM# 109 10 CENTS
2.4000 g., Copper-Nickel, 17.8 mm. **Ruler:** Elizabeth II **Obv:** Head with tiara right **Obv. Designer:** Ian Rank-Broadley **Rev:** Bermuda lily **Rev. Designer:** Michael Rizzello **Edge:** Reeded

Date	Mintage	F	VF	XF	Unc	BU
2001	1,400,000	—	—	—	0.85	1.00
2002	800,000	—	—	—	0.85	1.00
2003	600,000	—	—	—	0.85	1.00
2004	800,000	—	—	—	0.85	1.00
2005	800,000	—	—	—	0.85	1.00

KM# 110 25 CENTS
Copper-Nickel, 24 mm. **Ruler:** Elizabeth II **Obv:** Head with tiara right **Obv. Designer:** Ian Rank-Broadley **Rev:** Yellow-billed tropical bird right **Rev. Designer:** Michael Rizzello **Edge:** Reeded

Date	Mintage	F	VF	XF	Unc	BU
2001	800,000	—	—	—	1.50	2.00
2002	800,000	—	—	—	1.50	2.00
2003	800,000	—	—	—	1.50	2.00
2004	800,000	—	—	—	1.50	2.00
2005	1,440,000	—	—	—	1.50	2.00

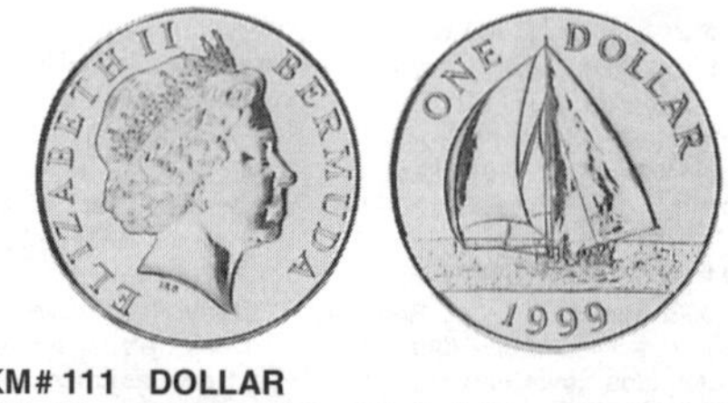

KM# 111 DOLLAR
Nickel-Brass, 26 mm. **Ruler:** Elizabeth II **Obv:** Head with tiara right **Obv. Designer:** Rank-Broadley **Rev:** Sailboat **Rev. Designer:** Eldron Trimingham III

Date	Mintage	F	VF	XF	Unc	BU
2001	—	—	—	—	3.00	3.50
2002	12,000	—	—	—	3.00	3.50
2003	12,000	—	—	—	3.00	3.50

Date	Mintage	F	VF	XF	Unc	BU
2004	12,000	—	—	—	3.00	3.50
2005	240,000	—	—	—	3.00	3.50

KM# 139 DOLLAR

28.2800 g., Copper-Nickel, 38.6 mm. **Obv:** Head with tiara right **Rev:** 4 Gombey dancers **Edge:** Reeded

Date	Mintage	F	VF	XF	Unc	BU
2001	—	—	—	—	10.00	12.00

KM# 124 DOLLAR

28.4100 g., Copper-Nickel, 38.5 mm. **Subject:** Queen's Jubilee **Obv:** Head with tiara right, denomination below **Obv. Designer:** Ian Rank-Broadley **Rev:** Stylized trumpeters above monogram and date **Edge:** Reeded

Date	Mintage	F	VF	XF	Unc	BU
2002	—	—	—	—	10.00	12.00

KM# 140 3 DOLLARS

33.6300 g., 0.9250 Silver 1.0000 oz. ASW, 35 mm. **Subject:** Shipwreck Series **Obv:** Elizabeth II **Rev:** The Mary Celestia gold plated image **Edge:** Plain **Shape:** Triangular

Date	Mintage	F	VF	XF	Unc	BU
2006 Proof	15,000	Value: 90.00				

KM# 141 3 DOLLARS

1.5550 g., 0.9990 Gold 0.0499 oz. AGW, 15 mm. **Subject:** Shipwreck Series **Obv:** Elizabeth II **Rev:** The Mary Celestia **Edge:** Plain **Shape:** Triangular

Date	Mintage	F	VF	XF	Unc	BU
2006 Proof	15,000	Value: 100				

KM# 148 3 DOLLARS

33.6300 g., 0.9250 Silver 1.0000 oz. ASW, 35 mm. **Subject:** Shipwreck Series **Obv:** Elizabeth II **Rev:** The Constellation in gold plated image **Edge:** Plain **Shape:** Triangular

Date	Mintage	F	VF	XF	Unc	BU
2006 Proof	15,000	Value: 90.00				

KM# 149 3 DOLLARS

1.5550 g., 0.9990 Gold 0.0499 oz. AGW, 15 mm. **Subject:** Shipwreck Series **Obv:** Elizabeth II **Rev:** The Constellation **Edge:** Plain **Shape:** Triangular

Date	Mintage	F	VF	XF	Unc	BU
2006 Proof	15,000	Value: 100				

KM# 157 3 DOLLARS

33.6300 g., 0.9250 Silver 1.0000 oz. ASW, 35 mm. **Subject:** Shipwrecks Series **Obv:** Elizabeth II **Rev:** Gold plated image of the Hunter Galley **Edge:** Plain

Date	Mintage	F	VF	XF	Unc	BU
2006 Proof	15,000	Value: 90.00				

KM# 158 3 DOLLARS

33.6300 g., 0.9250 Silver 1.0000 oz. ASW, 35 mm. **Subject:** Shipwrecks Series **Obv:** Elizabeth II **Rev:** Gold plated image of the North Carolina **Edge:** Plain

Date	Mintage	F	VF	XF	Unc	BU
2006 Proof	15,000	Value: 90.00				

KM# 159 3 DOLLARS

33.6300 g., 0.9250 Silver 1.0000 oz. ASW, 35 mm. **Subject:** Shipwrecks Series **Obv:** Elizabeth II **Rev:** Gold plated image of the Pollockshields **Edge:** Plain

Date	Mintage	F	VF	XF	Unc	BU
2006 Proof	15,000	Value: 90.00				

KM# 156 3 DOLLARS

33.6300 g., 0.9250 Silver 1.0000 oz. ASW, 35 mm. **Subject:** Shipwrecks Series **Obv:** Elizabeth II **Rev:** Gold plated image of the Sea Venture **Edge:** Plain

Date	Mintage	F	VF	XF	Unc	BU
2007 Proof	15,000	Value: 90.00				

KM# 120 5 DOLLARS

28.2800 g., 0.9250 Silver 0.8410 oz. ASW, 38.6 mm. **Subject:** Gombey Dancers **Obv:** Head with tiara right **Obv. Designer:** Ian Rank-Broadley **Rev:** Multicolor costumed dancers **Edge:** Reeded

Date	Mintage	F	VF	XF	Unc	BU
2001 Proof	3,500	Value: 50.00				

KM# 129 5 DOLLARS

28.2800 g., 0.9250 Silver 0.8410 oz. ASW, 38.6 mm. **Subject:** Queen's Jubilee **Obv:** Gold-plated head with tiara right, denomination below **Rev:** Trumpeters, monogram and date below **Edge:** Reeded

Date	Mintage	F	VF	XF	Unc	BU
2002 Proof	20,000	Value: 40.00				

KM# 130 5 DOLLARS

28.2800 g., 0.9250 Silver 0.8410 oz. ASW, 38.6 mm. **Subject:** Queen's Jubilee **Obv:** Gold-plated head with tiara right **Rev:** Royal visit scene **Edge:** Reeded

Date	Mintage	F	VF	XF	Unc	BU
2003 Proof	20,000	Value: 40.00				

KM# 128 5 DOLLARS

28.2800 g., 0.9250 Silver 0.8410 oz. ASW, 38.6 mm. **Obv:** Head with tiara right **Rev:** 2 fitted racing dinghys with multicolor sails **Edge:** Reeded

Date	Mintage	F	VF	XF	Unc	BU
ND (2003) Proof	3,500	Value: 60.00				

KM# 131 5 DOLLARS

28.2800 g., 0.9250 Silver 0.8410 oz. ASW, 38.6 mm. **Obv:** Head with tiara right **Rev:** Bermudan stone quarrying scene **Edge:** Reeded

Date	Mintage	F	VF	XF	Unc	BU
2004 Proof	3,500	Value: 60.00				

KM# 160 5 DOLLARS

14.5000 g., Silver, 30.89 mm. **Ruler:** Elizabeth II **Subject:** Bermuda Quincentennial **Obv:** Gold plated bust and rim **Rev:** Caravel type sailing ship in partially gold plated compass face and rim **Edge:** Gold plated plain **Shape:** Pentagonal

Date	Mintage	F	VF	XF	Unc	BU
2005 Proof	2,500	Value: 40.00				

KM# 160a 5 DOLLARS

, 30.89 mm. **Ruler:** Elizabeth II **Obv:** Queen Elizabeth II **Rev:** Caravel type sailing ship in compass face **Edge:** Plain **Shape:** Pentagonal **Note:** Bermuda Quincentennial

Date	Mintage	F	VF	XF	Unc	BU
2005	3,000	Value: 500				

KM# 142 9 DOLLARS

155.5200 g., 0.9990 Silver 4.9949 oz. ASW, 65 mm. **Subject:** Shipwreck Series **Obv:** Elizabeth II **Rev:** The Mary Celestia **Edge:** Plain **Shape:** Triangular

Date	Mintage	F	VF	XF	Unc	BU
2007 Proof	1,000	Value: 180				

KM# 150 9 DOLLARS

155.5200 g., 0.9990 Silver 4.9949 oz. ASW, 65 mm. **Subject:** Shipwreck Series **Obv:** Elizabeth II **Rev:** The Constellation **Edge:** Plain **Shape:** Triangular

Date	Mintage	F	VF	XF	Unc	BU
2007 Proof	1,000	Value: 180				

KM# 143 30 DOLLARS

31.4890 g., 0.9990 Gold 1.0113 oz. AGW, 35 mm. **Subject:** Shipwreck Series **Obv:** Elizabeth II **Rev:** The Mary Celestia **Edge:** Plain **Shape:** Triangular

Date	Mintage	F	VF	XF	Unc	BU
2006 Proof	750	Value: 900				

KM# 151 30 DOLLARS

31.4890 g., 0.9990 Gold 1.0113 oz. AGW, 35 mm. **Subject:** Shipwreck Series **Obv:** Elizabeth II **Rev:** The Constellation **Edge:** Plain **Shape:** Triangular

Date	Mintage	F	VF	XF	Unc	BU
2006 Proof	750	Value: 900				

KM# 144 60 DOLLARS

1000.0000 g., 0.9990 Silver 32.117 oz. ASW, 100 mm. **Subject:** Shipwreck Series **Obv:** Elizabeth II **Rev:** The Mary Celestia **Edge:** Plain

Date	Mintage	F	VF	XF	Unc	BU
2007 Proof	300	Value: 600				

KM# 152 60 DOLLARS

1000.0000 g., 0.9990 Silver 32.117 oz. ASW, 100 mm. **Subject:** Shipwreck Series **Obv:** Elizabeth II **Rev:** The Constellation **Edge:** Plain **Shape:** Triangular

Date	Mintage	F	VF	XF	Unc	BU
2007 Proof	300	Value: 600				

KM# 145 90 DOLLARS

155.5200 g., 0.9990 Gold 4.9949 oz. AGW, 65 mm. **Subject:** Shipwreck Series **Obv:** Elizabeth II **Rev:** The Mary Celestia **Edge:** Plain **Shape:** Triangular

Date	Mintage	F	VF	XF	Unc	BU
2006 Proof	90	Value: 4,500				

KM# 153 90 DOLLARS

155.5200 g., 0.9990 Gold 4.9949 oz. AGW, 65 mm. **Subject:** Shipwreck Series **Obv:** Elizabeth II **Rev:** The Constellation **Edge:** Plain **Shape:** Triangular

Date	Mintage	F	VF	XF	Unc	BU
2006 Proof	90	Value: 4,500				

KM# 146 300 DOLLARS

155.5200 g., 0.9995 Platinum 4.9974 oz. APW, 65 mm. **Subject:** Shipwrecks Series **Obv:** Elizabeth II **Rev:** The Mary Celestia **Edge:** Plain **Shape:** Triangular

Date	Mintage	F	VF	XF	Unc	BU
2006 Proof	60	Value: 8,000				

KM# 154 300 DOLLARS

155.5200 g., 0.9995 Platinum 4.9974 oz. APW, 65 mm. **Subject:** Shipwreck Series **Obv:** Elizabeth II **Rev:** The Constellation **Edge:** Plain **Shape:** Triangular

Date	Mintage	F	VF	XF	Unc	BU
2006 Proof	60	Value: 8,000				

KM# 147 600 DOLLARS

1096.0000 g., 0.9180 Gold 32.346 oz. AGW, 100 mm. **Subject:** Shipwreck Series **Obv:** Elizabeth II **Rev:** The Mary Celestia **Edge:** Plain **Shape:** Triangular

Date	Mintage	F	VF	XF	Unc	BU
2007 Proof	300	Value: 28,500				

KM# 155 600 DOLLARS

1096.0000 g., 0.9180 Gold 32.346 oz. AGW, 100 mm. **Subject:** Shipwreck Series **Obv:** Elizabeth II **Rev:** The Constellation **Edge:** Plain **Shape:** Triangular

Date	Mintage	F	VF	XF	Unc	BU
2007 Proof	300	Value: 28,500				

PIEFORTS

KM#	Date	Mintage	Identification	Mkt Val
P3	2005	250	5 Dollars. 0.9250 Silver. 29.0000 g. 30.89 mm. Gold plated bust and rim. Caravel type sailing ship in partially gold plated compass face and rim. Plain, gold plated edge.	—

BHUTAN

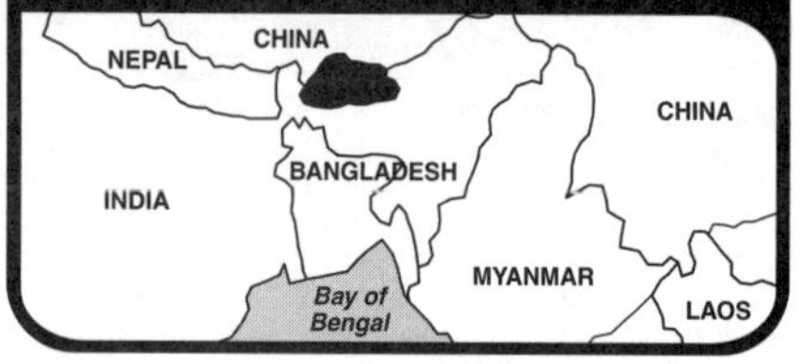

The Kingdom of Bhutan, a landlocked Himalayan country bordered by Tibet and India, has an area of 18,150 sq. mi. (47,000 sq. km.) and a population of *2.03 million. Capital: Thimphu. Virtually the entire population is engaged in agricultural and pastoral activities. Rice, wheat, barley, and yak butter are produced in sufficient quantity to make the country self-sufficient in food. The economy of Bhutan is primitive and many transactions are conducted on a barter basis.

RULER

Jigme Singye Wangchuk, 1972-

KINGDOM

REFORM COINAGE

Commencing 1974; 100 Chetrums (Paisa) = 1 Ngultrum (Rupee); 100 Ngultrums = 1 Sertum

KM# 105 5 CHHERTUM

3.8600 g., Brass, 21.9 mm. **Obv:** Monkey right, date below **Rev:** Effigy of the old "Ma-tam", value below **Edge:** Plain

Date	Mintage	F	VF	XF	Unc	BU
2003	—	—	—	—	0.25	0.35

BOLIVIA

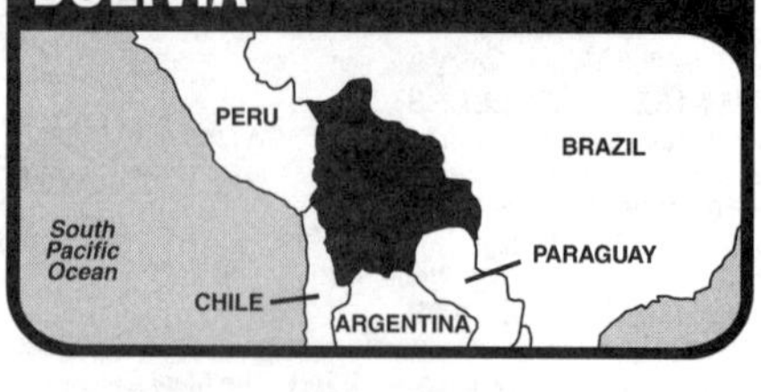

The Republic of Bolivia, a landlocked country in west central South America, has an area of 424,165 sq. mi. (1,098,580 sq. km.) and a population of *8.33 million. Its capitals are: La Paz (administrative) and Sucre (constitutional). Principal exports are tin, zinc, antimony, tungsten, petroleum, natural gas, cotton and coffee.

Much of present day Bolivia was first dominated by the Tiahuanaco Culture ca.400 BC. It had in turn been incorporated into the Inca Empire by 1440AD prior to the arrival of the Spanish, in 1535, who reduced the Indian population to virtual slavery. When Joseph Napoleon was placed upon the throne of occupied Spain in 1809, a fervor of revolutionary activity quickened throughout Alto Peru - culminating in the 1809 Proclamation of Liberty. Sixteen bloody years of struggle ensued before the republic, named for the famed liberator Simon Bolivar, was established on August 6, 1825. Since then Bolivia has survived more than 16 constitutions, 78 Presidents, 3 military juntas and over 160 revolutions.

MINT MARKS

A - Paris
(a) - Paris, privy marks only
CHI - Valcambia
H - Heaton
KN - Kings' Norton

REPUBLIC

REFORM COINAGE

1987-; 1,000,000 Peso Bolivianos = 1 Boliviano; 100 Centavos = 1 Boliviano

KM# 204 50 CENTAVOS

5.0800 g., Stainless Steel, 24 mm. **Obv:** National arms, star below **Rev:** Denomination within circle, date below **Edge:** Plain

Date	Mintage	F	VF	XF	Unc	BU
2001	—	—	—	—	0.75	1.00

KM# 212 5 BOLIVIANOS

Center Weight: 5.0000 g. **Center Composition:** Brass Clad Steel, 23 mm. **Obv:** National arms within inner circle **Rev:** Denomination within inner circle **Edge:** Reeded

Date	Mintage	F	VF	XF	Unc	BU
2001	—	—	—	—	3.50	5.00

BOSNIA AND HERZEGOVINA

The Republic of Bosnia and Herzegovina borders Croatia to the north and west, Serbia to the east and Montenegro in the southeast with only 12.4 mi. of coastline. The total land area is 19,735 sq. mi. (51,129 sq. km.). They have a population of *4.34 million. Capital: Sarajevo. Electricity, mining and agriculture are leading industries.

MONETARY SYSTEM

1 Convertible Marka = 100 Convertible Feniga = 1 Deutschemark 1998-

NOTE: German Euros circulate freely.

REPUBLIC

REFORM COINAGE

1998-

KM# 121 5 FENINGA

2.6600 g., Steel, 17.98 mm. **Obv:** Denomination on map **Rev:** Triangle and stars **Edge:** Reeded

Date	Mintage	F	VF	XF	Unc	BU
2005	—	—	—	—	1.00	1.25

KM# 115 10 FENINGA

3.9000 g., Copper-Plated-Steel, 19.98 mm. **Obv:** Denomination on map within circle **Rev:** Triangle and stars, date at left, within circle **Edge:** Plain

Date	Mintage	F	VF	XF	Unc	BU
2004	—	—	—	—	0.50	0.75

KM# 116 20 FENINGA

4.5000 g., Copper-Plated-Steel, 21.97 mm. **Obv:** Denomination on map within circle **Rev:** Triangle and stars, date at left, within circle

Date	Mintage	F	VF	XF	Unc	BU
2004	—	—	—	—	1.00	1.25

KM# 118 KONVERTIBLE MARKA

4.9000 g., Nickel Plated Steel, 23.23 mm. **Obv:** Denomination **Rev:** Coat of arms above date **Edge:** Reeded and plain sections

Date	Mintage	F	VF	XF	Unc	BU
2003	—	—	—	—	5.50	6.00
2006	—	—	—	—	—	5.00

KM# 119 2 KONVERTIBLE MARKA

6.9000 g., Bi-Metallic Copper-Nickel center in Nickel-Brass ring, 25.75 mm. **Obv:** Denomination within circle **Rev:** Dove of peace, date at right, within circle **Edge:** Reeded and plain sections

Date	Mintage	F	VF	XF	Unc	BU
2002	—	—	—	—	13.50	15.00
2003	—	—	—	—	13.50	15.00

KM# 120 5 KONVERTIBLE MARKA

10.3500 g., Bi-Metallic **Ring Composition:** Copper Nickel **Center Composition:** Brass, 29.99 mm. **Obv:** Denomination within circle **Rev:** Dove of Peace in flight

Date	Mintage	F	VF	XF	Unc	BU
2005	—	—	—	—	17.50	20.00

BOTSWANA

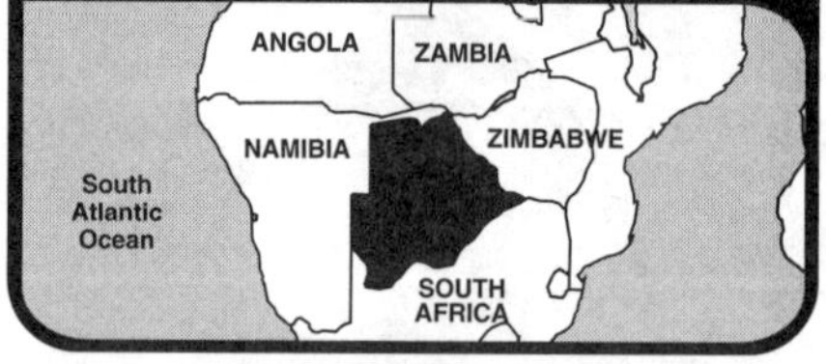

The Republic of Botswana (formerly Bechuanaland), located in south central Africa between Namibia and Zimbabwe, has an area of 224,607 sq. mi. (600,370 sq. km.) and a population of *1.62 million. Capital: Gaborone. Botswana is a member of a Customs Union with South Africa, Lesotho, and Swaziland. The economy is primarily pastoral with a rapidly developing mining industry, of which diamonds, copper and nickel are the chief elements. Meat products and diamonds comprise 85 percent of the exports.

Little is known of the origin of the peoples of Botswana. The early inhabitants, the Bushmen, did not develop a recorded history and are now dying out. The ancestors of the present Botswana residents probably arrived about 1600AD in Bantu migrations from the north and east. Bechuanaland was first united early in the 19th century under Chief Khama III to more effectively resist incursions by the Boer trekkers from Transvaal and by the neighboring Matabeles. As the Boer threat intensified, appeals for protection were made to the British Government, which proclaimed the whole of Bechuanaland a British protectorate in 1885. In 1895, the southern part of the protectorate was annexed to Cape Province. The northern part, known as the Bechuanaland Protectorate, remained under British administration until it became the independent Republic of Botswana on Sept. 30, 1966. Botswana is a member of the Commonwealth of Nations. The president is Chief of State and Head of government.

MINT MARK

B - Berne

MONETARY SYSTEM

100 Cents = 1 Thebe

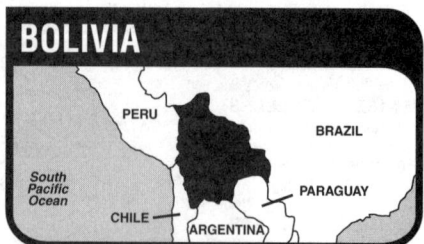

REPUBLIC

REFORM COINAGE

100 Thebe = 1 Pula

KM# 25a 2 PULA

Brass **Subject:** Wildlife **Obv:** National arms with supporters, date below **Rev:** Rhinoceros, left, denomination above **Shape:** 7-sided

Date	Mintage	F	VF	XF	Unc	BU
2004	—	—	—	—	2.75	3.50

The Federative Republic of Brazil, which comprises half the continent of South America and is the only Latin American country deriving its culture and language from Portugal, has an area of 3,286,488 sq. mi. (8,511,965 sq. km.) and a population of *169.2 million. Capital: Brasilia. The economy of Brazil is as varied and complex as any in the developing world. Agriculture is a mainstay of the economy, while only 4 percent of the area is under cultivation. Known mineral resources are almost unlimited in variety and size of reserves. A large, relatively sophisticated industry ranges from basic steel and chemical production to finished consumer goods. Coffee, cotton, iron ore and cocoa are the chief exports.

MINT MARKS

(a) - Paris, privy marks only
B - Bahia

REPUBLIC

REFORM COINAGE

1994-present

2750 Cruzeiros Reais = 1 Real; 100 Centavos = 1 Real

KM# 647 CENTAVO

Copper Plated Steel, 17 mm. **Obv:** Cabral bust at right **Rev:** Denomination on linear design at left, 3/4 globe with sash on right, date below **Edge:** Plain

Date	Mintage	F	VF	XF	Unc	BU
2001	—	—	—	—	0.10	0.20
2002	—	—	—	—	0.10	0.20
2003	—	—	—	—	0.10	0.20
2004	—	—	—	—	0.10	0.20

KM# 648 5 CENTAVOS

4.0500 g., Copper Plated Steel, 22 mm. **Obv:** Tiradente bust at right, dove at left **Rev:** Denomination on linear design at left, 3/4 globe with sash on right, date below **Edge:** Plain

Date	Mintage	F	VF	XF	Unc	BU
2001	—	—	—	—	0.45	0.65
2002	—	—	—	—	0.45	0.65
2003	—	—	—	—	0.45	0.65
2004	—	—	—	—	0.45	0.65
2005	—	—	—	—	0.45	0.65

KM# 649.2 10 CENTAVOS

4.8500 g., Brass Plated Steel, 20 mm. **Obv:** Bust of Pedro at right, horseman with sword in right hand at left **Rev:** Denomination on linear design at left, 3/4 globe with sash on right, date below **Edge:** Plain

Date	Mintage	F	VF	XF	Unc	BU
2001	—	—	—	—	0.60	0.80
2002	—	—	—	—	0.60	0.80
2003	—	—	—	—	0.60	0.80
2004	—	—	—	—	0.60	0.80

KM# 649.3 10 CENTAVOS

4.8000 g., Brass Plated Steel, 20 mm. **Obv:** Pedro I and horseman **Rev:** Value **Edge:** Reeded

Date	Mintage	F	VF	XF	Unc	BU
2006	—	—	—	—	0.50	0.75

KM# 650 25 CENTAVOS

7.6500 g., Brass Plated Steel, 25 mm. **Obv:** Deodoro bust at right, national arms at left **Rev:** Denomination on linear design at left, 3/4 globe with sash on right, date below **Edge:** Reeded

Date	Mintage	F	VF	XF	Unc	BU
2001	—	—	—	—	0.75	1.00
2002	—	—	—	—	0.75	1.00
2003	—	—	—	—	0.75	1.00
2004	—	—	—	—	0.75	1.00

KM# 651 50 CENTAVOS

9.2200 g., Copper-Nickel, 23 mm. **Obv:** Rio Branco bust at right, map at left **Rev:** Denomination on linear design at left, 3/4 globe with sash on right, date below **Edge Lettering:** BRASIL ORDEM E PROGRESSO

Date	Mintage	F	VF	XF	Unc	BU
2001	—	—	—	—	1.25	1.50
2002	—	—	—	—	1.25	1.50
2003	—	—	—	—	1.25	1.50
2005	—	—	—	—	1.25	1.50

KM# 651a 50 CENTAVOS

7.8600 g., Stainless Steel, 23.05 mm. **Obv:** Rio Branco bust at right, map at left **Rev:** Denomination on linear design at left, 3/4 globe with sash on right, date below

Date	Mintage	F	VF	XF	Unc	BU
2002	—	—	—	—	1.25	1.50

KM# 652 REAL

7.8700 g., Bi-Metallic **Ring Composition:** Brass **Center Composition:** Copper-Nickel, 27 mm. **Obv:** Allegorical portrait left **Rev:** Denomination on linear design at left, 3/4 globe with sash on right, date below **Edge:** Segmented reeding **Note:** Total coin weight 7.8 grams.

Date	Mintage	F	VF	XF	Unc	BU
2002	—	—	—	—	3.00	4.50

KM# 652a REAL

7.0000 g., Bi-Metallic **Ring Composition:** Brass-Plated Steel **Center Composition:** Stainless Steel, 26.9 mm. **Obv:** Allegorical portrait **Rev:** Denomination on linear design at left, 3/4 globe with sash on right, date below **Edge:** Segmented reeding

Date	Mintage	F	VF	XF	Unc	BU
2002	—	—	—	—	3.50	4.50
2004	—	—	—	—	3.50	4.50

KM# 656 REAL

7.0000 g., Bi-Metallic **Ring Composition:** Brass-Plated Steel **Center Composition:** Stainless Steel, 26.9 mm. **Subject:** Centennial of Juscelino Kubitschek, president **Obv:** Head left **Obv. Designer:** Alzira Duim **Rev:** Denomination on linear design at left, 3/4 globe with sash on right, date below **Edge:** Segmented reeding

Date	Mintage	F	VF	XF	Unc	BU
2002	50,000,000	—	—	—	3.50	4.50

KM# 668 REAL

6.9100 g., Bi-Metallic Stainless Steel center in Brass plated Stainless Steel ring, 27.1 mm. **Subject:** 40th Anniversary of Central Bank **Obv:** Monument **Rev:** Value on flag **Edge:** Segmented reeding

Date	Mintage	F	VF	XF	Unc	BU
2005	40,000	—	—	—	5.00	6.50

KM# 657 2 REAIS

28.0000 g., 0.9990 Silver 0.8993 oz. ASW, 40 mm. **Subject:** Centennial - Carlos Drummond de Andrade **Obv:** Denomination and writer **Rev:** Stylized portrait **Edge:** Reeded

Date	Mintage	F	VF	XF	Unc	BU
ND(2002) Proof	7,000	Value: 60.00				

KM# 658 2 REAIS

28.0000 g., 0.9990 Silver 0.8993 oz. ASW, 40 mm. **Subject:** Centennial - Juscelino Kubitschek **Obv:** Bust facing in upper right, initials at left **Rev:** Denomination **Edge:** Reeded

Date	Mintage	F	VF	XF	Unc	BU
2002 Proof	20,000	Value: 55.00				

KM# 663 2 REAIS

27.0000 g., 0.9250 Silver 0.8029 oz. ASW, 40 mm. **Obv:** Value and piano player **Rev:** Ary Barroso singing **Edge:** Reeded

Date	Mintage	F	VF	XF	Unc	BU
ND(2003) Proof	7,000	Value: 45.00				

KM# 665 2 REAIS

27.0000 g., 0.9250 Silver 0.8029 oz. ASW, 40 mm. **Subject:** Centennial - Portinari **Obv:** Starving family scene, value and country name **Rev:** Portinari's portrait, stars in squares design **Edge:** Reeded

Date	Mintage	F	VF	XF	Unc	BU
ND(2003) Proof	2,000	Value: 50.00				

KM# 666 2 REAIS

27.0000 g., 0.9250 Silver 0.8029 oz. ASW, 40 mm. **Subject:** FIFA Centennial **Obv:** Soccer ball and value **Rev:** Center part of a Brazilian flag and stars **Edge:** Reeded

Date	Mintage	F	VF	XF	Unc	BU
2004 Proof	—	Value: 55.00				

KM# 661 5 REAIS

28.0000 g., 0.9990 Silver 0.8993 oz. ASW, 40 mm. **Obv:** Soccer player and Brazilian flag **Rev:** Soccer ball and value **Edge:** Reeded

Date	Mintage	F	VF	XF	Unc	BU
2002 Proof	10,000	Value: 45.00				

KM# 659 20 REAIS

8.0000 g., 0.9000 Gold 0.2315 oz. AGW, 22 mm. **Obv:** Juscelino Kubitschek de Oliveira's portrait **Rev:** Value **Edge:** Reeded

Date	Mintage	F	VF	XF	Unc	BU
2002 Proof	2,500	Value: 245				

KM# 660 20 REAIS

8.0000 g., 0.9000 Gold 0.2315 oz. AGW, 22 mm. **Obv:** Carlos Drummond de Andrade portrait and value **Rev:** Andrade caricature, name and dates **Edge:** Reeded

Date	Mintage	F	VF	XF	Unc	BU
ND(2002) Proof	2,500	Value: 245				

KM# 662 20 REAIS

8.0000 g., 0.9000 Gold 0.2315 oz. AGW, 22 mm. **Obv:** Soccer player **Rev:** Value, inscription and shooting stars **Edge:** Reeded

Date	Mintage	F	VF	XF	Unc	BU
2002	2,500	Value: 245				

KM# 664 20 REAIS

8.0000 g., 0.9000 Gold 0.2315 oz. AGW, 22 mm. **Subject:** Centennial - Ary Barroso **Obv:** Piano keyboard and music above value **Rev:** Caricature of Ary Barroso **Edge:** Reeded

Date	Mintage	F	VF	XF	Unc	BU
ND(2003) Proof	2,500	Value: 245				

BRITISH VIRGIN ISLANDS

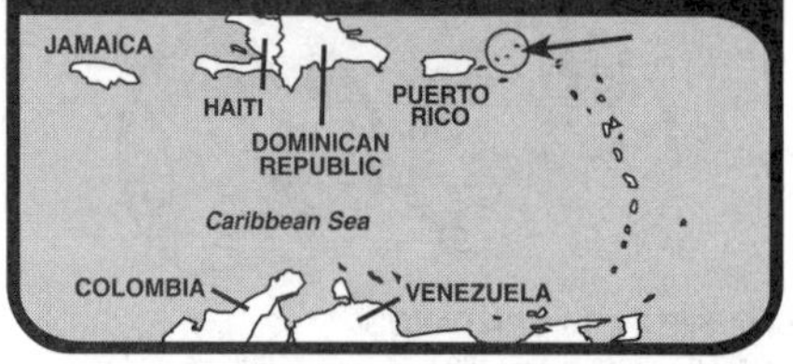

The Colony of the Virgin Islands, a British colony situated in the Caribbean Sea northeast of Puerto Rico and west of the Leeward Islands, has an area of 59 sq. mi. (155 sq. km.) and a population of 13,000. Capital: Road Town. The principal islands of the 36-island group are Tortola, Virgin Gorda, Anegada, and Jost Van Dyke. The chief industries are fishing and stock raising. Fish, livestock and bananas are exported. U.S. currency and Sterling circulate in common with the East Caribbean Dollar.

BRITISH COLONY

STANDARD COINAGE

KM# 196 DOLLAR

28.2800 g., Copper-Nickel, 38.6 mm. **Subject:** Queen's Golden Jubilee **Obv:** Queens portrait right **Obv. Designer:** Ian Rank-Broadley **Rev:** Carnival dancers **Edge:** Reeded

Date	Mintage	F	VF	XF	Unc	BU
2002	—	—	—	—	7.50	9.50

KM# 180 DOLLAR

28.2800 g., Copper-Nickel, 25.7 mm. **Subject:** Sir Francis Drake **Obv:** Queens portrait right **Obv. Designer:** Ian Rank-Broadley **Rev:** Ship, portrait and map **Edge:** Reeded

Date	Mintage	F	VF	XF	Unc	BU
2002	—	—	—	—	7.50	9.50

KM# 183 DOLLAR

28.2800 g., Copper-Nickel, 38.6 mm. **Subject:** Sir Walter Raleigh **Obv:** Queens portrait right **Obv. Designer:** Ian Rank-Broadley **Rev:** Ship, portrait and map **Edge:** Reeded

Date	Mintage	F	VF	XF	Unc	BU
2002	—	—	—	—	7.50	9.50

KM# 187 DOLLAR

28.2800 g., Copper-Nickel, 38.6 mm. **Subject:** Queen's Golden Jubilee **Obv:** Queens portrait right **Obv. Designer:** Ian Rank-Broadley **Rev:** Queen on horse **Edge:** Reeded

Date	Mintage	F	VF	XF	Unc	BU
2002	—	—	—	—	7.50	9.50

KM# 190 DOLLAR

28.2800 g., Copper-Nickel, 38.6 mm. **Subject:** Queen's Golden Jubilee **Obv:** Queens portrait right **Obv. Designer:** Ian Rank-Broadley **Rev:** Queen on throne **Edge:** Reeded

Date	Mintage	F	VF	XF	Unc	BU
2002	—	—	—	—	7.50	9.50

KM# 193 DOLLAR

28.2800 g., Copper-Nickel, 38.6 mm. **Subject:** Queen's Golden Jubilee **Obv:** Queens portrait right **Obv. Designer:** Ian Rank-Broadley **Rev:** Queen with President Ronald Reagan and First Lady Nancy Reagan **Edge:** Reeded

Date	Mintage	F	VF	XF	Unc	BU
2002	—	—	—	—	7.50	9.50

KM# 199 DOLLAR

28.2800 g., Copper-Nickel, 38.6 mm. **Subject:** Teddy Bear Centennial **Obv:** Queens portrait right **Obv. Designer:** Ian Rank-Broadley **Rev:** Teddy bear **Edge:** Reeded

Date	Mintage	F	VF	XF	Unc	BU
2002	—	—	—	—	8.50	10.00

KM# 204 DOLLAR

28.2800 g., Copper-Nickel, 38.6 mm. **Subject:** Princess Diana **Obv:** Queens portrait right **Obv. Designer:** Ian Rank-Broadley **Rev:** Diana's portrait **Edge:** Reeded

Date	Mintage	F	VF	XF	Unc	BU
2002	—	—	—	—	7.50	9.50

KM# 207 DOLLAR

28.2800 g., Copper-Nickel, 38.6 mm. **Subject:** September 11, 2001 **Obv:** Queens portrait right **Obv. Designer:** Ian Rank-Broadley **Rev:** World Trade Center twin towers **Edge:** Reeded

Date	Mintage	F	VF	XF	Unc	BU
2002	—	—	—	—	12.00	13.50

KM# 210 DOLLAR

28.2800 g., Copper-Nickel, 38.6 mm. **Subject:** September 11, 2001 **Obv:** Queens portrait right **Obv. Designer:** Ian Rank-Broadley **Rev:** Statue of Liberty **Edge:** Reeded

Date	Mintage	F	VF	XF	Unc	BU
2002	—	—	—	—	12.00	13.50

KM# 213 DOLLAR

28.2800 g., Copper-Nickel, 38.6 mm. **Subject:** Queen Mother **Obv:** Queens portrait right **Obv. Designer:** Ian Rank-Broadley **Rev:** Queen Mother and a young Prince Charles **Edge:** Reeded

Date	Mintage	F	VF	XF	Unc	BU
2002	—	—	—	—	10.00	12.00

KM# 216 DOLLAR

28.2800 g., Copper-Nickel, 38.6 mm. **Subject:** Queen Mother **Obv:** Queens portrait right **Obv. Designer:** Ian Rank-Broadley **Rev:** Queen Mother with four grandchildren **Edge:** Reeded

Date	Mintage	F	VF	XF	Unc	BU
2002	—	—	—	—	10.00	12.00

KM# 219 DOLLAR

28.2800 g., Copper-Nickel, 38.6 mm. **Subject:** Queen Mother Series **Obv:** Queens portrait right **Obv. Designer:** Ian Rank-Broadley **Rev:** Queen Mother with uniformed Prince Charles **Edge:** Reeded

Date	Mintage	F	VF	XF	Unc	BU
2002	—	—	—	—	10.00	12.00

KM# 222 DOLLAR

28.2800 g., Copper-Nickel, 38.6 mm. **Subject:** Queen Mother Series **Obv:** Queens portrait right **Obv. Designer:** Ian Rank-Broadley **Rev:** Queen Mother's coffin **Edge:** Reeded

Date	Mintage	F	VF	XF	Unc	BU
2002	—	—	—	—	10.00	12.00

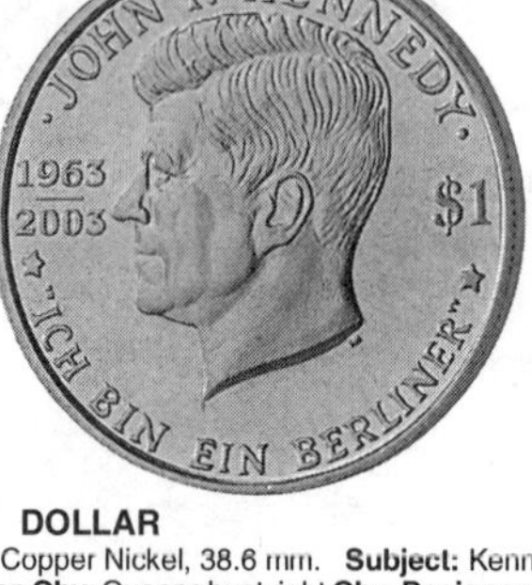

KM# 225 DOLLAR

28.4400 g., Copper Nickel, 38.6 mm. **Subject:** Kennedy Assassination **Obv:** Queens bust right **Obv. Designer:** Ian Rank-Broadley **Rev:** President Kennedy's portrait left **Edge:** Reeded

Date	Mintage	F	VF	XF	Unc	BU
2003	—	—	—	—	10.00	12.00

KM# 229 DOLLAR
28.2800 g., Copper-Nickel, 38.6 mm. **Subject:** Powered Flight Centennial **Obv:** Queens portrait right **Obv. Designer:** Ian Rank-Broadley **Rev:** Three historic airplanes and rocket **Edge:** Reeded

Date	Mintage	F	VF	XF	Unc	BU
2003	—	—	—	—	10.00	12.00

KM# 232 DOLLAR
28.2800 g., Copper-Nickel, 38.6 mm. **Obv:** Queens portrait right **Obv. Designer:** Ian Rank-Broadley **Rev:** Henry VIII and Elizabeth I **Edge:** Reeded

Date	Mintage	F	VF	XF	Unc	BU
2003	—	—	—	—	10.00	12.00

KM# 235 DOLLAR
28.2800 g., Copper-Nickel, 38.6 mm. **Obv:** Queens portrait right **Obv. Designer:** Ian Rank-Broadley **Rev:** Matthew Parker, Archbishop of Canterbury **Edge:** Reeded

Date	Mintage	F	VF	XF	Unc	BU
2003	—	—	—	—	10.00	12.00

KM# 238 DOLLAR
28.2800 g., Copper-Nickel, 38.6 mm. **Obv:** Queens portrait right **Obv. Designer:** Ian Rank-Broadley **Rev:** Sir Francis Drake and ships **Edge:** Reeded

Date	Mintage	F	VF	XF	Unc	BU
2003	—	—	—	—	10.00	12.00

KM# 241 DOLLAR
28.2800 g., Copper-Nickel, 38.6 mm. **Obv:** Queens portrait right **Obv. Designer:** Ian Rank-Broadley **Rev:** Sir Walter Raleigh **Edge:** Reeded

Date	Mintage	F	VF	XF	Unc	BU
2003	—	—	—	—	10.00	12.00

KM# 244 DOLLAR
28.2800 g., Copper-Nickel, 38.6 mm. **Obv:** Queens portrait right **Obv. Designer:** Ian Rank-Broadley **Rev:** Sir William Shakespeare **Edge:** Reeded

Date	Mintage	F	VF	XF	Unc	BU
2003	—	—	—	—	10.00	12.00

KM# 247 DOLLAR
28.2800 g., Copper-Nickel, 38.6 mm. **Obv:** Queens portrait right **Obv. Designer:** Ian Rank-Broadley **Rev:** Elizabeth I above her funeral procession **Edge:** Reeded

Date	Mintage	F	VF	XF	Unc	BU
2003	—	—	—	—	10.00	12.00

KM# 250 DOLLAR
28.2800 g., Copper-Nickel, 38.6 mm. **Subject:** Olympics **Obv:** Queens portrait right **Obv. Designer:** Ian Rank-Broadley **Rev:** Ancient bust, runners and coin **Edge:** Reeded

Date	Mintage	F	VF	XF	Unc	BU
2003	—	—	—	—	10.00	12.00

KM# 253 DOLLAR
28.2800 g., Copper-Nickel, 38.6 mm. **Subject:** Olympics **Obv:** Queens portrait right **Obv. Designer:** Ian Rank-Broadley **Rev:** Ancient bust, charioteer and coin **Edge:** Reeded

Date	Mintage	F	VF	XF	Unc	BU
2003	—	—	—	—	10.00	12.00

KM# 303 DOLLAR
28.2800 g., Copper-Nickel, 38.6 mm. **Subject:** 2004 Athens Olympics **Obv:** Queens portrait right **Obv. Designer:** Ian Rank-Broadley **Rev:** Ancient athlete's bust right, runners at lower right, ancient coin with owl at upper right coin **Edge:** Reeded

Date	Mintage	F	VF	XF	Unc	BU
2003	—	—	—	—	10.00	12.00

KM# 306 DOLLAR
28.2800 g., Copper-Nickel, 38.6 mm. **Subject:** 2004 Athens Olympics **Obv:** Queens portrait right **Obv. Designer:** Ian Rank-Broadley **Rev:** Ancient athlete bust left, chariot race at lower left, ancient coin at upper left **Edge:** Reeded

Date	Mintage	F	VF	XF	Unc	BU
2003	—	—	—	—	10.00	12.00

KM# 310 DOLLAR
28.2800 g., Copper-Nickel, 38.6 mm. **Subject:** Queen Elizabeth's Golden Coronation Jubilee **Obv:** Elizabeth II **Rev:** Cameo portraits above the ship "Gothic" **Edge:** Reeded

Date	Mintage	F	VF	XF	Unc	BU
2003	—	—	—	—	—	7.50

KM# 319 DOLLAR
28.2800 g., Copper-Nickel **Rev:** Queen riding in automobile

Date	Mintage	F	VF	XF	Unc	BU
2003	—	—	—	—	10.00	12.00

KM# 320 DOLLAR
28.2800 g., Copper-Nickel **Rev:** Sir. Edmond Hillary on Mt. Everest

Date	Mintage	F	VF	XF	Unc	BU
2003	—	—	—	—	10.00	12.00

KM# 321 DOLLAR
28.2800 g., Copper-Nickel **Rev:** Queen presenting Ascot Horse Racing prize

Date	Mintage	F	VF	XF	Unc	BU
2003	—	—	—	—	10.00	12.00

KM# 265 DOLLAR
28.2800 g., Copper-Nickel, 38.6 mm. **Obv:** Queens portrait right **Obv. Designer:** Ian Rank-Broadley **Rev:** Sir Francis Drake, ship and map **Edge:** Reeded

Date	Mintage	F	VF	XF	Unc	BU
2004	—	—	—	—	10.00	12.00

KM# 267.1 DOLLAR
28.2800 g., Copper-Nickel, 38.6 mm. **Obv:** Queens portrait right **Obv. Designer:** Ian Rank-Broadley **Rev:** Peter Rabbit **Edge:** Reeded

Date	Mintage	F	VF	XF	Unc	BU
2004	—	—	—	—	15.00	17.00

KM# 267.2 DOLLAR
28.2800 g., Copper-Nickel, 38.6 mm. **Obv:** Queens portrait right **Obv. Designer:** Ian Rank-Broadley **Rev:** Multicolor Peter Rabbit **Edge:** Reeded

Date	Mintage	F	VF	XF	Unc	BU
2004	—	—	—	—	20.00	22.00

KM# 268 DOLLAR
3.1100 g., 0.9990 Silver 0.0999 oz. ASW, 18 mm. **Obv:** Queens portrait right **Obv. Designer:** Ian Rank-Broadley **Rev:** Peter Rabbit **Edge:** Reeded

Date	Mintage	F	VF	XF	Unc	BU
2004 Proof	10,000	Value: 25.00				

KM# 281 DOLLAR
28.2800 g., Copper-Nickel, 38.6 mm. **Obv:** Queens portrait right **Obv. Designer:** Ian Rank-Broadley **Rev:** Sailor above two D-Day landing craft **Edge:** Reeded

Date	Mintage	F	VF	XF	Unc	BU
2004	—	—	—	—	10.00	12.00

KM# 286 DOLLAR
28.2800 g., Copper-Nickel, 38.6 mm. **Obv:** Queens portrait right **Obv. Designer:** Ian Rank-Broadley **Rev:** Dolphin **Edge:** Reeded

Date	Mintage	F	VF	XF	Unc	BU
2004	—	—	—	—	10.00	12.00

KM# 297 DOLLAR
28.2800 g., Copper-Nickel, 38.6 mm. **Obv:** Queens portrait right **Obv. Designer:** Ian Rank-Broadley **Rev:** Soldier above tank and jeeps **Edge:** Reeded

Date	Mintage	F	VF	XF	Unc	BU
2004	—	—	—	—	10.00	12.00

KM# 300 DOLLAR
28.2800 g., Copper-Nickel, 38.6 mm. **Obv:** Queens portrait right **Obv. Designer:** Ian Rank-Broadley **Rev:** Pilot and planes above D-Day landing **Edge:** Reeded

Date	Mintage	F	VF	XF	Unc	BU
2004	—	—	—	—	10.00	12.00

KM# 330 DOLLAR
Copper-Nickel **Ruler:** Elizabeth II **Rev:** Battle of Britain

Date	Mintage	F	VF	XF	Unc	BU
2005	—	—	—	—	15.00	17.00

KM# 331 DOLLAR
Copper-Nickel **Ruler:** Elizabeth II **Rev:** Battle of Berlin

Date	Mintage	F	VF	XF	Unc	BU
2005	—	—	—	—	15.00	17.00

KM# 312 DOLLAR
28.2800 g., Copper-Nickel, 38.6 mm. **Obv:** Bust of Queen Elizabeth II right **Rev:** Mother and baby dolphins **Edge:** Reeded

Date	Mintage	F	VF	XF	Unc	BU
2005	—	—	—	—	10.00	12.00

KM# 322 DOLLAR

28.2800 g., Copper-Nickel **Rev:** VJ Day, McArthur and U.S.S. Missiouri Battleship

Date	Mintage	F	VF	XF	Unc	BU
2005	—	—	—	—	10.00	12.00

KM# 323 DOLLAR

28.2800 g., Copper-Nickel **Rev:** Warships near Arlantic coast, West Indies islands

Date	Mintage	F	VF	XF	Unc	BU
2005	—	—	—	—	10.00	12.00

KM# 324 DOLLAR

28.2800 g., Copper-Nickel **Rev:** Death of Nelson

Date	Mintage	F	VF	XF	Unc	BU
2005	—	—	—	—	10.00	12.00

KM# 325 DOLLAR

28.2800 g., Copper-Nickel **Rev:** Nelson and Order Star above ships

Date	Mintage	F	VF	XF	Unc	BU
2005	—	—	—	—	10.00	12.00

KM# 326 DOLLAR

28.2800 g., Copper-Nickel **Rev:** Nelson and Napoleon

Date	Mintage	F	VF	XF	Unc	BU
2005	—	—	—	—	10.00	12.00

KM# 327 DOLLAR

28.2800 g., Copper-Nickel **Rev:** Nelson's Column, statue and ships

Date	Mintage	F	VF	XF	Unc	BU
2005	—	—	—	—	10.00	12.00

KM# 328 DOLLAR

28.2800 g., Copper-Nickel **Rev:** V.E. Day, Montgomery and Eisenhower

Date	Mintage	F	VF	XF	Unc	BU
2005	—	—	—	—	10.00	12.00

KM# 329 DOLLAR

Copper-Nickel **Rev:** Two dolphins

Date	Mintage	F	VF	XF	Unc	BU
2006	—	—	—	—	10.00	12.00

KM# 349 DOLLAR

28.2800 g., Copper Nickel, 38.60 mm. **Ruler:** Elizabeth II **Subject:** 5th Anniversary Attack on Twin Towers, New York City **Obv:** Crowned bust right **Obv. Legend:** BRITISH VIRGIN ISLANDS - QUEEN ELIZABETH II **Rev:** Twin Towers in sprays, remembrance ribbon privy marl at upper right **Rev. Inscription:** LEST WE FORGET **Edge:** Reeded

Date	Mintage	F	VF	XF	Unc	BU
2006	—	—	—	—	15.00	17.00

KM# 332 DOLLAR

28.2800 g., Copper-Nickel, 38.60 mm. **Ruler:** Elizabeth II **Subject:** 400th Anniversary Founding of Jamestown **Obv:** Bust with tiara right **Obv. Legend:** BRITISH VIRGIN ISLANDS - QUEEN ELIZABETH II **Rev:** British lion laying, American Eagle perched on sprays **Rev. Legend:** UNITED IN FRIENDSHIP **Edge:** Reeded

Date	Mintage	F	VF	XF	Unc	BU
2007	—	—	—	—	16.50	18.00

KM# 278 2 DOLLARS

58.0000 g., Bronze, 50 mm. **Obv:** Queens portrait right **Obv. Designer:** Ian Rank-Broadley **Rev:** 1896 Olympic medal design **Edge:** Reeded

Date	Mintage	F	VF	XF	Unc	BU
2004 Proof	3,500	Value: 20.00				

KM# 269.1 2.50 DOLLARS

7.7758 g., 0.9990 Silver 0.2497 oz. ASW, 26 mm. **Obv:** Queens portrait right **Obv. Designer:** Ian Rank-Broadley **Rev:** Peter Rabbit **Edge:** Reeded

Date	Mintage	F	VF	XF	Unc	BU
2004 Proof	—	Value: 15.00				

KM# 269.2 2.50 DOLLARS

7.7758 g., 0.9990 Silver 0.2497 oz. ASW, 26 mm. **Obv:** Queens portrait right **Obv. Designer:** Ian Rank-Broadley **Rev:** Multicolor Peter Rabbit **Edge:** Reeded

Date	Mintage	F	VF	XF	Unc	BU
2004 Proof	7,500	Value: 25.00				

KM# 284 5 DOLLARS

10.0000 g., 0.9900 Titanium 0.3183 oz., 36.1 mm. **Obv:** Queens portrait right **Obv. Designer:** Ian Rank-Broadley **Rev:** British Guiana stamp design **Edge:** Reeded

Date	Mintage	F	VF	XF	Unc	BU
2004 Proof	7,500	Value: 70.00				

KM# 340 5 DOLLARS

0.9999 Silver **Ring Composition:** 0.9167 Gold **Ruler:** Elizabeth II **Obv:** Conjoined busts with Philip right, within gold ring **Obv. Legend:** BRITISH VIRGIN ISLANDS — QUEEN ELIZABETH II **Rev:** Conjoined busts of Princess Elizabeth and Prince Philip right within gold ring **Rev. Legend:** WITH THIS RING, I THEE WED **Edge:** Reeded

Date	Mintage	F	VF	XF	Unc	BU
2007 Proof	—	Value: 450				

KM# 181 10 DOLLARS

28.2800 g., 0.9250 Silver 0.8410 oz. ASW, 38.6 mm. **Subject:** Sir Francis Drake **Obv:** Queens portrait right **Obv. Designer:** Ian Rank-Broadley **Rev:** Ship, portrait and map **Edge:** Reeded

Date	Mintage	F	VF	XF	Unc	BU
2002 Proof	—	Value: 40.00				

KM# 184 10 DOLLARS

28.2800 g., 0.9250 Silver 0.8410 oz. ASW, 38.6 mm. **Subject:** Sir Walter Raleigh **Obv:** Queens portrait right **Obv. Designer:** Ian Rank-Broadley **Rev:** Ship, portrait and map **Edge:** Reeded

Date	Mintage	F	VF	XF	Unc	BU
2002 Proof	—	Value: 40.00				

KM# 188 10 DOLLARS

28.2800 g., 0.9250 Gold Clad Silver 0.8410 oz., 38.6 mm. **Subject:** Queen's Golden Jubilee **Obv:** Queens portrait right **Obv. Designer:** Ian Rank-Broadley **Rev:** Queen on horse trotting left **Edge:** Reeded

Date	Mintage	F	VF	XF	Unc	BU
2002 Proof	10,000	Value: 42.50				

KM# 191 10 DOLLARS

28.2800 g., 0.9250 Gold Clad Silver 0.8410 oz., 38.6 mm. **Subject:** Queen's Golden Jubilee **Obv:** Queens portrait right **Obv. Designer:** Ian Rank-Broadley **Rev:** 3/4-length Queen seated on throne **Edge:** Reeded

Date	Mintage	F	VF	XF	Unc	BU
2002 Proof	10,000	Value: 45.00				

KM# 194 10 DOLLARS

28.2800 g., 0.9250 Gold Clad Silver 0.8410 oz., 38.6 mm. **Subject:** Queen's Golden Jubilee **Obv:** Queens portrait right **Obv. Designer:** Ian Rank-Broadley **Rev:** Queen with President Ronald Reagan and First Lady Nancy Reagan **Edge:** Reeded

Date	Mintage	F	VF	XF	Unc	BU
2002 Proof	10,000	Value: 45.00				

KM# 197 10 DOLLARS
28.2800 g., 0.9250 Gold Clad Silver 0.8410 oz., 38.6 mm. **Subject:** Queen's Golden Jubilee **Obv:** Queens portrait right **Obv. Designer:** Ian Rank-Broadley **Rev:** Carnival dancers **Edge:** Reeded

Date	Mintage	F	VF	XF	Unc	BU
2002 Proof	10,000	Value: 45.00				

KM# 200 10 DOLLARS
28.2800 g., 0.9250 Silver 0.8410 oz. ASW, 38.6 mm. **Subject:** Teddy Bear Centennial **Obv:** Queens portrait right **Obv. Designer:** Ian Rank-Broadley **Rev:** Teddy bear **Edge:** Reeded

Date	Mintage	F	VF	XF	Unc	BU
2002 Proof	10,000	Value: 40.00				

KM# 205 10 DOLLARS
28.2800 g., 0.9250 Silver 0.8410 oz. ASW, 38.6 mm. **Subject:** Princess Diana **Obv:** Queens portrait right **Obv. Designer:** Ian Rank-Broadley **Rev:** Diana's portrait **Edge:** Reeded

Date	Mintage	F	VF	XF	Unc	BU
2002 Proof	10,000	Value: 40.00				

KM# 208.1 10 DOLLARS
28.2800 g., 0.9250 Silver 0.8410 oz. ASW, 38.6 mm. **Subject:** September 11, 2001 **Obv:** Queens portrait right **Obv. Designer:** Ian Rank-Broadley **Rev:** World Trade Center twin towers **Edge:** Reeded

Date	Mintage	F	VF	XF	Unc	BU
2002 Proof	10,000	Value: 40.00				

KM# 208.2 10 DOLLARS
28.2800 g., 0.9250 Silver 0.8410 oz. ASW, 38.6 mm. **Subject:** September 11, 2001 **Obv:** Queens portrait right **Obv. Designer:** Ian Rank-Broadley **Rev:** Holographic multicolor World Trade Center twin towers **Edge:** Reeded

Date	Mintage	F	VF	XF	Unc	BU
2002 Proof	10,000	Value: 45.00				

KM# 211 10 DOLLARS
28.2800 g., 0.9250 Silver 0.8410 oz. ASW, 38.6 mm. **Subject:** September 11, 2001 **Obv:** Queens portrait right **Obv. Designer:** Ian Rank-Broadley **Rev:** Statue of Liberty **Edge:** Reeded

Date	Mintage	F	VF	XF	Unc	BU
2002 Proof	10,000	Value: 40.00				

KM# 214 10 DOLLARS
28.2800 g., 0.9250 Silver 0.8410 oz. ASW, 38.6 mm. **Subject:** Queen Mother **Obv:** Queens portrait right **Obv. Designer:** Ian Rank-Broadley **Rev:** Queen Mother with young Prince Charles **Edge:** Reeded

Date	Mintage	F	VF	XF	Unc	BU
2002 Proof	10,000	Value: 40.00				

KM# 217 10 DOLLARS
28.2800 g., 0.9250 Silver 0.8410 oz. ASW, 38.6 mm. **Subject:** Queen Mother Series **Obv:** Queens portrait right **Obv. Designer:** Ian Rank-Broadley **Rev:** Queen Mother with four grandchildren **Edge:** Reeded

Date	Mintage	F	VF	XF	Unc	BU
2002 Proof	10,000	Value: 40.00				

KM# 220 10 DOLLARS
28.2800 g., 0.9250 Silver 0.8410 oz. ASW, 38.6 mm. **Subject:** Queen Mother Series **Obv:** Queens portrait right **Obv. Designer:** Ian Rank-Broadley **Rev:** Queen Mother with uniformed Prince Charles **Edge:** Reeded

Date	Mintage	F	VF	XF	Unc	BU
2002 Proof	10,000	Value: 40.00				

KM# 223 10 DOLLARS
28.2800 g., 0.9250 Silver 0.8410 oz. ASW, 38.6 mm. **Subject:** Queen Mother Series **Obv:** Queens portrait right **Obv. Designer:** Ian Rank-Broadley **Rev:** Queen Mother's coffin **Edge:** Reeded

Date	Mintage	F	VF	XF	Unc	BU
2002 Proof	10,000	Value: 40.00				

KM# 226 10 DOLLARS
28.2800 g., 0.9250 Silver 0.8410 oz. ASW, 38.6 mm. **Subject:** Kennedy Assassination **Obv:** Queens portrait right **Obv. Designer:** Ian Rank-Broadley **Rev:** President Kennedy's head left **Edge:** Reeded

Date	Mintage	F	VF	XF	Unc	BU
2003 Proof	10,000	Value: 40.00				

KM# 230 10 DOLLARS
28.2800 g., 0.9250 Silver 0.8410 oz. ASW, 38.6 mm. **Subject:** Powered Flight Centennial **Obv:** Queens portrait right **Obv. Designer:** Ian Rank-Broadley **Rev:** Three historic airplanes and rocket **Edge:** Reeded

Date	Mintage	F	VF	XF	Unc	BU
2003 Proof	10,000	Value: 45.00				

KM# 233 10 DOLLARS
28.2800 g., 0.9250 Silver 0.8410 oz. ASW, 38.6 mm. **Obv:** Queens portrait right **Obv. Designer:** Ian Rank-Broadley **Rev:** Henry VIII and Elizabeth I **Edge:** Reeded

Date	Mintage	F	VF	XF	Unc	BU
2003 Proof	10,000	Value: 40.00				

KM# 236 10 DOLLARS
28.2800 g., 0.9250 Silver 0.8410 oz. ASW, 38.6 mm. **Obv:** Queens portrait right **Obv. Designer:** Ian Rank-Broadley **Rev:** Matthew Parker, Archbishop of Canterbury **Edge:** Reeded

Date	Mintage	F	VF	XF	Unc	BU
2003 Proof	10,000	Value: 40.00				

KM# 239 10 DOLLARS
28.2800 g., 0.9250 Silver 0.8410 oz. ASW, 38.6 mm. **Obv:** Queens portrait right **Obv. Designer:** Ian Rank-Broadley **Rev:** Sir Francis Drake and ships **Edge:** Reeded

Date	Mintage	F	VF	XF	Unc	BU
2003 Proof	10,000	Value: 40.00				

KM# 242 10 DOLLARS
28.2800 g., 0.9250 Silver 0.8410 oz. ASW, 38.6 mm. **Obv:** Queens portrait right **Obv. Designer:** Ian Rank-Broadley **Rev:** Sir Walter Raleigh **Edge:** Reeded

Date	Mintage	F	VF	XF	Unc	BU
2003 Proof	10,000	Value: 40.00				

KM# 245 10 DOLLARS
28.2800 g., 0.9250 Silver 0.8410 oz. ASW, 38.6 mm. **Obv:** Queens portrait right **Obv. Designer:** Ian Rank-Broadley **Rev:** Sir William Shakespeare **Edge:** Reeded

Date	Mintage	F	VF	XF	Unc	BU
2003 Proof	10,000	Value: 40.00				

KM# 248 10 DOLLARS
28.2800 g., 0.9250 Silver 0.8410 oz. ASW, 38.6 mm. **Obv:** Queens portrait right **Obv. Designer:** Ian Rank-Broadley **Rev:** Elizabeth I above her funeral procession **Edge:** Reeded

Date	Mintage	F	VF	XF	Unc	BU
2003 Proof	10,000	Value: 40.00				

KM# 251 10 DOLLARS
28.2800 g., 0.9250 Silver 0.8410 oz. ASW, 38.6 mm. **Subject:** Olympics **Obv:** Queens portrait right **Obv. Designer:** Ian Rank-Broadley **Rev:** Ancient bust, runners and coin **Edge:** Reeded

Date	Mintage	F	VF	XF	Unc	BU
2003 Proof	10,000	Value: 40.00				

KM# 254 10 DOLLARS
28.2800 g., 0.9250 Silver 0.8410 oz. ASW, 38.6 mm. **Subject:** Olympics **Obv:** Queens portrait right **Obv. Designer:** Ian Rank-Broadley **Rev:** Ancient bust, charioteer and coin **Edge:** Reeded

Date	Mintage	F	VF	XF	Unc	BU
2003 Proof	10,000	Value: 40.00				

KM# 311 10 DOLLARS
28.3000 g., 0.9250 Gold Clad Silver 0.8416 oz., 38.6 mm. **Subject:** Queen Elizabeth's Golden Coronation Jubilee **Obv:** Elizabeth II **Rev:** Cameo portrait above ship "Gothic" **Edge:** Reeded

Date	Mintage	F	VF	XF	Unc	BU
2003 Proof	—	Value: 50.00				

KM# 266 10 DOLLARS
28.2800 g., 0.9250 Silver 0.8410 oz. ASW, 38.6 mm. **Obv:** Queens portrait right **Obv. Designer:** Ian Rank-Broadley **Rev:** Sir Francis Drake, ship and map **Edge:** Reeded

Date	Mintage	F	VF	XF	Unc	BU
2004 Proof	10,000	Value: 45.00				

KM# 270.1 10 DOLLARS
28.2800 g., 0.9250 Silver 0.8410 oz. ASW, 38.6 mm. **Obv:** Queens portrait right **Obv. Designer:** Ian Rank-Broadley **Rev:** Peter Rabbit **Edge:** Reeded

Date	Mintage	F	VF	XF	Unc	BU
2004 Proof	5,000	Value: 47.50				

KM# 270.2 10 DOLLARS
28.2800 g., 0.9250 Silver 0.8410 oz. ASW, 38.6 mm. **Obv:** Queens portrait right **Obv. Designer:** Ian Rank-Broadley **Rev:** Multicolor Peter Rabbit **Edge:** Reeded

Date	Mintage	F	VF	XF	Unc	BU
2004 Proof	—	Value: 65.00				

KM# 274 10 DOLLARS
1.2440 g., 0.9999 Gold 0.0400 oz. AGW, 14 mm. **Obv:** Queens portrait right **Obv. Designer:** Ian Rank-Broadley **Rev:** Hernando Pizarro **Edge:** Reeded

Date	Mintage	F	VF	XF	Unc	BU
2004 Proof	350	Value: 75.00				

KM# 282 10 DOLLARS
28.2800 g., 0.9250 Silver 0.8410 oz. ASW, 38.6 mm. **Obv:** Queens portrait right **Obv. Designer:** Ian Rank-Broadley **Rev:** Sailor above two D-Day landing craft **Edge:** Reeded

Date	Mintage	F	VF	XF	Unc	BU
2004 Proof	10,000	Value: 50.00				

KM# 287 10 DOLLARS
31.1035 g., 0.9990 Silver 0.9990 oz. ASW, 38.6 mm. **Obv:** Queens portrait right **Obv. Designer:** Ian Rank-Broadley **Rev:** Dolphin **Edge:** Reeded

Date	Mintage	F	VF	XF	Unc	BU
2004 Proof	10,000	Value: 50.00				

KM# 288 10 DOLLARS
1.2440 g., 0.9999 Gold 0.0400 oz. AGW, 14 mm. **Obv:** Queens portrait right **Obv. Designer:** Ian Rank-Broadley **Rev:** Dolphin **Edge:** Reeded

Date	Mintage	F	VF	XF	Unc	BU
2004 Proof	10,000	Value: 55.00				

KM# 298 10 DOLLARS
28.2800 g., 0.9250 Silver 0.8410 oz. ASW, 38.6 mm. **Obv:** Queens portrait right **Obv. Designer:** Ian Rank-Broadley **Rev:** Soldier above tank and jeeps **Edge:** Reeded

Date	Mintage	F	VF	XF	Unc	BU
2004 Proof	10,000	Value: 50.00				

KM# 301 10 DOLLARS
28.2800 g., 0.9250 Silver 0.8410 oz. ASW, 38.6 mm. **Obv:** Queens portrait right **Obv. Designer:** Ian Rank-Broadley **Rev:** Pilot and planes above D-Day landing **Edge:** Reeded

Date	Mintage	F	VF	XF	Unc	BU
2004 Proof	10,000	Value: 50.00				

KM# 304 10 DOLLARS
28.2800 g., 0.9250 Silver 0.8410 oz. ASW, 38.6 mm. **Obv:** Queens portrait right **Obv. Designer:** Ian Rank-Broadley **Rev:** Ancient Olympic bust, runners and owl coin **Edge:** Reeded

Date	Mintage	F	VF	XF	Unc	BU
2004 Proof	10,000	Value: 50.00				

KM# 307 10 DOLLARS
28.2800 g., 0.9250 Silver 0.8410 oz. ASW, 38.6 mm. **Obv:** Queens portrait right **Obv. Designer:** Ian Rank-Broadley **Rev:** Ancient Olympic bust, charioteer and Zeus coin **Edge:** Reeded

Date	Mintage	F	VF	XF	Unc	BU
2004 Proof	10,000	Value: 50.00				

KM# 313 10 DOLLARS
31.1030 g., 0.9990 Silver 0.9989 oz. ASW, 38.6 mm. **Obv:** Bust of Queen Elizabeth II right **Rev:** Mother and baby dolphins **Edge:** Reeded

Date	Mintage	F	VF	XF	Unc	BU
2005 Proof	10,000	Value: 50.00				

KM# 314 10 DOLLARS
1.2440 g., 0.9999 Gold 0.0400 oz. AGW, 13.92 mm. **Obv:** Bust of Queen Elizabeth II right **Rev:** Mother and baby dolphins **Edge:** Reeded

Date	Mintage	F	VF	XF	Unc	BU
2005 Proof	10,000	Value: 50.00				

KM# 350 10 DOLLARS
28.2800 g., 0.9250 Silver 0.8410 oz. ASW, 38.60 mm. **Ruler:** Elizabeth II **Subject:** 5th Anniversary - Attack on Twin Towers, New York City **Obv:** Crowned bust right **Obv. Legend:** BRITISH VIRGIN ISLANDS - QUEEN ELIZABETH II **Rev:** Twin Towers in sprays, remembrance ribbon privy mark at upper right **Rev. Inscription:** LEST WE FORGET **Edge:** Reeded

Date	Mintage	F	VF	XF	Unc	BU
2006 Proof	10,000	Value: 77.50				

KM# 333 10 DOLLARS
28.2800 g., 0.9167 Silver ASW 0.8335 0.8334 oz. ASW, 38.60 mm. **Ruler:** Elizabeth II **Subject:** 400th Anniversary Founding of Jamestown **Obv:** Bust with tiara right **Obv. Legend:** BRITISH VIRGIN ISLANDS - QUEEN ELIZABETH II **Rev:** British lion laying, American Eagle perched on sprays **Rev. Legend:** UNITED IN FRIENDSHIP **Edge:** Reeded

Date	Mintage	F	VF	XF	Unc	BU
2007 Proof	25,000	Value: 75.00				

KM# 334 10 DOLLARS
1.2444 g., 0.9999 Gold AGW 0.0400 0.0400 oz. AGW, 13.92 mm. **Ruler:** Elizabeth II **Subject:** 400th Anniversary Founding of Jamestown **Obv:** Bust with tiara right **Obv. Legend:** BRITISH VIRGIN ISLANDS - QUEEN ELIZABETH II **Rev:** British lion laying, American Eagle perched on sprays **Rev. Legend:** UNITED IN FRIENDSHIP **Edge:** Reeded

Date	Mintage	F	VF	XF	Unc	BU
2007 Proof	20,000	Value: 75.00				

KM# 339 10 DOLLARS
Copper-Nickel **Ruler:** Elizabeth II **Subject:** 10th Anniversary Death of Princess Diana **Obv:** Bust with tiara right **Obv. Legend:** BRITISH VIRGIN ISLANDS - QUEEN ELIZABETH II **Rev:** Mother Teresa at left, Princess Diana at right **Rev. Legend:** MOTHER TERESA • IN LOVING MEMORY • PRINCESS DIANA **Edge:** Reeded

Date	Mintage	F	VF	XF	Unc	BU
2007	—	—	—	—	16.50	20.00

KM# 339a 10 DOLLARS
0.9167 Silver **Ruler:** Elizabeth II **Subject:** 10th Anniversary - Death of Princess Diana **Obv:** Bust with tiara right **Obv. Legend:** BRITISH VIRGIN ISLANDS - QUEEN ELIZABETH II **Rev:** Mother Teresa at left, Princess Diana at right **Rev. Legend:** MOTHER TERESA • IN LOVING MEMORY • PRINCESS DIANA **Edge:** Reeded

Date	Mintage	F	VF	XF	Unc	BU
2007 Proof	—	Value: 75.00				

KM# 341 10 DOLLARS
Copper-Nickel **Ruler:** Elizabeth II **Subject:** Diamond Wedding Anniversary **Obv:** Conjoined busts with Philip right **Obv. Legend:** BRITISH VIRGIN ISLANDS — QUEEN ELIZABETH II **Rev:** Bride to be and King George VI standing facing **Rev. Legend:** Diamond Wedding of H.M. Queen Elizabeth II & H.R.H. Prince Philip **Rev. Inscription:** THE GIVING AWAY **Edge:** Reeded

Date	Mintage	F	VF	XF	Unc	BU
2007	—	—	—	—	16.50	18.50

KM# 341A 10 DOLLARS
0.9167 Silver **Ruler:** Elizabeth II **Subject:** Diamond Wedding Anniversary **Obv:** Conjoined busts with Philip right **Obv. Legend:** BRITISH VIRGIN ISLANDS — QUEEN ELIZABETH II **Rev:** Bride to be and King George VI standing facing **Rev. Legend:** Diamond Wedding of H.M. Queen Elizabeth II & H.R.H. Prince Philip **Rev. Inscription:** THE GIVING AWAY **Edge:** Reeded

Date	Mintage	F	VF	XF	Unc	BU
2007 Proof	—	Value: 75.00				

KM# 342 10 DOLLARS
Copper-Nickel **Ruler:** Elizabeth II **Subject:** Diamond Wedding Anniversary **Obv:** Conjoined busts with Philip right **Obv. Legend:** BRITISH VIRGIN ISLANDS — QUEEN ELIZABETH II **Rev. Legend:** Diamond Wedding of H.M. Queen Elizabeth II & H.R.H. Prince Philip **Rev. Inscription:** THE GLASS COACH **Edge:** Reeded

Date	Mintage	F	VF	XF	Unc	BU
2007	—	—	—	—	16.50	18.50

KM# 342a 10 DOLLARS
0.9167 Silver **Ruler:** Elizabeth II **Subject:** Diamond Wedding Anniversary **Obv:** Conjoined busts with Philip right **Obv. Legend:** BRITISH VIRGIN ISLANDS — QUEEN ELIZABETH II **Rev. Legend:** Diamond Wedding of H.M. Queen Elizabeth II & H.R.H. Prince Philip **Rev. Inscription:** THE GLASS COACH **Edge:** Reeded

Date	Mintage	F	VF	XF	Unc	BU
2007 Proof	—	Value: 75.00				

KM# 343 10 DOLLARS
Copper-Nickel **Ruler:** Elizabeth II **Subject:** Diamond Wedding Anniversary **Obv:** Conjoined busts with Philip right **Obv. Legend:** BRITISH VIRGIN ISLANDS — QUEEN ELIZABETH II **Rev. Legend:** Diamond Wedding of H.M. Queen Elizabeth II & H.R.H. Prince Philip **Rev. Inscription:** THE HONEYMOON **Edge:** Reeded

Date	Mintage	F	VF	XF	Unc	BU
2007	—	—	—	—	16.50	18.50

KM# 343a 10 DOLLARS
0.9167 Silver **Ruler:** Elizabeth II **Subject:** Diamond Wedding Anniversary **Obv:** Conjoined busts with Philip right **Obv. Legend:** BRITISH VIRGIN ISLANDS — QUEEN ELIZABETH II **Rev. Legend:** Diamond Wedding of H.M. Queen Elizabeth II & H.R.H. Prince Philip **Rev. Inscription:** THE HONEYMOON **Edge:** Reeded

Date	Mintage	F	VF	XF	Unc	BU
2007 Proof	—	Value: 75.00				

KM# 344 10 DOLLARS
Copper-Nickel **Ruler:** Elizabeth II **Subject:** Diamond Wedding Anniversary **Obv:** Conjoined busts with Philip right **Obv. Legend:** BRITISH VIRGIN ISLANDS — QUEEN ELIZABETH II **Rev. Legend:** Diamond Wedding of H.M. Queen Elizabeth II & H.R.H. Prince Philip **Rev. Inscription:** THE WEDDING PROGRAM **Edge:** Reeded

Date	Mintage	F	VF	XF	Unc	BU
2007	—	—	—	—	16.50	—

KM# 344a 10 DOLLARS
0.9167 Silver **Ruler:** Elizabeth II **Subject:** Diamond Wedding Anniversary **Obv:** Conjoined busts with Philip right **Obv. Legend:** BRITISH VIRGIN ISLANDS ? QUEEN ELIZABETH II **Rev. Legend:** Diamond Wedding of H.M. Queen Elizabeth II & H.R.H. Prince Philip **Rev. Inscription:** THE WEDDING PROGRAM **Edge:** Reeded

Date	Mintage	F	VF	XF	Unc	BU
2007	—	Value: 75.00				

KM# 201 20 DOLLARS
1.2441 g., 0.9999 Gold 0.0400 oz. AGW, 13.92 mm. **Subject:** Teddy Bear Centennial **Obv:** Queens portrait right **Obv. Designer:** Ian Rank-Broadley **Rev:** Teddy bear **Edge:** Reeded

Date	Mintage	F	VF	XF	Unc	BU
2002 Proof	10,000	Value: 45.00				

KM# 227 20 DOLLARS
1.2400 g., 0.9999 Gold 0.0399 oz. AGW, 13.92 mm. **Subject:** Kennedy Assasination **Obv:** Queens portrait right **Obv. Designer:** Ian Rank-Broadley **Rev:** President Kennedy's portrait **Edge:** Reeded

Date	Mintage	F	VF	XF	Unc	BU
2003 Proof	10,000	Value: 45.00				

KM# 271 20 DOLLARS
1.2440 g., 0.9999 Gold 0.0400 oz. AGW, 14 mm. **Obv:** Queens portrait right **Obv. Designer:** Ian Rank-Broadley **Rev:** Peter Rabbit **Edge:** Reeded

Date	Mintage	F	VF	XF	Unc	BU
2004 Proof	5,000	Value: 50.00				

KM# 279 20 DOLLARS
58.0000 g., 0.9990 Silver 1.8628 oz. ASW, 50 mm. **Obv:** Queens portrait right **Obv. Designer:** Ian Rank-Broadley **Rev:** 1896 Olympic medal design **Edge:** Reeded

Date	Mintage	F	VF	XF	Unc	BU
2004 Proof	2,004	Value: 75.00				

KM# 345 20 DOLLARS
3.9600 g., 0.7500 Gold 0.0955 oz. AGW, 21.78 mm. **Ruler:** Elizabeth II **Subject:** 500th Anniversary - Death of Columbus **Obv:** Crowned bust right **Obv. Legend:** BRITISH VIRGIN ISLANDS - QUEEN ELIZABETH II **Rev:** Bust of Columbus facing 3/4 left at right, outlined map of the Americas at left **Rev. Legend:** 1451 - CHRISTOPHER COLUMBUS - 1506 **Edge:** Reeded **Note:** Struck in white gold.

Date	Mintage	F	VF	XF	Unc	BU
2006 Proof	1,506	Value: 95.00				

KM# 346 20 DOLLARS
4.0200 g., 0.7500 Gold 0.0969 oz. AGW, 21.78 mm. **Ruler:** Elizabeth II **Subject:** 500th Anniversary - Death of Columbus **Obv:** Crowned bust right **Obv. Legend:** BRITISH VIRGIN ISLANDS - QUEEN ELIZABETH II **Rev:** Sailing ship " Santa Maria" **Rev. Legend:** 1451 - CHRISTOPHER COLUMBUS - 1506 **Edge:** Reeded **Note:** Struck in rose gold.

Date	Mintage	F	VF	XF	Unc	BU
2006 Proof	1,506	Value: 100				

KM# 347 20 DOLLARS
3.9900 g., 0.7500 Gold 0.0962 oz. AGW, 21.78 mm. **Ruler:** Elizabeth II **Subject:** 500th Anniversary - Death of Columbus **Obv:** Crowned bust right **Obv. Legend:** BRITISH VIRGIN ISLANDS - QUEEN ELIZABETH II **Rev:** Sailing ships "Niña" and "Pinta" **Rev. Legend:** 1451 - CHRISTOPHER COLUMBUS - 1506 **Edge:** Reeded **Note:** Struck in yellow gold

Date	Mintage	F	VF	XF	Unc	BU
2006 Proof	1,506	Value: 95.00				

KM# 275 25 DOLLARS
3.1100 g., 0.9999 Gold 0.1000 oz. AGW, 18 mm. **Obv:** Queens portrait right **Obv. Designer:** Ian Rank-Broadley **Rev:** Hernando Pizarro portrait and life events pictorial **Edge:** Reeded

Date	Mintage	F	VF	XF	Unc	BU
2004 Proof	350	Value: 125				

KM# 289 25 DOLLARS
3.1100 g., 0.9999 Gold 0.1000 oz. AGW, 18 mm. **Obv:** Queens portrait right **Obv. Designer:** Ian Rank-Broadley **Rev:** Dolphin **Edge:** Reeded

Date	Mintage	F	VF	XF	Unc	BU
2004 Proof	6,000	Value: 115				

KM# 315 25 DOLLARS
3.1100 g., 0.9999 Gold 0.1000 oz. AGW, 18 mm. **Obv:** Bust of Queen Elizabeth II right **Rev:** Mother and baby dolphins **Edge:** Reeded

Date	Mintage	F	VF	XF	Unc	BU
2005 Proof	6,000	Value: 125				

KM# 335 25 DOLLARS
3.1120 g., 0.9999 Gold AGW 0.1004 0.1000 oz. AGW, 17.95 mm. **Ruler:** Elizabeth II **Subject:** 400th Anniversary Founding of Jamestown **Obv:** Bust with tiara right **Obv. Legend:** BRITISH VIRGIN ISLANDS - QUEEN ELIZABETH II **Rev:** British lion laying, American Eagle perched on sprays **Rev. Legend:** UNITED IN FRIENDSHIP **Edge:** Reeded

Date	Mintage	VG	F	VF	XF	Unc
2007 Proof	7,500	Value: 100				

KM# 202 50 DOLLARS
3.1104 g., 0.9999 Gold 0.1000 oz. AGW, 17.95 mm. **Subject:** Teddy Bear Centennial **Obv:** Queens portrait right **Obv. Designer:** Ian Rank-Broadley **Rev:** Teddy bear **Edge:** Reeded

Date	Mintage	F	VF	XF	Unc	BU
2002 Proof	7,000	Value: 95.00				

KM# 272 50 DOLLARS
3.1100 g., 0.9999 Gold 0.1000 oz. AGW, 18 mm. **Obv:** Queens portrait right **Obv. Designer:** Ian Rank-Broadley **Rev:** Peter Rabbit **Edge:** Reeded

Date	Mintage	F	VF	XF	Unc	BU
2004 Proof	3,000	Value: 110				

KM# 276 50 DOLLARS
6.2200 g., 0.9999 Gold 0.1999 oz. AGW, 22 mm. **Obv:** Queens portrait right **Obv. Designer:** Ian Rank-Broadley **Rev:** Treasure ship with blue color sail **Edge:** Reeded

Date	Mintage	F	VF	XF	Unc	BU
2004 Proof	350	Value: 225				

KM# 290 50 DOLLARS
6.2200 g., 0.9999 Gold 0.1999 oz. AGW, 22 mm. **Obv:** Queens portrait right **Obv. Designer:** Ian Rank-Broadley **Rev:** Dolphin **Edge:** Reeded

Date	Mintage	F	VF	XF	Unc	BU
2004 Proof	3,500	Value: 215				

KM# 316 50 DOLLARS
6.2200 g., 0.9999 Gold 0.1999 oz. AGW, 22 mm. **Obv:** Bust of Queen Elizabeth II right **Rev:** Mother and baby dolphins **Edge:** Reeded

Date	Mintage	F	VF	XF	Unc	BU
2005	3,500	Value: 250				

KM# 351 50 DOLLARS
6.2200 g., 0.9999 Gold 0.1999 oz. AGW, 22.00 mm. **Ruler:** Elizabeth II **Subject:** 5th Anniversary - Attack on Twin Towers, New York City **Obv:** Crowned bust right **Obv. Legend:** BRISH VIRGIN ISLANDS - QUEEN ELIZABETH II **Rev:** Twin Towers in sprays, remembrance ribbon privy mark at upper right **Rev. Inscription:** LEST WE FORGET **Edge:** Reeded

Date	Mintage	F	VF	XF	Unc	BU
2006 Proof	2,000	Value: 335				

KM# 336 50 DOLLARS
6.2230 g., 0.9999 Gold AGW 0.1999 0.2000 oz. AGW, 22.00 mm. **Ruler:** Elizabeth II **Subject:** 400th Anniversary Founding of Jamestown **Obv:** Bust with tiara right **Obv. Legend:** BRITISH VIRGIN ISLANDS - QUEEN ELIZABETH II **Rev:** British lion laying, American Eagle perched on sprays **Rev. Legend:** UNITED IN FRIENDSHIP **Edge:** Reeded

Date	Mintage	F	VF	XF	Unc	BU
2007 Proof	5,000	Value: 200				

KM# 285 75 DOLLARS
11.0000 g., Bi-Metallic .990 Titanium 2g center in .9999 Gold 9g ring, 36.5 mm. **Obv:** Queens portrait right **Obv. Designer:** Ian Rank-Broadley **Rev:** British Guiana stamp design **Edge:** Reeded

Date	Mintage	F	VF	XF	Unc	BU
2004 Proof	2,500	Value: 300				

KM# 182 100 DOLLARS
6.2200 g., 0.9990 Gold 0.1998 oz. AGW, 22 mm. **Subject:** Sir Francis Drake **Obv:** Queens portrait right **Obv. Designer:** Ian Rank-Broadley **Rev:** Ship, portrait and map **Edge:** Reeded

Date	Mintage	F	VF	XF	Unc	BU
2002 Proof	5,000	Value: 200				

KM# 185 100 DOLLARS
6.2200 g., 0.9990 Gold 0.1998 oz. AGW, 22 mm. **Subject:** Sir Walter Raleigh **Obv:** Queens portrait right **Obv. Designer:** Ian Rank-Broadley **Rev:** Ship, portrait and map **Edge:** Reeded

Date	Mintage	F	VF	XF	Unc	BU
2002 Proof	5,000	Value: 210				

KM# 189 100 DOLLARS
6.2208 g., 0.9999 Gold 0.2000 oz. AGW, 22 mm. **Subject:** Queen's Golden Jubilee **Obv:** Queens portrait right **Obv. Designer:** Ian Rank-Broadley **Rev:** Queen on horse **Edge:** Reeded

Date	Mintage	F	VF	XF	Unc	BU
2002 Proof	2,002	Value: 215				

KM# 192 100 DOLLARS
6.2208 g., 0.9999 Gold 0.2000 oz. AGW, 22 mm. **Subject:** Queen's Golden Jubilee **Obv:** Queens portrait right **Obv. Designer:** Ian Rank-Broadley **Rev:** Queen on throne **Edge:** Reeded

Date	Mintage	F	VF	XF	Unc	BU
2002 Proof	2,002	Value: 215				

KM# 195 100 DOLLARS
6.2208 g., 0.9999 Gold 0.2000 oz. AGW, 22 mm. **Subject:** Queen's Golden Jubilee **Obv:** Queens portrait right **Obv. Designer:** Ian Rank-Broadley **Rev:** Queen with President Ronald Reagan and Mrs. Nancy Reagan **Edge:** Reeded

Date	Mintage	F	VF	XF	Unc	BU
2002 Proof	2,002	Value: 215				

KM# 198 100 DOLLARS
6.2208 g., 0.9999 Gold 0.2000 oz. AGW, 22 mm. **Subject:** Queen's Golden Jubilee **Obv:** Queens portrait right **Obv. Designer:** Ian Rank-Broadley **Rev:** Carnival dancers **Edge:** Reeded

Date	Mintage	F	VF	XF	Unc	BU
2002 Proof	2,002	Value: 215				

KM# 203 100 DOLLARS
6.2200 g., 0.9999 Gold 0.1999 oz. AGW, 22 mm. **Subject:** Teddy Bear Centennial **Obv:** Queens portrait right **Obv. Designer:** Ian Rank-Broadley **Rev:** Teddy bear **Edge:** Reeded

Date	Mintage	F	VF	XF	Unc	BU
2002 Proof	5,000	Value: 200				

KM# 206 100 DOLLARS
6.2200 g., 0.9999 Gold 0.1999 oz. AGW, 22 mm. **Subject:** Princess Diana **Obv:** Queens portrait right **Obv. Designer:** Ian Rank-Broadley **Rev:** Diana's portrait **Edge:** Reeded

Date	Mintage	F	VF	XF	Unc	BU
2002 Proof	5,000	Value: 200				

KM# 209.1 100 DOLLARS
6.2200 g., 0.9999 Gold 0.1999 oz. AGW, 22 mm. **Subject:** September 11, 2001 **Obv:** Queens portrait right **Obv. Designer:** Ian Rank-Broadley **Rev:** World Trade Center twin towers **Edge:** Reeded

Date	Mintage	F	VF	XF	Unc	BU
2002 Proof	5,000	Value: 200				

KM# 209.2 100 DOLLARS
6.2200 g., 0.9999 Gold 0.1999 oz. AGW, 22 mm. **Subject:** September 11, 2001 **Obv:** Queens portrait right **Obv. Designer:** Ian Rank-Broadley **Rev:** Holographic multicolor World Trade Center twin towers **Edge:** Reeded

Date	Mintage	F	VF	XF	Unc	BU
2002 Proof	5,000	Value: 200				

KM# 212 100 DOLLARS
6.2200 g., 0.9999 Gold 0.1999 oz. AGW, 22 mm. **Subject:** September 11, 2001 **Obv:** Queens portrait right **Obv. Designer:** Ian Rank-Broadley **Rev:** Statue of Liberty **Edge:** Reeded

Date	Mintage	F	VF	XF	Unc	BU
2002 Proof	5,000	Value: 200				

KM# 215 100 DOLLARS
6.2200 g., 0.9999 Gold 0.1999 oz. AGW, 22 mm. **Subject:** Queen Mother Series **Obv:** Queens portrait right **Obv. Designer:** Ian Rank-Broadley **Rev:** Queen Mother with young Prince Charles **Edge:** Reeded

Date	Mintage	F	VF	XF	Unc	BU
2002 Proof	5,000	Value: 200				

KM# 218 100 DOLLARS
6.2200 g., 0.9999 Gold 0.1999 oz. AGW, 22 mm. **Subject:** Queen Mother Series **Obv:** Queens portrait right **Obv. Designer:** Ian Rank-Broadley **Rev:** Queen Mother with four grandchildren **Edge:** Reeded

Date	Mintage	F	VF	XF	Unc	BU
2002 Proof	5,000	Value: 200				

KM# 221 100 DOLLARS
6.2200 g., 0.9999 Gold 0.1999 oz. AGW, 22 mm. **Subject:** Queen Mother Series **Obv:** Queens portrait right **Obv. Designer:** Ian Rank-Broadley **Rev:** Queen Mother with uniformed Prince Charles **Edge:** Reeded

Date	Mintage	F	VF	XF	Unc	BU
2002 Proof	5,000	Value: 200				

KM# 224 100 DOLLARS
6.2200 g., 0.9999 Gold 0.1999 oz. AGW, 22 mm. **Subject:** Queen Mother Series **Obv:** Queens portrait right **Obv. Designer:** Ian Rank-Broadley **Rev:** Queen Mother's coffin **Edge:** Reeded

Date	Mintage	F	VF	XF	Unc	BU
2002 Proof	5,000	Value: 200				

KM# 228 100 DOLLARS
6.2200 g., 0.9999 Gold 0.1999 oz. AGW, 22 mm. **Subject:** Kennedy Assasination **Obv:** Queens portrait right **Obv. Designer:** Ian Rank-Broadley **Rev:** President Kennedy's portrait **Edge:** Reeded

Date	Mintage	F	VF	XF	Unc	BU
2003 Proof	5,000	Value: 200				

KM# 231 100 DOLLARS
15.5500 g., 0.9999 Gold 0.4999 oz. AGW, 30 mm. **Subject:** Powered Flight Centennial **Obv:** Queens portrait right **Obv. Designer:** Ian Rank-Broadley **Rev:** Three historic airplanes and rocket **Edge:** Reeded

Date	Mintage	F	VF	XF	Unc	BU
2003 Proof	—	Value: 450				

KM# 234 100 DOLLARS
6.2200 g., 0.9999 Gold 0.1999 oz. AGW, 22 mm. **Obv:** Queens portrait right **Obv. Designer:** Ian Rank-Broadley **Rev:** Henry VIII and Elizabeth I **Edge:** Reeded

Date	Mintage	F	VF	XF	Unc	BU
2003 Proof	5,000	Value: 200				

KM# 237 100 DOLLARS
6.2200 g., 0.9999 Gold 0.1999 oz. AGW, 22 mm. **Obv:** Queens portrait right **Obv. Designer:** Ian Rank-Broadley **Rev:** Matthew Parker, Archbishop of Canterbury **Edge:** Reeded

Date	Mintage	F	VF	XF	Unc	BU
2003 Proof	5,000	Value: 200				

KM# 240 100 DOLLARS
6.2200 g., 0.9999 Gold 0.1999 oz. AGW, 22 mm. **Obv:** Queens portrait right **Obv. Designer:** Ian Rank-Broadley **Rev:** Sir Francis Drake and ships **Edge:** Reeded

Date	Mintage	F	VF	XF	Unc	BU
2003 Proof	5,000	Value: 200				

KM# 243 100 DOLLARS
6.2200 g., 0.9999 Gold 0.1999 oz. AGW, 22 mm. **Obv:** Queens portrait right **Obv. Designer:** Ian Rank-Broadley **Rev:** Sir Walter Raleigh **Edge:** Reeded

Date	Mintage	F	VF	XF	Unc	BU
2003 Proof	5,000	Value: 200				

KM# 246 100 DOLLARS
6.2200 g., 0.9999 Gold 0.1999 oz. AGW, 22 mm. **Obv:** Queens portrait right **Obv. Designer:** Ian Rank-Broadley **Rev:** Sir William Shakespeare **Edge:** Reeded

Date	Mintage	F	VF	XF	Unc	BU
2003 Proof	5,000	Value: 200				

KM# 249 100 DOLLARS
6.2200 g., 0.9999 Gold 0.1999 oz. AGW, 22 mm. **Obv:** Queens portrait right **Obv. Designer:** Ian Rank-Broadley **Rev:** Elizabeth I above her funeral procession **Edge:** Reeded

Date	Mintage	F	VF	XF	Unc	BU
2003 Proof	5,000	Value: 200				

KM# 252 100 DOLLARS
6.2200 g., 0.9999 Gold 0.1999 oz. AGW, 22 mm. **Subject:** Olympics **Obv:** Queens portrait right **Obv. Designer:** Ian Rank-Broadley **Rev:** Ancient bust, runners and coin **Edge:** Reeded

Date	Mintage	F	VF	XF	Unc	BU
2003 Proof	5,000	Value: 200				

KM# 255 100 DOLLARS
6.2200 g., 0.9999 Gold 0.1999 oz. AGW, 22 mm. **Subject:** Olympics **Obv:** Queens portrait right **Obv. Designer:** Ian Rank-Broadley **Rev:** Ancient bust, charioteer and coin **Edge:** Reeded

Date	Mintage	F	VF	XF	Unc	BU
2003 Proof	5,000	Value: 200				

KM# 273.1 100 DOLLARS
6.2200 g., 0.9999 Gold 0.1999 oz. AGW, 22 mm. **Obv:** Queens portrait right **Obv. Designer:** Ian Rank-Broadley **Rev:** Peter Rabbit **Edge:** Reeded

Date	Mintage	F	VF	XF	Unc	BU
2004 Proof	2,000	Value: 220				

KM# 273.2 100 DOLLARS
6.2200 g., 0.9999 Gold 0.1999 oz. AGW, 22 mm. **Obv:** Queens portrait right **Obv. Designer:** Ian Rank-Broadley **Rev:** Multicolor Peter Rabbit **Edge:** Reeded

Date	Mintage	F	VF	XF	Unc	BU
2004 Proof	—	Value: 240				

KM# 283 100 DOLLARS
6.2200 g., 0.9999 Gold 0.1999 oz. AGW, 22 mm. **Obv:** Queens portrait right **Obv. Designer:** Ian Rank-Broadley **Rev:** Sailor above two D-Day landing craft **Edge:** Reeded

Date	Mintage	F	VF	XF	Unc	BU
2004 Proof	5,000	Value: 200				

KM# 299 100 DOLLARS
6.2200 g., 0.9999 Gold 0.1999 oz. AGW, 22 mm. **Obv:** Queens portrait right **Obv. Designer:** Ian Rank-Broadley **Rev:** Soldier above tank and jeeps **Edge:** Reeded

Date	Mintage	F	VF	XF	Unc	BU
2004 Proof	5,000	Value: 200				

KM# 302 100 DOLLARS
6.2200 g., 0.9999 Gold 0.1999 oz. AGW, 22 mm. **Obv:** Queens portrait right **Obv. Designer:** Ian Rank-Broadley **Rev:** Pilot and planes above D-Day landing **Edge:** Reeded

Date	Mintage	F	VF	XF	Unc	BU
2004 Proof	5,000	Value: 200				

KM# 305 100 DOLLARS
6.2200 g., 0.9999 Gold 0.1999 oz. AGW, 22 mm. **Obv:** Queens portrait right **Obv. Designer:** Ian Rank-Broadley **Rev:** Ancient Olympic bust, runners and owl coin **Edge:** Reeded

Date	Mintage	F	VF	XF	Unc	BU
2004 Proof	5,000	Value: 200				

KM# 308 100 DOLLARS
6.2200 g., 0.9999 Gold 0.1999 oz. AGW, 22 mm. **Obv:** Queens portrait right **Obv. Designer:** Ian Rank-Broadley **Rev:** Ancient Olympic bust, charioteer and Zeus coin **Edge:** Reeded

Date	Mintage	F	VF	XF	Unc	BU
2004 Proof	5,000	Value: 200				

KM# 317 125 DOLLARS
15.5510 g., 0.9999 Gold 0.4999 oz. AGW, 30 mm. **Obv:** Bust of Queen Elizabeth II right **Rev:** Mother and baby dolphins **Edge:** Reeded

Date	Mintage	F	VF	XF	Unc	BU
2005	1,500	Value: 465				

KM# 337 125 DOLLARS
15.5590 g., 0.9999 Gold AGW 0.5000 0.5002 oz. AGW, 30.00 mm. **Ruler:** Elizabeth II **Subject:** 400th Anniversary Founding of Jamestown **Obv:** Bust with tiara right **Obv. Legend:** BRITISH VIRGIN ISLANDS - QUEEN ELIZABETH II **Rev:** British lion laying, American Eagle perched on sprays **Rev. Legend:** UNITED IN FRIENDSHIP **Edge:** Reeded

Date	Mintage	F	VF	XF	Unc	BU
2007 Proof	3,000	—	—	—	—	—

KM# 309 250 DOLLARS
15.5517 g., 0.9990 Gold 0.4995 oz. AGW, 30 mm. **Obv:** Queens portrait right **Obv. Designer:** Ian Rank-Broadley **Rev:** Statue of Liberty and the date "11 Sept. 2001" **Edge:** Reeded

Date	Mintage	F	VF	XF	Unc	BU
2002	250	Value: 485				

KM# 280 250 DOLLARS
58.0000 g., 0.5000 Gold 0.9323 oz. AGW, 50 mm. **Obv:** Queens portrait right **Obv. Designer:** Ian Rank-Broadley **Rev:** 1896 Olympic medal design **Edge:** Reeded

Date	Mintage	F	VF	XF	Unc	BU
2004 Proof	1,000	Value: 850				

KM# 318 250 DOLLARS
31.1030 g., 0.9999 Gold 0.9998 oz. AGW, 32.7 mm. **Obv:** Bust of Queen Elizabeth II right **Rev:** Mother and baby dolphins **Edge:** Reeded

Date	Mintage	F	VF	XF	Unc	BU
2005 Proof	750	Value: 950				

KM# 338 250 DOLLARS
31.1030 g., 0.9999 Gold AGW 0.9999 0.9998 oz. AGW, 32.70 mm. **Ruler:** Elizabeth II **Subject:** 400th Anniversary Founding of Jamestown **Obv:** Bust with tiara right **Obv. Legend:** BRITISH VIRGIN ISLANDS - QUEEN ELIZABETH II **Rev:** British lion laying, American eagle perched on sprays **Rev. Legend:** UNITED IN FRIENDSHIP **Edge:** Reeded

Date	Mintage	F	VF	XF	Unc	BU
2007 Proof	1,000	Value: 900				

KM# 277 500 DOLLARS
5000.0000 g., 0.9999 Gold 160.73 oz. AGW, 150 mm. **Obv:** Queens portrait right **Obv. Designer:** Ian Rank-Broadley **Rev:** Gold-plated portrait of Hernando Pizarro, small inset emerald above Pizarro's life events pictoral **Edge:** Reeded **Note:** Photo reduced.

Date	Mintage	F	VF	XF	Unc	BU
2004 Proof	500	Value: 4,350				

KM# 348 500 DOLLARS
160.7562 g., 0.9990 Gold 5.1630 oz. AGW, 150.00 mm. **Ruler:** Elizabeth II **Subject:** 500th Anniversary - Death of Columbus **Obv:** Crowned bust right **Obv. Legend:** BRITISH VIRGIN ISLANDS - QUEEN ELIZABETH II **Rev:** Ship in background at left, Columbus standing at right with right arm outstreched looking right, compass below. **Rev. Legend:** 1451 - DISCOVERER OF AMERICA - CHRISTOPHER COLUMBUS - 1506 **Edge:** Reeded

Date	Mintage	F	VF	XF	Unc	BU
2006 Proof	1,506	Value: 4,350				

MINT SETS

KM#	Date	Mintage	Identification	Issue Price	Mkt Val
MS12	2007 (4)	—	KM# 341 - 344	65.00	65.00

PROOF SETS

KM#	Date	Mintage	Identification	Issue Price	Mkt Val
PS20	2007 (4)	—	KM# 341a - 344a	300	300

BRUNEI

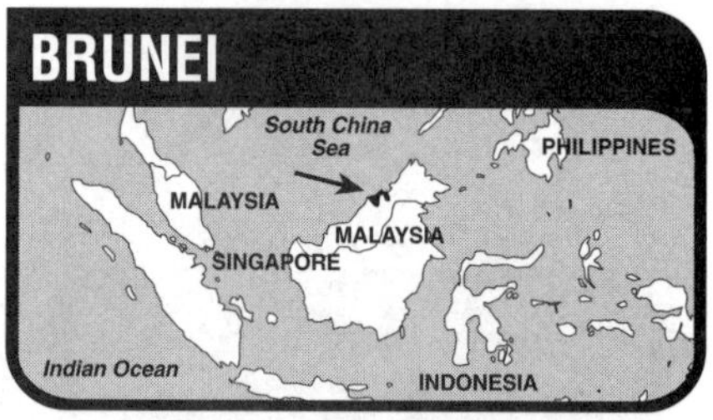

Negara Brunei Darussalam (State of Brunei), an independent sultanate on the northwest coast of the island of Borneo, has an area of 2,226 sq. mi. (5,765 sq. km.) and a population of *326,000. Capital: Bandar Seri Begawan. Crude oil and rubber are exported.

TITLES

نكري بروني

Negri Brunei

RULERS
Sultan Hassanal Bolkiah I, 1967-

SULTANATE

DECIMAL COINAGE

100 Sen = 1 Dollar (Ringgit)

KM# 34 SEN
Copper Clad Steel **Ruler:** Sultan Hassanal Bolkiah **Obv:** Uniformed bust facing **Rev:** Native design denomination below, date at right

Date	Mintage	F	VF	XF	Unc	BU
2001	576,000	—	—	—	0.35	0.50
2002	804,900	—	—	—	0.35	0.50
2005	—	—	—	—	0.35	0.50

KM# 35 5 SEN
Copper-Nickel **Ruler:** Sultan Hassanal Bolkiah **Obv:** Uniformed bust facing **Rev:** Native design, denomination below, date at right

Date	Mintage	F	VF	XF	Unc	BU
2001	808,000	—	—	—	0.50	0.75
2002	1,418,178	—	—	—	0.50	0.75
2005	—	—	—	—	0.50	0.75

KM# 36 10 SEN
Copper-Nickel **Ruler:** Sultan Hassanal Bolkiah **Obv:** Uniformed bust facing **Rev:** Native design, denomination below, date at right

Date	Mintage	F	VF	XF	Unc	BU
2001	164,000	—	—	—	0.65	1.00
2002	476,452	—	—	—	0.65	1.00
2005	—	—	—	—	0.65	1.00

KM# 37 20 SEN
5.6700 g., Copper-Nickel, 23.62 mm. **Ruler:** Sultan Hassanal Bolkiah **Obv:** Uniformed bust facing **Rev:** Native design, denomination below, date at right

Date	Mintage	F	VF	XF	Unc	BU
2001	270,647	—	—	—	1.00	1.50
2002	597,272	—	—	—	1.00	1.50
2004	—	—	—	—	1.00	1.50

KM# 38 50 SEN
Copper-Nickel, 27.5 mm. **Ruler:** Sultan Hassanal Bolkiah **Obv:** Uniformed bust facing **Rev:** National arms within circle, denomination below, date at right **Edge:** Reeded and security edge

Date	Mintage	F	VF	XF	Unc	BU
2001	50,000	—	—	—	2.50	3.00
2002	1,325	—	—	—	3.50	5.00
2005	—	—	—	—	2.50	3.00

KM# 80 2 DOLLARS
31.1000 g., Copper Nickel, 40.70 mm. **Ruler:** Sultan Hassanal Bolkiah **Subject:** 20th Anniversary of Independence **Obv:** Bust 3/4 left, facing **Obv. Legend:** SULTAN HAJI HASSANAL BOLKIAH **Rev:** National arms **Rev. Legend:** NEGARI BRUNEI DARUSSALAM

Date	Mintage	F	VF	XF	Unc	BU
2004 Proof	4,000	Value: 50.00				

KM# 86 2 DOLLARS
31.1000 g., Copper Nickel, 40.70 mm. **Ruler:** Sultan Hassanal Bolkiah **Subject:** 60th Birthday **Obv:** Bust 3/4 left, facing **Obv. Legend:** SULTAN HAJI HASSANAL BOLKIAH **Rev:** Multicolor 1/2 length figure in civilian clothes, facing

Date	Mintage	F	VF	XF	Unc	BU
2006 Proof	200	Value: 80.00				

KM# 77 3 DOLLARS
24.0000 g., Copper-Nickel, 40 mm. **Ruler:** Sultan Hassanal Bolkiah **Obv:** Uniformed bust facing **Obv. Legend:** SULTAN HAJI HASSANAL BOLKIAH **Rev:** Logo at center **Rev. Legend:** COMMONWEALTH FINANCE MINISTERS MEETING **Edge:** Reeded

Date	Mintage	F	VF	XF	Unc	BU
2003 Proof	3,500	Value: 30.00				

KM# 83 3 DOLLARS
31.1000 g., Copper Nickel, 40.70 mm. **Ruler:** Sultan Hassanal Bolkiah **Subject:** Royal Wedding **Obv:** Multicolor portraits of Royal couple

Date	Mintage	F	VF	XF	Unc	BU
2004 Proof	5,000	Value: 40.00				

KM# 81 20 DOLLARS
31.1000 g., 0.9990 Silver 0.9988 oz. ASW, 40.70 mm. **Ruler:** Sultan Hassanal Bolkiah **Subject:** 20th Anniversary of Independence **Obv:** Bust 3/4 left, facing **Obv. Legend:** SULTAN HAJI HASSANAL BOLKIAH **Rev:** National arms **Rev. Legend:** NEGARI BRUNEI DARUSSALAM

Date	Mintage	F	VF	XF	Unc	BU
2004 Proof	1,000	Value: 95.00				

KM# 87 20 DOLLARS
31.1000 g., 0.9990 Silver 0.9988 oz. ASW, 40.70 mm. **Ruler:** Sultan Hassanal Bolkiah **Subject:** 60th Birthday **Obv:** Bust 3/4 left, facing **Obv. Legend:** SULTAN HAJI HASSANAL BOLKIAH **Rev:** Multicolor 1/2 length figure in civilian clothes, facing

Date	Mintage	F	VF	XF	Unc	BU
2006 Proof	200	Value: 200				

KM# 78 30 DOLLARS
62.2000 g., 0.9990 Silver 1.9977 oz. ASW **Ruler:** Sultan Hassanal Bolkiah **Subject:** Commonwealth Finance Minister's Meeting **Obv:** Logo at upper left, multicolor bust of Sultan 3/4 left, facing at right **Obv. Legend:** SULTAN HAJI HASSANAL BOLIAH **Rev:** World map at left - center, national arms at upper right **Shape:** Rectangular, 65 x 31 mm

Date	Mintage	F	VF	XF	Unc	BU
2003 Proof	1,000	Value: 200				

KM# 84 30 DOLLARS
31.1000 g., 0.9990 Silver 0.9988 oz. ASW, 40.70 mm. **Ruler:** Sultan Hassanal Bolkiah **Subject:** Royal Wedding **Obv:** Multicolor portraits of Royal couple

Date	Mintage	F	VF	XF	Unc	BU
2004 Proof	1,000	Value: 160				

KM# 82 200 DOLLARS
31.1000 g., 0.9999 Gold 0.9997 oz. AGW, 32.12 mm. **Ruler:** Sultan Hassanal Bolkiah **Subject:** 2oth Anniversary of Independence **Obv:** Bust 3/4 left, facing **Obv. Legend:** SULTAN HAJI HASSANAL BOLKIAH **Rev:** National arms **Rev. Legend:** NEGARI BRUNEI DARUSSALAM

Date	Mintage	F	VF	XF	Unc	BU
2004 Proof	200	Value: 900				

KM# 85 200 DOLLARS
31.1000 g., 0.9999 Gold 0.9997 oz. AGW, 32.00 mm. **Ruler:** Sultan Hassanal Bolkiah **Subject:** Royal Wedding **Obv:** Multicolor portraits of Royal couple

Date	Mintage	F	VF	XF	Unc	BU
2004 Proof	200	Value: 900				

KM# 88 200 DOLLARS
31.1000 g., 0.9999 Gold 0.9997 oz. AGW, 32.12 mm. **Ruler:** Sultan Hassanal Bolkiah **Subject:** 60th Birthday **Obv:** Bust 3/4 left, facing **Obv. Legend:** SULTAN HAJI HASSANAL BOLKIAH **Rev:** Multicolor 1/2 length figure in civilian clothes, facing

Date	Mintage	F	VF	XF	Unc	BU
2006 Proof	200	Value: 1,500				

BULGARIA

The Republic of Bulgaria, formerly the Peoples Republic of Bulgaria, a Balkan country on the Black Sea in southeastern Europe, has an area of 42,855 sq. mi. (110,910 sq. km.) and a population of *8.31 million. Capital: Sofia. Agriculture remains a key component of the economy but industrialization, particularly heavy industry, has been emphasized since the late 1940s. Machinery, tobacco and cigarettes, wines and spirits, clothing and metals are the chief exports.

MONETARY SYSTEM
100 Stotinki = 1 Lev

REPUBLIC

REFORM COINAGE

KM# 237 STOTINKA
Brass, 16 mm. **Obv:** Madara horseman right, animal below **Rev:** Denomination above date **Edge:** Plain

Date	Mintage	F	VF	XF	Unc	BU
2002 Proof	10,000	Value: 1.00				

KM# 238 2 STOTINKI
Brass, 18 mm. **Obv:** Madara horseman right, animal below **Rev:** Denomination above date **Edge:** Plain

Date	Mintage	F	VF	XF	Unc	BU
2002 Proof	10,000	Value: 1.50				

KM# 239 5 STOTINKI
Brass, 20 mm. **Obv:** Madara horseman right, animal below **Rev:** Denomination above date **Edge:** Plain **Note:** Prev. KM#A239.

Date	Mintage	F	VF	XF	Unc	BU
2002 Proof	10,000	Value: 2.00				

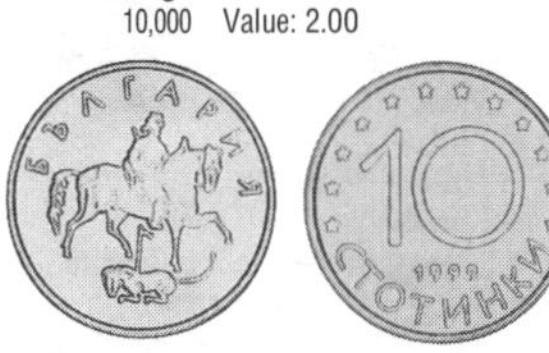

KM# 240 10 STOTINKI
Copper-Nickel, 18.5 mm. **Obv:** Madara horseman right, animal below **Rev:** Denomination above date **Edge:** Reeded

Date	Mintage	F	VF	XF	Unc	BU
2002 Proof	10,000	Value: 2.50				

KM# 241 20 STOTINKI
Copper-Nickel, 20.5 mm. **Obv:** Madara horseman right, animal below **Rev:** Denomination above date **Edge:** Reeded

Date	Mintage	F	VF	XF	Unc	BU
2002 Proof	10,000	Value: 3.00				

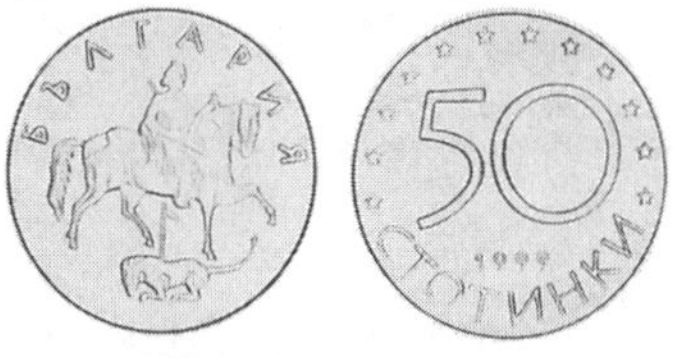

KM# 242 50 STOTINKI
Copper-Nickel, 22.5 mm. **Obv:** Madara horseman right, animal below **Rev:** Denomination above date **Edge:** Reeded

Date	Mintage	F	VF	XF	Unc	BU
2002 Proof	10,000	Value: 5.00				

KM# 272 50 STOTINKI
Copper-Nickel, 22.5 mm. **Obv:** Stylized Bulgarian arms, lion left, NATO - 2004 under lion **Rev:** Denomination above date **Edge:** Reeded

Date	Mintage	F	VF	XF	Unc	BU
2004	—	—	—	—	2.00	3.00

KM# 274 50 STOTINKI
5.0300 g., Copper-Nickel, 22.6 mm. **Obv:** European Union seated woman allegory **Rev:** Denomination above date **Edge:** Reeded

Date	Mintage	F	VF	XF	Unc	BU
2005	—	—	—	—	1.25	1.75

KM# 276 50 STOTINKI
5.0000 g., Copper-Zinc-Nickel, 22.5 mm. **Obv:** Value **Rev:** Pillar behind open book **Edge:** Reeded

Date	Mintage	F	VF	XF	Unc	BU
2007	500,000	—	—	—	—	1.50

KM# 254 LEV
7.0300 g., Bi-Metallic Copper-Nickel center in Brass ring, 24.3 mm. **Obv:** St. Ivan of Rila **Rev:** Denomination **Edge:** Reeded and plain sections

Date	Mintage	F	VF	XF	Unc	BU
2002	24,842,000	—	—	—	3.00	4.00
2002 Proof	10,000	Value: 10.00				

KM# 257 LEV
15.5500 g., 0.9990 Gold 0.4994 oz. AGW **Obv:** St. Ivan of Rila **Rev:** Large number one **Edge:** Plain

Date	Mintage	F	VF	XF	Unc	BU
2002 Proof	2,000	Value: 450				

KM# 258 5 LEVA
1.2400 g., 0.9990 Gold 0.0398 oz. AGW **Obv:** Denomination **Rev:** Olympic archer **Edge:** Plain

Date	Mintage	F	VF	XF	Unc	BU
2002 Proof	12,000	Value: 47.50				

KM# 259 5 LEVA
1.2400 g., 0.9990 Gold 0.0398 oz. AGW **Obv:** Denomination **Rev:** Olympic cyclist **Edge:** Plain

Date	Mintage	F	VF	XF	Unc	BU
2002 Proof	12,000	Value: 47.50				

KM# 260 5 LEVA
1.2400 g., 0.9990 Gold 0.0398 oz. AGW **Obv:** Denomination **Rev:** Olympic fencing **Edge:** Plain

Date	Mintage	F	VF	XF	Unc	BU
2002 Proof	12,000	Value: 47.50				

KM# 261 5 LEVA
1.2400 g., 0.9990 Gold 0.0398 oz. AGW **Obv:** Denomination **Rev:** Olympic wrestling **Edge:** Plain

Date	Mintage	F	VF	XF	Unc	BU
2002 Proof	12,000	Value: 47.50				

KM# 262 5 LEVA
1.2400 g., 0.9990 Gold 0.0398 oz. AGW, 14 mm. **Obv:** Denomination **Rev:** Olympic gymnastics **Edge:** Plain

Date	Mintage	F	VF	XF	Unc	BU
2002 Proof	12,000	Value: 47.50				

KM# 263 5 LEVA
1.2400 g., 0.9990 Gold 0.0398 oz. AGW, 14 mm. **Obv:** Denomination **Rev:** Olympics founder Pierre du Coubertin **Edge:** Plain

Date	Mintage	F	VF	XF	Unc	BU
2002 Proof	17,000	Value: 47.50				

KM# 264 5 LEVA
1.2400 g., 0.9990 Gold 0.0398 oz. AGW, 14 mm. **Obv:** Denomination **Rev:** Olympic running **Edge:** Plain

Date	Mintage	F	VF	XF	Unc	BU
2002 Proof	12,000	Value: 47.50				

KM# 265 5 LEVA
1.2400 g., 0.9990 Gold 0.0398 oz. AGW, 14 mm. **Obv:** Denomination **Rev:** Olympic swimming **Edge:** Plain

Date	Mintage	F	VF	XF	Unc	BU
2002 Proof	12,000	Value: 47.50				

KM# 266 5 LEVA
1.2400 g., 0.9990 Gold 0.0398 oz. AGW, 14 mm. **Obv:** Denomination **Rev:** Olympic tennis **Edge:** Plain

Date	Mintage	F	VF	XF	Unc	BU
2002 Proof	12,000	Value: 47.50				

KM# 267 5 LEVA
1.2400 g., 0.9990 Gold 0.0398 oz. AGW, 14 mm. **Obv:** Denomination **Rev:** Olympic weight lifting **Edge:** Plain

Date	Mintage	F	VF	XF	Unc	BU
2002 Proof	12,000	Value: 47.50				

KM# 268 5 LEVA
28.2800 g., 0.9250 Silver 0.8410 oz. ASW, 38.5 mm. **Obv:** Denomination **Rev:** FIFA Soccer trophy cup **Edge:** Plain

Date	Mintage	F	VF	XF	Unc	BU
2003 Proof	50,000	Value: 37.50				

KM# 275 5 LEVA
15.0000 g., Copper-Nickel, 34.2 mm. **Obv:** National arms, date and denomination below **Rev:** Multicolor child on rocking horse **Edge:** Plain

Date	Mintage	F	VF	XF	Unc	BU
2003 Proof	—	Value: 15.00				

KM# 247 10 LEVA
23.3300 g., 0.9250 Silver 0.6938 oz. ASW, 38.5 mm. **Subject:** Olympics **Obv:** National arms, date and denomination below **Rev:** Ski jumper **Edge:** Plain with serial number

Date	Mintage	F	VF	XF	Unc	BU
2001 Proof	25,000	Value: 45.00				

KM# 246 10 LEVA
23.6000 g., 0.9250 Silver 0.7018 oz. ASW, 38.5 mm. **Subject:** Higher Education **Obv:** National arms, date and denomination below **Rev:** Graduate before building **Edge:** Plain

Date	Mintage	F	VF	XF	Unc	BU
2001 Proof	10,000	Value: 40.00				

KM# 270 10 LEVA
23.3300 g., 0.9990 Silver 0.7493 oz. ASW, 38.6 mm. **Subject:** National Theater Centennial **Edge:** Plain

Date	Mintage	F	VF	XF	Unc	BU
2004 Proof	5,000	Value: 40.00				

KM# 273 10 LEVA
23.2000 g., 0.9250 Silver 0.6899 oz. ASW, 38.5 mm. **Obv:** National arms, date and denomination below **Rev:** St. Nikolay Mirlikiisky Chudofvorez with gold plated crosses and halo **Edge:** Plain

Date	Mintage	F	VF	XF	Unc	BU
2004 Proof	10,000	Value: 40.00				

KM# 277 10 LEVA
31.1000 g., 0.9990 Silver 0.9988 oz. ASW, 40.00 mm. **Subject:** Boris Christov **Obv:** National arms **Obv. Legend:** БЪЛГАРСКА НАРОДНА БАНКА **Rev:** Early regal 1/2 length male figure facing holding orb **Rev. Legend:** ИМЕНИТИ БЪГАРСКИ ГЛАСОВЕ

Date	Mintage	F	VF	XF	Unc	BU
2007 Proof	10,000					

KM# 269 20 LEVA
1.5500 g., 0.9990 Gold 0.0498 oz. AGW, 16 mm. **Obv:** Denomination **Rev:** Mother of God **Edge:** Plain

Date	Mintage	F	VF	XF	Unc	BU
2003 Proof	20,000	Value: 55.00				

KM# 271 125 LEVA
7.7800 g., 0.9990 Gold 0.2499 oz. AGW, 21 mm. **Subject:** Bulgarian National Bank 125th Anniversary

Date	Mintage	F	VF	XF	Unc	BU
2004 Proof	3,000	Value: 250				

PIEFORTS

KM#	Date	Mintage	Identification	Mkt Val
P4	2004	5,000	10 Leva. 0.9990 Silver. 46.6600 g. 100 Years - National Theatre, 38.61mm.	75.00

PROOF SETS

KM#	Date	Mintage	Identification	Issue Price	Mkt Val
PS8	2002 (7)	10,000	KM#237-242, 254	—	25.00

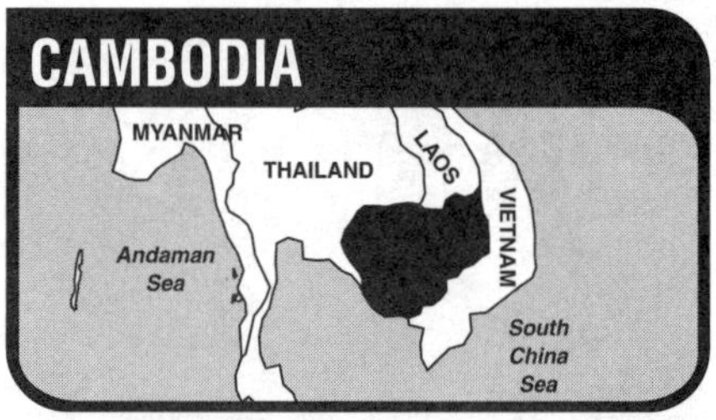

The State of Cambodia, formerly Democratic Kampuchea and the Khmer Republic, a land of paddy fields and forest-clad hills located on the Indo-Chinese peninsula, fronting on the Gulf of Thailand, has an area of 70,238 sq. mi. (181,040 sq. km.) and a population of *11.21 million. Capital: Phnom Penh. Agriculture is the basis of the economy, with rice the chief crop. Native industries include cattle breeding, weaving and rice milling. Rubber, cattle, corn, and timber are exported.

RULERS
Kings of Cambodia
Norodom Sihanouk, 1991-1993
Chairman, Supreme National Council
King, 1993-

KINGDOM OF CAMBODIA
1993 -

DECIMAL COINAGE

KM# 98 500 RIELS
19.9200 g., Brass, 38.7 mm. **Subject:** Angkor Wat **Obv:** Armless statue of Jayavarman VII **Rev:** View of Angkor Wat in center **Edge:** Reeded

Date	Mintage	F	VF	XF	Unc	BU
2001	28,000	—	—	—	7.50	10.00

KM# 99 3000 RIELS
1.2441 g., 0.9999 Gold 0.0400 oz. AGW, 13.92 mm. **Subject:** Angkor Wat **Obv:** Armless statue of Jayavarman VII **Rev:** View of Angkor Wat in center **Edge:** Reeded

Date	Mintage	F	VF	XF	Unc	BU
2001	28,000	—	—	—	45.00	55.00

KM# 100 3000 RIELS
20.0000 g., 0.9250 Silver 0.5948 oz. ASW, 38.7 mm. **Subject:** Buddha **Obv:** Armless statue of Jayavarman VII **Rev:** Radiant Buddha next to a carved Buddha face **Edge:** Reeded

Date	Mintage	F	VF	XF	Unc	BU
2001 Proof	10,000	Value: 45.00				

KM# 101 3000 RIELS
20.0000 g., 0.9250 Silver 0.5948 oz. ASW, 38.7 mm. **Subject:** Apsara Dance **Obv:** Armless statue of Jayavarman VII **Rev:** Dancer next to multicolor wall **Edge:** Reeded

Date	Mintage	F	VF	XF	Unc	BU
2001 Proof	10,000	Value: 50.00				

KM# 103 3000 RIELS
20.0000 g., 0.9990 Silver 0.6423 oz. ASW, 38.7 mm. **Obv:** King Jayavarman VII (1162-1201) **Rev:** Multicolor Tutankhamen's mask **Edge:** Reeded

Date	Mintage	F	VF	XF	Unc	BU
2004 Proof	9,100	Value: 50.00				

KM# 104 3000 RIELS
1.2440 g., 0.9990 Gold 0.0400 oz. AGW, 13.92 mm. **Obv:** King Jayavarman VII (1162-1201) **Rev:** Sphinx and pyramid **Edge:** Reeded

Date	Mintage	F	VF	XF	Unc	BU
2004 Proof	27,900	Value: 45.00				

KM# 102 10000 RIELS
31.1035 g., 0.9990 Silver 0.9990 oz. ASW **Center Weight:** 3.5000 g. **Center Composition:** 0.9999 Gold 0.1125 oz. AGW , 40.7 mm. **Subject:** Angkor Wat **Obv:** Armless statue of Jayavarman **Rev:** Multicolor holographic view of Angkor Wat in center **Edge:** Reeded

Date	Mintage	F	VF	XF	Unc	BU
2001 Proof	3,000	Value: 125				

KM# 105 10000 RIELS
31.1035 g., 0.9990 Silver 0.9990 oz. ASW, 40.7 mm. **Obv:** King Jayavarman VII (1162-1201) **Rev:** Sphinx and pyramid on holographic gold insert **Edge:** Reeded

Date	Mintage	F	VF	XF	Unc	BU
2004 Proof	2,100	Value: 80.00				

CANADA

CONFEDERATION

CIRCULATION COINAGE

KM# 289 CENT Comp.: Copper Plated Steel **Ruler:** Elizabeth II **Obv.:** Crowned head right **Obv. Des.:** Dora dePédery-Hunt **Rev.:** Maple twig design **Rev. Des.:** George E. Kruger-Gray **Edge:** Round and plain **Size:** 19.1 mm.

Date	Mintage	MS-60	MS-63	Proof
2001	919,358,000	—	0.10	—
2001P Proof	—	—	—	5.00
2003	92,219,775	—	0.10	—
2003P Proof	—	—	—	5.00
2003P	235,936,799	—	1.50	—

KM# 445 CENT Comp.: Copper Plated Steel **Ruler:** Elizabeth II **Subject:** Elizabeth II Golden Jubilee **Obv.:** Crowned head right, Jubilee commemorative dates 1952-2002 **Obv. Des.:** Dora dePédery-Hunt **Rev.:** Denomination above maple leaves **Rev. Des.:** George E. Kruger-Gray **Edge:** Plain **Size:** 19.1 mm.

Date	Mintage	MS-60	MS-63	Proof
ND(2002)	716,366,000	—	0.75	—
ND(2002)P	114,212,000	—	1.00	—
ND(2002)P	32,642	—	—	5.00

Note: In sets only

KM# 445a CENT Comp.: 0.9250 Silver **Ruler:** Elizabeth II **Subject:** Elizabeth II Golden Jubilee **Obv.:** Crowned head right, Jubilee commemorative dates 1952-2002 **Obv. Des.:** Dora dePédery-Hunt **Rev.:** Denomination above maple leaves **Rev. Des.:** George E. Kruger-Gray

Date	Mintage	MS-63	Proof
ND(2002)	21,537	—	3.00

Note: In sets only

KM# 490 CENT Comp.: Copper Plated Zinc **Ruler:** Elizabeth II **Obv.:** New effigy of Queen Elizabeth II right **Obv. Des.:** Susanna Blunt **Edge:** Plain **Size:** 19.1 mm.

Date	Mintage	MS-60	MS-63	Proof
2003	56,877,144	—	0.25	—
2004	645,220,000	—	0.25	—
2004 Proof	—	—	—	2.50
2005	—	—	0.25	—
2005 Proof	—	—	—	2.50
2006	—	—	0.25	—
2006 Proof	—	—	—	2.50
2007 (ml)	—	—	0.25	—
2007 (ml) Proof	—	—	—	2.50

KM# 468 CENT Comp.: Copper **Ruler:** Elizabeth II **Subject:** 50th Anniversary of the Coronation of Elizabeth II **Obv.:** 1953 effigy of the Queen, Jubilee commemorative dates 1952-2002 **Obv. Des.:** Mary Gillick

Date	Mintage	MS-63	Proof
ND(2002)	—	2.50	—

Note: In Coronation Proof sets only

KM# 410 3 CENTS Weight: 3.1100 g. **Comp.:** 0.9250 Gold Plated Silver 0.0925 oz. ASW AGW **Ruler:** Elizabeth II **Subject:** 1st Canadian Postage Stamp **Obv.:** Crowned head right

Obv. Des.: Dora dePédery-Hunt **Rev.:** Partial stamp design **Rev. Des.:** Sandford Fleming **Edge:** Plain **Size:** 21.3 mm.

Date	Mintage	MS-63	Proof
2001 Proof	90,000	—	12.50

KM# 182a 5 CENTS Weight: 5.3500 g. **Comp.:** 0.9250 Silver 0.1591 oz. ASW **Ruler:** Elizabeth II **Obv.:** Crowned head right **Obv. Des.:** Dora dePedery-Hunt **Rev.:** Beaver on rock divides date and denomination **Rev. Des.:** George E. Kruger-Gray **Size:** 21.2 mm.

Date	Mintage	MS-63	Proof
2001 Proof	—	—	5.00
2003 Proof	—	—	5.00

KM# 413 5 CENTS Weight: 5.3500 g. **Comp.:** 0.9250 Silver 0.1591 oz. ASW **Ruler:** Elizabeth II **Subject:** Royal Military College **Obv.:** Crowned head right **Rev.:** Marching cadets and arch **Rev. Des.:** Gerald T. Locklin **Edge:** Plain **Size:** 21.2 mm.

Date	Mintage	MS-63	Proof
2001 Proof	25,834	—	7.00

KM# 182 5 CENTS Weight: 4.6000 g. **Comp.:** Copper-Nickel **Ruler:** Elizabeth II **Obv.:** Crowned head right **Obv. Des.:** Dora dePedery-Hunt **Rev.:** Beaver on rock divides dates and denomination **Rev. Des.:** George E. Kruger-Gray **Edge:** Plain **Size:** 19.55 mm.

Date	Mintage	MS-60	MS-63	Proof
2001	30,035,000	6.50	12.50	—
2001P Proof	—	—	—	10.00
2003	—	0.15	0.30	—

KM# 182b 5 CENTS Weight: 3.9000 g. **Comp.:** Nickel Plated Steel **Ruler:** Elizabeth II **Obv.:** Crowned head right **Obv. Des.:** Dora dePedery-Hunt **Rev.:** Beaver on rock divides date and denomination **Rev. Des.:** George E. Kruger-Gray **Edge:** Plain **Size:** 21.2 mm.

Date	Mintage	MS-60	MS-63	Proof
2001 P	136,650,000	0.20	0.35	—
2003 P	31,388,921	—	0.35	—

KM# 446 5 CENTS Comp.: Nickel Plated Steel **Ruler:** Elizabeth II **Subject:** Elizabeth II Golden Jubilee **Obv.:** Crowned head right, Jubilee commemorative dates 1952-2002 **Obv. Des.:** Dora dePedery-Hunt **Rev. Des.:** George E. Kruger-Gray **Size:** 21.2 mm. **Note:** Magnetic.

Date	Mintage	MS-63	Proof
ND(2002)P	134,362,000	0.75	—
ND(2002)P Proof	32,642	—	10.00

KM# 446a 5 CENTS Comp.: 0.9250 Silver **Ruler:** Elizabeth II **Subject:** Elizabeth II Golden Jubilee **Obv.:** Queen, Jubilee commemorative dates 1952-2002 **Size:** 21.2 mm.

Date	Mintage	MS-63	Proof
ND(2002)	21,573	—	11.50

Note: In proof sets only

KM# 453 5 CENTS Comp.: 0.9250 Silver **Ruler:** Elizabeth II **Subject:** Vimy Ridge - WWI **Obv.:** Crowned head right **Rev.:** Vimy Ridge Memorial, allegorical figure and dates 1917-2002 **Rev. Des.:** S. A. Allward **Size:** 21.2 mm.

Date	Mintage	MS-63	Proof
ND(2002) Proof	22,646	—	11.50

KM# 491 5 CENTS Weight: 3.9300 g. **Comp.:** Nickel Plated Steel **Ruler:** Elizabeth II **Obv.:** Crowned head right **Obv. Des.:** Susanna Blunt **Rev.:** Beaver divides date and denomination **Rev. Des.:** George E. Kruger-Gray **Size:** 21.2 mm. **Note:** Magnetic.

Date	Mintage	MS-63	Proof
2003P	61,392,180	1.25	—
2004P	123,085,000	0.50	—
2004P Proof	—	—	2.50
2005P	—	0.50	—
2005P Proof	—	—	2.50
2006P	—	0.50	—
2006P Proof	—	—	2.50
2006(ml)	—	0.50	—
2006(ml) Proof	—	—	2.50

KM# 469 5 CENTS Comp.: 0.9250 Silver **Ruler:** Elizabeth II **Subject:** 50th Anniversary of the Coronation of Elizabeth II **Obv.:** Crowned head right, Jubilee commemorative dates 1952-2002 **Obv. Des.:** Mary Gillick **Size:** 21.2 mm.

Date	Mintage	MS-63	Proof
ND(2002)	30,000	11.50	—

Note: In Coronation Proof sets only

KM# 491a 5 CENTS Weight: 5.3500 g. **Comp.:** 0.9250 Silver 0.1591 oz. ASW **Ruler:** Elizabeth II **Obv.:** Crowned head right **Obv. Des.:** Susanna Blunt **Rev.:** Beaver divides date and denomination **Edge:** Plain **Size:** 21.1 mm.

Date	Mintage	MS-63	Proof
2004 Proof	—	—	3.50

KM# 506 5 CENTS Weight: 5.3500 g. **Comp.:** 0.9250 Silver 0.1591 oz. ASW **Ruler:** Elizabeth II **Obv.:** Bare head right **Rev.:** "Victory" design of the KM-40 reverse **Edge:** 12-sided plain **Size:** 21.3 mm.

Date	Mintage	MS-63	Proof
ND(2004) Proof	20,019	—	15.00

KM# 627 5 CENTS Comp.: Nickel **Ruler:** Elizabeth II **Subject:** 60th Anniversary, Victory in Europe 1945-2005 **Obv.:** Head right **Rev.:** Large V

Date	Mintage	MS-63	Proof
ND2005P	59,258,000	4.50	—

KM# 183b 10 CENTS Comp.: Nickel Plated Steel **Ruler:** Elizabeth II **Obv.:** Crowned head right **Obv. Des.:** Dora dePedery-Hunt **Rev.:** Bluenose sailing left, date at right, denomination below **Rev. Des.:** Emanuel Hahn **Edge:** Reeded **Size:** 18.03 mm.

Date	Mintage	MS-63	Proof
2001 P	266,000,000	0.45	—
2003 P	162,398,000	0.20	—

KM# 183a 10 CENTS Weight: 2.4000 g. **Comp.:** 0.9250 Silver 0.0714 oz. ASW **Ruler:** Elizabeth II **Obv.:** Crowned head right **Rev.:** Bluenose sailing left, date at right, denomination below **Size:** 18.03 mm.

Date	Mintage	MS-63	Proof
2001 Proof	—	—	5.00
2002 Proof	—	—	7.50
2003 Proof	—	—	7.50

KM# 412 10 CENTS Weight: 1.7700 g. **Comp.:** Nickel Plated Steel **Ruler:** Elizabeth II **Subject:** Year of the Volunteer **Obv.:** Crowned head right **Rev.:** Three portraits left and radiant sun **Rev. Des.:** R. C. M. Staff **Edge:** Reeded **Size:** 18 mm.

Date	Mintage	MS-63	Proof
2001P Proof	—	—	8.50

KM# 412a 10 CENTS Weight: 2.4000 g. **Comp.:** 0.9250 Silver 0.0714 oz. ASW **Ruler:** Elizabeth II **Subject:** Year of the Volunteer **Obv.:** Crowned head right **Rev.:** 3 portraits left above banner, radiant sun below **Edge:** Reeded **Size:** 18 mm.

Date	Mintage	MS-63	Proof
2001P Proof	40,634	—	9.00

KM# 447 10 CENTS Comp.: Nickel Plated Steel **Ruler:** Elizabeth II **Subject:** Elizabeth II Golden Jubilee **Obv.:** Crowned head right, Jubilee commemorative dates 1952-2002 **Size:** 18 mm.

Date	Mintage	MS-63	Proof
ND(2002)P	251,278,000	1.00	—
ND(2002) Proof	32,642	—	2.50

KM# 447a 10 CENTS Comp.: 0.9250 Silver **Ruler:** Elizabeth II **Subject:** Elizabeth II Golden Jubilee **Obv.:** Crowned head right, Jubilee commemorative dates 1952-2002 **Size:** 18 mm.

Date	Mintage	MS-63	Proof
ND(2002)	21,537	—	12.50

Note: In proof sets only

KM# 492 10 CENTS Comp.: Nickel Plated Steel **Ruler:** Elizabeth II **Obv.:** Crowned head right **Obv. Des.:** Susanna Blunt **Size:** 18 mm.

Date	Mintage	MS-63	Proof
2003P	—	1.25	—
2004P	211,924,000	0.60	—
2004P Proof	—	—	2.50
2005P	—	0.60	—
2005P Proof	—	—	2.50
2006P	—	0.60	—
2006P Proof	—	—	2.50
2007(ml)	—	0.60	—
2007(ml) Proof	—	—	2.50

KM# 492a 10 CENTS Weight: 2.4000 g. **Comp.:** 0.9250 Silver 0.0714 oz. ASW **Ruler:** Elizabeth II **Obv.:** Crowned head right **Obv. Des.:** Susanna Blunt **Rev.:** Sailboat **Edge:** Reeded **Size:** 18 mm.

Date	Mintage	MS-63	Proof
2004 Proof	—	—	5.00

KM# 470 10 CENTS **Comp.:** 0.9250 Silver **Ruler:** Elizabeth II **Subject:** 50th Anniversary of the Coronation of Elizabeth II

Date	Mintage	MS-63	Proof
ND(2003)	30,000	12.00	—

Note: In Coronation Proof sets only

KM# 524 10 CENTS **Weight:** 2.4000 g. **Comp.:** 0.9250 Silver 0.0714 oz. ASW **Ruler:** Elizabeth II **Subject:** Golf, Championship of Canada, Centennial. **Obv.:** Head right **Size:** 18 mm.

Date	Mintage	MS-63	Proof
2004	39,486	12.50	—

KM# 419 25 CENTS **Weight:** 5.0600 g. **Comp.:** Nickel Plated Steel **Ruler:** Elizabeth II **Subject:** Canada Day **Obv.:** Crowned head right **Rev.:** Maple leaf at center, children holding hands below **Rev. Des.:** Silke Ware **Edge:** Reeded **Size:** 23.9 mm.

Date	Mintage	MS-63	Proof
2001	96,352	7.00	—

KM# 184 25 CENTS **Weight:** 5.0700 g. **Comp.:** Nickel **Ruler:** Elizabeth II **Obv.:** Crowned head right **Obv. Des.:** Dora dePedery-Hunt **Rev.:** Caribou left, denomination above, date at right **Rev. Des.:** Emanuel Hahn **Size:** 23.88 mm.

Date	Mintage	MS-60	MS-63	Proof
2001	8,415,000	3.00	5.00	—
2001 Proof	—	—	—	7.50

KM# 184a 25 CENTS **Weight:** 5.9000 g. **Comp.:** 0.9250 Silver 0.1755 oz. ASW **Ruler:** Elizabeth II **Obv.:** Crowned head right **Rev.:** Caribou left, denomination above, date at right **Size:** 23.88 mm.

Date	Mintage	MS-63	Proof
2001 Proof	—	—	6.50
2003 Proof	—	—	6.50

KM# 184b 25 CENTS **Comp.:** Nickel Plated Steel **Ruler:** Elizabeth II **Obv.:** Crowned head right **Rev.:** Caribou left, denomination above, date at right **Size:** 23.88 mm.

Date	Mintage	MS-60	MS-63	Proof
2001 P	55,773,000	1.25	2.50	—
2001 P Proof	—	—	—	5.00
2002 P	—	—	2.50	—
2002 P Proof	—	—	—	5.00
2003 P	15,905,090	—	2.50	—
2003 p Proof	—	—	—	5.00

KM# 448 25 CENTS **Comp.:** Nickel Plated Steel **Ruler:** Elizabeth II **Subject:** Elizabeth II Golden Jubilee **Obv.:** Crowned head right **Size:** 23.9 mm. **Note:** Double-dated 1952-2002.

Date	Mintage	MS-63	Proof
ND(2002)P	152,485,000	2.00	—
ND(2002)P Proof	32,642	—	6.00

KM# 448a 25 CENTS **Comp.:** 0.9250 Silver **Ruler:** Elizabeth II **Subject:** Elizabeth II Golden Jubilee **Obv.:** Crowned head right, Jubilee commemorative dates 1952-2002 **Size:** 23.9 mm.

Date	Mintage	MS-63	Proof
ND(2002) Proof	100,000	—	12.50

KM# 451a 25 CENTS **Weight:** 4.4000 g. **Comp.:** Nickel Plated Steel **Ruler:** Elizabeth II **Subject:** Canada Day **Obv.:** Crowned head right **Rev.:** Human figures with large red maple leaf **Edge:** Reeded **Size:** 23.88 mm.

Date	Mintage	MS-63	Proof
ND2002P	49,903	6.00	—

KM# 493 25 CENTS **Weight:** 4.4500 g. **Comp.:** Nickel Plated Steel **Ruler:** Elizabeth II **Obv.:** Crowned head right **Obv. Des.:** Susanna Blunt **Size:** 23.9 mm.

Date	Mintage	MS-63	Proof
2003P	66,861,633	2.00	—
2003W	—	—	—
2004P	159,465,000	2.50	—
2004P Proof	—	—	5.00
2005P	—	2.50	—
2005P Proof	—	—	5.00
2006P	—	2.50	—
2006P Proof	—	—	5.00
2007(ml)	—	2.50	—
2007(ml) Proof	—	—	5.00

KM# 471 25 CENTS **Comp.:** 0.9250 Silver **Ruler:** Elizabeth II **Subject:** 50th Anniversary of the Coronation of Elizabeth II **Obv.:** 1953 effigy of the Queen, Jubilee commemorative dates 1952-2002 **Obv. Des.:** Mary Gillick **Size:** 23.9 mm.

Date	Mintage	MS-63	Proof
ND(2002)	30,000	12.50	—

Note: In Coronation Proof sets only

KM# 474 25 CENTS **Comp.:** 0.9250 Silver **Ruler:** Elizabeth II **Subject:** Canada Day **Obv.:** Queens head right **Rev.:** Polar bear and red colored maple leaves **Size:** 23.9 mm.

Date	Mintage	MS-63	Proof
2003 Proof	—	—	7.50

KM# 510 25 CENTS **Weight:** 4.4000 g. **Comp.:** Nickel Plated Steel **Ruler:** Elizabeth II **Obv.:** Crowned head right **Rev.:** Red Poppy in center of maple leaf **Edge:** Reeded **Size:** 23.9 mm.

Date	Mintage	MS-63	Proof
2004	28,500,000	5.00	—

KM# 510a 25 CENTS **Comp.:** 0.9250 Silver selectively gold plated **Ruler:** Elizabeth II **Obv.:** Crowned head right **Rev.:** Gold-plated poppy in maple leaf **Edge:** Reeded **Size:** 23.9 mm.

Date	Mintage	MS-63	Proof
2004 Proof	12,677	—	20.00

Note: Encased in cover of Annual Report

KM# 525 25 CENTS **Weight:** 4.4300 g. **Comp.:** Nickel Plated Steel **Ruler:** Elizabeth II **Obv.:** Crowned head right **Rev.:** Maple leaf, colorized

Date	Mintage	MS-63	Proof
2004	16,028	8.00	—

KM# 493a 25 CENTS **Weight:** 5.9000 g. **Comp.:** 0.9250 Silver 0.1755 oz. ASW **Ruler:** Elizabeth II **Obv.:** Crowned head right **Obv. Des.:** Suanne Blunt **Rev.:** Caribou **Edge:** Reeded **Size:** 23.9 mm.

Date	Mintage	MS-63	Proof
2004 Proof	—	—	6.50

KM# 628 25 CENTS **Weight:** 4.4600 g. **Comp.:** Nickel Plated Steel **Ruler:** Elizabeth II **Subject:** First Settlement, Ile Ste Croix 1604-2004 **Obv.:** Crowned head right **Rev.:** Sailing ship Bonne-Renommee

Date	Mintage	MS-63	Proof
ND2004P	15,400,000	5.00	—

KM# 529 25 CENTS **Weight:** 4.4300 g. **Comp.:** Nickel Plated Steel **Ruler:** Elizabeth II **Subject:** WWII, 60th Anniversary **Obv.:** Head right **Rev.:** Three soldiers and flag **Size:** 23.9 mm.

Date	Mintage	MS-63	Proof
2005	3,500	20.00	—

KM# 530 25 CENTS **Weight:** 4.4300 g. **Comp.:** Nickel Plated Steel **Ruler:** Elizabeth II **Subject:** Alberta **Obv.:** Head right **Size:** 23.9 mm.

Date	Mintage	MS-63	Proof
2005P	20,640,000	7.00	—

KM# 531 25 CENTS **Weight:** 4.4300 g. **Comp.:** Nickel Plated Steel **Ruler:** Elizabeth II **Subject:** Canada Day **Obv.:** Head right **Rev.:** Beaver, colorized **Size:** 23.9 mm.

Date	Mintage	MS-63	Proof
2005P	58,370	8.50	—

KM# 532 25 CENTS **Weight:** 4.4300 g. **Comp.:** Nickel Plated Steel **Ruler:** Elizabeth II **Subject:** Saskatchewan **Obv.:** Head right **Size:** 23.9 mm.

Date	Mintage	MS-63	Proof
2005P	19,290,000	7.00	—

KM# 533 25 CENTS **Weight:** 4.4300 g. **Comp.:** Nickel Plated Steel **Ruler:** Elizabeth II **Obv.:** Head right **Rev.:** Stuffed bear in Christmas stocking, colorized **Size:** 23.9 mm.

Date	Mintage	MS-63	Proof
2005P	72,831	10.00	—

KM# 535 25 CENTS **Weight:** 4.4300 g. **Comp.:** Nickel Plated Steel **Ruler:** Elizabeth II **Subject:** Year of the Veteran **Obv.:** Head right **Rev.:** Profile of young and old soldier **Size:** 23.9 mm.

Date	Mintage	MS-63	Proof
2005P	29,390,000	7.00	—

KM# 575 25 CENTS **Weight:** 4.4300 g. **Comp.:** Nickel Plated Steel **Ruler:** Elizabeth II **Subject:** Montreal Canadiens **Obv.:** Head right **Rev.:** Colorized logo **Size:** 23.9 mm.

Date	Mintage	MS-63	Proof
2006P	—	12.50	—

KM# 576 25 CENTS **Weight:** 4.4300 g. **Comp.:** Nickel Plated Steel **Ruler:** Elizabeth II **Subject:** Quebec Winter Carnival **Obv.:** Head right **Rev.:** Snowman, colorized **Size:** 23.9 mm.

Date	Mintage	MS-63	Proof
2006	8,095	10.00	—

KM# 534 25 CENTS **Weight:** 4.4300 g. **Comp.:** Nickel Plated Steel **Ruler:** Elizabeth II **Subject:** Toronto Maple Leafs **Obv.:** Head right **Rev.:** Colorized team logo **Size:** 23.9 mm.

Date	Mintage	MS-63	Proof
2006P	—	12.50	—

KM# 632 25 CENTS **Weight:** 12.6100 g. **Comp.:** Nickel Plated Steel **Ruler:** Elizabeth II **Subject:** Queen Elizabeth II 80th Birthday **Rev.:** Crown, colorized

Date	Mintage	MS-63	Proof
2006	—	25.00	—

KM# 633 25 CENTS **Weight:** 4.4300 g. **Comp.:** Nickel Plated Steel **Ruler:** Elizabeth II **Subject:** Canada Day **Obv.:** Crowned head right **Rev.:** Boy marching with flag, colorized

Date	Mintage	MS-63	Proof
2006P	29,760	6.00	—

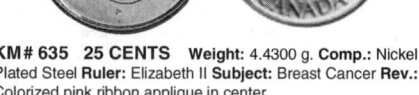

KM# 635 25 CENTS **Weight:** 4.4300 g. **Comp.:** Nickel Plated Steel **Ruler:** Elizabeth II **Subject:** Breast Cancer **Rev.:** Colorized pink ribbon applique in center.

Date	Mintage	MS-63	Proof
2006P	29,798,000	1.50	—

KM# 636 25 CENTS **Comp.:** Nickel Plated Steel **Ruler:** Elizabeth II **Subject:** Medal of Honor **Obv.:** Head right

Date	Mintage	MS-63	Proof
2006	—	7.00	—

KM# 637 25 CENTS **Weight:** 4.4300 g. **Comp.:** Nickel Plated Steel **Ruler:** Elizabeth II **Subject:** Wedding **Rev.:** Colorized flowers

Date	Mintage	MS-63	Proof
2007(ml)	—	5.00	—

KM# 644 25 CENTS **Weight:** 4.4300 g. **Comp.:** Nickel Plated Steel **Ruler:** Elizabeth II **Subject:** Calgary Flames **Obv.:** Head right **Rev.:** Logo

Date	Mintage	MS-63	Proof
2007(ml)	—	12.50	—

KM# 645 25 CENTS **Weight:** 4.4300 g. **Comp.:** Nickel Plated Steel **Ruler:** Elizabeth II **Subject:** Edmonton Oilers **Obv.:** Head right **Rev.:** Logo

Date	Mintage	MS-63	Proof
2007(ml)	—	12.50	—

KM# 647 25 CENTS **Weight:** 4.4300 g. **Comp.:** Nickel Plated Steel **Ruler:** Elizabeth II **Subject:** Santa and Rudolph **Rev.:** Colorized Santa in sled, lead by Rudolph

Date	Mintage	MS-63	Proof
2006P	99,258	5.00	—

KM# 629 25 CENTS **Weight:** 4.4300 g. **Comp.:** Nickel Plated Steel **Ruler:** Elizabeth II **Subject:** Bravery Medal **Obv.:** Crowned head right

Date	Mintage	MS-63	Proof
2006P	20,040,000	2.50	—

KM# 634 25 CENTS **Weight:** 4.4300 g. **Comp.:** Nickel Plated Steel **Ruler:** Elizabeth II **Subject:** Breast Cancer **Rev.:** Ribbons, all colorized **Note:** Sold housed in a bookmark.

Date	Mintage	MS-63	Proof
2006P	40,911	10.00	—

KM# 642 25 CENTS **Weight:** 4.4300 g. **Comp.:** Nickel Plated Steel **Ruler:** Elizabeth II **Subject:** Ottawa Senators **Obv.:** Head right **Rev.:** Logo

Date	Mintage	MS-63	Proof
2006P	—	12.50	—

KM# 643 25 CENTS **Weight:** 4.4300 g. **Comp.:** Nickel Plated Steel **Ruler:** Elizabeth II **Subject:** Vancouver Canucks **Obv.:** Head right **Rev.:** Logo

Date	Mintage	MS-63	Proof
2007(ml)	—	12.50	—

KM# 693 25 CENTS **Weight:** 12.6100 g. **Comp.:** Nickel Plated Steel **Ruler:** Elizabeth II **Obv.:** Elizabeth II **Rev.:** Multicolor Ruby-throated Hummingbird and flower **Edge:** Plain **Size:** 35 mm.

Date	Mintage	MS-63	Proof
2007	25,000	25.00	—

KM# 694 25 CENTS **Weight:** 12.6100 g. **Comp.:** Nickel Plated Steel **Ruler:** Elizabeth II **Subject:** Red-breasted Nuthatch **Obv.:** Head right **Obv. Leg.:** ELIZABETH II - D • G • REGINA **Obv. Des.:** Susanna Blunt **Rev.:** Nuthatch perched on pine branch multicolor **Rev. Leg.:** CANADA **Rev. Des.:** Arnold Nogy **Edge:** Plain **Size:** 35.0 mm.

Date	Mintage	MS-63	Proof
2007(ml)	—	25.00	—

KM# 682 25 CENTS **Weight:** 4.4300 g. **Comp.:** Nickel Plated Steel **Ruler:** Elizabeth II **Subject:** Curling **Obv.:** Head right

Date	Mintage	MS-63	Proof
2007	—	7.50	—

KM# 683 25 CENTS **Weight:** 4.4300 g. **Comp.:** Nickel Plated Steel **Ruler:** Elizabeth II **Subject:** Ice Hockey **Obv.:** Head right

Date	Mintage	MS-63	Proof
2007	—	7.50	—

KM# 684 25 CENTS **Weight:** 4.4300 g. **Comp.:** Nickel Plated Steel **Ruler:** Elizabeth II **Subject:** Paraolympic Winter Games **Obv.:** Head right **Rev.:** Wheelchair curling

Date	Mintage	MS-63	Proof
2007	—	7.50	—

KM# 685 25 CENTS **Weight:** 4.4300 g. **Comp.:** Nickel Plated Steel **Ruler:** Elizabeth II **Subject:** Biathlon **Obv.:** Head right

Date	Mintage	MS-63	Proof
2007	—	7.50	—

KM# 686 25 CENTS **Weight:** 4.4300 g. **Comp.:** Nickel Plated Steel **Ruler:** Elizabeth II **Subject:** Alpine Skiing **Obv.:** Head right

Date	Mintage	MS-63	Proof
2007	—	7.50	—

KM# 638 25 CENTS **Weight:** 4.4300 g. **Comp.:** Nickel Plated Steel **Ruler:** Elizabeth II **Subject:** Birthday **Rev.:** Colorized baloons

Date	Mintage	MS-63	Proof
2006(ml)	—	5.00	—

KM# 639 25 CENTS **Weight:** 4.4300 g. **Comp.:** Nickel Plated Steel **Ruler:** Elizabeth II **Subject:** Baby birth **Rev.:** Colorized baby rattle

Date	Mintage	MS-63	Proof
2006(ml)	—	5.00	—

KM# 640 25 CENTS **Weight:** 4.4300 g. **Comp.:** Nickel Plated Steel **Ruler:** Elizabeth II **Subject:** Oh Canada **Obv.:** Head right **Rev.:** Maple leaf, colorized

Date	Mintage	MS-63	Proof
2006(ml)	—	8.50	—

KM# 641 25 CENTS **Weight:** 4.4300 g. **Comp.:** Nickel Plated Steel **Ruler:** Elizabeth II **Subject:** Congratulations **Obv.:** Head right

Date	Mintage	MS-63	Proof
2006(ml)	—	8.00	—

KM# 290 50 CENTS **Weight:** 6.9000 g. **Comp.:** Nickel **Ruler:** Elizabeth II **Obv.:** Crowned head right **Obv. Des.:** Dora dePedery-Hunt **Rev.:** Redesigned arms **Rev. Des.:** Cathy Bursey-Sabourin **Size:** 27.13 mm.

Date	Mintage	MS-60	MS-63	Proof
2001P	—	—	1.50	—
2001P Proof	—	—	—	5.00
2003P	—	—	1.50	—
2003P Proof	—	—	—	5.00

KM# 421 50 CENTS **Weight:** 9.3000 g. **Comp.:** 0.9250 Silver 0.2766 oz. ASW **Series:** Festivals - Nunavut **Obv.:** Crowned head right **Rev.:** Dancer, dog sled and snowmobiles **Rev. Des.:** John Mardon **Edge:** Reeded **Size:** 27.13 mm.

Date	Mintage	MS-63	Proof
2001 Proof	58,123	—	8.50

KM# 422 50 CENTS **Weight:** 9.3000 g. **Comp.:** 0.9250 Silver 0.2766 oz. ASW **Series:** Festivals - Newfoundland **Obv.:** Crowned head right **Rev.:** Sailor and musical people **Rev. Des.:** David Craig **Edge:** Reeded **Size:** 27.13 mm.

Date	Mintage	MS-63	Proof
2001 Proof	58,123	—	8.50

KM# 290b 50 CENTS **Weight:** 6.9000 g. **Comp.:** Nickel Plated Steel **Ruler:** Elizabeth II **Obv.:** Crowned head right **Obv. Des.:** Dora dePedery-Hunt **Rev.:** Redesigned arms **Rev. Des.:** Cathy Bursey-Sabourin **Size:** 27.13 mm.

Date	Mintage	MS-63	Proof
2001 P	389,000	1.50	—
2003 P	—	5.00	—

KM# 290a 50 CENTS **Weight:** 11.6380 g. **Comp.:** 0.9250 Silver 0.3461 oz. ASW **Ruler:** Elizabeth II **Obv.:** Crowned head right **Obv. Des.:** Dora dePedery-Hunt **Rev.:** Redesigned arms **Rev. Des.:** Cathy Bursey-Sabourin **Size:** 27.13 mm.

Date	Mintage	MS-63	Proof
2001 Proof	—	—	10.00
2003 Proof	—	—	10.00

KM# 420 50 CENTS **Weight:** 9.3000 g. **Comp.:** 0.9250 Silver 0.2766 oz. ASW **Ruler:** Elizabeth II **Series:** Festivals - Quebec **Obv.:** Crowned head right **Rev.:** Snowman and Chateau Frontenac **Rev. Des.:** Sylvie Daigneault **Edge:** Reeded **Size:** 27.13 mm.

Date	Mintage	MS-63	Proof
2001 Proof	58,123	—	8.50

KM# 423 50 CENTS **Weight:** 9.3000 g. **Comp.:** 0.9250 Silver 0.2766 oz. ASW **Ruler:** Elizabeth II **Series:** Festivals - Prince Edward Island **Obv.:** Crowned head right **Rev.:** Family, juggler and building **Rev. Des.:** Brenda Whiteway **Edge:** Reeded **Size:** 27.13 mm.

Date	Mintage	MS-63	Proof
2001 Proof	58,123	—	8.50

KM# 424 50 CENTS **Weight:** 9.3000 g. **Comp.:** 0.9250 Silver 0.2766 oz. ASW **Ruler:** Elizabeth II **Series:** Folklore - The Sled **Obv.:** Crowned head right **Rev.:** Family scene **Rev. Des.:** Valentina Hotz-Entin **Edge:** Reeded **Size:** 27.13 mm.

Date	Mintage	MS-63	Proof
2001 Proof	28,979	—	9.00

KM# 425 50 CENTS **Weight:** 9.3000 g. **Comp.:** 0.9250 Silver 0.2766 oz. ASW **Ruler:** Elizabeth II **Series:** Folklore - The Maiden's Cave **Obv.:** Crowned head right **Rev.:** Woman shouting **Rev. Des.:** Peter Kiss **Edge:** Reeded **Size:** 27.13 mm.

Date	Mintage	MS-63	Proof
2001 Proof	28,979	—	9.00

KM# 426 50 CENTS **Weight:** 9.3000 g. **Comp.:** 0.9250 Silver 0.2766 oz. ASW **Ruler:** Elizabeth II **Series:** Folklore - The Small Jumpers **Obv.:** Crowned head right **Rev.:** Jumping children on seashore **Rev. Des.:** Miynki Tanobe **Edge:** Reeded **Size:** 27.13 mm.

Date	Mintage	MS-63	Proof
2001 Proof	28,979	—	9.00

KM# 509 50 CENTS **Weight:** 6.9000 g. **Comp.:** Nickel Plated Steel **Ruler:** Elizabeth II **Obv.:** Crowned head right **Rev.:** National arms **Edge:** Reeded **Size:** 27.13 mm.

Date	Mintage	MS-63	Proof
ND(2001) P	—	1.50	—

KM# 444 50 CENTS **Weight:** 6.9000 g. **Comp.:** Nickel Plated Steel **Ruler:** Elizabeth II **Subject:** Queen's Golden Jubilee **Obv.:** Coronation crowned head right and monogram **Rev.:** Canadian arms **Rev. Des.:** Bursey Sabourin **Edge:** Reeded **Size:** 27.13 mm.

Date	Mintage	MS-63	Proof
ND(2002)P	1,440,000	2.50	—

KM# 444a 50 CENTS **Weight:** 9.3000 g. **Comp.:** 0.9250 Silver 0.2766 oz. ASW **Ruler:** Elizabeth II **Subject:** Elizabeth II Golden Jubilee **Obv.:** Crowned head right, Jubilee commemorative dates 1952-2002 **Size:** 27.13 mm.

Date	Mintage	MS-63	Proof
ND(2002)	100,000	—	17.50

Note: In proof sets only

KM# 444b 50 CENTS **Weight:** 9.3000 g. **Comp.:** 0.9250 Gold Plated Silver 0.2766 oz. ASW AGW **Ruler:** Elizabeth II **Subject:** Queen's Golden Jubilee **Obv.:** Crowned head right and monogram **Rev.:** Canadian arms **Edge:** Reeded **Size:** 27.13 mm. **Note:** Special 24 karat gold plated issue of KM#444.

Date	Mintage	MS-63	Proof
ND(2002) Proof	32,642	—	35.00

KM# 454 50 CENTS **Weight:** 9.3000 g. **Comp.:** 0.9250 Silver 0.2766 oz. ASW **Ruler:** Elizabeth II **Subject:** Nova Scotia Annapolis Valley Apple Blossom Festival **Obv.:** Crowned head right **Rev. Des.:** Bonnie Ross **Size:** 27.13 mm.

Date	Mintage	MS-63	Proof
2002 Proof	59,998	—	8.50

KM# 455 50 CENTS **Weight:** 9.3000 g. **Comp.:** 0.9250 Silver 0.2766 oz. ASW **Ruler:** Elizabeth II **Subject:** Stratford Festival **Obv.:** Crowned head right **Rev.:** Couple with building in background **Rev. Des.:** Laurie McGaw **Size:** 27.13 mm.

Date	Mintage	MS-63	Proof
2002 Proof	59,998	—	8.50

KM# 456 50 CENTS **Weight:** 9.3000 g. **Comp.:** 0.9250 Silver 0.2766 oz. ASW **Ruler:** Elizabeth II **Subject:** Folklorama **Obv.:** Crowned head right **Rev. Des.:** William Woodruff **Size:** 27.13 mm.

Date	Mintage	MS-63	Proof
2002 Proof	59,998	—	8.50

KM# 457 50 CENTS **Weight:** 9.3000 g. **Comp.:** 0.9250 Silver 0.2766 oz. ASW **Ruler:** Elizabeth II **Subject:** Calgary Stampede **Obv.:** Crowned head right **Rev. Des.:** Stan Witten **Size:** 27.13 mm.

Date	Mintage	MS-63	Proof
2002 Proof	59,998	—	8.50

KM# 458 50 CENTS **Weight:** 9.3000 g. **Comp.:** 0.9250 Silver 0.2766 oz. ASW **Ruler:** Elizabeth II **Subject:** Squamish Days Logger Sports **Obv.:** Crowned head right **Rev. Des.:** Jose Osio **Size:** 27.13 mm.

Date	Mintage	MS-63	Proof
2002 Proof	59,998	—	8.50

KM# 459 50 CENTS **Weight:** 9.3000 g. **Comp.:** 0.9250 Silver 0.2766 oz. ASW **Ruler:** Elizabeth II **Series:** Folklore and Legends **Obv.:** Crowned head right **Rev.:** The Shoemaker in Heaven **Rev. Des.:** Francine Gravel **Size:** 27.13 mm.

Date	Mintage	MS-63	Proof
2002 Proof	19,267	—	9.50

KM# 460 50 CENTS **Weight:** 9.3000 g. **Comp.:** 0.9250 Silver 0.2766 oz. ASW **Ruler:** Elizabeth II **Series:** Folklore and Legends **Subject:** The Ghost Ship **Obv.:** Crowned head right **Rev. Des.:** Colette Boivin **Size:** 27.13 mm.

Date	Mintage	MS-63	Proof
2002 Proof	19,267	—	9.50

KM# 461 50 CENTS **Weight:** 9.3000 g. **Comp.:** 0.9250 Silver 0.2766 oz. ASW **Ruler:** Elizabeth II **Series:** Folklore and Legends **Subject:** The Pig That Wouldn't Get Over the Stile **Obv.:** Crowned head right **Rev. Des.:** Laura Jolicoeur **Size:** 27.13 mm.

Date	Mintage	MS-63	Proof
2002 Proof	19,267	—	9.50

KM# 494 50 CENTS **Weight:** 6.9000 g. **Comp.:** Nickel Plated Steel **Ruler:** Elizabeth II **Obv.:** Crowned head right **Obv. Des.:** Susanna Blunt **Rev. Des.:** Cathy Bursey-Sabourin **Size:** 27.13 mm.

Date	Mintage	MS-63	Proof
2003W	—	5.00	—
2003W Proof	—	—	7.50
2004P	—	5.00	—
2004P Proof	—	—	7.50
2005P	—	1.50	—
2005P Proof	—	—	5.00
2006P	—	1.50	—
2006P Proof	—	—	5.00
2006(ml)	—	1.50	—
2007(ml) Proof	—	—	5.00

KM# 472 50 CENTS **Weight:** 11.6200 g. **Comp.:** 0.9250 Silver 0.3456 oz. ASW **Ruler:** Elizabeth II **Subject:** 50th Anniversary of the Coronation of Elizabeth II **Obv.:** Crowned head right, Jubilee commemorative dates 1952-2002 **Obv. Des.:** Mary Gillick **Size:** 27.13 mm.

Date	Mintage	MS-63	Proof
ND(2003)	30,000	15.00	—

Note: In coronation proof sets only

KM# 475 50 CENTS **Comp.:** 0.9250 Silver **Ruler:** Elizabeth II **Obv.:** Crowned head right **Obv. Des.:** Dora dePédery-Hunt **Rev.:** Golden daffodil **Rev. Des.:** Christie Paquet, Stan Witten **Size:** 27.13 mm.

Date	Mintage	MS-63	Proof
2003 Proof	55,000	—	15.00

KM# 476 50 CENTS **Weight:** 9.3000 g. **Comp.:** 0.9250 Silver 0.2766 oz. ASW **Ruler:** Elizabeth II **Subject:** Yukon International Storytelling Festival **Obv.:** Crowned head right **Obv. Des.:** Dora dePédery-Hunt **Rev. Des.:** Ken Anderson, Jose Oslo **Size:** 27.13 mm.

Date	Mintage	MS-63	Proof
2003 Proof	—	—	11.00

KM# 477 50 CENTS **Weight:** 9.3000 g. **Comp.:** 0.9250 Silver 0.2766 oz. ASW **Ruler:** Elizabeth II **Subject:** Festival Acadien de Caraquet **Obv.:** Crowned head right **Obv. Des.:** Dora dePédery-Hunt **Rev.:** Sailboat and couple **Rev. Des.:** Susan Taylor, Hudson Design Group **Size:** 27.13 mm.

Date	Mintage	MS-63	Proof
2003 Proof	—	—	11.00

KM# 478 50 CENTS **Weight:** 9.3000 g. **Comp.:** 0.9250 Silver 0.2766 oz. ASW **Ruler:** Elizabeth II **Subject:** Back to Batoche **Obv.:** Crowned head right **Obv. Des.:** Dora dePédery-Hunt **Rev. Des.:** David Hannan, Stan Witten **Size:** 27.13 mm.

Date	Mintage	MS-63	Proof
2003 Proof	—	—	11.00

KM# 479 50 CENTS **Weight:** 9.3000 g. **Comp.:** 0.9250 Silver 0.2766 oz. ASW **Ruler:** Elizabeth II **Subject:** Great Northern Arts Festival **Obv.:** Crowned head right **Obv. Des.:** Dora dePédery-Hunt **Rev. Des.:** Dawn Oman, Susan Taylor **Size:** 27.13 mm.

Date	Mintage	MS-63	Proof
2003 Proof	—	—	11.00

KM# 526 50 CENTS **Weight:** 1.2700 g. **Comp.:** 0.9999 Gold 0.0408 oz. AGW **Ruler:** Elizabeth II **Subject:** Moose **Obv.:** Head right **Rev.:** Moose head facing right **Size:** 14 mm.

Date	Mintage	MS-63	Proof
2004 Proof	—	—	85.00

KM# 494a 50 CENTS **Weight:** 9.3000 g. **Comp.:** 0.9250 Silver 0.2766 oz. ASW **Ruler:** Elizabeth II **Obv.:** Crowned head right **Obv. Des.:** Susanna Blunt **Rev.:** Canadian coat of arms **Edge:** Reeded **Size:** 27.13 mm.

Date	Mintage	MS-63	Proof
2004 Proof	—	—	7.50

KM# 606 50 CENTS **Weight:** 9.3000 g. **Comp.:** 0.9250 Silver 0.2766 oz. ASW **Ruler:** Elizabeth II **Obv.:** Head right **Obv. Des.:** Susanna Blunt **Rev.:** Clouded Sulphur Butterfly, hologram **Rev. Des.:** Susan Taylor **Size:** 27.13 mm.

Date	Mintage	MS-63	Proof
2004 Proof	15,281	—	37.50

KM# 536 50 CENTS **Weight:** 9.3000 g. **Comp.:** 0.9250 Silver With Partial Gold Plating 0.2766 oz. **Ruler:** Elizabeth II **Subject:** Golden rose **Obv.:** Head right **Obv. Des.:** Susanna Blunt **Rev. Des.:** Christie Paquet **Size:** 27.13 mm.

Date	Mintage	MS-63	Proof
2005 Proof	17,418	—	19.00

KM# 537 50 CENTS **Weight:** 9.3000 g. **Comp.:** 0.9250 Silver 0.2766 oz. ASW **Ruler:** Elizabeth II **Subject:** Great Spangled Fritillary butterfly, hologram **Obv.:** Head right **Obv. Des.:** Susanna Blunt **Rev. Des.:** Jianping Yan **Size:** 27.13 mm.

Date	Mintage	MS-63	Proof
2005 Proof	20,000	—	37.50

KM# 538 50 CENTS **Weight:** 9.3000 g. **Comp.:** 0.9250 Silver 0.2766 oz. ASW **Ruler:** Elizabeth II **Subject:** Toronto Maple Leafs **Obv.:** Head right **Obv. Des.:** Susanna Blunt **Rev.:** Darryl Sittler **Size:** 27.13 mm.

Date	Mintage	MS-63	Proof
2005	25,000	17.50	—

KM# 539 50 CENTS **Weight:** 9.3000 g. **Comp.:** 0.9250 Silver 0.2766 oz. ASW **Ruler:** Elizabeth II **Subject:** Toronto Maple Leafs **Obv.:** Head right **Obv. Des.:** Susanna Blunt **Rev.:** Dave Keon **Size:** 27.13 mm.

Date	Mintage	MS-63	Proof
2005	25,000	17.50	—

KM# 540 50 CENTS **Weight:** 9.3000 g. **Comp.:** 0.9250 Silver 0.2766 oz. ASW **Ruler:** Elizabeth II **Subject:** Toronto Maple Leafs **Obv.:** Head right **Obv. Des.:** Susanna Blunt **Rev.:** Jonny Bover **Size:** 27.13 mm.

Date	Mintage	MS-63	Proof
2005	25,000	17.50	—

KM# 541 50 CENTS **Weight:** 9.3000 g. **Comp.:** 0.9250 Silver 0.2766 oz. ASW **Ruler:** Elizabeth II **Subject:** Toronto Maple Leafs **Obv.:** Head right **Obv. Des.:** Susanna Blunt **Rev.:** Tim Horton **Size:** 27.13 mm.

Date	Mintage	MS-63	Proof
2005	25,000	17.50	—

KM# 542 50 CENTS **Weight:** 1.2700 g. **Comp.:** 0.9999 Gold 0.0408 oz. AGW **Ruler:** Elizabeth II **Subject:** Voyageurs **Obv.:** Head right

Date	Mintage	MS-63	Proof
2005 Proof	—	—	65.00

KM# 543 50 CENTS **Comp.:** Silver **Ruler:** Elizabeth II **Subject:** WWII - Battle of Britain **Obv.:** Head right **Rev.:** Fighter plane in sky

Date	Mintage	MS-63	Proof
2005	—	22.50	—

KM# 544 50 CENTS **Weight:** 9.3000 g. **Comp.:** 0.9250 Silver 0.2766 oz. ASW **Ruler:** Elizabeth II **Subject:** WWII - Battle of Scheldt **Obv.:** Head right **Obv. Des.:** Susanna Blunt **Rev.:** Four soldiers walking down road **Rev. Des.:** Peter Mossman **Size:** 27.13 mm.

Date	Mintage	MS-63	Proof
2005	20,000	19.00	—

KM# 545 50 CENTS **Weight:** 9.3000 g. **Comp.:** 0.9250 Silver 0.2766 oz. ASW **Ruler:** Elizabeth II **Subject:** WWII - Battle of the Atlantic **Obv.:** Head right **Obv. Des.:** Susanna Blunt **Rev.:** Merchant ship sinking **Rev. Des.:** Peter Mossman **Size:** 27.13 mm.

Date	Mintage	MS-63	Proof
2005	20,000	19.00	—

KM# 546 50 CENTS **Weight:** 9.3000 g. **Comp.:** 0.9250 Silver 0.2766 oz. ASW **Ruler:** Elizabeth II **Subject:** WWII - Conquest of Sicily **Obv.:** Head right **Obv. Des.:** Susanna Blunt **Rev.:** Tank among town ruins **Rev. Des.:** Peter Mossman **Size:** 27.13 mm.

Date	Mintage	MS-63	Proof
2005	20,000	19.00	—

KM# 547 50 CENTS **Weight:** 9.3000 g. **Comp.:** 0.9250 Silver 0.2766 oz. ASW **Ruler:** Elizabeth II **Subject:** WWII - Liberation of the Netherlands **Obv.:** Head right **Obv. Des.:** Susanna Blunt **Rev.:** Soldiers in parade, one holding flag **Rev. Des.:** Peter Mossman **Size:** 27.13 mm.

Date	Mintage	MS-63	Proof
2005	20,000	19.00	—

KM# 548 50 CENTS **Weight:** 9.3000 g. **Comp.:** 0.9250 Silver 0.2766 oz. ASW **Ruler:** Elizabeth II **Subject:** WWII - Raid of Dieppe **Obv.:** Head right **Obv. Des.:** Susanna Blunt **Rev.:** Three soldiers exiting landing craft **Rev. Des.:** Peter Mossman **Size:** 27.13 mm.

Date	Mintage	MS-63	Proof
2005	20,000	19.00	—

KM# 577 50 CENTS **Weight:** 9.3000 g. **Comp.:** 0.9250 Silver 0.2766 oz. ASW **Ruler:** Elizabeth II **Subject:** Montreal Canadiens **Obv.:** Head right **Obv. Des.:** Susanna Blunt **Rev.:** Guy LaFleur **Size:** 27.13 mm.

Date	Mintage	MS-63	Proof
2005	25,000	17.50	—

KM# 578 50 CENTS **Weight:** 9.3000 g. **Comp.:** 0.9250 Silver 0.2766 oz. ASW **Ruler:** Elizabeth II **Subject:** Montreal Canadiens **Obv.:** Head right **Obv. Des.:** Susanna Blunt **Rev.:** Jaque Plante **Size:** 27.13 mm.

Date	Mintage	MS-63	Proof
2005	25,000	17.50	—

KM# 579 50 CENTS **Weight:** 9.3000 g. **Comp.:** 0.9250 Silver 0.2766 oz. ASW **Ruler:** Elizabeth II **Subject:** Montreal Canadiens **Obv.:** Head right **Obv. Des.:** Susanna Blunt **Rev.:** Jean Beliveau **Size:** 27.13 mm.

Date	Mintage	MS-63	Proof
2005	25,000	17.50	—

KM# 580 50 CENTS **Weight:** 9.3000 g. **Comp.:** 0.9250 Silver 0.2766 oz. ASW **Ruler:** Elizabeth II **Subject:** Montreal Canadiens **Obv.:** Head right **Obv. Des.:** Susanna Blunt **Rev.:** Maurice Richard **Size:** 27.13 mm.

Date	Mintage	MS-63	Proof
2005	25,000	17.50	—

KM# 599 50 CENTS **Weight:** 9.3000 g. **Comp.:** 0.9250 Silver 0.2766 oz. ASW **Ruler:** Elizabeth II **Subject:** Monarch Butterfly, colorized **Obv.:** Head right **Obv. Des.:** Susanna Blunt **Rev. Des.:** Susan Taylor **Size:** 27.13 mm.

Date	Mintage	MS-63	Proof
2005 Proof	20,000	—	37.50

KM# 648 50 CENTS **Weight:** 9.3000 g. **Comp.:** 0.9250 Silver With Partial Gold Plating 0.2766 oz. ASW **Ruler:** Elizabeth II **Subject:** Golden Daisy **Obv.:** Head right

Date	Mintage	MS-63	Proof
2006	17,771	10.00	—

KM# 649 50 CENTS **Weight:** 9.3000 g. **Comp.:** 0.9250 Silver 0.2766 oz. ASW **Ruler:** Elizabeth II **Subject:** Short tailed swallotail **Obv.:** Head right **Rev.:** Colorized butterfly

Date	Mintage	MS-63	Proof
2006	20,000	10.00	—

KM# 650 50 CENTS **Weight:** 9.3000 g. **Comp.:** 0.9250 Silver 0.2766 oz. ASW **Ruler:** Elizabeth II **Subject:** Butterfly hologram **Obv.:** Head right **Rev.:** Silvery blue hologram

Date	Mintage	MS-63	Proof
2006	16,000	10.00	—

KM# 651 50 CENTS **Weight:** 9.3000 g. **Comp.:** 0.9250 Silver 0.2766 oz. ASW **Ruler:** Elizabeth II **Subject:** Cowboy **Obv.:** Head right

Date	Mintage	MS-63	Proof
2006	—	17.50	—

KM# 704 50 CENTS **Comp.:** Silver **Ruler:** Elizabeth II **Rev.:** Forget-me-not flower

KM# 186 DOLLAR **Weight:** 7.0000 g. **Comp.:** Aureate-Bronze Plated Nickel **Ruler:** Elizabeth II **Obv.:** Crowned head right **Obv. Des.:** Dora dePedery-Hunt **Rev.:** Loon right, date and denomination **Rev. Des.:** Robert R. Carmichael **Shape:** 11-sided **Size:** 26.5 mm.

Date	Mintage	MS-63	Proof
2001	—	2.50	—
2001 Proof	—	—	8.00
2002	—	4.50	—
2002 Proof	—	—	7.50
2003	—	5.50	—
2003 Proof	100,000	—	12.00

KM# 414 DOLLAR **Weight:** 25.1750 g. **Comp.:** 0.9250 Silver 0.7487 oz. ASW **Ruler:** Elizabeth II **Subject:** National Ballet **Obv.:** Crowned head right **Rev.:** Ballet dancers **Rev. Des.:** Scott McKowen **Edge:** Reeded **Size:** 36 mm.

Date	Mintage	MS-63	P/L	Proof
2001	65,000	9.00	16.50	—
2001 Proof	225,000	—	—	21.50

KM# 434 DOLLAR **Weight:** 25.1750 g. **Comp.:** 0.9250 Silver 0.7487 oz. ASW **Ruler:** Elizabeth II **Obv.:** Crowned head right **Rev.:** Recycled 1911 pattern dollar design: denomination, country name and dates in crowned wreath. **Edge:** Reeded. **Size:** 36 mm.

Date	Mintage	MS-63	P/L	Proof
ND(2001) Proof	24,996	—	—	55.00

KM# 443 DOLLAR **Weight:** 25.1750 g. **Comp.:** 0.9250 Silver 0.7487 oz. ASW **Ruler:** Elizabeth II **Subject:** Queen's Golden Jubilee **Obv.:** Crowned head right, with anniversary date at left **Obv. Des.:** Dora dePédery-Hunt **Rev.:** Queen in her coach and a view of the coach, denomination below **Edge:** Reeded **Size:** 36 mm.

Date	Mintage	MS-63	P/L	Proof
ND(2002)	65,140	—	16.50	—
ND(2002) Proof	29,688	—	—	21.50

KM# 186a DOLLAR **Comp.:** Gold Plated Aureate-Bronze Plated Nickel **Ruler:** Elizabeth II **Subject:** Olympic Win **Size:** 26.5 mm.

Date	Mintage	MS-63	Proof
2002 Proof	—	—	40.00

KM# 443a DOLLAR **Weight:** 25.1800 g. **Comp.:** 0.9250 Gold Plated Silver 0.7488 oz. ASW AGW **Ruler:** Elizabeth II **Subject:** Queen's Golden Jubilee **Obv.:** Crowned head right with anniversary date **Rev.:** Queen in her coach and a view of the coach **Edge:** Reeded **Size:** 36 mm. **Note:** Special 24 karat gold plated issue of KM#443.

Date	Mintage	MS-63	Proof
ND(2002) Proof	32,642	—	40.00

KM# 462 DOLLAR **Weight:** 7.0000 g. **Comp.:** Aureate-Bronze Plated Nickel **Ruler:** Elizabeth II **Obv.:** Commemorative dates 1952-2002 **Obv. Des.:** Dora dePédery-Hunt **Rev.:** Family of Loons

Date	Mintage	MS-63	Proof
ND(2002)	67,672	10.00	—

Note: In Specimen Sets only

KM# 467 DOLLAR **Weight:** 7.0000 g. **Comp.:** Aureate-Bronze Plated Nickel **Ruler:** Elizabeth II **Subject:** Elizabeth II Golden Jubilee **Obv.:** Crowned head right, Jubilee commemorative dates 1952-2002 **Obv. Des.:** Dora dePédery-Hunt

Date	Mintage	MS-63	Proof
ND(2002)	—	2.50	—
ND(2002) Proof	—	—	8.00

KM# 503 DOLLAR **Weight:** 25.1750 g. **Comp.:** 0.9250 Silver 0.7487 oz. ASW **Ruler:** Elizabeth II **Subject:** Queen Mother **Obv.:** Crowned head right **Obv. Des.:** Dora de Pedery-Hunt **Rev.:** Queen Mother facing **Size:** 36 mm.

Date	Mintage	MS-63	Proof
2002 Proof	9,994	—	300

KM# 495 DOLLAR **Weight:** 7.0000 g. **Comp.:** Aureate-Bronze Plated Nickel **Ruler:** Elizabeth II **Obv.:** Crowned head right **Obv. Des.:** Susanna Blunt **Rev. Des.:** Robert R. Carmichael **Size:** 26.5 mm.

Date	Mintage	MS-63	Proof
2003	5,102,000	5.50	—
2003	—	—	7.50
2003W	—	7.50	—
2004	3,409,000	3.00	—
2004 Proof	—	—	12.00
2005	—	3.00	—
2005 Proof	—	—	7.50
2006	—	3.00	—
2006 Proof	—	—	7.50
2006(ml)	—	3.00	—
2006(ml) Proof	—	—	7.50

KM# 450 DOLLAR **Weight:** 25.1750 g. **Comp.:** 0.9999 Silver 0.8093 oz. ASW **Ruler:** Elizabeth II **Subject:** Cobalt Mining Centennial **Obv.:** Queens portrait right **Obv. Des.:** Dora dePédery-Hunt **Rev.:** Mine tower and fox **Edge:** Reeded **Size:** 36 mm.

Date	Mintage	MS-63	Proof
ND(2003)	51,130	20.00	—
ND(2003) Proof	88,536	—	28.00

KM# 473 DOLLAR **Weight:** 25.1750 g. **Comp.:** 0.9999 Silver 0.8093 oz. ASW **Ruler:** Elizabeth II **Subject:** 50th Anniversary of the Coronation of Elizabeth II **Obv.:** 1953 effigy of the Queen, Jubilee Commemorative dates 1953-2003 **Obv. Des.:** Mary Gillick **Rev.:** Voyageur, date and denomination below

Date	Mintage	MS-63	Proof
ND(2003)	29,586	35.00	—

Note: In Coronation Proof sets only

KM# 480 DOLLAR **Weight:** 25.1750 g. **Comp.:** 0.9999 Silver 0.8093 oz. ASW **Ruler:** Elizabeth II **Subject:** Coronation of Queen Elizabeth II **Obv.:** Head right **Rev.:** Voyaguers **Rev. Des.:** Emanuel Hahn

Date	Mintage	MS-63	Proof
ND2003 Proof	21,400	—	38.00

KM# 513 DOLLAR **Weight:** 7.0000 g. **Comp.:** Aureate-Bronze Plated Nickel **Ruler:** Elizabeth II **Subject:** Olympics **Obv.:** Crowned head right **Rev.:** Maple leaf, Olympic flame and rings above loon **Edge:** Plain **Shape:** 11-sided **Size:** 26.5 mm.

Date	Mintage	MS-63	Proof
2004	6,526,000	8.00	—

KM# 513a DOLLAR **Weight:** 9.3100 g. **Comp.:** 0.9250 Silver 0.2769 oz. ASW **Ruler:** Elizabeth II **Subject:** Olympics **Obv.:** Crowned head right **Rev.:** Multicolor maple leaf, Olympic flame and rings above loon **Edge:** Plain **Shape:** 11-sided **Size:** 26.5 mm.

Date	Mintage	MS-63	Proof
2004 Proof	19,994	—	50.00

KM# 507 DOLLAR **Weight:** 7.0000 g. **Comp.:** Aureate-Bronze Plated Nickel **Ruler:** Elizabeth II **Obv.:** Bare head right, date below **Obv. Des.:** Susanna Blunt **Rev.:** Loon **Edge:** Plain **Shape:** 11-sided **Size:** 26.5 mm.

Date	Mintage	MS-63	Proof
2004 Proof	12,550	—	12.50

KM# 512 DOLLAR **Weight:** 25.1750 g. **Comp.:** 0.9999 Silver 0.8093 oz. ASW **Ruler:** Elizabeth II **Subject:** First French Settlement in America **Obv.:** Crowned head right **Rev.:** Sailing ship **Edge:** Reeded **Size:** 36 mm.

Date	Mintage	MS-63	Proof
2004	42,582	30.00	—
2004 Fleur-dis-lis	8,315	50.00	—

Date	Mintage	MS-63	Proof
2004 Proof	106,974	—	40.00

KM# 552 DOLLAR **Weight:** 7.0000 g. **Comp.:** Aureate-Bronze Plated Nickel **Ruler:** Elizabeth II **Subject:** Terry Fox **Obv.:** Head right

Date	Mintage	MS-63	Proof
2005	1,290,900	3.50	—

KM# 549 DOLLAR **Weight:** 25.1750 g. **Comp.:** 0.9250 Silver 0.7487 oz. ASW **Ruler:** Elizabeth II **Subject:** 40th Anniversary of National Flag **Obv.:** Head right **Obv. Des.:** Susanna Blunt **Rev. Des.:** William Woodruff

Date	Mintage	MS-63	Proof
2005	50,948	22.50	—
2005 Proof	95,431	—	32.50

KM# 549a DOLLAR **Weight:** 7.0000 g. **Comp.:** 0.9250 Silver With Partial Gold Plating 0.2082 oz. **Ruler:** Elizabeth II **Subject:** 40th Anniversary of National Flag **Obv.:** Head right

Date	Mintage	MS-63	Proof
2005	62,483	65.00	—

KM# 553 DOLLAR **Weight:** 7.0000 g. **Comp.:** Aureate-Bronze Plated Nickel **Ruler:** Elizabeth II **Subject:** Tuffed Puffin **Obv.:** Head right **Obv. Des.:** Susanna Blunt

Date	Mintage	MS-63	Proof
2005	40,000	30.00	—

Note: In Specimen sets only

KM# 581 DOLLAR **Weight:** 7.0000 g. **Comp.:** 0.9250 Silver 0.2082 oz. ASW **Ruler:** Elizabeth II **Subject:** Lullabies Loonie **Obv.:** Head right **Obv. Des.:** Susanna Blunt **Rev.:** Loon and moon, teddy bear in stars

Date	Mintage	MS-63	Proof
2006	—	3.50	—

KM# 582 DOLLAR **Weight:** 7.0000 g. **Comp.:** Aureate-Bronze Plated Nickel **Ruler:** Elizabeth II **Subject:** Snowy owl **Obv.:** Head right **Obv. Des.:** Susanna Blunt **Rev.:** Snowy owl with year above

Date	Mintage	MS-63	Proof
2006	40,000	30.00	—

Note: In specimen sets only

KM# 653 DOLLAR **Weight:** 25.1750 g. **Comp.:** 0.9250 Silver 0.7487 oz. ASW **Ruler:** Elizabeth II **Subject:** Thayendanegea **Obv.:** Head right

Date	Mintage	MS-63	Proof
2006(ml)	35,000	30.00	—
2006(ml) Proof	65,000	—	40.00

KM# 656 DOLLAR **Weight:** 28.1750 g. **Comp.:** 0.9250 Silver 0.8379 oz. ASW **Ruler:** Elizabeth II **Subject:** Medal of Bravery **Obv.:** Head right

Date	Mintage	MS-63	Proof
2006	7,846	20.00	—

KM# 656a DOLLAR **Weight:** 28.1750 g. **Comp.:** 0.9250 Silver And Multi-Color Enamel 0.8379 oz. **Ruler:** Elizabeth II **Subject:** Medal of Bravery **Obv.:** Head right **Rev.:** Maple leaf within wreath. Colorized.

Date	Mintage	MS-63	Proof
2006	4,951	20.00	—

KM# 630 DOLLAR **Weight:** 7.0000 g. **Comp.:** 0.9250 Silver And Multi-Color Enamel 0.2082 oz. **Ruler:** Elizabeth II **Subject:** Olympic Games **Obv.:** Crowned head right

Date	Mintage	MS-63	Proof
2006	19,956	30.00	—

KM# 583 DOLLAR **Weight:** 25.1750 g. **Comp.:** 0.9250 Silver 0.7487 oz. ASW **Ruler:** Elizabeth II **Subject:** Victoria Cross **Obv.:** Head right

Date	Mintage	MS-63	Proof
2006	27,254	26.50	—
2006 Proof	54,835	—	35.00

KM# 583a DOLLAR **Weight:** 25.1750 g. **Comp.:** 0.9250 Silver With Partial Gold Plating 0.7487 oz. **Ruler:** Elizabeth II **Subject:** Victoria Cross **Obv.:** Head right

Date	Mintage	MS-63	Proof
2006 Proof	—	—	60.00

KM# 652 DOLLAR **Comp.:** Gold **Ruler:** Elizabeth II **Subject:** Gold Louis **Obv.:** Head right **Note:** Replica.

Date	Mintage	MS-63	Proof
2006	—	150	—

KM# 654 DOLLAR **Weight:** 7.0000 g. **Comp.:** 0.9250 Silver 0.2082 oz. ASW **Ruler:** Elizabeth II **Obv.:** Head right **Rev.:** Snowflake, colorized **Note:** Sold in a CD package.

Date	Mintage	MS-63	Proof
2006(ml)	—	30.00	—

KM# 655 DOLLAR **Weight:** 7.0000 g. **Comp.:** 0.9250 Silver 0.2082 oz. ASW **Ruler:** Elizabeth II **Subject:** Baby Rattle **Obv.:** Head right **Rev.:** Baby rattle, colorized

Date	Mintage	MS-63	Proof
2006	—	20.00	—

KM# 687 DOLLAR **Weight:** 28.1750 g. **Comp.:** 0.9250 Silver With Partial Gold Plating 0.8379 oz. **Ruler:** Elizabeth II **Subject:** Joseph Brant **Obv.:** Head right

Date	Mintage	MS-63	Proof
2007	—	20.00	—

KM# 688 DOLLAR **Weight:** 7.0000 g. **Comp.:** Aureate-Bronze Plated Nickel **Ruler:** Elizabeth II **Subject:** Trumpeter Swan **Obv.:** Head right **Rev.:** Loon

Date	Mintage	MS-63	Proof
2007(ml)	40,000	20.00	—

KM# 270 2 DOLLARS **Weight:** 7.3000 g. **Comp.:** Bi-Metallic Aluminumn-Bronze center in Nickel ring **Ruler:** Elizabeth II **Obv.:** Crowned head right within circle, date below **Obv. Des.:** Dora dePedery-Hunt **Rev.:** Polar bear right within circle, denomination below **Rev. Des.:** Brent Townsend **Size:** 28 mm.

Date	Mintage	MS-63	Proof
2001	27,008,000	5.00	—
2001 Proof	—	—	12.50
2002	11,910,000	5.00	—
2002 Proof	—	—	12.50
2003	—	5.00	—
2003 Proof	—	—	12.50

KM# 270c 2 DOLLARS **Weight:** 8.8300 g. **Comp.:** 0.9250 Silver Gold plated inner core 0.2626 oz. ASW **Ruler:** Elizabeth II **Obv.:** Crowned head right within circle, date below **Rev.:** Polar bear right within circle, denomination below **Edge:** 1.8mm thickness **Size:** 28 mm.

Date	Mintage	MS-63	Proof
2001 Proof	—	—	12.00

KM# 449 2 DOLLARS **Weight:** 7.3000 g. **Comp.:** Bi-Metallic Aluminum-Bronze center in Nickel ring **Ruler:** Elizabeth II **Subject:** Elizabeth II Golden Jubilee **Obv.:** Crowned head right, jubilee commemorative dates 1952-2002

Date	Mintage	MS-63	Proof
ND(2002)	27,008,000	4.00	—

KM# 449a 2 DOLLARS **Weight:** 8.8300 g. **Comp.:** 0.9250 Silver 24-Karat gold plated inner core 0.2626 oz. ASW **Ruler:** Elizabeth II **Subject:** Elizabeth II Golden Jubilee **Obv.:** Crowned head right, jubilee commemorative dates 1952-2002

Date	Mintage	MS-63	Proof
ND(2002) Proof	100,000	—	14.00

KM# 496 2 DOLLARS **Weight:** 7.3000 g. **Comp.:** Bi-Metallic Aluminum-Bronze center in Nickel ring **Ruler:** Elizabeth II **Obv.:** Head right **Obv. Des.:** Susanna Blunt **Rev. Des.:** Brent Townsend

Date	Mintage	MS-63	Proof
2003	—	5.00	—
2003W	—	—	18.00
2004	—	5.00	—
2004 Proof	—	—	12.50
2005	—	5.00	—
2005 Proof	—	—	12.50
2006	—	5.00	—
2006 Proof	—	—	12.50

KM# 270d 2 DOLLARS **Comp.:** Bi-Metallic gold plated inner core **Ruler:** Elizabeth II **Subject:** 100th Anniversary of the Cobalt Silver Strike **Obv.:** Crowned head right, within circle, date below **Rev.:** Polar bear right, within circle, denomination below

Date	Mintage	MS-63	Proof
2003 Proof	100,000	—	25.00

KM# 496a 2 DOLLARS **Weight:** 10.8414 g. **Comp.:** 0.9250 Bi-Metallic Gold And Silver Gold plated Silver center in Silver ring 0.3224 oz. **Ruler:** Elizabeth II **Obv.:** Head right **Obv. Des.:** Suanne Blunt **Rev.:** Polar Bear **Edge:** Segmented reeding **Size:** 28 mm.

Date	Mintage	MS-63	Proof
2004 Proof	—	—	25.00

KM# 631 2 DOLLARS **Comp.:** Bi-Metallic **Ruler:** Elizabeth II **Subject:** 10th Anniversary of $2 coin **Obv.:** Crowned head right

Date	Mintage	MS-63	Proof
ND(2006)(ml)	—	25.00	—
ND(2006)(ml) Proof	—	—	40.00

KM# 631a 2 DOLLARS **Comp.:** Bi-Metallic 22 Kt Gold ring around 4.1 Kt. Gold core **Ruler:** Elizabeth II **Subject:** 10th Anniversary of $2 coin **Obv.:** Crowned head right **Rev.:** Polar bear

Date	Mintage	MS-63	Proof
ND(2006) Proof	3,000	—	385

KM# 657 3 DOLLARS **Comp.:** 0.9250 Gold Plated Silver **Ruler:** Elizabeth II **Rev.:** Beaver within wreath **Shape:** Square **Size:** 27x27 mm.

Date	Mintage	MS-63	Proof
2006	19,963	—	200

KM# 435 5 DOLLARS **Weight:** 16.8600 g. **Comp.:** 0.9250 Silver 0.5014 oz. ASW **Ruler:** Elizabeth II **Subject:** Guglielmo Marconi **Obv.:** Crowned head right **Rev.:** Gold-plated cameo portrait of Marconi **Rev. Des.:** Cosme Saffioti **Edge:** Reeded **Size:** 28.4 mm. **Note:** Only issued in two coin set with British 2 pounds KM#1014a.

Date	Mintage	MS-63	Proof
ND(2001) Proof	30,000	—	22.00

KM# 519 5 DOLLARS **Weight:** 8.3600 g. **Comp.:** 0.9000 Gold 0.2419 oz. AGW **Ruler:** Elizabeth II **Obv.:** Crowned head right **Rev.:** National arms **Edge:** Reeded **Size:** 21.6 mm.

Date	Mintage	MS-63	Proof
ND (2002) Proof	2,002	—	245

KM# 518 5 DOLLARS **Weight:** 31.1200 g. **Comp.:** 0.9999 Silver 1.0004 oz. ASW **Ruler:** Elizabeth II **Subject:** F.I.F.A. World Cup Soccer, Germany 2006 **Obv.:** Crowned head right, denomination **Rev.:** Goalie on knees **Edge:** Reeded **Size:** 38 mm.

Date	Mintage	MS-63	Proof
2003 Proof	21,542	—	29.00

KM# 514 5 DOLLARS **Weight:** 31.1200 g. **Comp.:** 0.9999 Silver 1.0004 oz. ASW **Ruler:** Elizabeth II **Obv.:** Crowned head right **Rev.:** Moose **Edge:** Reeded **Size:** 38 mm.

Date	Mintage	MS-63	Proof
2004 Proof	25,555	—	120

KM# 607 5 DOLLARS **Weight:** 31.1200 g. **Comp.:** 0.9999 Silver 1.0004 oz. ASW **Ruler:** Elizabeth II **Obv.:** Head right **Rev.:** Maple leaf, winter colors

Date	Mintage	MS-63	Proof
2004	—	35.00	—

KM# 527 5 DOLLARS **Weight:** 31.1200 g. **Comp.:** 0.9999 Silver 1.0004 oz. ASW **Ruler:** Elizabeth II **Subject:** Golf, Championship of Canada, Centennial **Obv.:** Head right

Date	Mintage	MS-63	Proof
2004 Proof	18,750	—	25.00

KM# 556.1 5 DOLLARS **Weight:** 31.1200 g. **Comp.:** 0.9990 Silver 0.9995 oz. ASW **Ruler:** Elizabeth II **Subject:** WWII Veterans **Obv.:** Head right **Rev.:** Large V and three portraits **Size:** 38 mm.

Date	Mintage	MS-63	Proof
2005	25,000	35.00	—

KM# 554 5 DOLLARS **Weight:** 31.1200 g. **Comp.:** 0.9999 Silver 1.0004 oz. ASW **Ruler:** Elizabeth II **Subject:** Alberta **Obv. Des.:** Head right **Rev. Des.:** Michelle Grant

Date	Mintage	MS-63	Proof
2005 Proof	20,000	—	35.00

KM# 555 5 DOLLARS **Weight:** 31.1200 g. **Comp.:** 0.9999 Silver 1.0004 oz. ASW **Ruler:** Elizabeth II **Subject:** Saskatchewan **Obv.:** Head right **Obv. Des.:** Susanna Blunt **Rev. Des.:** Paulett Sapergia

Date	Mintage	MS-63	Proof
2005 Proof	20,000	—	35.00

KM# 556.2 5 DOLLARS **Weight:** 31.1200 g. **Comp.:** 0.9990 Silver 0.9995 oz. ASW **Ruler:** Elizabeth II **Subject:** WW II **Obv.:** Elizabeth II **Rev.:** Three military portraits and letter V on large maple leaf flanked by two small maple leaves **Edge:** Reeded **Size:** 38 mm.

Date	Mintage	MS-63	Proof
2005	10,000	50.00	—

KM# 557 5 DOLLARS **Weight:** 31.1200 g. **Comp.:** 0.9999 Silver 1.0004 oz. ASW **Ruler:** Elizabeth II **Subject:** Walrus and calf **Obv.:** Head right **Obv. Des.:** Susanna Blunt **Rev.:** Two walrusus and calf **Rev. Des.:** Pierre Leduc

Date	Mintage	MS-63	Proof
2005 Proof	5,519	—	35.00

KM# 558 5 DOLLARS **Weight:** 31.1200 g. **Comp.:** 0.9999 Silver 1.0004 oz. ASW **Ruler:** Elizabeth II **Subject:** White tailed deer **Obv.:** Head right **Obv. Des.:** Susanna Blunt **Rev.:** Two deer standing **Rev. Des.:** Xerxes Irani

Date	Mintage	MS-63	Proof
2005 Proof	6,439	—	35.00

KM# 585 5 DOLLARS **Weight:** 31.1200 g. **Comp.:** 0.9999 Silver 1.0004 oz. ASW **Ruler:** Elizabeth II **Obv.:** Head right **Obv. Des.:** Susanna Blunt **Rev.:** Peregrine Falcon feeding young ones **Rev. Des.:** Dwayne Harty

Date	Mintage	MS-63	Proof
2006 Proof	6,145	—	40.00

KM# 586 5 DOLLARS **Weight:** 31.1200 g. **Comp.:** 0.9999 Silver 1.0004 oz. ASW **Ruler:** Elizabeth II **Subject:** Sable Island horses **Obv.:** Head right **Obv. Des.:** Susanna Blunt **Rev.:** Horse and foal standing **Rev. Des.:** Christie Paquet

Date	Mintage	MS-63	Proof
2006 Proof	7,589	—	40.00

KM# 658 5 DOLLARS **Weight:** 31.1200 g. **Comp.:** 0.9999 Silver 1.0004 oz. ASW **Ruler:** Elizabeth II **Subject:** Breast Cancer Awareness **Rev.:** Colorized pink ribbon

Date	Mintage	MS-63	Proof
2006 Proof	11,048	—	50.00

KM# 659 5 DOLLARS **Weight:** 31.1200 g. **Comp.:** 0.9999 Silver 1.0004 oz. ASW **Ruler:** Elizabeth II **Subject:** C.A.F. Snowbirds Acrobatic Jet Flying Team

Date	Mintage	MS-63	Proof
2006 Proof	7,896	—	50.00

KM# 515 8 DOLLARS **Weight:** 28.8000 g. **Comp.:** 0.9250 Silver 0.8565 oz. ASW **Ruler:** Elizabeth II **Obv.:** Head right **Obv. Des.:** Susanna Blunt **Rev.:** Grizzly bear walking left **Edge:** Reeded **Size:** 39 mm.

Date	Mintage	MS-63	Proof
2004 Proof	12,942	—	60.00

KM# 597 8 DOLLARS **Weight:** 32.1500 g. **Comp.:** 0.9999 Silver 1.0335 oz. ASW **Ruler:** Elizabeth II **Subject:** Canadian Pacific Railway, 120th Anniversary **Obv.:** Head right **Obv. Des.:** Susanna Blunt **Rev.:** Railway bridge

Date	Mintage	MS-63	Proof
2005 Proof	12,942	—	50.00

KM# 598 8 DOLLARS **Weight:** 32.1500 g. **Comp.:** 0.9999 Silver 1.0335 oz. ASW **Ruler:** Elizabeth II **Subject:** Canadian Pacific Railway, 120th Anniversary **Obv.:** Head right **Rev.:** Railway memorial to the Chinese workers

Date	Mintage	MS-63	Proof
2005 Proof	9,892	—	50.00

KM# 520 10 DOLLARS **Weight:** 16.7200 g. **Comp.:** 0.9000 Gold 0.4838 oz. AGW **Ruler:** Elizabeth II **Obv.:** Crowned head right **Rev.:** National arms **Edge:** Reeded **Size:** 26.92 mm.

Date	Mintage	MS-63	Proof
ND (2002) Proof	2,002	—	475

KM# 559 10 DOLLARS **Weight:** 25.1750 g. **Comp.:** 0.9999 Silver 0.8093 oz. ASW **Ruler:** Elizabeth II **Subject:** Pope John Paul II **Obv.:** Head right

Date	Mintage	MS-63	Proof
2005 Proof	24,716	—	35.00

KM# 661 10 DOLLARS **Weight:** 25.1750 g. **Comp.:** 0.9999 Silver 0.8093 oz. ASW **Ruler:** Elizabeth II **Subject:** National Historic Sites **Obv.:** Head right **Rev.:** Fortress of Louisbourg

Date	Mintage	MS-63	Proof
2006	15,000	35.00	—

KM# 415 15 DOLLARS **Weight:** 33.6300 g. **Comp.:** 0.9250 Silver 1.0000 oz. ASW **Ruler:** Elizabeth II **Subject:** Year of the Snake **Obv.:** Crowned head right **Rev.:** Snake within circle of lunar calendar signs **Rev. Des.:** Harvey Chain **Edge:** Reeded **Size:** 40 mm.

Date	Mintage	MS-63	Proof
2001 Proof	60,754	—	35.00

KM# 463 15 DOLLARS **Weight:** 33.6300 g. **Comp.:** 0.9250 Silver 24-Karat Gold-plated central Cameo 1.0000 oz. ASW **Ruler:** Elizabeth II **Subject:** Year of the Horse **Obv.:** Crowned head right **Obv. Des.:** Dora dePédery-Hunt **Rev.:** Horse in center with Chinese Lunar calendar around **Rev. Des.:** Harvey Chain

Date	Mintage	MS-63	Proof
2002 Proof	59,395	—	65.00

KM# 481 15 DOLLARS **Weight:** 33.6300 g. **Comp.:** 0.9250 Silver 1.0000 oz. ASW **Ruler:** Elizabeth II **Subject:** Year of the Sheep **Obv.:** Crowned head right **Rev.:** Sheep in center with Chinese Lunar calendar around **Rev. Des.:** Harvey Chain **Size:** 40 mm.

Date	Mintage	MS-63	Proof
2003 Proof	53,714	—	60.00

KM# 610 15 DOLLARS **Weight:** 33.6300 g. **Comp.:** 0.9250 Silver Gold octagon applique in center 1.0000 oz. ASW **Ruler:** Elizabeth II **Subject:** Year of the Monkey **Obv.:** Crowned head right **Rev.:** Monkey in center with Chinese Lunar calendar around

Date	Mintage	MS-63	Proof
2004 Proof	46,175	—	75.00

KM# 560 15 DOLLARS **Weight:** 33.6300 g. **Comp.:** 0.9250 Silver Gold applique 1.0000 oz. ASW **Ruler:** Elizabeth II **Subject:** Year of the Rooster **Obv.:** Crowned head right **Rev.:** Rooster in center with Chinese Lunar calendar around

Date	Mintage	MS-63	Proof
2005 Proof	44,690	—	75.00

KM# 587 15 DOLLARS **Weight:** 33.6300 g. **Comp.:** 0.9250 Silver Gold applique 1.0000 oz. ASW **Ruler:** Elizabeth II **Subject:** Year of the Dog **Obv.:** Crowned head left **Rev.:** Dog in center with Chinese Lunar calendar around

Date	Mintage	MS-63	Proof
2006 Proof	41,617	—	65.00

KM# 662 15 DOLLARS **Weight:** 33.6300 g. **Comp.:** 0.9250 Silver Gold applique 1.0000 oz. ASW **Ruler:** Elizabeth II **Subject:** Year of the Pig **Obv.:** Crowned head right **Rev.:** Pig in center with Chinese Lunar calendar around

Date	Mintage	MS-63	Proof
2006 Proof	48,888	—	80.00

KM# 411 20 DOLLARS **Weight:** 31.1035 g. **Comp.:** 0.9250 Silver 0.9250 oz. ASW **Ruler:** Elizabeth II **Subject:** Transportation - Steam Locomotive **Obv.:** Crowned head right **Obv. Des.:** Dora dePédery-Hunt **Rev.:** First Canadian Steel Steam Locomotive and cameo hologram **Rev. Des.:** Don Curely **Edge:** Reeded and plain sections **Size:** 38 mm.

Date	Mintage	MS-63	Proof
2001 Proof	15,000	—	35.00

KM# 427 20 DOLLARS **Weight:** 31.1030 g. **Comp.:** 0.9250 Silver 0.9249 oz. ASW **Ruler:** Elizabeth II **Series:** Transportation - The Marco Polo **Obv.:** Crowned head right **Rev.:** Sailship with hologram cameo **Rev. Des.:** J. Franklin Wright **Edge:** Reeded and plain sections **Size:** 38 mm.

Date	Mintage	MS-63	Proof
2001 Proof	15,000	—	35.00

KM# 428 20 DOLLARS **Weight:** 31.1030 g. **Comp.:** 0.9250 Silver 0.9249 oz. ASW **Ruler:** Elizabeth II **Series:** Transportation - Russell Touring Car **Obv.:** Crowned head right **Rev.:** Russell touring car with hologram cameo **Rev. Des.:** John Mardon **Edge:** Reeded and plain sections **Size:** 38 mm.

Date	Mintage	MS-63	Proof
2001 Proof	15,000	—	35.00

KM# 464 20 DOLLARS **Weight:** 31.1030 g. **Comp.:** 0.9250 Silver 0.9249 oz. ASW **Ruler:** Elizabeth II **Obv.:** Crowned head right **Obv. Des.:** Dora dePédery-Hunt **Rev.:** Gray-Dort Model 25-SM with cameo hologram **Rev. Des.:** John Mardon

Date	Mintage	MS-63	Proof
2002 Proof	15,000	—	40.00

KM# 465 20 DOLLARS **Weight:** 31.1030 g. **Comp.:** 0.9250 Silver 0.9249 oz. ASW **Ruler:** Elizabeth II **Obv.:** Crowned head right **Obv. Des.:** Dora dePédery-Hunt **Rev.:** Sailing ship William D. Lawrence **Rev. Des.:** Bonnie Ross

Date	Mintage	MS-63	Proof
2002 Proof	15,000	—	40.00

KM# 523 20 DOLLARS **Weight:** 31.3900 g. **Comp.:** 0.9990 Silver 1.0082 oz. ASW **Ruler:** Elizabeth II **Subject:** Canadian Rockies, colorized **Obv.:** Crowned head right **Obv. Des.:** Dora dePédery-Hunt **Rev.:** Canadian Rockies

Date	Mintage	MS-63	Proof
2003 Proof	29,967	—	50.00

KM# 484 20 DOLLARS **Comp.:** 0.9250 Silver Selective gold plating **Ruler:** Elizabeth II **Subject:** Canadian National FA-1 diesel-electric locomotive **Obv.:** Crowned head right **Obv. Des.:** Dora dePédery-Hunt **Rev. Des.:** John Mardon, William Woodruff

Date	Mintage	MS-63	Proof
2003 Proof	15,000	—	40.00

KM# 485 20 DOLLARS **Weight:** 31.1030 g. **Comp.:** 0.9250 Silver With Partial Gold Plating 0.9249 oz. **Ruler:** Elizabeth II **Obv.:** Crowned head right **Obv. Des.:** Dora dePédery-Hunt **Rev.:** The Bricklin SV-1 **Rev. Des.:** Brian Hughes, José Oslo

Date	Mintage	MS-63	Proof
2003 Proof	15,000	—	45.00

KM# 482 20 DOLLARS **Weight:** 31.3900 g. **Comp.:** 0.9999 Silver 1.0091 oz. ASW **Ruler:** Elizabeth II **Obv.:** Crowned head right **Obv. Des.:** Dora dePédery-Hunt **Rev.:** Niagara Falls hologram **Rev. Des.:** Gary Corcoran

Date	Mintage	MS-63	Proof
2003 Proof	29,967	—	65.00

KM# 483 20 DOLLARS **Weight:** 31.1030 g. **Comp.:** 0.9250 Silver Selective gold plating 0.9249 oz. ASW **Ruler:** Elizabeth II **Subject:** The HMCS Bras d'or (FHE-400) **Obv.:** Crowned head right **Obv. Des.:** Dora dePédery-Hunt **Rev.:** Ship in water **Rev. Des.:** Donald Curley, Stan Witten

Date	Mintage	MS-63	Proof
2003 Proof	15,000	—	40.00

KM# 611 20 DOLLARS **Weight:** 31.3900 g. **Comp.:** 0.9999 Silver 1.0091 oz. ASW **Ruler:** Elizabeth II **Obv.:** Head right **Obv. Des.:** Susanna Blunt **Rev.:** Iceburg, hologram

Date	Mintage	MS-63	Proof
2004 Proof	24,879	—	55.00

KM# 561 20 DOLLARS **Weight:** 31.3900 g. **Comp.:** 0.9999 Silver 1.0091 oz. ASW **Ruler:** Elizabeth II **Subject:** Three-masted sailing ship, hologram **Obv.:** Head right **Obv. Des.:** Susanna Blunt **Rev. Des.:** Bonnie Ross

Date	Mintage	MS-63	Proof
2005 Proof	18,276	—	55.00

KM# 562 20 DOLLARS **Weight:** 31.3900 g. **Comp.:** 0.9999 Silver 1.0091 oz. ASW **Ruler:** Elizabeth II **Subject:** Northwest Territories Diamonds **Obv.:** Head right **Obv. Des.:** Susanna Blunt **Rev.:** Multicolor diamond hologram on landscape **Rev. Des.:** José Oslo **Edge:** Reeded **Size:** 38 mm.

Date	Mintage	MS-63	Proof
2005 Proof	35,000	—	45.00

KM# 563 20 DOLLARS **Weight:** 31.3900 g. **Comp.:** 0.9999 Silver 1.0091 oz. ASW **Ruler:** Elizabeth II **Subject:** Mingan Archepelago **Obv.:** Head right **Obv. Des.:** Susanna Blunt **Rev.:** Cliffs with whale tail out of water **Rev. Des.:** Pierre Leduc

Date	Mintage	MS-63	Proof
2005 Proof	—	—	60.00

KM# 564 20 DOLLARS **Weight:** 31.3900 g. **Comp.:** 0.9999 Silver 1.0091 oz. ASW **Ruler:** Elizabeth II **Subject:** Rainforests of the Pacific Northwest **Obv.:** Head right **Rev.:** Open winged bird

Date	Mintage	MS-63	Proof
2005 Proof	—	—	55.00

KM# 565 20 DOLLARS **Comp.:** Silver **Ruler:** Elizabeth II **Subject:** Toronto Island National Park **Obv.:** Head right **Rev.:** Toronto Island Lighthouse

Date	Mintage	MS-63	Proof
2005 Proof	—	—	62.50

KM# 588 20 DOLLARS **Weight:** 31.3900 g. **Comp.:** 0.9999 Silver 1.0091 oz. ASW **Ruler:** Elizabeth II **Subject:** Georgian Bay National Park **Obv.:** Head right **Rev.:** Canoe and small trees on island

Date	Mintage	MS-63	Proof
2006 Proof	—	—	60.00

KM# 589 20 DOLLARS **Weight:** 31.1000 g. **Comp.:** 0.9999 Silver 0.9997 oz. ASW **Ruler:** Elizabeth II **Subject:** Notre Dame Basilica, Montreal, as a hologram **Obv.:** Head right

Date	Mintage	MS-63	Proof
2006 Proof	15,000	—	60.00

KM# 663 20 DOLLARS **Weight:** 31.3900 g. **Comp.:** 0.9999 Silver 1.0091 oz. ASW **Ruler:** Elizabeth II **Subject:** Nahanni National Park **Obv.:** Head right **Rev.:** Bear walking along sream, cliff in background

Date	Mintage	MS-63	Proof
2006 Proof	—	—	60.00

KM# 664 20 DOLLARS **Weight:** 31.3900 g. **Comp.:** 0.9999 Silver 1.0091 oz. ASW **Ruler:** Elizabeth II **Subject:** Jasper National Park **Obv.:** Head right **Rev.:** Cowboy on horseback in majestic scene

Date	Mintage	MS-63	Proof
2006 Proof	—	—	60.00

KM# 665 20 DOLLARS **Weight:** 31.1000 g. **Comp.:** 0.9999 Silver 0.9997 oz. ASW **Ruler:** Elizabeth II **Subject:** CN Tower, Toronto **Obv.:** Head right **Rev.:** Holographic rendering of CN Tower

Date	Mintage	MS-63	Proof
2006 Proof	15,000	—	70.00

KM# 666 20 DOLLARS **Weight:** 31.1000 g. **Comp.:** 0.9999 Silver 0.9997 oz. ASW **Ruler:** Elizabeth II **Subject:** Pengrowth (Calgary Saddledome) **Obv.:** Head right **Rev.:** Holographic view of Saddledome

Date	Mintage	MS-63	Proof
2006 Proof	15,000	—	70.00

KM# 667 20 DOLLARS **Weight:** 31.3900 g. **Comp.:** 0.9999 Silver 1.0091 oz. ASW **Ruler:** Elizabeth II **Subject:** Tall Ship **Obv.:** Head right **Rev.:** Ketch and holographic image

Date	Mintage	MS-63	Proof
2006 Proof	10,299	—	70.00

KM# 590 30 DOLLARS **Weight:** 31.5000 g. **Comp.:** 0.9250 Silver 0.9368 oz. ASW **Ruler:** Elizabeth II **Subject:** Pacific Northwest Wood Carvings **Obv.:** Head right **Rev.:** Welcome figure totem pole

Date	Mintage	MS-63	Proof
2006 Proof	9,904	—	65.00

KM# 668 30 DOLLARS **Weight:** 31.5000 g. **Comp.:** 0.9250 Silver 0.9368 oz. ASW **Ruler:** Elizabeth II **Subject:** Canadarm and Col. C. Hadfield **Obv.:** Head right **Rev.:** Hologram of Canadarm

Date	Mintage	MS-63	Proof
2006 Proof	9,357	—	60.00

KM# 669 30 DOLLARS **Weight:** 31.5000 g. **Comp.:** 0.9250 Silver 0.9368 oz. ASW **Ruler:** Elizabeth II **Subject:** National War Memorial **Obv.:** Head right

Date	Mintage	MS-63	Proof
2006 Proof	15,000	—	80.00

KM# 670 30 DOLLARS **Weight:** 31.5000 g. **Comp.:** 0.9250 Silver 0.9368 oz. ASW **Ruler:** Elizabeth II **Subject:** Beaumont Hamel Newfoundland **Obv.:** Head right

Date	Mintage	MS-63	Proof
2006 Proof	15,000	—	80.00

KM# 671 30 DOLLARS **Weight:** 31.5000 g. **Comp.:** 0.9250 Silver 0.9368 oz. ASW **Ruler:** Elizabeth II **Subject:** Dog Sled Team **Obv.:** Head right **Rev.:** Colorized

Date	Mintage	MS-63	Proof
2006 Proof	6,797	—	80.00

KM# 566 50 DOLLARS **Weight:** 12.0000 g. **Comp.:** 0.5833 Gold 0.2250 oz. AGW **Ruler:** Elizabeth II **Subject:** WWII **Obv.:** Head right **Rev.:** Large V and three portraits

Date	Mintage	MS-63	Proof
2005 Proof	4,000	—	275

KM# 672 50 DOLLARS **Weight:** 31.1600 g. **Comp.:** 0.9995 Palladium 1.0013 oz. **Ruler:** Elizabeth II **Subject:** Constellation Spring **Rev.:** Large Bear at top

Date	Mintage	MS-63	Proof
2006 Proof	297	—	1,200

KM# 673 50 DOLLARS **Weight:** 31.1600 g. **Comp.:** 0.9995 Palladium 1.0013 oz. **Ruler:** Elizabeth II **Subject:** Constellation Summer **Rev.:** Large Bear at left.

Date	Mintage	MS-63	Proof
2006 Proof	296	—	1,200

KM# 674 50 DOLLARS **Weight:** 31.1600 g. **Comp.:** 0.9995 Palladium 1.0013 oz. **Ruler:** Elizabeth II **Subject:** Constellation Autumn **Rev.:** Large Bear towards bottom

Date	Mintage	MS-63	Proof
2006 Proof	296	—	1,200

KM# 675 50 DOLLARS **Weight:** 31.1600 g. **Comp.:** 0.9995 Palladium 1.0013 oz. **Ruler:** Elizabeth II **Subject:** Constellation Winter **Rev.:** Large Bear towards right.

Date	Mintage	MS-63	Proof
2006 Proof	293	—	1,200

KM# 567 75 DOLLARS **Weight:** 31.4400 g. **Comp.:** 0.4166 Gold 0.4211 oz. AGW **Ruler:** Elizabeth II **Subject:** Pope John Paul II **Obv.:** Head right

Date	Mintage	MS-63	Proof
2005 Proof	1,870	—	415

KM# 416 100 DOLLARS **Weight:** 13.3375 g. **Comp.:** 0.5830 Gold alloyed with 5.5579 g of .999 Silver, .1787 oz ASW 0.2500 oz. AGW **Ruler:** Elizabeth II **Subject:** Library of Parliament **Obv.:** Crowned head right **Obv. Des.:** Dora dePedery-Hunt **Rev.:** Statue in domed building **Rev. Des.:** Robert R. Carmichael **Edge:** Reeded **Size:** 27 mm.

Date	Mintage	MS-63	Proof
2001 Proof	8,080	—	235

KM# 452 100 DOLLARS **Weight:** 13.3375 g. **Comp.:** 0.5830 Gold 0.2500 oz. AGW **Ruler:** Elizabeth II **Subject:** Discovery of Oil in Alberta **Obv.:** Crowned head right **Rev.:** Oil well with black oil spill on ground **Rev. Des.:** John Marden **Edge:** Reeded **Size:** 27 mm.

Date	Mintage	MS-63	Proof
2002 Proof	9,994	—	250

KM# 486 100 DOLLARS **Weight:** 13.3375 g. **Comp.:** 0.5830 Gold 0.2500 oz. AGW **Ruler:** Elizabeth II **Subject:** 100th Anniversary of the Discovery of Marquis Wheat **Obv.:** Head right

Date	Mintage	MS-63	Proof
2003 Proof	9,993	—	230

KM# 528 100 DOLLARS **Weight:** 12.0000 g. **Comp.:** 0.5830 Gold 0.2249 oz. AGW **Ruler:** Elizabeth II **Subject:** St. Lawrence Seaway, 50th Anniversary **Obv.:** Head right

Date	Mintage	MS-63	Proof
2004 Proof	7,454	—	215

KM# 616 100 DOLLARS **Weight:** 12.0000 g. **Comp.:** 0.5833 Gold 0.2250 oz. AGW **Ruler:** Elizabeth II **Subject:** Supreme Court **Obv.:** Head right **Rev.:** Draped figure with sword

Date	Mintage	MS-63	Proof
2005 Proof	5,092	—	225

KM# 591 100 DOLLARS **Weight:** 12.0000 g. **Comp.:** 0.5833 Gold 0.2250 oz. AGW **Ruler:** Elizabeth II **Subject:** 75th Anniversary, Hockey Classic between Royal Military College and U.S. Military Academy **Obv.:** Head right

Date	Mintage	MS-63	Proof
2006 Proof	5,402	—	225

KM# 593 100 DOLLARS **Weight:** 12.0000 g. **Comp.:** 0.5833 Gold 0.2250 oz. AGW **Ruler:** Elizabeth II **Subject:** 130th Anniversary, Supreme Court **Obv.:** Head right

Date	Mintage	MS-63	Proof
2006 Proof	5,092	—	420

KM# 689 100 DOLLARS **Weight:** 12.0000 g. **Comp.:** 0.5833 Gold 0.2250 oz. AGW **Ruler:** Elizabeth II **Subject:** 140th Anniversary Dominion **Obv.:** Head right

Date	Mintage	MS-63	Proof
2007 Proof	5,000	—	225

KM# 417 150 DOLLARS **Weight:** 13.6100 g. **Comp.:** 0.7500 Gold 0.3282 oz. AGW **Ruler:** Elizabeth II **Subject:** Year of the Snake **Obv.:** Crowned head right **Obv. Des.:** Dora dePedery-Hunt **Rev.:** Multicolor snake hologram **Edge:** Reeded **Size:** 28 mm.

Date	Mintage	MS-63	Proof
2001 Proof	6,571	—	300

KM# 604 150 DOLLARS **Weight:** 13.6100 g. **Comp.:** 0.7500 Gold 0.3282 oz. AGW **Ruler:** Elizabeth II **Obv.:** Head right **Rev.:** Stylized horse left

Date	Mintage	MS-63	Proof
2002 Proof	6,843	—	320

KM# 487 150 DOLLARS **Weight:** 13.6100 g. **Comp.:** 0.7500 Gold 0.3282 oz. AGW **Ruler:** Elizabeth II **Subject:** Year of the Ram **Obv.:** Crowned head right **Rev.:** Stylized ram left **Rev. Des.:** Harvey Chan

Date	Mintage	MS-63	Proof
2003 Proof	3,927	—	325

KM# 614 150 DOLLARS **Weight:** 13.6100 g. **Comp.:** 0.7500 Gold 0.3282 oz. AGW **Ruler:** Elizabeth II **Obv.:** Head right **Rev.:** Year of the Monkey, hologram

Date	Mintage	MS-63	Proof
2004 Proof	3,392	—	345

KM# 568 150 DOLLARS **Weight:** 13.6100 g. **Comp.:** 0.7500 Gold 0.3282 oz. AGW **Ruler:** Elizabeth II **Subject:** Year of the Rooster **Obv.:** Head right **Rev.:** Rooster left

Date	Mintage	MS-63	Proof
2005 Proof	3,731	—	350

KM# 592 150 DOLLARS **Weight:** 13.6100 g. **Comp.:** 0.7500 Gold 0.3282 oz. AGW **Ruler:** Elizabeth II **Subject:** Year of the Dog, hologram **Obv.:** Head right **Rev.:** Stylized dog left

Date	Mintage	MS-63	Proof
2006 Proof	2,604	—	350

KM# 690 150 DOLLARS **Weight:** 13.6100 g. **Comp.:** 0.7500 Gold 0.3282 oz. AGW **Ruler:** Elizabeth II **Subject:** Year of the Pig **Obv.:** Head right **Rev.:** Pig in center with Chinese lunar calendar around

Date	Mintage	MS-63	Proof
2007 Proof	4,888	—	350

KM# 418 200 DOLLARS **Weight:** 17.1350 g. **Comp.:** 0.9166 Gold 0.5049 oz. AGW **Ruler:** Elizabeth II **Subject:** Cornelius D. Krieghoff's "The Habitant farm" **Obv.:** Queens head right **Edge:** Reeded **Size:** 29 mm.

Date	Mintage	MS-63	Proof
2001 Proof	5,406	—	445

KM# 466 200 DOLLARS **Weight:** 17.1350 g. **Comp.:** 0.9166 Gold 0.5049 oz. AGW **Ruler:** Elizabeth II **Subject:** Thomas Thompson "The Jack Pine" (1916-17) **Obv.:** Crowned head right **Size:** 29 mm.

Date	Mintage	MS-63	Proof
2002 Proof	5,264	—	450

KM# 488 200 DOLLARS **Weight:** 17.1350 g. **Comp.:** 0.9166 Gold 0.5049 oz. AGW **Ruler:** Elizabeth II **Subject:** Fitzgerald's "Houses" (1929) **Obv.:** Crowned head right **Rev.:** House with trees

Date	Mintage	MS-63	Proof
2003 Proof	4,118	—	460

KM# 516 200 DOLLARS **Weight:** 16.0000 g. **Comp.:** 0.9166 Gold 0.4715 oz. AGW **Ruler:** Elizabeth II **Subject:** "Fragments" **Obv.:** Crowned head right **Rev.:** Fragmented face **Edge:** Reeded **Size:** 29 mm.

Date	Mintage	MS-63	Proof
2004 Proof	3,917	—	425

KM# 569 200 DOLLARS **Weight:** 16.0000 g. **Comp.:** 0.9166 Gold 0.4715 oz. AGW **Ruler:** Elizabeth II **Subject:** Fur traders **Obv.:** Head right **Rev.:** Men in canoe riding wave

Date	Mintage	MS-63	Proof
2005 Proof	3,669	—	425

KM# 594 200 DOLLARS **Weight:** 16.0000 g. **Comp.:** 0.9166 Gold 0.4715 oz. AGW **Ruler:** Elizabeth II **Subject:** Timber trade **Obv.:** Head right **Rev.:** Lumberjacks felling tree

Date	Mintage	MS-63	Proof
2006 Proof	3,185	—	425

KM# 691 200 DOLLARS **Weight:** 16.0000 g. **Comp.:** 0.9166 Gold 0.4715 oz. AGW **Ruler:** Elizabeth II **Subject:** Fishing Trade **Obv.:** Head right

Date	Mintage	MS-63	Proof
2007 Proof	4,000	—	425

KM# 677 250 DOLLARS **Weight:** 45.0000 g. **Comp.:** 0.5833 Gold 0.8439 oz. AGW **Ruler:** Elizabeth II **Subject:** Dog Sled Team

Date	Mintage	MS-63	Proof
2006 Proof	900	—	775

KM# 501 300 DOLLARS **Weight:** 60.0000 g. **Comp.:** 0.5833 Gold 1.1252 oz. AGW **Ruler:** Elizabeth II **Obv.:** Triple cameo portraits of Queen Elizabeth II by Gillick, Machin and de Pedery-Hunt, each in 14K gold, rose in center **Rev.:** Dates "1952-2002" and denomination in legend, rose in center **Size:** 50 mm. **Note:** Housed in anodized gold-colored aluminum box with cherrywood stained siding

Date	Mintage	MS-63	Proof
ND(2002) Proof	999	—	1,050

KM# 517 300 DOLLARS **Weight:** 60.0000 g. **Comp.:** 0.5833 Gold 1.1252 oz. AGW **Ruler:** Elizabeth II **Obv.:** Four coinage portraits of Elizabeth II **Rev.:** Canadian arms above value **Edge:** Plain **Size:** 50 mm.

Date	Mintage	MS-63	Proof
2004 Proof	1,000	—	1,075

KM# 570 300 DOLLARS **Weight:** 60.0000 g. **Comp.:** 0.5833 Gold 1.1252 oz. AGW **Ruler:** Elizabeth II **Subject:** Standard Time **Obv.:** Head right **Rev.:** Roman numeral clock with world inside

Date	Mintage	MS-63	Proof
2005 Proof	—	—	1,000

KM# 596 300 DOLLARS **Weight:** 60.0000 g. **Comp.:** 0.5833 Gold 1.1252 oz. AGW **Ruler:** Elizabeth II **Subject:** Shinplaster **Obv.:** Head right **Rev.:** Britannia bust, spear over shoulder

Date	Mintage	MS-63	Proof
2005 Proof	994	—	1,075

KM# 600 300 DOLLARS **Weight:** 60.0000 g. **Comp.:** 0.5833 Gold 1.1252 oz. AGW **Ruler:** Elizabeth II **Subject:** Welcome Figure Totem Pole **Obv.:** Head right **Rev.:** Men with totem pole

Date	Mintage	MS-63	Proof
2005 Proof	948	—	1,000

KM# 678 300 DOLLARS **Weight:** 45.0000 g. **Comp.:** 0.5833 Gold 0.8439 oz. AGW **Ruler:** Elizabeth II **Subject:** Canadam and Col. C. Hadfield **Rev.:** Hologram of Canadarm

Date	Mintage	MS-63	Proof
2006 Proof	565	—	775

KM# 679 300 DOLLARS **Weight:** 60.0000 g. **Comp.:** 0.5833 Gold 1.1252 oz. AGW **Ruler:** Elizabeth II **Subject:** Queen Elizabeth's 80th Birthday **Rev.:** State Crown, colorized

Date	Mintage	MS-63	Proof
2006 Proof	996	—	1,050

KM# 680 300 DOLLARS **Weight:** 60.0000 g. **Comp.:** 0.5833 Gold 1.1252 oz. AGW **Ruler:** Elizabeth II **Subject:** Crystal Snowflake

Date	Mintage	MS-63	Proof
2006 Proof	861	—	1,050

KM# 595 300 DOLLARS **Weight:** 60.0000 g. **Comp.:** 0.5833 Gold 1.1252 oz. AGW **Ruler:** Elizabeth II **Subject:** The Shinplaster **Obv.:** Head right **Rev.:** Seated Britannia with shield

Date	Mintage	MS-63	Proof
2006 Proof	940	—	1,075

KM# 692 300 DOLLARS **Weight:** 60.0000 g. **Comp.:** 0.5833 Gold 1.1252 oz. AGW **Ruler:** Elizabeth II **Subject:** 1923 25 Cent Banknote

Date	Mintage	MS-63	Proof
2007 Proof	1,250	—	1,050

KM# 433 350 DOLLARS **Weight:** 38.0500 g. **Comp.:** 0.9999 Gold 1.2232 oz. AGW **Ruler:** Elizabeth II **Subject:** The Mayflower Flower **Obv.:** Crowned head right **Rev.:** Two flowers **Rev. Des.:** Bonnie Ross **Edge:** Reeded **Size:** 34 mm.

Date	Mintage	MS-63	Proof
2001 Proof	1,988	—	1,150

KM# 502 350 DOLLARS **Weight:** 38.0500 g. **Comp.:** 0.9999 Gold 1.2232 oz. AGW **Ruler:** Elizabeth II **Subject:** The Wild Rose **Obv.:** Crowned head right **Obv. Des.:** Dora de Pedery-Hunt **Rev.:** Wild rose plant **Rev. Des.:** Dr. Andreas Kare Hellum **Size:** 34 mm.

Date	Mintage	MS-63	Proof
2002 Proof	2,001	—	1,150

KM# 504 350 DOLLARS **Weight:** 38.0500 g. **Comp.:** 0.9999 Gold 1.2232 oz. AGW **Ruler:** Elizabeth II **Subject:** The White Trillium **Obv.:** Crowned head right **Obv. Des.:** Dora de Pedery-Hunt **Rev.:** White Trillium **Size:** 34 mm.

Date	Mintage	MS-63	Proof
2003 Proof	1,865	—	1,150

KM# 601 350 DOLLARS **Weight:** 38.0500 g. **Comp.:** 0.9999 Gold 1.2232 oz. AGW **Ruler:** Elizabeth II **Subject:** Western Red Lilly **Obv.:** Head right **Rev.:** Western Red Lilies

Date	Mintage	MS-63	Proof
2005 Proof	1,634	—	1,150

KM# 626 350 DOLLARS **Weight:** 38.0500 g. **Comp.:** 0.9999 Gold 1.2232 oz. AGW **Ruler:** Elizabeth II **Subject:** Iris Vericolor **Obv.:** Crowned head right **Rev.:** Iris **Size:** 34 mm.

Date	Mintage	MS-63	Proof
2006 Proof	1,969	—	1,150

SILVER BULLION COINAGE

KM# 617 DOLLAR **Weight:** 1.5550 g. **Comp.:** 0.9999 Silver 0.0500 oz. ASW **Ruler:** Elizabeth II **Obv.:** Crowned head right **Rev.:** Holographic Maple leaf **Edge:** Reeded **Size:** 16 mm.

Date	Mintage	MS-63	Proof
2003 Proof	—	—	4.50

KM# 621 DOLLAR **Weight:** 1.5550 g. **Comp.:** 0.9999 Silver 0.0500 oz. ASW **Ruler:** Elizabeth II **Obv.:** Crowned head right **Rev.:** Maple leaf and mint logo privy mark **Edge:** Reeded **Size:** 17 mm.

Date	Mintage	MS-63	Proof
2004 Proof	25,000	—	4.50

KM# 618 2 DOLLARS **Weight:** 3.1100 g. **Comp.:** 0.9999 Silver 0.1000 oz. ASW **Ruler:** Elizabeth II **Obv.:** Crowned head right **Rev.:** Holographic Maple leaf **Edge:** Reeded **Size:** 20.1 mm.

Date	Mintage	MS-63	Proof
2003 Proof	—	—	7.50

KM# 622 2 DOLLARS **Weight:** 3.1100 g. **Comp.:** 0.9999 Silver 0.1000 oz. ASW **Ruler:** Elizabeth II **Obv.:** Crowned head right **Rev.:** Maple leaf and mint logo privy mark **Edge:** Reeded **Size:** 21 mm.

Date	Mintage	MS-63	Proof
2004 Proof	25,000	—	7.50

KM# 571 2 DOLLARS **Weight:** 3.1050 g. **Comp.:** 0.9999 Silver 0.0998 oz. ASW **Ruler:** Elizabeth II **Obv.:** Head right **Rev.:** Lynx

Date	Mintage	MS-63	Proof
2005 Proof	—	—	7.50

KM# 619 3 DOLLARS **Weight:** 7.7760 g. **Comp.:** 0.9999 Silver 0.2500 oz. ASW **Ruler:** Elizabeth II **Obv.:** Crowned head right **Rev.:** Holographic Maple leaf **Edge:** Reeded **Size:** 26.9 mm.

Date	Mintage	MS-63	Proof
2003 Proof	—	—	15.00

KM# 623 3 DOLLARS **Weight:** 7.7760 g. **Comp.:** 0.9999 Silver 0.2500 oz. ASW **Ruler:** Elizabeth II **Obv.:** Crowned head right **Rev.:** Maple leaf and mint logo privy mark **Edge:** Reeded **Size:** 27 mm.

Date	Mintage	MS-63	Proof
2004 Proof	25,000	—	12.50

KM# 572 3 DOLLARS **Weight:** 7.7760 g. **Comp.:** 0.9999 Silver 0.2500 oz. ASW **Ruler:** Elizabeth II **Obv.:** Head right **Rev.:** Lynx

Date	Mintage	MS-63	Proof
2005 Proof	—	—	12.50

KM# 620 4 DOLLARS **Weight:** 15.5500 g. **Comp.:** 0.9999 Silver 0.4999 oz. ASW **Ruler:** Elizabeth II **Obv.:** Crowned head right **Rev.:** Holographic Maple leaf **Edge:** Reeded **Size:** 33.9 mm.

Date	Mintage	MS-63	Proof
2003 Proof	—	—	30.00

KM# 624 4 DOLLARS **Weight:** 15.5500 g. **Comp.:** 0.9999 Silver 0.4999 oz. ASW **Ruler:** Elizabeth II **Obv.:** Crowned head right **Rev.:** Maple leaf and mint logo privy mark **Edge:** Reeded **Size:** 34 mm.

Date	Mintage	MS-63	Proof
2004 Proof	25,000	—	25.00

KM# 573 4 DOLLARS **Weight:** 15.5500 g. **Comp.:** 0.9999 Silver 0.4999 oz. ASW **Ruler:** Elizabeth II **Obv.:** Head right **Rev.:** Lynx

Date	Mintage	MS-63	Proof
2005 Proof	—	—	22.50

KM# 187 5 DOLLARS **Weight:** 31.1000 g. **Comp.:** 0.9999 Silver 0.9997 oz. ASW **Ruler:** Elizabeth II **Obv.:** Crowned head right, date and denomination below **Obv. Des.:** Dora de Pedery-Hunt **Rev.:** Maple leaf flanked by 9999

Date	Mintage	MS-63	Proof
2001	398,563	16.00	—
2001 Snake privy mark	25,000	22.00	—
2002	576,196	16.00	—
2002 Horse privy mark	25,000	22.00	—
2003	—	16.00	—
2003 Sheep privy mark	25,000	18.00	—

KM# 436 5 DOLLARS **Weight:** 31.1035 g. **Comp.:** 0.9999 Silver 0.9999 oz. ASW **Ruler:** Elizabeth II **Obv.:** Crowned head right, date and denomination below **Rev.:** Three maple leaves in autumn colors, 9999 flanks **Rev. Des.:** Debbie Adams **Edge:** Reeded **Size:** 38 mm.

Date	Mintage	MS-63	Proof
2001 Proof	49,900	—	32.50

KM# 437 5 DOLLARS **Weight:** 31.1035 g. **Comp.:** 0.9999 Silver 0.9999 oz. ASW **Ruler:** Elizabeth II **Subject:** Multicolor Holographic Maple Leaf **Obv.:** Crowned head right, date and denomination below **Rev.:** Radiant maple leaf hologram with date privy mark **Edge:** Reeded **Size:** 38 mm.

Date	Mintage	MS-63	Proof
2001	29,906	75.00	—

KM# 505 5 DOLLARS **Weight:** 31.1035 g. **Comp.:** 0.9999 Silver 0.9999 oz. ASW **Ruler:** Elizabeth II **Obv.:** Crowned head right, date and denomination below **Rev.:** Two maple leaves in spring color (green) **Edge:** Reeded **Size:** 38 mm.

Date	Mintage	MS-63	Proof
2002 Proof	—	—	35.00

KM# 603 5 DOLLARS **Comp.:** 0.9999 Silver **Ruler:** Elizabeth II **Subject:** Loon, hologram **Obv.:** Head right

Date	Mintage	MS-63	Proof
2002 Satin Proof	30,000	—	45.00

KM# 521 5 DOLLARS **Weight:** 31.1035 g. **Comp.:** 0.9999 Silver 0.9999 oz. ASW **Ruler:** Elizabeth II **Obv.:** Head right **Rev.:** Maple leaf, summer colors

Date	Mintage	MS-63	Proof
2003 Proof	—	—	30.00

KM# 522 5 DOLLARS **Weight:** 31.1050 g. **Comp.:** 0.9999 Silver 0.9999 oz. ASW **Ruler:** Elizabeth II **Subject:** Colorized maple leaf **Obv.:** Head right

Date	Mintage	MS-63	Proof
2003	—	32.50	—

KM# 625 5 DOLLARS **Weight:** 31.1035 g. **Comp.:** 0.9999 Silver 0.9999 oz. ASW **Ruler:** Elizabeth II **Obv.:** Crowned head right **Rev.:** Maple leaf and mint logo privy mark **Edge:** Reeded **Size:** 38 mm.

Date	Mintage	MS-63	Proof
2004 Proof	25,000	—	35.00

KM# 508 5 DOLLARS **Weight:** 31.1035 g. **Comp.:** 0.9999 Silver 0.9999 oz. ASW **Ruler:** Elizabeth II **Obv.:** Crowned head right, date and denomination below **Obv. Des.:** Dora de Pedery-Hunt **Rev.:** Holographic Maple leaf flanked by 9999 **Edge:** Reeded **Size:** 38 mm.

Date	Mintage	MS-63	Proof
2003 Proof	—	—	35.00

KM# 550 5 DOLLARS **Weight:** 31.1035 g. **Comp.:** 0.9999 Silver 0.9999 oz. ASW **Ruler:** Elizabeth II **Subject:** Big Leaf Maple, colorized **Obv.:** Head right

Date	Mintage	MS-63	Proof
2005	25,000	30.00	—

KM# 574 5 DOLLARS **Weight:** 1.1035 g. **Comp.:** 0.9999 Silver 0.0355 oz. ASW **Ruler:** Elizabeth II **Obv.:** Head right **Rev.:** Lynx

Date	Mintage	MS-63	Proof
2005 Proof	—	—	35.00

KM# 660 5 DOLLARS **Weight:** 31.1035 g. **Comp.:** Silver **Ruler:** Elizabeth II **Subject:** Silver Maple **Rev.:** Colorized

Date	Mintage	MS-63	Proof
2006 Proof	—	—	35.00

KM# 676 250 DOLLARS **Weight:** 1000.0000 g. **Comp.:** 0.9999 Silver 32.146 oz. ASW **Ruler:** Elizabeth II **Subject:** Kilo

Date	Mintage	MS-63	Proof
2006	—	550	—

GOLD BULLION COINAGE

KM# 438 DOLLAR **Weight:** 1.5810 g. **Comp.:** 0.9990 Gold 0.0508 oz. AGW **Ruler:** Elizabeth II **Subject:** Holographic Maple Leaves **Obv.:** Crowned head right **Rev.:** Three maple leaves multicolor hologram **Edge:** Reeded. **Size:** 14.1 mm.

Date	Mintage	MS-63	Proof
2001 in sets only	600	75.00	—

KM# 439 5 DOLLARS **Weight:** 3.1310 g. **Comp.:** 0.9999 Gold 0.1006 oz. AGW **Ruler:** Elizabeth II **Subject:** Holographic Maple Leaves **Obv.:** Crowned head right **Rev.:** Three maple leaves multicolor hologram **Edge:** Reeded **Size:** 16 mm.

Date	Mintage	MS-63	Proof
2001 in sets only	600	150	—

KM# 440 10 DOLLARS **Weight:** 7.7970 g. **Comp.:** 0.9999 Gold 0.2506 oz. AGW **Ruler:** Elizabeth II **Subject:** Holographic Maples Leaves **Obv.:** Crowned head right **Rev.:** Three maple leaves multicolor hologram **Edge:** Reeded **Size:** 20 mm.

Date	Mintage	MS-63	Proof
2001	15,000	225	—

KM# 441 20 DOLLARS **Weight:** 15.5840 g. **Comp.:** 0.9999 Gold 0.5010 oz. AGW **Ruler:** Elizabeth II **Subject:** Holographic Maples Leaves **Obv.:** Crowned head right **Rev.:** Three maple leaves multicolor hologram **Edge:** Reeded **Size:** 25 mm.

Date	Mintage	MS-63	Proof
2001 in sets only	600	675	—

KM# 442 50 DOLLARS **Weight:** 31.1500 g. **Comp.:** 0.9999 Gold 1.0014 oz. AGW **Ruler:** Elizabeth II **Subject:** Holographic Maples Leaves **Obv.:** Crowned head right **Rev.:** Three maple leaves multicolor hologram **Edge:** Reeded **Size:** 30 mm.

Date	Mintage	MS-63	Proof
2001 in sets only	600	1,350	—

KM# 681 2500 DOLLARS **Weight:** 1000.0000 g. **Comp.:** 0.9999 Gold 32.146 oz. AGW **Ruler:** Elizabeth II **Subject:** Kilo **Rev.:** Common Characters, Early Canada

Date	Mintage	MS-63	Proof
2007	20	29,500	—

PLATINUM BULLION COINAGE

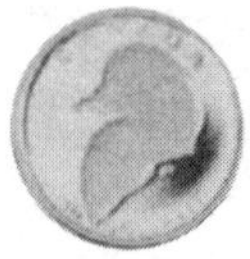

KM# 429 30 DOLLARS **Weight:** 3.1100 g. **Comp.:** 0.9995 Platinum 0.0999 oz. APW **Ruler:** Elizabeth II **Obv.:** Crowned head right **Rev.:** Harlequin duck's head **Rev. Des.:** Cosme Saffioti and Susan Taylor **Edge:** Reeded **Size:** 16 mm.

Date	Mintage	MS-63	Proof
2001 Proof	448	—	165

KM# 430 75 DOLLARS **Weight:** 7.7760 g. **Comp.:** 0.9995 Platinum 0.2499 oz. APW **Ruler:** Elizabeth II **Obv.:** Crowned head right **Rev.:** Harlequin duck in flight **Rev. Des.:** Cosme Saffioti and Susan Taylor **Edge:** Reeded **Size:** 20 mm.

Date	Mintage	MS-63	Proof
2001 Proof	448	—	400

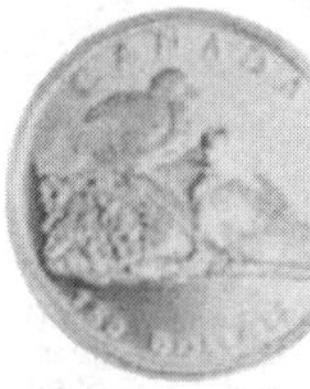

KM# 431 150 DOLLARS **Weight:** 15.5500 g. **Comp.:** 0.9995 Platinum 0.4997 oz. APW **Ruler:** Elizabeth II **Obv.:** Crowned head right **Rev.:** Two harlequin ducks **Rev. Des.:** Cosme Saffioti and Susan Taylor **Edge:** Reeded **Size:** 25 mm.

Date	Mintage	MS-63	Proof
2001 Proof	448	—	800

KM# 432 300 DOLLARS **Weight:** 31.1035 g. **Comp.:** 0.9995 Platinum 0.9995 oz. APW **Ruler:** Elizabeth II **Obv.:** Crowned head right **Rev.:** Two standing harlequin ducks **Rev. Des.:** Cosme Saffioti and Susan Taylor **Edge:** Reeded **Size:** 30 mm.

Date	Mintage	MS-63	Proof
2001 Proof	448	—	1,600

MINT SETS

KM	Date	Mintage	Identification	Issue Price	Mkt Val
MS8	2001	600	KM438-442	1,996	2,450
MS10	2002	—	KM#444-449, 467	17.00	16.00
MS11	2002	—	KM#444-449, 467	17.00	16.00
MS9	2002	135,000	Double-dated 1952-2002, KM#444-449, 467	11.75	11.00
MS12	2003	135,000	KM#289, 182b, 183b, 184b, 290, 186, 270	12.00	12.00
MS13	2003	75,000	KM#490-496	13.25	14.00
MS14	2003	—	KM#289, 182-184, 290, 186, 270	17.75	16.00
MS15	2003	—	KM#289, 182-184, 290, 186, 270	17.75	16.00

PROOF SETS

KM	Date	Mintage	Identification	Issue Price	Mkt Val
PS51	2001	—	KM429, 430, 431, 432	—	2,300
PS52	2002	100,000	KM#443, 444a,445,446a-449a, 467	60.00	70.00
PS54	2002	—	KM#519, 520	750	725
PS53	2002	—	KM#459-461	57.50	55.00
PS55	2003	100,000	KM#182a,183a,184a, 186, 270d, 289, 290a, 450	62.50	80.00
PS56	2003	30,000	KM#468-473	75.00	80.00
PS57	2004	—	KM#490, 491a-494a, 495, 496a, 512	—	85.00
PS58	2004	25,000	KM#621-625	—	125

SPECIMEN SETS (SS)

KM	Date	Mintage	Identification	Issue Price	Mkt Val
SS90	2002	75,000	KM#444-449,462	30.00	22.50
SS91	2003	75,000	KM#182-184, 186, 270, 289, 290	30.00	27.50

CAPE VERDE

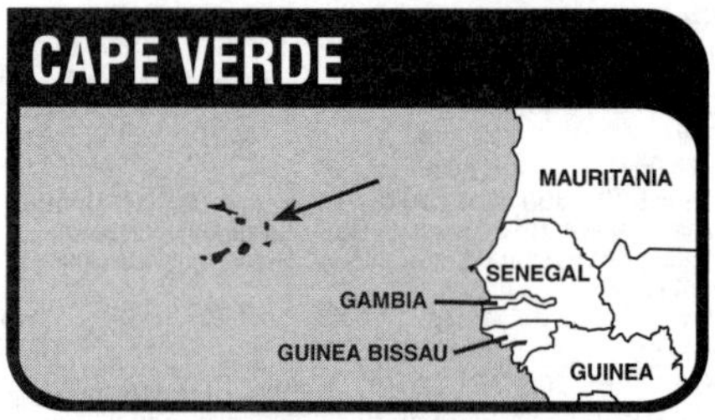

The Republic of Cape Verde, Africa's smallest republic, is located in the Atlantic Ocean, about 370 miles (595 km.) west of Dakar, Senegal, off the coast of Africa. The 14-island republic has an area of 1,557 sq. mi. (4,033 sq. km.) and a population of 435,983. Capital: Praia. The refueling of ships and aircraft is the chief economic function of the country. Fishing is important and agriculture is widely practiced, but the Cape Verdes are not self-sufficient in food. Fish products, salt, bananas, and shellfish are exported.

After 500 years of Portuguese rule, the Cape Verdes became independent on July 5, 1975. At the first general election, all seats of the new national assembly were won by the Party for the Independence of Guinea-Bissau and Cape Verde (PAIGC). The PAIGC linked the two former colonies into one state. Antonio Mascarenhas Monteiro won the first free presidential election in 1991.

RULER
Portuguese, until 1975

MONETARY SYSTEM
100 Centavos = 1 Escudo

REPUBLIC

DECIMAL COINAGE

KM# 46 25 ESCUDOS
15.5517 g., 0.9990 Silver 0.4995 oz. ASW, 30.4 mm. **Obv:** Value above national arms **Rev:** Jesus **Edge:** Plain

Date	Mintage	F	VF	XF	Unc	BU
2006 Proof	—	Value: 40.00				

KM# 47 50 ESCUDOS
1.5550 g., 0.9990 Gold 0.0499 oz. AGW, 16 mm. **Obv:** Value above national arms **Rev:** Jesus **Edge:** Plain

Date	Mintage	F	VF	XF	Unc	BU
2006 Proof	—	Value: 70.00				

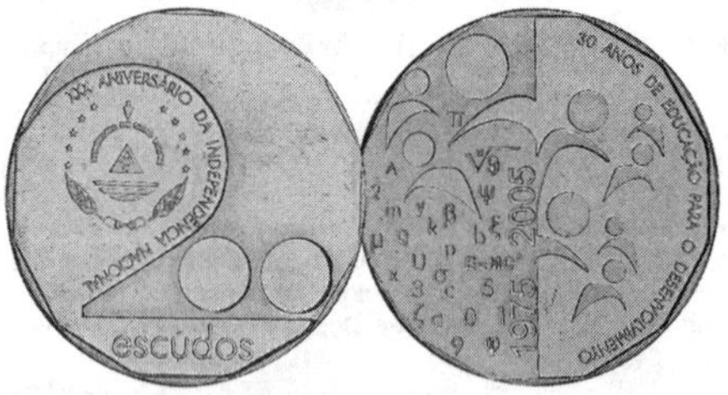

KM# 45 200 ESCUDOS
7.8000 g., Copper-Nickel, 29.5 mm. **Subject:** 30th Anniversary of Independence **Obv:** National arms in number 2 of 200 **Rev:** Symbolic education design **Edge:** Reeded **Shape:** Round

Date	Mintage	F	VF	XF	Unc	BU
2005	—	—	—	—	8.50	10.00

CAYMAN ISLANDS

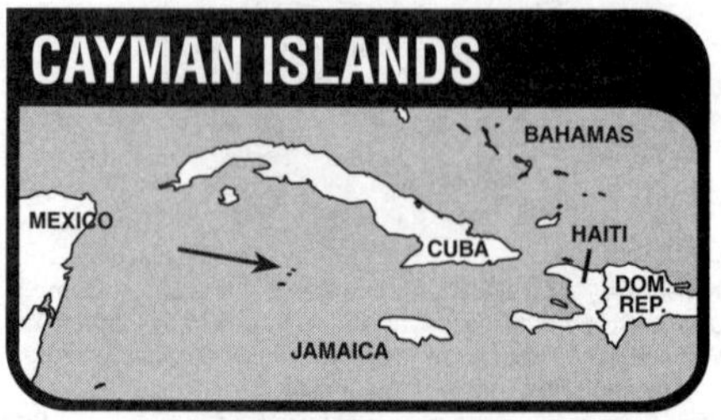

The Cayman Islands are a British Crown Colony situated about 180 miles (280 km) northwest of Jamaica. It consists of three islands: Grand Cayman, Little Cayman, and Cayman Brac. The islands have an area of 102 sq. mi. (259 sq. km.) and a population of 33,200. Capital: George Town. Seafaring, commerce, banking, and tourism are the principal industries. Rope, turtle shells, and sharkskins are exported.

RULER
British

MINT MARKS
CHI - Valcambi
FM - Franklin Mint, U.S.A.*

MONETARY SYSTEM
100 Cents = 1 Dollar

BRITISH COLONY

DECIMAL COINAGE

KM# 131 CENT

2.5300 g., Bronze Plated Steel, 17 mm. **Ruler:** Elizabeth II **Obv:** Crowned head right **Rev:** Great Caiman thrush **Rev. Designer:** Stuart Devlin

Date	Mintage	F	VF	XF	Unc	BU
2002	—	—	—	—	0.50	1.00

KM# 132 5 CENTS

2.0000 g., Nickel Clad Steel, 18 mm. **Ruler:** Elizabeth II **Obv:** Crowned head right **Rev:** Pink-spotted shrimp **Rev. Designer:** Stuart Devlin **Edge:** Plain

Date	Mintage	F	VF	XF	Unc	BU
2002	—	—	—	—	0.50	1.00
2005	—	—	—	—	0.50	1.00

KM# 136 2 DOLLARS

28.3400 g., 0.9250 Silver 0.8428 oz. ASW, 38.6 mm. **Ruler:** Elizabeth II **Obv:** Gold plated Queen Elizabeth II **Rev:** British crown and value **Edge:** Reeded

Date	Mintage	F	VF	XF	Unc	BU
2002 Proof	—	Value: 50.00				

KM# 135 2 DOLLARS

28.2800 g., 0.9250 Sterling Silver 0.8410 oz. ASW, 38.6 mm. **Subject:** 500th Anniversary - Christopher Columbus First Recorded Sighting of the Cayman Islands **Obv:** Crowned head right **Rev:** Quincentennial Celebrations Logo in color

Date	Mintage	F	VF	XF	Unc	BU
2003 Proof	1,500	Value: 75.00				

KM# 137 5 DOLLARS

0.9250 Silver **Ruler:** Elizabeth II **Subject:** Elizabeth II's 80th Birthday **Obv:** Crowned head right - gilt **Obv. Legend:** CAYMAN ISLANDS-ELIZABETH II **Obv. Designer:** Ian Rank-Broadley **Rev:** 1/2 length figures of Oueen Mother right crowning Elizabeth at left

Date	Mintage	F	VF	XF	Unc	BU
2006 Proof	—	Value: 40.00				

CENTRAL AFRICAN REPUBLIC

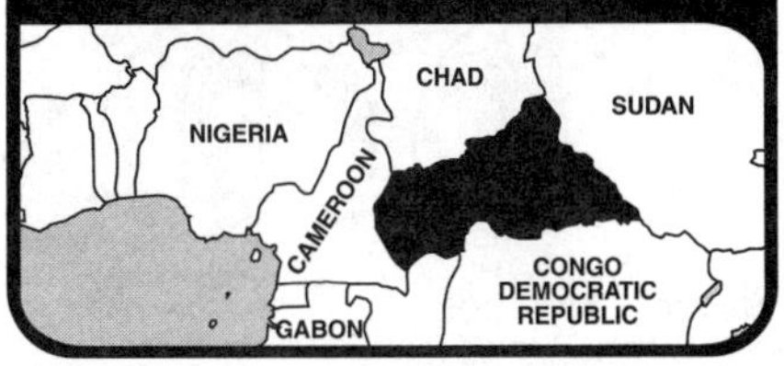

The Central African Republic, a landlocked country in Central Africa, bounded by Chad on the north, Cameroon on the west, Congo (Brazzaville) and Congo Democratic Republic, (formerly Zaire) on the south and the Sudan on the east, has an area of 240,324 sq. mi. (622,984 sq. km.) and a population of 3.2 million. Capital: Bangui. Deposits of uranium, iron ore, manganese and copper remain to be developed. Diamonds, cotton, timber and coffee are exported.

NOTE: For earlier coinage see French Equatorial Africa and Equatorial African States including later coinage as listed in Central African States.

MINT MARK
(a) - Paris, privy marks only

MONETARY SYSTEM
100 Centimes = 1 Franc

REPUBLIC

INSTITUT MONETAIRE

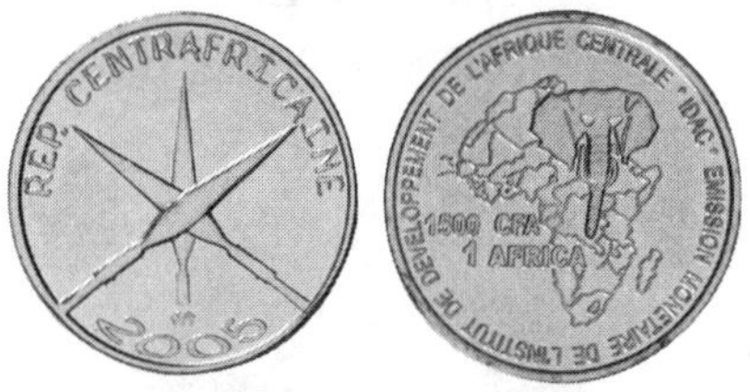

KM# 12 1500 CFA FRANCS-1 AFRICA

7.3200 g., Nickel Plated Iron, 25.9 mm. **Obv:** Crossed lances **Rev:** Elephant head on full Africa map **Edge:** Plain

Date	Mintage	F	VF	XF	Unc	BU
2005	2,005	—	—	—	20.00	—

KM# 12a 1500 CFA FRANCS-1 AFRICA

0.9990 Silver, 26 mm. **Obv:** Crossed lances **Rev:** Elephant head on full Africa map

Date	Mintage	F	VF	XF	Unc	BU
2005	25	—	—	—	250	—

KM# 13 4500 CFA-3 AFRICA

8.0000 g., Bi-Metallic Stainless Steel center in Brass ring, 26 mm. **Obv:** Pope John Paul II **Rev:** African Map **Edge:** Segmented reeding

Date	Mintage	F	VF	XF	Unc	BU
2007	2,007	—	—	—	—	65.00

KM# 13a 4500 CFA-3 AFRICA

10.0000 g., Bi-Metallic .999 Silver center in Gold plated Brass ring, 26 mm. **Obv:** Pope John Paul II **Rev:** African Map **Edge:** Segmented reeding

Date	Mintage	F	VF	XF	Unc	BU
2007	27	—	—	—	—	585

KM# 13b 4500 CFA-3 AFRICA

12.0000 g., 0.9990 Silver 0.3854 oz. ASW, 26 mm. **Obv:** Pope John Paul II **Rev:** African Map **Edge:** Segmented reeding

Date	Mintage	F	VF	XF	Unc	BU
2007	27	—	—	—	—	520

CENTRAL AFRICAN STATES

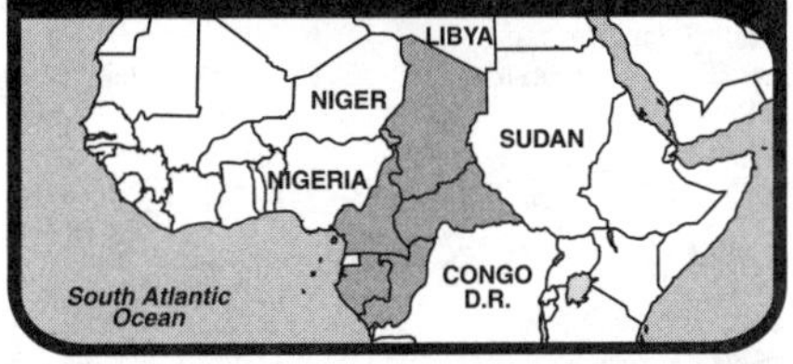

The Central African States, a monetary union comprised of Equatorial Guinea (a former Spanish possession), the former French possessions and now independent states of the Republic of Congo (Brazzaville), Gabon, Central African Republic, Chad and Cameroon, issues a common currency for the member states from a common central bank. The monetary unit, the African Financial Community franc, is tied to and supported by the French franc.

In 1960, an attempt was made to form a union of the newly independent republics of Chad, Congo, Central Africa and Gabon. The proposal was discarded when Chad refused to become a constituent member. The four countries then linked into an Equatorial Customs Unit, to which Cameroon became an associate member in 1961. A more extensive cooperation of the five republics, identified as the Central African Customs and Economic Union, was entered into force at the beginning of 1966.

In 1974 the Central Bank of the Equatorial African States, which had issued coins and paper currency in its own name and with the names of the constituent member nations, changed its name to the Bank of the Central African States. Equatorial Guinea converted to the CFA currency system issuing its first 100 Franc in 1985.

For earlier coinage see French Equatorial Africa.

Country Code Letters

To observe the movement of coinage throughout the states, the country of origin in which the coin is intended to circulate is designated by the following additional code letters:

A = Chad
B = Central African Republic
C = Congo
D = Gabon
E = Cameroon

By 1996 this practice was discontinued as the strategy had proved to be inconclusive.

MONETARY UNION

STANDARD COINAGE

KM# 16 FRANC

1.6100 g., Stainless Steel, 14.9 mm. **Obv:** Value above produce **Rev:** Value **Edge:** Plain

Date	Mintage	F	VF	XF	Unc	BU
2006(a)	—	—	—	—	0.15	0.25

KM# 17 2 FRANCS

2.4300 g., Stainless Steel, 17.9 mm. **Obv:** Value above produce **Rev:** Value **Edge:** Plain

Date	Mintage	F	VF	XF	Unc	BU
2006(a)	—	—	—	—	0.25	0.35

KM# 18 5 FRANCS

2.4100 g., Brass, 15.9 mm. **Obv:** Value above produce **Rev:** Value **Edge:** Reeded

Date	Mintage	F	VF	XF	Unc	BU
2006(a)	—	—	—	—	0.50	0.65

KM# 19 10 FRANCS

3.0000 g., Brass, 17.9 mm. **Obv:** Value above produce **Rev:** Value **Edge:** Reeded

Date	Mintage	F	VF	XF	Unc	BU
2006(a)	—	—	—	—	0.75	1.00

KM# 9 10 FRANCS

4.0000 g., Aluminum-Bronze, 23 mm. **Obv:** Three giant eland left, date below **Obv. Designer:** G.B.L. Bazor **Rev:** Denomination within wreath

Date	Mintage	F	VF	XF	Unc	BU
2003(a)	—	0.20	0.35	0.75	1.50	—

KM# 20 25 FRANCS

4.2000 g., Brass, 22.7 mm. **Obv:** Value above produce **Rev:** Value **Edge:** Reeded

Date	Mintage	F	VF	XF	Unc	BU
2006(a)	—	—	—	—	1.00	1.25

KM# 10 25 FRANCS
8.0000 g., Aluminum-Bronze, 27.1 mm. **Obv:** Three giant eland left, date below **Obv. Designer:** G.B.L. Bazor **Rev:** Denomination within wreath

Date	Mintage	F	VF	XF	Unc	BU
2003(a)	—	0.25	0.50	1.00	2.00	—

KM# 21 50 FRANCS
4.9000 g., Stainless Steel, 22 mm. **Obv:** Value above produce **Rev:** Value **Edge:** Reeded

Date	Mintage	F	VF	XF	Unc	BU
2006(a)	—	—	—	—	1.25	1.50

KM# 11 50 FRANCS
4.7000 g., Nickel, 21.5 mm. **Obv:** Three giant eland left, date below **Obv. Designer:** G.B.L. Bazor **Rev:** Denomination within flower design **Note:** Starting in 1996 an extra flora item was added where the mint mark was formerly located.

Date	Mintage	F	VF	XF	Unc	BU
2003(a) Cocoa bean	—	0.75	1.50	3.50	6.00	—

KM# 15 100 FRANCS
6.0000 g., Bi-Metallic Stainless Steel center in Brass ring, 23.9 mm. **Obv:** Denomination above initials within beaded circle **Rev:** Value above produce **Edge:** Reeded

Date	Mintage	F	VF	XF	Unc	BU
2006(a)	—	—	—	—	5.00	6.50

KM# 22 500 FRANCS
8.1000 g., Copper-Nickel, 26 mm. **Obv:** Value above produce **Rev:** Value **Edge:** Segmented reeding and lettering

Date	Mintage	F	VF	XF	Unc	BU
2006(a)	—	—	—	—	8.00	9.50

CHAD

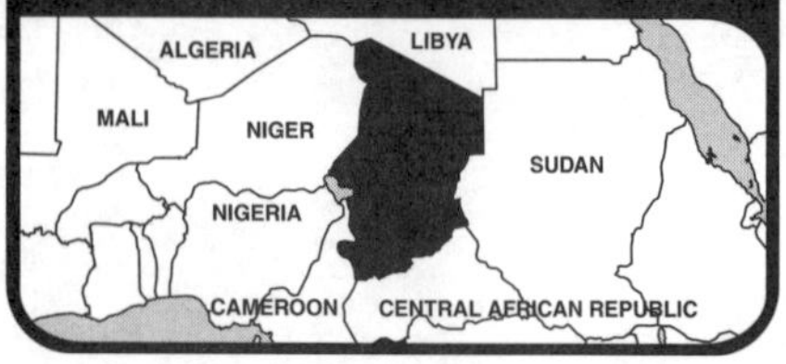

The Republic of Chad, a landlocked country of central Africa, is the largest country of former French Equatorial Africa. It has an area of 495,755 sq. mi. (1,284,000 sq. km.) and a population of *7.27 million. Capital: N'Djamena. An expanding livestock industry produces camels, cattle and sheep. Cotton (the chief product), ivory and palm oil are important exports.

NOTE: For earlier and related coinage see French Equatorial Africa and the Equatorial African States. For later coinage see Central African States.

MINT MARKS
(a) - Paris, privy marks only
(b) = Brussels
NI - Numismatic Italiana, Arezzo, Italy

REPUBLIC

DECIMAL COINAGE

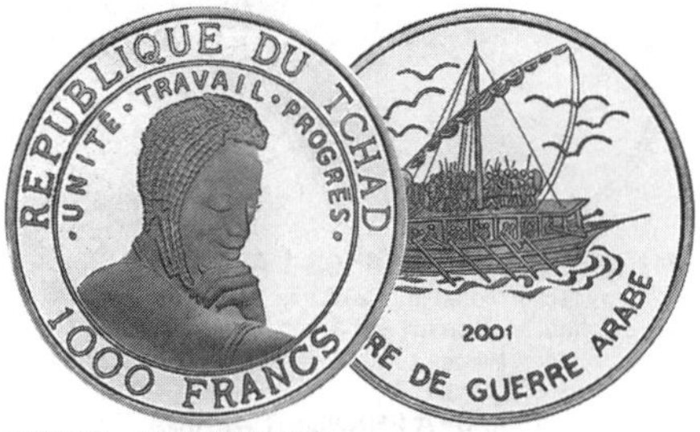

KM# 20 1000 FRANCS
15.0000 g., 0.9990 Silver 0.4818 oz. ASW, 35 mm. **Obv:** Native portrait within circle, denomination below **Rev:** Ancient Arabic war ship **Edge:** Plain

Date	Mintage	F	VF	XF	Unc	BU
2001 Proof	—	Value: 35.00				

KM# 21 1000 FRANCS
25.1000 g., 0.9990 Silver 0.8061 oz. ASW, 40 mm. **Obv:** Native portrait within circle, denomination below **Rev:** Soccer player and stadium **Edge:** Reeded

Date	Mintage	F	VF	XF	Unc	BU
2001 Proof	—	Value: 40.00				

KM# 22 1000 FRANCS
20.0000 g., 0.9990 Silver 0.6423 oz. ASW, 40 mm. **Obv:** Native portrait within circle, denomination below **Rev:** Horizontal soccer player above stadium **Edge:** Reeded

Date	Mintage	F	VF	XF	Unc	BU
2002 Proof	5,000	Value: 40.00				

KM# 23 1000 FRANCS
20.1500 g., 0.9990 Silver 0.6472 oz. ASW, 40 mm. **Obv:** Native portrait within circle, denomination below **Rev:** Soccer player and Arch of Triumph **Edge:** Reeded

Date	Mintage	F	VF	XF	Unc	BU
2002 Proof	—	Value: 40.00				

CHILE

The Republic of Chile, a ribbon-like country on the Pacific coast of southern South America, has an area of 292,135 sq. mi. (756,950 sq. km.) and a population of *15.21 million. Capital: Santiago. Historically, the economic base of Chile has been the rich mineral deposits of its northern provinces. Copper has accounted for more than 75 percent of Chile's export earnings in recent years. Other important mineral exports are iron ore, iodine and nitrate of soda. Fresh fruits and vegetables, as well as wine are increasingly significant in inter-hemispheric trade.

MINT MARK
So - Santiago

REPUBLIC

REFORM COINAGE

100 Centavos = 1 Peso; 1000 Old Escudos = 1 Peso

KM# 231 PESO
0.0830 g., Aluminum, 16.14 mm. **Obv:** Armored bust right **Rev:** Denomination above date within wreath **Edge:** Plain **Shape:** 8-sided **Note:** Varieties exist.

Date	Mintage	F	VF	XF	Unc	BU
2001	—	—	—	—	0.10	0.20
2002	—	—	—	—	0.10	0.20
2003	—	—	—	—	0.10	0.20
2004	—	—	—	—	0.10	0.20
2005	—	—	—	—	0.10	0.20

KM# 232 5 PESOS
2.1600 g., Aluminum-Bronze, 16.02 mm. **Obv:** Armored bust right **Rev:** Denomination above date within wreath **Edge:** Plain **Shape:** 8-sided **Note:** Varieties exist.

Date	Mintage	F	VF	XF	Unc	BU
2001 Narrow date	—	—	—	0.10	0.35	0.60
2001 (sa) Wide date	—	—	—	0.15	0.50	0.75
Note: Without name of sculptor						
2002 Narrow date	—	—	—	0.10	0.35	0.60
2002A Narrow date	—	—	—	0.15	0.50	0.75
2003	—	—	—	0.10	0.35	0.60
2004	—	—	—	0.10	0.35	0.60
2005	—	—	—	0.10	0.35	0.60

KM# 228.2 10 PESOS
3.5000 g., Nickel-Brass, 20.8 mm. **Obv:** Armored bust of Bernardo O'Higgins right, normal rim **Rev:** Denomination above date within wreath **Note:** All 9's are curl tail 9's except for the 1999 date, these are straight tail 9's.

Date	Mintage	F	VF	XF	Unc	BU
2002	—	—	0.10	0.20	0.50	0.65
2003	—	—	0.10	0.20	0.50	0.65
2004	—	—	0.10	0.20	0.50	0.65
2005	—	—	0.10	0.20	0.50	0.65
2006	—	—	0.10	0.20	0.50	0.65

KM# 219.2 50 PESOS
7.0000 g., Aluminum-Bronze, 25.75 mm. **Obv:** Armored bust right **Rev:** Denomination above date within wreath **Shape:** 10-sided **Note:** Narrow date.

Date	Mintage	F	VF	XF	Unc	BU
2001	—	—	0.25	0.50	1.25	1.50
2002	—	—	0.25	0.50	1.25	1.50
2005	—	—	0.25	0.50	1.00	1.25
2006	—	—	0.25	0.50	1.00	1.25

KM# 236 100 PESOS
Bi-Metallic Copper-nickel center in Brass ring, 23.5 mm. **Subject:** Native people **Obv:** Bust of native Mapuche girl facing **Rev:** National arms above denomination **Edge:** Reeded and striated sections

Date	Mintage	F	VF	XF	Unc	BU
2001	—	—	—	—	2.50	3.00
2003	—	—	—	—	2.50	3.00
2004	—	—	—	—	2.50	3.00
2005	—	—	—	—	2.50	3.00
2006	—	—	—	—	2.50	3.00

KM# 235 500 PESOS
6.5000 g., Bi-Metallic Aluminum-bronze center in Copper-nickel ring, 25.9 mm. **Subject:** Cardinal Raul Silva Henriquez **Obv:** Bust of Henriquez within inner ring facing left **Rev:** Denomination above date within wreath **Edge:** Reeded

Date	Mintage	F	VF	XF	Unc	BU
2001	—	—	—	—	6.00	6.50
2002 4.1mm date	—	—	—	—	6.00	6.50
2002 5.2mm date	—	—	—	—	6.00	6.50
2003	—	—	—	—	6.00	6.50

CHINA / Peoples Republic

The Peoples Republic of China, located in eastern Asia, has an area of 3,696,100 sq. mi. (9,596,960 sq. km.) (including Manchuria and Tibet) and a population of *1.20 billion. Capital: Peking (Beijing). The economy is based on agriculture, mining, and manufacturing. Textiles, clothing, metal ores, tea and rice are exported.

MONETARY SYSTEM

After 1949

10 Fen (Cents) = 1 Jiao
10 Jiao = 1 Renminbi Yuan

MINT MARKS

(b) - Beijing (Peking)
(s) - Shanghai
(y) - Shenyang (Mukden)

OBVERSE LEGENDS

中华人民共和国

ZHONGHUA RENMIN GONGHEGUO
(Peoples Republic of China)

中国人民银行

ZHONGGUO RENMIN YINHANG
(Peoples Bank of China)

PEOPLES REPUBLIC

STANDARD COINAGE

KM# 1210 JIAO
1.1200 g., Aluminum, 19 mm. **Obv:** Denomination, date below **Rev:** Orchid **Rev. Legend:** ZHONGGUA RENMIN YINHANG **Edge:** Plain **Note:** Prev.Prev. Y # 1068.

Date	Mintage	F	VF	XF	Unc	BU
2001	—	—	—	—	0.50	—
2002	—	—	—	—	0.50	—
2003	—	—	—	—	0.50	—

KM# 1210a JIAO
Copper-Nickel **Obv:** Denomination, date below **Note:** Prev. Y # 1068a.

Date	Mintage	F	VF	XF	Unc	BU
2005	—	—	—	—	0.50	—

KM# 1210b JIAO
3.2200 g., Steel, 19.03 mm. **Obv:** Value, date below **Rev:** Orchid **Rev. Legend:** ZHONGGUA RENMIN YINHANG **Edge:** Plain **Note:** Prev. Y # 1068b.

Date	Mintage	F	VF	XF	Unc	BU
2005	—	—	—	—	0.25	—
2006	—	—	—	—	0.25	—

KM# 336 5 JIAO
3.8300 g., Brass, 20.5 mm. **Obv:** National emblem, date below **Rev:** Denomination above flowers **Edge:** Segmented reeding **Note:** Prev. Y # 329.

Date	Mintage	F	VF	XF	Unc	BU
2001	—	—	—	—	1.00	—

KM# 1411 5 JIAO
3.8000 g., Brass, 20.5 mm. **Obv:** Denomination **Rev:** Flower **Rev. Legend:** ZHONGGUA RENMIN YINHANG **Edge:** Reeded and plain sections **Note:** Prev. Y # 1106.

Date	Mintage	F	VF	XF	Unc	BU
2002	—	—	—	—	1.50	—
2003	—	—	—	—	1.50	—

KM# 1212 YUAN
6.1000 g., Nickel Plated Steel, 24.9 mm. **Obv:** Denomination, date below **Rev:** Chrysanthemum **Rev. Legend:** ZHONGGUA RENMIN YINHANG **Edge:** "RMB" three times **Note:** Prev. Y # 1069.

Date	Mintage	F	VF	XF	Unc	BU
2001	—	—	—	—	2.00	—
2002	—	—	—	—	2.00	—
2003	—	—	—	—	2.00	—
2004	—	—	—	—	2.00	—

KM# 1465 YUAN
6.8500 g., Brass, 25 mm. **Obv:** Value **Rev:** Celebrating child and ram **Edge:** Lettered **Edge Lettering:** "R M B" three times **Note:** Prev. Y # 1125.

Date	Mintage	F	VF	XF	Unc	BU
2003	—	—	—	—	5.00	—

KM# 1521 YUAN
Nickel Clad Steel **Obv:** Denomination **Rev:** Celebrating Child **Note:** Prev. Y # 1247.

Date	Mintage	F	VF	XF	Unc	BU
2004	—	—	—	—	2.50	—

KM# 1522 YUAN
Nickel Clad Steel **Obv:** Palace **Rev:** Deng Xiao Ping 1904-2004 **Note:** Prev. Y # 1248.

Date	Mintage	F	VF	XF	Unc	BU
2004	—	—	—	—	3.50	—

KM# 1523 YUAN
Nickel Clad Steel **Subject:** 50th Year of Peoples Congress **Obv:** Congress building **Note:** Prev. Y # 1249.

Date	Mintage	F	VF	XF	Unc	BU
2004	—	—	—	—	3.50	—

KM# 1575 YUAN
Nickel Clad Steel **Subject:** Year of the Rooster **Obv:** Denomination **Rev:** Celebrating Child **Note:** Prev. Y # 1250.

Date	Mintage	F	VF	XF	Unc	BU
2005	—	—	—	—	3.00	—

KM# 1574 YUAN
5.9600 g., Nickel Clad Steel, 25 mm. **Obv:** Building **Rev:** Bust of Chenyun **Edge:** Lettered **Note:** Prev. Y # 1208.

Date	Mintage	F	VF	XF	Unc	BU
2005	—	—	—	—	3.50	—

KM# 1650 YUAN
Nickel Clad Steel **Subject:** Year of the Dog **Obv:** Denomination **Rev:** Celebrating Child **Note:** Prev. Y # 1251.

Date	Mintage	F	VF	XF	Unc	BU
2006	—	—	—	—	3.00	—

KM# 1675 YUAN
6.7500 g., Brass, 25 mm. **Subject:** 29th Olympics **Obv:** Stylized Olympics logo **Rev:** Cartoon swimmer **Edge:** Reeded **Note:** Prev. Y # 1256.

Date	Mintage	F	VF	XF	Unc	BU
2008 (2006)(y)	—	—	—	—	—	6.00

KM# 1676 YUAN
6.7500 g., Brass, 25 mm. **Subject:** 29th Olympics **Obv:** Stylized Olympics logo **Rev:** Cartoon Weight Lifter **Edge:** Reeded **Note:** Prev. Y # 1257.

Date	Mintage	F	VF	XF	Unc	BU
2008 (2006)	—	—	—	—	—	6.00

KM# 1364 5 YUAN
12.3000 g., Brass, 30 mm. **Subject:** Revolution: 90th Anniversary **Obv:** National emblem **Rev:** Battle scene **Edge:** Reeded **Note:** Prev. Y # 1109.

Date	Mintage	F	VF	XF	Unc	BU
2001	—	—	—	—	7.50	—

KM# 1363 5 YUAN
12.8000 g., Brass, 30 mm. **Subject:** 50th Anniversary - Chinese Occupation of Tibet **Obv:** National emblem **Rev:** Potala Palace, value and two dancers **Edge:** Reeded **Note:** Prev. Y # 1126.

Date	Mintage	F	VF	XF	Unc	BU
2001(y)	10,000,000	—	—	—	7.00	—

KM# 1412 5 YUAN
12.9000 g., Brass, 29.9 mm. **Subject:** The Great Wall **Obv:** State arms, icroscopic inscription repeated four times on the inner raised rim **Obv. Inscription:** SHI JIE WEN HUA YI CHAN **Rev:** Two views of the Great Wall **Edge:** Reeded **Note:** Prev. Y # 1107.

Date	Mintage	F	VF	XF	Unc	BU
2002	—	—	—	—	7.00	—

KM# 1413 5 YUAN
12.8200 g., Brass, 29.9 mm. **Subject:** Terra Cotta Army **Obv:** State arms and the microscopic inscription repeated four times on the raised inner rim. **Obv. Inscription:** SHI JIE WEN HUA YI CHAN **Rev:** Terra Cotta Soldier close-up with many more in background **Edge:** Reeded **Note:** Prev. Y # 1108.

Date	Mintage	F	VF	XF	Unc	BU
2002	—	—	—	—	7.00	—

KM# 1463 5 YUAN
12.8000 g., Brass, 30 mm. **Subject:** Chaotian Temple in Beijing **Obv:** State emblem **Rev:** Buildings **Edge:** Reeded **Note:** Prev. Y # 1230.

Date	Mintage	F	VF	XF	Unc	BU
2003	10,000,000	—	—	—	7.00	—

KM# 1464 5 YUAN
Brass, 30 mm. **Obv:** National emblem **Rev:** Imperial Palace **Note:** Prev. Y # 1252.

Date	Mintage	F	VF	XF	Unc	BU
2003	—	—	—	—	7.00	—

KM# 1461 5 YUAN
12.8000 g., Brass, 30 mm. **Obv:** National emblem **Rev:** Chaotian Temple in Beigang Taiwan **Edge:** Reeded **Note:** Prev. Y # 1127.

Date	Mintage	F	VF	XF	Unc	BU
2003	10,000,000	—	—	—	7.00	—

KM# 1462 5 YUAN
12.8000 g., Brass, 30 mm. **Obv:** National emblem **Rev:** Chikan Tower on Treasure Island Taiwan **Edge:** Reeded **Note:** Prev. Y # 1128.

Date	Mintage	F	VF	XF	Unc	BU
2003(y)	10,000,000	—	—	—	7.00	—

KM# 1526 5 YUAN
12.7000 g., Brass, 30 mm. **Obv:** National emblem **Rev:** Peking Man bust and discovery site view **Edge:** Reeded **Note:** Prev. Y#1201.

Date	Mintage	F	VF	XF	Unc	BU
2004	6,000,000	—	—	—	6.00	—

KM# 1527 5 YUAN
12.7000 g., Brass, 30 mm. **Obv:** National emblem **Rev:** Pavillion and bridge **Edge:** Reeded **Note:** Prev. Y # 1202.

Date	Mintage	F	VF	XF	Unc	BU
2004	6,000,000	—	—	—	6.00	—

KM# 1524 5 YUAN
Brass, 30 mm. **Obv:** National emblem **Rev:** Island scene **Note:** Prev. Y # 1253.

Date	Mintage	F	VF	XF	Unc	BU
2004	—	—	—	—	6.00	—

KM# 1525 5 YUAN
Brass, 30 mm. **Obv:** National emblem **Rev:** Lighthouse **Note:** Prev. Y # 1254.

Date	Mintage	F	VF	XF	Unc	BU
2004	—	—	—	—	6.00	—

KM# 1068 5 YUAN
22.0000 g., 0.9000 Silver 0.6366 oz. ASW, 36 mm. **Obv:** Great Wall **Rev:** Gymnast, denomination at right **Edge:** Reeded **Note:** Prev. Y # 1189.

Date	Mintage	F	VF	XF	Unc	BU
2005	—	—	—	—	22.50	—

KM# 1577 5 YUAN
12.8000 g., Brass, 30 mm. **Subject:** "Taiwan" **Obv:** State emblem **Rev:** Tower and terrace **Edge:** Reeded **Note:** Prev. Y # 1231.

Date	Mintage	F	VF	XF	Unc	BU
2005	—	—	—	—	6.00	—

KM# 1576 5 YUAN
12.9200 g., Brass, 30 mm. **Obv:** National emblem **Rev:** Lijiang building **Edge:** Reeded **Note:** Prev. Y # 1209.

Date	Mintage	F	VF	XF	Unc	BU
2005	—	—	—	—	6.00	—

KM# 1578 5 YUAN
12.9200 g., Brass, 30 mm. **Obv:** National emblem **Rev:** Green City Hall **Edge:** Reeded **Note:** Prev. Y # 1210.

Date	Mintage	F	VF	XF	Unc	BU
2005	—	—	—	—	6.00	—

KM# 1395 10 YUAN
31.1035 g., 0.9990 Silver 0.9990 oz. ASW, 40 mm. **Subject:** 2008 Olympics Beijing bid **Obv:** Gold-plated "V" design **Rev:** Radiant Temple of Heaven **Edge:** Reeded **Note:** Prev. Y # 1103.

Date	Mintage	F	VF	XF	Unc	BU
2001 Proof	60,000	Value: 50.00				

KM# 1455 10 YUAN
31.1035 g., 0.9990 Silver 0.9990 oz. ASW, 40 mm. **Subject:** Shanghai World Expo of 2010 **Obv:** Flower design with inset pearl **Rev:** 2010 Logo incorporating a tower **Edge:** Reeded **Note:** Prev. Y # 1233.

Date	Mintage	F	VF	XF	Unc	BU
2002 Proof	50,000	Value: 50.00				

KM# 1507 10 YUAN
31.1035 g., 0.9990 Silver 0.9990 oz. ASW, 40 mm. **Obv:** Stylized forest **Rev:** Cyclists in forest **Edge:** Reeded **Note:** Prev. Y # 1132.

Date	Mintage	F	VF	XF	Unc	BU
2003 Proof	30,000	Value: 50.00				

KM# 1508 10 YUAN
31.1035 g., 0.9990 Silver 0.9990 oz. ASW, 40 mm. **Obv:** Stylized forest **Rev:** Birds flying over forest **Edge:** Reeded **Note:** Prev. Y # 1133.

Date	Mintage	F	VF	XF	Unc	BU
2003(y) Proof	30,000	Value: 50.00				

KM# 1510 10 YUAN
31.1035 g., 0.9990 Silver 0.9990 oz. ASW, 40 mm. **Obv:** Solar system design **Rev:** Multicolor Chinese Astronaut **Edge:** Reeded **Note:** Prev. Y # 1134.

Date	Mintage	F	VF	XF	Unc	BU
2003(y) Proof	60,000	Value: 60.00				

KM# 1559 10 YUAN
31.1035 g., 0.9990 Silver 0.9990 oz. ASW, 40 mm. **Obv:** Monkey King leading the Master over bridge **Rev:** Multicolor Monkey King fighting the "Ox Fiend" **Edge:** Reeded **Note:** Prev. Y # 1214.

Date	Mintage	F	VF	XF	Unc	BU
2004 Proof	38,000	Value: 55.00				

KM# 1558 10 YUAN
31.1035 g., 0.9990 Silver 0.9990 oz. ASW, 40 mm. **Obv:** Monkey King leading the Master over bridge **Rev:** Multicolor Pig carrying Monkey King piggy-back style **Edge:** Reeded **Note:** Prev. Y # 1215.

Date	Mintage	F	VF	XF	Unc	BU
2004 Proof	38,000	Value: 55.00				

KM# 1566 10 YUAN
31.1035 g., 0.9990 Silver 0.9990 oz. ASW, 40 mm. **Obv:** Guangan Exposition Hall **Rev:** Deng Xiaoping and value **Edge:** Reeded **Note:** Prev. Y # 1240.

Date	Mintage	F	VF	XF	Unc	BU
2004 Proof	80,000	Value: 60.00				

KM# 1580 10 YUAN
31.1035 g., 0.9990 Silver 0.9990 oz. ASW, 40 mm. **Subject:** 600th Anniversary of Zheng He's voyage **Obv:** Multicolor stylized sailboat on water **Rev:** Ancient Chinese navigational instruments **Edge:** Reeded **Note:** Prev. Y # 1239.

Date	Mintage	F	VF	XF	Unc	BU
2005(y) Proof	—	Value: 50.00				

KM# 1670 10 YUAN
Silver **Subject:** World Cup Soccer **Obv:** Colorized logo **Rev:** Classically dressed athlete scoring goal **Note:** Prev. Y # 1255.

Date	Mintage	F	VF	XF	Unc	BU
2006 Proof	—	Value: 55.00				

KM# 1651 10 YUAN
31.1035 g., Silver **Obv:** Qing Yuan Gate of the China Great Wall **Rev:** 2 dogs at play **Shape:** 30° Fan **Note:** Prev. Y # 1219.

Date	Mintage	F	VF	XF	Unc	BU
2006 Proof	66,000	Value: 65.00				

KM# 1653 10 YUAN
31.1035 g., Silver, 40 mm. **Obv:** Belt-hook in dog shape from Chinese ancient bronze ware and a decorative design of dog tail-shaped plant leaves **Rev:** 2 dogs at play **Note:** Prev. Y # 1221.

Date	Mintage	F	VF	XF	Unc	BU
2006 Proof	100,000	Value: 50.00				

KM# 1655 10 YUAN
31.1035 g., Silver, 40 mm. **Obv:** Dog-shaped belt-hook depicted from ancient Chinese bronze ware and a decorative design of dog tail-shaped plant leaves **Rev:** 2 smart dogs **Shape:** Scalloped **Note:** Prev. Y # 1223.

Date	Mintage	F	VF	XF	Unc	BU
2006 Proof	60,000	Value: 55.00				

KM# 1388 20 YUAN
62.2070 g., 0.9990 Silver 1.9979 oz. ASW, 40 mm. **Subject:** Mogao Grottos **Obv:** 8-story building **Rev:** Buddha-like statue **Edge:** Reeded **Note:** Prev. Y # 1082.

Date	Mintage	F	VF	XF	Unc	BU
2001 Proof	30,000	Value: 100				

KM# 1390 50 YUAN
155.5175 g., 0.9990 Silver 4.9948 oz. ASW, 70 mm. **Subject:** Mogao Grottoes **Obv:** Eight story building **Rev:** Four musicians **Edge:** Reeded. **Note:** Prev. Y # 1083.

Date	Mintage	F	VF	XF	Unc	BU
2001 Proof	8,000	Value: 200				

KM# 1389 50 YUAN
3.1104 g., 0.9990 Gold 0.0999 oz. AGW **Subject:** Mogao Grottoes **Obv:** Eight story building **Rev:** Buddha-like statue **Edge:** Reeded. **Note:** Prev. Y # 1084.

Date	Mintage	F	VF	XF	Unc	BU
2001 Proof	50,000	Value: 95.00				

KM# 1394 50 YUAN
155.5175 g., 0.9990 Silver 4.9948 oz. ASW, 90 x 40 mm. **Subject:** Han Xizai's Dinner Party **Obv:** Tang dynasty buildings **Rev:** Multicolor "Five Dynasties" painting **Edge:** Plain **Shape:** Rectangular **Note:** Prev. Y # 1104.

Date	Mintage	F	VF	XF	Unc	BU
2001 Proof	18,800	Value: 175				

KM# 1514 50 YUAN
3.1104 g., 0.9990 Gold 0.0999 oz. AGW, 18 mm. **Obv:** Putuo Mountain Pilgrimage Gate **Rev:** Seated Kuanyin with holographic background **Edge:** Reeded **Note:** Prev. Y # 1234.

Date	Mintage	F	VF	XF	Unc	BU
2003 Proof	33,000	Value: 95.00				

KM# 1572 50 YUAN
3.1100 g., 0.9990 Gold 0.0999 oz. AGW, 18 mm. **Obv:** Putuo Mountain Pilgrimage Gate **Rev:** Kuanyin and value **Edge:** Reeded **Note:** Prev. Y # 1237.

Date	Mintage	F	VF	XF	Unc	BU
2004 Proof	33,000	Value: 95.00				

KM# 1560 50 YUAN
155.5175 g., 0.9990 Silver 4.9948 oz. ASW, 80x50 mm. **Obv:** Monkey King leading the Master over bridge **Rev:** Multicolor Monkey King fighting the Pig Demon of Bones **Edge:** Plain **Shape:** ingot **Note:** Prev. Y # 1216.

Date	Mintage	F	VF	XF	Unc	BU
2004 Proof	10,000	Value: 300				

KM# 1654 50 YUAN
3.1103 g., 0.9990 Gold 0.0999 oz. AGW, 18 mm. **Obv:** Dog-shaped belt-hook , an ancient Chinese bronze ware, decorative disign of dog tail-shaped plant leaves **Rev:** 2 dogs at play **Note:** Prev. Y # 1222.

Date	Mintage	F	VF	XF	Unc	BU
2006 Proof	30,000	Value: 95.00				

KM# 1534 100 YUAN
15.5500 g., 0.9990 Palladium 0.4994 oz., 27 mm. **Obv:** Temple of Heaven **Rev:** Panda mother and cub, "kissing pandas" **Edge:** Reeded **Note:** Prev. Y # 1211.

Date	Mintage	F	VF	XF	Unc	BU
2004 Proof	8,000	Value: 375				

KM# 1573 100 YUAN
3.1100 g., 0.9995 Platinum 0.0999 oz. APW, 18 mm. **Obv:** Putuo Mountain Pilgrimage Gate **Rev:** Kuanyin and value **Edge:** Reeded **Note:** Prev. Y # 1238.

Date	Mintage	F	VF	XF	Unc	BU
2004 Proof	33,000	Value: 165				

KM# 1391 200 YUAN
15.5518 g., 0.9990 Gold 0.4995 oz. AGW, 27 mm. **Subject:** Mogao Grottoes **Obv:** Eight story building **Rev:** Dancing drummer **Edge:** Reeded. **Note:** Prev. Y # 1085.

Date	Mintage	F	VF	XF	Unc	BU
2001 Proof	8,800	Value: 450				

KM# 1393 200 YUAN
15.5518 g., 0.9990 Gold 0.4995 oz. AGW, 27 mm. **Subject:** 50th Anniversary Chinese Occupation of Tibet **Obv:** Five stars **Rev:** Denomination in flower **Edge:** Reeded **Note:** Prev. Y # 1087.

Date	Mintage	F	VF	XF	Unc	BU
2001 Proof	15,000	Value: 435				

KM# 1434 200 YUAN
15.5500 g., 0.9990 Gold 0.4994 oz. AGW, 27 mm. **Subject:** Budda **Note:** Prev. Y # 1145.

Date	Mintage	F	VF	XF	Unc	BU
2002	8,800	—	—	—	—	450

KM# 1454 200 YUAN
15.5000 g., 0.9990 Gold 0.4978 oz. AGW **Subject:** Peking Opera **Note:** Prev. Y # 1146.

Date	Mintage	F	VF	XF	Unc	BU
2002	8,000	—	—	—	—	825

KM# 1446 200 YUAN
15.5000 g., 0.9990 Gold 0.4978 oz. AGW **Subject:** Dream of the Red Mansion **Shape:** Octagon **Note:** Prev. Y # 1147.

Date	Mintage	F	VF	XF	Unc	BU
2002 Proof	8,000	Value: 550				

KM# 1431 200 YUAN
15.5000 g., 0.9990 Gold 0.4978 oz. AGW **Subject:** Cave man art **Rev:** Multicolor. **Note:** Prev. Y # 1148.

Date	Mintage	F	VF	XF	Unc	BU
2002 Proof	8,800	Value: 525				

KM# 1440 200 YUAN
15.5000 g., 0.9990 Gold 0.4978 oz. AGW **Subject:** Ceremonial Mask **Note:** Prev. Y # 1149.

Date	Mintage	F	VF	XF	Unc	BU
2002	5,000	—	—	—	—	475

KM# 1504 200 YUAN
15.5519 g., 0.9999 Gold 0.4999 oz. AGW **Subject:** Pilgrimage to the West **Note:** Prev. Y # 1159.

Date	Mintage	F	VF	XF	Unc	BU
2003	—	—	—	—	—	450

KM# 1494 200 YUAN
15.5519 g., 0.9999 Gold 0.4999 oz. AGW **Subject:** Chinese Mythical Folk Tales **Note:** Prev. Y # 1160.

Date	Mintage	F	VF	XF	Unc	BU
2003	—	—	—	—	—	450

KM# 1571 200 YUAN
15.5500 g., 0.9990 Gold 0.4994 oz. AGW, 27 mm. **Obv:** National arms above People's Congress Hall and ornamental column **Rev:** Multicolor hologram depicting the hall's overhead lighting **Edge:** Reeded **Note:** Prev. Y # 1213.

Date	Mintage	F	VF	XF	Unc	BU
2004 Proof	5,000	Value: 550				

KM# 1561 200 YUAN
15.5500 g., 0.9990 Gold 0.4994 oz. AGW, 27 mm. **Obv:** Monkey King leading the Master over bridge **Rev:** Multicolor Monkey King on one knee meeting the Master **Edge:** Reeded **Note:** Prev. Y#1217.

Date	Mintage	F	VF	XF	Unc	BU
2004 Proof	11,800	Value: 475				

KM# 1567 200 YUAN
15.5518 g., 0.9990 Gold 0.4995 oz. AGW, 27 mm. **Obv:** Guangan Exposition Hall **Rev:** Deng Xiaoping and value **Edge:** Reeded **Note:** Prev. Y # 1241.

Date	Mintage	F	VF	XF	Unc	BU
2004 Proof	10,000	Value: 500				

KM# 1652 200 YUAN
15.6300 g., Gold **Obv:** Qing Yuan Gate of the China Great Wall **Rev:** 2 dogs at play **Shape:** 30° Fan **Note:** Prev. Y # 1220.

Date	Mintage	F	VF	XF	Unc	BU
2006 Proof	6,600	Value: 485				

KM# 1656 200 YUAN
15.6300 g., Gold, 27 mm. **Obv:** Dog-shaped belt-hook from ancient Chinese bronze ware, decorative design of dog tail-shaped plant leaves **Rev:** 2 smart dogs **Shape:** Scalloped **Note:** Prev. Y # 1224.

Date	Mintage	F	VF	XF	Unc	BU
2006 Proof	8,000	Value: 485				

KM# 1568 300 YUAN
1000.0000 g., 0.9990 Silver 32.117 oz. ASW, 100 mm. **Obv:** Guangan Exposition Hall **Rev:** Deng Xiaoping and value **Edge:** Reeded **Note:** Prev. Y # 1242.

Date	Mintage	F	VF	XF	Unc	BU
2004 Proof	5,000	Value: 650				

KM# 1659 300 YUAN
32.1500 g., Silver, 100 mm. **Obv:** Dog-shaped belt-hook from ancient Chinese bronze ware, decorative design of dog tail-shaped plant leaves **Rev:** 2 dogs **Note:** Prev. Y # 1227.

Date	Mintage	F	VF	XF	Unc	BU
2006 Proof	3,800	Value: 65.00				

KM# 1392 2000 YUAN
155.5175 g., 0.9990 Gold 4.9948 oz. AGW, 60 mm. **Subject:** Mogao Grottoes **Obv:** Eight story building **Rev:** Two dancers **Edge:** Reeded **Note:** Prev. Y # 1086.

Date	Mintage	F	VF	XF	Unc	BU
2001 Proof	288	Value: 4,650				

KM# 1436 2000 YUAN
155.5175 g., 0.9990 Gold 4.9948 oz. AGW, 60 mm. **Subject:** Buddest Ceremony **Note:** Prev. Y # 1151.

Date	Mintage	F	VF	XF	Unc	BU
2002	288	—	—	—	—	4,650

KM# 1565 2000 YUAN
155.5175 g., 0.9990 Gold 4.9948 oz. AGW, 60 mm. **Subject:** Maijishan Grottos **Obv:** Grotto view **Rev:** Buddha portrait within halo of flying devatas **Edge:** Reeded **Note:** Prev. Y # 1206.

Date	Mintage	F	VF	XF	Unc	BU
2004(y) Proof	288	Value: 4,650				

KM# 1562 2000 YUAN
155.5175 g., 0.9990 Gold 4.9948 oz. AGW, 64x40 mm. **Obv:** Monkey King leading Master over bridge **Rev:** Multicolor Monkey King fighting the Pig "Demon of Bones" **Edge:** Plain **Shape:** Ingot **Note:** Prev. Y # 1218.

Date	Mintage	F	VF	XF	Unc	BU
2004 Proof	500	Value: 5,300				

KM# 1569 2000 YUAN
155.5175 g., 0.9990 Gold 4.9948 oz. AGW, 60 mm. **Obv:** Guangan Exposition Hall **Rev:** Deng Xiaoping and value **Edge:** Reeded **Note:** Prev. Y # 1243.

Date	Mintage	F	VF	XF	Unc	BU
2004 Proof	600	Value: 5,000				

SILVER BULLION COINAGE

Lunar Series

KM# 1379 10 YUAN
30.8400 g., 0.9990 Silver 0.9905 oz. ASW, 39.9 mm. **Subject:** Year of the Snake **Obv:** Traditional style building **Rev:** Snake **Shape:** Scalloped **Note:** Prev. Y # 1041.

Date	Mintage	F	VF	XF	Unc	BU
2001 Proof	6,800	Value: 65.00				

KM# 1382 10 YUAN
31.1035 g., 0.9990 Silver 0.9990 oz. ASW **Subject:** Year of the Snake **Shape:** Fan-like **Note:** Prev. Y # 1042.

Date	Mintage	F	VF	XF	Unc	BU
2001	66,000	—	—	—	35.00	—

KM# 1418.1 10 YUAN
31.1035 g., 0.9990 Silver 0.9990 oz. ASW, 40 mm. **Subject:** Year of the Horse **Obv:** Da Zheng Hall **Rev:** Stylized horse head **Edge:** Reeded **Note:** Prev. Y # 1232.

Date	Mintage	F	VF	XF	Unc	BU
2002	50,000	—	—	—	—	50.00

KM# 1657 10 YUAN
31.1035 g., Silver, 40 mm. **Obv:** Dog-shaped belt-hook from ancient Chinese bronze ware, decorative design of dog tail-shaped plant leaves **Rev:** 2 smart dogs **Note:** Prev. Y # 1225.

Date	Mintage	F	VF	XF	Unc	BU
2006	80,000	—	—	—	—	45.00

KM# 1377 50 YUAN
155.4400 g., 0.9990 Silver 4.9923 oz. ASW, 80.6 x 50.5 mm. **Subject:** Year of the Snake **Obv:** Traditional style building **Rev:** Snake **Edge:** Plain **Shape:** Rectangle **Note:** Illustration reduced. Prev. Y # 1040.

Date	Mintage	F	VF	XF	Unc	BU
2001 Proof	1,888,000	Value: 245				

SILVER BULLION COINAGE

Panda Series

KM# 1365 10 YUAN
31.1035 g., 0.9990 Silver 0.9990 oz. ASW, 40 mm. **Obv:** Temple of Heaven with incuse legend **Rev:** Panda walking left through bamboo **Edge:** Reeded **Note:** Large and small date varieties exist. Prev. Y # 1111.

Date	Mintage	F	VF	XF	Unc	BU
2001	250,000	—	—	—	27.50	—
2001 D	—	—	—	—	27.50	—

Note: Domestic issue

KM# 1466 10 YUAN
31.1035 g., 0.9990 Silver 0.9990 oz. ASW, 40 mm. **Obv:** Temple of Heaven **Rev:** Panda eating bamboo in a frosted circle **Edge:** Slant reeded **Note:** Prev. Y # 1244.

Date	Mintage	F	VF	XF	Unc	BU
2003 Proof	—	Value: 55.00				

KM# 1528 10 YUAN
31.1035 g., 0.9990 Silver 0.9990 oz. ASW, 40 mm. **Obv:** Temple of Heaven **Rev:** Panda nuzzling her cub **Edge:** Slant reeded **Note:** Prev. Y # 1245.

Date	Mintage	F	VF	XF	Unc	BU
2004 Proof	—	Value: 55.00				

KM# 1416 300 YUAN
1007.7534 g., 0.9990 Silver 32.366 oz. ASW, 100 mm. **Subject:** Panda Coinage 20th Anniversary **Obv:** Temple of Heaven **Rev:** Two gold inserts with the 1982 and 2002 panda designs on bamboo leaves **Edge:** Plain **Note:** Large and small date varieties exist. Illustration reduced. Prev. Y # 1116.

Date	Mintage	F	VF	XF	Unc	BU
2002 Proof	6,000	Value: 775				

GOLD BULLION COINAGE

Panda Series

KM# 1366 20 YUAN
1.5600 g., 0.9990 Gold 0.0501 oz. AGW, 14 mm. **Obv:** Temple of Heaven **Rev:** Panda walking left through bamboo **Edge:** Reeded **Note:** Large and small date varieties exist. Prev. Y # 1112.

Date	Mintage	F	VF	XF	Unc	BU
2001	100,000	—	—	—	—	45.00
2001 D	200,000	—	—	—	—	45.00

KM# 1529 20 YUAN
1.5552 g., 0.9999 Gold 0.0500 oz. AGW **Subject:** Panda **Note:** Large and small date varieties exist. Prev. Y # 1172.

Date	Mintage	F	VF	XF	Unc	BU
2004	—	—	—	—	—	45.00

KM# 1367 50 YUAN
3.1103 g., 0.9990 Gold 0.0999 oz. AGW, 18 mm. **Obv:** Temple of Heaven **Rev:** Panda walking left through bamboo **Edge:** Reeded **Note:** Large and small date varieties exist. Prev. Y # 1113.

Date	Mintage	F	VF	XF	Unc	BU
2001	50,000	—	—	—	—	95.00
2001 D	150,000	—	—	—	—	95.00

KM# 1469 50 YUAN
3.1103 g., 0.9999 Gold 0.1000 oz. AGW **Subject:** Panda **Note:** Large and small date varieties exist. Prev. Y # 1157.

Date	Mintage	F	VF	XF	Unc	BU
2003	—	—	—	—	—	95.00

KM# 1531 50 YUAN
3.1103 g., 0.9999 Gold 0.1000 oz. AGW **Subject:** Panda **Note:** Large and small date varieties exist. Prev. Y # 1173.

Date	Mintage	F	VF	XF	Unc	BU
2004	—	—	—	—	—	95.00

KM# 1368 100 YUAN
7.7759 g., 0.9990 Gold 0.2497 oz. AGW, 22 mm. **Obv:** Temple of Heaven **Rev:** Panda walking left through bamboo **Edge:** Reeded **Note:** Large and small date varieties exist. Prev. Y # 1114.

Date	Mintage	F	VF	XF	Unc	BU
2001	30,000	—	—	—	—	225
2001 D	100,000	—	—	—	—	225

KM# 1471 100 YUAN
7.7759 g., 0.9999 Gold 0.2500 oz. AGW **Subject:** Panda **Note:** Large and small date varieties exist. Prev. Y # 1158.

Date	Mintage	F	VF	XF	Unc	BU
2003	—	—	—	—	—	225

KM# 1533 100 YUAN
7.7759 g., 0.9999 Gold 0.2500 oz. AGW **Subject:** Panda **Note:** Large and small date varieties exist. Prev. Y # 1174.

Date	Mintage	F	VF	XF	Unc	BU
2004	—	—	—	—	—	225

KM# 1369 200 YUAN
15.5518 g., 0.9990 Gold 0.4995 oz. AGW, 27 mm. **Obv:** Temple of Heaven **Rev:** Panda in bamboo forest **Edge:** Slanted reeding **Note:** Illustration reduced. Large and small date varieties exist. Prev. Y # 1105.

Date	Mintage	F	VF	XF	Unc	BU
2001	—	—	—	—	—	445
2001 D	100,000	—	—	—	—	445

KM# 1472 200 YUAN
15.5519 g., 0.9999 Gold 0.4999 oz. AGW **Subject:** Panda **Note:** Large and small date varieties exist. Prev. Y # 1162.

Date	Mintage	F	VF	XF	Unc	BU
2003	—	—	—	—	—	445

KM# 1535 200 YUAN
15.5519 g., 0.9990 Gold 0.4995 oz. AGW **Subject:** Panda **Note:** Large and small date varieties exist. Prev. Y # 1175.

Date	Mintage	F	VF	XF	Unc	BU
2004	—	—	—	—	—	445

KM# 1474 500 YUAN
31.1320 g., 0.9999 Gold 1.0008 oz. AGW **Subject:** Panda **Note:** Large and small date varieties exist. Prev. Y # 1164.

Date	Mintage	F	VF	XF	Unc	BU
2003	—	—	—	—	—	895

KM# 1537 500 YUAN
31.1035 g., 0.9999 Gold 0.9999 oz. AGW **Subject:** Panda **Note:** Large and small date varieties exist. Prev. Y # 1176.

Date	Mintage	F	VF	XF	Unc	BU
2004	—	—	—	—	—	895

KM# 1372 10000 YUAN
321.5000 g., 0.9999 Gold 10.335 oz. AGW **Subject:** Panda **Note:** Large and small date varieties exist. Prev. Y # 1138.

Date	Mintage	F	VF	XF	Unc	BU
2001	68	—	—	—	—	17,000

KM# 1467 10000 YUAN
1000.0000 g., 0.9999 Gold 32.146 oz. AGW **Subject:** Panda **Note:** Large and small date varieties exist. Prev. Y # 1165.

Date	Mintage	F	VF	XF	Unc	BU
2003	—	—	—	—	—	—BV+25%

KM# 1538 10000 YUAN
1000.0000 g., 0.9999 Gold 32.146 oz. AGW **Subject:** Panda **Note:** Large and small date varieties exist. Prev. Y # 1177.

Date	Mintage	F	VF	XF	Unc	BU
2004	68	—	—	—	—	—BV+25%

GOLD BULLION COINAGE

Lunar Series

KM# 1374 50 YUAN
3.1103 g., 0.9990 Gold 0.0999 oz. AGW **Subject:** Year of the Snake **Note:** Prev. Y # 1141.1; 1043.

Date	Mintage	F	VF	XF	Unc	BU
2001	48,000	—	—	—	—	110

KM# 1376 50 YUAN
3.1105 g., 0.9999 Gold 0.1000 oz. AGW **Subject:** Year of the Snake **Rev:** Multicolor. **Note:** Prev. Y # 1141.2.

Date	Mintage	F	VF	XF	Unc	BU
2001	30,000	—	—	—	—	145

KM# 1419.1 50 YUAN
3.1050 g., 0.9999 Gold 0.0998 oz. AGW **Subject:** Year of the Horse **Note:** Prev. Y # 1143.1.

Date	Mintage	F	VF	XF	Unc	BU
2002	48,000	—	—	—	—	140

KM# 1419.2 50 YUAN
3.1050 g., 0.9999 Gold 0.0998 oz. AGW **Subject:** Year of the Horse **Rev:** Multicolor. **Note:** Prev. Y # 1143.2.

Date	Mintage	F	VF	XF	Unc	BU
2002	30,000	—	—	—	—	275

KM# 1424 50 YUAN
15.5500 g., 0.9990 Gold 0.4994 oz. AGW **Subject:** Year of the Horse **Shape:** Fan **Note:** Prev. Y # 1144.

Date	Mintage	F	VF	XF	Unc	BU
2002	6,600	—	—	—	—	650

KM# 1478.1 50 YUAN
3.1103 g., 0.9999 Gold 0.1000 oz. AGW **Subject:** Year of the Goat **Note:** Prev. Y # 1155.1.

Date	Mintage	F	VF	XF	Unc	BU
2003	48,000	—	—	—	—	110

KM# 1478.2 50 YUAN
3.1105 g., 0.9999 Gold 0.1000 oz. AGW **Subject:** Year of the Goat **Rev:** Multicolor. **Note:** Prev. Y # 1155.2

Date	Mintage	F	VF	XF	Unc	BU
2003	30,000	—	—	—	—	200

KM# 1546.1 50 YUAN
3.1103 g., 0.9999 Gold 0.1000 oz. AGW **Subject:** Year of the Monkey **Note:** Prev. Y # 1167.1.

Date	Mintage	F	VF	XF	Unc	BU
2004	48,000	—	—	—	—	140

KM# 1546.2 50 YUAN
3.1103 g., 0.9999 Gold 0.1000 oz. AGW **Subject:** Year of the Monkey **Rev:** Multicolor. **Note:** Prev. Y # 1167.2

Date	Mintage	F	VF	XF	Unc	BU
2004	30,000	—	—	—	—	275

KM# 1658 50 YUAN
3.1103 g., 0.9990 Gold 0.0999 oz. AGW, 18 mm. **Obv:** Dog-shaped belt-hook from ancient Chinese bronze ware, decorative design of dog tail-shaped plant leaves **Rev:** 2 smart dogs **Note:** Prev. Y # 1226.

Date	Mintage	F	VF	XF	Unc	BU
2006	60,000	—	—	—	—	110

KM# 1383 200 YUAN
15.5518 g., 0.9990 Gold 0.4995 oz. AGW **Subject:** Year of the Snake **Rev:** Fan **Note:** Prev. Y # 1044.

Date	Mintage	F	VF	XF	Unc	BU
2001	6,600	—	—	—	—	450

KM# 1380 200 YUAN
15.5518 g., 0.9990 Gold 0.4995 oz. AGW **Subject:** Year of the Snake **Shape:** Scalloped **Note:** Prev. Y # 1045.

Date	Mintage	F	VF	XF	Unc	BU
2001 Proof	2,300	Value: 475				

KM# 1426 200 YUAN
15.5000 g., 0.9990 Gold 0.4978 oz. AGW **Subject:** Year of the Horse **Shape:** Scallop **Note:** Prev. Y # 1150.

Date	Mintage	F	VF	XF	Unc	BU
2002	2,300	—	—	—	—	700

KM# 1481 200 YUAN
15.5519 g., 0.9999 Gold 0.4999 oz. AGW **Subject:** Year of the Goat **Note:** Prev. Y # 1161.

Date	Mintage	F	VF	XF	Unc	BU
2003	2,300	—	—	—	—	525

KM# 1549 200 YUAN
15.5519 g., 0.9999 Gold 0.4999 oz. AGW **Subject:** Year of the Monkey **Note:** Prev. Y # 1169.

Date	Mintage	F	VF	XF	Unc	BU
2004	2,300	—	—	—	—	800

KM# 1371 500 YUAN
31.1035 g., 0.9990 Gold 0.9990 oz. AGW, 32 mm. **Obv:** Temple of Heaven **Rev:** Panda walking through bamboo **Edge:** Reeded **Note:** Prev. Y # 1088.

Date	Mintage	F	VF	XF	Unc	BU
2001	—	—	—	—	—	—BV+15%
2001 D	150,000	—	—	—	—	—BV+15%

KM# 1554 500 YUAN
15.5519 g., 0.9999 Gold 0.4999 oz. AGW **Subject:** Year of the Monkey **Shape:** Fan **Note:** Prev. Y # 1168.

Date	Mintage	F	VF	XF	Unc	BU
2004	6,600	—	—	—	—	550

KM# 1378 2000 YUAN
155.5175 g., 0.9990 Gold 4.9948 oz. AGW **Subject:** Year of the Snake **Shape:** Rectangle **Note:** Prev. Y # 1046.

Date	Mintage	F	VF	XF	Unc	BU
2001 Proof	118	Value: 4,750				

KM# 1422 2000 YUAN
155.5175 g., 0.9999 Gold 4.9993 oz. AGW **Subject:** Year of the Horse **Shape:** Rectangle **Note:** Prev. Y # 1152.

Date	Mintage	F	VF	XF	Unc	BU
2002	—	—	—	—	—	5,000

KM# 1483 2000 YUAN
155.5190 g., 0.9999 Gold 4.9993 oz. AGW **Subject:** Year of the Goat **Note:** Prev. Y # 1163.

Date	Mintage	F	VF	XF	Unc	BU
2003	—	—	—	—	—	4,800

KM# 1552 2000 YUAN
155.1750 g., 0.9999 Gold 4.9883 oz. AGW **Subject:** Year of the Monkey **Note:** Prev. Y # 1170.

Date	Mintage	F	VF	XF	Unc	BU
2004	—	—	—	—	—	5,000

KM# 1381 10000 YUAN
1000.2108 g., 0.9990 Gold 32.124 oz. AGW **Subject:** Year of the Snake **Shape:** Scalloped **Note:** Prev. Y # 1047.

Date	Mintage	F	VF	XF	Unc	BU
2001 Proof	15	Value: 28,500				

KM# 1427 10000 YUAN
1000.0000 g., 0.9999 Gold 32.146 oz. AGW **Subject:** Year of the Horse **Shape:** Scalloped **Note:** Prev. Y # 1153.

Date	Mintage	F	VF	XF	Unc	BU
2002	15	—	—	—	—	35,000

KM# 1482 10000 YUAN
1000.0000 g., 0.9999 Gold 32.146 oz. AGW **Subject:** Year of the Goat **Note:** Prev. Y # 1166.

Date	Mintage	F	VF	XF	Unc	BU
2003	15	—	—	—	—	35,000

KM# 1550 10000 YUAN
1000.0000 g., 0.9999 Gold 32.146 oz. AGW **Subject:** Year of the Monkey **Note:** Prev. Y # 1171.

Date	Mintage	F	VF	XF	Unc	BU
2004	15	—	—	—	—	35,000

PLATINUM BULLION COINAGE

Panda Series

KM# 1415 100 YUAN
3.1103 g., 0.9995 Platinum 0.0999 oz. APW, 18 mm. **Subject:** Panda Coinage 20th Anniversary **Obv:** Seated panda design of 1982 **Rev:** Walking panda design of 2002 **Edge:** Reeded **Note:** Prev. Y # 1115.

Date	Mintage	F	VF	XF	Unc	BU
2002 Proof	20,000	Value: 200				

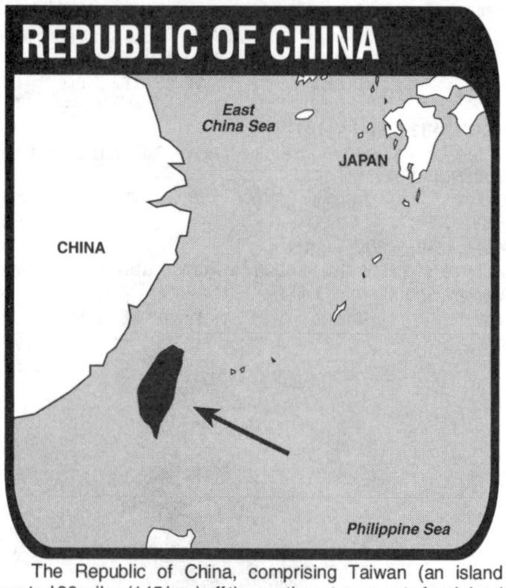

The Republic of China, comprising Taiwan (an island located 90 miles (145 km.) off the southeastern coast of mainland China), the offshore islands of Quemoy and Matsu and nearby islets of the Pescadores chain, has an area of 14,000 sq. mi. (35,980 sq. km.) and a population of 20.2 million. Capital: Taipei. During the past decade, manufacturing has replaced agriculture in importance. Fruits, vegetables, plywood, textile yarns and fabrics and clothing are exported.

The coins of Nationalist China do not carry A.D. dating, but are dated according to the year of the republic, which was established in 1911. However, republican years are added to 1911 to find the western year. Thus republican year 90 plus 1911 equals Gregorian calendar year 2001AD.

TAIWAN

REPUBLIC

STANDARD COINAGE

Y# 550 1/2 YUAN
3.0000 g., Bronze, 18 mm. **Obv:** Orchid **Rev:** Value and Chinese symbols **Edge:** Plain

Date	Mintage	F	VF	XF	Unc	BU
92(2003)	—	—	0.15	0.30	1.00	1.25
92(2003) Proof	—	Value: 10.00				

Y# 551 YUAN
3.8000 g., Bronze, 19.92 mm. **Obv:** Bust of Chiang Kai-shek left **Rev:** Chinese value in center, 1 below **Edge:** Reeded

Date	Mintage	F	VF	XF	Unc	BU
92(2003)	—	—	—	0.15	0.30	0.45
92(2003) Proof	—	Value: 12.50				

Y# 552 5 YUAN
Copper-Nickel **Obv:** Bust of Chiang Kai-shek left **Rev:** Chinese symbols in center, 5 below

Date	Mintage	F	VF	XF	Unc	BU
92(2003)	—	—	0.15	0.25	0.50	0.75
92(2003) Proof	—	Value: 12.50				

Y# 567 10 YUAN
7.4300 g., Copper-Nickel, 26 mm. **Subject:** 90th Anniversary of the Republic **Obv:** Bust of Sun Yat-sen facing **Rev:** Holographic design and denomination **Edge:** Reeded

Date	Mintage	F	VF	XF	Unc	BU
90 (2001)	30,000,000	—	—	—	2.50	3.00

Y# 553 10 YUAN
7.5000 g., Copper-Nickel, 26 mm. **Obv:** Bust of Chiang Kai-shek left **Rev:** Chinese symbols in center, 10 below

Date	Mintage	F	VF	XF	Unc	BU
92(2003)	—	—	0.25	0.45	0.75	1.00
92(2003) Proof	—	Value: 15.00				

Y# 565 20 YUAN
Ring Composition: Brass **Center Weight:** 8.4000 g. **Center Composition:** Copper-Nickel, 26.8 mm. **Obv:** Male portrait **Rev:** Three boats **Edge:** Reeded

Date	Mintage	F	VF	XF	Unc	BU
90 (2001)	—	—	—	—	3.50	4.50
92(2003)	—	—	—	—	3.50	4.50
92(2003) Proof	—	Value: 18.00				

Y# 570 50 YUAN
15.5680 g., 0.9990 Silver 0.5000 oz. ASW, 33 mm. **Subject:** World Cup Baseball **Obv:** Player at bat with ball background **Rev:** Mount Jade above denomination **Edge:** Reeded

Date	Mintage	F	VF	XF	Unc	BU
90 (2001)	130,000	—	—	—	25.00	27.50

Y# 568 50 YUAN
10.0000 g., Brass, 28 mm. **Obv:** Bust **Rev:** Denomination above latent image denomination **Edge:** Reeding and denomination

Date	Mintage	F	VF	XF	Unc	BU
91-2002	—	—	—	—	7.50	10.00
92-2003	—	—	—	—	7.50	10.00
92-2003 Proof	—	Value: 20.00				

Y# 569 50 YUAN
15.5680 g., 0.9990 Silver 0.5000 oz. ASW, 33 mm. **Subject:** 90th Anniversary of the Republic **Obv:** Portrait of Sun Yat-sen **Rev:** Latent image above denomination **Edge:** Reeded

Date	Mintage	F	VF	XF	Unc	BU
90(2001)	230,000	—	—	—	25.00	27.50

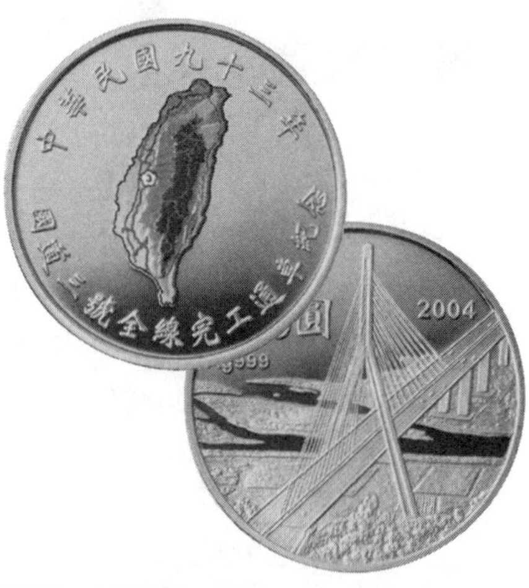

Y# 571 50 YUAN
31.1035 g., 0.9990 Silver 0.9990 oz. ASW, 38 mm. **Subject:** Third National Expressway **Obv:** Multicolor island map **Rev:** Kao Ping Hsi bridge **Edge:** Reeded

Date	Mintage	F	VF	XF	Unc	BU
Yr 93- 2004	20,000	—	—	—	40.00	—

MINT SETS

KM#	Date	Mintage	Identification	Issue Price	Mkt Val
MS9	92(2003) (6)	—	Y550-553, 565, 568 plus C-N Year of the Goat medal	—	20.00

PROOF SETS

KM#	Date	Mintage	Identification	Issue Price	Mkt Val
PS10	90(2001) (6)	210,000	Y#550-553, 565, 568 plus medal	29.40	50.00
PS12	92(2003) (6)	—	Y550-553, 565, 568 plus silver Year of the Goat Medal	—	100

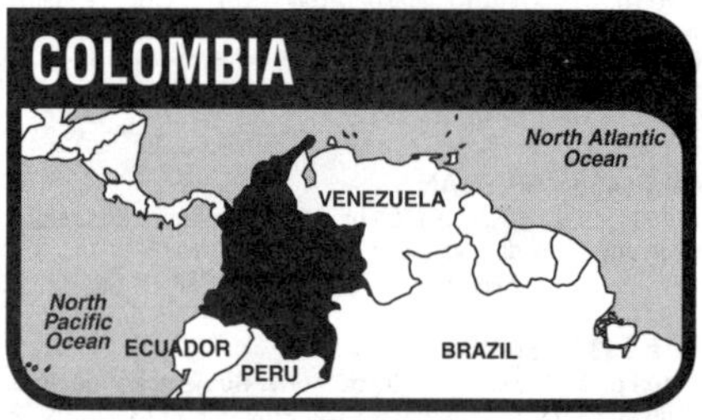

The Republic of Colombia, in the northwestern corner of South America, has an area of 440,831 sq. mi. (1,138,910 sq. km.) and a population of*42.3 million. Capital: Bogota. The economy is primarily agricultural with a mild, rich coffee being the chief crop. Colombia has the world's largest platinum deposits and important reserves of coal, iron ore, petroleum and limestone; other precious metals and emeralds are also mined. Coffee, crude oil, bananas, sugar and emeralds are exported.

MINT MARKS
A, M – Medellin (capital), Antioquia (state)
B - BOGOTA
(D) Denver, USA
H – Birmingham (Heaton & Sons)
(m) - Medellin, w/o mint mark
(Mo) - Mexico City
NI - Numismatica Italiana, Arezzo, Italy
mint marks stylized in wreath
(P) - Philadelphia
(S) - San Francisco, USA.
(W) - Waterbury, CT (USA, Scoville mint)

REPUBLIC

DECIMAL COINAGE

100 Centavos = 1 Peso

KM# 282.2 20 PESOS
3.6000 g., Copper-Aluminum-Nickel, 20.25 mm. **Obv:** Flagged arms, 68 beads circle around the rim **Rev:** Denomination within wreath

Date	Mintage	F	VF	XF	Unc	BU
2003	—	—	—	—	0.50	0.75

KM# 294 20 PESOS
2.0000 g., Brass, 17.2 mm. **Obv:** Simon Bolivar left **Rev:** Value **Edge:** Reeded

Date	Mintage	F	VF	XF	Unc	BU
2004	—	—	—	—	0.15	0.25

KM# 283.2 50 PESOS

4.5000 g., Copper-Nickel-Zinc, 21.8 mm. **Obv:** Flagged arms, date below **Rev:** Denomination within wreath, 72 beads circle around rim

Date	Mintage	F	VF	XF	Unc	BU
2003	—	—	—	—	1.00	1.25
2005	—	—	—	—	1.00	1.25

KM# 286 500 PESOS

7.4000 g., Bi-Metallic Aluminum-Bronze center in Copper-Nickel ring **Obv:** Guacari tree within circle **Rev:** Denomination within circle, date below

Date	Mintage	F	VF	XF	Unc	BU
2003	—	—	—	—	4.00	4.50
2004	—	—	—	—	4.00	4.50

COMOROS

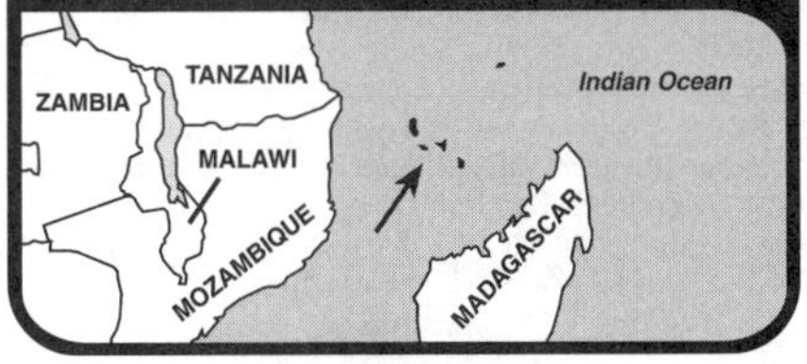

The Federal Islamic Republic of the Comoros, a volcanic archipelago located in the Mozambique Channel of the Indian Ocean 300 miles (483 km.) northwest of Madagascar, has an area of 719 sq. mi. (2,171 sq. km.) and a population of *714,000. Capital: Moroni. The economy of the islands is based on agriculture. There are practically no mineral resources. Vanilla, essence for perfumes, copra, and sisal are exported.

Ancient Phoenician traders were probably the first visitors to the Comoro Islands, but the first detailed knowledge of the area was gathered by Arab sailors. Arab dominion and culture were firmly established when the Portuguese, Dutch, and French arrived in the 16th century. In 1843 a Malagasy ruler ceded the island of Mayotte to France; the other three principal islands of the archipelago-Anjouan, Moheli, and Grand Comore came under French protection in 1886. The islands were joined administratively with Madagascar in 1912. The Comoros became partially autonomous, with the status of a French overseas territory, in 1946, and achieved complete internal autonomy in 1961. On Dec. 31, 1975, after 133 years of French association, the Comoro Islands became the independent Republic of the Comoros.

Mayotte retained the option of determining its future ties and in 1976 voted to remain French. Its present status is that of a French Territorial Collectivity. French currency now circulates there.

TITLES

Daulat Anjazanchiyah

RULER

French, 1886-1975

MINT MARKS

- Paris, privy marks only
- Paris, horseshoe privy mark (2001)

A - Paris

MONETARY SYSTEM

100 Centimes = 1 Franc

FEDERAL ISLAMIC REPUBLIC

BANQUE CENTRAL COINAGE

KM# 14 25 FRANCS

3.9700 g., Nickel, 20 mm. **Series:** F.A.O. **Obv:** Chickens **Rev:** Denomination above date

Date	Mintage	F	VF	XF	Unc	BU
2001(a) Horseshoe	—	0.20	0.40	0.80	2.00	—

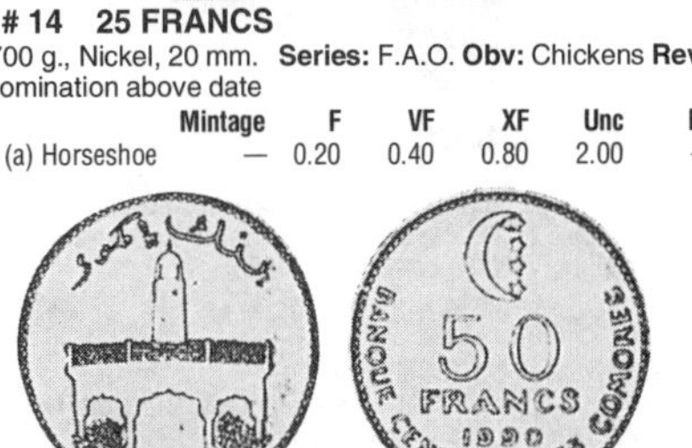

KM# 16 50 FRANCS

6.0300 g., Nickel, 24.1 mm. **Obv:** Building with tall tower **Rev:** Moon and stars above denomination, date below

Date	Mintage	F	VF	XF	Unc	BU
2001(a)	—	0.50	0.80	1.50	2.50	3.50

KM# 18 100 FRANCS

10.0000 g., Nickel, 28 mm. **Subject:** Circulation Type **Obv:** Denomination, moon and stars above, date below **Rev:** Boat and fish **Edge:** Plain

Date	Mintage	F	VF	XF	Unc	BU
2003	—	—	—	—	3.50	5.00

CONGO REPUBLIC

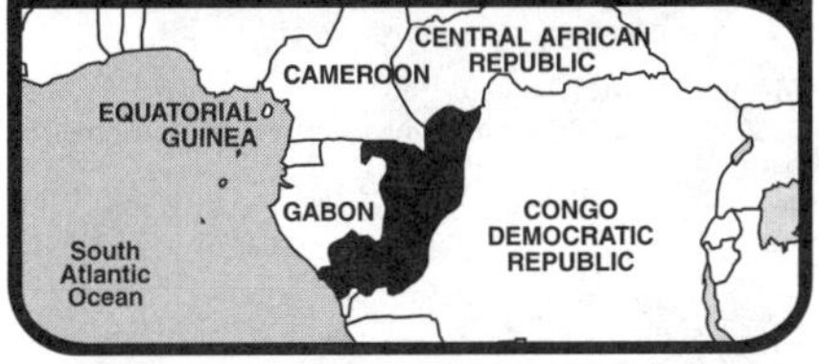

The Republic of the Congo (formerly the Peoples Republic of the Congo), located on the equator in west-central Africa, has an area of 132,047 sq. mi. (342,000 sq. km.) and a population of *2.98 million. Capital: Brazzaville. Agriculture forestry, mining, and food processing are the principal industries. Timber, industrial diamonds, potash, peanuts, and cocoa beans are exported.

NOTE: For earlier and related coinage see French Equatorial Africa and the Equatorial African States. For later coinage see Central African States.

RULER

French until 1960

MINT MARK

(a) - Paris, privy marks only

MONETARY SYSTEM

100 Centimes = 1 Franc

REPUBLIC

Republique du Congo

DECIMAL COINAGE

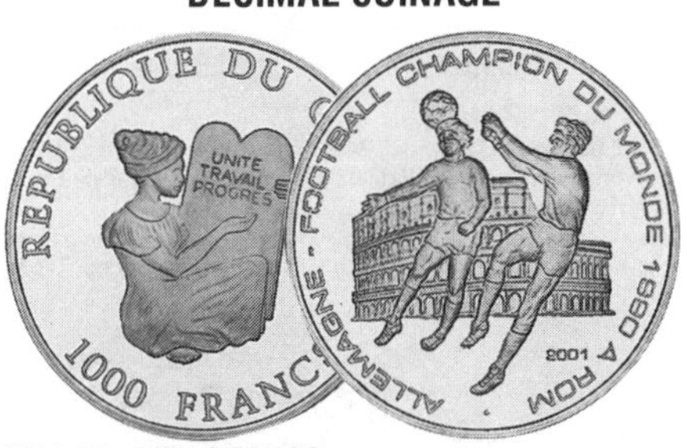

KM# 47 1000 FRANCS

15.0000 g., 0.9990 Silver 0.4818 oz. ASW, 35 mm. **Obv:** Seated woman with tablet **Rev:** Two soccer players and colosseum **Edge:** Plain

Date	Mintage	F	VF	XF	Unc	BU
2001 Proof	—	Value: 40.00				

KM# 48 1000 FRANCS

20.0000 g., 0.9990 Silver 0.6423 oz. ASW, 38 mm. **Obv:** Seated woman with tablet **Rev:** Two soccer players and Mexican pyramid **Edge:** Reeded

Date	Mintage	F	VF	XF	Unc	BU
2001 Proof	—	Value: 40.00				

INSTITUT MONETAIRE

KM# 46 1500 CFA FRANCS-1 AFRICA

7.3400 g., Nickel Plated Iron, 25.9 mm. **Obv:** Katanga Cross **Rev:** Elephant head on full Africa map **Edge:** Plain

Date	Mintage	F	VF	XF	Unc	BU
2005	2,005	—	—	—	25.00	—

KM# 46a 1500 CFA FRANCS-1 AFRICA

0.9990 Silver, 26 mm. **Obv:** Katanga Cross **Rev:** Elephant head on full Africa map

Date	Mintage	F	VF	XF	Unc	BU
2005	25	—	—	—	360	—

KM# 49 4500 CFA-3 AFRICA

8.0000 g., Bi-Metallic Stainless Steel center in Brass ring, 26 mm. **Obv:** Pope John Paul II **Rev:** African Map **Edge:** Segmented reeding

Date	Mintage	F	VF	XF	Unc	BU
2007	2,007	—	—	—	—	65.00

KM# 49a 4500 CFA-3 AFRICA

10.0000 g., Bi-Metallic .999 Silver center in Gold plated Brass ring, 26 mm. **Obv:** Pope John Paul II **Rev:** African Map **Edge:** Segmented reeding

Date	Mintage	F	VF	XF	Unc	BU
2007	27	—	—	—	—	585

KM# 49b 4500 CFA-3 AFRICA

12.0000 g., 0.9990 Silver 0.3854 oz. ASW, 26 mm. **Obv:** Pope John Paul II **Rev:** African Map **Edge:** Segmented reeding

Date	Mintage	F	VF	XF	Unc	BU
2007	27	—	—	—	—	520

CONGO DEMOCRATIC REPUBLIC

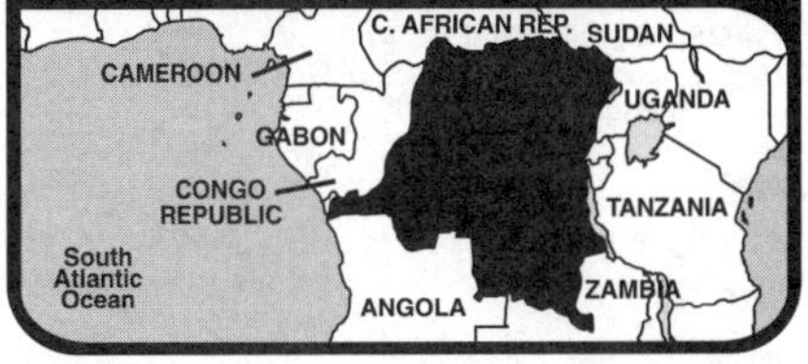

The Democratic Republic of the Congo (formerly the Republic of Zaire, and earlier the Belgian Congo), located in the south-central part of Africa, has an area of 905,568 sq. mi. (2,345,410 sq. km.) and a population of *47.4 million. Capital: Kinshasa. The mineral-rich country produces copper, tin, diamonds, gold, zinc, cobalt and uranium.

DECIMAL COINAGE

KM# 176 10 FRANCS

32.0000 g., 0.9990 Silver 1.0278 oz. ASW, 40 mm. **Obv:** Lion **Rev:** World Trade Center Twin Towers as they were before 9-11 **Edge:** Reeded

Date	Mintage	F	VF	XF	Unc	BU
2006 Proof	—	Value: 42.50				

REFORM COINAGE

Congo Francs replace Zaire; July 1998

KM# 76 25 CENTIMES

0.8800 g., Aluminum, 19.90 mm. **Obv:** Lion left **Rev:** Weasel **Edge:** Plain

Date	Mintage	F	VF	XF	Unc	BU
2002	—	—	—	—	0.75	1.00

KM# 77 25 CENTIMES

0.8500 g., Aluminum, 20 mm. **Obv:** Lion left **Rev:** Ram right, looking left **Edge:** Plain

Date	Mintage	F	VF	XF	Unc	BU
2002	—	—	—	—	0.75	1.00

KM# 83 25 CENTIMES
1.3000 g., Aluminum, 20 mm. **Obv:** Lion left **Rev:** Wild dog leaping right **Edge:** Plain

Date	Mintage	F	VF	XF	Unc	BU
2002	—	—	—	—	0.75	1.00

KM# 75 50 CENTIMES
2.2000 g., Aluminum, 26.97 mm. **Obv:** Lion left **Rev:** Soccer player right, bumping ball with head **Edge:** Plain

Date	Mintage	F	VF	XF	Unc	BU
2002	—	—	—	—	1.25	1.50

KM# 78 50 CENTIMES
2.1600 g., Aluminum, 27 mm. **Obv:** Lion left **Rev:** Giraffe right, looking left **Edge:** Plain

Date	Mintage	F	VF	XF	Unc	BU
2002	—	—	—	—	1.25	1.50

KM# 79 50 CENTIMES
2.2000 g., Aluminum, 26.92 mm. **Obv:** Lion left **Rev:** Gorilla facing, looking left **Edge:** Plain

Date	Mintage	F	VF	XF	Unc	BU
2002	—	—	—	—	1.00	1.25

KM# 80 50 CENTIMES
2.1600 g., Aluminum, 27 mm. **Obv:** Lion left **Rev:** Butterfly **Edge:** Plain

Date	Mintage	F	VF	XF	Unc	BU
2002	—	—	—	—	1.50	1.75

KM# 123 50 CENTIMES
3.9200 g., Stainless Steel, 22.3 mm. **Obv:** Lion left above denomination **Rev:** Verney L. Camereon **Edge:** Plain

Date	Mintage	F	VF	XF	Unc	BU
2002	—	—	—	—	1.00	1.25

KM# 81 FRANC
4.5700 g., Brass, 20.31 mm. **Obv:** Lion left **Rev:** Turtle **Edge:** Plain

Date	Mintage	F	VF	XF	Unc	BU
2002	—	—	—	—	1.25	1.50

KM# 82 FRANC
4.5200 g., Brass, 20.32 mm. **Obv:** Lion left **Rev:** Chicken **Edge:** Plain

Date	Mintage	F	VF	XF	Unc	BU
2002	—	—	—	—	1.50	1.75

KM# 156 FRANC
5.0000 g., Nickel Clad Steel, 24.8 mm. **Subject:** 25th Anniversary - Pope John Paul II's Visit **Obv:** Lion left **Rev:** Pope John Paul II as a priest in 1946 **Edge:** Plain

Date	Mintage	F	VF	XF	Unc	BU
2004	—	—	—	—	2.00	2.50

KM# 157 FRANC
5.0000 g., Nickel Clad Steel, 24.8 mm. **Subject:** 25th Anniversary - Pope John Paul II's Visit **Obv:** Lion left **Rev:** Pope John Paul II as a Cardinal in 1967 **Edge:** Plain

Date	Mintage	F	VF	XF	Unc	BU
2004	—	—	—	—	2.00	2.50

KM# 158 FRANC
5.0000 g., Nickel Clad Steel, 24.8 mm. **Subject:** 25th Anniversary - Pope John Paul II's Visit **Obv:** Lion left **Rev:** Pope John Paul II as newly elected pope in 1978 **Edge:** Plain

Date	Mintage	F	VF	XF	Unc	BU
2004	—	—	—	—	2.00	2.50

KM# 159 FRANC
5.0000 g., Nickel Clad Steel, 24.8 mm. **Subject:** 25th Anniversary - Pope John Paul II's Visit **Obv:** Lion left **Rev:** Pope John Paul II wearing a mitre **Edge:** Plain

Date	Mintage	F	VF	XF	Unc	BU
2004	—	—	—	—	2.00	2.50

KM# 174 FRANC
6.0000 g., Copper-Nickel, 21 mm. **Obv:** Lion left **Rev:** African Golden Cat right **Edge:** Plain

Date	Mintage	F	VF	XF	Unc	BU
2004	5,000	—	—	—	7.25	9.00

KM# 174a FRANC
8.0000 g., 0.9990 Silver 0.2569 oz. ASW, 21 mm. **Obv:** Lion left **Rev:** African Golden Cat right **Edge:** Plain

Date	Mintage	F	VF	XF	Unc	BU
2004	25	—	—	—	270	—

KM# 56 5 FRANCS
22.4000 g., Copper-Nickel, 39.8 mm. **Series:** Wild Life Protection **Obv:** Lion left **Rev:** Multicolor swallowtail butterfly hologram **Edge:** Reeded **Note:** Prev. KM#79.

Date	Mintage	F	VF	XF	Unc	BU
2002(2001)	20,000	—	—	—	35.00	—

KM# 57 5 FRANCS
22.4000 g., Copper Nickel, 39.8 mm. **Series:** Wild Life Protection **Obv:** Lion left **Rev:** Multicolor dark greenish butterfly hologram **Edge:** Reeded **Note:** Prev. KM#80.

Date	Mintage	F	VF	XF	Unc	BU
2002(2001)	20,000	—	—	—	35.00	—

KM# 58 5 FRANCS
22.4000 g., Copper Nickel, 39.8 mm. **Series:** Wild Life Protection **Obv:** Lion left **Rev:** Multicolor red and black butterfly hologram **Edge:** Reeded **Note:** Prev. KM#81.

Date	Mintage	F	VF	XF	Unc	BU
2002(2001)	20,000	—	—	—	35.00	—

KM# 170 5 FRANCS
24.3000 g., Copper-Nickel, 38.5 mm. **Obv:** Lion left **Rev:** Multicolor German 1 mark coin dated 2001 **Edge:** Reeded

Date	Mintage	F	VF	XF	Unc	BU
2002	—	—	—	—	15.00	—

KM# 128 5 FRANCS
8.0000 g., Iron, 27.26x14.13 mm. **Obv:** Country name, lion and date in the bowl part of the spoon; value on the handle part **Edge:** Reeded **Note:** This is the Spoon part of the Compass and Spoon set. (The spoon is the compass needle.)

Date	Mintage	F	VF	XF	Unc	BU
2004	5,000	—	—	—	15.00	—

KM# 146 5 FRANCS
27.0000 g., Copper-Nickel, 38.6 mm. **Obv:** Lion left **Rev:** Multicolor Quetzal bird **Edge:** Reeded

Date	Mintage	F	VF	XF	Unc	BU
2004 Proof	5,000	Value: 35.00				

KM# 147 5 FRANCS
27.0000 g., Copper-Nickel, 38.6 mm. **Obv:** Lion left **Rev:** Multicolor Bird of Paradise **Edge:** Reeded

Date	Mintage	F	VF	XF	Unc	BU
2004 Proof	5,000	Value: 35.00				

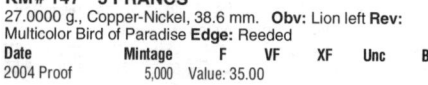

KM# 148 5 FRANCS

27.0000 g., Copper-Nickel, 38.6 mm. **Obv:** Lion left **Rev:** Multicolor Kingfisher bird **Edge:** Reeded

Date	Mintage	F	VF	XF	Unc	BU
2004 Proof	5,000	Value: 35.00				

KM# 164 5 FRANCS

25.4000 g., Copper-Nickel, 38.8 mm. **Subject:** Papal Visit **Obv:** Lion left **Rev:** Pope John Paul II with staff and mitre **Edge:** Reeded

Date	Mintage	F	VF	XF	Unc	BU
ND (2004) Proof	—	Value: 15.00				

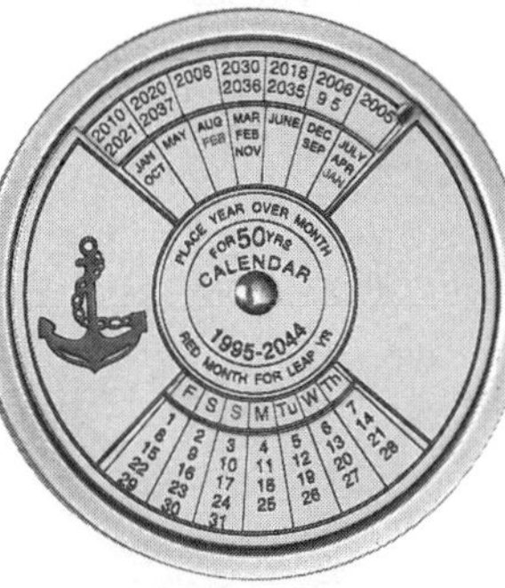

KM# 165 5 FRANCS

49.5000 g., Copper-Nickel, 45.1 mm. **Obv:** Lion left **Rev:** Rotating 50 year calender **Edge:** Reeded

Date	Mintage	F	VF	XF	Unc	BU
ND Matte	—	—	—	—	75.00	—

KM# 166 5 FRANCS

2.1600 g., Maple wood, 39.4 mm. **Obv:** Lion, brown ink **Rev:** Gorilla, brown ink **Edge:** Plain

Date	Mintage	F	VF	XF	Unc	BU
2005	2,000	—	—	—	20.00	—

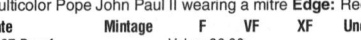

KM# 178 5 FRANCS

26.3000 g., Silver Plated Bronze, 38.6 mm. **Obv:** Lion **Rev:** Multicolor Pope John Paul II wearing a mitre **Edge:** Reeded

Date	Mintage	F	VF	XF	Unc	BU
2007 Proof	—	Value: 30.00				

KM# 72 10 FRANCS

20.0000 g., 0.9250 Silver 0.5948 oz. ASW, 40.1 mm. **Series:** Airplanes **Obv:** Lion left **Rev:** Mikoyan-Gurevich Mig 21 fighter flying left **Edge:** Reeded

Date	Mintage	F	VF	XF	Unc	BU
2001 Proof	—	Value: 40.00				

KM# 74 10 FRANCS

31.1035 g., 0.9990 Silver 0.9990 oz. ASW, 40 mm. **Subject:** 2004 Olympics **Obv:** Lion left **Rev:** Convex chariot **Edge:** Reeded

Date	Mintage	F	VF	XF	Unc	BU
2001 Antique Finish	15,000	—	—	—	37.50	—

KM# 167 10 FRANCS

20.0000 g., 0.9250 Silver 0.5948 oz. ASW, 40.1 mm. **Obv:** Lion left **Rev:** SS Bremen ship at sea **Edge:** Reeded

Date	Mintage	F	VF	XF	Unc	BU
2001 Proof	—	Value: 30.00				

KM# 168 10 FRANCS

20.0000 g., 0.9250 Silver 0.5948 oz. ASW, 40.1 mm. **Obv:** Lion left **Rev:** RMS Queen Elizabeth 2 at sea **Edge:** Reeded

Date	Mintage	F	VF	XF	Unc	BU
2001 Proof	—	Value: 30.00				

KM# 169 10 FRANCS

20.0000 g., 0.9250 Silver 0.5948 oz. ASW, 30 mm. **Obv:** Lion left **Rev:** Sail Ship America **Edge:** Reeded

Date	Mintage	F	VF	XF	Unc	BU
2001 Proof	—	Value: 30.00				

KM# 38 10 FRANCS

31.3000 g., 0.9250 Silver 0.9308 oz. ASW, 27 x 47.1 mm. **Subject:** Illusion **Obv:** Lion left **Rev:** Multicolor couple in flower picture **Edge:** Plain **Shape:** Rectangular **Note:** Prev. KM#61.

Date	Mintage	F	VF	XF	Unc	BU
2001 Proof	—	Value: 50.00				

KM# 59 10 FRANCS

25.9500 g., 0.9250 Silver 0.7717 oz. ASW, 39.9 mm. **Series:** Wild Life Protection **Obv:** Lion left **Rev:** Multicolor swallowtail butterfly hologram **Edge:** Reeded **Note:** Prev. KM#82.

Date	Mintage	F	VF	XF	Unc	BU
2002 (2001) Proof	15,000	Value: 65.00				

KM# 60 10 FRANCS

25.9500 g., 0.9250 Silver 0.7717 oz. ASW, 39.9 mm. **Series:** Wild Life Protection **Obv:** Lion left **Rev:** Multicolor dark greenish butterfly hologram **Edge:** Reeded **Note:** Prev. KM#83.

Date	Mintage	F	VF	XF	Unc	BU
2002 (2001) Proof	15,000	Value: 65.00				

KM# 61 10 FRANCS

25.9500 g., 0.9250 Silver 0.7717 oz. ASW, 39.9 mm. **Series:** Wild Life Protection **Obv:** Lion left **Rev:** Multicolor red and black butterfly hologram **Edge:** Reeded **Note:** Prev. KM#84.

Date	Mintage	F	VF	XF	Unc	BU
2002 (2001) Proof	15,000	Value: 65.00				

KM# 65 10 FRANCS

20.0000 g., 0.9250 Silver 0.5948 oz. ASW, 40.1 mm. **Series:** Airplanes **Obv:** Lion left **Rev:** Vickers Vimy twin engine biplane flying left **Edge:** Reeded **Note:** Prev. KM#88.

Date	Mintage	F	VF	XF	Unc	BU
2001 Proof	—	Value: 40.00				

KM# 66 10 FRANCS

20.0000 g., 0.9250 Silver 0.5948 oz. ASW, 40.1 mm. **Series:** Airplanes **Obv:** Lion left **Rev:** Fokker DR1 triplane flying left **Edge:** Reeded **Note:** Prev. KM#89.

Date	Mintage	F	VF	XF	Unc	BU
2001 Proof	—	Value: 40.00				

KM# 67 10 FRANCS
20.0000 g., 0.9250 Silver 0.5948 oz. ASW, 40.1 mm. **Series:** Airplanes **Obv:** Lion left **Rev:** Lockheed Vega flying left **Edge:** Reeded **Note:** Prev. KM#90.

Date	Mintage	F	VF	XF	Unc	BU
2001 Proof	—	Value: 40.00				

KM# 68 10 FRANCS
20.0000 g., 0.9250 Silver 0.5948 oz. ASW, 40.1 mm. **Series:** Airplanes **Obv:** Lion left **Rev:** Boeing 314 Clipper flying left **Edge:** Reeded **Note:** Prev. KM#91.

Date	Mintage	F	VF	XF	Unc	BU
2001 Proof	—	Value: 40.00				

KM# 69 10 FRANCS
20.0000 g., 0.9250 Silver 0.5948 oz. ASW, 40.1 mm. **Series:** Airplanes **Obv:** Lion left **Rev:** Junkers JU-87 Stuka in a dive **Edge:** Reeded **Note:** Prev. KM#92.

Date	Mintage	F	VF	XF	Unc	BU
2001 Proof	—	Value: 40.00				

KM# 70 10 FRANCS
20.0000 g., 0.9250 Silver 0.5948 oz. ASW, 40.1 mm. **Series:** Airplanes **Obv:** Lion left **Rev:** B-29 Enola Gay flying left **Edge:** Reeded **Note:** Prev. KM#93.

Date	Mintage	F	VF	XF	Unc	BU
2001 Proof	—	Value: 42.50				

KM# 71 10 FRANCS
20.0000 g., 0.9250 Silver 0.5948 oz. ASW, 40.1 mm. **Series:** Airplanes **Obv:** Lion left **Rev:** Bell X-1 rocket plane flying left **Edge:** Reeded **Note:** Prev. KM#94.

Date	Mintage	F	VF	XF	Unc	BU
2001 Proof	—	Value: 40.00				

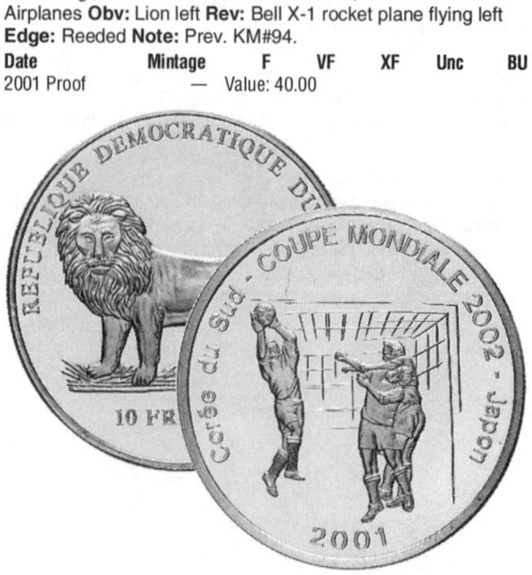

KM# 175 10 FRANCS
25.8300 g., Silver, 40 mm. **Obv:** Lion left **Rev:** 3 players **Edge:** Reeded

Date	Mintage	F	VF	XF	Unc	BU
2001	—	—	—	—	—	50.00

KM# 91 10 FRANCS
31.1000 g., 0.9990 Silver 0.9988 oz. ASW, 40 mm. **Subject:** Olympics **Obv:** Lion left **Rev:** Ancient athlete incuse design **Edge:** Plain **Note:** Design hubs with the design of the 500 sika coin KM-42 of Ghana

Date	Mintage	F	VF	XF	Unc	BU
2002 Antiqued finish	—	—	—	—	37.50	—

KM# 124 10 FRANCS
26.0000 g., 0.9250 Silver 0.7732 oz. ASW, 40 mm. **Subject:** Field Marshal Erwin Rommel **Obv:** Lion left above value **Rev:** Rommel, tank and map **Edge:** Reeded

Date	Mintage	F	VF	XF	Unc	BU
2002 Proof	15,000	Value: 42.50				

KM# 125 10 FRANCS
26.0000 g., 0.9250 Silver 0.7732 oz. ASW, 40 mm. **Subject:** Field Marshal Erwin Rommel **Obv:** Lion left above value **Rev:** Patton, tank and map **Edge:** Reeded

Date	Mintage	F	VF	XF	Unc	BU
2002 Proof	15,000	Value: 42.50				

KM# 162 10 FRANCS
20.2000 g., 0.9990 Silver 0.6488 oz. ASW, 40 mm. **Obv:** Lion left **Rev:** Space shuttle and five astronauts **Edge:** Reeded

Date	Mintage	F	VF	XF	Unc	BU
2002 Proof	—	Value: 40.00				

KM# 93 10 FRANCS
31.2300 g., 0.9990 Silver 1.0030 oz. ASW, 38.7 mm. **Obv:** Lion left **Rev:** Bearded portrait of Verney L. Camereon **Edge:** Reeded

Date	Mintage	F	VF	XF	Unc	BU
2002	—	—	—	—	35.00	40.00

KM# 94 10 FRANCS
26.1500 g., Copper-Nickel, 40.3 mm. **Subject:** Historic Automobiles **Obv:** Lion left **Rev:** 1908 Berliet car **Edge:** Reeded

Date	Mintage	F	VF	XF	Unc	BU
2002 Proof	—	Value: 18.00				

KM# 95 10 FRANCS
26.1500 g., Copper-Nickel, 40.3 mm. **Subject:** Historic Automobiles **Obv:** Lion left **Rev:** 1919 Hispano Suiza H6 car right **Edge:** Reeded

Date	Mintage	F	VF	XF	Unc	BU
2002 Proof	—	Value: 18.00				

KM# 96 10 FRANCS
32.0000 g., Silver Plated Copper, 40 mm. **Subject:** World Cup Soccer **Obv:** Lion left **Rev:** Soccer player and multicolor American flag **Edge:** Reeded

Date	Mintage	F	VF	XF	Unc	BU
2002 Proof	20,000	Value: 50.00				

KM# 97 10 FRANCS
32.0000 g., Silver Plated Copper, 40 mm. **Subject:** World Cup Soccer **Obv:** Lion left **Rev:** Two soccer players and multicolor flag of Ecuador **Edge:** Reeded

Date	Mintage	F	VF	XF	Unc	BU
2002 Proof	20,000	Value: 50.00				

KM# 103 10 FRANCS
19.0000 g., 0.9990 Silver 0.6102 oz. ASW, 40 mm. **Subject:** Gotha Ursinus G **Obv:** Lion left **Rev:** WWI German bomber flying left at 8 o'clock **Edge:** Reeded

Date	Mintage	F	VF	XF	Unc	BU
2002 Proof	—	Value: 40.00				

KM# 104 10 FRANCS
19.0000 g., 0.9990 Silver 0.6102 oz. ASW, 40 mm. **Obv:** Lion left **Rev:** WWII ME 109 German fighter plane flying left **Edge:** Reeded

Date	Mintage	F	VF	XF	Unc	BU
2002 Proof	—	Value: 40.00				

KM# 105 10 FRANCS
19.0000 g., 0.9990 Silver 0.6102 oz. ASW, 40 mm. **Obv:** Lion left **Rev:** Savoia-Marchetti S 55 seaplane flying left **Edge:** Reeded

Date	Mintage	F	VF	XF	Unc	BU
2002 Proof	—	Value: 40.00				

KM# 106 10 FRANCS
19.0000 g., 0.9990 Silver 0.6102 oz. ASW, 40 mm. **Obv:** Lion left **Rev:** B-58 Hustler Delta wing bomber flying left at 8 o'clock **Edge:** Reeded

Date	Mintage	F	VF	XF	Unc	BU
2002 Proof	—	Value: 40.00				

KM# 107 10 FRANCS
19.0000 g., 0.9990 Silver 0.6102 oz. ASW, 40 mm. **Obv:** Lion left **Rev:** CF-105 Arrow jet fighter plane flying right, nose up **Edge:** Reeded

Date	Mintage	F	VF	XF	Unc	BU
2002 Proof	—	Value: 40.00				

KM# 108 10 FRANCS
19.0000 g., 0.9990 Silver 0.6102 oz. ASW, 40 mm. **Obv:** Lion left **Rev:** XB-70 Valkyrie experimental jet bomber flying right **Edge:** Reeded

Date	Mintage	F	VF	XF	Unc	BU
2002 Proof	—	Value: 40.00				

KM# 109 10 FRANCS
19.0000 g., 0.9990 Silver 0.6102 oz. ASW, 40 mm. **Obv:** Lion left **Rev:** 14 BIS early aircraft in flight **Edge:** Reeded

Date	Mintage	F	VF	XF	Unc	BU
2003 Proof	—	Value: 40.00				

KM# 110 10 FRANCS
19.0000 g., 0.9990 Silver 0.6102 oz. ASW, 40 mm. **Obv:** Lion left **Rev:** WWI Sopwith Camel fighter plane flying right **Edge:** Reeded

Date	Mintage	F	VF	XF	Unc	BU
2003 Proof	—	Value: 40.00				

KM# 111 10 FRANCS
19.0000 g., 0.9990 Silver 0.6102 oz. ASW, 40 mm. **Obv:** Lion left **Rev:** Curtiss NC-4 early seaplane flying left **Edge:** Reeded

Date	Mintage	F	VF	XF	Unc	BU
2003 Proof	—	Value: 40.00				

KM# 112 10 FRANCS
19.0000 g., 0.9990 Silver 0.6102 oz. ASW, 40 mm. **Obv:** Lion left **Rev:** Macchi-Castoldi MC-72 seaplane flying left at 8 o'clock **Edge:** Reeded

Date	Mintage	F	VF	XF	Unc	BU
2003 Proof	—	Value: 40.00				

KM# 113 10 FRANCS
19.0000 g., 0.9990 Silver 0.6102 oz. ASW, 40 mm. **Obv:** Lion left **Rev:** WWII CA-12 Boomerang fighter plane flying above map at 10 o'clock **Edge:** Reeded

Date	Mintage	F	VF	XF	Unc	BU
2003 Proof	—	Value: 40.00				

KM# 114 10 FRANCS
19.0000 g., 0.9990 Silver 0.6102 oz. ASW, 40 mm. **Obv:** Lion left **Rev:** B-50A Superfortress bomber flying left **Edge:** Reeded

Date	Mintage	F	VF	XF	Unc	BU
2003 Proof	—	Value: 40.00				

KM# 115 10 FRANCS
19.0000 g., 0.9990 Silver 0.6102 oz. ASW, 40 mm. **Obv:** Lion left **Rev:** WWII Heinkel-178 German jet plane flying left **Edge:** Reeded

Date	Mintage	F	VF	XF	Unc	BU
2003 Proof	—	Value: 40.00				

KM# 116 10 FRANCS
19.0000 g., 0.9990 Silver 0.6102 oz. ASW, 40 mm. **Obv:** Lion left **Rev:** Early De Havilland Comet jet liner flying left **Edge:** Reeded

Date	Mintage	F	VF	XF	Unc	BU
2003 Proof	—	Value: 40.00				

KM# 117 10 FRANCS
19.0000 g., 0.9990 Silver 0.6102 oz. ASW, 40 mm. **Obv:** Lion left **Rev:** Panavia Tornado jet fighter-bomber flying left **Edge:** Reeded

Date	Mintage	F	VF	XF	Unc	BU
2003 Proof	—	Value: 40.00				

KM# 118 10 FRANCS
19.0000 g., 0.9990 Silver 0.6102 oz. ASW, 40 mm. **Obv:** Lion left **Rev:** Hindustan HF24 jet fighter flying left **Edge:** Reeded

Date	Mintage	F	VF	XF	Unc	BU
2003 Proof	—	Value: 40.00				

KM# 119 10 FRANCS
19.0000 g., 0.9990 Silver 0.6102 oz. ASW, 40 mm. **Obv:** Lion left **Rev:** Lockheed F-117 Stealth fighter flying left **Edge:** Reeded

Date	Mintage	F	VF	XF	Unc	BU
2003 Proof	—	Value: 40.00				

KM# 120 10 FRANCS
19.0000 g., 0.9990 Silver 0.6102 oz. ASW, 40 mm. **Obv:** Lion left **Rev:** North American X-15 experimental rocket plane flying right at 1 o'clock **Edge:** Reeded

Date	Mintage	F	VF	XF	Unc	BU
2003 Proof	—	Value: 40.00				

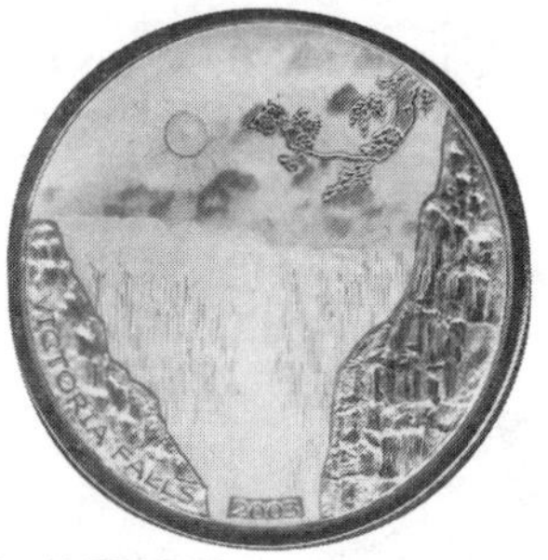

KM# 122 10 FRANCS

25.0000 g., 0.9250 Silver 0.7435 oz. ASW, 38.6 mm. **Obv:** Lion left **Rev:** Multicolor 3D hologram view of Victoria Falls **Edge:** Reeded

Date	Mintage	F	VF	XF	Unc	BU
2003 Proof	5,000	Value: 45.00				

KM# 99.1 10 FRANCS

24.9100 g., 0.9250 Silver 0.7408 oz. ASW, 38.6 mm. **Obv:** Lion left **Rev:** Chameleon **Edge:** Reeded

Date	Mintage	F	VF	XF	Unc	BU
2003 Proof	—	Value: 40.00				

KM# 99.2 10 FRANCS

24.9100 g., 0.9250 Silver 0.7408 oz. ASW, 38.6 mm. **Obv:** Lion left **Rev:** Multicolor chameleon **Edge:** Reeded

Date	Mintage	F	VF	XF	Unc	BU
2003 Proof	—	Value: 50.00				

KM# 100 10 FRANCS

24.9100 g., 0.9250 Silver 0.7408 oz. ASW, 38.6 mm. **Obv:** Lion left **Rev:** Bushy-tailed Mongoose left **Edge:** Reeded

Date	Mintage	F	VF	XF	Unc	BU
2003 Proof	—	Value: 45.00				

KM# 101 10 FRANCS

24.9100 g., 0.9250 Silver 0.7408 oz. ASW, 38.6 mm. **Obv:** Lion left **Rev:** Porcupine on rock, right **Edge:** Reeded

Date	Mintage	F	VF	XF	Unc	BU
2003 Proof	—	Value: 45.00				

KM# 102 10 FRANCS

24.9100 g., 0.9250 Silver 0.7408 oz. ASW, 38.6 mm. **Obv:** Lion left **Rev:** Pangolin on rock right **Edge:** Reeded

Date	Mintage	F	VF	XF	Unc	BU
2003 Proof	—	Value: 45.00				

KM# 132 10 FRANCS

25.0000 g., 0.9000 Silver 0.7234 oz. ASW, 40 mm. **Obv:** Lion left **Rev:** Multicolor dolphin leaping left **Edge:** Reeded

Date	Mintage	F	VF	XF	Unc	BU
2003 Proof	5,000	Value: 50.00				

KM# 133 10 FRANCS

25.0000 g., 0.9000 Silver 0.7234 oz. ASW, 40 mm. **Obv:** Lion left **Rev:** Multicolor sea turtle left **Edge:** Reeded

Date	Mintage	F	VF	XF	Unc	BU
2003 Proof	5,000	Value: 50.00				

KM# 134 10 FRANCS

25.0000 g., 0.9000 Silver 0.7234 oz. ASW, 40 mm. **Obv:** Lion left **Rev:** Multicolor killer whale jumping right **Edge:** Reeded

Date	Mintage	F	VF	XF	Unc	BU
2003 Proof	5,000	Value: 50.00				

KM# 135 10 FRANCS

26.0000 g., 0.9990 Silver 0.8350 oz. ASW, 40 mm. **Obv:** Lion left **Rev:** Pope John Paul II with staff and mitre, waving **Edge:** Reeded

Date	Mintage	F	VF	XF	Unc	BU
2003 Proof	—	Value: 50.00				

KM# 163 10 FRANCS

39.1000 g., Acrylic, 49.9 mm. **Obv:** Old World Swallowtail butterfly above lion and value **Rev:** Rear view of the obverse **Edge:** Plain

Date	Mintage	F	VF	XF	Unc	BU
2003	—	—	—	—	75.00	—

KM# 171 10 FRANCS

39.1000 g., Acrylic, 49.9 mm. **Obv:** Gorch Fock sail ship above lion and value **Rev:** Rear view of the obverse design **Edge:** Plain

Date	Mintage	F	VF	XF	Unc	BU
2003	1,000	—	—	—	75.00	—

KM# 126 10 FRANCS

25.0000 g., 0.9250 Silver 0.7435 oz. ASW, 38.6 mm. **Obv:** Lion left above value **Rev:** Sundial face with collapsible gnomon **Edge:** Reeded

Date	Mintage	F	VF	XF	Unc	BU
2004 Proof	5,000	Value: 50.00				

KM# 127 10 FRANCS

25.0000 g., 0.9250 Silver 0.7435 oz. ASW, 38.6 mm. **Obv:** Lion left above value **Rev:** Compass face **Edge:** Reeded **Note:** Compass part of the Compass and Spoon set

Date	Mintage	F	VF	XF	Unc	BU
2004 Proof	5,000	Value: 50.00				

KM# 141 10 FRANCS

25.0000 g., 0.9250 Silver 0.7435 oz. ASW, 38.6 mm. **Obv:** Lion left **Rev:** Multicolor Emperor fish swimming left **Edge:** Reeded

Date	Mintage	F	VF	XF	Unc	BU
2004 Proof	5,000	Value: 45.00				

KM# 142 10 FRANCS

25.0000 g., 0.9250 Silver 0.7435 oz. ASW, 38.6 mm. **Obv:** Lion left **Rev:** Multicolor octopus facing **Edge:** Reeded

Date	Mintage	F	VF	XF	Unc	BU
2004 Proof	5,000	Value: 50.00				

KM# 143 10 FRANCS

25.0000 g., 0.9250 Silver 0.7435 oz. ASW, 38.6 mm. **Obv:** Lion left **Rev:** Formula 1 and GT race cars **Edge:** Reeded

Date	Mintage	F	VF	XF	Unc	BU
2004 Proof	5,000	Value: 45.00				

KM# 145 10 FRANCS

25.0000 g., 0.9250 Silver 0.7435 oz. ASW, 27x47 mm. **Obv:** Lion left **Rev:** Pope with crucifix **Edge:** Plain **Shape:** Rectangular

Date	Mintage	F	VF	XF	Unc	BU
2004 Proof	5,000	Value: 45.00				

KM# 149 10 FRANCS
25.0000 g., 0.9250 Silver 0.7435 oz. ASW, 38.6 mm. **Obv:** Lion left **Rev:** Multicolor Quetzal bird **Edge:** Reeded

Date	Mintage	F	VF	XF	Unc	BU
2004 Proof	5,000	Value: 45.00				

KM# 150 10 FRANCS
25.0000 g., 0.9250 Silver 0.7435 oz. ASW, 38.6 mm. **Obv:** Lion left **Rev:** Multicolor Bird of Paradise on branch left **Edge:** Reeded

Date	Mintage	F	VF	XF	Unc	BU
2004 Proof	5,000	Value: 45.00				

KM# 151 10 FRANCS
25.0000 g., 0.9250 Silver 0.7435 oz. ASW, 38.6 mm. **Obv:** Lion left **Rev:** Multicolor Kingfisher bird left **Edge:** Reeded

Date	Mintage	F	VF	XF	Unc	BU
2004 Proof	5,000	Value: 45.00				

KM# 155 10 FRANCS
Acrylic Clear, 50 mm. **Obv:** Etched nine-masted sailing junk above lion, value and country name **Edge:** Plain

Date	Mintage	F	VF	XF	Unc	BU
2004	2,000	—	—	—	55.00	—

KM# 172 10 FRANCS
25.0000 g., Silver, 38.6 mm. **Obv:** Lion left **Rev:** Pope waving half facing at left, cross at upper right, Vatican at lower right

Date	Mintage	F	VF	XF	Unc	BU
2005 Proof	3,000	Value: 50.00				

KM# 136 20 FRANCS
1.2440 g., 0.9999 Gold 0.0400 oz. AGW, 13.92 mm. **Obv:** Lion left **Rev:** Pope John Paul II with staff and mitre, waving **Edge:** Plain

Date	Mintage	F	VF	XF	Unc	BU
2003 Proof	—	Value: 55.00				

KM# 137 20 FRANCS
1.2440 g., 0.9999 Gold 0.0400 oz. AGW, 13.92 mm. **Obv:** Lion left **Rev:** Skunk **Edge:** Plain

Date	Mintage	F	VF	XF	Unc	BU
2003 Proof	25,000	Value: 55.00				

KM# 138 20 FRANCS
1.2440 g., 0.9999 Gold 0.0400 oz. AGW, 13.92 mm. **Obv:** Lion left **Rev:** Giant anteater right **Edge:** Plain

Date	Mintage	F	VF	XF	Unc	BU
2003 Proof	25,000	Value: 55.00				

KM# 139 20 FRANCS
1.2440 g., 0.9999 Gold 0.0400 oz. AGW, 13.92 mm. **Obv:** Lion left **Rev:** Porcupine right **Edge:** Plain

Date	Mintage	F	VF	XF	Unc	BU
2003 Proof	25,000	Value: 55.00				

KM# 140 20 FRANCS
1.2440 g., 0.9999 Gold 0.0400 oz. AGW, 13.92 mm. **Obv:** Lion left **Rev:** Chameleon **Edge:** Plain

Date	Mintage	F	VF	XF	Unc	BU
2003 Proof	25,000	Value: 55.00				

KM# 144 20 FRANCS
1.2440 g., 0.9999 Gold 0.0400 oz. AGW, 13.92 mm. **Obv:** Lion left **Rev:** Ferrari coat of arms **Edge:** Plain

Date	Mintage	F	VF	XF	Unc	BU
2004 Proof	5,000	Value: 55.00				

KM# 173 20 FRANCS
1.5300 g., 0.9990 Gold 0.0491 oz. AGW, 13.9 mm. **Obv:** Lion left **Rev:** Pope waving at left, cross at upper right, Vatican at lower right

Date	Mintage	F	VF	XF	Unc	BU
2005 Proof	25,000	Value: 60.00				

KM# 129 100 FRANCS
31.1000 g., 0.9999 Gold 0.9997 oz. AGW, 40 mm. **Obv:** Lion left **Rev:** Reflective multicolor swallowtail butterfly **Edge:** Reeded

Date	Mintage	F	VF	XF	Unc	BU
2002 Proof	50	Value: 1,000				

KM# 130 100 FRANCS
31.1000 g., 0.9999 Gold 0.9997 oz. AGW, 40 mm. **Obv:** Lion left **Rev:** Reflective multicolor dark greenish butterfly **Edge:** Reeded

Date	Mintage	F	VF	XF	Unc	BU
2002 Proof	50	Value: 1,000				

KM# 131 100 FRANCS
31.1000 g., 0.9999 Gold 0.9997 oz. AGW, 40 mm. **Obv:** Lion left **Rev:** Reflective multicolor red and black butterfly **Edge:** Reeded

Date	Mintage	F	VF	XF	Unc	BU
2002 Proof	50	Value: 1,000				

KM# 152 100 FRANCS
31.1035 g., 0.9999 Gold 0.9999 oz. AGW, 38.6 mm. **Obv:** Lion left **Rev:** Multicolor Quetzal bird **Edge:** Reeded

Date	Mintage	F	VF	XF	Unc	BU
2004 Proof	25	Value: 1,200				

KM# 153 100 FRANCS
31.1035 g., 0.9999 Gold 0.9999 oz. AGW, 38.6 mm. **Obv:** Lion left **Rev:** Multicolor Bird of Paradise left **Edge:** Reeded

Date	Mintage	F	VF	XF	Unc	BU
2004 Proof	25	Value: 1,200				

KM# 154 100 FRANCS
31.1035 g., 0.9999 Gold 0.9999 oz. AGW, 38.6 mm. **Obv:** Lion left **Rev:** Multicolor Kingfisher bird **Edge:** Reeded

Date	Mintage	F	VF	XF	Unc	BU
2004 Proof	25	Value: 1,200				

MINT SETS

KM#	Date	Mintage	Identification	Issue Price	Mkt Val
MS2	2004 (4)	—	KM#156-159	—	8.50

COOK ISLANDS

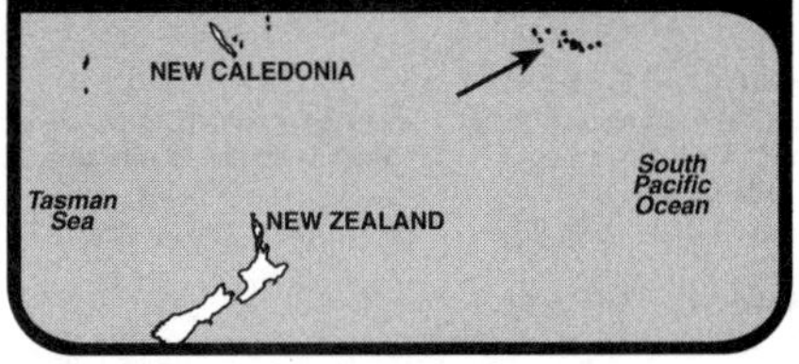

Cook Islands, a self-governing dependency of New Zealand consisting of 15 islands, is located in the South Pacific Ocean about 2,000 miles (3,218 km.) northeast of New Zealand. It has an area of 93 sq. mi. (234 sq. km.) and a population of 17,185. Capital: Avarua. The United States claims the islands of Danger, Manahiki, Penrhyn, and Rakahanga atolls. Citrus and canned fruits and juices, copra, clothing, jewelry, and mother-of-pearl shell are exported.

RULER
British

MINT MARK
PM - Pobjoy Mint

MONETARY SYSTEM
100 Cents = 1 Dollar

DEPENDENCY OF NEW ZEALAND

DECIMAL COINAGE

KM# 419 CENT
1.4400 g., Aluminum, 21.9 mm. **Ruler:** Elizabeth II **Obv:** Crowned head right, date below **Rev:** Bust of Capt. James Cook right, denomination below **Edge:** Plain

Date	Mintage	F	VF	XF	Unc	BU
2003	—	—	—	—	1.25	1.50

KM# 420 CENT
1.4400 g., Aluminum, 21.9 mm. **Ruler:** Elizabeth II **Obv:** Crowned head right, date below **Rev:** Collie dog right, denomination below **Edge:** Plain

Date	Mintage	F	VF	XF	Unc	BU
2003	—	—	—	—	0.75	1.00

KM# 421 CENT
1.4400 g., Aluminum, 21.9 mm. **Ruler:** Elizabeth II **Obv:** Crowned head right, date below **Rev:** Pointer dog right, denomination above **Edge:** Plain

Date	Mintage	F	VF	XF	Unc	BU
2003	—	—	—	—	0.75	1.00

KM# 422 CENT
1.4400 g., Aluminum, 21.9 mm. **Ruler:** Elizabeth II **Obv:** Crowned head right, date below **Rev:** Rooster right, denomination above **Edge:** Plain

Date	Mintage	F	VF	XF	Unc	BU
2003	—	—	—	—	0.75	1.00

KM# 423 CENT
1.4400 g., Aluminum, 22 mm. **Ruler:** Elizabeth II **Obv:** Crowned head right, date below **Rev:** Monkey on branch, denomination at left **Edge:** Plain

Date	Mintage	F	VF	XF	Unc	BU
2003	—	—	—	—	0.75	1.00

KM# 396 DOLLAR
24.8828 g., 0.9990 Silver with Acrylic capsule center containing tiny rubies, sapphires and cubic zirconias 0.7992 oz. ASW, 40.6 mm. **Ruler:** Elizabeth II **Subject:** Crown Jewels **Obv:** Crowned head right, legend **Rev:** Crowns and royal regalia **Edge:** Reeded

Date	Mintage	F	VF	XF	Unc	BU
2002 Proof	50,000	Value: 11.50				

KM# 416 DOLLAR
10.7500 g., Copper-Nickel, 28.5 mm. **Ruler:** Elizabeth II **Obv:** Queen's new portrait **Rev:** Tangaroa statue and value **Edge:** Scalloped

Date	Mintage	F	VF	XF	Unc	BU
2003	—	—	—	—	2.50	3.00

KM# 455 DOLLAR
23.9000 g., Copper-Nickel, 38.5 mm. **Ruler:** Elizabeth II **Obv:** Queen Elizabeth II **Rev:** 50th Anniversary - Playboy magazine logo **Edge:** Reeded

Date	Mintage	F	VF	XF	Unc	BU
2003	—	—	—	—	7.00	9.00

KM# 455a DOLLAR
25.2700 g., Copper-Nickel, Gold Plated, 38.3 mm. **Ruler:** Elizabeth II **Obv:** Elizabeth II **Rev:** Playboy magazine's 50th Anniversary logo **Edge:** Reeded

Date	Mintage	F	VF	XF	Unc	BU
2003 Proof	50,000	Value: 20.00				

KM# 455b DOLLAR
25.2700 g., 0.9990 Silver 0.8116 oz. ASW, 38.3 mm. **Ruler:** Elizabeth II **Obv:** Elizabeth II **Rev:** Playboy magazine's 50th Anniversary logo **Edge:** Reeded

Date	Mintage	F	VF	XF	Unc	BU
2003 Proof	—	Value: 40.00				

KM# 455c DOLLAR
25.2700 g., 0.9990 Gold Plated Silver 0.8116 oz. ASW AGW, 38.3 mm. **Ruler:** Elizabeth II **Obv:** Elizabeth II **Rev:** Playboy magazine's 50th Anniversary logo **Edge:** Reeded

Date	Mintage	F	VF	XF	Unc	BU
2003 Proof	—	Value: 50.00				

KM# 462 DOLLAR
Copper-Nickel, 41 mm. **Ruler:** Elizabeth II **Rev:** Face of 5 Euro Banknote

Date	Mintage	F	VF	XF	Unc	BU
2003	—	—	—	—	7.00	9.00

KM# 463 DOLLAR
Copper-Nickel, 41 mm. **Ruler:** Elizabeth II **Rev:** Face of 10 Euro Banknote

Date	Mintage	F	VF	XF	Unc	BU
2003	—	—	—	—	7.00	9.00

KM# 464 DOLLAR
Copper-Nickel, 41 mm. **Ruler:** Elizabeth II **Rev:** Face of 20 Euro Banknote

Date	Mintage	F	VF	XF	Unc	BU
2003	—	—	—	—	7.00	9.00

KM# 465 DOLLAR
Copper-Nickel, 41 mm. **Ruler:** Elizabeth II **Rev:** Face of 50 Euro Banknote

Date	Mintage	F	VF	XF	Unc	BU
2003	—	—	—	—	7.00	9.00

KM# 466 DOLLAR
Copper-Nickel, 41 mm. **Ruler:** Elizabeth II **Rev:** Face of 100 Euro Banknote

Date	Mintage	F	VF	XF	Unc	BU
2003	—	—	—	—	7.00	9.00

KM# 467 DOLLAR
Copper-Nickel, 41 mm. **Ruler:** Elizabeth II **Rev:** Face of 500 Euro Banknote

Date	Mintage	F	VF	XF	Unc	BU
2003	—	—	—	—	7.00	9.00

KM# 424 DOLLAR
8.5000 g., 0.9990 Silver 0.2730 oz. ASW, 25.1 mm. **Ruler:** Elizabeth II **Subject:** Zodiac Gemstones - Cancer **Obv:** Crowned head above ornamental center **Rev:** Encapsulated emeralds above Crab (Cancer) **Edge:** Reeded

Date	Mintage	F	VF	XF	Unc	BU
ND(2003) Proof	10,000	Value: 15.00				

KM# 424a DOLLAR
8.5000 g., 0.9990 Gold Plated Silver 0.2730 oz. ASW AGW, 25.1 mm. **Ruler:** Elizabeth II **Obv:** Crowned head above ornamental center **Rev:** Encapsulated emeralds above Crab (cancer)

Date	Mintage	F	VF	XF	Unc	BU
ND(2003) Proof	10,000	Value: 18.50				

KM# 425 DOLLAR
8.5000 g., 0.9990 Silver 0.2730 oz. ASW, 25.1 mm. **Ruler:** Elizabeth II **Subject:** Zodiac Gemstones - Aquarius **Obv:** Crowned head above ornamental center **Rev:** Encapsulated garnets with Aquarious in background **Edge:** Reeded

Date	Mintage	F	VF	XF	Unc	BU
ND(2004) Proof	10,000	Value: 15.00				

KM# 425a DOLLAR
8.5000 g., 0.9990 Gold Plated Silver 0.2730 oz. ASW AGW, 25.1 mm. **Ruler:** Elizabeth II **Obv:** Crowned head above ornamental center **Rev:** Encapsulated garnets with Aquarious in background

Date	Mintage	F	VF	XF	Unc	BU
ND(2003) Proof	10,000	Value: 18.50				

KM# 426 DOLLAR
8.5000 g., 0.9990 Silver 0.2730 oz. ASW, 25.1 mm. **Ruler:** Elizabeth II **Subject:** Zodiac Gemstones - Aries **Obv:** Crowned head above ornamental center **Rev:** Encapsulated Bloodstones in center with ram at left **Edge:** Reeded

Date	Mintage	F	VF	XF	Unc	BU
ND(2003) Proof	10,000	Value: 15.00				

KM# 426a DOLLAR
8.5000 g., 0.9990 Gold Plated Silver 0.2730 oz. ASW AGW, 25.1 mm. **Ruler:** Elizabeth II **Obv:** Crowned head above ornamental center **Rev:** Encapsulated Bloodstones in center with ram at left

Date	Mintage	F	VF	XF	Unc	BU
ND(2003) Proof	10,000	Value: 18.50				

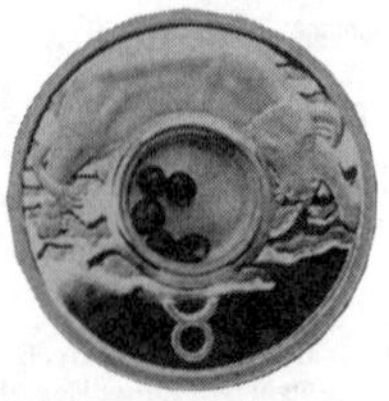

KM# 427 DOLLAR
8.5000 g., 0.9990 Silver 0.2730 oz. ASW, 25.1 mm. **Ruler:** Elizabeth II **Subject:** Zodiac Gemstones - Taurus **Obv:** Crowned head above ornamental center **Rev:** Encapsulated Sapphires with bull in background **Edge:** Reeded

Date	Mintage	F	VF	XF	Unc	BU
ND(2003) Proof	10,000	Value: 18.50				

KM# 427a DOLLAR
8.5000 g., 0.9990 Gold Plated Silver 0.2730 oz. ASW AGW, 25.1 mm. **Ruler:** Elizabeth II **Subject:** Zodiac Gemstones - Taurus **Obv:** Crowned head above ornamental center **Rev:** Encapsulated Sapphires with bull in background **Edge:** Reeded

Date	Mintage	F	VF	XF	Unc	BU
ND(2003) Proof	10,000	Value: 30.00				

KM# 428 DOLLAR
8.5000 g., 0.9990 Silver 0.2730 oz. ASW, 25.1 mm. **Ruler:** Elizabeth II **Obv:** Crowned head above ornamental center **Rev:** Encapsulated Agates between twins **Edge:** Reeded

Date	Mintage	F	VF	XF	Unc	BU
ND(2003) Proof	10,000	Value: 15.00				

KM# 428a DOLLAR
8.5000 g., 0.9990 Gold Plated Silver 0.2730 oz. ASW AGW, 25.1 mm. **Ruler:** Elizabeth II **Obv:** Crowned head above ornamental center **Rev:** Encapsulated Agates between twins **Edge:** Reeded

Date	Mintage	F	VF	XF	Unc	BU
ND(2003) Proof	10,000	Value: 18.50				

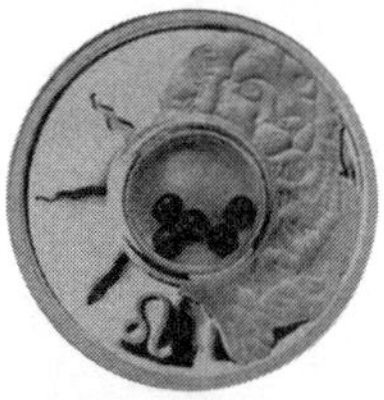

KM# 429 DOLLAR
8.5000 g., 0.9990 Silver 0.2730 oz. ASW, 25.1 mm. **Ruler:** Elizabeth II **Obv:** Crowned head above ornamental center **Rev:** Encapsulated Onyx stones with lion at right **Edge:** Reeded

Date	Mintage	F	VF	XF	Unc	BU
ND(2003) Proof	10,000	Value: 15.00				

KM# 429a DOLLAR
8.5000 g., 0.9990 Gold Plated Silver 0.2730 oz. ASW AGW, 25.1 mm. **Ruler:** Elizabeth II **Obv:** Crowned head above ornamental center **Rev:** Encapsulated Onyx stones with lion at right **Edge:** Reeded

Date	Mintage	F	VF	XF	Unc	BU
ND(2003) Proof	10,000	Value: 18.50				

KM# 430 DOLLAR
8.5000 g., 0.9990 Silver 0.2730 oz. ASW, 25.1 mm. **Ruler:** Elizabeth II **Subject:** Zodiac Gemstones - Virgo **Obv:** Crowned head above ornamented center **Rev:** Encapsulated Carnelian stones with woman at right **Edge:** Reeded

Date	Mintage	F	VF	XF	Unc	BU
ND(2003) Proof	10,000	Value: 15.00				

KM# 430a DOLLAR
8.5000 g., 0.9990 Gold Plated Silver 0.2730 oz. ASW AGW, 25.1 mm. **Ruler:** Elizabeth II **Subject:** Zodiac Gemstones - Virgo **Obv:** Crowned head above ornamented center **Rev:** Encapsulated Carnelian stones with Virgo at right **Edge:** Reeded

Date	Mintage	F	VF	XF	Unc	BU
ND(2003) Proof	10,000	Value: 18.50				

KM# 431 DOLLAR
8.5000 g., 0.9990 Silver 0.2730 oz. ASW, 25.1 mm. **Ruler:** Elizabeth II **Subject:** Zodiac Gemstones - Libra **Obv:** Crowned head above ornamental center **Rev:** Encapsulated Peridot stones with balance scale **Edge:** Reeded

Date	Mintage	F	VF	XF	Unc	BU
ND(2003) Proof	10,000	Value: 15.00				

KM# 431a DOLLAR
8.5000 g., 0.9990 Gold Plated Silver 0.2730 oz. ASW AGW, 25.1 mm. **Ruler:** Elizabeth II **Subject:** Zodiac Gemstones - Libra **Obv:** Crowned head above ornamented center **Rev:** Encapsulated Peridot stones with balance scale **Edge:** Reeded

Date	Mintage	F	VF	XF	Unc	BU
ND(2003) Proof	10,000	Value: 18.50				

KM# 432 DOLLAR
8.5000 g., 0.9990 Silver 0.2730 oz. ASW, 25.1 mm. **Ruler:** Elizabeth II **Subject:** Zodiac Gemstones - Scorpio **Obv:** Crowned head above ornamented center **Rev:** Encapsulated Aquamarine stones with scorpion at lower right **Edge:** Reeded

Date	Mintage	F	VF	XF	Unc	BU
ND(2003) Proof	10,000	Value: 15.00				

KM# 432a DOLLAR
8.5000 g., 0.9990 Gold Plated Silver 0.2730 oz. ASW AGW, 25.1 mm. **Ruler:** Elizabeth II **Subject:** Zodiac Gemstones - Scorpio **Obv:** Crowned head above ornamented center **Rev:** Encapsulated Aquamarine stones with scorpion at lower right **Edge:** Reeded

Date	Mintage	F	VF	XF	Unc	BU
ND(2003) Proof	10,000	Value: 18.50				

KM# 433 DOLLAR
8.5000 g., 0.9990 Silver 0.2730 oz. ASW, 25.1 mm. **Ruler:** Elizabeth II **Subject:** Zodiac Gemstones - Sagittarius **Obv:** Crowned head above ornamented center **Rev:** Encapsulated Topaz stones with centaur at right **Edge:** Reeded

Date	Mintage	F	VF	XF	Unc	BU
ND(2003) Proof	10,000	Value: 15.00				

KM# 433a DOLLAR
8.5000 g., 0.9990 Gold Plated Silver 0.2730 oz. ASW AGW, 25.1 mm. **Ruler:** Elizabeth II **Subject:** Zodiac Gemstones - Sagittarius **Obv:** Crowned head above ornamented center **Rev:** Encapsulated Topaz stones with centaur at right **Edge:** Reeded

Date	Mintage	F	VF	XF	Unc	BU
ND(2003) Proof	10,000	Value: 18.50				

KM# 434 DOLLAR
8.5000 g., 0.9990 Silver 0.2730 oz. ASW, 25.1 mm. **Ruler:** Elizabeth II **Subject:** Zodiac Gemstones - Capricorn **Obv:** Crowned head above ornamental center **Rev:** Encapsulated rubies with goat at right **Edge:** Reeded

Date	Mintage	F	VF	XF	Unc	BU
ND(2003) Proof	10,000	Value: 15.00				

KM# 434a DOLLAR
8.5000 g., 0.9990 Gold Plated Silver 0.2730 oz. ASW AGW, 25.1 mm. **Ruler:** Elizabeth II **Subject:** Zodiac Gemstones - Capricorn **Obv:** Crowned head above ornamented center **Rev:** Encapsulated Rubies with goat at right **Edge:** Reeded

Date	Mintage	F	VF	XF	Unc	BU
ND(2003) Proof	10,000	Value: 18.50				

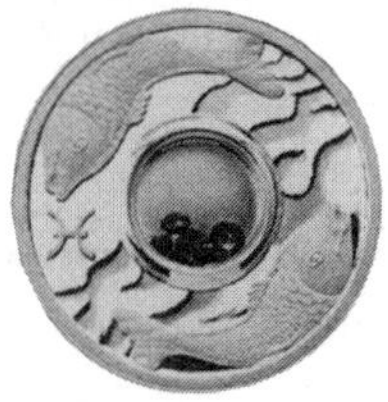

KM# 435 DOLLAR
8.5000 g., 0.9990 Silver 0.2730 oz. ASW, 25.1 mm. **Ruler:** Elizabeth II **Subject:** Zodiac Gemstones - Pices **Obv:** Crowned head above ornamented center **Rev:** Encapsulated Amethyst stones and two fish **Edge:** Reeded

Date	Mintage	F	VF	XF	Unc	BU
ND(2003) Proof	10,000	Value: 15.00				

KM# 435a DOLLAR
8.5000 g., 0.9990 Gold Plated Silver 0.2730 oz. ASW AGW, 25.1 mm. **Ruler:** Elizabeth II **Subject:** Zodiac Gemstones - Pices **Obv:** Crowned head above ornamented center **Rev:** Encapsulated Amethyst stones and 2 fish **Edge:** Reeded

Date	Mintage	F	VF	XF	Unc	BU
ND(2003) Proof	10,000	Value: 18.50				

KM# 438 DOLLAR
31.1035 g., 0.9990 Silver 0.9990 oz. ASW, 40.5 mm. **Ruler:** Elizabeth II **Obv:** Crowned head right **Rev:** Multicolor Deng Xiaoping on Chinese map **Edge:** Plain **Shape:** As a map

Date	Mintage	F	VF	XF	Unc	BU
2004	20,000	—	—	—	35.00	—

KM# 454 DOLLAR
27.5300 g., 0.9990 Silver Clad Copper-Nickel 0.8842 oz. ASW, 38.6 mm. **Ruler:** Elizabeth II **Subject:** 60th Anniversary - D-Day Invasion **Obv:** Crowned bust right, new portrait **Rev:** Invasion scene of soldiers storming the beaches (Sword, Gold, Juno, Omaha, and Utah) of Normandy

Date	Mintage	F	VF	XF	Unc	BU
2004	—	—	—	—	12.50	15.00

KM# 443 DOLLAR
23.9000 g., Copper-Nickel, 38.5 mm. **Ruler:** Elizabeth II **Subject:** Battle of Trafalgar **Obv:** Crowned bust right, new portrait **Rev:** HMS Victory and color portrait of Nelson **Edge:** Reeded

Date	Mintage	F	VF	XF	Unc	BU
2005	—	—	—	—	10.00	11.50

KM# 470 DOLLAR
30.1050 g., 0.9990 Silver 0.9669 oz. ASW **Obv:** Twin Towers and Statue of Liberty, Queens Head below **Obv. Legend:** COOK ISLANDS / WE WILL NEVER FORGET **Rev:** Freedoom Tower and Statue of Liberty **Rev. Legend:** ONE DOLLAR /LET FREEDOM RING /FREEDOM TOWER / 2006 **Edge:** Reeded and lettered **Edge Lettering:** 1 Troy Oz . 999 fine silver

Date	Mintage	F	VF	XF	Unc	BU
2006 Proof	—	Value: 25.00				

KM# 471 DOLLAR
35.8000 g., 0.9990 Silver 1.1498 oz. ASW **Ruler:** Elizabeth II **Subject:** Sputnik 50th Anniversary - 1957-2007 **Obv:** Small bust divides legend above, center globe with color applique **Rev:** Satellite orbiting Earth with color applique **Rev. Legend:** SPUTNIK 50th ANNIVERSARY 1957 - 2007 **Edge:** Plain **Note:** Center piece rotates freely

Date	Mintage	F	VF	XF	Unc	BU
ND(2007) Proof	—	Value: 72.50				

KM# 468 2 DOLLARS
Copper-Nickel **Ruler:** Elizabeth II **Rev:** Football championship

Date	Mintage	F	VF	XF	Unc	BU
2002	—	—	—	—	5.00	7.00

KM# 417 2 DOLLARS
7.5500 g., Copper-Nickel, 26 mm. **Ruler:** Elizabeth II **Obv:** Crowned bust right, new portrait **Rev:** Mortar and pestle from Atiu Island **Edge:** Triangular

Date	Mintage	F	VF	XF	Unc	BU
2003	—	—	—	—	3.00	3.50

KM# 418 5 DOLLARS
14.0000 g., Aluminum-Bronze, 31.5 mm. **Ruler:** Elizabeth II **Obv:** Crowned bust right, new portrait **Rev:** Conch shell and value **Shape:** 12-sided

Date	Mintage	F	VF	XF	Unc	BU
2003	—	—	—	—	6.00	8.00

KM# 469 5 DOLLARS
Copper-Nickel, 40 mm. **Obv:** USPS logo, Queens head above **Rev:** 5 cent 1847 Benjamin Franklin stamp

Date	Mintage	F	VF	XF	Unc	BU
2004	—	—	—	—	—	7.50

KM# 469a 5 DOLLARS
Silver, 40 mm. **Obv:** USPS logo, Queens head above **Rev:** 5 cent 1847 Benjamin Franklin stamp **Edge:** Reeded

Date	Mintage	F	VF	XF	Unc	BU
2004 Proof	—	Value: 20.00				

KM# 453 10 DOLLARS
186.8300 g., 0.9990 Gold Plated Silver 6.0005 oz. ASW AGW, 89 mm. **Ruler:** Elizabeth II **Obv:** Crowned bust right, unique portrait for Cook Islands **Rev:** Queen Victoria standing with lion **Rev. Designer:** W. Wyon **Edge:** Reeded **Note:** Illustration reduced.

Date	Mintage	F	VF	XF	Unc	BU
2003 Proof	198	Value: 300				

KM# 439 30 DOLLARS
10.0000 g., 0.9999 Gold 0.3215 oz. AGW, 16.1 mm. **Ruler:** Elizabeth II **Obv:** Crowned head right, date below **Rev:** Multicolor Peony flower and denomination **Edge:** Reeded

Date	Mintage	F	VF	XF	Unc	BU
2004	10,000	—	—	—	—	285

KM# 440 35 DOLLARS
10.0000 g., 0.9999 Gold 0.3215 oz. AGW, 16.1 mm. **Ruler:** Elizabeth II **Obv:** Crowned head right, date below **Rev:** Multicolor Chinese man beating a tiger and denomination **Edge:** Reeded

Date	Mintage	F	VF	XF	Unc	BU
2004	6,000	—	—	—	—	285

KM# 441 35 DOLLARS
10.0000 g., 0.9999 Gold 0.3215 oz. AGW, 16.1 mm. **Ruler:** Elizabeth II **Obv:** Crowned head right, date below **Rev:** Multicolor Chinese man riding a horse and denomination **Edge:** Reeded

Date	Mintage	F	VF	XF	Unc	BU
2004	10,000	—	—	—	—	285

KM# 442 35 DOLLARS
10.0000 g., 0.9999 Gold 0.3215 oz. AGW, 25 x 15 mm. **Ruler:** Elizabeth II **Obv:** Crowned head right, date below **Rev:** Multicolor "Eight immortals crossing the sea" and denomination **Edge:** Plain **Shape:** Ingot

Date	Mintage	F	VF	XF	Unc	BU
2004	3,000	—	—	—	—	285

KM# 397 100 DOLLARS
23.3276 g., 0.9999 Gold Acrylic capsule center containing tiny diamonds, rubies and sapphires 0.7499 oz. AGW, 32.1 mm. **Ruler:** Elizabeth II **Subject:** Crown Jewels **Obv:** Crowned bust right, legend **Rev:** Crowns and royal regalia **Edge:** Reeded

Date	Mintage	F	VF	XF	Unc	BU
2002 Proof	5,000	Value: 525				

KM# 389 500 DOLLARS
1723.1259 g., 0.9990 Silver 55.342 oz. ASW, 115.2 mm. **Ruler:** Elizabeth II **Subject:** Moby Dick **Obv:** Crowned head right **Rev:** Whale jumping over a six-man rowboat **Edge:** Plain **Note:** Illustration reduced.

Date	Mintage	F	VF	XF	Unc	BU
2001 Proof	—	Value: 900				

MAUNDY MONEY

Ceremonial Sterling Pence

KM# 449 PENNY
0.4800 g., 0.9990 Silver 0.0154 oz. ASW, 11.1 mm. **Ruler:** Elizabeth II **Subject:** Maundy **Obv:** Crowned bust right **Rev:** Crowned denomination divides date within wreath **Edge:** Plain

Date	Mintage	F	VF	XF	Unc	BU
2002 Proof	5,000	Value: 8.00				

KM# 450 2 PENCE
0.9400 g., 0.9990 Silver 0.0302 oz. ASW, 13.4 mm. **Ruler:** Elizabeth II **Subject:** Maundy **Obv:** Crowned bust right **Rev:** Crowned denomination divides date within wreath **Edge:** Plain

Date	Mintage	F	VF	XF	Unc	BU
2002 Proof	5,000	Value: 10.00				

KM# 451 3 PENCE
1.4400 g., 0.9990 Silver 0.0462 oz. ASW, 16.1 mm. **Ruler:** Elizabeth II **Subject:** Maundy **Obv:** Crowned bust right **Rev:** Crowned denomination divides date within wreath **Edge:** Plain

Date	Mintage	F	VF	XF	Unc	BU
2002 Proof	5,000	Value: 12.00				

KM# 452 4 PENCE
1.9300 g., 0.9990 Silver 0.0620 oz. ASW, 17.5 mm. **Ruler:** Elizabeth II **Subject:** Maundy **Obv:** Crowned bust right **Rev:** Crowned denomination divides date within wreath **Edge:** Plain

Date	Mintage	F	VF	XF	Unc	BU
2002 Proof	5,000	Value: 15.00				

PROOF SETS

KM#	Date	Mintage	Identification	Issue Price	Mkt Val
PS25	2002 (4)	5,000	KM449-452	—	45.00

COSTA RICA

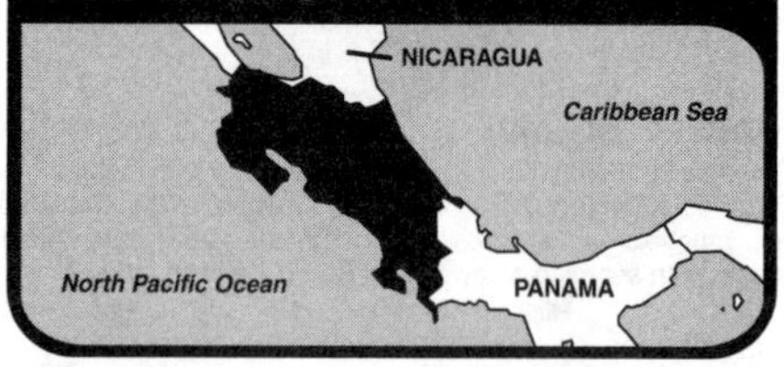

The Republic of Costa Rica, located in southern Central America between Nicaragua and Panama, has an area of 19,730 sq. mi. (51,100 sq. km.) and a population of 3.4 million. Capital: San Jose. Agriculture predominates; tourism and coffee, bananas, beef and sugar contribute heavily to the country's export earnings.

KEY TO MINT IDENTIFICATION

Key Letter	Mint
(a)	Armant Metalurgica, Santiago, Chile
(c)	Casa de Moneda, Mexico City Mint
(cc)	Casa de Moneda, Brazil
(co)	Colombia Republican Banko
(g)	Guatemala Mint
(i)	Italcambio Mint
(p) or (P)	Philadelphia Mint, USA
®	RCM – Royal Canadian Mint
(rm)	Royal Mint, London
(s)	San Francisco
(sj)	San Jose
(sm)	Sherrit Mint, Toronto
(v)	Vereingte Deutsche Metallwerke, Karlsruhe
(w)	Westain, Toronto

REPUBLIC

REFORM COINAGE

1920, 100 Centimos = 1 Colon

KM# 227a.2 5 COLONES
4.0000 g., Brass, 21.6 mm. **Obv:** National arms, date below, large letters in legend, large date, shield is not outlined **Rev:** Denomination above spray, B.C.C.R. below, large letters in legend, thick '5' **Edge:** Segmented reeding

Date	Mintage	F	VF	XF	Unc	BU
2001(a)	—	—	—	—	0.65	—

KM# 227b 5 COLONES
0.9000 g., Aluminum, 21.4 mm. **Obv:** National arms **Obv. Legend:** REPUBLICA DE COSTA RICA **Rev:** Denomination above sprays, B.C.C.R. **Edge:** Plain

Date	Mintage	F	VF	XF	Unc	BU
2005	—	—	—	—	—	0.50

KM# 228 10 COLONES
4.0200 g., Brass Plated Steel, 23.5 mm. **Obv:** National arms, date below **Rev:** Denomination above spray, B.C.C.R. below, thick numerals

Date	Mintage	F	VF	XF	Unc	BU
2002	—	—	—	0.35	1.25	—

KM# 228.2 10 COLONES
5.0000 g., Brass, 23.5 mm. **Obv:** National arms, date below, large legend and date, shield not outlined **Rev:** Denomination above spray, B.C.C.R. below **Edge:** Segmented reeding

Date	Mintage	F	VF	XF	Unc	BU
2002	—	—	—	—	1.15	—

KM# 228b 10 COLONES
1.1300 g., Aluminum, 22.97 mm. **Obv:** National arms **Obv. Legend:** REPUBLICA DE COSTA RICA **Rev:** Denomination above sprays, B.C.C.R. **Edge:** Reeded

Date	Mintage	F	VF	XF	Unc	BU
2005	—	—	—	—	—	0.75

KM# 229a 25 COLONES
7.0000 g., Brass, 25.4 mm. **Obv:** National arms **Obv. Legend:** REPUBLICA DE COSTA RICA **Rev:** Denomination above sprays, B.C.C.R. below **Edge:** Segmented reeding

Date	Mintage	F	VF	XF	Unc	BU
2001(a)	—	—	0.50	1.00	2.50	—
2003	—	—	0.50	1.00	2.50	—

KM# 231.2 50 COLONES
7.8000 g., Brass, 27.5 mm. **Obv:** National arms, date below, large legend and date, shield not outlined **Obv. Legend:** REPUBLICA DE COSTA RICA **Rev:** Value over spray **Rev. Legend:** B. C. C. R. **Edge:** Segmented reeding

Date	Mintage	F	VF	XF	Unc	BU
2003	—	—	—	—	3.00	—

KM# 239.1 500 COLONES
11.0000 g., Copper-Aluminum-Nickel, 32.9 mm. **Obv:** National arms **Obv. Legend:** REPUBLICA DE COSTA RICA **Rev:** Denomination above sprays, B.C.C.R. below, thick numerals **Edge:** Segmented reeding

Date	Mintage	F	VF	XF	Unc	BU
2003(a)	—	—	—	2.00	3.00	—
2005	—	—	—	2.00	3.00	—

KM# 239.2 500 COLONES
11.0000 g., Copper-Aluminum-Nickel, 32.9 mm. **Obv:** National arms, date below **Obv. Legend:** REPUBLICA DE COSTA RICA **Rev:** Denomination above sprays, B.C.C.R. below, thin numerals **Edge:** Segmented reeding

Date	Mintage	F	VF	XF	Unc	BU
2003	100	—	—	120	200	—

CROATIA

The Republic of Croatia, (Hrvatska) bordered on the west by the Adriatic Sea and the northeast by Hungary, has an area of 21,829 sq. mi. (56,538 sq. km.) and a population of 4.7 million. Capital: Zagreb.

NOTE: Coin dates starting with 1994 are followed with a period. Example: 1994.

REPUBLIC

REFORM COINAGE

May 30, 1994 - 1000 Dinara = 1 Kuna; 100 Lipa = 1 Kuna

For the circulating minor coins, the reverse legend (name of item) is in Croatian for odd dated years and Latin for even dated years.

KM# 3 LIPA
0.8000 g., Aluminum, 16 mm. **Obv:** Denomination above crowned arms **Rev:** Ears of corn, date below **Edge:** Plain **Designer:** Kuzma Kovacic

Date	Mintage	F	VF	XF	Unc	BU
2001.	2,000,000	—	—	0.20	0.50	—
2001. Proof	1,000	Value: 2.50				
2003.	1,500,000	—	—	0.20	0.50	—
2003. Proof	1,000	Value: 2.50				
2005.	—	—	—	0.20	0.50	—
2005. Proof	—	Value: 2.00				

KM# 12 LIPA
0.7000 g., Aluminum, 17 mm. **Obv:** Denomination above crowned arms **Rev:** Ears of corn, date below **Rev. Legend:** ZEA MAYS

Date	Mintage	F	VF	XF	Unc	BU
2002.	3,000,000	—	—	0.40	1.00	—
2002. Proof	1,000	Value: 2.50				
2004.	2,000,000	—	—	0.40	1.00	—
2004. Proof	2,000	Value: 1.50				
2006	—	—	—	0.40	1.00	—

KM# 4 2 LIPE
0.9000 g., Aluminum, 18.97 mm. **Obv:** Denomination above crowned arms on half braid **Rev:** Grapevine, date below **Edge:** Plain

Date	Mintage	F	VF	XF	Unc	BU
2001.	2,986,000	—	—	0.40	1.00	—
2001. Proof	1,000	Value: 3.00				
2003.	2,000,000	—	—	0.40	1.00	—
2003. Proof	1,000	Value: 3.00				
2005.	—	—	—	0.40	1.00	—
2005. Proof	—	Value: 3.00				

KM# 14 2 LIPE
0.9200 g., Aluminum, 19 mm. **Obv:** Denomination above crowned arms on half braid **Rev:** Grapevine, date below **Rev. Legend:** VITIS VINIFERA **Designer:** Kuzma Kovacic

Date	Mintage	F	VF	XF	Unc	BU
2002.	2,000,000	—	—	0.80	2.00	—
2002. Proof	1,000	Value: 3.00				
2004.	2,000,000	—	—	0.80	2.00	—
2004. Proof	2,000	Value: 2.50				
2006	—	—	—	0.80	2.00	—

KM# 5 5 LIPA
2.5000 g., Brass Plated Steel, 17.95 mm. **Obv:** Denomination above crowned arms **Rev:** Oak leaves, date below **Edge:** Plain **Designer:** Kuzma Kovacic

Date	Mintage	F	VF	XF	Unc	BU
2001.	6,598,000	—	—	0.40	1.00	—
2001. Proof	1,000	Value: 4.00				
2003.	13,000,000	—	—	0.40	1.00	—
2003. Proof	2,000	Value: 3.50				
2005.	—	—	—	0.40	1.00	—
2005. Proof	—	Value: 3.50				

KM# 15 5 LIPA
2.5000 g., Brass Plated Steel, 18 mm. **Obv:** Denomination above crowned arms **Rev:** Oak leaves, date below **Rev. Legend:** QUERCUS ROBUR **Designer:** Kuzma Kovacic

Date	Mintage	F	VF	XF	Unc	BU
2002.	3,500,000	—	—	0.80	2.00	—
2002. Proof	1,000	Value: 4.00				
2004.	2,000,000	—	—	0.80	2.00	—
2004. Proof	2,000	Value: 3.00				
2006	—	—	—	0.80	2.00	—

KM# 6 10 LIPA
3.3200 g., Brass Plated Steel, 20 mm. **Obv:** Denomination above crowned arms **Rev:** Tobacco plant, date below **Designer:** Kuzma Kovacic

Date	Mintage	F	VF	XF	Unc	BU
2001.	31,500,000	—	—	0.40	1.50	—
2001. Proof	1,000	Value: 5.00				
2003.	12,000,000	—	—	0.40	1.50	—
2003. Proof	1,000	Value: 5.00				
2005.	—	—	—	0.40	1.50	—
2005. Proof	—	Value: 5.00				

KM# 16 10 LIPA
Brass Plated Steel, 20 mm. **Obv:** Denomination above crowned arms on half braid **Rev:** Tobacco plant, date below **Rev. Legend:** NICOTIANA TABACUM **Designer:** Kuzma Kovacic

Date	Mintage	F	VF	XF	Unc	BU
2002.	2,000,000	—	—	0.80	2.50	—
2002. Proof	1,000	Value: 5.00				
2004.	2,000,000	—	—	0.80	2.50	—
2004. Proof	2,000	Value: 4.50				
2006	—	—	—	0.80	2.50	—

KM# 7 20 LIPA
2.9000 g., Nickel Plated Steel, 18.5 mm. **Obv:** Denomination above crowned arms on half braid **Rev:** Olive branch, date below **Designer:** Kuzma Kovacic

Date	Mintage	F	VF	XF	Unc	BU
2001.	23,000,000	—	—	0.45	1.50	—
2001. Proof	1,000	Value: 5.00				
2003.	12,500,000	—	—	0.45	1.50	—
2003. Proof	1,000	Value: 5.00				
2005.	—	—	—	0.45	1.50	—
2005. Proof	—	Value: 5.00				

KM# 17 20 LIPA
2.8800 g., Nickel Plated Steel, 18.5 mm. **Obv:** Denomination above crowned arms on half braid **Rev:** Olive branch, date below **Rev. Legend:** OLEA EUROPAEA

Date	Mintage	F	VF	XF	Unc	BU
2002.	2,000,000	—	—	0.80	2.50	—
2002. Proof	1,000	Value: 5.00				
2004.	2,000,000	—	—	0.80	2.50	—
2004. Proof	2,000	Value: 4.50				
2006	—	—	—	0.80	2.50	—

KM# 8 50 LIPA

3.6500 g., Nickel Plated Steel, 20.5 mm. **Obv:** Denomination above crowned arms on half braid **Rev:** Flowers, date below **Designer:** Kuzma Kovacic

Date	Mintage	F	VF	XF	Unc	BU
2001.	5,500,000	—	—	0.60	1.50	—
2001. Proof	1,000	Value: 5.50				
2003.	8,000,000	—	—	0.60	1.50	—
2003. Proof	1,000	Value: 5.50				
2005.	—	—	—	0.60	1.50	—
2005. Proof	—	Value: 5.00				

KM# 19 50 LIPA

3.6500 g., Nickel Plated Steel, 20.5 mm. **Obv:** Denomination above crowned arms on half braid **Rev:** Flowers, date below **Rev. Legend:** DEGENIA VELEBITICA **Designer:** Kuzma Kovacic

Date	Mintage	F	VF	XF	Unc	BU
2002.	2,000,000	—	—	0.80	2.50	—
2002. Proof	1,000	Value: 5.00				
2004.	2,000,000	—	—	0.80	2.50	—
2004. Proof	2,000	Value: 4.50				
2006	—	—	—	0.80	2.50	—

KM# 9.1 KUNA

5.0000 g., Copper-Nickel, 22.5 mm. **Obv:** Marten back of numeral, arms divide branches below **Rev:** Nightingale left, two dates **Designer:** Kusma Kovacic

Date	Mintage	F	VF	XF	Unc	BU
2001.	1,000,000	—	—	0.75	1.65	2.00
2001. Proof	1,000	Value: 4.50				
2003.	2,000,000	—	—	0.75	1.65	2.00
2003. Proof	1,000	Value: 4.50				
2005.	—	—	—	0.75	1.65	2.00
2005. Proof	—	Value: 4.50				

KM# 20.1 KUNA

5.0000 g., Copper-Nickel, 22.5 mm. **Obv:** Marten back of numeral, arms divide branches below **Rev:** Nightingale left, date below **Rev. Legend:** Error spelling "LUSCINNIA" MEGARHYNCHOS **Designer:** Kuzma Kovacic **Note:** Formerly KM-20

Date	Mintage	F	VF	XF	Unc	BU
2002.	—	—	—	—	—	2.00

KM# 20.2 KUNA

5.0000 g., Copper-Nickel, 22.5 mm. **Obv:** Marten back of numeral, arms divide branches below **Rev:** Nightingale left, date below **Rev. Legend:** Correct spelling "LUSCINIA" MEGARHYNCHOS **Edge:** Reeded **Designer:** Kuzma Kovacic

Date	Mintage	F	VF	XF	Unc	BU
2002.	1,000,000	—	—	1.00	3.00	2.00
2002. Proof	1,000	Value: 5.00				
2006	—	—	—	1.00	3.00	—

KM# 79 KUNA

5.0000 g., Copper Nickel, 22.5 mm. **Subject:** 10th Anniversary of National Currency **Obv:** Crowned arms flanked by sprays, denomination above on marten **Rev:** Nightingale left, date below

Date	Mintage	F	VF	XF	Unc	BU
ND(2004)	30,000	—	—	1.00	3.00	—
ND(2004) Proof	2,000	Value: 5.00				

KM# 10 2 KUNE

6.2000 g., Copper-Nickel, 24.5 mm. **Obv:** Marten back of numeral, arms divide branches below **Rev:** Bluefin tuna right, date below **Designer:** Kuzma Kovacic

Date	Mintage	F	VF	XF	Unc	BU
2001.	1,250,000	—	—	1.00	2.00	—
2001. Proof	1,000	Value: 6.50				
2003.	7,250,000	—	—	1.00	2.00	—
2003. Proof	1,000	Value: 6.50				
2005.	—	—	—	1.00	2.00	—
2005. Proof	—	Value: 6.50				

KM# 21 2 KUNE

6.2000 g., Copper-Nickel, 24.5 mm. **Obv:** Marten back of numeral, arms divide branches below **Rev:** Bluefin tuna right, date below **Rev. Legend:** THUNNUS - THYNNUS **Designer:** Kuzma Kovacic

Date	Mintage	F	VF	XF	Unc	BU
2002.	1,000,000	—	—	1.50	3.00	—
2002. Proof	1,000	Value: 6.00				
2004.	2,000,000	—	—	1.50	3.00	—
2004. Proof	2,000	Value: 5.50				
2006	—	—	—	1.50	3.00	—

KM# 11 5 KUNA

7.5000 g., Copper-Nickel, 26.7 mm. **Obv:** Marten back of numeral, arms divide branches below **Rev:** Brown bear left, date below

Date	Mintage	F	VF	XF	Unc	BU
2001.	17,300,000	—	—	1.50	5.00	8.00
2001. Proof	1,000	Value: 8.00				
2003.	1,000,000	—	—	1.50	5.00	8.00
2003. Proof	1,000	Value: 8.00				
2005.	—	—	—	1.50	5.00	8.00
2005. Proof	—	Value: 8.00				

KM# 23 5 KUNA

7.5000 g., Copper-Nickel, 26.7 mm. **Obv:** Marten back of numeral, arms divide branches below **Rev:** Brown bear left, date below **Rev. Legend:** URSUS ARCTOS

Date	Mintage	F	VF	XF	Unc	BU
2002.	2,000,000	—	—	2.00	5.00	7.50
2002. Proof	1,000	Value: 9.00				
2004.	2,000,000	—	—	2.00	5.00	7.50
2004. Proof	2,000	Value: 8.00				
2006	—	—	—	2.00	5.00	7.50

KM# 66 25 KUNA

Bi-Metallic Brass center in Copper-Nickel ring, 31 mm. **Subject:** 10th Anniversary of International Recognition **Obv:** Denomination in 3-D on outlined marten within circle, arms divide sprays below **Rev:** National map **Edge:** Plain **Shape:** 12-sided

Date	Mintage	F	VF	XF	Unc	BU
ND(2002)	200,000	—	—	—	8.50	—

KM# 78 25 KUNA

12.6500 g., Bi-Metallic, 31 mm. **Subject:** Croatian European Union Candidacy **Obv:** Denomination in 3-D on outlined marten within circle, arms divide sprays below **Rev:** Joined squares within circle of stars **Edge:** Plain **Shape:** 12-sided

Date	Mintage	F	VF	XF	Unc	BU
ND (2004)	30,000	—	—	—	10.00	—
ND (2004) Proof	—	Value: 25.00				

KM# 83 150 KUNA

24.0000 g., 0.9250 Silver 0.7137 oz. ASW, 37.00 mm. **Subject:** 2006 Winter Olympics - Italy **Obv:** National arms below denomination **Rev:** Slalom skiing

Date	Mintage	F	VF	XF	Unc	BU
ND(2006) Proof	15,000	Value: 40.00				

KM# 84 150 KUNA

24.0000 g., 0.9250 Silver 0.7137 oz. ASW, 37.00 mm. **Subject:** 2006 World Soccer Championship - Germany **Obv:** National arms below denomination **Rev:** Soccer player

Date	Mintage	F	VF	XF	Unc	BU
ND(2006) Proof	50,000	Value: 30.00				

KM# 85 150 KUNA

24.0000 g., 0.9250 Silver 0.7137 oz. ASW, 37.00 mm. **Subject:** 2006 World Soccer Championship - Germany **Obv:** National arms above denomination **Rev:** Vignette

Date	Mintage	F	VF	XF	Unc	BU
ND(2006) Proof	10,000	Value: 45.00				

KM# 86 150 KUNA

24.0000 g., 0.9250 Silver 0.7137 oz. ASW, 37.00 mm. **Subject:** 150th Anniversary Birth of Nikola Tesla **Obv:** National arms above induction motor and denomination **Rev:** Bust of Tesla

Date	Mintage	F	VF	XF	Unc	BU
2006 Proof	5,000	Value: 50.00				

KM# 87 150 KUNA

24.0000 g., 0.9250 Silver 0.7137 oz. ASW, 37.00 mm. **Subject:** 2008 Olympic Games - Peoples Republic of China **Obv:** National arms, value in laurel wreath **Rev:** T'ai-ho Tien gate in Beijing, athlete

Date	Mintage	F	VF	XF	Unc	BU
ND(2006) Proof	20,000	Value: 40.00				

MINT SETS

KM#	Date	Mintage	Identification	Issue Price	Mkt Val
MS2	2002 (9)	—	KM12,14-17, 19-21, 23	—	15.00

CUBA

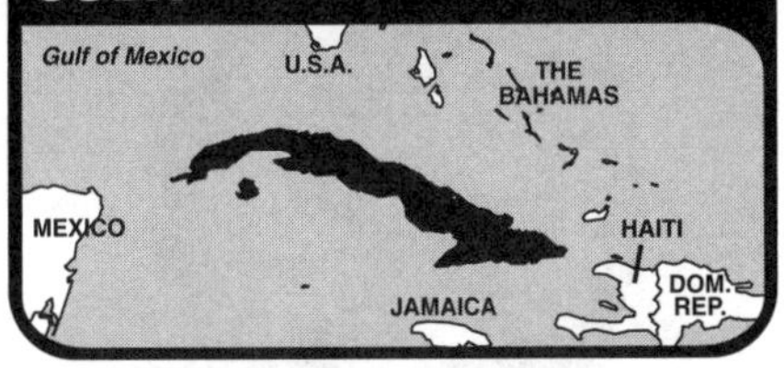

The Republic of Cuba, situated at the northern edge of the Caribbean Sea about 90 miles (145 km.) south of Florida, has an area of 42,804 sq. mi. (110,860 sq. km.) and a population of *11.2 million. Capital: Havana. The Cuban economy is based on the cultivation and refining of sugar, which provides 80 percent of export earnings.

MINT MARK

Key - Havana, 1977-

MONETARY SYSTEM

100 Centavos = 1 Peso

SECOND REPUBLIC

1962 - Present

DECIMAL COINAGE

KM# 33.3 CENTAVO

0.7500 g., Aluminum, 16.76 mm. **Obv:** Cuban arms within wreath, denomination below **Rev:** Roman denomination within circle of star, date below **Edge:** Plain

Date	Mintage	F	VF	XF	Unc	BU
2001	—	—	0.10	0.40	0.80	1.75
2002	—	—	0.10	0.40	0.80	1.75
2003	—	—	0.10	0.40	0.80	1.75
2004	—	—	0.10	0.40	0.80	1.75
2005	—	—	0.10	0.40	0.80	1.75

KM# 34 5 CENTAVOS

Aluminum, 21 mm. **Obv:** National arms within wreath, denomination below **Rev:** Roman denomination within circle of star, date below

Date	Mintage	F	VF	XF	Unc	BU
2001	—	—	0.10	0.25	0.75	1.50
2002	—	—	0.10	0.25	0.75	1.50
2003	—	—	0.10	0.25	0.75	1.50
2004	—	—	0.10	0.25	0.75	1.50
2006	—	—	0.10	0.25	0.75	1.50

KM# 35.1 20 CENTAVOS

2.0000 g., Aluminum, 24 mm. **Obv:** Cuban arms within wreath, denomination below **Rev:** Roman denomination within circle of star, date below

Date	Mintage	F	VF	XF	Unc	BU
2002	—	—	0.50	1.00	2.00	4.00
2003	—	—	0.50	1.00	2.00	4.00
2005	—	—	0.50	1.00	2.00	4.00
2006	—	—	0.50	1.00	2.00	4.00

KM# 347 PESO

5.5000 g., Brass Plated Steel, 24.4 mm. **Subject:** Jose Marti **Obv:** National arms within wreath, denomination below **Rev:** Bust facing, denomination at left **Rev. Legend:** PATRIA O MUERTE

Date	Mintage	F	VF	XF	Unc	BU
2001	—	—	—	1.00	2.00	4.00
2002	—	—	—	1.00	2.00	4.00

KM# 346a 3 PESOS

8.2000 g., Nickel Clad Steel, 26.3 mm. **Obv:** National arms within wreath, denomination below **Rev:** Head facing, date below

Date	Mintage	F	VF	XF	Unc	BU
2002	—	—	—	2.50	5.00	7.00

KM# 739 5 PESOS

1.2400 g., Gold, 14 mm. **Subject:** Wonders of the Ancient World **Obv:** Cuban arms **Rev:** Ancient lighthouse of Alexandria

Date	Mintage	F	VF	XF	Unc	BU
2005 Proof	5,000	Value: 40.00				

KM# 740 5 PESOS

1.2400 g., Gold, 14 mm. **Subject:** Wonders of the Ancient World **Obv:** Cuban arms **Rev:** Colossus of Rhodes

Date	Mintage	F	VF	XF	Unc	BU
2005 Proof	5,000	Value: 40.00				

KM# 741 5 PESOS

1.2400 g., Gold, 14 mm. **Subject:** Wonders of the Ancient World **Obv:** Cuban arms **Rev:** Hanging Gardens of Babylon

Date	Mintage	F	VF	XF	Unc	BU
2005 Proof	5,000	Value: 40.00				

KM# 742 5 PESOS

1.2400 g., Gold, 14 mm. **Subject:** Wonders of the Ancient World **Obv:** Cuban arms **Rev:** Egyptian Pyramids

Date	Mintage	F	VF	XF	Unc	BU
2005	5,000	Value: 40.00				

KM# 743 5 PESOS

1.2400 g., Gold, 14 mm. **Subject:** Wonders of the Ancient World **Obv:** Cuban arms **Rev:** Temple of Artemis

Date	Mintage	F	VF	XF	Unc	BU
2005 Proof	5,000	Value: 40.00				

KM# 744 5 PESOS

1.2400 g., Gold, 14 mm. **Subject:** Wonders of the Ancient World **Obv:** Cuban arms **Rev:** Statue of Jupiter

Date	Mintage	F	VF	XF	Unc	BU
2005	5,000	Value: 40.00				

KM# 745 5 PESOS

1.2400 g., Gold, 14 mm. **Subject:** Wonders of the Ancient World **Obv:** Cuban arms **Rev:** Mausoleum of Halicarnas

Date	Mintage	F	VF	XF	Unc	BU
2005 Proof	5,000	Value: 40.00				

KM# 746 5 PESOS

1.2400 g., Gold, 14 mm. **Obv:** Cuban arms **Rev:** Cortes, Montezuma and Aztec Pyramid

Date	Mintage	F	VF	XF	Unc	BU
2005 Proof	15,000	Value: 40.00				

KM# 763 10 PESOS

20.0000 g., 0.9990 Silver 0.6423 oz. ASW, 38 mm. **Subject:** Third Globalization Conference **Obv:** Cuban arms **Rev:** World map

Date	Mintage	F	VF	XF	Unc	BU
2001 Proof	100	Value: 200				

KM# 764 10 PESOS

20.0000 g., 0.9990 Silver 0.6423 oz. ASW, 38 mm. **Subject:** 40th Anniversary - Battle of Giron **Obv:** Cuban arms **Rev:** Soldiers on tank

Date	Mintage	F	VF	XF	Unc	BU
2001 Proof	3,000	Value: 45.00				

KM# 765 10 PESOS

31.1035 g., 0.9990 Silver 0.9990 oz. ASW, 38 mm. **Subject:** 106th Anniversary - Jose Marti's **Obv:** Cuban arms **Rev:** Monument

Date	Mintage	F	VF	XF	Unc	BU
2001 Proof	2,000	Value: 50.00				

KM# 762 10 PESOS

31.1035 g., 0.9990 Silver 0.9990 oz. ASW, 38 mm. **Obv:** Cuban arms **Rev:** Two Bee hummingbirds

Date	Mintage	F	VF	XF	Unc	BU
2001 Proof	20,000	Value: 40.00				

KM# 766 10 PESOS

15.0000 g., 0.9990 Silver 0.4818 oz. ASW, 35 mm. **Subject:** Cuban Fauna **Obv:** Cuban arms **Rev:** Red-splashed Sulphur butterfly

Date	Mintage	F	VF	XF	Unc	BU
2001 Proof	5,000	Value: 35.00				

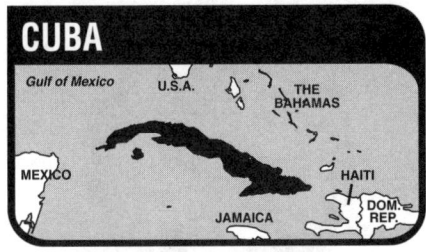

KM# 767 10 PESOS
15.0000 g., 0.9990 Silver 0.4818 oz. ASW, 35 mm. **Subject:** Cuban Fauna **Obv:** Cuban arms **Rev:** Cuban Parrot

Date	Mintage	F	VF	XF	Unc	BU
2001 Proof	5,000	Value: 35.00				

KM# 768 10 PESOS
15.0000 g., 0.9990 Silver 0.4818 oz. ASW, 35 mm. **Subject:** Cuban Fauna **Obv:** Cuban arms **Rev:** Cuban Red-bellied woodpecker

Date	Mintage	F	VF	XF	Unc	BU
2001 Proof	5,000	Value: 35.00				

KM# 769 10 PESOS
15.0000 g., 0.9990 Silver 0.4818 oz. ASW, 35 mm. **Obv:** Cuban arms **Rev:** Multicolor white orchid

Date	Mintage	F	VF	XF	Unc	BU
2001 Proof	5,000	Value: 35.00				

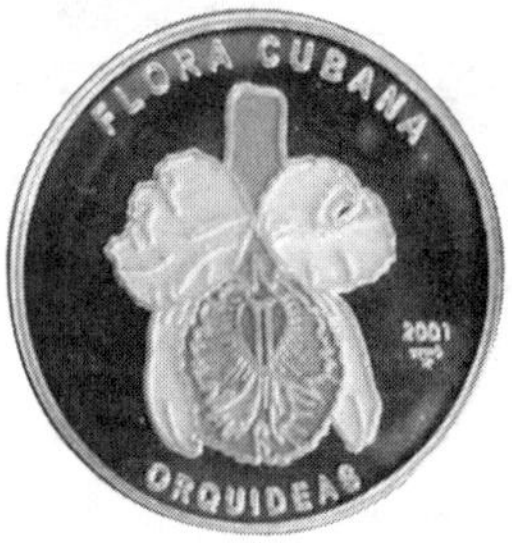

KM# 770 10 PESOS
15.0000 g., 0.9990 Silver 0.4818 oz. ASW, 35 mm. **Subject:** Cuban Flora **Obv:** Cuban arms **Rev:** Multicolor yellow orchid

Date	Mintage	F	VF	XF	Unc	BU
2001 Proof	5,000	Value: 35.00				

KM# 771 10 PESOS
15.0000 g., 0.9990 Silver 0.4818 oz. ASW, 35 mm. **Subject:** Cuban Flora **Obv:** Cuban arms **Rev:** Multicolor pink orchid

Date	Mintage	F	VF	XF	Unc	BU
2001 Proof	5,000	Value: 35.00				

KM# 772 10 PESOS
31.1035 g., 0.9990 Silver 0.9990 oz. ASW, 38 mm. **Obv:** Cuban arms **Rev:** Multicolor Santa Maria

Date	Mintage	F	VF	XF	Unc	BU
2001 Proof	4,000	Value: 50.00				

KM# 773 10 PESOS
15.0000 g., 0.9990 Silver 0.4818 oz. ASW, 35 mm. **Subject:** World Cup Soccer Champions **Obv:** Cuban arms **Rev:** Soccer player and stadium

Date	Mintage	F	VF	XF	Unc	BU
2001 Proof	7,500	Value: 35.00				

KM# 774 10 PESOS
20.0000 g., 0.9990 Silver 0.6423 oz. ASW, 38 mm. **Subject:** Cuban Monuments **Obv:** Cuban arms **Rev:** Trinidad street view

Date	Mintage	F	VF	XF	Unc	BU
2001 Proof	5,000	Value: 45.00				

KM# 775 10 PESOS
20.0000 g., 0.9990 Silver 0.6423 oz. ASW, 38 mm. **Subject:** Cuban Monuments **Obv:** Cuban arms **Rev:** Havana Cathedral

Date	Mintage	F	VF	XF	Unc	BU
2001 Proof	5,000	Value: 45.00				

KM# 776 10 PESOS
20.0000 g., 0.9990 Silver 0.6423 oz. ASW, 38 mm. **Subject:** Cuban Monuments **Obv:** Cuban arms **Rev:** Template building

Date	Mintage	F	VF	XF	Unc	BU
2001 Proof	5,000	Value: 45.00				

KM# 777 10 PESOS
31.1035 g., 0.9990 Silver 0.9990 oz. ASW, 38 mm. **Obv:** Cuban arms **Rev:** Bolivar standing at his birthplace

Date	Mintage	F	VF	XF	Unc	BU
2001 Proof	5,000	Value: 50.00				

KM# 778 10 PESOS
31.1035 g., 0.9990 Silver 0.9990 oz. ASW, 38 mm. **Obv:** Cuban arms **Rev:** Bolivar and map of South America

Date	Mintage	F	VF	XF	Unc	BU
2001 Proof	5,000	Value: 50.00				

KM# 779 10 PESOS
31.1035 g., 0.9990 Silver 0.9990 oz. ASW, 38 mm. **Subject:** 180th Anniversary of the Battle of Carabobo **Obv:** Cuban arms **Rev:** Bolivar leading troops

Date	Mintage	F	VF	XF	Unc	BU
2001 Proof	5,000	Value: 50.00				

KM# 734 10 PESOS
20.0000 g., 0.9990 Silver 0.6423 oz. ASW, 37.9 mm. **Subject:** Olympics **Obv:** Cuban arms **Rev:** Runner and ancient ruins **Edge:** Reeded

Date	Mintage	F	VF	XF	Unc	BU
2002 Proof	—	Value: 35.00				

KM# 780 10 PESOS
20.0000 g., 0.9990 Silver 0.6423 oz. ASW, 38 mm. **Subject:** World Cup Soccer Champions **Obv:** Cuban arms **Rev:** Soccer player and map above "CHILE 1962"

Date	Mintage	F	VF	XF	Unc	BU
2002 Proof	7,500	Value: 35.00				

KM# 781 10 PESOS
20.0000 g., 0.9990 Silver 0.6423 oz. ASW, 38 mm. **Subject:** World Cup Soccer Champions **Obv:** Cuban arms **Rev:** Soccer player and "CUAUHTEMOC" below "MEXICO 1970"

Date	Mintage	F	VF	XF	Unc	BU
2002 Proof	7,500	Value: 35.00				

KM# 782 10 PESOS
20.0000 g., 0.9990 Silver 0.6423 oz. ASW, 38 mm. **Obv:** Cuban arms **Rev:** Vasco De Gama and ship

Date	Mintage	F	VF	XF	Unc	BU
2002 Proof	5,000	Value: 45.00				

KM# 783 10 PESOS
20.0000 g., 0.9990 Silver 0.6423 oz. ASW, 38 mm. **Obv:** Cuban arms **Rev:** Americo Vespucio and ship

Date	Mintage	F	VF	XF	Unc	BU
2002 Proof	5,000	Value: 45.00				

KM# 784 10 PESOS
31.1035 g., 0.9990 Silver 0.9990 oz. ASW, 38 mm. **Subject:** Leaders of Communism **Obv:** Cuban arms **Rev:** Head of Mao Tse Tung left

Date	Mintage	F	VF	XF	Unc	BU
2002 Proof	2,000	Value: 50.00				

KM# 785 10 PESOS
31.1035 g., 0.9990 Silver 0.9990 oz. ASW, 38 mm. **Subject:** Leaders of Communism **Obv:** Cuban arms **Rev:** Head of Karl Marx 3/4 left

Date	Mintage	F	VF	XF	Unc	BU
2002 Proof	2,000	Value: 50.00				

KM# 786 10 PESOS
31.1035 g., 0.9990 Silver 0.9990 oz. ASW, 38 mm. **Subject:** Leaders of Communism **Obv:** Cuban arms **Rev:** Head of Vladimir Lenin right

Date	Mintage	F	VF	XF	Unc	BU
2002 Proof	2,000	Value: 50.00				

KM# 787 10 PESOS
31.1035 g., 0.9990 Silver 0.9990 oz. ASW, 38 mm. **Subject:** Leaders of Communism **Obv:** Cuban arms **Rev:** Head 3/4 right

Date	Mintage	F	VF	XF	Unc	BU
2002 Proof	2,000	Value: 50.00				

KM# 788 10 PESOS
27.0000 g., 0.9990 Silver 0.8672 oz. ASW, 40 mm. **Subject:** IBERO-AMERICA Series **Obv:** Circle of arms around Cuban arms **Rev:** Santisima Trinidad ship

Date	Mintage	F	VF	XF	Unc	BU
2002 Proof	14,000	Value: 75.00				

KM# 789 10 PESOS
31.1035 g., 0.9990 Silver 0.9990 oz. ASW, 38 mm. **Subject:** Jose Marti's 150th Birthday **Obv:** Cuban arms **Rev:** Numbered infield behind head right

Date	Mintage	F	VF	XF	Unc	BU
2003 Proof	150	Value: 50.00				

KM# 794 10 PESOS
20.0000 g., 0.9990 Silver 0.6423 oz. ASW, 38 mm. **Subject:** Endangered Wildlife **Obv:** Cuban arms **Rev:** Crocodile

Date	Mintage	F	VF	XF	Unc	BU
2003 Proof	5,000	Value: 45.00				

KM# 795 10 PESOS
20.0000 g., 0.9990 Silver 0.6423 oz. ASW, 38 mm. **Subject:** Endangered Wildlife **Obv:** Cuban arms **Rev:** Ocelot

Date	Mintage	F	VF	XF	Unc	BU
2003 Proof	5,000	Value: 50.00				

KM# 792 10 PESOS
20.0000 g., 0.9990 Silver 0.6423 oz. ASW, 38 mm. **Obv:** Cuban arms **Rev:** Che Guevara, 75th Anniversary of Birth

Date	Mintage	F	VF	XF	Unc	BU
2003 Proof	5,000	Value: 45.00				

KM# 791 10 PESOS
20.0000 g., 0.9990 Silver 0.6423 oz. ASW, 38 mm. **Obv:** Cuban arms **Rev:** Sailing ship, Sovereign of the Seas

Date	Mintage	F	VF	XF	Unc	BU
2003 Proof	5,000	Value: 45.00				

KM# 790 10 PESOS
20.0000 g., 0.9990 Silver 0.6423 oz. ASW, 38 mm. **Obv:** Cuban arms **Rev:** Ferdinand Magellan, ship, and astrolab

Date	Mintage	F	VF	XF	Unc	BU
2003 Proof	5,000	Value: 45.00				

KM# 793 10 PESOS
31.1000 g., 0.9990 Silver 0.9988 oz. ASW, 38 mm. **Subject:** World Cup Soccer - Germany 2006 **Obv:** Cuban arms **Rev:** 5 soccer players

Date	Mintage	F	VF	XF	Unc	BU
2003 Proof	50,000	Value: 50.00				

KM# 796 10 PESOS
20.0000 g., 0.9990 Silver 0.6423 oz. ASW, 38 mm. **Obv:** Cuban arms **Rev:** John Cabot's portrait in cameo above ship

Date	Mintage	F	VF	XF	Unc	BU
2004 Proof	5,000	Value: 45.00				

KM# 797 10 PESOS
15.0000 g., 0.9990 Silver 0.4818 oz. ASW, 35 mm. **Subject:** Hippocampus Kuda **Obv:** Cuban arms **Rev:** Spotted seahorse

Date	Mintage	F	VF	XF	Unc	BU
2004 Proof	5,000	Value: 45.00				

KM# 798 10 PESOS
20.0000 g., 0.9990 Silver 0.6423 oz. ASW, 38 mm. **Obv:** Cuban arms **Rev:** Murphy's Petrel bird on rock

Date	Mintage	F	VF	XF	Unc	BU
2004 Proof	5,000	Value: 45.00				

KM# 799 10 PESOS
20.0000 g., 0.9990 Silver 0.6423 oz. ASW, 38 mm. **Obv:** Cuban arms **Rev:** Iguana on branch

Date	Mintage	F	VF	XF	Unc	BU
2004 Proof	5,000	Value: 45.00				

KM# 800 10 PESOS
31.1000 g., 0.9990 Silver 0.9988 oz. ASW, 38 mm. **Obv:** Cuban arms **Rev:** Imperial eagle perched on branch

Date	Mintage	F	VF	XF	Unc	BU
2004 Proof	1,000	Value: 50.00				

KM# 801 10 PESOS
31.1000 g., 0.9990 Silver 0.9988 oz. ASW, 38 mm. **Obv:** Cuban arms **Rev:** Bearded vulture in flight

Date	Mintage	F	VF	XF	Unc	BU
2004 Proof	1,000	Value: 50.00				

KM# 802 10 PESOS
31.1000 g., 0.9990 Silver 0.9988 oz. ASW, 38 mm. **Obv:** Cuban arms **Rev:** Iberian Lynx

Date	Mintage	F	VF	XF	Unc	BU
2004 Proof	1,000	Value: 50.00				

KM# 803 10 PESOS
31.1000 g., 0.9990 Silver 0.9988 oz. ASW, 38 mm. **Obv:** Cuban arms **Rev:** 2 grey wolves

Date	Mintage	F	VF	XF	Unc	BU
2004 Proof	1,000	Value: 50.00				

KM# 804 10 PESOS
31.1000 g., 0.9990 Silver 0.9988 oz. ASW, 38 mm. **Obv:** Cuban arms **Rev:** Brown bear

Date	Mintage	F	VF	XF	Unc	BU
2004 Proof	1,000	Value: 50.00				

KM# 805 10 PESOS
31.1000 g., 0.9990 Silver 0.9988 oz. ASW, 38 mm. **Obv:** Cuban arms **Rev:** Peregrine Falcon perches on branch

Date	Mintage	F	VF	XF	Unc	BU
2004 Proof	1,000	Value: 50.00				

KM# 806 10 PESOS
20.0000 g., 0.9990 Silver 0.6423 oz. ASW, 38 mm. **Subject:** Monuments of Cuba **Obv:** Cuban arms **Rev:** University of Havana building

Date	Mintage	F	VF	XF	Unc	BU
2004 Proof	1,500	Value: 45.00				

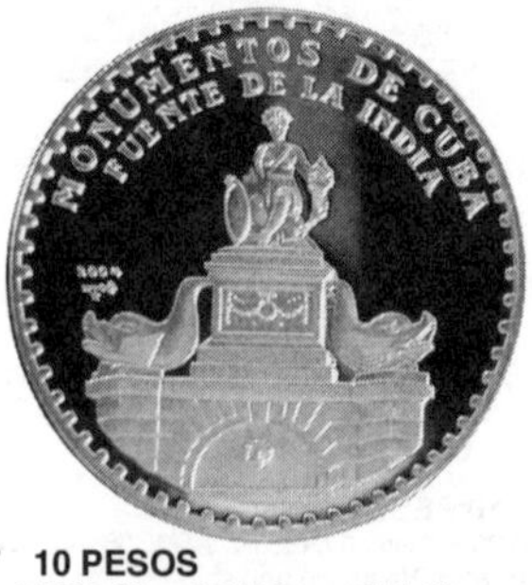

KM# 807 10 PESOS
20.0000 g., 0.9990 Silver 0.6423 oz. ASW, 38 mm. **Subject:** Monuments of Cuba **Obv:** Cuban arms **Rev:** Fountain of India

Date	Mintage	F	VF	XF	Unc	BU
2004 Proof	1,500	Value: 45.00				

KM# 808 10 PESOS
20.0000 g., 0.9990 Silver 0.6423 oz. ASW, 38 mm. **Subject:** Monuments of Cuba **Obv:** Cuban arms **Rev:** Plaza building

Date	Mintage	F	VF	XF	Unc	BU
2004 Proof	1,500	Value: 45.00				

KM# 809 10 PESOS
27.0000 g., 0.9250 Silver 0.8029 oz. ASW, 40 mm. **Obv:** Cuban arms within circle of arms **Rev:** Portions of the old Havana Wall

Date	Mintage	F	VF	XF	Unc	BU
2005 Proof	12,000	Value: 75.00				

KM# 810 10 PESOS
20.0000 g., 0.9990 Silver 0.6423 oz. ASW, 38 mm. **Subject:** Tobacco **Obv:** Cuban arms **Rev:** Indian showing tobacco to Columbus, ship in background

Date	Mintage	F	VF	XF	Unc	BU
2005 Proof	2,000	Value: 45.00				

KM# 811 10 PESOS
20.0000 g., 0.9250 Silver 0.5948 oz. ASW, 38 mm. **Subject:** Columbus' Ships **Obv:** Cuban arms **Rev:** The Santa Maria under sail

Date	Mintage	F	VF	XF	Unc	BU
2005 Proof	5,000	Value: 45.00				

KM# 812 10 PESOS
20.0000 g., 0.9250 Silver 0.5948 oz. ASW, 38 mm. **Subject:** Columbus' Ships **Obv:** Cuban arms **Rev:** The Nina under sail

Date	Mintage	F	VF	XF	Unc	BU
2005 Proof	5,000	Value: 45.00				

KM# 813 10 PESOS
20.0000 g., 0.9250 Silver 0.5948 oz. ASW, 38 mm. **Subject:** Columbus' Ships **Obv:** Cuban arms **Rev:** The Pinta under sail

Date	Mintage	F	VF	XF	Unc	BU
2005 Proof	5,000	Value: 45.00				

KM# 814 10 PESOS
20.0000 g., 0.9250 Silver 0.5948 oz. ASW, 38 mm. **Obv:** Cuban arms **Rev:** Cuban Solenodon on branch

Date	Mintage	F	VF	XF	Unc	BU
2005 Proof	5,000	Value: 45.00				

KM# 815 10 PESOS
15.0000 g., 0.9990 Silver 0.4818 oz. ASW, 35 mm. **Obv:** Cuban arms **Rev:** Multicolor Solenodon on branch

Date	Mintage	F	VF	XF	Unc	BU
2005 Proof	5,000	Value: 35.00				

KM# 816 10 PESOS
15.0000 g., 0.9250 Silver 0.4461 oz. ASW, 35 mm. **Subject:** Tropical Fish **Obv:** Cuban arms **Rev:** Picassofish (triggerfish)

Date	Mintage	F	VF	XF	Unc	BU
2005 Proof	2,000	Value: 35.00				

KM# 817 10 PESOS
15.0000 g., 0.9250 Silver 0.4461 oz. ASW, 35 mm. **Subject:** Tropical Fish **Obv:** Cuban arms **Rev:** Moorish Idol fish

Date	Mintage	F	VF	XF	Unc	BU
2005 Proof	2,000	Value: 35.00				

KM# 818 10 PESOS
15.0000 g., 0.9250 Silver 0.4461 oz. ASW, 35 mm. **Subject:** Tropical Fish **Obv:** Cuban arms **Rev:** Regal Angel fish

Date	Mintage	F	VF	XF	Unc	BU
2005 Proof	2,000	Value: 35.00				

KM# 819 10 PESOS
31.1000 g., 0.9250 Silver 0.9249 oz. ASW, 38 mm. **Subject:** 400 Years of Quijote **Obv:** Cuban arms **Rev:** Don Quijote and Sancho looking at two windmills

Date	Mintage	F	VF	XF	Unc	BU
2005 Proof	5,000	Value: 50.00				

KM# 820 10 PESOS
31.1000 g., 0.9990 Silver 0.9988 oz. ASW, 38 mm. **Subject:** Maximo Gomez Centennial of Death **Obv:** Cuban arms **Rev:** Bust 3/4 left, numbered behind neck

Date	Mintage	F	VF	XF	Unc	BU
2005 Proof	100	Value: 50.00				

KM# 821 10 PESOS
20.0000 g., 0.9250 Silver 0.5948 oz. ASW, 38 mm. **Subject:** XXIX Olympics **Obv:** Cuban arms **Rev:** Baseball player with bat, baseball background

Date	Mintage	F	VF	XF	Unc	BU
2006 Proof	15,000	Value: 45.00				

KM# 822 100 PESOS
31.1000 g., 0.9990 Gold 0.9988 oz. AGW, 38 mm. **Subject:** 100th Anniversary - Death of Marti **Obv:** Cuban arms **Rev:** Monument

Date	Mintage	F	VF	XF	Unc	BU
2001 Proof	100	Value: 900				

PESO CONVERTIBLE SERIES

KM# 733 CENTAVO
0.7500 g., Aluminum, 16.75 mm. **Obv:** Cuban arms **Rev:** Tower and denomination **Edge:** Plain

Date	Mintage	F	VF	XF	Unc	BU
2001	—	—	—	—	2.00	—
2002	—	—	—	—	2.00	—

Date	Mintage	F	VF	XF	Unc	BU
2003	—	—	—	—	2.00	—
2005	—	—	—	—	2.00	—

KM# 729 CENTAVO
1.7000 g., Copper Plated Steel, 15 mm. **Obv:** National arms within wreath, denomination below **Rev:** Tower and denomination **Edge:** Reeded

Date	Mintage	F	VF	XF	Unc	BU
2002	—	—	—	—	3.00	—

KM# 575.2 5 CENTAVOS
2.6500 g., Nickel-Plated Steel, 18 mm. **Obv:** National arms **Rev:** Casa Colonial **Note:** Coin alignment, recut designs.

Date	Mintage	F	VF	XF	Unc	BU
2002	—	—	—	—	1.00	—
2006	—	—	—	—	1.00	—

KM# 576.2 10 CENTAVOS
3.9400 g., Nickel Plated Steel **Obv:** National arms **Rev:** Castillo de la Fuerza **Note:** Coin alignment, recut designs.

Date	Mintage	F	VF	XF	Unc	BU
2002	—	—	—	—	2.00	—

KM# 577.2 25 CENTAVOS
5.7000 g., Nickel Plated Steel, 23 mm. **Obv:** National arms **Rev:** Trinidad **Note:** Coin alignment.

Date	Mintage	F	VF	XF	Unc	BU
2001	—	—	—	—	3.00	—
2002	—	—	—	—	3.00	—
2003	—	—	—	—	3.00	—
2006	—	—	—	—	3.00	—

KM# 578.2 50 CENTAVOS
7.5000 g., Nickel Plated Steel, 25 mm. **Obv:** Cuban arms **Rev:** Havana Cathedral **Note:** Coin alignment.

Date	Mintage	F	VF	XF	Unc	BU
2002	—	—	—	—	5.00	—

KM# 579.2 PESO
8.5000 g., Nickel Plated Steel, 27 mm. **Obv:** National arms **Rev:** Guama **Note:** Coin alignment.

Date	Mintage	F	VF	XF	Unc	BU
2001	—	—	—	—	5.00	—

CYPRUS

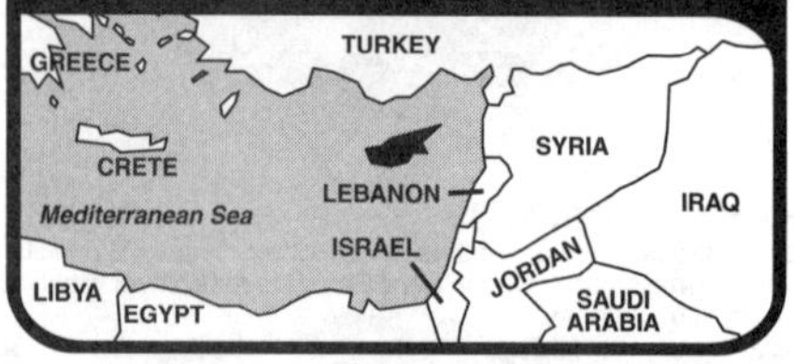

The island of Cyprus lies in the eastern Mediterranean Sea 44 miles (71 km.) south of Turkey and 60 miles (97 km.) off the Syrian coast. It is the third largest island in the Mediterranean Sea, having an area of 3,572 sq. mi. (9,251 sq. km.) and a population of 736,636. Capital: Nicosia. Agriculture, light manufacturing and tourism are the chief industries. Citrus fruit, potatoes, footwear and clothing are exported

Cyprus is a member of the Commonwealth of Nations. The president is Chief of State and Head of Government. Cyprus is also a member of the European Union.

MINT MARKS
no mint mark - Royal Mint, London, England
H - Birmingham, England

REPUBLIC

REFORM COINAGE

100 Cents = 1 Pound

KM# 53.3 CENT
2.0300 g., Nickel-Brass, 16.48 mm. **Obv:** Shielded arms within altered wreath, date below **Rev:** Stylized bird on a branch, denomination at left **Edge:** Plain

Date	Mintage	F	VF	XF	Unc	BU
2003	5,000,000	—	—	0.10	0.20	0.30
2004	—	—	—	0.10	0.20	0.30

KM# 54.3 2 CENTS
2.5800 g., Nickel-Brass, 18.95 mm. **Obv:** Shielded arms within altered wreath, date below **Rev:** Stylized goats, denomination upper right **Edge:** Plain

Date	Mintage	F	VF	XF	Unc	BU
2003	5,000,000	—	—	0.15	0.25	0.35
2004	—	—	—	0.15	0.25	0.35

KM# 55.3 5 CENTS
3.8000 g., Nickel-Brass, 20.37 mm. **Obv:** Altered wreath around arms **Rev:** Stylized bulls head above denomination **Edge:** Plain

Date	Mintage	F	VF	XF	Unc	BU
2001	15,000,000	—	—	0.20	0.50	0.75
2004	—	—	—	0.20	0.50	0.75

KM# 56.3 10 CENTS
5.5700 g., Nickel-Brass, 24.4 mm. **Obv:** Altered wreath around arms **Rev:** Decorative vase, denomination above

Date	Mintage	F	VF	XF	Unc	BU
2002	10,000,000	—	—	0.35	0.75	1.00
2004	—	—	—	0.35	0.75	1.00

KM# 62.2 20 CENTS
7.7500 g., Nickel-Brass, 27 mm. **Obv:** Altered wreath around arms **Rev:** Head left, denomination at right

Date	Mintage	F	VF	XF	Unc	BU
2001	15,000,000	—	—	—	1.00	1.50
2004	—	—	—	—	1.00	1.50

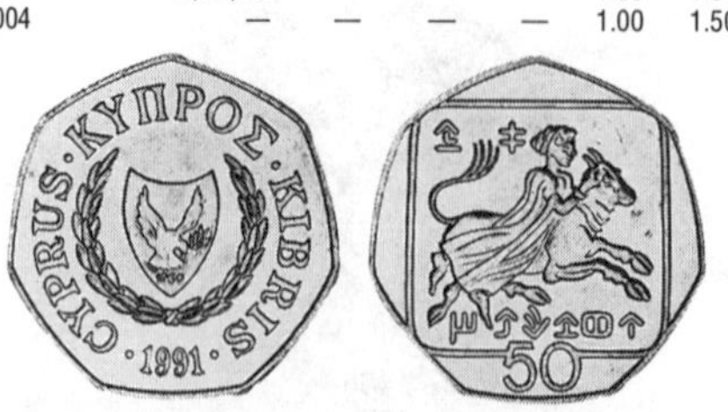

KM# 66 50 CENTS
7.0000 g., Copper-Nickel, 26 mm. **Subject:** Abduction of Europa **Obv:** Shielded arms within wreath, date below **Rev:** Figure riding bull within square, denomination below **Shape:** 7-sided

Date	Mintage	F	VF	XF	Unc	BU
2002	7,000,000	—	—	—	2.50	3.25
2004	—	—	—	—	2.50	3.25

KM# 75 POUND
28.2800 g., Copper-Nickel, 38.6 mm. **Subject:** Cyprus Joins the European Union **Obv:** National arms **Rev:** Map in center with Triton trumpeting through a seashell **Edge:** Plain

Date	Mintage	F	VF	XF	Unc	BU
2004	6,000	—	—	—	15.00	18.00

KM# 75a POUND
28.2800 g., 0.9250 Silver 0.8410 oz. ASW, 38.6 mm. **Subject:** Cyprus Joins the European Union **Obv:** National arms **Rev:** Map and Triton trumpeting through a sea shell **Edge:** Plain

Date	Mintage	F	VF	XF	Unc	BU
2004 Proof	3,000	Value: 45.00				

KM# 76 POUND
28.2700 g., Copper-Nickel, 38.5 mm. **Obv:** National arms **Rev:** Mediterranean Monk Seal **Edge:** Plain

Date	Mintage	F	VF	XF	Unc	BU
2005 Proof	40	Value: 35.00				

KM# 76a POUND
28.2800 g., 0.9250 Silver 0.8410 oz. ASW **Obv:** National arms **Rev:** Mediterranean Monk Seal **Edge:** Plain

Date	Mintage	F	VF	XF	Unc	BU
2005	4,000	Value: 50.00				

KM# 77a POUND
28.2800 g., 0.9250 Silver 0.8410 oz. ASW **Obv:** National arms **Rev:** Thistle-like flowers **Edge:** Plain

Date	Mintage	F	VF	XF	Unc	BU
2006	3,000	Value: 75.00				

KM# 77 POUND
28.2800 g., Copper-Nickel, 38.6 mm. **Obv:** National arms **Rev:** Thistle-like flowers **Edge:** Plain

Date	Mintage	F	VF	XF	Unc	BU
2006 Proof	6,000	Value: 20.00				

KM# 86 POUND
28.2800 g., Copper-Nickel, 38.61 mm. **Subject:** 50th Anniversary Treaty of Rome **Obv:** National arms **Rev:** Open Treaty Book **Edge:** Plain

Date	Mintage	F	VF	XF	Unc	BU
2007 Proof	10,000	—	—	—	—	—

EURO COINAGE

European Union Issues

KM# 78 EURO CENT
2.2700 g., Copper Plated Steel, 16.20 mm. **Obv:** Two Mouflons **Rev:** Large value at left, globe at lower right **Edge:** Plain

Date	Mintage	F	VF	XF	Unc	BU
2008	—	—	—	—	0.35	0.50

KM# 79 2 EURO CENT
3.0300 g., Copper Plated Steel, 18.70 mm. **Obv:** Two Mouflons **Rev:** Large value at left, globe at lower right **Edge:** Plain

Date	Mintage	F	VF	XF	Unc	BU
2008	—	—	—	—	0.50	0.75

KM# 80 5 EURO CENT
3.8600 g., Copper Plated Steel, 21.20 mm. **Obv:** Two Mouflons **Rev:** Large value at left, globe at lower right **Edge:** Plain

Date	Mintage	F	VF	XF	Unc	BU
2008	—	—	—	—	1.00	1.25

KM# 81 10 EURO CENT
4.0700 g., Brass, 19.70 mm. **Obv:** Early sailing boat **Rev:** Modified outline of Europe at left, large value at right

Date	Mintage	F	VF	XF	Unc	BU
2008	—	—	—	—	1.25	1.50

KM# 82 20 EURO CENT
5.7300 g., Brass, 22.10 mm. **Obv:** Early sailing boat **Rev:** Modified outline of Europe at left, large value at right **Edge:** Notched

Date	Mintage	F	VF	XF	Unc	BU
2008	—	—	—	—	1.50	2.00

KM# 83 50 EURO CENT
7.8100 g., Brass, 24.20 mm. **Obv:** Early sailing boat **Rev:** Modified outline of Europe at left, large value at right **Edge:** Reeded

Date	Mintage	F	VF	XF	Unc	BU
2008	—	—	—	—	2.00	2.50

KM# 84 EURO
7.5000 g., Bi-Metallic **Ring Composition:** Brass **Center Composition:** Copper Nickel, 23.20 mm. **Obv:** Ancient statue wearing a cross found in Soloi **Rev:** Large value at left, modified outline of Europe at right **Edge:** Segmented reeding

Date	Mintage	F	VF	XF	Unc	BU
2008	—	—	—	—	3.50	5.00

KM# 85 2 EURO
8.5200 g., Bi-Metallic, 25.70 mm. **Obv:** Ancient statue wearing a cross found in Soloi **Rev:** Large value at left, modified outline of Europe at right

Date	Mintage	F	VF	XF	Unc	BU
2008	—	—	—	—	5.00	7.00

CZECH REPUBLIC

The Czech Republic was formerly united with Slovakia as Czechoslovakia. It is bordered in the west by Germany, to the north by Poland, to the east by Slovakia and to the south by Austria. It consists of 3 major regions: Bohemia, Moravia and Silesia and has an area of 30,450 sq. mi. (78,864 sq. km.) and a population of 10.4 million. Capital: Prague (Praha). Agriculture and livestock are chief occupations while coal deposits are the main mineral resources.

NOTE: For earlier issues see Czechoslovakia, Bohemia and Moravia or Slovakia listings.

MINT MARKS

(c) - castle = Hamburg
(cr) - cross = British Royal Mint
(l) - leaf = Royal Canadian
(m) - crowned *b* or *CM* = Jablonec nad Nisou
(mk) - *MK* in circle = Kremnica
(o) - broken circle = Vienna (Wien)

MONETARY SYSTEM

1 Czechoslovak Koruna (Kcs) = 1 Czech Koruna (Kc)
1 Koruna = 100 Haleru

REPUBLIC

STANDARD COINAGE

KM# 6 10 HALERU
0.6000 g., Aluminum, 15.5 mm. **Obv:** Crowned Czech lion left, date below **Rev:** Denomination and stylized river **Edge:** Plain **Designer:** Jiri Pradler **Note:** Two varieties of mint marks exist for 1994.

Date	Mintage	F	VF	XF	Unc	BU
2001(m)	40,525,000	—	—	—	0.20	—
2001(m) Proof	2,500	Value: 2.00				
2002(m)	81,496,000	—	—	—	0.20	—
2002(m) Proof	3,490	Value: 2.00				
2003(m)	3,022,350	—	—	—	0.20	—
2003(l) Proof	3,000	Value: 2.00				
2004(m)	—	—	—	—	0.20	—
2004(m) Proof	3,000	Value: 2.00				

KM# 2.3 20 HALERU
0.7400 g., Aluminum **Obv:** Crowned Czech lion left, date above **Rev:** Open 2 in denomination, "h" above angle line **Note:** Medallic coin alignment.

Date	Mintage	F	VF	XF	Unc	BU
2001(m)	40,525,000	—	—	—	0.30	—
2001(m) Proof	2,500	Value: 3.00				
2002(m)	81,496,000	—	—	—	0.30	—
2002(m) Proof	3,490	Value: 3.00				
2003(m)	3,022,350	—	—	—	0.30	—
2003(m) Proof	3,000	Value: 3.00				
2004(m)	—	—	—	—	0.30	—
2004(m) Proof	3,000	Value: 3.00				

KM# 3.2 50 HALERU
0.9000 g., Aluminum, 19 mm. **Subject:** Outlined lettering and larger mint mark **Obv:** Crowned Czech lion right, date below **Rev:** Large denomination

Date	Mintage	F	VF	XF	Unc	BU
2001(m)	21,425,000	—	—	—	0.50	—
2001(m) Proof	2,500	Value: 3.00				
2002(m)	26,246,298	—	—	—	0.50	—
2002(m) Proof	3,490	Value: 3.00				
2003(m)	41,548,000	—	—	—	0.50	—
2003(m) Proof	3,000	Value: 3.00				
2004(m)	931,145	—	—	—	0.50	—
2004(m) Proof	4,000	Value: 3.00				
2005(m)	36,800	—	—	—	0.50	—
2005(m) Proof	3,000	Value: 3.00				
2006(m)	40,000	—	—	—	0.50	—
2006(m) Proof	3,500	Value: 3.00				

KM# 3.1 50 HALERU
0.9000 g., Aluminum, 19 mm. **Obv:** Crowned Czech lion left, date below **Rev:** Large denomination **Edge:** Part plain, part milled repeated **Designer:** Vladimir Oppl **Note:** Two styles of "9" exist for 1994; prev. KM#3.

Date	Mintage	F	VF	XF	Unc	BU
2001(m)	21,425,000	—	—	—	0.50	—
2001(m) Proof	2,500	Value: 3.00				

KM# 7 KORUNA
Nickel Clad Steel, 20 mm. **Obv:** Crowned Czech lion left, date below **Rev:** Denomination above crown **Edge:** Milled **Designer:** Jarmila Truhlikova-Spevakova **Note:** Two varieties of mint marks exist for 1996. 2000-03 have two varieties in the artisit monogram.

Date	Mintage	F	VF	XF	Unc	BU
2001(m)	15,938,353	—	—	—	0.60	—
2001(m) Proof	2,500	Value: 4.00				
2002(m)	26,244,666	—	—	—	0.60	—
2002(m) Proof	3,490	Value: 4.00				
2003(m)	36,877,440	—	—	—	0.60	—
2003(m) Proof	3,000	Value: 4.00				
2004(m)	30,500	—	—	—	0.60	—
2004(m) Proof	4,000	Value: 4.00				
2005(m)	—	—	—	—	0.60	—
2005(m) Proof	3,000	Value: 6.00				
2006(m)	35,864	—	—	—	0.60	—
2006(m) Proof	2,500	Value: 6.00				

KM# 9 2 KORUN
3.7000 g., Nickel Clad Steel, 21.5 mm. **Obv:** Crowned Czech lion left, date below **Rev:** Large denomination, pendant design at left **Edge:** Plain **Shape:** 11-sided **Designer:** Jarmila Truhlikova-Spevakova **Note:** Two varieties of designer monograms exist for 2001-04.

Date	Mintage	F	VF	XF	Unc	BU
2001(m)	26,117,000	—	—	—	0.65	—
2001(m) Proof	2,500	Value: 5.00				
2002(m)	20,941,084	—	—	—	0.65	—
2002(m) Proof	3,490	Value: 5.00				
2003(m)	20,955,000	—	—	—	0.65	—
2003(m) Proof	3,000	Value: 5.00				
2004(m)	15,658,556	—	—	—	0.65	—
2004(m) Proof	4,000	Value: 5.00				
2005(m)	—	—	—	—	0.65	—
2005(m) Proof	3,000	Value: 5.00				
2006(m)	—	—	—	—	0.65	—
2006(m) Proof	2,500	Value: 5.00				

KM# 8 5 KORUN
4.8000 g., Nickel Plated Steel, 23 mm. **Obv:** Crowned Czech lion left, date below **Rev:** Large denomination, Charles bridge and linden leaf **Edge:** Plain **Designer:** Jiri Harcuba

Date	Mintage	F	VF	XF	Unc	BU
2001(m)	25,000	—	—	—	1.00	—
2001(m) Proof	2,500	Value: 6.00				
2002(m)	21,344,995	—	—	—	1.00	—
2002(m) Proof	3,490	Value: 6.00				
2003(m)	22,000	—	—	—	1.00	—
2003(m) Proof	3,000	Value: 6.00				
2004(m)	34,940	—	—	—	1.00	—
2004(m) Proof	4,000	Value: 6.00				
2005(m)	—	—	—	—	1.00	—
2005(m) Proof	3,000	Value: 6.00				
2006(m)	25,000	—	—	—	1.00	—
2006(m) Proof	2,500	Value: 6.00				

KM# 4 10 KORUN
7.6200 g., Copper Plated Steel, 24.5 mm. **Obv:** Crowned Czech lion left, date below **Rev:** Brno Cathedral, denomination below **Edge:** Milled **Designer:** Ladislav Kozak **Note:** Position of designer's initials on reverse change during the 1995 strike.

Date	Mintage	F	VF	XF	Unc	BU
2001(m)	25,000	—	—	—	1.50	—
2001(m) Proof	2,500	Value: 7.00				
2002(m)	20,156	—	—	—	1.50	—
2002(m) Proof	3,490	Value: 7.00				
2003(m)	18,747,000	—	—	—	1.50	—
2003(m) Proof	3,000	Value: 7.00				
2004(m)	2,255,740	—	—	—	1.50	—
2004(m) Proof	4,000	Value: 7.00				
2005(m)	—	—	—	—	1.50	—
2005(m) Proof	3,000	Value: 7.00				
2006(m)	—	—	—	—	1.50	—
2006(m) Proof	2,500	Value: 7.00				

KM# 5 20 KORUN
8.4300 g., Brass Plated Steel, 26 mm. **Obv:** Crowned Czech lion left, date below **Rev:** St. Wenceslas (Duke Vaclav) on horse **Edge:** Plain **Shape:** 13-sided **Designer:** Vladimir Oppl **Note:** Two varieties of mint marks and style of 9's exist for 1997.

Date	Mintage	F	VF	XF	Unc	BU
2001(m)	25,000	—	—	—	2.50	—
2001(m) Proof	2,500	Value: 10.00				
2002(m)	20,996,500	—	—	—	2.50	—
2002(m) Proof	3,490	Value: 10.00				
2003(m)	22,000	—	—	—	2.50	—
2003(m) Proof	3,000	Value: 10.00				
2004(m)	8,249,507	—	—	—	2.50	—
2004(m) Proof	4,000	Value: 10.00				
2005(m)	—	—	—	—	2.50	—
2005(m) Proof	3,000	Value: 10.00				
2006(m)	—	—	—	—	2.50	—
2006(m) Proof	2,500	Value: 10.00				

KM# 1 50 KORUN

9.7000 g., Bi-Metallic Brass plated Steel center in Copper plated Steel ring, 27.5 mm. **Obv:** Crowned Czech lion left **Rev:** Prague city view **Edge:** Plain **Designer:** Ladislav Kozak

Date	Mintage	F	VF	XF	Unc	BU
2001(m)	16,000	—	—	—	9.00	—
2001(m) Proof	2,500	Value: 20.00				
2002(m)	16,771	—	—	—	9.00	—
2002(m) Proof	3,490	Value: 20.00				
2003(m)	22,000	—	—	—	9.00	—
2003(m) Proof	3,000	Value: 20.00				
2004(m)	34,555	—	—	—	9.00	—
2004(m) Proof	4,000	Value: 20.00				
2005(m)	—	—	—	—	9.00	—
2005(m) Proof	3,000	Value: 20.00				
2006(m)	—	—	—	—	9.00	—
2006(m) Proof	2,500	Value: 20.00				

KM# 58 200 KORUN

13.0000 g., 0.9000 Silver 0.3761 oz. ASW, 31 mm. **Subject:** Frantisek Skroup **Obv:** Quartered, elongated arms above date **Rev:** Portrait and name **Designer:** Jiri Harcuba **Note:** 1,480 pieces uncirculated and 13 proof remelted.

Date	Mintage	F	VF	XF	Unc	BU
ND(2001)	12,909	—	—	—	15.00	17.00
Note: Reeded edge						
ND(2001) Proof	3,200	Value: 30.00				
Note: CESKA NARODNI BANKA * 0.900 *						

KM# 51 200 KORUN

13.0000 g., 0.9000 Silver 0.3761 oz. ASW, 31 mm. **Subject:** Jaroslav Seifert **Obv:** Quartered arms above denomination **Rev:** Head right, dates at left **Designer:** Ladislav Kozak **Note:** 1,680 pieces uncirculated and 2 proof remelted.

Date	Mintage	F	VF	XF	Unc	BU
ND(2001)	12,870	—	—	—	15.00	17.00
Note: Reeded edge						
ND(2001) Proof	3,199	Value: 30.00				
Note: CESKA NARODNI BANKA * 0.900 *						

KM# 53 200 KORUN

13.0000 g., 0.9000 Silver 0.3761 oz. ASW, 31 mm. **Subject:** 250th Anniversary - Death of Kilian Ignac Dientzenhofer **Obv:** Quartered arms, denomination at right **Rev:** Doorway and caliper **Designer:** Petr Pyciak **Note:** 1,840 pieces uncirculated and 104 proof remelted.

Date	Mintage	F	VF	XF	Unc	BU
ND(2001)	12,744	—	—	—	15.00	17.00
Note: Reeded edge						
ND(2001) Proof	3,373	Value: 30.00				
Note: CESKA NARODNI BANKA * 0.900 *						

KM# 54 200 KORUN

13.0000 g., 0.9000 Silver 0.3761 oz. ASW, 31 mm. **Subject:** Euro Currency System **Obv:** National arms **Rev:** Prague gros coin design **Designer:** Josef Safarik **Note:** 134 pieces uncirculated and 1 proof remelted.

Date	Mintage	F	VF	XF	Unc	BU
ND(2001)	13,867	—	—	—	15.00	17.00
Note: Reeded edge						
ND(2001) Proof	4,000	Value: 28.00				
Note: CESKA NARODNI BANKA * 0.900 *						

KM# 52 200 KORUN

13.0000 g., 0.9000 Silver 0.3761 oz. ASW, 31 mm. **Subject:** Soccer **Obv:** Quartered arms on square, denomination below **Rev:** Rampant lion on soccer ball **Designer:** Milena Blaskova **Note:** 2,350 pieces uncirculated and 1 proof remelted.

Date	Mintage	F	VF	XF	Unc	BU
ND(2001)	13,324	—	—	—	15.00	17.00
Note: Reeded edge						
ND(2001) Proof	3,900	Value: 28.00				
Note: CESKA NARODNI BANKA * 0.900 *						

KM# 59 200 KORUN

13.0000 g., 0.9000 Silver 0.3761 oz. ASW, 31 mm. **Subject:** Mikolas Ales **Obv:** Four coats of arms above denomination **Rev:** Horse and rider **Edge:** Reeded **Designer:** Petr Pycian **Note:** 573 pieces uncirculated and 139 proof remelted.

Date	Mintage	F	VF	XF	Unc	BU
ND(2002)	12,473	—	—	—	15.00	17.00
ND(2002)(m) Proof	4,400	Value: 28.00				

KM# 57 200 KORUN

13.0000 g., 0.9000 Silver 0.3761 oz. ASW, 30.9 mm. **Subject:** Jiri of Podebrady **Obv:** Overlapped arms **Rev:** Head right **Designer:** Michal Vitanovswky **Note:** 1,200 pieces uncirculated and 5 proof remelted.

Date	Mintage	F	VF	XF	Unc	BU
ND(2002)	12,750	—	—	—	15.00	17.00
Note: Reeded edge						
ND(2002) Proof	3,600	Value: 28.00				
Note: CESKA NARDONI BANKA * 0.900 *						

KM# 56 200 KORUN

13.0000 g., 0.9000 Silver 0.3761 oz. ASW, 30.9 mm. **Subject:** Emil Holub **Obv:** National arms, eagles and lions, denomination below **Rev:** Traveler and African dancers **Designer:** Ladislav Kozak **Note:** 1,350 pieces uncirculated and 7 proof remelted.

Date	Mintage	F	VF	XF	Unc	BU
ND(2002)	12,635	—	—	—	15.00	17.00
Note: Reeded edge						
ND(2002) Proof	3,600	Value: 28.00				
Note: CESKA NARODNI BANKA * 0.900 *						

KM# 55 200 KORUN

13.0000 g., 0.9000 Silver 0.3761 oz. ASW, 31 mm. **Subject:** St. Zdislava **Obv:** Old and new arms form diamond above denomination **Rev:** Saint feeding sick person **Designer:** Michal Vitanovsky **Note:** 865 pieces uncirculated remelted.

Date	Mintage	F	VF	XF	Unc	BU
ND(2002)	12,706	—	—	—	15.00	17.00
Note: Reeded edge						
ND(2002) Proof	3,600	Value: 28.00				
Note: CESKA NARODNI BANKA * 0.900 *						

KM# 60 200 KORUN

13.1400 g., 0.9000 Silver 0.3802 oz. ASW, 31 mm. **Subject:** Jaroslav Vrchlicky **Obv:** Denomination and quill **Obv. Designer:** Jiri Harcuba **Rev:** Bust with hat facing **Rev. Designer:** Pavel Jekl **Note:** 889 pieces unciruclated and 5 proof remelted.

Date	Mintage	F	VF	XF	Unc	BU
ND(2003)	11,975	—	—	—	15.00	17.00
Note: Reeded						
ND(2003) Proof	3,700	Value: 28.00				
Note: Plain with CESKA NARODNI BANKA *Ag 0.900* 13g*						

KM# 62 200 KORUN

13.0000 g., 0.9000 Silver 0.3761 oz. ASW, 30.9 mm. **Subject:** Josef Thomayer **Obv:** National arms **Obv. Designer:** Ladislav Kozak **Rev:** Portrait **Rev. Designer:** Josef Oplistil **Edge:** Reeded **Note:** 783 uncirculated and 12 proof were remelted.

Date	Mintage	F	VF	XF	Unc	BU
ND(2003)	11,975	—	—	—	15.00	17.00
ND(2003) Proof	4,000	Value: 28.00				

KM# 63 200 KORUN

13.0000 g., 0.9000 Silver 0.3761 oz. ASW, 31 mm. **Subject:** Tabor-Bechyne Electric Railway **Obv:** Head left **Rev:** Railroad station scene **Designer:** Ladislav Kozak **Note:** 808 Uncirculated were remelted.

Date	Mintage	F	VF	XF	Unc	BU
ND(2003)	11,975	—	—	—	16.00	18.00
Note: Reeded edge						
ND(2003) Proof	4,100	Value: 28.00				
Note: Plain edge with CESKA NARODNI BANKA * Ag 0.900 * 13g						

KM# 64 200 KORUN
13.0000 g., 0.9000 Silver 0.3761 oz. ASW, 31 mm. **Subject:** Bohemian Skiers' Union **Obv:** Head 3/4 left **Rev:** Skier **Designer:** Ladislav Kozak **Note:** 680 Uncirculated and 13 proof were remelted.

Date	Mintage	F	VF	XF	Unc	BU
ND(2003)	11,975	—	—	—	16.00	18.00
Note: Reeded edge						
ND(2003) Proof	4,300	Value: 28.00				
Note: Plain edge with CESKA NARODNI BANKA * Ag 0.900 * 13g						

KM# 70 200 KORUN
13.1000 g., 0.9000 Silver 0.3790 oz. ASW, 30.8 mm. **Subject:** 300th Anniversary - Death of pond builder Jakub Krcin **Obv:** Coat of arms above value with reflected design below **Rev:** Two fishermen in boat with reflection on water below **Designer:** Vladimir Oppl **Note:** 656 uncirculated remelted.

Date	Mintage	F	VF	XF	Unc	BU
ND(2004)(m)	11,975	—	—	—	16.00	18.00
Note: Reeded						
ND(2004) Proof	4,000	Value: 28.00				
Note: Plain with CESKA NARODNI BANKA *Ag 0.900* 13g*						

KM# 77 200 KORUN
Silver, 31 mm. **Rev:** Lightening Conductor

Date	Mintage	F	VF	XF	Unc	BU
2004	—	—	—	—	16.00	18.00

KM# 71 200 KORUN
13.1000 g., 0.9000 Silver 0.3790 oz. ASW **Subject:** Entry into the European Union

Date	Mintage	F	VF	XF	Unc	BU
2004	10,000	—	—	—	16.00	18.00
Note: Reeded						
2004 Proof	8,800	Value: 28.00				

KM# 72 200 KORUN
13.1000 g., 0.9000 Silver 0.3790 oz. ASW **Subject:** Prokop Divis

Date	Mintage	F	VF	XF	Unc	BU
2004	10,975	—	—	—	16.00	18.00
Note: Reeded						
2004 Proof	3,900	Value: 28.00				

KM# 73 200 KORUN
13.1000 g., 0.9000 Silver 0.3790 oz. ASW **Subject:** Leos Janacek

Date	Mintage	F	VF	XF	Unc	BU
2004	10,975	—	—	—	16.00	18.00
Note: Reeded						
2004 Proof	4,100	Value: 28.00				

KM# 74 200 KORUN
13.1000 g., 0.9000 Silver 0.3790 oz. ASW **Subject:** Kralice Bible

Date	Mintage	F	VF	XF	Unc	BU
2004	10,975	—	—	—	16.00	18.00
Note: Reeded						
2004 Proof	5,000	Value: 28.00				

KM# 78 200 KORUN
Silver, 31 mm. **Subject:** 100th Anniversary of Jan Werich and Jiri Voskovec

Date	Mintage	F	VF	XF	Unc	BU
2005	—	—	—	—	16.00	18.00

KM# 79 200 KORUN
Silver, 31 mm. **Subject:** 100th Anniversary of Production of 1st Car in Malada Boleslov

Date	Mintage	F	VF	XF	Unc	BU
2005	—	—	—	—	16.00	18.00

KM# 80 200 KORUN
Silver, 31 mm. **Subject:** 450th Anniversary - Birth of Mikulas Dacicky

Date	Mintage	F	VF	XF	Unc	BU
2005	—	—	—	—	16.00	18.00

KM# 81 200 KORUN
Silver, 31 mm. **Subject:** 250th Anniversary - Birth of F.J. Gerstner

Date	Mintage	F	VF	XF	Unc	BU
2006	—	—	—	—	16.00	18.00

KM# 82 200 KORUN
13.0000 g., 0.9000 Silver 0.3761 oz. ASW, 31 mm. **Subject:** 150th Anniversary - School of Glass Making in Kamenicky Senov **Obv:** Image of National Arms within glass cube **Rev:** Artistic image within glass cube **Designer:** Zuzana Hubena

Date	Mintage	F	VF	XF	Unc	BU
2006	12,000	—	—	—	16.00	18.00
2006 Proof	7,500	Value: 28.00				

KM# 83 200 KORUN
Silver, 31 mm. **Subject:** 500th Anniversary - Death of Matej Rejsek

Date	Mintage	F	VF	XF	Unc	BU
2006	—	—	—	—	16.00	18.00

KM# 84 200 KORUN
13.0000 g., 0.9000 Silver 0.3761 oz. ASW, 31 mm. **Subject:** 700th Anniversary - Death of Wenceslas III **Obv:** Sword between two shields positioned top-to-top **Rev:** King Wenceslas III between two shields **Designer:** Vojtech Dostal

Date	Mintage	F	VF	XF	Unc	BU
2006	11,500	—	—	—	16.00	18.00
2006 Proof	7,500	Value: 28.00				

KM# 85 200 KORUN
13.0000 g., 0.9000 Silver 0.3761 oz. ASW, 31 mm. **Subject:** 100th Anniversary - Birth of Jaroslav Jezek **Obv:** Musical score **Rev:** Caricature looking at score **Designer:** Josef Oplistil

Date	Mintage	F	VF	XF	Unc	BU
2006	11,500	—	—	—	16.00	18.00
2006 Proof	20,000	Value: 28.00				

GOLD BULLION COINAGE

KM# 65 2000 KORUN
6.2200 g., 0.9999 Gold 0.1999 oz. AGW, 20 mm. **Subject:** Romanesque - Znojmo Rotunda **Obv:** Three heraldic animals **Rev:** Farmer and round building **Designer:** Jiri Harcuba

Date	Mintage	F	VF	XF	Unc	BU
ND(2001)	2,500	—	—	—	—	180
Note: Reeded edge						
ND(2001) Proof	2,997	Value: 200				
Note: Plain edge						

KM# 66 2000 KORUN
6.2200 g., 0.9999 Gold 0.1999 oz. AGW, 20 mm. **Subject:** Gothic - Cloister of the Vyssi Brod Monastery **Obv:** Three heraldic animals above Gothic design **Rev:** Man holding church building model **Designer:** Michal Vitanovsky

Date	Mintage	F	VF	XF	Unc	BU
2001	2,197	—	—	—	—	180
Note: Reeded edge						
2001 Proof	2,997	Value: 200				
Note: Plain edge						

KM# 67 2000 KORUN
6.2200 g., 0.9999 Gold 0.1999 oz. AGW, 20 mm. **Subject:** Gothic - Fountain in Kutna Hora **Obv:** Three heraldic animals **Rev:** Fountain enclosure **Designer:** Josef Oplistil

Date	Mintage	F	VF	XF	Unc	BU
2002	2,197	—	—	—	—	180
Note: Reeded edge						
2002	2,997	Value: 200				
Note: Plain edge						

KM# 61 2000 KORUN
6.2200 g., 0.9999 Gold 0.1999 oz. AGW, 20 mm. **Subject:** Renaissance - Litomysl Castle **Obv:** Three heraldic animals above mermaid **Rev:** Aerial castle view and mythical creature **Designer:** Jiri Venecek

Date	Mintage	F	VF	XF	Unc	BU
2002	2,097	—	—	—	—	180
Note: Reeded edge						
2002 Proof	3,097	Value: 200				
Note: Plain edge						

KM# 68 2000 KORUN
6.2200 g., 0.9999 Gold 0.1999 oz. AGW, 20 mm. **Subject:** Renaissance - Slavonice House Gables **Obv:** Three heraldic animals above city view **Rev:** City arms **Designer:** Jiri Harcuba

Date	Mintage	F	VF	XF	Unc	BU
2003	1,997	—	—	—	—	180
Note: Reeded edge						
2003 Proof	1,497	Value: 200				
Note: Plain edge						

KM# 69 2000 KORUN
6.2200 g., 0.9999 Gold 0.1999 oz. AGW, 20 mm. **Subject:** Baroque - Buchlovice Palace **Obv:** Three heraldic animals above palace **Rev:** Palace view **Designer:** Jakub Venecek

Date	Mintage	F	VF	XF	Unc	BU
2003	1,997	—	—	—	—	180
Note: Reeded edge						
2003 Proof	3,197	Value: 200				
Note: Plain edge						

KM# 75 2000 KORUN
6.2200 g., 0.9999 Gold 0.1999 oz. AGW, 20 mm. **Obv:** Ornamental porch below three heraldic animals **Rev:** Hluboka Castle with coat of arms in foreground

Date	Mintage	F	VF	XF	Unc	BU
2004	2,500	—	—	—	—	180
Note: Reeded edge						
2004 Proof	3,500	Value: 200				
Note: Plain edge						

KM# 76 2500 KORUN
31.1040 g., 0.9990 Bi-Metallic Gold And Silver .9999 Gold 7.776g center in .999 Silver 23.328g ring 0.9990 oz., 40 mm. **Subject:** Czech entry into the European Union **Obv:** Value within circle of shields **Rev:** "1.5.2004" within circle of dates and text **Edge:** Lettered **Edge Lettering:** "CNB * Ag 0.999 * 23,328 g * Au 999.9 * 7,776g * "

Date	Mintage	F	VF	XF	Unc	BU
ND (2004) Proof	10,000	Value: 285				

KM# 86 2500 KORUN
7.7850 g., 0.9990 Gold 0.2500 oz. AGW, 22 mm. **Subject:** Observatory at Prague Klementinum **Obv:** Sun's rays thru clouds **Obv. Designer:** Josef Oplistil **Rev:** Building tower, rays and moon **Rev. Designer:** Jesef Oplistil

Date	Mintage	F	VF	XF	Unc	BU
2006	2,100	—	—	—	—	225
2006 Proof	3,800	Value: 245				

MINT SETS

KM#	Date	Mintage	Identification	Issue Price	Mkt Val
MS12	2001 (9)	6,000	KM#1, 2.3, 3-9 International Monetary Fund	—	14.00

PROOF SETS

KM#	Date	Mintage	Identification	Issue Price	Mkt Val
PS6	2001 (9)	2,500	KM#1, 2.3, 3-9	35.00	60.00
PS7	2002 (9)	3,490	KM#1, 2.3, 3.2, 4, 5, 6, 7, 8, 9	35.00	60.00
PS8	2003 (9)	3,000	KM#1, 2.3, 3.2, 4, 5, 6, 7, 8, 9	35.00	60.00
PS9	2004 (9)	4,000	KM#1, 2.3, 3.2, 4, 5, 6, 7, 8, 9	35.00	60.00

DENMARK

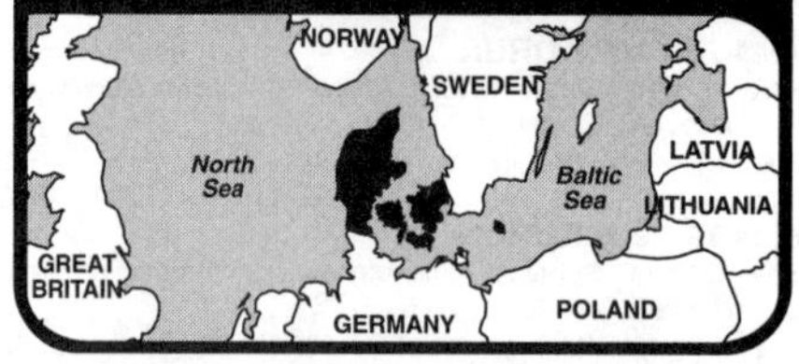

The Kingdom of Denmark (Danmark), a constitutional monarchy located at the mouth of the Baltic Sea, has an area of 16,639 sq. mi. (43,070 sq. km.) and a population of 5.2 million. Capital: Copenhagen. Most of the country is arable. Agriculture is conducted by large farms served by cooperatives. The largest industries are food processing, iron and metal, and shipping. Machinery, meats (chiefly bacon), dairy products and chemicals are exported.

As a result of a referendum held September 28, 2000, the currency of the European Monetary Union, the Euro, will not be introduced in Denmark in the foreseeable future.

RULER
Margrethe II, 1972—

MINT MARKS
(h) - Copenhagen, heart

MINT OFFICIALS' INITIALS

Copenhagen

Letter	Date	Name
LG	1989-2001	Laust Grove

MONEYERS' INITIALS

Copenhagen

Letter	Date	Name
A	1986-	Johan Alkjaer (designer)
HV	1986-	Hanne Varming (sculptor)
JP	1989-	Jan Petersen

MONETARY SYSTEM
100 Øre = 1 Krone

KINGDOM

DECIMAL COINAGE

100 Øre = 1 Krone; 1874-present

KM# 868.1 25 ORE
2.8000 g., Bronze, 17.5 mm. **Ruler:** Margrethe II **Obv:** Large crown divides date above, initial to right of country **Rev:** Denomination, small heart above, mint mark and initials LG-JP below **Note:** Beginning in 1996 and ending with 1998, the words "DANMARK" and "ØRE" have raised edges. Heart mint mark under "ØRE"; Prev. KM#868.

Date	Mintage	F	VF	XF	Unc	BU
2001 LG; JP; A	10,530,000	—	—	—	0.15	—

KM# 868.2 25 ORE
2.8000 g., Bronze, 17.5 mm. **Ruler:** Margrethe II **Obv:** Large crown divides date above **Rev:** Denomination, small heart above **Edge:** Plain **Note:** Without initials

Date	Mintage	F	VF	XF	Unc	BU
2002	12,000,000	—	—	—	0.15	—
2003	17,590,000	—	—	—	0.15	—
2004	7,040,304	—	—	—	0.15	—
2004 Proof	3,000	Value: 12.00				
2005	—	—	—	—	0.15	—
2005 Proof	—	Value: 12.00				
2006	—	—	—	—	0.15	—
2006 Proof	—	Value: 12.00				
2007	—	—	—	—	0.15	—

KM# 866.2 50 ORE
4.3000 g., Bronze **Ruler:** Margrethe II **Obv:** Large crown divides date above, initial to right of country name **Rev:** Large heart above value, mint mark and initials LG-JP below **Note:** Beginning in 1996 and ending with 1998, the words "DANMARK" and "ØRE" have raised edges. Heart mint mark under the word "ØRE".

Date	Mintage	F	VF	XF	Unc	BU
2001 LG; JP; A	12,270,000	—	—	—	0.25	—

KM# 866.3 50 ORE
4.3000 g., Bronze, 21.48 mm. **Ruler:** Margrethe II **Obv:** Large crown divides date above **Rev:** Small heart above denomination **Edge:** Plain **Note:** No initials

Date	Mintage	F	VF	XF	Unc	BU
2002	3,900,000	—	—	—	0.20	—
2003	8,817,000	—	—	—	0.20	—
2004	10,040,706	—	—	—	0.20	—
2004 Proof	3,000	Value: 15.00				
2005	—	—	—	—	0.20	—
2005 Proof	—	Value: 15.00				
2006	—	—	—	—	0.20	—
2006 Proof	—	Value: 15.00				
2007	—	—	—	—	0.20	—

KM# 873.1 KRONE
3.6000 g., Copper-Nickel **Ruler:** Margrethe II **Obv:** Wave design surrounds center hole, value above, hearts flank **Rev:** 3 crowned MII monograms around center hole, date, mint mark, and initials LG-JP-A below **Note:** Prev. KM#873.

Date	Mintage	F	VF	XF	Unc	BU
2001 LG; JP; A	14,640,000	—	—	—	0.60	—

KM# 873.2 KRONE
3.6000 g., Copper-Nickel, 20.29 mm. **Ruler:** Margrethe II **Obv:** 3 crowned MII monograms around center hole, date below **Rev:** Design surounds center hole, value above, hearts flank **Edge:** Reeded **Note:** Without initials

Date	Mintage	F	VF	XF	Unc	BU
2002	9,000,000	—	—	—	0.40	—
2003	5,231,000	—	—	—	0.40	—
2004	16,139,596	—	—	—	0.40	—
2004 Proof	3,000	Value: 18.00				
2005	—	—	—	—	0.40	—
2005 Proof	—	Value: 18.00				
2006	—	—	—	—	0.40	—
2006 Proof	—	Value: 18.00				
2007	—	—	—	—	40.00	—

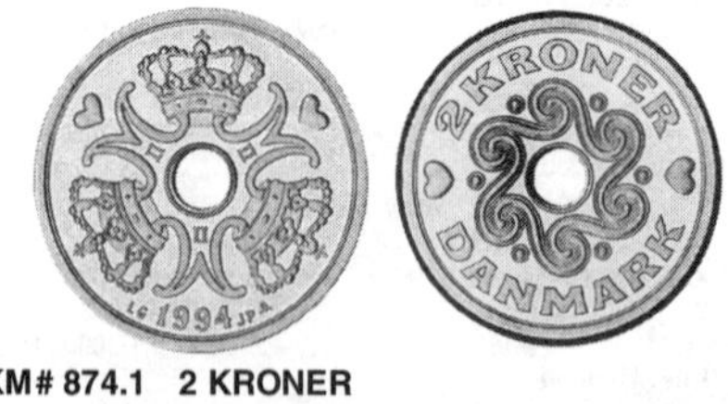

KM# 874.1 2 KRONER
Copper-Nickel **Ruler:** Margrethe II **Obv:** 3 crowned MII monograms around center hole, date and initials LG-JP-A below **Rev:** Design surrounds center hole, denomination above, hearts flank **Note:** Prev. KM#874.

Date	Mintage	F	VF	XF	Unc	BU
2001 LG; JP; A	11,180,000	—	—	—	0.60	—

KM# 874.2 2 KRONER
5.9400 g., Copper-Nickel, 24.37 mm. **Ruler:** Margrethe II **Obv:** 3 crowned MII monograms around center hole, date and initials LGpJP-A below **Rev:** Wave design surrounds center hole, denomination above, hearts flank **Edge:** Reeded and plain sections **Note:** Without initials

Date	Mintage	F	VF	XF	Unc	BU
2002	60,159,000	—	—	—	0.60	—
2004	7,381,531	—	—	—	0.60	—

Date	Mintage	F	VF	XF	Unc	BU
2004 Proof	3,000	Value: 22.00				
2005	—	—	—	—	0.60	—
2005 Proof	—	Value: 22.00				
2006	—	—	—	—	0.60	—
2006 Proof	—	Value: 22.00				
2007	—	—	—	—	0.60	—

KM# 869.1 5 KRONER

9.2000 g., Copper-Nickel, 28 mm. **Ruler:** Margrethe II **Obv:** 3 crowned MII monograms around center hole, date and initials LG-JP-A below **Rev:** Wave design surrounds center hole, denomination above, hearts flank **Note:** Large and small date varieties exist.

Date	Mintage	F	VF	XF	Unc	BU
2001 LG; JP; A	5,700,000	—	—	—	2.00	—

KM# 869.2 5 KRONER

9.2500 g., Copper Nickel, 28.52 mm. **Ruler:** Margrethe II **Obv:** 3 crowned MII monograms around center hole, date and initials LG-JP-A below **Rev:** Wave design surrounds center hole, denomination above, hearts flank **Edge:** Reeded **Note:** Without initials

Date	Mintage	F	VF	XF	Unc	BU
2002	5,980,000	—	—	—	2.00	—
2004	1,415,925	—	—	—	2.00	—
2004 Proof	3,000	Value: 25.00				
2005	—	—	—	—	2.00	—
2005 Proof	—	Value: 25.00				
2006	—	—	—	—	2.00	—
2006 Proof	—	Value: 25.00				
2007	—	—	—	—	2.00	—

KM# 887.1 10 KRONER

7.0000 g., Aluminum-Bronze, 23.4 mm. **Ruler:** Margrethe II **Obv:** Crowned head right within inner circle, date, initials LG-JP-A below, mint mark after II in title **Obv. Designer:** Mogens Moller **Rev:** Crowned arms within inner circle above denomination **Edge:** Plain

Date	Mintage	F	VF	XF	Unc	BU
2001 LG; JP; A	4,800,000	—	—	—	3.00	—

KM# 887.2 10 KRONER

7.1000 g., Aluminum-Bronze, 23.31 mm. **Ruler:** Margrethe II **Obv:** Crowned head right, mint mark after II in title **Obv. Legend:** MARGRETHE II - DANMARKS DRONNING **Obv. Designer:** Mogens Moller **Rev:** Crowned arms and denomination **Edge:** Plain **Note:** Without initials

Date	Mintage	F	VF	XF	Unc	BU
2002	7,299,900	—	—	—	3.00	—

KM# 896 10 KRONER

6.9500 g., Aluminum-Bronze, 23.39 mm. **Ruler:** Margrethe II **Obv:** Head right within circle, date below **Obv. Legend:** MARGRETHE II - DANMARKS DRONNING **Rev:** Crowned arms above denomination **Edge:** Plain **Designer:** Mogens Moller

Date	Mintage	F	VF	XF	Unc	BU
2004	5,835,426	—	—	—	2.75	—
2004 Proof	—	Value: 30.00				
2005	—	—	—	—	2.75	—
2005 Proof	—	Value: 30.00				
2006	—	—	—	—	2.75	—
2006 Proof	—	Value: 30.00				
2007	—	—	—	—	2.75	—

KM# 898 10 KRONER

7.0000 g., Aluminum-Bronze, 23.4 mm. **Ruler:** Margrethe II **Subject:** Hans Christian Andersen's Ugly duckling story **Obv:** Head right within circle, date below **Rev:** Swan and reflection on water within circle, value below **Rev. Designer:** Hans Pauli Olsen **Edge:** Plain

Date	Mintage	F	VF	XF	Unc	BU
2005	1,200,000	—	—	—	3.25	—

KM# 906 10 KRONER

31.1000 g., 0.9990 Silver 0.9988 oz. ASW, 38 mm. **Ruler:** Margrethe II **Subject:** Hans Christian Andersen's The Ugly Duckling **Obv:** Queen **Rev:** Swan and reflection on water **Rev. Designer:** Hans Pauli Olsen

Date	Mintage	F	VF	XF	Unc	BU
2005	75,000	—	—	—	—	45.00

KM# 907 10 KRONER

8.6500 g., 0.9000 Gold 0.2503 oz. AGW, 22 mm. **Ruler:** Margrethe II **Subject:** Hans Christian Andersen's The Ugly Duckling **Obv:** Queen **Rev:** Swan and reflection on water **Rev. Designer:** Hans Pauli Olsen

Date	Mintage	F	VF	XF	Unc	BU
2005	7,000	—	—	—	—	400

KM# 900 10 KRONER

7.0000 g., Aluminum-Bronze, 23.4 mm. **Ruler:** Margrethe II **Subject:** Hans Christian Andersen's Little Mermaid **Obv:** Head right within circle, date below **Rev:** Little Mermaid **Rev. Designer:** Tina Maria Nielsen **Edge:** Plain

Date	Mintage	F	VF	XF	Unc	BU
2005	1,200,000	—	—	—	3.25	—

KM# 908 10 KRONER

31.1000 g., 0.9990 Silver 0.9988 oz. ASW, 38 mm. **Ruler:** Margrethe II **Subject:** Hans Christian Andersen's Little Mermaid **Obv:** Queen **Rev:** Little Mermaid **Rev. Designer:** Tina Maria Nielsen

Date	Mintage	F	VF	XF	Unc	BU
2005	60,000	—	—	—	—	45.00

KM# 911 10 KRONER

8.6500 g., 0.9000 Gold 0.2503 oz. AGW, 22 mm. **Ruler:** Margrethe II **Subject:** Hans Christian Andersen's Little Mermaid **Obv:** Queen **Rev:** Little Mermaid **Rev. Designer:** Tina Maria Nielsen

Date	Mintage	F	VF	XF	Unc	BU
2005	6,000	—	—	—	—	400

KM# 903 10 KRONER

7.1000 g., Aluminum-Bronze, 23.31 mm. **Ruler:** Margrethe II **Subject:** H.C. Andersen's "The Snow Queen" **Obv:** Head right within circle, date below **Obv. Legend:** MARGRETHE II - DANMARKS DRONNING **Rev:** Stylized figures **Rev. Designer:** Bjørn Nørgaard **Edge:** Plain

Date	Mintage	F	VF	XF	Unc	BU
2006	1,200,000	—	—	—	3.25	—

KM# 909 10 KRONER

31.1000 g., 0.9990 Silver 0.9988 oz. ASW, 38 mm. **Ruler:** Margrethe II **Subject:** H.C. Andersen's "Skyggen (The Shadow) **Obv:** Queen **Rev:** Stylized figures **Rev. Designer:** Bjørn Nørgaard

Date	Mintage	F	VF	XF	Unc	BU
2006	50,000	—	—	—	—	45.00

KM# 910 10 KRONER

8.6500 g., 0.9000 Gold 0.2503 oz. AGW, 22 mm. **Ruler:** Margrethe II **Subject:** H.C. Andersen's "Skyggen" (The Shadow) **Obv:** Queen **Rev:** Stylized figures **Rev. Designer:** Bjørn Nørgaard

Date	Mintage	F	VF	XF	Unc	BU
2006	5,000	—	—	—	—	400

KM# 914 10 KRONER

31.1000 g., 0.9990 Silver 0.9988 oz. ASW, 38 mm. **Ruler:** Margrethe II **Subject:** The Snow Queen **Obv:** Queen **Obv. Designer:** Hans Christian Andersen **Rev:** Ice pieces **Rev. Designer:** Øivind Nygaard

Date	Mintage	F	VF	XF	Unc	BU
2006	40,000	—	—	—	—	45.00

KM# 915 10 KRONER

8.6500 g., 0.9000 Gold 0.2503 oz. AGW, 22 mm. **Ruler:** Margrethe II **Subject:** The Snow Queen **Obv:** Queen **Obv. Designer:** Mogens Møller **Rev:** Ice pieces **Rev. Designer:** Øivind Nygaard

Date	Mintage	F	VF	XF	Unc	BU
2006	4,000	—	—	—	—	400

KM# 916 10 KRONER

7.1000 g., Aluminum-Bronze, 23.31 mm. **Ruler:** Margrethe II **Subject:** Polar Year **Obv:** Crowned bust right **Obv. Legend:** MARGRETHE II - DANMARKS DRONNING **Rev:** Polar bear facing, walking on ice flow **Rev. Legend:** POLARÅR 2007-2009 **Edge:** Plain

Date	Mintage	F	VF	XF	Unc	BU
2007(h)	1,200,000	—	—	—	3.00	—

KM# 888.1 20 KRONER

9.3000 g., Aluminum-Bronze **Ruler:** Margrethe II **Obv:** Crowned head right within circle, date and initials LG-JP-A below, mint mark after II in legend **Rev:** Crowned arms within ornaments and value **Edge:** Alternate reeded and plain sections **Designer:** Mogens Moller

Date	Mintage	F	VF	XF	Unc	BU
2001(h) LG; JP; A	2,900,000	—	—	—	5.25	—

KM# 889 20 KRONER

9.3000 g., Aluminum-Bronze, 26.8 mm. **Ruler:** Margrethe II **Subject:** Danish Towers **Obv:** Head right within circle date below, mint mark after II in legend **Rev:** Aarhus City Hall **Rev. Designer:** Lis Nogel **Edge:** Reeded and plain sections

Date	Mintage	F	VF	XF	Unc	BU
2002	1,000,000	—	—	—	5.25	—
2003	—	—	—	—	—	—

KM# 888.2 20 KRONER

9.3000 g., Aluminum-Bronze, 26.9 mm. **Ruler:** Margrethe II **Obv:** Crowned head right within circle, mint mark after II in legend **Rev:** Crowned arms within ornaments and value **Edge:** Alternate reeded and plain sections **Designer:** Mogens Møller **Note:** Without initials.

Date	Mintage	F	VF	XF	Unc	BU
2002	5,500,000	—	—	—	5.25	—
2004	—	—	—	—	5.25	—

KM# 890 20 KRONER
9.3000 g., Aluminum-Bronze, 26.8 mm. **Ruler:** Margrethe II **Subject:** Danish towers **Obv:** Head right within circle, mint mark and date **Rev:** Copenhagen Old Stock Exchange spire with four intertwined dragon tails **Rev. Designer:** Karin Lorentzen **Edge:** Alternate reeded and plain sections

Date	Mintage	F	VF	XF	Unc	BU
2003	1,000,000	—	—	—	5.25	—

KM# 891 20 KRONER
9.3000 g., Aluminum-Bronze, 26.94 mm. **Ruler:** Margrethe II **Obv:** Head right within circle, mint mark and date **Obv. Legend:** MARGRETHE II - DANMARKS DRONNING **Rev:** Crowned arms above denomination **Rev. Designer:** Mogens M?ller **Edge:** Alternate reeded and plain sections

Date	Mintage	F	VF	XF	Unc	BU
2003	5,720,000	—	—	—	5.25	—
2004	6,922,182	—	—	—	5.25	—
2004 Proof	3,000	Value: 40.00				
2005	—	—	—	—	5.25	—
2005 Proof	—	Value: 45.00				
2006	—	—	—	—	5.25	—
2006 Proof	—	Value: 45.00				
2007	—	—	—	—	5.25	—

KM# 892 20 KRONER
9.3100 g., Aluminum-Bronze, 26.8 mm. **Ruler:** Margrethe II **Subject:** Danish towers **Obv:** Head right within circle, mint mark and date **Rev:** Christiansborg Castle (parliament) tower and Danish flag **Rev. Designer:** Hans Pauli Olsen **Edge:** Alternate reeded and plain sections

Date	Mintage	F	VF	XF	Unc	BU
2003	1,000,000	—	—	—	5.25	—

KM# 893 20 KRONER
9.3100 g., Aluminum-Bronze, 26.8 mm. **Ruler:** Margrethe II **Subject:** Danish towers **Obv:** Head right within circle, date below **Rev:** Gåsetårnet tower **Rev. Designer:** Tina Maria Nielsen **Edge:** Alternate reeded and plain sections

Date	Mintage	F	VF	XF	Unc	BU
2004	1,200,000	—	—	—	5.25	—

KM# 894 20 KRONER
9.3100 g., Aluminum-Bronze, 26.8 mm. **Ruler:** Margrethe II **Subject:** Crown Prince's Wedding **Obv:** Head right within circle, date below **Rev:** Crown Prince Frederik and Crown Princess Mary **Rev. Designer:** Karin Lorentzen **Edge:** Alternate reeded and plain sections

Date	Mintage	F	VF	XF	Unc	BU
2004	1,200,000	—	—	—	5.25	—

KM# 897 20 KRONER
Aluminum-Bronze, 26.8 mm. **Ruler:** Margrethe II **Subject:** Danish towers **Obv:** Head right within circle, date below **Rev:** Svaneke water tower, Bornholm **Rev. Designer:** Morten Straede **Edge:** Alternate reeded and plain sections

Date	Mintage	F	VF	XF	Unc	BU
2004	1,200,000	—	—	—	5.25	—

KM# 899 20 KRONER
9.3000 g., Aluminum-Bronze, 26.8 mm. **Ruler:** Margrethe II **Obv:** Head right within circle, date below **Rev:** Landet Kirke, with elements from the story of Elvira Madigan and Sixten Sparre, including a revolver among leaves of chestnut-trees **Rev. Designer:** Øivind Nygaard **Edge:** Segmented reeding

Date	Mintage	F	VF	XF	Unc	BU
2005	1,200,000	—	—	—	5.25	—

KM# 901 20 KRONER
9.3000 g., Aluminum-Bronze, 26.94 mm. **Ruler:** Margrethe II **Obv:** Head right within circle, date below **Obv. Legend:** MARGRETHE II - DANMARKS DRONNING **Rev:** Lighthouse of Nolsoy (Faeroe Islands) **Rev. Designer:** Hans Pauli Olsen **Edge:** Alternate plain and reeded segments

Date	Mintage	F	VF	XF	Unc	BU
2005	1,200,000	—	—	—	5.25	—

KM# 902 20 KRONER
9.3300 g., Aluminum-Bronze, 26.8 mm. **Ruler:** Margrethe II **Obv:** Head right within circle, date below **Rev:** Grasten Castle Bell Tower **Rev. Designer:** Sys Hindsbo **Edge:** Segmented reeding

Date	Mintage	F	VF	XF	Unc	BU
2006(h)	1,200,000	—	—	—	5.25	—

KM# 913 20 KRONER
9.3000 g., Aluminum-Bronze, 26.94 mm. **Ruler:** Margrethe II **Subject:** Danish Towers **Obv:** Margrethe II **Obv. Legend:** MARGRETHE II - DANMARKS DRONNING **Rev:** The Greenland Cairns: Nukaritt/Three Brothers **Rev. Legend:** TRE BRØDRE **Rev. Designer:** Niels Motzfeldt **Edge:** Alternate plain and reeded segments

Date	Mintage	F	VF	XF	Unc	BU
2006	1,200,000	—	—	—	5.25	—

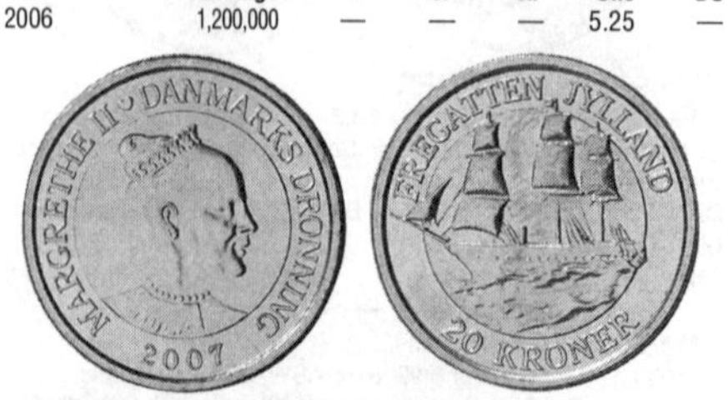

KM# 920 20 KRONER
9.3000 g., Aluminum-Bronze, 26.94 mm. **Ruler:** Margrethe II **Series:** Danish ships **Obv:** Crowned bust right **Obv. Legend:** MARGRETHE II - DANMARKS DRONNING **Rev:** Sailing ship Jylland **Rev. Legend:** FREGATTEN - JYLLAND **Edge:** Alternate plain and reeded segments

Date	Mintage	F	VF	XF	Unc	BU
2007(h)	—	—	—	—	—	4.50

KM# 921 20 KRONER
9.3000 g., Aluminum-Bronze, 26.94 mm. **Ruler:** Margrethe II **Series:** Danish ships **Obv:** Crowned bust right **Obv. Legend:** MARGRETHE II - DANMARKS DRONNING **Rev:** Ship Vaedderen, route map in background **Rev. Legend:** VAEDDEREN **Edge:** Alternate plain and reeded segments

Date	Mintage	F	VF	XF	Unc	BU
2007(h)	—	—	—	—	—	4.50

KM# 917 100 KRONER
Silver **Ruler:** Margrethe II **Subject:** Polar Year **Obv:** Crowned bust right **Obv. Legend:** MARGRETHE II - DANMARKS DRONNING **Rev:** Polar facing, walking on ice flow **Rev. Legend:** POLAR?R 2007-2009

Date	Mintage	F	VF	XF	Unc	BU
2007(h)	50,000	—	—	—	55.00	—

KM# 895 200 KRONER
31.1000 g., 0.9990 Silver 0.9988 oz. ASW, 38.3 mm. **Ruler:** Margrethe II **Subject:** Wedding of Crown Prince **Obv:** Head right within circle, date below **Rev:** Crown Prince Frederik and Crown Princess Mary **Rev. Designer:** Karin Lorentzen **Edge:** Plain **Note:** No initials.

Date	Mintage	F	VF	XF	Unc	BU
2004	125,000	—	—	—	60.00	—

KM# 918 1000 KRONER
Gold, 22.00 mm. **Ruler:** Margrethe II **Subject:** Polar Year **Obv:** Crowned bust right **Obv. Legend:** MARGRETHE II - DANMARKS DRONNING **Rev:** Polar bear facing, walking on ice flow **Rev. Legend:** POLAR?R 2007-2009 **Note:** Struck from gold from Greenland having a small polar bear to right of denomination.

Date	Mintage	F	VF	XF	Unc	BU
2007(h)	6,000	—	—	—	460	475

MINT SETS

KM#	Date	Mintage	Identification	Issue Price	Mkt Val
MS46	2001 (7)	28,000	KM866.2, 868, 869, 873, 874, 887, 888	15.00	27.50
MS47	2002 (7)	28,000	KM866.3, 868.2, 869.2, 873.2, 874.2, 887.2, 888.2	17.50	22.50
MS48	2003 (6)	35,000	KM866.3, 868.2, 873.2, 889, 890, 891	17.50	22.50
MS49	2004 (8)	35,000	KM#866.3, 868.2, 869.2, 873.2, 874.2, 891, 895, 896, plus medal in Nordic gold	34.50	45.00
MS50	2005 (8)	31,000	KM#866.3, 868.2, 869.2, 873.2, 874.2, 869.2, 896, 891, 898.	34.50	45.00
MS51	2006 (7)	35,000	KM#868.2, 866.3, 873.2, 874.2, 869.2, 896, 902, plus medal in Nordic Gold	40.00	45.00
MS52	2007 (7)	6,000	KM#866.3, 868.2, 869.2, 873.2, 874.2, 891, 896 Children's set with medal in .925 Silver	46.00	50.00

PROOF SETS

KM#	Date	Mintage	Identification	Issue Price	Mkt Val
PS1	2004 (8)	3,000	KM#866.3, 868.2, 869.2, 873.2, 874.2, 896, 891, plus Wedding medal in .925 Silver	150	190
PS2	2005 (8)	3,500	KM866.3, 868.2, 873.2, 874.2, 869.2, 896, 891 and 1801 Battle of Copenhagen medal in .925 Silver	150	165
PS3	2006 (7)	2,500	KM#868.2, 866.3, 873.2, 874.2, 869.2, 896, 891 and 1691 Floating Dock medal in .925 Silver	160	170

DJIBOUTI

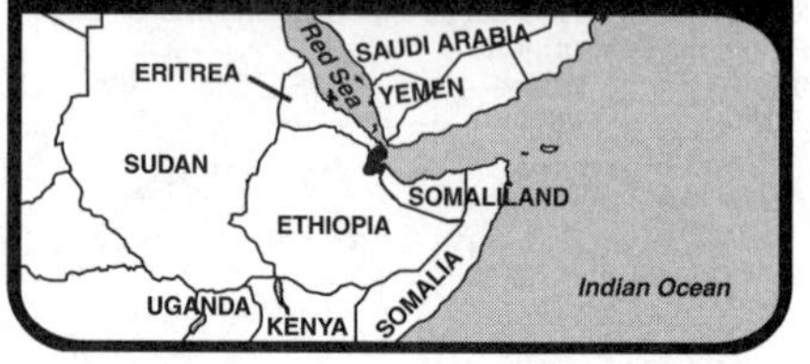

The Republic of Djibouti (formerly French Somaliland and the French Overseas Territory of Afars and Issas), located in northeast Africa at the Bab el Mandeb Strait connecting the Suez Canal and the Red Sea with the Gulf of Aden and the Indian Ocean, has an area of 8,950 sq. mi. (22,000 sq. km.) and a population of 421,320. Capital: Djibouti. The tiny nation has less than one sq. mi. of arable land, and no natural resources except salt, sand, and camels. The commercial activities of the transshipment port of Djibouti and the Addis Abada-Djibouti railroad are the basis of the economy. Salt, fish and hides are exported.

REPUBLIC

STANDARD COINAGE

KM# 34 10 FRANCS
3.4000 g., Copper-Nickel, 20.9 mm. **Obv:** National arms **Rev:** Chimpanzee **Edge:** Plain

Date	Mintage	F	VF	XF	Unc	BU
2003	—	—	—	—	1.50	2.50

KM# 26 100 FRANCS
12.0000 g., Copper-Nickel, 30 mm. **Obv:** National arms within wreath, date below **Rev:** Pair of dromedary camels right, denomination above

Date	Mintage	F	VF	XF	Unc	BU
2004(a)	—	—	—	2.25	7.00	9.00

DOMINICAN REPUBLIC

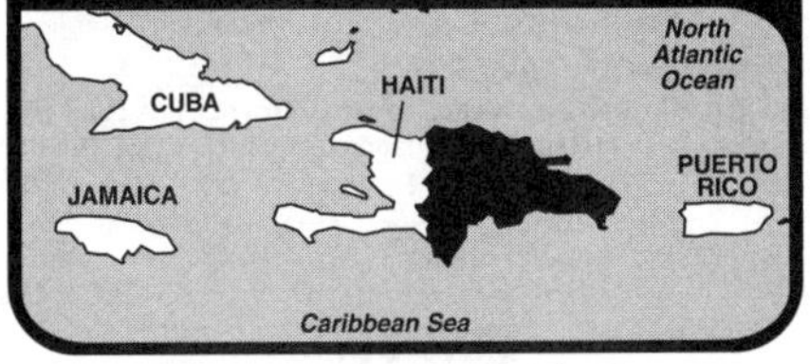

The Dominican Republic, which occupies the eastern two-thirds of the island of Hispaniola, has an area of 18,704 sq. mi. (48,734 sq. km.) and a population of 7.9 million. Capital: Santo Domingo. The largely agricultural economy produces sugar, coffee, tobacco and cocoa. Tourism and casino gaming are also a rising source of revenue.

REPUBLIC

REFORM COINAGE

1937

100 Centavos = 1 Peso Oro

KM# 80.2 PESO
Copper-Zinc, 25 mm. **Subject:** Juan Pablo Duarte **Obv:** National arms and denomination **Rev:** DUARTE below bust, date below **Note:** Coin die alignment.

Date	Mintage	F	VF	XF	Unc	BU
2002	—	—	—	—	2.00	2.50

KM# 90 PESO
12.5000 g., Copper-Nickel, 30.6 mm. **Obv:** Pan American Games logo **Rev:** National arms and denomination **Edge:** Reeded

Date	Mintage	F	VF	XF	Unc	BU
2003 Proof	—	Value: 15.00				

KM# 89 5 PESOS
5.9500 g., Bi-Metallic Stainless Steel center in Brass ring, 23 mm. **Subject:** Sanchez **Obv:** National arms and denomination **Rev:** Portrait facing within circle, date below **Edge:** Segmented reeding

Date	Mintage	F	VF	XF	Unc	BU
2002	—	—	—	—	2.50	3.00
2005	—	—	—	—	2.50	3.00

KM# 106 10 PESOS
8.0500 g., Bi-Metallic **Ring Composition:** Copper-Nickel **Center Composition:** Brass, 26.93 mm. **Obv:** Value at left of national arms **Obv. Legend:** • REPUBLICA DOMINICANA • **Rev:** Bust of General Mella facing **Rev. Legend:** BANCO CENTRAL DE LA REPUBLICA DOMINICANA **Edge:** Segmented reeding

Date	Mintage	F	VF	XF	Unc	BU
2005	—	—	—	—	6.00	8.00

KM# 107 25 PESOS
8.5600 g., Copper-Nickel, 28.82 mm. **Obv:** Value at left of national arms **Obv. Legend:** REPUBLICA DOMINICANA **Rev:** Bust of General Luperon facing **Rev. Legend:** BANCO CENTRAL DE LA REPUBLICA DOMINICANA **Rev. Inscription:** HEROE DE LA RESTAURACION **Edge:** Reeded

Date	Mintage	F	VF	XF	Unc	BU
2005	—	—	—	—	5.00	7.00

EAST CARIBBEAN STATES

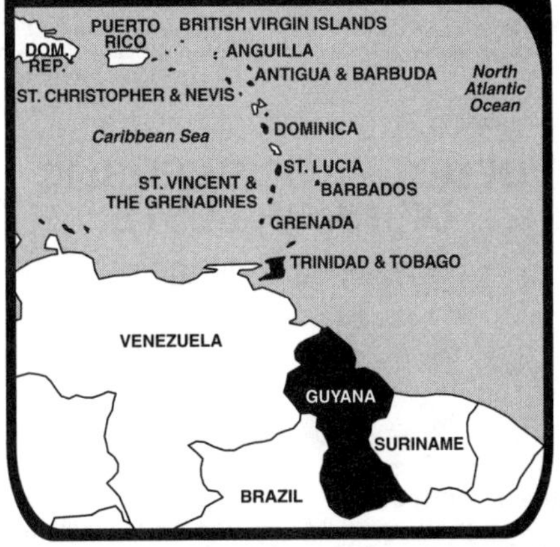

The East Caribbean States, formerly the British Caribbean Territories (Eastern Group), formed a currency board in 1950 to provide the constituent territories of Trinidad & Tobago, Barbados, British Guiana (now Guyana), British Virgin Islands, Anguilla, St. Kitts, Nevis, Antigua, Dominica, St. Lucia, St. Vincent and Grenada with a common currency, thereby permitting withdrawal of the regular British Pound currency. This was dissolved in 1965 and after the breakup, the East Caribbean Territories, a grouping including Barbados, the Leeward and Windward Islands, came into being. Coinage of the dissolved 'Eastern Group' continues to circulate. Paper currency of the East Caribbean Authority was first issued in 1965 and although Barbados withdrew from the group they continued using them prior to 1973 when Barbados issued a decimal coinage.

A series of 4-dollar coins tied to the FAO coinage program were released in 1970 under the name of the Caribbean Development Bank by eight loosely federated island groupings in the eastern Caribbean. These issues are listed individually in this volume under Antigua, Barbados, Dominica, Grenada, Montserrat, St. Kitts, St. Lucia and St. Vincent.

EAST CARIBBEAN STATES

STANDARD COINAGE

100 Cents = 1 Dollar

KM# 34 CENT
1.0300 g., Aluminum, 18.42 mm. **Ruler:** Elizabeth II **Obv:** Crowned head right **Obv. Designer:** Ian Rank-Broadley **Rev:** Denomination **Edge:** Plain

Date	Mintage	F	VF	XF	Unc	BU
2002	—	—	—	—	0.20	0.30
2004	—	—	—	—	0.20	0.30

KM# 35 2 CENTS
1.4200 g., Aluminum, 21.46 mm. **Ruler:** Elizabeth II **Obv:** Crowned head right **Obv. Designer:** Ian Rank-Broadley **Rev:** Denomination **Edge:** Plain

Date	Mintage	F	VF	XF	Unc	BU
2002	—	—	—	—	0.25	0.35

KM# 36 5 CENTS
1.7400 g., Aluminum, 23.11 mm. **Ruler:** Elizabeth II **Obv:** Crowned head right **Obv. Designer:** Ian Rank-Broadley **Rev:** Denomination **Edge:** Plain

Date	Mintage	F	VF	XF	Unc	BU
2002	—	—	—	—	0.30	0.45

KM# 37 10 CENTS
Copper-Nickel, 18.06 mm. **Ruler:** Elizabeth II **Obv:** Crowned head right **Obv. Designer:** Ian Rank-Broadley **Rev:** Sir Francis Drake's Golden Hind and denomination **Edge:** Reeded

Date	Mintage	F	VF	XF	Unc	BU
2002	—	—	—	—	0.40	0.60

KM# 38 25 CENTS
6.4800 g., Copper-Nickel, 23.98 mm. **Ruler:** Elizabeth II **Obv:** Crowned head right **Obv. Designer:** Ian Rank-Broadley **Rev:** Sir Francis Drake's Golden Hind and denomination **Edge:** Reeded

Date	Mintage	F	VF	XF	Unc	BU
2002	—	—	—	—	0.50	0.75

KM# 39 DOLLAR
7.9800 g., Copper-Nickel, 26.5 mm. **Ruler:** Elizabeth II **Obv:** Crowned head right **Obv. Designer:** Ian Rank-Broadley **Rev:** Sir Francis Drake's Golden Hind and denomination **Edge:** Alternating plain and reeded

Date	Mintage	F	VF	XF	Unc	BU
2002	—	—	—	—	2.00	3.00

KM# 40 DOLLAR
28.2800 g., Copper-Nickel, Gold Plated, 38.6 mm. **Ruler:** Elizabeth II **Subject:** Golden Jubilee Monarchs **Obv:** Crowned head right **Obv. Designer:** Ian Rank-Broadley **Rev:** Henry III (1216-1277) **Edge:** Reeded

Date	Mintage	F	VF	XF	Unc	BU
2002	5,000	—	—	—	22.50	25.00

KM# 42 DOLLAR
28.2800 g., Copper-Nickel, Gold Plated, 38.6 mm. **Ruler:** Elizabeth II **Subject:** Golden Jubilee Monarchs **Obv:** Crowned head right **Obv. Designer:** Ian Rank-Broadley **Rev:** Edward III (1327-1377) **Edge:** Reeded

Date	Mintage	F	VF	XF	Unc	BU
2002	5,000	—	—	—	22.50	25.00

KM# 44 DOLLAR
28.2800 g., Copper-Nickel, Gold Plated, 38.6 mm. **Ruler:** Elizabeth II **Subject:** Golden Jubilee Monarchs **Obv:** Crowned head right **Obv. Designer:** Ian Rank-Broadley **Rev:** George III (1760-1820) **Edge:** Reeded

Date	Mintage	F	VF	XF	Unc	BU
2002	5,000	—	—	—	22.50	25.00

KM# 46 DOLLAR
28.2800 g., Copper-Nickel, Gold Plated, 38.6 mm. **Ruler:** Elizabeth II **Subject:** Golden Jubilee Monarchs **Obv:** Crowned head right **Obv. Designer:** Ian Rank-Broadley **Rev:** Queen Victoria (1837-1901) **Edge:** Reeded

Date	Mintage	F	VF	XF	Unc	BU
2002	5,000	—	—	—	22.50	25.00

KM# 48 DOLLAR
28.2800 g., Copper-Nickel, Gold Plated, 38.6 mm. **Ruler:** Elizabeth II **Subject:** Golden Jubilee Monarchs **Obv:** Crowned head right **Obv. Designer:** Ian Rank-Broadley **Rev:** Queen Elizabeth II (1952-) **Edge:** Reeded

Date	Mintage	F	VF	XF	Unc	BU
2002	5,000	—	—	—	22.50	25.00

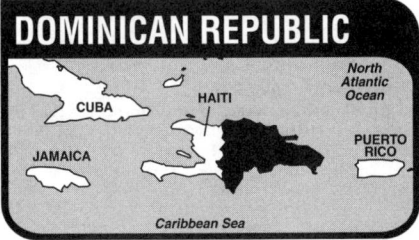

KM# 86 DOLLAR

27.7300 g., Copper-Nickel, 38.5 mm. **Ruler:** Elizabeth II **Subject:** Coronation Jubilee **Obv:** Crowned head right **Obv. Designer:** Ian Rank-Broadley **Rev:** Fireworks display above building **Edge:** Reeded

Date	Mintage	F	VF	XF	Unc	BU
2002	—	—	—	—	10.00	12.00

KM# 51 2 DOLLARS

56.5600 g., Copper-Nickel, Gold Plated, 38.6 mm. **Ruler:** Elizabeth II **Subject:** British Military Leaders **Obv:** Crowned head right **Obv. Designer:** Ian Rank-Broadley **Rev:** Wellington's portrait and battle scene **Edge:** Reeded

Date	Mintage	F	VF	XF	Unc	BU
2002 Proof	10,000	Value: 45.00				

KM# 54 2 DOLLARS

56.5600 g., Copper-Nickel, Gold Plated, 38.6 mm. **Ruler:** Elizabeth II **Subject:** British Military Leaders **Obv:** Crowned head right **Obv. Designer:** Ian Rank-Broadley **Rev:** Admiral Nelson's portrait and naval battle scene **Edge:** Reeded

Date	Mintage	F	VF	XF	Unc	BU
2003 Proof	10,000	Value: 45.00				

KM# 57 2 DOLLARS

56.5600 g., Copper-Nickel, Gold Plated, 38.6 mm. **Ruler:** Elizabeth II **Subject:** British Military Leaders **Obv:** Crowned head right **Obv. Designer:** Ian Rank-Broadley **Rev:** Churchill's portrait and air battle scene **Edge:** Reeded

Date	Mintage	F	VF	XF	Unc	BU
2003 Proof	10,000	Value: 45.00				

KM# 41 10 DOLLARS

28.2800 g., 0.9250 Silver with gold cameo 0.8410 oz. ASW, 38.6 mm. **Ruler:** Elizabeth II **Subject:** Golden Jubilee Monarchs **Obv:** Crowned head right **Obv. Designer:** Ian Rank-Broadley **Rev:** Henry III (1216-1272) **Edge:** Reeded

Date	Mintage	F	VF	XF	Unc	BU
2002 Proof	10,000	Value: 65.00				

KM# 41a 10 DOLLARS

39.9400 g., 0.9166 Gold 1.1770 oz. AGW, 38.6 mm. **Ruler:** Elizabeth II **Subject:** Golden Jubilee Monarchs **Obv:** Crowned head right **Obv. Designer:** Ian Rank-Broadley **Rev:** Henry III (1216-1272) **Edge:** Reeded

Date	Mintage	F	VF	XF	Unc	BU
2002 Proof	100	Value: 1,100				

KM# 43 10 DOLLARS

28.2800 g., 0.9250 Silver 0.8410 oz. ASW, 38.6 mm. **Ruler:** Elizabeth II **Subject:** Golden Jubile Monarchs **Obv:** Crowned head right **Obv. Designer:** Ian Rank-Broadley **Rev:** Edward III (1327-1377) **Edge:** Reeded

Date	Mintage	F	VF	XF	Unc	BU
2002 Proof	10,000	Value: 65.00				

KM# 43a 10 DOLLARS

39.9400 g., 0.9166 Gold 1.1770 oz. AGW, 38.6 mm. **Ruler:** Elizabeth II **Subject:** Golden Jubilee Monarchs **Obv:** Crowned head right **Obv. Designer:** Ian Rank-Broadley **Rev:** Edward III (1327-1377) **Edge:** Reeded

Date	Mintage	F	VF	XF	Unc	BU
2002 Proof	100	Value: 1,100				

KM# 45 10 DOLLARS

28.2800 g., 0.9250 Silver with gold cameo 0.8410 oz. ASW, 38.6 mm. **Subject:** Golden Jubilee Monarchs **Obv:** Crowned head right **Obv. Designer:** Ian Rank-Broadley **Rev:** George III (1760-1820) **Edge:** Reeded

Date	Mintage	F	VF	XF	Unc	BU
2002 Proof	10,000	Value: 65.00				

KM# 45a 10 DOLLARS

39.9400 g., 0.9166 Gold 1.1770 oz. AGW, 38.6 mm. **Ruler:** Elizabeth II **Subject:** Golden Jubilee Monarchs **Obv:** Crowned head right **Obv. Designer:** Ian Rank-Broadley **Rev:** George III (1760-1820) **Edge:** Reeded

Date	Mintage	F	VF	XF	Unc	BU
2002 Proof	100	Value: 1,100				

KM# 47 10 DOLLARS

28.2800 g., 0.9250 Silver With Partial Gold Plating 0.8410 oz., 38.6 mm. **Ruler:** Elizabeth II **Subject:** Golden Jubilee Monarchs **Obv:** Crowned head right **Obv. Designer:** Ian Rank-Broadley **Rev:** Queen Victoria (1837-1901) **Edge:** Reeded

Date	Mintage	F	VF	XF	Unc	BU
2002 Proof	10,000	Value: 65.00				

KM# 47a 10 DOLLARS

39.9400 g., 0.9166 Gold 1.1770 oz. AGW, 38.6 mm. **Ruler:** Elizabeth II **Subject:** Golden Jubilee Monarchs **Obv:** Crowned head right **Obv. Designer:** Ian Rank-Broadley **Rev:** Queen Victoria (1837-1901) **Edge:** Reeded

Date	Mintage	F	VF	XF	Unc	BU
2002 Proof	100	Value: 1,100				

KM# 49 10 DOLLARS

28.2800 g., 0.9250 Silver with gold cameo 0.8410 oz. ASW, 38.6 mm. **Ruler:** Elizabeth II **Subject:** Golden Jubilee Monarchs **Obv:** Crowned head right **Obv. Designer:** Ian Rank-Broadley **Rev:** Queen Elizabeth II (1952-) **Edge:** Reeded

Date	Mintage	F	VF	XF	Unc	BU
2002 Proof	10,000	Value: 65.00				

KM# 49a 10 DOLLARS

39.9400 g., 0.9166 Gold 1.1770 oz. AGW, 38.6 mm. **Ruler:** Elizabeth II **Subject:** Golden Jubilee Monarchs **Obv:** Crowned head right **Obv. Designer:** Ian Rank-Broadley **Rev:** Queen Elizabeth II (1952-) **Edge:** Reeded

Date	Mintage	F	VF	XF	Unc	BU
2002 Proof	100	Value: 1,100				

EAST TIMOR

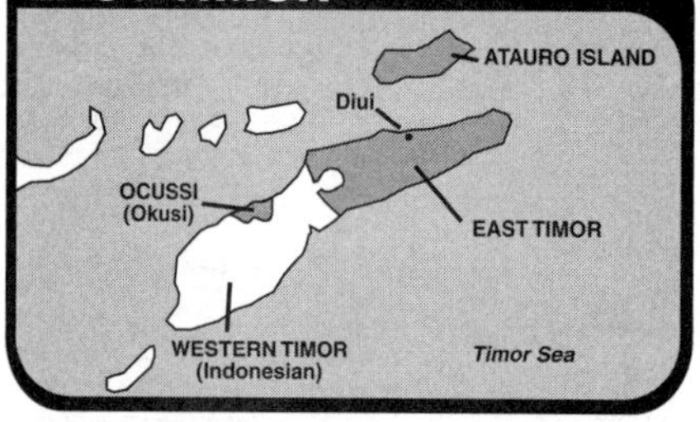

East Timor, population: 522,433, area: 7332 sq. miles, capital: Dili, is primarily located on the eastern half of the island of Timor, just northwest of Australia at the eastern end of the Indonesian archipelago. Formerly a Portuguese colony, Timor declared its independence from Portugal on November 28, 1975. After nine short days of fledgling autonomy, a guerilla faction sympathetic to the Indonesian territorial claim to East Timor seized the government. On July 17, 1976 the Provisional government enacted a law, which dissolved the free republic and made East Timor the 24th province of Indonesia. Violent rule and civil unrest plagued the province, with great loss of life and extreme damage to property and natural resources until independence was again achieved with United Nations assistance during a period from 1999 to 2002. Emerging as the Democratic Republic of Timor-Leste and commonly known as East Timor the country has worked, with international assistance to rebuild its decimated infrastructure. Natural resources waiting to be tapped include rich oil reserves, though current exports are most dependent on coffee, sandalwood and marble. The first coins of the new republic were issued in 2003.

DEMOCRATIC REPUBLIC OF TIMOR-LESTE

DECIMAL COINAGE

KM# 1 CENTAVO

3.1000 g., Nickel Clad Steel, 17 mm. **Obv:** Nautilus above date **Rev:** Denomination within circle **Edge:** Plain

Date	Mintage	F	VF	XF	Unc	BU
2003	1,500,000	—	—	—	1.50	2.50
2003 Proof	12,500	Value: 7.00				
2004	1,500,000	—	—	—	1.50	2.50

KM# 2 5 CENTAVOS

4.0500 g., Nickel Clad Steel, 18.8 mm. **Obv:** Rice plant above date **Rev:** Denomination within circle **Edge:** Plain

Date	Mintage	F	VF	XF	Unc	BU
2003	1,500,000	—	—	—	2.00	3.00
2003 Proof	12,500	Value: 9.00				
2004	1,500,000	—	—	—	2.00	3.00

KM# 3 10 CENTAVOS

5.1100 g., Nickel Clad Steel, 20.8 mm. **Obv:** Rooster left above date **Rev:** Denomination within circle **Edge:** Plain

Date	Mintage	F	VF	XF	Unc	BU
2003	2,500,000	—	—	—	2.50	4.00
2003 Proof	12,500	Value: 12.00				
2004	2,500,000	—	—	—	2.50	4.00

KM# 4 25 CENTAVOS

5.8700 g., Copper-Zinc-Nickel, 21.3 mm. **Obv:** Sail boat above date **Rev:** Denomination within circle **Edge:** Reeded

Date	Mintage	F	VF	XF	Unc	BU
2003	1,500,000	—	—	—	3.50	5.00
2003 Proof	12,500	Value: 15.00				
2004	1,500,000	—	—	—	3.50	5.00

KM# 5 50 CENTAVOS

6.5000 g., Copper-Zinc-Nickel, 25 mm. **Obv:** Coffee plant with beans above date **Rev:** Denomination within circle **Edge:** Reeded

Date	Mintage	F	VF	XF	Unc	BU
2003	1,000,000	—	—	—	5.00	7.00
2003 Proof	12,500	Value: 20.00				
2004	1,000,000	—	—	—	5.00	7.00

MINT SETS

KM#	Date	Mintage	Identification	Issue Price	Mkt Val
MS1	2003 (5)	25,000	KM#1 - KM#5	27.84	35.00

PROOF SETS

KM#	Date	Mintage	Identification	Issue Price	Mkt Val
PS1	2003 (5)	12,500	KM#1 - KM#5	57.25	65.00

ECUADOR

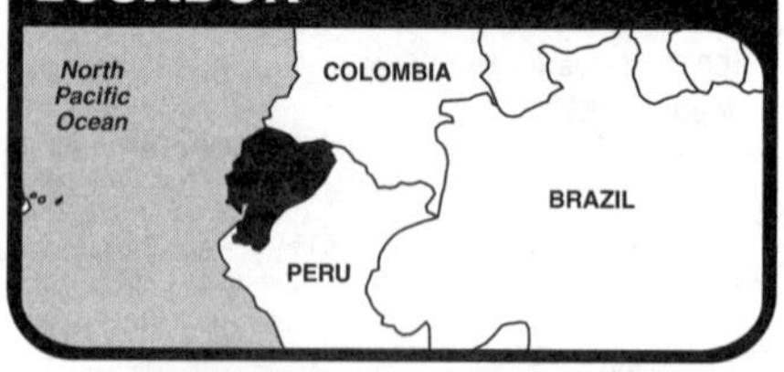

The Republic of Ecuador, located astride the equator on the Pacific Coast of South America, has an area of 105,037 sq. mi. (283,560 sq. km.) and a population of 10.9 million. Capital: Quito. Agriculture is the mainstay of the economy but there are appreciable deposits of minerals and petroleum. It is one of the world's largest exporters of bananas and balsa wood. Coffee, cacao, sugar and petroleum are also valuable exports.

REPUBLIC

DECIMAL COINAGE

10 Centavos = 1 Decimo; 10 Decimos = 1 Sucre;
25 Sucres = 1 Condor

KM# 115 SUCRE (Un)

8.3600 g., 0.9000 Gold 0.2419 oz. AGW, 22 mm. **Subject:** Homage to Jefferson Pérez Quezada **Obv:** National arms **Obv. Legend:** BANCO CENTRAL DEL ECUADOR **Rev:** 3/4 length figure of Perez running **Rev. Legend:** BICAMPEON MUNDIAL - CAMPEON OLIMPICO ATLANTA 1996

Date	Mintage	F	VF	XF	Unc	BU
2006	—	Value: 380				

KM# 112 25000 SUCRES
27.1000 g., 0.9250 Silver 0.8059 oz. ASW, 40 mm. **Subject:** IBERO-AMERICA Series **Obv:** Coats of arms **Rev:** Balsawood sailing raft **Edge:** Reeded

Date	Mintage	F	VF	XF	Unc	BU
2002 Proof	—	Value: 60.00				

KM# 113 25000 SUCRES
27.0000 g., 0.9250 Silver 0.8029 oz. ASW, 40 mm. **Obv:** National arms **Rev:** Capital building in Quito **Edge:** Reeded

Date	Mintage	F	VF	XF	Unc	BU
2004 Proof	1,000	Value: 50.00				

KM# 114 25000 SUCRES
27.2000 g., 0.9250 Silver 0.8089 oz. ASW, 40 mm. **Subject:** 2006 World Cup Soccer **Obv:** National arms **Rev:** Ecuadorian Soccer player torso holding a soccer ball **Edge:** Reeded

Date	Mintage	F	VF	XF	Unc	BU
ND(2006) Proof	—	Value: 40.00				

REFORM COINAGE

100 Centavos = 1 Dollar

KM# 104 CENTAVO (Un)
2.5200 g., Brass, 19 mm. **Obv:** Map of the Americas within circle **Rev:** Denomination **Edge:** Plain

Date	Mintage	F	VF	XF	Unc	BU
2003	—	—	—	—	0.20	0.40
2004	—	—	—	—	0.20	0.40

KM# 104a CENTAVO (Un)
2.4200 g., Copper Plated Steel, 19 mm. **Obv:** Map of the Americas **Rev:** Denomination **Edge:** Plain

Date	Mintage	F	VF	XF	Unc	BU
2003	—	—	—	—	0.30	0.50

EGYPT

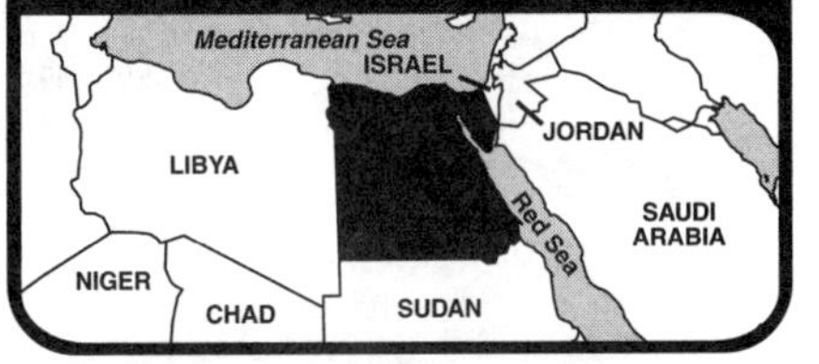

The Arab Republic of Egypt, located on the northeastern corner of Africa, has an area of 385,229 sq. mi. (1,1001,450 sq. km.) and a population of 62.4 million. Capital: Cairo. Although Egypt is an almost rainless expanse of desert, its economy is predominantly agricultural. Cotton, rice and petroleum are exported. Other main sources of income are revenues from the Suez Canal, remittances of Egyptian workers abroad and tourism.

ARAB REPUBLIC
AH1391- / 1971- AD

DECIMAL COINAGE

KM# 941 5 PIASTRES
1.9500 g., Brass, 18 mm. **Obv:** Denomination divides dates below, legend above **Rev:** Antique pottery vase **Edge:** Plain

Date	Mintage	F	VF	XF	Unc	BU
AH1425-2004	—	—	—	—	1.50	—

KM# 922 10 PIASTRES
4.5200 g., Copper-Nickel, 24.8 mm. **Subject:** National Women's Council **Obv:** Value **Rev:** Woman standing next to Sphinx **Edge:** Reeded

Date	Mintage	F	VF	XF	Unc	BU
AH1425-2004	—	—	—	—	1.50	—

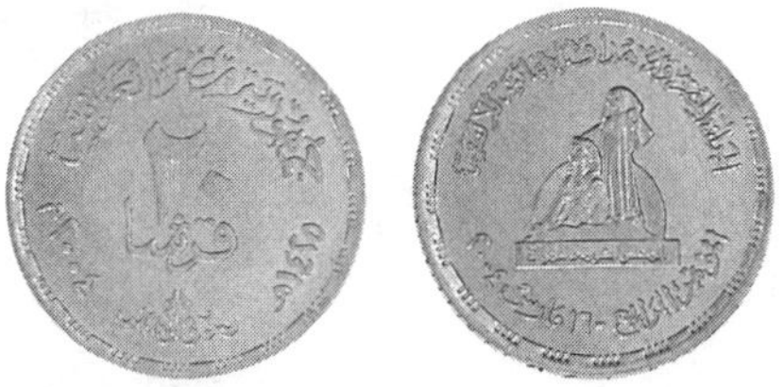

KM# 923 20 PIASTRES
6.0000 g., Copper-Nickel, 26.8 mm. **Subject:** National Women's Council **Obv:** Value **Rev:** Woman standing next to Sphinx **Edge:** Reeded

Date	Mintage	F	VF	XF	Unc	BU
AH1425-2004	—	—	—	—	2.50	—

KM# 939 50 PIASTRES
6.4400 g., Aluminum-Bronze, 24.8 mm. **Obv:** Value **Rev:** Cleopatra left **Edge:** Reeded

Date	Mintage	F	VF	XF	Unc	BU
AH1426-2005	—	—	—	—	2.00	—

KM# 942 50 PIASTRES
6.5000 g., Brass, 25 mm. **Rev:** Queen Cleopatra VII **Edge:** Milled

Date	Mintage	F	VF	XF	Unc	BU
AH1426-2005	—	—	—	—	—	—

KM# 903 1/2 POUND
4.0000 g., 0.8750 Gold 0.1125 oz. AGW, 18 mm. **Subject:** Egyptian Museum Centennial **Obv:** Value **Rev:** Building **Edge:** Reeded

Date	Mintage	F	VF	XF	Unc	BU
AH1423-2002	—	—	—	—	250	—

KM# 930 POUND
15.0000 g., 0.7200 Silver 0.3472 oz. ASW, 35 mm. **Subject:** National Women's Council **Obv:** Value **Rev:** Woman standing next to Sphinx **Edge:** Reeded

Date	Mintage	F	VF	XF	Unc	BU
AH1421-2001	600	—	—	—	45.00	—

KM# 936 POUND
8.0000 g., 0.8750 Gold 0.2250 oz. AGW, 24 mm. **Subject:** 50th Anniversary of Egyptian Revolution **Obv:** Value **Rev:** Soldier with flag, pyramids and radiant sun **Edge:** Reeded

Date	Mintage	F	VF	XF	Unc	BU
AH1423-2002	—	—	—	—	—	400

KM# 937 POUND
8.0000 g., 0.8750 Gold 0.2250 oz. AGW, 24 mm. **Subject:** 100th Anniversary of National Bank **Obv:** Value **Rev:** Flower through number 100 **Edge:** Reeded

Date	Mintage	F	VF	XF	Unc	BU
AH1423-2002	—	—	—	—	—	400

KM# 938 POUND
8.0000 g., 0.8750 Gold 0.2250 oz. AGW, 24 mm. **Subject:** Alexandria Library **Obv:** Cufic text in center **Rev:** Arched inscription above slanted library roof **Edge:** Reeded

Date	Mintage	F	VF	XF	Unc	BU
AH1423-2002	—	—	—	—	—	400

KM# 904 POUND
15.0000 g., 0.7200 Silver 0.3472 oz. ASW, 35 mm. **Subject:** Egyptian Museum Centennial **Obv:** Value **Rev:** Building, centennial numerals in background **Edge:** Reeded

Date	Mintage	F	VF	XF	Unc	BU
AH1423-2002	1,500	—	—	—	35.00	40.00

KM# 905 POUND
8.0000 g., 0.8750 Gold 0.2250 oz. AGW, 24 mm. **Subject:** Egyptian Museum Centennial **Obv:** Value **Rev:** Building, centennial numerals in background **Edge:** Reeded

Date	Mintage	F	VF	XF	Unc	BU
AH1423-2002	—	—	—	—	—	400

KM# 909 POUND
15.0000 g., 0.7200 Silver 0.3472 oz. ASW, 35 mm. **Subject:** International Ear, Nose and Throat Conference **Obv:** King Tut's Gold Mask **Rev:** "IFOS" on world map **Edge:** Reeded

Date	Mintage	F	VF	XF	Unc	BU
AH1423-2002	2,500	—	—	—	30.00	35.00

KM# 910 POUND
14.9400 g., 0.7200 Silver 0.3458 oz. ASW, 34.9 mm. **Subject:** 50th Anniversary of Egyptian Revolution **Obv:** Value **Rev:** Soldier with flag **Edge:** Reeded

Date	Mintage	F	VF	XF	Unc	BU
AH1423-2002	1,500	—	—	—	35.00	40.00

KM# 912 POUND
15.0000 g., 0.7200 Silver 0.3472 oz. ASW, 35 mm. **Obv:** Legend and inscription **Rev:** Inscribed arches above Alexandria library roof **Edge:** Reeded

Date	Mintage	F	VF	XF	Unc	BU
AH1423-2002	—	—	—	—	30.00	35.00

KM# 913 POUND
15.0000 g., 0.7200 Silver 0.3472 oz. ASW, 35 mm. **Subject:** Body Building Championships **Obv:** Arabic and English legends **Rev:** Mr. Universe cartoon **Edge:** Reeded

Date	Mintage	F	VF	XF	Unc	BU
AH1423-2002	800	—	—	—	30.00	35.00

KM# 915 POUND
15.0000 g., 0.7200 Silver 0.3472 oz. ASW, 35 mm. **Subject:** 30th Anniversary of the October War **Obv:** Value, dates and legend **Rev:** Soldier with flag above pyramids **Edge:** Reeded

Date	Mintage	F	VF	XF	Unc	BU
AH1424-2003	—	—	—	—	30.00	35.00

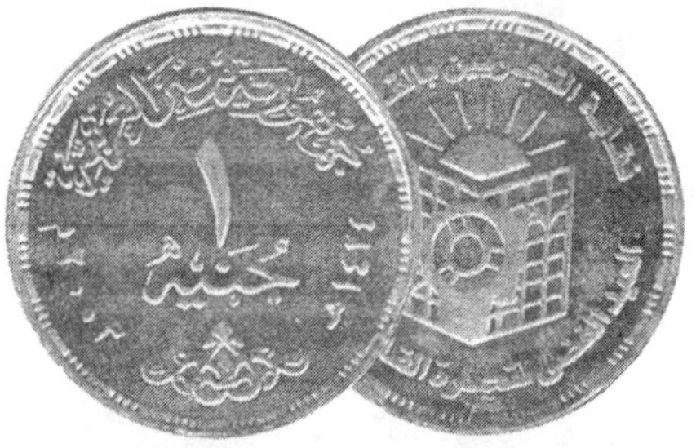

KM# 917 POUND
15.0000 g., 0.7200 Silver 0.3472 oz. ASW, 35 mm. **Subject:** 25th Anniversary of the Commerce Society **Obv:** Value, dates and legend **Rev:** Radiant sun above lattice work **Edge:** Reeded

Date	Mintage	F	VF	XF	Unc	BU
AH1424-2003	—	—	—	—	30.00	35.00

KM# 924 POUND
15.0000 g., 0.7200 Silver 0.3472 oz. ASW, 35 mm. **Obv:** Value **Rev:** Navy pilot's wings **Edge:** Reeded

Date	Mintage	F	VF	XF	Unc	BU
AH1425-2004	—	—	—	—	30.00	35.00

KM# 934 POUND
Silver, 35 mm. **Subject:** Golden Jubilee - Military Production Day

Date	Mintage	F	VF	XF	Unc	BU
AH1425-2004	—	—	—	—	30.00	35.00

KM# 940 POUND
8.5000 g., Bi-Metallic Brass center in Copper-Nickel ring, 25.1 mm. **Obv:** Value **Rev:** King Tut's gold mask **Edge:** Reeded

Date	Mintage	F	VF	XF	Unc	BU
AH1426-2005	—	—	—	—	3.00	5.00

KM# 943 POUND
8.5000 g., Bi-Metallic **Center Composition:** Brass, 25 mm. **Rev:** Tutankhamun's gold mask **Edge:** Milled

Date	Mintage	F	VF	XF	Unc	BU
AH1426-2005	—	—	—	—	—	—

KM# 931 5 POUNDS
17.5000 g., 0.7200 Silver 0.4051 oz. ASW, 37 mm. **Subject:** National Women's Council **Obv:** Value **Rev:** Woman standing next to Sphinx **Edge:** Reeded

Date	Mintage	F	VF	XF	Unc	BU
AH1421-2001	600	—	—	—	55.00	60.00

KM# 932 5 POUNDS
17.5000 g., 0.7200 Silver 0.4051 oz. ASW, 37 mm. **Subject:** 50th Anniversary of the National Police **Obv:** Value and police logo **Rev:** Ceremonial design **Edge:** Reeded

Date	Mintage	F	VF	XF	Unc	BU
AH1422-2002	—	—	—	—	45.00	50.00

KM# 906 5 POUNDS
17.5000 g., 0.7200 Silver 0.4051 oz. ASW, 37 mm. **Subject:** Egyptian Museum Centennial **Obv:** Value **Rev:** Building, centennial numerals in background **Edge:** Reeded

Date	Mintage	F	VF	XF	Unc	BU
AH1423-2002	1,500	—	—	—	40.00	45.00

KM# 907 5 POUNDS
26.0000 g., 0.8750 Gold 0.7314 oz. AGW, 33 mm. **Subject:** Egyptian Museum Centennial **Obv:** Value **Rev:** Building, centennial numerals in background **Edge:** Reeded

Date	Mintage	F	VF	XF	Unc	BU
AH1423-2002	—	—	—	—	650	675

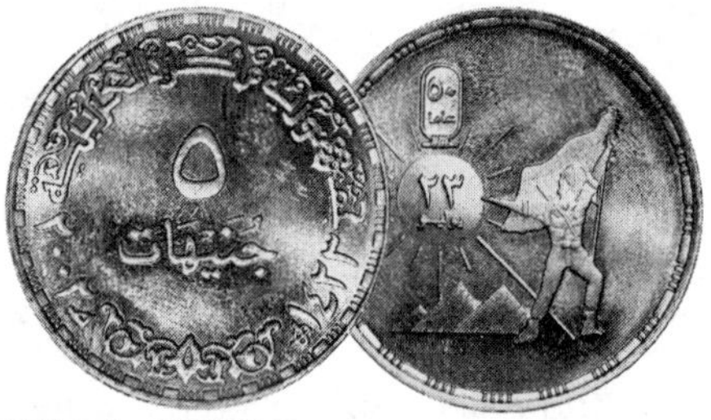

KM# 911 5 POUNDS
17.5500 g., 0.9250 Silver 0.5219 oz. ASW, 37 mm. **Subject:** 50th Anniversary of the Egyptian Revolution **Obv:** Value **Rev:** Soldier with flag **Edge:** Reeded

Date	Mintage	F	VF	XF	Unc	BU
AH1423-2002	1,500	—	—	—	40.00	45.00

KM# 914 5 POUNDS
17.5000 g., 0.7200 Silver 0.4051 oz. ASW, 37 mm. **Subject:** Body Building Championships **Obv:** Arabic and English legends **Rev:** Mr. Universe cartoon **Edge:** Reeded

Date	Mintage	F	VF	XF	Unc	BU
AH1423-2002	800	—	—	—	35.00	40.00

KM# 916 5 POUNDS
17.5000 g., 0.7200 Silver 0.4051 oz. ASW, 37 mm. **Subject:** 30th Anniversary of the October War **Obv:** Value and legend **Rev:** Soldier with flag above pyramids **Edge:** Reeded

Date	Mintage	F	VF	XF	Unc	BU
AH1424-2003	—	—	—	—	35.00	40.00

KM# 918 5 POUNDS
17.5000 g., 0.7200 Silver 0.4051 oz. ASW, 37 mm. **Obv:** Value and legend **Rev:** Geo-Physical Institute **Edge:** Reeded

Date	Mintage	F	VF	XF	Unc	BU
AH1424-2003	—	—	—	—	35.00	40.00

KM# 919 5 POUNDS
17.5000 g., 0.7200 Silver 0.4051 oz. ASW, 37 mm. **Subject:** 50th Anniversary of the Republic **Obv:** Value and legend **Rev:** Portrait and building **Edge:** Reeded

Date	Mintage	F	VF	XF	Unc	BU
AH1424-2003	—	—	—	—	35.00	40.00

KM# 920 5 POUNDS
17.5000 g., 0.7200 Silver 0.4051 oz. ASW, 37 mm. **Subject:** 25th Anniversary of the Delta Bank **Obv:** Value and legend **Rev:** Delta on world globe **Edge:** Reeded

Date	Mintage	F	VF	XF	Unc	BU
AH1424-2004	—	—	—	—	35.00	40.00

KM# 925 5 POUNDS
17.5000 g., 0.7200 Silver 0.4051 oz. ASW, 37 mm. **Obv:** Value **Rev:** Balance scale **Edge:** Reeded

Date	Mintage	F	VF	XF	Unc	BU
AH1425-2004	—	—	—	—	35.00	40.00

KM# 933 5 POUNDS
Silver, 37 mm. **Subject:** 90th Anniversary - Egyptian Scouts Organization - 1914-2004

Date	Mintage	F	VF	XF	Unc	BU
AH1425-2004	—	—	—	—	35.00	40.00

KM# 935 5 POUNDS
Silver, 37 mm. **Subject:** Golden Jubilee - Military Production Day

Date	Mintage	F	VF	XF	Unc	BU
AH1425-2004	—	—	—	—	35.00	40.00

KM# 908 10 POUNDS
40.0000 g., 0.8750 Gold 1.1252 oz. AGW, 37 mm. **Subject:** Egyptian Museum Centennial **Obv:** Denomination **Rev:** Building, centennial numerals in background **Edge:** Reeded

Date	Mintage	F	VF	XF	Unc	BU
AH1423-2002	—	—	—	—	1,100	1,150

EQUATORIAL GUINEA

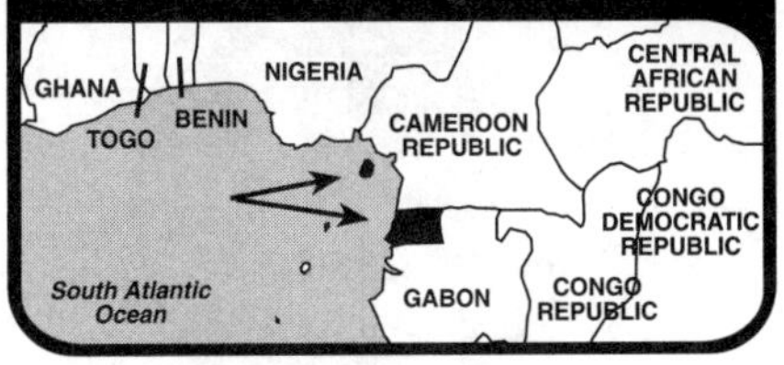

The Republic of Equatorial Guinea (formerly Spanish Guinea) consists of Rio Muni, located on the coast of West-Central Africa between Cameroon and Gabon, and the off-shore islands of Fernando Po, Annobon, Corisco, Elobey Grande and Elobey Chico. The equatorial country has an area of 10,831 sq. mi. (28,050 sq. km.) and a population of 420,293. Capital: Malabo. The economy is based on agriculture and forestry. Cacao, wood and coffee are exported.

MINT MARK
(a) - Paris, privy marks only

REPUBLIC

INSTITUT MONETAIRE

KM# 124 1500 CFA FRANCS-1 AFRICA
Nickel Plated Iron, 26 mm. **Obv:** Cowry shells **Rev:** Elephant head on full Africa map **Edge:** Plain

Date	Mintage	F	VF	XF	Unc	BU
2005	2,005	—	—	—	25.00	—

KM# 124a 1500 CFA FRANCS-1 AFRICA
0.9990 Silver, 26 mm. **Obv:** Cowry shells **Rev:** Elephant head on full Africa map

Date	Mintage	F	VF	XF	Unc	BU
2005	25	—	—	—	360	—

ESTONIA

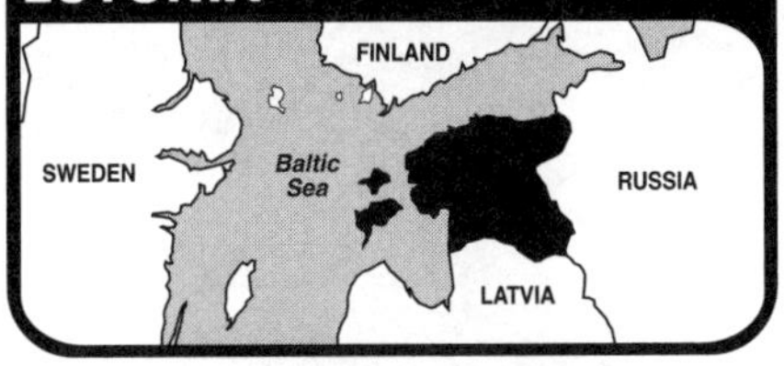

The Republic of Estonia (formerly the Estonian Soviet Socialist Republic of the U.S.S.R.) is the northernmost of the three Baltic States in Eastern Europe. It has an area of 17,462 sq. mi. (45,100 sq. km.) and a population of 1.6 million. Capital: Tallinn. Agriculture and dairy farming are the principal industries. Butter, eggs, bacon, timber and petroleum are exported.

MODERN REPUBLIC
1991 - present

STANDARD COINAGE

KM# 22 10 SENTI
1.8500 g., Copper-Aluminum-Nickel, 17.1 mm. **Obv:** Three Czech lions left divide date **Rev:** Denomination **Edge:** Plain

Date	Mintage	F	VF	XF	Unc	BU
2002	—	—	—	—	0.50	0.75
2006	—	—	—	—	0.50	0.75

KM# 23a 20 SENTI
2.0000 g., Nickel Plated Steel, 18.9 mm. **Obv:** Three Czech lions left divide date **Rev:** Denomination **Edge:** Plain

Date	Mintage	F	VF	XF	Unc	BU
2003	—	—	—	—	0.65	1.00
2004	—	—	—	—	0.65	1.00
2006	—	—	—	—	0.65	1.00

KM# 24 50 SENTI
2.9000 g., Brass, 19.5 mm. **Obv:** Three Czech lions left divide date **Rev:** Denomination **Edge:** Plain

Date	Mintage	F	VF	XF	Unc	BU
2004	—	—	—	—	1.00	1.25
2006	—	—	—	—	1.00	1.25

KM# 35 KROON
5.0000 g., Brass, 23.5 mm. **Obv:** Three Czech lions within shield divide date **Rev:** Large, thick denomination **Edge:** Three reeded and plain sections

Date	Mintage	F	VF	XF	Unc	BU
2001	—	—	—	—	1.50	1.75
2003	—	—	—	—	1.50	1.75

KM# 38 10 KROONI
28.2800 g., 0.9990 Silver 0.9083 oz. ASW, 38.6 mm. **Subject:** Tartu University **Obv:** National arms **Rev:** Building in oval, value at left **Edge:** Reeded

Date	Mintage	F	VF	XF	Unc	BU
2002 Proof	10,000	Value: 25.00				

KM# 40 10 KROONI
28.2800 g., 0.9990 Silver 0.9083 oz. ASW, 38.6 mm. **Subject:** Estonian Flag **Obv:** National arms **Rev:** Round multicolor flag design **Edge:** Reeded

Date	Mintage	F	VF	XF	Unc	BU
2004 Proof	10,000	Value: 25.00				

KM# 42 10 KROONI
28.2800 g., 0.9990 Silver 0.9083 oz. ASW, 38.6 mm. **Subject:** Torino Winter Olympics **Obv:** National arms **Rev:** Gold inset cross country skier in semi-circle above Olympic flame **Edge:** Reeded

Date	Mintage	F	VF	XF	Unc	BU
2006 Proof	5,000	Value: 42.50				

KM# 39 100 KROONI
7.7760 g., 0.9999 Gold 0.2500 oz. AGW **Subject:** Monetary Reform **Obv:** National arms **Rev:** Cross design **Edge:** Reeded

Date	Mintage	F	VF	XF	Unc	BU
2002	2,000	—	—	—	—	250

KM# 41 100 KROONI
7.7760 g., 0.9999 Gold 0.2500 oz. AGW, 21.9 mm. **Subject:** Olympic Games **Obv:** National arms **Rev:** Olympic flame above rings in center **Edge:** Reeded

Date	Mintage	F	VF	XF	Unc	BU
2004	5,000	—	—	—	—	225

KM# 43 100 KROONI
28.2800 g., 0.9990 Silver 0.9083 oz. ASW, 38.6 mm. **Subject:** National Opera **Obv:** National arms **Rev:** Building front **Edge:** Plain

Date	Mintage	F	VF	XF	Unc	BU
2006 Proof	10,000	Value: 42.50				

ETHIOPIA

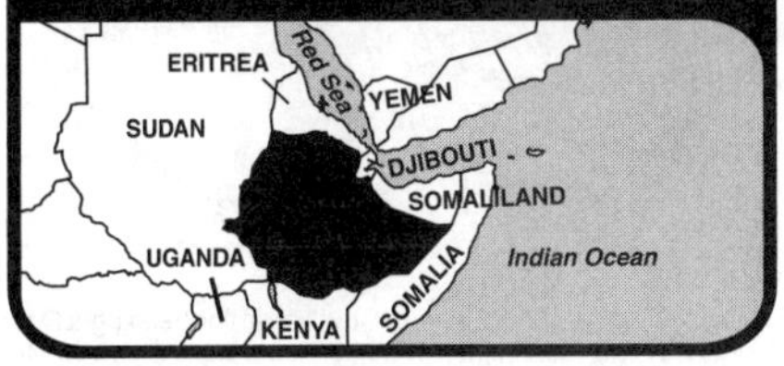

The People's Federal Republic of Ethiopia (formerly the Peoples Democratic Republic and the Empire of Ethiopia), Africa's oldest independent nation, faces the Red Sea in East-Central Africa. The country has an area of 424,214 sq. mi. (1,004,390 sq. km.) and a population of 56 million people who are divided among 40 tribes that speak some 270 languages and dialects. Capital: Addis Ababa. The economy is predominantly agricultural and pastoral. Gold and platinum are mined and petroleum fields are being developed. Coffee, oilseeds, hides and cereals are exported.

DATING

Ethiopian coinage is dated by the Ethiopian Era calendar (E.E.), which commenced 7 years and 8 months after the advent of A.D. dating.

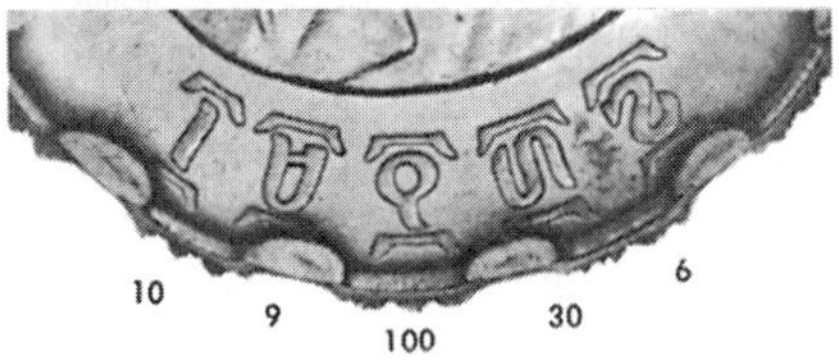

EXAMPLE
1900 (10 and 9 = 19 x 100)
36 (Add 30 and 6)
1936 E.E.
8 (Add)
1943/4 AD

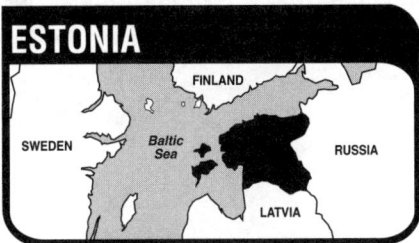

PEOPLES DEMOCRATIC REPUBLIC

We have two varieties for KM#43.1 to KM#46.1. One was minted at the British Royal Mint, the other at the Berlin Mint. The main difference is where the lion's chin whiskers end above the date (easiest to see on the 2nd, 3rd and 4th characters).

British Royal Mint

Berlin Mint

DECIMAL COINAGE

100 Santeems (Cents) = 1 Birr (Dollar)

100 Matonas = 100 Santeems

KM# 44.3 5 CENTS
3.0000 g., Copper-Zinc, 20 mm. **Obv:** Large lion head, right **Rev:** Denomination left of figure **Designer:** Stuart Devlin

Date	Mintage	F	VF	XF	Unc	BU
EE1996(2004)	—	—	—	—	—	1.00

KM# 45.3 10 CENTS
4.5000 g., Copper-Zinc, 23 mm. **Obv:** Large lion head right **Rev:** Mountain Nyala, denomination at right **Designer:** Stuart Devlin

Date	Mintage	F	VF	XF	Unc	BU
EE1996 (2004)	—	—	—	—	—	1.25

KM# 46.3 25 CENTS
3.7000 g., Copper-Nickel, 21.45 mm. **Obv:** Large lion head right **Rev:** Man and woman with arms raised divide denomination **Designer:** Stuart Devlin

Date	Mintage	F	VF	XF	Unc	BU
EE1996 (2004)	—	—	—	—	—	1.25

FALKLAND ISLANDS

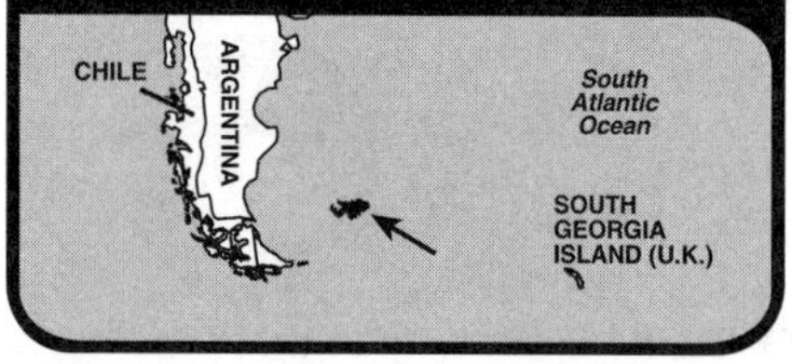

The Colony of the Falkland Islands and Dependencies, a British colony located in the South Atlantic about 500 miles north-east of Cape Horn, has an area of 4,700 sq. mi. (12,170 sq. km.) and a population of 2,121. East Falkland, West Falkland, South Georgia, and South Sandwich are the largest of the 200 islands. Capital: Stanley. Sheep grazing is the main industry. Wool, whale oil, and seal oil are exported.

RULER
British

MONETARY SYSTEM
100 Pence = 1 Pound

BRITISH COLONY

DECIMAL COINAGE

KM# 130 PENNY
Bronze **Ruler:** Elizabeth II **Obv:** Young bust right

Date	Mintage	F	VF	XF	Unc	BU
2004	—	—	—	—	0.50	0.75

KM# 131 2 PENCE
Bronze **Ruler:** Elizabeth II **Obv:** Young bust right

Date	Mintage	F	VF	XF	Unc	BU
2004	—	—	—	—	0.50	1.00

KM# 132 5 PENCE
Copper-Nickel **Ruler:** Elizabeth II **Obv:** Young bust right

Date	Mintage	F	VF	XF	Unc	BU
2004	—	—	—	—	0.75	1.00

KM# 133 10 PENCE
Copper-Nickel **Ruler:** Elizabeth II **Obv:** Young bust right

Date	Mintage	F	VF	XF	Unc	BU
2004	—	—	—	—	1.50	3.00

KM# 134 20 PENCE
Copper-Nickel **Ruler:** Elizabeth II **Obv:** Young bust right

Date	Mintage	F	VF	XF	Unc	BU
2004	—	—	—	—	2.00	4.00

KM# 70 50 PENCE
29.1000 g., Copper-Nickel, 38.6 mm. **Ruler:** Elizabeth II **Subject:** Centennial of Queen Victoria's Death **Obv:** Crowned bust right, denomination below **Obv. Designer:** Raphael Maklouf **Rev:** Crowned head left, three dates **Edge:** Reeded

Date	Mintage	F	VF	XF	Unc	BU
2001	—	—	—	—	6.00	7.00

KM# 70a 50 PENCE
28.2800 g., 0.9250 Silver 0.8410 oz. ASW, 38.6 mm. **Ruler:** Elizabeth II **Obv:** Crowned bust right, denomination below **Rev:** Crowned head left, three dates **Edge:** Reeded

Date	Mintage	F	VF	XF	Unc	BU
2001 Proof	10,000	Value: 50.00				

KM# 70b 50 PENCE
47.5400 g., 0.9166 Gold 1.4009 oz. AGW, 38.6 mm. **Ruler:** Elizabeth II **Subject:** Centennial of Queen Victoria's Death **Obv:** Crowned bust right, denomination below **Rev:** Victoria's crowned bust left, three dates **Edge:** Reeded

Date	Mintage	F	VF	XF	Unc	BU
2001 Proof	100	Value: 1,275				

KM# 71 50 PENCE
29.1000 g., Copper-Nickel, 38.6 mm. **Ruler:** Elizabeth II **Subject:** Queen Elizabeth's 75th Birthday **Obv:** Crowned bust right, denomination below **Obv. Designer:** Raphael Maklouf **Rev:** Bust of Queen Elizabeth II left **Edge:** Reeded

Date	Mintage	F	VF	XF	Unc	BU
2001	—	—	—	—	6.00	7.00

KM# 71b 50 PENCE
47.5400 g., 0.9160 Gold 1.4000 oz. AGW **Ruler:** Elizabeth II **Subject:** Queen Elizabeth's 75th Birthday **Obv:** Crowned bust right, denomination below **Rev:** Bust of Queen Elizabeth II left

Date	Mintage	F	VF	XF	Unc	BU
2001 Proof	Est. 100	Value: 1,275				

KM# 86 50 PENCE
28.2800 g., Copper-Nickel, 38.6 mm. **Ruler:** Elizabeth II **Obv:** Crowned bust right, denomination below **Rev:** Edward IV (1461-83) with Rose Ryal gold coin design **Rev. Designer:** Willem Vis **Edge:** Reeded

Date	Mintage	F	VF	XF	Unc	BU
2001	—	—	—	—	9.00	10.00

KM# 86a 50 PENCE
28.2800 g., 0.9250 Silver 0.8410 oz. ASW, 38.6 mm. **Ruler:** Elizabeth II **Obv:** Crowned bust right, denomination below **Rev:** Edward IV (1461-83) with gold-plated Rose Ryal gold coin design **Edge:** Reeded

Date	Mintage	F	VF	XF	Unc	BU
2001 Proof	5,000	Value: 50.00				

KM# 87 50 PENCE
28.2800 g., Copper-Nickel, 38.6 mm. **Ruler:** Elizabeth II **Obv:** Crowned bust right, denomination below **Rev:** Henry VII (1485-

1509) with 1489 Gold Sovereign coin design **Rev. Designer:** Willem Vis **Edge:** Reeded

Date	Mintage	F	VF	XF	Unc	BU
2001	—	—	—	—	9.00	10.00

KM# 87a 50 PENCE

28.2800 g., 0.9250 Silver 0.8410 oz. ASW, 38.6 mm. **Ruler:** Elizabeth II **Obv:** Crowned bust right, denomination below **Rev:** Henry VII (1485-1509) with gold-plated 1489 gold Sovereign coin design **Edge:** Reeded

Date	Mintage	F	VF	XF	Unc	BU
2001 Proof	5,000	Value: 50.00				

KM# 88 50 PENCE

28.2800 g., Copper-Nickel, 38.6 mm. **Ruler:** Elizabeth II **Obv:** Crowned bust right, denomination below **Rev:** Charles II (1660-85) with 1663 gold Guinea coin design **Rev. Designer:** Willem Vis **Edge:** Reeded

Date	Mintage	F	VF	XF	Unc	BU
2001	—	—	—	—	9.00	10.00

KM# 88a 50 PENCE

28.2800 g., 0.9250 Silver 0.8410 oz. ASW, 38.6 mm. **Ruler:** Elizabeth II **Obv:** Crowned bust right, denomination below **Rev:** Charles II (1660-85) with gold-plated Gold Guinea coin design **Edge:** Reeded

Date	Mintage	F	VF	XF	Unc	BU
2001 Proof	5,000	Value: 50.00				

KM# 89 50 PENCE

28.2800 g., Copper-Nickel, 38.6 mm. **Ruler:** Elizabeth II **Obv:** Crowned bust right, denomination below **Rev:** Queen Victoria with Gold Sovereign coin design **Rev. Designer:** Willem Vis **Edge:** Reeded

Date	Mintage	F	VF	XF	Unc	BU
2001	—	—	—	—	9.00	10.00

KM# 89a 50 PENCE

28.2800 g., 0.9250 Silver 0.8410 oz. ASW, 38.6 mm. **Ruler:** Elizabeth II **Obv:** Crowned bust right, denomination below **Rev:** Queen Victoria with gold-plated Gold Sovereign coin design **Edge:** Reeded

Date	Mintage	F	VF	XF	Unc	BU
2001 Proof	5,000	Value: 50.00				

KM# 73.1 50 PENCE

28.1300 g., Copper-Nickel, 38.6 mm. **Ruler:** Elizabeth II **Subject:** Queen's Golden Jubilee **Obv:** Crowned head right, denomination below **Rev:** Queen Elizabeth II on throne in inner circle below multicolor bunting **Edge:** Reeded

Date	Mintage	F	VF	XF	Unc	BU
2002(2001) Proof	—	Value: 8.00				

KM# 73.2 50 PENCE

Copper-Nickel **Ruler:** Elizabeth II **Subject:** Queen's Golden Jubilee **Obv:** Crowned bust right, denomination below **Rev:** With plain bunting

Date	Mintage	F	VF	XF	Unc	BU
2002	—	—	—	—	6.00	7.00

KM# 73a.1 50 PENCE

28.2800 g., 0.9250 Silver 0.8410 oz. ASW, 38.6 mm. **Ruler:** Elizabeth II **Subject:** Queen's Golden Jubilee **Obv:** Crowned bust right, denomination below **Rev:** Queen on throne below multicolor bunting **Edge:** Reeded

Date	Mintage	F	VF	XF	Unc	BU
2002 Proof	25,000	Value: 45.00				

KM# 73a.2 50 PENCE

Silver **Ruler:** Elizabeth II **Obv:** Crowned bust right, denomination below **Rev:** With plain bunting

Date	Mintage	F	VF	XF	Unc	BU
2002 Proof	—	Value: 45.00				

KM# 73b.1 50 PENCE

39.9400 g., 0.9166 Gold 1.1770 oz. AGW, 38.6 mm. **Ruler:** Elizabeth II **Obv:** Crowned bust right, denomination below **Rev:** Crowned queen with scepter and orb below multicolor bunting **Edge:** Reeded

Date	Mintage	F	VF	XF	Unc	BU
2002 Proof	150	Value: 1,100				

KM# 74.1 50 PENCE

28.1300 g., Copper-Nickel, 38.6 mm. **Ruler:** Elizabeth II **Subject:** Queen's Golden Jubilee **Obv:** Crowned bust right, denomination below **Obv. Designer:** Raphael Maklouf **Rev:** Queen on horse half left in inner circle below multicolor bunting **Edge:** Reeded

Date	Mintage	F	VF	XF	Unc	BU
2002(2001) Proof	—	Value: 8.00				

KM# 74.2 50 PENCE

Copper-Nickel **Ruler:** Elizabeth II **Subject:** Queen's Golden Jubilee **Obv:** Crowned bust right, denomination below **Rev:** With plain bunting

Date	Mintage	F	VF	XF	Unc	BU
2002	—	—	—	—	7.00	8.00

KM# 74a.1 50 PENCE

28.2800 g., 0.9250 Silver 0.8410 oz. ASW, 38.6 mm. **Ruler:** Elizabeth II **Subject:** Queen's Golden Jubilee **Obv:** Crowned bust right, denomination below **Rev. Designer:** Queen on horse below multicolor bunting **Edge:** Reeded

Date	Mintage	F	VF	XF	Unc	BU
2002 Proof	25,000	Value: 45.00				

KM# 74a.2 50 PENCE

0.9250 Silver **Ruler:** Elizabeth II **Subject:** Queen's Golden Jubilee **Obv:** Crowned bust right, denomination below **Rev:** With plain bunting

Date	Mintage	F	VF	XF	Unc	BU
2002 Proof	—	Value: 45.00				

KM# 74b.1 50 PENCE

39.9400 g., 0.9166 Gold 1.1770 oz. AGW, 38.6 mm. **Ruler:** Elizabeth II **Subject:** Queen's Golden Jubilee **Obv:** Crowned bust right, denomination below **Rev:** Queen on horseback below multicolored bunting **Edge:** Reeded

Date	Mintage	F	VF	XF	Unc	BU
2002 Proof	150	Value: 1,100				

KM# 74b.2 50 PENCE

Gold **Ruler:** Elizabeth II **Obv:** Crowned bust right, denomination below **Rev:** With plain bunting

Date	Mintage	F	VF	XF	Unc	BU
2002 Proof	—	Value: 1,100				

KM# 75.1 50 PENCE

28.1300 g., Copper-Nickel, 38.6 mm. **Ruler:** Elizabeth II **Subject:** Queen's Golden Jubilee **Obv:** Crowned bust right, denomination below **Rev:** Queen Elizabeth II talking into microphone below multicolor bunting **Edge:** Reeded

Date	Mintage	F	VF	XF	Unc	BU
2002(2001) Proof	—	Value: 8.00				

KM# 75.2 50 PENCE

Copper-Nickel **Ruler:** Elizabeth II **Subject:** Queen's Golden Jubilee **Obv:** Crowned bust right, denomination below **Rev:** With plain bunting

Date	Mintage	F	VF	XF	Unc	BU
2002	—	—	—	—	6.00	7.00

KM# 75a.1 50 PENCE

28.2800 g., 0.9250 Silver 0.8410 oz. ASW, 38.6 mm. **Ruler:** Elizabeth II **Subject:** Queen's Golden Jubilee **Obv:** Crowned bust right, denomination below **Rev:** Queen speaking into a radio microphone below multicolored bunting **Edge:** Reeded

Date	Mintage	F	VF	XF	Unc	BU
2002 Proof	25,000	Value: 45.00				

KM# 75a.2 50 PENCE

Silver **Ruler:** Elizabeth II **Subject:** Queen's Golden Jubilee **Obv:** Crowned bust right, denomination below **Rev:** With plain bunting

Date	Mintage	F	VF	XF	Unc	BU
2002 Proof	—	Value: 45.00				

KM# 75b.1 50 PENCE

39.9400 g., 0.9166 Gold 1.1770 oz. AGW, 38.6 mm. **Ruler:** Elizabeth II **Subject:** Queen's Golden Jubilee **Obv:** Crowned bust right, denomination below **Rev:** Elizabeth speaking into a radio microphone below multicolored bunting **Edge:** Reeded

Date	Mintage	F	VF	XF	Unc	BU
2002 Proof	50	Value: 1,100				

KM# 75b.2 50 PENCE

Gold **Ruler:** Elizabeth II **Subject:** Queen's Golden Jubilee **Obv:** Crowned bust right, denomination below **Rev:** With plain bunting

Date	Mintage	F	VF	XF	Unc	BU
2002 Proof	—	Value: 1,100				

KM# 76.1 50 PENCE

28.1300 g., Copper-Nickel, 38.6 mm. **Ruler:** Elizabeth II **Subject:** Queen's Golden Jubilee **Obv:** Crowned bust right, denomination below **Rev:** Queen walking to left in front of a crowd below multicolored bunting **Edge:** Reeded

Date	Mintage	F	VF	XF	Unc	BU
2002(2001) Proof	—	Value: 8.00				

KM# 76.2 50 PENCE

Copper-Nickel **Ruler:** Elizabeth II **Subject:** Queen's Golden Jubilee **Obv:** Crowned bust right, denomination below **Rev:** With plain bunting

Date	Mintage	F	VF	XF	Unc	BU
2002	—	—	—	—	6.00	7.00

KM# 76a.1 50 PENCE

28.2800 g., 0.9250 Silver 0.8410 oz. ASW, 38.6 mm. **Ruler:** Elizabeth II **Subject:** Queen's Golden Jubilee **Obv:** Crowned bust right, denomination below **Rev:** Queen standing before crowd below multicolored bunting **Edge:** Reeded

Date	Mintage	F	VF	XF	Unc	BU
2002 Proof	15,000	Value: 45.00				

KM# 76a.2 50 PENCE

Silver **Ruler:** Elizabeth II **Subject:** Queen's Golden Jubilee **Obv:** Crowned bust right, denomination below **Rev:** With plain bunting

Date	Mintage	F	VF	XF	Unc	BU
2002 Proof	—	Value: 45.00				

KM# 76b.1 50 PENCE

39.9400 g., 0.9166 Gold 1.1770 oz. AGW, 38.6 mm. **Ruler:** Elizabeth II **Subject:** Queen's Golden Jubilee **Obv:** Crowned bust right, denomination below **Rev:** Queen standing before a crowd below multicolored bunting **Edge:** Reeded

Date	Mintage	F	VF	XF	Unc	BU
2002 Proof	50	Value: 1,100				

KM# 76b.2 50 PENCE

Gold **Ruler:** Elizabeth II **Subject:** Queen's Golden Jubilee **Obv:** Crowned bust right, denomination below **Rev:** With plain bunting

Date	Mintage	F	VF	XF	Unc	BU
2002 Plain	—	Value: 1,100				

KM# 77.1 50 PENCE

28.1300 g., Copper-Nickel, 38.6 mm. **Ruler:** Elizabeth II **Subject:** Queen's Golden Jubilee **Obv:** Crowned bust right, denomination below **Obv. Designer:** Raphael Maklouf **Rev:** Conjoined busts of Queen Elizabeth, Prince Charles, Prince William facing left in inner circle below multicolor bunting **Edge:** Reeded

Date	Mintage	F	VF	XF	Unc	BU
2002(2001) Proof	—	Value: 8.00				

KM# 77.2 50 PENCE

Copper-Nickel **Ruler:** Elizabeth II **Subject:** Queen's Golden Jubilee **Obv:** Crowned bust right, denomination below **Rev:** With plain bunting

Date	Mintage	F	VF	XF	Unc	BU
2002	—	—	—	—	6.00	7.00

KM# 77a.1 50 PENCE

28.2800 g., 0.9250 Silver 0.8410 oz. ASW, 38.6 mm. **Ruler:** Elizabeth II **Subject:** Queen's Golden Jubilee **Obv:** Crowned bust right, denomination below **Rev:** Queen, Crown Prince and Prince William below multicolor bunting **Edge:** Reeded

Date	Mintage	F	VF	XF	Unc	BU
2002 Proof	15,000	Value: 45.00				

KM# 77a.2 50 PENCE

Silver **Ruler:** Elizabeth II **Subject:** Queen's Golden Jubilee **Obv:** Crowned bust right, denomination below **Rev:** With plain bunting

Date	Mintage	F	VF	XF	Unc	BU
2002 Proof	—	Value: 45.00				

KM# 77b.1 50 PENCE

39.9400 g., 0.9166 Gold 1.1770 oz. AGW, 38.6 mm. **Ruler:** Elizabeth II **Subject:** Queen's Golden Jubilee **Obv:** Crowned bust right, denomination below **Rev:** Elizabeth II, Prince Charles and his son William below multicolored bunting **Edge:** Reeded

Date	Mintage	F	VF	XF	Unc	BU
2002 Proof	50	Value: 1,100				

KM# 77b.2 50 PENCE

Gold **Ruler:** Elizabeth II **Obv:** Crowned bust right, denomination below **Rev:** With plain bunting

Date	Mintage	F	VF	XF	Unc	BU
2002 Proof	—	Value: 1,100				

KM# 78.1 50 PENCE

28.1300 g., Copper-Nickel, 38.6 mm. **Ruler:** Elizabeth II **Subject:** Queen's Golden Jubilee **Obv:** Crowned bust right, denomination below **Rev:** Royal coach below multicolor bunting **Edge:** Reeded

Date	Mintage	F	VF	XF	Unc	BU
2002 Proof	—	Value: 8.00				

KM# 78.2 50 PENCE

Copper-Nickel **Ruler:** Elizabeth II **Subject:** Queen's Golden Jubilee **Obv:** Crowned bust right, denomination below **Rev:** With plain bunting

Date	Mintage	F	VF	XF	Unc	BU
2002	—	—	—	—	6.00	7.00

KM# 78a.1 50 PENCE

28.2800 g., 0.9250 Silver 0.8410 oz. ASW, 38.6 mm. **Ruler:** Elizabeth II **Subject:** Queen's Golden Jubilee **Obv:** Crowned bust right, denomination below **Rev:** Coronation coach below multicolor bunting **Edge:** Reeded

Date	Mintage	F	VF	XF	Unc	BU
2002 Proof	15,000	Value: 45.00				

KM# 78a.2 50 PENCE

Gold **Ruler:** Elizabeth II **Subject:** Queen's Golden Jubilee **Obv:** Crowned bust right, denomination below **Rev:** With plain bunting

Date	Mintage	F	VF	XF	Unc	BU
2002 Proof	—	Value: 1,100				

KM# 78b.1 50 PENCE

39.9400 g., 0.9166 Gold 1.1770 oz. AGW, 38.6 mm. **Ruler:** Elizabeth II **Subject:** Queen's Golden Jubilee **Obv:** Crowned bust right, denomination below **Rev:** Coronation coach below multicolor bunting **Edge:** Reeded

Date	Mintage	F	VF	XF	Unc	BU
2002 Proof	150	Value: 1,100				

KM# 78b.2 50 PENCE

Gold **Ruler:** Elizabeth II **Subject:** Queen's Golden Jubilee **Obv:** Crowned bust right, denomination below **Rev:** With plain bunting

Date	Mintage	F	VF	XF	Unc	BU
2002 Proof	—	Value: 1,100				

KM# 79.1 50 PENCE

28.1300 g., Copper-Nickel, 38.6 mm. **Ruler:** Elizabeth II **Subject:** Queen's Golden Jubilee **Obv:** Crowned bust right, denomination below **Rev:** Scepter and orb below multicolor bunting **Edge:** Reeded

Date	Mintage	F	VF	XF	Unc	BU
2002 Proof	—	Value: 8.00				

KM# 79.2 50 PENCE

Copper-Nickel **Ruler:** Elizabeth II **Subject:** Queen's Golden Jubilee **Obv:** Crowned bust right, denomination below **Rev:** With plain bunting

Date	Mintage	F	VF	XF	Unc	BU
2002	—	—	—	—	6.00	7.00

KM# 79a.1 50 PENCE

28.2800 g., 0.9250 Silver 0.8410 oz. ASW, 38.6 mm. **Ruler:** Elizabeth II **Subject:** Queen's Golden Jubilee **Obv:** Crowned bust right, denomination below **Rev:** Orb and scepter below multicolor bunting **Edge:** Reeded

Date	Mintage	F	VF	XF	Unc	BU
2002 Proof	15,000	Value: 45.00				

KM# 79a.2 50 PENCE

Silver **Ruler:** Elizabeth II **Subject:** Queen's Golden Jubilee **Obv:** Crowned bust right, denomination below **Rev:** With plain bunting

Date	Mintage	F	VF	XF	Unc	BU
2002 Proof	—	Value: 45.00				

KM# 79b.1 50 PENCE

39.9400 g., 0.9166 Gold 1.1770 oz. AGW, 38.6 mm. **Ruler:** Elizabeth II **Subject:** Queen's Golden Jubilee **Obv:** Crowned bust right, denomination below **Rev:** Orb and scepter below multicolor bunting **Edge:** Reeded

Date	Mintage	F	VF	XF	Unc	BU
2002 Proof	150	Value: 1,100				

KM# 79b.2 50 PENCE

Gold **Ruler:** Elizabeth II **Subject:** Queen's Golden Jubilee **Obv:** Crowned bust right, denomination below **Rev:** With plain bunting

Date	Mintage	F	VF	XF	Unc	BU
2002 Proof	—	Value: 1,100				

KM# 80.1 50 PENCE

28.1300 g., Copper-Nickel, 38.6 mm. **Ruler:** Elizabeth II **Subject:** Queen's Golden Jubilee **Obv:** Crowned bust right, denomination below **Obv. Designer:** Raphael Maklouf **Rev:** Crown below multicolor bunting **Edge:** Reeded

Date	Mintage	F	VF	XF	Unc	BU
2002 Proof	—	Value: 8.00				

KM# 80.2 50 PENCE

Copper-Nickel **Ruler:** Elizabeth II **Subject:** Queen's Golden Jubilee **Obv:** Crowned bust right, denomination below **Rev:** With plain bunting

Date	Mintage	F	VF	XF	Unc	BU
2002	—	—	—	—	6.00	7.00

KM# 80a.1 50 PENCE

28.2800 g., 0.9250 Silver 0.8410 oz. ASW, 38.6 mm. **Ruler:** Elizabeth II **Subject:** Queen's Golden Jubilee **Obv:** Crowned bust right, denomination below **Rev:** Crown below multicolor bunting **Edge:** Reeded

Date	Mintage	F	VF	XF	Unc	BU
2002 Proof	15,000	Value: 45.00				

KM# 80a.2 50 PENCE

Silver **Ruler:** Elizabeth II **Subject:** Queen's Golden Jubilee **Obv:** Crowned bust right, denomination below **Rev:** With plain bunting

Date	Mintage	F	VF	XF	Unc	BU
2002 Proof	—	Value: 45.00				

KM# 80b.1 50 PENCE

39.9400 g., 0.9166 Gold 1.1770 oz. AGW, 38.6 mm. **Ruler:** Elizabeth II **Subject:** Queen's Golden Jubilee **Obv:** Crowned bust right, denomination below **Rev:** Crown below multicolor bunting **Edge:** Reeded

Date	Mintage	F	VF	XF	Unc	BU
2002 Proof	150	Value: 1,100				

KM# 80b.2 50 PENCE

Gold **Ruler:** Elizabeth II **Subject:** Queen's Golden Jubilee **Obv:** Crowned bust right, denomination below **Rev:** With plain bunting

Date	Mintage	F	VF	XF	Unc	BU
2002 Proof	—	Value: 1,100				

KM# 81.1 50 PENCE

28.1300 g., Copper-Nickel, 38.6 mm. **Ruler:** Elizabeth II **Subject:** Queen's Golden Jubilee **Obv:** Crowned bust right, denomination below **Rev:** Throne below multicolor bunting **Edge:** Reeded

Date	Mintage	F	VF	XF	Unc	BU
2002 Proof	—	Value: 8.00				

KM# 81.2 50 PENCE

Copper-Nickel **Ruler:** Elizabeth II **Subject:** Queen's Golden Jubilee **Obv:** Crowned bust right, denomination below **Rev:** With plain bunting

Date	Mintage	F	VF	XF	Unc	BU
2002	—	—	—	—	6.00	7.00

KM# 81a.1 50 PENCE

28.2800 g., 0.9250 Silver 0.8410 oz. ASW, 38.6 mm. **Ruler:** Elizabeth II **Subject:** Queen's Golden Jubilee **Obv:** Crowned bust right, denomination below **Rev:** Coronation throne below multicolor bunting **Edge:** Reeded

Date	Mintage	F	VF	XF	Unc	BU
2002 Proof	15,000	Value: 45.00				

KM# 81a.2 50 PENCE

Silver **Ruler:** Elizabeth II **Subject:** Queen's Golden Jubilee **Obv:** Crowned bust right, denomination below **Rev:** With plain bunting

Date	Mintage	F	VF	XF	Unc	BU
2002 Proof	—	Value: 45.00				

KM# 81b.1 50 PENCE

39.9400 g., 0.9166 Gold 1.1770 oz. AGW, 38.6 mm. **Ruler:** Elizabeth II **Subject:** Queen's Golden Jubilee **Obv:** Crowned bust right, denomination below **Rev:** Coronation Throne below multicolored bunting **Edge:** Reeded

Date	Mintage	F	VF	XF	Unc	BU
2002 Proof	150	Value: 1,100				

KM# 81b.2 50 PENCE

Gold **Ruler:** Elizabeth II **Obv:** Crowned bust right, denomination below **Rev:** With plain bunting

Date	Mintage	F	VF	XF	Unc	BU
2002 Proof	—	Value: 1,100				

KM# 82.1 50 PENCE

28.1300 g., Copper-Nickel, 38.6 mm. **Ruler:** Elizabeth II **Subject:** Queen's Golden Jubilee **Obv:** Crowned bust right, denomination below **Rev:** Queen on throne below multicolor bunting **Edge:** Reeded

Date	Mintage	F	VF	XF	Unc	BU
2002 Proof	—	—	—	—	6.00	7.00

KM# 82.2 50 PENCE

Copper-Nickel **Ruler:** Elizabeth II **Subject:** Queen's Golden Jubilee **Obv:** Crowned bust right, denomination below **Rev:** With plain bunting

Date	Mintage	F	VF	XF	Unc	BU
2002	—	—	—	—	6.00	7.00

KM# 82a.1 50 PENCE

28.2800 g., 0.9250 Silver 0.8410 oz. ASW, 38.6 mm. **Ruler:** Elizabeth II **Subject:** Queen's Golden Jubilee **Obv:** Crowned bust right, denomination below **Rev:** Queen on throne below multicolor bunting **Edge:** Reeded

Date	Mintage	F	VF	XF	Unc	BU
2002 Proof	15,000	Value: 45.00				

KM# 82a.2 50 PENCE

Silver **Ruler:** Elizabeth II **Subject:** Queen's Golden Jubilee **Obv:** Crowned bust right, denomination below **Rev:** With plain bunting

Date	Mintage	F	VF	XF	Unc	BU
2002 Proof	—	Value: 45.00				

KM# 82b.1 50 PENCE

39.9400 g., 0.9166 Gold 1.1770 oz. AGW, 38.6 mm. **Ruler:** Elizabeth II **Subject:** Queen's Golden Jubilee **Obv:** Crowned bust right, denomination below **Rev:** Queen seated on throne below multicolor bunting **Edge:** Reeded

Date	Mintage	F	VF	XF	Unc	BU
2002 Proof	50	Value: 1,100				

KM# 82b.2 50 PENCE

Gold **Ruler:** Elizabeth II **Subject:** Queen's Golden Jubilee **Obv:** Crowned bust right, denomination below **Rev:** With plain bunting

Date	Mintage	F	VF	XF	Unc	BU
2002 Proof	—	Value: 1,100				

KM# 83.1 50 PENCE

28.1300 g., Copper-Nickel, 38.6 mm. **Ruler:** Elizabeth II **Subject:** Queen's Golden Jubilee **Obv:** Crowned bust right, denomination below **Obv. Designer:** Raphael Maklouf **Rev:** Queen and young family below multicolor bunting **Edge:** Reeded

Date	Mintage	F	VF	XF	Unc	BU
2002 Proof	—	—	—	—	6.00	7.00

KM# 83.2 50 PENCE

Gold **Ruler:** Elizabeth II **Subject:** Queen's Golden Jubilee **Obv:** Crowned bust right, denomination below **Rev:** With plain bunting

Date	Mintage	F	VF	XF	Unc	BU
2002 Proof	—	Value: 1,100				

KM# 83a.1 50 PENCE

28.2800 g., 0.9250 Silver 0.8410 oz. ASW, 38.6 mm. **Ruler:** Elizabeth II **Subject:** Queen's Golden Jubilee **Obv:** Crowned bust right, denomination below **Rev:** Royal family below multicolor bunting **Edge:** Reeded

Date	Mintage	F	VF	XF	Unc	BU
2002 Proof	15,000	Value: 45.00				

KM# 83a.2 50 PENCE

Silver **Ruler:** Elizabeth II **Subject:** Queen's Golden Jubilee **Obv:** Crowned bust right, denomination below **Rev:** With plain bunting

Date	Mintage	F	VF	XF	Unc	BU
2002 Proof	—	Value: 45.00				

KM# 83b.1 50 PENCE

39.9400 g., 0.9166 Gold 1.1770 oz. AGW, 38.6 mm. **Ruler:** Elizabeth II **Subject:** Queen's Golden Jubilee **Obv:** Crowned bust right, denomination below **Rev:** Royal Family below multicolor bunting **Edge:** Reeded

Date	Mintage	F	VF	XF	Unc	BU
2002 Proof	50	Value: 1,100				

KM# 83b.2 50 PENCE

Gold **Ruler:** Elizabeth II **Subject:** Queen's Golden Jubilee **Obv:** Crowned bust right, denomination below **Rev:** With plain bunting

Date	Mintage	F	VF	XF	Unc	BU
2002 Proof	—	Value: 1,100				

KM# 84.1 50 PENCE

28.1300 g., Copper-Nickel, 38.6 mm. **Ruler:** Elizabeth II **Subject:** Queen's Golden Jubilee **Obv:** Crowned bust right, denomination below **Rev:** Queens head and tree house below multicolor bunting **Edge:** Reeded

Date	Mintage	F	VF	XF	Unc	BU
2002 Proof	—	Value: 8.00				

KM# 84.2 50 PENCE

Copper-Nickel **Ruler:** Elizabeth II **Subject:** Queen's Golden Jubilee **Obv:** Crowned bust right, denomination below **Rev:** With plain bunting

Date	Mintage	F	VF	XF	Unc	BU
2002	—	—	—	—	6.00	7.00

KM# 84a.1 50 PENCE
28.2800 g., 0.9250 Silver 0.8410 oz. ASW, 38.6 mm. **Ruler:** Elizabeth II **Subject:** Queen's Golden Jubilee **Obv:** Crowned bust right, denomination below **Rev:** Queen and tree house below multicolor bunting **Edge:** Reeded

Date	Mintage	F	VF	XF	Unc	BU
2002 Proof	25,000	Value: 45.00				

KM# 84a.2 50 PENCE
Silver **Ruler:** Elizabeth II **Subject:** Queen's Golden Jubilee **Obv:** Crowned bust right, denomination below **Rev:** With plain bunting

Date	Mintage	F	VF	XF	Unc	BU
2002 Proof	—	Value: 45.00				

KM# 84b.1 50 PENCE
39.9400 g., 0.9166 Gold 1.1770 oz. AGW, 38.6 mm. **Ruler:** Elizabeth II **Subject:** Queen's Golden Jubilee **Obv:** Crowned bust right, denomination below **Rev:** Queen and tree house below multicolor bunting **Edge:** Reeded

Date	Mintage	F	VF	XF	Unc	BU
2002 Proof	50	Value: 1,100				

KM# 84b.2 50 PENCE
Gold **Ruler:** Elizabeth II **Subject:** Queen's Golden Jubilee **Obv:** Crowned bust right, denomination below **Rev:** With plain bunting

Date	Mintage	F	VF	XF	Unc	BU
2002 Proof	—	Value: 1,100				

KM# 90 50 PENCE
28.2800 g., Copper-Nickel, 38.6 mm. **Ruler:** Elizabeth II **Obv:** Crowned bust right, denomination below **Rev:** Conjoined busts of Elizabeth and Philip below multicolor bunting **Edge:** Reeded

Date	Mintage	F	VF	XF	Unc	BU
2002	—	—	—	—	6.00	7.00

KM# 90a.1 50 PENCE
28.2800 g., 0.9250 Silver 0.8410 oz. ASW, 38.6 mm. **Ruler:** Elizabeth II **Obv:** Crowned bust right, denomination below **Rev:** Elizabeth and Philip below multicolor bunting **Edge:** Reeded

Date	Mintage	F	VF	XF	Unc	BU
2002 Proof	15,000	Value: 45.00				

KM# 90a.2 50 PENCE
28.2800 g., 0.9250 Silver 0.8410 oz. ASW, 38.6 mm. **Ruler:** Elizabeth II **Obv:** Crowned bust right, denomination below **Rev:** With plain bunting

Date	Mintage	F	VF	XF	Unc	BU
2002 Proof	—	Value: 45.00				

KM# 90b.1 50 PENCE
39.9400 g., 0.9160 Gold 1.1762 oz. AGW, 38.6 mm. **Ruler:** Elizabeth II **Obv:** Crowned bust right, denomination below **Rev:** Elizabeth and Philip below multicolor bunting **Edge:** Reeded

Date	Mintage	F	VF	XF	Unc	BU
2002 Proof	50	Value: 1,100				

KM# 90b.2 50 PENCE
39.9400 g., 0.9160 Gold 1.1762 oz. AGW, 38.6 mm. **Ruler:** Elizabeth II **Obv:** Crowned bust right, denomination below **Rev:** With plain bunting **Edge:** Reeded

Date	Mintage	F	VF	XF	Unc	BU
2002 Proof	—	Value: 1,100				

KM# 91 50 PENCE
28.2800 g., Copper-Nickel, 38.6 mm. **Ruler:** Elizabeth II **Obv:** Crowned bust right, denomination below **Rev:** Queen and Aborigine dancers below multicolor bunting **Edge:** Reeded

Date	Mintage	F	VF	XF	Unc	BU
2002	—	—	—	—	6.00	7.00

KM# 91a.1 50 PENCE
28.2800 g., 0.9250 Silver 0.8410 oz. ASW, 38.6 mm. **Ruler:** Elizabeth II **Obv:** Crowned bust right, denomination below **Rev:** Queen and Aborigine dancers below multicolor bunting **Edge:** Reeded

Date	Mintage	F	VF	XF	Unc	BU
2002 Proof	15,000	Value: 45.00				

KM# 91a.2 50 PENCE
28.2800 g., 0.9250 Silver 0.8410 oz. ASW, 38.6 mm. **Ruler:** Elizabeth II **Obv:** Crowned bust right, denomination below **Rev:** With plain bunting **Edge:** Reeded

Date	Mintage	F	VF	XF	Unc	BU
2002 Proof	—	Value: 45.00				

KM# 91b.1 50 PENCE
28.2800 g., 0.9160 Gold 0.8328 oz. AGW, 38.6 mm. **Ruler:** Elizabeth II **Obv:** Crowned bust right, denomination below **Rev:** Queen and Aborigine dancers below multicolor bunting **Edge:** Reeded

Date	Mintage	F	VF	XF	Unc	BU
2002 Proof	50	Value: 1,100				

KM# 91b.2 50 PENCE
39.9400 g., 0.9160 Gold 1.1762 oz. AGW, 38.6 mm. **Ruler:** Elizabeth II **Obv:** Crowned bust right, denomination below **Rev:** With plain bunting **Edge:** Reeded

Date	Mintage	F	VF	XF	Unc	BU
2002 Proof	—	Value: 1,100				

KM# 92 50 PENCE
28.2800 g., Copper-Nickel, 38.6 mm. **Ruler:** Elizabeth II **Obv:** Crowned bust right, denomination below **Rev:** Queen and St. Paul's Cathedral dome below multicolor bunting **Edge:** Reeded

Date	Mintage	F	VF	XF	Unc	BU
2002	—	—	—	—	6.00	7.00

KM# 92a.1 50 PENCE
28.2800 g., 0.9250 Silver 0.8410 oz. ASW, 38.6 mm. **Ruler:** Elizabeth II **Obv:** Crowned bust right, denomination below **Rev:** Queen and St. Paul's Cathedral dome below multicolor bunting **Edge:** Reeded

Date	Mintage	F	VF	XF	Unc	BU
2002 Proof	15,000	Value: 45.00				

KM# 92a.2 50 PENCE
28.2800 g., 0.9250 Silver 0.8410 oz. ASW, 38.6 mm. **Ruler:** Elizabeth II **Obv:** Crowned bust right, denomination below **Rev:** With plain bunting **Edge:** Reeded

Date	Mintage	F	VF	XF	Unc	BU
2002 Proof	—	Value: 45.00				

KM# 92b.1 50 PENCE
39.9400 g., 0.9160 Gold 1.1762 oz. AGW, 38.6 mm. **Ruler:** Elizabeth II **Obv:** Crowned bust right, denomination below **Rev:** Queen and St. Paul's Cathedral dome below multicolor bunting **Edge:** Reeded

Date	Mintage	F	VF	XF	Unc	BU
2002 Proof	50	Value: 1,100				

KM# 92b.2 50 PENCE
39.9400 g., 0.9160 Gold 1.1762 oz. AGW, 38.6 mm. **Ruler:** Elizabeth II **Obv:** Crowned bust right, denomination below **Rev:** With plain bunting **Edge:** Reeded

Date	Mintage	F	VF	XF	Unc	BU
2002 Proof	—	Value: 1,100				

KM# 93 50 PENCE
28.2800 g., Copper-Nickel, 38.6 mm. **Ruler:** Elizabeth II **Obv:** Crowned bust right, denomination below **Rev:** Elizabeth and Philip in coronation coach below multicolor bunting **Edge:** Reeded

Date	Mintage	F	VF	XF	Unc	BU
2002	—	—	—	—	6.00	7.00

KM# 93a.1 50 PENCE
28.2800 g., 0.9250 Silver 0.8410 oz. ASW, 38.6 mm. **Ruler:** Elizabeth II **Obv:** Crowned bust right, denomination below **Rev:** Elizabeth and Philip in coronation coach below multicolor bunting **Edge:** Reeded

Date	Mintage	F	VF	XF	Unc	BU
2002 Proof	15,000	Value: 45.00				

KM# 93a.2 50 PENCE
28.2800 g., 0.9250 Silver 0.8410 oz. ASW, 38.6 mm. **Ruler:** Elizabeth II **Obv:** Crowned bust right, denomination below **Rev:** With plain bunting **Edge:** Reeded

Date	Mintage	F	VF	XF	Unc	BU
2002 Proof	—	Value: 45.00				

KM# 93b.1 50 PENCE
39.9400 g., 0.9160 Gold 1.1762 oz. AGW, 38.6 mm. **Ruler:** Elizabeth II **Obv:** Crowned bust right, denomination below **Rev:** Elizabeth and Philip in coronation coach below multicolor bunting **Edge:** Reeded

Date	Mintage	F	VF	XF	Unc	BU
2002 Proof	50	Value: 1,100				

KM# 93b.2 50 PENCE
39.9400 g., 0.9160 Gold 1.1762 oz. AGW, 38.6 mm. **Ruler:** Elizabeth II **Obv:** Crowned bust right, denomination below **Rev:** With plain bunting **Edge:** Reeded

Date	Mintage	F	VF	XF	Unc	BU
2002 Proof	—	Value: 1,100				

KM# 94 50 PENCE
28.2800 g., Copper-Nickel, 38.6 mm. **Ruler:** Elizabeth II **Obv:** Crowned bust right, denomination below **Rev:** Elizabeth and Prince Charles at flower show below multicolor bunting **Edge:** Reeded

Date	Mintage	F	VF	XF	Unc	BU
2002	—	—	—	—	6.00	7.00

KM# 94a.1 50 PENCE
28.2800 g., 0.9250 Silver 0.8410 oz. ASW, 38.6 mm. **Ruler:** Elizabeth II **Obv:** Crowned bust right, denomination below **Rev:** Queen and Prince Charles at flower show below multicolor bunting **Edge:** Reeded

Date	Mintage	F	VF	XF	Unc	BU
2002 Proof	15,000	Value: 45.00				

KM# 94a.2 50 PENCE
28.2800 g., 0.9250 Silver 0.8410 oz. ASW, 38.6 mm. **Ruler:** Elizabeth II **Obv:** Crowned bust right, denomination below **Rev:** With plain bunting **Edge:** Reeded

Date	Mintage	F	VF	XF	Unc	BU
2002 Proof	—	Value: 45.00				

KM# 94b.1 50 PENCE
39.9400 g., 0.9160 Gold 1.1762 oz. AGW, 38.6 mm. **Ruler:** Elizabeth II **Obv:** Crowned bust right, denomination below **Rev:** Queen and Prince Charles at flower show below multicolor bunting **Edge:** Reeded

Date	Mintage	F	VF	XF	Unc	BU
2002 Proof	50	Value: 1,100				

KM# 94b.2 50 PENCE
39.9400 g., 0.9160 Gold 1.1762 oz. AGW, 38.6 mm. **Ruler:** Elizabeth II **Obv:** Crowned bust right, denomination below **Rev:** With plain bunting **Edge:** Reeded

Date	Mintage	F	VF	XF	Unc	BU
2002 Proof	—	Value: 1,100				

KM# 95 50 PENCE
28.2800 g., Copper-Nickel, 38.6 mm. **Ruler:** Elizabeth II **Obv:** Crowned bust right, denomination below **Rev:** Elizabeth and Philip on balcony below multicolor bunting **Edge:** Reeded

Date	Mintage	F	VF	XF	Unc	BU
2002	—	—	—	—	6.00	7.00

KM# 95a.1 50 PENCE
28.2800 g., 0.9250 Silver 0.8410 oz. ASW, 38.6 mm. **Ruler:** Elizabeth II **Obv:** Crowned bust right, denomination below **Rev:** Elizabeth and Philip on balcony below colored bunting **Edge:** Reeded

Date	Mintage	F	VF	XF	Unc	BU
2002 Proof	15,000	Value: 45.00				

KM# 95a.2 50 PENCE
28.2800 g., 0.9250 Silver 0.8410 oz. ASW, 38.6 mm. **Ruler:** Elizabeth II **Obv:** Crowned bust right, denomination below **Rev:** With plain bunting **Edge:** Reeded

Date	Mintage	F	VF	XF	Unc	BU
2002 Proof	—	Value: 45.00				

KM# 95b.1 50 PENCE
39.9400 g., 0.9160 Gold 1.1762 oz. AGW, 38.6 mm. **Ruler:** Elizabeth II **Obv:** Crowned bust right, denomination below **Rev:** Elizabeth and Philip on balcony below multicolor bunting **Edge:** Reeded

Date	Mintage	F	VF	XF	Unc	BU
2002 Proof	50	Value: 1,100				

KM# 95b.2 50 PENCE
39.9400 g., 0.9160 Gold 1.1762 oz. AGW, 38.6 mm. **Ruler:** Elizabeth II **Obv:** Crowned bust right, denomination below **Rev:** With plain bunting **Edge:** Reeded

Date	Mintage	F	VF	XF	Unc	BU
2002 Proof	—	Value: 1,100				

KM# 96 50 PENCE
28.2800 g., Copper-Nickel, 38.6 mm. **Ruler:** Elizabeth II **Obv:** Crowned bust right, denomination below **Rev:** Multicolor jets below multicolor bunting **Edge:** Reeded

Date	Mintage	F	VF	XF	Unc	BU
2002	—	—	—	—	6.00	7.00

KM# 96a.1 50 PENCE
28.2800 g., 0.9250 Silver 0.8410 oz. ASW, 38.6 mm. **Ruler:** Elizabeth II **Obv:** Crowned bust right, denomination below **Rev:** Multicolor jets below multicolor bunting **Edge:** Reeded

Date	Mintage	F	VF	XF	Unc	BU
2002 Proof	15,000	Value: 45.00				

KM# 96a.2 50 PENCE
28.2800 g., 0.9250 Silver 0.8410 oz. ASW, 38.6 mm. **Ruler:** Elizabeth II **Obv:** Crowned bust right, denomination below **Rev:** With plain bunting **Edge:** Reeded

Date	Mintage	F	VF	XF	Unc	BU
2002 Proof	—	Value: 45.00				

KM# 96b.1 50 PENCE
39.9400 g., 0.9160 Gold 1.1762 oz. AGW, 38.6 mm. **Ruler:** Elizabeth II **Obv:** Crowned bust right, denomination below **Rev:** Multicolor jets below multicolor bunting **Edge:** Reeded

Date	Mintage	F	VF	XF	Unc	BU
2002 Proof	50	Value: 1,100				

KM# 96b.2 50 PENCE
39.9400 g., 0.9160 Gold 1.1762 oz. AGW, 38.6 mm. **Ruler:** Elizabeth II **Obv:** Crowned bust right, denomination below **Rev:** With plain bunting **Edge:** Reeded

Date	Mintage	F	VF	XF	Unc	BU
2002 Proof	—	Value: 1,100				

KM# 97 50 PENCE
28.2800 g., Copper-Nickel, 38.6 mm. **Ruler:** Elizabeth II **Obv:** Crowned bust right, denomination below **Rev:** Queen and fireworks below multicolor bunting **Edge:** Reeded

Date	Mintage	F	VF	XF	Unc	BU
2002	—	—	—	—	6.00	7.00

KM# 97a.1 50 PENCE
28.2800 g., 0.9250 Copper-Nickel 0.8410 oz., 38.6 mm. **Ruler:** Elizabeth II **Obv:** Crowned bust right, denomination below **Rev:** Queen and fireworks below multicolor bunting **Edge:** Reeded

Date	Mintage	F	VF	XF	Unc	BU
2002 Proof	15,000	Value: 45.00				

KM# 97a.2 50 PENCE
28.2800 g., 0.9250 Silver 0.8410 oz. ASW, 38.6 mm. **Ruler:** Elizabeth II **Obv:** Crowned bust right, denomination below **Rev:** With plain bunting **Edge:** Reeded

Date	Mintage	F	VF	XF	Unc	BU
2002 Proof	—	Value: 45.00				

KM# 97b.1 50 PENCE
39.9400 g., 0.9160 Gold 1.1762 oz. AGW, 38.6 mm. **Ruler:** Elizabeth II **Obv:** Crowned bust right, denomination below **Rev:** Queen and fireworks below multicolor bunting **Edge:** Reeded

Date	Mintage	F	VF	XF	Unc	BU
2002 Proof	50	Value: 1,100				

KM# 97b.2 50 PENCE
39.9400 g., 0.9160 Gold 1.1762 oz. AGW, 38.6 mm. **Ruler:** Elizabeth II **Obv:** Crowned bust right, denomination below **Rev:** With plain bunting **Edge:** Reeded

Date	Mintage	F	VF	XF	Unc	BU
2002 Proof	—	Value: 1,100				

KM# 98 50 PENCE
28.2800 g., Copper-Nickel, 38.6 mm. **Ruler:** Elizabeth II **Obv:** Crowned bust right, denomination below **Rev:** UK map and flags below multicolor bunting **Edge:** Reeded

Date	Mintage	F	VF	XF	Unc	BU
2002	—	—	—	—	6.00	7.00

KM# 98a.1 50 PENCE
28.2800 g., 0.9250 Silver 0.8410 oz. ASW, 38.6 mm. **Ruler:** Elizabeth II **Obv:** Crowned bust right, denomination below **Rev:** UK and four flags below multicolor bunting **Edge:** Reeded

Date	Mintage	F	VF	XF	Unc	BU
2002 Proof	15,000	Value: 45.00				

KM# 98a.2 50 PENCE
28.2800 g., 0.9250 Silver 0.8410 oz. ASW, 38.6 mm. **Ruler:** Elizabeth II **Obv:** Crowned bust right, denomination below **Rev:** With plain bunting **Edge:** Reeded

Date	Mintage	F	VF	XF	Unc	BU
2002 Proof	—	Value: 45.00				

KM# 98b.1 50 PENCE
39.9400 g., 0.9160 Gold 1.1762 oz. AGW, 38.6 mm. **Ruler:** Elizabeth II **Obv:** Crowned bust right, denomination below **Rev:** UK map and four flags below multicolor bunting **Edge:** Reeded

Date	Mintage	F	VF	XF	Unc	BU
2002 Proof	50	Value: 1,100				

KM# 98b.2 50 PENCE
39.9400 g., 0.9160 Gold 1.1762 oz. AGW, 38.6 mm. **Ruler:** Elizabeth II **Obv:** Crowned bust right, denomination below **Rev:** With plain bunting **Edge:** Reeded

Date	Mintage	F	VF	XF	Unc	BU
2002 Proof	—	Value: 1,100				

KM# 99 50 PENCE
28.2800 g., Copper-Nickel, 38.6 mm. **Ruler:** Elizabeth II **Obv:** Crowned bust right, denomination below **Rev:** Queen and two Commonwealth Games athletes below multicolor bunting **Edge:** Reeded

Date	Mintage	F	VF	XF	Unc	BU
2002	—	—	—	—	6.00	7.00

KM# 99a.1 50 PENCE
28.2800 g., 0.9250 Silver 0.8410 oz. ASW, 38.6 mm. **Ruler:** Elizabeth II **Obv:** Crowned bust right, denomination below **Rev:** Queen and two Commonwealth Games athletes below multicolor bunting **Edge:** Reeded

Date	Mintage	F	VF	XF	Unc	BU
2002 Proof	15,000	Value: 45.00				

KM# 99a.2 50 PENCE
28.2800 g., 0.9250 Silver 0.8410 oz. ASW, 38.6 mm. **Ruler:** Elizabeth II **Obv:** Crowned bust right, denomination below **Rev:** With plain bunting **Edge:** Reeded

Date	Mintage	F	VF	XF	Unc	BU
2002 Proof	—	Value: 45.00				

KM# 99b.1 50 PENCE
39.9400 g., 0.9160 Gold 1.1762 oz. AGW, 38.6 mm. **Ruler:** Elizabeth II **Obv:** Crowned bust right, denomination below **Rev:** Queen and two Commonwealth Games athletes below multicolor bunting **Edge:** Reeded

Date	Mintage	F	VF	XF	Unc	BU
2002 Proof	50	Value: 1,100				

KM# 99b.2 50 PENCE
39.9400 g., 0.9160 Gold 1.1762 oz. AGW, 38.6 mm. **Ruler:** Elizabeth II **Obv:** Crowned bust right, denomination below **Rev:** With plain bunting **Edge:** Reeded

Date	Mintage	F	VF	XF	Unc	BU
2002 Proof	—	Value: 1,100				

KM# 100 50 PENCE
28.2800 g., Copper-Nickel, 38.6 mm. **Ruler:** Elizabeth II **Obv:** Crowned bust right, denomination below **Rev:** Royal Ascot Carriage scene below multicolor bunting **Edge:** Reeded

Date	Mintage	F	VF	XF	Unc	BU
2002	—	—	—	—	6.00	7.00

KM# 100a.1 50 PENCE
28.2800 g., 0.9250 Silver 0.8410 oz. ASW, 38.6 mm. **Ruler:** Elizabeth II **Obv:** Crowned bust right, denomination below **Rev:** Royal Ascot Carriage scene below multicolor bunting **Edge:** Reeded

Date	Mintage	F	VF	XF	Unc	BU
2002 Proof	15,000	Value: 45.00				

KM# 100a.2 50 PENCE
28.2800 g., 0.9250 Silver 0.8410 oz. ASW, 38.6 mm. **Ruler:** Elizabeth II **Obv:** Crowned bust right, denomination below **Rev:** With plain bunting **Edge:** Reeded

Date	Mintage	F	VF	XF	Unc	BU
2002 Proof	—	Value: 45.00				

KM# 100b.1 50 PENCE
39.9400 g., 0.9160 Gold 1.1762 oz. AGW, 38.6 mm. **Ruler:** Elizabeth II **Obv:** Crowned bust right, denomination below **Rev:** Royal Ascot Carriage scene below multicolor bunting **Edge:** Reeded

Date	Mintage	F	VF	XF	Unc	BU
2002 Proof	50	Value: 1,100				

KM# 100b.2 50 PENCE
39.9400 g., 0.9160 Gold 1.1762 oz. AGW, 38.6 mm. **Ruler:** Elizabeth II **Obv:** Crowned bust right, denomination below **Rev:** With plain bunting **Edge:** Reeded

Date	Mintage	F	VF	XF	Unc	BU
2002 Proof	—	Value: 1,100				

KM# 101 50 PENCE
28.2800 g., Copper-Nickel, 38.6 mm. **Ruler:** Elizabeth II **Obv:** Crowned bust right, denomination below **Rev:** Queen and two hockey players below multicolor bunting **Edge:** Reeded

Date	Mintage	F	VF	XF	Unc	BU
2002	—	—	—	—	6.00	7.00

KM# 101a.1 50 PENCE
28.2800 g., 0.9250 Silver 0.8410 oz. ASW, 38.6 mm. **Ruler:** Elizabeth II **Obv:** Crowned bust right, denomination below **Rev:** Queen and two hockey players below multicolor bunting **Edge:** Reeded

Date	Mintage	F	VF	XF	Unc	BU
2002 Proof	15,000	Value: 45.00				

KM# 101a.2 50 PENCE
28.2800 g., 0.9250 Silver 0.8410 oz. ASW, 38.6 mm. **Ruler:** Elizabeth II **Obv:** Crowned bust right, denomination below **Rev:** With plain bunting **Edge:** Reeded

Date	Mintage	F	VF	XF	Unc	BU
2002 Proof	—	Value: 45.00				

KM# 101b.1 50 PENCE
39.9400 g., 0.9160 Gold 1.1762 oz. AGW, 38.6 mm. **Ruler:** Elizabeth II **Obv:** Crowned bust right, denomination below **Rev:** Queen and two hockey players below multicolor bunting **Edge:** Reeded

Date	Mintage	F	VF	XF	Unc	BU
2002 Proof	50	Value: 1,100				

KM# 101b.2 50 PENCE
39.9400 g., 0.9160 Gold 1.1762 oz. AGW, 38.6 mm. **Ruler:** Elizabeth II **Obv:** Crowned bust right, denomination below **Rev:** With plain bunting **Edge:** Reeded

Date	Mintage	F	VF	XF	Unc	BU
2002 Proof	—	Value: 1,100				

KM# 102 50 PENCE
28.2800 g., Copper-Nickel, 38.6 mm. **Ruler:** Elizabeth II **Obv:** Crowned bust right, denomination below **Obv. Designer:** Raphael Maklouf **Rev:** Queen Mother as a young lady and as an elderly lady **Rev. Designer:** Willem Vis **Edge:** Reeded

Date	Mintage	F	VF	XF	Unc	BU
ND(2002)	—	—	—	—	9.00	10.00

KM# 102a 50 PENCE
28.2800 g., 0.9250 Silver 0.8410 oz. ASW, 38.6 mm. **Ruler:** Elizabeth II **Obv:** Crowned bust right, denomination below **Rev:** Queen Mother as a young lady and as an elderly lady **Edge:** Reeded

Date	Mintage	F	VF	XF	Unc	BU
ND(2002) Proof	10,000	Value: 45.00				

KM# 135 50 PENCE
Copper-Nickel **Ruler:** Elizabeth II **Obv:** Young bust right

Date	Mintage	F	VF	XF	Unc	BU
2004	—	—	—	—	5.00	7.50

KM# 149 50 PENCE
28.2800 g., 0.9250 Silver 0.8410 oz. ASW, 38.6 mm. **Ruler:** Elizabeth II **Subject:** Queen's 80th Birthday **Obv:** Head with tiara right - gilt **Obv. Legend:** QUEEN ELIZABETH II - FALKLAND ISLANDS **Obv. Designer:** Ian Rank-Broadley **Rev:** Elizabeth seated at left, Queen Mother at right holding baby

Date	Mintage	F	VF	XF	Unc	BU
2006 Proof	—	Value: 40.00				

KM# 136 POUND
Nickel-Brass **Ruler:** Elizabeth II **Obv:** Crowned bust right

Date	Mintage	F	VF	XF	Unc	BU
2004	—	—	—	—	3.50	5.00

KM# 137 2 POUNDS
Bi-Metallic **Ruler:** Elizabeth II **Obv:** Crowned bust right **Rev:** Sun and map

Date	Mintage	F	VF	XF	Unc	BU
2004	—	—	—	—	15.00	20.00

KM# 103 25 POUNDS
7.8100 g., 0.9999 Gold 0.2511 oz. AGW, 22 mm. **Ruler:** Elizabeth II **Obv:** Crowned bust right, denomination below **Obv. Designer:** Raphael Maklouf **Rev:** Queen Mother as a young lady and as an elderly lady **Rev. Designer:** Willem Vis **Edge:** Reeded

Date	Mintage	F	VF	XF	Unc	BU
ND(2002) Proof	1,000	Value: 185				

KM# 146a CROWN
0.9167 Silver **Ruler:** Elizabeth II **Subject:** 10th Anniversary Death of Princess Diana **Obv:** Bust with tiara right **Obv. Legend:** QUEEN ELIZABETH II - FALKLAND ISLANDS **Rev:** Bust of Princess Diana facing 3/4 right **Rev. Legend:** 1961 - 1997 ? DIANA ? PRINCESS OF WALES **Edge:** Reeded

Date	Mintage	F	VF	XF	Unc	BU
2007PM Proof	—	Value: 75.00				

CROWN COINAGE

KM# 141 1/5 CROWN
6.2200 g., 0.9999 Gold 0.1999 oz. AGW **Ruler:** Elizabeth II **Subject:** Diamond Wedding Anniversary **Obv:** Conjoined busts with Prince Philip right **Obv. Legend:** QUEEN ELIZABETH II - FALKLAND ISLANDS **Rev:** Bride and groom standing facing at wedding cake; .01 carat x 1.3mm diamond embedded at top **Rev. Legend:** Diamond Wedding of H.M. Queen Elizabeth II & H.R.H. Prince Philip **Edge:** Reeded

Date	Mintage	F	VF	XF	Unc	BU
2007PM Proof	—	Value: 450				

KM# 129 CROWN
Copper-Nickel **Ruler:** Elizabeth II **Rev:** Nelson and the H.M.S. Victory

Date	Mintage	F	VF	XF	Unc	BU
2005	—	—	—	—	10.00	12.00

KM# 138 CROWN
Copper-Nickel **Ruler:** Elizabeth II **Rev:** Winston Churchill

Date	Mintage	F	VF	XF	Unc	BU
2007	—	—	—	—	15.00	17.50

KM# 139 CROWN
Copper-Nickel **Ruler:** Elizabeth II **Rev:** Queen Elizabeth I

Date	Mintage	F	VF	XF	Unc	BU
2007	—	—	—	—	15.00	17.50

KM# 140 CROWN
Copper-Nickel **Ruler:** Elizabeth II **Rev:** Charles Darwin

Date	Mintage	F	VF	XF	Unc	BU
2007	—	—	—	—	15.00	17.50

KM# 142 CROWN
Copper-Nickel **Ruler:** Elizabeth II **Subject:** Diamond Wedding Anniversary **Obv:** Conjoined busts with Prince Philip right **Obv. Legend:** QUEEN ELIZABETH II - FALKLAND ISLANDS **Rev:** King George VI standing at left giving Philip standing at right his consent to a contract of matrimony **Rev. Legend:** Diamond Wedding of H.M. Queen Elizabeth II & H.R.H. Prince Philip **Edge:** Reeded

Date	Mintage	F	VF	XF	Unc	BU
2007PM	—	—	—	—	17.00	20.00

KM# 142a CROWN
0.9167 Silver **Ruler:** Elizabeth II **Subject:** Diamond Wedding Anniversary **Obv:** Conjoined busts with Prince Philip right **Obv. Legend:** QUEEN ELIZABETH II - FALKLAND ISLANDS **Rev:** King George VI, standing at left, giving Philip, standing at right, his consent to a contract of matrimony **Rev. Legend:** Diamond Wedding of H.M. Queen Elizabeth II & H.R.H. Prince Philip **Edge:** Reeded

Date	Mintage	F	VF	XF	Unc	BU
2007PM	—	Value: 35.00				

KM# 143 CROWN
Copper-Nickel **Ruler:** Elizabeth II **Subject:** Diamond Wedding Anniversary **Obv:** Conjoined busts with Prince Philip right **Obv. Legend:** QUEEN ELIZABETH II - FALKLAND ISLANDS **Rev:** Bride and groom standing facing at wedding cake **Rev. Legend:** Diamond Wedding of H.M. Queen Elizabeth II & H.R.H. Prince Philip **Edge:** Reeded

Date	Mintage	F	VF	XF	Unc	BU
2007PM	—	—	—	—	17.00	20.00

KM# 144 CROWN
Copper-Nickel **Ruler:** Elizabeth II **Subject:** Diamond Wedding Anniversary **Obv:** Conjoined busts with Prince Philip right **Obv. Legend:** QUEEN ELIZABETH II - FALKLAND ISLANDS **Rev:** Bride and groom standing at wedding cake **Rev. Legend:** Diamond Wedding of H.M. Queen Elizabeth II & H.R.H. Prince Philip **Edge:** Reeded

Date	Mintage	F	VF	XF	Unc	BU
2007PM	—	—	—	—	17.00	20.00

KM# 144a CROWN
0.9167 Silver **Ruler:** Elizabeth II **Subject:** Diamond Wedding Anniversary **Obv:** Conjoined busts with Prince Philip right **Obv. Legend:** QUEEN ELIZABETH II - FALKLAND ISLANDS **Rev:** Bride and groom standing at wedding cake **Rev. Legend:** Diamond Wedding of H.M. Queen Elizabeth II & H.R.H. Prince Philip **Edge:** Reeded

Date	Mintage	F	VF	XF	Unc	BU
2007PM Proof	—	Value: 35.00				

KM# 145 CROWN
Copper-Nickel **Ruler:** Elizabeth II **Subject:** Diamond Wedding Anniversary **Obv:** Conjoined busts with Prince Philip right **Obv. Legend:** QUEEN ELIZABETH II - FALKLAND ISLANDS **Rev:** Buckingham Palace facade **Rev. Legend:** Diamond Wedding of H.M. Queen Elizabeth II & H.R.H. Prince Philip **Edge:** Reeded

Date	Mintage	F	VF	XF	Unc	BU
2007PM	—	—	—	—	17.00	20.00

KM# 146 CROWN
Copper-Nickel **Ruler:** Elizabeth II **Subject:** 10th Anniversary - Death of Princess Diana **Obv:** Bust with tiara right **Obv. Legend:** QUEEN ELIZABETH II - FALKLAND ISLANDS **Rev:** Bust of Princess Diana facing 3/4 right **Rev. Legend:** 1961 - 1997 • DIANA — PRINCESS OF WALES **Edge:** Reeded

Date	Mintage	F	VF	XF	Unc	BU
2007PM	—	—	—	—	17.00	20.00

KM# 147 CROWN
Copper-Nickel, 38 mm. **Ruler:** Elizabeth II **Subject:** 20th Anniversary - Falkland Islands Fishery **Obv:** Bust right of Queen Elizabeth II **Rev:** Shortfin Squid (Illex Argentinca) **Edge:** Reeded

Date	Mintage	F	VF	XF	Unc	BU
2007PM	—	—	—	—	17.00	12.50

KM# 148 CROWN

Copper-Nickel, 39 mm. **Ruler:** Elizabeth II **Subject:** Scouting Centennial **Obv:** Crowned bust right **Obv. Legend:** QUEEN ELIZABETH II FALKLAND ISLANDS 2007 **Rev:** Baden-Powell bust 3/4 left, scout saluting, tent flanking within circle on animal tracks **Rev. Legend:** 1857 ROBERT BADEN-POWELL 1941 ONE CROWN **Edge:** Reeded

Date	Mintage	F	VF	XF	Unc	BU
2007PM	—	—	—	—	12.50	15.00

KM# 148a CROWN

28.2800 g., 0.9250 Silver 0.8410 oz. ASW, 38.5 mm. **Ruler:** Elizabeth II **Subject:** Scouting Centennial **Obv:** Crowned bust right **Obv. Legend:** QUEEN ELIZABETH II FALKLAND ISLANDS 2007 **Rev:** Baden-Powell bust 3/4 facing left, scout saluting and tent flanking, within circle of animal tracks and rope **Rev. Legend:** 1857 ROBERT BADEN-POWELL 1941 ONE CROWN **Edge:** Reeded

Date	Mintage	F	VF	XF	Unc	BU
2007PM Proof	10,000	Value: 65.00				

KM# 143a CROWN

0.9167 Silver **Ruler:** Elizabeth II **Subject:** Diamond Wedding Anniversary **Obv:** Conjoined busts with Prince Philip right **Obv. Legend:** QUEEN ELIZABETH II - FALKLAND ISLANDS **Rev:** Bride and groom standing facing at wedding cake **Rev. Legend:** Diamond Wedding of H.M. Queen Elizabeth II & H.R.H. Prince Philip **Edge:** Reeded

Date	Mintage	VG	F	VF	XF	Unc
2007PM Proof	—	Value: 35.00				

PIEFORTS

KM#	Date	Mintage	Identification	Mkt Val
P4	2001	500	50 Pence. 0.9250 Silver. 56.5600 g. 38.6 mm. Reeded edge.	100
P5	2001	500	50 Pence. 0.9250 Silver. 56.5600 g. 38.6 mm. Reeded edge. Proof KM#70a.	100

KM#	Date	Mintage	Identification	Mkt Val
P18	2001	500	50 Pence. 0.9250 Silver. 56.5600 g. 38.6 mm. Reeded edge. Proof KM#86a.	90.00
P19	2001	500	50 Pence. 0.9250 Silver. 56.5600 g. 38.6 mm. Reeded edge.	90.00
P20	2001	500	50 Pence. 0.9250 Silver. 56.5600 g. 38.6 mm. Reeded edge.	90.00
P21	2001	500	50 Pence. 0.9250 Silver. 56.5600 g. 38.6 mm. Reeded edge.	90.00
P22	ND(2002)	500	50 Pence. 0.9250 Silver. 56.5600 g. 38.6 mm. Reeded edge. Proof KM#102a.	90.00
P6	2002	500	50 Pence. 0.9250 Silver. 56.5600 g. 38.6 mm. Reeded edge. Proof KM#73a.	90.00
P7	2002	500	50 Pence. 0.9250 Silver. 56.5600 g. 38.6 mm. Reeded edge. Proof KM#74a.	90.00
P8	2002	500	50 Pence. 0.9250 Silver. 56.5600 g. 38.6 mm. Reeded edge. Proof KM#75a.	90.00
P9	2002	500	50 Pence. 0.9250 Silver. 56.5600 g. 38.6 mm. Reeded edge. Proof KM#76a.	90.00
P10	2002	500	50 Pence. 0.9250 Silver. 56.5600 g. 38.6 mm. Reeded edge. Proof KM#77a.	90.00

KM#	Date	Mintage	Identification	Mkt Val
P11	2002	500	50 Pence. 0.9250 Silver. 56.5600 g. 38.6 mm. Reeded edge. Proof KM#78a.	90.00
P12	2002	500	50 Pence. 0.9250 Silver. 56.5600 g. 38.6 mm. Reeded edge. Proof KM#79a.	90.00
P13	2002	500	50 Pence. 0.9250 Silver. 56.5600 g. 38.6 mm. Reeded edge. Proof KM#80a.	90.00
P14	2002	500	50 Pence. 0.9250 Silver. 56.5600 g. 38.6 mm. Reeded edge. Proof KM#81a.	90.00
P15	2002	500	50 Pence. 0.9250 Silver. 56.5600 g. 38.6 mm. Reeded edge. Proof KM#82a.	90.00
P16	2002	500	50 Pence. 0.9250 Silver. 56.5600 g. 38.6 mm. Reeded edge. Proof KM#83a.	90.00
P17	2002	500	50 Pence. 0.9250 Silver. 56.5600 g. 38.6 mm. Reeded edge. Proof KM#84a.	90.00

FIJI

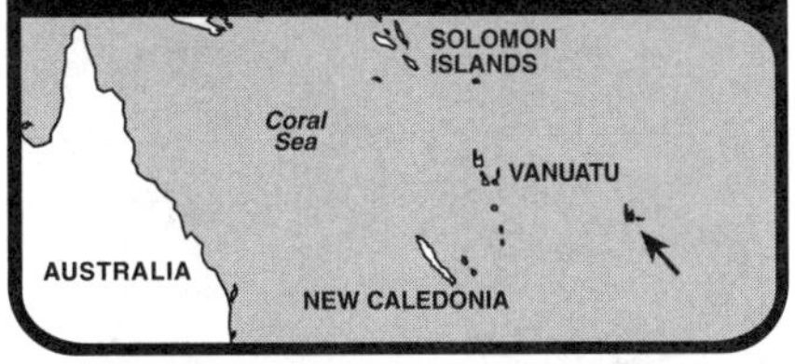

The Republic of Fiji consists of about 320 islands located in the southwestern Pacific 1,100 miles (1,770 km.) north of New Zealand. The islands have a combined area of 7,056 sq. mi. (18,274 sq. km.) and a population of 772,891. Capital: Suva. Fiji's economy is based on agriculture and mining. Sugar, coconut products, manganese, and gold are exported. Fiji is a member of the Commonwealth of Nations, but has been subject to periodic short suspensions.

MINT MARK

(o) - Royal Canadian Mint, Ottawa

REPUBLIC

British Administration until 1970

DECIMAL COINAGE

100 Cents = 1 Dollar

KM# 49a CENT

1.5400 g., Copper Plated Zinc, 17.5 mm. **Ruler:** Elizabeth II **Obv:** Crowned head right, date at right **Rev:** Tanoa kava bowl divides denomination

Date	Mintage	F	VF	XF	Unc	BU
2001	—	—	—	—	0.20	0.65
2002(o)	5,880,000	—	—	—	0.20	0.65
2003(o)	8,030,000	—	—	—	0.20	0.65
(o)	8,840,000	—	—	—	0.20	0.65
2005(o)	9,720,000	—	—	—	0.20	0.65

KM# 50a 2 CENTS

3.8500 g., Copper Plated Zinc, 21.1 mm. **Ruler:** Elizabeth II **Obv:** Crowned head right, date at right **Rev:** Palm fan and denomination

Date	Mintage	F	VF	XF	Unc	BU
2001(o)	2,830,000	—	—	—	0.30	0.85
2002(o)	5,000,000	—	—	—	0.30	0.85
2003(o)	6,410,000	—	—	—	0.30	0.85
2004(o)	7,050,000	—	—	—	0.30	0.85
2005(o)	7,760,000	—	—	—	0.30	0.85

KM# 95 20 CENTS

11.2400 g., Copper-Nickel, 28.5 mm. **Ruler:** Elizabeth II **Obv:** Crowned head right, date at right **Obv. Designer:** Raphael Maklouf **Rev:** South Pacific Games flame logo **Edge:** Reeded

Date	Mintage	F	VF	XF	Unc	BU
2003	1,540,000	—	—	—	1.50	2.50

KM# 93 5 DOLLARS

1.5550 g., 0.9999 Gold 0.0500 oz. AGW **Ruler:** Elizabeth II **Obv:** Crowned head right, date at right **Rev:** Arms

Date	Mintage	F	VF	XF	Unc	BU
2002	3,000	Value: 50.00				

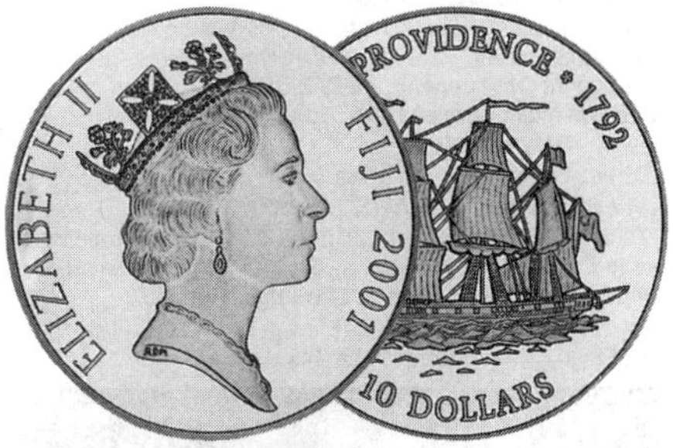

KM# 82 10 DOLLARS

31.6200 g., 0.9250 Silver 0.9403 oz. ASW, 38.6 mm. **Ruler:** Elizabeth II **Obv:** Crowned head right, date at right **Obv. Designer:** Raphael Maklouf **Rev:** William Bligh's - HMS Providence **Edge:** Reeded

Date	Mintage	F	VF	XF	Unc	BU
2001 Proof	—	Value: 18.50				

KM# 83 10 DOLLARS

28.2800 g., 0.9250 Silver 0.8410 oz. ASW, 38.6 mm. **Ruler:** Elizabeth II **Subject:** Queen Elizabeth II - 50 Years of Reign **Obv:** Queen's head right, gilded **Rev:** Cloth draped sword hilt, legend and denomination **Rev. Legend:** Defender of the Faith... **Rev. Designer:** Robert Low **Edge:** Reeded

Date	Mintage	F	VF	XF	Unc	BU
2002 Proof	15,000	Value: 17.50				

KM# 84 10 DOLLARS

28.2800 g., 0.9250 Silver 0.8410 oz. ASW, 38.6 mm. **Ruler:** Elizabeth II **Subject:** Queen Elizabeth II - 50th Year of Reign **Obv:** Head right, gilded **Rev:** Four man chorus, legend, and denomination **Rev. Legend:** Westminster Abbey June 1953. **Rev. Designer:** Robert Low **Edge:** Reeded

Date	Mintage	F	VF	XF	Unc	BU
2002 Proof	15,000	Value: 17.50				

KM# 94 10 DOLLARS

3.1100 g., 0.9999 Gold 0.1000 oz. AGW **Ruler:** Elizabeth II **Obv:** Crowned head right, date at right **Rev:** Arms **Edge:** Reeded

Date	Mintage	F	VF	XF	Unc	BU
2002 Proof	2,000	Value: 100				

KM# 101 10 DOLLARS
31.1000 g., 0.9990 Silver 0.9988 oz. ASW, 40 mm. **Ruler:** Elizabeth II **Series:** Save the Whales **Obv:** Crowned head right, date at right **Obv. Legend:** ELIZABETH II - FIJI **Rev:** Sperm Whale on mother-of-pearl inset **Edge:** Plain

Date	Mintage	F	VF	XF	Unc	BU
2002 Proof	2,000	Value: 50.00				

KM# 99 100 DOLLARS
7.7800 g., 0.5850 Gold 0.1463 oz. AGW **Ruler:** Elizabeth II **Subject:** 2006 FIFA World Cup - Germany **Obv:** Crowned head right, date at right **Rev:** World Cup **Edge:** Reeded

Date	Mintage	F	VF	XF	Unc	BU
2003 Proof	25,000	Value: 145				

FINLAND

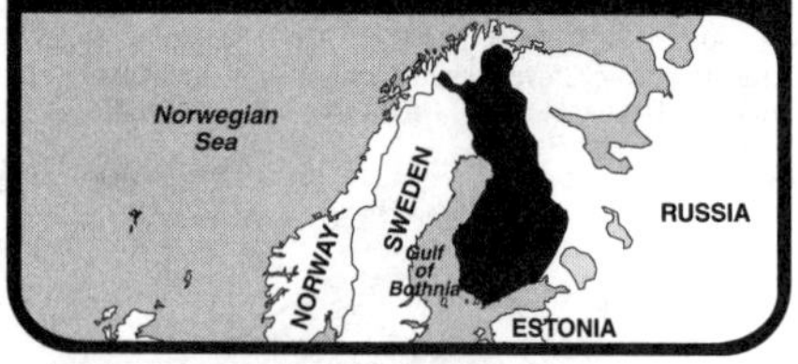

The Republic of Finland, the third most northerly state of the European continent, has an area of 130,559 sq. mi. (338,127 sq. km.) and a population of 5.1 million. Capital: Helsinki. Lumbering, shipbuilding, metal and woodworking are the leading industries. Paper, timber, wood pulp, plywood and metal products are exported.

MONETARY SYSTEM
100 Pennia = 1 Markka

MINT MARKS
H - Birmingham 1921
Heart (h) - Copenhagen 1922
No mm – Helsinki

MINT OFFICIALS' INITIALS

Letter	Date	Name
J-M	2002	Toivo Jaatinen & Raimo Makkonen
L-M	2003	Tero Lounas & Raimo Makkonen
K-M	2004	Heli Kauhanen & Raimo Makkonen
K-M	2005-2006	Tapio Kettunen & Raimo Makkonen
M-M	2002-2006	Pertti Mäkinen & Raimo Makkonen
N-M	2001	Antti Neuvonen & Raimo Makkonen
P-M	2003	Matti Peltokangas & Raimo Makkonen
P-M	2001, 2005-07	Reijo Paavilainen & Raimo Makkonen
S-M	2003	Anneli Sigriläinen & Raimo Makkonen
W-M	2002	Erkki Vainio & Hannu Veijalainen & Raimo Makkonen

REPUBLIC

REFORM COINAGE

100 Old Markka = 1 New Markka 1963

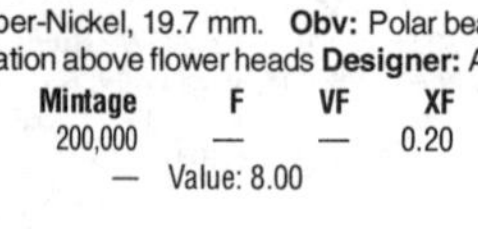

KM# 65 10 PENNIA
1.8000 g., Copper-Nickel, 16.3 mm. **Obv:** Flower pods and stems, date at right **Rev:** Denomination to right of honeycombs **Designer:** Antti Neuvonen

Date	Mintage	F	VF	XF	Unc	BU
2001 M	25,000,000	—	—	—	1.00	—
2001 M Proof	—	Value: 7.00				

KM# 66 50 PENNIA
3.3000 g., Copper-Nickel, 19.7 mm. **Obv:** Polar bear, date below **Rev:** Denomination above flower heads **Designer:** Antti Neuvonen

Date	Mintage	F	VF	XF	Unc	BU
2001 M	200,000	—	—	0.20	0.75	1.50
2001 M Proof	—	Value: 8.00				

KM# 76 MARKKA
4.9000 g., Aluminum-Bronze, 22 mm. **Obv:** Rampant lion left within circle, date below **Rev:** Ornaments flank denomination within circle

Date	Mintage	F	VF	XF	Unc	BU
2001 M	200,000	—	—	0.35	0.75	—
2001 M Proof	—	Value: 10.00				

KM# 95 MARKKA
8.6400 g., 0.7500 Gold 0.2083 oz. AGW, 22 mm. **Subject:** Last Markka Coin **Obv:** Rampant lion with sword left **Rev:** Stylized tree with roots **Edge:** Reeded **Designer:** Reijo Paavilainen

Date	Mintage	F	VF	XF	Unc	BU
2001 P-M Proof	55,000	Value: 215				

KM# 106 MARKKA
6.1000 g., Copper-Nickel, 24 mm. **Subject:** Remembrance Markka **Obv:** Rampant lion with sword left **Rev:** Denomination and pine tree **Edge:** Plain **Designer:** Antti Neuvonen **Note:** This coin is encased in acrylic resin and sealed in a display card.

Date	Mintage	F	VF	XF	Unc	BU
2001 N-M	500,000	—	—	—	5.00	6.50

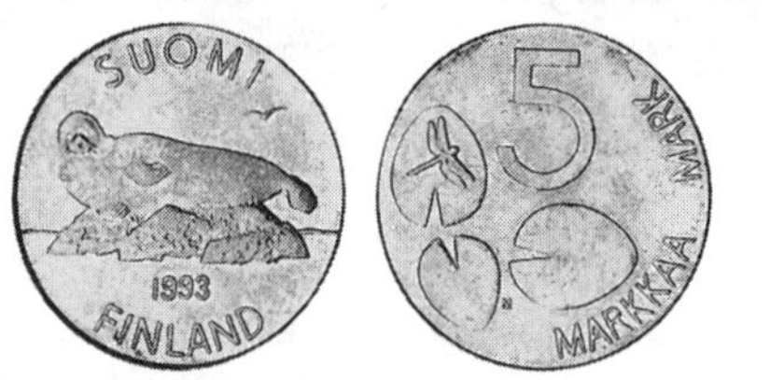

KM# 73 5 MARKKAA
5.5000 g., Copper-Aluminum-Nickel, 24.5 mm. **Obv:** Lake Saimaa ringed seal, date below **Rev:** Denomination, dragonfly and lily pad leaves

Date	Mintage	F	VF	XF	Unc	BU
2001 M	200,000	—	—	—	4.00	6.00
2001 M Proof	—	Value: 12.00				

KM# 77 10 MARKKAA
8.8000 g., Bi-Metallic Brass center in Copper-Nickel ring, 27.25 mm. **Obv:** Capercaillie bird within circle, date above **Rev:** Denomination and branches

Date	Mintage	F	VF	XF	Unc	BU
2001 M	200,000	—	—	3.00	5.00	6.00
2001 M Proof	—	Value: 18.00				

KM# 96 25 MARKKAA
20.2000 g., Bi-Metallic Brass center in Copper-Nickel ring, 35 mm. **Subject:** First Nordic Ski Championship, "Lahti 2001" **Obv:** Stylized woman's face **Rev:** Female torso, landscape **Edge:** Plain **Designer:** Jarkko Roth

Date	Mintage	F	VF	XF	Unc	BU
2001 Prooflike	100,000	—	—	—	—	25.00

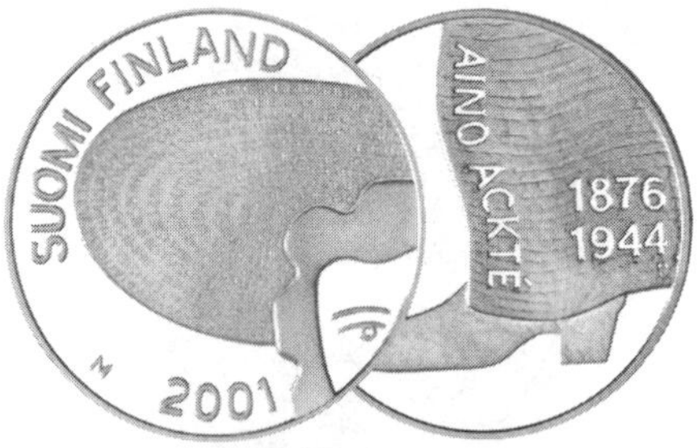

KM# 97 100 MARKKAA
31.0000 g., 0.9250 Silver 0.9219 oz. ASW, 35 mm. **Subject:** Aino Ackte **Obv:** Partial portrait **Rev:** High heel boot and trouser bottom **Edge:** Plain **Designer:** Timo Rytkönen.

Date	Mintage	F	VF	XF	Unc	BU
2001	33,000	—	—	—	35.00	40.00
2001 Proof	12,000	Value: 50.00				

EURO COINAGE

European Union Issues

KM# 98 EURO CENT
2.2700 g., Copper Plated Steel, 16.3 mm. **Obv:** Rampant lion left surrounded by stars, date at left **Obv. Designer:** Heikki Häiväoja **Rev:** Denomination and globe **Rev. Designer:** Luc Luycx **Edge:** Plain

Date	Mintage	F	VF	XF	Unc	BU
2001	500,000	—	—	—	10.00	—
2001 Proof	—	—	—	—	—	—
2002	659,000	—	—	—	5.00	—
2002 Proof	16,000	Value: 15.00				
2003	6,790,000	—	—	—	5.00	—
2003 Proof	—	Value: 15.00				
2004	9,690,000	—	—	—	5.00	—
2004 Proof	—	Value: 15.00				
2005	5,800,000	—	—	—	5.00	—
2005 Proof	—	Value: 15.00				
2006	—	—	—	—	5.00	—
2006 Proof	—	Value: 15.00				
2007	—	—	—	—	5.00	—
2008	—	—	—	—	5.00	—

KM# 99 2 EURO CENT
3.0000 g., Copper Plated Steel, 18.7 mm. **Obv:** Rampant lion surrounded by stars, date at left **Obv. Designer:** Heikki Häiväoja **Rev:** Denomination and globe **Rev. Designer:** Luc Luycx **Edge:** Grooved

Date	Mintage	F	VF	XF	Unc	BU
2001	500,000	—	—	—	10.00	—
2001 Proof	—	—	—	—	—	—
2002	659,000	—	—	—	5.00	—
2002 Proof	16,000	Value: 15.00				
2003	6,790,000	—	—	—	5.00	—
2003 Proof	—	Value: 15.00				
2004	8,024,000	—	—	—	5.00	—
2004 Proof	—	Value: 15.00				
2005	5,800,000	—	—	—	5.00	—
2005 Proof	—	Value: 15.00				
2006	—	—	—	—	5.00	—
2006 Proof	—	Value: 15.00				
2007	—	—	—	—	5.00	—
2008	—	—	—	—	5.00	—

KM# 100 5 EURO CENT
3.9400 g., Copper Plated Steel, 19.66 mm. **Obv:** Rampant lion left surrounded by stars, date at left **Obv. Designer:** Heikki Häiväoja **Rev:** Denomination and globe **Rev. Designer:** Luc Luycx **Edge:** Plain

Date	Mintage	F	VF	XF	Unc	BU
2001	213,756,000	—	—	—	0.50	—
2001 Proof	—	—	—	—	—	—
2002	101,824,000	—	—	—	0.50	—
2002 Proof	16,000	Value: 15.00				

Date	Mintage	F	VF	XF	Unc	BU
2003	790,000	—	—	—	1.00	—
2003 Proof	—	Value: 15.00				
2004	629,000	—	—	—	1.00	—
2004 Proof	—	Value: 15.00				
2005	800,000	—	—	—	1.00	—
2005 Proof	—	Value: 15.00				
2006	—	—	—	—	1.00	—
2006 Proof	—	Value: 15.00				
2007	—	—	—	—	1.00	—
2008	—	—	—	—	1.00	—

KM# 101 10 EURO CENT

4.0000 g., Brass, 19.7 mm. **Obv:** Rampant lion left surrounded by stars, date at left **Obv. Designer:** Heikki Häiväoja **Rev:** Denomination and map **Rev. Designer:** Luc Luycx **Edge:** Reeded

Date	Mintage	F	VF	XF	Unc	BU
2001	14,730,000	—	—	—	10.00	—
2001 Proof	—	—	—	—	—	—
2002	1,499,000	—	—	—	2.50	—
2002 Proof	16,000	Value: 18.00				
2003	790,000	—	—	—	2.50	—
2003 Proof	—	Value: 18.00				
2004	629,000	—	—	—	2.50	—
2004 Proof	—	Value: 18.00				
2005	800,000	—	—	—	2.50	—
2005 Proof	—	Value: 18.00				
2006	1,000,000	—	—	—	2.50	—
2006 Proof	—	Value: 18.00				

KM# 126 10 EURO CENT

4.0000 g., Brass, 19.7 mm. **Obv:** Rampant lion surrounded by stars **Obv. Designer:** Heikki Häiväoja **Rev:** Relief map of Western Europe, stars, lines and value **Rev. Designer:** Luc Luycx **Edge:** Reeded

Date	Mintage	F	VF	XF	Unc	BU
2007	—	—	—	—	2.50	—
2008	—	—	—	—	—	—

KM# 102 20 EURO CENT

5.7300 g., Brass, 22.2 mm. **Obv:** Rampant lion left surrounded by stars, date at left **Obv. Designer:** Heikki Häiväoja **Rev:** Denomination and map **Rev. Designer:** Luc Luycx **Edge:** Notched

Date	Mintage	F	VF	XF	Unc	BU
2001	121,763,000	—	—	—	1.75	—
2001 Proof	—	—	—	—	—	—
2002	100,759,000	—	—	—	1.75	—
2002 Proof	16,000	Value: 20.00				
2003	790,000	—	—	—	1.75	—
2003 Proof	—	Value: 20.00				
2004	629,000	—	—	—	1.75	—
2004 Proof	—	Value: 20.00				
2005	800,000	—	—	—	1.75	—
2005 Proof	—	Value: 20.00				
2006	1,000,000	—	—	—	1.75	—
2006 Proof	—	Value: 20.00				

KM# 127 20 EURO CENT

5.7300 g., Brass, 22.2 mm. **Obv:** Rampant lion surrounded by stars **Obv. Designer:** Heikki Häiväoja **Rev:** Relief map of Western Europe, stars, lines and value **Rev. Designer:** Luc Luycx **Edge:** Notched

Date	Mintage	F	VF	XF	Unc	BU
2007	—	—	—	—	1.75	—
2008	—	—	—	—	—	—

KM# 103 50 EURO CENT

7.8100 g., Brass, 24.2 mm. **Obv:** Rampant lion left surrounded by stars, date at left **Obv. Designer:** Heikki Häiväoja **Rev:** Denomination and map **Rev. Designer:** Luc Luycx **Edge:** Reeded

Date	Mintage	F	VF	XF	Unc	BU
2001	4,432,000	—	—	—	7.50	—
2001 Proof	—	—	—	—	—	—
2002	1,147,000	—	—	—	5.00	—
2002 Proof	16,000	Value: 22.00				
2003	790,000	—	—	—	5.00	—
2003 Proof	—	Value: 22.00				
2004	629,000	—	—	—	5.00	—
2004 Proof	—	Value: 22.00				
2005	4,800,000	—	—	—	5.00	—
2005 Proof	—	Value: 22.00				
2006	6,850,000	—	—	—	5.00	—
2006 Proof	—	Value: 22.00				

KM# 128 50 EURO CENT

7.8100 g., Brass, 24.2 mm. **Obv:** Rampant lion surrounded by stars **Obv. Designer:** Heikki Häiväoja **Rev:** Relief map of Western Europe, stars, lines and value **Rev. Designer:** Luc Luycx **Edge:** Reeded

Date	Mintage	F	VF	XF	Unc	BU
2007	—	—	—	—	5.00	—
2008	—	—	—	—	—	—

KM# 104 EURO

7.5000 g., Bi-Metallic Copper-nickel center in Brass ring, 23.2 mm. **Obv:** 2 flying swans, date below, surrounded by stars on outer ring **Obv. Designer:** Pertti Mäkinen **Rev:** Denomination and map **Rev. Designer:** Luc Luycx **Edge:** Reeded and plain sections

Date	Mintage	F	VF	XF	Unc	BU
2001	13,862,000	—	—	—	3.00	—
2001 Proof	—	—	—	—	—	—
2002	14,114,000	—	—	—	6.50	—
2002 Proof	16,000	Value: 25.00				
2003	790,000	—	—	—	6.50	—
2003 Proof	—	Value: 25.00				
2004	5,529,000	—	—	—	6.50	—
2004 Proof	—	Value: 25.00				
2005	7,935,000	—	—	—	6.50	—
2005 Proof	—	Value: 25.00				
2006	1,705,000	—	—	—	6.50	—
2006 Proof	—	Value: 25.00				

KM# 129 EURO

7.5000 g., Bi-Metallic Copper-Nickel center in Brass ring, 23.2 mm. **Obv:** 2 flying swans surrounded by stars on outer ring **Obv. Designer:** Pertti Mäekinen **Rev:** Relief map of western Europe, stars, lines and value **Rev. Designer:** Luc Luycx **Edge:** Reeded and plain sections

Date	Mintage	F	VF	XF	Unc	BU
2007	—	—	—	—	6.50	—
2008	—	—	—	—	—	—

KM# 105 2 EURO

8.5200 g., Bi-Metallic Brass center in Copper-nickel ring, 25.6 mm. **Obv:** 2 cloudberry flowers surrounded by stars on outer ring **Obv. Designer:** Raimo Heino **Rev:** Denomination and map **Rev. Designer:** Luc Luycx **Edge:** Reeded and lettered **Edge Lettering:** SUOMI FINLAND

Date	Mintage	F	VF	XF	Unc	BU
2001	29,132,000	—	—	—	4.00	—
2001 Proof	—	—	—	—	—	—
2002	1,386,000	—	—	—	7.50	—
2002 Proof	16,000	Value: 30.00				
2003	9,080,000	—	—	—	5.00	—
2003 Proof	—	Value: 30.00				
2004	10,029,000	—	—	—	5.00	—
2004 Proof	—	Value: 30.00				
2005	10,800,000	—	—	—	5.00	—
2005 Proof	—	Value: 30.00				
2006	11,000,000	—	—	—	5.00	—
2006 Proof	—	Value: 30.00				

KM# 114 2 EURO

8.5200 g., Bi-Metallic, 25.6 mm. **Subject:** EU Expansion **Obv:** Stylized flower **Obv. Designer:** Pertti Mäkinen **Rev:** Denomination and map **Rev. Designer:** Luc Luycx **Edge:** Reeded and lettered

Date	Mintage	F	VF	XF	Unc	BU
2004	1,000,000	—	—	—	10.00	11.50

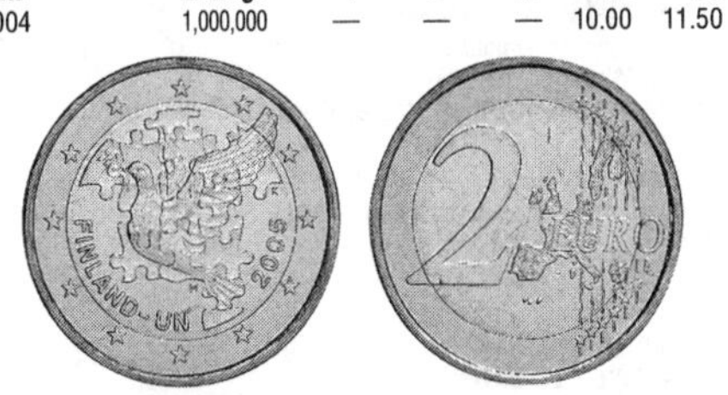

KM# 119 2 EURO

8.5200 g., Bi-Metallic Brass center in Copper-Nickel ring, 25.6 mm. **Subject:** 60th Anniversary - Finland - UN **Obv:** Dove on a puzzle **Rev:** Denomination over map **Edge:** Reeded and lettered **Edge Lettering:** "YK 1945-2005 FN"

Date	Mintage	F	VF	XF	Unc	BU
2005	2,000,000	—	—	—	6.00	7.50
2006	—	—	—	—	6.00	7.50

KM# 125 2 EURO

8.5200 g., Bi-Metallic Brass center in Copper-Nickel ring, 25.6 mm. **Obv:** Two faces **Obv. Designer:** Pertti Mäkinen **Rev:** Value and map **Rev. Designer:** Luc Luycx **Edge:** Reeded and lettered **Edge Lettering:** "SUOMI FINLAND" **Note:** Centennial of Universal Suffrage

Date	Mintage	F	VF	XF	Unc	BU
ND (2006) M-M	2,500,000	—	—	—	6.00	7.50

KM# 130 2 EURO

8.5200 g., Bi-Metallic Brass center in Copper-nickel ring, 25.6 mm. **Obv:** 2 cloudberry flowers surrounded by stars on outer ring **Obv. Designer:** Raimo Heino **Rev:** Relief map of Western Europe, stars, lines and value **Rev. Designer:** Luc Luycx **Edge:** Reeded and lettered **Edge Lettering:** SUOMI FINLAND

Date	Mintage	F	VF	XF	Unc	BU
2007	—	—	—	—	6.00	7.50

KM# 138 2 EURO

8.3200 g., Bi-Metallic Coper-Nickel center in Brass ring, 25.72 mm. **Subject:** 50th Anniversary Treaty of Rome **Obv:** Open treaty book **Rev:** Large value at left, modified outline of Europe at right **Edge:** Reeded and lettered

Date	Mintage	F	VF	XF	Unc	BU
2007	—	—	—	—	7.00	9.00

KM# 111 5 EURO

20.1000 g., Bi-Metallic Copper-Nickel center in Brass ring, 34.9 mm. **Subject:** Ice Hockey World Championships **Obv:** Summer landscape and denomination **Rev:** Three hockey sticks and a puck **Edge:** Plain **Designer:** Pertti Mäkinen

Date	Mintage	F	VF	XF	Unc	BU
2003 M-M	150,000	—	—	—	15.00	20.00

KM# 118 5 EURO

19.8000 g., Bi-Metallic Brass center in Copper-Nickel ring, 35 mm. **Obv:** Female javelin thrower, denomination **Rev:** Running feet **Edge:** Plain **Designer:** Tapio Kettunen

Date	Mintage	F	VF	XF	Unc	BU
2005 K-M	170,000	—	—	—	15.00	20.00
2005 K-M Proof	5,000	Value: 25.00				

KM# 123 5 EURO

18.7000 g., Copper, 35 mm. **Subject:** 150th Anniversary - Demilitarization of Aland **Obv:** Boat, Dove of Peace on the helm **Rev:** Tree **Edge Lettering:** AHVENANMAAN DEMILITARISOINTI 150 VUOTTA* **Designer:** Pertti Mäkinen

Date	Mintage	F	VF	XF	Unc	BU
2006 M-M	55,000	—	—	—	20.00	25.00

KM# 131 5 EURO

9.8100 g., Bi-Metallic Copper-Nickel center in Brass ring, 27.25 mm. **Subject:** Finland Presidency of European Union **Obv:** Letter decorations with 2006 and SUOMI-FINLAND **Rev:** 5 EURO below letter decoration **Designer:** Reijo Paavilainen

Date	Mintage	F	VF	XF	Unc	BU
2006 P-M	100,000	—	—	—	15.00	20.00

KM# 135 5 EURO

19.8000 g., Bi-Metallic Brass center in Copper-Nickel ring, 35 mm. **Subject:** Anniversary of Independence **Designer:** Reijo Paavilainen

Date	Mintage	F	VF	XF	Unc	BU
2007 P	—	—	—	—	15.00	20.00
2007 P Proof	—	Value: 25.00				

KM# 107 10 EURO

27.4000 g., 0.9250 Silver 0.8148 oz. ASW, 38.6 mm. **Subject:** 50th Anniversary - Helsinki Olympics **Obv:** Flames and denomination above globe with map of Finland **Obv. Designer:** Erkki Vainio **Rev:** Tower and partial coin design **Rev. Designer:** Hannu Veijalainen **Edge:** Plain

Date	Mintage	F	VF	XF	Unc	BU
2002 W-M	10,000	—	—	—	28.00	30.00
2002 W-M Proof	34,800	Value: 32.00				

KM# 108 10 EURO

27.4000 g., 0.9250 Silver 0.8148 oz. ASW, 38.6 mm. **Subject:** Elias Lönnrot **Obv:** Ribbon with stars **Rev:** Quill and signature **Edge:** Plain **Designer:** Pertti Mäkinen.

Date	Mintage	F	VF	XF	Unc	BU
2002 M-M	40,000	—	—	—	28.00	30.00
2002 M-M Proof	40,000	Value: 32.00				

KM# 110 10 EURO

27.4000 g., 0.9250 Silver 0.8148 oz. ASW, 38.6 mm. **Subject:** Anders Chydenius **Obv:** Stylized design **Rev:** Name and book **Edge:** Plain **Designer:** Tero Lounas

Date	Mintage	F	VF	XF	Unc	BU
2003 L-M	30,000	—	—	—	32.00	35.00
2003 Proof	30,000	Value: 40.00				

KM# 112 10 EURO

27.4000 g., 0.9250 Silver 0.8148 oz. ASW, 38.6 mm. **Subject:** Mannerheim and St. Petersburg **Obv:** Head 3/4 facing **Rev:** Fortress, denomination at right **Designer:** Anneli Sipiläinen

Date	Mintage	F	VF	XF	Unc	BU
2003 S-M	6,000	—	—	—	35.00	37.50
2003 S-M Proof	29,000	Value: 55.00				

KM# 115 10 EURO

27.4000 g., 0.9250 Silver 0.8148 oz. ASW, 38.6 mm. **Subject:** 200th Birthday of Johan Ludwig Runeberg **Obv:** Head of Runeberg **Rev:** Text of 1831 Helsingfors Tidningar newspaper **Designer:** Heli Kauhanen

Date	Mintage	F	VF	XF	Unc	BU
2004 K-M	6,400	—	—	—	32.00	35.00
2004 K-M Proof	600	Value: 45.00				

KM# 116 10 EURO

27.4000 g., 0.9250 Silver 0.8148 oz. ASW, 38.6 mm. **Subject:** Tove Jansson **Obv:** Three "muumi" figures **Rev:** Head of Tove Jansson **Edge:** Pertti Mäkinen

Date	Mintage	F	VF	XF	Unc	BU
2004 M-M	50,000	—	—	—	32.00	35.00
2004 M-M Proof	20,000	Value: 45.00				

KM# 120 10 EURO

25.5000 g., 0.9250 Silver 0.7583 oz. ASW, 38.6 mm. **Subject:** 60 years of Peace **Obv:** Dove of peace **Rev:** Flowering plant **Designer:** Pertti Mäkinen

Date	Mintage	F	VF	XF	Unc	BU
2005 M-M	55,000	—	—	—	32.00	35.00
2005 Proof	5,000	Value: 45.00				

KM# 122 10 EURO

25.5000 g., 0.9250 Silver 0.7583 oz. ASW, 38.6 mm. **Subject:** Unknown Soldier and Finnish Film Art **Obv:** Trench **Rev:** Soldier with helmet on top of a film **Designer:** Reijo Paavilainen

Date	Mintage	F	VF	XF	Unc	BU
2005 P-M	25,000	—	—	—	35.00	37.50
2005 P-M Proof	15,000	Value: 50.00				

KM# 132 10 EURO

25.5000 g., 0.9250 Silver 0.7583 oz. ASW, 38.6 mm. **Subject:** 100th Anniversary of Parliamentary Reform **Obv:** Two stylist heads female and male with text SUOMI FINLAND 10 EURO **Rev:** Male and female fingers inserting ballot paper into ballot box with text 100V EDUSKUNTAUUDISTUS 2006 **Rev. Designer:** Pertti Mäkinen **Edge Lettering:** LANTDAGSREFORMEN 1906

Date	Mintage	F	VF	XF	Unc	BU
2006 M-M	30,000	—	—	—	32.00	35.00
2006 M-M Proof	—	Value: 45.00				

KM# 124 10 EURO

25.5000 g., 0.9250 Silver 0.7583 oz. ASW, 38.6 mm. **Subject:** 200th Birthday - Johan Vilhelm Snellman **Obv:** Sun rising over the lake **Rev:** Snellman **Designer:** Tapio Kettunen

Date	Mintage	F	VF	XF	Unc	BU
2006 K-M	—	—	—	—	32.00	35.00
2006 K-M Proof	—	Value: 45.00				

KM# 134 10 EURO

25.5000 g., 0.9250 Silver 0.7583 oz. ASW, 38.6 mm. **Subject:** A.E. Nordenskiöld and the Northeast Passage **Designer:** Reijo Paavilainen

Date	Mintage	F	VF	XF	Unc	BU
2007 P	7,000	—	—	—	32.00	35.00
2007 P Proof	33,000	Value: 45.00				

KM# 136 10 EURO

25.5000 g., 0.9250 Silver 0.7583 oz. ASW, 38.6 mm. **Subject:** Mikael Agricola - Finnish Language **Designer:** Reijo Paavilainen

Date	Mintage	F	VF	XF	Unc	BU
2007 P	—	—	—	—	32.00	35.00
2007 P Proof	—	Value: 45.00				

KM# 121 20 EURO

1.7300 g., 0.9000 Gold 0.0501 oz. AGW, 13.9 mm. **Subject:** 10th Anniversary - IAAF World Championships in Athletics **Obv:** Helsinki Stadium **Rev:** Two faces **Designer:** Pertti Mäkinen

Date	Mintage	F	VF	XF	Unc	BU
2005 M-M Proof	30,000	Value: 100				

KM# 113 50 EURO

13.2000 g., Bi-Metallic Gold And Silver **Ring Composition:** 0.9250 Silver **Center Composition:** 0.7500 Gold, 27.25 mm. **Subject:** Finnish art and design **Obv:** Snowflake design within box, beaded circle surrounds **Rev:** Snowflake design within beaded circle **Designer:** Matti Peltokangas

Date	Mintage	F	VF	XF	Unc	BU
2003 P-M Proof	10,600	Value: 320				

KM# 133 50 EURO
12.8000 g., Tri-Metallic 0.750 Gold 0.125 Silver 0.125 Copper center in 0.925 Silver and 0.075 Copper ring, 27.25 mm. **Subject:** Finland Presidency of European Union **Obv:** Letter decorations with 2006 and SUOMI-FINLAND **Rev:** 50 EURO below letter decoration **Designer:** Reijo Paavilainen

Date	Mintage	F	VF	XF	Unc	BU
2006 P-M Proof	8,000	Value: 320				

KM# 109 100 EURO
8.6400 g., 0.9000 Gold 0.2500 oz. AGW, 22 mm. **Subject:** Lapland **Obv:** Small tree and mountain stream **Rev:** Lake landscape beneath the midnight sun **Edge:** Plain with serial number **Designer:** Toivo Jaatinen

Date	Mintage	F	VF	XF	Unc	BU
2002 J-M Proof	25,000	Value: 250				

KM# 117 100 EURO
8.6400 g., 0.9000 Gold 0.2500 oz. AGW, 22 mm. **Subject:** 150th Birthday of Albert Edelfelt **Obv:** Flower **Rev:** Head of Edelfelt **Designer:** Pertti Mäkinen

Date	Mintage	F	VF	XF	Unc	BU
2004 M-M Proof	8,500	Value: 280				

KM# 137 100 EURO
8.4800 g., 0.9170 Gold 0.2500 oz. AGW **Subject:** Anniversary of Independence **Designer:** Reijo Paavilainen

Date	Mintage	F	VF	XF	Unc	BU
2007 P	—	—	—	—	240	250
2007 P Proof	—	Value: 275				

MINT SETS

KM#	Date	Mintage	Identification	Issue Price	Mkt Val
MS58	2001 (5)	20,000	KM#65, 66, 73, 76, 77 plus 1865 coin design medal	18.00	20.00
MS59	2001 (5)	—	KM#65, 66, 73, 76, 77, medal (Johan Vilhelm Snellman)	—	22.50
MS60	2002 (8)	—	KM#98-105, medal (Church)	—	35.00
MS61	2003 (8)	—	KM#98-105	—	32.50
MS62	2004 (8)	—	KM#98-105, medal	—	32.50
MS63	2004/II (8)	—	KM#98-105, 114, medal	—	35.00
MS64	2005 (8)	—	KM#98-105, medal	—	32.50
MS65	2005/II (8)	—	KM#98-105, 118	—	35.00
MS66	2006 (9)	55,000	KM#98-105, 119	—	40.00
MS67	2006/II (9)	—	KM#98-105 and new 2 Euro	—	40.00

PROOF SETS

KM#	Date	Mintage	Identification	Issue Price	Mkt Val
PS9	2001 (5)	—	KM#65-66, 73, 76-77, medal (Suomen Markka 1864-2001)	—	60.00
PS10	2002 (8)	8,000	KM#98-105, gold medal (National Theater)	—	550
PS11	2002 (8)	—	KM#98-105, Silver medal	—	185
PS12	2003 (8)	—	KM#98-105	—	160
PS13	2004 (9)	5,000	KM#98-105, 116, medal	—	225
PS14	2005 (9)	3,000	KM#98-105, 118	—	200
PS15	2006 (9)	3,300	KM#98-105, medal (Salmon) and new 2 Euro	—	200

The French Republic, largest of the West European nations, has an area of 210,026 sq. mi. (547,030 sq. km.) and a population of 58.1 million. Capital: Paris. Agriculture, manufacturing, tourist industry and financial services are the most important elements of France's diversified economy. Textiles and clothing, steel products, machinery and transportation equipment, chemicals, pharmaceuticals, nuclear electricity, agricultural products and wine are exported.

RULER
Fifth Republic, 1959—

ENGRAVER GENERALS' PRIVY MARKS

Mark	Desc.	Date	Name
	Horseshoe	2000-2002	Gérard Buquoy
	SL Heart-shaped monogram	2002-2003	Serge Levet
	French horn w/starfish in water	2003	Hubert Lariviére

MINT DIRECTORS' PRIVY MARKS
Some modern coins struck from dies produced at the Paris Mint have the 'A' mint mark. In the absence of a mint mark, the cornucopia privy mark serves to attribute a coin to Paris design.

A – Paris, Central Mint

MONETARY SYSTEM
(Commencing 2002)
100 Euro Cents = 1 Euro

MODERN REPUBLICS
1870-

REFORM COINAGE
Commencing 1960

1 Old Franc = 1 New Centime;
100 New Centimes = 1 New Franc

KM# 928 CENTIME
1.6500 g., Chrome-Steel, 15 mm. **Obv:** Cursive legend surrounds grain sprig **Rev:** Cursive denomination, date at top **Edge:** Plain **Designer:** Atelier de Paris **Note:** 1991-1993 dated coins, non-Proof, exist in both coin and medal alignment. Values given here are for medal alignment examples. Pieces struck in coin alignment have been traded for as much as $50.00.

Date	Mintage	F	VF	XF	Unc	BU
2001	—	—	—	—	1.00	1.50
Note: In sets only						
2001 Proof	—	Value: 2.00				

KM# 928a CENTIME
2.5000 g., 0.7500 Gold 0.0603 oz. AGW **Obv:** Cursive legend surrounds grain sprig, medallic alignment **Rev:** Cursive denomination, date above, medallic alignment **Edge:** Plain **Note:** Last Centime.

Date	Mintage	F	VF	XF	Unc	BU
2001	Est. 7,492	—	—	—	—	110

KM# 933 5 CENTIMES
2.0000 g., Copper-Aluminum-Nickel, 17 mm. **Obv:** Liberty bust left **Obv. Designer:** Henri Lagriffoul **Rev:** Denomination above date, grain sprig below, laurel branch at left **Rev. Designer:** Adrien Dieudonne **Edge:** Plain **Note:** 1991-1993 dated coins, non-Proof exist in both coin and medal alignment.

Date	Mintage	F	VF	XF	Unc	BU
2001	—	—	—	—	1.50	2.50
Note: In sets only						
2001 Proof	—	Value: 1.00				

KM# 929 10 CENTIMES
3.0000 g., Copper-Aluminum-Nickel, 20 mm. **Obv:** Liberty bust left **Obv. Designer:** Henri Lagriffoul **Rev:** Denomination above date, grain sprig below, laurel branch at left **Rev. Designer:** Adrien Dieudonne **Edge:** Plain **Note:** Without mint mark. 1991-1993 dated coins, non-Proof, exist in both coin and medal alignment.

Date	Mintage	F	VF	XF	Unc	BU
2001	—	—	—	—	2.00	—
Note: In sets only						
2001 Proof	—	Value: 1.00				

KM# 930 20 CENTIMES
4.0000 g., Copper-Aluminum-Nickel, 23.5 mm. **Obv:** Liberty bust left **Obv. Designer:** Henri Lagriffoul **Rev:** Denomination above date, grain sprig below, laurel branch at left **Rev. Designer:** Adrien Dieudonne **Edge:** Plain **Note:** Without mint mark. 1991-1993 dated coins, non-Proof, exist in both coin and medal alignment.

Date	Mintage	F	VF	XF	Unc	BU
2001	—	—	—	—	2.00	—
Note: In sets only						
2001 Proof	—	Value: 1.00				

KM# 931.2 1/2 FRANC
4.5000 g., Nickel, 19.5 mm. **Obv:** Modified sower, engraver's signature: "O. ROTY" preceded by "D'AP" **Rev:** Laurel divides date and denomination **Edge:** Plain

Date	Mintage	F	VF	XF	Unc	BU
2001	—	—	—	—	0.40	0.60
2001 Proof	—	Value: 1.50				

KM# 931.1 1/2 FRANC
4.5000 g., Nickel, 19.5 mm. **Obv:** The seed sower **Rev:** Laurel divides denomination and date **Edge:** Reeded **Designer:** Louis Oscar Roty **Note:** Without mint mark.

Date	Mintage	F	VF	XF	Unc	BU
2001	—	—	—	—	2.00	3.00
Note: In sets only						

KM# 925.2 FRANC
6.0000 g., Nickel, 24 mm. **Obv:** Modified sower, engraver's signature: O. ROTY, preceded by D'AP **Rev:** Laurel divides date and denomination **Edge:** Plain

Date	Mintage	F	VF	XF	Unc	BU
2001	—	—	—	—	0.40	0.60
2001 Proof	—	Value: 2.50				

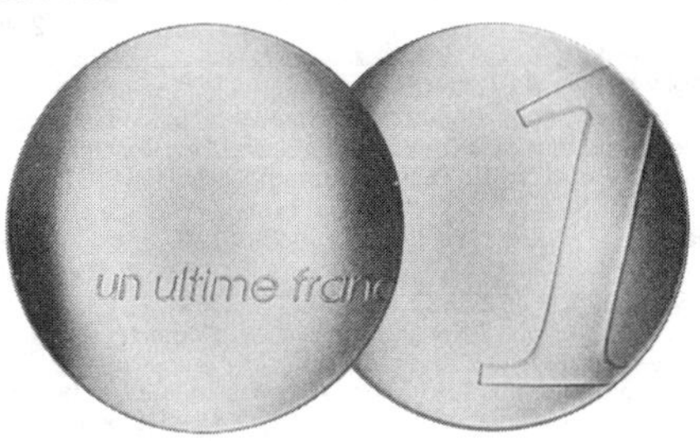

KM# 1290 FRANC
17.7700 g., 0.9800 Silver 0.5599 oz. ASW **Subject:** The Last

Franc **Obv:** Legend on polished field **Obv. Legend:** UN ULTIME FRANC **Rev:** Number "1" on polished field **Edge Lettering:** REPUBLIQUE FRANCAISE STARCK LIBERTE EGALITE FRATERNITE (2001). **Note:** The coin is intentionally warped and the edge inscription is very faint. Struck at Paris Mint.

Date	Mintage	F	VF	XF	Unc	BU
2001 Matte	49,838	Value: 75.00				

KM# 1290a FRANC
26.1000 g., 0.7500 Gold 0.6293 oz. AGW **Subject:** The Last Franc **Obv:** Legend on polished field **Obv. Legend:** UN ULTIME FRANC **Rev:** Number "1" on polished field **Edge Lettering:** REPUBLIQUE FRANCAISE. STARCK. LIBERTE. EGALITE. FRATERNITE (cornucopia) 2001 **Note:** This coin has an intentionally warped surface and the edge inscription is very weak.

Date	Mintage	F	VF	XF	Unc	BU
2001 Matte	4,963	—	—	—	625	650

KM# 925.1 FRANC
6.0000 g., Nickel, 24 mm. **Obv:** The seed sower **Obv. Designer:** Louis Oscar Roty **Rev:** Laurel branch divides denomination and date **Edge:** Reeded **Note:** Without mint mark.

Date	Mintage	F	VF	XF	Unc	BU
2001	20,000,000	—	—	—	0.40	0.60

KM# 925.1a FRANC
8.0000 g., 0.7500 Gold 0.1929 oz. AGW, 24 mm. **Obv:** The seed sower **Rev:** Laurel divides date and denomination **Edge:** Reeded **Designer:** Louis Oscar Roty **Note:** Medallic alignment.

Date	Mintage	F	VF	XF	Unc	BU
2001	Est. 9,941	—	—	—	230	275

KM# 942.1 2 FRANCS
7.5000 g., Nickel, 26.5 mm. **Obv:** The seed sower **Rev:** Denomination on branches, date below **Edge:** Plain **Designer:** Louis Oscar Roty

Date	Mintage	F	VF	XF	Unc	BU
2001 Bee	—	—	—	—	0.75	1.25

KM# 942.2 2 FRANCS
7.5000 g., Nickel, 26.5 mm. **Obv:** The seed sower **Rev:** Denomination on branches, date below **Edge:** Plain

Date	Mintage	F	VF	XF	Unc	BU
2001	—	—	—	—	0.75	1.25
2001 Proof	—	Value: 3.50				

KM# 926a.1 5 FRANCS
10.0000 g., Nickel Clad Copper-Nickel, 29 mm. **Obv:** The seed sower **Rev:** Branches divide denomination and date **Edge:** Reeded **Designer:** Raymond Joly

Date	Mintage	F	VF	XF	Unc	BU
2001	—	—	—	—	5.00	7.50

Note: In sets only

KM# 926a.2 5 FRANCS
6.5000 g., Nickel Clad Copper-Nickel, 29 mm. **Obv:** Modified sower, engraver's signature: "O. ROTY" preceded by "D'AP" **Rev:** Branches divide date and denomination **Edge:** Plain

Date	Mintage	F	VF	XF	Unc	BU
2001	—	—	—	—	1.65	2.50
2001 Proof	—	Value: 6.50				

KM# 1309 5 FRANCS
12.0000 g., 0.9000 Silver 0.3472 oz. ASW, 29 mm. **Subject:** Last Year of the Franc **Obv:** The seed sower **Rev:** Denomination and date **Edge:** Lettered **Edge Lettering:** "* LIBERTY * EGALITE * FRATERNITE * "

Date	Mintage	F	VF	XF	Unc	BU
2001	25,000	—	—	—	22.50	25.00

KM# 1265.1 6.55957 FRANCS
13.0000 g., 0.9000 Silver 0.3761 oz. ASW **Subject:** Last Year of the French Franc **Obv:** French and other European euro currency equivalents **Rev:** Europa allegorical portrait, date below, "last year of the franc" logo after the date **Edge:** Reeded

Date	Mintage	F	VF	XF	Unc	BU
2001	Est. 20,000	—	—	—	18.00	20.00

KM# 1265.2 6.55957 FRANCS
22.2000 g., 0.9000 Silver 0.6423 oz. ASW **Obv:** French and other European euro currency equivalents **Rev:** Europa allegorical portrait, date below, "last year of the franc" logo after the date **Edge:** Plain

Date	Mintage	F	VF	XF	Unc	BU
2001 Proof	Est. 10,000	Value: 35.00				

KM# 1276 6.55957 FRANCS
22.2000 g., 0.9000 Silver 0.6423 oz. ASW **Subject:** Mottos **Obv:** Denomination **Rev:** FRATERNITE in red letters **Edge:** Reeded

Date	Mintage	F	VF	XF	Unc	BU
2001 Proof	2,171	Value: 40.00				

KM# 1277 6.55957 FRANCS
22.2000 g., 0.9000 Silver 0.6423 oz. ASW **Subject:** Mottos **Obv:** Denomination **Rev:** EGALITE in white letters

Date	Mintage	F	VF	XF	Unc	BU
2001 Proof	2,190	Value: 40.00				

KM# 1278 6.55957 FRANCS
22.2000 g., 0.9000 Silver 0.6423 oz. ASW **Subject:** Mottos **Obv:** Denomination **Rev:** LIBERTE in white letters

Date	Mintage	F	VF	XF	Unc	BU
2001 Proof	2,259	Value: 40.00				

KM# 964.2 10 FRANCS
Aluminum-Bronze, 23 mm. **Obv:** Winged figure divides RF **Rev:** Patterned denomination above date **Edge:** Plain

Date	Mintage	F	VF	XF	Unc	BU
2001	—	—	—	—	6.00	7.50
2001 Proof	—	Value: 15.00				

KM# 1268 10 FRANCS
22.2000 g., 0.9000 Silver 0.6423 oz. ASW **Subject:** Monuments of France - Palace of Versailles **Obv:** Stylized French map **Rev:** 1/2 bust of Louis XIV at right, internal and external palace views at left **Edge:** Plain

Date	Mintage	F	VF	XF	Unc	BU
2001 Proof	Est. 2,561	Value: 35.00				

KM# 1270 10 FRANCS
22.2000 g., 0.9000 Silver 0.6423 oz. ASW **Subject:** Monuments of France - Arch of Triumph **Obv:** Stylized French map **Rev:** Arch of Triumph on the Champs Elysees partial close up and aerial views

Date	Mintage	F	VF	XF	Unc	BU
2001 Proof	Est. 2,882	Value: 35.00				

KM# 1272 10 FRANCS
22.2000 g., 0.9000 Silver 0.6423 oz. ASW **Subject:** Monuments of France - Notre Dame Cathedral **Obv:** Stylized French map **Rev:** Gargoyle at left, cathedral views at right

Date	Mintage	F	VF	XF	Unc	BU
2001 Proof	Est. 2,877	Value: 35.00				

KM# 1274 10 FRANCS
22.2000 g., 0.9000 Silver 0.6423 oz. ASW **Subject:** Monuments of France - Eiffel Tower **Obv:** Stylized French map **Rev:** Two tower views

Date	Mintage	F	VF	XF	Unc	BU
2001 Proof	Est. 3,888	Value: 35.00				

KM# 1008.2 20 FRANCS
9.0000 g., Tri-Metallic Copper-Aluminum-Nickel center plug, Nickel inner ring, Copper-Aluminum-Nickel outer ring, 27 mm. **Obv:** Mont St. Michel **Rev:** Patterned denomination above date **Edge:** 5 milled bands, reeded or plain

Date	Mintage	F	VF	XF	Unc	BU
2001	—	—	—	—	8.00	10.00
2001 Proof	—	Value: 25.00				

KM# 1266 65.5997 FRANCS
8.4500 g., 0.9200 Gold 0.2499 oz. AGW **Subject:** Last Year of the French Franc **Obv:** French and other European euro currency equivalents **Rev:** Europa allegorical portrait, date below, "last year of the franc" logo after the date **Edge:** Reeded

Date	Mintage	F	VF	XF	Unc	BU
2001 Proof	3,000	Value: 275				

KM# 1269 100 FRANCS
17.0000 g., 0.9200 Gold 0.5028 oz. AGW **Subject:** Palace of Versailles **Obv:** Stylized French map **Rev:** Louis XIV with internal and external palace views **Edge:** Plain

Date	Mintage	F	VF	XF	Unc	BU
2001 Proof	105	Value: 500				

KM# 1271 100 FRANCS
17.0000 g., 0.9200 Gold 0.5028 oz. AGW **Obv:** Champs-Elysees **Rev:** Arch of Triumph partial close up and aerial views

Date	Mintage	F	VF	XF	Unc	BU
2001 Proof	115	Value: 500				

KM# 1273 100 FRANCS
17.0000 g., 0.9200 Gold 0.5028 oz. AGW **Obv:** Notre-Dame Cathedral **Rev:** Gargoyle and cathedral views

Date	Mintage	F	VF	XF	Unc	BU
2001 Proof	116	Value: 500				

KM# 1275 100 FRANCS
17.0000 g., 0.9200 Gold 0.5028 oz. AGW **Obv:** Eiffel Tower **Rev:** Two tower views

Date	Mintage	F	VF	XF	Unc	BU
2001 Proof	170	Value: 500				

KM# 1267 655.957 FRANCS
31.1035 g., 0.9990 Gold 0.9990 oz. AGW **Subject:** Last Year of the French Franc **Obv:** French and other European euro currency equivalents **Rev:** Europa allegorical portrait, date below, "last year of the franc" logo after the date **Edge:** Plain

Date	Mintage	F	VF	XF	Unc	BU
2001 Proof	2,000	Value: 975				

KM# 1267.1 655.957 FRANCS
155.5175 g., 0.9990 Gold 4.9948 oz. AGW **Obv:** French and other European euro currency equivalents **Rev:** Europa allegorical portrait, date below, "last year of the franc" after the date **Edge:** Plain

Date	Mintage	F	VF	XF	Unc	BU
2001 Proof	99	Value: 4,850				

KM# 1279 655.957 FRANCS
17.0000 g., 0.9200 Gold 0.5028 oz. AGW **Subject:** Motto Series **Obv:** Denomination **Rev:** FRATERNITE **Edge:** Reeded

Date	Mintage	F	VF	XF	Unc	BU
2001 Proof	62	Value: 500				

KM# 1280 655.957 FRANCS
17.0000 g., 0.9200 Gold 0.5028 oz. AGW **Subject:** Motto Series **Obv:** Denomination **Rev:** EGALITE

Date	Mintage	F	VF	XF	Unc	BU
2001 Proof	64	Value: 500				

KM# 1281 655.957 FRANCS
17.0000 g., 0.9200 Gold 0.5028 oz. AGW **Subject:** Motto Series **Obv:** Denomination **Rev:** LIBERTE

Date	Mintage	F	VF	XF	Unc	BU
2001 Proof	63	Value: 500				

EURO COINAGE

European Union Issues

KM# 1282 EURO CENT
2.2700 g., Copper Plated Steel, 16.3 mm. **Obv:** Human face **Obv. Designer:** Fabienne Courtiade **Rev:** Denomination and globe **Rev. Designer:** Luc Luycx **Edge:** Plain

Date	Mintage	F	VF	XF	Unc	BU
2001	300,681,580	—	—	—	0.35	0.50
2001 Proof	15,000	Value: 10.00				

Date	Mintage	F	VF	XF	Unc	BU
2002	200,000	—	—	—	7.50	10.00
2002 Proof	40,000	Value: 8.00				
2003	160,175,000	—	—	—	1.00	1.50
2003 Proof	20,000	Value: 10.00				
2004	400,000,000	—	—	—	0.35	0.50
2005	240,200,000	—	—	—	0.35	0.50
2006	—	—	—	—	0.35	0.50
2007	—	—	—	—	0.35	0.50

KM# 1283 2 EURO CENT

3.0300 g., Copper-Plated-Steel, 18.7 mm. **Obv:** Human face **Obv. Designer:** Fabienne Courtiade **Rev:** Denomination and globe **Rev. Designer:** Luc Luycx **Edge:** Grooved

Date	Mintage	F	VF	XF	Unc	BU
2001	249,101,580	—	—	—	0.50	0.75
2001 Proof	15,000	Value: 10.00				
2002	100,000	—	—	—	10.00	12.50
Note: In sets only						
2002 Proof	40,000	Value: 8.00				
2003	160,175,000	—	—	—	1.25	2.00
2003 Proof	20,000	Value: 10.00				
2004	300,000,000	—	—	—	—	1.00
2005	260,200,000	—	—	—	—	1.00
2006	—	—	—	—	—	1.00
2007	—	—	—	—	—	1.00

KM# 1284 5 EURO CENT

3.8600 g., Copper-Plated-Steel, 21.2 mm. **Obv:** Human face **Obv. Designer:** Fabienne Courtiade **Rev:** Denomination and globe **Rev. Designer:** Luc Luycx

Date	Mintage	F	VF	XF	Unc	BU
2001	217,324,477	—	—	—	0.75	1.25
2001 Proof	15,000	Value: 12.00				
2002	186,400,000	—	—	—	0.75	1.25
2002 Proof	15,000	Value: 10.00				
2003	101,175,000	—	—	—	1.00	1.50
2003 Proof	20,000	Value: 12.00				
2004	60,000,000	—	—	—	—	1.25
2005	20,200,000	—	—	—	—	1.25
2006	—	—	—	—	—	1.25
2007	—	—	—	—	—	1.25

KM# 1285 10 EURO CENT

4.0700 g., Brass, 19.7 mm. **Obv:** The seed sower divides date and RF **Obv. Designer:** Laurent Jorb **Rev:** Denomination and map **Rev. Designer:** Luc Luycx **Edge:** Reeded

Date	Mintage	F	VF	XF	Unc	BU
2001	144,513,261	—	—	—	1.25	2.00
2001 Proof	15,000	Value: 12.00				
2002	206,700,000	—	—	—	0.75	1.25
2002 Proof	40,000	Value: 10.00				
2003	180,875,000	—	—	—	1.25	2.00
2003 Proof	20,000	Value: 12.00				
2004	—	—	—	—	—	1.50
2005	45,000,000	—	—	—	—	1.50
2006	—	—	—	—	—	1.50

KM# 1410 10 EURO CENT

4.0700 g., Brass, 19.7 mm. **Obv:** Sower **Obv. Designer:** Laurent Jorb **Rev:** Relief map of Western Europe, stars, lines and value **Rev. Designer:** Luc Luycx **Edge:** Reeded

Date	Mintage	F	VF	XF	Unc	BU
2007	—	—	—	—	—	1.50

KM# 1286 20 EURO CENT

5.7300 g., Brass, 22.2 mm. **Obv:** The seed sower divides date and RF **Obv. Designer:** Laurent Jorb **Rev:** Denomination and map **Rev. Designer:** Luc Luycx **Edge:** Notched

Date	Mintage	F	VF	XF	Unc	BU
2001	256,342,108	—	—	—	1.00	1.50
2001 Proof	15,000	Value: 14.00				
2002	192,100,000	—	—	—	1.00	1.50
2002 Proof	40,000	Value: 12.00				
2003	100,000	—	—	—	6.50	9.50
2003 Proof	20,000	Value: 14.00				
2004	—	—	—	—	—	1.50
2005	—	—	—	—	—	1.50
2006	—	—	—	—	—	1.50

KM# 1411 20 EURO CENT

5.7300 g., Brass, 22.2 mm. **Obv:** Sower **Obv. Designer:** Laurent Jorb **Rev:** Relief map of Western Europe, stars, lines and value **Rev. Designer:** Luc Luycx **Edge:** Notched

Date	Mintage	F	VF	XF	Unc	BU
2007	—	—	—	—	—	1.50

KM# 1293 1/4 EURO

12.5000 g., Copper-Aluminum-Nickel, 30 mm. **Subject:** Childrens Design **Obv:** Euro globe with children **Rev:** Denomination and stars **Edge:** Plain

Date	Mintage	F	VF	XF	Unc	BU
2002	1,000,000	—	—	—	6.50	8.50

KM# 1300 1/4 EURO

13.0000 g., 0.9000 Silver 0.3761 oz. ASW, 30 mm. **Subject:** Europa **Obv:** Eight French euro coin designs **Rev:** Portrait and flags design of 6.55957 francs coin KM-1265 **Edge:** Reeded

Date	Mintage	F	VF	XF	Unc	BU
2002	20,000	—	—	—	18.00	22.00

KM# 1293a 1/4 EURO

13.0000 g., 0.9000 Silver 0.3761 oz. ASW, 30 mm. **Subject:** Childrens Design **Obv:** Euro globe with children **Rev:** Denomination **Edge:** Plain

Date	Mintage	F	VF	XF	Unc	BU
2002 Proof	10,000	Value: 45.00				

KM# 1331 1/4 EURO

3.1100 g., 0.9990 Gold 0.0999 oz. AGW, 15 mm. **Subject:** Children's Design **Obv:** Euro globe with children **Rev:** Denomination **Edge:** Plain

Date	Mintage	F	VF	XF	Unc	BU
2002 Proof	5,000	Value: 125				

KM# 1350 1/4 EURO

3.1100 g., 0.9999 Gold 0.1000 oz. AGW, 15 mm. **Obv:** Obverse design of first one franc coin **Rev:** Reverse design of first one franc coin **Edge:** Plain

Date	Mintage	F	VF	XF	Unc	BU
2003 Proof	5,000	Value: 125				

KM# 1372 1/4 EURO

22.2000 g., 0.9000 Silver 0.6423 oz. ASW, 37 mm. **Obv:** Sammuel de Champlain **Rev:** Sail ship **Edge:** Plain

Date	Mintage	F	VF	XF	Unc	BU
2004	20,000	—	—	—	27.50	32.50

KM# 1390 1/4 EURO

13.0000 g., 0.9000 Silver 0.3761 oz. ASW, 30 mm. **Subject:** European Union Expansion **Obv:** Partial face and flags **Rev:** Puzzle map **Edge:** Plain

Date	Mintage	F	VF	XF	Unc	BU
2004	20,000	—	—	—	20.00	25.00

KM# 1402 1/4 EURO

11.0000 g., Copper-Aluminum-Nickel, 30 mm. **Subject:** Jules Verne **Obv:** Various scenes from Jules Verne's novels **Rev:** Jules Verne's portrait left of value and date

Date	Mintage	F	VF	XF	Unc	BU
2005	50,000	—	—	—	—	10.00

KM# 1442 1/4 EURO

22.2000 g., 0.9000 Silver 0.6423 oz. ASW, 37 mm. **Obv:** Bust of Franklin facing slightly right at left, his diplomatic and technical successes at right **Obv. Legend:** BENJAMIN FRANKLIN 1706-2006 **Obv. Inscription:** AMI DE LA FRANCE **Rev:** French flag at left, American flag at right **Rev. Inscription:** PHILOSOPHE / DIPLOMATE / ÉCRIVAIN / SAVANT

Date	Mintage	F	VF	XF	Unc	BU
2006	15,000	—	—	—	30.00	35.00

KM# 1445 1/4 EURO

22.2000 g., 0.9000 Silver 0.6423 oz. ASW, 37 mm. **Subject:** Marshall Bernadotte under Napoleon **Rev:** Military bust facing 3/4 right at left, building in backgound at right **Rev. Legend:** LIBERT? ?GALIT? FRATERNIT? - KARL XIV JOHAN ROI DE SU?DE

Date	Mintage	F	VF	XF	Unc	BU
2006 Proof	10,000	—	—	—	30.00	35.00

KM# 1457 1/4 EURO

22.2000 g., 0.9000 Silver 0.6423 oz. ASW, 37.00 mm. **Subject:** Hôpitaux de France Foundation **Obv:** Foundation logo **Rev:** TGV train, money box on outlined map of France

Date	Mintage	F	VF	XF	Unc	BU
2006	50,000	—	—	—	—	30.00

KM# 1415 1/4 EURO

22.2000 g., 0.9000 Silver 0.6423 oz. ASW, 37 mm. **Obv:** Jean de la Fontaine, value, Chinese astrological animals, date, Paris mint privy marks but without national identification **Rev:** Dog in wreath **Edge:** Reeded **Note:** Anonymous coinage

Date	Mintage	F	VF	XF	Unc	BU
2006	10,000	—	—	—	30.00	35.00

KM# 1417 1/4 EURO
22.2000 g., 0.9000 Silver 0.6423 oz. ASW, 37 mm. **Obv:** Jean de la Fontaine, value, Chinese astrological animals, date, Paris mint privy marks but without national identification **Rev:** Pig in wreath **Edge:** Reeded **Note:** anonymous issue

Date	Mintage	F	VF	XF	Unc	BU
2007	10,000	—	—	—	30.00	35.00

KM# 1419 1/4 EURO
13.0000 g., 0.9000 Silver 0.3761 oz. ASW, 30 mm. **Obv:** Military bust of Lafayette facing 3/4 left **Obv. Legend:** LA FAYETTE. HÉROS DELA RÉVOLUTION AMÉRICAINE **Obv. Inscription:** 1757/1854 at left, RF monogram at right **Rev:** Sailing ship L' Hermione **Rev. Legend:** LA FAYETTE, HERO OF THE AMERICAN REVOLUTION **Edge:** Plain

Date	Mintage	F	VF	XF	Unc	BU
2007 (a) Prooflike	5,000	—	—	—	—	30.00

KM# 1421 1/4 EURO
15.0000 g., 0.9000 Silver 0.4340 oz. ASW **Subject:** 90th Anniversary Death of Degas **Obv:** Ballerina "The Star" at left **Obv. Inscription:** *Degas* **Rev:** Paint brushes and oils multicolor at left, self portrait at right **Rev. Inscription:** LIBERTÉ / ÉGALITÉ / FRATERNITÉ **Shape:** rectangular, 30 x 21 mm

Date	Mintage	F	VF	XF	Unc	BU
2007	5,000	—	—	—	40.00	—

KM# 1287 50 EURO CENT
7.8100 g., Brass, 24.2 mm. **Obv:** The seed sower divides date and RF **Obv. Designer:** Laurent Jorb **Rev:** Denomination and map **Rev. Designer:** Luc Luycx **Edge:** Reeded

Date	Mintage	F	VF	XF	Unc	BU
2001	276,287,274	—	—	—	1.25	2.00
2001 Proof	15,000	Value: 15.00				
2002	226,500,000	—	—	—	1.25	2.00
2002 Proof	40,000	Value: 14.00				
2003	100,000	—	—	—	7.50	11.50
2003 Proof	20,000	Value: 15.00				
2004	—	—	—	—	—	2.00
2005	—	—	—	—	—	2.00
2006	—	—	—	—	—	2.00

KM# 1412 50 EURO CENT
7.8100 g., Brass, 24.2 mm. **Obv:** Sower **Obv. Designer:** Laurent Jorb **Rev:** Relief map of Western Europe, stars, lines and value **Rev. Designer:** Luc Luycx **Edge:** Reeded

Date	Mintage	F	VF	XF	Unc	BU
2007	—	—	—	—	—	2.00

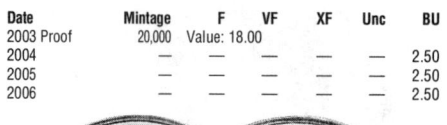

KM# 1288 EURO
7.5000 g., Bi-Metallic Copper-Nickel center in Brass ring, 23.3 mm. **Obv:** Stylized tree divides RF within circle, date below **Obv. Designer:** Joaquin Jimenez **Rev:** Denomination and map **Rev. Designer:** Luc Luycx **Edge:** Reeded and plain sections

Date	Mintage	F	VF	XF	Unc	BU
2001	150,251,624	—	—	—	2.75	4.00
2001 Proof	15,000	Value: 18.00				
2002	129,400,000	—	—	—	2.50	3.75
2002 Proof	40,000	Value: 16.00				
2003	100,000	—	—	—	8.00	12.50

Date	Mintage	F	VF	XF	Unc	BU
2003 Proof	20,000	Value: 18.00				
2004	—	—	—	—	—	2.50
2005	—	—	—	—	—	2.50
2006	—	—	—	—	—	2.50

KM# 1413 EURO
7.5000 g., Bi-Metallic Copper-Nickel center in Brass ring, 23.3 mm. **Obv:** Stylized tree **Obv. Designer:** Joaquin Jimenz **Rev:** Relief map of Western Europe, stars, lines and value **Rev. Designer:** Luc Luycx **Edge:** Reeded and plain sections

Date	Mintage	F	VF	XF	Unc	BU
2007	—	—	—	—	—	2.50

KM# 1332 1-1/2 EURO
22.2000 g., 0.9000 Silver 0.6423 oz. ASW, 37 mm. **Obv:** Victor Hugo, denomination and map **Rev:** Multicolor "Gavroche" **Edge:** Plain

Date	Mintage	F	VF	XF	Unc	BU
2002 Proof	10,000	Value: 52.50				

KM# 1301 1-1/2 EURO
22.2000 g., 0.9000 Silver 0.6423 oz. ASW, 37 mm. **Subject:** Europa **Obv:** Eight French euro coins design **Rev:** Portrait and flags design of 6.55957 francs KM-1265 **Edge:** Plain

Date	Mintage	F	VF	XF	Unc	BU
2002 Proof	50,000	Value: 40.00				

KM# 1305 1-1/2 EURO
22.2000 g., 0.9000 Silver 0.6423 oz. ASW, 37 mm. **Subject:** French Landmarks **Obv:** French map **Rev:** Le Mont St. Michel **Edge:** Plain

Date	Mintage	F	VF	XF	Unc	BU
2002 Proof	10,000	Value: 45.00				

KM# 1307 1-1/2 EURO
22.2000 g., 0.9000 Silver 0.6423 oz. ASW, 37 mm. **Subject:** French Landmarks **Obv:** French map **Rev:** La Butte Montmartre **Edge:** Plain

Date	Mintage	F	VF	XF	Unc	BU
2002 Proof	10,000	Value: 42.50				

KM# 1310 1-1/2 EURO
22.2000 g., 0.9000 Silver 0.6423 oz. ASW, 37 mm. **Subject:** First West to East Transatlantic Flight **Obv:** Denomination, map and Lindbergh portrait **Rev:** Spirit of St. Louis (airplane) and map **Edge:** Plain

Date	Mintage	F	VF	XF	Unc	BU
2002 Proof	10,000	Value: 45.00				

KM# 1321 1-1/2 EURO
22.2000 g., 0.9000 Silver 0.6423 oz. ASW, 37 mm. **Obv:** Tour de France logo **Rev:** Cyclist going left **Edge:** Plain

Date	Mintage	F	VF	XF	Unc	BU
2003 Proof	150,000	Value: 50.00				

KM# 1322 1-1/2 EURO
22.2000 g., 0.9000 Silver 0.6423 oz. ASW, 37 mm. **Obv:** Tour de France logo **Rev:** Group of cyclists and Arch de Triumph **Edge:** Plain

Date	Mintage	F	VF	XF	Unc	BU
2003A Proof	150,000	Value: 50.00				

KM# 1323 1-1/2 EURO
22.2000 g., 0.9000 Silver 0.6423 oz. ASW, 37 mm. **Obv:** Tour de France logo **Rev:** Two cyclists and spectators **Edge:** Plain

Date	Mintage	F	VF	XF	Unc	BU
2003A Proof	150,000	Value: 50.00				

KM# 1324 1-1/2 EURO
22.2000 g., 0.9000 Silver 0.6423 oz. ASW, 37 mm. **Obv:** Tour de France logo **Rev:** Two groups of cyclists **Edge:** Plain

Date	Mintage	F	VF	XF	Unc	BU
2003A Proof	150,000	Value: 50.00				

KM# 1325 1-1/2 EURO
22.2000 g., 0.9000 Silver 0.6423 oz. ASW, 37 mm. **Obv:** Tour de France logo **Rev:** Cyclists, stopwatch and gears **Edge:** Plain

Date	Mintage	F	VF	XF	Unc	BU
2003A Proof	150,000	Value: 50.00				

KM# 1336 1-1/2 EURO
22.2000 g., 0.9000 Silver 0.6423 oz. ASW, 37 mm. **Obv:** Jefferson and Napoleon with Louisiana Purchase map **Rev:** Jazz musician, mansion and river boat **Edge:** Plain

Date	Mintage	F	VF	XF	Unc	BU
2003 Proof	10,000	Value: 50.00				

KM# 1338 1-1/2 EURO
22.2000 g., 0.9000 Silver 0.6423 oz. ASW, 37 mm. **Obv:** Curved cross design with multiple values **Rev:** Goddess Europa and flags **Edge:** Plain

Date	Mintage	F	VF	XF	Unc	BU
2003 Proof	40,000	Value: 47.50				

KM# 1341 1-1/2 EURO
22.2000 g., 0.9000 Silver 0.6423 oz. ASW, 37 mm. **Obv:** Denomination and compass face **Rev:** SS Normandie and New York City **Edge:** Plain

Date	Mintage	F	VF	XF	Unc	BU
2003 Proof	15,000	Value: 50.00				

KM# 1343 1-1/2 EURO
22.2000 g., 0.9000 Silver 0.6423 oz. ASW, 37 mm. **Obv:** Denomination and compass face **Rev:** Airplane and Tokyo Geisha **Edge:** Plain

Date	Mintage	F	VF	XF	Unc	BU
2003 Proof	15,000	Value: 50.00				

KM# 1345 1-1/2 EURO
22.2000 g., 0.9000 Silver 0.6423 oz. ASW, 37 mm. **Obv:** Paul Gauguin **Rev:** Native woman **Edge:** Plain

Date	Mintage	F	VF	XF	Unc	BU
2003 Proof	15,000	Value: 50.00				

KM# 1351 1-1/2 EURO
22.2000 g., 0.9000 Silver 0.6423 oz. ASW, 37 mm. **Obv:** Obverse design of first one franc coin **Rev:** Reverse design of first one franc coin **Edge:** Plain

Date	Mintage	F	VF	XF	Unc	BU
2003 Proof	15,000	Value: 47.50				

KM# 1353 1-1/2 EURO
22.2000 g., 0.9000 Silver 0.6423 oz. ASW, 37 mm. **Obv:** Mona Lisa **Rev:** Leonardo da Vinci **Edge:** Plain

Date	Mintage	F	VF	XF	Unc	BU
2003 Proof	10,000	Value: 50.00				

KM# 1355 1-1/2 EURO
22.2000 g., 0.9000 Silver 0.6423 oz. ASW, 37 mm. **Obv:** Map and denomination **Rev:** Chateau Chambord **Edge:** Plain

Date	Mintage	F	VF	XF	Unc	BU
2003 Proof	10,000	Value: 47.50				

KM# 1357 1-1/2 EURO
22.2000 g., 0.9000 Silver 0.6423 oz. ASW, 37 mm. **Obv:** Denomination in swirling design **Rev:** Multicolor Hansel and Gretel, witch and house **Edge:** Plain

Date	Mintage	F	VF	XF	Unc	BU
2003 Proof	10,000	Value: 50.00				

KM# 1359 1-1/2 EURO
22.2000 g., 0.9000 Silver 0.6423 oz. ASW, 37 mm. **Obv:** Denomination in swirling design **Rev:** Multicolor Alice in Wonderland **Edge:** Plain

Date	Mintage	F	VF	XF	Unc	BU
2003 Proof	10,000	Value: 50.00				

KM# 1361 1-1/2 EURO
22.2000 g., 0.9000 Silver 0.6423 oz. ASW, 37 mm. **Obv:** Pierre de Coubertin **Rev:** Olympic runners **Edge:** Plain

Date	Mintage	F	VF	XF	Unc	BU
2003 Proof	50,000	Value: 47.50				

KM# 1364 1-1/2 EURO
22.2000 g., 0.9000 Silver 0.6423 oz. ASW, 37 mm. **Obv:** Map with denomination **Rev:** Avignon Popes Palace **Edge:** Plain

Date	Mintage	F	VF	XF	Unc	BU
2004 Proof	10,000	Value: 47.50				

KM# 1373 1-1/2 EURO
22.2000 g., 0.9000 Silver 0.6423 oz. ASW, 37 mm. **Obv:** Emile Loubet and King Edward VII **Rev:** Marianne and Britannia **Edge:** Plain

Date	Mintage	F	VF	XF	Unc	BU
2004 Proof	10,000	Value: 45.00				

KM# 1374 1-1/2 EURO
22.2000 g., 0.9000 Silver 0.6423 oz. ASW, 37 mm. **Obv:** Soccer ball and denomination **Rev:** Rooster and quill **Edge:** Plain

Date	Mintage	F	VF	XF	Unc	BU
2004 Proof	25,000	Value: 50.00				

KM# 1378 1-1/2 EURO
22.2000 g., 0.9000 Silver 0.6423 oz. ASW, 37 mm. **Obv:** Compass rose **Rev:** Ocean liner **Edge:** Plain

Date	Mintage	F	VF	XF	Unc	BU
2004 Proof	10,000	Value: 45.00				

KM# 1380 1-1/2 EURO
22.2000 g., 0.9000 Silver 0.6423 oz. ASW, 37 mm. **Obv:** Compass rose **Rev:** Trans-Siberian Railroad **Edge:** Plain

Date	Mintage	F	VF	XF	Unc	BU
2004 Proof	10,000	Value: 45.00				

KM# 1382 1-1/2 EURO
22.2000 g., 0.9000 Silver 0.6423 oz. ASW, 37 mm. **Obv:** Compass rose **Rev:** Half-track vehicle **Edge:** Plain

Date	Mintage	F	VF	XF	Unc	BU
2004 Proof	10,000	Value: 45.00				

KM# 1384 1-1/2 EURO
22.2000 g., 0.9000 Silver 0.6423 oz. ASW, 37 mm. **Obv:** Compass rose **Rev:** Biplane airliner **Edge:** Plain

Date	Mintage	F	VF	XF	Unc	BU
2004 Proof	10,000	Value: 45.00				

KM# 1379 1-1/2 EURO
17.0000 g., 0.9200 Gold 0.5028 oz. AGW, 31 mm. **Obv:** Compass rose **Rev:** Ocean liner **Edge:** Plain

Date	Mintage	F	VF	XF	Unc	BU
2004 Proof	1,000	Value: 550				

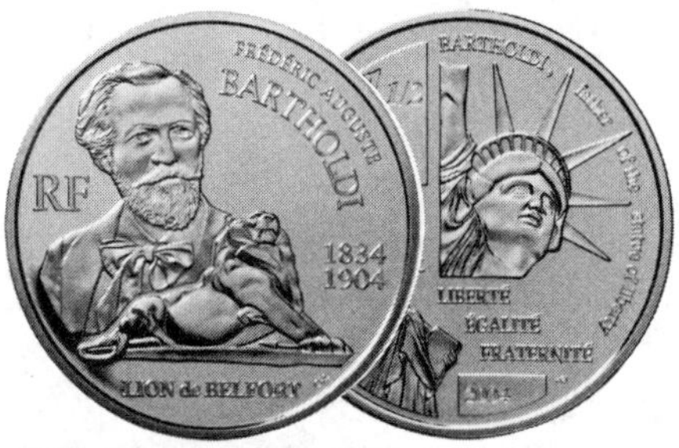

KM# 1386 1-1/2 EURO
22.2000 g., 0.9000 Silver 0.6423 oz. ASW, 37 mm. **Obv:** Statue of Liberty **Rev:** F.A. Bartholdi **Edge:** Plain

Date	Mintage	F	VF	XF	Unc	BU
2004 Proof	15,000	Value: 45.00				

KM# 1391 1-1/2 EURO
22.2000 g., 0.9000 Silver 0.6423 oz. ASW, 37 mm. **Subject:** European Union Expansion **Obv:** Partial face and flags **Rev:** Puzzle map **Edge:** Plain

Date	Mintage	F	VF	XF	Unc	BU
2004 Proof	40,000	Value: 40.00				

KM# 1366 1-1/2 EURO
22.2000 g., 0.9000 Silver 0.6423 oz. ASW, 37 mm. **Obv:** Book, eagle and denomination **Rev:** Napoleon and coronation scene in background **Edge:** Plain

Date	Mintage	F	VF	XF	Unc	BU
2004 Proof	20,000	Value: 45.00				

KM# 1369 1-1/2 EURO
22.2000 g., 0.9000 Silver 0.6423 oz. ASW, 37 mm. **Obv:** Soldiers and Normandy invasion scene **Rev:** "D-DAY" above denomination **Edge:** Plain

Date	Mintage	F	VF	XF	Unc	BU
2004 Proof	20,000	Value: 50.00				

KM# 1423 1-1/2 EURO
22.2000 g., 0.9000 Silver 0.6423 oz. ASW, 37 mm. **Subject:** Biathlon **Rev:** Skier at right facing 3/4 left, mountain peaks in background **Rev. Inscription:** JEUX D'HIVER

Date	Mintage	F	VF	XF	Unc	BU
2005 Proof	30,000	Value: 45.00				

KM# 1425 1-1/2 EURO
22.2000 g., 0.9000 Silver 0.6423 oz. ASW, 37 mm. **Series:** Jules Verne **Subject:** From the Earth to the Moon **Rev:** Crowd observing at lower left, volcano erupting above, moon at upper right, Verne in spaceship at lower right, factory chimneys belching smoke in bachground **Rev. Legend:** DE LA TERRE… LA LUNE

Date	Mintage	F	VF	XF	Unc	BU
2005 Proof	5,000	Value: 60.00				

KM# 1427 1-1/2 EURO
22.2000 g., 0.9000 Silver 0.6423 oz. ASW, 37 mm. **Rev:** Kitty and poodle at table at cafe, multicolor **Rev. Legend:** Hello Kitty

Date	Mintage	F	VF	XF	Unc	BU
2005 Proof	4,000	Value: 60.00				

KM# 1428 1-1/2 EURO
22.2000 g., 0.9000 Silver 0.6423 oz. ASW, 37 mm. **Rev:** Kitty on the Champs-Elysees, multicolor **Rev. Legend:** Hello Kitty

Date	Mintage	F	VF	XF	Unc	BU
2005 Proof	4,000	Value: 60.00				

KM# 1431 1-1/2 EURO
22.2000 g., 0.9000 Silver 0.6423 oz. ASW, 37 mm. **Subject:** Bicentennial Victory at Austerlitz **Rev:** Battle scene **Rev. Legend:** LIBERTÉ ÉGALITÉ FRATERNITÉ

Date	Mintage	F	VF	XF	Unc	BU
2005 Proof	15,000	Value: 50.00				

KM# 1434 1-1/2 EURO
22.2000 g., 0.9000 Silver 0.6423 oz. ASW, 37 mm. **Subject:** 50th Anniversary of the Europe flag **Rev:** Stars at left, partial flag at center right

Date	Mintage	F	VF	XF	Unc	BU
2005 Proof	15,000	Value: 50.00				

KM# 1436 1-1/2 EURO
, 37 mm. **Subject:** Centenary Law of Dec. 9, 1905 **Obv:** "Sower" left in ring of stars

Date	Mintage	F	VF	XF	Unc	BU
2005 Proof	15,000	Value: 50.00				
2006 Proof	10,000	Value: 50.00				

KM# 1438 1-1/2 EURO
22.2900 g., 0.9000 Silver 0.6449 oz. ASW, 37 mm. **Series:** Jules Verne **Subject:** 20,000 leagues under the sea **Rev:** Submarine above plants and divers **Rev. Legend:** VINGT MILLE LIEUES SOUS LES MERS

Date	Mintage	F	VF	XF	Unc	BU
2005 Proof	5,000	Value: 60.00				

KM# 1440 1-1/2 EURO
22.2000 g., 0.9000 Silver 0.6423 oz. ASW, 37 mm. **Subject:** 150th Anniversary of Classification of Bordeaux Wines **Rev:** Stylized female with grapes between various names of wines at her feet

Date	Mintage	F	VF	XF	Unc	BU
2005 Proof	5,000	Value: 60.00				

KM# 1441 1-1/2 EURO
22.2000 g., 0.9000 Silver 0.6423 oz. ASW, 37 mm. **Subject:** 50th Anniversary - End of World War II **Rev:** Doves in flight **Rev. Inscription:** L'EUROPE FAIT LA PAIX

Date	Mintage	F	VF	XF	Unc	BU
2005 Proof	50,000	Value: 40.00				

KM# 1453 1-1/2 EURO
22.2000 g., 0.9000 Silver 0.6423 oz. ASW, 37 mm. **Subject:** 100th Anniversary - Death of Paul Cézanne **Obv:** Self portrait **Obv. Inscription:** PAUL / CÉZANNE **Rev:** "The Card Players" **Rev. Legend:** LIBERTÉ ÉGALITÉ FRATERNITÉ

Date	Mintage	F	VF	XF	Unc	BU
2006 Proof	5,000	Value: 60.00				

KM# 1455 1-1/2 EURO
22.2000 g., 0.9000 Silver 0.6423 oz. ASW, 37 mm. **Obv:** Map of the Basilica **Rev:** Bust of Pope Benoît with arms outstretched facing 3/4 right at lower left, Basilica in background **Rev. Legend:** 500 ANS de la BASILIQUE SAINT-PIERRE

Date	Mintage	F	VF	XF	Unc	BU
2006 Proof	5,000	Value: 60.00				

KM# 1456 1-1/2 EURO
22.2000 g., 0.9000 Silver 0.6423 oz. ASW, 37 mm. **Rev:** Half of Arc at left, eternal flame above WW I plaque at right **Rev. Legend:** ARC DE TRIOMPHE

Date	Mintage	F	VF	XF	Unc	BU
2006 Proof	10,000	Value: 50.00				

KM# 1458 1-1/2 EURO
22.2000 g., 0.9000 Silver 0.6423 oz. ASW, 37 mm. **Subject:** 300th Anniversary - Completion of the Dome of Les Invalides **Rev:** Dome between Jules-Hardouin Mansart at left, Louis XIV at right **Rev. Legend:** SAINT-LOUIS - DES INVALIDES **Rev. Inscription:** 28/AOÛT - 1706

Date	Mintage	F	VF	XF	Unc	BU
2006 Proof	10,000	Value: 50.00				

KM# 1444 1-1/2 EURO
22.2000 g., 0.9200 Silver 0.6566 oz. ASW, 37 mm. **Subject:** 100th Anniversary - French Grand Prix **Obv:** Steering wheel with early race car in upper segment, two gauges at lower left, R / F at lower right **Obv. Legend:** LE MANS 1906 - CENTENAIRE du 1er GRAND PRIX de l'AUTOMOBILE CLUB de FRANCE **Rev:** Modern racing car's steering wheel **Rev. Legend:** MAGNY-COURS

Date	Mintage	F	VF	XF	Unc	BU
2006 Proof	5,000	Value: 60.00				

KM# 1447 1-1/2 EURO
22.2000 g., 0.9000 Silver 0.6423 oz. ASW, 37.00 mm. **Obv:** Strogoff horseback wielding sword, city at left, soldiers at lower left, calvalry at right **Obv. Legend:** MICHEL STROGOFF **Rev:** Head of Verne facing 3/4 right at left center, instruments and anchor in curved band **Rev. Legend:** 1828 JULES VERNE 1905 - LIBERTÉ . ÉGALITÉ . FRATERNITÉ

Date	Mintage	F	VF	XF	Unc	BU
2006 Proof	500	—	—	—	—	—

KM# 1450 1-1/2 EURO
22.2000 g., 0.9000 Silver 0.6423 oz. ASW, 37 mm. **Subject:** Jules Verne **Obv:** Hot air balloon, parrots at left, native masks at lower left, foliage at right, native huts below, map of Africa in background **Obv. Legend:** CINQ SEMAINES EN BALLOON **Rev:** Head of Verne facing 3/4 right at left center, instruments and anchor in curved band **Rev. Legend:** 1828 JULES VERNE 1905

Date	Mintage	F	VF	XF	Unc	BU
2006 Proof	5,000	Value: 60.00				

KM# 1452 1-1/2 EURO

22.2000 g., 0.9000 Silver 0.6423 oz. ASW, 37 mm. **Subject:** Formula 1 World Championship **Obv:** Race car outline on checker board background **Obv. Legend:** LIBERTÉ ÉGALITÉ FRATERNITÉ **Rev:** Race car outline in victory sprays with star **Rev. Legend:** RENAULT - CHAMPION DU MONDE FIA 2005 DESCONSTRUCTEURS DE FORMULE 1

Date	Mintage	F	VF	XF	Unc	BU
2006 Proof	10,000	Value: 50.00				

KM# 1289 2 EURO

8.5200 g., Bi-Metallic Brass center in Copper-Nickel ring, 25.6 mm. **Obv:** Stylized tree divides RF within circle, date below **Obv. Designer:** Joaquin Jimenez **Rev:** Denomination and map **Rev. Designer:** Luc Luycx **Edge:** Reeding with 2's and stars

Date	Mintage	F	VF	XF	Unc	BU
2001	237,950,793	—	—	—	3.75	6.00
2001 Proof	15,000	Value: 20.00				
2002	153,700,000	—	—	—	3.75	6.00
2002 Proof	40,000	Value: 18.00				
2003	100,000	—	—	—	8.50	13.50
2003 Proof	20,000	Value: 20.00				
2004	—	—	—	—	—	5.00
2005	—	—	—	—	—	5.00
2006	—	—	—	—	—	5.00

KM# 1414 2 EURO

8.5200 g., Bi-Metallic Brass center in Copper-Nickel ring, 25.6 mm. **Obv:** Stylized tree **Obv. Designer:** Joaquin Jimenez **Rev:** Relief map of Western Europe, stars, lines and value **Rev. Designer:** Luc Luycx **Edge:** Reeding with 2's and stars

Date	Mintage	F	VF	XF	Unc	BU
2007	—	—	—	—	—	6.00

KM# 1347 5 EURO

24.9000 g., 0.9000 Bi-Metallic Gold And Silver .900 Silver 22.2g planchet with .750 Gold 2.7 insert 0.7205 oz., 37 mm. **Obv:** The seed sower on gold insert **Rev:** Denomination and map **Edge:** Plain

Date	Mintage	F	VF	XF	Unc	BU
2003 Proof	10,000	Value: 475				

KM# 1371 5 EURO

24.9000 g., Bi-Metallic Gold And Silver .750 Gold 2.7 g insert on .900 Silver 22.2g planchet, 37 mm. **Obv:** The seed sower on gold insert **Rev:** French face map and denomination **Edge:** Plain

Date	Mintage	F	VF	XF	Unc	BU
2004 Proof	3,000	Value: 475				

KM# 1302 10 EURO

8.4500 g., 0.9990 Gold 0.2714 oz. AGW, 22 mm. **Subject:** Europa **Obv:** Eight French euro coin designs **Rev:** Portrait and flags design of 6.55957 francs KM-1265 **Edge:** Reeded

Date	Mintage	F	VF	XF	Unc	BU
2002 Proof	3,000	Value: 285				

KM# 1326 10 EURO

8.4500 g., 0.9200 Gold 0.2499 oz. AGW, 22 mm. **Obv:** Tour de France logo **Rev:** Cyclist going left **Edge:** Reeded

Date	Mintage	F	VF	XF	Unc	BU
2003A Proof	5,000	Value: 250				

KM# 1327 10 EURO

8.4500 g., 0.9200 Gold 0.2499 oz. AGW, 22 mm. **Obv:** Tour de France logo **Rev:** Group of cyclists and Arch de Triumph **Edge:** Reeded

Date	Mintage	F	VF	XF	Unc	BU
2003A Proof	5,000	Value: 250				

KM# 1328 10 EURO

8.4500 g., 0.9200 Gold 0.2499 oz. AGW, 22 mm. **Obv:** Tour de France logo **Rev:** Two cyclists and spectators **Edge:** Reeded

Date	Mintage	F	VF	XF	Unc	BU
2003A Proof	5,000	Value: 250				

KM# 1329 10 EURO

8.4500 g., 0.9200 Gold 0.2499 oz. AGW, 22 mm. **Obv:** Tour de France logo **Rev:** Two groups of cyclists **Edge:** Reeded

Date	Mintage	F	VF	XF	Unc	BU
2003A Proof	5,000	Value: 250				

KM# 1330 10 EURO

8.4500 g., 0.9200 Gold 0.2499 oz. AGW, 22 mm. **Obv:** Tour de France logo **Rev:** Cyclist, stop watch and gears **Edge:** Reeded

Date	Mintage	F	VF	XF	Unc	BU
2003A Proof	5,000	Value: 250				

KM# 1348 10 EURO

8.4500 g., 0.9200 Gold 0.2499 oz. AGW, 22 mm. **Obv:** The seed sower **Rev:** Denomination and map **Edge:** Plain

Date	Mintage	F	VF	XF	Unc	BU
2003 Proof	15,000	Value: 250				

KM# 1352 10 EURO

8.4500 g., 0.9200 Gold 0.2499 oz. AGW, 22 mm. **Obv:** Obverse design of first one franc coin **Rev:** Reverse design of first one franc coin **Edge:** Plain

Date	Mintage	F	VF	XF	Unc	BU
2003 Proof	10,000	Value: 250				

KM# 1362 10 EURO

8.4500 g., 0.9200 Gold 0.2499 oz. AGW, 22 mm. **Obv:** Pierre de Coubertin **Rev:** Olympic runners **Edge:** Plain

Date	Mintage	F	VF	XF	Unc	BU
2003 Proof	15,000	Value: 250				

KM# 1367 10 EURO

6.4100 g., 0.9000 Gold 0.1855 oz. AGW, 22 mm. **Obv:** Book, denomination and eagle **Rev:** Napoleon and coronation scene **Edge:** Plain

Date	Mintage	F	VF	XF	Unc	BU
2004 Proof	5,000	Value: 200				

KM# 1375 10 EURO

8.4500 g., 0.9200 Gold 0.2499 oz. AGW, 22 mm. **Obv:** Half soccer ball and denomination **Rev:** Eiffel tower and soccer balls **Edge:** Plain

Date	Mintage	F	VF	XF	Unc	BU
2004 Proof	10,000	Value: 300				

KM# 1392 10 EURO

8.4500 g., 0.9200 Gold 0.2499 oz. AGW, 22 mm. **Subject:** European Union Expansion **Obv:** Partial face and flags **Rev:** Puzzle map **Edge:** Reeded

Date	Mintage	F	VF	XF	Unc	BU
2004 Proof	5,000	Value: 245				

KM# 1403 10 EURO

8.4500 g., 0.9200 Gold 0.2499 oz. AGW, 22 mm. **Subject:** Jules Verne **Obv:** Various scenes from Verne's novel "Around The World in 80 Days" **Rev:** Jules Verne's portrait left of value and date

Date	Mintage	F	VF	XF	Unc	BU
2005 Proof	2,000	Value: 300				

KM# 1424 10 EURO

8.4500 g., 0.9200 Gold 0.2499 oz. AGW, 22 mm. **Subject:** Biathlon **Rev:** Skier at right facing 3/4 left, mountain peaks in background **Rev. Inscription:** JEUX D'HIVER

Date	Mintage	F	VF	XF	Unc	BU
2005 Proof	—	Value: 300				

KM# 1429 10 EURO

8.4500 g., 0.9200 Gold 0.2499 oz. AGW, 22 mm. **Rev:** Kitty at the Spectacle, multicolor **Rev. Legend:** Hello Kitty

Date	Mintage	F	VF	XF	Unc	BU
2005 Proof	1,000	Value: 325				

KM# 1432 10 EURO

6.4100 g., 0.9000 Gold 0.1855 oz. AGW, 21 mm. **Subject:** Bicentennial - Victory at Austerlitz **Rev:** Battle scene **Rev. Legend:** LIBERTÉ ÉGALITÉ FRATERNITÉ

Date	Mintage	F	VF	XF	Unc	BU
2005 Proof	3,000	Value: 300				

KM# 1435 10 EURO

8.4500 g., 0.9200 Gold 0.2499 oz. AGW, 22 mm. **Subject:** 50th Anniversary - Flag of Europe **Rev:** Stars at left, partial flag at center right

Date	Mintage	F	VF	XF	Unc	BU
2005 Proof	3,000	Value: 300				

KM# 1439 10 EURO

8.4500 g., 0.9200 Gold 0.2499 oz. AGW, 22 mm. **Series:** Jules Verne **Subject:** 20,000 Leagues Under the Sea **Rev:** Submarine above plants and divers **Rev. Legend:** VINGT MILE LIEUES SOUS LES MERS

Date	Mintage	F	VF	XF	Unc	BU
2005 Proof	2,000	Value: 300				

KM# 1426 10 EURO

8.4500 g., 0.9200 Gold 0.2499 oz. AGW, 22 mm. **Series:** Jules Verne **Subject:** From the earth to the moon **Rev:** Crowd observing at lower left, volcano erupting above, moon at upper right, Verne in spaceship at lower right, chimneys belching smoke in backgroud **Rev. Legend:** DE LA TERRE À LA LUNE

Date	Mintage	F	VF	XF	Unc	BU
2005 Proof	2,000	Value: 300				

KM# 1448 10 EURO

8.4500 g., 0.9200 Gold 0.2499 oz. AGW, 22 mm. **Subject:** 20,000 Leagues Under the Sea **Obv:** Strogoff horseback wielding a sword, city at left, soldiers at lower left, calvary at right - the Tartars, Siberia and the Tsar's Army **Obv. Legend:** MICHEL STROGOFF **Rev:** Head of Verne facing 3/4 right at left center, instruments and anchor in curved band **Rev. Legend:** 1828 JULES VERNE 1905

Date	Mintage	F	VF	XF	Unc	BU
2006 Proof	500	Value: 350				

KM# 1449 10 EURO

8.4500 g., 0.9200 Gold 0.2499 oz. AGW, 22 mm. **Subject:** 20,000 Leagues Under the Sea **Obv:** Hot air balloon, parrots at left, native masks below left, foliage at right, huts below, map of Africa in background. **Obv. Legend:** CINQ SEMAINES EN BALLON **Rev:** Head of Verne facing 3/4 right at left center, instruments and anchor in curved band **Rev. Legend:** 1828 JULES VERNE 1905 - LIBERTÉ . ÉGALITÉ . FRATERNITÉ

Date	Mintage	F	VF	XF	Unc	BU
2006 Proof	500	Value: 350				

KM# 1451 10 EURO

8.4500 g., 0.9200 Gold 0.2499 oz. AGW, 22 mm. **Subject:** 100th Anniversary - French Grand Prix **Obv:** Steering wheel with early race car in upper segment, two gauges at lower left, R / F at lower right **Obv. Legend:** LE MANS 1906 - CENTENAIRE du 1er GRAND PRIX de l'AUTOMOBILE CLUB de FRANCE **Rev. Legend:** MAGNY-COURS

Date	Mintage	F	VF	XF	Unc	BU
2006 Proof	500	Value: 350				

KM# 1446 10 EURO

8.4500 g., 0.9200 Gold 0.2499 oz. AGW, 22 mm. **Subject:** Marshal Bernadotte under Napoleon **Rev:** Military bust facing 3/4 right at left, building in backgound at right **Rev. Legend:** LIBERT? ?GALIT? FRATERNIT? - KARL XIV JOHAN ROI DE SU?DE

Date	Mintage	F	VF	XF	Unc	BU
2006 Proof	1,000	Value: 325				

KM# 1416 10 EURO

8.4500 g., 0.9200 Gold 0.2499 oz. AGW, 22 mm. **Obv:** Jean de la Fontaine, value, Chinese astrological animals, date, Paris mint privy marks but without national identification **Rev:** Dog in wreath **Edge:** Reeded **Note:** Anonymous issue

Date	Mintage	F	VF	XF	Unc	BU
2006 Proof	500	Value: 350				

KM# 1418 10 EURO

8.4500 g., 0.9200 Gold 0.2499 oz. AGW, 22 mm. **Obv:** Jean de la Fontaine, value, Chinese astrological animals, date, Paris mint privy marks but without national identification **Rev:** Pig in wreath **Edge:** Reeded **Note:** anonymous issue

Date	Mintage	F	VF	XF	Unc	BU
2007 Proof	500	Value: 350				

KM# 1420 10 EURO

8.4500 g., 0.9200 Gold 0.2499 oz. AGW, 22 mm. **Obv:** Military bust of Lafayette facing 3/4 left **Obv. Legend:** LA FAYETTE. HÉROS DELA RÉVOLUTION AMÉRICAINE **Obv. Inscription:** 1757/1854 at left, RF monogram at right **Rev:** Sailing ship L' Hermione **Rev. Legend:** LA FAYETTE, HERO OF THE AMERICAN REVOLUTION **Edge:** Plain

Date	Mintage	F	VF	XF	Unc	BU
2007 (a) Proof	500	Value: 350				

KM# 1306 20 EURO

17.0000 g., 0.9200 Gold 0.5028 oz. AGW, 31 mm. **Subject:** French Landmarks **Obv:** French map **Rev:** Le Mont St. Michel **Edge:** Plain

Date	Mintage	F	VF	XF	Unc	BU
2002 Proof	1,000	Value: 550				

KM# 1308 20 EURO

17.0000 g., 0.9200 Gold 0.5028 oz. AGW, 31 mm. **Subject:** French Landmarks **Obv:** French map **Rev:** La Butte Montmartre **Edge:** Plain

Date	Mintage	F	VF	XF	Unc	BU
2002 Proof	1,000	Value: 550				

KM# 1333 20 EURO

17.0000 g., 0.9200 Gold 0.5028 oz. AGW, 31 mm. **Obv:** Victor Hugo, denomination and map **Rev:** "Gavroche" **Edge:** Plain

Date	Mintage	F	VF	XF	Unc	BU
2002 Proof	2,000	Value: 500				

KM# 1334 20 EURO

17.0000 g., 0.9200 Gold 0.5028 oz. AGW, 31 mm. **Obv:** Tour de France logo **Rev:** Cyclist going left **Edge:** Plain

Date	Mintage	F	VF	XF	Unc	BU
2003 Proof	5,000	Value: 500				

KM# 1337 20 EURO

17.0000 g., 0.9200 Gold 0.5028 oz. AGW, 31 mm. **Obv:** Jefferson and Napoleon with Louisiana Purchase map **Rev:** Jazz musician, mansion and river boat **Edge:** Plain

Date	Mintage	F	VF	XF	Unc	BU
2003 Proof	1,000	Value: 525				

KM# 1339 20 EURO

17.0000 g., 0.9200 Gold 0.5028 oz. AGW, 31 mm. **Obv:** Curved cross design with multiple values **Rev:** Goddess Europa and flags **Edge:** Plain

Date	Mintage	F	VF	XF	Unc	BU
2003 Proof	3,000	Value: 525				

KM# 1342 20 EURO

17.0000 g., 0.9200 Gold 0.5028 oz. AGW, 31 mm. **Obv:** Denomination and compass face **Rev:** SS Normandie and New York City skyline **Edge:** Plain

Date	Mintage	F	VF	XF	Unc	BU
2003 Proof	1,000	Value: 525				

KM# 1344 20 EURO
17.0000 g., 0.9200 Gold 0.5028 oz. AGW, 31 mm. **Obv:** Denomination and compass face **Rev:** Airplane and Tokyo Geisha **Edge:** Plain

Date	Mintage	F	VF	XF	Unc	BU
2003 Proof	1,000	Value: 525				

KM# 1346 20 EURO
17.0000 g., 0.9200 Gold 0.5028 oz. AGW, 31 mm. **Obv:** Paul Gauguin **Rev:** Native woman **Edge:** Plain

Date	Mintage	F	VF	XF	Unc	BU
2003 Proof	2,000	Value: 545				

KM# 1349 20 EURO
17.0000 g., 0.9200 Gold 0.5028 oz. AGW, 31 mm. **Obv:** The seed sower **Rev:** Denomination and map **Edge:** Plain

Date	Mintage	F	VF	XF	Unc	BU
2003 Proof	5,000	Value: 575				

KM# 1354 20 EURO
17.0000 g., 0.9200 Gold 0.5028 oz. AGW, 31 mm. **Obv:** Mona Lisa **Rev:** Leonardo da Vinci and denomination **Edge:** Plain

Date	Mintage	F	VF	XF	Unc	BU
2003 Proof	1,000	Value: 545				

KM# 1356 20 EURO
17.0000 g., 0.9200 Gold 0.5028 oz. AGW, 31 mm. **Obv:** Map and denomination **Rev:** Chateau Chambord **Edge:** Plain

Date	Mintage	F	VF	XF	Unc	BU
2003 Proof	1,000	Value: 525				

KM# 1358 20 EURO
17.0000 g., 0.9200 Gold 0.5028 oz. AGW, 31 mm. **Obv:** Denomination in swirling design **Rev:** Hansel and Gretel, witch and house **Edge:** Plain

Date	Mintage	F	VF	XF	Unc	BU
2003 Proof	1,000	Value: 545				

KM# 1360 20 EURO
17.0000 g., 0.9200 Gold 0.5028 oz. AGW, 31 mm. **Obv:** Denomination in swirling design **Rev:** Alice in Wonderland **Edge:** Plain

Date	Mintage	F	VF	XF	Unc	BU
2003 Proof	1,000	Value: 545				

KM# 1363 20 EURO
17.0000 g., 0.9200 Gold 0.5028 oz. AGW, 31 mm. **Obv:** Pierre de Coubertin **Rev:** Olympic runners **Edge:** Plain

Date	Mintage	F	VF	XF	Unc	BU
2003 Proof	3,000	Value: 525				

KM# 1365 20 EURO
17.0000 g., 0.9200 Gold 0.5028 oz. AGW, 31 mm. **Obv:** Map with denomination **Rev:** Avignon Popes Palace **Edge:** Plain

Date	Mintage	F	VF	XF	Unc	BU
2004 Proof	1,000	Value: 600				

KM# 1370 20 EURO
17.0000 g., 0.9200 Gold 0.5028 oz. AGW, 31 mm. **Obv:** Soldiers and Normandy invasion scene **Rev:** "D-DAY" above denomination **Edge:** Plain

Date	Mintage	F	VF	XF	Unc	BU
2004 Proof	2,000	Value: 600				

KM# 1376 20 EURO
17.0000 g., 0.9200 Gold 0.5028 oz. AGW, 31 mm. **Subject:** Centenary Law of Dec. 9, 1905 **Obv:** "Sower" left in ring of stars **Rev:** Denomination and French map face design **Edge:** Plain

Date	Mintage	F	VF	XF	Unc	BU
2004 Proof	3,000	Value: 525				
2006 Proof	1,000	Value: 550				

KM# 1381 20 EURO
17.0000 g., 0.9200 Gold 0.5028 oz. AGW, 31 mm. **Obv:** Compass rose **Rev:** Trans-Siberian Railroad **Edge:** Plain

Date	Mintage	F	VF	XF	Unc	BU
2004 Proof	1,000	Value: 535				

KM# 1383 20 EURO
17.0000 g., 0.9200 Gold 0.5028 oz. AGW, 31 mm. **Obv:** Compass rose **Rev:** Half-track vehicle **Edge:** Plain

Date	Mintage	F	VF	XF	Unc	BU
2004 Proof	1,000	Value: 535				

KM# 1385 20 EURO
17.0000 g., 0.9200 Gold 0.5028 oz. AGW, 31 mm. **Obv:** Compass rose **Rev:** Biplane airliner **Edge:** Plain

Date	Mintage	F	VF	XF	Unc	BU
2004 Proof	1,000	Value: 535				

KM# 1387 20 EURO
155.5000 g., 0.9500 Silver 4.7493 oz. ASW, 50 mm. **Obv:** Statue of Liberty **Rev:** F. A. Bartholdi **Edge:** Plain

Date	Mintage	F	VF	XF	Unc	BU
2004 Proof	999	Value: 175				

KM# 1388 20 EURO
17.0000 g., 0.9200 Gold 0.5028 oz. AGW, 31 mm. **Obv:** Statue of Liberty **Rev:** F. A. Bartholdi **Edge:** Plain

Date	Mintage	F	VF	XF	Unc	BU
2004 Proof	2,000	Value: 550				

KM# 1393 20 EURO
17.0000 g., 0.9200 Gold 0.5028 oz. AGW, 31 mm. **Subject:** European Union Expansion **Obv:** Partial face and flags **Rev:** Puzzle map **Edge:** Plain

Date	Mintage	F	VF	XF	Unc	BU
2004 Proof	3,000	Value: 550				

KM# 1433 20 EURO
17.0000 g., 0.9200 Gold 0.5028 oz. AGW, 31.00 mm. **Subject:** Bicentennial Victory at Austerlitz **Rev:** Battle scene **Rev. Legend:** LIBERTÉ ÉGALITÉ FRATERNITÉ

Date	Mintage	F	VF	XF	Unc	BU
2005 Proof	5,000	—	—	—	—	—

KM# 1437 20 EURO
17.0000 g., 0.9200 Gold 0.5028 oz. AGW, 31 mm. **Subject:** Centenary - Law of Dec. 9, 1905 **Obv:** "Sower" at left in ring of stars

Date	Mintage	F	VF	XF	Unc	BU
2005 Proof	1,500	Value: 550				

KM# 1454 20 EURO
155.5000 g., 0.9500 Silver 4.7493 oz. ASW, 50 mm. **Subject:** 100th Anniversary - Paul Cézanne's death **Obv:** Self portrait **Rev:** "The Card Players" **Rev. Legend:** LIBERTÉ ÉGALITÉ FRATERNITÉ

Date	Mintage	F	VF	XF	Unc	BU
2006 Proof	500	Value: 200				

KM# 1443 20 EURO
155.5200 g., 0.9500 Silver 4.7499 oz. ASW, 50 mm. **Obv:** Bust of Franklin facing slightly right at left, his diplomatic and technical successes at right **Obv. Legend:** BENJAMIN FRANKLIN 1706-2006 **Obv. Inscription:** AMI DE LA FRANCE

Date	Mintage	F	VF	XF	Unc	BU
2006 Proof	500	Value: 200				

KM# 1422 20 EURO
17.0000 g., 0.9167 Gold 0.5010 oz. AGW **Subject:** 90th Anniversary - Death of Degas **Obv:** Ballerina "The Star" at left **Obv. Inscription:** *Degas* **Rev:** Paint brushes and oils at left, self portrait at right **Shape:** Rectangular, 30 x 21 mm

Date	Mintage	F	VF	XF	Unc	BU
2007	500	—	—	—	800	—

KM# 1303 50 EURO
31.0000 g., 0.9990 Gold 0.9956 oz. AGW, 37 mm. **Subject:** Europa **Obv:** Eight French euro coin designs **Rev:** Portrait and flags design of 6.55957 francs KM-1265 **Edge:** Plain

Date	Mintage	F	VF	XF	Unc	BU
2002 Proof	2,000	Value: 975				

KM# 1335 50 EURO
31.1000 g., 0.9990 Gold 0.9988 oz. AGW, 37 mm. **Obv:** Tour de France logo **Rev:** Cyclist going left **Edge:** Plain

Date	Mintage	F	VF	XF	Unc	BU
2003 Proof	5,000	Value: 975				

KM# 1340 50 EURO
1000.0000 g., 0.9500 Silver 30.541 oz. ASW, 100 mm. **Obv:** Curved cross design with multiple values **Rev:** Goddess Europa and flags **Edge:** Plain with three line inscription at six o'clock

Date	Mintage	F	VF	XF	Unc	BU
2003 Proof	2,000	Value: 650				

KM# 1368 50 EURO
31.1000 g., 0.9990 Gold 0.9988 oz. AGW, 37 mm. **Obv:** Book, denomination and eagle **Rev:** Napoleon and coronation scene **Edge:** Plain

Date	Mintage	F	VF	XF	Unc	BU
2004 Proof	2,000	Value: 990				

KM# 1394 50 EURO
31.1040 g., 0.9990 Gold 0.9990 oz. AGW, 37 mm. **Subject:** European Union Expansion **Obv:** Partial face and flags **Rev:** Puzzle map **Edge:** Plain

Date	Mintage	F	VF	XF	Unc	BU
2004 Proof	2,000	Value: 990				

KM# 1430 50 EURO
31.1040 g., 0.9990 Gold 0.9990 oz. AGW, 37 mm. **Rev:** Kitty and Daniel in Versailles **Rev. Legend:** Hello Kitty

Date	Mintage	F	VF	XF	Unc	BU
2005 Proof	1,000	Value: 1,000				

KM# 1304 100 EURO
155.5175 g., 0.9990 Gold 4.9948 oz. AGW, 50 mm. **Subject:** Europa **Obv:** Eight French euro coin designs **Rev:** Portrait and flags design of 6.55957 francs KM-1265 **Edge:** Plain

Date	Mintage	F	VF	XF	Unc	BU
2002 Proof	99	Value: 5,750				

KM# 1377 100 EURO
155.5175 g., 0.9990 Gold 4.9948 oz. AGW, 50 mm. **Subject:** D-Day 60th Anniversary **Obv:** Soldiers and Normandy invasion scene **Rev:** "D-Day" inscription above denomination **Edge:** Plain

Date	Mintage	F	VF	XF	Unc	BU
2004 Proof	299	Value: 4,850				

KM# 1389 100 EURO
155.5000 g., 0.9990 Gold 4.9942 oz. AGW, 50 mm. **Obv:** Statue of Liberty **Rev:** F. A. Bartholdi **Edge:** Plain

Date	Mintage	F	VF	XF	Unc	BU
2004 Proof	99	Value: 5,000				

KM# 1395 100 EURO
155.5500 g., 0.9990 Gold 4.9958 oz. AGW, 50 mm. **Subject:** European Union Expansion **Obv:** Partial face and flags **Rev:** Puzzle map **Edge:** Plain

Date	Mintage	F	VF	XF	Unc	BU
2004 Proof	99	Value: 5,000				

KM# 1396 500 EURO
1000.0000 g., 0.9990 Gold 32.117 oz. AGW, 85 mm. **Subject:** European Union Expansion **Obv:** Partial face and flags **Rev:** Puzzle map **Edge:** Plain

Date	Mintage	F	VF	XF	Unc	BU
2004 Proof, Rare	20	—	—	—	—	—

MINT SETS

KM#	Date	Mintage	Identification	Issue Price	Mkt Val
MS20	2001 (2)	10,000	KM#925.1a, 928a	—	350
MS21	2001 (8)	35,000	KM#1282-1289	20.25	25.00
MS22	2002 (8)	35,000	KM#1282-1289	20.25	40.00
MS23	2003 (8)	—	KM#1282-89	—	55.00
MS24	2004 (8)	—	KM#1282-1289	—	20.00
MS25	2005 (8)	—	KM#1282-1289	—	20.00
MS26	2005 (8)	40,000	KM#1282-1289 Moebius set plus token	45.00	40.00
MS27	2005 (8)	10,000	KM1282-1289, French Memories - Bordeaux	45.00	40.00
MS28	2006 (8)	70,000	KM#1282-1289	36.50	20.00
MS29	2006 (8)	500	KM#1282-1289, Denver, Colorado special ANA Coin Convention Set	45.00	70.00
MS30	2006 (8)	500	KM#1282-1289, Berlin set	45.00	55.00
MS31	2006 (8)	500	KM1282-1289, Pierre Curie set	45.00	50.00
MS32	2006 (8)	500	KM#1282-1289, Musee de la Monnaie set	45.00	50.00
MS33	2006 (8)	500	KM#1282-1289, Journees du Patrimoine set	45.00	50.00
MS34	2006 (8)	500	KM#1282-1289, Bourgogne set	45.00	50.00
MS35	2006 (8)	500	KM#1282-1289, "Coree set" (Korea)	45.00	50.00
MS36	2006 (8)	500	KM#1282-1289, Nord Pas-de-Calais set	45.00	50.00
MS37	2006 (8)	500	KM#1282-1289, Jacques Chirac set	45.00	55.00
MS38	2006 (8)	500	KM#1282-1289, Mitterand & Khol	45.00	50.00
MS39	2006 (8)	500	KM#1282-1289, Birthday 1 set	45.00	45.00
MS40	2006 (7)	500	KM#1282-1289, Birthday 2 set	45.00	45.00
MS41	2006 (8)	500	KM#1282-1289, Tokyo set	45.00	50.00
MS42	2006 (8)	500	KM#1282-1289, Viaduc de Millau set	45.00	50.00
MS43	2006 (8)	500	KM#1282-1289, Ile-de-France set	45.00	55.00

PROOF SETS

KM#	Date	Mintage	Identification	Issue Price	Mkt Val
PS21	2001 (8)	15,000	KM#1282-1289	59.00	150
PS22	2002 (8)	40,000	KM#1282-1289	59.00	110
PS23	2003 (5)	150,000	KM#1321, 1322, 1323, 1324, 1325	—	250
PS24	2003 (5)	5,000	KM#1326, 1327, 1328, 1329, 1330	—	1,250

FRENCH POLYNESIA

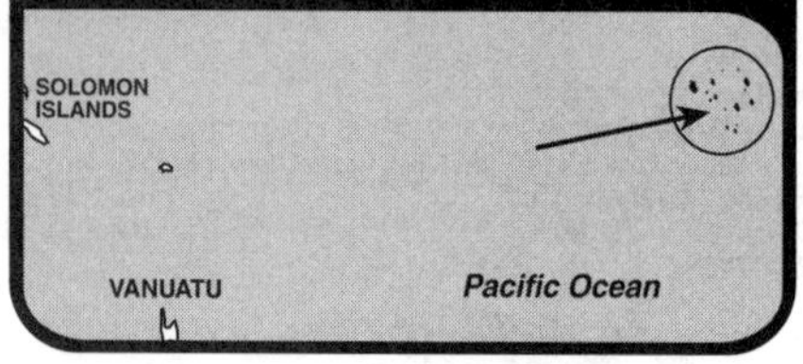

The Territory of French Polynesia (formerly French Oceania) has an area of 1,544 sq. mi. (3,941 sq. km.) and a population of 220,000. It is comprised of the same five archipelagoes that were grouped administratively to form French Oceania.

The colony of French Oceania became the Territory of French Polynesia by act of the French National Assembly in March, 1957. In Sept. of 1958 it voted in favor of the new constitution of the Fifth Republic, thereby electing to remain within the new French Community.

Picturesque, mountainous Tahiti, the setting of many tales of adventure and romance, is one of the most inspiringly beautiful islands in the world. Robert Louis Stevenson called it 'God's sweetest works'. It was there that Paul Gaugin, one of the pioneers of the Impressionist movement, painted the brilliant, exotic pictures that later made him famous. The arid coral atolls of Tuamotu comprise the most economically valuable area of French Polynesia. Pearl oysters thrive in the warm, limpid lagoons, and extensive portions of the atolls are valuable phosphate rock.

RULER

French

MINT MARK

(a) - Paris, privy marks only

MONETARY SYSTEM

100 Centimes = 1 Franc

FRENCH OVERSEAS TERRITORY

DECIMAL COINAGE

KM# 11 FRANC

1.3000 g., Aluminum, 23 mm. **Obv:** Seated Liberty with torch and cornucopia right, date below, legend added flanking figure's feet **Obv. Legend:** I. E. O. M. **Obv. Designer:** G.B.L. Bazor **Rev:** Legend and island scene divide denomination

Date	Mintage	F	VF	XF	Unc	BU
2001(a)	2,900,000	—	—	—	0.50	1.00
2002(a)	1,600,000	—	—	—	0.50	1.00
2003(a)	4,200,000	—	—	—	0.50	1.00

KM# 10 2 FRANCS

2.7000 g., Aluminum, 27 mm. **Obv:** Seated Liberty with torch and cornucopia right, date below, legend added flanking figure's feet **Obv. Legend:** I. E. O. M. **Obv. Designer:** G.B.L. Bazor **Rev:** Legend and island scene divide denomination

Date	Mintage	F	VF	XF	Unc	BU
2001(a)	2,400,000	—	—	—	0.75	1.50
2002(a)	2,500,000	—	—	—	0.75	1.50
2003(a)	3,200,000	—	—	—	0.75	1.50

KM# 12 5 FRANCS

3.7500 g., Aluminum, 31 mm. **Obv:** Seated Liberty with torch and cornucopia right, date below, legend added flanking figure's feet **Obv. Legend:** I. E. O. M. **Obv. Designer:** G.B.L. Bazor **Rev:** Legend and island scene divide denomination

Date	Mintage	F	VF	XF	Unc	BU
2001(a)	1,600,000	—	—	—	1.00	2.00
2002(a)	400,000	—	—	—	1.00	2.00
2003(a)	1,000,000	—	—	—	1.00	2.00

KM# 8 10 FRANCS

6.0000 g., Nickel, 24 mm. **Obv:** Capped head left, date and legend below **Obv. Legend:** I. E. O. M. **Obv. Designer:** R. Joly **Rev:** Native art, denomination below **Rev. Designer:** A. Guzman

Date	Mintage	F	VF	XF	Unc	BU
2001(a)	500,000	—	—	—	1.25	2.75
2002(a)	600,000	—	—	—	1.25	2.75
2003(a)	1,000,000	—	—	—	1.25	2.75

KM# 9 20 FRANCS

10.0000 g., Nickel, 28.3 mm. **Obv:** Capped head left, date and legend below **Obv. Legend:** I. E. O. M. **Obv. Designer:** R. Joly **Rev:** Flowers, vanilla shoots, bread fruit **Rev. Designer:** A. Guzman

Date	Mintage	F	VF	XF	Unc	BU
2001(a)	500,000	—	—	—	1.75	3.25
2002(a)	—	—	—	—	1.75	3.25
2003(a)	700,000	—	—	—	1.75	3.00

KM# 13 50 FRANCS

15.0000 g., Nickel, 33 mm. **Obv:** Capped head left, date and legend below **Obv. Legend:** I. E. O. M. **Obv. Designer:** R. Joly **Rev:** Denomination above Moorea Harbor **Rev. Designer:** A. Guzman

Date	Mintage	F	VF	XF	Unc	BU
2001(a)	300,000	—	—	—	2.00	4.00
2002(a)	—	—	—	—	2.00	4.00
2003(a)	240,000	—	—	—	2.00	4.00

KM# 14 100 FRANCS

10.0000 g., Nickel-Bronze, 30 mm. **Obv:** Capped head left, date below **Obv. Designer:** R. Joly **Rev:** Denomination above Moorea Harbor **Rev. Designer:** A. Guzman

Date	Mintage	F	VF	XF	Unc	BU
2001(a)	200,000	—	—	—	3.00	5.00
2002(a)	—	—	—	—	3.00	5.00
2003(a)	600,000	—	—	—	2.75	5.00

MINT SETS

KM#	Date	Mintage	Identification	Issue Price	Mkt Val
MS1	2001 (7)	3,000	KM#8-14	—	25.00
MS2	2002 (7)	5,000	KM#8-14	—	25.00
MS3	2003 (7)	3,000	KM#8-14	—	20.00

GEORGIA

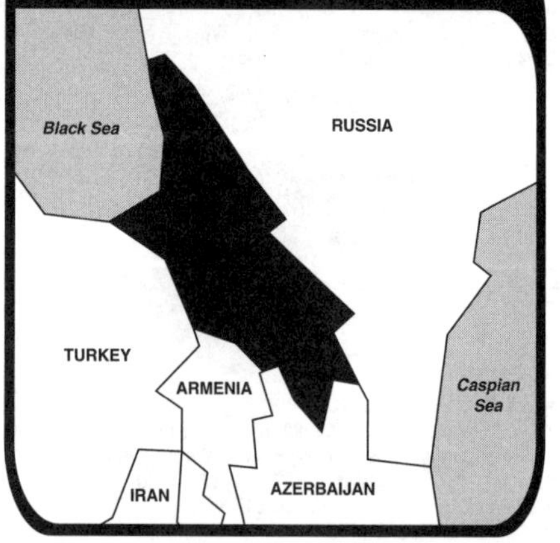

Georgia (formerly the Georgian Social Democratic Republic under the U.S.S.R.), is bounded by the Black Sea to the west and by Turkey, Armenia and Azerbaijan. It occupies the western part of Transcaucasia covering an area of 26,900 sq. mi. (69,700 sq. km.) and a population of 5.7 million. Capitol: Tbilisi. Hydro-electricity, minerals, forestry and agriculture are the chief industries.

Germano-- Georgian treaty was signed on May 28, 1918, followed by a Turko-Georgian peace treaty on June 4. The end of WW I and the collapse of the central powers allowed free The collapse of the U.S.S.R. allowed full transition to independence and on April 9, 1991 a unanimous vote declared the republic an independent state based on its original treaty of independence of May 1918.

MONETARY SYSTEM

100 Thetri = 1 Lari

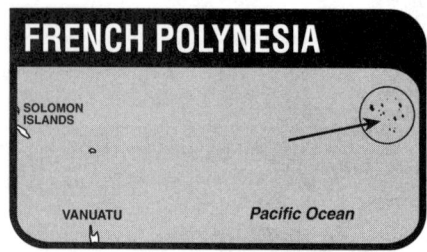

REPUBLIC

STANDARD COINAGE

100 Thetri = 1 Lari

KM# 89 50 THETRI

6.5200 g., Copper-Nickel, 24 mm. **Obv:** National arms **Rev:** Value **Edge:** Reeded and lettered

Date	Mintage	F	VF	XF	Unc	BU
2006	—	—	—	—	3.00	4.00

KM# 90 LARI

7.8500 g., Copper-Nickel, 26.2 mm. **Obv:** National arms **Rev:** Value **Edge:** Reeded and lettered

Date	Mintage	F	VF	XF	Unc	BU
2006	—	—	—	—	5.00	6.50

KM# 94 2 LARI

8.0600 g., Bi-Metallic **Ring Composition:** Copper Nickel **Center Composition:** Brass, 26.99 mm. **Obv:** National arms **Rev:** Large value **Edge:** Reeded and lettered

Date	Mintage	F	VF	XF	Unc	BU
2006	—	—	—	7.50	9.00	—

KM# 91 2 LARI

8.0500 g., Bi-Metallic Brass center in Copper-Nickel ring, 27 mm. **Obv:** National arms **Rev:** Value **Edge:** Reeded and lettered

Date	Mintage	F	VF	XF	Unc	BU
2006	—	—	—	—	6.00	7.50

KM# 92 2 LARI

12.9200 g., Copper-Nickel, 31 mm. **Obv:** Trophy cup, value and date **Rev:** UFFA Winners Cup and soccer player **Edge:** Plain

Date	Mintage	F	VF	XF	Unc	BU
2006 Proof	—	Value: 18.00				

KM# 93 3 LARI

13.1200 g., Copper-Nickel, 31 mm. **Obv:** Three oil wells **Rev:** Map with "Baku-Tbilisi-Ceyhan" route **Edge:** Lettered

Date	Mintage	F	VF	XF	Unc	BU
2006 Proof	—	Value: 25.00				

GERMANY-FEDERAL REPUBLIC

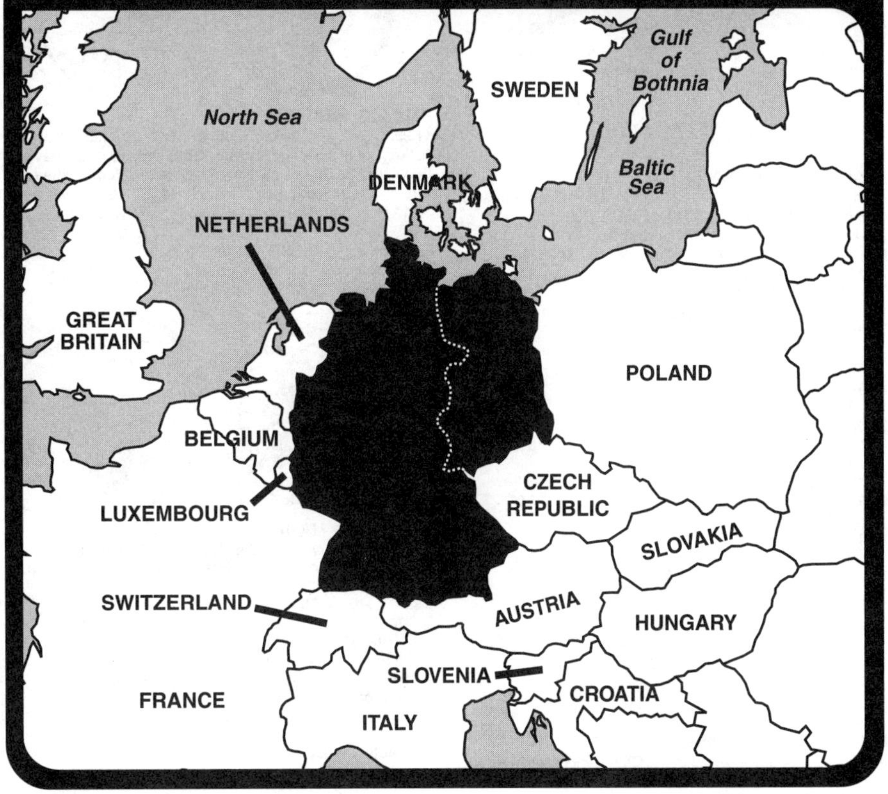

The Federal Republic of Germany, located in north-central Europe, has an area of 137,744 sq. mi. (356,910sq. km.) and a population of 81.1 million. Capital: Berlin. The economy centers about one of the world's foremost industrial establishments. Machinery, motor vehicles, iron, steel, yarns and fabrics are exported.

MINT MARKS

A - Berlin
D - Munich
F - Stuttgart
G - Karlsruhe
J - Hamburg

MONETARY SYSTEM

100 Pfennig = 1 Deutsche Mark (DM)

FEDERAL REPUBLIC

STANDARD COINAGE

KM# 105 PFENNIG

2.0000 g., Copper Plated Steel, 16.5 mm. **Obv:** Five oak leaves, date below **Obv. Legend:** BUNDES REPUBLIK DEUTSCHLAND **Rev:** Denomination

Date	Mintage	F	VF	XF	Unc	BU
2001A	130,000	—	—	—	5.00	—
Note: In sets only						
2001A Proof	78,000	Value: 5.00				
2001D	130,000	—	—	—	5.00	—
Note: In sets only						
2001D Proof	78,000	Value: 5.00				
2001F	130,000	—	—	—	5.00	—
Note: In sets only						
2001F Proof	78,000	Value: 5.00				
2001G	130,000	—	—	—	5.00	—
Note: In sets only						
2001G Proof	78,000	Value: 5.00				
2001J	130,000	—	—	—	5.00	—
Note: In sets only						
2001J Proof	78,000	Value: 5.00				

KM# 106a 2 PFENNIG

2.9000 g., Bronze Clad Steel, 19.25 mm. **Obv:** Five oak leaves, date below **Rev:** Denomination

Date	Mintage	F	VF	XF	Unc	BU
2001A	130,000	—	—	—	5.00	—
Note: In sets only						
2001A Proof	78,000	Value: 5.00				
2001D	130,000	—	—	—	5.00	—
Note: In sets only						
2001D Proof	78,000	Value: 5.00				
2001F	130,000	—	—	—	5.00	—
Note: In sets only						
2001F Proof	78,000	Value: 5.00				
2001G	130,000	—	—	—	5.00	—
Note: In sets only						
2001G Proof	78,000	Value: 5.00				
2001J	130,000	—	—	—	5.00	—
Note: In sets only						
2001J Proof	78,000	Value: 5.00				

KM# 107 5 PFENNIG

3.0000 g., Brass Plated Steel, 18.5 mm. **Obv:** Five oak leaves, date below **Obv. Legend:** BUNDES REPUBLIK DEUTSCHLAND **Rev:** Denomination

Date	Mintage	F	VF	XF	Unc	BU
2001A	130,000	—	—	—	5.00	—
Note: In sets only						
2001A Proof	78,000	Value: 5.00				
2001D	130,000	—	—	—	5.00	—
Note: In sets only						
2001D Proof	78,000	Value: 5.00				
2001F	130,000	—	—	—	5.00	—
Note: In sets only						
2001F Proof	78,000	Value: 5.00				
2001G	130,000	—	—	—	5.00	—
Note: In sets only						
2001G Proof	78,000	Value: 5.00				
2001J	130,000	—	—	—	5.00	—

Date	Mintage	F	VF	XF	Unc	BU
Note: In sets only						
2001J Proof	78,000	Value: 5.00				

KM# 108 10 PFENNIG

4.0000 g., Brass Plated Steel, 21.5 mm. **Obv:** Five oak leaves, date below **Obv. Legend:** BUNDES REPUBLIK DEUTSCHLAND **Rev:** Denomination **Edge:** Plain

Date	Mintage	F	VF	XF	Unc	BU
2001A	130,000	—	—	—	5.00	—
Note: In sets only						
2001A Proof	78,000	Value: 5.00				
2001D	130,000	—	—	—	5.00	—
Note: In sets only						
2001D Proof	78,000	Value: 5.00				
2001F	130,000	—	—	—	5.00	—
Note: In sets only						
2001F Proof	78,000	Value: 5.00				
2001G	130,000	—	—	—	5.00	—
Note: In sets only						
2001G Proof	78,000	Value: 5.00				
2001J	130,000	—	—	—	5.00	—
Note: In sets only						
2001J Proof	78,000	Value: 5.00				

KM# 109.2 50 PFENNIG

3.5000 g., Copper-Nickel, 20 mm. **Obv:** Denomination **Rev:** Woman planting an oak seedling **Edge:** Plain **Note:** Counterfeits of 1972 dated coins with reeded edges exist.

Date	Mintage	F	VF	XF	Unc	BU
2001A	130,000	—	—	—	10.00	—
Note: In sets only						
2001A Proof	78,000	Value: 10.00				
2001D	130,000	—	—	—	10.00	—
Note: In sets only						
2001D Proof	78,000	Value: 10.00				
2001F	130,000	—	—	—	10.00	—
Note: In sets only						
2001F Proof	78,000	Value: 10.00				
2001G	130,000	—	—	—	10.00	—
Note: In sets only						
2001G Proof	78,000	Value: 10.00				
2001J	130,000	—	—	—	10.00	—
Note: In sets only						
2001J Proof	78,000	Value: 10.00				

KM# 110 MARK

5.5000 g., Copper-Nickel, 23.5 mm. **Obv:** Eagle **Rev:** Denomination flanked by oak leaves, date below

Date	Mintage	F	VF	XF	Unc	BU
2001A	130,000	—	—	—	15.00	—
Note: In sets only						
2001A Proof	78,000	Value: 15.00				
2001D	130,000	—	—	—	15.00	—
Note: In sets only						
2001D Proof	78,000	Value: 15.00				
2001F	130,000	—	—	—	15.00	—
Note: In sets only						
2001F Proof	78,000	Value: 15.00				
2001G	130,000	—	—	—	15.00	—
Note: In sets only						
2001G Proof	78,000	Value: 15.00				
2001J	130,000	—	—	—	15.00	—
Note: In sets only						
2001J Proof	78,000	Value: 15.00				

KM# 203 MARK

11.8500 g., 0.9990 Gold 0.3806 oz. AGW, 23.5 mm. **Subject:** Retirement of the Mark Currency **Obv:** Imperial eagle **Rev:** Denomination flanked by leaves, date below **Edge:** Lettered

Date	Mintage	F	VF	XF	Unc	BU
2001A Proof	200,000	Value: 335				
2001D Proof	200,000	Value: 335				
2001G Proof	200,000	Value: 335				
2001J Proof	200,000	Value: 335				
2001F Proof	200,000	Value: 335				

KM# 170 2 MARK

7.0000 g., Copper-Nickel Clad Nickel, 26.75 mm. **Subject:** Ludwig Erhard **Obv:** Eagle above denomination **Rev:** Head facing divides dates

Date	Mintage	F	VF	XF	Unc	BU
2001A	130,000	—	—	—	10.00	—
Note: In sets only						
2001A Proof	78,000	Value: 10.00				
2001D	130,000	—	—	—	10.00	—
Note: In sets only						
2001D Proof	78,000	Value: 10.00				
2001F	130,000	—	—	—	10.00	—
Note: In sets only						
2001F Proof	78,000	Value: 10.00				
2001G	130,000	—	—	—	10.00	—
Note: In sets only						
2001G Proof	78,000	Value: 10.00				
2001J	130,000	—	—	—	10.00	—
Note: In sets only						
2001J Proof	78,000	Value: 10.00				

KM# 175 2 MARK

7.0000 g., Copper-Nickel Clad Nickel, 26.75 mm. **Subject:** Franz Joseph Strauss **Obv:** Eagle above denomination **Rev:** Head left divides dates

Date	Mintage	F	VF	XF	Unc	BU
2001A	130,000	—	—	—	10.00	—
Note: In sets only						
2001A Proof	78,000	Value: 10.00				
2001D	130,000	—	—	—	10.00	—
Note: In sets only						
2001D Proof	78,000	Value: 10.00				
2001F	130,000	—	—	—	10.00	—
Note: In sets only						
2001F Proof	78,000	Value: 10.00				
2001G	130,000	—	—	—	10.00	—
Note: In sets only						
2001G Proof	78,000	Value: 10.00				
2001J	130,000	—	—	—	10.00	—
Note: In sets only						
2001J Proof	78,000	Value: 10.00				

KM# 183 2 MARK

7.0000 g., Copper-Nickel Clad Nickel, 26.75 mm. **Subject:** Willy Brandt **Obv:** Eagle above denomination **Rev:** Head facing divides dates

Date	Mintage	F	VF	XF	Unc	BU
2001A	130,000	—	—	—	10.00	—
Note: In sets only						
2001A Proof	78,000	Value: 10.00				
2001D	130,000	—	—	—	10.00	—
Note: In sets only						
2001D Proof	78,000	Value: 10.00				
2001F	130,000	—	—	—	10.00	—
Note: In sets only						
2001F Proof	78,000	Value: 10.00				
2001G	130,000	—	—	—	10.00	—
Note: In sets only						
2001G Proof	78,000	Value: 10.00				
2001J	130,000	—	—	—	10.00	—
Note: In sets only						
2001J Proof	78,000	Value: 10.00				

KM# 140.1 5 MARK

10.0000 g., Copper-Nickel Clad Nickel, 29 mm. **Obv:** Denomination within rounded square **Rev:** Eagle above date

Date	Mintage	F	VF	XF	Unc	BU
2001A	130,000	—	—	—	30.00	—
Note: In sets only						
2001A Proof	78,000	Value: 30.00				
2001D	130,000	—	—	—	30.00	—
Note: In sets only						
2001D Proof	78,000	Value: 30.00				
2001F	130,000	—	—	—	30.00	—
Note: In sets only						
2001F Proof	78,000	Value: 30.00				
2001G	130,000	—	—	—	30.00	—
Note: In sets only						
2001G Proof	78,000	Value: 30.00				
2001J	130,000	—	—	—	30.00	—
Note: In sets only						
2001J Proof	78,000	Value: 30.00				

COMMEMORATIVE COINAGE

KM# 204 10 MARK

15.5000 g., 0.9250 Silver 0.4609 oz. ASW, 32.5 mm. **Obv:** Imperial eagle above denomination **Rev:** Naval Museum, Stralsund **Edge Lettering:** "OHNE WASSER KEIN LEBEN"

Date	Mintage	F	VF	XF	Unc	BU
2001A	2,500,000	—	—	—	9.00	11.00
2001A Proof	160,000	Value: 16.00				
2001D Proof	160,000	Value: 16.00				
2001F Proof	160,000	Value: 16.00				
2001G Proof	160,000	Value: 16.00				
2001J Proof	160,000	Value: 16.00				

KM# 205 10 MARK

15.5000 g., 0.9250 Silver 0.4609 oz. ASW, 32.5 mm. **Subject:** 200th Anniversary - Birth of Albert Gustav Lortzing **Obv:** Stylized eagle above denomination **Rev:** Portrait and music **Edge Lettering:** "WILDSCHUET * UNDINE" ZAR UND ZIMMERMANN"

Date	Mintage	F	VF	XF	Unc	BU
2001A Proof	160,000	Value: 16.00				
2001D Proof	160,000	Value: 16.00				
2001F Proof	160,000	Value: 16.00				
2001G Proof	160,000	Value: 16.00				
2001J	2,500,000	—	—	—	9.00	11.00
2001J Proof	160,000	Value: 16.00				

KM# 206 10 MARK

15.5000 g., 0.9250 Silver 0.4609 oz. ASW, 32.5 mm. **Subject:** Federal Court of Constitution: 50th Anniversary **Obv:** Stylized eagle above denomination **Rev:** Justice holding books and scale **Edge:** Lettered

Date	Mintage	F	VF	XF	Unc	BU
2001A Proof	160,000	Value: 16.00				
2001D Proof	160,000	Value: 16.00				
2001F Proof	160,000	Value: 16.00				
2001G	2,500,000	—	—	—	9.00	11.00
2001G Proof	160,000	Value: 16.00				
2001J Proof	160,000	Value: 16.00				

EURO COINAGE

European Union Issues

KM# 207 EURO CENT

2.2700 g., Copper Plated Steel, 16.3 mm. **Obv:** Oak leaves **Obv. Designer:** Rolf Lederbogen **Rev:** Denomination and globe **Rev. Designer:** Luc Luycx **Edge:** Plain

Date	Mintage	F	VF	XF	Unc	BU
2002A	770,000,000	—	—	—	0.35	—
2002A Proof	130,000	Value: 1.00				
2002D	805,350,000	—	—	—	0.35	—
2002D Proof	130,000	Value: 1.00				
2002F	902,660,000	—	—	—	0.35	—
2002F Proof	130,000	Value: 1.00				
2002G	537,100,000	—	—	—	0.35	—
2002G Proof	130,000	Value: 1.00				
2002J	833,100,000	—	—	—	0.35	—
2002J Proof	130,000	Value: 1.00				
2003A	180,000	—	—	—	4.50	—
2003A Proof	150,000	Value: 1.00				
2003D	180,000	—	—	—	4.50	—
2003D Proof	150,000	Value: 1.00				
2003F	180,000	—	—	—	4.50	—
2003F Proof	150,000	Value: 1.00				
2003G	180,000	—	—	—	4.50	—
2003G Proof	150,000	Value: 1.00				
2003J	180,000	—	—	—	4.50	—
2003J Proof	150,000	Value: 1.00				
2004A	—	—	—	—	2.50	—
2004A Proof	—	Value: 1.00				
2004D	—	—	—	—	2.50	—
2004D Proof	—	Value: 1.00				
2004F	—	—	—	—	2.50	—
2004F Proof	—	Value: 1.00				
2004G	—	—	—	—	2.50	—
2004G Proof	—	Value: 1.00				
2004J	—	—	—	—	2.50	—
2004J Proof	—	Value: 1.00				
2005A	—	—	—	—	0.35	—
2005A Proof	—	Value: 1.00				
2005D	—	—	—	—	0.35	—
2005D Proof	—	Value: 1.00				
2005F	—	—	—	—	0.35	—
2005F Proof	—	Value: 1.00				
2005G	—	—	—	—	0.35	—
2005G Proof	—	Value: 1.00				
2005J	—	—	—	—	0.35	—
2005J Proof	—	Value: 1.00				

KM# 208 2 EURO CENT

3.0000 g., Copper Plated Steel, 18.7 mm. **Obv:** Oak leaves **Obv. Designer:** Rolf Lederbogen **Rev:** Denomination and globe **Rev. Designer:** Luc Luycx **Edge:** Grooved

Date	Mintage	F	VF	XF	Unc	BU
2002A	460,000,000	—	—	—	0.50	—
2002A Proof	130,000	Value: 1.50				
2002D	436,100,000	—	—	—	0.50	—
2002D Proof	130,000	Value: 1.50				
2002F	495,960,000	—	—	—	0.50	—
2002F Proof	130,000	Value: 1.50				
2002G	311,900,000	—	—	—	0.50	—
2002G Proof	130,000	Value: 1.50				
2002J	419,274,000	—	—	—	0.50	—
2002J Proof	130,000	Value: 1.50				
2003A	100,000,000	—	—	—	0.50	—
2003A Proof	150,000	Value: 1.50				
2003D	151,855,000	—	—	—	0.50	—
2003D Proof	150,000	Value: 1.50				
2003F	175,400,000	—	—	—	0.50	—
2003F Proof	150,000	Value: 1.50				
2003G	80,200,000	—	—	—	0.50	—
2003G Proof	150,000	Value: 1.50				
2003J	168,681,000	—	—	—	0.50	—
2003J Proof	150,000	Value: 1.50				
2004A	—	—	—	—	0.50	—
2004A Proof	—	Value: 1.50				
2004D	—	—	—	—	0.50	—
2004D Proof	—	Value: 1.50				
2004F	—	—	—	—	0.50	—
2004F Proof	—	Value: 1.50				
2004G	—	—	—	—	0.50	—
2004G Proof	—	Value: 1.50				
2004J	—	—	—	—	0.50	—
2004J Proof	—	Value: 1.50				
2005A	—	—	—	—	0.50	—
2005A Proof	—	Value: 1.50				
2005D	—	—	—	—	0.50	—
2005D Proof	—	Value: 1.50				
2005F	—	—	—	—	0.50	—
2005F Proof	—	Value: 1.50				
2005G	—	—	—	—	0.50	—
2005G Proof	—	Value: 1.50				
2005J	—	—	—	—	0.50	—
2005J Proof	—	Value: 1.50				

KM# 209 5 EURO CENT

3.8600 g., Copper Plated Steel, 21.2 mm. **Obv:** Oak leaves **Obv. Designer:** Rolf Lederbogen **Rev:** Denomination and globe **Rev. Designer:** Luc Luycx **Edge:** Plain

Date	Mintage	F	VF	XF	Unc	BU
2002A	475,000,000	—	—	—	0.75	—
2002A Proof	130,000	Value: 2.00				
2002D	495,700,000	—	—	—	0.75	—
2002D Proof	130,000	Value: 2.00				
2002F	563,710,000	—	—	—	0.75	—
2002F Proof	130,000	Value: 2.00				
2002G	328,400,000	—	—	—	0.75	—
2002G Proof	130,000	Value: 2.00				
2002J	501,850,000	—	—	—	0.75	—
2002J Proof	130,000	Value: 2.00				
2003A	180,000	—	—	—	4.50	—
2003A Proof	150,000	Value: 2.00				
2003D	180,000	—	—	—	4.50	—
2003D Proof	150,000	Value: 2.00				
2003F	180,000	—	—	—	4.50	—
2003F Proof	150,000	Value: 2.00				
2003G	180,000	—	—	—	4.50	—
2003G Proof	150,000	Value: 2.00				
2003J	180,000	—	—	—	4.50	—
2003J Proof	150,000	Value: 2.00				
2004A	—	—	—	—	2.50	—
2004A Proof	—	Value: 2.00				
2004D	—	—	—	—	2.50	—
2004D Proof	—	Value: 2.00				
2004F	—	—	—	—	2.50	—
2004F Proof	—	Value: 2.00				
2004G	—	—	—	—	2.50	—
2004G Proof	—	Value: 2.00				
2004J	—	—	—	—	2.50	—
2004J Proof	—	Value: 2.00				
2005A	—	—	—	—	0.75	—
2005A Proof	—	Value: 2.00				
2005D	—	—	—	—	0.75	—
2005D Proof	—	Value: 2.00				
2005F	—	—	—	—	0.75	—
2005F Proof	—	Value: 2.00				
2005G	—	—	—	—	0.75	—
2005G Proof	—	Value: 2.00				
2005J	—	—	—	—	0.75	—
2005J Proof	—	Value: 2.00				

KM# 210 10 EURO CENT

4.0000 g., Brass, 19.7 mm. **Obv:** Brandenburg Gate **Obv. Designer:** Reinhard Heinsdorff **Rev:** Denomination and map **Rev. Designer:** Luc Luycx **Edge:** Reeded

Date	Mintage	F	VF	XF	Unc	BU
2002A	696,000,000	—	—	—	0.75	—
2002A Proof	130,000	Value: 2.00				
2002D	722,050,000	—	—	—	0.75	—
2002D Proof	130,000	Value: 2.00				
2002F	788,860,000	—	—	—	0.75	—
2002F Proof	130,000	Value: 2.00				
2002G	545,500,000	—	—	—	0.75	—
2002G Proof	130,000	Value: 2.00				
2002J	694,150,000	—	—	—	0.75	—
2002J Proof	130,000	Value: 2.00				
2003A	15,000,000	—	—	—	1.25	—
2003A Proof	150,000	Value: 2.00				
2003D	9,000,000	—	—	—	1.25	—
2003D Proof	150,000	Value: 2.00				
2003F	1,500,000	—	—	—	1.50	—
2003F Proof	150,000	Value: 2.00				
2003G	9,450,000	—	—	—	1.25	—
2003G Proof	150,000	Value: 2.00				
2003J	89,405,000	—	—	—	1.25	—
2003J Proof	150,000	Value: 2.00				
2004A	—	—	—	—	1.25	—
2004A Proof	—	Value: 2.00				
2004D	—	—	—	—	1.25	—
2004D Proof	—	Value: 2.00				
2004F	—	—	—	—	1.25	—
2004F Proof	—	Value: 2.00				
2004G	—	—	—	—	1.25	—
2004G Proof	—	Value: 2.00				
2004J	—	—	—	—	1.25	—
2004J Proof	—	Value: 2.00				
2005A	—	—	—	—	1.25	—
2005A Proof	—	Value: 2.00				
2005D	—	—	—	—	1.25	—
2005D Proof	—	Value: 2.00				
2005F	—	—	—	—	1.25	—
2005F Proof	—	Value: 2.00				
2005G	—	—	—	—	1.25	—
2005G Proof	—	Value: 2.00				
2005J	—	—	—	—	1.25	—
2005J Proof	—	Value: 2.00				
2006A	—	—	—	—	1.25	—
2006A Proof	—	Value: 2.00				
2006D	—	—	—	—	1.25	—
2006D Proof	—	Value: 2.00				
2006F	—	—	—	—	1.25	—
2006F Proof	—	Value: 2.00				
2006G	—	—	—	—	1.25	—
2006G Proof	—	Value: 2.00				
2006J	—	—	—	—	1.25	—
2006J Proof	—	Value: 2.00				

KM# 254 10 EURO CENT

4.0000 g., Brass, 19.7 mm. **Obv:** Brandenburg Gate **Obv. Designer:** Reinhard Heinsdorff **Rev:** Relief map of Western Europe, stars, lines and value **Rev. Designer:** Luc Luycx **Edge:** Reeded

Date	Mintage	F	VF	XF	Unc	BU
2007A	—	—	—	—	1.25	—
2007A Proof	—	Value: 2.00				
2007D	—	—	—	—	1.25	—
2007D Proof	—	Value: 2.00				
2007F	—	—	—	—	1.25	—
2007F Proof	—	Value: 2.00				
2007G	—	—	—	—	1.25	—
2007G Proof	—	Value: 2.00				
2007J	—	—	—	—	1.25	—
2007J Proof	—	Value: 2.00				

KM# 211 20 EURO CENT

5.7300 g., Brass, 22.2 mm. **Obv:** Brandenburg Gate **Obv. Designer:** Reinhard Heinsdorff **Rev:** Denomination and map **Rev. Designer:** Luc Luycx **Edge:** Notched

Date	Mintage	F	VF	XF	Unc	BU
2002A	378,000,000	—	—	—	1.00	—
2002A Proof	130,000	Value: 3.00				
2002D	367,100,000	—	—	—	1.00	—
2002D Proof	130,000	Value: 3.00				
2002F	423,760,000	—	—	—	1.00	—
2002F Proof	130,000	Value: 3.00				
2002G	252,100,000	—	—	—	1.00	—
2002G Proof	130,000	Value: 3.00				
2002J	441,000,000	—	—	—	1.00	—
2002J Proof	130,000	Value: 3.00				
2003A	42,000,000	—	—	—	1.00	—
2003A Proof	150,000	Value: 3.00				
2003D	24,100,000	—	—	—	1.00	—
2003D Proof	150,000	Value: 3.00				
2003F	82,000,000	—	—	—	1.00	—
2003F Proof	150,000	Value: 3.00				
2003G	24,829,000	—	—	—	1.00	—
2003G Proof	150,000	Value: 3.00				
2003J	180,000	—	—	—	4.50	—
2003J Proof	150,000	Value: 3.00				
2004A	—	—	—	—	2.50	—
2004A Proof	—	Value: 3.00				
2004D	—	—	—	—	2.50	—
2004D Proof	—	Value: 3.00				
2004F	—	—	—	—	2.50	—
2004F Proof	—	Value: 3.00				
2004G	—	—	—	—	2.50	—
2004G Proof	—	Value: 3.00				
2004J	—	—	—	—	2.50	—
2004J Proof	—	Value: 3.00				
2005A	—	—	—	—	1.00	—
2005A Proof	—	Value: 3.00				
2005D	—	—	—	—	1.00	—
2005D Proof	—	Value: 3.00				
2005F	—	—	—	—	1.00	—
2005F Proof	—	Value: 3.00				

Date	Mintage	F	VF	XF	Unc	BU
2005G	—	—	—	—	1.00	—
2005G Proof	—	Value: 3.00				
2005J	—	—	—	—	1.00	—
2005J Proof	—	Value: 3.00				
2006A	—	—	—	—	1.00	—
2006A Proof	—	Value: 3.00				
2006D	—	—	—	—	1.00	—
2006D Proof	—	Value: 3.00				
2006F	—	—	—	—	1.00	—
2006F Proof	—	Value: 3.00				
2006G	—	—	—	—	1.00	—
2006G Proof	—	Value: 3.00				
2006J	—	—	—	—	1.00	—
2006J Proof	—	Value: 3.00				

KM# 255 20 EURO CENT

5.7300 g., Brass, 22.2 mm. **Obv:** Brandenburg Gate **Obv. Designer:** Reinhard Heinsdorff **Rev:** Relief map of Western Europe, stars, lines and value **Rev. Designer:** Luc Luycx **Edge:** Notched

Date	Mintage	F	VF	XF	Unc	BU
2007A	—	—	—	—	1.00	—
2007A Proof	—	Value: 3.00				
2007D	—	—	—	—	1.00	—
2007D Proof	—	Value: 3.00				
2007F	—	—	—	—	1.00	—
2007F Proof	—	Value: 3.00				
2007G	—	—	—	—	1.00	—
2007G Proof	—	Value: 3.00				
2007J	—	—	—	—	1.00	—
2007J Proof	—	Value: 3.00				

KM# 212 50 EURO CENT

7.8100 g., Brass, 24.2 mm. **Obv:** Brandenburg Gate **Obv. Designer:** Reinhard Heinsdorff **Rev:** Denomination and map **Rev. Designer:** Luc Luycx **Edge:** Reeded

Date	Mintage	F	VF	XF	Unc	BU
2002A	337,600,000	—	—	—	1.75	—
2002A Proof	130,000	Value: 4.00				
2002D	370,340,000	—	—	—	1.75	—
2002D Proof	130,000	Value: 4.00				
2002F	432,000,000	—	—	—	1.75	—
2002F Proof	130,000	Value: 4.00				
2002G	257,860,000	—	—	—	1.75	—
2002G Proof	130,000	Value: 4.00				
2002J	375,467,000	—	—	—	1.75	—
2002J Proof	130,000	Value: 4.00				
2003A	180,000	—	—	—	4.50	—
2003A Proof	150,000	Value: 4.00				
2003D	180,000	—	—	—	4.50	—
2003D Proof	150,000	Value: 4.00				
2003F	180,000	—	—	—	4.50	—
2003F Proof	150,000	Value: 4.00				
2003G	180,000	—	—	—	4.50	—
2003G Proof	150,000	Value: 4.00				
2003J	54,400,000	—	—	—	1.75	—
2003J Proof	150,000	Value: 4.00				
2004A	—	—	—	—	1.75	—
2004A Proof	—	Value: 4.00				
2004D	—	—	—	—	1.75	—
2004D Proof	—	Value: 4.00				
2004F	—	—	—	—	1.75	—
2004F Proof	—	Value: 4.00				
2004G	—	—	—	—	1.75	—
2004G Proof	—	Value: 4.00				
2004J	—	—	—	—	1.75	—
2004J Proof	—	Value: 4.00				
2005A	—	—	—	—	1.00	—
2005A Proof	—	Value: 3.00				
2005D	—	—	—	—	1.00	—
2005D Proof	—	Value: 3.00				
2005F	—	—	—	—	1.00	—
2005F Proof	—	Value: 3.00				
2005G	—	—	—	—	1.00	—
2005G Proof	—	Value: 3.00				
2005J	—	—	—	—	1.00	—
2005J Proof	—	Value: 3.00				
2006A	—	—	—	—	1.00	—
2006A Proof	—	Value: 3.00				
2006D	—	—	—	—	1.00	—
2006D Proof	—	Value: 3.00				
2006F	—	—	—	—	1.00	—
2006F Proof	—	Value: 3.00				
2006G	—	—	—	—	1.00	—
2006G Proof	—	Value: 3.00				
2006J	—	—	—	—	1.00	—
2006J Proof	—	Value: 3.00				

KM# 256 50 EURO CENT

7.8100 g., Brass, 24.2 mm. **Obv:** Brandenburg Gate **Obv. Designer:** Reinhard Heinsdorff **Rev:** Relief map of Western Europe, stars, lines and value **Rev. Designer:** Luc Luycx **Edge:** Reeded

Date	Mintage	F	VF	XF	Unc	BU
2007A	—	—	—	—	1.00	—
2007A Proof	—	Value: 3.00				
2007D	—	—	—	—	1.00	—
2007D Proof	—	Value: 3.00				
2007F	—	—	—	—	1.00	—
2007F Proof	—	Value: 3.00				
2007G	—	—	—	—	1.00	—
2007G Proof	—	Value: 3.00				
2007J	—	—	—	—	1.00	—
2007J Proof	—	Value: 3.00				

KM# 213 EURO

7.5000 g., Bi-Metallic Copper-Nickel center in Brass ring, 23.3 mm. **Obv:** Stylized eagle **Obv. Designer:** Heinz Sneschana Russewa-Hover **Rev:** Denomination over map **Rev. Designer:** Luc Luycx **Edge:** Three normally reeded and three very finely reeded sections

Date	Mintage	F	VF	XF	Unc	BU
2002A	367,750,000	—	—	—	2.50	—
2002A Proof	130,000	Value: 6.50				
2002D	372,700,000	—	—	—	2.50	—
2002D Proof	130,000	Value: 6.50				
2002F	440,910,000	—	—	—	2.50	—
2002F Proof	130,000	Value: 6.50				
2002G	266,975,000	—	—	—	2.50	—
2002G Proof	130,000	Value: 6.50				
2002J	433,000,000	—	—	—	2.50	—
2002J Proof	130,000	Value: 6.50				
2003A	36,750,000	—	—	—	2.50	—
2003A Proof	150,000	Value: 6.50				
2003D	180,000	—	—	—	5.50	—
2003D Proof	150,000	Value: 6.50				
2003F	375,000	—	—	—	5.50	—
2003F Proof	150,000	Value: 6.50				
2003G	180,000	—	—	—	5.50	—
2003G Proof	150,000	Value: 6.50				
2003J	975,000	—	—	—	2.50	—
2003J Proof	150,000	Value: 6.50				
2004A	—	—	—	—	2.50	—
2004A Proof	—	Value: 6.50				
2004D	—	—	—	—	2.50	—
2004D Proof	—	Value: 6.50				
2004F	—	—	—	—	2.50	—
2004F Proof	—	Value: 6.50				
2004G	—	—	—	—	2.50	—
2004G Proof	—	Value: 6.50				
2004J	—	—	—	—	2.50	—
2004J Proof	—	Value: 6.50				
2005A	—	—	—	—	2.50	—
2005A Proof	—	Value: 5.00				
2005D	—	—	—	—	2.50	—
2005D Proof	—	Value: 5.00				
2005F	—	—	—	—	2.50	—
2005F Proof	—	Value: 5.00				
2005G	—	—	—	—	2.50	—
2005G Proof	—	Value: 5.00				
2005J	—	—	—	—	2.50	—
2005J Proof	—	Value: 5.00				
2006A	—	—	—	—	2.50	—
2006A Proof	—	Value: 5.00				
2006D	—	—	—	—	2.50	—
2006D Proof	—	Value: 5.00				
2006F	—	—	—	—	2.50	—
2006F Proof	—	Value: 5.00				
2006G	—	—	—	—	2.50	—
2006G Proof	—	Value: 5.00				
2006J	—	—	—	—	2.50	—
2006J Proof	—	Value: 5.00				

KM# 257 EURO

7.5000 g., Bi-Metallic Copper-Nickel center in Brass ring, 23.3 mm. **Obv:** Stylized eagle **Obv. Designer:** Heinz Sneschana Russewa-Hover **Rev:** Relief map of Western Europe, stars, lines and value **Rev. Designer:** Luc Luycx **Edge:** Three normally reeded and three very finely reeded sections

Date	Mintage	F	VF	XF	Unc	BU
2007A	—	—	—	—	2.50	—
2007A Proof	—	Value: 5.00				
2007D	—	—	—	—	2.50	—
2007D Proof	—	Value: 5.00				
2007F	—	—	—	—	2.50	—
2007F Proof	—	Value: 5.00				
2007G	—	—	—	—	2.50	—
2007G Proof	—	Value: 5.00				
2007J	—	—	—	—	2.50	—
2007J Proof	—	Value: 5.00				

KM# 214 2 EURO

8.5200 g., Bi-Metallic Brass center in Copper-Nickel ring, 25.6 mm. **Obv:** Stylized eagle **Obv. Designer:** Heinz Sneschana Russewa-Hover **Rev:** Denomination and map **Rev. Designer:** Luc Luycx **Edge:** Reeded and "EINIGKEIT UND RECHT UND FREIHEIT"

Date	Mintage	F	VF	XF	Unc	BU
2002A	238,775,000	—	—	—	4.50	—
2002A Proof	130,000	Value: 12.50				
2002D	231,400,000	—	—	—	4.50	—
2002D Proof	130,000	Value: 12.50				
2002F	264,610,000	—	—	—	4.50	—
2002F Proof	130,000	Value: 12.50				
2002G	181,050,000	—	—	—	4.50	—
2002G Proof	130,000	Value: 12.50				
2002J	257,718,000	—	—	—	4.50	—
2002J Proof	130,000	Value: 12.50				
2003A	20,475,000	—	—	—	4.50	—
2003A Proof	150,000	Value: 12.50				
2003D	30,300,000	—	—	—	4.50	—
2003D Proof	150,000	Value: 12.50				
2003F	74,000,000	—	—	—	4.50	—
2003F Proof	150,000	Value: 12.50				
2003G	13,950,000	—	—	—	4.50	—
2003G Proof	150,000	Value: 12.50				
2003J	6,450,000	—	—	—	4.50	—
2003J Proof	150,000	Value: 12.50				
2004A	—	—	—	—	4.50	—
2004A Proof	—	Value: 12.50				
2004D	—	—	—	—	4.50	—
2004D Proof	—	Value: 12.50				
2004F	—	—	—	—	4.50	—
2004F Proof	—	Value: 12.50				
2004G	—	—	—	—	4.50	—
2004G Proof	—	Value: 12.50				
2004J	—	—	—	—	4.50	—
2004J Proof	—	Value: 12.50				
2005A	—	—	—	—	4.50	—
2005A Proof	—	Value: 10.00				
2005D	—	—	—	—	4.50	—
2005D Proof	—	Value: 10.00				
2005F	—	—	—	—	4.50	—
2005F Proof	—	Value: 10.00				
2005G	—	—	—	—	4.50	—
2005G Proof	—	Value: 10.00				
2005J	—	—	—	—	4.50	—
2005J Proof	—	Value: 10.00				
2006A	—	—	—	—	4.50	—
2006A Proof	—	Value: 10.00				
2006D	—	—	—	—	4.50	—
2006D Proof	—	Value: 10.00				
2006	—	—	—	—	4.50	—
2006F Proof	—	Value: 10.00				
2006G	—	—	—	—	4.50	—
2006G Proof	—	Value: 10.00				
2006J	—	—	—	—	4.50	—
2006J Proof	—	Value: 10.00				

KM# 253 2 EURO

8.5200 g., Bi-Metallic Brass center in Copper-Nickel ring **Obv:** Towered city gate **Obv. Legend:** BUNDESREPULIK DEUTSCHLAND **Obv. Inscription:** SCHLESWIG- / HOLSTEIN **Rev:** Denomination over map

Date	Mintage	F	VF	XF	Unc	BU
2006A	6,000,000	—	—	—	5.00	—
2006A Proof	70,000	Value: 10.00				
2006D	6,300,000	—	—	—	5.00	—
2006D Proof	70,000	Value: 10.00				
2006F	7,250,000	—	—	—	5.00	—
2006F Proof	70,000	Value: 10.00				
2006G	4,200,000	—	—	—	5.00	—
2006G Proof	70,000	Value: 10.00				
2006J	6,300,000	—	—	—	5.00	—
2006J Proof	70,000	Value: 10.00				

KM# 258 2 EURO

8.5200 g., Bi-Metallic Brass center in Copper-Nickel ring, 25.6 mm. **Obv:** Stylized eagle **Obv. Designer:** Heinz Sneschana Russewa-Hover **Rev:** Relief map of Western Europe, stars, lines and value **Rev. Designer:** Luc Luycx **Edge:** Reeded and lettered **Edge Lettering:** EINIGKEIT UND RECHT UND FREIHEIT

Date	Mintage	F	VF	XF	Unc	BU
2007A	—	—	—	—	4.50	—
2007A Proof	—	Value: 10.00				
2007D	—	—	—	—	4.50	—
2007D Proof	—	Value: 10.00				
2007F	—	—	—	—	4.50	—
2007F Proof	—	Value: 10.00				
2007G	—	—	—	—	4.50	—
2007G Proof	—	Value: 10.00				
2007J	—	—	—	—	4.50	—
2007J Proof	—	Value: 10.00				

KM# 259 2 EURO

8.4500 g., Bi-Metallic Brass center in Copper-Nickel ring, 25.72 mm. **Subject:** 50th Anniversary Treaty of Rome **Obv:** Large value at left, modified outline of Europe at right **Rev:** Open Treaty book **Edge:** Reeded and lettered **Edge Lettering:** EINIGKEIT UND RECHT UND FREIHEIT

Date	Mintage	F	VF	XF	Unc	BU
2007F	—	—	—	—	—	9.00

KM# 260 2 EURO

8.4000 g., Bi-Metallic Brass center in Copper-Nickel ring, 25.72 mm. **Obv:** Large value at left, modified outline of Europe at right **Obv. Legend:** BUNDESREPUBLIK DEUTSCHLAND **Rev:** City buildings **Edge:** Reeded and lettered **Edge Lettering:** EINIGKEIT UND RECHT UND FREIHEIT

Date	Mintage	F	VF	XF	Unc	BU
2007F	—	—	—	—	—	9.00

KM# 215 10 EURO

18.0000 g., 0.9250 Silver 0.5353 oz. ASW, 32.5 mm. **Subject:** Introduction of the Euro Currency **Obv:** Stylized round eagle **Rev:** Euro symbol and map **Edge Lettering:** IM ZEICHEN DER EINIGUNG EUROPAS

Date	Mintage	F	VF	XF	Unc	BU
2002F	2,000,000	—	—	—	20.00	—
2002F Proof	400,000	Value: 25.00				

KM# 216 10 EURO

18.0000 g., 0.9250 Silver 0.5353 oz. ASW, 32.5 mm. **Subject:** Berlin Subway Centennial **Obv:** Stylized squarish eagle **Rev:** Elevated and subterranean train views **Edge Lettering:** HISTORISCH UND

Date	Mintage	F	VF	XF	Unc	BU
2002D	2,000,000	—	—	—	20.00	—
2002D Proof	400,000	Value: 25.00				

KM# 217 10 EURO

18.0000 g., 0.9250 Silver 0.5353 oz. ASW, 32.5 mm. **Subject:** "Documenta Kassel" Art Exposition **Obv:** Stylized eagle above inscription **Rev:** Exposition logo **Edge Lettering:** ART (in nine languages)

Date	Mintage	F	VF	XF	Unc	BU
2002J	2,000,000	—	—	—	20.00	—
2002J Proof	400,000	Value: 25.00				

KM# 218 10 EURO

18.0000 g., 0.9250 Silver 0.5353 oz. ASW, 32.5 mm. **Subject:** Museum Island, Berlin **Obv:** Stylized eagle **Rev:** Aerial view of museum complex **Edge:** Lettered

Date	Mintage	F	VF	XF	Unc	BU
2002A	2,000,000	—	—	—	20.00	—
2002A Proof	280,000	Value: 30.00				

KM# 219 10 EURO

18.0000 g., 0.9250 Silver 0.5353 oz. ASW, 32.5 mm. **Subject:** 50 Years - German Television **Obv:** Stylized eagle silhouette **Rev:** Television screen silhouette **Edge Lettering:** BILDUNG UNTERHALTUNG INFORMATION

Date	Mintage	F	VF	XF	Unc	BU
2002G	2,000,000	—	—	—	20.00	—
2002G Proof	290,000	Value: 30.00				

KM# 222 10 EURO

18.0000 g., 0.9250 Silver 0.5353 oz. ASW, 32.5 mm. **Subject:** Justus von Liebig **Obv:** Eagle above denomination **Rev:** Liebig's portrait **Edge Lettering:** FORSCHEN . LEHREN . ANWENDEN . .

Date	Mintage	F	VF	XF	Unc	BU
2003J	2,050,000	—	—	—	20.00	—
2003J Proof	350,000	Value: 30.00				

KM# 227 10 EURO

18.0000 g., 0.9250 Silver 0.5353 oz. ASW, 32.5 mm. **Obv:** Stylized eagle above denomination **Rev:** Gottfried Semper and floor plan **Edge:** Lettered **Edge Lettering:** "ARCHITEKT. FORSCHER. KOSMOPOLIT. DEMOKRAT."

Date	Mintage	F	VF	XF	Unc	BU
2003G	2,050,000	—	—	—	18.50	—
2003G Proof	350,000	Value: 22.50				

KM# 223 10 EURO

18.0000 g., 0.9250 Silver 0.5353 oz. ASW, 32.5 mm. **Subject:** World Cup Soccer **Obv:** Stylized round eagle above denomination **Rev:** German map on soccer ball **Edge:** Lettered **Edge Lettering:** "DIE WELT ZU GAST BEI FREUNDEN A. D. F. G.J ." **Note:** Mint is determined by which letter "E" in the edge inscription has a short center bar. If the first letter "E" has the short center bar the coin is from the Berlin mint. Second "E"= Munich, third "E"=Stuttgart, fourth "E"=Karlsruhe, fifth "E"=Hamburg

Date	Mintage	F	VF	XF	Unc	BU
2003A	710,000	—	—	—	20.00	—
2003A Proof	80,000	Value: 30.00				
2003D	710,000	—	—	—	20.00	—
2003D Proof	80,000	Value: 30.00				
2003F	710,000	—	—	—	20.00	—
2003F Proof	80,000	Value: 30.00				
2003G	710,000	—	—	—	20.00	—
2003G Proof	80,000	Value: 30.00				
2003J	710,000	—	—	—	20.00	—
2003J Proof	80,000	Value: 30.00				

KM# 224 10 EURO

18.0000 g., 0.9250 Silver 0.5353 oz. ASW, 32.5 mm. **Subject:** Ruhr Industrial District **Obv:** Stylized eagle, denomination below **Rev:** Various city views **Edge:** Lettered **Edge Lettering:** "RUHRPOTT KULTURLANDSCHAFT"

Date	Mintage	F	VF	XF	Unc	BU
2003F	2,050,000	—	—	—	20.00	—
2003F Proof	350,000	Value: 30.00				

KM# 225 10 EURO

18.0000 g., 0.9250 Silver 0.5353 oz. ASW, 32.5 mm. **Subject:** German Museum Centennial **Obv:** Stylized eagle, denomination at left **Rev:** Abstract design **Edge:** Lettered **Edge Lettering:** "SAMMELN. AUSSTELLEN. FORSCHEN. BILDEN."

Date	Mintage	F	VF	XF	Unc	BU
2003D Proof	350,000	Value: 30.00				

KM# 226 10 EURO

18.0000 g., 0.9250 Silver 0.5353 oz. ASW, 32.5 mm. **Subject:** 50th Anniversary of the Ill-fated East German Revolution **Obv:** Stylized eagle, denomination at left **Rev:** Tank tracks over slogans **Edge:** Lettered **Edge Lettering:** "ERINNERUNG AN DEN VOLKSAUFSTAND IN DER DDR"

Date	Mintage	F	VF	XF	Unc	BU
2003A	2,050,000	—	—	—	20.00	—
2003A Proof	350,000	Value: 30.00				

KM# 232 10 EURO

18.0000 g., 0.9250 Silver 0.5353 oz. ASW, 32.5 mm. **Obv:** Stylized eagle and denomination **Rev:** Geese flying over Wattenmeer National Park **Edge:** Lettered **Edge Lettering:** "MEERESGRUND TRIFFT HORIZONT"

Date	Mintage	F	VF	XF	Unc	BU
2004J	—	—	—	—	20.00	—
2004J Proof	—	Value: 20.00				

KM# 233 10 EURO

18.0000 g., 0.9250 Silver 0.5353 oz. ASW, 32.5 mm. **Obv:** Stylized eagle **Rev:** Eduard Moerike **Edge:** Lettered **Edge Lettering:** "OHNE DAS SCHONE WAS SOLL DER GEWINN"

Date	Mintage	F	VF	XF	Unc	BU
2004F	—	—	—	—	20.00	—
2004F Proof	—	Value: 20.00				

KM# 234 10 EURO

18.0000 g., 0.9250 Silver 0.5353 oz. ASW, 32.5 mm. **Obv:** Stylized eagle, denomination below **Rev:** Space station above the earth **Edge:** Lettered **Edge Lettering:** "RAUMFAHRT VERBINDET DIE WELT"

Date	Mintage	F	VF	XF	Unc	BU
2004D	1,800,000	—	—	—	20.00	—
2004D Proof	300,000	Value: 20.00				

KM# 230 10 EURO

18.0000 g., 0.9250 Silver 0.5353 oz. ASW, 32.5 mm. **Obv:** Stylized eagle, stars and denomination **Rev:** Bauhaus Dessau geometric shapes design **Edge:** Lettered **Edge Lettering:** "KUNST TECHNIK LEHRE"

Date	Mintage	F	VF	XF	Unc	BU
2004A	1,800,000	—	—	—	20.00	—
2004A Proof	300,000	Value: 20.00				

KM# 231 10 EURO

18.0000 g., 0.9250 Silver 0.5353 oz. ASW, 32.5 mm. **Obv:** Stylized eagle above denomination **Rev:** European Union country names and dates **Edge:** Lettered **Edge Lettering:** "FREUDE SCHONER GOTTERFUNKEN"

Date	Mintage	F	VF	XF	Unc	BU
2004F	—	—	—	—	20.00	—
2004F Proof	—	Value: 20.00				
2004G	—	—	—	—	20.00	—
2004G Proof	—	Value: 20.00				

KM# 229 10 EURO

18.0000 g., 0.9250 Silver 0.5353 oz. ASW, 32.5 mm. **Obv:** Stylized eagle, denomination below **Rev:** Soccer ball orbiting the earth **Edge:** Lettered **Edge Lettering:** "DIE WELT ZU GAST BEI FREUNDEN A D F G J" **Note:** Soccer Series: Mint determination same as KM-223

Date	Mintage	F	VF	XF	Unc	BU
2004A	800,000	—	—	—	20.00	—
2004A Proof	80,000	Value: 20.00				
2004D	800,000	—	—	—	20.00	—
2004D Proof	80,000	Value: 20.00				
2004F	800,000	—	—	—	20.00	—
2004F Proof	80,000	Value: 20.00				
2004G	800,000	—	—	—	20.00	—
2004G Proof	80,000	Value: 20.00				
2004J	800,000	—	—	—	20.00	—
2004J Proof	80,000	Value: 20.00				

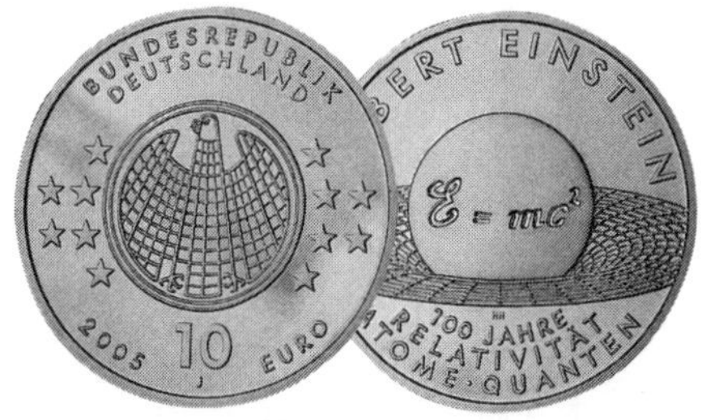

KM# 238 10 EURO

18.0000 g., 0.9250 Silver 0.5353 oz. ASW, 32.5 mm. **Subject:** Albert Einstein **Obv:** Stylized eagle within circle, denomination below **Rev:** E=mc2 on a sphere resting on a net **Edge Lettering:** "NICHT AUFHOREN ZU FRAGEN"

Date	Mintage	F	VF	XF	Unc	BU
2005J	1,800,000	—	—	—	15.00	—
2005J Proof	300,000	Value: 20.00				

KM# 239 10 EURO

18.0000 g., 0.9250 Silver 0.5353 oz. ASW, 32.5 mm. **Subject:** Friedrich von Schiller **Obv:** Stylized eagle **Rev:** Schiller portrait **Edge Lettering:** "ERNST IST DAS LEBEN. HEITER IST DIE KUNST"

Date	Mintage	F	VF	XF	Unc	BU
2005G	1,800,000	—	—	—	15.00	—
2005G Proof	300,000	Value: 20.00				

KM# 240 10 EURO

18.0000 g., 0.9250 Silver 0.5353 oz. ASW, 32.5 mm. **Subject:** Magdeburg **Obv:** Stylized eagle, denomination below **Rev:** Church flanked by landmarks and objects **Edge Lettering:** MAGADOBURG 805..MAGDEBURG 2005..

Date	Mintage	F	VF	XF	Unc	BU
2005A	1,800,000	—	—	—	15.00	—
2005A Proof	300,000	Value: 20.00				

KM# 241 10 EURO

18.0000 g., 0.9250 Silver 0.5353 oz. ASW, 32.5 mm. **Subject:** Bavarian Forest National Park **Obv:** Stylized eagle **Rev:** Various park scenes **Edge:** Lettered

Date	Mintage	F	VF	XF	Unc	BU
2005D	1,800,000	—	—	—	15.00	—
2005D Proof	300,000	Value: 20.00				

KM# 242 10 EURO

18.0000 g., 0.9250 Silver 0.5353 oz. ASW, 32.5 mm. **Subject:** Bertha von Suttner **Obv:** Stylized eagle above stars **Rev:** Suttner's portrait **Edge:** Lettered **Edge Lettering:** "EIPHNH PAX FRIEDEN" twice

Date	Mintage	F	VF	XF	Unc	BU
2005F	1,800,000	—	—	—	15.00	—
2005F Proof	300,000	Value: 20.00				

KM# 243 10 EURO

18.0000 g., 0.9250 Silver 0.5353 oz. ASW, 32.5 mm. **Subject:** World Cup Soccer **Obv:** Round stylized eagle **Rev:** Ball and legs seen through a net **Edge Lettering:** DIE WELT ZU GAST BEI FREUNDEN

Date	Mintage	F	VF	XF	Unc	BU
2005A	800,000	—	—	—	15.00	—
2005A Proof	80,000	Value: 20.00				
2005D	800,000	—	—	—	15.00	—
2005D Proof	80,000	Value: 20.00				
2005F	800,000	—	—	—	15.00	—
2005F Proof	80,000	Value: 20.00				
2005G	800,000	—	—	—	15.00	—
2005G Proof	80,000	Value: 20.00				
2005J	800,000	—	—	—	15.00	—
2005J Proof	80,000	Value: 20.00				

KM# 245 10 EURO

18.0000 g., 0.9250 Silver 0.5353 oz. ASW, 32.5 mm. **Subject:** Karl Friedrich Schinkel **Obv:** Stylized eagle **Rev:** Kneeling brick layer **Edge Lettering:** DER MENSCH BILDE SICH IN ALLEM SCHON

Date	Mintage	F	VF	XF	Unc	BU
2006F	1,600,000	—	—	—	20.00	—
2006F Proof	300,000	Value: 25.00				

KM# 246 10 EURO

18.0000 g., 0.9250 Silver 0.5353 oz. ASW, 32.5 mm. **Subject:** Dresden **Obv:** Stylized eagle **Rev:** City view and reflection **Edge Lettering:** 1206 1485 1547 1697 1832 1945 1989 2006

Date	Mintage	F	VF	XF	Unc	BU
2006A	1,600,000	—	—	—	15.00	—
2006A Proof	300,000	Value: 20.00				

KM# 247 10 EURO

18.0000 g., 0.9250 Silver 0.5353 oz. ASW, 32.5 mm. **Subject:** Hanseatic League **Obv:** Stylized eagle **Rev:** Old sail boat **Edge Lettering:** Wandel durch Handel - von der Hanse nach Europa

Date	Mintage	F	VF	XF	Unc	BU
2006J	1,600,000	—	—	—	15.00	—
2006J Proof	300,000	Value: 20.00				

KM# 248 10 EURO

18.0000 g., 0.9250 Silver 0.5353 oz. ASW, 32.5 mm. **Subject:** Mozart **Obv:** Stylized eagle, music and denomination above **Rev:** Bust left, dates above **Edge Lettering:** -- MOZART -- DIE WELT HAT EINEN SINN

Date	Mintage	F	VF	XF	Unc	BU
2006D	—	—	—	—	15.00	—
2006D Proof	—	Value: 20.00				

KM# 249 10 EURO

18.0000 g., 0.9250 Silver 0.5353 oz. ASW, 32.5 mm. **Subject:** World Cup Soccer **Obv:** Stylized eagle **Rev:** Brandenburg Gate on ball on globe

Date	Mintage	F	VF	XF	Unc	BU
2006A	800,000	—	—	—	15.00	—
2006A Proof	80,000	Value: 20.00				
2006D	800,000	—	—	—	15.00	—
2006D Proof	80,000	Value: 20.00				
2006F	800,000	—	—	—	15.00	—
2006F Proof	80,000	Value: 20.00				
2006G	800,000	—	—	—	15.00	—
2006G Proof	80,000	Value: 20.00				
2006J	800,000	—	—	—	15.00	—
2006J Proof	80,000	Value: 20.00				

KM# 220 100 EURO

15.5500 g., 0.9990 Gold 0.4994 oz. AGW, 28 mm. **Subject:** Introduction of the Euro Currency **Obv:** Stylized round eagle **Rev:** Euro symbol and arches **Edge:** Reeded

Date	Mintage	F	VF	XF	Unc	BU
2002A Proof	100,000	Value: 500				
2002D Proof	100,000	Value: 500				
2002F Proof	100,000	Value: 500				
2002G Proof	100,000	Value: 500				
2002J Proof	100,000	Value: 500				

KM# 228 100 EURO

15.5000 g., 0.9999 Gold 0.4983 oz. AGW, 28 mm. **Obv:** Stylized eagle, denomination below **Rev:** Quedlinburg Abbey in monogram **Edge:** Reeded

Date	Mintage	F	VF	XF	Unc	BU
2003A Proof	100,000	Value: 500				
2003D Proof	100,000	Value: 500				
2003F Proof	100,000	Value: 500				
2003G Proof	100,000	Value: 500				
2003J Proof	100,000	Value: 500				

KM# 235 100 EURO

15.5500 g., 0.9999 Gold 0.4999 oz. AGW, 28 mm. **Obv:** Stylized eagle, denomination below **Rev:** Bamberg city view **Edge:** Reeded

Date	Mintage	F	VF	XF	Unc	BU
2004A Proof	80,000	Value: 500				
2004D Proof	80,000	Value: 500				
2004F Proof	80,000	Value: 500				
2004G Proof	80,000	Value: 500				
2004J Proof	80,000	Value: 500				

KM# 236 100 EURO

15.5500 g., 0.9990 Gold 0.4994 oz. AGW **Subject:** UNESCO - Weimar **Obv:** Stylized eagle **Rev:** Historical City of Weimar buildings

Date	Mintage	F	VF	XF	Unc	BU
2006A	80,000	—	—	—	—	500
2006D	80,000	—	—	—	—	500
2006F	80,000	—	—	—	—	500
2006G	80,000	—	—	—	—	500
2006J	80,000	—	—	—	—	500

KM# 237 100 EURO

15.5500 g., 0.9990 Gold 0.4994 oz. AGW, 28 mm. **Subject:** Soccer - Germany 2006 **Obv:** Round stylized eagle **Rev:** Aerial view of stadium

Date	Mintage	F	VF	XF	Unc	BU
2005A	70,000	—	—	—	—	500
2005D	70,000	—	—	—	—	500
2005F	70,000	—	—	—	—	500
2005G	70,000	—	—	—	—	500
2005J	70,000	—	—	—	—	500

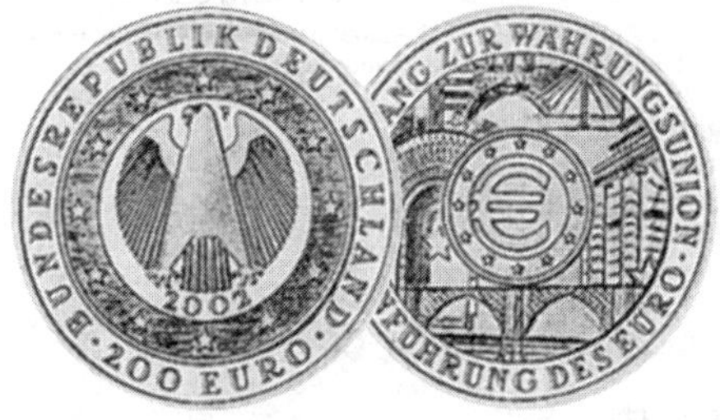

KM# 221 200 EURO

31.1000 g., 0.9990 Gold 0.9988 oz. AGW, 32.5 mm. **Subject:** Introduction of the Euro Currency **Obv:** Stylized round eagle **Rev:** Euro symbol and arches **Edge Lettering:** IM...ZEICHEN...DER... EINIGUNG...EUROPAS

Date	Mintage	F	VF	XF	Unc	BU
2002A Proof	20,000	Value: 1,250				
2002D Proof	20,000	Value: 1,250				
2002F Proof	20,000	Value: 1,250				
2002G Proof	20,000	Value: 1,250				
2002J Proof	20,000	Value: 1,250				

KM# 250 200 EURO

31.1000 g., 0.9990 Gold 0.9988 oz. AGW **Subject:** Quedlinburg Abbey

Date	Mintage	F	VF	XF	Unc	BU
2003A Proof	—	Value: 1,000				
2003D Proof	—	Value: 1,000				
2003F Proof	—	Value: 1,000				
2003G Proof	—	Value: 1,000				
2003J Proof	—	Value: 1,000				

KM# 251 200 EURO

31.1000 g., 0.9990 Gold 0.9988 oz. AGW **Subject:** City of Bamberg

Date	Mintage	F	VF	XF	Unc	BU
2004A Proof	—	Value: 1,000				
2004D Proof	—	Value: 1,000				
2004F Proof	—	Value: 1,000				
2004G Proof	—	Value: 1,000				
2004J Proof	—	Value: 1,000				

KM# 252 200 EURO

31.1000 g., 0.9990 Gold 0.9988 oz. AGW **Subject:** 2006 World Cup - Soccer

Date	Mintage	F	VF	XF	Unc	BU
2005A Proof	—	Value: 1,000				
2005D Proof	—	Value: 1,000				
2005F Proof	—	Value: 1,000				
2005G Proof	—	Value: 1,000				
2005J Proof	—	Value: 1,000				

MINT SETS

KM#	Date	Mintage	Identification	Issue Price	Mkt Val
MS119	2001A (10)	130,000	KM105,106a,107-108,109.2,110,140.1,17 0,175,183	—	40.00
MS120	2001D (10)	130,000	KM105,106a,107-108,109.2,110,140.1,17 0,175,183	—	40.00
MS121	2001F (10)	130,000	KM105,106a,107-108,109.2,110,140.1,17 0,175,183	—	40.00
MS122	2001G (10)	130,000	KM105,106a,107-108,109.2,110,140.1,17 0,175,183	—	40.00
MS123	2001J (10)	130,000	KM105,106a,107-108,109.2,110,140.1,17 0,175,183	—	40.00
MS124	2002A (8)	145,000	KM#207-214	—	20.00
MS125	2002D (8)	145,000	KM#207-214	—	20.00
MS126	2002F (8)	145,000	KM#207-214	—	20.00
MS127	2002G (8)	145,000	KM#207-214	—	20.00
MS128	2002J (8)	145,000	KM#207-214	—	20.00
MS129	2003A (8)	180,000	KM#207-214	—	20.00
MS130	2003D (8)	180,000	KM#207-214	—	20.00
MS131	2003F (8)	180,000	KM#207-214	—	20.00
MS132	2003G (8)	180,000	KM#207-214	—	20.00
MS133	2003J (8)	180,000	KM#207-214	—	20.00
MS134	2004A (8)	—	KM#207-214	—	20.00
MS135	2004D (8)	—	KM#207-214	—	20.00
MS136	2004F (8)	—	KM#207-214	—	20.00
MS137	2004G (8)	—	KM#207-214	—	20.00
MS138	2004J (8)	—	KM#207-214	—	20.00
MS139	2005A (8)	—	KM#207-214	—	25.00
MS140	2005D (8)	—	KM#207-214	—	25.00
MS141	2005F (8)	—	KM#207-214	—	25.00
MS142	2005G (8)	—	KM#207-214	—	25.00
MS143	2005J (8)	—	KM#207-214	—	25.00

PROOF SETS

KM#	Date	Mintage	Identification	Issue Price	Mkt Val
PS150	2001A (10)	78,000	KM105,106a,107-108,109.2,110,140.1,17 0,175,183	—	50.00
PS151	2001D (10)	78,000	KM105,106a,107-108,109.2,110,140.1,17 0,175,183	—	50.00
PS152	2001F (10)	78,000	KM105,106a,107-108,110,140.1,170,175, 183	—	50.00
PS153	2001G (10)	78,000	KM105,106a,107-108,109.2,110,140.1,17 0,175,183	—	50.00
PS154	2001J (10)	78,000	KM105,106a,107-108,109.2,110,140.1,17 0,175,183	—	50.00
PS155	2002A (8)	130,000	KM#207-214	—	35.00
PS156	2002D (8)	130,000	KM#207-214	—	35.00
PS157	2002F (8)	130,000	KM#207-214	—	35.00
PS158	2002G (8)	130,000	KM#207-214	—	35.00
PS159	2002J (8)	130,000	KM#207-214	—	35.00
PS160	2003A (8)	150,000	KM#207-214	—	20.00
PS161	2003D (8)	150,000	KM#207-214	—	20.00
PS162	2003F (8)	150,000	KM#207-214	—	20.00
PS163	2003G (8)	150,000	KM#207-214	—	20.00
PS164	2003J (8)	150,000	KM#207-214	—	20.00
PS165	2004A (8)	—	KM#207-214	—	20.00
PS166	2004D (8)	—	KM#207-214	—	20.00
PS167	2004F (8)	—	KM#207-214	—	20.00
PS168	2004G (8)	—	KM#207-214	—	20.00
PS169	2004J (8)	—	KM#207-214	—	20.00
PS170	2005A (8)	—	KM#207-214	—	30.00
PS171	2005D (8)	—	KM#207-214	—	35.00
PS172	2005D (8)	—	KM#207-214	—	30.00
PS173	2005F (8)	—	KM#207-214	—	30.00
PS174	2005G (8)	—	KM#207-214	—	30.00
PS175	2005J (8)	—	KM#207-214	—	30.00

GHANA

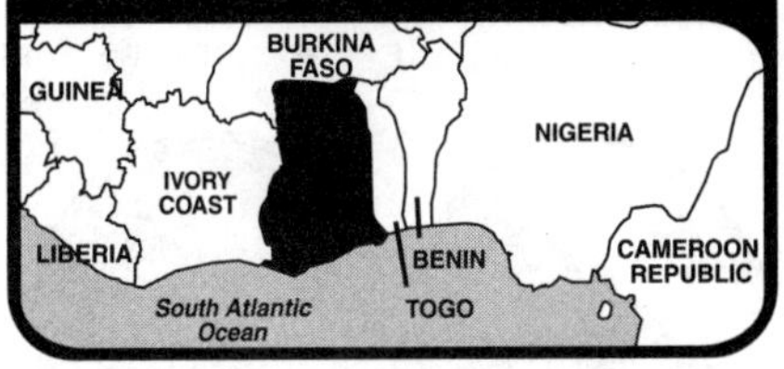

The Republic of Ghana, a member of the Commonwealth of Nations situated on the West Coast of Africa between Ivory Coast and Togo, has an area of 92,100 sq. mi. (238,540 sq. km.) and a population of 14 million, almost entirely African. Capital: Accra. Cocoa (the major crop), coconuts, palm kernels and coffee are exported. Mining, second in importance to agriculture, is concentrated on gold, manganese and industrial diamonds.

MONETARY SYSTEM

1 Cedi = 100 Pesewas, 1965-2007

1 (new) Cedi = 10,000 (old) Cedis, 2007-

REPUBLIC

DECIMAL COINAGE

KM# 36 10 CEDIS
4.4100 g., Copper-Nickel, 22.9 mm. **Obv:** National arms divides date and denomination **Rev:** Gorilla family **Edge:** Plain

Date	Mintage	F	VF	XF	Unc	BU
2003	—	—	—	—	1.50	2.00

REFORM COINAGE

2007-

KM# 37 PESEWA
1.8200 g., Copper Clad Steel, 16.97 mm. **Obv:** National arms **Obv. Legend:** GHANA **Rev:** Modern arch bridge **Edge:** Plain

Date	Mintage	F	VF	XF	Unc	BU
2007	—	—	—	—	—	0.75

KM# 38 5 PESEWAS
2.5200 g., Nickel Clad Steel, 17.98 mm. **Obv:** National arms **Obv. Legend:** GHANA **Rev:** Native male blowing horn **Edge:** Plain

Date	Mintage	F	VF	XF	Unc	BU
2007	—	—	—	—	—	1.25

KM# 39 10 PESEWAS
3.2200 g., Nickel Clad Steel, 20.43 mm. **Obv:** National arms **Obv. Legend:** GHANA **Rev:** Open book, pen **Edge:** Reeded

Date	Mintage	F	VF	XF	Unc	BU
2007	—	—	—	—	—	2.50

KM# 40 20 PESEWAS
4.3600 g., Nickel Clad Steel, 23.47 mm. **Obv:** National arms **Obv. Legend:** GHANA **Rev:** Split open fruit **Edge:** Plain

Date	Mintage	F	VF	XF	Unc	BU
2007	—	—	—	—	—	3.50

KM# 41 50 PESEWAS
6.0800 g., Nickel, 26.40 mm. **Obv:** National arms **Obv. Legend:** GHANA **Rev:** 1/2 length figure of native woman facing **Edge:** Reeded

Date	Mintage	F	VF	XF	Unc	BU
2007	—	—	—	—	—	6.00

KM# 42 CEDI
7.3000 g., Bi-Metallic Brass center in Nickel Clad Steel ring, 27.98 mm. **Obv:** National arms **Obv. Legend:** GHANA **Rev:** Balance scale in sprays **Edge:** Segmented reeding

Date	Mintage	F	VF	XF	Unc	BU
2007	—	—	—	—	—	10.00

GIBRALTAR

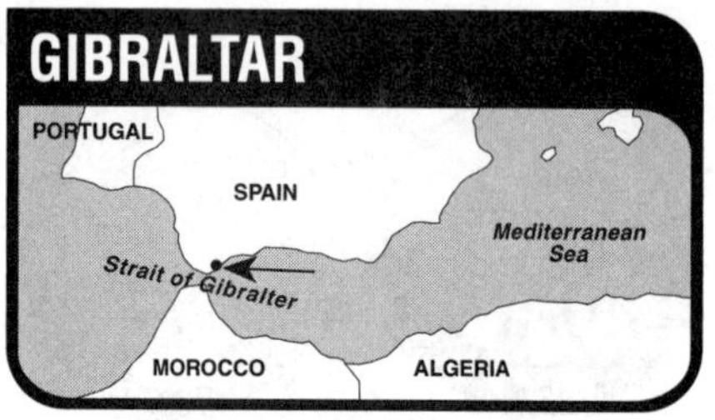

The British Colony of Gibraltar, located at the southernmost point of the Iberian Peninsula, has an area of 2.25 sq. mi. (6.5 sq. km.) and a population of 29,651. Capital (and only town): Gibraltar. Aside from its strategic importance as guardian of the western entrance to the Mediterranean Sea, Gibraltar is also a free port and a British naval base.

RULERS
British

MINT MARKS
PM - Pobjoy Mint
PMM – Pobjoy Mint (only appears on coins dated 2000)

NOTE: ALL coins for 1988 –2003 include the PM mint mark except the 2000 dated circulation pieces which instead have PMM.

MINT PRIVY MARKS
U - Unc finish

MONETARY SYSTEM
100 Pence = 1 Pound

BRITISH COLONY

DECIMAL COINAGE

100 Pence = 1 Pound

KM# 773 PENNY
3.5200 g., Bronze Plated Steel, 20.4 mm. **Ruler:** Elizabeth II **Obv:** Head with tiara right **Obv. Designer:** Ian Rank-Broadley **Rev:** Barbary partridge left divides denomination

Date	Mintage	F	VF	XF	Unc	BU
2001 AA	—	—	—	—	0.35	0.50
2002 AA	—	—	—	—	0.35	0.50
2003 AA	—	—	—	—	0.35	0.50

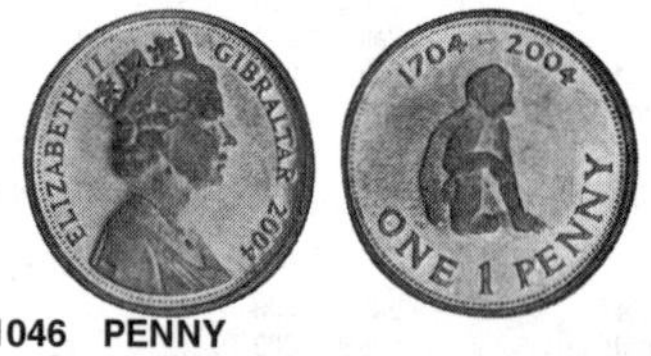

KM# 1046 PENNY
3.5400 g., Copper-Plated-Steel, 20.02 mm. **Ruler:** Elizabeth II **Subject:** 300th Anniversary **Obv:** Crowned bust right **Rev:** Monkey **Edge:** Plain

Date	Mintage	F	VF	XF	Unc	BU
2004	—	—	—	—	0.30	0.50

KM# 774 2 PENCE
Bronze Plated Steel, 20.4 mm. **Ruler:** Elizabeth II **Obv:** Head with tiara right **Obv. Designer:** Ian Rank-Broadley

Date	Mintage	F	VF	XF	Unc	BU
2001 AA	—	—	—	—	0.50	0.85
2001PM AB	—	—	—	—	0.50	0.85

KM# 1044 2 PENCE
7.0400 g., Copper-Plated-Steel, 25.4 mm. **Ruler:** Elizabeth II **Subject:** 200th Anniversary **Obv:** Crowned bust right **Rev:** Four old keys **Edge:** Plain

Date	Mintage	F	VF	XF	Unc	BU
2004	—	—	—	—	0.50	0.65

KM# 775 5 PENCE
3.1000 g., Copper-Nickel, 18 mm. **Ruler:** Elizabeth II **Obv:** Head with tiara right **Obv. Designer:** Ian Rank-Broadley **Rev:** Barbary Ape left divides denomination

Date	Mintage	F	VF	XF	Unc	BU
2001	—	—	—	—	0.60	0.75

KM# 1049 5 PENCE
3.2500 g., Copper-Nickel, 18 mm. **Ruler:** Elizabeth II **Subject:** Tercentenary 1704-2004 **Obv:** Elizabeth II **Rev:** British Royal Sceptre **Edge:** Reeded

Date	Mintage	F	VF	XF	Unc	BU
2004PM	—	—	—	—	—	1.50

KM# 776 10 PENCE
6.5000 g., Copper-Nickel, 24.5 mm. **Ruler:** Elizabeth II **Obv:** Head with tiara right, date below **Obv. Designer:** Ian Rank-Broadley **Rev:** Denomination below building

Date	Mintage	F	VF	XF	Unc	BU
2001	—	—	—	—	1.00	1.25

KM# 1047 10 PENCE
6.4200 g., Copper-Nickel, 24.4 mm. **Ruler:** Elizabeth II **Subject:** 300th Anniversary **Obv:** Elizabeth II **Rev:** Three military officers planning Operation Torch 1942 **Edge:** Reeded

Date	Mintage	F	VF	XF	Unc	BU
2004	—	—	—	—	0.75	1.00

KM# 777 20 PENCE
5.0000 g., Copper-Nickel, 21.4 mm. **Ruler:** Elizabeth II **Obv:** Head with tiara right, date below **Obv. Designer:** Ian Rank-Broadley **Rev:** Our Lady of Europa, denomination below and right **Rev. Designer:** Alfred Ryman **Shape:** 7-sided

Date	Mintage	F	VF	XF	Unc	BU
2001 AA	—	—	—	—	1.50	2.00

KM# 1048 20 PENCE
4.9400 g., Copper-Nickel, 21.4 mm. **Ruler:** Elizabeth II **Subject:** 300th Anniversary **Obv:** Crowned buat right **Rev:** Neanderthal skull found in Gibraltar in 1848 **Edge:** Plain **Shape:** 7-sided

Date	Mintage	F	VF	XF	Unc	BU
2004	—	—	—	—	1.00	1.50

KM# 971 50 PENCE
8.0000 g., Copper-Nickel, 27.3 mm. **Ruler:** Elizabeth II **Subject:** Christmas **Obv:** Head with tiara right, date below **Obv. Designer:** Ian Rank-Broadley **Rev:** Three wise men **Edge:** Plain **Shape:** 7-sided

Date	Mintage	F	VF	XF	Unc	BU
2001 BB	30,000	—	—	—	10.00	12.00

KM# 971a 50 PENCE
8.0000 g., 0.9250 Silver 0.2379 oz. ASW, 27.3 mm. **Ruler:** Elizabeth II **Obv:** Head with tiara right, date below **Obv. Designer:** Ian Rank-Broadley **Rev:** Three wise men **Edge:** Plain **Shape:** 7-sided

Date	Mintage	F	VF	XF	Unc	BU
2001 Proof	5,000	Value: 35.00				

KM# 971b 50 PENCE
8.0000 g., 0.9167 Gold 0.2358 oz. AGW, 27.3 mm. **Ruler:** Elizabeth II **Obv:** Head with tiara right, date below **Obv. Designer:** Ian Rank-Broadley **Rev:** Three wise men **Edge:** Plain **Shape:** 7-sided

Date	Mintage	F	VF	XF	Unc	BU
2001 Proof	250	Value: 645				

KM# 778 50 PENCE
8.0000 g., Copper-Nickel, 27.3 mm. **Ruler:** Elizabeth II **Obv:** Head with tiara right **Obv. Designer:** Ian Rank-Broadley **Rev:** Dolphins surround denomination **Edge:** Plain **Shape:** 7-sided

Date	Mintage	F	VF	XF	Unc	BU
2001 AA	—	—	—	—	4.50	5.50
2001 AB	—	—	—	—	4.50	5.50

KM# 1026 50 PENCE
8.0000 g., Copper-Nickel, 27.3 mm. **Ruler:** Elizabeth II **Subject:** Christmas **Obv:** Head with tiara right, date below **Obv. Designer:** Ian Rank-Broadley **Rev:** Shepherds **Edge:** Plain **Shape:** 7-sided

Date	Mintage	F	VF	XF	Unc	BU
2002PM BB	30,000	—	—	—	10.00	12.00

KM# 1026a 50 PENCE
8.0000 g., 0.9250 Silver 0.2379 oz. ASW, 27.3 mm. **Ruler:** Elizabeth II **Subject:** Christmas **Obv:** Head with tiara right, date below **Obv. Designer:** Ian Rank-Broadley **Rev:** Two Shepherds **Edge:** Plain **Shape:** 7-sided

Date	Mintage	F	VF	XF	Unc	BU
2002PM Proof	2,002	Value: 35.00				

KM# 1050 50 PENCE
8.0000 g., Copper-Nickel, 27.3 mm. **Ruler:** Elizabeth II **Subject:** Tercentenary 1704-2004 **Obv:** Elizabeth II **Rev:** HMS Victory sailing past Gibraltar **Edge:** Plain **Shape:** Seven sided

Date	Mintage	F	VF	XF	Unc	BU
2004PM	—	—	—	—	—	3.00

KM# 988 1/25 CROWN
1.2240 g., 0.9990 Gold 0.0393 oz. AGW, 13.92 mm. **Ruler:** Elizabeth II **Subject:** Peter Rabbit Centennial **Obv:** Crowned bust right **Rev:** Peter Rabbit **Edge:** Reeded

Date	Mintage	F	VF	XF	Unc	BU
2002 Proof	5,000	Value: 55.00				

KM# 988a 1/25 CROWN
1.2240 g., 0.9990 Platinum 0.0393 oz. APW, 13.92 mm. **Ruler:** Elizabeth II **Subject:** Peter Rabbit Centennial **Obv:** Crowned bust right **Rev:** Peter Rabbit **Edge:** Reeded

Date	Mintage	F	VF	XF	Unc	BU
2002 Proof	3,000	Value: 95.00				

KM# 1016 1/25 CROWN
1.2441 g., 0.9999 Gold 0.0400 oz. AGW, 13.92 mm. **Ruler:** Elizabeth II **Subject:** Peter Pan **Obv:** Crowned bust right **Rev:** Peter Pan and Tinkerbell flying above city **Edge:** Reeded

Date	Mintage	F	VF	XF	Unc	BU
2002 Proof	10,000	Value: 50.00				

KM# 989 1/10 CROWN
3.1100 g., 0.9990 Gold 0.0999 oz. AGW, 17.95 mm. **Ruler:** Elizabeth II **Subject:** Peter Rabbit Centennial **Obv:** Crowned bust right **Rev:** Peter Rabbit **Edge:** Reeded

Date	Mintage	F	VF	XF	Unc	BU
2002 Proof	5,000	Value: 110				

KM# 989a 1/10 CROWN
3.1100 g., 0.9990 Platinum 0.0999 oz. APW, 17395 mm. **Ruler:** Elizabeth II **Subject:** Peter Rabbit Centennial **Obv:** Crowned bust right **Rev:** Peter Rabbit **Edge:** Reeded

Date	Mintage	F	VF	XF	Unc	BU
2002 Proof	2,000	Value: 225				

KM# 1017 1/10 CROWN
3.1104 g., 0.9999 Gold 0.1000 oz. AGW, 17.95 mm. **Ruler:** Elizabeth II **Subject:** Peter Pan **Obv:** Crowned bust right **Rev:** Peter Pan and Tinkerbell flying above city **Edge:** Reeded

Date	Mintage	F	VF	XF	Unc	BU
2002 Proof	7,500	Value: 110				

KM# 902 1/5 CROWN
6.2200 g., 0.9999 Gold 0.1999 oz. AGW, 22 mm. **Ruler:** Elizabeth II **Subject:** Queen Mother **Obv:** Bust with tiara right **Obv. Designer:** Ian Rank-Broadley **Rev:** 1953 Coronation scene **Edge:** Reeded

Date	Mintage	F	VF	XF	Unc	BU
2001 Proof	5,000	Value: 200				

KM# 903 1/5 CROWN
6.2200 g., 0.9999 Gold 0.1999 oz. AGW **Ruler:** Elizabeth II **Obv:** Bust with tiara right **Obv. Designer:** Ian Rank-Broadley **Rev:** Queen Mother and Prince Charles in 1954

Date	Mintage	F	VF	XF	Unc	BU
2001 Proof	5,000	Value: 200				

KM# 909 1/5 CROWN
6.2200 g., 0.9999 Gold 0.1999 oz. AGW, 22 mm. **Ruler:** Elizabeth II **Series:** Victorian Era - Victoria's Coronation 1838 **Obv:** Bust with tiara right **Obv. Designer:** Ian Rank-Broadley **Rev:** 1838 Coronation scene **Edge:** Reeded

Date	Mintage	F	VF	XF	Unc	BU
2001 Proof	5,000	Value: 200				

KM# 909.1 1/5 CROWN
6.2200 g., 0.9999 Gold 0.1999 oz. AGW, 22 mm. **Ruler:** Elizabeth II **Series:** Victorian Era **Obv:** Bust with tiara right **Obv. Designer:** Ian Rank-Broadley **Rev:** 1838 Coronation scene with a tiny emerald set in the field below the 1838 date **Edge:** Reeded

Date	Mintage	F	VF	XF	Unc	BU
2001 Proof	2,001	Value: 215				

KM# 911.1 1/5 CROWN
6.2200 g., 0.9999 Gold 0.1999 oz. AGW, 22 mm. **Ruler:** Elizabeth II **Series:** Victorian Era - Empress of India 1876 **Obv:** Bust with tiara right **Obv. Designer:** Ian Rank-Broadley **Rev:** Crowned portrait of Victoria and two elephants **Edge:** Reeded

Date	Mintage	F	VF	XF	Unc	BU
2001 Proof	5,000	Value: 200				

KM# 911.2 1/5 CROWN
6.2200 g., 0.9999 Gold 0.1999 oz. AGW, 22 mm. **Ruler:** Elizabeth II **Series:** Victorian Era - Empress of India 1876 **Obv:** Bust with tiara right **Obv. Designer:** Ian Rank-Broadley **Rev:** Tiny ruby set in the field behind Victoria's head **Edge:** Reeded

Date	Mintage	F	VF	XF	Unc	BU
2001 Proof	2,001	Value: 215				

KM# 913.1 1/5 CROWN
6.2200 g., 0.9999 Gold 0.1999 oz. AGW, 22 mm. **Ruler:** Elizabeth II **Series:** Victorian Era - Diamond Jubilee 1897 **Obv:** Bust with tiara right **Obv. Designer:** Ian Rank-Broadley **Rev:** Victoria's cameo portrait above naval ships **Edge:** Reeded

Date	Mintage	F	VF	XF	Unc	BU
2001 Proof	5,000	Value: 200				

KM# 913.2 1/5 CROWN
6.2200 g., 0.9999 Gold 0.1999 oz. AGW, 22 mm. **Ruler:** Elizabeth II **Series:** Victorian Era - Diamond Jubilee 1897 **Obv:** Bust with tiara right **Obv. Designer:** Ian Rank-Broadley **Rev:** Tiny diamond set at the top of the fourth mast **Edge:** Reeded

Date	Mintage	F	VF	XF	Unc	BU
2001 Proof	2,001	Value: 215				

KM# 915.1 1/5 CROWN
6.2200 g., 0.9999 Gold 0.1999 oz. AGW, 22 mm. **Ruler:** Elizabeth II **Series:** Victorian Era - Victoria's Death 1901 **Obv:** Bust with tiara right **Obv. Designer:** Ian Rank-Broadley **Rev:** Victoria's cameo portrait and Osborne Manor **Edge:** Reeded

Date	Mintage	F	VF	XF	Unc	BU
2001 Proof	5,000	Value: 200				

KM# 915.2 1/5 CROWN
6.2200 g., 0.9999 Gold 0.1999 oz. AGW, 22 mm. **Ruler:** Elizabeth II **Series:** Victorian Era - Victoria's Death 1901 **Obv:** Bust with tiara right **Obv. Designer:** Ian Rank-Broadley **Rev:** Tiny sapphire set in the field between the towers **Edge:** Reeded

Date	Mintage	F	VF	XF	Unc	BU
2001 Proof	2,001	Value: 215				

KM# 917 1/5 CROWN
6.2200 g., 0.9999 Gold 0.1999 oz. AGW, 22 mm. **Ruler:** Elizabeth II **Series:** Victorian Era - Prince Albert and the Great Exhibition 1851 **Obv:** Bust with tiara right **Obv. Designer:** Ian Rank-Broadley **Rev:** Albert's cameo portrait and the exhibit hall **Edge:** Reeded

Date	Mintage	F	VF	XF	Unc	BU
2001 Proof	5,000	Value: 200				

KM# 919 1/5 CROWN
6.2200 g., 0.9999 Gold 0.1999 oz. AGW, 22 mm. **Ruler:** Elizabeth II **Series:** Victorian Era - Isambard K. Brunel **Obv:** Bust with tiara right **Obv. Designer:** Ian Rank-Broadley **Rev:** Portrait in top hat and railroad bridge **Edge:** Reeded

Date	Mintage	F	VF	XF	Unc	BU
2001 Proof	5,000	Value: 200				

KM# 921 1/5 CROWN
6.2200 g., 0.9999 Gold 0.1999 oz. AGW, 22 mm. **Ruler:** Elizabeth II **Series:** Victorian Era - Charles Dickens **Obv:** Bust with tiara right **Obv. Designer:** Ian Rank-Broadley **Rev:** Portrait and scene from "Oliver Twist" **Edge:** Reeded

Date	Mintage	F	VF	XF	Unc	BU
2001 Proof	5,000	Value: 200				

KM# 923 1/5 CROWN
6.2200 g., 0.9999 Gold 0.1999 oz. AGW, 22 mm. **Ruler:** Elizabeth II **Series:** Victorian Era - Charles Darwin **Obv:** Bust with tiara right **Obv. Designer:** Ian Rank-Broadley **Rev:** Portrait, ship and a squatting aboriginal figure **Edge:** Reeded

Date	Mintage	F	VF	XF	Unc	BU
2001 Proof	5,000	Value: 200				

KM# 925 1/5 CROWN
6.2200 g., 0.9999 Gold 0.1999 oz. AGW, 22 mm. **Ruler:** Elizabeth II **Series:** Mythology of the Solar System **Obv:** Queens portrait **Rev:** Standing goddess with snake basket **Edge:** Reeded

Date	Mintage	F	VF	XF	Unc	BU
2001 Proof	5,000	Value: 200				

KM# 926 1/5 CROWN
Bi-Metallic 0.925 Silver center in 0.999 Gold ring, 32.25 mm. **Ruler:** Elizabeth II **Series:** Mythology of the Solar System **Obv:** Bust with tiara right **Obv. Designer:** Ian Rank-Broadley **Rev:** Standing goddess with snake basket **Edge:** Reeded

Date	Mintage	F	VF	XF	Unc	BU
2001 In Proof sets only	999	Value: 375				

KM# 929.1 1/5 CROWN
6.2200 g., 0.9999 Gold 0.1999 oz. AGW, 22 mm. **Ruler:** Elizabeth II **Series:** Mythology of the Solar System - Sun **Obv:** Bust with tiara right **Obv. Designer:** Ian Rank-Broadley **Rev:** Helios in chariot and the sun **Edge:** Reeded

Date	Mintage	F	VF	XF	Unc	BU
2001 Proof	5,000	Value: 200				

KM# 929.2 1/5 CROWN
6.2200 g., 0.9999 Gold 0.1999 oz. AGW, 22 mm. **Ruler:** Elizabeth II **Series:** Mythology of the Solar System **Obv:** Bust with tiara right **Obv. Designer:** Ian Rank-Broadley **Rev:** Fiery hologram in the sun **Edge:** Reeded

Date	Mintage	F	VF	XF	Unc	BU
2001 In Proof sets only	999	Value: 350				

KM# 931.1 1/5 CROWN
6.2200 g., 0.9999 Gold 0.1999 oz. AGW, 22 mm. **Ruler:** Elizabeth II **Series:** Mythology of the Solar System - Moon **Obv:** Bust with tiara right **Obv. Designer:** Ian Rank-Broadley **Rev:** Goddess Diana and the moon **Edge:** Reeded

Date	Mintage	F	VF	XF	Unc	BU
2001 Proof	5,000	Value: 200				

KM# 931.2 1/5 CROWN
6.2200 g., 0.9999 Gold 0.1999 oz. AGW, 22 mm. **Ruler:** Elizabeth II **Series:** Mythology of the Solar System - Moon **Obv:** Bust with tiara right **Obv. Designer:** Ian Rank-Broadley **Rev:** Small pearl set in the moon **Edge:** Reeded

Date	Mintage	F	VF	XF	Unc	BU
2001 In Proof sets only	999	Value: 350				

KM# 933.1 1/5 CROWN
6.2200 g., 0.9999 Gold 0.1999 oz. AGW, 22 mm. **Ruler:** Elizabeth II **Series:** Mythology of the Solar System - Atlas **Obv:** Bust with tiara right **Obv. Designer:** Ian Rank-Broadley **Rev:** Atlas carrying the earth **Edge:** Reeded

Date	Mintage	F	VF	XF	Unc	BU
2001 Proof	5,000	Value: 200				

KM# 933.2 1/5 CROWN
6.2200 g., 0.9999 Gold 0.1999 oz. AGW, 22 mm. **Ruler:** Elizabeth II **Series:** Mythology of the Solar System - Atlas **Obv:** Bust with tiara right **Obv. Designer:** Ian Rank-Broadley **Rev:** Tiny diamond set in the earth **Edge:** Reeded

Date	Mintage	F	VF	XF	Unc	BU
2001 In Proof sets only	999	Value: 350				

KM# 935 1/5 CROWN
6.2200 g., 0.9999 Gold 0.1999 oz. AGW, 22 mm. **Ruler:** Elizabeth II **Series:** Mythology of the Solar System - Neptune **Obv:** Bust with tiara right **Obv. Designer:** Ian Rank-Broadley **Rev:** Seated god with trident and ringed planet **Edge:** Reeded

Date	Mintage	F	VF	XF	Unc	BU
2001 Proof	5,000	Value: 200				

KM# 937 1/5 CROWN
6.2200 g., 0.9999 Gold 0.1999 oz. AGW, 22 mm. **Ruler:** Elizabeth II **Series:** Mythology of the Solar System - Jupiter **Obv:** Bust with tiara right **Obv. Designer:** Ian Rank-Broadley **Rev:** Seated god with lightning bolts and a planet **Edge:** Reeded

Date	Mintage	F	VF	XF	Unc	BU
2001 Proof	5,000	Value: 200				

KM# 939 1/5 CROWN
6.2200 g., 0.9999 Gold 0.1999 oz. AGW, 22 mm. **Ruler:** Elizabeth II **Series:** Mythology of the Solar System - Mars **Obv:** Bust with tiara right **Obv. Designer:** Ian Rank-Broadley **Rev:** Standing Roman solider and a planet **Edge:** Reeded

Date	Mintage	F	VF	XF	Unc	BU
2001 Proof	5,000	Value: 200				

KM# 941 1/5 CROWN
6.2200 g., 0.9999 Gold 0.1999 oz. AGW, 22 mm. **Ruler:** Elizabeth II **Series:** Mythology of the Solar System - Mercury **Obv:** Bust with tiara right **Obv. Designer:** Ian Rank-Broadley **Rev:** Seated god with caduceus and a planet **Edge:** Reeded

Date	Mintage	F	VF	XF	Unc	BU
2001 Proof	5,000	Value: 200				

KM# 943 1/5 CROWN
6.2200 g., 0.9999 Gold 0.1999 oz. AGW, 22 mm. **Ruler:** Elizabeth II **Series:** Mythology of the Solar System - Uranus **Obv:** Bust with tiara right **Obv. Designer:** Ian Rank-Broadley **Rev:** Seated god with scepter **Edge:** Reeded

Date	Mintage	F	VF	XF	Unc	BU
2001 Proof	5,000	Value: 200				

KM# 945 1/5 CROWN
6.2200 g., 0.9999 Gold 0.1999 oz. AGW, 22 mm. **Ruler:** Elizabeth II **Series:** Mythology of the Solar System - Saturn **Obv:** Bust with tiara right **Obv. Designer:** Ian Rank-Broadley **Rev:** Seated god with long handled sickle and a ringed planet **Edge:** Reeded

Date	Mintage	F	VF	XF	Unc	BU
2001 Proof	5,000	Value: 200				

KM# 947 1/5 CROWN
6.2200 g., 0.9999 Gold 0.1999 oz. AGW, 22 mm. **Ruler:** Elizabeth II **Series:** Mythology of the Solar System - Pluto **Obv:** Bust with tiara right **Obv. Designer:** Ian Rank-Broadley **Rev:** Seated god with dogs and a planet **Edge:** Reeded

Date	Mintage	F	VF	XF	Unc	BU
2001 Proof	5,000	Value: 200				

KM# 949 1/5 CROWN
6.2200 g., 0.9999 Gold 0.1999 oz. AGW, 22 mm. **Ruler:** Elizabeth II **Series:** Mythology of the Solar System - Venus **Obv:** Bust with tiara right **Obv. Designer:** Ian Rank-Broadley **Rev:** Goddess seated on a half shell **Edge:** Reeded

Date	Mintage	F	VF	XF	Unc	BU
2001 Proof	5,000	Value: 200				

KM# 951 1/5 CROWN
6.2200 g., 0.9999 Gold 0.1999 oz. AGW, 22 mm. **Ruler:** Elizabeth II **Subject:** Queen's 76th Birthday **Obv:** Bust with tiara right **Obv. Designer:** Ian Rank-Broadley **Rev:** Queen in Order of the Garter robes with a tiny inset diamond **Edge:** Reeded

Date	Mintage	F	VF	XF	Unc	BU
2001 Proof	2,001	Value: 215				

KM# 954 1/5 CROWN
6.2200 g., 0.9999 Gold 0.1999 oz. AGW, 22 mm. **Ruler:** Elizabeth II **Series:** Victorian Age Part II - Victoria's Accession to the Throne **Obv:** Bust with tiara right **Obv. Designer:** Ian Rank-Broadley **Rev:** Victoria learning of her accession **Edge:** Reeded

Date	Mintage	F	VF	XF	Unc	BU
2001 Proof	5,000	Value: 200				

KM# 956 1/5 CROWN
6.2200 g., 0.9999 Gold 0.1999 oz. AGW, 22 mm. **Ruler:** Elizabeth II **Series:** Victorian Age Part II - Royal Family **Rev:** Victoria and Albert seated with children **Edge:** Reeded

Date	Mintage	F	VF	XF	Unc	BU
2001 Proof	5,000	Value: 200				

KM# 958 1/5 CROWN
6.2200 g., 0.9999 Gold 0.1999 oz. AGW, 22 mm. **Ruler:** Elizabeth II **Series:** Victorian Age Part II - Victoria in Scotland **Obv:** Bust with tiara right **Obv. Designer:** Ian Rank-Broadley **Rev:** Victoria on horse and servant **Edge:** Reeded

Date	Mintage	F	VF	XF	Unc	BU
2001 Proof	5,000	Value: 200				

KM# 960 1/5 CROWN
6.2200 g., 0.9999 Gold 0.1999 oz. AGW, 22 mm. **Ruler:** Elizabeth II **Series:** Victorian Age Part II **Obv:** Bust with tiara right **Obv. Designer:** Ian Rank-Broadley **Rev:** Portraits of Gladstone and Disaraeli **Edge:** Reeded

Date	Mintage	F	VF	XF	Unc	BU
2001 Proof	5,000	Value: 200				

KM# 962 1/5 CROWN
6.2200 g., 0.9999 Gold 0.1999 oz. AGW, 22 mm. **Ruler:** Elizabeth II **Series:** Victorian Age Part II **Obv:** Bust with tiara right **Obv. Designer:** Ian Rank-Broadley **Rev:** Florence Nightingale holding lantern **Edge:** Reeded

Date	Mintage	F	VF	XF	Unc	BU
2001 Proof	5,000	Value: 200				

KM# 964 1/5 CROWN
6.2200 g., 0.9999 Gold 0.1999 oz. AGW, 22 mm. **Ruler:** Elizabeth II **Series:** Victorian Age Part II **Obv:** Bust with tiara right **Obv. Designer:** Ian Rank-Broadley **Rev:** Lord Tennyson with the Light Brigade in background **Edge:** Reeded

Date	Mintage	F	VF	XF	Unc	BU
2001 Proof	5,000	Value: 200				

KM# 966 1/5 CROWN
6.2200 g., 0.9999 Gold 0.1999 oz. AGW, 22 mm. **Ruler:** Elizabeth II **Series:** Victorian Age Part II **Obv:** Bust with tiara right **Obv. Designer:** Ian Rank-Broadley **Rev:** Stanley meeting Dr. Livingstone **Edge:** Reeded

Date	Mintage	F	VF	XF	Unc	BU
2001 Proof	5,000	Value: 200				

KM# 968 1/5 CROWN
6.2200 g., 0.9999 Gold 0.1999 oz. AGW, 22 mm. **Ruler:** Elizabeth II **Series:** Victorian Age Part II **Obv:** Bust with tiara right **Rev:** Bronte sisters **Edge:** Reeded

Date	Mintage	F	VF	XF	Unc	BU
2001 Proof	5,000	Value: 200				

KM# 978 1/5 CROWN
6.2200 g., 0.9990 Gold 0.1998 oz. AGW, 22 mm. **Ruler:** Elizabeth II **Subject:** Queen Mother's Life **Obv:** Bust right **Rev:** Prince William's christening scene **Edge:** Reeded

Date	Mintage	F	VF	XF	Unc	BU
2002 Proof	5,000	Value: 200				

KM# 980 1/5 CROWN
6.2200 g., 0.9999 Gold 0.1999 oz. AGW, 22 mm. **Ruler:** Elizabeth II **Subject:** World Cup Soccer **Obv:** Bust right **Rev:** Two players about to collide **Edge:** Reeded

Date	Mintage	F	VF	XF	Unc	BU
2002 Proof	5,000	Value: 200				

KM# 982 1/5 CROWN
6.2200 g., 0.9999 Gold 0.1999 oz. AGW, 22 mm. **Ruler:** Elizabeth II **Subject:** World Cup Soccer **Obv:** Bust right **Rev:** Two players facing viewer **Edge:** Reeded

Date	Mintage	F	VF	XF	Unc	BU
2002 Proof	5,000	Value: 200				

KM# 984 1/5 CROWN
6.2200 g., 0.9999 Gold 0.1999 oz. AGW, 22 mm. **Ruler:** Elizabeth II **Subject:** World Cup Soccer **Obv:** Bust right **Rev:** Two horizontal players **Edge:** Reeded

Date	Mintage	F	VF	XF	Unc	BU
2002 Proof	5,000	Value: 200				

KM# 986 1/5 CROWN
6.2200 g., 0.9999 Gold 0.1999 oz. AGW, 22 mm. **Ruler:** Elizabeth II **Subject:** World Cup Soccer **Obv:** Bust right **Rev:** Two players moving to the left **Edge:** Reeded

Date	Mintage	F	VF	XF	Unc	BU
2002 Proof	5,000	Value: 200				

KM# 990 1/5 CROWN
6.2200 g., 0.9990 Gold 0.1998 oz. AGW, 22 mm. **Ruler:** Elizabeth II **Subject:** Peter Rabbit Centennial **Obv:** Bust right **Rev:** Peter Rabbit **Edge:** Reeded

Date	Mintage	F	VF	XF	Unc	BU
2002 Proof	3,500	Value: 200				

KM# 990a 1/5 CROWN
6.2200 g., 0.9990 Platinum 0.1998 oz. APW, 22 mm. **Ruler:** Elizabeth II **Subject:** Peter Rabbit Centennial **Obv:** Bust right **Rev:** Peter Rabbit **Edge:** Reeded

Date	Mintage	F	VF	XF	Unc	BU
2002 Proof	1,500	Value: 450				

KM# 993 1/5 CROWN
6.2200 g., 0.3750 Gold 0.0750 oz. AGW, 22 mm. **Ruler:** Elizabeth II **Subject:** Queen's Golden Jubilee **Obv:** Bust with tiara right **Obv. Designer:** Ian Rank-Broadley **Rev:** Royal couple and tree house **Edge:** Reeded

Date	Mintage	F	VF	XF	Unc	BU
2002 Proof	5,000	Value: 85.00				

KM# 993a 1/5 CROWN
6.2200 g., 0.9999 Gold 0.1999 oz. AGW, 22 mm. **Ruler:** Elizabeth II **Subject:** Queen's Golden Jubilee **Obv:** Bust with tiara right **Obv. Designer:** Ian Rank-Broadley **Rev:** Royal couple and tree house **Edge:** Reeded

Date	Mintage	F	VF	XF	Unc	BU
2002 Proof	2,002	Value: 200				

KM# 995 1/5 CROWN
6.2200 g., 0.3750 Gold 0.0750 oz. AGW, 22 mm. **Ruler:** Elizabeth II **Subject:** Queen's Golden Jubilee **Obv:** Bust with tiara right **Obv. Designer:** Ian Rank-Broadley **Rev:** Royal coach **Edge:** Reeded

Date	Mintage	F	VF	XF	Unc	BU
2002 Proof	5,000	Value: 85.00				

KM# 995a 1/5 CROWN
6.2200 g., 0.9999 Gold 0.1999 oz. AGW, 22 mm. **Ruler:** Elizabeth II **Subject:** Queen's Golden Jubilee **Obv:** Bust with tiara right **Obv. Designer:** Ian Rank-Broadley **Rev:** Royal coach **Edge:** Reeded

Date	Mintage	F	VF	XF	Unc	BU
2002 Proof	2,002	Value: 200				

KM# 997 1/5 CROWN
6.2200 g., 0.3750 Gold 0.0750 oz. AGW, 22 mm. **Ruler:** Elizabeth II **Subject:** Queen's Golden Jubilee **Obv:** Bust with tiara right **Obv. Designer:** Ian Rank-Broadley **Rev:** Queen holding baby **Edge:** Reeded

Date	Mintage	F	VF	XF	Unc	BU
2002 Proof	5,000	Value: 85.00				

KM# 997a 1/5 CROWN
6.2200 g., 0.9999 Gold 0.1999 oz. AGW, 22 mm. **Ruler:** Elizabeth II **Subject:** Queen's Golden Jubilee **Obv:** Bust with tiara right **Obv. Designer:** Ian Rank-Broadley **Rev:** Queen holding baby **Edge:** Reeded

Date	Mintage	F	VF	XF	Unc	BU
2002 Proof	2,002	Value: 200				

KM# 999 1/5 CROWN
6.2200 g., 0.3750 Gold 0.0750 oz. AGW, 22 mm. **Ruler:** Elizabeth II **Subject:** Queen's Golden Jubilee **Obv:** Bust with tiara right **Obv. Designer:** Ian Rank-Broadley **Rev:** Yacht under Tower bridge **Edge:** Reeded

Date	Mintage	F	VF	XF	Unc	BU
2002 Proof	5,000	Value: 85.00				

KM# 999a 1/5 CROWN
6.2200 g., 0.9999 Gold 0.1999 oz. AGW, 22 mm. **Ruler:** Elizabeth II **Subject:** Queen's Golden Jubilee **Obv:** Bust with tiara right **Obv. Designer:** Ian Rank-Broadley **Rev:** Yacht under Tower bridge **Edge:** Reeded

Date	Mintage	F	VF	XF	Unc	BU
2002 Proof	2,002	Value: 200				

KM# 1001 1/5 CROWN
6.2200 g., 0.9999 Gold 0.1999 oz. AGW, 22 mm. **Ruler:** Elizabeth II **Subject:** Queen's Golden Jubilee **Obv:** Bust with tiara right **Obv. Designer:** Ian Rank-Broadley **Rev:** Crown jewels inset with a tiny diamond, ruby, sapphire and emerald **Edge:** Reeded

Date	Mintage	F	VF	XF	Unc	BU
2002 Proof	2,002	Value: 200				

KM# 1003 1/5 CROWN
6.2200 g., Electrum Special alloy of equal parts of gold and silver, 22 mm. **Ruler:** Elizabeth II **Series:** Ancient Coins **Obv:** Bust with tiara right **Obv. Designer:** Ian Rank-Broadley **Rev:** Head of Athena left **Edge:** Reeded **Note:** From a Mysia electrum coin c.520BC.

Date	Mintage	F	VF	XF	Unc	BU
2002 Proof	3,500	Value: 100				

KM# 1005 1/5 CROWN
6.2200 g., Electrum Special alloy of equal parts of gold and silver., 22 mm. **Ruler:** Elizabeth II **Series:** Ancient Coins **Obv:** Bust with tiara right **Obv. Designer:** Ian Rank-Broadley **Rev:** Head of Hercules right **Edge:** Reeded **Note:** From a Lesbos coin c. 480-450 BC.

Date	Mintage	F	VF	XF	Unc	BU
2002 Proof	3,500	Value: 100				

KM# 1007 1/5 CROWN
6.2200 g., 0.9990 Electrum Special alloy of equal parts of gold and silver. 0.1998 oz., 22 mm. **Ruler:** Elizabeth II **Series:** Ancient Coins **Obv:** Bust with tiara right **Obv. Designer:** Ian Rank-Broadley **Rev:** Pegasus **Edge:** Reeded **Note:** From a Lampsakos electrum coin c. 450 BC.

Date	Mintage	F	VF	XF	Unc	BU
2002 Proof	3,500	Value: 100				

KM# 1009 1/5 CROWN
6.2200 g., Electrum Special Alloy of equal parts of gold and silver., 22 mm. **Ruler:** Elizabeth II **Series:** Ancient Coins **Obv:** Bust with tiara right **Obv. Designer:** Ian Rank-Broadley **Rev:** Lion and bull facing **Edge:** Reeded **Note:** From a Kroisos "sic" coin c. 560-546 BC.

Date	Mintage	F	VF	XF	Unc	BU
2002 Proof	3,500	Value: 100				

KM# 1012 1/5 CROWN
6.2200 g., 0.9999 Gold 0.1999 oz. AGW, 22 mm. **Ruler:** Elizabeth II **Subject:** Queen Mother **Obv:** Bust with tiara right **Obv. Designer:** Ian Rank-Broadley **Rev:** Queen Mother trout fishing **Edge:** Reeded

Date	Mintage	F	VF	XF	Unc	BU
2002 Proof	5,000	Value: 200				

KM# 1014 1/5 CROWN
6.2200 g., 0.9999 Gold 0.1999 oz. AGW, 22 mm. **Ruler:** Elizabeth II **Subject:** Princess Diana **Obv:** Bust right **Rev:** Diana's portrait **Edge:** Reeded

Date	Mintage	F	VF	XF	Unc	BU
2002 Proof	5,000	Value: 200				

KM# 1018 1/5 CROWN
6.2200 g., 0.9999 Gold 0.1999 oz. AGW, 22 mm. **Ruler:** Elizabeth II **Subject:** Peter Pan **Obv:** Bust right **Rev:** Peter Pan and Tinkerbell flying above city **Edge:** Reeded

Date	Mintage	F	VF	XF	Unc	BU
2002 Proof	5,000	Value: 200				

KM# 1020 1/5 CROWN
6.2200 g., 0.9999 Gold 0.1999 oz. AGW, 22 mm. **Ruler:** Elizabeth II **Subject:** Grand Masonic Lodge **Obv:** Bust right **Rev:** Masonic seal above Gibraltar **Edge:** Reeded

Date	Mintage	F	VF	XF	Unc	BU
2002 Proof	5,000	Value: 200				

KM# 991 1/2 CROWN
15.5500 g., 0.9990 Gold 0.4994 oz. AGW, 30 mm. **Ruler:** Elizabeth II **Subject:** Peter Rabbit Centennial **Obv:** Bust right **Rev:** Peter Rabbit **Edge:** Reeded

Date	Mintage	F	VF	XF	Unc	BU
2002 Proof	1,000	Value: 500				

KM# 1002 1/2 CROWN
15.5500 g., 0.9999 Gold 0.4999 oz. AGW, 30 mm. **Ruler:** Elizabeth II **Subject:** Queen's Golden Jubilee **Obv:** Bust with tiara right **Obv. Designer:** Ian Rank-Broadley **Rev:** Crown jewels inset with a tiny diamond, ruby, sapphire and emerald **Edge:** Reeded

Date	Mintage	F	VF	XF	Unc	BU
2002 Proof	999	Value: 500				

KM# 1004 1/2 CROWN
15.5500 g., Electrum Special alloy of equal parts of gold and silver., 32.2 mm. **Ruler:** Elizabeth II **Series:** Ancient Coins **Obv:** Bust with tiara right **Obv. Designer:** Ian Rank-Broadley **Rev:** Head of Athena left **Edge:** Reeded **Note:** From a Mysia electrum coin c. 520 BC.

Date	Mintage	F	VF	XF	Unc	BU
2002 Proof	2,000	Value: 220				

KM# 1006 1/2 CROWN
15.5500 g., Electrum Special alloy of equal parts of gold and silver., 32.2 mm. **Ruler:** Elizabeth II **Series:** Ancient Coins **Obv:** Bust with tiara right **Obv. Designer:** Ian Rank-Broadley **Rev:** Head of Hercules right **Edge:** Reeded **Note:** From a Lesbos coin c. 480-450 BC.

Date	Mintage	F	VF	XF	Unc	BU
2002 Proof	2,000	Value: 220				

KM# 1008 1/2 CROWN
15.5500 g., Gold-Silver Special alloy of equal parts of gold and silver., 32.2 mm. **Ruler:** Elizabeth II **Series:** Ancient Coins **Obv:** Bust with tiara right **Obv. Designer:** Ian Rank-Broadley **Rev:** Pegasus **Edge:** Reeded **Note:** From a Lampsakos electrum coin c. 450 BC.

Date	Mintage	F	VF	XF	Unc	BU
2002 Proof	2,000	Value: 220				

KM# 1010 1/2 CROWN
15.5500 g., Electrum Special alloy of equal parts of gold and silver., 32.2 mm. **Ruler:** Elizabeth II **Series:** Ancient Coins **Obv:** Bust with tiara right **Obv. Designer:** Ian Rank-Broadley **Rev:** Lion and bull facing **Edge:** Reeded **Note:** From a Kroisos [sic] coin c. 560-546 BC.

Date	Mintage	F	VF	XF	Unc	BU
2002 Proof	2,000	Value: 220				

KM# 1056 CROWN
31.1000 g., 0.9990 Tri-Metallic Center: silver, Ring: silver-gilt, Outer ring: silver-pearl black 0.9988 oz., 38.60 mm. **Ruler:** Elizabeth II **Subject:** 21st Century **Obv:** Crowned bust right **Obv. Legend:** GIBRALTER • ELIZABETH II **Rev:** Helmeted cross at center flanked by satellites, archaic sailing ship below **Rev. Legend:** 21st CENTURY **Edge:** Reeded

Date	Mintage	F	VF	XF	Unc	BU
2001 Proof	2,001	Value: 600				

KM# 904 CROWN
28.2800 g., Copper-Nickel, 38.6 mm. **Ruler:** Elizabeth II **Subject:** The Life of Queen Elizabeth - The Queen Mother **Obv:** Bust with tiara right **Obv. Designer:** Ian Rank-Broadley **Rev:** 1953 Coronation scene **Edge:** Reeded

Date	Mintage	F	VF	XF	Unc	BU
2001	—	—	—	—	10.00	12.00

KM# 904a CROWN
28.2800 g., 0.9250 Silver 0.8410 oz. ASW, 38.6 mm. **Ruler:** Elizabeth II **Subject:** The Life of Queen Elizabeth - The Queen Mother **Obv:** Bust with tiara right **Obv. Designer:** Ian Rank-Broadley **Rev:** 1953 Coronation scene **Edge:** Reeded

Date	Mintage	F	VF	XF	Unc	BU
2001 Proof	10,000	Value: 47.50				

KM# 905 CROWN
28.2800 g., Copper-Nickel, 38.6 mm. **Ruler:** Elizabeth II **Subject:** The Life of Queen Elizabeth - The Queen Mother **Obv:** Bust with tiara right **Obv. Designer:** Ian Rank-Broadley **Rev:** Queen Mother with Prince Charles in 1954 **Edge:** Reeded

Date	Mintage	F	VF	XF	Unc	BU
2001	—	—	—	—	10.00	12.00

KM# 905a CROWN
28.2800 g., 0.9250 Silver 0.8410 oz. ASW, 38.6 mm. **Ruler:** Elizabeth II **Subject:** The Life of Queen Elizabeth - The Queen Mother **Obv:** Bust with tiara right **Obv. Designer:** Ian Rank-Broadley **Rev:** Queen Mother with Prince Charles in 1954 **Edge:** Reeded

Date	Mintage	F	VF	XF	Unc	BU
2001 Proof	10,000	Value: 47.50				

KM# 906 CROWN
28.2800 g., Copper-Nickel, 38.6 mm. **Ruler:** Elizabeth II **Subject:** 21st Century **Obv:** Crowned bust right, date below **Obv. Designer:** Raphael Maklouf **Rev:** Celtic cross, Viking ship and modern technological items **Edge:** Reeded

Date	Mintage	F	VF	XF	Unc	BU
2001	—	—	—	—	10.00	12.00

KM# 906a CROWN
31.1035 g., 0.9990 Silver 0.9990 oz. ASW, 38.6 mm. **Ruler:** Elizabeth II **Subject:** 21st Century **Obv:** Crowned bust right, date below **Obv. Designer:** Raphael Maklouf **Rev:** Celtic cross, Viking ship and modern technological items **Edge:** Reeded **Note:** 31.1035 .999 Silver, 1.0000 ASW with a gold plated inner ring and a blackened outer ring.

Date	Mintage	F	VF	XF	Unc	BU
2001 Proof	2,001	Value: 47.50				

KM# 906b CROWN
31.1000 g., Tri-Metallic Center .9995 Platinum 5.2g. Inner Ring .9999 Gold 14.2g. Outer Ring .999 Silver 11.7g **Ruler:** Elizabeth II **Subject:** 21st Century **Obv:** Crowned bust right, date below **Obv. Designer:** Raphael Maklouf **Rev:** Celtic cross, Viking ship and modern technological items

Date	Mintage	F	VF	XF	Unc	BU
2001 Proof	999	Value: 600				

KM# 910 CROWN
28.2800 g., Copper-Nickel, 38.6 mm. **Ruler:** Elizabeth II **Series:** The Victorian Age **Obv:** Bust with tiara right **Obv. Designer:** Ian Rank-Broadley **Rev:** 1838 Coronation of Queen Victoria **Edge:** Reeded

Date	Mintage	F	VF	XF	Unc	BU
2001	—	—	—	—	10.00	12.00

KM# 910a CROWN
28.2800 g., 0.9250 Silver 0.8410 oz. ASW, 38.6 mm. **Ruler:** Elizabeth II **Series:** Victorian Era **Obv:** Bust with tiara right **Obv. Designer:** Ian Rank-Broadley **Rev:** 1838 Coronation scene **Edge:** Reeded

Date	Mintage	F	VF	XF	Unc	BU
2001 Proof	10,000	Value: 47.50				

KM# 912 CROWN
Copper-Nickel, 38.6 mm. **Ruler:** Elizabeth II **Series:** Victorian Era - Empress of India 1876 **Obv:** Bust with tiara right **Obv. Designer:** Ian Rank-Broadley **Rev:** Crowned portrait of Victoria and two elephants

Date	Mintage	F	VF	XF	Unc	BU
2001	—	—	—	—	10.00	12.00

KM# 912a CROWN
28.2800 g., 0.9250 Silver 0.8410 oz. ASW **Ruler:** Elizabeth II **Series:** The Victorian Age - Empress of India 1876 **Obv:** Bust with tiara right **Obv. Designer:** Ian Rank-Broadley **Rev:** Crowned portrait of Victoria and two elephants

Date	Mintage	F	VF	XF	Unc	BU
2001 Proof	10,000	Value: 47.50				

KM# 914 CROWN
Copper-Nickel, 38.6 mm. **Ruler:** Elizabeth II **Series:** Victorian Era - Diamond Jubilee **Obv:** Bust with tiara right **Obv. Designer:** Ian Rank-Broadley **Rev:** Victoria's cameo portrait above naval ships

Date	Mintage	F	VF	XF	Unc	BU
2001	—	—	—	—	10.00	12.00

KM# 914a CROWN
28.2800 g., 0.9250 Silver 0.8410 oz. ASW **Ruler:** Elizabeth II **Series:** The Victorian Age - Diamond Jubilee 1897 **Obv:** Bust with tiara right **Obv. Designer:** Ian Rank-Broadley **Rev:** Victoria's cameo above naval ships, Spithead Review

Date	Mintage	F	VF	XF	Unc	BU
2001 Proof	10,000	Value: 47.50				

KM# 916 CROWN
Copper-Nickel, 38.6 mm. **Ruler:** Elizabeth II **Series:** The Victorian Age - Victoria's Death 1901 **Obv:** Bust with tiara right **Obv. Designer:** Ian Rank-Broadley **Rev:** Victoria's cameo portrait and Osborne Manor

Date	Mintage	F	VF	XF	Unc	BU
2001	—	—	—	—	10.00	12.00

KM# 916a CROWN
28.2800 g., 0.9250 Silver 0.8410 oz. ASW, 38.6 mm. **Ruler:** Elizabeth II **Series:** The Victorian Age - Victoria's Death 1901 **Obv:** Bust with tiara right **Obv. Designer:** Ian Rank-Broadley **Rev:** Victoria's cameo portrait and Osborne Manor

Date	Mintage	F	VF	XF	Unc	BU
2001 Proof	10,000	Value: 47.50				

KM# 918 CROWN
Copper-Nickel, 38.6 mm. **Ruler:** Elizabeth II **Series:** The Victorian Age - Prince Albert and the Great Exhibition 1851 **Obv:** Bust with tiara right **Obv. Designer:** Ian Rank-Broadley **Rev:** Albert's cameo portrait and the exhibit hall

Date	Mintage	F	VF	XF	Unc	BU
2001 Proof	5,000	Value: 175				

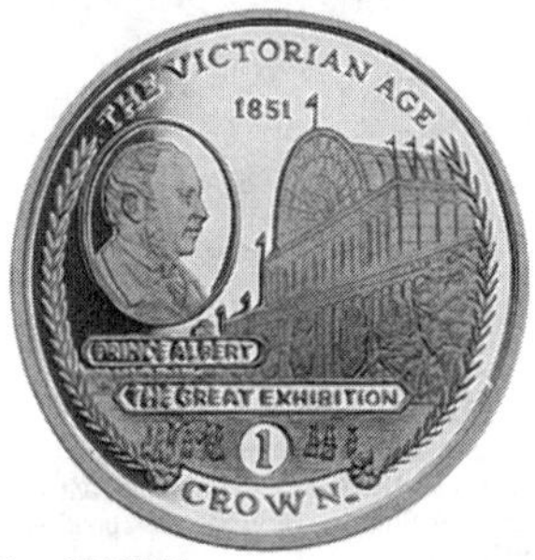

KM# 918a CROWN
28.2800 g., 0.9250 Silver 0.8410 oz. ASW, 38.6 mm. **Ruler:** Elizabeth II **Series:** The Victorian Age - Prince Albert and the Great Exhibition 1851 **Obv:** Bust with tiara right **Obv. Designer:** Ian Rank-Broadley **Rev:** Albert's cameo portrait and the exhibit hall

Date	Mintage	F	VF	XF	Unc	BU
2001 Proof	10,000	Value: 47.50				

KM# 920 CROWN

Copper-Nickel, 38.6 mm. **Ruler:** Elizabeth II **Series:** The Victorian Age **Obv:** Bust with tiara right **Obv. Designer:** Ian Rank-Broadley **Rev:** 1/2 bust of Isambard K. Brunel half left in front of railroad bridge

Date	Mintage	F	VF	XF	Unc	BU
2001	—	—	—	—	10.00	12.00

KM# 920a CROWN

28.2800 g., 0.9250 Silver 0.8410 oz. ASW, 38.6 mm. **Ruler:** Elizabeth II **Series:** Victorian Era **Obv:** Bust with tiara right **Rev:** 1/2 bust of Isambard K. Brunel half left in front of railroad bridge

Date	Mintage	F	VF	XF	Unc	BU
2001 Proof	10,000	Value: 47.50				

KM# 922 CROWN

Copper-Nickel, 38.6 mm. **Ruler:** Elizabeth II **Series:** The Victorian Age **Obv:** Bust with tiara right **Obv. Designer:** Ian Rank-Broadley **Rev:** 1/2 length bust of Charles Dickens half left, scene from "Oliver Twist" in background

Date	Mintage	F	VF	XF	Unc	BU
2001	—	—	—	—	10.00	12.00

KM# 922a CROWN

28.2800 g., 0.9250 Silver 0.8410 oz. ASW, 38.6 mm. **Series:** The Victorian Age **Obv:** Bust with tiara right **Obv. Designer:** Ian Rank-Broadley **Rev:** 1/2 length bust of Charles Dickens half left, scene from "Oliver Twist" in background

Date	Mintage	F	VF	XF	Unc	BU
2001 Proof	10,000	Value: 47.50				

KM# 924 CROWN

Copper-Nickel, 38.6 mm. **Ruler:** Elizabeth II **Series:** The Victorian Age **Obv:** Bust with tiara right **Obv. Designer:** Ian Rank-Broadley **Rev:** 3/4-length figure of Charles Darwin right, ship and a squatting aboriginal figure

Date	Mintage	F	VF	XF	Unc	BU
2001	—	—	—	—	10.00	12.00

KM# 924a CROWN

28.2800 g., 0.9250 Silver 0.8410 oz. ASW, 38.6 mm. **Ruler:** Elizabeth II **Series:** The Victorian Age **Obv:** Bust with tiara right **Obv. Designer:** Ian Rank-Broadley **Rev:** 3/4-length figure of Charles Darwin right, ship and a squatting aboriginal figure

Date	Mintage	F	VF	XF	Unc	BU
2001 Proof	10,000	Value: 47.50				

KM# 927 CROWN

28.2800 g., Copper-Nickel, 38.6 mm. **Ruler:** Elizabeth II **Series:** Mythology of the Solar System **Obv:** Bust with tiara right **Obv. Designer:** Ian Rank-Broadley **Rev:** Standing goddess with snake basket **Edge:** Reeded

Date	Mintage	F	VF	XF	Unc	BU
2001	—	—	—	—	10.00	12.00

KM# 927a CROWN

28.2800 g., 0.9250 Silver 0.8410 oz. ASW, 38.6 mm. **Ruler:** Elizabeth II **Series:** Mythology of the Solar System **Obv:** Bust with tiara right **Obv. Designer:** Ian Rank-Broadley **Rev:** Standing goddess with snake basket **Edge:** Reeded

Date	Mintage	F	VF	XF	Unc	BU
2001 Proof	10,000	Value: 47.50				

KM# 928 CROWN

Bi-Metallic Titanium center in Silver ring, 32.25 mm. **Ruler:** Elizabeth II **Series:** Mythology of the Solar System **Obv:** Bust with tiara right **Obv. Designer:** Ian Rank-Broadley **Rev:** Standing goddess with snake basket **Edge:** Reeded

Date	Mintage	F	VF	XF	Unc	BU
2001 In Proof sets only	2,001	Value: 100				

KM# 930 CROWN

Copper-Nickel, 38.6 mm. **Ruler:** Elizabeth II **Series:** Mythology of the Solar System - Sun **Obv:** Bust with tiara right **Obv. Designer:** Ian Rank-Broadley **Rev:** Helios in chariot and the sun

Date	Mintage	F	VF	XF	Unc	BU
2001	—	—	—	—	10.00	12.00

KM# 930a CROWN

28.2800 g., 0.9250 Silver 0.8410 oz. ASW, 38.6 mm. **Ruler:** Elizabeth II **Series:** Mythology of the Solar System - Sun **Obv:** Bust with tiara right **Obv. Designer:** Ian Rank-Broadley **Rev:** Helios in chariot and the sun

Date	Mintage	F	VF	XF	Unc	BU
2001 Proof	10,000	Value: 47.50				

KM# 930a.1 CROWN

28.2800 g., 0.9250 Silver 0.8410 oz. ASW **Ruler:** Elizabeth II **Series:** Mythology of the Solar System - Sun **Obv:** Bust with tiara right **Obv. Designer:** Ian Rank-Broadley **Rev:** Fiery hologram in the sun

Date	Mintage	F	VF	XF	Unc	BU
2001 In Proof sets only	2,001	Value: 87.50				

KM# 932 CROWN

Copper-Nickel, 38.6 mm. **Ruler:** Elizabeth II **Series:** Mythology of the Solar System - Moon **Obv:** Bust with tiara right **Obv. Designer:** Ian Rank-Broadley **Rev:** Goddess Diana and the moon

Date	Mintage	F	VF	XF	Unc	BU
2001	—	—	—	—	10.00	12.00

KM# 932a CROWN

28.2800 g., 0.9250 Silver 0.8410 oz. ASW, 38.6 mm. **Ruler:** Elizabeth II **Series:** Mythology of the Solar System - Moon **Obv:** Bust with tiara right **Obv. Designer:** Ian Rank-Broadley **Rev:** Goddess Diana and the moon

Date	Mintage	F	VF	XF	Unc	BU
2001 Proof	10,000	Value: 47.50				

KM# 932a.1 CROWN

28.2800 g., 0.9250 Silver 0.8410 oz. ASW, 38.6 mm. **Ruler:** Elizabeth II **Series:** Mythology of the Solar System - Moon **Obv:** Bust with tiara right **Obv. Designer:** Ian Rank-Broadley **Rev:** Small pearl set in the moon

Date	Mintage	F	VF	XF	Unc	BU
2001 In Proof sets only	2,001	Value: 87.50				

KM# 934 CROWN

Copper-Nickel **Ruler:** Elizabeth II **Series:** Mythology of the Solar System - Atlas **Obv:** Bust with tiara right **Obv. Designer:** Ian Rank-Broadley **Rev:** Atlas carrying the earth

Date	Mintage	F	VF	XF	Unc	BU
2001	—	—	—	—	10.00	12.00

KM# 934a CROWN

28.2800 g., 0.9250 Silver 0.8410 oz. ASW, 38.6 mm. **Ruler:** Elizabeth II **Series:** Mythology of the Solar System - Atlas **Obv:** Bust with tiara right **Obv. Designer:** Ian Rank-Broadley **Rev:** Atlas carrying the earth

Date	Mintage	F	VF	XF	Unc	BU
2001 Proof	10,000	Value: 47.50				

KM# 934a.1 CROWN

28.2800 g., 0.9250 Silver 0.8410 oz. ASW, 38.6 mm. **Ruler:** Elizabeth II **Series:** Mythology of the Solar System - Atlas **Obv:** Bust with tiara right **Rev:** Fancy diamond set in the earth

Date	Mintage	F	VF	XF	Unc	BU
2001 In Proof sets only	2,001	Value: 87.50				

KM# 936 CROWN

Copper-Nickel, 38.6 mm. **Ruler:** Elizabeth II **Series:** Mythology of the Solar System **Obv:** Bust with tiara right **Obv. Designer:** Ian Rank-Broadley **Rev:** Seated Neptune with trident and ringed planet

Date	Mintage	F	VF	XF	Unc	BU
2001	—	—	—	—	10.00	12.00

KM# 936a CROWN

28.2800 g., 0.9250 Silver 0.8410 oz. ASW, 38.6 mm. **Ruler:** Elizabeth II **Series:** Mythology of the Solar System **Obv:** Bust with tiara right **Obv. Designer:** Ian Rank-Broadley **Rev:** Seated Neptune with trident and ringed planet

Date	Mintage	F	VF	XF	Unc	BU
2001 Proof	10,000	Value: 47.50				

KM# 938 CROWN

Copper-Nickel, 38.6 mm. **Ruler:** Elizabeth II **Series:** Mythology of the Solar System **Obv:** Bust with tiara right **Obv. Designer:** Ian Rank-Broadley **Rev:** Seated Jupiter with lightening bolts and a planet

Date	Mintage	F	VF	XF	Unc	BU
2001	—	—	—	—	10.00	12.00

KM# 938a CROWN

28.2800 g., 0.9250 Silver 0.8410 oz. ASW, 38.6 mm. **Ruler:** Elizabeth II **Series:** Mythology of the Solar System **Obv:** Bust with tiara right **Obv. Designer:** Ian Rank-Broadley **Rev:** Seated Jupiter with lightening bolts and a planet

Date	Mintage	F	VF	XF	Unc	BU
2001 Proof	10,000	Value: 47.50				

KM# 940 CROWN

Copper-Nickel, 38.6 mm. **Ruler:** Elizabeth II **Series:** Mythology of the Solar System - Mars **Obv:** Bust with tiara right **Obv. Designer:** Ian Rank-Broadley **Rev:** Standing Roman soldier and a planet

Date	Mintage	F	VF	XF	Unc	BU
2001	—	—	—	—	10.00	12.00

KM# 940a CROWN

28.2800 g., 0.9250 Silver 0.8410 oz. ASW, 38.6 mm. **Ruler:** Elizabeth II **Series:** Mythology of the Solar System - Mars **Obv:** Bust with tiara right **Obv. Designer:** Ian Rank-Broadley **Rev:** Standing Roman soldier and a planet

Date	Mintage	F	VF	XF	Unc	BU
2001 Proof	10,000	Value: 47.50				

KM# 942 CROWN

Copper-Nickel, 38.6 mm. **Ruler:** Elizabeth II **Series:** Mythology of the Solar System **Obv:** Bust with tiara right **Obv. Designer:** Ian Rank-Broadley **Rev:** Seated Mercury with caduceus and a planet

Date	Mintage	F	VF	XF	Unc	BU
2001	—	—	—	—	10.00	12.00

KM# 942a CROWN

28.2800 g., 0.9250 Silver 0.8410 oz. ASW, 38.6 mm. **Ruler:** Elizabeth II **Series:** Mythology of the Solar System **Obv:** Bust with tiara right **Obv. Designer:** Ian Rank-Broadley **Rev:** Seated Mercury with caduceus and a planet

Date	Mintage	F	VF	XF	Unc	BU
2001 Proof	10,000	Value: 47.50				

KM# 944 CROWN

Copper-Nickel, 38.6 mm. **Ruler:** Elizabeth II **Series:** Mythology of the Solar System **Obv:** Bust with tiara right **Obv. Designer:** Ian Rank-Broadley **Rev:** Seated Uranus with scepter

Date	Mintage	F	VF	XF	Unc	BU
2001	—	—	—	—	10.00	12.00

KM# 944a CROWN
28.2800 g., 0.9250 Silver 0.8410 oz. ASW, 38.6 mm. **Ruler:** Elizabeth II **Series:** Mythology of the Solar System **Obv:** Bust with tiara right **Obv. Designer:** Ian Rank-Broadley **Rev:** Seated Uranus with scepter

Date	Mintage	F	VF	XF	Unc	BU
2001 Proof	10,000	Value: 47.50				

KM# 946 CROWN
Copper-Nickel, 38.6 mm. **Ruler:** Elizabeth II **Series:** Mythology of the Solar System **Obv:** Bust with tiara right **Obv. Designer:** Ian Rank-Broadley **Rev:** Seated Saturn with long handled sickle and a ringed planet

Date	Mintage	F	VF	XF	Unc	BU
2001	—	—	—	—	10.00	12.00

KM# 946a CROWN
28.2800 g., 0.9250 Silver 0.8410 oz. ASW, 38.6 mm. **Ruler:** Elizabeth II **Series:** Mythology of the Solar System **Obv:** Bust with tiara right **Obv. Designer:** Ian Rank-Broadley **Rev:** Seated Saturn with long handled sickle and a ringed planet

Date	Mintage	F	VF	XF	Unc	BU
2001 Proof	10,000	Value: 47.50				

KM# 948 CROWN
Copper-Nickel, 38.6 mm. **Ruler:** Elizabeth II **Series:** Mythology of the Solar System **Obv:** Bust with tiara right **Obv. Designer:** Ian Rank-Broadley **Rev:** Seated Pluto with dogs and planet

Date	Mintage	F	VF	XF	Unc	BU
2001	—	—	—	—	10.00	12.00

KM# 948a CROWN
28.2800 g., 0.9250 Silver 0.8410 oz. ASW, 38.6 mm. **Ruler:** Elizabeth II **Series:** Mythology of the Solar System **Obv:** Bust with tiara right **Obv. Designer:** Ian Rank-Broadley **Rev:** Seated Pluto with dogs and planet

Date	Mintage	F	VF	XF	Unc	BU
2001 Proof	10,000	Value: 47.50				

KM# 950 CROWN
Copper-Nickel, 38.6 mm. **Ruler:** Elizabeth II **Series:** Mythology of the Solar System **Obv:** Bust with tiara right **Obv. Designer:** Ian Rank-Broadley **Rev:** Venus seated on a half shell

Date	Mintage	F	VF	XF	Unc	BU
2001	—	—	—	—	10.00	12.00

KM# 950a CROWN
28.2800 g., 0.9250 Silver 0.8410 oz. ASW, 38.6 mm. **Ruler:** Elizabeth II **Series:** Mythology of the Solar System **Obv:** Bust with tiara right **Obv. Designer:** Ian Rank-Broadley **Rev:** Venus seated on a half shell

Date	Mintage	F	VF	XF	Unc	BU
2001 Proof	10,000	Value: 47.50				

KM# 952 CROWN
28.2800 g., Copper-Nickel, 38.6 mm. **Ruler:** Elizabeth II **Subject:** Queen's 75th Birthday **Obv:** Bust with tiara right **Obv. Designer:** Ian Rank-Broadley **Rev:** Queen in Order of Garter robes **Edge:** Reeded

Date	Mintage	F	VF	XF	Unc	BU
2001	—	—	—	—	10.00	12.00

KM# 952a CROWN
28.2800 g., 0.9250 Silver 0.8410 oz. ASW, 38.6 mm. **Ruler:** Elizabeth II **Subject:** Queen's 75th Birthday **Obv:** Bust with tiara right **Obv. Designer:** Ian Rank-Broadley **Rev:** Queen in Order of Garter robes **Edge:** Reeded

Date	Mintage	F	VF	XF	Unc	BU
2001 Proof	10,000	Value: 47.50				

KM# 955 CROWN
28.2800 g., Copper-Nickel, 38.6 mm. **Ruler:** Elizabeth II **Series:** Victorian Age Part II **Obv:** Bust with tiara right **Obv. Designer:** Ian Rank-Broadley **Rev:** Victoria learning of her accession **Edge:** Reeded

Date	Mintage	F	VF	XF	Unc	BU
2001	—	—	—	—	10.00	12.00

KM# 955a CROWN
28.2800 g., 0.9250 Silver 0.8410 oz. ASW, 38.6 mm. **Ruler:** Elizabeth II **Series:** Victorian Age Part II **Obv:** Bust with tiara right **Obv. Designer:** Ian Rank-Broadley **Rev:** Victoria learning of her accession **Edge:** Reeded

Date	Mintage	F	VF	XF	Unc	BU
2001 Proof	10,000	Value: 47.50				

KM# 957 CROWN
Copper-Nickel, 38.6 mm. **Ruler:** Elizabeth II **Series:** Victorian Age Part II - Royal Family **Obv:** Bust with tiara right **Obv. Designer:** Ian Rank-Broadley **Rev:** Victoria and Albert seated with children **Edge:** Reeded

Date	Mintage	F	VF	XF	Unc	BU
2001	—	—	—	—	10.00	12.00

KM# 957a CROWN
28.2800 g., 0.9250 Silver 0.8410 oz. ASW, 38.6 mm. **Ruler:** Elizabeth II **Series:** Victorian Age Part II - Royal Family **Obv:** Bust with tiara right **Obv. Designer:** Ian Rank-Broadley **Rev:** Victoria and Albert seated with children **Edge:** Reeded

Date	Mintage	F	VF	XF	Unc	BU
2001 Proof	10,000	Value: 47.50				

KM# 959 CROWN
Copper-Nickel, 38.6 mm. **Ruler:** Elizabeth II **Series:** Victorian Age Part II - Victoria in Scotland **Obv:** Bust with tiara right **Obv. Designer:** Ian Rank-Broadley **Rev:** Victoria on horse with servant **Edge:** Reeded

Date	Mintage	F	VF	XF	Unc	BU
2001	2,001	—	—	—	10.00	12.00

KM# 959a CROWN
28.2800 g., 0.9250 Silver 0.8410 oz. ASW, 38.6 mm. **Ruler:** Elizabeth II **Series:** Victorian Age Part II - Victoria in Scotland **Obv:** Bust with tiara right **Obv. Designer:** Ian Rank-Broadley **Rev:** Victoria on horse with servant **Edge:** Reeded

Date	Mintage	F	VF	XF	Unc	BU
2001 Proof	10,000	Value: 47.50				

KM# 961 CROWN
Copper-Nickel, 38.6 mm. **Ruler:** Elizabeth II **Series:** Victorian Age Part II - Gladstone and Disraeli **Obv:** Bust with tiara right **Obv. Designer:** Ian Rank-Broadley **Rev:** Portraits of both politicians **Edge:** Reeded

Date	Mintage	F	VF	XF	Unc	BU
2001	—	—	—	—	10.00	12.00

KM# 961a CROWN
28.2800 g., 0.9250 Silver 0.8410 oz. ASW, 38.6 mm. **Ruler:** Elizabeth II **Series:** Victorian Age Part II - Gladstone and Disraeli **Obv:** Bust with tiara right **Obv. Designer:** Ian Rank-Broadley **Rev:** Portraits of both politicians **Edge:** Reeded

Date	Mintage	F	VF	XF	Unc	BU
2001 Proof	10,000	Value: 47.50				

KM# 963 CROWN
Copper-Nickel, 38.6 mm. **Ruler:** Elizabeth II **Series:** Victorian Age Part II **Obv:** Bust with tiara right **Obv. Designer:** Ian Rank-Broadley **Rev:** Florence Nightingale holding lantern **Edge:** Reeded

Date	Mintage	F	VF	XF	Unc	BU
2001	—	—	—	—	10.00	12.00

KM# 963a CROWN
28.2800 g., 0.9250 Silver 0.8410 oz. ASW, 38.6 mm. **Ruler:** Elizabeth II **Series:** Victorian Age Part II **Obv:** Bust with tiara right **Obv. Designer:** Ian Rank-Broadley **Rev:** Florence Nightingale holding lantern **Edge:** Reeded

Date	Mintage	F	VF	XF	Unc	BU
2001 Proof	10,000	Value: 47.50				

KM# 965 CROWN
Copper-Nickel, 38.6 mm. **Ruler:** Elizabeth II **Series:** Victorian Age Part II **Obv:** Bust with tiara right **Obv. Designer:** Ian Rank-Broadley **Rev:** Lord Tennyson with the Light Brigade in background **Edge:** Reeded

Date	Mintage	F	VF	XF	Unc	BU
2001	—	—	—	—	10.00	12.00

KM# 965a CROWN
28.2800 g., 0.9250 Silver 0.8410 oz. ASW, 38.6 mm. **Ruler:** Elizabeth II **Series:** Victorian Age Part II **Obv:** Bust with tiara right **Obv. Designer:** Ian Rank-Broadley **Rev:** Lord Tennyson with the Light Brigade in background **Edge:** Reeded

Date	Mintage	F	VF	XF	Unc	BU
2001 Proof	10,000	Value: 47.50				

KM# 967 CROWN
Copper-Nickel, 38.6 mm. **Ruler:** Elizabeth II **Series:** Victorian Age Part II **Obv:** Bust with tiara right **Obv. Designer:** Ian Rank-Broadley **Rev:** Stanley meeting Dr. Livingstone **Edge:** Reeded

Date	Mintage	F	VF	XF	Unc	BU
2001	—	—	—	—	10.00	12.00

KM# 967a CROWN
28.2800 g., 0.9250 Silver 0.8410 oz. ASW, 38.6 mm. **Ruler:** Elizabeth II **Series:** Victorian Age Part II **Obv:** Bust with tiara right **Obv. Designer:** Ian Rank-Broadley **Rev:** Stanley meeting Dr. Livingstone **Edge:** Reeded

Date	Mintage	F	VF	XF	Unc	BU
2001 Proof	10,000	Value: 47.50				

KM# 969 CROWN
Copper-Nickel, 38.6 mm. **Ruler:** Elizabeth II **Series:** Victorian Age Part II **Obv:** Bust with tiara right **Obv. Designer:** Ian Rank-Broadley **Rev:** Bronte sisters **Edge:** Reeded

Date	Mintage	F	VF	XF	Unc	BU
2001	—	—	—	—	10.00	12.00

KM# 969a CROWN
28.2800 g., 0.9250 Silver 0.8410 oz. ASW, 38.6 mm. **Ruler:** Elizabeth II **Series:** Victorian Age Part II **Obv:** Bust with tiara right **Obv. Designer:** Ian Rank-Broadley **Rev:** Bronte sisters **Edge:** Reeded

Date	Mintage	F	VF	XF	Unc	BU
2001 Proof	10,000	Value: 47.50				

KM# 1061 CROWN
31.1000 g., Electrum Special alloy of equal parts of gold and silver. **Ruler:** Elizabeth II **Series:** Ancient Coins **Obv:** Crowned bust right **Rev:** Lion and bull facing **Note:** From a Kroisos [sic] coin c. 560-546 BC.

Date	Mintage	F	VF	XF	Unc	BU
2002 Proof	—	Value: 600				

KM# 1060 CROWN
31.1000 g., Electrum Special alloy of equal parts of gold and silver. **Ruler:** Elizabeth II **Series:** Ancient Coins. **Obv:** Crowned bust right **Rev:** Lion and bull facing **Note:** From a Lampsakos electrum coin c. 450 BC.

Date	Mintage	F	VF	XF	Unc	BU
2002 Proof	—	Value: 600				

KM# 1059 CROWN

31.1000 g., Electrum Special alloy of equal parts of gold and silver. **Ruler:** Elizabeth II **Series:** Ancient Coins **Obv:** Crowned bust right **Rev:** Hercules head right **Note:** From a Lesbos coin c. 480-450 BC.

Date	Mintage	F	VF	XF	Unc	BU
2002 Proof	—	Value: 600				

KM# 1058 CROWN

31.1000 g., 1.0000 Electrum Special alloy of equal parts of gold and silver. 0.9998 oz. **Ruler:** Elizabeth II **Series:** Ancient Coins **Obv:** Crowned head right **Rev:** Head of Athena left **Note:** From a Mysia electrum coin c. 520 BC.

Date	Mintage	F	VF	XF	Unc	BU
2002 Proof	—	Value: 600				

KM# 992.2 CROWN

Copper-Nickel **Ruler:** Elizabeth II **Obv:** Bust with tiara right **Obv. Designer:** Ian Rank-Broadley **Rev:** Peter Rabbit in multi-color

Date	Mintage	F	VF	XF	Unc	BU
2002	—	—	—	—	10.00	12.00

KM# 979 CROWN

28.2800 g., Copper-Nickel, 38.6 mm. **Ruler:** Elizabeth II **Subject:** Queen Mother's Life **Obv:** Bust with tiara right **Obv. Designer:** Ian Rank-Broadley **Rev:** Christening of Prince William **Edge:** Reeded

Date	Mintage	F	VF	XF	Unc	BU
2002	—	—	—	—	10.00	12.00

KM# 979a CROWN

28.2800 g., 0.9250 Silver 0.8410 oz. ASW, 38.6 mm. **Ruler:** Elizabeth II **Subject:** Queen Mother's Life **Obv:** Bust with tiara right **Obv. Designer:** Ian Rank-Broadley **Rev:** Prince William's christening **Edge:** Reeded

Date	Mintage	F	VF	XF	Unc	BU
2002 Proof	10,000	Value: 47.50				

KM# 981 CROWN

28.2800 g., Copper-Nickel, 38.6 mm. **Ruler:** Elizabeth II **Subject:** World Cup Soccer **Obv:** Bust with tiara right **Obv. Designer:** Ian Rank-Broadley **Rev:** Two players about to collide **Edge:** Reeded

Date	Mintage	F	VF	XF	Unc	BU
2002	—	—	—	—	10.00	11.50

KM# 981a CROWN

28.2800 g., 0.9250 Silver 0.8410 oz. ASW, 38.6 mm. **Ruler:** Elizabeth II **Subject:** World Cup Soccer **Obv:** Bust with tiara right **Obv. Designer:** Ian Rank-Broadley **Rev:** Two players about to collide **Edge:** Reeded

Date	Mintage	F	VF	XF	Unc	BU
2002 Proof	10,000	Value: 47.50				

KM# 983 CROWN

28.2800 g., Copper-Nickel, 38.6 mm. **Ruler:** Elizabeth II **Subject:** World Cup Soccer **Obv:** Bust with tiara right **Obv. Designer:** Ian Rank-Broadley **Rev:** Two players facing viewer **Edge:** Reeded

Date	Mintage	F	VF	XF	Unc	BU
2002	—	—	—	—	10.00	11.50

KM# 983a CROWN

28.2800 g., 0.9250 Silver 0.8410 oz. ASW, 38.6 mm. **Ruler:** Elizabeth II **Subject:** World Cup Soccer **Obv:** Bust with tiara right **Obv. Designer:** Ian Rank-Broadley **Rev:** Two players facing viewer **Edge:** Reeded

Date	Mintage	F	VF	XF	Unc	BU
2002 Proof	10,000	Value: 47.50				

KM# 985 CROWN

28.2800 g., Copper-Nickel, 38.6 mm. **Ruler:** Elizabeth II **Subject:** World Cup Soccer **Obv:** Bust with tiara right **Obv. Designer:** Ian Rank-Broadley **Rev:** Two horizontal players **Edge:** Reeded

Date	Mintage	F	VF	XF	Unc	BU
2002	—	—	—	—	10.00	11.50

KM# 985a CROWN

28.2800 g., 0.9250 Silver 0.8410 oz. ASW, 38.6 mm. **Ruler:** Elizabeth II **Subject:** World Cup Soccer **Obv:** Bust with tiara right **Obv. Designer:** Ian Rank-Broadley **Rev:** Two horizontal players **Edge:** Reeded

Date	Mintage	F	VF	XF	Unc	BU
2002 Proof	10,000	Value: 47.50				

KM# 987 CROWN

28.2800 g., Copper-Nickel, 38.6 mm. **Ruler:** Elizabeth II **Subject:** World Cup Soccer **Obv:** Bust with tiara right **Obv. Designer:** Ian Rank-Broadley **Rev:** Two players moving to left **Edge:** Reeded

Date	Mintage	F	VF	XF	Unc	BU
2002	—	—	—	—	10.00	11.50

KM# 987a CROWN

28.2800 g., 0.9250 Silver 0.8410 oz. ASW, 38.6 mm. **Ruler:** Elizabeth II **Subject:** World Cup Soccer **Obv:** Bust with tiara right **Obv. Designer:** Ian Rank-Broadley **Rev:** Two players moving to left **Edge:** Reeded

Date	Mintage	F	VF	XF	Unc	BU
2002 Proof	10,000	Value: 47.50				

KM# 992.1 CROWN

28.2800 g., Copper-Nickel, 38.6 mm. **Ruler:** Elizabeth II **Subject:** Peter Rabbit Centennial **Obv:** Bust with tiara right **Obv. Designer:** Ian Rank-Broadley **Rev:** Peter Rabbit **Edge:** Reeded

Date	Mintage	F	VF	XF	Unc	BU
2002	—	—	—	—	10.00	12.00

KM# 992a CROWN

28.2800 g., 0.9250 Silver 0.8410 oz. ASW, 38.6 mm. **Ruler:** Elizabeth II **Subject:** Peter Rabbit Centennial **Obv:** Bust with tiara right **Obv. Designer:** Ian Rank-Broadley **Rev:** Peter Rabbit **Edge:** Reeded

Date	Mintage	F	VF	XF	Unc	BU
2002 Proof	10,000	Value: 47.50				

KM# 994 CROWN

28.2800 g., Copper-Nickel, 38.6 mm. **Ruler:** Elizabeth II **Subject:** Queen's Golden Jubilee **Obv:** Bust with tiara right **Obv. Designer:** Ian Rank-Broadley **Rev:** Royal couple and tree house **Edge:** Reeded

Date	Mintage	F	VF	XF	Unc	BU
2002	—	—	—	—	10.00	12.00

KM# 994a CROWN

Yellow Brass, 38.6 mm. **Ruler:** Elizabeth II **Subject:** Queen's Golden Jubilee **Obv:** Bust with tiara right **Obv. Designer:** Ian Rank-Broadley **Rev:** Royal couple and tree house **Edge:** Reeded

Date	Mintage	F	VF	XF	Unc	BU
2002 Proof	15,000	Value: 20.00				

KM# 994b CROWN

28.2800 g., 0.9250 Gold Clad Silver 0.8410 oz., 38.6 mm. **Ruler:** Elizabeth II **Subject:** Queen's Golden Jubilee **Obv:** Bust with tiara right **Obv. Designer:** Ian Rank-Broadley **Rev:** Royal couple and tree house **Edge:** Reeded

Date	Mintage	F	VF	XF	Unc	BU
2002 Proof	10,000	Value: 50.00				

KM# 996 CROWN

28.2800 g., Copper-Nickel, 38.6 mm. **Ruler:** Elizabeth II **Subject:** Queen's Golden Jubilee **Obv:** Bust with tiara right **Obv. Designer:** Ian Rank-Broadley **Rev:** Royal coach **Edge:** Reeded

Date	Mintage	F	VF	XF	Unc	BU
2002	—	—	—	—	10.00	12.00

KM# 996a CROWN

Yellow Brass, 38.6 mm. **Ruler:** Elizabeth II **Subject:** Queen's Golden Jubilee **Obv:** Bust with tiara right **Obv. Designer:** Ian Rank-Broadley **Rev:** Royal coach **Edge:** Reeded

Date	Mintage	F	VF	XF	Unc	BU
2002 Proof	15,000	Value: 20.00				

KM# 996b CROWN

28.2800 g., 0.9250 Gold Clad Silver 0.8410 oz., 38.6 mm. **Ruler:** Elizabeth II **Subject:** Queen's Golden Jubilee **Obv:** Bust with tiara right **Obv. Designer:** Ian Rank-Broadley **Rev:** Royal coach **Edge:** Reeded

Date	Mintage	F	VF	XF	Unc	BU
2002 Proof	10,000	Value: 50.00				

KM# 998 CROWN

28.2800 g., Copper-Nickel, 38.6 mm. **Ruler:** Elizabeth II **Subject:** Queen's Golden Jubilee **Obv:** Bust with tiara right **Obv. Designer:** Ian Rank-Broadley **Rev:** Royal couple with baby **Edge:** Reeded

Date	Mintage	F	VF	XF	Unc	BU
2002	—	—	—	—	10.00	12.00

KM# 998a CROWN

Yellow Brass, 38.6 mm. **Ruler:** Elizabeth II **Subject:** Queen's Golden Jubilee **Obv:** Bust with tiara right **Obv. Designer:** Ian Rank-Broadley **Rev:** Royal couple with baby **Edge:** Reeded

Date	Mintage	F	VF	XF	Unc	BU
2002 Proof	15,000	Value: 20.00				

KM# 998b CROWN

28.2800 g., 0.9250 Gold Clad Silver 0.8410 oz., 38.6 mm. **Ruler:** Elizabeth II **Subject:** Queen's Golden Jubilee **Obv:** Bust with tiara right **Obv. Designer:** Ian Rank-Broadley **Rev:** Royal couple with baby **Edge:** Reeded

Date	Mintage	F	VF	XF	Unc	BU
2002 Proof	1,000	Value: 50.00				

KM# 1000 CROWN

28.2800 g., Copper-Nickel, 38.6 mm. **Ruler:** Elizabeth II **Subject:** Queen's Golden Jubilee **Obv:** Bust with tiara right **Obv. Designer:** Ian Rank-Broadley **Rev:** Royal yacht under Tower bridge **Edge:** Reeded

Date	Mintage	F	VF	XF	Unc	BU
2002	—	—	—	—	10.00	12.00

KM# 1000a CROWN

Yellow Brass, 38.6 mm. **Ruler:** Elizabeth II **Subject:** Queen's Golden Jubilee **Obv:** Bust with tiara right **Obv. Designer:** Ian Rank-Broadley **Rev:** Royal yacht under Tower bridge **Edge:** Reeded

Date	Mintage	F	VF	XF	Unc	BU
2002 Proof	15,000	Value: 20.00				

KM# 1000b CROWN

28.2800 g., 0.9250 Gold Clad Silver 0.8410 oz., 38.6 mm. **Ruler:** Elizabeth II **Subject:** Queen's Golden Jubilee **Obv:** Bust with tiara right **Obv. Designer:** Ian Rank-Broadley **Rev:** Royal yacht under Tower bridge **Edge:** Reeded

Date	Mintage	F	VF	XF	Unc	BU
2002 Proof	10,000	Value: 50.00				

KM# 1013 CROWN

28.2800 g., Copper-Nickel, Blackened, 38.6 mm. **Ruler:** Elizabeth II **Subject:** Death of Queen Mother **Obv:** Bust with tiara right **Obv. Designer:** Ian Rank-Broadley **Rev:** Queen Mother trout fishing **Edge:** Reeded

Date	Mintage	F	VF	XF	Unc	BU
2002	—	—	—	—	10.00	12.00

KM# 1013a CROWN

28.2800 g., 0.9250 Silver 0.8410 oz. ASW, 38.6 mm. **Ruler:** Elizabeth II **Subject:** Queen Mother **Obv:** Bust with tiara right **Obv. Designer:** Ian Rank-Broadley **Rev:** Queen Mother trout fishing **Edge:** Reeded **Note:** Obv. and rev. have blackened legends.

Date	Mintage	F	VF	XF	Unc	BU
2002 Proof	5,000	Value: 175				

KM# 1015 CROWN

28.2800 g., Copper-Nickel, 38.6 mm. **Ruler:** Elizabeth II **Subject:** Princess Diana **Obv:** Bust with tiara right **Obv. Designer:** Ian Rank-Broadley **Rev:** Diana's portrait **Edge:** Reeded

Date	Mintage	F	VF	XF	Unc	BU
2002	—	—	—	—	10.00	12.00

KM# 1015a CROWN

28.2800 g., 0.9250 Silver 0.8410 oz. ASW, 38.6 mm. **Ruler:** Elizabeth II **Subject:** Princess Diana **Obv:** Bust with tiara right **Obv. Designer:** Ian Rank-Broadley **Rev:** Diana's portrait **Edge:** Reeded

Date	Mintage	F	VF	XF	Unc	BU
2002 Proof	10,000	Value: 47.50				

KM# 1019 CROWN

28.2800 g., Copper-Nickel, 38.6 mm. **Ruler:** Elizabeth II **Subject:** Peter Pan **Obv:** Bust with tiara right **Obv. Designer:** Ian Rank-Broadley **Rev:** Peter Pan and Tinkerbell flying above city **Edge:** Reeded

Date	Mintage	F	VF	XF	Unc	BU
2002	—	—	—	—	10.00	12.00

KM# 1019a CROWN

28.2800 g., 0.9250 Silver 0.8410 oz. ASW, 38.6 mm. **Ruler:** Elizabeth II **Subject:** Peter Pan **Obv:** Bust with tiara right **Obv. Designer:** Ian Rank-Broadley **Rev:** Peter Pan and Tinkerbell flying above city **Edge:** Reeded

Date	Mintage	F	VF	XF	Unc	BU
2002 Proof	10,000	Value: 47.50				

KM# 1021 CROWN

28.2800 g., Copper-Nickel, 38.6 mm. **Ruler:** Elizabeth II **Subject:** Grand Masonic Lodge **Obv:** Bust with tiara right **Obv. Designer:** Ian Rank-Broadley **Rev:** Masonic seal above Gibraltar **Edge:** Reeded

Date	Mintage	F	VF	XF	Unc	BU
2002 Proof	5,000	Value: 10.00				

KM# 1021a CROWN

28.2800 g., 0.9250 Silver 0.8410 oz. ASW, 38.6 mm. **Ruler:** Elizabeth II **Subject:** Grand Masonic Lodge **Obv:** Bust with tiara right **Obv. Designer:** Ian Rank-Broadley **Rev:** Masonic seal above Gibraltar **Edge:** Reeded

Date	Mintage	F	VF	XF	Unc	BU
2002 Proof	10,000	Value: 47.50				

KM# 1025 CROWN

28.2800 g., Copper Nickel, 38.6 mm. **Ruler:** Elizabeth II **Subject:** Calpe Conference **Obv:** Bust with tiara right **Obv. Designer:** Ian Rank-Broadley **Rev:** Crossed flags and arms **Edge:** Reeded

Date	Mintage	F	VF	XF	Unc	BU
2002PM	—	—	—	—	10.00	12.00

KM# 1025a CROWN

28.2800 g., 0.9250 Silver 0.8410 oz. ASW, 38.6 mm. **Ruler:** Elizabeth II **Subject:** Calpe Conference **Obv:** Bust with tiara right **Obv. Designer:** Ian Rank-Broadley **Rev:** Crossed flags and arms **Edge:** Reeded

Date	Mintage	F	VF	XF	Unc	BU
2002PM Proof	10,000	Value: 47.50				

KM# 1052 CROWN

Copper-Nickel **Ruler:** Elizabeth II **Subject:** 2004 Athens Olympics **Rev:** Horse jumping left

Date	Mintage	F	VF	XF	Unc	BU
2003	—	—	—	—	10.00	12.00

KM# 1053 CROWN

Copper-Nickel **Ruler:** Elizabeth II **Subject:** 2004 Athens Olympics **Rev:** Javelin thrower

Date	Mintage	F	VF	XF	Unc	BU
2003	—	—	—	—	10.00	12.00

KM# 1054 CROWN

Copper-Nickel **Ruler:** Elizabeth II **Subject:** 2004 Athens Olympics **Rev:** Field Hockey

Date	Mintage	F	VF	XF	Unc	BU
2003	—	—	—	—	10.00	12.00

KM# 1055 CROWN

Copper-Nickel **Ruler:** Elizabeth II **Subject:** 2004 Athens Olympics **Rev:** Wrestlers

Date	Mintage	F	VF	XF	Unc	BU
2003	—	—	—	—	10.00	12.00

KM# 1035 CROWN

28.2800 g., Copper-Nickel, 38.6 mm. **Ruler:** Elizabeth II **Subject:** 1700th Anniversary - Death of St. George **Obv:** Bust with tiara right **Obv. Designer:** Ian Rank-Broadley **Rev:** St. George and the dragon **Edge:** Reeded

Date	Mintage	F	VF	XF	Unc	BU
2003	—	—	—	—	9.00	10.00

KM# 1035a CROWN

28.2800 g., 0.9250 Silver 0.8410 oz. ASW, 38.6 mm. **Ruler:** Elizabeth II **Subject:** 1700th Anniversary - Death of St. George **Obv:** Bust with tiara right **Obv. Designer:** Ian Rank-Broadley **Rev:** St. George and the dragon **Edge:** Reeded

Date	Mintage	F	VF	XF	Unc	BU
2003 Proof	10,000	Value: 47.50				

KM# 1039 CROWN

28.3000 g., Copper-Nickel, 38.6 mm. **Ruler:** Elizabeth II **Subject:** Peter Rabbit **Obv:** Bust with tiara right **Obv. Designer:** Ian Rank-Broadley **Rev:** Peter Rabbit holding carrot **Edge:** Reeded

Date	Mintage	F	VF	XF	Unc	BU
2003PM	—	—	—	—	9.00	10.00

KM# 1040 CROWN

28.2800 g., Copper-Nickel, 38.6 mm. **Ruler:** Elizabeth II **Subject:** Centennial of Powered Flight **Obv:** Queens portrait **Rev:** Stealth bomber within circles of WWI and WWII planes **Edge:** Reeded

Date	Mintage	F	VF	XF	Unc	BU
2003PM	—	—	—	—	10.00	12.00

KM# 1040a CROWN

31.1000 g., Tri-Metallic .9995 Platinum 5.2g center in .9999 Gold 14.2 g ring within .999 Silver 11.7 g outer ring, 38.6 mm. **Ruler:** Elizabeth II **Subject:** Centennial of Powered Flight **Obv:** Queens portrait **Rev:** Stealth bomber within circles of WWI and WWII planes **Edge:** Reeded

Date	Mintage	F	VF	XF	Unc	BU
2003PM Proof	999	Value: 850				

KM# 1041 CROWN
28.2800 g., Copper-Nickel, 38.6 mm. **Ruler:** Elizabeth II **Subject:** 50th Anniversary of Coronation **Obv:** Queens portrait **Rev:** Buckingham Palace **Edge:** Reeded

Date	Mintage	F	VF	XF	Unc	BU
2003PM	—	—	—	—	10.00	12.00

KM# 1034 2 CROWN
41.5000 g., Bi-Metallic .999 Silver 11.5g. star shaped center in Copper outer ring, 50 mm. **Ruler:** Elizabeth II **Subject:** Euro's First Anniversary **Obv:** Crowned bust right within star silhouette **Rev:** Europa riding a bull, stars and star silhouette in background **Edge:** Reeded

Date	Mintage	F	VF	XF	Unc	BU
2003PM Proof	3,500	Value: 100				

KM# 1034a 2 CROWN
50.0000 g., Bi-Metallic .9999 Gold 20g star shaped center in Copper outer ring, 50 mm. **Ruler:** Elizabeth II **Subject:** 1st Anniversary - Euro **Obv:** Crowned bust right within star silhouette **Rev:** Europa riding the bull, stars and star silhouette in background **Edge:** Reeded

Date	Mintage	F	VF	XF	Unc	BU
2003PM Proof	2,003	Value: 775				

KM# 1034b 2 CROWN
56.3000 g., Bi-Metallic .9999 Gold 20.8g star shaped center in a .999 Silver 35.5g outer ring, 50 mm. **Ruler:** Elizabeth II **Subject:** 1st Anniversary - Euro **Obv:** Crowned bust right within star silhouette **Rev:** Europa riding the bull, stars and star silhouette in background **Edge:** Reeded

Date	Mintage	F	VF	XF	Unc	BU
2003PM Proof	2,003	Value: 800				

KM# 907 5 CROWN
Tri-Metallic Center .9995 Platinum 26.9g. Inner Ring .9999 Gold 73.41g. Outer Ring .999 Silver 55.19g, 50 mm. **Ruler:** Elizabeth II **Subject:** 21st Century **Obv:** Crowned bust right, date below **Obv. Designer:** Raphael Maklouf **Rev:** Celtic cross, Viking ship and modern technological items **Edge:** Reeded

Date	Mintage	F	VF	XF	Unc	BU
2001 Proof	199	Value: 4,500				

KM# 1042 5 CROWN
155.5500 g., 0.9990 Silver 4.9958 oz. ASW, 65 mm. **Ruler:** Elizabeth II **Subject:** 50th Anniversary of Coronation **Obv:** Queens portrait **Rev:** Buckingham Palace with tiny .01ct ruby, diamond and sapphire inserts above the main entrance **Edge:** Reeded

Date	Mintage	F	VF	XF	Unc	BU
2003PM Proof	2,003	Value: 175				

KM# 1045 32 CROWNS
1000.0000 g., 0.9990 Silver 32.117 oz. ASW **Ruler:** Elizabeth II **Subject:** Beatrix Potter's Peter Rabbit **Obv:** Bust with tiara right **Obv. Designer:** Ian Rank-Broadley **Rev:** Multicolor Peter Rabbit holding carrot, with blue coat and red slippers

Date	Mintage	F	VF	XF	Unc	BU
2003 Proof	1,000	Value: 750				

KM# 869 POUND
9.5000 g., Nickel-Brass, 22.5 mm. **Ruler:** Elizabeth II **Obv:** Head with tiara right **Obv. Designer:** Ian Rank-Broadley **Rev:** Gibraltar castle and key

Date	Mintage	F	VF	XF	Unc	BU
2001 AA	—	—	—	—	3.50	4.50
2001 AB	—	—	—	—	3.50	4.50
2002 AC	—	—	—	—	3.50	4.50

KM# 1036 POUND
9.5000 g., Nickel-Brass, 22 mm. **Ruler:** Elizabeth II **Subject:** 1700th Anniversary - Death of St. George **Obv:** Bust with tiara right **Rev:** St. George and the dragon **Edge:** Reeded

Date	Mintage	F	VF	XF	Unc	BU
2003	—	—	—	—	9.00	10.00

KM# 1051 POUND
9.5000 g., Nickel-Brass, 22.5 mm. **Ruler:** Elizabeth II **Subject:** Tercentenary 1704-2004 **Obv:** Elizabeth II **Rev:** Old cannon set for a downhill target **Edge:** Reeded

Date	Mintage	F	VF	XF	Unc	BU
2004PM	—	—	—	—	—	4.00

KM# 970 2 POUNDS
Bi-Metallic Steel Copper-Nickel center in Brass ring, 28.4 mm. **Ruler:** Elizabeth II **Subject:** Bicentennial of the Union Jack **Obv:** Head with tiara right **Obv. Designer:** Ian Rank-Broadley **Rev:** Standing Britannia wearing flag as a cape **Edge:** Reeded

Date	Mintage	F	VF	XF	Unc	BU
2001 AA	—	—	—	—	10.00	12.00

KM# 970a 2 POUNDS
12.0000 g., 0.9990 Bi-Metallic Silver center in Gold plated Silver ring 0.3854 oz., 28.4 mm. **Ruler:** Elizabeth II **Subject:** Bicentennial of the Union Jack **Obv:** Head with tiara right **Obv. Designer:** Ian Rank-Broadley **Rev:** Standing Britannia wearing flag as a cape **Edge:** Reeded

Date	Mintage	F	VF	XF	Unc	BU
2001	7,500	—	—	—	30.00	35.00

KM# 1043 2 POUNDS
12.0600 g., Bi-Metallic Copper-Nickel center in Brass ring, 28.3 mm. **Ruler:** Elizabeth II **Obv:** Head with tiara right **Obv. Designer:** Ian Rank-Broadley **Rev:** Old cannon **Edge:** Reeded

Date	Mintage	F	VF	XF	Unc	BU
2003PM	—	—	—	—	10.00	12.00

KM# 1057 2 POUNDS
9.5000 g., Nickel-Brass, 22.5 mm. **Ruler:** Elizabeth II **Subject:** Tercentenary 1704-2004 **Obv:** Elizabeth II **Rev:** Old cannon set for a downhill target **Edge:** Reeded

Date	Mintage	F	VF	XF	Unc	BU
2004PM	—	—	—	—	—	4.00

KM# 953 5 POUNDS
20.0000 g., Virenium, 36.1 mm. **Ruler:** Elizabeth II **Subject:** Gibraltar Chronicle 200 Years **Obv:** Head with tiara right **Obv. Designer:** Ian Rank-Broadley **Rev:** Naval battle scene with newspaper in background **Edge:** Reeded

Date	Mintage	F	VF	XF	Unc	BU
2001	—	—	—	—	15.00	18.00

KM# 953a 5 POUNDS
23.5000 g., 0.9250 Silver 0.6988 oz. ASW, 36.1 mm. **Ruler:** Elizabeth II **Subject:** Gibraltar Chronicle 200 Years **Obv:** Head with tiara right **Obv. Designer:** Ian Rank-Broadley **Rev:** Naval battle scene with newspaper in background **Edge:** Reeded

Date	Mintage	F	VF	XF	Unc	BU
2001 Proof	10,000	Value: 50.00				

KM# 953b 5 POUNDS
39.8300 g., 0.9167 Gold 1.1738 oz. AGW, 36.1 mm. **Ruler:** Elizabeth II **Subject:** Gibraltar Chronicle 200 Years **Obv:** Head with tiara right **Obv. Designer:** Ian Rank-Broadley **Rev:** Naval battle scene with newspaper in background **Edge:** Reeded

Date	Mintage	F	VF	XF	Unc	BU
2001 Proof	850	Value: 1,150				

KM# 1011 5 POUNDS
20.0000 g., Virenium, 36.1 mm. **Ruler:** Elizabeth II **Subject:** Queen's Golden Jubilee **Obv:** Head with tiara right **Obv. Designer:** Ian Rank-Broadley **Rev:** Coronation scene **Edge:** Reeded

Date	Mintage	F	VF	XF	Unc	BU
2002	—	—	—	—	15.00	18.00

KM# 1011a 5 POUNDS
23.5000 g., 0.9250 Silver 0.6988 oz. ASW, 36.1 mm. **Ruler:** Elizabeth II **Subject:** Queen's Golden Jubilee **Obv:** Head with tiara right **Obv. Designer:** Ian Rank-Broadley **Rev:** Coronation scene **Edge:** Reeded

Date	Mintage	F	VF	XF	Unc	BU
2002 Proof	10,000	Value: 50.00				

KM# 1011b 5 POUNDS
39.8300 g., 0.9166 Gold 1.1737 oz. AGW, 36.1 mm. **Ruler:** Elizabeth II **Subject:** Queen's Golden Jubilee **Obv:** Head with tiara right **Obv. Designer:** Ian Rank-Broadley **Rev:** Coronation scene **Edge:** Reeded

Date	Mintage	F	VF	XF	Unc	BU
2002 Proof	850	Value: 1,150				

SOVEREIGN COINAGE

KM# 1037 1/5 SOVEREIGN
1.2200 g., 0.9999 Gold 0.0392 oz. AGW, 13.92 mm. **Ruler:** Elizabeth II **Subject:** Death of St. George **Obv:** Bust with tiara right **Obv. Designer:** Ian Rank-Broadley **Rev:** St. George and the dragon **Edge:** Reeded

Date	Mintage	F	VF	XF	Unc	BU
2003 Proof	10,000	Value: 55.00				

KM# 1038 SOVEREIGN
6.2200 g., 0.9999 Gold 0.1999 oz. AGW, 22 mm. **Ruler:** Elizabeth II **Subject:** Death of St. George **Obv:** Bust with tiara right **Obv. Designer:** Ian Rank-Broadley **Rev:** St. George and the dragon **Edge:** Reeded

Date	Mintage	F	VF	XF	Unc	BU
2003 Proof	5,000	Value: 215				

ROYAL COINAGE

KM# 896 1/25 ROYAL
1.2441 g., 0.9999 Gold 0.0400 oz. AGW, 13.92 mm. **Ruler:** Elizabeth II **Subject:** Bullion **Obv:** Bust with tiara right **Obv. Designer:** Ian Rank-Broadley **Rev:** Two cherubs **Edge:** Reeded

Date	Mintage	F	VF	XF	Unc	BU
2001	—	—	—	—	40.00	—
2001 In Proof sets only	1,000	Value: 55.00				

KM# 972 1/25 ROYAL
1.2440 g., 0.9990 Gold 0.0400 oz. AGW, 13.92 mm. **Ruler:** Elizabeth II **Subject:** Cherubs **Obv:** Bust with tiara right **Obv. Designer:** Ian Rank-Broadley **Rev:** Two cherubs shooting arrows **Edge:** Reeded

Date	Mintage	F	VF	XF	Unc	BU
2002	—	—	—	—	40.00	—
2002 Proof	1,000	Value: 55.00				

KM# 1027 1/25 ROYAL
1.2440 g., 0.9999 Gold 0.0400 oz. AGW, 13.92 mm. **Ruler:** Elizabeth II **Obv:** Bust with tiara right **Obv. Designer:** Ian Rank-Broadley **Rev:** Cherub with crossed arms **Edge:** Reeded

Date	Mintage	F	VF	XF	Unc	BU
2003PM	—	—	—	—	40.00	—
2003PM Proof	—	Value: 55.00				

KM# 897 1/10 ROYAL
3.1100 g., 0.9999 Gold 0.1000 oz. AGW, 18 mm. **Ruler:** Elizabeth II **Subject:** Bullion **Obv:** Bust with tiara right **Obv. Designer:** Ian Rank-Broadley **Rev:** Two cherubs **Edge:** Reeded

Date	Mintage	F	VF	XF	Unc	BU
2001	—	—	—	—	95.00	—
2001 Proof	1,000	Value: 110				

KM# 973 1/10 ROYAL
3.1100 g., 0.9990 Gold 0.0999 oz. AGW, 17.95 mm. **Ruler:** Elizabeth II **Subject:** Cherubs **Obv:** Bust with tiara right **Obv. Designer:** Ian Rank-Broadley **Rev:** Two cherubs shooting arrows **Edge:** Reeded

Date	Mintage	F	VF	XF	Unc	BU
2002	—	—	—	—	95.00	—
2002 Proof	1,000	Value: 110				

KM# 1028 1/10 ROYAL
3.1100 g., 0.9999 Gold 0.1000 oz. AGW, 17.95 mm. **Ruler:** Elizabeth II **Obv:** Bust with tiara right **Obv. Designer:** Ian Rank-Broadley **Rev:** Cherub with crossed arms **Edge:** Reeded

Date	Mintage	F	VF	XF	Unc	BU
2003PM	—	—	—	—	95.00	—
2003PM Proof	—	Value: 110				

KM# 898 1/5 ROYAL
6.2200 g., 0.9990 Gold 0.1998 oz. AGW, 22 mm. **Ruler:** Elizabeth II **Subject:** Bullion **Obv:** Bust with tiara right **Obv. Designer:** Ian Rank-Broadley **Rev:** Two cherubs **Edge:** Reeded

Date	Mintage	F	VF	XF	Unc	BU
2001	—	—	—	—	195	—
2001 Proof	1,000	Value: 225				

KM# 974 1/5 ROYAL
6.2200 g., 0.9990 Gold 0.1998 oz. AGW, 22 mm. **Ruler:** Elizabeth II **Obv:** Bust with tiara right **Obv. Designer:** Ian Rank-Broadley **Rev:** Two cherubs shooting arrows **Edge:** Reeded

Date	Mintage	F	VF	XF	Unc	BU
2002	—	—	—	—	195	—
2002 Proof	1,000	Value: 225				

KM# 1029 1/5 ROYAL
6.2200 g., 0.9999 Gold 0.1999 oz. AGW, 22 mm. **Ruler:** Elizabeth II **Obv:** Bust with tiara right **Obv. Designer:** Ian Rank-Broadley **Rev:** Cherub with crossed arms **Edge:** Reeded

Date	Mintage	F	VF	XF	Unc	BU
2003PM	—	—	—	—	195	—
2003PM Proof	—	Value: 225				

KM# 899 1/2 ROYAL
15.5517 g., 0.9999 Gold 0.4999 oz. AGW, 30 mm. **Ruler:** Elizabeth II **Subject:** Bullion **Obv:** Bust with tiara right **Obv. Designer:** Ian Rank-Broadley **Rev:** Two cherubs **Edge:** Reeded

Date	Mintage	F	VF	XF	Unc	BU
2001	—	—	—	—	485	—
2001 Proof	1,000	Value: 515				

KM# 975 1/2 ROYAL
15.5510 g., 0.9990 Gold 0.4995 oz. AGW, 30 mm. **Ruler:** Elizabeth II **Obv:** Bust with tiara right **Obv. Designer:** Ian Rank-Broadley **Rev:** Two cherubs shooting arrows **Edge:** Reeded

Date	Mintage	F	VF	XF	Unc	BU
2002	—	—	—	—	485	—
2002 Proof	1,000	Value: 515				

KM# 1030 1/2 ROYAL
15.5510 g., 0.9999 Gold 0.4999 oz. AGW, 30 mm. **Ruler:** Elizabeth II **Obv:** Bust with tiara right **Obv. Designer:** Ian Rank-Broadley **Rev:** Cherub with crossed arms **Edge:** Reeded

Date	Mintage	F	VF	XF	Unc	BU
2003PM	—	—	—	—	485	—
2003PM Proof	—	Value: 515				

KM# 900 ROYAL
28.2800 g., Copper-Nickel, 38.6 mm. **Ruler:** Elizabeth II **Obv:** Bust with tiara right **Obv. Designer:** Ian Rank-Broadley **Rev:** Two cherubs **Edge:** Reeded

Date	Mintage	F	VF	XF	Unc	BU
2001	—	—	—	—	10.00	12.00

KM# 900a ROYAL
31.1035 g., 0.9990 Silver 0.9990 oz. ASW **Ruler:** Elizabeth II **Obv:** Bust with tiara right **Obv. Designer:** Ian Rank-Broadley **Rev:** Two cherubs

Date	Mintage	F	VF	XF	Unc	BU
2001 Proof	10,000	Value: 47.50				

KM# 901 ROYAL
31.1035 g., 0.9999 Gold 0.9999 oz. AGW, 32.7 mm. **Ruler:** Elizabeth II **Subject:** Bullion **Obv:** Bust with tiara right **Obv. Designer:** Ian Rank-Broadley **Rev:** Two cherubs **Edge:** Reeded

Date	Mintage	F	VF	XF	Unc	BU
2001	—	—	—	—	950	975
2001 In Proof sets only	1,000	Value: 1,050				

KM# 976 ROYAL
28.2800 g., Copper-Nickel, 38.6 mm. **Ruler:** Elizabeth II **Obv:** Bust with tiara right **Obv. Designer:** Ian Rank-Broadley **Rev:** Two cherubs shooting arrows **Edge:** Reeded

Date	Mintage	F	VF	XF	Unc	BU
2002	—	—	—	—	10.00	12.00

KM# 976a ROYAL
31.1035 g., 0.9990 Silver 0.9990 oz. ASW **Ruler:** Elizabeth II **Obv:** Bust with tiara right **Obv. Designer:** Ian Rank-Broadley **Rev:** Two cherubs shooting arrows **Edge:** Reeded

Date	Mintage	F	VF	XF	Unc	BU
2002 Proof	1,000	Value: 47.50				

KM# 977 ROYAL
31.1035 g., 0.9990 Gold 0.9990 oz. AGW, 32.7 mm. **Ruler:** Elizabeth II **Obv:** Bust with tiara right **Obv. Designer:** Ian Rank-Broadley **Rev:** Two cherubs shooting arrows **Edge:** Reeded

Date	Mintage	F	VF	XF	Unc	BU
2002	—	—	—	—	950	975
2002 Proof	1,000	Value: 1,050				

KM# 1031 ROYAL
28.2800 g., Copper-Nickel, 38.6 mm. **Ruler:** Elizabeth II **Obv:** Bust with tiara right **Obv. Designer:** Ian Rank-Broadley **Rev:** Cherub with crossed arms **Edge:** Reeded

Date	Mintage	F	VF	XF	Unc	BU
2003PM	—	—	—	—	10.00	12.00

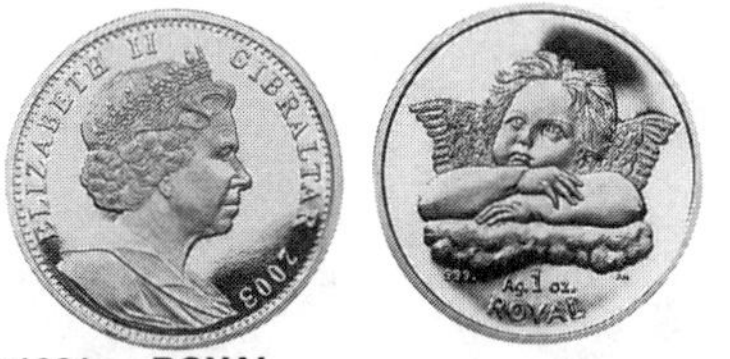

KM# 1031a ROYAL
28.2800 g., 0.9990 Silver 0.9083 oz. ASW, 38.6 mm. **Ruler:** Elizabeth II **Obv:** Bust with tiara right **Obv. Designer:** Ian Rank-Broadley **Rev:** Cherub with crossed arms **Edge:** Reeded

Date	Mintage	F	VF	XF	Unc	BU
2003PM Proof	10,000	Value: 47.50				

KM# 1032 ROYAL
31.1035 g., 0.9999 Gold 0.9999 oz. AGW, 32.7 mm. **Ruler:** Elizabeth II **Obv:** Bust with tiara right **Obv. Designer:** Ian Rank-Broadley **Rev:** Cherub with crossed arms **Edge:** Reeded

Date	Mintage	F	VF	XF	Unc	BU
2003PM	—	—	—	—	950	975
2003PM Proof	—	Value: 1,050				

PROOF SETS

KM#	Date	Mintage	Identification	Issue Price	Mkt Val
PS29	2001 (5)	1,000	KM#896-899, 901	—	1,350
PS30	2003 (5)	1,000	KM#1027-30, 1032	—	1,400

GREAT BRITAIN

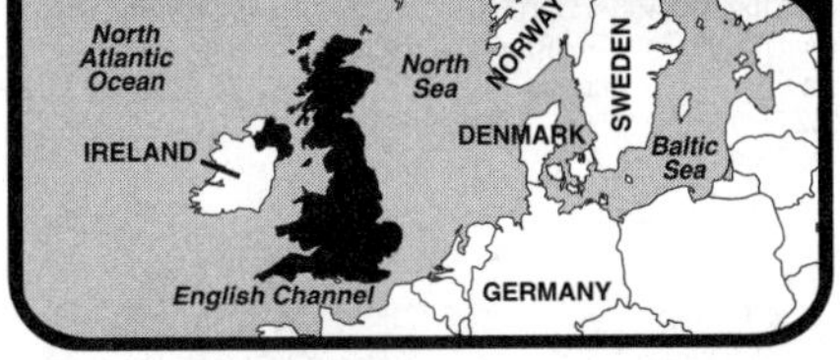

The United Kingdom of Great Britain and Northern Ireland, located off the northwest coast of the European continent, has an area of 94,227 sq. mi. (244,820 sq. km.) and a population of 54 million. Capital: London. The economy is based on industrial activity and trading. Machinery, motor vehicles, chemicals, and textile yarns and fabrics are exported.

By the mid-20th century, most of the territories formerly comprising the British Empire had gained independence, and the empire had evolved into the Commonwealth of Nations, an association of equal and autonomous states, which enjoy special trade interests. The Commonwealth is presently composed of 54 member nations, including the United Kingdom. All recognize the British monarch as head of the Commonwealth. Sixteen continue to recognize the British monarch as Head of State. They are: United Kingdom, Antigua and Barbuda, Australia, Bahamas, Barbados, Belize, Canada, Grenada, Jamaica, New Zealand, Papua New Guinea, St. Christopher & Nevis, Saint Lucia, Saint Vincent and the Grenadines, Solomon Islands, and Tuvalu. Elizabeth II is personally, and separately, the Queen of the sovereign, independent countries just mentioned. There is no other British connection between the several individual, national sovereignties, except that High Commissioners represent them each instead of ambassadors in each other's countries.

RULERS
Elizabeth II, 1952--

MINT MARKS
H - Heaton
KN - King's Norton

KINGDOM
PRE-DECIMAL COINAGE

KM# 898 PENNY
0.4713 g., 0.9250 Silver 0.0140 oz. ASW **Ruler:** Elizabeth II **Series:** Maundy **Obv:** Laureate bust right **Obv. Designer:** Mary Gillick **Rev:** Crowned value in sprays divides date within wreath

Date	Mintage	F	VF	XF	Unc	BU
2001 Prooflike	1,132	—	—	—	50.00	55.00
2002 Prooflike	1,681	—	—	—	50.00	55.00
2003 Prooflike	1,608	—	—	—	55.00	60.00
2004 Prooflike	1,613	—	—	—	55.00	60.00
2005 Prooflike	1,685	—	—	—	55.00	60.00
2006 Prooflike	—	—	—	—	55.00	60.00
2007 Prooflike	—	—	—	—	55.00	60.00

KM# 898a PENNY
0.9167 Gold **Ruler:** Elizabeth II **Series:** Maundy Sets **Obv:** Laureate bust right **Obv. Designer:** Mary Gillick **Rev:** Crowned denomination divides date within wreath

Date	Mintage	F	VF	XF	Unc	BU
2002 Proof	—	Value: 1,000				

KM# 899 2 PENCE
0.9426 g., 0.9250 Silver 0.0280 oz. ASW **Ruler:** Elizabeth II **Series:** Maundy **Obv:** Laureate bust right **Obv. Legend:** Without BRITT OMN **Obv. Designer:** Mary Gillick **Rev:** Crowned value in sprays divides date within wreath

Date	Mintage	F	VF	XF	Unc	BU
2001 Prooflike	1,132	—	—	—	55.00	60.00
2002 Prooflike	1,681	—	—	—	55.00	60.00
2003 Prooflike	1,608	—	—	—	60.00	65.00
2004 Prooflike	1,613	—	—	—	60.00	65.00
2005 Prooflike	1,685	—	—	—	60.00	65.00
2006 Prooflike	—	—	—	—	60.00	65.00
2007 Prooflike	—	—	—	—	60.00	65.00

KM# 899a 2 PENCE
0.9167 Gold **Ruler:** Elizabeth II **Series:** Maundy Sets **Obv:** Laureate bust right **Obv. Legend:** Without BRITT OMN **Obv. Designer:** Mary Gillick **Rev:** Crowned denomination divides date within wreath

Date	Mintage	F	VF	XF	Unc	BU
2002 Proof	—	Value: 1,100				

KM# 901 3 PENCE
1.4138 g., 0.9250 Silver 0.0420 oz. ASW **Ruler:** Elizabeth II **Series:** Maundy **Obv:** Laureate bust right **Obv. Legend:** without BRITT OMN **Obv. Designer:** Mary Gillick **Rev:** Crowned value in sprays divides date within wreath

Date	Mintage	F	VF	XF	Unc	BU
2001 Prooflike	1,132	—	—	—	58.00	62.00
2002 Prooflike	1,681	—	—	—	58.00	62.00
2003 Prooflike	1,608	—	—	—	60.00	65.00
2004 Prooflike	1,613	—	—	—	60.00	65.00
2005 Prooflike	1,685	—	—	—	60.00	65.00
2006 Prooflike	—	—	—	—	60.00	65.00
2007 Prooflike	—	—	—	—	60.00	65.00

KM# 901a 3 PENCE
0.9167 Gold **Ruler:** Elizabeth II **Series:** Maundy Sets **Obv:** Laureate bust right **Obv. Legend:** Without RITT OMN **Obv. Designer:** Mary Gillick **Rev:** Crowned denomination divides date within wreath

Date	Mintage	F	VF	XF	Unc	BU
2002 Proof	—	Value: 1,150				

KM# 902 4 PENCE (Groat)

1.8851 g., 0.9250 Silver 0.0561 oz. ASW **Ruler:** Elizabeth II **Obv:** Laureate bust right **Obv. Inscription:** without BRITT OMN **Rev:** Crowned denomination divides date within wreath

Date	Mintage	F	VF	XF	Unc	BU
2001 Prooflike	1,132	—	—	—	58.00	62.00
2002 Prooflike	1,681	—	—	—	58.00	62.00
2003 Prooflike	1,608	—	—	—	60.00	65.00
2004 Prooflike	1,613	—	—	—	60.00	65.00
2005 Prooflike	1,685	—	—	—	60.00	65.00
2006 Prooflike	—	—	—	—	60.00	65.00
2007 Prooflike	—	—	—	—	60.00	65.00

KM# 902a 4 PENCE

0.9167 Gold **Ruler:** Elizabeth II **Series:** Maundy sets **Obv:** Laureate bust right **Obv. Inscription:** Without BRITT OMN **Rev:** Crowned denomination divides date within wreath

Date	Mintage	F	VF	XF	Unc	BU
2002 Proof	—	Value: 1,250				

DECIMAL COINAGE

1971-1981, 100 New Pence = 1 Pound;
1982, 100 Pence = 1 Pound

KM# 986 PENNY

3.5900 g., Copper Plated Steel, 20.34 mm. **Ruler:** Elizabeth II **Obv:** Head with tiara right **Obv. Designer:** Ian Rank-Broadley **Rev:** Crowned portcullis **Rev. Designer:** Christopher Ironside **Edge:** Plain

Date	Mintage	F	VF	XF	Unc	BU
2001	928,802,000	—	—	—	0.20	—
2002	601,446,000	—	—	—	0.20	—
2003	539,436,000	—	—	—	0.20	—
2004	739,764,000	—	—	—	0.20	—
2004 Proof	—	Value: 3.25				
2005	584,916,000	—	—	—	0.20	—
2005 Proof	—	Value: 3.25				
2006	—	—	—	—	0.20	—
2006 Proof	—	Value: 3.25				
2007	—	—	—	—	0.20	—
2007 Proof	—	Value: 3.25				

KM# 986a PENNY

3.5000 g., Bronze, 20.3 mm. **Ruler:** Elizabeth II **Obv:** Head with tiara right **Obv. Designer:** Ian Rank-Broadley **Rev:** Crowned portcullis **Edge:** Plain **Note:** Issued in sets only

Date	Mintage	F	VF	XF	Unc	BU
2001	—	—	—	—	0.20	—
2001 Proof	100,000	Value: 2.50				
2002 Proof	—	Value: 2.00				
2003 Proof	—	Value: 2.00				
2004 Proof	100,000	Value: 2.00				

KM# 986c PENNY

0.9167 Gold **Ruler:** Elizabeth II **Subject:** Queen's Golden Jubilee - 1952-2002 **Obv:** Head with tiara right **Obv. Designer:** Ian Rank-Broadley **Rev:** Crowned portcullis **Rev. Designer:** Christopher Ironside

Date	Mintage	F	VF	XF	Unc	BU
2002 Proof	—	Value: 700				

Note: In sets only

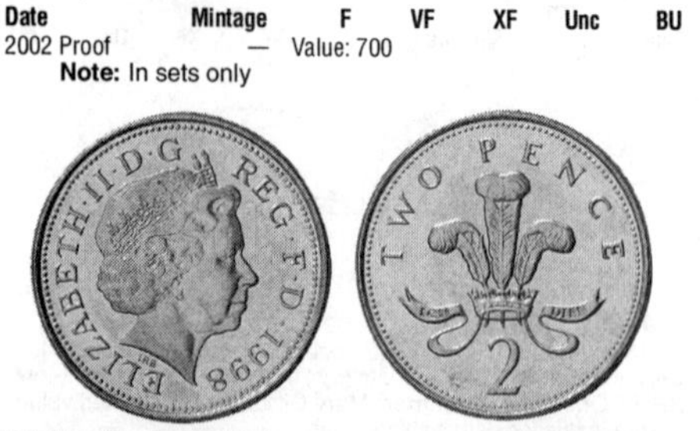

KM# 987 2 PENCE

7.1400 g., Copper Plated Steel, 25.86 mm. **Ruler:** Elizabeth II **Obv:** Head with tiara right **Obv. Designer:** Ian Rank-Broadley **Rev:** Welsh plumes and crown **Rev. Designer:** Christopher Ironside **Edge:** Plain

Date	Mintage	F	VF	XF	Unc	BU
2001	551,886,000	—	—	—	0.25	—
2002	168,556,000	—	—	—	0.25	—
2003	260,225,000	—	—	—	0.25	—
2004	356,396,000	—	—	—	0.25	—
2004 Proof	—	Value: 3.25				
2005	243,325,000	—	—	—	0.25	—
2005 Proof	—	Value: 3.25				
2006	—	—	—	—	0.25	—
2006 Proof	—	Value: 3.25				

Date	Mintage	F	VF	XF	Unc	BU
2007	—	—	—	—	0.25	—
2007 Proof	—	Value: 3.25				

KM# 987a 2 PENCE

Bronze, 25.91 mm. **Ruler:** Elizabeth II **Obv:** Head with tiara right **Obv. Designer:** Ian Rank-Broadley **Rev:** Welsh plumes and crown **Rev. Designer:** Christopher Ironside

Date	Mintage	F	VF	XF	Unc	BU
2001	—	—	—	—	0.25	—
2001 Proof	Est. 100,000	Value: 2.50				
2002 Proof	—	Value: 2.50				
2003 Proof	—	Value: 2.50				
2004 Proof	100,000	Value: 2.50				

KM# 987c 2 PENCE

0.9167 Gold, 25.91 mm. **Ruler:** Elizabeth II **Subject:** Queen's Golden Jubilee - 1952-2002 **Obv:** Head with tiara right **Obv. Designer:** Ian Rank-Broadley **Rev:** Welsh plumes and crown **Rev. Designer:** Christopher Ironside

Date	Mintage	F	VF	XF	Unc	BU
2002 Proof	—	Value: 800				

Note: In sets only

KM# 988 5 PENCE

3.2500 g., Copper-Nickel, 18 mm. **Ruler:** Elizabeth II **Obv:** Head with tiara right **Obv. Designer:** Ian Rank-Broadley **Rev:** Crowned thistle

Date	Mintage	F	VF	XF	Unc	BU
2001	320,330,000	—	—	—	0.30	—
2001 Proof	Est. 100,000	Value: 3.00				
2002	219,258,000	—	—	—	0.30	—
2002 Proof	—	Value: 3.00				
2003	333,230,000	—	—	—	0.30	—
2003 Proof	—	Value: 3.00				
2004	271,810,000	—	—	—	0.30	—
2004 Proof	100,000	Value: 3.00				
2005	264,412,000	—	—	—	0.30	—
2005 Proof	—	Value: 3.00				
2006	—	—	—	—	0.30	—
2006 Proof	—	Value: 3.00				
2007	—	—	—	—	0.30	—
2007 Proof	—	Value: 3.00				

KM# 988b 5 PENCE

0.9167 Gold, 18 mm. **Ruler:** Elizabeth II **Obv:** Head with tiara right **Obv. Designer:** Ian Rank-Broadley **Rev:** Crowned thistle

Date	Mintage	F	VF	XF	Unc	BU
2002 Proof	—	Value: 350				

Note: In sets only

KM# 989 10 PENCE

6.5000 g., Copper-Nickel, 24.5 mm. **Ruler:** Elizabeth II **Obv:** Head with tiara right **Obv. Designer:** Ian Rank-Broadley **Rev:** Crowned lion prancing left **Rev. Designer:** Christopher Ironside

Date	Mintage	F	VF	XF	Unc	BU
2001	82,081,000	—	—	—	0.40	—
2001 Proof	Est. 100,000	Value: 3.25				
2002	80,934,000	—	—	—	0.40	—
2002 Proof	—	Value: 3.25				
2003	88,118,000	—	—	—	0.40	—
2003 Proof	—	Value: 3.25				
2004	99,602,000	—	—	—	0.40	—
2004 Proof	100,000	Value: 3.25				
2005	89,839,000	—	—	—	0.40	—
2005 Proof	—	Value: 3.25				
2006	—	—	—	—	0.40	—
2006 Proof	—	Value: 3.25				
2007	—	—	—	—	0.40	—
2007 Proof	—	Value: 3.25				

KM# 989b 10 PENCE

0.9167 Gold, 24.5 mm. **Ruler:** Elizabeth II **Obv:** Head with tiara right **Obv. Designer:** Ian Rank-Broadley **Rev:** Crowned lion prancing left **Rev. Designer:** Christopher Ironside

Date	Mintage	F	VF	XF	Unc	BU
2002 Proof	—	Value: 600				

Note: In sets only

KM# 990 20 PENCE

5.0000 g., Copper-Nickel, 21.4 mm. **Ruler:** Elizabeth II **Obv:** Head with tiara right **Obv. Designer:** Ian Rank-Broadley **Rev:** Crowned rose **Rev. Designer:** William Gardner **Shape:** 7-sided

Date	Mintage	F	VF	XF	Unc	BU
2001	148,122,500	—	—	—	0.60	—
2001 Proof	Est. 100,000	Value: 3.25				
2002	93,360,000	—	—	—	0.60	—
2002 Proof	100,000	Value: 3.25				
2003	153,383,750	—	—	—	0.60	—
2003 Proof	—	Value: 3.25				
2004	120,212,500	—	—	—	0.60	—
2004 Proof	100,000	Value: 3.25				
2005	104,016,000	—	—	—	0.60	—
2005 Proof	—	Value: 3.25				
2006	—	—	—	—	0.60	—
2006 Proof	—	Value: 3.25				
2007	—	—	—	—	0.60	—
2007 Proof	—	Value: 3.25				

KM# 990b 20 PENCE

0.9167 Gold, 21.4 mm. **Ruler:** Elizabeth II **Obv:** Head with tiara right **Obv. Designer:** Ian Rank-Broadley **Rev:** Crowned rose **Rev. Designer:** William Gardner **Shape:** 7-sided

Date	Mintage	F	VF	XF	Unc	BU
2002 Proof	—	Value: 400				

Note: In sets only

KM# 991 50 PENCE

8.0000 g., Copper-Nickel, 27.3 mm. **Ruler:** Elizabeth II **Obv:** Head with tiara right **Obv. Designer:** Ian Rank-Broadley **Rev:** Britannia seated right **Rev. Designer:** Christopher Ironside **Shape:** 7-sided

Date	Mintage	F	VF	XF	Unc	BU
2001	84,999,500	—	—	—	1.75	—
2001 Proof	Est. 100,000	Value: 2.50				
2002	23,907,500	—	—	—	1.75	—
2002 Proof	—	Value: 2.50				
2003	26,557,030	—	—	—	1.75	—
2003 Proof	—	Value: 2.50				
2004	Est. 33,478,000	—	—	—	1.75	—
2004 Proof	100,000	Value: 2.50				
2005	30,254,500	—	—	—	1.75	—
2005 Proof	—	Value: 2.50				
2006	—	—	—	—	1.75	—
2006 Proof	—	Value: 2.50				
2007	—	—	—	—	1.75	—
2007 Proof	—	Value: 2.50				

KM# 1017 50 PENCE

8.1100 g., 0.9584 Silver 0.2499 oz. ASW, 27.3 mm. **Ruler:** Elizabeth II **Subject:** Britannia Bullion **Obv:** Head with tiara right **Obv. Designer:** Ian Rank-Broadley **Rev:** Stylized "Britannia and the Lion" **Edge:** Reeded

Date	Mintage	F	VF	XF	Unc	BU
2001 Proof	5,000	Value: 25.00				

KM# 991b 50 PENCE

0.9167 Gold, 27.3 mm. **Ruler:** Elizabeth II **Obv:** Head with tiara right **Obv. Designer:** Ian Rank-Broadley **Rev:** Britannia seated right **Rev. Designer:** Christopher Ironside **Shape:** 7-sided

Date	Mintage	F	VF	XF	Unc	BU
2002 Proof	—	Value: 500				

Note: In sets only

KM# 1036 50 PENCE

8.0000 g., Copper-Nickel, 27.3 mm. **Ruler:** Elizabeth II **Subject:** Woman's Suffrage **Obv:** Head with tiara right **Obv. Designer:** Ian Rank-Broadley **Rev:** Standing woman with banner **Edge:** Plain **Shape:** 7-sided

Date	Mintage	F	VF	XF	Unc	BU
2003	Est. 5,000,000	—	—	—	2.50	—
2003 Proof	—	Value: 9.50				

KM# 1036a 50 PENCE

8.0000 g., 0.9250 Silver 0.2379 oz. ASW, 27.3 mm. **Ruler:** Elizabeth II **Obv:** Head with tiara right **Obv. Designer:** Ian Rank-Broadley **Rev:** Standing woman with banner **Edge:** Plain **Shape:** 7-sided

Date	Mintage	F	VF	XF	Unc	BU
2003 Proof	15,000	Value: 45.00				

KM# 1036b 50 PENCE
15.5000 g., 0.9166 Gold 0.4568 oz. AGW, 27.3 mm. **Ruler:** Elizabeth II **Obv:** Head with tiara right **Obv. Designer:** Ian Rank-Broadley **Rev:** Standing woman with banner **Edge:** Plain **Shape:** 7-sided

Date	Mintage	F	VF	XF	Unc	BU
2003 Proof	1,000	Value: 475				

KM# 1047 50 PENCE
8.0000 g., Copper-Nickel, 27.3 mm. **Ruler:** Elizabeth II **Subject:** The First Four Minute Mile **Obv:** Head with tiara right **Obv. Designer:** Ian Rank-Broadley **Rev:** Running legs, stop watch and value **Edge:** Plain

Date	Mintage	F	VF	XF	Unc	BU
2004	Est. 5,000,000	—	—	—	5.00	6.00
2004 Proof	100,000	Value: 7.50				

KM# 1050 50 PENCE
8.0000 g., Copper-Nickel, 27.3 mm. **Ruler:** Elizabeth II **Obv:** Head with tiara right **Obv. Designer:** Ian Rank-Broadley **Rev:** Text from the first English dictionary by Samuel Johnson **Edge:** Plain

Date	Mintage	F	VF	XF	Unc	BU
2005	36,125,000	—	—	—	2.50	3.50
2005 Proof	50,000	Value: 6.00				

KM# 1050a 50 PENCE
8.0000 g., 0.9250 Silver 0.2379 oz. ASW, 27.3 mm. **Ruler:** Elizabeth II **Subject:** First English Dictionary **Obv:** Head with tiara right **Obv. Designer:** Ian Rank-Broadley **Rev:** Sample page from Johnson's 1755 dictionary **Edge:** Plain **Shape:** 7-sided

Date	Mintage	F	VF	XF	Unc	BU
2005 Proof	7,500	Value: 45.00				

KM# 1050b 50 PENCE
15.5000 g., 0.9167 Gold 0.4568 oz. AGW, 27.3 mm. **Ruler:** Elizabeth II **Subject:** 1st English Dictionary **Obv:** Head with tiara right **Obv. Designer:** Ian Rank-Broadley **Rev:** Sample page from Johnson's 1755 dictionary **Edge:** Plain **Shape:** 7-sided

Date	Mintage	F	VF	XF	Unc	BU
2005 Proof	1,000	Value: 550				

KM# 1057 50 PENCE
8.0000 g., Copper-Nickel, 27.3 mm. **Ruler:** Elizabeth II **Obv:** Head with tiara right **Obv. Designer:** Ian Rank-Broadley **Rev:** Victoria Cross obverse and reverse views **Edge:** Plain **Shape:** 7-sided

Date	Mintage	F	VF	XF	Unc	BU
2006	—	—	—	—	5.00	6.00
2006 Proof	50,000	Value: 7.50				

KM# 1058 50 PENCE
8.0000 g., Copper-Nickel, 27.3 mm. **Ruler:** Elizabeth II **Obv:** Head with tiara right **Obv. Designer:** Ian Rank-Broadley **Rev:** Heroic Act scene with cross shape in background **Edge:** Plain **Shape:** 7-sided

Date	Mintage	F	VF	XF	Unc	BU
2006	—	—	—	—	5.00	6.00
2006 Proof	50,000	Value: 7.50				

KM# 1073 50 PENCE
8.0000 g., Copper-Nickel, 27.3 mm. **Ruler:** Elizabeth II **Subject:** Centennial of Scouting **Obv:** Bust right **Rev:** Fleur de Lis Scouting emblem superimposed on globe **Edge:** Plain **Shape:** Seven sided

Date	Mintage	F	VF	XF	Unc	BU
2007	—	—	—	—	—	5.00
2007 Proof	50,000	Value: 7.50				

KM# 1073a 50 PENCE
8.0000 g., 0.9250 Silver 0.2379 oz. ASW, 27.3 mm. **Ruler:** Elizabeth II **Subject:** Scouting Centennial **Obv:** Elizabeth II **Rev:** Fleur de Lis Scouting emblem superimposed on globe **Edge:** Plain **Shape:** 7-sided

Date	Mintage	F	VF	XF	Unc	BU
2007 Proof	12,500	Value: 60.00				

KM# 1073b 50 PENCE
15.5000 g., 0.9166 Gold 0.4568 oz. AGW, 27.3 mm. **Ruler:** Elizabeth II **Subject:** Scouting Centennial **Obv:** Elizabeth II **Rev:** Fleur de Lis Scouting emblem superimposed on globe **Edge:** Plain **Shape:** 7-sided

Date	Mintage	F	VF	XF	Unc	BU
2007 Proof	1,250	Value: 675				

KM# 1013 POUND
9.5000 g., Nickel-Brass, 22.5 mm. **Ruler:** Elizabeth II **Subject:** Northern Ireland **Obv:** Head with tiara right **Obv. Designer:** Ian Rank-Broadley **Rev:** Celtic style cross **Rev. Designer:** Norman Sillman **Edge:** Reeding **Edge Lettering:** DECUS ET TUTAMEN

Date	Mintage	F	VF	XF	Unc	BU
2001	58,093,731	—	—	—	4.00	5.00
2001 Proof	—	Value: 6.00				

KM# 1013a POUND
9.5000 g., 0.9250 Silver 0.2825 oz. ASW, 22.5 mm. **Ruler:** Elizabeth II **Subject:** Northern Ireland **Obv:** Head with tiara right **Obv. Designer:** Ian Rank-Broadley **Rev:** Celtic cross design **Edge:** Reeded **Edge Lettering:** DECUS ET TUTAMEN

Date	Mintage	F	VF	XF	Unc	BU
2001 Proof	25,000	Value: 40.00				

KM# 1030 POUND
9.5000 g., Nickel-Brass, 22.5 mm. **Ruler:** Elizabeth II **Obv:** Head with tiara right **Obv. Designer:** Ian Rank-Broadley **Rev:** Three lions **Rev. Designer:** Norman Sillman **Edge:** Reeded **Edge Lettering:** DECUS ET TUTAMEN

Date	Mintage	F	VF	XF	Unc	BU
2002	77,818,000	—	—	—	5.00	6.00
2002 Proof	100,000	Value: 6.00				

KM# 1030a POUND
9.5000 g., 0.9250 Silver 0.2825 oz. ASW, 22.5 mm. **Ruler:** Elizabeth II **Obv:** Head with tiara right **Obv. Designer:** Ian Rank-Broadley **Rev:** Three lions **Edge:** Reeded **Edge Lettering:** DECUS ET TUTAMEN

Date	Mintage	F	VF	XF	Unc	BU
2002 Proof	—	Value: 40.00				

KM# 1030b POUND
0.9167 Gold, 22.5 mm. **Ruler:** Elizabeth II **Obv:** Head with tiara right **Obv. Designer:** Ian Rank-Broadley **Rev:** Three lions left **Rev. Designer:** Norman Sillman **Edge:** Reeded **Edge Lettering:** DECUS ET TUTAMEN

Date	Mintage	F	VF	XF	Unc	BU
2002 Proof	—	Value: 600				

KM# 993 POUND
9.5000 g., Nickel-Brass, 22.5 mm. **Ruler:** Elizabeth II **Obv:** Head with tiara right **Obv. Designer:** Ian Rank-Broadley **Rev:** Shield of Great Britain within Garter, crowned and supported **Rev. Designer:** Eric Sewell **Edge Lettering:** DECUS ET TUTAMEN

Date	Mintage	F	VF	XF	Unc	BU
2003	61,596,500	—	—	—	5.00	6.00
2003 Proof	—	Value: 7.50				

KM# 1048b POUND
19.6190 g., 0.9166 Gold 0.5781 oz. AGW, 22.5 mm. **Ruler:** Elizabeth II **Obv:** Elizabeth II **Rev:** Forth Rail Bridge **Edge:** Ornamented and reeded

Date	Mintage	F	VF	XF	Unc	BU
2004 Proof	1,500	Value: 650				

KM# 1048a POUND
9.5000 g., 0.9250 Silver 0.2825 oz. ASW, 22.5 mm. **Obv:** Elizabeth II **Rev:** Forth Rail Bridge **Edge:** Ornamented and reeded

Date	Mintage	F	VF	XF	Unc	BU
2004 Proof	20,000	Value: 45.00				

KM# 1048 POUND
9.5000 g., Nickel-Brass, 22.5 mm. **Ruler:** Elizabeth II **Obv:** Head with tiara right **Obv. Designer:** Ian Rank-Broadley **Rev:** "Forth Rail Bridge" in Scotland **Edge:** Reeded and lettered **Edge Lettering:** "NEMO ME IMPUNE LACESSIT"

Date	Mintage	F	VF	XF	Unc	BU
2004	39,162,000	—	—	—	6.00	7.50
2004 Proof	100,000	Value: 9.00				

KM# 1051 POUND
9.5000 g., Nickel-Brass, 22.5 mm. **Ruler:** Elizabeth II **Obv:** Head with tiara right **Obv. Designer:** Ian Rank-Broadley **Rev:** Menai Bridge in Wales **Edge:** Reeded and lettered **Edge Lettering:** "PLEIDOL WYF I'M GWLAD"

Date	Mintage	F	VF	XF	Unc	BU
2005	70,763,000	—	—	—	5.00	6.00
2005 Proof	50,000	Value: 5.00				

KM# 1051a POUND
9.5000 g., 0.9250 Silver 0.2825 oz. ASW, 22.5 mm. **Ruler:** Elizabeth II **Obv:** Head with tiara right **Obv. Designer:** Ian Rank-Broadley **Rev:** Menai Bridge **Edge Lettering:** 'PLEIDOL WYF I'M GWLAD"

Date	Mintage	F	VF	XF	Unc	BU
2005 Proof	15,000	Value: 45.00				

KM# 1051b POUND
19.6190 g., 0.9167 Gold 0.5782 oz. AGW, 22.5 mm. **Ruler:** Elizabeth II **Obv:** Head with tiara right **Obv. Designer:** Ian Rank-Broadley **Rev:** Menai Bridge **Edge Lettering:** 'PLEIDOL WYF I'M GWLAD"

Date	Mintage	F	VF	XF	Unc	BU
2005 Proof	1,500	Value: 725				

KM# 1051a.2 POUND
9.5000 g., 0.9250 Silver 0.2825 oz. ASW, 22.5 mm. **Ruler:** Elizabeth II **Obv:** Elizabeth II **Rev:** Menai Suspension Bridge **Edge:** Ornamented and reeded

Date	Mintage	F	VF	XF	Unc	BU
2005 Proof	20,000	Value: 45.00				

KM# 1051b.2 POUND
19.6190 g., 0.9166 Gold 0.5781 oz. AGW, 22.5 mm. **Ruler:** Elizabeth II **Obv:** Elizabeth II **Rev:** Menai Suspension Bridge **Edge:** Ornamented and reeded

Date	Mintage	F	VF	XF	Unc	BU
2005 Proof	1,500	Value: 650				

KM# 1059b.2 POUND
19.6190 g., 0.9166 Gold 0.5781 oz. AGW, 22.5 mm. **Ruler:** Elizabeth II **Obv:** Elizabeth II **Rev:** Egyptian Arch Bridge **Edge:** Ornamented and reeded

Date	Mintage	F	VF	XF	Unc	BU
2006 Proof	1,500	Value: 650				

KM# 1059a.2 POUND
9.5000 g., 0.9250 Silver 0.2825 oz. ASW, 22.5 mm. **Ruler:** Elizabeth II **Obv:** Elizabeth II **Rev:** Egyptian Arch Bridge **Edge:** Ornamented and reeded

Date	Mintage	F	VF	XF	Unc	BU
2006 Proof	20,000	Value: 45.00				

KM# 1059a POUND
9.5000 g., 0.9250 Silver 0.2825 oz. ASW, 22.5 mm. **Ruler:** Elizabeth II **Obv:** Head with tiara right **Obv. Designer:** Ian Rank-Broadley **Rev:** Egyptian Arch Bridge **Edge Lettering:** "DECUS ET TUTAMEN"

Date	Mintage	F	VF	XF	Unc	BU
2006 Proof	20,000	Value: 50.00				

KM# 1059b POUND
19.6190 g., 0.9167 Gold 0.5782 oz. AGW, 22.5 mm. **Ruler:** Elizabeth II **Obv:** Head with tiara right **Obv. Designer:** Ian Rank-Broadley **Rev:** Egyptian Arch Bridge **Edge Lettering:** "DECUS ET TUTAMEN"

Date	Mintage	F	VF	XF	Unc	BU
2006 Proof	—	Value: 725				

KM# 1059 POUND
9.5000 g., Nickel-Brass, 22.5 mm. **Ruler:** Elizabeth II **Obv:** Head with tiara right **Obv. Designer:** Ian Rank-Broadley **Rev:** Egyptian Arch Bridge at Newry, Northern Ireland **Edge:** Reeded and lettered

Date	Mintage	F	VF	XF	Unc	BU
2006	—	—	—	—	8.00	9.00
2006 Proof	50,000	Value: 10.00				

KM# 1074 POUND
9.5000 g., Nickel-Brass, 22.5 mm. **Ruler:** Elizabeth II **Obv:** Head with tiara right **Obv. Designer:** Ian Rank-Broadley **Rev:** Gateshead Millennium Bridge **Edge:** Reeded and lettered

Date	Mintage	F	VF	XF	Unc	BU
2007	—	—	—	—	—	8.00
2007 Proof	50,000	Value: 10.00				

KM# 1074a POUND
9.5000 g., 0.9250 Silver 0.2825 oz. ASW, 22.5 mm. **Ruler:** Elizabeth II **Obv:** Elizabeth II **Rev:** Gateshead Millennium Bridge **Edge:** Ornamented and reeded

Date	Mintage	F	VF	XF	Unc	BU
2007 Proof	20,000	Value: 45.00				

KM# 1074b POUND
19.6190 g., 0.9166 Gold 0.5781 oz. AGW, 22.5 mm. **Ruler:** Elizabeth II **Obv:** Elizabeth II **Rev:** Gateshead Millennium Bridge **Edge:** Ornamented and reeded

Date	Mintage	F	VF	XF	Unc	BU
2007 Proof	1,500	Value: 700				

KM# 994 2 POUNDS
12.0000 g., Bi-Metallic Copper-Nickel center in Nickel-Brass ring, 28.35 mm. **Ruler:** Elizabeth II **Obv:** Head with tiara right within circle **Obv. Designer:** Ian Rank-Broadley **Rev:** Celtic design within circle **Rev. Designer:** Bruce Rushin **Edge Lettering:** STANDING ON THE SHOULDERS OF GIANTS

Date	Mintage	F	VF	XF	Unc	BU
2001	37,843,500	—	—	—	6.00	8.50
2001 Proof	—	Value: 10.00				
2002	15,521,000	—	—	—	6.00	8.50
2002 Proof	—	Value: 10.00				
2003	21,830,250	—	—	—	6.00	8.50
2003 Proof	—	Value: 10.00				
2004	13,904,500	—	—	—	6.00	8.50
2004 Proof	100,000	Value: 10.00				
2005	20,507,000	—	—	—	6.00	8.50
2005 Proof	—	Value: 10.00				
2006	—	—	—	—	6.00	8.50
2006 Proof	—	Value: 10.00				
2007	—	—	—	—	6.00	8.50
2007 Proof	—	Value: 10.00				

KM# 1014 2 POUNDS
11.9700 g., Bi-Metallic Copper-Nickel center in Nickel-Brass ring, 28.4 mm. **Ruler:** Elizabeth II **Subject:** First Transatlantic Radio Transmission **Obv:** Head with tiara right within circle **Obv. Designer:** Ian Rank-Broadley **Rev:** Symbolic design **Rev. Designer:** Robert Evans **Edge:** Reeded and inscribed **Edge Lettering:** WIRELESS BRIDGES THE ATLANTIC... MARCONI... 1901

Date	Mintage	F	VF	XF	Unc	BU
2001	5,000,000	—	—	—	6.00	7.00
2001 Proof	—	Value: 10.00				

KM# 1014a 2 POUNDS
24.0000 g., 0.9250 Silver Gold plated ring 0.7137 oz. ASW, 28.4 mm. **Ruler:** Elizabeth II **Subject:** First Transatlantic Radio Transmission **Obv:** Head with tiara right within circle **Obv. Designer:** Ian Rank-Broadley **Rev:** Symbolic design **Rev. Designer:** Robert Evans **Edge:** Reeded and inscribed **Edge Lettering:** "WIRELESS BRIDGES THE ATLANTIC...MARCONI 1901..."

Date	Mintage	F	VF	XF	Unc	BU
2001 Proof	25,000	Value: 33.50				

KM# 1014b 2 POUNDS
15.9700 g., 0.9166 Gold Yellow gold plated Red Gold center in Red Gold ring 0.4706 oz. AGW, 28.4 mm. **Ruler:** Elizabeth II **Subject:** First Transatlantic Radio Transmission **Obv:** Head with tiara right **Obv. Designer:** Ian Rank-Broadley **Rev:** Symbolic design **Rev. Designer:** Robert Evans

Date	Mintage	F	VF	XF	Unc	BU
2001 Proof	1,500	Value: 500				

KM# 1019 2 POUNDS
32.4500 g., 0.9584 Silver 0.9998 oz. ASW, 40 mm. **Ruler:** Elizabeth II **Subject:** Britannia Bullion **Obv:** Head with tiara right **Obv. Designer:** Ian Rank-Broadley **Rev:** Stylized "Britannia and the Lion" **Edge:** Reeded

Date	Mintage	F	VF	XF	Unc	BU
2001	100,000	—	—	—	25.00	30.00
2001 Proof	10,000	Value: 55.00				

KM# 994c 2 POUNDS
15.9800 g., 0.9167 Gold 0.4710 oz. AGW, 28.35 mm. **Ruler:** Elizabeth II **Obv:** Head with tiara right within circle **Obv. Designer:** Ian Rank-Broadley **Rev:** Celtic design within circle **Rev. Designer:** Bruce Rushin

Date	Mintage	F	VF	XF	Unc	BU
2002 Proof	—	Value: 750				

KM# 1031 2 POUNDS
12.0000 g., Bi-Metallic Copper-Nickel center in Nickel-Brass ring, 28.4 mm. **Ruler:** Elizabeth II **Subject:** 17th Commonwealth Games - Manchester, England **Obv:** Head with tiara right **Obv. Designer:** Ian Rank-Broadley **Rev:** Runner breaking ribbon at finish line, national flag of England in circle behind athlete **Rev. Designer:** Matthew Bonaccorsi **Edge:** Reeded and lettered **Edge Lettering:** SPIRIT OF FRIENDSHIP MANCHESTER 2002

Date	Mintage	F	VF	XF	Unc	BU
2002	—	—	—	—	6.00	7.00
2002 Proof	—	Value: 8.75				

KM# 1031a 2 POUNDS
12.0000 g., Silver Gold plated ring, 28.4 mm. **Ruler:** Elizabeth II **Subject:** Commonwealth Games - England **Obv:** Head with tiara right **Obv. Designer:** Ian Rank-Broadley **Rev:** Runner breaking ribbon at finish line **Rev. Designer:** Matthew Bonaccorsi **Edge:** Reeded and lettered

Date	Mintage	F	VF	XF	Unc	BU
2002 Proof	10,000	—	—	—	30.00	35.00

KM# 1031b 2 POUNDS
15.9800 g., 0.9160 Gold Yellow gold center in Red Gold ring 0.4706 oz. AGW, 28.4 mm. **Ruler:** Elizabeth II **Subject:** Commonwealth Games - England **Obv:** Head with tiara right **Obv. Designer:** Ian Rank-Broadley **Rev:** Runner breaking ribbon at finish line **Rev. Designer:** Matthew Bonaccorsi **Edge:** Reeded and lettered

Date	Mintage	F	VF	XF	Unc	BU
2002 Proof	500	Value: 550				

KM# 1032 2 POUNDS
12.0000 g., Bi-Metallic Copper-Nickel center in Nickel-Brass ring, 28.4 mm. **Ruler:** Elizabeth II **Subject:** 17th Commonwealth Games - Manchester, England **Obv:** Head with tiara right **Obv. Designer:** Ian Rank-Broadley **Rev:** Runner breaking ribbon at finish line, national flag of Scotland in circle behind athlete **Rev. Designer:** Matthew Bonaccorsi **Edge:** Reeded and lettered

Date	Mintage	F	VF	XF	Unc	BU
2002	—	—	—	—	5.00	6.00
2002 Proof	—	Value: 8.75				

KM# 1032a 2 POUNDS
Bi-Metallic Silver center with Gold plated ring, 28.4 mm. **Ruler:** Elizabeth II **Subject:** Commonwealth Games - Scotland **Obv:** Head with tiara right **Obv. Designer:** Ian Rank-Broadley **Rev:** Runner breaking ribbon at finish line **Rev. Designer:** Matthew Bonaccorsi **Edge:** Reeded and lettered

Date	Mintage	F	VF	XF	Unc	BU
2002 Proof	10,000	Value: 30.00				

KM# 1032b 2 POUNDS
15.9800 g., 0.9160 Gold Yellow gold center in Red Gold ring 0.4706 oz. AGW, 28.4 mm. **Ruler:** Elizabeth II **Subject:** Commonwealth Games - Scotland **Obv:** Head with tiara right **Obv. Designer:** Ian Rank-Broadley **Rev:** Runner breaking ribbon at finish line **Rev. Designer:** Matthew Bonaccorsi **Edge:** Reeded and lettered

Date	Mintage	F	VF	XF	Unc	BU
2002 Proof	500	Value: 550				

KM# 1033 2 POUNDS
12.0000 g., Bi-Metallic Copper-Nickel center in Nickel-Brass ring, 28.4 mm. **Ruler:** Elizabeth II **Subject:** 17th Commonwealth Games - Manchester, England **Obv:** Head with tiara right **Obv. Designer:** Ian Rank-Broadley **Rev:** Runner breaking ribbon at finish line, national flag of Wales in circle behind athlete **Rev. Designer:** Matthew Bonaccorsi **Edge:** Reeded and lettered **Edge Lettering:** SPIRIT OF FRIENDSHIP MANCHESTER 2002

Date	Mintage	F	VF	XF	Unc	BU
2002	—	—	—	—	6.00	7.00
2002 Proof	—	Value: 8.75				

KM# 1033a 2 POUNDS
12.0000 g., Silver Silver center in Gold plated ring, 28.4 mm. **Ruler:** Elizabeth II **Subject:** Commonwealth Games - Wales **Obv:** Head with tiara right **Obv. Designer:** Ian Rank-Broadley **Rev:** Runner breaking ribbon at finish line **Rev. Designer:** Matthew Bonaccorsi **Edge:** Reeded and lettered

Date	Mintage	F	VF	XF	Unc	BU
2002 Proof	10,000	Value: 30.00				

KM# 1033b 2 POUNDS
15.9800 g., 0.9160 Gold Yellow Gold center in Red Gold ring 0.4706 oz. AGW, 28.4 mm. **Ruler:** Elizabeth II **Subject:** Commonwealth Games - Wales **Obv:** Head with tiara right **Obv. Designer:** Ian Rank-Broadley **Rev:** Runner breaking ribbon at finish line **Rev. Designer:** Matthew Bonaccorsi **Edge:** Reeded and lettered

Date	Mintage	F	VF	XF	Unc	BU
2002 Proof	500	Value: 550				

KM# 1034 2 POUNDS
12.0000 g., Bi-Metallic Copper-Nickel center in Nickel-Brass ring, 28.4 mm. **Ruler:** Elizabeth II **Subject:** 17th Commonwealth Games - Manchester, England **Obv:** Head with tiara right **Obv. Designer:** Ian Rank-Broadley **Rev:** Runner breaking ribbon at finish line, national flag of Northern Ireland in circle behind athlete **Rev. Designer:** Matthew Bonaccorsi **Edge:** Reeded and lettered **Edge Lettering:** SPIRIT OF FRIENDSHIP MANCHESTER 2002

Date	Mintage	F	VF	XF	Unc	BU
2002	—	—	—	—	6.00	7.00
2002 Proof	—	Value: 8.75				

KM# 1034a 2 POUNDS
12.0000 g., Silver Silver center in Gold plated ring, 28.4 mm. **Ruler:** Elizabeth II **Subject:** Commonwealth Games - Northern Ireland **Obv:** Head with tiara right **Obv. Designer:** Ian Rank-Broadley **Rev:** Runner breaking ribbon at finish line **Rev. Designer:** Matthew Bonaccorsi **Edge:** Reeded and lettered

Date	Mintage	F	VF	XF	Unc	BU
2002 Proof	10,000	Value: 30.00				

KM# 1034b 2 POUNDS
15.9800 g., 0.9160 Gold Yellow Gold center in Red Gold ring 0.4706 oz. AGW, 28.4 mm. **Ruler:** Elizabeth II **Subject:** Commonwealth Games - Northern Ireland **Obv:** Head with tiara right **Obv. Designer:** Ian Rank-Broadley **Rev:** Runner breaking ribbon at finish line **Rev. Designer:** Matthew Bonaccorsi **Edge:** Reeded and lettered

Date	Mintage	F	VF	XF	Unc	BU
2002 Proof	500	Value: 550				

KM# 1037 2 POUNDS
12.0000 g., Bi-Metallic Copper-Nickel center in Nickel-Brass ring, 28.4 mm. **Ruler:** Elizabeth II **Subject:** 50th Anniversary of the Discovery of DNA **Obv:** Head with tiara right **Obv. Designer:** Ian Rank-Broadley **Rev:** DNA Double Helix **Rev. Designer:** John Mills **Edge:** Reeded and inscribed **Edge Lettering:** DEOXYRIBONUCLEIC ACID

Date	Mintage	F	VF	XF	Unc	BU
ND(2003)	—	—	—	—	7.00	8.00
ND(2003) Proof	—	Value: 10.00				

KM# 1037a 2 POUNDS
12.0000 g., 0.9250 Silver Silver center in Gold plated silver ring 0.3569 oz. ASW, 28.4 mm. **Ruler:** Elizabeth II **Obv:** Head with tiara right **Obv. Designer:** Ian Rank-Broadley **Rev:** DNA Double Helix **Rev. Designer:** John Mills **Edge:** Reeded and lettered

Date	Mintage	F	VF	XF	Unc	BU
ND(2003) Proof	10,000	Value: 30.00				

KM# 1037b 2 POUNDS
15.9800 g., 0.9167 Gold Yellow gold center in Red gold ring 0.4710 oz. AGW, 28.4 mm. **Ruler:** Elizabeth II **Obv:** Head with tiara right **Obv. Designer:** Ian Rank-Broadley **Rev:** DNA Double Helix **Rev. Designer:** John Mills **Edge:** Reeded and lettered

Date	Mintage	F	VF	XF	Unc	BU
ND(2003)	6,250	Value: 550				

KM# 1049 2 POUNDS
12.0000 g., Bi-Metallic Nickel-Brass center in Copper-Nickel ring, 28.4 mm. **Ruler:** Elizabeth II **Subject:** Richard Trevithick, Inventor of the First Steam Locomotive **Obv:** Head with tiara right **Obv. Designer:** Ian Rank-Broadley **Rev:** First steam locomotive **Edge:** Reeded and lettered **Edge Lettering:** 2004 R. TREVITHICK 1804 INVENTION-INDUSTRY-PROGRESS

Date	Mintage	F	VF	XF	Unc	BU
2004	—	—	—	—	7.50	8.50
2004 Proof	100,000	Value: 10.00				

KM# 1049a 2 POUNDS
12.0000 g., 0.9250 Bi-Metallic .925 Silver center in Gold Plated .925 Silver ring 0.3569 oz., 28.4 mm. **Ruler:** Elizabeth II **Obv:** Head with tiara right **Obv. Designer:** Ian Rank-Broadley **Rev:** First steam locomotive **Edge:** Reeded and lettered

Date	Mintage	F	VF	XF	Unc	BU
2004 Proof	25,000	Value: 30.00				

KM# 1049b 2 POUNDS
15.9800 g., 0.9166 Bi-Metallic .9166 Yellow Gold center in .9166 Red Gold ring 0.4709 oz., 28.4 mm. **Ruler:** Elizabeth II **Obv:** Head with tiara right **Obv. Designer:** Ian Rank-Broadley **Rev:** First steam locomotive **Edge:** Reeded and lettered

Date	Mintage	F	VF	XF	Unc	BU
2004 Proof	1,500	Value: 550				

KM# 1052 2 POUNDS
12.0000 g., Bi-Metallic Nickel-Brass center in Copper-Nickel ring, 28.4 mm. **Ruler:** Elizabeth II **Subject:** 400th Anniversary - The Gunpowder Plot **Obv:** Head with tiara right **Obv. Designer:** Ian Rank-Broadley **Rev:** Circular design of Royal scepters, swords and crosiers **Rev. Designer:** Peter Forster **Edge:** Reeded and lettered **Edge Lettering:** REMEMBER REMEMBER THE FIFTH OF NOVEMBER

Date	Mintage	F	VF	XF	Unc	BU
ND(2005)	—	—	—	—	6.00	7.00
ND(2005) Proof	50,000	Value: 9.00				

KM# 1056 2 POUNDS
Copper-Nickel Nickel-Brass outer ring, 28.4 mm. **Ruler:** Elizabeth II **Subject:** 60th Anniversary of the End of WW II **Obv:** Head with tiara right **Obv. Designer:** Ian Rank-Broadley **Rev:** St. Paul's Cathedral amid search light beams **Rev. Designer:** Robert Elderton **Edge:** Reeded and lettered **Edge Lettering:** "IN VICTORY MAGNANIMITY IN PEACE GOODWILL"

Date	Mintage	F	VF	XF	Unc	BU
ND (2005)	—	Value: 30.00				

KM# 1056a 2 POUNDS
12.0000 g., 0.9250 Silver with Gold-plated outer ring 0.3569 oz. ASW, 28.4 mm. **Ruler:** Elizabeth II **Subject:** 60th Anniversary of the End of WWII **Obv:** Crowned head right **Obv. Designer:** Ian Rank-Broadley **Rev:** St. Paul's Cathedral amid search light beams **Rev. Designer:** Robert Elderton **Edge:** Reeded and lettered **Edge Lettering:** "IN VICTORY MAGNANIMITY IN PEACE GOODWILL"

Date	Mintage	F	VF	XF	Unc	BU
ND(2005) Proof	25,000	Value: 30.00				

KM# 1060 2 POUNDS
12.0000 g., Bi-Metallic Copper-Nickel center in Nickel-Brass ring, 28.4 mm. **Ruler:** Elizabeth II **Subject:** 200th Birthday of Engineer Isambard Kingdom Brunel **Obv:** Head with tiara right **Obv. Designer:** Ian Rank-Broadley **Rev:** Isambard Brunel **Edge:** Lettered

Date	Mintage	F	VF	XF	Unc	BU
2006	—	—	—	—	16.00	18.00
2006 Proof	50,000	Value: 35.00				

KM# 1061 2 POUNDS
12.0000 g., Bi-Metallic Copper-Nickel center in Nickel-Brass ring, 28.4 mm. **Ruler:** Elizabeth II **Subject:** Engineering Achievements of Isambard Kingdom Brunel **Obv:** Head with tiara right **Obv. Designer:** Ian Rank-Broadley **Rev:** Paddington Station structural supports **Edge:** Lettered

Date	Mintage	F	VF	XF	Unc	BU
2006	—	—	—	—	16.00	17.50
2006 Proof	50,000	Value: 20.00				

KM# 1075 2 POUNDS
12.0000 g., Bi-Metallic Copper-Nickel center in Brass ring, 28.4 mm. **Ruler:** Elizabeth II **Subject:** 200th Anniversary of the Abolition of the Slave Trade **Obv:** Bust right **Rev:** Chain crossing 1807 date **Edge:** Reeded and lettered

Date	Mintage	F	VF	XF	Unc	BU
2007	—	—	—	—	—	6.00
2007 Proof	50,000	Value: 9.00				

KM# 1075a 2 POUNDS
12.0000 g., 0.9250 Silver Gold plated outer ring 0.3569 oz. ASW, 28.4 mm. **Ruler:** Elizabeth II **Subject:** Abolition of the Slave Trade **Obv:** Elizabeth II right **Rev:** Zero in 1807 date as a broken chain link **Edge:** Reeded and lettered

Date	Mintage	F	VF	XF	Unc	BU
2007 Proof	10,000	Value: 55.00				

KM# 1075b 2 POUNDS
15.9700 g., 0.9166 Gold Bimetallic with yellow gold center in red gold ring 0.4706 oz. AGW, 28.4 mm. **Ruler:** Elizabeth II **Subject:** Abolition of the Slave Trade **Obv:** Elizabeth II right **Rev:** Zero in 1807 date as a broken chain link **Edge:** Reeded and lettered

Date	Mintage	F	VF	XF	Unc	BU
2007 Proof	1,000	Value: 765				

KM# 1076 2 POUNDS
12.0000 g., Bi-Metallic Copper-Nickel center in Brass ring, 28.4 mm. **Ruler:** Elizabeth II **Subject:** 300th Anniversary of the Act of Union of England and Scotland **Obv:** Bust right **Rev:** Combination of British and Scottish arms **Edge:** Reeded and lettered

Date	Mintage	F	VF	XF	Unc	BU
2007	—	—	—	—	—	6.00
2007 Proof	50,000	Value: 9.00				

KM# 1076a 2 POUNDS
12.0000 g., 0.9250 Bi-Metallic .925 Silver center in Gold Plated .925 Silver ring 0.3569 oz., 28.4 mm. **Ruler:** Elizabeth II **Subject:** 300th Anniv. Union of Scotland and England **Obv:** Elizabeth II **Rev:** Combined English and Scottish arms **Edge:** Reeded and lettered **Edge Lettering:** "TVEATVR VNITA DEUS"

Date	Mintage	F	VF	XF	Unc	BU
2007 Proof	10,000	Value: 55.00				

KM# 1076b 2 POUNDS
15.9800 g., 0.9166 Bi-Metallic .9166 Yellow Gold center in .9166 Red Gold ring 0.4709 oz., 28.4 mm. **Ruler:** Elizabeth II **Subject:** 300th Anniv. Union of Scotland and England **Obv:** Elizabeth II **Rev:** Combined English and Scottish arms **Edge:** Reeded and lettered **Edge Lettering:** "TVEATVR VNITA DEUS"

Date	Mintage	F	VF	XF	Unc	BU
2007 Proof	750	Value: 765				

KM# 1015 5 POUNDS
28.2800 g., Copper-Nickel, 38.6 mm. **Ruler:** Elizabeth II **Subject:** Centennial of Queen Victoria **Obv:** Head with tiara right **Obv. Designer:** Ian Rank-Broadley **Rev:** Queen Victoria's portrait within "V" **Rev. Designer:** Mary Milner Dickens, William Wyon **Edge:** Reeded

Date	Mintage	F	VF	XF	Unc	BU
2001	851,491	—	—	—	14.00	16.00
2001 Proof	—	Value: 20.00				

KM# 1015a 5 POUNDS

28.2800 g., 0.9250 Silver 0.8410 oz. ASW, 38.6 mm. **Ruler:** Elizabeth II **Subject:** Centennial of Queen Victoria **Obv:** Head with tiara right **Obv. Designer:** Ian Rank-Broadley **Rev:** Queen Victoria's portrait within "V" **Rev. Designer:** Mary Milner Dickens

Date	Mintage	F	VF	XF	Unc	BU
2001 Proof	—	Value: 65.00				

KM# 1015b 5 POUNDS

39.9400 g., 0.9167 Gold 1.1771 oz. AGW **Ruler:** Elizabeth II **Subject:** Centennial of Queen Victoria **Obv:** Head with tiara right **Obv. Designer:** Ian Rank-Broadley **Rev:** Queen Victoria's portrait within "V" **Rev. Designer:** Mary Milner Dickens

Date	Mintage	F	VF	XF	Unc	BU
2001 Proof	1,000	Value: 1,150				

KM# 1024 5 POUNDS

28.2800 g., Copper-Nickel, 38.6 mm. **Ruler:** Elizabeth II **Subject:** Queen's Golden Jubilee of Reign **Obv:** Crowned bust in royal garb right **Rev:** Queen on horse **Edge:** Reeded

Date	Mintage	F	VF	XF	Unc	BU
2002	3,468,210	—	—	—	12.50	14.50
2002 Proof	—	Value: 20.00				

KM# 1024a 5 POUNDS

28.2800 g., 0.9250 Silver 0.8410 oz. ASW, 38.6 mm. **Ruler:** Elizabeth II **Subject:** Queen's Golden Jubilee of Reign **Obv:** Crowned bust in royal garb right **Rev:** Queen on horse **Edge:** Reeded

Date	Mintage	F	VF	XF	Unc	BU
2002 Proof	—	Value: 50.00				

KM# 1024b 5 POUNDS

39.9400 g., 0.9167 Gold 1.1771 oz. AGW, 38.6 mm. **Ruler:** Elizabeth II **Subject:** Queen's Golden Jubilee of Reign **Obv:** Crowned bust in royal garb right **Rev:** Queen on horse left **Edge:** Reeded

Date	Mintage	F	VF	XF	Unc	BU
2002 Proof	—	Value: 1,150				

KM# 1035 5 POUNDS

28.2800 g., Copper Nickel, 38.6 mm. **Ruler:** Elizabeth II **Subject:** Queen Mother **Obv:** Head with tiara right **Obv. Designer:** Ian Rank-Broadley **Rev:** Queen Mother's portrait in wreath **Rev. Designer:** Avril Vaughan **Edge:** Reeded

Date	Mintage	F	VF	XF	Unc	BU
	—	—	—	—	15.00	—
ND(2002) Proof	—	Value: 20.00				

KM# 1035a 5 POUNDS

28.2800 g., Silver, 38.6 mm. **Ruler:** Elizabeth II **Subject:** Queen Mother **Obv:** Head with tiara right **Obv. Designer:** Ian Rank-Broadley **Rev:** Queen Mother's portrait in wreath **Rev. Designer:** Avril Vaughan **Edge:** Reeded

Date	Mintage	F	VF	XF	Unc	BU
ND(2002) Proof	25,000	Value: 50.00				

KM# 1035b 5 POUNDS

39.9400 g., 0.9167 Gold 1.1771 oz. AGW, 38.6 mm. **Ruler:** Elizabeth II **Subject:** Queen Mother **Obv:** Head with tiara right **Obv. Designer:** Ian Rank-Broadley **Rev:** Queen Mother's portrait in wreath **Rev. Designer:** Avril Vaughan **Edge:** Reeded

Date	Mintage	F	VF	XF	Unc	BU
ND(2002) Proof	3,000	Value: 1,150				

KM# 1038 5 POUNDS

28.2800 g., Copper Nickel, 38.6 mm. **Ruler:** Elizabeth II **Subject:** Queen's Golden Jubilee **Obv:** Queen's stylized portrait **Rev:** Childlike lettering **Edge:** Reeded **Designer:** Tom Phillips

Date	Mintage	F	VF	XF	Unc	BU
2003	1,307,010	—	—	—	12.50	14.50
2003 Proof	—	Value: 20.00				

KM# 1038a 5 POUNDS

28.2800 g., 0.9250 Silver 0.8410 oz. ASW, 38.6 mm. **Ruler:** Elizabeth II **Subject:** Queen's Golden Jubilee **Obv:** Stylized Queens portrait **Rev:** Childlike lettering **Edge:** Reeded **Designer:** Tom Phillips

Date	Mintage	F	VF	XF	Unc	BU
2003 Proof	50,000	Value: 50.00				

KM# 1038b 5 POUNDS

39.9400 g., 0.9166 Gold 1.1770 oz. AGW, 38.6 mm. **Ruler:** Elizabeth II **Subject:** Queen's Golden Jubilee **Obv:** Stylized Queens portrait **Rev:** Childlike lettering **Edge:** Reeded **Designer:** Tom Phillips

Date	Mintage	F	VF	XF	Unc	BU
2003 Proof	2,750	Value: 1,150				

KM# 1055 5 POUNDS

28.2800 g., Copper-Nickel, 38.6 mm. **Ruler:** Elizabeth II **Subject:** Entente Cordiale **Obv:** Head with tiara right **Obv. Designer:** Ian Rank-Broadley **Rev:** Britannia and Marianne **Edge:** Reeded

Date	Mintage	F	VF	XF	Unc	BU
2004	1,205,158	—	—	—	15.00	17.50
2004 Proof	—	Value: 20.00				

KM# 1055a 5 POUNDS

28.2800 g., 0.9250 Silver 0.8410 oz. ASW, 38.6 mm. **Ruler:** Elizabeth II **Subject:** Entente Cordiale **Obv:** Head with tiara right **Obv. Designer:** Ian Rank-Broadley **Rev:** Britannia and Marianne **Edge:** Reeded

Date	Mintage	F	VF	XF	Unc	BU
2004 Proof	15,000	Value: 50.00				

KM# 1055b 5 POUNDS

39.9400 g., 0.9167 Gold 1.1771 oz. AGW, 38.6 mm. **Ruler:** Elizabeth II **Subject:** Entente Cordiale **Obv:** Head with tiara right **Obv. Designer:** Ian Rank-Broadley **Rev:** Britannia and Marianne **Edge:** Reeded

Date	Mintage	F	VF	XF	Unc	BU
2004 Proof	1,500	Value: 1,150				

KM# 1055c 5 POUNDS

94.2000 g., 0.9995 Platinum 3.0270 oz. APW, 38.6 mm. **Ruler:** Elizabeth II **Subject:** Entente Cordiale **Obv:** Head with tiara right **Obv. Designer:** Ian Rank-Broadley **Rev:** Britannia and Marianne **Edge:** Reeded

Date	Mintage	F	VF	XF	Unc	BU
2004 Proof	501	Value: 7,000				

KM# 1053 5 POUNDS

28.2800 g., Copper-Nickel, 38.6 mm. **Ruler:** Elizabeth II **Subject:** Battle of Trafalgar **Obv:** Head with tiara right **Obv. Legend:** ELIZABETH • II D•G•REG•F•D **Obv. Designer:** Ian Rank-Broadley **Rev:** HMS Victory and HMS Temeraire at Trafalgar **Rev. Legend:** TRAFALGAR **Rev. Designer:** Clive Duncan **Edge:** Reeded

Date	Mintage	F	VF	XF	Unc	BU
2005	—	—	—	—	12.50	16.50
2005 Proof	50,000	Value: 18.50				

KM# 1054 5 POUNDS

28.2800 g., Copper-Nickel, 38.6 mm. **Ruler:** Elizabeth II **Obv:** Head with tiara right **Obv. Legend:** ELIZABETH • II D • G • REG • F • D **Obv. Designer:** Ian Rank-Broadley **Rev:** Uniformed facing 1/2 bust of Admiral Horatio Nelson **Rev. Legend:** HORATIO NELSON **Edge:** Reeded

Date	Mintage	F	VF	XF	Unc	BU
2005	—	—	—	—	15.00	16.50
2005 Proof	50,000	Value: 18.50				

KM# 1053a 5 POUNDS

28.2800 g., 0.9250 Silver 0.8410 oz. ASW, 38.6 mm. **Ruler:** Elizabeth II **Subject:** Battle of Trafalgar **Obv:** Head with tiara right **Obv. Legend:** ELIZABETH • II D • G • REG • F • D **Obv. Designer:** Ian Rank-Broadley **Rev:** Ships HMS Victory and Temeraire at Trafalgar **Rev. Legend:** TRAFALGAR **Rev. Designer:** Clive Duncan **Edge:** Reeded

Date	Mintage	F	VF	XF	Unc	BU
2005 Proof	30,000	Value: 60.00				

KM# 1053b 5 POUNDS

39.9400 g., 0.9167 Gold 1.1771 oz. AGW, 38.6 mm. **Ruler:** Elizabeth II **Subject:** Battle of Trafalgar **Obv:** Head with tiara right **Obv. Legend:** ELIZABETH • II D • G • REG • F • D **Obv. Designer:** Ian Rank-Broadley **Rev:** Ships HMS Victory and Temeraire at Trafalgar **Rev. Legend:** TRAFALGAR **Rev. Designer:** Clive Duncan **Edge:** Reeded

Date	Mintage	F	VF	XF	Unc	BU
2005 Proof	1,805	Value: 1,200				

KM# 1054a 5 POUNDS

28.2800 g., 0.9250 Silver 0.8410 oz. ASW, 38.6 mm. **Ruler:** Elizabeth II **Obv:** Queen's head with tiara right **Obv. Legend:** ELIZABETH ? II D ? G ? REG ? F ? D **Obv. Designer:** Ian Rank-Broadley **Rev:** Uniformed facing 1/2 bust of Admiral Horatio Nelson **Rev. Legend:** HORATIO NELSON

Date	Mintage	F	VF	XF	Unc	BU
2005 Proof	—	Value: 60.00				

KM# 1054b 5 POUNDS

39.9400 g., 0.9167 Gold 1.1771 oz. AGW, 38.6 mm. **Ruler:** Elizabeth II **Subject:** Battle of Trafalgar **Obv:** Queen's head with tiara right **Obv. Legend:** ELIZABETH • II D • G • REG • F • D **Rev:** Uniformed facing 1/2 bust of Admiral Horatio Nelson **Rev. Legend:** HORATIO NELSON

Date	Mintage	F	VF	XF	Unc	BU
2005 Proof	—	Value: 1,200				

KM# 1062a 5 POUNDS

28.2800 g., 0.9250 Silver 0.8410 oz. ASW **Ruler:** Elizabeth II **Subject:** Queen's 80th Birthday Celebration **Obv:** Queens head right **Obv. Legend:** ELIZABETH ? II D ? G ? REG ? F ? D **Obv. Designer:** Ian Rank-Broadley **Rev:** Three bannered trumpets **Rev. Legend:** VIVAT REGINA **Edge:** Reeded

Date	Mintage	F	VF	XF	Unc	BU
2006 Proof	—	Value: 65.00				

KM# 1062b 5 POUNDS

39.9400 g., 0.9167 Gold 1.1771 oz. AGW, 38.6 mm. **Ruler:** Elizabeth II **Subject:** Queen's 80th Birthday Celebration **Obv:** Queen's head with tiara right **Obv. Legend:** ELIZABETH ? II D ? G ? REG ? F ? D **Obv. Designer:** Ian Rank-Broadley **Rev:** Three bannered trumpets **Rev. Legend:** VIVAT REGINA **Edge:** Reeded

Date	Mintage	F	VF	XF	Unc	BU
2006 Proof	—	Value: 1,200				

KM# 1062 5 POUNDS

28.2800 g., Copper-Nickel, 38.6 mm. **Ruler:** Elizabeth II **Obv:** Head with tiara right **Obv. Designer:** Ian Rank-Broadley **Rev:** Three bannered trumpets **Edge:** Reeded

Date	Mintage	F	VF	XF	Unc	BU
2006	—	—	—	—	20.00	22.00
2006 Proof	50,000	Value: 27.00				

KM# 1077 5 POUNDS
28.2800 g., Copper-Nickel, 38.6 mm. **Ruler:** Elizabeth II **Subject:** Queen's 60th Wedding Anniversary **Obv:** Queen Elizabeth II and Prince Philip **Rev:** North Rose Window of Westminster Abby **Edge:** Reeded

Date	Mintage	F	VF	XF	Unc	BU
2007	—	—	—	—	—	20.00
2007 Proof	50,000	Value: 30.00				

KM# 1077a 5 POUNDS
28.2800 g., 0.9250 Silver 0.8410 oz. ASW, 38.6 mm. **Ruler:** Elizabeth II **Subject:** 60th Wedding Anniversary **Obv:** Elizabeth II and Prince Philip **Rev:** Westminster Abbey's North Rose Window **Edge Lettering:** "MY STRENGTH AND STAY"

Date	Mintage	F	VF	XF	Unc	BU
ND (2007) Proof	35,000	Value: 70.00				

KM# 1077b 5 POUNDS
39.9400 g., 0.9166 Gold 1.1770 oz. AGW, 28.4 mm. **Ruler:** Elizabeth II **Subject:** 60th Wedding Anniversary **Obv:** Elizabeth II and Prince Philip **Rev:** Westminster Abbey's North Rose Window **Edge Lettering:** "MY STRENGTH AND STAY"

Date	Mintage	F	VF	XF	Unc	BU
ND (2007) Proof	2,500	Value: 1,475				

SOVEREIGN COINAGE

KM# 1001 1/2 SOVEREIGN
3.9900 g., 0.9170 Gold 0.1176 oz. AGW **Ruler:** Elizabeth II **Obv:** Head with tiara right **Obv. Designer:** Ian Rank-Broadley **Rev:** St. George slaying the dragon

Date	Mintage	F	VF	XF	Unc	BU
2001	94,763	—	—	—	90.00	120
2001 Proof	10,000	Value: 145				
2002	61,347	—	—	—	90.00	120
2003	47,818	—	—	—	90.00	120
2003 Proof	14,750	Value: 145				
2004	34,924	—	—	—	90.00	120
2005	30,299	—	—	—	95.00	120
2006	—	—	—	—	100	125
2006 Proof	8,500	Value: 170				
2007	75,000	—	—	—	—	125
2007 Proof	7,500	Value: 195				

KM# 1025 1/2 SOVEREIGN
3.9900 g., 0.9167 Gold 0.1176 oz. AGW, 19.3 mm. **Ruler:** Elizabeth II **Subject:** Queen Elizabeth II's Golden Jubilee **Obv:** Head with tiara right **Obv. Designer:** Ian Rank-Broadley **Rev:** Crowned arms within wreath, date below **Edge:** Reeded

Date	Mintage	F	VF	XF	Unc	BU
2002 Proof	18,000	Value: 145				

KM# 1064 1/2 SOVEREIGN
3.9940 g., 0.9167 Gold 0.1177 oz. AGW, 19.3 mm. **Ruler:** Elizabeth II **Obv:** Head with tiara right **Obv. Designer:** Ian Rank-Broadley **Rev:** Knight fighting dragon with sword **Edge:** Reeded

Date	Mintage	F	VF	XF	Unc	BU
2005 Proof	12,500	Value: 175				

KM# 1002 SOVEREIGN
7.9881 g., 0.9170 Gold 0.2355 oz. AGW **Ruler:** Elizabeth II **Obv:** Head with tiara right **Obv. Designer:** Ian Rank-Broadley **Rev:** St. George slaying the dragon

Date	Mintage	F	VF	XF	Unc	BU
2001	49,462	—	—	—	175	230
2001 Proof	15,000	Value: 245				
2002	75,264	—	—	—	175	230
2003	43,230	—	—	—	165	230
2003 Proof	19,750	Value: 245				
2004	30,688	—	—	—	175	230
2005	45,542	—	—	—	165	230
2006	—	—	—	—	195	230
2006 Proof	16,000	Value: 325				
2007	75,000	—	—	—	—	230
2007 Proof	12,500	Value: 345				

KM# 1026 SOVEREIGN
7.9800 g., 0.9167 Gold 0.2352 oz. AGW, 22 mm. **Ruler:** Elizabeth II **Subject:** Queen Elizabeth II's Golden Jubilee **Obv:** Head with tiara right **Obv. Designer:** Ian Rank-Broadley **Rev:** Crowned arms within wreath, date below **Edge:** Reeded

Date	Mintage	F	VF	XF	Unc	BU
2002	71,815	—	—	—	225	—
2002 Proof	20,500	Value: 250				

KM# 1065 SOVEREIGN
7.9880 g., 0.9176 Gold 0.2356 oz. AGW, 22.05 mm. **Ruler:** Elizabeth II **Obv:** Head with tiara right **Obv. Designer:** Ian Rank-Broadley **Rev:** Knight fighting dragon with sword **Edge:** Reeded

Date	Mintage	F	VF	XF	Unc	BU
2005	75,000	—	—	—	—	240
2005 Proof	17,500	Value: 275				

KM# 1027 2 POUNDS
15.9700 g., 0.9167 Gold 0.4707 oz. AGW, 28.4 mm. **Ruler:** Elizabeth II **Subject:** Queen Elizabeth II's Golden Jubilee **Obv:** Head with tiara right **Obv. Designer:** Ian Rank-Broadley **Rev:** Crowned arms within wreath, date below **Edge:** Reeded **Note:** In proof sets only.

Date	Mintage	F	VF	XF	Unc	BU
2002	8,000	Value: 465				

KM# 1066 2 POUNDS
15.9760 g., 0.9167 Gold 0.4708 oz. AGW, 28.4 mm. **Ruler:** Elizabeth II **Obv:** Head with tiara right **Obv. Designer:** Ian Rank-Broadley **Rev:** Knight fighting dragon with sword **Edge:** Reeded

Date	Mintage	F	VF	XF	Unc	BU
2005 Proof	5,000	Value: 475				

KM# 1072 2 POUNDS
15.9700 g., 0.9167 Gold 0.4707 oz. AGW, 28.4 mm. **Ruler:** Elizabeth II **Obv:** Head with tiara right **Obv. Designer:** Ian Rank-Broadley **Rev:** St. George slaying the Dragon **Edge:** Reeded

Date	Mintage	F	VF	XF	Unc	BU
2006 Proof	3,500	Value: 475				
2007 Proof	2,500	Value: 620				

KM# 1003 5 POUNDS
39.9400 g., 0.9170 Gold 1.1775 oz. AGW, 36 mm. **Ruler:** Elizabeth II **Obv:** Head with tiara right **Obv. Designer:** Ian Rank-Broadley **Rev:** St. George slaying dragon **Edge:** Reeded

Date	Mintage	F	VF	XF	Unc	BU
2001 Proof	1,000	Value: 1,250				
2003 Proof	2,250	Value: 1,200				
2004	1,000	—	—	—	1,500	1,500
2006	1,000	—	—	—	1,425	1,425
2006 Proof	1,750	Value: 1,200				
2007 Proof	1,750	Value: 1,650				

KM# 1028 5 POUNDS
39.9400 g., 0.9167 Gold 1.1771 oz. AGW, 36 mm. **Ruler:** Elizabeth II **Subject:** Queen Elizabeth II's Golden Jubilee **Obv:** Head with tiara right **Obv. Designer:** Ian Rank-Broadley **Rev:** Crowned arms within wreath **Edge:** Reeded

Date	Mintage	F	VF	XF	Unc	BU
2002	3,000	Value: 1,200				

KM# 1067 5 POUNDS
39.9400 g., 0.9167 Gold 1.1771 oz. AGW, 36 mm. **Ruler:** Elizabeth II **Obv:** Head with tiara right **Obv. Designer:** Ian Rank-Broadley **Rev:** Knight fighting dragon with sword **Edge:** Reeded

Date	Mintage	F	VF	XF	Unc	BU
2005 Proof	2,500	Value: 1,200				

BULLION COINAGE

Until 1990, .917 Gold was commonly alloyed with copper by the British Royal Mint.

All proof issues have designers name as P. Nathan. The uncirculated issues use only Nathan.

KM# 1016 20 PENCE
3.2400 g., 0.9584 Silver 0.0998 oz. ASW, 16.5 mm. **Ruler:** Elizabeth II **Subject:** Britannia Bullion **Obv:** Head with tiara right **Obv. Designer:** Ian Rank-Broadley **Rev:** Stylized "Britannia and the Lion" **Edge:** Reeded

Date	Mintage	F	VF	XF	Unc	BU
2001 Proof	15,000	Value: 25.00				

KM# 1044 20 PENCE
3.2400 g., 0.9584 Silver 0.0998 oz. ASW, 16.5 mm. **Ruler:** Elizabeth II **Obv:** Head with tiara right **Obv. Designer:** Ian Rank-Broadley **Rev:** Britannia portrait behind wavy lines **Edge:** Reeded

Date	Mintage	F	VF	XF	Unc	BU
2003 Proof	5,000	Value: 35.00				

KM# 1045 50 PENCE
8.1100 g., 0.9584 Silver 0.2499 oz. ASW, 22 mm. **Ruler:** Elizabeth II **Obv:** Head with tiara right **Obv. Designer:** Ian Rank-Broadley **Rev:** Britannia portrait behind wavy lines **Edge:** Reeded

Date	Mintage	F	VF	XF	Unc	BU
2003 Proof	5,000	Value: 35.00				

KM# 1018 POUND
16.2200 g., 0.9584 Silver 0.4998 oz. ASW, 27 mm. **Ruler:** Elizabeth II **Subject:** Britannia Bullion **Obv:** Head with tiara right **Obv. Designer:** Ian Rank-Broadley **Rev:** Stylized "Britannia and the Lion" **Edge:** Reeded

Date	Mintage	F	VF	XF	Unc	BU
2001 Proof	5,000	Value: 40.00				

KM# 1046 POUND
16.2200 g., 0.9584 Silver 0.4998 oz. ASW, 22.5 mm. **Ruler:** Elizabeth II **Obv:** Head with tiara right **Obv. Designer:** Ian Rank-Broadley **Rev:** Britannia portrait behind wavy lines **Edge:** Reeded

Date	Mintage	F	VF	XF	Unc	BU
2003 Proof	5,000	Value: 50.00				

KM# 1029 2 POUNDS
32.5400 g., 0.9580 Silver 1.0022 oz. ASW, 40 mm. **Ruler:** Elizabeth II **Obv:** Head with tiara right **Obv. Designer:** Ian Rank-Broadley **Rev:** Standing Britannia **Rev. Designer:** Philip Nathan **Edge:** Reeded

Date	Mintage	F	VF	XF	Unc	BU
2002	36,543	—	—	—	22.50	25.00
2004	100,000	—	—	—	22.50	25.00
2006	100,000	—	—	—	22.50	25.00

KM# 1039 2 POUNDS
32.4500 g., 0.9580 Silver 0.9994 oz. ASW, 40 mm. **Ruler:** Elizabeth II **Subject:** Britannia Bullion **Obv:** Head with tiara right **Obv. Designer:** Ian Rank-Broadley **Rev:** Britannia portrait behind wavy puzzle-like lines **Rev. Designer:** Philip Nathan **Edge:** Reeded

Date	Mintage	F	VF	XF	Unc	BU
2003	73,271	—	—	—	—	25.00
2003 Proof	1,833	Value: 60.00				

KM# 1063 2 POUNDS
32.4500 g., 0.9580 Silver 0.9994 oz. ASW, 40 mm. **Ruler:** Elizabeth II **Obv:** Head with tiara right **Obv. Designer:** Ian Rank-Broadley **Rev:** Seated Britannia **Rev. Designer:** Philip Nathan **Edge:** Reeded

Date	Mintage	F	VF	XF	Unc	BU
2005	100,000	—	—	—	—	25.00
2005 Proof	2,500	Value: 65.00				

KM# 1000a 2 POUNDS
32.4500 g., 0.9580 Silver 0.9994 oz. ASW, 40 mm. **Ruler:** Elizabeth II **Subject:** Golden Silhouette Britannias **Obv:** Head with tiara right **Obv. Designer:** Ian Rank-Broadley **Rev:** Gold plated Britannia in chariot **Rev. Designer:** Philip Nathan **Edge:** Reeded

Date	Mintage	F	VF	XF	Unc	BU
2006 Proof	3,000	Value: 100				

KM# 1029a 2 POUNDS
32.4500 g., 0.9580 Silver 0.9994 oz. ASW, 40 mm. **Ruler:** Elizabeth II **Subject:** Golden Silhouette Britannias **Obv:** Head with tiara right **Obv. Designer:** Ian Rank-Broadley **Rev:** Gold plated Britannia standing with shield **Edge:** Reeded

Date	Mintage	F	VF	XF	Unc	BU
2006 Proof	3,000	Value: 100				

KM# 1018a 2 POUNDS
32.4500 g., 0.9580 Silver 0.9994 oz. ASW, 40 mm. **Ruler:** Elizabeth II **Subject:** Golden Silhouette Britannias **Obv:** Head with tiara right **Obv. Designer:** Ian Rank-Broadley **Rev:** Gold plated Britannia and Lion **Edge:** Reeded

Date	Mintage	F	VF	XF	Unc	BU
2006 Proof	3,000	Value: 100				

KM# 1039a 2 POUNDS
32.4500 g., 0.9580 Silver 0.9994 oz. ASW, 40 mm. **Ruler:** Elizabeth II **Subject:** Golden Silhouette Britannias **Obv:** Head with tiara right **Obv. Designer:** Ian Rank-Broadley **Rev:** Gold plated Britannia head **Edge:** Reeded

Date	Mintage	F	VF	XF	Unc	BU
2006 Proof	3,000	Value: 100				

KM# 1063a 2 POUNDS
32.4500 g., 0.9580 Gold 0.9994 oz. AGW, 40 mm. **Ruler:** Elizabeth II **Subject:** Golden Silhouette Britannias **Obv:** Head with tiara right **Obv. Designer:** Ian Rank-Broadley **Rev:** Gold plated Britannia seated **Edge:** Reeded

Date	Mintage	F	VF	XF	Unc	BU
2006 Proof	3,000	Value: 100				

KM# 1078 2 POUNDS
32.4500 g., 0.9580 Silver 0.9994 oz. ASW, 40 mm. **Ruler:** Elizabeth II **Subject:** Britannia series **Obv:** Elizabeth II **Rev:** Seated, bareheaded Britannia with a recumbent lion at her feet **Edge:** Reeded

Date	Mintage	F	VF	XF	Unc	BU
2007	100,000	—	—	—	—	35.00
2007 Proof	—	Value: 65.00				

KM# 1020 10 POUNDS (1/10 Ounce - Britannia)
3.4100 g., 0.9167 Gold 0.1005 oz. AGW, 16.5 mm. **Ruler:** Elizabeth II **Subject:** Britannia Bullion **Obv:** Head with tiara right **Obv. Designer:** Ian Rank-Broadley **Rev:** Stylized "Britannia and the Lion" **Rev. Designer:** Philip Nathan **Edge:** Reeded

Date	Mintage	F	VF	XF	Unc	BU
2001	1,100	—	—	—	BV+16%	—
2001 Proof	1,557	Value: 115				

KM# 1008 10 POUNDS (1/10 Ounce - Britannia)
3.4100 g., 0.9167 Gold 0.1005 oz. AGW **Ruler:** Elizabeth II **Obv:** Head with tiara right **Obv. Designer:** Ian Rank-Broadley **Rev:** Britannia standing **Rev. Designer:** Philip Nathan **Edge:** Reeded

Date	Mintage	F	VF	XF	Unc	BU
2002 Proof	1,500	Value: 115				
2004	—	—	—	—	—	BV+16%
2004 Proof	—	Value: 200				

KM# 1040 10 POUNDS (1/10 Ounce - Britannia)
3.4100 g., 0.9167 Gold 0.1005 oz. AGW, 16.5 mm. **Ruler:** Elizabeth II **Obv:** Head with tiara right **Obv. Designer:** Ian Rank-Broadley **Rev:** Britannia portrait behind wavy lines **Rev. Designer:** Philip Nathan **Edge:** Reeded

Date	Mintage	F	VF	XF	Unc	BU
2003	—	—	—	—	BV+16%	—
2003 Proof	—	Value: 115				
2003 Proof	4,000	Value: 115				

KM# 1068 10 POUNDS (1/10 Ounce - Britannia)
3.4100 g., 0.9167 Gold 0.1005 oz. AGW, 16.5 mm. **Ruler:** Elizabeth II **Obv:** Head with tiara right **Obv. Designer:** Ian Rank-Broadley **Rev:** Seated Britannia **Rev. Designer:** Philip Nathan **Edge:** Reeded

Date	Mintage	F	VF	XF	Unc	BU
2005 Proof	3,500	Value: 150				

KM# 1021 25 POUNDS (1/4 Ounce - Britannia)
8.5100 g., 0.9167 Gold 0.2508 oz. AGW, 22 mm. **Ruler:** Elizabeth II **Subject:** Britannia Bullion **Obv:** Head with tiara right **Obv. Designer:** Ian Rank-Broadley **Rev:** Stylized "Britannia and the Lion" **Rev. Designer:** Philip Nathan **Edge:** Reeded

Date	Mintage	F	VF	XF	Unc	BU
2001	1,100	—	—	—	BV+25%	—
2001 Proof	1,500	Value: 275				

KM# 1009 25 POUNDS (1/4 Ounce - Britannia)
8.5100 g., 0.9167 Gold 0.2508 oz. AGW **Ruler:** Elizabeth II **Obv:** Head with tiara right **Obv. Designer:** Ian Rank-Broadley **Rev:** Britannia standing **Rev. Designer:** Philip Nathan **Edge:** Reeded

Date	Mintage	F	VF	XF	Unc	BU
2002 Proof	750	Value: 275				
2004	—	—	—	—	BV+15%	—
2004 Proof	—	Value: 350				

KM# 1041 25 POUNDS (1/4 Ounce - Britannia)
8.5100 g., 0.9167 Gold 0.2508 oz. AGW, 22 mm. **Ruler:** Elizabeth II **Obv:** Head with tiara right **Obv. Designer:** Ian Rank-Broadley **Rev:** Britannia portrait behind wavy lines **Rev. Designer:** Philip Nathan **Edge:** Reeded

Date	Mintage	F	VF	XF	Unc	BU
2003	604	—	—	—	BV+25%	—
2003 Proof	3,250	Value: 275				

KM# 1069 25 POUNDS (1/4 Ounce - Britannia)
8.5100 g., 0.9167 Gold 0.2508 oz. AGW, 22 mm. **Ruler:** Elizabeth II **Obv:** Head with tiara right **Obv. Designer:** Ian Rank-Broadley **Rev:** Seated Britannia **Rev. Designer:** Philip Nathan **Edge:** Reeded

Date	Mintage	F	VF	XF	Unc	BU
2005 Proof	2,750	Value: 300				

KM# 1022 50 POUNDS (1/2 Ounce - Britannia)
17.0200 g., 0.9167 Gold 0.5016 oz. AGW, 27 mm. **Ruler:** Elizabeth II **Subject:** Britannia Bullion **Obv:** Head with tiara right **Obv. Designer:** Ian Rank-Broadley **Rev:** Stylized "Britannia and the Lion" **Rev. Designer:** Philip Nathan **Edge:** Reeded

Date	Mintage	F	VF	XF	Unc	BU
2001	600	—	—	—	BV+25%	—
2001 Proof	1,000	Value: 550				

KM# 1010 50 POUNDS (1/2 Ounce - Britannia)
17.0300 g., 0.9167 Gold 0.5019 oz. AGW **Ruler:** Elizabeth II **Obv:** Head with tiara right **Obv. Designer:** Ian Rank-Broadley **Rev:** Britannia standing **Rev. Designer:** Philip Nathan **Edge:** Reeded

Date	Mintage	F	VF	XF	Unc	BU
2002 Proof	1,000	Value: 550				
2004	—	—	—	—	—	BV+15%
2004 Proof	—	Value: 600				

KM# 1042 50 POUNDS (1/2 Ounce - Britannia)
17.0200 g., 0.9167 Gold 0.5016 oz. AGW, 27 mm. **Ruler:** Elizabeth II **Obv:** Head with tiara right **Obv. Designer:** Ian Rank-Broadley **Rev:** Britannia portrait behind wavy lines **Rev. Designer:** Philip Nathan **Edge:** Reeded

Date	Mintage	F	VF	XF	Unc	BU
2003	—	—	—	—	BV+15%	—
2003 Proof	2,500	Value: 550				

KM# 1070 50 POUNDS (1/2 Ounce - Britannia)
17.0300 g., 0.9167 Gold 0.5019 oz. AGW, 27 mm. **Ruler:** Elizabeth II **Obv:** Head with tiara right **Obv. Designer:** Ian Rank-Broadley **Rev:** Seated Britannia **Rev. Designer:** Philip Nathan **Edge:** Reeded

Date	Mintage	F	VF	XF	Unc	BU
2005 Proof	2,000	Value: 550				

KM# 1023 100 POUNDS (1 Ounce - Britannia)
34.0500 g., 0.9167 Gold 1.0035 oz. AGW, 32.7 mm. **Ruler:** Elizabeth II **Subject:** Britannia Bullion **Obv:** Head with tiara right **Obv. Designer:** Ian Rank-Broadley **Rev:** Stylized "Britannia and the Lion" **Rev. Designer:** Philip Nathan **Edge:** Reeded

Date	Mintage	F	VF	XF	Unc	BU
2001	900	—	—	—	BV+15%	—
2001 Proof	1,000	Value: 1,100				

KM# 1011 100 POUNDS (1 Ounce - Britannia)
34.0500 g., 0.9167 Gold 1.0035 oz. AGW **Ruler:** Elizabeth II **Obv:** Head with tiara right **Obv. Designer:** Ian Rank-Broadley **Rev:** Britannia standing **Rev. Designer:** Philip Nathan **Edge:** Reeded

Date	Mintage	F	VF	XF	Unc	BU
2002 Proof	1,000	Value: 1,100				
2004	—	—	—	—	—	BV+15%
2004 Proof	—	Value: 1,100				

KM# 1043 100 POUNDS (1 Ounce - Britannia)
34.0500 g., 0.9167 Gold 1.0035 oz. AGW, 32.7 mm. **Ruler:** Elizabeth II **Obv:** Head with tiara right **Obv. Designer:** Ian Rank-Broadley **Rev:** Britannia portrait behind wavy lines **Rev. Designer:** Philip Nathan **Edge:** Reeded

Date	Mintage	F	VF	XF	Unc	BU
2003	—	—	—	—	BV+15%	—
2003 Proof	1,500	Value: 1,150				

KM# 1071 100 POUNDS (1 Ounce - Britannia)
34.0500 g., 0.9167 Gold 1.0035 oz. AGW, 32.7 mm. **Ruler:** Elizabeth II **Obv:** Head with tiara right **Obv. Designer:** Ian Rank-Broadley **Rev:** Seated Britannia **Edge:** Reeded

Date	Mintage	F	VF	XF	Unc	BU
2005 Proof	1,500	Value: 1,100				

PIEFORTS

KM#	Date	Mintage	Identification	Mkt Val
P32	2004	10,000	2 Pounds. 0.9250 Bi-Metallic. 24.0000 g. 28.4 mm. Queen Elizabeth II. First steam locomotive. Reeded and lettered edge.	—
P33	2007	—	50 Pence. 0.9250 Silver. 16.0000 g. 27.3 mm. Elizabeth II. Fleur de Lis Scouting emblem. Plain edge.	—
P34	2007	250	5 Pounds. 0.9995 Platinum. 94.2000 g. 38.6 mm. Elizabeth II and Prince Philip. North Rose window of Westminster Abbey.	7,500
P35	2007	5,000	5 Pounds. 0.9250 Silver. 56.5600 g. 38.6 mm. Elizabeth II and Prince Philip. Westminster Abbey's North Rose Window. KM#1075a.	150
P36	2007	3,000	Pound. 0.9250 Silver. 19.0000 g. 22.5 mm. Elizabeth II. Gateshead Millennium Bridge. KM#1074a.	75.00
P37	2007	3,000	2 Pounds. 0.9250 Silver. 24.0000 g. 28.4 mm. Elizabeth II. 1807 Date and broken chain. KM#1075a.	80.00
P38	2007	3,000	2 Pounds. 0.9250 Silver. 24.0000 g. 28.4 mm. Elizabeth II. Combined English and Scottish arms. KM#1076a.	80.00
P39	2005	—	5 Pounds. 0.9250 Silver. KM#1053a.	150
P40	2005	—	5 Pounds. 0.9250 Silver. KM#1054a.	150
P41	2006	—	5 Pounds. 0.9250 Silver. KM#1062a.	170

MAUNDY SETS

KM#	Date	Mintage	Identification	Issue Price	Mkt Val
MDS260	2001 (4)	1,132	KM#898-899, 901-902. Westminster Abbey	—	200
MDS261	2002 (4)	1,681	KM#898-899, 901-902. Canterbury Cathedral	—	225
MDS262	2003 (4)	1,601	KM#898-899, 901-902. Gloucester Cathedral	—	245
MDS263	2004 (4)	1,613	KM#898-899, 901-902. Liverpool Cathedral	—	245
MDS264	2005 (4)	1,685	KM#898-899,901-902 Wakefield Cathedral	—	250
MDS265	2006 (4)	—	KM#898-899, 901-902	—	250

MINT SETS

KM#	Date	Mintage	Identification	Issue Price	Mkt Val
MS129	2001 (9)	57,741	KM#986-991, 994, 1013-1015 B.U. set	22.50	28.00
MS130	2001 (9)	—	KM#986-991, 994, 1013-1014 Wedding Collection	27.50	30.00
MS131	2001 (9)	—	KM#986-991, 994, 1013-1014 Baby Gift Set	27.50	30.00
MS132	2002 (8)	60,539	KM#986-991, 994, 1030	22.50	25.00
MS133	2002 (8)	—	KM#986-991, 994, 1030 Wedding Collection	27.50	28.00
MS134	2002 (8)	—	KM#986-991, 994, 1030 Baby Gift Set	27.50	28.00
MS135	2003 (10)	—	KM#986-991, 993, 994, 1036-1037 Brilliant Uncirculated Set	22.50	28.00
MS136	2003 (10)	—	KM#986-991, 993, 994, 1036-1037 Wedding Collection	27.50	30.00
MS137	2003 (10)	—	KM#986-991, 993, 994, 1036-1037 Baby Gift Set	27.50	30.00
MS138	2005 (10)	—	KM#986-991, 994, 1050-1052	26.50	29.00
MS139	2005 (10)	—	KM#986-991, 994, 1050-1052 Baby Gift Set	36.50	37.50
MS140	2005 (3)	—	KM#1050-1052 New Coinage Set	16.25	17.50
MS141	2005 (2)	—	KM#1053-1054 Trafalgar Set	36.00	40.00
MS142	2006 (10)	—	KM#986-990, 1057-1061	30.00	29.00
MS143	2006 (10)	—	KM#986-990, 1057-1061 Baby Gift Set	38.50	38.50

PROOF SETS

KM#	Date	Mintage	Identification	Issue Price	Mkt Val
PS117	2001 (4)	1,000	KM#1001-1003,1014a	1,645	1,675
PS118	2001 (4)	5,000	KM#1016-1019	—	140
PS127	2001 (10)	10,000	KM#986-991, 994, 1013-1015 Executive Proof Set in display case	115	150
PS128	2001 (10)	30,000	KM#986-991, 994, 1013-1015 Deluxe Proof Set in red leather case	72.50	95.00
PS129	2001 (10)	28,244	KM#986-991, 994, 1013-1015 Standard Proof Set in simple case	50.00	65.00
PS130	2001 (10)	1,351	KM#986-991, 994, 1013-1015 Gift Proof Set with a pack of occasion cards	65.00	85.00
PS119	2001 (4)	1,000	KM#1020-1023	1,595	2,000
PS116	2001 (3)	1,500	KM#1001-1002, 1014a	795	450
PSA119	2001 (3)	1,500	KM#1001, 1002, 1014b	—	425
PSB119	2001 (4)	1,000	KM#1001, 1002, 1014b, 1015b	—	2,050
PS120	2002 (3)	5,000	KM#1025-1027	795	850
PS121	2002 (3)	3,000	KM#1025-1028	1,645	1,800
PS126	2002 (4)	1,000	KM#1008-1011	1,600	2,000
PS131	2002 (9)	5,000	KM#986-991, 994, 1024, 1030 Executive Proof Set	100	100
PS132	2002 (9)	30,000	KM#986-991, 994, 1024, 1030 Deluxe Proof Set	70.00	75.00
PS133	2002 (9)	30,884	KM#986-991, 994, 1024, 1030 Standard Proof Set	48.00	50.00
PS134	2002 (9)	1,544	KM#986-991, 994, 1024, 1030 Gift Proof Set	62.40	65.00
PSA135	2002 (13)	—	KM#898a, 899a, 901a, 902a, 986c, 987c, 988b, 989b, 990b, 991b, 1030b, 994c, 1024b Queen Elizabeth II - Golden Jubilee 1952-2002, set is struck in gold (including Maundy set), in presentation box	—	7,850
PS122	2002 (4)	3,358	KM#1031-1034; Standard Set	34.95	35.00
PS123	2002 (4)	673	KM#1031-1034; Display Set	44.95	45.00
PS124	2002 (4)	2,553	KM#1031a-1034a; Display Set	120	125
PS125	2002 (4)	315	KM#1031b-1034b; Display Set	1,675	2,200
PS135	2003 (11)	—	KM#986-991, 993, 994, 1036-1038 Executive Proof Set	100	125
PS136	2003 (11)	—	KM#986-991, 993, 994, 1036-1038 Deluxe Proof Set	72.00	90.00
PS137	2003 (11)	23,305	KM#986-991, 993, 994, 1036-1038 Standard Proof Set	50.00	65.00
PSA138	2003 (4)	5,000	KM#1039, 1044-1046	—	180
PS138	2005 (12)	5,000	KM#986-991, 994, 1050-1054 Executive Set	146	150
PS139	2005 (12)	20,000	KM#986-991, 994, 1050-1054 Deluxe Proof Set	80.00	90.00
PS140	2005	25,000	KM#986-991, 994, 1050-1054	60.00	70.00
PS141	2005 (3)	2,000	KM#1068-1070	850	875
PS142	2005 (4)	1,500	KM#1068-1071	1,895	1,900
PS143	2005 (3)	2,500	KM#1064-1066	820	825
PS144	2005 (4)	2,500	KM#1064-1067	1,925	1,950
PS145	2005 (2)	—	P39, P40	—	300
PS146	2006 (13)	5,000	KM#986-991, 994, 1057-1062 Executive Proof Set, wooden case	—	100
PS147	2006 (13)	15,000	KM#986-991, 994, 1057-1062 Deluxe Proof Set	82.50	85.00
PS148	2006 (13)	30,000	KM#986-991, 994, 1057-1062 Standard Proof Set	65.00	65.00
PS149	2006 (5)	3,000	KM#1000a, 1012a, 1018a, 1039, 1063a	475	500
PS150	2006 (3)	1,750	KM#1001, 1002, 1072	1,015	1,025
PS151	2006 (4)	1,750	KM#1001-1003, 1072	2,091	2,100
PS152	2007	30,000		65.00	65.00

GREECE

The Hellenic (Greek) Republic is situated in southeastern Europe on the southern tip of the Balkan Peninsula. The republic includes many islands, the most important of which are Crete and the Ionian Islands. Greece (including islands) has an area of 50,944 sq. mi. (131,940 sq. km.) and a population of 10.3 million. Capital: Athens. Greece is still largely agricultural. Tobacco, cotton, fruit and wool are exported.

MINT MARKS
(a) - Paris, privy marks only
A - Paris
B - Vienna
BB – Strassburg
E – Madrid
F - Pessac
H - Heaton, Birmingham
K - Bordeaux
KN - King's Norton
(p) - Poissy – Thunderbolt
S – Vantaa (Suomi)
Anthemion – Greek National Mint, Athens

MONETARY SYSTEM
Commencing 1831
100 Lepta = 1 Drachma

REPUBLIC

DECIMAL COINAGE

KM# 132 10 DRACHMES
7.6000 g., Copper-Nickel, 26 mm. **Obv:** Atom design **Rev:** Head of Democritus left

Date	Mintage	F	VF	XF	Unc	BU
2002	—	—	0.25	0.50	1.25	2.50

EURO COINAGE

European Union Issues

The Greek Euro coinage series contains the denomination in Lepta as well.

KM# 181 EURO CENT
2.2700 g., Copper Plated Steel, 16.2 mm. **Subject:** Euro Coinage **Obv:** Ancient Athenian trireme **Obv. Designer:** George Stamatopoulos **Rev:** Denomination and globe **Rev. Designer:** Luc Luycx **Edge:** Plain

Date	Mintage	F	VF	XF	Unc	BU
2002	88,000,000	—	—	—	0.35	—
2002 F in star	15,000,000	—	—	—	1.25	—
2003	7,000,000	—	—	—	0.35	—
2003 Proof	—	—	—	—	—	—
2004	45,000,000	—	—	—	0.35	—
2005	—	—	—	—	0.35	—
2006	—	—	—	—	0.35	—
2007	—	—	—	—	0.35	—

KM# 182 2 EURO CENT
3.0300 g., Copper Plated Steel, 18.7 mm. **Subject:** Euro Coinage **Obv:** Corvette sailing ship **Obv. Designer:** George Stamatopoulos **Rev:** Denomination and globe **Rev. Designer:** Luc Luycx **Edge:** Grooved

Date	Mintage	F	VF	XF	Unc	BU
2002	172,000,000	—	—	—	0.50	—
2002 F in star	18,000,000	—	—	—	1.00	—
2003	9,000,000	—	—	—	0.50	—

Date	Mintage	F	VF	XF	Unc	BU
2003 Proof	—	—	—	—	—	—
2004	25,000,000	—	—	—	0.50	—
2005	—	—	—	—	0.50	—
2006	—	—	—	—	0.50	—
2007	—	—	—	—	0.50	—

KM# 183 5 EURO CENT
3.8600 g., Copper Plated Steel, 21.2 mm. **Subject:** Euro Coinage **Obv:** Freighter **Obv. Designer:** George Stamatopoulos **Rev:** Denomination and globe **Rev. Designer:** Luc Luyx **Edge:** Plain

Date	Mintage	F	VF	XF	Unc	BU
2002	288,000,000	—	—	—	1.00	—
2002 F in star	18,000,000	—	—	—	1.25	—
2003	400,000	—	—	—	1.00	—
2003 Proof	—	—	—	—	—	—
2004	250,000	—	—	—	1.00	—
2005	—	—	—	—	1.00	—
2006	—	—	—	—	1.00	—
2007	—	—	—	—	1.00	—

KM# 184 10 EURO CENT
4.0700 g., Brass, 19.7 mm. **Subject:** Euro Coinage **Obv:** Bust of Rhgas Feriaou's half right **Obv. Designer:** George Stamatopoulos **Rev:** Denomination and map **Rev. Designer:** Luc Luycx **Edge:** Reeded

Date	Mintage	F	VF	XF	Unc	BU
2002	257,000,000	—	—	—	1.25	—
2002 F in star	24,000,000	—	—	—	2.00	—
2003	330,000	—	—	—	1.25	—
2003 Proof	—	—	—	—	—	—
2004	—	—	—	—	1.25	—
2005	—	—	—	—	1.25	—
2006	—	—	—	—	1.25	—

KM# 211 10 EURO CENT
4.0700 g., Brass, 19.7 mm. **Subject:** Euro Coinage **Obv:** Bust of Rhgas Feriaou's half right **Obv. Designer:** George Stamatopoulos **Rev:** Relief map of Western Europe, stars, lines and value **Rev. Designer:** Luc Luycx **Edge:** Reeded

Date	Mintage	F	VF	XF	Unc	BU
2007	—	—	—	—	1.25	—

KM# 185 20 EURO CENT
5.7300 g., Brass, 22.1 mm. **Subject:** Euro Coinage **Obv:** Bust of John Kapodistrias half right **Obv. Designer:** George Stamatopoulos **Rev:** Denomination and map **Rev. Designer:** Luc Luycx **Edge:** Notched

Date	Mintage	F	VF	XF	Unc	BU
2002	370,000,000	—	—	—	1.25	—
2002 E in star	21,000,000	—	—	—	2.25	—
2003	330,000	—	—	—	1.25	—
2003 Proof	—	—	—	—	—	—
2004	400,000	—	—	—	1.25	—
2005	—	—	—	—	1.25	—
2006	—	—	—	—	1.25	—

KM# 212 20 EURO CENT
5.7300 g., Brass, 22.1 mm. **Subject:** Euro Coinage **Obv:** Bust of John Kapodistrias' half right **Obv. Designer:** George Stamatopoulos **Rev:** Relief map of Western Europe, stars, lines and value **Rev. Designer:** Luc Luycx **Edge:** Notched

Date	Mintage	F	VF	XF	Unc	BU
2007	—	—	—	—	1.25	—

KM# 186 50 EURO CENT
7.8100 g., Brass, 24.2 mm. **Subject:** Euro Coinage **Obv:** Bust of El. Venizelos half left **Obv. Designer:** George Stamatopoulos **Rev:** Denomination and map **Rev. Designer:** Luc Luycx **Edge:** Reeded

Date	Mintage	F	VF	XF	Unc	BU
2002	145,000,000	—	—	—	1.50	—
2002 F in star	18,000,000	—	—	—	2.50	—
2003	330,000	—	—	—	1.50	—
2003 Proof	—	—	—	—	—	—
2004	400,000	—	—	—	1.50	—
2005	—	—	—	—	1.50	—
2006	—	—	—	—	1.50	—

KM# 213 50 EURO CENT
7.8100 g., Brass, 24.2 mm. **Subject:** Euro Coinage **Obv:** Bust of El. Venizelos half left **Obv. Designer:** George Stamatopoulos **Rev:** Relief map of Western Europe, stars, lines and value **Rev. Designer:** Luc Luycx **Edge:** Reeded

Date	Mintage	F	VF	XF	Unc	BU
2007	—	—	—	—	1.50	—

KM# 187 EURO
7.5000 g., Bi-Metallic Copper-Nickel center in Brass ring, 23.2 mm. **Subject:** Euro Coinage **Obv:** Ancient Athenian coin design **Obv. Designer:** George Stamatopoulos **Rev:** Denomination and map **Rev. Designer:** Luc Luycx **Edge:** Reeded and plain sections

Date	Mintage	F	VF	XF	Unc	BU
2002	118,000,000	—	—	—	4.00	—
2002 S in star	15,000,000	—	—	—	6.00	—
2003	1,650,000	—	—	—	7.50	—
2003 Proof	—	—	—	—	—	—
2004	10,000,000	—	—	—	5.00	—
2005	—	—	—	—	5.00	—
2006	—	—	—	—	5.00	—

KM# 214 EURO
7.5000 g., Bi-Metallic Copper-Nickel center in Brass ring, 23.2 mm. **Subject:** Euro Coinage **Obv:** Ancient Athenian coin design **Obv. Designer:** George Stamatopoulos **Rev:** Relief map of Western Europe, stars, lines and value **Rev. Designer:** Luc Luycx **Edge:** Reeded and plain sections

Date	Mintage	F	VF	XF	Unc	BU
2007	—	—	—	—	4.00	—

KM# 188 2 EURO
8.5200 g., Bi-Metallic Brass center in Copper-Nickel ring, 25.7 mm. **Subject:** Euro Coinage **Obv:** Europa seated on a bull **Obv. Designer:** George Stamatopoulos **Rev:** Denomination and map **Rev. Designer:** Luc Luycx **Edge:** Reeded with Greek letters and stars

Date	Mintage	F	VF	XF	Unc	BU
2002	162,000,000	—	—	—	4.00	—
2002 S in star	6,000,000	—	—	—	6.50	—
2003	540,000	—	—	—	4.00	—
2003 Proof	—	—	—	—	—	—
2004	—	—	—	—	4.00	—
Note: In sets only						
2005	—	—	—	—	4.00	—
2006	—	—	—	—	4.00	—

KM# 209 2 EURO
8.5200 g., Bi-Metallic **Ring Composition:** Copper Nickel **Center Composition:** Brass, 25.7 mm. **Subject:** 2004 Olympics **Obv:** Discus thrower **Rev:** Denomination and map **Edge:** Reeded and lettered **Edge Lettering:** Greek

Date	Mintage	F	VF	XF	Unc	BU
2004	50,000,000	—	—	—	4.00	6.00

KM# 215 2 EURO
8.5200 g., Bi-Metallic Brass center in Copper-Nickel ring, 25.7 mm. **Subject:** Euro Coinage **Obv:** Europa seated on a bull **Obv. Designer:** George Stamatopoulos **Rev:** Relief map of Western Europe, stars, lines and value **Rev. Designer:** Luc Luycx **Edge:** Reeded with Greek letters and stars

Date	Mintage	F	VF	XF	Unc	BU
2007	—	—	—	—	—	9.00
Note: In sets only						

KM# 216 2 EURO
8.5500 g., Bi-Metallic Brass center in Copper-Nickel ring, 25.72 mm. **Subject:** 50th Anniversary - Treaty of Rome **Obv:** Open treaty book **Rev:** Large value at left, modified outline of Europe at right **Edge:** Reeded and lettered

Date	Mintage	F	VF	XF	Unc	BU
2007	—	—	—	—	—	9.00

KM# 191 10 EURO
34.0000 g., 0.9250 Silver 1.0111 oz. ASW, 40 mm. **Subject:** Olympics **Obv:** Olympic rings in wreath above value within circle of stars **Rev:** Ancient and modern discus throwers **Edge:** Plain

Date	Mintage	F	VF	XF	Unc	BU
ND(2003) Proof	68,000	Value: 60.00				

KM# 193 10 EURO
34.0000 g., 0.9250 Silver 1.0111 oz. ASW, 40 mm. **Subject:** Olympics **Obv:** Olympic rings in wreath above value within circle of stars **Rev:** Ancient and modern javelin throwers **Edge:** Plain

Date	Mintage	F	VF	XF	Unc	BU
ND(2003) Proof	68,000	Value: 60.00				

KM# 194 10 EURO
34.0000 g., 0.9250 Silver 1.0111 oz. ASW, 40 mm. **Subject:** Olympics **Obv:** Olympic rings in wreath above value within circle of stars **Rev:** Ancient and modern long jumpers **Edge:** Plain

Date	Mintage	F	VF	XF	Unc	BU
ND(2003) Proof	68,000	Value: 60.00				

KM# 196 10 EURO
34.0000 g., 0.9250 Silver 1.0111 oz. ASW, 40 mm. **Subject:** Olympics **Obv:** Olympic rings in wreath above value within circle of stars **Rev:** Ancient and modern relay runners **Edge:** Plain

Date	Mintage	F	VF	XF	Unc	BU
ND(2003) Proof	68,000	Value: 60.00				

KM# 197 10 EURO
34.0000 g., 0.9250 Silver 1.0111 oz. ASW, 40 mm. **Subject:** Olympics **Obv:** Olympic rings in wreath above value within circle of stars **Rev:** Ancient and modern horsemen **Edge:** Plain

Date	Mintage	F	VF	XF	Unc	BU
ND(2003) Proof	68,000	Value: 60.00				

KM# 199 10 EURO
34.0000 g., 0.9250 Silver 1.0111 oz. ASW, 40 mm. **Subject:** Olympics **Obv:** Olympic rings in wreath above value within circle of stars **Rev:** Modern ribbon dancer and two ancient female acrobats **Edge:** Plain

Date	Mintage	F	VF	XF	Unc	BU
ND(2003) Proof	68,000	Value: 60.00				

KM# 200 10 EURO
34.0000 g., 0.9250 Silver 1.0111 oz. ASW, 40 mm. **Subject:** Olympics **Obv:** Olympic rings in wreath above value within a circle of stars **Rev:** Ancient and modern female swimmers **Edge:** Plain

Date	Mintage	F	VF	XF	Unc	BU
ND(2003) Plain	68,000	Value: 60.00				

KM# 208 10 EURO
9.7500 g., 0.9250 Silver 0.2899 oz. ASW, 28.25 mm. **Subject:** Greek Presidency of E. U. **Obv:** National arms in wreath above value **Rev:** Stylized document design **Edge:** Notched

Date	Mintage	F	VF	XF	Unc	BU
2003 Proof	50,000	Value: 55.00				

KM# 190 10 EURO
34.0000 g., 0.9250 Silver 1.0111 oz. ASW, 40 mm. **Subject:** Olympics **Obv:** Olympic rings in wreath above value within circle of stars **Rev:** Ancient and modern runners **Edge:** Plain **Note:** Olympics

Date	Mintage	F	VF	XF	Unc	BU
ND (2003) Proof	68,000	Value: 60.00				

KM# 202 10 EURO
34.0000 g., 0.9250 Silver 1.0111 oz. ASW, 40 mm. **Subject:** Olympics **Obv:** Olympic rings in wreath above value within circle of stars **Rev:** Ancient and modern weight lifters **Edge:** Plain

Date	Mintage	F	VF	XF	Unc	BU
ND(2004) Proof	68,000	Value: 60.00				

KM# 203 10 EURO
34.0000 g., 0.9250 Silver 1.0111 oz. ASW, 40 mm. **Subject:** Olympics **Obv:** Olympic rings in wreath above value within circle of stars **Rev:** Ancient and modern wrestlers **Edge:** Plain

Date	Mintage	F	VF	XF	Unc	BU
ND(2004) Proof	68,000	Value: 60.00				

KM# 205 10 EURO
34.0000 g., 0.9250 Silver 1.0111 oz. ASW, 40 mm. **Subject:** Olympics **Obv:** Olympic rings in wreath above value within circle of stars **Rev:** Ancient and modern handball players **Edge:** Plain

Date	Mintage	F	VF	XF	Unc	BU
ND(2004) Proof	68,000	Value: 60.00				

KM# 206 10 EURO
34.0000 g., 0.9250 Silver 1.0111 oz. ASW, 40 mm. **Subject:** Olympics **Obv:** Olympic rings in wreath above value within circle of stars **Rev:** Ancient and modern soccer players **Edge:** Plain

Date	Mintage	F	VF	XF	Unc	BU
ND(2004) Proof	68,000	Value: 60.00				

KM# 217 10 EURO
9.7500 g., 0.9250 Silver 0.2899 oz. ASW **Obv:** National arms above stylized flowers **Rev:** Four Titans above flowers in camp

Date	Mintage	F	VF	XF	Unc	BU
2005 Proof	25,000	Value: 45.00				

KM# 218 10 EURO
9.7500 g., 0.9250 Silver 0.2899 oz. ASW, 28.25 mm. **Subject:** PATRA - European Capitol of Culture - Achaia **Obv:** National arms at upper right, stylized bridge below **Rev:** PATRA logo **Edge:** Plain

Date	Mintage	F	VF	XF	Unc	BU
2006 Proof	—	Value: 50.00				

KM# 219 10 EURO
34.0000 g., 0.9250 Silver 1.0111 oz. ASW, 40.00 mm. **Obv:** National arms above stylizes flowers **Rev:** Outline of Greece at left, statue of Zeus, flowers at right **Edge:** Plain

Date	Mintage	F	VF	XF	Unc	BU
2006 Proof	5,000	Value: 55.00				

KM# 220 10 EURO
34.0000 g., 0.9250 Silver 1.0111 oz. ASW, 40.00 mm. **Subject:** National Parks - Mount Olympus _ International Biosphere Reserve **Obv:** National arms above stylized flowers **Rev:** Archaeological outline of Dion City above landscape **Edge:** Plain

Date	Mintage	F	VF	XF	Unc	BU
2006 Proof	5,000	Value: 55.00				

KM# 221 10 EURO

34.0000 g., 0.9250 Silver 1.0111 oz. ASW, 40.00 mm. **Subject:** National Parks - Arkoudorema River in Southern Pindos - Valia Kalda **Obv:** National arms on stylized tree **Rev:** Outlined map at upper left, bird perched on stalk, flowers at center right **Edge:** Plain

Date	Mintage	F	VF	XF	Unc	BU
2007 Proof	5,000	Value: 60.00				

KM# 222 10 EURO

34.0000 g., 0.9250 Silver 1.0111 oz. ASW, 40.00 mm. **Subject:** National Parks - Valia Kalda - Southern Pindos **Obv:** National arms on stylized tree **Rev:** Tree line **Edge:** Plain

Date	Mintage	F	VF	XF	Unc	BU
2007 Proof	5,000	—	—	—	—	—

KM# 223 10 EURO

9.7500 g., 0.9250 Silver 0.2899 oz. ASW, 28.25 mm. **Subject:** 30th Anniversary Death of Maria Callas, Operatic Soprano **Obv:** National arms above denomination, facsimile signature below, music scores in background **Rev:** Bust of M. Callas right **Edge:** Plain **Shape:** Spanish Flower

Date	Mintage	F	VF	XF	Unc	BU
2007 Proof	5,000	—	—	—	—	—

KM# 224 10 EURO

9.7500 g., 0.9250 Silver 0.2899 oz. ASW, 28.25 mm. **Subject:** 50th Anniversary death of Nikos Kazantzakis, Author **Obv:** National arms above denomination, facsimile signature below **Rev:** Head of N. Kazantzakis facing 3/4 left **Edge:** Plain **Shape:** Spanish Flower

Date	Mintage	F	VF	XF	Unc	BU
2007 Proof	5,000	—	—	—	—	—

KM# 210 20 EURO

24.0000 g., 0.9250 Silver 0.7137 oz. ASW, 37 mm. **Subject:** Bank of Greece 75th Anniversary **Obv:** Value **Rev:** Flag

Date	Mintage	F	VF	XF	Unc	BU
2003	10,000	—	—	—	—	27.00
2003 Proof	1,000	Value: 55.00				

KM# 192 100 EURO

0.9999 Gold, 25 mm. **Subject:** Olympics **Obv:** Olympic rings in wreath above value within circle of stars **Rev:** Knossos Palace **Edge:** Plain

Date	Mintage	F	VF	XF	Unc	BU
ND(2003) Proof	28,000	Value: 570				

KM# 195 100 EURO

10.0000 g., 0.9999 Gold 0.3215 oz. AGW, 25 mm. **Subject:** Olympics **Obv:** Olympic rings in wreath above value within circle of stars **Rev:** Krypte archway **Edge:** Plain

Date	Mintage	F	VF	XF	Unc	BU
ND(2003) Proof	28,000	Value: 570				

KM# 198 100 EURO

10.0000 g., 0.9999 Gold 0.3215 oz. AGW, 25 mm. **Subject:** Olympics **Obv:** Olympic rings in wreath above value within circle of stars **Rev:** Panathenean Stadium **Edge:** Plain

Date	Mintage	F	VF	XF	Unc	BU
ND(2003) Proof	28,000	Value: 570				

KM# 201 100 EURO

10.0000 g., 0.9999 Gold 0.3215 oz. AGW, 25 mm. **Subject:** Olympics **Obv:** Olympic rings in wreath above value within circle of stars **Rev:** Zappeion Mansion **Edge:** Plain

Date	Mintage	F	VF	XF	Unc	BU
ND(2003) Proof	28,000	Value: 570				

KM# 204 100 EURO

10.0000 g., 0.9999 Gold 0.3215 oz. AGW, 25 mm. **Subject:** Olympics **Obv:** Olympic rings in wreath above value within circle of stars **Rev:** Acropolis **Edge:** Plain

Date	Mintage	F	VF	XF	Unc	BU
ND(2004) Proof	28,000	Value: 570				

KM# 207 100 EURO

10.0000 g., 0.9999 Gold 0.3215 oz. AGW, 25 mm. **Subject:** Olympics **Obv:** Olympic rings in wreath above value within circle of stars **Rev:** Academy of Athens **Edge:** Plain

Date	Mintage	F	VF	XF	Unc	BU
ND(2004) Proof	28,000	Value: 570				

MINT SETS

KM#	Date	Mintage	Identification	Issue Price	Mkt Val
MS6	2002 (8)	50,000	KM#181-188	—	50.00
MS7	2002F (8)	5,000	KM#181-188 Issued by Ministry of Finance	—	—
MS8	2003 (8)	—	KM#181-188	—	45.00
MS9	2003 (9)	—	KM#181-188, 208	—	—
MS11	2004 (8)	20,000	KM#181-188 2004 Discobole commemorating Olympic Games in Athens	—	45.00
MS12	2005 (8)	25,000	KM#181-188	—	45.00
MS13	2005 (9)	25,000	KM#181-188, 220 Mount Olympus as a National Park	—	—
MS14	2006 (9)	25,000	KM#181-188 (2005), 220 Aegina - Korinth set	28.00	—
MS15	2006 (9)	25,000	KM#181-188, 218 Patras - Cultural Capital of Europe	50.00	—
MS16	2007 (8)	15,000	KM#181-183, 211-215, 224 Ancient Coins of the Aegean Sea	—	—
MS17	2007 (9)	15,000	KM#181-183, 211-215, 224 Nikos Kazantzakis, 1885-1957, Author - Zorba the Greek	50.00	—
MS18	2007 (9)	15,000	KM#181-183, 211-215, 223 Maria Callas, 1923-1977, Greek Operatic Soprano	50.00	—

FRENCH OVERSEAS DEPARTMENT

ESSAIS

KM# E8 20 EURO

7.8000 g., 0.9990 Gold 0.2505 oz. AGW, 27 mm. **Obv:** Sun across sugar cane **Rev:** Brown pelican **Edge:** Reeded

Date	Mintage
	300 Value: 350

MINT SETS

KM#	Date	Mintage	Identification	Issue Price	Mkt Val
XMS1	2005 (8)	2,500	X#Pn1-Pn8	—	30.00

GUATEMALA

The Republic of Guatemala, the northernmost of the five Central American republics, has an area of 42,042 sq. mi. (108,890 sq. km.) and a population of 10.7 million. Capital: Guatemala City. The economy of Guatemala is heavily dependent on agriculture, however, the country is rich in nickel resources which are being developed. Coffee, cotton and bananas are exported.

Guatemala, once the site of an ancient Mayan civilization, was conquered by Pedro de Alvarado, the resourceful lieutenant of Cortes who undertook the conquest from Mexico. Cruel but strategically skillful, he progressed rapidly along the Pacific coastal lowlands to the highland plain of Quetzaltenango where the decisive battle for Guatemala was fought. After routing the Indian forces, he established the city of Guatemala in 1524. The Spanish Captaincy-General of Guatemala included all Central America but Panama. Guatemala declared its independence of Spain in 1821 and was absorbed into the Mexican empire of Augustin Iturbide (1822-23). From 1823 to 1839 Guatemala was a constituent state of the Central American Republic. Upon dissolution of that confederation, Guatemala proclaimed itself an independent republic. Like El Salvador, Guatemala suffered from internal strife between right-wing, US-backed military government and leftist indigenous peoples from ca. 1954 to ca. 1997.

MINT MARKS

H, (H) - Heaton, Birmingham
(KN) – Birmingham, King's Norton Mint
(L) – London, Royal Mint
(P) – Philadelphia, USA
NG - ??? 1992
(S) – San Francisco, USA

REPUBLIC

REFORM COINAGE

100 Centavos = 1 Quetzal

KM# 283 50 CENTAVOS

5.5400 g., Brass, 24.2 mm. **Obv:** National arms **Rev:** Whitenun orchid (lycaste skinneri var. alba orchidaceae) **Edge:** Reeded

Date	Mintage	F	VF	XF	Unc	BU
2001	—	—	—	0.50	1.25	1.75

KM# 284 QUETZAL

11.1000 g., Brass, 28.9 mm. **Obv:** National arms **Rev:** PAX above stylized dove **Edge:** Reeded

Date	Mintage	F	VF	XF	Unc	BU
2001 Small letters	—	—	—	1.00	2.50	3.00

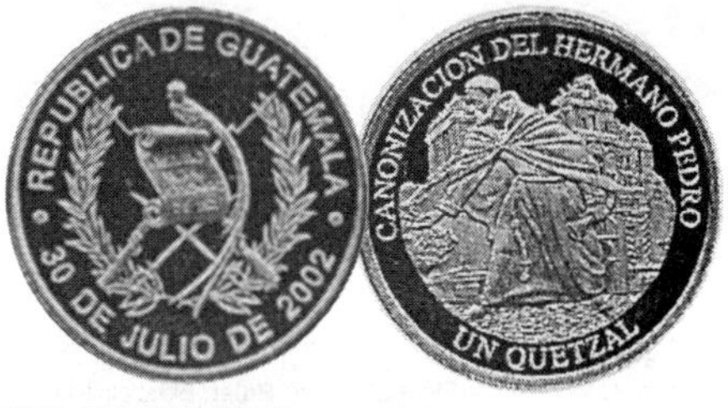

KM# 287 QUETZAL

31.1035 g., 0.9999 Silver 0.9999 oz. ASW, 30 mm. **Subject:** Canonization of Brother Pedro Betancourt **Obv:** National arms **Rev:** Standing monk **Edge:** Plain

Date	Mintage	F	VF	XF	Unc	BU
ND(2002) Proof	6,000	Value: 50.00				

KM# 288 QUETZAL

Silver **Subject:** Discovery of the Americas **Obv:** Shields **Rev:** Nature with fish in canoe

Date	Mintage	F	VF	XF	Unc	BU
2002 Proof	—	Value: 55.00				

GUERNSEY

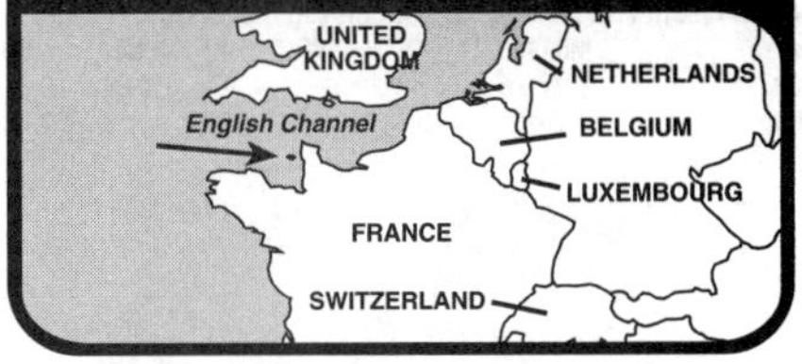

The Bailiwick of Guernsey, a British crown dependency located in the English Channel 30 miles (48 km.) west of Normandy, France, has an area of 30 sq. mi. (194 sq. km.)(including the isles of Alderney, Jethou, Herm, Brechou, and Sark), and a population of 54,000. Capital: St. Peter Port. Agriculture and cattle breeding are the main occupations.

Militant monks from the duchy of Normandy established the first permanent settlements on Guernsey prior to the Norman invasion of England, but the prevalence of prehistoric monuments suggests an earlier occupancy. The island, the only part of the duchy of Normandy belonging to the British crown, has been a possession of Britain since the Norman Conquest of 1066. During the Anglo-French wars, the harbors of Guernsey were employed in the building and out-fitting of ships for the English privateers preying on French shipping. Guernsey is administered by its own laws and customs. Unless the island is mentioned specifically, acts passed by the British Parliament are not applicable to Guernsey. During World War II, German troops occupied the island from June 30, 1940 till May 9,1945.

RULERS

British

MINT MARKS

H - Heaton, Birmingham

MONETARY SYSTEM

8 Doubles = 1 Penny
12 Pence = 1 Shilling
5 Shillings = 1 Crown
20 Shillings = 1 Pound

1 Stem

3 Stems

BRITISH DEPENDENCY

DECIMAL COINAGE

100 Pence = 1 Pound

KM# 89 PENNY

3.5500 g., Copper Plated Steel, 20.3 mm. **Ruler:** Elizabeth II **Obv:** Head with tiara right **Obv. Designer:** Ian Rank-Broadley **Rev:** Edible crab **Rev. Designer:** Robert Elderton

Date	Mintage	F	VF	XF	Unc	BU
2003	1,302,600	—	—	—	0.35	1.00
2006	1,731,000	—	—	—	0.35	0.75

KM# 96 2 PENCE
7.2000 g., Copper Plated Steel, 25.9 mm. **Ruler:** Elizabeth II **Obv:** Head with tiara, shield at left **Obv. Designer:** Ian Rank-Broadley **Rev:** Guernsey cows **Rev. Designer:** Robert Elderton **Edge:** Plain

Date	Mintage	F	VF	XF	Unc	BU
2003	662,600	—	—	—	0.50	1.00
2006	1,322,000	—	—	—	0.50	1.00

KM# 97 5 PENCE
3.2600 g., Copper-Nickel, 18 mm. **Ruler:** Elizabeth II **Obv:** Head with tiara right **Obv. Designer:** Ian Rank-Broadley **Rev:** Sailboat **Rev. Designer:** Robert Elderton **Edge:** Reeded

Date	Mintage	F	VF	XF	Unc	BU
2003	292,600	—	—	—	0.45	0.65
2006	1,217,000	—	—	—	0.45	0.65

KM# 149 10 PENCE
6.5000 g., Copper-Nickel, 24.5 mm. **Ruler:** Elizabeth II **Obv:** Head with tiara right **Obv. Designer:** Ian Rank-Broadley **Rev:** Tomato plant **Rev. Designer:** Robert Elderton **Edge:** Reeded

Date	Mintage	F	VF	XF	Unc	BU
2003	32,600	—	—	—	0.60	0.85
2006	26,000	—	—	—	0.60	0.85

KM# 90 20 PENCE
5.1000 g., Copper-Nickel, 21.4 mm. **Ruler:** Elizabeth II **Obv:** Head with tiara right, small arms at left **Obv. Designer:** Ian Rank-Broadley **Rev:** Island map within cogwheel **Rev. Designer:** Robert Elderton **Shape:** 7-sided

Date	Mintage	F	VF	XF	Unc	BU
2003	732,600	—	—	—	0.90	1.25
2006	16,250	—	—	—	0.90	1.25

KM# 145 50 PENCE
7.9700 g., Copper-Nickel, 27.3 mm. **Ruler:** Elizabeth II **Subject:** Coronation Jubilee **Obv:** Head with tiara right **Obv. Designer:** Ian Rank-Broadley **Rev:** Queen on horseback **Edge:** Plain **Shape:** 7-sided

Date	Mintage	F	VF	XF	Unc	BU
2003	—	—	—	—	1.50	2.50

KM# 145a 50 PENCE
8.1000 g., 0.9250 Silver 0.2409 oz. ASW, 27.3 mm. **Ruler:** Elizabeth II **Subject:** Coronation Jubilee **Obv:** Head with tiara right **Obv. Designer:** Ian Rank-Broadley **Rev:** Queen on horseback **Edge:** Plain **Shape:** 7-sided

Date	Mintage	F	VF	XF	Unc	BU
2003 Proof	—	Value: 25.00				

KM# 146 50 PENCE
7.9700 g., Copper-Nickel, 27.3 mm. **Ruler:** Elizabeth II **Subject:** Coronation Jubilee **Obv:** Head with tiara right **Rev:** Queen on throne **Edge:** Plain **Shape:** 7-sided

Date	Mintage	F	VF	XF	Unc	BU
2003	—	—	—	—	1.50	2.50

KM# 146a 50 PENCE
8.1000 g., 0.9250 Silver 0.2409 oz. ASW, 27.3 mm. **Ruler:** Elizabeth II **Subject:** Coronation Jubilee **Obv:** Head with tiara right **Rev:** Queen on throne **Edge:** Plain **Shape:** 7-sided

Date	Mintage	F	VF	XF	Unc	BU
2003 Proof	—	Value: 25.00				

KM# 147 50 PENCE
7.9700 g., Copper-Nickel, 27.3 mm. **Ruler:** Elizabeth II **Subject:** Coronation Jubilee **Obv:** Head with tiara right **Rev:** Crown **Edge:** Plain **Shape:** 7-sided

Date	Mintage	F	VF	XF	Unc	BU
2003	—	—	—	—	1.50	2.50
2006	—	—	—	—	1.50	2.50

KM# 147a 50 PENCE
8.1000 g., 0.9250 Silver 0.2409 oz. ASW, 27.3 mm. **Ruler:** Elizabeth II **Subject:** Coronation Jubilee **Obv:** Head with tiara right **Rev:** Crown **Edge:** Plain **Shape:** 7-sided

Date	Mintage	F	VF	XF	Unc	BU
2003 Proof	—	Value: 25.00				

KM# 148 50 PENCE
7.9700 g., Copper-Nickel, 27.3 mm. **Ruler:** Elizabeth II **Subject:** Coronation Jubilee **Obv:** Head with tiara right **Rev:** Crowned ERII monogram **Edge:** Plain **Shape:** 7-sided

Date	Mintage	F	VF	XF	Unc	BU
2003	—	—	—	—	1.50	2.50

KM# 148a 50 PENCE
8.1000 g., 0.9250 Silver 0.2409 oz. ASW, 27.3 mm. **Ruler:** Elizabeth II **Subject:** Coronation Jubilee **Obv:** Head with tiara right **Rev:** Crowned ERII monogram **Edge:** Plain **Shape:** 7-sided

Date	Mintage	F	VF	XF	Unc	BU
2003 Proof	—	Value: 25.00				

KM# 156 50 PENCE
7.9700 g., Copper-Nickel, 27.3 mm. **Ruler:** Elizabeth II **Obv:** Head with tiara right **Rev:** Crossed flowers **Edge:** Plain **Shape:** 7-sided

Date	Mintage	F	VF	XF	Unc	BU
2003	—	—	—	—	1.75	2.75
2006	19,000	—	—	—	1.75	2.75

KM# 110 POUND
9.5000 g., Nickel-Brass, 22.5 mm. **Ruler:** Elizabeth II **Subject:** Circulation Type **Obv:** Head with tiara right **Obv. Designer:** Ian Rank-Broadley **Rev:** Denomination **Edge:** Reeded

Date	Mintage	F	VF	XF	Unc	BU
2001	175,000	—	—	—	2.50	3.50
2003	46,600	—	—	—	2.50	3.50
2006	11,000	—	—	—	2.50	3.50

KM# 111 POUND
9.5000 g., 0.9250 Silver 0.2825 oz. ASW, 22.5 mm. **Subject:** Queen's 75th Birthday **Obv:** Head with tiara right **Rev:** Queen's portrait in wreath **Edge:** Reeded

Date	Mintage	F	VF	XF	Unc	BU
2001 Proof	50,000	Value: 25.00				

KM# 142 POUND
30.9300 g., 0.9250 Silver 0.9198 oz. ASW, 38.6 mm. **Ruler:** Elizabeth II **Obv:** Head with tiara right **Obv. Designer:** Ian Rank-Broadley **Rev:** 1/2-bust of William, Duke of Normandy holding sword at left **Edge:** Reeded

Date	Mintage	F	VF	XF	Unc	BU
2002	—	—	—	—	35.00	45.00

KM# 83 2 POUNDS
12.0000 g., Bi-Metallic Copper-Nickel center in Nickel-Brass ring, 28.35 mm. **Ruler:** Elizabeth II **Obv:** Head with tiara right **Obv. Designer:** Ian Rank-Broadley **Rev:** Latent image arms on cross **Edge:** BAILIWICK OF GUERNSEY

Date	Mintage	F	VF	XF	Unc	BU
2003	19,600	—	—	—	8.50	10.00
2006	9,500	—	—	—	8.50	10.00

KM# 106 5 POUNDS
28.2800 g., Copper-Nickel, 38.6 mm. **Ruler:** Elizabeth II **Subject:** Queen Victoria Centennial **Obv:** Head with tiara right **Obv. Designer:** Ian Rank-Broadley **Rev:** Bust of Queen Victoria left **Edge:** Reeded

Date	Mintage	F	VF	XF	Unc	BU
2001	12,754	—	—	—	7.50	8.50
2001 Proof	30,000	Value: 20.00				

KM# 106a 5 POUNDS
28.2800 g., 0.9250 Silver 0.8410 oz. ASW, 38.6 mm. **Ruler:** Elizabeth II **Subject:** Queen Victoria 1837-1901 **Obv:** Head with tiara right **Obv. Designer:** Ian Rank-Broadley **Rev:** Bust of Queen Victoria left **Edge:** Reeded

Date	Mintage	F	VF	XF	Unc	BU
2001 Proof	10,000	Value: 47.50				

KM# 108 5 POUNDS
28.0000 g., Copper-Nickel, 38.6 mm. **Ruler:** Elizabeth II **Subject:** Queen Elizabeth's 75th Birthday **Obv:** Head with tiara right **Obv. Designer:** Ian Rank-Broadley **Rev:** Queen's portrait in wreath **Edge:** Reeded

Date	Mintage	F	VF	XF	Unc	BU
2001	14,000	—	—	—	6.00	7.00

KM# 108a 5 POUNDS
28.2800 g., 0.9250 Silver 0.8410 oz. ASW, 38.6 mm. **Ruler:** Elizabeth II **Subject:** Queen's 75th Birthday **Obv:** Head with tiara right **Obv. Designer:** Ian Rank-Broadley **Rev:** Queen's portrait in wreath **Edge:** Reeded

Date	Mintage	F	VF	XF	Unc	BU
2001 Proof	20,000	Value: 55.00				

KM# 114 5 POUNDS
28.2800 g., Copper-Nickel, 38.6 mm. **Ruler:** Elizabeth II **Subject:** 19th Century Monarchy **Obv:** Head with tiara right **Obv. Designer:** Ian Rank-Broadley **Rev:** Four portraits **Edge:** Reeded

Date	Mintage	F	VF	XF	Unc	BU
2001	5,700	—	—	—	11.50	12.50

KM# 114a 5 POUNDS
28.2800 g., 0.9250 Silver 0.8410 oz. ASW, 38.6 mm. **Ruler:** Elizabeth II **Obv:** Head with tiara right **Obv. Designer:** Ian Rank-Broadley **Rev:** Four portraits **Edge:** Reeded

Date	Mintage	F	VF	XF	Unc	BU
2001 Proof	10,000	Value: 55.00				

KM# 115 5 POUNDS
1.1300 g., 0.9170 Gold 0.0333 oz. AGW, 13.9 mm. **Ruler:** Elizabeth II **Subject:** 19th Century Monarchy **Obv:** Head with tiara right **Obv. Designer:** Ian Rank-Broadley **Rev:** Four portraits **Edge:** Reeded

Date	Mintage	F	VF	XF	Unc	BU
2001 Proof	—	Value: 65.00				

KM# 117 5 POUNDS
1.1300 g., 0.9170 Gold 0.0333 oz. AGW, 13.9 mm. **Ruler:** Elizabeth II **Subject:** Queen Victoria 1837-1901 **Obv:** Head with tiara right **Obv. Designer:** Ian Rank-Broadley **Rev:** Queen Victoria's portrait **Edge:** Reeded

Date	Mintage	F	VF	XF	Unc	BU
2001 Proof	300	Value: 65.00				

KM# 118 5 POUNDS
1.1300 g., 0.9170 Gold 0.0333 oz. AGW, 13.9 mm. **Ruler:** Elizabeth II **Subject:** Queen's 75th Birthday **Obv:** Head with tiara right **Obv. Designer:** Ian Rank-Broadley **Rev:** Queen's portrait in wreath **Edge:** Reeded

Date	Mintage	F	VF	XF	Unc	BU
2001 Proof	250	Value: 65.00				

KM# 114b 5 POUNDS
39.9400 g., 0.9166 Gold 1.1770 oz. AGW, 38.6 mm. **Ruler:** Elizabeth II **Subject:** 19th Century Monarchy **Obv:** Head with tiara right **Obv. Designer:** Ian Rank-Broadley **Rev:** Four royal portraits **Edge:** Reeded

Date	Mintage	F	VF	XF	Unc	BU
2001 Proof	200	Value: 900				

KM# 119 5 POUNDS
27.7100 g., Copper-Nickel, 38.6 mm. **Ruler:** Elizabeth II **Subject:** The Golden Jubilee **Obv:** Head with tiara right **Obv. Designer:** Ian Rank-Broadley **Rev:** The queen in her coach **Edge:** Reeded

Date	Mintage	F	VF	XF	Unc	BU
2002	9,250	—	—	—	16.50	18.00

KM# 119a 5 POUNDS
28.2800 g., Gold-Plated Base Metal Gold plated copper-nickel, 38.6 mm. **Ruler:** Elizabeth II **Subject:** Golden Jubilee **Obv:** Head with tiara right **Obv. Designer:** Ian Rank-Broadley **Rev:** Queen in coach **Edge:** Reeded

Date	Mintage	F	VF	XF	Unc	BU
2002	50,000	—	—	—	15.00	16.50

KM# 119b 5 POUNDS
28.2800 g., 0.9250 Silver 0.8410 oz. ASW, 38.6 mm. **Ruler:** Elizabeth II **Subject:** Queen's Golden Jubilee **Obv:** Head with tiara right **Obv. Designer:** Ian Rank-Broadley **Rev:** Queen in her coach **Edge:** Reeded **Note:** Previous KM#119a.

Date	Mintage	F	VF	XF	Unc	BU
2002 Proof	20,000	Value: 50.00				

KM# 119c 5 POUNDS
39.9400 g., 0.9166 Gold 1.1770 oz. AGW, 38.6 mm. **Ruler:** Elizabeth II **Subject:** Golden Jubilee **Obv:** Head with tiara right **Obv. Designer:** Ian Rank-Broadley **Rev:** Queen in coach **Edge:** Reeded

Date	Mintage	F	VF	XF	Unc	BU
2002 Proof	250	Value: 875				

KM# 121 5 POUNDS
27.7100 g., Copper Nickel, 38.6 mm. **Ruler:** Elizabeth II **Subject:** Queen's Golden Jubilee **Obv:** Head with tiara right **Obv. Designer:** Ian Rank-Broadley **Rev:** Trooping the Colors scene **Edge:** Reeded

Date	Mintage	F	VF	XF	Unc	BU
2002	2,000	—	—	—	17.50	20.00

KM# 121a 5 POUNDS
28.2800 g., 0.9250 Silver 0.8410 oz. ASW, 38.6 mm. **Ruler:** Elizabeth II **Subject:** Queen's Golden Jubilee **Obv:** Head with tiara right **Obv. Designer:** Ian Rank-Broadley **Rev:** Trooping the Colors scene **Edge:** Reeded

Date	Mintage	F	VF	XF	Unc	BU
2002 Proof	20,000	Value: 50.00				

KM# 121b 5 POUNDS
39.9400 g., 0.9166 Gold 1.1770 oz. AGW, 38.6 mm. **Ruler:** Elizabeth II **Subject:** Golden Jubilee **Obv:** Head with tiara right **Obv. Designer:** Ian Rank-Broadley **Rev:** Trooping the Colors scene **Edge:** Reeded

Date	Mintage	F	VF	XF	Unc	BU
2002 Proof	250	Value: 875				

KM# 122 5 POUNDS
28.2800 g., Copper Nickel, 38.6 mm. **Ruler:** Elizabeth II **Subject:** Princess Diana **Obv:** Head with tiara right **Obv. Designer:** Ian Rank-Broadley **Rev:** World and children behind cameo portrait of Diana **Edge:** Reeded

Date	Mintage	F	VF	XF	Unc	BU
2002	4,231	—	—	—	13.50	15.00

KM# 122a 5 POUNDS
28.2800 g., 0.9250 Silver 0.8410 oz. ASW **Ruler:** Elizabeth II **Subject:** Princess Diana **Obv:** Head with tiara right **Obv. Designer:** Ian Rank-Broadley **Rev:** World and children behind Diana's cameo portrait **Edge:** Reeded

Date	Mintage	F	VF	XF	Unc	BU
2002 Proof	20,000	Value: 45.00				

KM# 122b 5 POUNDS
39.9400 g., 0.9167 Gold 1.1771 oz. AGW, 1.1771 mm. **Ruler:** Elizabeth II **Subject:** Princess Diana **Obv:** Head with tiara right **Obv. Designer:** Ian Rank-Broadley **Rev:** World and children behind Diana's cameo portrait **Edge:** Reeded

Date	Mintage	F	VF	XF	Unc	BU
2002 Proof	100	Value: 950				

KM# 124 5 POUNDS
28.2800 g., Copper Nickel, 38.6 mm. **Ruler:** Elizabeth II **Subject:** 18th Century British Monarchy **Obv:** Head with tiara right **Obv. Designer:** Ian Rank-Broadley **Rev:** Five royal portraits **Edge:** Reeded

Date	Mintage	F	VF	XF	Unc	BU
2002	1,300	—	—	—	15.00	16.50

KM# 124a 5 POUNDS
28.2800 g., 0.9250 Silver 0.8410 oz. ASW, 38.6 mm. **Ruler:** Elizabeth II **Subject:** 18th Century British Monarchy **Obv:** Head with tiara right **Obv. Designer:** Ian Rank-Broadley **Rev:** Five royal portraits **Edge:** Reeded

Date	Mintage	F	VF	XF	Unc	BU
2002 Proof	10,000	Value: 50.00				

KM# 124b 5 POUNDS
39.9400 g., 0.9166 Gold 1.1770 oz. AGW, 38.6 mm. **Ruler:** Elizabeth II **Subject:** 18th Century British Monarchy **Obv:** Head with tiara right **Obv. Designer:** Ian Rank-Broadley **Rev:** Five royal portraits **Edge:** Reeded

Date	Mintage	F	VF	XF	Unc	BU
2002 Proof	200	Value: 900				

KM# 125 5 POUNDS
1.1300 g., 0.9166 Gold 0.0333 oz. AGW, 13.9 mm. **Ruler:** Elizabeth II **Subject:** 18th Century British Monarchy **Obv:** Head with tiara right **Obv. Designer:** Ian Rank-Broadley **Rev:** Five royal portraits **Edge:** Reeded **Note:** Prev. KM#124b.

Date	Mintage	F	VF	XF	Unc	BU
2002 Proof	55	Value: 70.00				

KM# 127 5 POUNDS
28.2800 g., Copper-Nickel, 38.6 mm. **Ruler:** Elizabeth II **Subject:** Queen Mother **Obv:** Head with tiara right **Obv. Designer:** Ian Rank-Broadley **Rev:** The late Queen Mother's portrait **Edge:** Reeded

Date	Mintage	F	VF	XF	Unc	BU
2002	1,750	—	—	—	15.00	16.50
2002 Proof	1,680	Value: 20.00				

KM# 127a 5 POUNDS
28.2800 g., 0.9250 Silver 0.8410 oz. ASW, 38.6 mm. **Ruler:** Elizabeth II **Subject:** Queen Mother **Obv:** Head with tiara right **Obv. Designer:** Ian Rank-Broadley **Rev:** The late Queen Mother's portrait **Edge:** Reeded

Date	Mintage	F	VF	XF	Unc	BU
2002 Proof	15,000	Value: 50.00				

KM# 127b 5 POUNDS
39.9400 g., 0.9166 Gold 1.1770 oz. AGW, 38.6 mm. **Ruler:** Elizabeth II **Subject:** Queen Mother **Obv:** Head with tiara right **Obv. Designer:** Ian Rank-Broadley **Rev:** Queen Mother's portrait **Edge:** Reeded

Date	Mintage	F	VF	XF	Unc	BU
2002 Proof	250	Value: 875				

KM# 128 5 POUNDS
1.1300 g., 0.9166 Gold 0.0333 oz. AGW, 13.9 mm. **Ruler:** Elizabeth II **Subject:** Queen Mother **Obv:** Head with tiara right **Obv. Designer:** Ian Rank-Broadley **Rev:** The late Queen Mother's portrait **Edge:** Reeded

Date	Mintage	F	VF	XF	Unc	BU
2002 Proof	—	Value: 65.00				

KM# 129 5 POUNDS
28.2800 g., Copper-Nickel, 38.6 mm. **Ruler:** Elizabeth II **Subject:** The Duke of Wellington **Obv:** Head with tiara right **Obv. Designer:** Ian Rank-Broadley **Rev:** Portrait with mounted dragoons in background **Edge:** Reeded

Date	Mintage	F	VF	XF	Unc	BU
2002	675	—	—	—	22.50	25.00

KM# 129a 5 POUNDS
28.2800 g., 0.9250 Silver 0.8410 oz. ASW, 38.6 mm. **Ruler:** Elizabeth II **Subject:** The Duke of Wellington **Obv:** Head with tiara right **Obv. Designer:** Ian Rank-Broadley **Rev:** Portrait with multicolor mounted dragoons in background **Rev. Designer:** Willem Vis **Edge:** Reeded

Date	Mintage	F	VF	XF	Unc	BU
2002 Proof	15,000	Value: 50.00				

KM# 129b 5 POUNDS
39.9400 g., 0.9166 Gold 1.1770 oz. AGW, 38.6 mm. **Ruler:** Elizabeth II **Subject:** Duke of Wellington **Obv:** Head with tiara right **Obv. Designer:** Ian Rank-Broadley **Rev:** Wellington's portrait with multicolor cavalry scene **Edge:** Reeded

Date	Mintage	F	VF	XF	Unc	BU
2002 Proof	200	Value: 900				

KM# 130 5 POUNDS
1.1300 g., 0.9166 Gold 0.0333 oz. AGW, 13.9 mm. **Ruler:** Elizabeth II **Subject:** The Duke of Wellington **Obv:** Head with tiara right **Obv. Designer:** Ian Rank-Broadley **Rev:** Portrait with mounted dragoons in background **Edge:** Reeded

Date	Mintage	F	VF	XF	Unc	BU
2002 Proof	—	Value: 65.00				

KM# 143 5 POUNDS
28.2800 g., Copper-Nickel, 38.6 mm. **Ruler:** Elizabeth II **Obv:** Head with tiara right **Obv. Designer:** Ian Rank-Broadley **Rev:** Prince William wearing sweater **Edge:** Reeded

Date	Mintage	F	VF	XF	Unc	BU
2003	3,700	—	—	—	17.50	20.00

KM# 143a 5 POUNDS
28.2800 g., 0.9250 Silver 0.8410 oz. ASW, 38.6 mm. **Ruler:** Elizabeth II **Obv:** Head with tiara right **Obv. Designer:** Ian Rank-Broadley **Rev:** Prince William wearing sweater **Edge:** Reeded

Date	Mintage	F	VF	XF	Unc	BU
2003 Proof	5,000	Value: 47.50				

KM# 143b 5 POUNDS
39.9400 g., 0.9166 Gold 1.1770 oz. AGW, 38.6 mm. **Ruler:** Elizabeth II **Obv:** Head with tiara right **Obv. Designer:** Ian Rank-Broadley **Rev:** Prince William wearing sweater **Edge:** Reeded

Date	Mintage	F	VF	XF	Unc	BU
2003 Proof	200	Value: 900				

KM# 158 5 POUNDS
28.2800 g., Copper-Nickel, 38.7 mm. **Ruler:** Elizabeth II **Subject:** Golden Hind **Obv:** Head with tiara right **Obv. Designer:** Ian Rank-Broadley **Rev:** The Golden Hind ship **Edge:** Reeded

Date	Mintage	F	VF	XF	Unc	BU
2003	300	—	—	—	—	25.00

KM# 159 5 POUNDS
Copper-Nickel **Ruler:** Elizabeth II **Subject:** 17th Century Monarchs **Obv:** Head with tiara right **Obv. Designer:** Ian Rank-Broadley

Date	Mintage	F	VF	XF	Unc	BU
2003	500	—	—	—	—	22.50

KM# 160 5 POUNDS
Copper-Nickel **Ruler:** Elizabeth II **Subject:** Royal Navy - H. Nelson **Obv:** Head with tiara right **Obv. Designer:** Ian Rank-Broadley

Date	Mintage	F	VF	XF	Unc	BU
2003	550	—	—	—	—	22.50

KM# 161 5 POUNDS
Copper-Nickel **Ruler:** Elizabeth II **Subject:** 16th Century Monarchs **Obv:** Head with tiara right **Obv. Designer:** Ian Rank-Broadley

Date	Mintage	F	VF	XF	Unc	BU
2004	500	—	—	—	—	22.50

KM# 162 5 POUNDS
Copper-Nickel **Ruler:** Elizabeth II **Subject:** Mallard Locomotive **Obv:** Head with tiara right **Obv. Designer:** Ian Rank-Broadley

Date	Mintage	F	VF	XF	Unc	BU
2004	2,193	—	—	—	—	17.50

KM# 163 5 POUNDS
Copper-Nickel **Ruler:** Elizabeth II **Subject:** City of Truro Train **Obv:** Head with tiara right **Obv. Designer:** Ian Rank-Broadley

Date	Mintage	F	VF	XF	Unc	BU
2004	500	—	—	—	—	22.50

KM# 164 5 POUNDS
Copper-Nickel **Ruler:** Elizabeth II **Subject:** The Boat Train **Obv:** Head with tiara right **Obv. Designer:** Ian Rank-Broadley

Date	Mintage	F	VF	XF	Unc	BU
2004	250	—	—	—	—	25.00

KM# 165 5 POUNDS
Copper-Nickel **Ruler:** Elizabeth II **Subject:** Train Spotter **Obv:** Head with tiara right **Obv. Designer:** Ian Rank-Broadley

Date	Mintage	F	VF	XF	Unc	BU
2004	300	—	—	—	—	25.00

KM# 166 5 POUNDS
Copper-Nickel **Ruler:** Elizabeth II **Subject:** Royal Navy - Henry VIII **Obv:** Head with tiara right **Obv. Designer:** Ian Rank-Broadley

Date	Mintage	F	VF	XF	Unc	BU
2004	300	—	—	—	—	25.00

KM# 167 5 POUNDS
Copper-Nickel **Ruler:** Elizabeth II **Subject:** Royal Navy - Invincible **Obv:** Head with tiara right **Obv. Designer:** Ian Rank-Broadley

Date	Mintage	F	VF	XF	Unc	BU
2004	300	—	—	—	—	25.00

KM# 150 5 POUNDS
28.2800 g., Copper-Nickel, 38.6 mm. **Ruler:** Elizabeth II **Subject:** D-Day **Obv:** Head with tiara right **Obv. Designer:** Ian Rank-Broadley **Rev:** British troops storming ashore **Edge:** Reeded

Date	Mintage	F	VF	XF	Unc	BU
2004	65,611	—	—	—	15.00	16.50

KM# 154 5 POUNDS
28.2800 g., 0.9250 Silver 0.8410 oz. ASW, 38.6 mm. **Ruler:** Elizabeth II **Subject:** D-Day **Obv:** Head with tiara right **Obv. Designer:** Ian Rank-Broadley **Rev:** British soldier advancing to left **Edge:** Reeded

Date	Mintage	F	VF	XF	Unc	BU
2004 Proof	10,000	Value: 85.00				

KM# 154a 5 POUNDS
39.9400 g., 0.9167 Gold 1.1771 oz. AGW, 38.6 mm. **Ruler:** Elizabeth II **Subject:** D-Day **Obv:** Head with tiara right **Obv. Designer:** Ian Rank-Broadley **Rev:** British soldier advancing to left **Edge:** Reeded

Date	Mintage	F	VF	XF	Unc	BU
2004 Proof	500	Value: 1,000				

KM# 155 5 POUNDS
28.2800 g., Copper-Nickel, 38.6 mm. **Ruler:** Elizabeth II **Obv:** Head with tiara right **Obv. Designer:** Ian Rank-Broadley **Rev:** Sgt. Luke O'Connor , first army Victoria Cross winner, above Battle of Alma scene with multicolor flag **Edge:** Reeded

Date	Mintage	F	VF	XF	Unc	BU
2004	1,060	—	—	—	25.00	27.50

KM# 155a 5 POUNDS
28.2800 g., 0.9250 Silver 0.8410 oz. ASW, 38.6 mm. **Ruler:** Elizabeth II **Obv:** Head with tiara right **Obv. Designer:** Ian Rank-Broadley **Rev:** Sgt. Luke O'Conner, first army Victoria Cross winner, above Battle of Alma scene with multicolor flag **Edge:** Reeded

Date	Mintage	F	VF	XF	Unc	BU
2004 Proof	10,000	Value: 85.00				

KM# 155b 5 POUNDS
39.9400 g., 0.9166 Gold 1.1770 oz. AGW, 38.6 mm. **Ruler:** Elizabeth II **Obv:** Head with tiara right **Obv. Designer:** Ian Rank-Broadley **Rev:** Sgt. Luke O'Connor, first army Victoria Cross winner, above Battle of Alma scene with multicolor flag **Edge:** Reeded

Date	Mintage	F	VF	XF	Unc	BU
2004 Proof	500	Value: 1,000				

KM# 168a 5 POUNDS
28.2800 g., 0.9250 Silver 0.8410 oz. ASW, 38.6 mm. **Ruler:** Elizabeth II **Subject:** End of WWII **Obv:** Head with tiara right **Obv. Designer:** Ian Rank-Broadley **Rev:** Churchill and George VI **Edge:** Reeded

Date	Mintage	F	VF	XF	Unc	BU
2005 Proof	5,000	Value: 85.00				

KM# 168b 5 POUNDS
39.9400 g., 0.9167 Gold 1.1771 oz. AGW, 38.6 mm. **Ruler:** Elizabeth II **Subject:** End of WWII **Obv:** Head with tiara right **Obv. Designer:** Ian Rank-Broadley **Rev:** Churchill and George VI **Edge:** Reeded

Date	Mintage	F	VF	XF	Unc	BU
2005 Proof	150	Value: 1,000				

KM# 169a 5 POUNDS
39.9400 g., 0.9167 Gold 1.1771 oz. AGW, 38.6 mm. **Ruler:** Elizabeth II **Subject:** WWII Liberation **Obv:** Head with tiara right **Obv. Designer:** Ian Rank-Broadley **Rev:** Soldiers and waving crowd **Edge:** Reeded

Date	Mintage	F	VF	XF	Unc	BU
2005 Proof	150	Value: 1,000				

KM# 170 5 POUNDS
28.2800 g., 0.9250 Silver 0.8410 oz. ASW, 38.6 mm. **Ruler:** Elizabeth II **Subject:** Queen's 80th Birthday **Obv:** Head with tiara right - gilt **Obv. Legend:** ELIZABETH II BAILIWICK OF GUERNSEY **Obv. Designer:** Ian Rank-Broadley **Rev:** Bust at left looking upwards, tower and florals at upper right

Date	Mintage	F	VF	XF	Unc	BU
2006 Proof	—	Value: 40.00				

KM# 116 10 POUNDS
141.7500 g., 0.9990 Silver 4.5526 oz. ASW, 65 mm. **Ruler:** Elizabeth II **Subject:** 19th Century Monarchy **Obv:** Head with tiara right **Obv. Designer:** Ian Rank-Broadley **Rev:** Four portraits **Edge:** Reeded

Date	Mintage	F	VF	XF	Unc	BU
2001 Proof	950	Value: 200				

KM# 126 10 POUNDS
155.5175 g., 0.9990 Silver 4.9948 oz. ASW, 65 mm. **Ruler:** Elizabeth II **Subject:** British Monarchy 18th Century **Obv:** Head with tiara right **Obv. Designer:** Ian Rank-Broadley **Rev:** Five royal portraits **Edge:** Reeded

Date	Mintage	F	VF	XF	Unc	BU
2002 Proof	950	Value: 200				

KM# 151 10 POUNDS
155.5170 g., 0.9250 Silver 4.6248 oz. ASW, 65 mm. **Ruler:** Elizabeth II **Subject:** D-Day **Obv:** Head with tiara right **Obv. Designer:** Ian Rank-Broadley **Rev:** British troops storming ashore **Edge:** Reeded

Date	Mintage	F	VF	XF	Unc	BU
2004 Proof	1,944	Value: 400				

KM# 107 25 POUNDS
7.8100 g., 0.9170 Gold 0.2302 oz. AGW, 22 mm. **Ruler:** Elizabeth II **Subject:** Queen Victoria Centennial **Obv:** Head with tiara right **Obv. Designer:** Ian Rank-Broadley **Rev:** Queen Victoria's portrait **Edge:** Reeded

Date	Mintage	F	VF	XF	Unc	BU
2001 Proof	2,500	Value: 270				

KM# 112 25 POUNDS
7.8100 g., 0.9170 Gold 0.2302 oz. AGW, 22 mm. **Ruler:** Elizabeth II **Subject:** Queen's 75th Birthday **Obv:** Head with tiara right **Obv. Designer:** Ian Rank-Broadley **Rev:** Queen's portrait in wreath **Edge:** Reeded

Date	Mintage	F	VF	XF	Unc	BU
2001 Proof	5,000	Value: 235				

KM# 123 25 POUNDS
7.9800 g., 0.9167 Gold 0.2352 oz. AGW, 22.05 mm. **Ruler:** Elizabeth II **Subject:** Princess Diana **Obv:** Head with tiara right **Obv. Designer:** Ian Rank-Broadley **Rev:** Diana's cameo portrait in wreath **Edge:** Reeded

Date	Mintage	F	VF	XF	Unc	BU
2002 Proof	2,500	Value: 285				

KM# 131 25 POUNDS
7.8100 g., 0.9166 Gold 0.2301 oz. AGW, 22 mm. **Ruler:** Elizabeth II **Subject:** The Duke of Wellington **Obv:** Head with tiara right **Obv. Designer:** Ian Rank-Broadley **Rev:** Portrait with mounted dragoons in the background **Edge:** Reeded

Date	Mintage	F	VF	XF	Unc	BU
2002 Proof	2,500	Value: 235				

KM# 139 25 POUNDS
7.9800 g., 0.9166 Gold 0.2352 oz. AGW, 22 mm. **Ruler:** Elizabeth II **Subject:** Golden Jubilee **Obv:** Head with tiara right **Obv. Designer:** Ian Rank-Broadley **Rev:** Queen in coach **Edge:** Reeded

Date	Mintage	F	VF	XF	Unc	BU
2002 Proof	5,000	Value: 300				

KM# 140 25 POUNDS
7.9800 g., 0.9166 Gold 0.2352 oz. AGW, 22 mm. **Ruler:** Elizabeth II **Subject:** Queen Mother **Obv:** Head with tiara right **Obv. Designer:** Ian Rank-Broadley **Rev:** Queen Mother's portrait **Edge:** Reeded

Date	Mintage	F	VF	XF	Unc	BU
2002 Proof	2,500	Value: 300				

KM# 141 25 POUNDS
7.9800 g., 0.9166 Gold 0.2352 oz. AGW, 22 mm. **Ruler:** Elizabeth II **Subject:** Golden Jubilee **Obv:** Head with tiara right **Obv. Designer:** Ian Rank-Broadley **Rev:** Trooping the Colors scene **Edge:** Reeded

Date	Mintage	F	VF	XF	Unc	BU
2003 Proof	5,000	Value: 300				

KM# 152 25 POUNDS
7.9800 g., 0.9167 Gold 0.2352 oz. AGW, 22 mm. **Ruler:** Elizabeth II **Subject:** D-Day **Obv:** Head with tiara right **Obv. Designer:** Ian Rank-Broadley **Rev:** Advancing British soldier **Edge:** Reeded

Date	Mintage	F	VF	XF	Unc	BU
2004 Proof	500	Value: 325				

KM# 144 50 POUNDS
1000.0000 g., 0.9250 Silver 29.738 oz. ASW, 100 mm. **Ruler:** Elizabeth II **Obv:** Head with tiara right **Obv. Designer:** Ian Rank-Broadley **Rev:** Prince William wearing sweater **Edge:** Reeded

Date	Mintage	F	VF	XF	Unc	BU
2003 Proof	500	Value: 995				

KM# 153 50 POUNDS
1000.0000 g., 0.9250 Silver 29.738 oz. ASW, 100 mm. **Ruler:** Elizabeth II **Subject:** D-Day **Obv:** Head with tiara right **Obv. Designer:** Ian Rank-Broadley **Rev:** British troops storming ashore **Edge:** Reeded

Date	Mintage	F	VF	XF	Unc	BU
2004 Proof	600	Value: 1,200				

PIEFORTS

KM#	Date	Mintage	Identification	Mkt Val
P3	2002	100	5 Pounds. 0.9166 Gold. 56.5600 g. 38.6 mm. Queen's portrait. Queen in coach. Reeded edge. Not a full weight piefort.	1,400
	2004	300	5 Euro. Silver. X#Pn9a.	65.00

MINT SETS

KM#	Date	Mintage	Identification	Issue Price	Mkt Val
MS10	2003 (8)	—	KM#89,96,97,149,90,148,11 0,83	—	20.00

GUYANA

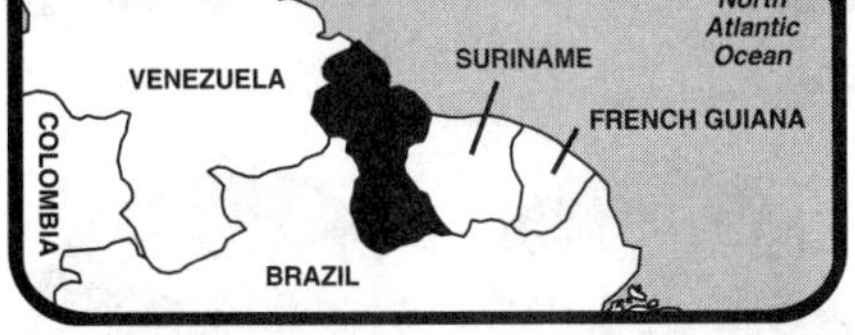

The Cooperative Republic of Guyana, is situated on the northeast coast of South America, has an area of 83,000 sq. mi. (214,970 sq. km.) and a population of 729,000. Capital: Georgetown. The economy is basically agrarian. Sugar, rice and bauxite are exported.

The original area of Essequibo and Demerary, which included present-day Suriname, French Guiana, and parts of Brazil and Venezuela was sighted by Columbus in 1498. Guyana became a republic on Feb. 23, 1970. It is a member of the Commonwealth of Nations. The president is the Chief of State. The prime minister is the Head of Government. Guyana is a member of the Caribbean Community and Common Market (CARICOM).

REPUBLIC

DECIMAL COINAGE

KM# 50 DOLLAR
2.4600 g., Copper Plated Steel, 16.92 mm. **Obv:** Helmeted and supported arms **Obv. Designer:** Sean Thomas **Rev:** Hand gathering rice **Rev. Designer:** Jean Thomas **Edge:** Reeded

Date	Mintage	F	VF	XF	Unc	BU
2001	—	—	—	0.30	0.50	0.65
2002	—	—	—	0.30	0.50	0.65

KM# 51 5 DOLLARS
3.7500 g., Copper Plated Steel, 20.5 mm. **Obv:** Helmeted and supported arms **Rev:** Sugar cane **Rev. Designer:** Selayn Cambridge

Date	Mintage	F	VF	XF	Unc	BU
2002	—	—	—	—	0.75	1.00

HONDURAS

The Republic of Honduras, situated in Central America alongside El Salvador, between Nicaragua and Guatemala, has an area of 43,277 sq. mi. (112,090 sq. km.) and a population of 5.6 million. Capital: Tegucigalpa. Agriculture, mining (gold and silver), and logging are the major economic activities, with increasing tourism and emerging petroleum resource discoveries. Precious metals, bananas, timber and coffee are exported.

From 1933 to 1940 General Tiburcio Carias Andino was dictator president of the Republic. Since 1990 democratic practices have become more consistent.

MINT MARKS
T.G. - Yoro
T.L. – Comayagua

MONETARY SYSTEM
100 Centavos = 1 Lempira

REPUBLIC

REFORM COINAGE

KM# 72.4 5 CENTAVOS
3.2500 g., Brass, 19.21 mm. **Obv:** National arms, without clouds behind pyramids **Rev:** Denomination within circle, wreath surrounds **Edge:** Plain

Date	Mintage	F	VF	XF	Unc	BU
2003	—	—	0.10	0.15	0.35	—

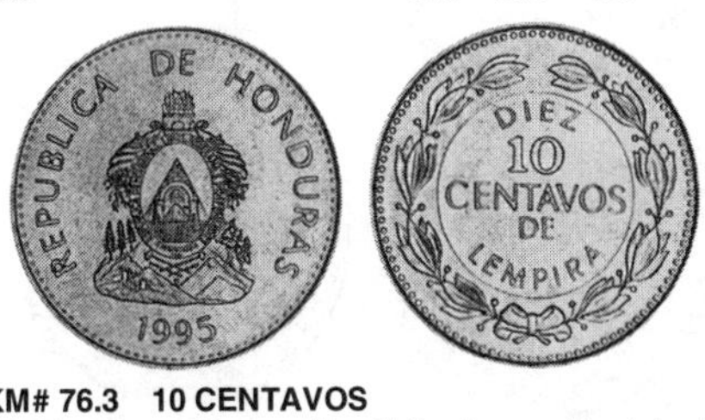

KM# 76.3 10 CENTAVOS
5.9700 g., Brass, 26 mm. **Obv:** National arms, without clouds behind pyramid **Rev:** Denomination within circle, wreath surrounds

Date	Mintage	F	VF	XF	Unc	BU
2002	—	—	0.10	0.20	0.45	—

HONG KONG

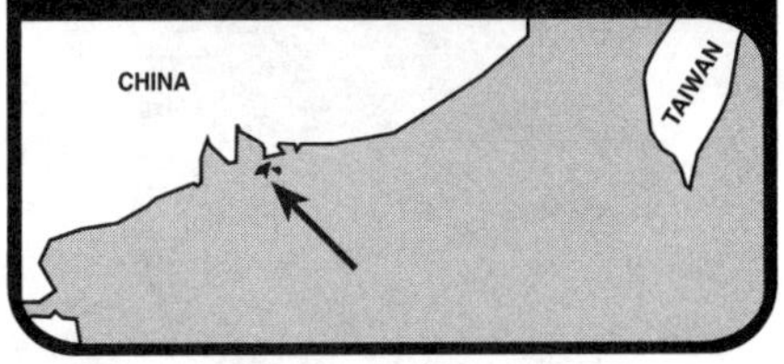

Hong Kong, a former British colony, reverted to control of the People's Republic of China on July 1, 1997 as a Special Administrative Region. It is situated at the mouth of the Canton or Pearl River 90 miles (145 km.) southeast of Canton, has an area of 403 sq. mi. (1,040 sq. km.) and an estimated population of 6.3 million. Capital: Victoria. The free port of Hong Kong, the commercial center of the Far East, is a trans-shipment point for goods destined for China and the countries of the Pacific Rim. Light manufacturing and tourism are important components of the economy.

SPECIAL ADMINISTRATION REGION (S.A.R.)

DECIMAL COINAGE

KM# 80 50 DOLLARS
35.4300 g., 0.9250 Silver Gold plated center 1.0536 oz. ASW, 40 mm. **Subject:** "May your wishes come true" **Obv:** Bauhinia flower **Rev:** Jade Ju-I

Date	Mintage	F	VF	XF	Unc	BU
2002 Proof	60,000	Value: 60.00				

KM# 81 50 DOLLARS
35.4300 g., 0.9250 Silver Gold plated center 1.0536 oz. ASW, 40 mm. **Obv:** Bauhinia flower **Rev:** Fish

Date	Mintage	F	VF	XF	Unc	BU
2002 Proof	60,000	Value: 60.00				

KM# 82 50 DOLLARS
35.2500 g., 0.9250 Silver Gold plated center 1.0483 oz. ASW, 40 mm. **Obv:** Bauhinia flower **Rev:** Horses

Date	Mintage	F	VF	XF	Unc	BU
2002 Proof	60,000	Value: 60.00				

KM# 83 50 DOLLARS
35.3400 g., 0.9250 Silver Gold plated center 1.0509 oz. ASW, 40 mm. **Obv:** Bauhinia flower **Rev:** Peony flower

Date	Mintage	F	VF	XF	Unc	BU
2002 Proof	60,000	Value: 60.00				

KM# 84 50 DOLLARS
35.1400 g., 0.9250 Silver Gold plated center 1.0450 oz. ASW, 40 mm. **Obv:** Bauhinia flower **Rev:** Windmills

Date	Mintage	F	VF	XF	Unc	BU
2002 Proof	60,000	Value: 60.00				

PROOF SETS

KM#	Date	Mintage	Identification	Issue Price	Mkt Val
PS8	2002 (5)	60,000	KM#80-84 plus gold medal	370	360

HUNGARY

The Republic of Hungary, located in central Europe, has an area of 35,929 sq. mi. (93,030 sq. km.) and a population of 10.7 million. Capital: Budapest. The economy is based on agriculture, bauxite and a rapidly expanding industrial sector. Machinery, chemicals, iron and steel, and fruits and vegetables are exported.

MINT MARKS
B, K, KB - Kremnitz (Kormoczbanya)
BP - Budapest

MONETARY SYSTEM

Commencing 1946
100 Filler = 1 Forint

SECOND REPUBLIC
1989-present
DECIMAL COINAGE

KM# 692 FORINT
2.0500 g., Brass, 16.5 mm. **Obv:** Crowned shield **Rev:** Denomination

Date	Mintage	F	VF	XF	Unc	BU
2001BP	—	—	—	—	0.10	0.25
2001BP Proof	3,000	Value: 3.75				
2002BP	—	—	—	—	0.10	0.25
2002BP Proof	3,000	Value: 3.75				
2003BP	—	—	—	—	0.10	0.25
2003BP Proof	7,000	Value: 3.50				
2004BP	—	—	—	—	0.10	0.25
2004BP Proof	7,000	Value: 3.50				
2005BP	—	—	—	—	0.10	0.25
2005BP Proof	—	Value: 3.50				
2006BP	—	—	—	—	0.10	0.25
2006BP Proof	—	Value: 3.50				

KM# 693 2 FORINT
3.1000 g., Copper-Nickel, 19 mm. **Obv:** Native flower: Colchicum Hungaricum **Rev:** Denomination

Date	Mintage	F	VF	XF	Unc	BU
2001BP	—	—	—	—	0.20	0.35
2001BP Proof	3,000	Value: 4.25				
2002BP	—	—	—	—	0.20	0.35
2002BP Proof	3,000	Value: 4.25				
2003BP	—	—	—	—	0.20	0.35
2003BP Proof	7,000	Value: 4.00				
2004BP	—	—	—	—	0.20	0.35
2004BP Proof	7,000	Value: 4.00				
2005BP	—	—	—	—	0.20	0.35
2005BP Proof	—	Value: 4.00				
2006BP	—	—	—	—	0.20	0.35
2006BP Proof	—	Value: 4.00				

KM# 694 5 FORINT
4.2000 g., Brass, 21.5 mm. **Obv:** Great White Egret **Rev:** Denomination

Date	Mintage	F	VF	XF	Unc	BU
2001BP	—	—	—	—	1.00	1.50
2001BP Proof	3,000	Value: 5.00				
2002BP	—	—	—	—	1.00	1.50
2002BP Proof	3,000	Value: 5.00				
2003BP	—	—	—	—	1.00	1.50
2003BP Proof	7,000	Value: 4.50				
2004BP	—	—	—	—	1.00	1.50
2004BP Proof	7,000	Value: 4.50				
2005BP	—	—	—	—	1.00	1.50
2005BP Proof	—	Value: 4.50				
2006BP	—	—	—	—	1.00	1.50
2006BP Proof	—	Value: 4.50				

KM# 695 10 FORINT
6.1000 g., Copper-Nickel Clad Brass, 25 mm. **Obv:** Crowned shield **Rev:** Denomination

Date	Mintage	F	VF	XF	Unc	BU
2001BP	—	—	—	—	1.00	2.50
2001BP Proof	3,000	Value: 5.50				
2002BP	—	—	—	—	1.00	2.50
2002BP Proof	3,000	Value: 5.50				
2003BP	—	—	—	—	1.00	2.50
2003BP Proof	7,000	Value: 5.00				
2004BP	—	—	—	—	1.00	2.50
2004BP Proof	7,000	Value: 5.00				
2005BP	—	—	—	—	1.00	2.50
2005BP Proof	—	Value: 5.00				
2006BP	—	—	—	—	1.00	2.50
2006BP Proof	—	Value: 5.00				

KM# 779 10 FORINT
6.1000 g., Copper-Nickel, 24.8 mm. **Obv:** Jozsef Attila **Rev:** Value **Edge:** Segmented reeding

Date	Mintage	F	VF	XF	Unc	BU
2005BP	20,000	—	—	—	2.50	3.00
2005BP Proof	7,000	Value: 3.50				

KM# 696 20 FORINT
6.9000 g., Nickel-Brass, 26.3 mm. **Obv:** Hungarian Iris **Rev:** Denomination

Date	Mintage	F	VF	XF	Unc	BU
2001BP	—	—	—	—	1.50	2.00
2001BP Proof	3,000	Value: 4.50				
2002BP	—	—	—	—	1.50	2.00
2002BP Proof	3,000	Value: 4.50				
2003BP	—	—	—	—	1.50	2.00
2003BP Proof	7,000	Value: 4.00				
2004BP	—	—	—	—	1.50	2.00
2004BP Proof	7,000	Value: 4.00				
2005BP	—	—	—	—	1.50	2.00
2005BP Proof	—	Value: 4.00				
2006BP	—	—	—	—	1.50	2.00
2006BP Proof	—	Value: 4.00				

KM# 768 20 FORINT
6.9400 g., Nickel-Brass, 26.4 mm. **Obv:** Deak Ferenc **Rev:** Denomination **Edge:** Reeded

Date	Mintage	F	VF	XF	Unc	BU
2003BP	993,000	—	—	—	1.50	2.00
2003BP Proof	7,000	Value: 4.00				

KM# 697 50 FORINT
7.7000 g., Copper-Nickel Clad Brass, 27.5 mm. **Obv:** Saker falcon **Rev:** Denomination

Date	Mintage	F	VF	XF	Unc	BU
2001BP	—	—	—	—	3.00	4.00
2001BP Proof	3,000	Value: 6.00				
2002BP	—	—	—	—	3.00	3.50
2002BP Proof	3,000	Value: 5.50				
2003BP	—	—	—	—	3.00	3.50
2003BP Proof	7,000	Value: 5.00				
2004BP	—	—	—	—	3.00	3.50
2004BP Proof	7,000	Value: 5.00				
2005BP	—	—	—	—	3.00	3.50
2005BP Proof	—	Value: 5.00				
2006BP	—	—	—	—	3.00	3.50
2006BP Proof	—	Value: 5.00				

KM# 773 50 FORINT
7.7000 g., Copper-Nickel Clad Brass, 27.5 mm. **Obv:** National arms above Euro Union star circle **Rev:** Denomination **Edge:** Plain

Date	Mintage	F	VF	XF	Unc	BU
2004BP	993,000	—	—	—	3.00	3.50
2004BP Proof	7,000	Value: 6.00				

KM# 780 50 FORINT
7.7000 g., Copper-Nickel, 27.4 mm. **Subject:** International Childrens Safety Service **Obv:** Stylized crying child **Rev:** Denomination **Edge:** Plain

Date	Mintage	F	VF	XF	Unc	BU
2005BP	2,000,000	—	—	—	3.00	3.50

KM# 788 50 FORINT
7.7000 g., Copper-Nickel, 27.4 mm. **Obv:** Hungarian Red Cross 125th Anniversary seal above date and country name **Rev:** Value **Edge:** Plain

Date	Mintage	F	VF	XF	Unc	BU
2006BP	2,000,000	—	—	—	—	3.50

KM# 789 50 FORINT
7.7000 g., Copper-Nickel, 27.4 mm. **Subject:** 1956 Revolution **Obv:** Holed flag with Parliament building in background **Rev:** Value **Edge:** Plain

Date	Mintage	F	VF	XF	Unc	BU
2006BP	2,000,000	—	—	—	—	3.50

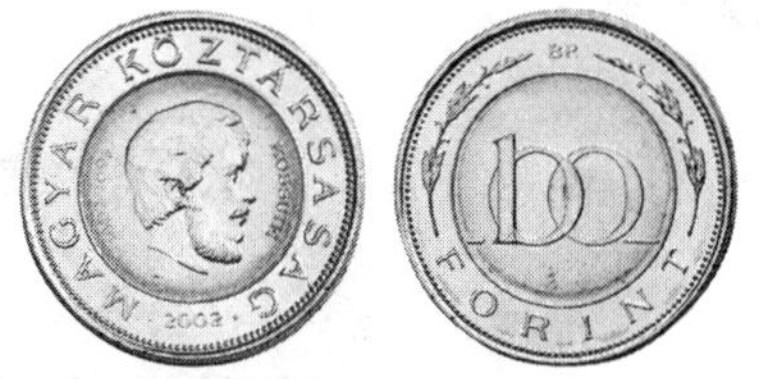

KM# 760 100 FORINT
8.0000 g., Bi-Metallic Stainless Steel center in Brass plated Steel ring, 23.7 mm. **Subject:** Lajos Kossuth **Obv:** Head right within circle **Rev:** Denomination within circle **Edge:** Reeded

Date	Mintage	F	VF	XF	Unc	BU
2002BP	997,000	—	—	—	2.00	2.50
2002BP Proof	3,000	Value: 5.00				

KM# 721 100 FORINT (Szaz)
Bi-Metallic Brass plated Steel center in Stainless Steel ring, 23.6 mm. **Obv:** Crowned shield **Rev:** Denomination

Date	Mintage	F	VF	XF	Unc	BU
2001BP	—	—	—	—	3.50	5.00
2001BP Proof	3,000	Value: 8.00				
2002BP	—	—	—	—	3.50	5.00
2002BP Proof	3,000	Value: 8.00				
2003BP	—	—	—	—	3.50	5.00
2003BP Proof	7,000	Value: 7.50				
2004BP	—	—	—	—	3.50	5.00
2004BP Proof	7,000	Value: 7.50				
2005BP	—	—	—	—	3.50	5.00
2005BP Proof	—	Value: 7.50				
2006BP	—	—	—	—	3.50	5.00
2006BP Proof	—	Value: 7.50				

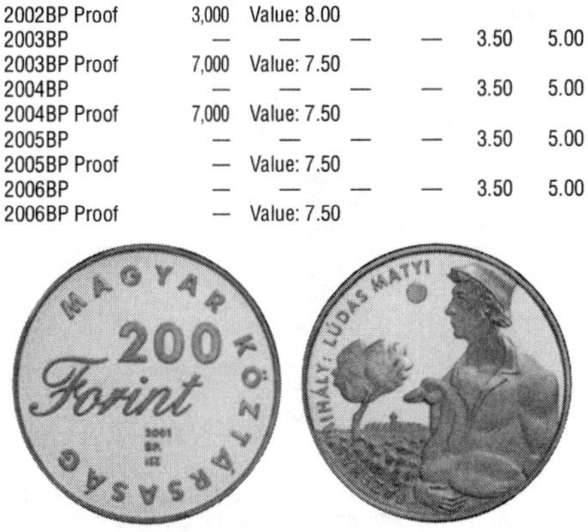

KM# 754 200 FORINT
9.4000 g., Brass, 29.2 mm. **Subject:** Childrens Literature: Ludas Matyi **Obv:** Denomination **Rev:** Man holding a goose **Edge:** Plain

Date	Mintage	F	VF	XF	Unc	BU
2001BP	12,000	—	—	—	6.50	7.50
2001BP Proof	5,000	Value: 12.50				

KM# 755 200 FORINT
Brass, 29.2 mm. **Subject:** Childrens Literature: Janos Vitez **Obv:** Denomination **Rev:** Soldier riding a flying bird **Edge:** Plain

Date	Mintage	F	VF	XF	Unc	BU
2001BP	12,000	—	—	—	6.50	7.50
2001BP Proof	5,000	Value: 12.50				

KM# 756 200 FORINT
Brass, 29.2 mm. **Subject:** Childrens Literature: Toldi **Obv:** Denomination **Rev:** Knight kicking a boat off the shore **Edge:** Plain

Date	Mintage	F	VF	XF	Unc	BU
2001BP	12,000	—	—	—	6.50	7.50
2001BP Proof	5,000	Value: 12.50				

KM# 757 200 FORINT
Brass, 29.2 mm. **Subject:** Childrens Literature: A Pal Utcai Fiuk **Obv:** Denomination **Rev:** Two men and cordwood **Edge:** Plain

Date	Mintage	F	VF	XF	Unc	BU
2001	12,000	—	—	—	6.50	7.50
2001 Proof	5,000	Value: 12.50				

KM# 764 500 FORINT
13.9000 g., Copper Nickel **Subject:** Farkas Kempelen's Chess Machine **Obv:** Denomination, letters A-H and numbers 1-8 repeated along edges **Rev:** Robotic human form chess playing machine built in 1769 **Edge:** Plain **Shape:** Square, 28.43 x 28.43 mm

Date	Mintage	F	VF	XF	Unc	BU
2002BP	5,000	—	—	—	12.50	—
2002BP Proof	5,000	Value: 25.00				

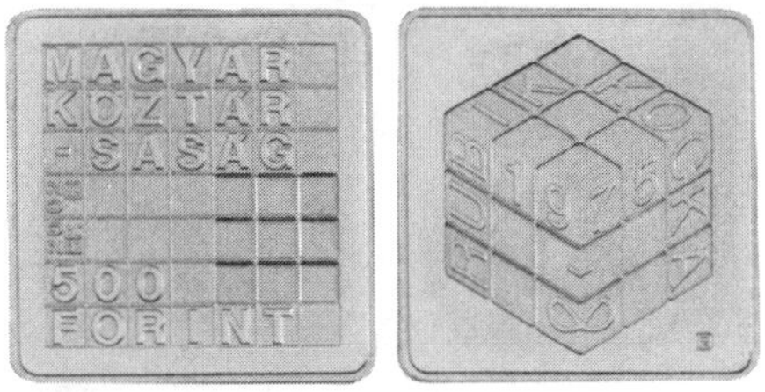

KM# 765 500 FORINT
13.8000 g., Copper Nickel **Subject:** Rubik's Cube **Obv:** Inscription on Rubik's Cube design **Rev:** Rubik's Cube with inscription **Edge:** Plain **Shape:** Square, 28.43 x 28.43 mm

Date	Mintage	F	VF	XF	Unc	BU
2002BP Proof	5,000	Value: 25.00				
2002BP	5,000	—	—	—	12.50	—

KM# 781 500 FORINT
14.0000 g., Copper-Nickel **Obv:** Old wheel **Rev:** First Hungarian Post Office motor vehicle **Edge:** Plain **Shape:** Square **Note:** 28.43 x 28.43mm

Date	Mintage	F	VF	XF	Unc	BU
2005BP	5,000	—	—	—	—	15.00
2005BP Proof	10,000	Value: 25.00				

KM# 766 1000 FORINT
19.5000 g., Bronze Hollow coin unscrews to open **Obv:** Denomination and satellite dish **Rev:** Mercury

Date	Mintage	F	VF	XF	Unc	BU
2002BP	15,000	—	—	—	15.00	16.50

KM# 787 1000 FORINT
13.8100 g., Copper-Nickel, 28.3 mm. **Obv:** Value and partial front view of antique automobile **Rev:** Model T Ford **Edge:** Plain **Shape:** Square

Date	Mintage	F	VF	XF	Unc	BU
2006BP Proof	10,000	Value: 20.00				
2006BP	10,000	—	—	—	—	10.00

KM# 797 1000 FORINT
14.0000 g., Copper Nickel **Subject:** 125th Anniversary - Birth of Janos Adorjan **Obv:** Early two cylinder aircraft motor with propeller **Obv. Inscription:** MAGYAR / KOZTARSASAG **Obv. Designer:** Balozs Bi **Rev:** Early monoplane **Rev. Inscription:** ADORJAN JANOS /AZ ELSO SIKERES MAGYAR / REPULOGEP TERVEZOJE **Shape:** Square 28.43 x 28.43

Date	Mintage	F	VF	XF	Unc	BU
2007BP	10,000	—	—	—	—	12.00
2007BP Proof	10,000	Value: 22.00				

KM# 752 3000 FORINT
31.4600 g., 0.9250 Silver 0.9356 oz. ASW, 28.5 mm. **Subject:** Hungarian Silver Coinage Millennium **Obv:** Denomination in ornamental frame **Rev:** Thaler design circa 1500 portraying Ladislaus I (1077-95) with the title of saint **Edge:** Reeding over "1001-2001" **Edge Lettering:** "BP.NX.KB.HX.GY.F.AF.MM.C+"

Date	Mintage	F	VF	XF	Unc	BU
2001BP	5,000	—	—	—	35.00	37.50
2001BP Proof	5,000	Value: 40.00				

KM# 759 3000 FORINT
31.8000 g., 0.9250 Silver 0.9457 oz. ASW, 38.7 mm. **Subject:** Centennial of First Hungarian Film "The Dance" **Obv:** Denomination **Rev:** Two dancers on film **Edge:** Reeded

Date	Mintage	F	VF	XF	Unc	BU
2001BP	3,500	—	—	—	37.50	40.00
2001BP Proof	3,500	Value: 45.00				

KM# 761 3000 FORINT
31.3300 g., 0.9250 Silver 0.9317 oz. ASW, 38.6 mm. **Subject:** Hortobagy National Park **Obv:** Landscape, denomination **Rev:** Hungarian Grey Longhorn bull **Edge:** Reeded

Date	Mintage	F	VF	XF	Unc	BU
2002BP	5,000	—	—	—	32.00	35.00
2002BP Proof	5,000	Value: 45.00				

KM# 767 3000 FORINT
31.4600 g., 0.9250 Silver 0.9356 oz. ASW **Subject:** 100th Anniversary - Birth of Kovacs Margit (1902-1977) **Obv:** Denomination **Rev:** The "Trumpet of Judgement Day"

Date	Mintage	F	VF	XF	Unc	BU
2002BP	4,000	—	—	—	38.00	40.00
2002BP Proof	4,000	Value: 48.00				

KM# 762 3000 FORINT
31.4600 g., 0.9250 Silver 0.9356 oz. ASW, 38.5 mm. **Subject:** 200th Anniversary - National Library **Obv:** Small coat of arms in ornate frame **Rev:** Interior view of library **Edge:** Reeded

Date	Mintage	F	VF	XF	Unc	BU
2002BP Proof	3,000	Value: 40.00				
2002BP	3,000	—	—	—	35.00	37.50

KM# 763 3000 FORINT
31.4600 g., 0.9250 Silver 0.9356 oz. ASW, 38.5 mm. **Subject:** Janos Bolyai's publication of his "Appendix" **Obv:** Circular graph **Rev:** Signature above 7-line inscription, name and dates **Edge:** Reeded

Date	Mintage	F	VF	XF	Unc	BU
2002BP Proof	3,000	Value: 40.00				
2002BP	3,000	—	—	—	35.00	37.50

KM# 751 4000 FORINT
31.4600 g., 0.9250 Silver 0.9356 oz. ASW, 26.4 x 39.6 mm. **Subject:** Godollo Artist Colony Centennial **Obv:** Denomination **Rev:** "Sisters" stained glass window design **Edge:** Plain **Shape:** 4-sided

Date	Mintage	F	VF	XF	Unc	BU
2001BP	4,000	—	—	—	40.00	42.50
2001BP Proof	4,000	Value: 50.00				

KM# 769 5000 FORINT
31.4600 g., 0.9250 Silver 0.9356 oz. ASW, 38.6 mm. **Subject:** Budapest Philharmonic Orchestra **Obv:** Crowned arms in wreath **Rev:** Four coin-like portraits of Erkel, Dohnanyi, Bartók and Kodaly **Edge:** Reeded

Date	Mintage	F	VF	XF	Unc	BU
2003BP Proof	4,000	Value: 42.50				
2003BP	4,000	—	—	—	37.50	40.00

KM# 770 5000 FORINT
31.4600 g., 0.9250 Silver 0.9356 oz. ASW, 38.6 mm. **Subject:** 100th Anniversary - Birth of Neumann Janos **Obv:** Denomination and binary number date **Rev:** Neumann Janos **Edge:** Reeded

Date	Mintage	F	VF	XF	Unc	BU
2003BP Proof	3,000	Value: 45.00				
2003BP	3,000	—	—	—	40.00	42.50

KM# 771 5000 FORINT
31.4600 g., 0.9250 Silver 0.9356 oz. ASW, 38.6 mm. **Subject:** Rakoczi's War of Liberation **Obv:** Transylvanian ducat design above country name, value and date **Rev:** Kuruc cavalryman with sword and trumpet **Edge:** Reeded

Date	Mintage	F	VF	XF	Unc	BU
2003BP	3,000	—	—	—	45.00	47.50
2003BP Proof	3,000	Value: 50.00				

KM# 772 5000 FORINT
31.4600 g., 0.9250 Silver 0.9356 oz. ASW, 38.6 mm. **Subject:** World Heritage in Hungary - Holloko **Obv:** Holloko castle ruins above country name, value and date **Rev:** Village view behind woman in folk costume **Edge:** Reeded

Date	Mintage	F	VF	XF	Unc	BU
2003BP	5,000	—	—	—	42.50	45.00
2003BP Proof	5,000	Value: 50.00				

KM# 774 5000 FORINT
31.4600 g., 0.9250 Silver 0.9356 oz. ASW, 38.6 mm. **Obv:** Value **Rev:** Two Olympic boxers **Edge:** Reeded

Date	Mintage	F	VF	XF	Unc	BU
2004BP	3,000	—	—	—	45.00	47.50
2004BP Proof	9,000	Value: 50.00				

KM# 775 5000 FORINT
31.4600 g., 0.9250 Silver 0.9356 oz. ASW, 38.6 mm. **Obv:** "Solomon Tower" above value **Rev:** Visegrad Castle with the Solomon Tower **Edge:** Reeded

Date	Mintage	F	VF	XF	Unc	BU
2004BP	4,000	—	—	—	45.00	47.50
2004BP Proof	4,000	Value: 50.00				

KM# 776 5000 FORINT
31.4600 g., 0.9250 Silver 0.9356 oz. ASW, 38.6 mm. **Obv:** Value and country name above Euro Union stars **Rev:** Mythical stag seen through an ornate window **Edge:** Reeded

Date	Mintage	F	VF	XF	Unc	BU
2004BP Proof	10,000	Value: 50.00				

KM# 778 5000 FORINT
31.4600 g., 0.9250 Silver 0.9356 oz. ASW, 38.6 mm. **Subject:** Ancient Christian Necropolis at Pecs **Obv:** Value and ancient artifact **Rev:** Interior view of tomb **Edge:** Reeded

Date	Mintage	F	VF	XF	Unc	BU
2004BP	5,000	—	—	—	40.00	42.00
2004BP Proof	5,000	Value: 45.00				

KM# 782 5000 FORINT
31.4600 g., 0.9250 Silver 0.9356 oz. ASW, 38.6 mm. **Obv:** Bat flying above value **Rev:** Interior cave view **Edge:** Reeded

Date	Mintage	F	VF	XF	Unc	BU
2005BP	5,000	—	—	—	45.00	50.00
2005BP Proof	5,000	Value: 55.00				

KM# 783 5000 FORINT
31.4600 g., 0.9250 Silver 0.9356 oz. ASW, 38.6 mm. **Obv:** Hungarian National Bank building **Rev:** Ignac Alpar and life dates **Edge:** Reeded

Date	Mintage	F	VF	XF	Unc	BU
ND (2005)BP	3,000	—	—	—	45.00	47.50
ND (2005)BP Proof	3,000	Value: 50.00				

KM# 784 5000 FORINT
31.4600 g., 0.9250 Silver 0.9356 oz. ASW, 38.6 mm. **Obv:** Knight on horse with lance **Rev:** Diosgyor Castle **Edge:** Reeded

Date	Mintage	F	VF	XF	Unc	BU
2005BP	4,000	—	—	—	45.00	47.50
2005BP Proof	4,000	Value: 50.00				

KM# 785 5000 FORINT
31.4600 g., 0.9250 Silver 0.9356 oz. ASW, 38.6 mm. **Obv:** Large building above value **Rev:** Karoli Gaspar Reformed (Calvinist) University seal **Edge:** Reeded

Date	Mintage	F	VF	XF	Unc	BU
2005BP	3,000	—	—	—	45.00	47.50
2005BP Proof	3,000	Value: 50.00				

KM# 786 5000 FORINT
31.4600 g., 0.9250 Silver 0.9356 oz. ASW, 38.6 mm. **Obv:** Coin design of a Transylvanian KM-10 thaler reverse dated 1605 **Rev:** Stephan Bocskai (1557-1606) **Edge:** Reeded

Date	Mintage	F	VF	XF	Unc	BU
2005BP	3,000	—	—	—	—	45.00
2005BP Proof	3,000	Value: 50.00				

KM# 790 5000 FORINT
31.4600 g., 0.9250 Silver 0.9356 oz. ASW, 38.61 mm. **Series:** Masterpieces of Ecclesiastical Architecture **Obv:** View of interior of dome **Obv. Legend:** MAGYAR KÖZTÁRSASÁG **Obv. Designer:** István Péter Bartos **Rev:** Basilica facade **Rev. Legend:** ESZTERGOMI BAZILIKA

Date	Mintage	F	VF	XF	Unc	BU
2006BP	2,500	—	—	—	—	50.00
2006BP Proof	3,500	Value: 55.00				

KM# 791 5000 FORINT
31.4600 g., 0.9250 Silver 0.9356 oz. ASW, 38.61 mm. **Subject:** 125th Anniversary - Birth of Béla Bartók **Obv:** Transylvanian woodcarving **Obv. Legend:** MAGYAR KÖZTÁRSASÁG **Obv. Designer:** György Kiss **Rev:** Bust of Bartók right, Euro star behind **Edge:** Reeded and lettered **Edge Lettering:** Bartók Béla repeated three times

Date	Mintage	F	VF	XF	Unc	BU
2006BP Proof	25,000	Value: 35.00				

KM# 792 5000 FORINT
31.4600 g., 0.9250 Silver 0.9356 oz. ASW, 38.61 mm. **Series:** Heritage Sites **Obv:** Great White Egret in flight **Obv. Legend:** MAGYAR - KÖZTÁRSASÁG **Obv. Designer:** Virág Szabó **Rev:** Landscape, Schneeberg Mountain above Esterházy palace facade

Date	Mintage	F	VF	XF	Unc	BU
2006BP	5,000	—	—	—	—	45.00
2006BP Proof	5,000	Value: 50.00				

KM# 793 5000 FORINT
31.4600 g., 0.9250 Silver 0.9356 oz. ASW, 38.61 mm. **Series:** Hungarian Castles **Subject:** Hungarian Castles **Obv:** Portrait of Ilona Zrinyi **Obv. Legend:** MAGYAR KÖZTÁRSASÁG **Obv. Designer:** Enikö Szöllössy **Rev:** Munkács Castle

Date	Mintage	F	VF	XF	Unc	BU
2006BP	4,000	—	—	—	—	45.00
2006BP Proof	4,000	Value: 50.00				

KM# 794 5000 FORINT
31.4600 g., 0.9250 Silver 0.9356 oz. ASW, 38.61 mm. **Subject:** 500th Anniversary - Victory in Nándorfehévár **Obv:** Decorative sword hilt **Obv. Legend:** MAGYAR KÖZTÁRSASÁG **Obv. Designer:** E. Tamás Soltra **Rev:** János Hunyadi in armor at left, John Capistrano in monk's garb at right **Rev. Inscription:** NÁNDORFEHÉRVÁRI / DIADAL

Date	Mintage	F	VF	XF	Unc	BU
2006BP	2,500	—	—	—	—	45.00
2006BP Proof	3,500	Value: 50.00				

KM# 795 5000 FORINT
31.4600 g., 0.9250 Silver 0.9356 oz. ASW, 38.61 mm. **Subject:** 50th Anniversary - Hungarian Revolution **Obv:** 1956 repeated in stone blocks at right **Obv. Legend:** MAGYAR KÖZTÁRSASÁG **Obv. Designer:** Attila Rónay **Rev:** 1956 repeated in stone blocks at left, freedom fighter's flag at center **Rev. Legend:** MAGYAR FORRADALOM ÉS SZABADSÁGHARC

Date	Mintage	F	VF	XF	Unc	BU
2006BP	5,000	—	—	—	—	45.00
2006BP Proof	5,000	Value: 50.00				

KM# 798 5000 FORINT
31.4600 g., 0.9250 Silver 0.9356 oz. ASW, 38.61 mm. **Series:** Hungarian Castles **Obv:** Walled tower **Obv. Inscription:** MAGYAR / KÖZTÁRSASÁG **Obv. Designer:** György Kiss **Rev:** Gyula castle **Rev. Inscription:** GYULAI / VÁR

Date	Mintage	F	VF	XF	Unc	BU
2007BP	4,000	—	—	—	—	45.00
2007BP Proof	4,000	Value: 50.00				

KM# 799 5000 FORINT
31.4600 g., 0.9250 Silver 0.9356 oz. ASW, 38.61 mm. **Subject:** 200th Anniversary - Birth of Count Lajos Batthyány **Obv:** Seal dated 1848 with crowned arms above Batthyány's autograph **Obv. Legend:** MAGYAR KÖZTÁRASÁG **Obv. Designer:** Márta Csikai **Rev:** 1/2 length figure of Batthyány facing **Rev. Legend:** BATTHYÁNY LAJOS

Date	Mintage	F	VF	XF	Unc	BU
2007BP Proof	20,000	Value: 35.00				

KM# 800 5000 FORINT
31.4600 g., 0.9250 Silver 0.9356 oz. ASW, 38.61 mm. **Subject:** 125th Anniversary - Birth of Zoltán Kodály **Obv:** Gramaphone **Obv. Legend:** MAGYAR KÖZTÁRSASÁG **Obv. Designer:** Gábor Gáti **Rev:** Bust of Kodály facing 3/4 right

Date	Mintage	F	VF	XF	Unc	BU
2007BP	4,000	—	—	—	—	45.00
2007BP Proof	6,000	Value: 50.00				

KM# 802 5000 FORINT
31.4600 g., 0.9250 Silver 0.9356 oz. ASW, 38.61 mm. **Subject:** 8ooth Anniversary - Birth of St. Elizabeth **Obv:** Stylized image of St. Elizabeth feeding the hungry **Obv. Inscription:** Magyar / Köztárszág **Rev:** 3/4 length figure of St. Elizabeth seated facing holding roses and bread rolls in her lap

Date	Mintage	F	VF	XF	Unc	BU
2007BP	4,000	—	—	—	—	55.00
2007BP Proof	4,000	Value: 57.50				

KM# 753 20000 FORINT
6.9820 g., 0.9860 Gold 0.2213 oz. AGW, 22 mm. **Subject:** Hungarian Coinage Millennium **Obv:** Denomination **Rev:** Hammered coinage minting scene above old coin design **Edge:** Plain

Date	Mintage	F	VF	XF	Unc	BU
2001BP Proof	3,000	Value: 235				

KM# 777 50000 FORINT
13.9640 g., 0.9860 Gold 0.4426 oz. AGW, 25 mm. **Obv:** Value and country name above Euro Union stars **Rev:** Mythical stag seen through ornate window **Edge:** Reeded

Date	Mintage	F	VF	XF	Unc	BU
2004BP Proof	7,000	Value: 450				

KM# 758 100000 FORINT
31.1040 g., 0.9860 Gold 0.9860 oz. AGW, 37 mm. **Subject:** Saint Stephen **Obv:** Angels crowning coat of arms **Rev:** King seated on throne **Edge:** Reeded

Date	Mintage	F	VF	XF	Unc	BU
2001BP Proof	3,000	Value: 975				

KM# 796 100000 FORINT
20.9460 g., 0.9860 Gold 0.6640 oz. AGW, 38.61 mm. **Subject:** 50th Anniversary - Hungarian Revolution **Obv:** 1956 repeated in cut out stone **Obv. Legend:** MAGYAR KÖZTÁRSASÁG **Obv. Designer:** Attila Rónay **Rev:** 1956 repeated in cut out stone with two freedom fighter's flags **Rev. Legend:** MAGYAR FORRADALOM ÉS SZABADSÁGHARC

Date	Mintage	F	VF	XF	Unc	BU
2006BP Proof	5,000	Value: 675				

MINT SETS

KM#	Date	Mintage	Identification	Issue Price	Mkt Val
MS32	2001 (7)	—	KM#692-697, 721	—	16.50
MS33	2002 (8)	—	KM#692, 693, 694, 695, 696, 697, 721, 760	—	17.50
MS34	2003 (8)	—	KM#692, 693, 694, 695, 696, 697, 721, 768	—	16.50
MS35	2004 (8)	—	KM#692, 693, 694, 695, 696, 697, 721, 773	—	16.50
MS37	2006 (7)	—	KM#692-697, 721	—	15.00

PROOF SETS

KM#	Date	Mintage	Identification	Issue Price	Mkt Val
PS26	2001 (7)	—	KM#692-697, 721	35.00	37.50
PS27	2002 (8)	—	KM#692-697, 721, 760	—	42.50
PS28	2003 (8)	—	KM#692-697, 721, 768	—	37.50
PS29	2004 (8)	—	KM#692-697, 721, 773	—	40.00
PS30	2005 (8)	7,000	KM#692-697, 721, 779	—	37.50
PS31	2006 (7)	—	KM#692-697, 721	—	35.00

ICELAND

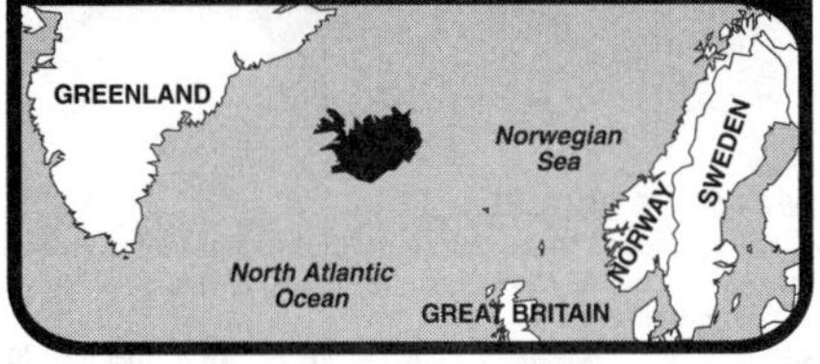

The Republic of Iceland, an island of recent volcanic origin in the North Atlantic east of Greenland and immediately south of the Arctic Circle, has an area of 39,768 sq. mi. (103,000 sq. km.) and a population of just over 300,000. Capital: Reykjavik. Fishing is the chief industry and accounts for a little less than 60 percent of the exports.

REPUBLIC

REFORM COINAGE

100 Old Kronur = 1 New Krona

KM# 27a KRONA
4.0000 g., Nickel Plated Steel, 19.79 mm. **Obv:** Giant facing **Rev:** Cod **Edge:** Reeded

Date	Mintage	F	VF	XF	Unc	BU
2003	5,144,000	—	—	—	0.75	1.50
2005	5,000,000	—	—	—	0.75	1.50
2006	10,000,000	—	—	—	0.75	1.50

KM# 28a 5 KRONUR
5.6000 g., Nickel Clad Steel, 24.5 mm. **Obv:** Quartered design of Eagle, dragon, bull and giant **Rev:** Two dolphins leaping left **Edge:** Reeded

Date	Mintage	F	VF	XF	Unc	BU
2005	2,000,000	—	—	—	2.00	3.00

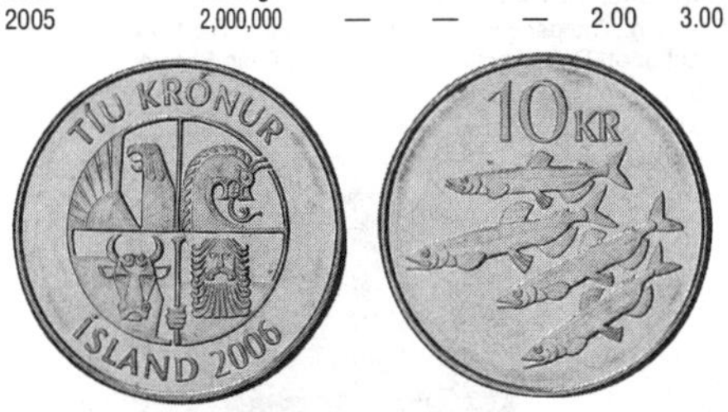

KM# 29.1a 10 KRONUR
8.0000 g., Nickel Clad Steel, 27.5 mm. **Obv:** Quartered design of Eagle, dragon, bull and giant **Rev:** Four capelins left **Edge:** Reeded

Date	Mintage	F	VF	XF	Unc	BU
2004	2,000,000	—	—	—	1.75	2.50
2005	4,505,000	—	—	—	1.75	2.50
2006	6,000,000	—	—	—	1.75	2.50

KM# 31 50 KRONUR
8.2500 g., Nickel-Brass, 23 mm. **Obv:** Quartered design of eagle, dragon, bull and giant **Rev:** Crab **Edge:** Reeded

Date	Mintage	F	VF	XF	Unc	BU
2001	2,000,000	—	—	—	4.00	5.00
2005	2,000,000	—	—	—	4.00	5.00

KM# 35 100 KRONUR
8.5000 g., Nickel-Brass, 25.5 mm. **Obv:** Quartered design of Eagle, dragon, bull and giant **Rev:** Lumpfish left **Edge:** Reeded

Date	Mintage	F	VF	XF	Unc	BU
2001	2,140,000	—	—	—	6.00	7.00
2004	2,400,000	—	—	—	6.00	7.00
2006	2,000,000	—	—	—	6.00	7.00

INDIA - REPUBLIC

The Republic of India, a subcontinent jutting southward from the mainland of Asia, has an area of 1,269,346 sq. mi. (3,287,590 sq. km.) and a population of over 900 million, second only to that of the People's Republic of China. Capital: New Delhi. India's economy is based on agriculture and industrial activity. Engineering goods, cotton apparel and fabrics, handicrafts, tea, iron and steel are exported.

The Republic of India is a member of the Common-wealth of Nations. The president is the Chief of State. The prime minister is the Head of Government.

MINT MARKS

(Mint marks usually appear directly below the date.)
B - Mumbai (Bombay), proof issues only
(B) - Mumbai (Bombay), diamond
(1985 25 Paise; 1988 10, 25 & 50 Paise)
(C) - Calcutta, no mint mark
(H) - Hyderabad, star (1963--)
(Hd) - Hyderabad, diamond split vertically (1953-1960)
(Hy) - Hyderabad, incuse dot in diamond (1960-1968)
M - Mumbai (Bombay), proof only after 1996
(N) - Noida, dot
(T) - Taegu (Korea), star below first or last date digit

REPUBLIC

DECIMAL COINAGE

KM# 54 25 PAISE
2.8200 g., Stainless Steel, 19 mm. **Obv:** Small Asoka lion pedestal **Rev:** Rhinoceros left **Edge:** Plain **Note:** Varieties of date size exist.

Date	Mintage	F	VF	XF	Unc	BU
2001(B)	—	—	0.10	0.20	1.00	—
2001(C)	—	—	0.10	0.20	1.00	—
2001(H)	—	—	0.15	0.25	1.00	—
2002(B)	—	—	0.15	0.25	1.00	—
2002(C)	—	—	0.15	0.25	1.00	—
2002(H)	—	—	0.25	0.40	1.00	—

KM# 69 50 PAISE
3.8000 g., Stainless Steel, 22 mm. **Subject:** Parliament Building in New Delhi **Obv:** Denomination **Rev:** Building

Date	Mintage	F	VF	XF	Unc	BU
2001(B)	—	—	0.15	0.25	0.50	—
2001(C)	—	—	0.15	0.25	0.50	—
2001(H)	—	—	0.20	0.40	0.75	—
2001(N)	—	—	0.15	0.25	0.50	—
2002(B)	—	—	0.15	0.25	0.50	—
2002(C)	—	—	0.15	0.25	0.50	—
2002(H)	—	—	0.15	0.25	0.50	—
2002(N)	—	—	0.15	0.25	0.50	—
2003(B)	—	—	0.15	0.25	0.50	—
2003(N)	—	—	0.15	0.25	0.50	—
2003(C)	—	—	0.15	0.25	0.50	—

KM# 92.2 RUPEE
4.8500 g., Stainless Steel, 25 mm. **Obv:** Asoka lion pedestal **Rev:** Denomination and date, grain ears flank **Edge:** Plain **Note:** Mintmark varieties exist.

Date	Mintage	F	VF	XF	Unc	BU
2001(H)	—	—	0.15	0.30	0.45	—
Note: Small and large mint mark exist, doubled left or right of wheat stalks						
2001(B)	—	—	0.15	0.30	0.45	—
2001(C)	—	—	0.15	0.30	0.45	—
2001(K)	—	—	0.15	0.30	0.45	—
2002(B)	—	—	0.15	0.30	0.45	—
2002(C)	—	—	0.15	0.30	0.45	—
2002(H)	—	—	0.15	0.30	0.45	—
2003(B)	—	—	0.15	0.30	0.45	—
2003(C)	—	—	0.15	0.30	0.45	—
2003(H)	—	—	0.15	0.30	0.45	—
2004(B)	—	—	0.15	0.30	0.45	—
2004(C)	—	—	0.15	0.30	0.45	—

KM# 313 RUPEE
4.9500 g., Stainless Steel, 25 mm. **Subject:** 100th Anniversary Birth of Jaya Prakash Narayan **Obv:** Asoka column **Rev:** Bust of Jaya Prakash Narayan slightly left **Edge:** Plain

Date	Mintage	F	VF	XF	Unc	BU
2002(B)	—	—	0.45	0.75	1.00	—
2002(B)	—	—	—	—	—	3.00
Note: In sets only						
2002(H)	—	—	0.45	0.75	1.00	—

KM# 314 RUPEE
4.9500 g., Stainless Steel, 25 mm. **Subject:** Maharana Pratap **Edge:** Plain

Date	Mintage	F	VF	XF	Unc	BU
2003(B)	—	—	0.45	0.75	1.00	—
2003(B)	—	—	—	—	—	2.50
Note: In sets only						
2003(H)	—	—	0.45	0.75	1.00	—

KM# 316 RUPEE
4.8500 g., Stainless Steel, 25 mm. **Obv:** Asoka lions **Rev:** 3/4 length military figure Veer Durgadass with spear left **Edge:** Plain

Date	Mintage	F	VF	XF	Unc	BU
2003(B)	—	—	0.50	0.80	1.25	—
2003(B)	—	—	—	—	—	2.50
Note: In sets only						
2003(H)	—	—	0.50	0.80	1.25	—

KM# 321 RUPEE
5.0000 g., Stainless Steel, 24.9 mm. **Subject:** 150th Anniversary of the Indian Postal Service **Obv:** Asoka lions above value **Rev:** Partial postage stamp design **Edge:** Grooved

Date	Mintage	F	VF	XF	Unc	BU
2004	—	—	—	—	2.00	—
2004	—	—	—	—	—	3.50
Note: In sets only						

KM# 322 RUPEE
4.9500 g., Stainless Steel, 24.8 mm. **Obv:** Asoka lions and value **Rev:** Cross dividing four dots **Edge:** Plain

Date	Mintage	F	VF	XF	Unc	BU
2005(C)	—	—	—	—	2.00	—
2007(H)	—	—	—	—	2.00	—

KM# 331 RUPEE
4.9300 g., Stainless Steel, 24.98 mm. **Subject:** Bharata Natyam Dance Expressions **Obv:** Asoka lion pedestal **Rev:** Jesture of hand with thumb up **Edge:** Plain

Date	Mintage	F	VF	XF	Unc	BU
2007(N)	—	—	—	—	2.00	—

KM# 121.5 2 RUPEES
6.0600 g., Copper-Nickel, 26 mm. **Subject:** National Integration **Obv:** Type C **Rev:** Flag on map **Edge:** Plain **Note:** 11-sided

Date	Mintage	F	VF	XF	Unc	BU
2001(B)	—	—	0.30	0.50	1.00	—
2001(C)	—	—	0.30	0.50	1.00	—
2001(H)	—	—	0.30	0.50	1.00	—
2002(B)	—	—	0.30	0.50	1.00	—
2002(C)	—	—	0.30	0.50	1.00	—
2002(H)	—	—	0.30	0.50	1.00	—
2002(N)	—	—	0.30	0.50	1.00	—
2003(B)	—	—	0.30	0.50	1.00	—
2003(C)	—	—	0.30	0.50	1.00	—
2003(H)	—	—	0.30	0.50	1.00	—

KM# 121.3 2 RUPEES
6.0000 g., Copper-Nickel, 26 mm. **Subject:** National Integration **Obv:** Type A **Rev:** Flag on map **Edge:** Plain **Shape:** 11-sided **Note:** Reduced size, non magnetic.

Date	Mintage	F	VF	XF	Unc	BU
2001(B)	—	—	0.30	0.50	1.00	—
2001(C)	—	—	0.30	0.50	1.00	—
2002(C)	—	—	0.30	0.50	1.00	—
2003(C)	—	—	0.30	0.50	1.00	—

KM# 303 2 RUPEES
6.2400 g., Copper-Nickel, 25.7 mm. **Subject:** 100th Anniversary Birth of Dr. Syama P. Mookerjee **Obv:** Asoka lion pedestal above denomination, type B **Rev:** Bust of Dr. Mookerjeeright **Edge:** Plain

Date	Mintage	F	VF	XF	Unc	BU
2001(C)	—	—	1.25	2.00	3.00	—
2001(C) Proof	—	Value: 7.50				

KM# 305 2 RUPEES
6.1000 g., Copper-Nickel, 25.7 mm. **Subject:** St. Tukaram **Obv:** Asoka column above value **Rev:** Seated musician **Shape:** Eleven sided

Date	Mintage	F	VF	XF	Unc	BU
2002(B)	—	—	0.75	1.25	2.00	—
2002(C)	—	—	0.75	1.25	2.00	—

KM# 346 2 RUPEES
6.0000 g., Copper-Nickel, 26 mm. **Subject:** Sant Tukaram (film about poet) **Obv:** Asoka column **Edge:** Plain **Shape:** 11-sided

Date	Mintage	F	VF	XF	Unc	BU
2002(C)	—	—	—	2.00	3.00	—
2002(C)	—	Value: 5.00				

KM# 307 2 RUPEES
6.0500 g., Copper-Nickel **Subject:** 150th Anniversary - Indian Railways **Obv:** Asoka column above value **Rev:** Cartoon elephant holding railroad lantern **Edge:** Plain **Shape:** 11-sided

Date	Mintage	F	VF	XF	Unc	BU
2003(B)	—	—	0.75	1.25	2.00	—
2003(C)	—	—	0.75	1.25	2.00	—
2003(C) Proof	—	Value: 5.00				

KM# 334 2 RUPEES
6.0000 g., Copper-Nickel, 26 mm. **Subject:** 150th Anniversary Telecommunications **Obv:** Asoka lions **Rev:** Cartoon bird standing holding cell phone **Edge:** Plain **Shape:** 11-sided

Date	Mintage	F	VF	XF	Unc	BU
2004(B)	—	—	—	—	2.00	—
2004(B) Proof	—	—	—	—	—	5.00

KM# 326 2 RUPEES
5.8000 g., Stainless Steel **Obv:** Asoka Pillar and value in center **Rev:** Cross with U-shaped arms and dots **Edge:** Plain **Note:** Size varies 26.75 - 27.07 mm

Date	Mintage	F	VF	XF	Unc	BU
2005(B)	—	—	—	0.50	1.35	—
2005(C)	—	—	—	0.50	1.35	—
2006(B) small date	—	—	—	0.40	1.00	—
2006(B) large date	—	—	—	0.40	1.00	—
2006(H)	—	—	—	0.40	1.00	—
2006(N)	—	—	—	0.40	1.00	—
2007(B)	—	—	—	0.40	1.00	—
2007(H)	—	—	—	0.40	1.00	—

KM# 350 2 RUPEES
6.0000 g., Copper-Nickel, 26 mm. **Subject:** 75th Anniversary Indian Air Force **Obv:** Asoka column **Edge:** Plain **Shape:** 11-sided

Date	Mintage	F	VF	XF	Unc	BU
2007(C)	—	—	—	—	3.00	1.25
2007(C) Proof	—	Value: 5.00				

KM# 327 2 RUPEES
5.8000 g., Stainless Steel, 26.97 mm. **Obv:** Asoka Pillar at center **Obv. Inscription:** INDIA in Hindi and English **Rev:** Hasta Mudra - hand gesture from the dance Bharata Natyam **Edge:** Plain

Date	Mintage	F	VF	XF	Unc	BU
2007(B)	—	—	—	0.40	1.00	—
2007(C)	—	—	—	0.40	1.00	—

KM# 154.2 5 RUPEES
8.9100 g., Copper-Nickel, 23 mm. **Obv:** Asoka lion pedestal **Rev:** Denomination flanked by flowers **Edge:** Milled

Date	Mintage	F	VF	XF	Unc	BU
2001(C)	—	—	8.00	10.00	15.00	—
2002(C)	—	—	8.00	10.00	15.00	—
2003(C)	—	—	8.00	10.00	15.00	—

KM# 154.4 5 RUPEES
Copper-Nickel, 23 mm. **Obv:** Asoka lion pedestal as seen on 2 Rupees, KM#121.5 **Rev:** Denomination flanked by flowers

Date	Mintage	F	VF	XF	Unc	BU
2001(B)	—	—	0.25	0.50	1.00	—
2002(B)	—	—	0.25	0.50	1.00	—
2003(B)	—	—	0.25	0.50	1.00	—
2004(B)	—	—	0.25	0.50	1.00	—

KM# 154.1 5 RUPEES
9.0000 g., Copper-Nickel, 35 mm. **Obv:** Asoka lion pedestal **Rev:** Denomination flanked by flowers **Note:** (C) - Calcutta mint has issued 2 distinctly different security edge varieties every year 1992-2003 with large dots and thick center line, w/small dots and narrow center line.

Date	Mintage	F	VF	XF	Unc	BU
2001(B)	—	—	0.25	0.50	1.00	—
2001(C) Plain 1	—	—	0.25	0.50	1.00	—
2001(C) Serif 1	—	—	1.00	2.00	3.00	—
2001(H)	—	—	0.35	0.60	1.50	—
2002(C)	—	—	0.25	0.50	1.00	—
2002(N)	—	—	0.25	0.50	1.00	—
2003(C)	—	—	0.25	0.50	1.00	—

KM# 304 5 RUPEES
9.0700 g., Copper-Nickel, 23.19 mm. **Subject:** 2600th Anniversary Birth of Bhagwan Mahavir **Obv:** Asoka column above denomination **Rev:** Swastika above hand in irregular frame **Edge:** Security

Date	Mintage	F	VF	XF	Unc	BU
2001(B)	—	—	1.00	2.00	3.00	5.00
2001(B) Proof	—	Value: 6.50				
2001(N)	—	—	1.00	2.00	3.00	5.00

KM# 308 5 RUPEES
8.9200 g., Copper-Nickel, 23.1 mm. **Subject:** Dadabhai Naroji **Obv:** Asoka column above value **Rev:** Bust of Dadabhai Naroji 3/4 right **Edge:** Security

Date	Mintage	F	VF	XF	Unc	BU
ND(2003)(B)	—	—	1.00	1.75	3.00	5.00

KM# 317.2 5 RUPEES
8.8000 g., Copper-Nickel, 23.1 mm. **Obv:** Asoka lion pedestal **Rev:** K. Kamaraj above life dates **Edge:** Reeded

Date	Mintage	F	VF	XF	Unc	BU
ND (2003)(H)	—	—	5.00	7.00	11.00	—

KM# 341 5 RUPEES
9.0000 g., Copper-Nickel, 23 mm. **Subject:** 100th Anniversary Birth of Kumaraswami Kamaraj **Obv:** Asoka column **Edge:** Security

Date	Mintage	F	VF	XF	Unc	BU
ND(2003)	—	—	—	—	3.50	—
ND(2003) Proof	—	Value: 6.00				

KM# 317.1 5 RUPEES
8.8000 g., Copper-Nickel, 23.1 mm. **Obv:** Asoka lions **Rev:** K. Kamaraj above life dates **Edge:** Security

Date	Mintage	F	VF	XF	Unc	BU
ND(2003)(B)	—	—	1.00	1.75	3.00	5.00
ND(2003)(H)	—	—	1.25	2.00	3.50	5.50
ND(2003)(C)	—	—	1.00	1.75	3.00	5.00

KM# 336 5 RUPEES
9.0000 g., Copper-Nickel, 23 mm. **Subject:** 100th Anniversary Birth of Lal Bahadur Shastri **Obv:** Asoka lions **Rev:** Bust of Lal Bahadur Shastri 3/4 right **Edge:** Security

Date	Mintage	F	VF	XF	Unc	BU
ND(2004)(C)	—	—	—	—	3.50	—
ND(2004)(C) Proof	—	Value: 8.00				

KM# 329 5 RUPEES
9.0700 g., Bi-Metallic Brass center in Copper-Nickel ring, 23.25 mm. **Obv:** Asoka column, value below **Rev:** Bust of Shastri 3/4 left **Rev. Legend:** LALBAHADUR SHASTRI BIRTH CENTENARY **Edge:** Security

Date	Mintage	F	VF	XF	Unc	BU
ND(2004)	—	—	—	—	3.50	5.00

KM# 325 5 RUPEES
8.8500 g., Copper-Nickel, 23 mm. **Subject:** 75th Anniversary Dandi March **Obv:** Asoka column **Rev:** Ghandi leading marchers **Edge:** Security type

Date	Mintage	F	VF	XF	Unc	BU
ND (2005)(B)	—	—	—	—	3.00	—
ND(2005)(B)	—	—	—	—	—	5.00

Note: In sets only

KM# 324 5 RUPEES
8.8500 g., Copper-Nickel, 23 mm. **Obv:** Asoka column **Rev:** Bust of Mahatma Basaveshwara slightly left **Edge:** Security

Date	Mintage	F	VF	XF	Unc	BU
ND(2006)(B)	—	—	0.40	1.00	3.00	5.00
ND(2006)(B)	—	Value: 6.00				

KM# 328 5 RUPEES
9.5000 g., Copper-Nickel, 23.10 mm. **Subject:** 150th Anniversary Birth of L. B. G. Tilak **Obv:** Asoka Lion pedestal **Rev:** Bust of Tilak facing slightly right **Edge:** Security

Date	Mintage	F	VF	XF	Unc	BU
2007(B)	—	—	—	—	3.50	5.00

KM# 330 5 RUPEES
6.0300 g., Stainless Steel, 22.88 mm. **Obv:** Asoka column **Rev:** Waves **Edge:** Security

Date	Mintage	F	VF	XF	Unc	BU
2007(B)	—	—	—	—	4.00	5.00
2007(H)	—	—	—	—	4.00	5.00

KM# 309 10 RUPEES
12.5000 g., Copper-Nickel, 31 mm. **Subject:** 100th Anniversary Birth of Dr. Syama P. Mookerjee **Obv:** Asoka lion pedestal **Rev:** Bust of Dr. Mookerjee 1/2 right **Edge:** Reeded

Date	Mintage	F	VF	XF	Unc	BU
2001(C)	—	—	—	—	9.00	—
2001(C) Proof	—	Value: 15.00				

KM# 344 10 RUPEES
12.5000 g., Copper-Nickel, 31 mm. **Subject:** 100th Anniversary Birth of Jaya Prakash Narayan **Obv:** Asoka column **Rev:** Bust of Jaya Prakash Narayan slightly left **Edge:** Reeded

Date	Mintage	F	VF	XF	Unc	BU
2002(B)	—	—	—	—	9.00	—
2002(B) Proof	—	Value: 15.00				

KM# 347 10 RUPEES
12.5000 g., Copper-Nickel, 31 mm. **Subject:** Sant Tukaram (film about poet) **Obv:** Asoka column **Edge:** Reeded

Date	Mintage	F	VF	XF	Unc	BU
2002(C)	—	—	—	—	9.00	—
2002(C) Proof	—	Value: 15.00				

KM# 319 10 RUPEES
12.5000 g., Copper-Nickel, 31 mm. **Obv:** Asoka lion pedestal **Rev:** Bust of Maharana Pratap left

Date	Mintage	F	VF	XF	Unc	BU
2003(B)	—	—	—	—	9.00	—
2003(B) Proof	—	Value: 15.00				

KM# 332 10 RUPEES
12.5000 g., Copper-Nickel, 31 mm. **Obv:** Asoka lions **Rev:** 3/4 length military figure Veer Durgadass with spear left **Edge:** Reeded

Date	Mintage	F	VF	XF	Unc	BU
2003(B)	—	—	—	—	9.00	—
2003(B) Proof	—	Value: 15.00				

KM# 310 50 RUPEES
30.0000 g., Copper-Nickel, 39 mm. **Subject:** 100th Anniversary Birth of Dr. Syama P. Mookerjee **Obv:** Asoka lion pedestal **Rev:** Bust of Dr. Mookerjee 1/2 right **Edge:** Reeded

Date	Mintage	F	VF	XF	Unc	BU
2001(C)	—	—	—	—	18.00	—
2001(C) Proof	—	Value: 30.00				

KM# 348 50 RUPEES
30.0000 g., Copper-Nickel, 39 mm. **Subject:** Sant Tukaram (film about poet) **Obv:** Asoka column **Edge:** Reeded

Date	Mintage	F	VF	XF	Unc	BU
2002(C)	—	—	—	—	15.00	—
2002(C) Proof	—	Value: 35.00				

KM# 311 100 RUPEES
35.0000 g., 0.5000 Silver 0.5626 oz. ASW, 44 mm. **Subject:** 10th Anniversary Dr, Syama P. Mookerjee **Obv:** Asoka lion pedestal **Rev:** Bust of Dr. Mookerjee1/2 right **Edge:** Reeded

Date	Mintage	F	VF	XF	Unc	BU
2001(C)	—	—	—	—	35.00	—
2001(C) Proof	—	Value: 50.00				

KM# 312 100 RUPEES
35.0000 g., 0.5000 Silver 0.5626 oz. ASW, 44 mm. **Subject:** 2600th Anniversary Birth of Bhagwan Mahavir **Obv:** Asoka lion pedestal **Rev:** Swastika above hand in irregular frame **Edge:** Reeded

Date	Mintage	F	VF	XF	Unc	BU
2001(B)	—	—	—	—	35.00	—
2001(B) Proof	—	Value: 50.00				

KM# 315 100 RUPEES
35.0000 g., 0.5000 Silver 0.5626 oz. ASW, 44 mm. **Subject:** 2600th Anniversary - Bhagwan Mahavir **Edge:** Reeded

Date	Mintage	F	VF	XF	Unc	BU
2002(B)	—	—	—	—	30.00	—
2002(B) Proof	—	Value: 50.00				

KM# 345 100 RUPEES
35.0000 g., 0.5000 Silver 0.5626 oz. ASW, 44 mm. **Subject:** 100th Anniversary Birth of Jaya Prakash Narayan **Obv:** Asoka column **Rev:** Bust of Jaya Prakash Narayan slightly left **Edge:** Reeded

Date	Mintage	F	VF	XF	Unc	BU
2002(B)	—	—	—	—	35.00	—
2002(B) Proof	—	Value: 50.00				

KM# 349 100 RUPEES
35.0000 g., 0.5000 Silver 0.5626 oz. ASW, 44 mm. **Subject:** Sant Tukaram (film about poet) **Obv:** Asoka column **Edge:** Reeded

Date	Mintage	F	VF	XF	Unc	BU
2002(C)	—	—	—	—	35.00	—
2002(C) Proof	—	Value: 50.00				

KM# 342 100 RUPEES
35.0000 g., 0.5000 Silver 0.5626 oz. ASW, 44 mm. **Subject:** 100th Anniversary Birth of Kumaraswami Kamaraj **Obv:** Asoka column **Edge:** Reeded

Date	Mintage	F	VF	XF	Unc	BU
ND(2003)	—	—	—	—	35.00	—
ND(2003) Proof	—	Value: 50.00				

KM# 340 100 RUPEES
35.0000 g., 0.5000 Silver 0.5626 oz. ASW, 44 mm. **Subject:** 150th Anniversary Indian Railways **Obv:** Asoka column **Rev:** Cartoon elephant holding railroad lantern **Edge:** Reeded

Date	Mintage	F	VF	XF	Unc	BU
2003	—	—	—	—	—	35.00
2003 Proof	—	Value: 50.00				

KM# 318 100 RUPEES
35.0000 g., 0.5000 Silver 0.5626 oz. ASW, 44 mm. **Obv:** Asoka lion pedestal **Rev:** K. Kamaraj above life dates **Edge:** Reeded

Date	Mintage	F	VF	XF	Unc	BU
ND(2003)(B)	—	—	—	—	35.00	—
ND(2003)(B) Proof	—	Value: 50.00				

KM# 320 100 RUPEES
35.0000 g., 0.5000 Silver 0.5626 oz. ASW, 44 mm. **Obv:** Asoka lion pedestal **Rev:** Bust of Maharana Pratap left **Edge:** Reeded

Date	Mintage	F	VF	XF	Unc	BU
2003(B)	—	—	—	—	30.00	—
2003(B) Proof	—	Value: 50.00				

KM# 333 100 RUPEES
35.0000 g., 0.5000 Silver 0.5626 oz. ASW, 44 mm. **Obv:** Asoka lions **Rev:** 3/4 length military figure Veer Durgadass with spear left **Edge:** Reeded

Date	Mintage	F	VF	XF	Unc	BU
2003(B)	—	—	—	—	35.00	—
2003(B) Proof	—	Value: 50.00				

KM# 335 100 RUPEES
35.0000 g., 0.5000 Silver 0.5626 oz. ASW, 44 mm. **Subject:** 150th Anniversary Telecommunications **Obv:** Asoka lions **Rev:** Cartoon bird standing holding cell phone **Edge:** Reeded

Date	Mintage	F	VF	XF	Unc	BU
2004(B)	—	—	—	—	35.00	—
2004(B) Proof	—	Value: 50.00				

KM# 337 100 RUPEES
35.0000 g., 0.5000 Silver 0.5626 oz. ASW, 44 mm. **Subject:** 100th Anniversary Birth of Lal Bahadur Shasti **Obv:** Asoka lions **Rev:** Bust of Lal Bahadur Shastri 3/4 left **Edge:** Reeded

Date	Mintage	F	VF	XF	Unc	BU
ND(2004)(C)	—	—	—	—	35.00	—
ND(2004)(C) Proof	—	Value: 50.00				

KM# 343 100 RUPEES
35.0000 g., 0.5000 Silver 0.5626 oz. ASW, 44 mm. **Subject:** 150th Anniversary Indian Postal Service **Obv:** Asoka column **Rev:** Partial postage stamp design **Edge:** Reeded

Date	Mintage	F	VF	XF	Unc	BU
2004	—	—	—	—	35.00	—
2004 Proof	—	Value: 50.00				

KM# 339 100 RUPEES
35.0000 g., 0.5000 Silver 0.5626 oz. ASW, 44 mm. **Obv:** Asoka column **Rev:** Bust of Mahatma Basaveshwara slightly left **Edge:** Reeded

Date	Mintage	F	VF	XF	Unc	BU
ND(2006)B	—	—	—	—	35.00	—
ND(2006)B Proof	—	Value: 50.00				

KM# 351 100 RUPEES
35.0000 g., 0.5000 Silver 0.5626 oz. ASW, 44 mm. **Subject:** 75th Anniversary Indian Air Force **Obv:** Asoka column **Edge:** Reeded

Date	Mintage	F	VF	XF	Unc	BU
2007(C)	—	—	—	—	35.00	—
2007(C) Proof	—	Value: 50.00				

PROOF SETS

KM#	Date	Mintage	Identification	Issue Price	Mkt Val
PS56	2001 (4)	—	KM#303, 309, 310, 311	—	100
PS57	2001 (2)	—	KM#304, 312	—	55.00
PS58	2002B (3)	—	KM#313, 344, 345	—	65.00
PS59	2002(C) (4)	—	KM#346-349	—	70.00
PS60	2003 (3)	—	KM#314, 319, 320	—	65.00
PS61	2003B (3)	—	KM#316, 332, 333	—	65.00
PS62	2003(C) (2)	—	KM#307, 340	—	55.00
PS63	ND(2003) (2)	—	KM#341, 342	—	60.00
PS64	2004 (2)	—	KM#321, 343	—	55.00
PS65	2004B (2)	—	KM#334, 335	—	55.00
PS66	2005(C) (2)	—	KM#336, 337	—	55.00
PS67	2005B (2)	—	KM#325, 338	—	55.00
PS68	2006B (2)	—	KM#324, 339	—	55.00
PS69	2007 (2)	—	KM#350, 351	—	55.00

INDONESIA

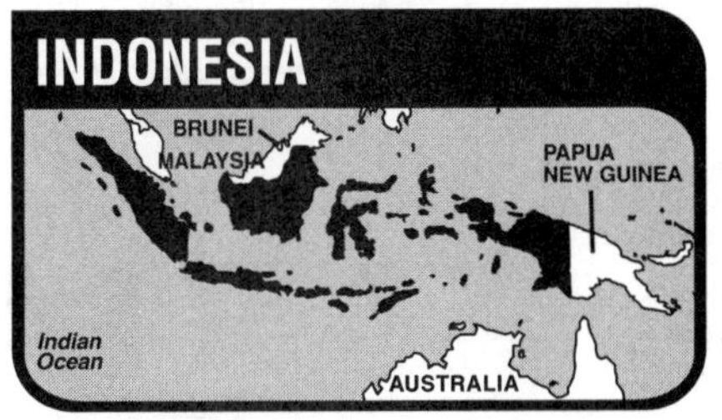

The Republic of Indonesia, the world's largest archipelago, extends for more than 3,000 miles (4,827 km.) along the equator from the mainland of southeast Asia to Australia. The 17,508 islands comprising the archipelago have a combined area of 788,425 sq. mi. (1,919,440 sq. km.) and a population of 205 million, including East Timor. On August 30, 1999, the Timorese majority voted for independence. The Inter FET (International Forces for East Timor) is now in charge of controlling the chaotic situation. Capitol: Jakarta. Petroleum, timber, rubber, and coffee are exported.

Modern coinage issued by the Republic of Indonesia includes separate series for West Irian and for the Riau Archipelago, an area of small islands between Singapore and Sumatra.

MONETARY SYSTEM
100 Sen = 1 Rupiah

REPUBLIC

STANDARD COINAGE

100 Sen = 1 Rupiah

KM# 60 50 RUPIAH
1.3600 g., Aluminum, 19.95 mm. **Obv:** National emblem **Rev:** Black-naped Oriole **Edge:** Plain

Date	Mintage	F	VF	XF	Unc	BU
2001	—	—	—	—	0.30	1.00
2002	—	—	—	—	0.30	1.00

KM# 61 100 RUPIAH
1.7900 g., Aluminum, 23 mm. **Obv:** National emblem **Rev:** Palm Cockatoo **Edge:** Plain

Date	Mintage	F	VF	XF	Unc	BU
2001	—	—	—	—	0.75	1.25
2002	—	—	—	—	0.75	1.25
2003	—	—	—	—	0.75	1.25
2004	—	—	—	—	0.75	1.25

KM# 66 200 RUPIAH
2.4000 g., Aluminum, 25 mm. **Obv:** National arms **Rev:** Balinese starling bird above value **Edge:** Plain

Date	Mintage	F	VF	XF	Unc	BU
2003	—	—	—	—	1.00	1.50

KM# 59 500 RUPIAH
5.3200 g., Aluminum-Bronze, 24 mm. **Obv:** National emblem **Rev:** Denomination

Date	Mintage	F	VF	XF	Unc	BU
2001	—	—	—	—	2.00	2.50
2002	—	—	—	—	2.00	2.50
2003	—	—	—	—	2.00	2.50

KM# 67 500 RUPIAH
3.1100 g., Aluminum, 27.2 mm. **Obv:** National arms **Rev:** Jasmine flower above value **Edge:** Segmented reeding

Date	Mintage	F	VF	XF	Unc	BU
2003	—	—	—	—	2.00	2.50

KM# 64 25000 RUPIAH
28.2800 g., 0.9250 Silver 0.8410 oz. ASW, 38.6 mm. **Subject:** Centennial of Sukarno's Birth **Obv:** National arms **Rev:** Uniformed bust of Sukarno **Edge:** Reeded

Date	Mintage	F	VF	XF	Unc	BU
2001 Proof	500	Value: 100				

KM# 65 500,000 RUPIAH
15.0000 g., 0.9990 Gold 0.4818 oz. AGW, 28.2 mm. **Subject:** Centennial of Sukarno's Birth **Obv:** National arms **Rev:** Head left **Edge:** Reeded

Date	Mintage	F	VF	XF	Unc	BU
2001 Proof	500	Value: 500				

IRAN

The Islamic Republic of Iran, located between the Caspian Sea and the Persian Gulf in southwestern Asia, has an area of 636,296 sq. mi. (1,648,000 sq. km.) and a population of 59.7 million. Capital: Tehran. Although predominantly an agricultural state, Iran depends heavily on oil for foreign exchange. Crude oil, carpets and agricultural products are exported.

In 1931 the Kingdom of Persia became known as the Kingdom of Iran. In 1979 the monarchy was toppled and an Islamic Republic proclaimed.

TITLES

دار الخلافة

Dar al-Khilafat

RULERS
Islamic Republic, SH1358-/1979-AD

MINT NAME

طهران

Tehran

تفليس

Tiflis

MINT MARKS
H - Heaton (Birmingham)
L - Leningrad (St. Petersburg)

COIN DATING

Iranian coins were dated according to the Moslem lunar calendar until March 21, 1925 (AD), when dating was switched to a new calendar based on the solar year, indicated by the notation SH. The monarchial calendar system was adopted in 1976 = MS2535 and was abandoned in 1978 = MS2537. The previously used solar year calendar was restored at that time.

MONETARY SYSTEM

1932-Date (SH1310-Date)
5 Dinars = 1 Shahi
20 Shahis = 1 Rial (100 Dinars)
10 Rials = 1 Toman

SILVER AND GOLD COINAGE

The precious metal monetary system of Qajar Persia prior to the reforms of 1878 was the direct descendant of the Mongol system introduced by Ghazan Mahmud in 1297AD, and was the last example of a medieval islamic coinage. It is not a modern system, and cannot be understood as such. It is not possible to list types, dates, and mints as for other countries, both because of the nature of the coinage, and because very little research has been done on the series. The following comments should help elucidate its nature.

STANDARDS: The weight of the primary silver and gold coins was set by law and was expressed in terms of the Mesqal (about 4.61 g) and the Nokhod (24 Nokhod = 1 Mesqal). The primary silver coin was the Rupee from AH1211-1212, the Riyal from AH1212-1241, and the Gheran from AH1241-1344. The standard gold coin was the Toman. Currently the price of gold is quoted in Mesqals.

DENOMINATIONS: In addition to the primary denominations, noted in the last paragraph, fractional pieces were coined, valued at one-eighth, one-fourth, and one-half the primary denomination, usually in much smaller quantities. These were ordinarily struck from the same dies as the larger pieces, sometimes on broad, thin flans, sometimes on thick, dumpy flans. On the smaller coins, the denomination can best be determined only by weighing the coin. The denomination is almost never expressed on the coin!

DEVALUATIONS: From time to time, the standard for silver and gold was reduced, and the old coin recalled and replaced with lighter coin, the difference going to the government coffers. The effect was that of a devaluation of the primary silver and gold coins, or inversely regarded, an increase in the price of silver and gold. The durations of each standard varied from about 2 to 20 years. The standards are given for each ruler, as the denomination can only be determined when the standard is known.

LIGHTWEIGHT AND ALLOYED PIECES: Most of the smaller denomination coins were issued at lighter weights than those prescribed by law, with the difference going to the pockets of the mintmasters. Other mints, notably Hamadan, added excessive amounts of alloy to the coins, and some mintmasters lost their heads as a result. Discrepancies in weight of as much as 15 percent and more are observed, with the result that it is often quite impossible to determine the denomination of a coin!

OVERSIZE COINS: Occasionally, multiples of the primary denominations were produced, usually on special occasions for presentation by the Shah to his favorites. These 'coins' did not circulate (except as bullion), and were usually worn as ornaments. They were the 'NCLT's' of their day.

MINTS & EPITHETS: Qajar coinage was struck at 34 mints (plus at least a dozen others striking only copper Falus), which are listed previously, with drawings of the mintnames in Persian, as they appear on the coins. However, the Persian script admits of infinite variation and stylistic whimsy, so the forms given are only guides, and not absolute. Only a knowledge of the script will assure correct reading. In addition to the city name, most mintnames were given identifying epithets, which occasionally appear in lieu of the mintname, particularly at Iravan and Mashhad.

TYPES: There were no types in the modern sense, but the arrangement of the legends and the ornamental borders were frequently changed. These changes do not coincide with changes in standards, and cannot be used to determine the mint, which must be found by actually reading the reverse inscriptions.

ARRANGEMENT

The following listings are arranged first by ruler, with various standards explained. Then, the coins are listed by denomination within each reign. For each denomination, one or more pieces, when available, are illustrated, with the mint and date noted beneath each photo. For each type, a date range is given, but this range indicates the years during which the particular type was current, and does not imply that every year of the interval is known on actual coins. Because dates were carelessly engraved, and old dies were used until they wore out or broke, we occasionally find coins of a particular type dated before or after the indicated interval. Such coins command no premium. No attempt has been made to determine which mints actually exist for which types.

KRAN STANDARD
AH1293-1344, SH1304-1309,
1876-1931AD
50 Dinars = 1 Shahi
1000 Dinars = 20 Shahis = 1 Kran (Qiron)
10 Krans = 1 Toman

Special Gold Issue
AH1337/1918-1919AD
1 Ashrafi (= 1 Toman)
SH1305-1309/1927-1931AD

Toman replaced by Pahlavi (light standard). Relationship of Pahlavi to Kran not known.

NOTE: Dated reverse dies lacking the ruler's name were not discarded at the end of a reign (especially from Nasir al-Din to Muzaffar al-Din), but remained in use until broken or worn out. Sometimes the old date was scratched out or changed, but often the die was used with the old date unaltered. Some dies with date below wreath retained the old date but had the new date engraved among the lion's legs.

SHAHI SEFID
(White Shahi)

Called the White (i.e. silver) Shahi to distinguish it from the Black or Copper Shahi, the Shahi Sefid was actually worth 3 Shahis (150 Dinars) or 3 1/8 Shahis (156 ¼ Dinars). It was used primarily for distribution on New Year's Day (now RUZ) as good-luck gifts. Since 1926 special privately struck tokens, having no monetary value, have been used instead of coins. The Shahi Sefid was broader, but much thinner than the ¼ Kran (Rob'l), worth 250 Dinars.

Milled Gold Coinage:

Modern imitations exist of many types, particularly the small 1/5, 1/2, and 1 Toman coins. These are usually underweight (or rarely overweight), and are sold in the bazaars at a small premium over bullion. They are usually crude and probably not intended to deceive collectors, but some are sold for jewelry and some are dated outside the reign of the ruler whose name or portrait they bear. A few deceptive counterfeits are known of the large 10 Toman pieces.

ISLAMIC REPUBLIC

MILLED COINAGE

KM# 1260 50 RIALS

Copper-Nickel, 26 mm. **Subject:** Shrine of Hazrat Masumah **Obv:** Value and date **Rev:** Shrine within beaded circle **Edge:** Reeded

Date	Mintage	F	VF	XF	Unc	BU
SH1380 (2001)	—	—	2.50	3.50	5.00	—
SH1382 (2003)	—	—	2.50	3.50	5.00	—

KM# 1266 50 RIALS

3.5100 g., Aluminum-Bronze, 20.1 mm. **Obv:** Value and date **Rev:** Hazrat Masumah Shrine **Edge:** Reeded **Mint:** Tehran

Date	Mintage	F	VF	XF	Unc	BU
SH1382(2003)	—	—	—	—	50.00	—
SH1383(2004)	—	—	—	—	2.50	—
SH1384(2005)	—	—	—	—	2.50	—
SH1385(2006)	—	—	—	—	2.50	—

KM# 1261.2 100 RIALS

Copper-Nickel, 29 mm. **Obv:** Value and date **Rev:** Shrine within designed border **Note:** Thick denomination and numerals

Date	Mintage	F	VF	XF	Unc	BU
SH1380 (2001)	—	—	—	—	6.50	—
SH1382 (2003)	—	—	—	—	6.50	—

KM# 1267 100 RIALS

4.6200 g., Aluminum-Bronze, 22.9 mm. **Obv:** Value, date divides wreath below **Rev:** Imam Reza Shrine **Edge:** Reeded **Mint:** Tehran

Date	Mintage	F	VF	XF	Unc	BU
SH1382(2003)	—	—	—	—	50.00	—
SH1383(2004)	—	—	—	—	3.50	—
SH1384(2005)	—	—	—	—	3.50	—
SH1385(2006)	—	—	—	—	3.50	—

KM# 1262 250 RIALS

Bi-Metallic Copper-Nickel center in Brass ring, 28 mm. **Obv:** Value within circle, inscription and date divide wreath **Rev:** Stylized flower within circle and wreath

Date	Mintage	F	VF	XF	Unc	BU
SH1381 (2002)	—	—	—	—	7.50	—
SH1382 (2003)	—	—	—	—	7.50	—

KM# 1268 250 RIALS

5.5000 g., Copper-Nickel, 24.6 mm. **Obv:** Value, date below divides sprays **Rev:** Stylized flower within sprays **Edge:** Plain **Mint:** Tehran

Date	Mintage	F	VF	XF	Unc	BU
SH1382(2003)	—	—	—	—	50.00	—
SH1383(2004)	—	—	—	—	4.50	—
SH1384(2005)	—	—	—	—	4.50	—
SH1385(2006)	—	—	—	—	4.50	—

KM# 1268a 250 RIALS

Aluminum-Bronze **Obv:** Value, date below divides sprays **Rev:** Stylized flower within sprays **Mint:** Tehran

Date	Mintage	F	VF	XF	Unc	BU
SH1386(2007)	—	—	—	—	4.50	—

KM# 1269 500 RIALS

8.9100 g., Bi-Metallic Aluminum-Bronze center in Copper-Nickel ring, 27.1 mm. **Obv:** Value **Rev:** Bird and flowers **Edge:** Reeded **Mint:** Tehran

Date	Mintage	F	VF	XF	Unc	BU
SH1382(2003)	—	—	—	—	50.00	—
SH1383(2004)	—	—	—	—	6.00	—
SH1384(2005)	—	—	—	—	6.00	—
SH1385(2006)	—	—	—	—	6.00	—

KM# 1269a 500 RIALS

Aluminum-Bronze **Obv:** Value in ornamental circle **Rev:** Bird and flowers **Mint:** Tehran

Date	Mintage	F	VF	XF	Unc	BU
SH1386(2007)	—	—	—	—	6.00	—

BULLION COINAGE

Issued by the National Bank of Iran

KM# 1250.2 1/2 AZADI

4.0680 g., 0.9000 Gold 0.1177 oz. AGW **Obv:** Legend larger **Obv. Legend:** "Spring of Freedom"

Date	Mintage	F	VF	XF	Unc	BU
SH1381 (2002)	—	—	—	—	150	—

IRAQ

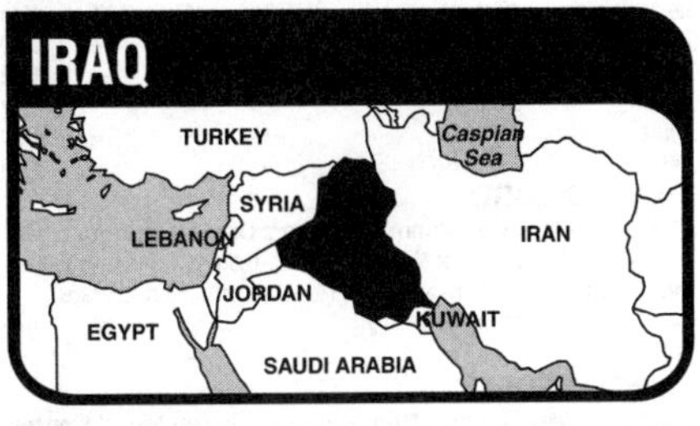

The Republic of Iraq, historically known as Mesopotamia, is located in the Near East and is bordered by Kuwait, Iran, Turkey, Syria, Jordan and Saudi Arabia. It has an area of 167,925 sq. mi. (434,920 sq. km.) and a population of 19 million. Capital: Baghdad. The economy of Iraq is based on agriculture and petroleum. Crude oil accounted for 94 percent of the exports before the war with Iran began in 1980.

Mesopotamia was the site of a number of flourishing civilizations of antiquity - Sumeria, Assyria, Babylonia, Parthia, Persia and the Biblical cities of Ur, Ninevehand and Babylon. Desired because of its favored location, which embraced the fertile alluvial plains of the Tigris and Euphrates Rivers, Mesopotamia - 'land between the rivers'- was conquered by Cyrus the Great of Persia, Alexander of Macedonia and by Arabs who made the legendary city of Baghdad the capital of the ruling caliphate. Suleiman the Magnificent conquered Mesopotamia for Turkey in1534, and it formed part of the Ottoman Empire until 1623, and from 1638 to 1917. Great Britain, given a League of Nations mandate over the territory in 1920, recognized Iraq as a kingdom in 1922. Iraq became an independent constitutional monarchy presided over by the Hashemite family, direct descendants of the prophet Mohammed, in 1932. In 1958, the army-led revolution of July 14 overthrew the monarchy and proclaimed a republic.

NOTE: The 'I' mintmark on 1938 and 1943 issues appears on the obverse near the point of the bust. Some of the issues of 1938 have a dot to denote a composition change from nickel to copper-nickel.

MONETARY SYSTEM

Falus, Fulus — Fals, Fils — Falsan

50 Fils = 1 Dirham
200 Fils = 1 Riyal
1000 Fils = 1 Dinar (Pound)

REPUBLIC

DECIMAL COINAGE

KM# 175 25 DINARS

2.5000 g., Copper-Plated-Steel, 17.4 mm. **Obv:** Value **Rev:** Map **Edge:** Plain

Date	Mintage	F	VF	XF	Unc	BU
AH1425-2004	—	—	—	—	1.00	—

KM# 176 50 DINARS

3.4300 g., Brass-Plated Steel, 19.9 mm. **Obv:** Value and legend **Rev:** Map **Edge:** Plain

Date	Mintage	F	VF	XF	Unc	BU
AH1425-2004	—	—	—	—	—	1.50

KM# 177 100 DINARS

4.3000 g., Stainless Steel, 22 mm. **Obv:** Value **Rev:** Map **Edge:** Reeded

Date	Mintage	F	VF	XF	Unc	BU
AH1425-2004	—	—	—	—	2.00	—

IRELAND

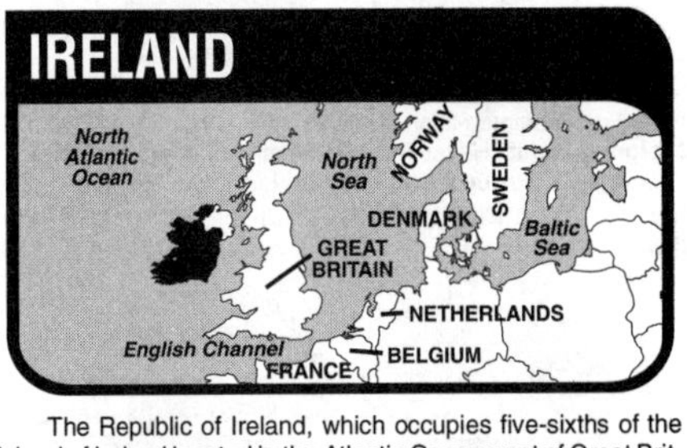

The Republic of Ireland, which occupies five-sixths of the island of Ireland located in the Atlantic Ocean west of Great Britain, has an area of 27,136 sq. mi. (70,280 sq. km.) and a population of 4.3 million. Capital: Dublin. Agriculture and dairy farming are the principal industries. Meat, livestock, dairy products and textiles are exported.

REPUBLIC

EURO COINAGE

European Union Issues

KM# 32 EURO CENT

2.2700 g., Copper Plated Steel, 16.25 mm. **Obv:** Harp **Obv. Designer:** Jarlath Hayes **Rev:** Denomination and globe **Rev. Designer:** Luc Luycx **Edge:** Plain

Date	Mintage	VG	F	VF	XF	Unc
2002	404,339,788	—	—	—	—	0.35
2003	67,902,182	—	—	—	—	0.35
2004	174,833,634	—	—	—	—	0.35

Date	Mintage	VG	F	VF	XF	Unc
2005	127,019	—	—	—	—	0.35
2006	—	—	—	—	—	0.35
2007	—	—	—	—	—	0.35

KM# 33 2 EURO CENT

3.0000 g., Copper Plated Steel, 18.75 mm. **Obv:** Harp **Obv. Designer:** Jarlath Hayes **Rev:** Denomination and globe **Rev. Designer:** Luc Luycx **Edge:** Plain with groove

Date	Mintage	VG	F	VF	XF	Unc
2002	354,643,386	—	—	—	—	0.50
2003	177,290,034	—	—	—	—	0.50
2004	143,004,694	—	—	—	—	0.50
2005	72,600	—	—	—	—	0.50
2006	—	—	—	—	—	0.50
2007	—	—	—	—	—	0.50

KM# 34 5 EURO CENT

4.0000 g., Copper-Plated-Steel, 19.60 mm. **Obv:** Harp **Obv. Designer:** Jarlath Hayes **Rev:** Denomination and globe **Rev. Designer:** Luc Luycx **Edge:** Plain

Date	Mintage	VG	F	VF	XF	Unc
2002	456,270,848	—	—	—	—	0.75
2003	48,352,370	—	—	—	—	0.75
2004	80,354,322	—	—	—	—	0.75
2005	42,224	—	—	—	—	0.75
2006	—	—	—	—	—	0.75
2007	—	—	—	—	—	0.75

KM# 35 10 EURO CENT

4.0700 g., Aluminum-Bronze, 19.75 mm. **Obv:** Harp **Obv. Designer:** Jarlath Hayes **Rev:** Denomination and map **Rev. Designer:** Luc Luycx **Edge:** Reeded

Date	Mintage	VG	F	VF	XF	Unc
2002	275,913,000	—	—	—	—	1.00
2003	133,815,907	—	—	—	—	1.00
2004	16,922,898	—	—	—	—	1.00
2005	4,707	—	—	—	—	1.00
2006	—	—	—	—	—	1.00

KM# 47 10 EURO CENT

4.0700 g., Aluminum-Bronze, 19.75 mm. **Obv:** Harp **Obv. Designer:** Jarlath Hayes **Rev:** Relief map of Western Europe, stars, lines and value **Rev. Designer:** Luc Luycz **Edge:** Reeded

Date	Mintage	VG	F	VF	XF	Unc
2007	—	—	—	—	—	1.00

KM# 36 20 EURO CENT

5.7300 g., Aluminum-Bronze, 22.25 mm. **Obv:** Harp **Obv. Designer:** Jarlath Hayes **Rev:** Denomination and map **Rev. Designer:** Luc Luycx **Edge:** Notched

Date	Mintage	VG	F	VF	XF	Unc
2002	234,575,562	—	—	—	—	1.25
2003	57,142,221	—	—	—	—	1.25
2004	32,421,447	—	—	—	—	1.25
2005	30,675	—	—	—	—	1.25
2006	—	—	—	—	—	1.25

KM# 48 20 EURO CENT

5.7300 g., Aluminum-Bronze, 22.25 mm. **Obv:** Harp **Obv. Designer:** Jarlath Hayes **Rev:** Relief map of Western Europe, stars, lines and value **Rev. Designer:** Luc Luycz **Edge:** Notched

Date	Mintage	F	VF	XF	Unc	BU
2007	—	—	—	—	1.25	—

KM# 37 50 EURO CENT

7.8100 g., Aluminum-Bronze, 24.25 mm. **Obv:** Harp **Obv. Designer:** Jarlath Hayes **Rev. Designer:** Denomination and map **Edge:** Reeded

Date	Mintage	VG	F	VF	XF	Unc
2002	144,144,592	—	—	—	—	1.50
2003	11,811,926	—	—	—	—	1.50
2004	6,748,912	—	—	—	—	1.50
2005	7,529	—	—	—	—	1.50
2006	—	—	—	—	—	1.50

KM# 49 50 EURO CENT

7.8100 g., Aluminum-Bronze, 24.25 mm. **Obv:** Harp **Obv. Designer:** Jarlath Hayes **Rev:** Relief map of Western Europe, stars, lines and value **Rev. Designer:** Luc Luycx **Edge:** Reeded

Date	Mintage	F	VF	XF	Unc	BU
2007	—	—	—	—	1.50	—

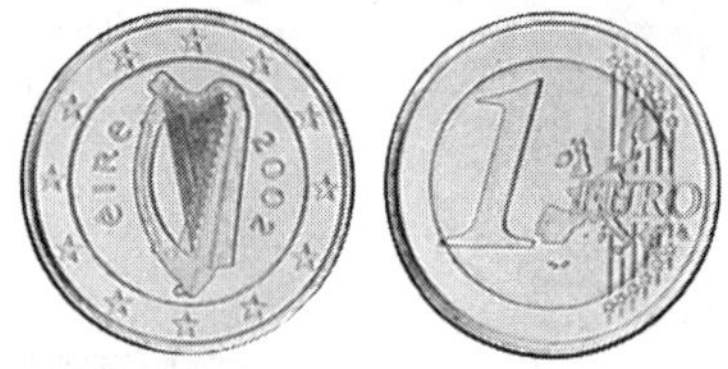

KM# 38 EURO

7.5000 g., Bi-Metallic Copper-Nickel center in Brass ring, 23.25 mm. **Obv:** Harp **Obv. Designer:** Jarlath Hayes **Rev:** Denomination and map **Rev. Designer:** Luc Luycx **Edge:** Reeded and plain sections

Date	Mintage	VG	F	VF	XF	Unc
2002	135,139,737	—	—	—	—	2.75
2003	2,520,000	—	—	—	—	2.75
2004	1,632,990	—	—	—	—	2.75
2005	6,024	—	—	—	—	2.75
2006	—	—	—	—	—	2.75

KM# 50 EURO

7.5000 g., Bi-Metallic, 23.25 mm. **Obv:** Harp **Obv. Designer:** Jarlath Hayes **Rev:** Relief map of Western Europe, stars, lines and value **Rev. Designer:** Luc Luycz **Edge:** Reeded and plain sections

Date	Mintage	VG	F	VF	XF	Unc
2007	—	—	—	—	—	2.75

KM# 39 2 EURO

8.5200 g., Bi-Metallic Brass center in Copper-Nickel ring, 25.7 mm. **Obv:** Harp **Obv. Designer:** Jarlath Hayes **Rev:** Denomination and map **Rev. Designer:** Luc Luycx **Edge:** Reeded with 2's and stars

Date	Mintage	VG	F	VF	XF	Unc
2002	90,548,166	—	—	—	—	4.00
2003	2,631,076	—	—	—	—	4.00
2004	3,738,186	—	—	—	—	4.00
2005	11,714	—	—	—	—	4.00
2006	—	—	—	—	—	4.00

KM# 51 2 EURO

8.5200 g., Bi-Metallic, 25.7 mm. **Obv:** Harp **Obv. Designer:** Jarlath Hayes **Rev:** Relief map of Western Europe, stars, lines and value **Rev. Designer:** Luc Luycx **Edge:** Reeded with 2's and stars

Date	Mintage	VG	F	VF	XF	Unc
2007	—	—	—	—	—	4.00

KM# 53 2 EURO

8.4500 g., Bi-Metallic **Ring Composition:** Copper Nickel **Center Composition:** Brass, 25.72 mm. **Subject:** 50th Anniversary Treaty of Rome **Obv:** Open treaty book **Rev:** Large value at left, modified outline of Europe at right **Edge:** Reeded with stars and 2's

Date	Mintage	F	VF	XF	Unc	BU
2007	—	—	—	—	—	9.00

KM# 40 5 EURO

14.1900 g., Copper-Nickel, 28.4 mm. **Subject:** Special Olympics **Obv:** 2003, Erie, Harp **Obv. Designer:** Jarlath Hayes **Rev:** Multicolor games logo **Edge:** Reeded

Date	Mintage	F	VF	XF	Unc	BU
2003	35,000	—	—	—	15.00	18.00
2003 Proof	25,000	Value: 25.00				

KM# 41 10 EURO

28.3000 g., 0.9250 Silver 0.8416 oz. ASW, 38.6 mm. **Subject:** Special Olympics **Obv:** Gold highlighted harp, 2003, Erie **Obv. Designer:** Jarlath Hayes **Rev:** Gold highlighted games logo **Edge:** Reeded

Date	Mintage	F	VF	XF	Unc	BU
2003 Proof	30,000	Value: 40.00				

KM# 42 10 EURO

28.3400 g., 0.9250 Silver 0.8428 oz. ASW, 38.6 mm. **Obv:** 2004, Erie, Harp **Rev:** Stylized Celtic swan **Edge:** Reeded

Date	Mintage	F	VF	XF	Unc	BU
2004 Proof	50,000	Value: 40.00				

KM# 44 10 EURO

28.2800 g., 0.9250 Silver 0.8410 oz. ASW, 38.6 mm. **Subject:** Sir William R. Hamilton **Obv:** Eire, 2005, Harp **Rev:** Triangle in circle of Greek letters used as math symbols **Edge:** Reeded

Date	Mintage	F	VF	XF	Unc	BU
2005 Proof	30,000	Value: 40.00				

KM# 45 10 EURO
28.5000 g., 0.9250 Silver 0.8475 oz. ASW, 38.6 mm. **Subject:** Samuel Beckett 1906-1989 **Obv:** 2006, Erie, Harp **Rev:** Face, value and play scene **Edge:** Reeded

Date	Mintage	F	VF	XF	Unc	BU
2006 Proof	35,000	Value: 40.00				

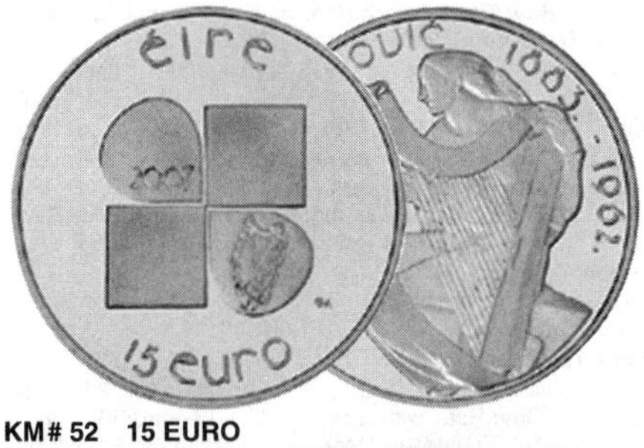

KM# 52 15 EURO
24.0000 g., 0.9250 Silver 0.7137 oz. ASW, 37 mm. **Obv:** Stylized clover with date and harp **Rev:** Ivan Mestroviae's Seated Woman with Harp design **Note:** Illustration reduced.

Date	Mintage	F	VF	XF	Unc	BU
2007 Proof	10,000	Value: 65.00				

KM# 46 20 EURO
1.2400 g., 0.9990 Gold 0.0398 oz. AGW, 14 mm. **Subject:** Samuel Beckett 1906-1989 **Obv:** 2006, Erie, Harp **Rev:** Face, value and play **Edge:** Reeded

Date	Mintage	F	VF	XF	Unc	BU
2006 Proof	20,000	Value: 65.00				

MINT SETS

KM#	Date	Mintage	Identification	Issue Price	Mkt Val
MS10	2002 (8)	20,000	KM#32,33,34,35,36,37,38,39	16.00	200
MS11	2003 (8)	30,000	KM#32-39	20.00	75.00
MS12	2003 (9)	35,000	KM#32-40 Special Olympics	25.00	90.00
MS13	2004 (8)	40,000	KM#32-39	25.00	45.00
MS14	2005 (8)	50,000	KM#32-39 Heywood Gardens	29.00	40.00
MS15	2006 (8)	40,000	KM#32-39 Glenveagh National Park and Castle	26.00	40.00
MS16	2006 (8)	—	KM#32-39 Boy Baby Set	35.00	42.50
MS17	2006 (8)	—	KM#32-39 Girl Baby Set	35.00	42.50
MS18	2007 (8)	20,000	KM#32-34, 47-51	29.00	30.00

PROOF SETS

KM#	Date	Mintage	Identification	Issue Price	Mkt Val
PS6	2006 (8)	5,000	KM#32-39	125	150
PS7	2006 (2)	—	KM#45-46	—	110

ISLE OF MAN

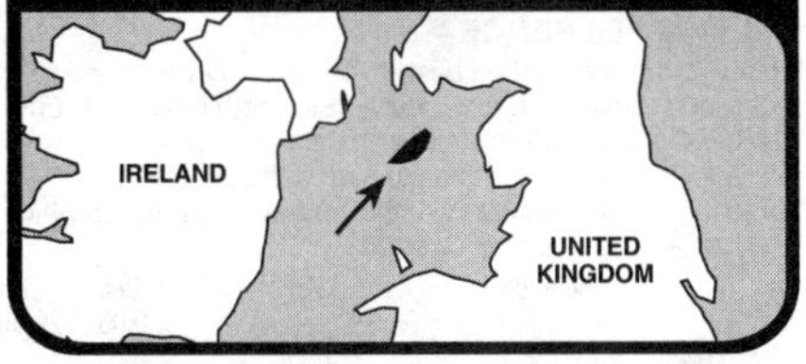

The Isle of Man, a dependency of the British Crown located in the Irish Sea equidistant from Ireland, Scotland and England, has an area of 227 sq. mi. (588 sq. km.) and a population of 68,000. Capital: Douglas. Agriculture, dairy farming, fishing and tourism are the chief industries.

MINT MARK
PM - Pobjoy Mint

BRITISH DEPENDENCY

DECIMAL COINAGE

100 Pence = 1 Pound

KM# 1036 PENNY
3.5600 g., Bronze-Plated Steel, 20.32 mm. **Ruler:** Elizabeth II **Obv:** Head with tiara right with small triskeles dividing legend **Obv. Designer:** Ian Rank-Broadley **Rev:** Ruins **Edge:** Plain

Date	Mintage	F	VF	XF	Unc	BU
2001PM AA	—	—	—	—	0.25	0.45
2001PM AC	—	—	—	—	0.25	0.45
2002PM AA	—	—	—	—	0.25	0.45
2002PM AE	—	—	—	—	0.25	0.45
2003PM AA	—	—	—	—	0.25	0.45
2003PM AE	—	—	—	—	0.25	0.45

KM# 1253 PENNY
3.5600 g., Copper-Plated-Steel, 20.3 mm. **Ruler:** Elizabeth II **Obv:** Head with tiara right **Rev:** Stanton War Memorial **Edge:** Reeded

Date	Mintage	F	VF	XF	Unc	BU
2004PM AA	—	—	—	—	0.25	0.45
2004PM AB	—	—	—	—	0.25	0.45
2005PM AA	—	—	—	—	0.25	0.45
2005PM AB	—	—	—	—	0.25	0.45
2006PM AA	—	—	—	—	0.25	0.45
2006PM AB	—	—	—	—	0.25	0.45
2007PM AA	—	—	—	—	0.25	0.45
2007PM AB	—	—	—	—	0.25	0.45

KM# 1037 2 PENCE
7.1650 g., Brass-Plated Steel, 25.86 mm. **Ruler:** Elizabeth II **Obv:** Head with tiara right **Obv. Designer:** Ian Rank-Broadley **Rev:** Sailboat **Edge:** Plain

Date	Mintage	F	VF	XF	Unc	BU
2001PM AA	—	—	—	—	0.40	0.60
2001PM AB	—	—	—	—	0.40	0.60
2002PM AA	—	—	—	—	0.40	0.60
2002PM AB	—	—	—	—	0.40	0.60
2002PM AC	—	—	—	—	0.40	0.60
2002PM AF	—	—	—	—	0.40	0.60
2003PM AA	—	—	—	—	0.40	0.60
2003PM AF	—	—	—	—	0.40	0.60

KM# 1254 2 PENCE
7.1200 g., Copper-Plated-Steel, 25.9 mm. **Ruler:** Elizabeth II **Obv:** Head with tiara right **Obv. Designer:** Ian Rank-Broadley **Rev:** Albert Tower **Edge:** Reeded

Date	Mintage	F	VF	XF	Unc	BU
2004PM AA	—	—	—	—	0.40	0.60
2004PM AB	—	—	—	—	0.40	0.60
2005PM AA	—	—	—	—	0.40	0.60
2005PM AB	—	—	—	—	0.40	0.60
2006PM AA	—	—	—	—	0.40	0.60
2006PM AB	—	—	—	—	0.40	0.60
2007PM AA	—	—	—	—	0.40	0.60
2007PM AB	—	—	—	—	0.40	0.60

KM# 1038 5 PENCE
3.2500 g., Copper-Nickel, 18 mm. **Ruler:** Elizabeth II **Obv:** Head with tiara right **Obv. Designer:** Ian Rank-Broadley **Rev:** Gaut's Cross **Edge:** Reeded

Date	Mintage	F	VF	XF	Unc	BU
2001PM AA	—	—	—	—	0.75	1.00
2002PM AA	—	—	—	—	0.75	1.00
2002PM AC	—	—	—	—	0.75	1.00
2003PM AA	—	—	—	—	0.75	1.00
2003PM AD	—	—	—	—	0.75	1.00

KM# 1255 5 PENCE
3.2500 g., Copper-Nickel, 18 mm. **Ruler:** Elizabeth II **Obv:** Head with tiara right **Obv. Designer:** Ian Rank-Broadley **Rev:** Tower of Refuge **Edge:** Reeded

Date	Mintage	F	VF	XF	Unc	BU
2004PM AA	—	—	—	—	0.75	1.00
2004PM AB	—	—	—	—	0.75	1.00
2005PM AA	—	—	—	—	0.75	1.00
2005PM AB	—	—	—	—	0.75	1.00
2006PM AA	—	—	—	—	0.75	1.00
2006PM AB	—	—	—	—	0.75	1.00
2007PM AA	—	—	—	—	0.75	1.00
2007PM AB	—	—	—	—	0.75	1.00

KM# 1039 10 PENCE
6.5000 g., Copper-Nickel, 24.5 mm. **Ruler:** Elizabeth II **Obv:** Head with tiara right **Obv. Designer:** Ian Rank-Broadley **Rev:** Cathedral **Edge:** Reeded

Date	Mintage	F	VF	XF	Unc	BU
2001PM AA	—	—	—	—	1.00	1.50
2002PM AA	—	—	—	—	1.00	1.50
2003PM AA	—	—	—	—	1.00	1.50

KM# 1256 10 PENCE
6.5000 g., Copper-Nickel, 24.5 mm. **Ruler:** Elizabeth II **Obv:** Head with tiara right **Obv. Designer:** Ian Rank-Broadley **Rev:** Chicken Rock Lighthouse **Edge:** Reeded

Date	Mintage	F	VF	XF	Unc	BU
2004PM AA	—	—	—	—	1.00	1.50
2004PM AB	—	—	—	—	1.00	1.50
2005PM AA	—	—	—	—	1.00	1.50
2005PM AB	—	—	—	—	1.00	1.50
2006PM AA	—	—	—	—	1.00	1.50
2006PM AB	—	—	—	—	1.00	1.50
2007PM AA	—	—	—	—	1.00	1.50
2007PM AB	—	—	—	—	1.00	1.50

KM# 1040 20 PENCE
5.0000 g., Copper-Nickel, 21.4 mm. **Ruler:** Elizabeth II **Subject:** Rushen Abbey **Obv:** Head with tiara right **Obv. Designer:** Ian Rank-Broadley **Rev:** Monk writing **Edge:** Plain **Shape:** 7-sided

Date	Mintage	F	VF	XF	Unc	BU
2001PM AA	—	—	—	—	1.50	2.00
2002PM AA	—	—	—	—	1.50	2.00
2002PM AB	—	—	—	—	1.50	2.00
2003PM AA	—	—	—	—	1.50	2.00
2003PM BA	—	—	—	—	1.50	2.00

KM# 1257 20 PENCE
5.0000 g., Copper-Nickel, 21.5 mm. **Ruler:** Elizabeth II **Obv:** Head with tiara right **Obv. Designer:** Ian Rank-Broadley **Rev:** Castle Rushen Clock **Edge:** Plain **Shape:** 7-sided

Date	Mintage	F	VF	XF	Unc	BU
2004PM AA	—	—	—	—	1.50	2.00
2004PM AB	—	—	—	—	1.50	2.00
2005PM AA	—	—	—	—	1.50	2.00
2005PM AB	—	—	—	—	1.50	2.00
2006PM AA	—	—	—	—	1.50	2.00
2006PM AB	—	—	—	—	1.50	2.00
2007PM AA	—	—	—	—	1.50	2.00
2007PM AB	—	—	—	—	1.50	2.00

KM# 1041 50 PENCE
8.0000 g., Copper-Nickel, 27.3 mm. **Ruler:** Elizabeth II **Obv:** Head with tiara right **Obv. Designer:** Ian Rank-Broadley **Rev:** Stylized crucifix **Edge:** Plain **Shape:** 7-sided

Date	Mintage	F	VF	XF	Unc	BU
2001PM AA	—	—	—	—	2.25	2.75
2002PM AA	—	—	—	—	2.25	2.75
2003PM AA	—	—	—	—	2.25	2.75

KM# 1105 50 PENCE
8.0000 g., Copper-Nickel, 27.3 mm. **Ruler:** Elizabeth II **Subject:** Christmas **Obv:** Head with tiara right **Obv. Designer:** Ian Rank-Broadley **Rev:** Postman and children **Edge:** Plain **Shape:** 7-sided

Date	Mintage	F	VF	XF	Unc	BU
2001PM BB	30,000	—	—	—	4.50	6.00

KM# 1105a 50 PENCE
8.0000 g., 0.9250 Silver 0.2379 oz. ASW, 27.3 mm. **Ruler:** Elizabeth II **Obv:** Head with tiara right **Rev:** Postman and children **Edge:** Plain **Shape:** 7-sided

Date	Mintage	F	VF	XF	Unc	BU
2001PM Proof	5,000	Value: 35.00				

KM# 1105b 50 PENCE
8.0000 g., 0.9167 Gold 0.2358 oz. AGW, 27.3 mm. **Ruler:** Elizabeth II **Obv:** Head with tiara right **Rev:** Postman and children **Edge:** Plain **Shape:** 7-sided

Date	Mintage	F	VF	XF	Unc	BU
2001PM Proof	250	Value: 500				

KM# 1160 50 PENCE
8.0000 g., Copper Nickel, 27.3 mm. **Ruler:** Elizabeth II **Subject:** Christmas **Obv:** Head with tiara right **Obv. Designer:** Ian Rank-Broadley **Rev:** Scrooge in bed **Edge:** Plain **Shape:** 7-sided

Date	Mintage	F	VF	XF	Unc	BU
2002BB PM	30,000	—	—	—	4.50	6.00

KM# 1160a 50 PENCE
8.0000 g., 0.9250 Silver 0.2379 oz. ASW, 27.3 mm. **Ruler:** Elizabeth II **Subject:** Christmas **Obv:** Head with tiara right **Rev:** Scrooge in bed **Edge:** Plain **Shape:** 7-sided

Date	Mintage	F	VF	XF	Unc	BU
2002PM Proof	5,000	Value: 35.00				

KM# 1160b 50 PENCE
8.0000 g., 0.9167 Gold 0.2358 oz. AGW, 27.3 mm. **Ruler:** Elizabeth II **Subject:** Christmas **Obv:** Head with tiara right **Rev:** Scrooge in bed **Edge:** Plain **Shape:** 7-sided

Date	Mintage	F	VF	XF	Unc	BU
2002PM Proof	250	Value: 500				

KM# 1183 50 PENCE
8.0000 g., Copper-Nickel, 27.3 mm. **Ruler:** Elizabeth II **Obv:** Head with tiara right **Obv. Designer:** Ian Rank-Broadley **Rev:** "The Snowman and James" **Edge:** Plain **Shape:** 7-sided

Date	Mintage	F	VF	XF	Unc	BU
2003PM BB	10,000	—	—	—	6.50	8.00

KM# 1183a 50 PENCE
8.0000 g., 0.9250 Silver 0.2379 oz. ASW, 27.3 mm. **Ruler:** Elizabeth II **Subject:** Christmas **Obv:** Head with tiara right **Rev:** "The Snowman and James" **Edge:** Plain **Shape:** 7-sided

Date	Mintage	F	VF	XF	Unc	BU
2003PM Proof	3,000	Value: 35.00				

KM# 1183b 50 PENCE
8.0000 g., 0.9167 Gold 0.2358 oz. AGW, 27.3 mm. **Ruler:** Elizabeth II **Obv:** Head with tiara right **Rev:** "The Snowman and James" **Edge:** Plain **Shape:** 7-sided

Date	Mintage	F	VF	XF	Unc	BU
2003PM Proof	100	Value: 500				

KM# 1258 50 PENCE
8.0000 g., Copper-Nickel, 21.5 mm. **Ruler:** Elizabeth II **Obv:** Head with tiara right **Obv. Designer:** Ian Rank-Broadley **Rev:** Milner's Tower **Edge:** Plain **Shape:** 7-sided

Date	Mintage	F	VF	XF	Unc	BU
2004PM AA	—	—	—	—	2.25	2.75
2004PM AB	—	—	—	—	2.25	2.75
2005PM AA	—	—	—	—	2.25	2.75
2005PM AB	—	—	—	—	2.25	2.75
2006PM AA	—	—	—	—	2.25	2.75
2006PM AB	—	—	—	—	2.25	2.75
2007PM AA	—	—	—	—	2.25	2.75
2007PM AB	—	—	—	—	2.25	2.75

KM# 1262a 50 PENCE
9.1852 g., 0.9250 Silver 0.2732 oz. ASW, 27.3 mm. **Ruler:** Elizabeth II **Subject:** Christmas **Obv:** Head with tiara right **Rev:** Laxey Wheel **Edge:** Plain **Shape:** 7-sided

Date	Mintage	F	VF	XF	Unc	BU
2004PM Proof	5,000	Value: 35.00				

KM# 1262b 50 PENCE
15.4074 g., 0.9167 Gold 0.4541 oz. AGW, 27.3 mm. **Ruler:** Elizabeth II **Subject:** Christmas **Obv:** Head with tiara right **Rev:** Laxey Wheel **Edge:** Plain **Shape:** 7-sided

Date	Mintage	F	VF	XF	Unc	BU
2004PM Proof	250	Value: 625				

KM# 1293 50 PENCE
Copper-Nickel **Ruler:** Elizabeth II **Obv:** Queen's new portrait **Rev:** Tourist Trophy

Date	Mintage	F	VF	XF	Unc	BU
2004	—	—	—	—	6.00	7.00

KM# 1262 50 PENCE
8.0000 g., Copper-Nickel, 27.3 mm. **Ruler:** Elizabeth II **Subject:** Christmas **Obv:** Head with tiara right **Obv. Designer:** Ian Rank-Broadley **Rev:** Laxey Wheel **Edge:** Plain **Shape:** 7-sided

Date	Mintage	F	VF	XF	Unc	BU
2004PM AA	—	—	—	—	6.00	7.00
2004PM BA	30,000	—	—	—	6.00	7.00

KM# 1294 50 PENCE
Copper-Nickel **Ruler:** Elizabeth II **Obv:** Queen's new portrait **Rev:** Christmas scene

Date	Mintage	F	VF	XF	Unc	BU
2005	—	—	—	—	6.50	8.00

KM# 1320.1 50 PENCE
8.0000 g., Copper-Nickel, 27.3 mm. **Ruler:** Elizabeth II **Series:** 12 Days of Christmas **Obv:** Head with tiara right **Obv. Legend:** ISLE OF MAN - ELIZABETH II **Obv. Designer:** Ian Rank-Broadley **Rev:** Partridge in a Pear Tree **Rev. Legend:** CHRISTMAS **Edge:** Plain **Shape:** 7-sided

Date	Mintage	F	VF	XF	Unc	BU
2005PM	30,000	—	—	—	—	16.00

KM# 1320.2 50 PENCE
8.0000 g., Copper-Nickel, 27.3 mm. **Ruler:** Elizabeth II **Series:** 12 Days of Christmas **Obv:** Head with tiara right **Obv. Legend:** ISLE OF MAN - ELIZABETH II **Obv. Designer:** Ian Rank-Broadley **Rev:** Partidge in a Pear Tree multicolor **Rev. Legend:** CHRISTMAS **Edge:** Plain **Shape:** 7-sided

Date	Mintage	F	VF	XF	Unc	BU
2005PM	Inc. above	—	—	—	—	20.00

KM# 1320.1a 50 PENCE
9.1825 g., 0.9250 Silver 0.2731 oz. ASW, 27.3 mm. **Ruler:** Elizabeth II **Series:** 12 Days of Christmas **Obv:** Head with tiara right **Obv. Legend:** ISLE OF MAN - ELIZABETH II **Obv. Designer:** Ian Rank-Broadley **Rev:** Partridge in a Pear Tree **Rev. Legend:** CHRISTMAS **Edge:** Plain **Shape:** 7-sided

Date	Mintage	F	VF	XF	Unc	BU
2005PM Proof	—	Value: 35.00				

KM# 1320.2a 50 PENCE
8.0000 g., 0.9250 Silver 0.2379 oz. ASW, 27.3 mm. **Ruler:** Elizabeth II **Series:** 12 Days of Christmas **Obv:** Head with tiara right **Obv. Legend:** ISLE OF MAN - ELIZABETH II **Obv. Designer:** Ian Rank-Broadley **Rev:** Partridge in a Pear Tree multicolor **Rev. Legend:** CHRISTMAS **Edge:** Plain **Shape:** 7-sided

Date	Mintage	F	VF	XF	Unc	BU
2005PM Proof	—	Value: 35.00				

KM# 1320b 50 PENCE
0.9167 Gold, 27.3 mm. **Ruler:** Elizabeth II **Series:** 12 Days of Christmas **Obv:** Head with tiara right **Obv. Legend:** ISLE OF MAN - ELIZABETH II **Obv. Designer:** Ian Rank-Broadley **Rev:** Partridge in a Pear Tree **Rev. Legend:** CHRISTMAS **Edge:** Plain **Shape:** 7-sided

Date	Mintage	F	VF	XF	Unc	BU
2005PM Proof	—	Value: 600				

KM# 1321.1 50 PENCE
8.0000 g., Copper-Nickel, 27.3 mm. **Ruler:** Elizabeth II **Series:** 12 Days of Christmas **Obv:** Head with tiara right **Obv. Legend:** ISLE OF MAN - ELIZABETH II **Obv. Designer:** Ian Rank-Broadley **Rev:** Two Turtle Doves **Rev. Legend:** CHRISTMAS **Edge:** Plain **Shape:** 7-sided

Date	Mintage	F	VF	XF	Unc	BU
2006PM	—	—	—	—	6.00	7.00

KM# 1321.2 50 PENCE
8.0000 g., Copper-Nickel, 27.3 mm. **Ruler:** Elizabeth II **Series:** 12 Days of Christmas **Obv:** Head with tiara right **Obv. Legend:** ISLE OF MAN - ELIZABETH II **Obv. Designer:** Ian Rank-Broadley **Rev:** Two Turtle Doves multicolor **Rev. Legend:** CHRISTMAS **Edge:** Plain **Shape:** 7-sided

Date	Mintage	F	VF	XF	Unc	BU
2006PM	—	—	—	—	8.00	10.00

KM# 1321.1a 50 PENCE
0.9250 Silver, 27.3 mm. **Ruler:** Elizabeth II **Series:** 12 Days of Christmas **Obv:** Head with tiara right **Obv. Legend:** ISLE OF MAN - ELIZABETH II **Obv. Designer:** Ian Rank-Broadley **Rev:** Two Turtle Doves **Rev. Legend:** CHRISTMAS **Edge:** Plain **Shape:** 7-sided

Date	Mintage	F	VF	XF	Unc	BU
2006PM Proof	—	Value: 35.00				

KM# 1321.2a 50 PENCE
0.9250 Silver, 27.3 mm. **Ruler:** Elizabeth II **Series:** 12 Days of Christmas **Obv:** Head with tiara right **Obv. Legend:** ISLE OF MAN - ELIZABETH II **Obv. Designer:** Ian Rank-Broadley **Rev:** Two Turtle Doves multicolor **Rev. Legend:** CHRISTMAS **Edge:** Plain **Shape:** 7-sided

Date	Mintage	F	VF	XF	Unc	BU
2006PM Proof	—	Value: 40.00				

KM# 1321b 50 PENCE
0.9167 Gold, 27.3 mm. **Ruler:** Elizabeth II **Series:** 12 Days of Christmas **Obv:** Head with tiara right **Obv. Legend:** ISLE OF MAN - ELIZABETH II **Obv. Designer:** Ian Rank-Broadley **Rev:** Two Turtle Doves **Rev. Legend:** CHRISTMAS **Edge:** Plain **Shape:** 7-sided

Date	Mintage	F	VF	XF	Unc	BU
2006PM Proof	—	Value: 600				

KM# 1322.1 50 PENCE
8.0000 g., Copper-Nickel, 27.3 mm. **Ruler:** Elizabeth II **Series:** 12 Days of Christmas **Obv:** Head with tiara right **Obv. Legend:** ISLE OF MAN - ELIZABETH II **Obv. Designer:** Ian Rank-Broadley **Rev:** Three French Hens **Rev. Legend:** CHRISTMAS **Edge:** Plain **Shape:** 7-sided

Date	Mintage	F	VF	XF	Unc	BU
2007PM	—	—	—	—	6.00	7.00

KM# 1322.2 50 PENCE
8.0000 g., Copper-Nickel, 27.3 mm. **Ruler:** Elizabeth II **Series:** 12 Days of Christmas **Obv:** Head with tiara right **Obv. Legend:** ISLE OF MAN - ELIZABETH II **Obv. Designer:** Ian Rank-Broadley **Rev:** Three French Hens multicolor **Rev. Legend:** CHRISTMAS **Edge:** Plain **Shape:** 7-sided

Date	Mintage	F	VF	XF	Unc	BU
2007PM	—	—	—	—	8.00	10.00

KM# 1322.1a 50 PENCE
0.9250 Silver, 27.3 mm. **Ruler:** Elizabeth II **Series:** 12 Days of Christmas **Obv:** Head with tiara right **Obv. Legend:** ISLE OF MAN - ELIZABETH II **Obv. Designer:** Ian Rank-Broadley **Rev:** Three French Hens **Rev. Legend:** CHRISTMAS **Edge:** Plain **Shape:** 7-sided

Date	Mintage	F	VF	XF	Unc	BU
2007PM Proof	—	Value: 35.00				

KM# 1322.2a 50 PENCE
0.9250 Silver, 27.3 mm. **Ruler:** Elizabeth II **Series:** 12 Days of Christmas **Obv:** Head with tiara right **Obv. Legend:** ISLE OF MAN - ELIZABETH II **Obv. Designer:** Ian Rank-Broadley **Rev:** Three French Hens multicolor **Rev. Legend:** CHRISTMAS **Edge:** Plain **Shape:** 7-sided

Date	Mintage	F	VF	XF	Unc	BU
2007PM Proof	—	Value: 40.00				

KM# 1322b 50 PENCE
0.9167 Gold, 27.3 mm. **Ruler:** Elizabeth II **Series:** 12 Days of Christmas **Obv:** Head with tiara right **Obv. Legend:** ISLE OF MAN - ELIZABETH II **Obv. Designer:** Ian Rank-Broadley **Rev:** Three French Hens **Rev. Legend:** CHRISTMAS **Edge:** Plain **Shape:** 7-sided

Date	Mintage	F	VF	XF	Unc	BU
2007PM Proof	250	Value: 600				

KM# 1128 60 PENCE
Bi-Metallic Bronze finished base metal with a silver finished rotator on reverse., 38.6 mm. **Ruler:** Elizabeth II **Subject:** Euro Currency Converter **Obv:** Head with tiara right **Obv. Designer:** Ian Rank-Broadley **Rev:** Rotating map with cut out arrow revealing the Euro equivalent of the country's currency to which the arrow is pointed **Edge:** Reeded

Date	Mintage	F	VF	XF	Unc	BU
2002	15,000	—	—	—	20.00	22.50

KM# 1042 POUND
9.5000 g., Brass, 22.5 mm. **Ruler:** Elizabeth II **Subject:** Millennium Bells **Obv:** Head with tiara right **Obv. Designer:** Ian Rank-Broadley **Rev:** Triskeles and three bells **Edge:** Reeded and plain sections

Date	Mintage	F	VF	XF	Unc	BU
2001PM AA	—	—	—	—	4.00	5.00
2002PM AA	—	—	—	—	4.00	5.00
2003PM AA	—	—	—	—	4.00	5.00

KM# 1259 POUND

9.5000 g., Nickel-Brass, 22.5 mm. **Ruler:** Elizabeth II **Obv:** Head with tiara right **Obv. Designer:** Ian Rank-Broadley **Rev:** St. John's Chapel **Edge:** Reeded and Plain Sections

Date	Mintage	F	VF	XF	Unc	BU
2004PM AA	—	—	—	—	4.00	5.00
2004PM AB	—	—	—	—	4.00	5.00
2004PM AC	—	—	—	—	4.00	5.00
2005PM AA	—	—	—	—	4.00	5.00
2005PM AB	—	—	—	—	4.00	5.00
2006PM AA	—	—	—	—	4.00	5.00
2006PM AB	—	—	—	—	4.00	5.00
2007PM AA	—	—	—	—	4.00	5.00
2007PM AB	—	—	—	—	4.00	5.00

KM# 1043 2 POUNDS

12.0000 g., Bi-Metallic Copper-Nickel center in Brass ring, 28.4 mm. **Ruler:** Elizabeth II **Subject:** Thorwald's Cross **Obv:** Head with tiara right within beaded circle **Obv. Designer:** Ian Rank-Broadley **Rev:** Ancient drawing within circle **Edge:** Reeded

Date	Mintage	F	VF	XF	Unc	BU
2001PM AA	—	—	—	—	6.50	7.50
2002PM AA	—	—	—	—	6.50	7.50
2003PM AA	—	—	—	—	6.50	7.50

KM# 1260 2 POUNDS

12.0000 g., Bi-Metallic Copper-Nickel center in Brass ring, 28.4 mm. **Ruler:** Elizabeth II **Obv:** Head with tiara right **Obv. Designer:** Ian Rank-Broadley **Rev:** Round Tower of Peel Castle **Edge:** Reeded

Date	Mintage	F	VF	XF	Unc	BU
2004PM AA	—	—	—	—	6.50	7.50
2005PM AA	—	—	—	—	6.50	7.50
2006PM AA	—	—	—	—	6.50	7.50
2007PM AA	—	—	—	—	6.50	7.50
2007PM AB	—	—	—	—	6.50	7.50

KM# 1044 5 POUNDS

20.1000 g., Virenium, 36.5 mm. **Ruler:** Elizabeth II **Subject:** St. Patrick's Hymn **Obv:** Head with tiara right **Obv. Designer:** Ian Rank-Broadley **Rev:** Stylized cross design **Edge:** Reeded and plain sections

Date	Mintage	F	VF	XF	Unc	BU
2001PM AA	—	—	—	—	15.00	16.50
2002PM AA	—	—	—	—	15.00	16.50
2003PM AA	—	—	—	—	15.00	16.50

KM# 1261 5 POUNDS

20.1000 g., Virenium, 36 mm. **Ruler:** Elizabeth II **Obv:** Head with tiara right **Obv. Designer:** Ian Rank-Broadley **Rev:** Laxey Wheel **Edge:** Reeded

Date	Mintage	F	VF	XF	Unc	BU
2004PM AA	—	—	—	—	15.00	16.50
2005PM AA	—	—	—	—	15.00	16.50
2006PM AA	—	—	—	—	15.00	16.50
2007PM AA	—	—	—	—	15.00	16.50
2007PM AB	—	—	—	—	15.00	16.50

CROWN SERIES

Pobjoy Mint Key

(M) MATTE - Normal circulation strike

(U) SPECIAL UNCIRCULATED - Polished or prooflike in appearance, slightly frosted features.

(P) PROOF - The highest quality obtainable having mirror-like fields and frosted features.

KM# 1129 1/32 CROWN

1.0000 g., 0.9720 Gold 0.0312 oz. AGW, 9.8 mm. **Ruler:** Elizabeth II **Subject:** Queen's Golden Jubilee **Obv:** Head with tiara right **Obv. Designer:** Ian Rank-Broadley **Rev:** Seated crowned Queen holding sceptre at her coronation **Edge:** Plain

Date	Mintage	F	VF	XF	Unc	BU
2002 Prooflike	—	—	—	—	—	35.00

KM# 1058 1/25 CROWN

1.2440 g., 0.9999 Gold 0.0400 oz. AGW, 13.92 mm. **Ruler:** Elizabeth II **Subject:** Year of the Snake **Obv:** Bust with tiara right **Obv. Designer:** Ian Rank-Broadley **Rev:** Snake **Edge:** Reeded

Date	Mintage	F	VF	XF	Unc	BU
2001 Proof	20,000	Value: 45.00				

KM# 1067 1/25 CROWN

1.2440 g., 0.9999 Gold 0.0400 oz. AGW, 13.9 mm. **Ruler:** Elizabeth II **Subject:** Somali Kittens **Obv:** Head with tiara right **Obv. Designer:** Ian Rank-Broadley **Rev:** Two kittens **Edge:** Reeded

Date	Mintage	F	VF	XF	Unc	BU
2001	—	—	—	—	—	45.00
2001 Proof	1,000	Value: 50.00				

KM# 1067a 1/25 CROWN

1.2441 g., 0.9995 Platinum 0.0400 oz. APW, 13.9 mm. **Ruler:** Elizabeth II **Subject:** Somali Kittens **Obv:** Head with tiara right **Obv. Designer:** Ian Rank-Broadley **Rev:** Two kittens **Edge:** Reeded

Date	Mintage	F	VF	XF	Unc	BU
2001	—	—	—	—	—	95.00

KM# 1086 1/25 CROWN

1.2441 g., 0.9999 Gold 0.0400 oz. AGW, 13.9 mm. **Ruler:** Elizabeth II **Subject:** Harry Potter **Obv:** Bust with tiara right **Obv. Designer:** Ian Rank-Broadley **Rev:** Boy with magic wand **Edge:** Reeded

Date	Mintage	F	VF	XF	Unc	BU
2001 Proof	10,000	Value: 49.50				

KM# 1088 1/25 CROWN

1.2441 g., 0.9999 Gold 0.0400 oz. AGW, 13.9 mm. **Ruler:** Elizabeth II **Series:** Harry Potter **Subject:** Journey to Hogwarts School **Obv:** Bust with tiara right **Obv. Designer:** Ian Rank-Broadley **Rev:** Boat full of children going to Hogwarts School **Edge:** Reeded

Date	Mintage	F	VF	XF	Unc	BU
2001 Proof	10,000	Value: 49.50				

KM# 1090 1/25 CROWN

1.2441 g., 0.9999 Gold 0.0400 oz. AGW, 13.9 mm. **Ruler:** Elizabeth II **Series:** Harry Potter **Subject:** First Quidditch Match **Obv:** Bust with tiara right **Obv. Designer:** Ian Rank-Broadley **Rev:** Harry flying a broom **Edge:** Reeded

Date	Mintage	F	VF	XF	Unc	BU
2001 Proof	10,000	Value: 49.50				

KM# 1092 1/25 CROWN

1.2441 g., 0.9999 Gold 0.0400 oz. AGW, 13.9 mm. **Ruler:** Elizabeth II **Series:** Harry Potter **Subject:** Birth of Norbert **Obv:** Bust with tiara right **Obv. Designer:** Ian Rank-Broadley **Edge:** Reeded

Date	Mintage	F	VF	XF	Unc	BU
2001 Proof	10,000	Value: 49.50				

KM# 1094 1/25 CROWN

1.2441 g., 0.9999 Gold 0.0400 oz. AGW, 13.9 mm. **Ruler:** Elizabeth II **Series:** Harry Potter **Subject:** School **Obv:** Bust with tiara right **Obv. Designer:** Ian Rank-Broadley **Rev:** Harry in Potions class **Edge:** Reeded

Date	Mintage	F	VF	XF	Unc	BU
2001 Proof	10,000	Value: 49.50				

KM# 1096 1/25 CROWN

1.2441 g., 0.9999 Gold 0.0400 oz. AGW, 13.9 mm. **Ruler:** Elizabeth II **Series:** Harry Potter **Subject:** Keys **Obv:** Bust with tiara right **Obv. Designer:** Ian Rank-Broadley **Rev:** Harry chasing a quidditch **Edge:** Reeded

Date	Mintage	F	VF	XF	Unc	BU
2001 Proof	10,000	Value: 49.50				

KM# 1098 1/25 CROWN

1.2441 g., 0.9999 Gold 0.0400 oz. AGW, 13.9 mm. **Ruler:** Elizabeth II **Subject:** Year of the Horse **Obv:** Bust with tiara right **Obv. Designer:** Ian Rank-Broadley **Rev:** Two horses **Edge:** Reeded

Date	Mintage	F	VF	XF	Unc	BU
2002 Proof	20,000	Value: 49.50				

KM# 1107 1/25 CROWN

1.2440 g., 0.9990 Gold 0.0400 oz. AGW, 13.92 mm. **Ruler:** Elizabeth II **Subject:** Bengal Cat **Obv:** Head with tiara right **Obv. Designer:** Ian Rank-Broadley **Rev:** Cat and kitten **Edge:** Reeded

Date	Mintage	F	VF	XF	Unc	BU
2002	—	—	—	—	—	45.00
2002 Proof	1,000	Value: 50.00				

KM# 1107a 1/25 CROWN

1.2440 g., 0.9990 Platinum 0.0400 oz. APW, 13.92 mm. **Ruler:** Elizabeth II **Subject:** Bengal Cat **Obv:** Head with tiara right **Obv. Designer:** Ian Rank-Broadley **Rev:** Cat and kitten **Edge:** Reeded

Date	Mintage	F	VF	XF	Unc	BU
2002 Proof	—	Value: 85.00				

KM# 1145 1/25 CROWN

1.2440 g., 0.9999 Gold 0.0400 oz. AGW, 13.92 mm. **Ruler:** Elizabeth II **Subject:** Harry Potter Series **Obv:** Bust with tiara right **Obv. Designer:** Ian Rank-Broadley **Rev:** Harry and friends making Polyjuice potion **Edge:** Reeded

Date	Mintage	F	VF	XF	Unc	BU
2002PM Proof	10,000	Value: 55.00				

KM# 1143 1/25 CROWN

1.2440 g., 0.9999 Gold 0.0400 oz. AGW, 13.92 mm. **Ruler:** Elizabeth II **Subject:** Harry Potter **Obv:** Bust with tiara right **Obv. Designer:** Ian Rank-Broadley **Rev:** Tom Riddle twirling Harry's magic wand **Edge:** Reeded

Date	Mintage	F	VF	XF	Unc	BU
2002PM Proof	10,000	Value: 55.00				

KM# 1147 1/25 CROWN

1.2440 g., 0.9999 Gold 0.0400 oz. AGW **Ruler:** Elizabeth II **Subject:** Harry Potter **Obv:** Bust with tiara right **Obv. Designer:** Ian Rank-Broadley **Rev:** Harry arrives at the Burrow in a flying car **Edge:** Reeded

Date	Mintage	F	VF	XF	Unc	BU
2002PM Proof	10,000	Value: 55.00				

KM# 1149 1/25 CROWN

1.2440 g., 0.9999 Gold 0.0400 oz. AGW, 13.92 mm. **Ruler:** Elizabeth II **Subject:** Harry Potter Series **Obv:** Bust with tiara right **Obv. Designer:** Ian Rank-Broadley **Rev:** Harry retrieves Gryffindor sword from snake **Edge:** Reeded

Date	Mintage	F	VF	XF	Unc	BU
2002PM Proof	10,000	Value: 55.00				

KM# 1151 1/25 CROWN

1.2240 g., 0.9999 Gold 0.0393 oz. AGW, 13.92 mm. **Ruler:** Elizabeth II **Series:** Harry Potter **Obv:** Bust with tiara right **Obv. Designer:** Ian Rank-Broadley **Rev:** Harry and Ron encounter the spider Aragog **Edge:** Reeded

Date	Mintage	F	VF	XF	Unc	BU
2002PM Proof	10,000	Value: 55.00				

KM# 1153 1/25 CROWN

1.2440 g., 0.9999 Gold 0.0400 oz. AGW, 13.92 mm. **Ruler:** Elizabeth II **Series:** Harry Potter **Obv:** Bust with tiara right **Obv. Designer:** Ian Rank-Broadley **Rev:** Harry in hospital **Edge:** Reeded

Date	Mintage	F	VF	XF	Unc	BU
2002PM Proof	10,000	Value: 55.00				

KM# 1186 1/25 CROWN

1.2440 g., 0.9999 Gold 0.0400 oz. AGW, 13.9 mm. **Ruler:** Elizabeth II **Subject:** Lord of the Rings **Obv:** Bust with tiara right **Obv. Designer:** Ian Rank-Broadley **Rev:** Man with short sword **Edge:** Reeded

Date	Mintage	F	VF	XF	Unc	BU
2003PM Proof	6,000	Value: 50.00				

KM# 1161 1/25 CROWN

1.2440 g., 0.9999 Gold 0.0400 oz. AGW, 13.92 mm. **Ruler:** Elizabeth II **Subject:** Cat **Obv:** Head with tiara right **Obv. Designer:** Ian Rank-Broadley **Rev:** Two Balinese kittens **Edge:** Reeded

Date	Mintage	F	VF	XF	Unc	BU
2003PM	—	—	—	—	—	45.00
2003PM Proof	—	Value: 50.00				

KM# 1161a 1/25 CROWN

1.2440 g., 0.9995 Platinum 0.0400 oz. APW, 13.92 mm. **Ruler:** Elizabeth II **Subject:** Cat **Obv:** Head with tiara right **Obv. Designer:** Ian Rank-Broadley **Rev:** Two Balinese kittens **Edge:** Reeded

Date	Mintage	F	VF	XF	Unc	BU
2003PM Proof	—	Value: 85.00				

KM# 1167 1/25 CROWN

1.2441 g., 0.9999 Gold 0.0400 oz. AGW, 13.9 mm. **Ruler:** Elizabeth II **Subject:** Year of the Goat **Obv:** Head with tiara right **Obv. Designer:** Ian Rank-Broadley **Rev:** Three goats **Edge:** Reeded

Date	Mintage	F	VF	XF	Unc	BU
2003PM Proof	20,000	Value: 49.50				

KM# 1203 1/25 CROWN

1.2440 g., 0.9999 Gold 0.0400 oz. AGW, 14 mm. **Ruler:** Elizabeth II **Obv:** Bust with tiara right **Obv. Designer:** Ian Rank-Broadley **Rev:** Harry Potter and patron fighting off a spectre **Edge:** Reeded

Date	Mintage	F	VF	XF	Unc	BU
2004PM Proof	2,500	Value: 50.00				

KM# 1205 1/25 CROWN

1.2440 g., 0.9999 Gold 0.0400 oz. AGW, 14 mm. **Ruler:** Elizabeth II **Obv:** Bust with tiara right **Obv. Designer:** Ian Rank-Broadley **Rev:** Harry Potter in the shrieking shack **Edge:** Reeded

Date	Mintage	F	VF	XF	Unc	BU
2004PM Proof	2,500	Value: 50.00				

KM# 1207 1/25 CROWN

1.2440 g., 0.9999 Gold 0.0400 oz. AGW, 14 mm. **Ruler:** Elizabeth II **Obv:** Bust with tiara right **Obv. Designer:** Ian Rank-Broadley **Rev:** Harry Potter and Professor Dumbledore **Edge:** Reeded

Date	Mintage	F	VF	XF	Unc	BU
2004PM Proof	2,500	Value: 50.00				

KM# 1209 1/25 CROWN

1.2440 g., 0.9999 Gold 0.0400 oz. AGW, 14 mm. **Ruler:** Elizabeth II **Obv:** Bust with tiara right **Obv. Designer:** Ian Rank-Broadley **Rev:** Sirius Black on flying griffin **Edge:** Reeded

Date	Mintage	F	VF	XF	Unc	BU
2004PM Proof	2,500	Value: 50.00				

KM# 1211 1/25 CROWN

1.2440 g., 0.9999 Gold 0.0400 oz. AGW, 14 mm. **Ruler:** Elizabeth II **Obv:** Head with tiara right **Obv. Designer:** Ian Rank-Broadley **Rev:** Three Olympic Swimmers **Edge:** Reeded

Date	Mintage	F	VF	XF	Unc	BU
2004PM Proof	5,000	Value: 50.00				

KM# 1213 1/25 CROWN

1.2440 g., 0.9999 Gold 0.0400 oz. AGW, 14 mm. **Ruler:** Elizabeth II **Obv:** Head with tiara right **Obv. Designer:** Ian Rank-Broadley **Rev:** Three Olympic Cyclists **Edge:** Reeded

Date	Mintage	F	VF	XF	Unc	BU
2004PM Proof	5,000	Value: 50.00				

KM# 1215 1/25 CROWN

1.2440 g., 0.9999 Gold 0.0400 oz. AGW, 14 mm. **Ruler:** Elizabeth II **Obv:** Head with tiara right **Obv. Designer:** Ian Rank-Broadley **Rev:** Three Olympic Runners **Edge:** Reeded

Date	Mintage	F	VF	XF	Unc	BU
2004PM Proof	5,000	Value: 50.00				

KM# 1217 1/25 CROWN

1.2440 g., 0.9999 Gold 0.0400 oz. AGW, 14 mm. **Ruler:** Elizabeth II **Obv:** Head with tiara right **Obv. Designer:** Ian Rank-Broadley **Rev:** Three Olympic Sail Boarders **Edge:** Reeded

Date	Mintage	F	VF	XF	Unc	BU
2004PM Proof	5,000	Value: 50.00				

KM# 1240 1/25 CROWN

1.2440 g., 0.9999 Gold 0.0400 oz. AGW, 14 mm. **Ruler:** Elizabeth II **Obv:** Head with tiara right **Obv. Designer:** Ian Rank-Broadley **Rev:** Monkey **Edge:** Reeded

Date	Mintage	F	VF	XF	Unc	BU
2004PM Proof	20,000	Value: 50.00				

KM# 1247 1/25 CROWN
1.2440 g., 0.9999 Gold 0.0400 oz. AGW, 14 mm. **Ruler:** Elizabeth II **Obv:** Head with tiara right **Obv. Designer:** Ian Rank-Broadley **Rev:** Two Tonkinese cats **Edge:** Reeded

Date	Mintage	F	VF	XF	Unc	BU
2004PM	—	—	—	—	—	45.00
2004PM Proof	1,000	Value: 50.00				

KM# 1269 1/25 CROWN
1.2440 g., 0.9999 Gold 0.0400 oz. AGW, 13.92 mm. **Ruler:** Elizabeth II **Obv:** Bust with tiara right **Obv. Designer:** Ian Rank-Broadley **Rev:** Himalayan cat and two kittens **Edge:** Reeded

Date	Mintage	F	VF	XF	Unc	BU
2005PM Proof	—	Value: 50.00				

KM# 1269a 1/25 CROWN
1.2440 g., 0.9950 Platinum 0.0398 oz. APW, 13.92 mm. **Ruler:** Elizabeth II **Obv:** Bust with tiara right **Obv. Designer:** Ian Rank-Broadley **Rev:** Himalayan cat and two kittens **Edge:** Reeded

Date	Mintage	F	VF	XF	Unc	BU
2005PM Proof	—	Value: 90.00				

KM# 1340 1/25 CROWN
1.2441 g., 0.9999 Gold 0.0400 oz. AGW **Ruler:** Elizabeth II **Obv:** Bust with tiara right **Obv. Designer:** Ian Rank-Broadley **Rev:** Three Exotic Shorthair cats sitting facing **Edge:** Reeded

Date	Mintage	F	VF	XF	Unc	BU
2006PM	—	—	—	—	—	100

KM# 1343 1/25 CROWN
1.2441 g., 0.9999 Gold 0.0400 oz. AGW **Ruler:** Elizabeth II **Obv:** Bust with tiara right **Obv. Legend:** ELIZABETH II - ISLE OF MAN **Obv. Designer:** Ian Rank-Broadley **Rev:** Ragdoll cat with two kittens sitting facing **Edge:** Reeded

Date	Mintage	F	VF	XF	Unc	BU
2007PM	—	—	—	—	—	100

KM# 1349 1/25 CROWN
1.2440 g., 0.9999 Gold 0.0400 oz. AGW **Ruler:** Elizabeth II **Subject:** The tale of Peter Rabbit **Obv:** Bust with tiara right **Obv. Legend:** ELIZABETH II - ISLE OF MAN **Obv. Designer:** Ian Rank-Broadley **Rev:** Peter walking with friends **Edge:** Reeded

Date	Mintage	F	VF	XF	Unc	BU
2007PM	—	—	—	—	—	110

KM# 1308 1/25 CROWN
1.2441 g., 0.9999 Gold 0.0400 oz. AGW **Ruler:** Elizabeth II **Subject:** 100th Anniversary of Scouting **Obv:** Bust with tiara right **Obv. Legend:** ELIZABETH II - ISLE OF MAN **Rev:** 3/4 length figure of Robert Baden-Powell standing facing 3/4 left, Fleur-de-lys below, images of scouting at left and right **Rev. Legend:** CENTENARY OF SCOUTING **Edge:** Reeded

Date	Mintage	F	VF	XF	Unc	BU
2007PM Proof	—	Value: 300				

KM# 1314 1/25 CROWN
1.2200 g., 0.9999 Gold AGW 0.0400 0.0392 oz. AGW, 13.92 mm. **Ruler:** Elizabeth II **Obv:** Bust with tiara right **Obv. Legend:** ELIZABETH II - ISLE OF MAN **Rev:** Two swans facing **Edge:** Reeded

Date	Mintage	F	VF	XF	Unc	BU
2007 Proof	10,000	Value: 50.00				

KM# 1059 1/10 CROWN
3.1100 g., 0.9999 Gold 0.1000 oz. AGW, 17.95 mm. **Ruler:** Elizabeth II **Subject:** Year of the Snake **Obv:** Bust with tiara right **Obv. Designer:** Ian Rank-Broadley **Rev:** Snake **Edge:** Reeded

Date	Mintage	F	VF	XF	Unc	BU
2001 Proof	15,000	Value: 115				

KM# 1068 1/10 CROWN
3.1100 g., 0.9999 Gold 0.1000 oz. AGW, 18 mm. **Ruler:** Elizabeth II **Obv:** Head with tiara right **Obv. Designer:** Ian Rank-Broadley **Rev:** Somali kittens **Edge:** Reeded

Date	Mintage	F	VF	XF	Unc	BU
2001	—	—	—	—	—	110
2001 Proof	1,000	Value: 120				

KM# 1068a 1/10 CROWN
3.1100 g., 0.9995 Platinum 0.0999 oz. APW, 18 mm. **Ruler:** Elizabeth II **Obv:** Head with tiara right **Obv. Designer:** Ian Rank-Broadley **Rev:** Somali kittens **Edge:** Reeded

Date	Mintage	F	VF	XF	Unc	BU
2001 Proof	—	Value: 220				

KM# 1328 1/10 CROWN
3.1100 g., 0.9990 Gold 0.0999 oz. AGW **Ruler:** Elizabeth II **Subject:** Harry Potter **Obv:** Bust right **Obv. Designer:** Ian Rank-Broadley **Rev:** Boy with magic wand **Edge:** Reeded

Date	Mintage	F	VF	XF	Unc	BU
2001 Proof	7,500	Value: 115				

KM# 1329 1/10 CROWN
3.1100 g., 0.9990 Gold 0.0999 oz. AGW **Ruler:** Elizabeth II **Subject:** Harry Potter - Journey to Hogwarts **Obv:** Bust right **Rev:** Boat full of children going to Hogwarts School **Edge:** Reeded

Date	Mintage	F	VF	XF	Unc	BU
2001 Proof	7,500	Value: 115				

KM# 1330 1/10 CROWN
3.1100 g., 0.9990 Gold 0.0999 oz. AGW **Ruler:** Elizabeth II **Subject:** Harry Potter **Obv:** Bust right **Obv. Designer:** Ian Rank-Broadley **Rev:** Harry flying on a broomstick **Edge:** Reeded

Date	Mintage	F	VF	XF	Unc	BU
2001 Proof	7,500	Value: 115				

KM# 1331 1/10 CROWN
3.1100 g., 0.9990 Gold 0.0999 oz. AGW **Ruler:** Elizabeth II **Subject:** Harry Potter **Obv:** Bust right **Obv. Designer:** Ian Rank-Broadley **Rev:** Birth of Norbert the dragon **Edge:** Reeded

Date	Mintage	F	VF	XF	Unc	BU
2001 Proof	7,500	Value: 115				

KM# 1332 1/10 CROWN
3.1100 g., 0.9990 Gold 0.0999 oz. AGW **Ruler:** Elizabeth II **Subject:** Harry Potter **Obv:** Bust right **Obv. Designer:** Ian Rank-Broadley **Rev:** Harry in Potions class **Edge:** Reeded

Date	Mintage	F	VF	XF	Unc	BU
2001 Proof	7,500	Value: 115				

KM# 1333 1/10 CROWN
3.1100 g., 0.9990 Gold 0.0999 oz. AGW **Ruler:** Elizabeth II **Subject:** Harry Potter **Obv:** Bust right **Obv. Designer:** Ian Rank-Broadley **Rev:** Harry chasing a snitch **Edge:** Reeded

Date	Mintage	F	VF	XF	Unc	BU
2001 Proof	7,500	Value: 115				

KM# 1155 1/10 CROWN
3.1100 g., 0.9990 Gold 0.0999 oz. AGW, 17.95 mm. **Ruler:** Elizabeth II **Subject:** Queen's Golden Jubilee **Obv:** Queen's portrait **Rev:** Queen on horse **Edge:** Reeded

Date	Mintage	F	VF	XF	Unc	BU
2002PM Proof	500	Value: 115				

KM# 1099 1/10 CROWN
3.1100 g., 0.9999 Gold 0.1000 oz. AGW, 17.95 mm. **Ruler:** Elizabeth II **Subject:** Year of the Horse **Obv:** Bust with tiara right **Obv. Designer:** Ian Rank-Broadley **Rev:** Two horses **Edge:** Reeded

Date	Mintage	F	VF	XF	Unc	BU
2002 Proof	15,000	Value: 115				

KM# 1108 1/10 CROWN
3.1100 g., 0.9990 Gold 0.0999 oz. AGW, 17.95 mm. **Ruler:** Elizabeth II **Subject:** Bengal Cat **Obv:** Head with tiara right **Obv. Designer:** Ian Rank-Broadley **Rev:** Cat and kitten **Edge:** Reeded

Date	Mintage	VG	F	VF	XF	Unc
2002	—	—	—	—	—	—
2002 Proof	—	Value: 115				

KM# 1108a 1/10 CROWN
3.1100 g., 0.9990 Platinum 0.0999 oz. APW, 17.95 mm. **Ruler:** Elizabeth II **Subject:** Bengal Cat **Obv:** Head with tiara right **Obv. Designer:** Ian Rank-Broadley **Rev:** Cat and kitten **Edge:** Reeded

Date	Mintage	F	VF	XF	Unc	BU
2002	—	—	—	—	—	225

KM# 1162 1/10 CROWN
3.1100 g., 0.9999 Gold 0.1000 oz. AGW, 17.95 mm. **Ruler:** Elizabeth II **Subject:** Cat **Obv:** Head with tiara right **Obv. Designer:** Ian Rank-Broadley **Rev:** Two Balinese kittens **Edge:** Reeded

Date	Mintage	F	VF	XF	Unc	BU
2003PM	—	—	—	—	—	115
2003PM Proof	—	Value: 120				

KM# 1162a 1/10 CROWN
3.1100 g., 0.9995 Platinum 0.0999 oz. APW, 17.95 mm. **Ruler:** Elizabeth II **Subject:** Cat **Obv:** Head with tiara right **Obv. Designer:** Ian Rank-Broadley **Rev:** Two Balinese kittens **Edge:** Reeded

Date	Mintage	F	VF	XF	Unc	BU
2003PM	—	—	—	—	225	—

KM# 1187 1/10 CROWN
3.1100 g., 0.9999 Gold 0.1000 oz. AGW, 18 mm. **Ruler:** Elizabeth II **Subject:** Lord of the Rings **Obv:** Bust with tiara right **Obv. Designer:** Ian Rank-Broadley **Rev:** Aragorn with broad sword **Edge:** Reeded

Date	Mintage	F	VF	XF	Unc	BU
2003PM Proof	4,500	Value: 115				

KM# 1241 1/10 CROWN
3.1100 g., 0.9999 Gold 0.1000 oz. AGW, 18 mm. **Ruler:** Elizabeth II **Obv:** Head with tiara right **Obv. Designer:** Ian Rank-Broadley **Rev:** Monkey **Edge:** Reeded

Date	Mintage	F	VF	XF	Unc	BU
2004PM Proof	15,000	Value: 115				

KM# 1248 1/10 CROWN
3.1100 g., 0.9999 Gold 0.1000 oz. AGW, 18 mm. **Ruler:** Elizabeth II **Obv:** Head with tiara right **Obv. Designer:** Ian Rank-Broadley **Rev:** Two Tonkinese cats **Edge:** Reeded

Date	Mintage	F	VF	XF	Unc	BU
2004PM	—	—	—	—	—	110
2004PM Proof	1,000	Value: 115				

KM# 1270 1/10 CROWN
3.1100 g., 0.9999 Gold 0.1000 oz. AGW, 18 mm. **Ruler:** Elizabeth II **Obv:** Bust with tiara right **Obv. Designer:** Ian Rank-Broadley **Rev:** Himalayan cat and two kittens **Edge:** Reeded

Date	Mintage	F	VF	XF	Unc	BU
2005PM Proof	—	Value: 115				

KM# 1270a 1/10 CROWN
3.1100 g., 0.9950 Platinum 0.0995 oz. APW, 18 mm. **Ruler:** Elizabeth II **Obv:** Queen Elizabeth II **Rev:** Himalayan cat and two kittens **Edge:** Reeded

Date	Mintage	F	VF	XF	Unc	BU
2005PM Proof	—	Value: 245				

KM# 1341 1/10 CROWN
3.1100 g., 0.9999 Gold 0.1000 oz. AGW **Ruler:** Elizabeth II **Obv:** Bust with tiara right **Obv. Designer:** Ian Rank-Broadley **Rev:** Three Exotic Shorthair cats sitting facing **Edge:** Reeded

Date	Mintage	F	VF	XF	Unc	BU
2006PM	—	—	—	—	—	170

KM# 1344 1/10 CROWN
3.1100 g., 0.9999 Gold 0.1000 oz. AGW **Ruler:** Elizabeth II **Obv:** Bust with tiara right **Obv. Legend:** ELIZABETH II - ISLE OF MAN **Obv. Designer:** Ian Rank-Broadley **Rev:** Ragdoll cat with two kittens sitting facing **Edge:** Reeded

Date	Mintage	F	VF	XF	Unc	BU
2007PM	—	—	—	—	—	170

KM# 1350 1/10 CROWN
3.1100 g., 0.9999 Gold 0.1000 oz. AGW **Ruler:** Elizabeth II **Subject:** The tale of Peter Rabbit **Obv:** Bust with tiara right **Obv. Legend:** ELIZABETH II - ISLE OF MAN **Obv. Designer:** Ian Rank-Broadley **Rev:** Peter walking with friends **Edge:** Reeded

Date	Mintage	F	VF	XF	Unc	BU
2007PM	—	—	—	—	—	180

KM# 1168 1/10 CROWN
3.1100 g., 0.9999 Gold 0.1000 oz. AGW, 17.95 mm. **Ruler:** Elizabeth II **Subject:** Year of the Goat **Obv:** Bust with tiara right **Obv. Designer:** Ian Rank-Broadley **Rev:** Three goats **Edge:** Reeded

Date	Mintage	F	VF	XF	Unc	BU
2003PM Proof	—	Value: 115				

KM# 1060 1/5 CROWN
6.2200 g., 0.9999 Gold 0.1999 oz. AGW, 22 mm. **Ruler:** Elizabeth II **Subject:** Year of the Snake **Obv:** Bust with tiara right **Obv. Designer:** Ian Rank-Broadley **Rev:** Snake **Edge:** Reeded

Date	Mintage	F	VF	XF	Unc	BU
2001 Proof	12,000	Value: 215				

KM# 1069 1/5 CROWN
6.2200 g., 0.9999 Gold 0.1999 oz. AGW, 22 mm. **Ruler:** Elizabeth II **Obv:** Head with tiara right **Obv. Designer:** Ian Rank-Broadley **Rev:** Two Somali kittens **Edge:** Reeded

Date	Mintage	F	VF	XF	Unc	BU
2001	—	—	—	—	—	215
2001 Proof	1,000	Value: 225				

KM# 1069a 1/5 CROWN
6.2200 g., 0.9995 Platinum 0.1999 oz. APW, 22 mm. **Ruler:** Elizabeth II **Obv:** Head with tiara right **Obv. Designer:** Ian Rank-Broadley **Rev:** Somali kittens **Edge:** Reeded

Date	Mintage	F	VF	XF	Unc	BU
2001	—	—	—	—	—	450

KM# 1074 1/5 CROWN
6.2200 g., 0.9999 Gold 0.1999 oz. AGW, 22 mm. **Ruler:** Elizabeth II **Subject:** Queen Mother **Obv:** Head with tiara right **Obv. Designer:** Ian Rank-Broadley **Rev:** 1948 Silver wedding anniversary **Edge:** Reeded

Date	Mintage	F	VF	XF	Unc	BU
2001 Proof	5,000	Value: 215				

KM# 1075 1/5 CROWN
6.2200 g., 0.9999 Gold 0.1999 oz. AGW, 22 mm. **Ruler:** Elizabeth II **Subject:** Queen Mother **Obv:** Head with tiara right **Obv. Designer:** Ian Rank-Broadley **Rev:** 1948 holding baby Prince Charles **Edge:** Reeded

Date	Mintage	F	VF	XF	Unc	BU
2001 Proof	5,000	Value: 215				

KM# 1078 1/5 CROWN
6.2200 g., 0.9999 Gold 0.1999 oz. AGW, 22 mm. **Ruler:** Elizabeth II **Subject:** Martin Frobisher **Obv:** Head with tiara right **Obv. Designer:** Ian Rank-Broadley **Rev:** Portrait, ship and map **Edge:** Reeded

Date	Mintage	F	VF	XF	Unc	BU
2001 Proof	5,000	Value: 215				

KM# 1079 1/5 CROWN
6.2200 g., 0.9999 Gold 0.1999 oz. AGW, 22 mm. **Ruler:** Elizabeth II **Subject:** Ronald Amundsen **Obv:** Head with tiara right **Obv. Designer:** Ian Rank-Broadley **Rev:** Portrait, ship and dirigible **Edge:** Reeded

Date	Mintage	F	VF	XF	Unc	BU
2001 Proof	5,000	Value: 215				

KM# 1082 1/5 CROWN
6.2200 g., 0.9999 Gold 0.1999 oz. AGW, 22 mm. **Ruler:** Elizabeth II **Subject:** Queen's 75th Birthday **Obv:** Head with tiara right **Obv. Designer:** Ian Rank-Broadley **Rev:** Flower bouquet with a tiny diamond mounted on the bow of the ribbon **Edge:** Reeded

Date	Mintage	F	VF	XF	Unc	BU
2001 Proof	2,000	Value: 300				

KM# 1334 1/5 CROWN
6.1500 g., 0.9990 Gold 0.1975 oz. AGW, 21.78 mm. **Ruler:** Elizabeth II **Subject:** Harry Potter **Obv:** Bust right **Obv. Designer:** Ian Rank-Broadley **Rev:** Boy with magic wand **Edge:** Reeded

Date	Mintage	F	VF	XF	Unc	BU
2001 Proof	5,000	Value: 210				

KM# 1335 1/5 CROWN
6.1500 g., 0.9990 Gold 0.1975 oz. AGW, 21.78 mm. **Ruler:** Elizabeth II **Subject:** Harry Potter - Journey to Hogwarts School **Obv:** Bust right **Obv. Designer:** Ian Rank-Broadley **Rev:** Boat full of children going to Hogwarts School **Edge:** Reeded

Date	Mintage	F	VF	XF	Unc	BU
2001 Proof	5,000	Value: 210				

KM# 1336 1/5 CROWN
6.1500 g., 0.9990 Gold 0.1975 oz. AGW, 21.78 mm. **Ruler:** Elizabeth II **Subject:** Harry Potter - First Quidditch Match **Obv:** Bust right **Obv. Designer:** Ian Rank-Broadley **Rev:** Harry flying a broom in a quidditch match **Edge:** Reeded

Date	Mintage	F	VF	XF	Unc	BU
2001 Proof	5,000	Value: 210				

KM# 1337 1/5 CROWN
6.1500 g., 0.9990 Gold 0.1975 oz. AGW, 21.78 mm. **Ruler:** Elizabeth II **Subject:** Harry Potter **Obv:** Bust right **Obv. Designer:** Ian Rank-Broadley **Rev:** Birth of Norbert, the dragon **Edge:** Reeded

Date	Mintage	F	VF	XF	Unc	BU
2001 Proof	5,000	Value: 210				

KM# 1338 1/5 CROWN
6.1500 g., 0.9990 Gold 0.1975 oz. AGW, 21.78 mm. **Ruler:** Elizabeth II **Subject:** Harry Potter **Obv:** Bust right **Obv. Designer:** Ian Rank-Broadley **Rev:** Harry in Potions class **Edge:** Reeded

Date	Mintage	F	VF	XF	Unc	BU
2001 Proof	5,000	Value: 210				

KM# 1339 1/5 CROWN
6.1500 g., 0.9990 Gold 0.1975 oz. AGW, 21.78 mm. **Ruler:** Elizabeth II **Subject:** Harry Potter **Obv:** Bust right **Obv. Designer:** Ian Rank-Broadley **Rev:** Harry chasing a jeweled snitch **Edge:** Reeded

Date	Mintage	F	VF	XF	Unc	BU
2001 Proof	5,000	Value: 210				

KM# 1156 1/5 CROWN
6.2200 g., 0.9990 Gold 0.1998 oz. AGW, 22 mm. **Ruler:** Elizabeth II **Subject:** Queen's Golden Jubilee **Obv:** Queen's portrait **Rev:** Queen on horse **Edge:** Reeded

Date	Mintage	F	VF	XF	Unc	BU
2002PM Proof	500	Value: 220				

KM# 1117 1/5 CROWN
6.2200 g., 0.9990 Gold 0.1998 oz. AGW, 22 mm. **Ruler:** Elizabeth II **Subject:** Queen Mother's Love of Horses **Obv:** Bust with tiara right **Obv. Designer:** Ian Rank-Broadley **Rev:** Queen Mother and horse **Edge:** Reeded

Date	Mintage	F	VF	XF	Unc	BU
2002 Proof	5,000	Value: 215				

KM# 1109 1/5 CROWN
6.2200 g., 0.9990 Gold 0.1998 oz. AGW, 22 mm. **Ruler:** Elizabeth II **Subject:** Bengal Cat **Obv:** Head with tiara right **Obv. Designer:** Ian Rank-Broadley **Rev:** Cat and kitten **Edge:** Reeded

Date	Mintage	VG	F	VF	XF	Unc
2002	—	—	—	—	—	—
2002 Proof	1,000	Value: 225				

KM# 1109a 1/5 CROWN
6.2200 g., 0.9990 Platinum 0.1998 oz. APW, 22 mm. **Ruler:** Elizabeth II **Subject:** Bengal Cat **Obv:** Head with tiara right **Obv. Designer:** Ian Rank-Broadley **Rev:** Cat and kitten **Edge:** Reeded

Date	Mintage	F	VF	XF	Unc	BU
2002	—	—	—	—	—	450

KM# 1100 1/5 CROWN
6.2200 g., 0.9999 Gold 0.1999 oz. AGW, 22 mm. **Ruler:** Elizabeth II **Subject:** Year of the Horse **Obv:** Bust with tiara right **Obv. Designer:** Ian Rank-Broadley **Rev:** Two horses **Edge:** Reeded

Date	Mintage	F	VF	XF	Unc	BU
2002 Proof	12,000	Value: 215				

KM# 1113 1/5 CROWN
6.2200 g., 0.9990 Gold 0.1998 oz. AGW, 22 mm. **Ruler:** Elizabeth II **Subject:** Olympics - Salt Lake City **Obv:** Bust with tiara right **Obv. Designer:** Ian Rank-Broadley **Rev:** Skier, torch and flag **Edge:** Reeded

Date	Mintage	F	VF	XF	Unc	BU
2002 Proof	5,000	Value: 215				

KM# 1114 1/5 CROWN
6.2200 g., 0.9990 Gold 0.1998 oz. AGW **Ruler:** Elizabeth II **Subject:** Olympics - Salt Lake City **Obv:** Bust with tiara right **Obv. Designer:** Ian Rank-Broadley **Rev:** Bobsled, torch and stadium **Edge:** Reeded

Date	Mintage	F	VF	XF	Unc	BU
2002 Proof	5,000	Value: 215				

KM# 1120 1/5 CROWN
6.2200 g., 0.9990 Gold 0.1998 oz. AGW, 22 mm. **Ruler:** Elizabeth II **Subject:** World Cup 2002 Japan - Korea **Obv:** Bust with tiara right **Obv. Designer:** Ian Rank-Broadley **Rev:** Player running right **Edge:** Reeded

Date	Mintage	F	VF	XF	Unc	BU
2002 Proof	5,000	Value: 215				

KM# 1122 1/5 CROWN
6.2200 g., 0.9990 Gold 0.1998 oz. AGW, 22 mm. **Ruler:** Elizabeth II **Subject:** World Cup 2002 Japan - Korea **Obv:** Bust with tiara right **Obv. Designer:** Ian Rank-Broadley **Rev:** Player kicking to right **Edge:** Reeded

Date	Mintage	F	VF	XF	Unc	BU
2002 Proof	5,000	Value: 215				

KM# 1124 1/5 CROWN
6.2200 g., 0.9990 Gold 0.1998 oz. AGW, 22 mm. **Ruler:** Elizabeth II **Subject:** World Cup 2002 Japan - Korea **Obv:** Head with tiara right **Obv. Designer:** Ian Rank-Broadley **Rev:** Player kicking to left **Edge:** Reeded

Date	Mintage	F	VF	XF	Unc	BU
2002 Proof	5,000	Value: 215				

KM# 1126 1/5 CROWN
6.2200 g., 0.9990 Gold 0.1998 oz. AGW, 22 mm. **Ruler:** Elizabeth II **Subject:** World Cup 2002 Japan - Korea **Obv:** Head with tiara right **Obv. Designer:** Ian Rank-Broadley **Rev:** Player running to left **Edge:** Reeded

Date	Mintage	F	VF	XF	Unc	BU
2002 Proof	5,000	Value: 215				

KM# 1130 1/5 CROWN
6.2200 g., 0.3750 Gold 0.0750 oz. AGW, 22 mm. **Ruler:** Elizabeth II **Subject:** Elizabeth II's Golden Jubilee **Obv:** Bust with tiara right **Obv. Designer:** Ian Rank-Broadley **Rev:** Seated crowned Queen holding scepter at her coronation **Edge:** Reeded

Date	Mintage	F	VF	XF	Unc	BU
2002 Proof	2,002	Value: 85.00				

KM# 1132 1/5 CROWN
6.2200 g., 0.3750 Gold 0.0750 oz. AGW, 22 mm. **Ruler:** Elizabeth II **Subject:** Elizabeth II's Golden Jubilee **Obv:** Bust with tiara right **Obv. Designer:** Ian Rank-Broadley **Rev:** Queen on horse **Edge:** Reeded

Date	Mintage	F	VF	XF	Unc	BU
2002 Proof	2,002	Value: 85.00				

KM# 1134 1/5 CROWN
6.2200 g., 0.3750 Gold 0.0750 oz. AGW, 22 mm. **Ruler:** Elizabeth II **Subject:** Elizabeth II's Golden Jubilee **Obv:** Head with tiara right **Obv. Designer:** Ian Rank-Broadley **Rev:** Queen with dog **Edge:** Reeded

Date	Mintage	F	VF	XF	Unc	BU
2002 Proof	2,002	Value: 85.00				

KM# 1136 1/5 CROWN
6.2200 g., 0.3750 Gold 0.0750 oz. AGW, 22 mm. **Ruler:** Elizabeth II **Subject:** Elizabeth II's Golden Jubilee **Obv:** Bust with tiara right **Obv. Designer:** Ian Rank-Broadley **Rev:** Queen at war memorial **Edge:** Reeded

Date	Mintage	F	VF	XF	Unc	BU
2002 Proof	2,002	Value: 85.00				

KM# 1138 1/5 CROWN
6.2200 g., 0.9990 Gold 0.1998 oz. AGW, 22 mm. **Ruler:** Elizabeth II **Subject:** Queen Mother **Obv:** Bust with tiara right **Obv. Designer:** Ian Rank-Broadley **Rev:** Queen Mother and Castle May **Edge:** Reeded

Date	Mintage	F	VF	XF	Unc	BU
2002 Proof	5,000	Value: 215				

KM# 1140 1/5 CROWN
6.2200 g., 0.9999 Gold 0.1999 oz. AGW, 22 mm. **Ruler:** Elizabeth II **Subject:** Princess Diana **Obv:** Bust with tiara right **Obv. Designer:** Ian Rank-Broadley **Rev:** Diana's portrait **Edge:** Reeded

Date	Mintage	F	VF	XF	Unc	BU
2002 Proof	5,000	Value: 215				

KM# 1163 1/5 CROWN
6.2200 g., 0.9999 Gold 0.1999 oz. AGW, 22 mm. **Ruler:** Elizabeth II **Subject:** Cat **Obv:** Head with tiara right **Obv. Designer:** Ian Rank-Broadley **Rev:** Two Balinese kittens **Edge:** Reeded

Date	Mintage	F	VF	XF	Unc	BU
2003PM	—	—	—	—	—	210
2003PM Proof	—	Value: 215				

KM# 1163a 1/5 CROWN
6.2200 g., 0.9995 Platinum 0.1999 oz. APW, 22 mm. **Ruler:** Elizabeth II **Subject:** Cat **Obv:** Head with tiara right **Obv. Designer:** Ian Rank-Broadley **Rev:** Two Balinese kittens **Edge:** Reeded

Date	Mintage	F	VF	XF	Unc	BU
2003PM	—	—	—	—	—	450

KM# 1169 1/5 CROWN
6.2200 g., 0.9999 Gold 0.1999 oz. AGW, 22 mm. **Ruler:** Elizabeth II **Subject:** Year of the Goat **Obv:** Bust with tiara right **Obv. Designer:** Ian Rank-Broadley **Rev:** Three goats **Edge:** Reeded

Date	Mintage	F	VF	XF	Unc	BU
2003PM Proof	—	Value: 215				

KM# 1175 1/5 CROWN
6.2200 g., 0.9999 Gold 0.1999 oz. AGW, 22 mm. **Ruler:** Elizabeth II **Subject:** Olympics **Obv:** Bust with tiara right **Obv. Designer:** Ian Rank-Broadley **Rev:** Swimmers **Edge:** Reeded

Date	Mintage	F	VF	XF	Unc	BU
2003PM Proof	5,000	Value: 200				

KM# 1177 1/5 CROWN
6.2200 g., 0.9999 Gold 0.1999 oz. AGW, 22 mm. **Ruler:** Elizabeth II **Subject:** Olympics **Obv:** Bust with tiara right **Obv. Designer:** Ian Rank-Broadley **Rev:** Runners **Edge:** Reeded

Date	Mintage	F	VF	XF	Unc	BU
2003PM Proof	5,000	Value: 215				

KM# 1179 1/5 CROWN
6.2200 g., 0.9999 Gold 0.1999 oz. AGW, 22 mm. **Ruler:** Elizabeth II **Subject:** Olympics **Obv:** Bust with tiara right **Obv. Designer:** Ian Rank-Broadley **Rev:** Bicyclists **Edge:** Reeded

Date	Mintage	F	VF	XF	Unc	BU
2003PM Proof	5,000	Value: 215				

KM# 1181 1/5 CROWN
6.2200 g., 0.9999 Gold 0.1999 oz. AGW, 22 mm. **Ruler:** Elizabeth II **Subject:** Olympics **Obv:** Head with tiara right **Obv. Designer:** Ian Rank-Broadley **Rev:** Sail Boarders **Edge:** Reeded

Date	Mintage	F	VF	XF	Unc	BU
2003PM Proof	—	Value: 215				

KM# 1188 1/5 CROWN
6.2200 g., 0.9999 Gold 0.1999 oz. AGW, 22 mm. **Ruler:** Elizabeth II **Subject:** Lord of the Rings **Obv:** Bust with tiara right **Obv. Designer:** Ian Rank-Broadley **Rev:** Legolas **Edge:** Reeded

Date	Mintage	F	VF	XF	Unc	BU
2003PM Proof	3,500	Value: 215				

KM# 1223 1/5 CROWN
6.2200 g., 0.9999 Gold 0.1999 oz. AGW, 22 mm. **Ruler:** Elizabeth II **Obv:** Bust with tiara right **Obv. Designer:** Ian Rank-Broadley **Rev:** D-Day Invasion Plan Map **Edge:** Reeded

Date	Mintage	F	VF	XF	Unc	BU
2004PM Proof	5,000	Value: 215				

KM# 1225 1/5 CROWN
6.2200 g., 0.9999 Gold 0.1999 oz. AGW, 22 mm. **Ruler:** Elizabeth II **Obv:** Bust with tiara right **Obv. Designer:** Ian Rank-Broadley **Rev:** Victoria Cross and battle scene **Edge:** Reeded

Date	Mintage	F	VF	XF	Unc	BU
2004PM Proof	5,000	Value: 215				

KM# 1227 1/5 CROWN
6.2200 g., 0.9999 Gold 0.1999 oz. AGW, 22 mm. **Ruler:** Elizabeth II **Obv:** Bust with tiara right **Obv. Designer:** Ian Rank-Broadley **Rev:** Silver Star and battle scene **Edge:** Reeded

Date	Mintage	F	VF	XF	Unc	BU
2004PM Proof	5,000	Value: 215				

KM# 1229 1/5 CROWN
6.2200 g., 0.9999 Gold 0.1999 oz. AGW, 22 mm. **Ruler:** Elizabeth II **Obv:** Bust with tiara right **Obv. Designer:** Ian Rank-Broadley **Rev:** George Cross and rescue scene **Edge:** Reeded

Date	Mintage	F	VF	XF	Unc	BU
2004PM Proof	5,000	Value: 215				

KM# 1231 1/5 CROWN
6.2200 g., 0.9999 Gold 0.1999 oz. AGW, 22 mm. **Ruler:** Elizabeth II **Obv:** Bust with tiara right **Obv. Designer:** Ian Rank-Broadley **Rev:** White Rose of Finland Medal and battle scene **Edge:** Reeded

Date	Mintage	F	VF	XF	Unc	BU
2004PM Proof	5,000	Value: 215				

KM# 1233 1/5 CROWN
6.2200 g., 0.9999 Gold 0.1999 oz. AGW, 22 mm. **Ruler:** Elizabeth II **Obv:** Bust with tiara right **Obv. Designer:** Ian Rank-Broadley **Rev:** The Norwegian War Medal and naval battle scene **Edge:** Reeded

Date	Mintage	F	VF	XF	Unc	BU
2004PM Proof	5,000	Value: 215				

KM# 1235 1/5 CROWN
6.2200 g., 0.9999 Gold 0.1999 oz. AGW, 22 mm. **Ruler:** Elizabeth II **Obv:** Bust with tiara right **Obv. Designer:** Ian Rank-Broadley **Rev:** French Croix de Guerre and Partisan battle scene **Edge:** Reeded

Date	Mintage	F	VF	XF	Unc	BU
2004PM Proof	5,000	Value: 215				

KM# 1249.1 1/5 CROWN
6.2200 g., 0.9999 Gold 0.1999 oz. AGW, 22 mm. **Ruler:** Elizabeth II **Obv:** Head with tiara right **Obv. Designer:** Ian Rank-Broadley **Rev:** Two Tonkinese cats **Edge:** Reeded

Date	Mintage	F	VF	XF	Unc	BU
2004PM Proof	1,000	Value: 215				
2004PM	—	—	—	—	—	210

KM# 1249.2 1/5 CROWN
6.2200 g., 0.9999 Gold 0.1999 oz. AGW, 22 mm. **Ruler:** Elizabeth II **Obv:** Head with tiara right **Obv. Designer:** Ian Rank-Broadley **Rev:** Two multicolor Tonkinese cats **Edge:** Reeded

Date	Mintage	F	VF	XF	Unc	BU
2004PM Proof	—	Value: 215				

KM# 1198 1/5 CROWN
6.2200 g., 0.9990 Palladium 0.1998 oz., 22 mm. **Ruler:** Elizabeth II **Subject:** Palladium Bicentennial **Obv:** Head with tiara right **Obv. Designer:** Ian Rank-Broadley **Rev:** Athena **Edge:** Reeded

Date	Mintage	F	VF	XF	Unc	BU
2004PM Proof	999	Value: 300				

KM# 1271 1/5 CROWN
6.2200 g., 0.9999 Gold 0.1999 oz. AGW, 22 mm. **Ruler:** Elizabeth II **Obv:** Bust with tiara right **Obv. Designer:** Ian Rank-Broadley **Rev:** Himalayan cat and two kittens **Edge:** Reeded

Date	Mintage	F	VF	XF	Unc	BU
2005PM Proof	—	Value: 225				

KM# 1271a 1/5 CROWN
6.2200 g., 0.9950 Platinum 0.1990 oz. APW, 22 mm. **Ruler:** Elizabeth II **Obv:** Bust with tiara right **Obv. Designer:** Ian Rank-Broadley **Rev:** Himalayan cat and two kittens **Edge:** Reeded

Date	Mintage	F	VF	XF	Unc	BU
2005PM Proof	—	Value: 450				

KM# 1295 1/5 CROWN
6.2200 g., 0.9999 Gold 0.1999 oz. AGW, 22 mm. **Ruler:** Elizabeth II **Subject:** Battles that Changed the World **Obv:** Elizabeth II **Rev:** Trojan War scene **Edge:** Reeded

Date	Mintage	F	VF	XF	Unc	BU
2006PM Proof	5,000	Value: 215				

KM# 1297 1/5 CROWN
6.2200 g., 0.9999 Gold 0.1999 oz. AGW, 22 mm. **Ruler:** Elizabeth II **Subject:** Battles that Changed the World **Obv:** Elizabeth II **Rev:** Battle of Arbela scene **Edge:** Reeded

Date	Mintage	F	VF	XF	Unc	BU
2006PM Proof	5,000	Value: 215				

KM# 1299 1/5 CROWN
6.2200 g., 0.9999 Gold 0.1999 oz. AGW, 22 mm. **Ruler:** Elizabeth II **Subject:** Battles that Changed the World **Obv:** Elizabeth II **Rev:** Battle of Thapsus scene **Edge:** Reeded

Date	Mintage	F	VF	XF	Unc	BU
2006PM Proof	5,000	Value: 215				

KM# 1301 1/5 CROWN
6.2200 g., 0.9999 Gold 0.1999 oz. AGW, 22 mm. **Ruler:** Elizabeth II **Subject:** Battles that Changed the World **Obv:** Elizabeth II **Rev:** Battle of Cologne scene **Edge:** Reeded

Date	Mintage	F	VF	XF	Unc	BU
2006PM Proof	5,000	Value: 215				

KM# 1303 1/5 CROWN
6.2200 g., 0.9999 Gold 0.1999 oz. AGW, 22 mm. **Ruler:** Elizabeth II **Subject:** Battles that Changed the World **Obv:** Elizabeth II **Rev:** Siege of Valencia scene **Edge:** Reeded

Date	Mintage	F	VF	XF	Unc	BU
2006PM Proof	5,000	Value: 215				

KM# 1305 1/5 CROWN
6.2200 g., 0.9999 Gold 0.1999 oz. AGW, 22 mm. **Ruler:** Elizabeth II **Subject:** Battles that Changed the World **Obv:** Elizabeth II **Rev:** Battle of Agincourt scene **Edge:** Reeded

Date	Mintage	F	VF	XF	Unc	BU
2006PM Proof	5,000	Value: 215				

KM# 1342 1/5 CROWN
6.2200 g., 0.9999 Gold 0.1999 oz. AGW **Ruler:** Elizabeth II **Obv:** Bust with tiara right **Obv. Designer:** Ian Rank-Broadley **Rev:** Three Exotic Shorthair cats sitting facing **Edge:** Reeded

Date	Mintage	F	VF	XF	Unc	BU
2006PM	—	—	—	—	—	330

KM# 1345 1/5 CROWN
6.2200 g., 0.9999 Gold 0.1999 oz. AGW **Ruler:** Elizabeth II **Obv:** Bust with tiara right **Obv. Legend:** ELIZABETH II - ISLE OF MAN **Obv. Designer:** Ian Rank-Broadley **Rev:** Ragdoll cat with two kittens sitting facing **Edge:** Reeded

Date	Mintage	F	VF	XF	Unc	BU
2007PM	—	—	—	—	—	330

KM# 1351.1 1/5 CROWN

6.2200 g., 0.9999 Gold 0.1999 oz. AGW **Ruler:** Elizabeth II **Subject:** The tale of Peter Rabbit **Obv:** Bust with tiara right **Obv. Legend:** ELIZABETH II - ISLE OF MAN **Obv. Designer:** Ian Rank-Broadley **Rev:** Peter walking with friends **Edge:** Reeded

Date	Mintage	F	VF	XF	Unc	BU
2007PM	—	—	—	—	—	340

KM# 1351.2 1/5 CROWN

6.2200 g., 0.9999 Gold 0.1999 oz. AGW **Ruler:** Elizabeth II **Subject:** The tale of Peter Rabbit **Obv:** Bust with tiara right **Obv. Legend:** ELIZABETH II - ISLE OF MAN **Obv. Designer:** Ian Rank-Broadley **Rev:** Peter walking with friends **Edge:** Reeded

Date	Mintage	F	VF	XF	Unc	BU
2007PM	—	—	—	—	—	355

KM# 1309 1/5 CROWN

6.2200 g., 0.9999 Gold 0.1999 oz. AGW **Ruler:** Elizabeth II **Subject:** 100th Anniversary of Scouting **Obv:** Bust with tiara right **Obv. Legend:** ELIZABETH II - ISLE OF MAN **Rev:** 3/4 length figure of Robert Baden-Powell standing facing 3/4 left, Fleur-de-lys below, images of scouting at left and right **Rev. Legend:** CENTERARY OF SCOUTING **Edge:** Reeded

Date	Mintage	F	VF	XF	Unc	BU
2007 Proof	—	Value: 215				

KM# 1061 1/2 CROWN

15.5517 g., 0.9999 Gold 0.4999 oz. AGW, 30 mm. **Ruler:** Elizabeth II **Subject:** Year of the Snake **Obv:** Bust with tiara right **Obv. Designer:** Ian Rank-Broadley **Rev:** Snake **Edge:** Reeded

Date	Mintage	F	VF	XF	Unc	BU
2001 Proof	6,000	Value: 500				

KM# 1070 1/2 CROWN

15.5517 g., 0.9999 Gold 0.4999 oz. AGW, 30 mm. **Ruler:** Elizabeth II **Obv:** Head with tiara right **Obv. Designer:** Ian Rank-Broadley **Rev:** Two Somali kittens **Edge:** Reeded

Date	Mintage	F	VF	XF	Unc	BU
2001	—	—	—	—	—	485
2001 Proof	1,000	Value: 500				

KM# 1071 1/2 CROWN

15.5517 g., 0.9995 Platinum 0.4997 oz. APW, 27 mm. **Ruler:** Elizabeth II **Obv:** Head with tiara right **Obv. Designer:** Ian Rank-Broadley **Rev:** Two Somali kittens **Edge:** Reeded

Date	Mintage	F	VF	XF	Unc	BU
2001	—	—	—	—	—	1,000

KM# 1157 1/2 CROWN

15.5510 g., 0.9990 Gold 0.4995 oz. AGW, 30 mm. **Ruler:** Elizabeth II **Subject:** Queen's Golden Jubilee **Obv:** Queen's portrait **Rev:** Queen on horse **Edge:** Reeded

Date	Mintage	F	VF	XF	Unc	BU
2002PM Proof	500	Value: 500				

KM# 1110 1/2 CROWN

15.5510 g., 0.9990 Gold 0.4995 oz. AGW, 30 mm. **Ruler:** Elizabeth II **Subject:** Bengal Cat **Obv:** Head with tiara right **Obv. Designer:** Ian Rank-Broadley **Rev:** Cat and kitten **Edge:** Reeded

Date	Mintage	VG	F	VF	XF	Unc
2002	—	—	—	—	—	—
2002 Proof	1,000	Value: 500				

KM# 1101 1/2 CROWN

15.5500 g., 0.9999 Gold 0.4999 oz. AGW, 30 mm. **Ruler:** Elizabeth II **Subject:** Year of the Horse **Obv:** Bust with tiara right **Obv. Designer:** Ian Rank-Broadley **Rev:** Two horses **Edge:** Reeded

Date	Mintage	F	VF	XF	Unc	BU
2002 Proof	6,000	Value: 500				

KM# 1110a 1/2 CROWN

6.2200 g., 0.9990 Platinum 0.1998 oz. APW, 30 mm. **Ruler:** Elizabeth II **Subject:** Bengal Cat **Obv:** Head with tiara right **Obv. Designer:** Ian Rank-Broadley **Rev:** Cat and kitten **Edge:** Reeded

Date	Mintage	F	VF	XF	Unc	BU
2002	—	—	—	—	—	475

KM# 1164 1/2 CROWN

15.5510 g., 0.9999 Gold 0.4999 oz. AGW, 30 mm. **Ruler:** Elizabeth II **Subject:** Cat **Obv:** Head with tiara right **Obv. Designer:** Ian Rank-Broadley **Rev:** Two Balinese kittens **Edge:** Reeded

Date	Mintage	F	VF	XF	Unc	BU
2003PM	—	—	—	—	—	485
2003PM Proof	—	Value: 500				

KM# 1164a 1/2 CROWN

15.5510 g., 0.9995 Platinum 0.4997 oz. APW, 30 mm. **Ruler:** Elizabeth II **Subject:** Cat **Obv:** Head with tiara right **Obv. Designer:** Ian Rank-Broadley **Rev:** Two Balinese kittens **Edge:** Reeded

Date	Mintage	F	VF	XF	Unc	BU
2003PM	—	—	—	—	—	1,000

KM# 1170 1/2 CROWN

15.5500 g., 0.9999 Gold 0.4999 oz. AGW, 30 mm. **Ruler:** Elizabeth II **Subject:** Year of the Goat **Obv:** Bust with tiara right **Obv. Designer:** Ian Rank-Broadley **Rev:** Three goats **Edge:** Reeded

Date	Mintage	F	VF	XF	Unc	BU
2003PM Proof	—	Value: 500				

KM# 1189 1/2 CROWN

15.5510 g., 0.9999 Gold 0.4999 oz. AGW, 30 mm. **Ruler:** Elizabeth II **Subject:** Lord of the Rings **Obv:** Bust with tiara right **Obv. Designer:** Ian Rank-Broadley **Rev:** Gimli with two battle axes **Edge:** Reeded

Date	Mintage	F	VF	XF	Unc	BU
2003PM Proof	1,000	Value: 500				

KM# 1243 1/2 CROWN

15.5520 g., 0.9999 Gold 0.4999 oz. AGW, 30 mm. **Ruler:** Elizabeth II **Obv:** Head with tiara right **Obv. Designer:** Ian Rank-Broadley **Rev:** Monkey **Edge:** Reeded

Date	Mintage	F	VF	XF	Unc	BU
2004PM Proof	6,000	Value: 500				

KM# 1250 1/2 CROWN

15.5520 g., 0.9999 Gold 0.4999 oz. AGW, 30 mm. **Ruler:** Elizabeth II **Obv:** Head with tiara right **Obv. Designer:** Ian Rank-Broadley **Rev:** Two Tonkinese cats **Edge:** Reeded

Date	Mintage	F	VF	XF	Unc	BU
2004PM Proof	1,000	Value: 500				
2004PM	—	—	—	—	—	485

KM# 1199 1/2 CROWN

15.5500 g., 0.9990 Bi-Metallic .999 Palladium 6.3g center in .9999 Gold 9.25 g ring 0.4994 oz., 30 mm. **Ruler:** Elizabeth II **Subject:** Palladium Bicentennial **Obv:** Bust with tiara right **Obv. Designer:** Ian Rank-Broadley **Rev:** Athena **Edge:** Reeded

Date	Mintage	F	VF	XF	Unc	BU
2004PM Proof	500	Value: 750				

KM# 1272 1/2 CROWN

15.5510 g., 0.9999 Gold 0.4999 oz. AGW, 27 mm. **Ruler:** Elizabeth II **Obv:** Bust with tiara right **Obv. Designer:** Ian Rank-Broadley **Rev:** Himalayan cat and two kittens **Edge:** Reeded

Date	Mintage	F	VF	XF	Unc	BU
2005PM Proof	—	Value: 500				

KM# 1272a 1/2 CROWN

15.5510 g., 0.9950 Platinum 0.4975 oz. APW, 27 mm. **Ruler:** Elizabeth II **Obv:** Bust with tiara right **Obv. Designer:** Ian Rank-Broadley **Rev:** Himalayan cat and two kittens **Edge:** Reeded

Date	Mintage	F	VF	XF	Unc	BU
2005PM	—	—	—	—	—	1,050
2005PM Proof	—	Value: 1,100				

KM# 1346 1/2 CROWN

15.5500 g., 0.9999 Gold 0.4999 oz. AGW **Ruler:** Elizabeth II **Obv:** Bust with tiara right **Obv. Legend:** ELIZABETH II - ISLE OF MAN **Obv. Designer:** Ian Rank-Broadley **Rev:** Ragdoll cat with two kittens sitting facing **Edge:** Reeded

Date	Mintage	F	VF	XF	Unc	BU
2007PM	—	—	—	—	—	670

KM# 1062 CROWN

28.2800 g., Copper-Nickel, 38.6 mm. **Ruler:** Elizabeth II **Subject:** Year of the Snake **Obv:** Bust with tiara right **Obv. Designer:** Ian Rank-Broadley **Rev:** Snake **Edge:** Reeded

Date	Mintage	F	VF	XF	Unc	BU
2001	—	—	—	—	10.00	14.00

KM# 1062a CROWN

28.2800 g., 0.9250 Silver 0.8410 oz. ASW, 38.6 mm. **Ruler:** Elizabeth II **Subject:** Year of the Snake **Obv:** Head with tiara right **Obv. Designer:** Ian Rank-Broadley **Rev:** Snake **Edge:** Reeded

Date	Mintage	F	VF	XF	Unc	BU
2001 Proof	30,000	Value: 47.50				

KM# 1063 CROWN

31.1035 g., 0.9999 Gold 0.9999 oz. AGW, 32.7 mm. **Ruler:** Elizabeth II **Subject:** Year of the Snake **Obv:** Bust with tiara right **Obv. Designer:** Ian Rank-Broadley **Rev:** Snake **Edge:** Reeded

Date	Mintage	F	VF	XF	Unc	BU
2001 Proof	2,000	Value: 1,000				

KM# 1072 CROWN

28.2800 g., Copper-Nickel, 38.6 mm. **Ruler:** Elizabeth II **Subject:** Somali Kittens **Obv:** Bust with tiara right **Obv. Designer:** Ian Rank-Broadley **Rev:** Two kittens **Edge:** Reeded

Date	Mintage	F	VF	XF	Unc	BU
2001	—	—	—	—	9.00	12.50

KM# 1072a CROWN

31.1035 g., 0.9990 Silver 0.9990 oz. ASW, 38.6 mm. **Ruler:** Elizabeth II **Subject:** Somali Kittens **Obv:** Bust with tiara right **Obv. Designer:** Ian Rank-Broadley **Rev:** Two kittens **Edge:** Reeded

Date	Mintage	F	VF	XF	Unc	BU
2001 Proof	50,000	Value: 47.50				

KM# 1073 CROWN

31.1035 g., 0.9999 Gold 0.9999 oz. AGW, 32.7 mm. **Ruler:** Elizabeth II **Subject:** Somali Kittens **Obv:** Bust with tiara right **Obv. Designer:** Ian Rank-Broadley **Rev:** Two kittens **Edge:** Reeded

Date	Mintage	F	VF	XF	Unc	BU
2001	—	—	—	—	—	985
2001 Proof	1,000	Value: 1,000				

KM# 1076 CROWN

28.2800 g., Copper-Nickel, 38.6 mm. **Ruler:** Elizabeth II **Subject:** Queen Mother **Obv:** Bust with tiara right **Obv. Designer:** Ian Rank-Broadley **Rev:** 1948 Silver wedding anniversary **Edge:** Reeded

Date	Mintage	F	VF	XF	Unc	BU
2001	—	—	—	—	10.00	12.00

KM# 1076a CROWN

28.2800 g., 0.9250 Silver 0.8410 oz. ASW, 38.6 mm. **Ruler:** Elizabeth II **Subject:** Queen Mother **Obv:** Bust with tiara right **Obv. Designer:** Ian Rank-Broadley **Rev:** 1948 Silver wedding anniversary **Edge:** Reeded

Date	Mintage	F	VF	XF	Unc	BU
2001 Proof	10,000	Value: 47.50				

KM# 1077 CROWN

Copper-Nickel, 38.6 mm. **Ruler:** Elizabeth II **Subject:** Queen Mother **Obv:** Bust with tiara right **Obv. Designer:** Ian Rank-Broadley **Rev:** 1948 holding baby Prince Charles **Edge:** Reeded

Date	Mintage	F	VF	XF	Unc	BU
2001	—	—	—	—	10.00	12.00

KM# 1077a CROWN

28.2800 g., 0.9250 Silver 0.8410 oz. ASW, 38.6 mm. **Ruler:** Elizabeth II **Subject:** Queen Mother **Obv:** Head with tiara right **Obv. Designer:** Ian Rank-Broadley **Rev:** 1948 holding baby Prince Charles **Edge:** Reeded

Date	Mintage	F	VF	XF	Unc	BU
2001 Proof	10,000	Value: 47.50				

KM# 1080 CROWN

Copper-Nickel, 38.6 mm. **Ruler:** Elizabeth II **Subject:** Martin Frobisher **Obv:** Bust with tiara right **Obv. Designer:** Ian Rank-Broadley **Rev:** Bust at left, ship at right and map below **Edge:** Reeded

Date	Mintage	F	VF	XF	Unc	BU
2001	—	—	—	—	10.00	12.00

KM# 1080a CROWN

28.2800 g., 0.9250 Silver 0.8410 oz. ASW, 38.6 mm. **Ruler:** Elizabeth II **Subject:** Martin Frobisher **Obv:** Bust of Queen Elizabeth II right **Obv. Designer:** Ian Rank-Broadley **Edge:** Reeded

Date	Mintage	F	VF	XF	Unc	BU
2001 Proof	10,000	Value: 47.50				

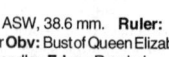

KM# 1081 CROWN
Copper-Nickel, 38.6 mm. **Ruler:** Elizabeth II **Subject:** Roald Amundsen **Obv:** Bust with tiara right **Obv. Designer:** Ian Rank-Broadley **Rev:** Bust at right, ship at center, dirigible above at left **Edge:** Reeded

Date	Mintage	F	VF	XF	Unc	BU
2001	—	—	—	—	10.00	12.00

KM# 1081a CROWN
28.2800 g., 0.9250 Silver 0.8410 oz. ASW, 38.6 mm. **Ruler:** Elizabeth II **Subject:** Roald Amundsen **Obv:** Bust with tiara right **Obv. Designer:** Ian Rank-Broadley **Rev:** Bust at right, ship at center, dirigible at upper left **Edge:** Reeded

Date	Mintage	F	VF	XF	Unc	BU
2001 Proof	10,000	Value: 47.50				

KM# 1085 CROWN
28.2800 g., Copper-Nickel, 38.6 mm. **Ruler:** Elizabeth II **Subject:** Joey Dunlop (1952-2000) **Obv:** Bust with tiara right **Obv. Designer:** Ian Rank-Broadley **Rev:** Motorcycle racer **Edge:** Reeded

Date	Mintage	F	VF	XF	Unc	BU
2001 Black finish	—	—	—	—	10.00	12.00

KM# 1085a CROWN
28.2800 g., 0.9250 Silver 0.8410 oz. ASW, 38.6 mm. **Ruler:** Elizabeth II **Subject:** Joey Dunlop (1952-2000) **Obv:** Bust with tiara right **Obv. Designer:** Ian Rank-Broadley **Rev:** Motorcycle racer **Edge:** Reeded

Date	Mintage	F	VF	XF	Unc	BU
2001 Proof	10,000	Value: 47.50				

KM# 1083 CROWN
28.2800 g., Copper-Nickel, 38.6 mm. **Ruler:** Elizabeth II **Subject:** Queen's 75th Birthday **Obv:** Bust with tiara right **Obv. Designer:** Ian Rank-Broadley **Rev:** Flower bouquet **Edge:** Reeded

Date	Mintage	F	VF	XF	Unc	BU
2001	—	—	—	—	14.00	16.00

KM# 1083a CROWN
28.2800 g., 0.9250 Silver 0.8410 oz. ASW, 38.6 mm. **Ruler:** Elizabeth II **Subject:** Queen's 75th Birthday **Obv:** Bust with tiara right **Obv. Designer:** Ian Rank-Broadley **Rev:** Flower bouquet **Edge:** Reeded

Date	Mintage	F	VF	XF	Unc	BU
2001 Proof	10,000	Value: 50.00				

KM# 1087 CROWN
28.2800 g., Copper-Nickel, 38.6 mm. **Ruler:** Elizabeth II **Series:** Harry Potter **Obv:** Bust with tiara right **Obv. Designer:** Ian Rank-Broadley **Rev:** Harry with magic wand **Edge:** Reeded

Date	Mintage	F	VF	XF	Unc	BU
2001	—	—	—	—	10.00	12.00

KM# 1087a CROWN
28.2800 g., 0.9250 Silver 0.8410 oz. ASW, 38.6 mm. **Ruler:** Elizabeth II **Series:** Harry Potter **Obv:** Bust with tiara right **Obv. Designer:** Ian Rank-Broadley **Rev:** Harry with magic wand **Edge:** Reeded

Date	Mintage	F	VF	XF	Unc	BU
2001 Proof	15,000	Value: 47.50				

KM# 1089 CROWN
28.2800 g., Copper-Nickel, 38.6 mm. **Ruler:** Elizabeth II **Series:** Harry Potter **Subject:** Journey to Hogwart's **Obv:** Bust with tiara right **Obv. Designer:** Ian Rank-Broadley **Rev:** Boat full of children going to Hogwart's **Edge:** Reeded

Date	Mintage	F	VF	XF	Unc	BU
2001	—	—	—	—	10.00	12.00

KM# 1089a CROWN
28.2800 g., 0.9250 Silver 0.8410 oz. ASW, 38.6 mm. **Ruler:** Elizabeth II **Series:** Harry Potter **Obv:** Bust with tiara right **Obv. Designer:** Ian Rank-Broadley **Rev:** Boat full of children going to Hogwart's **Edge:** Reeded

Date	Mintage	F	VF	XF	Unc	BU
2001 Proof	15,000	Value: 47.50				

KM# 1091 CROWN
Copper-Nickel **Ruler:** Elizabeth II **Series:** Harry Potter **Subject:** First Quidditch Match **Obv:** Bust with tiara right **Obv. Designer:** Ian Rank-Broadley **Rev:** Harry flying his Nimbus 2000

Date	Mintage	F	VF	XF	Unc	BU
2001	—	—	—	—	10.00	12.00

KM# 1091a CROWN
28.2800 g., 0.9250 Silver 0.8410 oz. ASW **Ruler:** Elizabeth II **Series:** Harry Potter **Subject:** First Quidditch Match **Obv:** Bust with tiara right **Obv. Designer:** Ian Rank-Broadley **Rev:** Harry flying his Nimbus 2000

Date	Mintage	F	VF	XF	Unc	BU
2001 Proof	15,000	Value: 47.50				

KM# 1093 CROWN
Copper-Nickel **Ruler:** Elizabeth II **Series:** Harry Potter **Subject:** Birth of Norbert **Obv:** Bust with tiara right **Obv. Designer:** Ian Rank-Broadley **Rev:** Hagrid and children watching Norbert hatch

Date	Mintage	F	VF	XF	Unc	BU
2001	—	—	—	—	10.00	14.00

KM# 1093a CROWN
28.2800 g., 0.9250 Silver 0.8410 oz. ASW **Ruler:** Elizabeth II **Series:** Harry Potter **Subject:** Birth of Norbert **Obv:** Bust with tiara right **Obv. Designer:** Ian Rank-Broadley **Rev:** Hagrid and children watching Norbert hatch

Date	Mintage	F	VF	XF	Unc	BU
2001 Proof	15,000	Value: 47.50				

KM# 1095 CROWN
Copper-Nickel **Ruler:** Elizabeth II **Series:** Harry Potter **Subject:** School **Obv:** Bust with tiara right **Obv. Designer:** Ian Rank-Broadley **Rev:** Harry in Potions class

Date	Mintage	F	VF	XF	Unc	BU
2001	—	—	—	—	10.00	12.00

KM# 1095a CROWN
28.2800 g., 0.9250 Silver 0.8410 oz. ASW **Ruler:** Elizabeth II **Series:** Harry Potter **Subject:** School **Obv:** Bust with tiara right **Obv. Designer:** Ian Rank-Broadley **Rev:** Harry in Potions class

Date	Mintage	F	VF	XF	Unc	BU
2001 Proof	15,000	Value: 47.50				

KM# 1097 CROWN
Copper-Nickel, 38.72 mm. **Ruler:** Elizabeth II **Series:** Harry Potter **Obv:** Bust with tiara right **Obv. Designer:** Ian Rank-Broadley **Rev:** Harry catching a flying jeweled snitch **Edge:** Reeded

Date	Mintage	F	VF	XF	Unc	BU
2001	—	—	—	—	10.00	12.00

KM# 1097a CROWN
28.2800 g., 0.9250 Silver 0.8410 oz. ASW, 38.71 mm. **Ruler:** Elizabeth II **Series:** Harry Potter **Obv:** Bust with tiara right **Obv. Designer:** Ian Rank-Broadley **Rev:** Harry catching a flying jeweled snitch **Edge:** Reeded

Date	Mintage	F	VF	XF	Unc	BU
2001 Proof	15,000	Value: 47.50				

KM# 1102 CROWN
28.2800 g., Copper-Nickel, 38.6 mm. **Ruler:** Elizabeth II **Subject:** Year of the Horse **Obv:** Bust with tiara right **Obv. Designer:** Ian Rank-Broadley **Rev:** Two horses **Edge:** Reeded

Date	Mintage	F	VF	XF	Unc	BU
2002	—	—	—	—	12.00	14.00

KM# 1102a CROWN
28.2800 g., 0.9250 Silver 0.8410 oz. ASW, 38.6 mm. **Ruler:** Elizabeth II **Subject:** Year of the Horse **Obv:** Bust with tiara right **Obv. Designer:** Ian Rank-Broadley **Rev:** Two horses **Edge:** Reeded

Date	Mintage	F	VF	XF	Unc	BU
2002 Proof	30,000	Value: 47.50				

KM# 1103 CROWN
31.1000 g., 0.9999 Gold 0.9997 oz. AGW **Ruler:** Elizabeth II **Subject:** Year of the Horse **Obv:** Bust with tiara right **Obv. Designer:** Ian Rank-Broadley

Date	Mintage	F	VF	XF	Unc	BU
2002 Proof	2,000	Value: 1,000				

KM# 1111 CROWN
28.2800 g., Copper-Nickel, 38.6 mm. **Ruler:** Elizabeth II **Subject:** Bengal Cat **Obv:** Bust with tiara right **Obv. Designer:** Ian Rank-Broadley **Rev:** Cat and kitten **Edge:** Reeded

Date	Mintage	F	VF	XF	Unc	BU
2002	—	—	—	—	12.50	14.00

KM# 1111a CROWN
31.1035 g., 0.9990 Silver 0.9990 oz. ASW, 38.6 mm. **Ruler:** Elizabeth II **Subject:** Bengal Cat **Obv:** Bust with tiara right **Obv. Designer:** Ian Rank-Broadley **Rev:** Cat and kitten **Edge:** Reeded

Date	Mintage	F	VF	XF	Unc	BU
2002 Proof	10,000	Value: 47.50				

KM# 1112 CROWN
31.1035 g., 0.9990 Gold 0.9990 oz. AGW **Ruler:** Elizabeth II **Subject:** Bengal Cat **Obv:** Bust with tiara right **Obv. Designer:** Ian Rank-Broadley **Rev:** Cat and kitten **Edge:** Reeded

Date	Mintage	F	VF	XF	Unc	BU
2002	—	—	—	—	—	985
2002 Proof	1,000	Value: 1,000				

KM# 1115 CROWN
28.2800 g., Copper-Nickel, 38.6 mm. **Ruler:** Elizabeth II **Subject:** Olympics - Salt Lake City **Obv:** Bust with tiara right **Obv. Designer:** Ian Rank-Broadley **Rev:** Skier, torch and flag **Edge:** Reeded

Date	Mintage	F	VF	XF	Unc	BU
2002	—	—	—	—	10.00	12.00

KM# 1115a CROWN
28.2800 g., 0.9250 Silver 0.8410 oz. ASW, 38.6 mm. **Ruler:** Elizabeth II **Subject:** Olympics - Salt Lake City **Obv:** Bust with tiara right **Obv. Designer:** Ian Rank-Broadley **Rev:** Skier, torch and flag **Edge:** Reeded

Date	Mintage	F	VF	XF	Unc	BU
2002 Proof	10,000	Value: 47.50				

KM# 1116 CROWN
28.2800 g., Copper-Nickel, 38.6 mm. **Ruler:** Elizabeth II **Subject:** Olympics - Salt Lake City **Obv:** Bust with tiara right **Obv. Designer:** Ian Rank-Broadley **Rev:** Bobsled, torch and stadium **Edge:** Reeded

Date	Mintage	F	VF	XF	Unc	BU
2002	—	—	—	—	10.00	12.00

KM# 1116a CROWN
28.2800 g., 0.9250 Silver 0.8410 oz. ASW, 38.6 mm. **Ruler:** Elizabeth II **Subject:** Olympics - Salt Lake City **Obv:** Bust with tiara right **Obv. Designer:** Ian Rank-Broadley **Rev:** Bobsled, torch and stadium **Edge:** Reeded

Date	Mintage	F	VF	XF	Unc	BU
2002 Proof	10,000	Value: 47.50				

KM# 1118 CROWN
28.2800 g., Copper-Nickel, 38.6 mm. **Ruler:** Elizabeth II **Subject:** Queen Mother's Love of Horses **Obv:** Bust with tiara right **Obv. Designer:** Ian Rank-Broadley **Rev:** Queen Mother and horse **Edge:** Reeded

Date	Mintage	F	VF	XF	Unc	BU
2002	—	—	—	—	10.00	12.00

KM# 1118a CROWN
28.2800 g., Silver, 38.6 mm. **Ruler:** Elizabeth II **Subject:** Queen Mother's Love of Horses **Obv:** Bust with tiara right **Obv. Designer:** Ian Rank-Broadley **Rev:** Queen Mother and horse **Edge:** Reeded

Date	Mintage	F	VF	XF	Unc	BU
2002 Proof	10,000	Value: 47.50				

KM# 1119 CROWN
35.0000 g., 0.7500 Gold 0.8439 oz. AGW, 38.6 mm. **Ruler:** Elizabeth II **Subject:** Golden Jubilee **Obv:** Bust with tiara right **Obv. Designer:** Ian Rank-Broadley **Rev:** Queen Elizabeth II's young laureate bust right **Rev. Designer:** Mary Gillick **Edge:** Reeded **Note:** Red Gold center in a White Gold inner ring within a Yellow Gold outer ring.

Date	Mintage	F	VF	XF	Unc	BU
2002 Proof	999	Value: 875				

KM# 1121 CROWN
28.2800 g., Copper-Nickel, 38.6 mm. **Ruler:** Elizabeth II **Subject:** World Cup 2002 Japan - Korea **Obv:** Bust with tiara right **Obv. Designer:** Ian Rank-Broadley **Rev:** Player running right **Edge:** Reeded

Date	Mintage	F	VF	XF	Unc	BU
2002	—	—	—	—	10.00	12.00

KM# 1121a CROWN
28.2800 g., 0.9250 Silver 0.8410 oz. ASW, 38.6 mm. **Ruler:** Elizabeth II **Subject:** World Cup 2002 Japan - Korea **Obv:** Bust with tiara right **Obv. Designer:** Ian Rank-Broadley **Rev:** Player running right **Edge:** Reeded

Date	Mintage	F	VF	XF	Unc	BU
2002 Proof	10,000	Value: 47.50				

KM# 1123 CROWN
28.2800 g., Copper-Nickel, 38.6 mm. **Ruler:** Elizabeth II **Subject:** World Cup 2002 Japan - Korea **Obv:** Bust with tiara right **Obv. Designer:** Ian Rank-Broadley **Rev:** Player kicking to right **Edge:** Reeded

Date	Mintage	F	VF	XF	Unc	BU
2002	—	—	—	—	10.00	12.00

KM# 1123a CROWN
28.2800 g., 0.9250 Silver 0.8410 oz. ASW, 38.6 mm. **Ruler:** Elizabeth II **Subject:** World Cup 2002 Japan - Korea **Obv:** Bust with tiara right **Obv. Designer:** Ian Rank-Broadley **Rev:** Player kicking to right **Edge:** Reeded

Date	Mintage	F	VF	XF	Unc	BU
2002 Proof	10,000	Value: 47.50				

KM# 1125 CROWN
28.2800 g., Copper-Nickel, 38.6 mm. **Ruler:** Elizabeth II **Subject:** World Cup 2002 Japan - Korea **Obv:** Bust with tiara right **Obv. Designer:** Ian Rank-Broadley **Rev:** Player kicking to left **Edge:** Reeded

Date	Mintage	F	VF	XF	Unc	BU
2002	—	—	—	—	10.00	12.00

KM# 1125a CROWN
28.2800 g., 0.9250 Silver 0.8410 oz. ASW, 38.6 mm. **Ruler:** Elizabeth II **Subject:** World Cup 2002 Japan - Korea **Obv:** Bust with tiara right **Rev:** Player kicking to left **Edge:** Reeded

Date	Mintage	F	VF	XF	Unc	BU
2002 Proof	10,000	Value: 47.50				

KM# 1127 CROWN
28.2800 g., Copper-Nickel, 38.6 mm. **Ruler:** Elizabeth II **Subject:** World Cup 2002 Japan - Korea **Obv:** Bust with tiara right **Obv. Designer:** Ian Rank-Broadley **Rev:** Player running to left **Edge:** Reeded

Date	Mintage	F	VF	XF	Unc	BU
2002	—	—	—	—	10.00	12.00

KM# 1127a CROWN
28.2800 g., 0.9250 Silver 0.8410 oz. ASW, 38.6 mm. **Ruler:** Elizabeth II **Subject:** World Cup 2002 Japan - Korea **Obv:** Bust with tiara right **Obv. Designer:** Ian Rank-Broadley **Rev:** Player running to left **Edge:** Reeded

Date	Mintage	F	VF	XF	Unc	BU
2002 Proof	10,000	Value: 47.50				

KM# 1131 CROWN
28.2800 g., Copper-Nickel, 38.6 mm. **Ruler:** Elizabeth II **Subject:** Queen Elizabeth II's Golden Jubilee **Obv:** Bust with tiara right **Obv. Designer:** Ian Rank-Broadley **Rev:** Seated crowned Queen holding scepter at her coronation **Edge:** Reeded

Date	Mintage	F	VF	XF	Unc	BU
2002	—	—	—	—	10.00	12.00

KM# 1131a CROWN
28.2800 g., Gold Color Base Metal, 38.6 mm. **Ruler:** Elizabeth II **Subject:** Queen Elizabeth II's Golden Jubilee **Obv:** Bust with tiara right **Obv. Designer:** Ian Rank-Broadley **Rev:** Seated crowned Queen holding scepter at her coronation **Edge:** Reeded

Date	Mintage	F	VF	XF	Unc	BU
2002	15,000	—	—	—	10.00	12.00

KM# 1131b CROWN
28.2800 g., 0.9250 Gold Clad Silver 0.8410 oz., 38.6 mm. **Ruler:** Elizabeth II **Subject:** Queen Elizabeth II's Golden Jubilee **Obv:** Bust with tiara right **Obv. Designer:** Ian Rank-Broadley **Rev:** Seated crowned Queen holding scepter at her coronation **Edge:** Reeded

Date	Mintage	F	VF	XF	Unc	BU
2002 Proof	10,000	Value: 47.50				

KM# 1133 CROWN
28.2800 g., Copper-Nickel, 38.6 mm. **Ruler:** Elizabeth II **Subject:** Queen Elizabeth II's Golden Jubilee **Obv:** Bust with tiara right **Obv. Designer:** Ian Rank-Broadley **Rev:** Queen on horse **Edge:** Reeded

Date	Mintage	F	VF	XF	Unc	BU
2002	—	—	—	—	10.00	12.00

KM# 1133a CROWN
28.2800 g., Gold Color Base Metal, 38.6 mm. **Ruler:** Elizabeth II **Subject:** Queen Elizabeth II's Golden Jubilee **Obv:** Bust with tiara right **Obv. Designer:** Ian Rank-Broadley **Rev:** Queen on horse **Edge:** Reeded

Date	Mintage	F	VF	XF	Unc	BU
2002	15,000	—	—	—	10.00	12.00

KM# 1133b CROWN
28.2800 g., 0.9250 Gold Clad Silver 0.8410 oz., 38.6 mm. **Ruler:** Elizabeth II **Subject:** Queen Elizabeth II's Golden Jubilee **Obv:** Bust with tiara right **Obv. Designer:** Ian Rank-Broadley **Rev:** Queen on horse half left **Edge:** Reeded

Date	Mintage	F	VF	XF	Unc	BU
2002 Proof	10,000	Value: 47.50				

KM# 1135 CROWN
28.2800 g., Copper-Nickel, 38.6 mm. **Ruler:** Elizabeth II **Subject:** Queen Elizabeth II's Golden Jubilee **Obv:** Bust with tiara right **Obv. Designer:** Ian Rank-Broadley **Rev:** Queen with her pet Corgi **Edge:** Reeded

Date	Mintage	F	VF	XF	Unc	BU
2002	—	—	—	—	10.00	12.00

KM# 1135a CROWN
28.2800 g., Gold Color Base Metal, 38.6 mm. **Ruler:** Elizabeth II **Subject:** Queen Elizabeth II's Golden Jubilee **Obv:** Bust with tiara right **Obv. Designer:** Ian Rank-Broadley **Rev:** Seated Queen with her pet Corgi **Edge:** Reeded

Date	Mintage	F	VF	XF	Unc	BU
2002	15,000	—	—	—	10.00	12.00

KM# 1135b CROWN
28.2800 g., 0.9250 Gold Clad Silver 0.8410 oz., 38.6 mm. **Ruler:** Elizabeth II **Subject:** Queen Elizabeth II's Golden Jubilee **Obv:** Bust with tiara right **Obv. Designer:** Ian Rank-Broadley **Rev:** Queen with her pet Corgi **Edge:** Reeded

Date	Mintage	F	VF	XF	Unc	BU
2002 Proof	10,000	Value: 47.50				

KM# 1137 CROWN
28.2800 g., Copper-Nickel, 38.6 mm. **Ruler:** Elizabeth II **Subject:** Queen Elizabeth II's Golden Jubilee **Obv:** Bust with tiara right **Obv. Designer:** Ian Rank-Broadley **Rev:** Queen at war memorial **Edge:** Reeded

Date	Mintage	F	VF	XF	Unc	BU
2002	—	—	—	—	10.00	12.00

KM# 1137a CROWN
28.2800 g., Gold Color Base Metal, 38.6 mm. **Ruler:** Elizabeth II **Subject:** Queen Elizabeth II's Golden Jubilee **Obv:** Bust with tiara right **Obv. Designer:** Ian Rank-Broadley **Rev:** Queen at war memorial **Edge:** Reeded

Date	Mintage	F	VF	XF	Unc	BU
2002	15,000	—	—	—	10.00	12.00

KM# 1137b CROWN
28.2800 g., Gold Clad Silver, 38.6 mm. **Ruler:** Elizabeth II **Subject:** Queen Elizabeth II's Golden Jubilee **Obv:** Bust with tiara right **Obv. Designer:** Ian Rank-Broadley **Rev:** Queen at war memorial **Edge:** Reeded

Date	Mintage	F	VF	XF	Unc	BU
2002 Proof	10,000	Value: 47.50				

KM# 1139 CROWN
Copper-Nickel, Blackened, 38.6 mm. **Ruler:** Elizabeth II **Subject:** Queen Mother **Obv:** Bust with tiara right **Obv. Designer:** Ian Rank-Broadley **Rev:** Queen Mother and Castle May **Edge:** Reeded

Date	Mintage	F	VF	XF	Unc	BU
2002	—	—	—	—	10.00	12.00

KM# 1139a CROWN
28.2800 g., 0.9250 Silver 0.8410 oz. ASW, 38.6 mm. **Ruler:** Elizabeth II **Obv:** Head with tiara right with blackened legends **Obv. Designer:** Ian Rank-Broadley **Rev:** Queen Mother standing at left in front of Castle May with blackened legends

Date	Mintage	F	VF	XF	Unc	BU
2002 Proof	10,000	Value: 47.50				

KM# 1141 CROWN
28.2800 g., Copper-Nickel, 38.6 mm. **Ruler:** Elizabeth II **Subject:** Princess Diana **Obv:** Bust with tiara right **Obv. Designer:** Ian Rank-Broadley **Rev:** Diana's bust facing **Edge:** Reeded

Date	Mintage	F	VF	XF	Unc	BU
2002	—	—	—	—	10.00	12.00

KM# 1141a CROWN
28.2800 g., 0.9250 Silver 0.8410 oz. ASW, 38.6 mm. **Ruler:** Elizabeth II **Subject:** Princess Diana **Obv:** Bust with tiara right **Obv. Designer:** Ian Rank-Broadley **Rev:** Diana facing **Edge:** Reeded

Date	Mintage	F	VF	XF	Unc	BU
2002 Proof	10,000	Value: 47.50				

KM# 1144 CROWN
28.2800 g., Copper Nickel, 38.6 mm. **Ruler:** Elizabeth II **Series:** Harry Potter **Obv:** Bust with tiara right **Obv. Designer:** Ian Rank-Broadley **Rev:** Tom Riddle twirling Harry's magic wand **Edge:** Reeded

Date	Mintage	F	VF	XF	Unc	BU
2002PM	—	—	—	—	10.00	12.00

KM# 1144a CROWN
28.2800 g., 0.9250 Silver 0.8410 oz. ASW, 28.6 mm. **Ruler:** Elizabeth II **Series:** Harry Potter **Obv:** Bust with tiara right **Obv. Designer:** Ian Rank-Broadley **Rev:** Tom Riddle twirling Harry's magic wand **Edge:** Reeded

Date	Mintage	F	VF	XF	Unc	BU
2002PM Proof	15,000	Value: 50.00				

KM# 1146 CROWN
28.2800 g., Copper-Nickel, 38.6 mm. **Ruler:** Elizabeth II **Series:** Harry Potter **Obv:** Bust with tiara right **Obv. Designer:** Ian Rank-Broadley **Rev:** Harry and friends making Polyjuice potion **Edge:** Reeded

Date	Mintage	F	VF	XF	Unc	BU
2002PM	—	—	—	—	10.00	12.00

KM# 1146a CROWN
28.2800 g., 0.9250 Silver 0.8410 oz. ASW, 38.6 mm. **Ruler:** Elizabeth II **Series:** Harry Potter **Obv:** Bust with tiara right **Obv. Designer:** Ian Rank-Broadley **Rev:** Harry Potter and friends making Polyjuice potion **Edge:** Reeded

Date	Mintage	F	VF	XF	Unc	BU
2002PM Proof	15,000	Value: 50.00				

KM# 1148 CROWN
28.2800 g., Copper-Nickel, 38.6 mm. **Ruler:** Elizabeth II **Series:** Harry Potter **Obv:** Bust with tiara right **Obv. Designer:** Ian Rank-Broadley **Rev:** Harry arrives at the Burrow in a flying car **Edge:** Reeded

Date	Mintage	F	VF	XF	Unc	BU
2002PM	—	—	—	—	10.00	12.00

KM# 1148a CROWN
28.2800 g., 0.9250 Silver 0.8410 oz. ASW, 38.6 mm. **Ruler:** Elizabeth II **Series:** Harry Potter **Obv:** Bust with tiara right **Obv. Designer:** Ian Rank-Broadley **Rev:** Harry arrives at the Burrow in a flying car **Edge:** Reeded

Date	Mintage	F	VF	XF	Unc	BU
2002PM Proof	15,000	Value: 50.00				

KM# 1150 CROWN
28.2800 g., Copper-Nickel, 38.6 mm. **Ruler:** Elizabeth II **Series:** Harry Potter **Obv:** Bust with tiara right **Obv. Designer:** Ian Rank-Broadley **Rev:** Harry retrieves Gryffindor sword from sorting hat **Edge:** Reeded

Date	Mintage	F	VF	XF	Unc	BU
2002PM	—	—	—	—	10.00	12.00

KM# 1150a CROWN
28.2800 g., 0.9250 Silver 0.8410 oz. ASW, 38.6 mm. **Ruler:** Elizabeth II **Series:** Harry Potter **Obv:** Bust with tiara right **Obv. Designer:** Ian Rank-Broadley **Rev:** Harry retrieves Gryffindor sword from sorting hat **Edge:** Reeded

Date	Mintage	F	VF	XF	Unc	BU
2002PM Proof	15,000	Value: 50.00				

KM# 1152 CROWN
28.2800 g., Copper-Nickel, 38.6 mm. **Ruler:** Elizabeth II **Series:** Harry Potter **Obv:** Bust with tiara right **Obv. Designer:** Ian Rank-Broadley **Rev:** Harry and Ron encounter the spider Aragog **Edge:** Reeded

Date	Mintage	F	VF	XF	Unc	BU
2002PM	—	—	—	—	10.00	12.00

KM# 1152a CROWN
28.2800 g., 0.9250 Silver 0.8410 oz. ASW, 38.6 mm. **Ruler:** Elizabeth II **Series:** Harry Potter **Obv:** Bust with tiara right **Obv. Designer:** Ian Rank-Broadley **Rev:** Harry and Ron encounter the spider Aragog **Edge:** Reeded

Date	Mintage	F	VF	XF	Unc	BU
2002PM Proof	15,000	Value: 50.00				

KM# 1154 CROWN
28.2800 g., Copper-Nickel, 38.6 mm. **Ruler:** Elizabeth II **Series:** Harry Potter **Obv:** Bust with tiara right **Obv. Designer:** Ian Rank-Broadley **Rev:** Harry in hospital with Dobby **Edge:** Reeded

Date	Mintage	F	VF	XF	Unc	BU
2002PM	—	—	—	—	10.00	12.00

KM# 1154a CROWN
28.2800 g., 0.9250 Silver 0.8410 oz. ASW, 38.6 mm. **Ruler:** Elizabeth II **Series:** Harry Potter **Obv:** Bust with tiara right **Obv. Designer:** Ian Rank-Broadley **Rev:** Harry in hospital with Dobby **Edge:** Reeded

Date	Mintage	F	VF	XF	Unc	BU
2002PM Proof	15,000	Value: 50.00				

KM# 1185 CROWN
28.2800 g., Copper-Nickel, 38.6 mm. **Ruler:** Elizabeth II **Obv:** Bust with tiara right **Obv. Designer:** Ian Rank-Broadley **Rev:** Lord of the Rings characters
Edge: Reeded

Date	Mintage	F	VF	XF	Unc	BU
2003PM	100,000	—	—	—	12.50	14.50

KM# 1185a CROWN
28.2800 g., 0.9250 Silver 0.8410 oz. ASW, 38.6 mm. **Ruler:** Elizabeth II **Obv:** Bust with tiara right **Obv. Designer:** Ian Rank-Broadley **Rev:** Lord of the Rings characters **Edge:** Reeded

Date	Mintage	F	VF	XF	Unc	BU
2003PM Proof	10,000	Value: 50.00				

KM# 1190 CROWN
31.1035 g., 0.9999 Gold 0.9999 oz. AGW, 32.7 mm. **Ruler:** Elizabeth II **Subject:** Lord of the Rings **Obv:** Bust with tiara right **Obv. Designer:** Ian Rank-Broadley **Rev:** Man on horse **Edge:** Reeded

Date	Mintage	F	VF	XF	Unc	BU
2003PM Proof	1,000	Value: 1,000				

KM# 1191 CROWN
28.2800 g., 0.9250 Silver 0.8410 oz. ASW, 38.6 mm. **Ruler:** Elizabeth II **Subject:** Lord of the Rings **Obv:** Bust with tiara right **Obv. Designer:** Ian Rank-Broadley **Rev:** Man with short sword **Edge:** Reeded

Date	Mintage	F	VF	XF	Unc	BU
2003PM Proof	5,000	Value: 47.50				

KM# 1192 CROWN
28.2800 g., 0.9250 Silver 0.8410 oz. ASW, 38.6 mm. **Ruler:** Elizabeth II **Subject:** Lord of the Rings **Obv:** Bust with tiara right **Obv. Designer:** Ian Rank-Broadley **Rev:** Aragorn with broadsword **Edge:** Reeded

Date	Mintage	F	VF	XF	Unc	BU
2003PM Proof	5,000	Value: 47.50				

KM# 1193 CROWN
28.2800 g., 0.9250 Silver 0.8410 oz. ASW, 38.6 mm. **Ruler:** Elizabeth II **Subject:** Lord of the Rings **Obv:** Bust with tiara right **Obv. Designer:** Ian Rank-Broadley **Rev:** Legolas **Edge:** Reeded

Date	Mintage	F	VF	XF	Unc	BU
2003PM Proof	5,000	Value: 47.50				

KM# 1194 CROWN
28.2800 g., 0.9250 Silver 0.8410 oz. ASW, 38.6 mm. **Ruler:** Elizabeth II **Subject:** Lord of the Rings **Obv:** Bust with tiara right **Obv. Designer:** Ian Rank-Broadley **Rev:** Gimli with two battle axes **Edge:** Reeded

Date	Mintage	F	VF	XF	Unc	BU
2003PM Proof	5,000	Value: 47.50				

KM# 1195 CROWN
28.2800 g., 0.9250 Silver 0.8410 oz. ASW, 38.6 mm. **Ruler:** Elizabeth II **Subject:** Lord of the Rings **Obv:** Bust with tiara right **Obv. Designer:** Ian Rank-Broadley **Rev:** Man on horse **Edge:** Reeded

Date	Mintage	F	VF	XF	Unc	BU
2003PM Proof	5,000	Value: 47.50				

KM# 1165 CROWN
28.2800 g., Copper-Nickel, 38.6 mm. **Ruler:** Elizabeth II **Subject:** Cat **Obv:** Bust with tiara right **Obv. Designer:** Ian Rank-Broadley **Rev:** Two Balinese kittens **Edge:** Reeded

Date	Mintage	F	VF	XF	Unc	BU
2003PM	—	—	—	—	12.00	14.00

KM# 1165a CROWN
31.1035 g., 0.9990 Silver 0.9990 oz. ASW, 38.6 mm. **Ruler:** Elizabeth II **Subject:** Cat **Obv:** Head with tiara right **Obv. Designer:** Ian Rank-Broadley **Rev:** Two Balinese kittens **Edge:** Reeded

Date	Mintage	F	VF	XF	Unc	BU
2003PM Proof	50,000	Value: 47.50				

KM# 1166 CROWN
31.1035 g., 0.9999 Gold 0.9999 oz. AGW, 32.7 mm. **Ruler:** Elizabeth II **Subject:** Cat **Obv:** Head with tiara right **Obv. Designer:** Ian Rank-Broadley **Rev:** Two Balinese kittens **Edge:** Reeded

Date	Mintage	F	VF	XF	Unc	BU
2003PM	—	—	—	—	—	985
2003PM Proof	—	Value: 1,000				

KM# 1171 CROWN
28.2800 g., Copper-Nickel, 38.6 mm. **Ruler:** Elizabeth II **Subject:** Year of the Goat **Obv:** Bust with tiara right **Obv. Designer:** Ian Rank-Broadley **Rev:** Three goats **Edge:** Reeded

Date	Mintage	F	VF	XF	Unc	BU
2003PM	—	—	—	—	12.00	14.00

KM# 1171a CROWN
28.2800 g., 0.9250 Silver 0.8410 oz. ASW, 38.6 mm. **Ruler:** Elizabeth II **Subject:** Year of the Goat **Obv:** Bust with tiara right **Obv. Designer:** Ian Rank-Broadley **Rev:** Three goats **Edge:** Reeded

Date	Mintage	F	VF	XF	Unc	BU
2003PM Proof	30,000	Value: 47.50				

KM# 1172 CROWN
31.1035 g., 0.9999 Gold 0.9999 oz. AGW, 32.7 mm. **Ruler:** Elizabeth II **Subject:** Year of the Goat **Obv:** Bust with tiara right **Obv. Designer:** Ian Rank-Broadley **Rev:** Three goats **Edge:** Reeded

Date	Mintage	F	VF	XF	Unc	BU
2003PM Proof	2,000	Value: 1,000				

KM# 1174 CROWN
28.5300 g., Copper-Nickel, 38.6 mm. **Ruler:** Elizabeth II **Obv:** Bust with tiara right **Obv. Designer:** Ian Rank-Broadley **Rev:** The Star of India sailing ship **Edge:** Reeded

Date	Mintage	F	VF	XF	Unc	BU
2003PM	—	—	—	—	10.00	12.00

KM# 1176 CROWN
28.2800 g., Copper-Nickel, 38.6 mm. **Ruler:** Elizabeth II **Subject:** Olympics **Obv:** Bust with tiara right **Obv. Designer:** Ian Rank-Broadley **Rev:** Swimmers **Edge:** Reeded

Date	Mintage	F	VF	XF	Unc	BU
2003PM	—	—	—	—	10.00	12.00

KM# 1176a CROWN
28.2800 g., 0.9250 Silver 0.8410 oz. ASW, 38.6 mm. **Ruler:** Elizabeth II **Subject:** Olympics **Obv:** Bust with tiara right **Obv. Designer:** Ian Rank-Broadley **Rev:** Swimmers **Edge:** Reeded

Date	Mintage	F	VF	XF	Unc	BU
2003PM Proof	10,000	Value: 47.50				

KM# 1178 CROWN
28.2800 g., Copper-Nickel, 38.6 mm. **Ruler:** Elizabeth II **Subject:** Olympics **Obv:** Bust with tiara right **Obv. Designer:** Ian Rank-Broadley **Rev:** Runners **Edge:** Reeded

Date	Mintage	F	VF	XF	Unc	BU
2003PM	—	—	—	—	10.00	12.00

KM# 1178a CROWN
28.2800 g., 0.9250 Silver 0.8410 oz. ASW, 38.6 mm. **Ruler:** Elizabeth II **Subject:** Olympics **Obv:** Bust with tiara right **Obv. Designer:** Ian Rank-Broadley **Rev:** Runners **Edge:** Reeded

Date	Mintage	F	VF	XF	Unc	BU
2003PM Proof	10,000	Value: 47.50				

KM# 1180 CROWN
28.2800 g., Copper-Nickel, 38.6 mm. **Ruler:** Elizabeth II **Subject:** Olympics **Obv:** Bust with tiara right **Obv. Designer:** Ian Rank-Broadley **Rev:** Bicyclists **Edge:** Reeded

Date	Mintage	F	VF	XF	Unc	BU
2003PM	—	—	—	—	10.00	12.00

KM# 1180a CROWN
28.2800 g., 0.9250 Silver 0.8410 oz. ASW, 38.6 mm. **Ruler:** Elizabeth II **Subject:** Olympics **Obv:** Bust with tiara right **Obv. Designer:** Ian Rank-Broadley **Rev:** Bicyclists **Edge:** Reeded

Date	Mintage	F	VF	XF	Unc	BU
2003PM Proof	10,000	Value: 47.50				

KM# 1182 CROWN
28.2800 g., Copper-Nickel, 38.6 mm. **Ruler:** Elizabeth II **Subject:** Olympics **Obv:** Bust with tiara right **Obv. Designer:** Ian Rank-Broadley **Rev:** Sail Boarders **Edge:** Reeded

Date	Mintage	F	VF	XF	Unc	BU
2003PM	—	—	—	—	10.00	12.00

KM# 1182a CROWN
28.2800 g., 0.9250 Silver 0.8410 oz. ASW, 38.6 mm. **Ruler:** Elizabeth II **Subject:** Olympics **Obv:** Bust with tiara right **Obv. Designer:** Ian Rank-Broadley **Rev:** Sail Boarders **Edge:** Reeded

Date	Mintage	F	VF	XF	Unc	BU
2003PM Proof	10,000	Value: 47.50				

KM# 1196 CROWN
28.4400 g., Copper-Nickel, 38.6 mm. **Ruler:** Elizabeth II **Obv:** Bust with tiara right **Obv. Designer:** Ian Rank-Broadley **Rev:** Four pre-1918 airplanes **Edge:** Reeded

Date	Mintage	F	VF	XF	Unc	BU
2003PM	—	—	—	—	10.00	12.00

KM# 1197 CROWN
28.4400 g., Copper-Nickel, 38.6 mm. **Obv:** Bust with tiara right **Obv. Designer:** Ian Rank-Broadley **Rev:** Propeller plain, Zeppelin and two jet airliners **Edge:** Reeded

Date	Mintage	F	VF	XF	Unc	BU
2003PM	—	—	—	—	10.00	12.00

KM# 1201 CROWN
28.2800 g., Copper-Nickel, 38.6 mm. **Ruler:** Elizabeth II **Obv:** Bust with tiara right **Obv. Designer:** Ian Rank-Broadley **Rev:** European Union map within hand held rope circle **Edge:** Reeded

Date	Mintage	F	VF	XF	Unc	BU
2004PM	—	—	—	—	10.00	12.00

KM# 1201a CROWN
28.2800 g., 0.9250 Silver 0.8410 oz. ASW, 38.6 mm. **Ruler:** Elizabeth II **Obv:** Bust with tiara right **Obv. Designer:** Ian Rank-Broadley **Rev:** European Union map within a hand held rope circle **Edge:** Reeded

Date	Mintage	F	VF	XF	Unc	BU
2004PM Proof	10,000	Value: 50.00				

KM# 1202 CROWN
28.2800 g., Copper-Nickel, 38.6 mm. **Ruler:** Elizabeth II **Obv:** Bust with tiara right **Obv. Designer:** Ian Rank-Broadley **Rev:** Harry Potter and patron fighting off a spectre **Edge:** Reeded

Date	Mintage	F	VF	XF	Unc	BU
2004PM	—	—	—	—	15.00	17.00

KM# 1202a CROWN
28.2800 g., 0.9250 Silver 0.8410 oz. ASW, 38.6 mm. **Ruler:** Elizabeth II **Obv:** Bust with tiara right **Obv. Designer:** Ian Rank-Broadley **Rev:** Harry Potter and patron fighting off a spectre **Edge:** Reeded

Date	Mintage	F	VF	XF	Unc	BU
2004PM Proof	10,000	Value: 50.00				

KM# 1204 CROWN
28.2800 g., Copper-Nickel, 38.6 mm. **Ruler:** Elizabeth II **Obv:** Bust with tiara right **Obv. Designer:** Ian Rank-Broadley **Rev:** Harry Potter in the shrieking shed **Edge:** Reeded

Date	Mintage	F	VF	XF	Unc	BU
2004PM	—	—	—	—	15.00	17.00

KM# 1204a CROWN
28.2800 g., 0.9250 Silver 0.8410 oz. ASW, 38.6 mm. **Ruler:** Elizabeth II **Obv:** Bust with tiara right **Obv. Designer:** Ian Rank-Broadley **Rev:** Harry Potter in the shrieking shack **Edge:** Reeded

Date	Mintage	F	VF	XF	Unc	BU
2004PM Proof	10,000	Value: 50.00				

KM# 1206 CROWN
28.2800 g., Copper-Nickel, 38.6 mm. **Ruler:** Elizabeth II **Obv:** Bust with tiara right **Obv. Designer:** Ian Rank-Broadley **Rev:** Harry Potter and Professor Dumbledore **Edge:** Reeded

Date	Mintage	F	VF	XF	Unc	BU
2004PM	—	—	—	—	15.00	17.00

KM# 1206a CROWN

28.2800 g., 0.9250 Silver 0.8410 oz. ASW, 38.6 mm. **Ruler:** Elizabeth II **Obv:** Bust with tiara right **Obv. Designer:** Ian Rank-Broadley **Rev:** Harry Potter and Professor Dumbledore **Edge:** Reeded

Date	Mintage	F	VF	XF	Unc	BU
2004PM Proof	10,000	Value: 50.00				

KM# 1208 CROWN

28.2800 g., Copper-Nickel, 38.6 mm. **Ruler:** Elizabeth II **Obv:** Bust with tiara right **Obv. Designer:** Ian Rank-Broadley **Rev:** Sirius Black on flying griffin **Edge:** Reeded

Date	Mintage	F	VF	XF	Unc	BU
2004PM	—	—	—	—	15.00	17.00

KM# 1208a CROWN

28.2800 g., 0.9250 Silver 0.8410 oz. ASW, 38.6 mm. **Ruler:** Elizabeth II **Obv:** Bust with tiara right **Obv. Designer:** Ian Rank-Broadley **Rev:** Sirius Black on flying griffin **Edge:** Reeded

Date	Mintage	F	VF	XF	Unc	BU
2004PM Proof	10,000	Value: 50.00				

KM# 1210 CROWN

28.2800 g., Copper-Nickel, 38.6 mm. **Ruler:** Elizabeth II **Obv:** Bust with tiara right **Obv. Designer:** Ian Rank-Broadley **Rev:** Three Olympic Swimmers **Edge:** Reeded

Date	Mintage	F	VF	XF	Unc	BU
2004PM	—	—	—	—	10.00	12.00

KM# 1210a CROWN

28.2800 g., 0.9250 Silver 0.8410 oz. ASW, 38.6 mm. **Ruler:** Elizabeth II **Obv:** Bust with tiara right **Obv. Designer:** Ian Rank-Broadley **Rev:** Three Olympic Swimmers **Edge:** Reeded

Date	Mintage	F	VF	XF	Unc	BU
2004PM Proof	10,000	Value: 50.00				

KM# 1212 CROWN

28.2800 g., Copper-Nickel, 38.6 mm. **Ruler:** Elizabeth II **Obv:** Bust with tiara right **Obv. Designer:** Ian Rank-Broadley **Rev:** Three Olympic Cyclists **Edge:** Reeded

Date	Mintage	F	VF	XF	Unc	BU
2004PM	—	—	—	—	10.00	12.00

KM# 1212a CROWN

28.2800 g., 0.9250 Silver 0.8410 oz. ASW, 38.6 mm. **Ruler:** Elizabeth II **Obv:** Bust with tiara right **Obv. Designer:** Ian Rank-Broadley **Rev:** Three Olympic Cyclists **Edge:** Reeded

Date	Mintage	F	VF	XF	Unc	BU
2004PM Proof	10,000	Value: 50.00				

KM# 1214 CROWN

28.2800 g., Copper-Nickel, 38.6 mm. **Ruler:** Elizabeth II **Obv:** Bust with tiara right **Obv. Designer:** Ian Rank-Broadley **Rev:** Three Olympic Runners **Edge:** Reeded

Date	Mintage	F	VF	XF	Unc	BU
2004PM	—	—	—	—	10.00	12.00

KM# 1214a CROWN

28.2800 g., 0.9250 Silver 0.8410 oz. ASW, 38.6 mm. **Ruler:** Elizabeth II **Obv:** Bust with tiara right **Obv. Designer:** Ian Rank-Broadley **Rev:** Three Olympic Runners **Edge:** Reeded

Date	Mintage	F	VF	XF	Unc	BU
2004PM Proof	10,000	Value: 50.00				

KM# 1216 CROWN

28.2800 g., Copper-Nickel, 38.6 mm. **Ruler:** Elizabeth II **Obv:** Bust with tiara right **Obv. Designer:** Ian Rank-Broadley **Rev:** Three Olympic Sail Boarders **Edge:** Reeded

Date	Mintage	F	VF	XF	Unc	BU
2004PM	—	—	—	—	10.00	12.00

KM# 1216a CROWN

28.2800 g., 0.9250 Silver 0.8410 oz. ASW, 38.6 mm. **Ruler:** Elizabeth II **Obv:** Bust with tiara right **Obv. Designer:** Ian Rank-Broadley **Rev:** Three Olympic Sail Boarders **Edge:** Reeded

Date	Mintage	F	VF	XF	Unc	BU
2004PM Proof	10,000	Value: 50.00				

KM# 1218 CROWN

28.2800 g., Copper-Nickel, 38.6 mm. **Ruler:** Elizabeth II **Obv:** Bust with tiara right **Obv. Designer:** Ian Rank-Broadley **Rev:** Ocean Liner Queen Mary 2 **Edge:** Reeded

Date	Mintage	F	VF	XF	Unc	BU
2004PM	—	—	—	—	15.00	17.00

KM# 1220 CROWN

28.2800 g., Copper-Nickel, 38.6 mm. **Ruler:** Elizabeth II **Obv:** Bust with tiara right **Obv. Designer:** Ian Rank-Broadley **Rev:** Lt. Quillan portrait above Battle of Trafalgar scene **Edge:** Reeded

Date	Mintage	F	VF	XF	Unc	BU
2004PM	—	—	—	—	15.00	17.00

KM# 1220a CROWN

28.2800 g., 0.9250 Silver 0.8410 oz. ASW, 38.6 mm. **Ruler:** Elizabeth II **Obv:** Bust with tiara right **Obv. Designer:** Ian Rank-Broadley **Rev:** Lt. Quillan portrait above Battle of Trafalgar scene **Edge:** Reeded

Date	Mintage	F	VF	XF	Unc	BU
2004PM Proof	10,000	Value: 50.00				

KM# 1221 CROWN

28.2800 g., Copper-Nickel, 38.6 mm. **Ruler:** Elizabeth II **Obv:** Bust with tiara right **Obv. Designer:** Ian Rank-Broadley **Rev:** Napoleon and Nelson portraits above Battle of Trafalgar scene **Edge:** Reeded

Date	Mintage	F	VF	XF	Unc	BU
2004PM	—	—	—	—	15.00	17.00

KM# 1221a CROWN

28.2800 g., 0.9990 Silver 0.9083 oz. ASW, 38.6 mm. **Ruler:** Elizabeth II **Obv:** Bust with tiara right **Obv. Designer:** Ian Rank-Broadley **Rev:** Napoleon and Nelson portraits above Battle of Trafalgar scene **Edge:** Reeded

Date	Mintage	F	VF	XF	Unc	BU
2004PM Proof	10,000	Value: 50.00				

KM# 1222 CROWN

28.2800 g., Copper-Nickel, 38.6 mm. **Ruler:** Elizabeth II **Obv:** Bust with tiara right **Obv. Designer:** Ian Rank-Broadley **Rev:** D-Day Invasion Plan Map **Edge:** Reeded

Date	Mintage	F	VF	XF	Unc	BU
2004PM	—	—	—	—	15.00	17.00

KM# 1222a CROWN

28.2800 g., 0.9250 Silver 0.8410 oz. ASW, 38.6 mm. **Ruler:** Elizabeth II **Obv:** Bust with tiara right **Obv. Designer:** Ian Rank-Broadley **Rev:** D-Day Invasion Plan Map **Edge:** Reeded

Date	Mintage	F	VF	XF	Unc	BU
2004PM Proof	10,000	Value: 50.00				

KM# 1224 CROWN

28.2800 g., Copper-Nickel, 38.6 mm. **Ruler:** Elizabeth II **Obv:** Bust with tiara right **Obv. Designer:** Ian Rank-Broadley **Rev:** Victoria Cross and battle scene **Edge:** Reeded

Date	Mintage	F	VF	XF	Unc	BU
2004PM	—	—	—	—	15.00	17.00

KM# 1224a CROWN

28.2800 g., 0.9250 Silver 0.8410 oz. ASW, 38.6 mm. **Ruler:** Elizabeth II **Obv:** Bust with tiara right **Obv. Designer:** Ian Rank-Broadley **Rev:** Victoria Cross and battle scene **Edge:** Reeded

Date	Mintage	F	VF	XF	Unc	BU
2004PM Proof	10,000	Value: 50.00				

KM# 1226 CROWN

28.2800 g., Copper-Nickel, 38.6 mm. **Ruler:** Elizabeth II **Obv:** Bust with tiara right **Obv. Designer:** Ian Rank-Broadley **Rev:** Silver Star and battle scene **Edge:** Reeded

Date	Mintage	F	VF	XF	Unc	BU
2004PM	—	—	—	—	15.00	17.00

KM# 1226a CROWN

28.2800 g., 0.9250 Silver 0.8410 oz. ASW, 38.6 mm. **Ruler:** Elizabeth II **Obv:** Bust with tiara right **Obv. Designer:** Ian Rank-Broadley **Rev:** Silver Star and battle scene **Edge:** Reeded

Date	Mintage	F	VF	XF	Unc	BU
2004PM Proof	10,000	Value: 50.00				

KM# 1228 CROWN

28.2800 g., Copper-Nickel, 38.6 mm. **Ruler:** Elizabeth II **Obv:** Bust with tiara right **Obv. Designer:** Ian Rank-Broadley **Rev:** George Cross and rescue scene **Edge:** Reeded

Date	Mintage	F	VF	XF	Unc	BU
2004PM	—	—	—	—	15.00	17.00

KM# 1228a CROWN

28.2800 g., 0.9250 Silver 0.8410 oz. ASW, 38.6 mm. **Ruler:** Elizabeth II **Obv:** Bust with tiara right **Obv. Designer:** Ian Rank-Broadley **Rev:** George Cross and rescue scene **Edge:** Reeded

Date	Mintage	F	VF	XF	Unc	BU
2004PM Proof	10,000	Value: 50.00				

KM# 1230 CROWN

28.2800 g., Copper-Nickel, 38.6 mm. **Ruler:** Elizabeth II **Obv:** Bust with tiara right **Obv. Designer:** Ian Rank-Broadley **Rev:** White Rose of Finland Medal and battle scene **Edge:** Reeded

Date	Mintage	F	VF	XF	Unc	BU
2004PM	—	—	—	—	15.00	17.00

KM# 1230a CROWN

28.2800 g., 0.9250 Silver 0.8410 oz. ASW, 38.6 mm. **Ruler:** Elizabeth II **Obv:** Bust with tiara right **Obv. Designer:** Ian Rank-Broadley **Rev:** White Rose of Finland Medal and battle scene **Edge:** Reeded

Date	Mintage	F	VF	XF	Unc	BU
2004PM Proof	10,000	Value: 50.00				

KM# 1232 CROWN

28.2800 g., Copper-Nickel, 38.6 mm. **Ruler:** Elizabeth II **Obv:** Bust with tiara right **Obv. Designer:** Ian Rank-Broadley **Rev:** The Norwegian War Medal and naval battle scene **Edge:** Reeded

Date	Mintage	F	VF	XF	Unc	BU
2004PM	—	—	—	—	15.00	17.00

KM# 1232a CROWN

28.2800 g., 0.9250 Silver 0.8410 oz. ASW, 38.6 mm. **Ruler:** Elizabeth II **Obv:** Bust with tiara right **Obv. Designer:** Ian Rank-Broadley **Rev:** The Norwegian War Medal and a naval battle scene **Edge:** Reeded

Date	Mintage	F	VF	XF	Unc	BU
2004PM Proof	10,000	Value: 50.00				

KM# 1234 CROWN

28.2800 g., Copper-Nickel, 38.6 mm. **Ruler:** Elizabeth II **Obv:** Bust with tiara right **Obv. Designer:** Ian Rank-Broadley **Rev:** French Croix de Guerre and partisan battle scene **Edge:** Reeded

Date	Mintage	F	VF	XF	Unc	BU
2004PM	—	—	—	—	15.00	17.00

KM# 1234a CROWN

28.2800 g., 0.9250 Silver 0.8410 oz. ASW, 38.6 mm. **Ruler:** Elizabeth II **Obv:** Bust with tiara right **Obv. Designer:** Ian Rank-Broadley **Rev:** French Croix de Guerre and partisan battle scene **Edge:** Reeded

Date	Mintage	F	VF	XF	Unc	BU
2004PM Proof	10,000	Value: 50.00				

KM# 1236 CROWN

28.2800 g., Copper-Nickel, 38.6 mm. **Ruler:** Elizabeth II **Obv:** Bust with tiara right **Obv. Designer:** Ian Rank-Broadley **Rev:** Multicolor cartoon soccer player **Edge:** Reeded

Date	Mintage	F	VF	XF	Unc	BU
2004PM	—	—	—	—	10.00	12.00

KM# 1236a CROWN

28.2800 g., 0.9250 Silver 0.8410 oz. ASW, 38.6 mm. **Ruler:** Elizabeth II **Obv:** Bust with tiara right **Obv. Designer:** Ian Rank-Broadley **Rev:** Multicolor cartoon soccer player **Edge:** Reeded

Date	Mintage	F	VF	XF	Unc	BU
2004PM Proof	7,500	Value: 50.00				

KM# 1237 CROWN

28.2800 g., Copper-Nickel, 38.6 mm. **Ruler:** Elizabeth II **Obv:** Bust with tiara right **Obv. Designer:** Ian Rank-Broadley **Rev:** Soccer ball in flight **Edge:** Reeded

Date	Mintage	F	VF	XF	Unc	BU
2004PM	—	—	—	—	10.00	12.00

KM# 1237a CROWN

28.2800 g., 0.9250 Silver 0.8410 oz. ASW, 38.6 mm. **Ruler:** Elizabeth II **Obv:** Bust with tiara right **Obv. Designer:** Ian Rank-Broadley **Rev:** Soccer ball in flight **Edge:** Reeded

Date	Mintage	F	VF	XF	Unc	BU
2004PM Proof	7,500	Value: 50.00				

KM# 1238 CROWN

28.2800 g., Copper-Nickel, 38.6 mm. **Ruler:** Elizabeth II **Obv:** Bust with tiara right **Obv. Designer:** Ian Rank-Broadley **Rev:** Gibbon monkey **Edge:** Reeded

Date	Mintage	F	VF	XF	Unc	BU
2004PM	—	—	—	—	10.00	15.00

KM# 1238a CROWN

28.2800 g., 0.9250 Silver 0.8410 oz. ASW, 38.6 mm. **Ruler:** Elizabeth II **Obv:** Bust with tiara right **Obv. Designer:** Ian Rank-Broadley **Rev:** Monkey **Edge:** Reeded

Date	Mintage	F	VF	XF	Unc	BU
2004PM Proof	30,000	Value: 50.00				

KM# 1239 CROWN

31.1035 g., 0.9999 Gold 0.9999 oz. AGW, 32.7 mm. **Ruler:** Elizabeth II **Obv:** Bust with tiara right **Obv. Designer:** Ian Rank-Broadley **Rev:** Monkey **Edge:** Reeded

Date	Mintage	F	VF	XF	Unc	BU
2004PM Proof	2,000	Value: 1,000				

KM# 1242 CROWN

6.2200 g., 0.9999 Gold 0.1999 oz. AGW, 22 mm. **Ruler:** Elizabeth II **Obv:** Bust with tiara right **Obv. Designer:** Ian Rank-Broadley **Rev:** Monkey **Edge:** Reeded

Date	Mintage	F	VF	XF	Unc	BU
2004PM Proof	12,000	Value: 215				

KM# 1245 CROWN

28.2800 g., Copper-Nickel, 38.6 mm. **Ruler:** Elizabeth II **Subject:** Lord of the Rings **Obv:** Bust with tiara right **Obv. Designer:** Ian Rank-Broadley **Rev:** Nine characters **Edge:** Reeded

Date	Mintage	F	VF	XF	Unc	BU
2004PM	100,000	—	—	—	15.00	17.00

KM# 1245a CROWN

28.2800 g., 0.9250 Silver 0.8410 oz. ASW, 38.6 mm. **Ruler:** Elizabeth II **Subject:** Lord of the Rings **Obv:** Bust with tiara right **Obv. Designer:** Ian Rank-Broadley **Rev:** Nine characters **Edge:** Reeded

Date	Mintage	F	VF	XF	Unc	BU
2004PM Proof	10,000	Value: 50.00				

KM# 1246 CROWN

28.2800 g., Copper-Nickel, 38.6 mm. **Ruler:** Elizabeth II **Obv:** Head with tiara right **Obv. Designer:** Ian Rank-Broadley **Rev:** Two Tonkinese cats **Edge:** Reeded

Date	Mintage	F	VF	XF	Unc	BU
2004PM	—	—	—	—	14.00	16.00

KM# 1246a CROWN

31.1035 g., 0.9990 Silver 0.9990 oz. ASW, 38.6 mm. **Ruler:** Elizabeth II **Obv:** Head with tiara right **Obv. Designer:** Ian Rank-Broadley **Rev:** Two Tonkinese cats **Edge:** Reeded

Date	Mintage	F	VF	XF	Unc	BU
2004PM Proof	50,000	Value: 50.00				

KM# 1246a.1 CROWN

31.1035 g., 0.9990 Silver 0.9990 oz. ASW, 38.6 mm. **Ruler:** Elizabeth II **Obv:** Head with tiara right **Obv. Designer:** Ian Rank-Broadley **Rev:** Two multicolor Tonkinese cats **Edge:** Reeded

Date	Mintage	F	VF	XF	Unc	BU
2004PM Proof	—	Value: 55.00				

KM# 1251 CROWN

31.1035 g., 0.9999 Gold 0.9999 oz. AGW, 32.7 mm. **Ruler:** Elizabeth II **Obv:** Head with tiara right **Obv. Designer:** Ian Rank-Broadley **Rev:** Two Tonkinese cats **Edge:** Reeded

Date	Mintage	F	VF	XF	Unc	BU
2004PM	—	—	—	—	—	985
2004PM Proof	1,000	Value: 1,000				

KM# 1266 CROWN

28.3300 g., Copper-Nickel, 38.7 mm. **Ruler:** Elizabeth II **Obv:** Bust with tiara right **Obv. Designer:** Ian Rank-Broadley **Rev:** Himalayan cat with two kittens **Edge:** Reeded

Date	Mintage	F	VF	XF	Unc	BU
2005PM	—	—	—	—	12.00	14.00

KM# 1266a CROWN

31.1030 g., 0.9990 Silver 0.9989 oz. ASW, 38.6 mm. **Ruler:** Elizabeth II **Obv:** Bust with tiara right **Obv. Designer:** Ian Rank-Broadley **Rev:** Himalayan cat and two kittens **Edge:** Reeded

Date	Mintage	F	VF	XF	Unc	BU
2005PM Proof	50,000	Value: 50.00				

KM# 1268 CROWN

31.1030 g., 0.9999 Gold 0.9998 oz. AGW, 32.7 mm. **Ruler:** Elizabeth II **Obv:** Bust with tiara right **Obv. Designer:** Ian Rank-Broadley **Rev:** Himalayan cat and two kittens **Edge:** Reeded

Date	Mintage	F	VF	XF	Unc	BU
2005PM Proof	—	Value: 1,000				

KM# 1273 CROWN

28.2800 g., Copper-Nickel, 38.6 mm. **Ruler:** Elizabeth II **Obv:** Bust with tiara right **Obv. Designer:** Ian Rank-Broadley **Rev:** Harry Potter and the Hungarian Horn Tail, Tri-Wizard Tournament feat **Edge:** Reeded

Date	Mintage	F	VF	XF	Unc	BU
2005PM	—	—	—	—	15.00	17.00

KM# 1274 CROWN

28.2800 g., Copper-Nickel **Subject:** 60th Anniversary - End of WW II **Obv:** Bust with tiara right **Obv. Designer:** Ian Rank-Broadley **Rev:** Sir Winston Churchill

Date	Mintage	F	VF	XF	Unc	BU
2005	—	—	—	—	10.00	12.00

KM# 1275 CROWN

28.2800 g., Copper-Nickel **Ruler:** Elizabeth II **Subject:** 400th Anniversary - Gunpowder plot **Obv:** Bust with tiara right **Obv. Designer:** Ian Rank-Broadley **Rev:** Tower of London, Beefeaters

Date	Mintage	F	VF	XF	Unc	BU
2005	—	—	—	—	10.00	12.00

KM# 1276 CROWN

28.2800 g., Copper-Nickel **Ruler:** Elizabeth II **Obv:** Bust with tiara right **Obv. Designer:** Ian Rank-Broadley **Rev:** Harry Potter and Tri-Wizard Tournament feat - Underwater retrieval

Date	Mintage	F	VF	XF	Unc	BU
2005	—	—	—	—	10.00	12.00

KM# 1277 CROWN

Copper-Nickel **Ruler:** Elizabeth II **Obv:** Bust with tiara right **Obv. Designer:** Ian Rank-Broadley **Rev:** Harry Potter and pensive

Date	Mintage	F	VF	XF	Unc	BU
2005	—	—	—	—	10.00	12.00

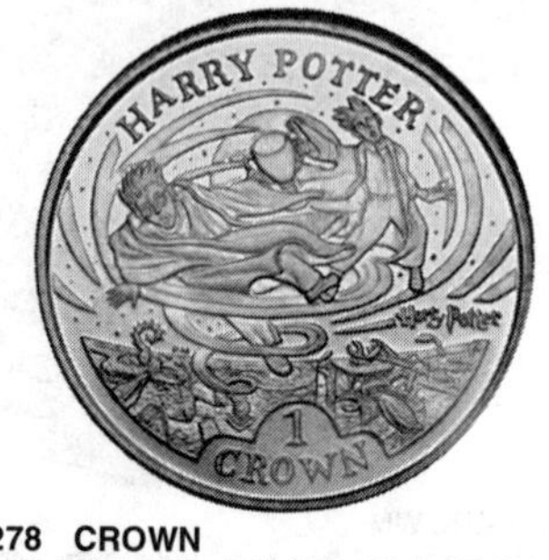

KM# 1278 CROWN

Copper-Nickel **Ruler:** Elizabeth II **Obv:** Bust with tiara right **Obv. Designer:** Ian Rank-Broadley **Rev:** Harry Potter and portkey

Date	Mintage	F	VF	XF	Unc	BU
2005	—	—	—	—	10.00	12.00

KM# 1291 CROWN

28.2800 g., Copper-Nickel **Ruler:** Elizabeth II **Subject:** Trafalgar - 300th Anniversary **Obv:** Bust with tiara right **Obv. Designer:** Ian Rank-Broadley **Rev:** Nelson at Battle of Copenhagen

Date	Mintage	F	VF	XF	Unc	BU
2005	—	—	—	—	10.00	12.00

KM# 1279 CROWN

Copper-Nickel **Subject:** The Battle of Cape St. Vincent **Obv:** Bust with tiara right **Obv. Designer:** Ian Rank-Broadley **Rev:** Naval battle scene

Date	Mintage	F	VF	XF	Unc	BU
2005	—	—	—	—	10.00	12.00

KM# 1280 CROWN

Copper-Nickel **Ruler:** Elizabeth II **Subject:** Nelson Funeral Procession **Obv:** Bust with tiara right **Obv. Designer:** Ian Rank-Broadley **Rev:** Thames and Greenwich view

Date	Mintage	F	VF	XF	Unc	BU
2005	—	—	—	—	10.00	12.00

KM# 1281 CROWN

Copper-Nickel **Ruler:** Elizabeth II **Subject:** Battle of the Nile **Obv:** Bust with tiara right **Obv. Designer:** Ian Rank-Broadley **Rev:** Naval battle

Date	Mintage	F	VF	XF	Unc	BU
2005	—	—	—	—	10.00	12.00

KM# 1282 CROWN

Copper-Nickel **Ruler:** Elizabeth II **Subject:** Norway Independence **Obv:** Bust with tiara right **Obv. Designer:** Ian Rank-Broadley **Rev:** Three swords

Date	Mintage	F	VF	XF	Unc	BU
2005	—	—	—	—	10.00	12.00

KM# 1283 CROWN

Copper-Nickel **Ruler:** Elizabeth II **Subject:** Nelson - Trafalgar 300th Anniversary **Obv. Designer:** Ian Rank-Broadley **Rev:** Nelson portrait

Date	Mintage	F	VF	XF	Unc	BU
2005	—	—	—	—	10.00	12.00

KM# 1284 CROWN

Copper-Nickel **Ruler:** Elizabeth II **Subject:** Battle of Trafalgar **Obv. Designer:** Ian Rank-Broadley **Rev:** Naval battle scene

Date	Mintage	F	VF	XF	Unc	BU
2005	—	—	—	—	10.00	12.00

KM# 1285 CROWN

Copper-Nickel **Ruler:** Elizabeth II **Subject:** Steam Packet - King Orry III **Obv:** Bust with tiara right **Obv. Designer:** Ian Rank-Broadley **Rev:** Ship view

Date	Mintage	F	VF	XF	Unc	BU
2005	—	—	—	—	10.00	12.00

KM# 1286 CROWN

Copper-Nickel **Ruler:** Elizabeth II **Subject:** Isle of Man Steam Packet Company - 175th Anniversary **Obv:** Bust with tiara right **Obv. Designer:** Ian Rank-Broadley **Rev:** Modern and early ferry

Date	Mintage	F	VF	XF	Unc	BU
2005	—	—	—	—	10.00	12.00

KM# 1287 CROWN

Copper-Nickel **Ruler:** Elizabeth II **Rev:** Motorcycle right

Date	Mintage	F	VF	XF	Unc	BU
2005	—	—	—	—	10.00	12.00

KM# 1288 CROWN

Copper-Nickel **Ruler:** Elizabeth II **Rev:** Motorcycle forward

Date	Mintage	F	VF	XF	Unc	BU
2005	—	—	—	—	10.00	12.00

KM# 1289 CROWN

Copper-Nickel **Ruler:** Elizabeth II **Subject:** Ugly Duckling story **Obv:** Bust with tiara right **Obv. Designer:** Ian Rank-Broadley **Rev:** Farm animals

Date	Mintage	F	VF	XF	Unc	BU
2005	—	—	—	—	12.00	14.00

KM# 1290.2 CROWN

Copper-Nickel **Ruler:** Elizabeth II **Obv:** Bust with tiara right **Obv. Designer:** Ian Rank-Broadley **Rev:** Three Exotic Shorthair cats sitting facing, multi-colored **Edge:** Reeded

Date	Mintage	F	VF	XF	Unc	BU
2006	—	—	—	—	15.00	25.00

KM# 1296 CROWN

28.2800 g., Copper Nickel, 38.6 mm. **Ruler:** Elizabeth II **Subject:** Battles that Changed the World **Obv:** Elizabeth II **Rev:** Trojan War scene **Edge:** Reeded

Date	Mintage	F	VF	XF	Unc	BU
2006PM	—	—	—	—	10.00	12.00

KM# 1296a CROWN

28.2800 g., 0.9250 Silver 0.8410 oz. ASW, 38.6 mm. **Ruler:** Elizabeth II **Subject:** Battles that Changed the World **Obv:** Elizabeth II **Rev:** Trojan War scene **Edge:** Reeded

Date	Mintage	F	VF	XF	Unc	BU
2006PM Proof	10,000	Value: 47.50				

KM# 1298 CROWN

28.2800 g., Copper-Nickel, 38.6 mm. **Ruler:** Elizabeth II **Subject:** Battles that Changed the World **Obv:** Elizabeth II **Rev:** Battle of Arbela scene **Edge:** Reeded

Date	Mintage	F	VF	XF	Unc	BU
2006PM	—	—	—	—	10.00	12.00

KM# 1298a CROWN

28.2800 g., 0.9250 Silver 0.8410 oz. ASW, 38.6 mm. **Ruler:** Elizabeth II **Subject:** Battles that Changed the World **Obv:** Elizabeth II **Rev:** Battle of Arbela scene **Edge:** Reeded

Date	Mintage	F	VF	XF	Unc	BU
2006PM Proof	10,000	Value: 47.50				

KM# 1300 CROWN

28.2800 g., Copper-Nickel, 38.6 mm. **Ruler:** Elizabeth II **Subject:** Battles that Changed the World **Obv:** Elizabeth II **Rev:** Battle of Thapsus scene **Edge:** Reeded

Date	Mintage	F	VF	XF	Unc	BU
2006PM	—	—	—	—	10.00	12.00

KM# 1300a CROWN

28.2800 g., 0.9250 Silver 0.8410 oz. ASW, 38.6 mm. **Ruler:** Elizabeth II **Subject:** Battles that Changed the World **Obv:** Elizabeth II **Rev:** Battle of Thapsus scene **Edge:** Reeded

Date	Mintage	F	VF	XF	Unc	BU
2006PM Proof	10,000	Value: 47.50				

KM# 1302 CROWN

28.2800 g., Copper-Nickel, 38.6 mm. **Ruler:** Elizabeth II **Subject:** Battles that Changed the World **Obv:** Elizabeth II **Rev:** Battle of Cologne scene **Edge:** Reeded

Date	Mintage	F	VF	XF	Unc	BU
2006PM	—	—	—	—	10.00	12.00

KM# 1302a CROWN

28.2800 g., 0.9250 Silver 0.8410 oz. ASW, 38.6 mm. **Ruler:** Elizabeth II **Subject:** Battles that Changed the World **Obv:** Elizabeth II **Rev:** Battle of Cologne scene **Edge:** Reeded

Date	Mintage	F	VF	XF	Unc	BU
2006PM Proof	10,000	Value: 47.50				

KM# 1304 CROWN

28.2800 g., Copper-Nickel, 38.6 mm. **Ruler:** Elizabeth II **Subject:** Battles that Changed the World **Obv:** Elizabeth II **Rev:** Siege of Valencia scene **Edge:** Reeded

Date	Mintage	F	VF	XF	Unc	BU
2006PM	—	—	—	—	10.00	12.00

KM# 1304a CROWN

28.2800 g., 0.9250 Silver 0.8410 oz. ASW, 38.6 mm. **Ruler:** Elizabeth II **Subject:** Battles that Changed the World **Obv:** Elizabeth II **Rev:** Siege of Valencia scene **Edge:** Reeded

Date	Mintage	F	VF	XF	Unc	BU
2006PM Proof	10,000	Value: 47.50				

KM# 1306 CROWN

28.2800 g., Copper-Nickel, 38.6 mm. **Ruler:** Elizabeth II **Subject:** Battles that Changed the World **Obv:** Elizabeth II **Rev:** Battle of Agincourt scene **Edge:** Reeded

Date	Mintage	F	VF	XF	Unc	BU
2006PM	—	—	—	—	10.00	12.00

KM# 1306a CROWN

28.2800 g., 0.9250 Silver 0.8410 oz. ASW, 38.6 mm. **Ruler:** Elizabeth II **Subject:** Battles that Changed the World **Obv:** Elizabeth II **Rev:** Battle of Agincourt scene **Edge:** Reeded

Date	Mintage	F	VF	XF	Unc	BU
2006PM Proof	10,000	Value: 47.50				

KM# 1290.1 CROWN

Copper-Nickel **Ruler:** Elizabeth II **Obv:** Bust with tiara right **Obv. Designer:** Ian Rank-Broadley **Rev:** Three Exotic Shorthair cats sitting facing **Edge:** Reeded

Date	Mintage	F	VF	XF	Unc	BU
2006	—	—	—	—	12.00	14.00

KM# 1290.2a CROWN
31.1030 g., 0.9999 Gold 0.9998 oz. AGW **Ruler:** Elizabeth II **Obv:** Bust with tiara right **Obv. Designer:** Ian Rank-Broadley **Rev:** Three Exotic Shorthair cats sitting facing, multicolor **Edge:** Reeded

Date	Mintage	F	VF	XF	Unc	BU
2006PM	—	—	—	—	—	1,350

KM# 1323.1 CROWN
28.2800 g., Copper Nickel, 38.60 mm. **Ruler:** Elizabeth II **Subject:** Hans Christian Anderson's fairy tales **Obv:** Bust with tiarra righ **Obv. Legend:** ELIZABETH II - ISLE OF MAN **Obv. Designer:** Ian Rank-Broadley **Rev:** Three bears startling Goldilocks in bed **Rev. Legend:** Goldilocks and the Three Bears **Edge:** Reeded

Date	Mintage	F	VF	XF	Unc	BU
2006PM	—	—	—	—	—	35.00

KM# 1323.2 CROWN
28.2800 g., Copper Nickel, 38.60 mm. **Ruler:** Elizabeth II **Subject:** Hans Christian Anderson's fairy tales **Obv:** Bust with tiara right **Obv. Legend:** ELIZABETH II - ISLE OF MAN **Obv. Designer:** Ian Rank-Broadley **Rev:** Three bears startling Goldilocks in bed multicolor **Rev. Legend:** Goldilocks and the Three Bears **Edge:** Reeded

Date	Mintage	F	VF	XF	Unc	BU
2006PM	—	—	—	—	—	40.00

KM# 1323.1a CROWN
28.2800 g., 0.9250 Silver 0.8410 oz. ASW, 38.60 mm. **Ruler:** Elizabeth II **Subject:** Hans Christian Anderson's Fairy Tales **Obv:** Bust with tiara right **Obv. Legend:** ELIZABETH II - ISLE OF MAN **Obv. Designer:** Ian Rank-Broadley **Rev:** Three bears startling Goldilocks in bed **Rev. Legend:** Goldilocks and the Three Bears **Edge:** Reeded

Date	Mintage	F	VF	XF	Unc	BU
2006PM Proof	—	Value: 80.00				

KM# 1323.2a CROWN
28.2800 g., 0.9250 Silver 0.8410 oz. ASW, 38.60 mm. **Ruler:** Elizabeth II **Subject:** Hans Christian Anderson's fairy tales **Obv:** Bust with tiara right **Obv. Legend:** ELIZABETH II - ISLE OF MAN **Obv. Designer:** Ian-Rank-Broadley **Rev:** Three bears startling Goldilocks in bed multicolor **Rev. Legend:** Goldilocks and the Three Bears **Edge:** Reeded

Date	Mintage	F	VF	XF	Unc	BU
2006PM Proof	—	Value: 100				

KM# 1324.1 CROWN
28.2800 g., Copper-Nickel, 38.60 mm. **Ruler:** Elizabeth II **Subject:** Hans Christian Anderson's fairy tales **Obv:** Bust with tiara right **Obv. Legend:** ELIZABETH II - ISLE OF MAN **Obv. Designer:** Ian Rank-Broadley **Rev:** Prince awakening Sleeping Beauty, castle in background **Rev. Legend:** Sleeping Beauty **Edge:** Reeded

Date	Mintage	F	VF	XF	Unc	BU
2007PM	—	—	—	—	—	35.00

KM# 1347 CROWN
31.1030 g., 0.9999 Gold 0.9998 oz. AGW **Ruler:** Elizabeth II **Obv:** Bust with tiara right **Obv. Legend:** ELIZABETH II - ISLE OF MAN **Obv. Designer:** Ian Rank-Broadley **Rev:** Ragdoll cat with two kittens sitting facing **Edge:** Reeded

Date	Mintage	F	VF	XF	Unc	BU
CS2007PM	—	—	—	—	—	1,350

KM# 1348.1 CROWN
Copper-Nickel **Ruler:** Elizabeth II **Subject:** The tale of Peter Rabbit **Obv:** Bust with tiara right **Obv. Legend:** ELIZABETH II - ISLE OF MAN **Obv. Designer:** Ian Rank-Broadley **Rev:** Peter walking with friends **Edge:** Reeded

Date	Mintage	F	VF	XF	Unc	BU
2007PM	—	—	—	—	—	30.00

KM# 1348.2 CROWN
Copper-Nickel **Ruler:** Elizabeth II **Subject:** The tale of Peter Rabbit **Obv:** Bust with tiara right **Obv. Legend:** ELIZABETH II - ISLE OF MAN **Obv. Designer:** Ian Rank-Broadley **Rev:** Peter walking with friends, multicolor **Edge:** Reeded

Date	Mintage	F	VF	XF	Unc	BU
2007PM	—	—	—	—	—	35.00

KM# 1348.1a CROWN
0.9250 Silver **Ruler:** Elizabeth II **Subject:** The tale of Peter Rabbit **Obv:** Bust with tiara right **Obv. Legend:** ELIZABETH II - ISLE OF MAN **Obv. Designer:** Ian Rank-Broadley **Rev:** Peter walking with friends **Edge:** Reeded

Date	Mintage	F	VF	XF	Unc	BU
2007PM Proof	—	Value: 85.00				

KM# 1348.2a CROWN
0.9250 Silver **Ruler:** Elizabeth II **Subject:** The tale of Peter Rabbit **Obv:** Bust with tiara right **Obv. Legend:** ELIZABETH II - ISLE OF MAN **Obv. Designer:** Ian Rank-Broadley **Rev:** Peter walking with friends, multicolor **Edge:** Reeded

Date	Mintage	F	VF	XF	Unc	BU
2007PM Proof	—	Value: 100				

KM# 1307 CROWN
Copper-Nickel **Ruler:** Elizabeth II **Rev:** Ragdoll cat and kittens

Date	Mintage	F	VF	XF	Unc	BU
2007	—	—	—	—	15.00	18.00

KM# 1310 CROWN
Copper-Nickel **Ruler:** Elizabeth II **Subject:** 100th Anniversary of Scouting **Obv:** Bust with tiara right **Obv. Legend:** ELIZABETH II - ISLE OF MAN **Rev:** 3/4 length figure of Robert Baden-Powell standing facing 3/4 left, Fleur-de-lys below, images of scouting at left and right **Rev. Legend:** CENTENARY OF SCOUTING **Edge:** Reeded

Date	Mintage	F	VF	XF	Unc	BU
2007	—	—	—	—	17.00	20.00

KM# 1311 CROWN
28.2800 g., 0.9167 Silver 0.8334 oz. ASW **Ruler:** Elizabeth II **Subject:** 100th Anniversary of Scouting **Obv:** Bust with tiara right **Obv. Legend:** ELIZABETH II - ISLE OF MAN **Rev:** 3/4 length figure of Robert Baden-Powell standing facing 3/4 left, Fleur-de-lys below, images of scouting at left and right **Rev. Legend:** CENTENARY OF SCOUTING **Edge:** Reeded

Date	Mintage	F	VF	XF	Unc	BU
2007 Proof	—	Value: 75.00				

KM# 1312 CROWN
0.7500 Tri-Metallic Gold - yellow, white and red **Ruler:** Elizabeth II **Subject:** Diamond Wedding Anniversary **Obv:** Bust with tiara right **Obv. Legend:** ELIZABETH II - ISLE OF MAN **Rev:** Crowned pair of doves surrounded by a leek, thistle, rose and shamrock **Edge:** Reeded

Date	Mintage	F	VF	XF	Unc	BU
2007 Proof	—	Value: 2,000				

KM# 1313 CROWN
28.2800 g., Copper-Nickel, 38.60 mm. **Ruler:** Elizabeth II **Obv:** Bust with tiara right **Obv. Legend:** ELIZABETH II - ISLE OF MAN **Rev:** Two swans facing **Edge:** Reeded

Date	Mintage	F	VF	XF	Unc	BU
2007	—	—	—	—	15.00	18.00

KM# 1315 CROWN
28.2800 g., 0.9167 Silver ASW 0.8335 0.8334 oz. ASW, 38.60 mm. **Ruler:** Elizabeth II **Obv:** Bust with tiara right **Obv. Legend:** ELIZABETH II - ISLE OF MAN **Rev:** Two swans facing **Edge:** Reeded

Date	Mintage	F	VF	XF	Unc	BU
2007 Proof	10,000	Value: 75.00				

KM# 1316 CROWN
28.2800 g., Copper-Nickel **Ruler:** Elizabeth II **Subject:** Diamond Wedding Anniversary **Obv:** Conjoined busts with Philip right **Obv. Legend:** ELIZABETH II - ISLE OF MAN **Rev:** Bridal bouquet of white orchids **Rev. Legend:** Diamond Wedding of H.M. Queen Elizabeth II & H.R.H. Prince Philip **Edge:** Reeded

Date	Mintage	F	VF	XF	Unc	BU
2007	—	—	—	—	15.00	18.00

KM# 1316a CROWN
28.2800 g., 0.9167 Silver ASW 0.8335 0.8334 oz. ASW **Ruler:** Elizabeth II **Subject:** Diamond Wedding Anniversary **Obv:** Conjoined busts with Philip right **Obv. Legend:** ELIZABETH II - ISLE OF MAN **Rev:** Bridal bouquet of white orchids **Rev. Legend:** Diamond Wedding of H.M. Queen Elizabeth II & H.R.H. Prince Philip **Edge:** Reeded

Date	Mintage	F	VF	XF	Unc	BU
2007 Proof	—	Value: 75.00				

KM# 1317 CROWN
28.2800 g., Copper-Nickel **Ruler:** Elizabeth II **Subject:** Diamond Wedding Anniversary **Obv:** Conjoined busts with Philip right **Obv. Legend:** ELIZABETH II - ISLE OF MAN **Rev:** Westminster Abbey **Rev. Legend:** Diamond Wedding of H.M. Queen Elizabeth II & H.R.H. Prince Philip **Edge:** Reeded

Date	Mintage	F	VF	XF	Unc	BU
2007	—	—	—	—	15.00	18.00

KM# 1317a CROWN
28.2800 g., 0.9167 Silver ASW 0.8335 0.8334 oz. ASW **Ruler:** Elizabeth II **Subject:** Diamond Wedding Anniversary **Obv:** Conjoined busts with Philip right **Obv. Legend:** ELIZABETH II - ISLE OF MAN **Rev:** Westminster Abbey **Rev. Legend:** Diamond Wedding of H.M. Queen Elizabeth II & H.R.H. Prince Philip **Edge:** Reeded

Date	Mintage	F	VF	XF	Unc	BU
2007 Proof	—	Value: 75.00				

KM# 1318 CROWN
28.2800 g., Copper-Nickel **Ruler:** Elizabeth II **Subject:** Diamond Wedding Anniversary **Obv:** Conjoined busts with Philip right **Obv. Legend:** ELIZABETH II - ISLE OF MAN **Rev:** Royal Family of five standing facing **Rev. Legend:** Diamond Wedding of H.M. Queen Elizabeth II & H.R.H. Prince Philip **Edge:** Reeded

Date	Mintage	F	VF	XF	Unc	BU
2007	—	—	—	—	15.00	18.00

KM# 1318a CROWN
28.2800 g., 0.9167 Silver ASW 0.8335 0.8334 oz. ASW **Ruler:** Elizabeth II **Subject:** Diamond Wedding Anniversary **Obv:** Conjoined busts with Philip right **Obv. Legend:** ELIZABETH II - ISLE OF MAN **Rev:** Royal Family of five standing facing **Rev. Legend:** Diamond Wedding of H.M. Queen Elizabeth II & H.R.H. Prince Philip **Edge:** Reeded

Date	Mintage	F	VF	XF	Unc	BU
2007 Proof	—	Value: 75.00				

KM# 1319 CROWN
28.2800 g., Copper-Nickel **Ruler:** Elizabeth II **Subject:** Diamond Wedding Anniversary **Obv:** Conjoined busts with Philip right **Obv. Legend:** ELIZABETH II - ISLE OF MAN **Rev:** Bride and groom standing facing **Rev. Legend:** Diamond Wedding of H.M. Queen Elizabeth II & H.R.H. Prince Philip **Edge:** Reeded

Date	Mintage	F	VF	XF	Unc	BU
2007	—	—	—	—	15.00	18.00

KM# 1319a CROWN
28.2800 g., 0.9167 Silver ASW 0.8335 0.8334 oz. ASW **Ruler:** Elizabeth II **Subject:** Diamond Wedding Anniversary **Obv:** Conjoined busts with Philip right **Obv. Legend:** ELIZABETH II - ISLE OF MAN **Rev:** Bride and groom standing facing **Rev. Legend:** Diamond Wedding of H.M. Queen Elizabeth II & H.R.H. Prince Philip **Edge:** Reeded

Date	Mintage	F	VF	XF	Unc	BU
2007 Proof	—	Value: 75.00				

KM# 1324.2 CROWN
28.2800 g., Copper-Nickel, 38.60 mm. **Ruler:** Elizabeth II **Subject:** Hans Christian Anderson's fairy tales **Obv:** Bust with tiara right **Obv. Legend:** ELIZABET II - ISLE OF MAN **Obv. Designer:** Ian Rank-Broadley **Rev:** Prince awakening Sleeping Beauty, castle in background multicolor **Rev. Legend:** Sleeping Beauty **Edge:** Reeded

Date	Mintage	F	VF	XF	Unc	BU
2007PM	—	—	—	—	—	40.00

KM# 1324.1a CROWN
28.2800 g., 0.9250 Silver 0.8410 oz. ASW, 38.60 mm. **Ruler:** Elizabeth II **Subject:** Hans Christian Anderson's fairy tales **Obv:** Bust with tiara right **Obv. Legend:** ELIZABETH II - ISLE OF MAN **Obv. Designer:** Ian Rank-Broadley **Rev:** Prince wakening Sleeping Beauty, castle in background **Rev. Legend:** Sleeping Beauty **Edge:** Reeded

Date	Mintage	F	VF	XF	Unc	BU
2007PM Proof	—	Value: 80.00				

KM# 1324.2a CROWN
28.2800 g., 0.9250 Silver 0.8410 oz. ASW, 38.60 mm. **Ruler:** Elizabeth II **Subject:** Hans Christian Anderson's fairy tales **Obv:** Bust with tiara right **Obv. Legend:** ELIZABETH II - ISLE OF MAN **Obv. Designer:** Ian Rank-Broadley **Rev:** Prince awakening Sleeping Beauty, castle in background multicolor **Rev. Legend:** Sleeping Beauty **Edge:** Reeded

Date	Mintage	F	VF	XF	Unc	BU
2007PM Proof	—	Value: 100				

KM# 1325.1 CROWN
28.2800 g., Copper-Nickel, 38.60 mm. **Ruler:** Elizabeth II **Subject:** Hans Christian Anderson's fairy tales **Obv:** Bust with tiara right **Obv. Legend:** ELIZABETH II - ISLE OF MAN **Obv. Designer:** Ian Rank-Broadley **Rev:** Wolf at right trying to blow pig's house down, two pigs fleeing above in background **Rev. Legend:** Three Little Pigs **Edge:** Reeded

Date	Mintage	F	VF	XF	Unc	BU
2007PM	—	—	—	—	—	35.00

KM# 1325.2 CROWN
28.2800 g., Copper-Nickel, 38.60 mm. **Ruler:** Elizabeth II **Subject:** Hans Christian Anderson's fairy tales **Obv:** Bust with tiara right **Obv. Legend:** ELIZABETH II - ISLE OF MAN **Obv. Designer:** Ian Rank-Broadley **Rev:** Wolf at right trying to blow pig's house down, two pigs fleeing above in backgound multicolor **Rev. Legend:** Three Little Pigs **Edge:** Reeded

Date	Mintage	F	VF	XF	Unc	BU
2007PM	—	—	—	—	—	40.00

KM# 1325.1a CROWN
28.2800 g., 0.9250 Silver 0.8410 oz. ASW, 38.60 mm. **Ruler:** Elizabeth II **Subject:** Hans Christian Anderson's fairey tales **Obv:** Bust with tiara right **Obv. Legend:** ELIZABETH II - ISLE OF MAN **Obv. Designer:** Ian Rank-Broadley **Rev:** Wolf at right trying to blow pig's house down, two pigs fleeing above in background **Rev. Legend:** Three Little Pigs **Edge:** Reeded

Date	Mintage	F	VF	XF	Unc	BU
2007PM Proof	—	Value: 80.00				

KM# 1325.2a CROWN
28.2800 g., 0.9250 Silver 0.8410 oz. ASW, 38.60 mm. **Ruler:** Elizabeth II **Subject:** Hans Christian Anderson's fairey tales **Obv:** Bust with tiara right **Obv. Legend:** ELIZABETH II - ISLE OF MAN **Obv. Designer:** Ian Rank-Broadley **Rev:** Wolf at right trying to blow pig's house down, two pigs fleeing above in background multicolor **Rev. Legend:** Three Little Pigs **Edge:** Reeded

Date	Mintage	F	VF	XF	Unc	BU
2007PM Proof	—	Value: 100				

KM# 1200 2 CROWNS
62.2000 g., 0.9990 Palladium 1.9977 oz., 40 mm. **Ruler:** Elizabeth II **Subject:** Discovery of Palladium Bicentennial **Obv:** Bust with tiara right **Obv. Designer:** Ian Rank-Broadley **Rev:** Pallas Athena left **Edge:** Reeded

Date	Mintage	F	VF	XF	Unc	BU
2004PM Proof	300	Value: 1,100				

KM# 1064 5 CROWN
155.5175 g., 0.9999 Gold 4.9993 oz. AGW, 65 mm. **Ruler:** Elizabeth II **Subject:** Year of the Snake **Obv:** Bust with tiara right **Obv. Designer:** Ian Rank-Broadley **Rev:** Snake **Edge:** Reeded

Date	Mintage	F	VF	XF	Unc	BU
2001 Proof	250	Value: 5,000				

KM# 1104 5 CROWN
155.5100 g., 0.9999 Gold 4.9991 oz. AGW, 65 mm. **Ruler:** Elizabeth II **Subject:** Year of the Horse **Obv:** Bust with tiara right **Obv. Designer:** Ian Rank-Broadley **Rev:** Two horses **Edge:** Reeded

Date	Mintage	F	VF	XF	Unc	BU
2002 Proof	250	Value: 5,000				

KM# 1173 5 CROWN
155.5100 g., 0.9999 Gold 4.9991 oz. AGW, 65 mm. **Ruler:** Elizabeth II **Subject:** Year of the Goat **Obv:** Bust with tiara right **Obv. Designer:** Ian Rank-Broadley **Rev:** Three goats **Edge:** Reeded

Date	Mintage	F	VF	XF	Unc	BU
2003PM Proof	250	Value: 5,000				

KM# 1244 5 CROWN
155.5175 g., 0.9999 Gold 4.9993 oz. AGW, 65 mm. **Ruler:** Elizabeth II **Obv:** Bust with tiara right **Obv. Designer:** Ian Rank-Broadley **Rev:** Monkey **Edge:** Reeded

Date	Mintage	F	VF	XF	Unc	BU
2004PM Proof	250	Value: 5,000				

KM# 1219 64 CROWNS
2000.0000 g., 0.9990 Silver 64.234 oz. ASW, 140 mm. **Ruler:** Elizabeth II **Obv:** Bust with tiara right **Obv. Designer:** Ian Rank-Broadley **Rev:** Ocean Liner Queen Mary 2 **Edge:** Reeded

Date	Mintage	F	VF	XF	Unc	BU
2004PM Proof	500	Value: 1,350				

KM# 1142 100 CROWNS
3000.0000 g., 0.9999 Silver 96.438 oz. ASW, 130 mm. **Ruler:** Elizabeth II **Subject:** Queen's Golden Jubilee **Obv:** Bust with tiara right **Obv. Designer:** Ian Rank-Broadley **Rev:** Queen on horse **Edge:** Reeded **Note:** Illustration reduced.

Date	Mintage	F	VF	XF	Unc	BU
2002 Proof	500	Value: 1,950				

KM# 1184 130 CROWNS
4000.0000 g., 0.9990 Silver 128.46 oz. ASW, 130 mm. **Ruler:** Elizabeth II **Obv:** Bust with tiara right **Obv. Designer:** Ian Rank-Broadley **Rev:** Gold clad cameo portrait of Elizabeth I with a .035ct ruby inset on her forehead all within a circle of portraits **Edge:** Reeded

Date	Mintage	F	VF	XF	Unc	BU
2003PM Proof	500	Value: 2,650				

GOLD BULLION COINAGE

Angel Issues

KM# 1106 1/20 ANGEL
1.5552 g., 0.9999 Gold 0.0500 oz. AGW, 15 mm. **Ruler:** Elizabeth II **Obv:** Bust with tiara right **Obv. Designer:** Ian Rank-Broadley **Rev:** St. Michael slaying dragon, three crown privy mark at right **Edge:** Reeded

Date	Mintage	F	VF	XF	Unc	BU
2001 (3c) Proof	1,000	Value: 55.00				
2002 Proof	—	Value: 55.00				
Note: With candy cane privy mark						

KM# 393 1/20 ANGEL
1.5551 g., 0.9999 Gold 0.0500 oz. AGW **Ruler:** Elizabeth II **Obv:** Crowned bust right **Obv. Designer:** Raphael Maklouf **Rev:** Archangel Michael slaying dragon right

Date	Mintage	F	VF	XF	Unc	BU
2001	—	—	—	—	—	55.00
2001 Proof	—	Value: 60.00				
2001 Proof	—	Value: 65.00				
Note: Privy mark: 3 Kings						
2002	—	—	—	—	—	55.00
2002 Proof	—	Value: 60.00				
2002 Proof	—	Value: 65.00				
Note: Privy mark: Candy						
2003	—	—	—	—	—	55.00
2003 Proof	—	Value: 60.00				
2003 Proof	—	Value: 65.00				
Note: Privy mark: Candy						
2004	—	—	—	—	—	55.00
2004 Proof	—	Value: 60.00				
2004 Proof	—	Value: 65.00				
Note: Privy mark: Partridge in a Pear Tree						
2005	—	—	—	—	—	55.00
2005 Proof	—	Value: 60.00				
2005 Proof	—	Value: 65.00				
Note: Privy mark: 2 Turtle doves						
2006	—	—	—	—	—	55.00
2006 Proof	—	Value: 60.00				
2006 Proof	—	Value: 65.00				
Note: Privy mark: 4 Calling birds						
2007	—	—	—	—	—	55.00
2007 Proof	—	Value: 60.00				
2007 Proof	—	Value: 65.00				
Note: Privy mark: 4 Calling birds						

KM# 1252 1/20 ANGEL
1.5550 g., 0.9999 Gold 0.0500 oz. AGW, 15 mm. **Ruler:** Elizabeth II **Obv:** Bust with tiara right **Obv. Designer:** Ian Rank-Broadley **Rev:** St. Michael and Christmas privy mark **Edge:** Reeded

Date	Mintage	F	VF	XF	Unc	BU
2004PM Proof	1,000	Value: 60.00				

KM# 394 1/10 ANGEL
3.1103 g., 0.9999 Gold 0.1000 oz. AGW **Ruler:** Elizabeth II **Obv:** Crowned bust right **Obv. Designer:** Raphael Maklouf **Rev:** Archangel Michael

Date	Mintage	F	VF	XF	Unc	BU
2001 Proof	—	Value: 110				
2001	—	—	—	—	—	100
2002 Proof	—	Value: 110				
2002	—	—	—	—	—	100
2003 Proof	—	Value: 110				
2003	—	—	—	—	—	100
2004 Proof	—	Value: 110				
2004	—	—	—	—	—	100
2005 Proof	—	Value: 110				
2005	—	—	—	—	—	100

KM# 395 1/4 ANGEL
7.7758 g., 0.9999 Gold 0.2500 oz. AGW **Ruler:** Elizabeth II **Obv:** Crowned bust right **Obv. Designer:** Raphael Maklouf **Rev:** Archangel Michael slaying dragon

Date	Mintage	F	VF	XF	Unc	BU
2001 Proof	—	Value: 250				
2001	—	—	—	—	—	240
2002 Proof	—	Value: 250				
2002	—	—	—	—	—	240
2003 Proof	—	Value: 250				
2003	—	—	—	—	—	240
2004 Proof	—	Value: 250				
2004	—	—	—	—	—	240
2005 Proof	—	Value: 250				
2005	—	—	—	—	—	240

KM# 397 ANGEL
31.1035 g., 0.9999 Gold 0.9999 oz. AGW **Ruler:** Elizabeth II **Obv:** Crowned bust right **Obv. Designer:** Raphael Maklouf **Rev:** Archangel Michael slaying dragon right

Date	Mintage	F	VF	XF	Unc	BU
2001 Proof	—	Value: 1,000				
2001	—	—	—	—	—	985
2002 Proof	—	Value: 1,000				
2002	—	—	—	—	—	985
2003 Proof	—	Value: 1,000				
2003	—	—	—	—	—	985
2004 Proof	—	Value: 1,000				
2004	—	—	—	—	—	985
2005 Proof	—	Value: 1,000				
2005	—	—	—	—	—	985
2006 Proof	500	Value: 1,000				
2006	—	—	—	—	—	985
2007 Proof	—	Value: 1,000				
2007	—	—	—	—	—	985

KM# 397.1 ANGEL
31.1035 g., 0.9990 Gold 0.9990 oz. AGW **Ruler:** Elizabeth II **Obv:** Crowned bust right **Obv. Designer:** Raphael Maklouf **Rev:** Archangel Michael slaying dragon right

Date	Mintage	F	VF	XF	Unc	BU
2006 Proof, High Relief	Est. 1,000	Value: 1,100				
2007 Proof, High Relief	Est. 1,000	Value: 1,100				

MINT SETS

KM#	Date	Mintage	Identification	Issue Price	Mkt Val
MS30	2001 (8)	—	KM#1036, 1037, 1038, 1039, 1040, 1041, 1042, 1043	—	20.00
MS31	2001 (9)	—	KM#1036, 1037, 1038, 1039, 1040 1041, 1042, 1043, 1044	—	35.00
MS32	2002 (8)	—	KM#1036, 1037, 1038, 1039, 1040, 1041, 1042, 1043	—	20.00
MS33	2002 (9)	—	KM#1036, 1037, 1038, 1039, 1040, 1041, 1042, 1043, 1044	—	35.00
MS34	2003 (8)	—	KM#1036, 1037, 1038, 1039, 1040, 1041, 1042, 1043	—	20.00
MS35	2003 (9)	—	KM#1036, 1037, 1038, 1039, 1040, 1041, 1042, 1043, 1044	—	35.00
MS36	2004 (8)	—	KM#1253, 1254, 1255, 1256, 1257, 1258, 1259, 1260	—	28.00
MS37	2004 (9)	—	KM#1253, 1254, 1255, 1256, 1257, 1258, 1259, 1260, 1261	—	45.00
MS38	2005 (8)	—	KM#1253, 1254, 1255, 1256, 1257, 1258, 1259, 1260	—	20.00
MS39	2005 (9)	—	KM#1253, 1254, 1255, 1256, 1257, 1258, 1259, 1260, 1261	—	37.50
MS40	2006 (8)	—	MS#1253, 1254, 1255, 1256, 1257, 1258, 1259, 1260	35.00	32.00
MS41	2006 (9)	—	KM1253, 1254, 1255, 1256, 1257, 1258, 1259, 1260, 1261	42.50	40.00
MS42	2007 (8)	—	KM#1253, 1254, 1255, 1256, 1257, 1258, 1259, 1260	35.00	32.00
MS43	2007 (9)	—	KM1253, 1254, 1255, 1256, 1257, 1258, 1259, 1260 and 1261	42.50	40.00

PROOF SETS

KM#	Date	Mintage	Identification	Issue Price	Mkt Val
PS55	2001 (5)	1,000	KM#1067-1070, 1073	—	1,410
PS60	2003 (3)	—	KM#1186, 1187, 1188	—	320
PS61	2003 (5)	—	KM#1186, 1187, 1188, 1189, 1190 w/gold ring	—	1,400
PS62	2003 (5)	—	KM#1191, 1192, 1193, 1194, 1195 w/gold-plated silver ring	—	240
PS63	2004 (5)	1,000	KM#1247, 1248, 1249.1, 1250, 1251	—	1,425

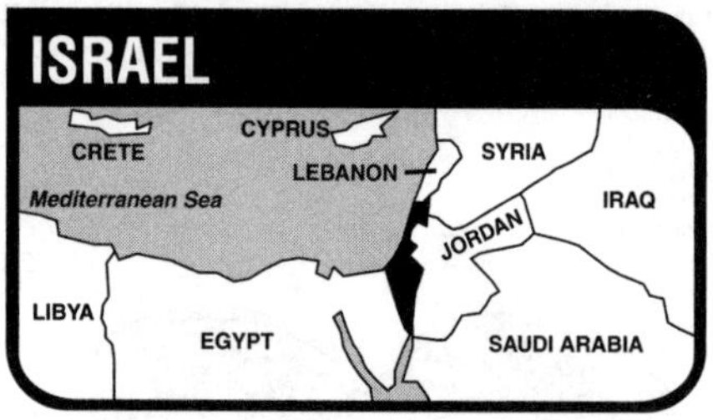

The state of Israel, a Middle Eastern republic at the eastern end of the Mediterranean Sea, bounded by Lebanon on the north, Syria on the northeast, Jordan on the east, and Egypt on the southwest, has an area of 9,000sq. mi. (20,770 sq. km.) and a population of 6 million. Capital: Jerusalem. Finished diamonds, chemicals, citrus, textiles, minerals, electronic and transportation equipment are exported.

HEBREW COIN DATING

Modern Israel's coins carry Hebrew dating formed from a combination of the 22 consonant letters of the Hebrew alphabet and read from right to left. The Jewish calendar dates back more than 5700 years; but five millenniums are assumed in the dating of coins (until 1981). Thus, the year 5735 (1975AD) appears as 735, with the first two characters from the right indicating the number of years in hundreds; tav (400), plus shin (300). The next is lamedh (30), followed by a separation mark which has the appearance of double quotation marks, then heh (5).

The Star of David is not a mintmark. It appears only on some coins sold by the Israel Government Coins and Medals Corporation Ltd., which is owned by the Israel government, and is a division of the Prime Minister's office and sole distributor to collectors. The Star of David was first used in 1971 on the science coin to signify that it was minted in Jerusalem, but was later used by different mint facilities.

AD Date		Jewish Era
2001	התשס"א	5761
2002	התשס"ב	5762
2003	התשס"ג	5763
2004	התשס"ד	5764
2005	התשס"ה	5765
2006	התשס"ו	5766
2007	התשס"ז	5767
2008	התשס"ח	5768
2009	התשס"ט	5769
2010	התש"ע	5770

MINT MARKS

(o) - Ottawa
(s) - San Francisco
None – Jerusalem

REPUBLIC

REFORM COINAGE

100 Agorot = 1 New Sheqel

September 4, 1985

KM# 157 5 AGOROT

2.9500 g., Aluminum-Bronze, 19.45 mm. **Obv:** Ancient coin **Rev:** Value within lined square **Edge:** Plain

Date	Mintage	F	VF	XF	Unc	BU
JE5761 (2001)(sl)	6,144,000	—	—	—	0.15	—
JE5762 (2002)(sl)	6,144,000	—	—	—	0.15	—
JE5764 (2004)	—	—	—	—	0.15	—
JE5765 (2005)	—	—	—	—	0.15	—
JE5766 (2006)	—	—	—	—	0.15	—
JE5767 (2007)	—	—	—	—	0.15	—

KM# 172 5 AGOROT

Aluminum-Bronze, 20.5 mm. **Subject:** Hanukkah **Obv:** Ancient coin **Rev:** Value within lined square **Note:** JE5754-5767 coins contain the Star of David mint mark; the JE5747-5753 coins do not.

Date	Mintage	F	VF	XF	Unc	BU
JE5761 (2001)(u)	4,000	—	—	—	2.50	—
Note: In sets only						
JE5762 (2002)(u)	4,000	—	—	—	2.50	—
Note: In sets only						
JE5763 (2003)(u)	3,000	—	—	—	2.50	—
Note: In sets only						
JE5764 (2004)(u)	3,000	—	—	—	2.50	—
Note: In sets only						
JE5765 (2005)(u)	2,500	—	—	—	2.50	—
Note: In sets only						
JE5766 (2006)(u)	3,000	—	—	—	2.50	—
Note: In sets only						
JE5767 (2007)(u)	3,000	—	—	—	2.50	—
Note: In sets only						
JE5768 (2008)(u)	3,000	—	—	—	2.50	—
Note: In sets only						

KM# 158 10 AGOROT

4.0000 g., Aluminum-Bronze, 22 mm. **Obv:** Menorah **Rev:** Value within lined square **Edge:** Plain

Date	Mintage	F	VF	XF	Unc	BU
JE5761 (2001)(sl)	46,140,000	—	—	—	0.20	—
Note: Sides of central part of zero are rounded.						
JE5761 (2001)(so)	32,256,000	—	—	—	0.20	—
Note: Sides of central part of zero are straight.						
JE5762 (2002)(w)	4,608,000	—	—	—	0.20	—
JE5763 (2003)(sl)	22,980,000	—	—	—	0.20	—
JE5764 (2004)	—	—	—	—	0.20	—
JE5765 (2005)	—	—	—	—	0.20	—
JE5766 (2006)	—	—	—	—	0.20	—
JE5767 (2007)	—	—	—	—	0.20	—

KM# 173 10 AGOROT

4.0700 g., Aluminum-Bronze, 22 mm. **Subject:** Hanukkah **Obv:** Menorah **Rev:** Value within lined square **Note:** JE5754-5768 have the Star of David mint mark, JE5747-5753 coins do not.

Date	Mintage	F	VF	XF	Unc	BU
JE5761 (2001)(u)	4,000	—	—	—	2.50	—
Note: In sets only						
JE5762 (2002)(u)	4,000	—	—	—	2.50	—
Note: In sets only						
JE5763 (2003)(u)	3,000	—	—	—	2.50	—
Note: In sets only						
JE5764 (2004)(u)	3,000	—	—	—	2.50	—
Note: In sets only						
JE5765 (2005)(u)	2,500	—	—	—	2.50	—
Note: In sets only						
JE5766 (2006)(u)	3,000	—	—	—	2.50	—
Note: In sets only						
JE5767 (2007)(u)	3,000	—	—	—	2.50	—
Note: In sets only						
JE5768 (2009)(u)	3,000	—	—	—	2.50	—
Note: In sets only						

KM# 354 1/2 NEW SHEQEL

6.5000 g., Copper-Aluminum-Nickel, 25.5 mm. **Subject:** Hanukka **Obv:** Denomination **Rev:** Curacao Hanukka lamp **Edge:** Plain **Shape:** 12-sided

Date	Mintage	F	VF	XF	Unc	BU
JE5761 (2001)(u)	4,000	—	—	—	8.00	—

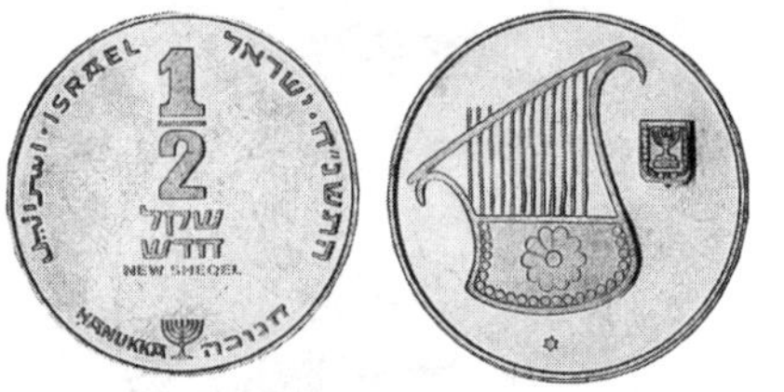

KM# 174 1/2 NEW SHEQEL

6.5000 g., Aluminum-Bronze, 26 mm. **Subject:** Hanukka **Obv:** Value **Rev:** Lyre **Note:** Coins dated JE5754-5768 have the Star of David mint mark; the coins dated JE5747-5753 do not.

Date	Mintage	F	VF	XF	Unc	BU
JE5761 (2001)(u)	4,000	—	—	—	2.50	—
Note: In sets only						
JE5762 (2002)(u)	4,000	—	—	—	2.50	—
Note: In sets only						
JE5763 (2003)(u)	3,000	—	—	—	2.50	—
Note: In sets only						
JE5764 (2004)(u)	3,000	—	—	—	2.50	—
Note: In sets only						
JE5765 (2005)(u)	2,500	—	—	—	2.50	—
Note: In sets only						
JE5766 (2006)(u)	3,000	—	—	—	2.50	—
Note: In sets only						
JE5767 (2007)(u)	3,000	—	—	—	2.50	—
Note: In sets only						
JE5768 (2008)(u)	3,000	—	—	—	2.50	—
Note: In sets only						

KM# 355 1/2 NEW SHEQEL

6.5000 g., Copper-Aluminum-Nickel, 25.5 mm. **Obv:** Value **Rev:** Yemenite Hanukka Lamp **Edge:** Twelve plain sections

Date	Mintage	F	VF	XF	Unc	BU
JE5762 (2002)(u)	4,000	—	—	—	8.00	—

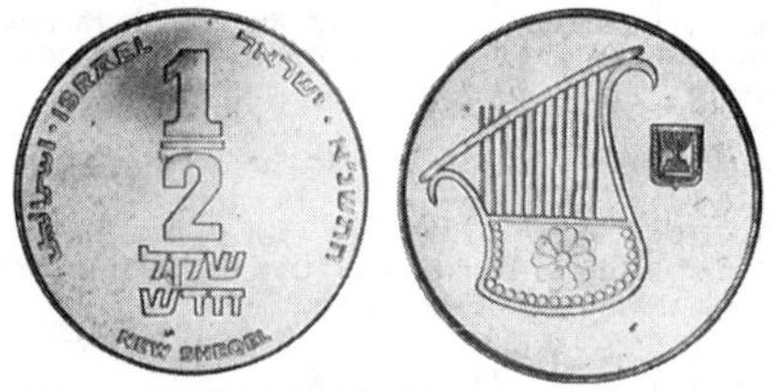

KM# 159 1/2 NEW SHEQEL

6.5200 g., Aluminum-Bronze, 25.95 mm. **Obv:** Value **Rev:** Lyre **Edge:** Plain

Date	Mintage	F	VF	XF	Unc	BU
JE5762 (2002)(so)	2,880,000	—	—	—	0.75	—
JE5762 (2002)(v)	5,760,000	—	—	—	0.75	—
Note: Length of fraction line is 4 or 4.5 mm. But which mint is which is not known.						
JE5763 (2003)	—	—	—	—	0.75	—
JE5764 (2004)(so)	2,640,000	—	—	—	0.75	—
JE5765 (2005)	—	—	—	—	0.75	—
JE5766 (2006)	—	—	—	—	0.75	—
JE5767 (2007)	—	—	—	—	0.75	—

KM# 389 1/2 NEW SHEQEL

6.5000 g., Copper-Aluminum-Nickel, 25.5 mm. **Obv:** Value **Rev:** Polish Hanukka Lamp **Edge:** Plain **Shape:** 12-sided

Date	Mintage	F	VF	XF	Unc	BU
JE5763 (2003)(u)	3,000	—	—	—	8.00	—
Note: In sets only						

KM# 390 1/2 NEW SHEQEL

6.5000 g., Copper-Aluminum-Nickel, 25.5 mm. **Obv:** Value **Rev:** Iraqi Hanukka Lamp **Edge:** Plain **Shape:** 12-sided

Date	Mintage	F	VF	XF	Unc	BU
JE5764 (2004)(u)	3,000	—	—	—	8.00	—
Note: In sets only						

KM# 391 1/2 NEW SHEQEL

6.5000 g., Copper-Aluminum-Nickel, 25.5 mm. **Obv:** Value **Rev:** Syrian Hanukka Lamp **Edge:** Plain **Shape:** 12-sided

Date	Mintage	F	VF	XF	Unc	BU
JE5765 (2005)(u)	2,500	—	—	—	8.00	—
Note: In sets only						

KM# 415 1/2 NEW SHEQEL

6.5000 g., Copper-Aluminum-Nickel, 25.5 mm. **Obv:** Value and mini-Hanukka Lamp **Rev:** Dutch Hanukka Lamp **Edge:** Plain **Shape:** 12-sided

Date	Mintage	F	VF	XF	Unc	BU
JE5766 (2006)	3,000	—	—	—	8.00	—
Note: In sets only						

KM# 422 1/2 NEW SHEQEL

6.5000 g., Copper-Aluminum-Nickel, 25.5 mm. **Obv:** Value and mini-Hanukka Lamp **Rev:** Corfu (Greek) Hanukka Lamp **Edge:** Plain **Shape:** 12-sided

Date	Mintage	F	VF	XF	Unc	BU
JE5767 (2007)	3,000	—	—	—	8.00	—
Note: In sets only						

KM# 434 1/2 NEW SHEQEL

6.5000 g., Copper-Aluminum-Nickel, 26 mm. **Subject:** Hanukka **Obv:** Value, date, inscriptions and menorah **Rev:** Egyptian Hanukka lamp **Shape:** 12-sided

Date	Mintage	F	VF	XF	Unc	BU
JE5768 (2008)	3,000	—	—	—	8.00	—
Note: In sets only						

KM# 160a NEW SHEQEL

3.4500 g., Nickel-Clad Steel, 17.97 mm. **Obv:** Value **Rev:** Lilly, state emblem and ancient Hebrew inscription **Edge:** Plain

Date	Mintage	F	VF	XF	Unc	BU
JE5761 (2001)(h)	9,648,000	—	—	—	1.00	—
JE5762 (2002)(h)	18,816,000	—	—	—	1.00	—
JE5763 (2003)(v)	10,198,500	—	—	—	1.00	—
JE5765 (2005)	—	—	—	—	1.00	—
JE5766 (2006)	—	—	—	—	1.00	—
Note: Coin alignment error exists. Value: $200.						
JE5767 (2007)	—	—	—	—	1.00	—

KM# 344 NEW SHEQEL

14.4000 g., 0.9250 Silver 0.4282 oz. ASW, 30 mm. **Subject:** Anniversary - Independence Day and Education **Obv:** Denomination **Rev:** Pomegranate full of symbols - Hebrew 'ABC-123', etc. **Rev. Designer:** Asher Kalderon **Edge:** Plain

Date	Mintage	F	VF	XF	Unc	BU
JE5761-2001(u) Prooflike	1,653	—	—	—	—	35.00

KM# 351 NEW SHEQEL

14.4000 g., 0.9250 Silver 0.4282 oz. ASW, 30 mm. **Subject:** Music **Obv:** National arms and denomination **Rev:** Musical instruments **Edge:** Plain

Date	Mintage	F	VF	XF	Unc	BU
JE5761-2001(u)	1,182	—	—	—	—	30.00

KM# 163 NEW SHEQEL

4.0500 g., Copper-Nickel, 18 mm. **Subject:** Hanukka **Obv:** Value **Rev:** Lilly **Note:** Coins dated JE5754-5768 have the Star of David mint mark; the JE5746-5753 coins do not.

Date	Mintage	F	VF	XF	Unc	BU
JE5761 (2001)(u)	4,000	—	—	—	2.50	—
Note: In sets only						
JE5762 (2002)(u)	4,000	—	—	—	2.50	—
Note: In sets only						
JE5763 (2003)(u)	3,000	—	—	—	2.50	—
Note: In sets only						
JE5764 (2004)(u)	3,000	—	—	—	2.50	—
Note: In sets only						
JE5765 (2005)(u)	2,500	—	—	—	2.50	—
Note: In sets only						
JE5766 (2006)(u)	3,000	—	—	—	2.50	—
Note: In sets only						
JE5767 (2007)(u)	3,000	—	—	—	2.50	—
Note: In sets only						
JE5768 (2008)	3,000	—	—	—	2.50	—
Note: In sets only.						

KM# 356 NEW SHEQEL

14.4000 g., 0.9250 Silver 0.4282 oz. ASW, 30 mm. **Subject:** Independence - Volunteering **Obv:** Denomination **Rev:** Heart in hands **Edge:** Plain

Date	Mintage	F	VF	XF	Unc	BU
JE5762-2002(o) Prooflike	1,364	—	—	—	—	30.00

KM# 359 NEW SHEQEL

14.4000 g., 0.9250 Silver 0.4282 oz. ASW, 30 mm. **Subject:** Tower of Babel **Obv:** National arms in spiral inscription **Rev:** Tower of Hebrew verses **Edge:** Plain

Date	Mintage	F	VF	XF	Unc	BU
JE5762 (2002)(o) Prooflike	1,312	—	—	—	—	30.00

KM# 371 NEW SHEQEL

14.4000 g., 0.9250 Silver 0.4282 oz. ASW, 30 mm. **Subject:** Space Exploration **Obv:** "Ofeq" satellite in orbit **Rev:** "Shavit" rocket **Edge Lettering:** Hebrew: "In memory of Ilan Ramon and his colleagues in the Columbia"

Date	Mintage	F	VF	XF	Unc	BU
JE5763-2003(v)	Est. 1,500	—	—	—	—	40.00

KM# 374 NEW SHEQEL

14.4000 g., 0.9250 Silver 0.4282 oz. ASW, 30 mm. **Obv:** Value **Rev:** Jacob and Rachel floating in air **Edge:** Plain

Date	Mintage	F	VF	XF	Unc	BU
JE5763-2003(v)	Est. 2,000	—	—	—	—	30.00

KM# 380 NEW SHEQEL

14.4000 g., 0.9250 Silver 0.4282 oz. ASW, 30 mm. **Obv:** Value **Rev:** Parent and child **Edge:** Plain

Date	Mintage	F	VF	XF	Unc	BU
JE5764-2004(u)	Est. 1,800	—	—	—	—	30.00

KM# 383 NEW SHEQEL

14.4000 g., 0.9250 Silver 0.4282 oz. ASW, 30 mm. **Obv:** Four windsurfers, value and national arms **Rev:** Eight windsurfers **Edge:** Plain

Date	Mintage	F	VF	XF	Unc	BU
JE5764-2004(v) Prooflike	Est. 2,000	—	—	—	—	30.00

KM# 386 NEW SHEQEL

14.4000 g., 0.9250 Silver 0.4282 oz. ASW, 30 mm. **Subject:** Biblical Burning Bush **Obv:** Burning twig and value **Rev:** Burning Bush **Edge:** Plain

Date	Mintage	F	VF	XF	Unc	BU
JE5764-2004(v)	Est. 1,800	—	—	—	—	30.00

KM# 377 NEW SHEQEL

14.4000 g., 0.9250 Silver 0.4282 oz. ASW, 30 mm. **Obv:** Value **Rev:** Architectural design **Edge:** Plain **Note:** With enamel.

Date	Mintage	F	VF	XF	Unc	BU
JE5764-2004(u)	Est. 1,300	—	—	—	—	30.00

KM# 405 NEW SHEQEL

1.2440 g., 0.9990 Gold 0.0400 oz. AGW, 13.92 mm. **Obv:** Value **Rev:** Jacob and Rachel floating in air **Edge:** Reeded

Date	Mintage	F	VF	XF	Unc	BU
JE5764 (2004) Proof	—	Value: 75.00				

KM# 405a NEW SHEQEL

1.2440 g., 0.9990 Gold 0.0400 oz. AGW, 13.92 mm. **Obv:** Value **Rev:** Arabic legend Israel is mispelled **Edge:** Reeded

Date	Mintage	F	VF	XF	Unc	BU
JE5764 (2004) Proof	682	Value: 200				

KM# 406 NEW SHEQEL

14.4000 g., 0.9250 Silver 0.4282 oz. ASW, 30 mm. **Subject:** FIFA 2006 World Cup **Obv:** Value and soccer ball **Rev:** Map and soccer ball **Edge:** Plain

Date	Mintage	F	VF	XF	Unc	BU
JE5764-2004(u)	Est. 2,800	—	—	—	—	40.00
Note: Issued in 2006						

KM# 412 NEW SHEQEL

14.4000 g., 0.9250 Silver 0.4282 oz. ASW, 30 mm. **Subject:** Naomi Shemer **Obv:** Value **Rev:** Portrait of Naomi Shemer **Edge:** Plain

Date	Mintage	F	VF	XF	Unc	BU
JE5765-2005(u)	Est. 1,800	—	—	—	—	45.00

KM# 396 NEW SHEQEL

14.4000 g., 0.9250 Silver 0.4282 oz. ASW, 30 mm. **Subject:** Einstein's Relativity Theory **Obv:** Concentric circles above equation **Rev:** Value above signature

Date	Mintage	F	VF	XF	Unc	BU
JE5765-2005(v) Prooflike	2,800	—	—	—	—	40.00

KM# 399 NEW SHEQEL

14.4000 g., 0.9250 Silver 0.4282 oz. ASW, 30 mm. **Subject:** Moses and Ten Commandments **Obv:** Ten Commandments and value **Rev:** Moses and Ten Commandments

Date	Mintage	F	VF	XF	Unc	BU
JE5765-2005(u) Prooflike	Est. 2,800	—	—	—	—	40.00

KM# 402 NEW SHEQEL

14.4000 g., 0.9250 Silver 0.4282 oz. ASW, 30 mm. **Subject:** Israel 57th Anniversary **Obv:** Value and olive branch **Rev:** Twisted olive tree

Date	Mintage	F	VF	XF	Unc	BU
JE5765-2005(u) Prooflike	Est. 1,800	—	—	—	—	45.00

KM# 409 NEW SHEQEL

14.4000 g., 0.9250 Silver 0.4282 oz. ASW, 30 mm. **Series:** Biblical Art **Subject:** Abraham and the Three Angels **Obv:** Value and stars **Rev:** Abraham and the three angels **Edge:** Reeded

Date	Mintage	F	VF	XF	Unc	BU
JE5766-2006(ig)	Est. 1,800	—	—	—	—	45.00

KM# 416 NEW SHEQEL

14.4000 g., 0.9250 Silver 0.4282 oz. ASW, 30 mm. **Series:** Independence Day **Subject:** Higher Education in Israel **Obv:** Value and design **Rev:** Symbols of Science, Humanities, Technology and Mathematics **Edge:** Plain

Date	Mintage	F	VF	XF	Unc	BU
JE5766-2006(ig)	Est. 1,200	—	—	—	—	45.00

KM# 419 NEW SHEQEL

14.4000 g., 0.9250 Silver 0.4282 oz. ASW, 30 mm. **Subject:** UNESCO World Heritage Site; White City of Tel Aviv **Obv:** Value and Bauhaus building **Rev:** Fall of Bauhaus style building and UNESCO symbol **Edge:** Plain

Date	Mintage	F	VF	XF	Unc	BU
JE5766-2006	Est. 1,200	—	—	—	—	50.00

KM# 423 NEW SHEQEL

14.4000 g., 0.9250 Silver 0.4282 oz. ASW, 30 mm. **Subject:** Independence Day - Performing Arts in Israel **Obv:** Value, state emblem and inscriptions **Rev:** Stylized actor, dancer and musician and inscription in Hebrew, English and Arabic **Rev. Inscription:** Performing Arts in Israel **Edge:** Plain

Date	Mintage	F	VF	XF	Unc	BU
JE5767-2007	Est. 1,200	—	—	—	—	50.00

KM# 426 NEW SHEQEL

14.4000 g., 0.9250 Silver 0.4282 oz. ASW, 30 mm. **Subject:** 2008 Olympics - Judo **Obv:** Value, state emblem, judo belt and inscriptions **Rev:** 2 judo athletes and inscriptions in Hebrew, English and Arabic **Rev. Inscription:** "The Olympic Delegation of Israel" and "Judo" **Edge:** Plain

Date	Mintage	F	VF	XF	Unc	BU
JE5767-2007	Est. 2,800	—	—	—	—	50.00

KM# 429 NEW SHEQEL

14.4000 g., 0.9250 Silver 0.4282 oz. ASW, 30 mm. **Subject:** Biblical Art - Isaiah, Wold with the Lamb **Obv:** Value, state emblem and inscriptions in Hebrew, English and Arabic **Obv. Inscription:** "And the Wolf shall dwell with the lamb" **Rev:** Wolf and lamb lying together under a tree **Edge:** Plain

Date	Mintage	F	VF	XF	Unc	BU
JE5767-2007	Est. 1,800	—	—	—	—	55.00

KM# 345 2 NEW SHEQALIM
28.8000 g., 0.9250 Silver 0.8565 oz. ASW, 38.7 mm. **Subject:** Independence Day and Education **Obv:** Denomination **Rev:** Pomegranate full of symbols **Edge:** Reeded **Designer:** Asher Kalderon

Date	Mintage	F	VF	XF	Unc	BU
JE5761-2001(u) Proof	1,847	Value: 55.00				

KM# 360 2 NEW SHEQALIM
28.8000 g., 0.9250 Silver 0.8565 oz. ASW, 38.7 mm. **Subject:** Tower of Babel **Obv:** National arms in spiral inscription **Rev:** Tower of Hebrew verses **Edge:** Reeded

Date	Mintage	F	VF	XF	Unc	BU
JE5762-2002(o) Proof	1,295	Value: 55.00				

KM# 378 2 NEW SHEQALIM
28.8000 g., 0.9250 Silver 0.8565 oz. ASW, 38.7 mm. **Obv:** Value and enameled shapes **Rev:** Architectural design **Edge:** Reeded

Date	Mintage	F	VF	XF	Unc	BU
JE5764-2004(u) Proof	Est. 1,300	Value: 55.00				

KM# 349 2 NEW SHEQALIM
28.8000 g., 0.9250 Silver 0.8565 oz. ASW, 38.7 mm. **Subject:** Wildlife **Obv:** Acacia tree **Rev:** Ibex **Edge:** Reeded

Date	Mintage	F	VF	XF	Unc	BU
JE5762-2000(u) Proof	2,000	Value: 55.00				

KM# 352 2 NEW SHEQALIM
28.8000 g., 0.9250 Silver 0.8565 oz. ASW, 38.7 mm. **Subject:** Music **Obv:** National arms and denomination **Rev:** Musical instruments **Edge:** Reeded

Date	Mintage	F	VF	XF	Unc	BU
JE5761-2001(u) Proof	1,747	Value: 55.00				

KM# 372 2 NEW SHEQALIM
28.8000 g., 0.9250 Silver 0.8565 oz. ASW, 38.7 mm. **Subject:** Space Exploration **Obv:** "Amos" satellite in orbit **Rev:** "Shavit" rocket **Edge Lettering:** Hebrew: "In memory of Ilan Ramon and his colleagues in the Columbia"

Date	Mintage	F	VF	XF	Unc	BU
JE5763-2003(v) Proof	Est. 1,500	Value: 60.00				

KM# 381 2 NEW SHEQALIM
28.8000 g., 0.9250 Silver 0.8565 oz. ASW, 38.7 mm. **Obv:** Value and stylized human shapes **Rev:** Stylized parent and child **Edge:** Reeded

Date	Mintage	F	VF	XF	Unc	BU
JE5764-2004(u) Proof	Est. 1,800	Value: 55.00				

KM# 357 2 NEW SHEQALIM
28.8000 g., 0.9250 Silver 0.8565 oz. ASW, 38.7 mm. **Subject:** Independence - Volunteering **Obv:** Denomination **Rev:** Heart in hands **Edge:** Reeded

Date	Mintage	F	VF	XF	Unc	BU
JE5762-2002(o) Proof	1,426	Value: 55.00				

KM# 375 2 NEW SHEQALIM
28.8000 g., 0.9250 Silver 0.8565 oz. ASW, 38.7 mm. **Obv:** Value **Rev:** Figures floating in air above flower and sheep **Edge:** Reeded

Date	Mintage	F	VF	XF	Unc	BU
JE5763-2003(u) Proof	Est. 2,000	Value: 55.00				

KM# 384 2 NEW SHEQALIM
28.8000 g., 0.9250 Silver 0.8565 oz. ASW, 38.7 mm. **Obv:** Four windsurfers, value and national arms **Rev:** Eight windsurfers **Edge:** Reeded

Date	Mintage	F	VF	XF	Unc	BU
JE5764-2004(v) Proof	2,800	Value: 55.00				

KM# 387 2 NEW SHEQALIM
28.8000 g., 0.9250 Silver 0.8565 oz. ASW, 38.7 mm. **Subject:** Biblical Burning Bush **Obv:** Burning twig and value **Rev:** Burning Bush **Edge:** Reeded

Date	Mintage	F	VF	XF	Unc	BU
JE5764-2004(v) Proof	Est. 1,800	Value: 55.00				

KM# 407 2 NEW SHEQALIM
28.8000 g., 0.9250 Silver 0.8565 oz. ASW, 38.7 mm. **Subject:** FIFA 2006 World Cup **Obv:** Value and soccer ball **Rev:** Map and soccer ball **Edge:** Reeded

Date	Mintage	F	VF	XF	Unc	BU
JE5764-2004(u) Proof	Est. 5,000	Value: 65.00				
Note: Issued in 2006						

KM# 413 2 NEW SHEQALIM
28.8000 g., 0.9250 Silver 0.8565 oz. ASW, 38.7 mm. **Subject:** Noami Shemer **Obv:** Value **Rev:** Portrait of Naomi Shemer **Edge:** Reeded

Date	Mintage	F	VF	XF	Unc	BU
JE5765-2005 Proof	Est. 1,800	Value: 60.00				

KM# 397 2 NEW SHEQALIM
28.8000 g., 0.9250 Silver 0.8565 oz. ASW, 38.7 mm. **Subject:** Einstein's Relativity Theory **Obv:** Concentric circles above equation **Rev:** Value above signature

Date	Mintage	F	VF	XF	Unc	BU
JE5765-2005(v) Proof	2,800	Value: 60.00				

KM# 400 2 NEW SHEQALIM
28.8000 g., 0.9250 Silver 0.8565 oz. ASW, 38.7 mm. **Subject:** Moses and Ten Commandments **Obv:** Ten Commandments and value **Rev:** Moses and Ten Commandments

Date	Mintage	F	VF	XF	Unc	BU
JE5765-2005(u) Proof	Est. 1,800	Value: 60.00				

KM# 403 2 NEW SHEQALIM
28.8000 g., 0.9250 Silver 0.8565 oz. ASW, 38.7 mm. **Subject:** Israel 57th Anniversary **Obv:** Value and olive branch **Rev:** Twisted olive tree **Edge:** Reeded

Date	Mintage	F	VF	XF	Unc	BU
JE5765-2005(u) Proof	Est. 1,800	Value: 60.00				

KM# 435 2 NEW SHEQALIM
5.6000 g., Nickel Plated Steel, 21.48 mm. **Obv:** Large value **Rev:** Small national arms above stylized double cornucopiae **Edge:** Segmented reeding

Date	Mintage	F	VF	XF	Unc	BU
JE5765(2005)	—	—	—	—	1.50	—

KM# 417 2 NEW SHEQALIM
28.8000 g., 0.9250 Silver 0.8565 oz. ASW, 38.7 mm. **Series:** Independence Day **Subject:** Higher Education in Israel **Obv:** Value and design **Rev:** Symbols of Science, Humanities, Technology and Mathematics **Edge:** Reeded

Date	Mintage	F	VF	XF	Unc	BU
JE5766-2006(ig) Proof	Est. 1,200	Value: 65.00				

KM# 410 2 NEW SHEQALIM
28.8000 g., 0.9250 Silver 0.8565 oz. ASW, 38.7 mm. **Series:** Biblical Art **Subject:** Abraham and the Three Angels **Obv:** Value and stars **Rev:** Abraham and the three angels **Edge:** Reeded

Date	Mintage	F	VF	XF	Unc	BU
JE5766-2006(ig) Proof	Est. 2,800	Value: 65.00				

KM# 420 2 NEW SHEQALIM
28.8000 g., 0.9250 Silver 0.8565 oz. ASW, 38.7 mm. **Subject:** UNESCO World Heritage Site, White Cityof Tel Aviv **Obv:** Value and Bauhaus building **Rev:** Fall of Bauhaus building and UNESCO symbl **Edge:** Reeded

Date	Mintage	F	VF	XF	Unc	BU
JE5766-2006 Proof	Est. 1,200	Value: 75.00				

KM# 424 2 NEW SHEQALIM
Silver, 38.7 mm. **Subject:** Performing Arts in Israel **Obv:** Value, state emblem and inscriptions **Rev:** Stylized actor, dancer and musician and inscription in Hebrew, English and Arabiv **Rev. Inscription:** Performing Arts in Israel **Edge:** Reeded

Date	Mintage	F	VF	XF	Unc	BU
JE5767-2007 Proof	Est. 1,200	Value: 75.00				

KM# 427 2 NEW SHEQALIM
28.8000 g., 0.8565 Silver 0.7930 oz. ASW, 38.7 mm. **Subject:** 2008 Olympics - Judo **Obv:** Value, state emblem, judo belt and inscriptions **Rev:** 2 judo athletes and inscriptions **Rev. Inscription:** The Olympic Delegation of Israel and "Judo" in Hebrew, English and Arabic **Edge:** Reeded

Date	Mintage	F	VF	XF	Unc	BU
JE5767-2007 Proof	Est. 6,000	Value: 75.00				

KM# 430 2 NEW SHEQALIM
28.8000 g., 0.8565 Silver 0.7930 oz. ASW, 38.7 mm. **Subject:** Biblical Art - Isaiah, Wolf with the Lamb **Obv:** Value, state emblem and inscriptions in Hebrew, English and Arabic **Obv. Inscription:** And the Wolf shall dwell with the lamb **Rev:** Wolf and lamb lying together under a tree **Edge:** Reeded

Date	Mintage	F	VF	XF	Unc	BU
JE5767-2007 Proof	Est. 2,800	Value: 80.00				

KM# 432 2 NEW SHEQALIM
5.7000 g., Nickel-Plated Steel, 21.6 mm. **Subject:** Hanukka **Obv:** Value, date, inscriptions and menorah **Rev:** Double cornucopiae (horns of plenty) draped in ribbons and filled with fruit and grain including a pomegranate **Edge:** Plain with 4 notches

Date	Mintage	F	VF	XF	Unc	BU
JE5768 (2008)	3,000	—	—	—	3.00	—
Note: In sets only						

KM# 433 2 NEW SHEQALIM
5.7000 g., Nickel-Plated Steel, 21.6 mm. **Obv:** Value, date and inscriptions **Rev:** Double cornucopiae (horns of plenty) draped in ribbons and filled with fruit and grain including a pomegranate **Edge:** Plain with 4 notches

Date	Mintage	F	VF	XF	Unc	BU
JE5768 (2008)	—	—	—	—	1.50	—

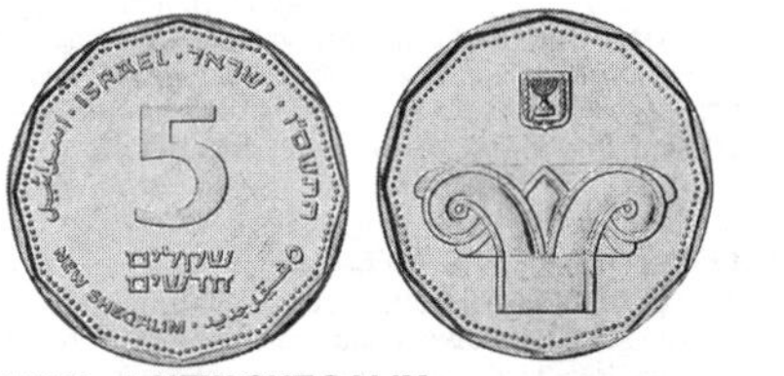

KM# 207 5 NEW SHEQALIM
8.1800 g., Copper-Nickel, 24 mm. **Obv:** Value **Rev:** Ancient column capitol **Edge:** Plain **Shape:** 12-sided

Date	Mintage	F	VF	XF	Unc	BU
JE5762 (2002)(o)	4,464,000	—	—	—	3.75	—
Note: The JE5762 coins are practically round.						
JE5765 (2005)	—	—	—	—	3.00	—
JE5766 (2006)	—	—	—	—	3.00	—

KM# 217 5 NEW SHEQALIM
Copper-Nickel, 24 mm. **Obv:** Value **Rev:** Ancient column capitol **Note:** Coins dated JE5754-5768 have the Star of David mint mark; the JE5751-5753 coins do not.

Date	Mintage	F	VF	XF	Unc	BU
JE5762 (2002)(u)	4,000	—	—	—	3.75	—
Note: In sets only						
JE5763 (2003)(u)	3,000	—	—	—	3.75	—
Note: In sets only						
JE5764 (2004)(u)	3,000	—	—	—	3.75	—
Note: In sets only						
JE5765 (2005)(u)	2,500	—	—	—	3.75	—
Note: In sets only						
JE5766 (2006)(u)	3,000	—	—	—	3.75	—
Note: In sets only						
JE5767 (2007)(u)	3,000	—	—	—	3.75	—
Note: In sets only						
JE5768 (2008)	3,000	—	—	—	3.75	—
Note: In sets only						

KM# 408 5 NEW SHEQALIM
7.7770 g., 0.9990 Gold 0.2498 oz. AGW, 27 mm. **Subject:** FIFA 2006 World Cup **Obv:** Value and soccer ball **Rev:** Map and soccer ball **Edge:** Reeded **Note:** Issued in 2006

Date	Mintage	F	VF	XF	Unc	BU
JE5764-2004 Proof	Est. 777	Value: 350				

KM# 315 10 NEW SHEQALIM
Bi-Metallic Aureate bonded Bronze center in Nickel bonded Steel ring, 22.5 mm. **Subject:** Hanukkah **Obv:** Value, text and menorah within circle and vertical lines **Rev:** Palm tree and baskets within half beaded circle

Date	Mintage	F	VF	XF	Unc	BU
JE5761 (2001)(u)	4,000	—	—	—	8.00	—
Note: In sets only						
JE5762 (2002)(u)	4,000	—	—	—	8.00	—
Note: In sets only						
JE5763 (2003)(u)	3,000	—	—	—	8.00	—
Note: In sets only						
JE5764 (2004)(u)	3,000	—	—	—	8.00	—
Note: In sets only						
JE5765 (2005)(u)	2,500	—	—	—	8.00	—
Note: In sets only						

Date	Mintage	F	VF	XF	Unc	BU
JE5766 (2006)(u)	3,000	—	—	—	8.00	—
Note: In sets only						
JE5766 (2008)(u)	3,000	—	—	—	8.00	—
Note: In sets only						
JE5765 (2007)(u)	3,000	—	—	—	8.00	—
Note: In sets only						

KM# 346 10 NEW SHEQALIM
16.9600 g., 0.9170 Gold 0.5000 oz. AGW, 30 mm. **Subject:** Independence Day and Education **Obv:** Value **Rev:** Pomegranate full of symbols - Hebrew for 'ABC - 123', etc. **Edge:** Reeded **Designer:** Asher Kalderon

Date	Mintage	F	VF	XF	Unc	BU
JE5761-2001(u) Proof	660	Value: 650				

KM# 353 10 NEW SHEQALIM
16.9600 g., 0.9170 Gold 0.5000 oz. AGW, 30 mm. **Subject:** Music **Obv:** National arms and value **Rev:** Musical instruments **Edge:** Reeded

Date	Mintage	F	VF	XF	Unc	BU
JE5761-2001(u) Proof	766	Value: 700				

KM# 358 10 NEW SHEQALIM
16.9600 g., 0.9166 Gold 0.4998 oz. AGW, 30 mm. **Subject:** Independence - Volunteering **Obv:** Value **Rev:** Heart in hands **Edge:** Reeded

Date	Mintage	F	VF	XF	Unc	BU
JE5762-2002 Proof	617	Value: 650				

KM# 361 10 NEW SHEQALIM
16.9600 g., 0.9170 Gold 0.5000 oz. AGW, 30 mm. **Subject:** Tower of Babel **Obv:** National arms in spiral inscription **Rev:** Tower of Hebrew verses **Edge:** Reeded

Date	Mintage	F	VF	XF	Unc	BU
JE5762-2002(o) Proof	750	Value: 700				

KM# 270 10 NEW SHEQALIM
7.0000 g., Bi-Metallic Aureate bonded Bronze center in Nickel bonded Steel ring, 22.95 mm. **Obv:** Value, vertical lines and text within circle **Rev:** Palm tree and baskets within half beaded circle **Edge:** Reeded

Date	Mintage	F	VF	XF	Unc	BU
JE5762 (2002)(h)	4,749,000	—	—	—	5.00	—
JE5765 (2005)	—	—	—	—	5.00	—
Note: Coin alignment error exists. Value: $500.						
JE5766 (2006)	—	—	—	—	5.00	—

KM# 373 10 NEW SHEQALIM
16.9600 g., 0.9170 Gold 0.5000 oz. AGW, 30 mm. **Subject:** Space Exploration **Obv:** "Eros" satellite in orbit **Rev:** "Shavit" rocket **Edge Lettering:** Hebrew: In memory of Ilan Ramon and his colleagues in the Columbia"

Date	Mintage	F	VF	XF	Unc	BU
JE5763-2003(v) Proof	575	Value: 650				

KM# 376 10 NEW SHEQALIM
16.9600 g., 0.9170 Gold 0.5000 oz. AGW, 30 mm. **Obv:** Value **Rev:** Jacob and Rachel floating in air above tree and sheep **Edge:** Reeded

Date	Mintage	F	VF	XF	Unc	BU
JE5763-2003(u) Proof	686	Value: 700				

KM# 379 10 NEW SHEQALIM

16.9600 g., 0.9170 Gold 0.5000 oz. AGW, 30 mm. **Obv:** Value **Rev:** Architectural design **Edge:** Reeded

Date	Mintage	F	VF	XF	Unc	BU
JE5764-2004(u) Proof	555	Value: 700				

KM# 382 10 NEW SHEQALIM

16.9600 g., 0.9170 Gold 0.5000 oz. AGW, 30 mm. **Obv:** Value **Rev:** Stylized parent and child **Edge:** Reeded

Date	Mintage	F	VF	XF	Unc	BU
JE5764-2004(u) Proof	555	Value: 700				

KM# 385 10 NEW SHEQALIM

16.9600 g., 0.9170 Gold 0.5000 oz. AGW, 30 mm. **Obv:** Four windsurfers, value and national arms **Rev:** Eight windsurfers **Edge:** Reeded

Date	Mintage	F	VF	XF	Unc	BU
JE5764-2004(v) Proof	555	Value: 700				

KM# 388 10 NEW SHEQALIM

16.9600 g., 0.9170 Gold 0.5000 oz. AGW, 30 mm. **Subject:** Biblical Burning Bush **Obv:** Burning twig and value **Rev:** Burning Bush **Edge:** Reeded

Date	Mintage	F	VF	XF	Unc	BU
JE5764-2004(v) Proof	555	Value: 700				

KM# 398 10 NEW SHEQALIM

16.9600 g., 0.9166 Gold 0.4998 oz. AGW, 30 mm. **Subject:** Einstein's Relativity Theory **Obv:** Concentric circles above equation **Rev:** Value above signature

Date	Mintage	F	VF	XF	Unc	BU
JE5765-2005(v) Proof	555	Value: 750				

KM# 401 10 NEW SHEQALIM

16.9600 g., 0.9166 Gold 0.4998 oz. AGW, 30 mm. **Series:** Biblical Art **Subject:** Moses and Ten Commandments **Obv:** Ten Commandments and value **Rev:** Moses and Ten Commandments

Date	Mintage	F	VF	XF	Unc	BU
JE5765-2005(u) Proof	555	Value: 700				

KM# 404 10 NEW SHEQALIM

16.9600 g., 0.9166 Gold 0.4998 oz. AGW, 30 mm. **Series:** Independence Day **Subject:** Israel 57th Anniversary **Obv:** Value and olive branch **Rev:** Twisted olive tree **Edge:** Reeded

Date	Mintage	F	VF	XF	Unc	BU
JE5765-2005(u) Proof	555	Value: 600				

KM# 414 10 NEW SHEQALIM

16.9600 g., 0.9170 Gold 0.5000 oz. AGW, 30 mm. **Subject:** Naomi Shemer **Obv:** Value **Rev:** Portrait of Naomi Shemer **Edge:** Reeded

Date	Mintage	F	VF	XF	Unc	BU
JE5765-2005 Proof	Est. 555	Value: 600				

KM# 418 10 NEW SHEQALIM

16.9600 g., 0.9170 Gold 0.5000 oz. AGW, 30 mm. **Series:** Independence Day **Subject:** Higher Education in Israel **Obv:** Value and design **Rev:** Symbols of Science, Humanities, Technology and Mathamatics **Edge:** Reeded

Date	Mintage	F	VF	XF	Unc	BU
JE5766-2006 Proof	Est. 444	Value: 650				

KM# 411 10 NEW SHEQALIM

16.9600 g., 0.9170 Gold 0.5000 oz. AGW, 30 mm. **Subject:** Abraham and the Three Angels **Obv:** Value and stars **Rev:** Abraham and the three angels **Edge:** Reeded

Date	Mintage	F	VF	XF	Unc	BU
JE5766-2006 Proof	Est. 555	Value: 725				

KM# 421 10 NEW SHEQALIM

16.9600 g., 0.9170 Gold 0.5000 oz. AGW, 30 mm. **Subject:** UNESCO World Heritage Site, White City Tel Aviv **Obv:** Value and Bauhaus building **Rev:** Face of Bauhaus building and UNESCO symbol **Edge:** Reeded

Date	Mintage	F	VF	XF	Unc	BU
JE5766-2006 Proof	Est. 555	Value: 660				

KM# 425 10 NEW SHEQALIM

16.9600 g., 0.9170 Gold 0.5000 oz. AGW, 30 mm. **Subject:** Independence Day - Performing Arts in Israel **Obv:** Value, state emblem and inscriptions **Rev:** Stylized actor, dancer and musician and inscription in Hebrew, English and Arabic **Rev. Inscription:** Performing Arts in Israel **Edge:** Reeded

Date	Mintage	F	VF	XF	Unc	BU
JE5767-2007 Proof	Est. 444	Value: 750				

KM# 428 10 NEW SHEQALIM

16.9600 g., 0.9170 Gold 0.5000 oz. AGW, 30 mm. **Subject:** 2008 Olympics - Judo **Obv:** Value, state emblem, judo belt and inscriptions **Rev:** 2 judo athletes and inscriptions in Hebrew, English and Arabic **Rev. Inscription:** "The Olympic Delegation of Israel" and "Judo" **Edge:** Reeded

Date	Mintage	F	VF	XF	Unc	BU
5767-2007 Proof	Est. 555	Value: 750				

KM# 431 10 NEW SHEQALIM

16.9600 g., 0.9170 Gold 0.5000 oz. AGW, 30 mm. **Subject:** Biblical Art - Isaiah, Wolf with the Lamb **Obv:** Value, state emblem and inscriptions in Hebrew, English and Arabic **Obv. Inscription:** "and the Wolf shall dwell with the lamb" **Rev:** Wolf and lamb lying together under a tree **Edge:** Reeded

Date	Mintage	F	VF	XF	Unc	BU
JE5767-2007 Proof	Est. 555	Value: 800				

MINT SETS

KM#	Date	Mintage	Identification	Issue Price	Mkt Val
MS60	JE5761 (2001) (7)	—	KM#163, 172-174, 217, 315, 354 (plastic case)	38.00	40.00
MS62	JE5762 (2002) (7)	—	KM#163, 172-174, 217, 315, 355 (plastic case)	38.00	40.00
MS63	JE5761-5762 (2001-02) (9)	3,000	KM#157, 158, 160 (5761), 159-159, 160a, 207, 270 (5762)	—	25.00
MS65	JE5763 (2003) (7)	—	KM#163, 172-174, 217, 315, 389 (plastic case)	38.00	38.00
MS67	JE5764 (2004) (7)	—	KM#163, 172-174, 217, 315, 390 (plastic case)	38.00	38.00
MS69	JE5765 (2005) (7)	—	KM#163, 172-174, 317, 315, 391 (plastic case)	38.00	38.00
MS70	JE5764-5765 (2004-05) (6)	3,000	KM#158, 159 (5764), 157, 160a, 207, 270 (5765)	35.00	35.00
MS71	JE5766 (2006) (7)	3,000	KM#163, 172-174, 217, 315 (folder)	39.00	39.00
MS72	JE5766 (2006) (7)	—	KM#163, 172-174, 217, 315 (plastic case)	38.00	38.00
MS73	JE5766 (2006) (6)	2,000	KM#157-159, 160a, 207, 270	35.00	35.00
MS74	JE5767 (2007) (7)	3,000	KM#163, 172-174, 217, 315 (folder)	39.00	39.00

MINT SETS NON-STANDARD METALS

KM#	Date	Mintage	Identification	Issue Price	Mkt Val
MS58	JE5761-62 (2001-02) (9)	3,000	KM#157 (2 pcs), 158 (2 pcs), 159, 160a (2 pcs), 207, 270 mixed date set	—	—
MS56	JE5760 (2000) (4)	3,000	KM#157, 158, 160A, 207 Contains 2001 ANA issue	—	—
MS57	JE5760 (2000) (7)	5,000	KM163, 172-174, 217, 315, 332	—	30.00
MS59	JE5761 (2001) (7)	4,000	KM#163, 172-174, 217, 315, 354 (folder)	39.00	39.00
MS61	JE5762 (2002) (7)	4,000	KM#163, 172-174, 217, 315, 355 (folder)	39.00	40.00
MS64	JE5763 (2003) (7)	3,000	KM#163, 172-174, 217, 315, 389 (folder)	39.00	39.00
MS66	JE5764 (2004) (7)	3,000	KM#163, 172-174, 217, 315, 390 (folder)	39.00	39.00
MS68	JE5765 (2005) (7)	2,500	KM#163, 172-174, 217, 315, 391 (folder)	39.00	39.00

ITALY

The Italian Republic, a 700-mile-long peninsula extending into the heart of the Mediterranean Sea, has an area of 116,304 sq. mi. (301,230 sq. km.) and a population of 60 million. Capital: Rome. The economy centers around agriculture, manufacturing, forestry and fishing. Machinery, textiles, clothing and motor vehicles are exported.

MINT

R - Rome

REPUBLIC

DECIMAL COINAGE

KM# 91 LIRA

0.6200 g., Aluminum, 17 mm. **Obv:** Balance scales **Rev:** Cornucopia, value and date **Designer:** Giuseppe Romagnoli **Note:** The 1968-1969 and 1982-2001 dates were issued in sets only.

Date	Mintage	F	VF	XF	Unc	BU
2001R Proof	10,000	Value: 40.00				
2001R	100,000	—	—	—	30.00	—

KM# 219 LIRA

11.0000 g., 0.8350 Silver 0.2953 oz. ASW, 29 mm. **Subject:** History of the Lira - Lira of 1946 (KM#87) **Obv:** Head with laureate left within circle **Rev:** Apple on branch within circle flanked by sprigs **Edge:** Reeded **Note:** This is a Lira Series reproducing an old coin design in the center of each coin.

Date	Mintage	F	VF	XF	Unc	BU
2001R	50,000	—	—	—	50.00	—
2001R Proof	6,100	Value: 170				

KM# 220 LIRA

6.0000 g., 0.8350 Silver 0.1611 oz. ASW, 24 mm. **Subject:** History of the Lira - Lira of 1951 (KM#91) **Obv:** Balance scale within circle **Rev:** Value and cornucopia within circle **Edge:** Reeded **Note:** This is a Lira Series reproducing an old coin design in the center of each coin.

Date	Mintage	F	VF	XF	Unc	BU
2001R	50,000	—	—	—	50.00	—
2001R Proof	6,100	Value: 170				

KM# 87a LIRA

8.0000 g., 0.9000 Gold 0.2315 oz. AGW, 21.6 mm. **Obv:** Ceres **Rev:** Orange on branch **Edge:** Plain **Note:** Official Restrike

Date	Mintage	F	VF	XF	Unc	BU
1946 (2006)R Proof	1,999	Value: 400				

KM# 91a LIRA
4.0000 g., 0.9000 Gold 0.1157 oz. AGW, 17.2 mm. **Obv:** Balance scale **Rev:** Cornucopia, date and value **Edge:** Plain **Note:** Official Restrike

Date	Mintage	F	VF	XF	Unc	BU
1951 (2006)R Proof	1,999	Value: 250				

KM# 94 2 LIRE
0.8000 g., Aluminum **Obv:** Honey bee **Rev:** Olive branch and value **Note:** The 1968-1969 and 1982-2001 dates were issued in sets only.

Date	Mintage	F	VF	XF	Unc	BU
2001R Proof	10,000	Value: 40.00				
2001R	100,000	—	—	—	18.00	—

KM# 88a 2 LIRE
11.0000 g., 0.9000 Gold 0.3183 oz. AGW, 24.1 mm. **Obv:** Farmer plowing field **Rev:** Wheat ear **Edge:** Plain **Note:** Official Restrike

Date	Mintage	F	VF	XF	Unc	BU
1946 (2006)R Proof	1,999	Value: 700				

KM# 94a 2 LIRE
5.0000 g., 0.9000 Gold 0.1447 oz. AGW, 18.3 mm. **Obv:** Honey bee **Rev:** Olive branch **Edge:** Reeded **Note:** Official Restrike

Date	Mintage	F	VF	XF	Unc	BU
1953 (2006)R Proof	1,999	Value: 300				

KM# 92 5 LIRE
1.0350 g., Aluminum, 20.12 mm. **Obv:** Rudder **Rev:** Dolphin and value **Edge:** Plain **Designer:** Giuseppe Romagnoli

Date	Mintage	F	VF	XF	Unc	BU
2001R	100,000	—	—	—	12.00	—
2001R Proof	10,000	Value: 20.00				

KM# 89a 5 LIRE
16.0000 g., 0.9000 Gold 0.4630 oz. AGW, 26.7 mm. **Obv:** Italia with torch **Rev:** Bunch of grapes **Edge:** Reeded **Note:** Official Restrike

Date	Mintage	F	VF	XF	Unc	BU
1946 (2006)R Proof	1,999	Value: 1,000				

KM# 92a 5 LIRE
6.0000 g., 0.9000 Gold 0.1736 oz. AGW, 20.2 mm. **Obv:** Rudder **Rev:** Dolphin and value **Edge:** Plain **Note:** Official Restrike

Date	Mintage	F	VF	XF	Unc	BU
1951 (2006)R Proof	1,999	Value: 400				

KM# 93 10 LIRE
1.6000 g., Aluminum, 23.25 mm. **Obv:** Plow **Rev:** Value within wheat ears **Edge:** Plain **Designer:** Giuseppe Romagnoli

Date	Mintage	F	VF	XF	Unc	BU
2001R Proof	10,000	Value: 35.00				
2001R	100,000	—	—	—	12.00	—

KM# 90a 10 LIRE
19.0000 g., 0.9000 Gold 0.5498 oz. AGW, 29 mm. **Obv:** Pegasus **Rev:** Olive branch **Edge:** Lettered **Edge Lettering:** REPVBBLICA ITALIANA **Note:** Official Restrike

Date	Mintage	F	VF	XF	Unc	BU
1946 (2006)R Proof	1,999	Value: 1,000				

KM# 93a 10 LIRE
10.0000 g., 0.9000 Gold 0.2893 oz. AGW, 23.3 mm. **Obv:** Plow **Rev:** Value within wheat ears **Edge:** Plain **Note:** Official Restrike

Date	Mintage	F	VF	XF	Unc	BU
1951 (2006)R Proof	1,999	Value: 600				

KM# 97.2 20 LIRE
3.6000 g., Aluminum-Bronze, 19.63 mm. **Obv:** Wheat sprigs within head left **Rev:** Oak leaves divide value and date **Edge:** Plain **Designer:** Pietro Giampaoli

Date	Mintage	F	VF	XF	Unc	BU
2001R Proof	10,000	Value: 35.00				
2001R	100,000	—	—	—	12.00	—

KM# 97.1a 20 LIRE
8.0000 g., 0.9000 Gold 0.2315 oz. AGW, 21.3 mm. **Obv:** Head laureate left **Rev:** Oak leaves divides date and value **Edge:** Reeded **Note:** Official Restrike

Date	Mintage	F	VF	XF	Unc	BU
1957 (2006)R Proof	1,999	Value: 500				

KM# 183 50 LIRE
Copper-Nickel, 19 mm. **Obv:** Turreted head left **Rev:** Large value within wreath of produce **Designer:** L. Cretara

Date	Mintage	F	VF	XF	Unc	BU
2001R Proof	10,000	Value: 35.00				
2001R	100,000	—	—	—	12.00	—

KM# 95.1a 50 LIRE
14.0000 g., 0.9000 Gold 0.4051 oz. AGW, 24.8 mm. **Obv:** Italia **Rev:** Vulcan **Edge:** Reeded **Note:** Official Restrike

Date	Mintage	F	VF	XF	Unc	BU
1954 (2006)R Proof	1,999	Value: 500				

KM# 183a 50 LIRE
9.0000 g., 0.9000 Gold 0.2604 oz. AGW, 19.2 mm. **Obv:** Roma **Rev:** Value within wreath **Edge:** Plain **Note:** Official Restrike

Date	Mintage	F	VF	XF	Unc	BU
1996 (2006)R Proof	1,999	Value: 500				

KM# 159 100 LIRE
Copper-Nickel, 22 mm. **Obv:** Turreted head left **Rev:** Large value within circle flanked by sprigs **Designer:** Laura Cretara

Date	Mintage	F	VF	XF	Unc	BU
2001R	100,000	—	—	—	12.00	—
2001R Proof	10,000	Value: 35.00				

KM# 96.1a 100 LIRE
18.0000 g., 0.9000 Gold 0.5208 oz. AGW, 27.8 mm. **Obv:** Ancient athlete **Rev:** Minerva standing **Edge:** Reeded **Note:** Official Restrike

Date	Mintage	F	VF	XF	Unc	BU
1955 (2006)R Proof	1,999	Value: 1,000				

KM# 159a 100 LIRE
9.0000 g., 0.9000 Gold 0.2604 oz. AGW, 22 mm. **Obv:** Turreted head left **Rev:** Large value within circle flanked by sprigs **Edge:** Segmented reeding **Note:** Official Restrike

Date	Mintage	F	VF	XF	Unc	BU
1993 (2006)R Proof	1,999	Value: 500				

KM# 105 200 LIRE
5.0000 g., Aluminum-Bronze, 24 mm. **Obv:** Head right **Rev:** Value within gear **Designer:** M. Vallucci

Date	Mintage	F	VF	XF	Unc	BU
2001R Proof	10,000	Value: 35.00				
2001R	100,000	—	—	—	18.00	—

KM# 105a 200 LIRE
11.0000 g., 0.9000 Gold 0.3183 oz. AGW, 24 mm. **Obv:** Head right **Rev:** Value within gear **Edge:** Reeded **Note:** Official Restrike

Date	Mintage	F	VF	XF	Unc	BU
1977 (2006)R Proof	1,999	Value: 700				

KM# 98 500 LIRE
11.0000 g., 0.8350 Silver 0.2953 oz. ASW, 29.3 mm. **Obv:** Columbus' ships **Obv. Designer:** Guido Veroi **Rev:** Bust left within wreath **Rev. Designer:** Pietro Giampaoli **Edge:** Dates in raised lettering

Date	Mintage	F	VF	XF	Unc	BU
2001R	100,000	—	—	—	40.00	—
2001R Proof	10,000	Value: 200				

KM# 111 500 LIRE
6.8000 g., Bi-Metallic Bronzital center in Acmonital ring, 25.8 mm. **Obv:** Head left within circle **Rev:** Plaza within circle flanked by sprigs **Designer:** Cretara

Date	Mintage	F	VF	XF	Unc	BU
2001R	100,000	—	—	—	12.00	—
2001R Proof	10,000	Value: 35.00				

KM# 98a 500 LIRE
18.0000 g., 0.9000 Gold 0.5208 oz. AGW, 29 mm. **Obv:** Columbus' ships **Rev:** Bust left within wreath **Edge:** Lettered **Edge Lettering:** REPVBBLICA ITALIANA *** 1958*** **Note:** Official Restrike

Date	Mintage	F	VF	XF	Unc	BU
1958 (2006)R Proof	1,999	Value: 1,000				

KM# 99a 500 LIRE
18.0000 g., 0.9000 Gold 0.5208 oz. AGW, 29 mm. **Obv:** Seated Italia **Rev:** Lady **Edge:** Lettered **Edge Lettering:** "1 CENTENARIO VNITA'D'ITALIA * 1861-1961* " **Note:** Official Restrike

Date	Mintage	F	VF	XF	Unc	BU
1961 (2006)R Proof	1,999	Value: 1,000				

KM# 100a 500 LIRE
18.0000 g., 0.9000 Gold 0.5208 oz. AGW, 29 mm. **Obv:** Dante **Rev:** Hell **Edge:** Lettered **Edge Lettering:** "7 CENTENARIO DELLA NASCITA DI DANTE" **Note:** Official Restrike

Date	Mintage	F	VF	XF	Unc	BU
1965 (2006)R Proof	1,999	Value: 1,000				

KM# 111a 500 LIRE
14.0000 g., Bi-Metallic .750 Gold center in .900 Gold ring, 25.8 mm. **Obv:** Head left within circle **Rev:** Plaza within circle flanked by sprigs **Edge:** Segmented reeding **Note:** Official Restrike

Date	Mintage	F	VF	XF	Unc	BU
1982 (2006)R Proof	1,999	Value: 270				

KM# 194 1000 LIRE
Bi-Metallic Copper-Nickel center in Aluminum-Bronze ring, 27 mm. **Subject:** European Union **Obv:** Head left within circle **Obv. Designer:** Laura Cretara **Rev:** Corrected map with United Germany within globe design **Rev. Designer:** Pernazza

Date	Mintage	F	VF	XF	Unc	BU
2001R	100,000	—	—	—	10.00	—
2001R Proof	10,000	Value: 35.00				

KM# 236 1000 LIRE
14.6000 g., 0.8350 Silver 0.3919 oz. ASW, 31.4 mm. **Obv:** Giuseppe Verdi **Rev:** Building

Date	Mintage	F	VF	XF	Unc	BU
2001R Proof	10,000	Value: 250				
2001R	115,000	—	—	—	80.00	—

KM# 101a 1000 LIRE
24.0000 g., 0.9000 Gold 0.6944 oz. AGW, 31.4 mm. **Obv:** Concordia **Rev:** Geometric shape above value **Edge:** Lettered **Edge Lettering:** "REPVBBLICA ITALIANA"

Date	Mintage	F	VF	XF	Unc	BU
1970 (2006)R Proof	1,999	Value: 1,200				

KM# 190a 1000 LIRE
17.0000 g., 0.9000 Gold 0.4919 oz. AGW, 27 mm. **Obv:** Roma **Rev:** European map **Edge:** Segmented reeding **Note:** Official Restrike

Date	Mintage	F	VF	XF	Unc	BU
1997 (2006)R Proof	1,999	Value: 475				

KM# 234 50000 LIRE
7.5000 g., 0.9000 Gold 0.2170 oz. AGW, 20 mm. **Subject:** 250th Anniversary - Palace of Caserta **Obv:** Front view of palace **Rev:** Fountain, date and denomination

Date	Mintage	F	VF	XF	Unc	BU
2001R Proof	6,200	Value: 450				

KM# 233 100000 LIRE
15.0000 g., 0.9000 Gold 0.4340 oz. AGW, 25 mm. **Subject:** 700th Anniversary - Pulpit at the Church of St. Andrea a Pistoia **Obv:** Full pulpit **Rev:** Enlarged detail of the pulpit

Date	Mintage	F	VF	XF	Unc	BU
2001R Proof	4,500	Value: 600				

EURO COINAGE

European Union Issues

KM# 210 EURO CENT

2.3000 g., Copper Plated Steel, 16.2 mm. **Obv:** Castle del Monte **Obv. Designer:** Eugenio Drutti **Rev:** Value and globe **Rev. Designer:** Luc Luycx **Edge:** Plain

Date	Mintage	F	VF	XF	Unc	BU
2002R	1,348,899,500	—	—	—	0.25	—
2003R	9,629,000	—	—	—	0.35	—
2003R Proof	12,000	Value: 10.00				
2004R	100,000,000	—	—	—	0.25	—
2004R Proof	—	Value: 7.00				
2005R	180,000,000	—	—	—	0.35	—
2005R Proof	12,000	Value: 5.00				
2006R	159,000,000	—	—	—	0.25	—
2006R Proof	—	Value: 5.00				
2007R	140,000,000	—	—	—	0.25	—
2007R Proof	—	Value: 5.00				
2008R	—	—	—	—	0.25	—
2008R Proof	—	Value: 5.00				

KM# 211 2 EURO CENT

3.0300 g., Copper Plated Steel, 18.7 mm. **Obv:** Observation tower in Turin **Obv. Designer:** Luciana de Simoni **Rev:** Value and globe **Rev. Designer:** Luc Luycx **Edge:** Plain

Date	Mintage	F	VF	XF	Unc	BU
2002R	1,099,166,250	—	—	—	0.25	—
2003R	21,817,000	—	—	—	0.25	—
2003R Proof	12,000	Value: 10.00				
2004R	120,000,000	—	—	—	0.25	—
2004R Proof	—	Value: 7.00				
2005R	120,000,000	—	—	—	0.25	—
2005R Proof	12,000	Value: 5.00				
2006R	196,000,000	—	—	—	0.25	—
2006R Proof	—	Value: 5.00				
2007R	140,000,000	—	—	—	0.25	—
2007R Proof	—	Value: 5.00				
2008R	—	—	—	—	0.25	—
2008R Proof	—	Value: 5.00				

KM# 212 5 EURO CENT

3.9500 g., Copper Plated Steel, 19.64 mm. **Obv:** Colosseum **Obv. Designer:** Lorenzo Frapiccini **Rev:** Value and globe **Rev. Designer:** Luc Luycx **Edge:** Plain

Date	Mintage	F	VF	XF	Unc	BU
2002R	1,341,742,204	—	—	—	0.25	—
2003R	1,960,000	—	—	—	0.50	—
2003R Proof	12,000	Value: 12.00				
2004R	10,000,000	—	—	—	0.50	—
2004R Proof	—	Value: 8.00				
2005R	70,000,000	—	—	—	0.50	—
2005R Proof	12,000	Value: 6.00				
2006R	119,000,000	—	—	—	0.50	—
2006R Proof	—	Value: 6.00				
2007R	85,000,000	—	—	—	0.50	—
2007R Proof	—	Value: 6.00				
2008R	—	—	—	—	0.50	—
2008R Proof	—	Value: 6.00				

KM# 213 10 EURO CENT

4.0700 g., Brass, 19.7 mm. **Obv:** Venus by Botticelli **Obv. Designer:** Claudia Momoni **Rev:** Value and map **Rev. Designer:** Luc Luycx **Edge:** Reeded

Date	Mintage	F	VF	XF	Unc	BU
2002R	1,142,383,000	—	—	—	0.25	—
2003R	29,976,000	—	—	—	0.50	—
2003R Proof	12,000	Value: 15.00				
2004R	5,000,000	—	—	—	0.50	—
2004R Proof	—	Value: 12.00				
2005R	100,000,000	—	—	—	0.50	—
2005R Proof	12,000	Value: 7.00				
2006R	180,000,000	—	—	—	0.50	—
2006R Proof	—	Value: 7.00				
2007R	105,000,000	—	—	—	0.50	—
2007R Proof	—	Value: 7.00				

KM# 247 10 EURO CENT

4.0700 g., Brass, 19.7 mm. **Obv:** Venus by Botticelli **Obv. Designer:** Claudia Momoni **Rev:** Relief Map of Western Europe, stars, lines and value **Rev. Designer:** Luc Luycx **Edge:** Reeded

Date	Mintage	F	VF	XF	Unc	BU
2008R	—	—	—	—	0.25	—

KM# 214 20 EURO CENT

5.7300 g., Brass, 22.1 mm. **Obv:** Futuristic sculpture **Obv. Designer:** Maria Cassol **Rev:** Value and map **Rev. Designer:** Luc Luycx **Edge:** Notched

Date	Mintage	F	VF	XF	Unc	BU
2002R	1,411,836,000	—	—	—	0.30	—
2003R	26,155,000	—	—	—	0.50	—
2003R Proof	12,000	Value: 16.00				
2004R	5,000,000	—	—	—	0.50	—
2004R Proof	—	Value: 14.00				
2005R	5,000,000	—	—	—	0.50	—
2005R Proof	12,000	Value: 8.00				
2006R	5,000,000	—	—	—	0.50	—
2006R Proof	—	Value: 8.00				
2007R	5,000,000	—	—	—	0.50	—
2007R Proof	—	Value: 8.00				

KM# 248 20 EURO CENT

5.7300 g., Brass, 22.1 mm. **Obv:** Futuristic sculpture **Obv. Designer:** Maria Cassoll **Rev:** Relief map of Western Europe, stars, lines and value **Rev. Designer:** Luc Luycx **Edge:** Reeded

Date	Mintage	F	VF	XF	Unc	BU
2008R	—	—	—	—	1.00	—

KM# 215 50 EURO CENT

7.8100 g., Brass, 24.2 mm. **Obv:** Sculpture of Marcus Aurelius on horseback **Obv. Designer:** Roberto Mauri **Rev:** Value and map **Rev. Designer:** Luc Luycx **Edge:** Reeded

Date	Mintage	F	VF	XF	Unc	BU
2002R	1,136,718,000	—	—	—	0.80	—
2003R	44,825,000	—	—	—	1.00	—
2003R Proof	12,000	Value: 18.00				
2004R	5,000,000	—	—	—	1.00	—
2004R Proof	—	Value: 16.00				
2005R	5,000,000	—	—	—	1.00	—
2005R Proof	12,000	Value: 10.00				
2006R	5,000,000	—	—	—	1.00	—
2006R Proof	—	Value: 10.00				
2007R	5,000,000	—	—	—	1.00	—
2007R Proof	—	Value: 10.00				

KM# 249 50 EURO CENT

7.8100 g., Brass, 24.2 mm. **Obv:** Sculpture of Marcus Aurelius on horseback **Obv. Designer:** Roberto Mauri **Rev:** Relief map of Western Europe, stars, lines and value **Rev. Designer:** Luc Luycx **Edge:** Reeded

Date	Mintage	F	VF	XF	Unc	BU
2008R	—	—	—	—	1.25	—

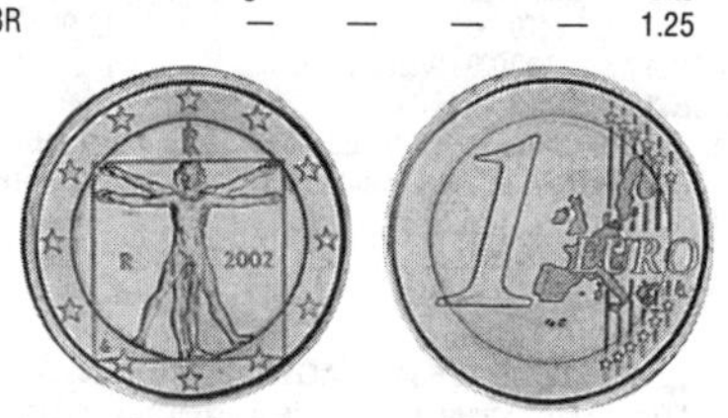

KM# 216 EURO

7.5000 g., Bi-Metallic Copper-Nickel center in Brass ring, 23.2 mm. **Obv:** Male figure drawing by Leonardo da Vinci within circle of stars **Obv. Designer:** Laura Cretara **Rev:** Value and map within circle **Rev. Designer:** Luc Luycx **Edge:** Reeded and plain sections

Date	Mintage	F	VF	XF	Unc	BU
2002R	966,025,300	—	—	—	1.60	—
2003R	66,474,000	—	—	—	2.00	—
2003R Proof	12,000	Value: 20.00				
2004R	5,000,000	—	—	—	2.00	—
2004R Proof	—	Value: 18.00				
2005R	5,000,000	—	—	—	2.00	—
2005R Proof	12,000	Value: 15.00				
2006R	108,000,000	—	—	—	2.00	—
2006R Proof	—	Value: 15.00				
2007R	135,000,000	—	—	—	2.00	—
2007R Proof	—	Value: 15.00				

KM# 250 EURO

7.5000 g., Bi-Metallic Copper-Nickel center in Brass ring, 23.2 mm. **Obv:** Male figure drawing by Leonardo da Vinci **Obv. Designer:** Laura Cretara **Rev:** Relief map of Western Europe, stars, lines and value **Rev. Designer:** Luc Luycx **Edge:** Reeded and plain sections

Date	Mintage	F	VF	XF	Unc	BU
2008R	—	—	—	—	2.50	—

KM# 217 2 EURO

8.5200 g., Bi-Metallic Brass center in Copper-Nickel ring, 25.7 mm. **Obv:** Head left within circle **Obv. Designer:** Maria Colanieri **Rev:** Value and map within circle **Rev. Designer:** Luc Luycx **Edge:** Reeded **Edge Lettering:** 2's and stars

Date	Mintage	F	VF	XF	Unc	BU
2002R	463,702,000	—	—	—	3.00	—
2003R	36,160,000	—	—	—	3.00	—
2003R Proof	12,000	Value: 25.00				
2004R	2,000,000	—	—	—	3.00	—
2004R Proof	—	Value: 22.00				
2005R	80,000,000	—	—	—	3.00	—
2005R Proof	12,000	Value: 20.00				
2006R	50,000,000	—	—	—	3.00	—
2006R Proof	—	Value: 20.00				
2007R	5,000,000	—	—	—	3.00	—
2007R Proof	—	Value: 20.00				

KM# 237 2 EURO

8.5300 g., Bi-Metallic Aluminum-Bronze center in Copper-Nickel ring, 25.7 mm. **Obv:** World Food Program globe within circle **Rev:** Value and map within circle **Edge:** Reeded and lettered **Edge Lettering:** 2's and stars

Date	Mintage	F	VF	XF	Unc	BU
2004R	160,000,000	—	—	—	3.50	—

KM# 245 2 EURO

8.5200 g., Bi-Metallic Brass center in Copper-Nickel ring, 25.6 mm. **Subject:** European Constitution **Obv:** Europa holding an open book while sitting on a bull within circle **Rev:** Value and map within circle **Edge:** Reeding over stars and 2's

Date	Mintage	F	VF	XF	Unc	BU
2005R	—	—	—	—	4.50	—

KM# 246 2 EURO

8.5100 g., Bi-Metallic Brass center in Copper-Nickel ring, 25.7 mm. **Subject:** Torino Winter Olympics **Obv:** Skier and other designs within circle **Rev:** Value and map within circle **Edge:** Reeded with stars and 2's

Date	Mintage	F	VF	XF	Unc	BU
2006R	—	—	—	—	6.00	—

KM# 251 2 EURO

8.5200 g., Bi-Metallic Brass center in Copper-Nickel ring, 25.7 mm. **Obv:** Bust of Danta Aligheri **Obv. Designer:** Maria Colanieri **Rev:** Relief map of Western Europe, stars, lines and value **Rev. Designer:** Luc Luycx **Edge:** Reeded **Edge Lettering:** 2's and stars

Date	Mintage	F	VF	XF	Unc	BU
2008R	—	—	—	—	3.75	—

KM# 253 5 EURO

18.0000 g., 0.9250 Silver 0.5353 oz. ASW, 32 mm. **Subject:** Work in Europe

Date	Mintage	F	VF	XF	Unc	BU
2003R	50,000	—	—	—	30.00	—
2003R Proof	12,000	Value: 65.00				

KM# 252 5 EURO

18.0000 g., 0.9250 Silver 0.5353 oz. ASW, 32 mm. **Subject:** People in Europe

Date	Mintage	F	VF	XF	Unc	BU
2003R	25,000	—	—	—	75.00	—

KM# 254 5 EURO

18.0000 g., 0.9250 Silver 0.5353 oz. ASW, 32 mm. **Subject:** 50th Anniversary of Italian Television

Date	Mintage	F	VF	XF	Unc	BU
2004R	40,000	—	—	—	30.00	—
2004R Proof	15,000	Value: 65.00				

KM# 238 5 EURO

18.0000 g., 0.9250 Silver 0.5353 oz. ASW, 32 mm. **Subject:** World Cup Soccer - Germany 2006 **Obv:** St. Croce Square in Florence **Rev:** Soccer ball and world globe design

Date	Mintage	F	VF	XF	Unc	BU
2004R Proof	35,000	Value: 95.00				

KM# 239 5 EURO

18.0000 g., 0.9250 Silver 0.5353 oz. ASW, 32 mm. **Subject:** Madam Butterfly **Obv:** Large building **Rev:** Geisha

Date	Mintage	F	VF	XF	Unc	BU
2004R Proof	12,000	Value: 30.00				
2004R	30,000	—	—	—	25.00	—

KM# 255 5 EURO

18.0000 g., 0.9250 Silver 0.5353 oz. ASW, 32 mm. **Subject:** 85th Birthday of Fed. Fellini

Date	Mintage	F	VF	XF	Unc	BU
2005R	35,000	—	—	—	30.00	—
2005R Proof	22,000	Value: 60.00				

KM# 256 5 EURO

18.0000 g., 0.9250 Silver 0.5353 oz. ASW, 32 mm. **Subject:** 2006 Olympic Winter Games Torino Ski Jump

Date	Mintage	F	VF	XF	Unc	BU
2005R	35,000	—	—	—	30.00	—
2005R Proof	40,000	Value: 50.00				

KM# 257 5 EURO

18.0000 g., 0.9250 Silver 0.5353 oz. ASW, 32 mm. **Subject:** 2006 Olympic Winter Games Cross Country Skiing

Date	Mintage	F	VF	XF	Unc	BU
2005R	35,000	—	—	—	30.00	—
2005R Proof	40,000	Value: 50.00				

KM# 266 5 EURO

18.0000 g., 0.9250 Silver 0.5353 oz. ASW, 32 mm. **Subject:** 2006 Olympic Games Torino Figure Skating

Date	Mintage	F	VF	XF	Unc	BU
2005	40,000	—	—	—	30.00	—

KM# 258 10 EURO

22.0000 g., 0.9250 Silver 0.6542 oz. ASW, 34 mm. **Subject:** People In Europe

Date	Mintage	F	VF	XF	Unc	BU
2003R Proof	8,000	Value: 140				

KM# 259 10 EURO

22.0000 g., 0.9250 Silver 0.6542 oz. ASW, 34 mm. **Subject:** Italian Presidenty of E.U.

Date	Mintage	F	VF	XF	Unc	BU
2003R	40,000	—	—	—	42.00	—
2003R Proof	8,000	Value: 120				

KM# 240 10 EURO

22.0000 g., 0.9250 Silver 0.6542 oz. ASW, 34 mm. **Subject:** City of Genoa **Obv:** Sculpture and art works **Rev:** Tower and harbor map

Date	Mintage	F	VF	XF	Unc	BU
2004R Proof	12,000	Value: 60.00				
2004R	30,000	—	—	—	50.00	—

KM# 241 10 EURO

22.0000 g., 0.9250 Silver 0.6542 oz. ASW, 34 mm. **Subject:** Giacomo Puccini **Obv:** Pucini wearing hat **Rev:** Stage, music and quill

Date	Mintage	F	VF	XF	Unc	BU
2004R	30,000	—	—	—	35.00	—
2004R Proof	12,000	Value: 40.00				

KM# 260 10 EURO

22.0000 g., 0.9250 Silver 0.6542 oz. ASW, 34 mm. **Subject:** 2006 Olympic Winter Games Torino Alpine Skiing

Date	Mintage	F	VF	XF	Unc	BU
2005R	40,000	—	—	—	60.00	—
2005R Proof	40,000	Value: 70.00				

KM# 261 10 EURO

22.0000 g., 0.9250 Silver 0.6542 oz. ASW, 34 mm. **Subject:** 2006 Olympic Winter Games Torino Ice Hockey

Date	Mintage	F	VF	XF	Unc	BU
2005R	35,000	—	—	—	60.00	—
2005R Proof	40,000	Value: 70.00				

KM# 262 10 EURO

22.0000 g., 0.9250 Silver 0.6542 oz. ASW, 34 mm. **Subject:** 2006 Olympic Winter Games Torino Speed Skating

Date	Mintage	F	VF	XF	Unc	BU
2005R	35,000	—	—	—	65.00	—
2005R Proof	40,000	Value: 70.00				

KM# 268 10 EURO

22.0000 g., 0.9250 Silver 0.6542 oz. ASW, 34 mm. **Subject:** 60th Anniversary UN "ONU"

Date	Mintage	F	VF	XF	Unc	BU
2005	25,000	—	—	—	40.00	—

KM# 271 10 EURO

22.0000 g., 0.9250 Silver 0.6542 oz. ASW, 34 mm. **Subject:** Peace and Freedom In Europe

Date	Mintage	F	VF	XF	Unc	BU
2005 Proof	20,000	Value: 55.00				

KM# 263 20 EURO

6.4510 g., 0.9000 Gold 0.1867 oz. AGW, 21 mm. **Subject:** Arts in Europe - Italy

Date	Mintage	F	VF	XF	Unc	BU
2003R Proof	6,000	Value: 360				

KM# 242 20 EURO

6.4510 g., 0.9000 Gold 0.1867 oz. AGW, 21 mm. **Obv:** Arts In Europe: Belgium **Rev:** Flying bird obscuring a man's face

Date	Mintage	F	VF	XF	Unc	BU
2004R Proof	6,000	Value: 300				

KM# 243 20 EURO

6.4510 g., 0.9000 Gold 0.1867 oz. AGW, 21 mm. **Subject:** World Cup Soccer - Germany 2006 **Obv:** Mascot **Rev:** Soccer ball and world globe

Date	Mintage	F	VF	XF	Unc	BU
2004R Proof	7,500	Value: 300				

KM# 265 20 EURO

6.4510 g., 0.9000 Gold 0.1867 oz. AGW, 54 mm. **Subject:** 2006 Olympic Winter Games Torino Porte Palatine Gate

Date	Mintage	F	VF	XF	Unc	BU
2005R Proof	10,000	Value: 250				

KM# 267 20 EURO

6.4510 g., 0.9000 Gold 0.1867 oz. AGW, 21 mm. **Subject:** 2006 Olympic Games Torino Madama Palace

Date	Mintage	F	VF	XF	Unc	BU
2005 Proof	10,000	Value: 250				

KM# 269 20 EURO

6.4510 g., 0.9000 Gold 0.1867 oz. AGW, 21 mm. **Subject:** 2006 Olympic Games Torino Stupinigi Palace

Date	Mintage	F	VF	XF	Unc	BU
2005 Proof	10,000	Value: 250				

KM# 272 20 EURO

6.4510 g., 0.9000 Gold 0.1867 oz. AGW, 21 mm. **Subject:** Art In Europe - Finland

Date	Mintage	F	VF	XF	Unc	BU
2005 Proof	5,000	Value: 250				

KM# 264 50 EURO

16.1300 g., 0.9900 Gold 0.5134 oz. AGW, 28 mm. **Subject:** Arts in Europe - Austria

Date	Mintage	F	VF	XF	Unc	BU
2003R Proof	6,000	Value: 600				

KM# 244 50 EURO

16.1300 g., 0.9000 Gold 0.4667 oz. AGW, 28 mm. **Obv:** Arts In Europe: Denmark **Rev:** Angel carrying away two children

Date	Mintage	F	VF	XF	Unc	BU
2004R Proof	6,000	Value: 600				

KM# 270 50 EURO

16.1300 g., 0.9000 Gold 0.4667 oz. AGW, 28 mm. **Subject:** 2006 Olympic Games Torino Emanuele Filiberto

Date	Mintage	F	VF	XF	Unc	BU
2005 Proof	6,000	Value: 600				

KM# 273 50 EURO

16.1300 g., 0.9000 Gold 0.4667 oz. AGW, 28 mm. **Subject:** Art In Europe - France

Date	Mintage	F	VF	XF	Unc	BU
2005 Proof	5,000	Value: 600				

KM# 274 50 EURO

16.1300 g., 0.9000 Gold 0.4667 oz. AGW, 28 mm. **Subject:** 2006 Olympic Games Torino Olympic Torch

Date	Mintage	F	VF	XF	Unc	BU
2006 Proof	5,000	Value: 600				

MINT SETS

KM#	Date	Mintage	Identification	Issue Price	Mkt Val
MS39	2001 (12)	125,200	KM#91-94, 97.2, 98, 105, 111, 159, 183, 194, 236	—	100
MS40	2002 (8)	50,000	KM#210-217	—	20.00
MS41	2003 (8)	50,000	KM#210-217	—	20.00
MS42	2003 (9)	50,000	KM#210-217, 253	—	70.00
MS43	2004 (8)	40,000	KM#210-217	—	35.00
MS44	2004 (9)	40,000	KM#210-217, 254	—	70.00
MS45	2005 (8)	35,000	KM#210-217	—	28.00
MS46	2005 (9)	35,000	KM#210-217, 255	—	64.00
MS47	2006 (8)	25,000	KM#210-217	—	28.00
MS48	2007 (8)	—	KM#210-217	—	28.00

PROOF SETS

KM#	Date	Mintage	Identification	Issue Price	Mkt Val
PS25	2001 (12)	10,000	KM#91-94, 97.2, 98, 105, 111, 159, 183, 194, 236	—	450
PS26	2003 (9)	12,000	KM#210-217, 253	—	175
PS27	2004 (9)	15,000	KM#210-217, 254	—	160
PS28	2005 (9)	12,000	KM#210-217, 255	—	135
PS29	2006 (8)	10,000	KM#210-217	—	75.00
PS30	2007 (8)	—	KM#210-217	—	75.00

JAMAICA

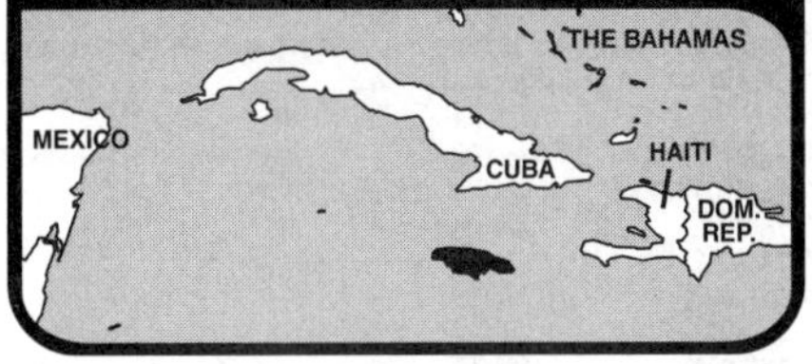

Jamaica is situated in the Caribbean Sea 90 miles south of Cuba, has an area of 4,244 sq. mi. (10,990 sq. km.) and a population of 2.1 million. Capital: Kingston. The economy is founded chiefly on mining, tourism and agriculture. Aluminum, bauxite, sugar, rum and molasses are exported.

Jamaica is a member of the Commonwealth of Nations. Elizabeth II is the Head of State, as Queen of Jamaica.

RULER

British, until 1962

MINT MARKS

C - Royal Canadian Mint, Ottawa
H - Heaton

MONETARY SYSTEM

(Commencing 1969)
100 Cents = 1 Dollar

COMMONWEALTH

DECIMAL COINAGE

The Franklin Mint and Royal Mint have both been striking the 1 Cent through 1 Dollar coinage. The 1970 issues were all struck with dies similar to/or Royal Mint without the FM mint mark. The Royal Mint issues have the name JAMAICA extending beyond the native headdress feathers. Those struck after 1970 by the Franklin Mint have the name JAMAICA within the headdress feathers.

KM# 64 CENT

1.2000 g., Aluminum, 20.05 mm. **Ruler:** Elizabeth II **Series:** F.A.O. **Obv:** Arms with supporters **Rev:** Ackee fruit above value **Edge:** Plain **Shape:** 12-sided **Designer:** Christopher Ironside

Date	Mintage	F	VF	XF	Unc	BU
2002 Proof	500	Value: 1.00				
2002	—	—	—	0.25	0.50	0.75

KM# 146.2 10 CENTS

2.4500 g., Copper Plated Steel, 17 mm. **Ruler:** Elizabeth II **Subject:** Paul Bogle **Obv:** Arms with supporters **Rev:** Bust facing **Edge:** Plain **Note:** Reduced size.

Date	Mintage	F	VF	XF	Unc	BU
2002 Proof	500	Value: 2.00				
2002	—	—	—	0.25	0.50	0.75

KM# 167 25 CENTS

3.6500 g., Copper Plated Steel, 19.97 mm. **Ruler:** Elizabeth II **Subject:** Marcus Garvey **Obv:** Arms with supporters **Rev:** Head 1/4 right **Edge:** Plain

Date	Mintage	F	VF	XF	Unc	BU
2002 Proof	500	Value: 3.00				
2002	—	—	—	0.25	0.50	0.75

KM# 164 DOLLAR

2.9400 g., Nickel Clad Steel, 18.47 mm. **Ruler:** Elizabeth II **Obv:** Arms with supporters **Rev:** Bust facing **Edge:** Plain **Shape:** 7-sided

Date	Mintage	F	VF	XF	Unc	BU
2002 Proof	500	Value: 4.00				
2002	—	—	—	1.00	1.25	1.50
2005	—	—	—	1.00	1.25	1.50

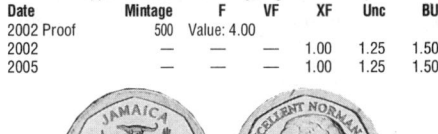

KM# 163 5 DOLLARS

Steel, 21.5 mm. **Ruler:** Elizabeth II **Obv:** Arms with supporters **Rev:** Head left

Date	Mintage	F	VF	XF	Unc	BU
2002 Proof	500	Value: 5.00				
2002	—	—	—	1.50	2.50	3.50

KM# 181 10 DOLLARS

6.1000 g., Stainless Steel **Ruler:** Elizabeth II **Obv:** Arms with supporters **Rev:** Bust facing **Shape:** Scalloped

Date	Mintage	F	VF	XF	Unc	BU
2002	—	—	—	1.50	3.00	4.00
2002 Proof	500	Value: 9.00				

KM# 182 20 DOLLARS

Center Weight: 7.8000 g. **Center Composition:** Bi-Metallic Copper-Nickel center with Brass Ring, 23 mm. **Ruler:** Elizabeth II **Obv:** Value above arms with supporters within circle **Rev:** Head 1/4 right within circle **Edge:** Alternate reeding and plain

Date	Mintage	F	VF	XF	Unc	BU
2001	—	—	—	1.50	3.00	4.00
2002	—	—	—	1.50	3.00	4.00
2002 Proof	500	Value: 15.00				

KM# 186 25 DOLLARS

28.2800 g., 0.9250 Silver 0.8410 oz. ASW, 38.6 mm. **Ruler:** Elizabeth II **Subject:** UNICEF **Obv:** Arms with supporters **Rev:** Two boys above "Pals" **Edge:** Reeded

Date	Mintage	F	VF	XF	Unc	BU
2001 Proof	—	Value: 50.00				

KM# 185 25 DOLLARS

28.2800 g., 0.9250 Silver 0.8410 oz. ASW, 38.6 mm. **Ruler:** Elizabeth II **Subject:** IAAF World Junior Championships **Obv:** Arms with supporters and value **Rev:** Female runner **Edge:** Reeded

Date	Mintage	F	VF	XF	Unc	BU
2002 Proof	5,500	Value: 50.00				

KM# 184 50 DOLLARS

28.4500 g., 0.9250 Silver 0.8461 oz. ASW, 38.6 mm. **Ruler:** Elizabeth II **Subject:** Millennium **Obv:** Arms with supporters **Rev:** Family within radiant sun **Edge:** Reeded

Date	Mintage	F	VF	XF	Unc	BU
ND(2002) Proof	5,000	Value: 50.00				

PROOF SETS

KM#	Date	Mintage	Identification	Issue Price	Mkt Val
PS33	2002 (8)	500	KM#64, 146.2, 163, 164, 167, 181, 182, 185	99.00	100

JAPAN

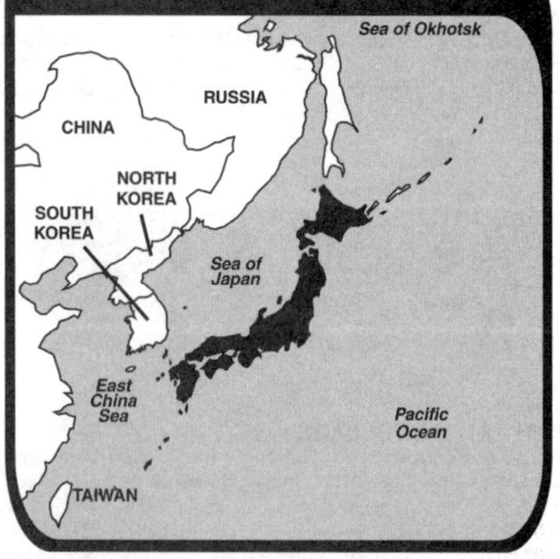

Japan, a constitutional monarchy situated off the east coast of Asia, has an area of 145,809 sq. mi. (377,835 sq. km.) and a population of 123.2 million. Capital: Tokyo. Japan, one of the major industrial nations of the world, exports machinery, motor vehicles, electronics and chemicals.

Japanese coinage of concern to this catalog includes those issued for the Ryukyu Islands (also called Liuchu), a chain of islands extending southwest from Japan toward Taiwan (Formosa), before the Japanese government converted the islands into a prefecture under the name Okinawa. Many of the provinces of Japan issued their own definitive coinage under the Shogunate.

RULERS

Emperors

Akihito (Heisei), 1989-

平成

Years 1 –

NOTE: The personal name of the emperor is followed by the name that he chose for his regnal era.

MONETARY UNITS

Rin 厘

Sen 銭

Yen 円 or 圓 or 圓

DATING

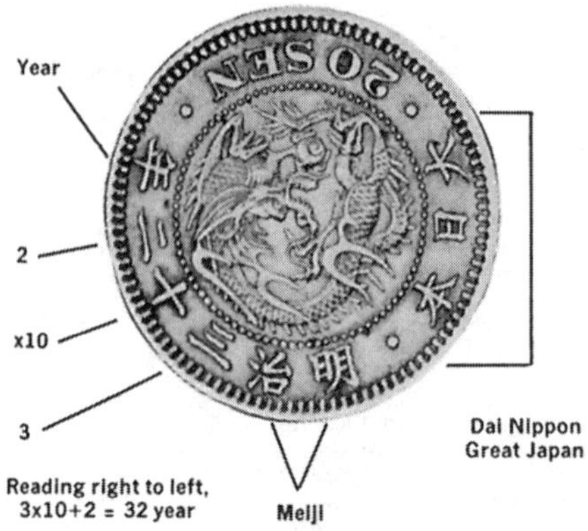

EMPIRE

REFORM COINAGE

Y# 95.2 YEN

1.0000 g., Aluminum, 20 mm. **Ruler:** Akihito (Heisei) **Obv:** Sprouting branch divides authority and value **Rev:** Value within circles above date **Edge:** Plain

Date	Mintage	F	VF	XF	Unc	BU
Yr,13(2001)	7,786,000	—	—	0.70	—	1.50
Yr.13(2001) Proof	8,024,000	Value: 3.00				
Yr.14(2002)	9,425,000	—	—	—	—	0.50
Yr.14(2002) Proof	242,000	Value: 3.00				
Yr.15(2003)	117,131,000	—	—	—	—	0.50
Yr.15(2003) Proof	275,000	Value: 3.00				
Yr.16(2004)	52,623,000	—	—	—	—	0.50
Yr.16(2004) Proof	280,000	Value: 3.00				
Yr.17(2005)	29,761,000	—	—	—	—	0.50
Yr.17(2005) Proof	258,000	Value: 3.00				
Yr.18(2006)	—	—	—	—	—	0.50
Yr.18(2006) Proof	246,000	Value: 3.00				
Yr.19(2007)	—	—	—	—	—	0.50
Yr.19(2007) Proof	—	Value: 3.00				

Y# 96.2 5 YEN

3.7500 g., Brass, 22 mm. **Ruler:** Akihito (Heisei) **Obv:** Hole in center flanked by a seed leaf with authority on top and date below **Rev:** Gear design around center hole with bending rice stalk above value in horizontal lines below

Date	Mintage	F	VF	XF	Unc	BU
Yr.13(2001)	78,025,000	—	—	—	—	0.35
Yr.13(2001) Proof	238,000	Value: 1.75				
Yr.14(2002)	143,423,000	—	—	—	—	0.35
Yr.14(2002) Proof	242,000	Value: 1.75				
Yr.15(2003)	102,406,000	—	—	—	—	0.35
Yr.15(2003) Proof	275,000	Value: 1.75				
Yr.16(2004)	70,623,000	—	—	—	—	0.35
Yr.16(2004) Proof	280,000	Value: 1.75				
Yr.17(2005)	15,761,000	—	—	—	—	0.35
Yr.17(2005) Proof	258,000	Value: 1.75				
Yr.18(2006)	—	—	—	—	—	0.35
Yr.18(2006) Proof	246,000	Value: 1.75				
Yr.19(2007)	—	—	—	—	—	0.35
Yr.19(2007) Proof	—	Value: 1.75				

Y# 97.2 10 YEN

4.5000 g., Bronze, 23.5 mm. **Ruler:** Akihito (Heisei) **Obv:** Temple divides authority and value **Rev:** Value within wreath

Date	Mintage	F	VF	XF	Unc	BU
Yr.13(2001)	542,024,000	—	—	—	—	0.45
Yr.13(2001) Proof	238,000	Value: 1.75				
Yr.14(2002)	455,667,000	—	—	—	—	0.45
Yr.14(2002) Proof	242,000	Value: 1.75				
Yr.15(2003)	551,406,000	—	—	—	—	0.45
Yr.15(2003) Proof	275,000	Value: 1.75				
Yr.16(2004)	592,623,000	—	—	—	—	0.45
Yr.16(2004) Proof	280,000	Value: 1.75				
Yr.17(2005)	503,761,000	—	—	—	—	0.45
Yr.17(2005) Proof	258,000	Value: 1.75				
Yr.18(2006)	—	—	—	—	—	0.45
Yr.18(2006) Proof	246,000	Value: 1.75				
Yr.19(2007)	—	—	—	—	—	0.45
Yr.19(2007) Proof	—	Value: 1.75				

Y# 101.2 50 YEN

4.0000 g., Copper-Nickel, 21 mm. **Ruler:** Akihito (Heisei) **Obv:** Center hole flanked by chrysanthemums, authority at top and value below **Rev:** Value above hole in center

Date	Mintage	F	VF	XF	Unc	BU
Yr.13(2001)	8,024,000	—	—	—	—	3.00
Yr.13(2001) Proof	238,000	Value: 4.00				
Yr.14(2002)	11,667,000	—	—	—	—	5.00
Yr.14(2002) Proof	242,000	Value: 7.00				
Yr.15(2003)	10,406,000	—	—	—	—	5.00
Yr.15(2003) Proof	275,000	Value: 7.00				
Yr.16(2004)	9,623,000	—	—	—	—	5.00
Yr.16(2004) Proof	280,000	Value: 7.00				
Yr.17(2005)	9,761,000	—	—	—	—	5.00
Yr.17(2005) Proof	258,000	Value: 7.00				
Yr.18(2006)	—	—	—	—	—	5.00
Yr.18(2006) Proof	246,000	Value: 7.00				
Yr.19(2007)	—	—	—	—	—	5.00
Yr.19(2007) Proof	—	Value: 7.00				

Y# 98.2 100 YEN

9.8000 g., Copper-Nickel, 22.6 mm. **Ruler:** Akihito (Heisei) **Obv:** Cherry blossoms **Rev:** Large numeral 100

Date	Mintage	F	VF	XF	Unc	BU
Yr.13(2001)	8,024,000	—	—	—	—	7.50
Yr.13(2001) Proof	238,000	Value: 10.00				
Yr.14(2002)	10,667,000	—	—	—	—	5.00
Yr.14(2002) Proof	242,000	Value: 8.00				
Yr.15(2003)	98,406,000	—	—	—	—	2.00
Yr.15(2003) Proof	275,000	Value: 5.00				
Yr.16(2004)	204,623,000	—	—	—	—	2.00
Yr.16(2004) Proof	280,000	Value: 5.00				
Yr.17(2005)	299,761,000	—	—	—	—	2.00
Yr.17(2005) Proof	258,000	Value: 5.00				
Yr.18(2006)	—	—	—	—	—	2.00
Yr.18(2006) Proof	246,000	Value: 5.00				
Yr.19(2007)	—	—	—	—	—	2.00
Yr.19(2007) Proof	—	Value: 5.00				

Y# 125 500 YEN

7.0000 g., Nickel-Brass, 26.5 mm. **Ruler:** Akihito (Heisei) **Obv:** Pawlownia flower and highlighted legends **Rev:** Value with latent zeros **Edge:** Slanted reeding

Date	Mintage	F	VF	XF	Unc	BU
Yr.13(2001)	607,813,000	—	—	—	—	9.00
Yr.13(2001) Proof	238,000	Value: 15.00				
Yr.14(2002)	504,419,000	—	—	—	—	9.00
Yr.14(2002) Proof	242,000	Value: 15.00				
Yr.15(2003)	438,130,000	—	—	—	—	9.00
Yr.15(2003) Proof	275,000	Value: 15.00				
Yr.16(2004)	356,623,000	—	—	—	—	9.00
Yr.16(2004) Proof	280,000	Value: 15.00				
Yr.17(2005)	334,762,000	—	—	—	—	9.00

Date	Mintage	F	VF	XF	Unc	BU
Yr.17(2005) Proof	258,000	Value: 15.00				
Yr.18(2006)	—	—	—	—	—	9.00
Yr.18(2006) Proof	246,000	Value: 15.00				
Yr.19(2007)	—	—	—	—	—	9.00
Yr.19(2007) Proof	—	Value: 15.00				

Y# 126 500 YEN
7.0000 g., Copper-Zinc-Nickel, 26.5 mm. **Ruler:** Akihito (Heisei) **Subject:** World Cup Soccer - Europe & Africa **Obv:** Four players and map background **Rev:** Games logo within shooting star wreath **Edge:** Reeded

Date	Mintage	VG	F	VF	XF	BU
Yr.14(2002)	10,000,000	—	—	—	—	10.00

Y# 127 500 YEN
7.0000 g., Copper-Zinc-Nickel, 26.5 mm. **Ruler:** Akihito (Heisei) **Subject:** World Cup Soccer - Asia & Oceania **Obv:** Three players and map background **Rev:** Games logo within shooting star wreath **Edge:** Reeded

Date	Mintage	VG	F	VF	XF	BU
Yr. 14(2002)	10,000,000	—	—	—	—	10.00

Y# 128 500 YEN
7.0000 g., Copper-Zinc-Nickel, 26.5 mm. **Ruler:** Akihito (Heisei) **Subject:** World Cup Soccer - North & South America **Obv:** Four players and map background **Rev:** Games logo **Edge:** Reeded

Date	Mintage	VG	F	VF	XF	BU
Yr. 14 (2002)	10,000,000	—	—	—	—	10.00

Y# 133 500 YEN
7.0000 g., Copper-Zinc-Nickel, 26.5 mm. **Ruler:** Akihito (Heisei) **Subject:** Expo 2005 - Aichi, Japan **Obv:** Pacific map **Rev:** Expo logo

Date	Mintage	VG	F	VF	XF	BU
Yr. 17(2005)	8,241,000	—	—	—	—	10.00

Y# 134 500 YEN
15.6000 g., 0.9990 Silver 0.5010 oz. ASW, 28 mm. **Ruler:** Akihito (Heisei) **Subject:** Chubu National Airport **Obv:** Aircraft wing in flight over airport **Rev:** Aircraft silhouettes over maps

Date	Mintage	F	VF	XF	Unc	BU
Yr. 17(2005) Proof	50,000	Value: 85.00				

Y# 137 500 YEN
7.0000 g., Copper-Zinc-Nickel, 26.5 mm. **Ruler:** Akihito (Heisei) **Subject:** 50th Anniversary of Japanese Antarctic Research **Obv:** Ship and two dogs **Rev:** Map of Antarctica

Date	Mintage	F	VF	XF	Unc	BU
Yr.19(2007)	6,600,000	—	—	—	—	10.00

Y# 129 1000 YEN
31.1000 g., 0.9990 Silver 0.9988 oz. ASW, 40 mm. **Ruler:** Akihito (Heisei) **Subject:** World Cup Soccer **Obv:** Trophy within flower sprigs **Rev:** Games logo flanked by players **Edge:** Reeded

Date	Mintage	F	VF	XF	Unc	BU
Yr. 14 (2002) Proof	100,000	Value: 200				

Y# 132 1000 YEN
31.1000 g., 0.9990 Silver 0.9988 oz. ASW **Ruler:** Akihito (Heisei) **Subject:** 50th Anniversary of the reversion of the Amami Islands **Obv:** Lily and bird in multicolor enamel **Rev:** Map of the Amami-shoto

Date	Mintage	F	VF	XF	Unc	BU
Proof	50,000	Value: 200				

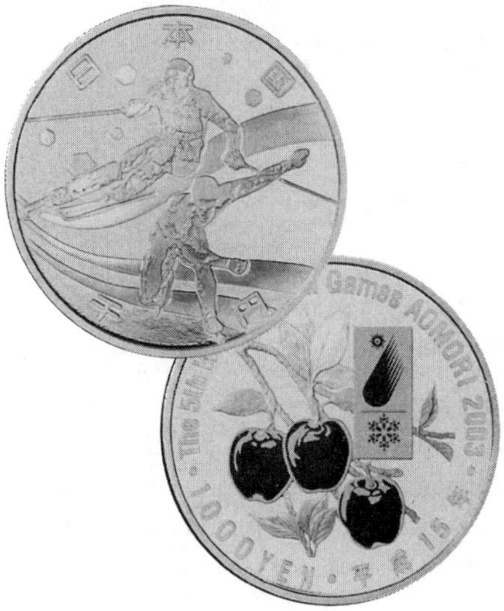

Y# 131 1000 YEN
31.1000 g., 0.9990 Silver 0.9988 oz. ASW **Ruler:** Akihito (Heisei) **Subject:** 5th Winter Asian Games, Aomori **Obv:** Skier and skater **Rev:** Three red apples and multicolor games logo

Date	Mintage	VG	F	VF	XF	BU
Yr.15 (2003) Proof	50,000	Value: 625				

Y# 135 1000 YEN
31.1000 g., 0.9990 Silver 0.9988 oz. ASW, 40 mm. **Ruler:** Akihito (Heisei) **Subject:** Expo 2005 **Obv:** Blue and white enamel Pacific map in wreath **Rev:** Expo logo

Date	Mintage	F	VF	XF	Unc	BU
Yr. 16(2004) Proof	70,000	Value: 165				

Y# 138 1000 YEN
31.1000 g., 1.0000 Silver 0.9998 oz. ASW, 40 mm. **Ruler:** Akihito (Heisei) **Subject:** 50th Anniversary of Japan's Entry into the United Nations **Obv:** Globe and plum blossom wreath (enameled blue, pink and green) **Rev:** UN emblem

Date	Mintage	F	VF	XF	Unc	BU
Yr.18(2006) Proof	70,000	Value: 165				

KM# 142 1000 YEN
31.1000 g., 0.9990 Silver 0.9988 oz. ASW, 40.0 mm. **Ruler:** Akihito (Heisei) **Obv:** Dual multicolor rainbows **Obv. Inscription:** SKILLS / 2007 **Rev:** Mount Fuji **Rev. Legend:** International Skills Festival for All, Japan

Date	Mintage	F	VF	XF	Unc	BU
Yr.19(2007) Proof	80,000	Value: 100				

Y# 130 10000 YEN
15.6000 g., 0.9990 Gold 0.5010 oz. AGW, 26 mm. **Ruler:** Akihito (Heisei) **Subject:** World Cup Soccer **Obv:** Two soccer players **Rev:** Games logo **Edge:** Reeded

Date	Mintage	F	VF	XF	Unc	BU
Yr.14(2002) Proof	100,000	Value: 550				

Y# 136 10000 YEN
15.6000 g., 0.9990 Gold 0.5010 oz. AGW, 26 mm. **Ruler:** Akihito (Heisei) **Subject:** Expo 2005 **Obv:** Two owls on globe **Rev:** Expo logo

Date	Mintage	F	VF	XF	Unc	BU
Yr. 16(2004) Proof	70,000	Value: 700				

MINT SETS

KM#	Date	Mintage	Identification	Issue Price	Mkt Val
MS125	2001 (6)	8,000	Y#95.2-98.2, 101.2, 125 Mint exhibition in Fukuoka	16.00	30.00
MS126	2001 (6)	85,000	Y#95.2-98.2, 101.2, 125 Osaka cherry blossoms box	17.00	30.00
MS127	2001 (6)	10,000	Y#95.2-98.2, 101.2, 125 Hiroshima cherry blossoms box	17.00	33.00
MS128	2001 (6)	10,000	Y#95.2-98.2, 101.2, 125 12th Tokyo International Coin Convention	17.00	30.00
MS129	2001 (6)	5,000	Y#95.2-98.2, 101.2, 125 Beautiful Future Exposition	17.00	30.00
MS130	2001 (6)	8,000	Y#95.2-98.2, 101.2, 125 Kagoshima Coin and Stamp Show	17.00	30.00
MS131	2001 (6)	5,000	Y#95.2-98.2, 101.2, 125 Tokyo Mint Fair	17.00	33.00
MS132	2001 (6)	5,000	Y#95.2-98.2, 101.2, 125 Yamaguchi Mica Exposition	17.00	40.00
MS133	2001 (6)	193,600	Y#95.2-98.2, 101.2, 125 21st Century Commemorative Respect for the Aged	17.00	27.00
MS134	2001 (6)	190,300	Y#95.2-98.2, 101.2, 125 Ryukyu World Cultural Sites	17.00	27.00
MS135	2001 (6)	8,300	Y#95.2-98.2, 101.2, 125 Birthday folder	18.00	33.00
MS136	2001 (1)	4,000	Y#125 Mint Visit Commemorative	8.00	10.00
MS137	2001 (6)	224,000	Y#95.2-98.2, 101.2, 125 Mint Bureau Box	15.00	27.00
MS138	2001 (6)	7,300	Y#95.2-98.2, 101.2, 125 "Japan Coins"	17.00	30.00
MS139	2001 (2)	5,000	Y#96.2, 125 "Japan Coins" (short set)	8.50	13.00
MS140	2001 (6)	128,700	Y#95.2-98.2, 101.2, 125 World Intangible Heritage - Nogaku	17.00	27.00
MS141	2002 (1)	3,000	Y#125 Mint Visit Commemorative	7.50	10.00
MS142	2002 (6)	7,000	Y#95.2-98.2, 102.2, 125 Birthday folder	18.00	27.00
MS143	2002 (2)	4,000	Y#96.2, 125. "Japan Coins" (short set)	8.50	13.00
MS144	2002 (6)	6,000	Y#95.2-98.2, 101.2, 125 "Japan Coins"	17.00	23.00
MS145	2002 (6)	4,000	Y#95.2-98.2, 101.2, 125 Mint exhibition in Takamatsu	16.00	33.00
MS146	2002 (6)	80,000	Y#95.2-98.2, 101.2, 125 Osaka cherry blossoms	16.00	20.00
MS147	2002 (6)	10,000	Y#95.2-98.2, 101.2, 125 Hiroshima cherry blossoms	16.00	23.00
MS148	2002 (6)	10,000	Y#95.2-98.2, 101.2, 125 13th Tokyo Int'l Coin Convention	16.00	20.00

KM#	Date	Mintage	Identification	Issue Price	Mkt Val
MS149	2002 (6)	6,000	Y#95.2-98.2, 101.2, 125 Mint exhibition in Sendai	16.00	23.00
MS150	2002 (6)	194,000	Y#95.2-98.2, 101.2, 125 Respect for the Aged	19.00	20.00
MS151	2002 (6)	6,000	Y#95.2-98.2, 101.2, 125 Matsuyama Coin and Stamp Show	16.00	23.00
MS152	2002 (6)	3,000	Y395.2-98.2, 101.2, 125 Tokyo Mint Fair	16.00	120
MS153	2002 (6)	2,000	Y#95.2-98.2, 101.2, 125 Birthday folder (with sound recording function)	25.00	40.00
MS154	2002 (6)	214,800	Y395.2-98.2, 101.2, 125 Mint Bureau box	15.00	20.00
MS155	2003 (6)	8,000	Y#95.2-98.2, 101.2, 125 "Japan Coins"	17.00	20.00
MS156	2003 (6)	7,000	Y#95.2-98.2, 101.2, 125 Birthday folder	18.00	20.00
MS157	2003 (6)	7,000	Y#95.2-98.2, 101.2, 125 Birthday folder (with sound recording function)	25.00	27.00
MS158	2003 (6)	6,000	Y#95.2-98.2, 101.2, 125 Mint exhibition in Okayama	16.00	30.00
MS159	2003 (6)	80,000	Y#95.2-98.2, 101.2, 125 Osaka cherry blossoms	16.00	20.00
MS160	2003 (6)	10,000	Y#95.2-98.2, 101.2, 125 Hiroshima cherry blossoms	16.00	20.00
MS161	2003 (6)	10,000	Y#95.2-98.2, 101.2, 125 14th Tokyo Int'l Coin Convention	16.00	20.00
MS162	2003 (6)	6,000	Y#95.2-98.2, 101.2, 125 First Osaka Coin Show	16.00	20.00
MS163	2003 (6)	235,000	Y#95.2-98.2, 101.2, 125 Birth of Astro Boy	19.00	20.00
MS164	2003 (6)	130,000	Y#95.2-98.2, 101.2, 125 Respect for the Aged	19.00	17.00
MS165	2003 (6)	5,000	Y#95.2-98.2, 101.2, 125 Tokyo Mint Fair - Mint Collection in Omote-sando	17.00	30.00
MS166	2003 (6)	5,000	Y#95.2-98.2, 101.2, 125 Mint exhibition in Sapporo	17.00	27.00
MS167	2003 (6)	5,000	Y#95.2-98.2, 101.2, 125 Yonago Coin and Stamp Show	17.00	23.00
MS168	2003 (6)	205,000	Y#95.2-98.2, 101.2, 125 Mint Bureau box	17.00	16.00
MS169	2003 (6)	100,000	Y#95.2-98.2, 101.2, 125 2003 Central League Champions - Hanshin Tigers	22.00	27.00
MS170	2003 (6)	100,000	Y#95.2-98.2, 101.2, 125 2003 Pacific league Champions - Fukuoka Daiei Hawks	22.00	16.00
MS171	2003 (6)	5,000	Y#95.2-98.2, 101.2, 126 400th Anniversary of the Estabelishmtn of Government in Edo	22.00	200
MS172	2004	8,000	Y#95.2-98.2, 101.2, 125 Japan Coins	19.00	20.00
MS173	2004 (6)	5,000	Y#95.2-98.2, 101.2, 125 Birthday folder	20.00	22.00
MS174	2004 (6)	5,000	Y#95.2-98.2, 101.2, 125 Birthday folder (with sound recording function)	28.50	27.00
MS175	2004 (6)	4,000	Y#95.2-98.2, 101.2, 125 Mint exhibition in Fukui	18.00	53.00
MS176	2004 (6)	70,000	Y#95.2-98.2, 101.2, 125 Osaka cherry blossoms	18.00	20.00
MS177	2004 (6)	10,000	Y#95.2-98.2, 101.2, 125 Hiroshima cherry blossoms	18.00	20.00
MS178	2004 (6)	10,000	Y#95.2-98.2, 101.2, 125 15th Tokyo Int'l Coin Convention	18.00	20.00
MS179	2004 (6)	6,000	Y#95.2-98.2, 101.2, 125 Second Osaka Coin Show	18.00	20.00
MS180	2004 (6)	100,000	Y#95.2-98.2, 101.2, 125 World Intangible Heritage series: Bunraku puppets	19.00	20.00
MS181	2004 (6)	122,500	Y#95.2-98.2, 101.2, 125 Respect for the Aged	20.00	20.00
MS182	2004 (6)	5,000	Y#95.2-98.2, 101.2, 125 Mint exhibition in Tosu	18.00	23.00
MS183	2004 (6)	189,000	Y#95.2-98.2, 101.2, 125 Mint Bureau box	16.00	17.00
MS184	2004 (6)	5,000	Y#95.2-98.2, 101.2, 125 Gifu Coin and Stamp Show	17.00	23.00
MS185	2004 (6)	226,000	Y#95.2-98.2, 101.2, 125 30th Birthday of Hello Kitty (cartoon character)	22.00	23.00
MS186	2004 (6)	5,000	Y#95.2-98.2, 101.2, 125 Tokyo Mint Fair - 40th Anniversary - Issue of Commemorative Coins	17.00	33.00
MS187	2004 (6)	44,000	Y#95.2-98.2, 101.2, 125 2004 Central League Champions - Chunichi Dragons	21.00	17.00
MS188	2004 (6)	38,500	Y#95.2-98.2, 101.2, 125 2004 Pacific League Champions - Seibu Lions	21.00	17.00
MS189	2005 (6)	200,000	Y#95.2-98.2, 101.2, 133 Expo 2005, Aichi	22.00	23.00
MS190	2005 (6)	8,000	Y#95.2-98.2, 101.2, 125 Japan Coin Set	17.00	16.00
MS191	2005 (6)	5,000	Y#95.2-98.2, 101.2, 125 Birthday folder	19.00	20.00
MS192	2005 (6)	2,000	Y#95.2-98.2, 101.2, 125 Birthday folder (with sound recording function)	27.50	27.00
MS193	2005 (6)	5,000	Y#95.2-98.2, 101.2, 125 Mint exhibition in Shizuoka	17.00	33.00
MS194	2005 (6)	60,000	Y#95.2-98.2, 101.2, 125 Osaka cherry blossoms	17.00	23.00
MS195	2005 (6)	10,000	Y#95.2-98.2, 101.2, 125 Hiroshima Flower Tour	17.00	20.00
MS196	2005 (6)	10,000	Y#95.2-98.2, 101.2, 125 16th Tokyo International Coin Convention	17.00	20.00
MS197	2005 (6)	5,000	Y#95.2-98.2, 101.2, 125 Third Osaka Coin Show	17.00	20.00
MS198	2005 (6)	126,500	Y#95.2-98.2, 101.2, 125 World Intangible Heritage Series: Kii Hills Sacred Places and Pilgrimage Trails	18.00	20.00
MS199	2005 (6)	104,500	Y#95.2-98.2, 101.2, 125 Respect for the Aged	19.00	20.00
MS200	2005 (6)	5,000	Y#95.2-98.2, 101.2, 125 Mint Exhibition in Morioka	18.00	23.00
MS201	2005 (6)	5,000	Y#95.2-98.2, 101.2, 125 Koriyama Coin and Stamp Show	17.00	23.00
MS202	2005 (6)	182,000	Y#95.2-98.2, 101.2, 125 35th Anniversary of Doraemon (cartoon character)	17.00	30.00
MS203	2005 (6)	141,000	Y#95.2-98.2, 101.2, 125 Mint Bureau Box	16.00	18.00
MS204	2005 (6)	75,800	Y#95.2-98.2, 101.2, 125 World Natural Heritage	18.00	20.00
MS205	2005 (6)	5,000	Y#95.2-98.2, 101.2, 125 Mint Bureau Tokyo Fair / 50th Anniversary of One-Yen Aluminum Coin	17.00	40.00
MS206	2005 (6)	83,600	Y#95.2-98.2, 101.2, 125 2005 Central League Champions - Hanshin Tigers	21.00	20.00
MS207	2005 (6)	56,600	Y#95.2-98.2, 101.2, 125 2005 Pacific League Champions - Chiba Lotte Marines	21.00	20.00
MS208	2006 (6)	5,000	Y#95.2-98.2, 101.2, 125 Mint exhibition in Oita	17.00	17.50
MS209	2006 (6)	—	Y#95.2-98.2, 101.2, 125 Japan Coin Set	18.00	18.00
MS210	2006 (6)	—	Y#95.2-98.2, 101.2, 125 Birthday Folder	19.00	20.00
MS211	2006 (6)	189,000	Y#95.2-98.2, 101.2, 125 Mint Bureau box	16.00	17.00
MS212	2006 (6)	66,500	Y#95.2-98.2, 101.2, 125 World Intangible Heritage Series: Kabuki Theater	18.00	18.00
MS213	2006 (6)	60,000	Y#95.2-98.2, 101.2, 125 Osaka Cherry Blossoms	17.00	17.50
MS214	2006 (6)	8,000	Y#95.2-98.2, 101.2, 125 Hiroshima Flower Tour	17.00	17.50
MS215	2006 (6)	8,000	Y#95.2-98.2, 101.2, 125 16th Tokyo International Coin Convention	17.00	18.50
MS216	2006 (6)	85,500	Y#95.2-98.2, 101.2, 125 Respect for the Aged	19.00	20.00
MS217	2006 (6)	4,000	Y#95.2-98.2, 101.2, 125 Third Osaka Coin Show	17.00	18.50
MS218	2006 (6)	4,000	Y#95.2-98.2, 101.2, 125 Mint Exhibition in Kofu	17.00	17.50
MS219	2006 (6)	200,000	Y#95.2-98.2, 101.2, 125 80th Anniversary of Pooh-Bear	22.00	22.50
MS220	2006 (6)	3,500	Y#95.2-98.2, 101.2, 125 Nagasaki Coin and Stamp Show	17.00	17.50
MS221	2007 (6)	100,000	Y#95.2-98.2, 101.2, 125 plus medal	—	45.00

PROOF SETS

KM#	Date	Mintage	Identification	Issue Price	Mkt Val
PS32	2001 (6)	138,000	Y#95.2-98.2, 101.2, 125 Mint Bureau Box	62.50	47.00
PS33	2001 (6)	100,000	Y#95.2-98.2, 101.2, 125 Old Type Coin Series	62.50	53.00
PS37	2002 (3)	200,000	Y#126-128 World Cup	26.00	20.00
PS38	2002 (2)	50,000	Y#129, 130 World Cup	385	550
PS34	2002 (6)	144,000	Y#95.2-98.2, 101.2, 125 Mint Bureau box	62.50	53.00
PS35	2002 (6)	3,000	Y#95.2-98.2, 101.2, 125 15th Anniversary of Proof Sets	62.50	100
PS36	2002 (6)	95,000	Y#95.2-98.2, 101.2, 125 Techno medal set	62.50	53.00
PS39	2003 (6)	105,000	Y#95.2-98.2, 101.2, 125 Mint Bureau box, with date plaquette	67.50	53.00
PS40	2003 (6)	90,000	Y#95.2-98.2, 101.2, 125 Astro Boy	115	100
PS41	2003 (6)	5,000	Y#95.2-98.2, 101.2, 125 Tokyo Mint Fair - Mint Collection in Omote-Sando	67.50	100
PS42	2003 (6)	70,000	Y#95.2-98.2, 101.2, 125 Mickey Mouse	125	120
PS43	2003 (6)	5,000	Y#95.2-98.2, 101.2, 125 400th Anniversary - Establishment of Government in Edo	67.50	165
PS50	2004 (2)	35,000	Y#135-136 Expo 2005, Aichi	425	500
PS44	2004 (6)	108,000	Y#95.2-98.2, 101.2, 125 Mint Bureau box with date plaquette	71.00	60.00
PS45	2004 (6)	—	Y#95.2-98.2, 101.2, 125 Mint Bureau box without date plaquette	70.00	67.00
PS46	2004 (6)	60,000	Y#95.2-98.2, 101.2, 125 70h Anniversary - Pro Baseball	120	145
PS47	2004 (6)	50,000	Y#95.2-98.2, 101.2, 125 Techno Medal Series 2	71.00	60.00
PS48	2004 (6)	50,000	Y#95.2-98.2, 101.2, 125 30th Birthday of Hello Kitty (cartoon character)	120	150
PS49	2004 (6)	5,000	Y#95.2-98.2, 101.2, 125 Tokyo Mint Fair - 40th Anniversary - Issue of Commemorative Coins	71.00	100
PSA40	2003 (6)	—	Y#95.2-98.2, 101.2, 125 Mint Bureau Box without Date Plaquette	66.00	67.00
PS51	2005 (6)	86,700	Y#95.2-98.2, 101.2, 125 Mint Bureau Box with date plaquette	71.00	65.00
PS52	2005 (6)	—	Y#95.2-98.2, 101.2, 125 Mint Bureau Box without date plaquette	70.00	65.00
PS53	2005 (6)	60,000	Y#95.2-98.2, 101.2, 125 35th Anniversary of Doraemon (cartoon character)	125	170
PS54	2005 (6)	34,000	Y#95.2-98.2, 101.2, 125 50th Anniversary of One-Yen Aluminum Coin	125	170
PS55	2005 (6)	30,000	Y#95.2-98.2, 101.2, 125 50th Anniversary of the Pencil Rocket	125	100
PS56	2005 (6)	47,300	Y#95.2-98.2, 101.2, 125 Techno Medal Series #3	71.00	65.00
PS57	2006 (6)	85,000	Y#95.2-98.2, 101.2, 125 Mint Bureau box with date plaquette	71.00	65.00
PS58	2006 (6)	—	Y#95.2-98.2, 101.2, 125 Mint Bureau Box without date plaquette	70.00	65.00
PS59	2006 (6)	35,000	Y#95.2-98.2, 101.2, 125 125th Anniversary of Cherry Blossom Viewing at the Mint	125	125
PS60	2006 (6)	46,000	Y#95.2-98.2, 101.2, 125 includes Australian 1oz Silver coin Australia-Japan Year of Exchange	128	145
PS61	2006 (6)	80,000	Y#95.2-98.2, 101.2, 125 50th Anniversary of Debut of Ishihara Yujiro (film actor)	125	120
PS62	2007 (6)	50,000	Y#95.2-98.2, 101.2, 125 plus medal	—	175
PS63	2007 (7)	—	Y#95.2, 96.2, 97.2, 98.2, 101.2, 125 plus New Zealand KM#232, Aoraki	—	120
PS64	2007 (7)	—	Y#95.2, 96.2, 97.2, 98.2, 101.2, 125, plus medal 11th IAAF World Championships in Athletics, Osaka, plastic display case w/leather	—	95.00

JERSEY

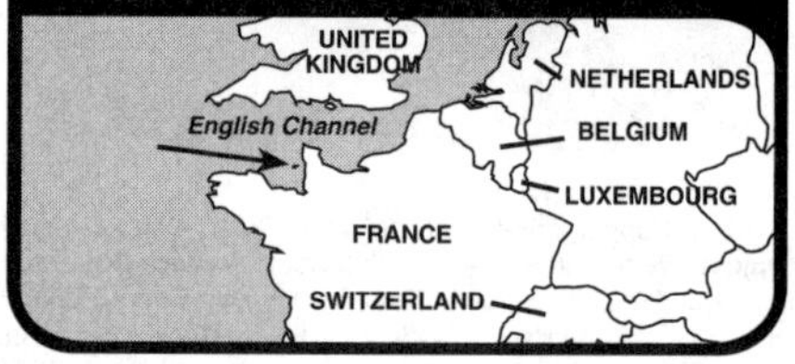

The Bailiwick of Jersey, a British Crown dependency located in the English Channel 12 miles (19 km.) west of Normandy, France, has an area of 45 sq. mi. (117 sq. km.) and a population of 74,000. Capital: St. Helier. The economy is based on agriculture and cattle breeding – the importation of cattle is prohibited to protect the purity of the island's world-famous strain of milk cows.

The island together with the Bailiwick of Guernsey, is the only part of the Dutchy of Normandy belonging to the British Crown, has been a possession of Britain since the Norman conquest of 1066. Jersey is administered by its own laws and customs. Unless the island is mentioned specifically, acts passed by the British Parliament are not applicable to Jersey. During WW II, German troops occupied the island from 1940 to 1945.

RULER

British

MINT MARK

H - Heaton, Birmingham

BRITISH DEPENDENCY

DECIMAL COINAGE

100 New Pence = 1 Pound

Many of the following coins are also struck in silver, gold, and platinum for collectors

KM# 103 PENNY

3.5500 g., Copper Plated Steel, 20.27 mm. **Ruler:** Elizabeth II **Obv:** Crowned head right **Obv. Designer:** Ian Rank-Broadley **Rev:** Le Hoeq Watch Tower, St. Clement **Edge:** Plain

Date	Mintage	F	VF	XF	Unc	BU
2002	1,500,000	—	—	0.10	0.50	—
2003	1,485,000	—	—	0.10	0.50	—

Date	Mintage	F	VF	XF	Unc	BU
2005	—	—	—	0.10	0.50	—
2006	—	—	—	0.10	0.50	—

KM# 104 2 PENCE

7.1000 g., Copper Plated Steel, 25.91 mm. **Ruler:** Elizabeth II **Obv:** Head with tiara right **Obv. Designer:** Ian Rank-Broadley **Rev:** L'Hermitage, St. Helier **Edge:** Plain

Date	Mintage	F	VF	XF	Unc	BU
2002	1,250,000	—	—	0.15	0.50	—
2003	10,000	—	—	0.15	0.50	—
2005	—	—	—	0.15	0.50	—
2006	—	—	—	0.15	0.50	—

KM# 105 5 PENCE

3.2900 g., Copper-Nickel, 18 mm. **Ruler:** Elizabeth II **Obv:** Head with tiara right **Obv. Designer:** Ian Rank-Broadley **Rev:** Seymour Tower, Grouville, L'Avathigon

Date	Mintage	F	VF	XF	Unc	BU
2002	1,200,000	—	—	0.15	0.50	—
2003	1,002,000	—	—	0.15	0.50	—
2005	—	—	—	0.15	0.50	—

KM# 106 10 PENCE

Copper-Nickel, 24.5 mm. **Ruler:** Elizabeth II **Obv:** Head with tiara right **Obv. Designer:** Ian Rank-Broadley **Rev:** La Hougne Bie, Faldouet, St. Martin

Date	Mintage	F	VF	XF	Unc	BU
2002	500,000	—	—	—	1.00	—
2003	10,000	—	—	—	1.00	—
2005	—	—	—	—	1.00	—

KM# 57.2 10 PENCE

Copper-Nickel, 24.5 mm. **Ruler:** Elizabeth II **Obv:** Young bust right **Rev:** La Houque Bie, Faldouet, St. Martin **Note:** Reduced size.

Date	Mintage	F	VF	XF	Unc	BU
2002	—	—	—	—	1.00	—

KM# 66 20 PENCE

5.0000 g., Copper-Nickel, 21.4 mm. **Ruler:** Elizabeth II **Subject:** 100th Anniversary of Lighthouse at Corbiere **Obv:** Young bust right **Rev:** Written value below lighthouse **Rev. Designer:** Robert Lowe **Shape:** 7-sided

Date	Mintage	F	VF	XF	Unc	BU
2002	—	—	—	0.50	1.00	—

KM# 107 20 PENCE

Copper-Nickel, 21.4 mm. **Ruler:** Elizabeth II **Obv:** Head with tiara right **Obv. Designer:** Ian Rank-Broadley

Date	Mintage	F	VF	XF	Unc	BU
2002	515,000	—	—	—	1.00	—
2003	10,000	—	—	—	1.00	—
2005	—	—	—	—	1.00	—

KM# 108 50 PENCE

Copper-Nickel, 27.3 mm. **Ruler:** Elizabeth II **Obv:** Crowned bust right **Obv. Designer:** Ian Rank-Broadley

Date	Mintage	F	VF	XF	Unc	BU
2003	—	—	—	1.00	2.50	—
2005	—	—	—	1.00	2.50	—
2006	—	—	—	1.00	2.50	—

KM# 123 50 PENCE

8.0000 g., Copper-Nickel, 27.3 mm. **Ruler:** Elizabeth II **Subject:** Golden Coronation Anniversary **Obv:** Crowned head right **Rev:** Coronation scene **Edge:** Plain **Shape:** 7-sided

Date	Mintage	F	VF	XF	Unc	BU
2003	10,000	—	—	—	2.50	—

KM# 123a 50 PENCE

8.0000 g., 0.9250 Silver 0.2379 oz. ASW, 27.3 mm. **Ruler:** Elizabeth II **Subject:** Golden Coronation Anniversary **Obv:** Crowned head right **Rev:** Coronation scene **Edge:** Plain **Shape:** 7-sided

Date	Mintage	F	VF	XF	Unc	BU
2003 Proof	15,000	Value: 25.00				

KM# 101 POUND

9.5000 g., Nickel-Brass, 22.5 mm. **Ruler:** Elizabeth II **Obv:** Head with tiara right **Obv. Designer:** Ian Rank-Broadley **Rev:** Schooner, Resolute **Rev. Designer:** Robert Evans **Edge Lettering:** CAESAREA INSULA

Date	Mintage	F	VF	XF	Unc	BU
2003	10,000	—	—	—	4.00	—
2005	—	—	—	—	4.00	—

KM# 102 2 POUNDS

12.0000 g., Bi-Metallic Copper-Nickel center in Nickel-Brass ring, 28.35 mm. **Ruler:** Elizabeth II **Obv:** Head with tiara right **Obv. Designer:** Ian Rank-Broadley **Rev:** Latent image value within circle of assorted shields **Rev. Designer:** Alan Copp **Edge Lettering:** CAESAREA INSULA

Date	Mintage	F	VF	XF	Unc	BU
2003	10,000	—	—	—	10.00	—

KM# 111 5 POUNDS

28.2800 g., Copper-Nickel, 38.6 mm. **Ruler:** Elizabeth II **Subject:** Princess Diana **Obv:** Crowned head right **Rev:** Diana's cameo above people **Edge:** Reeded

Date	Mintage	F	VF	XF	Unc	BU
2002	—	—	—	—	13.50	—

KM# 111a 5 POUNDS

28.2800 g., 0.9250 Silver 0.8410 oz. ASW, 38.6 mm. **Ruler:** Elizabeth II **Subject:** Princess Diana **Obv:** Crowned head right **Rev:** Diana's cameo above people **Edge:** Reeded

Date	Mintage	F	VF	XF	Unc	BU
2002 Proof	20,000	Value: 45.00				

KM# 111b 5 POUNDS

39.9400 g., 0.9167 Gold 1.1771 oz. AGW, 38.6 mm. **Ruler:** Elizabeth II **Subject:** Princess Diana **Obv:** Crowned head right **Rev:** Diana's cameo above people **Edge:** Reeded

Date	Mintage	F	VF	XF	Unc	BU
2002 Proof	100	Value: 1,200				

KM# 113 5 POUNDS

28.2800 g., Copper-Nickel, 38.6 mm. **Ruler:** Elizabeth II **Subject:** Queen Mother **Obv:** Crowned head right **Obv. Designer:** Ian Rank-Broadley **Rev:** Queen Mother's bust right (circa 1918) **Rev. Legend:** HER MAJESTY QUEEN ELIZABETH THE QUEEN MOTHER **Edge:** Reeded

Date	Mintage	F	VF	XF	Unc	BU
2002	—	—	—	—	13.50	—

KM# 113a 5 POUNDS

28.2800 g., 0.9250 Silver 0.8410 oz. ASW, 38.6 mm. **Ruler:** Elizabeth II **Subject:** Queen Mother **Obv:** Crowned head right **Obv. Designer:** Ian Rank-Broadley **Rev:** Queen Mother's bust right, (circa 1918) **Rev. Legend:** HER MAJESTY QUEEN ELIZABETH THE QUEEN MOTHER **Edge:** Reeded

Date	Mintage	F	VF	XF	Unc	BU
2002 Proof	15,000	Value: 50.00				

KM# 113b 5 POUNDS

39.9400 g., 0.9166 Gold 1.1770 oz. AGW, 38.6 mm. **Ruler:** Elizabeth II **Subject:** Queen Mother **Obv:** Crowned head right **Obv. Designer:** Ian Rank-Broadley **Rev:** Queen Mother's bust right, (circa 1918) **Rev. Legend:** HER MAJESTY QUEEN ELIZABETH THE QUEEN MOTHER **Edge:** Reeded

Date	Mintage	F	VF	XF	Unc	BU
2002 Proof	250	Value: 1,175				

KM# 115 5 POUNDS

28.2800 g., Copper-Nickel, 38.6 mm. **Ruler:** Elizabeth II **Subject:** Golden Jubilee **Obv:** Crowned head right **Rev:** Abbey procession scene **Rev. Designer:** Robert Evans **Edge:** Reeded

Date	Mintage	F	VF	XF	Unc	BU
2002	—	—	—	—	13.50	—

KM# 115a 5 POUNDS

28.2800 g., 0.9250 Silver 0.8410 oz. ASW, 38.6 mm. **Ruler:** Elizabeth II **Subject:** Golden Jubilee **Obv:** Crowned head right **Rev:** Abbey procession scene **Edge:** Reeded

Date	Mintage	F	VF	XF	Unc	BU
2002 Proof	20,000	Value: 50.00				

KM# 115b 5 POUNDS

39.9400 g., 0.9166 Gold 1.1770 oz. AGW, 38.6 mm. **Ruler:** Elizabeth II **Subject:** Golden Jubilee **Obv:** Crowned head right **Rev:** Abbey procession scene **Edge:** Reeded

Date	Mintage	F	VF	XF	Unc	BU
2002 Proof	100	Value: 1,200				

KM# 117 5 POUNDS

28.2800 g., Copper-Nickel, 38.6 mm. **Ruler:** Elizabeth II **Subject:** Duke of Wellington **Obv:** Crowned head right **Rev:** Wellington's portrait with multicolor infantry scene **Rev. Designer:** Willem Vis **Edge:** Reeded

Date	Mintage	F	VF	XF	Unc	BU
2002	—	—	—	—	13.50	—

KM# 117a 5 POUNDS

28.2800 g., 0.9250 Silver 0.8410 oz. ASW, 38.6 mm. **Ruler:** Elizabeth II **Subject:** Duke of Wellington **Obv:** Crowned head right **Rev:** Wellington's portrait with multicolor infantry scene **Edge:** Reeded

Date	Mintage	F	VF	XF	Unc	BU
2002 Proof	15,000	Value: 50.00				

KM# 117b 5 POUNDS

39.9400 g., 0.9166 Gold 1.1770 oz. AGW, 38.6 mm. **Ruler:** Elizabeth II **Subject:** Duke of Wellington **Obv:** Crowned head right **Rev:** Wellington's portrait with multicolor infantry scene **Edge:** Reeded

Date	Mintage	F	VF	XF	Unc	BU
2002 Proof	200	Value: 1,175				

KM# 119 5 POUNDS

28.2800 g., Copper-Nickel, 38.6 mm. **Ruler:** Elizabeth II **Subject:** Golden Jubilee **Obv:** Crowned head right **Rev:** Honor guard and memorial **Edge:** Reeded

Date	Mintage	F	VF	XF	Unc	BU
2003	—	—	—	—	13.50	—

KM# 119a 5 POUNDS

28.2800 g., 0.9250 Silver 0.8410 oz. ASW, 38.6 mm. **Ruler:** Elizabeth II **Subject:** Golden Jubilee **Obv:** Crowned head right **Rev:** Honor guard and monument **Edge:** Reeded

Date	Mintage	F	VF	XF	Unc	BU
2003 Proof	20,000	Value: 50.00				

KM# 119b 5 POUNDS

39.9400 g., 0.9166 Gold 1.1770 oz. AGW, 38.6 mm. **Ruler:** Elizabeth II **Subject:** Golden Jubilee **Obv:** Crowned head right **Rev:** Honor guard and monument **Edge:** Reeded

Date	Mintage	F	VF	XF	Unc	BU
2003 Proof	250	Value: 1,175				

KM# 121 5 POUNDS

28.2800 g., Copper-Nickel, 38.6 mm. **Ruler:** Elizabeth II **Obv:** Crowned head right **Rev:** Bust facing and crowned arms with supporters **Edge:** Reeded

Date	Mintage	F	VF	XF	Unc	BU
2003	—	—	—	—	16.50	—

KM# 121a 5 POUNDS

28.2800 g., 0.9250 Silver 0.8410 oz. ASW, 38.6 mm. **Ruler:** Elizabeth II **Obv:** Crowned head right **Rev:** Bust facing and crowned arms with supporters **Edge:** Reeded

Date	Mintage	F	VF	XF	Unc	BU
2003 Proof	5,000	Value: 47.50				

KM# 121b 5 POUNDS

39.9400 g., 0.9166 Gold 1.1770 oz. AGW, 38.6 mm. **Ruler:** Elizabeth II **Obv:** Crowned head right **Rev:** Bust facing and crowned arms with supporters **Edge:** Reeded

Date	Mintage	F	VF	XF	Unc	BU
2003 Proof	200	Value: 1,175				

KM# 144 5 POUNDS

28.2800 g., 0.9250 Silver 0.8410 oz. ASW, 38.61 mm. **Ruler:** Elizabeth II **Subject:** History of the Royal Navy **Obv:** Head left with tiarra **Obv. Legend:** ELIZABETH II BALIWICK - OF JERSEY **Rev:** Five heads of King Alfred the Great, Sir Francis Drake, Admiral Lord Horatio Nelson, admiral Sir John Fisher and Admiral Sir John Woodward at left and ships "Mary Rose", HMS "Victory", HMS "Warspite", HMS "Ark Royal" and submarine HMS "Conquerer" at **Edge:** Reeded

Date	Mintage	F	VF	XF	Unc	BU
2003 Proof	—	Value: 75.00				

KM# 130 5 POUNDS

28.2800 g., 0.9250 Silver 0.8410 oz. ASW, 38.6 mm. **Ruler:** Elizabeth II **Subject:** Drake **Obv:** Crowned head right **Rev:** Naval leader Sir Francis Drake

Date	Mintage	F	VF	XF	Unc	BU
2003 Proof	—	Value: 75.00				

KM# 131 5 POUNDS

28.2800 g., 0.9250 Silver 0.8410 oz. ASW, 38.6 mm. **Ruler:** Elizabeth II **Subject:** Sovereign Of The Seas **Obv:** Crowned head right **Rev:** The Sovereign of the Seas ship

Date	Mintage	F	VF	XF	Unc	BU
2003 Proof	—	Value: 75.00				

KM# 132 5 POUNDS
28.2800 g., 0.9250 Silver 0.8410 oz. ASW, 38.6 mm. **Ruler:** Elizabeth II **Subject:** John Fisher **Obv:** Crowned head right **Rev:** WWI Naval leader Sir John Fisher

Date	Mintage	F	VF	XF	Unc	BU
2003 Proof	—	Value: 75.00				

KM# 133 5 POUNDS
28.2800 g., 0.9250 Silver 0.8410 oz. ASW, 38.6 mm. **Ruler:** Elizabeth II **Subject:** HMS Victory **Obv:** Crowned head right **Rev:** Nelson's flag ship HMS Victory

Date	Mintage	F	VF	XF	Unc	BU
2003 Proof	—	Value: 75.00				

KM# 134 5 POUNDS
28.2800 g., 0.9250 Silver 0.8410 oz. ASW, 38.6 mm. **Ruler:** Elizabeth II **Subject:** Cunningham **Obv:** Crowned head right **Rev:** WWII Admiral Andrew B. Cunningham

Date	Mintage	F	VF	XF	Unc	BU
2003 Proof	—	Value: 75.00				

KM# 135 5 POUNDS
28.2800 g., 0.9250 Silver 0.8410 oz. ASW, 38.6 mm. **Ruler:** Elizabeth II **Subject:** Conqueror **Obv:** Crowned head right **Rev:** Submarine HMS Conqueror

Date	Mintage	F	VF	XF	Unc	BU
2003 Proof	—	Value: 75.00				

KM# 136 5 POUNDS
28.2800 g., 0.9250 Silver 0.8410 oz. ASW, 38.6 mm. **Ruler:** Elizabeth II **Subject:** Coronation **Obv:** Crowned head right **Rev:** The Pacific Class Coronation

Date	Mintage	F	VF	XF	Unc	BU
2004 Proof	—	Value: 75.00				

KM# 137 5 POUNDS
28.2800 g., 0.9250 Silver 0.8410 oz. ASW, 38.6 mm. **Ruler:** Elizabeth II **Subject:** Flying Scotsman **Obv:** Crowned head right **Rev:** Famous Flying Scotsman Locomotive, designed by Sir Nigel Gresley

Date	Mintage	F	VF	XF	Unc	BU
2004 Proof	—	Value: 75.00				

KM# 138 5 POUNDS
28.2800 g., 0.9250 Silver 0.8410 oz. ASW, 38.6 mm. **Ruler:** Elizabeth II **Subject:** Golden Arrow **Obv:** Crowned head right **Rev:** The Golden Arrow, which ran from London to Dover en route to Paris

Date	Mintage	F	VF	XF	Unc	BU
2004 Proof	—	Value: 75.00				

KM# 139 5 POUNDS
28.2800 g., 0.9250 Silver 0.8410 oz. ASW, 38.6 mm. **Ruler:** Elizabeth II **Subject:** Driver and Fireman **Obv:** Crowned head right **Rev:** Familiar image from the Golden Age of Steam: the driver and fireman

Date	Mintage	F	VF	XF	Unc	BU
2004 Proof	—	Value: 75.00				

KM# 140 5 POUNDS
28.2800 g., 0.9250 Silver 0.8410 oz. ASW, 38.6 mm. **Ruler:** Elizabeth II **Subject:** Tunnel **Obv:** Crowned head right **Rev:** Familiar image from the Golden Age of Steam: A locomotive storming out of a tunnel

Date	Mintage	F	VF	XF	Unc	BU
2004	—	Value: 75.00				

KM# 141 5 POUNDS
28.2800 g., 0.9250 Silver 0.8410 oz. ASW, 38.6 mm. **Ruler:** Elizabeth II **Subject:** Evening Star **Obv:** Crowned head right **Rev:** The Evening Star - representing the last British Rail Steam Locomotive

Date	Mintage	F	VF	XF	Unc	BU
2004 Proof	—	Value: 75.00				

KM# 124 5 POUNDS
28.2800 g., Copper-Nickel, 38.6 mm. **Ruler:** Elizabeth II **Obv:** Crowned head right **Rev:** British Horsa gliders in flight **Rev. Designer:** David Cornell **Edge:** Reeded **Note:** D-Day

Date	Mintage	F	VF	XF	Unc	BU
2004	—	—	—	—	15.00	—

KM# 124a 5 POUNDS
28.2800 g., 0.9250 Silver 0.8410 oz. ASW, 38.6 mm. **Ruler:** Elizabeth II **Obv:** Crowned head right **Rev:** British Horsa gliders in flight

Date	Mintage	F	VF	XF	Unc	BU
2004 Proof	10,000	Value: 85.00				

KM# 124b 5 POUNDS
39.9400 g., 0.9167 Gold 1.1771 oz. AGW, 38.6 mm. **Ruler:** Elizabeth II **Obv:** Crowned head right **Rev:** British Horsa gliders in flight

Date	Mintage	F	VF	XF	Unc	BU
2004 Proof	500	Value: 1,175				

KM# 126 5 POUNDS
28.2800 g., Copper-Nickel, 38.6 mm. **Ruler:** Elizabeth II **Obv:** Crowned head right **Rev:** Charge of the Light Brigade scene with one blue uniform behind the Earl of Cardigan **Edge:** Reeded

Date	Mintage	F	VF	XF	Unc	BU
2004	—	—	—	—	25.00	—

KM# 126a 5 POUNDS
28.2800 g., 0.9250 Silver 0.8410 oz. ASW, 38.6 mm. **Ruler:** Elizabeth II **Obv:** Crowned head right **Rev:** Charge of the Light Brigade scene with one blue uniform behind the Earl of Cardigan **Edge:** Reeded

Date	Mintage	F	VF	XF	Unc	BU
2004 Proof	10,000	Value: 85.00				

KM# 126b 5 POUNDS
39.9400 g., 0.9166 Gold 1.1770 oz. AGW, 38.6 mm. **Ruler:** Elizabeth II **Obv:** Crowned head right **Rev:** Charge of the Light Brigade scene with one blue uniform behind the Earl of Cardigan **Edge:** Reeded

Date	Mintage	F	VF	XF	Unc	BU
2004 Proof	500	Value: 1,175				

KM# 127 5 POUNDS
Copper Nickel **Ruler:** Elizabeth II **Subject:** Battle of Trafalgar **Obv:** Crowned head right

Date	Mintage	F	VF	XF	Unc	BU
2005	—	—	—	—	7.50	—

KM# 128 5 POUNDS
Copper Nickel **Ruler:** Elizabeth II **Subject:** 60th Anniversary - End of WW II **Obv:** Crowned head right **Obv. Designer:** Ian Rank-Broadley **Rev:** Big Ben Tower

Date	Mintage	F	VF	XF	Unc	BU
2005	—	—	—	—	7.50	—

KM# 128a 5 POUNDS
28.2800 g., 0.9250 Silver 0.8410 oz. ASW, 38.6 mm. **Ruler:** Elizabeth II **Subject:** WWII Liberation **Obv:** Crowned head right **Rev:** Big Ben Tower **Edge:** Reeded

Date	Mintage	F	VF	XF	Unc	BU
2005 Proof	5,000	Value: 85.00				

KM# 128b 5 POUNDS
39.9400 g., 0.9167 Gold 1.1771 oz. AGW, 38.6 mm. **Ruler:** Elizabeth II **Subject:** WWII Liberation **Obv:** Crowned head right **Rev:** Big Ben Tower **Edge:** Reeded

Date	Mintage	F	VF	XF	Unc	BU
2005 Proof	150	Value: 1,200				

KM# 129a 5 POUNDS
39.9400 g., 0.9167 Gold 1.1771 oz. AGW, 38.6 mm. **Ruler:** Elizabeth II **Subject:** WWII Liberation **Obv:** Crowned head right **Rev:** Returning evacuees **Edge:** Reeded

Date	Mintage	F	VF	XF	Unc	BU
2005 Proof	150	Value: 1,200				

KM# 129 5 POUNDS
Copper Nickel **Ruler:** Elizabeth II **Subject:** WW II Liberation **Obv:** Crowned head right **Rev:** Returning evacuees **Edge:** Reeded

Date	Mintage	F	VF	XF	Unc	BU
2005	—	—	—	—	7.50	—

KM# 127a 5 POUNDS
28.2800 g., 0.9250 Silver 0.8410 oz. ASW, 38.6 mm. **Ruler:** Elizabeth II **Subject:** Nelson Trafalger **Obv:** Crowned head right **Rev:** 200th Anniversary of the Battle of Trafalgar, image of Nelson with a gilded ship in the background

Date	Mintage	F	VF	XF	Unc	BU
2005 Proof	—	Value: 75.00				

KM# 142 5 POUNDS
28.2800 g., 0.9250 Silver 0.8410 oz. ASW, 38.6 mm. **Ruler:** Elizabeth II **Subject:** Queen's 80th Birthday **Obv:** Head with tiara right - gilt **Obv. Legend:** ELIZABETH II BAILIWICK - OF JERSEY **Obv. Designer:** Ian Rank-Broadley **Rev:** Queen horseback facing

Date	Mintage	F	VF	XF	Unc	BU
2006 Proof	—	Value: 40.00				

KM# 145 5 POUNDS
28.2800 g., 0.9250 Silver 0.8410 oz. ASW, 38.6 mm. **Ruler:** Elizabeth II **Subject:** Elizabeth II's 80th Birthday **Obv:** Head with tiara right **Obv. Legend:** ELIZABETH II BALIWIWICK - OF JERSEY **Obv. Designer:** Ian Rank-Broadley **Rev:** Queen on horseback **Edge:** Reeded

Date	Mintage	F	VF	XF	Unc	BU
2006 Proof	—	Value: 40.00				

KM# 143 10 POUNDS
Silver Partially Gold plated, 65 mm. **Ruler:** Elizabeth II **Subject:** 50th Anniversary of Coronation **Obv:** Queens silver portrait on gold plated fields **Rev:** Crown and scepter above arms, gold plated **Rev. Designer:** Marcel Canioni

Date	Mintage	F	VF	XF	Unc	BU
2003	2,000	—	—	—	30.00	—

KM# 114 25 POUNDS
7.9800 g., 0.9166 Gold 0.2352 oz. AGW, 22 mm. **Ruler:** Elizabeth II **Subject:** Queen Mother **Obv:** Crowned head right **Rev:** Queen Mother's portrait circa 1918 **Edge:** Reeded

Date	Mintage	F	VF	XF	Unc	BU
2002 Proof	2,500	Value: 300				

KM# 116 25 POUNDS
7.9800 g., 0.9166 Gold 0.2352 oz. AGW, 22 mm. **Ruler:** Elizabeth II **Subject:** Golden Jubilee **Obv:** Crowned head right **Rev:** Abbey procession scene **Edge:** Reeded

Date	Mintage	F	VF	XF	Unc	BU
2002 Proof	2,500	Value: 300				

KM# 118 25 POUNDS
7.9800 g., 0.9166 Gold 0.2352 oz. AGW, 22 mm. **Ruler:** Elizabeth II **Subject:** Duke of Wellington **Obv:** Crowned head right **Rev:** Wellington's portrait with infantry scene **Edge:** Reeded

Date	Mintage	F	VF	XF	Unc	BU
2002 Proof	2,500	Value: 300				

KM# 112 25 POUNDS
7.9800 g., 0.9167 Gold 0.2352 oz. AGW, 22.05 mm. **Ruler:** Elizabeth II **Subject:** Princess Diana **Obv:** Crowned head right **Rev:** Diana's portrait **Edge:** Reeded

Date	Mintage	F	VF	XF	Unc	BU
2002 Proof	2,500	Value: 300				

KM# 120 25 POUNDS
7.9800 g., 0.9166 Gold 0.2352 oz. AGW, 22 mm. **Ruler:** Elizabeth II **Subject:** Golden Jubilee **Obv:** Crowned head right **Rev:** Honor guard and monument **Edge:** Reeded

Date	Mintage	F	VF	XF	Unc	BU
2003 Proof	5,000	Value: 300				

KM# 125 25 POUNDS

7.9800 g., 0.9167 Gold 0.2352 oz. AGW, 22 mm. **Ruler:** Elizabeth II **Obv:** Crowned head right **Rev:** British Horsa gliders in flight **Edge:** Reeded **Note:** D-Day

Date	Mintage	F	VF	XF	Unc	BU
2004 Proof	500	Value: 300				

KM# 122 50 POUNDS

1000.0000 g., 0.9250 Silver 29.738 oz. ASW, 100 mm. **Ruler:** Elizabeth II **Obv:** Crowned head right **Rev:** Bust facing and crowned arms with supporters **Edge:** Reeded

Date	Mintage	F	VF	XF	Unc	BU
2003 Proof	500	Value: 995				

PIEFORTS

KM#	Date	Mintage	Identification	Mkt Val
P3	2002	100	5 Pounds. 0.9166 Gold. 56.5600 g. 38.6 mm. Queen's portrait. Abbey procession scene. Reeded edge. Underweight piefort	1,400

JORDAN

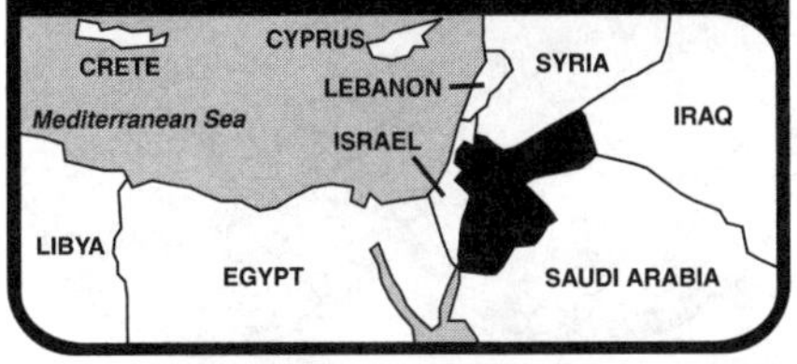

The Hashemite Kingdom of Jordan, a constitutional monarchy in southwest Asia, has an area of 37,738 sq. mi.(91,880 sq. km.) and a population of 3.5 million. Capital: Amman. Agriculture and tourism comprise Jordan's economic base. Chief exports are phosphates, tomatoes and oranges.

TITLES

المملكة الاردنية الهاشمية

el-Mamlaka(t) el-Urduniya(t) el-Hashemiya(t)

RULERS

Abdullah Ibn Al-Hussein, 1999-

MONETARY SYSTEM

Commencing 1992

100 Piastres = 1 Dinar

KINGDOM

REFORM COINAGE

1992

KM# 73 5 PIASTRES

5.0000 g., Nickel-Clad Steel, 25.8 mm. **Ruler:** Abdullah Ibn Al-Hussein **Obv:** Bust right **Rev:** Value to left within lines below date with written value at lower right **Edge:** Milled

Date	Mintage	F	VF	XF	Unc	BU
AH1427-2006	—	—	—	—	2.00	2.50

KM# 74 10 PIASTRES

8.0000 g., Nickel Clad Steel, 27.9 mm. **Ruler:** Abdullah Ibn Al-Hussein **Obv:** Bust right **Rev:** Value at left within lines below date with written value at lower right **Edge:** Milled

Date	Mintage	F	VF	XF	Unc	BU
AH1425-2004	—	—	—	—	4.00	5.00

KM# 83 1/4 DINAR

7.4000 g., Nickel-Brass **Ruler:** Abdullah Ibn Al-Hussein **Obv:** Bust right **Edge:** Plain

Date	Mintage	F	VF	XF	Unc	BU
AH1425-2004	—	—	—	—	3.00	4.00

KM# 75 3 DINARS

28.5000 g., Brass, 40 mm. **Ruler:** Abdullah Ibn Al-Hussein **Subject:** Amman: Arabic Culture Capital **Obv:** Bust right **Rev:** Building **Edge:** Milled

Date	Mintage	F	VF	XF	Unc	BU
AH1423//2002	2,000	—	—	—	100	—

Note: Only 500 sold to collectors. Rest were taken by Amman municipality as official gifts

KM# 84 10 DINARS

120.0000 g., 0.9990 Silver 3.8541 oz. ASW, 60 mm. **Subject:** 60th Anniversary of Jordan's Independence **Obv:** King Abdullah I and Independence speech **Rev:** The National Assembly building **Edge:** Milled

Date	Mintage	F	VF	XF	Unc	BU
2006 Proof	250	Value: 200				

Note: Issued primarily for use as official state gifts

KM# 85 60 DINARS

72.7500 g., 0.9170 Gold 2.1447 oz. AGW, 40 mm. **Subject:** 60th Anniversary of Jordan's Independence **Obv:** King Abdullah II **Rev:** Treasury in Petra **Edge:** Milled

Date	Mintage	F	VF	XF	Unc	BU
2006 Proof	250	Value: 2,150				

Note: Issued primarily for use as official state gifts

MINT SETS

KM#	Date	Mintage	Identification	Issue Price	Mkt Val
MS4	2000-2004 (5)	—	KM#73-74, 78.1, 79, 83	—	20.00

PROOF SETS

KM#	Date	Mintage	Identification	Issue Price	Mkt Val
PS14	2006 (2)	250	KM#84-85	—	2,350

KAZAKHSTAN

The Republic of Kazakhstan (formerly Kazakhstan S.S.R.) is bordered to the west by the Caspian Sea and Russia, to the north by Russia, in the east by the Peoples Republic of China and in the south by Uzbekistan and Kirghizia. It has an area of 1,049,155 sq. mi. (2,717,300 sq. km.) and a population of 16.7 million. Capital: Astana. Rich in mineral resources including coal, tungsten, copper, lead, zinc and manganese with huge oil and natural gas reserves. Agriculture is very important, (it previously represented 20 percent of the total arable acreage of the combined U.S.S.R.) Non-ferrous metallurgy, heavy engineering and chemical industries are leaders in its economy.

MONETARY SYSTEM

100 Tyin = 1 Tenge

REPUBLIC

DECIMAL COINAGE

KM# 23 TENGE

1.6000 g., Brass, 14.60 mm. **Obv:** National emblem **Rev:** Value flanked by designs **Edge:** Plain

Date	Mintage	F	VF	XF	Unc	BU
2002	—	—	—	—	0.50	0.85
2004	—	—	—	—	0.50	0.85
2005	—	—	—	—	0.50	0.85

KM# 64 2 TENGE

1.8200 g., Brass, 16 mm. **Obv:** National emblem **Rev:** Value flanked by designs **Edge:** Plain

Date	Mintage	F	VF	XF	Unc	BU
2005	—	—	—	—	0.65	1.20

KM# 8 3 TENGE

Copper-Nickel **Obv:** Mythical animal within circle **Rev:** Star design with value and date within

Date	Mintage	F	VF	XF	Unc	BU
2005	—	—	—	—	0.75	1.25

KM# 24 5 TENGE

Brass **Obv:** National emblem **Rev:** Value flanked by designs

Date	Mintage	F	VF	XF	Unc	BU
2002	—	—	—	—	0.50	0.85
2004	—	—	—	—	0.50	0.85
2005	—	—	—	—	0.50	0.85

KM# 25 10 TENGE

Brass **Obv:** National emblem **Rev:** Value above design

Date	Mintage	F	VF	XF	Unc	BU
2002	—	—	—	—	0.75	1.25
2004	—	—	—	—	0.75	1.25
2005	—	—	—	—	0.75	1.25

KM# 26 20 TENGE

2.8600 g., Copper-Nickel, 18.3 mm. **Obv:** National emblem **Rev:** Value above design **Edge:** Segmented reeding **Edge Lettering:** * CTO TENGE * Y 3 TENGE

Date	Mintage	F	VF	XF	Unc	BU
2002	—	—	—	—	1.00	1.75
2004	—	—	—	—	1.00	1.75
2006	—	—	—	—	1.00	1.75

KM# 40 50 TENGE

11.5000 g., Copper-Nickel, 31 mm. **Obv:** Eagle superimposed on ornate 10 **Edge:** Reeded and plain sections

Date	Mintage	F	VF	XF	Unc	BU
2001	—	—	—	—	4.00	6.50

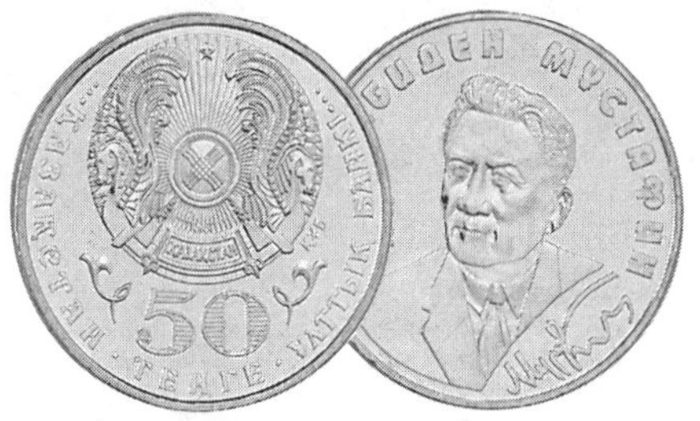

KM# 41 50 TENGE

11.2000 g., Copper Nickel, 31.1 mm. **Subject:** Gabiden Mustafin **Obv:** National emblem above value **Rev:** Bust 1/4 left **Edge:** Segmented reeding

Date	Mintage	F	VF	XF	Unc	BU
ND(2002)	—	—	—	—	4.00	6.50

KM# 69 50 TENGE
Copper-Nickel, 31 mm. **Subject:** Gabit Mosrepov **Obv:** Symbol and value

Date	Mintage	F	VF	XF	Unc	BU
2002	—	—	—	—	4.00	6.50

KM# 27 50 TENGE
Copper-Nickel **Obv:** National emblem **Rev:** Value above design

Date	Mintage	F	VF	XF	Unc	BU
2002	—	—	—	—	2.00	3.50

KM# 70 50 TENGE
Copper-Nickel, 31 mm. **Subject:** 200th Anniversary of Makhambet Utemisov **Obv:** Symbol and value

Date	Mintage	F	VF	XF	Unc	BU
2003	—	—	—	—	4.00	6.50

KM# 54 50 TENGE
11.5000 g., Copper-Nickel, 31.1 mm. **Obv:** National emblem above value **Rev:** Painter Abylichan Kasteev (1904-1973) **Edge:** Reeded and plain sections

Date	Mintage	F	VF	XF	Unc	BU
2004	—	—	—	—	4.00	6.50

KM# 65 50 TENGE
11.5000 g., Copper-Nickel, 31.1 mm. **Subject:** Alken Margulan **Obv:** National emblem above value **Rev:** Bust facing **Edge:** Segmented reeding

Date	Mintage	F	VF	XF	Unc	BU
2004	—	—	—	—	4.00	6.50

KM# 58 50 TENGE
11.5000 g., Copper-Nickel, 31.1 mm. **Subject:** 10th Anniversary of the Constitution **Obv:** National emblem above value **Rev:** National emblem within circle above book **Edge:** Segmented reeding

Date	Mintage	F	VF	XF	Unc	BU
2005	—	—	—	—	4.00	6.50

KM# 71 50 TENGE
Copper-Nickel, 31 mm. **Subject:** 60 Years Victory WWII **Obv:** Symbol and value

Date	Mintage	F	VF	XF	Unc	BU
2005	—	—	—	—	4.00	6.50

KM# 79 50 TENGE
11.2200 g., Copper-Nickel, 31 mm. **Subject:** 20th Anniversary **Obv:** National arms above value **Rev:** Happy woman **Edge:** Segmented reeding

Date	Mintage	F	VF	XF	Unc	BU
ND (2006)	—	—	—	—	4.00	6.50

KM# 73 50 TENGE
11.3700 g., Copper-Nickel, 31 mm. **Obv:** Human figure and solar system **Rev:** Astronaut and solar system **Edge:** Segmented reeding

Date	Mintage	F	VF	XF	Unc	BU
2006	50,000	—	—	—	4.00	6.00

KM# 74 50 TENGE
11.3700 g., Copper-Nickel, 31 mm. **Obv:** National arms on tapestry **Rev:** Woman with baby in cradle **Edge:** Segmented reeding

Date	Mintage	F	VF	XF	Unc	BU
2006	—	—	—	—	4.00	6.00

KM# 75 50 TENGE
11.3700 g., Copper-Nickel, 31 mm. **Obv:** National arms **Rev:** Tetraogallus Altaicus birds **Edge:** Segmented reeding

Date	Mintage	F	VF	XF	Unc	BU
2006	50,000	—	—	—	4.00	6.00

KM# 76 50 TENGE
11.3700 g., Copper-Nickel, 31 mm. **Obv:** National arms **Rev:** Altyn Kyran Order Grand Collar and Badge **Edge:** Segmented reeding

Date	Mintage	F	VF	XF	Unc	BU
2006	50,000	—	—	—	4.00	6.00

KM# 77 50 TENGE
11.3700 g., Copper-Nickel, 31 mm. **Obv:** National arms **Rev:** Altyn Kyran Order Breast Star **Edge:** Segmented reeding

Date	Mintage	F	VF	XF	Unc	BU
2006	50,000	—	—	—	4.00	6.00

KM# 78 50 TENGE
11.3700 g., Copper-Nickel, 31 mm. **Obv:** National arms **Rev:** Zhubanov bust and music score **Edge:** Segmented reeding

Date	Mintage	F	VF	XF	Unc	BU
2006	50,000	—	—	—	4.00	6.00

KM# 80 50 TENGE
10.8900 g., Copper-Nickel, 31.10 mm. **Subject:** 50th Anniversary Launch of Sputnik I **Obv:** Stylized view of solar system **Obv. Legend:** REPUBLIC OF KAZAKHSTAN **Rev:** Sputnik I in space, earth in background **Rev. Legend:** THE FIRST SPACE SATELLITE OF THE EARTH **Edge:** Segmented reeding

Date	Mintage	F	VF	XF	Unc	BU
ND(2007)	—	—	—	—	4.00	6.00

KM# 81 50 TENGE
11.1100 g., Copper-Nickel, 31 mm. **Obv:** National arms, value below **Obv. Legend:** КАЗАКСТАН.... **Rev:** Ibise - Pure White Crested Spoonbill standing left **Rev. Legend:** ... • PLATALEA LEUCORODIA **Edge:** Segmented reeding

Date	Mintage	F	VF	XF	Unc	BU
2007	—	—	—	—	4.00	6.00

KM# 39 100 TENGE
6.2300 g., Bi-Metallic Copper-Nickel center in Brass ring, 24.4 mm. **Obv:** National emblem **Rev:** Value within lined circle flanked by designs **Edge:** Reeding over incuse value

Date	Mintage	F	VF	XF	Unc	BU
2002	—	—	—	—	3.50	5.50
2004	—	—	—	—	3.50	5.50
2006	—	—	—	—	3.50	5.50
2007	—	—	—	—	3.50	5.50

KM# 49 100 TENGE
6.4000 g., Bi-Metallic Copper-Nickel center in Brass ring, 24.5 mm. **Obv:** Stylized chicken **Rev:** Value within lined circle flanked by designs **Edge:** Reeded and lettered

Date	Mintage	F	VF	XF	Unc	BU
2003	100,000	—	—	—	4.00	6.50

KM# 50 100 TENGE
6.4000 g., Bi-Metallic Copper-Nickel center in Brass ring, 24.5 mm. **Obv:** Stylized panther **Rev:** Value within lined circle flanked by designs **Edge:** Reeded and lettered

Date	Mintage	F	VF	XF	Unc	BU
2003	100,000	—	—	—	4.00	6.50

KM# 51 100 TENGE
6.4000 g., Bi-Metallic Copper-Nickel center in Brass ring, 24.5 mm. **Obv:** Stylized wolf's head **Rev:** Value within lined circle flanked by designs **Edge:** Reeded and lettered

Date	Mintage	F	VF	XF	Unc	BU
2003	100,000	—	—	—	4.00	6.50

KM# 52 100 TENGE
6.4000 g., Bi-Metallic Copper-Nickel center in Brass ring, 24.5 mm. **Obv:** Stylized sheep's head **Rev:** Value within lined circle flanked by designs **Edge:** Reeded and lettered

Date	Mintage	F	VF	XF	Unc	BU
2003	100,000	—	—	—	4.00	6.50

KM# 57 100 TENGE
6.4000 g., Bi-Metallic Copper-Nickel center in Brass ring, 24.5 mm. **Subject:** 60th Anniversary of the UN **Obv:** UN logo as part of the number 60 **Rev:** Value within lined circle flanked by designs **Edge:** Reeded and lettered

Date	Mintage	F	VF	XF	Unc	BU
2005	—	—	—	—	5.00	7.50

KM# 37 500 TENGE
23.9000 g., 0.9250 Silver 0.7107 oz. ASW, 37 mm. **Subject:** Wildlife **Obv:** Value **Rev:** Female Saiga with two babies **Edge:** Plain

Date	Mintage	F	VF	XF	Unc	BU
2001 Proof	—	Value: 50.00				

KM# 38 500 TENGE
23.8100 g., 0.9250 Silver 0.7081 oz. ASW, 36.9 mm. **Subject:** 10 Years of Independence **Obv:** Monument and flag **Rev:** National emblem within design above value **Edge:** Plain

Date	Mintage	F	VF	XF	Unc	BU
2001 Proof	3,000	Value: 42.50				

KM# 55 500 TENGE
24.0000 g., 0.9250 Silver 0.7137 oz. ASW, 37 mm. **Obv:** Value **Rev:** Altai Mountain petroglyph **Edge:** Plain

Date	Mintage	F	VF	XF	Unc	BU
2001 Proof	3,000	Value: 45.00				

KM# 66 500 TENGE
24.0000 g., 0.9250 Silver 0.7137 oz. ASW, 37 mm. **Obv:** Seated musician, tree and value **Rev:** Stringed instrument and musical notes **Edge:** Plain

Date	Mintage	F	VF	XF	Unc	BU
2001 Proof	—	Value: 45.00				

KM# 42 500 TENGE
23.9000 g., 0.9250 Silver 0.7107 oz. ASW, 37 mm. **Subject:** Music **Obv:** Musician and value divided by tree **Rev:** Musical instruments **Edge:** Plain

Date	Mintage	F	VF	XF	Unc	BU
2002 Proof	—	Value: 45.00				

KM# 43 500 TENGE
23.9000 g., 0.9250 Silver 0.7107 oz. ASW, 37 mm. **Subject:** Prehistoric Art **Obv:** Value **Rev:** Prehistoric cave art **Edge:** Plain

Date	Mintage	F	VF	XF	Unc	BU
2002 Proof	—	Value: 40.00				

KM# 44 500 TENGE
23.9000 g., 0.9250 Silver 0.7107 oz. ASW, 37 mm. **Subject:** Bighorn Sheep **Obv:** Value **Rev:** Kazakhstan Argali Ram **Edge:** Plain

Date	Mintage	F	VF	XF	Unc	BU
2002 Proof	—	Value: 50.00				

KM# 56 500 TENGE
24.0000 g., 0.9250 Silver 0.7137 oz. ASW, 37 mm. **Subject:** Applied Arts **Obv:** Folk Dancer **Rev:** Cultural artifacts **Edge:** Plain

Date	Mintage	F	VF	XF	Unc	BU
2003 Proof	3,000	Value: 45.00				

KM# 53 500 TENGE
24.0000 g., 0.9250 Silver 0.7137 oz. ASW, 37 mm. **Obv:** Value **Rev:** Great Bustard bird standing on ground **Edge:** Plain

Date	Mintage	F	VF	XF	Unc	BU
2003 Proof	3,000	Value: 60.00				

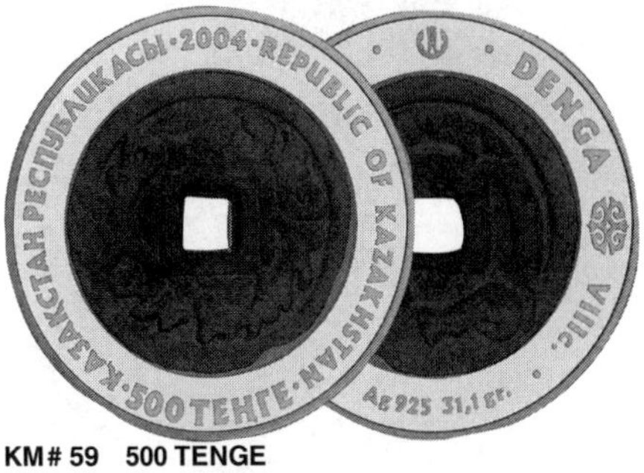

KM# 59 500 TENGE
31.1000 g., 0.9250 Bi-Metallic Blackend silver center in proof silver ring 0.9249 oz., 38.6 mm. **Subject:** "Denga" **Obv:** Black square holed coin design above value **Rev:** Black square holed coin design and metal content statement **Edge:** Reeded

Date	Mintage	F	VF	XF	Unc	BU
2004 Proof	5,000	Value: 50.00				

KM# 60 500 TENGE

24.0000 g., 0.9250 Silver 0.7137 oz. ASW, 37 mm. **Obv:** Value **Rev:** Prehistoric art horseman **Edge:** Plain

Date	Mintage	F	VF	XF	Unc	BU
2005 Proof	3,000	Value: 50.00				

KM# 61 500 TENGE

24.0000 g., 0.9250 Silver 0.7137 oz. ASW, 37 mm. **Obv:** Value **Rev:** Two Goitered Gazelles **Edge:** Plain

Date	Mintage	F	VF	XF	Unc	BU
2005 Proof	3,000	Value: 50.00				

KM# 62 500 TENGE

31.1000 g., 0.9250 Silver 0.9249 oz. ASW, 38.6 mm. **Obv:** Horse race and value **Rev:** Gold plated tiger **Edge:** Plain **Shape:** 12-sided

Date	Mintage	F	VF	XF	Unc	BU
2005 Proof	5,000	Value: 50.00				

KM# 63 500 TENGE

31.1000 g., 0.9250 Bi-Metallic Blackend Silver center in Proof Silver ring 0.9249 oz., 38.6 mm. **Subject:** "Drakhma" **Obv:** Old coin design above value **Rev:** Old coin design **Edge:** Reeded

Date	Mintage	F	VF	XF	Unc	BU
2005 Proof	5,000	Value: 50.00				

KM# 72 500 TENGE

31.1000 g., 0.9250 Silver 0.9249 oz. ASW, 38.6 mm. **Obv:** Horse race and value **Rev:** Gold plated rider **Edge:** Plain

Date	Mintage	F	VF	XF	Unc	BU
2005 Proof	5,000	Value: 50.00				

KM# 82 500 TENGE

41.4000 g., Bi-Metallic**Ring Weight:** 14.6000 g. **Ring Composition:** 0.9250 Silver 0.4342 oz. ASW , 38.61 mm. **Subject:** 50th Anniversary Launch of Sputnik I **Obv:** Stylized view of our solar system, multicolor **Obv. Legend:** REPUBLIC OF KAZAKHSTAN **Rev:** Sputnik I in space, earth in background, multicolor **Rev. Legend:** THE FIRST SPACE SATELLITE OF THE EARTH **Edge:** Reeded

Date	Mintage	F	VF	XF	Unc	BU
ND(2007) Proof	—	Value: 100				

KM# 68 1000 TENGE

7.7800 g., 0.9990 Gold 0.2499 oz. AGW, 20 mm. **Obv:** Two winged ibexes **Rev:** Ancient warrior **Edge:** Reeded

Date	Mintage	F	VF	XF	Unc	BU
2001 Proof	—	Value: 350				

KM# 67 5000 TENGE

1000.0000 g., 0.9250 Silver 29.738 oz. ASW, 100 mm. **Subject:** 10th Anniversary of Independence **Obv:** National arms above value **Rev:** Monument statue

Date	Mintage	F	VF	XF	Unc	BU
2001 Proof	—	Value: 650				

KENYA

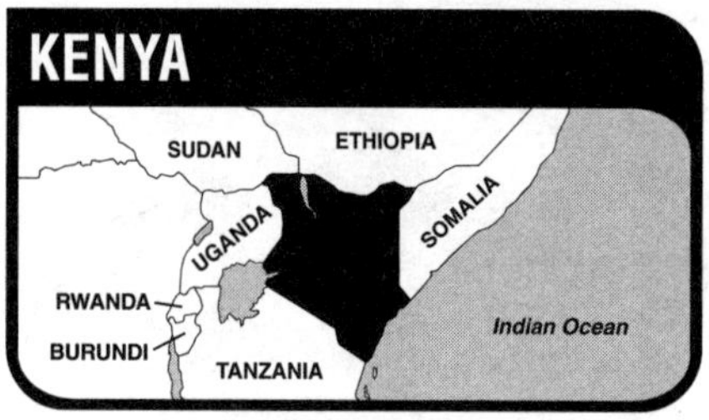

The Republic of Kenya, located on the east coast of Central Africa, has an area of 224,961 sq. mi (582,650 sq. km.) and a population of 20.1 million. Capital: Nairobi. The predominantly agricultural country exports coffee, tea and petroleum products.

Independence was attained on Dec. 12, 1963. Kenya became a republic in 1964. It is a member of the Commonwealth of Nations. The president is Chief of State and Head of Government.

MONETARY SYSTEM

100 Cents = 1 Shilling

REPUBLIC

STANDARD COINAGE

KM# 34 SHILLING

5.4600 g., Nickel Clad Steel, 23.9 mm. **Obv:** Value and national arms **Rev:** Jomo Kenyata **Edge:** Reeded and plain sections

Date	Mintage	F	VF	XF	Unc	BU
2005	—	—	—	—	—	1.00

KM# 35 10 SHILLINGS

5.0300 g., Bi-Metallic **Ring Composition:** Brass **Center Composition:** Copper-Nickel, 22.95 mm. **Subject:** First President **Obv:** Value above national arms **Obv. Legend:** REPUBLIC OF KENYA **Rev:** Bust of Mzee Jomo Kenyatta left **Edge:** Reeded

Date	Mintage	F	VF	XF	Unc	BU
2005	—	—	—	—	—	4.00

KM# 36 20 SHILLINGS

9.0200 g., Bi-Metallic **Ring Composition:** Copper-Nickel **Center Composition:** Brass, 25.97 mm. **Subject:** First President **Obv:** Large value above national arms **Obv. Legend:** REPUBLIC OF KENYA **Rev:** Bust of Mzee Jomo Kenyatta left **Edge:** Segmented reeding

Date	Mintage	F	VF	XF	Unc	BU
2005	—	—	—	—	—	5.00

KM# 33 40 SHILLINGS

11.1000 g., Bi-Metallic Copper-Nickel center in Brass ring, 27.4 mm. **Obv:** Bust facing within circle **Rev:** Arms with supporters and value within circle **Edge:** Reeding over lettering **Edge Lettering:** "40 YEARS OF INDEPENDENCE" **Note:** Issued December 11, 2003.

Date	Mintage	F	VF	XF	Unc	BU
ND(2003)	—	—	—	—	6.00	7.50

KIRIBATI

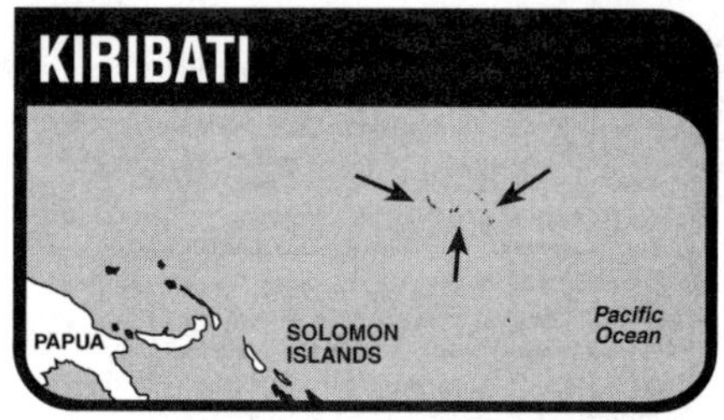

The Republic of Kiribati (formerly the Gilbert Islands), consists of 30 coral atolls and islands spread over more than one million sq. mi. (2,590,000 sq. km.) of the southwest Pacific Ocean, has an area of 332 sq. mi. (717 sq. km.) and a population of 64,200. Capital: Bairiki, on Tarawa. In addition to the Gilbert Islands proper, Kiribati includes Ocean Island, the Central and Southern Line Islands, and the Phoenix Islands, though possession of Canton and Enderbury of the Phoenix Islands is disputed with the United States. Most families engage in subsistence fishing. Copra and phosphates are exported, mostly to Australia and New Zealand.

Kiribati is a member of the Commonwealth of Nations. The President is the Head of State and Head of Government.

MONETARY SYSTEM

100 Cents = 1 Dollar

REPUBLIC

DECIMAL COINAGE

KM# 40 5 CENTS

4.2400 g., Brass, 22.9 mm. **Obv:** National arms **Rev:** Gorilla **Edge:** Reeded

Date	Mintage	F	VF	XF	Unc	BU
2003	—	—	—	—	1.00	1.50

KOREA-NORTH

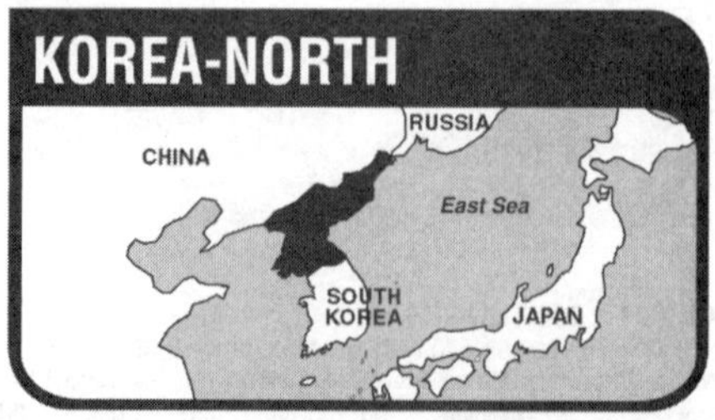

The Democratic Peoples Republic of Korea, situated in northeastern Asia on the northern half of the Korean peninsula between the Peoples Republic of China and the Republic of Korea, has an area of 46,540 sq. mi. (120,540 sq. km.) and a population of 20 million. Capital: Pyongyang. The economy is based on heavy industry and agriculture. Metals, minerals and farm produce are exported.

NOTE: For earlier coinage see Korea.

MONETARY SYSTEM

100 Chon = 1 Won

MINT

Pyongyang

DATING

In the year 2001 the North Korean adopted the "Juche" dating system which is based on the birth year of Kim Il Sung, founder of North Korea. He was born in 1911. "Quel" refers to month and "Quil" refers to day. 9 Quel 3 Quil refers to September 3rd. The western dates on these coins follow the "Juche" date in parenthesis.

PEOPLES REPUBLIC

DECIMAL COINAGE

KM# 183 1/2 CHON

2.1600 g., Aluminum, 27.02 mm. **Obv:** State arms **Rev:** Horse **Edge:** Plain

Date	Mintage	F	VF	XF	Unc	BU
2002	—	—	—	—	1.25	1.50

KM# 184 1/2 CHON

2.1600 g., Aluminum, 27.02 mm. **Obv:** State arms **Rev:** Orangutan **Edge:** Plain

Date	Mintage	F	VF	XF	Unc	BU
2002	—	—	—	—	1.25	1.50

KM# 185 1/2 CHON

2.1600 g., Aluminum, 27.02 mm. **Obv:** State arms **Rev:** Leopard **Edge:** Plain

Date	Mintage	F	VF	XF	Unc	BU
2002	—	—	—	—	1.25	1.50

KM# 186 1/2 CHON

2.1600 g., Aluminum, 27.02 mm. **Obv:** State arms **Rev:** Two giraffes **Edge:** Plain

Date	Mintage	F	VF	XF	Unc	BU
2002	—	—	—	—	1.25	1.50

KM# 187 1/2 CHON

2.1600 g., Aluminum, 27.02 mm. **Obv:** State arms **Rev:** Helmeted guineafowl **Edge:** Plain

Date	Mintage	F	VF	XF	Unc	BU
2002	—	—	—	—	1.25	1.50

KM# 188 1/2 CHON

2.1600 g., Aluminum, 27.02 mm. **Obv:** State arms **Rev:** Mamushi pit viper **Edge:** Plain

Date	Mintage	F	VF	XF	Unc	BU
2002	—	—	—	—	1.25	1.50

KM# 189 1/2 CHON

2.1600 g., Aluminum, 27.02 mm. **Obv:** State arms **Rev:** Bighorn sheep **Edge:** Plain

Date	Mintage	F	VF	XF	Unc	BU
2002	—	—	—	—	1.25	1.50

KM# 190 1/2 CHON

2.1600 g., Aluminum, 27.02 mm. **Obv:** State arms **Rev:** Hippopotamus **Edge:** Plain

Date	Mintage	F	VF	XF	Unc	BU
2002	—	—	—	—	1.25	1.50

KM# 191 1/2 CHON

2.1600 g., Aluminum, 27.02 mm. **Subject:** FAO **Obv:** State arms **Rev:** Ancient ship **Edge:** Plain

Date	Mintage	F	VF	XF	Unc	BU
2002	—	—	—	—	1.25	1.50

KM# 192 1/2 CHON

2.1600 g., Aluminum, 27.02 mm. **Subject:** FAO **Obv:** State arms **Rev:** Archaic ship **Edge:** Plain

Date	Mintage	F	VF	XF	Unc	BU
2002	—	—	—	—	1.25	1.50

KM# 193 1/2 CHON

2.1600 g., Aluminum, 27.02 mm. **Subject:** FAO **Obv:** State arms **Rev:** Modern train **Edge:** Plain

Date	Mintage	F	VF	XF	Unc	BU
2002	—	—	—	—	1.25	1.50

KM# 194 1/2 CHON

2.1600 g., Aluminum, 27.02 mm. **Subject:** FAO **Obv:** State arms **Rev:** Jet airliner **Edge:** Plain

Date	Mintage	F	VF	XF	Unc	BU
2002	—	—	—	—	1.25	1.50

KM# 195 CHON

4.6300 g., Brass, 21.7 mm. **Subject:** FAO **Obv:** State arms **Rev:** Antique steam locomotive **Edge:** Plain

Date	Mintage	F	VF	XF	Unc	BU
2002	—	—	—	—	1.50	1.75

KM# 196 CHON

4.6300 g., Brass, 21.7 mm. **Subject:** FAO **Obv:** State arms **Rev:** Antique automobile **Edge:** Plain

Date	Mintage	F	VF	XF	Unc	BU
2002	—	—	—	—	1.50	1.75

KM# 197 2 CHON

6.0400 g., Copper Nickel, 24.2 mm. **Subject:** FAO **Obv:** State arms **Rev:** Antique touring car **Edge:** Plain

Date	Mintage	F	VF	XF	Unc	BU
2002	—	—	—	—	2.00	2.50

KM# 162.2 WON

7.0000 g., Aluminum, 40 mm. **Obv:** State arms, date above value **Rev:** Radiant Korean map and landmarks **Edge:** Plain

Date	Mintage	F	VF	XF	Unc	BU
2001 Proof	—	Value: 15.00				

KM# 351 WON

7.0000 g., Aluminum, 40 mm. **Obv:** State arms, date and value below **Rev:** North Korean Arch of Triumph **Edge:** Plain

Date	Mintage	F	VF	XF	Unc	BU
2001 Proof	—	Value: 15.00				

KM# 352 WON

28.6000 g., Brass, 40.1 mm. **Obv:** State arms, value below **Rev:** North Korean Arch of Triumph **Edge:** Plain

Date	Mintage	F	VF	XF	Unc	BU
2001 Proof	—	Value: 17.50				

KM# 353 WON

6.4500 g., Aluminum, 40 mm. **Obv:** State arms, value below **Rev:** N. Korean landmarks and tourists above ship **Edge:** Plain

Date	Mintage	F	VF	XF	Unc	BU
2001 Proof	—	Value: 15.00				

KM# 354 WON

27.6300 g., Brass, 40 mm. **Obv:** State arms, date and value below **Rev:** N. Korean landmarks and tourists above ship **Edge:** Plain

Date	Mintage	F	VF	XF	Unc	BU
2001 Proof	—	Value: 17.50				

KM# 355 WON

6.7500 g., Aluminum, 40 mm. **Obv:** State arms, value below **Rev:** Temple of Heaven above Hong Kong city view below **Edge:** Plain

Date	Mintage	F	VF	XF	Unc	BU
ND Proof	—	Value: 15.00				

KM# 356 WON

28.1000 g., Brass, 40 mm. **Obv:** State arms, date and value below **Rev:** Temple of Heaven above, Hong Kong city view below **Edge:** Plain

Date	Mintage	F	VF	XF	Unc	BU
2001 Proof	—	Value: 17.50				

KM# 294a WON

6.7500 g., Aluminum, 40 mm. **Obv:** State arms **Rev:** Antique ceramics **Edge:** Plain

Date	Mintage	F	VF	XF	Unc	BU
2001 Proof	—	Value: 15.00				

KM# 358 WON

6.7500 g., Aluminum, 40 mm. **Obv:** State arms **Rev:** Old fort **Edge:** Plain

Date	Mintage	F	VF	XF	Unc	BU
2001 Proof	—	Value: 15.00				

KM# 358a WON

28.1000 g., Brass, 40 mm. **Obv:** State arms **Rev:** Old fort **Edge:** Plain

Date	Mintage	F	VF	XF	Unc	BU
2001 Proof	—	Value: 17.50				

KM# 359 WON

7.0000 g., Aluminum, 40.1 mm. **Obv:** State arms **Rev:** Old couple above dates1945-2000 **Edge:** Plain

Date	Mintage	F	VF	XF	Unc	BU
2001 Proof	—	Value: 15.00				

KM# 359a WON

27.8000 g., Brass, 40.1 mm. **Obv:** State arms **Rev:** Old couple above dates 1945-2000 **Edge:** Plain

Date	Mintage	F	VF	XF	Unc	BU
2001 Proof	—	Value: 17.50				

KM# 360 WON

27.8000 g., Brass, 40.1 mm. **Obv:** State arms **Rev:** Blue Dragon **Edge:** Plain

Date	Mintage	F	VF	XF	Unc	BU
2001 Proof	—	Value: 20.00				

KM# 361 WON
7.0000 g., Aluminum, 40.1 mm. **Obv:** State arms **Rev:** Head 3/4 left divides dates (1904-1997) flanked by sprigs **Edge:** Plain

Date	Mintage	F	VF	XF	Unc	BU
2001 Proof	—	Value: 15.00				

KM# 361a WON
27.8000 g., Brass, 40.1 mm. **Obv:** State arms **Rev:** Head 3/4 left divides dates(1904-1997) flanked by sprigs **Edge:** Plain

Date	Mintage	F	VF	XF	Unc	BU
2001 Proof	—	Value: 17.50				

KM# 362 WON
7.0000 g., Aluminum, 40.1 mm. **Obv:** State arms **Rev:** Children flying a kite **Edge:** Plain

Date	Mintage	F	VF	XF	Unc	BU
2001 Proof	—	Value: 15.00				

KM# 362a WON
27.8000 g., Brass, 40.1 mm. **Obv:** State arms **Rev:** Children flying a kite **Edge:** Plain

Date	Mintage	F	VF	XF	Unc	BU
2001 Proof	—	Value: 17.50				

KM# 363 WON
7.0000 g., Aluminum, 40.1 mm. **Obv:** State arms **Rev:** Children on seesaw **Edge:** Plain

Date	Mintage	F	VF	XF	Unc	BU
2001 Proof	—	Value: 15.00				

KM# 363a WON
27.8000 g., Brass, 40.1 mm. **Obv:** State arms **Rev:** Children on seesaw **Edge:** Plain

Date	Mintage	F	VF	XF	Unc	BU
2001 Proof	—	Value: 17.50				

KM# 364 WON
7.0000 g., Aluminum, 40.1 mm. **Obv:** State arms **Rev:** Children wrestling **Edge:** Plain

Date	Mintage	F	VF	XF	Unc	BU
2001 Proof	—	Value: 15.00				

KM# 364a WON
27.8000 g., Brass, 40.1 mm. **Obv:** State arms **Rev:** Children wrestling **Edge:** Plain

Date	Mintage	F	VF	XF	Unc	BU
2001 Proof	—	Value: 17.50				

KM# 365 WON
7.0000 g., Aluminum, 40.1 mm. **Obv:** State arms **Rev:** Girl on swing **Edge:** Plain

Date	Mintage	F	VF	XF	Unc	BU
2001 Proof	—	Value: 15.00				

KM# 365a WON
27.8000 g., Brass, 40.1 mm. **Obv:** State arms **Rev:** Girl on swing **Edge:** Plain

Date	Mintage	F	VF	XF	Unc	BU
2001 Proof	—	Value: 17.50				

KM# 366 WON
7.0000 g., Aluminum, 40.1 mm. **Obv:** State arms **Rev:** Girls jumping rope **Edge:** Plain

Date	Mintage	F	VF	XF	Unc	BU
2001 Proof	—	Value: 15.00				

KM# 366a WON
27.8000 g., Brass, 40.1 mm. **Obv:** State arms **Rev:** Girls jumping rope **Edge:** Plain

Date	Mintage	F	VF	XF	Unc	BU
2001 Proof	—	Value: 17.50				

KM# 367 WON
8.7000 g., Aluminum, 40.4 mm. **Obv:** State arms **Rev:** "Kumdang-2 Injection" in center square on leaves **Edge:** Plain

Date	Mintage	F	VF	XF	Unc	BU
2001 Proof	—	Value: 15.00				

KM# 367a WON
26.5400 g., Brass, 40.2 mm. **Obv:** State arms **Rev:** "Kumdang-2 Injection" in center square on leaves **Edge:** Plain

Date	Mintage	F	VF	XF	Unc	BU
2001 Proof	—	Value: 17.50				

KM# 368 WON
27.6100 g., Brass, 40.2 mm. **Obv:** State arms **Rev:** Bust facing divides dates(1912-1994) above sprigs **Edge:** Plain

Date	Mintage	F	VF	XF	Unc	BU
JU90-2001 Proof	—	Value: 17.50				

KM# 369 WON
6.5500 g., Aluminum, 40.4 mm. **Obv:** State arms **Rev:** Train at left, couple below jet plane at right **Edge:** Plain

Date	Mintage	F	VF	XF	Unc	BU
2001 Proof	—	Value: 15.00				

KM# 370 WON
27.5600 g., Brass, 40.1 mm. **Obv:** State arms **Rev:** Train at left, couple below jet plane at right **Edge:** Plain

Date	Mintage	F	VF	XF	Unc	BU
2001 Proof	—	Value: 17.50				

KM# 371 WON
5.0500 g., Aluminum, 35 mm. **Obv:** State arms **Rev:** Hong Kong city view **Edge:** Plain

Date	Mintage	F	VF	XF	Unc	BU
2001 Proof	—	Value: 10.00				

KM# 372 WON
6.4000 g., Aluminum, 40 mm. **Obv:** State arms **Rev:** Bust with beard facing flanked by text **Edge:** Plain

Date	Mintage	F	VF	XF	Unc	BU
2001 Proof	—	Value: 15.00				

KM# 372a WON
27.7000 g., Brass, 40 mm. **Obv:** State arms **Rev:** Bust with beard facing flanked by text **Edge:** Plain

Date	Mintage	F	VF	XF	Unc	BU
2001 Proof	—	Value: 17.50				

KM# 373 WON
6.9000 g., Aluminum, 40 mm. **Subject:** 1996 Olympics **Obv:** State arms **Rev:** Two green gymnasts and multicolor flame **Edge:** Plain

Date	Mintage	F	VF	XF	Unc	BU
2001 Proof	—	Value: 15.00				

KM# 374 WON
7.0000 g., Aluminum, 40 mm. **Obv:** State arms **Rev:** Taedong Gatehouse **Edge:** Plain

Date	Mintage	F	VF	XF	Unc	BU
2001 Proof	—	Value: 15.00				

KM# 375 WON
8.5000 g., Aluminum, 40.2 mm. **Obv:** State arms **Rev:** Tourists above volcano crater **Edge:** Plain

Date	Mintage	F	VF	XF	Unc	BU
JU90-2001 Proof	—	Value: 15.00				

KM# 238a WON
7.1400 g., Aluminum, 40.1 mm. **Obv:** State arms **Rev:** Tiger and cub **Edge:** Plain

Date	Mintage	F	VF	XF	Unc	BU
2001 Proof	—	Value: 17.00				

KM# 376 WON
7.1000 g., Aluminum, 40.1 mm. **Subject:** 1996 Olympics **Obv:** State arms **Rev:** Horse jumping **Edge:** Plain

Date	Mintage	F	VF	XF	Unc	BU
2001 Proof	—	Value: 15.00				

KM# 377 WON
7.0000 g., Aluminum, 40.1 mm. **Subject:** 1996 Olympics **Obv:** State arms **Rev:** Four runners **Edge:** Plain

Date	Mintage	F	VF	XF	Unc	BU
2001 Proof	—	Value: 15.00				

KM# 378 WON
6.8400 g., Aluminum, 40.1 mm. **Obv:** State arms **Rev:** Monument flanked by multicolor flags and flowers **Edge:** Plain

Date	Mintage	F	VF	XF	Unc	BU
2001 Proof	—	Value: 15.00				

KM# 379 WON
6.6000 g., Aluminum, 40.1 mm. **Obv:** State arms **Rev:** Olympic diver **Edge:** Plain

Date	Mintage	F	VF	XF	Unc	BU
2001 Proof	—	Value: 15.00				

KM# 380 WON
6.9100 g., Aluminum, 40.1 mm. **Obv:** State arms **Rev:** Olympic handball player **Edge:** Plain

Date	Mintage	F	VF	XF	Unc	BU
2001 Proof	—	Value: 15.00				

KM# 381 WON
7.1100 g., Aluminum, 40.2 mm. **Obv:** State arms **Rev:** Olympic high bar gymnast **Edge:** Plain

Date	Mintage	F	VF	XF	Unc	BU
2001 Proof	—	Value: 15.00				

KM# 381a WON
28.8200 g., Brass, 40.1 mm. **Obv:** State arms **Rev:** Olympic high bar gymnast **Edge:** Plain

Date	Mintage	F	VF	XF	Unc	BU
2001 Proof	—	Value: 17.50				

KM# 382 WON
6.5000 g., Aluminum, 40.1 mm. **Obv:** State arms **Rev:** Olympic archer **Edge:** Plain

Date	Mintage	F	VF	XF	Unc	BU
2001 Proof	—	Value: 15.00				

KM# 382a WON
27.4100 g., Brass, 40.2 mm. **Obv:** State arms **Rev:** Olympic archer **Edge:** Plain

Date	Mintage	F	VF	XF	Unc	BU
2001 Proof	—	Value: 17.50				

KM# 383 WON
7.1000 g., Aluminum, 40.1 mm. **Obv:** State arms **Rev:** Olympic hurdler **Edge:** Plain

Date	Mintage	F	VF	XF	Unc	BU
2001 Proof	—	Value: 15.00				

KM# 383a WON
28.0000 g., Brass, 40.1 mm. **Obv:** State arms **Rev:** Olympic hurdler **Edge:** Plain

Date	Mintage	F	VF	XF	Unc	BU
2001 Proof	—	Value: 17.50				

KM# 384 WON
7.1500 g., Aluminum, 40.1 mm. **Obv:** State arms **Rev:** Kim Il Sung's birthplace side view **Edge:** Plain

Date	Mintage	F	VF	XF	Unc	BU
JU90-2001 Proof	—	Value: 15.00				

KM# 385 WON
7.0000 g., Aluminum, 40.1 mm. **Obv:** State arms **Rev:** Mt. Kumgang Fairy playing flute **Edge:** Plain

Date	Mintage	F	VF	XF	Unc	BU
2001 Proof	—	Value: 15.00				

KM# 385a WON
28.1600 g., Brass, 40.2 mm. **Obv:** State arms **Rev:** Mt. Kumgang Fairy playing flute **Edge:** Plain

Date	Mintage	F	VF	XF	Unc	BU
2001 Proof	—	Value: 17.50				

KM# 290 WON
28.2000 g., Brass, 40.1 mm. **Obv:** State arms **Rev:** Bust facing above flower sprigs **Edge:** Plain

Date	Mintage	F	VF	XF	Unc	BU
JU90-2001 Proof	—	Value: 20.00				

KM# 291 WON
28.2000 g., Brass, 40.1 mm. **Obv:** State arms **Rev:** Bust facing divides dates (1917-1949) above flower sprigs **Edge:** Plain

Date	Mintage	F	VF	XF	Unc	BU
JU90-2001 Proof	—	Value: 20.00				

KM# 293 WON
28.2000 g., Brass, 40.2 mm. **Obv:** State arms **Rev:** Olympic runners **Edge:** Crude reeding

Date	Mintage	F	VF	XF	Unc	BU
2001 Proof	—	Value: 20.00				

KM# 294 WON
28.2000 g., Brass, 40.2 mm. **Obv:** State arms **Rev:** Antique porcelain objects **Edge:** Plain

Date	Mintage	F	VF	XF	Unc	BU
2001 Proof	—	Value: 20.00				

KM# 236a WON
7.0000 g., Aluminum, 40 mm. **Obv:** State arms **Rev:** "Hyonmu" **Edge:** Plain

Date	Mintage	F	VF	XF	Unc	BU
2001 Proof	—	Value: 15.00				

KM# 452 WON
27.4400 g., Brass, 40.13 mm. **Obv:** State arms **Rev:** Early sailing ship **Rev. Legend:** • HISTORY OF SEAFARING • MERCHANTMAN - THE DPR KOREA . KORYO PERIOD . 918-1392 **Edge:** Plain

Date	Mintage	F	VF	XF	Unc	BU
2001 Proof	—	Value: 9.00				

KM# 157 WON

6.7000 g., Aluminum, 40 mm. **Subject:** Seafaring Ships **Obv:** State arms **Rev:** Cruise ship below sryilized head left profile **Edge:** Plain

Date	Mintage	F	VF	XF	Unc	BU
JU90-2001 Proof	—	Value: 9.00				

KM# 157a WON

29.0500 g., Brass, 40.2 mm. **Obv:** State arms **Rev:** Cruise ship below styilized head profile left **Edge:** Plain

Date	Mintage	F	VF	XF	Unc	BU
2001 Proof	—	Value: 17.50				

KM# 158 WON

16.2000 g., Brass, 35 mm. **Subject:** First Nobel Prize Winner in Literature **Obv:** State arms **Rev:** Half length seated bust left flanked by shelves and books **Edge:** Plain

Date	Mintage	F	VF	XF	Unc	BU
ND(2001) Proof	—	Value: 10.00				

KM# 158a WON

17.0000 g., Copper-Nickel, 35 mm. **Subject:** First Nobel Prize Winner in Literature - Sully Prudhomme **Obv:** State arms **Rev:** Half length seated bust left flanked by shelves and books **Edge:** Plain

Date	Mintage	F	VF	XF	Unc	BU
ND(2001) Proof	2,000	Value: 100				

KM# 159 WON

16.2000 g., Brass, 35 mm. **Subject:** First Nobel Prize in Physics **Obv:** State arms **Rev:** Bust 3/4 right at left with same person seated in lab at right **Edge:** Plain

Date	Mintage	F	VF	XF	Unc	BU
ND(2001) Proof	—	Value: 10.00				

KM# 159a WON

17.0000 g., Copper-Nickel, 35 mm. **Subject:** First Nobel Prize Winner in Physics - Wilhelm C. Roentgen **Obv:** State arms **Rev:** Bust 3/4 right at left with same person seated in lab at right **Edge:** Plain

Date	Mintage	F	VF	XF	Unc	BU
ND(2001) Proof	2,000	Value: 100				

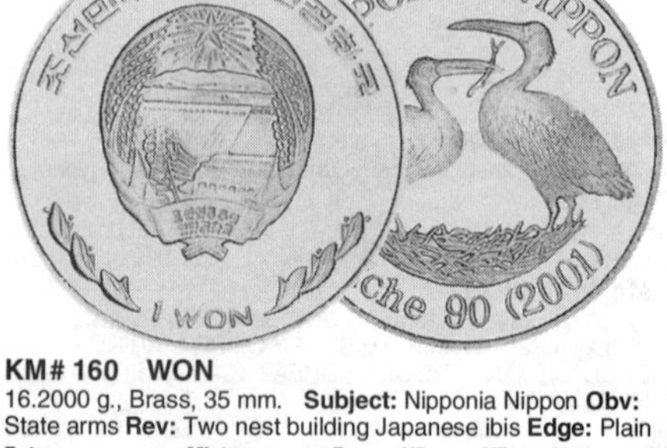

KM# 160 WON

16.2000 g., Brass, 35 mm. **Subject:** Nipponia Nippon **Obv:** State arms **Rev:** Two nest building Japanese ibis **Edge:** Plain

Date	Mintage	F	VF	XF	Unc	BU
JU90-2001 Proof	—	Value: 15.00				

KM# 160a WON

17.0000 g., Copper-Nickel, 35 mm. **Subject:** Wildlife **Obv:** State arms **Rev:** Two nesting Japanese Ibis birds **Edge:** Plain

Date	Mintage	F	VF	XF	Unc	BU
JU2001 Proof	200	Value: 100				

KM# 160b WON

5.3500 g., Aluminum, 35.1 mm. **Obv:** State arms **Rev:** Two nest building Japanese Ibis birds **Edge:** Plain

Date	Mintage	F	VF	XF	Unc	BU
JU90-2001 Proof	—	Value: 15.00				

KM# 202 WON

17.0000 g., Copper-Nickel, 35 mm. **Subject:** School Ships **Obv:** State arms **Rev:** SS Krusenstern **Edge:** Plain

Date	Mintage	F	VF	XF	Unc	BU
ND(2001) Proof	200	Value: 100				

KM# 204 WON

17.0000 g., Copper-Nickel, 35 mm. **Subject:** Wildlife **Obv:** State arms **Rev:** Two standing Japanese Ibis birds **Edge:** Plain

Date	Mintage	F	VF	XF	Unc	BU
JU90-2001 Proof	100	Value: 150				

KM# 207 WON

17.0000 g., Copper-Nickel, 35 mm. **Subject:** Wildlife **Obv:** State arms **Rev:** Two Korean Longtail Gorals **Edge:** Plain

Date	Mintage	F	VF	XF	Unc	BU
JU90-2001 Proof	200	Value: 100				

KM# 207a WON

16.0500 g., Brass, 35 mm. **Obv:** State arms **Rev:** Two Longtail Gorals **Edge:** Plain

Date	Mintage	F	VF	XF	Unc	BU
JU90-2001 Proof	—	Value: 18.50				

KM# 207b WON

5.3500 g., Aluminum, 35.1 mm. **Obv:** State arms **Rev:** Two Longtail Gorals **Edge:** Plain

Date	Mintage	F	VF	XF	Unc	BU
JU90-2001 Proof	—	Value: 15.00				

KM# 209 WON

17.0000 g., Copper-Nickel, 35 mm. **Subject:** First Nobel Prize Winner in Medicine - Emil A. von Behring **Obv:** State arms **Rev:** Lab beaker divides half length figures facing each other **Edge:** Plain

Date	Mintage	F	VF	XF	Unc	BU
ND(2001) Proof	2,000	Value: 100				

KM# 210 WON

17.0000 g., Copper-Nickel, 35 mm. **Subject:** First Nobel Prize Winner in Peace - Henri Dunant **Obv:** State arms **Rev:** Bust facing at left, war wounded at right **Edge:** Plain

Date	Mintage	F	VF	XF	Unc	BU
ND(2001) Proof	2,000	Value: 100				

KM# 211 WON

17.0000 g., Copper-Nickel, 35 mm. **Subject:** First Nobel Prize Winner in Chemistry - Jacobus Van't Hoff **Obv:** State arms **Rev:** Standing figures in lab scene **Edge:** Plain

Date	Mintage	F	VF	XF	Unc	BU
ND(2001) Proof	2,000	Value: 100				

KM# 212 WON

17.0000 g., Copper-Nickel, 35 mm. **Subject:** First Nobel Prize Winner in Peace - Frederic Passy **Obv:** State arms **Rev:** Head left at right with allegorical scene at left **Edge:** Plain

Date	Mintage	F	VF	XF	Unc	BU
ND(2001) Proof	2,000	Value: 100				

KM# 232 WON

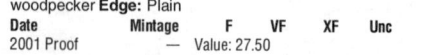

28.1100 g., Brass, 40 mm. **Obv:** State arms **Rev:** White-bellied woodpecker **Edge:** Plain

Date	Mintage	F	VF	XF	Unc	BU
2001 Proof	—	Value: 27.50				

KM# 233 WON
28.1100 g., Brass, 40 mm. **Obv:** State arms **Rev:** Black grouse **Edge:** Plain

Date	Mintage	F	VF	XF	Unc	BU
2001 Proof	—	Value: 27.50				

KM# 234 WON
28.1100 g., Brass, 40 mm. **Obv:** State arms **Rev:** Sand grouse **Edge:** Plain

Date	Mintage	F	VF	XF	Unc	BU
2001 Proof	—	Value: 27.50				

KM# 235 WON
28.1100 g., Brass, 40 mm. **Obv:** State arms **Rev:** Fairy Pitta bird **Edge:** Plain

Date	Mintage	F	VF	XF	Unc	BU
2001 Proof	—	Value: 27.50				

KM# 236 WON
28.1100 g., Brass, 40 mm. **Obv:** State arms **Rev:** Mythical "Hyonmu" **Edge:** Plain

Date	Mintage	F	VF	XF	Unc	BU
2001 Proof	—	Value: 27.50				

KM# 237 WON
28.1100 g., Brass, 40 mm. **Obv:** State arms **Rev:** Blue Dragon **Edge:** Plain

Date	Mintage	F	VF	XF	Unc	BU
2001 Proof	—	Value: 27.50				

KM# 238 WON
28.1100 g., Brass, 40 mm. **Obv:** State arms **Rev:** Two tigers **Edge:** Plain

Date	Mintage	F	VF	XF	Unc	BU
2001 Proof	—	Value: 27.50				

KM# 239 WON
28.1100 g., Brass, 40 mm. **Obv:** State arms **Rev:** Brontosaurus **Edge:** Plain

Date	Mintage	F	VF	XF	Unc	BU
2001 Proof	—	Value: 27.50				

KM# 247 WON
26.9500 g., Brass, 40 mm. **Obv:** State arms **Rev:** Soldier watching an air raid on a Yalu River bridge **Edge:** Plain

Date	Mintage	F	VF	XF	Unc	BU
2001 Proof	—	Value: 20.00				

KM# 248 WON
7.0000 g., Aluminum, 40 mm. **Obv:** State arms **Rev:** Multicolor rabbit and hearts **Edge:** Plain **Note:** Year of the Rabbit

Date	Mintage	F	VF	XF	Unc	BU
2001 Proof	—	Value: 20.00				

KM# 305 WON
28.2000 g., Brass, 40.2 mm. **Obv:** State arms **Rev:** Tomb of King Kong Min **Edge:** Plain

Date	Mintage	F	VF	XF	Unc	BU
JU91-2002 Proof	—	Value: 20.00				

KM# 306 WON
7.1000 g., Aluminum, 40 mm. **Obv:** State arms **Rev:** Two horses within circle of animals **Edge:** Plain **Note:** Prev. KM#398.

Date	Mintage	F	VF	XF	Unc	BU
2002 Proof	—	Value: 20.00				

KM# 306a WON
28.2000 g., Brass, 40.2 mm. **Obv:** State arms **Rev:** Two horses within circle of animals **Edge:** Plain

Date	Mintage	F	VF	XF	Unc	BU
2002 Proof	—	Value: 20.00				

KM# 308 WON
6.9000 g., Aluminum, 40 mm. **Obv:** State arms **Rev:** Arirang dancer with cranes flying above **Edge:** Plain **Note:** Prev. KM#390.

Date	Mintage	F	VF	XF	Unc	BU
JU91-(2002) Proof	—	Value: 15.00				

KM# 308a WON
28.2000 g., Brass, 40.2 mm. **Subject:** Arirang **Obv:** State arms **Rev:** Performers and flying cranes **Edge:** Plain

Date	Mintage	F	VF	XF	Unc	BU
JU91-(2002) Proof	—	Value: 20.00				

KM# 310 WON
28.2000 g., Brass, 40.2 mm. **Obv:** State arms **Rev:** Tomb of King Tongmyong **Edge:** Plain

Date	Mintage	F	VF	XF	Unc	BU
JU91-2002 Proof	—	Value: 20.00				

KM# 313 WON
6.7000 g., Aluminum, 40 mm. **Obv:** State arms **Rev:** Arirang dancer **Edge:** Plain **Note:** Prev. KM#389.

Date	Mintage	F	VF	XF	Unc	BU
JU91-(2002) Proof	—	Value: 15.00				

KM# 313a WON

28.2000 g., Brass, 40.2 mm. **Subject:** Arirang **Obv:** State arms **Rev:** Dancer with upheld arms **Edge:** Plain

Date	Mintage	F	VF	XF	Unc	BU
JU91-(2002) Proof	—	Value: 20.00				

KM# 388 WON

7.1000 g., Aluminum, 40 mm. **Obv:** State arms **Rev:** Arirang dancer Silhouette **Edge:** Plain

Date	Mintage	F	VF	XF	Unc	BU
2002 Proof	—	Value: 15.00				

KM# 391 WON

7.1000 g., Aluminum, 40 mm. **Obv:** State arms **Rev:** Arirang ribbon dancer **Edge:** Plain

Date	Mintage	F	VF	XF	Unc	BU
JU91-2002 Proof	—	Value: 15.00				

KM# 392 WON

7.0000 g., Aluminum, 40 mm. **Obv:** State arms **Rev:** May Day Stadium **Edge:** Plain

Date	Mintage	F	VF	XF	Unc	BU
JU91-2002 Proof	—	Value: 15.00				

KM# 392a WON

28.5000 g., Brass, 40.1 mm. **Obv:** State arms **Rev:** May Day Stadium **Edge:** Plain

Date	Mintage	F	VF	XF	Unc	BU
JU91-2002 Proof	—	Value: 17.50				

KM# 393 WON

7.1000 g., Aluminum, 40 mm. **Obv:** State arms **Rev:** Woman floating above stadium **Edge:** Plain

Date	Mintage	F	VF	XF	Unc	BU
JU91-2002 Proof	—	Value: 15.00				

KM# 393a WON

28.2000 g., Brass, 40 mm. **Obv:** State arms **Rev:** Woman floating above stadium **Edge:** Plain

Date	Mintage	F	VF	XF	Unc	BU
JU91-2002 Proof	—	Value: 17.50				

KM# 394 WON

27.5000 g., Brass, 40 mm. **Obv:** State arms **Rev:** Ribbon dancer with Korea shaped ribbon **Edge:** Plain

Date	Mintage	F	VF	XF	Unc	BU
JU91-2002 Proof	—	Value: 17.50				

KM# 395 WON

27.5000 g., Brass, 40 mm. **Obv:** State arms **Rev:** Dancer in the shape of Korea **Edge:** Plain

Date	Mintage	F	VF	XF	Unc	BU
JU91-2002 Proof	—	Value: 17.50				

KM# 396 WON

7.0000 g., Aluminum, 40 mm. **Obv:** State arms **Rev:** Bust with hat facing divides dates(1337-1392) above building foundation **Edge:** Plain

Date	Mintage	F	VF	XF	Unc	BU
JU91-2002 Proof	—	Value: 15.00				

KM# 397 WON

7.0000 g., Aluminum, 40 mm. **Obv:** State arms **Rev:** Victorious athletes hugging **Edge:** Plain

Date	Mintage	F	VF	XF	Unc	BU
JU91-(2002) Proof	—	Value: 15.00				

KM# 397a WON

28.2400 g., Brass, 40 mm. **Obv:** State arms **Rev:** Victorious athletes hugging **Edge:** Plain

Date	Mintage	F	VF	XF	Unc	BU
JU91-(2002) Proof	—	Value: 17.50				

KM# 399 WON

4.8600 g., Aluminum, 35 mm. **Obv:** State arms **Rev:** Cantering horse **Edge:** Plain

Date	Mintage	F	VF	XF	Unc	BU
JU91-(2002) Proof	—	Value: 15.00				

KM# 399a WON

16.9300 g., Brass, 35 mm. **Obv:** State arms **Rev:** Cantering horse **Edge:** Plain

Date	Mintage	F	VF	XF	Unc	BU
JU91-(2002) Proof	—	Value: 15.00				

KM# 400 WON

5.1000 g., Aluminum, 35 mm. **Obv:** State arms **Rev:** Two wrestlers **Edge:** Plain

Date	Mintage	F	VF	XF	Unc	BU
JU91-(2002) Proof	—	Value: 12.50				

KM# 400a WON

16.5000 g., Brass, 35 mm. **Obv:** State arms **Rev:** Two wrestlers **Edge:** Plain

Date	Mintage	F	VF	XF	Unc	BU
JU91-(2002) Proof	—	Value: 15.00				

KM# 323 WON

6.9400 g., Aluminum, 40 mm. **Obv:** State arms **Rev:** Turtle shaped armoured ship of 1592 **Edge:** Plain

Date	Mintage	F	VF	XF	Unc	BU
JU92-2003 Proof	—	Value: 15.00				

KM# 319 WON

9.6200 g., Aluminum, 40 mm. **Obv:** State arms **Rev:** Helmeted head with two antenna-like horns on the helmet **Edge:** Plain

Date	Mintage	F	VF	XF	Unc	BU
JU92-2003 Proof	—	Value: 15.00				

KM# 403a WON

22.1000 g., Brass, 40 mm. **Obv:** State arms **Rev:** Armored bust facing wearing winged helmet (948-1031) **Edge:** Plain

Date	Mintage	F	VF	XF	Unc	BU
JU92-2003 Proof	—	Value: 17.50				

KM# 404 WON
9.6300 g., Aluminum, 40 mm. **Obv:** State arms **Rev:** Armored bust wearing a horned helmet **Edge:** Plain

Date	Mintage	F	VF	XF	Unc	BU
JU92-2003 Proof	—	Value: 15.00				

KM# 404a WON
22.2500 g., Brass, 40 mm. **Obv:** State arms **Rev:** Armored bust wearing a horned helmet **Edge:** Plain

Date	Mintage	F	VF	XF	Unc	BU
JU92-2003 Proof	—	Value: 17.50				

KM# 405 WON
7.0000 g., Aluminum, 40 mm. **Obv:** State arms **Rev:** Ram within circle of animals **Edge:** Plain

Date	Mintage	F	VF	XF	Unc	BU
2003 Proof	—	Value: 15.00				

KM# 405a WON
28.4400 g., Brass, 40 mm. **Obv:** State arms **Rev:** Ram within circle of animals **Edge:** Plain

Date	Mintage	F	VF	XF	Unc	BU
2003 Proof	—	Value: 17.50				

KM# 406 WON
10.1500 g., Aluminum, 40 mm. **Obv:** State arms **Rev:** Children kicking a shuttlecock **Edge:** Plain

Date	Mintage	F	VF	XF	Unc	BU
JU92-2003 Proof	—	Value: 15.00				

KM# 406a WON
24.6300 g., Brass, 40 mm. **Obv:** State arms **Rev:** Children kicking a shuttlecock **Edge:** Plain

Date	Mintage	F	VF	XF	Unc	BU
JU92-2003 Proof	—	Value: 17.50				

KM# 407a WON
23.1000 g., Brass, 40 mm. **Obv:** State arms **Rev:** Children playing jacks **Edge:** Plain

Date	Mintage	F	VF	XF	Unc	BU
JU92-2003 Proof	—	Value: 17.50				

KM# 408a WON
24.5600 g., Brass, 40 mm. **Obv:** State arms **Rev:** Children spinning tops **Edge:** Plain

Date	Mintage	F	VF	XF	Unc	BU
JU92-2003 Proof	—	Value: 17.50				

KM# 410a WON
24.6400 g., Brass, 40 mm. **Obv:** State arms **Rev:** Large dome building **Edge:** Plain

Date	Mintage	F	VF	XF	Unc	BU
JU92-2003 Proof	—	Value: 17.50				

KM# 319a WON
28.2000 g., Brass, 40.2 mm. **Obv:** State arms **Rev:** Helmeted head with two antenna-like horns on helmet **Edge:** Plain

Date	Mintage	F	VF	XF	Unc	BU
JU92-(2003) Proof	—	Value: 20.00				

KM# 323a WON
28.1000 g., Brass, 40.2 mm. **Obv:** State arms **Rev:** Turtle-shaped armoured ship of 1592 **Edge:** Plain

Date	Mintage	F	VF	XF	Unc	BU
JU92-2003 Proof	—	Value: 20.00				

KM# 264 WON
28.4700 g., Brass, 40 mm. **Obv:** State arms **Rev:** Sheep within circle of animals **Edge:** Plain

Date	Mintage	F	VF	XF	Unc	BU
2003 Proof	—	Value: 22.00				

KM# 265 WON
17.7000 g., Brass, 23.2 x 40.1 mm. **Obv:** State arms **Rev:** Callithrix Jacchus monkey **Edge:** Plain

Date	Mintage	F	VF	XF	Unc	BU
2004	—	Value: 27.50				

KM# 266 WON
17.7000 g., Brass, 23.2 x 40.1 mm. **Obv:** State arms **Rev:** Cercopjthecus Mitis monkey **Edge:** Plain

Date	Mintage	F	VF	XF	Unc	BU
2004 Proof	—	Value: 27.50				

KM# 267 WON
17.7000 g., Brass, 23.2 x 40.1 mm. **Obv:** State arms **Rev:** Two Saguinus Midas monkeys **Edge:** Plain

Date	Mintage	F	VF	XF	Unc	BU
2004 Proof	—	Value: 27.50				

KM# 330 WON
9.9200 g., Aluminum, 45 mm. **Obv:** State arms **Rev:** Mountain cabin **Edge:** Plain **Note:** Prev. KM#411.

Date	Mintage	F	VF	XF	Unc	BU
JU93-(2004) Proof	—	Value: 15.00				

KM# 330a WON
26.4500 g., Brass, 45 mm. **Obv:** State arms **Rev:** Mountain cabin **Edge:** Plain

Date	Mintage	F	VF	XF	Unc	BU
JU93-(2004) Proof	—	Value: 20.00				

KM# 331 WON
10.0000 g., Aluminum, 45 mm. **Obv:** State arms **Rev:** Kim Il Sung's birthplace, front view **Edge:** Plain **Note:** Prev. KM#412.

Date	Mintage	F	VF	XF	Unc	BU
JU93-(2004) Proof	—	Value: 15.00				

KM# 331a WON
26.4500 g., Brass, 45 mm. **Obv:** State arms **Rev:** Sung's birth place, front view **Edge:** Plain

Date	Mintage	F	VF	XF	Unc	BU
JU93-(2004) Proof	—	Value: 20.00				

KM# 332 WON

10.0000 g., Aluminum, 45 mm. **Obv:** State arms **Rev:** Kim Il Sung's birthplace, side view **Edge:** Plain **Note:** Prev. KM#413.

Date	Mintage	F	VF	XF	Unc	BU
JU93-(2004) Proof	—	Value: 15.00				

KM# 332a WON

26.4500 g., Brass, 45 mm. **Obv:** State arms **Rev:** Sung's birthplace, side view **Edge:** Plain

Date	Mintage	F	VF	XF	Unc	BU
JU93-(2004) Proof	—	Value: 20.00				

KM# 333 WON

26.4500 g., Brass, 45 mm. **Obv:** State arms **Rev:** Kim Jung Sook facing **Edge:** Plain

Date	Mintage	F	VF	XF	Unc	BU
JU93-2004 Proof	—	Value: 20.00				

KM# 334 WON

26.4500 g., Brass, 45 mm. **Obv:** State arms **Rev:** Uniformed bust facing **Edge:** Plain

Date	Mintage	F	VF	XF	Unc	BU
JU93-2004 Proof	—	Value: 20.00				

KM# 335 WON

26.4500 g., Brass, 45 mm. **Obv:** State arms **Rev:** Uniformed bust facing **Edge:** Plain

Date	Mintage	F	VF	XF	Unc	BU
JU93-2004 Proof	—	Value: 20.00				

KM# 336 WON

10.1000 g., Aluminum, 45 mm. **Obv:** State arms **Rev:** Kim Il Sung flower, orchid **Edge:** Plain **Note:** Prev. KM#414.

Date	Mintage	F	VF	XF	Unc	BU
JU93-(2004) Proof	—	Value: 15.00				

KM# 336a WON

26.4500 g., Brass, 45 mm. **Obv:** State arms **Rev:** Orchids **Edge:** Plain

Date	Mintage	F	VF	XF	Unc	BU
JU93-(2004) Proof	—	Value: 20.00				

KM# 337 WON

10.1000 g., Aluminum, 45 mm. **Obv:** State arms **Rev:** Kim Jong Il flower, peony **Edge:** Plain **Note:** Prev. KM#415.

Date	Mintage	F	VF	XF	Unc	BU
JU93-2004 Proof	—	Value: 15.00				

KM# 337a WON

26.4500 g., Brass, 45 mm. **Obv:** State arms **Rev:** Peony flower **Edge:** Plain

Date	Mintage	F	VF	XF	Unc	BU
JU93-(2004) Proof	—	Value: 20.00				

KM# 338 WON

9.9300 g., Aluminum, 45 mm. **Obv:** State arms **Rev:** Jin Dal Lae flower, Rose of Sharon **Edge:** Plain **Note:** Prev. KM#416.

Date	Mintage	F	VF	XF	Unc	BU
JU93-(2004) Proof	—	Value: 15.00				

KM# 338a WON

26.4500 g., Brass, 45 mm. **Obv:** State arms **Rev:** Rose of Sharon flowers **Edge:** Plain

Date	Mintage	F	VF	XF	Unc	BU
JU93-(2004) Proof	—	Value: 20.00				

KM# 249 2 WON

7.0000 g., 0.9990 Silver 0.2248 oz. ASW, 30 mm. **Obv:** State arms **Rev:** Two multicolor pandas **Edge:** Plain

Date	Mintage	F	VF	XF	Unc	BU
2003 Proof	—	Value: 30.00				

KM# 417 2 WON

24.6600 g., Brass, 31.6x45.75 mm. **Obv:** State arms **Rev:** Half length uniformed figure standing in land rover saluting below dates 1904-2004 **Edge:** Plain **Shape:** Rectangle

Date	Mintage	F	VF	XF	Unc	BU
ND(2004) Proof	—	Value: 18.00				

KM# 339 3 WON

12.5500 g., Aluminum, 50.1 mm. **Obv:** Korean map **Rev:** Huh Jun, Chosun doctor with books **Edge:** Plain

Date	Mintage	F	VF	XF	Unc	BU
JU93-2004 Proof	—	Value: 20.00				

KM# 339a 3 WON

40.5300 g., Brass, 50.2 mm. **Obv:** Korean map **Rev:** Bust facing to left of books **Edge:** Plain

Date	Mintage	F	VF	XF	Unc	BU
JU93-(2004) Proof	—	Value: 25.00				

KM# 203 5 WON

15.0000 g., 0.9990 Silver 0.4818 oz. ASW, 35 mm. **Subject:** School Ships **Obv:** State arms **Rev:** SS Krusenstern **Edge:** Plain

Date	Mintage	F	VF	XF	Unc	BU
ND(2001) Proof	500	Value: 75.00				

KM# 205 5 WON
15.0000 g., 0.9990 Silver 0.4818 oz. ASW, 35 mm. **Subject:** Wildlife **Obv:** State arms **Rev:** Two standing Japanese Ibis birds **Edge:** Plain

Date	Mintage	F	VF	XF	Unc	BU
JU90-2001 Proof	100	Value: 200				

KM# 206 5 WON
15.0000 g., 0.9990 Silver 0.4818 oz. ASW, 35 mm. **Subject:** Wildlife **Obv:** State arms **Rev:** Two nesting Japanese Ibis birds **Edge:** Plain

Date	Mintage	F	VF	XF	Unc	BU
JU90-2001 Proof	3,000	Value: 50.00				

KM# 208 5 WON
15.0000 g., 0.9990 Silver 0.4818 oz. ASW, 35 mm. **Subject:** Wildlife **Obv:** State arms **Rev:** Two Korean Longtail Gorals **Edge:** Plain

Date	Mintage	F	VF	XF	Unc	BU
JU90-2001 Proof	3,000	Value: 50.00				

KM# 219 5 WON
14.9600 g., 0.9990 Silver 0.4805 oz. ASW, 35 mm. **Obv:** State arms **Rev:** Dragon ship **Edge:** Plain

Date	Mintage	F	VF	XF	Unc	BU
2001 Proof	5,000	Value: 35.00				

KM# 226 5 WON
20.0000 g., 0.9990 Silver 0.6423 oz. ASW, 33.8 mm. **Subject:** Olympics **Obv:** State arms **Rev:** Hurdler **Edge:** Reeded

Date	Mintage	F	VF	XF	Unc	BU
2001 proof	—	Value: 35.00				

KM# 240 5 WON
14.9400 g., 0.9990 Silver 0.4798 oz. ASW, 35 mm. **Obv:** State arms **Rev:** "Orca" (Killer Whale) **Edge:** Plain

Date	Mintage	F	VF	XF	Unc	BU
2001 Proof	—	Value: 60.00				

KM# 241 5 WON
14.9200 g., 0.9990 Silver 0.4792 oz. ASW, 35 mm. **Obv:** State arms **Rev:** Orca and Eco-Tourists in boat **Edge:** Plain

Date	Mintage	F	VF	XF	Unc	BU
2001 Proof	—	Value: 60.00				

KM# 242 5 WON
14.8700 g., 0.9990 Silver 0.4776 oz. ASW, 35 mm. **Obv:** State arms **Rev:** "Pottwal" (Sperm Whale) **Edge:** Plain

Date	Mintage	F	VF	XF	Unc	BU
2001 Proof	—	Value: 60.00				

KM# 243 5 WON
14.9500 g., 0.9990 Silver 0.4802 oz. ASW, 35 mm. **Obv:** State arms **Rev:** "Buckelwal" (Humpback Whale) **Edge:** Plain

Date	Mintage	F	VF	XF	Unc	BU
2001 Proof	—	Value: 60.00				

KM# 244 5 WON
14.9300 g., 0.9990 Silver 0.4795 oz. ASW, 35 mm. **Obv:** State arms **Rev:** "Groenlandwal" (Greenland Whale) **Edge:** Plain

Date	Mintage	F	VF	XF	Unc	BU
2001 Proof	—	Value: 60.00				

KM# 245 5 WON
14.9500 g., 0.9990 Silver 0.4802 oz. ASW, 35 mm. **Obv:** State arms **Rev:** "Blauwal" (Blue Whale) **Edge:** Plain

Date	Mintage	F	VF	XF	Unc	BU
2001 Proof	—	Value: 60.00				

KM# 246 5 WON
14.9600 g., 0.9990 Silver 0.4805 oz. ASW, 35 mm. **Obv:** State arms **Rev:** "Grindwal" (Pilot Whale) **Edge:** Plain

Date	Mintage	F	VF	XF	Unc	BU
2001 Proof	—	Value: 60.00				

KM# 250 5 WON
14.9600 g., 0.9990 Silver 0.4805 oz. ASW, 35 mm. **Subject:** Return of Hong Kong to China **Obv:** State arms **Rev:** City view **Edge:** Plain

Date	Mintage	F	VF	XF	Unc	BU
2001 Proof	—	Value: 16.00				

KM# 251 5 WON
14.9000 g., 0.9990 Silver 0.4785 oz. ASW, 35 mm. **Subject:** Year of the Horse **Obv:** State arms **Rev:** Cantering horse **Edge:** Plain

Date	Mintage	F	VF	XF	Unc	BU
2002 Proof	—	Value: 30.00				

KM# 252 5 WON
14.9200 g., 0.9990 Silver 0.4792 oz. ASW, 35 mm. **Subject:** Korean Games **Obv:** State arms **Rev:** Two wrestlers **Edge:** Plain

Date	Mintage	F	VF	XF	Unc	BU
JU91-2002 Proof	—	Value: 16.00				

KM# 303 5 WON
15.0000 g., 0.9990 Silver 0.4818 oz. ASW, 35 mm. **Obv:** State arms **Rev:** Janggo dancer **Edge:** Segmented reeding

Date	Mintage	F	VF	XF	Unc	BU
JU91-2002 Proof	—	Value: 30.00				

KM# 304 5 WON
15.0000 g., 0.9990 Silver 0.4818 oz. ASW, 35 mm. **Obv:** State arms **Rev:** Armored Knight **Edge:** Segmented reeding

Date	Mintage	F	VF	XF	Unc	BU
JU91-2002 Proof	—	Value: 30.00				

KM# 327 5 WON
20.0000 g., 0.9990 Silver 0.6423 oz. ASW, 35 mm. **Obv:** State arms **Rev:** "Turtle Boat " of 1592 **Edge:** Segmented reeding

Date	Mintage	F	VF	XF	Unc	BU
JU92-2003 Proof	—	Value: 30.00				

KM# 328 5 WON
20.0000 g., 0.9990 Silver 0.6423 oz. ASW, 35 mm. **Obv:** State arms **Rev:** Olympic fencers **Edge:** Segmented reeding

Date	Mintage	F	VF	XF	Unc	BU
JU92-2003 Proof	—	Value: 30.00				

KM# 329 5 WON
20.0000 g., 0.9990 Silver 0.6423 oz. ASW, 35 mm. **Obv:** State arms **Rev:** Three wild horses **Edge:** Segmented reeding

Date	Mintage	F	VF	XF	Unc	BU
JU92-2003 Proof	—	Value: 30.00				

KM# 220 7 WON
20.0000 g., 0.9990 Silver 0.6423 oz. ASW, 38 mm. **Subject:** 2002 Olympics **Obv:** State arms **Rev:** Two speed skaters **Edge:** Plain

Date	Mintage	F	VF	XF	Unc	BU
2001 Proof	10,000	Value: 40.00				

KM# 221 7 WON
20.0000 g., 0.9990 Silver 0.6423 oz. ASW, 38 mm. **Subject:** Endangered Wildlife **Obv:** State arms **Rev:** White-tailed sea Eagle **Edge:** Plain

Date	Mintage	F	VF	XF	Unc	BU
2001 Proof	10,000	Value: 30.00				

KM# 292 10 WON
31.0000 g., 0.9990 Silver 0.9956 oz. ASW, 40.2 mm. **Obv:** State arms **Rev:** Bust facing flanked by dates (1912-1994) above flower sprigs **Edge:** Plain

Date	Mintage	F	VF	XF	Unc	BU
JU90-2001 Proof	—	Value: 35.00				

KM# 295 10 WON
31.0000 g., 0.9990 Silver 0.9956 oz. ASW, 40.2 mm. **Obv:** State arms **Rev:** Mountain cabin **Edge:** Plain

Date	Mintage	F	VF	XF	Unc	BU
JU90-2001 Proof	—	Value: 35.00				

KM# 296 10 WON
31.0000 g., 0.9990 Silver 0.9956 oz. ASW, 40.2 mm. **Obv:** State arms **Rev:** "KUMDANG - 2 INJECTION" in center of leaves **Edge:** Plain

Date	Mintage	F	VF	XF	Unc	BU
2001 Proof	—	Value: 35.00				

KM# 297 10 WON
31.0000 g., 0.9990 Silver 0.9956 oz. ASW, 40.2 mm. **Obv:** State arms **Rev:** Train scene and a couple below a jet liner **Rev. Legend:** ...1945 - 2001... **Edge:** Plain

Date	Mintage	F	VF	XF	Unc	BU
ND(2001) Proof	—	Value: 35.00				

KM# 298 10 WON
31.0000 g., 0.9990 Silver 0.9956 oz. ASW, 40.2 mm. **Obv:** State arms **Rev:** Cruise ship below stylized head left profile **Edge:** Plain

Date	Mintage	F	VF	XF	Unc	BU
JU90-2001 Proof	—	Value: 35.00				

KM# 299 10 WON
31.0000 g., 0.9990 Silver 0.9956 oz. ASW, 40.2 mm. **Obv:** State arms **Rev:** Old fortress **Edge:** Plain

Date	Mintage	F	VF	XF	Unc	BU
JU90-2001 Proof	—	Value: 35.00				

KM# 300 10 WON
31.0000 g., 0.9990 Silver 0.9956 oz. ASW, 40.2 mm. **Obv:** State arms **Rev:** Landmarks, flag and tourist couple above cruise ship **Edge:** Plain

Date	Mintage	F	VF	XF	Unc	BU
JU90-2001 Proof	—	Value: 35.00				

KM# 301 10 WON
31.0000 g., 0.9990 Silver 0.9956 oz. ASW, 40.2 mm. **Obv:** State arms **Rev:** Conjoined half length figures facing shaking hands **Edge:** Plain

Date	Mintage	F	VF	XF	Unc	BU
JU90-2001 Proof	—	Value: 35.00				

KM# 302 10 WON
31.0000 g., 0.9990 Silver 0.9956 oz. ASW, 40.1 mm. **Obv:** State arms **Rev:** Great East Gate **Edge:** Plain

Date	Mintage	F	VF	XF	Unc	BU
JU90-2001 Proof	—	Value: 35.00				

KM# 357 10 WON
31.0000 g., 0.9990 Silver 0.9956 oz. ASW, 40.2 mm. **Obv:** State arms **Rev:** Antique ceramic items **Edge:** Plain

Date	Mintage	F	VF	XF	Unc	BU
2001 Proof	—	Value: 35.00				

KM# 386 10 WON
30.7600 g., 0.9990 Silver 0.9879 oz. ASW, 40.1 mm. **Obv:** State arms **Rev:** Kim Jung Sook facing flanked by dates (1917-1949) above flower sprigs **Edge:** Plain

Date	Mintage	F	VF	XF	Unc	BU
JU90-2001 Proof	—	Value: 35.00				

KM# 387 10 WON
30.7600 g., 0.9990 Silver 0.9879 oz. ASW, 40.1 mm. **Obv:** State arms **Rev:** Bust facing above flower sprigs **Edge:** Plain

Date	Mintage	F	VF	XF	Unc	BU
JU90-2001 Proof	—	Value: 35.00				

KM# 152 10 WON
31.0000 g., 0.9990 Silver 0.9956 oz. ASW, 39.8 mm. **Subject:** Asian Money Fair **Obv:** State arms **Rev:** Two snakes **Edge:** Reeded and plain sections

Date	Mintage	F	VF	XF	Unc	BU
2001 Proof	—	Value: 50.00				

KM# 153 10 WON
31.0000 g., 0.9990 Silver 0.9956 oz. ASW, 39.8 mm. **Subject:** Tortoise-Serpent **Obv:** State arms **Rev:** Mythical creature **Edge:** Reeded and plain sections

Date	Mintage	F	VF	XF	Unc	BU
2001 Proof	—	Value: 50.00				

KM# 227 10 WON
31.0600 g., 0.9250 Silver 0.9237 oz. ASW, 39.9 mm. **Subject:** General Ri Sun Sin **Obv:** State arms **Rev:** Helmeted head 1/4 left **Edge:** Reeded

Date	Mintage	F	VF	XF	Unc	BU
2001	—	—	—	—	35.00	—

KM# 253 10 WON
31.1100 g., 0.9990 Silver 0.9992 oz. ASW, 40.2 mm. **Obv:** State arms **Rev:** Head 3/4 left flanked by dates (1904-1997) above flower sprigs **Edge:** Plain

Date	Mintage	F	VF	XF	Unc	BU
2001	—	Value: 25.00				

KM# 254 10 WON
30.7700 g., 0.9990 Silver 0.9882 oz. ASW, 40.15 mm. **Obv:** State arms **Rev:** Bust facing and his tomb **Edge:** Plain

Date	Mintage	F	VF	XF	Unc	BU
JU91-2002 Proof	—	Value: 25.00				

KM# 255 10 WON
30.9400 g., 0.9990 Silver 0.9937 oz. ASW, 40.2 mm. **Subject:** Jongmongju and Sonjukgyo **Obv:** State arms **Rev:** Head with hat facing above building foundation **Edge:** Plain

Date	Mintage	F	VF	XF	Unc	BU
JU91-2002 Proof	—	Value: 25.00				

KM# 231 10 WON
31.0000 g., 0.9990 Silver 0.9956 oz. ASW, 39.9 mm. **Subject:** Kim Il Sung **Obv:** State arms **Rev:** Bust facing **Edge:** Segmented reeding

Date	Mintage	F	VF	XF	Unc	BU
JU91-2002 Proof	—	Value: 40.00				

KM# 401 10 WON
31.0000 g., 0.9990 Silver 0.9956 oz. ASW, 40.1 mm. **Obv:** State arms **Rev:** Arirang dancer **Edge:** Plain

Date	Mintage	F	VF	XF	Unc	BU
JU91-2002 Proof	—	Value: 35.00				

KM# 402 10 WON
31.0000 g., 0.9990 Silver 0.9956 oz. ASW, 40.1 mm. **Obv:** State arms **Rev:** Arirang ribbon dancer **Edge:** Plain

Date	Mintage	F	VF	XF	Unc	BU
JU91-2002 Proof	—	Value: 35.00				

KM# 307 10 WON
31.0000 g., 0.9990 Silver 0.9956 oz. ASW, 40.1 mm. **Obv:** State arms **Rev:** Two horses within a circle of animals **Edge:** Plain

Date	Mintage	F	VF	XF	Unc	BU
2002 Proof	—	Value: 35.00				

KM# 309 10 WON
31.0000 g., 0.9990 Silver 0.9956 oz. ASW, 40.2 mm. **Subject:** Arirang **Obv:** State arms **Rev:** Performers and flying cranes **Edge:** Plain

Date	Mintage	F	VF	XF	Unc	BU
JU91-2002 Proof	—	Value: 35.00				

KM# 311 10 WON
31.0000 g., 0.9990 Silver 0.9956 oz. ASW, 40.2 mm. **Obv:** State arms **Rev:** Tomb of King Tongmyong **Edge:** Plain

Date	Mintage	F	VF	XF	Unc	BU
JU91-2002 Proof	—	Value: 35.00				

KM# 312 10 WON
31.0000 g., 0.9990 Silver 0.9956 oz. ASW, 40.2 mm. **Obv:** State arms **Rev:** Tomb of King Kong Min **Edge:** Plain

Date	Mintage	F	VF	XF	Unc	BU
JU91-2002 Proof	—	Value: 35.00				

KM# 314 10 WON
31.0000 g., 0.9990 Silver 0.9956 oz. ASW, 40.2 mm. **Subject:** Arirang **Obv:** State arms **Rev:** Stylized dancer **Edge:** Plain

Date	Mintage	F	VF	XF	Unc	BU
2002 Proof	—	Value: 35.00				

KM# 315 10 WON
31.0000 g., 0.9990 Silver 0.9956 oz. ASW, 40.2 mm. **Obv:** State arms **Rev:** Korean map shaped dancer **Edge:** Plain

Date	Mintage	F	VF	XF	Unc	BU
JU91-2002 Proof	—	Value: 35.00				

KM# 316 10 WON
31.0000 g., 0.9990 Silver 0.9956 oz. ASW, 40.2 mm. **Obv:** State arms **Rev:** Korean map shaped ribbon dancer **Edge:** Plain

Date	Mintage	F	VF	XF	Unc	BU
JU91-2002 Proof	—	Value: 35.00				

KM# 317 10 WON
31.0000 g., 0.9990 Silver 0.9956 oz. ASW, 40.2 mm. **Obv:** State arms **Rev:** Victorious athletes hugging **Edge:** Plain

Date	Mintage	F	VF	XF	Unc	BU
JU91-2002 Proof	—	Value: 35.00				

KM# 318 10 WON
31.0000 g., 0.9990 Silver 0.9956 oz. ASW, 40.2 mm. **Obv:** State arms **Rev:** Woman floating above arena **Edge:** Plain

Date	Mintage	F	VF	XF	Unc	BU
JU91-2002 Proof	—	Value: 35.00				

KM# 320 10 WON
31.0000 g., 0.9990 Silver 0.9956 oz. ASW, 40.2 mm. **Obv:** State arms **Rev:** Helmeted head with two antenna-like horns on helmet **Edge:** Plain

Date	Mintage	F	VF	XF	Unc	BU
JU92-2003 Proof	—	Value: 35.00				

KM# 321 10 WON
31.0000 g., 0.9990 Silver 0.9956 oz. ASW, 40.2 mm. **Obv:** State arms **Rev:** Helmeted head with horns **Edge:** Plain

Date	Mintage	F	VF	XF	Unc	BU
JU92-2003 Proof	—	Value: 35.00				

KM# 322 10 WON
31.0000 g., 0.9990 Silver 0.9956 oz. ASW, 40.2 mm. **Obv:** State arms **Rev:** Armored bust facing (948-1031) wearing winged helmet **Edge:** Plain

Date	Mintage	F	VF	XF	Unc	BU
JU92-2003 Proof	—	Value: 35.00				

KM# 324 10 WON
31.0000 g., 0.9990 Silver 0.9956 oz. ASW, 40.2 mm. **Obv:** State arms **Rev:** Turtle-shaped armoured ship of 1592 **Edge:** Plain

Date	Mintage	F	VF	XF	Unc	BU
JU92-2003 Proof	—	Value: 35.00				

KM# 325 10 WON
31.0000 g., 0.9990 Silver 0.9956 oz. ASW, 40.2 mm. **Obv:** State arms **Rev:** Children playing jacks **Edge:** Plain

Date	Mintage	F	VF	XF	Unc	BU
JU92-2003 Proof	—	Value: 35.00				

KM# 326 10 WON
31.0000 g., 0.9990 Silver 0.9956 oz. ASW, 40.2 mm. **Obv:** State arms **Rev:** Children kicking a shuttlecock **Edge:** Plain

Date	Mintage	F	VF	XF	Unc	BU
JU92-2003 Proof	—	Value: 35.00				

KM# 409 10 WON
30.9400 g., 0.9990 Silver 0.9937 oz. ASW, 40 mm. **Obv:** State arms **Rev:** Children spinning tops **Edge:** Plain

Date	Mintage	F	VF	XF	Unc	BU
JU92-2003 Proof	—	Value: 35.00				

KM# 418 10 WON
31.0000 g., 0.9990 Silver 0.9956 oz. ASW, 39.7 mm. **Obv:** State arms **Rev:** Ibis standing in water **Edge:** Segmented reeding

Date	Mintage	F	VF	XF	Unc	BU
JU93-2004 Proof	—	Value: 40.00				

KM# 342 10 WON
31.0000 g., 0.9990 Silver 0.9956 oz. ASW, 40 mm. **Obv:** State arms **Rev:** Domed building **Edge:** Plain

Date	Mintage	F	VF	XF	Unc	BU
JU93-2004 Proof	—	Value: 37.50				

KM# 343 10 WON
31.0000 g., 0.9990 Silver 0.9956 oz. ASW, 40 mm. **Obv:** State arms **Rev:** Pigeon on branch **Edge:** Segmented reeding

Date	Mintage	F	VF	XF	Unc	BU
JU93-2004 Proof	—	Value: 37.50				

KM# 344 10 WON
31.0000 g., 0.9990 Silver 0.9956 oz. ASW, 40 mm. **Obv:** State arms **Rev:** Two Leiothrix birds **Edge:** Segmented reeding

Date	Mintage	F	VF	XF	Unc	BU
JU93-2004 Proof	—	Value: 37.50				

KM# 345 10 WON
31.0000 g., 0.9990 Silver 0.9956 oz. ASW, 40 mm. **Obv:** State arms **Rev:** Two cranes standing in water **Edge:** Segmented reeding

Date	Mintage	F	VF	XF	Unc	BU
JU93-2004 Proof	—	Value: 40.00				

KM# 346 10 WON
31.0000 g., 0.9990 Silver 0.9956 oz. ASW, 40 mm. **Obv:** State arms **Rev:** Curlew bird **Edge:** Segmented reeding

Date	Mintage	F	VF	XF	Unc	BU
JU93-2004 Proof	—	Value: 37.50				

KM# 347 10 WON
31.0000 g., 0.9990 Silver 0.9956 oz. ASW, 40 mm. **Obv:** State arms **Rev:** Goshawk on branch **Edge:** Segmented reeding

Date	Mintage	F	VF	XF	Unc	BU
JU93-2004 Proof	—	Value: 37.50				

KM# 420 10 WON
30.9100 g., 0.9990 Silver 0.9927 oz. ASW, 40 mm. **Subject:** End of WWII 60th Anniversary **Obv:** State arms **Rev:** Multicolor radiant map, doves, rainbow and inscription **Edge:** Plain

Date	Mintage	F	VF	XF	Unc	BU
JU94-2005 Proof	—	Value: 35.00				

KM# 425 10 WON
Aluminum, 23 mm. **Obv:** State arms **Rev:** Value

Date	Mintage	F	VF	XF	Unc	BU
2005	—	—	—	—	—	0.50

KM# 256 20 WON
42.0600 g., 0.9990 Silver 1.3509 oz. ASW, 45.1 mm. **Obv:** State arms **Rev:** Rose of sharon flower **Edge:** Plain

Date	Mintage	F	VF	XF	Unc	BU
JU93-2004 Proof	—	Value: 45.00				

KM# 257 20 WON
42.0100 g., 0.9990 Silver 1.3492 oz. ASW, 45.1 mm. **Obv:** State arms **Rev:** Peony flower **Edge:** Plain

Date	Mintage	F	VF	XF	Unc	BU
JU93-2004 Proof	—	Value: 45.00				

KM# 258 20 WON
41.9200 g., 0.9990 Silver 1.3464 oz. ASW, 45.1 mm. **Obv:** State arms **Rev:** Orchid flowers **Edge:** Plain

Date	Mintage	F	VF	XF	Unc	BU
JU93-2004 Proof	—	Value: 45.00				

KM# 259 20 WON
42.0000 g., 0.9990 Silver 1.3489 oz. ASW, 45.1 mm. **Obv:** State arms **Rev:** Kim Il Sung's birth place, side view **Edge:** Plain

Date	Mintage	F	VF	XF	Unc	BU
JU93-2004 Proof	—	Value: 45.00				

KM# 260 20 WON
41.6200 g., 0.9990 Silver 1.3367 oz. ASW, 45.1 mm. **Obv:** State arms **Rev:** Mountain cabin **Edge:** Plain

Date	Mintage	F	VF	XF	Unc	BU
JU93-2004 Proof	—	Value: 45.00				

KM# 261 20 WON
41.9100 g., 0.9990 Silver 1.3460 oz. ASW, 45.1 mm. **Obv:** State arms **Rev:** Kim Il Sung's birth place, front view **Edge:** Plain

Date	Mintage	F	VF	XF	Unc	BU
JU93-2004 Proof	—	Value: 45.00				

KM# 340 20 WON
31.0000 g., 0.9990 Silver 0.9956 oz. ASW, 39.8 mm. **Obv:** State arms **Rev:** Conjoined half length figures facing shaking hands **Edge:** Segmented reeding

Date	Mintage	F	VF	XF	Unc	BU
2004 Proof	—	Value: 45.00				

KM# 341 20 WON
31.0000 g., 0.9990 Silver 0.9956 oz. ASW, 39.8 mm. **Obv:** State arms **Rev:** Bust facing **Edge:** Segmented reeding

Date	Mintage	F	VF	XF	Unc	BU
2004 Proof	—	Value: 45.00				

KM# 419 20 WON
31.0000 g., 0.9990 Silver 0.9956 oz. ASW, 39.75 mm. **Subject:** Historic Pyongyang Meeting **Obv:** State arms **Rev:** Half length figures facing each other shaking hands, English legend **Edge:** Segmented reeding

Date	Mintage	F	VF	XF	Unc	BU
2004 Proof	—	Value: 45.00				

KM# 262 50 WON
69.6300 g., 0.9990 Silver 2.2363 oz. ASW, 50 mm. **Obv:** Korean map **Rev:** Huh Jun Chosun doctor with books **Edge:** Plain

Date	Mintage	F	VF	XF	Unc	BU
JU93-2004 Proof	—	Value: 75.00				

KM# 426 50 WON
Aluminum, 25 mm. **Obv:** State arms **Rev:** Value

Date	Mintage	F	VF	XF	Unc	BU
2005	—	—	—	—	—	0.75

KM# 427 100 WON
Aluminum, 27 mm. **Obv:** State arms **Rev:** Value

Date	Mintage	F	VF	XF	Unc	BU
2005	—	—	—	—	—	1.00

KM# 445 200 WON
5.1900 g., 0.9990 Silver 0.1667 oz. ASW, 30.00 mm. **Series:** Endangered Wildlife **Obv:** Fortress Gate **Rev:** Polar Bear standing facing **Rev. Legend:** URSUS MARITIMUS **Edge:** Plain

Date	Mintage	F	VF	XF	Unc	BU
2007 Proof	5,000	Value: 28.00				

KM# 441 500 WON
12.0000 g., 0.9990 Silver 0.3854 oz. ASW, 38.00 mm. **Subject:** 170th Anniversary First Public Railway St. Petersburg - Zarskoje Selo **Obv:** Fortress Gate **Rev:** First train arriving **Edge:** Plain

Date	Mintage	F	VF	XF	Unc	BU
ND(2007) Proof	5,000	Value: 70.00				

KM# 447 500 WON
12.0000 g., 0.9990 Silver 0.3854 oz. ASW, 38.00 mm. **Subject:** 150th Anniversay Birth of Ziolkowski and 50th Anniversary Launch of Sputnik I **Obv:** Fortress Gate **Rev:** Bust of Ziolkowski facing 3/4 right at lower left, Sputnik circling earth at upper right **Edge:** Plain

Date	Mintage	F	VF	XF	Unc	BU
ND(2007) Proof	5,000	Value: 65.00				

KM# 443 500 WON
12.0000 g., 0.9990 Silver 0.3854 oz. ASW, 38.00 mm. **Subject:** Lunar Year of the Rat **Obv:** Fortress Gate **Rev:** Two rats within circle of Lunar figures **Edge:** Plain

Date	Mintage	F	VF	XF	Unc	BU
2008	5,000	Value: 70.00				
2008 Proof	5,000	Value: 70.00				

KM# 428 700 WON
15.5500 g., 0.9990 Silver 0.4994 oz. ASW, 30.00 mm. **Series:** European Union Euro Commemoratives **Obv:** National arms **Rev:** Schleswig-Holstein City gate in relief in tigereye **Edge:** Plain

Date	Mintage	F	VF	XF	Unc	BU
2006 Proof	3,000	Value: 70.00				

KM# 429 700 WON
15.5500 g., 0.9990 Silver 0.4994 oz. ASW, 30.00 mm. **Series:** European Union Euro Commemoratives **Obv:** National arms **Rev:** Vatican in relief in tigereye **Edge:** Plain

Date	Mintage	F	VF	XF	Unc	BU
2006 Proof	3,000	Value: 70.00				

KM# 430 700 WON
15.5500 g., 0.9990 Silver 0.4994 oz. ASW, 30.00 mm. **Series:** European Union Euro Commemoratives **Obv:** National arms **Rev:** Male Olympic statue - discus - Athens in relief in tigereye **Edge:** Plain

Date	Mintage	F	VF	XF	Unc	BU
2006 Proof	3,000	Value: 70.00				

KM# 431 700 WON
15.5500 g., 0.9990 Silver 0.4994 oz. ASW, 30.00 mm. **Series:** European Union Euro Commemoratives **Obv:** National arms **Rev:** 50th Anniversary Austrian States Treaty in relief in tigereye **Edge:** Plain

Date	Mintage	F	VF	XF	Unc	BU
2006 Proof	3,000	Value: 70.00				

KM# 432 700 WON
15.5500 g., 0.9990 Silver 0.4994 oz. ASW, 30.00 mm. **Series:** European Union Euro Commemoratives **Obv:** National arms **Rev:** Don Quixote in relief in tigereye **Edge:** Plain

Date	Mintage	F	VF	XF	Unc	BU
2006 Proof	3,000	Value: 70.00				

KM# 433 700 WON
15.5500 g., 0.9990 Silver 0.4994 oz. ASW, 30.00 mm. **Series:** European Union Euro Commemoratives **Obv:** National arms **Rev:** Head of Henri, Grand Duke of Luxembourg at left facing right, crowned H at right in relief in tigereye **Edge:** Plain

Date	Mintage	F	VF	XF	Unc	BU
2006 Proof	3,000	Value: 70.00				

KM# 434 700 WON
15.5500 g., 0.9990 Silver 0.4994 oz. ASW, 30.00 mm. **Series:** European Union Euro Commemoratives **Obv:** National arms **Rev:** Italian FAO logo in relief in tigereye **Edge:** Plain

Date	Mintage	F	VF	XF	Unc	BU
2006 Proof	3,000	Value: 70.00				

KM# 435 700 WON
15.5500 g., 0.9990 Silver 0.4994 oz. ASW, 30.00 mm. **Series:** European Union Euro Commemoratives **Obv:** National arms **Rev:** Finland - stylized flower in relief in tigereye **Edge:** Plain

Date	Mintage	F	VF	XF	Unc	BU
2006 Proof	3,000	Value: 70.00				

KM# 436 700 WON
15.5500 g., 0.9990 Silver 0.4994 oz. ASW, 30.00 mm. **Series:** European Union Euro Commemoratives **Obv:** National arms **Rev:** Conjoined heads of Grand Duke Henri of Luxembourg and King Albert of Belgium left in relief in tigereye **Edge:** Plain

Date	Mintage	F	VF	XF	Unc	BU
2006 Proof	3,000	Value: 70.00				

KM# 437 700 WON
15.5500 g., 0.9990 Silver 0.4994 oz. ASW, 30.00 mm. **Series:** European Union Euro Commemoratives **Obv:** National arms **Rev:** San Marino - bust of Bartolomeo Borghesi slightly right in relief in tigereye **Edge:** Plain

Date	Mintage	F	VF	XF	Unc	BU
2006 Proof	3,000	Value: 70.00				

KM# 439 700 WON
15.5500 g., 0.9990 Silver 0.4994 oz. ASW, 30.00 mm. **Series:** European Union Euro Commemoratives **Obv:** National arms **Rev:** San Marino - Year of Physics design in relief in tigereye **Edge:** Plain

Date	Mintage	F	VF	XF	Unc	BU
2006 Proof	3,000	Value: 70.00				

KM# 438 700 WON
15.5500 g., 0.9990 Silver 0.4994 oz. ASW, 30.00 mm. **Series:** European Union Euro Commemoratives **Obv:** National arms **Rev:** Vatican - World Youth Day in Cologne **Edge:** Plain

Date	Mintage	F	VF	XF	Unc	BU
2006 Proof	3,000	Value: 70.00				

KM# 440 1000 WON
20.0000 g., 0.9990 Silver 0.6423 oz. ASW, 38 mm. **Obv:** National arms **Rev:** Arctic animals with map of North Pole in background **Rev. Legend:** INTERNATIONAL POLAR YEAR / ARCTIC ANIMALS **Edge:** Plain

Date	Mintage	F	VF	XF	Unc	BU
ND(2007) Proof	—	Value: 85.00				

KM# 446 1000 WON
20.0000 g., 0.9990 Silver 0.6423 oz. ASW, 38.00 mm. **Series:** Endangered Wildlife **Obv:** Fortress Gate **Rev:** Polar Bear standing facing **Rev. Legend:** URSUS MAITIMUS **Edge:** Plain

Date	Mintage	F	VF	XF	Unc	BU
2007 Proof	5,000	Value: 70.00				

KM# 442 15000 WON
7.7800 g., 0.9990 Gold 0.2499 oz. AGW, 26 mm. **Subject:** 170th Anniversary First Public Railway St. Petersburg - Zarskoje Selo **Obv:** Fortress Gate **Rev:** First train arriving **Edge:** Plain

Date	Mintage	F	VF	XF	Unc	BU
ND(2007) Proof	2,000	Value: 425				

KM# 448 15000 WON
7.7800 g., 0.9990 Gold 0.2499 oz. AGW, 26 mm. **Subject:** 150th Anniversary Birth of Ziolkowski and 50th Anniversary Launch of Sputnik I **Obv:** Fortress Gate **Rev:** Bust of Ziolkowski facing 3/4 right at lower left, Sputnik circling earth at top right **Edge:** Plain

Date	Mintage	F	VF	XF	Unc	BU
ND(2007) Proof	2,000	Value: 425				

KM# 444 15000 WON
7.7800 g., 0.9990 Gold 0.2499 oz. AGW, 26 mm. **Subject:** Lunar Year of the Rat **Obv:** Fortress Gate **Rev:** Two rats within circle of Lunar figures **Edge:** Plain

Date	Mintage	F	VF	XF	Unc	BU
2008 Proof	2,000	Value: 425				

KOREA-SOUTH

The Republic of Korea, situated in northeastern Asia on the southern half of the Korean peninsula between North Korea and the Korean Strait, has an area of 38,025 sq. mi. (98,480 sq. km.) and a population of 42.5 million. Capital: Seoul. The economy is based on agriculture and light and medium industry. Some of the world's largest oil tankers are built here. Automobiles, plywood, electronics, and textile products are exported.

NOTE: For earlier coinage see Korea.

MONETARY SYSTEM
100 Chon = 1 Hwan

MINT
KOMSCO - Korea Minting and Security Printing Corporation

REPUBLIC

REFORM COINAGE

10 Hwan = 1 Won

KM# 31 WON
0.7290 g., Aluminum, 17.2 mm. **Obv:** Rose of Sharon **Rev:** Value and date

Date	Mintage	F	VF	XF	Unc	BU
2001	—	—	—	—	0.15	0.25
2002	—	—	—	—	0.15	0.25
2003	—	—	—	—	0.15	0.25
2004	—	—	—	—	0.15	0.25
2005	—	—	—	—	0.15	0.25
2006	—	—	—	—	0.15	0.25

KM# 32 5 WON
2.9500 g., Brass, 20.4 mm. **Obv:** Iron-clad turtle boat **Rev:** Value and date

Date	Mintage	F	VF	XF	Unc	BU
2001	—	—	—	0.10	0.20	0.30
2002	—	—	—	0.10	0.20	0.30
2003	—	—	—	0.10	0.20	0.30
2004	—	—	—	0.10	0.20	0.30
2005	—	—	—	0.10	0.20	0.30
2006	—	—	—	0.10	0.20	0.30

KM# 33.2 10 WON
4.0600 g., Brass **Obv:** Pagoda at Pul Guk Temple **Rev:** Value below date

Date	Mintage	F	VF	XF	Unc	BU
2001	345,000,000	—	—	0.10	0.35	0.50
2002	100,000,000	—	—	0.10	0.35	0.50
2003	128,000,000	—	—	0.10	0.35	0.50
2004	135,000,000	—	—	0.10	0.35	0.50
2005	250,000,000	—	—	0.10	0.35	0.50
2006	40,800,000	—	—	0.10	0.35	0.50

KM# 33.2a 10 WON
1.2200 g., Aluminum-Bronze, 18 mm. **Obv:** Pagoda at Pul Guk Temple **Rev:** Value below date

Date	Mintage	F	VF	XF	Unc	BU
2006	109,200,000	—	—	—	0.10	0.35
2007	—	—	—	—	0.10	0.35
2008	—	—	—	—	0.10	0.35

KM# 34 50 WON
4.1600 g., Copper-Nickel, 21.16 mm. **Series:** F.A.O. **Obv:** Text below sagging oat sprig **Rev:** Value and date **Note:** Die varieties exist.

Date	Mintage	F	VF	XF	Unc	BU
2001	102,000,000	—	—	0.10	0.35	0.50
2002	10,000,000	—	—	0.10	0.35	0.50
2003	169,000,000	—	—	0.10	0.35	0.50
2004	100,000,000	—	—	0.10	0.45	1.00
2005	90,000,000	—	—	0.10	0.35	0.50
2006	120,000,000	—	—	0.10	0.35	0.50
2007	50,000,000	—	—	0.10	0.35	0.50
2008	—	—	—	0.10	0.35	0.50

KM# 35.2 100 WON
5.4200 g., Copper-Nickel, 24 mm. **Obv:** Bust with hat facing **Rev:** Value and date

Date	Mintage	F	VF	XF	Unc	BU
2001	470,000,000	—	0.15	0.25	0.55	0.75
2002	490,000,000	—	0.15	0.25	0.55	0.75
2003	415,000,000	—	0.15	0.25	0.55	0.75
2004	250,000,000	—	0.15	0.25	0.55	0.75
2005	205,000,000	—	0.15	0.25	0.55	0.75
2006	310,000,000	—	0.15	0.25	0.55	0.75
2007	240,000,000	—	0.15	0.25	0.55	0.75
2008	—	—	0.15	0.25	0.55	0.75

KM# 27 500 WON
7.7000 g., Copper-Nickel, 26.5 mm. **Obv:** Manchurian crane **Rev:** Value and date

Date	Mintage	F	VF	XF	Unc	BU
2001	113,000,000	—	—	1.00	2.50	5.00
2002	110,000,000	—	—	1.00	2.50	5.00
2003	122,000,000	—	—	1.00	2.50	5.00
2004	45,000,000	—	—	1.00	2.50	5.00
2005	105,000,000	—	—	1.00	2.50	5.00
2006	170,000,000	—	—	1.00	2.50	5.00
2007	70,000,000	—	—	1.00	2.50	5.00
2008	—	—	—	1.00	2.50	5.00

KM# 89 1000 WON
12.0000 g., Brass, 32 mm. **Series:** World Cup Soccer **Obv:** FIFA World Cup logo **Rev:** Mascot soccer player **Edge:** Reeded **Mint:** Seoul

Date	Mintage	F	VF	XF	Unc	BU
2001	102,000	—	—	—	8.50	10.00

KM# 90 10000 WON
31.1035 g., 0.9990 Silver 0.9990 oz. ASW, 35 mm. **Series:** World Cup Soccer **Subject:** Gwangju Stadium **Obv:** Multicolor soccer logo **Rev:** Player heading the ball **Edge:** Reeded **Mint:** Seoul

Date	Mintage	F	VF	XF	Unc	BU
2001 Proof	37,000	Value: 40.00				

KM# 91 10000 WON
31.1035 g., 0.9990 Silver 0.9990 oz. ASW, 35 mm. **Series:** World Sup Soccer **Subject:** Busan Stadium **Obv:** Multicolor soccer logo **Rev:** Player kicking the ball **Edge:** Reeded **Mint:** Seoul

Date	Mintage	F	VF	XF	Unc	BU
2001 Proof	37,000	Value: 40.00				

KM# 93 10000 WON
31.1035 g., 0.9990 Silver 0.9990 oz. ASW, 35 mm. **Series:** World Cup Soccer **Subject:** Suwon Stadium **Obv:** Multicolor soccer logo **Rev:** Player kicking the ball **Edge:** Reeded **Mint:** Seoul

Date	Mintage	F	VF	XF	Unc	BU
2001 Proof	37,000	Value: 40.00				

KM# 98 10000 WON
31.1035 g., 0.9990 Silver 0.9990 oz. ASW, 35 mm. **Obv:** Multicolor FIFA World Cup logo **Rev:** Player "Heading" ball **Edge:** Reeded **Mint:** Seoul

Date	Mintage	F	VF	XF	Unc	BU
2002 Proof	—	Value: 40.00				

KM# 99 10000 WON
31.1035 g., 0.9990 Silver 0.9990 oz. ASW, 35 mm. **Obv:** Multicolor FIFA World Cup logo **Rev:** Goalie catching ball **Edge:** Reeded **Mint:** Seoul

Date	Mintage	F	VF	XF	Unc	BU
2002 Proof	—	Value: 40.00				

KM# 100 10000 WON
31.1035 g., 0.9990 Silver 0.9990 oz. ASW, 35 mm. **Obv:** Multicolor FIFA World Cup logo **Rev:** Player's legs kicking ball **Edge:** Reeded **Mint:** Seoul

Date	Mintage	F	VF	XF	Unc	BU
2002 Proof	—	Value: 40.00				

KM# 101 10000 WON
31.1035 g., 0.9990 Silver 0.9990 oz. ASW, 35 mm. **Obv:** Multicolor FIFA World Cup logo **Rev:** Two players legs and ball **Edge:** Reeded **Mint:** Seoul

Date	Mintage	F	VF	XF	Unc	BU
2002 Proof	—	Value: 40.00				

KM# 94 20000 WON
15.5518 g., 0.9990 Gold 0.4995 oz. AGW, 28 mm. **Series:** World Cup Soccer **Obv:** Soccer logo **Rev:** World Cup soccer trophy **Edge:** Reeded **Mint:** Seoul

Date	Mintage	F	VF	XF	Unc	BU
2001 Proof	20,000	Value: 500				

KM# 97 20000 WON
20.7000 g., Silver, 35 mm. **Obv:** Blue circle with APEC, 2005 Korea at bottom at upper center, Vista Pacific Economic Cooperation and value below **Rev:** APEC on World map at upper center, building below with Korean words below it

Date	Mintage	F	VF	XF	Unc	BU
2005 Proof	10,000	Value: 35.00				

KM# 103 20000 WON
20.7000 g., 0.9990 Silver 0.6648 oz. ASW **Subject:** 60th Anniversary of Independence **Mint:** KOMSCO - Seoul

Date	Mintage	F	VF	XF	Unc	BU
2005 Proof	10,000	Value: 60.00				

KM# 104 20000 WON
19.0000 g., 0.9990 Silver 0.6102 oz. ASW **Subject:** 560th Year of Hangeul - Alphabet **Obv:** Early alphabet characters **Obv. Legend:** THE BANK OF KOREA **Rev:** Modern alphabet characters **Shape:** Round with square center hole **Mint:** KOMSCO - Seoul

Date	Mintage	F	VF	XF	Unc	BU
2006 Proof	—	Value: 75.00				

KM# 105 20000 WON
19.0000 g., 0.9990 Silver 0.6102 oz. ASW **Series:** Traditional Folk Game **Subject:** Talchum - Mask Dances **Obv. Legend:** THE BANK OF KOREA **Mint:** KOMSCO - Seoul

Date	Mintage	F	VF	XF	Unc	BU
2006 Proof	—	Value: 75.00				

KM# 102 20000 WON
19.0000 g., 0.9990 Silver 0.6102 oz. ASW, 33.00 mm. **Series:** Traditional Folk Game **Subject:** Talchum - Mask Dances **Obv:** Mask at center surrounded by 6 other masks **Obv. Legend:** THE BANK OF KOREA **Rev:** Mask dancer at left center **Edge:** Plain **Shape:** 12-sided **Mint:** KOMSCO - Seoul

Date	Mintage	F	VF	XF	Unc	BU
2007 Proof	50,000	Value: 75.00				

KM# 95 30000 WON
31.1035 g., 0.9990 Gold 0.9990 oz. AGW, 35 mm. **Series:** World Cup Soccer **Obv:** Soccer logo **Rev:** Nude soccer player flanked by other players **Edge:** Reeded **Mint:** Seoul

Date	Mintage	F	VF	XF	Unc	BU
2001 Proof	12,000	Value: 1,000				

MINT SETS

KM#	Date	Mintage	Identification	Issue Price	Mkt Val
MS8	2001 (7)	—	KM#27, 31, 32, 33.2, 34, 35.2, 89	10.00	16.00

PROOF SETS

KM#	Date	Mintage	Identification	Issue Price	Mkt Val
PS10	2001 (6)	2,002	KM#90-95	—	1,650

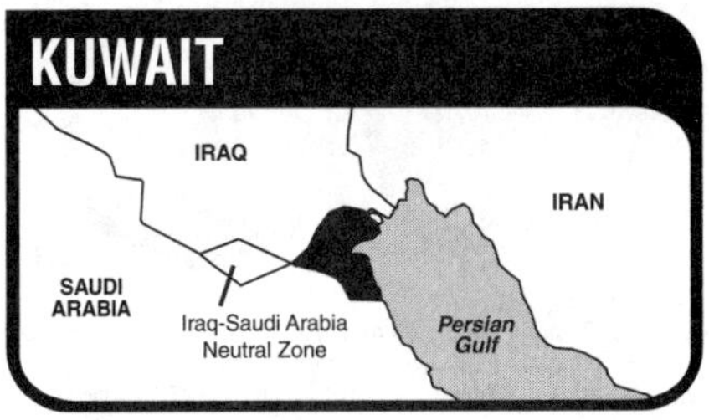

The State of Kuwait, a constitutional monarchy located on the Arabian Peninsula at the northwestern corner of the Persian Gulf, has an area of 6,880 sq. mi. (17,820 sq. km.) and a population of 1.7 million. Capital: Kuwait. Petroleum, the basis of the economy, provides 95 percent of the exports.

TITLES

الكويت

al-Kuwait

RULERS

LOCAL

Al Sabah Dynasty

Jabir Ibn Ahmad, 1977-2006
Sabah Al Ahmad Al Sabah, 2006-

MONETARY SYSTEM
1000 Fils = 1 Dinar

SOVEREIGN EMIRATE

MODERN COINAGE

KM# 10 5 FILS
2.5000 g., Nickel-Brass, 19.5 mm. **Ruler:** Jabir Ibn Ahmad **Obv:** Value within circle **Rev:** Dhow, dates below

Date	Mintage	F	VF	XF	Unc	BU
AH1422-2001	—	—	0.10	0.20	0.40	—
AH1424-2003	—	—	0.10	0.20	0.40	—
AH1426-2005	—	—	0.10	0.20	0.40	—

KM# 11 10 FILS
3.7500 g., Nickel-Brass, 21 mm. **Ruler:** Jabir Ibn Ahmad **Obv:** Value within circle **Rev:** Dhow, dates below

Date	Mintage	F	VF	XF	Unc	BU
AH1422-2001	—	—	0.15	0.25	0.75	—
AH1424-2003	—	—	0.15	0.25	0.75	—
AH1426-2005	—	—	0.15	0.25	0.75	—

KM# 12c 20 FILS
Stainless Steel, 20 mm. **Ruler:** Jabir Ibn Ahmad **Obv:** Value **Rev:** Dhow, dates below

Date	Mintage	F	VF	XF	Unc	BU
AH1422-2001	—	—	—	—	1.00	—
AH1424-2003	—	—	—	—	1.00	—
AH1426-2005	—	—	—	—	1.00	—

KM# 12 20 FILS
3.0000 g., Copper-Nickel, 20 mm. **Ruler:** Jabir Ibn Ahmad **Obv:** Value within circle **Rev:** Dhow, dates below **Note:** Varieties exist.

Date	Mintage	F	VF	XF	Unc	BU
AH1424-2003	—	—	0.20	0.45	2.00	—
AH1426-2005	—	—	0.20	0.45	2.00	—

KM# 13 50 FILS
4.5000 g., Copper-Nickel, 23 mm. **Ruler:** Jabir Ibn Ahmad **Obv:** Value within circle **Rev:** Dhow, dates below

Date	Mintage	F	VF	XF	Unc	BU
AH1424-2003	—	—	0.25	0.35	1.00	—
AH1426-2005	—	—	0.25	0.35	1.00	—
AH1427-2006	—	—	0.25	0.35	1.00	—

KM# 14 100 FILS
6.5000 g., Copper-Nickel, 26 mm. **Ruler:** Jabir Ibn Ahmad **Obv:** Value within circle **Rev:** Dhow, dates below

Date	Mintage	F	VF	XF	Unc	BU
AH1424-2003	—	—	0.50	0.75	1.50	—
AH1426-2005	—	—	0.50	0.75	1.50	—

The Republic of Kyrgyzstan, (formerly Kirghiz S.S.R., a Union Republic of the U.S.S.R.), is an independent state since Aug. 31, 1991, a member of the United Nations and of the C.I.S. It was the last state of the Union Republics to declare its sovereignty. Capital: Bishkek (formerly Frunze).

REPUBLIC

STANDARD COINAGE

KM# 3 10 SOM
28.2800 g., 0.9250 Silver 0.8410 oz. ASW, 38.6 mm. **Subject:** Tenth Anniversary of Republic **Obv:** National arms within circle **Rev:** Value and mountain **Edge:** Reeded

Date	Mintage	F	VF	XF	Unc	BU
2001 Proof	1,000	Value: 60.00				

KM# 4 10 SOM
28.2800 g., 0.9250 Silver 0.8410 oz. ASW, 38.6 mm. **Subject:** Flora and Fauna **Obv:** National arms **Rev:** Edelweiss flower and mountain **Edge:** Reeded

Date	Mintage	F	VF	XF	Unc	BU
2002 Proof	1,000	Value: 60.00				

KM# 5 10 SOM
28.2800 g., 0.9250 Silver 0.8410 oz. ASW, 38.6 mm. **Subject:** Flora and Fauna **Obv:** National arms **Rev:** Ram head and mountain **Edge:** Reeded

Date	Mintage	F	VF	XF	Unc	BU
2002 Proof	1,000	Value: 60.00				

KM# 6 10 SOM
28.2800 g., 0.9250 Silver 0.8410 oz. ASW, 38.6 mm. **Subject:** 60 Years of Great Victory

Date	Mintage	F	VF	XF	Unc	BU
2005 Proof	1,000	Value: 60.00				

KM# 7 10 SOM
28.2800 g., 0.8250 Silver 0.7501 oz. ASW, 38.6 mm. **Subject:** The Great Silk Road: Tashrabat

Date	Mintage	F	VF	XF	Unc	BU
2005 Proof	1,500	Value: 60.00				

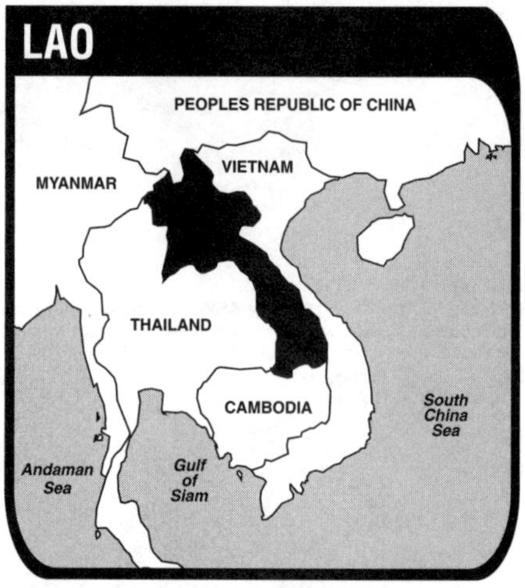

The Lao Peoples Democratic Republic, located on the Indo-Chinese Peninsula between the Socialist Republic of Vietnam and the Kingdom of Thailand, has an area of 91,428 sq. mi. (236,800 km.) and a population of 3.6 million. Capital Vientiane. Agriculture employs 95 per cent of the people. Tin, lumber and coffee are exported.

NOTE: For earlier coinage see French Indo-China.

RULERS
Sisavang Vong, 1904-1959
Savang Vatthana, 1959-1975

MONETARY SYSTEM
100 Cents = 1 Piastre
Commencing 1955
100 Att = 1 Kip

MINT MARKS
(a) - Paris, privy marks only
Key - Havana
None - Berlin

PEOPLES DEMOCRATIC REPUBLIC

STANDARD COINAGE

100 Att = 1 Kip

KM# 85 1000 KIP
31.5000 g., 0.9990 Silver 1.0117 oz. ASW, 38.5 mm. **Subject:** Olympics **Obv:** State emblem **Rev:** Freestyle skier **Edge:** Reeded

Date	Mintage	F	VF	XF	Unc	BU
2001 Proof	—	Value: 40.00				

KM# 96 1000 KIP
31.4500 g., 0.9990 Silver 1.0101 oz. ASW, 38.5 mm. **Obv:** State emblem **Rev:** Soccer player **Edge:** Reeded

Date	Mintage	F	VF	XF	Unc	BU
2001 Proof	—	Value: 40.00				

KM# 86 15000 KIP
20.0000 g., 0.9250 Silver 0.5948 oz. ASW, 38.7 mm. **Subject:** Year of the Horse **Obv:** State emblem **Rev:** Multicolor horse **Edge:** Reeded

Date	Mintage	F	VF	XF	Unc	BU
2002 Proof	9,500	Value: 40.00				

KM# 87 15000 KIP
20.0000 g., 0.9250 Silver 0.5948 oz. ASW, 38.7 mm. **Subject:** Year of the Horse **Obv:** State emblem **Rev:** Horse with multicolor holographic background **Edge:** Reeded

Date	Mintage	F	VF	XF	Unc	BU
2002 Proof	9,500	Value: 45.00				

KM# 94 15000 KIP
20.0000 g., 0.9990 Silver 0.6423 oz. ASW, 38.7 mm. **Obv:** State emblem **Rev:** Multicolor Golden Monkey **Edge:** Reeded

Date	Mintage	F	VF	XF	Unc	BU
2004 Proof	2,300	Value: 45.00				

KM# 98 15000 KIP
Silver, 38.7 mm. **Issuer:** Bank of Lao PDR **Obv:** National arms **Obv. Legend:** THE LAO PEOPLE'S DEMOCRATIC REPUBLIC **Rev:** Statue of Mazu with stylized Phoenix at left and right **Rev. Legend:** GODDESS OF THE SEA **Edge:** Reeded

Date	Mintage	F	VF	XF	Unc	BU
2006 Proof	6,888	Value: 50.00				

KM# 88 60000 KIP
155.5175 g., 0.9250 Silver 4.6248 oz. ASW, 65 mm. **Subject:** Year of the Horse **Obv:** State emblem **Rev:** Multicolor horse **Edge:** Reeded

Date	Mintage	F	VF	XF	Unc	BU
2002 Proof	1,000	Value: 200				

KM# 89 100000 KIP
15.5518 g., 0.9999 Gold 0.4999 oz. AGW, 27 mm. **Subject:** Year of the Horse **Obv:** State emblem **Rev:** Horse **Edge:** Reeded

Date	Mintage	F	VF	XF	Unc	BU
2002	2,000	Value: 500				

KM# 95 100000 KIP
15.5518 g., 0.9990 Gold 0.4995 oz. AGW, 27 mm. **Obv:** State emblem **Rev:** Black Gibbon on holographic background **Edge:** Reeded

Date	Mintage	F	VF	XF	Unc	BU
2004 Proof	888	Value: 520				

KM# 90 1000000 KIP
155.5175 g., 0.9999 Gold 4.9993 oz. AGW, 55 mm. **Subject:** Year of the Horse **Obv:** State emblem **Rev:** Horse with multicolor holographic background **Edge:** Reeded

Date	Mintage	F	VF	XF	Unc	BU
2002 Proof	500	Value: 5,000				

KM# 99 1000000 KIP
155.5150 g., 0.9999 Gold 4.9992 oz. AGW, 55.0 mm. **Issuer:** Bank of Lao PDR **Obv:** National arms **Obv. Legend:** THE LAO PEOPLE'S DEMOCRATIC REPUBLIC **Rev:** Multi-latent color bust of Lord Buddha "Fo Guang Pu Zhao" facing with diamond insert in forehead **Edge:** Reeded

Date	Mintage	F	VF	XF	Unc	BU
2006 Proof	99	Value: 5,250				

PROOF SETS

KM#	Date	Mintage	Identification	Issue Price	Mkt Val
PS7	2000-2001 (3)	3,500	KM#74-76	138	200
PS8	2000-2001 (3)	500	KM#74-76	214	300
PS9	2000-2001 (2)	800	KM#78, 83	—	700

LATVIA

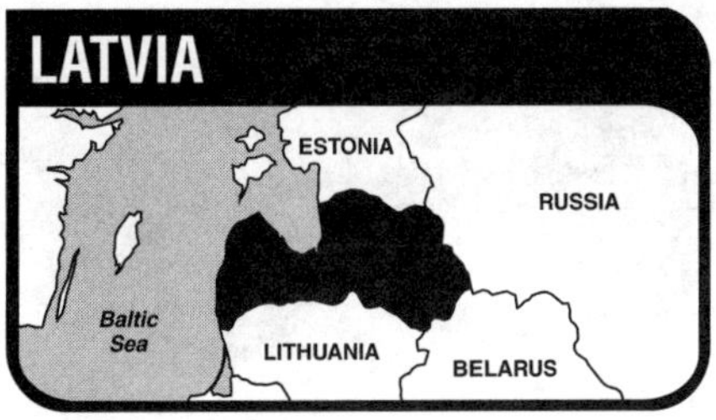

The Republic of Latvia, the central Baltic state in east Europe, has an area of 24,749 sq. mi. (43,601 sq. km.) and a population of *2.6 million. Capital: Riga. Livestock raising and manufacturing are the chief industries. Butter, bacon, fertilizers and telephone equipment are exported.

MONETARY SYSTEM
100 Santimu = 1 Lats

MODERN REPUBLIC
1991-present

STANDARD COINAGE
100 Santimu = 1 Lats

KM# 15 SANTIMS
1.6200 g., Copper-Clad Steel, 15.67 mm. **Obv:** National arms **Rev:** Value flanked by diamonds below lined arch **Edge:** Plain

Date	Mintage	F	VF	XF	Unc	BU
2003	—	—	—	—	0.30	0.50
2005	—	—	—	—	0.30	0.50
2007	—	—	—	—	0.30	0.50

KM# 21 2 SANTIMI
Bronze-Plated Steel, 17 mm. **Obv:** National arms **Rev:** Lined arch above value flanked by diamonds

Date	Mintage	F	VF	XF	Unc	BU
2003	—	—	—	—	0.50	1.00
2006	—	—	—	—	0.50	1.00

KM# 16 5 SANTIMI
2.5200 g., Brass, 18.5 mm. **Obv:** National arms **Obv. Legend:** LATVIJAS REPUBLIKA **Rev:** Lined arch above value flanked by diamonds **Edge:** Plain

Date	Mintage	F	VF	XF	Unc	BU
2006	—	—	—	—	1.00	2.00

KM# 70 100 SANTIMU
31.4700 g., 0.9250 Silver 0.9359 oz. ASW, 38.6 mm. **Obv:** Baron von Muenchausen with chain of birds around a dog with a lantern hanging from its tail. **Rev:** Baron von Muenchausen and dog hunting a circle of animals **Edge Lettering:** "LATVIJAS BANKA LATVIJAS REPUBLIKA"

Date	Mintage	F	VF	XF	Unc	BU
2005 Proof	Est. 5,000	Value: 45.00				

KM# 54 LATS
4.8000 g., Copper-Nickel, 21.7 mm. **Obv:** Arms with supporters **Rev:** Stork above value **Edge Lettering:** "LATVIJAS BANKA" twice

Date	Mintage	F	VF	XF	Unc	BU
2001	250,000	—	—	—	6.00	7.00

KM# 49 LATS
31.4700 g., 0.9250 Silver 0.9359 oz. ASW, 38.6 mm. **Subject:** Hanseatic City of Cesis **Obv:** City arms **Rev:** Sailing ship above, inverted walled city view below **Edge Lettering:** "LATVIJAS REPUBLIKA.LATVIJAS BANKA"

Date	Mintage	F	VF	XF	Unc	BU
2001 Proof	Est. 15,000	Value: 70.00				

KM# 50 LATS
31.4700 g., 0.9250 Silver 0.9359 oz. ASW **Series:** Ice Hockey **Obv:** Arms with supporters **Rev:** Hockey player

Date	Mintage	F	VF	XF	Unc	BU
2001 Proof	Est. 25,000	Value: 90.00				

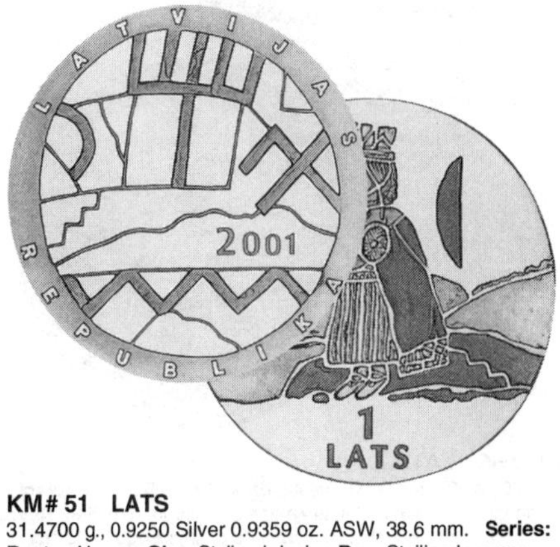

KM# 51 LATS
31.4700 g., 0.9250 Silver 0.9359 oz. ASW, 38.6 mm. **Series:** Roots - Heaven **Obv:** Stylized design **Rev:** Styilized woman holding sun **Edge:** Plain

Date	Mintage	F	VF	XF	Unc	BU
2001 Proof	Est. 5,000	Value: 50.00				

KM# 52 LATS
31.4700 g., 0.9250 Silver 0.9359 oz. ASW, 38.6 mm. **Series:** Roots - Destiny **Obv:** Stylized design **Rev:** Apple tree and landscape **Edge:** Plain

Date	Mintage	F	VF	XF	Unc	BU
2002 Proof	Est. 5,000	Value: 85.00				

KM# 53 LATS
31.4700 g., 0.9250 Silver 0.9359 oz. ASW, 38.6 mm. **Subject:** Hanseatic City of Kuldiga **Obv:** City arms **Rev:** City view and ships **Edge:** Lettered

Date	Mintage	F	VF	XF	Unc	BU
2002 Proof	Est. 15,000	Value: 80.00				

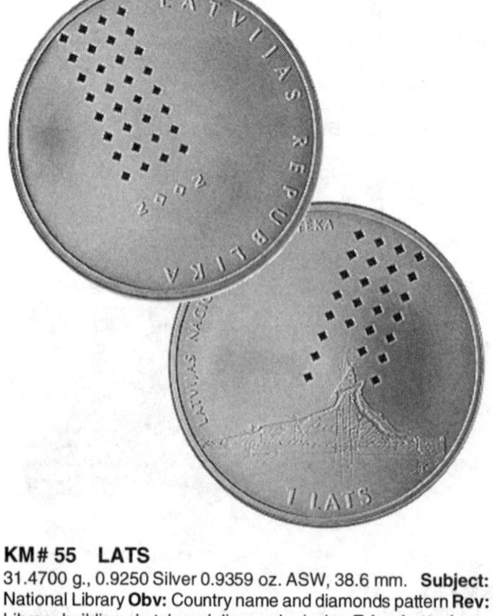

KM# 55 LATS
31.4700 g., 0.9250 Silver 0.9359 oz. ASW, 38.6 mm. **Subject:** National Library **Obv:** Country name and diamonds pattern **Rev:** Library building sketch and diamonds design **Edge Lettering:** "GAISMU SAUCA-GAISMA AUSA"

Date	Mintage	F	VF	XF	Unc	BU
2002 Proof	Est. 5,000	Value: 80.00				

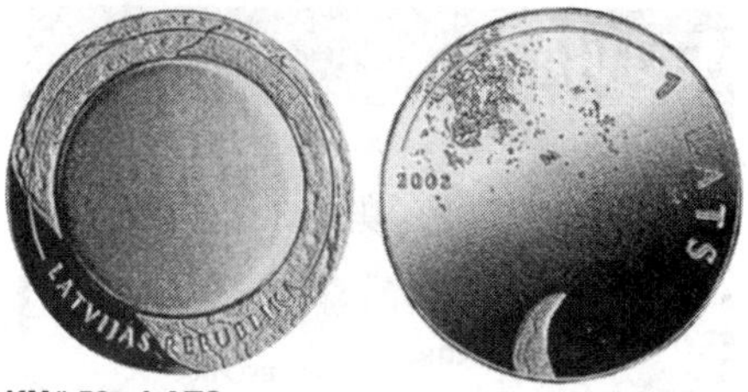

KM# 56 LATS
15.0000 g., 0.9250 Silver 0.4461 oz. ASW, 28 mm. **Subject:** "Fortune" **Obv:** Totally gold plated sun above country name **Rev:** Waning moon, date and value **Edge:** Plain

Date	Mintage	F	VF	XF	Unc	BU
2002 Proof	Est. 5,000	Value: 45.00				

KM# 57 LATS
31.4700 g., 0.9250 Silver 0.9359 oz. ASW, 38.6 mm. **Subject:** Olympics 2004 **Obv:** Arms with supporters **Rev:** Ancient wrestlers **Edge:** Lettered **Edge Lettering:** LATVIJAS BANKA repeated twice

Date	Mintage	F	VF	XF	Unc	BU
2002 Proof	Est. 26,000	Value: 70.00				

KM# 58 LATS
4.8000 g., Copper Nickel, 21.75 mm. **Obv:** Arms with supporters **Rev:** Ant above value **Edge:** Lettered **Edge Lettering:** LATVIJAS BANKA

Date	Mintage	F	VF	XF	Unc	BU
2003	254,000	—	—	—	5.00	7.50

KM# 71 LATS
31.4700 g., 0.9250 Silver 0.9359 oz. ASW, 38.6 mm. **Subject:** Vidzeme **Obv:** Crowned arms above horse drawn wagon **Rev:** Two men sawing wood **Edge Lettering:** "Rahapaja Oy"

Date	Mintage	F	VF	XF	Unc	BU
ND (2003) Proof	—	Value: 50.00				
2004 Proof	Est. 5,000	Value: 50.00				

KM# 72 LATS
31.4700 g., 0.9250 Silver 0.9359 oz. ASW, 38.6 mm. **Subject:** Latgale **Obv:** Madonna and Child above landscape **Rev:** Man sowing seeds and an angel **Edge Lettering:** "Rahapaja Oy"

Date	Mintage	F	VF	XF	Unc	BU
ND (2003) Proof	—	Value: 50.00				
2004 Proof	Est. 5,000	Value: 50.00				

KM# 75 LATS
31.4700 g., 0.9250 Silver 0.9359 oz. ASW, 38.61 mm. **Obv:** Coat of arms **Rev:** St. Simanis Church with VALMIERA and reflection of sailing ship **Edge:** LATVIJAS REPUBLIKA and LATVIJAS BANKA separted by dots

Date	Mintage	F	VF	XF	Unc	BU
2003 Proof	Est. 15,000	Value: 50.00				

KM# 60 LATS
31.4700 g., 0.9250 Silver 0.9359 oz. ASW, 38.6 mm. **Obv:** Crowned arms above partially built ship **Rev:** Hemp weighing scene with Iron foundry and brick wall in background **Edge:** Lettered **Edge Lettering:** "REPUBLIKA LATVIJAS BANKA LATVIJA" **Note:** Western Latvia formerly Courland

Date	Mintage	F	VF	XF	Unc	BU
2003 Proof	Est. 5,000	Value: 70.00				

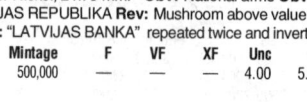

KM# 67 LATS
4.8000 g., Copper-Nickel, 21.75 mm. **Obv:** National arms **Obv. Legend:** LATVIJAS REPUBLIKA **Rev:** Mushroom above value **Edge Lettering:** "LATVIJAS BANKA" repeated twice and inverted

Date	Mintage	F	VF	XF	Unc	BU
2004	500,000	—	—	—	4.00	5.00

KM# 61 LATS

4.8000 g., Copper-Nickel, 21.75 mm. **Obv:** Arms with supporters **Rev:** Child with shovel above value **Edge:** Lettered **Edge Lettering:** "LATVIJAS BANKA" twice

Date	Mintage	F	VF	XF	Unc	BU
2004	500,000	—	—	—	5.50	6.00

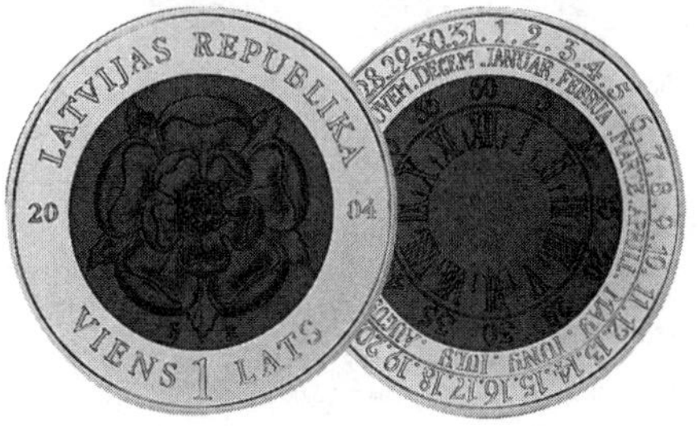

KM# 62 LATS

17.1500 g., Bi-Metallic Dark Blue Niobium 7.15g center in .900 Silver 10g ring, 34 mm. **Obv:** Heraldic Rose **Rev:** Astronomical Clock **Edge:** Plain

Date	Mintage	F	VF	XF	Unc	BU
2004	Est. 5,000	—	—	—	50.00	55.00

KM# 63 LATS

31.4700 g., 0.9250 Silver 0.9359 oz. ASW, 38.6 mm. **Obv:** Arms with supporters **Rev:** World Cup Soccer player **Edge:** "LATVIJA" three times

Date	Mintage	F	VF	XF	Unc	BU
2004 Proof	Est. 50,000	Value: 70.00				

KM# 64 LATS

31.4700 g., 0.9250 Silver 0.9359 oz. ASW, 38.6 mm. **Subject:** Latvian European Union Membership **Obv:** Arms with supporters **Rev:** "P.S. LATVIJA-ES 2004" above value **Edge:** Lettered **Edge Lettering:** "LATVIJAS BANKA" twice

Date	Mintage	F	VF	XF	Unc	BU
2004 Proof	Est. 15,000	Value: 80.00				

KM# 65 LATS

4.8000 g., Copper-Nickel, 21.75 mm. **Obv:** Arms with supporters **Rev:** Chicken above value **Edge:** Lettered **Edge Lettering:** :LATVIJAS BANKA" twice

Date	Mintage	F	VF	XF	Unc	BU
2005	500,000	—	—	—	6.00	7.00

KM# 66 LATS

4.8000 g., Copper-Nickel, 21.7 mm. **Obv:** Arms with supporters **Rev:** Pretzel above value **Edge Lettering:** "LATVIJAS BANKA"

Date	Mintage	F	VF	XF	Unc	BU
2005	500,000	—	—	—	5.00	6.00

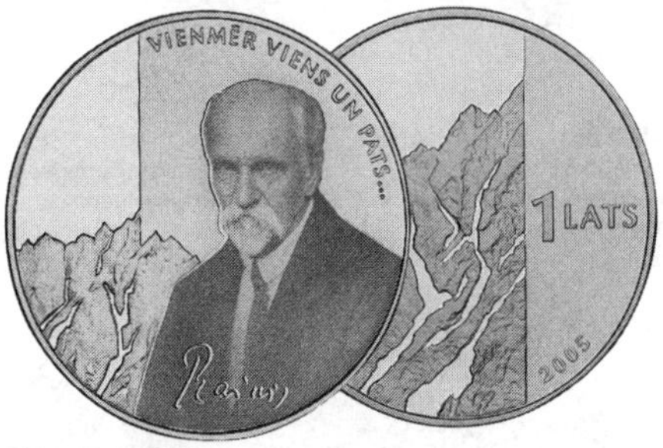

KM# 68 LATS

31.4700 g., 0.9250 Silver 0.9359 oz. ASW, 38.6 mm. **Obv:** Mountains and value **Rev:** Laser picture of Janis Plieksans, pseudonym "Rainis" the mountain climbing poet, dramatist and patriot. **Edge Lettering:** "LATVIJAS BANKA LATVIJAS REPUBLIKA"

Date	Mintage	F	VF	XF	Unc	BU
2005 Proof	Est. 5,000	Value: 45.00				

KM# 69 LATS

31.4700 g., 0.9250 Silver 0.9359 oz. ASW, 38.6 mm. **Obv:** National arms **Rev:** Bobsled **Edge Lettering:** "LATVIJA" repeated 3 times

Date	Mintage	F	VF	XF	Unc	BU
2005 Proof	Est. 15,000	Value: 45.00				

KM# 81 LATS

1.1500 g., Gold, 13.91 mm. **Obv:** Ribbon design **Obv. Legend:** RIGAS / LATVIJAS REPUBLIKA **Rev:** Stone face **Edge:** Reeded

Date	Mintage	F	VF	XF	Unc	BU
2005 Proof	—	Value: 65.00				

KM# 76 LATS

31.4700 g., 0.9250 Silver 0.9359 oz. ASW, 38.61 mm. **Obv:** Large coat of arms, date below **Rev:** Two hockey players viewed from above, RIGA 2006 on either side with hockey puck in center **Edge:** LATVIJA seperated by rhombic dots

Date	Mintage	F	VF	XF	Unc	BU
2005 Proof	Est. 5,000	Value: 50.00				

KM# 77 LATS

31.4700 g., 9.2500 Silver 9.3586 oz. ASW, 38.61 mm. **Obv:** Coat of arms **Rev:** Koknese castle on top with moon and sun on sides, reflection of Hanseatic Castle and ship on bottom **Edge Lettering:** LATVIJAS REPUBLIKA and LATVIJAS BANKA seperated by dots

Date	Mintage	F	VF	XF	Unc	BU
2005 Proof	Est. 15,000	Value: 45.00				

KM# 78 LATS

31.4700 g., 0.9250 Silver 0.9359 oz. ASW, 38.61 mm. **Obv:** Stylized bonfire flames **Obv. Legend:** janvāris 1991 **Rev:** Latvian mythological hero with raised sword against the background of concrete block barricades, rising sun behind **Edge Lettering:** LATVIJAS BANKA seperated by dots

Date	Mintage	F	VF	XF	Unc	BU
2006 Proof	—	Value: 45.00				

KM# 79 LATS

31.4700 g., 0.9250 Silver 0.9359 oz. ASW, 38.61 mm. **Obv:** Starry sky on left with value on right side **Rev:** Portrait of Krisjanis Barons on right side and starry sky on left **Edge Lettering:** LATVIJAS BANKA and LATVIJAS REPUBLIKA seperated by a dot

Date	Mintage	F	VF	XF	Unc	BU
2006 Proof	—	Value: 45.00				

KM# 80 LATS

31.4700 g., 0.9250 Silver 0.9359 oz. ASW, 38.61 mm. **Obv:** Seagul flying above water on left, value on right **Rev:** Portrait of Krisjanis Valdemars on right with sea on left **Edge Lettering:** LATVIJAS BANKA and LATVIJAS REPUBLIKA seperated by a dot

Date	Mintage	F	VF	XF	Unc	BU
2006 Proof	—	Value: 45.00				

KM# 82 LATS

31.4700 g., 0.9250 Silver 0.9359 oz. ASW, 38.61 mm. **Obv:** Outline of Latvia with three stars above **Obv. Inscription:** LATVIJAS REPUBLIKA **Rev:** Two crossed swords outlined against the sun **Rev. Inscription:** NO ZOBENA SAULE LECA **Edge:** Plain

Date	Mintage	F	VF	XF	Unc	BU
2006 Proof	—	Value: 45.00				

KM# 83 LATS

31.4700 g., 0.9250 Silver 0.9359 oz. ASW, 38.61 mm. **Obv:** Coat of arms, date and value below **Obv. Inscription:** ROOP top, 1 LATS bottom **Rev:** Lielstraupe castle church top, reflection of Hanseatic ship with trees on both sides on bottom **Edge Lettering:** LATVIJAS REPUBLIKA AND LATVIJAS BANKA seperated by dots

Date	Mintage	F	VF	XF	Unc	BU
2006 Proof	—	Value: 45.00				

KM# 74 LATS

4.8200 g., Copper-Nickel, 21.75 mm. **Obv:** National arms **Rev:** Pine cone above value **Edge Lettering:** "LATVIJAS BANKA" twice

Date	Mintage	F	VF	XF	Unc	BU
2006	—	—	—	—	5.00	6.00

KM# 73 LATS

4.8100 g., Copper-Nickel, 21.8 mm. **Subject:** Summer Solstice **Obv:** National arms **Rev:** Head wearing leaves above value **Edge Lettering:** "LATVIJAS BANKA"

Date	Mintage	F	VF	XF	Unc	BU
2006	—	—	—	—	5.00	6.00

KM# 59 5 LATI

1.2442 g., 0.9999 Gold 0.0400 oz. AGW, 13.92 mm. **Obv:** Bust right **Rev:** Arms with supporters above value **Edge:** Reeded **Note:** Remake of the popular KM-9 design

Date	Mintage	F	VF	XF	Unc	BU
2003 Proof	Est. 20,000	Value: 120				

LEBANON

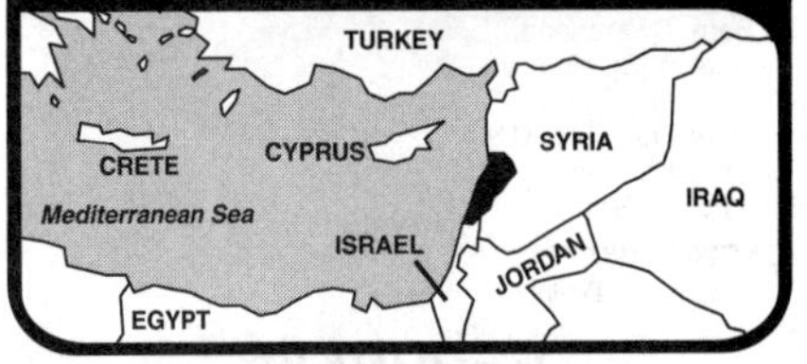

The Republic of Lebanon, situated on the eastern shore of the Mediterranean Sea between Syria and Israel, has an area of 4,015 sq. mi. (10,400 sq. km.) and a population of 3.5 million. Capital: Beirut. The economy is based on agriculture, trade and tourism. Fruit, other foodstuffs and textiles are exported.

TITLES

الجمهورية اللبنانية

al-Jomhuriya(t) al-Lubnaniya(t)

MINT MARKS

(a) - Paris, privy marks only
(u) - Utrecht, privy marks only

MONETARY SYSTEM

100 Piastres = 1 Livre (Pound)

REPUBLIC

STANDARD COINAGE

KM# 40 25 LIVRES
2.8200 g., Nickel Plated Steel, 20.5 mm. **Obv:** Value on tree **Rev:** Value within square design **Edge:** Plain

Date	Mintage	F	VF	XF	Unc	BU
2002	—	—	—	—	1.00	2.00

KM# 38a 100 LIVRES
4.0500 g., Stainless Steel, 22.5 mm. **Obv:** Value on tree **Rev:** Value above date **Edge:** Plain

Date	Mintage	F	VF	XF	Unc	BU
2003	—	—	—	—	1.50	2.50

KM# 36 250 LIVRES
5.0100 g., Brass, 23.5 mm. **Obv:** Arabic legend above value within tree **Rev:** French legend within beaded circle and value

Date	Mintage	F	VF	XF	Unc	BU
2003	—	—	—	0.75	2.00	2.50

LIBERIA

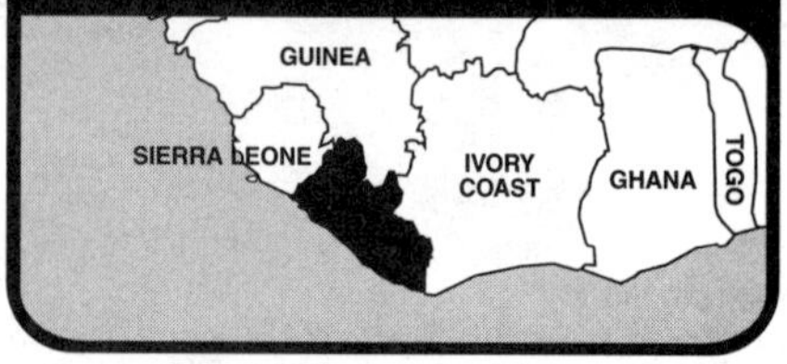

The Republic of Liberia, located on the southern side of the West African bulge between Sierra Leone and Ivory Coast, has an area of 38,250 sq. mi. (111,370 sq. km) and a population of 2.2 million. Capital: Monrovia. The major industries are agriculture, mining and lumbering. Iron ore, diamonds, rubber, coffee and coca are exported.

MINT MARKS
B - Bern, Switzerland
H - Heaton, Birmingham
(l) - London
(s) - San Francisco, U.S.
FM - Franklin Mint, U.S.A.*
PM - Pobjoy Mint

MONETARY SYSTEM
100 Cents = 1 Dollar

REPUBLIC

STANDARD COINAGE

100 Cents = 1 Dollar

KM# 618 5 CENTS
5.0200 g., Copper-Nickel, 23.8 mm. **Obv:** National arms **Rev:** Chimpanzee family **Edge:** Plain

Date	Mintage	F	VF	XF	Unc	BU
2003	—	—	—	—	1.50	2.00

KM# 568 5 DOLLARS
14.6300 g., Copper-Nickel, 33.1 mm. **Subject:** Battle of Gettysburg **Obv:** National arms **Rev:** Cannon and crossed flags divides busts facing **Edge:** Reeded

Date	Mintage	F	VF	XF	Unc	BU
2001B	—	—	—	—	12.00	14.00

KM# 651 5 DOLLARS
14.5600 g., Copper-Nickel, 33.1 mm. **Obv:** National arms **Rev:** Japanese "Zero" flying over Pearl Harbor **Edge:** Reeded

Date	Mintage	F	VF	XF	Unc	BU
2001	—	—	—	—	10.00	12.00

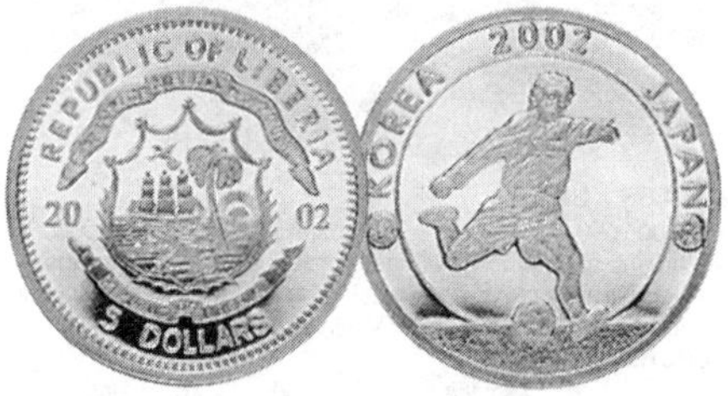

KM# 494 5 DOLLARS
8.5000 g., 0.9999 Silver 0.2732 oz. ASW, 30 mm. **Subject:** Soccer **Obv:** National arms **Rev:** Soccer player divides circle **Edge:** Reeded

Date	Mintage	F	VF	XF	Unc	BU
2002 Proof	3,000	Value: 30.00				

KM# 664 5 DOLLARS
6.4000 g., Bi-Metallic Brass center in Copper-Nickel ring, 25.7 mm. **Obv:** National arms **Rev:** Pope and cathedral within circle **Edge:** Reeded

Date	Mintage	F	VF	XF	Unc	BU
2005	—	—	—	—	12.00	14.00

KM# 724 5 DOLLARS
26.3000 g., Silver Plated Bronze, 38.6 mm. **Obv:** National arms **Rev:** Multicolor Pope John Paul II with cross **Edge:** Reeded

Date	Mintage	F	VF	XF	Unc	BU
2007 Proof	—	Value: 30.00				

KM# 733 5 DOLLARS
27.0000 g., Copper-Nickel Silvered and Gilt, 38.61 mm. **Subject:** The Black Madonna of Czestochowa **Obv:** Arms **Obv. Legend:** REPUBLIC OF LIBERIA **Rev:** 1/2 length figure of Madonna facing with child

Date	Mintage	F	VF	XF	Unc	BU
2007 Proof	1,000	Value: 40.00				

KM# 491 10 DOLLARS
25.2500 g., 0.9250 Silver 0.7509 oz. ASW, 36.8 mm. **Subject:** Illusion **Obv:** National arms **Rev:** Stylized head with glasses facing **Edge:** Plain **Shape:** 10-sided

Date	Mintage	F	VF	XF	Unc	BU
2001 Proof	5,000	Value: 35.00				

KM# 513 10 DOLLARS
Copper-Nickel, 38.6 mm. **Subject:** Hungarian Revolution of 1848 **Obv:** National arms **Rev:** Multicolor heroic scene **Edge:** Reeded

Date	Mintage	F	VF	XF	Unc	BU
2001 Proof	9,999	Value: 10.00				

KM# 537 10 DOLLARS
28.5000 g., Copper-Nickel, 38.6 mm. **Subject:** "Moments of Freedom" Series **Obv:** National arms **Rev:** Multicolor Buddha, spelled "Budha" on the coin **Edge:** Reeded

Date	Mintage	F	VF	XF	Unc	BU
2001 Proof	9,999	Value: 10.00				

KM# 538 10 DOLLARS
28.5000 g., Copper-Nickel, 38.6 mm. **Subject:** "Moments of Freedom" Series **Obv:** National arms **Rev:** Multicolor Battle of Marathon scene **Edge:** Reeded

Date	Mintage	F	VF	XF	Unc	BU
2001 Proof	9,999	Value: 10.00				

KM# 539 10 DOLLARS
28.5000 g., Copper-Nickel, 38.6 mm. **Series:** "Moments of Freedom" **Obv:** National arms **Rev:** Multicolor founding of Liberia design **Edge:** Reeded

Date	Mintage	F	VF	XF	Unc	BU
2001 Proof	9,999	Value: 10.00				

KM# 540 10 DOLLARS
28.5000 g., Copper-Nickel, 38.6 mm. **Series:** "Moments of Freedom" **Obv:** National arms **Rev:** Multicolor portrait of Constantine I **Edge:** Reeded

Date	Mintage	F	VF	XF	Unc	BU
2001 Proof	9,999	Value: 10.00				

KM# 541 10 DOLLARS
28.5000 g., Copper-Nickel, 38.6 mm. **Series:** "Moments of Freedom" **Obv:** National arms **Rev:** Multicolor William Tell statue **Edge:** Reeded

Date	Mintage	F	VF	XF	Unc	BU
2001 Proof	9,999	Value: 10.00				

KM# 542 10 DOLLARS
28.5000 g., Copper-Nickel, 38.6 mm. **Series:** "Moments of Freedom" **Obv:** National arms **Rev:** Multicolor bust facing **Edge:** Reeded

Date	Mintage	F	VF	XF	Unc	BU
2001 Proof	9,999	Value: 10.00				

KM# 544 10 DOLLARS
28.5000 g., Copper-Nickel, 38.6 mm. **Series:** "Moments of Freedom" **Subject:** Fall of Berlin Wall **Obv:** National arms **Rev:** Multicolor Brandenburg Gate scene **Edge:** Reeded

Date	Mintage	F	VF	XF	Unc	BU
2001 Proof	9,999	Value: 10.00				

KM# 545 10 DOLLARS
28.5000 g., Copper-Nickel, 38.6 mm. **Series:** "Moments of Freedom" **Obv:** National arms **Rev:** Multicolor half length figure facing **Edge:** Reeded

Date	Mintage	F	VF	XF	Unc	BU
2001 Proof	9,999	Value: 10.00				

KM# 546 10 DOLLARS
28.5000 g., Copper Nickel, 38.6 mm. **Subject:** "Moments of Freedom" Series **Obv:** National arms **Rev:** Multicolor Sitting Bull portrait **Edge:** Reeded

Date	Mintage	F	VF	XF	Unc	BU
Proof	9,999	Value: 10.00				

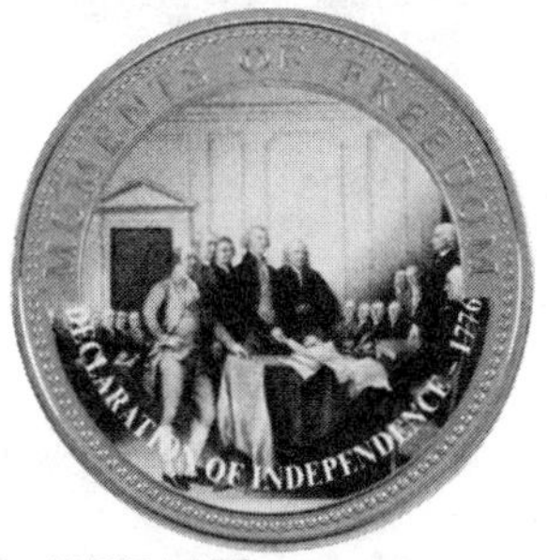

KM# 547 10 DOLLARS
28.5000 g., Copper-Nickel, 38.6 mm. **Series:** "Moments of Freedom" **Obv:** National arms **Rev:** Multicolor Declaration of Independence scene **Edge:** Reeded

Date	Mintage	F	VF	XF	Unc	BU
2001 Proof	9,999	Value: 10.00				

KM# 548 10 DOLLARS
28.5000 g., Copper-Nickel, 38.6 mm. **Series:** "Moments of Freedom" **Subject:** Women's Rights **Obv:** National arms **Rev:** Multicolor allegorical woman **Edge:** Reeded

Date	Mintage	F	VF	XF	Unc	BU
2001 Proof	9,999	Value: 10.00				

KM# 549 10 DOLLARS
28.5000 g., Copper-Nickel, 38.6 mm. **Series:** "Moments of Freedom" **Obv:** National arms **Rev:** Multicolor bust looking down **Edge:** Reeded

Date	Mintage	F	VF	XF	Unc	BU
2001 Proof	9,999	Value: 10.00				

KM# 550 10 DOLLARS
28.5000 g., Copper-Nickel, 38.6 mm. **Series:** "Moments of Freedom" **Subject:** Spanish Civil War **Obv:** National arms **Rev:** Multicolor picture of a soldier at the moment he is shot in battle **Edge:** Reeded

Date	Mintage	F	VF	XF	Unc	BU
2001 Proof	9,999	Value: 10.00				

KM# 551 10 DOLLARS
28.5000 g., Copper-Nickel, 38.6 mm. **Series:** "Moments of Freedom" **Subject:** End of Holocaust **Obv:** National arms **Rev:** Multicolor inmates behind wire fence scene **Edge:** Reeded

Date	Mintage	F	VF	XF	Unc	BU
2001 Proof	9,999	Value: 10.00				

KM# 552 10 DOLLARS
28.5000 g., Copper-Nickel, 38.6 mm. **Series:** "Moments of Freedom" **Subject:** End of WWII **Obv:** National arms **Rev:** Multicolor Iwo Jima flag raising scene **Edge:** Reeded

Date	Mintage	F	VF	XF	Unc	BU
2001 Proof	9,999	Value: 10.00				

KM# 553 10 DOLLARS
28.5000 g., Copper-Nickel, 38.6 mm. **Series:** "Moments of Freedom" **Subject:** United Nations **Obv:** National arms **Rev:** Multicolor UN logo and dove **Edge:** Reeded

Date	Mintage	F	VF	XF	Unc	BU
2001 Proof	9,999	Value: 10.00				

KM# 554 10 DOLLARS
28.5000 g., Copper-Nickel, 38.6 mm. **Series:** "Moments of Freedom" **Obv:** National arms **Rev:** Multicolor Solzhenitsyn portrait **Edge:** Reeded

Date	Mintage	F	VF	XF	Unc	BU
2001 Proof	9,999	Value: 10.00				

KM# 555 10 DOLLARS
28.5000 g., Copper-Nickel, 38.6 mm. **Series:** "Moments of Freedom" **Obv:** National arms **Rev:** Multicolor Spartacus and troops **Edge:** Reeded

Date	Mintage	F	VF	XF	Unc	BU
2001 Proof	9,999	Value: 12.00				

KM# 556 10 DOLLARS
28.5000 g., Copper-Nickel, 38.6 mm. **Series:** "Moments of Freedom" **Subject:** Czechoslovakia 1968 **Obv:** National arms **Rev:** Multicolor Soviet tank in Prague **Edge:** Reeded

Date	Mintage	F	VF	XF	Unc	BU
2001 Proof	9,999	Value: 10.00				

KM# 557 10 DOLLARS
28.5000 g., Copper Nickel, 38.6 mm. **Subject:** "Moments of Freedom" Series - French Revolution **Obv:** National arms **Rev:** Multicolor Bastille scene **Edge:** Reeded.

Date	Mintage	F	VF	XF	Unc	BU
2001 Proof	9,999	Value: 10.00				

KM# 558 10 DOLLARS
28.5000 g., Copper-Nickel, 38.6 mm. **Series:** "Moments of Freedom" **Obv:** National arms **Rev:** Multicolor Nelson Mandela and fist **Edge:** Reeded

Date	Mintage	F	VF	XF	Unc	BU
2001 Proof	9,999	Value: 10.00				

KM# 559 10 DOLLARS
28.5000 g., Copper-Nickel, 38.6 mm. **Series:** "Moments of Freedom" **Subject:** Freedom of Communication **Obv:** National arms **Rev:** Multicolor circuit board and world globe **Edge:** Reeded

Date	Mintage	F	VF	XF	Unc	BU
2001 Proof	9,999	Value: 10.00				

KM# 777 10 DOLLARS
14.5500 g., Copper Nickel, 32 mm. **Subject:** 43rd President of USA **Obv:** National arms **Obv. Legend:** REPUBLIC OF LIBERIA **Rev:** George W. Bush, flag in background

Date	Mintage	F	VF	XF	Unc	BU
2001 Proof	—	Value: 10.00				

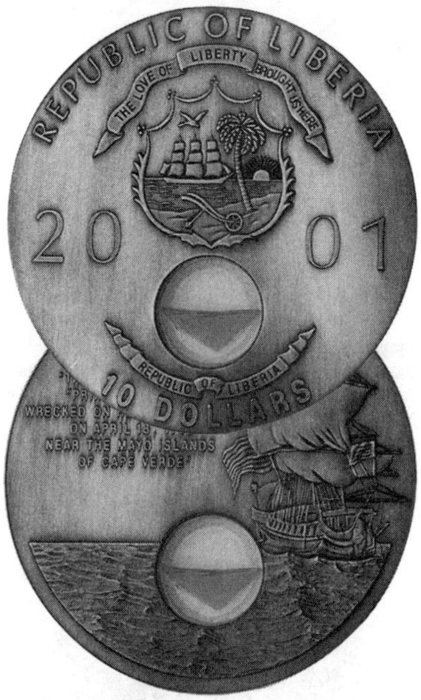

KM# 493 10 DOLLARS
770.0000 g., Copper, 100 mm. **Subject:** "The Wreck of the Princess Louisa" **Obv:** National arms **Rev:** Sailing ship **Edge:** Reeded **Note:** Illustration reduced. With an encased glass shard recovered from the wreck site of the Princess Louisa.

Date	Mintage	F	VF	XF	Unc	BU
2001	2,000	—	—	—	200	—

KM# 510 10 DOLLARS
33.2400 g., Gold-Plated Copper, 40.1 mm. **Subject:** American Eagle **Obv:** National arms **Rev:** Multicolor holographic eagle **Edge:** Reeded **Note:** The American Mint is not an actual mint.

Date	Mintage	F	VF	XF	Unc	BU
2001	20,000	—	—	—	—	35.00

KM# 543 10 DOLLARS
28.5000 g., Copper-Nickel, 38.6 mm. **Series:** "Moments of Freedom" **Subject:** Liberation of Vienna **Obv:** National arms **Rev:** Multicolor head with headdress and battle scene **Edge:** Reeded **Note:** Vienna was never captured by the Turks.

Date	Mintage	F	VF	XF	Unc	BU
2001 Proof	9,999	Value: 10.00				

KM# 654 10 DOLLARS
15.3300 g., Copper-Nickel, 33.2 mm. **Obv:** National arms **Rev:** "GEORGE W. BUSH..." No value at bottom **Edge:** Reeded

Date	Mintage	F	VF	XF	Unc	BU
2002	—	—	—	—	—	10.00

KM# 705 10 DOLLARS

31.1035 g., 0.9990 Silver 0.9990 oz. ASW, 38.6 mm. **Subject:** 2002 World Football Championship - Japan - South Korea **Obv:** National arms **Rev:** Pagoda superimposed on a soccer ball, legend around **Edge:** Reeded

Date	Mintage	F	VF	XF	Unc	BU
2002 Proof	—	Value: 45.00				

KM# 708 10 DOLLARS

25.1000 g., 0.9250 Silver 0.7464 oz. ASW, 38.6 mm. **Obv:** National arms **Rev:** Clipper ship "Flying Cloud" **Edge:** Reeded

Date	Mintage	F	VF	XF	Unc	BU
2003 Proof	—	Value: 35.00				

KM# 602 10 DOLLARS

25.0000 g., 0.9250 Silver 0.7435 oz. ASW, 38.6 mm. **Obv:** National arms **Rev:** Icarus and Daedalus in flight **Edge:** Reeded

Date	Mintage	F	VF	XF	Unc	BU
2003 Proof	—	Value: 35.00				

KM# 603 10 DOLLARS

25.0000 g., 0.9250 Silver 0.7435 oz. ASW, 38.6 mm. **Obv:** National arms **Rev:** First parachute **Edge:** Reeded

Date	Mintage	F	VF	XF	Unc	BU
2003 Proof	—	Value: 35.00				

KM# 604 10 DOLLARS

25.0000 g., 0.9250 Silver 0.7435 oz. ASW, 38.6 mm. **Obv:** National arms **Rev:** Montgolfier ballon **Edge:** Reeded

Date	Mintage	F	VF	XF	Unc	BU
2003 Proof	—	Value: 35.00				

KM# 605 10 DOLLARS

25.0000 g., 0.9250 Silver 0.7435 oz. ASW, 38.6 mm. **Obv:** National arms **Rev:** Otto v. Lillenthal **Edge:** Reeded

Date	Mintage	F	VF	XF	Unc	BU
2003 Proof	—	Value: 35.00				

KM# 606 10 DOLLARS

25.0000 g., 0.9250 Silver 0.7435 oz. ASW, 38.6 mm. **Obv:** National arms **Rev:** Wright Brothers **Edge:** Reeded

Date	Mintage	F	VF	XF	Unc	BU
2003 Proof	—	Value: 35.00				

KM# 607 10 DOLLARS

25.0000 g., 0.9250 Silver 0.7435 oz. ASW, 38.6 mm. **Obv:** National arms **Rev:** Mach 1- Bell X **Edge:** Reeded

Date	Mintage	F	VF	XF	Unc	BU
2003 Proof	—	Value: 35.00				

KM# 608 10 DOLLARS

25.0000 g., 0.9250 Silver 0.7435 oz. ASW, 38.6 mm. **Obv:** National arms **Rev:** The Concorde **Edge:** Reeded

Date	Mintage	F	VF	XF	Unc	BU
2003 Proof	—	Value: 35.00				

KM# 611 10 DOLLARS

62.2070 g., 0.9990 Silver 1.9979 oz. ASW, 50 mm. **Obv:** National arms left of window design with Tiffany Glass inlay **Rev:** Window design with Tiffany Glass inlay **Edge:** Plain

Date	Mintage	F	VF	XF	Unc	BU
2004	999	—	—	—	—	85.00

KM# 740 10 DOLLARS

20.0000 g., 0.9990 Silver And Gold 0.6423 oz., 38.00 mm. **Series:** Endangered Wildlife **Obv:** National arms **Obv. Legend:** REPUBLIC OF LIBERIA **Rev:** Gilt Siberian Tiger with diamonds inset in eyes **Rev. Legend:** RUSSIA **Edge:** Plain

Date	Mintage	F	VF	XF	Unc	BU
2004 Proof	5,000	Value: 165				

KM# 741 10 DOLLARS

20.0000 g., 0.9990 Silver And Gold 0.6423 oz., 38.00 mm. **Series:** Endangered Wildlife **Obv:** National arms **Obv. Legend:** REPUBLIC OF LIBERIA **Rev:** Two gilt Hyacinth Macaws perched on branch with diamond insets in eyes **Rev. Legend:** BRAZIL **Edge:** Plain

Date	Mintage	F	VF	XF	Unc	BU
2004 Proof	5,000	Value: 165				

KM# 742 10 DOLLARS

20.0000 g., 0.9990 Silver And Gold 0.6423 oz., 38.00 mm. **Series:** Endangered Wildlife **Obv:** National arms **Obv. Legend:** REPUBLIC OF LIBERIA **Rev:** Gilt young Giant Panda seated eating bamboo shoots **Rev. Legend:** CHINA **Edge:** Plain

Date	Mintage	F	VF	XF	Unc	BU
2004 Proof	5,000	Value: 165				

KM# 743 10 DOLLARS

20.0000 g., 0.9990 Silver And Gold 0.6423 oz., 38.00 mm. **Subject:** Endangered Wildlife **Obv:** National arms **Obv. Legend:** REPUBLIC OF LIBERIA **Rev:** Two gilt Bald Eagles. one perched at left, one alighting at center right **Rev. Legend:** USA **Edge:** Plain

Date	Mintage	F	VF	XF	Unc	BU
2004 Proof	5,000	Value: 165				

KM# 744 10 DOLLARS

20.0000 g., 0.9990 Silver And Gold 0.6423 oz., 38.00 mm. **Series:** Endangered Wildlife **Obv:** National arms **Obv. Legend:** REPUBLIC OF LIBERIA **Rev:** Gilt Puma standing with diamonds inset in eyes **Rev. Legend:** MEXICO **Edge:** Plain

Date	Mintage	F	VF	XF	Unc	BU
2004 Proof	5,000	Value: 165				

KM# 745 10 DOLLARS

20.0000 g., 0.9990 Silver And Gold 0.6423 oz., 38.00 mm. **Series:** Endangered Wildlife **Obv:** National arms **Obv. Legend:** REPUBLIC OF LIBERIA **Rev:** Gilt Red-ruffedLemur on branch with diamonds inset in eyes **Rev. Legend:** MADAGASCAR **Edge:** Plain

Date	Mintage	F	VF	XF	Unc	BU
2004 Proof	5,000	Value: 165				

KM# 746 10 DOLLARS

20.0000 g., 0.9990 Silver And Gold 0.6423 oz., 38.00 mm. **Series:** Endangered Wildlife **Obv:** National arms **Obv. Legend:** REPUBLIC OF LIBERIA **Rev:** Two gilt Andean Condors, one lifting off at center, one perched at right **Rev. Legend:** CHILE **Edge:** Plain

Date	Mintage	F	VF	XF	Unc	BU
2004 Proof	5,000	Value: 165				

KM# 747 10 DOLLARS

20.0000 g., 0.9990 Silver And Gold 0.6423 oz., 38.00 mm. **Series:** Endangered Wildlife **Obv:** National arms **Obv. Legend:** REPUBLIC OF LIBERIA **Rev:** Two gilt Yellow-eyed Penguins standin facing with diamonds inset in eyes **Rev. Legend:** NEW ZEALAND **Edge:** Plain

Date	Mintage	F	VF	XF	Unc	BU
2004 Proof	5,000	Value: 165				

KM# 748 10 DOLLARS

20.0000 g., 0.9990 Silver And Gold 0.6423 oz., 38.00 mm. **Series:** Endangered Wildlife **Obv:** National arms **Obv. Legend:** REPUBLIC OF LIBERIA **Rev:** Gilt African lion standing facing with diamonds inset in eyes **Rev. Legend:** SOUTH AFRICA **Edge:** Plain

Date	Mintage	F	VF	XF	Unc	BU
2004 Proof	5,000	Value: 165				

KM# 749 10 DOLLARS

20.0000 g., 0.9990 Silver And Gold 0.6423 oz., 38.00 mm. **Series:** Endangered Wildlife **Obv:** National arms **Obv. Legend:** REPUBLIC OF LIBERIA **Rev:** Two gilt perched Kookaburras with diamonds inset in eyes **Rev. Legend:** AUSTRALIA **Edge:** Plain

Date	Mintage	F	VF	XF	Unc	BU
2004 Proof	5,000	Value: 165				

KM# 750 10 DOLLARS

20.0000 g., 0.9990 Silver And Gold 0.6423 oz., 38.00 mm. **Series:** Endangered Wildlife **Obv:** National arms **Obv. Legend:** REPUBLIC OF LIBERIA **Rev:** Gilt Polar Bear standing facing with diamonds inset in eyes **Rev. Legend:** CANADA **Edge:** Plain

Date	Mintage	F	VF	XF	Unc	BU
2004 Proof	5,000	Value: 165				

KM# 751 10 DOLLARS

20.0000 g., 0.9990 Silver And Gold 0.6423 oz. **Series:** Endangered Wildlife **Obv:** National arms **Obv. Legend:** REPUBLIC OF LIBERIA **Rev:** Gilt perched Blakiston's Fish-owl with diamonds inset in eyes **Rev. Legend:** JAPAN

Date	Mintage	F	VF	XF	Unc	BU
2004 Proof	5,000	Value: 165				

KM# 738 10 DOLLARS

27.1900 g., Copper Nickel, 43 mm. **Subject:** Death of Pope John-Paul II **Edge:** Reeded

Date	Mintage	F	VF	XF	Unc	BU
2005	—	—	—	—	12.00	14.00

KM# 739.1 10 DOLLARS

25.0000 g., 0.9250 Silver 0.7435 oz. ASW **Subject:** Death of Pope John-Paul II **Rev:** Silhouette of John-Paul gilt, backgound in Ruthenium

Date	Mintage	F	VF	XF	Unc	BU
2005	7,500	—	—	—	—	60.00

KM# 739.2 10 DOLLARS

25.0000 g., 0.9250 Silver 0.7435 oz. ASW **Subject:** Death of Pope John-Paul II **Rev:** Silhouette of John-Paul gilt, blackened background

Date	Mintage	F	VF	XF	Unc	BU
2005	7,500	—	—	—	—	47.50

KM# 752 10 DOLLARS

20.0000 g., 0.9990 Silver And Gold 0.6423 oz., 38.00 mm. **Series:** Endangered Wildlife **Obv:** National arms **Obv. Legend:** REPUBLIC OF LIBERIA **Rev:** Gilt Koala perched on branch with diamonds inset in eyes **Rev. Legend:** AUSTRALIA **Edge:** Plain

Date	Mintage	F	VF	XF	Unc	BU
2005 Proof	5,000	Value: 165				

KM# 753 10 DOLLARS

20.0000 g., 0.9990 Silver And Gold 0.6423 oz., 38.00 mm. **Series:** Endangered Wildlife **Obv:** National arms **Obv. Legend:** REPUBLIC OF LIBERIA **Rev:** Two perched gilt Yellow-eared Conures with diamonds inset in eyes **Rev. Legend:** COLOMBIA **Edge:** Plain

Date	Mintage	F	VF	XF	Unc	BU
2005 Proof	5,000	Value: 165				

KM# 754 10 DOLLARS

20.0000 g., 0.9990 Silver And Gold 0.6423 oz., 38.00 mm. **Series:** Endangered Wildlife **Obv:** National arms **Obv. Legend:** REPUBLIC OF LIBERIA **Rev:** Gilt Iberian Lynx standing facing with diamonds inset in eyes **Rev. Legend:** SPAIN **Edge:** Plain

Date	Mintage	F	VF	XF	Unc	BU
2005 Proof	5,000	Value: 165				

KM# 755 10 DOLLARS

20.0000 g., 0.9990 Silver And Gold 0.6423 oz., 38.00 mm. **Series:** Endangered Wildlife **Obv:** National arms **Obv. Legend:** REPUBLIC OF LIBERIA **Rev:** Two perched gilt Yellow-crested Cockatoos **Rev. Legend:** INDONESIA **Edge:** Plain

Date	Mintage	F	VF	XF	Unc	BU
2005 Proof	5,000	Value: 165				

KM# 756 10 DOLLARS

20.0000 g., 0.9990 Silver And Gold 0.6423 oz., 38.00 mm. **Series:** Endangered Wildlife **Obv:** National arms **Obv. Legend:** R$EPUBLIC OF LIBERIA **Rev:** Gilt Jaguar resting on branch with diamonds inset in eyes **Rev. Legend:** BELIZE **Edge:** Plain

Date	Mintage	F	VF	XF	Unc	BU
2005 Proof	5,000	Value: 165				

KM# 757 10 DOLLARS

20.0000 g., 0.9990 Silver And Gold 0.6423 oz., 38.00 mm. **Series:** Endangered Wildlife **Obv:** National arms **Obv. Legend:** REPUBLIC OF LIBERIA **Rev:** Two perched gilt Plate-billed Mountain Toucans with diamons inset in eyes **Rev. Legend:** ECUADOR **Edge:** Plain

Date	Mintage	F	VF	XF	Unc	BU
2005 Proof	5,000	Value: 165				

KM# 758 10 DOLLARS

20.0000 g., 0.9990 Silver And Gold 0.6423 oz., 38.00 mm. **Series:** Endangered Wildlife **Obv:** National arms **Obv. Legend:** REPUBLIC OF LIBERIA **Rev:** Gilt Red Panda resting facing with diamonds inset in eyes **Rev. Legend:** INDIA **Edge:** Plain

Date	Mintage	F	VF	XF	Unc	BU
2005 Proof	5,000	Value: 165				

KM# 759 10 DOLLARS

20.0000 g., 0.9990 Silver And Gold 0.6423 oz., 38.00 mm. **Series:** Endangered Wildlife **Obv:** National arms **Obv. Legend:** REPUBLIC OF LIBERIA **Rev:** Two perched gilt Resplendent Quetzals with diamonds inset in eyes **Rev. Legend:** GUATEMALA **Edge:** Plain

Date	Mintage	F	VF	XF	Unc	BU
2005 Proof	5,000	Value: 165				

KM# 760 10 DOLLARS

20.0000 g., 0.9990 Silver And Gold 0.6423 oz., 38.00 mm. **Series:** Endangered Wildlife **Obv:** National arms **Obv. Legend:** REPUBLIC OF LIBERIA **Rev:** Gilt Snow Leopard standing left looking back with diamonds inset in eyes **Rev. Legend:** NEPAL **Edge:** Plain

Date	Mintage	F	VF	XF	Unc	BU
2005 Proof	5,000	Value: 165				

KM# 761 10 DOLLARS

20.0000 g., 0.9990 Silver And Gold 0.6423 oz., 38.00 mm. **Series:** Endangered Wildlife **Obv:** National arms **Obv. Legend:** REPUBLIC OF LIBERIA **Rev:** Gilt Fossa standing right on branch facing with diamonds inset in eyes **Rev. Legend:** MADAGASCAR **Edge:** Plain

Date	Mintage	F	VF	XF	Unc	BU
2005 Proof	5,000	Value: 165				

KM# 762 10 DOLLARS

20.0000 g., 0.9990 Silver And Gold 0.6423 oz., 38.00 mm. **Series:** Endangered Wildlife **Obv:** National arms **Obv. Legend:** REPUBLIC OF LIBERIA **Rev:** Two gilt Chilean Flamingos standing left with diamonds inset in eyes **Rev. Legend:** ARGENTINA **Edge:** Plain

Date	Mintage	F	VF	XF	Unc	BU
2005 Proof	5,000	Value: 165				

KM# 763 10 DOLLARS

20.0000 g., 0.9990 Silver And Gold 0.6423 oz., 38.00 mm. **Series:** Endangered Wildlife **Obv:** National arms **Obv. Legend:** REPUBLIC OF LIBERIA **Rev:** Two gilt White-winged ducks, one standing, one swimming right with diamonds inset in eyes **Rev. Legend:** THAILAND **Edge:** Plain

Date	Mintage	F	VF	XF	Unc	BU
2005 Proof	5,000	Value: 165				

KM# 764 10 DOLLARS

20.0000 g., 0.9990 Silver And Gold 0.6423 oz., 38.00 mm. **Series:** Endangered Wildlife **Obv:** National arms **Obv. Legend:** REPUBLIC OF LIBERIA **Rev:** Gilt Crested Genet on branch facing with diamonds inset in eyes **Rev. Legend:** CAMEROON **Edge:** Plain

Date	Mintage	F	VF	XF	Unc	BU
2006 Proof	5,000	Value: 165				

KM# 765 10 DOLLARS

20.0000 g., 0.9990 Silver And Gold 0.6423 oz., 38.00 mm. **Series:** Endangered Wildlife **Obv:** National arms **Obv. Legend:** REPUBLIC OF LIBERIA **Rev:** Two gilt Dalmatian Pelicans, one swimming, one standing with diamonds inset in eyes **Rev. Legend:** MONTENEGRO **Edge:** Plain

Date	Mintage	F	VF	XF	Unc	BU
2006 Proof	5,000	Value: 165				

KM# 766 10 DOLLARS

20.0000 g., 0.9990 Silver And Gold 0.6423 oz., 38.00 mm. **Series:** Endangered Wildlife **Obv:** National arms **Obv. Legend:** REPUBLIC OF LIBERIA **Rev:** Gilt Hairy-bared Dwarf Lemue standing on branch with diamonds inset in eyes **Rev. Legend:** MADAGASCAR **Edge:** Plain

Date	Mintage	F	VF	XF	Unc	BU
2006 Proof	5,000	Value: 165				

KM# 767 10 DOLLARS

20.0000 g., 0.9990 Silver And Gold 0.6423 oz., 38.00 mm. **Series:** Endangered Wildlife **Obv:** National arms **Obv. Legend:** REPUBLIC OF LIBERIA **Rev:** Two gilt Visayan Tarictics perched on branches with diamonds inset in eyes **Rev. Legend:** Philippines **Edge:** Plain

Date	Mintage	F	VF	XF	Unc	BU
2006 Proof	5,000	Value: 165				

KM# 768 10 DOLLARS

20.0000 g., 0.9990 Silver And Gold 0.6423 oz., 38.00 mm. **Series:** Endangered Wildlife **Obv:** National arms **Obv. Legend:** REPUBLIC OF LIBERIA **Rev:** Two gilt Ethiopian Wolves, one seated, one laying with diamonds inset in eyes **Rev. Legend:** ETHIOPIA **Edge:** Plain

Date	Mintage	F	VF	XF	Unc	BU
2006 Proof	5,000	Value: 165				

KM# 769 10 DOLLARS

20.0000 g., 0.9990 Silver And Gold 0.6423 oz., 38.00 mm. **Series:** Endangered Wildlife **Obv:** National arms **Obv. Legend:** REPUBLIC OF LIBERIA **Rev:** Two gilt Kakapos perched on a branch with diamonds inset in eyes **Rev. Legend:** NEW ZEALAND **Edge:** Plain

Date	Mintage	F	VF	XF	Unc	BU
2006 Proof	5,000	Value: 165				

KM# 770 10 DOLLARS

20.0000 g., 0.9990 Silver And Gold 0.6423 oz., 38.00 mm. **Series:** Endangered Wildlife **Obv:** National arms **Obv. Legend:** REPUBLIC OF LIBERIA **Rev:** Gilt Spectacled Bear standing with diamonds inset in eyes **Rev. Legend:** BOLIVIA **Edge:** Plain

Date	Mintage	F	VF	XF	Unc	BU
2006 Proof	5,000	Value: 165				

KM# 771 10 DOLLARS

20.0000 g., 0.9990 Silver And Gold 0.6423 oz., 38.00 mm. **Series:** Endangered Wildlife **Obv:** National arms **Obv. Legend:** REPUBLIC OF LIBERIA **Rev:** Two gilt Mauritius Kestrels perched on branch with diamonds inset in eyes **Rev. Legend:** MAURITIUS **Edge:** Plain

Date	Mintage	F	VF	XF	Unc	BU
2006 Proof	5,000	Value: 165				

KM# 772 10 DOLLARS

20.0000 g., 0.9990 Silver And Gold 0.6423 oz., 38.00 mm. **Series:** Endangered Wildlife **Obv:** National arms **Obv. Legend:** REPUBLIC OF LIBERIA **Rev:** Two gilt Mhorr Gazelles, one standing, one resting with diamonds inset in eyes **Rev. Legend:** MALI **Edge:** Plain

Date	Mintage	F	VF	XF	Unc	BU
2006 Proof	5,000	Value: 165				

KM# 773 10 DOLLARS

20.0000 g., 0.9990 Silver And Gold 0.6423 oz., 38.00 mm. **Series:** Endangered Wildlife **Obv:** National arms **Obv. Legend:** REPUBLIC OF LIBERIA **Rev:** Two gilt Blue Lorikeets perched on branches with diamonds inset in eyes **Rev. Legend:** FRENCH POLYNESIA **Edge:** Plain

Date	Mintage	F	VF	XF	Unc	BU
2006 Proof	5,000	Value: 165				

KM# 774 10 DOLLARS

20.0000 g., 0.9990 Silver And Gold 0.6423 oz., 38.00 mm. **Series:** Endangered Wildlife **Obv:** National arms **Obv. Legend:** REPUBLIC OF LIBERIA **Rev:** Gilt resting Arabian Leopard with diamonds inset in eyes **Rev. Legend:** SAUDI ARABIA **Edge:** Plain

Date	Mintage	F	VF	XF	Unc	BU
2006 Proof	5,000	Value: 165				

KM# 775 10 DOLLARS

20.0000 g., 0.9990 Silver And Gold 0.6423 oz., 38.00 mm. **Series:** Endangered Wildlife **Obv:** National arms **Obv. Legend:** REPUBLIC OF LIBERIA **Rev:** Two gilt Hawaiian Geese standing with diamonds inset in eyes **Rev. Legend:** USA **Edge:** Plain

Date	Mintage	F	VF	XF	Unc	BU
2006 Proof	5,000	Value: 165				

KM# 725 10 DOLLARS

3.1100 g., 0.9990 Gold 0.0999 oz. AGW, 16 mm. **Obv:** National arms **Rev:** Leopard head **Edge:** Reeded

Date	Mintage	F	VF	XF	Unc	BU
2007 Proof	120	Value: 150				

KM# 734 10 DOLLARS

25.0000 g., 0.9250 Silver 0.7435 oz. ASW, 38.61 mm. **Subject:** The Black Madonna of Czestochowa **Obv:** Arms **Obv. Legend:** REPUBLIC OF LIBERIA **Rev:** 1/2 length figure of Madonna facing with child

Date	Mintage	F	VF	XF	Unc	BU
2007 Proof	1,000	Value: 60.00				

KM# 643 20 DOLLARS

15.5500 g., 0.9990 Silver 0.4994 oz. ASW, 30.4 mm. **Obv:** St. Peter's Basilica **Rev:** Bust of Pope facing **Edge:** Reeded

Date	Mintage	F	VF	XF	Unc	BU
2001S Proof	—	Value: 25.00				

KM# 650 20 DOLLARS

19.9100 g., 0.9990 Silver 0.6395 oz. ASW, 40 mm. **Obv:** National arms **Rev:** Bust of Charles Lindbergh facing and plane **Edge:** Reeded

Date	Mintage	F	VF	XF	Unc	BU
2001 Proof	—	Value: 40.00				

KM# 715 20 DOLLARS

20.0000 g., 0.9990 Silver 0.6423 oz. ASW, 40.3 mm. **Subject:** American History Series **Obv:** National arms **Rev:** First Continental Congress in prayer **Edge:** Reeded

Date	Mintage	F	VF	XF	Unc	BU
2001 Proof	20,000	Value: 25.00				

KM# 716 20 DOLLARS

20.0000 g., 0.9990 Silver 0.6423 oz. ASW, 40.3 mm. **Subject:** American History Series **Obv:** National arms **Rev:** U.S. Constitution Ratification, text in stars of folded flag **Edge:** Reeded

Date	Mintage	F	VF	XF	Unc	BU
2001 Proof	20,000	Value: 25.00				

KM# 717 20 DOLLARS

20.0000 g., 0.9990 Silver 0.6423 oz. ASW, 40.3 mm. **Subject:** American History Series **Obv:** National arms **Rev:** Washington's Inauguration scene **Edge:** Reeded

Date	Mintage	F	VF	XF	Unc	BU
2001 Proof	20,000	Value: 25.00				

KM# 719 20 DOLLARS

20.0000 g., 0.9990 Silver 0.6423 oz. ASW, 40.3 mm. **Subject:** American History Series **Obv:** National arms **Rev:** Prohibition, hatchet, barrels and bottles destruction **Edge:** Reeded

Date	Mintage	F	VF	XF	Unc	BU
2001 Proof	20,000	Value: 25.00				

KM# 720 20 DOLLARS

20.0000 g., 0.9990 Silver 0.6423 oz. ASW, 40.3 mm. **Subject:** American History Series **Obv:** National arms **Rev:** Cuban Missile Crisis, Castro, Khrushchev, Kennedy, missiles and map **Edge:** Reeded

Date	Mintage	F	VF	XF	Unc	BU
2001 Proof	20,000	Value: 25.00				

KM# 721 20 DOLLARS

20.0000 g., 0.9990 Silver 0.6423 oz. ASW, 40.3 mm. **Subject:** American History Series **Obv:** National arms **Rev:** First Man on Moon, Armstrong and Lander **Edge:** Reeded

Date	Mintage	F	VF	XF	Unc	BU
2001 Proof	20,000	Value: 25.00				

KM# 722 20 DOLLARS

20.0000 g., 0.9990 Silver 0.6423 oz. ASW, 40.3 mm. **Subject:** American History Series **Obv:** National arms **Rev:** Desert Storm, soldier, helicopter, rocket launcher etc. **Edge:** Reeded

Date	Mintage	F	VF	XF	Unc	BU
2001 Proof	20,000	Value: 25.00				

KM# 718 20 DOLLARS

20.0000 g., 0.9990 Silver 0.6423 oz. ASW, 40.3 mm. **Subject:** American History Series **Obv:** National arms **Rev:** Appomattox surrender scene with Lee and Grant **Edge:** Reeded

Date	Mintage	F	VF	XF	Unc	BU
2001 Proof	20,000	Value: 25.00				

KM# 514 20 DOLLARS

31.1035 g., 0.9990 Silver 0.9990 oz. ASW, 38.2 mm. **Subject:** Bush-Cheney Inauguration **Obv:** White House **Rev:** Conjoined busts right **Edge:** Reeded

Date	Mintage	F	VF	XF	Unc	BU
2001 Proof	—	Value: 45.00				

KM# 616 20 DOLLARS
31.2000 g., 0.9990 Gold Plated Silver 1.0021 oz. ASW AGW, 38.7 mm. **Obv:** National arms **Rev:** Diamond studded scorpion (scorpio) **Edge:** Reeded

Date	Mintage	F	VF	XF	Unc	BU
2002 Proof	—	Value: 60.00				

KM# 617 20 DOLLARS
31.2000 g., 0.9990 Gold Plated Silver 1.0021 oz. ASW AGW, 38.7 mm. **Obv:** National arms **Rev:** Diamond studded archer (sagittarius) **Edge:** Reeded

Date	Mintage	F	VF	XF	Unc	BU
2002 Proof	—	Value: 60.00				

KM# 730 25 DOLLARS
0.0234 g., 0.9990 Gold 0.0008 oz. AGW **Obv:** Shield **Rev:** Map of Germany and stars

Date	Mintage	F	VF	XF	Unc	BU
2003B Proof	—	Value: 35.00				

KM# 495 50 DOLLARS
907.0000 g., 0.9990 Silver 29.130 oz. ASW, 100 mm. **Subject:** Wreck of the Princess Louisa **Obv:** National arms and value **Rev:** Ship under sail **Edge:** Reeded **Note:** Each coin has a cob coin recovered from the wreck site encased in a hole with clear resin. Illustration reduced.

Date	Mintage	F	VF	XF	Unc	BU
2001	500	—	—	—	625	—

KM# 731 50 DOLLARS
222.0800 g., 0.9990 Silver 7.1326 oz. ASW, 80.04 mm. **Subject:** Japanese Attack on Pearl Harbor **Obv:** National arms **Obv. Legend:** REPUBLIC OF LIBERIA **Rev:** USA flag hologram at upper left, bust of Franklin D. Roosevelt facing above Japanese aircraft attacking ship in harbor **Rev. Legend:** REMEMBERING PEARL HARBOR - DECEMBER 7, 1941

Date	Mintage	F	VF	XF	Unc	BU
2001 Proof	—	Value: 175				

KM# 776 50 DOLLARS
93.3000 g., 0.9990 Silver And Gold 2.9965 oz., 65.00 mm. **Series:** Endangered Wildlife **Obv:** National arms **Obv. Legend:** REPUBLIC OF LIBERIA **Rev:** Two gilt Cheetahs, one sitting, one resting with diamonds inst in eyes **Rev. Legend:** TANZANIA **Edge:** Plain

Date	Mintage	F	VF	XF	Unc	BU
2005 Proof	999	Value: 450				

KM# 726 50 DOLLARS
62.2070 g., 0.9990 Silver 1.9979 oz. ASW, 50 mm. **Obv:** National arms **Rev:** Leopard lying across a map of Africa **Edge:** Reeded

Date	Mintage	F	VF	XF	Unc	BU
2007 Proof	500	Value: 85.00				

KM# 727 2500 DOLLARS
155.5175 g., 0.9990 Gold 4.9948 oz. AGW, 60 mm. **Obv:** National arms **Rev:** Leopard lying across a map of Africa **Edge:** Reeded

Date	Mintage	F	VF	XF	Unc	BU
2007 Proof	48	Value: 5,000				

PATTERNS

Including off metal strikes

KM#	Date	Mintage	Identification	Mkt Val
Pn58	2001	—	10 Dollars. Copper Nickel. 29.2500 g. 38.2 mm. National arms. "9-11" Flag raising scene. Plain edge.	100
Pn59	2001	—	20 Dollars. Silver-Plated Base Metal. 5.3100 g. 20 mm. National arms. "9-11" Flag raising scene. Plain edge.	60.00
Pn60	2001	—	100 Dollars. Gold-Plated Base Metal. 3.4200 g. 16 mm. National arms. "9-11" Flag raising scene. Plain edge.	40.00

LIBYA

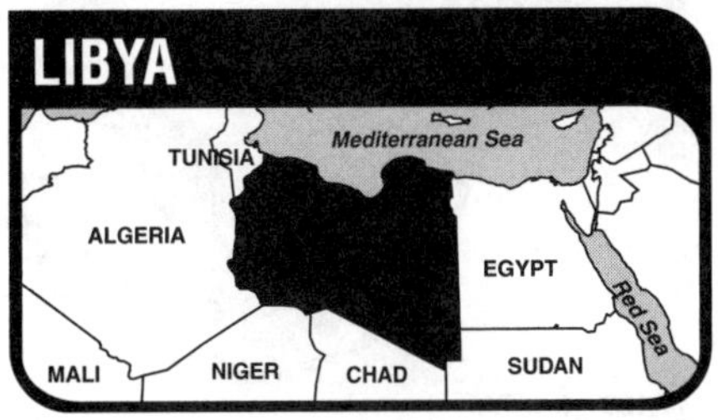

The Socialist People's Libyan Arab Jamahariya, located on the north-central coast of Africa between Tunisia and Egypt, has an area of 679,358 sq. mi. (1,759,540 sq. km.) and a population of 3.9 million. Capital: Tripoli. Crude oil, which accounts for 90 per cent of the export earnings, is the mainstay of the economy.

TITLES

المملكة الليبية

al-Mamlaka(t) al-Libiya(t)

الجمهورية البية

al-Jomhuriya(t) al-Arabiya(t) al-Libiya(t)

MONETARY SYSTEM
10 Milliemes = 1 Piastre
100 Piastres = 1 Pound

SOCIALIST PEOPLE'S REPUBLIC

STANDARD COINAGE

1000 Dirhams = 1 Dinar

KM# 26 1/4 DINAR
11.1500 g., Nickel-Brass, 28 mm. **Obv:** Man on horse with gun 1/2 left, ornamental legend with date **Rev:** Value in Arabic script above wheat ears in ornamented frame **Edge:** Ten alternating reeded and plain flat sections **Shape:** 10-sided

Date	Mintage	F	VF	XF	Unc	BU
AH1369	—	—	—	6.00	10.00	15.00

Note: Restruck in 2001-2002

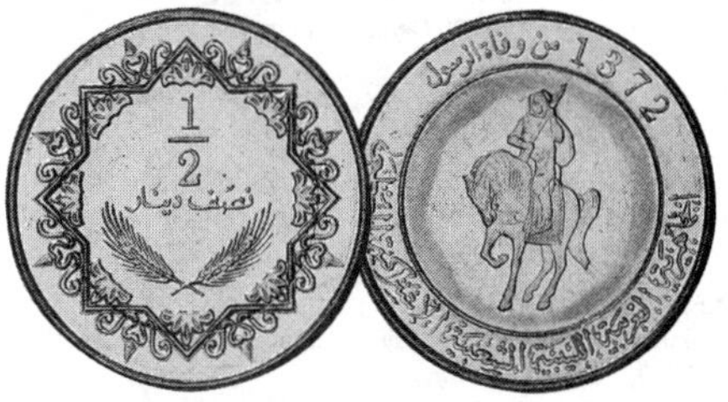

KM# 27 1/2 DINAR
11.5000 g., Bi-Metallic, 30 mm. **Obv:** Man on horse with gun 1/2 left, ornamental legend with date **Rev:** Value in Arabic script above wheat ears in ornamented frame **Edge:** Reeded

Date	Mintage	F	VF	XF	Unc	BU
ND(2004)(AH1372)	—	—	—	—	—	15.00

Note: Restruck in 2004-2005.

LIECHTENSTEIN

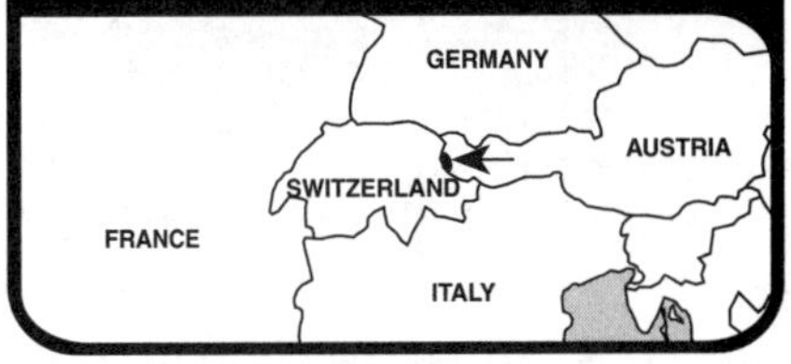

The Principality of Liechtenstein, located in central Europe on the east bank of the Rhine between Austria and Switzerland, has an area of 62 sq. mi. (160 sq. km.) and a population of 27,200. Capital: Vaduz. The economy is based on agriculture and light manufacturing. Canned goods, textiles, ceramics and precision instruments are exported.

RULERS
Prince Hans Adam II, 1990-

MINT MARKS
A - Vienna
B - Bern
M - Munich (restrikes)

MONETARY SYSTEM
100 Heller = 1 Krone

PRINCIPALITY

REFORM COINAGE

100 Rappen = 1 Frank

Y# 24 10 FRANKEN
29.9500 g., 0.9000 Silver 0.8666 oz. ASW, 37.3 mm. **Ruler:** Prince Hans Adam II **Subject:** 200 Years of Sovereignty **Obv:** Vertical inscription between crowned arms and value **Rev:** Johann I (1760-1836) **Edge:** Reeded

Date	Mintage	F	VF	XF	Unc	BU
ND (2006)B Proof	—	Value: 50.00				

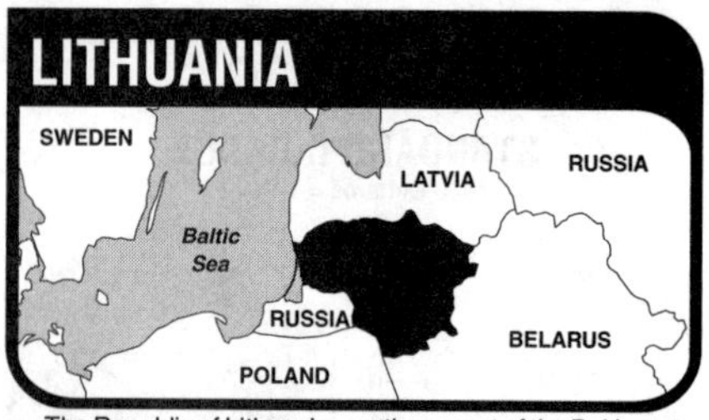

The Republic of Lithuania, southernmost of the Baltic states in east Europe, has an area of 25,174 sq. mi. (65,201 sq. km.) and a population of *3.6 million. Capital: Vilnius. The economy is based on livestock raising and manufacturing. Hogs, cattle, hides and electric motors are exported.

Lithuania declared its independence March 11, 1990 and it was recognized by the United States on Sept. 2, 1991, followed by the Soviet government in Moscow on Sept. 6. They were seated in the UN General Assembly on Sept. 17, 1991.

MODERN REPUBLIC

1991-present

REFORM COINAGE

100 Centas = 1 Litas

KM# 106 10 CENTU

2.6700 g., Brass, 17 mm. **Obv:** National arms **Rev:** Value **Edge:** Reeded

Date	Mintage	F	VF	XF	Unc	BU
2003	—	—	—	—	0.40	—
2003 Proof	10,000	Value: 0.75				
2006	—	—	—	—	0.40	—
2006 Proof	2,000	Value: 45.00				
2007	—	—	—	—	0.40	—

KM# 107 20 CENTU

4.7700 g., Brass, 20.43 mm. **Obv:** National arms **Rev:** Value **Edge:** Reeded

Date	Mintage	F	VF	XF	Unc	BU
2003	—	—	—	—	0.75	—
2003 Proof	10,000	Value: 1.00				
2007	—	—	—	—	0.75	—

KM# 108 50 CENTU

6.0000 g., Brass **Obv:** National arms **Rev:** Value within designed circle

Date	Mintage	F	VF	XF	Unc	BU
2003	—	—	—	—	1.00	—
2003 Proof	10,000	Value: 1.50				

KM# 111 LITAS

6.1800 g., Copper-Nickel, 22.3 mm. **Obv:** National arms **Rev:** Value within circle above lined designs **Edge:** Reeded

Date	Mintage	F	VF	XF	Unc	BU
2001	—	—	—	—	1.50	—
2002	—	—	—	—	1.50	—
2003	—	—	—	—	1.50	—
2003 Proof	10,000	Value: 2.00				

KM# 137 LITAS

6.1500 g., Copper-Nickel, 22.2 mm. **Subject:** 425th Anniversary - University of Vilnius **Obv:** Knight on horse within rope wreath **Rev:** Building within court yard **Edge:** Segmented reeding

Date	Mintage	F	VF	XF	Unc	BU
2004	200,000	1.00	2.00	3.00	5.00	—

KM# 142 LITAS

6.4100 g., Copper-Nickel, 22.35 mm. **Obv:** Knight on horse within circle **Rev:** Palace **Edge:** Segmented reeding

Date	Mintage	F	VF	XF	Unc	BU
2005	1,000,000	—	—	2.00	4.00	—

KM# 112 2 LITAI

7.5000 g., Bi-Metallic Copper-Nickel ring in Brass center, 25 mm. **Obv:** National arms within circle **Rev:** Value within circle **Edge:** Segmented reeding

Date	Mintage	F	VF	XF	Unc	BU
2001	—	—	—	—	3.00	—
2002	—	—	—	—	3.00	—
2003	—	—	—	—	3.00	—
2003 Proof	10,000	Value: 3.50				

KM# 132 5 LITAI

28.2800 g., 0.9250 Silver 0.8410 oz. ASW, 38.6 mm. **Series:** Endangered Wildlife **Obv:** Knight on horse **Rev:** Owl in flight **Edge Lettering:** LIETUVOS BANKAS

Date	Mintage	F	VF	XF	Unc	BU
2002 Proof	3,000	Value: 50.00				

KM# 113 5 LITAI

10.2600 g., Bi-Metallic Copper-Nickel ring in Brass center, 22.5 mm. **Obv:** National arms within circle **Rev:** Value within circle **Edge Lettering:** PENKI LITAI

Date	Mintage	F	VF	XF	Unc	BU
2003	—	—	—	—	6.00	7.50
2003 Proof	10,000	Value: 9.00				

KM# 131 10 LITU

13.1500 g., Copper-Nickel, 28.7 mm. **Obv:** Knight on horse on shield within aerial harbor view **Rev:** Shield within city view **Edge Lettering:** KLAIPEDAI - 75 (twice)

Date	Mintage	F	VF	XF	Unc	BU
2002 Proof	5,000	Value: 25.00				

KM# 129 50 LITU

28.2800 g., 0.9250 Silver 0.8410 oz. ASW, 38.61 mm. **Subject:** Motiejus Valancius' 200th Birthday **Obv:** Knight on horse within shield above church and landscape **Rev:** Bust facing **Edge Lettering:** LIETUVISKAS ZODIS RASTAS IR TIKEJMAS TAUTOS GYVASTIS

Date	Mintage	F	VF	XF	Unc	BU
2001 Proof	2,000	Value: 100				

KM# 130 50 LITU

28.2800 g., 0.9250 Silver 0.8410 oz. ASW, 38.61 mm. **Subject:** Jonas Basanavicius (1851-1927) **Obv:** Knight on horse **Rev:** Jonas Basanavicius **Edge Lettering:** KAD AUSRAI AUSTANT PRAVISTU IR LIETUVOS DVASIA

Date	Mintage	F	VF	XF	Unc	BU
2001 Proof	2,000	Value: 90.00				

KM# 133 50 LITU

28.2800 g., 0.9250 Silver 0.8410 oz. ASW **Series:** Historical Architecture **Obv:** Republic of Lithuania coat of arms **Rev:** Trakai Island Castle **Edge Lettering:** ISTORIJOS IR ARCHITEKTUROS PAMINKLAI

Date	Mintage	F	VF	XF	Unc	BU
2002 Proof	1,500	Value: 100				

KM# 134 50 LITU
28.2800 g., 0.9250 Silver 0.8410 oz. ASW, 38.6 mm. **Obv:** Knight on horse above value **Rev:** Vilnius Cathedral **Edge Lettering:** ISTORIJOS IR ARCHITEKTUROS PAMINKLAI

Date	Mintage	F	VF	XF	Unc	BU
2003 Proof	1,500	Value: 110				

KM# 135 50 LITU
28.2800 g., 0.9250 Silver 0.8410 oz. ASW, 38.6 mm. **Subject:** Olympics **Obv:** Knight on horse above value **Rev:** Stylized cyclists **Edge Lettering:** XXVIII OLIMPIADOS ZAIDYNEMS

Date	Mintage	F	VF	XF	Unc	BU
2003 Proof	2,000	Value: 140				

KM# 138 50 LITU
28.2800 g., 0.9250 Silver 0.8410 oz. ASW, 38.6 mm. **Series:** Historical Architecture **Subject:** 425th Anniversary - University of Vilnius **Obv:** Knight on horse **Rev:** Old university buildings **Edge:** Lettered **Edge Lettering:** ISTORIJOS IR ARCHITEKTUROS PAMINKLAI

Date	Mintage	F	VF	XF	Unc	BU
2004 Proof	2,000	Value: 120				

KM# 139 50 LITU
28.2800 g., 0.9250 Silver 0.8410 oz. ASW, 38.6 mm. **Obv:** Knight on horse **Rev:** Pazaislis Monastery **Edge:** Lettered **Edge Lettering:** ISTORIJOS IR ARCHITEKTUROS PAMINKLAI

Date	Mintage	F	VF	XF	Unc	BU
2004 Proof	1,500	Value: 140				

KM# 140 50 LITU
28.2800 g., 0.9250 Silver 0.8410 oz. ASW, 38.6 mm. **Subject:** First Lithuanian Statute of 1529 **Obv:** Knight on horse **Rev:** Seated and kneeling figures **Edge:** Lettered **Edge Lettering:** "BUKIME TEISES VERGAI, KAD GALETUME NAUDOTIS LAISVEMIS"

Date	Mintage	F	VF	XF	Unc	BU
2004 Proof	1,000	Value: 200				

KM# 141 50 LITU
28.2800 g., 0.9250 Silver 0.8410 oz. ASW, 38.6 mm. **Subject:** Curonian Spit **Obv:** Knight on horse **Rev:** Shifting sand dunes design **Edge:** Ornamented pattern from Neringa emblem

Date	Mintage	F	VF	XF	Unc	BU
2004 Proof	2,000	Value: 170				

KM# 143 50 LITU
28.2800 g., 0.9250 Silver ASW 0.8410 0.8410 oz. ASW, 38.6 mm. **Series:** Historical Architecture **Obv:** Denar coin with Knight on horse **Rev:** Kernavé hill fort **Edge Lettering:** ISTORIJOS IR ARCHITEKTUROS PAMINKLAI

Date	Mintage	F	VF	XF	Unc	BU
2005 Proof	2,000	Value: 140				

KM# 147 50 LITU
28.2800 g., 0.9250 Silver 0.8410 oz. ASW, 38.6 mm. **Subject:** 1905 Lithuanian Congress **Obv:** Knight on horse **Rev:** Legend and inscription **Edge:** Ornamented

Date	Mintage	F	VF	XF	Unc	BU
2005 Proof	1,500	Value: 220				

KM# 144 50 LITU
28.2800 g., 0.9250 Silver 0.8410 oz. ASW, 38.6 mm. **Subject:** 150th Anniversary - National Museum **Obv:** Trio of ancient Lithuanian coins **Rev:** Man blowing horn **Edge Lettering:** PRO PUBLICO BONO

Date	Mintage	F	VF	XF	Unc	BU
2005 Proof	1,500	Value: 75.00				

KM# 145 50 LITU
28.2800 g., 0.9250 Silver 0.8410 oz. ASW, 38.6 mm. **Subject:** Knight on horse and cross **Rev:** Cardinal Vincentas Sladkevicius **Edge Lettering:** LET OUR LIFE BE BUILT ON GOODNESS AND HOPE

Date	Mintage	F	VF	XF	Unc	BU
2005 Proof	2,000	Value: 90.00				

KM# 148 50 LITU
28.2800 g., 0.9250 Silver 0.8410 oz. ASW, 38.6 mm. **Obv:** National arms on forest background **Rev:** Lynx prowling **Edge:** Stylized lynx paw prints

Date	Mintage	F	VF	XF	Unc	BU
2006 Proof	3,000	Value: 200				

KM# 149 50 LITU
28.2800 g., 0.9250 Silver 0.8410 oz. ASW, 38.6 mm. **Obv:** National arms against castle wall background **Rev:** Medininkai Castle **Edge Lettering:** "ISTORIJOS IR ARCHITEKTUROS PAMINKLAI"

Date	Mintage	F	VF	XF	Unc	BU
2006 Proof	2,500	Value: 80.00				

KM# 151 50 LITU
28.2800 g., 0.9250 Silver 0.8410 oz. ASW, 38.61 mm. **Subject:** 1831 Uprising **Obv:** Small national arms above battle scene **Obv. Legend:** LIETUVA **Rev:** Bust of Pliaterytė facing **Rev. Legend:** EMILIJA PLIATERYTĖ **Edge Lettering:** 1831 * SUKILIMAS **Designer:** Giedrius Paulauskis

Date	Mintage	F	VF	XF	Unc	BU
2006 Proof	2,500	Value: 80.00				

KM# 136 200 LITU
15.0000 g., Bi-Metallic .900 Gold 7.9g. center in a .925 Silver 7.1g. ring, 27 mm. **Subject:** 750th Anniversary - King Mindaugas **Obv:** Knight on horse **Obv. Legend:** LIETUVA **Rev:** Seated King **Rev. Legend:** MINDAUGO KARUNAVIMAS **Edge Lettering:** LIETUVOS KARALYSTE 1253

Date	Mintage	F	VF	XF	Unc	BU
2003 Proof	2,000	Value: 1,200				

KM# 146 500 LITU
31.1000 g., 0.9999 Gold 0.9997 oz. AGW, 32.5 mm. **Obv:** Knight on horse **Rev:** Palace **Edge:** Plain

Date	Mintage	F	VF	XF	Unc	BU
2005 Proof	1,000	Value: 1,400				

MINT SETS

KM#	Date	Mintage	Identification	Issue Price	Mkt Val
MS4	2003 (6)	10,000	KM#106-108, 111-113	7.50	14.50

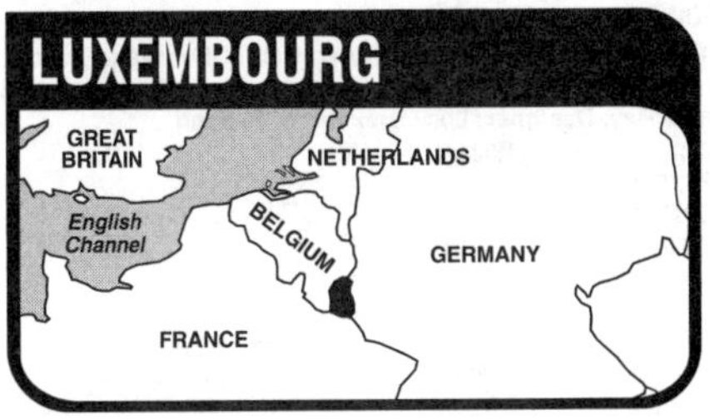

The Grand Duchy of Luxembourg is located in western Europe between Belgium, Germany and France, has an area of 1,103 sq. mi. (2,586 sq. km.) and a population of 377,100. Capital: Luxembourg. The economy is based on steel.

RULER
Henri, 2000-

MINT MARKS
A - Paris
(b) - Brussels, privy marks only
H – Gunzburg
(n) – lion - Namur
(u) - Utrecht, privy marks only

GRAND DUCHY

EURO COINAGE

European Economic Community Issues

KM# 75 EURO CENT
2.2700 g., Copper Plated Steel, 16.2 mm. **Ruler:** Henri **Obv:** Head right **Obv. Designer:** Yvette Gastauer-Claire **Rev:** Value and globe **Rev. Designer:** Luc Luycx **Edge:** Plain

Date	Mintage	F	VF	XF	Unc	BU
2002(u)	34,517,500	—	—	—	0.35	—
2002(u) Proof	1,500	—	—	—	—	—
2003(u)	1,500,000	—	—	—	0.50	—
2003(u) Proof	1,500	—	—	—	—	—
2004(u)	21,001,000	—	—	—	0.35	—
2004(u) Proof	1,500	—	—	—	—	—
2005(u)	7,000,000	—	—	—	0.35	—
2006(u)	4,000,000	—	—	—	0.35	—
2007(a)	—	—	—	—	0.35	—

KM# 76 2 EURO CENT
3.0300 g., Copper Plated Steel, 18.7 mm. **Ruler:** Henri **Obv:** Head right **Obv. Designer:** Yvette Gastauer-Claire **Rev:** Value and globe **Rev. Designer:** Luc Luycx **Edge:** Grooved

Date	Mintage	F	VF	XF	Unc	BU
2002(u)	35,917,500	—	—	—	0.50	—
2002(u) Proof	1,500	—	—	—	—	—
2003(u)	1,500,000	—	—	—	0.65	—
2003(u) Proof	1,500	—	—	—	—	—
2004(u)	20,001,000	—	—	—	0.50	—
2004(u) Proof	1,500	—	—	—	—	—
2005(u)	13,000,000	—	—	—	0.50	—
2006(u)	4,000,000	—	—	—	0.50	—
2007(a)	—	—	—	—	0.50	—

KM# 77 5 EURO CENT
3.8600 g., Copper Plated Steel, 21.2 mm. **Ruler:** Henri **Obv:** Head right **Obv. Designer:** Yvette Gastauer-Claire **Rev:** Value and globe **Rev. Designer:** Luc Luycx **Edge:** Plain

Date	Mintage	F	VF	XF	Unc	BU
2002(u)	28,917,500	—	—	—	0.75	—
2002(u) Proof	1,500	—	—	—	—	—
2003(u)	4,500,000	—	—	—	1.00	—
2003(u) Proof	1,500	—	—	—	—	—
2004(u)	16,001,000	—	—	—	0.75	—
2004(u) Proof	1,500	—	—	—	—	—
2005(u)	6,000,000	—	—	—	0.75	—
2006(u)	5,000,000	—	—	—	0.75	—
2007(a)	—	—	—	—	0.75	—

KM# 78 10 EURO CENT

4.0700 g., Brass, 19.7 mm. **Ruler:** Henri **Obv:** Grand Duke's portrait **Obv. Designer:** Yvette Gastauer-Claire **Rev:** Value and map **Rev. Designer:** Luc Luycx **Edge:** Reeded

Date	Mintage	F	VF	XF	Unc	BU
2002(u)	25,117,500	—	—	—	0.75	—
2002(u) Proof	1,500	—	—	—	—	—
2003(u)	1,500,000	—	—	—	1.00	—
2003(u) Proof	1,500	—	—	—	—	—
2004(u)	12,001,000	—	—	—	0.75	—
2004(u) Proof	1,500	—	—	—	—	—
2005(u)	2,000,000	—	—	—	0.75	—
2006(u)	4,000,000	—	—	—	0.75	—

KM# 89 10 EURO CENT

4.0700 g., Brass, 19.7 mm. **Ruler:** Henri **Obv:** Prince's portrait **Obv. Designer:** Yvette Gastauer-Claire **Rev:** Relief map of Western Europe, stars, lines and value **Rev. Designer:** Luc Luycx **Edge:** Reeded

Date	Mintage	F	VF	XF	Unc	BU
2007(u)	—	—	—	—	0.75	—

KM# 79 20 EURO CENT

5.7300 g., Brass, 22.1 mm. **Ruler:** Henri **Obv:** Grand Duke's portrait **Obv. Designer:** Yvette Gastauer-Claire **Rev:** Value and map **Rev. Designer:** Luc Luycx **Edge:** Notched

Date	Mintage	F	VF	XF	Unc	BU
2002(u)	25,717,500	—	—	—	1.00	—
2002(u) Proof	1,500	—	—	—	—	—
2003(u)	1,500,000	—	—	—	1.25	—
2003(u) Proof	1,500	—	—	—	—	—
2004(u)	14,001,000	—	—	—	1.00	—
2004(u) Proof	1,500	—	—	—	—	—
2005(u)	6,000,000	—	—	—	1.00	—
2006(u)	7,000,000	—	—	—	1.00	—

KM# 90 20 EURO CENT

5.7300 g., Brass, 22.1 mm. **Ruler:** Henri **Obv:** Prince's portrait **Obv. Designer:** Yvette Gastauer-Claire **Rev:** Relief map of Western Europe, stars, lines and value **Rev. Designer:** Luc Luycx **Edge:** Notched

Date	Mintage	F	VF	XF	Unc	BU
2007(u)	—	—	—	—	1.00	—

KM# 80 50 EURO CENT

7.8100 g., Brass, 24.1 mm. **Ruler:** Henri **Obv:** Grand Duke's portrait **Obv. Designer:** Yvette Gastauer-Claire **Rev:** Value and map **Rev. Designer:** Luc Luycx **Edge:** Reeded

Date	Mintage	F	VF	XF	Unc	BU
2002(u)	21,917,500	—	—	—	1.25	—
2002(u) Proof	1,500	—	—	—	—	—
2003(u)	2,500,000	—	—	—	1.50	—
2003(u) Proof	1,500	—	—	—	—	—
2004(u)	10,001,000	—	—	—	1.25	—
2004(u) Proof	1,500	—	—	—	—	—
2005(u)	3,000,000	—	—	—	1.25	—
2006(u)	3,000,000	—	—	—	1.25	—

KM# 91 50 EURO CENT

7.8100 g., Brass, 24.1 mm. **Ruler:** Henri **Obv:** Prince's portrait **Obv. Designer:** Yvette Gastauer-Claire **Rev:** Relief map of Western Europe, stars, lines and value **Rev. Designer:** Luc Luycx **Edge:** Reeded

Date	Mintage	F	VF	XF	Unc	BU
2007(u)	—	—	—	—	1.25	—

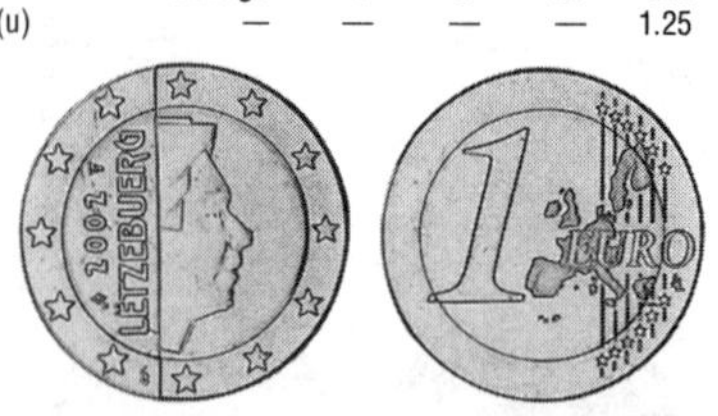

KM# 81 EURO

7.5000 g., Bi-Metallic Copper-Nickel center in Brass ring, 23.2 mm. **Ruler:** Henri **Obv:** Grand Duke's portrait **Obv. Designer:** Yvette Gastauer-Claire **Rev:** Value and map within divided circle **Rev. Designer:** Luc Luycx **Edge:** Reeded and plain sections

Date	Mintage	F	VF	XF	Unc	BU
2002(u)	21,318,525	—	—	—	2.50	—
2002(u) Proof	1,500	—	—	—	—	—
2003(u)	1,500,000	—	—	—	2.75	—
2003(u) Proof	1,500	—	—	—	—	—
2004(u)	9,001,000	—	—	—	2.50	—
2004(u) Proof	1,500	—	—	—	—	—
2005(u)	2,000,000	—	—	—	2.50	—
2006(u)	1,000,000	—	—	—	2.50	—

KM# 92 EURO

7.5000 g., Bi-Metallic Copper-Nickel center in Brass ring, 23.2 mm. **Ruler:** Henri **Obv:** Prince's portrait **Obv. Designer:** Yvette Gastauer-Claire **Rev:** Relief map of Western Europe, stars, lines and value **Rev. Designer:** Luc Luycx **Edge:** Reeded and plain sections

Date	Mintage	F	VF	XF	Unc	BU
2007(a)	—	—	—	—	2.50	—

KM# 82 2 EURO

8.5200 g., Bi-Metallic Brass center in Copper-Nickel ring, 25.7 mm. **Ruler:** Henri **Obv:** Grand Duke's portrait **Obv. Designer:** Yvette Gastauer-Claire **Rev:** Value and map within divided circle **Rev. Designer:** Luc Luycx **Edge:** Reeded with 2's and stars

Date	Mintage	F	VF	XF	Unc	BU
2002(u)	18,517,500	—	—	—	3.75	—
2002(u) Proof	1,500	—	—	—	—	—
2003(u)	3,500,000	—	—	—	4.50	—
2003(u) Proof	1,500	—	—	—	—	—
2004(u)	7,553,200	—	—	—	4.00	—
2004(u) Proof	1,500	—	—	—	—	—
2005(u)	3,500,000	—	—	—	4.00	—
2006(u)	2,000,000	—	—	—	4.00	—

KM# 85 2 EURO

8.5200 g., Bi-Metallic Brass center in Copper-Nickel ring, 25.7 mm. **Ruler:** Henri **Obv:** Head right and crowned monogram within 1/2 star circle **Rev:** Value and map within divided circle

Date	Mintage	F	VF	XF	Unc	BU
2004(u)	2,447,800	—	—	—	5.50	—
2004(u) Proof	1,500	—	—	—	—	—

KM# 87 2 EURO

8.5200 g., Bi-Metallic Brass center in Copper-Nickel ring, 25.7 mm. **Ruler:** Henri **Obv:** Conjoined heads right within circle **Rev:** Value and map within divided circle **Edge:** Reeding over stars and 2's

Date	Mintage	F	VF	XF	Unc	BU
2005(u)	2,720,000	—	—	—	5.00	—

KM# 88 2 EURO

8.5000 g., Bi-Metallic, 25.7 mm. **Ruler:** Henri **Obv:** Conjoined heads right within circle and star border **Rev:** Value and map within divided circle **Edge:** Reeding over 2's and stars

Date	Mintage	F	VF	XF	Unc	BU
2006(u)	1,000,000	—	—	—	5.00	—

KM# 93 2 EURO

8.5200 g., Bi-Metallic Brass center in Copper-Nickel ring, 25.7 mm. **Ruler:** Henri **Obv:** Prince's portrait **Obv. Designer:** Yvette Gastauer-Claire **Rev:** Relief map of Western Europe, stars, lines and value **Rev. Designer:** Luc Luycx **Edge:** Reeded with 2's and stars

Date	Mintage	F	VF	XF	Unc	BU
2007(u)	1,000,000	—	—	—	4.00	—

KM# 94 2 EURO

Bi-Metallic Brass center in Copper-Nickel ring, 25.71 mm. **Ruler:** Henri **Subject:** 50th Anniversary Treaty of Rome **Obv:** Open treaty book with latent image on left hand page **Obv. Legend:** LËTZEBUERG **Rev:** Large value at left, modified outline of Europe at right **Edge:** Reeded with 2's and stars

Date	Mintage	F	VF	XF	Unc	BU
2007(a)	—	—	—	—	—	9.00

KM# 95 2 EURO

8.5400 g., Bi-Metallic Brass center in Copper-Nickel ring, 25.71 mm. **Ruler:** Henri **Obv:** Palace in background at left, head 3/4 left at right **Obv. Legend:** LËTZEBUERG **Rev:** Large value at left, modified outline of Europe at right **Edge:** Reeded with 2's and stars

Date	Mintage	F	VF	XF	Unc	BU
2007(a)	—	—	—	—	—	9.00

KM# 84 5 EURO

6.2200 g., 0.9990 Gold 0.1998 oz. AGW, 20 mm. **Ruler:** Henri **Subject:** European Central Bank **Obv:** Grand Duke Henri **Rev:** Building

Date	Mintage	F	VF	XF	Unc	BU
2003(u) Proof	20,000	Value: 225				

KM# 83 25 EURO

22.8500 g., 0.9250 Silver 0.6795 oz. ASW, 37 mm. **Ruler:** Henri **Subject:** European Court System **Obv:** Grand Duke Henri **Rev:** Sword scale on law book

Date	Mintage	F	VF	XF	Unc	BU
2002(u) Proof	20,000	Value: 100				

KM# 86 25 EURO

22.8500 g., 0.9250 Silver 0.6795 oz. ASW, 37 mm. **Ruler:** Henri **Subject:** European Parliament **Obv:** Grand Duke Henri **Rev:** Parliament

Date	Mintage	F	VF	XF	Unc	BU
2004(u) Proof	20,000	Value: 100				

MINT SETS

KM#	Date	Mintage	Identification	Issue Price	Mkt Val
MS7	2005 (9)	20,000	KM#75-82, 87	40.00	45.00
MS8	2006 (9)	15,000	KM#75-82, 88	40.00	45.00

MACAO

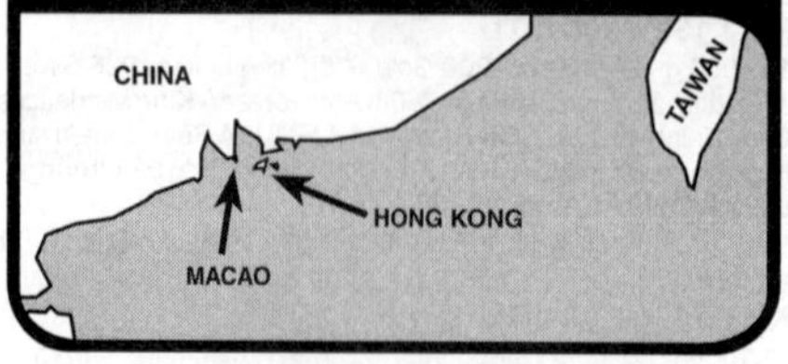

The Province of Macao, a Portuguese overseas province located in the South China Sea 40 miles southwest of Hong Kong, consists of the peninsula of Macao and the islands of Taipa and Coloane. It has an area of 6.2 sq. mi.(16 sq. km.) and a population of 500,000. Capital: Macao. Macao's economy is based on light industry, commerce, tourism, fishing, and gold trading - Macao is one of the entirely free markets for gold in the world. Cement, textiles, fireworks, vegetable oils, and metal products are exported.

In 1987, Portugal and China agreed that Macao would become a Chinese Territory in 1999. In December of 1999, Macao became a special administrative zone of China.

RULERS

Portuguese 1887-1999

MINT MARKS

(p) - Pobjoy Mint
(s) - Singapore Mint

Pobjoy Mint   Singapore Mint

MONETARY SYSTEM

100 Avos = 1 Pataca

PORTUGUESE COLONY

STANDARD COINAGE

100 Avos = 1 Pataca

KM# 70 10 AVOS

1.3800 g., Brass, 17 mm. **Obv:** MACAU written at center with date below **Rev:** Crowned design above value flanked by mint marks

Date	Mintage	F	VF	XF	Unc	BU
2005	—	—	—	—	0.75	1.25

KM# 72 50 AVOS

4.5900 g., Brass, 23 mm. **Obv:** MACAU written across center of globe with date below **Rev:** Figure in ceremonial dragon costume being led by a man

Date	Mintage	F	VF	XF	Unc	BU
2003	—	—	—	—	1.50	2.50
2005	—	—	—	—	1.50	2.50

KM# 57 PATACA

9.1800 g., Copper-Nickel, 25.98 mm. **Obv:** MACAU written across center of globe with date below **Rev:** Lighthouse above value **Edge:** Reeded

Date	Mintage	F	VF	XF	Unc	BU
2003	—	—	—	—	2.50	4.00
2005	—	—	—	—	2.50	4.00

KM# 56 5 PATACAS

10.1000 g., Copper-Nickel **Obv:** MACAU written across center of globe with date below **Rev:** Sailing ship and building scene **Edge:** Plain **Shape:** 12-sided

Date	Mintage	F	VF	XF	Unc	BU
2003	—	—	—	—	6.50	10.00

SPECIAL ADMINISTRATIVE REGION (S.A.R.)

STANDARD COINAGE

100 Avos = 1 Pataca

KM# 128 50 PATACAS

28.2800 g., 0.9250 Silver 0.8410 oz. ASW **Subject:** 1st World Championship Grand Prix **Rev:** Two race cars - gilt

Date	Mintage	F	VF	XF	Unc	BU
2003 Proof	5,000	Value: 75.00				

KM# 102 100 PATACAS
28.2800 g., 0.9250 Silver 0.8410 oz. ASW **Subject:** Year of the Snake **Obv:** Church facade **Rev:** Snake

Date	Mintage	F	VF	XF	Unc	BU
2001 Proof	4,000	Value: 55.00				

KM# 107 100 PATACAS
28.2800 g., 0.9250 Silver 0.8410 oz. ASW, 38.6 mm. **Subject:** Year of the Horse **Obv:** Church facade flanked by stars **Rev:** Horse above value **Edge:** Reeded

Date	Mintage	F	VF	XF	Unc	BU
2002 Proof	4,000	Value: 45.00				

KM# 122 100 PATACAS
28.2800 g., 0.9250 Silver 0.8410 oz. ASW **Subject:** 5th Anniversary Return of Macao to China

Date	Mintage	F	VF	XF	Unc	BU
2004 Proof	10,000	Value: 60.00				

KM# 130 100 PATACAS
28.2800 g., 0.9250 Silver 0.8410 oz. ASW **Series:** Lunar **Subject:** Year of the Monkey

Date	Mintage	F	VF	XF	Unc	BU
2004	1,000	—	—	—	—	60.00
2004 Proof	4,000	Value: 75.00				

KM# 134 100 PATACAS
28.2800 g., 0.9250 Silver 0.8410 oz. ASW **Series:** Lunar **Subject:** Year of the Rooster **Rev:** Stylized rooster walking left

Date	Mintage	F	VF	XF	Unc	BU
2005 Proof	—	Value: 90.00				

KM# 137 100 PATACAS
28.2800 g., 0.9250 Silver 0.8410 oz. ASW **Subject:** IV East Asian Games - FRIENDSHIP

Date	Mintage	F	VF	XF	Unc	BU
2005 Proof	6,000	Value: 75.00				

KM# 139 100 PATACAS
28.2800 g., 0.9250 Silver 0.8410 oz. ASW **Series:** Lunar **Subject:** Year of the Dog **Rev:** Stylized dog standing left

Date	Mintage	F	VF	XF	Unc	BU
2006 Proof	—	Value: 90.00				

KM# 123 200 PATACAS
28.2800 g., 0.9250 Silver With gilt subject 0.8410 oz. ASW **Subject:** 5th Anniversary Return of Macao to China

Date	Mintage	F	VF	XF	Unc	BU
2004 Proof	10,000	Value: 75.00				

KM# 138 200 PATACAS
28.2800 g., 0.9250 Silver With gilt subject. 0.8410 oz. ASW **Subject:** IV East Asian Games **Rev:** U-N-I-T-Y in blocks at left - bottom. logo at upper right

Date	Mintage	F	VF	XF	Unc	BU
2005 Proof	6,000	Value: 90.00				

KM# 103 250 PATACAS
3.9900 g., 0.9167 Gold 0.1176 oz. AGW **Subject:** Year of the Snake **Obv:** Church facade **Rev:** Snake

Date	Mintage	F	VF	XF	Unc	BU
2001 Proof	2,500	Value: 140				

KM# 108 250 PATACAS
3.9900 g., 0.9167 Gold 0.1176 oz. AGW, 19.3 mm. **Subject:** Year of the Horse **Obv:** Church of St. Paul facade **Rev:** Horse above value **Edge:** Reeded

Date	Mintage	F	VF	XF	Unc	BU
2002 Proof	2,500	Value: 140				

KM# 119 250 PATACAS
3.9900 g., 0.9167 Gold 0.1176 oz. AGW, 19.3 mm. **Subject:** Year of the Goat **Obv:** Church facade **Rev:** Goat above value **Edge:** Reeded

Date	Mintage	F	VF	XF	Unc	BU
2003 Proof	2,500	Value: 140				

KM# 131 250 PATACAS
3.9900 g., 0.9167 Gold 0.1176 oz. AGW **Series:** Lunar **Subject:** Year of the Monkey

Date	Mintage	F	VF	XF	Unc	BU
2004 Proof	2,500	Value: 225				

KM# 135 250 PATACAS
2.8300 g., 0.9990 Gold 0.0909 oz. AGW **Series:** Lunar **Subject:** Year of the Rooster **Rev:** Stylized rooster walking left

Date	Mintage	F	VF	XF	Unc	BU
2005 Proof	—	Value: 225				

KM# 140 250 PATACAS
3.1100 g., 0.9990 Gold 0.0999 oz. AGW **Series:** Lunar **Subject:** Year of the Dog **Rev:** Stylized dog standing left - multicolor

Date	Mintage	F	VF	XF	Unc	BU
2006 Proof	—	Value: 225				

KM# 104 500 PATACAS
7.9900 g., 0.9167 Gold 0.2355 oz. AGW **Subject:** Year of the Snake **Obv:** Church facade **Rev:** Snake

Date	Mintage	F	VF	XF	Unc	BU
2001 Proof	2,500	Value: 250				

KM# 109 500 PATACAS
7.9800 g., 0.9167 Gold 0.2352 oz. AGW, 22.05 mm. **Subject:** Year of the Horse **Obv:** Church facade **Rev:** Horse above value **Edge:** Reeded

Date	Mintage	F	VF	XF	Unc	BU
2002 Proof	2,500	Value: 250				

KM# 120 500 PATACAS
7.9800 g., 0.9167 Gold 0.2352 oz. AGW, 22 mm. **Subject:** Year of the Goat **Obv:** Church facade **Rev:** Goat above value **Edge:** Reeded

Date	Mintage	F	VF	XF	Unc	BU
2003 Proof	2,500	Value: 250				

KM# 129 500 PATACAS
7.9600 g., 0.9167 Gold 0.2346 oz. AGW **Subject:** 1st World Championship Grand Prix **Rev:** Two race cars

Date	Mintage	F	VF	XF	Unc	BU
2003 Proof	2,000	Value: 300				

KM# 132 500 PATACAS
7.9800 g., 0.9167 Gold 0.2352 oz. AGW **Series:** Lunar **Subject:** Year of the Monkey

Date	Mintage	F	VF	XF	Unc	BU
2004 Proof	2,500	Value: 375				

KM# 124 500 PATACAS
62.2060 g., 0.9990 Silver With gilt subject 1.9979 oz. ASW **Subject:** 5th Anniversary Return of Macao to China

Date	Mintage	F	VF	XF	Unc	BU
2004 Proof	1,000	Value: 120				

KM# 136 500 PATACAS
7.9600 g., 0.9990 Gold 0.2557 oz. AGW **Series:** Lunar **Subject:** Year of the Rooster **Rev:** Stylized rooster walking left

Date	Mintage	F	VF	XF	Unc	BU
2005 Proof	—	Value: 600				

KM# 141 500 PATACAS
7.9600 g., 0.9990 Gold 0.2557 oz. AGW **Series:** Lunar **Subject:** Year of the Dog **Rev:** Stylized dog standing left

Date	Mintage	F	VF	XF	Unc	BU
2006 Proof	—	Value: 600				

KM# 105 1000 PATACAS
16.9760 g., 0.9167 Gold 0.5003 oz. AGW **Subject:** Year of the Snake **Obv:** Church facade flanked by stars **Rev:** Snake

Date	Mintage	F	VF	XF	Unc	BU
2001 Proof	4,000	Value: 460				

KM# 110 1000 PATACAS
15.9700 g., 0.9167 Gold 0.4707 oz. AGW, 28.4 mm. **Subject:** Year of the Horse **Obv:** Church facade **Rev:** Horse above value **Edge:** Reeded

Date	Mintage	F	VF	XF	Unc	BU
2002 Proof	4,000	Value: 450				

KM# 118 1000 PATACAS
28.2800 g., 0.9250 Silver 0.8410 oz. ASW, 38.6 mm. **Subject:** Year of the Goat **Obv:** Church facade **Rev:** Goat above value **Edge:** Reeded

Date	Mintage	F	VF	XF	Unc	BU
2002 Proof	4,000	Value: 45.00				

KM# 121 1000 PATACAS
15.9760 g., 0.9170 Gold 0.4710 oz. AGW **Subject:** Year of the Goat **Obv:** Church facade flanked by stars **Rev:** Goat above value **Edge:** Reeded

Date	Mintage	F	VF	XF	Unc	BU
2003 Proof	4,000	Value: 450				

KM# 125 1000 PATACAS
155.5150 g., 0.9990 Silver 4.9947 oz. ASW **Subject:** 5th Anniversary Return of Macao to China

Date	Mintage	F	VF	XF	Unc	BU
2004 Proof	3,000	Value: 300				

KM# 133 1000 PATACAS
15.9800 g., 0.9167 Gold 0.4710 oz. AGW **Series:** Lunar **Subject:** Year of the Monkey

Date	Mintage	F	VF	XF	Unc	BU
2004	500	—	—	—	550	—
2004 Proof	4,000	Value: 600				

KM# 126 2000 PATACAS
155.5150 g., 0.9990 Silver With gilt subject 4.9947 oz. ASW **Subject:** 5th Anniversary Return of Macao to China

Date	Mintage	F	VF	XF	Unc	BU
2004 Proof	1,500	Value: 300				

PROOF SETS

KM#	Date	Mintage	Identification	Issue Price	Mkt Val
PS16	2001 (3)	2,500	KM#103-105	849	825
PS17	2002 (3)	4,000	KM#108-110	849	825
PS18	2003 (3)	2,500	KM#119-121	849	825

MACEDONIA

The Republic of Macedonia is land-locked, and is bordered in the north by Yugoslavia, to the east by Bulgaria, in the south by Greece and to the west by Albania and has an area of 9,781 sq. mi. (25,713 sq. km.) and a population at the 1991 census was 2,038,847, of which the predominating ethnic groups were Macedonians. The capital is Skopje.

On Nov. 20, 1991 parliament promulgated a new constitution, and declared its independence on Nov.20, 1992, but failed to secure EC and US recognition owing to Greek objections to use of the name *Macedonia*. On Dec. 11, 1992, the UN Security Council authorized the expedition of a small peacekeeping force to prevent hostilities spreading into Macedonia.

There is a 120-member single-chamber National Assembly.

REPUBLIC

STANDARD COINAGE

KM# 2 DENAR
5.1500 g., Brass, 23.7 mm. **Obv:** Sheepdog **Obv. Legend:** РЕПУБЛИКА МАКЕДОНИЈА **Rev:** Radiant value **Edge:** Plain

Date	Mintage	F	VF	XF	Unc	BU
2001	12,874,000	—	0.20	0.35	1.50	4.00
2006	—	—	—	—	1.25	3.75

KM# 3 2 DENARI
5.1500 g., Brass, 23.7 mm. **Obv:** Trout above water **Obv. Legend:** РЕПУБЛИКА МАКЕДОНИЈА **Rev:** Radiant value **Edge:** Plain

Date	Mintage	F	VF	XF	Unc	BU
2001	11,672,000	—	0.25	0.50	1.25	3.00
2006	—	—	0.25	0.50	1.00	2.50

KM# 4 5 DENARI
7.2500 g., Brass, 27.5 mm. **Obv:** European lynx **Obv. Legend:** РЕПУБЛИКА МАКЕДОНИЈА **Rev:** Radiant value **Edge:** Plain

Date	Mintage	F	VF	XF	Unc	BU
2001	6,921,000	—	0.35	0.75	1.75	3.50
2006	—	—	—	—	1.50	3.00

KM# 13 10 DENARI
10.0000 g., 0.9160 Gold 0.2945 oz. AGW, 27 mm. **Subject:** 10th Anniversary of Independence **Obv:** Value in circle within radiant map **Rev:** Grape vine

Date	Mintage	F	VF	XF	Unc	BU
2001	1,000	—	—	—	285	300

KM# 22 60 DENARI
6.0000 g., 0.9160 Gold 0.1767 oz. AGW, 23.8 mm. **Subject:** 100th Anniversary - Statehood **Obv:** Monument above value within circle **Rev:** Djorce Petrov

Date	Mintage	F	VF	XF	Unc	BU
2003	500	—	—	—	175	195

KM# 23 60 DENARI
6.0000 g., 0.9160 Gold 0.1767 oz. AGW, 23.8 mm. **Subject:** 100th Anniversary - Statehood **Obv:** Monument above value within circle **Rev:** Krste Petkov-Misirkov

Date	Mintage	F	VF	XF	Unc	BU
2003	500	—	—	—	175	195

KM# 24 60 DENARI
6.0000 g., 0.9160 Gold 0.1767 oz. AGW, 23.8 mm. **Subject:** 100th Anniversary - Statehood **Obv:** Monument above value within circle **Rev:** Metodije Andonov

Date	Mintage	F	VF	XF	Unc	BU
2003	500	—	—	—	175	195

KM# 25 60 DENARI
6.0000 g., 0.9160 Gold 0.1767 oz. AGW, 23.8 mm. **Subject:** 100th Anniversary - Statehood **Obv:** Monument above value within circle **Rev:** Mihailo Apostolski

Date	Mintage	F	VF	XF	Unc	BU
2003	500	—	—	—	175	195

KM# 26 60 DENARI
6.0000 g., 0.9160 Gold 0.1767 oz. AGW, 23.8 mm. **Subject:** 100th Anniversary - Statehood **Obv:** Monument above value within circle **Rev:** Blaze Koneski

Date	Mintage	F	VF	XF	Unc	BU
2003	500	—	—	—	175	195

KM# 21 60 DENARI
8.0000 g., 0.9160 Gold 0.2356 oz. AGW, 23.8 mm. **Subject:** 50th Anniversary of separation from Greece **Obv:** The Monifest **Rev:** Monastery

Date	Mintage	F	VF	XF	Unc	BU
2004	500	—	—	—	225	250

KM# 14 100 DENARI
16.0000 g., 0.9250 Silver 0.4758 oz. ASW, 32 mm. **Subject:** 100th Anniversary of Statehood **Obv:** Monument above value within circle **Rev:** Cherry tree canon divides circle

Date	Mintage	F	VF	XF	Unc	BU
2003	500	—	—	—	460	490

KM# 14a 100 DENARI
18.0000 g., 0.9160 Gold 0.5301 oz. AGW, 32 mm. **Subject:** 100th Anniversary of Statehood **Obv:** Monument above value within circle **Rev:** Cherry tree canon divides circle

Date	Mintage	F	VF	XF	Unc	BU
2003	500	—	—	—	500	525

KM# 15 100 DENARI
6.0000 g., 0.9160 Gold 0.1767 oz. AGW, 23.8 mm. **Subject:** 100th Anniversary of Statehood **Obv:** Monument above value within circle **Rev:** Bust facing within circle

Date	Mintage	F	VF	XF	Unc	BU
2003	500	—	—	—	175	195

KM# 16 100 DENARI
6.0000 g., 0.9160 Gold 0.1767 oz. AGW, 23.8 mm. **Subject:** 100th Anniversary of Statehood **Obv:** Monument above value within circle **Rev:** Head with hat facing within circle

Date	Mintage	F	VF	XF	Unc	BU
2003	500	—	—	—	175	195

KM# 17 100 DENARI
6.0000 g., 0.9160 Gold 0.1767 oz. AGW, 23.8 mm. **Subject:** 100th Anniversary of Statehood **Obv:** Monument above value within circle **Rev:** Head facing within circle

Date	Mintage	F	VF	XF	Unc	BU
2003	500	—	—	—	175	195

KM# 18 100 DENARI
6.0000 g., 0.9160 Gold 0.1767 oz. AGW, 23.8 mm. **Subject:** 100th Anniversary of Statehood **Obv:** Monument above value within circle **Rev:** Bust left within circle

Date	Mintage	F	VF	XF	Unc	BU
2003	500	—	—	—	175	195

KM# 19 100 DENARI
6.0000 g., 0.9160 Gold 0.1767 oz. AGW, 23.8 mm. **Subject:** 100th Anniversary of Statehood **Obv:** Monument above value within circle **Rev:** Bust right within circle

Date	Mintage	F	VF	XF	Unc	BU
2003	500	—	—	—	175	195

MADAGASCAR

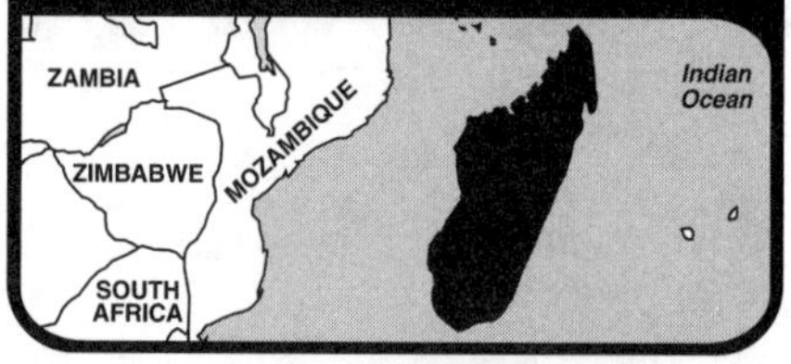

The Democratic Republic of Madagascar, an independent member of the French Community located in the Indian Ocean 250 miles (402 km.) off the southeast coast of Africa, has an area of 226,656 sq. mi. (587,040 sq. km.) and a population of 10 million. Capital: Antananarivo. The economy is primarily agricultural; large bauxite deposits are being developed. Coffee, vanilla, graphite, and rice are exported.

MONETARY SYSTEM
100 Centimes = 1 Franc

MINT MARKS
(a) - Paris, privy marks only
SA - Pretoria

MALAGASY REPUBLIC

STANDARD COINAGE

KM# 8 FRANC
2.4000 g., Stainless Steel **Obv:** Poinsettia **Rev:** Value within horns of ox head above sprigs

Date	Mintage	F	VF	XF	Unc	BU
2002(a)	—	0.15	0.20	0.40	1.45	—

REPUBLIC

Madagasikara Republic

STANDARD COINAGE

KM# 25.2 50 ARIARY
Stainless Steel, 30.5 mm. **Obv:** Star above value within 3/4 wreath **Rev:** Avenue of the Baobabs **Rev. Legend:** Motto C **Shape:** 11-sided

Date	Mintage	F	VF	XF	Unc	BU
2005	—	—	—	—	8.00	12.00

STANDARD COINAGE

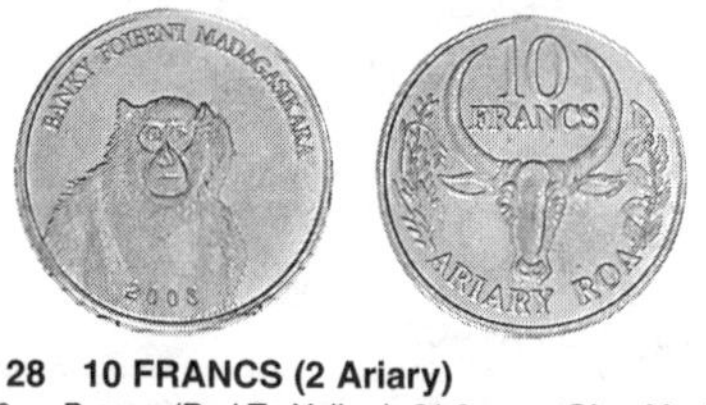

KM# 28 10 FRANCS (2 Ariary)
4.3400 g., Bronze (Red To Yellow), 21.9 mm. **Obv:** Monkey **Rev:** Value within steer horns flanked by sprigs **Edge:** Plain

Date	Mintage	F	VF	XF	Unc	BU
2003	—	—	—	—	2.50	3.50

KM# 29 ARIARY
4.9300 g., Stainless Steel, 22 mm. **Obv:** Flower **Rev:** Value within steer horns above sprigs **Edge:** Plain

Date	Mintage	F	VF	XF	Unc	BU
2004(a)	—	—	—	—	2.00	3.00

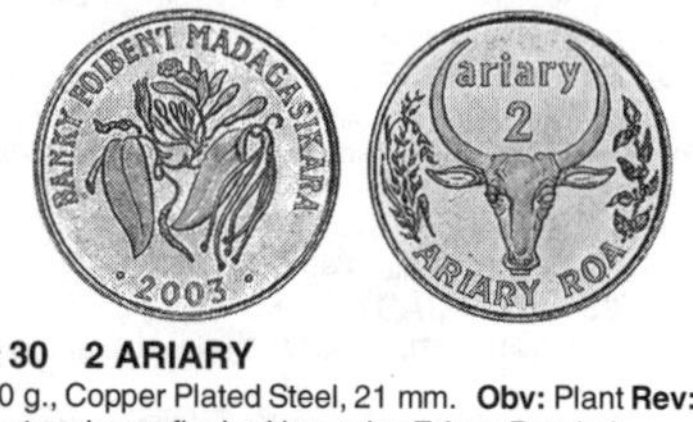

KM# 30 2 ARIARY
3.2300 g., Copper Plated Steel, 21 mm. **Obv:** Plant **Rev:** Value within steer horns flanked by sprigs **Edge:** Reeded

Date	Mintage	F	VF	XF	Unc	BU
2003	—	—	—	—	2.00	3.00

MALAWI

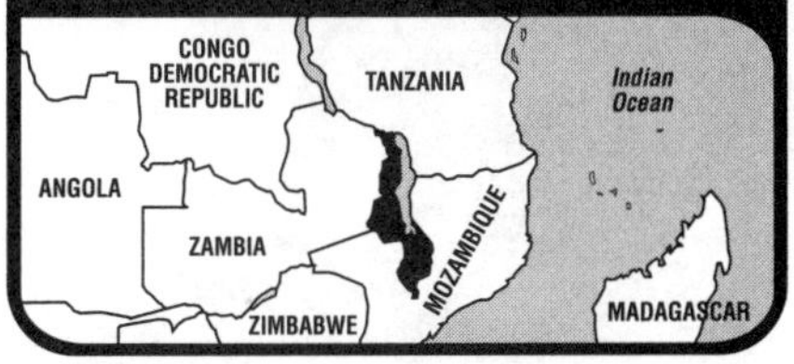

The Republic of Malawi (formerly Nyasaland), located in southeastern Africa to the west of Lake Malawi (Nyasa), has an area of 45,745 sq. mi. (118,480 sq. km.) and a population of 7 million. Capital: Lilongwe. The economy is predominantly agricultural. Tobacco, tea, peanuts and cotton are exported.

REPUBLIC

DECIMAL COINAGE

100 Tambala = 1 Kwacha

KM# 33a TAMBALA

Copper-Plated-Steel, 17.3 mm. **Obv:** Arms with supporters **Rev:** 2 Talapia fish **Edge:** Plain

Date	Mintage	F	VF	XF	Unc	BU
2003	—	—	—	—	1.00	1.50

KM# 34a 2 TAMBALA

Copper-Plated-Steel, 20.3 mm. **Obv:** Arms with supporters **Rev:** Paradise whydah bird divides date and value, designer's initials "P.V." **Edge:** Plain

Date	Mintage	F	VF	XF	Unc	BU
2003	—	—	—	—	1.00	1.50

KM# 32.2 5 TAMBALA

Nickel-Plated Steel, 19.35 mm. **Obv:** Arms with supporters **Rev:** Purple heron, value, designer's initials "P.V."

Date	Mintage	F	VF	XF	Unc	BU
2003	—	—	—	—	2.50	3.00

KM# 27 10 TAMBALA

5.6200 g., Nickel Plated Steel, 23.6 mm. **Obv:** Bust right **Rev:** Bundled corncobs divide date and value

Date	Mintage	F	VF	XF	Unc	BU
2003	—	—	—	—	2.25	3.00

KM# 30 50 TAMBALA

4.4000 g., Brass Plated Steel, 22 mm. **Obv:** Bust right **Rev:** Arms with supporters **Shape:** 7-sided

Date	Mintage	F	VF	XF	Unc	BU
2003	—	—	—	—	4.50	5.00

KM# 66 50 TAMBALA

4.4000 g., Brass-Plated Steel, 22 mm. **Obv:** State arms and supporters with country name below **Rev:** Zebras with date above and value below **Shape:** 7-sided

Date	Mintage	F	VF	XF	Unc	BU
2004	—	—	—	—	4.50	5.00

KM# 28 KWACHA

9.0000 g., Brass Plated Steel, 26 mm. **Obv:** Bust right **Rev:** Fish eagle

Date	Mintage	F	VF	XF	Unc	BU
2003	—	—	—	—	7.00	10.00

KM# 65 KWACHA

Brass-Plated Steel, 26 mm. **Obv:** State arms, country name **Rev:** Fish eagle, date

Date	Mintage	F	VF	XF	Unc	BU
2004	—	—	—	—	2.50	3.50

KM# 59 5 KWACHA

Brass, 45x27.5 mm. **Obv:** National arms, date and value **Rev:** USS Coral Sea aircraft carrier **Edge:** Plain

Date	Mintage	F	VF	XF	Unc	BU
2005 Proof	—	Value: 20.00				

KM# 62 5 KWACHA

Brass, 45x27.5 mm. **Obv:** National arms,date and value **Rev:** Ship USSR Molotov **Edge:** Plain

Date	Mintage	F	VF	XF	Unc	BU
2005 Proof	—	Value: 20.00				

KM# 63 5 KWACHA

Brass, 45x27.5 mm. **Obv:** National arms,date and value **Rev:** Ship USS Missouri **Edge:** Plain

Date	Mintage	F	VF	XF	Unc	BU
2005 Proof	—	Value: 20.00				

KM# 64 5 KWACHA

Brass, 45x27.5 mm. **Obv:** National arms,date and value **Rev:** Ship HMS Hood **Edge:** Plain

Date	Mintage	F	VF	XF	Unc	BU
2005 Proof	—	Value: 20.00				

KM# 44 5 KWACHA

22.0000 g., Silver-Plated Copper-Nickel, 40 mm. **Subject:** Asian Zodiac Animals **Obv:** Queen Elizabeth II above Zambian arms **Rev:** Multicolor stylized rat **Edge:** Reeded

Date	Mintage	F	VF	XF	Unc	BU
2005 Prooflike	835	—	—	—	—	20.00

KM# 45 5 KWACHA

22.0000 g., Silver-Plated Copper-Nickel, 40 mm. **Subject:** Asian Zodiac Animals **Obv:** Queen Elizabeth II above Zambian arms **Rev:** Multicolor stylized ox **Edge:** Reeded

Date	Mintage	F	VF	XF	Unc	BU
2005 Prooflike	835	—	—	—	—	20.00

KM# 46 5 KWACHA

22.0000 g., Silver-Plated Copper-Nickel, 40 mm. **Subject:** Asian Zodiac Animals **Obv:** Queen Elizabeth II above Zambian arms **Rev:** Multicolor stylized tiger **Edge:** Reeded

Date	Mintage	F	VF	XF	Unc	BU
2005 Prooflike	835	—	—	—	—	20.00

KM# 47 5 KWACHA

22.0000 g., Silver-Plated Copper-Nickel, 40 mm. **Subject:** Asian Zodiac Animals **Obv:** Queen Elizabeth II above Zambian arms **Rev:** Multicolor stylized rabbit **Edge:** Reeded

Date	Mintage	F	VF	XF	Unc	BU
2005 Prooflike	835	—	—	—	—	20.00

KM# 48 5 KWACHA

22.0000 g., Silver-Plated Copper-Nickel, 40 mm. **Subject:** Asian Zodiac Animals **Obv:** Queen Elizabeth II above Zambian arms **Rev:** Multicolor stylized dragon **Edge:** Reeded

Date	Mintage	F	VF	XF	Unc	BU
2005 Prooflike	835	—	—	—	—	20.00

KM# 49 5 KWACHA

22.0000 g., Silver-Plated Copper-Nickel, 40 mm. **Subject:** Asian Zodiac Animals **Obv:** Queen Elizabeth II above Zambian arms **Rev:** Multicolor stylized snake **Edge:** Reeded

Date	Mintage	F	VF	XF	Unc	BU
2005 Prooflike	835	—	—	—	—	20.00

KM# 50 5 KWACHA

22.0000 g., Silver-Plated Copper-Nickel, 40 mm. **Subject:** Asian Zodiac Animals **Obv:** Queen Elizabeth II above Zambian arms **Rev:** Multicolor stylized horse **Edge:** Reeded

Date	Mintage	F	VF	XF	Unc	BU
2005 Prooflike	835	—	—	—	—	20.00

KM# 51 5 KWACHA

22.0000 g., Silver-Plated Copper-Nickel, 40 mm. **Subject:** Asian Zodiac Animals **Obv:** Queen Elizabeth II above Zambian arms **Rev:** Multicolor stylized goat **Edge:** Reeded

Date	Mintage	F	VF	XF	Unc	BU
2005 Prooflike	835	—	—	—	—	20.00

KM# 52 5 KWACHA

22.0000 g., Silver-Plated Copper-Nickel, 40 mm. **Subject:** Asian Zodiac Animals **Obv:** Queen Elizabeth II above Zambian arms **Rev:** Multicolor stylized monkey **Edge:** Reeded

Date	Mintage	F	VF	XF	Unc	BU
2005 Proolike	835	—	—	—	—	20.00

KM# 53 5 KWACHA

22.0000 g., Silver-Plated Copper-Nickel, 40 mm. **Subject:** Asian Zodiac Animals **Obv:** Queen Elizabeth II above Zambian arms **Rev:** Multicolor stylized rooster **Edge:** Reeded

Date	Mintage	F	VF	XF	Unc	BU
2005 Prooflike	835	—	—	—	—	20.00

KM# 54 5 KWACHA

22.0000 g., Silver-Plated Copper-Nickel, 40 mm. **Subject:** Asian Zodiac Animals **Obv:** Queen Elizabeth II above Zambian arms **Rev:** Multicolor stylized dog **Edge:** Reeded

Date	Mintage	F	VF	XF	Unc	BU
2005 Prooflike	835	—	—	—	—	20.00

KM# 55 5 KWACHA

22.0000 g., Silver-Plated Copper-Nickel, 40 mm. **Subject:** Asian Zodiac Animals **Obv:** Queen Elizabeth II above Zambian arms **Rev:** Multicolor stylized pig **Edge:** Reeded

Date	Mintage	F	VF	XF	Unc	BU
2005 Prooflike	835	—	—	—	—	20.00

KM# 57 5 KWACHA

10.2500 g., Bi-Metallic Copper-Nickel ring and Nickel-Brass center, 27.05 mm. **Subject:** Fishing **Obv:** State arms and supporters with country name below **Obv. Legend:** MALAWI **Rev:** Fisherman at work with date above and value below **Edge:** Reeded

Date	Mintage	F	VF	XF	Unc	BU
2006	—	—	—	—	—	6.00

KM# 39 10 KWACHA

29.1000 g., Copper-Nickel, 38.7 mm. **Subject:** Soccer World Championship **Obv:** Arms with supporters **Rev:** Soccer players **Edge:** Reeded

Date	Mintage	F	VF	XF	Unc	BU
2002 Proof	—	Value: 50.00				

KM# 42 10 KWACHA

19.7400 g., 0.9990 Silver 0.6340 oz. ASW, 29.9 mm. **Subject:** XXVII Olympic Games - Athens 2004 **Obv:** Arms with supporters divides date **Obv. Legend:** REPUBLIC OF MALAWI **Rev:** Two rowers within circle flanked by sprigs **Edge:** Reeded

Date	Mintage	F	VF	XF	Unc	BU
2003 Proof	—	Value: 40.00				

KM# 60 10 KWACHA

29.4000 g., Copper-Nickel, 38.7 mm. **Obv:** National arms **Rev:** multicolor zebra mother and child **Edge:** Reeded

Date	Mintage	F	VF	XF	Unc	BU
2004 Proof	—	Value: 20.00				

KM# 61 10 KWACHA

29.2000 g., Copper-Nickel, 39 mm. **Obv:** National arms **Rev:** Multicolor leopard mother and cub **Edge:** reeded

Date	Mintage	F	VF	XF	Unc	BU
2004 Proof	—	Value: 20.00				

KM# 58 10 KWACHA

15.1000 g., Bi-Metallic Copper-Nickel center with Nickel-Brass ring, 28.04 mm. **Obv:** State arms and supporters with country name below **Obv. Legend:** MALAWI **Rev:** Farm worker harvesting **Edge:** Coarse reeding

Date	Mintage	F	VF	XF	Unc	BU
2006	—	—	—	—	—	7.00

KM# 56 20 KWACHA

31.1000 g., 0.9250 Silver 0.9249 oz. ASW, 38.6 mm. **Obv:** National arms **Rev:** Two water buffalo on green malachite center insert

Date	Mintage	F	VF	XF	Unc	BU
2004 Proof	—	Value: 50.00				

KM# 43 50 KWACHA

141.2100 g., Bronze with Gold Plated center and Silver Plated ring, 65 mm. **Subject:** Republic of China **Obv:** Large building above value within circle **Rev:** Conjoined busts facing within circle **Edge:** Reeded **Note:** Illustration reduced.

Date	Mintage	F	VF	XF	Unc	BU
2004 Proof	1,000	Value: 75.00				

PATTERNS

Including off metal strikes

KM#	Date	Mintage	Identification	Mkt Val
Pn3	2002	—	10 Kwacha. Copper-Nickel. 29.0200 g. 38.7 mm. National arms. Olympic torch under two world globes. Reeded edge.	—

KM#	Date	Mintage	Identification	Mkt Val
Pn4	2002	—	10 Kwacha. Copper-Nickel. 29.0200 g. 38.7 mm. National arms. "MILLENNIUM" above Mona Lisa like portrait. Reeded edge.	—

KM#	Date	Mintage	Identification	Mkt Val
Pn2	2002	—	10 Kwacha. Copper-Nickel. 29.0200 g. 38.7 mm. National arms. Alexander the Great. Reeded edge.	—

KM#	Date	Mintage	Identification	Mkt Val
Pn5	2003	—	10 Kwacha. Silver Plated. 29.4500 g. 38.7 mm. National arms. Trans-Siberian Express train. Reeded edge.	—

KM#	Date	Mintage	Identification	Mkt Val
Pn6	2003	—	10 Kwacha. Silver Plated. 29.4500 g. 38.7 mm. National arms. Blesbok antelope. Reeded edge.	—

KM#	Date	Mintage	Identification	Mkt Val
Pn7	2003	—	10 Kwacha. Copper-Nickel. 29.0200 g. 38.7 mm. National arms. Eland antelope. Reeded edge.	—

KM#	Date	Mintage	Identification	Mkt Val
Pn8	2003	—	10 Kwacha. Copper-Nickel. 29.0200 g. 38.7 mm. National arms. Kudu antelope. Reeded edge.	—

KM#	Date	Mintage	Identification	Mkt Val
Pn9	ND (2004)	—	10 Kwacha. Copper-Nickel. 29.1500 g. 38.7 mm. National arms. Multicolor Leopard with cub. Reeded edge.	—

KM#	Date	Mintage	Identification	Mkt Val
Pn10	ND (2004)	—	10 Kwacha. Copper-Nickel. 29.1500 g. 38.7 mm. National arms. Multicolor Lion and cub. Reeded edge.	—

KM#	Date	Mintage	Identification	Mkt Val
Pn11	ND (2004)	—	10 Kwacha. Silver Plated. 29.2200 g. 38.7 mm. National arms. Multicolor Zebra and colt. Reeded edge.	—

KM#	Date	Mintage	Identification	Mkt Val
Pn12	ND (2004)	—	10 Kwacha. Silver Plated. 29.2200 g. 38.7 mm. National arms. Multicolor elephant and calf. Reeded edge.	—

KM#	Date	Mintage	Identification	Mkt Val

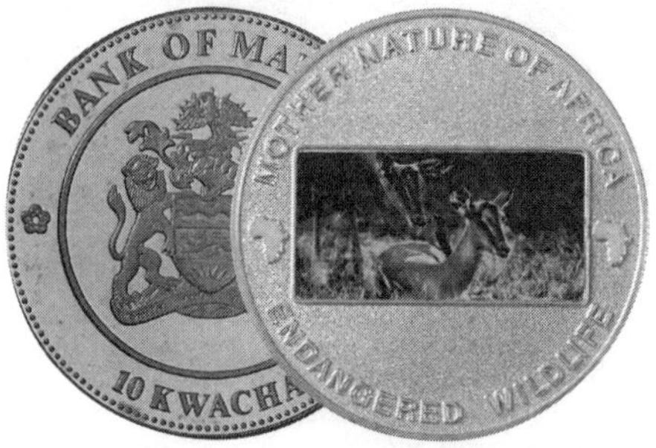

KM#	Date	Mintage	Identification	Mkt Val
Pn13	ND (2004)	—	10 Kwacha. Silver Plated. 29.2200 g. 38.7 mm. National arms. Multicolor Deer and fawn. Reeded edge.	—

KM#	Date	Mintage	Identification	Mkt Val
Pn14	ND (2004)	—	10 Kwacha. Silver Plated. 29.2200 g. 38.7 mm. National arms. Multicolor Giraffe and her calf. Reeded edge.	—

KM#	Date	Mintage	Identification	Mkt Val
Pn15	ND (2004)	—	10 Kwacha. Silver Plated. 29.2200 g. 38.7 mm. National arms. Multicolor pair of birds with chick. Reeded edge.	—

MALAYSIA

The independent limited constitutional monarchy of Malaysia, which occupies the southern part of the Malay Peninsula in Southeast Asia and the northern part of the island of Borneo, has an area of 127,316 sq. mi. (329,750 sq. km.) and a population of 15.4 million. Capital: Kuala Lumpur. The economy is based on agriculture, mining and forestry. Rubber, tin, timber and palm oil are exported.

Malaysia came into being on Sept. 16, 1963, as a federation of Malaya (Johore, Kelantan, Kedah, Perlis, Trengganu, Negri-Sembilan, Pahang, Perak, Selangor, Penang, Malacca), Singapore, Sabah (British North Borneo) and Sarawak. Following two serious racial riots involving Malays and Chinese, Singapore withdrew from the federation on Aug. 9, 1965. Malaysia is a member of the Commonwealth of Nations.

MINT MARK

FM - Franklin Mint, U.S.A.

CONSTITUTIONAL MONARCHY

STANDARD COINAGE

100 Sen = 1 Ringgit (Dollar)

KM# 49 SEN

1.8000 g., Bronze Clad Steel, 17.66 mm. **Obv:** Value divides date below flower blossom **Obv. Legend:** BANK NEGARA MALAYSIA **Rev:** Drum **Edge:** Plain

Date	Mintage	F	VF	XF	Unc	BU
2001	213,645,000	—	—	—	0.15	0.25
2002	185,220,000	—	—	—	0.15	0.25
2003	235,350,000	—	—	—	0.15	0.25
2004	227,700,000	—	—	—	0.15	0.25
2005	437,400,000	—	—	—	0.15	0.25
2006	328,050,000	—	—	—	0.15	0.25

KM# 162 SEN

Brass **Subject:** 200th Anniversary Malaysian Police Force **Obv:** Police badge **Obv. Legend:** BANK NEGARA MALAYSIA **Rev:** Two hands clasped in sprays

Date	Mintage	F	VF	XF	Unc	BU
2007	20,000	—	—	—	—	5.50

KM# 50 5 SEN

1.4000 g., Copper-Nickel, 16.28 mm. **Obv:** Value divides date below flower blossom **Obv. Legend:** BANK NEGARA MALAYSIA **Rev:** Top with string **Edge:** Reeded

Date	Mintage	F	VF	XF	Unc	BU
2001	94,617,472	—	—	—	0.15	0.25
2002	85,316,000	—	—	—	0.15	0.25
2003	75,690,000	—	—	—	0.15	0.25
2004	11,520,000	—	—	—	0.15	0.25
2005	119,520,000	—	—	—	0.15	0.25
2006	87,120,000	—	—	—	0.15	0.25

KM# 51 10 SEN

2.8200 g., Copper-Nickel, 19.43 mm. **Obv:** Value divides date below flower blossom **Obv. Legend:** BANK NEGARA MALAYSIA **Rev:** Ceremonial table **Edge:** Reeded

Date	Mintage	F	VF	XF	Unc	BU
2001	313,422,000	—	—	—	0.25	0.40
2002	290,451,948	—	—	—	0.25	0.40
2003	8,640,000	—	—	—	0.25	0.40
2004	170,640,000	—	—	—	0.25	0.40
2005	316,800,000	—	—	—	0.25	0.40
2006	304,560,000	—	—	—	0.25	0.40
2007	—	—	—	—	0.25	0.40

KM# 52 20 SEN

5.6900 g., Copper-Nickel, 23.57 mm. **Obv:** Value divides date below flower blossom **Obv. Legend:** BANK NEGARA MALAYSIA **Rev:** Basket with food and utensils **Edge:** Reeded

Date	Mintage	F	VF	XF	Unc	BU
2001	278,802,000	—	—	—	0.35	0.50
2002	131,279,881	—	—	—	0.35	0.50
2003	—	—	—	—	0.35	0.50
2004	96,840,000	—	—	—	0.35	0.50
2005	209,700,000	—	—	—	0.35	0.50
2006	155,880,000	—	—	—	0.35	0.50
2007	—	—	—	—	0.35	0.50

KM# 77 25 SEN

9.1400 g., Brass, 30 mm. **Series:** Endangered Species **Obv:** Logo left, value right **Rev:** Rhinoceros **Edge:** Reeded

Date	Mintage	F	VF	XF	Unc	BU
2003	—	—	—	—	—	12.50

KM# 78 25 SEN

9.1400 g., Brass, 30 mm. **Series:** Endangered Species **Obv:** Logo left, value right **Rev:** Elephant **Edge:** Reeded

Date	Mintage	F	VF	XF	Unc	BU
2003	—	—	—	—	—	12.50

KM# 79 25 SEN

9.1400 g., Brass, 30 mm. **Series:** Endangered Species **Obv:** Logo left, value right **Rev:** Orangutan **Edge:** Reeded

Date	Mintage	F	VF	XF	Unc	BU
2003	—	—	—	—	—	12.50

KM# 80 25 SEN

9.1400 g., Brass, 30 mm. **Series:** Endangered Species **Obv:** Logo left, value right **Rev:** Tiger **Edge:** Reeded

Date	Mintage	F	VF	XF	Unc	BU
2003	—	—	—	—	—	12.50

KM# 81 25 SEN

9.1400 g., Brass, 30 mm. **Series:** Endangered Species **Obv:** Logo left, value right **Rev:** Lemur on branch **Edge:** Reeded

Date	Mintage	F	VF	XF	Unc	BU
2003	—	—	—	—	—	12.50

KM# 82 25 SEN

9.1400 g., Brass, 30 mm. **Series:** Endangered Species **Obv:** Logo left, value right **Rev:** Barking Deer **Edge:** Reeded

Date	Mintage	F	VF	XF	Unc	BU
2003	—	—	—	—	—	12.50

KM# 83 25 SEN

9.1400 g., Brass, 30 mm. **Series:** Endangered Species **Obv:** Logo left, value right **Rev:** Tapir **Edge:** Reeded

Date	Mintage	F	VF	XF	Unc	BU
2003	—	—	—	—	—	12.50

KM# 84 25 SEN
9.1400 g., Brass, 30 mm. **Series:** Endangered Species **Obv:** Logo left, value right **Rev:** Serow **Edge:** Reeded

Date	Mintage	F	VF	XF	Unc	BU
2003	—	—	—	—	—	12.50

KM# 85 25 SEN
9.1400 g., Brass, 30 mm. **Series:** Endangered Species **Obv:** Logo left, value right **Rev:** Sambar Deer **Edge:** Reeded

Date	Mintage	F	VF	XF	Unc	BU
2003	—	—	—	—	—	12.50

KM# 86 25 SEN
9.1400 g., Brass, 30 mm. **Series:** Endangered Species **Obv:** Logo left, value right **Rev:** Seated monkey flanked by sprigs **Edge:** Reeded

Date	Mintage	F	VF	XF	Unc	BU
2003	—	—	—	—	—	12.50

KM# 87 25 SEN
9.1400 g., Brass, 30 mm. **Series:** Endangered Species **Obv:** Logo left, value right **Rev:** Gaur **Edge:** Reeded

Date	Mintage	F	VF	XF	Unc	BU
2003	—	—	—	—	—	12.50

KM# 88 25 SEN
9.1400 g., Brass, 30 mm. **Series:** Endangered Species **Obv:** Logo left, value right **Rev:** Clouded Leopard **Edge:** Reeded

Date	Mintage	F	VF	XF	Unc	BU
2003	—	—	—	—	—	12.50

KM# 89 25 SEN
9.1400 g., Brass, 30 mm. **Series:** Endangered Species **Obv:** Logo left, value right **Rev:** Straw-headed Bulbul bird **Edge:** Reeded

Date	Mintage	F	VF	XF	Unc	BU
2004	—	—	—	—	—	12.50

KM# 90 25 SEN
9.1400 g., Brass, 30 mm. **Series:** Endangered Species **Obv:** Logo left, value right **Rev:** Great Argus bird **Edge:** Reeded

Date	Mintage	F	VF	XF	Unc	BU
2004	—	—	—	—	—	12.50

KM# 91 25 SEN
9.1400 g., Brass, 30 mm. **Series:** Endangered Species **Obv:** Logo left, value right **Rev:** Collared Kingfisher **Edge:** Reeded

Date	Mintage	F	VF	XF	Unc	BU
2004	—	—	—	—	—	12.50

KM# 92 25 SEN
9.1400 g., Brass, 30 mm. **Series:** Endangered Species **Obv:** Logo left, value right **Rev:** Sea Eagle perched on branch **Edge:** Reeded

Date	Mintage	F	VF	XF	Unc	BU
2004	—	—	—	—	—	12.50

KM# 93 25 SEN
9.1600 g., Brass, 30 mm. **Series:** Endangered Species **Obv:** Logo left, value right **Rev:** Bluebird **Edge:** Reeded

Date	Mintage	F	VF	XF	Unc	BU
2004	40,000	—	—	—	—	12.50

KM# 94 25 SEN
9.1600 g., Brass, 30 mm. **Series:** Endangered Species **Obv:** Logo left, value right **Rev:** Rhinoceros Hornbill bird **Edge:** Reeded

Date	Mintage	F	VF	XF	Unc	BU
2004	40,000	—	—	—	—	12.50

KM# 95 25 SEN
9.1600 g., Brass, 30 mm. **Series:** Endangered Species **Obv:** Logo left, value right **Rev:** Nicobar Pigeon **Edge:** Reeded

Date	Mintage	F	VF	XF	Unc	BU
2004	40,000	—	—	—	—	12.50

KM# 96 25 SEN
9.1600 g., Brass, 30 mm. **Series:** Endangered Species **Obv:** Logo left, value right **Rev:** Two Crested Wood Partridges **Edge:** Reeded

Date	Mintage	F	VF	XF	Unc	BU
2004	40,000	—	—	—	—	12.50

KM# 97 25 SEN
9.1600 g., Brass, 30 mm. **Series:** Endangered Species **Obv:** Logo left, value right **Rev:** Black and Red Broadbill bird **Edge:** Reeded

Date	Mintage	F	VF	XF	Unc	BU
2004	40,000	—	—	—	—	12.50

KM# 98 25 SEN
9.1600 g., Brass, 30 mm. **Series:** Endangered Species **Obv:** Logo left, value right **Rev:** Green Imperial Pigeon on branch **Edge:** Reeded

Date	Mintage	F	VF	XF	Unc	BU
2004	40,000	—	—	—	—	12.50

KM# 99 25 SEN
9.1600 g., Brass, 30 mm. **Series:** Endangered Species **Obv:** Logo left, value right **Rev:** Great Egret **Edge:** Re eded

Date	Mintage	F	VF	XF	Unc	BU
2004	40,000	—	—	—	—	12.50

KM# 100 25 SEN
9.1600 g., Brass, 30 mm. **Series:** Endangered Species **Obv:** Logo left, value right **Rev:** Brown Shrike on branch **Edge:** Reeded

Date	Mintage	F	VF	XF	Unc	BU
2004	40,000	—	—	—	—	12.50

KM# 117 25 SEN
Brass, 30 mm. **Series:** Endangered Species **Obv:** Logo and value **Obv. Legend:** BANK NEGARA MALAYSIA - SIRI HAIWAN TERANCAM **Rev:** Barau-Barau (Straw-headed Bulbul)

Date	Mintage	F	VF	XF	Unc	BU
2005	40,000	—	—	—	—	4.00

KM# 118 25 SEN
Brass, 30 mm. **Series:** Endangered Species **Obv:** Logo and value **Obv. Legend:** BANK NEGARA MALAYSIA - SIRI HAIWAN TERANCAM **Rev:** Kuang Raya (Great Argus Pheasant) alighting

Date	Mintage	F	VF	XF	Unc	BU
2005	40,000	—	—	—	—	4.00

KM# 119 25 SEN
Brass, 30 mm. **Series:** Endangered Species **Obv:** Logo and value **Obv. Legend:** BANK NEGARA MALAYSIA - SIRI HAIWAN TERANCAM **Rev:** Lang Siput (White-bellied Sea-eagle)

Date	Mintage	F	VF	XF	Unc	BU
2005	40,000	—	—	—	—	4.00

KM# 120 25 SEN
Brass, 30 mm. **Series:** Endangered Species **Obv:** Logo and value **Obv. Legend:** BANK NEGARA MALAYSIA - SIRI HAIWAN TERANCAM **Rev:** Pekaka Sungai (White-collared Kingfisher)

Date	Mintage	F	VF	XF	Unc	BU
2005	40,000	—	—	—	—	4.00

KM# 124 25 SEN
Brass, 30 mm. **Series:** Endangered Species **Obv:** Logo and value **Obv. Legend:** BANK NEGARA MALAYSIA - SIRI HAIWAN TERANCAM **Rev:** Dendang Gajah (Asian Fairy Bluebird)

Date	Mintage	F	VF	XF	Unc	BU
2005	40,000	—	—	—	—	4.00

KM# 125 25 SEN
Brass, 30 mm. **Series:** Endangered Species **Obv:** Logo and value **Obv. Legend:** BANK NEGARA MALAYSIA - SIRI HAIWAN TERANCAM **Rev:** Enggang Badak (Rhinoceros Hornbill)

Date	Mintage	F	VF	XF	Unc	BU
2005	40,000	—	—	—	—	4.00

KM# 126 25 SEN
Brass, 30 mm. **Series:** Endangered Species **Obv:** Logo and value **Obv. Legend:** BANK NEGARA MALAYSIA - SIRI HAIWAN TERANCAM **Rev:** Merpati Emas (Nicobar Pigeon)

Date	Mintage	F	VF	XF	Unc	BU
2005	40,000	—	—	—	—	4.00

KM# 127 25 SEN

Brass, 30 mm. **Series:** Endangered Species **Obv:** Logo and value **Obv. Legend:** BANK NEGARA MALAYSIA - SIRI HAIWAN TERANCAM **Rev:** Siul Berjambul (Crested Wood Partridge)

Date	Mintage	F	VF	XF	Unc	BU
2005	40,000	—	—	—	—	4.00

KM# 128 25 SEN

Brass, 30 mm. **Series:** Endangered Species **Obv:** Logo and value **Obv. Legend:** BANK NEGARA MALAYSIA - SIRI HAIWAN TERANCAM **Rev:** Takau Rakit (Black and Red Broadbill)

Date	Mintage	F	VF	XF	Unc	BU
2005	40,000	—	—	—	—	4.00

KM# 129 25 SEN

Brass, 30 mm. **Series:** Endangered Species **Obv:** Logo and value **Obv. Legend:** BANK NEGARA MALAYSIA - SIRI HAIWAN TERANCAN **Rev:** Bangau Besar (Great Egret)

Date	Mintage	F	VF	XF	Unc	BU
2005	40,000	—	—	—	—	4.00

KM# 130 25 SEN

Brass, 30 mm. **Series:** Endangered Species **Obv:** Logo and value **Obv. Legend:** BANK NEGARA MALAYSIA - SIRI HAIWAN TERANCAM **Rev:** Pergam Besar (Green Imperial Pigeon)

Date	Mintage	F	VF	XF	Unc	BU
2005	40,000	—	—	—	—	4.00

KM# 131 25 SEN

Brass, 30 mm. **Series:** Endangered Species **Obv:** Logo and value **Obv. Legend:** BANK NEGARA MALAYSIA - SIRI HAIWAN TERANCAM **Rev:** Tirjup Tanah (Brown Shrike)

Date	Mintage	F	VF	XF	Unc	BU
2005	40,000	—	—	—	—	4.00

KM# 150 25 SEN

Brass, 34 mm. **Series:** Endangered Species **Obv:** Logo and value **Obv. Legend:** BANK NEGARA MALAYSIA - SIRI HAIWAN TERANCAN **Rev:** Penyu Agar (Green Turtle)

Date	Mintage	F	VF	XF	Unc	BU
2006	40,000	—	—	—	—	4.00

KM# 104 25 SEN

Brass **Rev:** Hawksbill turtle

Date	Mintage	F	VF	XF	Unc	BU
2006	—	—	—	—	—	15.00

KM# 103 25 SEN

Brass **Rev:** Green turtle

Date	Mintage	F	VF	XF	Unc	BU
2006	—	—	—	—	—	15.00

KM# 102 25 SEN

Brass **Rev:** Leatherback turtle

Date	Mintage	F	VF	XF	Unc	BU
2006	—	—	—	—	—	15.00

KM# 101 25 SEN

Brass **Rev:** Olive ridley turtle

Date	Mintage	F	VF	XF	Unc	BU
2006	—	—	—	—	—	15.00

KM# 105 25 SEN

15.5000 g., Brass, 34 mm. **Obv:** Logo and value **Rev:** Dugong manatee **Edge:** Reeded

Date	Mintage	F	VF	XF	Unc	BU
2006	40,000	—	—	—	—	15.00

KM# 106 25 SEN

15.5000 g., Brass, 34 mm. **Obv:** Logo and value **Rev:** Whale Shark **Edge:** Reeded

Date	Mintage	F	VF	XF	Unc	BU
2006	40,000	—	—	—	—	15.00

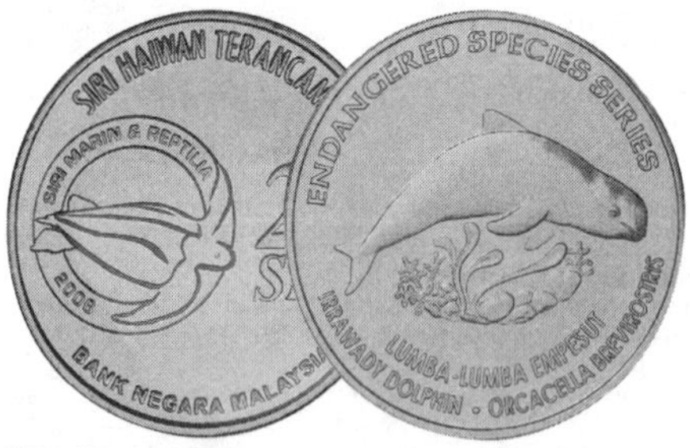

KM# 107 25 SEN

15.5000 g., Brass, 34 mm. **Obv:** Logo and value **Rev:** Irraddy Dolphin **Edge:** Reeded

Date	Mintage	F	VF	XF	Unc	BU
2006	40,000	—	—	—	—	15.00

KM# 108 25 SEN

15.5000 g., Brass, 34 mm. **Obv:** Logo and value **Rev:** Bottlenose Dolphin **Edge:** Reeded

Date	Mintage	F	VF	XF	Unc	BU
2006	40,000	—	—	—	—	15.00

KM# 109 25 SEN

15.5000 g., Brass, 34 mm. **Obv:** Logo and value **Rev:** Siamese Crocodile **Edge:** Reeded

Date	Mintage	F	VF	XF	Unc	BU
2006	40,000	—	—	—	—	15.00

KM# 110 25 SEN

15.5000 g., Brass, 34 mm. **Obv:** Logo and value **Rev:** Indopacific Crocodile **Edge:** Reeded

Date	Mintage	F	VF	XF	Unc	BU
2006	40,000	—	—	—	—	15.00

KM# 111 25 SEN

15.5000 g., Brass, 34 mm. **Obv:** Logo and value **Rev:** Malayan Gharial **Edge:** Reeded

Date	Mintage	F	VF	XF	Unc	BU
2006	40,000	—	—	—	—	15.00

KM# 112 25 SEN

15.5000 g., Brass, 34 mm. **Obv:** Logo and value **Rev:** Painted Terrapin turtle **Edge:** Reeded

Date	Mintage	F	VF	XF	Unc	BU
2006	40,000	—	—	—	—	15.00

KM# 151 25 SEN

Brass, 34 mm. **Series:** Endangered Species **Obv:** Logo and value **Obv. Legend:** BANK NEGARA MALAYSIA - SIRI HAIWAN TERANCAN **Rev:** Penyu Karah (Hawksbill Turtle)

Date	Mintage	F	VF	XF	Unc	BU
2006	40,000	—	—	—	—	4.00

KM# 152 25 SEN

Brass, 34 mm. **Series:** Endangered Species **Obv:** Logo and value **Obv. Legend:** BANK NEGARA MALAYSIA - SIRI HAIWAN TERANCAN **Rev:** Lumba Lumba (Bottlenose Dolphin)

Date	Mintage	F	VF	XF	Unc	BU
2006	40,000	—	—	—	—	4.00

KM# 153 25 SEN

Brass, 34 mm. **Series:** Endangered Species **Obv:** Logo and value **Obv. Legend:** Bank Negara Malaysia - SIRI HAIWAN TERANCAN **Rev:** Tuntung laut (Painted Terrapin)

Date	Mintage	F	VF	XF	Unc	BU
2006	40,000	—	—	—	—	4.00

KM# 154 25 SEN

Brass, 34 mm. **Series:** Endangered species **Obv:** Logo and value **Obv. Legend:** BANK NEGARA MALAYSIA - SIRI HAIWAN TERANCAN **Rev:** Pengu Lipas (Olive Ridley Turtle)

Date	Mintage	F	VF	XF	Unc	BU
2006	40,000	—	—	—	—	4.00

KM# 155 25 SEN

Brass, 34 mm. **Series:** Endangered species **Obv:** Logo and value **Obv. Legend:** BANK NEGARA MALAYSIA - SIRI HAIWAN TERANCAN **Rev:** Penyu Belimbing (Leatherneck Turtle)

Date	Mintage	F	VF	XF	Unc	BU
2006	40,000	—	—	—	—	4.00

KM# 156 25 SEN

Brass, 34 mm. **Series:** Endangered species **Obv:** Logo and value **Obv. Legend:** BANK NEGARA MALAYSIA - SIRI HAIWAN TERANCAN **Rev:** Duyung (Dugong)

Date	Mintage	F	VF	XF	Unc	BU
2006	40,000	—	—	—	—	4.00

KM# 157 25 SEN

Brass, 34 mm. **Series:** Endangered species **Obv:** Logo and value **Obv. Legend:** BANK NEGARA MALAYSIA - SIRI HAIWAN TERANCAN **Rev:** Buaya Siam (Siamese Crocodile)

Date	Mintage	F	VF	XF	Unc	BU
2006	40,000	—	—	—	—	4.00

KM# 158 25 SEN

Brass, 34 mm. **Series:** Endangered species **Obv:** Logo and value **Obv. Legend:** BANK NEGARA MALAYSIA - SIRI HAIWAN TERANCAN **Rev:** Jerung Paus (Whale Shark)

Date	Mintage	F	VF	XF	Unc	BU
2006	40,000	—	—	—	—	4.00

KM# 159 25 SEN

Brass, 34 mm. **Series:** Endangered species **Obv:** Logo and value **Obv. Legend:** BANK NEGARA MALAYSIA - SIRI HAIWAN TERANCAN **Rev:** Buaya Julong (Malayan Gharial)

Date	Mintage	F	VF	XF	Unc	BU
2006	40,000	—	—	—	—	4.00

KM# 160 25 SEN

Brass, 34 mm. **Series:** Endangered species **Obv:** Logo and value **Obv. Legend:** BANK NEGARA MALAYSIA - SIRI HAIWAN TERANCAN **Rev:** Buaya Tembaga (Estuarine Crocodile)

Date	Mintage	F	VF	XF	Unc	BU
2006	40,000	—	—	—	—	4.00

KM# 161 25 SEN

Brass, 34 mm. **Series:** Endangered species **Obv:** Logo and value **Obv. Legend:** BANK NEGARA MALAYSIA - SIRI HAIWAN TERANCAN **Rev:** Lumba-Lumba Empesut (Irrawady Dolphin)

Date	Mintage	F	VF	XF	Unc	BU
2006	40,000	—	—	—	—	4.00

KM# 53 50 SEN

9.2800 g., Copper-Nickel, 27.78 mm. **Obv:** Value divides date below flower blossom **Obv. Legend:** BANK NEGARA MALAYSIA **Rev:** Ceremonial kite **Edge:** Lettered **Edge Lettering:** BANK NEGARA MALAYSIA (twice)

Date	Mintage	F	VF	XF	Unc	BU
2001	67,371,000	—	—	—	0.65	0.85
2002	61,928,000	—	—	—	0.65	0.85
2003	32,580,000	—	—	—	0.65	0.85
2004	37,890,000	—	—	—	0.65	0.85
2005	691,680,006	—	—	—	0.65	0.85
2006	19,480,006	—	—	—	0.65	0.85

KM# 71 RINGGIT

16.8000 g., Copper Nickel, 33.7 mm. **Subject:** XXI SEA Games **Obv:** Games logo **Rev:** Cartoon mascot **Edge:** Reeded

Date	Mintage	F	VF	XF	Unc	BU
2001	200,000	—	—	—	3.00	5.00

KM# 165 RINGGIT

Copper Plated Zinc **Subject:** 10th Men's Hockey World Cup **Obv:** Logo **Obv. Legend:** BANK NEGARA MALAYSIA **Rev:** 2 stylized players **Rev. Legend:** KEJOHANAN HOKI LELAKI PIALA DUNIA **Edge:** Reeded

Date	Mintage	F	VF	XF	Unc	BU
2002	100,000	—	—	—	—	6.00

KM# 168 RINGGIT

Brass **Subject:** 45th National Day **Obv:** Buildings, tower, metro liner **Obv. Legend:** BANK NEGARA MALAYSIA **Rev:** Stylized waving flag **Rev. Legend:** 45 TAHUN MERDEKA

Date	Mintage	F	VF	XF	Unc	BU
2002	10,000	—	—	—	—	5.50

KM# 74 RINGGIT

16.8000 g., Copper-Nickel, 33.7 mm. **Subject:** Coronation of Agong XII **Obv:** Head with headdress facing **Rev:** Arms with supporters within sprigs **Edge:** Reeded **Note:** Prev. KM#72.

Date	Mintage	F	VF	XF	Unc	BU
ND(2002)	100,000	—	—	—	4.00	6.00

KM# 171 RINGGIT

Brass **Subject:** XIII NAM Summit **Obv:** Modern building, plaza **Obv. Legend:** MALAYSIA - BANK NEGARA MALAYSIA **Rev:** Stylized dove in rays **Rev. Legend:** XIII CONFERENCE OF HEADS OF STATE OR GOVERNMENT OF THE NON-ALIGNED MOVEMENT

Date	Mintage	F	VF	XF	Unc	BU
2003	9,400	—	—	—	—	5.50

KM# 174 RINGGIT

Brass **Subject:** LIMA - 7th Bi-annual Langkawi Island Trade Fair **Obv:** Jet fighter plane above naval missile corvette **Obv. Legend:** BANK NEGARA MALAYSIA **Rev:** Logo **Rev. Legend:** LANGKAWI INTERNATIONAL MARITIME & AEROSPACE

Date	Mintage	F	VF	XF	Unc	BU
2003	25,000	—	—	—	—	5.50

KM# 177 RINGGIT

Brass **Subject:** 10th Session Islamic Summit Conference **Obv:** Circular Arabic text **Obv. Legend:** BANK NEGARA MALAYSIA **Rev:** Symmetrical design **Rev. Legend:** PERSIDANGAN KETUA-KETUA NEGARASLAM

Date	Mintage	F	VF	XF	Unc	BU
2003	25,000	—	—	—	—	5.50

KM# 114 RINGGIT

Copper-Nickel **Subject:** Century of Tunku Abdul Rahman **Obv:** National arms **Obv. Legend:** BANK NEGARA MALAYSIA - BAPA KEMERDEKAAN **Rev:** 3/4 length figure of Tunku Abdul Rahman left with right hand raised **Rev. Legend:** Y. T. M. TUNKU ABDUL RAHMAN PUTRA AL-HAJ

Date	Mintage	F	VF	XF	Unc	BU
2005	25,000	—	—	—	—	4.00

KM# 132 RINGGIT

Brass **Subject:** 30th Annual Meeting Islamic Development Bank **Obv:** Circular Arabic text **Obv. Legend:** BANK NEGARA MALYSIA - MESYUARAT TAHUNAN BANK PEMBANCUNAN ISLAM KE - 30 **Rev:** Logo

Date	Mintage	F	VF	XF	Unc	BU
2005	20,000	—	—	—	—	6.00

KM# 135 RINGGIT

Copper-Nickel **Subject:** 11th ASEAN Summit **Obv:** Twin towers center right **Obv. Legend:** BANK NEGARA MALAYSIA - SIDANG KEMUNCAK ASEAN KE-11 **Rev:** Logo

Date	Mintage	F	VF	XF	Unc	BU
2005	20,000	—	—	—	—	5.00

KM# 138 RINGGIT

Bi-Metallic **Subject:** Songket - The Regal Heritage **Obv:** Stylized flower - Bunga Ketola **Obv. Legend:** BANK NEGARA MALAYSIA **Rev:** Floral pattern below inscription

Date	Mintage	F	VF	XF	Unc	BU
2005	20,000	—	—	—	—	5.00

KM# 141 RINGGIT

Brass **Subject:** 50th Anniversary Mara Technology University **Obv:** Large "50" with horizontal lines in background **Obv. Legend:** BANK NEGARA MALAYSIA - JUBLI EMAS UITM **Rev:** Logo **Rev. Legend:** Universiti Teknologi Mara

Date	Mintage	F	VF	XF	Unc	BU
ND(2006)	12,050	—	—	—	—	5.00

KM# 144 RINGGIT

Brass **Subject:** 50th Anniversary P. Felda **Obv:** 1/2 length figure of Felda 3/4 right **Obv. Legend:** BANK NEGARA MALYSIA **Rev:** Two opposed hands holding symbol **Rev. Legend:** MENEMPA KEJAYAAN

Date	Mintage	F	VF	XF	Unc	BU
2006	10,000	—	—	—	—	5.00

KM# 147 RINGGIT

Brass **Subject:** 9th Malaysian Plan **Obv:** Bust 3/4 right **Obv. Legend:** BANK NEGARA MALAYSIA - CEMERLANG GEMILANG TERBILANg **Rev:** Globe logo **Rev. Legend:** RANCANGAN MALAYSIA KE SEMBILAN

Date	Mintage	F	VF	XF	Unc	BU
2006	10,000	—	—	—	—	5.50

KM# 72 10 RINGGIT

21.7000 g., 0.9250 Silver 0.6453 oz. ASW, 35.7 mm. **Subject:** XXI SEA Games **Obv:** Games logo **Rev:** Cartoon mascot **Edge:** Reeded

Date	Mintage	F	VF	XF	Unc	BU
Proof	3,000	Value: 50.00				

KM# 75 10 RINGGIT

21.7000 g., 0.9250 Silver 0.6453 oz. ASW, 35.7 mm. **Subject:** Coronation of Agong XII **Obv:** Head with headdress facing **Rev:** Arms with supporters within sprigs **Edge:** Reeded

Date	Mintage	F	VF	XF	Unc	BU
ND(2002) Proof	10,000	Value: 50.00				

KM# 166 10 RINGGIT

0.9250 Silver **Subject:** 10th Men's Hockey World Cup **Obv:** Logo **Obv. Legend:** BANK NEGARA MALAYSIA **Rev:** 2 stylized players **Rev. Legend:** KEJOHANAN HOKI LELAKI PIALA

Date	Mintage	F	VF	XF	Unc	BU
2002 Proof	3,000	Value: 65.00				

KM# 169 10 RINGGIT

0.9250 Silver **Subject:** 45th National Day **Obv:** Buildings, tower, metro liner **Obv. Legend:** BANK NEGARA MALAYSIA **Rev:** Stylized waving flag **Rev. Legend:** 45 TAHUN MERDEKA

Date	Mintage	F	VF	XF	Unc	BU
2002 Proof	1,800	Value: 60.00				

KM# 172 10 RINGGIT

0.9250 Silver **Subject:** XIII NAM Summit **Obv:** Modern building, plaza **Obv. Legend:** MALAYSIA - BANK NEGARA MALAYSIA **Rev:** Stylized dove in rays **Rev. Legend:** XIII CONFERENCE OF HEADS OF STATE OR GOVERNMENT OF THE NON-ALIGNED MOVEMENT

Date	Mintage	F	VF	XF	Unc	BU
2003 Proof	—	Value: 60.00				

KM# 175 10 RINGGIT

0.9250 Silver **Subject:** LIMA - 7th bi-annual Langkawi Island Trade Fair **Obv:** Jet fighter plane above naval missile corvette **Obv. Legend:** BANK NEGARA MALAYSIA **Rev:** Logo **Rev. Legend:** LANGKAWI INTERNATIONAL MARITIME & SPACE

Date	Mintage	F	VF	XF	Unc	BU
2003 Proof	—	Value: 60.00				

KM# 178 10 RINGGIT

0.9250 Silver **Subject:** 10th Session Islamic Summit Conference **Obv:** Circular Arabic Text **Obv. Legend:** BANK NEGARA MALAYSIA **Rev:** Symmetrical pattern **Rev. Legend:** PERSIDANGAN KETUA - KETUA NEGARA ISLAM

Date	Mintage	F	VF	XF	Unc	BU
2003 Proof	—	Value: 60.00				

KM# 115 10 RINGGIT

0.9250 Silver **Subject:** Century of Tunku Abdul Rahman **Obv:** National arms **Obv. Legend:** BANK NEGARA MALAYSIA - BAPA KEMERDEKAAN **Rev:** 3/4 length figure of Tunku Abdul Rahman left with right hand raised **Rev. Legend:** Y. T. M. TUNKU ABDUL RAHMAN PUTRA AL-HAJ

Date	Mintage	F	VF	XF	Unc	BU
2005 Proof	—	Value: 50.00				

KM# 136 10 RINGGIT

21.7000 g., Silver, 35.7 mm. **Subject:** 11th ASEAN Summit **Obv:** Twin towers center right **Obv. Legend:** BANK NEGARA MALAYSIA - SIDANG KEMUNCAK ASEAN KE-11 **Rev:** Logo

Date	Mintage	F	VF	XF	Unc	BU
2005 Proof	250	Value: 68.00				

KM# 139 10 RINGGIT

21.7000 g., Silver, 35.7 mm. **Subject:** Songket - The Regal Heritage **Obv:** Uniform pattern - Bunga Bintang **Obv. Legend:** BANK NEGARA MALAYSIA **Rev:** Floral pattern below inscription

Date	Mintage	F	VF	XF	Unc	BU
2005 Proof	—	Value: 65.00				

KM# 142 10 RINGGIT

21.7000 g., Silver, 35.7 mm. **Subject:** 50th Anniversary Mara Technology Universit **Obv:** Large "50" with horizontal lines in background **Obv. Legend:** BANK NEGARA MALAYSIA - JUBLI EMAS UITM **Rev:** Logo **Rev. Legend:** Universiti Teknologi Mara

Date	Mintage	F	VF	XF	Unc	BU
ND(2006) Proof	—	Value: 65.00				

KM# 145 10 RINGGIT

31.1100 g., Silver, 40 mm. **Subject:** 50th Anniversary P. Felda **Obv:** Outlined map of South East Asia above logo **Obv. Legend:** BANK NEGARA MALAYSIA **Rev:** Monument at left, Felda with 4 others at right **Rev. Legend:** MENEMPA KEJAYAAN

Date	Mintage	F	VF	XF	Unc	BU
2006 Proof	—	Value: 60.00				

KM# 148 10 RINGGIT

21.0000 g., Silver, 35.7 mm. **Subject:** 9th Malaysian Plan **Obv:** Bust 3/4 right **Obv. Legend:** BANK NEGARA MALAYSIA - CEMERLANG GEMILANG TERBILANG **Rev:** Globe logo **Rev. Legend:** RANCANGAN MALAYSIA KE SEMBILAN

Date	Mintage	F	VF	XF	Unc	BU
2006 Proof	—	Value: 55.00				

KM# 163 10 RINGGIT

21.0000 g., Silver, 35.70 mm. **Subject:** 200th Anniversary Malaysian Police Force **Obv:** Police badge **Obv. Legend:** BANK NEGARA MALAYSIA **Rev:** Two hands clasped in sprays

Date	Mintage	F	VF	XF	Unc	BU
2007 Proof	—	Value: 55.00				

KM# 133 20 RINGGIT

31.1000 g., Silver, 40 mm. **Subject:** 30th Annual Meeting Islamic Development Bank **Obv:** Mosque **Obv. Legend:** BANK NEGARA MALAYSIA **Rev:** Logo

Date	Mintage	F	VF	XF	Unc	BU
2005 Proof	1,000	Value: 70.00				

KM# 73 100 RINGGIT

8.6000 g., 0.9160 Gold 0.2533 oz. AGW, 22 mm. **Subject:** XXI SEA Games **Obv:** Games logo **Rev:** Cartoon mascot **Edge:** Reeded

Date	Mintage	F	VF	XF	Unc	BU
Proof	500	Value: 400				

KM# 76 100 RINGGIT

8.6000 g., 0.9160 Gold 0.2533 oz. AGW, 22 mm. **Subject:** Coronation of Agong XII **Obv:** Head with headdress facing **Rev:** Arms with supporters within sprigs **Edge:** Reeded

Date	Mintage	F	VF	XF	Unc	BU
ND(2002) Proof	300	Value: 400				

KM# 167 100 RINGGIT

9.0000 g., 0.9000 Gold 0.2604 oz. AGW **Subject:** 10th Men's Hockey World Cup **Obv:** Logo **Obv. Legend:** BANK NEGARA MALAYSIA **Rev:** 2 stylized players **Rev. Legend:** KEJOHANAN HOKI LELAKI PIALA

Date	Mintage	F	VF	XF	Unc	BU
2002 Proof	1,000	Value: 425				

KM# 170 100 RINGGIT

8.6000 g., 0.9999 Gold 0.2765 oz. AGW **Subject:** 45th National Day **Obv:** Buildings, tower, metro liner **Obv. Legend:** BANK NEGARA MALAYSIA **Rev:** Stylized waving flag **Rev. Legend:** 45 TAHUN MERDEKA

Date	Mintage	F	VF	XF	Unc	BU
2002 Proof	300	Value: 425				

KM# 173 100 RINGGIT

8.6000 g., 0.9999 Gold 0.2765 oz. AGW, 22 mm. **Subject:** XIII NAM Summit **Obv:** Modern building, plaza **Obv. Legend:** MALAYSIA - BANK NEGARA MALAYSIA **Rev:** Stylized dove in rays **Rev. Legend:** XIII CONFERENCE OF HEADS OF STATE OR GOVERNMENT OF THE NON-ALIGNED MOVEMENT

Date	Mintage	F	VF	XF	Unc	BU
2003 Proof	—	Value: 425				

KM# 176 100 RINGGIT

8.6000 g., 0.9999 Gold 0.2765 oz. AGW, 22 mm. **Subject:** LIMA - 7th bi-annual Langkawi Island Trade Fair **Obv:** Jet fighter plane above naval missile corvette **Obv. Legend:** BANK NEGARA MALAYSIA **Rev:** Logo **Rev. Legend:** LANGKAWI INTERNATIONAL MARITIME & AEROSPACE

Date	Mintage	F	VF	XF	Unc	BU
2003 Proof	50	Value: 800				

KM# 179 100 RINGGIT

8.6000 g., 0.9999 Gold 0.2765 oz. AGW, 22 mm. **Obv:** Circular Arabic text **Obv. Legend:** BANK NEGARA MALAYSIA **Rev:** Symmetrical design **Rev. Legend:** PERSIDANGAN KETUA - KETUA NEGARA ISLAM

Date	Mintage	F	VF	XF	Unc	BU
2003 Proof	—	Value: 425				

KM# 116 100 RINGGIT

0.9999 Gold **Subject:** Century of Tunku Abdul Rahman **Obv:** National arms **Obv. Legend:** BANK NEGARA MALAYSIA - BAPA KEMERDEKAAN **Rev:** 3/4 length figure of Tunku Abdul Rahman left with right hand raised **Rev. Legend:** Y. T. M. TUNKU ABDUL RAHMAN PUTRA AL-HAJ

Date	Mintage	F	VF	XF	Unc	BU
2005 Proof	—	Value: 500				

KM# 137 100 RINGGIT

8.6000 g., Gold, 22 mm. **Subject:** 11th ASEAN Summit **Obv:** Twin towers center right **Obv. Legend:** BANK NEGARA MALAYSIA - SIDANG KEMUNCAK ASEAN KE-11 **Rev:** Logo

Date	Mintage	F	VF	XF	Unc	BU
2005 Proof	150	Value: 400				

KM# 140 100 RINGGIT

8.6000 g., Gold, 22 mm. **Subject:** Songket - The Regal Heritage **Obv:** Uniform pattern - Tampur Kesemak **Obv. Legend:** BANK NEGARA MALAYSIA **Rev:** Floral pattern below inscription

Date	Mintage	F	VF	XF	Unc	BU
2005 Proof	—	Value: 400				

KM# 143 100 RINGGIT

8.6000 g., Gold, 22 mm. **Subject:** 50th Anniversary Mara Technology University **Obv:** Large "50" with horizontal lines in background **Obv. Legend:** BANK NEGARA MALAYSIA - JUBLI EMAS UITM **Rev:** Logo **Rev. Legend:** Universiti Teknologi Mara

Date	Mintage	F	VF	XF	Unc	BU
ND(2006) Proof	—	Value: 400				

KM# 146 100 RINGGIT

9.0000 g., Gold, 22 mm. **Subject:** 50th Anniversary P. Felda **Obv:** 1/2 length figure of Felda 3/4 right **Obv. Legend:** BANK NEGARA MALAYSIA **Rev:** Stylized palm tree at left, rubber tree trunk at right **Rev. Legend:** MENEMPA KEJAYAAN

Date	Mintage	F	VF	XF	Unc	BU
2006 Proof	—	Value: 425				

KM# 149 100 RINGGIT

7.9600 g., Gold, 22 mm. **Subject:** 9th Malaysian Plan **Obv:** Bust 3/4 right **Obv. Legend:** BANK NEGARA MALAYSIA - CEMERLANG GEMILANG TERBILANG **Rev:** Globe logo **Rev. Legend:** RANCANGAN MALAYSIA KE SEMBILAN

Date	Mintage	F	VF	XF	Unc	BU
2006 Proof	—	Value: 425				

KM# 164 100 RINGGIT

7.9600 g., Gold, 22 mm. **Subject:** 200th Anniversary Malaysian Police Force **Obv:** Police badge **Obv. Legend:** BANK NEGARA MALAYSIA **Rev:** Two hands clasped in sprays

Date	Mintage	F	VF	XF	Unc	BU
2007 Proof	—	Value: 425				

KM# 134 200 RINGGIT

15.5500 g., Gold, 28 mm. **Subject:** 30th Annual Meeting Islamic Development Bank **Obv:** Mosque in rays **Obv. Legend:** BANK NEGARA MALAYSIA **Rev:** Logo

Date	Mintage	F	VF	XF	Unc	BU
2005 Proof	500	Value: 600				

PROOF SETS

KM#	Date	Mintage	Identification	Issue Price	Mkt Val
PS19	2003 (2)	300	KM#171, 172	—	65.00
PS20	2003 (3)	300	KM#171-173	—	490
PS21	2003 (2)	300	KM#174, 175	—	65.00
PS22	2003 (3)	100	KM#174-176	—	865
PS23	2003 (2)	500	KM#177, 178	—	65.00
PS24	2003 (3)	250	KM#177-179	—	565
PS25	2005 (2)	300	KM#114, 115	—	65.00
PS26	2005 (3)	100	KM#114-116	—	490
PS27	2005 (2)	1,000	KM#132, 133	—	75.00
PS28	2005 (3)	500	KM#132-134	—	675
PS29	2005 (2)	200	KM#135, 136	—	72.00
PS30	2005 (3)	150	KM#135-137	—	480
PS31	2005 (2)	150	KM#138, 139	—	72.00
PS32	2005 (3)	150	KM#138-140	—	480
PS33	2006 (2)	300	KM#141, 142	—	70.00
PS34	2006 (3)	300	KM#141-143	—	480
PS35	2006 (2)	500	KM#144, 145	—	65.00
PS36	2006 (3)	500	KM#144-146	—	480
PS37	2006 (2)	300	KM#147, 148	—	60.00
PS38	2006 (3)	500	KM#147-149	—	460
PS39	2007 (2)	200	KM#162, 163	—	60.00
PS40	2007 (3)	200	KM#162-164	—	460

MALTA

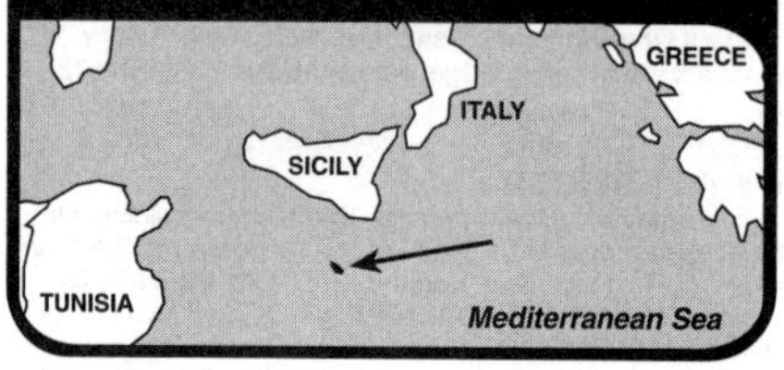

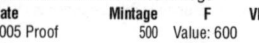

The Republic of Malta, an independent parliamentary democracy, is situated in the Mediterranean Sea between Sicily and North Africa. With the islands of Gozo and Comino, Malta has an area of 124 sq. mi. (320 sq. km.) and a population of 386,000.Capital: Valletta. Malta has no proven mineral resources, agriculture insufficient to its needs, and a small, but expanding, manufacturing facility. Clothing, textile yarns and fabrics, and knitted wear are exported.

Malta became a republic on Dec. 13, 1974, but remained a member of the Commonwealth of Nations. The president is Chief of State. The prime minister is the Head of Government. Malta is also a member of the European Union since May 2004.

RULERS

Fr. Andreas Bertie, 1988-2008

MINT MARKS

Order of Malta Mint in Rome – SMOM in angles of a cross - 1964-

REPUBLIC

REFORM COINAGE

1982 - Present

10 Mils = 1 Cent; 100 Cents = 1 Lira = (Pound)

KM# 5 2 MILS

0.9500 g., Aluminum, 20.3 mm. **Obv:** Maltese cross **Rev:** Value within 3/4 wreath **Shape:** Scalloped

Date	Mintage	F	VF	XF	Unc	BU
2005	—	—	—	—	4.00	—
Note: In sets only, not issued for circulation						
2006	—	—	—	—	4.00	—
2007	—	—	—	—	4.00	—

KM# 93 CENT

2.8000 g., Copper-Zinc, 18.53 mm. **Obv:** Crowned shield within sprigs **Obv. Designer:** Galea Bason **Rev:** Common Weasel below value

Date	Mintage	F	VF	XF	Unc	BU
2001	—	—	0.40	0.50	1.00	—
2002	—	—	0.40	0.50	1.00	—
Note: In sets only, not issued for circulation						
2004	—	—	0.40	0.50	0.75	—
2005	—	—	—	—	0.75	—
Note: In sets only, not issued for circulation						
2006	—	—	—	—	0.75	—
Note: In sets only, not issued for circulation						
2007	—	—	—	—	0.75	—

KM# 94 2 CENTS

2.2400 g., Copper-Zinc, 17.8 mm. **Obv:** Crowned shield within sprigs **Obv. Designer:** Galea Bason **Rev:** Olive branch and value

Date	Mintage	F	VF	XF	Unc	BU
2002	—	—	0.75	1.00	1.25	—
2004	—	—	0.75	1.00	1.25	—
2005	—	—	—	—	1.25	—
2006	—	—	—	—	1.25	—
Note: Not in circulation						
2007	—	—	—	—	1.25	—
Note: Not in circulation						

KM# 95 5 CENTS

3.5100 g., Copper-Nickel, 20 mm. **Obv:** Crowned shield within sprigs **Obv. Designer:** Galea Bason **Rev:** Crab and value

Date	Mintage	F	VF	XF	Unc	BU
2001	—	—	0.75	1.00	1.25	2.00
2005	—	—	—	—	1.25	2.00
Note: In sets only, not issued for circulation						
2006	—	—	—	—	1.25	2.00
Note: In sets only, not issued for circulation						
2007	—	—	—	—	1.25	2.00
Note: In sets only, not issued for circulation						

KM# 96 10 CENTS

5.0000 g., Copper-Nickel, 22 mm. **Obv:** Crowned shield within sprigs **Obv. Designer:** Galea Bason **Rev:** Dolphin fish and value

Date	Mintage	F	VF	XF	Unc	BU
2005	—	—	1.25	1.50	2.00	—
2006	—	—	—	—	2.00	—
Note: In sets only, not issued for circulation						
2007	—	—	—	—	2.00	—
Note: In sets only, not issued for circulation						

KM# 97 25 CENTS

6.2300 g., Copper-Nickel, 25 mm. **Obv:** Crowned shield within sprigs **Obv. Designer:** Galea Bason **Rev:** Ghirlanda flower and value

Date	Mintage	F	VF	XF	Unc	BU
2005	—	—	2.25	2.50	3.00	—
2006	—	—	—	—	3.00	—
Note: In sets only						
2007	—	—	—	—	3.00	—
Note: Not in circulation						

KM# 98 50 CENTS

7.9500 g., Copper-Nickel, 26.9 mm. **Obv:** Crowned shield within sprigs **Obv. Designer:** Galea Bason **Rev:** Tulliera plant and value

Date	Mintage	F	VF	XF	Unc	BU
2001	—	—	2.50	5.00	10.00	—
2005	—	—	—	—	10.00	—
Note: In sets only, not issued for circulation						
2006	—	—	—	—	10.00	—
Note: In sets only, not issued for circulation						
2007	—	—	—	—	10.00	—
Note: In sets only, not issued for circulation						

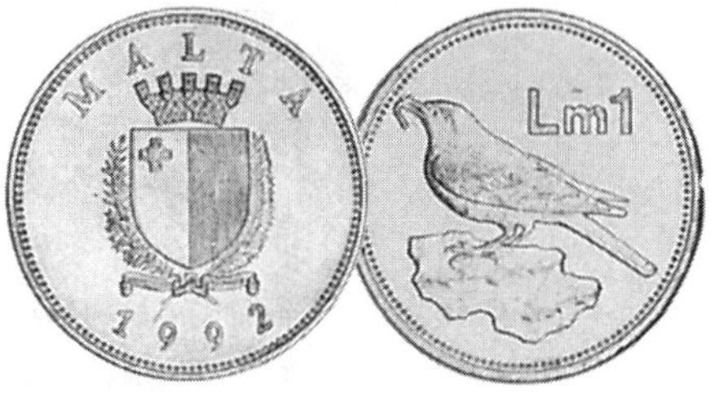

KM# 99 LIRA
Nickel **Obv:** Crowned shield within sprigs **Obv. Designer:** Galea Bason **Rev:** Merill bird and value **Rev. Designer:** Noel Galea

Date	Mintage	F	VF	XF	Unc	BU
2005	—	—	—	4.50	6.50	12.00
2006	—	—	—	—	—	12.00
Note: In sets only						
2007	—	—	—	—	—	12.00

KM# 117 5 LIRI
28.2800 g., 0.9250 Silver 0.8410 oz. ASW, 38.6 mm. **Obv:** Crowned shield within sprigs **Rev:** Enrico Mizzi right **Edge:** Reeded

Date	Mintage	F	VF	XF	Unc	BU
2001 Proof	2,000	Value: 60.00				

KM# 118 5 LIRI
28.2800 g., 0.9250 Silver 0.8410 oz. ASW, 38.6 mm. **Obv:** Crowned shield within sprigs **Rev:** Nicolo Isouard left **Edge:** Reeded

Date	Mintage	F	VF	XF	Unc	BU
2002 Proof	2,000	Value: 60.00				

KM# 120 5 LIRI
28.2800 g., 0.9250 Silver 0.8410 oz. ASW, 38.6 mm. **Obv:** Crowned shield within sprigs **Rev:** Sir Adriano Dingli as Grand Commander of the St. Michael and George Order **Edge:** Reeded

Date	Mintage	F	VF	XF	Unc	BU
2003 Proof	2,000	Value: 60.00				

KM# 121 5 LIRI
28.2800 g., 0.9250 Silver 0.8410 oz. ASW, 38.6 mm. **Obv:** Crowned shield within sprigs **Rev:** Painter Giuseppe Cali with palette **Edge:** Reeded

Date	Mintage	F	VF	XF	Unc	BU
2004 Proof	2,000	Value: 90.00				

KM# 123 5 LIRI
28.2800 g., 0.9250 Silver 0.8410 oz. ASW, 38.61 mm. **Subject:** 450th Anniversary of Jean de la Valette appointed Grand master **Rev:** de la Vallete standing facing left, city of Valletta map at lower left

Date	Mintage	F	VF	XF	Unc	BU
ND(2007) Proof	25,000	Value: 50.00				

KM# 119 10 LIRI
1.2400 g., 0.9990 Gold 0.0398 oz. AGW, 13.92 mm. **Obv:** Crowned shield within sprigs **Rev:** Xprunara sailboat **Edge:** Reeded

Date	Mintage	F	VF	XF	Unc	BU
2002 Prooflike	Est. 25,000	—	—	—	—	110

KM# 122 25 LIRI
3.9940 g., 0.9167 Gold 0.1177 oz. AGW, 19.3 mm. **Subject:** Accession to the European Union **Obv:** Crowned shield within sprigs **Rev:** Maltese flag under European Union star circle **Edge:** Reeded

Date	Mintage	F	VF	XF	Unc	BU
2004 Proof	6,000	Value: 245				

KM# 124 25 LIRI
6.5000 g., 0.9200 Gold 0.1923 oz. AGW, 21.00 mm. **Subject:** 450th Anniversary Jean de la Valette Appointed as Grand Master **Rev:** de la Valette standing facing left, city of Valletta map at lower left

Date	Mintage	F	VF	XF	Unc	BU
ND(2007) Proof	2,500	Value: 300				

EURO COINAGE

KM# 125 EURO CENT
Copper Plated Steel **Obv:** Doorway **Rev:** Denomination and globe

Date	Mintage	F	VF	XF	Unc	BU
2008	—	—	—	—	—	0.35

KM# 126 2 EURO CENT
Copper Plated Steel **Obv:** Doorway **Rev:** Denomination and globe

Date	Mintage	F	VF	XF	Unc	BU
2008	—	—	—	—	—	0.50

KM# 127 5 EURO CENT
Copper Plated Steel **Obv:** Doorway **Rev:** Denomination and globe

Date	Mintage	F	VF	XF	Unc	BU
2008	—	—	—	—	—	0.75

KM# 128 10 EURO CENT
Aluminum-Bronze **Obv:** Crowned shield within wreath

Date	Mintage	F	VF	XF	Unc	BU
2008	—	—	—	—	—	1.00

KM# 129 20 EURO CENT
Aluminum-Brass **Obv:** Crowned shield within wreath **Rev:** Denomination and Map of Western Europe

Date	Mintage	F	VF	XF	Unc	BU
2008	—	—	—	—	—	1.25

KM# 130 50 EURO CENT
Aluminum-Brass **Obv:** Crowned shield within wreath **Rev:** Relief map of Western Europe

Date	Mintage	F	VF	XF	Unc	BU
2008	—	—	—	—	—	1.50

KM# 131 EURO
Bi-Metallic Copper-Nickel center in Brass ring **Obv:** Maltese Cross **Rev:** Value and relief map of Europe

Date	Mintage	F	VF	XF	Unc	BU
2008	—	—	—	—	—	2.75

KM# 132 2 EURO
Bi-Metallic Brass center in Copper-Nickel ring **Obv:** Maltese Cross **Rev:** Value and Relief Map of Western Europe

Date	Mintage	F	VF	XF	Unc	BU
2008	—	—	—	—	—	4.00

MINT SETS

KM#	Date	Mintage	Identification	Issue Price	Mkt Val
MS26	2005 (8)	—	KM#5, 93-99	—	35.00
MS27	2006 (8)	—	KM#5, 93-99	—	35.00
MS28	2007 (8)	—	KM#5, 93-99	—	56.00

MAURITANIA

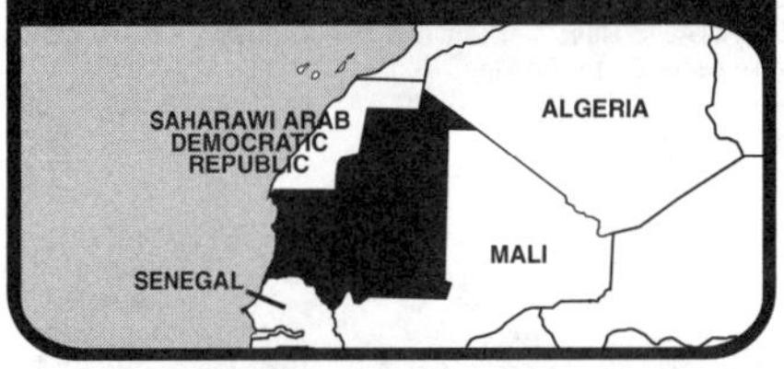

The Islamic Republic of Mauritania, located in northwest Africa bounded by Western Sahara, Mali, Algeria, Senegal and the Atlantic Ocean, has an area of 397,955 sq. mi.(1,030,700 sq. km.) and a population of 1.9 million. Capital: Nouakchott. The economy centers on herding, agriculture, fishing and mining. Iron ore, copper concentrates and fish products are exported.

On June 28, 1973, in a move designed to emphasize its non-alignment with France, Mauritania converted its currency from the old French-supported C.F.A. franc unit to a new unit called the Ouguiya.

MONETARY SYSTEM
5 Khoums = 1 Ouguiya

REPUBLIC

STANDARD COINAGE

KM# 6 OUGUIYA
3.6000 g., Copper-Nickel-Aluminum, 21 mm. **Obv:** National emblem divides date above value **Obv. Legend:** BANQUE CENTRALE DE MAURITANIE **Rev:** Star and crescent divide sprigs with legend below value, all within circle

Date	Mintage	VG	F	VF	XF	Unc
AH1423//2003	—	—	0.50	1.00	2.00	4.00

KM# 3 5 OUGUIYA
5.8800 g., Copper-Nickel-Aluminum, 25 mm. **Obv:** National emblem divides date above value **Obv. Legend:** BANQUE CENTRALE DE MAURITANIE **Rev:** Star and crescent divide sprigs below value within circle

Date	Mintage	VG	F	VF	XF	Unc
AH1423//2003	—	—	0.50	1.00	2.00	4.00

KM# 3a 5 OUGUIYA
Copper Plated Steel Galvanized steel., 25 mm. **Obv:** National emblem divides date above value **Obv. Legend:** BANQUE CENTRALE DE MAURITANIE **Rev:** Star and crescent divides sprigs below value within circle

Date	Mintage	F	VF	XF	Unc	BU
AH1425//2004	—	—	0.50	1.00	2.00	—
AH1426//2005	—	—	0.50	1.00	2.00	—

KM# 4 10 OUGUIYA
6.0000 g., Copper-Nickel, 25 mm. **Obv:** National emblem divides date above value **Obv. Legend:** BANQUE CENTRALE DE MAURITANIE **Rev:** Crescent and star divide sprigs below value within circle

Date	Mintage	VG	F	VF	XF	Unc
AH1423//2003	—	—	0.75	1.50	2.50	4.50

KM# 4a 10 OUGUIYA

Nickel-Plated Steel, 25 mm. **Obv:** National emblem divides date above value **Obv. Legend:** BANQUE CENTRALE DE MAURITANIE **Rev:** Crescent and star divide sprigs below value within circle **Edge:** Reeded

Date	Mintage	VG	F	VF	XF	Unc
AH1425//2004	—	—	—	1.50	2.50	4.50
AH1426//2005	—	—	—	1.50	2.50	4.50

KM# 5 20 OUGUIYA

8.0000 g., Copper-Nickel, 28 mm. **Obv:** National emblem divides date above value **Obv. Legend:** BANQUE CENTRALE DE MAURITANIE **Rev:** Star and crescent divide sprigs below value within circle

Date	Mintage	VG	F	VF	XF	Unc
AH1423//2003	—	—	1.75	3.00	6.00	10.00

KM# 5a 20 OUGUIYA

Nickel Plated Steel , 28 mm. **Obv:** National emblem divides date above value **Obv. Legend:** BANQUE CENTRALE DE MAURITANIE **Rev:** Star and crescent divide sprigs below value within circle

Date	Mintage	F	VF	XF	Unc	BU
AH1425//2004	—	1.75	3.00	6.00	10.00	—
AH1426//2005	—	1.75	3.00	6.00	10.00	—

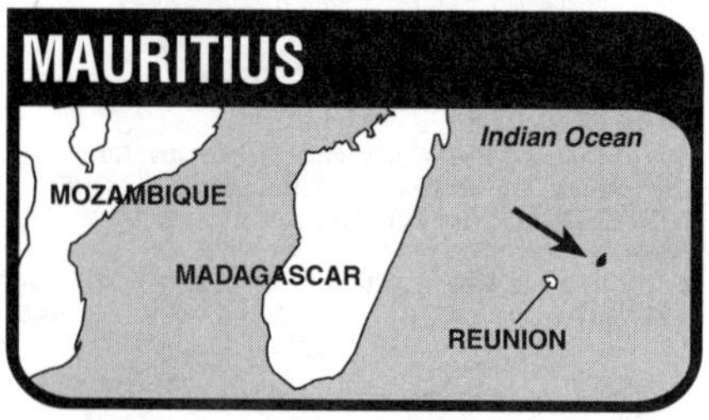

The Republic of Mauritius, is located in the Indian Ocean 500 miles (805 km.) east of Madagascar, has an area of 790 sq. mi. (1,860 sq. km.) and a population of 1 million. Capital: Port Louis. Sugar provides 90 percent of the export revenue.

Mauritius became independent on March 12, 1968. It is a member of the Commonwealth of Nations.

RULER

British, until 1968

MINT MARKS

H - Heaton, Birmingham
SA - Pretoria Mint

MONETARY SYSTEM

100 Cents = 1 Rupee

REPUBLIC

STANDARD COINAGE

100 Cents = 1 Rupee

KM# 52 5 CENTS

3.0000 g., Copper Plated Steel **Obv:** Value within beaded circle **Rev:** Bust of Sir Seewoosagur Ramgoolam 3/4 right

Date	Mintage	F	VF	XF	Unc	BU
2003	—	—	—	—	0.30	0.50
2004	—	—	—	—	0.30	0.50

KM# 53 20 CENTS

3.0000 g., Nickel Plated Steel **Obv:** Value within beaded circle **Rev:** Bust of Sir Seewoosagur Ramgoolam 3/4 right

Date	Mintage	F	VF	XF	Unc	BU
2001	—	—	—	—	0.50	0.75
2003	—	—	—	—	0.50	0.75

KM# 54 1/2 RUPEE

6.0000 g., Nickel Plated Steel **Obv:** Stag left **Rev:** Bust of Sir Seewoosagur Ramgoolam 3/4 right **Rev. Designer:** G.E. Kruger-Gray

Date	Mintage	F	VF	XF	Unc	BU
2002	—	—	—	—	1.50	3.00
2003	—	—	—	—	1.50	3.00

KM# 55 RUPEE

Copper-Nickel **Obv:** Shield divides date above value **Rev:** Bust of Sir Seewoosagur Ramgoolam 3/4 right **Rev. Designer:** G.E. Kruger-Gray

Date	Mintage	F	VF	XF	Unc	BU
2002	—	—	—	—	1.65	2.75
2004	—	—	—	—	1.65	2.75
2005	—	—	—	—	1.65	2.75

KM# 65 100 RUPEES

28.2800 g., 0.9250 Silver 0.8410 oz. ASW **Subject:** Mohandas Karamchand "Mahatma" Gandi **Obv:** National arms

Date	Mintage	F	VF	XF	Unc	BU
2001 Proof	—	Value: 85.00				

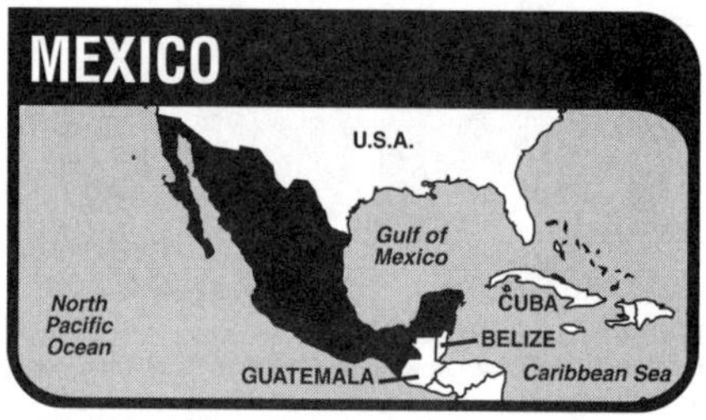

The United States of Mexico, located immediately south of the United States has an area of 759,529 sq. mi. (1,967,183 sq. km.) and an estimated population of 100 million. Capital: Mexico City. The economy is based on agriculture, manufacturing and mining. Oil, cotton, silver, coffee, and shrimp are exported.

UNITED STATES

REFORM COINAGE

1 New Peso = 1000 Old Pesos

KM# 546 5 CENTAVOS

1.5900 g., Stainless Steel, 15.58 mm. **Obv:** National arms, eagle left **Rev:** Value **Edge:** Plain

Date	Mintage	F	VF	XF	Unc	BU
2001Mo	34,811,000	—	—	0.15	0.20	0.25
2002Mo	14,901,000	—	—	0.15	0.20	0.25
2003	—	—	—	0.15	0.20	0.25
2004	—	—	—	0.15	0.20	0.25
2005	—	—	—	0.15	0.20	0.25
2006	—	—	—	0.15	0.20	0.25

KM# 547 10 CENTAVOS

2.0300 g., Stainless Steel, 17 mm. **Obv:** National arms, eagle left **Rev:** Value

Date	Mintage	F	VF	XF	Unc	BU
2001	618,061,000	—	—	0.20	0.25	0.30
2002	463,968,000	—	—	0.20	0.25	0.30
2003Mo	378,938,000	—	—	0.20	0.25	0.30
2004	393,705,000	—	—	0.20	0.25	0.30
2005	488,773,000	—	—	0.20	0.25	0.30
2006	473,104,000	—	—	0.20	0.25	0.30

KM# 548 20 CENTAVOS

Aluminum-Bronze, 19 mm. **Obv:** National arms, eagle left **Rev:** Value and date within 3/4 wreath **Shape:** 12-sided

Date	Mintage	F	VF	XF	Unc	BU
2001	234,360,000	—	—	0.25	0.35	0.40
2002Mo	229,256,000	—	—	0.25	0.35	0.40
2003Mo	149,518,000	—	—	0.25	0.35	0.40
2004	174,351,000	—	—	0.25	0.35	0.40
2005	204,444,000	—	—	0.25	0.35	0.40
2006	233,989,000	—	—	0.25	0.35	0.40

KM# 549 50 CENTAVOS

Aluminum-Bronze, 22 mm. **Obv:** National arms, eagle left **Rev:** Value and date within 1/2 designed wreath **Shape:** 12-sided

Date	Mintage	F	VF	XF	Unc	BU
2001	199,006,000	—	—	0.45	0.75	1.00
2002	94,552,000	—	—	0.45	0.75	1.00
2003Mo	124,522,000	—	—	0.45	0.75	1.00
2004	154,434,000	—	—	0.45	0.75	1.00
2005	179,304,000	—	—	0.45	0.75	1.00
2006	233,786,000	—	—	0.45	0.75	1.00

KM# 603 PESO

3.9500 g., Bi-Metallic Stainless-steel ring in Aluminum Bronze center, 21 mm. **Obv:** National arms, eagle left within circle **Rev:** Value and date within circle **Note:** Similar to KM#550 but without N.

Date	Mintage	F	VF	XF	Unc	BU
2001Mo	208,576,000	—	—	—	1.25	2.25
2002Mo	119,541,000	—	—	—	1.25	2.25
2003Mo	169,320,000	—	—	—	1.25	2.25
2004	208,611,000	—	—	—	1.25	2.25
2005	253,924,000	—	—	—	1.25	2.25
2006	289,717,000	—	—	—	1.25	2.25

KM# 604 2 PESOS

5.2100 g., Bi-Metallic Aluminum-Bronze center in Stainless Steel ring, 23 mm. **Obv:** National arms, eagle left within circle **Rev:** Value and date within center circle of assorted emblems **Note:** Similar to KM#551, but denomination without N.

Date	Mintage	F	VF	XF	Unc	BU
2001Mo	74,563,000	—	—	—	2.35	2.50
2002Mo	74,547,000	—	—	—	2.35	2.50
2003Mo	39,814,000	—	—	—	2.35	2.50
2004	89,496,000	—	—	—	2.35	2.50
2005	94,532,000	—	—	—	2.35	2.50
2006	143,919,000	—	—	—	2.35	2.50

KM# 651 5 PESOS

31.1710 g., 0.9990 Silver 1.0011 oz. ASW, 40 mm. **Series:** Endangered Wildlife **Obv:** National arms in center of past and present arms **Rev:** Manatee, value and date **Edge:** Reeded

Date	Mintage	F	VF	XF	Unc	BU
2001	50,000	—	—	—	35.00	—

KM# 653 5 PESOS

31.1710 g., 0.9990 Silver 1.0011 oz. ASW, 40 mm. **Subject:** Aguila Arpia **Obv:** National arms in center of past and present arms **Rev:** Crowned Harpy Eagle perched on branch

Date	Mintage	F	VF	XF	Unc	BU
2001	50,000	—	—	—	35.00	—

KM# 654 5 PESOS

31.1710 g., 0.9990 Silver 1.0011 oz. ASW, 40 mm. **Series:** Endangered Wildlife **Subject:** Oso Negro **Obv:** National arms in center of past and present arms **Rev:** Black bear, value and date

Date	Mintage	F	VF	XF	Unc	BU
2001	50,000	—	—	—	35.00	—

KM# 658 5 PESOS

31.1710 g., 0.9990 Silver 1.0011 oz. ASW, 40 mm. **Series:** Endangered Wildlife **Obv:** National arms in center of past and present arms **Rev:** Jaguar, value and date

Date	Mintage	F	VF	XF	Unc	BU
2001	50,000	—	—	—	35.00	—

KM# 659 5 PESOS

31.1710 g., 0.9990 Silver 1.0011 oz. ASW, 40 mm. **Series:** Endangered Wildlife **Obv:** National arms in center of past and present arms **Rev:** Prairie dog, value and date

Date	Mintage	F	VF	XF	Unc	BU
2001	50,000	—	—	—	35.00	—

KM# 660 5 PESOS

31.1710 g., 0.9990 Silver 1.0011 oz. ASW, 40 mm. **Series:** Endangered Wildlife **Obv:** National arms in center of past and present arms **Rev:** Volcano rabbit, value and date

Date	Mintage	F	VF	XF	Unc	BU
2001	50,000	—	—	—	35.00	—

KM# 605 5 PESOS

Bi-Metallic Aluminum-Bronze center in Stainless Steel ring, 25.5 mm. **Obv:** National arms, eagle left within circle **Rev:** Value within circle **Note:** Similar to KM#552 but denomination without N.

Date	Mintage	F	VF	XF	Unc	BU
2001Mo	79,169,000	—	—	3.00	4.00	5.00
2002Mo	34,754,000	—	—	3.00	4.00	5.00
2003Mo	54,676,000	—	—	3.00	4.00	5.00
2004	89,518,000	—	—	3.00	4.00	5.00
2005	94,482,000	—	—	3.00	4.00	5.00
2006	89,189,000	—	—	3.00	4.00	5.00

KM# 678 5 PESOS

27.0000 g., 0.9250 Silver 0.8029 oz. ASW, 40 mm. **Subject:** Ibero-America: Acapulco Galleon **Obv:** National arms in center of past and present arms **Rev:** Spanish galleon with Pacific Ocean background and trading scene in foreground **Edge:** Reeded

Date	Mintage	F	VF	XF	Unc	BU
2003Mo Proof	5,000	Value: 65.00				

KM# 765 5 PESOS

31.1035 g., 0.9250 Silver 0.9250 oz. ASW, 40 mm. **Subject:** Palacio de Bellas Artes **Obv:** Mexican Eagle and Snake **Rev:** Palace of Fine Arts **Edge:** Reeded

Date	Mintage	F	VF	XF	Unc	BU
2005Mo Proof	—	Value: 40.00				

KM# 769 5 PESOS

15.5518 g., 0.9990 Silver 0.4995 oz. ASW, 33 mm. **Subject:** Monetary Reform of 1905 **Obv:** Mexican Eagle and Snake **Rev:** Cap and rays coin design

Date	Mintage	F	VF	XF	Unc	BU
2005Mo Proof	—	Value: 30.00				

KM# 770 5 PESOS

31.1035 g., 0.9990 Silver 0.9990 oz. ASW, 40 mm. **Subject:** World Cup Soccer **Obv:** Mexican Eagle and Snake **Rev:** Mayan Pelota player and soccer ball

Date	Mintage	F	VF	XF	Unc	BU
2006Mo Proof	40,000	Value: 40.00				

KM# 805 5 PESOS

Silver **Obv:** Eagle on cactus **Rev:** Mayan ball game

Date	Mintage	F	VF	XF	Unc	BU
2006 Proof	—	Value: 55.00				

KM# 636 10 PESOS

10.3500 g., Bi-Metallic Copper-Nickel center in Brass ring, 28 mm. **Series:** Millennium **Obv:** National arms **Obv. Legend:** ESTADOS UNIDOS MEXICANOS **Rev:** Aztec carving **Edge:** Lettered **Edge Lettering:** ANO and date repeated 3 times

Date	Mintage	F	VF	XF	Unc	BU
2001Mo	44,768,000	—	—	—	5.00	6.50
2002Mo	44,721,000	—	—	—	5.00	6.50
2004Mo	74,739,000	—	—	—	5.00	6.50
2005Mo	64,635,000	—	—	—	5.00	6.50
2006Mo	84,480,000	—	—	—	5.00	6.50

KM# 739 10 PESOS

31.1040 g., 0.9990 Bi-Metallic 0.9990 oz., 39.9 mm. **Series:** First **Subject:** 180th Anniversary of Federation **Obv:** National arms **Obv. Legend:** ESTADOS UNIDOS MEXICANOS **Rev:** State arms **Rev. Legend:** ESTADO DE OAXACA **Edge:** Reeded

Date	Mintage	F	VF	XF	Unc	BU
2004 Proof	10,000	Value: 75.00				

KM# 766 10 PESOS

31.1035 g., 0.9990 Silver 0.9990 oz. ASW, 40 mm. **Subject:** Cervantes Festival **Obv:** Mexican Eagle and Snake **Rev:** Don Quixote **Edge:** Reeded

Date	Mintage	F	VF	XF	Unc	BU
2005Mo Proof	—	Value: 55.00				

KM# 768 10 PESOS

31.1035 g., 0.9990 Silver 0.9990 oz. ASW, 40 mm. **Subject:** 470th Anniversary - Mexico City Mint **Obv:** Mexican Eagle and Snake **Rev:** Antique coin press

Date	Mintage	F	VF	XF	Unc	BU
2005Mo Proof	—	Value: 45.00				

KM# 755 10 PESOS

31.1040 g., 0.9990 Silver 0.9990 oz. ASW, 40 mm. **Obv:** National arms **Rev:** Baja California del Norte arms

Date	Mintage	F	VF	XF	Unc	BU
2005 Proof	—	Value: 55.00				

KM# 763 10 PESOS

31.1040 g., 0.9990 Silver 0.9990 oz. ASW, 40 mm. **Obv:** National arms **Rev:** Benito Juarez **Edge:** Reeded

Date	Mintage	F	VF	XF	Unc	BU
2006Mo Proof	—	Value: 55.00				

KM# 637 20 PESOS

Bi-Metallic Copper-Nickel center within Brass ring, 32 mm. **Subject:** Xiuhtecuhtli **Obv:** National arms, eagle left within circle **Rev:** Aztec with torch within spiked circle

Date	Mintage	F	VF	XF	Unc	BU
2001	2,478,000	—	—	—	15.00	17.50

KM# 638 20 PESOS

Bi-Metallic Copper-Nickel center within Brass ring, 32 mm. **Obv:** National arms, eagle left within circle **Rev:** Head 1/4 right within circle

Date	Mintage	F	VF	XF	Unc	BU
2001	2,515,000	—	—	—	15.00	17.50

KM# 704 20 PESOS

62.4000 g., 0.9990 Silver 2.0041 oz. ASW, 48.1 mm. **Subject:** 400th Anniversary of Don Quijote de la Manchia **Obv:** National arms **Rev:** Skeletal figure horseback with spear galloping right **Edge:** Plain

Date	Mintage	F	VF	XF	Unc	BU
ND(2005)Mo Proof	10,000	Value: 85.00				

KM# 767 20 PESOS

62.4000 g., 0.9990 Silver 2.0041 oz. ASW, 48 mm. **Subject:** 80th Anniversary - Bank of Mexico **Obv:** National arms **Rev:** 100 Peso banknote design of 1925

Date	Mintage	F	VF	XF	Unc	BU
2005Mo	—	—	—	—	—	45.00
2005Mo Proof	—	Value: 90.00				

KM# 705 100 PESOS

33.7400 g., Bi-Metallic .925 Silver center in Aluminum-Bronze ring, 39 mm. **Subject:** 400th Anniversary of Don Quijote de la Manchia **Obv:** National arms **Obv. Legend:** ESTADOS UNIDOS MEXICANOS **Rev:** Sekeletal figure Horseback with spear galloping right **Edge:** Segmented reeding

Date	Mintage	F	VF	XF	Unc	BU
2005Mo	726,833	—	—	—	35.00	45.00
2005Mo Proof	3,761	Value: 75.00				

KM# 730 100 PESOS

33.8250 g., Bi-Metallic .925 Silver 20.1753g center in Aluminum-Bronze ring, 39.9 mm. **Subject:** Monetary Reform Centennial **Obv:** National arms **Rev:** Radiant Liberty Cap divides date above value within circle **Edge:** Segmented reeding

Date	Mintage	F	VF	XF	Unc	BU
2005Mo	49,716	—	—	—	35.00	45.00

KM# 731 100 PESOS

33.8250 g., Bi-Metallic .925 Silver 20.1753g center in Aluminum-Bronze ring, 39.9 mm. **Subject:** Mexico City Mint's 470th Anniversary **Obv:** National arms **Rev:** Screw press, value and date within circle **Edge:** Segmented reeding

Date	Mintage	F	VF	XF	Unc	BU
2005Mo	49,895	—	—	—	35.00	45.00

KM# 732 100 PESOS

33.8250 g., Bi-Metallic .925 Silver 20.1753g center in Aluminum-Bronze ring, 39.9 mm. **Subject:** Bank of Mexico's 80th Anniversary **Obv:** National arms **Rev:** Back design of the 1925 hundred peso note **Edge:** Segmented reeding

Date	Mintage	F	VF	XF	Unc	BU
2005Mo	49,712	—	—	—	35.00	45.00

KM# 680 10 PESOS

31.1040 g., 0.9990 Silver 0.9990 oz. ASW, 39.9 mm. **Series:** First **Subject:** 180th Anniversary of Federation **Obv:** National arms **Obv. Legend:** ESTADO UNIDOS MEXICANOS **Rev:** State arms **Rev. Legend:** ESTADO DE YUCATÁN **Edge:** Reeded

Date	Mintage	F	VF	XF	Unc	BU
2003Mo Proof	10,000	Value: 75.00				

KM# 683 10 PESOS

31.1040 g., 0.9990 Silver 0.9990 oz. ASW, 39.9 mm. **Series:** First **Subject:** 180th Anniversary of Federation **Obv:** National arms **Obv. Legend:** ESTADOS UNIDOS MEXICANOS **Rev:** State arms **Rev. Legend:** ESTADO DE TAMAULIPAS **Edge:** Reeded

Date	Mintage	F	VF	XF	Unc	BU
2004Mo Proof	10,000	Value: 75.00				

KM# 764 100 PESOS

33.7000 g., Bi-Metallic .925 Silver 20.1753g center in Aluminum-Bronze ring **Subject:** 200th Anniversary Birth of Benito Juarez Garcia **Obv:** National arms **Rev:** Bust 1/4 left within circle

Date	Mintage	F	VF	XF	Unc	BU
2006Mo	49,913	—	—	—	35.00	45.00

KM# 771 50000 PESOS

0.9990 Gold, 23 mm. **Subject:** World Cup Soccer **Obv:** Mexican Eagle and Snake **Rev:** Kneeling Mayan Pelota player and soccer ball

Date	Mintage	F	VF	XF	Unc	BU
2006Mo Proof	—	Value: 600				

REFORM COINAGE

State Commemoratives

KM# 679 10 PESOS

31.1040 g., 0.9990 Silver 0.9990 oz. ASW, 39.9 mm. **Series:** First **Subject:** 180th Anniversary of Federation **Obv:** National arms **Obv. Legend:** ESTADOS UNIDOS MEXICANOS **Rev:** State Arms **Rev. Legend:** ESTADO DE ZACATECAS **Edge:** Reeded

Date	Mintage	F	VF	XF	Unc	BU
2003Mo Proof	10,000	Value: 75.00				

KM# 681 10 PESOS

31.1040 g., 0.9990 Silver 0.9990 oz. ASW, 39.9 mm. **Series:** First **Subject:** 180th Anniversary of Federation **Obv:** National arms **Obv. Legend:** ESTADOS UNIDOS MEXICANOS **Rev:** State arms **Rev. Legend:** ESTADO DE VERACRUZ-LLAVE **Edge:** Reeded

Date	Mintage	F	VF	XF	Unc	BU
2003Mo Proof	10,000	Value: 75.00				

KM# 682 10 PESOS

31.1040 g., 0.9990 Silver 0.9990 oz. ASW, 39.9 mm. **Series:** First **Subject:** 180th Anniversary of Frederation **Obv:** National arms **Obv. Legend:** ESTADOS UNIDOS MEXICANOS **Rev:** State arms **Rev. Legend:** ESTADO DE TLAXCALA **Edge:** Reeded

Date	Mintage	F	VF	XF	Unc	BU
2003Mo Proof	10,000	Value: 75.00				

KM# 684 10 PESOS

31.1040 g., 0.9990 Silver 0.9990 oz. ASW, 39.9 mm. **Series:** First **Subject:** 180th Anniversary of Federation **Obv:** National arms **Obv. Legend:** ESTADOS UNIDOS DE MEXICANOS **Rev:** State arms **Rev. Legend:** ESTADO DE TABASCO **Edge:** Reeded

Date	Mintage	F	VF	XF	Unc	BU
2004Mo Proof	10,000	Value: 75.00				

KM# 685 10 PESOS

31.1040 g., 0.9990 Silver 0.9990 oz. ASW, 39.9 mm. **Series:** First **Subject:** 180th Anniversary of Federation **Obv:** National arms **Obv. Legend:** ESTADOS UNIDOS MEXICANOS **Rev:** State arms **Rev. Legend:** ESTADO DE SONORA **Edge:** Reeded **Note:** Mexican States: Sonora

Date	Mintage	F	VF	XF	Unc	BU
2004Mo Proof	10,000	Value: 75.00				

KM# 686 10 PESOS
31.1040 g., 0.9990 Silver 0.9990 oz. ASW, 39.9 mm. **Series:** First **Subject:** 180th Anniversary of Federation **Obv:** National arms **Obv. Legend:** ESTADOS UNIDOS DE MEXICANOS **Rev:** State arms **Rev. Legend:** ESTADO DE SINALOA **Edge:** Reeded **Note:** Mexican States: Sinaloa

Date	Mintage	F	VF	XF	Unc	BU
2004Mo Proof	10,000	Value: 75.00				

KM# 687 10 PESOS
31.1040 g., 0.9990 Silver 0.9990 oz. ASW, 39.9 mm. **Series:** First **Subject:** 180th Anniversary of Federation **Obv:** National arms **Obv. Legend:** ESTADOS UNIDOS MEXICANOS **Rev:** State arms **Rev. Legend:** ESTADO DE SAN LUIS POTOSÍ **Edge:** Reeded

Date	Mintage	F	VF	XF	Unc	BU
2004Mo Proof	10,000	Value: 75.00				

KM# 735 10 PESOS
31.1040 g., 0.9990 Silver 0.9990 oz. ASW, 39.9 mm. **Series:** First **Subject:** 180th Anniversary of Federation **Obv:** National arms **Obv. Legend:** ESTADOS UNIDOS MEXICANOS **Rev:** State arms **Rev. Legend:** ESTADO DE QUINTANA ROO

Date	Mintage	F	VF	XF	Unc	BU
2004 Proof	10,000	Value: 75.00				

KM# 733 10 PESOS
31.1040 g., 0.9990 Silver 0.9990 oz. ASW, 39.9 mm. **Series:** First **Subject:** 180th Anniversary of Federation **Obv:** National arms **Obv. Legend:** ESTADOS UNIDOS MEXICANOS **Rev:** State arms **Rev. Legend:** ESTADO DE QUERÉTARO ARTEAGA **Edge:** Reeded

Date	Mintage	F	VF	XF	Unc	BU
2004 Proof	10,000	Value: 75.00				

KM# 737 10 PESOS
31.1040 g., 0.9990 Silver 0.9990 oz. ASW, 39.9 mm. **Series:** First **Subject:** 180th Anniversary of Federation **Obv:** National arms **Obv. Legend:** ESTADOS UNIDOS MEXICANOS **Rev:** State arms **Rev. Legend:** ESTADO DE PUEBLA **Edge:** Reeded

Date	Mintage	F	VF	XF	Unc	BU
2004 Proof	10,000	Value: 75.00				

KM# 741 10 PESOS
31.1040 g., 0.9990 Silver 0.9990 oz. ASW, 39.9 mm. **Series:** First **Subject:** 180th Anniversary of Federation **Obv:** National arms **Obv. Legend:** ESTADOS UNIDOS MEXICANOS **Rev:** State arms **Rev. Legend:** ESTADO DE NUEVO LEÓN **Edge:** Reeded

Date	Mintage	F	VF	XF	Unc	BU
2004 Proof	10,000	Value: 75.00				

KM# 743 10 PESOS
31.1040 g., 0.9990 Silver 0.9990 oz. ASW, 39.9 mm. **Series:** First **Subject:** 180th Anniversary of Federation **Obv:** National arms **Obv. Legend:** ESTADOS UNIDOS MEXICANOS **Rev:** State arms **Rev. Legend:** ESTADO DE NAYARIT **Edge:** Reeded

Date	Mintage	F	VF	XF	Unc	BU
2004 Proof	10,000	Value: 75.00				

KM# 745 10 PESOS
31.1040 g., 0.9990 Silver 0.9990 oz. ASW, 39.9 mm. **Series:** First **Subject:** 180th Anniversary of Federation **Obv:** National arms **Obv. Legend:** ESTADOS UNIDOS MEXICANOS **Rev:** State arms **Rev. Legend:** ESTADO DE MORELOS **Edge:** Reeded

Date	Mintage	F	VF	XF	Unc	BU
2004 Proof	10,000	Value: 75.00				

KM# 796 10 PESOS
31.1040 g., 0.9990 Silver 0.9990 oz. ASW, 39.9 mm. **Series:** First **Subject:** 180th Anniversary of Federation **Obv:** National arms **Obv. Legend:** ESTADOS UNIDOS MEXICANOS **Rev:** State arms **Rev. Legend:** ESTADO DE MICHOACÁN DE OCAMPO **Edge:** Reeded

Date	Mintage	F	VF	XF	Unc	BU
2004Mo Proof	10,000	Value: 75.00				

KM# 747 10 PESOS
31.1040 g., 0.9990 Silver 0.9990 oz. ASW, 39.9 mm. **Series:** First **Subject:** 180th Anniversary of Federation **Obv:** National arms **Obv. Legend:** ESTADOS UNIDOS MEXICANOS **Rev:** State arms **Rev. Legend:** ESTADO DE MÉXICO **Edge:** Reeded

Date	Mintage	F	VF	XF	Unc	BU
2004 Proof	10,000	Value: 75.00				

KM# 749 10 PESOS
31.1040 g., 0.9990 Silver 0.9990 oz. ASW, 39.9 mm. **Series:** First **Subject:** 180th Anniversary of Federation **Obv:** National arms **Obv. Legend:** ESTADOS UNIDOS MEXICANOS **Rev:** State arms **Rev. Legend:** ESTADO DE JALISCO **Edge:** Reeded

Date	Mintage	F	VF	XF	Unc	BU
2004 Proof	10,000	Value: 75.00				

KM# 711 10 PESOS
31.1040 g., 0.9990 Silver 0.9990 oz. ASW, 39.9 mm. **Series:** First **Subject:** 180th Anniversary of Federation **Obv:** National arms **Obv. Legend:** ESTADOS UNIDOS MEXICANOS **Rev:** State arms **Rev. Legend:** ESTADO DE HIDALGO **Edge:** Reeded

Date	Mintage	F	VF	XF	Unc	BU
2005Mo Proof	10,000	Value: 75.00				

KM# 710 10 PESOS
31.1040 g., 0.9990 Silver 0.9990 oz. ASW, 39.9 mm. **Series:** First **Subject:** 180th Anniversary of Federation **Obv:** National arms **Obv. Legend:** ESTADOS UNIDOS MEXICANOS **Rev:** State arms **Rev. Legend:** ESTADO DE GUERRERO **Edge:** Reeded

Date	Mintage	F	VF	XF	Unc	BU
2005Mo Proof	10,000	Value: 75.00				

KM# 709 10 PESOS
31.1040 g., 0.9990 Silver 0.9990 oz. ASW, 39.9 mm. **Series:** First **Subject:** 180th Anniversary of Federation **Obv:** National arms **Obv. Legend:** ESTADOS UNIDOS MEXICANOS **Rev:** State arms **Rev. Legend:** ESTADO DE GUANAJUATO **Edge:** Reeded

Date	Mintage	F	VF	XF	Unc	BU
2005Mo Proof	10,000	Value: 75.00				

KM# 708 10 PESOS
31.1040 g., 0.9990 Silver 0.9990 oz. ASW, 39.9 mm. **Series:** First **Subject:** 180th Anniversary of Federation **Obv:** National arms **Obv. Legend:** ESTADOS UNIDOS MEXICANOS **Rev:** State arms **Rev. Legend:** ESTADO DE DURANGO **Edge:** Reeded

Date	Mintage	F	VF	XF	Unc	BU
2005Mo Proof	10,000	Value: 75.00				

KM# 707 10 PESOS
31.1040 g., 0.9990 Silver 0.9990 oz. ASW, 39.9 mm. **Series:** First **Subject:** 180th Anniversary of Federation **Obv:** National arms **Obv. Legend:** ESTADOS UNIDOS MEXICANOS **Rev:** Federal District arms **Rev. Legend:** DISTRITO FEDERAL **Edge:** Reeded

Date	Mintage	F	VF	XF	Unc	BU
2005Mo Proof	10,000	Value: 75.00				

KM# 753 10 PESOS
31.1040 g., 0.9990 Silver 0.9990 oz. ASW, 39.9 mm. **Series:** First **Subject:** 180th Anniversary of Federation **Obv:** National arms **Obv. Legend:** ESTADOS UNIDOS MEXICANOS **Rev:** State arms **Rev. Legend:** ESTADO DE CHIHUAHUA **Edge:** Reeded

Date	Mintage	F	VF	XF	Unc	BU
2005 Proof	10,000	Value: 75.00				

KM# 706 10 PESOS
31.1040 g., 0.9990 Silver 0.9990 oz. ASW, 39.9 mm. **Series:** First **Subject:** 180th Anniversary of Federation **Obv:** National arms **Obv. Legend:** ESTADOS UNIDOS MEXICANOS **Rev:** State arms **Rev. Legend:** ESTADO DE CHIAPAS **Edge:** Reeded

Date	Mintage	F	VF	XF	Unc	BU
2005Mo Proof	10,000	Value: 75.00				

KM# 728 10 PESOS
31.1040 g., 0.9990 Silver 0.9990 oz. ASW, 39.9 mm. **Series:** First **Subject:** 180th Anniversary of Federation **Obv:** National arms **Obv. Legend:** ESTADOS UNIDOS MEXICANOS **Rev:** State arms **Rev. Legend:** ESTADO DE COLIMA **Edge:** Reeded

Date	Mintage	F	VF	XF	Unc	BU
2005Mo Proof	10,000	Value: 75.00				

KM# 751 10 PESOS
31.1040 g., 0.9990 Silver 0.9990 oz. ASW, 39.9 mm. **Series:** First **Subject:** 180th Anniversary of Federation **Obv:** National arms **Obv. Legend:** ESTADOS UNIDOS MEXICANOS **Rev:** State arms **Rev. Legend:** ESTADO DE COAHUILA DE ZARAGOZA **Edge:** Reeded

Date	Mintage	F	VF	XF	Unc	BU
2005 Proof	10,000	Value: 75.00				

KM# 726 10 PESOS
31.1040 g., 0.9990 Silver 0.9990 oz. ASW, 39.9 mm. **Series:** First **Subject:** 180th Anniversary of Federation **Obv:** National arms **Obv. Legend:** ESTADOS UNIDOS MEXICANOS **Rev:** State arms **Rev. Legend:** ESTADO DE CAMPECHE **Edge:** Reeded

Date	Mintage	F	VF	XF	Unc	BU
2005Mo Proof	10,000	Value: 75.00				

KM# 724 10 PESOS
31.1040 g., 0.9990 Silver 0.9990 oz. ASW, 39.9 mm. **Series:** First **Subject:** 180th Anniversary of Federation **Obv:** National arms **Obv. Legend:** ESTADOS UNIDOS MEXICANOS **Rev:** State arms **Rev. Legend:** ESTADO DE BAJA CALIFORNIA SUR **Edge:** Reeded

Date	Mintage	F	VF	XF	Unc	BU
2005Mo Proof	10,000	Value: 75.00				

KM# 722 10 PESOS
31.1040 g., 0.9990 Silver 0.9990 oz. ASW, 39.9 mm. **Series:** First **Subject:** 180th Anniversary of Federation **Obv:** National arms **Obv. Legend:** ESTADOS UNIDOS MEXICANOS **Rev:** State arms **Rev. Legend:** ESTADO DE BAJA CALIFORNIA **Edge:** Reeded

Date	Mintage	F	VF	XF	Unc	BU
2005Mo Proof	10,000	Value: 75.00				

KM# 720 10 PESOS
31.1040 g., 0.9990 Silver 0.9990 oz. ASW, 39.9 mm. **Series:** First **Subject:** 180th Anniversary of Federation **Obv:** National arms **Obv. Legend:** ESTADOS UNIDOS MEXICANOS **Rev:** State arms **Rev. Legend:** ESTADO DE AGUASCALIENTES **Edge:** Reeded

Date	Mintage	F	VF	XF	Unc	BU
2005Mo Proof	10,000	Value: 75.00				

KM# 718 10 PESOS
31.1040 g., 0.9990 Silver 0.9990 oz. ASW, 40 mm. **Series:** Second **Obv:** National arms **Obv. Legend:** ESTADOS UNIDOS MEXICANOS **Rev:** Facade of the San Marcos garden above sculpture of national emblem at left, San Antonio Temple at right **Rev. Legend:** AGUASCALIENTES **Edge:** Reeded

Date	Mintage	F	VF	XF	Unc	BU
2005Mo Proof	6,000	Value: 75.00				

KM# 757 10 PESOS
31.1040 g., 0.9990 Silver 0.9990 oz. ASW, 40 mm. **Series:** Second **Obv:** National arms **Obv. Legend:** ESTADOS UNIDOS MEXICANOS **Rev:** Rams head, mountain outline in background **Rev. Legend:** BAJA CALIFORNIA - GOBIERNO DEL ESTADO **Edge:** Reeded

Date	Mintage	F	VF	XF	Unc	BU
2005Mo Proof	6,000	Value: 75.00				

KM# 761 10 PESOS
31.1040 g., 0.9990 Silver 0.9990 oz. ASW, 40 mm. **Series:** Second **Obv:** National arms **Obv. Legend:** ESTADOS UNIDOS MEXICANOS **Rev:** Outlined map of peninsula at center, cave painting of deer behind, cactus at right **Rev. Legend:** ESTADO DE BAJA CALIFORNIA SUR **Edge:** Reeded

Date	Mintage	F	VF	XF	Unc	BU
2006Mo Proof	6,000	Value: 75.00				

KM# 759 10 PESOS
31.1040 g., 0.9990 Silver 0.9990 oz. ASW, 40 mm. **Series:** Second **Obv:** National arms **Obv. Legend:** ESTADOS UNIDOS MEXICANOS **Rev:** Jade mask - Calakmul, Campeche **Rev. Legend:** ESTADO DE CAMPECHE **Edge:** Reeded

Date	Mintage	F	VF	XF	Unc	BU
2006Mo Proof	6,000	Value: 75.00				

KM# 780 10 PESOS
31.1040 g., 0.9990 Silver 0.9990 oz. ASW, 40 mm. **Series:** Second **Obv:** National arms **Obv. Legend:** ESTADOS UNIDOS MEXICANOS **Rev:** Outlined map with turtle, mine cart above grapes at center, Friendship dam above Christ of the Nodas at left, chimneys above crucibles and bell tower of Santiago's cathedral at right **Rev. Inscription:** COAHUILA DE ZARAGOZA **Edge:** Reeded

Date	Mintage	F	VF	XF	Unc	BU
2006Mo Proof	6,000	Value: 75.00				

KM# 776 10 PESOS
31.1040 g., 0.9990 Silver 0.9990 oz. ASW, 40 mm. **Series:** Second **Obv:** National arms **Obv. Legend:** ESTADOS UNIDOS MEXICANOS **Rev:** State arms at lower center, Nevado de Colima and Volcan de Fuego volcanos in background **Rev. Legend:** *Colima* **Rev. Inscription:** GENEROSO **Edge:** Reeded

Date	Mintage	F	VF	XF	Unc	BU
2006Mo Proof	6,000	Value: 75.00				

KM# 772 10 PESOS
31.1040 g., 0.9990 Silver 0.9990 oz. ASW, 40 mm. **Series:** Second **Obv:** National arms **Obv. Legend:** ESTADOS UNIDOS MEXICANOS **Rev:** Head of Pakal, ancient Mayan king, Palenque **Rev. Legend:** ESTADO DE CHIAPAS - CABEZA MAYA DEL REY PAKAL, PALENQUE **Edge:** Reeded

Date	Mintage	F	VF	XF	Unc	BU
2006Mo Proof	6,000	Value: 75.00				

KM# 774 10 PESOS
31.1040 g., 0.9990 Silver 0.9990 oz. ASW, 40 mm. **Series:** Second **Obv:** National arms **Obv. Legend:** ESTADOS UNIDOS MEXICANOS **Rev:** Angel of Liberty **Rev. Legend:** MÉXICO - ANGEL DE LA LIBERTAD, CHIHUAHUA **Edge:** Reeded

Date	Mintage	F	VF	XF	Unc	BU
2006Mo Proof	6,000	Value: 75.00				

KM# 778 10 PESOS
31.1040 g., 0.9990 Silver 0.9990 oz. ASW, 40 mm. **Series:** Second **Obv:** National arms **Obv. Legend:** ESTADOS UNIDOS MEXICANOS **Rev:** National Palace **Rev. Legend:** DISTRITO FEDERAL - ANTIGUO AYUNTAMIENTO **Edge:** Reeded

Date	Mintage	F	VF	XF	Unc	BU
2006Mo Proof	6,000	Value: 75.00				

KM# 786 10 PESOS
31.1040 g., 0.9990 Silver 0.9990 oz. ASW, 40 mm. **Series:** Second **Obv:** National arms **Obv. Legend:** ESTADOS UNIDOS MEXICANOS **Rev:** Tree **Rev. Legend:** PRIMERA RESERVA NACIONAL FORESTAL - DURANGO **Edge:** Reeded

Date	Mintage	F	VF	XF	Unc	BU
2006Mo Proof	6,000	Value: 75.00				

KM# 788 10 PESOS
31.1040 g., 0.9990 Silver 0.9990 oz. ASW, 40 mm. **Series:** Second **Obv:** National arms **Obv. Legend:** ESTADOS UNIDOS MEXICANOS **Rev:** State arms at center, statue of Miguel Hidalgo at left, monument to Pípila at lower right **Rev. Inscription:** *Guanajuato* **Edge:** Reeded

Date	Mintage	F	VF	XF	Unc	BU
2006Mo Proof	6,000	Value: 75.00				

KM# 790 10 PESOS
31.1040 g., 0.9990 Silver 0.9990 oz. ASW, 40 mm. **Series:** Second **Obv:** National arms **Obv. Legend:** ESTADOS UNIDOS MEXICANOS **Rev:** Stylized portrait of Vicente Guerrero at left, church of Taxco at upper center, Acapulco's la Quebrada with diver above Christmas Eve flower and mask **Rev. Legend:** GUERRERO **Edge:** Reeded

Date	Mintage	F	VF	XF	Unc	BU
2006Mo Proof	6,000	Value: 75.00				

KM# 792 10 PESOS
31.1040 g., 0.9990 Silver 0.9990 oz. ASW, 40 mm. **Series:** Second **Obv:** National arms **Obv. Legend:** ESTADOS UNIDOS MEXICANOS **Rev:** Monument of Pachuca Hidalgo **Rev. Inscription:** *RELOJ / MONUMENTAL / DE / PACHUCA / HIDALGO - La / Bella / Airosa* **Edge:** Reeded

Date	Mintage	F	VF	XF	Unc	BU
2006Mo Proof	6,000	Value: 75.00				

KM# 794 10 PESOS
31.1040 g., 0.9990 Silver 0.9990 oz. ASW, 40 mm. **Series:** Second **Obv:** National arms **Obv. Legend:** ESTADOS UNIDOS MEXICANOS **Rev:** Hospicio Cabañas orphanage **Rev. Legend:** ESTADO DE JALISCCO **Edge:** Reeded

Date	Mintage	F	VF	XF	Unc	BU
2006Mo Proof	6,000	Value: 75.00				

KM# 830 10 PESOS
31.1040 g., 0.9990 Silver 0.9990 oz. ASW, 40 mm. **Series:** Second **Obv:** National arms **Obv. Legend:** ESTADOS UNIDOS MEXICANOS **Rev:** Pyramid de la Loona (Moon) **Rev. Legend:** ESTADO DE MÉXICO **Edge:** Reeded

Date	Mintage	F	VF	XF	Unc	BU
2006Mo Proof	6,000	Value: 75.00				

KM# 831 10 PESOS
31.1040 g., 0.9990 Silver 0.9990 oz. ASW, 40 mm. **Series:** Second **Obv:** National arms **Obv. Legend:** ESTADOS UNIDOS MEXICANOS **Rev:** Four Monarch butterflies **Rev. Legend:** ESTADO DE MICHOACÁN **Edge:** Reeded

Date	Mintage	F	VF	XF	Unc	BU
2006Mo Proof	6,000	Value: 75.00				

KM# 832 10 PESOS
31.1040 g., 0.9990 Silver 0.9990 oz. ASW, 40 mm. **Series:** Second **Obv:** National arms **Obv. Legend:** ESTADOS UNIDOS MEXICANOS **Rev:** 1/2 length figure of Chinelo (local dancer) at right, Palacio de Cortes in background **Rev. Inscription:** ESTADO DE / MORELOS **Edge:** Reeded

Date	Mintage	F	VF	XF	Unc	BU
2006Mo Proof	6,000	Value: 75.00				

KM# 833 10 PESOS
31.1040 g., 0.9990 Silver 0.9990 oz. ASW, 40 mm. **Series:** Second **Obv:** National arms **Obv. Legend:** ESTADOS UNIDOS MEXICANOS **Rev:** Isle de Mexcaltitlán **Rev. Legend:** ESTADO DE NAYARIT **Edge:** Reeded

Date	Mintage	F	VF	XF	Unc	BU
2007Mo Proof	6,000	Value: 75.00				

KM# 834 10 PESOS
31.1040 g., 0.9990 Silver 0.9990 oz. ASW, 40 mm. **Series:** Second **Obv:** National arms **Obv. Legend:** ESTADOS UNIDOS MEXICANOS **Rev:** Old foundry in Pargue Fundidora (public park) at right, Cerro de la Silla (Saddle Hill) in background **Rev. Legend:** ESTADO DE NUEVO LEÓN **Edge:** Reeded

Date	Mintage	F	VF	XF	Unc	BU
2007Mo Proof	6,000	Value: 75.00				

KM# 835 10 PESOS
31.1040 g., 0.9990 Silver 0.9990 oz. ASW, 40 mm. **Series:** Second **Obv:** National arms **Obv. Legend:** ESTADOS UNIDOS MEXICANOS **Rev:** Teatro Macedonio Alcala (theater) **Rev. Legend:** OAXACA **Edge:** Reeded

Date	Mintage	F	VF	XF	Unc	BU
2007Mo Proof	6,000	Value: 75.00				

KM# 836 10 PESOS
31.1040 g., 0.9990 Silver 0.9990 oz. ASW, 40 mm. **Series:** Second **Obv:** National arms **Obv. Legend:** ESTADOS UNIDOS MEXICANOS **Rev:** Talavera porcelain dish **Rev. Legend:** ESTADO DE PUEBLA **Edge:** Reeded

Date	Mintage	F	VF	XF	Unc	BU
2007Mo Proof	6,000	Value: 75.00				

KM# 837 10 PESOS
31.1040 g., 0.9990 Silver 0.9990 oz. ASW, 40 mm. **Series:** Second **Obv:** National arms **Obv. Legend:** ESTADOS UNIDOS MEXICANOS **Rev:** Mask at left, rays above state arms at center, Mayan ruins at right **Rev. Legend:** QUINTANA ROO **Edge:** Reeded

Date	Mintage	F	VF	XF	Unc	BU
2007Mo Proof	6,000	Value: 75.00				

KM# 838 10 PESOS
31.1040 g., 0.9990 Silver 0.9990 oz. ASW, 40 mm. **Series:** Second **Obv:** National arms **Obv. Legend:** ESTADOS UNIDOS MEXICANOS **Rev:** Acueduct of Querétaro at left, church of Santa Rosa de Viterbo at right **Rev. Legend:** ESTADO DE QUERÉTARO ARTEAGA **Edge:** Reeded

Date	Mintage	F	VF	XF	Unc	BU
2007Mo Proof	6,000	Value: 75.00				

KM# 839 10 PESOS
31.1040 g., Silver, 40 mm. **Series:** Second **Obv:** National arms **Obv. Legend:** ESTADOS UNIDOS MEXICANOS **Rev:** Facade of Caja Real **Rev. Legend:** • SAN LUIS POTOSÍ • **Edge:** Reeded

Date	Mintage	F	VF	XF	Unc	BU
2007Mo Proof	6,000	Value: 75.00				

KM# 840 10 PESOS
31.1040 g., 0.9990 Silver 0.9990 oz. ASW, 40 mm. **Series:** Second **Obv:** National arms **Obv. Legend:** ESTADOS UNIDOS MEXICANOS **Rev:** Shield on pile of cactus fruits **Rev. Legend:** ESTADO DE SINALOA - LUGAR DE PITAHAYAS **Edge:** Reeded

Date	Mintage	F	VF	XF	Unc	BU
2007Mo Proof	6,000	Value: 75.00				

KM# 841 10 PESOS
31.1040 g., 0.9990 Silver 0.9990 oz. ASW, 40 mm. **Series:** Second **Obv:** National arms **Obv. Legend:** ESTADOS UNIDOS MEXICANOS **Rev:** Local in Dance of the Deer at left, cactus at right, mountains in background **Rev. Legend:** ESTADO DE SONORA **Edge:** Reeded

Date	Mintage	F	VF	XF	Unc	BU
2007Mo Proof	6,000	Value: 75.00				

KM# 842 10 PESOS
31.1040 g., 0.9990 Silver 0.9990 oz. ASW, 40 mm. **Series:** Second **Obv:** National arms **Obv. Legend:** ESTADOS UNIDOS MEXICANOS **Rev:** Fuente de los Pescadores (fisherman fountain) at lower left, giant head from the Olmec-pre-Hispanic culture at right, Planetario Tabasco in background **Rev. Legend:** TABASCO **Edge:** Reeded

Date	Mintage	F	VF	XF	Unc	BU
2007Mo Proof	6,000	Value: 75.00				

KM# 843 10 PESOS
31.1040 g., 0.9990 Silver 0.9990 oz. ASW, 40 mm. **Series:** Second **Obv:** National arms **Obv. Legend:** ESTADOS UNIDOS MEXICANOS **Rev:** Ridge - Cerro Del Bernal, Gonzáles **Rev. Legend:** TAMAULIPAS **Edge:** Reeded

Date	Mintage	F	VF	XF	Unc	BU
2007Mo Proof	6,000	Value: 75.00				

KM# 844 10 PESOS
31.1040 g., 0.9990 Silver 0.9990 oz. ASW, 40 mm. **Series:** Second **Obv:** National arms **Obv. Legend:** ESTADOS UNIDOS MEXICANOS **Rev:** Basilica de Ocotlán at left, state arms above Capilla Abierta, Plaza de Toros Ranchero Aguilar below, Exconvento de San Francisco at right **Rev. Legend:** ESTADO DE TLAXCALA **Edge:** Reeded

Date	Mintage	F	VF	XF	Unc	BU
2007Mo Proof	6,000	Value: 75.00				

KM# 845 10 PESOS
31.1040 g., 0.9990 Silver 0.9990 oz. ASW, 40 mm. **Series:** Second **Obv:** National arms **Obv. Legend:** ESTADOS UNIDOS MEXICANOS **Rev:** Pyramid of El Tajín **Rev. Legend:** • VERACRUZ • - • DE IGNACIO DE LA LLAVE • **Edge:** Reeded

Date	Mintage	F	VF	XF	Unc	BU
2007Mo Proof	6,000	Value: 75.00				

KM# 846 10 PESOS
31.1030 g., 0.9990 Silver 0.9989 oz. ASW, 40 mm. **Series:** Second **Obv:** National arms **Obv. Legend:** ESTADOS UNIDOS MEXICANOS **Rev:** Stylized pyramid of Chichén-Itzá **Rev. Legend:** Castillo de Chichén Itzá **Rev. Inscription:** YUCATÁN **Edge:** Reeded

Date	Mintage	F	VF	XF	Unc	BU
2007Mo Proof	6,000	Value: 75.00				

KM# 847 10 PESOS
31.1040 g., 0.9990 Silver 0.9990 oz. ASW, 40 mm. **Series:** Second **Obv:** National arms **Obv. Legend:** ESTADOS UNIDOS MEXICANOS **Rev:** Cable car above Monumento al Minero at left, Catedral de Zacatecas at center right **Rev. Legend:** Zacatecas **Edge:** Reeded

Date	Mintage	F	VF	XF	Unc	BU
2007Mo Proof	6,000	Value: 75.00				

KM# 688 100 PESOS
33.9400 g., Bi-Metallic .925 Silver 20.1753g center in Aluminum-Bronze ring, 39.04 mm. **Series:** First **Subject:** 180th Anniversary of Federation **Obv:** National arms **Obv. Legend:** ESTADOS UNIDOS MEXICANOS **Rev:** State arms **Rev. Legend:** ESTADO DE ZACATECAS **Edge:** Segmented reeding

Date	Mintage	F	VF	XF	Unc	BU
2003Mo	244,900	—	—	—	35.00	45.00

KM# 696 100 PESOS
29.1690 g., Bi-Metallic .999 Gold 17.154g center in .999 Silver 12.015g ring, 34.5 mm. **Series:** First **Subject:** 180th Anniversary of Federation **Obv:** National arms **Obv. Legend:** ESTADOS UNIDOS MEXICANOS **Rev:** State arms **Rev. Legend:** ESTADO DE ZACATECAS **Edge:** Segmented reeding

Date	Mintage	F	VF	XF	Unc	BU
2003Mo Proof	1,000	Value: 775				

KM# 689 100 PESOS
33.9400 g., Bi-Metallic .925 Silver 20.1753g center in Aluminum-Bronze ring, 39.04 mm. **Series:** First **Subject:** 180th Anniversary of Federation **Obv:** National arms **Obv. Legend:** ESTADOS UNIDOS MEXICANOS **Rev:** State arms **Rev. Legend:** ESTADO DE YUCATÁN **Edge:** Segmented reeding

Date	Mintage	F	VF	XF	Unc	BU
2003Mo	235,763	—	—	—	35.00	45.00

KM# 697 100 PESOS
29.1690 g., Bi-Metallic .999 Gold 17.154g center in .999 Silver 12.015g ring, 34.5 mm. **Series:** First **Subject:** 180th Anniversary of Federation **Obv:** National arms **Obv. Legend:** ESTADOS UNIDOS MEXICANOS **Rev:** State arms **Rev. Legend:** ESTADO DE YUCATÁN **Edge:** Segmented reeding

Date	Mintage	F	VF	XF	Unc	BU
2003Mo Proof	1,000	Value: 775				

KM# 690 100 PESOS
33.9400 g., Bi-Metallic .925 Silver 20.1753g center in Aluminum-Bronze ring, 39.04 mm. **Series:** First **Subject:** 180th Anniversary of Federation **Obv:** National arms **Obv. Legend:** ESTADOS UNIDOS MEXICANOS **Rev:** State arms **Rev. Legend:** ESTADO DE VERACRUZ-LLAVE **Edge:** Segmented reeding

Date	Mintage	F	VF	XF	Unc	BU
2003Mo	248,810	—	—	—	35.00	45.00

KM# 698 100 PESOS

29.1690 g., Bi-Metallic .999 Gold 17.154g center in .999 Silver 12.015g ring, 34.5 mm. **Series:** First **Subject:** 180th Anniversary of Federation **Obv:** National arms **Obv. Legend:** ESTADOS UNIDOS MEXICANOS **Rev:** State arms **Rev. Legend:** ESTADO DE VERACRUZ-LLAVE **Edge:** Segmented reeding

Date	Mintage	F	VF	XF	Unc	BU
2003Mo Proof	1,000	Value: 775				

KM# 691 100 PESOS

33.9400 g., Bi-Metallic .925 Silver 20.1753g center in Aluminum-Bronze ring, 39.9 mm. **Series:** First **Subject:** 180th Anniversary of Federation **Obv:** National arms **Obv. Legend:** ESTADOS UNIDOS MEXICANOS **Rev:** State arms **Rev. Legend:** ESTADO DE TLAXCALA **Edge:** Segmented reeding

Date	Mintage	F	VF	XF	Unc	BU
2003Mo	248,976	—	—	—	35.00	45.00

KM# 699 100 PESOS

29.1690 g., Bi-Metallic .999 Gold 17.154g center in .999 Silver 12.015g ring, 34.5 mm. **Series:** First **Subject:** 180th Anniversary of Federation **Obv:** National arms **Obv. Legend:** ESTADOS UNIDOS MEXICANOS **Rev:** State arms **Rev. Legend:** ESTADO DE TLAXCALA **Edge:** Segmented reeding

Date	Mintage	F	VF	XF	Unc	BU
2003Mo Proof	1,000	Value: 775				

KM# 692 100 PESOS

33.9400 g., Bi-Metallic .925 Silver 20.1753g center in Aluminum-Bronze ring, 39.04 mm. **Series:** First **Subject:** 180th Anniversary of Federation **Obv:** National arms **Obv. Legend:** ESTADOS UNIDOS MEXICANOS **Rev:** State arms **Rev. Legend:** ESTADO DE TAMAULIPAS **Edge:** Segmented reeding

Date	Mintage	F	VF	XF	Unc	BU
2004Mo	249,398	—	—	—	35.00	45.00

KM# 700 100 PESOS

29.1690 g., Bi-Metallic .999 Gold 17.154g center in .999 Silver 12.015g ring, 34.5 mm. **Series:** First **Subject:** 180th Anniversary of Federation **Obv:** National arms **Obv. Legend:** ESTADOS UNIDOS MEXICANOS **Rev:** State arms **Rev. Legend:** ESTADO DE TAMAULIPAS **Edge:** Segmented reeding

Date	Mintage	F	VF	XF	Unc	BU
2004Mo Proof	1,000	Value: 775				

KM# 693 100 PESOS

33.9400 g., Bi-Metallic .925 Silver 20.1753g center in Aluminum-Bronze ring, 39.04 mm. **Series:** First **Subject:** 180th Anniversary of Federation **Obv:** National arms **Obv. Legend:** ESTADOS UNIDOS MEXICANOS **Rev:** State arms **Rev. Legend:** ESTADO DE TABASCO **Edge:** Segmented reeding

Date	Mintage	F	VF	XF	Unc	BU
2004Mo	249,318	—	—	—	35.00	45.00

KM# 701 100 PESOS

29.1690 g., Bi-Metallic .999 Gold 17.154g center in .999 Silver 12.015g ring, 34.5 mm. **Series:** First **Subject:** 180th Anniversary of Federation **Obv:** National arms **Obv. Legend:** ESTADOS UNIDOS MEXICANOS **Rev:** State arms **Rev. Legend:** ESTADO DE TABASCO **Edge:** Segmented reeding

Date	Mintage	F	VF	XF	Unc	BU
2004Mo Proof	1,000	Value: 775				

KM# 694 100 PESOS

33.9400 g., Bi-Metallic .925 Silver 20.1753g center in Aluminum-Bronze ring, 39.04 mm. **Series:** First **Subject:** 180th Anniversary of Federation **Obv:** National arms **Obv. Legend:** ESTADOS UNIDOS MEXICANOS **Rev:** State arms **Rev. Legend:** ESTADO DE SONORA **Edge:** Segmented reeding

Date	Mintage	F	VF	XF	Unc	BU
2004Mo	249,300	—	—	—	—	30.00

KM# 702 100 PESOS

29.1690 g., Bi-Metallic .999 Gold 17.154g center in .999 Silver 12.015g ring, 34.5 mm. **Series:** First **Subject:** 180th Anniversary of Federation **Obv:** National arms **Obv. Legend:** ESTADOS UNIDOS MEXICANOS **Rev:** State arms **Rev. Legend:** ESTADO DE SONORA **Edge:** Segmented reeding

Date	Mintage	F	VF	XF	Unc	BU
2004Mo Proof	1,000	Value: 775				

KM# 695 100 PESOS

33.9400 g., Bi-Metallic .925 Silver 20.1753g center in Aluminum-Bronze ring, 39.04 mm. **Series:** First **Subject:** 180th Anniversary of Federation **Obv:** National arms **Obv. Legend:** ESTADOS UNIDOS MEXICANOS **Rev:** State arms **Rev. Legend:** ESTADO DE SINALOA **Edge:** Segmented reeding

Date	Mintage	F	VF	XF	Unc	BU
2004Mo	244,722	—	—	—	35.00	45.00

KM# 703 100 PESOS

29.1690 g., Bi-Metallic .999 Gold 17.154g center in .999 Silver 12.015g ring, 34.5 mm. **Series:** First **Subject:** 180th Anniversary of Federation **Obv:** National arms **Obv. Legend:** ESTADOS UNIDOS MEXICANOS **Rev:** State arms **Rev. Legend:** ESTADO DE SINALOA **Edge:** Segmented reeding

Date	Mintage	F	VF	XF	Unc	BU
2004Mo Proof	1,000	Value: 775				

KM# 803 100 PESOS

33.9400 g., Bi-Metallic .925 Silver 20.1753g center in Aluminum-Bronze ring, 39.04 mm. **Series:** First **Subject:** 180th Anniversary of Federation **Obv:** National arms **Obv. Legend:** ESTADOS UNIDOS MEXICANOS **Rev:** State arms **Rev. Legend:** ESTADO DE SAN LUIS POTOSÍ **Edge:** Segmented reeding

Date	Mintage	F	VF	XF	Unc	BU
2004Mo	249,662	—	—	—	35.00	45.00

KM# 806 100 PESOS

29.1690 g., Bi-Metallic .999 Gold 17.154g center in .999 silver 12.015 ring, 34.5 mm. **Series:** First **Subject:** 180th Anniversary of Federation **Obv:** National arms **Obv. Legend:** ESTADOS UNIDOS MEXICANOS **Rev:** State arms **Rev. Legend:** ESTADO DE SAN LUIS POTOSÍ **Edge:** Segmented reeding

Date	Mintage	F	VF	XF	Unc	BU
2004Mo Proof	1,000	Value: 775				

KM# 736 100 PESOS

33.9400 g., Bi-Metallic .925 Silver 20.1753g center in Aluminum-Bronze ring, 39.04 mm. **Series:** First **Subject:** 180th Anniversary of Federation **Obv:** National arms **Obv. Legend:** ESTADOS UNIDOS MEXICANOS **Rev:** State arms **Rev. Legend:** ESTADO DE QUINTANA ROO **Edge:** Segmented reeding

Date	Mintage	F	VF	XF	Unc	BU
2004Mo	249,134	—	—	—	35.00	45.00

KM# 807 100 PESOS

29.1690 g., Bi-Metallic .999 Gold 17.154g center in .999 Silver 12.015g ring, 34.5 mm. **Series:** First **Subject:** 180th Anniversary of Federation **Obv:** National arms **Obv. Legend:** ESTADOS UNIDOS MEXICANOS **Rev:** State arms **Rev. Legend:** ESTADO DE QUINTANA ROO **Edge:** Segmented reeding

Date	Mintage	F	VF	XF	Unc	BU
2004Mo Proof	1,000	Value: 775				

KM# 734 100 PESOS

33.9400 g., Bi-Metallic .925 Silver 20.1753g center in Aluminum-Bronze ring, 39.04 mm. **Series:** First **Subject:** 180th Anniversary of Federation **Obv:** National arms **Obv. Legend:** ESTADOS UNIDOS MEXICANOS **Rev:** State arms **Rev. Legend:** ESTADO DE QUERÉTARO ARTEAGA **Edge:** Segmented reeding

Date	Mintage	F	VF	XF	Unc	BU
2004Mo	249,263	—	—	—	35.00	45.00

KM# 808 100 PESOS

29.1690 g., Bi-Metallic .999 Gold 17.154g center in .999 Silver 12.015g ring, 34.5 mm. **Series:** First **Subject:** 180th Anniversary of Federation **Obv:** National arms **Obv. Legend:** ESTADOS UNIDOS MEXICANOS **Rev:** State arms **Rev. Legend:** ESTADO DE QUERÉTARO ARTEAGA **Edge:** Segmented reeding

Date	Mintage	F	VF	XF	Unc	BU
2004Mo Proof	1,000	Value: 775				

KM# 740 100 PESOS

33.9400 g., Bi-Metallic .925 Silver 20.1753g center in Aluminum-Bronze ring, 39.04 mm. **Series:** First **Subject:** 180th Anniversary of Federation **Obv:** National arms **Obv. Legend:** ESTADOS UNIDOS MEXICANOS **Rev:** State arms **Rev. Legend:** ESTADO DE OAXACA **Edge:** Segmented reeding

Date	Mintage	F	VF	XF	Unc	BU
2004Mo	249,589	—	—	—	35.00	45.00

KM# 810 100 PESOS

29.1690 g., Bi-Metallic .999 Gold 17.154g center in .999 Silver 12.015g ring, 34.5 mm. **Series:** First **Subject:** 180th Anniversary of Federation **Obv:** National arms **Obv. Legend:** ESTADOS UNIDOS MEXICANOS **Rev:** State arms **Rev. Legend:** ESTADO DE OAXACA **Edge:** Segmented reeding

Date	Mintage	F	VF	XF	Unc	BU
2004Mo Proof	1,000	Value: 775				

KM# 744 100 PESOS

33.9400 g., Bi-Metallic .925 Silver 20.1753g center in Aluminum-Bronze ring, 39.04 mm. **Series:** First **Subject:** 180th Anniversary of Federation **Obv:** National arms **Obv. Legend:** ESTADOS UNIDOS MEXICANOS **Rev:** State arms **Rev. Legend:** ESTADO DE NAYARIT **Edge:** Segmented reeding

Date	Mintage	F	VF	XF	Unc	BU
2004Mo	248,305	—	—	—	35.00	45.00

KM# 812 100 PESOS

29.1690 g., Bi-Metallic .999 Gold 17.154g center in .999 Silver 12.015g ring, 34.5 mm. **Series:** First **Subject:** 180th Anniversary of Federation **Obv:** National arms **Obv. Legend:** ESTADOS UNIDOS MEXICANOS **Rev:** State arms **Rev. Legend:** ESTADO DE NAYARIT **Edge:** Segmented reeding

Date	Mintage	F	VF	XF	Unc	BU
2004Mo Proof	1,000	Value: 775				

KM# 738 100 PESOS

33.9400 g., Bi-Metallic .925 Silver 20.1753g center in Aluminum-Bronze ring, 39.04 mm. **Series:** First **Subject:** 180th Anniversary of Federation **Obv:** National arms **Obv. Legend:** ESTADOS UNIDOS MEXICANOS **Rev:** State arms **Rev. Legend:** ESTADO DE PUEBLA **Edge:** Segmented reeding

Date	Mintage	F	VF	XF	Unc	BU
2004Mo	248,850	—	—	—	35.00	45.00

KM# 809 100 PESOS

Bi-Metallic .999 Gold 17.154g center in .999 Silver 12.015g ring, 34.5 mm. **Series:** First **Subject:** 180th Anniversary of Federation **Obv:** National arms **Obv. Legend:** ESTADOS UNIDOS MEXICANOS **Rev:** State arms **Rev. Legend:** ESTADO DE PUEBLA **Edge:** Segmented reeding

Date	Mintage	F	VF	XF	Unc	BU
2004Mo Proof	1,000	Value: 775				

KM# 742 100 PESOS

33.9400 g., Bi-Metallic .925 Silver 20.1753g center in Aluminum-Bronze ring, 39.04 mm. **Series:** First **Subject:** 180th Anniversary of Federation **Obv:** National arms **Obv. Legend:** ESTADOS UNIDOS MEXICANOS **Rev:** State arms **Rev. Legend:** ESTADO DE NUEVO LEÓN **Edge:** Segmented reeding

Date	Mintage	F	VF	XF	Unc	BU
2004Mo	249,199	—	—	—	35.00	45.00

KM# 811 100 PESOS

29.1690 g., Bi-Metallic .999 Gold 17.154g center in .999 Silver 12.015g ring, 34.5 mm. **Series:** First **Subject:** 180th Anniversary of Federation **Obv:** National arms **Obv. Legend:** ESTADOS UNIDOS MEXICANOS **Rev:** State arms **Rev. Legend:** ESTADO DE NUEVO LEÓN **Edge:** Segmented reeding

Date	Mintage	F	VF	XF	Unc	BU
2004Mo Proof	1,000	Value: 775				

KM# 746 100 PESOS

33.9400 g., Bi-Metallic .925 Silver 20.1753g center in Aluminum-Bronze ring, 39.04 mm. **Series:** First **Subject:** 180th Anniversary of Federation **Obv:** National arms **Obv. Legend:** ESTADOS UNIDOS MEXICANOS **Rev:** State arms **Rev. Legend:** ESTADO DE MORELOS **Edge:** Segmented reeding

Date	Mintage	F	VF	XF	Unc	BU
2004Mo	249,260	—	—	—	35.00	45.00

KM# 813 100 PESOS

29.1690 g., Bi-Metallic .999 Gold 17.154g center in .999 Silver 12.015g ring, 34.5 mm. **Series:** First **Subject:** 180th Anniversary of Federation **Obv:** National arms **Obv. Legend:** ESTADOS UNIDOS MEXICANOS **Rev:** State arms **Rev. Legend:** ESTADO DE MORELOS **Edge:** Segmented reeding

Date	Mintage	F	VF	XF	Unc	BU
2004Mo Proof	1,000	Value: 775				

KM# 804 100 PESOS

33.9400 g., Bi-Metallic o.925 Silver 20.1763g center in Aluminum-Bronze ring, 39.04 mm. **Series:** First **Subject:** 180th Anniversary of Federation **Obv:** National arms **Obv. Legend:** ESTADOS UNIDOS MEXICANOS **Rev:** State arms **Rev. Legend:** ESTADO DE MICHOACÁN DE OCAMPO **Edge:** Segmented reeding

Date	Mintage	F	VF	XF	Unc	BU
2004Mo	249,492	—	—	—	35.00	45.00

KM# 814 100 PESOS

29.1690 g., Bi-Metallic .999 Gold 17.154g center in .999 12.015g ring, 34.5 mm. **Series:** First **Subject:** 180th Anniversary of Federation **Obv:** National arms **Obv. Legend:** ESTADOS UNIDOS MEXICANOS **Rev:** State arms **Rev. Legend:** ESTADO DE MICHOACÁN DE OCAMPO **Edge:** Segmented reeding

Date	Mintage	F	VF	XF	Unc	BU
2004Mo Proof	1,000	Value: 775				

KM# 750 100 PESOS

33.9400 g., Bi-Metallic .925 Silver 20.1753g center in Aluminum-Bronze ring, 39.04 mm. **Series:** First **Subject:** 180th Anniversary of Federation **Obv:** National arms **Obv. Legend:** ESTADOS UNIDOS MEXICANOS **Rev:** State arms **Rev. Legend:** ESTADO DE JALISCO **Edge:** Segmented reeding

Date	Mintage	F	VF	XF	Unc	BU
2004Mo	249,115	—	—	—	35.00	45.00

KM# 816 100 PESOS

29.1690 g., Bi-Metallic .999 Gold 17.154g center in .999 Silver 12.015g ring, 34.5 mm. **Series:** First **Subject:** 180th Anniversary of Federation **Obv:** National arms **Obv. Legend:** ESTADOS UNIDOS MEXICANOS **Rev:** State arms **Rev. Legend:** ESTADO DE JALISCO **Edge:** Segmented reeding

Date	Mintage	F	VF	XF	Unc	BU
2004Mo Proof	1,000	Value: 775				

KM# 716 100 PESOS

33.9400 g., Bi-Metallic .925 Silver center in Brass ring, 39.04 mm. **Series:** First **Subject:** 180th Anniversary of Federation **Obv:** National arms **Obv. Legend:** ESTADOS UNIDOS MEXICANOS **Rev:** State arms **Rev. Legend:** ESTADO DE GUERRERO **Edge:** Segmented reeding

Date	Mintage	F	VF	XF	Unc	BU
2005Mo	248,850	—	—	—	35.00	45.00

KM# 818 100 PESOS

29.1690 g., Bi-Metallic .999 Gold 17.154g center in .999 Silver 12.015 ring, 34.5 mm. **Series:** First **Subject:** 180th Anniversary of Federation **Obv:** National arms **Obv. Legend:** ESTADOS UNIDOS MEXICANOS **Rev:** State arms **Rev. Legend:** ESTADO DE GUERRERO **Edge:** Segmented reeding

Date	Mintage	F	VF	XF	Unc	BU
2005Mo Proof	1,000	Value: 775				

KM# 748 100 PESOS

33.9400 g., Bi-Metallic .925 Silver 20.1753g center in Aluminum-Bronze ring, 39.04 mm. **Series:** First **Subject:** 180th Anniversary of Federation **Obv:** National arms **Obv. Legend:** ESTADOS UNIDOS MEXICANOS **Rev:** State arms **Rev. Legend:** ESTADO DE MÉXICO **Edge:** Segmented reeding

Date	Mintage	F	VF	XF	Unc	BU
2004Mo	249,800	—	—	—	35.00	45.00

KM# 815 100 PESOS

29.1690 g., Bi-Metallic .999 Gold 17.154 center in .999 Silver 12.015 ring, 34.5 mm. **Series:** First **Subject:** 180th Anniversary of Federation **Obv:** National arms **Obv. Legend:** ESTADOS UNIDOS MEXICANOS **Rev:** State arms **Rev. Legend:** ESTADO DE MÉXICO **Edge:** Segmented reeding

Date	Mintage	F	VF	XF	Unc	BU
2004Mo Proof	1,000	Value: 775				

KM# 717 100 PESOS

33.9400 g., Bi-Metallic .925 Silver center in Brass ring, 39.04 mm. **Series:** First **Subject:** 180th Anniversary of Federation **Obv:** National arms **Obv. Legend:** ESTADOS UNIDOS MEXICANOS **Rev:** State arms **Rev. Legend:** ESTADO DE HIDALGO **Edge:** Segmented reeding

Date	Mintage	F	VF	XF	Unc	BU
2005Mo	249,820	—	—	—	35.00	45.00

KM# 817 100 PESOS

29.1690 g., Bi-Metallic .999 Gold 17.154g center in .999 Silver 12.015g ring, 34.5 mm. **Series:** First **Subject:** 180th Anniversary of Federation **Obv:** National arms **Obv. Legend:** ESTADOS UNIDOS MEXICANOS **Rev:** State arms **Rev. Legend:** ESTADO DE HIDALGO **Edge:** Segmented reeding

Date	Mintage	F	VF	XF	Unc	BU
2005Mo Proof	1,000	Value: 775				

KM# 715 100 PESOS

33.9400 g., Bi-Metallic .925 Silver center in Brass ring, 39.04 mm. **Series:** First **Subject:** 180th Anniversary of Federation **Obv:** National arms **Obv. Legend:** ESTADOS UNIDOS MEXICANOS **Rev:** State arms **Rev. Legend:** ESTADO DE GUANAJUATO **Edge:** Segmented reeding

Date	Mintage	F	VF	XF	Unc	BU
2005Mo	249,489	—	—	—	35.00	45.00

KM# 819 100 PESOS

29.1690 g., Bi-Metallic .999 Gold 17.154g center in .999 Silver 12.015g ring, 34.5 mm. **Series:** First **Subject:** 180th Anniversary of Federation **Obv:** National arms **Obv. Legend:** ESTADOS UNIDOS MEXICANOS **Rev:** State arms **Rev. Legend:** ESTADO DE GUANAJUATO **Edge:** Segmented reeding

Date	Mintage	F	VF	XF	Unc	BU
2005Mo Proof	1,000	Value: 775				

KM# 714 100 PESOS
33.9400 g., Bi-Metallic .925 Silver center in Brass ring, 39.04 mm. **Series:** First **Subject:** 180th Anniversary of Federation **Obv:** National arms **Obv. Legend:** ESTADOS UNIDOS MEXICANOS **Rev:** State arms **Rev. Legend:** ESTADO DE DURANGO **Edge:** Segmented reeding

Date	Mintage	F	VF	XF	Unc	BU
2005Mo	249,774	—	—	—	35.00	45.00

KM# 820 100 PESOS
29.1690 g., Bi-Metallic .999 Gold 17.154g center in .999 silver 12.015g ring, 34.5 mm. **Series:** First **Subject:** 180th Anniversary of Federation **Obv:** National arms **Obv. Legend:** ESTADOS UNIDOS MEXICANOS **Rev:** State arms **Rev. Legend:** ESTADO DE DURANGO **Edge:** Segmented reeding

Date	Mintage	F	VF	XF	Unc	BU
2005Mo Proof	1,000	Value: 775				

KM# 713 100 PESOS
33.9400 g., Bi-Metallic .925 Silver 20.1753g center in Brass ring, 39.04 mm. **Series:** First **Subject:** 180th Anniversary of Federation **Obv:** National arms **Obv. Legend:** ESTADOS UNIDOS MEXICANOS **Rev:** Federal District arms **Rev. Legend:** DISTRITO FEDERAL **Edge:** Segmented reeding

Date	Mintage	F	VF	XF	Unc	BU
2005Mo	249,461	—	—	—	35.00	45.00

KM# 821 100 PESOS
29.1690 g., Bi-Metallic .999 Gold 17.154g center in .999 Silver 12.015g ring, 34.5 mm. **Series:** First **Subject:** 180th Anniversary of Federation **Obv:** National arms **Obv. Legend:** ESTADOS UNIDOS MEXICANOS **Rev:** Federal District arms **Rev. Legend:** DISTRITO FEDERAL **Edge:** Segmented reeding

Date	Mintage	F	VF	XF	Unc	BU
2005Mo Proof	1,000	Value: 775				

KM# 754 100 PESOS
33.9400 g., Bi-Metallic .925 Silver 20.1753g center in Aluminum-Bronze ring, 39.04 mm. **Series:** First **Subject:** 180th Anniversary of Federation **Obv:** National arms **Obv. Legend:** ESTADOS UNIDOS MEXICANOS **Rev:** State arms **Rev. Legend:** ESTADO DE CHIHUAHUA **Edge:** Segmented reeding

Date	Mintage	F	VF	XF	Unc	BU
2005	249,102	—	—	—	35.00	45.00

KM# 822 100 PESOS
29.1690 g., Bi-Metallic .999 Gold 17.154g center in .999 Silver 12.015g ring, 34.5 mm. **Series:** First **Subject:** 180th Anniversary of Federation **Obv:** National arms **Obv. Legend:** ESTADOS UNIDOS MEXICANOS **Rev:** State arms **Rev. Legend:** ESTADO DE CHIHUAHUA **Edge:** Segmented reeding

Date	Mintage	F	VF	XF	Unc	BU
2005Mo Proof	1,000	Value: 775				

KM# 712 100 PESOS
33.9400 g., Bi-Metallic .925 Silver 20.1753g center in Brass ring, 39.04 mm. **Series:** First **Subject:** 180th Anniversary of Federation **Obv:** National arms **Obv. Legend:** ESTADOS UNIDOS MEXICANOS **Rev:** State arms **Rev. Legend:** ESTADO DE CHIAPAS **Edge:** Segmented reeding

Date	Mintage	F	VF	XF	Unc	BU
2005Mo	249,417	—	—	—	35.00	45.00

KM# 823 100 PESOS
29.1690 g., Bi-Metallic .999 Gold 17.154g center in .999 Silver 12.015g ring, 34.5 mm. **Series:** First **Subject:** 180th Anniversary of Federation **Obv:** National arms **Obv. Legend:** ESTADOS UNIDOS MEXICANOS **Rev:** State arms **Rev. Legend:** ESTADO DE CHIAPAS **Edge:** Segmented reeding

Date	Mintage	F	VF	XF	Unc	BU
2005Mo Proof	1,000	Value: 775				

KM# 729 100 PESOS
33.8250 g., Bi-Metallic .925 Silver 20.1753g center in Aluminum-Bronze ring, 39.04 mm. **Series:** First **Subject:** 180th Anniversary of Federation **Obv:** National arms **Obv. Legend:** ESTADOS UNIDOS MEXICANOS **Rev:** State arms **Rev. Legend:** ESTADO DE COLIMA **Edge:** Segmented reeding

Date	Mintage	F	VF	XF	Unc	BU
2005Mo	248,850	—	—	—	35.00	45.00

KM# 824 100 PESOS
29.1690 g., Bi-Metallic .999 Gold 17.154g center in .999 Silver 12.015g ring, 34.5 mm. **Series:** First **Subject:** 180th Anniversary of Federation **Obv:** National arms **Obv. Legend:** ESTADOS UNIDOS MEXICANOS **Rev:** State arms **Rev. Legend:** ESTADO DE COLIMA **Edge:** Segmented reeding

Date	Mintage	F	VF	XF	Unc	BU
2005Mo Proof	1,000	Value: 775				

KM# 752 100 PESOS
33.9400 g., Bi-Metallic .925 Silver 20.1753g center in Aluminum-Bronze ring, 39.04 mm. **Series:** First **Subject:** 180th Anniversary of Federation **Obv:** National arms **Obv. Legend:** ESTADOS UNIDOS MEXICANOS **Rev:** State arms **Rev. Legend:** ESTADO DE COAHUILA DE ZARAGOZA **Edge:** Segmented reeding

Date	Mintage	F	VF	XF	Unc	BU
2005Mo	247,991	—	—	—	35.00	45.00

KM# 825 100 PESOS
29.1690 g., Bi-Metallic .999 Gold 17.154g center in .999 Silver 12.015g ring, 34.5 mm. **Series:** First **Subject:** 180th Anniversary of Federation **Obv:** National arms **Obv. Legend:** ESTADOS UNIDOS MEXICANOS **Rev:** State arms **Rev. Legend:** ESTADO DE COAHUILA DE ZARAGOZA **Edge:** Segmented reeding

Date	Mintage	F	VF	XF	Unc	BU
2005Mo Proof	1,000	Value: 775				

KM# 727 100 PESOS
33.9400 g., Bi-Metallic .925 Silver 20.1753g center in Aluminum-Bronze ring, 39.04 mm. **Series:** First **Subject:** 180th Anniversary of Federation **Obv:** National arms **Obv. Legend:** ESTADOS UNIDOS MEXICANOS **Rev:** State arms **Rev. Legend:** ESTADO DE CAMPECHE **Edge:** Segmented reeding

Date	Mintage	F	VF	XF	Unc	BU
2005Mo	249,040	—	—	—	35.00	45.00

KM# 826 100 PESOS
29.1690 g., Bi-Metallic .999 Gold 17.154g center in .999 Silver 12.015g ring, 34.5 mm. **Series:** First **Subject:** 180th Anniversary of Federation **Obv:** National arms **Obv. Legend:** ESTADOS UNIDOS MEXICANOS **Rev:** State arms **Rev. Legend:** ESTADO DE CAMPECHE **Edge:** Segmented reeding

Date	Mintage	F	VF	XF	Unc	BU
2005Mo Proof	1,000	Value: 775				

KM# 725 100 PESOS

33.9400 g., Bi-Metallic .925 Silver 20.1753g center in Aluminum-Bronze ring, 39.04 mm. **Series:** First **Subject:** 180th Anniversary of Federation **Obv:** National arms **Obv. Legend:** ESTADOS UNIDOS MEXICANOS **Rev:** State arms **Rev. Legend:** ESTADO DE BAJA CALIFORNIA SUR **Edge:** Segmented reeding

Date	Mintage	F	VF	XF	Unc	BU
2005Mo	249,585	—	—	—	35.00	45.00

KM# 827 100 PESOS

29.1690 g., Bi-Metallic .999 Gold 17.154g center in .999 Silver 12.015g ring, 34.5 mm. **Series:** First **Subject:** 180th Anniversary of Federation **Obv:** National arms **Obv. Legend:** ESTADOS UNIDOS MEXICANOS **Rev:** State arms **Rev. Legend:** ESTADO DE BAJA CALIFORNIA SUR **Edge:** Segmented reeding

Date	Mintage	F	VF	XF	Unc	BU
2005Mo Proof	—	Value: 775				

KM# 721 100 PESOS

33.9400 g., Bi-Metallic .925 Silver 20.1753g center in Aluminum-Bronze ring, 39.04 mm. **Series:** First **Subject:** 180th Anniversary of Federation **Obv:** National arms **Obv. Legend:** ESTADOS UNIDOS MEXICANOS **Rev:** Estados de Aguascalientes state arms **Rev. Legend:** ESTADO DE AGUASCALIENTES **Edge:** Segmented reeding

Date	Mintage	F	VF	XF	Unc	BU
2005Mo	248,410	—	—	—	35.00	45.00

KM# 829 100 PESOS

29.1690 g., Bi-Metallic .999 Gold 17.154g center in .999 Silver 12.015g ring, 34.5 mm. **Series:** First **Subject:** 180th Anniversary of Federation **Obv:** National arms **Obv. Legend:** ESTADOS UNIDOS MEXICANOS **Rev:** State arms **Rev. Legend:** ESTADO DE AGUASCALIENTES **Edge:** Segmented reeding

Date	Mintage	F	VF	XF	Unc	BU
2005Mo Proof	1,000	Value: 775				

KM# 758 100 PESOS

33.9400 g., Bi-Metallic .925 Silver 20.1753g center in Aluminum-Bronze ring, 39.04 mm. **Series:** Second **Obv:** National arms **Obv. Legend:** ESTADOS UNIDOS MEXICANOS **Rev:** Ram's head and value within circle **Rev. Legend:** BAJA CALIFORNIA - GOBIERNO DEL ESTADO **Edge:** Segmented reeding

Date	Mintage	F	VF	XF	Unc	BU
2005Mo	—	—	—	—	25.00	30.00

KM# 863 100 PESOS

29.1690 g., Bi-Metallic .999 Gold 17.154g center in .999 Silver 12.015g ring, 34.5 mm. **Series:** Second **Obv:** National arms **Obv. Legend:** ESTTADOS UNIDOS MEXICANOS **Rev:** Ram's head, mountain outline in background **Rev. Legend:** BAJA CALIFORNIA - GOBIERNO DEL ESTADO **Edge:** Segmented reeding

Date	Mintage	F	VF	XF	Unc	BU
2005Mo Proof	600	Value: 775				

KM# 723 100 PESOS

33.9400 g., Bi-Metallic .925 Silver 20.1753g center in Aluminum-Bronze ring, 39.04 mm. **Series:** First **Subject:** 180th Anniversary of Federation **Obv:** National arms **Obv. Legend:** ESTADOS UNIDOS MEXICANOS **Rev:** State arms **Rev. Legend:** ESTADO DE BAJA CALIFORNIA **Edge:** Segmented reeding

Date	Mintage	F	VF	XF	Unc	BU
2005Mo	249,263	—	—	—	35.00	45.00

KM# 828 100 PESOS

29.1690 g., Bi-Metallic .999 Gold 17.154g center in .999 Silver 12.015g ring, 34.5 mm. **Series:** First **Subject:** 180th Anniversary of Federation **Obv:** National arms **Obv. Legend:** ESTADOS UNIDOS MEXICANOS **Rev:** State arms **Rev. Legend:** ESTADO DE BAJA CALIFORNIA **Edge:** Segmented reeding

Date	Mintage	F	VF	XF	Unc	BU
2005Mo Proof	1,000	Value: 775				

KM# 719 100 PESOS

33.8250 g., Bi-Metallic .925 Silver 20.1753g center in Aluminum-Bronze ring, 39.04 mm. **Series:** Second **Obv:** National arms **Obv. Legend:** ESTADOS UNIDOS MEXICANOS **Rev:** Facade of the San Marcos garden above sculpture of national emblem at left, San Antonio Temple at right **Rev. Legend:** AGUASCALIENTES **Edge:** Segmented reeding

Date	Mintage	F	VF	XF	Unc	BU
2005Mo	149,705	—	—	—	35.00	45.00

KM# 862 100 PESOS

29.1690 g., Bi-Metallic .999 Gold 17.154g center in .999 Silver 12.015g ring, 34.5 mm. **Series:** Second **Obv:** National arms **Obv. Legend:** ESTADOS UNIDOS MEXICANOS **Rev:** Facade of the San Marcos garden above sculpture of national emblem at left, San Antonio temple at right **Rev. Legend:** AGUASCALUENTES **Edge:** Segmented reeding

Date	Mintage	F	VF	XF	Unc	BU
2005Mo Proof	600	Value: 775				

KM# 762 100 PESOS

33.9400 g., Bi-Metallic .925 Silver 20.175g center in Aluminum-Bronze ring, 39.04 mm. **Series:** Second **Obv:** National arms **Obv. Legend:** ESTADOS UNIDOS MEXICANOS **Rev:** Outlined map of peninsula at center, cave painting of deer behind, cactus at right **Rev. Legend:** ESTADO DE BAJA CALIFORNIA SUR **Edge:** Segmented reeding

Date	Mintage	F	VF	XF	Unc	BU
2005Mo	149,152	—	—	—	—	25.00

KM# 864 100 PESOS

29.1690 g., Bi-Metallic .999 Gold 17.154g center in .999 Silver 12.015g ring, 34.5 mm. **Series:** Second **Obv:** National arms **Obv. Legend:** ESTADOS UNIDOS MEXICANOS **Rev:** Outlined map of peninsula at center, cave painting of deer behind, cactus at right **Rev. Legend:** ESTADO DE BAJA CALIFORNIA SUR **Edge:** Segmented reeding

Date	Mintage	F	VF	XF	Unc	BU
2006Mo Proof	600	Value: 775				

KM# 760 100 PESOS
33.9400 g., Bi-Metallic .925 Silver 20.1753g center in Aluminum-Bronze ring, 39.04 mm. **Series:** Second **Subject:** Estado de Campeche **Obv:** National arms **Obv. Legend:** ESTADOS UNIDOS MEXICANOS **Rev:** Jade mask - Calakmul, Campeche **Rev. Legend:** ESTADO DE CAMPECHE **Edge:** Segmented reeding

Date	Mintage	F	VF	XF	Unc	BU
2006Mo	—	—	—	—	—	25.00

KM# 865 100 PESOS
29.1690 g., Bi-Metallic .999 Gold 17.154g center in .999 Silver 12.015g ring, 34.5 mm. **Series:** Second **Obv:** National arms **Obv. Legend:** ESTADOS UNIDOS MEXICANOS **Rev:** Jade mask - Calakmul, Campeche **Rev. Legend:** ESTADO DE CAMPECHE **Edge:** Segmented reeding

Date	Mintage	F	VF	XF	Unc	BU
2006Mo Proof	600	Value: 775				

KM# 781 100 PESOS
33.7000 g., Bi-Metallic .925 Silver 20.1753g center in Aluminum-Bronze ring, 39.04 mm. **Series:** Second **Obv:** National arms **Obv. Legend:** ESTADOS UNIDOS MEXICANOS **Rev:** Outlined map with turtle, mine cart above grapes at center, Friendship Dam above Christ of the Nodas at left, chimneys above crucibles and bell tower of Santiago's cathedral at right **Rev. Legend:** COAHUILA DE ZARAGOZA **Edge:** Segmented reeding

Date	Mintage	F	VF	XF	Unc	BU
2006Mo	—	—	—	—	35.00	45.00

KM# 866 100 PESOS
29.1690 g., Bi-Metallic .999 Gold 17.154g center in .999 Silver 12.015g ring, 34.5 mm. **Series:** Second **Obv:** National arms **Obv. Legend:** ESTADOS UNIDOS MEXICANOS **Rev:** Outlined map with turtle, mine cart above grapes at center, Friendship dam above Christ of the Nodas at left, chimneys above crucibles and bell tower of Santiago's cathedral at right **Rev. Inscription:** COAHUILA DE ZARAGOZA **Edge:** Segmented reeding

Date	Mintage	F	VF	XF	Unc	BU
2006Mo Proof	600	Value: 775				

KM# 777 100 PESOS
33.9400 g., Bi-Metallic .925 Silver 20.1753g center in Aluminum-Bronze ring, 39.04 mm. **Series:** Second **Obv:** National arms **Obv. Legend:** ESTADOS UNIDOS MEXICANOS **Rev:** State arms at lower center, Nevado de Colima and Volcan de Fuego volcanos in background **Rev. Legend:** *Colima* **Rev. Inscription:** GENEROSO **Edge:** Segmented reeding

Date	Mintage	F	VF	XF	Unc	BU
2006Mo	149,041	—	—	—	35.00	45.00

KM# 867 100 PESOS
29.1690 g., Bi-Metallic .999 Gold 17.154g center in .999 Silver 12.015 ring, 34.5 mm. **Series:** Second **Obv:** National arms **Obv. Legend:** ESTADOS UNIDOS MEXICANOS **Rev:** State arms at lower center, Nevado de Colima and Volcan de Fuego volcanos in background **Rev. Legend:** *Colima* **Rev. Inscription:** GENEROSO **Edge:** Segmented reeding

Date	Mintage	F	VF	XF	Unc	BU
2006Mo Proof	600	Value: 775				

KM# 773 100 PESOS
33.9400 g., Bi-Metallic .925 Silver 20.1753g center in Aluminum-Bronze ring, 39.04 mm. **Series:** Second **Obv:** National arms **Obv. Legend:** ESTADOS UNIDOS MEXICANOS **Rev:** Head of Pakal, ancient Mayan king, Palenque **Rev. Legend:** ESTADO DE CHIAPAS - CABEZA MAYA DEL REY PAKAL, PALENQUE **Edge:** Segmented reeding

Date	Mintage	F	VF	XF	Unc	BU
2006Mo	149,491	—	—	—	35.00	45.00

KM# 868 100 PESOS
29.1690 g., Bi-Metallic .999 Gold 17.154g center in .999 Silver 12.015g ring, 34.5 mm. **Series:** Second **Obv:** National arms **Obv. Legend:** ESTADOS UNIDOS MEXICANOS **Rev:** Head of Pakal, ancient Mayan king, Palenque **Rev. Legend:** ESTADO DE CHIAPAS - CABEZA MAYA DEL REY PAKAL, PALENQUE **Edge:** Segmented reeding

Date	Mintage	F	VF	XF	Unc	BU
2006Mo Proof	600	Value: 775				

KM# 775 100 PESOS
33.9400 g., Bi-Metallic .925 Silver 20.1753g center in Aluminum-Bronze ring, 39.04 mm. **Series:** Second **Obv:** National arms **Obv. Legend:** ESTADOS UNIDOS MEXICANOS **Rev:** Angel of Liberty **Rev. Legend:** MÉXICO - ANGEL DE LA LIBERTAD, CHIHUAHUA **Edge:** Segmented reeding

Date	Mintage	F	VF	XF	Unc	BU
2006Mo	149,557	—	—	—	35.00	45.00

KM# 869 100 PESOS
29.1690 g., Bi-Metallic .999 Gold 17.154g center in .999 Silver 12.015g ring, 34.5 mm. **Series:** Second **Obv:** National arms **Obv. Legend:** ESTADOS UNIDOS MEXICANOS **Rev:** Angel of Liberty **Rev. Legend:** MÉXICO - ANGEL DE LA LIBERTAD, CHIHUAHUA **Edge:** Segmented reeding

Date	Mintage	F	VF	XF	Unc	BU
2006Mo Proof	600	Value: 775				

KM# 779 100 PESOS
33.9400 g., Bi-Metallic .925 Silver 20.1753g center in Aluminum-Bronze ring, 39.04 mm. **Series:** Second **Obv:** National arms **Obv. Legend:** ESTADOS UNIDOS MEXICANOS **Rev:** National Palace **Rev. Legend:** DISTRITO FEDERAL - ANTIGUO AYUNTAMIENTO **Edge:** Segmented reeding

Date	Mintage	F	VF	XF	Unc	BU
2006Mo	149,525	—	—	—	35.00	45.00

KM# 870 100 PESOS
29.1690 g., Bi-Metallic .999 Gold 17.154g center in .999 Silver 12.015g ring, 34.5 mm. **Series:** Second **Obv:** National arms **Obv. Legend:** ESTADOS UNIDOS MEXICANOS **Rev:** National palace **Rev. Legend:** DISTRITO FEDERAL - ANTIGUO AYUNTAMIENTO **Edge:** Segmented reeding

Date	Mintage	F	VF	XF	Unc	BU
2006Mo Proof	600	Value: 775				

KM# 787 100 PESOS
33.9400 g., Bi-Metallic .925 Silver 20.1753g center in Brass ring, 39.04 mm. **Series:** Second **Obv:** National arms **Obv. Legend:** ESTADOS UNIDOS MEXICANOS **Rev:** Tree **Rev. Legend:** PRIMERA RESERVA NACIONAL FORESTAL - DURANGO **Edge:** Segmented reeding

Date	Mintage	F	VF	XF	Unc	BU
2006Mo	149,034	—	—	—	35.00	45.00

KM# 871 100 PESOS
29.1690 g., Bi-Metallic .999 Gold 17.154g center in .999 Silver 12.015g ring, 34.5 mm. **Series:** Second **Obv:** National arms **Obv. Legend:** ESYADOS UNIDOS MEXICANOS **Rev:** Tree **Rev. Legend:** PRIMERA RESERVA NACIONAL RORESTAL - DURANGO **Edge:** Segmented reeding

Date	Mintage	F	VF	XF	Unc	BU
2006Mo Proof	600	Value: 775				

KM# 789 100 PESOS

33.9400 g., Bi-Metallic .925 Silver 20.1753g center in Brass ring, 39.04 mm. **Series:** Second **Obv:** National arms **Obv. Legend:** ESTADOS UNIDOS MEXICANOS **Rev:** State arms at center, statue of Miguel Hidalgo at left, monument to Pipla at lower right **Rev. Inscription:** *Guanajuato* **Edge:** Segmented reeding

Date	Mintage	F	VF	XF	Unc	BU
2006Mo	149,921	—	—	—	—	25.00

KM# 872 100 PESOS

29.1690 g., Bi-Metallic .999 Gold 17.154g center in .999 Silver 12.015g ring, 34.50 mm. **Series:** Second **Obv:** National arms **Obv. Legend:** ESTADOS UNIDOS MEXICANOS **Rev:** State arms at lower center, statue of Miguel Hidalgo at left, monument to Pipila at lower right **Rev. Inscription:** *Guanajauto* **Edge:** Segmented reeding

Date	Mintage	F	VF	XF	Unc	BU
2006Mo Proof	600	Value: 775				

KM# 791 100 PESOS

33.9400 g., Bi-Metallic .925 Silver 20.1753g center in Brass ring, 39.04 mm. **Series:** Second **Obv:** National arms **Obv. Legend:** ESTADOS UNIDOS MEXICANOS **Rev:** Stylized portrait of Vicente Guerrero at left, church of Taxco at upper center, Acapulco's la Quebrada with diver above Christmas Eve flower and mask **Rev. Legend:** GUERRERO **Edge:** Segmented reeding

Date	Mintage	F	VF	XF	Unc	BU
2006Mo	149,675	—	—	—	35.00	45.00

KM# 873 100 PESOS

29.1690 g., Bi-Metallic .999 Gold 17.154g center in .999 Silver 12.015g ring, 34.5 mm. **Series:** Second **Obv:** National arms **Obv. Legend:** ESTADOS UNIDOS MEXICANOS **Rev:** Stylized portrait of Vicente Guerrero at left, church of Taxco at upper center, Acapulco's la Quebrada with diver over Christmas Eve flower and mask **Rev. Legend:** GUERRERO **Edge:** Segmented reeding

Date	Mintage	F	VF	XF	Unc	BU
2006Mo Proof	600	Value: 775				

KM# 793 100 PESOS

33.9400 g., Bi-Metallic .925 Silver 20.1753g center in Aluminum-Bronze ring, 39.04 mm. **Series:** Second **Obv:** National arms **Obv. Legend:** ESTADOS UNIDOS MEXICANOS **Rev:** Monument of Pachuca Hidalgo **Rev. Inscription:** *RELOJ / MONUMENTAL / DE / PACHUCA / HIDALGO - La / Bella / Airosa* **Edge:** Segmented reeding

Date	Mintage	F	VF	XF	Unc	BU
2006Mo	149,273	—	—	—	35.00	45.00

KM# 874 100 PESOS

29.1690 g., Bi-Metallic .999 Gold 17.154g center in .999 Silver 12.015g ring, 34.5 mm. **Series:** Second **Obv:** National arms **Obv. Legend:** ESTADOS UNIDOS MEXICANOS **Rev:** Monument of Pachuca Hidalgo **Rev. Inscription:** *RELOJ / MONUMENTAL / DE / PACHUCA / HIDALGO* **Edge:** Segmented reeding

Date	Mintage	F	VF	XF	Unc	BU
2006Mo Proof	600	Value: 775				

KM# 795 100 PESOS

33.9400 g., Bi-Metallic .925 Silver 20.1753g center in Brass ring, 39.04 mm. **Series:** Second **Obv:** National arms **Obv. Legend:** ESTADOS UNIDOS MEXICANOS **Rev:** Hospicio Cabañas orphanage **Rev. Legend:** ESTADO DE JALISCO **Edge:** Segmented reeding

Date	Mintage	F	VF	XF	Unc	BU
2006Mo	149,750	—	—	—	—	25.00

KM# 875 100 PESOS

29.1690 g., Bi-Metallic .999 Gold 17.154g center in .999 Silver 12.015g ring, 34.5 mm. **Series:** Second **Obv:** National arms **Obv. Legend:** ESTADOS UNIDOS MEXICANOS **Rev:** Hospicio Cabañas orphanage **Rev. Legend:** ESTADO DE JALISCO **Edge:** Segmented reeding

Date	Mintage	F	VF	XF	Unc	BU
2006Mo Proof	600	Value: 775				

KM# 802 100 PESOS

33.9400 g., Bi-Metallic .925 Silver 20.1753g center in Aluminum-Bronze ring, 33.7, 39.04 mm. **Series:** Second **Obv:** National arms **Obv. Legend:** ESTADOS UNIDOS MEXICANOS **Rev:** Pyramid de la Loona (moon) **Rev. Legend:** ESTADO DE MÉXICO **Edge:** Segmented reeding

Date	Mintage	F	VF	XF	Unc	BU
2006Mo	149,377	—	—	—	—	25.00

KM# 876 100 PESOS

29.1690 g., Bi-Metallic .999 Gold 17.154g center in .999 Silver 12.015g ring, 34.5 mm. **Series:** Second **Obv:** National arms **Obv. Legend:** ESTADOS UNIDOS MEXICANOS **Rev:** Pyramid de la Looona (moon) **Rev. Legend:** ESTADO DE MÉXICO **Edge:** Segmented reeding

Date	Mintage	F	VF	XF	Unc	BU
2006Mo Proof	600	Value: 775				

KM# 785 100 PESOS

33.9400 g., Bi-Metallic .925 Silver 20.1753g center in Aluminum-Bronze ring, 33.7, 39.04 mm. **Series:** Second **Obv:** National arms **Obv. Legend:** ESTADOS UNIDOS MEXICANOS **Rev:** Four Monarch butterflies **Rev. Legend:** ESTADO DE MICHOACÁN **Edge:** Segmented reeding

Date	Mintage	F	VF	XF	Unc	BU
2006Mo	149,730	—	—	—	—	25.00

KM# 877 100 PESOS

29.1690 g., Bi-Metallic .999 Gold 17.154g center in .999 Silver 12.015g ring, 34.5 mm. **Series:** Second **Obv:** National arms **Obv. Legend:** ESTADOS UNIDOS MEXICANOS **Rev:** Four Monarch butterflies **Rev. Legend:** ESTADO DE MICHOACÁN **Edge:** Segmented reeding

Date	Mintage	F	VF	XF	Unc	BU
2006Mo Proof	600	Value: 775				

KM# 800 100 PESOS

33.9400 g., Bi-Metallic .925 Silver 20.1753g center in Aluminum-Bronze ring, 33.7, 39.04 mm. **Series:** Second **Obv:** National arms **Obv. Legend:** ESTADOS UNIDOS MEXICANOS **Rev:** 1/2 length figure of Chinelo (local dancer) at right, Palacio de Cortes in background **Rev. Inscription:** ESTADO DE / MORELOS **Edge:** Segmented reeding

Date	Mintage	F	VF	XF	Unc	BU
2006Mo	149,648	—	—	—	—	25.00

KM# 878 100 PESOS

29.1690 g., Bi-Metallic .999 Gold 17.154g center in .999 Silver 12.015g ring, 34.5 mm. **Series:** Second **Obv:** National arms **Obv. Legend:** ESTADOS UNIDOS MEXICANOS **Rev:** 1/2 length figure of Chinelo (local dancer) at right, Palacio de Cortes in background **Rev. Inscription:** ESTADO DE / MORELOS **Edge:** Segmented reeding

Date	Mintage	F	VF	XF	Unc	BU
2006Mo Proof	600	Value: 775				

KM# 798 100 PESOS

33.9400 g., 33.8250 Bi-Metallic 0.925 Silver 20.1753g center in Aluminum-Bronze ring 36.908 oz., 39.04 mm. **Series:** Second **Obv:** National arms **Obv. Legend:** ESTADOS UNIDOS MEXICANOS **Rev:** Isle de Mexcaltitlán **Rev. Legend:** ESTADO DE NAYARIT **Edge:** Segmented reeding

Date	Mintage	F	VF	XF	Unc	BU
2007Mo	149,560	—	—	—	—	25.00

KM# 879 100 PESOS

29.1690 g., Bi-Metallic .999 Gold 17.154g center in .999 12.015g ring, 34.5 mm. **Series:** Second **Obv:** National arms **Obv. Legend:** ESTADOS UNIDOS MEXICANOS **Rev:** Isle de Mexcaltitlán **Rev. Legend:** ESTADO DE NAYARIT **Edge:** Segmented reeding

Date	Mintage	F	VF	XF	Unc	BU
2007Mo Proof	600	Value: 775				

KM# 848 100 PESOS
33.9400 g., Bi-Metallic .925 Silver 20.1753 center in Aluminum-Bronze ring, 39.04 mm. **Series:** Second **Obv:** National arms **Obv. Legend:** ESTADOS UNIDOS MEXICANOE **Rev:** Old foundry in Parque Fundidora (public park) at right, Cerro de la Silla (Saddle Hill) in background **Rev. Legend:** ESTADO DE NUEVO LÉON **Edge:** Segmented reeding

Date	Mintage	F	VF	XF	Unc	BU
2007Mo	—	—	—	—	—	25.00

KM# 880 100 PESOS
29.1690 g., Bi-Metallic .999 Gold 17.154g center in .999 Silver 12.015g ring, 34.5 mm. **Series:** Second **Obv:** National arms **Obv. Legend:** ESTADOS UNIDOS MEXICANOS **Rev:** Old foundry in Parque Fundidora (public park) at right, Cerro de la Silla (Saddle hill) in background **Rev. Legend:** ESTADO DE NUEVO LEÓN **Edge:** Segmented reeding

Date	Mintage	F	VF	XF	Unc	BU
2007Mo Proof	600	Value: 775				

KM# 849 100 PESOS
33.9400 g., Bi-Metallic .925 Silver 20.1753g center in Aluminum-Bronze ring, 39.04 mm. **Series:** Second **Obv:** National arms **Obv. Legend:** ESTADOS UNIDOS MEXICANOS **Rev:** Teatro Macedonio Alcala (theater) **Rev. Legend:** OAXACA **Edge:** Segmented reeding

Date	Mintage	F	VF	XF	Unc	BU
2007Mo	—	—	—	—	—	25.00

KM# 881 100 PESOS
29.1690 g., Bi-Metallic .999 Gold 17.154g center in .999 Silver 12.015g ring, 34.50 mm. **Series:** Second **Obv:** National arms **Obv. Legend:** ESTADOS UNIDOS MEXICANOS **Rev:** Teatro Macedonio Alcala (theater) **Rev. Legend:** OAXACA **Edge:** Segmented reeding

Date	Mintage	F	VF	XF	Unc	BU
2007Mo Proof	600	Value: 775				

KM# 850 100 PESOS
33.9400 g., Bi-Metallic .925 Silver 20.1753g center in Aluminum-Bronze ring, 39.04 mm. **Series:** Second **Obv:** National arms **Obv. Legend:** ESTADOS UNIDOS MEXICANOS **Rev:** Talavera porcelain dish **Rev. Legend:** ESTADO DE PUEBLA **Edge:** Segmented reeding

Date	Mintage	F	VF	XF	Unc	BU
2007Mo	—	—	—	—	—	25.00

KM# 882 100 PESOS
29.1690 g., Bi-Metallic .999 Gold 17.154g center in .999 Silver 12.015g ring, 34.5 mm. **Series:** Second **Obv:** National arms **Obv. Legend:** ESTADOS UNIDOS MEXICANOS **Rev:** Talavera porcelain dish **Rev. Legend:** ESTADO DE PUEBLA **Edge:** Segmented reeding

Date	Mintage	F	VF	XF	Unc	BU
2007Mo Proof	600	Value: 775				

KM# 851 100 PESOS
33.9400 g., Bi-Metallic .925 Silver 20.1753g center in Aluminum-Bronze ring, 39.04 mm. **Series:** Second **Obv:** National arms **Obv. Legend:** ESTADOS UNIDOS MEXICANOS **Rev:** Mask at left, rays above state arms at center, Mayan ruins at right **Rev. Legend:** QUINTANA ROO **Edge:** Segmented reeding

Date	Mintage	F	VF	XF	Unc	BU
2007Mo	—	—	—	—	—	25.00

KM# 883 100 PESOS
29.1690 g., Gold .999 Gold 17.154g center in .999 Silver 12.015g ring, 34.5 mm. **Series:** Second **Obv:** National arms **Obv. Legend:** ESTADOS UNIDOS MEXICANOS **Rev:** Mask at left, rays above state arms at center, Mayan ruins at right **Rev. Legend:** QUINTANA ROO **Edge:** Segmented reeding

Date	Mintage	F	VF	XF	Unc	BU
2007Mo Proof	600	Value: 775				

KM# 852 100 PESOS
33.9400 g., Bi-Metallic .925 Silver 20.1753 center in Aluminum-Bronze ring, 39.04 mm. **Series:** Second **Obv:** National arms **Obv. Legend:** ESTADOS UNIDOS MEXICANOS **Rev:** Acueduct of Querétaro at left, church of Santa Rosa de Viterbo at right **Rev. Legend:** ESTADO DE QUERÉTARO ARTEAGA **Edge:** Segmented reeding

Date	Mintage	F	VF	XF	Unc	BU
2007Mo	—	—	—	—	—	25.00

KM# 884 100 PESOS
29.1690 g., Bi-Metallic .999 Gold 17.154g center in .999 Silver 12.015g ring, 34.5 mm. **Series:** Second **Obv:** National arms **Obv. Legend:** ESTADOS UNIDOS MEXICANOS **Rev:** Acueduct of Querétaro at left, church of Santa Rosa de Viterbo at right **Rev. Legend:** ESTADO DE QUERÉTARO ARTEAGA **Edge:** Segmented reeding

Date	Mintage	F	VF	XF	Unc	BU
2007Mo Proof	600	—	—	—	—	775

KM# 853 100 PESOS
33.9400 g., Bi-Metallic .925 Silver 20.1753g center in Aluminum-Bronze ring, 39.04 mm. **Series:** Second **Obv:** National arms **Obv. Legend:** ESRADOS UNIDOS MEXICANOS **Rev:** Facade of Caja Real **Rev. Legend:** • SAN LUIS POTOSÍ • **Edge:** Segmented reeding

Date	Mintage	F	VF	XF	Unc	BU
2007Mo	—	—	—	—	—	25.00

KM# 885 100 PESOS
29.1690 g., Bi-Metallic .999 Gold 17.154g center in .999 Silver 12.015 ring, 34.5 mm. **Series:** Second **Obv:** National arms **Obv. Legend:** ESTADOS UNIDOS MEXICANOS **Rev:** Facade of Caja Real **Rev. Legend:** • SAN LUIS POTOSÍ • **Edge:** Segmented reeding

Date	Mintage	F	VF	XF	Unc	BU
2007Mo Proof	600	Value: 775				

KM# 854 100 PESOS
33.9400 g., Bi-Metallic .925 Silver 20.1753g center in Aluminum-Bronze ring, 39.04 mm. **Series:** Second **Obv:** National arms **Obv. Legend:** ESTADOS UNIDOS MEXICANOS **Rev:** Shield on pile of cactus fruits **Rev. Legend:** ESTADO DE SINALOA - LUGAR DE PITAHAYAS **Edge:** Segmented reeding

Date	Mintage	F	VF	XF	Unc	BU
2007Mo	—	—	—	—	—	25.00

KM# 886 100 PESOS
29.1690 g., Bi-Metallic .999 Gold 17.154 center in .999 Silver 12.015g ring, 34.5 mm. **Series:** Second **Obv:** National arms **Obv. Legend:** ESTADOS UNIDOS MEXICANOS **Rev:** Shield on pile of cactus fruits **Rev. Legend:** ESTADO DE SINALOA - LUGAR DE PITAHAYES **Edge:** Segmented reeding

Date	Mintage	F	VF	XF	Unc	BU
2007Mo Proof	600	Value: 775				

KM# 855 100 PESOS
33.9400 g., Bi-Metallic .925 Silver 20.1753g center in Aluminum-Bronze ring, 39.04 mm. **Series:** Second **Obv:** National arms **Obv. Legend:** ESTADOS UNIDOS MEXICANOS **Rev:** Local in Dance of the Deer at left, cactus at right, mountains in background **Rev. Legend:** ESTADO DE SONORA **Edge:** Segmented reeding

Date	Mintage	F	VF	XF	Unc	BU
2007Mo	—	—	—	—	—	25.00

KM# 887 100 PESOS
29.1690 g., Bi-Metallic .999 Gold 17.154g center in .999 Silver 12.015g ring, 34.5 mm. **Series:** Second **Obv:** National arms **Obv. Legend:** ESTADOS UNIDOS MEXICANOS **Rev:** Local in Dance of the Deer at left, cactus at right, mountains in background **Rev. Legend:** ESTADO DE SONORA **Edge:** Segmented reeding

Date	Mintage	F	VF	XF	Unc	BU
2007Mo Proof	600	Value: 775				

KM# 856 100 PESOS
33.9400 g., Bi-Metallic .925 Silver 20.1753 center in Aluminum-Bronze ring, 39.04 mm. **Series:** Second **Obv:** National arms **Obv. Legend:** ESTADOS UNIDOS MEXICANOS **Rev:** Fuente de los Pescadores (fisherman fountain) at lower left, giant head from the Olmec-pre-Hispanic culture at right, Planetario Tabasco in background **Rev. Legend:** TABASCO **Edge:** Segmented reeding

Date	Mintage	F	VF	XF	Unc	BU
2007Mo	—	—	—	—	—	25.00

KM# 888 100 PESOS
29.1690 g., Bi-Metallic .999 Gold 17.154g center in .999 Silver 12.015g ring, 34.5 mm. **Series:** Second **Obv:** National arms **Obv. Legend:** ESTADOS UNIDOS MEXICANOE **Rev:** Fuente de los Pescadores (fisherman fountain) at lower left, giant head from the Olmec-pre-Hispanic culture at right, Planetario Tabasco in background **Rev. Legend:** TABASCO **Edge:** Segmented reeding

Date	Mintage	F	VF	XF	Unc	BU
2007Mo Proof	600	Value: 775				

KM# 857 100 PESOS
33.9400 g., Bi-Metallic .925 Silver 20.1753g center in Aluminum-Bronze ring, 39.04 mm. **Series:** Second **Obv:** National arms **Obv. Legend:** ESTADOS UNIDOS MEXICANOS **Rev:** Ridge - Cerro Del Bermal, Gonzáles **Rev. Legend:** TAMAULIPAS **Edge:** Segmented reeding

Date	Mintage	F	VF	XF	Unc	BU
2007Mo	—	—	—	—	—	25.00

KM# 889 100 PESOS
29.1690 g., Bi-Metallic .999 Gold 17.154g center in .999 Silver 12.015g ring, 34.5 mm. **Series:** Second **Obv:** National arms **Obv. Legend:** ESTADOS DE MEXICANOS **Rev:** Ridge - Cerro Del Bemal, Gonzáles **Rev. Legend:** TAMAULIPAS **Edge:** Segmented reeding

Date	Mintage	F	VF	XF	Unc	BU
2007Mo Proof	600	Value: 775				

KM# 858 100 PESOS
33.9400 g., Bi-Metallic .925 Silver 20.1753g center in Aluminum-Bronze ring, 39.04 mm. **Series:** Second **Obv:** National arms **Obv. Legend:** ESTADOS UNIDOS MEXICANOS **Rev:** Basilica de Ocotlán at left, state arms above Capilla Abierta, Plaza de Toros Ranchero Aguilar below, Exconvento de San Francisco at right **Rev. Legend:** ESTADO DE TLAXCALA **Edge:** Segmented reeding

Date	Mintage	F	VF	XF	Unc	BU
2007Mo	—	—	—	—	—	25.00

KM# 890 100 PESOS
29.1690 g., Bi-Metallic .999 Gold 17.154g center in .999 Silver 12.015g ring, 34.5 mm. **Series:** Second **Obv:** National arms **Obv. Legend:** ESTADOS UNIDOS MEXICANOS **Rev:** Basilica de Ocotlán at left, state arms above Capilla Abierta, Plaza de Toros Ranchero Aguilar below, Exconvento de San Francisco at right **Rev. Legend:** ESTADO DE TLAXCALA **Edge:** Segmented reeding

Date	Mintage	F	VF	XF	Unc	BU
2007Mo Proof	600	Value: 775				

KM# 859 100 PESOS
33.9400 g., Bi-Metallic .912 Silver 20.1753g center in Aluminum-Bronze ring, 39.04 mm. **Series:** Second **Obv:** National arms **Obv. Legend:** ESTADOS UNIDOS MEXICANOS **Rev:** Pyramid of El Tajín **Rev. Legend:** • VERACRUZ • - • DE IGNACIO DE LA LLAVE • **Edge:** Segmented reeding

Date	Mintage	F	VF	XF	Unc	BU
2007Mo	—	—	—	—	—	25.00

KM# 891 100 PESOS
29.1690 g., Bi-Metallic .999 Gold 17.154g center in .999 Silver 12.015g ring, 34.5 mm. **Series:** Second **Obv:** National arms **Obv. Legend:** ESTADOS UNIDOS MEXICANOS **Rev:** Pyramid of El Tajin **Rev. Legend:** • VERACRUZ • - • DE IGNACIO DE LA LLAVE • **Edge:** Segmented reeding

Date	Mintage	F	VF	XF	Unc	BU
2007Mo Proof	600	Value: 775				

KM# 860 100 PESOS
33.9400 g., Bi-Metallic .925 Silver 20.1753 center in Aluminum-Bronze ring, 39.04 mm. **Series:** Second **Obv:** National arms **Obv. Legend:** ESTADOS UNIDOS MEXICANOS **Rev:** Stylized pryamid of Chichén Itzá **Rev. Legend:** Castillo de Chichén Itzá **Edge:** Segmented reeding

Date	Mintage	F	VF	XF	Unc	BU
2007Mo	—	—	—	—	—	25.00

KM# 892 100 PESOS
29.1690 g., Bi-Metallic .999 Gold 17.154g center in .999 Silver 12.015g ring, 34.5 mm. **Series:** Second **Obv:** National arms **Obv. Legend:** ESTADOS UNIDOS MEXICANOS **Rev:** Stylized pyramid of Chichén-Itzá **Rev. Inscription:** YUCATÁN **Edge:** Segmented reeding

Date	Mintage	F	VF	XF	Unc	BU
2007Mo Proof	600	Value: 775				

KM# 861 100 PESOS
33.9400 g., Bi-Metallic .925 Silver 20.1753g center in Aluminum-Bronze ring, 39.04 mm. **Series:** Second **Obv:** National arms **Obv. Legend:** ESTADOS UNIDOS MEXICANOS **Rev:** Cable car above Monumento al Minero at left, Catedral de Zacatecas at center right **Rev. Legend:** ZACATEXAS **Edge:** Segmented reeding

Date	Mintage	F	VF	XF	Unc	BU
2007Mo	—	—	—	—	—	25.00

KM# 893 100 PESOS
29.1690 g., Bi-Metallic .999 Gold 17.154g center in .999 Silver 12.015g ring, 34.5 mm. **Series:** Second **Obv:** National arms **Obv. Legend:** ESTADOS UNIDOS MEXICANOS **Rev:** Cable car above Monumento al Minero at left, Catedral de Zacatecas at center right **Rev. Legend:** Zacatecas **Edge:** Segmented reeding

Date	Mintage	F	VF	XF	Unc	BU
2007Mo Proof	600	Value: 775				

SILVER BULLION COINAGE

Libertad Series

KM# 609 1/20 ONZA (1/20 Troy Ounce of Silver)
1.5551 g., 0.9990 Silver 0.0499 oz. ASW **Obv:** National arms, eagle left **Rev:** Winged Victory

Date	Mintage	F	VF	XF	Unc	BU
2001Mo	25,000	—	—	—	—	12.00
2001Mo Proof	1,500	Value: 15.00				
2002Mo	45,000	—	—	—	—	8.00
2002Mo Proof	2,800	Value: 13.00				
2003Mo	35,000	—	—	—	—	8.00
2003Mo Proof	3,015	Value: 13.00				
2004Mo	35,000	—	—	—	—	8.00
2004Mo Proof	5,285	Value: 13.00				
2005Mo	16,525	—	—	—	—	8.00
2005Mo Proof	1,500	Value: 12.00				
2006Mo	20,000	—	—	—	—	8.00
2006Mo Proof	3,300	Value: 12.00				
2007Mo	—	—	—	—	—	8.00
2007Mo Proof	—	Value: 12.00				

KM# 610 1/10 ONZA (1/10 Troy Ounce of Silver)
3.1103 g., 0.9990 Silver 0.0999 oz. ASW **Obv:** National arms, eagle left **Rev:** Winged Victory

Date	Mintage	F	VF	XF	Unc	BU
2001Mo	25,000	—	—	—	—	14.00
2001Mo Proof	1,500	Value: 18.00				
2002Mo	35,000	—	—	—	—	10.00
2002Mo Proof	2,800	Value: 15.00				
2003Mo	5,000	—	—	—	—	10.00
2003Mo Proof	4,500	Value: 15.00				
2004Mo	22,277	—	—	—	—	10.00
2004Mo Proof	3,500	Value: 15.00				
2005Mo	7,086	—	—	—	—	10.00
2005Mo Proof	2,500	Value: 14.00				
2006Mo	15,000	—	—	—	—	10.00
2006Mo Proof	3,000	Value: 14.00				
2007Mo	—	—	—	—	—	10.00
2007Mo Proof	—	Value: 14.00				

KM# 611 1/4 ONZA (1/4 Troy Ounce of Silver)
7.7758 g., 0.9990 Silver 0.2497 oz. ASW **Obv:** National arms, eagle left **Rev:** Winged Victory

Date	Mintage	F	VF	XF	Unc	BU
2001Mo	25,000	—	—	—	—	18.00
2001Mo Proof	1,000	Value: 22.00				
2002Mo	35,000	—	—	—	—	13.50
2002Mo Proof	2,800	Value: 20.00				
2003Mo	7,000	—	—	—	—	13.50
2003Mo Proof	3,500	Value: 20.00				
2004Mo	30,000	—	—	—	—	13.50
2004Mo Proof	3,900	Value: 20.00				
2005Mo	1,901	—	—	—	—	13.50
2005Mo Proof	1,500	Value: 18.50				
2006Mo	15,000	—	—	—	—	13.00
2006Mo Proof	3,000	Value: 18.50				
2007Mo	—	—	—	—	—	13.00
2007Mo Proof	—	Value: 18.50				

KM# 612 1/2 ONZA (1/2 Troy Ounce of Silver)
15.5517 g., 0.9990 Silver 0.4995 oz. ASW **Obv:** National arms, eagle left **Rev:** Winged Victory

Date	Mintage	F	VF	XF	Unc	BU
2001Mo	20,000	—	—	—	—	22.00
2001Mo Proof	1,000	Value: 30.00				
2002Mo	35,000	—	—	—	—	18.00
2002Mo Proof	2,800	Value: 25.00				
2003Mo	13,000	—	—	—	—	18.00
2003Mo Proof	3,000	Value: 25.00				
2004Mo	24,000	—	—	—	—	18.00
2004Mo Proof	4,300	Value: 25.00				
2005Mo	8,126	—	—	—	—	18.00
2005Mo Proof	1,500	Value: 22.00				
2006Mo	15,000	—	—	—	—	18.00
2006Mo Proof	2,900	Value: 22.00				
2007Mo	—	—	—	—	—	18.00
2007Mo Proof	—	Value: 22.00				

KM# 639 ONZA (Troy Ounce of Silver)
31.1000 g., 0.9990 Silver 0.9988 oz. ASW **Subject:** Libertad **Obv:** National arms, eagle left within center of past and present arms **Rev:** Winged Victory **Edge:** Reeded

Date	Mintage	F	VF	XF	Unc	BU
2001Mo	650,000	—	—	—	—	28.00
2001Mo Proof	2,000	Value: 60.00				
2002Mo	850,000	—	—	—	—	28.00
2002Mo Proof	3,800	Value: 60.00				
2003Mo	678,869	—	—	—	—	28.00
2003Mo Proof	5,000	Value: 60.00				
2004Mo	560,412	—	—	—	—	35.00
2004Mo Proof	5,300	Value: 60.00				
2005Mo	300,000	—	—	—	—	45.00
2005Mo Proof	4,000	Value: 60.00				
2006Mo	—	—	—	—	—	28.00
2006Mo Proof	—	Value: 60.00				
2007Mo	—	—	—	—	—	28.00
2007Mo Proof	—	Value: 60.00				

KM# 614 2 ONZAS (2 Troy Ounces of Silver)
62.2070 g., 0.9990 Silver 1.9979 oz. ASW, 48 mm. **Subject:** Libertad **Obv:** National arms, eagle left within center of past and present arms **Rev:** Winged Victory **Edge:** Reeded

Date	Mintage	F	VF	XF	Unc	BU
2001Mo	1,700	—	—	—	—	60.00
2001Mo Proof	500	Value: 75.00				
2002Mo	8,700	—	—	—	—	55.00
2002Mo Proof	1,000	Value: 70.00				
2003Mo	9,000	—	—	—	—	55.00
2003Mo Proof	400	Value: 70.00				
2004Mo	11,349	—	—	—	—	45.00
2004Mo Proof	1,360	Value: 70.00				
2005Mo	1,200	—	—	—	—	45.00
2005Mo Proof	740	Value: 70.00				
2006Mo	5,800	—	—	—	—	45.00
2006Mo Proof	1,100	Value: 70.00				
2007Mo	—	—	—	—	—	45.00
2007Mo Proof	—	Value: 70.00				

KM# 615 5 ONZAS (5 Troy Ounces of Silver)
155.5175 g., 0.9990 Silver 4.9948 oz. ASW, 65 mm. **Subject:** Libertad **Obv:** National arms, eagle left within center of past and present arms **Rev:** Winged Victory **Edge:** Reeded **Note:** Illustration reduced.

Date	Mintage	F	VF	XF	Unc	BU
2001Mo	4,000	—	—	—	—	110
2001Mo Proof	600	Value: 200				
2002Mo	5,200	—	—	—	—	110
2002Mo Proof	1,000	Value: 200				
2003Mo	5,500	—	—	—	—	100
2003Mo Proof	495	Value: 115				
2004Mo	6,324	—	—	—	—	100
2004Mo Proof	1,805	Value: 135				
2005Mo	790	—	—	—	—	100
2005Mo Proof	900	Value: 125				
2006Mo	3,000	—	—	—	—	100
2006Mo Proof	1,000	Value: 125				
2007Mo	—	—	—	—	—	100
2007Mo Proof	—	Value: 125				

KM# 677 KILO (32.15 Troy Ounces of Silver)
999.9775 g., 0.9990 Silver 32.116 oz. ASW, 110 mm. **Subject:** Collector Bullion **Obv:** National arms in center of past and present arms **Rev:** Winged Victory **Edge:** Reeded

Date	Mintage	F	VF	XF	Unc	BU
2002Mo Prooflike	1,100	—	—	—	—	750
2003Mo Proof	2,234	Value: 650				
2004Mo Prooflike	500	—	—	—	—	650
2005Mo Proof	874	Value: 675				

GOLD BULLION COINAGE

KM# 671 1/20 ONZA (1/20 Ounce of Pure Gold)
1.5551 g., 0.9990 Gold 0.0499 oz. AGW, 16 mm. **Obv:** National arms, eagle left **Rev:** Winged Victory **Edge:** Reeded **Note:** Design similar to KM#609. Value estimates do not include the high taxes and surcharges added to the issue prices by the Mexican Government.

Date	Mintage	F	VF	XF	Unc	BU
2002Mo	5,000	—	—	—	—	BV+30%
2004Mo	—	—	—	—	—	BV+30%
2005Mo	—	—	—	—	—	BV+30%
2006Mo	—	—	—	—	—	BV+30%
2007Mo	—	—	—	—	—	—

KM# 672 1/10 ONZA (1/10 Ounce of Pure Gold)
3.1103 g., 0.9990 Gold 0.0999 oz. AGW, 20 mm. **Obv:** National arms, eagle left **Rev:** Winged Victory **Edge:** Reeded **Note:** Design similar to KM#610. Value estimates do not include the high taxes and surcharges added to the issue prices by the Mexican Government.

Date	Mintage	F	VF	XF	Unc	BU
2002Mo	5,000	—	—	—	—	BV+20%
2004Mo	—	—	—	—	—	BV+20%
2005Mo	—	—	—	—	—	BV+20%
2006Mo	—	—	—	—	—	BV+20%
2006Mo Proof	—	BV+22%				
2007Mo	—	—	—	—	—	BV+20%

KM# 673 1/4 ONZA (1/4 Ounce of Pure Gold)
7.7758 g., 0.9990 Gold 0.2497 oz. AGW, 26.9 mm. **Obv:** National arms, eagle left **Rev:** Winged Victory **Edge:** Reeded **Note:** Design similar to KM#611. Value estimates do not include the high taxes and surcharges added to the issue prices by the Mexican Government.

Date	Mintage	F	VF	XF	Unc	BU
2002Mo	—	—	—	—	—	BV+12%
2004Mo	—	—	—	—	—	BV+12%
2004Mo Proof	—	BV+15%				
2005Mo	—	—	—	—	—	BV+12%
2005Mo Proof	—	BV+15%				
2006Mo	—	—	—	—	—	BV+12%
2006Mo Proof	—	BV+12%				
2007Mo	—	—	—	—	—	BV+12%

KM# 674 1/2 ONZA (1/2 Ounce of Pure Gold)
15.5517 g., 0.9990 Gold 0.4995 oz. AGW, 32.9 mm. **Obv:** National arms, eagle left **Rev:** Winged Victory **Edge:** Reeded **Note:** Design similar to KM#612. Value estimates do not include the high taxes and surcharges added to the issue prices by the Mexican Government.

Date	Mintage	F	VF	XF	Unc	BU
2002Mo	—	—	—	—	—	BV+8%
2004Mo	—	—	—	—	—	BV+8%
2005Mo	—	—	—	—	—	BV+8%
2005Mo Proof	—	BV+12%				
2006Mo	—	—	—	—	—	BV+8%
2006Mo Proof	—	BV+12%				
2007Mo	—	—	—	—	—	BV+8%

KM# 675 ONZA (Ounce of Pure Gold)
31.1035 g., 0.9990 Gold 0.9990 oz. AGW, 40 mm. **Obv:** National arms, eagle left **Rev:** Winged Victory **Edge:** Reeded **Note:** Design similar to KM#639. Value estimates do not include the high taxes and surcharges added to the issue prices by the Mexican Government.

Date	Mintage	F	VF	XF	Unc	BU
2002Mo	—	—	—	—	—	BV+3%
2004Mo	—	—	—	—	—	BV+3%
2005Mo	—	—	—	—	—	BV+3%
2005Mo Proof	—	BV+5%				
2006Mo	—	—	—	—	—	BV+3%
2006Mo Proof	—	BV+5%				

BANK SETS

Hard Case Sets unless otherwise noted.

KM#	Date	Mintage	Identification	Issue Price	Mkt Val
BS38	2001 (10)	—	KM#546-549, 603-605, 636-638 Set in folder	—	30.00
BS39	2002 (8)	—	KM#546-549, 603-605, 616 Set in folder	—	30.00
BS40	2003 (6)	—	KM#547-549, 603-605 Set in folder	—	30.00

MOLDOVA

The Republic of Moldova (formerly the Moldavian S.S.R.) is bordered in the north, east and south by the Ukraine and on the west by Romania. It has an area of 13,000 sq.mi. (33,700 sq.km.) and a population of 4.4 million. The capital is Chisinau. Agricultural products are mainly cereals, grapes, tobacco, sugar beets and fruits. Food processing, clothing, building materials and agricultural machinery manufacturing dominate industry.

MONETARY SYSTEM
100 Bani = 1 Leu

REPUBLIC

DECIMAL COINAGE

KM# 1 BAN
0.6800 g., Aluminum, 14.5 mm. **Obv:** National arms **Rev:** Value divides date above monogram **Edge:** Plain

Date	Mintage	F	VF	XF	Unc	BU
2004	—	—	—	—	0.25	0.50

KM# 2 5 BANI
0.8000 g., Aluminum, 16 mm. **Obv:** National arms **Rev:** Monogram divides sprigs below value and date **Edge:** Plain

Date	Mintage	F	VF	XF	Unc	BU
2001	—	—	—	—	0.30	0.50
2002	—	—	—	—	0.30	0.50
2003	—	—	—	—	0.30	0.50
2005	—	—	—	—	0.30	0.50

KM# 7 10 BANI
0.8400 g., Aluminum, 16.6 mm. **Obv:** National arms **Rev:** Value, date and monogram **Edge:** Plain

Date	Mintage	F	VF	XF	Unc	BU
2001	—	—	—	—	0.40	0.60
2002	—	—	—	—	0.40	0.60
2003	—	—	—	—	0.40	0.60
2005	—	—	—	—	0.40	0.60

KM# 3 25 BANI
0.9200 g., Aluminum, 17.5 mm. **Obv:** National arms **Rev:** Monogram divides sprigs below value and date **Edge:** Plain

Date	Mintage	F	VF	XF	Unc	BU
2001	—	—	—	—	0.50	0.75
2002	—	—	—	—	0.50	0.75
2003	—	—	—	—	0.50	0.75
2004	—	—	—	—	0.50	0.75

KM# 10 50 BANI
3.1000 g., Brass-Clad Steel, 19 mm. **Obv:** National arms **Rev:** Value and date within grapevine **Edge:** Reeded

Date	Mintage	F	VF	XF	Unc	BU
2003	—	—	—	—	1.50	2.00
2005	—	—	—	—	1.50	2.00

KM# 12 10 LEI
13.5000 g., 0.9250 Silver 0.4015 oz. ASW, 24.5 mm. **Obv:** National arms above value **Rev:** European wildcat within circle **Edge:** Plain

Date	Mintage	F	VF	XF	Unc	BU
20001 Proof	1,000	Value: 55.00				

KM# 13 10 LEI
13.5000 g., 0.9250 Silver 0.4015 oz. ASW, 24.5 mm. **Obv:** National arms above value **Rev:** Woodpecker on tree within circle **Edge:** Plain

Date	Mintage	F	VF	XF	Unc	BU
2001 Proof	1,000	Value: 50.00				

KM# 19 10 LEI
13.4500 g., 0.9250 Silver 0.4000 oz. ASW, 24.5 mm. **Obv:** National arms above value **Rev:** Mink within circle **Edge:** Plain

Date	Mintage	F	VF	XF	Unc	BU
2003 Proof	500	Value: 55.00				

KM# 20 10 LEI
13.4500 g., 0.9250 Silver 0.4000 oz. ASW, 24.5 mm. **Obv:** National arms above value **Rev:** Storks within circle **Edge:** Plain

Date	Mintage	F	VF	XF	Unc	BU
2003 Proof	500	Value: 55.00				

KM# 25 10 LEI
25.0000 g., Nickel Plated Brass, 30 mm. **Subject:** Wine Holiday **Obv:** National arms above value **Rev:** Wine grapes, goblet and flask **Edge:** Plain

Date	Mintage	F	VF	XF	Unc	BU
2003 Proof	—	Value: 12.50				

KM# 22 10 LEI
13.5000 g., 0.9250 Silver 0.4015 oz. ASW, 24.5 mm. **Obv:** National arms above value **Rev:** Wood Marten within circle **Edge:** Plain

Date	Mintage	F	VF	XF	Unc	BU
2004 Proof	500	Value: 55.00				

KM# 29 10 LEI
25.0000 g., Nickel Plated Brass, 30 mm. **Subject:** European Women's Chess Championship **Obv:** Arms, date at top, value at bottom **Obv. Legend:** REPUBLICA - 2005 - MOLDOVA **Rev:** 2 chess figures on board at left, map at right **Rev. Inscription:** 2005 CHISINAU **Edge:** Plain

Date	Mintage	F	VF	XF	Unc	BU
2005 Proof	—	Value: 12.50				

KM# 30 10 LEI
13.5000 g., 0.9250 Silver 0.4015 oz. ASW, 24.5 mm. **Obv:** Arms, value below **Obv. Legend:** REPUBLICA MOLDOVA **Rev:** Golden eagle on branch, legend follows the coin circumference **Edge:** Plain

Date	Mintage	F	VF	XF	Unc	BU
2005 Proof	—	Value: 35.00				

KM# 33 10 LEI
13.5000 g., 0.9250 Silver 0.4015 oz. ASW, 24.5 mm. **Obv:** Arms, value below **Obv. Legend:** REPUBLICA - 2006 - MOLDOVA **Rev:** Bustard on vegetal background, legend around circumference using Latin name **Edge:** Plain

Date	Mintage	F	VF	XF	Unc	BU
2006 Proof	—	Value: 35.00				

KM# 17 50 LEI
16.5000 g., 0.9250 Silver 0.4907 oz. ASW, 30 mm. **Obv:** National arms above value **Rev:** Constantin Brancusi and building **Edge:** Plain

Date	Mintage	F	VF	XF	Unc	BU
2001 Proof	1,000	Value: 35.00				

KM# 18 50 LEI
16.5000 g., 0.9250 Silver 0.4907 oz. ASW, 30 mm. **Obv:** National arms above value **Rev:** Vasile Alecsandri with book and landscape **Edge:** Plain

Date	Mintage	F	VF	XF	Unc	BU
2001 Proof	1,000	Value: 35.00				

KM# 21 50 LEI
16.5000 g., 0.9250 Silver 0.4907 oz. ASW, 29.8 mm. **Subject:** Effigy of Dimitrie Cantemir **Obv:** National arms above value **Rev:** Bust facing flanked by dates and scroll **Edge:** Plain

Date	Mintage	F	VF	XF	Unc	BU
2003 Proof	500	Value: 35.00				

KM# 14 50 LEI
16.5500 g., 0.9250 Silver 0.4922 oz. ASW, 29.9 mm. **Subject:** Effigy of Miron Costin **Obv:** National arms above value **Rev:** Bust with hat 1/4 right flanked by dates and books **Edge:** Plain

Date	Mintage	F	VF	XF	Unc	BU
2003 Proof	500	Value: 50.00				

KM# 23 50 LEI
16.5000 g., 0.9250 Silver 0.4907 oz. ASW, 30 mm. **Obv:** National arms above value **Rev:** Bust of Bishop facing holding scepter **Edge:** Plain

Date	Mintage	F	VF	XF	Unc	BU
2004 Proof	500	Value: 40.00				

KM# 31 50 LEI
16.5000 g., 0.9250 Silver 0.4907 oz. ASW, 30 mm. **Subject:** 415th Anniversary - Birth of Grigore Ureche **Obv:** Arms, date divides legend at top, value below, **Obv. Legend:** REPUBLICA MOLDOVA **Rev:** Bust faces right, scroll with feather pen at right, inscription on scroll **Rev. Legend:** GRIGORE URECHE **Rev. Inscription:** Letopisetul Tarii Moldovei **Edge:** Plain

Date	Mintage	F	VF	XF	Unc	BU
2005 Proof	—	Value: 40.00				

KM# 34 50 LEI
16.5000 g., 0.9250 Silver 0.4907 oz. ASW, 30 mm. **Subject:** 200th Anniversary - Birth of Alexandru Donici **Obv:** Arms, date divides legend above, value below **Obv. Legend:** REPUBLICA MOLDOVA **Rev:** Bust of Donici facing, life dates on ribbon below **Rev. Legend:** ALEXANDRU DONICI

Date	Mintage	F	VF	XF	Unc	BU
2006 Proof	—	Value: 40.00				

KM# 16 100 LEI
31.1000 g., 0.9250 Silver 0.9249 oz. ASW, 37 mm. **Subject:** 10th Anniversary of Independence **Obv:** National arms above value **Rev:** Arch monument within circle above value and sprigs **Edge:** Plain

Date	Mintage	F	VF	XF	Unc	BU
2001 Proof	1,000	Value: 60.00				

KM# 26 100 LEI

7.8000 g., 0.9999 Gold 0.2507 oz. AGW, 24 mm. **Obv:** National arms above value **Rev:** King Stephan the Great (1456-1504) **Edge:** Plain

Date	Mintage	F	VF	XF	Unc	BU
2004 Proof	—	Value: 350				

KM# 32 100 LEI

31.1000 g., 0.9250 Silver 0.9249 oz. ASW, 37 mm. **Subject:** Burebista - King of Dacians **Obv:** Arms, date divides legend at top, value below **Obv. Legend:** REPUBLICA MOLDOVA **Rev:** Bust of Burebista at left, battle scene of Geto-Dacians with Romans at right **Rev. Legend:** BUREBISTA REGELE DACILOR **Edge:** Plain

Date	Mintage	F	VF	XF	Unc	BU
2005 Proof	—	Value: 60.00				

KM# 35 100 LEI

31.1000 g., 0.9250 Silver 0.9249 oz. ASW, 37 mm. **Subject:** 15th Anniversary - Independence Proclamation of the Republic of Moldova **Obv:** Arms, date divides legend above, value below **Obv. Legend:** REPUBLICA MOLDOVA **Rev:** Map of Moldova within stars in inner circle, legend around **Rev. Legend:** PROCLAMAREA INDEPENDENTEI / 1991-2006 **Edge:** Plain

Date	Mintage	F	VF	XF	Unc	BU
2006 Proof	—	Value: 60.00				

MONACO

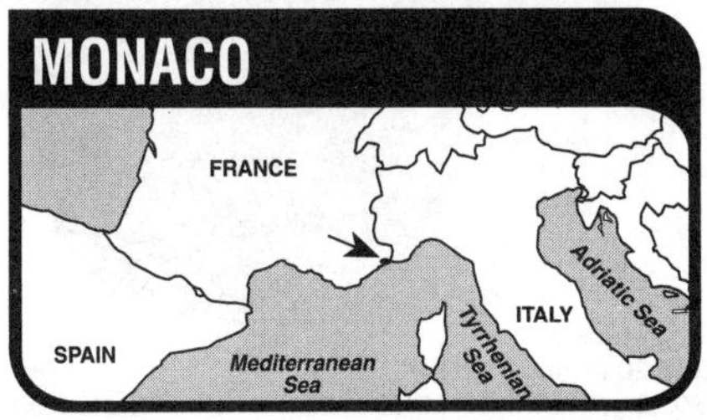

The Principality of Monaco, located on the Mediterranean coast nine miles from Nice, has an area of 0.58 sq. mi. (1.9 sq. km.) and a population of 26,000. Capital: Monaco-Ville. The economy is based on tourism and the manufacture of cosmetics, gourmet foods and highly specialized electronics. Monaco also derives its revenue from a tobacco monopoly and the sale of postage stamps for philatelic purpose. Gambling in Monte Carlo accounts for only a small fraction of the country's revenue.

RULERS

Rainier III, 1949-2005
Albert II, 2005-

MINT PRIVY MARKS

(a) - Paris (privy marks only)
Horseshoe - 2001 and 2002
Heart – 2002-2003
French Horn with starfish in water – 2003-
(p) - Thunderbolt - Poissy

MONETARY SYSTEM

100 Euro Cents = 1 Euro

PRINCIPALITY

EURO COINAGE

KM# 167 EURO CENT

2.2700 g., Copper Plated Steel, 16.2 mm. **Ruler:** Rainier III **Obv:** Crowned arms **Obv. Designer:** Robert Cochet **Rev:** Value and globe **Rev. Designer:** Luc Luycx **Edge:** Plain

Date	Mintage	F	VF	XF	Unc	BU
2001 (a)	347	—	—	—	20.00	30.00
2001 (a) Proof	3,500	Value: 75.00				
2002 (a)	Est. 40,000	—	—	—	—	65.00
Note: Initially available only in sets						
2003 (a)	—	—	—	—	—	—
2004 (a) Proof	14,999	Value: 25.00				
2005 (a) Proof	35,000	Value: 50.00				

KM# 168 2 EURO CENT

3.0300 g., Copper Plated Steel, 18.7 mm. **Ruler:** Rainier III **Obv:** Crowned arms **Obv. Designer:** Robert Cochet **Rev:** Value and globe **Rev. Designer:** Luc Luycx **Edge:** Grooved **Note:** Initially available only in sets

Date	Mintage	F	VF	XF	Unc	BU
2001 (a)	393,400	—	—	—	15.00	25.00
2001 (a) Proof	3,500	Value: 85.00				
2002 (a)	Est. 40,000	—	—	—	—	65.00
Note: Initially available only in sets						
2003 (a)	—	—	—	—	—	—
2004 (a) Proof	14,999	Value: 35.00				
2005 (a) Proof	35,000	Value: 50.00				

KM# 169 5 EURO CENT

3.8600 g., Copper-Nickel Plated Steel, 21.2 mm. **Ruler:** Rainier III **Obv:** Crowned arms **Obv. Designer:** Robert Cochet **Rev:** Value and globe **Rev. Designer:** Luc Luycx **Edge:** Plain **Note:** Initially available only in sets

Date	Mintage	F	VF	XF	Unc	BU
2001 (a)	320,000	—	—	—	20.00	30.00
2001 (a) Proof	3,500	Value: 95.00				
2002 (a)	Est. 40,000	—	—	—	—	70.00
Note: Initially available only in sets						
2003 (a)	—	—	—	—	—	—

Date	Mintage	F	VF	XF	Unc	BU
2004 (a) Proof	14,999	Value: 45.00				
2004 (a) Proof	35,000	Value: 55.00				

KM# 170 10 EURO CENT

4.0700 g., Brass, 19.7 mm. **Ruler:** Rainier III **Obv:** Knight on horse **Obv. Designer:** R. Baron **Rev:** Value and map **Rev. Designer:** Luc Luycx **Edge:** Reeded

Date	Mintage	F	VF	XF	Unc	BU
2001 (a)	320,000	—	—	—	15.00	20.00
2001 (a) Proof	3,500	Value: 110				
2002 (a)	407,200	—	—	—	8.00	12.00
2003 (a)	100,800	—	—	—	12.00	16.00
2004 (a) Proof	14,999	Value: 50.00				

KM# 181 10 EURO CENT

4.0700 g., Brass, 19.7 mm. **Ruler:** Albert II **Obv:** Charging knight **Obv. Designer:** R. Baron **Rev:** Relief map of Western Europe, stars, lines and value **Rev. Designer:** Luc Luycx **Edge:** Reeded

Date	Mintage	F	VF	XF	Unc	BU
2007 (a)	—	—	—	—	12.00	16.00

KM# 171 20 EURO CENT

5.7300 g., Brass, 22.1 mm. **Ruler:** Rainier III **Obv:** Knight on horse **Rev:** Value and map **Edge:** Notched **Designer:** R. Baron

Date	Mintage	F	VF	XF	Unc	BU
2001(a)	386,400	—	—	—	15.00	20.00
2001 (a) Proof	3,500	Value: 120				
2002 (a)	376,000	—	—	—	12.00	16.00
2003 (a)	100,000	—	—	—	12.00	16.00
2004 (a) Proof	14,999	Value: 60.00				

KM# 182 20 EURO CENT

5.7300 g., Brass, 22.1 mm. **Ruler:** Albert II **Obv:** Charging knight **Rev:** Relief map of Western Europe, stars, lines and value **Edge:** Notched **Designer:** R. Baron

Date	Mintage	F	VF	XF	Unc	BU
2007 (a)	—	—	—	—	12.00	16.00

KM# 172 50 EURO CENT

7.8100 g., Brass **Ruler:** Rainier III **Obv:** Knight on horse **Obv. Designer:** R. Baron **Rev:** Value and map **Rev. Designer:** Luc Luycx **Edge:** Reeded

Date	Mintage	F	VF	XF	Unc	BU
2001 (a)	320,000	—	—	—	15.00	20.00
2001 (a) Proof	3,500	Value: 130				
2002 (a)	364,000	—	—	—	8.00	12.00
2003 (a)	100,000	—	—	—	12.00	16.00
2004 (a) Proof	14,999	Value: 65.00				

KM# 183 50 EURO CENT

7.8100 g., Brass **Ruler:** Albert II **Obv:** Charging knight **Obv. Designer:** R. Baron **Rev:** Relief map of Western Europe, stars, lines and value **Rev. Designer:** Luc Luycx **Edge:** Reeded

Date	Mintage	F	VF	XF	Unc	BU
2007 (a)	—	—	—	—	12.00	16.00

KM# 173 EURO

7.5000 g., Bi-Metallic Copper- Nickel center in Brass ring, 23.2 mm. **Ruler:** Rainier III **Obv:** Conjoined heads of Prince Ranier and Crown Prince Albert right within circle **Obv. Designer:** Pierre Rodier **Rev:** Value and map **Rev. Designer:** Luc Luycx **Edge:** Reeded and plain sections

Date	Mintage	F	VF	XF	Unc	BU
2001 (a)	991,100	—	—	—	10.00	12.00
2001 (a) Proof	3,500	Value: 145				
2002 (a)	512,500	—	—	—	11.00	14.00
2003 (a)	135,000	—	—	—	13.50	18.50
2004 (a) Proof	14,999	Value: 75.00				

KM# 184 EURO

7.5000 g., Bi-Metallic Copper-Nickel center in Brass ring, 23.2 mm. **Ruler:** Albert II **Obv:** Conjoined heads of Prince Rainier and Crown Prince Albert right **Obv. Designer:** Pierre Rodier **Rev:** Relief map of Western Europe, stars, lines and value **Rev. Designer:** Luc Luycx **Edge:** Reeded and plain sections

Date	Mintage	F	VF	XF	Unc	BU
2007 (a)	—	—	—	—	13.50	18.50

KM# 174 2 EURO

8.5200 g., Bi-Metallic Brass center in Copper-Nickel ring, 25.7 mm. **Ruler:** Rainier III **Obv:** Head right within circle flanked by stars **Obv. Designer:** Pierre Rodier **Rev:** Value and map **Rev. Designer:** Luc Luycx **Edge:** Reeding over "2's" and stars

Date	Mintage	F	VF	XF	Unc	BU
2001 (a)	919,800	—	—	—	14.00	16.00
2001 (a) Proof	3,500	Value: 165				

Date	Mintage	F	VF	XF	Unc	BU
2002 (a)	496,000	—	—	—	15.00	18.00
2003 (a)	228,000	—	—	—	17.50	22.50
2004 (a) Proof	14,999	Value: 95.00				

KM# 185 2 EURO

8.5200 g., Bi-Metallic Brass center in Copper-Nickel ring, 25.7 mm. **Ruler:** Albert II **Obv:** Prince Rainer's portrait right **Obv. Designer:** Pierre Rodier **Rev:** Relief map of Western Europe, stars, lines and value **Rev. Designer:** Luc Luycx **Edge:** Reeding over 2's and stars

Date	Mintage	F	VF	XF	Unc	BU
2007 (a)	—	—	—	—	17.50	22.50

KM# 186 2 EURO

8.5200 g., Bi-Metallic Copper-Nickel center with brass ring, 25.75 mm. **Ruler:** Albert II **Subject:** 25th Anniversary Death of Princess Grace **Obv:** Head of Princess Grace left **Rev:** Relief map of Western Europe, stars, lines and value **Edge:** Reeded

Date	Mintage	F	VF	XF	Unc	BU
2007 (a)	20,000	—	—	—	—	—

KM# 180 5 EURO

12.0000 g., 0.9000 Silver 0.3472 oz. ASW, 29 mm. **Ruler:** Rainier III **Obv:** Bust right **Rev:** Saint standing

Date	Mintage	F	VF	XF	Unc	BU
2004 (a) Proof	14,999	Value: 125				

KM# 187 5 EURO

3.2200 g., 0.9000 Gold 0.0932 oz. AGW **Ruler:** Albert II **Subject:** Death of Rainier III **Obv:** Principality arms **Rev:** Head of Rainier III right

Date	Mintage	F	VF	XF	Unc	BU
2005 (a) Proof	3,313	Value: 550				

KM# 178 10 EURO

25.0000 g., 0.9250 Silver 0.7435 oz. ASW, 37 mm. **Ruler:** Rainier III **Obv:** Conjoined busts of Prince Ranier and Crown Prince Albert right **Rev:** Arms

Date	Mintage	F	VF	XF	Unc	BU
2003 (a) Proof	4,000	Value: 465				

KM# 177 20 EURO

18.0000 g., 0.9250 Gold 0.5353 oz. AGW, 32 mm. **Ruler:** Rainier III **Obv:** Bust right **Rev:** Arms

Date	Mintage	F	VF	XF	Unc	BU
2002 (a) Proof	10,000	Value: 1,100				

KM# 179 100 EURO

29.0000 g., 0.9000 Gold 0.8391 oz. AGW **Ruler:** Rainier III **Obv:** Bust right **Rev:** Knight on horse

Date	Mintage	F	VF	XF	Unc	BU
2003 (a) Proof	1,000	Value: 3,250				

MINT SETS

KM#	Date	Mintage	Identification	Issue Price	Mkt Val
MS1	2001 (8)	20,000	KM#167-174, exercise caution, as privately packaged and deceptively false sets are known	35.00	450
MS2	2002 (8)	40,000	KM#167-174, exercise caution, as partial sets, privately packaged and deceptively false sets are known	35.00	375

PROOF SETS

KM#	Date	Mintage	Identification	Issue Price	Mkt Val
PS1	2001 (8)	3,500	KM#167-174	—	1,000
PS2	2004 (9)	14,999	KM#167-174, 180	—	575
PS3	2005 (3)	35,000	KM#167-169	—	150

MONGOLIA

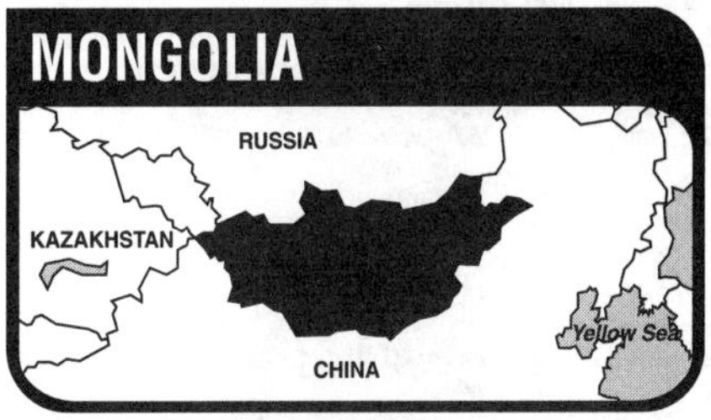

The State of Mongolia, (formerly the Mongolian Peoples Republic) a landlocked country in central Asia between Russia and the People's Republic of China, has an area of 604,250 sq. mi. (1,565,000 sq. km.) and a population of 2.26 million. Capital: Ulaan Baator. Animal herds and flocks are the chief economic asset. Wool, cattle, butter, meat and hides are exported.

For earlier issues see Russia - Tannu Tuva.

MONETARY SYSTEM

100 Mongo = 1 Tugrik

STATE

DECIMAL COINAGE

KM# 189 500 TUGRIK
25.0000 g., 0.9250 Silver 0.7435 oz. ASW, 38.7 mm. **Obv:** National emblem above value **Rev:** Protoceratops Andrewsi **Edge:** Reeded

Date	Mintage	F	VF	XF	Unc	BU
2001 Proof	2,500	Value: 40.00				

KM# 190 500 TUGRIK
25.0000 g., 0.9250 Silver 0.7435 oz. ASW **Obv:** National emblem above value **Rev:** Velociraptor Mongoliensis

Date	Mintage	F	VF	XF	Unc	BU
2001 Proof	2,500	Value: 40.00				

KM# 191 500 TUGRIK
25.0000 g., 0.9250 Silver 0.7435 oz. ASW **Series:** Olympics **Obv:** National emblem above value **Rev:** Speed skater

Date	Mintage	F	VF	XF	Unc	BU
2001 Proof	15,000	Value: 42.50				

KM# 192 500 TUGRIK
25.0000 g., 0.9250 Silver 0.7435 oz. ASW **Series:** Olympics **Obv:** National emblem above value **Rev:** Cross-country skiers

Date	Mintage	F	VF	XF	Unc	BU
2001 Proof	20,000	Value: 32.50				

KM# 195 500 TUGRIK
Copper-Nickel, 22.1 mm. **Subject:** Sukhe-Bataar **Obv:** National emblem and value **Rev:** Crowned head facing **Edge:** Plain

Date	Mintage	F	VF	XF	Unc	BU
2001	—	—	—	—	2.50	3.00

KM# 200 500 TUGRIK
25.5700 g., 0.9250 Silver 0.7604 oz. ASW, 38.5 mm. **Subject:** Marco Polo, Homeward **Obv:** National emblem above value **Rev:** Five-masted sailing junk **Edge:** Reeded

Date	Mintage	F	VF	XF	Unc	BU
2003 Proof	5,000	Value: 45.00				

KM# 205 500 TUGRIK
25.0000 g., 0.9250 Silver 0.7435 oz. ASW, 38.6 mm. **Obv:** National emblem above value **Rev:** Medallion divides busts **Edge:** Reeded

Date	Mintage	F	VF	XF	Unc	BU
2003 Proof	5,000	Value: 50.00				

KM# 206 500 TUGRIK
1.2440 g., 0.9999 Gold 0.0400 oz. AGW, 13.92 mm. **Obv:** National emblem above value **Rev:** Five masted sailing junk **Edge:** Reeded

Date	Mintage	F	VF	XF	Unc	BU
2003 Proof	25,000	Value: 50.00				

KM# 207 500 TUGRIK
1.2440 g., 0.9999 Gold 0.0400 oz. AGW, 13.92 mm. **Obv:** National emblem above value **Rev:** Medallion divides busts **Edge:** Reeded

Date	Mintage	F	VF	XF	Unc	BU
2003 Proof	25,000	Value: 50.00				

KM# 204 500 TUGRIK
25.0000 g., 0.9250 Silver 0.7435 oz. ASW, 38 mm. **Obv:** National emblem above value **Rev:** Wolf within full moon **Edge:** Reeded

Date	Mintage	F	VF	XF	Unc	BU
2003 Proof	10,000	Value: 50.00				

KM# 208 500 TUGRIK
25.0000 g., 0.9250 Silver 0.7435 oz. ASW, 38 mm. **Obv:** National emblem above value **Rev:** Holographic Osprey catching fish **Edge:** Reeded

Date	Mintage	F	VF	XF	Unc	BU
2004 Proof	5,000	Value: 50.00				

KM# 209 500 TUGRIK
24.9300 g., 0.9250 Bi-Metallic Niobium Leopard shape center in .925 Silver oval 0.7414 oz., 30 mm. **Obv:** National emblem above value **Rev:** Snow Leopard **Edge:** Reeded

Date	Mintage	F	VF	XF	Unc	BU
2005 Proof	5,000	Value: 70.00				

KM# 210 500 TUGRIK

31.1035 g., 0.9990 Silver 0.9990 oz. ASW, 35x35 mm. **Obv:** Bronze plated horse and rider on antiqued silver with national emblem and value **Rev:** Bronze plated horse and rider on antiqued silver above date **Edge:** Reeded **Shape:** Square

Date	Mintage	F	VF	XF	Unc	BU
2005	2,500	—	—	—	50.00	55.00

KM# 210a 500 TUGRIK

31.1035 g., 0.9990 Silver 0.9990 oz. ASW, 35x35 mm. **Obv:** Gold plated horse and rider with national emblem and value **Rev:** Gold plated horse and rider above date **Edge:** Reeded

Date	Mintage	F	VF	XF	Unc	BU
2005 Proof	2,500	Value: 65.00				

KM# 212 500 TUGRIK

31.1050 g., 0.9990 Silver 0.9990 oz. ASW, 38 mm. **Obv:** Arms and value **Rev:** Wolverine head facing with diamonds in eyes **Rev. Inscription:** WILDLIFE PROTECTION GULO GULO

Date	Mintage	F	VF	XF	Unc	BU
2007	—	—	—	—	—	50.00

KM# 213 500 TUGRIK

31.1000 g., 0.9990 Silver 0.9988 oz. ASW, 39mm mm. **Subject:** Year of the Rat **Obv:** National emblem, value below **Rev:** Three rats in grass **Edge:** Reeded

Date	Mintage	F	VF	XF	Unc	BU
2008	20,000	—	—	—	—	45.00

KM# 213a 500 TUGRIK

31.1000 g., 0.9990 Silver 0.9988 oz. ASW, 39.0 mm. **Subject:** Year of the Rat **Obv:** National emblem, value below **Rev:** Three gilt rats in grass **Edge:** Reeded

Date	Mintage	F	VF	XF	Unc	BU
2008 Proof	5,000	Value: 50.00				

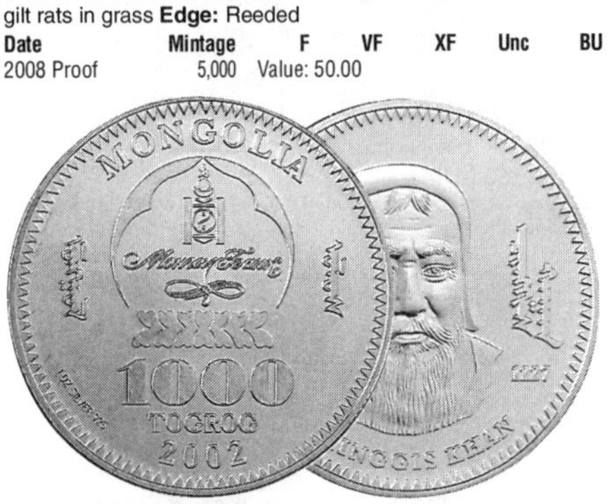

KM# 199 1000 TUGRIK

31.1100 g., 0.9250 Silver 0.9252 oz. ASW, 38.6 mm. **Obv:** National emblem above value **Obv. Inscription:** Denomination spelled "TOGROG" **Rev:** Head facing **Edge:** Reeded

Date	Mintage	F	VF	XF	Unc	BU
2002	17,000	—	—	—	35.00	40.00

KM# 214 1000 TUGRIK

1.2400 g., 0.9990 Gold 0.0398 oz. AGW, 14.0 mm. **Subject:** Year of the Rat **Obv:** National emblem, value below **Edge:** Reeded

Date	Mintage	F	VF	XF	Unc	BU
2008 Proof	10,000	Value: 50.00				

KM# 198 5000 TUGRIK

155.5000 g., 0.9990 Silver 4.9942 oz. ASW, 40x90 mm. **Subject:** Year of the Horse **Obv:** National emblem above value to left of Palace Museum **Rev:** Five multicolor running horses **Edge:** Plain **Note:** Round-cornered rectangle. Photo reduced.

Date	Mintage	F	VF	XF	Unc	BU
2002 Proof	—	Value: 175				

KM# 215 100000 TUGRIK

3000.0000 g., 0.9990 Silver 96.351 oz. ASW, 130.0 mm. **Subject:** Year of the Rat **Obv:** National emblem, value below **Rev:** Three rats in grass **Edge:** Reeded **Note:** Sreial number on edge.

Date	Mintage	F	VF	XF	Unc	BU
2008 Proof	500	Value: 2,250				

MOROCCO

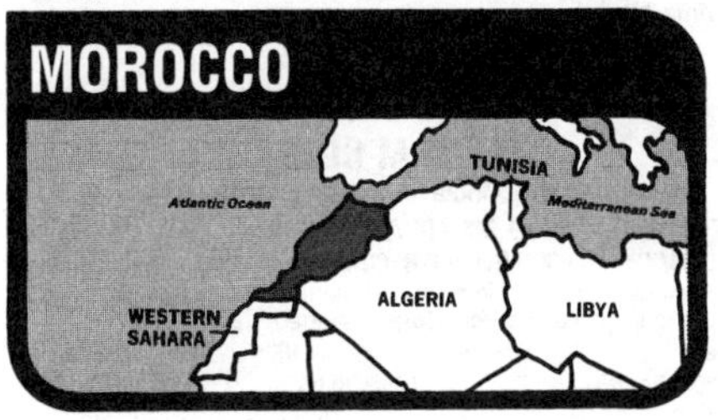

The Kingdom of Morocco, situated on the northwest corner of Africa, has an area of 432,620 sq. mi. (710,850 sq. km.) and a population of 36 million. Capital: Rabat. The economy is essentially agricultural. Phosphates, fresh and preserved vegetables, canned fish, and raw materials are exported.

TITLES

المعربية

Al-Maghribiya(t)

المملكة المغربية

Al-Mamlaka(t) al-Maghribiya(t)

المحمدية الشريفة

Al-Mohammediya(t) esh-Sherifiya(t)

RULERS

Kingdom

Mohammed VI, AH1420- /1999- AD

KINGDOM

1956-

Mohammed VI

AH1420/1999AD

REFORM COINAGE

100 Santimat = 1 Dirham

Y# 116 1/2 DIRHAM

4.0000 g., Copper-Nickel, 21 mm. **Obv:** Crowned arms with supporters **Rev:** Value, design theme "telecommunications and new technologies" **Edge:** Reeded

Date	Mintage	F	VF	XF	Unc	BU
AH1423-2002	—	—	—	—	2.00	—

Y# 117 DIRHAM

6.0000 g., Copper-Nickel, 24 mm. **Obv:** Head 3/4 left **Rev:** Crowned arms with supporters above value **Edge:** Reeded

Date	Mintage	F	VF	XF	Unc	BU
AH1423-2002	—	—	—	—	3.00	—

Y# 112 5 SANTIMAT

2.5000 g., Brass, 17.5 mm. **Obv:** Crowned arms with supporters **Rev:** Value, flower and dates **Edge:** Plain

Date	Mintage	F	VF	XF	Unc	BU
AH1423-2002	—	—	—	—	0.50	—

Y# 114 10 SANTIMAT

3.0000 g., Brass, 19.8 mm. **Obv:** Crowned arms with supporters **Rev:** Value, design of "sport and solidarity" **Edge:** Reeded

Date	Mintage	F	VF	XF	Unc	BU
AH1423-2002	—	—	—	—	1.00	—

Y# 115 20 SANTIMAT

4.0000 g., Brass, 23 mm. **Obv:** Crowned arms with supporters **Rev:** Value, design of "tourist and craftsmen trade" **Edge:** Reeded

Date	Mintage	F	VF	XF	Unc	BU
AH1423-2002	—	—	—	—	1.50	—

Y# 118 2 DIRHAMS

7.3000 g., Copper-Nickel, 25.9 mm. **Obv:** Head 3/4 left within octagon shape **Rev:** Crowned arms with supporters above value within octogon shape **Edge:** Reeded

Date	Mintage	F	VF	XF	Unc	BU
AH1423-2002	—	—	—	—	4.00	—

Y# 109 5 DIRHAMS

7.5300 g., Bi-Metallic Brass center in Copper-Nickel ring, 25 mm. **Obv:** Head 3/4 left **Rev:** Crowned arms with supporters above value **Edge:** Segmented reeding

Date	Mintage	F	VF	XF	Unc	BU
AH1423-2002	—	—	—	—	6.00	—

Y# 124 5 DIRHAMS

Bi-Metallic **Obv:** King Hassan II 1903-2000 **Rev:** Coat of arms

Date	Mintage	F	VF	XF	Unc	BU
2002	—	—	—	—	6.00	—

Y# 110 10 DIRHAMS

9.0000 g., Bi-Metallic Copper-Nickel center in Brass ring, 26.9 mm. **Obv:** Head 3/4 left **Rev:** Crowned arms with supporters above value **Edge:** Reeded

Date	Mintage	F	VF	XF	Unc	BU
AH1423-2002	—	—	—	—	10.00	—

Y# 107 250 DIRHAMS

25.0000 g., 0.9250 Silver 0.7435 oz. ASW, 37 mm. **Subject:** Inauguration of Mohammed VI 2nd Anniversary **Obv:** Head 3/4 left **Rev:** Crowned arms with supporters above value **Edge:** Reeded

Date	Mintage	F	VF	XF	Unc	BU
AH1422-2001	—	—	—	—	55.00	—

Y# 95 250 DIRHAMS

25.0000 g., 0.9250 Silver 0.7435 oz. ASW, 37 mm. **Subject:** World Children's Day **Obv:** Head 3/4 left **Rev:** Children standing on open book within globe **Edge:** Reeded

Date	Mintage	F	VF	XF	Unc	BU
AH1422-2001	—	—	—	—	55.00	—
AH1422-2001 Proof	—	Value: 90.00				

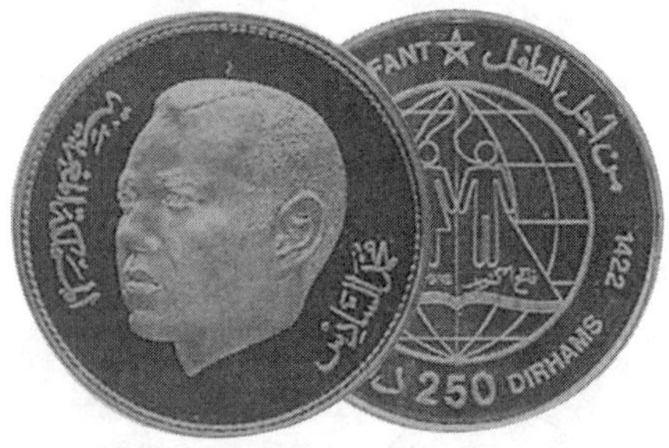

Y# 95a 250 DIRHAMS

25.0000 g., 0.9999 Gold 0.8037 oz. AGW, 37 mm. **Subject:** World Children's Day **Obv:** Head 3/4 left **Rev:** Two children standing on an open book within globe **Edge:** Reeded **Note:** Prev. Y#95.

Date	Mintage	F	VF	XF	Unc	BU
AH1422-2001 Proof	2,800	Value: 650				

Y# 108 250 DIRHAMS

25.0000 g., 0.9250 Silver 0.7435 oz. ASW, 37 mm. **Subject:** Mohammed VI's Inauguration 3rd Anniversary **Obv:** Head 3/4 left **Rev:** Crowned arms with supporters above value **Edge:** Reeded **Note:** Slightly different legend of Y-107

Date	Mintage	F	VF	XF	Unc	BU
AH1423-2002	—	—	—	—	55.00	—
AH1423-2002 Proof	—	Value: 90.00				

Y# 113 250 DIRHAMS

25.0000 g., 0.9250 Silver 0.7435 oz. ASW, 37 mm. **Obv:** Head 3/4 left **Rev:** Crown above radiant flowers **Edge:** Reeded

Date	Mintage	F	VF	XF	Unc	BU
ND(2002) Proof	—	Value: 90.00				

Y# 119 250 DIRHAMS

25.0000 g., Silver, 37 mm. **Subject:** Birth of Crown Prince Moulay Al Hassan **Obv:** Head 3/4 left **Rev:** Crowned arms with supporters above value

Date	Mintage	F	VF	XF	Unc	BU
ND(2003) Proof	—	Value: 90.00				

Y# 120 250 DIRHAMS

25.0000 g., Silver, 37 mm. **Subject:** 50th Anniversary - Kingdom **Obv:** Conjoined heads right **Rev:** Crowned arms with supporters above value

Date	Mintage	F	VF	XF	Unc	BU
AH1424-2003	—	—	—	—	55.00	—
AH1424-2003 Proof	—	Value: 90.00				

Y# 111 250 DIRHAMS

25.0000 g., 0.9250 Silver 0.7435 oz. ASW, 37 mm. **Subject:** Mohammed VI's Inauguration 4th Anniversary **Obv:** Head 3/4 left **Rev:** Crowned arms with supporters above value **Edge:** Reeded **Note:** Virtually identical to Y-107 and Y-108.

Date	Mintage	F	VF	XF	Unc	BU
AH1424-2003	—	—	—	—	55.00	—

Y# 122 250 DIRHAMS

25.0000 g., 0.9250 Silver 0.7435 oz. ASW, 37 mm. **Subject:** 5th Anniversary of Mohammed VI's Reign **Obv:** Head 3/4 left, national arms **Rev:** Crowned arms with supporters above value **Edge:** Reeded **Note:** Vitually identical to Y-107, 108 and 111.

Date	Mintage	F	VF	XF	Unc	BU
AH1425-2004	—	—	—	—	55.00	—

Y# 121 250 DIRHAMS

25.0000 g., Silver, 37 mm. **Subject:** Year of Handicapped Persons **Obv:** Head 3/4 left **Rev:** Stylized figures

Date	Mintage	F	VF	XF	Unc	BU
AH1425-2004	—	—	—	—	55.00	—

Y# 123 250 DIRHAMS

25.0000 g., Silver, 37 mm. **Subject:** 30th Anniversary - Green March **Obv:** Head 3/4 left **Rev:** Men marching left with flags aloft

Date	Mintage	F	VF	XF	Unc	BU
AH1426-2005	—	—	—	—	55.00	—

MOZAMBIQUE

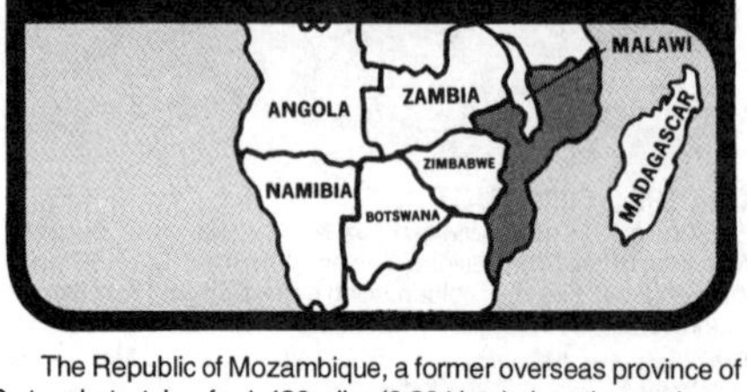

The Republic of Mozambique, a former overseas province of Portugal, stretches for 1,430 miles (2,301 km.) along the southeast coast of Africa, has an area of 302,330 sq. mi. (801,590 sq. km.) and a population of 14.1 million, 99 % of whom are native Africans of the Bantu tribes. Capital: Maputo. Agriculture is the chief industry. Cashew nuts, cotton, sugar, copra and tea are exported.

Mozambique became a member of the Commonwealth of Nations in November 1995. The President is Head of State; the Prime Minister is Head of Government.

REPUBLIC

REFORM COINAGE

100 Centavos = 1 Metical; 1994

KM# 130 1000 METICAIS

25.7100 g., 0.9800 Silver 0.8100 oz. ASW, 38.5 mm. **Subject:** Pedro De Covilha, 1498 **Obv:** National arms within circle **Rev:** Sailing ship within circle **Edge:** Reeded

Date	Mintage	F	VF	XF	Unc	BU
2003 Proof	—	Value: 40.00				

KM# 131 10000 METICAIS

8.0400 g., Bi-Metallic Stainless Steel center in Brass ring, 26.6 mm. **Obv:** National arms within circle **Rev:** Rhino within circle **Edge:** Segmented reeding

Date	Mintage	F	VF	XF	Unc	BU
2003	—	—	3.50	5.00	7.50	12.00

REFORM COINAGE

(New) Metical = 1,000 Meticals; 2005

KM# 132 1 CENTAVO

2.0000 g., Copper-Plated-Steel, 15 mm. **Obv:** Bank logo, date **Obv. Legend:** BANCO DE MOÇAMBIQUE **Rev:** Rhinoceros, value **Edge:** Reeded

Date	Mintage	F	VF	XF	Unc	BU
2006	—	—	—	—	0.15	0.25

KM# 133 5 CENTAVOS

2.3000 g., Copper-Plated-Steel, 19 mm. **Obv:** Bank logo, date **Obv. Legend:** BANCO DE MOÇAMBIQUE **Rev:** Cheetah, value **Edge:** Reeded

Date	Mintage	F	VF	XF	Unc	BU
2006	—	—	—	—	0.25	0.35

KM# 134 10 CENTAVOS

3.0600 g., Brass-Plated Steel, 17 mm. **Obv:** Bank logo, date **Obv. Legend:** BANCO DE MOÇAMBIQUE **Rev:** Tractor, value **Edge:** Reeded

Date	Mintage	F	VF	XF	Unc	BU
2006	—	—	—	—	0.35	0.50

KM# 135 20 CENTAVOS

4.1000 g., Brass-Plated Steel, 20 mm. **Obv:** Bank logo, date **Obv. Legend:** BANCO DE MOÇAMBIQUE **Rev:** Cotton, value **Edge:** Reeded

Date	Mintage	F	VF	XF	Unc	BU
2006	—	—	—	—	0.50	0.75

KM# 136 50 CENTAVOS

5.7400 g., Brass-Plated Steel, 23 mm. **Obv:** Bank logo, date **Obv. Legend:** BANCO DE MOÇAMBIQUE **Rev:** Woodpecker, value **Edge:** Reeded

Date	Mintage	F	VF	XF	Unc	BU
2006	—	—	—	—	0.75	1.00

KM# 137 METICAL

5.3000 g., Nickel-Plated Steel, 21 mm. **Obv:** Bank logo, date **Obv. Legend:** BANCO DE MOÇAMBIQUE **Rev:** Woman writing, value **Edge:** Plain **Shape:** 7-sided

Date	Mintage	F	VF	XF	Unc	BU
2006	—	—	—	—	1.00	1.50

KM# 138 2 METICAIS

6.0000 g., Nickel-Plated Steel, 24 mm. **Obv:** Bank logo, date **Obv. Legend:** BANCO DE MO?AMBIQUE **Rev:** Coelacanth fish, value **Edge:** 4 segmented reeded and plain sections

Date	Mintage	F	VF	XF	Unc	BU
2006	—	—	—	—	2.00	2.50

KM# 139 5 METICAIS

6.5000 g., Nickel-Plated Steel, 27 mm. **Obv:** Bank logo, date **Obv. Legend:** BANCO DE MO?AMBIQUE **Rev:** Timbila (similar to a xylophone), value **Edge:** Reeded

Date	Mintage	F	VF	XF	Unc	BU
2006	—	—	—	—	3.50	4.00

KM# 140 10 METICAIS

7.5100 g., Bi-Metallic **Ring Composition:** Brass **Center Composition:** Nickel Clad Steel, 24.92 mm. **Obv:** Bank logo **Obv. Legend:** BANCO • DE • MOCAMBIQUE **Rev:** Modern bank building, value below **Edge:** Reeded

Date	Mintage	F	VF	XF	Unc	BU
2006	—	—	—	—	—	6.00

NAGORNO-KARABAKH

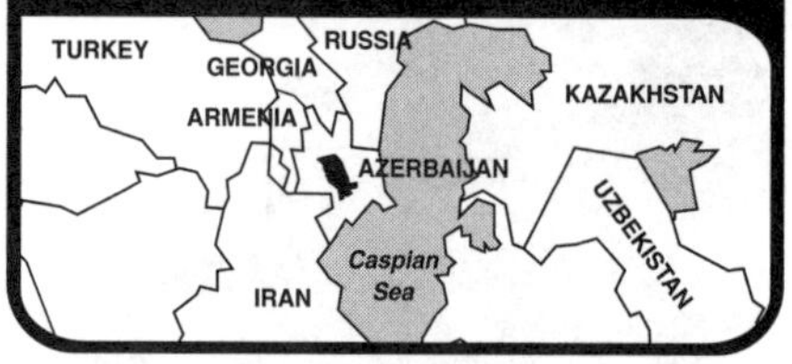

Nagorno-Karabakh, an ethnically Armenian enclave inside Azerbaijan (pop., 1991 est.: 193,000), SW region. It occupies an area of 1,700 sq mi (4,400 square km) on the NE flank of the Karabakh Mountain Range, with the capital city of Stepanakert.

Russia annexed the area from Persia in 1813, and in 1923 it was established as an autonomous province of the Azerbaijan S.S.R. In 1988 the region's ethnic Armenian majority demonstrated against Azerbaijani rule, and in 1991, after the breakup of the U.S.S.R. brought independence to Armenia and Azerbaijan, war broke out between the two ethnic groups. On January 8, 1992 the leaders of Nagorno-Karabakh declared independence as the Republic of Mountainous Karabakh (RMK). Since 1994, following a cease-fire, ethnic Armenians have held Karabakh, though officially it remains part of Azerbaijan. Karabakh remains sovereign, but the political and military condition is volatile and tensions frequently flare into skirmishes.

Its marvelous nature and geographic situation, have all facilitated Karabakh to be a center of science, poetry and, especially, of the musical culture of Azerbaijan.

MONETARY SYSTEM

100 Luma = 1 Dram

REPUBLIC

STANDARD COINAGE

KM# 6 50 LUMA

0.9500 g., Aluminum, 19.8 mm. **Obv:** National arms **Rev:** Horse cantering left **Edge:** Plain

Date	Mintage	F	VF	XF	Unc	BU
2004	—	—	—	—	1.00	1.25

KM# 7 50 LUMA

0.9500 g., Aluminum, 19.8 mm. **Obv:** National arms **Rev:** Gazelle **Edge:** Plain

Date	Mintage	F	VF	XF	Unc	BU
2004	—	—	—	—	1.00	1.25

KM# 8 DRAM

1.1300 g., Aluminum, 21.7 mm. **Obv:** National arms **Rev:** Pheasant **Edge:** Plain

Date	Mintage	F	VF	XF	Unc	BU
2004	—	—	—	—	1.00	1.25

KM# 9 DRAM

1.1200 g., Aluminum, 21.7 mm. **Obv:** National arms **Rev:** 1/2-length Saint facing **Edge:** Plain

Date	Mintage	F	VF	XF	Unc	BU
2004	—	—	—	—	1.00	1.25

KM# 10 DRAM

1.1300 g., Aluminum, 21.7 mm. **Obv:** National arms **Rev:** Cheetah facing **Edge:** Plain

Date	Mintage	F	VF	XF	Unc	BU
2004	—	—	—	—	1.00	1.25

KM# 11 5 DRAMS

4.4000 g., Brass, 21.8 mm. **Obv:** National arms **Rev:** Church **Edge:** Plain

Date	Mintage	F	VF	XF	Unc	BU
2004	—	—	—	—	1.00	1.50

KM# 12 5 DRAMS

4.5000 g., Brass, 21.8 mm. **Obv:** National arms **Rev:** Monument faces **Edge:** Plain

Date	Mintage	F	VF	XF	Unc	BU
2004	—	—	—	—	1.00	1.50

KM# 23 1000 DRAMS

31.4300 g., 0.9990 Silver 1.0094 oz. ASW, 38.9 mm. **Obv:** National arms **Rev:** Archer **Edge:** Plain

Date	Mintage	F	VF	XF	Unc	BU
2003 Proof	—	Value: 60.00				

KM# 19 1000 DRAMS

31.3700 g., 0.9990 Silver 1.0075 oz. ASW, 38.9 mm. **Obv:** National arms **Rev:** Leopard head facing **Edge:** Plain

Date	Mintage	F	VF	XF	Unc	BU
2004 Proof	—	Value: 60.00				

KM# 19a 1000 DRAMS

31.3700 g., 0.9990 Gold Plated Silver 1.0075 oz. ASW AGW, 38.9 mm. **Obv:** National arms **Rev:** Leopard head facing **Edge:** Plain

Date	Mintage	F	VF	XF	Unc	BU
2004 Proof	—	Value: 75.00				

KM# 20 1000 DRAMS

31.3700 g., 0.9990 Silver 1.0075 oz. ASW, 38.9 mm. **Obv:** National arms **Rev:** Standing Brown Bear **Edge:** Plain

Date	Mintage	F	VF	XF	Unc	BU
2004 Proof	—	Value: 60.00				

KM# 20a 1000 DRAMS

31.3700 g., 0.9990 Gold Plated Silver 1.0075 oz. ASW AGW, 38.9 mm. **Obv:** National arms **Rev:** Standing Brown Bear **Edge:** Plain

Date	Mintage	F	VF	XF	Unc	BU
2004 Proof	—	Value: 75.00				

KM# 21 1000 DRAMS

31.3700 g., 0.9990 Silver 1.0075 oz. ASW, 38.9 mm. **Obv:** National arms **Rev:** Eagle head within circle **Edge:** Plain

Date	Mintage	F	VF	XF	Unc	BU
2004 Proof	—	Value: 60.00				

KM# 21a 1000 DRAMS

31.3700 g., 0.9990 Gold Plated Silver 1.0075 oz. ASW AGW, 38.9 mm. **Obv:** National arms **Rev:** Eagle head within circle **Edge:** Plain

Date	Mintage	F	VF	XF	Unc	BU
2004 Proof	—	Value: 75.00				

KM# 22 1000 DRAMS

31.1200 g., 0.9990 Silver 0.9995 oz. ASW, 38.9 mm. **Obv:** National arms **Rev:** 1918 Genocide Victims Monument **Edge:** Plain

Date	Mintage	F	VF	XF	Unc	BU
2004 Proof	—	Value: 50.00				

NAMIBIA

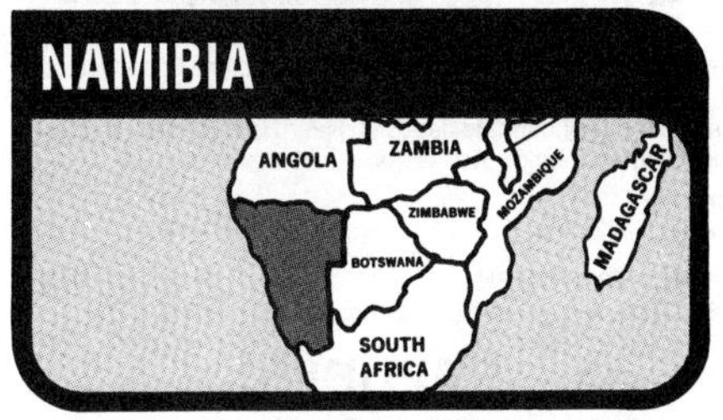

The Republic of Namibia, once the German colonial territory of German South West Africa, and later South West Africa, is situated on the Atlantic coast of southern Africa, bounded on the north by Angola, on the east by Botswana, and on the south by South Africa. It has an area of 318,261 sq. mi. (824,290 sq. km.) and a population of *1.4 million. Capital: Windhoek. Diamonds, copper, lead, zinc, and cattle are exported.

On June 17, 1985 the Transitional Government of National Unity was installed. Negotiations were held in 1988 between Angola, Cuba, and South Africa reaching a peaceful settlement on Aug. 5, 1988. By April 1989 Cuban troops were to withdraw from Angola and South African troops from Namibia. The Transitional Government resigned on Feb. 28, 1988 for the upcoming elections of the constituent assembly in Nov. 1989. Independence was finally achieved on March 12, 1990 within the Commonwealth of Nations. The President is the Head of State; the Prime Minister is Head of Government.

MONETARY SYSTEM

100 Cents = 1 Namibia Dollar

REPUBLIC

1990 - present

DECIMAL COINAGE

KM# 1 5 CENTS

2.2000 g., Nickel Plated Steel, 16.9 mm. **Obv:** Arms with supporters **Rev:** Value left, aloe plant within 3/4 sun design

Date	Mintage	F	VF	XF	Unc	BU
2002	—	—	—	0.20	0.50	0.75

KM# 2 10 CENTS

3.3900 g., Nickel Plated Steel, 21.5 mm. **Obv:** Arms with supporters **Rev:** Camelthorn tree right, partial sun design left, value below

Date	Mintage	F	VF	XF	Unc	BU
2002	—	—	—	0.35	1.00	1.25

KM# 4 DOLLAR

4.9600 g., Brass, 22.3 mm. **Obv:** Arms with supporters **Rev:** Value divides Bateleur eagle at right, partial sun design at left

Date	Mintage	F	VF	XF	Unc	BU
2002	—	—	—	1.25	3.50	6.00

NAURU

The Republic of Nauru, formerly Pleasant Island, is an island republic in the western Pacific Ocean west of the Gilbert Islands. It has an area of 8-1/2 sq. mi. and a population of 7,254. It is known for its phosphate deposits. Nauru is a special member of the Commonwealth of Nations.

RULER
British, until 1968

MONETARY SYSTEM
100 Cents = 1 (Australian) Dollar

REPUBLIC

DECIMAL COINAGE

KM# 18 10 DOLLARS
31.1000 g., 0.9990 Silver 0.9988 oz. ASW **Subject:** Discontinuation of the German Mark **Obv:** National arms **Obv. Legend:** BANK OF NAURU

Date	Mintage	F	VF	XF	Unc	BU
2001 Proof	—	Value: 50.00				

KM# 13 10 DOLLARS
31.2500 g., 0.9990 Silver 71.5 x 72 1.0037 oz. ASW, 72 mm. **Subject:** First Euro Coinage **Obv:** National arms, matte finish **Rev:** Denomination, inscription and partially gold-plated 1 Euro reverse coin design, Proof finish **Edge:** Plain **Shape:** Like a map

Date	Mintage	F	VF	XF	Unc	BU
2002 Proof	—	Value: 55.00				

KM# 15 10 DOLLARS
31.1000 g., 0.9990 Silver 0.9988 oz. ASW, 40 mm. **Series:** Save the Whales **Obv:** National arms **Obv. Legend:** BANK OF NAURU **Rev:** Blue Whale on mother-of-pearl insert **Edge:** Plain

Date	Mintage	F	VF	XF	Unc	BU
2002 Proof	2,000	Value: 60.00				

KM# 14 10 DOLLARS
34.6000 g., 0.9250 Silver with gold plated or gold attachment 1.0289 oz. ASW, 38.5 mm. **Subject:** Brandenburg Gate **Obv:** National arms **Rev:** Brandenburg Gate **Edge:** Plain **Note:** Gold color 1mm thick

Date	Mintage	F	VF	XF	Unc	BU
2002 Proof/Matte	—	Value: 110				

KM# 19 10 DOLLARS
31.1000 g., 0.9990 Silver 0.9988 oz. ASW **Subject:** European Union - Mark and Euro **Obv:** National arms **Obv. Legend:** BANK OF NAURU

Date	Mintage	F	VF	XF	Unc	BU
2003 Proof	5,000	Value: 60.00				

KM# 20 10 DOLLARS
1.2400 g., 0.9990 Gold 0.0398 oz. AGW **Subject:** European Union - Europa **Obv:** National arms **Obv. Legend:** BANK OF NAURU

Date	Mintage	F	VF	XF	Unc	BU
2003 Proof	—	Value: 75.00				

KM# 21 10 DOLLARS
1.2400 g., 0.9990 Gold 0.0398 oz. AGW **Subject:** Treasure of Priamos in Troja **Obv:** National arms **Obv. Legend:** BANK OF NAURU

Date	Mintage	F	VF	XF	Unc	BU
2003 Proof	—	Value: 75.00				

KM# 22 10 DOLLARS
1.2400 g., 0.9990 Gold 0.0398 oz. AGW **Subject:** Treasure of Nibelungen **Obv:** National arms **Obv. Legend:** BANK OF NAURU

Date	Mintage	F	VF	XF	Unc	BU
2003 Proof	—	Value: 75.00				

KM# 23 10 DOLLARS
30.9500 g., Silver With removable gold or gilt 2.6g Reichstag building attachment with 2004/ NAURU 0077 on reverse **Subject:** European Monuments **Obv:** National arms **Obv. Legend:** BANK OF NAURU **Rev. Legend:** GERMANY - DEUTSCHER REICHSTAG **Edge:** Plain

Date	Mintage	F	VF	XF	Unc	BU
2003 Proof/Matte	—	Value: 110				

KM# 24 10 DOLLARS
Silver With removable gold or gilt attachment **Series:** European Monuments **Subject:** Palazzo Pubblico in San Marino **Obv:** National arms **Obv. Legend:** BANK OF NAURU **Edge:** Plain

Date	Mintage	F	VF	XF	Unc	BU
2005 Proof/Matte	—	Value: 110				

KM# 25 10 DOLLARS
1.2400 g., 0.9990 Gold 0.0398 oz. AGW **Subject:** East Gothic stylized eagle broach from Domagnano, Italy in National Museum in Nuremburg **Obv:** National arms **Obv. Legend:** BANK OF NAURU

Date	Mintage	F	VF	XF	Unc	BU
2005 Proof	25,000	Value: 75.00				

KM# 26 10 DOLLARS
1.2400 g., 0.9990 Gold 0.0398 oz. AGW **Subject:** Angela Dorothea Merkel, Chancellor of Germany **Obv:** National arms **Obv. Legend:** BANK OF NAURU

Date	Mintage	F	VF	XF	Unc	BU
2005 Proof	—	Value: 75.00				

KM# 27 10 DOLLARS
1.2400 g., 0.9990 Gold 0.0398 oz. AGW **Subject:** Konrad Adenauer at 1949 demonstration **Obv:** National arms **Obv. Legend:** BANK OF NAURU

Date	Mintage	F	VF	XF	Unc	BU
2006 Proof	15,000	Value: 75.00				

KM# 28 10 DOLLARS
1.2400 g., 0.9990 Gold 0.0398 oz. AGW **Subject:** Volkswagen **Obv:** National arms **Obv. Legend:** BANK OF NAURU

Date	Mintage	F	VF	XF	Unc	BU
2006 Proof	—	Value: 75.00				

KM# 29 10 DOLLARS
1.2400 g., 0.9990 Gold 0.0398 oz. AGW **Subject:** Conrad Schumann in Berlin 1961 **Obv:** National arms **Obv. Legend:** BANK OF NAURU

Date	Mintage	F	VF	XF	Unc	BU
2006 Proof	—	Value: 75.00				

KM# 30 10 DOLLARS
1.2400 g., 0.9990 Gold 0.0398 oz. AGW **Subject:** Olympic Stadium in Munich 1972 **Obv:** National arms **Obv. Legend:** BANK OF NAURU

Date	Mintage	F	VF	XF	Unc	BU
2006 Proof	—	Value: 75.00				

KM# 31 10 DOLLARS
1.2400 g., 0.9990 Gold 0.0398 oz. AGW **Subject:** Independent Activists 1980 **Obv:** National arms **Obv. Legend:** BANK OF NAURU

Date	Mintage	F	VF	XF	Unc	BU
2006 Proof	—	Value: 75.00				

KM# 32 10 DOLLARS
1.2400 g., 0.9990 Gold 0.0398 oz. AGW **Subject:** Brandenburg Gate in Berlin 1990 **Obv. Legend:** BANK OF NAURU

Date	Mintage	F	VF	XF	Unc	BU
2006 Proof	—	Value: 75.00				

KM# 33 10 DOLLARS
1.2400 g., 0.9990 Gold 0.0398 oz. AGW **Subject:** European Union 2002 **Obv:** National arms **Obv. Legend:** BANK OF NAURU

Date	Mintage	F	VF	XF	Unc	BU
2006 Proof	—	Value: 75.00				

KM# 34 10 DOLLARS
1.2400 g., 0.9990 Gold 0.0398 oz. AGW **Subject:** Johannes Rau, German President, 1999-2004 **Obv:** National arms **Obv. Legend:** BANK OF NAURU

Date	Mintage	F	VF	XF	Unc	BU
2006 Proof	—	Value: 75.00				

NEPAL

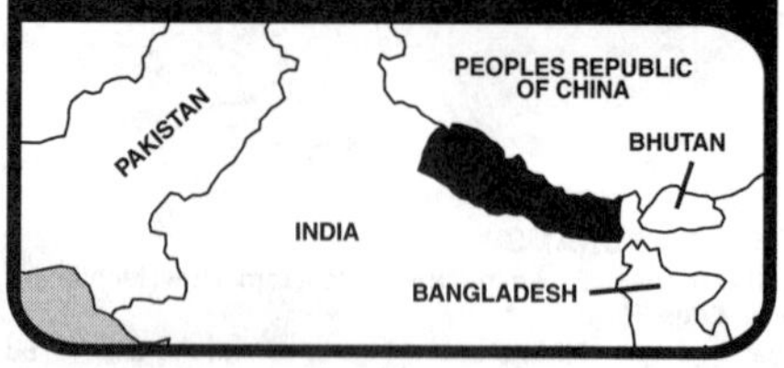

The Kingdom of Nepal, the world's only surviving Hindu kingdom, is a landlocked country occupying the southern slopes of the Himalayas. It has an area of 56,136 sq. mi. (140,800 sq. km.) and a population of 18 million. Capital: Kathmandu. Nepal has deposits of coal, copper, iron and cobalt, but they are largely unexploited. Agriculture is the principal economic activity. Rice, timber and jute are exported, with tourism being the other major foreign exchange earner.

On June 2, 2001 tragedy struck the royal family when Crown Prince Dipendra used an assault rifle to kill his father, mother and other members of the royal family as the result of a dispute over his current lady friend. He died 48 hours later, as King, from self inflicted gunshot wounds. Gyanendra began his second reign as King (his first was a short time as a toddler, 1950-51).

DATING

Bikram Samvat Era (VS)

From 1888AD most copper coins were dated in the Bikram Samvat (VS) era. To convert take VS date - 57 =AD date. Coins with this era have VS before the year in the listing. With the exception of a few gold coins struck in 1890 & 1892, silver and gold coins only changed to the VS era in 1911AD, but now this era is used for all coins struck in Nepal.

RULERS

SHAH DYNASTY

त्रिभुवनवीर विक्रम

Tribhuvana Bir Bikram
VS1968-2007, 2007-2011/1911-1950, 1951-1955AD (first reign)
VS2058- / 2001- AD (second reign)

वीरेन्द्र वीर विक्रम

Birendra Bir Bikram
VS2028-2058 /1971-2001AD

ऐश्वर्य राज्य लक्ष्मी देवी

Queen of Birendra Bir Bikram: Aishvarya Rajya Lakshmi
VS2028-2058 /1971-2001AD

Dipendra Bir Bikram
VS2058 / 2001AD (reign of 48 hours)

ज्ञानेन्द्र वीर विक्रम

Gyanendra Bir Bikram
VS2058-/2001-AD

MONETARY SYSTEM

Many of the mohars circulated in Tibet as well as in Nepal, and on a number of occasions coins were struck from bullion supplied by the Tibetan authorities. The smaller denominations never circulated in Tibet, but some of the mohars were cut for use as small change in Tibet.

With a few exceptions, most all coins were struck at Kathmandu.

COPPER

Initially the copper paisa was not fixed in value relative to the silver coins, and generally fluctuated in value from1/32 mohar in 1865AD to around 1/50 mohar after 1880AD, and was fixed at that value in 1903AD.

4 Dam = 1 Paisa
2 Paisa = 1 Dyak, Adhani

COPPER and SILVER

Decimal Series

100 Paisa = 1 Rupee

Although the value of the copper paisa was fixed at 100 paisa to the rupee in 1903, it was not until 1932 that silver coins were struck in the decimal system.

GOLD COINAGE

Nepalese gold coinage, until recently, did not carry any denominations and was traded for silver, etc. at the local bullion exchange rate. The three basic weight standards used in the following listing are distinguished for convenience, although all were known as Asarphi (gold coin) locally as follows:

GOLD MOHAR

5.60 g multiples and fractions

TOLA

12.48 g multiples and fractions

GOLD RUPEE or ASHRPHI/ASARFI

11.66 g multiples and fractions
(Reduced to 10.00 g in 1966)

NOTE: In some instances the gold and silver issues were struck from the same dies.

NUMERALS

Nepal has used more variations of numerals on their coins than any other nation. The most common are illustrated in the numeral chart in the introduction. The chart below illustrates some variations encompassing the last four centuries.

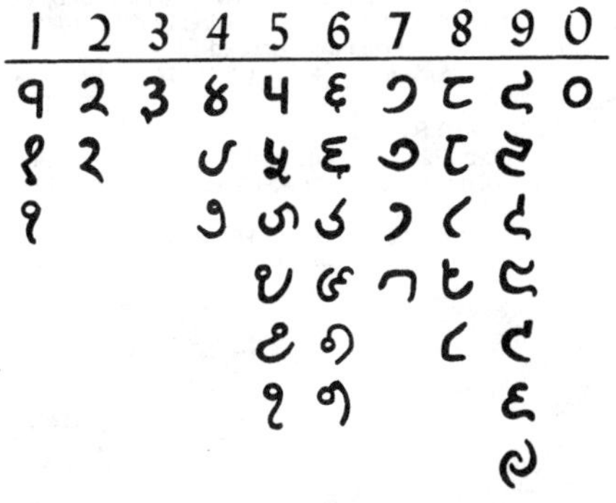

NUMERICS

Half	आधा
One	एक
Two	दुइ
Four	चार
Five	पाच
Ten	दश
Twenty	बिस
Twenty-five	पचीस
Fifty	पचास
Hundred	सय

DENOMINATIONS

Paisa	पैसा
Dam	दाम
Mohar	मोहर
Rupee	रूपैयाँ
Ashrapi	असर्फी
Asarphi (Asarfi)	अश्रफी

DIE VARIETIES

Although the same dies were usually used both for silver and gold minor denominations, the gold Mohar is easily recognized being less ornate. The following illustrations are of a silver Mohar, KM#602 and a gold Mohar KM#615 issued by Surendra Bikram Saha Deva in the period SE1769-1803/1847-1881AD. Note the similar reverse legend. The obverse usually will start with the character for the word Shri either in single or multiples, the latter as Shri Shri Shri or Shri 3.

OBVERSE

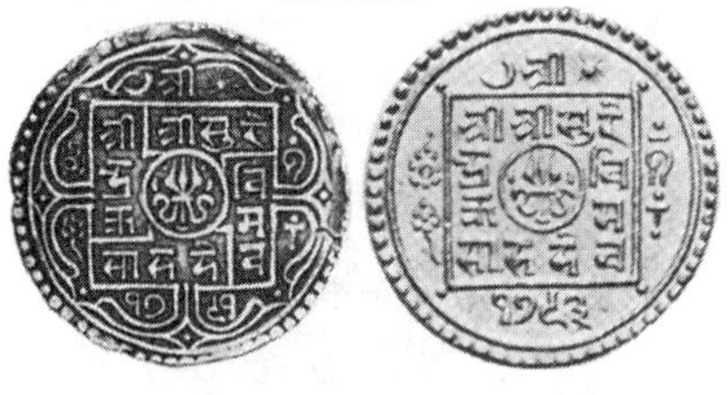

SILVER SE1791 GOLD SE1793

LEGEND

श्री श्रीश्री सुरेन्द्र बिक्रम साहदेव

Shri Shri Shri Surendra Bikrama Saha Deva (date).

REVERSE

SILVER GOLD

LEGEND
(in center)

श्री ३ भवानी

Shri 3 Bhavani
(around outer circle)

श्री श्री श्री गोरषनाथ

Shri Shri Shri Gorakhanatha

KINGDOM

Shah Dynasty

Gyanendra Bir Bikram

VS2058-2064 / 2001- 2007AD

DECIMAL COINAGE

100 Paisa = 1 Rupee

KM# 1173 10 PAISA

Aluminum, 17 mm. **Obv:** Royal crown **Edge:** Plain

Date	Mintage	F	VF	XF	Unc	BU
VS2058 (2001)	—	—	—	—	1.00	—

KM# 1148 25 PAISA

Aluminum, 20 mm. **Obv:** Royal crown **Edge:** Plain

Date	Mintage	F	VF	XF	Unc	BU
VS2058 (2001)	—	—	—	—	0.50	—
VS2059 (2002)	—	—	—	—	0.50	—
VS2060 (2003)	—	—	—	—	0.50	—

KM# 1149 50 PAISA

Aluminum, 22.5 mm. **Obv:** Royal crown **Rev:** Swayambhunath **Edge:** Plain

Date	Mintage	F	VF	XF	Unc	BU
VS2058 (2001)	—	—	—	—	0.50	—
VS2059 (2002)	—	—	—	—	0.50	—

KM# 1179 50 PAISA

1.4100 g., Aluminum, 22.5 mm. **Obv:** Crown above crossed flags **Rev:** Swayambhunath **Edge:** Plain

Date	Mintage	F	VF	XF	Unc	BU
VS2060 (2003)	—	—	—	—	—	—
VS2061 (2004)	—	—	—	—	0.40	0.50

KM# 1150.2 RUPEE

Brass Plated Steel **Obv:** Traditional design **Rev:** Small (7mm high) temple, small (4mm) "1" **Edge:** Plain **Note:** Magnetic.

Date	Mintage	F	VF	XF	Unc	BU
VS2058 (2001)	—	—	—	—	1.00	—
VS2059 (2002)	—	—	—	—	1.00	—
VS2060 (2003)	—	—	—	—	1.00	—

KM# 1150.1 RUPEE

Brass Plated Steel **Rev:** Large (8mm) temple, medium (4.5mm) **Edge:** Reeded **Note:** Non-magnetic.

Date	Mintage	F	VF	XF	Unc	BU
VS2058 (2001)	—	—	—	—	1.00	—

KM# 1150.3 RUPEE

3.9600 g., Brass, 20 mm. **Obv:** Traditional design **Rev:** Small (6.5mm high) temple, small (4mm) "1" **Edge:** Plain

Date	Mintage	F	VF	XF	Unc	BU
VS2058 (2001)	—	—	—	—	0.50	—

KM# 1150.4 RUPEE

3.9600 g., Brass Plated Steel, 20 mm. **Obv:** Traditional design **Rev:** Small (7mm high) temple, large (5.5mm) "1" **Note:** Magnetic.

Date	Mintage	F	VF	XF	Unc	BU
VS2059 (2002)	—	—	—	—	1.00	—
VS2060 (2003)	—	—	—	—	1.00	—

KM# 1180 RUPEE

3.9600 g., Brass-Plated Steel, 20 mm. **Obv:** Traditional design **Rev:** Sri Talbarahi Temple in Pokhara **Edge:** Plain **Note:** "1" in denomination different style.

Date	Mintage	F	VF	XF	Unc	BU
VS2061 (2004)	—	—	—	—	0.75	1.00

KM# 1181 RUPEE

4.0000 g., Brass Plated Steel, 20 mm. **Obv:** Traditional design **Rev:** Sri Talbarahi Temple with outline mountain scene behind **Edge:** Reeded

Date	Mintage	F	VF	XF	Unc	BU
VS 2062 (2005)	—	—	—	—	—	1.00

KM# 1187 RUPEE

3.9400 g., Brass Plated Steel, 19.95 mm. **Obv:** Traditional design **Rev:** Temple **Edge:** Plain

Date	Mintage	F	VF	XF	Unc	BU
VS2062(2005)	—	—	—	—	—	0.75

KM# 1170 2 RUPEES

4.9400 g., Brass, 25 mm. **Obv:** Traditional square design **Rev:** People with flag celebrating 50 Years of Democracy **Edge:** Plain

Date	Mintage	F	VF	XF	Unc	BU
VS2058(2001)	—	—	—	—	0.50	—

KM# 1151.2 2 RUPEES

Brass, 25 mm. **Obv:** Traditional design **Rev:** Three domed building **Edge:** Plain

Date	Mintage	F	VF	XF	Unc	BU
VS2058 (2001)	—	—	—	—	1.50	—
VS2059 (2002)	—	—	—	—	1.50	—
VS2060 (2003)	—	—	—	—	1.50	—

KM# 1151.1 2 RUPEES

5.0700 g., Brass Plated Steel, 25 mm. **Obv:** Traditional design **Rev:** Three domed building **Edge:** Plain **Note:** Edge varieties exist. Prev. KM#1151. Magnetic.

Date	Mintage	F	VF	XF	Unc	BU
VS2060 (2003)	—	—	—	—	1.50	—

KM# 1151.1a 2 RUPEES

6.7000 g., Silver, 25 mm. **Obv:** Traditional design **Rev:** Three domed building **Edge:** Plain

Date	Mintage	F	VF	XF	Unc	BU
VS2060(2003)	—	—	—	—	100	—

KM# 1188 2 RUPEES

5.0000 g., Brass Plated Steel, 24.93 mm. **Obv:** Farmer plowing with water buffalos **Rev:** Mount Everest **Edge:** Plain

Date	Mintage	F	VF	XF	Unc	BU
VS2063(2006)	—	—	—	—	—	1.50

KM# 1164 5 RUPEE

8.5300 g., Copper-Nickel, 29.2 mm. **Obv:** Crowned bust right **Rev:** Traditional design **Edge:** Plain

Date	Mintage	F	VF	XF	Unc	BU
VS2058 (2001)	—	—	—	—	3.50	5.00

KM# 1159 25 RUPEE

8.3600 g., Copper Nickel, 29.1 mm. **Obv:** Crowned bust right **Rev:** Sword in round design **Edge:** Plain

Date	Mintage	F	VF	XF	Unc	BU
VS2059 (2002)	—	—	—	—	4.00	5.00

KM# 1183 25 RUPEE

8.5500 g., Copper-Nickel, 29.1 mm. **Subject:** World Hindu Federation **Obv:** Traditional design **Edge:** Plain

Date	Mintage	F	VF	XF	Unc	BU
VS2062 (2005)	—	—	—	—	4.00	5.00

KM# 1160 50 RUPEE

20.1000 g., Brass, 37.7 mm. **Subject:** 50th Anniversary of Scouting in Nepal **Obv:** Traditional design **Rev:** Scouting emblem within beaded wreath **Edge:** Plain

Date	Mintage	F	VF	XF	Unc	BU
VS2059 (2002)	—	—	—	—	9.00	10.00

KM# 1182 50 RUPEE

8.6000 g., Copper-Nickel, 29 mm. **Subject:** Golden Jubilee of Supreme Court **Obv:** Traditional design **Rev:** Supreme Court building **Edge:** Plain

Date	Mintage	F	VF	XF	Unc	BU
VS2063 (2006)	—	—	—	—	5.00	9.00

KM# 1157 100 RUPEE

20.0000 g., Brass, 38.7 mm. **Subject:** Buddha **Obv:** Traditional design **Rev:** Seated Buddha teaching five seated monks **Edge:** Reeded

Date	Mintage	F	VF	XF	Unc	BU
VS2058 (2001)	30,000	—	—	—	10.00	12.00

KM# 1162 200 RUPEE

18.1000 g., 0.5000 Silver 0.2910 oz. ASW, 29.6 mm. **Subject:** 50th Anniversary of Civil Service **Obv:** Traditional design **Rev:** Crown above flags and value **Edge:** Plain

Date	Mintage	F	VF	XF	Unc	BU
VS2058 (2001)	—	—	—	—	20.00	25.00

KM# 1161 200 RUPEE

18.1000 g., 0.5000 Silver 0.2910 oz. ASW, 29.6 mm. **Subject:** 50th Anniversary of the Nepal Chamber of Commerce **Obv:** Traditional design **Rev:** Swastika within rotary gear **Edge:** Plain

Date	Mintage	F	VF	XF	Unc	BU
VS2059 (2002)	—	—	—	—	20.00	25.00

KM# 1171 250 RUPEE

18.0000 g., 0.5000 Silver 0.2893 oz. ASW, 29 mm. **Subject:** 2600th Anniversary of Bhagawan Mahavir **Obv:** Traditional design **Rev:** Haloed head above value **Edge:** Plain

Date	Mintage	F	VF	XF	Unc	BU
VS2058 (2001)	—	—	—	—	25.00	30.00

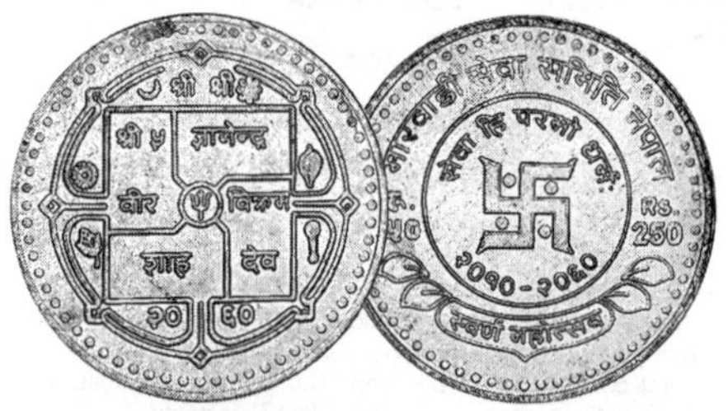

KM# 1176 250 RUPEE

17.8300 g., 0.5000 Silver 0.2866 oz. ASW, 31.6 mm. **Subject:** Marwadi, non-profit making organization **Obv:** Traditional design **Rev:** Swastika within circle **Edge:** Reeded

Date	Mintage	F	VF	XF	Unc	BU
VS2060 (2003)	—	—	—	—	25.00	30.00

KM# 1184 250 RUPEE

18.0000 g., Silver, 32 mm. **Subject:** 400th Anniversary of Guru Granth Sahib **Obv:** Traditional design **Rev:** Holy Book of Sikhs **Edge:** Reeded

Date	Mintage	F	VF	XF	Unc	BU
VS2061	—	—	—	—	25.00	30.00

KM# 1174 300 RUPEE

Silver, 31.8 mm. **Subject:** Economic Growth Through Export **Obv:** Traditional design **Rev:** Two joined hands in front of globe **Edge:** Reeded

Date	Mintage	F	VF	XF	Unc	BU
VS2060 (2003)	—	—	—	—	20.00	25.00

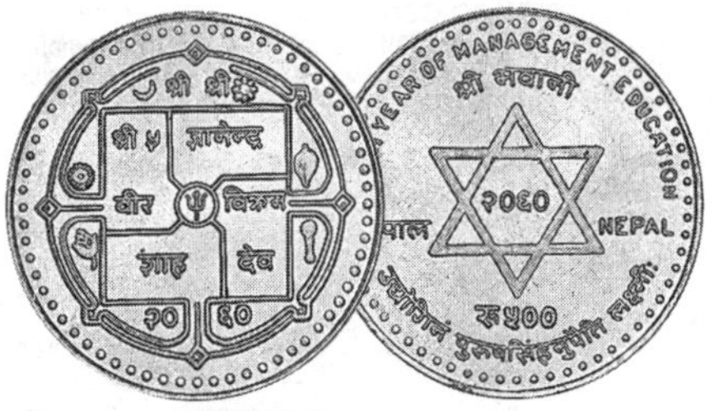

KM# 1177 500 RUPEE
23.0000 g., 0.9000 Silver 0.6655 oz. ASW, 31.7 mm. **Subject:** Management Education 50th Anniversary **Obv:** Traditional design **Rev:** Six point star outline **Edge:** Reeded

Date	Mintage	F	VF	XF	Unc	BU
VS2060 (2003)	—	—	—	—	25.00	30.00

KM# 1163 500 RUPEE
23.3400 g., 0.9000 Silver 0.6753 oz. ASW, 32 mm. **Subject:** 50th Anniversary of the Conquest of Mt. Everest **Obv:** Traditional design **Rev:** Mountain and map above value **Edge:** Reeded

Date	Mintage	F	VF	XF	Unc	BU
VS2060 (2003)	—	—	—	—	25.00	30.00

KM# 1185 500 RUPEE
20.1000 g., Silver, 32 mm. **Subject:** 50th Anniversary of Nepal-United Nations **Obv:** Traditional design **Rev:** Head of the late King Mahendra Bir Birkam **Edge:** Reeded

Date	Mintage	F	VF	XF	Unc	BU
VS2062	—	—	—	—	25.00	30.00

KM# 1175 1000 RUPEE
35.0000 g., Silver, 40 mm. **Subject:** 100 Years - Rotary Club **Edge:** Reeded

Date	Mintage	F	VF	XF	Unc	BU
VS2062 (2005)	—	—	—	—	45.00	50.00

KM# 1178 1000 RUPEE
35.2000 g., 0.5000 Silver 0.5658 oz. ASW, 40 mm. **Subject:** Rastriya Bank 50th Anniversary **Obv:** Traditional square design **Rev:** Bank seal above value **Edge:** Reeded

Date	Mintage	F	VF	XF	Unc	BU
VS2062 (2005)	—	—	—	—	25.00	30.00

KM# 1158 1500 RUPEE
20.0000 g., 0.9250 Silver 0.5948 oz. ASW, 38.7 mm. **Subject:** Buddha **Obv:** Traditional design **Rev:** Seated Buddha teaching five seated monks **Edge:** Reeded

Date	Mintage	F	VF	XF	Unc	BU
VS2058 (2001) Proof	15,000	Value: 31.50				

KM# 1172 2000 RUPEE
31.2000 g., 0.7200 Silver 0.7222 oz. ASW, 40 mm. **Obv:** Crowned bust right **Rev:** Upright sword above value in circular design **Edge:** Reeded

Date	Mintage	F	VF	XF	Unc	BU
VS2058 (2001)	—	—	—	—	40.00	45.00

ASARFI GOLD COINAGE

(Asarphi)

Fractional designations are approximate for this series. Actual Gold Weight (AGW) is used to identify each type.

KM# 1153 0.3G ASARPHI
0.3000 g., 0.9999 Gold 0.0096 oz. AGW, 7 mm. **Subject:** Buddha **Obv:** Traditional design **Rev:** Seated Buddha **Edge:** Plain

Date	Mintage	VG	F	VF	XF	BU
VS2058 (2001)	30,000	—	—	—	—	16.00

KM# 1154 1/25-OZ. ASARFI
1.2441 g., 0.9999 Gold 0.0400 oz. AGW, 13.92 mm. **Subject:** Buddha **Obv:** Traditional design **Rev:** Seated Buddha **Edge:** Reeded

Date	Mintage	VG	F	VF	XF	BU
VS2058 (2001)	25,000	—	—	—	—	40.00

KM# 1155 1/10-OZ. ASARFI
3.1104 g., 0.9999 Gold 0.1000 oz. AGW, 17.95 mm. **Subject:** Buddha **Obv:** Traditional design **Rev:** Seated Buddha **Edge:** Reeded

Date	Mintage	VG	F	VF	XF	BU
VS2058 (2001)	15,000	—	—	—	—	100

KM# 1156 1/2-OZ. ASARFI
15.5518 g., 0.9999 Gold 0.4999 oz. AGW, 27 mm. **Subject:** Buddha **Obv:** Traditional design **Rev:** Seated Buddha **Edge:** Reeded

Date	Mintage	VG	F	VF	XF	BU
VS2058 (2001) Proof	2,500	Value: 500				

SECULAR STATE

Gyanendra Bir Bikram
VS2058-2064 / 2001- 2007AD

DECIMAL COINAGE

100 Paisa = 1 Rupee

KM# 1186 25 RUPEE
8.5000 g., Copper-Nickel, 29 mm. **Subject:** 125th Anniversary - First Nepal Postal Stamp Issue **Obv:** Features image of legendary 1 Anna stamp **Rev:** Traditional mailman on the reverse **Note:** First coin without King Gyanendra's royal seal

Date	Mintage	F	VF	XF	Unc	BU
VS2064 (2007)	—	—	—	—	9.00	10.00

FEDERAL DEMOCRATIC REPUBLIC

DECIMAL COINAGE

100 Paisa = 1 Rupee

KM# 1189 50 RUPEE
8.6000 g., Copper-Nickel, 29 mm. **Subject:** 250th Anniversary Hindu festival "Kimari Jatra" **Obv:** Bust of Goddess Kumari facing **Rev:** Kumari temple in Kathmandu **Edge:** Plain

Date	Mintage	F	VF	XF	Unc	BU
VS2064	—	—	—	—	10.00	12.00

KM# 1190 500 RUPEE
14.1900 g., 0.5000 Silver 0.2281 oz. ASW, 32 mm. **Subject:** 250th Anniversary Hindu festival "Kimari Jatra" **Obv:** Bust of Goddess Kumari facing **Rev:** Kumari temple in Kathmandu **Edge:** Reeded

Date	Mintage	F	VF	XF	Unc	BU
VS2064	—	—	—	—	25.00	30.00

NETHERLANDS

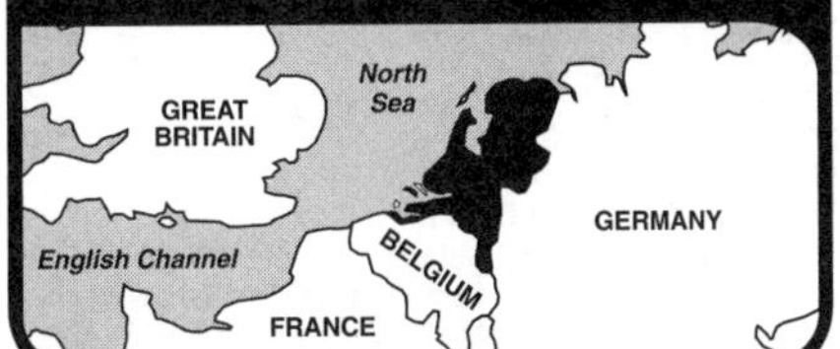

The Kingdom of the Netherlands, a country of western Europe fronting on the North Sea and bordered by Belgium and Germany, has an area of 15,770 sq. mi. (41,500 sq. km.) and a population of 16.1 million. Capital: Amsterdam, but the seat of government is at The Hague. The economy is based on dairy farming and a variety of industrial activities. Chemicals, yarns and fabrics, and meat products are exported.

NOTE: Excepting the World War II issues struck at U.S. mints, all of the modern coins were struck at the Utrecht Mint and bear the caduceus mint mark of that facility. They also bear the mintmasters' marks.

RULERS

KINGDOM OF THE NETHERLANDS

Beatrix, 1980—

MINT PRIVY MARKS

Utrecht

Date	Privy Mark
1806-present	Caduceus

MINTMASTERS' PRIVY MARKS

Utrecht Mint

Date	Privy Mark
2001	Wine tendril w/grapes
2002	Wine tendril w/grapes and star
2003	Sails of a clipper

NOTE: A star adjoining the privy mark indicates that the piece was struck at the beginning of the term of office of a successor. (The star was used only if the successor had not chosen his own mark yet.)

NOTE: Since October 1999, the Dutch Mint has taken the title of Royal Dutch Mint.

MONETARY SYSTEM

Until January 29, 2002
100 Cents = 1 Gulden
Since January 1, 2002
100 Euro Cents = 1 Euro

KINGDOM

DECIMAL COINAGE

KM# 202 5 CENTS
3.5000 g., Bronze, 21 mm. **Ruler:** Beatrix **Obv:** Head left with vertical inscription **Rev:** Value within vertical lines **Edge:** Plain **Designer:** Bruno Ninaber von Eyben

Date	Mintage	F	VF	XF	Unc	BU
2001 Proof	17,000	Value: 4.00				
2001	16,060,000	—	—	—	—	0.40

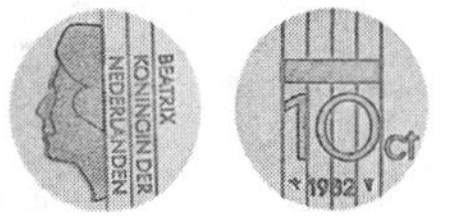

KM# 203 10 CENTS
1.5000 g., Nickel, 15 mm. **Ruler:** Beatrix **Obv:** Head left with vertical inscription **Rev:** Value and vertical lines **Edge:** Reeded **Designer:** Bruno Ninaber von Eyben

Date	Mintage	F	VF	XF	Unc	BU
2001	26,140,000	—	—	—	—	0.50
2001 Proof	17,000	Value: 4.00				

KM# 204 25 CENTS
3.0000 g., Nickel, 19 mm. **Ruler:** Beatrix **Obv:** Head left with vertical inscription **Obv. Inscription:** Beatrix/Konincin Der/Nederlanden **Rev:** Value within vertical and horizontal lines **Edge:** Reeded **Designer:** Bruno Ninaber van Eyben

Date	Mintage	F	VF	XF	Unc	BU
2001	11,800,000	—	—	—	0.20	0.60
2001 Proof	17,000	Value: 6.00				

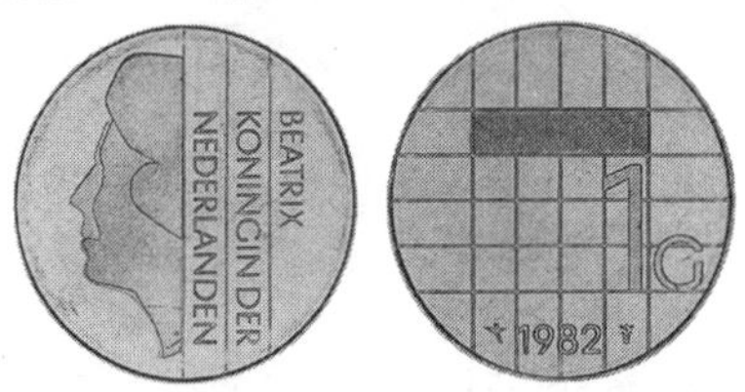

KM# 205 GULDEN
6.0000 g., Nickel, 25 mm. **Ruler:** Beatrix **Obv:** Head left with vertical inscription **Rev:** Value within vertical and horizontal lines **Edge Lettering:** GOD * ZIJ * MET * ONS * **Designer:** Bruno Ninaber von Eyben

Date	Mintage	F	VF	XF	Unc	BU
2001 Proof	17,000	Value: 7.50				
2001	6,650,000	—	—	—	—	1.25

KM# 233 GULDEN
6.0400 g., Nickel, 25 mm. **Ruler:** Beatrix **Obv:** Head left within inscription **Obv. Designer:** Geerten Verheus and Michael Raedecker **Rev:** Child art design **Rev. Designer:** Tim van Melis **Edge Lettering:** GOD ZIJ MET ONS

Date	Mintage	F	VF	XF	Unc	BU
2001	16,045,000	—	—	—	—	4.00
2001 Prooflike	32,000	—	—	—	—	6.00

KM# 233a GULDEN
7.1000 g., 0.9250 Silver 0.2111 oz. ASW, 25 mm. **Ruler:** Beatrix **Obv:** Head left within inscription **Rev:** Child art design **Edge Lettering:** GOD * ZIJ * MET * ONS *

Date	Mintage	F	VF	XF	Unc	BU
2001 Prooflike	360	—	—	—	—	1,000

Note: Given as gifts to workers at the mint

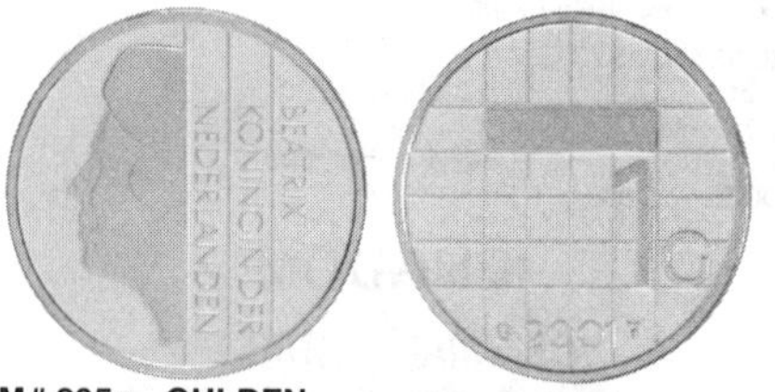

KM# 205a GULDEN
7.1000 g., 0.9250 Silver 0.2111 oz. ASW **Ruler:** Beatrix **Obv:** Head left with vertical inscription **Rev:** Value within vertical and horizontal lines **Edge Lettering:** GOD*ZIJ*MET*OMS*

Date	Mintage	F	VF	XF	Unc	BU
2001 Prooflike	200,000	—	—	—	—	17.50

KM# 233b GULDEN
13.2000 g., 0.9990 Gold 0.4239 oz. AGW, 25 mm. **Ruler:** Beatrix **Obv:** Head left within inscription **Obv. Designer:** G. Verheus and M. Raedecker **Rev:** Child art design **Rev. Designer:** T. van Malis **Note:** 98 of 100 pieces melted down, with 2 known in museum collections.

Date	Mintage	F	VF	XF	Unc	BU
2001 Prooflike; Rare	100	—	—	—	—	—

KM# 205b GULDEN
13.2000 g., 0.9990 Gold 0.4239 oz. AGW **Ruler:** Beatrix **Obv:** Head left with vertical inscription **Rev:** Value within vertical and horizontal lines **Edge Lettering:** GOD*ZIJ*MET*ONS* **Note:** Prev. KM#205a.

Date	Mintage	F	VF	XF	Unc	BU
2001 Prooflike	25,000	—	—	—	—	325

KM# 205c GULDEN
13.2000 g., 0.9990 Gold 0.4239 oz. AGW **Ruler:** Beatrix **Obv:** Head left with vertical inscription **Rev:** Value within vertical and horizontal lines **Edge:** Plain, missing lettering

Date	Mintage	F	VF	XF	Unc	BU
2001 Prooflike	Est. 500	—	—	—	—	550

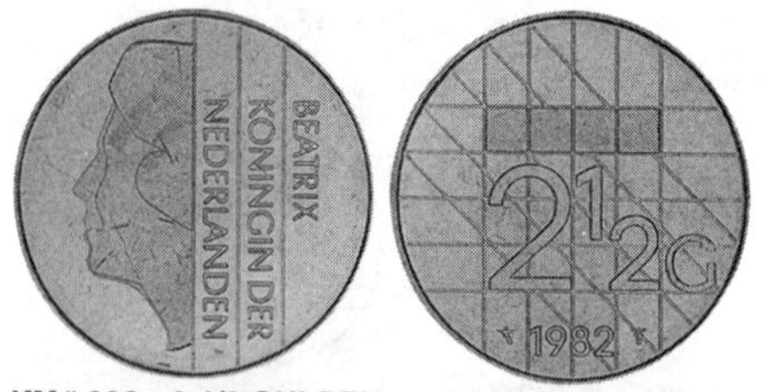

KM# 206 2-1/2 GULDEN
10.0000 g., Nickel, 29 mm. **Ruler:** Beatrix **Obv:** Head left with vertical inscription **Rev:** Value within horizontal, vertical and diagonal lines **Edge Lettering:** GOD * ZIJ * MET * ONS * **Designer:** Bruno Ninaber van Eyben

Date	Mintage	F	VF	XF	Unc	BU
2001	560,000	—	—	—	—	12.00
2001 Proof	17,000	Value: 16.00				

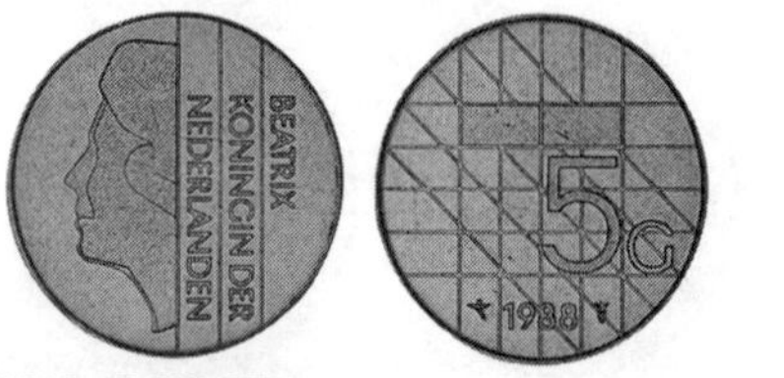

KM# 210 5 GULDEN
9.2500 g., Bronze Clad Nickel, 23.5 mm. **Ruler:** Beatrix **Obv:** Head left with vertical inscription **Rev:** Value within horizontal, vertical and diagonal lines **Edge:** GOD * ZIJ * MET * ONS * **Designer:** Bruno Ninaber van Eyben

Date	Mintage	F	VF	XF	Unc	BU
2001 Proof	17,000	Value: 15.50				
2001	360,000	—	—	—	—	10.00

EURO COINAGE

European Union Issues

KM# 234 EURO CENT
2.3000 g., Copper Plated Steel, 16.2 mm. **Ruler:** Beatrix **Obv:** Head left among stars **Obv. Designer:** Bruno Ninaber van Eyben **Rev:** Value and globe **Rev. Designer:** Luc Luycx **Edge:** Plain

Date	Mintage	F	VF	XF	Unc	BU
2001	179,300,000	—	—	—	0.35	0.50
2001 Proof	16,500	—	—	—	—	—
2002	800,000	—	—	—	1.00	1.25
2002 Proof	16,500	—	—	—	—	—
2003	58,100,000	—	—	—	0.50	0.75
2003 Proof	13,000	—	—	—	—	—
2004	113,900,000	—	—	—	0.50	0.75
2004 Proof	5,000	—	—	—	—	—
2005	413,000	—	—	—	1.50	2.00
2005 Proof	5,000	—	—	—	—	—
2006	200,000	—	—	—	1.50	2.00
2006 Proof	3,500	—	—	—	—	—
2007	225,000	—	—	—	1.50	2.00
2007 Proof	10,000	—	—	—	—	—
2008	—	—	—	—	1.50	2.00
2008 Proof	—	—	—	—	—	—

KM# 235 2 EURO CENT
3.0000 g., Copper Plated Steel, 18.7 mm. **Ruler:** Beatrix **Obv:** Head left among stars **Obv. Designer:** Bruno Ninaber van Eyben **Rev:** Value and globe **Rev. Designer:** Luc Luycx **Edge:** Grooved

Date	Mintage	F	VF	XF	Unc	BU
2001	145,800,000	—	—	—	0.50	0.75
2001 Proof	16,500	—	—	—	—	—
2002	53,100,000	—	—	—	0.75	1.00
2002 Proof	16,500	—	—	—	—	—
2003	151,200,000	—	—	—	0.50	0.75
2003 Proof	13,000	—	—	—	—	—
2004	115,622,000	—	—	—	0.50	0.75
2004 Proof	5,000	—	—	—	—	—
2005	413,000	—	—	—	1.50	2.00
2005 Proof	5,000	—	—	—	—	—
2006	200,000	—	—	—	1.50	2.00
2006 Proof	3,500	—	—	—	—	—
2007	225,000	—	—	—	1.50	2.00
2007 Proof	10,000	—	—	—	—	—
2008	—	—	—	—	1.50	2.00
2008 Proof	—	—	—	—	—	—

KM# 236 5 EURO CENT
3.9000 g., Copper Plated Steel, 21.25 mm. **Ruler:** Beatrix **Obv:** Head left among stars **Obv. Designer:** Bruno Ninaber van Eyben **Rev:** Value and globe **Rev. Designer:** Luc Luycx **Edge:** Plain

Date	Mintage	F	VF	XF	Unc	BU
2001	205,900,000	—	—	—	0.50	0.75
2001 Proof	16,500	—	—	—	—	—
2002	900,000	—	—	—	1.75	2.25
2002 Proof	16,500	—	—	—	—	—
2003	1,400,000	—	—	—	1.50	2.00
2003 Proof	13,000	—	—	—	—	—
2004	306,000	—	—	—	2.00	2.50
2004 Proof	5,000	—	—	—	—	—
2005	80,413,000	—	—	—	1.00	1.25
2005 Proof	5,000	—	—	—	—	—
2006	60,100,000	—	—	—	1.00	1.25
2006 Proof	3,500	—	—	—	—	—
2007	50,225,000	—	—	—	1.00	1.25
2007 Proof	10,000	—	—	—	—	—
2008	—	—	—	—	1.00	1.25
2008 Proof	—	—	—	—	—	—

KM# 237 10 EURO CENT
4.1000 g., Brass, 19.7 mm. **Ruler:** Beatrix **Obv:** Head left among stars **Obv. Designer:** Bruno Ninaber van Eyben **Rev:** Value and map **Rev. Designer:** Luc Luycx

Date	Mintage	F	VF	XF	Unc	BU
2001	193,500,000	—	—	—	0.75	1.00
2001 Proof	16,500	—	—	—	—	—
2002	800,000	—	—	—	1.50	2.00
2002 Proof	16,500	—	—	—	—	—
2003	1,200,000	—	—	—	1.50	2.00
2003 Proof	13,000	—	—	—	—	—
2004	262,000	—	—	—	2.00	2.50
2004 Proof	5,000	—	—	—	—	—
2005	363,000	—	—	—	1.75	2.25
2005 Proof	5,000	—	—	—	—	—
2006	150,000	—	—	—	1.75	2.25
2006 Proof	3,500	—	—	—	—	—

KM# 268 10 EURO CENT
4.1000 g., Brass, 19.7 mm. **Ruler:** Beatrix **Obv:** Head of Queen Beatrix left **Obv. Designer:** Bruno Ninaber van Eybew **Rev:** Relief map of Western Europe, stars, lines and value **Rev. Designer:** Luc Luycx

Date	Mintage	F	VF	XF	Unc	BU
2007	180,000	—	—	—	1.75	2.25
2007 Proof	10,000	—	—	—	—	—
2008	—	—	—	—	1.75	2.50
2008 Proof	—	—	—	—	—	—

KM# 238 20 EURO CENT
5.7000 g., Brass, 22.2 mm. **Ruler:** Beatrix **Obv:** Head left among stars **Obv. Designer:** Bruno Ninaber van Eyben **Rev:** Value and map **Rev. Designer:** Luc Luycx **Edge:** Notched

Date	Mintage	F	VF	XF	Unc	BU
2001	97,600,000	—	—	—	1.00	1.25
2001 Proof	16,500	—	—	—	—	—
2002	51,200,000	—	—	—	1.75	2.25
2002 Proof	16,500	—	—	—	—	—
2003	58,200,000	—	—	—	1.75	2.25
2003 Proof	13,000	—	—	—	—	—
2004	20,430,000	—	—	—	2.00	2.50
2004 Proof	5,000	—	—	—	—	—
2005	363,000	—	—	—	2.50	3.00
2005 Proof	5,000	—	—	—	—	—
2006	150,000	—	—	—	2.50	3.00
2006 Proof	3,500	—	—	—	—	—

KM# 269 20 EURO CENT
5.7000 g., Brass, 22.2 mm. **Ruler:** Beatrix **Obv:** Head of Queen Beatrix left **Obv. Designer:** Bruno Ninaber van Eybew **Rev:** Relief map of Western Europe, stars, lines and value **Rev. Designer:** Luc Luycx **Edge:** Notched

Date	Mintage	F	VF	XF	Unc	BU
2007	180,000	—	—	—	2.50	3.00
2007 Proof	10,000	—	—	—	—	—
2008	—	—	—	—	2.50	3.00
2008 Proof	—	—	—	—	—	—

KM# 239 50 EURO CENT
7.8000 g., Brass, 24.2 mm. **Ruler:** Beatrix **Obv:** Head left among stars **Obv. Designer:** Bruno Ninaber van Eyben **Rev:** Value and map **Rev. Designer:** Luc Luycx **Edge:** Notched

Date	Mintage	F	VF	XF	Unc	BU
2001	94,500,000	—	—	—	1.25	1.50
2001 Proof	16,500	—	—	—	—	—
2002	80,900,000	—	—	—	1.25	1.50
2002 Proof	16,500	—	—	—	—	—
2003	1,200,000	—	—	—	2.00	2.50
2003 Proof	13,000	—	—	—	—	—
2004	269,000	—	—	—	2.25	2.75
2004 Proof	5,000	—	—	—	—	—
2005	363,000	—	—	—	2.00	2.50
2005 Proof	5,964	—	—	—	—	—
2006	150,000	—	—	—	2.00	2.50
2006 Proof	3,500	—	—	—	—	—

KM# 270 50 EURO CENT
7.8000 g., Brass, 24.2 mm. **Ruler:** Beatrix **Obv:** Head of Quen Beatrix left **Obv. Designer:** Bruno Ninaber van Eybew **Rev:** Relief map of Western Europe, stars, lines and value **Rev. Designer:** Luc Luycx **Edge:** Notched

Date	Mintage	F	VF	XF	Unc	BU
2007	180,000	—	—	—	2.00	2.50
2007 Proof	10,000	—	—	—	—	—
2008	—	—	—	—	2.00	2.75
2008 Proof	—	—	—	—	—	—

KM# 240 EURO
7.5000 g., Bi-Metallic Copper-Nickel center in Brass ring, 23.2 mm. **Ruler:** Beatrix **Obv:** Half head left within 1/2 circle and star border, name within vertical lines **Obv. Designer:** Bruno Ninaber van Eyben **Rev:** Value and map within circle **Rev. Designer:** Luc Luycx **Edge:** Plain and reeded sections

Date	Mintage	F	VF	XF	Unc	BU
2001	67,900,000	—	—	—	2.50	3.00
2001 Proof	16,500	—	—	—	—	—
2002	20,100,000	—	—	—	3.25	3.75
2002 Proof	16,500	—	—	—	—	—
2003	1,400,000	—	—	—	3.50	4.00
2003 Proof	13,000	—	—	—	—	—
2004	235,000	—	—	—	5.00	6.00
2004 Proof	5,000	—	—	—	—	—
2005	288,000	—	—	—	4.00	5.00
2005 Proof	5,964	—	—	—	—	—
2006	100,000	—	—	—	4.00	5.00
2006 Proof	3,500	—	—	—	—	—

KM# 271 EURO
7.5000 g., Bi-Metallic Copper-Nickel center in Brass ring, 23.2 mm. **Ruler:** Beatrix **Obv:** Queen's profile left **Obv. Designer:** Bruno Ninaber van Eybew **Rev:** Relief map of Western Europe, stars, lines and value **Edge:** Plain and reeded sections

Date	Mintage	F	VF	XF	Unc	BU
2007	42,500	—	—	—	4.00	5.00
2007 Proof	10,000	—	—	—	—	—

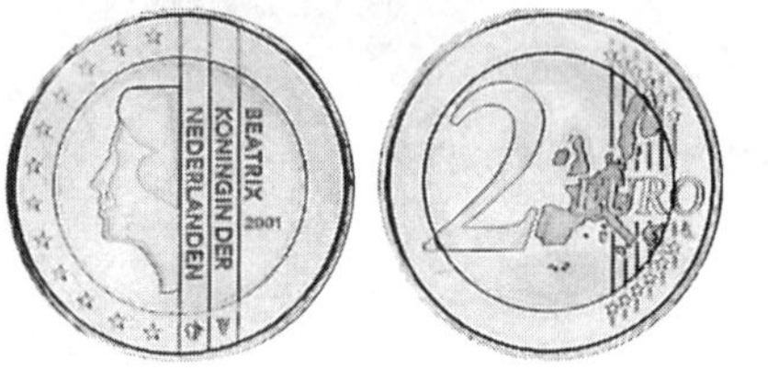

KM# 241 2 EURO
8.5000 g., Bi-Metallic Brass center in Copper-Nickel ring, 25.7 mm. **Ruler:** Beatrix **Obv:** Profile left within 1/2 circle and star border, name within vertical lines **Obv. Designer:** Bruno Ninaber van Eyben **Rev:** Value and map within circle **Rev. Designer:** Luc Luycx **Edge:** Reeded **Edge Lettering:** "GOD*ZIJ*MET*ONS*"

Date	Mintage	F	VF	XF	Unc	BU
2001	140,500,000	—	—	—	4.00	5.00
2001 Proof	16,500	—	—	—	—	—
2002	37,200,000	—	—	—	4.50	5.50
2002 Proof	16,500	—	—	—	—	—
2003	1,200,000	—	—	—	5.50	6.50
2003 Proof	13,000	—	—	—	—	—
2004	245,000	—	—	—	7.00	9.00
2004 Proof	5,000	—	—	—	—	—
2005	288,000	—	—	—	6.00	8.00
2005 Proof	5,964	—	—	—	—	—
2006	100,000	—	—	—	6.00	8.00
2006 Proof	3,500	—	—	—	—	—

KM# 273 2 EURO
8.5100 g., Bi-Metallic Brass center in Copper-Nickel ring, 25.69 mm. **Ruler:** Beatrix **Subject:** 50th Anniversary Treaty of Rome **Obv:** Open treaty book **Rev:** Large value at left, modified outline of Europe at right **Edge:** Reeded and lettered **Edge Lettering:** GOD ZU MET ONS

Date	Mintage	F	VF	XF	Unc	BU
2007	112,500	—	—	—	6.00	8.00
2007 Proof	10,000	—	—	—	—	—

KM# 272 2 EURO
8.5000 g., Bi-Metallic Brass center in Copper-Nickel ring, 25.7 mm. **Ruler:** Beatrix **Obv:** Queen's profile left **Obv. Designer:** Bruno Ninaber van Eybew **Rev:** Relief map of Western Europe, stars, lines and value **Rev. Designer:** Luc Luycx **Edge:** Reeded **Edge Lettering:** "GOD*ZIJ*MET*ONS*"

Date	Mintage	F	VF	XF	Unc	BU
2008	—	—	—	—	6.00	8.00
2008 Proof	—	—	—	—	—	—

KM# 245 5 EURO
11.9900 g., 0.9250 Silver 0.3566 oz. ASW, 29 mm. **Ruler:** Beatrix **Subject:** Vincent Van Gogh **Obv:** Head facing **Rev:** Tilted head facing **Edge:** Lettered **Edge Lettering:** GOD ZIJ MET ONS **Designer:** K. Martens

Date	Mintage	F	VF	XF	Unc	BU
ND(2003)	1,000,000	—	—	—	7.00	8.00
ND(2003) Prooflike	100,000	—	—	—	—	20.00

KM# 252 5 EURO
11.9000 g., 0.9250 Silver 0.3539 oz. ASW **Ruler:** Beatrix **Obv:** Head left **Obv. Designer:** M. Mieras and H. Mieras **Rev:** Names of old and new member countries

Date	Mintage	F	VF	XF	Unc	BU
2004	600,000	—	—	—	—	10.00
2004 Proof	55,000	Value: 45.00				

KM# 253 5 EURO
11.9000 g., 0.9250 Silver 0.3539 oz. ASW **Ruler:** Beatrix **Subject:** 50th Anniversary - End of colonization of Netherlands Antilles **Obv:** Head left **Obv. Designer:** R. Luijters **Rev:** Fruit and date within beaded circle **Edge Lettering:** GOD*ZIJ*MET*ONS*

Date	Mintage	F	VF	XF	Unc	BU
2004	650,000	—	—	—	10.00	12.00
2004 Proof	26,900	Value: 35.00				

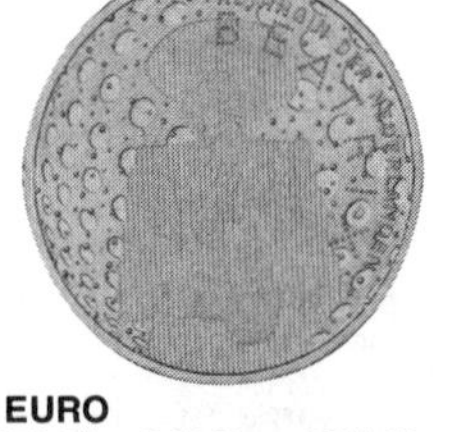

KM# 254 5 EURO
11.9100 g., 0.9250 Silver 0.3542 oz. ASW, 29 mm. **Ruler:** Beatrix **Subject:** 60th Anniversary of Liberation **Obv:** Queen's image **Rev:** Value and dots **Edge:** GOD*ZIJ*MET*ONS* **Designer:** Suzan Drummen

Date	Mintage	F	VF	XF	Unc	BU
2005	630,000	—	—	—	12.00	15.00
2005 Proof	40,000	Value: 45.00				

KM# 255 5 EURO
11.9100 g., 0.9250 Silver 0.3542 oz. ASW, 29 mm. **Ruler:** Beatrix **Obv:** Queen's silhouette centered on a world globe **Rev:** Value above Australia on a world globe **Edge Lettering:** GOD*ZIJ*MET*ONS **Designer:** Irma Boom

Date	Mintage	F	VF	XF	Unc	BU
2006	500,000	—	—	—	15.00	18.00
2006 Proof	22,500	Value: 40.00				

KM# 266 5 EURO
11.9100 g., 0.9250 Silver 0.3542 oz. ASW, 28.9 mm. **Ruler:** Beatrix **Obv:** Queen Beatrix **Rev:** Rembrandt **Edge Lettering:** GOD * Z IJ * MET * ONS * **Designer:** Berend Strik

Date	Mintage	F	VF	XF	Unc	BU
ND (2006)	651,000	—	—	—	10.00	45.00
ND(2006) Proof	35,000	Value: 35.00				

KM# 267 5 EURO
Silver, 29 mm. **Ruler:** Beatrix **Subject:** 200th Anniversary of Taxes **Obv:** Queen's portrait **Rev:** Circles with dates 1806-2006

Date	Mintage	F	VF	XF	Unc	BU
2006	359,189	—	—	—	10.00	—
2006 Proof	16,000	Value: 35.00				

KM# 243 10 EURO
17.8000 g., 0.9250 Silver 0.5293 oz. ASW, 33 mm. **Ruler:** Beatrix **Subject:** Crown Prince's Wedding **Obv:** Head left **Rev:** Two facing silhouettes **Edge:** Plain **Designer:** H. van Houwelingen

Date	Mintage	F	VF	XF	Unc	BU
2002	1,000,000	—	—	—	15.00	40.00
2002 Prooflike	80,000	—	—	—	—	55.00

KM# 244 10 EURO
6.7200 g., 0.9000 Gold 0.1944 oz. AGW, 22.5 mm. **Ruler:** Beatrix **Subject:** Crown Prince's Wedding **Obv:** Head left **Rev:** Two facing silhouettes **Edge:** Reeded **Designer:** J. van Houwelingen

Date	Mintage	F	VF	XF	Unc	BU
2002 Prooflike	33,000	—	—	—	—	200

KM# 246 10 EURO
6.7200 g., 0.9000 Gold 0.1944 oz. AGW, 22.5 mm. **Ruler:** Beatrix **Subject:** Vincent Van Gogh **Obv:** Head facing **Rev:** Tilted head facing **Edge:** Reeded **Designer:** K. Martens

Date	Mintage	F	VF	XF	Unc	BU
ND(2003) Prooflike	20,000	—	—	—	—	200

KM# 247 10 EURO
6.7200 g., 0.9000 Gold 0.1944 oz. AGW, 22.5 mm. **Ruler:** Beatrix **Subject:** New EEC members **Obv:** Head left **Rev:** Value and legend **Edge:** Reeded **Designer:** M. Mieras and H. Mieras

Date	Mintage	F	VF	XF	Unc	BU
2004 Proof	6,000	Value: 450				

KM# 251 10 EURO
Gold **Ruler:** Beatrix **Subject:** 50 Years of Domestic Autonomy, 1954-2004 (for Netherlands Antilles) **Obv:** Small head left **Rev:** Fruit and date within beaded circle **Edge:** Reeded **Designer:** R. L. Luijters

Date	Mintage	F	VF	XF	Unc	BU
2004 Proof	3,800	Value: 350				

KM# 248 10 EURO
0.9250 Silver **Ruler:** Beatrix **Obv:** Head left **Rev:** Multi-views of Prince Willem-Alexander, Princess Catherina-Amalia and Princess Maxima

Date	Mintage	F	VF	XF	Unc	BU
2004	1,000,000	—	—	—	—	18.00
2004 Proof	50,000	Value: 40.00				

KM# 261 10 EURO
17.8000 g., 0.9250 Silver 0.5293 oz. ASW, 33 mm. **Ruler:** Beatrix **Subject:** Silver Jubilee of Reign **Obv:** Queen's photo **Rev:** Queen taking oath photo **Edge Lettering:** GOD*ZIJ*MET*ONS* **Designer:** Germaine Kuip

Date	Mintage	F	VF	XF	Unc	BU
2005	1,000,000	—	—	—	—	20.00
2005 Proof	59,754	Value: 45.00				

KM# 264 10 EURO
6.7200 g., 0.9000 Gold 0.1944 oz. AGW, 22.5 mm. **Ruler:** Beatrix **Subject:** 60th Anniversary of Liberation **Obv:** Queen and dots **Rev:** Value and dots **Edge:** Reeded **Designer:** Suzan Drummen

Date	Mintage	F	VF	XF	Unc	BU
2005 Proof	6,000	Value: 300				

KM# 249 20 EURO
8.5000 g., 0.9000 Gold 0.2459 oz. AGW, 25 mm. **Ruler:** Beatrix **Subject:** Birth of Crown-Princess - Catharina-Amalia - July 12, 2003 **Obv:** Bust left **Rev:** Holographic images: left, Princess Maxima; front, Princess Catharina-Amalia; right, Prince Willem-Alexander **Edge:** Reeded

Date	Mintage	F	VF	XF	Unc	BU
2004 Proof	5,345	Value: 300				

KM# 262 20 EURO
8.5000 g., 0.9000 Gold 0.2459 oz. AGW, 25 mm. **Ruler:** Beatrix **Subject:** Silver Jubilee of Reign **Obv:** Queen's photo **Rev:** Queen taking oath photo **Edge:** Reeded **Designer:** Germaine Kuip

Date	Mintage	F	VF	XF	Unc	BU
2005 Proof	5,001	Value: 345				

KM# 250 50 EURO
13.4400 g., 0.9000 Gold 0.3889 oz. AGW, 27 mm. **Ruler:** Beatrix **Subject:** Birth of Crown-Princess - Catharina-Amalia - July 12, 2003 **Obv:** Bust left **Rev:** Holographic images: left, Princess Maxima; front, Princess Catharina-Amalia; right, Prince Willem-Alexander **Edge:** Reeded

Date	Mintage	F	VF	XF	Unc	BU
2004 Proof	3,500	Value: 500				

KM# 263 50 EURO
13.4400 g., 0.9000 Gold 0.3889 oz. AGW, 27 mm. **Ruler:** Beatrix **Subject:** Silver Jubilee of Reign **Obv:** Queen's photo **Rev:** Queen taking oath photo **Edge:** Reeded **Designer:** Germaine Kuip

Date	Mintage	F	VF	XF	Unc	BU
2005 Proof	3,500	Value: 575				

TRADE COINAGE

KM# 190.2 DUCAT
3.4940 g., 0.9830 Gold 0.1104 oz. AGW **Ruler:** Beatrix **Obv:** Knight divides date with larger letters in legend **Rev:** Inscription within decorated square

Date	Mintage	F	VF	XF	Unc	BU
2001 Proof	7,500	Value: 125				
2002 Proof	3,400	Value: 145				
2003 Proof	2,650	Value: 145				
2004 Proof	2,120	Value: 200				
2005 Proof	2,243	Value: 150				
2006 Proof	2,092	Value: 150				
2007 Proof	2,500	Value: 145				
2008	—	Value: 145				

KM# 211 2 DUCAT
6.9880 g., 0.9830 Gold 0.2208 oz. AGW, 26 mm. **Ruler:** Beatrix **Obv:** Knight divides date within beaded circle **Rev:** Inscription within decorated square

Date	Mintage	F	VF	XF	Unc	BU
2002 Proof	6,650	Value: 215				
2003 Proof	3,350	Value: 235				
2004 Proof	2,015	Value: 245				
2005 Proof	3,500	Value: 235				
2006 Proof	1,800	Value: 235				
2007 Proof	2,500	Value: 235				
2008	—	Value: 235				

SILVER BULLION COINAGE

KM# 242 SILVER DUCAT

28.2500 g., 0.8730 Silver 0.7929 oz. ASW, 40 mm. **Ruler:** Beatrix **Obv:** Crowned shield **Rev:** Armored Knight with sword divides date and circle, shield in front **Edge:** Reeded **Note:** Utrecht coin design circa 1659 based on KM#48.

Date	Mintage	F	VF	XF	Unc	BU
2001 Proof	9,000	Value: 40.00				

KM# 256 SILVER DUCAT

28.2500 g., 0.8730 Silver 0.7929 oz. ASW, 40 mm. **Ruler:** Beatrix **Obv:** Crowned shield **Rev:** Armored Knight with Gelderland arms **Edge:** Reeded

Date	Mintage	F	VF	XF	Unc	BU
2002 Proof	9,400	Value: 45.00				

KM# 257 SILVER DUCAT

28.2500 g., 0.8730 Silver 0.7929 oz. ASW, 40 mm. **Ruler:** Beatrix **Obv:** Crowned shield **Rev:** Armored Knight with sword holding arms of Holland **Edge:** Reeded

Date	Mintage	F	VF	XF	Unc	BU
2003 Proof	4,100	Value: 45.00				

KM# 258 SILVER DUCAT

28.2500 g., 0.8730 Silver 0.7929 oz. ASW, 40 mm. **Ruler:** Beatrix **Obv:** Crowned shield **Rev:** Armored Knight holding sword with Zeeland arms **Edge:** Reeded

Date	Mintage	F	VF	XF	Unc	BU
2004 Proof	2,500	Value: 45.00				

KM# 259 SILVER DUCAT

28.2500 g., 0.8730 Silver 0.7929 oz. ASW, 40 mm. **Ruler:** Beatrix **Obv:** Crowned shield **Rev:** Armored Knight holding sword with Friesland arms **Edge:** Reeded

Date	Mintage	F	VF	XF	Unc	BU
2005 Proof	4,109	Value: 45.00				

KM# 260 SILVER DUCAT

28.2500 g., 0.8730 Silver 0.7929 oz. ASW, 40 mm. **Ruler:** Beatrix **Obv:** Crowned shield **Rev:** Armored Knight holding sword with Groningen arms **Edge:** Reeded

Date	Mintage	F	VF	XF	Unc	BU
2006 Proof	4,000	Value: 45.00				
2007	—	—	—	—	—	—

PATTERNS

Including off metal strikes

KM#	Date	Mintage	Identification	Mkt Val
Pn165	2001	—	2 Euro Cent. Nickel.	100
Pn166	2001	—	Euro. Brass. KM240	—
Pn162	2001	—	Gulden. Nickel. Medal rotation	—

MINT SETS

KM#	Date	Mintage	Identification	Issue Price	Mkt Val
MS4	2001 (6)	85,000	KM#202-206, 210	12.00	15.00
MS5	2001 (8)	68,000	KM#234-241 Charity set, Disabled Sports	15.00	17.00
MS6	2002 (8)	105,000	KM#234-241 Charity set, Blind Escort Dogs Fund	15.00	17.00
MS7	2002 (8)	59,500	KM#234-241 Last FDC set	15.00	17.00
MS8	2002 (8)	25,000	KM#234-241 plus bear medal Baby set	15.50	25.00
MS9	2002 (8)	10,000	KM#234-241 plus medal Wedding Set	15.50	35.00
MS10	2002 (8)	3,500	KM#234-241 plus medal Queen Beatrix set	20.00	110
MS11	2002 (8)	2,002	KM#234-241 plus medal 10th Day of the Mint	22.00	150
MS12	2002 (8)	10,000	KM#234-241 plus medal VOC set I	22.00	35.00
MS13	2002 (8)	10,000	KM#234-241 plus medal VOC set II	22.00	25.00
MS14	2002 (8)	10,000	KM#234-241 plus medal VOC set III	22.00	25.00
MS15	2002 (8)	10,000	KM#234-241 plus medal VOC set IV	22.00	25.00
MS16	2002 (8)	3,000	KM#234-241 plus medal BVC	30.00	40.00
MS17	2002 (1)	9,200	KM#243 plus stamp	30.00	30.00
MS17A	2002 (8)	2,500	KM#234-241 VVV - Irisgiftset	20.00	40.00
MS18	2002 (8)	1,000	KM#234-241 plus medal Theo Peters (Christmas)	99.00	99.00
MS19	2003 (8)	75,000	KM#234-241 Charity set, Epilepsy fund	15.50	17.00
MS20	2003 (8)	15,000	KM#234-241 Information set Denmark	20.00	40.00
MS21	2003 (8)	10,000	KM#234-241 VVV - Irisgiftset	15.50	17.00
MS22	2003 (8)	10,000	KM#234-241 plus medal VOC set V	22.00	25.00
MS23	2003 (8)	10,000	KM#234-241 plus medal VOC set VI	42.00	45.00
MS24	2003 (8)	2,003	KM#234-241 plus medal Day of the Mint	25.00	120
MS25	2003 (8)	1,000	KM#234-241 plus bi-color medal Theo Peters Jubilee set	—	30.00
MS26	2003 (8)	100	KM#234-241 plus silver medal Theo Peters Jubilee set	70.00	70.00
MS27	2003 (8)	25	KM#234-241 plus golden medal Theo Peters Jubilee set	400	410
MS28	2003 (8)	25,000	KM#234-241 plus bear medal Baby set	20.00	25.00
MS29	2003 (8)	15,000	KM#234-241 plus medal Wedding set	20.00	25.00
MS30	2003 (8)	1,000	KM#234-241 plus silver medal Theo Peters Christmas set	—	30.00
MS31	2003 (8)	150	KM#234-241 plus silver medal Theo Peters Christmas set	70.00	70.00
MS32	2003 (8)	50	KM#234-241 plus golden medal Theo Peters Christmas set	400	400
MS33	2003	3,500	KM#234-241 plus medal Mintmasters I	20.00	60.00
MS34	2003 (8)	1,000	KM#234-241 World Money Fair	20.00	110
MS35	2003 (8)	15,000	KM234-241 Information Set Hungaria	20.00	40.00
MS36	2003 (8)	20,000	KM#234-241 plus silver medal Royal Birth of Princess Catharina-Amalia	22.00	25.00
MS37	2003 (16)	10,000	KM#234-241 and Luxembourg KM#75-81, 40 Benelux Set	40.00	45.00
MS38	2003 (40)	10,000	KM#224-231 plus Germany KM#207-214 plus Spain KM#1040-1047 plus Belgium KM#224-231 and Austria KM#3082-3089 Charles V Set	85.00	85.00
MS39	2004 (8)	3,500	KM#234-241 plus medal Mintmasters II	20.00	60.00
MS40	2004 (8)	10,000	KM#234-241 Wedding set plus medal	18.00	—
MS41	2004 (9)	20,000	KM#234-241 Baby set plus bear medal	20.00	25.00
MS42	2004 (8)	1,000	KM#234-241 Basel World Money Fair	20.00	110
MS43	2004 (24)	35,000	KM#234-241 and Luxembourg KM#75-81 plus Belgium KM#224-231 Benelux set with silver medal	60.00	60.00
MS44	2004 (10)	10,000	KM#234-241 Queen Juliana set plus silver guilder, KM#184 and 30mm silver medal	25.00	28.00
MS45	2004 (9)	1,500	KM#234-241 Theo Peters Christmas set plus bi-color medal	30.00	30.00
MS46	2004 (8)	3,500	KM#234-241 VVV - Iris gift set	20.00	25.00
MS47	2004 (9)	150	KM#234-241 Theo Peters Christmas set plus silver medal	100	—
MS48	2004 (9)	50	KM#234-241 Theo Peters Christmas set plus golden medal	500	—
MS49	2004 (8)	50,000	KM#234-241 Fire - Burn Centre Charity set	18.00	22.00
MS50	2004 (9)	—	KM#234-241 Day of the Mint plus medal	25.00	150
MS51	2005 (9)	3,500	KM#234-241 Mintmasters III plus medal	20.00	60.00
MS52	2005 (9)	—	KM#234-241 Day of the Mint plus medal	25.00	150
MS53	2005 (9)	10,000	KM#234-241 Wedding set plus medal	18.00	—
MS54	2005 (9)	20,000	KM#234-241 Baby set plus bear medal	20.00	25.00
MS55	2005 (9)	20,000	KM#234-241 Nijntje set (Dick Bruna) plus medal	18.00	—
MS56	2005 (8)	55,000	KM#234-241 Charity set: Princess Beatrix Fonds	18.00	22.00
MS57	2005 (24)	20,000	KM#234-241, Belgium 224-231, Luxembourg 75-81 Benelux set: Belgium, Netherlands plus Luxembourg with silver medal	60.00	60.00
MS58	2005 (8)	1,000	KM#234-241 World Money Fair, Basel	25.00	110
MS59	2005 (8)	15,000	KM#234-241 60th Anniversary Liberation plus Canadian 25 cent	35.00	35.00
MS60	2005 (9)	1,000	KM#234-241 Theo Peters Christmas set plus bi-color medal	30.00	30.00
MS61	2005 (9)	100	KM#234-241 Theo Peters Christmas set plus silver medal	120	—
MS62	2005 (9)	25	KM#234-241 Theo Peters Christmas set plus golden medal	550	—
MS63	2006 (10)	3,500	KM#234-241 Mintmasters IV plus medal	20.00	40.00
MS64	2006 (10)	4,000	KM#234-241 5 sets plus a Rembrandt silver medal and 1 set with a Rembrandt 5 Euro coin (6x8)	250	—
MS65	2006 (10)	500	KM#234-241 5 sets with Rembrandt silver medal and one set with Rembrandt 10 euro coin (6x8)	900	—
MS66	2006 (8)	45,000	KM#234-241 Charity set: Kika	18.00	22.00
MS67	2006 (9)	2,750	KM#231-241 Baby set boy plus bear medal	20.00	25.00
MS68	2006 (9)	100	KM#234-241 Baby set boy plus silver medal	—	95.00
MS69	2006 (8)	25	KM#234-241 Baby set boy plus gold medal	—	500
MS70	2006 (9)	2,750	KM#234-241 Baby set girl plus bear medal	20.00	25.00
MS71	2006 (8)	100	KM#234-241 Baby set girl plus silver medal	—	95.00
MS72	2006 (9)	25	KM#234-241 Baby set girl, plus gold medal	—	500
MS73	2006 (9)	15,000	KM#234-241 Benelux set: Belgium, 224-231, Luxembourg 75-81 plus Netherlands	65.00	65.00
MS74	2006 (9)	1,050	KM#234-241 Wedding set plus medal	22.00	25.00
MS75	2006 (8)	1,500	KM#234-241 Royal Dutch Mint Christmas set	30.00	—
MS76	2006 (9)	600	KM#234-241 Theo Peters Christmas set plus bi-color medal	35.00	40.00
MS77	2006 (9)	100	KM#234-241 Christmas set plus silver medal	150	—
MS78	2006 (9)	25	KM#234-241 Christmas set plus golden medal	650	—
MS79	2006 (8)	1,000	KM#234-241 Berlin Coin Fair	25.00	45.00
MS80	2006 (9)	—	KM#234-241 Day of the Mint set plus medal	25.00	120
MS81	2006 (8)	10,000	KM#234-241 200 Years of Coins in Kingdom of Holland	25.00	20.00
MS82	2007 (9)	3,500	KM#234-241 Mintmasters V plus medal	20.00	40.00
MS83	2007 (9)	100	KM#234-241 Mintmasters V plus silver medal	—	500
MS84	2007 (8)	3,500	KM#234-241 (6 sets) Michiel de Ruyter sets, 1 plus silver medal and 1 set with Ruyter's 5 euro coin	—	250
MS85	2007 (8)	500	KM#234-241, (6 sets) Michiel de Ruyter sets, 1 set with silver medal and 1 set with Ruyter's 10 euro coin	900	—
MS86	2007 (8)	40,000	KM#234-241 Charity set	18.00	22.00
MS87	2007 (9)	3,000	KM#234-241 Baby set boy plus bear medal	20.00	25.00
MS88	2007 (9)	100	KM#234-241 Baby set boy plus silver medal	—	95.00
MS89	2007 (9)	3,000	KM#234-241 Baby set girl plus bear medal	20.00	25.00
MS90	2007 (9)	100	KM#234-241 Baby set girl plus silver medal	—	95.00
MS92	2007 (9)	1,050	KM#234-241 Wedding set plus medal	22.00	25.00
MS93	2007 (9)	1,000	KM#234-241 Christmas set plus bi-color medal	35.00	40.00
MS94	2007 (9)	100	KM#234-241 Christmas set plus silver medal	150	—
MS95	2007 (9)	25	KM#234-241 Christmas set plus golden medal	650	—
MS96	2007 (8)	1,000	KM#234-241 Berlin Coin Fair	25.00	75.00
MS97	2007 (9)	—	KM#234-241 Day of the Mint plus medal	25.00	100
MS98	2007 (8)	5,000	KM#234-241 200 Years of Royal Predicate	25.00	28.00
MS99	2007 (8)	—	KM#234-236, 268-272	—	—

PROOF SETS

KM#	Date	Mintage	Identification	Issue Price	Mkt Val
PS54	2001 (6)	17,000	KM#202-206, 210 Booklet 5 Guilder	50.00	60.00
PS55	2001 (2)	500	KM#190.2, 242 Gold and Silver Ducat	50.00	60.00
PS56	2002 (2)	—	KM#190.2, 211 Golden Ducats	—	230
PS57	2002 (3)	—	KM#190.2, 211, 232 Golden Ducats and Silver Ducat	—	270
PS58	2003 (2)	—	KM#190.2, 211 Golden ducats in wooden box	230	230
PS59	2003 (8)	2,000	KM#234-241 Frigate "The Netherland" and silber medal and numbered ingot	85.00	125

PROOF-LIKE SETS (PL)

KM#	Date	Mintage	Identification	Issue Price	Mkt Val
PL3	2001 (8)	16,500	KM#234-241	50.00	50.00
PL4	2002 (2)	—	KM#243, 244 Wedding set (10 Euro in silver and gold) in plastic box	145	150
PL5	2002 (2)	—	KM#243, 244 Wedding set in wooden box	145	160
PL6	2002 (8)	15,500	KM#234-241	50.00	45.00
PL7	2003 (8)	10,000	KM#234-241	50.00	45.00
PL8	2004 (8)	10,000	KM#234-241	—	75.00
PL9	2005 (8)	10,000	KM#234-241	—	75.00

SELECT SETS (FLEUR DE COIN)

KM#	Date	Mintage	Identification	Issue Price	Mkt Val
SS90	2001 (6)	120,000	KM#202-206, 210 Introduction to Euro Coins	15.00	16.00

KM#	Date	Mintage	Identification	Issue Price	Mkt Val
SS91	2001 (6)	3,400	KM#202-206, 210 Queen Julianna Medal	17.50	40.00
SS92	2001 (6)	100	KM#202-206, 210 Queen Julianna Medal; some coins dated 2000 in error	17.50	150
SS93	2001 (6)	1,000	KM#202-206, 210 BOLEGO - VOK	—	60.00
SS94	2001 (7)	1,000	KM#202-206, 210, 2 Stuiver coin from the wreck of the De Akerendam II	125	145
SS95	2001 (6)	1,000	KM#202-206, 210 United Provinces, Groningen Medal	40.00	40.00
SS96	2001 (6)	21,000	KM#202-206, 210 Baby set plus bear medal	15.50	17.50
SS97	2001 (6)	1,015	KM#202-206, 210 Onderlinge "'s-Gravenhage"	70.00	70.00

SPECIMEN FDC SETS (FLEUR DE COIN)

KM#	Date	Mintage	Identification	Issue Price	Mkt Val
SS95A	2001 (6)	1,000	KM202-206, 210 United Provinces, Utrecht Medal	40.00	40.00

NETHERLANDS ANTILLES

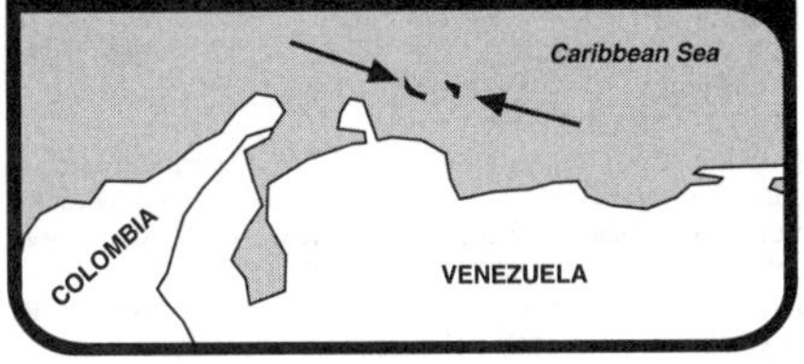

The Netherlands Antilles, comprises two groups of islands in the West Indies: Aruba (until 1986), Bonaire and Curacao and their dependencies near the Venezuelan coast and St. Eustatius, Saba, and the southern part of St. Martin (*St. Maarten*) southeast of Puerto Rico. The island group has an area of 371 sq. mi. (960 sq. km.) and a population of 225,000. Capital: Willemstad. Chief industries are the refining of crude oil and tourism. Petroleum products and phosphates are exported.

RULERS

Beatrix, 1980-

MINT MARKS

Y - York Mint

Utrecht Mint

(privy marks only)

Date	Privy Mark
2001	Wine tendril with grapes
2002	Wine tendril with grapes and star
2003	Sails of a clipper

FM - Franklin Mint, U.S.A.

NOTE: See Kingdom of the Netherlands for more details.

MONETARY SYSTEM

100 Cents = 1 Gulden

DUTCH ADMINISTRATION

DECIMAL COINAGE

KM# 32 CENT

0.7000 g., Aluminum, 14 mm. **Ruler:** Beatrix **Obv:** Orange blossom within circle **Rev:** Value within circle of geometric designed border **Edge:** Reeded

Date	Mintage	F	VF	XF	Unc	BU
2001(u)	12,806,500	—	—	0.10	0.20	0.50
2002(u)	6,000	—	—	0.50	1.00	1.25
Note: In sets only						
2003(u)	19,604,000	—	—	0.10	0.20	0.50
2004(u)	7,100	—	—	0.10	0.20	0.50
2005(u)	—	—	—	0.10	0.20	0.50
2006(u)	—	—	—	0.10	0.20	0.50
2007(u)	—	—	—	0.10	0.20	0.50

KM# 33 5 CENTS

1.1600 g., Aluminum, 16 mm. **Ruler:** Beatrix **Obv:** Orange blossom within circle **Rev:** Value within circle, geometric designed border **Edge:** Reeded

Date	Mintage	F	VF	XF	Unc	BU
2001	2,006,500	—	—	0.20	0.60	0.75
2002	6,000	—	—	0.20	2.00	2.50
Note: In sets only						
2003	3,104,000	—	—	0.30	0.60	0.75
2004	2,402,100	—	—	0.30	0.50	0.75
2005	—	—	—	0.30	0.50	0.75
2006	—	—	—	0.30	0.50	0.75
2007	—	—	—	0.30	0.50	0.75

KM# 34 10 CENTS

3.0000 g., Nickel Bonded Steel, 18 mm. **Ruler:** Beatrix **Obv:** Orange blossom within circle **Rev:** Value within circle, geometric designed border **Edge:** Reeded

Date	Mintage	F	VF	XF	Unc	BU
2001	11,500	—	—	0.50	1.25	2.00
2002	6,000	—	—	0.50	2.00	3.00
Note: In sets only						
2003	2,104,000	—	—	0.50	1.00	1.75
2004	2,202,100	—	—	0.50	1.00	1.75
2005	—	—	—	0.50	1.00	1.75
2006	—	—	—	0.50	1.00	1.75
2007	—	—	—	0.50	1.00	1.75

KM# 35 25 CENTS

3.5000 g., Nickel Bonded Steel, 20.2 mm. **Ruler:** Beatrix **Obv:** Orange blossom within circle **Rev:** Value within circle, geometric designed border **Edge:** Reeded

Date	Mintage	F	VF	XF	Unc	BU
2001	11,500	—	—	0.50	1.25	1.50
2002	6,000	—	—	0.50	2.00	3.00
Note: In sets only						
2003	1,404,000	—	—	0.50	1.25	1.50
2004	1,502,100	—	—	0.50	1.25	1.50
2005	—	—	—	0.50	1.25	1.50
2006	—	—	—	0.50	1.25	1.50
2007	—	—	—	0.50	1.25	1.50

KM# 36 50 CENTS

5.0000 g., Aureate Steel, 24 mm. **Ruler:** Beatrix **Obv:** Orange blossom within circle, designed border **Rev:** Value within circle of pearls and shell border **Edge:** Plain **Shape:** 4-sided

Date	Mintage	F	VF	XF	Unc	BU
2001	11,500	—	—	0.75	3.00	4.00
2002	6,000	—	—	0.75	4.50	6.00
Note: In sets only						
2003	9,000	—	—	0.75	3.00	4.00
2004	7,100	—	—	0.75	3.00	4.00
2005	—	—	—	0.75	3.00	4.00
2006	—	—	—	0.75	3.00	4.00
2007	—	—	—	0.75	3.00	4.00

KM# 37 GULDEN

6.0000 g., Aureate Steel **Ruler:** Beatrix **Obv:** Head left **Rev:** Crowned shield divides value above date and ribbon **Edge Lettering:** GOD * ZIJ * MET * ONS *

Date	Mintage	F	VF	XF	Unc	BU
2001	11,500	—	—	0.75	3.00	4.00
2002	6,000	—	—	0.75	5.00	6.00
Note: In sets only						
2003	504,000	—	—	0.75	3.00	4.00
2004	7,100	—	—	0.75	5.00	6.00
2005	—	—	—	0.75	3.00	4.00
2006	—	—	—	0.75	3.00	4.00
2007	—	—	—	0.75	3.00	4.00

KM# 38 2-1/2 GULDEN

9.0000 g., Aureate Steel, 28 mm. **Ruler:** Beatrix **Obv:** Head left **Rev:** Crowned shield divides value above date and ribbon **Edge Lettering:** GOD * ZIJ * MET * ONS *

Date	Mintage	F	VF	XF	Unc	BU
2001	11,500	—	—	1.00	5.00	6.00
2002	6,000	—	—	1.00	7.00	8.00
Note: In sets only						
2003	9,000	—	—	1.00	5.00	6.00
2004	7,100	—	—	1.00	5.00	6.00
2005	—	—	—	1.00	5.00	6.00
2006	—	—	—	1.00	5.00	6.00
2007	—	—	—	1.00	5.00	6.00

KM# 43 5 GULDEN

11.0000 g., Brass Plated Steel, 26 mm. **Ruler:** Beatrix **Obv:** Head left **Rev:** Crowned shield divides value above date and ribbon **Edge Lettering:** GOD * ZIJ * MET * ONS *

Date	Mintage	F	VF	XF	Unc	BU
2001	9,500	—	—	1.00	4.00	5.00
2002	6,000	—	—	1.00	5.00	6.00
Note: In sets only						
2003	7,000	—	—	1.00	4.00	5.00
2004	102,100	—	—	1.00	4.00	5.00
2005	—	—	—	1.00	4.00	5.00
2006	—	—	—	1.00	4.00	5.00
2007	—	—	—	1.00	4.00	5.00

KM# 74 5 GULDEN

11.9000 g., 0.9250 Silver 0.3539 oz. ASW, 29 mm. **Ruler:** Beatrix **Subject:** 50th Anniversary - End to Dutch Colonial Rule **Obv:** Head left **Rev:** Triangular signatures around value **Edge Lettering:** GOD*ZIJ*MET*ONS* **Designer:** Ans Mezas-Hummelink

Date	Mintage	F	VF	XF	Unc	BU
2004 Proof	4,000	Value: 30.00				

KM# 74.1 5 GULDEN

11.0000 g., Aureate Bonded Steel, 26 mm. **Ruler:** Beatrix **Subject:** 50th Anniversary - End To Dutch Colonial Rule **Obv:** Head left **Rev:** Triangular signatures around value **Edge Lettering:** GOD*ZIJ*MET*ONS*

Date	Mintage	F	VF	XF	Unc	BU
2004 Proof	10,000	Value: 8.00				

KM# 76.1 5 GULDEN

11.0000 g., Aureate Bonded Steel, 26 mm. **Ruler:** Beatrix **Subject:** Queen's Silver Jubilee **Obv:** Head left **Rev:** Child art and value **Edge Lettering:** GOD*ZIJ*MET*ONS*

Date	Mintage	F	VF	XF	Unc	BU
2005 Proof	10,000	Value: 8.00				

KM# 76 5 GULDEN

11.9000 g., 0.9250 Silver 0.3539 oz. ASW, 29 mm. **Ruler:** Beatrix **Subject:** Queen's Silver Jubilee **Obv:** Head left **Rev:** Child art and value **Edge Lettering:** GOD*ZIJ*MET*ONS*

Date	Mintage	F	VF	XF	Unc	BU
2005(u) Proof	4,000	Value: 32.00				

KM# 49 10 GULDEN

31.1035 g., 0.9250 Silver 0.9250 oz. ASW, 40 mm. **Ruler:** Beatrix **Subject:** Gold Trade Coins: Sulla Aureus **Obv:** Crowned shield divides value above date and ribbon **Rev:** Bust facing with two gold coins at lower left **Edge:** Plain

Date	Mintage	F	VF	XF	Unc	BU
2001(u) Proof	589	Value: 50.00				

KM# 50 10 GULDEN

31.1035 g., 0.9250 Silver 0.9250 oz. ASW, 40 mm. **Ruler:** Beatrix **Subject:** Gold Trade Coins: Constantin I Solidus **Obv:** Crowned shield divides value above date and ribbon **Rev:** Bust facing with two gold coins at lower right **Edge:** Plain

Date	Mintage	F	VF	XF	Unc	BU
2001(u) Proof	578	Value: 50.00				

KM# 51 10 GULDEN

31.1035 g., 0.9250 Silver 0.9250 oz. ASW, 40 mm. **Ruler:** Beatrix **Subject:** Gold Trade Coins: Clovis I Tremissisfiorino d'oro **Obv:** Crowned shield divides value above date and ribbon **Rev:** Bust facing with two gold coins **Edge:** Plain

Date	Mintage	F	VF	XF	Unc	BU
2001(u) Proof	566	Value: 50.00				

KM# 52 10 GULDEN

31.1035 g., 0.9250 Silver 0.9250 oz. ASW, 40 mm. **Ruler:** Beatrix **Subject:** Gold Trade Coins: Cosimo de'Medici Fiorino d'oro **Obv:** Crowned shield divides value above date and ribbon **Rev:** Bust facing with two gold coins **Edge:** Plain

Date	Mintage	F	VF	XF	Unc	BU
2001(u) Proof	575	Value: 50.00				

KM# 53 10 GULDEN

31.1035 g., 0.9250 Silver 0.9250 oz. ASW, 40 mm. **Ruler:** Beatrix **Subject:** Gold Trade Coins: Dandolo Ducato d'Oro **Obv:** Crowned shield divides value above date and ribbon **Rev:** Bust facing with two gold coins **Edge:** Plain

Date	Mintage	F	VF	XF	Unc	BU
2001(u) Proof	490	Value: 50.00				

KM# 54 10 GULDEN

31.1035 g., 0.9250 Silver 0.9250 oz. ASW, 40 mm. **Ruler:** Beatrix **Subject:** Gold Trade Coins: Philips IV Ecu d'or la chaise **Obv:** Crowned shield divides value above date and ribbon **Rev:** Bust facing with two gold coins **Edge:** Plain

Date	Mintage	F	VF	XF	Unc	BU
2001(u) Proof	460	Value: 50.00				

KM# 55 10 GULDEN

31.1035 g., 0.9250 Silver 0.9250 oz. ASW, 40 mm. **Ruler:** Beatrix **Subject:** Gold Trade Coins: Edward III Nobel **Obv:** Crowned shield divides value above date and ribbon **Rev:** Crowned bust facing with two gold coins **Edge:** Plain

Date	Mintage	F	VF	XF	Unc	BU
2001(u) Proof	575	Value: 50.00				

KM# 56 10 GULDEN

31.1035 g., 0.9250 Silver 0.9250 oz. ASW, 40 mm. **Ruler:** Beatrix **Subject:** Gold Trade Coins: Carolus IV Rhine Gold Guilder **Obv:** Crowned shield divides value above date and ribbon **Rev:** Bust facing with two gold coins **Edge:** Plain

Date	Mintage	F	VF	XF	Unc	BU
2001(u) Proof	430	Value: 50.00				

KM# 57 10 GULDEN

31.1035 g., 0.9250 Silver 0.9250 oz. ASW, 40 mm. **Ruler:** Beatrix **Subject:** Gold Trade Coins: John II Franc d'or a cheval **Obv:** Crowned shield divides value above date and ribbon **Rev:** Bust facing with two gold coins **Edge:** Plain

Date	Mintage	F	VF	XF	Unc	BU
2001(u) Proof	464	Value: 50.00				

KM# 58 10 GULDEN

31.1035 g., 0.9250 Silver 0.9250 oz. ASW, 40 mm. **Ruler:** Beatrix **Subject:** Gold Trade Coins: Philip the Good Adriesguilder **Obv:** Crowned shield divides value above date and ribbon **Rev:** Bust facing with two gold coins **Edge:** Plain

Date	Mintage	F	VF	XF	Unc	BU
2001(u) Proof	250	Value: 50.00				

KM# 59 10 GULDEN

31.1035 g., 0.9250 Silver 0.9250 oz. ASW, 40 mm. **Ruler:** Beatrix **Subject:** Gold Trade Coins: Louis XI Ecu d'or au soleil **Obv:** Crowned shield divides value above date and ribbon **Rev:** Bust facing with two gold coins **Edge:** Plain

Date	Mintage	F	VF	XF	Unc	BU
2001(u) Proof	450	Value: 50.00				

KM# 60 10 GULDEN

31.1035 g., 0.9250 Silver 0.9250 oz. ASW, 40 mm. **Ruler:** Beatrix **Subject:** Gold Trade Coins: Elisabeth I Sovereign **Obv:** Crowned shield divides value above date and ribbon **Rev:** Bust facing with two gold coins **Edge:** Plain

Date	Mintage	F	VF	XF	Unc	BU
2001(u) Proof	450	Value: 50.00				

KM# 61 10 GULDEN

31.1035 g., 0.9250 Silver 0.9250 oz. ASW, 40 mm. **Ruler:** Beatrix **Subject:** Gold Trade Coins: Carolus V Carolus Guilder **Obv:** Crowned shield divides value above date and ribbon **Rev:** Bust facing with two gold coins **Edge:** Plain

Date	Mintage	F	VF	XF	Unc	BU
2001(u) Proof	440	Value: 50.00				

KM# 62 10 GULDEN

31.1035 g., 0.9250 Silver 0.9250 oz. ASW, 40 mm. **Ruler:** Beatrix **Subject:** Gold Trade Coins: Philips II Real **Obv:** Crowned shield divides value above date and ribbon **Rev:** Bust facing with two gold coins **Edge:** Plain

Date	Mintage	F	VF	XF	Unc	BU
2001(u) Proof	440	Value: 50.00				

KM# 63 10 GULDEN

31.1035 g., 0.9250 Silver 0.9250 oz. ASW, 40 mm. **Ruler:** Beatrix **Subject:** Gold Trade Coins: Maurits Ducat **Obv:** Crowned shield divides value above date and ribbon **Rev:** Bust facing with two gold coins **Edge:** Plain

Date	Mintage	F	VF	XF	Unc	BU
2001(u) Proof	443	Value: 50.00				

KM# 64 10 GULDEN

31.1035 g., 0.9250 Silver 0.9250 oz. ASW, 40 mm. **Ruler:** Beatrix **Subject:** Gold Trade Coins: Isabella and Albrecht Double Albertin **Obv:** Crowned shield divides value above date and ribbon **Rev:** Conjoined busts facing with two gold coins **Edge:** Plain

Date	Mintage	F	VF	XF	Unc	BU
2001(u) Proof	490	Value: 50.00				

KM# 65 10 GULDEN

31.1035 g., 0.9250 Silver 0.9250 oz. ASW, 40 mm. **Ruler:** Beatrix **Subject:** Gold Trade Coins: William III Golden Rider **Obv:** Crowned shield divides value above date and ribbon **Rev:** Bust facing with two gold coins **Edge:** Plain

Date	Mintage	F	VF	XF	Unc	BU
2001(u) Proof	440	Value: 50.00				

KM# 66 10 GULDEN

31.1035 g., 0.9250 Silver 0.9250 oz. ASW, 40 mm. **Ruler:** Beatrix **Subject:** Gold Trade Coins: Louis XIII Louis d'or **Obv:** Crowned shield divides value above date and ribbon **Rev:** Bust facing with two gold coins **Edge:** Plain

Date	Mintage	F	VF	XF	Unc	BU
2001(u) Proof	440	Value: 50.00				

KM# 67 10 GULDEN

31.1035 g., 0.9250 Silver 0.9250 oz. ASW, 40 mm. **Ruler:** Beatrix **Subject:** Gold Trade Coins: Catharina the Great Rubel **Obv:** Crowned shield divides value above date and ribbon **Rev:** Crowned laureate bust facing with two gold coins **Edge:** Plain

Date	Mintage	F	VF	XF	Unc	BU
2001(u) Proof	560	Value: 50.00				

KM# 68 10 GULDEN

31.1035 g., 0.9250 Silver 0.9250 oz. ASW, 40 mm. **Ruler:** Beatrix **Subject:** Gold Trade Coins: Maria Theresia Double Sovereign **Obv:** Crowned shield divides value above date and ribbon **Rev:** Bust facing with two gold coins **Edge:** Plain

Date	Mintage	F	VF	XF	Unc	BU
2001(u) Proof	440	Value: 50.00				

KM# 69 10 GULDEN

31.1035 g., 0.9250 Silver 0.9250 oz. ASW, 40 mm. **Ruler:** Beatrix **Subject:** Gold Trade Coins: Napolean Bonaparte 20 Franc **Obv:** Crowned shield divides value above date and ribbon **Rev:** Bust facing with two gold coins **Edge:** Plain

Date	Mintage	F	VF	XF	Unc	BU
2001(u) Proof	555	Value: 50.00				

KM# 70 10 GULDEN

31.1035 g., 0.9250 Silver 0.9250 oz. ASW, 40 mm. **Ruler:** Beatrix **Series:** Gold Trade Coins: Wilhelmina Golden 10 Guilder **Obv:** Crowned shield divides value above date and ribbon **Rev:** Bust facing with two gold coins **Edge:** Plain

Date	Mintage	F	VF	XF	Unc	BU
2001(u) Proof	440	Value: 50.00				

KM# 71 10 GULDEN

31.1035 g., 0.9250 Silver 0.9250 oz. ASW, 40 mm. **Ruler:** Beatrix **Subject:** Gold Trade Coins: George III Sovereign **Obv:** Crowned shield divides value above date and ribbon **Rev:** Bust facing with two gold coins **Edge:** Plain

Date	Mintage	F	VF	XF	Unc	BU
2001(u) Proof	440	Value: 50.00				

KM# 72 10 GULDEN

31.1035 g., 0.9250 Silver 0.9250 oz. ASW, 40 mm. **Ruler:** Beatrix **Subject:** Gold Trade Coins: Albert I Belgium 20 Franc **Obv:** Crowned shield divides value above date and ribbon **Rev:** Bust facing with two gold coins **Edge:** Plain

Date	Mintage	F	VF	XF	Unc	BU
2001(u) Proof	490	Value: 50.00				

KM# 75 10 GULDEN

6.7200 g., 0.9000 Gold 0.1944 oz. AGW **Ruler:** Beatrix **Subject:** 50th Anniversary - End to Dutch Colonial Rule **Obv:** Head left **Rev:** Triangular signatures around value **Edge:** Reeded **Designer:** Ans Mezas-Hummelink

Date	Mintage	F	VF	XF	Unc	BU
2004 Proof	1,000	Value: 200				

KM# 77 10 GULDEN

6.7200 g., 0.9000 Gold 0.1944 oz. AGW, 22.5 mm. **Ruler:** Beatrix **Subject:** Queen's Silver Jubilee **Obv:** Head left **Rev:** Child art and value **Edge:** Reeded

Date	Mintage	F	VF	XF	Unc	BU
2005(u) Proof	1,500	Value: 195				

KM# 78 10 GULDEN

1.2442 g., 0.9990 Gold 0.0400 oz. AGW, 13.92 mm. **Ruler:** Beatrix **Subject:** Year of the dolphin **Obv:** Head left **Obv. Legend:** BEATRIX KONINGIN DER NEDERLANDEN **Rev:** Stylized outlines of birds above dolphins at sunset **Rev. Legend:** NEDERLANDSE ANTILLEN - JAAR VAN DE DOLFIJN **Edge:** Reeded

Date	Mintage	F	VF	XF	Unc	BU
2007(u) Proof	5,000	Value: 65.00				

MINT SETS

KM#	Date	Mintage	Identification	Issue Price	Mkt Val
MS22	2001 (8)	6,500	KM#32-38, 43	15.00	18.50
MS23	2002 (8)	6,000	KM#32-38, 43	15.00	27.50
MS24	2003 (8)	4,000	KM#32-38, 43	15.00	20.00
MS25	2004 (8)	2,100	KM32-38, 43	15.00	20.00
MS26	2005 (8)	3,500	KM32-38, 43	17.00	17.50
MS27	2006 (8)	2,000	KM#32-38, 43	20.00	20.00
MS28	2007 (8)	2,000	KM#32-38, 43	20.00	20.00

NEW CALEDONIA

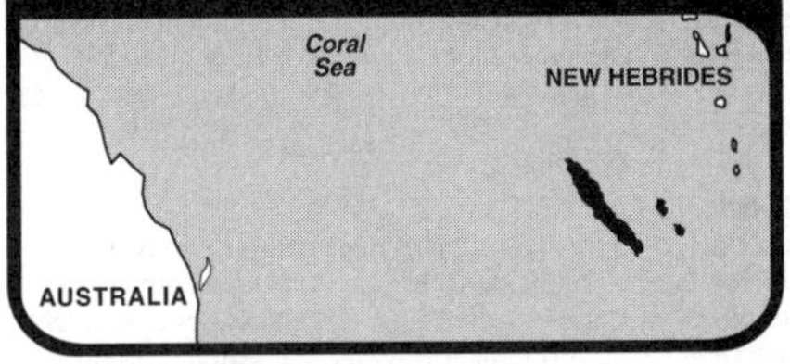

The French Associated State of New Caledonia is a group of about 25 islands in the South Pacific. They are situated about 750 miles (1,207 km.) east of Australia. The territory, which includes the dependencies of Isle des Pins, Loyalty Islands, Isle Huon, Isles Belep, Isles Chesterfield, Isle Walpole, Wallis and Futuna Islands and has a total land area of 7,358 sq. mi.(19,060 sq. km.) and a population of *156,000. Capital: Noumea. The islands are rich in minerals; New Caledonia has some of the world's largest known deposit of nickel. Nickel, nickel castings, coffee and copra are exported.

MINT MARK

Paris, privy marks only

MONETARY SYSTEM

100 Centimes = 1 Franc

FRENCH OVERSEAS TERRITORY

1958-1998

DECIMAL COINAGE

KM# 10 FRANC

1.3000 g., Aluminum, 23 mm. **Obv:** Seated figure holding torch, legend added **Obv. Legend:** I. E. O. M. **Rev:** Kagu bird within sprigs below value **Designer:** G.B.L. Bazor

Date	Mintage	F	VF	XF	Unc	BU
2001(a)	100,000	—	—	0.15	0.50	1.25
2002(a)	1,200,000	—	—	0.15	0.50	1.25
2003(a)	2,000,000	—	—	0.15	0.50	1.25
2004(a)	1,200,000	—	—	0.15	0.50	1.25
2005(a)	700,000	—	—	0.15	0.50	1.25

KM# 14 2 FRANCS

2.2000 g., Aluminum, 27 mm. **Obv:** Seated figure holding torch, legend added **Obv. Legend:** I. E. O. M. **Rev:** Kagu bird and value within sprigs

Date	Mintage	F	VF	XF	Unc	BU
2001(a)	800,000	—	—	0.25	0.75	1.50
2002(a)	1,200,000	—	—	0.25	0.75	1.50
2003(a)	2,400,000	—	—	0.20	0.65	1.50
2004(a)	200,000	—	—	0.20	0.65	1.50
2005(a)	530,000	—	—	0.20	0.65	1.50

KM# 16 5 FRANCS

3.7500 g., Aluminum, 31 mm. **Obv:** Seated figure holding torch, legend added **Obv. Legend:** I. E. O. M. **Rev:** Kagu bird and value within sprigs **Designer:** G.B.L. Bazor

Date	Mintage	F	VF	XF	Unc	BU
2001(a)	600,000	—	—	0.50	1.00	2.00
2002(a)	480,000	—	—	0.50	1.00	2.00
2003(a)	700,000	—	—	0.40	1.00	2.00
2004(a)	1,000,000	—	—	0.40	1.00	2.00
2005(a)	360,000	—	—	0.40	1.00	2.00

KM# 11 10 FRANCS

6.0000 g., Nickel, 24 mm. **Obv:** Liberty head left **Obv. Legend:** I. E. O. M. **Rev:** Sailboat above value **Designer:** R. Joly

Date	Mintage	F	VF	XF	Unc	BU
2001(a)	100,000	—	—	0.65	1.25	2.75
2002(a)	200,000	—	—	0.65	1.25	2.75
2003(a)	800,000	—	—	0.65	1.25	2.75
2004(a)	600,000	—	—	0.65	1.25	2.75
2005(a)	64,000	—	—	0.65	1.25	2.75

KM# 12 20 FRANCS

10.0000 g., Nickel, 28.5 mm. **Obv:** Liberty head left **Obv. Legend:** I. O. E. M. **Rev:** Three ox heads above value **Designer:** R. Joly

Date	Mintage	F	VF	XF	Unc	BU
2001(a)	150,000	—	—	1.00	1.75	3.25
2002(a)	250,000	—	—	1.00	1.75	3.25
2003(a)	250,000	—	—	1.00	1.75	3.25
2004(a)	500,000	—	—	1.00	1.75	3.25
2005(a)	300,000	—	—	1.00	1.75	3.25

KM# 13 50 FRANCS

15.0000 g., Nickel, 33 mm. **Obv:** Liberty head left **Obv. Legend:** I. E. O. M. **Rev:** Hut above value in center of palm and pine trees **Designer:** R. Joly

Date	Mintage	F	VF	XF	Unc	BU
2001(a)	100,000	—	—	1.25	2.00	4.00
2002(a)	—	—	—	1.25	2.00	4.00
2003(a)	75,000	—	—	1.25	2.00	4.00
2004(a)	150,000	—	—	1.25	2.00	4.00
2005(a)	54,000	—	—	1.25	2.00	4.00

KM# 15 100 FRANCS

10.0000 g., Nickel-Bronze, 30 mm. **Obv:** Liberty head left **Rev:** Hut above value in center of palm and pine trees **Designer:** R. Joly

Date	Mintage	F	VF	XF	Unc	BU
2001(a)	100,000	—	—	1.50	3.00	5.00
2002(a)	620,000	—	—	1.50	3.00	6.00
2003(a)	500,000	—	—	1.50	3.00	5.00
2004(a)	500,000	—	—	1.50	3.00	5.00
2005(a)	180,000	—	—	1.50	3.00	5.00

MINT SETS

KM#	Date	Mintage	Identification	Issue Price	Mkt Val
MS1	2001 (7)	3,000	KM#10-16	—	30.00
MS2	2002 (7)	5,000	KM#10-16	—	25.00
MS3	2004 (7)	3,000	KM#10-16	—	30.00

NEW ZEALAND

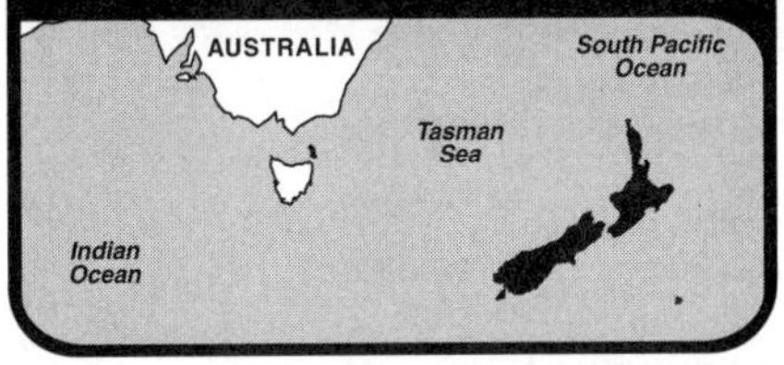

New Zealand, a parliamentary state located in the Southwest Pacific 1,250 miles (2,011 km.) east of Australia, has an area of 103,883 sq. mi. (268,680 sq. km.) and a population of *3.4 million. Capital: Wellington. Wool, meat, dairy products and some manufactured items are exported.

Decimal Currency was introduced in 1967 with special sets commemorating the last issues of pound sterling (1965) and the first of the decimal issues. Since then dollars and sets of coins have been issued nearly every year.

New Zealand is a founding member of the Commonwealth of Nations. Elizabeth II is the Head of State as the Queen of New Zealand; the Prime Minister is the Head of Government.

RULER

British

STATE

1907 - present

DECIMAL COINAGE

100 Cents = 1 Dollar

(c) Royal Australian Mint, Canberra

(l) Royal Mint, Llantrisant

(o) Royal Canadian Mint, Ottawa

(m) B.H. Mayer, Germany

(n) Norwegian Mint, Kongsberg

(p) South African Mint, Pretoria

(v) Valcambi SA, Switzerland

(w) Perth Mint, Western Australia

KM# 116 5 CENTS

2.8300 g., Copper-Nickel, 19.43 mm. **Ruler:** Elizabeth II **Obv:** Head with tiara right **Obv. Designer:** Ian Rank-Broadley **Rev:** Value below tuatara **Rev. Designer:** James Berry **Edge:** Reeded **Note:** Many recalled and melted in 2006.

Date	Mintage	F	VF	XF	Unc	BU
2001(l)	20,000,000	—	—	0.10	0.50	1.00
2001(c)	Est. 52,910,000	—	—	—	4.00	5.00
Note: In sets only						
2001(c) Proof	Est. 1,364	Value: 3.00				
2002(l)	40,500,000	—	—	0.10	0.50	1.00
2002(c)	3,000	—	—	—	5.00	6.00
Note: In sets only						
2002(c) Proof	1,500	Value: 3.00				
2003(l)	30,000,000	—	—	—	0.50	1.00
2003(c)	1,496	—	—	—	5.00	6.00
Note: In sets only						
2003 Proof	3,000	Value: 3.00				
2004(l)	15,000,000	—	—	—	25.00	50.00
Note: All but 48,000 melted						
2004(c)	2,800	—	—	—	20.00	30.00
Note: In sets only						
2004(c) Proof	1,750	Value: 3.00				
2005(c)	3,000	—	—	—	8.00	12.00
Note: In sets only						
2005(c) Proof	2,250	Value: 3.00				

KM# 117 10 CENTS

5.6600 g., Copper-Nickel, 23.62 mm. **Ruler:** Elizabeth II **Obv:** Head with tiara right **Obv. Designer:** Ian Rank-Broadley **Rev:** Value above koruru **Rev. Designer:** James Berry **Note:** Many recalled and melted in 2006.

Date	Mintage	F	VF	XF	Unc	BU
2001(l)	10,000,000	—	—	0.10	0.30	0.50
2001(c)	2,910	—	—	—	6.00	8.00

Date	Mintage	F	VF	XF	Unc	BU
Note: In sets only						
2001(c) Proof	1,364	Value: 4.00				
2002(l)	10,000,000	—	—	0.10	0.30	0.50
2002(c)	3,000	—	—	—	3.00	5.00
Note: In sets only						
2002(c) Proof	1,500	Value: 4.00				
2003(l)	13,000,000	—	—	0.10	0.30	0.50
2003(c)	3,000	—	—	—	5.00	8.00
Note: In sets only						
2003(l) Proof	1,496	Value: 4.00				
2004(l)	6,500,000	—	—	—	0.30	0.50
2004(c)	—	—	—	—	5.00	8.00
Note: In sets only						
2004(c) Proof	1,750	Value: 4.00				
2005	2,000,000	—	—	—	30.00	40.00
Note: All but 28,000 melted						
2005(c)	3,000	—	—	—	20.00	30.00
Note: In sets only						
2005(c) Proof	2,250	Value: 4.00				
2006(c)	3,000	—	—	—	10.00	15.00
Note: In sets only						
2006(c) Proof	2,100	Value: 4.00				

KM# 117a 10 CENTS

Copper Plated Steel, 20.5 mm. **Ruler:** Elizabeth II **Obv:** Head with tiara right **Obv. Designer:** Ian Rank-Broadley **Rev:** Value above koruru

Date	Mintage	F	VF	XF	Unc	BU
2006(o)	140,200,000	—	—	—	0.20	0.40
2007(c)	5,000	—	—	—	3.00	5.00
Note: In sets only						
2007(c) Proof	4,000	Value: 4.00				

KM# 118 20 CENTS

11.3100 g., Copper-Nickel, 28.58 mm. **Ruler:** Elizabeth II **Obv:** Head with tiara right **Obv. Designer:** Ian Rank-Broadley **Rev:** Value below Hei Tiki **Note:** Many recalled and melted in 2006.

Date	Mintage	F	VF	XF	Unc	BU
2001(c)	2,910	—	—	—	—	4.00
Note: In sets only						
2001(c) Proof	1,364	Value: 10.00				
2002(l)	7,000,000	—	—	—	0.50	—
2002(c)	3,000	—	—	—	—	5.00
Note: In sets only						
2002(c) Proof	1,500	Value: 10.00				
2003(c)	3,000	—	—	—	—	4.00
Note: In sets only						
2003(c) Proof	3,000	Value: 10.00				
2004(l)	8,500,000	—	—	—	0.50	—
2004(c)	2,800	—	—	—	—	5.00
Note: In sets only						
2004(c) Proof	1,750	Value: 10.00				
2005(l)	4,000,000	—	—	—	—	15.00
Note: All but 178,000 melted						
2005(c)	3,000	—	—	—	—	5.00
Note: In sets only						
2005(c) Proof	2,250	Value: 10.00				
2006(c)	3,000	—	—	—	—	5.00
Note: In sets only						
2006(c) Proof	2,100	Value: 10.00				

KM# 118a 20 CENTS

4.0000 g., Nickel Plated Steel, 21.75 mm. **Ruler:** Elizabeth II **Obv:** Head with tiara right **Obv. Designer:** Ian Rank-Broadley **Rev:** Value below Hei Tiki

Date	Mintage	F	VF	XF	Unc	BU
2006(o)	116,600,000	—	—	—	0.40	0.65
2007(c)	5,000	—	—	—	5.00	7.00
Note: In sets only						
2007(c) Proof	4,000	Value: 8.00				

KM# 119 50 CENTS

13.6100 g., Copper-Nickel, 31.75 mm. **Ruler:** Elizabeth II **Obv:** Head with tiara right **Obv. Designer:** Ian Rank-Broadley **Rev:** Ship, H.M.S. Endeavour **Rev. Designer:** James Berry **Note:** Many recalled and melted in 2006.

Date	Mintage	F	VF	XF	Unc	BU
2001(l)	5,000,000	—	—	—	1.00	—
2001(c)	2,910	—	—	—	—	4.00
Note: In sets only						
2001(c) Proof	1,364	Value: 5.00				
2002(l)	3,000,000	—	—	0.50	1.00	—
2002(c)	3,000	—	—	—	—	4.00
Note: In sets only						
2002(c) Proof	1,500	Value: 5.00				
2003(l)	2,500,000	—	—	0.50	1.00	—
2003(c)	3,000	—	—	—	—	4.00
Note: In sets only						
2003(c) Proof	1,496	Value: 5.00				
2004(l)	2,000,000	—	—	—	1.00	—
2004(c)	2,800	—	—	—	—	4.00
Note: In sets only						
2004(c) Proof	1,750	Value: 5.00				
2005(l)	1,000,000	—	—	—	7.50	—
Note: All but 503,800 melted						
2005(c)	3,000	—	—	—	—	4.00
Note: In sets only						
2005(c) Proof	2,250	Value: 5.00				
2006(c)	3,000	—	—	—	—	4.00
Note: In sets only.						
2006(c) Proof	2,100	Value: 5.00				

KM# 135 50 CENTS

13.6100 g., Copper-Nickel, 31.75 mm. **Ruler:** Elizabeth II **Subject:** Lord of the Rings **Obv:** Head with tiara right **Obv. Designer:** Ian Rank-Broadley **Rev:** Frodo's head facing to left of vine and value **Rev. Designer:** Matthew Bonaccorsi **Edge:** Reeded

Date	Mintage	F	VF	XF	Unc	BU
2003	—	—	—	—	4.00	—
Note: In sets only						

KM# 136 50 CENTS

13.6100 g., Copper-Nickel, 31.75 mm. **Ruler:** Elizabeth II **Subject:** Lord of the Rings **Obv:** Head with tiara right **Obv. Designer:** Ian Rank-Broadley **Rev:** Head of Gandolf with hat facing and value **Rev. Designer:** Matthew Bonaccorsi **Edge:** Reeded

Date	Mintage	F	VF	XF	Unc	BU
2003	—	—	—	—	4.00	—
Note: In sets only						

KM# 137 50 CENTS

13.6100 g., Copper-Nickel, 31.75 mm. **Ruler:** Elizabeth II **Subject:** Lord of the Rings **Obv:** Head with tiara right **Obv. Designer:** Ian Rank-Broadley **Rev:** Head of Aragorn facing and value **Rev. Designer:** Matthew Bonaccorsi **Edge:** Reeded

Date	Mintage	F	VF	XF	Unc	BU
2003	—	—	—	—	4.00	—
Note: In sets only						

KM# 138 50 CENTS

13.6100 g., Copper-Nickel, 31.75 mm. **Ruler:** Elizabeth II **Subject:** Lord of the Rings **Obv:** Head with tiara right **Obv. Designer:** Ian Rank-Broadley **Rev:** Head of Gollom facing and value **Rev. Designer:** Matthew Bonaccorsi **Edge:** Reeded

Date	Mintage	F	VF	XF	Unc	BU
2003	—	—	—	—	4.00	—
Note: In sets only						

KM# 139 50 CENTS

13.6100 g., Copper-Nickel, 31.75 mm. **Ruler:** Elizabeth II **Subject:** Lord of the Rings **Obv:** Head with tiara right **Obv. Designer:** Ian Rank-Broadley **Rev:** View of Mordor, value **Rev. Designer:** Matthew Bonaccorsi **Edge:** Reeded

Date	Mintage	F	VF	XF	Unc	BU
2003	—	—	—	—	4.00	—
Note: In sets only						

KM# 140 50 CENTS

13.6100 g., Copper-Nickel, 31.75 mm. **Ruler:** Elizabeth II **Subject:** Lord of the Rings **Obv:** Head with tiara right **Obv. Designer:** Ian Rank-Broadley **Rev:** Head of Sauron 1/4 left and value **Rev. Designer:** Matthew Bonaccorsi **Edge:** Reeded

Date	Mintage	F	VF	XF	Unc	BU
2003	—	—	—	—	4.00	—
Note: In sets only						

KM# 119a 50 CENTS

5.0000 g., Nickel Plated Steel, 24.75 mm. **Ruler:** Elizabeth II **Obv:** Head with tiara right **Rev:** Ship, H.M.S. Endeavour **Rev. Designer:** James Berry

Date	Mintage	F	VF	XF	Unc	BU
2006(o)	70,200,000	—	—	—	0.75	1.00
2007(c)	5,000	Value: 8.00				
Note: In sets only						

KM# 120 DOLLAR

8.0000 g., Aluminum-Bronze **Ruler:** Elizabeth II **Obv:** Head with tiara right **Obv. Designer:** Ian Rank-Broadley **Rev:** Kiwi bird within sprigs **Rev. Designer:** R. Maurice Conly

Date	Mintage	F	VF	XF	Unc	BU
2001(c)	2,910	—	—	—	1.00	2.50
Note: In sets only						
2001(c) Proof	1,364	Value: 5.00				
2002(l)	8,000,000	—	—	—	1.00	2.50
2002(c)	4,000	—	—	—	—	4.00
Note: In sets only						
2002(c) Proof	1,500	Value: 5.00				
2003(l)	4,000,000	—	—	—	1.00	2.50
2003(c)	5,000	—	—	—	—	4.00
Note: In sets only						
2003(c) Proof	1,750	Value: 5.00				
2004(l)	2,700,000	—	—	—	1.00	2.50
2004(c)	3,500	—	—	—	—	4.00
Note: In sets only						
2004(c) Proof	2,250	Value: 5.00				
2005(l)	2,000,000	—	—	—	1.00	2.50
2005(c)	4,000	—	—	—	—	4.00

Date	Mintage	F	VF	XF	Unc	BU
Note: In sets only						
2005(c) Proof	2,250	Value: 5.00				
2006(c)	3,000	—	—	—	—	4.00
Note: In sets only.						
2006(c) Proof	2,100	Value: 5.00				
2007(c)	—	—	—	—	—	4.00
2007(c) Proof	—	Value: 5.00				

KM# 141 DOLLAR

28.2800 g., Nickel-Brass, 38.61 mm. **Ruler:** Elizabeth II **Subject:** Lord of the Rings **Obv:** Head with tiara right **Obv. Designer:** Ian Rank-Broadley **Rev:** Inscribed ring around value **Rev. Designer:** Matthew Bonaccorsi **Edge:** Reeded

Date	Mintage	F	VF	XF	Unc	BU
2003	—	—	—	—	15.00	—

KM# 141a DOLLAR

28.2800 g., 0.9250 Silver 0.8410 oz. ASW, 38.61 mm. **Ruler:** Elizabeth II **Obv:** Head with tiara right **Obv. Designer:** Ian Rank-Broadley **Rev:** Gold-plated ring and edge **Edge:** Reeded

Date	Mintage	F	VF	XF	Unc	BU
2003 Proof	150,000	Value: 30.00				

KM# 142 DOLLAR

28.2800 g., Nickel-Brass, 38.61 mm. **Ruler:** Elizabeth II **Subject:** Lord of the Rings **Obv:** Head with tiara right **Obv. Designer:** Ian Rank-Broadley **Rev:** Head of Frodo looking down above inscription **Rev. Designer:** Matthew Bonaccorsi **Edge:** Reeded

Date	Mintage	F	VF	XF	Unc	BU
2003	—	—	—	—	10.00	—
Note: In sets only						

KM# 143 DOLLAR

28.2800 g., Nickel-Brass, 38.61 mm. **Ruler:** Elizabeth II **Subject:** Lord of the Rings **Obv:** Head with tiara right **Obv. Designer:** Ian Rank-Broadley **Rev:** View of Mordor, value **Rev. Designer:** Matthew Bonaccorsi **Edge:** Reeded

Date	Mintage	F	VF	XF	Unc	BU
2003	—	—	—	—	10.00	—
Note: In sets only						

KM# 152 DOLLAR

31.1000 g., 0.9990 Silver 0.9988 oz. ASW, 40 mm. **Ruler:** Elizabeth II **Obv:** Crowned head right **Rev:** Spotted kiwi **Edge:** Reeded

Date	Mintage	F	VF	XF	Unc	BU
2004(c)	2,500	—	—	—	—	45.00
2004(c) Proof	1,500	Value: 50.00				

KM# 154 DOLLAR

1.0000 g., 0.9990 Silver 0.0321 oz. ASW, 40 mm. **Ruler:** Elizabeth II **Subject:** ANZAC **Obv:** Crowned head right **Rev:** Soldiers superimposed on a colored flag **Edge:** Reeded

Date	Mintage	F	VF	XF	Unc	BU
2005(w)	15,000	—	—	—	—	30.00

KM# 155 DOLLAR

20.0000 g., Aluminum-Bronze, 38.74 mm. **Ruler:** Elizabeth II **Subject:** ANZAC **Obv:** Crowned head right **Rev:** New Zealand soldier playing bugle in front of War Memorial **Edge:** Reeded

Date	Mintage	F	VF	XF	Unc	BU
2005	15,000	—	—	—	—	25.00

KM# 153 DOLLAR

Silver, 40 mm. **Ruler:** Elizabeth II **Obv:** Crowned head right **Rev:** Kiwi **Edge:** Reeded

Date	Mintage	F	VF	XF	Unc	BU
2005	4,000	—	—	—	—	60.00
2005 Proof	2,200	Value: 70.00				

KM# 156 DOLLAR

28.2800 g., Aluminum-Bronze, 40 mm. **Ruler:** Elizabeth II **Subject:** Lions Rugby Tour **Obv:** Crowned head right

Date	Mintage	F	VF	XF	Unc	BU
2005(l)	15,000	—	—	—	—	25.00

KM# 163 DOLLAR

31.1350 g., 0.9990 Silver Gilt 100000 oz. ASW, 40.6 mm. **Ruler:** Elizabeth II **Subject:** King Kong **Obv:** Crowned head right **Edge:** Reeded

Date	Mintage	F	VF	XF	Unc	BU
2005(w) Proof	3,000	Value: 60.00				

KM# 159 DOLLAR

20.0000 g., Aluminum-Bronze, 38.74 mm. **Ruler:** Elizabeth II **Subject:** King Kong **Obv:** Crowned head right **Edge:** Reeded

Date	Mintage	F	VF	XF	Unc	BU
2005(w)	7,000	—	—	—	—	25.00

KM# 160 DOLLAR

20.0000 g., Aluminum-Bronze, 38.74 mm. **Ruler:** Elizabeth II **Subject:** King Kong **Obv:** Crowned head right **Rev:** Multicolored King Kong **Edge:** Reeded

Date	Mintage	F	VF	XF	Unc	BU
2005(w)	4,000	—	—	—	—	30.00

KM# 161 DOLLAR

20.0000 g., Aluminum-Bronze, 38.74 mm. **Ruler:** Elizabeth II **Subject:** King Kong **Obv:** Crowned head right **Rev:** Carl Denham and camera on reverse in multicolor **Edge:** Reeded

Date	Mintage	F	VF	XF	Unc	BU
2005	4,000	—	—	—	—	30.00

KM# 162 DOLLAR

20.0000 g., Aluminum-Bronze, 38.74 mm. **Ruler:** Elizabeth II **Subject:** King Kong **Obv:** Crowned head right **Rev:** Ann Darrow and Jack Driscoll multicolored **Edge:** Reeded

Date	Mintage	F	VF	XF	Unc	BU
2005	4,000	—	—	—	—	30.00

KM# 164 DOLLAR

Silver **Ruler:** Elizabeth II **Subject:** King Kong **Obv:** Crowned head right **Note:** Gold plated King Kong.

Date	Mintage	F	VF	XF	Unc	BU
2005 Proof	—	Value: 60.00				

KM# 156a DOLLAR

28.2800 g., 0.9990 Silver 0.9083 oz. ASW, 38.61 mm. **Ruler:** Elizabeth II **Subject:** Lions Rugby Tour **Obv:** Crowned head right **Edge:** Reeded

Date	Mintage	F	VF	XF	Unc	BU
2005(l) Proof	5,000	Value: 60.00				

KM# 158 DOLLAR

28.2800 g., 0.9990 Silver 0.9083 oz. ASW, 38.61 mm. **Ruler:** Elizabeth II **Subject:** FIFA **Obv:** Crowned head right **Rev. Designer:** Michael McHalick

Date	Mintage	F	VF	XF	Unc	BU
2006	7,500	—	—	—	—	50.00

KM# 232 DOLLAR

31.1000 g., 0.9990 Silver 0.9988 oz. ASW, 40.00 mm. **Ruler:** Elizabeth II **Subject:** Aoraki - Mount Cook in Japan **Obv:** Head with tiara right **Obv. Legend:** NEW ZEALAND - ELIZABETH II **Rev:** Flowers in bloom, Mount Cook in background multicolor **Note:** Also released in a Japanese proof set.

Date	Mintage	F	VF	XF	Unc	BU
2007 Proof	—	Value: 60.00				

KM# 121 2 DOLLARS

10.0000 g., Aluminum-Bronze, 26.5 mm. **Ruler:** Elizabeth II **Obv:** Head with tiara right **Obv. Designer:** Ian Rank-Broadley **Rev:** Heron above value **Rev. Designer:** R. Maurice Conley

Date	Mintage	F	VF	XF	Unc	BU
2001(l)	3,000,000	—	—	—	2.50	5.00
2001(c)	2,910	—	—	—	—	6.00
Note: In sets only						
2001(c) Proof	2,000	Value: 7.50				
2002(l)	6,000,000	—	—	—	2.50	5.00
2002(c)	3,000	—	—	—	—	6.00
Note: In sets only						
2002(c) Proof	2,000	Value: 7.50				
2003(l)	6,000,000	—	—	—	2.50	5.00
2003(c)	3,000	—	—	—	—	6.00
Note: In sets only						
2003(c) Proof	3,000	Value: 7.50				
2004(c)	2,800	—	—	—	2.50	5.00
Note: In sets only						
2004 Proof	3,500	Value: 7.50				
2005(l)	5,000,000	—	—	—	2.50	5.00
2005(c)	3,000	—	—	—	—	6.00
Note: In sets only						
2005(c) Proof	3,000	Value: 7.50				
2006(c)	3,000	—	—	—	—	6.00
Note: In sets only.						
2006(c) Proof	2,100	Value: 7.50				
2007(c)	—	—	—	—	—	6.00
2007(c) Proof	4,000	Value: 7.50				

KM# 128 5 DOLLARS

28.2800 g., Copper-Nickel, 38.6 mm. **Ruler:** Elizabeth II **Subject:** Kereru Bird **Obv:** Head with tiara right **Obv. Designer:** Ian Rank-Broadley **Rev:** Pigeon on branch **Edge:** Reeded

Date	Mintage	F	VF	XF	Unc	BU
2001(l)	1,500	—	—	—	25.00	—
2001 Proof	—	Value: 40.00				

KM# 128a 5 DOLLARS

28.2800 g., 0.9990 Silver 0.9083 oz. ASW **Ruler:** Elizabeth II **Obv:** Head with tiara right **Obv. Designer:** Ian Rank-Broadley **Rev:** Pigeon on branch

Date	Mintage	F	VF	XF	Unc	BU
2001 Proof	1,000	Value: 80.00				

KM# 149 5 DOLLARS

28.2800 g., Copper-Nickel, 38.6 mm. **Ruler:** Elizabeth II **Subject:** Royal Visit (canceled after coin issue) **Obv:** Crowned head right **Obv. Designer:** Ian Rank-Broadley **Rev:** Queen with flowers and two girls **Edge:** Reeded

Date	Mintage	F	VF	XF	Unc	BU
2001	—	—	—	—	—	20.00

KM# 149a 5 DOLLARS

28.2800 g., 0.9250 Silver 0.8410 oz. ASW, 38.6 mm. **Ruler:** Elizabeth II **Subject:** Royal Visit (canceled after coin issue) **Obv:** Head with tiara right **Obv. Designer:** Ian Rank-Broadley **Rev:** Queen with flowers and two girls **Edge:** Reeded

Date	Mintage	F	VF	XF	Unc	BU
2001 Proof	2,000	Value: 100				
Note: 200 issued in stamp cover						

KM# 145a 5 DOLLARS

27.2220 g., 0.9990 Silver 0.8743 oz. ASW **Ruler:** Elizabeth II **Obv:** Head with tiara right **Obv. Designer:** Ian Rank-Broadley **Rev:** Two Hector's Dolphins jumping out of the water **Edge:** Reeded

Date	Mintage	F	VF	XF	Unc	BU
2002(c)	Est. 2,000	—	—	—	—	100
Note: 500 in stamp covers						

KM# 151 5 DOLLARS

28.2800 g., 0.9250 Silver 0.8410 oz. ASW, 38.61 mm. **Ruler:** Elizabeth II **Subject:** Queen's Jubilee **Obv:** Crowned head right **Rev. Designer:** Robert Lowe **Note:** Queens bust is gold plated.

Date	Mintage	F	VF	XF	Unc	BU
2002(l)	25,000	—	—	—	—	50.00
Note: 100 in stamp covers						

KM# 131 5 DOLLARS

28.2800 g., Copper-Nickel, 38.6 mm. **Ruler:** Elizabeth II **Subject:** Architectural Heritage **Obv:** Head with tiara right **Obv. Designer:** Ian Rank-Broadley **Rev:** Auckland Sky Tower **Edge:** Reeded

Date	Mintage	F	VF	XF	Unc	BU
2002(l)	3,000	—	—	—	12.50	—
Note: 500 of which are issued in Numismatic-Philatelic covers.						

KM# 131a 5 DOLLARS

28.2800 g., 0.9250 Silver 0.8410 oz. ASW, 38.6 mm. **Ruler:** Elizabeth II **Subject:** Architectural Heritage **Obv:** Head with tiara right **Obv. Designer:** Ian Rank-Broadley **Rev:** Auckland Sky Tower **Edge:** Reeded

Date	Mintage	F	VF	XF	Unc	BU
2002(l)	2,000	Value: 37.50				
Note: 500 of which are issued in Numismatic-Philatelic covers						

KM# 145 5 DOLLARS
27.2200 g., Copper-Nickel, 38.74 mm. **Ruler:** Elizabeth II **Obv:** Head with tiara right **Obv. Designer:** Ian Rank-Broadley **Rev:** Dolphins jumping out of the water **Rev. Designer:** Michael McHalick **Edge:** Reeded

Date	Mintage	F	VF	XF	Unc	BU
2002(c)	4,000	—	—	—	30.00	—

Note: 500 in stamp covers

KM# 147 5 DOLLARS
28.2300 g., 0.9250 Silver 0.8395 oz. ASW, 38.6 mm. **Ruler:** Elizabeth II **Subject:** 50th Anniversary of Coronation **Obv:** Gold plated crowned head right **Obv. Designer:** Ian Rank-Broadley **Rev:** Crown above fern and flowers **Edge:** Reeded

Date	Mintage	F	VF	XF	Unc	BU
2003 Proof	25,000	Value: 80.00				

Note: 100 in stamp covers

KM# 132 5 DOLLARS
26.7000 g., Copper-Nickel, 38.6 mm. **Ruler:** Elizabeth II **Obv:** Head with tiara right **Rev:** Giant Kokopu fish divides circle **Edge:** Reeded **Designer:** Michael McHalick

Date	Mintage	F	VF	XF	Unc	BU
2003(c)	2,400	—	—	—	12.00	27.50

Note: 400 in stamp covers

KM# 132a 5 DOLLARS
28.2800 g., 0.9990 Silver Gold plated 0.9083 oz. ASW, 38.6 mm. **Ruler:** Elizabeth II **Obv:** Head with tiara right **Obv. Designer:** Ian Rank-Broadley **Rev:** Giant Kokopu fish **Edge:** Reeded

Date	Mintage	F	VF	XF	Unc	BU
2003(c)	1,700	—	—	—	—	75.00

Note: 200 in stamp covers

KM# 133 5 DOLLARS
26.7200 g., Copper-Nickel, 38.6 mm. **Ruler:** Elizabeth II **Subject:** Chatham Island Taiko **Obv:** Head with tiara right **Obv. Designer:** Ian Rank-Broadley **Rev:** Bird **Edge:** Reeded

Date	Mintage	F	VF	XF	Unc	BU
2004(2003)	1,350	—	—	—	27.50	—
2004(2003) Proof	1,300	Value: 50.00				

KM# 133a 5 DOLLARS
28.2800 g., 0.9990 Silver 0.9083 oz. ASW, 38.74 mm. **Ruler:** Elizabeth II **Obv:** Head with tiara right **Obv. Designer:** Ian Rank-Broadley **Rev:** Chatham Island Taiko

Date	Mintage	F	VF	XF	Unc	BU
2004 Proof	1,300	Value: 60.00				

KM# 146 5 DOLLARS
27.2200 g., Copper-Nickel, 38.74 mm. **Ruler:** Elizabeth II **Obv:** Head with tiara right **Obv. Designer:** Ian Rank-Broadley **Rev:** Fiordland Crested Penguin **Edge:** Reeded

Date	Mintage	F	VF	XF	Unc	BU
2005(2004)	4,000	—	—	—	25.00	30.00

KM# 146a 5 DOLLARS
27.2200 g., 0.9990 Silver 0.8742 oz. ASW, 38.74 mm. **Ruler:** Elizabeth II **Obv:** Head with tiara right **Obv. Designer:** Ian Rank-Broadley **Rev:** Fiordland Crested Penguin **Edge:** Reeded

Date	Mintage	F	VF	XF	Unc	BU
2005	3,500	—	—	—	—	50.00

KM# 148 5 DOLLARS
27.2200 g., Copper-Nickel, 38.74 mm. **Ruler:** Elizabeth II **Obv:** Head with tiara right **Obv. Designer:** Ian Rank-Broadley **Rev:** Falcon on tree stump **Edge:** Reeded

Date	Mintage	F	VF	XF	Unc	BU
2006	4,000	—	—	—	—	30.00

KM# 148a 5 DOLLARS
28.2800 g., 0.9990 Silver 0.9083 oz. ASW, 38.74 mm. **Ruler:** Elizabeth II **Obv:** Head with tiara right **Obv. Designer:** Ian Rank-Broadley **Rev:** New Zealand Falcon on tree stump **Edge:** Reeded

Date	Mintage	F	VF	XF	Unc	BU
2006 Proof	2,500	Value: 50.00				

KM# 150 5 DOLLARS
27.2200 g., Copper-Nickel, 38.7 mm. **Ruler:** Elizabeth II **Obv:** Head with tiara right **Obv. Designer:** Ian Rank-Broadley **Rev:** Tuatara (Sphenodon punctatus), a lizard-like reptile **Edge:** Reeded

Date	Mintage	F	VF	XF	Unc	BU
2007	3,000	—	—	—	—	30.00

KM# 233 5 DOLLARS
28.2800 g., Copper-Nickel **Ruler:** Elizabeth II **Subject:** Hamilton's frog **Obv:** Head with tiara right **Obv. Legend:** NEW ZEALAND - ELIZABETH II **Obv. Designer:** Ian Rank-Broadley **Rev:** Frog perched on branch at left center

Date	Mintage	F	VF	XF	Unc	BU
2008	4,000	—	—	—	—	30.00

KM# 129 10 DOLLARS
3.8879 g., 0.9990 Gold 0.1249 oz. AGW, 18 mm. **Ruler:** Elizabeth II **Obv:** Head with tiara right **Obv. Designer:** Ian Rank-Broadley **Rev:** Salvage ship above value **Edge:** Reeded

Date	Mintage	F	VF	XF	Unc	BU
2001 Proof	600	Value: 125				

KM# 130 10 DOLLARS
7.7759 g., 0.9990 Gold 0.2497 oz. AGW, 22 mm. **Ruler:** Elizabeth II **Obv:** Head with tiara right **Obv. Designer:** Ian Rank-Broadley **Rev:** Ship above value **Edge:** Reeded

Date	Mintage	F	VF	XF	Unc	BU
2001 Proof	600	Value: 245				

KM# 144 10 DOLLARS
39.9400 g., 0.9166 Gold 1.1770 oz. AGW, 38.61 mm. **Ruler:** Elizabeth II **Subject:** Lord of the Rings **Obv:** Head with tiara right **Obv. Designer:** Ian Rank-Broadley **Rev:** Inscribed ring around value **Rev. Designer:** Matthew Bonaccorsi **Edge:** Reeded

Date	Mintage	F	VF	XF	Unc	BU
2003 Proof	—	Value: 1,000				

KM# 157 10 DOLLARS
7.7700 g., 0.9990 Gold 0.2496 oz. AGW, 20.1 mm. **Ruler:** Elizabeth II **Subject:** ANZAC **Obv:** Crowned head right **Rev:** Soldiers from Chun uk Bair battle with rifles and bayonets **Edge:** Reeded

Date	Mintage	F	VF	XF	Unc	BU
2005 Proof	1,000	Value: 250				

KM# 165 10 DOLLARS
7.9880 g., 0.9170 Gold 0.2355 oz. AGW, 22.05 mm. **Ruler:** Elizabeth II **Subject:** Lions Rugby Tour **Obv:** Crowned head right **Edge:** Reeded

Date	Mintage	F	VF	XF	Unc	BU
2005 Proof	1,000	Value: 250				

MINT SETS

KM#	Date	Mintage	Identification	Issue Price	Mkt Val
MS50	2001 (7)	2,910	KM#116-121, 128	18.50	20.00
MS51	2002 (5)	3,000	KM#116-121, 128	18.00	20.00
MS52	2003 (4)	3,000	KM#116-121, 128	18.00	20.00
MS53	2003 (6)	—	KM#135, 136, 137, 138, 139, 140 Light vs Dark Set	19.95	25.00
MS54	2003 (3)	—	KM141, 142, 143 Battle for the Ring Set	29.95	35.00

PROOF SETS

KM#	Date	Mintage	Identification	Issue Price	Mkt Val
PS45	2001 (7)	1,366	KM#116-121, 128	49.25	60.00
PS46	2001 (2)	600	KM#129-130	400	450
PS47	2002 (5)	1,500	KM#116-121, 128	60.00	55.00
PS48	2003 (7)	1,496	KM#116-121, 132a	60.00	55.00
PS49	2004 (7)	1,750	KM#116-121, 133 Chatham Islands Taiko	—	85.00

NICARAGUA

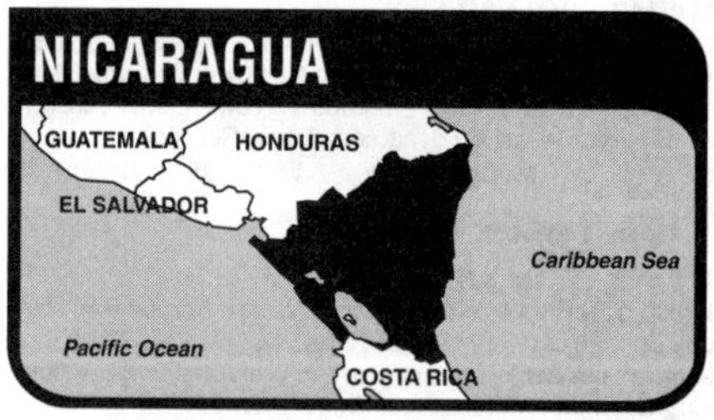

The Republic of Nicaragua, situated in Central America between Honduras and Costa Rica, has an area of 50,193 sq. mi. (129,494 sq. km.) and a population of *3.7 million. Capital: Managua. Agriculture, mining (gold and silver) and hardwood logging are the principal industries. Cotton, meat, coffee and sugar are exported.

MONETARY SYSTEM
100 Centavos = 1 Cordoba

REPUBLIC

DECIMAL COINAGE

KM# 97 5 CENTAVOS
3.0000 g., Copper Plated Steel, 18.5 mm. **Obv:** National arms **Rev:** Value within circle **Edge:** Plain

Date	Mintage	F	VF	XF	Unc	BU
2002	—	—	—	—	0.25	0.50

KM# 98 10 CENTAVOS
4.0000 g., Brass Plated Steel, 20.5 mm. **Obv:** National arms **Rev:** Value within circle **Edge:** Reeded and plain sections

Date	Mintage	F	VF	XF	Unc	BU
2002	—	—	—	—	0.45	0.85

KM# 99 25 CENTAVOS
5.0000 g., Brass Plated Steel, 23.25 mm. **Obv:** National arms **Rev:** Value within circle **Edge:** Reeded and plain sections

Date	Mintage	F	VF	XF	Unc	BU
2002	—	—	—	—	0.65	1.25

KM# 89 CORDOBA
6.2500 g., Nickel Clad Steel, 25 mm. **Obv:** National emblem **Rev:** Value above sprigs within circle

Date	Mintage	F	VF	XF	Unc	BU
2002	—	—	—	—	2.50	3.00

KM# 100 10 CORDOBAS
27.1200 g., 0.9250 Silver 0.8065 oz. ASW, 40 mm. **Subject:** Ibero-America **Obv:** National arms in circle of arms **Rev:** Sail boat **Edge:** Reeded

Date	Mintage	F	VF	XF	Unc	BU
2002 Proof	—	Value: 50.00				

NIGERIA

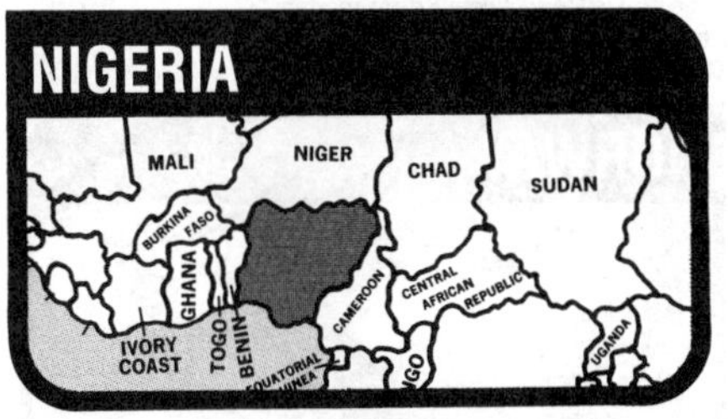

Nigeria, situated on the Atlantic coast of West Africa has an area of 356,669 sq. mi. (923,770 sq. km.). Nigeria is a member of the Commonwealth of Nations. The President is the Head of State and the Head of Government.

FEDERAL REPUBLIC

DECIMAL COINAGE

100 Kobo = 1 Naira

KM# 17 KOBO
4.6700 g., Brass, 23.2 mm. **Obv:** Arms with supporters **Rev:** Monkey musicians below value **Edge:** Reeded

Date	Mintage	F	VF	XF	Unc	BU
2003	—	—	—	—	1.50	2.00

KM# 13.3 50 KOBO
3.5000 g., Nickel Clad Steel, 19.44 mm. **Obv:** Arms with supporters **Obv. Legend:** FEDERAL REPUBLIC of NIGERIA **Rev:** Value at left, corn cob and stalk at right **Edge:** Plain **Note:** Reduced size.

Date	Mintage	F	VF	XF	Unc	BU
2006	—	—	—	—	1.00	1.35

KM# 18 NAIRA
5.4300 g., Bi-Metallic Brass center in Stainless Steel ring, 21.48 mm. **Obv:** National arms **Obv. Legend:** FEDERAL REPUBLIC OF NIGERIA **Rev:** Small bust of Herbert Macaulay above value **Edge:** Plain

Date	Mintage	F	VF	XF	Unc	BU
2006	—	—	—	—	—	4.00

KM# 19 2 NAIRA
7.4800 g., Bi-Metallic Stainless Steel center in Copper-Brass ring, 25.99 mm. **Obv:** National arms **Obv. Legend:** FEDERAL REPUBLIC OF NIGERIA **Rev:** Large value, National Assembly in background **Edge:** Coarse reeding

Date	Mintage	F	VF	XF	Unc	BU
2006	—	—	—	—	—	5.00

NIUE

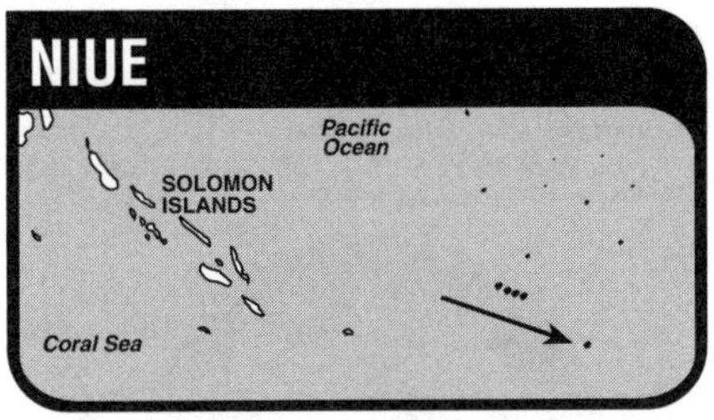

Niue, or Savage Island, a dependent state of New Zealand is located in the Pacific Ocean east of Tonga and southeast of Samoa. The size is 100 sq. mi. (260 sq. km.) with a population of *2,000. Chief village and port is Alofi. Bananas and copra are exported.

MINT MARK
PM - Pobjoy Mint

NEW ZEALAND DEPENDENT STATE

DECIMAL COINAGE

KM# 123 DOLLAR
28.2800 g., Copper-Nickel, 38.6 mm. **Ruler:** Elizabeth II **Subject:** Snoopy as an Ace **Obv:** Crowned head right **Rev:** Snoopy flying his dog house **Edge:** Reeded

Date	Mintage	F	VF	XF	Unc	BU
2001	100,000	—	—	—	3.00	4.50

KM# 128 DOLLAR
28.2800 g., Copper-Nickel, 38.6 mm. **Ruler:** Elizabeth II **Series:** Pokemon **Obv:** Crowned shield within sprigs **Rev:** "Bulbasaur" **Edge:** Reeded

Date	Mintage	F	VF	XF	Unc	BU
2001	100,000	—	—	—	12.00	14.00

KM# 129 DOLLAR
7.7700 g., 0.9990 Silver 0.2496 oz. ASW, 22 mm. **Ruler:** Elizabeth II **Series:** Pokemon **Obv:** Crowned shield within sprigs **Rev:** "Bulbasaur" **Edge:** Reeded

Date	Mintage	F	VF	XF	Unc	BU
2001 Proof	20,000	Value: 7.00				

KM# 131 DOLLAR
28.2800 g., Copper-Nickel, 38.6 mm. **Ruler:** Elizabeth II **Series:** Pokemon **Obv:** Crowned shield within sprigs **Rev:** "Charmander" **Edge:** Reeded

Date	Mintage	F	VF	XF	Unc	BU
2001	100,000	—	—	—	12.00	14.00

KM# 132 DOLLAR
7.7700 g., 0.9990 Silver 0.2496 oz. ASW, 22 mm. **Ruler:** Elizabeth II **Series:** Pokemon **Obv:** Crowned shield within sprigs **Rev:** "Charmander" **Edge:** Reeded

Date	Mintage	F	VF	XF	Unc	BU
2001 Proof	20,000	Value: 7.00				

KM# 134 DOLLAR
28.2800 g., Copper-Nickel, 38.6 mm. **Ruler:** Elizabeth II **Series:** Pokemon **Obv:** Crowned shield within sprigs **Rev:** "Meowth" **Edge:** Reeded

Date	Mintage	F	VF	XF	Unc	BU
2001	100,000	—	—	—	12.00	14.00

KM# 135 DOLLAR
7.7700 g., 0.9990 Silver 0.2496 oz. ASW, 22 mm. **Ruler:** Elizabeth II **Series:** Pokemon **Obv:** Crowned shield within sprigs **Rev:** "Meowth" **Edge:** Reeded

Date	Mintage	F	VF	XF	Unc	BU
2001 Proof	20,000	Value: 7.00				

KM# 137 DOLLAR
28.2800 g., Copper-Nickel, 38.6 mm. **Ruler:** Elizabeth II **Series:** Pokemon **Obv:** Crowned shield within sprigs **Rev:** "Pikachu" **Edge:** Reeded

Date	Mintage	F	VF	XF	Unc	BU
2001	100,000	—	—	—	12.00	14.00

KM# 138 DOLLAR
7.7700 g., 0.9990 Silver 0.2496 oz. ASW, 22 mm. **Ruler:** Elizabeth II **Series:** Pokemon **Obv:** Crowned shield within sprigs **Rev:** "Pikachu" **Edge:** Reeded

Date	Mintage	F	VF	XF	Unc	BU
2001 Proof	20,000	Value: 7.00				

KM# 140 DOLLAR
28.2800 g., Copper-Nickel, 38.6 mm. **Ruler:** Elizabeth II **Series:** Pokemon **Obv:** Crowned shield within sprigs **Rev:** "Squirtle" **Edge:** Reeded

Date	Mintage	F	VF	XF	Unc	BU
2001	100,000	—	—	—	12.00	14.00

KM# 141 DOLLAR
7.7700 g., 0.9990 Silver 0.2496 oz. ASW, 22 mm. **Ruler:** Elizabeth II **Series:** Pokemon **Obv:** Crowned shield within sprigs **Rev:** "Squirtle" **Edge:** Reeded

Date	Mintage	F	VF	XF	Unc	BU
2001 Proof	20,000	Value: 7.00				

KM# 146 DOLLAR
28.2800 g., Copper-Nickel, 38.6 mm. **Ruler:** Elizabeth II **Subject:** Pokemon Series **Obv:** Crowned shield within sprigs **Rev:** Pikachu **Edge:** Reeded

Date	Mintage	F	VF	XF	Unc	BU
2002PM	100,000	—	—	—	3.00	4.50

KM# 151 DOLLAR
28.2800 g., Copper-Nickel, 38.6 mm. **Ruler:** Elizabeth II **Subject:** Pokemon Series **Obv:** Crowned shield within sprigs **Rev:** Pichu **Edge:** Reeded

Date	Mintage	F	VF	XF	Unc	BU
2002PM	100,000	—	—	—	3.00	4.50

KM# 156 DOLLAR
28.2800 g., Copper-Nickel, 38.6 mm. **Ruler:** Elizabeth II **Subject:** Pokemon Series **Obv:** Crowned shield within sprigs **Rev:** Mewtwo **Edge:** Reeded

Date	Mintage	F	VF	XF	Unc	BU
2002PM	100,000	—	—	—	3.00	4.50

KM# 161 DOLLAR
28.2800 g., Copper-Nickel, 38.6 mm. **Ruler:** Elizabeth II **Subject:** Pokemon Series **Obv:** Crowned shield within sprigs **Rev:** Entei **Edge:** Reeded

Date	Mintage	F	VF	XF	Unc	BU
2002PM	100,000	—	—	—	3.00	4.50

KM# 166 DOLLAR
28.2800 g., Copper Nickel, 38.6 mm. **Ruler:** Elizabeth II **Subject:** Pokemon Series **Obv:** Crowned shield within sprigs **Rev:** Celebi **Edge:** Reeded

Date	Mintage	F	VF	XF	Unc	BU
2002PM	100,000	—	—	—	3.00	4.50

KM# 176 DOLLAR
28.2800 g., 0.9250 Silver 0.8410 oz. ASW **Ruler:** Elizabeth II **Obv:** Tiarra head of Elizabeth II right at left, multicolor Van Gogh's painting "Starry Night" with 3 zircon crystals as stars at center right. **Obv. Inscription:** ELIZABETH II - NIUE ISLAND **Rev:** Van Gogh's painting "Vase with Twelve Sunflowers" at left, self portrait of artist with brush at upper right **Rev. Inscription:** VAN GOGH / Vincent **Edge:** Plain **Shape:** Rectangular, 39.94 x 27.97 mm

Date	Mintage	F	VF	XF	Unc	BU
2007 Proof	10,000	Value: 60.00				

KM# 124 10 DOLLARS
28.2800 g., 0.9250 Silver 0.8410 oz. ASW, 38.6 mm. **Ruler:** Elizabeth II **Subject:** Snoopy as an Ace **Obv:** Crowned head right **Rev:** Snoopy flying his dog house **Edge:** Reeded

Date	Mintage	F	VF	XF	Unc	BU
2001 Proof	10,000	Value: 17.50				

KM# 130 10 DOLLARS
28.2800 g., 0.9250 Silver 0.8410 oz. ASW, 38.6 mm. **Ruler:** Elizabeth II **Series:** Pokeman **Obv:** Crowned shield within sprigs **Rev:** "Bulbasaur" **Edge:** Reeded

Date	Mintage	F	VF	XF	Unc	BU
2001 Proof	10,000	Value: 16.50				

KM# 133 10 DOLLARS
28.2800 g., 0.9250 Silver 0.8410 oz. ASW, 38.6 mm. **Ruler:** Elizabeth II **Series:** Pokeman **Obv:** Crowned shield within sprigs **Rev:** "Charmander" **Edge:** Reeded

Date	Mintage	F	VF	XF	Unc	BU
2001 Proof	10,000	Value: 16.50				

KM# 136 10 DOLLARS
28.2800 g., 0.9250 Silver 0.8410 oz. ASW, 38.6 mm. **Ruler:** Elizabeth II **Series:** Pokeman **Obv:** Crowned shield within sprigs **Rev:** "Meowth" **Edge:** Reeded

Date	Mintage	F	VF	XF	Unc	BU
2001 Proof	10,000	Value: 16.50				

KM# 139 10 DOLLARS
28.2800 g., 0.9250 Silver 0.8410 oz. ASW, 38.6 mm. **Ruler:** Elizabeth II **Series:** Pokeman **Obv:** Crowned shield within sprigs **Rev:** "Pikachu" **Edge:** Reeded

Date	Mintage	F	VF	XF	Unc	BU
2001 Proof	10,000	Value: 16.50				

KM# 142 10 DOLLARS
28.2800 g., 0.9250 Silver 0.8410 oz. ASW, 38.6 mm. **Ruler:** Elizabeth II **Series:** Pokeman **Obv:** Crowned shield within sprigs **Rev:** "Squirtle" **Edge:** Reeded

Date	Mintage	F	VF	XF	Unc	BU
2001 Proof	10,000	Value: 16.50				

KM# 147 10 DOLLARS
28.2800 g., 0.9250 Silver 0.8410 oz. ASW, 38.6 mm. **Ruler:** Elizabeth II **Subject:** Pokémon Series **Obv:** Crowned shield within sprigs **Rev:** Pikachu **Edge:** Reeded

Date	Mintage	F	VF	XF	Unc	BU
2002PM Proof	10,000	Value: 16.50				

KM# 152 10 DOLLARS
28.2800 g., 0.9250 Silver 0.8410 oz. ASW, 38.6 mm. **Ruler:** Elizabeth II **Subject:** Pokémon Series **Obv:** Crowned shield within sprigs **Rev:** Pichu **Edge:** Reeded

Date	Mintage	F	VF	XF	Unc	BU
2002PM Proof	10,000	Value: 16.50				

KM# 157 10 DOLLARS
28.2800 g., 0.9250 Silver 0.8410 oz. ASW, 38.6 mm. **Ruler:** Elizabeth II **Subject:** Pokémon Series **Obv:** Crowned shield within sprigs **Rev:** Mewtwo **Edge:** Reeded

Date	Mintage	F	VF	XF	Unc	BU
2002PM Proof	10,000	Value: 16.50				

KM# 162 10 DOLLARS
28.2800 g., 0.9250 Silver 0.8410 oz. ASW, 38.6 mm. **Ruler:** Elizabeth II **Subject:** Pokémon Series **Obv:** Crowned shield within sprigs **Rev:** Entei **Edge:** Reeded

Date	Mintage	F	VF	XF	Unc	BU
2002PM Proof	10,000	Value: 16.50				

KM# 167 10 DOLLARS
28.2800 g., 0.9250 Silver 0.8410 oz. ASW, 38.6 mm. **Ruler:** Elizabeth II **Subject:** Pokémon Series **Obv:** Crowned shield within sprigs **Rev:** Celebi **Edge:** Reeded

Date	Mintage	F	VF	XF	Unc	BU
2002PM Proof	10,000	Value: 14.00				

KM# 125 20 DOLLARS
1.2400 g., 0.9999 Gold 0.0399 oz. AGW, 13.9 mm. **Ruler:** Elizabeth II **Subject:** Snoopy as an Ace **Obv:** Crowned head right **Rev:** Snoopy flying his dog house **Edge:** Reeded

Date	Mintage	F	VF	XF	Unc	BU
2001 Proof	10,000	Value: 38.00				

KM# 148 20 DOLLARS
1.2400 g., 0.9999 Gold 0.0399 oz. AGW, 13.92 mm. **Ruler:** Elizabeth II **Subject:** Pokémon Series **Obv:** Crowned shield within sprigs **Rev:** Pikachu **Edge:** Reeded

Date	Mintage	F	VF	XF	Unc	BU
2002PM Proof	10,000	Value: 38.00				

KM# 153 20 DOLLARS
1.2400 g., 0.9999 Gold 0.0399 oz. AGW, 13.9 mm. **Ruler:** Elizabeth II **Subject:** Pokémon Series **Obv:** Crowned shield within sprigs **Rev:** Pichu **Edge:** Reeded

Date	Mintage	F	VF	XF	Unc	BU
2001PM Proof	10,000	Value: 38.00				

KM# 158 20 DOLLARS
1.2400 g., 0.9999 Gold 0.0399 oz. AGW, 13.92 mm. **Ruler:** Elizabeth II **Subject:** Pokémon Series **Obv:** Crowned shield within sprigs **Rev:** Mewtwo **Edge:** Reeded

Date	Mintage	F	VF	XF	Unc	BU
2002PM Proof	10,000	Value: 38.00				

KM# 163 20 DOLLARS
1.2400 g., 0.9999 Gold 0.0399 oz. AGW, 13.9 mm. **Ruler:** Elizabeth II **Subject:** Pokémon Series **Obv:** Crowned shield within sprigs **Rev:** Entei **Edge:** Reeded

Date	Mintage	F	VF	XF	Unc	BU
2002PM Proof	10,000	Value: 38.00				

KM# 168 20 DOLLARS
1.2400 g., 0.9999 Gold 0.0399 oz. AGW, 13.9 mm. **Ruler:** Elizabeth II **Subject:** Pokémon Series **Obv:** Crowned shield within sprigs **Rev:** Celebi **Edge:** Reeded

Date	Mintage	F	VF	XF	Unc	BU
2002PM Proof	10,000	Value: 38.00				

KM# 126 50 DOLLARS
3.1100 g., 0.9999 Gold 0.1000 oz. AGW, 17.9 mm. **Ruler:** Elizabeth II **Subject:** Snoopy as an Ace **Obv:** Crowned head right **Rev:** Snoopy flying his dog house **Edge:** Reeded

Date	Mintage	F	VF	XF	Unc	BU
2001 Proof	7,500	Value: 95.00				

KM# 149 50 DOLLARS
3.1100 g., 0.9999 Gold 0.1000 oz. AGW, 17.9 mm. **Ruler:** Elizabeth II **Subject:** Pokémon Series **Obv:** Crowned shield within sprigs **Rev:** Pikachu **Edge:** Reeded

Date	Mintage	F	VF	XF	Unc	BU
2002PM Proof	7,500	Value: 95.00				

KM# 154 50 DOLLARS
3.1100 g., 0.9999 Gold 0.1000 oz. AGW, 17.9 mm. **Ruler:** Elizabeth II **Subject:** Pokémon Series **Obv:** Crowned shield within sprigs **Rev:** Pichu **Edge:** Reeded

Date	Mintage	F	VF	XF	Unc	BU
2002PM Proof	7,500	Value: 95.00				

KM# 159 50 DOLLARS
3.1100 g., 0.9999 Gold 0.1000 oz. AGW, 17.9 mm. **Ruler:** Elizabeth II **Subject:** Pokémon Series **Obv:** Crowned shield within sprigs **Rev:** Mewtwo **Edge:** Reeded

Date	Mintage	F	VF	XF	Unc	BU
2002PM Proof	7,500	Value: 95.00				

KM# 164 50 DOLLARS
3.1100 g., 0.9999 Gold 0.1000 oz. AGW, 17.9 mm. **Ruler:** Elizabeth II **Subject:** Pokémon Series **Obv:** Crowned shield within sprigs **Rev:** Entei **Edge:** Reeded

Date	Mintage	F	VF	XF	Unc	BU
2002PM Proof	7,500	Value: 95.00				

KM# 169 50 DOLLARS
3.1100 g., 0.9999 Gold 0.1000 oz. AGW, 17.9 mm. **Ruler:** Elizabeth II **Subject:** Pokémon Series **Obv:** Crowned shield within sprigs **Rev:** Celebi **Edge:** Reeded

Date	Mintage	F	VF	XF	Unc	BU
2002PM Proof	7,500	Value: 95.00				

KM# 127 100 DOLLARS
6.2200 g., 0.9999 Gold 0.1999 oz. AGW, 22 mm. **Ruler:** Elizabeth II **Subject:** Snoopy as an Ace **Obv:** Crowned head right **Rev:** Snoopy flying his dog house **Edge:** Reeded

Date	Mintage	F	VF	XF	Unc	BU
2001 Proof	5,000	Value: 190				

KM# 150 100 DOLLARS
6.2200 g., 0.9999 Gold 0.1999 oz. AGW, 22 mm. **Ruler:** Elizabeth II **Subject:** Pokémon Series **Obv:** Crowned shield within sprigs **Rev:** Pikachu **Edge:** Reeded

Date	Mintage	F	VF	XF	Unc	BU
2002PM Proof	5,000	Value: 190				

KM# 155 100 DOLLARS
6.2200 g., 0.9999 Gold 0.1999 oz. AGW, 22 mm. **Ruler:** Elizabeth II **Subject:** Pokémon Series **Obv:** Crowned shield within sprigs **Rev:** Pichu **Edge:** Reeded

Date	Mintage	F	VF	XF	Unc	BU
2002PM Proof	5,000	Value: 190				

KM# 160 100 DOLLARS
6.2200 g., 0.9999 Gold 0.1999 oz. AGW, 22 mm. **Ruler:** Elizabeth II **Subject:** Pokémon Series **Obv:** Crowned shield within sprigs **Rev:** Mewtwo **Edge:** Reeded

Date	Mintage	F	VF	XF	Unc	BU
2002PM Proof	5,000	Value: 195				

KM# 165 100 DOLLARS
6.2200 g., 0.9999 Gold 0.1999 oz. AGW, 22 mm. **Ruler:** Elizabeth II **Subject:** Pokémon Series **Obv:** Crowned shield within sprigs **Rev:** Entei **Edge:** Reeded

Date	Mintage	F	VF	XF	Unc	BU
2002PM Proof	5,000	Value: 190				

KM# 170 100 DOLLARS
6.2200 g., 0.9999 Gold 0.1999 oz. AGW, 22 mm. **Ruler:** Elizabeth II **Subject:** Pokémon Series **Obv:** Crowned shield within sprigs **Rev:** Celebi **Edge:** reeded

Date	Mintage	F	VF	XF	Unc	BU
2002PM Proof	5,000	Value: 190				

NORWAY

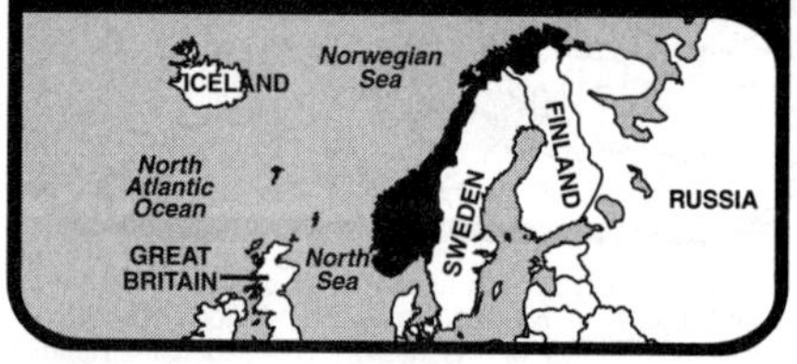

The Kingdom of Norway (*Norge, Noreg*), a constitutional monarchy located in northwestern Europe, has an area of 150,000sq. mi. (324,220 sq. km.), including the island territories of Spitzbergen (Svalbard) and Jan Mayen, and a population of *4.2 million. Capital: Oslo (Christiania). The diversified economic base of Norway includes shipping, fishing, forestry, agriculture, and manufacturing. Nonferrous metals, paper and paperboard, paper pulp, iron, steel and oil are exported.

RULER
Harald V, 1991-

MINT MARK
(h) - Crossed hammers – Kongsberg

MONETARY SYSTEM
100 Ore = 1 Krone (30 Skilling)

KINGDOM

DECIMAL COINAGE

KM# 460 50 ORE
3.6000 g., Bronze, 18.49 mm. **Ruler:** Harald V **Obv:** Crown **Rev:** Stylized animal and value **Edge:** Plain **Designer:** Grazyna Jolanta Linday

Date	Mintage	VG	F	VF	XF	BU
2001 with star	13,291,750	—	—	—	—	0.40
2001 without star	16,848,250	—	—	—	—	0.40
2001 Proof	—	Value: 10.00				
2002	—	—	—	—	—	0.40

Date	Mintage	VG	F	VF	XF	BU
2002 Proof	—	Value: 10.00				
2003	—	—	—	—	—	0.40
2003 Proof	—	Value: 10.00				
2004	—	—	—	—	—	0.40
2004 Proof	—	Value: 10.00				
2005	—	—	—	—	—	0.40
2005 Proof	—	Value: 10.00				
2006	—	—	—	—	—	0.40

KM# 462 KRONE

4.3000 g., Copper-Nickel, 21 mm. **Ruler:** Harald V **Obv:** Crowned monograms form cross within circle with center hole **Rev:** Bird on vine above center hole date and value below

Date	Mintage	VG	F	VF	XF	BU
2001 with star	7,355,350	—	—	—	—	0.75
2001 without star	43,128,650	—	—	—	—	0.65
2001 Proof	—	Value: 10.00				
2002	—	—	—	—	—	0.65
2002 Proof	—	Value: 10.00				
2003	—	—	—	—	—	0.65
2003 Proof	—	Value: 10.00				
2004	—	—	—	—	—	0.65
2004 Proof	—	Value: 10.00				
2005	—	—	—	—	—	0.65
2005 Proof	—	Value: 10.00				
2006	—	—	—	—	—	0.65

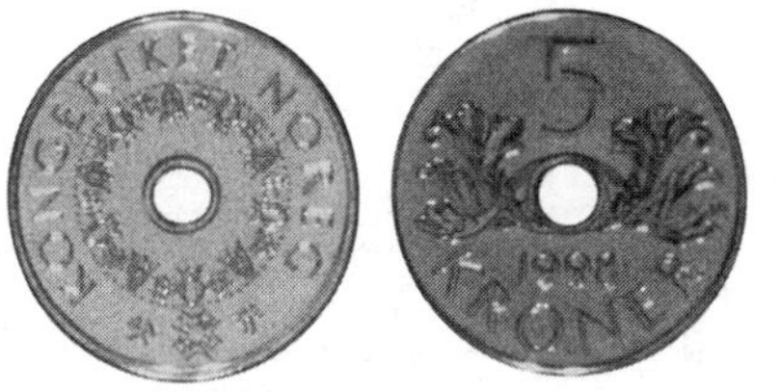

KM# 463 5 KRONER

7.8500 g., Copper-Nickel **Ruler:** Harald V **Subject:** Order of St. Olaf **Obv:** Hole at center of order chain **Rev:** Center hole divides sprigs, value above and date below

Date	Mintage	VG	F	VF	XF	BU
2001	460,000	—	—	—	—	2.00
2001 Proof	—	Value: 12.50				
2002	—	—	—	—	—	1.50
2002 Proof	—	Value: 12.50				
2003	—	—	—	—	—	1.50
2003 Proof	—	Value: 12.50				
2004	—	—	—	—	—	1.50
2004 Proof	—	Value: 12.50				
2005	—	—	—	—	—	1.50
2005 Proof	—	Value: 12.50				
2006	—	—	—	—	—	1.50

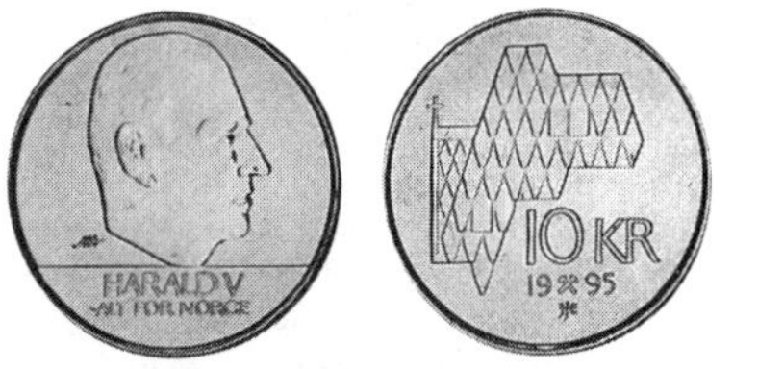

KM# 457 10 KRONER

6.8000 g., Copper-Zinc-Nickel **Ruler:** Harald V **Obv:** Head right **Rev:** Stylized church rooftop, value and date **Designer:** Ingrid Austlid Rise

Date	Mintage	VG	F	VF	XF	BU
2001 without star	9,837,500	—	—	—	—	3.50
2001 with star	10,000	—	—	—	—	7.50
2001 Proof	—	Value: 10.00				
2002	—	—	—	—	—	3.50
2002 Proof	—	Value: 10.00				
2003	—	—	—	—	—	3.50
2003 Proof	—	Value: 10.00				
2004	—	—	—	—	—	3.50
2004 Proof	—	Value: 10.00				
2005	—	—	—	—	—	3.50
2005 Proof	—	Value: 10.00				
2006	—	—	—	—	—	3.50

KM# 478 20 KRONER (5 Speciedaler)

9.9000 g., Copper-Zinc-Nickel, 27.5 mm. **Ruler:** Harald V **Subject:** First Norwegian Railroad **Obv:** Head right **Rev:** Switch track and value **Edge:** Plain

Date	Mintage	F	VF	XF	Unc	BU
2004	10,000	—	—	—	17.50	20.00
2004 Proof	—	Value: 25.00				

KM# 453 20 KRONER

8.7000 g., Copper-Zinc-Nickel **Ruler:** Harald V **Obv:** Head right **Rev:** Value above 1/2 ancient boat **Designer:** Ingrid Austlid Rise

Date	Mintage	VG	F	VF	XF	BU
2001	4,178,010	—	—	—	—	6.50
2001 Proof	—	Value: 25.00				
2001 Proof	—	Value: 25.00				
2002	—	—	—	—	—	6.50
2002 Proof	—	—	—	—	—	6.50
2003 Proof	—	Value: 25.00				
2004	—	—	—	—	—	6.50
2004 Proof	—	Value: 25.00				
2005	—	—	—	—	—	6.50
2005 Proof	—	Value: 25.00				

KM# 471 20 KRONER

9.7300 g., Nickel-Brass, 27.4 mm. **Ruler:** Harald V **Subject:** Niels Henrik Abel **Obv:** Head right **Rev:** Pair of glasses, dates and value within mathematical graphs **Edge:** Plain

Date	Mintage	F	VF	XF	Unc	BU
2002	—	—	—	—	10.00	12.50

KM# 479 20 KRONER

9.7300 g., Copper-Zinc-Nickel, 27.4 mm. **Ruler:** Harald V **Obv:** Harold V **Edge:** Plain

Date	Mintage	F	VF	XF	Unc	BU
2006	10,000	—	—	—	—	12.50

KM# 469 100 KRONER

33.6000 g., 0.9250 Silver 0.9992 oz. ASW, 39 mm. **Ruler:** Harald V **Subject:** Nobel Peace Prize Centennial **Obv:** Rampant crowned lion left holding axe **Rev:** Head left **Edge:** Plain

Date	Mintage	F	VF	XF	Unc	BU
2001 Proof	Est. 50,000	Value: 85.00				

KM# 472 100 KRONER

33.8000 g., 0.9250 Silver 1.0052 oz. ASW, 39 mm. **Ruler:** Harald V **Subject:** 1905 Liberation **Obv:** Three kings **Rev:** Farm field **Edge:** Plain

Date	Mintage	F	VF	XF	Unc	BU
2003 Proof	65,000	Value: 70.00				

KM# 474 100 KRONER

33.8000 g., 0.9250 Silver 1.0052 oz. ASW, 39 mm. **Ruler:** Harald V **Subject:** 1905 Liberation **Obv:** Three kings **Rev:** Off shore ocean oil well **Edge:** Plain

Date	Mintage	F	VF	XF	Unc	BU
2004 Proof	65,000	Value: 70.00				

KM# 476 100 KRONER

33.8000 g., 0.9250 Silver 1.0052 oz. ASW, 39 mm. **Ruler:** Harald V **Obv:** Three kings **Rev:** Circuit board **Edge:** Plain

Date	Mintage	F	VF	XF	Unc	BU
2005 Proof	—	Value: 70.00				

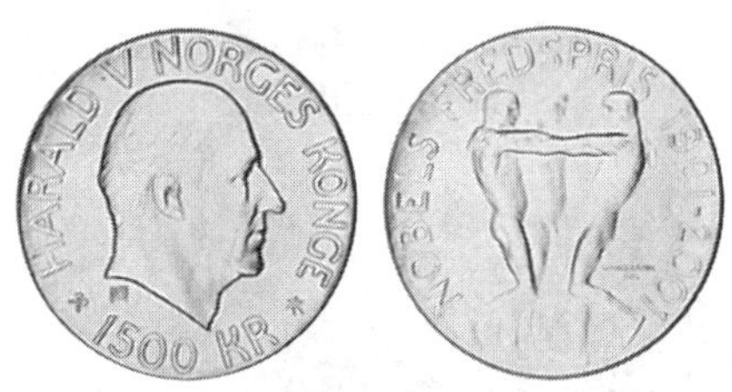

KM# 470 1500 KRONER

16.9600 g., 0.9170 Gold 0.5000 oz. AGW, 27 mm. **Ruler:** Harald V **Subject:** Nobel Peace Prize Centennial **Obv:** Head right **Rev:** Reverse design of the prize medal **Edge:** Plain

Date	Mintage	VG	F	VF	XF	BU
ND(2001) Matte Proof	7,500	Value: 485				

KM# 473 1500 KRONER

16.9600 g., 0.9170 Gold 0.5000 oz. AGW, 27 mm. **Ruler:** Harald V **Subject:** 1905 Liberation **Obv:** Three kings **Rev:** Various leaf types **Edge:** Plain

Date	Mintage	F	VF	XF	Unc	BU
2003 Proof	10,000	Value: 525				

KM# 475 1500 KRONER

16.9600 g., 0.9170 Gold 0.5000 oz. AGW, 27 mm. **Ruler:** Harald V **Subject:** 1905 Liberation **Obv:** Three kings **Rev:** Liquid drops on hard surface **Edge:** Plain

Date	Mintage	F	VF	XF	Unc	BU
2004 Proof	10,000	Value: 525				

KM# 477 1500 KRONER

16.9600 g., 0.9170 Gold 0.5000 oz. AGW, 27 mm. **Ruler:** Harald V **Obv:** Three kings **Rev:** Binary language **Edge:** Plain

Date	Mintage	F	VF	XF	Unc	BU
2005 Proof	—	Value: 525				

MINT SETS

KM#	Date	Mintage	Identification	Issue Price	Mkt Val
MS59	2001 (5)	55,000	KM453, 457, 460, 462, 463. Folder.	20.00	25.00
MS60	2001 (5)	30,000	KM453, 457, 460, 462, 463. Baby gift set.	18.00	30.00
MS61	2001 (5)	2,000	KM453, 457, 460, 462, 463 plus medal.	27.00	27.00
MS62	2001 (5)	—	KM453, 457, 460, 462, 463. Sandhill.	—	30.00
MS63	2002 (6)	55,000	KM#453, 457, 460, 462, 463, 471	—	32.00
MS64	2003 (5)	55,000	KM#453, 457, 460, 462, 463	—	30.00
MS65	2004 (6)	55,000	KM#453, 457, 460, 462, 463, 478	—	32.00
MS66	2005 (5)	55,000	KM#453, 457, 460, 462, 463	—	30.00

PROOF SETS

KM#	Date	Mintage	Identification	Issue Price	Mkt Val
PS13	2002 (6)	10,000	KM#453, 457, 460, 462, 463, 471	—	110
PS14	2003 (5)	10,000	KM#453, 457, 460, 42, 463	—	100
PS15	2004 (6)	10,000	KM#453, 457, 460, 462, 463, 478	—	110
PS16	2005 (5)	10,000	KM#453, 457, 460, 462, 463	—	100

OMAN

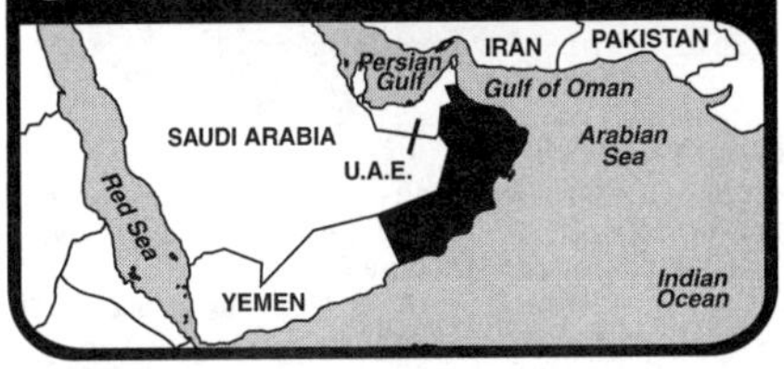

The Sultanate of Oman (formerly Muscat and Oman), an independent monarchy located in the southeastern part of the Arabian Peninsula, has an area of 82,030 sq. mi. (212,460 sq. km.) and a population of *1.3 million. Capital: Muscat. The economy is based on agriculture, herding and petroleum. Petroleum products, dates, fish and hides are exported.

TITLES

Muscat	مسقط
Oman	عمان

SULTANATE

REFORM COINAGE

1000 Baisa = 1 Omani Rial

KM# 154 OMANI RIAL

28.2800 g., 0.9250 Silver 0.8410 oz. ASW, 38.6 mm. **Ruler:** Qabus bin Sa'id AH1390-/1970AD- **Subject:** 31st National Day and Environment Year **Obv:** National arms **Rev:** Multicolor map design **Edge:** Reeded

Date	Mintage	F	VF	XF	Unc	BU
2001	500	—	—	—	60.00	—
2001 Proof	105	Value: 100				

KM# 154a OMANI RIAL

37.8000 g., 0.9160 Gold 1.1132 oz. AGW, 38.6 mm. **Ruler:** Qabus bin Sa'id AH1390-/1970AD- **Subject:** 31st National Day and Environment Year **Obv:** National arms **Rev:** Multicolor map design **Edge:** Reeded

Date	Mintage	F	VF	XF	Unc	BU
2001	350	—	—	—	1,100	—
2001 Proof	105	Value: 1,200				

KM# 155 OMANI RIAL

28.2800 g., 0.9250 Silver 0.8410 oz. ASW, 38.6 mm. **Ruler:** Qabus bin Sa'id AH1390-/1970AD- **Obv:** National arms **Rev:** Sailing ship below map within circle **Edge:** Reeded

Date	Mintage	F	VF	XF	Unc	BU
2003 Proof	—	Value: 50.00				

PAKISTAN

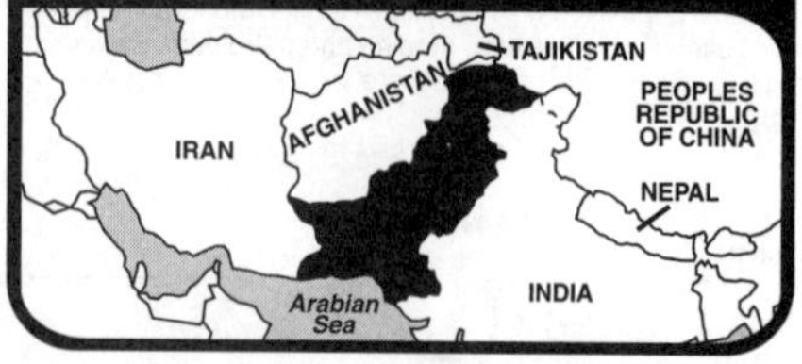

The Islamic Republic of Pakistan, located on the Indian subcontinent between India and Afghanistan, has an area of 310,404 sq. mi. (803,940 sq. km.) and a population of130 million. Capital: Islamabad. Pakistan is mainly an agricultural land although the industrial base is expanding rapidly. Yarn, textiles, cotton, rice, medical instruments, sports equipment and leather are exported.

TITLE

پاکستان

Pakistan

ISLAMIC REPUBLIC

DECIMAL COINAGE

100 Paisa = 1 Rupee

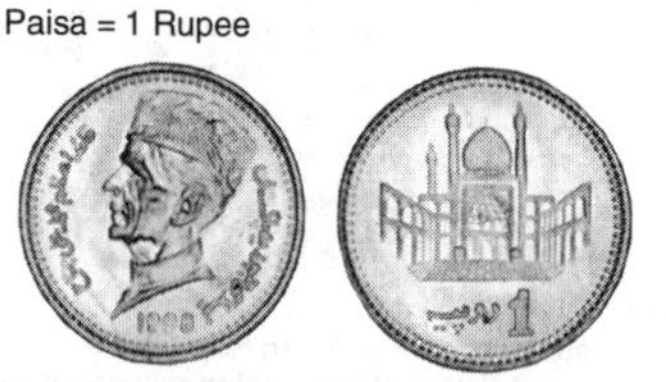

KM# 62 RUPEE

4.0000 g., Bronze, 20 mm. **Obv:** Head left **Rev:** Mosque above value **Edge:** Reeded

Date	Mintage	F	VF	XF	Unc	BU
2001	—	0.20	0.25	0.35	0.65	0.75
2002	—	0.20	0.25	0.35	0.65	0.75
2003	—	0.20	0.25	0.35	0.65	0.75
2004	—	0.20	0.25	0.35	0.65	0.75
2005	—	0.20	0.25	0.35	0.65	0.75
2006	—	0.20	0.25	0.35	0.65	0.75

KM# 64 2 RUPEES

5.0000 g., Nickel-Brass, 22.5 mm. **Obv:** Crescent, star and date above sprigs **Rev:** Value below mosque and clouds **Edge:** Reeded

Date	Mintage	F	VF	XF	Unc	BU
2001	—	0.20	0.30	0.45	0.85	1.00
2002	—	0.20	0.30	0.45	0.85	1.00
2003	—	0.20	0.30	0.45	0.85	1.00
2004	—	0.20	0.30	0.45	0.85	1.00
2005	—	0.20	0.30	0.45	0.85	1.00
2006	—	0.20	0.30	0.45	0.85	1.00

KM# 65 5 RUPEES

6.5000 g., Copper-Nickel, 24 mm. **Obv:** Cresent, star and date above sprays **Rev:** Value within star design and sprigs **Edge:** Reeded

Date	Mintage	F	VF	XF	Unc	BU
2002	—	0.50	1.00	1.50	3.00	3.25
2003	—	0.50	1.00	1.50	3.00	3.25
2004	—	0.50	1.00	1.50	3.00	3.25
2005	—	0.50	1.00	1.50	3.00	3.25

KM# 66 10 RUPEES

7.5000 g., Copper-Nickel, 27.5 mm. **Obv:** Cresent, star and date above sprays **Rev:** Flowers and inscription **Rev. Inscription:** Year of Fatima Jinnah **Edge:** Reeded

Date	Mintage	F	VF	XF	Unc	BU
2003	200,000	—	—	4.00	6.50	7.50

PALAU

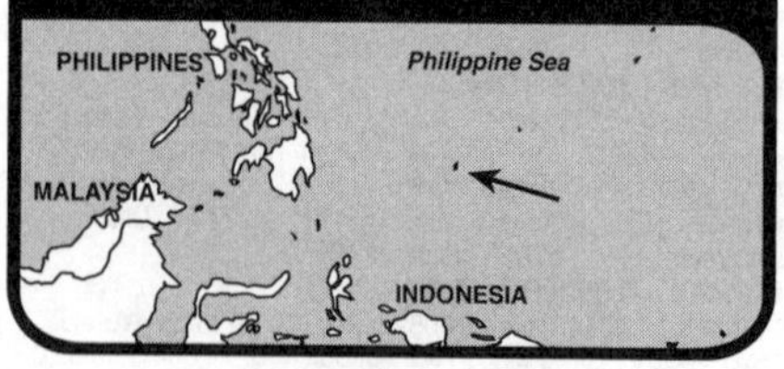

The Republic of Palau, a group of about 100 islands and islets, is generally considered a part of the Caroline Islands. It is located about 1,000 miles southeast of Manila and about the same distance southwest of Saipan and has an area of 179 sq. mi. and a population of 12,116. Capital: Koror.

REPUBLIC

MILLED COINAGE

KM# 86 DOLLAR

1.2441 g., 0.9999 Gold 0.0400 oz. AGW, 13.94 mm. **Subject:** Marine Life Protection **Obv:** Prone Mermaid **Rev:** Two fish

Date	Mintage	F	VF	XF	Unc	BU
2001 Proof	—	Value: 45.00				

KM# 87 DOLLAR

1.2441 g., 0.9999 Gold 0.0400 oz. AGW, 13.94 mm. **Subject:** Marine Life Protection **Obv:** Seated Mermaid with raised arm above value **Rev:** Two glittering fish

Date	Mintage	F	VF	XF	Unc	BU
2001 Proof	—	Value: 45.00				

KM# 88 DOLLAR

1.2441 g., 0.9999 Gold 0.0400 oz. AGW, 13.94 mm. **Subject:** Marine Life Protection **Obv:** Figurehead Mermaid and value **Rev:** Moorish Idol fish

Date	Mintage	F	VF	XF	Unc	BU
2001 Proof	—	Value: 45.00				

KM# 89 DOLLAR

1.2441 g., 0.9999 Gold 0.0400 oz. AGW, 13.94 mm. **Subject:** Marine Life Protection **Obv:** Figurehead Mermaid and value **Rev:** Moorish Idol fish

Date	Mintage	F	VF	XF	Unc	BU
2001 Proof	—	Value: 45.00				

KM# 60 DOLLAR

26.8000 g., Copper-Nickel, 37.2 mm. **Subject:** Marine Life Protection **Obv:** Seated Mermaid with raised arm above value **Rev:** Two glittering fish **Edge:** Reeded

Date	Mintage	F	VF	XF	Unc	BU
2001 Proof	—	Value: 37.50				

KM# 61 DOLLAR

26.8000 g., Copper-Nickel, 37.2 mm. **Subject:** Marine Life Protection **Obv:** Prone Mermaid above value **Rev:** Two glittering fish **Edge:** Reeded

Date	Mintage	F	VF	XF	Unc	BU
2001 Proof	—	Value: 37.50				

KM# 62 DOLLAR

26.8000 g., Copper-Nickel, 37.2 mm. **Subject:** Marine Life Protection **Obv:** Figurehead mermaid and value **Rev:** Moorish-Idol fish **Edge:** Reeded

Date	Mintage	F	VF	XF	Unc	BU
2001 Proof	—	Value: 35.00				

KM# 52 DOLLAR

26.8600 g., Copper Nickel, 37.3 mm. **Subject:** Marine Life Protection **Obv:** Mermaid figurehead and value **Rev:** Multicolor jellyfish **Edge:** Reeded

Date	Mintage	F	VF	XF	Unc	BU
2001 Proof	—	Value: 35.00				

KM# 56 DOLLAR
26.8000 g., Copper-Nickel, 37.2 mm. **Subject:** Marine Life Protection **Obv:** Mermaid figurehead and value **Rev:** Multicolor fish scene **Edge:** Reeded

Date	Mintage	F	VF	XF	Unc	BU
2002 Proof	—	Value: 35.00				

KM# 57 DOLLAR
26.8000 g., Copper-Nickel, 37.2 mm. **Subject:** Marine Life Protection **Obv:** Mermaid figurehead on approaching ship **Rev:** Multicolor reflective fish scene under an acrylic layer **Edge:** Reeded

Date	Mintage	F	VF	XF	Unc	BU
2002 Proof	—	Value: 40.00				

KM# 63 DOLLAR
26.8000 g., Copper-Nickel, 37.2 mm. **Subject:** Marine Life Protection **Obv:** Figurehead mermaid and value **Rev:** Blue Tang Fish **Edge:** Reeded

Date	Mintage	F	VF	XF	Unc	BU
2002 Proof	—	Value: 37.50				

KM# 64 DOLLAR
26.8000 g., Copper-Nickel, 37.2 mm. **Subject:** Marine Life Protection **Obv:** Figurehead mermaid and value **Rev:** Multicolor whales **Edge:** Reeded

Date	Mintage	F	VF	XF	Unc	BU
2002 Proof	—	Value: 37.50				

KM# 65 DOLLAR
26.8000 g., Copper-Nickel, 37.2 mm. **Subject:** Marine Life Protection **Obv:** Mermaid washing hair and value **Rev:** Multicolor jellyfish **Edge:** Reeded

Date	Mintage	F	VF	XF	Unc	BU
2002 Proof	—	Value: 37.50				

KM# 90 DOLLAR
1.2441 g., 0.9999 Gold 0.0400 oz. AGW, 13.94 mm. **Subject:** Marine Life Protection **Obv:** Figurehead Mermaid and value **Rev:** Multicolor whales

Date	Mintage	F	VF	XF	Unc	BU
2002 Proof	—	Value: 45.00				

KM# 91 DOLLAR
1.2441 g., 0.9999 Gold 0.0400 oz. AGW, 13.94 mm. **Subject:** Marine Life Protection **Obv:** Figurehead Mermaid and value **Rev:** Pufferfish

Date	Mintage	F	VF	XF	Unc	BU
2002 Proof	—	Value: 45.00				

KM# 92 DOLLAR
1.2441 g., 0.9999 Gold 0.0400 oz. AGW, 13.94 mm. **Subject:** Marine Life Protection **Obv:** Seated Mermaid with both arms raised and value **Rev:** Jellyfish

Date	Mintage	F	VF	XF	Unc	BU
2002 Proof	—	Value: 45.00				

KM# 93 DOLLAR
1.2441 g., 0.9999 Gold 0.0400 oz. AGW, 13.94 mm. **Subject:** Marine Life Protection **Obv:** Figurehead Mermaid and value **Rev:** Blue Tang Fish

Date	Mintage	F	VF	XF	Unc	BU
2002 Proof	—	Value: 45.00				

KM# 94 DOLLAR
1.2441 g., 0.9999 Gold 0.0400 oz. AGW, 13.94 mm. **Subject:** Marine Life Protection **Obv:** Figurehead mermaid and value **Rev:** Lionfish

Date	Mintage	F	VF	XF	Unc	BU
2002 Proof	—	Value: 45.00				

KM# 95 DOLLAR
1.2441 g., 0.9999 Gold 0.0400 oz. AGW, 13.94 mm. **Subject:** Marine Life Protection **Obv:** Mermaid riding dolphin and value **Rev:** Starfish

Date	Mintage	F	VF	XF	Unc	BU
2003 Proof	—	Value: 45.00				

KM# 96 DOLLAR
1.2441 g., 0.9999 Gold 0.0400 oz. AGW, 13.94 mm. **Subject:** Marine Life Protection **Obv:** Seated Mermaid on shell and value **Rev:** Multicolor Orca **Edge:** Reeded Proof

Date	Mintage	F	VF	XF	Unc	BU
2003 Proof	—	Value: 45.00				

KM# 97 DOLLAR
1.2441 g., 0.9999 Gold 0.0400 oz. AGW, 13.94 mm. **Subject:** Marine Life Protection **Obv:** Mermaid under radiant sun and value **Rev:** Crab

Date	Mintage	F	VF	XF	Unc	BU
2003 Proof	—	Value: 45.00				

KM# 98 DOLLAR
1.2441 g., 0.9999 Gold 0.0400 oz. AGW, 13.94 mm. **Subject:** Marine Life Protection **Obv:** Mermaid riding turtle and value **Rev:** Two glittering fish

Date	Mintage	F	VF	XF	Unc	BU
2003 Proof	—	Value: 45.00				

KM# 66 DOLLAR
26.8000 g., Copper-Nickel, 37.2 mm. **Subject:** Marine Life Protection **Obv:** Mermaid under sun and value **Rev:** Orange crab **Edge:** Reeded

Date	Mintage	F	VF	XF	Unc	BU
2003 Proof	—	Value: 32.00				

KM# 67 DOLLAR
26.8000 g., Copper-Nickel, 37.2 mm. **Subject:** Marine Life Protection **Obv:** Mermaid riding turtle and value **Rev:** Two glittering fish **Edge:** Reeded

Date	Mintage	F	VF	XF	Unc	BU
2003 Proof	—	Value: 35.00				

KM# 68 DOLLAR

26.8000 g., Copper-Nickel, 37.2 mm. **Subject:** Marine Life Protection **Obv:** Seated Mermaid on shell and value **Rev:** Multicolor Orca **Edge:** Reeded

Date	Mintage	F	VF	XF	Unc	BU
2003 Proof	—	Value: 37.50				

KM# 69 DOLLAR

26.8000 g., Copper-Nickel, 37.2 mm. **Subject:** Marine Life Protection **Obv:** Mermaid playing shell guitar and value **Rev:** Green fish **Edge:** Reeded

Date	Mintage	F	VF	XF	Unc	BU
2003 Proof	—	Value: 35.00				

KM# 70 DOLLAR

26.8000 g., Copper-Nickel, 37.2 mm. **Subject:** Marine Life Protection **Obv:** Seated Mermaid on rock and value **Rev:** School of blue fish **Edge:** Reeded

Date	Mintage	F	VF	XF	Unc	BU
2004 Proof	—	Value: 37.50				

KM# 71 DOLLAR

26.8000 g., Copper-Nickel, 37.2 mm. **Subject:** Marine Life Protection **Obv:** Side view of Mermaid facing right and value **Rev:** Clownfish **Edge:** Reeded

Date	Mintage	F	VF	XF	Unc	BU
2004 Proof	—	Value: 37.50				

KM# 72 DOLLAR

26.8000 g., Copper-Nickel, 37.2 mm. **Subject:** Marine Life Protection **Obv:** Mermaid flanked by dolphins **Rev:** Multicolor dolphin head **Edge:** Reeded

Date	Mintage	F	VF	XF	Unc	BU
2004 Proof	—	Value: 37.50				

KM# 123 DOLLAR

Copper-Nickel, 37.2 mm. **Subject:** Marine Life Protection **Obv:** Mermaid seated inside a giant conch shell **Rev:** Puffer fish **Edge:** Reeded

Date	Mintage	F	VF	XF	Unc	BU
2004 Proof	—	Value: 37.50				

KM# 124 DOLLAR

Copper-Nickel, 37.2 mm. **Subject:** Marine Life Protection **Obv:** Seated Mermaid **Rev:** Sea turtle **Edge:** Reeded

Date	Mintage	F	VF	XF	Unc	BU
2004 Proof	—	Value: 37.50				

KM# 99 DOLLAR

1.2441 g., 0.9999 Gold 0.0400 oz. AGW, 13.94 mm. **Subject:** Marine Life Protection **Obv:** Mermaid under radiant sun and value **Rev:** Clownfish

Date	Mintage	F	VF	XF	Unc	BU
2004 Proof	—	Value: 45.00				

KM# 100 DOLLAR

1.2441 g., 0.9999 Gold 0.0400 oz. AGW, 13.94 mm. **Subject:** Marine Life Protection **Obv:** Mermaid flanked by dolphins **Rev:** Multicolor dolphin head

Date	Mintage	F	VF	XF	Unc	BU
2004 Proof	—	Value: 45.00				

KM# 101 DOLLAR

1.2441 g., 0.9999 Gold 0.0400 oz. AGW, 13.94 mm. **Subject:** Marine Life Protection **Obv:** Mermaid sitting in a shell listening to a conch shell **Rev:** Sea Horse

Date	Mintage	F	VF	XF	Unc	BU
2005 Proof	—	Value: 45.00				

KM# 125 DOLLAR

Copper-Nickel, 37.2 mm. **Subject:** Marine Life Protection **Obv:** Mermaid with head tilted back **Rev:** Barracuda

Date	Mintage	F	VF	XF	Unc	BU
2006 Proof	—	Value: 37.50				

KM# 126 DOLLAR
Copper-Nickel, 37.2 mm. **Subject:** Marine Life Protection **Obv:** Two mermaids **Rev:** Parrot fish

Date	Mintage	F	VF	XF	Unc	BU
2006 Proof	—	Value: 37.50				

KM# 127 DOLLAR
Copper-Nickel, 37.2 mm. **Subject:** Marine Life Protection **Obv:** Mermaid swimming downward **Rev:** Hog Fish **Edge:** Reeded

Date	Mintage	F	VF	XF	Unc	BU
2006 Proof	—	Value: 37.50				

KM# 128 DOLLAR
Copper-Nickel, 37.2 mm. **Subject:** Marine Life Protection **Obv:** Seated mermaid with bird perched on outstretched hand **Rev:** Mahi Mahi **Edge:** Reeded

Date	Mintage	F	VF	XF	Unc	BU
2006 Proof	—	Value: 37.50				

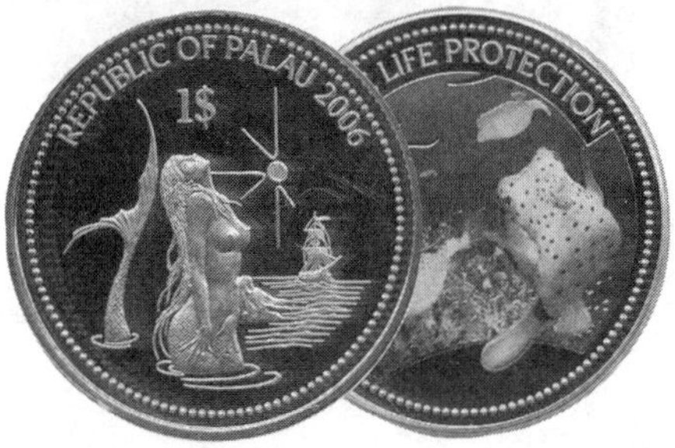

KM# 129 DOLLAR
Copper-Nickel, 37.2 mm. **Subject:** Marine Life Protection **Obv:** Mermaid, sailing ship and sun **Rev:** Box Fish **Edge:** Reeded

Date	Mintage	F	VF	XF	Unc	BU
2006 Proof	—	Value: 37.50				

KM# 116 DOLLAR
25.7300 g., Silver Plated Bronze, 38.6 mm. **Obv:** National arms **Rev:** Multicolor Pope John Paul II with cross **Edge:** Reeded

Date	Mintage	F	VF	XF	Unc	BU
2007 Proof	—	Value: 30.00				

KM# 118 DOLLAR
27.0000 g., Copper Nickel, 38.61 mm. **Series:** Marine Life Protection **Obv:** Neptune reclining with trident, mermaid at his side **Obv. Legend:** REPUBLIC OF PALAU **Rev:** Multicolor Doctor Fish

Date	Mintage	F	VF	XF	Unc	BU
2007 Proof	5,000	Value: 30.00				

KM# 121 DOLLAR
27.0000 g., Copper-Nickel, 38.61 mm. **Obv:** Shield with Neptune holding trident, mermaid reclining at his side, RAINBOW'S / END below **Obv. Legend:** REPUBLIC OF PALAU **Rev:** Red racing car 3/4 left **Rev. Legend:** FERRARI - 60 YEARS ANNIVERSARY

Date	Mintage	F	VF	XF	Unc	BU
ND(2007) Proof	5,000	Value: 37.50				

KM# 120 DOLLAR
0.5000 g., 0.9990 Gold 0.0161 oz. AGW, 11.0 mm. **Obv:** Shield with Neptune holding trident, mermaid reclining at his side, RAINBOW'S / END below **Obv. Legend:** REPUBLIC OF PALAU **Shape:** 4-leaf clover **Note:** Uniface

Date	Mintage	F	VF	XF	Unc	BU
2007 Proof	25,000	Value: 45.00				

KM# 130 2 DOLLARS
10.0000 g., 0.9990 Silver 0.3212 oz. ASW, 30.0 mm. **Obv:** Shield with Neptune holding trident, mermaid reclining at his side **Obv. Legend:** REPUBLIC OF PALAU **Rev:** Red racing car 3/4 right **Rev. Legend:** FERRARI - 60 YEARS ANNIVERSARY

Date	Mintage	F	VF	XF	Unc	BU
ND(2007) Proof	2,500	Value: 60.00				

KM# 131 2 DOLLARS
10.0000 g., 0.9990 Silver 0.3212 oz. ASW, 30.0 mm. **Obv:** Shield with Neptune holding trident, mermaid reclining at his side **Obv. Legend:** REPUBLIC OF PALAU **Rev:** Red racing car 3/4 right **Rev. Legend:** FERRARI - 60 YEARS ANNIVERSARY

Date	Mintage	F	VF	XF	Unc	BU
ND(2007) Proof	2,500	Value: 60.00				

KM# 132 2 DOLLARS
10.0000 g., 0.9990 Silver 0.3212 oz. ASW, 30.00 mm. **Obv:** Shield with Neptune holding trident, mermaid reclining at his side **Obv. Legend:** REPUBLIC OF PALAU **Rev:** Red racing car front view **Rev. Legend:** FERRARI - 60 YEARS ANNIVERSARY

Date	Mintage	F	VF	XF	Unc	BU
ND(2007) Proof	2,500	Value: 60.00				

KM# 133 2 DOLLARS
10.0000 g., 0.9990 Silver 0.3212 oz. ASW, 30.0 mm. **Obv:** Shield with Neptune holding trident, mermaid reclining at his side **Obv. Legend:** REPUBLIC OF PALAU **Rev:** Looking down on red racing car approaching in turn **Rev. Legend:** FERRARI - 60 YEARS ANNIVERSARY

Date	Mintage	F	VF	XF	Unc	BU
ND(2007) Proof	2,500	Value: 60.00				

KM# 134 2 DOLLARS
10.0000 g., 0.9990 Silver 0.3212 oz. ASW, 30.0 mm. **Obv:** Shield with Neptune holding trident, reclining mermaid at his side **Obv. Legend:** REPUBLIC OF PALAU **Rev:** Front view of red racing car **Rev. Legend:** FERRARI - 60 YEARS ANNIVERSARY

Date	Mintage	F	VF	XF	Unc	BU
ND(2007) Proof	2,500	Value: 60.00				

KM# 135 2 DOLLARS
10.0000 g., 0.9990 Silver 0.3212 oz. ASW, 30.0 mm. **Obv:** Shield with Neptune holding trident, mermaid reclining at his side **Obv. Legend:** REPUBLIC OF PALAU **Rev:** Red racing car approaching 3/4 right **Rev. Legend:** FERRARI - 60 YEARS ANNIVERSARY

Date	Mintage	F	VF	XF	Unc	BU
ND(2007) Proof	2,500	Value: 60.00				

KM# 53 5 DOLLARS
25.0000 g., 0.9000 Silver 0.7234 oz. ASW, 37.2 mm. **Series:** Marine Life Protection **Obv:** Neptune **Rev:** Multicolor jellyfish **Edge:** Reeded

Date	Mintage	F	VF	XF	Unc	BU
2001 Proof	—	Value: 75.00				

KM# 75 5 DOLLARS
25.0000 g., 0.9000 Silver 0.7234 oz. ASW, 37.2 mm. **Subject:** Marine Life Protection **Obv:** Neptune behind Polynesian ship and value **Rev:** Moorish-Idol fish **Edge:** Reeded

Date	Mintage	F	VF	XF	Unc	BU
2001 Proof	—	Value: 75.00				

KM# 76 5 DOLLARS
Silver, 37.2 mm. **Subject:** Marine Life Protection **Obv:** Neptune riding seahorse and value **Rev:** Fish **Edge:** Reeded

Date	Mintage	F	VF	XF	Unc	BU
2001 Proof	—	Value: 75.00				

KM# 115 5 DOLLARS
25.0000 g., 0.9000 Silver 0.7234 oz. ASW, 37.2 mm. **Subject:** Marine Life Protection **Obv:** Neptune waist deep in water above value with mermaid to the left and behind **Rev:** Multicolor iridescent fish scene **Edge:** Reeded

Date	Mintage	F	VF	XF	Unc	BU
2001 Proof	—	Value: 70.00				

KM# 77 5 DOLLARS
25.0000 g., 0.9000 Silver 0.7234 oz. ASW, 37.2 mm. **Subject:** Marine Life Protection **Obv:** Neptune in shell boat **Rev:** Blue Tang Fish **Edge:** Reeded

Date	Mintage	F	VF	XF	Unc	BU
2002 Proof	—	Value: 75.00				

KM# 78 5 DOLLARS
25.0000 g., 0.9000 Silver 0.7234 oz. ASW, 37.2 mm. **Subject:** Marine Life Protection **Obv:** Neptune in sea chariot **Rev:** Multicolor whales **Edge:** Reeded

Date	Mintage	F	VF	XF	Unc	BU
2002 Proof	—	Value: 75.00				

KM# 79 5 DOLLARS
25.0000 g., 0.9000 Silver 0.7234 oz. ASW, 37.2 mm. **Subject:** Marine Life Protection **Obv:** Zeus and value **Rev:** Multicolor puffer fish **Edge:** Reeded

Date	Mintage	F	VF	XF	Unc	BU
2002 Proof	—	Value: 75.00				

KM# 80 5 DOLLARS
25.0000 g., 0.9000 Silver 0.7234 oz. ASW, 37.2 mm. **Subject:** Marine Life Protection **Obv:** Neptune standing behind Polynesian ship **Rev:** Multicolor Jellyfish **Edge:** Reeded

Date	Mintage	F	VF	XF	Unc	BU
2002 Proof	—	Value: 70.00				

KM# 102 5 DOLLARS
25.0000 g., 0.9000 Silver 0.7234 oz. ASW, 32 mm. **Subject:** Marine Life Protection **Obv:** Neptune in sea chariot with two merhorses **Rev:** Two multicolor reflective fish

Date	Mintage	F	VF	XF	Unc	BU
2002 Proof	—	Value: 60.00				

KM# 103 5 DOLLARS
25.0000 g., 0.9000 Silver 0.7234 oz. ASW, 32 mm. **Subject:** Marine Life Protection **Obv:** Neptune standing in waves **Rev:** Multicolor starfish

Date	Mintage	F	VF	XF	Unc	BU
2003 Proof	—	Value: 60.00				

KM# 104 5 DOLLARS
25.0000 g., 0.9000 Silver 0.7234 oz. ASW, 32 mm. **Subject:** Marine Life Protection **Obv:** Neptune standing in sea chariot **Rev:** Two multicolor reflective fish

Date	Mintage	F	VF	XF	Unc	BU
2003 Proof	—	Value: 60.00				

KM# 105 5 DOLLARS
25.0000 g., 0.9000 Silver 0.7234 oz. ASW, 32 mm. **Subject:** Marine Life Protection **Rev:** Multicolor Orca

Date	Mintage	F	VF	XF	Unc	BU
2003 Proof	—	Value: 60.00				

KM# 106 5 DOLLARS
25.0000 g., 0.9000 Silver 0.7234 oz. ASW, 32 mm. **Subject:** Marine Life Protection **Obv:** Neptune in sea chariot **Rev:** Multicolor Napoleon Fish

Date	Mintage	F	VF	XF	Unc	BU
2003 Proof	—	Value: 60.00				

KM# 107 5 DOLLARS
25.0000 g., 0.9000 Silver 0.7234 oz. ASW, 32 mm. **Subject:** Marine Life Protection **Obv:** Neptune seated behind mermaid **Rev:** Multicolor school of sweetlips fish

Date	Mintage	F	VF	XF	Unc	BU
2004 Proof	—	Value: 60.00				

KM# 108 5 DOLLARS
25.0000 g., 0.9000 Silver 0.7234 oz. ASW, 32 mm. **Subject:** Marine Life Protection **Obv:** Standing Neptune and ship **Rev:** Multicolor Porcupine fish

Date	Mintage	F	VF	XF	Unc	BU
2004 Proof	—	Value: 75.00				

KM# 109 5 DOLLARS
25.0000 g., 0.9000 Silver 0.7234 oz. ASW, 32 mm. **Subject:** Marine Life Protection **Obv:** Neptune in sea chariot **Rev:** Multicolor Loggerhead turtle

Date	Mintage	F	VF	XF	Unc	BU
2004 Proof	—	Value: 75.00				

KM# 110 5 DOLLARS
25.0000 g., 0.9000 Silver 0.7234 oz. ASW, 32 mm. **Subject:** Marine Life Protection **Obv:** Neptune and merhorse **Rev:** Multicolor dolphin head

Date	Mintage	F	VF	XF	Unc	BU
2004 Proof	—	Value: 75.00				

KM# 81 5 DOLLARS
25.0000 g., 0.9000 Silver 0.7234 oz. ASW, 37.2 mm. **Subject:** Marine Life Protection **Obv:** Neptune with treasure chest **Rev:** Clownfish **Edge:** Reeded

Date	Mintage	F	VF	XF	Unc	BU
2004 Proof	—	Value: 75.00				

KM# 111 5 DOLLARS
25.0000 g., 0.9000 Silver 0.7234 oz. ASW, 32 mm. **Subject:** Marine Life Protection **Obv:** Neptune flanked by mermaids **Rev:** Multicolor sea horse

Date	Mintage	F	VF	XF	Unc	BU
2005 Proof	—	Value: 75.00				

KM# 113 5 DOLLARS
25.0000 g., 0.9000 Silver 0.7234 oz. ASW, 32 mm. **Subject:** Marine Life Protection **Obv:** Neptune flanked by mermaids **Rev:** Multicolor fish with ring-like stripes **Edge:** Reeded

Date	Mintage	F	VF	XF	Unc	BU
2005 Proof	—	Value: 75.00				

KM# 114 5 DOLLARS
25.0000 g., 0.9000 Silver 0.7234 oz. ASW, 32 mm. **Subject:** Marine Life Protection **Obv:** Neptune in shell boat talking to a dolphin **Rev:** Multicolor reef fish scene **Edge:** Reeded

Date	Mintage	F	VF	XF	Unc	BU
2006 Proof	—	Value: 75.00				

KM# 117 5 DOLLARS
Copper-Nickel, 38.5 mm. **Obv:** Outrigger canoe above shield **Obv. Legend:** REPUBLIC OF PALAU / 5$ **Rev:** Pearl in colorized shell **Rev. Legend:** MARINE LIFE PROTECTION / PINETADA MAXIMA / 2007 **Edge:** Reeded

Date	Mintage	F	VF	XF	Unc	BU
2007 Proof	—	Value: 35.00				

KM# 119 5 DOLLARS
25.0000 g., 0.9000 Silver 0.7234 oz. ASW, 38.61 mm. **Series:** Marine Life Protection **Obv:** Neptune reclining with trident, mermaid at his side **Obv. Legend:** REPUBLIC OF PALAU **Rev:** Multicolor Doctor Fish

Date	Mintage	F	VF	XF	Unc	BU
2007 Proof	1,500	Value: 60.00				

KM# 122 5 DOLLARS
25.0000 g., 0.5000 Silver 0.4019 oz. ASW, 38.61 mm. **Obv:** Shield with Neptune holding trident, mermaid reclining at his side, RAINBOW'S / End below **Obv. Legend:** REPUBLIC OF PALAU **Rev:** Red racing car 3/4 right **Rev. Legend:** FERRARI - 60 YEARS ANNIVERSARY

Date	Mintage	F	VF	XF	Unc	BU
ND(2007) Proof	2,500	Value: 70.00				

KM# 136 5 DOLLARS
25.0000 g., 0.9250 Silver 0.7435 oz. ASW **Series:** Pacific Wildlife **Obv:** National arms **Obv. Legend:** REPUBLIC OF PALAU **Rev:** Saltwater Crocodile with green crystal eye

Date	Mintage	F	VF	XF	Unc	BU
2007 Proof	2,500	Value: 70.00				

PROOF SETS

KM#	Date	Mintage	Identification	Issue Price	Mkt Val
PS4	2007 (6)	2,500	KM#130-135	—	360

PANAMA

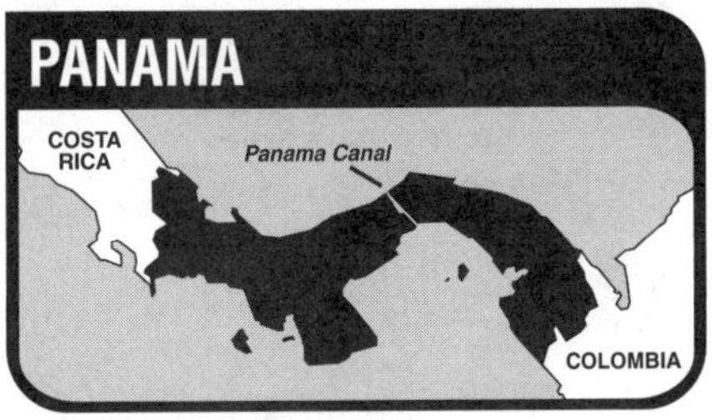

The Republic of Panama, a Central American country situated between Costa Rica and Colombia, has an area of 29,762 sq. mi. (78,200 sq. km.) and a population of *2.4 million. Capital: Panama City. The Panama Canal is the country's biggest asset; servicing world related transit trade and international commerce. Bananas, refined petroleum, sugar and shrimp are exported.

MONETARY SYSTEM
100 Centesimos = 1 Balboa

REPUBLIC

DECIMAL COINAGE

KM# 125 CENTESIMO
2.4400 g., Copper Plated Zinc, 18.96 mm. **Obv:** Written value **Obv. Legend:** REPUBLICA DE PANAMA **Rev:** Native Urraca bust left **Edge:** Plain

Date	Mintage	F	VF	XF	Unc	BU
2001 (RCM)	160,000,000	—	—	—	0.50	1.00

KM# 133 5 CENTESIMOS
5.0000 g., Copper Nickel, 21.15 mm. **Subject:** Sara Sotillo **Obv:** National coat of arms **Obv. Legend:** REPUBLICA DE PANAMA **Rev:** Head of Sotillo 3/4 right **Edge:** Plain

Date	Mintage	F	VF	XF	Unc	BU
2001 (RCM)	8,000,000	—	—	—	0.25	0.30

KM# 127 1/10 BALBOA
2.2800 g., Copper-Nickel Clad Copper, 17.9 mm. **Obv:** National coat of arms **Obv. Legend:** REPUBLICA DE PANAMA **Rev:** Armored bust of Balboa left **Edge:** Reeded

Date	Mintage	F	VF	XF	Unc	BU
2001 (RCM)	15,000,000	—	—	—	0.25	0.50

KM# 135 25 CENTESIMOS
5.5600 g., Copper-Nickel Clad Copper, 24.2 mm. **Obv:** National coat of arms **Rev:** Tower and Spanish ruins **Edge:** Reeded **Note:** Released in 2004

Date	Mintage	F	VF	XF	Unc	BU
2003 (RCM)	6,000,000	—	—	—	0.75	1.50
2003 (RCM) Proof	2,000	Value: 15.00				

KM# 128 1/4 BALBOA
5.6500 g., Copper-Nickel Clad Copper, 24.25 mm. **Obv:** National coat of arms **Rev:** Armored bust left **Edge:** Reeded

Date	Mintage	F	VF	XF	Unc	BU
2001 (RCM)	12,000,000	—	—	—	0.50	1.00

KM# 129 1/2 BALBOA
11.3000 g., Copper-Nickel Clad Copper, 30.54 mm. **Obv:** National coat of arms **Obv. Legend:** REPUBLICA DE PANAMA **Rev:** Armored bust of Balboa left **Edge:** Reeded

Date	Mintage	F	VF	XF	Unc	BU
2001 (RCM)	600,000	—	—	1.00	2.00	3.50

KM# 134 BALBOA
22.7700 g., Copper-Nickel, 38 mm. **Obv:** Bust left **Rev:** Flag and canal scene **Edge:** Reeded

Date	Mintage	F	VF	XF	Unc	BU
ND(2004) (RCM)	348,000	—	—	—	3.00	5.00
ND(2004) (RCM)(P)	2,000	Value: 50.00				

PAPUA NEW GUINEA

Papua New Guinea occupies the eastern half of the island of New Guinea. It lies north of Australia near the equator and borders on West Irian. The country, which includes nearby Bismark archipelago, Buka and Bougainville, has an area of 178,260 sq. mi. (461,690 sq. km.) and a population of 3.7 million that is divided into more than 1,000 separate tribes, speaking more than 700 mutually unintelligible languages. Capital: Port Moresby. The economy is agricultural, and exports copra, rubber, cocoa, coffee, tea, gold and copper

Papua New Guinea is a member of the Commonwealth of Nations. Elizabeth II is Head of State, as Queen of Papua New Guinea.

CONSTITUTIONAL MONARCHY

Commonwealth of Nations

STANDARD COINAGE

100 Toea = 1 Kina

KM# 1 TOEA
2.0000 g., Bronze, 17.65 mm. **Obv:** National emblem **Rev:** Butterfly and value

Date	Mintage	F	VF	XF	Unc	BU
2001	—	—	—	—	1.00	1.25
2002	—	—	—	—	1.00	1.25

KM# 2 2 TOEA
4.0000 g., Bronze, 21.72 mm. **Obv:** National emblem **Rev:** Lion fish

Date	Mintage	F	VF	XF	Unc	BU
2001	—	—	—	—	0.50	1.25

Date	Mintage	F	VF	XF	Unc	BU
2002	—	—	—	—	0.50	1.25
2004	—	—	—	—	0.50	1.25

KM# 3a 5 TOEA

Nickel Plated Steel, 19.53 mm. **Obv:** National emblem **Rev:** Plateless turtle

Date	Mintage	F	VF	XF	Unc	BU
2002	—	—	—	—	0.75	1.50

KM# 4 10 TOEA

5.6700 g., Copper-Nickel, 23.72 mm. **Obv:** National emblem **Rev:** Cuscus and value

Date	Mintage	F	VF	XF	Unc	BU
2001	—	—	—	—	1.50	2.00

KM# 4a 10 TOEA

Nickel Plated Steel, 23.72 mm. **Obv:** National emblem **Rev:** Cuscus and value

Date	Mintage	F	VF	XF	Unc	BU
2002	—	—	—	—	1.50	2.00
2004	—	—	—	—	1.50	2.00

KM# 5a 20 TOEA

Nickel Plated Steel, 28.65 mm. **Obv:** National emblem **Rev:** Bennett's Cassowary and value

Date	Mintage	F	VF	XF	Unc	BU
2004	—	—	0.25	0.50	1.25	1.50

KM# 6a KINA

Nickel Plated Steel, 33 mm. **Obv:** Symbolic design around center hole **Rev:** Crocidiles flank center hole

Date	Mintage	F	VF	XF	Unc	BU
2002	—	—	—	—	3.50	6.00
2004	—	—	—	—	3.50	6.00

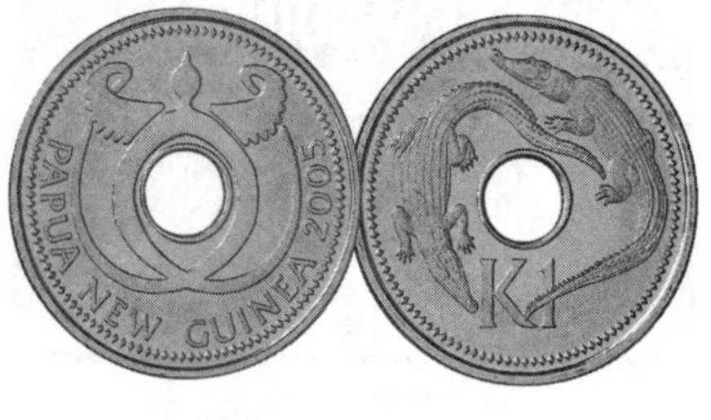

KM# 6.1 KINA

11.1300 g., Nickel Plated Steel, 30 mm. **Obv:** Native design **Rev:** Two Salt Water Crocodiles **Edge:** Reeded

Date	Mintage	F	VF	XF	Unc	BU
2005	—	—	—	—	5.00	7.00

PARAGUAY

The Republic of Paraguay, a landlocked country in the heart of South America surrounded by Argentina, Bolivia and Brazil, has an area of 157,048 sq. mi. (406,750 sq. km.) and a population of *4.5 million, 95 percent of whom are of mixed Spanish and Indian descent. Capital: Asuncion. The country is predominantly agrarian, with no important mineral deposits or oil reserves. Meat, timber, hides, oilseeds, tobacco and cotton account for 70 percent of Paraguay's export revenue.

During the Triple Alliance War (1864-1870) in which Paraguay faced Argentina, Brazil and Uruguay, Asuncion's ladies gathered in an Assembly on Feb. 24, 1867 and decided to give up their jewelry in order to help the national defense. The President of the Republic, Francisco Solano Lopez accepted the offering and ordered one twentieth of it be used to mint the first Paraguayan gold coins according to the Decree of the 11th of Sept.1867.

Two dies were made, one by Bouvet, and another by an American, Leonard Charles, while only the die made by Bouvet was eventually used.

MONETARY SYSTEM

100 Centavos (Centesimos) = 1 Peso

MINT MARK

HF – LeLocle (Swiss)

REPUBLIC

REFORM COINAGE

100 Centimos = 1 Guarani

KM# 197 GUARANI

27.0000 g., 0.9250 Silver 0.8029 oz. ASW, 39.7 mm. **Subject:** 50th Anniversary of the Central Bank **Obv:** Naval gunship **Obv. Legend:** REPUBLICA DEL PARAGUAY **Obv. Inscription:** CAÑONERO PARAGUAY **Rev:** Bank building within circle **Rev. Legend:** BANCO CENTRAL DEL PARAGUAY **Edge:** Reeded

Date	Mintage	F	VF	XF	Unc	BU
2002 Proof	3,000	Value: 55.00				

KM# 199 GUARANI

26.8600 g., 0.9250 Silver 0.7988 oz. ASW, 40.03 mm. **Series:** 5th Ibero-America **Subject:** Encounter of the Two Worlds **Obv:** National arms in center with ten national arms in outer circle **Obv. Legend:** REPUBLICA DEL PARAGUAY **Rev:** Native in canoe with outline of South America in background at left, early sailing ship at loewer right. **Rev. Legend:** ENCUENTRO DE DOS MUNDOS **Edge:** Reeded

Date	Mintage	F	VF	XF	Unc	BU
2002 Proof	—	Value: 60.00				

KM# 200 GUARANI

27.0000 g., 0.9250 Silver 0.8029 oz. ASW **Subject:** 60th Anniversary of Currency Reform **Obv:** National arms **Obv. Legend:** REPUBLICA DEL PARAGUAY **Rev:** Outline map of Paraguay **Edge:** Reeded

Date	Mintage	F	VF	XF	Unc	BU
2003 Proof	—	Value: 60.00				

KM# 201 GUARANI

27.0000 g., 0.9250 Silver 0.8029 oz. ASW **Subject:** XVIII World Football Championship - Germany 2006 **Obv:** National arms **Obv. Legend:** REPUBLICA DEL PARAGUAY **Rev:** Two opponents after ball **Rev. Legend:** COPA MUNDIAL DE LA FIFA - ALEMANIA **Edge:** Reeded

Date	Mintage	F	VF	XF	Unc	BU
2003 Proof	50,000	Value: 60.00				

KM# 202 GUARANI

27.0000 g., 0.9250 Silver 0.8029 oz. ASW **Subject:** XVIII World Football Championship - Germany 2006 **Obv:** National arms **Obv. Legend:** REPUBLICA DEL PARAGUAY **Rev:** Ball in goal **Edge:** Reeded

Date	Mintage	F	VF	XF	Unc	BU
2004 Proof	50,000	Value: 60.00				

KM# 204 GUARANI

27.0000 g., 0.9250 Silver 0.8029 oz. ASW **Series:** 6th Ibero-America **Subject:** Encounter of the Two Worlds **Obv:** National arms in center with ten national arms in outer circle **Obv. Legend:** REPUBLICA DEL PARAGUAY **Rev:** Church of the Most Holy, Trinidad in Yaguarón **Rev. Legend:** ENCUENTRO DE DOS MUNDOS - IGLESIA DE LA SANTISIMA TRINIDAD **Edge:** Reeded

Date	Mintage	F	VF	XF	Unc	BU
2005 Proof	—	Value: 65.00				

KM# 191a 50 GUARANIES

Brass Plated Steel **Obv:** Uniformed bust facing **Rev:** Value above river dam **Note:** Magnetic

Date	Mintage	F	VF	XF	Unc	BU
2005	—	—	—	—	0.75	1.00

KM# 191b 50 GUARANIES

1.0100 g., Aluminum, 18.98 mm. **Obv:** Bust of Major General J.F. Estigarribia facing **Obv. Legend:** REPUBLICA DEL PARAGUAY **Rev:** Acaray River Dam **Rev. Inscription:** REPRESA ACARAY **Edge:** Plain **Note:** Reduced size

Date	Mintage	F	VF	XF	Unc	BU
2006	25,000,000	—	—	—	1.00	2.00

KM# 177a 100 GUARANIES

5.4500 g., Brass Plated Steel **Obv:** Bust of General Jose E. Dias facing **Obv. Legend:** REPUBLICA DEL PARAGUAY **Rev:** Ruins of Humaita **Rev. Inscription:** RUINAS DE HUMAITA 1865/70 **Note:** Reduced weight and thickness.

Date	Mintage	F	VF	XF	Unc	BU
2004	15,000,000	—	—	—	1.50	2.00
2005	10,000,000	—	—	—	1.50	2.00

KM# 177b 100 GUARANIES

3.7200 g., Nickel-Steel, 20.94 mm. **Obv:** Bust of General Jose E. Dias facing **Obv. Legend:** REPUBLICA DEL PARAGUAY **Rev:** Ruins of Humaita **Rev. Inscription:** RUINAS DE HUMAITA 1865/70 **Edge:** Plain

Date	Mintage	F	VF	XF	Unc	BU
2006	30,000,000	—	—	—	1.50	2.00

KM# 195 500 GUARANIES

7.8200 g., Brass Plated Steel **Obv:** Head of General Bernardino Caballero facing **Obv. Legend:** REPUBLICA DEL PARAGUAY **Rev:** Bank above value within circle **Rev. Legend:** BANCO CENTRAL DEL PARAGUAY

Date	Mintage	F	VF	XF	Unc	BU
2002	15,000,000	—	—	—	2.50	3.00
2005	5,000,000	—	—	—	2.50	3.00

KM# 195a 500 GUARANIES

4.8000 g., Nickel-Steel, 23 mm. **Obv:** Head of General Bernardino Caballero facing **Obv. Legend:** REPUBLICA DEL PARAGUAY **Rev:** Bank above value in circle **Rev. Legend:** BANCO CENTRAL DEL PARAGUAY **Edge:** Plain

Date	Mintage	F	VF	XF	Unc	BU
2006	12,000,000	—	—	—	2.00	2.50

KM# 198 MIL (1000) GUARANIES

6.0700 g., Nickel-Steel, 25 mm. **Obv:** Bust of Major General Francisco Solano Lopez facing **Obv. Legend:** REPUBLICA DEL PARAGUAY **Rev:** National Heroes Pantheon **Rev. Legend:** BANCO CENTRAL DEL PARAGUAY **Rev. Inscription:** PANTEON NACIONAL / DE LOS HEROES **Edge:** Plain

Date	Mintage	F	VF	XF	Unc	BU
2006	25,000,000	—	—	—	4.00	6.00

KM# 203 1500 GUARANIES
7.7800 g., 0.9990 Gold 0.2499 oz. AGW **Subject:** XVIII World Football Championship - Germany 2006 **Obv:** National arms **Obv. Legend:** REPUBLICA DEL PARAGUAY **Rev:** Ball in goal

Date	Mintage	F	VF	XF	Unc	BU
2004 Proof	25,000	Value: 450				

The Republic of Peru, located on the Pacific coast of South America, has an area of 496,225 sq. mi. (1,285,220sq. km.) and a population of *21.4 million. Capital: Lima. The diversified economy includes mining, fishing and agriculture. Fishmeal, copper, sugar, zinc and iron ore are exported.

MINT MARKS
L, LIMAE (monogram), Lima
(monogram), LIMA = Lima

NOTE: The LIMAE monogram appears in three forms. The early LM monogram form looks like a dotted L with M. The later LIMAE monogram has all the letters of LIMAE more readily distinguishable. The third form appears as an M monogram during early Republican issues.

REPUBLIC

DECIMAL COINAGE

100 Centavos (10 Dineros) = 1 Sol; 10 Soles = 1 Libra

KM# 303.4a CENTIMO
0.8300 g., Aluminum, 15.96 mm. **Obv:** National arms **Edge:** Plain **Note:** LIMA monogram is mint mark.

Date	Mintage	F	VF	XF	Unc	BU
2006	—	—	—	—	0.50	—
2007	—	—	—	—	0.50	—

KM# 304.4a 5 CENTIMOS
1.0200 g., Aluminum, 18 mm. **Obv:** National arms **Edge:** Plain **Note:** LIMA monogram is mint mark.

Date	Mintage	F	VF	XF	Unc	BU
2007	—	—	—	—	0.50	—

REFORM COINAGE

1/M Intis = 1 Nuevo Sol; 100 (New) Centimos = 1 Nuevo Sol

KM# 303.4 CENTIMO
1.8800 g., Brass, 15.9 mm. **Obv:** National arms, accent mark above "u" **Rev:** Without Braille dots, no Chavez **Edge:** Plain **Note:** LIMA monogram is mint mark.

Date	Mintage	F	VF	XF	Unc	BU
2001	—	—	—	—	0.25	0.40
2002	—	—	—	—	0.25	0.40
2004	—	—	—	—	0.25	0.40
2005	—	—	—	—	0.25	0.40
2005LIMA	—	—	—	—	0.25	0.40
2006	—	—	—	—	0.25	0.40
2006LIMA	—	—	—	—	0.25	0.40

KM# 303.5 CENTIMO
Aluminum **Obv:** National arms **Rev:** Value flanked by designs **Note:** LIMA monogram mint mark.

Date	Mintage	F	VF	XF	Unc	BU
2005	—	—	—	—	0.25	0.40
2006	—	—	—	—	0.25	0.40

KM# 304.4 5 CENTIMOS
2.6900 g., Brass, 18.01 mm. **Obv:** National arms, accent above "u" **Rev:** Without Braille dots, with accent above "e" **Edge:** Plain **Note:** LIMA monogram is mint mark.

Date	Mintage	F	VF	XF	Unc	BU
2001	—	—	—	—	0.35	0.50
2002	—	—	—	—	0.35	0.50
2005	—	—	—	—	0.35	0.50
2006	—	—	—	—	0.35	0.50
2007	—	—	—	—	0.35	0.50

KM# 305.4 10 CENTIMOS
3.5000 g., Brass, 20.47 mm. **Obv:** National arms, accent above "u" **Rev:** Without braille dots, accent above "e" **Edge:** Plain **Note:** LIMA monogram is mint mark.

Date	Mintage	F	VF	XF	Unc	BU
2001LIMA	—	—	—	—	0.65	0.85
2002LIMA	—	—	—	—	0.65	0.85
2003LIMA	—	—	—	—	0.65	0.85
2004LIMA	—	—	—	—	0.65	0.85
2005LIMA	—	—	—	—	0.65	0.85
2006LIMA	—	—	—	—	0.65	0.85
2007LIMA	—	—	—	—	0.65	0.85

KM# 306.4 20 CENTIMOS
4.5300 g., Brass, 23 mm. **Obv:** National arms, accent above "u" **Rev:** Without braille dots, accent above "e" **Edge:** Plain **Note:** LIMA monogram is mint mark.

Date	Mintage	F	VF	XF	Unc	BU
2001LIMA	—	—	—	—	0.85	1.20
2002LIMA	—	—	—	—	0.85	1.20
2004LIMA	—	—	—	—	0.85	1.20
2006LIMA	—	—	—	—	0.85	1.20
2007LIMA	—	—	—	—	0.85	1.20

KM# 307.4 50 CENTIMOS
5.5200 g., Copper-Nickel, 22 mm. **Obv:** National arms, accent above "u" **Rev:** Without braille, accent above "e" **Edge:** Reeded **Note:** LIMA monogram is mint mark.

Date	Mintage	F	VF	XF	Unc	BU
2001LIMA	—	—	—	—	1.50	1.75
2002LIMA	—	—	—	—	1.50	1.75
2003LIMA	—	—	—	—	1.50	1.75
2004LIMA	—	—	—	—	1.50	1.75
2006LIMA	—	—	—	—	1.50	1.75
2007LIMA	—	—	—	—	1.50	1.75

KM# 308.4 NUEVO SOL
7.3000 g., Copper-Nickel, 25.48 mm. **Obv:** National arms, accent above "u" **Rev:** Without braille, accent above "e" **Edge:** Reeded **Note:** LIMA monogram is mint mark.

Date	Mintage	F	VF	XF	Unc	BU
2001LIMA	—	—	—	—	4.00	4.50
2002LIMA	—	—	—	—	4.00	4.50
2003LIMA	—	—	—	—	4.00	4.50
2004LIMA	—	—	—	—	4.00	4.50
2005LIMA	—	—	—	—	4.00	4.50
2006LIMA	—	—	—	—	4.00	4.50
2007LIMA	—	—	—	—	4.00	4.50

KM# 329 NUEVO SOL
33.6250 g., 0.9250 Silver 0.9999 oz. ASW, 37 mm. **Subject:** 450th Anniversary - San Marcos University **Obv:** National arms **Rev:** University seal and building **Edge:** Reeded **Note:** LIMA monogram is mint mark.

Date	Mintage	F	VF	XF	Unc	BU
2001 Proof	—	Value: 55.00				

KM# 330 NUEVO SOL
33.6250 g., 0.9250 Silver 0.9999 oz. ASW, 37 mm. **Subject:** 50th Anniversary - Numismatic Society of Peru **Obv:** National arms **Rev:** Stylized design within circle **Edge:** Reeded **Note:** LIMA monogram is mint mark.

Date	Mintage	F	VF	XF	Unc	BU
2001 Proof	—	Value: 45.00				

KM# 331 NUEVO SOL
33.6250 g., 0.9250 Silver 0.9999 oz. ASW, 37 mm. **Subject:** 200th Anniversary - von Humboldt's visit to Peru **Obv:** National arms **Rev:** Seated figure 1/4 left **Edge:** Reeded **Note:** LIMA monogram is mint mark.

Date	Mintage	F	VF	XF	Unc	BU
2002 Proof	—	Value: 55.00				

KM# 334 NUEVO SOL

27.0800 g., 0.9250 Silver 0.8053 oz. ASW, 40 mm. **Series:** Fifth Ibero-America **Obv:** National arms in center with ten national arms in outer circle **Obv. Legend:** BANCO CENTRAL DE RESERVA DEL PERÚ **Rev:** Ceramic - Indians in reed boats **Rev. Legend:** PERÚ **Edge:** Reeded

Date	Mintage	F	VF	XF	Unc	BU
2002 Proof	—	Value: 75.00				

KM# 332 NUEVO SOL

33.6250 g., 0.9250 Silver 0.9999 oz. ASW, 37 mm. **Subject:** 125th Anniversary of the Inmaculate Jesuitas - Lima College **Obv:** National arms **Rev:** Statue and 3/4 crowned shield **Edge:** Reeded **Note:** LIMA monogram is mint mark.

Date	Mintage	F	VF	XF	Unc	BU
2003 Proof	—	Value: 50.00				

KM# 333 NUEVO SOL

33.6250 g., 0.9250 Silver 0.9999 oz. ASW, 37 mm. **Subject:** 180th Anniversary of Peru's Congress **Obv:** National arms **Rev:** Statue in front of building **Edge:** Reeded **Note:** LIMA monogram is mint mark.

Date	Mintage	F	VF	XF	Unc	BU
2003 Proof	—	Value: 55.00				

KM# 335 NUEVO SOL

Silver **Subject:** FIFA World Cup Soccer **Obv:** Arms within wreath **Rev:** Action scene beneath globe

Date	Mintage	F	VF	XF	Unc	BU
2004 Proof	—	Value: 55.00				

KM# 339 NUEVO SOL

27.0000 g., 0.9250 Silver 0.8029 oz. ASW, 40 mm. **Series:** 6th Ibero-America **Subject:** Lost city of the Incas **Obv:** National arms in center with ten national arms in outer ring **Obv. Legend:** BANCO CENTRAL DE RESERVA DEL PERÚ **Rev:** Village ruins **Rev. Legend:** MACHU PICCHU . PERÚ **Edge:** Reeded

Date	Mintage	F	VF	XF	Unc	BU
2005 Proof	—	Value: 65.00				

KM# 313 2 NUEVOS SOLES

5.5800 g., Bi-Metallic Brass center in Steel ring, 22.22 mm. **Obv:** National arms within circle **Rev:** Stylized bird in flight to left of value within circle **Edge:** Plain **Note:** LIMA monogram is mint mark.

Date	Mintage	F	VF	XF	Unc	BU
2002LIMA	—	—	—	—	4.50	5.00
2003LIMA	—	—	—	—	4.50	5.00
2004LIMA	—	—	—	—	4.50	5.00
2005LIMA	—	—	—	—	4.50	5.00
2006LIMA	—	—	—	—	4.50	5.00

KM# 316 5 NUEVOS SOLES

6.6700 g., Bi-Metallic Brass center in Steel ring, 24.27 mm. **Obv:** National arms within circle **Rev:** Stylized bird in flight to left of value within circle **Edge:** Plain **Note:** LIMA monogram is mint mark.

Date	Mintage	F	VF	XF	Unc	BU
2001LIMA	—	—	—	—	6.50	7.00
2002LIMA	—	—	—	—	6.50	7.00
2004LIMA	—	—	—	—	6.50	7.00
2005LIMA	—	—	—	—	6.50	7.00
2006LIMA	—	—	—	—	6.50	7.00

PHILIPPINES

The Republic of the Philippines, an archipelago in the western Pacific 500 miles (805 km.) from the southeast coast of Asia, has an area of 115,830 sq. mi. (300,000 sq. km.) and a population of *64.9 million. Capital: Manila. The economy of the 7,000-island group is based on agriculture, forestry and fishing. Timber, coconut products, sugar and hemp are exported.

MINT MARKS

BSP - Bangko Sentral Pilipinas

M, MA - Manila

MONETARY SYSTEM

100 Sentimos = 1 Piso

REPUBLIC

REFORM COINAGE

100 Sentimos = 1 Piso

KM# 270.2 10 CENTIMOS

2.4600 g., Bronze-Plated Steel, 16.9 mm. **Obv:** Value high on coin, different font, date **Rev:** Central Bank seal within circle and gear design **Edge:** Reeded

Date	Mintage	F	VF	XF	Unc	BU
2006	—	—	—	—	0.25	0.50

KM# 273 SENTIMO

2.0000 g., Copper Plated Steel **Obv:** Value and date **Rev:** Central bank seal within circle and gear design, 1993 (date Cenral Bank was established) below

Date	Mintage	F	VF	XF	Unc	BU
2004	—	—	—	—	0.35	0.50
2005	—	—	—	—	0.35	0.50
2006	—	—	—	—	0.35	0.50

KM# 268 5 SENTIMOS

1.9000 g., Copper Plated Steel, 15.43 mm. **Obv:** Numeral value around center hole **Rev:** Hole in center with date, bank and name around border, 1993 (date Cenral Bank was established) below **Rev. Legend:** 1993 BANGKO CENTRAL NG PILIPINAS **Edge:** Plain

Date	Mintage	F	VF	XF	Unc	BU
2002	—	—	—	—	0.50	0.75
2005	—	—	—	—	0.50	1.00
2006	—	—	—	—	0.50	1.00

KM# 270.1 10 SENTIMOS

2.4600 g., Bronze Plated Steel, 16.9 mm. **Obv:** Value and date **Rev:** Central Bank seal within circle and gear design, 1993 (date Cenral Bank was established) below **Edge:** Reeded

Date	Mintage	F	VF	XF	Unc	BU
2002	—	—	—	—	0.25	0.40
2004	—	—	—	—	0.25	0.40
2005	—	—	—	—	0.25	0.50

KM# 271.1 25 SENTIMOS

3.8000 g., Brass, 20 mm. **Obv:** Value and date **Rev:** Central Bank seal within circle and gear design, 1993 (date Cenral Bank was established) below **Edge:** Plain

Date	Mintage	F	VF	XF	Unc	BU
2001	—	—	—	—	1.00	1.25
2002	—	—	—	—	1.00	1.25
2003	—	—	—	—	1.00	1.25
2006	—	—	—	—	1.00	1.25

KM# 271.2 25 SENTIMOS

Brass-Plated Steel, 20 mm. **Obv:** Value and date **Rev:** Central Bank seal within circle and gear design **Edge:** Plain

Date	Mintage	F	VF	XF	Unc	BU
2004	—	—	—	—	1.00	1.25
2005	—	—	—	—	1.00	1.25

KM# 269.1 PISO

Copper-Nickel, 24 mm. **Obv:** Head of Jose Rizal right, value and date **Rev:** Bank seal within circle and gear design, 1993 (date Cenral Bank was established) below

Date	Mintage	F	VF	XF	Unc	BU
2001	—	—	—	—	1.25	1.75
2002	—	—	—	—	1.25	1.75
2003	—	—	—	—	1.25	1.75
2004	—	—	—	—	2.50	5.00
2006	—	—	—	—	1.50	2.00

KM# 269.2 2 PISO

Nickel-Plated Steel, 24 mm. **Obv:** Head of Jose Rizal right, value and date **Rev:** Bank seal within circle and gear design

Date	Mintage	F	VF	XF	Unc	BU
2004	—	—	—	—	1.25	2.00
2005	—	—	—	—	1.25	2.00

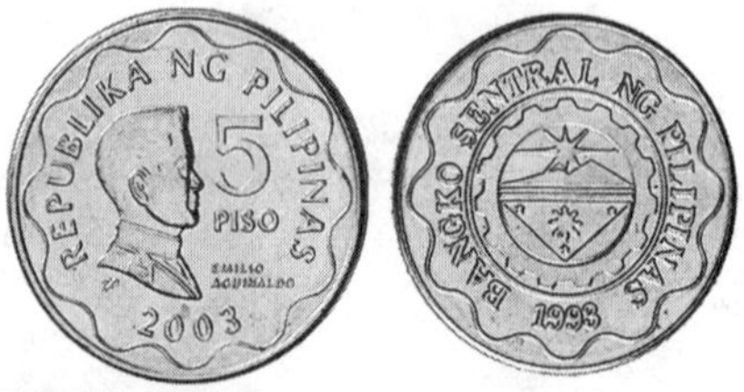

KM# 272 5 PISO

7.6700 g., Nickel-Brass, 25.5 mm. **Obv:** Head of Emilio Aguinaldo right, value and date within scalloped border **Rev:** Central Bank seal within circle and gear design within scalloped border, 1993 (date Cenral Bank was established) below **Edge:** Plain

Date	Mintage	F	VF	XF	Unc	BU
2001BSP	—	—	—	—	1.50	3.00
2002	—	—	—	—	1.50	3.00

Date	Mintage	F	VF	XF	Unc	BU
2003	—	—	—	—	1.50	3.00
2004	—	—	—	—	1.50	3.00
2005	—	—	—	—	1.75	4.00
2006	—	—	—	—	1.50	3.00

KM# 278 10 PISO
8.7000 g., Bi-Metallic Brass center in Copper-Nickel ring, 26.5 mm. **Obv:** Conjoined heads right within circle **Rev:** Bank seal within circle and gear design, 1993 (date Cenral Bank was established) below **Edge:** Plain and reeded sections

Date	Mintage	F	VF	XF	Unc	BU
2001	—	—	—	—	3.00	4.50
2002	—	—	—	—	3.00	4.00
2003	—	—	—	—	3.00	4.00
2004	—	—	—	—	5.00	7.00
2005	—	—	—	—	3.00	5.00
2006	—	—	—	—	3.00	4.00

MINT SETS

KM#	Date	Mintage	Identification	Issue Price	Mkt Val
MS39	2005 (7)	—	KM#268-273, 278 plus medal	10.00	15.00

PITCAIRN ISLANDS

A small volcanic island, along with the uninhabited islands of Oeno, Henderson, and Ducie, constitute the British Colony of Pitcairn Islands. The main island has an area of about 2 sq. mi. (5 sq. km.) and a population of *68. It is located 1350 miles southeast of Tahiti. The islanders subsist on fishing, garden produce and crops. The sale of postage stamps and carved curios to passing ships brings cash income.

New Zealand currency has been used since July 10, 1967.

BRITISH COLONY

REGULAR COINAGE

KM# 14 DOLLAR
Copper-Nickel **Obv:** Bust facing right **Rev:** Queen Mum, Elizabeth II and Margaret facing **Rev. Legend:** 80th Birthday of H.M. Queen Elizabeth II

Date	Mintage	F	VF	XF	Unc	BU
2006	—	—	—	—	—	15.00

KM# 12 5 DOLLARS
31.1000 g., 0.9990 Silver 0.9988 oz. ASW, 40 mm. **Series:** Save the Whales **Obv:** Crowned bust right **Obv. Legend:** ELIZABETH II • PITCAIRN ISLANDS **Rev:** Humpback Whale and date on mother-of-pearl inset **Edge:** Plain

Date	Mintage	F	VF	XF	Unc	BU
2002 Proof	2,000	Value: 65.00				

POLAND

The Republic of Poland, located in central Europe, has an area of 120,725 sq. mi. (312,680 sq. km.) and a population of *38.2 million. Capital: Warszawa (Warsaw). The economy is essentially agricultural, but industrial activity provides the products for foreign trade. Machinery, coal, coke, iron, steel and transport equipment are exported.

MINT MARKS
MV, MW, MW-monogram - Warsaw Mint, 1965-
CHI - Valcambi, Switzerland

Other letters appearing with date denote the Mintmaster at the time the coin was struck.

REPUBLIC

Democratic

REFORM COINAGE

100 Old Zlotych = 1 Grosz; 10,000 Old Zlotych = 1 Zloty

As far back as 1990, production was initiated for the new 1 Grosz - 1 Zlotych coins for a forthcoming monetary reform. It wasn't announced until the Act of July 7, 1994 and was enacted on January 1, 1995.

Y# 276 GROSZ
1.6400 g., Brass, 15.5 mm. **Obv:** National arms **Obv. Legend:** RZECZPOSPOLITA POLSKA **Rev:** Drooping oak leaf over value **Edge:** Reeded

Date	Mintage	F	VF	XF	Unc	BU
2001MW	210,000,020	—	—	—	0.10	0.20
2002MW	240,000,000	—	—	—	0.10	0.20
2003MW	250,000,000	—	—	—	0.10	0.20
2004MW	300,000,000	—	—	—	0.10	0.20
2005MW	375,000,000	—	—	—	0.10	0.20
2007MW	—	—	—	—	0.10	0.20

Y# 277 2 GROSZE
2.1300 g., Brass, 17.5 mm. **Obv:** National arms **Obv. Legend:** RZECZPOSPOLITA POLSKA **Rev:** Drooping oak leaves above value

Date	Mintage	F	VF	XF	Unc	BU
2001MW	86,100,000	—	—	—	0.15	0.25
2002MW	83,910,000	—	—	—	0.15	0.25
2003MV	80,000,000	—	—	—	0.15	0.25
2004MW	100,000,000	—	—	—	0.15	0.25
2005MW	163,003,250	—	—	—	0.15	0.25
2007MW	—	—	—	—	0.15	0.25

Y# 278 5 GROSZY
2.5900 g., Brass, 19.5 mm. **Obv:** National arms **Obv. Legend:** RZECZPOSPOLITA POLSKA **Rev:** Value at upper left of oak leaves **Edge:** Segmented reeding

Date	Mintage	F	VF	XF	Unc	BU
2001MW	67,368,000	—	—	—	0.25	0.45
2002MW	67,200,000	—	—	—	0.25	0.45
2003MW	48,000,000	—	—	—	0.25	0.45
2004MW	62,500,000	—	—	—	0.25	0.45
2005MW	113,000,000	—	—	—	0.25	0.45
2006MW	—	—	—	—	0.25	0.45
2007MW	—	—	—	—	0.25	0.45

Y# 279 10 GROSZY
2.5100 g., Copper-Nickel, 16.5 mm. **Obv:** National arms **Obv. Legend:** RZECZPOSPOLITA POLSKA **Rev:** Value within wreath

Date	Mintage	F	VF	XF	Unc	BU
2001MW	62,820,000	—	—	—	0.40	0.60
2002MW	10,500,000	—	—	—	0.40	0.60
2003MW	31,500,000	—	—	—	0.40	0.60
2004MW	70,500,000	—	—	—	0.40	0.60
2005MW	94,000,000	—	—	—	0.40	0.60
2007MW	—	—	—	—	0.40	0.60

Y# 280 20 GROSZY
3.2200 g., Copper-Nickel, 18.5 mm. **Obv:** National arms **Obv. Legend:** RZECZPOSPOLITA POLSKA **Rev:** Value within artistic design **Edge:** Reeded

Date	Mintage	F	VF	XF	Unc	BU
2001MW	41,980,001	—	—	—	0.65	0.85
2002MW	10,500,000	—	—	—	0.65	0.85
2003MW	20,400,000	—	—	—	0.65	0.85
2004MV	40,000,025	—	—	—	0.65	0.85
2005MW	37,000,000	—	—	—	0.65	0.85
2006MW	—	—	—	—	0.65	0.85

Y# 421 2 ZLOTE
8.1000 g., Brass, 26.8 mm. **Subject:** Michal Siedlecki **Obv:** Crowned eagle with wings open **Rev:** Bust left and art work **Edge:** "NBP" eight times

Date	Mintage	F	VF	XF	Unc	BU
2001	600,000	—	—	—	3.00	5.00

Y# 422 2 ZLOTE
Brass, 26.8 mm. **Subject:** Koledicy **Obv:** Crowned eagle with wings open **Rev:** Christmas celebration scene

Date	Mintage	F	VF	XF	Unc	BU
2001	600,000	—	—	—	3.00	5.00

Y# 408 2 ZLOTE
8.1500 g., Brass, 26.8 mm. **Subject:** Wieliczka Salt Mine **Obv:** Crowned eagle with wings open **Rev:** Ancient salt miners

Date	Mintage	F	VF	XF	Unc	BU
2001	500,000	—	—	—	3.00	5.00

Y# 410 2 ZLOTE
8.1500 g., Brass, 26.8 mm. **Subject:** Amber Route **Obv:** Crowned eagle with wings open **Rev:** Ancient Roman coin and map with route marked in stars

Date	Mintage	F	VF	XF	Unc	BU
2001	500,000	—	—	—	3.00	5.00

Y# 412 2 ZLOTE
8.1500 g., Brass, 27 mm. **Subject:** 15 Years of the Constitutional Court **Obv:** Crowned eagle with wings open **Rev:** Crowned eagle head and scale **Edge:** "*NBP*" eight times

Date	Mintage	F	VF	XF	Unc	BU
2001	500,000	—	—	—	3.00	5.00

Y# 414 2 ZLOTE
8.1500 g., Brass, 27 mm. **Obv:** Crowned eagle with wings open **Rev:** Butterfly **Edge:** "*NBP*" eight times

Date	Mintage	F	VF	XF	Unc	BU
2001	600,000	—	—	—	7.00	8.00

Y# 418 2 ZLOTE
8.1500 g., Brass, 27 mm. **Subject:** Cardinal Stefan Wyszynski **Obv:** Crowned eagle with wings open **Rev:** Bust left wearing mitre **Edge:** "NBP" eight times

Date	Mintage	F	VF	XF	Unc	BU
2001	1,200,000	—	—	—	3.00	5.00

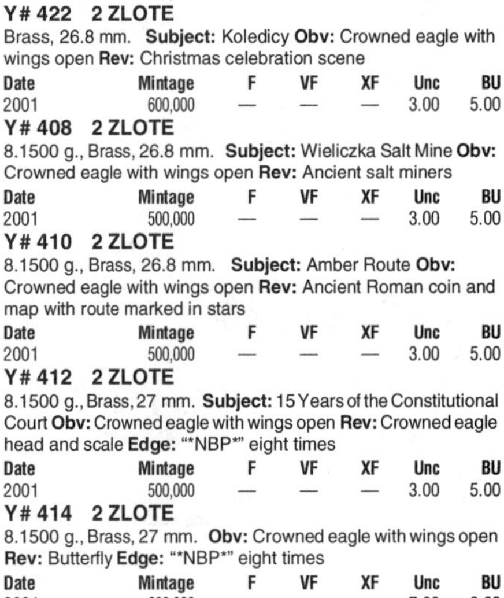

Y# 423 2 ZLOTE
8.1500 g., Brass, 26.8 mm. **Subject:** Jan III Sobieski **Obv:** Crowned eagle with wings open **Rev:** Bust facing **Edge Lettering:** *NBP* repeated

Date	Mintage	F	VF	XF	Unc	BU
2001	500,000	—	—	—	3.00	5.00

Y# 426 2 ZLOTE

8.1500 g., Brass, 26.8 mm. **Subject:** Henryk Wieniawski **Obv:** Crowned eagle with wings open **Rev:** Bust left and violin **Edge Lettering:** *NBP* repeated

Date	Mintage	F	VF	XF	Unc	BU
2001	600,000	—	—	—	3.00	5.00

Y# 427 2 ZLOTE

8.1000 g., Brass, 26.7 mm. **Obv:** Crowned eagle with wings open **Rev:** Turtles **Edge:** Lettered **Edge Lettering:** "NBP" repeatedly

Date	Mintage	F	VF	XF	Unc	BU
2002	750,000	—	—	—	6.00	10.00

Y# 431 2 ZLOTE

8.1500 g., Brass, 27 mm. **Subject:** Bronislaw Malinowski **Obv:** Crowned eagle with wings open **Rev:** Bust facing and Trobriand Islanders **Edge Lettering:** "NBP" eight times

Date	Mintage	F	VF	XF	Unc	BU
2002	680,000	—	—	—	3.50	5.50

Y# 433 2 ZLOTE

8.1500 g., Brass, 27 mm. **Subject:** World Cup Soccer **Obv:** National arms **Rev:** Soccer players **Edge Lettering:** "NBP" eight times

Date	Mintage	F	VF	XF	Unc	BU
2002	1,000,000	—	—	—	3.50	5.50

Y# 439 2 ZLOTE

8.1000 g., Brass, 26.8 mm. **Subject:** August II (1697-1706, 1709-1733) **Obv:** National arms **Rev:** Head facing **Edge Lettering:** NBP* repeated

Date	Mintage	F	VF	XF	Unc	BU
2002MW	620,000	—	—	—	3.00	5.00

Y# 440 2 ZLOTE

8.1300 g., Brass, 26.7 mm. **Subject:** Gen. Wladyslaw Anders **Obv:** Crowned eagle with wings open **Rev:** Uniformed bust facing and cross **Edge:** "NBP" repeated eight times

Date	Mintage	F	VF	XF	Unc	BU
2002MW	680,000	—	—	—	3.00	5.00

Y# 443 2 ZLOTE

8.1500 g., Brass, 26.8 mm. **Subject:** Zamek W. Malborku **Obv:** Crowned eagle with wings open **Rev:** Castle **Edge:** "*NBP*" repeatedly

Date	Mintage	F	VF	XF	Unc	BU
2002MW	680,000	—	—	—	3.00	5.00

Y# 444 2 ZLOTE

8.1300 g., Brass, 26.8 mm. **Subject:** Jan Matejko **Obv:** Denomination, crowned eagle and artist's palette **Rev:** Jester behind portrait **Edge:** "NBP" repeatedly

Date	Mintage	F	VF	XF	Unc	BU
2002MW	700,000	—	—	—	3.00	5.00

Y# 445 2 ZLOTE

8.1300 g., Brass, 26.8 mm. **Subject:** Eels **Obv:** Crowned eagle with wings open **Rev:** Two eels **Edge:** "NBP" repeatedly

Date	Mintage	F	VF	XF	Unc	BU
2003MW	—	—	—	—	5.00	9.00

Y# 446 2 ZLOTE

7.7500 g., Brass, 26.7 mm. **Subject:** Children **Obv:** Children and square design above crowned eagle, date and value **Rev:** Children on square design **Edge:** "NBP" repeatedly **Note:** minted with center hole

Date	Mintage	F	VF	XF	Unc	BU
2003MW	—	—	—	—	4.50	6.50

Y# 447 2 ZLOTE

8.1500 g., Brass, 26.8 mm. **Subject:** City of Poznan (Posen) **Obv:** Crowned eagle with wings open **Rev:** Clock face and tower flanked by goat heads **Edge:** NBP repeated eight times

Date	Mintage	F	VF	XF	Unc	BU
2003MW	—	—	—	—	4.50	6.50

Y# 451 2 ZLOTE

8.2100 g., Brass, 26.8 mm. **Subject:** Easter Monday Festival **Obv:** Crowned eagle with wings open **Rev:** Festival scene **Edge:** Lettered **Edge Lettering:** NBP eight times

Date	Mintage	F	VF	XF	Unc	BU
2003MW	—	—	—	—	3.00	5.00

Y# 455 2 ZLOTE

8.1400 g., Brass, 26.7 mm. **Subject:** Petroleum and Gas Industry 150th Anniversary **Obv:** Crowned eagle with wings open **Rev:** Portrait and refinery **Edge:** "NBP" repeated eight times

Date	Mintage	F	VF	XF	Unc	BU
2003MW	—	—	—	—	3.50	5.50

Y# 456 2 ZLOTE

8.1400 g., Brass, 26.7 mm. **Subject:** General B. S. Maczek **Obv:** Crowned eagle with wings open **Rev:** Military uniformed portrait **Edge:** "NBP" repeated eight times

Date	Mintage	F	VF	XF	Unc	BU
2003MW	600,000	—	—	—	3.00	5.00

Y# 465 2 ZLOTE

8.1700 g., Aluminum-Bronze, 26.7 mm. **Subject:** Pope John-Paul II **Obv:** Small national arms at lower right with cross in background **Obv. Inscription:** RZECZPOSPOLITA POLSKA **Rev:** Pope in prayer at left, cross in background **Edge:** Lettered **Edge Lettering:** "NBP" repeated 8 times

Date	Mintage	F	VF	XF	Unc	BU
2003MW	2,000,000	—	—	—	3.00	5.00

Y# 473 2 ZLOTE

8.1500 g., Brass, 27 mm. **Obv:** Crowned eagle with wings open **Rev:** Stanislaus Leszcywski **Edge:** Lettered **Edge Lettering:** "NBP" repeated eight times

Date	Mintage	F	VF	XF	Unc	BU
2003MW	600,000	—	—	—	3.50	5.50

Y# 477 2 ZLOTE

8.1500 g., Brass, 27 mm. **Obv:** Crowned eagle with wings open and artist's palette **Rev:** Self portrait of Jacek Malczewski **Edge:** Lettered **Edge Lettering:** "NBP" repeated eight times

Date	Mintage	F	VF	XF	Unc	BU
2003MW	600,000	—	—	—	3.50	5.50

Y# 479 2 ZLOTE

8.1500 g., Brass, 27 mm. **Subject:** 80th Anniversary of the Modern Zloty Currency **Obv:** Crowned eagle with wings open above value **Rev:** Bust left **Edge:** Lettered **Edge Lettering:** "NBP" eight times

Date	Mintage	F	VF	XF	Unc	BU
2004MW	800,000	—	—	—	3.00	5.00

Y# 481 2 ZLOTE

8.1500 g., Brass, 27 mm. **Subject:** Poland Joining the European Union **Obv:** Crowned eagle with wings open above value **Rev:** Map and stars **Edge:** Lettered **Edge Lettering:** "NBP" eight times

Date	Mintage	F	VF	XF	Unc	BU
2004MW	1,000,000	—	—	—	3.00	5.00

Y# 484 2 ZLOTE

8.1500 g., Brass, 27 mm. **Subject:** Dolnoslaskie (Lower Silesian) District **Obv:** Crowned eagle with wings open on map **Rev:** Silesian eagle on shield **Edge:** Lettered **Edge Lettering:** "NBP" eight times

Date	Mintage	F	VF	XF	Unc	BU
2004MW	700,000	—	—	—	3.00	5.00

Y# 485 2 ZLOTE

8.1500 g., Brass, 27 mm. **Subject:** Kujawsko-Pomorskie District **Obv:** Crowned eagle with wings open on map **Rev:** Shield with crowned half eagle and griffin **Edge:** Lettered **Edge Lettering:** "NBP" eight times

Date	Mintage	F	VF	XF	Unc	BU
2004MW	750,000	—	—	—	3.00	5.00

Y# 486 2 ZLOTE

8.1500 g., Brass, 27 mm. **Subject:** Lubuskie District **Obv:** Crowned eagle with wings open on map **Rev:** Shield with half eagle and two stars **Edge:** Lettered **Edge Lettering:** "NBP" eight times

Date	Mintage	F	VF	XF	Unc	BU
2004MW	820,000	—	—	—	3.00	5.00

Y# 487 2 ZLOTE

8.1500 g., Brass, 27 mm. **Subject:** Lodzkie District **Obv:** Crowned eagle with wings open on map **Rev:** Shield with two creatures above an eagle **Edge:** Lettered **Edge Lettering:** "NBP" eight times

Date	Mintage	F	VF	XF	Unc	BU
2004MW	920,000	—	—	—	3.00	5.00

Y# 488 2 ZLOTE

8.1500 g., Brass, 27 mm. **Subject:** Malopolskie District **Obv:** Crowned eagle with wings open on map **Rev:** Shield with crowned eagle **Edge:** Lettered **Edge Lettering:** "NBP" eight times

Date	Mintage	F	VF	XF	Unc	BU
2004MW	920,000	—	—	—	3.00	5.00

Y# 489 2 ZLOTE

8.1500 g., Brass, 27 mm. **Subject:** Mazowieckie District **Obv:** Crowned eagle with wings open on map **Rev:** Eagle on shield **Edge:** Lettered **Edge Lettering:** "NBP" eight times

Date	Mintage	F	VF	XF	Unc	BU
2004MW	920,000	—	—	—	3.00	5.00

Y# 490 2 ZLOTE

8.1500 g., Brass, 27 mm. **Subject:** Podkarpackie District **Obv:** Crowned eagle with wings open on map **Rev:** Shield with iron cross above griffin and lion **Edge:** Lettered **Edge Lettering:** "NBP" eight times

Date	Mintage	F	VF	XF	Unc	BU
2004MW	920,000	—	—	—	3.00	5.00

Y# 491 2 ZLOTE
8.1500 g., Brass, 27 mm. **Subject:** Podlaskie District **Obv:** Crowned eagle with wings open on map **Rev:** Shield with Polish eagle above Lithuanian knight **Edge:** Lettered **Edge Lettering:** "NBP" eight times

Date	Mintage	F	VF	XF	Unc	BU
2004MW	900,000	—	—	—	3.00	5.00

Y# 492 2 ZLOTE
8.1500 g., Brass, 27 mm. **Subject:** Pomorskie District **Obv:** Crowned eagle with wings open on map **Rev:** Griffin on shield **Edge:** Lettered **Edge Lettering:** "NBP" eight times

Date	Mintage	F	VF	XF	Unc	BU
2004MW	900,000	—	—	—	3.00	5.00

Y# 493 2 ZLOTE
8.1500 g., Brass, 27 mm. **Subject:** Slaskie (Silesia) District **Obv:** Crowned eagle with wings open on map **Rev:** Eagle on shield **Edge:** Lettered **Edge Lettering:** "NBP" eight times

Date	Mintage	F	VF	XF	Unc	BU
2004MW	960,000	—	—	—	3.00	5.00

Y# 496 2 ZLOTE
8.1500 g., Brass, 27 mm. **Subject:** Warsaw Uprising 60th Anniversary **Obv:** Crowned eagle with wings open **Rev:** Resistance symbol on brick wall **Edge Lettering:** "NBP" eight times

Date	Mintage	F	VF	XF	Unc	BU
2004MW	900,000	—	—	—	3.00	5.00

Y# 499 2 ZLOTE
8.1500 g., Brass, 27 mm. **Obv:** Crowned eagle with wings open **Rev:** Gen. Stanislaw F. Sosabowski **Edge:** Lettered **Edge Lettering:** "NBP" eight times

Date	Mintage	F	VF	XF	Unc	BU
2004MW	850,000	—	—	—	3.00	5.00

Y# 501 2 ZLOTE
8.1500 g., Brass, 27 mm. **Subject:** Polish Police 85th Anniversary **Obv:** Crowned eagle with wings open **Rev:** Police badge **Edge:** Lettered **Edge Lettering:** "NBP" eight times

Date	Mintage	F	VF	XF	Unc	BU
2004MW	760,000	—	—	—	3.00	5.00

Y# 503 2 ZLOTE
8.1500 g., Brass, 27 mm. **Subject:** Polish Senate **Obv:** Crowned eagle with wings open **Rev:** Senate eagle and speaker's staff **Edge:** Lettered **Edge Lettering:** "NBP" eight times

Date	Mintage	F	VF	XF	Unc	BU
2004MW	760,000	—	—	—	3.00	5.00

Y# 505 2 ZLOTE
8.1500 g., Brass, 27 mm. **Obv:** Crowned eagle with wings open **Rev:** Aleksander Czekanowski (1833-1876) **Edge:** Lettered **Edge Lettering:** "NBP" eight times

Date	Mintage	F	VF	XF	Unc	BU
2004MW	700,000	—	—	—	3.00	5.00

Y# 507 2 ZLOTE
8.1500 g., Brass, 26.83 mm. **Obv:** National arms **Obv. Legend:** RZECZPOSPOLITA POLSKA **Rev:** Harvest fest couple in folk costume at left, large group in background at right **Rev. Inscription:** DOZYNKI **Edge:** Lettered **Edge Lettering:** "NBP" eight times

Date	Mintage	F	VF	XF	Unc	BU
2004MW	850,000	—	—	—	3.00	5.00

Y# 509 2 ZLOTE
8.1500 g., Brass, 27 mm. **Subject:** Warsaw Fine Arts Academy Centennial **Obv:** Crowned eagle with wings open **Rev:** Painter's hands **Edge:** Lettered **Edge Lettering:** "NBP" eight times

Date	Mintage	F	VF	XF	Unc	BU
2004MW	850,000	—	—	—	3.00	5.00

Y# 512 2 ZLOTE
8.1500 g., Brass, 27 mm. **Obv:** Crowned eagle with wings open and artist's palette **Rev:** Stanislaw Wyspianski (1869-1907) **Edge:** Lettered **Edge Lettering:** "NBP" eight times

Date	Mintage	F	VF	XF	Unc	BU
2004MW	900,000	—	—	—	3.00	5.00

Y# 516 2 ZLOTE
8.1500 g., Brass, 27 mm. **Subject:** Olympics **Obv:** Crowned eagle with wings open **Rev:** Ancient runners **Edge:** Lettered **Edge Lettering:** "NBP" eight times

Date	Mintage	F	VF	XF	Unc	BU
2004MW	1,000,000	—	—	—	3.00	5.00

Y# 464 2 ZLOTE
8.1300 g., Brass, 26.8 mm. **Obv:** Crowned eagle with wings open **Rev:** Two dolphins **Edge:** Lettered **Edge Lettering:** "NBP" repeated

Date	Mintage	F	VF	XF	Unc	BU
2004MW	—	—	—	—	4.00	6.00

Y# 607 2 ZLOTE
8.1500 g., Brass, 26.79 mm. **Obv:** National arms on outlined map **Obv. Legend:** RZECZPOSPOLITA POLSKA **Rev:** Region arms **Rev. Legend:** WOJEWODZTWO - OPOLSKIE **Edge Lettering:** NBP repeated

Date	Mintage	F	VF	XF	Unc	BU
2004MW	—	—	—	—	3.00	5.00

Y# 514 2 ZLOTE
8.1500 g., Brass, 27 mm. **Obv:** National arms on outlined map **Rev:** Wojewodztwo-Lubelskie arms with stag on shield **Edge Lettering:** "NBP" eight times

Date	Mintage	F	VF	XF	Unc	BU
2004MW	—	—	—	—	—	5.00

Y# 541 2 ZLOTE
8.1500 g., Brass, 27 mm. **Obv:** Eagle, value, palette and paint brushes **Rev:** Painter Tadeusz Makowski **Edge Lettering:** "NBP" repeated eight times

Date	Mintage	F	VF	XF	Unc	BU
2005MW	900,000	—	—	—	3.00	5.00

Y# 608 2 ZLOTE
8.0600 g., Brass, 26.80 mm. **Subject:** 500th Anniversary Birth of Nikolaja Reja **Obv:** National arms **Obv. Legend:** RZECZPOSPOLITA POLSKA **Rev:** Bust of Reja facing 3/4 right **Edge Lettering:** NBP repeated

Date	Mintage	F	VF	XF	Unc	BU
2005	—	—	—	—	3.00	5.00

Y# 283 2 ZLOTE
5.2100 g., Bi-Metallic Copper-Nickel center in Brass ring, 21.5 mm. **Obv:** National arms within circle **Obv. Legend:** RZECZPOSPOLITA POLSKA **Rev:** Value flanked by oak leaves

Date	Mintage	F	VF	XF	Unc	BU
2005MW	5,000,000	—	—	—	4.00	4.50
2006MW	—	—	—	—	4.00	4.50

Y# 558 2 ZLOTE
Brass, 26.7 mm. **Subject:** 60th Anniversary of WWII **Obv:** National arms

Date	Mintage	F	VF	XF	Unc	BU
2005MW	—	—	—	—	3.00	5.00

Y# 559 2 ZLOTE
Brass, 26.7 mm. **Subject:** 500th Anniversary of Mikolaja Reja **Obv:** National arms

Date	Mintage	F	VF	XF	Unc	BU
2005MW	—	—	—	—	3.00	5.00

Y# 560 2 ZLOTE
8.0600 g., Brass, 26.79 mm. **Obv:** National arms on outline map **Obv. Legend:** RZECZPOSPOLITA POLSKA **Rev:** Region arms **Rev. Legend:** WOJEWÓDZTWO SWIETOKRZYSKIE **Edge Lettering:** NBP repeated

Date	Mintage	F	VF	XF	Unc	BU
2005MW	—	—	—	—	3.00	5.00

Y# 561 2 ZLOTE
Brass **Obv:** National arms **Rev:** Wojewodztwo Mazurskie

Date	Mintage	F	VF	XF	Unc	BU
2005MW	—	—	—	—	3.00	5.00

Y# 562 2 ZLOTE
Brass, 26.7 mm. **Obv:** National arms **Rev:** Region Wielkopolskie

Date	Mintage	F	VF	XF	Unc	BU
2005	—	—	—	—	3.00	5.00

Y# 563 2 ZLOTE
8.1100 g., Brass, 26.81 mm. **Obv:** National arms on outlined map **Obv. Legend:** RZECZPOSPOLITA POLSKA **Rev:** Region arms **Rev. Legend:** WOJEWODZTWO ZACHODIOPOMORSKIE **Edge Lettering:** NBP repeated

Date	Mintage	F	VF	XF	Unc	BU
2005MW	—	—	—	—	3.00	5.00

Y# 564 2 ZLOTE
Brass, 26.7 mm. **Obv:** National arms **Rev:** City of Gniezno

Date	Mintage	F	VF	XF	Unc	BU
2005MW	—	—	—	—	3.00	5.00

Y# 565 2 ZLOTE
Brass, 26.7 mm. **Obv:** National arms **Rev:** Solidarity

Date	Mintage	F	VF	XF	Unc	BU
2005MW	—	—	—	—	3.00	5.00

Y# 520 2 ZLOTE
8.1500 g., Brass, 26.8 mm. **Obv:** Crowned eagle with wings open **Rev:** Owl on nest with chicks **Edge:** Lettered **Edge Lettering:** "NBP" repeated eight times

Date	Mintage	F	VF	XF	Unc	BU
2005MW	990,000	—	—	—	3.50	5.50

Y# 521 2 ZLOTE
8.1500 g., Brass, 26.8 mm. **Obv:** Crowned eagle with wings open **Rev:** Ship within circle **Edge:** Lettered **Edge Lettering:** "NBP" repeatedly

Date	Mintage	F	VF	XF	Unc	BU
2005MW	—	—	—	—	3.50	5.50

Y# 522 2 ZLOTE
8.1500 g., Brass, 26.8 mm. **Subject:** Japan's Aichi Expo **Obv:**

Crowned eagle with wings open **Rev:** Two cranes flying over Mt. Fuji with rising sun background **Edge:** Lettered **Edge Lettering:** "NBP" repeatedly

Date	Mintage	F	VF	XF	Unc	BU
2005MW	—	—	—	—	3.50	5.50

Y# 524 2 ZLOTE
8.1300 g., Brass, 26.7 mm. **Subject:** Obrony Jasnej Cory **Obv:** Crowned eagle with wings open **Rev:** Half length figure left and city scene **Edge:** Lettered **Edge Lettering:** "NBP" repeatedly

Date	Mintage	F	VF	XF	Unc	BU
2005MW	—	—	—	—	4.00	6.00

Y# 525 2 ZLOTE
8.1300 g., Brass, 26.7 mm. **Subject:** Pope John-Paul II **Obv:** National arms **Obv. Legend:** RZECZPOSPOLITA POLSKA **Rev:** Bust right at left, outline of church steeple at center right **Edge:** Lettered **Edge Lettering:** "NBP" repeated 8 times

Date	Mintage	F	VF	XF	Unc	BU
2005MW	4,000,000	—	—	—	4.00	6.00

Y# 527 2 ZLOTE
8.2000 g., Brass, 26.7 mm. **Obv:** Crowned eagle with wings open **Rev:** Bust 1/4 left with horse head and goose at left **Edge Lettering:** "NBP" repeatedly

Date	Mintage	F	VF	XF	Unc	BU
2005MW	—	—	—	—	3.00	5.00

Y# 528 2 ZLOTE
8.2000 g., Brass, 26.7 mm. **Obv:** Crowned eagle above wall **Rev:** Kolobrzeg Lighthouse **Edge Lettering:** "NBP" repeatedly

Date	Mintage	F	VF	XF	Unc	BU
2005MW	—	—	—	—	3.00	5.00

Y# 529 2 ZLOTE
8.2000 g., Brass, 26.7 mm. **Obv:** Crowned eagle with wings open above wall **Rev:** Cathedral **Edge Lettering:** "NBP" repeatedly

Date	Mintage	F	VF	XF	Unc	BU
2005MW	—	—	—	—	3.00	5.00

Y# 530 2 ZLOTE
8.2000 g., Brass, 26.7 mm. **Obv:** Crowned eagle with wings open **Rev:** Bust right **Edge Lettering:** "NBP" repeatedly

Date	Mintage	F	VF	XF	Unc	BU
2005MW	990,000	—	—	—	3.00	5.00

Y# 532 2 ZLOTE
8.1500 g., Copper-Aluminum-Zinc-Tin, 27 mm. **Obv:** National arms **Rev:** St. John's Night dancer **Edge Lettering:** NBP repeated

Date	Mintage	F	VF	XF	Unc	BU
2006MW	1,000,000	—	—	—	—	4.00

Y# 534 2 ZLOTE
8.1500 g., Copper-Aluminum-Zinc-Tin, 27 mm. **Obv:** National arms **Rev:** Alpine Marmot standing **Edge Lettering:** NBP repeated eight times

Date	Mintage	F	VF	XF	Unc	BU
2006MW	1,400,000	—	—	—	—	4.00

Y# 566 2 ZLOTE
Brass, 26.7 mm. **Obv:** National arms **Rev:** City of Jaroslaw

Date	Mintage	F	VF	XF	Unc	BU
2006MW	—	—	—	—	3.00	5.00

Y# 567 2 ZLOTE
Brass, 26.7 mm. **Obv:** National arms **Rev:** 2006 Olympic Games Turin

Date	Mintage	F	VF	XF	Unc	BU
2006MW	—	—	—	—	3.00	5.00

Y# 569 2 ZLOTE
Brass, 26.7 mm. **Obv:** National arms **Rev:** Castle Zagan

Date	Mintage	F	VF	XF	Unc	BU
2006MW	—	—	—	—	3.00	5.00

Y# 570 2 ZLOTE
Brass, 26.7 mm. **Obv:** National arms above gateway **Rev:** City of Nysa **Edge Lettering:** NBP repeated

Date	Mintage	F	VF	XF	Unc	BU
2006MW	—	—	—	—	5.00	3.00

Y# 571 2 ZLOTE
Brass, 26.7 mm. **Subject:** 30th Anniversary of June 1976 **Obv:** National arms

Date	Mintage	F	VF	XF	Unc	BU
2006MW	—	—	—	—	3.00	5.00

Y# 575 2 ZLOTE
8.1300 g., Brass, 26.78 mm. **Subject:** Aleksander Gierymski (painter) **Obv:** Palette, brushes at left, national arms at right **Obv. Legend:** RZECZPOSPOLITA POLSKA **Rev:** Bust of Gierymski facing at left, coastline village in background **Edge Lettering:** NBP repeated

Date	Mintage	F	VF	XF	Unc	BU
2006MW	—	—	—	—	3.00	5.00

Y# 609 2 ZLOTE
8.1300 g., Brass, 26.79 mm. **Subject:** 100th Anniversary Warsaw School of Economics **Obv:** National arms **Obv. Legend:** RZECZPOSPOLITA POLSKA **Rev:** School facade **Rev. Legend:** SZKOLA CLOWNA HANDLOWA W WARSZAWIE **Rev. Inscription:** Large SGH **Edge Lettering:** NBP repeated

Date	Mintage	F	VF	XF	Unc	BU
2006MW	—	—	—	—	3.00	5.00

Y# 543 2 ZLOTE
8.1300 g., Brass, 26.7 mm. **Obv:** Polish Eagle above castle gate **Rev:** Bochnia church **Edge Lettering:** NBP repeatedly

Date	Mintage	F	VF	XF	Unc	BU
2006MW	1,100,000	—	—	—	3.00	5.00

Y# 544 2 ZLOTE
8.1300 g., Brass, 26.7 mm. **Obv:** Polish Eagle above castle gate **Rev:** Chelm church **Edge Lettering:** NBP repeatedly

Date	Mintage	F	VF	XF	Unc	BU
2006MW	1,100,000	—	—	—	3.00	5.00

Y# 545 2 ZLOTE
8.1300 g., Brass, 26.7 mm. **Obv:** Polish Eagle above castle gate **Rev:** Chelmno Palace **Edge Lettering:** NBP repeatedly

Date	Mintage	F	VF	XF	Unc	BU
2006MW	1,100,000	—	—	—	3.00	5.00

Y# 546 2 ZLOTE
8.1300 g., Brass, 26.7 mm. **Obv:** Polish Eagle above castle gate **Rev:** Elblag tower **Edge Lettering:** NBP repeatedly

Date	Mintage	F	VF	XF	Unc	BU
2006MW	1,100,000	—	—	—	3.00	5.00

Y# 547 2 ZLOTE
8.1300 g., Brass, 26.7 mm. **Obv:** Polish Eagle above castle gate **Rev:** Kosciol W. Haczowie church **Edge Lettering:** NBP repeatedly

Date	Mintage	F	VF	XF	Unc	BU
2006MW	—	—	—	—	3.00	5.00

Y# 548 2 ZLOTE
8.1300 g., Brass, 26.7 mm. **Obv:** Polish Eagle above castle gate **Rev:** Legnica tower and building **Edge Lettering:** NBP repeatedly

Date	Mintage	F	VF	XF	Unc	BU
2006MW	—	—	—	—	3.00	5.00

Y# 549 2 ZLOTE

8.1300 g., Brass, 26.7 mm. **Obv:** Polish Eagle above castle gate **Rev:** Pszczyna palace **Edge Lettering:** NBP repeatedly

Date	Mintage	F	VF	XF	Unc	BU
2006MW	1,100,000	—	—	—	3.00	5.00

Y# 550 2 ZLOTE

8.1300 g., Brass, 26.7 mm. **Obv:** Polish Eagle above castle gate **Rev:** Sandomierz palace **Edge Lettering:** NBP repeatedly

Date	Mintage	F	VF	XF	Unc	BU
2006MW	1,100,000	—	—	—	3.00	5.00

Y# 551 2 ZLOTE

8.1300 g., Brass, 26.7 mm. **Obv:** National arms above castle gate **Rev:** Soccer ball **Edge Lettering:** NBP repeatedly

Date	Mintage	F	VF	XF	Unc	BU
2006MW	—	—	—	—	3.00	5.00

Y# 576 2 ZLOTE

8.2000 g., Brass, 26.7 mm. **Obv:** National arms **Rev:** Knight on horseback **Edge Lettering:** NBP repeated

Date	Mintage	F	VF	XF	Unc	BU
2006MW	—	—	—	—	3.00	5.00

Y# 582 2 ZLOTE

8.1300 g., Brass, 26.8 mm. **Obv:** National arms **Obv. Legend:** RZECZPOSPOLITA POLSKA **Rev:** Old Y-20 Queen's fead left coin design from the 1930's **Edge Lettering:** "NPB" repeatedly

Date	Mintage	F	VF	XF	Unc	BU
2006MW	—	—	—	—	3.00	5.00

Y# 573 2 ZLOTE

8.1600 g., Brass, 26.7 mm. **Obv:** Polish eagle above wall **Rev:** Nowy Sacz church **Edge Lettering:** "NBP" eight times

Date	Mintage	F	VF	XF	Unc	BU
2006MW	—	—	—	—	3.00	5.00

Y# 574 2 ZLOTE

8.1600 g., Brass, 26.7 mm. **Subject:** 500th Anniversary of the Publication of the Statute by Laski **Obv:** Polish eagle above value **Rev:** Jan Lashjego and book **Edge Lettering:** "NBP" eight times

Date	Mintage	F	VF	XF	Unc	BU
2006MW	—	—	—	—	3.00	5.00

Y# 580 2 ZLOTE

8.1600 g., Brass, 26.7 mm. **Obv:** Polish eagle above wall **Rev:** Kalisz building **Edge Lettering:** "NBP" eight times

Date	Mintage	F	VF	XF	Unc	BU
2006MW	—	—	—	—	3.00	5.00

Y# 605 2 ZLOTE

8.2000 g., Brass, 26.80 mm. **Obv:** National arms **Obv. Legend:** RZECZPOSPOLITA POLSKA **Rev:** Skier and marksman standing **Rev. Legend:** XX ZIMOWE IGAZYSKA OLIMPIJSKIE **Rev. Inscription:** TURYN **Edge:** NBP repeatedly

Date	Mintage	F	VF	XF	Unc	BU
2006MW	—	—	—	—	3.00	5.00

Y# 606 2 ZLOTE

8.3000 g., Brass, 26.81 mm. **Obv:** National arms **Obv. Legend:** RZECZPOSPOLITA POLSKA **Rev:** Large soccer ball with fancy linked date 2006 **Rev. Legend:** MISTRZOSTWA SWIATA W PItCE NOZNEJ NIEMCY - FIFA **Edge:** NBP repeatedly

Date	Mintage	F	VF	XF	Unc	BU
2006MW	—	—	—	—	3.00	5.00

Y# 577 2 ZLOTE

8.1500 g., Brass, 27 mm. **Obv:** Crowned eagle **Rev:** Kwidzyn Castle **Edge Lettering:** "NBP" eight times

Date	Mintage	F	VF	XF	Unc	BU
2007MW	1,000,000	—	—	—	3.00	5.00

Y# 578 2 ZLOTE

8.1500 g., Brass, 27 mm. **Obv:** Crowned eagle **Rev:** Grey Seal and silhouette **Edge Lettering:** "NBP" eight times

Date	Mintage	F	VF	XF	Unc	BU
2007MW	1,000,000	—	—	—	3.00	5.00

Y# 590 2 ZLOTE

8.0200 g., Brass, 26.80 mm. **Obv:** National arms **Obv. Legend:** RZECZPOSPOLITA POLSKA **Rev:** Bust of Dozmeyko facing **Rev. Legend:** IGNACY DOMEYKO 1802 - 1889 **Edge Lettering:** NBP repeated

Date	Mintage	F	VF	XF	Unc	BU
2007MW	—	—	—	—	3.00	5.00

Y# 592 2 ZLOTE

8.1500 g., Brass, 26.77 mm. **Subject:** History of Zloty **Obv:** Nike at left, obverse of 5 Zlotych, Y#18, national arms below **Obv. Legend:** RZECZPOLPOLITA POLSKA **Rev:** Spray at left of reverse of 5 Zlotych, Y# 18 **Edge Lettering:** NBP repeated

Date	Mintage	F	VF	XF	Unc	BU
2007MW	—	—	—	—	3.00	5.00

Y# 594 2 ZLOTE

8.0800 g., Brass, 26.78 mm. **Subject:** 750th Anniversary Municipality of Krakau **Obv:** National arms **Obv. Legend:** RZECZPOSPOLITA POLSKA **Rev:** Knight standing facing with spear and shield **Edge Lettering:** NBP repeated

Date	Mintage	F	VF	XF	Unc	BU
2007MW	—	—	—	—	3.00	5.00

Y# 610 2 ZLOTE

8.1800 g., Brass, 26.78 mm. **Subject:** Artic Explorers Antoni B. Dombrowolski and Henryk Arctowski **Obv:** National arms **Obv. Legend:** RZCEZPOSPOLITA POLSKA **Rev:** Explorer's bust facing at bottom, sailing ship in background **Edge Lettering:** NBP repeated

Date	Mintage	F	VF	XF	Unc	BU
2007MW	—	—	—	—	3.00	5.00

Y# 611 2 ZLOTE

8.1400 g., Brass, 26.77 mm. **Obv:** National arms **Obv. Legend:** RZECZPOSPOLIYA POLSKA **Rev:** Ciezkozbrojny in armor, horseback left **Rev. Legend:** RYCERZ CIEZKOZBROJNY-XV **Edge Lettering:** NBP repeated

Date	Mintage	F	VF	XF	Unc	BU
2007MW	—	—	—	—	3.00	5.00

Y# 612 2 ZLOTE

8.2400 g., Brass, 26.79 mm. **Subject:** 70th Anniversary Death of Szymanowskiego **Obv:** National arms **Obv. Legend:** RZECZPOSPOLITA POLSKA **Rev:** Bust facing 3/4 right at left, music score in background **Rev. Legend:** ROCZNICA URODZIN KAROLA SYMANOWSKIEGO **Edge Lettering:** NBP repeated

Date	Mintage	F	VF	XF	Unc	BU
2007MW	—	—	—	—	3.00	5.00

Y# 613 2 ZLOTE

8.2600 g., Brass, 26.79 mm. **Obv:** National arms above gateway **Obv. Legend:** RZECZPOSPOLITA POLSKA **Rev:** Buildings **Rev. Legend:** STARGARD - SZCZECINSKI **Edge Lettering:** NBP repeated

Date	Mintage	F	VF	XF	Unc	BU
2007MW	—	—	—	—	3.00	5.00

Y# 614 2 ZLOTE

8.1100 g., Brass, 26.78 mm. **Obv:** National arms on outlined map **Obv. Legend:** RZECZPOSPOLITA POLSKA **Rev:** Region arms **Rev. Legend:** WOJEWÓDZTWO WARMINSKO-MAZURSKIE **Edge Lettering:** NBP repeated

Date	Mintage	F	VF	XF	Unc	BU
2007MW	—	—	—	—	3.00	5.00

Y# 615 2 ZLOTE

8.2000 g., Brass, 26.80 mm. **Obv:** National arms above gateway **Obv. Legend:** RZECZPOSPOLITA POLSKA **Rev:** Building with branches at left and right **Rev. Legend:** BRZEG **Edge Lettering:** NBP repeated

Date	Mintage	F	VF	XF	Unc	BU
2007MW	—	—	—	—	3.00	5.00

Y# 616 2 ZLOTE

8.2300 g., Brass, 26.80 mm. **Obv:** National arms above gateway **Obv. Legend:** RZECZPOSPOLITA POLSKA **Rev:** Church **Rev. Legend:** LOMZA **Edge Lettering:** NBP repeated

Date	Mintage	F	VF	XF	Unc	BU
2007MW	—	—	—	—	3.00	5.00

Y# 617 2 ZLOTE

8.1900 g., Brass, 26.80 mm. **Obv:** National arms above gateway **Obv. Legend:** RZECZPOSPOLITA POLSKA **Rev:** Church **Rev. Legend:** PLOCK **Edge Lettering:** NBP repeated

Date	Mintage	F	VF	XF	Unc	BU
2007MW	—	—	—	—	3.00	5.00

Y# 618 2 ZLOTE

8.0700 g., Brass, 26.79 mm. **Obv:** National arms above gateway **Obv. Legend:** RZECZPOSPOLITA POLSKA **Rev:** Church **Rev. Legend:** PRZEMYSL **Edge Lettering:** NBP repeated

Date	Mintage	F	VF	XF	Unc	BU
2007MW	—	—	—	—	3.00	5.00

Y# 619 2 ZLOTE

8.0900 g., Brass, 26.81 mm. **Obv:** National arms above gateway **Obv. Legend:** RZECZPOSPOLITA POLSKA **Rev:** Towered gateway **Rev. Inscription:** RACIBÓRZ **Edge Lettering:** NBP repeated

Date	Mintage	F	VF	XF	Unc	BU
2007MW	—	—	—	—	3.00	5.00

Y# 620 2 ZLOTE

8.2100 g., Brass, 26.79 mm. **Obv:** National arms above gateway **Obv. Legend:** RZECZPOSPOLITA POLSKA **Rev:** Church **Rev. Legend:** SLUPSK **Edge Lettering:** NBP repeated

Date	Mintage	F	VF	XF	Unc	BU
2007MW	—	—	—	—	3.00	5.00

Y# 621 2 ZLOTE

8.0700 g., Brass, 26.78 mm. **Obv:** National arms above gateway **Obv. Legend:** RZECZPOSPOLITA POLSKA **Rev:** Church **Rev. Inscription:** SWIDNICA **Edge Lettering:** NBP repeated

Date	Mintage	F	VF	XF	Unc	BU
2007MW	—	—	—	—	3.00	5.00

Y# 622 2 ZLOTE

8.0200 g., Brass, 26.78 mm. **Obv:** National arms **Obv. Legend:** RZECZPOSPOLITA POLSKE **Rev:** Chuches **Rev. Legend:** MIASTO SREDNIOWIECZNE - W TORUNIU **Edge Lettering:** NBP repeated

Date	Mintage	F	VF	XF	Unc	BU
2007MW	—	—	—	—	3.00	5.00

Y# 623 2 ZLOTE

8.0700 g., Brass, 26.80 mm. **Obv:** National arms above gateway **Obv. Legend:** RZECZPOSPOLITA POLSKA **Rev:** Church **Rev. Legend:** GORZÓW WIELKOPOLSKI **Edge Lettering:** NBP repeated

Date	Mintage	F	VF	XF	Unc	BU
2007MW	—	—	—	—	3.00	5.00

Y# 624 2 ZLOTE

8.2000 g., Brass, 26.78 mm. **Obv:** National arms above gateway **Obv. Legend:** RZECZPOSPOLITA POLSKA **Rev:** Church at lower right, houses to left, fortress in upper background **Rev. Inscription:** KLODZKO **Edge Lettering:** NBP repeated

Date	Mintage	F	VF	XF	Unc	BU
2007MW	—	—	—	—	3.00	5.00

Y# 625 2 ZLOTE

8.2200 g., Brass, 26.77 mm. **Obv:** National arms above gateway **Obv. Legend:** RZECZPOSPOLITA POLSKE **Rev:** Church **Rev. Legend:** TARNÓW **Edge Lettering:** BNP repeated

Date	Mintage	F	VF	XF	Unc	BU
2007MW	—	—	—	—	3.00	5.00

Y# 626 2 ZLOTE

8.2200 g., Brass, 26.79 mm. **Subject:** Leon Wyczótkowski **Obv:** Artist's palette, brushes at left, national arms at right **Obv. Legend:** RZECZPOSPOLITA POLSKE **Rev:** Bust facing **Edge Lettering:** NBP repeated

Date	Mintage	F	VF	XF	Unc	BU
2007MW	—	—	—	—	3.00	5.00

Y# 406 10 ZLOTYCH

14.1400 g., 0.9250 Silver 0.4205 oz. ASW **Subject:** Year 2001 **Obv:** Crowned eagle with wings open **Rev:** Printed circuit board

Date	Mintage	F	VF	XF	Unc	BU
2001MW Proof	35,000	Value: 30.00				

Y# 413 10 ZLOTYCH

14.1400 g., 0.9250 Silver 0.4205 oz. ASW, 32 mm. **Subject:** 15 Years of the Constitutional Court **Obv:** Crowned eagle suspended from a judge's neck chain **Rev:** Crowned eagle head and balance scale **Edge Lettering:** "TRYBUNAL KONSTYTUCYJNY W SLUZBIE PANSTWA PRAWA"

Date	Mintage	F	VF	XF	Unc	BU
2001MW Proof	25,000	Value: 28.00				

Y# 419 10 ZLOTYCH
14.1400 g., 0.9250 Silver 0.4205 oz. ASW, 32 mm. **Subject:** Cardinal Stefan Wyszynski **Obv:** Crowned eagle with wings open above ribbon **Rev:** Half length figure facing with raised hands **Edge Lettering:** "100.ROCZNIA URODZIN"

Date	Mintage	F	VF	XF	Unc	BU
2001MW Proof	60,000	Value: 30.00				

Y# 425 10 ZLOTYCH
14.2100 g., 0.9250 Silver 0.4226 oz. ASW, 32 mm. **Subject:** Jan III Sobieski **Obv:** Crowned eagle with wings open **Rev:** 3/4 armored bust facing with army in background **Edge:** Plain

Date	Mintage	F	VF	XF	Unc	BU
2001MW Proof	24,000	Value: 32.50				

Y# 458 10 ZLOTYCH
14.1400 g., 0.9250 Silver 0.4205 oz. ASW, 32 mm. **Obv:** Crowned eagle with wings open **Rev:** Jan Sobieski, type II **Edge:** Plain

Date	Mintage	F	VF	XF	Unc	BU
2001MW Proof	17,000	Value: 45.00				

Y# 459 10 ZLOTYCH
14.1400 g., 0.9250 Silver 0.4205 oz. ASW, 32 mm. **Obv:** Three violins **Rev:** Henryk Wieniawski **Edge:** Plain

Date	Mintage	F	VF	XF	Unc	BU
2001MW Proof	28,000	Value: 40.00				

Y# 460 10 ZLOTYCH
14.1400 g., 0.9250 Silver 0.4205 oz. ASW, 32 mm. **Obv:** Crowned eagle with wings open above fish **Rev:** Michal Siedlecki **Edge:** Plain

Date	Mintage	F	VF	XF	Unc	BU
2001MW Proof	26,000	Value: 40.00				

Y# 461 10 ZLOTYCH
14.1400 g., 0.9250 Silver 0.4205 oz. ASW, 32 mm. **Obv:** Crowned eagle with wings open **Rev:** August II **Edge:** Plain

Date	Mintage	F	VF	XF	Unc	BU
2002MW Proof	30,000	Value: 30.00				

Y# 432 10 ZLOTYCH
14.1400 g., 0.9250 Silver 0.4205 oz. ASW, 32 mm. **Subject:** Bronislaw Malinowski **Obv:** Small crowned eagle with wings open to right of bust facing **Rev:** Trobriand Islands village scene **Edge Lettering:** "etnolog, antropolog kultury"

Date	Mintage	F	VF	XF	Unc	BU
2002MW Proof	33,500	Value: 25.00				

Y# 434 10 ZLOTYCH
14.1400 g., 0.9250 Silver 0.4205 oz. ASW, 32 mm. **Subject:** World Cup Soccer **Obv:** Crowned eagle with wings open **Rev:** Soccer player **Edge Lettering:** "etnolog, antropolog kultury"

Date	Mintage	F	VF	XF	Unc	BU
2002MW Proof	55,000	Value: 22.50				

Y# 435 10 ZLOTYCH
14.1400 g., 0.9250 Silver 0.4205 oz. ASW, 32 mm. **Subject:** World Cup Soccer **Obv:** Amber soccer ball inset entering goal net **Rev:** Two soccer players with amber soccer ball inset **Edge Lettering:** "etnolog, antropolog kultury"

Date	Mintage	F	VF	XF	Unc	BU
2002MW Proof	65,000	Value: 25.00				

Y# 437 10 ZLOTYCH
14.1400 g., 0.9250 Silver 0.4205 oz. ASW, 32 mm. **Subject:** Pope John Paul II **Obv:** Crowned eagle with wings open within two views of praying Pope **Rev:** Pope facing radiant Holy Door **Edge:** Plain

Date	Mintage	F	VF	XF	Unc	BU
2002MW Proof	80,000	Value: 27.50				

Y# 441 10 ZLOTYCH
14.2000 g., 0.9250 Silver 0.4223 oz. ASW, 32 mm. **Subject:** Gen. Wladyslaw Anders **Obv:** Crowned eagle with wings open, cross and multicolor flowers **Rev:** Uniformed bust right **Edge:** Plain

Date	Mintage	F	VF	XF	Unc	BU
2002MW Proof	40,000	Value: 35.00				

Y# 450 10 ZLOTYCH
14.1400 g., 0.9250 Silver 0.4205 oz. ASW, 32 mm. **Subject:** August II (1697-1706, 1709-1735) **Obv:** Crowned eagle with wings open **Rev:** Portrait and Order of the White Eagle **Edge:** Plain

Date	Mintage	F	VF	XF	Unc	BU
2002MW Proof	—	Value: 25.00				

Y# 453 10 ZLOTYCH
14.1400 g., 0.9250 Silver 0.4205 oz. ASW, 32 mm. **Subject:** Great Orchestra of Christmas Charity **Obv:** Large inscribed heart above crowned eagle with wings open **Rev:** Boy playing flute **Edge:** Plain

Date	Mintage	F	VF	XF	Unc	BU
2003MW Proof	47,000	Value: 25.00				

Y# 468 10 ZLOTYCH
14.1400 g., 0.9250 Silver 0.4205 oz. ASW, 32 mm. **Obv:** Tanks on battlefield **Rev:** General Maczek **Edge:** Plain

Date	Mintage	F	VF	XF	Unc	BU
2003MW Proof	44,000	Value: 25.00				

Y# 469 10 ZLOTYCH
14.1400 g., 0.9250 Silver 0.4205 oz. ASW, 32 mm. **Subject:** Gas and Oil Industry **Obv:** Crowned eagle and highway leading to city view **Rev:** Portrait and refinery **Edge:** Plain

Date	Mintage	F	VF	XF	Unc	BU
2003MW Proof	43,000	Value: 25.00				

Y# 474 10 ZLOTYCH
14.1400 g., 0.9250 Silver 0.4205 oz. ASW, 32 mm. **Obv:** Crowned eagle with wings open **Rev:** Stanislaus I and wife's portrait **Edge:** Plain

Date	Mintage	F	VF	XF	Unc	BU
2003MW Proof	45,000	Value: 25.00				

Y# 475 10 ZLOTYCH
14.1400 g., 0.9250 Silver 0.4205 oz. ASW, 32 mm. **Obv:** Crowned eagle with wings open **Rev:** Half-length figure of Stanislaus I with his wife in background **Edge:** Plain

Date	Mintage	F	VF	XF	Unc	BU
2003MW Proof	40,000	Value: 25.00				

Y# 448 10 ZLOTYCH
14.1400 g., 0.9250 Silver 0.4205 oz. ASW, 32 mm. **Subject:** City of Poznan (Posen) **Obv:** Old coin design and arched door **Rev:** Old coin design and city view **Edge:** Plain

Date	Mintage	F	VF	XF	Unc	BU
2003MW Proof	—	Value: 25.00				

Y# 480 10 ZLOTYCH
14.1400 g., 0.9250 Silver 0.4205 oz. ASW, 32 mm. **Subject:** 80th Anniversary of the Modern Zloty Currency **Obv:** Man wearing glasses behind crowned eagle with wings open **Rev:** Bust left **Edge:** Plain

Date	Mintage	F	VF	XF	Unc	BU
2004MW Proof	55,000	Value: 25.00				

Y# 482 10 ZLOTYCH
14.1400 g., 0.9250 Silver 0.4205 oz. ASW, 32 mm. **Subject:** Poland Joining the European Union **Obv:** Crowned eagle in blue circle with yellow stars **Rev:** Multicolor European Union and Polish flags **Edge:** Plain

Date	Mintage	F	VF	XF	Unc	BU
2004MW Proof	78,000	Value: 25.00				

Y# 497 10 ZLOTYCH
14.1400 g., 0.9250 Silver 0.4205 oz. ASW, 32 mm. **Subject:** Warsaw Uprising 60th Anniversary **Obv:** Crowned eagle and value on resistance symbol **Rev:** Polish soldier wearing captured German helmet **Edge:** Plain

Date	Mintage	F	VF	XF	Unc	BU
2004MW Proof	92,000	Value: 25.00				

Y# 500 10 ZLOTYCH
14.1400 g., 0.9250 Silver 0.4205 oz. ASW, 32 mm. **Obv:** Polish paratrooper badge **Rev:** Gen. Sosabowski and descending paratrooper **Edge:** Plain

Date	Mintage	F	VF	XF	Unc	BU
2004MW Proof	56,000	Value: 25.00				

Y# 502 10 ZLOTYCH
14.1400 g., 0.9250 Silver 0.4205 oz. ASW, 32 mm. **Subject:** Polish Police 85th Anniversary **Obv:** Crowned eagle with wings open **Rev:** Seal partially overlapping police badge **Edge:** Plain

Date	Mintage	F	VF	XF	Unc	BU
2004MW Proof	65,000	Value: 25.00				

Y# 506 10 ZLOTYCH
14.1400 g., 0.9250 Silver 0.4205 oz. ASW, 32 mm. **Obv:** Siberian landscape above crowned eagle and value **Rev:** Aleksander Czekanowski (1833-1876) **Edge:** Plain

Date	Mintage	F	VF	XF	Unc	BU
2004MW Proof	45,000	Value: 25.00				

Y# 510 10 ZLOTYCH

14.1400 g., 0.9250 Silver 0.4205 oz. ASW, 32 mm. **Subject:** Warsaw Fine Arts Academy Centennial **Obv:** Crowned eagle with wings open within city square **Rev:** Art studio **Edge:** Plain

Date	Mintage	F	VF	XF	Unc	BU
2004MW Proof	75,000	Value: 25.00				

Y# 517 10 ZLOTYCH

14.1400 g., 0.9250 Silver 0.4205 oz. ASW, 32 mm. **Subject:** Olympics **Obv:** Crowned eagle with wings open and woman **Rev:** Fencers in front of Parthenon **Edge:** Plain

Date	Mintage	F	VF	XF	Unc	BU
2004MW Proof	70,000	Value: 25.00				

Y# 518 10 ZLOTYCH

14.1400 g., 0.9250 Silver 0.4205 oz. ASW, 32 mm. **Subject:** Olympics **Obv:** Crowned eagle with wings open within gold plated center **Rev:** Ancient athlete within gold plated circle **Edge:** Plain

Date	Mintage	F	VF	XF	Unc	BU
2004MW Proof	90,000	Value: 35.00				

Y# 523 10 ZLOTYCH

14.2300 g., 0.9250 Silver 0.4232 oz. ASW, 43.2 x 29.2 mm. **Subject:** Japan's Aichi Expo **Obv:** Monument **Rev:** Two cranes **Edge:** Plain **Shape:** Quarter of circle

Date	Mintage	F	VF	XF	Unc	BU
2005MW Proof	—	Value: 50.00				

Y# 526 10 ZLOTYCH

14.1400 g., 0.9250 Silver 0.4205 oz. ASW, 32.1 mm. **Obv:** Crowned eagle with wings open above date and grasping hands **Rev:** Gold plated bust right and church **Edge:** Plain, Gold plated

Date	Mintage	F	VF	XF	Unc	BU
2005MW Proof	—	Value: 30.00				

Y# 537 10 ZLOTYCH

14.1400 g., 0.9250 Silver 0.4205 oz. ASW, 32 mm. **Obv:** Horse drawn carriage **Rev:** Green duck and Konstanty Ildefons Galczynski in top hat **Edge:** Plain

Date	Mintage	F	VF	XF	Unc	BU
2005MW Proof	62,000	Value: 25.00				

Y# 539 10 ZLOTYCH

14.1400 g., 0.9250 Silver 0.4205 oz. ASW, 32 mm. **Obv:** Baptismal font and Polish eagle **Rev:** Pope John Paul II and St. Peters Basilica **Edge:** Plain

Date	Mintage	F	VF	XF	Unc	BU
2005MW Proof	170,000	Value: 30.00				

Y# 552 10 ZLOTYCH

14.1400 g., 0.9250 Silver 0.4205 oz. ASW, 32 mm. **Obv:** Crowned eagle above value **Rev:** Stanislaw August Poniatowski and shadow **Edge:** Plain

Date	Mintage	F	VF	XF	Unc	BU
2005MW Proof	—	Value: 30.00				

Y# 553 10 ZLOTYCH

14.1400 g., 0.9250 Silver 0.4205 oz. ASW, 32 mm. **Obv:** Crowned eagle above value **Rev:** Stanislaw August Poniatowski and crowned monogram **Edge:** Plain

Date	Mintage	F	VF	XF	Unc	BU
2005MW Proof	—	Value: 30.00				

Y# 554 10 ZLOTYCH

14.1400 g., 0.9250 Silver 0.4205 oz. ASW, 32 mm. **Subject:** End of WWII 60th Anniversary **Obv:** Crowned eagle above soldier silhouettes and value **Rev:** City view in ruins above bird with green sprig **Edge:** Plain

Date	Mintage	F	VF	XF	Unc	BU
2005MW Proof	—	Value: 35.00				

Y# 568 10 ZLOTYCH

14.1400 g., 0.9250 Silver 0.4205 oz. ASW, 32 mm. **Obv:** Sail ship and obverse design of Y-31 **Rev:** Reverse design of Y-31 on radiant design **Edge:** Lettered

Date	Mintage	F	VF	XF	Unc	BU
2005MW Proof	—	Value: 30.00				

Y# 596 10 ZLOTYCH

14.1800 g., 0.9250 Silver 0.4217 oz. ASW, 32.06 mm. **Subject:** 500th Anniversary Birth of M. Reja **Obv:** National arms in oval, value below **Obv. Legend:** RZECZPOSPOLITA POLSKA **Rev:** Bust of Reja 3/4 right **Rev. Legend:** 500. ROCZNICA URODZIN MIKOLAJA REJA **Edge:** Plain

Date	Mintage	F	VF	XF	Unc	BU
2005MW Proof	—	Value: 25.00				

Y# 598 10 ZLOTYCH

14.1500 g., 0.9250 Silver 0.4208 oz. ASW, 32.05 mm. **Subject:** 3oth Anniversary June 1976 **Obv:** National arms divides denomination, split railroad tracks below **Obv. Legend:** RZECZPOSPOLITA POLSKA **Rev:** 3/4 length woman standing with child, outlined row of shielded forces in background **Rev. Legend:** 30. ROCZNICA - CZERWCA 1976 **Edge:** Plain

Date	Mintage	F	VF	XF	Unc	BU
2006MW Proof	—	Value: 30.00				

Y# 599 10 ZLOTYCH

14.1800 g., 0.9250 Silver 0.4217 oz. ASW, 32.07 mm. **Series:** History of the Zloty **Obv:** National arms at upper left, 1932 dated 10 Zlotych obverse at lower right, building facade in background **Obv. Legend:** RZECZPOSPOLITA POLSKA **Rev:** Reverse of 1932 dated coin with head of Queen Jadwiga **Rev. Legend:** DZIEJE ZLOTEGO **Edge:** Plain

Date	Mintage	F	VF	XF	Unc	BU
2006MW Proof	—	Value: 30.00				

Y# 583 10 ZLOTYCH

Subject: 30th Anniversary of June 1976 **Obv:** National arms **Rev:** Mother and child in front of riot police line **Edge:** Plain

Date	Mintage	F	VF	XF	Unc	BU
2006MW Proof	—	Value: 30.00				

Y# 555 10 ZLOTYCH

14.1400 g., 0.9250 Silver 0.4205 oz. ASW, 32 mm. **Subject:** 2006 Winter Olympics **Obv:** Snow boarder above crowned eagle **Rev:** Snow boarder **Edge:** Plain

Date	Mintage	F	VF	XF	Unc	BU
2006MW Proof	—	Value: 30.00				

Y# 556 10 ZLOTYCH

14.1400 g., 0.9250 Silver 0.4205 oz. ASW, 32.03 mm. **Subject:** 2006 Winter Olympics **Obv:** Small national arms at left, figure skating couple at center **Obv. Legend:** RZECZPOSPOLITA POLSKA **Rev:** Female figure skater **Rev. Legend:** XX ZIMOWE IGRZYSKA OLIMPIJSKIE **Edge:** Plain

Date	Mintage	F	VF	XF	Unc	BU
2006MW Proof	—	Value: 30.00				

Y# 585 10 ZLOTYCH

14.1400 g., 0.9250 Silver 0.4205 oz. ASW, 32 mm. **Obv:** Mountains, Polish Eagle and value **Rev:** Ignacy Domeyko **Edge:** Plain

Date	Mintage	F	VF	XF	Unc	BU
2007MW Proof	—	Value: 30.00				

Y# 587 10 ZLOTYCH

14.1400 g., 0.9250 Silver 0.4205 oz. ASW, 32 mm. **Subject:** 75th Anniversary breaking the Enigma Code **Obv:** Polish Eagle on circuit board **Rev:** Segmented letters **Edge:** Lettered

Date	Mintage	F	VF	XF	Unc	BU
2007MW Proof	—	Value: 30.00				

Y# 589 10 ZLOTYCH

14.1400 g., 0.9250 Silver 0.4205 oz. ASW, 32 mm. **Obv:** Angel, Polish Eagle and obverse coin design of Y-18 **Rev:** Reverse coin design of Y-18 on wheat ears **Edge:** Plain

Date	Mintage	F	VF	XF	Unc	BU
2007MW Proof	—	Value: 30.00				

Y# 595 10 ZLOTYCH

14.1400 g., 0.9250 Silver ASW 0.4205 0.4205 oz. ASW **Subject:** 750th Anniversary Munincipality of Krakau **Obv:** City gate tower, national arms at lower right **Obv. Legend:** RZECZPOSPOLITA POLSKA **Rev:** Knight with shield standing facing

Date	Mintage	F	VF	XF	Unc	BU
2007MW Proof	—	Value: 30.00				

Y# 600 10 ZLOTYCH

14.1000 g., 0.9250 Silver 0.4193 oz. ASW, 32.07 mm. **Subject:**

125th Anniversary Birth of Szymanowskiego **Obv:** Holgram dates of birth and death at left, national arms on music composition **Obv. Legend:** RZECZPOSPOLITA POLSKA **Rev:** Bust of Szymanowskiego 3/4 left, music composition behind face and over upper body **Rev. Legend:** 125. ROCZNICA URODZIN KAROLA SZYMANOWSKIEGO **Edge:** Plain

Date	Mintage	F	VF	XF	Unc	BU
2007MW Proof	—	Value: 30.00				

Y# 601 10 ZLOTYCH

14.3000 g., 0.9250 Silver 0.4253 oz. ASW, 14.30 mm. **Subject:** Arctic Explorers **Obv:** Sailing ship at center, national arms at right with denomination below **Obv. Legend:** RZECZPOSPOLITA POLSKA **Rev:** Busts of Henryk Arctowski and Antoni Dobrowolski facing, polar outline map at lower left **Edge:** plain

Date	Mintage	F	VF	XF	Unc	BU
2007MW Proof	—	Value: 30.00				

Y# 602 10 ZLOTYCH

14.0500 g., 0.9250 Silver 0.4178 oz. ASW **Obv:** Helmeted national arms, sword and denomination below **Obv. Legend:** RZECZPOSPOLITA - POLSKA **Rev:** Chivarous knight horseback jousting right **Rev. Inscription:** RYCERZ - CIEZKOZBROJNY **Edge:** Plain **Shape:** Rectangular, 31.95 x 22.39 mm

Date	Mintage	F	VF	XF	Unc	BU
2007MW Proof	—	Value: 30.00				

Y# 409 20 ZLOTYCH

28.2800 g., 0.9250 Silver 0.8410 oz. ASW, 38.6 mm. **Subject:** Wieliezce Salt Mine **Obv:** Crowned eagle with wings open in center of rock **Rev:** Ancient salt miners **Edge:** Plain

Date	Mintage	F	VF	XF	Unc	BU
2001 Proof	25,000	Value: 60.00				

Y# 411 20 ZLOTYCH

28.2800 g., 0.9250 Silver 0.8410 oz. ASW, 38.6 mm. **Subject:** Amber Route **Obv:** Crowned eagle and two ancient Roman silver cups **Rev:** Piece of amber mounted above an ancient Roman coin design and map with the route marked with stars **Edge:** Plain

Date	Mintage	F	VF	XF	Unc	BU
2001	30,000	—	—	—	85.00	—

Note: Antiqued finish

Y# 415 20 ZLOTYCH

28.2800 g., 0.9250 Silver 0.8410 oz. ASW, 38.6 mm. **Obv:** Crowned eagle with wings open flanked by flags **Rev:** Butterfly **Edge:** Plain

Date	Mintage	F	VF	XF	Unc	BU
2001 Proof	27,000	Value: 220				

Y# 424 20 ZLOTYCH

28.7700 g., 0.9250 Silver 0.8556 oz. ASW, 38.6 mm. **Subject:** Christmas **Obv:** Ornate city view **Rev:** Celebration scene including an attached zirconia star **Edge:** Plain **Note:** Antiqued finish.

Date	Mintage	F	VF	XF	Unc	BU
2001	55,000	—	—	—	50.00	—

Y# 457 20 ZLOTYCH

28.2800 g., 0.9250 Silver 0.8410 oz. ASW, 38.6 mm. **Obv:** Crowned eagle and castle **Rev:** Malborku castle and ceramic applique **Edge:** Plain **Note:** Antiqued finish

Date	Mintage	F	VF	XF	Unc	BU
2002MW	51,000	—	—	—	50.00	—

Antiqued finish

Y# 428 20 ZLOTYCH

28.2800 g., 0.9250 Silver 0.8410 oz. ASW, 38.6 mm. **Obv:** Crowned eagle with wings open flanked by flags **Rev:** Turtles **Edge:** Plain

Date	Mintage	F	VF	XF	Unc	BU
2002 Proof	35,000	Value: 90.00				

Y# 442 20 ZLOTYCH

28.0500 g., 0.9250 Silver 0.8342 oz. ASW **Subject:** Jan Matejko **Obv:** Seated figure with crowned eagle at lower right **Rev:** Head facing with multicolor artist's palette **Edge:** Plain **Shape:** Rectangular **Note:** Actual size 40 x 37.9mm.

Date	Mintage	F	VF	XF	Unc	BU
2002MW Proof	57,000	Value: 45.00				

Y# 449 20 ZLOTYCH

28.4700 g., 0.9250 Silver 0.8466 oz. ASW, 38.6 mm. **Obv:** Crowned eagle with wings open **Rev:** Eels and world globe **Edge:** Plain

Date	Mintage	F	VF	XF	Unc	BU
2003MW Proof	—	Value: 90.00				

Y# 452 20 ZLOTYCH

28.2800 g., 0.9250 Silver 0.8410 oz. ASW, 38.6 mm. **Subject:** Easter Monday Festival **Obv:** Crowned eagle on lace curtain above lamb and multicolor Easter eggs **Rev:** Festival scene **Edge:** Plain

Date	Mintage	F	VF	XF	Unc	BU
2003MW Proof	44,000	Value: 50.00				

Y# 471 20 ZLOTYCH

28.2800 g., 0.9250 Silver 0.8410 oz. ASW, 40 x 40 mm. **Obv:** Standing Pope John Paul II **Rev:** Pope"s portrait **Edge:** Plain **Shape:** Square

Date	Mintage	F	VF	XF	Unc	BU
2003MW Proof	83,000	Value: 60.00				

Y# 478 20 ZLOTYCH

28.2800 g., 0.9250 Silver 0.8410 oz. ASW, 28 mm. **Obv:** "Death" allegory closing an old man's eyes **Rev:** Self portrait of Jacek Malczewski **Edge:** Plain **Shape:** Rectangular

Date	Mintage	F	VF	XF	Unc	BU
2003MW Proof	64,000	Value: 50.00				

Y# 498 20 ZLOTYCH

28.2800 g., 0.9250 Silver 0.8410 oz. ASW, 38.6 mm. **Subject:** Lodz Ghetto (1940-1944) **Obv:** Silhouette on wall **Rev:** Child with a pot **Edge:** Plain

Date	Mintage	F	VF	XF	Unc	BU
2004MW Matte	64,000	—	—	—	—	75.00

Y# 504 20 ZLOTYCH

28.2800 g., 0.9250 Silver 0.8410 oz. ASW, 38.6 mm. **Subject:** Polish Senate **Obv:** Crowned eagle above Senate chamber **Rev:** Senate eagle and speaker's staff **Edge:** Plain

Date	Mintage	F	VF	XF	Unc	BU
2004MW Proof	67,000	Value: 50.00				

Y# 508 20 ZLOTYCH

28.2800 g., 0.9250 Silver 0.8410 oz. ASW, 38.6 mm. **Obv:** Crowned eagle in harvest wreath **Rev:** Harvest fest parade **Edge:** Plain

Date	Mintage	F	VF	XF	Unc	BU
2004MW Proof	74,000	Value: 50.00				

Y# 513 20 ZLOTYCH

28.2800 g., 0.9250 Silver 0.8410 oz. ASW, 40x28 mm. **Obv:** Mother and children **Rev:** Stanislaw Wyspianski (1869-1907) **Edge:** Plain

Date	Mintage	F	VF	XF	Unc	BU
2004MW Proof	80,000	Value: 60.00				

Y# 515 20 ZLOTYCH

28.2800 g., 0.9250 Silver 0.8410 oz. ASW, 38.6 mm. **Obv:** Crowned eagle with wings open **Rev:** Baltic Sea Whales **Edge:** Plain

Date	Mintage	F	VF	XF	Unc	BU
2004MW Proof	56,000	Value: 120				

Y# 597 20 ZLOTYCH

28.5000 g., 0.9250 Silver 0.8475 oz. ASW, 38.55 mm. **Subject:** 350 Years, Defence of Góry **Obv:** National arms to right of outlined Góry **Obv. Legend:** RZECZPOSPOLITA POLSKA **Obv. Inscription:** Tutaj zawsze / bylismy woini / JAN PAWEL II **Rev:** 1/2 length figure of man at lower right, Góry under bombardment in background **Rev. Legend:** 350 - LECIE OBRONY JASNEJ GÓRY **Edge:** Lettered **Edge Lettering:** CZESTOCHOWA 2005 repeated three times

Date	Mintage	F	VF	XF	Unc	BU
2005MW Proof	—	Value: 60.00				

Y# 531 20 ZLOTYCH

28.8400 g., 0.9250 Silver 0.8576 oz. ASW, 38.6 mm. **Obv:** Polish eagle above value **Rev:** Eagle Owl with nestlings **Edge:** Plain

Date	Mintage	F	VF	XF	Unc	BU
2005MW Proof	61,000	Value: 175				

Y# 542 20 ZLOTYCH

28.2800 g., 0.9250 Silver 0.8410 oz. ASW, 28 x 40 mm. **Obv:** Sneak thief stealing from a miser **Rev:** Painter Tadeusz Makowski **Edge:** Plain **Shape:** Rectangular

Date	Mintage	F	VF	XF	Unc	BU
2005MW Proof	70,000	Value: 60.00				

Y# 557 20 ZLOTYCH

28.2800 g., 0.9250 Silver 0.8410 oz. ASW, 38.6 mm. **Obv:** Crowned eagle **Rev:** Marmots **Edge:** Plain

Date	Mintage	F	VF	XF	Unc	BU
2006MW Proof	—	Value: 135				

Y# 535 20 ZLOTYCH

28.8400 g., 0.9250 Silver 0.8576 oz. ASW, 38.6 mm. **Obv:** Polish eagle above value **Rev:** Alpine Marmot standing **Edge:** Plain

Date	Mintage	F	VF	XF	Unc	BU
2006MW Proof	60,000	Value: 125				

Y# 584 20 ZLOTYCH

28.4700 g., 0.9250 Silver 0.8466 oz. ASW, 38.6 mm. **Obv:** Polish Eagle on old wood **Rev:** Multi-color wood behind Haczowie church **Edge:** Plain

Date	Mintage	F	VF	XF	Unc	BU
2006MW Proof	—	Value: 50.00				

Y# 533 20 ZLOTYCH

28.8400 g., 0.9250 Silver 0.8576 oz. ASW, 38.6 mm. **Obv:** Polish eagle above value **Rev:** Multicolor holographic spider web **Edge:** Plain

Date	Mintage	F	VF	XF	Unc	BU
2006MW Proof	65,000	Value: 115				

Y# 603 20 ZLOTYCH

28.2500 g., 0.9250 Silver 0.8401 oz. ASW, 38.53 mm. **Subject:** Medieval Principality of Sredniowiecznew in Torin **Obv:** City arms at right, national arms below walled city gate in background **Obv. Legend:** RZECZPOSPOLITA POLSKA **Rev:** City view **Rev. Legend:** MIASTO SREDNIOWIECZNEW W TORUNIU **Edge:** Plain

Date	Mintage	F	VF	XF	Unc	BU
2007MW Proof	—	Value: 50.00				

Y# 579 20 ZLOTYCH

28.2800 g., 0.9250 Silver 0.8410 oz. ASW, 38.6 mm. **Obv:** Crowned eagle **Rev:** Two Grey Seal females and cub with two silhouettes in background **Edge:** Plain

Date	Mintage	F	VF	XF	Unc	BU
2007MW Proof	58,000	Value: 65.00				

Y# 292 50 ZLOTYCH

3.1000 g., 0.9999 Gold 0.0997 oz. AGW, 18 mm. **Obv:** Crowned eagle with wings open, all within circle **Rev:** Golden eagle

Date	Mintage	F	VF	XF	Unc	BU
2002	500	—	—	—	BV	150

Y# 416 100 ZLOTYCH

8.0000 g., 0.9000 Gold 0.2315 oz. AGW, 21 mm. **Subject:** Wladyslaw I (1320-33) **Obv:** Crowned eagle with wings open **Rev:** Crowned bust facing **Edge:** Plain

Date	Mintage	F	VF	XF	Unc	BU
2001 Proof	2,000	Value: 275				

Y# 417 100 ZLOTYCH

8.0000 g., 0.9000 Gold 0.2315 oz. AGW, 21 mm. **Subject:** Boleslaw III (1102-1138) **Obv:** Crowned eagle with wings open **Rev:** Pointed crowned bust facing **Edge:** Plain

Date	Mintage	F	VF	XF	Unc	BU
2001 Proof	2,000	Value: 275				

Y# 462 100 ZLOTYCH

8.0000 g., 0.9000 Gold 0.2315 oz. AGW, 21 mm. **Obv:** Crowned eagle with wings open **Rev:** Jan Sobieski III **Edge:** Plain

Date	Mintage	F	VF	XF	Unc	BU
2001MV Proof	2,200	Value: 275				

Y# 293 100 ZLOTYCH

7.7800 g., 0.9999 Gold 0.2501 oz. AGW, 22 mm. **Obv:** Crowned eagle with wings open, all within circle **Rev:** Golden eagle

Date	Mintage	F	VF	XF	Unc	BU
2002	800	—	—	—	BV	250

Y# 436 100 ZLOTYCH

8.0000 g., 0.9000 Gold 0.2315 oz. AGW, 21 mm. **Subject:** World Cup Soccer **Obv:** Crowned eagle with wings open and world background **Rev:** Soccer player **Edge:** Plain

Date	Mintage	F	VF	XF	Unc	BU
2002 Proof	4,500	Value: 275				

Y# 429 100 ZLOTYCH

8.0000 g., 0.9000 Gold 0.2315 oz. AGW, 21 mm. **Obv:** Crowned eagle with wings open **Rev:** Crowned bust facing **Edge:** Plain

Date	Mintage	F	VF	XF	Unc	BU
2002 Proof	2,400	Value: 275				

Y# 430 100 ZLOTYCH

8.0000 g., 0.9000 Gold 0.2315 oz. AGW, 21 mm. **Obv:** Crowned eagle with wings open **Rev:** Crowned bust 1/4 left **Edge:** Plain

Date	Mintage	F	VF	XF	Unc	BU
2002 Proof	2,200	Value: 275				

Y# 454 100 ZLOTYCH

8.0000 g., 0.9000 Gold 0.2315 oz. AGW, 21 mm. **Obv:** Crowned eagle with wings open **Rev:** Uniformed bust 1/4 left **Edge:** Plain

Date	Mintage	F	VF	XF	Unc	BU
2003MW Proof	2,000	Value: 275				

Y# 466 100 ZLOTYCH

8.0000 g., 0.9000 Gold 0.2315 oz. AGW, 21 mm. **Subject:** 750th Anniversary - City Charter **Obv:** Door knocker and church **Rev:** Clock face and tower **Edge:** Plain

Date	Mintage	F	VF	XF	Unc	BU
2003MW Proof	2,100	Value: 275				

Y# 467 100 ZLOTYCH

8.0000 g., 0.9000 Gold 0.2315 oz. AGW, 21 mm. **Obv:** Crowned eagle with wings open **Rev:** Kazimierz IV (1447-1492) **Edge:** Plain

Date	Mintage	F	VF	XF	Unc	BU
2003MW Proof	2,300	Value: 275				

Y# 476 100 ZLOTYCH

8.0000 g., 0.9000 Gold 0.2315 oz. AGW, 21 mm. **Obv:** Crowned eagle with wings open **Rev:** Stanislaus I and eagle **Edge:** Plain

Date	Mintage	F	VF	XF	Unc	BU
2003MW Proof	2,500	Value: 275				

Y# 494 100 ZLOTYCH

8.0000 g., 0.9000 Gold 0.2315 oz. AGW, 21 mm. **Obv:** Crowned eagle with wings open **Rev:** King Przemysi II (1295-1296) **Edge:** Plain

Date	Mintage	F	VF	XF	Unc	BU
2004MW Proof	3,400	Value: 260				

Y# 495 100 ZLOTYCH

8.0000 g., 0.9000 Gold 0.2315 oz. AGW, 21 mm. **Obv:** Crowned eagle with wings open **Rev:** King Zygmunt I (1506-1548) **Edge:** Plain

Date	Mintage	F	VF	XF	Unc	BU
2004MW Proof	3,400	Value: 260				

Y# 540 100 ZLOTYCH

8.0000 g., 0.9000 Gold 0.2315 oz. AGW, 21 mm. **Obv:** St. Peters Basilica dome **Rev:** Pope John Paul II and baptismal font **Edge:** Plain

Date	Mintage	F	VF	XF	Unc	BU
2005MW Proof	18,700	Value: 375				

Y# 581 100 ZLOTYCH

8.0000 g., 0.9000 Gold 0.2315 oz. AGW, 21 mm. **Obv:** Line of soccer players on soccer ball surface with Polish eagle in one of the sections **Rev:** Two soccer players **Edge:** Plain

Date	Mintage	F	VF	XF	Unc	BU
2006MW Proof	—	Value: 300				

Y# 407 200 ZLOTYCH

Tri-Metallic Gold with Palladium center, Gold with Silver ring, Gold with Copper outer limit, 27 mm. **Subject:** Year 2001 **Obv:** Crowned eagle with wings open within a swirl **Rev:** Couple looking into the future **Edge:** Plain

Date	Mintage	F	VF	XF	Unc	BU
2001 Proof	4,000	Value: 300				

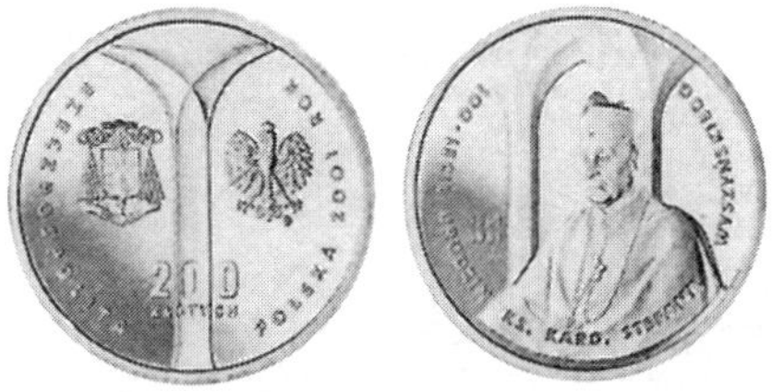

Y# 420 200 ZLOTYCH

15.5000 g., 0.9000 Gold 0.4485 oz. AGW, 27 mm. **Subject:** Cardinal Stefan Wyszynski **Obv:** Pillar divides arms and eagle **Rev:** Bust left within arch **Edge Lettering:** "100 ROCZNIA URODZIN"

Date	Mintage	F	VF	XF	Unc	BU
2001 Proof	4,500	Value: 375				

Y# 463 200 ZLOTYCH

15.5000 g., 0.9000 Gold 0.4485 oz. AGW, 27 mm. **Obv:** Standing violinist **Rev:** Henry Wieniawski **Edge:** Lettered **Edge Lettering:** "XII MIEDZYNARODOWY KONKURS SKRZYPCOWY IM HENRYKA WIENIAWSKIEGO"

Date	Mintage	F	VF	XF	Unc	BU
2001MW Proof	2,000	Value: 375				

Y# 294 200 ZLOTYCH

15.5000 g., 0.9000 Gold 0.4485 oz. AGW, 27 mm. **Obv:** Crowned eagle with wings open within beaded circle **Rev:** Golden eagle

Date	Mintage	F	VF	XF	Unc	BU
2002	500	—	—	—	BV	500

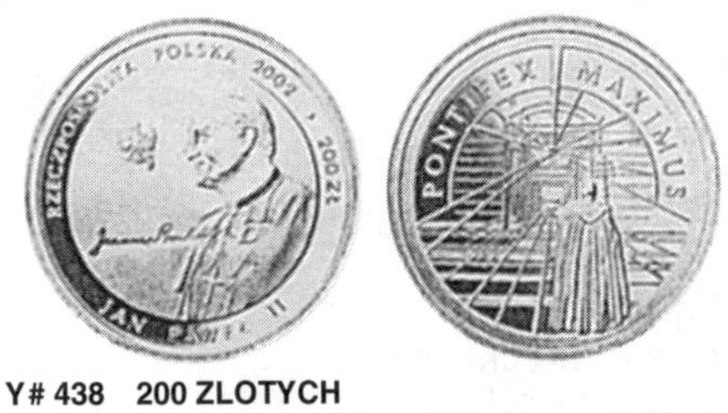

Y# 438 200 ZLOTYCH

15.5000 g., 0.9000 Gold 0.4485 oz. AGW, 27 mm. **Subject:** Pope John Paul II **Obv:** Bust left and small eagle with wings open **Rev:** Pope facing radiant Holy Door **Edge:** Plain

Date	Mintage	F	VF	XF	Unc	BU
2002 Proof	5,000	Value: 475				

Y# 470 200 ZLOTYCH

15.5000 g., 0.9000 Gold 0.4485 oz. AGW, 27 mm. **Subject:** Gas and Oil Industry **Obv:** Crowned eagle, oil wells and refinery **Rev:** Scientist at work **Edge:** Plain

Date	Mintage	F	VF	XF	Unc	BU
2003MW Proof	2,100	Value: 475				

Y# 472 200 ZLOTYCH

15.5000 g., 0.9000 Gold 0.4485 oz. AGW, 27 mm. **Obv:** Standing Pope John Paul II **Rev:** Seated Pope **Edge:** Plain

Date	Mintage	F	VF	XF	Unc	BU
2003MW Proof	4,900	Value: 385				

Y# 483 200 ZLOTYCH

15.5000 g., 0.9000 Gold 0.4485 oz. AGW, 27 mm. **Subject:** Poland Joining the European Union **Obv:** Polish euro coin design elements **Rev:** Polish euro coin design elements **Edge:** Plain

Date	Mintage	F	VF	XF	Unc	BU
2004MW Proof	4,400	Value: 475				

Y# 511 200 ZLOTYCH

15.5000 g., 0.9000 Gold 0.4485 oz. AGW, 27 mm. **Subject:** Warsaw Fine Arts Academy Centennial **Obv:** Campus view **Rev:** Statue and building **Edge:** Plain

Date	Mintage	F	VF	XF	Unc	BU
2004MW Proof	5,000	Value: 475				

Y# 519 200 ZLOTYCH

15.5000 g., 0.9000 Gold 0.4485 oz. AGW, 27 mm. **Subject:** Olympics **Obv:** Woman and crowned eagle **Rev:** Ancient runners painted on pottery **Edge:** Plain

Date	Mintage	F	VF	XF	Unc	BU
2004MW Proof	6,000	Value: 475				

Y# 538 200 ZLOTYCH

15.5000 g., 0.9000 Gold 0.4485 oz. AGW, 27 mm. **Obv:** Horse drawn carriage **Rev:** Konstanty Ildefons Galczynski in top hat **Edge:** Plain

Date	Mintage	F	VF	XF	Unc	BU
2005MW Proof	3,500	Value: 475				

Y# 536 200 ZLOTYCH

15.5000 g., 0.9000 Gold 0.4485 oz. AGW, 27 mm. **Obv:** Chopin **Rev:** Nagoya Castle roof tops and Mt. Fuji **Edge:** Plain **Note:** Aichi Expo Japan

Date	Mintage	F	VF	XF	Unc	BU
2005MW Proof	4,200	Value: 375				

MINT SETS

KM#	Date	Mintage	Identification	Issue Price	Mkt Val
MS5	2007 (11)	2,000	Y#276-284, 465, 525, mixed date set - 1995-2007	39.95	—

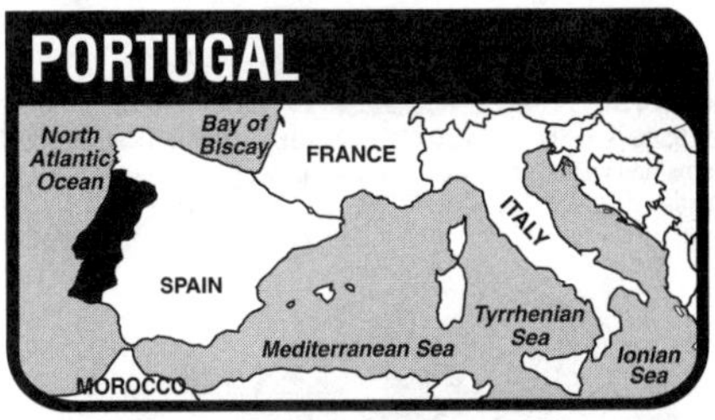

The Portuguese Republic, located in the western part of the Iberian Peninsula in southwestern Europe, has an area of 35,553 sq. mi. (92,080 sq. km.) and a population of *10.5 million. Capital: Lisbon. Portugal's economy is based on agriculture, tourism, minerals, fisheries and a rapidly expanding industrial sector. Textiles account for 33% of the exports and Portuguese wine is world famous. Portugal has become Europe's number one producer of copper and the world's largest producer of cork.

RULER

Republic, 1910 to date

MONETARY SYSTEM

100 Cents = 1 Euro

REPUBLIC

DECIMAL COINAGE

New denominations, all expressed in terms of Reis were introduced by Maria II in 1836, to bring Portugal's currency into decimal form. Some of the coins retained old names, as follows:

1000 Reis Silver - Coroa

100 Reis Silver - Tostao

The diameter of the new copper coins, first minted by Maria II in 1837, was smaller than the earlier coinage, but the weight was unaltered. However, in 1882, Luis I reduced the size and weight of the copper currency.

The Real and 2 Reis pieces dated 1853 were issued for circulation in Mozambique and will be found in those listings.

KM# 631a ESCUDO

4.6000 g., 0.9167 Gold 0.1356 oz. AGW, 16 mm. **Subject:** Last Escudo **Obv:** Design above shield with "Au" above top left corner of shield **Rev:** Flower design above value **Edge:** Plain

Date	Mintage	F	VF	XF	Unc	BU
2001INCM	50,000	—	—	—	145	—

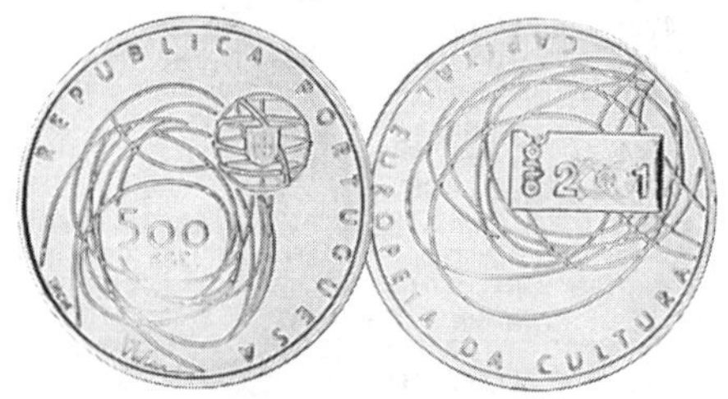

KM# 733 500 ESCUDOS
13.9600 g., 0.5000 Silver 0.2244 oz. ASW, 30.1 mm. **Subject:** Porto, European Culture Capital **Obv:** National arms and value **Rev:** Stylized design **Edge:** Reeded

Date	Mintage	F	VF	XF	Unc	BU
2001INCM	—	—	—	—	6.50	7.50

KM# 734 1000 ESCUDOS
26.9500 g., 0.5000 Silver 0.4332 oz. ASW, 40 mm. **Obv:** National arms and value **Rev:** Soccer ball within net **Edge:** Reeded

Date	Mintage	F	VF	XF	Unc	BU
2001	—	—	—	—	13.50	15.00

KM# 768 10 EURO
27.0000 g., 0.5000 Silver 0.4340 oz. ASW, 40 mm. **Obv:** National arms above value in circle of multi-national coats of arms **Rev:** Church **Edge:** Reeded

Date	Mintage	F	VF	XF	Unc	BU
2005INCM	—	—	—	—	—	30.00

EURO COINAGE

European Union Issues

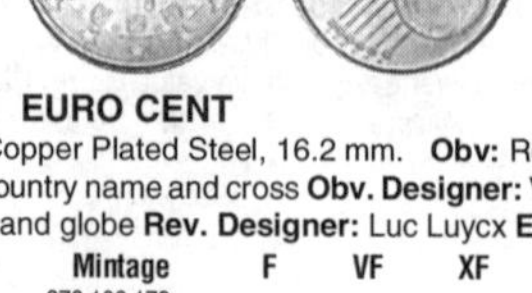

KM# 740 EURO CENT
2.2700 g., Copper Plated Steel, 16.2 mm. **Obv:** Royal seal of 1134 with country name and cross **Obv. Designer:** Vitor Santos **Rev:** Value and globe **Rev. Designer:** Luc Luycx **Edge:** Plain

Date	Mintage	F	VF	XF	Unc	BU
2002INCM	278,106,172	—	—	—	0.35	0.50
2002INCM Proof	15,000	Value: 7.00				
2003INCM	50,000	—	—	—	0.35	0.50
2003INCM Proof	15,000	Value: 7.00				
Note: in sets only						
2004INCM	75,000,000	—	—	—	0.35	0.50
2004INCM Proof	15,000	Value: 7.00				
2005INCM	40,000,000	—	—	—	0.35	0.50
2005INCM Proof	10,000	Value: 7.00				
2006INCM	30,000,000	—	—	—	0.35	0.50
2006INCM Proof	3,000	Value: 7.00				

KM# 741 2 EURO CENT
3.0300 g., Copper Plated Steel, 18.7 mm. **Obv:** Royal seal of 1134 with country name and cross **Obv. Designer:** Vitor Santos **Rev:** Value and globe **Rev. Designer:** Luc Luycx **Edge:** Grooved

Date	Mintage	F	VF	XF	Unc	BU
2002INCM	324,376,590	—	—	—	0.50	0.65
2002INCM Proof	15,000	Value: 9.00				
2003INCM	50,000	—	—	—	—	—
Note: In sets only						
2003INCM Proof	15,000	Value: 9.00				
Note: In sets only						
2004INCM	1,000,000	—	—	—	0.50	0.65
2004INCM Proof	15,000	Value: 9.00				
2005INCM	10,000,000	—	—	—	0.50	0.65
2005INCM Proof	10,000	Value: 9.00				
2006INCM	1,000,000	—	—	—	0.50	0.65
2006INCM Proof	3,000	Value: 9.00				

KM# 742 5 EURO CENT
3.8600 g., Copper Plated Steel, 21.2 mm. **Obv:** Royal seal of 1134 with country name and cross **Obv. Designer:** Vitor Santos **Rev:** Value and globe **Rev. Designer:** Luc Luycx **Edge:** Plain

Date	Mintage	F	VF	XF	Unc	BU
2002INCM	234,512,047	—	—	—	0.75	1.00
2002INCM Proof	15,000	Value: 10.00				
2003INCM	50,000	—	—	—	—	—
Note: In sets only						
2003INCM Proof	15,000	Value: 10.00				
Note: In sets only						
2004INCM	40,000,000	—	—	—	0.75	1.00
2004INCM Proof	15,000	Value: 10.00				
2005INCM	30,000,000	—	—	—	0.75	1.00
2005INCM Proof	10,000	Value: 10.00				
2006INCM	20,000,000	—	—	—	0.75	1.00
2006INCM Proof	3,000	Value: 10.00				

KM# 743 10 EURO CENT
4.0700 g., Brass, 19.7 mm. **Obv:** Royal seal of 1142, country name in circular design **Obv. Designer:** Vitor Santos **Rev:** Value and map **Rev. Designer:** Luc Luycx **Edge:** Reeded

Date	Mintage	F	VF	XF	Unc	BU
2002INCM	220,289,835	—	—	—	0.75	1.00
2002INCM Proof	15,000	Value: 12.00				
2003INCM	50,000	—	—	—	1.00	1.50
Note: In sets only						
2003INCM Proof	15,000	Value: 12.00				
Note: In sets only						
2004INCM	1,000,000	—	—	—	1.50	2.00
2004INCM Proof	15,000	Value: 12.00				
2005INCM	1,000,000	—	—	—	1.50	2.00
2005INCM Proof	10,000	Value: 12.00				
2006INCM	1,000,000	—	—	—	1.50	2.00
2006INCM Proof	3,000	Value: 12.00				
2007INCM	—	—	—	—	1.50	2.00

KM# 763 10 EURO CENT
4.0700 g., Brass, 19.7 mm. **Obv:** Royal seal of 1142, country name in circular design **Obv. Designer:** Vitor Santos **Rev:** Relief map of Western Europe, stars, lines and value **Rev. Designer:** Luc Luycx **Edge:** Reeded

Date	Mintage	F	VF	XF	Unc	BU
2008INCM	—	—	—	—	1.50	2.00

KM# 744 20 EURO CENT
5.7300 g., Brass, 22.1 mm. **Obv:** Royal seal of 1142, country name in circular design **Obv. Designer:** Vitor Santos **Rev:** Value and map **Rev. Designer:** Luc Luycx **Edge:** Notched

Date	Mintage	F	VF	XF	Unc	BU
2002INCM	147,411,038	—	—	—	1.00	1.25
2002INCM Proof	15,000	Value: 14.00				
2003INCM	50,000	—	—	—	1.25	1.50
Note: In sets only						
2003INCM Proof	15,000	Value: 14.00				
Note: In sets only						
2004INCM	1,000,000	—	—	—	1.50	2.00
2004INCM Proof	15,000	Value: 14.00				
2005INCM	25,000,000	—	—	—	1.50	2.00
2005INCM Proof	10,000	Value: 14.00				
2006INCM	20,000,000	—	—	—	1.50	2.00
2006INCM Proof	3,000	Value: 14.00				
2007INCM	—	—	—	—	1.50	2.00

KM# 764 20 EURO CENT
5.7300 g., Brass, 22.1 mm. **Obv:** Royal seal of 1142, country name in circular design **Obv. Designer:** Vitor Santos **Rev:** Relief map of Western Europe, stars, lines and value **Rev. Designer:** Luc Luycx **Edge:** Notched

Date	Mintage	F	VF	XF	Unc	BU
2008INCM	—	—	—	—	1.50	2.00

KM# 777 1/4 EURO
1.5600 g., 0.9990 Gold 0.0501 oz. AGW, 14 mm. **Subject:** King Alfons I, the Conqueror **Obv:** National arms, value **Obv. Legend:** REPÚBLICA PORTUGUESA **Rev:** Stylized 3/4 length armored figure standing facing

Date	Mintage	F	VF	XF	Unc	BU
2006INCM	30,000	—	—	—	90.00	—

KM# 745 50 EURO CENT
7.8100 g., Brass, 24.2 mm. **Obv:** Royal seal of 1142, country name in circular design **Obv. Designer:** Vitor Santos **Rev:** Value and map **Rev. Designer:** Luc Luycx **Edge:** Reeded

Date	Mintage	F	VF	XF	Unc	BU
2002INCM	151,947,133	—	—	—	1.50	2.00
2002INCM Proof	15,000	Value: 16.00				
2003INCM	50,000	—	—	—	1.50	2.00
Note: In sets only						
2003INCM Proof	15,000	Value: 16.00				
Note: In sets only						
2004INCM	1,000,000	—	—	—	2.50	3.00
2004INCM Proof	15,000	Value: 16.00				
2005INCM	1,000,000	—	—	—	2.50	3.00
2005INCM Proof	10,000	Value: 16.00				
2006INCM	1,000,000	—	—	—	2.50	3.00
2006INCM Proof	3,000	Value: 16.00				
2007INCM	—	—	—	—	2.50	3.00

KM# 765 50 EURO CENT
7.8100 g., Brass, 24.2 mm. **Obv:** Royal seal of 1142, country name in circular design **Obv. Designer:** Vitor Santos **Rev:** Relief map of Western Europe, stars, lines and value **Rev. Designer:** Luc Luycx **Edge:** Reeded

Date	Mintage	F	VF	XF	Unc	BU
2008INCM	—	—	—	—	2.50	3.00

KM# 746 EURO
7.5000 g., Bi-Metallic Copper-Nickel center in Brass ring, 23.2 mm. **Obv:** Royal seal of 1144, country name in looped design **Obv. Designer:** Vitor Santos **Rev:** Value and map **Rev. Designer:** Luc Luycx **Edge:** Reeded and plain sections

Date	Mintage	F	VF	XF	Unc	BU
2002INCM	100,228,135	—	—	—	2.00	2.50
2002INCM Proof	15,000	Value: 18.00				
2003INCM	50,000	—	—	—	2.00	2.50
Note: In sets only						
2003INCM Proof	15,000	Value: 18.00				
Note: In sets only						
2004INCM	20,000,000	—	—	—	2.00	2.50
2004INCM Proof	15,000	Value: 18.00				
2005INCM	20,000,000	—	—	—	2.00	2.50
2005INCM Proof	10,000	Value: 18.00				
2006INCM	20,000,000	—	—	—	2.00	2.50
2006INCM Proof	3,000	Value: 18.00				
2007INCM	—	—	—	—	2.00	2.50

KM# 766 EURO
7.5000 g., Bi-Metallic Copper-Nickel center in Brass ring, 23.2 mm. **Obv:** Royal seal of 1144, country name in looped design **Obv. Designer:** Vitor Santos **Rev:** Relief map of Western Europe, stars, lines and value **Rev. Designer:** Luc Luycx **Edge:** Reeded and plain sections

Date	Mintage	F	VF	XF	Unc	BU
2008INCM	—	—	—	—	2.75	3.50

KM# 747 2 EURO
8.5200 g., Bi-Metallic Brass center in Copper-Nickel ring, 25.7 mm. **Obv:** Royal seal of 1144, country name in looped design **Obv. Designer:** Vitor Santos **Rev:** Value and map **Rev. Designer:** Luc Luycx **Edge:** Reeding over castles and shields

Date	Mintage	F	VF	XF	Unc	BU
2002INCM	61,930,775	—	—	—	3.50	4.00
2002INCM Proof	15,000	Value: 22.00				
2003INCM	50,000	—	—	—	4.25	5.00
Note: In sets only						
2003INCM Proof	15,000	Value: 22.00				
Note: In sets only						
2004INCM	1,000,000	—	—	—	5.50	6.00
2004INCM Proof	15,000	Value: 22.00				
2005INCM	1,000,000	—	—	—	5.50	6.00
2005INCM Proof	10,000	Value: 22.00				
2006INCM	1,000,000	—	—	—	5.50	6.00
2006INCM Proof	3,000	Value: 22.00				
2007INCM	—	—	—	—	5.50	6.00

KM# 771 2 EURO
8.4700 g., Bi-Metallic Brass center in Copper-Nickel ring, 25.74 mm. **Subject:** 50th Anniversary Treaty of Rome **Obv:** Open treaty book **Rev:** Large value at left, modified outline of Europe at right **Edge:** Reeded and lettered

Date	Mintage	F	VF	XF	Unc	BU
2007	—	—	—	—	—	9.00

KM# 772 2 EURO
8.4000 g., Bi-Metallic Brass center in Copper-Nickel ring, 25.73 mm. **Subject:** European Union President **Obv:** Large tree, small national arms at lower left **Obv. Inscription:** POR / TV / GAL **Rev:** Large value at left, revised map of Europe at right **Edge:** Reeded with repeated symbols

Date	Mintage	F	VF	XF	Unc	BU
2007	—	—	—	—	4.25	5.00

KM# 767 2 EURO
8.5200 g., Bi-Metallic Brass center in Copper-Nickel ring, 25.7 mm. **Obv:** Royal seal of 1144, country name in looped design **Obv. Designer:** Vitor Santos **Rev:** Relief map of Western Europe, stars, lines and value **Rev. Designer:** Luc Luycx **Edge:** Reeding over castles and shields

Date	Mintage	F	VF	XF	Unc	BU
2008INCM	—	—	—	—	5.50	6.00

KM# 749 5 EURO
14.0000 g., 0.5000 Silver 0.2250 oz. ASW, 30 mm. **Subject:** 150th Anniversary - First Portuguese Postage Stamp **Obv:** National arms and value within partial stamp design **Rev:** Partial postal stamp design **Edge:** Reeded

Date	Mintage	F	VF	XF	Unc	BU
2003INCM	300,000	—	—	—	30.00	32.50

KM# 749a 5 EURO
14.0000 g., 0.9250 Silver 0.4163 oz. ASW, 30 mm. **Obv:** National arms and value within partial stamp design **Rev:** Partial postal stamp design

Date	Mintage	F	VF	XF	Unc	BU
2003INCM Proof	20,000	Value: 40.00				

KM# 749b 5 EURO
17.5000 g., 0.9166 Gold 0.5157 oz. AGW, 30 mm. **Obv:** National arms and value within partial stamp design **Rev:** Partial postal stamp design

Date	Mintage	F	VF	XF	Unc	BU
2003INCM Proof	—	Value: 550				

KM# 754 5 EURO
14.0000 g., 0.5000 Silver 0.2250 oz. ASW, 30 mm. **Subject:** Convent of Christ **Obv:** National arms above value flanked by designs **Rev:** Ornate convent window **Edge:** Reeded

Date	Mintage	F	VF	XF	Unc	BU
2004INCM	300,000	—	—	—	30.00	32.50

KM# 754a 5 EURO
14.0000 g., 0.9250 Silver 0.4163 oz. ASW, 30 mm. **Subject:** Convent of Christ **Obv:** National arms above value flanked by designs **Rev:** Ornate convent window **Edge:** Reeded

Date	Mintage	F	VF	XF	Unc	BU
2004INCM Proof	10,000	Value: 50.00				

KM# 755 5 EURO
14.0000 g., 0.5000 Silver 0.2250 oz. ASW, 30 mm. **Subject:** Historic City of Evora **Obv:** National arms and value on city map silhouette **Rev:** Architectural highlights **Edge:** Reeded

Date	Mintage	F	VF	XF	Unc	BU
2004INCM	300,000	—	—	—	30.00	32.50

KM# 755a 5 EURO
14.0000 g., 0.9250 Silver 0.4163 oz. ASW, 30 mm. **Subject:** Historic City of Evora **Obv:** National arms and value on city map silhouette **Rev:** Architectural highlights **Edge:** Reeded

Date	Mintage	F	VF	XF	Unc	BU
2004INCM Proof	10,000	Value: 50.00				

KM# 760 5 EURO
14.0000 g., 0.5000 Silver 0.2250 oz. ASW, 30 mm. **Obv:** National arms within circle **Obv. Legend:** REPUBLICA POTUGUESA **Rev:** Angra do Heroismo - Azores Terceira, emblem above **Rev. Legend:** CENTRO HISTÓRICO DE ANGRA DO HEROISMA **Edge:** Reeded

Date	Mintage	F	VF	XF	Unc	BU
2005	300,000	—	—	—	30.00	—

KM# 761 5 EURO
14.0000 g., 0.5000 Silver 0.2250 oz. ASW, 30 mm. **Obv:** Design divides national arms and value **Obv. Legend:** REPUBLICA PORTUGUESA **Rev:** Batalha monastery and emblem **Rev. Legend:** MONTEIRO DA BATALHA **Edge:** Reeded

Date	Mintage	F	VF	XF	Unc	BU
2005	300,000	—	—	—	30.00	—

KM# 762 5 EURO
14.0000 g., 0.5000 Silver 0.2250 oz. ASW, 30 mm. **Subject:** 800th Anniversary Birth of Pope John XXI **Obv:** National arms at lower right with archways in backgound **Obv. Legend:** REPUBLICA PORTUGUESA **Rev:** 1/2 length figure of Pope facing at right with staff dividing dates, small shield at left **Edge:** Reeded

Date	Mintage	F	VF	XF	Unc	BU
2005INCM	300,000	—	—	—	30.00	—

KM# 762a 5 EURO
14.0000 g., 0.9250 Silver 0.4163 oz. ASW, 30 mm. **Subject:** 800th Anniversary Birth of Pope John XXI **Obv:** National arms at lower right with archways in backgound **Obv. Legend:** REPUBLICA PORTUGUESA **Rev:** 1/2 length figure of Pope facing at right with staff dividing dates, small shield at left **Edge:** Reeded

Date	Mintage	F	VF	XF	Unc	BU
2005INCM Proof	15,000	Value: 65.00				

KM# 762b 5 EURO
17.5000 g., 0.9167 Gold 0.5157 oz. AGW, 30 mm. **Subject:** 800th Anniversary Birth of Pope John XXI **Obv:** National arms at lower right, archways in background **Obv. Legend:** REPUBLICA PORTUGUESA **Edge:** Reeded

Date	Mintage	F	VF	XF	Unc	BU
2005INCM Proof	7,500	Value: 600				

KM# 760a 5 EURO
14.0000 g., 0.9250 Silver 0.4163 oz. ASW, 30 mm. **Obv:** National arms within circle **Obv. Legend:** REPUBLICA PORTUGUESA **Rev:** Angra do Heroisma - Azores Terceira, emblem above **Rev. Legend:** CENTRO HISTÓRICO DE ANGRA DO HEROISMA **Edge:** Reeded

Date	Mintage	F	VF	XF	Unc	BU
2005 Proof	10,000	Value: 60.00				

KM# 761a 5 EURO
14.0000 g., 0.9250 Silver 0.4163 oz. ASW, 30 mm. **Obv:** Design divides national arms and value **Obv. Legend:** REPUBLICA PORTUGUESA **Rev:** Batalha monastery and emblem **Rev. Legend:** MONTEIRO DA BATALHA **Edge:** Reeded

Date	Mintage	F	VF	XF	Unc	BU
2005 Proof	10,000	Value: 60.00				

KM# 769 5 EURO
14.0000 g., 0.5000 Silver 0.2250 oz. ASW, 30 mm. **Subject:** UNESCO - Cultural preservation **Obv:** National arms above value **Obv. Legend:** REPUBLICA PORTUGUESA **Rev:** Outlined view **Rev. Legend:** PAISAGEM CULTURAL DE SINTRA **Edge:** Reeded

Date	Mintage	F	VF	XF	Unc	BU
2006INCM	300,000	—	—	—	30.00	32.50

KM# 769a 5 EURO
14.0000 g., 0.9250 Silver 0.4163 oz. ASW, 30 mm. **Subject:** UNESCO - Cultural preservation **Obv:** National arms above value **Obv. Legend:** REPUBLICA PORTUGUESA **Rev:** Outlined view **Rev. Legend:** PAISAGEM CULTURAL DE SINTRA **Edge:** Reeded

Date	Mintage	F	VF	XF	Unc	BU
2006INCM Proof	10,000	Value: 55.00				

KM# 779 5 EURO
14.0000 g., 0.5000 Silver 0.2250 oz. ASW **Subject:** Alcobaça Monestary **Obv:** National arms **Obv. Legend:** REPÚBLICA PORTUGUESA **Edge:** Reeded

Date	Mintage	F	VF	XF	Unc	BU
2006INCM	300,000	—	—	—	20.00	22.50

KM# 779a 5 EURO
14.0000 g., 0.9250 Silver 0.4163 oz. ASW **Subject:** Alcobaça Monestary **Obv:** National arms **Obv. Legend:** REPÚBLICA PORTUGUESA **Edge:** Reeded

Date	Mintage	F	VF	XF	Unc	BU
2006INCM Proof	10,000	Value: 50.00				

KM# 770a 5 EURO
14.0000 g., 0.9250 Silver 0.4163 oz. ASW, 30 mm. **Subject:** World Scouting Centennial **Obv:** National arms, World Scouting emblem **Obv. Legend:** REPUBLICA POTUGUESA 1907 - 2007 CENTENARIO DO ESCUTISMO MUNDIAL **Rev:** Linear portrait of Lord Robert Baden-Powell **Rev. Legend:** UM MUNDO UMA PROMESA **Edge:** Reeded **Designer:** Joao Calvina

Date	Mintage	F	VF	XF	Unc	BU
ND(2007) Proof	10,000	Value: 60.00				

KM# 770 5 EURO
14.0000 g., 0.5000 Silver 0.2250 oz. ASW, 30 mm. **Subject:** World Scouting Centennial **Obv:** Portuguese Arms, World Scouting emblem **Obv. Legend:** REPUBLICA PORTUGUESA 1907-2007 CENTENARIO DO ESCUTISMO MUNDIAL **Rev:** Linear portrait of Lord Robert Baden-Powell **Rev. Legend:** UM MUNDO UMA PROMESA **Edge:** Reeded **Designer:** Joao Calvino

Date	Mintage	F	VF	XF	Unc	BU
ND(2007)	70,000	—	—	—	20.00	22.50

KM# 781a 5 EURO
14.0000 g., 0.9250 Silver 0.4163 oz. ASW, 30 mm. **Subject:** Equal Opportunities **Obv:** Small national arms above moon shaped arc **Obv. Legend:** República Portuguesa **Rev:** Small 3 persons logo above 12 stars along rim **Rev. Legend:** Ano Europeu da Igualdade de Oportunidades para Todos **Edge:** Reeded

Date	Mintage	F	VF	XF	Unc	BU
2007INCM Proof	6,000	Value: 60.00				

KM# 781 5 EURO
14.0400 g., 0.5000 Silver 0.2257 oz. ASW, 30 mm. **Subject:** Equal Opportunities **Obv:** Small national arms above moon shaped arc **Obv. Legend:** República Portuguesa **Rev:** Small 3 persons logo above 12 stars along rim **Rev. Legend:** Ano Europeu da Igualdade de Oportunidades para Todos **Edge:** Reeded

Date	Mintage	F	VF	XF	Unc	BU
2007INCM	75,000	—	—	—	20.00	22.50

KM# 782 5 EURO

13.9500 g., 0.5000 Silver 0.2242 oz. ASW, 30 mm. **Series:** UNESCO - World Heritage **Subject:** National Forest Reserve in Madeira Nature Park **Obv:** National arms **Obv. Legend:** REPÚBLICA POTUGUESA **Rev:** Foliage with small UNESCO World Heritage logo at lower right **Rev. Legend:** FLORESTA LAURISSILVA DA MADEIRA **Edge:** Reeded

Date	Mintage	F	VF	XF	Unc	BU
2007INCM	70,000	—	—	—	20.00	22.50

KM# 782a 5 EURO

14.0000 g., 0.9250 Silver 0.4163 oz. ASW, 30 mm. **Series:** UNESCO - World Heritage **Subject:** National Forest Reserve in Madeira Nature Park **Obv:** National arms **Obv. Legend:** REPÚBLICA PORTUGUESA **Rev:** Foliage with small UNESCO World Heritage logo at lower right **Rev. Legend:** FLORESTA LAURISSILVA DA MADEIRA **Edge:** Reeded

Date	Mintage	F	VF	XF	Unc	BU
2007INCM Proof	7,500	Value: 60.00				

KM# 750 8 EURO

21.1000 g., 0.5000 Silver 0.3392 oz. ASW, 36 mm. **Obv:** National arms, value and flag-covered globe **Rev:** Flag-covered globe and "Euro 2004" soccer games logo **Edge:** Reeded

Date	Mintage	F	VF	XF	Unc	BU
2003INCM	1,500,000	—	—	—	35.00	37.50

KM# 750a 8 EURO

31.1000 g., 0.9250 Silver 0.9249 oz. ASW, 36 mm. **Obv:** National arms, value and flag-covered globe **Rev:** Flag-covered globe and "Euro 2004" soccer games logo

Date	Mintage	F	VF	XF	Unc	BU
2003INCM Proof	—	Value: 45.00				

KM# 750b 8 EURO

31.1000 g., 0.9166 Gold 0.9165 oz. AGW, 36 mm. **Obv:** National arms, value and flag-covered globe **Rev:** Flag-covered globe and "Euro 2004" soccer games logo

Date	Mintage	F	VF	XF	Unc	BU
2003INCM Proof	—	Value: 950				

KM# 751 8 EURO

21.1000 g., 0.5000 Silver 0.3392 oz. ASW, 36 mm. **Obv:** National arms and value below many bubbles **Rev:** "Euro 2004" soccer games logo below many hearts **Edge:** Reeded

Date	Mintage	F	VF	XF	Unc	BU
2003INCM	1,500,000	—	—	—	35.00	37.50

KM# 751a 8 EURO

31.1000 g., 0.9250 Silver 0.9249 oz. ASW, 36 mm. **Obv:** National arms and value below many bubbles **Rev:** "Euro 2004" soccer games logo below many hearts

Date	Mintage	F	VF	XF	Unc	BU
2003INCM Proof	—	Value: 45.00				

KM# 751b 8 EURO

31.1000 g., 0.9166 Gold 0.9165 oz. AGW, 36 mm. **Obv:** National arms and value below many bubbles **Rev:** "Euro 2004" soccer games logo below many hearts

Date	Mintage	F	VF	XF	Unc	BU
2003INCM Proof	—	Value: 950				

KM# 752 8 EURO

21.1000 g., 0.5000 Silver 0.3392 oz. ASW, 36 mm. **Obv:** National arms and value **Rev:** "Euro 2004" soccer games logo in center with partial text background **Edge:** Reeded

Date	Mintage	F	VF	XF	Unc	BU
2003INCM	1,500,000	—	—	—	35.00	37.50

KM# 752a 8 EURO

31.1000 g., 0.9250 Silver 0.9249 oz. ASW, 36 mm. **Obv:** National arms and value **Rev:** "Euro 2004" soccer games logo in center with partial text background

Date	Mintage	F	VF	XF	Unc	BU
2003INCM Proof	—	Value: 45.00				

KM# 752b 8 EURO

31.1000 g., 0.9166 Gold 0.9165 oz. AGW, 36 mm. **Obv:** National arms and value **Rev:** "Euro 2004" soccer games logo in center with partial text background

Date	Mintage	F	VF	XF	Unc	BU
2003INCM Proof	—	Value: 950				

KM# 753 8 EURO

21.2200 g., 0.5000 Silver 0.3411 oz. ASW, 36 mm. **Subject:** Expansion of the European Union **Obv:** Radiant national arms and value **Rev:** European map **Edge:** Reeded

Date	Mintage	F	VF	XF	Unc	BU
2004INCM	300,000	—	—	—	20.00	22.50

KM# 753a 8 EURO

31.1000 g., 0.9250 Silver 0.9249 oz. ASW, 36 mm. **Subject:** Expansion of the European Union **Obv:** Radiant national arms and value **Rev:** European map **Edge:** Reeded

Date	Mintage	F	VF	XF	Unc	BU
2004INCM Proof	35,000	Value: 50.00				

KM# 756 8 EURO

21.0000 g., 0.5000 Silver 0.3376 oz. ASW, 36 mm. **Subject:** Euro 2004 Soccer **Obv:** National arms **Rev:** Stylized goal keeper **Edge:** Reeded

Date	Mintage	F	VF	XF	Unc	BU
2004INCM	1,500,000	—	—	—	12.50	15.00

KM# 756a 8 EURO

31.1000 g., 0.9250 Silver 0.9249 oz. ASW, 36 mm. **Subject:** Euro 2004 Soccer **Obv:** National arms **Rev:** Stylized goal keeper **Edge:** Reeded

Date	Mintage	F	VF	XF	Unc	BU
2004INCM	30,000	—	—	—	—	30.00
2004INCM Proof	15,000	Value: 50.00				

KM# 756b 8 EURO

31.1000 g., 0.9166 Gold 0.9165 oz. AGW, 36 mm. **Subject:** Euro 2004 Soccer **Obv:** National arms **Rev:** Stylized goal keeper **Edge:** Reeded

Date	Mintage	F	VF	XF	Unc	BU
2004INCM Proof	10,000	Value: 950				

KM# 757 8 EURO

21.0000 g., 0.9250 Silver 0.6245 oz. ASW, 36 mm. **Subject:** Euro 2004 Soccer **Obv:** National arms **Rev:** Face of player making shot **Edge:** Reeded

Date	Mintage	F	VF	XF	Unc	BU
2004INCM	1,500,000	—	—	—	12.50	15.00

KM# 757a 8 EURO

31.1000 g., 0.9250 Silver 0.9249 oz. ASW, 36 mm. **Subject:** Euro 2004 Soccer **Obv:** National arms **Rev:** Face of player making a shot **Edge:** Reeded

Date	Mintage	F	VF	XF	Unc	BU
2004INCM	30,000	—	—	—	—	30.00
2004INCM Proof	15,000	Value: 50.00				

KM# 757b 8 EURO

31.1000 g., 0.9166 Gold 0.9165 oz. AGW, 36 mm. **Subject:** Euro 2004 Soccer **Obv:** National arms **Rev:** Face of player making a shot **Edge:** Reeded

Date	Mintage	F	VF	XF	Unc	BU
2004INCM Proof	10,000	Value: 950				

KM# 758 8 EURO

21.0000 g., 0.5000 Silver 0.3376 oz. ASW, 36 mm. **Subject:** Euro 2004 Soccer **Obv:** National arms **Rev:** Symbolic explosion of a goal **Edge:** Reeded

Date	Mintage	F	VF	XF	Unc	BU
2004INCM	1,500,000	—	—	—	12.50	15.00

KM# 758a 8 EURO

31.1000 g., 0.9250 Silver 0.9249 oz. ASW, 36 mm. **Subject:** Euro 2004 Soccer **Obv:** National arms **Rev:** Symbolic explosion of a goal **Edge:** Reeded

Date	Mintage	F	VF	XF	Unc	BU
2004INCM	30,000	—	—	—	—	30.00
2004INCM Proof	15,000	Value: 50.00				

KM# 758b 8 EURO

31.1000 g., 0.9166 Gold 0.9165 oz. AGW, 36 mm. **Subject:** Euro 2004 Soccer **Obv:** National arms **Rev:** Symbolic explosion of a goal **Edge:** Reeded

Date	Mintage	F	VF	XF	Unc	BU
2004INCM Proof	10,000	Value: 950				

KM# 773 8 EURO

21.0000 g., 0.5000 Silver 0.3376 oz. ASW, 36 mm. **Subject:** 50th Anniversary End of WW II **Obv:** Quill pens horizontal at left center, national arms at lower righr **Obv. Inscription:** REPÚBLICA PORTUGUESA **Rev:** Four quill pens upright, outlined map of Europe in background **Rev. Inscription:** FIM DA II GUERRA MUNDIAL **Edge:** Reeded

Date	Mintage	F	VF	XF	Unc	BU
2005INCM	300,000	—	—	—	25.00	—

KM# 773a 8 EURO

31.1000 g., 0.9250 Silver 0.9249 oz. ASW, 36 mm. **Subject:** 50th Anniversary End of WW II **Obv:** Quill pens horizontal at left center, national arms at lower right **Obv. Inscription:** REPÚBLICA PORTUGUESA **Rev:** Four quill pens upright, outlined map of Europe in background **Rev. Inscription:** FIM DA II GUERRA MUNDIAL **Edge:** Reeded

Date	Mintage	F	VF	XF	Unc	BU
2005INCM Proof	35,000	Value: 70.00				

KM# 776 8 EURO

21.0000 g., 0.5000 Silver 0.3376 oz. ASW, 35 mm. **Subject:** Prince Henry the Navigator **Obv:** Small national arms and shield **Obv. Legend:** REPÚBLICA PORTUGUESA **Edge:** Reeded

Date	Mintage	F	VF	XF	Unc	BU
2006INCM	100,000	—	—	—	25.00	—

KM# 776a 8 EURO

31.1000 g., 0.9250 Silver 0.9249 oz. ASW, 35 mm. **Subject:** Prince Henry the Navigator **Obv:** Small national arms and shield **Obv. Legend:** REPÚBLICA PORTUGUESA **Edge:** Reeded

Date	Mintage	F	VF	XF	Unc	BU
2006INCM Proof	35,000	Value: 65.00				

KM# 778 8 EURO

21.0000 g., 0.5000 Silver 0.3376 oz. ASW, 36 mm. **Subject:** 150th Anniversary Railroad Lisbon - Carregado **Obv:** National arms on wavy flag **Obv. Legend:** REPÚBLICA PORTUGUESA **Rev:** Vertical railroad track divides two shields **Rev. Legend:** 150 ANOS DA PRIMEIRA LINHA FERREA LISBOA CARREGADO **Edge:** Reeded

Date	Mintage	F	VF	XF	Unc	BU
2006INCM	100,000	—	—	—	25.00	—

KM# 778a 8 EURO

31.1000 g., 0.9250 Silver 0.9249 oz. ASW, 36 mm. **Subject:** 150th Anniversary Railroad Lisbon - Carregado **Obv:** National srms on wavy flag **Obv. Legend:** REPÚBLICA PORTUGUESA **Rev:** Vertical railroad track divides two shields **Rev. Legend:** 150 ANOSDA PRIMEIRA LINHA FERREA LISBOA CARREGADO **Edge:** Reeded

Date	Mintage	F	VF	XF	Unc	BU
2006INCM Proof	35,000	Value: 75.00				

KM# 748 10 EURO
27.0000 g., 0.5000 Silver 0.4340 oz. ASW, 40 mm. **Subject:** Nautica **Obv:** National arms within circle of assorted shields **Rev:** Sailing ship and sextant **Edge:** Reeded

Date	Mintage	F	VF	XF	Unc	BU
2003INCM	350,000	—	—	—	20.00	22.50

KM# 748a 10 EURO
27.0000 g., 0.9250 Silver 0.8029 oz. ASW, 40 mm. **Obv:** National arms within circle of assorted shields **Rev:** Sailing ship and sextant **Edge:** Reeded

Date	Mintage	F	VF	XF	Unc	BU
2003INCM Proof	10,000	Value: 50.00				

KM# 759 10 EURO
27.0000 g., 0.5000 Silver 0.4340 oz. ASW, 40 mm. **Subject:** Olympics **Obv:** National arms above stylized value **Rev:** Stylized sail above Olympic rings **Edge:** Reeded

Date	Mintage	F	VF	XF	Unc	BU
2004INCM	350,000	—	—	—	25.00	27.50

KM# 759a 10 EURO
27.0000 g., 0.9250 Silver 0.8029 oz. ASW, 40 mm. **Subject:** Olympics **Obv:** National arms above stylized value **Rev:** Stylized sail above Olympic rings **Edge:** Reeded

Date	Mintage	F	VF	XF	Unc	BU
2004INCM Proof	15,000	Value: 55.00				

KM# 774 10 EURO
27.0000 g., 0.5000 Silver 0.4340 oz. ASW, 40 mm. **Subject:** XVIII World Championship Football Games - Germany 2006 **Obv:** National arms above stadium **Obv. Inscription:** REPÚBLICA PORTUGUESA **Rev:** Circular legend above sticks representing stadium fans **Edge:** Reeded

Date	Mintage	F	VF	XF	Unc	BU
2006INCM	100,000	—	—	—	25.00	27.50

KM# 774a 10 EURO
27.0000 g., 0.9250 Silver 0.8029 oz. ASW, 40 mm. **Subject:** XVIII World Championship Football Games - Germany 2006 **Obv:** National arms above stadium **Obv. Inscription:** REPÚBLICA PORTUGUESA **Rev:** Circular legend above sticks representing stadium fans **Edge:** Reeded

Date	Mintage	F	VF	XF	Unc	BU
2006INCM Proof	25,000	Value: 85.00				

KM# 775 10 EURO
27.0000 g., 0.5000 Silver 0.4340 oz. ASW, 40 mm. **Subject:** 20th Anniversary of Spain and Portugal's membership in the European Union **Obv:** National arms **Obv. Legend:** REPÚBLICA PORTUGUESA **Rev:** Viaduct, outlined map of Europe above **Rev. Legend:** ADESÃO AS COMUNIDADES EUROPIAS **Edge:** Reeded

Date	Mintage	F	VF	XF	Unc	BU
2006INCM	100,000	—	—	—	25.00	27.50

KM# 775a 10 EURO
27.0000 g., 0.9250 Silver 0.8029 oz. ASW, 40 mm. **Subject:** 20th Anniversary of Spain and Portugal's membership in European Union **Obv:** National arms **Obv. Legend:** REPÚBLICA PORTUGUESA **Rev:** Viaduct, outlined map of Europe above **Rev. Legend:** ADESÃO AS COMUNIDADES EUROPIAS **Edge:** Reeded

Date	Mintage	F	VF	XF	Unc	BU
2006INCM Proof	25,000	Value: 70.00				

MINT SETS

KM#	Date	Mintage	Identification	Issue Price	Mkt Val
MS32	2002 (8)	50,000	KM#740-747	—	55.00
MS33	2003 (8)	50,000	KM#740-747	—	55.00
MS34	2004 (8)	50,000	KM#740-747	—	50.00
MS35	2005 (8)	30,000	KM#740-747	—	50.00
MS36	2006 (8)	12,500	KM#740-747	—	50.00

PROOF SETS

KM#	Date	Mintage	Identification	Issue Price	Mkt Val
PS45	2002 (8)	15,000	KM#740-747	—	120
PS46	2003 (8)	15,000	kM#740-747	—	100
PS47	2004 (8)	15,000	KM#740-747	—	100
PS48	2005 (8)	10,000	KM#740-747	—	100
PS49	2006 (8)	3,000	KM#740-747	—	110

QATAR

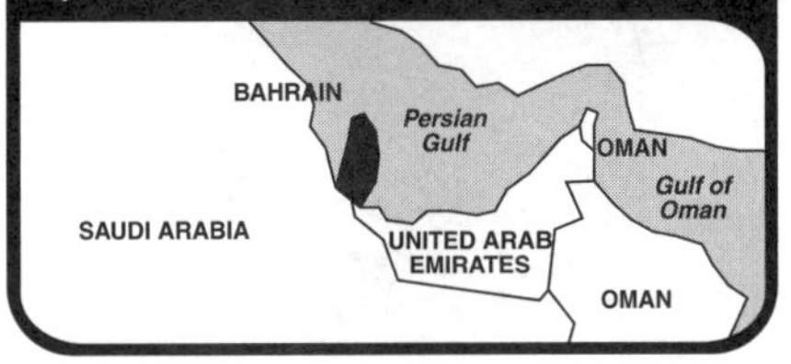

The State of Qatar, an emirate in the Persian Gulf between Bahrain and Trucial Oman, has an area of 4,247sq. mi. (11,000 sq. km.) and a population of *469,000. Capital: Doha. Oil is the chief industry and export.

TITLES

دولة قطر

Daulat Qatar

RULERS

Al-Thani Dynasty

Hamad bin Khalifah, 1995-

MONETARY SYSTEM

100 Dirhem = 1 Riyal

STATE

STANDARD COINAGE

KM# 12 5 DIRHAMS
3.8000 g., Bronze, 22 mm. **Ruler:** Hamad bin Khalifah **Obv:** Arms **Rev:** Value **Edge:** Plain

Date	Mintage	F	VF	XF	Unc	BU
AH1427-2006	—	—	—	—	0.75	1.25

KM# 13 10 DIRHAMS
7.5000 g., Bronze, 26 mm. **Ruler:** Hamad bin Khalifah **Obv:** Arms **Rev:** Value **Edge:** Plain

Date	Mintage	F	VF	XF	Unc	BU
AH1427-2006	—	—	—	—	1.25	2.00

KM# 8 25 DIRHAMS
3.5000 g., Copper-Nickel, 19 mm. **Ruler:** Hamad bin Khalifah **Obv:** Value **Obv. Legend:** STATE OF QATAR **Rev:** Sail boat and palm trees flanked by beads **Edge:** Reeded

Date	Mintage	F	VF	XF	Unc	BU
AH1424-2003	—	—	0.30	0.65	1.50	2.50

KM# 14 25 DIRHAMS
3.5000 g., Copper-Nickel, 19 mm. **Ruler:** Hamad bin Khalifah **Obv:** Arms **Rev:** Value **Edge:** Reeded

Date	Mintage	F	VF	XF	Unc	BU
AH1427-2006	—	—	—	—	1.50	2.50

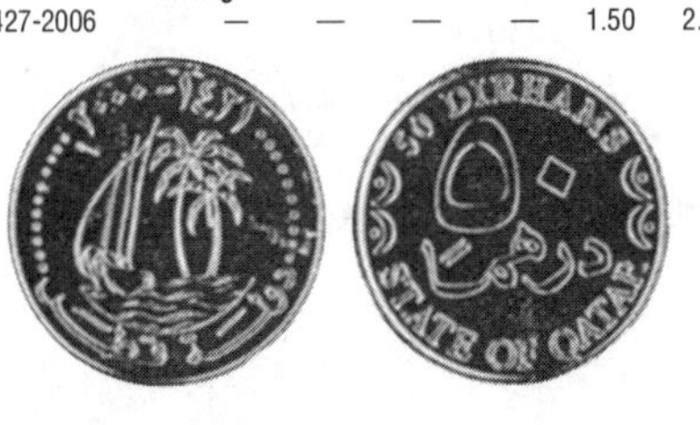

KM# 9 50 DIRHAMS
6.5000 g., Copper-Nickel, 24 mm. **Ruler:** Hamad bin Khalifah **Obv:** Arms **Rev:** Value **Edge:** Reeded

Date	Mintage	F	VF	XF	Unc	BU
AH1424-2003	—	—	—	—	2.00	3.00

KM# 15 50 DIRHAMS
6.5000 g., Copper-Nickel, 24 mm. **Ruler:** Hamad bin Khalifah **Obv:** Arms **Rev:** Value **Edge:** Reeded

Date	Mintage	F	VF	XF	Unc	BU
AH1427-2006	—	—	—	—	1.75	2.75

KM# 16 RIYAL
Aluminum-Bronze **Ruler:** Hamad bin Khalifah **Subject:** 15th Asian Games **Obv:** Arms above value **Rev:** Multicolor Fox on Bicycle, cartoon character

Date	Mintage	F	VF	XF	Unc	BU
2006	—	—	—	—	3.50	4.25

KM# 34 RIYAL
Aluminum-Bronze, 38.74 mm. **Ruler:** Hamad bin Khalifah **Subject:** 15th Asian Games **Obv:** Arms **Rev:** Multicolor mascot with flag

Date	Mintage	F	VF	XF	Unc	BU
2006	25,000	—	—	—	—	15.00

KM# 35 RIYAL
Aluminum-Bronze, 38.74 mm. **Ruler:** Hamad bin Khalifah **Subject:** 15th Asian Games **Obv:** Arms **Rev:** Multicolor mascot kicking soccer ball

Date	Mintage	F	VF	XF	Unc	BU
2006	25,000	—	—	—	—	15.00

KM# 36 RIYAL
Aluminum-Bronze, 38.74 mm. **Ruler:** Hamad bin Khalifah **Subject:** 15th Asian Games **Obv:** Arms **Rev:** Three multicolor torches

Date	Mintage	F	VF	XF	Unc	BU
2006	25,000	—	—	—	—	15.00

KM# 37 RIYAL
Aluminum-Bronze, 38.74 mm. **Ruler:** Hamad bin Khalifah **Subject:** 15th Asian Games **Obv:** Arms **Rev:** Two figures with linked arms

Date	Mintage	F	VF	XF	Unc	BU
2006	25,000	—	—	—	—	15.00

KM# 38 RIYAL
Aluminum-Bronze, 38.74 mm. **Ruler:** Hamad bin Khalifah **Subject:** 15th Asian Games **Obv:** Arms **Rev:** Figure with outstretched arms

Date	Mintage	F	VF	XF	Unc	BU
2006	25,000	—	—	—	—	15.00

KM# 25 10 RIYALS
31.1035 g., 0.9990 Silver 0.9990 oz. ASW, 40.5 mm. **Ruler:** Hamad bin Khalifah **Subject:** 15th Asian Games **Obv:** Arms **Rev:** Runner trailing green color

Date	Mintage	F	VF	XF	Unc	BU
2006 Proof	25,000	Value: 75.00				

KM# 26 10 RIYALS
31.1035 g., 0.9990 Silver 0.9990 oz. ASW, 40.5 mm. **Ruler:** Hamad bin Khalifah **Subject:** 15th Asian Games **Obv:** Arms **Rev:** Cyclist trailing red color

Date	Mintage	F	VF	XF	Unc	BU
2006 Proof	25,000	Value: 75.00				

KM# 27 10 RIYALS
31.1035 g., 0.9990 Silver 0.9990 oz. ASW, 40.5 mm. **Ruler:** Hamad bin Khalifah **Subject:** 15th Asian Games **Obv:** Arms **Rev:** Soccer player legs on green color

Date	Mintage	F	VF	XF	Unc	BU
2006 Proof	25,000	Value: 75.00				

KM# 28 10 RIYALS
31.1035 g., 0.9990 Silver 0.9990 oz. ASW, 40.5 mm. **Ruler:** Hamad bin Khalifah **Subject:** 15th Asian Games **Obv:** Arms **Rev:** Ribbon dancer trailing red color

Date	Mintage	F	VF	XF	Unc	BU
2006 Proof	25,000	Value: 75.00				

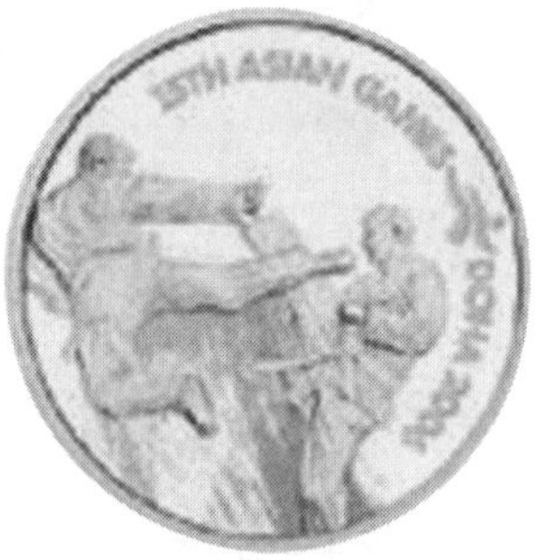

KM# 29 10 RIYALS
31.1035 g., 0.9990 Silver 0.9990 oz. ASW, 40.5 mm. **Ruler:** Hamad bin Khalifah **Subject:** 15th Asian Games **Obv:** Arms **Rev:** Karate contestants and dark yellow color

Date	Mintage	F	VF	XF	Unc	BU
2006 Proof	25,000	Value: 75.00				

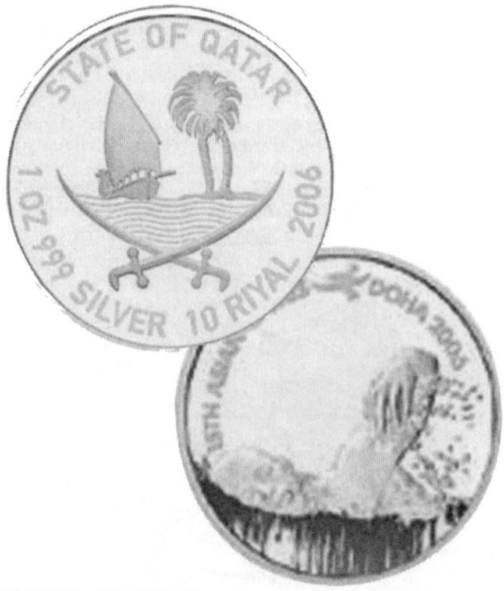

KM# 30 10 RIYALS
31.1035 g., 0.9990 Silver 0.9990 oz. ASW, 40.5 mm. **Ruler:** Hamad bin Khalifah **Subject:** 15th Asian Games **Obv:** Arms **Rev:** Swimmer in aqua colored water

Date	Mintage	F	VF	XF	Unc	BU
2006 Proof	25,000	Value: 75.00				

KM# 31 10 RIYALS
31.1035 g., 0.9990 Silver 0.9990 oz. ASW, 40.5 mm. **Ruler:** Hamad bin Khalifah **Subject:** 15th Asian Games **Obv:** Arms **Rev:** Table tennis player and orange-brownish color

Date	Mintage	F	VF	XF	Unc	BU
2006 Proof	25,000	Value: 75.00				

KM# 32 10 RIYALS
31.1035 g., 0.9990 Silver 0.9990 oz. ASW, 40.5 mm. **Ruler:** Hamad bin Khalifah **Subject:** 15th Asian Games **Obv:** Arms **Rev:** Tennis player and aqua color

Date	Mintage	F	VF	XF	Unc	BU
2006 Proof	25,000	Value: 75.00				

KM# 33 10 RIYALS
31.1035 g., 0.9990 Silver 0.9990 oz. ASW, 40.5 mm. **Ruler:** Hamad bin Khalifah **Subject:** 15th Asian Games **Obv:** Arms **Rev:** Volleyball player trailing purple color

Date	Mintage	F	VF	XF	Unc	BU
2006 Proof	25,000	Value: 75.00				

KM# 17 100 RIYALS
Gold **Ruler:** Hamad bin Khalifah **Subject:** 15th Asian Games **Obv:** Arms above value **Rev:** Games mascot Fox on Bicycle cartoon character

Date	Mintage	F	VF	XF	Unc	BU
2006 Proof	Est. 10,000	Value: 525				

KM# 18 100 RIYALS
17.0000 g., 0.9200 Gold 0.5028 oz. AGW, 31 mm. **Ruler:** Hamad bin Khalifah **Obv:** Arms **Rev:** Central Bank building **Edge:** Reeded

Date	Mintage	F	VF	XF	Unc	BU
2006 Proof	300	Value: 1,200				

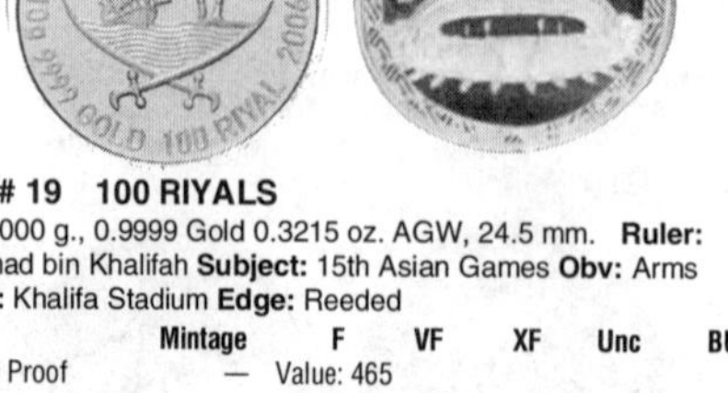

KM# 19 100 RIYALS
10.0000 g., 0.9999 Gold 0.3215 oz. AGW, 24.5 mm. **Ruler:** Hamad bin Khalifah **Subject:** 15th Asian Games **Obv:** Arms **Rev:** Khalifa Stadium **Edge:** Reeded

Date	Mintage	F	VF	XF	Unc	BU
2006 Proof	—	Value: 465				

KM# 20 100 RIYALS
10.0000 g., 0.9999 Gold 0.3215 oz. AGW, 24.5 mm. **Ruler:** Hamad bin Khalifah **Subject:** 15th Asian Games **Obv:** Arms **Rev:** Two fighting oryxes **Edge:** Reeded

Date	Mintage	F	VF	XF	Unc	BU
2006 Proof	—	Value: 465				

KM# 21 100 RIYALS
10.0000 g., 0.9999 Gold 0.3215 oz. AGW, 24.5 mm. **Ruler:** Hamad bin Khalifah **Subject:** 15th Asian Games **Obv:** Arms **Rev:** Falcon bust **Edge:** Reeded

Date	Mintage	F	VF	XF	Unc	BU
2006 Proof	—	Value: 465				

KM# 22 100 RIYALS
10.0000 g., 0.9999 Gold 0.3215 oz. AGW, 24.5 mm. **Ruler:** Hamad bin Khalifah **Subject:** 15th Asian Games **Obv:** Arms **Rev:** Coffee pot **Edge:** Reeded

Date	Mintage	F	VF	XF	Unc	BU
2006 Proof	—	Value: 465				

KM# 23 100 RIYALS
10.0000 g., 0.9999 Gold 0.3215 oz. AGW, 24.5 mm. **Ruler:** Hamad bin Khalifah **Subject:** 15th Asian Games **Obv:** Arms **Rev:** Radiant sun **Edge:** Reeded

Date	Mintage	F	VF	XF	Unc	BU
2006 Proof	—	Value: 465				

KM# 11 250 RIYALS
Silver **Ruler:** Hamad bin Khalifah **Subject:** 4th WTO Conference **Obv:** National arms **Rev:** WTO logo, value, date, and legend in English and Islamic

Date	Mintage	F	VF	XF	Unc	BU
AH1422 (2001) Proof	—	Value: 250				

KM# 39 300 RIYALS
1000.0000 g., 0.9990 Silver 32.117 oz. ASW, 100.0 mm. **Ruler:** Hamad bin Khalifah **Obv.** National arms **Obv. Legend:** STATE OF QATAR **Rev:** Sports montage around game's logo **Rev. Inscription:** 15TH ASIAN GAMES / DOHA 2006 **Edge:** Plain

Date	Mintage	F	VF	XF	Unc	BU
2006 Proof	5,000	Value: 675				

KM# 24 10000 RIYALS
1000.0000 g., 0.9999 Gold 32.146 oz. AGW, 75.3 mm. **Ruler:** Hamad bin Khalifah **Subject:** 15th Asian Games **Obv:** Arms **Rev:** Radiant sun **Edge:** Reeded **Note:** Illustration reduced.

Date	Mintage	F	VF	XF	Unc	BU
2006 Proof	—	Value: 35,000				

ROMANIA

Romania (formerly the Socialist Republic of Romania), a country in southeast Europe, has an area of 91,699 sq. mi. (237,500 sq. km.) and a population of 23.2 million. Capital: Bucharest. Machinery, foodstuffs, raw minerals and petroleum products are exported. Heavy industry and oil have become increasingly important to the economy since 1959. Romania joined the European Union in January 2007.

MONETARY SYSTEM
100 Bani = 1 Leu

REPUBLIC

STANDARD COINAGE

KM# 115 LEU
2.5200 g., Copper Clad Steel, 19 mm. **Obv:** Value flanked by sprigs **Rev:** Shield divides date

Date	Mintage	F	VF	XF	Unc	BU
2002 Proof	1,500	Value: 5.00				
2003 Proof	2,000	Value: 5.00				
2004 Proof	2,000	Value: 5.00				
2005	—	—	—	—	1.00	—
2005 Proof	—	Value: 6.00				
2006 Proof	1,000	Value: 6.00				

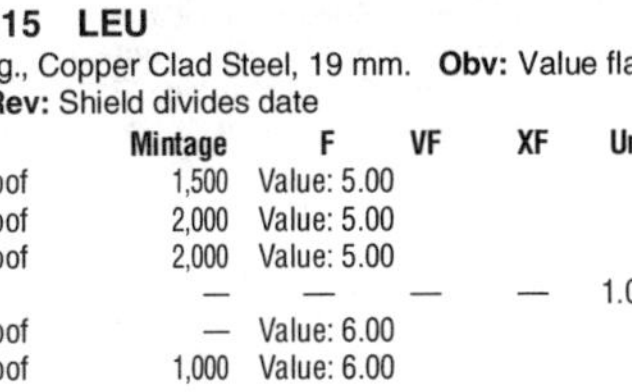

KM# 114 5 LEI
3.3000 g., Nickel Plated Steel, 20.99 mm. **Obv:** Value flanked by oak leaves **Rev:** Shield divides date **Edge:** Plain

Date	Mintage	F	VF	XF	Unc	BU
2002 Proof	1,500	Value: 5.00				
2003 Proof	2,000	Value: 5.00				
2004 Proof	—	Value: 5.00				
2005 Proof	—	Value: 5.00				

KM# 116 10 LEI
4.7000 g., Nickel-Clad Steel, 23 mm. **Obv:** Value within sprigs **Rev:** Shield divides date **Edge:** Plain

Date	Mintage	F	VF	XF	Unc	BU
2002 Proof	1,500	Value: 6.00				
2003 Proof	2,000	Value: 6.00				

KM# 109 20 LEI
5.0000 g., Brass Clad Steel, 24 mm. **Obv:** Crowned bust of Prince Stefan Cel Mare facing, flanked by dots **Rev:** Value and date within half sprigs and dots **Edge:** Plain **Designer:** Constantin Dumitrescu **Note:** Date varieties exist.

Date	Mintage	F	VF	XF	Unc	BU
2002 Proof	1,500	Value: 7.50				
2003 Proof	2,000	Value: 7.50				

KM# 159 50 LEI
15.5510 g., 0.9990 Silver 0.4995 oz. ASW, 31.1 mm. **Series:** Romanian Aviation **Obv:** AVIONUL VUIA 1 - 1906 airplane **Rev:** Traian Vuia **Edge:** Plain **Shape:** Octagonal

Date	Mintage	F	VF	XF	Unc	BU
2001 Proof	500	Value: 100				

KM# 160 50 LEI
15.5510 g., 0.9990 Silver 0.4995 oz. ASW, 31.1 mm. **Series:** Romanian Aviation **Obv:** Avionul Coanda 1910, world's first (?) jet airplane **Rev:** Portrait of Henri Coanda **Edge:** Plain **Shape:** Octagonal

Date	Mintage	F	VF	XF	Unc	BU
2001 Proof	500	Value: 100				

KM# 161 50 LEI
15.5510 g., 0.9990 Silver 0.4995 oz. ASW, 31.1 mm. **Series:** Romanian Aviation **Obv:** IAR CV-11 airplane **Rev:** Elie Carafoli **Edge:** Plain **Shape:** Octagonal

Date	Mintage	F	VF	XF	Unc	BU
2001 Proof	500	Value: 100				

KM# 110 50 LEI
5.9000 g., Brass Clad Steel, 26 mm. **Obv:** Bust left flanked by dots **Rev:** Sprig divides date and value **Edge:** Plain **Designer:** Vasile Gabor

Date	Mintage	F	VF	XF	Unc	BU
2002 Proof	1,500	Value: 8.00				
2003 Proof	2,000	Value: 8.00				

KM# 167 50 LEI
15.5510 g., 0.9990 Silver 0.4995 oz. ASW, 27 mm. **Subject:** National Parks: Retezzf **Obv:** National arms in triangular design **Rev:** Chamois **Edge:** Plain **Shape:** Rounded triangle

Date	Mintage	F	VF	XF	Unc	BU
2002 Proof	500	Value: 85.00				

KM# 168 50 LEI
15.5510 g., 0.9990 Silver 0.4995 oz. ASW, 27 mm. **Subject:** National Parks: Pictrosul Mare **Obv:** National arms in triangular design **Rev:** Eagle **Edge:** Plain **Shape:** Rounded triangle

Date	Mintage	F	VF	XF	Unc	BU
2002 Proof	500	Value: 85.00				

KM# 169 50 LEI
15.5510 g., 0.9990 Silver 0.4995 oz. ASW, 27 mm. **Subject:** National Parks: Piztra Crzivtvi **Obv:** National arms in triangular design **Rev:** Lynx **Edge:** Plain **Shape:** Rounded triangle

Date	Mintage	F	VF	XF	Unc	BU
2002 Proof	500	Value: 85.00				

KM# 186 50 LEI
15.5510 g., 0.9990 Silver 0.4995 oz. ASW, 26.8 mm. **Subject:** Birds **Obv:** Stylized water drop **Rev:** Pelicans within circle **Edge:** Plain

Date	Mintage	F	VF	XF	Unc	BU
2003 Proof	500	Value: 75.00				

KM# 187 50 LEI
15.5510 g., 0.9990 Silver 0.4995 oz. ASW, 26.8 mm. **Subject:** Birds **Obv:** Stylized water drop **Rev:** Great Egret within circle **Edge:** Plain

Date	Mintage	F	VF	XF	Unc	BU
2003 Proof	500	Value: 75.00				

KM# 188 50 LEI
15.5510 g., 0.9990 Silver 0.4995 oz. ASW, 26.8 mm. **Subject:** Birds **Obv:** Stylized water drop **Rev:** Kingfisher within circle **Edge:** Plain

Date	Mintage	F	VF	XF	Unc	BU
2003 Proof	500	Value: 80.00				

KM# 111 100 LEI
8.7500 g., Nickel Plated Steel, 29 mm. **Obv:** Bust with headdress 1/4 right **Rev:** Value within sprigs **Edge Lettering:** ROMANIA **Designer:** Vasile Gabor

Date	Mintage	F	VF	XF	Unc	BU
2002 Proof	1,500	Value: 8.00				
2003 Proof	2,000	Value: 8.00				
2004 Proof	2,000	Value: 8.00				
2005	—	—	—	—	2.50	—
2005 Proof	2,000	Value: 9.00				
2006 Proof	1,000	Value: 9.00				

KM# 165 100 LEI
1.2240 g., 0.9990 Gold 0.0393 oz. AGW **Subject:** History of Gold - "The Apahida Eagle" **Obv:** National arms in ornamental circle above value **Edge:** Plain

Date	Mintage	F	VF	XF	Unc	BU
2003 Proof	2,000	Value: 125				

KM# 166 100 LEI
1.2240 g., 0.9990 Gold 0.0393 oz. AGW, 14 mm. **Subject:** History of Gold **Obv:** National arms and country name above two stylized birds and value **Rev:** Jeweled double headed eagle pendant

Date	Mintage	F	VF	XF	Unc	BU
2004 Proof	1,000	Value: 165				

KM# 170 500 LEI
6.2200 g., 0.9990 Gold 0.1998 oz. AGW, 12 mm. **Subject:** History of Gold - Treasure of Pietroasa **Rev:** "Big clip" of Pietroasa

Date	Mintage	F	VF	XF	Unc	BU
	250	—	—	—	—	250

KM# 171 500 LEI
6.2200 g., 0.9990 Gold 0.1998 oz. AGW **Subject:** History of Gold - Treasure of Pietroasa **Rev:** "Medium Clip" of Pietroasa

Date	Mintage	F	VF	XF	Unc	BU
2001	250	—	—	—	—	250

KM# 172 500 LEI
6.2200 g., 0.9990 Gold 0.1998 oz. AGW **Subject:** History of Gold - Treasure of Pietroasa **Rev:** 12-sided golden bowl

Date	Mintage	F	VF	XF	Unc	BU
2001	250	—	—	—	—	250

KM# 173 500 LEI
6.2200 g., 0.9990 Gold 0.1998 oz. AGW **Subject:** History of Gold - Treasure of Pietroasa **Rev:** Pitcher

Date	Mintage	F	VF	XF	Unc	BU
2001	250	—	—	—	—	250

KM# 176 500 LEI
6.2200 g., 0.9990 Gold 0.1998 oz. AGW, 23 mm. **Subject:** Christian Monuments **Rev:** Mogosoaia Palace **Shape:** Square

Date	Mintage	F	VF	XF	Unc	BU
2001	250	—	—	—	—	250

KM# 145 500 LEI
3.7000 g., Aluminum, 25 mm. **Obv:** Shield within sprigs **Rev:** Value within 3/4 wreath **Edge:** Lettered **Edge Lettering:** ROMANIA (three times)

Date	Mintage	F	VF	XF	Unc	BU
2001	—	—	—	0.75	2.00	—
2002 Proof	1,500	Value: 7.00				
2003 Proof	2,000	Value: 7.00				
2004 Proof	2,000	Value: 7.00				
2005	—	—	—	—	3.00	—
2005 Proof	1,000	Value: 8.00				
2006	—	—	—	—	3.00	—
2006 Proof	—	Value: 8.00				

KM# 174 500 LEI
6.2200 g., 0.9990 Gold 0.1998 oz. AGW **Subject:** Christian Monuments **Rev:** Bistritz Monastery

Date	Mintage	F	VF	XF	Unc	BU
2002	250	—	—	—	—	250

KM# 175 500 LEI
6.2200 g., 0.9990 Gold 0.1998 oz. AGW **Subject:** Christian Monuments **Rev:** Coltea Church

Date	Mintage	F	VF	XF	Unc	BU
2002	250	—	—	—	—	225

KM# 177 500 LEI
31.1030 g., 0.9990 Silver 0.9989 oz. ASW, 37 mm. **Subject:** 150th Anniversary - Birth of Ciprian Porumbescu, Composer **Obv:** Partial piano and violin left of National arms and value **Rev:** Portrait and musical score **Edge:** Plain

Date	Mintage	F	VF	XF	Unc	BU
2003 Proof	500	Value: 80.00				

KM# 178 500 LEI
31.1030 g., 0.9990 Silver 0.9989 oz. ASW, 37 mm. **Subject:** 500th Anniversary - Establishment of Bishopric of Ramnic **Obv:** National arms and value above inscription **Rev:** Bishopric's coat-of-arms **Edge:** Plain

Date	Mintage	F	VF	XF	Unc	BU
2003 Proof	500	Value: 80.00				

KM# 179 500 LEI
31.1030 g., 0.9990 Silver 0.9989 oz. ASW, 37 mm. **Subject:** Romanian Numismatic Society Centennial **Obv:** Cornucopia above value **Rev:** Minerva and torch

Date	Mintage	F	VF	XF	Unc	BU
2003 Proof	1,000	Value: 75.00				

KM# 180 500 LEI
31.1030 g., 0.9990 Silver 0.9989 oz. ASW, 37 mm. **Subject:** 140th Anniversary - University of Bucharest **Obv:** National arms, value and date at left. University emblem at right **Rev:** Cameo and crowned arms above University Building **Edge:** Plain

Date	Mintage	F	VF	XF	Unc	BU
2004 Proof	500	Value: 100				

KM# 193 500 LEI
31.1035 g., 0.9990 Silver 0.9990 oz. ASW, 37 mm. **Subject:** 150th Anniversary - Birth of Anghel Saligny **Obv:** Cernavoda bridge **Rev:** Bridge builder Anghel Saligny **Edge:** Plain

Date	Mintage	F	VF	XF	Unc	BU
2004 Proof	500	Value: 80.00				

KM# 163 500 LEI
31.1030 g., 0.9990 Silver 0.9989 oz. ASW, 37 mm. **Subject:** Christian Feudal Art Monuments **Obv:** National arms and value left of church tower **Rev:** Cotroceni Monastery church **Edge:** Plain **Shape:** 10-sided

Date	Mintage	F	VF	XF	Unc	BU
2004 Proof	500	Value: 80.00				

KM# 164 500 LEI
31.1030 g., 0.9990 Silver 0.9989 oz. ASW, 37 mm. **Subject:** Christian Feudal Art Monuments **Obv:** National arms, bell and value **Rev:** St. Trei Ierarhi church in Iasi **Edge:** Plain **Shape:** 10-sided

Date	Mintage	F	VF	XF	Unc	BU
2004 Proof	500	Value: 80.00				

KM# 194 500 LEI
31.1035 g., 0.9990 Silver 0.9990 oz. ASW, 37 mm. **Subject:** 125th Anniversary - National Bank **Obv:** National arms and coin design of 5 Lei dated 1880 **Rev:** Bank building **Edge:** Plain

Date	Mintage	F	VF	XF	Unc	BU
2005 Proof	—	Value: 300				

KM# 153 1000 LEI
2.0000 g., Aluminum, 22.2 mm. **Subject:** Constantin Brancoveanu **Obv:** Value above shield within lined circle **Rev:** Bust with headdress facing **Edge:** Plain with serrated sections

Date	Mintage	VG	F	VF	XF	Unc
2001	—	—	—	—	0.25	2.50
2002	—	—	—	—	0.25	2.50
2002 Proof	1,500	Value: 12.00				
Note: In proof sets only						
2003	—	—	—	—	0.25	2.50
2003 Proof	2,000	Value: 12.00				
Note: In proof sets only						
2004	—	—	—	—	0.25	2.50
2004 Proof	2,000	Value: 12.00				
Note: In proof sets only						
2005	—	—	—	—	0.25	2.50
2005 Proof	—	Value: 13.00				
Note: In proof sets only						
2006 Proof	1,000	Value: 13.00				

KM# 156 1000 LEI
15.5510 g., 0.9990 Gold 0.4995 oz. AGW, 27 mm. **Subject:** 1900th Anniversary of the First Roman-Dacian War **Obv:** Traian's column and shield **Rev:** Monument divides cameos **Edge:** Plain

Date	Mintage	VG	F	VF	XF	Unc
2001 Proof	500	Value: 575				

KM# 181 2000 LEI
25.0000 g., Bi-Metallic .999 Silver, 10g center in .999 Gold, 15g ring, 35 mm. **Subject:** Ion Heliade Radulescu (1802-1872) **Obv:** Lyre at left, national arms at right in divided circle design **Rev:** Ion Heliade Radulescu above signature **Edge:** Reeded

Date	Mintage	F	VF	XF	Unc	BU
2002 Proof	500	Value: 700				

KM# 158 5000 LEI
2.5200 g., Aluminum, 23.5 mm. **Obv:** Value and country name **Rev:** Sprig divides date and shield **Edge:** Plain **Shape:** 12-sided

Date	Mintage	F	VF	XF	Unc	BU
2001	—	—	—	—	0.50	—
2002	—	—	—	—	0.50	—
2002 Proof	1,500	Value: 15.00				
2003	—	—	—	—	0.25	—
2003 Proof	2,000	Value: 15.00				
2004	—	—	—	—	0.25	—
2004 Proof	2,000	Value: 16.00				
2005	—	—	—	—	0.25	—
2005 Proof	2,000	Value: 17.00				
2006 Proof	1,000	Value: 17.00				

KM# 162 5000 LEI
31.1035 g., 0.9990 Gold 0.9990 oz. AGW, 35 mm. **Subject:** Constantin Brancusi 125th Anniversary of Birth **Obv:** National arms, value and sculpture **Rev:** Bearded portrait and signature **Edge:** Plain

Date	Mintage	F	VF	XF	Unc	BU
2001 Proof	500	Value: 1,100				

KM# 183 5000 LEI
31.1030 g., 0.9990 Gold 0.9989 oz. AGW, 35 mm. **Subject:** Ion Luca Caragiale, playright (1852-1912) **Obv:** National arms, value and masks of Comedy and Tragedy **Rev:** Portrait **Edge:** Plain

Date	Mintage	F	VF	XF	Unc	BU
2002 Proof	250	Value: 1,150				

KM# 184 5000 LEI
31.1030 g., 0.9990 Gold 0.9989 oz. AGW, 35 mm. **Subject:** Bran Castle (1378-2003) **Obv:** Two coats of arms on shield above value **Rev:** Castle view **Edge:** Plain

Date	Mintage	F	VF	XF	Unc	BU
2003 Proof	250	Value: 1,150				

KM# 185 5000 LEI
31.1030 g., 0.9990 Gold 0.9989 oz. AGW, 35 mm. **Subject:** Stephen the Great **Obv:** National arms, value above coin design in wall **Rev:** Portrait of Stephen and Putna Monastery

Date	Mintage	F	VF	XF	Unc	BU
2004 Proof	250	Value: 1,150				

REFORM COINAGE - 2005

10,000 Old Leu = 1 New Leu

KM# 189 BAN
2.4000 g., Copper-Plated-Steel, 16.8 mm. **Subject:** Monetary Reform of 2005 **Obv:** National arms flanked by stars **Rev:** Value **Edge:** Plain

Date	Mintage	F	VF	XF	Unc	BU
2005	—	—	—	—	0.30	0.50
2005 Proof	—	Value: 2.50				
2006	—	—	—	—	0.30	0.50
2006 Proof	—	Value: 2.50				
2007	—	—	—	—	0.30	0.50
2007 Proof	—	Value: 2.50				

KM# 190 5 BANI
2.8100 g., Copper Plated Steel, 18.2 mm. **Subject:** Monetary Reform of 2005 **Obv:** National arms flanked by stars **Obv. Legend:** ROMANIA **Rev:** Value **Edge:** Reeded

Date	Mintage	F	VF	XF	Unc	BU
2005	—	—	—	—	0.50	0.75
2005 Proof	—	Value: 5.00				
2006	—	—	—	—	0.50	0.65
2006 Proof	—	Value: 5.00				
2007	—	—	—	—	0.50	0.65
2007 Proof	—	Value: 5.00				

KM# 191 10 BANI
4.0000 g., Nickel Plated Steel, 20.4 mm. **Subject:** Monetary Reform of 2005 **Obv:** National arms flanked by stars **Obv. Legend:** ROMANIA **Rev:** Value **Edge:** Segmented reeding

Date	Mintage	F	VF	XF	Unc	BU
2005	—	—	—	—	0.65	0.85
2005 Proof	—	Value: 7.00				
2006	—	—	—	—	0.60	0.75
2006 Proof	—	Value: 7.00				
2007	—	—	—	—	0.50	0.65
2007 Proof	—	Value: 7.00				

KM# 192 50 BANI
6.1200 g., Brass, 23.6 mm. **Subject:** Monetary Reform of 2005 **Obv:** National arms flanked by stars **Obv. Legend:** ROMANIA **Rev:** Value **Edge:** Lettered **Edge Lettering:** "ROMANIA' twice

Date	Mintage	F	VF	XF	Unc	BU
2005	—	—	—	—	0.85	1.00
2005 Proof	—	Value: 10.00				
2006	—	—	—	—	0.75	0.85
2006 Proof	—	Value: 10.00				
2007	—	—	—	—	0.65	0.75
2007 Proof	—	Value: 10.00				

KM# 209 LEU
23.5000 g., Copper-Plated Brass, 37 mm. **Subject:** 140th Anniversary Founding Romanian Academy **Edge:** Plain

Date	Mintage	F	VF	XF	Unc	BU
2006 Proof	35	Value: 125				

KM# 220 LEU
23.5000 g., Bronze, 37 mm. **Subject:** Centennial - Birth of Mircea Eliade **Edge:** Reeded

Date	Mintage	F	VF	XF	Unc	BU
2007 Proof	250	Value: 85.00				

KM# 223 LEU
23.5000 g., Bronze, 37 mm. **Subject:** Dimitric Cantemir, (Prince of Moldavia 1710-1711), Scientist **Edge:** Reeded

Date	Mintage	F	VF	XF	Unc	BU
2007 Proof	250	Value: 85.00				

KM# 226 LEU
23.5000 g., Bronze, 37 mm. **Subject:** Dimitric Cantemir, (Prince of Moldavia 1710-1711), Scientist **Edge:** Reeded

Date	Mintage	F	VF	XF	Unc	BU
2007 Proof	250	Value: 85.00				

KM# 208 5 LEI
31.1000 g., 0.9990 Silver 0.9988 oz. ASW, 37 mm. **Subject:** 100th Anniversary - Birth of Grigore Vasiliu-Birlic **Edge:** Plain

Date	Mintage	F	VF	XF	Unc	BU
2005 Proof	150	Value: 250				

KM# 210 5 LEI
31.1000 g., 0.9990 Silver 0.9988 oz. ASW, 30 mm. **Subject:** 140th Anniversary Founding Romanian Academy **Edge:** Plain

Date	Mintage	F	VF	XF	Unc	BU
2006 Proof	500	Value: 195				

KM# 212 5 LEI
31.1000 g., 0.9990 Silver 0.9988 oz. ASW, 37 mm. **Subject:** Christian Feudal Art - "Wooden Church from Ieud-Deal" **Obv:** Fragment of mural in Ieud Church depicting Isaac, Abraham and Jacob at top, inscription, value and date in lower half **Obv. Inscription:** ROMANIA **Rev:** Front view of Ieud Church against frosted background **Rev. Inscription:** BISERICA DE LEMN IEUD DEAL **Edge:** Plain **Designer:** Cristian Ciornci, Vasilc Gabor

Date	Mintage	F	VF	XF	Unc	BU
2006 Proof	500	Value: 200				

KM# 213 5 LEI
31.1030 g., Silver, 37 mm. **Subject:** 150th Anniversary - Establishment of the European Commission of the Danube **Edge:** Plain

Date	Mintage	F	VF	XF	Unc	BU
2006 Proof	500	Value: 200				

KM# 216 5 LEI
31.1030 g., 0.9990 Silver 0.9989 oz. ASW, 37 mm. **Subject:** Church from Densus **Obv:** 14th century icon on which "The Holy Trinity of Densus" was painted at left, arms with value below at center, inscription at right **Obv. Inscription:** ROMANIA **Obv. Designer:** Cristian Ciornei and Vasile Gabor **Rev:** Image of Densus Church as from the altar apse, central pillar at right **Rev. Inscription:** BISERICA DE LA DENSUS **Edge:** Plain

Date	Mintage	F	VF	XF	Unc	BU
2006 Proof	500	Value: 200				

KM# 217 5 LEI
31.1030 g., 0.9990 Silver 0.9989 oz. ASW, 37 mm. **Subject:** Designation of Sibiu as the "European Capital of Culture in 2007" **Obv:** 2 city towers in Sibiu at left, fortress wall connecting them, Potter's Tower in background, coat of arms at right **Obv. Inscription:** ROMANIA **Obv. Designer:** Cristian Ciornci and Vasile Gabor **Rev:** City of Sibiu's logo at bottom, 2 line inscription at left, 3 line inscription at right, 4 famous edifices at center **Rev. Inscription:** SIBIU/2007 and CAPITALA / CULTURALA / EUROPEANA **Edge:** Plain

Date	Mintage	F	VF	XF	Unc	BU
2007 Proof	500	Value: 200				

KM# 221 5 LEI
15.5500 g., 0.9990 Silver 0.4994 oz. ASW, 30 mm. **Subject:** Centennial - Birth of Mircea Eliade **Edge:** Reeded

Date	Mintage	F	VF	XF	Unc	BU
2007 Proof	250	Value: 175				

KM# 224 5 LEI
15.5500 g., 0.9000 Silver 0.4499 oz. ASW, 30 mm. **Subject:** Dimitric Cantemir, (Prince of Moldavia 1710-1711), Scientist **Edge:** Reeded

Date	Mintage	F	VF	XF	Unc	BU
2007 Proof	250	Value: 175				

KM# 227 5 LEI
15.5000 g., 0.9990 Silver 0.4978 oz. ASW, 30 mm. **Subject:** Dimitric Cantemir, (Prince of Moldavia 1710-1711), Scientist **Edge:** Reeded

Date	Mintage	F	VF	XF	Unc	BU
2007 Proof	250	Value: 175				

KM# 202 5 LEI
31.1034 g., 0.9990 Silver 0.9990 oz. ASW, 37 mm. **Obv:** National arms and fortified city wall **Rev:** Sibiu (Hermannstadt) city view above city arms **Edge:** Plain

Date	Mintage	F	VF	XF	Unc	BU
2007 Proof	500	Value: 300				

KM# 207 10 LEI
1.2200 g., 0.9990 Gold 0.0392 oz. AGW, 13.92 mm. **Subject:** History of Gold - The Persinari Hoard **Edge:** Plain

Date	Mintage	F	VF	XF	Unc	BU
2005 Proof	1,000	Value: 200				

KM# 215 10 LEI
1.2200 g., 0.9990 Gold 0.0392 oz. AGW, 13.92 mm. **Subject:** Histoy of Gold - The Cuculeni Báiceni Hoard **Edge:** Plain

Date	Mintage	F	VF	XF	Unc	BU
2006 Proof	500	Value: 200				

KM# 203 10 LEI
1.2240 g., 0.9990 Gold 0.0393 oz. AGW **Subject:** Cucuteni Romania **Obv:** Romania's Coat of Arms with denomination **Rev:** Cheekpiece of the gold helmet in the Cucuteni-Baiceni hoard **Edge:** Milled **Designer:** Cristian Ciornei

Date	Mintage	F	VF	XF	Unc	BU
2006 Proof	500	Value: 220				

KM# 229 10 LEI
31.1030 g., 0.9990 Silver 0.9989 oz. ASW, 37 mm. **Subject:** 50th Anniversary - Treaty of Rome **Edge:** Reeded

Date	Mintage	F	VF	XF	Unc	BU
2007 Proof	—	Value: 250				

KM# 211 50 LEI
6.4500 g., 0.9000 Gold 0.1866 oz. AGW, 21 mm. **Subject:** 140th Anniversary Founding Romanian Academy **Edge:** Plain

Date	Mintage	F	VF	XF	Unc	BU
2006 Proof	35	Value: 550				

KM# 222 100 LEI
6.4500 g., 0.9000 Gold 0.1866 oz. AGW, 21 mm. **Subject:** Centennial - Birth of Mircea Eliade **Edge:** Reeded

Date	Mintage	F	VF	XF	Unc	BU
2007 Proof	250	Value: 400				

KM# 225 100 LEI
6.4500 g., 0.9000 Gold 0.1866 oz. AGW, 21 mm. **Subject:** Dimitric Cantemir, (Prince of Moldavia 1710-1711), Scientist **Edge:** Reeded

Date	Mintage	F	VF	XF	Unc	BU
2007 Proof	250	Value: 400				

KM# 228 100 LEI
6.4520 g., 0.9000 Gold 0.1867 oz. AGW, 21 mm. **Subject:** 550th Anniversary - Ascension Prince Stephen the Great into Moldavia **Edge:** Reeded

Date	Mintage	F	VF	XF	Unc	BU
2007 Proof	250	Value: 400				

KM# 206 500 LEI
31.1000 g., 0.9990 Gold 0.9988 oz. AGW, 35 mm. **Subject:** 50th Anniversary - Death of George Enescu **Edge:** Plain

Date	Mintage	F	VF	XF	Unc	BU
2005 Proof	250	Value: 2,000				

KM# 214 500 LEI
31.1030 g., 0.9990 Gold 0.9989 oz. AGW, 35 mm. **Subject:** 350th Anniversary - Establishment of the Patriarchal Cathedral **Edge:** Plain

Date	Mintage	F	VF	XF	Unc	BU
2006 Proof	250	Value: 2,000				

KM# 218 500 LEI
31.1030 g., 0.9990 Gold 0.9989 oz. AGW, 35 mm. **Subject:** The Accession of Romania to the European Union **Edge:** Plain

Date	Mintage	F	VF	XF	Unc	BU
2007 Proof	250	Value: 2,000				

KM# 219 500 LEI
31.1000 g., 0.9990 Gold 0.9988 oz. AGW, 37 mm. **Subject:** Nicolze Ba'lceseu **Edge:** Plain

Date	Mintage	F	VF	XF	Unc	BU
2007 Proof	—	—	—	—	—	2,000

KM# 204 500 LEI
31.1035 g., 0.9990 Gold 0.9990 oz. AGW **Subject:** Romania's Accession to European Union, January 1 2007 **Obv:** Romania's Coat of Arms surrounded by 12 stars of European Union **Rev:** Map of the European Union including Romania **Edge:** Plain **Designer:** Cristian Ciornei

Date	Mintage	F	VF	XF	Unc	BU
2007 Proof	250	Value: 1,750				

KM# 205 500 LEI
31.1035 g., 0.9990 Gold 0.9990 oz. AGW **Subject:** Nicolae Balcescu (1819-1852) **Obv:** Romania's Coat of Arms and **Obv. Inscription:** Justice and Brotherhood **Rev:** Portrait of Nicolae Balcescu **Edge:** Plain

Date	Mintage	F	VF	XF	Unc	BU
2007 Proof	250	Value: 1,850				

MINT SETS

KM#	Date	Mintage	Identification	Issue Price	Mkt Val
MS4	2006 (4)	—	KM189-192, plus medal	—	12.50
MS5	2007 (4)	—	KM189-192, plus medal	—	10.00

PROOF SETS

KM#	Date	Mintage	Identification	Issue Price	Mkt Val
PS4	2001 (3)	500	KM#159,160,161	80.00	250
PS5	2002 (9)	1,500	KM#109-111, 114-116, 145, 153, 158	20.00	50.00
PS6	2003 (9)	2,000	KM#109-111, 114-116, 145, 153, 158	20.00	50.00
PS7	2003 (3)	500	KM#186-188	—	225
PS8	2004 (2)	500	KM#163, 164	—	120
PS9	2005 (10)	—	KM#111, 115, 145, 153, 158, 189-192 plus medal	—	20.00
PS10	2006 (10)	—	KM#111, 115, 145, 153, 158, 189-192	—	20.00
PS11	2006 (3)	—	KM#209-211	—	925
PS12	2007 (3)	—	KM#220-222	—	650
PS13	2007 (3)	—	KM#223-225	—	650
PS14	2007 (3)	—	KM#226-228	—	650
PS15	2007 (5)	—	KM#189-192 plus Silver 75th Anniversary of Rodna Mountains National Park medal	—	50.00

RUSSIA (U.S.S.R.)

Russia, formerly the central power of the Union of Soviet Socialist Republics and now of the Commonwealth of Independent States occupies the northern part of Asia and the eastern part of Europe, has an area of 17,075,400 sq. km. Capital: Moscow. Exports include iron and steel, crude oil, timber, and nonferrous metals.

In the fall of 1991, events moved swiftly in the Soviet Union. Estonia, Latvia and Lithuania won their independence and were recognized by Moscow, Sept. 6. The Commonwealth of Independent States was formed Dec. 8, 1991 in Mensk by Belarus, Russia and Ukraine. It was expanded at a summit Dec. 21, 1991 to include 11 of the 12 remaining republics (excluding Georgia) of the old U.S.S.R.

RUSSIAN FEDERATION

Issued by РОССИJСКИJ БАНК (Russian Bank)

REFORM COINAGE

January 1, 1998

1,000 Old Roubles = 1 New Rouble

Y# 600 KOPEK

1.5000 g., Nickel Plated Steel, 15.54 mm. **Obv:** St. George **Obv. Legend:** БАНК РОССИИ **Rev:** Value above vine sprig **Edge:** Plain

Date	Mintage	F	VF	XF	Unc	BU
2001М	—	—	—	—	0.30	0.40
2001СП	—	—	—	—	0.30	0.40
2002М	—	—	—	—	0.30	0.40
2002СП	—	—	—	—	0.30	0.40
2003М	—	—	—	—	0.30	0.40
2003СП	—	—	—	—	0.30	0.40
2004М	—	—	—	—	0.30	0.40

Y# 601 5 KOPEKS

2.5000 g., Nickel Plated Steel, 19 mm. **Obv:** St. George **Obv. Legend:** БАНК РОССИИ **Rev:** Value above vine sprig **Edge:** Plain

Date	Mintage	F	VF	XF	Unc	BU
2001М	—	—	—	—	0.40	0.50
2001СП	—	—	—	—	0.40	0.50
2002	—	—	—	—	15.00	17.00
2002М	—	—	—	—	0.40	0.50
2002СП	—	—	—	—	0.40	0.50
2003	—	—	—	—	10.00	12.00
2003М	—	—	—	—	0.35	0.50
2003СП	—	—	—	—	0.35	0.50
2004М	—	—	—	—	0.35	0.50
2004СП	—	—	—	—	0.35	0.50
2005М	—	—	—	—	0.35	0.50
2005СП	—	—	—	—	0.35	0.50
2006СП	—	—	—	—	0.35	0.50

KM# 601a 5 KOPEKS

Brass Plated Steel **Obv:** St. George on horseback slaying dragon right **Obv. Legend:** БАНК; РОССИИ **Rev:** Value above vine sprig **Edge:** Plain

Date	Mintage	F	VF	XF	Unc	BU
2006СП	—	—	—	—	0.35	0.50

Y# 602 10 KOPEKS

2.0000 g., Brass **Obv:** St. George horseback right slaying dragon **Rev:** Value above vine sprig **Edge:** Reeded

Date	Mintage	F	VF	XF	Unc	BU
2001М	—	—	—	—	0.50	0.80
2001СП	—	—	—	—	0.50	0.80
2002М	—	—	—	—	0.50	0.80
2002СП	—	—	—	—	0.50	0.80
2003М	—	—	—	—	0.50	0.80
2003СП	—	—	—	—	0.50	0.80
2004М	—	—	—	—	0.50	0.80
2004СП	—	—	—	—	0.50	0.80
2005М	—	—	—	—	0.50	0.80
2005СП	—	—	—	—	0.50	0.80
2006М	—	—	—	—	0.50	0.80
2006СП	—	—	—	—	0.50	0.80
2007М	—	—	—	—	1.00	3.00
2007СП	—	—	—	—	1.00	3.00

Y# 602a 10 KOPEKS

Brass Plated Steel **Obv:** St. George on horseback slaying dragon to right **Obv. Legend:** БАНК РОССИИ **Rev:** Denomination above vine sprig **Edge:** Plain

Date	Mintage	F	VF	XF	Unc	BU
2006М	—	—	—	—	0.50	0.80
2006СП	—	—	—	—	0.50	0.80
2007М	—	—	—	—	0.50	0.80
2007СП	—	—	—	—	0.50	0.80

Y# 603 50 KOPEKS

2.9000 g., Brass, 19.5 mm. **Obv:** St. George on horseback slaying dragon right **Rev:** Value above vine sprig **Edge:** Reeded

Date	Mintage	F	VF	XF	Unc	BU
2001М Rare	—	—	—	—	—	—
2002М	—	—	—	—	0.80	1.00
2002СП	—	—	—	—	0.80	1.00
2003М	—	—	—	—	0.80	1.00
2003СП	—	—	—	—	0.80	1.00
2004М	—	—	—	—	0.80	1.00
2004СП	—	—	—	—	0.80	1.00
2005СП	—	—	—	—	0.80	1.00
2006М	—	—	—	—	0.80	1.00
2006СП	—	—	—	—	0.80	1.00
2007М	—	—	—	—	2.50	4.00
2007СП	—	—	—	—	2.50	4.00

Y# 603a 50 KOPEKS

Brass Plated Steel **Obv:** St. George on horseback slaying dragon right **Rev:** Value above vine sprig **Edge:** Plain

Date	Mintage	F	VF	XF	Unc	BU
2006М	—	—	—	—	0.80	1.00
2006СП	—	—	—	—	0.80	1.00
2007М	—	—	—	—	0.80	1.00
2007СП	—	—	—	—	0.80	1.00

Y# 745 ROUBLE

17.4000 g., 0.9000 Silver 0.5035 oz. ASW, 32.8 mm. **Obv:** Double-headed eagle within beaded circle **Rev:** Ram **Edge:** Reeded

Date	Mintage	F	VF	XF	Unc	BU
2001(sp) Proof	7,500	Value: 50.00				

Y# 746 ROUBLE

17.4000 g., 0.9000 Silver 0.5035 oz. ASW, 32.8 mm. **Obv:** Double-headed eagle within beaded circle **Rev:** Beavers **Edge:** Reeded

Date	Mintage	F	VF	XF	Unc	BU
2001(sp) Proof	7,500	Value: 50.00				

Y# 604 ROUBLE

3.2500 g., Copper-Nickel-Zinc, 20.6 mm. **Obv:** Double-headed eagle **Rev:** Value **Edge:** Reeded

Date	Mintage	F	VF	XF	Unc	BU
2001 (m) Rare	—	—	—	—	—	—

Y# 731 ROUBLE
3.2100 g., Copper-Nickel, 20.7 mm. **Obv:** Double-headed eagle **Rev:** Stylized design above hologram **Edge:** Reeded

Date	Mintage	F	VF	XF	Unc	BU
2001СПМД	100,000,000	—	—	—	1.50	2.00

Y# 732 ROUBLE
17.4300 g., 0.9000 Silver 0.5043 oz. ASW, 32.8 mm. **Subject:** Sturgeon **Obv:** Double-headed eagle within beaded circle **Rev:** Sakhalin sturgeon and other fish **Edge:** Reeded

Date	Mintage	F	VF	XF	Unc	BU
2001 Proof	7,500	Value: 50.00				

Y# 797 ROUBLE
3.2500 g., Copper-Nickel, 20.7 mm. **Obv:** Curved bank name below eagle

Date	Mintage	F	VF	XF	Unc	BU
2002	—	—	—	—	1.00	2.00

Y# 758 ROUBLE
17.4400 g., 0.9000 Silver 0.5046 oz. ASW, 33 mm. **Obv:** Double-headed eagle within beaded circle **Rev:** Chinese Goral **Edge:** Reeded

Date	Mintage	F	VF	XF	Unc	BU
2002(sp) Proof	10,000	Value: 45.00				

Y# 759 ROUBLE
17.4400 g., 0.9000 Silver 0.5046 oz. ASW, 33 mm. **Obv:** Double-headed eagle within beaded circle **Rev:** Whale **Edge:** Reeded

Date	Mintage	F	VF	XF	Unc	BU
2002(sp) Proof	10,000	Value: 45.00				

Y# 760 ROUBLE
17.4400 g., 0.9000 Silver 0.5046 oz. ASW, 33 mm. **Subject:** Golden Eagle **Obv:** Double-headed eagle within beaded circle **Rev:** Golden Eagle with nestling **Edge:** Reeded

Date	Mintage	F	VF	XF	Unc	BU
2002(sp) Proof	10,000	Value: 45.00				

Y# 770 ROUBLE
8.5300 g., 0.9250 Silver 0.2537 oz. ASW, 25 mm. **Subject:** Ministry of Education **Obv:** Double-headed eagle within beaded circle **Rev:** Seedling within open book **Edge:** Reeded

Date	Mintage	F	VF	XF	Unc	BU
2002(m) Proof	3,000	Value: 50.00				

Y# 771 ROUBLE
8.5300 g., 0.9250 Silver 0.2537 oz. ASW, 25 mm. **Subject:** Ministry of Finances **Obv:** Double-headed eagle within beaded circle **Rev:** Caduceus in monogram **Edge:** Reeded

Date	Mintage	F	VF	XF	Unc	BU
2002(sp) Proof	3,000	Value: 50.00				

Y# 772 ROUBLE
8.5300 g., 0.9250 Silver 0.2537 oz. ASW, 25 mm. **Subject:** Ministry of Economic Development **Obv:** Double-headed eagle within beaded circle **Rev:** Crowned double-headed eagle with cornucopia and caduceus **Edge:** Reeded

Date	Mintage	F	VF	XF	Unc	BU
2002(sp) Proof	3,000	Value: 50.00				

Y# 773 ROUBLE
8.5300 g., 0.9250 Silver 0.2537 oz. ASW, 25 mm. **Subject:** Ministry of Foreign Affairs **Obv:** Double-headed eagle within beaded circle **Rev:** Crowned two-headed eagle above crossed sprigs **Edge:** Reeded

Date	Mintage	F	VF	XF	Unc	BU
2002(sp) Proof	3,000	Value: 50.00				

Y# 774 ROUBLE
8.5300 g., 0.9250 Silver 0.2537 oz. ASW, 25 mm. **Subject:** Ministry of Internal Affairs **Obv:** Double-headed eagle within beaded circle **Rev:** Crowned two-headed eagle with round breast **Edge:** Reeded

Date	Mintage	F	VF	XF	Unc	BU
2002(sp) Proof	3,000	Value: 50.00				

Y# 775 ROUBLE
8.5300 g., 0.9250 Silver 0.2537 oz. ASW, 25 mm. **Subject:** Ministry of Justice **Obv:** Double-headed eagle within beaded circle **Rev:** Crowned double-headed eagle with column on breast shield **Edge:** Reeded

Date	Mintage	F	VF	XF	Unc	BU
2002(sp) Proof	3,000	Value: 50.00				

Y# 776 ROUBLE
8.5300 g., 0.9250 Silver 0.2537 oz. ASW, 25 mm. **Subject:** Russian Armed Forces **Obv:** Double-headed eagle within beaded circle **Rev:** Double-headed eagle with crowned top pointed breast shield **Edge:** Reeded

Date	Mintage	F	VF	XF	Unc	BU
2002(m) Proof	3,000	Value: 50.00				

Y# 833 ROUBLE
3.2500 g., Copper-Nickel-Zinc, 20.6 mm. **Obv:** Two headed eagle above curved inscription **Rev:** Value and flower **Edge:** Reeded

Date	Mintage	F	VF	XF	Unc	BU
2002(sp)	—	—	—	—	2.00	3.00
2005(m)	—	—	—	—	2.00	3.00
2005(sp)	—	—	—	—	2.00	3.00
2006(m)	—	—	—	—	2.00	3.00

Y# A834 ROUBLE
7.7800 g., 0.9250 Silver 0.2314 oz. ASW, 0.25 mm. **Subject:** St. Petersburg **Obv:** Double-headed eagle within beaded circle **Rev:** Angel on steeple of Cathedral in fortress

Date	Mintage	F	VF	XF	Unc	BU
2002 Proof	5,000	Value: 25.00				

Y# 835 ROUBLE
7.7800 g., 0.9250 Silver 0.2314 oz. ASW, 25 mm. **Subject:** St. Petersburg **Obv:** Double-headed eagle within beaded circle **Rev:** Sphinx

Date	Mintage	F	VF	XF	Unc	BU
2002 Proof	5,000	Value: 25.00				

Y# 836 ROUBLE
7.7800 g., 0.9250 Silver 0.2314 oz. ASW, 25 mm. **Subject:** St. Petersburg **Obv:** Double-headed eagle within beaded circle **Rev:** Small ship

Date	Mintage	F	VF	XF	Unc	BU
2002 Proof	5,000	Value: 25.00				

Y# 837 ROUBLE
7.7800 g., 0.9250 Silver 0.2314 oz. ASW, 25 mm. **Subject:** St. Petersburg **Obv:** Double-headed eagle within beaded circle **Rev:** Lion

Date	Mintage	F	VF	XF	Unc	BU
2002 Proof	5,000	Value: 25.00				

Y# 838 ROUBLE
7.7800 g., 0.9250 Silver 0.2314 oz. ASW, 25 mm. **Subject:** St. Petersburg **Obv:** Double-headed eagle within beaded circle **Rev:** Horse sculpture

Date	Mintage	F	VF	XF	Unc	BU
2002 Proof	5,000	Value: 25.00				

Y# 839 ROUBLE
7.7800 g., 0.9250 Silver 0.2314 oz. ASW, 25 mm. **Subject:** St. Petersburg **Obv:** Double-headed eagle within beaded circle **Rev:** Griffin

Date	Mintage	F	VF	XF	Unc	BU
2002 Proof	5,000	Value: 25.00				

Y# 814 ROUBLE
17.4000 g., 0.9000 Silver 0.5035 oz. ASW, 32.8 mm. **Obv:** Double-headed eagle within beaded circle **Rev:** Arctic foxes **Edge:** Reeded

Date	Mintage	F	VF	XF	Unc	BU
2003(sp) Proof	10,000	Value: 45.00				

Y# 816 ROUBLE

17.4000 g., 0.9000 Silver 0.5035 oz. ASW, 32.8 mm. **Obv:** Double-headed eagle within beaded circle **Rev:** Pygmy Cormorant drying its wings **Edge:** Reeded

Date	Mintage	F	VF	XF	Unc	BU
2003(sp) Proof	10,000	Value: 45.00				

Y# 815 ROUBLE

17.4000 g., 0.9000 Silver 0.5035 oz. ASW, 32.8 mm. **Obv:** Double-headed eagle within beaded circle **Rev:** Chinese Softshell turtle **Edge:** Reeded

Date	Mintage	F	VF	XF	Unc	BU
2003(sp) Proof	10,000	Value: 50.00				

Y# 828 ROUBLE

17.2800 g., 0.9000 Silver 0.5000 oz. ASW, 33 mm. **Obv:** Two headed eagle within beaded circle **Rev:** Amur Forest Cat on branch **Edge:** Reeded

Date	Mintage	F	VF	XF	Unc	BU
2004(sp) Proof	10,000	Value: 45.00				

Y# 881 ROUBLE

7.4300 g., 0.9000 Silver 0.2150 oz. ASW, 32.8 mm. **Obv:** Double-headed eagle within beaded circle **Rev:** Toads **Edge:** Reeded

Date	Mintage	F	VF	XF	Unc	BU
2004 Proof	—	Value: 60.00				

Y# 882 ROUBLE

7.0100 g., 0.9250 Silver 0.2085 oz. ASW, 32.8 mm. **Obv:** Double-headed eagle within beaded circle **Rev:** Two Marbled Murrelet sea birds **Edge:** Reeded

Date	Mintage	F	VF	XF	Unc	BU
2005 Proof	—	Value: 45.00				

Y# 883 ROUBLE

7.0100 g., 0.9250 Silver 0.2085 oz. ASW, 32.8 mm. **Obv:** Double-headed eagle within beaded circle **Rev:** Asiatic Wild Dog **Edge:** Reeded

Date	Mintage	F	VF	XF	Unc	BU
2005 Proof	—	Value: 50.00				

Y# 884 ROUBLE

7.0100 g., 0.9250 Silver 0.2085 oz. ASW, 32.8 mm. **Obv:** Double-headed eagle within beaded circle **Rev:** Volkhov Whitefish **Edge:** Reeded

Date	Mintage	F	VF	XF	Unc	BU
2005 Proof	—	Value: 45.00				

Y# 916 ROUBLE

8.5300 g., 0.9250 Silver 0.2537 oz. ASW, 25 mm. **Obv:** Double-headed eagle **Rev:** Russian Navy Emblem **Edge:** Reeded

Date	Mintage	F	VF	XF	Unc	BU
2005 Proof	10,000	Value: 25.00				

Y# 917 ROUBLE

8.5300 g., 0.9250 Silver 0.2537 oz. ASW, 25 mm. **Obv:** Double-headed eagle **Rev:** Russian Marine circa 1705 **Edge:** Reeded

Date	Mintage	F	VF	XF	Unc	BU
2005 Proof	10,000	Value: 25.00				

Y# 918 ROUBLE

8.5300 g., 0.9250 Silver 0.2537 oz. ASW, 25 mm. **Obv:** Double-headed eagle **Rev:** Russian Marine circa 2005 **Edge:** Reeded

Date	Mintage	F	VF	XF	Unc	BU
2005 Proof	10,000	Value: 25.00				

Y# 605 2 ROUBLES

5.1000 g., Copper-Nickel-Zinc, 23 mm. **Obv:** Double-headed eagle **Rev:** Value and vine sprig **Edge:** Alternating reeded and smooth

Date	Mintage	F	VF	XF	Unc	BU
2001(m)	—	—	—	—	5.00	7.00

Y# 730 2 ROUBLES

17.0000 g., 0.9250 Silver 0.5055 oz. ASW, 33 mm. **Subject:** V.I. Dal **Obv:** Double-headed eagle **Rev:** Portrait, book, signature, figures **Edge:** Reeded

Date	Mintage	F	VF	XF	Unc	BU
2001(m) Proof	7,500	Value: 40.00				

Y# 675 2 ROUBLES

5.2000 g., Copper-Nickel, 23 mm. **Subject:** Yuri Gagarin **Obv:** Value and date to left of vine sprig **Rev:** Uniformed bust facing **Edge:** Segmented reeding

Date	Mintage	F	VF	XF	Unc	BU
2001	—	—	—	—	15.00	18.00
2001(m)	10,000,000	—	—	—	2.00	4.00
2001(sp)	10,000,000	—	—	—	2.00	4.00

Y# 742 2 ROUBLES

17.0000 g., 0.9250 Silver 0.5055 oz. ASW, 33 mm. **Subject:** Zodiac Signs **Obv:** Double-headed eagle within beaded circle **Rev:** Leo **Edge:** Reeded

Date	Mintage	F	VF	XF	Unc	BU
2002 Proof	20,000	Value: 35.00				

Y# 798 2 ROUBLES

5.1000 g., Copper-Nickel, 23 mm. **Obv:** Curved bank name below eagle

Date	Mintage	F	VF	XF	Unc	BU
2002	—	—	—	—	2.00	3.00

Y# 834 2 ROUBLES

5.1000 g., Copper-Nickel, 23 mm. **Obv:** Two headed eagle above curved inscription **Rev:** Value and flower **Edge:** Segmented reeding

Date	Mintage	F	VF	XF	Unc	BU
2002(sp)	—	—	—	—	4.00	5.00

Y# 747 2 ROUBLES

17.0000 g., 0.9250 Silver 0.5055 oz. ASW, 33 mm. **Subject:** Zodiac Signs **Obv:** Double-headed eagle within beaded circle **Rev:** Virgo and stars **Edge:** Reeded

Date	Mintage	F	VF	XF	Unc	BU
2002(m) Proof	20,000	Value: 30.00				

Y# 761 2 ROUBLES

17.0000 g., 0.9250 Silver 0.5055 oz. ASW, 33 mm. **Subject:** Zodiac Signs **Obv:** Double-headed eagle within beaded circle **Rev:** Capricorn **Edge:** Reeded

Date	Mintage	F	VF	XF	Unc	BU
2002(sp) Proof	20,000	Value: 35.00				

Y# 762 2 ROUBLES

17.0000 g., 0.9250 Silver 0.5055 oz. ASW, 33 mm. **Subject:** Zodiac Signs **Obv:** Double-headed eagle within beaded circle **Rev:** Sagittarius **Edge:** Reeded

Date	Mintage	F	VF	XF	Unc	BU
2002(sp) Proof	20,000	Value: 30.00				

Y# 766 2 ROUBLES

17.0000 g., 0.9250 Silver 0.5055 oz. ASW, 33 mm. **Subject:** Zodiac Signs **Obv:** Double-headed eagle within beaded circle **Rev:** Scorpion **Edge:** Reeded

Date	Mintage	F	VF	XF	Unc	BU
2002(m) Proof	20,000	Value: 35.00				

Y# 768 2 ROUBLES

17.0000 g., 0.9250 Silver 0.5055 oz. ASW, 33 mm. **Subject:** Zodiac Signs **Obv:** Double-headed eagle **Rev:** Balance scale **Edge:** Reeded

Date	Mintage	F	VF	XF	Unc	BU
2002(sp) Proof	20,000	Value: 30.00				

Y# 793 2 ROUBLES

17.0000 g., 0.9250 Silver 0.5055 oz. ASW, 33 mm. **Subject:** L.P. Orlova **Obv:** Double-headed eagle **Rev:** Head facing **Edge:** Reeded

Date	Mintage	F	VF	XF	Unc	BU
2002(m) Proof	10,000	Value: 25.00				

Y# 803 2 ROUBLES

17.1000 g., 0.9250 Silver 0.5085 oz. ASW, 32.8 mm. **Subject:** Zodiac signs **Obv:** Double-headed eagle within beaded circle **Rev:** Pisces **Edge:** Reeded

Date	Mintage	F	VF	XF	Unc	BU
2003(sp) Proof	20,000	Value: 35.00				

Y# 804 2 ROUBLES

17.1000 g., 0.9250 Silver 0.5085 oz. ASW, 32.8 mm. **Subject:** Zodiac signs **Obv:** Double-headed eagle within beaded circle **Rev:** Aquarius **Edge:** Reeded

Date	Mintage	F	VF	XF	Unc	BU
2003(m) Proof	20,000	Value: 35.00				

Y# 820 2 ROUBLES

17.0000 g., 0.9250 Silver 0.5055 oz. ASW, 33 mm. **Subject:** Zodiac signs **Obv:** Double-headed eagle within beaded circle **Rev:** Cancer **Edge:** Reeded

Date	Mintage	F	VF	XF	Unc	BU
2003(sp) Proof	20,000	Value: 35.00				

Y# 840 2 ROUBLES

16.8100 g., 0.9250 Silver 0.4999 oz. ASW, 33 mm. **Rev:** Guil Yarovsky

Date	Mintage	F	VF	XF	Unc	BU
2003(m) Proof	10,000	Value: 20.00				

Y# 841 2 ROUBLES

16.8100 g., 0.9250 Silver 0.4999 oz. ASW, 33 mm. **Rev:** Fedor Tyutchev

Date	Mintage	F	VF	XF	Unc	BU
2003(sp) Proof	10,000	Value: 20.00				

Y# 844 2 ROUBLES

17.0000 g., 0.9250 Silver 0.5055 oz. ASW, 33 mm. **Subject:** Zodiac Signs **Obv:** Double-headed eagle within beaded circle **Rev:** Aries

Date	Mintage	F	VF	XF	Unc	BU
2003 Proof	20,000	Value: 25.00				

Y# 845 2 ROUBLES

17.0000 g., 0.9250 Silver 0.5055 oz. ASW **Subject:** Zodiac Signs **Obv:** Double-headed eagle within beaded circle **Rev:** Taurus

Date	Mintage	F	VF	XF	Unc	BU
2003 Proof	20,000	Value: 25.00				

Y# 846 2 ROUBLES

17.0000 g., 0.9250 Silver 0.5055 oz. ASW, 33 mm. **Subject:** Zodiac Signs **Obv:** Double-headed eagle within beaded circle **Rev:** Gemini

Date	Mintage	F	VF	XF	Unc	BU
2003 Proof	20,000	Value: 22.50				

Y# 842 2 ROUBLES

16.8100 g., 0.9250 Silver 0.4999 oz. ASW, 33 mm. **Rev:** V. P. Tchkalov

Date	Mintage	F	VF	XF	Unc	BU
2004(m) Proof	7,000	Value: 20.00				

Y# 843 2 ROUBLES

16.8100 g., 0.9250 Silver 0.4999 oz. ASW, 33 mm. **Rev:** Mikhail Glinka

Date	Mintage	F	VF	XF	Unc	BU
2004(m) Proof	7,000	Value: 20.00				

Y# 897 2 ROUBLES

17.0000 g., 0.9250 Silver 0.5055 oz. ASW, 33 mm. **Obv:** Double-headed eagle **Rev:** Gemini twins **Edge:** Reeded

Date	Mintage	F	VF	XF	Unc	BU
2005 Proof	20,000	Value: 25.00				

Y# 899 2 ROUBLES

17.0000 g., 0.9250 Silver 0.5055 oz. ASW, 33 mm. **Obv:** Double-headed eagle **Rev:** Cancer crawfish **Edge:** Reeded

Date	Mintage	F	VF	XF	Unc	BU
2005 Proof	20,000	Value: 30.00				

Y# 901 2 ROUBLES

17.0000 g., 0.9250 Silver 0.5055 oz. ASW, 33 mm. **Obv:** Double-headed eagle **Rev:** Leo lion **Edge:** Reeded

Date	Mintage	F	VF	XF	Unc	BU
2005 Proof	20,000	Value: 30.00				

Y# 905 2 ROUBLES

17.0000 g., 0.9250 Silver 0.5055 oz. ASW, 33 mm. **Obv:** Double-headed eagle **Rev:** Mikhail Sholokhov with pen in hand **Edge:** Reeded

Date	Mintage	F	VF	XF	Unc	BU
2005 Proof	10,000	Value: 25.00				

Y# 909 2 ROUBLES

17.0000 g., 0.9250 Silver 0.5055 oz. ASW, 33 mm. **Obv:** Double-headed eagle **Rev:** Peter Klodt viewing man and horse statue **Edge:** Reeded

Date	Mintage	F	VF	XF	Unc	BU
2005 Proof	10,000	Value: 25.00				

Y# 914 2 ROUBLES

17.0000 g., 0.9250 Silver 0.5055 oz. ASW, 33 mm. **Obv:** Double-headed eagle **Rev:** Virgo standing lady **Edge:** Reeded

Date	Mintage	F	VF	XF	Unc	BU
2005 Proof	20,000	Value: 25.00				

Y# 919 2 ROUBLES

17.0000 g., 0.9250 Silver 0.5055 oz. ASW, 33 mm. **Obv:** Double-headed eagle **Rev:** Libra - 2 stylized birds forming a balance scale **Edge:** Reeded

Date	Mintage	F	VF	XF	Unc	BU
2005 Proof	20,000	Value: 25.00				

Y# 921 2 ROUBLES

17.0000 g., 0.9250 Silver 0.5055 oz. ASW, 33 mm. **Obv:** Double-headed eagle **Rev:** Scorpio scorpion **Edge:** Reeded

Date	Mintage	F	VF	XF	Unc	BU
2005 Proof	25	Value: 30.00				

Y# 926 2 ROUBLES

17.0000 g., 0.9250 Silver 0.5055 oz. ASW, 33 mm. **Obv:** Double-headed eagle **Rev:** Sagittarius the archer **Edge:** Reeded

Date	Mintage	F	VF	XF	Unc	BU
2005 Proof	20,000	Value: 25.00				

Y# 928 2 ROUBLES

17.0000 g., 0.9250 Silver 0.5055 oz. ASW, 33 mm. **Obv:** Double-headed eagle **Rev:** Capricorn as half goat and fish **Edge:** Reeded

Date	Mintage	F	VF	XF	Unc	BU
2005 Proof	20,000	Value: 30.00				

Y# 930 2 ROUBLES

17.0000 g., 0.9250 Silver 0.5055 oz. ASW, 33 mm. **Obv:** Double-headed eagle **Rev:** Pisces as catfish and sturgeon **Edge:** Reeded

Date	Mintage	F	VF	XF	Unc	BU
2005 Proof	20,000	Value: 25.00				

Y# 932 2 ROUBLES

17.0000 g., 0.9250 Silver 0.5055 oz. ASW, 33 mm. **Obv:** Double-headed eagle **Rev:** Aries ram **Edge:** Reeded

Date	Mintage	F	VF	XF	Unc	BU
2005 Proof	20,000	Value: 25.00				

Y# 934 2 ROUBLES

17.0000 g., 0.9250 Silver 0.5055 oz. ASW, 33 mm. **Obv:** Double-headed eagle **Rev:** Taurus bull **Edge:** Reeded

Date	Mintage	F	VF	XF	Unc	BU
2005 Proof	20,000	Value: 30.00				

Y# 936 2 ROUBLES

17.0000 g., 0.9250 Silver 0.5055 oz. ASW, 33 mm. **Obv:** Double-headed eagle **Rev:** Aquarius water carrier **Edge:** Reeded

Date	Mintage	F	VF	XF	Unc	BU
2005 Proof	20,000	Value: 25.00				

Y# 967 2 ROUBLES

17.0000 g., 0.9250 Silver 0.5055 oz. ASW, 33.0 mm. **Subject:** 100th Anniversary Birth of Gerasimov **Obv:** Two-headed eagle **Rev:** Gerasimov recreating a man's face **Rev. Legend:** М. М. ГЕРАСИМОВ

Date	Mintage	F	VF	XF	Unc	BU
2007(m) Proof	10,000	Value: 30.00				

Y# 968 2 ROUBLES

17.0000 g., 0.9250 Silver 0.5055 oz. ASW, 33.0 mm. **Subject:** 150th Anniversary Birth of Tsiolkovsky **Rev:** Bust of Tsiolkovsky 3/4 right at left, scheme of two flight vehicles with earth in background at upper right **Rev. Legend:** К. Э. ЦИОЛКОВСКИЈ **Edge:** Reeded

Date	Mintage	F	VF	XF	Unc	BU
2007(m) Proof	10,000	Value: 30.00				

Y# 677 3 ROUBLES

34.8800 g., 0.9000 Silver 1.0092 oz. ASW, 39 mm. **Subject:** 225 Years - Bolshoi Theater **Obv:** Double-headed eagle **Rev:** Standing figures facing **Edge:** Reeded

Date	Mintage	F	VF	XF	Unc	BU
2001 Proof	7,500	Value: 40.00				

Y# 680 3 ROUBLES

34.8800 g., 0.9000 Silver 1.0092 oz. ASW, 39 mm. **Subject:** 40th Anniversary of Manned Space Flight - Yuri Gagarin **Obv:** Double-headed eagle **Rev:** Uniformed bust holding dove **Edge:** Reeded

Date	Mintage	F	VF	XF	Unc	BU
2001 Proof	7,500	Value: 40.00				

Y# 682 3 ROUBLES
34.8800 g., 0.9000 Silver 1.0092 oz. ASW, 39 mm. **Subject:** Siberian Exploration **Obv:** Double-headed eagle **Rev:** Men riding horses, deer and sleds **Edge:** Reeded

Date	Mintage	F	VF	XF	Unc	BU
2001 Proof	5,000	Value: 45.00				

Y# 733 3 ROUBLES
34.8800 g., 0.9000 Silver 1.0092 oz. ASW, 39 mm. **Subject:** 200th Anniversary of Navigation School **Obv:** Double-headed eagle **Rev:** Navigational tools and building **Edge:** Reeded

Date	Mintage	F	VF	XF	Unc	BU
2001 Proof	5,000	Value: 42.50				

Y# 734 3 ROUBLES
34.8800 g., 0.9000 Silver 1.0092 oz. ASW, 39 mm. **Subject:** First Moscow Savings Bank **Obv:** Double-headed eagle **Rev:** Beehive above building within circle **Edge:** Reeded

Date	Mintage	F	VF	XF	Unc	BU
2001 Proof	17,500	Value: 40.00				

Y# 735 3 ROUBLES
34.8800 g., 0.9000 Silver 1.0092 oz. ASW, 39 mm. **Subject:** State Labor Savings Bank **Obv:** Double-headed eagle **Rev:** Dam, passbook and tractor **Edge:** Reeded

Date	Mintage	F	VF	XF	Unc	BU
2001 Proof	17,500	Value: 40.00				

Y# 736 3 ROUBLES
34.8800 g., 0.9000 Silver 1.0092 oz. ASW, 39 mm. **Subject:** Savings Bank of the Russian Federation **Obv:** Double-headed eagle **Rev:** Chevrons above building **Edge:** Reeded

Date	Mintage	F	VF	XF	Unc	BU
2001 Proof	17,500	Value: 40.00				

Y# 737 3 ROUBLES
34.8800 g., 0.9000 Silver 1.0092 oz. ASW, 39 mm. **Subject:** 10th Anniversary - Commonwealth of Independent States **Obv:** Double-headed eagle **Rev:** Hologram below logo **Edge:** Reeded

Date	Mintage	F	VF	XF	Unc	BU
2001 Proof	7,500	Value: 45.00				

Y# 738 3 ROUBLES
34.8800 g., 0.9000 Silver 1.0092 oz. ASW, 39 mm. **Subject:** Olympics **Obv:** Double-headed eagle **Rev:** Cross-country skiers **Edge:** Reeded

Date	Mintage	F	VF	XF	Unc	BU
2002 Proof	25,000	Value: 40.00				

Y# 744 3 ROUBLES
34.8800 g., 0.9000 Silver 1.0092 oz. ASW, 39 mm. **Subject:** St. John's Nunnery, St. Petersburg **Obv:** Double-headed eagle **Rev:** Nunnery and cameo **Edge:** Reeded

Date	Mintage	F	VF	XF	Unc	BU
2002 Proof	5,000	Value: 45.00				

Y# 778 3 ROUBLES
34.8800 g., 0.9000 Silver 1.0092 oz. ASW, 39 mm. **Subject:** Kideksha **Obv:** Double-headed eagle **Rev:** Three churches on river bank **Edge:** Reeded

Date	Mintage	F	VF	XF	Unc	BU
2002(sp) Proof	10,000	Value: 42.50				

Y# 779 3 ROUBLES
34.8800 g., 0.9000 Silver 1.0092 oz. ASW, 39 mm. **Subject:** Iversky Monastery, Valdaiy **Obv:** Double-headed eagle **Rev:** Building complex on an island in Lake Valdaiy **Edge:** Reeded

Date	Mintage	F	VF	XF	Unc	BU
2002(sp) Proof	10,000	Value: 42.50				

Y# 780 3 ROUBLES
34.8800 g., 0.9000 Silver 1.0092 oz. ASW, 39 mm. **Subject:** Miraculous Savior Church **Obv:** Double-headed eagle **Rev:** Church with separate bell tower **Edge:** Reeded

Date	Mintage	F	VF	XF	Unc	BU
2002(m) Proof	5,000	Value: 50.00				

Y# 781 3 ROUBLES
34.8800 g., 0.9000 Silver 1.0092 oz. ASW, 39 mm. **Subject:** Works of Dionissy **Obv:** Double-headed eagle **Rev:** "The Crucifix" **Edge:** Reeded

Date	Mintage	F	VF	XF	Unc	BU
2002(sp) Proof	10,000	Value: 40.00				

Y# 755 3 ROUBLES
34.8800 g., 0.9000 Silver 1.0092 oz. ASW, 39 mm. **Subject:** Admiral Nakhimov **Obv:** Double-headed eagle **Rev:** Monument, Admiral with cannon and naval battle scene **Edge:** Reeded

Date	Mintage	F	VF	XF	Unc	BU
2002(sp) Proof	10,000	Value: 40.00				

Y# 787 3 ROUBLES
34.8800 g., 0.9000 Silver 1.0092 oz. ASW, 39 mm. **Subject:** World Cup Soccer **Obv:** Double-headed eagle **Rev:** Soccer ball within circle of players **Edge:** Reeded

Date	Mintage	F	VF	XF	Unc	BU
2002(sp) Proof	25,000	Value: 35.00				

Y# 756 3 ROUBLES
34.8800 g., 0.9000 Silver 1.0092 oz. ASW, 39 mm. **Subject:** Hermitage **Obv:** Double-headed eagle **Rev:** Statues and arch **Edge:** Reeded

Date	Mintage	F	VF	XF	Unc	BU
2002(sp) Proof	10,000	Value: 42.50				

Y# 885 3 ROUBLES
34.8000 g., 0.9000 Silver 1.0069 oz. ASW, 38.7 mm. **Subject:** City of Pskov 1100th Anniversary **Obv:** Double-headed eagle **Rev:** Walled city view **Edge:** Reeded

Date	Mintage	F	VF	XF	Unc	BU
2003(sp) Proof	—	Value: 55.00				

Y# 801 3 ROUBLES
34.8000 g., 0.9000 Silver 1.0069 oz. ASW, 38.7 mm. **Subject:** Veborg **Obv:** Double-headed eagle **Rev:** Sailing ships and buildings **Edge:** Reeded

Date	Mintage	F	VF	XF	Unc	BU
2003(sp) Proof	10,000	Value: 50.00				

Y# 802 3 ROUBLES
34.7500 g., 0.9000 Silver 1.0055 oz. ASW, 38.7 mm. **Subject:** Lunar Calendar **Obv:** National emblem **Rev:** Mountain goat in crescent **Edge:** Reeded

Date	Mintage	F	VF	XF	Unc	BU
2003(m) Proof	15,000	Value: 50.00				

Y# 805 3 ROUBLES
34.8400 g., 0.9000 Silver 1.0081 oz. ASW, 38.8 mm. **Subject:** Zodiac signs **Obv:** Double-headed eagle within beaded circle **Rev:** Leo **Edge:** Reeded

Date	Mintage	F	VF	XF	Unc	BU
2003(m) Proof	30,000	Value: 50.00				

Y# 806 3 ROUBLES
34.7400 g., 0.9000 Silver 1.0052 oz. ASW, 38.8 mm. **Subject:** St. Daniel's Monastery **Obv:** Double-headed eagle **Rev:** Statue and monastery **Edge:** Reeded

Date	Mintage	F	VF	XF	Unc	BU
2003(m) Proof	10,000	Value: 45.00				

Y# 807 3 ROUBLES
34.7400 g., 0.9000 Silver 1.0052 oz. ASW, 38.8 mm. **Subject:** World Biathlon Championships **Obv:** Double-headed eagle **Rev:** Rifleman and archer on skis **Edge:** Reeded

Date	Mintage	F	VF	XF	Unc	BU
2003(m) Proof	7,500	Value: 40.00				

Y# 808 3 ROUBLES
34.7400 g., 0.9000 Silver 1.0052 oz. ASW, 38.8 mm. **Obv:** Double-headed eagle **Rev:** Monastery **Edge:** Reeded

Date	Mintage	F	VF	XF	Unc	BU
2003(m) Proof	10,000	Value: 42.50				

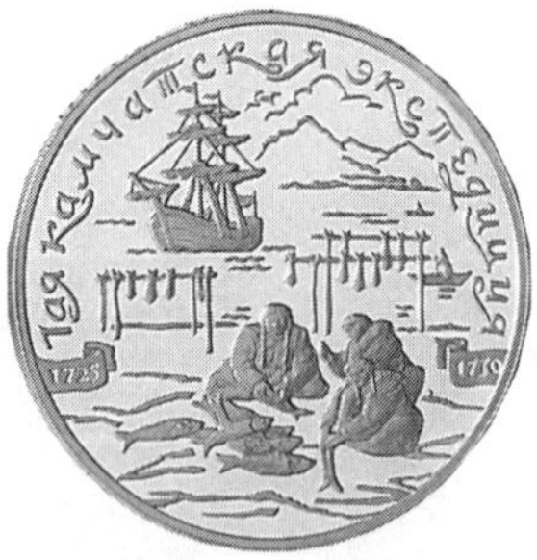

Y# 809 3 ROUBLES
34.7400 g., 0.9000 Silver 1.0052 oz. ASW, 38.8 mm. **Subject:** First Kamchatka Expedition **Obv:** Double-headed eagle **Rev:** Natives, fish and ship **Edge:** Reeded

Date	Mintage	F	VF	XF	Unc	BU
2003(sp) Proof	10,000	Value: 37.50				

Y# 810 3 ROUBLES
34.7400 g., 0.9000 Silver 1.0052 oz. ASW, 38.8 mm. **Subject:** Zodiac signs **Obv:** Double-headed eagle within beaded circle **Rev:** Virgo **Edge:** Reeded

Date	Mintage	F	VF	XF	Unc	BU
2003(sp)	30,000	Value: 35.00				

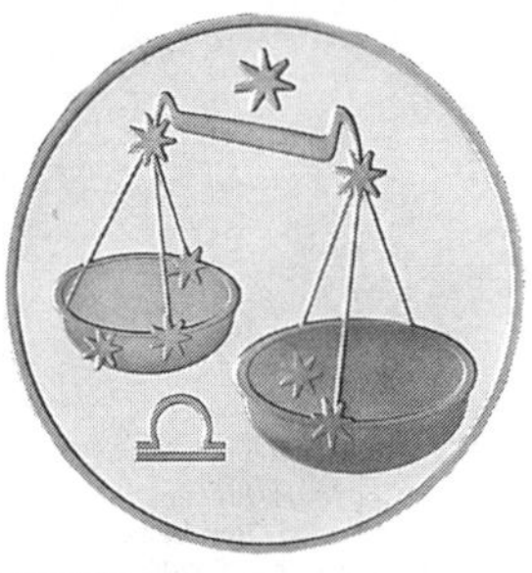

Y# 811 3 ROUBLES
34.7400 g., 0.9000 Silver 1.0052 oz. ASW, 38.8 mm. **Subject:** Zodiac signs **Obv:** Double-headed eagle within beaded circle **Rev:** Libra **Edge:** Reeded

Date	Mintage	F	VF	XF	Unc	BU
2003(m) Proof	30,000	Value: 35.00				

Y# 812 3 ROUBLES
34.7400 g., 0.9000 Silver 1.0052 oz. ASW, 38.8 mm. **Subject:** Diveyevsky Monastery **Obv:** Double-headed eagle **Rev:** Cameo above churches **Edge:** Reeded

Date	Mintage	F	VF	XF	Unc	BU
2003(sp) Proof	10,000	Value: 42.50				

Y# 813 3 ROUBLES
34.7400 g., 0.9000 Silver 1.0052 oz. ASW, 38.8 mm. **Subject:** Zodiac Signs **Obv:** Double-headed eagle within beaded circle **Rev:** Scorpio **Edge:** Reeded

Date	Mintage	F	VF	XF	Unc	BU
2003(m) Proof	30,000	Value: 35.00				

Y# 847 3 ROUBLES
34.5600 g., 0.9000 Silver 100000 oz. ASW, 39 mm. **Rev:** St. Trinity Monastery

Date	Mintage	F	VF	XF	Unc	BU
2003(sp) Proof	10,000	Value: 40.00				

Y# 848 3 ROUBLES
34.5600 g., 0.9000 Silver 100000 oz. ASW, 39 mm. **Subject:** Zodiac Signs **Obv:** Double-headed eagle within beaded circle **Rev:** Sagittarius

Date	Mintage	F	VF	XF	Unc	BU
2003(sp) Proof	30,000	Value: 35.00				

Y# 849 3 ROUBLES
34.5600 g., 0.9000 Silver 100000 oz. ASW, 39 mm. **Subject:** Zodiac Signs **Obv:** Double-headed eagle within beaded circle **Rev:** Capricorn

Date	Mintage	F	VF	XF	Unc	BU
2003(m) Proof	30,000	Value: 35.00				

Y# 850 3 ROUBLES
34.5600 g., 0.9000 Silver 100000 oz. ASW, 39 mm. **Subject:** Lunar Calendar **Rev:** Monkey

Date	Mintage	F	VF	XF	Unc	BU
2004(m) Proof	15,000	Value: 37.50				

Y# 851 3 ROUBLES
34.5600 g., 0.9000 Silver 100000 oz. ASW, 39 mm. **Subject:** Zodiac Signs **Obv:** Double-headed eagle within beaded circle **Rev:** Aquarius

Date	Mintage	F	VF	XF	Unc	BU
2004(sp) Proof	30,000	Value: 35.00				

Y# 852 3 ROUBLES
34.5600 g., 0.9000 Silver 100000 oz. ASW, 39 mm. **Rev:** Tomsk

Date	Mintage	F	VF	XF	Unc	BU
2004(m) Proof	8,000	Value: 35.00				

Y# 853 3 ROUBLES
34.5600 g., 0.9000 Silver 100000 oz. ASW, 39 mm. **Subject:** Zodiac Signs **Obv:** Double-headed eagle within beaded circle **Rev:** Pisces

Date	Mintage	F	VF	XF	Unc	BU
2004(m) Proof	30,000	Value: 35.00				

Y# 854 3 ROUBLES
34.5600 g., 0.9000 Silver 100000 oz. ASW, 39 mm. **Rev:** Epiphany Cathedral, Moscow

Date	Mintage	F	VF	XF	Unc	BU
2004(m) Proof	8,000	Value: 35.00				

Y# 855 3 ROUBLES
34.5600 g., 0.9000 Silver 100000 oz. ASW, 39 mm. **Subject:** Zodiac Signs **Obv:** Double-headed eagle within beaded circle **Rev:** Aries

Date	Mintage	F	VF	XF	Unc	BU
2004(sp) Proof	30,000	Value: 35.00				

Y# 856 3 ROUBLES
34.5600 g., 0.9000 Silver 100000 oz. ASW, 39 mm. **Rev:** Soccer

Date	Mintage	F	VF	XF	Unc	BU
2004(sp) Proof	10,000	Value: 30.00				

Y# 857 3 ROUBLES
34.5600 g., 0.9000 Silver 100000 oz. ASW, 39 mm. **Subject:** Zodiac Signs **Obv:** Double-headed eagle within beaded circle **Rev:** Taurus

Date	Mintage	F	VF	XF	Unc	BU
2004(sp) Proof	30,000	Value: 35.00				

Y# 858 3 ROUBLES
34.5600 g., 0.9000 Silver 100000 oz. ASW, 39 mm. **Rev:** Olympic torch

Date	Mintage	F	VF	XF	Unc	BU
2004(m) Proof	20,000	Value: 32.50				

Y# 859 3 ROUBLES
34.5600 g., 0.9000 Silver 100000 oz. ASW, 39 mm. **Subject:** Zodiac Signs **Obv:** Double-headed eagle within beaded circle **Rev:** Gemini

Date	Mintage	F	VF	XF	Unc	BU
2004(m) Proof	30,000	Value: 35.00				

Y# 860 3 ROUBLES
34.5600 g., 0.9000 Silver 100000 oz. ASW, 39 mm. **Subject:** Zodiac Signs **Obv:** Double-headed eagle within beaded circle **Rev:** Cancer

Date	Mintage	F	VF	XF	Unc	BU
2004(sp) Proof	30,000	Value: 35.00				

Y# 861 3 ROUBLES
34.5600 g., 0.9000 Silver 100000 oz. ASW, 39 mm. **Rev:** Church of the Sign of the Holy Mother of God

Date	Mintage	F	VF	XF	Unc	BU
2004(m) Proof	8,000	Value: 35.00				

Y# 862 3 ROUBLES
34.5600 g., 0.9000 Silver 100000 oz. ASW, 39 mm. **Rev:** Transfiguration icon

Date	Mintage	F	VF	XF	Unc	BU
2004(m) Proof	8,000	Value: 35.00				

Y# 863 3 ROUBLES
34.5600 g., 0.9000 Silver 100000 oz. ASW, 39 mm. **Rev:** Peter I's monetary reform

Date	Mintage	F	VF	XF	Unc	BU
2004(sp) Proof	8,000	Value: 75.00				

Y# 892 3 ROUBLES
33.9400 g., 0.9250 Silver 1.0093 oz. ASW, 39 mm. **Obv:** Double-headed eagle **Rev:** Rooster and crescent moon **Edge:** Reeded

Date	Mintage	F	VF	XF	Unc	BU
2005 Proof	15,000	Value: 35.00				

Y# 893 3 ROUBLES
33.9400 g., 0.9250 Silver 1.0093 oz. ASW, 39 mm. **Subject:** 60th Anniversary - Victory Over Germany **Obv:** Double-headed eagle **Rev:** Soldier and wife circa 1945 **Edge:** Reeded

Date	Mintage	F	VF	XF	Unc	BU
2005 Proof	35,000	Value: 35.00				

Y# 903 3 ROUBLES
33.9400 g., 0.9250 Silver 1.0093 oz. ASW, 39 mm. **Obv:** Double-headed eagle **Rev:** St. Nicholas Cathedral in Kaliningrad **Edge:** Reeded

Date	Mintage	F	VF	XF	Unc	BU
2005 Proof	10,000	Value: 35.00				

Y# 904 3 ROUBLES
33.9400 g., 0.9250 Silver 1.0093 oz. ASW, 39 mm. **Obv:** Double-headed eagle **Rev:** Kropotkin Metro Station in Moscow **Edge:** Reeded

Date	Mintage	F	VF	XF	Unc	BU
2005 Proof	10,000	Value: 35.00				

Y# 906 3 ROUBLES
33.9400 g., 0.9250 Silver 1.0093 oz. ASW, 39 mm. **Subject:** Helsinki Games **Obv:** Double-headed eagle **Rev:** Stylized track and field athletes **Edge:** Reeded

Date	Mintage	F	VF	XF	Unc	BU
2005 Proof	10,000	Value: 32.50				

Y# 908 3 ROUBLES
33.9400 g., 0.9250 Silver 1.0093 oz. ASW, 39 mm. **Obv:** Double-headed eagle **Rev:** Virgin Monastery in Raifa, Tatarstan **Edge:** Reeded

Date	Mintage	F	VF	XF	Unc	BU
2005 Proof	10,000	Value: 35.00				

Y# 910 3 ROUBLES
33.9400 g., 0.9250 Silver 1.0093 oz. ASW, 39 mm. **Obv:** Double-headed eagle **Rev:** Kazan Theater Building **Edge:** Reeded

Date	Mintage	F	VF	XF	Unc	BU
2005 Proof	10,000	Value: 35.00				

Y# 923 3 ROUBLES
33.9400 g., 0.9250 Silver 1.0093 oz. ASW, 39 mm. **Subject:** 625th Anniversary - Battle of Kulikovo **Obv:** Double-headed eagle **Rev:** Carved Lion and Griffin between opposing armies **Edge:** Reeded

Date	Mintage	F	VF	XF	Unc	BU
2005 Proof	10,000	Value: 35.00				

Y# 955 3 ROUBLES
33.9400 g., 0.9250 Silver 1.0093 oz. ASW, 39 mm. **Subject:** Moscow's Lomonosov University **Obv:** Two headed eagle **Rev:** Lomonosov statue before university building and Moscow skyline **Edge:** Reeded

Date	Mintage	F	VF	XF	Unc	BU
2005(m) Proof	10,000	Value: 32.50				

Y# 966 3 ROUBLES
33.9400 g., 0.9250 Silver 1.0093 oz. ASW, 39.0 mm. **Subject:** 250th Anniversary Academy of the Arts **Obv:** Two-headed eagle **Rev:** Relief image of Minerva group **Rev. Legend:** РОССИЙСКАЯ - АКАДЕМИЯ ХУДОЖЕСТВ **Edge:** Reeded

Date	Mintage	F	VF	XF	Unc	BU
2007(m) Proof	10,000	Value: 32.50				

Y# 799 5 ROUBLES
6.4500 g., Copper-Nickel Clad Copper, 25 mm. **Obv:** Curved bank name below eagle **Edge:** Segmented reeding

Date	Mintage	F	VF	XF	Unc	BU
2002	—	—	—	—	3.00	4.00

Y# 829 5 ROUBLES
47.2400 g., 0.9000 Bi-Metallic Gold And Silver .900 Silver 21.34g center in .900 Gold 25.9g ring 1.3669 oz., 39.5 mm. **Obv:** Double-headed eagle **Rev:** Uglich city view **Edge:** Reeded

Date	Mintage	F	VF	XF	Unc	BU
2004(sp) Proof	5,000	Value: 850				

Y# 676 10 ROUBLES
8.2200 g., Bi-Metallic Copper-Nickel center in Brass ring, 27 mm. **Subject:** Yuri Gagarin **Obv:** Value with latent image in zero within circle and sprigs **Rev:** Helmeted bust 1/4 right **Edge:** Reeding over denomination

Date	Mintage	F	VF	XF	Unc	BU
2001(m)	10,000,000	—	—	—	4.00	5.00
2001(sp)	10,000,000	—	—	—	4.00	5.00

Y# 686 10 ROUBLES
1.6100 g., 0.9990 Gold 0.0517 oz. AGW, 12 mm. **Subject:** Bolshoi Theater 225 Years **Obv:** Double-headed eagle within circle **Rev:** Building above number 225 **Edge:** Reeded

Date	Mintage	F	VF	XF	Unc	BU
2001 Proof	3,000	Value: 65.00				

Y# 739 10 ROUBLES
8.2200 g., Bi-Metallic Copper-Nickel center in Brass ring, 27 mm. **Subject:** Ancient Towns - Derbent **Obv:** Value with latent image in zero within circle and sprigs **Rev:** Shield above walled city view **Edge:** Reeding over denomination

Date	Mintage	F	VF	XF	Unc	BU
2002	5,000,000	—	—	—	4.00	5.00

Y# 740 10 ROUBLES
8.2200 g., Bi-Metallic Copper-Nickel center in Brass ring, 27 mm. **Subject:** Ancient Towns - Kostroma **Obv:** Value with latent image in zero within circle and sprigs **Rev:** Cupola, shield and river view **Edge:** Reeding over denomination

Date	Mintage	F	VF	XF	Unc	BU
2002	5,000,000	—	—	—	4.00	6.00

Y# 741 10 ROUBLES
8.2200 g., Bi-Metallic Copper-Nickel center in Brass ring, 27 mm. **Subject:** Ancient Towns - Staraya Russa **Obv:** Value with latent image in zero within circle and sprigs **Rev:** Shield and cathedral **Edge:** Reeding over denomination

Date	Mintage	F	VF	XF	Unc	BU
2002(sp)	5,000,000	—	—	—	4.00	6.00

Y# 748 10 ROUBLES
8.2200 g., Bi-Metallic Copper-Nickel center in Brass ring, 27 mm. **Subject:** Ministry of Education **Obv:** Value with latent image in zero within circle and sprigs **Rev:** Seedling within open book **Edge:** Reeding over denomination

Date	Mintage	F	VF	XF	Unc	BU
2002(m)	5,000,000	—	—	—	4.00	6.00

Y# 749 10 ROUBLES
8.2200 g., Bi-Metallic Copper-Nickel center in Brass ring, 27 mm. **Subject:** Ministry of Finance **Obv:** Value with latent image in zero within circle and sprigs **Rev:** Caduceus within monogram **Edge:** Reeding over denomination

Date	Mintage	F	VF	XF	Unc	BU
2002(sp)	5,000,000	—	—	—	4.00	6.00

Y# 750 10 ROUBLES
8.2200 g., Bi-Metallic Copper-Nickel center in Brass ring, 27 mm. **Subject:** Ministry of Economic Development **Obv:** Value with latent image in zero within circle and sprigs **Rev:** Crowned double-headed eagle with cornucopia and caduceus **Edge:** Reeding over denomination

Date	Mintage	F	VF	XF	Unc	BU
2002(sp)	5,000,000	—	—	—	4.00	6.00

Y# 751 10 ROUBLES
8.2200 g., Bi-Metallic Copper-Nickel center in Brass ring, 27 mm. **Subject:** Ministry of Foreign Affairs **Obv:** Value with latent image in zero within circle and sprigs **Rev:** Crowned double-headed eagle above crossed sprigs **Edge:** Reeding over denomination

Date	Mintage	F	VF	XF	Unc	BU
2002(sp)	5,000,000	—	—	—	4.00	6.00

Y# 752 10 ROUBLES
8.2200 g., Bi-Metallic Copper-Nickel center in Brass ring, 27 mm. **Subject:** Ministry of Internal Affairs **Obv:** Value with latent image in zero within circle and sprigs **Rev:** Crowned double-headed eagle with round breast shield **Edge:** Reeding over denomination

Date	Mintage	F	VF	XF	Unc	BU
2002(sp)	5,000,000	—	—	—	4.00	6.00

Y# 753 10 ROUBLES
8.2200 g., Bi-Metallic Copper-Nickel center in Brass ring, 27 mm. **Subject:** Ministry of Justice **Obv:** Value with latent image in zero within circle and sprigs **Rev:** Crowned double-headed eagle with column on breast shield **Edge:** Reeding over denomination

Date	Mintage	F	VF	XF	Unc	BU
2002(sp)	5,000,000	—	—	—	4.00	6.00

Y# 754 10 ROUBLES
8.2200 g., Bi-Metallic Copper-Nickel center in Brass ring, 27 mm. **Subject:** Russian Armed Forces **Obv:** Value with latent image in zero within circle and sprigs **Rev:** Crowned double-headed eagle with crowned pointed top shield **Edge:** Reeding over denomination

Date	Mintage	F	VF	XF	Unc	BU
2002(m)	5,000,000	—	—	—	4.00	6.00

Y# 817 10 ROUBLES
8.3400 g., Bi-Metallic Copper-Nickel center in Brass ring, 27 mm. **Obv:** Value with latent image in zero within circle and sprigs **Rev:** Murom city view and tilted oval shields within circle **Edge:** Reeded and lettered

Date	Mintage	F	VF	XF	Unc	BU
2003(sp)	5,000,000	—	—	—	4.00	6.00

Y# 818 10 ROUBLES
8.3400 g., Bi-Metallic Copper-Nickel center in Brass ring, 27 mm. **Obv:** Value with latent image in zero within circle and sprigs **Rev:** Kasimov city view and shield within circle **Edge:** Reeded and lettered

Date	Mintage	F	VF	XF	Unc	BU
2003(sp)	5,000,000	—	—	—	4.00	6.00

Y# 819 10 ROUBLES
8.3400 g., Bi-Metallic Copper-Nickel center in Brass ring, 27 mm. **Obv:** Value with latent image in zero within circle and sprigs **Rev:** Monument, city view and shield within circle **Edge:** Reeded and lettered

Date	Mintage	F	VF	XF	Unc	BU
2003(m)	5,000,000	—	—	—	4.00	6.00

Y# 800 10 ROUBLES
8.4400 g., Bi-Metallic Copper-Nickel center in Brass ring, 27.1 mm. **Obv:** Value with latent image in zero within circle and sprigs **Rev:** Shield above walled city **Edge:** Reeding over lettering

Date	Mintage	F	VF	XF	Unc	BU
2003(sp)	—	—	—	—	4.00	6.00

Y# 824 10 ROUBLES
8.4600 g., Bi-Metallic Copper-Nickel center in Brass ring, 27.08 mm. **Subject:** Town of Ryazhsk **Obv:** Value with latent image in zero within circle and sprigs **Obv. Legend:** БАНК РОССИИ **Rev:** City view and crowned shield within circle **Edge:** Reeded and lettered

Date	Mintage	F	VF	XF	Unc	BU
2004ММД	—	—	—	—	4.00	6.00

Y# 825 10 ROUBLES
8.4600 g., Bi-Metallic, 27.08 mm. **Subject:** Town of Dmitrov **Obv:** Value with latent image in zero within circle and sprigs **Obv. Legend:** БАНК РОССИИ **Rev:** City view and crowned shield within circle **Edge:** Reeded and lettered

Date	Mintage	F	VF	XF	Unc	BU
2004ММД	—	—	—	—	4.00	6.00

Y# 826 10 ROUBLES
8.4600 g., Bi-Metallic, 27.08 mm. **Subject:** Town of Kem **Obv:** Value with latent image in zero within circle and sprigs **Obv. Legend:** БАНК РОССИИ **Rev:** City view and crowned shield within circle **Edge:** Reeded and lettered

Date	Mintage	F	VF	XF	Unc	BU
2004СПМД	—	—	—	—	4.00	6.00

Y# 827 10 ROUBLES
8.4000 g., Bi-Metallic Copper-Nickel center in brass ring, 27 mm. **Obv:** Value with latent image in zero within circle and sprigs **Rev:** WWII eternal flame monument above date and sprig within circle **Edge:** Reeded and Lettered

Date	Mintage	F	VF	XF	Unc	BU
2005(sp)	—	—	—	—	4.00	6.00

Y# 886 10 ROUBLES
8.2300 g., Bi-Metallic Copper-Nickel center in Brass ring, 27 mm. **Obv:** Value with latent image in zero within circle and sprigs **Rev:** Moscow coat of arms within circle **Edge:** Reeded and lettered

Date	Mintage	F	VF	XF	Unc	BU
2005	—	—	—	—	4.00	6.00

Y# 887 10 ROUBLES
8.2300 g., Bi-Metallic Copper-Nickel center in Brass ring, 27 mm. **Obv:** Value with latent image in zero within circle and sprigs **Rev:** Leningrad Oblast coat of arms within circle **Edge:** Reeded and lettered

Date	Mintage	F	VF	XF	Unc	BU
2005	—	—	—	—	4.00	6.00

Y# 888 10 ROUBLES
8.2300 g., Bi-Metallic Copper-Nickel center in Brass ring, 27 mm. **Obv:** Value with latent image in zero within circle and sprigs **Rev:** Tverskaya arms within circle **Edge:** Reeded and lettered

Date	Mintage	F	VF	XF	Unc	BU
2005	—	—	—	—	4.00	6.00

Y# 889 10 ROUBLES
8.2300 g., Bi-Metallic Copper-Nickel center in Brass ring, 27 mm. **Obv:** Value with latent image in zero within circle and sprigs **Rev:** Krasnodarskiy Kray coat of arms **Edge:** Reeded and lettered

Date	Mintage	F	VF	XF	Unc	BU
2005	—	—	—	—	4.00	6.00

Y# 890 10 ROUBLES
8.2300 g., Bi-Metallic Copper-Nickel center in Brass ring, 27 mm. **Obv:** Value with latent image in zero within circle and sprigs **Rev:** Orlovskaya Oblast coat of arms within circle **Edge:** Reeded and lettered

Date	Mintage	F	VF	XF	Unc	BU
2005	—	—	—	—	4.00	6.00

Y# 891 10 ROUBLES
8.2300 g., Bi-Metallic Copper-Nickel center in Brass ring, 27 mm. **Obv:** Value with latent image in zero within circle and sprigs **Rev:** Tatarstan Republic coat of arms within circle **Edge:** Reeded and lettered

Date	Mintage	F	VF	XF	Unc	BU
2005	—	—	—	—	4.00	6.00

Y# 943 10 ROUBLES
Bi-Metallic Copper-Nickel center in Brass ring **Obv:** Double-headed eagle **Rev:** City of Kazan

Date	Mintage	F	VF	XF	Unc	BU
2005	—	—	—	—	4.00	6.00

Y# 944 10 ROUBLES
Bi-Metallic Copper-Nickel center in Brass ring **Obv:** Double-headed eagle **Rev:** City of Borobesk

Date	Mintage	F	VF	XF	Unc	BU
2005	—	—	—	—	4.00	6.00

Y# 945 10 ROUBLES
Bi-Metallic **Obv:** Double-headed eagle **Rev:** City of Machensk

Date	Mintage	F	VF	XF	Unc	BU
2005	—	—	—	—	4.00	6.00

Y# 946 10 ROUBLES
Bi-Metallic Copper-Nickel center in Brass ring **Obv:** Double-headed eagle **Rev:** City of Kaliningrad

Date	Mintage	F	VF	XF	Unc	BU
2005	—	—	—	—	4.00	6.00

Y# 956 10 ROUBLES
8.3000 g., Bi-Metallic Copper-Nickel center in Brass ring, 27 mm. **Obv:** Value with latent image in zero within circle and sprays **Rev:** Kaliningrad arms **Edge:** Reeded and lettered

Date	Mintage	F	VF	XF	Unc	BU
2005	—	—	—	—	4.00	6.00

Y# 957 10 ROUBLES
8.3000 g., Bi-Metallic Copper-Nickel center in Brass ring, 27 mm. **Obv:** Value with latent image in zero within circle and sprays **Rev:** Kasan arms **Edge:** Reeded and lettered

Date	Mintage	F	VF	XF	Unc	BU
2005	—	—	—	—	4.00	6.00

Y# 958 10 ROUBLES
8.3000 g., Bi-Metallic Copper-Nickel center in Brass ring, 27 mm. **Obv:** Value with latent image in zero within circle and sprays **Rev:** Mzensk arms **Edge:** Reeded and lettered

Date	Mintage	F	VF	XF	Unc	BU
2005	—	—	—	—	4.00	6.00

Y# 959 10 ROUBLES
8.3000 g., Bi-Metallic Copper-Nickel center in Brass ring, 27 mm. **Obv:** Value with latent image in zero within circle and sprays **Rev:** Borovsk arms **Edge:** Reeded and lettered

Date	Mintage	F	VF	XF	Unc	BU
2005	—	—	—	—	4.00	6.00

Y# 960 10 ROUBLES
8.3000 g., Bi-Metallic, 27 mm. **Obv:** Value with latent image in zero within circle and sprays **Rev:** Belgorod arms **Edge:** Reeded and lettered

Date	Mintage	F	VF	XF	Unc	BU
2006	—	—	—	—	4.00	6.00

Y# 961 10 ROUBLES
8.3000 g., Bi-Metallic Copper-Nickel center in Brass ring, 27 mm. **Obv:** Value with latent image in zero within circle and sprays **Rev:** Torzhok arms **Edge:** Reeded and lettered

Date	Mintage	F	VF	XF	Unc	BU
2006	—	—	—	—	4.00	6.00

Y# 962 10 ROUBLES
8.3000 g., Bi-Metallic Copper-Nickel center in Brass ring, 27 mm. **Obv:** Value with latent image in zero within circle and sprays **Rev:** Kargopol arms **Edge:** Reeded and lettered

Date	Mintage	F	VF	XF	Unc	BU
2006	—	—	—	—	4.00	6.00

Y# 947 10 ROUBLES
Bi-Metallic Copper-Nickel center in Brass ring **Obv:** Double-headed eagle **Rev:** City of Belgorod

Date	Mintage	F	VF	XF	Unc	BU
2006	—	—	—	—	4.00	6.00

Y# 948 10 ROUBLES
Bi-Metallic Copper-Nickel center in Brass ring **Obv:** Double-headed eagle **Rev:** City of Kargopol

Date	Mintage	F	VF	XF	Unc	BU
2006	—	—	—	—	4.00	6.00

Y# 949 10 ROUBLES
Bi-Metallic Copper-Nickel center in Brass ring **Obv:** Double-headed eagle **Rev:** City of Turzhok

Date	Mintage	F	VF	XF	Unc	BU
2006	—	—	—	—	4.00	6.00

Y# 950 10 ROUBLES
Bi-Metallic **Obv:** Double-headed eagle **Rev:** Coat of arms, Primorski Krai

Date	Mintage	F	VF	XF	Unc	BU
2006	—	—	—	—	4.00	6.00

Y# 951 10 ROUBLES
Bi-Metallic Copper-Nickel center in Brass ring **Obv:** Double-headed eagle **Rev:** Coat of arms, Chitinskaya Oblast

Date	Mintage	F	VF	XF	Unc	BU
2006	—	—	—	—	4.00	6.00

Y# 952 10 ROUBLES
Bi-Metallic Copper-Nickel center in Brass ring **Obv:** Double-headed eagle **Rev:** Coat of arms, Republic of Sakha (Yakotia)

Date	Mintage	F	VF	XF	Unc	BU
2006	—	—	—	—	4.00	6.00

Y# 953 10 ROUBLES
Bi-Metallic Copper-Nickel center in Brass ring **Obv:** Double-headed eagle **Rev:** Coat of arms, Republic of Altay

Date	Mintage	F	VF	XF	Unc	BU
2006	—	—	—	—	4.00	6.00

Y# 938 10 ROUBLES
8.2300 g., Bi-Metallic Copper-Nickel center in Brass ring, 27 mm. **Obv:** Value with latent image in zero within circle and sprigs **Rev:** Republic of Altai arms **Edge:** Lettered and reeded

Date	Mintage	F	VF	XF	Unc	BU
2006(sp)	10,000,000	—	—	—	4.00	6.00

Y# 939 10 ROUBLES
8.2300 g., Bi-Metallic Copper-Nickel center in Brass ring, 27 mm. **Obv:** Value with latent image in zero within circle and sprigs **Rev:** Chita Region arms **Edge:** Lettered and reeded

Date	Mintage	F	VF	XF	Unc	BU
2006(sp)	10,000,000	—	—	—	4.00	6.00

Y# 940 10 ROUBLES
8.2300 g., Bi-Metallic Copper-Nickel center in Brass ring, 27 mm. **Obv:** Value with latent image in zero within circle and sprigs **Rev:** Primorskij Kraj Maritime Territory coat of arms **Edge:** Lettered and reeded

Date	Mintage	F	VF	XF	Unc	BU
2006(sp)	10,000,000	—	—	—	4.00	6.00

Y# 941 10 ROUBLES
8.2300 g., Bi-Metallic Copper-Nickel center in Brass ring, 27 mm. **Obv:** Value with latent image in zero within circle and sprigs **Rev:** Sakha Republic coat of arms **Edge:** Lettered and reeded

Date	Mintage	F	VF	XF	Unc	BU
2006(sp)	10,000,000	—	—	—	4.00	6.00

Y# 942 10 ROUBLES
8.2300 g., Bi-Metallic **Ring Composition:** Brass **Center Composition:** Copper-Nickel, 27 mm. **Obv:** Value with latent image in zero within circle and sprigs **Rev:** Sakhalin Region coat of arms **Edge:** Lettered and reeded

Date	Mintage	F	VF	XF	Unc	BU
2006(sp)	10,000,000	—	—	—	4.00	6.00

Y# 963 10 ROUBLES
8.3000 g., Bi-Metallic, 27 mm. **Obv:** Value with latent image in zero within circle and sprays **Rev:** Vologda arms **Edge:** Reeded and lettered

Date	Mintage	F	VF	XF	Unc	BU
2007	—	—	—	—	4.00	6.00

Y# 964 10 ROUBLES
8.3000 g., Bi-Metallic, 27 mm. **Obv:** Value with latent image in zero within circle and sprays **Rev:** Veliky Ustyug arms **Edge:** Reeded and lettered

Date	Mintage	F	VF	XF	Unc	BU
2007	—	—	—	—	4.00	6.00

Y# 965 10 ROUBLES
8.3000 g., Bi-Metallic, 27 mm. **Obv:** Value with latent image in zero within circle and sprays **Rev:** Gdov arms **Edge:** Reeded and lettered

Date	Mintage	F	VF	XF	Unc	BU
2007	—	—	—	—	4.00	6.00

Y# 970 10 ROUBLES
8.5700 g., Bi-Metallic, 27.08 mm. **Obv:** Value with latent image in zero within circle and sprays **Obv. Legend:** БАНК РОССИИ **Rev:** Rostov Region arms **Edge:** Reeded and lettered

Date	Mintage	F	VF	XF	Unc	BU
2007(sp)	—	—	—	—	4.00	6.00

Y# 971 10 ROUBLES
8.5700 g., Bi-Metallic, 27.08 mm. **Obv:** Value with latent image in zero within circle and sprays **Obv. Legend:** БАНК РОССИИ **Rev:** Caucasia Republic arms **Edge:** Reeded and lettered

Date	Mintage	F	VF	XF	Unc	BU
2007(sp)	—	—	—	—	4.00	6.00

Y# 972 10 ROUBLES
8.5700 g., Bi-Metallic, 27.08 mm. **Obv:** Value with latent image in zero within circle and sprays **Obv. Legend:** БАНК РОССИИ **Rev:** Bashkiria Republic arms **Edge:** Reeded and lettered

Date	Mintage	F	VF	XF	Unc	BU
2007(sp)	—	—	—	—	4.00	6.00

Y# 973 10 ROUBLES
8.5700 g., Bi-Metallic, 27.08 mm. **Obv:** Value with latent image in zero within circle and sprays **Obv. Legend:** БАНК РОССИИ **Rev:** Archangel region arms **Edge:** Reeded and lettered

Date	Mintage	F	VF	XF	Unc	BU
2007(sp)	—	—	—	—	4.00	6.00

Y# 974 10 ROUBLES
8.5700 g., Bi-Metallic, 27.08 mm. **Obv:** Value with latent image in zero within circle and sprays **Obv. Legend:** БАНК РОССИИ **Rev:** Novosibirsk region arms **Edge:** Reeded and lettered

Date	Mintage	F	VF	XF	Unc	BU
2007(sp)	—	—	—	—	4.00	6.00

Y# 678 25 ROUBLES
173.2900 g., 0.9000 Silver 5.0141 oz. ASW, 60 mm. **Subject:** Bolshoi Theater 225 Years **Obv:** Double-headed eagle **Rev:** Dancing couple scene **Edge:** Reeded **Note:** Illustration reduced.

Date	Mintage	F	VF	XF	Unc	BU
2001 Proof	2,000	Value: 165				

Y# 683 25 ROUBLES
173.2900 g., 0.9000 Silver 5.0141 oz. ASW, 60 mm. **Subject:** Siberian Exploration **Obv:** Double-headed eagle **Rev:** Standing king and river boats **Edge:** Reeded **Note:** Illustration reduced.

Date	Mintage	F	VF	XF	Unc	BU
2001 Proof	1,000	Value: 175				

Y# 794 25 ROUBLES
173.1300 g., 0.9000 Silver 5.0094 oz. ASW, 60.2 mm. **Subject:** Foundation of Russian Savings Banks **Obv:** Double-headed eagle **Rev:** Czar Nicholas I and document **Edge:** Reeded

Date	Mintage	F	VF	XF	Unc	BU
2001(m) Proof	10,500	Value: 150				

Y# 687 25 ROUBLES
3.2000 g., 0.9990 Gold 0.1028 oz. AGW, 16 mm. **Subject:** Bolshoi Theater **Obv:** Double-headed eagle **Rev:** Ballerina **Edge:** Reeded

Date	Mintage	F	VF	XF	Unc	BU
2001 Proof	2,500	Value: 145				

Y# 777 25 ROUBLES
173.2900 g., 0.9000 Silver 5.0141 oz. ASW, 60 mm. **Subject:** Czar Alexander I **Obv:** Double-headed eagle **Rev:** Head right and crowned double-headed eagle above document text **Edge:** Reeded **Note:** Illustration reduced.

Date	Mintage	F	VF	XF	Unc	BU
2002(m) Proof	1,500	Value: 185				

Y# 785 25 ROUBLES
173.2900 g., 0.9000 Silver 5.0141 oz. ASW, 60 mm. **Subject:** Admiral Nakhimov **Obv:** Double-headed eagle **Rev:** Admiral watching naval battle **Edge:** Reeded **Note:** Illustration reduced.

Date	Mintage	F	VF	XF	Unc	BU
2002(sp) Proof	2,000	Value: 165				

Y# 790 25 ROUBLES
173.2900 g., 0.9000 Silver 5.0141 oz. ASW, 60 mm. **Subject:** Hermitage **Obv:** Double-headed eagle **Rev:** Staircase viewed through doorway **Edge:** Reeded **Note:** Illustration reduced.

Date	Mintage	F	VF	XF	Unc	BU
2002(sp) Proof	2,000	Value: 165				

Y# 743 25 ROUBLES
3.2000 g., 0.9990 Gold 0.1028 oz. AGW, 16 mm. **Subject:** Zodiac Signs: **Obv:** Double-headed eagle within beaded circle **Rev:** Leo **Edge:** Reeded

Date	Mintage	F	VF	XF	Unc	BU
2002 Proof	10,000	Value: 145				

Y# 763 25 ROUBLES
3.2000 g., 0.9990 Gold 0.1028 oz. AGW, 16 mm. **Subject:** Zodiac Signs **Obv:** Double-headed eagle within beaded circle **Rev:** Capricorn **Edge:** Reeded

Date	Mintage	F	VF	XF	Unc	BU
2002(m)	10,000	—	—	—	—	200

Y# 764 25 ROUBLES
3.2000 g., 0.9990 Gold 0.1028 oz. AGW, 16 mm. **Subject:** Zodiac Signs **Obv:** Double-headed eagle within beaded circle **Rev:** Virgo **Edge:** Reeded

Date	Mintage	F	VF	XF	Unc	BU
2002(sp)	10,000	—	—	—	—	200

Y# 765 25 ROUBLES
3.2000 g., 0.9990 Gold 0.1028 oz. AGW, 16 mm. **Subject:** Zodiac Signs **Obv:** Double-headed eagle within beaded circle **Rev:** Sagittarius **Edge:** Reeded

Date	Mintage	F	VF	XF	Unc	BU
2002(SP)	10,000	—	—	—	—	200

Y# 767 25 ROUBLES
3.2000 g., 0.9990 Gold 0.1028 oz. AGW, 16 mm. **Subject:** Zodiac signs **Obv:** Double-headed eagle within beaded circle **Rev:** Scorpio **Edge:** Reeded

Date	Mintage	F	VF	XF	Unc	BU
2002(m)	10,000	—	—	—	—	200

Y# 769 25 ROUBLES
3.2000 g., 0.9990 Gold 0.1028 oz. AGW **Subject:** Zodiac Signs **Obv:** Double-headed eagle within beaded circle **Rev:** Libra **Edge:** Reeded

Date	Mintage	F	VF	XF	Unc	BU
2002(sp)	10,000	—	—	—	—	200

Y# 821 25 ROUBLES
3.2000 g., 0.9990 Gold 0.1028 oz. AGW, 16 mm. **Subject:** Zodiac signs **Obv:** Double-headed eagle within beaded circle **Rev:** Cancer **Edge:** Reeded

Date	Mintage	F	VF	XF	Unc	BU
2003(sp)	50,000	—	—	—	—	200

Y# 864 25 ROUBLES
172.8000 g., 0.9000 Silver 4.9999 oz. ASW, 60 mm. **Rev:** St. Sercius Monastery

Date	Mintage	F	VF	XF	Unc	BU
2003 Proof	2,000	Value: 165				

Y# 865 25 ROUBLES
172.8000 g., 0.9000 Silver 4.9999 oz. ASW, 60 mm. **Rev:** Shlisselburg

Date	Mintage	F	VF	XF	Unc	BU
2003(m) Proof	2,000	Value: 145				

Y# 866 25 ROUBLES
172.8000 g., 0.9000 Silver 4.9999 oz. ASW, 60 mm. **Rev:** Kamchatka

Date	Mintage	F	VF	XF	Unc	BU
2003	2,000	Value: 165				

Y# 830 25 ROUBLES
177.9600 g., 0.9000 Bi-Metallic Gold And Silver .900 Silver 172.78g planchet with .900 Gold 5.18g insert 5.1492 oz., 60 mm. **Subject:** Monetary reform of Peter the Great **Obv:** Double-headed eagle **Rev:** Gold insert replicating the obverse and reverse designs of a 1704 one rouble coin **Edge:** Reeded **Note:** Illustration reduced.

Date	Mintage	F	VF	XF	Unc	BU
2004(sp) Proof	1,000	Value: 335				

Y# 867 25 ROUBLES
172.8000 g., 0.9000 Silver 4.9999 oz. ASW, 60 mm. **Rev:** Valaam Church

Date	Mintage	F	VF	XF	Unc	BU
2004	1,500	Value: 165				

Y# 898 25 ROUBLES
3.2000 g., 0.9990 Gold 0.1028 oz. AGW, 16 mm. **Obv:** Double-headed eagle **Rev:** Gemini twins **Edge:** Reeded

Date	Mintage	F	VF	XF	Unc	BU
2005	10,000	—	—	—	—	200

Y# 900 25 ROUBLES
3.2000 g., 0.9990 Gold 0.1028 oz. AGW, 16 mm. **Obv:** Double-headed eagle **Rev:** Cancer crawfish **Edge:** Reeded

Date	Mintage	F	VF	XF	Unc	BU
2005 Proof	10,000	Value: 145				

Y# 902 25 ROUBLES
3.2000 g., 0.9990 Gold 0.1028 oz. AGW, 16 mm. **Obv:** Double-headed eagle **Rev:** Leo lion **Edge:** Reeded

Date	Mintage	F	VF	XF	Unc	BU
2005	10,000	—	—	—	—	200

Y# 915 25 ROUBLES
3.2000 g., 0.9990 Gold 0.1028 oz. AGW, 16 mm. **Obv:** Double-headed eagle **Rev:** Virgos standing lady **Edge:** Reeded

Date	Mintage	F	VF	XF	Unc	BU
2005 Proof	10,000	Value: 145				

Y# 920 25 ROUBLES
3.2000 g., 0.9990 Gold 0.1028 oz. AGW, 16 mm. **Obv:** Double-headed eagle **Rev:** Two stylized birds forming balance scale **Edge:** Reeded

Date	Mintage	F	VF	XF	Unc	BU
2005	10,000	—	—	—	—	200

Y# 922 25 ROUBLES
3.2000 g., 0.9990 Gold 0.1028 oz. AGW, 16 mm. **Obv:** Double-headed eagle **Rev:** Scorpio scorpion **Edge:** Reeded

Date	Mintage	F	VF	XF	Unc	BU
2005	10,000	—	—	—	—	200

Y# 927 25 ROUBLES
3.2000 g., 0.9990 Gold 0.1028 oz. AGW, 16 mm. **Obv:** Double-headed eagle **Rev:** Sagittarius the archer **Edge:** Reeded

Date	Mintage	F	VF	XF	Unc	BU
2005	10,000	—	—	—	—	200

Y# 929 25 ROUBLES
3.2000 g., 0.9990 Gold 0.1028 oz. AGW, 16 mm. **Obv:** Double-headed eagle **Rev:** Capricorn as half goat and fish **Edge:** Reeded

Date	Mintage	F	VF	XF	Unc	BU
2005	10,000	—	—	—	—	200

Y# 931 25 ROUBLES
3.2000 g., 0.9990 Gold 0.1028 oz. AGW, 16 mm. **Obv:** Double-headed eagle **Rev:** Pisces as catfish and sturgeon **Edge:** Reeded

Date	Mintage	F	VF	XF	Unc	BU
2005	10,000	—	—	—	—	200

Y# 933 25 ROUBLES
3.2000 g., 0.9990 Gold 0.1028 oz. AGW, 16 mm. **Obv:** Double-headed eagle **Rev:** Aries ram **Edge:** Reeded

Date	Mintage	F	VF	XF	Unc	BU
2005	10,000	—	—	—	—	200

Y# 935 25 ROUBLES
3.2000 g., 0.9990 Gold 0.1028 oz. AGW, 16 mm. **Obv:** Double-headed eagle **Rev:** Taurus bull **Edge:** Reeded

Date	Mintage	F	VF	XF	Unc	BU
2005	10,000	—	—	—	—	200

Y# 937 25 ROUBLES
3.2000 g., 0.9990 Gold 0.1028 oz. AGW, 16 mm. **Obv:** Double-headed eagle **Rev:** Aquarius water carrier **Edge:** Reeded

Date	Mintage	F	VF	XF	Unc	BU
2005	10,000	—	—	—	—	200

Y# 924 25 ROUBLES
169.0000 g., 0.9250 Silver 5.0258 oz. ASW, 60 mm. **Subject:** 625th Anniversary - Battle of Kulikovo **Obv:** Double-headed eagle **Rev:** Mounted warriors above and below crossed swords **Edge:** Reeded **Note:** Illustration reduced.

Date	Mintage	F	VF	XF	Unc	BU
2005 Proof	1,500	Value: 185				

Y# 969 25 ROUBLES
169.0000 g., 0.9250 Silver 5.0258 oz. ASW, 60.00 mm. **Obv:** Two-headed eagle **Rev:** Vyatka St. Trifon Monastery of the Assumption, Kirov **Edge:** Reeded **Note:** Illustration reduced

Date	Mintage	F	VF	XF	Unc	BU
2007(sp) (l) Proof	2,000	Value: 165				

Y# 679 50 ROUBLES
8.7500 g., 0.9990 Gold 0.2810 oz. AGW, 22.6 mm. **Subject:** Bolshoi Theater **Obv:** Double-headed eagle within beaded circle **Rev:** Dueling figures **Edge:** Reeded

Date	Mintage	F	VF	XF	Unc	BU
2001 Proof	2,000	Value: 320				

Y# 684 50 ROUBLES
8.7500 g., 0.9000 Gold 0.2532 oz. AGW, 22.6 mm. **Subject:** Siberian Exploration **Obv:** Double-headed eagle within beaded circle **Rev:** Head with hat 1/4 right and boat **Edge:** Reeded

Date	Mintage	F	VF	XF	Unc	BU
2001 Proof	1,500	Value: 300				

Y# 757 50 ROUBLES
8.6444 g., 0.9000 Gold 0.2501 oz. AGW, 22.6 mm. **Subject:** Olympics **Obv:** Double-headed eagle within beaded circle **Rev:** Figure skater and flying eagle **Edge:** Reeded

Date	Mintage	F	VF	XF	Unc	BU
2002 Proof	3,000	Value: 300				

Y# 782 50 ROUBLES
7.8900 g., 0.9990 Gold 0.2534 oz. AGW, 22.6 mm. **Subject:** Works of Dionissy **Obv:** Double-headed eagle within beaded circle **Rev:** Half-length figure holding child flanked by double headed eagle and church **Edge:** Reeded

Date	Mintage	F	VF	XF	Unc	BU
2002(m) Proof	1,500	Value: 300				

Y# 786 50 ROUBLES
8.7500 g., 0.9000 Gold 0.2532 oz. AGW, 22.6 mm. **Subject:** Admiral Nakhimov **Obv:** Double-headed eagle within beaded circle **Rev:** Bust facing within circle above flags and anchor **Edge:** Reeded

Date	Mintage	F	VF	XF	Unc	BU
2002(sp) Proof	1,500	Value: 300				

Y# 788 50 ROUBLES
8.7500 g., 0.9000 Gold 0.2532 oz. AGW, 22.6 mm. **Subject:** World Cup Soccer **Obv:** Double-headed eagle within beaded circle **Rev:** Stylized player kicking soccer ball **Edge:** Reeded

Date	Mintage	F	VF	XF	Unc	BU
2002(m) Proof	3,000	Value: 300				

Y# 822 50 ROUBLES
7.8900 g., 0.9990 Gold 0.2534 oz. AGW, 22.6 mm. **Subject:** Zodiac Signs **Obv:** Double-headed eagle within beaded circle **Rev:** Virgo **Edge:** Reeded

Date	Mintage	F	VF	XF	Unc	BU
2003(sp)	30,000	—	—	—	—	300

Y# 823 50 ROUBLES
7.8900 g., 0.9990 Gold 0.2534 oz. AGW, 22.6 mm. **Subject:** Zodiac signs **Obv:** Double-headed eagle within beaded circle **Rev:** Libra **Edge:** Reeded

Date	Mintage	F	VF	XF	Unc	BU
2003(m)	30,000	—	—	—	—	300

Y# 868 50 ROUBLES
8.6400 g., 0.9000 Gold 0.2500 oz. AGW, 23 mm. **Rev:** Peter I monetary reform

Date	Mintage	F	VF	XF	Unc	BU
2003(m) Proof	1,500	Value: 300				

Y# 869 50 ROUBLES
8.6400 g., 0.9000 Gold 0.2500 oz. AGW, 23 mm. **Rev:** Ski race

Date	Mintage	F	VF	XF	Unc	BU
2003(m) Proof	1,500	Value: 300				

Y# 870 50 ROUBLES
8.6400 g., 0.9000 Gold 0.2500 oz. AGW, 23 mm. **Rev:** Soccer player

Date	Mintage	F	VF	XF	Unc	BU
2004(sp) Proof	1,000	Value: 300				

Y# 871 50 ROUBLES
8.6400 g., 0.9000 Gold 0.2500 oz. AGW, 23 mm. **Rev:** Olympic athletes

Date	Mintage	F	VF	XF	Unc	BU
2004(m) Proof	2,000	Value: 300				

Y# 872 50 ROUBLES
8.6400 g., 0.9000 Gold 0.2500 oz. AGW, 23 mm. **Rev:** Virgin of the Son Icon

Date	Mintage	F	VF	XF	Unc	BU
2004(m) Proof	1,500	Value: 300				

Y# 894 50 ROUBLES
7.8900 g., 0.9990 Gold 0.2534 oz. AGW, 22.6 mm. **Subject:** 60th Anniversary - Victory Over Germany **Obv:** Double-headed eagle **Rev:** 60th Anniversary - Victory Over Germany medal **Edge:** Reeded

Date	Mintage	F	VF	XF	Unc	BU
2005 Proof	7,000	Value: 300				

Y# 907 50 ROUBLES
7.8900 g., 0.9990 Gold 0.2534 oz. AGW, 22.6 mm. **Subject:** Helsinki Games **Obv:** Double-headed eagle **Rev:** Stylized track and field athletes **Edge:** Reeded

Date	Mintage	F	VF	XF	Unc	BU
2005 Proof	1,500	Value: 300				

Y# 911 50 ROUBLES
7.8900 g., 0.9990 Gold 0.2534 oz. AGW, 22.6 mm. **Obv:** Double-headed eagle **Rev:** Kazan University Building **Edge:** Reeded

Date	Mintage	F	VF	XF	Unc	BU
2005 Proof	1,500	Value: 300				

Y# 795 100 ROUBLES
1111.1200 g., 0.9000 Silver 32.149 oz. ASW, 100 mm. **Subject:** The Bark Sedov **Obv:** Double-headed eagle **Rev:** Ship flanked by compass and cameo **Edge:** Reeded **Note:** Illustration reduced.

Date	Mintage	F	VF	XF	Unc	BU
2001(m) Proof	500	Value: 800				

Y# 681 100 ROUBLES
1111.1000 g., 0.9000 Silver 32.149 oz. ASW, 100 mm. **Subject:** 40th Anniversary of Manned Space Flight - Yuri Gagarin **Obv:** Double-headed eagle **Rev:** Astronaut and rocket in space **Edge:** Reeded **Note:** Illustration reduced.

Date	Mintage	F	VF	XF	Unc	BU
2001 Proof	750	Value: 800				

Y# 689 100 ROUBLES
1111.1000 g., 0.9000 Silver 32.149 oz. ASW, 100 mm. **Subject:** Bolshoi Theater 225 Years **Obv:** Double-headed eagle **Rev:** Casino gambling scene **Edge:** Reeded **Note:** Illustration reduced.

Date	Mintage	F	VF	XF	Unc	BU
2001 Proof	500	Value: 1,000				

Y# 685 100 ROUBLES
17.4500 g., 0.9000 Gold 0.5049 oz. AGW, 30 mm. **Subject:** Siberian Exploration **Obv:** Double-headed eagle within beaded circle **Rev:** Head and silhouette left, sailboat and other designs **Edge:** Reeded

Date	Mintage	F	VF	XF	Unc	BU
2001 Proof	1,000	Value: 600				

Y# 688 100 ROUBLES
15.7200 g., 0.9990 Gold 0.5049 oz. AGW, 30 mm. **Subject:** Bolshoi Theater 225 Years **Obv:** Double-headed eagle within beaded circle **Rev:** Three dancers with swords **Edge:** Reeded

Date	Mintage	F	VF	XF	Unc	BU
2001 Proof	1,500	Value: 600				

Y# 783 100 ROUBLES
1111.1200 g., 0.9000 Silver 32.149 oz. ASW, 100 mm. **Subject:** Works of Dionissy **Obv:** Double-headed eagle **Rev:** St. Ferapont Monastery in the center of a fresco covered cross **Edge:** Reeded **Note:** Illustration reduced.

Date	Mintage	F	VF	XF	Unc	BU
2002(sp) Prooflike	500	—	—	—	—	900

Y# 789 100 ROUBLES

1111.1200 g., 0.9000 Silver 32.149 oz. ASW, 100 mm. **Subject:** World Cup Soccer **Obv:** Double-headed eagle **Rev:** Soccer ball design with map and players **Edge:** Reeded **Note:** Illustration reduced.

Date	Mintage	F	VF	XF	Unc	BU
2002(sp) Proof	500	Value: 900				

Y# 791 100 ROUBLES

1111.1200 g., 0.9000 Silver 32.149 oz. ASW, 100 mm. **Subject:** Hermitage **Obv:** Double-headed eagle **Rev:** Statues and arches **Edge:** Reeded **Note:** Illustration reduced.

Date	Mintage	F	VF	XF	Unc	BU
2002(sp) Proof	1,000	Value: 800				

Y# 792 100 ROUBLES

17.4500 g., 0.9000 Gold 0.5049 oz. AGW, 30 mm. **Subject:** Hermitage **Obv:** Double-headed eagle within beaded circle **Rev:** Ancient battle scene sculpted on comb **Edge:** Reeded

Date	Mintage	F	VF	XF	Unc	BU
2002(sp) Proof	1,000	Value: 600				

Y# 873 100 ROUBLES

1111.1200 g., 0.9000 Silver 32.149 oz. ASW, 100 mm. **Rev:** St. Petersburg

Date	Mintage	F	VF	XF	Unc	BU
2003(m) Proof	1,000	Value: 750				

Y# 874 100 ROUBLES

17.4500 g., 0.9000 Gold 0.5049 oz. AGW, 30 mm. **Rev:** Petrozavodsk

Date	Mintage	F	VF	XF	Unc	BU
2003(m) Proof	1,000	Value: 600				

Y# 875 100 ROUBLES

17.4500 g., 0.9000 Gold 0.5049 oz. AGW, 30 mm. **Rev:** Kamchatka

Date	Mintage	F	VF	XF	Unc	BU
2003(sp) Proof	1,500	Value: 600				

Y# 832 100 ROUBLES

17.2800 g., 0.9000 Gold 0.5000 oz. AGW, 30 mm. **Subject:** 2nd Kamchatka Expedition **Obv:** Double-headed eagle **Rev:** Shaman and two seated men **Edge:** Reeded

Date	Mintage	F	VF	XF	Unc	BU
2004(sp) Proof	1,500	Value: 600				

Y# 831 100 ROUBLES

1000.0000 g., 0.9250 Silver 28.934 oz. ASW, 100 mm. **Obv:** Double-headed eagle **Rev:** Panel of icons painted by Theophanes the Greek **Edge:** Reeded **Note:** Illustration reduced.

Date	Mintage	F	VF	XF	Unc	BU
2004(sp) Proof	500	Value: 750				

Y# 876 100 ROUBLES

1111.1200 g., 0.9000 Silver 32.149 oz. ASW, 100 mm. **Rev:** Annunciation Cathedral Iconostasis

Date	Mintage	F	VF	XF	Unc	BU
2004(sp) Proof	500	Value: 800				

Y# 895 100 ROUBLES

1083.7400 g., 0.9250 Silver 32.228 oz. ASW, 100 mm. **Subject:** 60th Anniversary Victory Over Germany **Obv:** Double-headed eagle **Rev:** Decorated locomotive returning soldiers circa 1945 **Edge:** Reeded **Note:** Illustration reduced.

Date	Mintage	F	VF	XF	Unc	BU
2005 Proof	2,000	Value: 750				

Y# 912 100 ROUBLES

1083.7400 g., 0.9250 Silver 32.228 oz. ASW, 100 mm. **Obv:** Double-headed eagle **Rev:** Kazan city view with mausoleums **Edge:** Reeded **Note:** Illustration reduced.

Date	Mintage	F	VF	XF	Unc	BU
2005 Proof	500	Value: 750				

Y# 925 100 ROUBLES

1083.7400 g., 0.9250 Silver 32.228 oz. ASW, 100 mm. **Subject:** 625th Anniversary - Battle of Kulikovo **Obv:** Double-headed eagle **Rev:** Battle of Kulikovo beginning scene **Edge:** Reeded **Note:** Illustration reduced.

Date	Mintage	F	VF	XF	Unc	BU
2005 Proof	500	Value: 750				

Y# 877 200 ROUBLES

3342.3899 g., 0.9000 Silver 96.710 oz. ASW, 130 mm. **Rev:** Peter I monetary reform

Date	Mintage	F	VF	XF	Unc	BU
2003(sp) Proof	300	Value: 4,000				

Y# 796 1000 ROUBLES

156.4000 g., 0.9990 Gold 5.0231 oz. AGW, 50 mm. **Subject:** The Bark Sedov **Obv:** Double-headed eagle **Rev:** Four-masted sailing ship **Edge:** Reeded

Date	Mintage	F	VF	XF	Unc	BU
2001(m) Proof	250	Value: 5,000				

Y# 878 1000 ROUBLES

156.4000 g., 0.9990 Gold 5.0231 oz. AGW, 50 mm. **Rev:** Cronstadt

Date	Mintage	F	VF	XF	Unc	BU
2003(m) Proof	250	Value: 5,000				

Y# 784 10000 ROUBLES

1001.1000 g., 0.9990 Gold 32.152 oz. AGW, 100 mm. **Subject:** Works of Dionissy **Obv:** Double-headed eagle **Rev:** Interior view of the carved portal of the Virgin of the Nativity Church **Edge:** Reeded **Note:** Illustration reduced.

Date	Mintage	F	VF	XF	Unc	BU
2002(sp) Proof	100	Value: 32,000				

Y# 879 10000 ROUBLES

1001.1000 g., 0.9990 Gold 32.152 oz. AGW, 100 mm. **Rev:** St. Petersburg area map

Date	Mintage	F	VF	XF	Unc	BU
2003 Proof	200	Value: 32,000				

Y# 880 10000 ROUBLES

1001.1000 g., 0.9990 Gold 32.152 oz. AGW, 100 mm. **Rev:** Church of the Transfiguration of the Savior, Novgorod

Date	Mintage	F	VF	XF	Unc	BU
2004 Proof	100	Value: 32,000				

Y# 896 10000 ROUBLES
1001.1000 g., 0.9990 Gold 32.152 oz. AGW, 100 mm. **Subject:** 60th Anniversary - Victory Over Germany **Obv:** Double-headed eagle **Rev:** Soldiers dishonoring captured Nazi flags and standards **Edge:** Reeded **Note:** Illustration reduced.

Date	Mintage	F	VF	XF	Unc	BU
2005 Proof	250	Value: 32,000				

Y# 913 10000 ROUBLES
1001.1000 g., 0.9990 Gold 32.152 oz. AGW, 100 mm. **Obv:** Two headed eagle **Rev:** Kazan Kremlin view **Edge:** Reeded **Note:** Illustration reduced.

Date	Mintage	F	VF	XF	Unc	BU
2005 Proof	150	Value: 32,000				

MINT SETS

KM#	Date	Mintage	Identification	Issue Price	Mkt Val
MS44	2002 (7)	—	Y#600-603, 797-799, plus mint medal	7.50	10.00

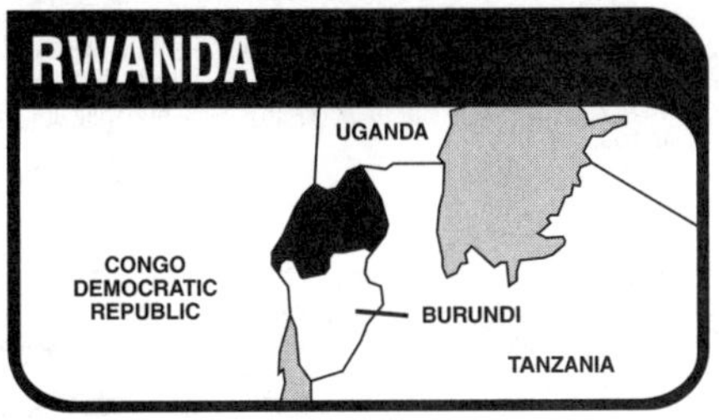

The Republic of Rwanda, located in central Africa between the Republic of the Congo and Tanzania, has an area of 10,169 sq. mi. (26,340 sq. km.) and a population of 7.3 million. Capital: Kigali. The economy is based on agriculture and mining. Coffee and tin are exported.

For earlier coinage see Belgian Congo, and Rwanda and Burundi.

MINT MARKS
(a) - Paris, privy marks only
(b) - Brussels, privy marks only

MONETARY SYSTEM
100 Centimes = 1 Franc

REPUBLIC

STANDARD COINAGE

KM# 22 FRANC
0.0700 g., Aluminum, 16 mm. **Obv:** National arms **Rev:** Sorghum plant **Edge:** Plain

Date	Mintage	F	VF	XF	Unc	BU
2003(a)	—	—	—	0.25	0.65	1.00

KM# 23 5 FRANCS
2.9600 g., Brass Plated Steel, 20 mm. **Obv:** National arms **Rev:** Coffee plant **Edge:** Plain

Date	Mintage	F	VF	XF	Unc	BU
2003(a)	—	—	—	0.25	0.65	1.00

KM# 24 10 FRANCS
5.0000 g., Brass Plated Steel, 23.9 mm. **Obv:** National arms **Rev:** Banana tree **Edge:** Plain

Date	Mintage	F	VF	XF	Unc	BU
2003(a)	—	—	—	0.45	1.00	1.50

KM# 25 20 FRANCS
3.5000 g., Nickel Clad Steel, 20 mm. **Obv:** National arms **Rev:** Coffee plant seedling **Edge:** Reeded

Date	Mintage	F	VF	XF	Unc	BU
2003(a)	—	—	—	—	1.75	2.00

KM# 26 50 FRANCS
5.8000 g., Nickel Clad Steel, 24 mm. **Obv:** National arms **Rev:** Ear of corn within husks **Edge:** Reeded

Date	Mintage	F	VF	XF	Unc	BU
2003(a)	—	—	—	—	4.50	5.00

KM# 28 200 FRANCS
1.0000 g., 0.9990 Gold 0.0321 oz. AGW, 13.92 mm. **Subject:** 75th Birthday Dian Fossey **Obv:** National arms **Obv. Legend:** BANKI NASIYONALI Y'U RWANDA **Rev:** Fossey facing holding monkey **Edge:** Plain

Date	Mintage	F	VF	XF	Unc	BU
2007 Proof	15,000	Value: 115				

KM# 30 500 FRANCS
22.2000 g., 0.9000 Silver 0.6423 oz. ASW **Obv:** National arms **Obv. Legend:** BANQUE NATIONALE DU RWANDA **Rev:** Stalk of bananas on leaves

Date	Mintage	F	VF	XF	Unc	BU
2002(a) Proof	500	Value: 90.00				

KM# 27 500 FRANCS
20.0000 g., 0.9990 Silver 0.6423 oz. ASW, 38.00 mm. **Subject:** OlympicGames 2008 - Peking, marathon races **Obv:** National arms **Obv. Legend:** BANKI NASIYONALI Y'U RWANDA **Rev:** Three male marathon runners, Rwanda Olympic logo at right **Rev. Legend:** JEUX OLYMPIQUES **Edge:** Plain

Date	Mintage	F	VF	XF	Unc	BU
2006 Proof	—	Value: 115				

KM# 29 1000 FRANCS
93.3000 g., 0.9990 Silver And Gold 2.9965 oz., 65.00 mm. **Obv:** National arms **Obv. Legend:** BANKI NASIYONALI Y'U RWANDA **Rev:** Gilt elephant family of four with diamonds inset in eyes **Rev. Legend:** AFRICAN ELEPHANT **Edge:** Plain

Date	Mintage	F	VF	XF	Unc	BU
2007	1,500	—	—	—	—	420
2007 Proof	500	Value: 500				

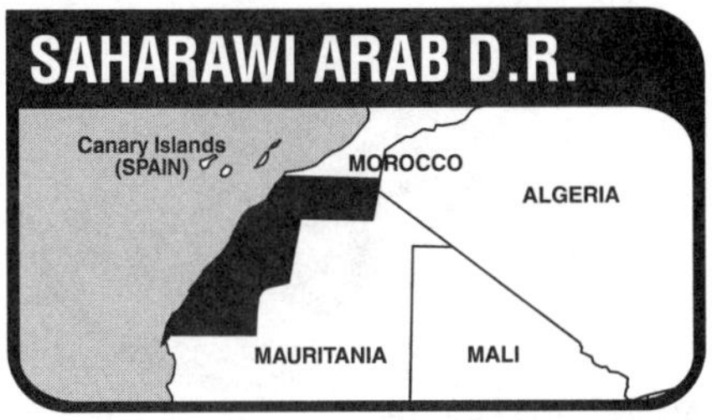

The Saharawi Arab Democratic Republic, located in northwest Africa has an area of 102,703 sq. mi. and a population (census taken 1974) of 76,425. Formerly known as Spanish Sahara, the area is bounded on the north by Morocco, on the east and southeast by Mauritania, on the northeast by Algeria, and on the west by the Atlantic Ocean. Capital: El Aaium. Agriculture, fishing and mining are the three main industries. Exports are barley, livestock and phosphates. The SADR is a "government in exile". It currently controls about 20% of its claimed territory, the former Spanish colony of Western Sahara; Morocco controls and administers the majority of the territory as its Southern Provinces. SADR claims control over a zone largely bordering Mauritania, described as "the Free Zone," although characterized by Morocco as a buffer zone.

DEMOCRATIC REPUBLIC

NON-CIRCULATING COLLECTOR COINAGE

KM# 51 500 PESETAS
Bi-Metallic Stainless Steel center in Brass ring, 26 mm. **Obv:** National arms within circle **Rev:** Two Fennec foxes within circle **Edge:** Segmented reeding

Date	Mintage	F	VF	XF	Unc	BU
2004	5,000	—	—	—	27.50	32.50

KM# 51a 500 PESETAS
Bi-Metallic .999Silver center in .999 Gold plated .999 Silver ring, 26 mm. **Obv:** National arms within circle **Rev:** Two Fennec foxes within circle **Edge:** Segmented reeded

Date	Mintage	F	VF	XF	Unc	BU
2004	25	—	—	—	235	250

KM# 51b 500 PESETAS
0.9990 Silver, 26 mm. **Obv:** National arms within circle **Rev:** Two Fennec foxes within circle **Edge:** Segmented reeding

Date	Mintage	F	VF	XF	Unc	BU
2004	25	—	—	—	210	225

KM# 52 500 PESETAS
Bi-Metallic Stainless Steel center in Brass ring, 26 mm. **Obv:** National arms within circle **Rev:** Independence map divides circle **Edge:** Segmented reeding

Date	Mintage	F	VF	XF	Unc	BU
2004	5,000	—	—	—	30.00	35.00

KM# 52a 500 PESETAS
Bi-Metallic .999 Silver center in .999 Gold plated .999 Silver ring, 26 mm. **Obv:** National arms within circle **Rev:** Independence map divides circle **Edge:** Segmented reeding

Date	Mintage	F	VF	XF	Unc	BU
2004	25	—	—	—	235	250

KM# 52b 500 PESETAS
0.9990 Silver, 26 mm. **Obv:** National arms within circle **Rev:** Independence map divides circle **Edge:** Segmented reeding

Date	Mintage	F	VF	XF	Unc	BU
2004	25	—	—	—	210	225

KM# 54 1000 PESETAS
19.9400 g., 0.9990 Silver 0.6404 oz. ASW, 38.1 mm. **Obv:** National arms **Rev:** Soccer player and stadium **Edge:** Plain

Date	Mintage	F	VF	XF	Unc	BU
2002 Proof	—	Value: 30.00				

SAINT HELENA

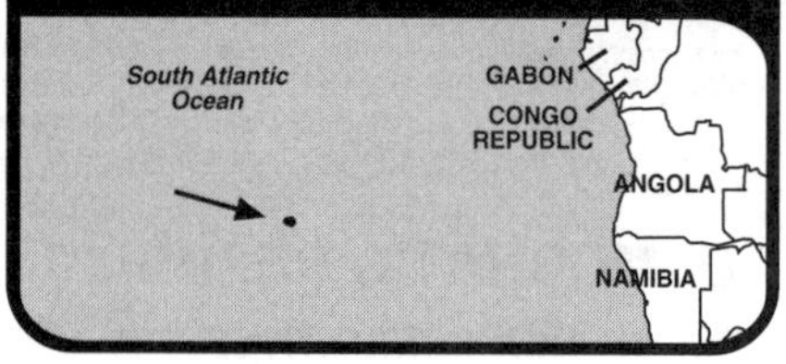

Saint Helena, a British colony located about 1,150 miles (1,850 km.) from the west coast of Africa, has an area of 47 sq. mi. (410 sq. km.) and a population of *7,000. Capital: Jamestown. Flax, lace, and rope are produced for export. Ascension and Tristan da Cunha are dependencies of Saint Helena.

MONETARY SYSTEM
12 Pence = 1 Shilling
100 Pence = 1 Pound

BRITISH COLONY
STANDARD COINAGE

KM# 19 50 PENCE
38.6000 g., Copper-Nickel, 38.6 mm. **Ruler:** Elizabeth II **Subject:** 75th Birthday of Queen Elizabeth II **Obv:** Crowned bust right **Obv. Designer:** Raphael Maklouf **Rev:** Bust facing within circle and rose sprigs **Edge:** Reeded

Date	Mintage	VG	F	VF	XF	Unc
2001	—	—	—	—	—	8.00

KM# 19a 50 PENCE
28.2800 g., 0.9250 Silver 0.8410 oz. ASW, 38.6 mm. **Ruler:** Elizabeth II **Subject:** 75th Birthday of Queen Elizabeth II **Obv:** Crowned bust right **Rev:** Bust facing within circle and rose sprigs **Edge:** Reeded

Date	Mintage	F	VF	XF	Unc	BU
2001 Proof	10,000	Value: 50.00				

KM# 19b 50 PENCE
47.5400 g., 0.9166 Gold 1.4009 oz. AGW, 38.6 mm. **Ruler:** Elizabeth II **Subject:** 75th Birthday of Queen Elizabeth II **Obv:** Crowned bust right **Rev:** Bust facing within circle and rose sprigs **Edge:** Reeded

Date	Mintage	F	VF	XF	Unc	BU
2001 Proof	75	Value: 1,450				

KM# 20 50 PENCE
28.5500 g., Copper-Nickel, 38.6 mm. **Ruler:** Elizabeth II **Subject:** Queen Victoria's Death **Obv:** Crowned bust right **Obv. Designer:** Raphael Maklouf **Rev:** Half-length figure facing and ship within circle **Edge:** Reeded

Date	Mintage	VG	F	VF	XF	Unc
2001	—	—	—	—	—	8.00

KM# 20a 50 PENCE
28.2800 g., 0.9250 Silver 0.8410 oz. ASW, 38.6 mm. **Ruler:** Elizabeth II **Subject:** Centennial - Death of Queen Victoria **Obv:** Crowned bust right **Rev:** Half-length figure facing and ship within circle **Edge:** Reeded

Date	Mintage	F	VF	XF	Unc	BU
2001 Proof	10,000	Value: 50.00				

KM# 20b 50 PENCE
47.5400 g., 0.9166 Gold 1.4009 oz. AGW, 38.6 mm. **Ruler:** Elizabeth II **Subject:** Centennial - Death of Queen Victoria **Obv:** Crowned bust right **Rev:** Half-length figure facing and ship within circle **Edge:** Reeded

Date	Mintage	F	VF	XF	Unc	BU
2001 Proof	100	Value: 1,350				

KM# 23 50 PENCE
28.2800 g., Copper-Nickel, 38.6 mm. **Ruler:** Elizabeth II **Subject:** 50th Anniversary - Queen Elizabeth II's Accession **Obv:** Crowned bust right **Obv. Designer:** Raphael Maklouf **Rev:** Crown on pillow within circle **Edge:** Reeded

Date	Mintage	F	VF	XF	Unc	BU
ND(2002)	—	—	—	—	10.00	12.00

KM# 23a 50 PENCE
28.2800 g., 0.9250 Silver 0.8410 oz. ASW, 38.6 mm. **Ruler:** Elizabeth II **Subject:** 50th Anniversary - Queen Elizabeth's Accession **Obv:** Crowned bust right **Rev:** Crown on pillow within circle **Edge:** Reeded

Date	Mintage	F	VF	XF	Unc	BU
ND(2002) Proof	10,000	Value: 50.00				

KM# 24 50 PENCE
28.2800 g., Copper-Nickel, 38.6 mm. **Ruler:** Elizabeth II **Subject:** To Celebrate a Life of Duty, Dignity and Love, 1900-2002 **Obv:** Crowned bust right **Obv. Designer:** Raphael Maklouf **Rev:** Conjoined busts right **Rev. Designer:** Willem Vis **Edge:** Reeded

Date	Mintage	F	VF	XF	Unc	BU
ND(2002)	—	—	—	—	10.00	12.00

KM# 24a 50 PENCE
28.2800 g., 0.9250 Silver 0.8410 oz. ASW, 38.6 mm. **Ruler:** Elizabeth II **Subject:** To Celebrate a Life of Duty, Dignity and Love, 1900-2002 **Obv:** Crowned bust right **Rev:** Conjoined busts right **Edge:** Reeded

Date	Mintage	F	VF	XF	Unc	BU
ND(2002) Proof	10,000	Value: 50.00				

KM# 25 50 PENCE
28.2800 g., Copper-Nickel, 38.6 mm. **Ruler:** Elizabeth II **Subject:** 500th Anniversary - Discovery of St. Helena **Obv:** Crowned bust right **Obv. Designer:** Raphael Maklouf **Rev:** Half length figure right and ship above 1502 date **Rev. Designer:** Willem Vis **Edge:** Reeded

Date	Mintage	F	VF	XF	Unc	BU
ND(2002)	—	—	—	—	10.00	12.00

KM# 25a 50 PENCE
28.2800 g., 0.9250 Silver 0.8410 oz. ASW, 38.6 mm. **Ruler:** Elizabeth II **Subject:** 500th Anniversary - Discovery of St. Helena **Obv:** Crowned bust right **Rev:** Half length figure right and ship above 1502 date **Edge:** Reeded

Date	Mintage	F	VF	XF	Unc	BU
ND(2002) Proof	5,000	Value: 50.00				

KM# 26 50 PENCE
28.2800 g., Copper-Nickel, 38.6 mm. **Ruler:** Elizabeth II **Obv:** Crowned bust right **Obv. Designer:** Raphael Maklouf **Rev:** Bust 1/4 left, ship HMS Paramour and a comet **Rev. Designer:** Willem Vis **Edge:** Reeded

Date	Mintage	F	VF	XF	Unc	BU
ND(2002)	—	—	—	—	10.00	12.00

KM# 26a 50 PENCE
28.2800 g., 0.9250 Silver 0.8410 oz. ASW, 38.6 mm. **Ruler:** Elizabeth II **Obv:** Crowned bust right **Rev:** Bust 1/4 left, ship HMS Paramour and a comet **Edge:** Reeded

Date	Mintage	F	VF	XF	Unc	BU
ND(2002) Proof	5,000	Value: 50.00				

KM# 27 50 PENCE

28.2800 g., Copper-Nickel, 38.6 mm. **Ruler:** Elizabeth II **Obv:** Crowned bust right **Obv. Designer:** Raphael Maklouf **Rev:** Bust 1/4 right and the HMS Resolution **Rev. Designer:** Willem Vis **Edge:** Reeded

Date	Mintage	F	VF	XF	Unc	BU
ND(2002)	—	—	—	—	10.00	12.00

KM# 27a 50 PENCE

28.2800 g., 0.9250 Silver 0.8410 oz. ASW, 38.6 mm. **Ruler:** Elizabeth II **Obv:** Crowned bust right **Rev:** Bust 1/4 right and the HMS Resolution **Edge:** Reeded

Date	Mintage	F	VF	XF	Unc	BU
ND(2002) Proof	5,000	Value: 50.00				

KM# 28 50 PENCE

28.2800 g., Copper-Nickel, 38.6 mm. **Ruler:** Elizabeth II **Obv:** Crowned bust right **Obv. Designer:** Raphael Maklouf **Rev:** Half length figure facing and the ship HMS Northumberland **Rev. Designer:** Willem Vis **Edge:** Reeded

Date	Mintage	F	VF	XF	Unc	BU
ND(2002)	—	—	—	—	10.00	12.00

KM# 29 50 PENCE

28.2800 g., Copper-Nickel, 38.6 mm. **Ruler:** Elizabeth II **Obv:** Crowned bust right **Obv. Designer:** Raphael Maklouf **Rev:** Four conjoined busts left plus the HMS Vanguard **Rev. Designer:** Willem Vis **Edge:** Reeded

Date	Mintage	F	VF	XF	Unc	BU
ND(2002)	—	—	—	—	10.00	12.00

KM# 29a 50 PENCE

28.2800 g., 0.9250 Silver 0.8410 oz. ASW, 38.6 mm. **Ruler:** Elizabeth II **Obv:** Crowned bust right **Rev:** Four conjoined busts left plus the HMS Vanguard **Edge:** Reeded

Date	Mintage	F	VF	XF	Unc	BU
ND(2002) Proof	5,000	Value: 50.00				

KM# 30 50 PENCE

28.2800 g., Copper-Nickel, 38.6 mm. **Ruler:** Elizabeth II **Subject:** 50th Anniversary of Queen Elizabeth's Coronation **Obv:** Crowned bust right **Obv. Designer:** Raphael Maklouf **Rev:** Crowned Queen facing with scepter and orb **Edge:** Reeded

Date	Mintage	F	VF	XF	Unc	BU
ND(2003)	—	—	—	—	10.00	12.00

KM# 30a 50 PENCE

28.2800 g., 0.9250 Silver 0.8410 oz. ASW, 38.6 mm. **Ruler:** Elizabeth II **Subject:** 50th Anniversary - Queen Elizabeth's Coronation **Obv:** Crowned bust right **Rev:** Crowned Queen facing with scepter and orb **Edge:** Reeded

Date	Mintage	F	VF	XF	Unc	BU
ND(2003) Proof	5,000	Value: 50.00				

KM# 30b 50 PENCE

39.9400 g., 0.9166 Gold 1.1770 oz. AGW, 38.6 mm. **Ruler:** Elizabeth II **Subject:** 50th Anniversary of Queen's Coronation **Obv:** Crowned bust right **Rev:** Crowned Queen facing with scepter and orb **Edge:** Reeded

Date	Mintage	F	VF	XF	Unc	BU
ND(2003) Proof	50	Value: 1,350				

KM# 31 50 PENCE

28.2800 g., Copper-Nickel, 38.6 mm. **Ruler:** Elizabeth II **Subject:** 50th Anniversary of Coronation **Obv:** Crowned bust right **Obv. Designer:** Raphael Maklouf **Rev:** Coronation implements **Edge:** Reeded

Date	Mintage	F	VF	XF	Unc	BU
ND(2003)	—	—	—	—	10.00	12.00

KM# 31a 50 PENCE

28.2800 g., 0.9250 Silver 0.8410 oz. ASW, 38.6 mm. **Ruler:** Elizabeth II **Subject:** 50th Anniversary - Queen Elizabeth II's Coronation **Obv:** Crowned bust right **Rev:** Coronation implements **Edge:** Reeded

Date	Mintage	F	VF	XF	Unc	BU
ND(2003) Proof	5,000	Value: 50.00				

KM# 31b 50 PENCE

39.9400 g., 0.9166 Gold 1.1770 oz. AGW, 38.6 mm. **Ruler:** Elizabeth II **Subject:** 50th Anniversary of Coronation **Obv:** Crowned bust right **Rev:** Coronation implements **Edge:** Reeded

Date	Mintage	F	VF	XF	Unc	BU
ND(2003) Proof	50	Value: 1,350				

KM# 28a 50 PENCE

28.2800 g., 0.9250 Silver 0.8410 oz. ASW, 38.6 mm. **Ruler:** Elizabeth II **Obv:** Queen Elizabeth II **Rev:** Napoleon and the ship HMS Northumberland **Edge:** Reeded

Date	Mintage	F	VF	XF	Unc	BU
ND(2002) Proof	5,000	Value: 50.00				

PIEFORTS

KM#	Date	Mintage	Identification	Mkt Val
P3	ND(2002)	500	50 Pence. 0.9250 Silver. 56.5600 g. 38.6 mm. Reeded edge. Proof.	100

SAINT HELENA & ASCENSION

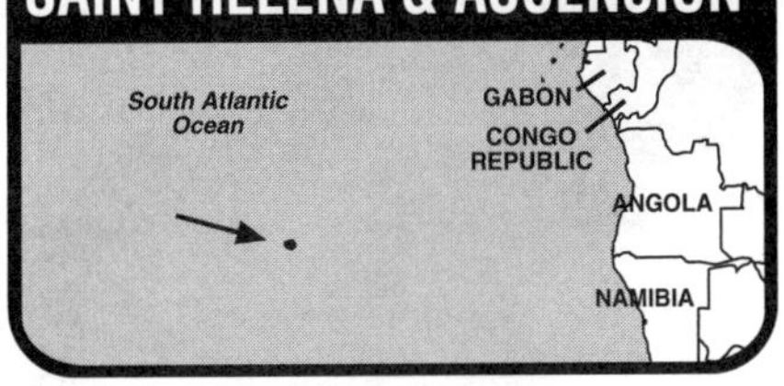

BRITISH OVERSEAS TERRITORY

STANDARD COINAGE

100 Pence = 1 Pound

KM# 13a PENNY

3.5000 g., Copper Plated Steel Galvanized steel, 20.28 mm. **Ruler:** Queen Elizabeth II **Obv:** Crowned head right **Obv. Designer:** Raphael David Maklouf **Rev:** Tuna above value **Edge:** Plain

Date	Mintage	F	VF	XF	Unc	BU
2003	—	—	—	0.15	0.35	0.75

KM# 12a 2 PENCE

Copper Plated Steel **Ruler:** Queen Elizabeth II **Obv:** Crowned head right **Obv. Designer:** Raphael David Maklouf **Rev:** Value below donkey **Shape:** 25.91

Date	Mintage	F	VF	XF	Unc	BU
2003	—	—	—	0.20	0.60	1.25

KM# 22 5 PENCE

Copper-Nickel, 18 mm. **Ruler:** Queen Elizabeth II **Obv:** Crowned head right **Rev:** Giant tortoise

Date	Mintage	F	VF	XF	Unc	BU
2003	—	—	—	1.00	2.50	4.50

KM# 23 10 PENCE

Copper-Nickel, 24.5 mm. **Ruler:** Queen Elizabeth II **Obv:** Crowned head right **Obv. Designer:** Raphael David Maklouf **Rev:** Dolphins

Date	Mintage	F	VF	XF	Unc	BU
2003	—	—	—	1.00	3.00	5.00

KM# 21 20 PENCE

Copper-Nickel, 21.4 mm. **Ruler:** Queen Elizabeth II **Obv:** Crowned head right **Rev:** Flower **Shape:** 7-sided

Date	Mintage	F	VF	XF	Unc	BU
2003	—	—	—	0.75	1.50	2.50

KM# 16 50 PENCE

13.5000 g., Copper-Nickel, 30 mm. **Ruler:** Queen Elizabeth II **Obv:** Crowned head right **Obv. Designer:** Raphael David Maklouf **Rev:** Green sea turtle **Shape:** 7-sided

Date	Mintage	F	VF	XF	Unc	BU
2003	—	—	—	1.50	3.50	5.00

KM# 17 POUND

9.5000 g., Nickel-Brass, 22.5 mm. **Ruler:** Queen Elizabeth II **Obv:** Crowned head right **Obv. Designer:** Raphael David Maklouf **Rev:** Two birds in flight left

Date	Mintage	F	VF	XF	Unc	BU
2003	—	—	—	2.25	5.00	7.50

KM# 26 2 POUNDS

11.8100 g., Nickel-Brass, 28.3 mm. **Obv:** Crowned bust right **Obv. Designer:** Raphael Maklouf **Rev:** National arms above value **Edge:** Reeded and lettered **Edge Lettering:** "500TH ANNIVERSARY"

Date	Mintage	F	VF	XF	Unc	BU
2002	—	—	—	6.00	10.00	12.50

KM# 25 2 POUNDS
12.0000 g., Bi-Metallic Copper-Nickel center in Brass ring, 28.4 mm. **Obv:** Crowned bust right **Obv. Designer:** Raphael Maklouf **Rev:** National Arms **Edge:** Reeded and lettered **Edge Lettering:** "LOYAL AND FAITHFUL"

Date	Mintage	F	VF	XF	Unc	BU
2003	—	—	—	9.00	15.00	17.50

SAMOA

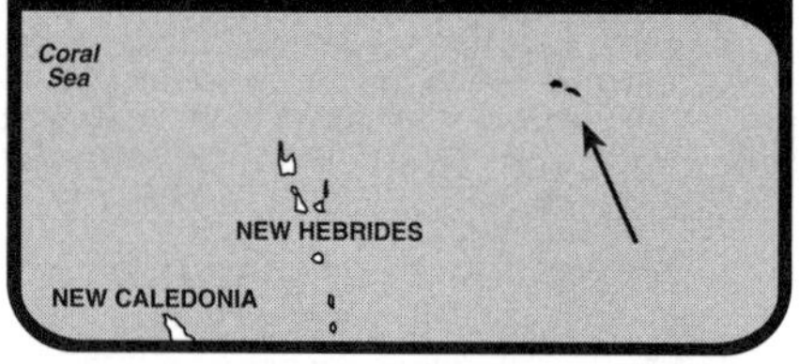

The Independent State of Samoa (formerly Western Samoa), located in the Pacific Ocean 1,600 miles (2,574 km.) northeast of New Zealand, has an area of 1,097 sq. mi. (2,860 sq. km.) and a population of *182,000. Capital: Apia. The economy is based on agriculture, fishing and tourism. Copra, cocoa and bananas are exported.

Samoa is a member of the Commonwealth of Nations. The Chief Executive is Chief of State. The prime minister is the Head of Government. The present Head of State, Malietoa Tanumafili II, holds his position for life. The Legislative Assembly will elect future Heads of State for 5-year terms.

Samoa, which had used New Zealand coinage, converted to a decimal coinage in 1967.

RULER
Malietoa Tanumafili II, 1962-2007
Tuiatua Tupua Tamasese Efi, 2007-

MONETARY SYSTEM
100 Sene = 1 Tala

CONSTITUTIONAL MONARCHY
Commonwealth of Nations
STANDARD COINAGE

KM# 131 5 SENE
2.8400 g., Copper-Nickel, 19.5 mm. **Obv:** Head left **Obv. Designer:** T.H. Paget **Rev:** Pineapple and value **Rev. Designer:** James Berry **Edge:** Reeded **Note:** "Western" dropped from country name

Date	Mintage	F	VF	XF	Unc	BU
2002	—	—	—	—	0.50	0.75

KM# 132 10 SENE
5.6500 g., Copper-Nickel, 23.6 mm. **Obv:** Head left **Rev:** Taro leaves and value **Rev. Designer:** James Berry **Edge:** Reeded **Note:** "Western" dropped from country name

Date	Mintage	F	VF	XF	Unc	BU
2002	—	—	—	—	0.75	1.00

KM# 133 20 SENE
11.4000 g., Copper-Nickel, 28.45 mm. **Obv:** Head left **Obv. Designer:** T.H. Paget **Rev:** Breadfruits and value **Rev. Designer:** James Berry **Edge:** Reeded **Note:** "Western" dropped from country name

Date	Mintage	F	VF	XF	Unc	BU
2002	—	—	—	—	1.00	1.25

KM# 134 50 SENE
14.1300 g., Copper-Nickel, 32.3 mm. **Obv:** Head left **Rev:** Banana tree and value **Edge:** Reeded **Note:** "Western" dropped from country name

Date	Mintage	F	VF	XF	Unc	BU
2002	—	—	—	—	1.75	2.00

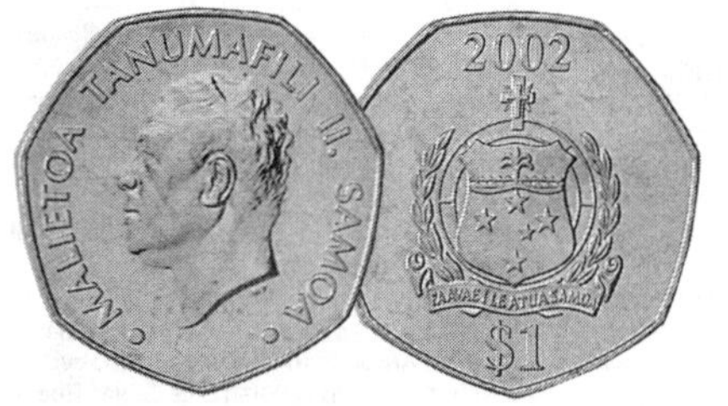

KM# 135 TALA
9.5000 g., Brass, 30 mm. **Obv:** Head left **Obv. Designer:** T.H. Paget **Rev:** National arms above value and banner flanked by sprigs **Rev. Designer:** Nelson Eustis **Edge:** Reeded **Note:** "Western" dropped from country name

Date	Mintage	F	VF	XF	Unc	BU
2002	—	—	—	—	2.50	3.00

KM# 137 10 TALA
31.1000 g., 0.9990 Silver 0.9988 oz. ASW, 40 mm. **Series:** Save the Whales **Obv:** National arms above value and banner flanked by sprigs **Obv. Legend:** SAMOA I SISIFO **Rev:** Bowhead Whale on mother-of-pearl insert **Edge:** Plain

Date	Mintage	F	VF	XF	Unc	BU
2002 Proof	2,000	Value: 60.00				

KM# 139 10 TALA
31.4700 g., 0.9250 Silver 0.9359 oz. ASW **Subject:** XXVIII Summer Olympics - Athens **Obv:** National arms **Obv. Legend:** SAMOA I SISIFO **Rev:** Swimming - two divers

Date	Mintage	F	VF	XF	Unc	BU
2003 Proof	—	Value: 60.00				

KM# 140 10 TALA
1.2400 g., 0.9990 Gold 0.0398 oz. AGW **Series:** World Statesmen **Subject:** Mahatma Gandhi **Obv:** National arms **Obv. Legend:** SAMOA I SISIFO

Date	Mintage	F	VF	XF	Unc	BU
2003 Proof	—	Value: 75.00				

KM# 141 10 TALA
1.2400 g., 0.9990 Gold 0.0398 oz. AGW **Series:** World Statesmen **Subject:** Konrad Adenauer **Obv:** National arms **Obv. Legend:** SAMOA I SISIFO

Date	Mintage	F	VF	XF	Unc	BU
2003 Proof	—	Value: 75.00				

KM# 143 10 TALA
28.5800 g., Silver, 38.61 mm. **Obv:** National arms **Obv. Legend:** SAMOA I SISIFO **Rev:** Sailing ship "La Récherche" **Rev. Legend:** JEAN FRANCOIS GALAUP - COMTE DE LA PEROUSE **Edge:** Reeded

Date	Mintage	F	VF	XF	Unc	BU
2004 Proof	—	Value: 50.00				

KM# 142 10 TALA
1.2400 g., 0.9990 Gold 0.0398 oz. AGW **Subject:** Death of Pope John-Paul II **Obv:** National arms

Date	Mintage	F	VF	XF	Unc	BU
2005	15,000	—	—	—	65.00	—
2005 Proof	3,300	Value: 75.00				

SAN MARINO

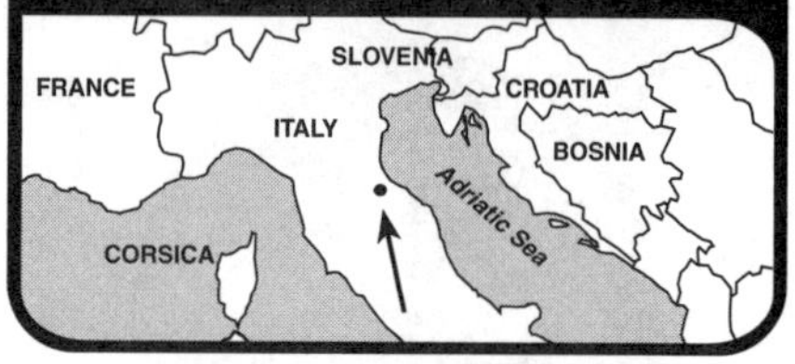

The Republic of San Marino, the oldest and smallest republic in the world is located in north central Italy entirely surrounded by the Province of Emilia-Romagna. It has an area of 24 sq. mi. (60 sq. km.) and a population of *23,000. Capital: San Marino. The principal economic activities are farming, livestock raising, cheese making, tourism and light manufacturing. Building stone, lime, wheat, hides and baked goods are exported. The government derives most of its revenue from the sale of postage stamps for philatelic purposes.

San Marino has its own coinage, but Italian and Vatican City coins and currency are also in circulation.

MINT MARKS
R - Rome

MONETARY SYSTEM
100 Centesimi = 1 Lira

REPUBLIC
STANDARD COINAGE

KM# 424 10 LIRE
1.6000 g., Aluminum, 23.3 mm. **Obv:** Three towers within circle **Rev:** Wheat stalks and value **Edge:** Plain

Date	Mintage	F	VF	XF	Unc	BU
2001R	—	—	—	—	0.35	—

KM# 425 20 LIRE
3.6000 g., Aluminum-Bronze, 21.8 mm. **Obv:** Three towers within circle **Rev:** Two dolphins and value **Edge:** Plain

Date	Mintage	F	VF	XF	Unc	BU
2001R	—	—	—	—	0.75	2.00

KM# 426 50 LIRE
4.5000 g., Stainless Steel, 19.2 mm. **Obv:** Three towers within circle **Rev:** Tree and value **Edge:** Plain

Date	Mintage	F	VF	XF	Unc	BU
2001R	—	—	—	—	0.85	—

KM# 427 100 LIRE
4.5000 g., Copper-Nickel, 22 mm. **Obv:** Three towers within circle **Rev:** Grasping hands and value **Edge:** Plain and reeded sections

Date	Mintage	F	VF	XF	Unc	BU
2001R	—	—	—	—	1.25	—

KM# 428 200 LIRE
5.0000 g., Aluminum-Bronze, 24 mm. **Obv:** Three towers within circle **Rev:** Broken chain, leaves, vines and value **Edge:** Reeded

Date	Mintage	F	VF	XF	Unc	BU
2001R	—	—	—	—	1.50	—

KM# 429 500 LIRE
Bi-Metallic Aluminum-Bronze center in Stainless Steel ring, 25.8 mm. **Obv:** Three towers within circle **Rev:** Three different plant stalks and value **Edge:** Reeded and plain sections **Note:** 6.8 grams.

Date	Mintage	F	VF	XF	Unc	BU
2001R	—	—	—	—	3.00	—

KM# 430 1000 LIRE
8.8000 g., Bi-Metallic Stainless-Steel center in Aluminum-Bronze ring, 27 mm. **Obv:** Three towers within circle **Rev:** Value within circle of birds **Edge:** Reeded and plain sections

Date	Mintage	F	VF	XF	Unc	BU
2001R	—	—	—	—	7.50	—

KM# 431 5000 LIRE
18.0000 g., 0.8350 Silver 0.4832 oz. ASW, 32 mm. **Obv:** Three towers within circle **Rev:** Dove on laurel branch above value **Edge:** Reeded and plain sections

Date	Mintage	F	VF	XF	Unc	BU
2001R	—	—	—	—	17.50	20.00

KM# 436 5000 LIRE
18.0000 g., 0.8350 Silver 0.4832 oz. ASW, 32 mm. **Subject:** Last Lire Coinage **Obv:** Crowned arms within sprigs **Rev:** Feather above six old coin designs with value below, all within beaded border **Edge:** Lettered

Date	Mintage	F	VF	XF	Unc	BU
2001R Proof	20,000	Value: 20.00				

KM# 432 10000 LIRE
22.0000 g., 0.8350 Silver 0.5906 oz. ASW, 34 mm. **Subject:** Ferrari **Obv:** Crowned arms within sprigs **Rev:** Race car with "FERRARI" background **Edge:** Reeded and plain sections

Date	Mintage	F	VF	XF	Unc	BU
2001R Proof	20,000	Value: 25.00				

KM# 437 10000 LIRE
22.0000 g., 0.8350 Silver 0.5906 oz. ASW, 34 mm. **Subject:** Last Lire Coinage **Obv:** Crowned arms within sprigs **Rev:** Feather above six old coin designs with value below, all within star border **Edge:** Reeded and plain sections

Date	Mintage	F	VF	XF	Unc	BU
2001R Proof	20,000	Value: 30.00				

KM# 438 10000 LIRE
22.0000 g., 0.8350 Silver 0.5906 oz. ASW, 34 mm. **Subject:** 2nd International Chambers of Commerce Convention **Obv:** Crowned arms within sprigs **Rev:** Mercury running by a computer **Edge:** Reeded and plain sections.

Date	Mintage	F	VF	XF	Unc	BU
2001R Proof	20,000	Value: 20.00				

KM# 433 1/2 SCUDO
1.6100 g., 0.9000 Gold 0.0466 oz. AGW, 13.8 mm. **Subject:** Cavaliere **Obv:** Crowned arms within sprigs **Rev:** Horse and rider **Edge:** Reeded

Date	Mintage	F	VF	XF	Unc	BU
2001R Proof	4,500	Value: 50.00				

KM# 434 SCUDO
3.2200 g., 0.9000 Gold 0.0932 oz. AGW, 16 mm. **Subject:** Tiziano **Obv:** Crowned arms within sprigs **Rev:** Bearded bust left **Edge:** Reeded

Date	Mintage	F	VF	XF	Unc	BU
2001R Proof	4,500	Value: 100				

KM# 435 2 SCUDI
6.4400 g., 0.9000 Gold 0.1863 oz. AGW, 21 mm. **Subject:** Flora **Obv:** Crowned arms within sprigs **Rev:** Bust 1/4 left and value **Edge:** Reeded

Date	Mintage	F	VF	XF	Unc	BU
2001R Proof	4,500	Value: 180				

KM# 457 2 SCUDI
6.4516 g., 0.9000 Gold 0.1867 oz. AGW, 21 mm. **Obv:** Crowned arms within sprigs **Rev:** Madonna and Child **Edge:** Reeded

Date	Mintage	F	VF	XF	Unc	BU
2002R Proof	3,000	Value: 180				

KM# 459 2 SCUDI
6.4516 g., 0.9000 Gold 0.1867 oz. AGW, 21 mm. **Obv:** Crowned arms within sprigs **Rev:** Nostradamus above value **Edge:** Reeded

Date	Mintage	F	VF	XF	Unc	BU
2003R Proof	7,500	Value: 180				

KM# 464 2 SCUDI
6.4516 g., 0.9000 Gold 0.1867 oz. AGW, 21 mm. **Subject:** The Domagnano Treasure **Obv:** Crowned arms within sprigs **Rev:** Gothic Eagle Brooch, 5 Mark coin of 1952 **Edge:** Reeded

Date	Mintage	F	VF	XF	Unc	BU
2004R Proof	6,500	Value: 180				

KM# 439 5 SCUDI
16.9655 g., 0.9166 Gold 0.4999 oz. AGW, 28 mm. **Subject:** San Marino's World Bank Membership **Obv:** Crowned arms within sprigs **Rev:** Orchid and bee within globe **Edge:** Reeded

Date	Mintage	F	VF	XF	Unc	BU
2001R Proof	4,000	Value: 475				

EURO COINAGE

KM# 440 EURO CENT
2.2700 g., Copper Plated Steel, 16.2 mm. **Obv:** "Il Montale" **Obv. Designer:** M. Frantisek Chochola **Rev:** Value and globe **Rev. Designer:** Luc Luycx **Edge:** Plain

Date	Mintage	F	VF	XF	Unc	BU
2002R	120,000	—	—	—	—	40.00
2003R	70,000	—	—	—	—	42.00
2004R	1,500,000	—	—	—	—	20.00
2005R	70,000	—	—	—	—	20.00
2006R	2,730,000	—	—	—	—	18.00
2007R	—	—	—	—	—	18.00
2008R	—	—	—	—	—	18.00

KM# 441 2 EURO CENT
3.0300 g., Copper Plated Steel, 18.7 mm. **Obv:** Stefano Gallietti, Liberty fighter **Obv. Designer:** M. Frantisek Chochola **Rev:** Value and globe **Rev. Designer:** Luc Luycx **Edge:** Grooved

Date	Mintage	F	VF	XF	Unc	BU
2002R	120,000	—	—	—	—	40.00
2003R	70,000	—	—	—	—	42.00
2004R	1,395,000	—	—	—	—	20.00
2005R	150,000	—	—	—	—	20.00
2006R	2,730,000	—	—	—	—	18.00
2007R	—	—	—	—	—	18.00
2008R	—	—	—	—	—	18.00

KM# 442 5 EURO CENT
3.8600 g., Copper Plated Steel, 21.2 mm. **Obv:** "Guaita" tower **Obv. Designer:** M. Frantisek Chochola **Rev:** Value and globe **Rev. Designer:** Luc Luycx **Edge:** Plain

Date	Mintage	F	VF	XF	Unc	BU
2002R	120,000	—	—	—	—	40.00
2003R	70,000	—	—	—	—	42.00
2004R	1,000,000	—	—	—	—	20.00
2005R	70,000	—	—	—	—	20.00
2006R	2,880,000	—	—	—	—	18.00
2007R	—	—	—	—	—	18.00
2008R	—	—	—	—	—	18.00

KM# 443 10 EURO CENT
4.0700 g., Brass, 19.7 mm. **Obv:** Building Basilica del Santo Marinus **Obv. Designer:** M. Frantisek Chochola **Rev:** Map and value **Rev. Designer:** Luc Luycx **Edge:** Reeded

Date	Mintage	F	VF	XF	Unc	BU
2002R	120,000	—	—	—	—	40.00
2003R	70,000	—	—	—	—	42.00
2004R	180,000	—	—	—	—	22.00
2005R	70,000	—	—	—	—	22.00
2006R	65,000	—	—	—	—	20.00
2007R	—	—	—	—	—	18.00

KM# 444 20 EURO CENT
5.7300 g., Brass, 22.1 mm. **Obv:** St. Marinus from a portrait by van Guercino **Obv. Designer:** M. Frantisek Chochola **Rev:** Map and value **Rev. Designer:** Luc Luycx **Edge:** Notched

Date	Mintage	F	VF	XF	Unc	BU
2002R	302,400	—	—	—	18.00	20.00
2003R	430,000	—	—	—	15.00	18.00
2004R	70,000	—	—	—	15.00	18.00
2005R	310,000	—	—	—	15.00	18.00
2006R	65,000	—	—	—	15.00	18.00
2007R	—	—	—	—	14.00	16.00

KM# 445 50 EURO CENT
7.8100 g., Brass, 24.2 mm. **Obv:** Fortress of San Marino **Obv. Designer:** M. Frantisek Chochola **Rev:** Map and value **Rev. Designer:** Luc Luycx **Edge:** Reeded

Date	Mintage	F	VF	XF	Unc	BU
2002R	230,400	—	—	—	20.00	22.50
2003R	415,000	—	—	—	17.50	20.00

Date	Mintage	F	VF	XF	Unc	BU
2004R	70,000	—	—	—	17.50	20.00
2005R	179,000	—	—	—	17.50	20.00
2006R	343,880	—	—	—	15.00	18.00
2007R	—	—	—	—	14.00	16.00

KM# 446 EURO
7.5000 g., Bi-Metallic Copper-Nickel center in Brass ring, 23.2 mm. **Obv:** Crowned arms within sprigs and circle within star border **Obv. Designer:** M. Frantisek Chochola **Rev:** Value and map **Rev. Designer:** Luc Luycx **Edge:** Reeded and plain sections

Date	Mintage	F	VF	XF	Unc	BU
2002R	360,800	—	—	—	22.00	25.00
2003R	70,000	—	—	—	—	45.00
2004R	180,000	—	—	—	—	25.00
2005R	70,000	—	—	—	—	25.00
2006R	150,000	—	—	—	—	20.00
2007R	—	—	—	—	—	18.00

KM# 447 2 EURO
8.5200 g., Bi-Metallic Brass center in Copper-Nickel ring, 25.7 mm. **Obv:** Government building **Obv. Designer:** M. Frantisek Chochola **Rev:** Value and map **Rev. Designer:** Luc Luycx **Edge:** Reeded with 2's and stars

Date	Mintage	F	VF	XF	Unc	BU
2002R	255,760	—	—	—	25.00	28.00
2003R	70,000	—	—	—	—	45.00
2004R	70,000	—	—	—	—	28.00
2005R	150,000	—	—	—	—	28.00
2006R	120,000	—	—	—	—	22.00
2007R	—	—	—	—	—	20.00

KM# 467 2 EURO
8.5000 g., Bi-Metallic Brass center in Copper-Nickel ring, 25.75 mm. **Obv:** Crowned arms within sprigs **Rev:** Bartolomeo Borghesi **Edge:** Alternating stars and 2's

Date	Mintage	F	VF	XF	Unc	BU
2004R	110,000	—	—	—	17.50	30.00

KM# 469 2 EURO
8.5000 g., Bi-Metallic, 25.75 mm. **Obv:** Galileo Galilei at telescope

Date	Mintage	F	VF	XF	Unc	BU
2005R	130,000	—	—	—	35.00	45.00

KM# 448 5 EURO
18.0000 g., 0.9250 Silver 0.5353 oz. ASW, 32 mm. **Subject:** Welcome Euro **Obv:** Three plumed towers **Rev:** Circle of roses

Date	Mintage	F	VF	XF	Unc	BU
2002R Proof	37,000	Value: 75.00				

KM# 450 5 EURO
18.0000 g., 0.9250 Silver 0.5353 oz. ASW, 32 mm. **Subject:** 1600th Anniversary of Ravenna **Obv:** National arms **Rev:** Bas-relief wall design **Edge:** Reeded

Date	Mintage	F	VF	XF	Unc	BU
2002R Proof	—	Value: 60.00				

KM# 453 5 EURO
18.0000 g., 0.9250 Silver 0.5353 oz. ASW, 32 mm. **Subject:** 2004 Olympics **Obv:** Stylized three towers **Rev:** Ancient Olympians **Edge:** Reeded

Date	Mintage	F	VF	XF	Unc	BU
2003R Proof	37,766	Value: 50.00				

KM# 452 5 EURO
18.0000 g., 0.9250 Silver 0.5353 oz. ASW, 32 mm. **Obv:** National arms **Rev:** Allegorical depiction of Independence, Tolerance and Liberty

Date	Mintage	F	VF	XF	Unc	BU
2003R	—	—	—	—	35.00	40.00

KM# 468 5 EURO
18.0000 g., 0.9250 Silver 0.5353 oz. ASW, 32 mm. **Obv:** Three towers **Rev:** Antonio Onofri and value

Date	Mintage	F	VF	XF	Unc	BU
2004R	—	—	—	—	45.00	50.00
2005R	—	—	—	—	45.00	50.00

KM# 458 5 EURO
18.0000 g., 0.9250 Silver 0.5353 oz. ASW, 32 mm. **Obv:** National arms **Rev:** Value behind Bartolomeo Borghesi

Date	Mintage	F	VF	XF	Unc	BU
2004R	—	—	—	—	—	35.00
2004R Proof	—	Value: 45.00				

KM# 462 5 EURO
18.0000 g., 0.9250 Silver 0.5353 oz. ASW, 32 mm. **Obv:** Three stylized plumed towers **Rev:** Two soccer players

Date	Mintage	F	VF	XF	Unc	BU
2004R Proof	35,000	Value: 45.00				

KM# 472 5 EURO
18.0000 g., 0.9250 Silver 0.5353 oz. ASW, 32 mm. **Obv:** Portrait of Melchiorie Delfico

Date	Mintage	F	VF	XF	Unc	BU
2006R	65,000	—	—	—	—	35.00

KM# 474 5 EURO
18.0000 g., 0.9250 Silver 0.5353 oz. ASW, 32.00 mm. **Subject:** 50th Anniversary Death of Toscanini **Obv:** Stylized national arms **Obv. Legend:** REPUBBLICA DI SAN MARINO **Rev:** Head of Toscanini left **Edge:** Reeded

Date	Mintage	F	VF	XF	Unc	BU
ND(2007)R Proof	18,000	Value: 32.50				

KM# 473 5 EURO
18.0000 g., 0.9250 Silver 0.5353 oz. ASW, 32.0 mm. **Subject:** Equal Opportunity between the sexes **Obv:** Three plumed towers **Obv. Legend:** REPUBLICA DI SAN MARINO **Rev:** Nude female at left, nude male at right, ribbon across symbols within circle above, value below **Rev. Inscription:** PARI OPPORTITA **Edge:** Reeded

Date	Mintage	F	VF	XF	Unc	BU
2008R	—	—	—	—	—	30.00

KM# 449 10 EURO
22.0000 g., 0.9250 Silver 0.6542 oz. ASW, 34 mm. **Subject:** Welcome Euro **Obv:** Three plumed towers **Rev:** Infant sleeping in flower

Date	Mintage	F	VF	XF	Unc	BU
2002R Proof	37,000	Value: 100				

KM# 451 10 EURO
22.0000 g., 0.9250 Silver 0.6542 oz. ASW, 34 mm. **Subject:** 1600th Anniversary of Ravenna **Obv:** National arms **Rev:** Wall painting

Date	Mintage	F	VF	XF	Unc	BU
2002R Proof	—	Value: 95.00				

KM# 454 10 EURO
22.0000 g., 0.9250 Silver 0.6542 oz. ASW, 34 mm. **Subject:** 2004 Olympics **Obv:** Three stylized towers **Rev:** Modern Olympians **Edge:** Segmented reeding

Date	Mintage	F	VF	XF	Unc	BU
2003R Proof	37,766	Value: 75.00				

KM# 463 10 EURO
22.0000 g., 0.9250 Silver 0.6542 oz. ASW, 34 mm. **Obv:** Three stylized plumed towers **Rev:** Two soccer players

Date	Mintage	F	VF	XF	Unc	BU
2004R Proof	30,000	Value: 60.00				

KM# 475 10 EURO
22.0000 g., 0.9250 Silver 0.6542 oz. ASW, 34.00 mm. **Subject:** 100th Anniversary Death of Giosuè Carducci **Obv:** Stylized national arms **Obv. Legend:** REPPUBLICA DISAN MARINO **Rev:** 1/2 length figure of Carducci facing with quill pen in hand at table **Rev. Legend:** CARDUCCI **Edge:** Plain and reeded segments

Date	Mintage	F	VF	XF	Unc	BU
ND(2007)R Proof	16,000	Value: 37.50				

KM# 460 20 EURO
6.4510 g., 0.9000 Gold 0.1867 oz. AGW, 21 mm. **Subject:** 1600th Anniversary of Ravenna **Obv:** National arms **Rev:** Bas-relief wall design **Edge:** Reeded

Date	Mintage	F	VF	XF	Unc	BU
2002R Proof	4,550	Value: 375				

KM# 455 20 EURO
6.4516 g., 0.9000 Gold 0.1867 oz. AGW, 21 mm. **Obv:** Three plumes **Rev:** Giotto's "Presentation of Jesus at the Temple" **Edge:** Reeded

Date	Mintage	F	VF	XF	Unc	BU
2003R Proof	7,300	Value: 245				

KM# 465 20 EURO
6.4510 g., 0.9000 Gold 0.1867 oz. AGW, 21 mm. **Obv:** Three plumes **Rev:** Marco Polo meeting Kublai Khan **Edge:** Reeded

Date	Mintage	F	VF	XF	Unc	BU
2004R Proof	7,300	Value: 255				

KM# 470 20 EURO
6.4510 g., 0.9000 Gold 0.1867 oz. AGW, 21 mm. **Subject:** International Day of Peace **Obv:** Stylized faces and leaves

Date	Mintage	F	VF	XF	Unc	BU
2005R Proof	5,300	Value: 300				

KM# 461 50 EURO
16.1290 g., 0.9000 Gold 0.4667 oz. AGW, 28 mm. **Subject:** 1600th Anniversary of Ravenna **Obv:** National arms **Rev:** Wall painting **Edge:** Reeded

Date	Mintage	F	VF	XF	Unc	BU
2002R Proof	4,550	Value: 775				

KM# 456 50 EURO
16.1290 g., 0.9000 Gold 0.4667 oz. AGW, 28 mm. **Obv:** Three plumes **Rev:** Giotto's "The Pentecost" **Edge:** Reeded

Date	Mintage	F	VF	XF	Unc	BU
2003R Proof	7,300	Value: 500				

KM# 466 50 EURO
16.1290 g., 0.9000 Gold 0.4667 oz. AGW, 28 mm. **Obv:** Three plumes **Rev:** Marco Polo **Edge:** Reeded

Date	Mintage	F	VF	XF	Unc	BU
2004R Proof	7,300	Value: 525				

KM# 471 50 EURO
16.1290 g., 0.9000 Gold 0.4667 oz. AGW, 28 mm. **Subject:** International Day of Peace **Obv:** Group of people gathering

Date	Mintage	F	VF	XF	Unc	BU
2005R Proof	5,300	Value: 500				

MINT SETS

KM#	Date	Mintage	Identification	Issue Price	Mkt Val
MS61	2001 (8)	2,000	KM424-431	18.00	40.00
MS62	2002 (8)	120,000	KM440 - 447	—	300
MS63	2003 (9)	—	KM#440-447, 452	55.00	350
MS64	2004 (9)	—	KM#440-447, 458	55.00	220
MS65	2005 (9)	—	KM#440-447, 468	55.00	225
MS66	2006 (9)	65,000	KM#440-447, 472	—	185
MS67	2007 (3)	—	KM#443-444,447	27.50	50.00
MS68	2007 (9)	—	KM#440-447, 473	120	165

PROOF SETS

KM#	Date	Mintage	Identification	Issue Price	Mkt Val
PS14	2001 (3)	4,500	KM433-435	179	180
PSA15	2001 (2)	—	KM#436-437	—	—
PS15	2002 (2)	37,000	KM448-449	—	175
PS16	2002 (2)	4,550	KM#460-461	—	1,150
PS17	2003 (2)	7,300	KM#455-456	—	750
PS18	2004 (2)	7,300	KM#465-466	—	780
PS19	2005 (2)	5,300	KM#470-471	—	800

SAUDI ARABIA

UNITED KINGDOMS

The Kingdom of Saudi Arabia, an independent and absolute hereditary monarchy comprising the former sultanate of Nejd, the old kingdom of Hejaz, Asir and Al Hasa, occupies four-fifths of the Arabian peninsula. The kingdom has an area of 830,000 sq. mi. (2,149,690 sq. km.) and a population of *16.1 million. Capital: Riyadh. The economy is based on oil, which provides 85 percent of Saudi Arabia's revenue.

TITLES

العربية السعودية

Al-Arabiya(t) as-Sa'udiya(t)

المملكة العربية السعودية

Al-Mamlaka(t) al-'Arabiya(t) as-Sa'udiya(t)

RULERS

al Sa'ud Dynasty

Fahad bin Abd Al-Aziz, AH1403-1426/1982-2005AD
Abdullah bin Abdul Aziz, AH1426-/2005AD

KINGDOM

REFORM COINAGE

5 Halala = 1 Ghirsh; 100 Halala = 1 Riyal

KM# 62 10 HALALA (2 Ghirsh)

4.0000 g., Copper-Nickel, 21 mm. **Ruler:** Fahad Bin Abd Al-Aziz AH1403-1426/1982-2005AD **Obv:** National emblem at center, legend above and below **Rev:** Legend above inscription in circle dividing value, date below

Date	Mintage	F	VF	XF	Unc	BU
AH1423 (2002)	—	—	0.30	0.60	1.25	—

KM# 63 25 HALALA (1/4 Riyal)

5.0000 g., Copper-Nickel, 23 mm. **Ruler:** Fahad Bin Abd Al-Aziz AH1403-1426/1982-2005AD **Obv:** National emblem at center, legend above and below **Rev:** Legend above inscription in circle dividing value, date below

Date	Mintage	F	VF	XF	Unc	BU
AH1423 (2002)	—	—	0.40	0.70	1.50	—

KM# 64 50 HALALA (1/2 Riyal)

6.5000 g., Copper-Nickel, 26 mm. **Ruler:** Fahad Bin Abd Al-Aziz AH1403-1426/1982-2005AD **Obv:** National emblem at center, legend above and below **Rev:** Legend above inscription in circle dividing value, date below

Date	Mintage	F	VF	XF	Unc	BU
AH1423 (2002)	—	0.20	0.50	2.25	3.50	—

KM# 68 50 HALALA (1/2 Riyal)

6.5000 g., Copper-Nickel **Ruler:** Abdullah bin Abdul Aziz AH1426-/2005-AD **Obv:** National emblem at center **Rev:** Legend above inscription in circle, dividing value, date below

Date	Mintage	F	VF	XF	Unc	BU
AH1428 (2007)	—	0.20	0.50	2.25	3.50	—

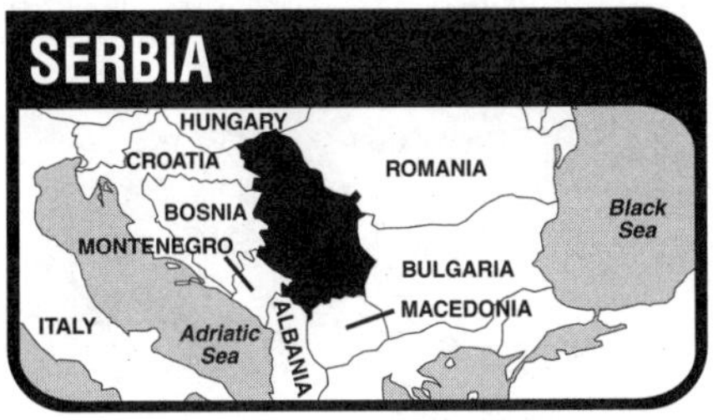

Serbia, a former inland Balkan kingdom has an area of 34,116 sq. mi. (88,361 sq. km.). Capital: Belgrade.

MINT MARKS

A - Paris
(a) - Paris, privy mark only
(g) - Gorham Mfg. Co., Providence, R.I.
H - Birmingham
V - Vienna
БП - (BP) Budapest

MONETARY SYSTEM

100 Para = 1 Dinara

DENOMINATIONS

ПАРА = Para
ПАРЕ = Pare
ДИНАР = Dinar
ДИНАРА = Dinara

REPUBLIC

STANDARD COINAGE

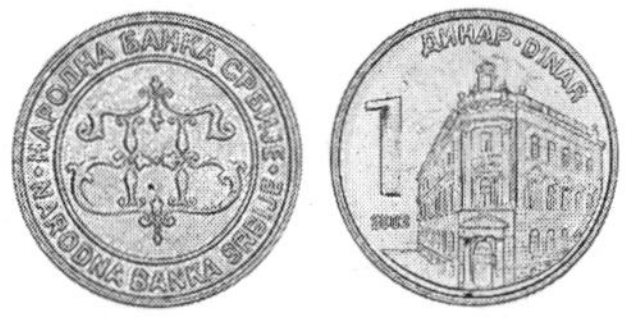

KM# 34 DINAR

4.3300 g., Copper-Zinc-Nickel, 20 mm. **Obv:** National Bank emblem within circle **Rev:** Bank building and value **Edge:** Reeded

Date	Mintage	F	VF	XF	Unc	BU
2003	10,320,000	—	—	0.25	1.00	1.50
2004	—	—	—	0.25	1.00	1.50
2005	—	—	—	0.25	1.00	1.50

KM# 39 DINAR

4.2600 g., Copper-Zinc-Nickel, 20 mm. **Obv:** Crowned and mantled arms **Rev:** National Bank and value **Edge:** Segmented reeding

Date	Mintage	F	VF	XF	Unc	BU
2005	—	—	—	0.25	1.00	1.50
2006	—	—	—	0.25	1.00	1.50
2007	—	—	—	0.25	1.00	1.50

KM# 35 2 DINARA

5.2400 g., Copper-Zinc-Nickel, 22 mm. **Obv:** National Bank emblem within circle **Rev:** Gracanica Monastery and value **Edge:** Reeded

Date	Mintage	F	VF	XF	Unc	BU
2003	4,688,500	—	—	0.50	2.00	2.50

KM# 46 2 DINARA

5.0000 g., Brass, 22 mm. **Obv:** Crowned and mantled arms **Rev:** Gracanica Monastery and value **Edge:** Segmented reeding

Date	Mintage	F	VF	XF	Unc	BU
2006	—	—	—	0.50	2.00	2.50
2007	—	—	—	0.50	2.00	2.50

KM# 36 5 DINARA

5.2400 g., Copper-Zinc-Nickel, 22 mm. **Obv:** National Bank emblem within circle **Rev:** Krusedol Monastery and value **Edge:** Reeded

Date	Mintage	F	VF	XF	Unc	BU
2003	15,170,000	—	0.50	1.00	2.25	3.25

KM# 40 5 DINARA

5.2500 g., Copper-Zinc-Nickel, 22 mm. **Obv:** Crowned and mantled arms **Rev:** Krusedol Monastery and value **Edge:** Segmented reeding

Date	Mintage	F	VF	XF	Unc	BU
2005	—	—	—	0.75	2.00	3.00
2006	—	—	—	0.75	2.00	3.00
2007	—	—	—	0.75	2.00	3.00

KM# 37 10 DINARA

7.7700 g., Copper-Zinc-Nickel, 26 mm. **Obv:** National Bank emblem within circle **Rev:** Studenica Monastery and value **Edge:** Reeded

Date	Mintage	F	VF	XF	Unc	BU
2003	10,160,500	—	0.50	1.00	2.50	3.50

KM# 41 10 DINARA

7.7700 g., Copper-Zinc-Nickel, 26 mm. **Obv:** Crowned and mantled arms **Rev:** Studenica Monastery and value **Edge:** Segmented reeding

Date	Mintage	F	VF	XF	Unc	BU
2005	—	—	—	0.75	2.25	3.50
2006	—	—	—	0.75	2.25	3.50
2007	—	—	—	—	2.00	3.25

KM# 38 20 DINARA

9.0000 g., Copper-Zinc-Nickel, 28 mm. **Obv:** National Bank emblem within circle **Rev:** Temple of St. Sava and value **Edge:** Reeded

Date	Mintage	F	VF	XF	Unc	BU
2003	25,491,500	—	—	0.75	2.00	3.00

KM# 42 20 DINARA

9.0000 g., Copper-Nickel-Zinc, 28 mm. **Obv:** Crowned and mantled Serbian royal arms **Rev:** Nikola Tesla **Edge:** Segmented reeding

Date	Mintage	F	VF	XF	Unc	BU
2006	1,000,000	—	—	0.75	2.25	3.50
2007	—	—	—	0.75	2.25	3.50

KM# 47 20 DINARA

9.1200 g., Copper-Nickel-Zinc, 27.93 mm. **Subject:** Dositej Obradovic, 1742-1811 **Obv:** National arms **Obv. Legend:** РЕПУБЛИКА СРБИЈА - REPUBLIKA SRBIJA **Rev:** Bast facing slightly left **Edge:** Segmented reeding

Date	Mintage	F	VF	XF	Unc	BU
2007	—	—	—	0.75	2.00	3.00

KM# 43 1000 DINARA
13.0000 g., 0.9250 Silver 0.3866 oz. ASW, 30 mm. **Obv:** Crowned and mantled Serbian royal arms **Rev:** Nikola Tesla **Edge:** Segmented reeding

Date	Mintage	F	VF	XF	Unc	BU
2006 Proof	2,000	Value: 20.00				

KM# 44 5000 DINARA
3.4550 g., 0.9000 Gold 0.1000 oz. AGW, 20 mm. **Obv:** Crowned and mantled Serbian royal arms **Rev:** Nikola Tesla

Date	Mintage	F	VF	XF	Unc	BU
2006 Proof	2,000	Value: 125				

KM# 45 10000 DINARA
8.6400 g., 0.9000 Gold 0.2500 oz. AGW, 25 mm. **Obv:** Crowned and mantled Serbian royal arms **Rev:** Nikola Tesla

Date	Mintage	F	VF	XF	Unc	BU
2006 Proof	1,000	Value: 285				

MINT SETS

KM#	Date	Mintage	Identification	Issue Price	Mkt Val
MS1	2003 (5)	—	KM34-38	—	10.00
MS2	2005 (3)	—	KM39-41	—	10.00
MS3	2006 (5)	—	KM#39-42, 46	—	12.00

PROOF SETS

KM#	Date	Mintage	Identification	Issue Price	Mkt Val
PS1	2006 (3)	—	KM#43-45	—	500

SEYCHELLES

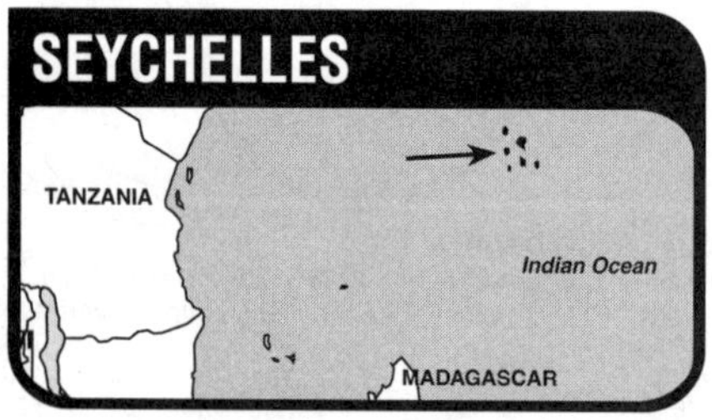

The Republic of Seychelles, an archipelago of 85 granite and coral islands situated in the Indian Ocean 600 miles (965 km.) northeast of Madagascar, has an area of 156 sq. mi. (455 sq. km.) and a population of *70,000. Among these islands are the Aldabra Islands, the Farquhar Group, and Ile Desroches, which the United Kingdom ceded to the Seychelles upon its independence. Capital: Victoria, on Mahe. The economy is based on fishing, a plantation system of agriculture, and tourism. Copra, cinnamon and vanilla are exported.

Seychelles is a member of the Commonwealth of Nations. The president is the Head of State and of the Government.

RULER
British, until 1976

MINT MARKS
(sa) - M in oval – South African Mint Co. (starting in 2000, not PM)
None - British Royal Mint

MONETARY SYSTEM
100 Cents = 1 Rupee

REPUBLIC

STANDARD COINAGE

KM# 46.2 CENT
1.3500 g., Brass, 16.03 mm. **Obv:** Altered coat of arms **Rev:** Mud Crab **Edge:** Plain

Date	Mintage	F	VF	XF	Unc	BU
2004PM	—	—	—	0.15	0.50	1.50

KM# 47.2 5 CENTS
1.9500 g., Brass, 18 mm. **Obv:** Altered coat of arms **Rev:** Tapioca plant

Date	Mintage	F	VF	XF	Unc	BU
2003PM	—	—	—	0.10	0.30	0.50

KM# 48.2 10 CENTS
3.2500 g., Brass, 21 mm. **Obv:** Altered coat of arms **Rev:** Yellowfin tuna **Edge:** Plain

Date	Mintage	F	VF	XF	Unc	BU
2003PM	—	—	0.10	0.25	1.00	1.50

KM# 49.3 25 CENTS
2.8000 g., Nickel Clad Steel, 19 mm. **Obv:** Arms with supporters **Rev:** Black Parrot and value

Date	Mintage	F	VF	XF	Unc	BU
2003PM	—	—	0.25	0.75	2.25	4.00

KM# 118 5 RUPEES
28.2800 g., Copper-Nickel, 38.6 mm. **Subject:** John Paul II memorial **Obv:** National Arms **Rev:** John Paul II in mitre waving

Date	Mintage	F	VF	XF	Unc	BU
2005	—	—	—	—	—	10.00

KM# 119 5 RUPEES
28.2800 g., Copper-Nickel, 38.6 mm. **Obv:** National Arms **Rev:** Benedict XVI blessing crowd at St. Peter's Square

Date	Mintage	F	VF	XF	Unc	BU
2005	—	—	—	—	—	10.00

KM# 121 25 RUPEES
28.2800 g., 0.9250 Silver 0.8410 oz. ASW, 38.6 mm. **Obv:** National arms **Rev:** Benedict XVI blessing crowd at St. Peter's Square **Edge:** Reeded

Date	Mintage	F	VF	XF	Unc	BU
2005	—	Value: 50.00				

KM# 120 25 RUPEES
28.2800 g., 0.9250 Silver 0.8410 oz. ASW, 38.6 mm. **Obv:** National arms **Rev:** Description John Paul II in mitre waving **Edge:** Reeded

Date	Mintage	F	VF	XF	Unc	BU
2005 Proof	—	Value: 50.00				

KM# 122 250 RUPEES
6.2200 g., 0.9999 Gold 0.1999 oz. AGW, 22 mm. **Obv:** National arms **Rev:** Description John Paul II in mitre waving **Edge:** Reeded

Date	Mintage	F	VF	XF	Unc	BU
2005 Proof	—	Value: 220				

KM# 123 250 RUPEES
6.2200 g., 0.9999 Gold 0.1999 oz. AGW, 22 mm. **Obv:** National arms **Rev:** Benedict XVI blessing crowd at St. Peter's Square **Edge:** Reeded

Date	Mintage	F	VF	XF	Unc	BU
2005 Proof	—	Value: 220				

SIERRA LEONE

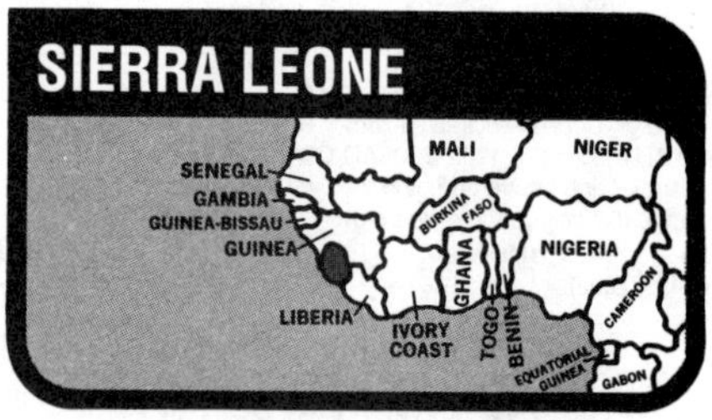

The Republic of Sierra Leone is located in western Africa between Guinea and Liberia, has an area of 27,699 sq. mi. (71,740 sq. km.) and a population of *4.1 million. Capital: Freetown. The economy is predominantly agricultural but mining contributes significantly to export revenues. Diamonds, iron ore, palm kernels, cocoa, and coffee are exported.

Sierra Leone is a member of the Commonwealth of Nations. The president is Chief of State and Head of Government.

MONETARY SYSTEM
Beginning 1964
100 Cents = 1 Leone

NOTE: Sierra Leone's official currency is the Leone. For previously listed Dollar Denominated Coinage, see the 5th Edition of Unusual World Coins.

REPUBLIC

STANDARD COINAGE

KM# 295 20 LEONES
3.9200 g., Copper-Nickel, 21.7 mm. **Obv:** Value within fish and beaded circle **Rev:** Chimpanzee facing **Edge:** Plain

Date	Mintage	F	VF	XF	Unc	BU
2003	—	—	—	—	0.50	1.25

KM# 302 100 LEONES
28.2800 g., Copper-Nickel, 38.6 mm. **Subject:** 40th Anniversary - Bank of Sierra Leone **Obv:** Bank President Kabbah **Rev:** Lion **Edge:** Reeded

Date	Mintage	F	VF	XF	Unc	BU
ND (2004)PM	5,000	—	—	—	15.00	18.00

KM# 296 500 LEONES
7.2000 g., Bi-Metallic Stainless Steel center in Brass ring, 24 mm. **Obv:** Building within circle **Rev:** Bust with hat facing within circle **Edge:** Plain **Shape:** 10-sided

Date	Mintage	F	VF	XF	Unc	BU
2004	—	—	—	—	7.50	9.00

KM# 346 500 LEONES
28.2800 g., Bronze, 38.6 mm. **Subject:** 40th Anniversary - Bank of Sierra Leone **Obv:** Bank President Kabbah **Rev:** Lion, denomination as "Le 500" **Edge:** Reeded

Date	Mintage	F	VF	XF	Unc	BU
ND(2004)PM	10,000	—	—	—	15.00	18.00

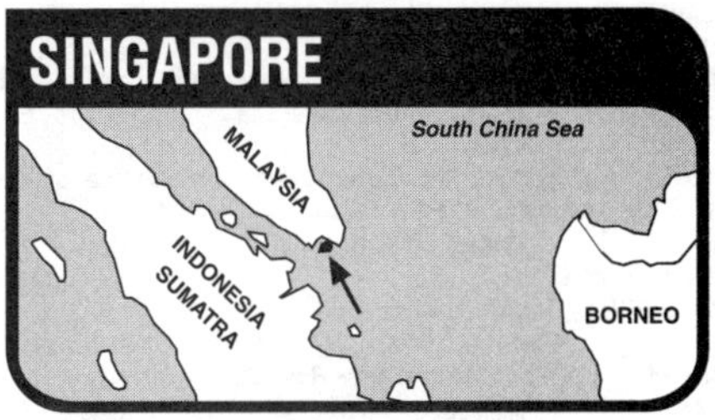

The Republic of Singapore, a member of the Commonwealth of Nations situated off the southern tip of the Malay peninsula, has an area of 224 sq. mi. (633 sq. km.) and a population of *2.7 million. Capital: Singapore. The economy is based on entrepôt trade, manufacturing and oil. Rubber, petroleum products, machinery and spices are exported.

The President is Chief of State. The prime minister is Head of Government.

MINT MARK

sm = "*sm*" - Singapore Mint monogram

MONETARY SYSTEM

100 Cents = 1 Dollar

REPUBLIC

STANDARD COINAGE

100 Cents = 1 Dollar

KM# 98 CENT

1.2750 g., Copper Plated Zinc, 15.96 mm. **Obv:** National arms **Rev:** Value divides plants **Edge:** Plain **Note:** Similar to KM#49 but motto ribbon on arms curves down at center.

Date	Mintage	F	VF	XF	Unc	BU
2001sm	56,220,000	—	—	—	0.10	0.15
2002sm	19,003,000	—	—	—	0.10	0.15
2003sm	—	—	—	—	0.10	0.15
2003sm Proof	—	Value: 2.00				
2004sm	—	—	—	—	0.10	0.15
2004sm Proof	20,000	Value: 2.00				
2005sm	—	—	—	—	0.10	0.15
2006sm	—	—	—	—	0.10	0.15
2007sm	—	—	—	—	0.10	0.15

KM# 98a CENT

1.8100 g., 0.9250 Silver 0.0538 oz. ASW, 17.8 mm. **Obv:** National arms **Rev:** Value divides plants

Date	Mintage	F	VF	XF	Unc	BU
2001sm Proof	10,000	Value: 2.25				
2002sm Proof	10,000	Value: 2.25				
2003sm Proof	—	Value: 2.25				
2004sm Proof	—	Value: 2.25				
2005sm Proof	—	Value: 2.25				
2006sm Proof	—	Value: 2.25				
2007sm Proof	—	Value: 2.25				

KM# 99 5 CENTS

1.6000 g., Aluminum-Bronze, 16.25 mm. **Obv:** National arms **Rev:** Fruit salad plant **Edge:** Reeded **Note:** Similar to KM#50 but motto ribbon on arms curves down at center.

Date	Mintage	F	VF	XF	Unc	BU
2001sm	35,005,000	—	—	—	0.20	0.30
2002sm	33,556,000	—	—	—	0.20	0.30
2003sm	35,930,000	—	—	—	0.20	0.30
2003sm Proof	—	Value: 3.00				
2004sm	38,040,000	—	—	—	0.20	0.30
2004sm Proof	20,000	Value: 3.00				
2005sm	56,832,000	—	—	—	0.20	0.30
2006sm	—	—	—	—	0.20	0.30
2007sm	—	—	—	—	0.20	0.30

KM# 99a 5 CENTS

2.0000 g., 0.9250 Silver 0.0595 oz. ASW, 16.25 mm. **Obv:** National arms **Rev:** Fruit salad plant

Date	Mintage	F	VF	XF	Unc	BU
2001sm Proof	10,000	Value: 2.50				
2002sm Proof	10,000	Value: 2.50				
2003sm Proof	—	Value: 2.50				
2004sm Proof	—	Value: 2.50				
2005sm Proof	—	Value: 2.50				
2006sm Proof	—	Value: 2.50				
2007sm Proof	—	Value: 2.50				

KM# 100 10 CENTS

2.8500 g., Copper-Nickel, 19.4 mm. **Obv:** National arms **Rev:** Star Jasmine plant **Edge:** Reeded **Note:** Similar to KM#51 but motto ribbon on arms curves down at center.

Date	Mintage	F	VF	XF	Unc	BU
2001sm	70,600,000	—	—	—	0.20	0.30
2002sm	61,670,000	—	—	—	0.20	0.30
2003sm	58,990,000	—	—	—	0.20	0.30
2003sm Proof	—	Value: 4.00				
2004sm	59,670,000	—	—	—	0.20	0.30
2004sm Proof	20,000	Value: 4.00				
2005sm	49,960,000	—	—	—	0.20	0.30
2006sm	—	—	—	—	0.20	0.30
2007sm	—	—	—	—	0.20	0.30

KM# 100a 10 CENTS

3.0500 g., 0.9250 Silver 0.0907 oz. ASW, 19.4 mm. **Obv:** National arms **Rev:** Star Jasmine plant **Edge:** Reeded

Date	Mintage	F	VF	XF	Unc	BU
2001sm Proof	10,000	Value: 4.00				
2002sm Proof	10,000	Value: 4.00				
2003sm Proof	—	Value: 4.00				
2004sm Proof	—	Value: 4.00				
2005sm Proof	—	Value: 4.00				
2006sm Proof	—	Value: 4.00				
2007sm Proof	—	Value: 4.00				

KM# 101 20 CENTS

5.6500 g., Copper-Nickel, 23.6 mm. **Obv:** National arms **Rev:** Powder puff plant above value **Edge:** Reeded **Note:** Similar to KM#52 but motto ribbon on arms curves down at center.

Date	Mintage	F	VF	XF	Unc	BU
2001sm	52,050,000	—	—	—	0.60	0.75
2002sm	48,120,000	—	—	—	0.60	0.75
2003sm	45,470,000	—	—	—	0.60	0.75
2003sm	—	Value: 5.00				
2004sm	44,870,000	—	—	—	0.60	0.75
2004sm	20,000	Value: 5.00				
2005sm	—	—	—	—	0.60	0.75
2006sm	23,310,000	—	—	—	0.60	0.75
2007sm	—	—	—	—	0.60	0.75

KM# 101a 20 CENTS

5.2400 g., 0.9250 Silver 0.1558 oz. ASW, 23.6 mm. **Obv:** National arms **Rev:** Powder puff plant above value **Edge:** Reeded

Date	Mintage	F	VF	XF	Unc	BU
2001sm Proof	10,000	Value: 6.50				
2002sm Proof	10,000	Value: 6.50				
2003sm Proof	—	Value: 6.50				
2004sm Proof	—	Value: 6.50				
2005sm Proof	—	Value: 6.50				
2006sm Proof	—	Value: 6.50				
2007sm Proof	—	Value: 6.50				

KM# 102 50 CENTS

7.1900 g., Copper-Nickel, 24 mm. **Obv:** National arms **Rev:** Yellow Allamanda plant above value **Edge:** Plain **Edge Lettering:** REPUBLIC OF SINGAPORE (lion's head) **Note:** Similar to KM#53 but motto ribbon on arms curves down at center.

Date	Mintage	F	VF	XF	Unc	BU
2001sm	30,020,000	—	—	—	0.75	1.00
2002sm	27,420,000	—	—	—	0.75	1.00
2003sm	23,650,000	—	—	—	0.75	1.00
2003sm Proof	—	Value: 6.00				
2004sm	24,640,000	—	—	—	0.75	1.00
2004sm Proof	20,000	Value: 6.00				
2005sm	24,996,000	—	—	—	0.75	1.00
2006sm	—	—	—	—	0.75	1.00
2007sm	7,680,000	—	—	—	0.75	1.00

KM# 102a 50 CENTS

8.5600 g., 0.9250 Silver 0.2546 oz. ASW **Obv:** National arms **Rev:** Yellow Allamanda plant above value

Date	Mintage	F	VF	XF	Unc	BU
2001sm Proof	10,000	Value: 12.00				
2002sm Proof	10,000	Value: 12.00				
2003sm Proof	—	Value: 12.00				
2004sm Proof	—	Value: 12.00				
2005sm Proof	—	Value: 12.00				
2006sm Proof	—	Value: 12.00				
2007sm Proof	—	Value: 12.00				

KM# 103 DOLLAR

6.2900 g., Aluminum-Bronze, 22.3 mm. **Obv:** National arms **Rev:** Periwinkle flower **Edge:** Reeded **Note:** Similar to KM#54 but motto ribbon on arms curves down at center.

Date	Mintage	F	VF	XF	Unc	BU
2001sm	40,840,000	—	—	—	1.50	2.25
2002sm	35,660,000	—	—	—	1.50	2.25
2003sm	31,900,000	—	—	—	1.50	2.25
2003sm Proof	—	Value: 10.00				
2004sm	34,380,000	—	—	—	1.50	2.25
2004sm Proof	20,000	Value: 10.00				
2005sm	—	—	—	—	1.50	2.25
2006sm	25,488,000	—	—	—	1.50	2.25
2007sm	—	—	—	—	1.50	2.25

KM# 103a DOLLAR

8.4273 g., 0.9250 Silver 0.2506 oz. ASW **Obv:** National arms **Rev:** Periwinkle flower

Date	Mintage	F	VF	XF	Unc	BU
2001sm Proof	10,000	Value: 15.00				
2002sm Proof	10,000	Value: 15.00				
2003sm Proof	—	Value: 15.00				
2004sm Proof	—	Value: 15.00				
2005sm Proof	—	Value: 15.00				
2006sm Proof	—	Value: 15.00				
2007sm Proof	—	Value: 15.00				

KM# 222 DOLLAR

0.3000 g., 0.9999 Gold 0.0096 oz. AGW, 7 mm. **Series:** Lunar **Subject:** Year of the Goat **Obv:** National arms **Rev:** Stylized goat standing right facing left

Date	Mintage	F	VF	XF	Unc	BU
2003sm Prooflike	8,000	—	—	—	—	32.50

KM# 184 DOLLAR

Copper-Nickel, 24.6 mm. **Subject:** Old World Charm - Balestier **Obv:** Arms with supporters **Rev:** Old buildings **Edge:** Reeded

Date	Mintage	F	VF	XF	Unc	BU
2004sm Prooflike	—	—	—	—	—	10.00

KM# 184a DOLLAR

0.9990 Silver, 24.6 mm. **Subject:** Old World Charm - Balestier **Obv:** Arms with supporters **Rev:** Old buildings

Date	Mintage	F	VF	XF	Unc	BU
2004sm Proof	8,000	Value: 27.50				

KM# 186 DOLLAR

0.3000 g., 0.9999 Gold 0.0096 oz. AGW, 7 mm. **Series:** Lunar **Subject:** Year of the Monkey **Obv:** National arms **Rev:** Stylized monkey sitting left **Edge:** Plain

Date	Mintage	F	VF	XF	Unc	BU
2004 Prooflike	8,000	—	—	—	—	32.50

KM# 190 DOLLAR

Copper-Nickel, 24.6 mm. **Subject:** Old World Charm - Jalan Besar

Date	Mintage	F	VF	XF	Unc	BU
2004sm Prooflike	—	—	—	—	—	10.00

KM# 190a DOLLAR

0.9990 Silver, 24.6 mm. **Subject:** Old World Charm - Jalan Besar

Date	Mintage	F	VF	XF	Unc	BU
2004sm Proof	8,000	Value: 27.50				

KM# 191 DOLLAR

Copper-Nickel, 24.6 mm. **Subject:** Old World Charm - Joo Chiat

Date	Mintage	F	VF	XF	Unc	BU
2004sm Prooflike	—	—	—	—	—	10.00

KM# 191a DOLLAR

0.9990 Silver, 24.6 mm. **Subject:** Old World Charm - Joo Chiat

Date	Mintage	F	VF	XF	Unc	BU
2004sm Proof	8,000	Value: 27.50				

KM# 192 DOLLAR

Copper-Nickel, 24.6 mm. **Subject:** Old World Charm - Tanjong Katong

Date	Mintage	F	VF	XF	Unc	BU
2004sm Prooflike	—	—	—	—	—	10.00

KM# 192a DOLLAR

0.9990 Silver, 24.6 mm. **Subject:** Old World Charm - Tanjong Katong

Date	Mintage	F	VF	XF	Unc	BU
2004sm Proof	8,000	Value: 27.50				

KM# 233 DOLLAR

0.3000 g., 0.9999 Gold 0.0096 oz. AGW, 7 mm. **Series:** Lunar **Subject:** Year of the Rooster **Obv:** National arms **Rev:** Stylized rooster standing right

Date	Mintage	F	VF	XF	Unc	BU
2005sm Prooflike	8,000	—	—	—	—	32.50

KM# 244 DOLLAR
Copper-Nickel **Series:** Urban Redevelopment **Obv:** National arms **Rev:** Anak Bukit

Date	Mintage	F	VF	XF	Unc	BU
2005sm Prooflike	—	Value: 12.00				

KM# 244a DOLLAR
0.9999 Silver **Series:** Urban Redevelopment **Obv:** National arms **Rev:** Anak Bukit - multicolor

Date	Mintage	F	VF	XF	Unc	BU
2005sm Proof	8,000	Value: 45.00				

KM# 245 DOLLAR
Copper-Nickel **Series:** Urban Redevelopment **Obv:** National arms **Rev:** Coronation

Date	Mintage	F	VF	XF	Unc	BU
2005sm Prooflike	—	Value: 12.00				

KM# 245a DOLLAR
0.9999 Silver **Series:** Urban Redevelopment **Obv:** National arms **Rev:** Coronation - multicolor

Date	Mintage	F	VF	XF	Unc	BU
2005sm Proof	8,000	Value: 45.00				

KM# 246 DOLLAR
Copper-Nickel **Series:** Urban Redevelopment **Obv:** National arms **Rev:** Jalan Leban and Casuarina Road

Date	Mintage	F	VF	XF	Unc	BU
2005sm Prooflike	—	Value: 12.00				

KM# 246a DOLLAR
0.9999 Silver **Series:** Urban Redevelopment **Obv:** National arms **Rev:** Jalan Leban and Casuarina Road - multicolor

Date	Mintage	F	VF	XF	Unc	BU
2005sm Proof	8,000	Value: 45.00				

KM# 247 DOLLAR
Copper-Nickel **Series:** Urban Redevelopment **Obv:** National arms **Rev:** Springleaf

Date	Mintage	F	VF	XF	Unc	BU
2005sm Prooflike	—	Value: 12.00				

KM# 247a DOLLAR
0.9999 Silver **Series:** Urban Redevelopment **Obv:** National arms **Rev:** Springleaf - multicolor

Date	Mintage	F	VF	XF	Unc	BU
2005sm Proof	8,000	Value: 45.00				

KM# 248 DOLLAR
Copper-Nickel **Series:** Urban Redevelopment **Obv:** National arms **Rev:** Thomson Village

Date	Mintage	F	VF	XF	Unc	BU
2005sm Prooflike	—	Value: 12.00				

KM# 248a DOLLAR
0.9999 Silver **Series:** Urban Redevelopment **Obv:** National arms **Rev:** Thomson Village - multicolor

Date	Mintage	F	VF	XF	Unc	BU
2005sm Proof	8,000	Value: 45.00				

KM# 249 DOLLAR
0.3000 g., 0.9999 Gold 0.0096 oz. AGW **Series:** Lunar **Subject:** Year of the Dog **Obv:** National arms **Rev:** Stylized dog standing left

Date	Mintage	F	VF	XF	Unc	BU
2006sm Prooflike	5,000	—	—	—	—	32.50

KM# 259 DOLLAR
Copper-Nickel **Series:** Urban Redevelopment **Obv:** National arms **Rev:** Changi Village - multicolor

Date	Mintage	F	VF	XF	Unc	BU
2007sm Prooflike	—	—	—	—	—	12.50

KM# 262 DOLLAR
Copper-Nickel **Series:** Urban Redevelopment **Obv:** National arms **Rev:** Punggoi Point and Coney Island - multicolor

Date	Mintage	F	VF	XF	Unc	BU
2007sm Prooflike	—	—	—	—	—	12.50

KM# 259a DOLLAR
0.9990 Silver **Series:** Urban Redevelopment **Obv:** National arms **Rev:** Changi Village - multicolor

Date	Mintage	F	VF	XF	Unc	BU
2007sm Proof	8,000	Value: 32.50				

KM# 260 DOLLAR
Copper-Nickel **Series:** Urban Redevelopment **Obv:** National arms **Rev:** Pasir Ris Park - multicolor

Date	Mintage	F	VF	XF	Unc	BU
2007sm Prooflike	—	—	—	—	—	12.50

KM# 260a DOLLAR
0.9990 Silver **Series:** Urban Redevelopment **Obv:** National arms **Rev:** Pasir Ris Park - multicolor

Date	Mintage	F	VF	XF	Unc	BU
2007sm Proof	8,000	Value: 32.50				

KM# 261 DOLLAR
Copper-Nickel **Series:** Urban Redevelopment **Obv:** National arms **Rev:** Pulau Ubin - multicolor

Date	Mintage	F	VF	XF	Unc	BU
2007sm Prooflike	—	—	—	—	—	12.50

KM# 261a DOLLAR
0.9990 Silver **Series:** Urban Redevelopment **Obv:** National arms **Rev:** Pulau Ubin - multicolor

Date	Mintage	F	VF	XF	Unc	BU
2007sm Proof	8,000	Value: 32.50				

KM# 262a DOLLAR
0.9990 Silver **Series:** Urban Redevelopment **Obv:** National arms **Rev:** Punggoi Point and Coney Island - multicolor

Date	Mintage	F	VF	XF	Unc	BU
2007sm Proof	8,000	Value: 32.50				

KM# 263 DOLLAR
0.3000 g., 0.9999 Gold 0.0096 oz. AGW **Series:** Lunar **Subject:** Year of the Boar **Obv:** National arms **Rev:** Stylized boar running right

Date	Mintage	F	VF	XF	Unc	BU
2007sm Prooflike	5,000	—	—	—	—	32.50

KM# 269 DOLLAR
0.3000 g., 0.9999 Gold 0.0096 oz. AGW **Series:** Lunar **Subject:** Year of the Rat **Obv:** National arms **Rev:** Stylized rat lying left

Date	Mintage	F	VF	XF	Unc	BU
2008sm	3,000	—	—	—	—	30.00

KM# 196 2 DOLLARS
Copper-Nickel **Subject:** Tribute to Healthcare Givers **Obv:** National arms **Rev:** Five 3/4 length people standing facing, clinic in background

Date	Mintage	F	VF	XF	Unc	BU
2003sm	—	—	—	—	—	15.00

KM# 196a 2 DOLLARS
0.9990 Silver **Subject:** Tribute to Healthcare Givers **Obv:** National arms **Rev:** Five 3/4 length people standing facing, clinic in background

Date	Mintage	F	VF	XF	Unc	BU
2003sm Proof	10,000	Value: 60.00				

KM# 223 2 DOLLARS
20.0000 g., 0.9990 Silver 0.6423 oz. ASW, 38.70 mm. **Series:** Lunar **Subject:** Year of the Goat **Obv:** National arms **Rev:** Stylized goat standing right facing left

Date	Mintage	F	VF	XF	Unc	BU
2003sm Proof	30,000	Value: 60.00				

KM# 229 2 DOLLARS
20.0000 g., 0.9990 Silver 0.6423 oz. ASW, 38.7 mm. **Series:** Lunar **Subject:** Year of the Monkey **Obv:** National arms **Rev:** Stylized monkey sitting left

Date	Mintage	F	VF	XF	Unc	BU
2004sm Proof	30,000	Value: 60.00				

KM# 234 2 DOLLARS
20.0000 g., Copper-Nickel, 38.7 mm. **Series:** Lunar **Subject:** Year of the Rooster **Obv:** National arms **Rev:** Rooster standing right

Date	Mintage	F	VF	XF	Unc	BU
2005sm Prooflike	—	—	—	—	—	15.00

KM# 234a 2 DOLLARS
20.0000 g., 0.9999 Silver 0.6429 oz. ASW, 38.7 mm. **Series:** Lunar **Subject:** Year of the Rooster **Obv:** National arms **Rev:** Stylized rooster standing right

Date	Mintage	F	VF	XF	Unc	BU
2005sm Proof	10,000	Value: 42.50				

KM# 242 2 DOLLARS
Copper-Nickel **Subject:** 40th National Day Parade **Obv:** National arms **Rev:** Fireworks, parade in government plaza, multicolor

Date	Mintage	F	VF	XF	Unc	BU
2005sm Prooflike	—	Value: 15.00				

KM# 242a 2 DOLLARS
20.0000 g., 0.9999 Silver 0.6429 oz. ASW **Subject:** 40th National Day Parade **Obv:** National arms **Rev:** Fireworks, parade in government plaza

Date	Mintage	F	VF	XF	Unc	BU
2005sm Proof	—	Value: 60.00				

KM# 258 2 DOLLARS
Copper-Nickel **Subject:** 41st National Day **Obv:** National arms **Rev:** People in stadium, emblem - multicolor

Date	Mintage	F	VF	XF	Unc	BU
2006sm Prooflike	—	Value: 15.00				

KM# 258a 2 DOLLARS
20.0000 g., 0.9990 Silver 0.6423 oz. ASW **Subject:** 41st National Day **Obv:** National arms **Rev:** People in stadium, emblem - multicolor

Date	Mintage	F	VF	XF	Unc	BU
2006sm Proof	8,000	Value: 60.00				

KM# 250 2 DOLLARS
20.0000 g., Copper-Nickel **Series:** Lunar **Subject:** Year of the Dog **Obv:** National arms **Rev:** Stylized dog standing left

Date	Mintage	F	VF	XF	Unc	BU
2006sm Prooflike	—	Value: 15.00				

KM# 250a 2 DOLLARS
20.0000 g., 0.9999 Silver 0.6429 oz. ASW **Series:** Lunar **Subject:** Year of the Dog **Obv:** National arms **Rev:** Stylized dog standing left

Date	Mintage	F	VF	XF	Unc	BU
2006sm Proof	6,000	Value: 60.00				

KM# 264 2 DOLLARS
Copper-Nickel **Series:** Lunar **Subject:** Year of the Boar **Obv:** National arms **Rev:** Stylized boar running right

Date	Mintage	F	VF	XF	Unc	BU
2007sm Prooflike	—	—	—	—	—	12.00

KM# 193 2 DOLLARS
20.0000 g., Copper-Nickel, 38.70 mm. **Subject:** 42nd National Day Parade **Obv:** Arms with supporters **Obv. Legend:** SINGAPURA - SINGAPORE **Rev:** Colored overlay with four children above Marina Bay floating platform **Edge:** Reeded

Date	Mintage	F	VF	XF	Unc	BU
2007 Prooflike	—	—	—	—	—	13.50

KM# 193a 2 DOLLARS
20.0000 g., 0.9990 Silver 0.6423 oz. ASW, 38.70 mm. **Subject:** 42nd National Day Parade **Obv:** Arms with supporters **Obv. Legend:** SINGAPURA - SINGAPORE **Rev:** Colored overlay with four children above Marina Bay floating platform **Edge:** Reeded

Date	Mintage	F	VF	XF	Unc	BU
2007 Proof	8,000	Value: 42.50				

KM# 264a 2 DOLLARS
20.0000 g., 0.9990 Silver 0.6423 oz. ASW **Series:** Lunar **Subject:** Year of the Boar **Obv:** National arms **Rev:** Stylized boar running right

Date	Mintage	F	VF	XF	Unc	BU
2007sm Proof	6,000	Value: 40.00				

KM# 270 2 DOLLARS
20.0000 g., Copper-Nickel **Series:** Lunar **Subject:** Year of the Rat **Obv:** National arms **Rev:** Stylized rat lying left

Date	Mintage	F	VF	XF	Unc	BU
2008sm Prooflike	—	—	—	—	—	12.50

KM# 270a 2 DOLLARS
20.0000 g., 0.9990 Silver 0.6423 oz. ASW **Series:** Lunar **Subject:** Year of the Rat **Obv:** National arms **Rev:** Stylized rat lying left

Date	Mintage	F	VF	XF	Unc	BU
2008sm Proof	6,000	Value: 42.50				

KM# 177a 5 DOLLARS
20.0000 g., 0.9250 Silver 0.5948 oz. ASW, 38.6 mm. **Subject:** Productivity Movement **Obv:** Arms with supporters **Rev:** Spiral design **Edge:** Reeded

Date	Mintage	F	VF	XF	Unc	BU
2001sm Proof	10,000	Value: 50.00				

KM# 177 5 DOLLARS
Copper-Nickel, 38.6 mm. **Subject:** Productivity Movement **Obv:** Arms with supporters **Rev:** Spiral design **Edge:** Reeded

Date	Mintage	F	VF	XF	Unc	BU
2001sm	20,000	—	—	—	12.50	15.00

KM# 181 5 DOLLARS
20.0000 g., Copper-Nickel, 38.7 mm. **Subject:** Esplanade Theaters on the Bay **Obv:** Arms with supporters **Rev:** Stylized symbolic design **Edge:** Reeded

Date	Mintage	F	VF	XF	Unc	BU
2002sm	—	—	—	—	13.50	16.50

KM# 181a 5 DOLLARS
20.0000 g., 0.9990 Silver 0.6423 oz. ASW, 38.7 mm. **Subject:** Esplanade Theaters on the Bay **Obv:** Arms with supporters **Rev:** Stylized symbolic design **Edge:** Reeded

Date	Mintage	F	VF	XF	Unc	BU
2002sm Proof	10,000	Value: 45.00				

KM# 104.1 5 DOLLARS
Bi-Metallic Aluminum-Bronze center in Copper-Nickel ring **Subject:** Vanda Miss Joaquim **Obv:** National arms, date and BCCS logo **Rev:** Flower and value within beaded circle **Shape:** Scalloped

Date	Mintage	F	VF	XF	Unc	BU
2002sm	—	—	—	—	—	15.00

KM# 104.1a 5 DOLLARS
8.2500 g., 0.9250 Silver 0.2453 oz. ASW **Subject:** Vanda Miss Joaquim **Obv:** National arms, date and BCCS logo **Rev:** Flower and value within beaded circle

Date	Mintage	F	VF	XF	Unc	BU
2001sm Proof	—	Value: 25.00				
2002sm Proof	—	Value: 25.00				

KM# 104.2 5 DOLLARS
Bi-Metallic **Ring Composition:** Copper-Nickel **Center Composition:** Aluminum-Bronze **Obv:** National arms, date and MAS logo **Rev:** Flower above value **Edge:** Plain

Date	Mintage	F	VF	XF	Unc	BU
2001sm	—	—	—	—	—	12.00
Note: In mint sets only						
2002sm	—	—	—	—	—	12.00
Note: In mint sets only						
2003sm	—	—	—	—	—	12.00
2004sm	—	—	—	—	—	12.00
2005sm	—	—	—	—	—	12.00
2006sm	—	—	—	—	—	12.00

KM# 104.2a 5 DOLLARS
8.2500 g., 0.9250 Silver 0.2453 oz. ASW **Obv:** National arms, date and MAS logo **Rev:** Flower above value **Edge:** Plain

Date	Mintage	F	VF	XF	Unc	BU
2001sm Proof	10,000	Value: 25.00				
2002sm Proof	10,000	Value: 25.00				
2003sm Proof	—	Value: 25.00				
2004sm Proof	—	Value: 25.00				
2005sm Proof	—	Value: 25.00				
2006sm Proof	—	Value: 25.00				

KM# 104.3 5 DOLLARS
Bi-Metallic Aluminum-Bronze center in Copper-Nickel ring **Obv:** National arms above latent image "MAS" **Rev:** Flower and value **Shape:** Scalloped

Date	Mintage	F	VF	XF	Unc	BU
2002sm	—	—	—	—	—	10.00
2003sm	—	—	—	—	—	10.00
2003sm Proof	—	Value: 15.00				
2004sm	—	—	—	—	—	10.00
2004sm Proof	20,000	Value: 15.00				
2005sm	—	—	—	—	—	10.00
2006sm	—	—	—	—	—	10.00
2007sm	—	—	—	—	—	10.00

KM# 104.3a 5 DOLLARS
8.2500 g., 0.9250 Silver 0.2453 oz. ASW **Obv:** National arms above latent image "MAS" **Rev:** Flower and value **Shape:** Scalloped

Date	Mintage	F	VF	XF	Unc	BU
2003sm Proof	—	Value: 25.00				
2004sm Proof	—	Value: 25.00				
2005sm Proof	—	Value: 25.00				
2006sm Proof	—	Value: 25.00				
2007sm Proof	—	Value: 25.00				

KM# 224 5 DOLLARS
7.7760 g., 0.9999 Gold 0.2500 oz. AGW, 21.9 mm. **Series:** Lunar **Subject:** Year of the Goat **Obv:** National arms **Rev:** Stylized goat standing right facing left

Date	Mintage	F	VF	XF	Unc	BU
2003sm Proof	8,000	Value: 265				

KM# 230 5 DOLLARS
7.7760 g., 0.9999 Gold 0.2500 oz. AGW, 21.9 mm. **Series:** Lunar **Subject:** Year of the Monkey **Obv:** National arms **Rev:** Stylized monkey sitting left

Date	Mintage	F	VF	XF	Unc	BU
2004sm Proof	8,000	Value: 265				

KM# 235 5 DOLLARS
7.7760 g., 0.9999 Gold 0.2500 oz. AGW, 21.9 mm. **Series:** Lunar **Subject:** Year of the Rooster **Obv:** National arms **Rev:** Stylized rooster standing right

Date	Mintage	F	VF	XF	Unc	BU
2005sm Proof	8,000	Value: 265				

KM# 194 5 DOLLARS
20.0000 g., 0.9990 Silver 0.6423 oz. ASW, 38.7 mm. **Obv:** Arms with supporters **Obv. Legend:** SINGAPURA - SINGAPORE **Rev:** Multicolor Singapore's skyline above world map, golden lion symbol below pointing to location of Singapore **Rev. Legend:** BOARD OF GOVERNORS ANNUAL MEETINGS • SINGAPORE 2006 • INTERNATIONAL MONETARY FUND • - WORLD BANK GROUP •

Date	Mintage	F	VF	XF	Unc	BU
2006sm Proof	1,000	Value: 60				

KM# 251 5 DOLLARS
7.7750 g., 0.9999 Gold 0.2499 oz. AGW **Series:** Lunar **Subject:** Year of the Dog **Obv:** National arms **Rev:** Stylized dog standing left

Date	Mintage	F	VF	XF	Unc	BU
2006sm Proof	5,000	Value: 265				

KM# 256 5 DOLLARS
20.0000 g., 0.9990 Silver 0.6423 oz. ASW **Series:** Heritage Orchids **Obv:** National arms **Rev:** Vanda Tan Chay Yan - multicolor

Date	Mintage	F	VF	XF	Unc	BU
2006sm Proof	8,000	Value: 60.00				

KM# 257 5 DOLLARS
20.0000 g., 0.9990 Silver 0.6423 oz. ASW **Series:** Heritage Orchids **Obv:** National arms **Rev:** Aranda Majula - multicolor

Date	Mintage	F	VF	XF	Unc	BU
2006sm Proof	8,000	Value: 60.00				

KM# 265 5 DOLLARS
7.7750 g., 0.9999 Gold 0.2499 oz. AGW **Series:** Lunar **Subject:** Year of the Boar **Obv:** National arms **Rev:** Stylized boar running right

Date	Mintage	F	VF	XF	Unc	BU
2007sm Proof	5,000	Value: 360				

KM# 275 5 DOLLARS
20.0000 g., 0.9990 Silver 0.6423 oz. ASW, 38.7 mm. **Series:** Heritage Orchids **Obv:** National arms **Rev:** Dendrobium Singa Mas - multicolor

Date	Mintage	F	VF	XF	Unc	BU
2007sm Proof	8,000	Value: 45.00				

Note: In sets only

KM# 276 5 DOLLARS
20.0000 g., 0.9990 Silver 0.6423 oz. ASW, 38.7 mm. **Series:** Heritage Orchids **Obv:** National arms **Rev:** Vanda Mimi Palmar - multicolor

Date	Mintage	F	VF	XF	Unc	BU
2007sm Proof	8,000	Value: 45.00				

Note: In sets only

KM# 271 5 DOLLARS
7.7750 g., 0.9999 Gold 0.2499 oz. AGW **Series:** Lunar **Subject:** Year of the Rat **Obv:** National arms **Rev:** Stylized rat lying left

Date	Mintage	F	VF	XF	Unc	BU
2008sm Proof	2,000	Value: 350				

KM# 179 10 DOLLARS
28.0000 g., Copper-Nickel, 40.7 mm. **Series:** Lunar **Subject:** Year of the Snake **Obv:** National arms **Rev:** Stylized snake **Edge:** Reeded

Date	Mintage	F	VF	XF	Unc	BU
2001sm Prooflike	—	—	—	—	—	20.00

KM# 179a 10 DOLLARS
62.2060 g., 0.9990 Silver 1.9979 oz. ASW, 40.7 mm. **Series:** Lunar **Subject:** Year of the Snake **Obv:** National arms **Rev:** Stylized snake **Edge:** Reeded

Date	Mintage	F	VF	XF	Unc	BU
2001sm Proof	35,000	Value: 85.00				

KM# 182 10 DOLLARS
28.0000 g., Copper-Nickel, 40.7 mm. **Series:** Lunar **Subject:** Year of the Horse **Obv:** National arms **Rev:** Stylized horse standing left **Edge:** Reeded

Date	Mintage	F	VF	XF	Unc	BU
2002sm Prooflike	—	—	—	—	—	20.00

KM# 182a 10 DOLLARS
62.2060 g., 0.9990 Silver 1.9979 oz. ASW, 40.7 mm. **Series:** Lunar **Subject:** Year of the Horse **Obv:** National arms **Rev:** Stylized horse standing left **Edge:** Reeded

Date	Mintage	F	VF	XF	Unc	BU
2002sm Proof	35,000	Value: 85.00				

KM# 225 10 DOLLARS
28.0000 g., Copper-Nickel, 40.7 mm. **Series:** Lunar **Subject:** Year of the Goat **Obv:** National arms **Rev:** Stylized goat standing right facing left

Date	Mintage	F	VF	XF	Unc	BU
2003sm Prooflike	—	—	—	—	—	20.00

KM# 225a 10 DOLLARS
62.2060 g., 0.9990 Silver 1.9979 oz. ASW, 40.7 mm. **Series:** Lunar **Subject:** Year of the Goat **Obv:** National arms **Rev:** Stylized goat standing right facing left

Date	Mintage	F	VF	XF	Unc	BU
2003sm Proof	35,000	Value: 85.00				

KM# 185 10 DOLLARS
31.1040 g., 0.9999 Gold 0.9999 oz. AGW, 32.1 mm. **Subject:** 10th Anniversary China-Singapore Suzhou Industrial Park **Obv:** National arms **Rev:** "Harmony" Sculpture **Edge:** Lettered edge

Date	Mintage	F	VF	XF	Unc	BU
2004sm Proof	500	Value: 1,000				

KM# 187 10 DOLLARS
28.0000 g., Copper-Nickel, 40.7 mm. **Series:** Lunar **Subject:** Year of the Monkey **Obv:** National arms **Rev:** Stylized monkey sitting left **Edge:** Reeded

Date	Mintage	F	VF	XF	Unc	BU
2004sm Prooflike	—	Value: 85.00				

KM# 189 10 DOLLARS
28.0000 g., Copper-Nickel, 40.7 mm. **Subject:** 10th Anniversary China-Singapore Suzhou Industrial Park **Obv:** National arms **Rev:** "Harmony" Sculpture **Edge:** Reeded

Date	Mintage	F	VF	XF	Unc	BU
2004sm Prooflike	7,000	—	—	—	—	20.00

KM# 189a 10 DOLLARS
0.9990 Silver, 40.7 mm. **Subject:** 10th Anniversary China-Singapore Suzhou Industrial Park **Obv:** National arms **Rev:** "Harmony" sculpture **Edge:** Reeded

Date	Mintage	F	VF	XF	Unc	BU
2004sm Proof	5,000	Value: 55.00				

KM# 187a 10 DOLLARS
62.2060 g., 0.9990 Silver 1.9979 oz. ASW, 40.7 mm. **Series:** Lunar **Subject:** Year of the Monkey **Obv:** National arms **Rev:** Stylized monkey sitting left **Edge:** Reeded

Date	Mintage	F	VF	XF	Unc	BU
2004sm Proof	35,000	Value: 85.00				

KM# 236 10 DOLLARS
62.2060 g., 0.9999 Silver 1.9997 oz. ASW, 45 mm. **Series:** Lunar **Subject:** Year of the Rooster **Obv:** National arms **Rev:** Stylized rooster standing right

Date	Mintage	F	VF	XF	Unc	BU
2005sm Proof	30,000	Value: 85.00				

KM# 240 10 DOLLARS
Copper-Nickel **Subject:** National University of Singapore **Obv:** National arms **Rev:** Person, globe and emblem

Date	Mintage	F	VF	XF	Unc	BU
2005sm Prooflike	20,000	—	—	—	—	22.50

KM# 240a 10 DOLLARS
20.0000 g., 0.9999 Silver 0.6429 oz. ASW **Subject:** National University of Singapore **Obv:** National arms **Rev:** Person, globe and emblem

Date	Mintage	F	VF	XF	Unc	BU
2005sm Proof	10,000	Value: 60.00				

KM# 243 10 DOLLARS
31.1030 g., 0.9999 Silver Inlay 0.9999 gold 2.3g 0.9998 oz. ASW **Subject:** 40th National Day parade **Obv:** National arms **Rev:** Fireworks, parade in government plaza

Date	Mintage	F	VF	XF	Unc	BU
2005sm Proof	1,500	Value: 225				

KM# 252 10 DOLLARS
62.2030 g., 0.9990 Silver 1.9978 oz. ASW **Series:** Lunar **Subject:** Year of the Dog **Obv:** National arms **Rev:** Stylized dog standing left

Date	Mintage	F	VF	XF	Unc	BU
2006sm Proof	30,000	Value: 90.00				

KM# 266 10 DOLLARS
62.2060 g., 0.9990 Silver 1.9979 oz. ASW **Series:** Lunar **Subject:** Year of the Boar **Obv:** National arms **Rev:** Stylized boar running right - multicolor

Date	Mintage	F	VF	XF	Unc	BU
2007sm Proof	30,000	Value: 100				

KM# 272 10 DOLLARS
62.2060 g., 0.9990 Silver 1.9979 oz. ASW **Series:** Lunar **Subject:** Year of the Rat **Obv:** National arms **Rev:** Stylized rat lying left - multicolor

Date	Mintage	F	VF	XF	Unc	BU
2008sm Proof	20,000	Value: 100				

KM# 226 25 DOLLARS
155.5200 g., 0.9990 Silver 4.9949 oz. ASW, 65.00 mm. **Series:** Lunar **Subject:** Year of the Goat **Obv:** National arms **Rev:** Stylized goat standing right facing left

Date	Mintage	F	VF	XF	Unc	BU
2003sm Proof	250	Value: 300				

KM# 231 25 DOLLARS
155.5200 g., 0.9990 Silver 4.9949 oz. ASW, 65 mm. **Series:** Lunar **Subject:** Year of the Monkey **Obv:** National arms **Rev:** Stylized monkey sitting left

Date	Mintage	F	VF	XF	Unc	BU
2004sm Proof	250	Value: 300				

KM# 237 25 DOLLARS
155.5200 g., 0.9999 Silver 4.9994 oz. ASW, 65 mm. **Series:** Lunar **Subject:** Year of the Rooster **Obv:** National arms **Rev:** Stylized rooster standing right

Date	Mintage	F	VF	XF	Unc	BU
2005sm Proof	250	Value: 300				

KM# 253 25 DOLLARS
155.5150 g., 0.9990 Silver 4.9947 oz. ASW **Series:** Lunar **Subject:** Year of the Dog **Obv:** National arms **Rev:** Stylized dog standing right

Date	Mintage	F	VF	XF	Unc	BU
2006sm Proof	250	Value: 350				

KM# 267 25 DOLLARS
155.5150 g., 0.9990 Silver 4.9947 oz. ASW **Series:** Lunar **Subject:** Year of the Boar **Obv:** National arms **Rev:** Stylized boar running right

Date	Mintage	F	VF	XF	Unc	BU
2007sm Proof	250	Value: 360				

KM# 273 25 DOLLARS
155.5150 g., 0.9990 Silver 4.9947 oz. ASW **Series:** Lunar **Subject:** Year of the Rat **Obv:** National arms **Rev:** Stylized rat lying left

Date	Mintage	F	VF	XF	Unc	BU
2008sm Proof	250	Value: 375				

KM# 238 100 DOLLARS
31.1030 g., 0.9999 Gold 0.9998 oz. AGW, 33 mm. **Series:** Lunar **Subject:** Year of the Rooster **Obv:** National arms **Rev:** Stylized rooster standing right

Date	Mintage	F	VF	XF	Unc	BU
2005sm Proof	5,000	Value: 1,000				

KM# 241 100 DOLLARS
31.1030 g., 0.9999 Gold 0.9998 oz. AGW **Subject:** National University of Singapore **Obv:** National arms **Rev:** Person, globe and emblem

Date	Mintage	F	VF	XF	Unc	BU
2005sm Proof	500	Value: 1,100				

KM# 254 100 DOLLARS
31.1030 g., 0.9999 Gold 0.9998 oz. AGW **Series:** Lunar **Subject:** Year of the Dog **Obv:** National arms **Rev:** Stylized dog standing left

Date	Mintage	F	VF	XF	Unc	BU
2006sm Proof	3,000	Value: 1,100				

KM# 268 100 DOLLARS
31.1030 g., 0.9999 Gold 0.9998 oz. AGW **Series:** Lunar **Subject:** Year of the Boar **Obv:** National arms **Rev:** Stylized boar running right

Date	Mintage	F	VF	XF	Unc	BU
2007sm Proof	3,000	Value: 1,250				

KM# 274 100 DOLLARS
31.1030 g., 0.9999 Gold 0.9998 oz. AGW **Series:** Lunar **Subject:** Year of the Rat **Obv:** National arms **Rev:** Stylized rat lying left

Date	Mintage	F	VF	XF	Unc	BU
2008sm Proof	2,000	Value: 1,275				

KM# 239 200 DOLLARS
155.5200 g., 0.9999 Gold 4.9994 oz. AGW, 60 mm. **Series:** Lunar **Subject:** Year of the Rooster **Obv:** National arms **Rev:** Stylized rooster standing right

Date	Mintage	F	VF	XF	Unc	BU
2005sm Proof	200	Value: 4,850				

KM# 255 200 DOLLARS
155.1500 g., 0.9999 Gold 4.9875 oz. AGW **Series:** Lunar **Subject:** Year of the Dog **Obv:** National arms **Rev:** Stylized dog standing left

Date	Mintage	F	VF	XF	Unc	BU
2006sm Proof	200	Value: 4,850				

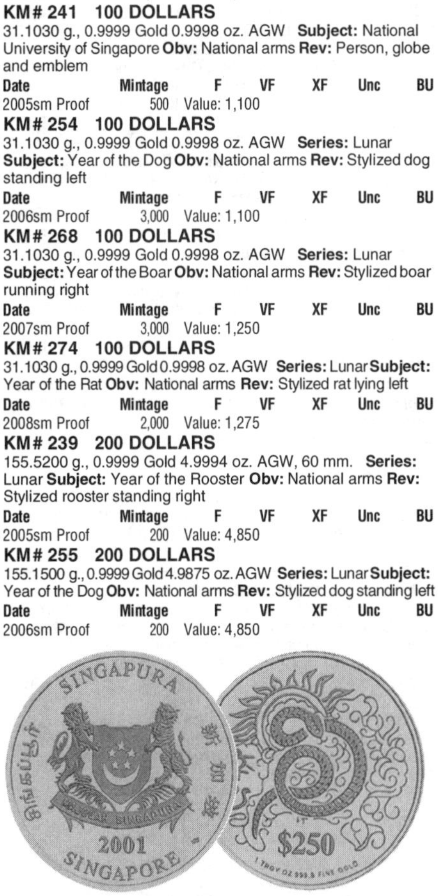

KM# 178 250 DOLLARS
31.1035 g., 0.9990 Gold 0.9990 oz. AGW, 32.1 mm. **Subject:** Year of the Snake **Obv:** National arms **Rev:** Stylized snake **Edge:** Reeded

Date	Mintage	F	VF	XF	Unc	BU
2001sm Proof	7,000	Value: 1,100				

KM# 183 250 DOLLARS
31.1035 g., 0.9999 Gold 0.9999 oz. AGW, 32.1 mm. **Subject:** Year of the Horse **Obv:** National arms **Rev:** Horse **Edge:** Reeded

Date	Mintage	F	VF	XF	Unc	BU
2002sm Proof	7,600	Value: 1,100				

KM# 227 250 DOLLARS
31.1030 g., 0.9999 Gold 0.9998 oz. AGW, 32.1 mm. **Series:** Lunar **Subject:** Year of the Goat **Obv:** National arms **Rev:** Stylized goat standing right facing left

Date	Mintage	F	VF	XF	Unc	BU
2003sm Proof	7,000	Value: 1,000				

KM# 188 250 DOLLARS
31.1030 g., 0.9999 Gold 0.9998 oz. AGW, 32.1 mm. **Series:** Lunar **Subject:** Year of the Monkey **Obv:** National arms **Rev:** Stylized monkey sitting left **Edge:** Reeded

Date	Mintage	F	VF	XF	Unc	BU
2004sm Proof	7,000	Value: 1,150				

KM# 228 500 DOLLARS
155.5200 g., 0.9999 Gold 4.9994 oz. AGW, 55 mm. **Series:** Lunar **Subject:** Year of the Goat **Obv:** National arms **Rev:** Stylized goat standing right facing left

Date	Mintage	F	VF	XF	Unc	BU
2003sm Proof	200	Value: 4,850				

KM# 232 500 DOLLARS
155.5200 g., 0.9999 Gold 4.9994 oz. AGW, 55 mm. **Series:** Lunar **Subject:** Year of the Monkey **Obv:** National arms **Rev:** Stylized monkey sitting left

Date	Mintage	F	VF	XF	Unc	BU
2004sm Proof	200	Value: 4,850				

BULLION COINAGE

KM# 212 DOLLAR
1.5550 g., 0.9999 Gold 0.0500 oz. AGW, 13.9 mm. **Series:** Lunar **Subject:** Year of the Snake **Obv:** National arms **Rev:** Stylized lion's head right, snake privy mark at lower left

Date	Mintage	F	VF	XF	Unc	BU
2001sm Proof	—	—	—	—	—	BV+20

KM# 217 DOLLAR
1.5550 g., 0.9999 Gold 0.0500 oz. AGW, 13.9 mm. **Series:** Lunar **Subject:** Year of the Horse **Obv:** National arms **Rev:** Stylized lion's head right, horse privy mark at lower left

Date	Mintage	F	VF	XF	Unc	BU
2002sm Proof	—	—	—	—	—	BV+20

KM# 213 5 DOLLARS
3.1100 g., 0.9999 Gold 0.1000 oz. AGW, 17.9 mm. **Series:** Lunar **Subject:** Year of the Snake **Obv:** National arms **Rev:** Stylized lion's head right, snake privy mark at lower left

Date	Mintage	F	VF	XF	Unc	BU
2001sm Proof	—	—	—	—	—	BV+15

KM# 218 5 DOLLARS
7.7750 g., 0.9999 Gold 0.2499 oz. AGW, 17.9 mm. **Series:** Lunar **Subject:** Year of the Horse **Obv:** National arms **Rev:** Stylized lion's head right, horse privy mark at lower left

Date	Mintage	F	VF	XF	Unc	BU
2002sm Proof	—	—	—	—	—	BV+10

KM# 214 10 DOLLARS
7.7750 g., 0.9999 Gold 0.2499 oz. AGW, 21.9 mm. **Series:** Lunar **Subject:** Year of the Snake **Obv:** National arms **Rev:** Stylized lion's head right, snake privy mark at lower left

Date	Mintage	F	VF	XF	Unc	BU
2001sm Proof	—	—	—	—	—	BV+10

KM# 219 10 DOLLARS
7.7750 g., 0.9999 Gold 0.2499 oz. AGW, 21.9 mm. **Series:** Lunar **Subject:** Year of the Horse **Obv:** National arms **Rev:** Stylized lion's head right, horse privy mark at lower left

Date	Mintage	F	VF	XF	Unc	BU
2002sm Proof	—	—	—	—	—	BV+10

KM# 215 20 DOLLARS
15.5520 g., 0.9999 Gold 0.4999 oz. AGW, 27 mm. **Series:** Lunar **Subject:** Year of the Snake **Obv:** National arms **Rev:** Stylized lion's head right, snake privy mark at lower left

Date	Mintage	F	VF	XF	Unc	BU
2001sm Proof	—	—	—	—	—	BV+8

KM# 220 20 DOLLARS
15.5520 g., 0.9999 Gold 0.4999 oz. AGW, 27 mm. **Series:** Lunar **Subject:** Year of the Horse **Obv:** National arms **Rev:** Stylized lion's head right, horse privy mark at lower left

Date	Mintage	F	VF	XF	Unc	BU
2002sm Proof	—	—	—	—	—	BV+8

KM# 216 50 DOLLARS
31.1030 g., 0.9999 Gold 0.9998 oz. AGW, 32.1 mm. **Series:** Lunar **Subject:** Year of the Snake **Obv:** National arms **Rev:** Stylized lion's head right, snake privy mark at lower left

Date	Mintage	F	VF	XF	Unc	BU
2001sm Proof	—	—	—	—	—	BV+5

KM# 221 50 DOLLARS
31.1030 g., 0.9999 Gold 0.9998 oz. AGW, 32.1 mm. **Series:** Lunar **Subject:** Year of the Horse **Obv:** National arms **Rev:** Stylized lion's head right, horse privy mark at lower left

Date	Mintage	F	VF	XF	Unc	BU
2002sm Proof	—	—	—	—	—	BV+5

MINT SETS

KM#	Date	Mintage	Identification	Issue Price	Mkt Val
MS39	2002 (7)	—	KM#98-103, 104.3 Hongbao	—	11.00
MS40	2003 (7)	—	KM#98-103, 104.3 Hongbao	—	11.00
MS41	2004 (7)	—	KM#98-103, 104.3 Hongbao	—	11.00
MS42	2005 (7)	—	KM#98-103, 104.3 Hongbao	—	11.00
MS43	2006 (7)	—	KM#98-103, 104.3 Hongbao	—	11.00
MS44	2007 (7)	—	KM98-103, 104.3 Hongbao	10.78	11.00

PROOF SETS

KM#	Date	Mintage	Identification	Issue Price	Mkt Val
PS61	2001 (2)	3,000	KM#179-180 plus copper-nickel ingot	—	100
PS62	2001 (3)	2,000	KM#178-180 plus copper-nickel ingot	—	1,100
PS63	2001 (4)	—	KM#212-215	—	—
PS64	2001 (6)	—	KM#212-216, plus ingot	—	—
PS65	2001 (2)	2,001	KM#177, 177a	—	60.00
PS66	2001 (7)	10,000	KM#98a-103a, 104.2a	—	70.00
PS67	2002 (2)	3,000	KM#182, 182a	—	100
PS68	2002 (3)	2,000	KM#182, 182a, 183	—	1,100
PS69	2002 (2)	2,001	KM#181, 181a	—	60.00
PS70	2002 (3)	2,001	KM#181, 181a, 217	—	100
PS71	2002 (4)	—	KM#217-220	—	—
PS72	2002 (6)	—	KM#217-221 plus ingot	—	—
PS73	2002 (7)	10,000	KM#98a-103a, 104.2a	—	70.00
PS74	2003 (2)	2,003	KM#196, 196a	—	75.00
PS75	2003 (7)	10,000	KM#98a-103a, 104.3a	—	70.00
PS76	2003 (8)	1,000	KM#98a-103a, 104.3a, 196a	—	130
PS77	2003 (2)	88	KM#226, 228	—	5,150
PS78	2003 (2)	3,000	KM#225, 225a	—	100
PS79	2003 (3)	2,000	KM#225, 225a, 227	—	1,100
PS80	2004 (2)	1,000	KM#189, 189a	—	85.00
PS81	2004 (3)	88	KM#185, 189, 189a	—	1,050
PS82	2004 (7)	10,000	KM#98a-103a, 104.3a	—	70.00
PS83	2004 (2)	1,000	KM#184, 184a	—	40.00
PS84	2004 (2)	1,000	KM#190, 190a	—	40.00
PS85	2004 (2)	1,000	KM#191, 191a	—	40.00
PS86	2004 (2)	1,000	KM#192, 192a	—	40.00
PS87	2004 (4)	800	KM#184a, 190a-192a	—	110
PS88	2004 (8)	88	KM#184, 184a, 190, 190a, 191, 191a, 192, 192a	—	150
PS89	2004 (2)	80	KM#231, 232	—	5,150
PS90	2004 (2)	3,000	KM#187, 187a	—	100
PS91	2004 (3)	2,000	KM#187, 187a, 188	—	1,250
PS92	2005 (7)	—	KM#98a-103a, 104.3a	—	70.00
PS93	2005 (2)	3,000	KM#234, 236	—	100
PS94	2005 (2)	88	KM#237, 239	—	5,150
PS95	2005 (3)	2,000	KM#234, 236, 238	—	1,100
PS96	2006 (7)	—	KM#98a-103a, 104.3a	—	70.00
PS97	2006 (2)	8,000	KM#256, 257	—	120
PS98	2007 (7)	—	KM#98a-103a, 104.3a	—	70.00
PS99	2007 (4)	800	KM#259a-262a	—	130
PS100	2007 (2)	8,000	KM#275, 276	90.00	90.00
PS101	2007 (2)	3,000	KM#193, 193a	65.00	65.00

PROOF-LIKE SETS (PL)

KM#	Date	Mintage	Identification	Issue Price	Mkt Val
PL1	2004 (4)	800	KM#184, 190, 191, 192	—	40.00
PL2	2007 (4)	800	KM#259-262	—	50.00

SLOVAKIA

The Republic of Slovakia has an area of 18,923 sq. mi. (49,035 sq. km.) and a population of 4.9 million. Capital: Bratislava. Textiles, steel, and wood products are exported.

MINT MARK

Kremnica Mint

REPUBLIC

STANDARD COINAGE

100 Halierov = 1 Slovak Koruna (Sk)

KM# 17 10 HALIEROV
0.7200 g., Aluminum, 17 mm. **Obv:** Double cross on shield above inscription **Rev:** Church steeple **Edge:** Plain **Designer:** Drahomir Zobek

Date	Mintage	F	VF	XF	Unc	BU
2001	20,330,000	—	—	—	0.35	—
2001 Proof	12,500	Value: 2.50				
2002	37,640,000	—	—	—	0.35	—
2002 Proof	16,100	Value: 1.50				
2003	3,000	—	—	—	2.50	—

Note: Mint sets only

KM# 18 20 HALIEROV
0.9500 g., Aluminum, 19.5 mm. **Obv:** Double cross on shield above inscription **Rev:** Mountain peak and value **Edge:** Reeded **Designer:** Drahomir Zobek

Date	Mintage	F	VF	XF	Unc	BU
2001	21,920,000	—	—	—	0.45	—
2001 Proof	12,500	Value: 2.50				
2002	36,300,000	—	—	—	0.45	—
2002 Proof	16,100	Value: 1.50				
2003	3,000	—	—	—	2.50	—

Note: Mint set only

KM# 35 50 HALIEROV
2.8000 g., Copper Plated Steel, 18.7 mm. **Obv:** Double cross on shield above inscription **Rev:** Watch tower and value **Edge:** Milled and plain **Designer:** Drahomir Zobek

Date	Mintage	F	VF	XF	Unc	BU
2001	10,400,000	—	—	—	0.60	—
2001 Proof	12,500	Value: 2.50				
2002	11,000,000	—	—	—	0.60	—
2002 Proof	16,100	Value: 1.50				
2003	11,000,000	—	—	—	0.60	—
2004	16,500,000	—	—	—	0.60	—
2005	17,000,000	—	—	—	0.60	—
2006	22,050,000	—	—	—	0.60	—
2007	—	—	—	—	0.60	—

KM# 12 KORUNA
3.8500 g., Bronze Clad Steel, 21 mm. **Subject:** 15th Century of Madonna and Child **Obv:** Double cross on shield above inscription **Rev:** Madonna holding child and value **Edge:** Milled **Designer:** Drahomir Zobek

Date	Mintage	F	VF	XF	Unc	BU
2001	12,500	—	—	—	1.50	—
Note: In sets only						
2001 Proof	—	Value: 3.00				
2002	11,000,000	—	—	—	0.75	—
2002 Proof	16,100	Value: 2.50				
2003	14,000	—	—	—	1.50	—
Note: In sets only						
2004	—	—	—	—	1.50	—
Note: In sets only						
2005	10,000,000	—	—	—	0.75	—
2006	9,605,000	—	—	—	0.75	—
2007	—	—	—	—	0.75	—

KM# 13 2 KORUNA
4.4000 g., Nickel Clad Steel, 21.5 mm. **Obv:** Double cross on shield above inscription **Rev:** Venus statue and value **Designer:** Drahomir Zobek

Date	Mintage	F	VF	XF	Unc	BU
2001	10,668,000	—	—	—	0.85	—
2001 Proof	12,500	Value: 5.00				
2002	11,000,000	—	—	—	0.85	—
2002 Proof	16,100	Value: 2.50				
2003	11,000,000	—	—	—	0.85	—
2004	—	—	—	—	2.00	—
Note: In sets only						
2005	—	—	—	—	2.00	—
Note: In sets only						
2006	—	—	—	—	2.00	—
Note: In sets only						
2007	—	—	—	—	2.00	—
Note: In sets only						

KM# 14 5 KORUNA
5.4000 g., Nickel Clad Steel, 24.75 mm. **Obv:** Double cross on shield above inscription **Rev:** Celtic coin of BIATEC at upper left of value **Edge:** Milled **Designer:** Drahomir Zobek

Date	Mintage	F	VF	XF	Unc	BU
2001 Proof	12,500	Value: 6.00				
2002 Proof	16,100	Value: 5.00				
2003	14,000	—	—	—	2.00	—
Note: In sets only						
2004	—	—	—	—	2.00	—
Note: In sets only						
2005	—	—	—	—	2.00	—
Note: In sets only						
2006	—	—	—	—	2.00	—
Note: In sets only						
2007	—	—	—	—	2.00	—
Note: In sets only						

KM# 11.1 10 KORUNA
6.6000 g., Brass, 26.5 mm. **Obv:** Double cross on shield above inscription **Rev:** Bronze cross and value **Designer:** Drahomir Zobek

Date	Mintage	F	VF	XF	Unc	BU
2001 Proof	12,500	Value: 12.50				
2002 Proof	16,100	Value: 10.00				
2003	10,923,000	—	—	—	2.50	—
Note: In sets only						
2004	—	—	—	—	4.00	—
Note: In sets only						
2005	—	—	—	—	4.00	—
Note: In sets only						
2006	—	—	—	—	4.00	—
Note: In sets only						
2007	—	—	—	—	4.00	—

KM# 67 20 KORUN
24.4800 g., 0.9250 Silver 0.7280 oz. ASW, 27.1 x 50.6 mm. **Series:** Banknotes **Obv:** Prince Pribina (800-861) **Rev:** Nitra Castle **Edge:** Plain

Date	Mintage	F	VF	XF	Unc	BU
2003 Proof	6,000	Value: 20.00				

KM# 68 50 KORUN
26.6300 g., 0.9250 Silver 0.7919 oz. ASW, 28.2 x 52.8 mm. **Series:** Banknotes **Obv:** Saints Cyril and Methodius (814-885) **Rev:** Two hands **Edge:** Plain

Date	Mintage	F	VF	XF	Unc	BU
2003 Proof	6,000	Value: 25.00				

KM# 69 100 KORUN
28.8700 g., 0.9250 Silver 0.8585 oz. ASW, 29.3 x 55 mm. **Series:** Banknotes **Obv:** The Levoca Madonna **Rev:** St. James Church in Levoca **Edge:** Plain

Date	Mintage	F	VF	XF	Unc	BU
2003 Proof	—	Value: 30.00				

KM# 59 200 KORUN
20.0000 g., 0.7500 Silver 0.4822 oz. ASW, 34 mm. **Subject:** Alexander Dubcek **Obv:** Double cross on shield and tree **Obv. Designer:** Anton Gabrik **Rev:** Head left **Rev. Designer:** Ladislav Kozak **Edge Lettering:** BUDSKOST SLOBODA DEMOKRACIA

Date	Mintage	F	VF	XF	Unc	BU
2001	12,800	—	—	—	15.00	—
2001 Proof	3,000	Value: 50.00				

Note: Unc. examples without edge lettering exist. Value $800.00.

KM# 60 200 KORUN
20.0000 g., 0.7500 Silver 0.4822 oz. ASW, 34 mm. **Subject:** Ludovit Fulla **Obv:** Modern art **Rev:** Head facing in national colstume, value and dates **Edge:** Lettered **Designer:** Emil Fulka **Note:** 1,800 pieces melted.

Date	Mintage	F	VF	XF	Unc	BU
2002	11,300	—	—	—	20.00	—
2002 Proof	2,400	Value: 35.00				

KM# 62 200 KORUN
20.3500 g., 0.7500 Silver 0.4907 oz. ASW, 34 mm. **Subject:** UNESCO World Heritage site - Vlkolínec **Obv:** Log building and double cross on shield **Rev:** Wooden tower and value **Edge Lettering:** WORLD HERITAGE PATRIMONE MONDIAL **Designer:** Pavol Karoly **Note:** 900 pieces melted.

Date	Mintage	F	VF	XF	Unc	BU
2002	11,500	—	—	—	15.00	—
2002 Proof	2,800	Value: 35.00				

KM# 66 200 KORUN
20.0000 g., 0.7500 Silver 0.4822 oz. ASW, 34 mm. **Obv:** Building below double cross within shield **Rev:** Head facing and value **Edge:** Lettered **Edge Lettering:** VYTRVALOST A VERNOST NARODNEMU IDEALU **Note:** 500 pieces uncirculated melted.

Date	Mintage	F	VF	XF	Unc	BU
2003	8,800	—	—	—	15.00	—
2003 Proof	2,700	Value: 30.00				

KM# 65 200 KORUN
20.0000 g., 0.7500 Silver 0.4822 oz. ASW, 34 mm. **Subject:** Imrich Karvas **Obv:** Building, national arms and value **Rev:** Portrait **Edge:** Lettered **Edge Lettering:** NARODOHOSPODAR HUMANISTA EUROPAN **Designer:** Miroslav Ronai **Note:** 500 pieces uncirculated melted.

Date	Mintage	F	VF	XF	Unc	BU
2003	9,800	—	—	—	15.00	—
2003 Proof	3,000	Value: 30.00				

KM# 70 200 KORUN
31.2100 g., 0.9250 Silver 0.9281 oz. ASW, 30.4 x 57.2 mm. **Series:** Banknotes **Obv:** Head facing and value **Rev:** 18th Century city view and value **Edge:** Plain

Date	Mintage	F	VF	XF	Unc	BU
2003 Proof	6,000	Value: 37.50				

KM# 75 200 KORUN
20.0000 g., 0.7500 Silver 0.4822 oz. ASW, 34 mm. **Obv:** Kempelen's Chess Machine (1770) **Rev:** Inventor Wolfgang Kemelen (1734-1804) above Bratislava city view **Edge Lettering:** VYNALEZCA - TECHNIK - KONSTRUKTER **Designer:** Miroslav Ronai

Date	Mintage	F	VF	XF	Unc	BU
2004	8,000	—	—	—	15.00	—
2004 Proof	3,200	Value: 35.00				

KM# 76 200 KORUN
20.0000 g., 0.7500 Silver 0.4822 oz. ASW, 34 mm. **Obv:** Church and town hall below double cross within shield **Rev:** Aerial view of Bardejov circa 1768 **Edge Lettering:** WORLD HERITAGE - PATRIMOINE MONDIAL **Designer:** Jan Cernaj

Date	Mintage	F	VF	XF	Unc	BU
2004	8,400	—	—	—	15.00	—
2004 Proof	3,600	Value: 35.00				

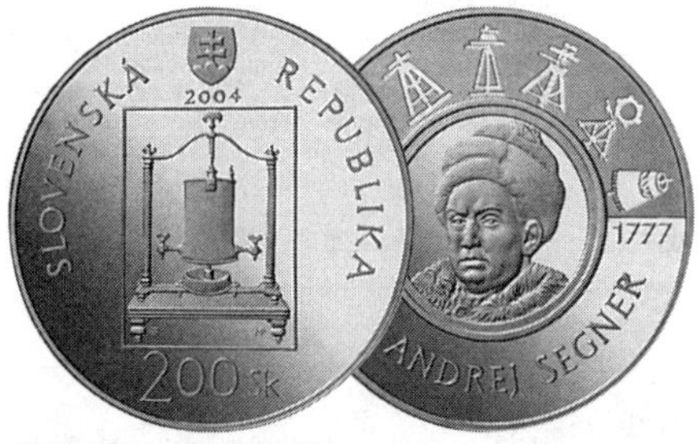

KM# 77 200 KORUN
18.0000 g., 0.9000 Silver 0.5208 oz. ASW, 34 mm. **Obv:** "The Segner Wheel" model **Rev:** Bust with fur hat facing within circle of designs **Edge Lettering:** VYNALEZCA - FYZIK - MATEMATIK - PEDAGOG **Designer:** Maria Poldaufova

Date	Mintage	F	VF	XF	Unc	BU
2004	10,500	—	—	—	15.00	—
2004 Proof	4,700	Value: 30.00				

KM# 78 200 KORUN
20.0000 g., 0.7500 Silver 0.4822 oz. ASW, 34 mm. **Subject:** Slovakian entry into the European Union **Obv:** Circle of stars in arch above national arms **Rev:** Map in arch above value **Edge Lettering:** ROZSIRENIE EUROPSKEJ UNIE O DESAT KRAJIN **Designer:** Patrik Kovacovsky

Date	Mintage	F	VF	XF	Unc	BU
2004	10,100	—	—	—	15.00	—
2004 Proof	4,700	Value: 30.00				

KM# 81 200 KORUN
18.0000 g., 0.9000 Silver 0.5208 oz. ASW, 34 mm. **Subject:** Leopold I Coronation 350th Anniversary **Obv:** Value and partial castle view **Rev:** Coin design of Leopold I in large size legend **Edge Lettering:** BRATISLAVSKE KORUNOVACIE **Designer:** Maria Poldaufova

Date	Mintage	F	VF	XF	Unc	BU
2005	8,900	—	—	—	—	20.00
2005 Proof	4,800	Value: 40.00				

KM# 82 200 KORUN
18.0000 g., 0.9000 Silver 0.5208 oz. ASW, 34 mm. **Subject:** Treaty of Pressburg **Obv:** Primate's Palace behind French military standard **Rev:** Napoleon and Francis I of Austria **Edge Lettering:** 26 DECEMBER. 5 MIVOSE AN 14 **Designer:** Pavel Karoly

Date	Mintage	F	VF	XF	Unc	BU
2005	5,100	—	—	—	—	20.00
2005 Proof	3,400	Value: 40.00				

KM# 87 200 KORUN
18.0000 g., 0.9000 Silver 0.5208 oz. ASW, 34 mm. **Subject:** 200th Anniversary Birth of Karol Kuzmány **Obv:** Small national arms at upper left, denomination at center **Obv. Inscription:** SLOVENSKÁ / REPUBLIKA **Rev:** Partial medallic head of Kuzmány facing

Date	Mintage	F	VF	XF	Unc	BU
2006	—	—	—	—	20.00	—

KM# 88 200 KORUN
18.0000 g., 0.9000 Silver 0.5208 oz. ASW, 34 mm. **Subject:** 100th Anniversary Birth of Andrej Kmet **Obv:** Small national arms above stylized M-shaped memorial representing the Slovak Museum. **Obv. Legend:** SLOVENSKÁ REPUBLIKA **Obv. Designer:** Stefan Novotny **Rev:** Head of Kmet 3/4 left **Rev. Designer:** Dalibor Schmidt **Edge:** Lettered **Edge Lettering:** POZNÁVAJME KRAJE SVOJE A POZNÁME SAMYCH SEBA

Date	Mintage	F	VF	XF	Unc	BU
2008	8,500	—	—	—	20.00	—

KM# 56 500 KORUN
33.6300 g., 0.9250 Silver 1.0000 oz. ASW, 40 mm. **Subject:** Mala Fatra National Park **Obv:** National arms center of cross formed by beetles **Rev:** Orchid with mountain background **Edge Lettering:** OCHRANA PRIRODY A KRAJINY **Designer:** Patrik Kovacovsky **Note:** 400 pieces uncirculated melted.

Date	Mintage	F	VF	XF	Unc	BU
2001	10,200	—	—	—	45.00	—
2001 Proof	1,800	Value: 65.00				

KM# 57 500 KORUN
31.1035 g., 0.9990 Silver 0.9990 oz. ASW, 45 mm. **Subject:** Third Millennium **Obv:** "The Universe" **Rev:** Three hands **Edge:** Plain **Shape:** 3-sided **Designer:** Patrik Kovacovsky **Note:** 400 pieces uncirculated melted.

Date	Mintage	F	VF	XF	Unc	BU
2001	13,000	—	—	—	45.00	—
2001 Proof	4,000	Value: 65.00				

KM# 71 500 KORUN
33.6300 g., 0.9250 Silver 1.0000 oz. ASW, 31.5 x 59.4 mm. **Series:** Banknotes **Obv:** Head facing and value **Rev:** Bratislava Castle view and value **Edge:** Plain

Date	Mintage	F	VF	XF	Unc	BU
2003 Proof	6,000	Value: 40.00				

KM# 85 500 KORUN
33.6300 g., 0.9250 Silver 1.0000 oz. ASW, 40 mm. **Subject:** Slovensky Kras National Park **Obv:** Two Emberiza cia birds above value **Rev:** Dogs Tooth violet flowers in front of Karst cave interior view **Edge Lettering:** OCHRANA PRIRODY A KRAJINY **Designer:** Maria Poldaufova

Date	Mintage	F	VF	XF	Unc	BU
2005	8,500	—	—	—	—	40.00
2005 Proof	3,600	Value: 60.00				

KM# 84 500 KORUN
33.6300 g., 0.9250 Silver 1.0000 oz. ASW, 40 mm. **Subject:** Muranska Planina National Park **Obv:** Wildflowers and Muran castle ruins **Rev:** Two wild horses **Edge Lettering:** OCHRANA PRIRODY A KRAJINY [flower] **Designer:** Karol Licko

Date	Mintage	F	VF	XF	Unc	BU
2006	4,300	—	—	—	—	40.00
2006 Proof	2,800	Value: 60.00				

KM# 86 500 KORUN
33.6300 g., 0.9250 Silver 1.0000 oz. ASW, 40 mm. **Subject:** 450th Anniversary - Construction Fortress at Komárno **Obv:** Early ships, fortress in background, national arms at lower right **Obv. Legend:** SLOVENSKÁ REPUBLIKA **Obv. Designer:** Karol Licko **Rev:** Layout of fortress, horses in battle against Turks below **Rev. Legend:** PEVNOST - KOMÁRNO **Rev. Designer:** Mária Poldaufová **Edge Lettering:** NEC ARTE NEC MARTE - COMORRA in relief

Date	Mintage	F	VF	XF	Unc	BU
2007	4,600	—	—	—	40.00	—
2007 Proof	2,600	Value: 65.00				

KM# 63 1000 KORUN
62.2070 g., 0.9990 Silver 1.9979 oz. ASW, 43.6 x 43.6 mm. **Subject:** 10th Anniversary of Republic **Obv:** National arms between hands **Rev:** Value above map **Edge:** Segmented reeding **Shape:** Square **Designer:** Milos Vavro

Date	Mintage	F	VF	XF	Unc	BU
2003 Proof	10,000	Value: 65.00				

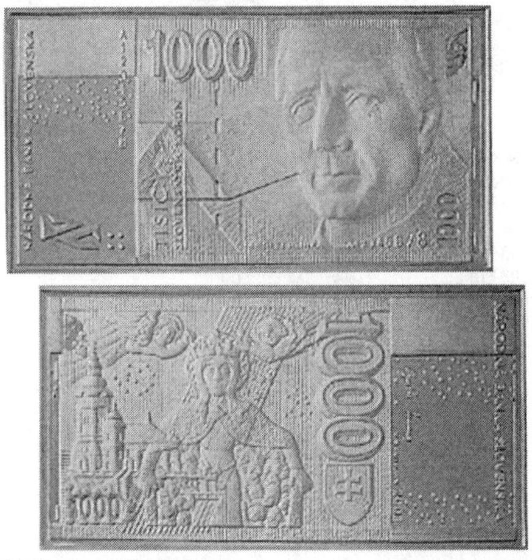

KM# 72 1000 KORUN
43.9100 g., Bi-Metallic Gold And Silver .925 Silver 43.91g with .999 Gold .28g insert, 32.6 x 61.6 mm. **Series:** Banknotes **Obv:** Head facing and value **Rev:** The Madonna Protector facing and church of Liptovske Sliace **Edge:** Plain **Note:** Illustration reduced.

Date	Mintage	F	VF	XF	Unc	BU
2003 Proof	6,000	Value: 70.00				

KM# 58 5000 KORUN
Tri-Metallic 31.1035, .999 Silver, 1.00 oz ASW with 6.22, .999 Gold, .20 oz AGW and .31, .999 Platinum, .10 oz. APW, 50 mm. **Series:** Third Millennium **Obv:** "The Universe" **Rev:** Three hands **Edge:** Plain **Shape:** Triangular **Designer:** Patrik Kovacovsky

Date	Mintage	F	VF	XF	Unc	BU
2001 Proof	8,000	Value: 400				

KM# 61 5000 KORUN
9.5000 g., 0.9000 Gold 0.2749 oz. AGW, 26 mm. **Subject:** Vikolinec village - UNESCO historic site **Obv:** Enclosed communal well **Rev:** Window and fence **Edge:** Reeded **Designer:** Maria Poldaufova

Date	Mintage	F	VF	XF	Unc	BU
2002 Proof	7,200	Value: 325				

KM# 73 5000 KORUN
47.6340 g., Bi-Metallic Gold And Silver .925 Silver 46.65g with two .9999 Gold inserts .964g in total, 33.4 x 63.8 mm. **Series:** Banknotes **Obv:** Head facing and value **Rev:** Stefanik's grave monument **Edge:** Plain **Note:** Illustration reduced.

Date	Mintage	F	VF	XF	Unc	BU
2003 Proof	6,000	Value: 125				

KM# 80 5000 KORUN
9.5000 g., 0.9000 Gold 0.2749 oz. AGW, 26 mm. **Subject:** Bardejov - UNESCO historic site **Obv:** National arms and value left of Town Hall **Rev:** Zachariah in window frame left of St. Aegidius Church, Bardejov **Edge:** Reeded

Date	Mintage	F	VF	XF	Unc	BU
2004 Proof	9,000	Value: 300				

KM# 83 5000 KORUN
9.5000 g., 0.9000 Gold 0.2749 oz. AGW, 26 mm. **Subject:** Leopold I Coronation **Obv:** Mounted Herald with Bratislava Castile in background **Rev:** Leopold I and Crown of St. Stephan **Edge:** Reeded

Date	Mintage	F	VF	XF	Unc	BU
2005 Proof	7,500	Value: 350				

KM# 64 10000 KORUN
18.8350 g., Bi-Metallic 1.555g, .999 Palladium round center in a 15.55g, .900 Gold square, 29.5 x 29.5 mm. **Subject:** 10th Anniversary of the Republic **Obv:** Young head left within circular inscription above double cross within shield **Rev:** Bratislava castle above value **Edge:** Segmented reeding **Shape:** Square **Designer:** Ludmila Cvengrosova

Date	Mintage	F	VF	XF	Unc	BU
2003 Proof	6,000	Value: 750				

KM# 79 10000 KORUN
24.8828 g., Bi-Metallic .999 Gold 12.4414g 23mm round center in .999 Palladium 12.4414g 40mm pentagon, 40 mm. **Subject:** Slovakian entry into the European Union **Obv:** National arms above date in center **Obv. Designer:** Stefan Novotny **Rev:** European map with entry date **Rev. Designer:** Jan Cernaj **Edge:** Plain

Date	Mintage	F	VF	XF	Unc	BU
2004 Proof	7,200	Value: 800				

MINT SETS

KM#	Date	Mintage	Identification	Issue Price	Mkt Val
MS9	2001 (7)	—	KM#11.1-14, 17-18, 35, plus medal	—	12.00
MS10	2002 (7)	—	KM#11-1-14, 17-18, 35, plus medal	—	12.00
MS11	2003 (7)	—	KM#11.1-14, 17-18, 35, plus medal	—	12.00

PROOF SETS

KM#	Date	Mintage	Identification	Issue Price	Mkt Val
PS2	2001 (7)	12,500	KM#11.1-14, 17-18, 35	—	30.00
PS3	2002 (7)	16,500	KM#11.1-14, 17-18, 35	—	25.00

SLOVENIA

The Republic of Slovenia is located northwest of Yugoslavia in the valleys of the Danube River. It has an area of 7,819 sq. mi. and a population of *1.9 million. Capital: Ljubljana. Agriculture is the main industry with large amounts of hops and fodder crops grown as well as many varieties of fruit trees. Sheep raising, timber production and the mining of mercury from one of the country's oldest mines are also very important to the economy. Slovenia joined the European Union in May 2004.

MINT MARKS
Based on last digit in date.
(K) - Kremnitz (Slovakia): open 4, upturned 5
(BP) - Budapest (Hungary): closed 4, down-turned 5

MONETARY SYSTEM
100 Stotinov = 1 Tolar
100 Euro Cents = 1 Euro

REPUBLIC

STANDARD COINAGE

100 Stotinow = 1 Tolar

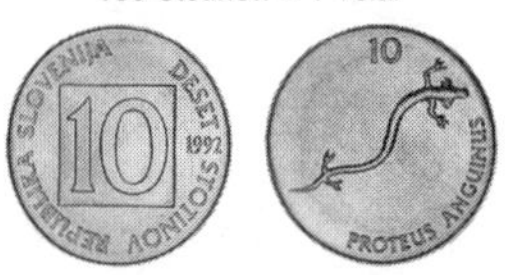

KM# 7 10 STOTINOV
0.5500 g., Aluminum, 16 mm. **Obv:** Value within square **Rev:** Olm salamander **Edge:** Plain **Note:** Varieties exist.

Date	Mintage	F	VF	XF	Unc	BU
2001	1,000	—	—	—	—	3.00
Note: In sets only						
2001 Proof	800	Value: 5.00				

Date	Mintage	F	VF	XF	Unc	BU
2002	1,000	—	—	—	—	3.00
Note: In sets only						
2002 Proof	800	Value: 5.00				
2003	1,000	—	—	—	—	3.00
Note: In sets only						
2003 Proof	800	Value: 5.00				
2004	1,000	—	—	—	—	3.00
Note: In sets only						
2004 Proof	800	Value: 5.00				
2005	3,000	—	—	—	—	2.00
Note: In sets only						
2005 Proof	1,000	Value: 5.00				
2006	4,000	—	—	—	—	2.00
Note: In sets only						
2006 Proof	1,000	Value: 5.00				

KM# 8 20 STOTINOV

0.7000 g., Aluminum, 18 mm. **Obv:** Value within square **Rev:** Small owl and value **Edge:** Plain

Date	Mintage	F	VF	XF	Unc	BU
2001	1,000	—	—	—	—	4.00
Note: In sets only						
2001 Proof	800	Value: 6.00				
2002	1,000	—	—	—	—	4.00
Note: In sets only						
2002 Proof	800	Value: 6.00				
2003	1,000	—	—	—	—	4.00
Note: In sets only						
2003 Proof	800	Value: 6.00				
2004	1,000	—	—	—	—	4.00
Note: In sets only						
2004 Proof	500	Value: 6.00				
2005	3,000	—	—	—	—	3.00
Note: In sets only						
2005 Proof	1,000	Value: 6.00				
2006	4,000	—	—	—	—	3.00
Note: In sets only						
2006 Proof	1,000	Value: 6.00				

KM# 3 50 STOTINOV

0.8500 g., Aluminum, 19.9 mm. **Obv:** Value within square **Rev:** Bee and value **Edge:** Plain

Date	Mintage	F	VF	XF	Unc	BU
2001	1,000	—	—	—	—	6.00
Note: In sets only						
2001 Proof	800	Value: 7.50				
2002	1,000	—	—	—	—	6.00
Note: In sets only						
2002 Proof	800	Value: 7.50				
2003	1,000	—	—	—	—	6.00
Note: In sets only						
2003 Proof	800	Value: 7.50				
2004	1,000	—	—	—	—	6.00
Note: In sets only						
2004 Proof	500	Value: 12.00				
2005	3,000	—	—	—	—	4.00
Note: In sets only						
2005 Proof	1,000	Value: 7.00				
2006	4,000	—	—	—	—	4.00
Note: In sets only						
2006 Proof	1,000	Value: 7.00				

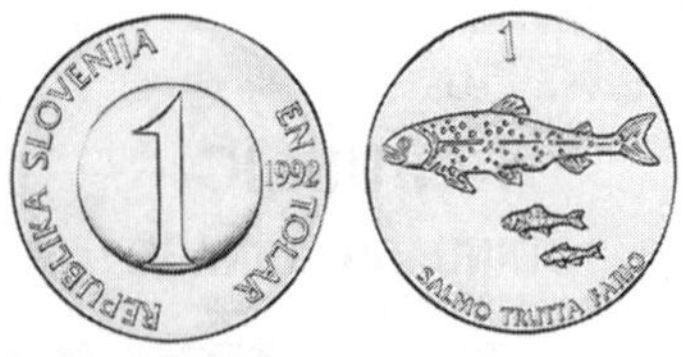

KM# 4 TOLAR

4.5000 g., Brass, 21.9 mm. **Obv:** Value within circle **Rev:** Three brown trout **Edge:** Reeded **Note:** Date varieties exist: 1994 = closed or open "4"; 1995 = serif up and serif down in "5".

Date	Mintage	F	VF	XF	Unc	BU
2001	10,001,000	—	—	—	0.75	1.25
2001 Proof	800	Value: 7.50				
2002	1,000	—	—	—	—	5.00
Note: In sets only						
2002 Proof	800	Value: 7.50				
2003	1,000	—	—	—	—	5.00
Note: In sets only						
2003 Proof	800	Value: 7.50				
2004	10,001,000	—	—	—	0.75	1.25

Date	Mintage	F	VF	XF	Unc	BU
2004 (K)	1,000	—	—	—	—	5.00
Note: 4 open to right; in sets only						
2004 Proof	500	Value: 8.50				
2005	3,000	—	—	—	—	4.00
Note: In sets only						
2005 Proof	1,000	Value: 7.50				
2006	4,000	—	—	—	—	4.00
Note: In sets only						
2006 Proof	1,000	Value: 7.50				

KM# 5 2 TOLARJA

5.4000 g., Brass, 24 mm. **Obv:** Value within circle **Rev:** Barn swallow in flight **Edge:** Reeded **Note:** Date varieties exist: 1994 = closed or open "4"; 1995 = serif up and serif down in "5".

Date	Mintage	F	VF	XF	Unc	BU
2001	10,001,000	—	—	—	0.75	1.75
2001 Proof	800	Value: 8.50				
2002	1,000	—	—	—	—	7.00
Note: In sets only						
2002 Proof	800	Value: 8.50				
2003	1,000	—	—	—	—	7.00
Note: In sets only						
2003 Proof	800	Value: 8.50				
2004	10,001,000	—	—	—	0.75	1.50
2004 Proof	500	Value: 8.50				
2005	3,000	—	—	—	—	7.00
Note: In sets only						
2005 Proof	1,000	Value: 8.50				
2006	4,000	—	—	—	—	7.00
Note: In sets only						
2006 Proof	1,000	Value: 8.50				

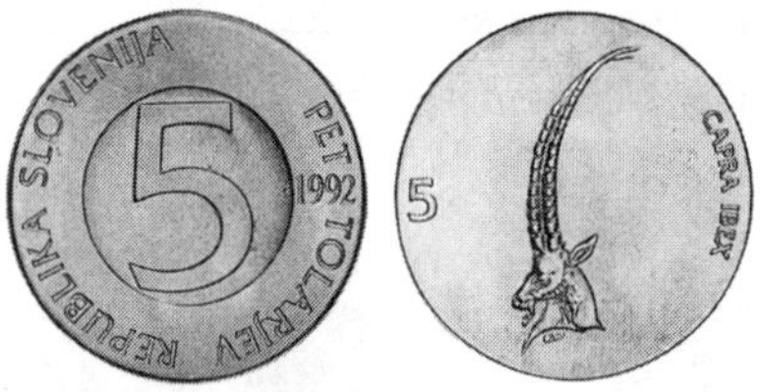

KM# 6 5 TOLARJEV

6.3900 g., Brass, 26 mm. **Obv:** Value within circle **Rev:** Head and horns of ibex **Edge:** Reeded **Note:** Date varieties exist: 1994 = closed or open "4"; 1995 = serif up and serif down in "5".

Date	Mintage	F	VF	XF	Unc	BU
2001	1,000	—	—	—	—	8.00
Note: In sets only						
2001 Proof	800	Value: 10.00				
2002	1,000	—	—	—	—	8.00
Note: In sets only						
2002 Proof	800	Value: 10.00				
2003	1,000	—	—	—	—	8.00
Note: In sets only						
2003 Proof	800	Value: 10.00				
2004	1,000	—	—	—	—	8.00
Note: In sets only						
2004 Proof	500	Value: 15.00				
2005	3,000	—	—	—	—	7.00
Note: In sets only						
2005 Proof	1,000	Value: 10.00				
2006	4,000	—	—	—	—	7.00
Note: In sets only						
2006 Proof	1,000	Value: 10.00				

KM# 41 10 TOLARJEV

5.7500 g., Copper Nickel, 22 mm. **Obv:** Value within circle **Rev:** Stylized rearing horse **Edge:** Reeded

Date	Mintage	F	VF	XF	Unc	BU
2001	29,441,000	—	—	—	1.00	2.00
2001 Proof	800	Value: 12.00				
2002	10,037,000	—	—	—	1.00	2.00
2002 Proof	800	Value: 12.00				
2003	1,000	—	—	—	—	4.00
Note: In sets only						
2003 Proof	800	Value: 12.00				
2004	10,001,000	—	—	—	1.00	2.00
2004 Proof	500	Value: 12.00				
2005	6,003,000	—	—	—	1.00	2.00
2005 Proof	1,000	Value: 12.00				

Date	Mintage	F	VF	XF	Unc	BU
2006	6,001,000	—	—	—	1.00	2.00
2006 Proof	1,000	Value: 12.00				

KM# 51 20 TOLARJEV

6.8500 g., Copper-Nickel, 24 mm. **Obv:** Value within circle **Rev:** White Stork **Edge:** Reeded

Date	Mintage	F	VF	XF	Unc	BU
2003	10,001,000	—	—	—	3.50	5.00
2003 Proof	800	Value: 15.00				
2004	5,001,000	—	—	—	3.00	5.00
2004 Proof	500	Value: 15.00				
2005	8,003,000	—	—	—	3.50	5.00
2005 Proof	1,000	Value: 15.00				
2006	4,004,000	—	—	—	3.50	5.00
2006 Proof	1,000	Value: 15.00				

KM# 52 50 TOLARJEV

8.0000 g., Copper-Nickel, 26 mm. **Obv:** Value within circle **Rev:** Stylized bull **Edge:** Reeded and plain sections

Date	Mintage	F	VF	XF	Unc	BU
2003	10,001,000	—	—	—	2.00	4.00
2003 Proof	800	Value: 12.00				
2004	5,001,000	—	—	—	2.00	4.00
2004 Proof	500	Value: 15.00				
2005	8,003,000	—	—	—	2.00	4.00
2005 Proof	1,000	Value: 12.00				
2006	4,000	—	—	—	—	6.00
Note: In sets only						
2006 Proof	1,000	Value: 12.00				

KM# 42 100 TOLARJEV

9.1000 g., Copper-Nickel, 28 mm. **Subject:** 10th Anniversary of Slovenia and the Tolar **Obv:** Value **Rev:** Tree rings and inscription **Edge:** Reeded

Date	Mintage	F	VF	XF	Unc	BU
2001	500,000	—	—	—	3.00	4.00
2001 Proof	800	Value: 10.00				

KM# 45 500 TOLARJEV

8.5400 g., Bi-Metallic Copper-Nickel center in Brass ring, 28.1 mm. **Subject:** Soccer **Obv:** Value **Rev:** Soccer player and radiant sun **Edge:** Reeded

Date	Mintage	F	VF	XF	Unc	BU
2002	500,000	—	—	—	5.50	7.50
2002 Proof	800	Value: 12.50				

KM# 50 500 TOLARJEV

8.7200 g., Bi-Metallic Copper-Nickel center in Brass ring, 27.9 mm. **Subject:** European Year of the Disabled **Obv:** Stylized wheelchair **Rev:** Value **Edge:** Reeded

Date	Mintage	F	VF	XF	Unc	BU
2003	200,000	—	—	—	6.00	8.00
2003 Proof	800	Value: 13.50				

KM# 57 500 TOLARJEV

8.6000 g., Bi-Metallic Copper-Nickel center in Brass ring, 28 mm. **Obv:** Value **Rev:** Profile left looking down within mathematical graph **Edge:** Reeded

Date	Mintage	F	VF	XF	Unc	BU
2004	200,000	—	—	—	6.00	8.00
2004 Proof	500	Value: 20.00				

KM# 63 500 TOLARJEV

8.6500 g., Bi-Metallic Copper-Nickel center in Brass ring, 27.9 mm. **Obv:** Perched falcon and value **Rev:** Horizontal line in center divides partial suns **Edge:** Reeded

Date	Mintage	F	VF	XF	Unc	BU
2005	103,000	—	—	—	6.25	8.50
2005	1,000	Value: 12.00				

KM# 65 500 TOLARJEV

8.6000 g., Bi-Metallic Copper-Nickel center in Brass ring, 28 mm. **Obv:** Value **Rev:** Anton Tomaz Linhart's silhouette above life dates **Edge:** Reeded

Date	Mintage	F	VF	XF	Unc	BU
2006	104,000	—	—	—	—	6.00
2006 Proof	1,000	Value: 12.00				

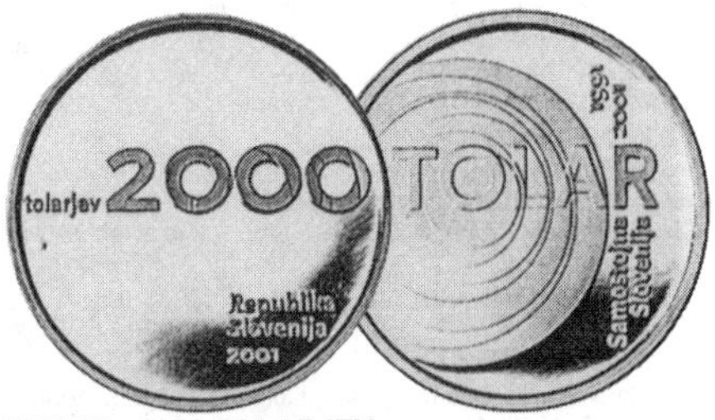

KM# 43 2000 TOLARJEV

15.0000 g., 0.9250 Silver 0.4461 oz. ASW, 32 mm. **Subject:** 10th Anniversary of Slovenia and the Tolar **Obv:** Value **Rev:** Tree rings and inscription **Edge:** Reeded

Date	Mintage	F	VF	XF	Unc	BU
2001 Proof	3,000	Value: 35.00				

KM# 46 2500 TOLARJEV

15.0000 g., 0.9250 Silver 0.4461 oz. ASW, 32 mm. **Subject:** Soccer **Obv:** Value **Rev:** Soccer player and radiant sun **Edge:** Reeded

Date	Mintage	F	VF	XF	Unc	BU
2002 Proof	2,500	Value: 35.00				

KM# 48 2500 TOLARJEV

15.0000 g., 0.9250 Silver 0.4461 oz. ASW, 32 mm. **Subject:** 35th Chess Olympiad **Obv:** Rearing horse and reflection **Rev:** Chess pieces in starting positions and reflection **Edge:** Reeded **Designer:** MNiljenko Licul and Jan Cernaj

Date	Mintage	F	VF	XF	Unc	BU
2002 Proof	1,000	Value: 40.00				

KM# 53 2500 TOLARJEV

15.0000 g., 0.9250 Silver 0.4461 oz. ASW, 32 mm. **Subject:** European Year of the Disabled **Obv:** Value **Rev:** Stylized wheel chair **Edge:** Reeded

Date	Mintage	F	VF	XF	Unc	BU
2003 Proof	1,500	Value: 30.00				

KM# 55 5000 TOLARJEV

15.0000 g., 0.9250 Silver 0.4461 oz. ASW, 32 mm. **Subject:** 60th Anniversary of the Slovenian Assembly **Obv:** Value in partial star design **Rev:** Dates in partial star design **Edge:** Reeded

Date	Mintage	F	VF	XF	Unc	BU
2003 Proof	1,500	Value: 35.00				

KM# 58 5000 TOLARJEV

15.0000 g., 0.9250 Silver 0.4461 oz. ASW, 32 mm. **Obv:** Value **Rev:** Facial profile left looking down within mathematical graph **Edge:** Reeded

Date	Mintage	F	VF	XF	Unc	BU
2004 Proof	1,500	Value: 50.00				

KM# 60 5000 TOLARJEV

15.0000 g., 0.9250 Silver 0.4461 oz. ASW, 32 mm. **Subject:** 1000th Anniversary Town of Bled **Obv:** Value **Rev:** Castle and towers silhouette **Edge:** Reeded

Date	Mintage	F	VF	XF	Unc	BU
2004 Proof	1,500	Value: 50.00				

KM# 62 5000 TOLARJEV

15.1000 g., 0.9250 Silver 0.4490 oz. ASW, 32 mm. **Subject:** Slovenian Film Centennial **Obv:** Value above a director's clapboard **Rev:** Film segment **Edge:** Reeded

Date	Mintage	F	VF	XF	Unc	BU
2005 Proof	—	Value: 45.00				

KM# 64 5000 TOLARJEV

15.1000 g., 0.9250 Silver 0.4490 oz. ASW, 32 mm. **Obv:** Perched falcon above value **Rev:** Diagonal center line divides partial suns **Edge:** Reeded

Date	Mintage	F	VF	XF	Unc	BU
2005 Proof	—	Value: 45.00				

KM# 44 20000 TOLARJEV

7.0000 g., 0.9000 Gold 0.2025 oz. AGW, 24 mm. **Subject:** 10th Anniversary of Slovenia and the Tolar **Obv:** Value **Rev:** Tree rings and inscription **Edge:** Reeded

Date	Mintage	F	VF	XF	Unc	BU
2001 Proof	1,000	Value: 275				

KM# 47 20000 TOLARJEV

7.0000 g., 0.9000 Gold 0.2025 oz. AGW, 24 mm. **Subject:** World Cup Soccer **Obv:** Value **Rev:** Soccer player and rising sun **Edge:** Reeded

Date	Mintage	F	VF	XF	Unc	BU
2002 Proof	500	Value: 275				

KM# 49 20000 TOLARJEV

7.0000 g., 0.9000 Gold 0.2025 oz. AGW, 24 mm. **Subject:** 35th Chess Olympiad **Obv:** Rearing horse and reflection **Rev:** Chess pieces in starting positions and reflection **Edge:** Reeded

Date	Mintage	F	VF	XF	Unc	BU
2002 Proof	500	Value: 300				

KM# 54 25000 TOLARJEV

7.0000 g., 0.9000 Gold 0.2025 oz. AGW, 24 mm. **Subject:** European Year of the Disabled **Obv:** Value **Rev:** Stylized wheel chair **Edge:** Reeded

Date	Mintage	F	VF	XF	Unc	BU
2003 Proof	300	Value: 300				

KM# 56 25000 TOLARJEV
7.0000 g., 0.9000 Gold 0.2025 oz. AGW, 24 mm. **Subject:** 60th Anniversary of the Slovenian Assembly **Obv:** Value in partial star design **Rev:** Dates in partial star design **Edge:** Reeded

Date	Mintage	F	VF	XF	Unc	BU
2003 Proof	300	Value: 300				

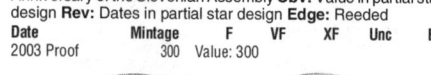

KM# 59 25000 TOLARJEV
7.0000 g., 0.9000 Gold 0.2025 oz. AGW, 24 mm. **Subject:** 250th Anniversary of Jurij Vega's Birth **Obv:** Value **Rev:** Facial profile left looking down within mathematical graph **Edge:** Reeded

Date	Mintage	F	VF	XF	Unc	BU
2004 Proof	300	Value: 300				

KM# 61 25000 TOLARJEV
7.0000 g., 0.9000 Gold 0.2025 oz. AGW, 24 mm. **Subject:** 1000th Anniversary Town of Bled **Obv:** Value **Rev:** Castle and towers silhouette **Edge:** Reeded

Date	Mintage	F	VF	XF	Unc	BU
2004 Proof	300	Value: 300				

KM# 66 25000 TOLARJEV
7.0000 g., 0.9000 Gold 0.2025 oz. AGW, 24 mm. **Subject:** Centennial of Slovene Sokol Association **Obv:** Perched falcon above value **Rev:** Rising sun and reflection **Edge:** Reeded

Date	Mintage	F	VF	XF	Unc	BU
2005 Proof	1,000	Value: 300				

KM# 67 25000 TOLARJEV
7.0000 g., 0.9000 Gold 0.2025 oz. AGW, 24 mm. **Subject:** Centennial of Slovene Film **Obv:** Value above clapboard **Rev:** Film segment **Edge:** Reeded

Date	Mintage	F	VF	XF	Unc	BU
2005 Proof	1,000	Value: 300				

EURO COINAGE

KM# 68 EURO CENT
2.2700 g., Copper Plated Steel, 16.2 mm. **Obv:** White Stork **Obv. Legend:** SLOVENIJA, star between each letter **Rev:** Value and globe **Edge:** Plain

Date	Mintage	F	VF	XF	Unc	BU
2007	—	—	—	—	0.25	—

KM# 69 2 EURO CENT
3.0000 g., Copper Plated Steel, 18.7 mm. **Obv:** Princely stone of power in consciousness **Obv. Legend:** SLOVENIJA, star between each letter **Rev:** Value and globe **Edge:** Grooved

Date	Mintage	F	VF	XF	Unc	BU
2007	—	—	—	—	0.50	—

KM# 70 5 EURO CENT
3.8600 g., Copper-Plated-Steel, 21.3 mm. **Obv:** Sower of Seeds - and stars **Obv. Legend:** SLOVENIJA, star between each letter **Rev:** Value and globe **Edge:** Plain

Date	Mintage	F	VF	XF	Unc	BU
2007	—	—	—	—	0.75	—

KM# 71 10 EURO CENT
4.0000 g., Brass, 19.7 mm. **Obv:** Plecnik's unrealised plans for Parliament building **Obv. Legend:** SLOVENIJA, star between each letter **Rev:** Value and map **Edge:** Reeded

Date	Mintage	F	VF	XF	Unc	BU
2007	—	—	—	—	1.00	—

KM# 72 20 EURO CENT
5.7300 g., Brass, 22.3 mm. **Obv:** Two Lipizzaner horses prancing left **Obv. Legend:** SLOVENIJA, star between each letter **Rev:** Value and map **Edge:** Notched

Date	Mintage	F	VF	XF	Unc	BU
2007	—	—	—	—	1.25	—

KM# 73 50 EURO CENT
7.8100 g., Brass, 24.2 mm. **Obv:** Mountain and stars **Rev:** Value and map **Edge:** Reeded

Date	Mintage	F	VF	XF	Unc	BU
2007	—	—	—	—	1.50	—

KM# 74 EURO
7.5000 g., Bi-Metallic Copper-Nickel center in Brass ring, 23.2 mm. **Obv:** Bearded Primoz Trubar **Rev:** Value and map **Edge:** Segmented reeding

Date	Mintage	F	VF	XF	Unc	BU
2007	—	—	—	—	2.50	—

KM# 75 2 EURO
8.5200 g., Bi-Metallic Brass center in Copper-Nickel ring, 25.7 mm. **Obv:** France Preseren silhouette and signature **Rev:** Value and map **Edge:** Reeded and lettered

Date	Mintage	F	VF	XF	Unc	BU
2007	—	—	—	—	4.00	—

PROOF SETS

KM#	Date	Mintage	Identification	Issue Price	Mkt Val
PS13	2001 (8)	—	KM#3, 4, 5, 6, 7, 8, 41, 42	—	55.00
PS14	2002 (8)	—	KM#3, 4, 5, 6, 7, 8, 41, 45	—	58.00
PS15	2003 (10)	—	KM#3, 4, 5, 6, 7, 8, 41, 50, 51, 52	—	80.00

The Solomon Islands are made up of about 200 islands. They are located in the southwest Pacific east of Papua New Guinea, have an area of 10,983 sq. mi. (28,450 sq. km.) and a population of *552,000. Capital: Honiara. The most important islands of the Solomon chain are Guadalcanal (scene of some of the fiercest fighting of World War II), Malaitia, New Georgia, Florida, Vella Lavella, Choiseul, Rendova, San Cristobal, the Lord Howe group, the Santa Cruz islands, and the Duff group. Copra is the only important cash crop but it is hoped that timber will become an economic factor.

Solomon Islands is a member of the Commonwealth of Nations. Queen Elizabeth II is Head of State, as Queen of the Solomon Islands.

RULER
British
Queen Elizabeth II (see above)

MONETARY SYSTEM
100 Cents = 1 Dollar

COMMONWEALTH NATION

STANDARD COINAGE

KM# 24 CENT
2.3000 g., Bronze Plated Steel, 17.53 mm. **Ruler:** Elizabeth II **Obv:** Crowned head right **Obv. Legend:** ELIZABETH II - SOLOMON ISLANDS **Rev:** Food bowl divides value **Edge:** Plain

Date	Mintage	F	VF	XF	Unc	BU
2005	—	—	—	—	0.35	0.75

KM# 25 2 CENTS
Bronze Plated Steel, 21.6 mm. **Ruler:** Elizabeth II **Obv:** Crowned head right **Obv. Legend:** ELIZABETH II - SOLOMON ISLANDS **Rev:** Eagle spirit below value **Edge:** Plain

Date	Mintage	F	VF	XF	Unc	BU
2005	—	—	—	—	0.35	0.75
2006	—	—	—	—	0.35	0.75

KM# 26a 5 CENTS
Nickel Plated Steel Galvanized steel planchet., 18.40 mm. **Ruler:** Elizabeth II **Obv:** Crowned bust right **Obv. Legend:** ELIZABETH II - SOLOMON ISLANDS **Rev:** Value at left, native mask at center right

Date	Mintage	F	VF	XF	Unc	BU
2005	—	—	—	—	0.50	1.00

KM# 27a 10 CENTS
Nickel Plated Steel Galvanized steel planchet., 23.6 mm. **Ruler:** Elizabeth II **Subject:** Ngorieru **Obv:** Crowned head right **Obv. Legend:** ELIZABETH II - SOLOMON ISLANDS **Rev:** Sea spirit divides value **Edge:** Reeded

Date	Mintage	F	VF	XF	Unc	BU
2005	—	—	—	—	0.65	1.00

KM# 28 20 CENTS
11.2500 g., Nickel Plated Steel Galvanized steel planchet., 28.5 mm. **Ruler:** Elizabeth II **Obv:** Crowned head right **Obv. Legend:** ELIZABETH II _ SOLOMON ISLANDS **Rev:** Malaita pendant design within circle, denomination appears twice in legend **Edge:** Reeded

Date	Mintage	F	VF	XF	Unc	BU
2005	—	—	—	—	0.85	1.25

KM# 29 50 CENTS
10.0000 g., Copper-Nickel, 29.5 mm. **Ruler:** Elizabeth II **Obv:** Crowned head right **Obv. Legend:** ELIZABETH II - SOLOMON ISLANDS **Rev:** Arms with supporters **Edge:** Plain **Shape:** 12-sided **Note:** Circulation type.

Date	Mintage	F	VF	XF	Unc	BU
2005	—	—	—	—	2.00	3.00

KM# 72 DOLLAR
13.4500 g., Copper-Nickel, 30 mm. **Ruler:** Elizabeth II **Obv:** Crowned head right **Obv. Legend:** ELIZABETH II - SOLOMON ISLANDS **Rev:** Sea spirit statue divides value **Edge:** Plain **Shape:** 7-sided

Date	Mintage	F	VF	XF	Unc	BU
2005	—	—	—	—	2.50	4.00

KM# 83 2 DOLLARS
62.2700 g., 0.9990 Silver 1.9999 oz. ASW, 50.3 mm. **Subject:** Regional Assistance Mission to Solomon Islands **Obv:** Crowned head right **Rev:** Dove outline over multicolor islands in a sea of country names **Edge:** Reeded

Date	Mintage	F	VF	XF	Unc	BU
2005 Proof	2,500	Value: 80.00				

KM# 75 5 DOLLARS
28.2800 g., Copper-Nickel, 38.6 mm. **Obv:** Crowned head right **Obv. Designer:** Raphael Maklouf **Rev:** F-117A Nighthawk Stealth fighter plane **Edge:** Reeded

Date	Mintage	F	VF	XF	Unc	BU
2003	—	—	—	—	4.00	6.00

KM# 76 5 DOLLARS
28.2800 g., Copper-Nickel, 38.6 mm. **Obv:** Crowned head right **Obv. Designer:** Raphael Maklouf **Rev:** Concorde supersonic airliner **Edge:** Reeded

Date	Mintage	F	VF	XF	Unc	BU
2003	—	—	—	—	4.00	6.00

KM# 84 5 DOLLARS
31.1035 g., 0.9990 Silver 0.9990 oz. ASW, 38.6 mm. **Obv:** Maklouf's portrait of Elizabeth II **Rev:** Gold plated pig **Edge:** Reeded **Note:** Year of the Pig

Date	Mintage	F	VF	XF	Unc	BU
2007	10,000	—	—	—	—	50.00

KM# 85 5 DOLLARS
31.1035 g., 0.9990 Silver 0.9990 oz. ASW, 38.6 mm. **Obv:** Maklouf's portrait of Elizabeth II **Rev:** Dark red pig and piglet **Edge:** Reeded **Note:** Year of the Pig

Date	Mintage	F	VF	XF	Unc	BU
2007	10,000	—	—	—	—	50.00

KM# 86 10 DOLLARS
28.3600 g., Silver, 38.6 mm. **Obv:** Crowned bust right **Obv. Legend:** ELIZABETH II - SOLOMON ISLANDS **Rev:** Bust of Mendana facing at left, early sailing ship at center - right **Rev. Legend:** ALVARO DE MENDANA **Edge:** Reeded

Date	Mintage	F	VF	XF	Unc	BU
2004 Proof	—	Value: 45.00				

KM# 87 25 DOLLARS
0.9250 Silver **Ruler:** Elizabeth II **Obv:** Crowned bust right **Obv. Legend:** ELIZABETH II - SOLOMON ISLANDS **Rev:** 3/4 length figures of Elizabeth and Prince Philip facing

Date	Mintage	F	VF	XF	Unc	BU
2006 Proof	—	Value: 40.00				

SOMALIA

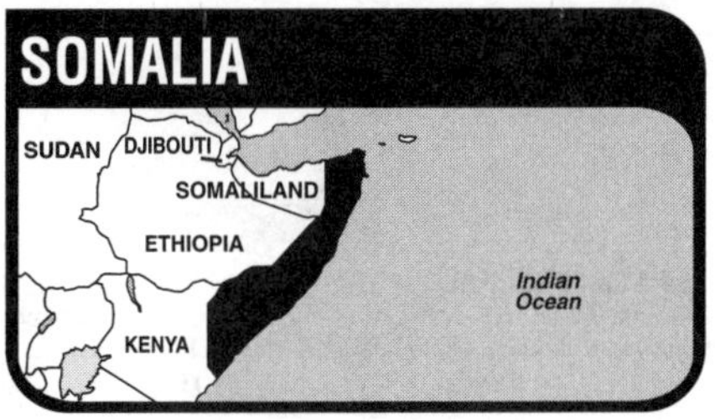

The Somali Democratic Republic, comprised of the former Italian Somaliland, is located on the coast of the eastern projection of the African continent commonly referred to as the "Horn". It has an area of 178,201 sq. mi. (461,657 sq. km.) and a population of *8.2 million. Capital: Mogadishu. The economy is pastoral and agricultural. Livestock, bananas and hides are exported.

The Northern Somali National Movement (SNM) declared a secession of the northwestern Somaliland Republic on May 17, 1991, which is not recognized by the Somali Democratic Republic.

TITLE
Al-Jumhuriya(t)as - Somaliya(t)

REPUBLIC OF SOMALIA

STANDARD COINAGE

100 Centesimi = 1 Scellino

KM# 45 5 SHILLING / SCELLINI
1.2900 g., Aluminum, 21 mm. **Series:** F.A.O. **Obv:** Crowned arms with supporters **Rev:** Elephant **Edge:** Plain

Date	Mintage	F	VF	XF	Unc	BU
2002	—	—	—	—	1.50	1.75

KM# 103 25 SHILLINGS / SCELLINI
4.3700 g., Brass, 21.8 mm. **Subject:** Soccer **Obv:** Crowned arms with supporters **Rev:** Soccer player **Edge:** Plain

Date	Mintage	F	VF	XF	Unc	BU
2001	—	—	—	—	1.25	1.50

KM# 111 50 SHILLINGS
3.9000 g., Nickel-Clad Steel, 21.9 mm. **Obv:** Crowned arms with supporters **Rev:** Mandrill **Edge:** Plain

Date	Mintage	F	VF	XF	Unc	BU
2002	—	—	—	—	0.85	1.25

KM# 109 100 SHILLINGS
10.5000 g., 0.9990 Silver 0.3372 oz. ASW, 30.1 mm. **Subject:** Soccer **Obv:** Crowned arms with supporters **Rev:** Multicolor soccer player and Brandenburg Gate **Edge:** Reeded

Date	Mintage	F	VF	XF	Unc	BU
2001 Proof	—	Value: 25.00				

KM# 112 100 SHILLINGS
3.5400 g., Brass, 18.8 mm. **Obv:** Crowned arms with supporters above value **Rev:** Bust with headdress facing **Edge:** Plain

Date	Mintage	F	VF	XF	Unc	BU
2002	—	—	—	—	1.50	2.50

KM# 110 250 SHILLINGS
31.1500 g., 0.9990 Silver 1.0005 oz. ASW, 39.9 mm. **Subject:** Queen of Sheba **Obv:** Crowned arms with supporters **Rev:** Crowned bust 1/4 right **Edge:** Reeded

Date	Mintage	F	VF	XF	Unc	BU
2002	—	—	—	—	35.00	40.00

REPUBLIC OF SOMALI

STANDARD COINAGE

100 Centesimi = 1 Scellino

KM# 155 25 SHILLINGS
28.1000 g., Copper Nickel, 38.73 mm. **Subject:** The life of Pope John-Paul II **Obv:** National arms **Obv. Legend:** SOMALI REPUBLIC **Rev:** Pope John-Paul II in window at the Vatican **Edge:** Plain

Date	Mintage	F	VF	XF	Unc	BU
2004	—	—	—	—	—	6.00

KM# 156 25 SHILLINGS
28.1000 g., Copper Nickel, 38.73 mm. **Subject:** Life of Pope John Paul II **Obv:** National arms **Obv. Legend:** SOMALI REPUBLIC **Rev:** Pope traveling in special vehicle **Edge:** Plain

Date	Mintage	F	VF	XF	Unc	BU
2004	—	—	—	—	—	6.00

KM# 157 25 SHILLINGS
28.1000 g., Copper Nickel, 38.73 mm. **Subject:** The life of Pope John-Paul II **Obv:** National arms **Obv. Legend:** SOMALI REPUBLIC **Rev:** Pope blessing Mother Teresa **Edge:** Plain

Date	Mintage	F	VF	XF	Unc	BU
2004	—	—	—	—	—	6.00

KM# 121 250 SHILLINGS
20.1200 g., Silver-Plated Base Metal, 38.5 mm. **Obv:** Crowned arms with supporters **Rev:** Multicolor Pope John Paul II and mountains **Edge:** Reeded

Date	Mintage	F	VF	XF	Unc	BU
2005 Proof	—	Value: 18.00				

KM# 123 250 SHILLINGS
20.1200 g., Silver-Plated Base Metal, 38.5 mm. **Obv:** Crowned arms with supporters **Rev:** Multicolor Pope John Paul II kissing bible **Edge:** Reeded

Date	Mintage	F	VF	XF	Unc	BU
2005 Proof	—	Value: 18.00				

KM# 125 250 SHILLINGS
20.1200 g., Silver-Plated Base Metal, 38.5 mm. **Obv:** Crowned arms with supporters **Rev:** Multicolor Pope John Paul II with flowers **Edge:** Reeded

Date	Mintage	F	VF	XF	Unc	BU
2005 Proof	—	Value: 18.00				

KM# 127 250 SHILLINGS
20.1200 g., Silver-Plated Base Metal, 38.5 mm. **Obv:** Crowned arms with supporters **Rev:** Multicolor Pope John Paul II saying mass **Edge:** Reeded

Date	Mintage	F	VF	XF	Unc	BU
2005 Proof	—	Value: 18.00				

KM# 129 250 SHILLINGS
20.1200 g., Silver-Plated Base Metal, 38.5 mm. **Obv:** Crowned arms with supporters **Rev:** Multicolor Pope John Paul II with cardinals **Edge:** Reeded

Date	Mintage	F	VF	XF	Unc	BU
2005 Proof	—	Value: 18.00				

KM# 131 250 SHILLINGS
20.1200 g., Silver-Plated Base Metal, 38.5 mm. **Obv:** Crowned arms with supporters **Rev:** Pope John Paul II with red vestments **Edge:** Reeded

Date	Mintage	F	VF	XF	Unc	BU
2005 Proof	—	Value: 18.00				

KM# 133 250 SHILLINGS
20.1200 g., Silver-Plated Base Metal, 38.5 mm. **Obv:** Crowned arms with supporters **Rev:** Pope John Paul II in white with skull cap **Edge:** Reeded

Date	Mintage	F	VF	XF	Unc	BU
2005 Proof	—	Value: 18.00				

KM# 135 250 SHILLINGS
20.1200 g., Silver-Plated Base Metal, 38.5 mm. **Obv:** Crowned arms with supporters **Rev:** Multicolor Pope John Paul II leaning head on staff **Edge:** Reeded

Date	Mintage	F	VF	XF	Unc	BU
2005 Proof	—	Value: 18.00				

KM# 137 250 SHILLINGS
20.1200 g., Silver-Plated Base Metal, 38.5 mm. **Obv:** Crowned arms with supporters **Rev:** Multicolor Pope John Paul II with staff facing left **Edge:** Reeded

Date	Mintage	F	VF	XF	Unc	BU
2005 Proof	—	Value: 18.00				

KM# 139 250 SHILLINGS
20.1200 g., Silver-Plated Base Metal, 38.5 mm. **Obv:** Crowned arms with supporters **Rev:** Multicolor Pope John Paul II with staff facing half right **Edge:** Reeded

Date	Mintage	F	VF	XF	Unc	BU
2005 Proof	—	Value: 18.00				

KM# 143 250 SHILLINGS
Copper-Nickel **Obv:** Crowned shield **Obv. Legend:** SOMALI REPUBLIC / 250 SHILLINGS **Rev:** Color applique, German Shephard **Rev. Legend:** YEAR OF THE DOG / 2006 **Edge:** Reeded

Date	Mintage	F	VF	XF	Unc	BU
2006	—	—	—	—	—	10.00

KM# 144 250 SHILLINGS
Copper-Nickel **Obv:** Crowned shield **Obv. Legend:** SOMALI REPUBLIC / 250 SHILLINGS **Rev:** Color applique, Dachsund **Rev. Legend:** YEAR OF THE DOG / 2006 **Edge:** Reeded

Date	Mintage	F	VF	XF	Unc	BU
2006	—	—	—	—	—	10.00

KM# 145 250 SHILLINGS
Copper-Nickel **Obv:** Crowned shield **Obv. Legend:** SOMALI REPUBLIC / 250 SHILLINGS **Rev:** Color applique, Yorkshire Terrier **Rev. Legend:** YEAR OF THE DOG / 2006 **Edge:** Reeded

Date	Mintage	F	VF	XF	Unc	BU
2006	—	—	—	—	—	10.00

KM# 146 250 SHILLINGS
Copper-Nickel **Obv:** Crowned shield **Obv. Legend:** SOMALI REPUBLIC / 250 SHILLINGS **Rev:** Color applique, Scottie (small white) **Rev. Legend:** YEAR OF THE DOG / 2006 **Edge:** Reeded

Date	Mintage	F	VF	XF	Unc	BU
2006	—	—	—	—	—	10.00

KM# 147 250 SHILLINGS
Copper-Nickel **Obv:** Crowned shield **Obv. Legend:** SOMALI REPUBLIC / 250 SHILLINGS **Rev:** Color applique, Wire-haired Terrier **Rev. Legend:** YEAR OF THE DOG / 2006 **Edge:** Reeded

Date	Mintage	F	VF	XF	Unc	BU
2006	—	—	—	—	—	10.00

KM# 148 250 SHILLINGS
Copper-Nickel **Obv:** Crowned shield **Obv. Legend:** SOMALI REPUBLIC / 250 SHILLINGS **Rev:** Color applique, Bulldog **Rev. Legend:** YEAR OF THE DOG / 2006 **Edge:** Reeded

Date	Mintage	F	VF	XF	Unc	BU
2006	—	—	—	—	—	10.00

KM# 149 250 SHILLINGS
Copper-Nickel **Obv:** Crowned shield **Obv. Legend:** SOMALI REPUBLIC / 250 SHILLINGS **Rev:** Color applique, Golden Retriever **Rev. Legend:** YEAR OF THE DOG **Edge:** Reeded

Date	Mintage	F	VF	XF	Unc	BU
2006	—	—	—	—	—	10.00

KM# 150 250 SHILLINGS
Copper-Nickel **Obv:** Crowned shield **Obv. Legend:** SOMALI REPUBLIC / 250 SHILLINGS **Rev:** Color applique, St. Bernard **Rev. Legend:** YEAR OF THE DOG / 2006 **Edge:** Reeded

Date	Mintage	F	VF	XF	Unc	BU
2006	—	—	—	—	—	10.00

KM# 151 250 SHILLINGS
Copper-Nickel **Obv:** Crowned shield **Obv. Legend:** SOMALI REPUBLIC / 250 SHILLINGS **Rev:** Color applique, Rottweiler **Rev. Legend:** YEAR OF THE DOG / 2006 **Edge:** Reeded

Date	Mintage	F	VF	XF	Unc	BU
2006	—	—	—	—	—	10.00

KM# 152 250 SHILLINGS
Copper-Nickel **Obv:** Crowned shield **Obv. Legend:** SOMALI REPUBLIC / 250 SHILLINGS **Rev:** Color applique, Basset Hound **Rev. Legend:** YEAR OF THE DOG / 2006 **Edge:** Reeded

Date	Mintage	F	VF	XF	Unc	BU
2006	—	—	—	—	—	10.00

KM# 153 250 SHILLINGS
Copper-Nickel **Obv:** Crowned shield **Obv. Legend:** SOMALI REPUBLIC / 250 SHILLINGS **Rev:** Color applique, Sheep Dog **Rev. Legend:** YEAR OF THE DOG / 2006 **Edge:** Reeded

Date	Mintage	F	VF	XF	Unc	BU
2006	—	—	—	—	—	10.00

KM# 154 250 SHILLINGS
Copper-Nickel **Obv:** Crowned shield **Obv. Legend:** SOMALI REPUBLIC / 250 SHILLINGS **Rev:** Color applique, Cocker Spaniel **Rev. Legend:** YEAR OF THE DOG / 2006 **Edge:** Reeded

Date	Mintage	F	VF	XF	Unc	BU
2006	—	—	—	—	—	10.00

KM# 122 500 SHILLINGS
18.8400 g., Silver-Plated Base Metal, 34.1 mm. **Obv:** Crowned arms with supporters **Rev:** Multicolor Pope John Paul II and mountains **Edge:** Plain **Shape:** Square with round corners

Date	Mintage	F	VF	XF	Unc	BU
2005 Proof	—	Value: 20.00				

KM# 124 500 SHILLINGS
18.8400 g., Silver-Plated Base Metal, 34.1 mm. **Obv:** Crowned arms with supporters **Rev:** Multicolor Pope John Paul II kissing bible **Edge:** Plain **Shape:** Square with round corners

Date	Mintage	F	VF	XF	Unc	BU
2005 Proof	—	Value: 20.00				

KM# 126 500 SHILLINGS
18.8400 g., Silver-Plated Base Metal, 34.1 mm. **Obv:** Crowned arms with supporters **Rev:** Multicolor Pope John Paul II with flowers **Edge:** Plain **Shape:** Square with round corners

Date	Mintage	F	VF	XF	Unc	BU
2005 Proof	—	Value: 20.00				

KM# 128 500 SHILLINGS
18.1400 g., Silver-Plated Base Metal, 34.1 mm. **Obv:** Crowned arms with supporters **Rev:** Multicolor Pope John Paul II saying mass **Edge:** Plain **Shape:** Square with round corners

Date	Mintage	F	VF	XF	Unc	BU
2005 Proof	—	Value: 20.00				

KM# 130 500 SHILLINGS
18.8400 g., Silver-Plated Base Metal, 34.1 mm. **Obv:** Crowned arms with supporters **Rev:** Multicolor Pope John Paul II with cardinals **Edge:** Plain **Shape:** Square with round corners

Date	Mintage	F	VF	XF	Unc	BU
2005 Proof	—	Value: 20.00				

KM# 132 500 SHILLINGS
18.8400 g., Silver-Plated Base Metal, 34.1 mm. **Obv:** Crowned arms with supporters **Rev:** Pope John Paul II with red vestments **Edge:** Plain **Shape:** Square with round corners

Date	Mintage	F	VF	XF	Unc	BU
2005 Proof	—	Value: 20.00				

KM# 134 500 SHILLINGS
18.8400 g., Silver-Plated Base Metal, 34.1 mm. **Obv:** Crowned arms with supporters **Rev:** Pope John Paul II in white with skull cap **Edge:** Plain **Shape:** Square with round corners

Date	Mintage	F	VF	XF	Unc	BU
2005 Proof	—	Value: 20.00				

KM# 136 500 SHILLINGS
18.8400 g., Silver-Plated Base Metal, 34.1 mm. **Obv:** Crowned arms with supporters **Rev:** Multicolor Pope John Paul II leaning head on staff **Edge:** Plain **Shape:** Square with round corners

Date	Mintage	F	VF	XF	Unc	BU
2005 Proof	—	Value: 20.00				

KM# 138 500 SHILLINGS
18.8400 g., Silver-Plated Base Metal, 34.1 mm. **Obv:** Crowned arms with supporters **Rev:** Multicolor Pope John Paul II with staff facing left **Edge:** Plain **Shape:** Square with round corners

Date	Mintage	F	VF	XF	Unc	BU
2005 Proof	—	Value: 20.00				

KM# 140 500 SHILLINGS
18.8400 g., Silver-Plated Base Metal, 34.1 mm. **Obv:** Crowned arms with supporters **Rev:** Multicolor Pope John Paul II with staff facing half right **Edge:** Plain **Shape:** Square with round corners

Date	Mintage	F	VF	XF	Unc	BU
2005 Proof	—	Value: 20.00				

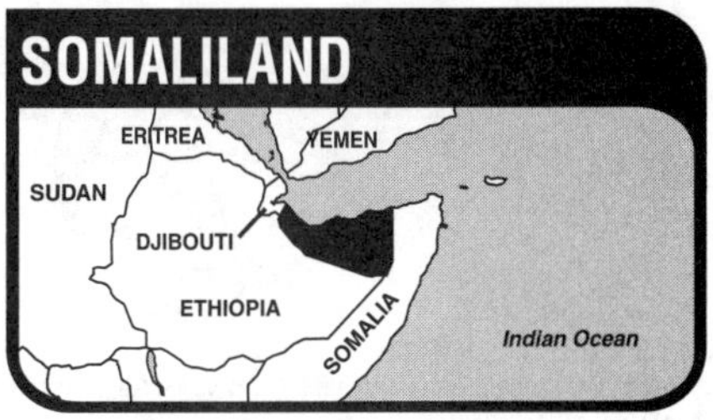

The Somaliland Republic, comprised of the former British Somaliland Protectorate, is located on the coast of the north-eastern projection of the African continent commonly referred to as the "Horn" on the southwestern end of the Gulf of Aden. Bordered by Ethiopia to the west and south and Somalia to the east. It has an area of 68,000* sq. mi. (176,000* sq. km). Capital: Hargeysa. It is mostly arid and mountainous except for the gulf shoreline.

The northern Somali National Movement (SNM) declared a secession of the Somaliland Republic on May 17, 1991, which is not recognized by the Somali Democratic Republic.

REPUBLIC

SHILLING COINAGE

KM# 4 5 SHILLINGS
1.4500 g., Aluminum, 21.9 mm. **Obv:** Value **Rev:** Bust of Sir Richard F. Burton - explorer, divides dates **Edge:** Plain

Date	Mintage	F	VF	XF	Unc	BU
2002	—	—	—	—	1.25	1.50

KM# 5 5 SHILLINGS
1.4500 g., Aluminum, 21.9 mm. **Obv:** Value **Rev:** Rooster **Edge:** Plain

Date	Mintage	F	VF	XF	Unc	BU
2002	—	—	—	—	1.00	1.25

KM# 19 5 SHILLINGS
1.2400 g., Aluminum, 22 mm. **Obv:** Elephant with calf walking right **Obv. Legend:** REPUBLIC OF SOMALILAND **Rev:** Value **Rev. Legend:** BAANKA SOMALILAND **Edge:** Plain

Date	Mintage	F	VF	XF	Unc	BU
2005	—	—	—	—	1.25	1.50

KM# 3 10 SHILLINGS
3.5100 g., Brass, 17.7 mm. **Obv:** Vervet Monkey **Rev:** Value **Edge:** Plain

Date	Mintage	F	VF	XF	Unc	BU
2002	—	—	—	—	0.65	1.25

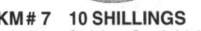

KM# 7 10 SHILLINGS
4.8000 g., Stainless Steel, 24.9 mm. **Obv:** Value **Rev:** Aquarius the water carrier **Edge:** Plain

Date	Mintage	F	VF	XF	Unc	BU
2006	—	—	—	—	1.00	1.25

KM# 8 10 SHILLINGS
4.8000 g., Stainless Steel, 24.9 mm. **Obv:** Value **Rev:** Pisces the two fish **Edge:** Plain

Date	Mintage	F	VF	XF	Unc	BU
2006	—	—	—	—	1.00	1.25

KM# 9 10 SHILLINGS
4.8000 g., Stainless Steel, 24.9 mm. **Obv:** Value **Rev:** Aries the ram **Edge:** Plain

Date	Mintage	F	VF	XF	Unc	BU
2006	—	—	—	—	1.00	1.25

KM# 10 10 SHILLINGS
4.8000 g., Stainless Steel, 24.9 mm. **Obv:** Value **Rev:** Taurus the bull **Edge:** Plain

Date	Mintage	F	VF	XF	Unc	BU
2006	—	—	—	—	1.00	1.25

KM# 11 10 SHILLINGS
4.8000 g., Stainless Steel, 24.9 mm. **Obv:** Value **Rev:** Gemini twins **Edge:** Plain

Date	Mintage	F	VF	XF	Unc	BU
2006	—	—	—	—	1.00	1.25

KM# 12 10 SHILLINGS
4.8000 g., Stainless Steel, 24.9 mm. **Obv:** Value **Rev:** Cancer the crab **Edge:** Plain

Date	Mintage	F	VF	XF	Unc	BU
2006	—	—	—	—	1.00	1.25

KM# 13 10 SHILLINGS
4.8000 g., Stainless Steel, 24.9 mm. **Obv:** Value **Rev:** Leo the lion **Edge:** Plain

Date	Mintage	F	VF	XF	Unc	BU
2006	—	—	—	—	1.00	1.25

KM# 14 10 SHILLINGS
4.8000 g., Stainless Steel, 24.9 mm. **Obv:** Value **Rev:** Virgo as a winged woman **Edge:** Plain

Date	Mintage	F	VF	XF	Unc	BU
2006	—	—	—	—	1.00	1.25

KM# 15 10 SHILLINGS
4.8000 g., Stainless Steel, 24.9 mm. **Obv:** Value **Rev:** Libra balance scale **Edge:** Plain

Date	Mintage	F	VF	XF	Unc	BU
2006	—	—	—	—	1.00	1.25

KM# 16 10 SHILLINGS
4.8000 g., Stainless Steel, 24.9 mm. **Obv:** Value **Rev:** Scorpio the scorpion **Edge:** Plain

Date	Mintage	F	VF	XF	Unc	BU
2006	—	—	—	—	1.00	1.25

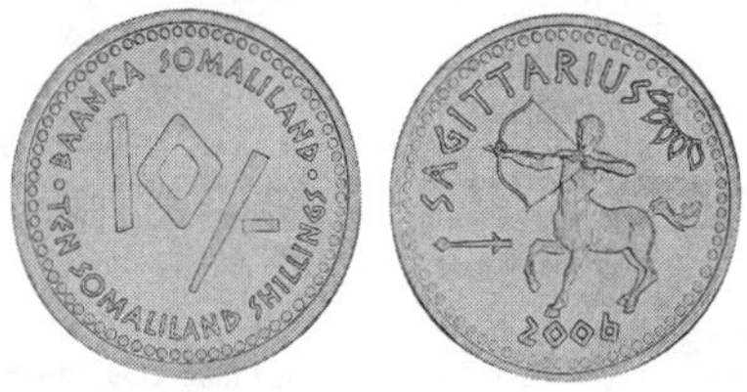

KM# 17 10 SHILLINGS
4.8000 g., Stainless Steel, 24.9 mm. **Obv:** Value **Rev:** Sagittarius the archer **Edge:** Plain

Date	Mintage	F	VF	XF	Unc	BU
2006	—	—	—	—	1.00	1.25

KM# 18 10 SHILLINGS
4.8000 g., Stainless Steel, 24.9 mm. **Obv:** Value **Rev:** Capricorn the goat **Edge:** Plain

Date	Mintage	F	VF	XF	Unc	BU
2006	—	—	—	—	1.00	1.25

KM# 6 20 SHILLINGS
3.8700 g., Stainless Steel, 21.8 mm. **Obv:** Value **Rev:** Greyhound dog **Edge:** Plain

Date	Mintage	F	VF	XF	Unc	BU
2002	—	—	—	—	1.00	1.50

KM# 2 1000 SHILLINGS
31.2700 g., 0.9990 Silver 1.0043 oz. ASW, 38.8 mm. **Obv:** Crowned arms with supporters **Rev:** Bust with hat 3/4 right **Edge:** Reeded

Date	Mintage	F	VF	XF	Unc	BU
2002	—	—	—	—	40.00	45.00

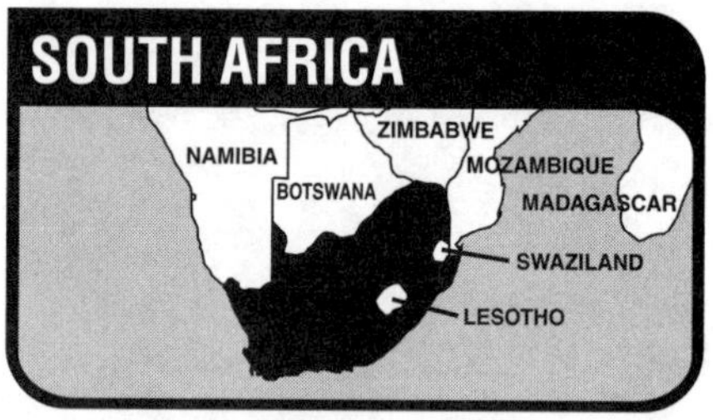

The Republic of South Africa, located at the southern tip of Africa, has an area of 471,445 sq. mi. (1,221,043 sq. km.) and a population of *30.2 million. Capitals: Administrative, Pretoria; Legislative, Cape Town; Judicial, Bloemfontein. Manufacturing, mining and agriculture are the principal industries. Exports include wool, diamonds, gold, and metallic ores.

The apartheid era ended April 27, 1994 with the first democratic election for all people of South Africa. Nelson Mandela was inaugurated President May 10, 1994, and South Africa was readmitted into the Commonwealth of Nations.

South African coins and currency bear inscriptions in tribal languages, Afrikaans and English.

MONETARY SYSTEM

Commencing 1961

100 Cents = 1 Rand

REPUBLIC

STANDARD COINAGE

100 Cents = 1 Rand

KM# 221 CENT
1.5000 g., Copper Plated Steel, 15 mm. **Obv:** Crowned arms **Obv. Designer:** A.L. Sutherland **Rev:** Value divides sparrows **Rev. Designer:** W. Lumley **Edge:** Plain

Date	Mintage	F	VF	XF	Unc	BU
2001	—	—	—	—	0.35	0.50

KM# 222 2 CENTS
3.0000 g., Copper Plated Steel, 18 mm. **Obv:** Crowned arms **Rev:** Eagle with fish in talons divides value **Edge:** Plain **Designer:** A.L. Sutherland

Date	Mintage	F	VF	XF	Unc	BU
2001	—	—	—	—	0.50	0.75

KM# 242 2-1/2 CENTS
1.4140 g., 0.9250 Silver 0.0420 oz. ASW, 16.3 mm. **Obv:** Crowned arms **Rev:** Dolphin **Edge:** Reeded

Date	Mintage	F	VF	XF	Unc	BU
2002 Proof	—	Value: 27.50				

KM# 282 2-1/2 CENTS
1.4140 g., 0.9250 Silver 0.0420 oz. ASW, 16.3 mm. **Obv:** Protea flower **Rev:** Southern Right Whale **Edge:** Plain

Date	Mintage	F	VF	XF	Unc	BU
2002 Proof	3,000	Value: 27.50				

KM# 285 2-1/2 CENTS
1.4140 g., 0.9250 Silver 0.0420 oz. ASW, 16.3 mm. **Obv:** Protea flower **Rev:** Martial and Bateleur Eagles **Edge:** Plain

Date	Mintage	F	VF	XF	Unc	BU
2003 Proof	—	Value: 25.00				

KM# 283 2-1/2 CENTS
1.4140 g., 0.9250 Silver 0.0420 oz. ASW, 16.3 mm. **Obv:** Protea flower **Rev:** Spotted Owl **Edge:** Plain

Date	Mintage	F	VF	XF	Unc	BU
2004 Proof	2,000	Value: 25.00				

KM# 223 5 CENTS
4.4300 g., Copper Plated Steel, 21 mm. **Obv:** Crowned arms **Obv. Designer:** A.L. Sutherland **Rev:** Blue crane **Rev. Designer:** G. Richard **Edge:** Plain

Date	Mintage	F	VF	XF	Unc	BU
2001	—	—	—	—	0.50	1.00

KM# 243 5 CENTS
8.4560 g., 0.9250 Silver 0.2515 oz. ASW, 26.7 mm. **Obv:** Water buffalo head **Rev:** Two buffalo heads within circle below value **Edge:** Reeded

Date	Mintage	F	VF	XF	Unc	BU
2001 Proof	—	Value: 25.00				

KM# 268 5 CENTS
4.5000 g., Copper Plated Steel, 21 mm. **Obv:** Crowned arms **Obv. Legend:** Ningizimu Afrika **Obv. Designer:** A.L. Sutherland **Rev:** Blue Crane and value **Rev. Designer:** G. Richard **Edge:** Plain **Note:** Change in legend.

Date	Mintage	F	VF	XF	Unc	BU
2002	—	—	—	—	0.50	1.00
2002 Proof	—	Value: 2.00				

KM# 324 5 CENTS
4.5000 g., Copper-Plated-Steel, 21 mm. **Obv:** Crowned arms **Obv. Legend:** Afrika-Dzonga **Rev:** Blue crane and denomination

Date	Mintage	F	VF	XF	Unc	BU
2003	—	—	—	—	0.50	1.00

KM# 325 5 CENTS
4.5000 g., Copper-Plated-Steel, 21 mm. **Obv:** Crowned arms **Obv. Legend:** South Africa **Rev:** Blue crane and denomination

Date	Mintage	F	VF	XF	Unc	BU
2004	—	—	—	—	0.50	1.00

KM# 320 5 CENTS
8.6000 g., 0.9250 Silver 0.2557 oz. ASW, 27.12 mm. **Series:** Hunters of Africa **Subject:** African Wild Dog **Obv:** National arms **Rev:** Painted Dog's head facing slightly left **Rev. Designer:** L. Guerra **Edge:** Reeded

Date	Mintage	F	VF	XF	Unc	BU
2005 Proof	1,500	Value: 20.00				

KM# 291 5 CENTS
4.5000 g., Copper-Plated-Steel, 21 mm. **Obv:** Crowned arms **Obv. Legend:** Aforika Borwa **Rev:** Crane and value **Edge:** Plain

Date	Mintage	F	VF	XF	Unc	BU
2005	—	—	—	—	—	1.00

KM# 316 5 CENTS
8.4060 g., 0.9250 Silver 0.2500 oz. ASW, 27 mm. **Obv:** National arms **Obv. Legend:** South Africa **Rev:** Black-backed jackal drinking **Edge:** Reeded

Date	Mintage	F	VF	XF	Unc	BU
2006 Proof	1,500	Value: 20.00				

KM# 224 10 CENTS
2.0000 g., Brass Plated Steel, 16 mm. **Obv:** Crowned arms **Obv. Legend:** South Africa **Obv. Designer:** A.L. Sutherland **Rev:** Arum Lily and value **Rev. Designer:** R.C. McFarlane **Edge:** Reeded

Date	Mintage	F	VF	XF	Unc	BU
2001	—	—	—	—	0.60	0.85

KM# 244 10 CENTS
16.8630 g., 0.9250 Silver 0.5015 oz. ASW, 32.7 mm. **Obv:** Water buffalo and country name **Rev:** Two water buffalo bulls fighting **Edge:** Reeded

Date	Mintage	F	VF	XF	Unc	BU
2001 Proof	—	Value: 25.00				

KM# 269 10 CENTS
2.0000 g., Copper Plated Steel, 16 mm. **Obv:** Crowned arms **Obv. Legend:** Afrika Dzonga **Obv. Designer:** A.L. Sutherland **Rev:** Arum Lily **Rev. Designer:** R.C. McFarlane **Edge:** Reeded **Note:** Change in legend.

Date	Mintage	F	VF	XF	Unc	BU
2002	—	—	—	—	0.60	1.00
2002 Proof	—	Value: 3.00				

KM# 326 10 CENTS
2.0000 g., Brass Plated Steel, 16 mm. **Obv:** Crowned arms **Obv. Legend:** Aforika Borwa **Rev:** Arum lily and denomination

Date	Mintage	F	VF	XF	Unc	BU
2004	—	—	—	—	0.40	0.60

KM# 321 10 CENTS
16.8100 g., 0.9250 Silver 0.4999 oz. ASW, 32.82 mm. **Series:** Hunters of Africa **Subject:** African Wild Dog **Obv:** National arms **Rev:** Two Painted Dogs walking right **Rev. Designer:** L. Guerra **Edge:** Reeded

Date	Mintage	F	VF	XF	Unc	BU
2005 Proof	1,500	Value: 25.00				

KM# 292 10 CENTS
2.0000 g., Brass Plated Steel, 16 mm. **Obv:** Crowned arms **Obv. Legend:** Afrika Borwa **Rev:** Lily and value **Edge:** Reeded **Shape:** Round

Date	Mintage	F	VF	XF	Unc	BU
2005	—	—	—	—	—	0.60

KM# 317 10 CENTS
16.8130 g., 0.9250 Silver 0.5000 oz. ASW, 32.7 mm. **Obv:** National arms **Rev:** Black-backed jackal chasing birds **Edge:** Reeded

Date	Mintage	F	VF	XF	Unc	BU
2006 Proof	1,500	Value: 25.00				

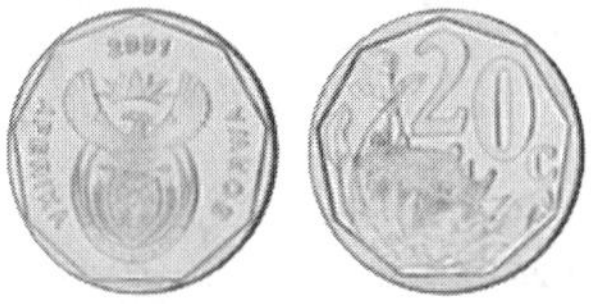

KM# 225 20 CENTS
3.5000 g., Brass Plated Steel, 19 mm. **Obv:** Crowned arms **Obv. Designer:** A.L. Sutherland **Rev:** Protea flower within sprigs and value **Edge:** Reeded

Date	Mintage	F	VF	XF	Unc	BU
2001	—	—	—	—	0.75	1.00

KM# 245 20 CENTS
33.7260 g., 0.9250 Silver 1.0030 oz. ASW, 38.3 mm. **Obv:** Water buffalo and country name **Rev:** Water buffalo heads facing **Edge:** Reeded

Date	Mintage	F	VF	XF	Unc	BU
2001 Proof	—	Value: 60.00				

KM# 270 20 CENTS
3.5000 g., Bronze Plated Steel, 19 mm. **Obv:** Crowned arms **Obv. Legend:** South Africa **Obv. Designer:** A.L. Sutherland **Rev:** Protea flower and value **Rev. Designer:** S. Erasmus **Edge:** Reeded **Note:** Change in legend.

Date	Mintage	F	VF	XF	Unc	BU
2002	—	—	—	—	0.75	1.25
2002 Proof	—	Value: 4.00				

KM# 327 20 CENTS
3.5000 g., Brass Plated Steel, 19 mm. **Obv:** Crowned arms **Obv. Legend:** Aforika Borwa **Rev:** Protea flower within sprigs and value

Date	Mintage	F	VF	XF	Unc	BU
2003	—	—	—	—	—	0.75

KM# 328 20 CENTS
3.5000 g., Brass Plated Steel, 19 mm. **Obv:** Crowned arms **Obv. Legend:** Afrika Borwa **Rev:** Protea flower within sprigs and value

Date	Mintage	F	VF	XF	Unc	BU
2004	—	—	—	—	—	0.75

KM# 322 20 CENTS
33.7500 g., 0.9250 Silver 1.0037 oz. ASW, 38.67 mm. **Series:** Hunters of Africa **Subject:** African Wild Dog **Obv:** National arms **Rev:** Three Painted Dogs **Rev. Designer:** L. Guerra **Edge:** Reeded

Date	Mintage	F	VF	XF	Unc	BU
2005 Proof	1,500	Value: 60.00				

KM# 293 20 CENTS
3.5000 g., Brass Plated Steel, 19 mm. **Obv:** Crowned arms **Obv. Legend:** Suid-Afrika **Rev:** Protea flower and value **Edge:** Reeded **Shape:** Round

Date	Mintage	F	VF	XF	Unc	BU
2005	—	—	—	—	—	0.75

KM# 318 20 CENTS
33.6260 g., 0.9250 Silver 100000 oz. ASW, 38.7 mm. **Obv:** National arms **Rev:** Two Black-backed jackals **Edge:** Reeded

Date	Mintage	F	VF	XF	Unc	BU
2006 Proof	1,500	Value: 60.00				

KM# 226 50 CENTS
5.0000 g., Brass Plated Steel, 22 mm. **Obv:** Crowned arms **Obv. Designer:** A.L. Sutherland **Rev:** Plant and value **Rev. Designer:** C. Cogle **Edge:** Reeded

Date	Mintage	F	VF	XF	Unc	BU
2001	—	—	—	—	1.00	1.25

KM# 246 50 CENTS
76.4020 g., 0.9250 Silver 2.2721 oz. ASW, 50 mm. **Obv:** Water buffalo and country name **Rev:** Water buffalo head and value **Edge:** Reeded

Date	Mintage	F	VF	XF	Unc	BU
2001 Proof	—	Value: 80.00				

KM# 287 50 CENTS
5.0000 g., Brass Plated Steel, 22 mm. **Obv:** Crowned arms **Rev:** Soccer player

Date	Mintage	F	VF	XF	Unc	BU
2002	—	—	—	—	2.25	2.50

KM# 329 50 CENTS
5.0000 g., Brass-Plated Steel, 22 mm. **Obv:** Crowned arms **Obv. Legend:** Aforika Borwa **Rev:** Cricket player diving towards the wicket **Edge:** Reeded

Date	Mintage	F	VF	XF	Unc	BU
2002	—	—	—	—	2.25	2.50

KM# 271 50 CENTS
5.0000 g., Brass-Plated Steel, 22 mm. **Obv:** Crowned arms **Obv. Legend:** Aforika Borwa **Obv. Designer:** A.L. Sutherland **Rev:** Strelitzia plant **Rev. Designer:** C. Cogle **Edge:** Reeded **Note:** Change in legend.

Date	Mintage	F	VF	XF	Unc	BU
2002	—	—	—	—	1.00	1.50
2002 Proof	—	Value: 5.00				

KM# 330 50 CENTS
5.0000 g., Brass-Plated Steel, 22 mm. **Obv:** Crowned arms **Obv. Legend:** Afrika Borwa **Rev:** Stelitzia plant and denomination

Date	Mintage	F	VF	XF	Unc	BU
2003	—	—	—	—	2.25	2.50

KM# 276 50 CENTS
5.0000 g., Brass-Plated Steel, 22 mm. **Obv:** Crowned arms **Obv. Legend:** Afrika Borwa **Obv. Designer:** A.L. Sutherland **Rev:** Cricket player diving towards the wicket **Edge:** Reeded

Date	Mintage	F	VF	XF	Unc	BU
2003	—	—	—	—	2.25	2.50

KM# 331 50 CENTS
5.0000 g., Brass-Plated Steel, 22 mm. **Obv:** Crowned arms **Obv. Legend:** Suid Afrika **Rev:** Stelitzia plant and denomination

Date	Mintage	F	VF	XF	Unc	BU
2004	—	—	—	—	2.25	2.50

KM# 323 50 CENTS
76.8600 g., 0.9250 Silver 2.2857 oz. ASW, 50.48 mm. **Series:** Hunters of Africa **Subject:** African Wild Dog **Obv:** National arms **Rev:** Two painted Dog's heads facing **Rev. Designer:** L. Guerra **Edge:** Reeded

Date	Mintage	F	VF	XF	Unc	BU
2005 Proof	1,500	Value: 100				

KM# 294 50 CENTS
5.0000 g., Brass Plated Steel, 22 mm. **Obv:** Crowned arms **Obv. Legend:** uMzantsi Afrika **Rev:** Plant and value **Edge:** Reeded **Shape:** Round

Date	Mintage	F	VF	XF	Unc	BU
2005	—	—	—	—	—	1.00

KM# 319 50 CENTS
76.2520 g., 0.9250 Silver 2.2676 oz. ASW, 50 mm. **Obv:** National arms **Rev:** Two black-backed jackals fighting over a carcass **Edge:** Reeded

Date	Mintage	F	VF	XF	Unc	BU
2006 Proof	1,500	Value: 100				

KM# 227 RAND
4.0000 g., Nickel Plated Steel, 20 mm. **Obv:** Crowned arms **Obv. Designer:** A.L. Sutherland **Rev:** Springbok and value **Rev. Designer:** L. Lotriet **Edge:** Reeded and plain sections

Date	Mintage	F	VF	XF	Unc	BU
2001	—	—	—	—	1.75	2.75

KM# 231 RAND

15.0000 g., 0.9250 Silver 0.4461 oz. ASW, 32.7 mm. **Subject:** Tourism **Obv:** Protea flower **Rev:** Steam locomotive and flower **Edge:** Reeded

Date	Mintage	F	VF	XF	Unc	BU
2001 Proof	3,000	Value: 30.00				

KM# 247 RAND

3.1103 g., 0.9999 Gold 0.1000 oz. AGW, 16.5 mm. **Obv:** Crowned arms **Obv. Designer:** A.L. Sutherland **Rev:** Seated figure with headdress **Edge:** Reeded

Date	Mintage	F	VF	XF	Unc	BU
2001 Proof	—	Value: 115				

KM# 272 RAND

4.0000 g., Nickel Plated Copper, 20 mm. **Obv:** Crowned arms **Obv. Legend:** Suid-Afrika Afrika Borwa **Obv. Designer:** A.L. Sutherland **Rev:** Springbok **Rev. Designer:** L. Lotriet **Edge:** Reeded **Note:** Change in legend.

Date	Mintage	F	VF	XF	Unc	BU
2002	—	—	—	—	1.75	2.50
2002 Proof	—	Value: 6.00				

KM# 275 RAND

4.0000 g., Nickel-Plated Steel, 20 mm. **Subject:** Johannesburg World Summit on Sustainable Development **Obv:** Crowned arms **Obv. Designer:** A.L. Sutherland **Rev:** World globe and logo **Edge:** Reeded and plain sections

Date	Mintage	F	VF	XF	Unc	BU
2002	—	—	—	—	3.00	4.00

KM# 277 RAND

15.0000 g., 0.9250 Silver 0.4461 oz. ASW, 32.7 mm. **Subject:** Soccer **Obv:** Protea flower **Obv. Designer:** A.L. Sutherland **Rev:** Goalkeeper in action **Edge:** Reeded

Date	Mintage	F	VF	XF	Unc	BU
2002	—	—	—	—	30.00	32.50

KM# 298 RAND

15.0500 g., 0.9250 Silver 0.4476 oz. ASW, 32.8 mm. **Obv:** Protea flower **Rev:** Cricket player **Edge:** Reeded

Date	Mintage	F	VF	XF	Unc	BU
2003	—	—	—	—	30.00	32.50

KM# 332 RAND

4.0000 g., Nickel Plated Copper, 20 mm. **Obv:** Crowned arms **Obv. Legend:** uMzantsi Afrika Suid-Afrika **Rev:** Springbok and denomination

Date	Mintage	F	VF	XF	Unc	BU
2003	—	—	—	—	—	1.75

KM# 333 RAND

4.0000 g., Nickel Plated Copper, 20 mm. **Obv:** Crowned arms **Obv. Legend:** iNingizimu Afrika uMzantsi Afrika **Rev:** Springbok and Denomination

Date	Mintage	F	VF	XF	Unc	BU
2004	—	—	—	—	—	1.75

KM# 288 RAND

15.0000 g., 0.9250 Silver 0.4461 oz. ASW, 32.7 mm. **Subject:** 10th Anniversary of South African Democracy **Obv:** Protea flower **Rev:** Flora and fawna **Edge:** Reeded

Date	Mintage	F	VF	XF	Unc	BU
2004 Proof	6,000	Value: 25.00				

KM# 295 RAND

4.0000 g., Nickel Plated Copper, 20 mm. **Obv:** Crowned arms **Obv. Legend:** iSewula Afrika iNingizimu Afrika **Rev:** Springbok and value **Edge:** Segmented reeding **Shape:** Round

Date	Mintage	F	VF	XF	Unc	BU
2005	—	—	—	—	—	1.75

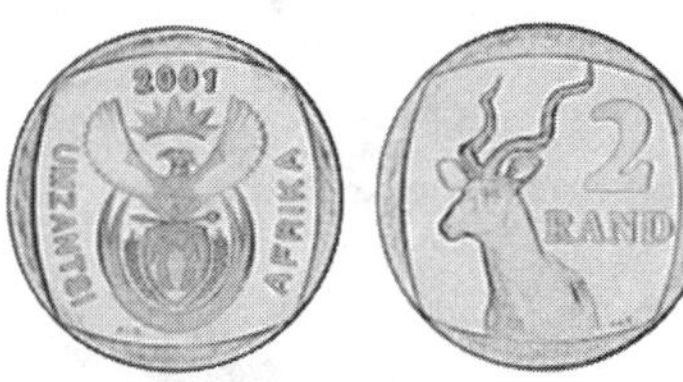

KM# 228 2 RAND

5.5000 g., Nickel Plated Steel, 23 mm. **Obv:** Crowned arms **Obv. Legend:** UMZANSTI AFRIKA, Xhosha legend **Rev:** Kudu and value **Edge:** Reeded and plain sections **Designer:** A.L. Sutherland

Date	Mintage	F	VF	XF	Unc	BU
2001	—	—	—	—	2.00	3.00

KM# 248 2 RAND

33.6260 g., 0.9250 Silver 1.0000 oz. ASW, 38.7 mm. **Obv:** Crowned arms **Rev:** Dolphins **Edge:** Reeded

Date	Mintage	F	VF	XF	Unc	BU
2001 Proof	—	Value: 60.00				

KM# 249 2 RAND

7.7770 g., 0.9999 Gold 0.2500 oz. AGW, 22 mm. **Obv:** Crowned arms **Obv. Designer:** A.L. Sutherland **Rev:** Gondwana theoretical landmass and dinosaur **Edge:** Reeded

Date	Mintage	F	VF	XF	Unc	BU
2001 Proof	—	Value: 270				

KM# 280 2 RAND

33.8000 g., 0.9250 Silver 1.0052 oz. ASW, 38.7 mm. **Obv:** Crowned arms and country name in eight languages **Rev:** Southern Right Whale **Edge:** Reeded

Date	Mintage	F	VF	XF	Unc	BU
2002 Proof	3,000	Value: 50.00				

KM# 273 2 RAND

5.5000 g., Nickel Plated Copper, 23 mm. **Obv:** Crowned arms **Obv. Legend:** iNingizimu Afrika uMzantsi Afrika **Rev:** Kudu and value **Edge:** Reeded and plain sections **Designer:** A.L. Sutherland **Note:** Change in legend.

Date	Mintage	F	VF	XF	Unc	BU
2002	—	—	—	—	2.00	3.50
2002 Proof	—	Value: 8.00				

KM# 286 2 RAND

33.7300 g., 0.9250 Silver 1.0031 oz. ASW, 38.7 mm. **Obv:** Crowned arms and country name in ten languages **Rev:** Martial and Bateleur Eagles **Edge:** Reeded

Date	Mintage	F	VF	XF	Unc	BU
2003 Proof	—	Value: 60.00				

KM# 335 2 RAND

5.5000 g., Nickel Plated Copper, 23 mm. **Obv:** Crowned arms **Obv. Legend:** iNingizimu Afrika iSewula Afrika **Rev:** Kudu and denomination

Date	Mintage	F	VF	XF	Unc	BU
2003	—	—	—	—	2.00	3.50

KM# 336 2 RAND

5.5000 g., Nickel Plated Copper, 23 mm. **Obv:** Crowned arms **Obv. Legend:** Afurika Tshipembe iSewula Afrika **Rev:** Kudu and denomination

Date	Mintage	F	VF	XF	Unc	BU
2004	—	—	—	—	2.00	3.50

KM# 284 2 RAND

33.6260 g., 0.9250 Silver 1.0000 oz. ASW, 38.7 mm. **Obv:** Crowned arms and country name in ten languages **Rev:** Verreaux's Eagle Owl face and value **Edge:** Reeded

Date	Mintage	F	VF	XF	Unc	BU
2004 Proof	3,000	Value: 50.00				

KM# 334 2 RAND

5.5000 g., Nickel Plated Copper, 23 mm. **Subject:** 10 Years of Freedom - 1994-2004 **Obv:** National arms, date and country name in English **Rev:** Denomination, flag logo and many people

Date	Mintage	F	VF	XF	Unc	BU
2004	—	—	—	—	—	2.00

KM# 296 2 RAND

5.5000 g., Nickel Plated Copper, 23 mm. **Obv:** Crowned arms **Obv. Legend:** Ningizimu Afrika Afurika Tshipembe **Rev:** Greater Kudu and value **Edge:** Segmented reeding **Shape:** Round

Date	Mintage	F	VF	XF	Unc	BU
2005	—	—	—	—	—	2.00

KM# 229 5 RAND

7.0000 g., Nickel Plated Steel, 26 mm. **Obv:** Crowned arms **Obv. Legend:** ININGIZIMU AFRIKA, Zulu legend **Rev:** Wildebeest and value **Edge:** Reeded and plain sections **Designer:** A.L. Sutherland

Date	Mintage	F	VF	XF	Unc	BU
2001	—	—	—	—	4.50	5.50

KM# 274 5 RAND

7.0000 g., Nickel Plated Copper, 26 mm. **Obv:** Crowned arms with Venda legend left, Ndebele legend right **Obv. Legend:** AFURIKA TSHIPEMBE - ISEWULA AFRIKA **Rev:** Wildebeest and value **Edge:** Reeded and plain sections **Designer:** A.L. Sutherland **Note:** Change in legend.

Date	Mintage	F	VF	XF	Unc	BU
2002	—	—	—	—	4.50	6.00
2002 Proof	—	Value: 10.00				

KM# 278 5 RAND

3.1104 g., 0.9999 Gold 0.1000 oz. AGW, 16.5 mm. **Obv:** Protea flower **Rev:** Soccer player heading the ball **Edge:** Reeded

Date	Mintage	F	VF	XF	Unc	BU
2002 Proof	—	Value: 115				

KM# 337 5 RAND

7.0000 g., Nickel Plated Copper, 26 mm. **Obv:** Crowned arms **Obv. Legend:** Afurika Tshipembe Ningizimu Afrika **Rev:** Wildebeest and denomination

Date	Mintage	F	VF	XF	Unc	BU
2003	—	—	—	—	4.50	6.00

KM# 281 5 RAND

9.5000 g., Bi-Metallic Brass center in Copper-Nickel ring, 26 mm. **Obv:** Crowned arms with Tsonga legend left, Zulu legend right **Obv. Legend:** AFRIKA DZONGA - NINGIZIMU AFRIKA **Rev:** Wildebeest and value **Edge:** Security type with lettering **Edge Lettering:** "SARB R5" repeated ten times

Date	Mintage	F	VF	XF	Unc	BU
2004	—	—	—	—	5.00	6.50

KM# 289 5 RAND

3.1100 g., 0.9999 Gold 0.1000 oz. AGW, 16.5 mm. **Subject:** 10th Anniversary of South African Democracy **Obv:** Protea flower **Rev:** Inscription covered flag **Edge:** Reeded

Date	Mintage	F	VF	XF	Unc	BU
2004 Proof	1,000	Value: 115				

KM# 297 5 RAND

9.5000 g., Bi-Metallic Brass center in Copper-Nickel ring, 26 mm. **Obv:** Crowned arms **Obv. Legend:** Afrika Dzonga South Africa **Rev:** Wildebeest and value **Edge:** Security type with lettering **Edge Lettering:** "SARB R5" repeated ten times

Date	Mintage	F	VF	XF	Unc	BU
2005	—	—	—	—	—	5.00

KM# 279 25 RAND

31.1035 g., 0.9999 Gold 0.9999 oz. AGW, 32.7 mm. **Obv:** Protea flower **Rev:** Soccer player kicking ball **Edge:** Reeded

Date	Mintage	F	VF	XF	Unc	BU
2002 Proof	—	Value: 1000				

KM# 290 25 RAND

31.1035 g., 0.9999 Gold 0.9999 oz. AGW, 32.7 mm. **Subject:** 10th Anniversary of South African Democracy **Obv:** Protea flower **Rev:** Two images of Nelson Mandela **Edge:** Reeded

Date	Mintage	F	VF	XF	Unc	BU
2004 Proof	5,000	Value: 1000				

BULLION COINAGE

Mint mark: GRC - Gold Reef City

KM# 105 1/10 KRUGERRAND

3.3930 g., 0.9170 Gold .1000 AGW 0.1000 oz. AGW, 16.50 mm. **Obv:** Bust of Paul Kruger left **Rev:** Springbok walking right divides date **Edge:** Reeded **Edge Lettering:** 180 serrations for uncirculated. 220 serrations for proof

Date	Mintage	F	VF	XF	Unc	BU
2001	17,936	—	—	—	BV+15%	—
2001 Proof	4,058	Value: 115				
2002	12,890	—	—	—	BV+15%	—
2002 Proof	3,110	Value: 115				
2003	15,893	—	—	—	BV+15%	—
2003 Proof	1,893	Value: 115				
2004	—	—	—	—	BV+15%	—
2004 Proof	3,811	Value: 115				
2005	—	—	—	—	BV+15%	—
2005 Proof	—	Value: 115				
2006	—	—	—	—	BV+15%	—
2006 Proof	—	Value: 115				
2007	—	—	—	—	BV+15%	—
2007 Proof	—	Value: 115				
2008	—	—	—	—	BV+15%	—
2008 Proof	—	Value: 115				

KM# 106 1/4 KRUGERRAND

8.4820 g., 0.9170 Gold 0.2501 oz. AGW, 22 mm. **Obv:** Bust of Paul Kruger left **Obv. Legend:** SUID — AFRIKA • SOUTH AFRICA **Rev:** Springbok bounding right divides date **Rev. Designer:** Coert L. Steynberg **Edge:** Reeded **Edge Lettering:** 180 serrations for uncirculated, 220 serrations for proof

Date	Mintage	F	VF	XF	Unc	BU
2001	10,607	—	—	—	BV+10%	—
2001 Proof	3,841	Value: 275				
2002	10,558	—	—	—	BV+10%	—
2002 Proof	2,442	Value: 275				
2003	11,468	—	—	—	BV+10%	—
2003 Proof	2,450	Value: 275				
2004	—	—	—	—	BV+10%	—
2004 Proof	4,570	Value: 275				
2005	—	—	—	—	BV+10%	—
2005 Proof	—	Value: 275				
2006	—	—	—	—	BV+10%	—
2006 Proof	—	Value: 275				
2007	—	—	—	—	BV+10%	—
2007 Proof	—	Value: 275				
2008	—	—	—	—	BV+10%	—
2008 Proof	—	Value: 275				

KM# 107 1/2 KRUGERRAND

16.9650 g., 0.9170 Gold 0.5001 oz. AGW, 27 mm. **Obv:** Bust of Paul Kruger left **Obv. Legend:** SUID ? AFRIKA ? SOUTH AFRICA **Rev:** Springbok walking right divides date **Rev. Designer:** Coert L. Steynberg **Edge:** Reeded **Edge Lettering:** 180 serrations for uncirculated, 220 serrations for proof

Date	Mintage	F	VF	XF	Unc	BU
2001	6,429	—	—	—	BV+8%	—
2001 Proof	3,696	Value: 525				
2002 Proof	2,295	Value: 525				
2003	11,588	—	—	—	BV+8%	—
2003 Proof	1,285	Value: 525				
2004	—	—	—	—	BV+8%	—
2004 Proof	3,288	Value: 525				
2005	—	—	—	—	BV+8%	—
2005 Proof	—	Value: 525				
2006	—	—	—	—	BV+8%	—
2006 Proof	—	Value: 525				
2007	—	—	—	—	BV+8%	—
2007 Proof	—	Value: 525				
2008	—	—	—	—	BV+8%	—
2008 Proof	—	Value: 525				

KM# 73 KRUGERRAND

33.9300 g., 0.9170 Gold 1.0003 oz. AGW, 32.7 mm. **Obv:** Bust of Paul Kruger left **Obv. Legend:** SUID — AFRIKA • SOUTH AFRICA **Rev:** Springbok walking right divides date **Rev. Designer:** Coert L. Steynberg **Edge:** Reeded **Edge Lettering:** 180 serrations for uncirculated, 220 serrations for proof

Date	Mintage	F	VF	XF	Unc	BU
2001	5,889	—	—	—	—	BV+5%
2001 Proof	5,563	Value: 1000				
2002	16,469	—	—	—	—	BV+5%
2002 Proof	3,531	Value: 1000				
2003	47,789	—	—	—	—	BV+5%
2003 Proof	2,136	Value: 1000				
2004	71,269	—	—	—	—	BV+5%
2004 Proof	3,492	Value: 1000				
2004 W/MM Proof	500	Value: 1000				
2005	—	—	—	—	—	BV+5%
2005 Proof	—	Value: 1000				
2006	—	—	—	—	—	BV+5%
2006 Proof	—	Value: 1000				
2007	—	—	—	—	—	BV+5%
2007 Proof	—	Value: 1000				

Date	Mintage	F	VF	XF	Unc	BU
2008	—	—	—	—	—	BV+5%
2008 Proof	—	Value: 1000				

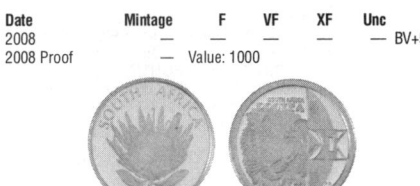

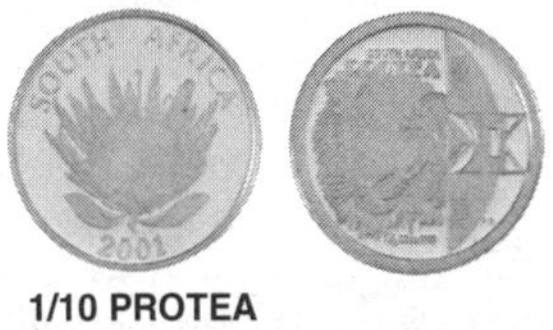

KM# 262 1/10 PROTEA

3.1103 g., 0.9999 Gold 0.1000 oz. AGW, 16.5 mm. **Obv:** Protea flower **Rev:** Lion and partial shield **Edge:** Reeded

Date	Mintage	F	VF	XF	Unc	BU
2001 Proof	—	Value: 115				

KM# 263 PROTEA

31.1035 g., 0.9999 Gold 0.9999 oz. AGW, 32.7 mm. **Obv:** Protea flower **Rev:** Child on sandy beach and partial sun **Edge:** Reeded

Date	Mintage	F	VF	XF	Unc	BU
2001 Proof	—	Value: 1000				

NATURA GOLD BULLION COINAGE

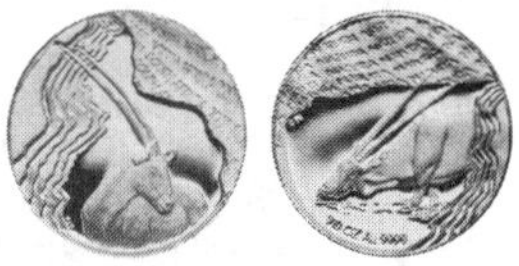

KM# 264 1/10 OUNCE

3.1103 g., 0.9999 Gold 0.1000 oz. AGW, 16.5 mm. **Obv:** Gemsbok head **Rev:** Gemsbok drinking **Edge:** Reeded

Date	Mintage	F	VF	XF	Unc	BU
2001 Proof	—	Value: 115				

KM# 265 1/4 OUNCE

7.7770 g., 0.9999 Gold 0.2500 oz. AGW, 22 mm. **Obv:** Gemsbok head **Rev:** Two Gemsbok males facing off **Edge:** Reeded

Date	Mintage	F	VF	XF	Unc	BU
2001 Proof	—	Value: 275				

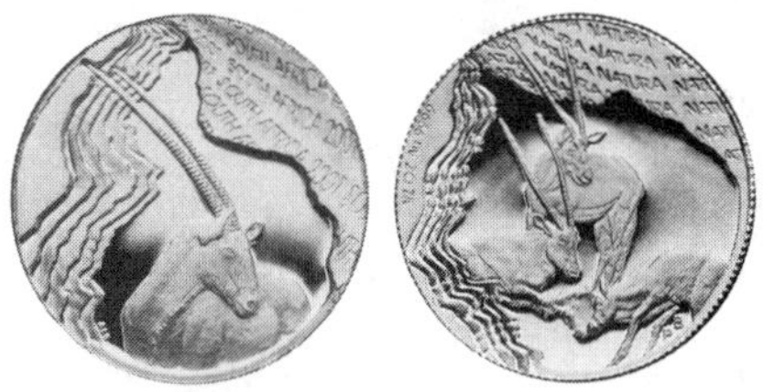

KM# 266 1/2 OUNCE

15.5518 g., 0.9990 Gold 0.4995 oz. AGW, 27 mm. **Obv:** Gemsbok head **Rev:** Gemsbok grazing **Edge:** Reeded

Date	Mintage	F	VF	XF	Unc	BU
2001 Proof	—	Value: 525				

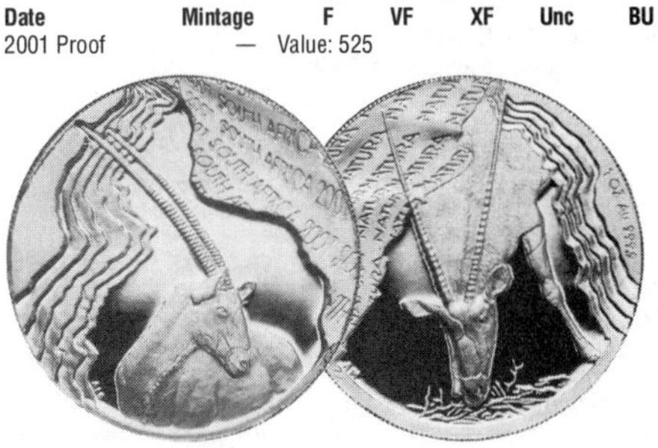

KM# 267 OUNCE

31.1035 g., 0.9990 Gold 0.9990 oz. AGW, 32.7 mm. **Obv:** Gemsbok head **Rev:** Gemsbok grazing **Edge:** Reeded

Date	Mintage	F	VF	XF	Unc	BU
2001 Proof	—	Value: 1000				

MINT SETS

KM#	Date	Mintage	Identification	Issue Price	Mkt Val
MS38	2002 (7)	—	KM#268-274 plus 1- and 2-cent medals	30.00	32.50

PROOF SETS

KM#	Date	Mintage	Identification	Issue Price	Mkt Val
PS170	2002 (7)	—	KM#268-274 plus 1- and 2-cent medals	40.00	42.50
PS171	2005 (4)	1,500	KM#320-323	—	200

S. GEORGIA & THE S. SANDWICH IS.

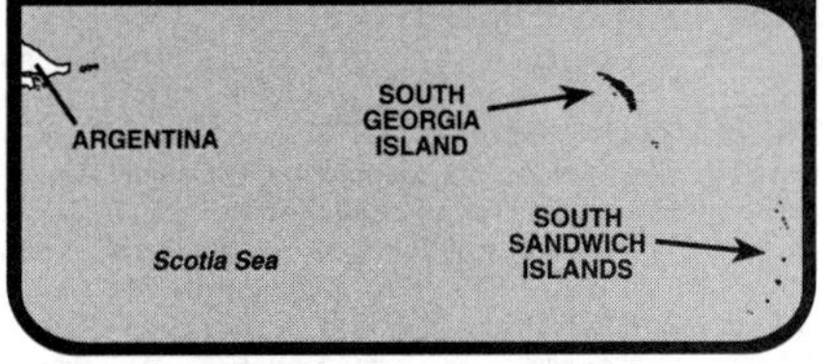

South Georgia and the South Sandwich Islands are a dependency of the Falkland Islands, and located about 800 miles east of them. South Georgia is 1,450 sq. mi. (1,770 sq. km.), and the South Sandwich Islands are 120 sq. mi. (311 sq. km.) Fishing and Antarctic research are the main industries. The islands were claimed for Great Britain in 1775 by Captain James Cook.

RULER

British since 1775

BRITISH OVERSEAS TERRITORY

STANDARD COINAGE

KM# 7 2 POUNDS

28.2800 g., Copper-Nickel, 38.6 mm. **Subject:** Sir Ernest H. Shackleton **Obv:** Crowned bust right **Obv. Designer:** Ian Rank-Broadley **Rev:** Bust facing and ship "Endurance" **Edge:** Reeded

Date	Mintage	F	VF	XF	Unc	BU
2001	—	—	—	—	10.00	12.00

KM# 7a 2 POUNDS

28.2800 g., 0.9250 Silver 0.8410 oz. ASW **Obv:** Crowned bust right **Rev:** Bust facing and ship "Endurance"

Date	Mintage	F	VF	XF	Unc	BU
2001 Proof	Est. 10,000	Value: 50.00				

KM# 9 2 POUNDS

Copper-Nickel **Subject:** Sir Joseph Banks **Obv:** Crowned bust right **Obv. Designer:** Ian Rank-Broadley **Rev:** Cameo and ship

Date	Mintage	F	VF	XF	Unc	BU
2001	—	—	—	—	10.00	12.00

KM# 9a 2 POUNDS

28.2800 g., 0.9250 Silver 0.8410 oz. ASW **Obv:** Crowned bust right **Rev:** Ship and cameo

Date	Mintage	F	VF	XF	Unc	BU
2001 Proof	Est. 10,000	Value: 50.00				

KM# 11 2 POUNDS

28.2800 g., Copper-Nickel, 38.6 mm. **Subject:** Queen Elizabeth II's Golden Jubilee **Obv:** Crowned bust right **Obv. Designer:** Ian Rank-Broadley **Rev:** Young crowned bust right **Edge:** Reeded

Date	Mintage	F	VF	XF	Unc	BU
2002	—	—	—	—	10.00	12.00

KM# 11a 2 POUNDS

28.2800 g., 0.9250 Gold Clad Silver 0.8410 oz., 38.6 mm. **Subject:** Queen Elizabeth II's Golden Jubilee **Obv:** Crowned bust right **Rev:** Young crowned bust right **Edge:** Reeded

Date	Mintage	F	VF	XF	Unc	BU
2002 Proof	10,000	Value: 50.00				

KM# 13 2 POUNDS

28.2800 g., Copper-Nickel, 38.6 mm. **Subject:** Queen Elizabeth II's Golden Jubilee **Obv:** Crowned bust right **Obv. Designer:** Ian Rank-Broadley **Rev:** Small crown above shield flanked by flower sprigs **Edge:** Reeded

Date	Mintage	F	VF	XF	Unc	BU
2002	—	—	—	—	10.00	12.00

KM# 13a 2 POUNDS

28.2800 g., 0.9250 Gold Clad Silver 0.8410 oz., 38.6 mm. **Subject:** Queen Elizabeth II's Golden Jubilee **Obv:** Crowned bust right **Rev:** Small crown above shield flanked by flower sprigs **Edge:** Reeded

Date	Mintage	F	VF	XF	Unc	BU
2002 Proof	10,000	Value: 50.00				

KM# 15 2 POUNDS

28.2800 g., Copper-Nickel, 38.6 mm. **Subject:** Diana, Princess of Wales - The Work Continues **Obv:** Crowned bust right **Obv. Designer:** Ian Rank-Broadley **Rev:** Head 1/4 left **Edge:** Reeded

Date	Mintage	F	VF	XF	Unc	BU
2002	—	—	—	—	—	12.00

KM# 17 2 POUNDS

28.2800 g., Copper-Nickel, 38.6 mm. **Subject:** Prince William's 21st Birthday **Obv:** Crowned bust right **Obv. Designer:** Ian Rank-Broadley **Rev:** Arms of Prince William of Wales **Edge:** Reeded

Date	Mintage	F	VF	XF	Unc	BU
2003PM	—	—	—	—	10.00	12.00

KM# 17a 2 POUNDS

28.2800 g., 0.9250 Silver 0.8410 oz. ASW, 38.6 mm. **Subject:** Prince William's 21st Birthday **Obv:** Crowned bust right **Rev:** Arms of Prince William of Wales **Edge:** Reeded

Date	Mintage	F	VF	XF	Unc	BU
2003PM Proof	—	Value: 50.00				

KM# 18 2 POUNDS

28.2800 g., Copper-Nickel, 38.6 mm. **Obv:** Crowned bust right **Rev:** Capt. Cook, ship and map **Edge:** Reeded

Date	Mintage	F	VF	XF	Unc	BU
2003PM	—	—	—	—	10.00	12.00

KM# 18a 2 POUNDS

28.2800 g., 0.9250 Silver 0.8410 oz. ASW, 38.6 mm. **Obv:** Crowned bust right **Rev:** Capt. Cook, ship and map **Edge:** Reeded

Date	Mintage	F	VF	XF	Unc	BU
2003PM Proof	—	Value: 47.50				

KM# 20 2 POUNDS

28.2800 g., Copper-Nickel, 38.6 mm. **Obv:** Crowned bust right **Obv. Designer:** Ian Rank-Broadley **Rev:** Sir Ernest Shackleton and icebound ship **Edge:** Reeded

Date	Mintage	F	VF	XF	Unc	BU
2004	—	—	—	—	15.00	16.50

KM# 20a 2 POUNDS

28.2800 g., 0.9250 Silver 0.8410 oz. ASW, 38.6 mm. **Obv:** Crowned bust right **Rev:** Sir Ernest Shackleton and icebound ship **Edge:** Reeded

Date	Mintage	F	VF	XF	Unc	BU
2004 Proof	10,000	Value: 50.00				

KM# 21 2 POUNDS

28.2800 g., Copper-Nickel, 38.6 mm. **Subject:** Centennial of Grytviken **Obv:** Crowned bust right **Obv. Designer:** Ian Rank-Broadley **Rev:** Portrait above ship in harbor **Edge:** Reeded

Date	Mintage	F	VF	XF	Unc	BU
2004	—	—	—	—	15.00	16.50

KM# 21a 2 POUNDS

28.2800 g., 0.9250 Silver 0.8410 oz. ASW, 38.6 mm. **Subject:** Centennial of Grytviken **Obv:** Crowned bust right **Rev:** Portrait above ship in harbor **Edge:** Reeded

Date	Mintage	F	VF	XF	Unc	BU
2004 Proof	—	Value: 50.00				

KM# 25 2 POUNDS

Copper-Nickel **Subject:** Marriage of Charles to Parker Bowles **Rev:** Arms of Prince of Wales

Date	Mintage	F	VF	XF	Unc	BU
2005	—	—	—	—	8.50	10.00

KM# 22 2 POUNDS

28.3700 g., Copper-Nickel, 38.5 mm. **Obv:** Elizabeth II **Rev:** Rockhopper Penguin and chick **Edge:** Reeded

Date	Mintage	F	VF	XF	Unc	BU
2006	—	—	—	—	7.50	9.00

KM# 23 2 POUNDS

28.3700 g., Copper-Nickel, 38.5 mm. **Obv:** Elizabeth II **Rev:** Elephant Seal and cub **Edge:** Reeded

Date	Mintage	F	VF	XF	Unc	BU
2006	—	—	—	—	7.50	9.00

KM# 24 2 POUNDS

28.3700 g., Copper-Nickel, 38.5 mm. **Obv:** Elizabeth II **Rev:** Humpback Whale and calf **Edge:** Reeded

Date	Mintage	F	VF	XF	Unc	BU
2006	—	—	—	—	7.50	9.00

KM# 26 2 POUNDS

Copper-Nickel **Subject:** Queen Elizabeth's II 80th Birthday **Rev:** Queen on horseback taking part in Trouping of the Color ceremony

Date	Mintage	F	VF	XF	Unc	BU
2006	—	—	—	—	16.50	—

KM# 26a 2 POUNDS

28.2800 g., 0.9167 Silver 0.8334 oz. ASW **Subject:** Queen Elizabeth's II 80th Birthday **Rev:** Queen on horseback taking part in Trouping of the Color ceremony

Date	Mintage	F	VF	XF	Unc	BU
2006 Proof	25,000	Value: 75.00				

KM# 27 2 POUNDS

Copper-Nickel **Rev:** Albatros

Date	Mintage	F	VF	XF	Unc	BU
2006	—	—	—	—	16.50	—

KM# 28 2 POUNDS

Copper-Nickel **Subject:** Queen Elizabeth's II 80th Birthday **Rev:** 1953 Royal family

Date	Mintage	F	VF	XF	Unc	BU
2006	—	—	—	—	16.50	—

KM# 28a 2 POUNDS

28.2800 g., 0.9167 Silver 0.8334 oz. ASW **Subject:** Queen Elizabeth's II 80th Birthday **Rev:** 1953 Royal family

Date	Mintage	F	VF	XF	Unc	BU
2006 Proof	25,000	Value: 75.00				

KM# 29 2 POUNDS

Copper-Nickel **Subject:** Queen Elizabeth's II 80th Birthday **Rev:** Wedding of Queen Elizabeth II and Prince Philip

Date	Mintage	F	VF	XF	Unc	BU
2006	—	—	—	—	16.50	—

KM# 29a 2 POUNDS

28.2800 g., 0.9167 Silver 0.8334 oz. ASW **Subject:** Queen Elizabeth's 80th Birthday **Rev:** Wedding of Queen Elizabeth II and Prince Philip

Date	Mintage	F	VF	XF	Unc	BU
2006 Proof	25,000	Value: 75.00				

KM# 30 2 POUNDS

Copper-Nickel **Subject:** Queen Elizabeth's II 80th Birthday **Rev:** Queen in Robes of Garter

Date	Mintage	F	VF	XF	Unc	BU
2006	—	—	—	—	16.50	—

KM# 30a 2 POUNDS

28.2800 g., 0.9167 Silver 0.8334 oz. ASW **Subject:** Queen Elizabeth's II 80th Birthday **Rev:** Queen in Robes of Garter

Date	Mintage	F	VF	XF	Unc	BU
2006 Proof	25,000	Value: 75.00				

KM# 37 2 POUNDS

28.2800 g., Copper-Nickel, 38.60 mm. **Ruler:** Elizabeth II **Subject:** Diamond Wedding Anniversary **Obv:** Conjoined busts with Prince Philip right **Obv. Legend:** SOUTH GEORGIA & SOUTH SANDWICH ISLANDS **Rev:** Bust of Princess Elizabeth facing **Rev. Legend:** Diamond Wedding of H.M. Queen Elizabeth II & H.R.H. Prince Philip **Rev. Inscription:** THE BRIDE **Edge:** Reeded

Date	Mintage	F	VF	XF	Unc	BU
2007	—	—	—	—	15.00	16.50

KM# 37a 2 POUNDS

28.2800 g., 0.9167 Silver ASW 0.8335 0.8334 oz. ASW, 38.60 mm. **Ruler:** Elizabeth II **Subject:** Diamond Wedding Anniversary **Obv:** Conjoined busts with Prince Philip right **Obv. Legend:** SOUTH GEORGIA & SOUTH SANDWICH ISLANDS **Rev:** Bust of Princess Elizabeth facing **Rev. Legend:** Diamond Wedding of H.M. Queen Elizabeth II & H.R.H. Prince Philip **Rev. Inscription:** THE BRIDE **Edge:** Reeded

Date	Mintage	F	VF	XF	Unc	BU
2007 Proof	25,000	—	—	75.00	—	—

KM# 38 2 POUNDS

28.2800 g., Copper-Nickel, 38.60 mm. **Ruler:** Elizabeth II **Subject:** Diamond Wedding Anniversary **Obv:** Conjoined busts with Prince Philip right **Obv. Legend:** SOUTH GEORGIA & SOUTH SANDWICH ISLANDS **Rev:** Bust of the bridegroom facing **Rev. Legend:** Diamond Wedding of H.M. Queen Elizabeth II & H.R.H. Prince Philip **Rev. Inscription:** THE BRIDEGROOM **Edge:** Reeded

Date	Mintage	F	VF	XF	Unc	BU
2007	—	—	—	—	15.00	16.50

KM# 38a 2 POUNDS

28.2800 g., 0.9167 Silver ASW 0.8335 0.8334 oz. ASW, 38.60 mm. **Ruler:** Elizabeth II **Subject:** Diamond Wedding Anniversary **Obv:** Conjoined busts with Prince Philip right **Obv. Legend:** SOUTH GEORGIA & SOUTH SANDWICH ISLANDS **Rev:** Bust of the bridegroom facing **Rev. Legend:** Diamond Wedding of H.M. Queen Elizabeth II & H.R.H. Prince Philip **Rev. Inscription:** THE BRIDEGROOM **Edge:** Reeded

Date	Mintage	F	VF	XF	Unc	BU
2007 Proof	25,000	—	—	75.00	—	—

KM# 39 2 POUNDS

28.2800 g., Copper-Nickel, 38.60 mm. **Ruler:** Elizabeth II **Subject:** Diamond Wedding Anniversary **Obv:** Conjoined busts with Prince Philip right **Obv. Legend:** SOUTH GEORGIA & SOUTH SANDWICH ISLANDS **Rev:** 1/2 length figures of royal engaged couple looking at each other **Rev. Legend:** Diamond Wedding of H.M. Queen Elizabeth II & H.R.H. Prince Philip **Rev. Inscription:** ROYAL ENGAGEMENT • JULY • 10 • 1947 **Edge:** Reeded

Date	Mintage	F	VF	XF	Unc	BU
2007	—	—	—	—	15.00	16.50

KM# 39a 2 POUNDS

28.2800 g., 0.9167 Silver ASW 0.8335 0.8334 oz. ASW, 38.60 mm. **Ruler:** Elizabeth II **Subject:** Diamond Wedding Anniversary **Obv:** Conjoined busts with Prince Philip right **Obv. Legend:** SOUTH GEORGIA & SOUTH SANDWICH ISLANDS **Rev:** 1/2 length figures of royal engaged couple looking at each other **Rev. Legend:** Diamond Wedding of H.M. Queen Elizabeth II & H.R.H. Prince Philip **Rev. Inscription:** ROYAL ENGAGEMENT • JULY • 10 • 1947 **Edge:** Reeded

Date	Mintage	F	VF	XF	Unc	BU
2007 Proof	25,000	—	—	75.00	—	—

KM# 40 2 POUNDS

28.2800 g., Copper-Nickel, 38.60 mm. **Ruler:** Elizabeth II **Subject:** Diamond Wedding Anniversary **Obv:** Conjoined busts with Prince Philip right **Obv. Legend:** SOUTH GEORGIA & SOUTH SANDWICH ISLANDS **Rev:** Marriage license, jubilant crowd scene **Rev. Legend:** Diamond Wedding of H.M. Queen Elizabeth II & H.R.H. Prince Philip **Rev. Inscription:** THE MARRIAGE LICENSE **Edge:** Reeded

Date	Mintage	F	VF	XF	Unc	BU
2007	—	—	—	—	15.00	16.50

KM# 40a 2 POUNDS

28.2800 g., 0.9167 Silver ASW 0.8335 0.8334 oz. ASW, 38.60 mm. **Ruler:** Elizabeth II **Subject:** Diamond Wedding Anniversary **Obv:** Conjoined busts with Prince Philip right **Obv. Legend:** SOUTH GEORGIA & SOUTH SANDWICH ISLANDS **Rev:** Marriage license, jubilant crowd scene **Rev. Legend:** Diamond Wedding of H.M. Queen Elizabeth II & H.R.H. Prince Philip **Rev. Inscription:** THE MARRIAGE LICENSE **Edge:** Reeded

Date	Mintage	F	VF	XF	Unc	BU
2007 Proof	25,000	—	—	75.00	—	—

KM# 31 2 POUNDS

Copper-Nickel **Rev:** Queen Elizabeth II 1926 (1953 portrait)

Date	Mintage	F	VF	XF	Unc	BU
2007	—	—	—	—	15.00	16.50

KM# 32 2 POUNDS

Copper-Nickel **Subject:** 25th Anniversary of Liberation **Rev:** Warship and helicopters

Date	Mintage	F	VF	XF	Unc	BU
2007	—	—	—	—	15.00	16.50

KM# 33 2 POUNDS

Copper-Nickel **Rev:** Trans Artic Expedition

Date	Mintage	F	VF	XF	Unc	BU
2007	—	—	—	—	15.00	16.50

KM# 34 2 POUNDS

Copper-Nickel **Subject:** International Polar Year **Rev:** Shackelton Expedition

Date	Mintage	F	VF	XF	Unc	BU
2007	—	—	—	—	15.00	16.50

KM# 35 2 POUNDS

Copper-Nickel **Rev:** Ernest Shacketon

Date	Mintage	F	VF	XF	Unc	BU
2007	—	—	—	—	15.00	16.50

KM# 36 2 POUNDS

Copper-Nickel **Rev:** James Cook

Date	Mintage	F	VF	XF	Unc	BU
2007	—	—	—	—	15.00	16.50

KM# 19 10 POUNDS

155.5100 g., 0.9990 Silver 4.9946 oz. ASW, 65 mm. **Obv:** Crowned bust right **Obv. Designer:** Ian Rank-Broadley **Rev:** Capt. Cook, ship and map **Edge:** Reeded

Date	Mintage	F	VF	XF	Unc	BU
2003PM Proof	2,003	Value: 175				

KM# 8 20 POUNDS

6.2200 g., 0.9999 Gold 0.1999 oz. AGW, 22 mm. **Obv:** Crowned bust right **Obv. Designer:** Ian Rank-Broadley **Rev:** Sir Ernest H. Shackleton and ship **Edge:** Reeded

Date	Mintage	F	VF	XF	Unc	BU
2001 Proof	Est. 2,000	Value: 25				

KM# 10 20 POUNDS

6.2200 g., 0.9999 Gold 0.1999 oz. AGW **Obv:** Crowned bust right **Obv. Designer:** Ian Rank-Broadley **Rev:** Sir Joseph Banks cameo and ship

Date	Mintage	F	VF	XF	Unc	BU
2001 Proof	Est. 2,000	Value: 225				

KM# 16 20 POUNDS

6.2200 g., 0.9999 Gold 0.1999 oz. AGW, 22 mm. **Subject:** Princess Diana **Obv:** Crowned bust right **Obv. Designer:** Ian Rank-Broadley **Rev:** Diana's portrait **Edge:** reeded

Date	Mintage	F	VF	XF	Unc	BU
2002PM Proof	—	Value: 225				

KM# 12 20 POUNDS

6.2200 g., 0.9990 Gold 0.1998 oz. AGW, 22 mm. **Subject:** Queen Elizabeth II's Golden Jubilee **Obv:** Crowned bust right **Obv. Designer:** Ian Rank-Broadley **Rev:** Young crowned bust right **Edge:** Reeded

Date	Mintage	F	VF	XF	Unc	BU
2002 Proof	2,002	Value: 225				

KM# 14 20 POUNDS

6.2200 g., 0.9990 Gold 0.1998 oz. AGW, 22 mm. **Subject:** Queen Elizabeth II's Golden Jubilee **Obv:** Crowned bust right **Obv. Designer:** Ian Rank-Broadley **Rev:** National arms **Edge:** Reeded

Date	Mintage	F	VF	XF	Unc	BU
2002 Proof	2,002	Value: 225				

SPAIN

The Spanish State, forming the greater part of the Iberian Peninsula of southwest Europe, has an area of 195,988 sq. mi. (504,714 sq. km.) and a population of 39.4 million including the Balearic and the Canary Islands. Capital: Madrid. The economy is based on agriculture, industry and tourism. Machinery, fruit, vegetables and chemicals are exported.

RULER

Juan Carlos I, 1975-

MINT MARK

After 1982

Crowned M – Madrid

KINGDOM
1949 - Present

DECIMAL COINAGE

Peseta System

100 Centimos = 1 Peseta

KM# 832 PESETA

Aluminum, 14 mm. **Ruler:** Juan Carlos I **Obv:** Vertical line divides head left from value **Rev:** Crowned shield flanked by pillars with banner **Edge:** Plain

Date	Mintage	F	VF	XF	Unc	BU
2001	—	—	—	0.10	0.30	0.50

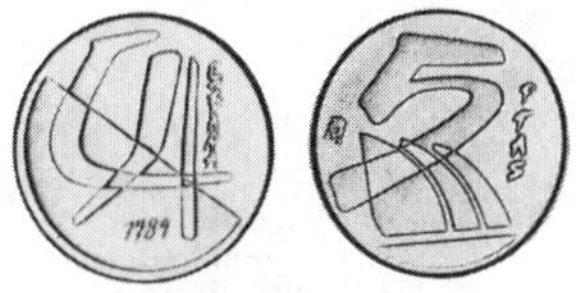

KM# 833 5 PESETAS

3.0500 g., Aluminum-Bronze, 18 mm. **Ruler:** Juan Carlos I **Obv:** Stylized design and date **Rev:** Value above stylized sailboats **Edge:** Plain

Date	Mintage	F	VF	XF	Unc	BU
2001	—	—	—	0.10	0.25	0.35

KM# 1013 25 PESETAS

4.2000 g., Nickel-Brass, 19.5 mm. **Ruler:** Juan Carlos I **Subject:** Navarra **Obv:** Center hole divides bust left and vertical letters **Rev:** Crowned above center hole, order collar at right, value at left **Edge:** Plain

Date	Mintage	F	VF	XF	Unc	BU
2001	—	—	—	—	1.50	2.00

KM# 1016 100 PESETAS

9.8000 g., Aluminum-Bronze, 24.4 mm. **Ruler:** Juan Carlos I **Subject:** 132nd Anniversary of the Peseta **Obv:** Head left **Rev:** Seated allegorical figure from an old coin design **Edge:** Ornamented

Date	Mintage	F	VF	XF	Unc	BU
2001	—	—	—	—	1.50	2.00

KM# 924 500 PESETAS

11.9000 g., Copper-Aluminum-Nickel **Ruler:** Juan Carlos I **Obv:** Conjoined heads of Juan Carlos and Sofia left **Rev:** Crowned shield flanked by pillars with banner, vertical value at right

Date	Mintage	F	VF	XF	Unc	BU
2001	—	—	—	—	12.00	15.00

KM# 1131 500 PESETAS

6.7300 g., Silver, 26.96 mm. **Ruler:** Juan Carlos I **Obv:** Minting equipment **Obv. Legend:** ESPAÑA **Rev:** Copy of Charles II silver reales coin **Rev. Legend:** CASA DE LA MONEDA DE SEGOVIA **Edge:** Reeded **Note:** Aqueduct and crowned M mintmarks appear on obverse

Date	Mintage	F	VF	XF	Unc	BU
2001 Proof	—	Value: 20.00				

KM# 1017 2000 PESETAS

18.0000 g., 0.9250 Silver 0.5353 oz. ASW, 32.9 mm. **Ruler:** Juan Carlos I **Subject:** 132nd Anniversary of the Peseta **Obv:** Conjoined heads left **Rev:** Seated allegorical design from the 1869 Spanish coin series **Edge:** Plain

Date	Mintage	F	VF	XF	Unc	BU
2001	—	—	—	—	22.00	25.00

KM# 1038 2000 PESETAS

27.0000 g., 0.9250 Silver 0.8029 oz. ASW, 40 mm. **Ruler:** Juan Carlos I **Subject:** Segovia Mint's 500th Anniversary **Obv:** Hammer coining scene within beaded circle **Rev:** Segovia Mint 8 reales coin design of 1588 **Edge:** Reeded

Date	Mintage	F	VF	XF	Unc	BU
2001 Proof	15,000	Value: 55.00				

EURO COINAGE

European Union Issues

KM# 1040 EURO CENT

2.2700 g., Copper Plated Steel, 16.2 mm. **Ruler:** Juan Carlos I **Obv:** Cathedral of Santiago de Compostela **Obv. Designer:** Garcilano Rollan **Rev:** Value and globe **Rev. Designer:** Luc Luycx **Edge:** Plain

Date	Mintage	F	VF	XF	Unc	BU
2001	130,900,000	—	—	—	0.25	0.30
2002	141,100,000	—	—	—	0.25	0.30
2003	670,500,000	—	—	—	0.25	0.30
2004	206,700,000	—	—	—	0.25	0.30
2005	444,200,000	—	—	—	0.25	0.30
2006	383,900,000	—	—	—	0.25	0.35
2007	—	—	—	—	0.25	0.35

KM# 1041 2 EURO CENT

3.0300 g., Copper Plated Steel, 18.7 mm. **Ruler:** Juan Carlos I **Obv:** Cathedral of Santiago de Compostela **Obv. Designer:** Garcilano Rollan **Rev:** Value and globe **Rev. Designer:** Luc Luycx **Edge:** Grooved

Date	Mintage	F	VF	XF	Unc	BU
2001	463,100,000	—	—	—	0.25	0.30
2002	4,100,000	—	—	—	1.25	1.50
2003	31,600,000	—	—	—	1.00	1.25
2004	206,700,000	—	—	—	0.25	0.30
2005	275,100,000	—	—	—	0.25	0.30
2006	262,200,000	—	—	—	0.25	0.30
2007	—	—	—	—	0.25	0.30

KM# 1042 5 EURO CENT

3.8600 g., Copper Plated Steel, 21.2 mm. **Ruler:** Juan Carlos I **Obv:** Cathedral of Santiago de Compostela **Obv. Designer:** Garcilano Rollan **Rev:** Value and globe **Rev. Designer:** Luc Luycx **Edge:** Plain

Date	Mintage	F	VF	XF	Unc	BU
2001	216,100,000	—	—	—	0.50	0.60
2002	8,300,000	—	—	—	1.00	1.50
2003	327,600,000	—	—	—	0.50	0.60
2004	258,700,000	—	—	—	0.40	0.50
2005	411,400,000	—	—	—	0.40	0.50
2006	142,800,000	—	—	—	0.40	0.50
2007	—	—	—	—	0.40	0.50

KM# 1043 10 EURO CENT

4.0700 g., Brass, 19.7 mm. **Ruler:** Juan Carlos I **Obv:** Head of Cervantes with ruffed collar 1/4 left within star border **Rev:** Value and map **Edge:** Reeded

Date	Mintage	F	VF	XF	Unc	BU
2001	160,100,000	—	—	—	0.60	0.75
2002	113,100,000	—	—	—	0.60	0.75
2003	292,500,000	—	—	—	0.75	0.90
2004	121,900,000	—	—	—	0.40	0.50
2005	321,300,000	—	—	—	0.40	0.50
2006	91,800,000	—	—	—	0.40	0.50

KM# 1070 10 EURO CENT

4.0700 g., Brass, 19.7 mm. **Ruler:** Juan Carlos I **Obv:** Cervantes **Rev:** Relief map of Western Europe, stars, lines and value **Edge:** Reeded

Date	Mintage	F	VF	XF	Unc	BU
2007	—	—	—	—	0.75	1.00

KM# 1044 20 EURO CENT
5.7300 g., Brass, 22.1 mm. **Ruler:** Juan Carlos I **Obv:** Head of Cervantes with ruffed collar 1/4 left within star border **Obv. Designer:** Begoña Castellanos **Rev:** Value and map **Rev. Designer:** Luc Luycx **Edge:** Notched

Date	Mintage	F	VF	XF	Unc	BU
2001	146,600,000	—	—	—	1.00	1.25
2002	91,500,000	—	—	—	0.60	0.75
2003	4,100,000	—	—	—	1.25	1.50
2004	3,900,000	—	—	—	0.60	0.75
2005	4,000,000	—	—	—	0.60	0.75
2006	102,000,000	—	—	—	0.60	0.75

KM# 1071 20 EURO CENT
5.7300 g., Brass, 22.1 mm. **Ruler:** Juan Carlos I **Obv:** Cervantes **Obv. Designer:** Begoña Castellanos **Rev:** Relief map of Western Europe, stars, lines and value **Rev. Designer:** Luc Luycx **Edge:** Notched

Date	Mintage	F	VF	XF	Unc	BU
2007	—	—	—	—	1.00	1.25

KM# 1045 50 EURO CENT
7.8100 g., Brass, 24.2 mm. **Ruler:** Juan Carlos I **Obv:** Head of Cervantes with ruffed collar 1/4 left within star border **Obv. Designer:** Begoña Castellanos **Rev:** Value and map **Rev. Designer:** Luc Luycx **Edge:** Reeded

Date	Mintage	F	VF	XF	Unc	BU
2001	351,100,000	—	—	—	1.00	1.25
2002	9,800,000	—	—	—	3.00	3.50
2003	6,000,000	—	—	—	3.00	3.50
2004	4,400,000	—	—	—	1.50	2.00
2005	3,900,000	—	—	—	1.25	1.50
2006	4,000,000	—	—	—	1.25	1.50

KM# 1072 50 EURO CENT
7.8100 g., Brass, 24.2 mm. **Ruler:** Juan Carlos I **Obv:** Cervantes **Obv. Designer:** Begoña Castellanos **Rev:** Relief map of Western Europe, stars, lines and value **Rev. Designer:** Luc Luycx **Edge:** Reeded

Date	Mintage	F	VF	XF	Unc	BU
2007	—	—	—	—	1.25	1.50

KM# 1046 EURO
7.5000 g., Bi-Metallic Copper-Nickel center in Brass ring, 23.2 mm. **Ruler:** Juan Carlos I **Obv:** Head 1/4 left within circle and star border **Obv. Designer:** Luiz Jose Diaz **Rev:** Value and map within circle **Rev. Designer:** Luc Luycx **Edge:** Reeded and plain sections

Date	Mintage	F	VF	XF	Unc	BU
2001	259,100,000	—	—	—	3.00	4.00
2002	335,600,000	—	—	—	2.00	2.50
2003	297,400,000	—	—	—	2.00	2.50
2004	9,870,000	—	—	—	2.00	2.50
2005	77,800,000	—	—	—	2.00	2.50
2006	101,600,000	—	—	—	2.00	2.50

KM# 1073 EURO
7.5000 g., Bi-Metallic Copper-Nickel center in Brass ring, 23.2 mm. **Ruler:** Juan Carlos I **Obv:** King's portrait **Obv. Designer:** Luiz Jose Diaz **Rev:** Relief map of Western Europe, stars, lines and value **Rev. Designer:** Luc Luycx **Edge:** Reeded and plain sections

Date	Mintage	F	VF	XF	Unc	BU
2007	—	—	—	—	3.00	3.50

KM# 1047 2 EURO
8.5200 g., Bi-Metallic Brass center in Copper-Nickel ring, 25.7 mm. **Ruler:** Juan Carlos I **Obv:** Head 1/4 left within circle and star border **Obv. Designer:** Luis Jose Diaz **Rev:** Value and map within circle **Rev. Designer:** Luc Luycx **Edge:** Reeded **Edge Lettering:** 2's and stars

Date	Mintage	F	VF	XF	Unc	BU
2001	140,200,000	—	—	—	4.50	5.00
2002	164,000,000	—	—	—	3.50	4.00
2003	44,500,000	—	—	—	4.50	5.00
2004	4,100,000	—	—	—	4.50	5.00
2005	4,000,000	—	—	—	4.50	5.00
2006	4,000,000	—	—	—	4.50	5.00

KM# 1063 2 EURO
8.5200 g., Bi-Metallic Brass center in Copper-Nickel ring, 25.7 mm. **Ruler:** Juan Carlos I **Obv:** Stylizec half length figure with hat holding spear within circle and star border **Rev:** Value and map within circle **Edge:** Reeding over stars and 2's **Note:** Mint mark: Crowned M.

Date	Mintage	F	VF	XF	Unc	BU
2005	8,000,000	—	—	—	5.00	6.00

KM# 1074 2 EURO
8.5200 g., Bi-Metallic Brass center in Copper-Nickel ring, 25.7 mm. **Ruler:** Juan Carlos I **Obv:** King's portrait **Obv. Designer:** Luis Jose Diaz **Rev:** Relief map of Western Europe, stars, lines and value **Rev. Designer:** Luc Luycx **Edge:** Reeded **Edge Lettering:** 2's and stars

Date	Mintage	F	VF	XF	Unc	BU
2007	—	—	—	—	4.75	5.00

KM# 1130 2 EURO
8.5300 g., Bi-Metallic **Ring Composition:** Copper-Nickel **Center Composition:** Brass, 25.70 mm. **Ruler:** Juan Carlos I **Subject:** 50th Anniversary Treaty of Rome **Obv:** Open treaty book **Obv. Legend:** ESPAÑA **Rev:** Large value at left, modified outline of Europe at right **Edge:** Reeded with 2's and stars

Date	Mintage	F	VF	XF	Unc	BU
2007	—	—	—	—	—	9.00

KM# 1048 10 EURO
27.0000 g., 0.9250 Silver 0.8029 oz. ASW, 40 mm. **Ruler:** Juan Carlos I **Subject:** Spanish Presidency of the European Union **Obv:** Head left **Rev:** Map of Europe **Edge:** Reeded

Date	Mintage	F	VF	XF	Unc	BU
2002 Proof	30,000	Value: 50.00				

KM# 1078 10 EURO
27.0000 g., Silver **Ruler:** Juan Carlos I **Subject:** XIX Winter Olympics - Salt Lake City **Obv:** Head left **Obv. Legend:** JUAN CARLOS I REY DE ESPAÑA **Rev:** Cross country skier right, stylized snowflake at right **Rev. Legend:** JUEGOS OLIMPICOS DE - INVERNO 2002

Date	Mintage	F	VF	XF	Unc	BU
2002Crowned M Proof	—	Value: 60.00				

KM# 1079 10 EURO
27.0000 g., Silver **Ruler:** Juan Carlos I **Subject:** XVII Football World Games 2002 - South Korea and Japan **Obv. Legend:** MUNDIAL DE FUTBOL/2002 - ESPANA **Rev:** Football against net

Date	Mintage	F	VF	XF	Unc	BU
2002Crowned M Proof	25,000	Value: 60.00				

KM# 1080 10 EURO
27.0000 g., Silver **Ruler:** Juan Carlos I **Subject:** XVII Football World Games 2002 - South Korea and Japan **Obv. Legend:** MUNDIAL DE FUTBOL/2002 - ESPANA **Rev:** Glove

Date	Mintage	F	VF	XF	Unc	BU
2002Crowned M Proof	25,000	Value: 60.00				

KM# 1087 10 EURO
27.0000 g., 0.9250 Silver 0.8029 oz. ASW **Ruler:** Juan Carlos I **Subject:** 100th Anniversary birth of Luis Cernuda **Obv:** Head left

Date	Mintage	F	VF	XF	Unc	BU
2002Crowned M Proof	25,000	Value: 60.00				

KM# 1088 10 EURO
27.0000 g., 0.9250 Silver 0.8029 oz. ASW **Ruler:** Juan Carlos I **Subject:** 100th Anniversary - Birth of Rafael Alberti **Obv:** Head left **Obv. Legend:** JUAN CARLOS I REY DE ESPANA **Rev:** Bust of Alberti facing 3/4 right

Date	Mintage	F	VF	XF	Unc	BU
2002 Crowned M Proof	25,000	Value: 60.00				

KM# 1089 10 EURO
27.0000 g., 0.9250 Silver 0.8029 oz. ASW **Ruler:** Juan Carlos I **Series:** Ibero-America V - ships **Obv:** Crowned arms in center circle, 10 participating country arms in outer circle **Obv. Legend:** JUAN CARLOS I REY DE ESPNA **Rev:** Galleon of the Spanish Armada **Rev. Legend:** ENCUENTRO DE DOS MUNDOS

Date	Mintage	F	VF	XF	Unc	BU
2002Crowned M Proof	12,000	Value: 135				

KM# 1082 10 EURO
27.0000 g., 0.9250 Silver 0.8029 oz. ASW, 40.0 mm. **Ruler:** Juan Carlos I **Subject:** 150th Anniversary Birth of Antoni Gaudi **Obv:** Bust of Gaudi at right facing **Obv. Legend:** Año Internacional **Rev:** Casa Milà

Date	Mintage	F	VF	XF	Unc	BU
2002Crowned M Proof	25,000	Value: 55.00				

KM# 1083 10 EURO
27.0000 g., 0.9250 Silver 0.8029 oz. ASW, 40.0 mm. **Ruler:** Juan Carlos I **Subject:** 150th Anniversary Birth of Antoni Gaudi **Obv:** Bust of Gaudi at right facing **Obv. Legend:** Año Internacional **Rev:** El Capricho

Date	Mintage	F	VF	XF	Unc	BU
2002Crowned M Proof	25,000	Value: 55.00				

KM# 1084 10 EURO
27.0000 g., 0.9250 Silver 0.8029 oz. ASW, 40.0 mm. **Ruler:** Juan Carlos I **Subject:** 150th Anniversary - Birth of Antoni Gaudi **Obv:** Bust of Gaudi at right facing **Obv. Legend:** Año Internacional **Rev:** Parque Güell

Date	Mintage	F	VF	XF	Unc	BU
2002Crowned M Proof	25,000	Value: 55.00				

KM# 1050 10 EURO
27.0000 g., 0.9250 Silver 0.8029 oz. ASW, 40 mm. **Ruler:** Juan Carlos I **Subject:** Annexation of Minorca **Obv:** Conjoined heads left **Rev:** Uniformed equestrians shaking hands flanked by ships **Edge:** Reeded **Note:** Mint mark: Crowned M.

Date	Mintage	F	VF	XF	Unc	BU
2002 Proof	30,000	Value: 50.00				

KM# 1076 10 EURO
27.0000 g., 0.9250 Silver 0.8029 oz. ASW **Ruler:** Juan Carlos I **Subject:** FIFA World Cup **Obv:** Kings head left **Rev:** Goalie jumping for ball by net

Date	Mintage	F	VF	XF	Unc	BU
2003 Proof	50,000	Value: 55.00				

KM# 1090 10 EURO
27.0000 g., 0.9250 Silver 0.8029 oz. ASW **Ruler:** Juan Carlos I **Obv:** Conjoined heads left **Obv. Legend:** JUAN CARLOS I Y SOFIA **Rev:** Ediface of Parliament building in Madrid **Rev. Legend:** CONSTITUCION ESPANOLA

Date	Mintage	F	VF	XF	Unc	BU
2003Crowned M Proof	30,000	Value: 60.00				

KM# 1092 10 EURO
27.0000 g., 0.9250 Silver 0.8029 oz. ASW, 40.0 mm. **Ruler:** Juan Carlos I **Subject:** !st Anniversary of Euro **Obv:** Conjoined heads left **Obv. Legend:** PREMIER ANIVERSARIO EURO ? JUAN CARLOS I Y SOFIA **Rev:** Europa riding steer left

Date	Mintage	F	VF	XF	Unc	BU
2003Crowned M Proof	50,000	Value: 60.00				

KM# 1052 10 EURO
27.0000 g., 0.9250 Silver 0.8029 oz. ASW, 40 mm. **Ruler:** Juan Carlos I **Obv:** Head left **Rev:** Bust facing flanked by ship and value **Edge:** Reeded

Date	Mintage	F	VF	XF	Unc	BU
2003 Proof	50,000	Value: 50.00				

KM# 1053 10 EURO
27.0000 g., 0.9250 Silver 0.8029 oz. ASW, 40 mm. **Ruler:** Juan Carlos I **Obv:** Juan Carlos I **Rev:** Miguel Lopez de Legazpi **Edge:** Reeded

Date	Mintage	F	VF	XF	Unc	BU
2003 Proof	25,000	Value: 50.00				

KM# 1054 10 EURO
27.0000 g., 0.9250 Silver 0.8029 oz. ASW, 40 mm. **Ruler:** Juan Carlos I **Obv:** Head facing **Rev:** Seated female figure and Swan **Edge:** Reeded

Date	Mintage	F	VF	XF	Unc	BU
2003 Proof	25,000	Value: 50.00				

KM# 1055 10 EURO
27.0000 g., 0.9250 Silver 0.8029 oz. ASW, 40 mm. **Ruler:** Juan Carlos I **Obv:** Head facing **Rev:** Dali's painting "El gran masturbador" of 1929 **Edge:** Reeded

Date	Mintage	F	VF	XF	Unc	BU
2004 Proof	25,000	Value: 50.00				

KM# 1056 10 EURO
27.0000 g., 0.9250 Silver 0.8029 oz. ASW, 40 mm. **Ruler:** Juan Carlos I **Obv:** Head facing **Rev:** Dali's self portrait with bacon strip **Edge:** Reeded

Date	Mintage	F	VF	XF	Unc	BU
2004 Proof	25,000	Value: 50.00				

KM# 1059 10 EURO
27.0000 g., 0.9250 Silver 0.8029 oz. ASW, 40 mm. **Ruler:** Juan Carlos I **Obv:** Conjoined heads left **Rev:** Bust of St. James facing **Edge:** Reeded

Date	Mintage	F	VF	XF	Unc	BU
2004 Proof	20,000	Value: 50.00				

KM# 1060 10 EURO
27.0000 g., 0.9250 Silver 0.8029 oz. ASW, 40 mm. **Ruler:** Juan Carlos I **Obv:** Conjoined heads left within beaded circle **Rev:** Bust 1/4 left within beaded circle (1451-1504) **Edge:** Reeded

Date	Mintage	F	VF	XF	Unc	BU
2004 Proof	20,000	Value: 50.00				

KM# 1099 10 EURO
27.0000 g., 0.9250 Silver 0.8029 oz. ASW **Ruler:** Juan Carlos I **Subject:** Expansion of the European Union **Obv:** Head left **Obv. Legend:** JUAN CARLOS I Y SOFIA **Rev:** Outlined map of European Union

Date	Mintage	F	VF	XF	Unc	BU
2004Crowned M Proof	50,000	Value: 75.00				

KM# 1101 10 EURO
27.0000 g., 0.9250 Silver 0.8029 oz. ASW **Ruler:** Juan Carlos I **Subject:** XXVIII Summer Olympics - Athens 2004 **Obv:** Conjoined heads left **Obv. Legend:** JUAN CARLOS I Y SOFIA **Rev:** Broad jumper, outlined world map in backgound **Rev. Legend:** JUEGOS OLIMICOS

Date	Mintage	F	VF	XF	Unc	BU
2004Crowned M Proof	30,000	Value: 60.00				

KM# 1102 10 EURO
27.0000 g., 0.9250 Silver 0.8029 oz. ASW **Ruler:** Juan Carlos I **Subject:** XVIII World Football games - Germany 2006 **Obv:** Head left **Obv. Legend:** JUAN CARLOS I REY DE ESPANA **Rev:** Goalie deflecting ball at net

Date	Mintage	F	VF	XF	Unc	BU
2004Crowned M Proof	50,000	Value: 60.00				

KM# 1097 10 EURO
27.0000 g., 0.9250 Silver 0.8029 oz. ASW, 40.0 mm. **Ruler:** Juan Carlos I **Subject:** Wedding of Prince Philip and Letizia Ortiz Rocasolano **Obv:** Conjoined heads left **Obv. Legend:** JUAN CARLOS I T SOFÍA **Rev:** Busts of wedding couple facing 3/4 right, crowned shield below **Rev. Legend:** FELIPE Y LETIZIA - 22.V.2004

Date	Mintage	F	VF	XF	Unc	BU
2004Crowned M Proof	100,000	Value: 55.00				

KM# 1104 10 EURO
27.0000 g., 0.9250 Silver 0.8029 oz. ASW, 40.0 mm. **Ruler:** Juan Carlos I **Obv:** Quixote seated reading a large book **Obv. Legend:** ESPAÑA - IV CENTENARIO DE LA PRIMERA EDICIÓN DE " EL QUIJOTE" **Rev:** Quixote being knocked off his horse by windmill blade **Rev. Legend:** LA AVENTURA - DE LOS - MOLINOS DE VIENTO

Date	Mintage	F	VF	XF	Unc	BU
2005Crowned M Proof	18,000	Value: 65.00				

KM# 1105 10 EURO
27.0000 g., 0.9250 Silver 0.8029 oz. ASW, 40.0 mm. **Ruler:** Juan Carlos I **Obv:** Quixote esated reading a large book **Obv. Legend:** ESPAÑA - IV CENTENARIO DE LA PREMERA EDICIÓN DE LA "EL QUIJOTE" **Rev:** Quixote thrusting his sword into an animal skin wine sack **Rev. Legend:** CON UNOS CUEROS DE VINO - BATALLA

Date	Mintage	F	VF	XF	Unc	BU
2005Crowned M Proof	18,000	Value: 65.00				

KM# 1106 10 EURO
27.0000 g., 0.9250 Silver 0.8029 oz. ASW, 40.0 mm. **Ruler:** Juan Carlos I **Obv:** Quixote seated reading a large book **Obv. Legend:** ESPAÑA - IV CENTENARIO DE LA PRIMERA EDICIÓN DE "EL QUIJOTE" **Rev:** Boy mounting a hobby horse with Quixote on it **Rev. Legend:** LA VENIDA DE CLAVAILEÑO CON...DILATADA AVENTURA

Date	Mintage	F	VF	XF	Unc	BU
2005Crowned M Proof	18,000	Value: 65.00				

KM# 1110 10 EURO
27.0000 g., 0.9250 Silver 0.8029 oz. ASW, 40.0 mm. **Ruler:** Juan Carlos I **Rev:** Crowned shield at left, head of Prince Philip at right **Rev. Legend:** XXV ANIVERSARIO - PREMIOS PRÍNCIPE DE ASTURIAS

Date	Mintage	F	VF	XF	Unc	BU
2005Crowned M Proof	35,000	Value: 60.00				

KM# 1109 10 EURO
27.0000 g., 0.9250 Silver 0.8029 oz. ASW **Ruler:** Juan Carlos I **Series:** Ibero-America VI - Architecture **Obv:** Crowned arms in center circle, 10 participating country arms in outer circle **Obv. Legend:** JUAN CARLOS I REY DE ESPAÑA **Rev:** General Archives building of West Indes in Seville **Rev. Legend:** ENCUENTRO DE DOS MUNDOS

Date	Mintage	F	VF	XF	Unc	BU
2005Crowned M Proof	12,000	Value: 90.00				

KM# 1064 10 EURO
27.0000 g., 0.9250 Silver 0.8029 oz. ASW, 40 mm. **Ruler:** Juan Carlos I **Subject:** 2006 Winter Olympics **Obv:** Juan Carlos **Rev:** Skier **Edge:** Reeded

Date	Mintage	F	VF	XF	Unc	BU
2005 Proof	25,000	Value: 45.00				

KM# 1065 10 EURO
27.0000 g., 0.9250 Silver 0.8029 oz. ASW, 40 mm. **Ruler:** Juan Carlos I **Subject:** European Peace and Freedom **Obv:** Juan Carlos **Rev:** European map on clasped hands **Edge:** Reeded

Date	Mintage	F	VF	XF	Unc	BU
2005 Proof	40,000	Value: 40.00				

KM# 1114 10 EURO
26.8000 g., 0.9250 Silver 0.7970 oz. ASW, 39.98 mm. **Ruler:** Juan Carlos I **Subject:** 500th Anniversary Death of Columbus **Obv:** Bust of Columbus facing at right, astrolabe at lower left **Obv. Legend:** ESPAÑA **Rev:** Sailing ship "Santa Maria" **Rev. Legend:** CRISTOBAL COLON **Edge:** Reeded

Date	Mintage	F	VF	XF	Unc	BU
2006Crowned M Proof	12,000	Value: 65.00				

KM# 1119 10 EURO
27.0000 g., 0.9250 Silver 0.8029 oz. ASW, 40.0 mm. **Ruler:** Juan Carlos I **Subject:** 20th Anniversay of Spain and Portugal membership in European Union **Obv:** Juan Carlos I **Rev:** Outlined map of Europe, bridge below **Rev. Legend:** ADHESIÓN A LAS COMUNIDADES EUROPEAS **Rev. Inscription:** ESPAÑA - PORTUGAL

Date	Mintage	F	VF	XF	Unc	BU
2006Crowned M Proof	12,000	Value: 60.00				

KM# 1122 10 EURO
27.0000 g., 0.9250 Silver 0.8029 oz. ASW, 40.0 mm. **Ruler:** Juan Carlos I **Obv:** Head left **Obv. Legend:** JUAN CARLOS I REY DE ESPAÑA **Rev:** Charles I (V) standing facing 3/4 right in front of portal **Rev. Legend:** CAROLVS IMPERATOR

Date	Mintage	F	VF	XF	Unc	BU
2006Crowned M Proof	35,000	Value: 65.00				

KM# 1115 10 EURO
18.0000 g., 0.9250 Silver 0.5353 oz. ASW, 39.98 mm. **Ruler:** Juan Carlos I **Subject:** 500th Anniversary - Death of Columbus **Obv:** Bust of Colombus facing at left, astrolabe at lower right **Obv. Legend:** ESPAÑA **Rev:** Sailing ship "Pinta" **Rev. Legend:** CRISTOBAL COLON **Edge:** Reeded

Date	Mintage	F	VF	XF	Unc	BU
2006Crowned M Proof	12,000	Value: 65.00				

KM# 1116 10 EURO
26.8000 g., 0.9250 Silver 0.7970 oz. ASW, 39.98 mm. **Ruler:** Juan Carlos I **Subject:** 500th Anniversary - Death of Columbus **Obv:** Bust of Columbus facing at right, astrolabe at lower left **Obv. Legend:** ESPAÑA **Rev:** Sailing ship "Niña" **Rev. Legend:** CRISTOBAL COLON **Edge:** Reeded

Date	Mintage	F	VF	XF	Unc	BU
2006Crowned M Proof	12,000	Value: 65.00				

KM# 1124 10 EURO
27.0000 g., 0.9250 Silver 0.8029 oz. ASW, 40 mm. **Ruler:** Juan Carlos I **Rev:** Two ornate portals **Rev. Legend:** V ANIVERSARIO DEL EURO

Date	Mintage	F	VF	XF	Unc	BU
2007 Proof	12,000	Value: 65.00				

KM# 1125 10 EURO
27.0000 g., 0.9250 Silver 0.8029 oz. ASW, 40 mm. **Ruler:** Juan Carlos I **Rev:** Stone arch bridge **Rev. Legend:** V ANIVERSARIO DEL EURO

Date	Mintage	F	VF	XF	Unc	BU
2007 Proof	12,000	Value: 65.00				

KM# 1126 10 EURO
27.0000 g., 0.9250 Silver 0.8029 oz. ASW, 40 mm. **Ruler:** Juan Carlos I **Rev:** Stone archway **Rev. Legend:** V ANIVERSARIO DEL EURO

Date	Mintage	F	VF	XF	Unc	BU
2007 Proof	12,000	Value: 65.00				

KM# 1132 10 EURO
27.0000 g., 0.9250 Silver 0.8029 oz. ASW, 40 mm. **Ruler:** Juan Carlos I **Obv:** Conjoined heads left **Obv. Legend:** JUAN CARLOS I Y SOFÍA - AÑO DE ESPAÑa EN CHINA **Rev:** Early silver "Pillar" reales coin with Chinese characters to left and right of pillars **Rev. Legend:** VTRAQUE VNVM

Date	Mintage	F	VF	XF	Unc	BU
2007 Proof	20,000	Value: 60.00				

KM# 1134 10 EURO
27.0000 g., 0.9250 Silver 0.8029 oz. ASW, 40 mm. **Ruler:** Juan Carlos I **Obv:** Head left **Obv. Legend:** JUAN CARLOS I REY DE ESPAÑA **Rev:** Basketball player shooting basket **Rev. Legend:** EUROBASKET 2007

Date	Mintage	F	VF	XF	Unc	BU
2007 Proof	12,000	Value: 65.00				

KM# 1049 12 EURO
18.0000 g., 0.9250 Silver 0.5353 oz. ASW, 33 mm. **Ruler:** Juan Carlos I **Subject:** Spanish European Union Presidency **Obv:** Conjoined heads left **Rev:** Distorted star design **Edge:** Reeded

Date	Mintage	F	VF	XF	Unc	BU
2002	1,500,000	—	—	—	20.00	22.50
2002 Special select	25,000	—	—	—	—	30.00
2002 Proof	50,000	Value: 50.00				

KM# 1051 12 EURO
18.0000 g., 0.9250 Silver 0.5353 oz. ASW, 33 mm. **Ruler:** Juan Carlos I **Subject:** 25th Anniversary of Constitution **Obv:** Conjoined heads left **Rev:** National arms above denomination **Edge:** Plain

Date	Mintage	F	VF	XF	Unc	BU
2003	1,469,000	—	—	—	25.00	27.50

KM# 1069 12 EURO
Silver **Ruler:** Juan Carlos I **Obv:** Juan Carlos and Sofia **Rev:** Felipe and Letizia

Date	Mintage	F	VF	XF	Unc	BU
2004M	—	—	—	—	25.00	27.50

KM# 1095 12 EURO
18.0000 g., 0.9250 Silver 0.5353 oz. ASW, 32.93 mm. **Ruler:** Juan Carlos I **Subject:** 6ooth Anniversary - Death of Isabel **Obv:** Conjoined heads left **Obv. Legend:** JUAN CARLOS I Y SOFIA **Rev:** Bust of Isabella I left **Rev. Legend:** ISABEL I DE CASTILLA / 1481-1404 **Edge:** Plain

Date	Mintage	F	VF	XF	Unc	BU
2004Crowned M	1,500,000	—	—	—	—	30.00

KM# 1096 12 EURO
18.0000 g., 0.9250 Silver 0.5353 oz. ASW, 32.94 mm. **Ruler:** Juan Carlos I **Subject:** Wedding of Prince Philip and Letizia Ortiz Rocasolano **Obv:** Conjoined heads left **Obv. Legend:** JUAN CARLOS I Y SOFIA **Rev:** Busts of wedding couple facing 3/4 right **Rev. Legend:** FELIPE Y LETIZIA - 22.V.2004 **Edge:** Plain

Date	Mintage	F	VF	XF	Unc	BU
2004Crowned M	4,000,000	—	—	—	22.50	30.00

KM# 1067 12 EURO
18.0000 g., 0.9250 Silver 0.5353 oz. ASW, 33 mm. **Ruler:** Juan Carlos I **Subject:** Don Quixote **Obv:** Conjoined heads left **Rev:** Man seated on books **Edge:** Reeded

Date	Mintage	F	VF	XF	Unc	BU
2005	4,000,000	—	—	—	22.50	25.00

KM# 1113 12 EURO
18.0000 g., 0.9250 Silver 0.5353 oz. ASW, 32.95 mm. **Ruler:** Juan Carlos I **Subject:** 500th Anniversary - Death of Columbus **Obv:** Conjoined heads left **Obv. Legend:** JUAN CARLOS I Y SOFIA **Rev:** Bust of Columbus facing 3/4 right, latitude and longitude lines with three small sailing ships in background **Edge:** Plain

Date	Mintage	F	VF	XF	Unc	BU
2006Crowned M	4,000,000	—	—	—	22.50	25.00

KM# 1129 12 EURO
18.0000 g., 0.9250 Silver 0.5353 oz. ASW, 32 mm. **Ruler:** Juan Carlos I **Rev:** Hand with pen **Rev. Legend:** 50 ANIVERSARIO • TRATADO DE ROMA **Rev. Inscription:** EUROPA

Date	Mintage	F	VF	XF	Unc	BU
2007 Proof	25,000	Value: 30.00				

KM# 1133 20 EURO
1.2400 g., 0.9990 Gold 0.0398 oz. AGW, 13.92 mm. **Ruler:** Juan Carlos I **Obv:** National arms **Obv. Legend:** JUAN CARLOS I REY DE ESPAÑA - AÑO DE ESPAÑA EN CHINA **Rev:** Early silver "Pillar" reales coin with Chinese chpmarks

Date	Mintage	F	VF	XF	Unc	BU
2007 Proof	15,000	Value: 65.00				

KM# 1085 50 EURO
168.7500 g., 0.9250 Silver 5.0183 oz. ASW, 73 mm. **Ruler:** Juan Carlos I **Subject:** 150th Anniversary - Birth of Antoni Gaudi **Obv:** Bust of Gaudi at right facing **Obv. Legend:** Año Internacional **Rev:** Sagrada Familia

Date	Mintage	F	VF	XF	Unc	BU
2002Crowned M Proof	8,000	Value: 200				

KM# 1093 50 EURO
168.7500 g., 0.9250 Silver 5.0183 oz. ASW, 73 mm. **Ruler:** Juan Carlos I **Subject:** 1st Anniversary of Euro **Obv:** Conjoined heads left **Obv. Legend:** PREMIER ANIVERSARIO EURO • JUAN CARLOS I Y SOFÍA **Rev:** National arms at center surrounded by various items of achitecture

Date	Mintage	F	VF	XF	Unc	BU
2003 Proof	20,000	Value: 550				

KM# 1057 50 EURO
168.7500 g., 0.9250 Silver with removeable gold plated silver insert 5.0183 oz. ASW, 73 mm. **Ruler:** Juan Carlos I **Obv:** Dali's "Dream State" painting **Rev:** Dali's "Rhinocerotic Disintegration..." painting **Edge:** Reeded **Note:** Illustration reduced.

Date	Mintage	F	VF	XF	Unc	BU
2004 Proof	12,000	Value: 175				

KM# 1061 50 EURO
168.7300 g., 0.9250 Silver 5.0177 oz. ASW, 73 mm. **Ruler:** Juan Carlos I **Obv:** Crowned bust left(1451-1504) and castle within beaded circle **Rev:** Surrender of Grenada scene within beaded circle **Edge:** Reeded **Note:** Illustration reduced.

Date	Mintage	F	VF	XF	Unc	BU
2004 Proof	8,000	Value: 180				

KM# 1107 50 EURO

168.7500 g., 0.9250 Silver 5.0183 oz. ASW, 73 mm. **Ruler:** Juan Carlos I **Obv:** 1/2 length figure of Miguel de Cervantes Saavedra facing writing in manuscript with quill pen **Obv. Legend:** ESPAÑA - IV CENTENARIO DE LA PRIMERA EDICIÓn DE "EL QUIJOTE" **Rev:** Quixote

Date	Mintage	F	VF	XF	Unc	BU
2005Crowned M Proof	12,000	Value: 225				

KM# 1117 50 EURO

168.2500 g., 0.9250 Silver 5.0035 oz. ASW, 73.95 mm. **Ruler:** Juan Carlos I **Subject:** 500th Anniversary - Death of Columbus **Obv:** Landing party at Guanahani **Obv. Legend:** ESPAÑA **Rev:** Columbus standing facing 3/4 left with right arm outstretched standing on outline of the northern part of South America **Rev. Legend:** CRISTOBAL COLON **Edge:** Plain **Note:** Illustration reduced.

Date	Mintage	F	VF	XF	Unc	BU
2006Crowned M Proof	6,000	Value: 225				

KM# 1127 50 EURO

168.7500 g., 0.9250 Silver 5.0183 oz. ASW, 73 mm. **Ruler:** Juan Carlos I **Rev:** Euro seated on resting bull left **Rev. Legend:** V ANIVERSARIO DEL EURO

Date	Mintage	F	VF	XF	Unc	BU
2007 Proof	6,000	Value: 220				

KM# 1077 100 EURO

6.7500 g., 0.9990 Gold 0.2168 oz. AGW **Ruler:** Juan Carlos I **Obv:** Head left **Obv. Legend:** JUAN CARLOS I REY DE ESPANA **Rev:** Player running right kicking ball **Rev. Legend:** ALEMANIA 2006 at bottom

Date	Mintage	F	VF	XF	Unc	BU
2003Crowned M Proof	25,000	Value: 375				

KM# 1103 100 EURO

6.7500 g., 0.9990 Gold 0.2168 oz. AGW **Ruler:** Juan Carlos I **Subject:** XVIII World Football Games - Germany 2006 **Obv:** Head left **Obv. Legend:** JUAN CARLOS I REY DE ESPANA **Rev:** Goalie deflecting ball at net **Rev. Inscription:** COPA MUNDIAL DE LA FIFA

Date	Mintage	F	VF	XF	Unc	BU
2004Crowned M Proof	25,000	Value: 350				

KM# 1081 200 EURO

13.5000 g., 0.9990 Gold 0.4336 oz. AGW **Ruler:** Juan Carlos I **Subject:** XVII Football World Games 2002 - South Korea and Japan **Obv. Legend:** MUNDIAL DE FUTBOL/2002 - ESPANA **Rev:** Ball hitting net

Date	Mintage	F	VF	XF	Unc	BU
2002Crowned M Proof	4,000	Value: 600				

KM# 1091 200 EURO

13.5000 g., 0.9990 Gold 0.4336 oz. AGW **Ruler:** Juan Carlos I **Obv:** Conjoined heads left **Obv. Legend:** JUAN CARLOS I Y SOFIA **Rev:** Ediface of Parliament Building in Madrid **Rev. Legend:** CONSTITUCION ESPANOLA

Date	Mintage	F	VF	XF	Unc	BU
2003Crowned M Proof	4,000	Value: 550				

KM# 1075 200 EURO

13.5000 g., 0.9990 Gold 0.4336 oz. AGW, 30 mm. **Ruler:** Juan Carlos I **Subject:** Birth of the Euro **Obv:** Spanish King and Queen left **Rev:** Mythological Europa riding on the back of a bull

Date	Mintage	F	VF	XF	Unc	BU
2003 Proof	20,000	Value: 500				

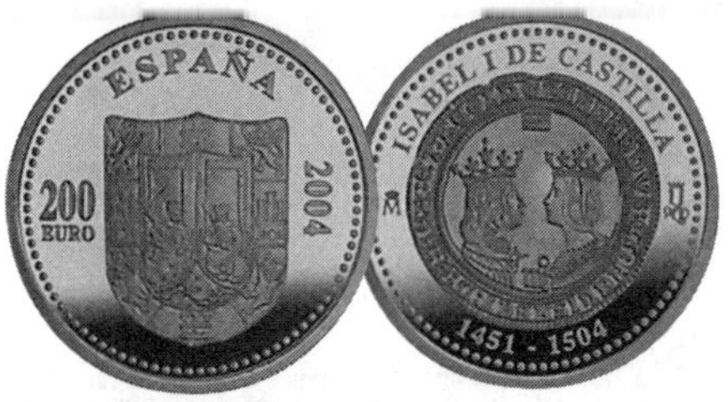

KM# 1062 200 EURO

13.5000 g., 0.9990 Gold 0.4336 oz. AGW, 30 mm. **Ruler:** Juan Carlos I **Obv:** Seated crowned figures on shield flanked by date and value **Rev:** Crowned busts facing each other on coin design **Edge:** Reeded

Date	Mintage	F	VF	XF	Unc	BU
2004 Proof	5,000	Value: 550				

KM# 1100 200 EURO

13.5000 g., 0.9990 Gold 0.4336 oz. AGW **Ruler:** Juan Carlos I **Subject:** Expansion of the European Union **Obv:** Head left **Obv. Legend:** JUAN CARLOS I Y SOFIA **Rev:** Outlined map of the European Union

Date	Mintage	F	VF	XF	Unc	BU
2004Crowned M Proof	5,000	Value: 600				

KM# 1098 200 EURO

13.5000 g., 0.9990 Gold 0.4336 oz. AGW, 30 mm. **Ruler:** Juan Carlos I **Subject:** Wedding of Prince Philip and Letizia Ortiz Rocasolano **Obv:** Conjoined heads left **Obv. Legend:** JUAN CARLOS I Y SOF?a **Rev:** Busts of wedding couple facing 3/4 right at center left, crowned shield at right **Rev. Legend:** FELIPE Y LETIZIA - 22.V.2004

Date	Mintage	F	VF	XF	Unc	BU
2004Crowned M Proof	30,000	Value: 550				

KM# 1111 200 EURO

13.5000 g., 0.9990 Gold 0.4336 oz. AGW, 30 mm. **Ruler:** Juan Carlos I **Rev:** Crowned shield at left, head of Prince Philip left at right **Rev. Legend:** XXV ANIVERSAIO - PREMIOS PRÍNCIPE DE ASTURIAS

Date	Mintage	F	VF	XF	Unc	BU
2005Crowned M Proof	3,500	Value: 650				

KM# 1066 200 EURO

13.5000 g., 0.9990 Gold 0.4336 oz. AGW, 30 mm. **Ruler:** Juan Carlos I **Subject:** European Peace and Freedom **Obv:** Juan Carlos **Rev:** European map on clasped hands **Edge:** Reeded

Date	Mintage	F	VF	XF	Unc	BU
2005 Proof	4,000	Value: 650				

KM# 1123 200 EURO

13.5000 g., 0.9990 Gold 0.4336 oz. AGW, 30 mm. **Ruler:** Juan Carlos I **Obv:** Head left **Obv. Legend:** JUAN CARLOS I REY DE ESPAÑA **Rev:** Charles I (V) standing facing 3/4 right in front of portal **Rev. Legend:** CAROLVS IMPERATOR

Date	Mintage	F	VF	XF	Unc	BU
2006Crowned M Proof	5,000	Value: 600				

KM# 1112 300 EURO

Ring Weight: 11.5400 g. **Ring Composition:** 0.9250 Silver 0.3432 oz. ASW **Center Weight:** 17.2600 g. **Center Composition:** 0.9990 Gold 0.5543 oz. AGW , 40 mm. **Ruler:** Juan Carlos I **Subject:** XVIII World Championship Football Games - Germany 2006 **Obv:** Football player facing kicking ball **Obv. Legend:** ESPAÑA **Rev:** Football player kicking ball into net at foreground **Rev. Legend:** COPA MUNDIAL DE LA FIFA - ALEMANIA **Shape:** 12-sided

Date	Mintage	F	VF	XF	Unc	BU
2005Crowned M Proof	2,006	Value: 900				

KM# 1121 300 EURO

Ring Composition: 0.9250 Silver **Center Composition:** 0.9990 Gold, 40 mm. **Ruler:** Juan Carlos I **Rev:** Basketball player facing tossing ball **Rev. Legend:** CAMPEONES DEL MUNDO - JAPÓn 2006 **Shape:** 12-sided

Date	Mintage	F	VF	XF	Unc	BU
2006Crowned M Proof	2,000	Value: 900				

KM# 1086 400 EURO

27.0000 g., 0.9990 Gold 0.8672 oz. AGW, 38 mm. **Ruler:** Juan Carlos I **Subject:** 150th Anniversary - Birth of Antoni Gaudi **Obv:** Bust of Gaudi at right facing **Obv. Legend:** Año Internacional **Rev:** Casa Batlló

Date	Mintage	F	VF	XF	Unc	BU
2002Crowned M Proof	3,000	Value: 1,100				

KM# 1058 400 EURO

27.0000 g., 0.9990 Gold 0.8672 oz. AGW, 38 mm. **Ruler:** Juan Carlos I **Obv:** Bust facing **Rev:** Dali's painting "Girl at the Window" **Edge:** Reeded

Date	Mintage	F	VF	XF	Unc	BU
2004 Proof	5,000	Value: 975				

KM# 1108 400 EURO

27.0000 g., 0.9990 Gold 0.8672 oz. AGW, 38 mm. **Ruler:** Juan Carlos I **Obv:** Quixote seated reading a large book **Obv. Legend:** ESPAÑA - IV CENTENARIO DE LA PRIMERA EDICIÓN DE "EL QUIJOTE" **Rev:** Quixote on horseback 3/4 right followed by his friend on a burro **Rev. Legend:** DON QUIJOTE DE LA MANCHA SANCHO PANZA

Date	Mintage	F	VF	XF	Unc	BU
2005Crowned M Proof	3,000	Value: 1,150				

KM# 1118 400 EURO

27.0000 g., 0.9990 Gold 0.8672 oz. AGW **Ruler:** Juan Carlos I **Subject:** 500th Anniversary - Death of Columbus **Obv:** Columbus **Rev:** Audience with Ferdinand and Isabella

Date	Mintage	F	VF	XF	Unc	BU
2006Crowned M Proof	3,000	Value: 1,150				

KM# 1128 400 EURO

27.0000 g., 0.9990 Gold 0.8672 oz. AGW, 38 mm. **Ruler:** Juan Carlos I **Rev:** Large ring of stars around globe **Rev. Legend:** V ANIVERSARIO DEL EURO

Date	Mintage	F	VF	XF	Unc	BU
2007 Proof	3,000	Value: 1,150				

MINT SETS

KM#	Date	Mintage	Identification	Issue Price	Mkt Val
MS27	2000-01 (8)	49,426	KM#832-833, 924, 991-992 (both dated 2000), 1012-1013, 1016	15.50	20.00
MS28	2002 (8)	99,301	KM#1040-1047	—	15.00
MS29	2003 (8)	149	KM#1040-1047	—	15.00
MS30	2004 (8)	43,000	KM#1040-1047	—	70.00
MS31	2005 (8)	49,923	KM#1040-1047	—	30.00
MS32	2006 (8)	49,996	KM#1040-1047	—	12.50
MS33	2007 (8)	—	KM#1040-1042, 1070-1074	—	30.00

PROOF SETS

KM#	Date	Mintage	Identification	Issue Price	Mkt Val
PS34	2002 (8)	23,000		—	—
PS35	2003 (3)	—	KM#1186, 1187, 1188	—	320
PS36	2007 (2)	—	KM#1132-1133	—	65.00

SRI (SHRI) LANKA

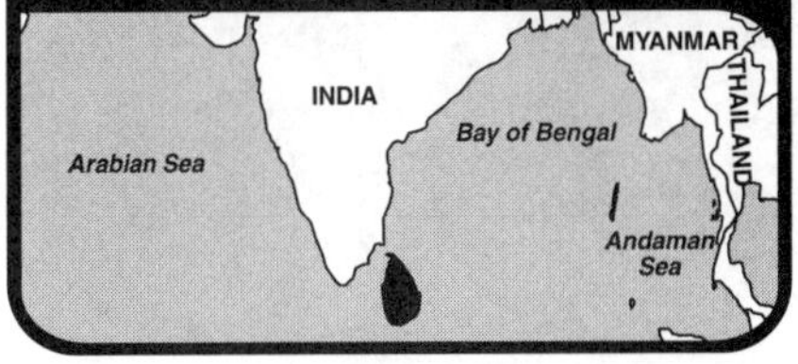

The Democratic Socialist Republic of Sri Lanka (formerly Ceylon) situated in the Indian Ocean 18 miles (29 km.) southeast of India, has an area of 25,332 sq. mi. (65,610 sq. km.) and a population of *16.9 million. Capital: Colombo. The economy is chiefly agricultural. Tea, coconut products and rubber are exported.

Sri Lanka is a member of the Commonwealth of Nations. The president is Chief of State. The prime minister is Head of Government. The present leaders of the country have reverted the country name back to Sri Lanka.

RULER

British, 1796-1948

DEMOCRATIC SOCIALIST REPUBLIC

DECIMAL COINAGE

100 Cents = 1 Rupee

KM# 141.2a 25 CENTS

Nickel Clad Steel **Obv:** Value above designs within wreath **Rev:** Navy emblem **Edge:** Reeded

Date	Mintage	F	VF	XF	Unc	BU
2001	10,000,000	—	—	0.10	0.25	0.45
2002	10,000,000	—	—	0.10	0.25	0.45

KM# 141.2b 25 CENTS

Copper Plated Steel, 16 mm. **Obv:** Denomination **Rev:** National arms

Date	Mintage	F	VF	XF	Unc	BU
2005	—	—	—	—	0.25	0.45

KM# 135.2a 50 CENTS

Nickel Clad Steel **Obv:** Value above designs within wreath **Rev:** Navy emblem **Edge:** Reeded

Date	Mintage	F	VF	XF	Unc	BU
2001	30,000,000	—	0.10	0.25	0.65	1.00
2002	10,000,000	—	0.10	0.25	0.65	1.00

KM# 135.2b 50 CENTS

Copper -clad Steel **Obv:** Value above designs within wreath **Rev:** Navy emblem **Edge:** Reeded

Date	Mintage	F	VF	XF	Unc	BU
2005	—	—	0.10	0.25	0.65	1.00

KM# 166 RUPEE
7.1300 g., Copper Nickel, 25.4 mm. **Subject:** Air Force's 50th Anniversary **Obv:** Badge of the Sri Lanka Air Force **Rev:** Two jets above propeller plane within circle **Edge:** Reeded

Date	Mintage	F	VF	XF	Unc	BU
2001 Proof	2,000	Value: 100				

KM# 136.2a RUPEE
Nickel Clad Steel **Obv:** Inscription below designs within wreath **Rev:** Navy emblem **Edge:** Reeded

Date	Mintage	F	VF	XF	Unc	BU
2002	50,000,000	—	0.25	0.50	1.00	1.50

KM# 136.2 RUPEE
Copper-Nickel **Obv:** Inscriptions below designs within wreath **Rev:** Navy emblem **Edge:** Reeded

Date	Mintage	F	VF	XF	Unc	BU
2004	—	—	—	0.50	1.00	1.50

KM# 136.3 RUPEE
3.6200 g., Brass-Plated Steel, 20 mm. **Obv:** National emblem **Rev:** Value and date **Edge:** Segmented reeding

Date	Mintage	F	VF	XF	Unc	BU
2005	—	—	—	—	1.00	—
2006	—	—	—	—	1.00	—

KM# 147 2 RUPEES
Copper-Nickel **Obv:** Value within inscription above date **Rev:** National emblem

Date	Mintage	F	VF	XF	Unc	BU
2001	10,000,000	—	0.30	0.60	1.35	1.75
2002	40,000,000	—	0.30	0.60	1.35	1.75

KM# 167 2 RUPEES
8.2500 g., Copper Nickel, 28.5 mm. **Subject:** Colombo Plan's 50th Anniversary **Obv:** Value within inscription above date **Rev:** Gear wheel **Edge:** Reeded

Date	Mintage	F	VF	XF	Unc	BU
2001	10,000,000	—	—	—	2.00	3.00

KM# 147a 2 RUPEES
7.0000 g., Nickel Clad Steel, 28.5 mm. **Obv:** Value **Rev:** National arms

Date	Mintage	F	VF	XF	Unc	BU
2005	—	—	—	—	1.35	1.75

KM# 148.2 5 RUPEES
9.5000 g., Aluminum-Bronze **Obv:** Value within inscription, legend around border **Rev:** National arms **Edge:** Lettered **Edge Lettering:** CBSL - Central Bank of Sri Lanka

Date	Mintage	F	VF	XF	Unc	BU
2002	30,000,000	—	0.35	0.65	2.00	2.75
2004	—	—	—	0.65	2.00	2.75

KM# 148.2a 5 RUPEES
Bronzeplated Steel **Obv:** Value within inscription, legend around border **Rev:** National arms **Edge:** Lettered **Edge Lettering:** CBSL - Central Bank of Sri Lanka

Date	Mintage	F	VF	XF	Unc	BU
2005	—	—	—	0.65	2.00	2.75

KM# 168 5 RUPEES
9.5200 g., Aluminum-Bronze, 23.4 mm. **Subject:** 250th Annniversary of the "Upasampada" Rite **Obv:** Value **Rev:** 1/2-length figure facing divides dates

Date	Mintage	F	VF	XF	Unc	BU
2003	—	—	—	—	3.00	4.50

KM# 169 5 RUPEES
9.5200 g., Aluminum-Bronze, 23.4 mm. **Subject:** 250th Anniversary - Upasampada **Obv:** Value **Rev:** Bust facing standing behind shield **Edge:** Reeded and lettered

Date	Mintage	F	VF	XF	Unc	BU
2003	—	—	—	—	3.00	4.50

KM# 148.2a 5 RUPEES
Bronze Plated Steel **Obv:** Value **Rev:** National arms

Date	Mintage	F	VF	XF	Unc	BU
2005	—	—	—	0.65	2.00	2.75

KM# 170 5 RUPEES
7.6500 g., Brass, 23.5 mm. **Subject:** 2550th Anniversary of Buddha **Obv:** Value **Rev:** "Buddha Jayanthi", wheel above mountain **Edge:** Reeded and lettered

Date	Mintage	F	VF	XF	Unc	BU
2006	—	—	—	—	3.00	4.00

SUDAN

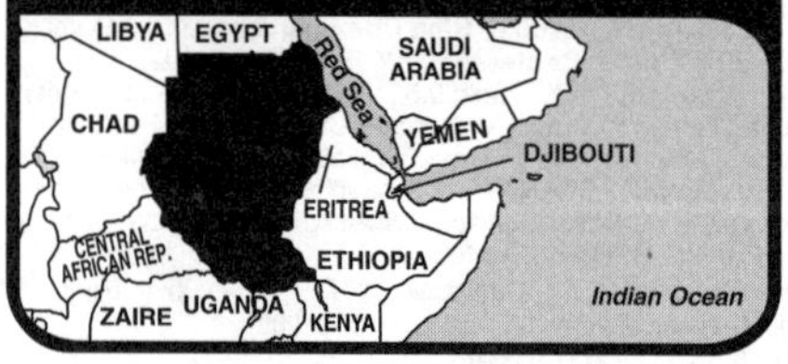

The Democratic Republic of the Sudan, located in northeast Africa on the Red Sea between Egypt and Ethiopia, has an area of 967,500 sq. mi. (2,505,810 sq. km.) and a population of *24.5 million. Capital: Khartoum. Agriculture and livestock raising are the chief occupations. Cotton, gum arabic and peanuts are exported.

REPUBLIC

REFORM COINAGE

100 Qurush (Piastres) = 1 Dinar

10 Pounds = 1 Dinar

KM# 119 5 DINARS
3.3500 g., Brass, 19 mm. **Obv:** Value **Rev:** Central Bank building

Date	Mintage	F	VF	XF	Unc	BU
AH1424-2003	—	—	0.75	1.50	3.00	5.00

KM# 120.1 10 DINARS
4.6800 g., Brass, 22 mm. **Rev:** Central Bank building, "a" above "n" at the left end of the Arabic inscription, 64 border beads

Date	Mintage	F	VF	XF	Unc	BU
AH1424-2003	—	—	1.00	2.00	3.50	6.00

KM# 120.2 10 DINARS
4.5600 g., Brass, 22 mm. **Obv:** Value **Rev:** Larger Central Bank building, "a" to right of "n" at the left end of the Arabic inscription, 72 border beads

Date	Mintage	F	VF	XF	Unc	BU
AH1424-2003	—	—	1.00	2.00	3.50	6.00

KM# 121 50 DINARS
Copper-Nickel, 24 mm. **Rev:** Central Bank building

Date	Mintage	F	VF	XF	Unc	BU
AH1423-2002	—	—	2.00	3.50	6.00	9.00

REFORM COINAGE

100 Piastres = 1 Pound

2005 -

KM# 124 20 PIASTRES
5.0200 g., Bi-Metallic **Ring Composition:** Brass **Center Composition:** Copper Nickel, 22.19 mm. **Obv:** Water Buffalo **Obv. Legend:** CENTRAL BANK OF SUDAN **Rev:** large value **Edge:** Reeded

Date	Mintage	F	VF	XF	Unc	BU
2006	—	—	—	—	—	5.00

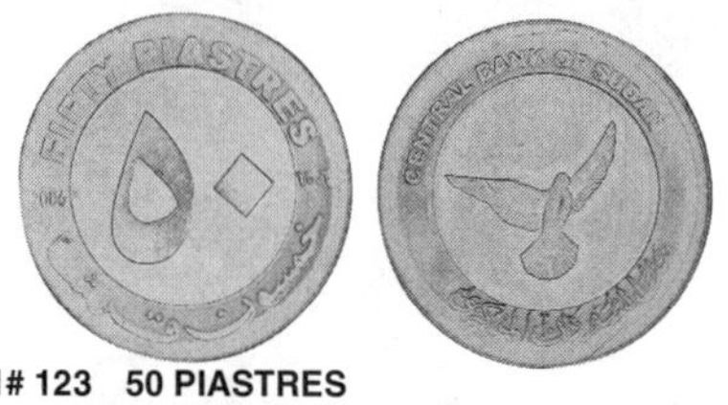

KM# 123 50 PIASTRES
5.8600 g., Bi-Metallic **Ring Composition:** Copper Nickel **Center Composition:** Brass, 24.27 mm. **Obv:** Dove in flight **Obv. Legend:** CENTRAL BANK OF SUDAN **Rev:** Value **Edge:** Reeded

Date	Mintage	F	VF	XF	Unc	BU
2006	—	—	—	—	—	7.00

SURINAME

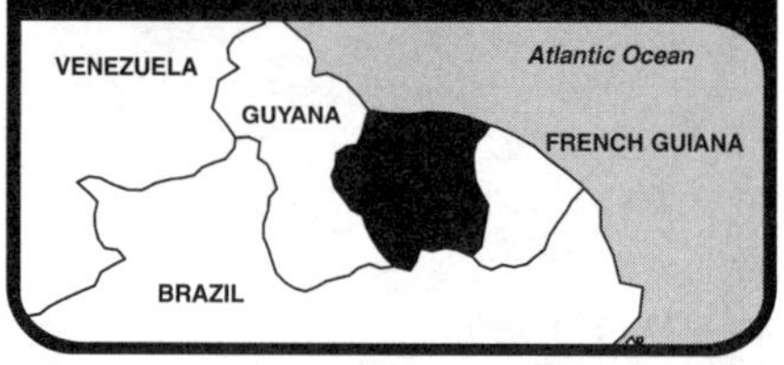

The Republic of Suriname also known as Dutch Guiana, located on the north central coast of South America between Guyana and French Guiana has an area of 63,037 sq. mi. (163,270 sq. km.) and a population of *433,000. Capital: Paramaribo. The country is rich in minerals and forests, and self-sufficient in rice, the staple food crop. The mining, processing and exporting of bauxite is the principal economic activity.

Lieutenants of Amerigo Vespucci sighted the Guiana coast in 1499. Spanish explorers of the 16th century, disappointed at finding no gold, departed leaving the area to be settled by the British in 1652. The colony prospered and the Netherlands acquired it in 1667 in exchange for the Dutch rights in Nieuw Nederland (state of New York). During the European wars of the 18th and 19th centuries, which were fought in part in the new world, Suriname was occupied by the British from 1781-1784 and 1796-1814.Suriname became an autonomous part of the Kingdom of the Netherlands on Dec. 15, 1954. Full independence was achieved on Nov. 25, 1975. In 1980, a coup installed a military government, which has since been dissolved.

MINT MARKS

(u) - Utrecht (privy marks only)

MONETARY SYSTEM

After January, 2004

1 Dollar = 100 Cents

REPUBLIC

MODERN COINAGE

KM# 11b CENT
2.5000 g., Copper Plated Steel, 18 mm. **Obv:** Arms with supporters within wreath **Rev:** Value divides date within circle **Edge:** Plain

Date	Mintage	F	VF	XF	Unc	BU
2004(u)	4,000	—	—	—	1.00	1.50
Note: In sets only						
2005(u)	1,500	—	—	—	1.00	1.50
Note: In sets only						
2006(u)	1,500	—	—	—	1.00	1.50
Note: In sets only						
2007(u)	—	—	—	—	1.00	1.50
2008(u)	—	—	—	—	1.00	1.50

KM# 12.1b 5 CENTS

3.0000 g., Copper Plated Steel, 18 mm. **Obv:** Arms with supporters within circle **Rev:** Value divides date within circle **Edge:** Plain **Shape:** Square

Date	Mintage	F	VF	XF	Unc	BU
2004(u)	4,000	—	—	—	1.00	1.50
Note: In sets only						
2005(u)	1,500	—	—	—	1.00	1.50
Note: In sets only						
2006(u)	1,500	—	—	—	1.00	1.50
Note: In sets only						
2007(u)	—	—	—	—	1.00	1.50
2008(u)	—	—	—	—	1.00	1.50

KM# 13a 10 CENTS

2.0000 g., Nickel Plated Steel, 16 mm. **Obv:** Arms with supporters within wreath **Rev:** Value and date within circle **Edge:** Reeded

Date	Mintage	F	VF	XF	Unc	BU
2004(u)	4,000	—	—	—	1.00	2.50
Note: In sets only						
2005(u)	1,500	—	—	—	1.00	2.50
Note: In sets only						
2006(u)	1,500	—	—	—	1.00	2.50
Note: In sets only						
2007(u)	—	—	—	—	1.00	2.50
2008(u)	—	—	—	—	1.00	2.50

KM# 14a 25 CENTS

3.5000 g., Nickel Plated Steel, 20 mm. **Obv:** Arms with supporters within wreath **Rev:** Value and date within circle **Edge:** Reeded

Date	Mintage	F	VF	XF	Unc	BU
2004(u)	4,000	—	—	—	2.00	4.00
Note: In sets only						
2005(u)	1,500	—	—	—	2.00	4.00
Note: In sets only						
2006(u)	1,500	—	—	—	2.00	4.00
Note: In sets only						
2007(u)	—	—	—	—	2.00	4.00
2008(u)	—	—	—	—	2.00	4.00

KM# 23 100 CENTS

Copper-Nickel, 23 mm. **Obv:** Arms with supporters within wreath **Rev:** Value and date within circle **Edge:** Reeded

Date	Mintage	F	VF	XF	Unc	BU
2004(u)	4,000	—	—	—	4.00	7.00
Note: In sets only						
2005(u)	1,500	—	—	—	4.00	7.00
Note: In sets only						
2006(u)	1,500	—	—	—	4.00	7.00
Note: In sets only						
2007(u)	—	—	—	—	4.00	7.00
2008(u)	—	—	—	—	4.00	7.00

KM# 24 250 CENTS

9.5700 g., Copper-Nickel, 28 mm. **Obv:** Arms with supporters within wreath **Rev:** Value and date within circle

Date	Mintage	F	VF	XF	Unc	BU
2004(u)	4,000	—	—	—	6.00	10.00
Note: In sets only						
2005(u)	1,500	—	—	—	6.00	10.00
Note: In sets only						
2006(u)	1,500	—	—	—	6.00	10.00
Note: In sets only						
2007(u)	—	—	—	—	6.00	10.00
2008(u)	—	—	—	—	6.00	10.00

KM# 64 400 DOLLARS

Gold **Subject:** 30 Years of Independence

Date	Mintage	F	VF	XF	Unc	BU
2006	—	—	—	—	—	500

MINT SETS

KM#	Date	Mintage	Identification	Issue Price	Mkt Val
MS1	2004 (6)	4,000	KM#11b, 12.1b, 13a, 14a, 23, 24	25.00	26.00
MS2	2005 (6)	1,500	KM#11b, 12.1b, 13a-14a, 23-24	25.00	25.00
MS3	2006 (6)	1,500	KM#11b, 12.1b, 13a-14a, 23-24	25.00	25.00
MS4	2007 (6)	1,500	KM#11b, 12.1b, 13a-14a, 23-24	25.00	25.00
MS5	2008 (6)	—	KM#11b, 12.1b, 13a-14a, 23-24	25.00	25.00

SWAZILAND

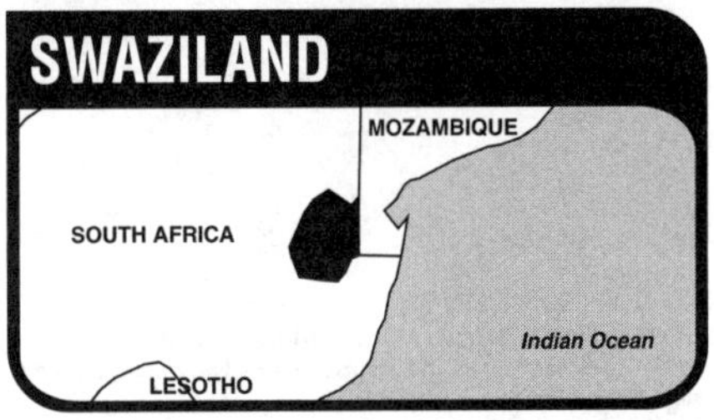

The Kingdom of Swaziland, located in southeastern Africa, has an area of 6,704 sq. mi. (17,360 sq. km.) and a population of *756,000. Capital: Mbabane (administrative); Lobamba (legislative). The diversified economy includes mining, agriculture, and light industry. Asbestos, iron ore, wood pulp, and sugar are exported.

The Kingdom is a member of the Commonwealth of Nations. King Mswati III is Head of State. The prime minister is Head of Government.

RULER

King Msawati III, 1986-

MONETARY SYSTEM

100 Cents = 1 Luhlanga
25 Luhlanga = 1 Lilangeni
(plural - Emalangeni)

KINGDOM

DECIMAL COINAGE

100 Cents = 1 Lilangeni (plural emelangeni)

KM# 48 5 CENTS

2.1000 g., Nickel Plated Steel, 18.5 mm. **Ruler:** King Msawati III **Obv:** Head 1/4 right **Rev:** Arum lily and value **Edge:** Plain **Shape:** Scalloped

Date	Mintage	F	VF	XF	Unc	BU
2001	—	—	—	—	0.50	0.75
2002	—	—	—	—	0.50	0.75
2006	—	—	—	—	0.50	0.75

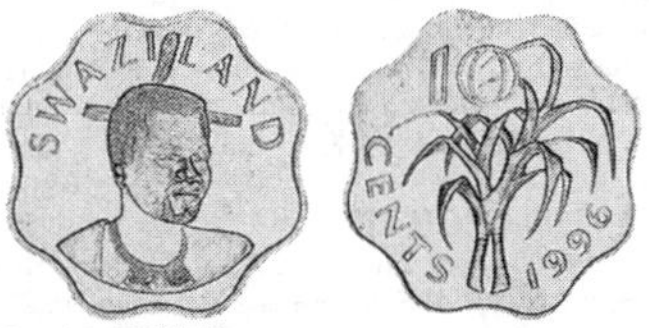

KM# 49 10 CENTS

Copper-Nickel, 22 mm. **Ruler:** King Msawati III **Obv:** Head 1/4 right **Rev:** Sugar cane and value **Shape:** Scalloped

Date	Mintage	F	VF	XF	Unc	BU
2001	—	—	—	—	0.50	0.75
2002	—	—	—	—	0.50	0.75
2006	—	—	—	—	0.50	0.75

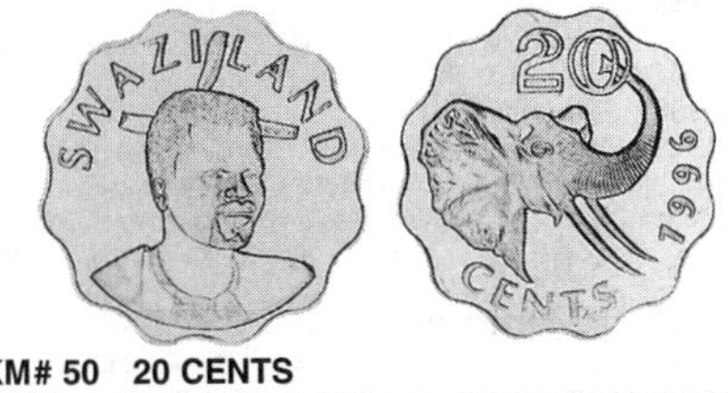

KM# 50 20 CENTS

5.6000 g., Copper-Nickel, 25.2 mm. **Ruler:** King Msawati III **Obv:** Head 1/4 right **Rev:** Elephant head and value **Shape:** Scalloped **Note:** "Lg bust and legend": right tusk closer to rim; "Sm bust and legend": right tusk further from rim.

Date	Mintage	F	VF	XF	Unc	BU
2001	—	—	0.40	0.80	3.00	5.00
Note: Small bust and legend						
2002	—	—	0.40	0.80	3.00	5.00
Note: Small bust and legend						
2003	—	—	0.40	0.80	3.00	5.00
Note: Small bust and legend						

KM# 52 50 CENTS

8.9000 g., Copper-Nickel, 29.45 mm. **Ruler:** King Msawati III **Obv:** Head 1/4 right **Rev:** Arms with supporters

Date	Mintage	F	VF	XF	Unc	BU
2001	—	—	—	—	3.75	4.50
2003	—	—	—	—	3.75	4.50

KM# 45 LILANGENI

9.5000 g., Brass, 22.5 mm. **Ruler:** King Msawati III **Obv:** Head 1/4 right **Rev:** Bust facing

Date	Mintage	F	VF	XF	Unc	BU
2002	—	—	—	1.50	3.25	3.75
2003	—	—	—	1.50	3.25	3.75

KM# 46 2 EMALANGENI

5.0000 g., Brass **Ruler:** King Msawati III **Obv:** Head 1/4 right **Rev:** Lilies and value

Date	Mintage	F	VF	XF	Unc	BU
2003 sm. bust	—	—	—	—	3.75	4.25

KM# 47 5 EMALANGENI

7.6000 g., Brass **Ruler:** King Msawati III **Obv:** Head 1/4 right **Rev:** Arms with supporters above value that divides date

Date	Mintage	F	VF	XF	Unc	BU
2003 sm. bust	—	—	—	—	6.00	7.00

SWEDEN

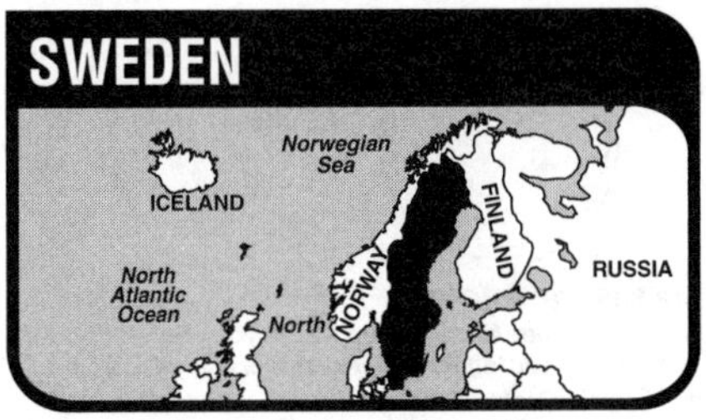

The Kingdom of Sweden, a limited constitutional monarchy located in northern Europe between Norway and Finland, has an area of 173,732 sq. mi. (449,960 sq. km.) and a population of *8.5 million. Capital: Stockholm. Mining, lumbering and a specialized machine industry dominate the economy. Machinery, paper, iron and steel, motor vehicles and wood pulp are exported.

RULER

Carl XVI Gustaf, 1973-

MINT OFFICIALS' INITIALS

Letter	Date	Name
B	1992-2005	Stefan Ingves
D	1986-2005	Bengt Dennis
SI	2006-	Stefan Ingves

MONETARY SYSTEM

100 Ore = 1 Krona

KINGDOM

REFORM COINAGE

1873 - present

KM# 878 50 ORE

3.7000 g., Bronze, 18.7 mm. **Ruler:** Carl XVI Gustaf **Obv:** Value **Rev:** Three crowns and date **Edge:** Reeded

Date	Mintage	F	VF	XF	Unc	BU
2001 B	30,120,532	—	—	0.10	0.15	0.25
2002 B	—	—	—	0.10	0.15	0.25
2003 B	—	—	—	0.10	0.15	0.25
2004 B	25,958,649	—	—	0.10	0.15	0.25
2005 B	—	—	—	0.10	0.15	0.25
2006 SI	—	—	—	0.10	0.15	0.25
2007 SI	—	—	—	0.10	0.15	0.25

KM# 894 KRONA

6.9800 g., Copper-Nickel, 24.9 mm. **Ruler:** Carl XVI Gustaf **Obv:** Head left **Rev:** Crown and value **Edge:** Reeded

Date	Mintage	F	VF	XF	Unc	BU
2001 B	23,905,454	—	—	—	0.65	1.00
2002 B	—	—	—	—	0.65	1.00
2003 B	—	—	—	—	0.65	1.00
2004 B	42,060,252	—	—	—	0.65	1.00
2005 B	—	—	—	—	0.65	1.00
2007 B	—	—	—	—	0.65	1.00

KM# 853a 5 KRONOR

9.6000 g., Copper-Nickel Clad Nickel, 28.5 mm. **Ruler:** Carl XVI Gustaf **Obv:** Crowned monogram **Rev:** Value

Date	Mintage	F	VF	XF	Unc	BU
2001 B	6,001,481	—	—	—	1.00	1.25
2002 B	—	—	—	—	1.00	1.25
2003 B	—	—	—	—	1.00	1.25
2004 B	6,732,730	—	—	—	1.00	1.25

KM# 895 10 KRONOR

6.5700 g., Copper-Aluminum-Zinc, 20.4 mm. **Ruler:** Carl XVI Gustaf **Obv:** Head left **Rev:** Three crowns and value **Edge:** Reeded and plain sections

Date	Mintage	F	VF	XF	Unc	BU
2001 B	4,171,757	—	—	—	1.75	2.00
2002 B	—	—	—	—	1.75	2.00
2003 B	—	—	—	—	1.75	2.00
2004 B	9,045,581	—	—	—	1.75	2.00
2005 B	—	—	—	—	1.75	2.00

KM# 910 50 KRONOR

22.0000 g., Brass, 36 mm. **Ruler:** Carl XVI Gustaf **Obv:** Playful young girl **Rev:** Astrid Lindgren **Edge:** Plain

Date	Mintage	F	VF	XF	Unc	BU
ND (2002)	100,000	—	—	—	—	8.50

KM# 915 50 KRONOR

22.0000 g., Brass, 36 mm. **Ruler:** Carl XVI Gustaf **Obv:** Winged letter flying over landscape **Rev:** Sweden's first postage stamp design **Edge:** Plain

Date	Mintage	F	VF	XF	Unc	BU
ND (2005)	100,000	—	—	—	—	8.50

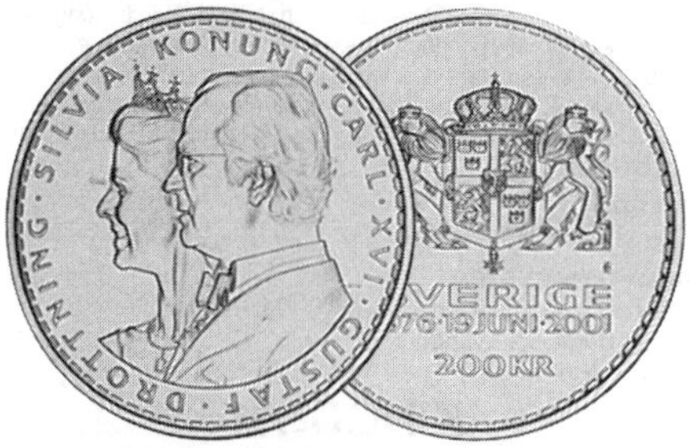

KM# 896 200 KRONOR

27.2500 g., 0.9250 Silver 0.8104 oz. ASW, 36 mm. **Ruler:** Carl XVI Gustaf **Subject:** 25th Wedding Anniversary **Obv:** Conjoined busts left **Rev:** Crowned arms with supporters **Edge:** Plain

Date	Mintage	F	VF	XF	Unc	BU
ND(2001)	50,000	—	—	—	35.00	45.00

KM# 908 200 KRONOR

27.0000 g., 0.9250 Silver 0.8029 oz. ASW, 36 mm. **Ruler:** Carl XVI Gustaf **Subject:** 750th Anniversary of Stockholm **Obv:** City seal with three towers and gate **Rev:** Three towers of city hall **Edge:** Plain

Date	Mintage	F	VF	XF	Unc	BU
ND (2002) Proof	25,000	Value: 35.00				

KM# 902 200 KRONOR

Silver **Ruler:** Carl XVI Gustaf **Subject:** 30th Anniversary of Reign

Date	Mintage	F	VF	XF	Unc	BU
2003	—	—	—	—	35.00	45.00

KM# 904 200 KRONOR

27.0300 g., 0.9250 Silver 0.8038 oz. ASW, 36 mm. **Ruler:** Carl XVI Gustaf **Subject:** 700th Anniversary, St. Birgitta **Obv:** Cross in circle above value **Rev:** St. Birgitta **Edge:** Plain

Date	Mintage	F	VF	XF	Unc	BU
ND (2003)	60,000	—	—	—	35.00	45.00

KM# 911 200 KRONOR

27.0000 g., 0.9250 Silver 0.8029 oz. ASW, 36 mm. **Ruler:** Carl XVI Gustaf **Subject:** Royal Palace in Stockholm 250th Anniversary **Obv:** Two antique keys over map **Rev:** Royal Palace in Stockholm **Edge:** Plain

Date	Mintage	F	VF	XF	Unc	BU
ND (2004) Proof	35,000	Value: 35.00				

KM# 913 200 KRONOR

27.0000 g., 0.9250 Silver 0.8029 oz. ASW, 36 mm. **Ruler:** Carl XVI Gustaf **Obv:** Stylized flames **Rev:** Dag Hammarskjold **Edge:** Plain

Date	Mintage	F	VF	XF	Unc	BU
ND (2005) Proof	35,000	Value: 35.00				

KM# 906 200 KRONOR

27.0300 g., 0.9250 Silver 0.8038 oz. ASW, 36 mm. **Ruler:** Carl XVI Gustaf **Subject:** Centennial of the end of the Union between Norway and Sweden **Obv:** Split disc **Rev:** Flag on pole and two clouds

Date	Mintage	F	VF	XF	Unc	BU
2005	35,000	—	—	—	35.00	45.00

KM# 909 2000 KRONOR

12.0000 g., 0.9000 Gold 0.3472 oz. AGW, 26 mm. **Ruler:** Carl XVI Gustaf **Subject:** 750th Anniversary of Stockholm **Obv:** City seal with three towers and gate **Rev:** Three towers of city hall **Edge:** Plain

Date	Mintage	F	VF	XF	Unc	BU
ND (2002) Proof	5,000	Value: 375				

KM# 903 2000 KRONOR

12.0000 g., 0.9990 Gold 0.3854 oz. AGW **Ruler:** Carl XVI Gustaf **Subject:** 30th Anniversary of Reign

Date	Mintage	F	VF	XF	Unc	BU
2003	—	—	—	—	375	400

KM# 905 2000 KRONOR

12.0000 g., 0.9000 Gold 0.3472 oz. AGW, 26 mm. **Ruler:** Carl XVI Gustaf **Subject:** St. Birgitta's 700th Anniversary of birth **Obv:** Gothic letter B above value **Rev:** St. Birgitta **Edge:** Plain

Date	Mintage	F	VF	XF	Unc	BU
ND (2003)	8,000	—	—	—	365	385

KM# 912 2000 KRONOR

12.0000 g., 0.9000 Gold Royal Palace in Stockholm 250th Anniversary 0.3472 oz. AGW, 26 mm. **Ruler:** Carl XVI Gustaf **Subject:** Two antique keys over map **Rev:** Royal Palace in Stockholm **Edge:** Plain

Date	Mintage	F	VF	XF	Unc	BU
ND (2004) Proof	5,243	Value: 375				

KM# 914 2000 KRONOR

12.0000 g., 0.9000 Gold 0.3472 oz. AGW, 26 mm. **Ruler:** Carl XVI Gustaf **Obv:** Stylized flames **Rev:** Dag Hammarskjold **Edge:** Plain

Date	Mintage	F	VF	XF	Unc	BU
ND (2005) Proof	5,000	Value: 375				

KM# 907 2000 KRONOR

12.0000 g., 0.9000 Gold 0.3472 oz. AGW, 26 mm. **Ruler:** Carl XVI Gustaf **Subject:** Centennial of the end of the Union between Norway and Sweden **Obv:** Split disc **Rev:** Flag pole dividing two clouds

Date	Mintage	F	VF	XF	Unc	BU
2005	5,000	—	—	—	365	385

MINT SETS

KM#	Date	Mintage	Identification	Issue Price	Mkt Val
MS107	2002 (4)	—	KM#853a, 878, 894, 895 plus medal	—	10.00

SWITZERLAND

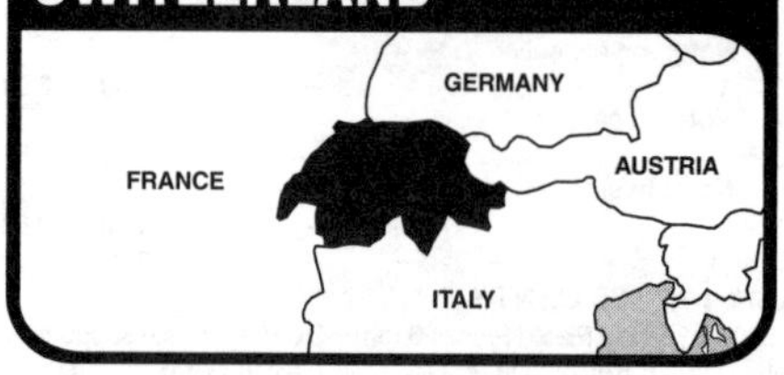

The Swiss Confederation, located in central Europe north of Italy and south of Germany, has an area of 15,941 sq. mi. (41,290 sq. km.) and a population of *6.6 million. Capital: Bern. The economy centers about a well-developed manufacturing industry. Machinery, chemicals, watches and clocks, and textiles are exported.

The Swiss Constitutions of 1848 and 1874 established a union modeled upon that of the United States.

MINT MARK

B - Bern

CONFEDERATION

Confoederatio Helvetica

MONETARY SYSTEM

100 Rappen (Centimes) = 1 Franc

DECIMAL COINAGE

KM# 46 RAPPEN

1.5400 g., Bronze, 15.95 mm. **Obv:** Cross **Rev:** Value and oat sprig **Edge:** Plain

Date	Mintage	F	VF	XF	Unc	BU
2001B	1,522,000	—	—	—	0.50	1.00
2001B Proof	6,000	Value: 2.00				
2002B	2,024,000	—	—	—	0.50	1.00
2002B Proof	5,500	Value: 2.00				
2003B	1,522,000	—	—	—	0.50	1.00
2003B Proof	5,500	Value: 2.00				
2004B	1,526,000	—	—	—	0.50	1.00
2004B Proof	5,000	Value: 2.00				
2005B	1,524,000	—	—	—	0.50	1.00
2005B Proof	4,500	Value: 2.00				
2006B	26,000	—	—	—	—	135

Note: In sets only, circulatin strikes not released

Date	Mintage	F	VF	XF	Unc	BU
2006B Proof	4,000	Value: 175				

KM# 26c 5 RAPPEN

2.0000 g., Aluminum-Brass, 17.1 mm. **Obv:** Crowned head right **Rev:** Value within wreath **Edge:** Plain

Date	Mintage	F	VF	XF	Unc	BU
2001B	5,022,000	—	—	—	0.50	1.00
2001B Proof	6,000	Value: 2.00				
2002B	12,024,000	—	—	—	0.50	1.00
2002B Proof	6,000	Value: 2.00				

Date	Mintage	F	VF	XF	Unc	BU
2003B	10,022,000	—	—	—	0.50	1.00
2003B Proof	5,500	Value: 2.00				
2004B	10,026,000	—	—	—	0.50	1.00
2004B Proof	5,000	Value: 2.00				
2005B	13,024,000	—	—	—	0.50	1.00
2005B Proof	4,500	Value: 2.00				
2006B	12,026,000	—	—	—	0.50	1.00
2006B Proof	4,000	Value: 2.00				
2007B	13,024,000	—	—	—	0.50	1.00
2007B Proof	4,000	Value: 2.00				

KM# 27 10 RAPPEN
3.0000 g., Copper-Nickel, 19.1 mm. **Obv:** Crowned head right **Obv. Legend:** CONFOEDERATIO HELVETICA **Rev:** Value within wreath **Edge:** Plain

Date	Mintage	F	VF	XF	Unc	BU
2001B	7,022,000	—	—	—	0.50	1.00
2001B Proof	6,000	Value: 2.00				
2002B	15,024,000	—	—	—	0.50	1.00
2002B Proof	6,000	Value: 2.00				
2003B	12,022,000	—	—	—	0.50	1.00
2003B Proof	5,500	Value: 2.00				
2004B	5,026,000	—	—	—	0.50	1.00
2004B Proof	5,000	Value: 2.00				
2005B	7,024,000	—	—	—	0.50	1.00
2005B Proof	4,500	Value: 2.00				
2006B	2,026,000	—	—	—	0.50	1.00
2006B Proof	4,000	Value: 2.00				
2007B	18,024,000	—	—	—	0.50	1.00
2007B Proof	4,000	Value: 2.00				

KM# 29a 20 RAPPEN
4.2000 g., Copper-Nickel, 21 mm. **Obv:** Crowned head right **Rev:** Value within wreath **Edge:** Plain

Date	Mintage	F	VF	XF	Unc	BU
2001B	7,022,000	—	—	—	1.00	2.00
2001B Proof	6,000	Value: 3.00				
2002B	12,024,000	—	—	—	1.00	2.00
2002B Proof	6,000	Value: 3.00				
2003B	10,022,000	—	—	—	1.00	2.00
2003B Proof	5,500	Value: 3.00				
2004B	10,026,000	—	—	—	1.00	2.00
2004B Proof	5,000	Value: 3.00				
2005B	6,024,000	—	—	—	1.00	2.00
2005B Proof	4,500	Value: 3.00				
2006B	5,026,000	—	—	—	1.00	2.00
2006B Proof	4,000	Value: 3.00				
2007B	22,024,000	—	—	—	1.00	2.00
2007B Proof	4,000	Value: 3.00				

KM# 23a.3 1/2 FRANC
2.2000 g., Copper-Nickel, 18.1 mm. **Obv:** 23 Stars around figure **Rev:** Value within wreath **Edge:** Reeded **Designer:** A. Bovy

Date	Mintage	F	VF	XF	Unc	BU
2001B	6,022,000	—	—	—	2.50	3.50
2001B Proof	6,000	Value: 5.00				
2002B	2,024,000	—	—	—	2.50	3.50
2002B Proof	6,000	Value: 5.00				
2003B	2,022,000	—	—	—	2.50	3.50
2003B Proof	5,500	Value: 5.00				
2004B	2,026,000	—	—	—	2.50	3.50
2004B Proof	5,000	Value: 5.00				
2005B	1,024,000	—	—	—	2.50	3.50
2005B Proof	4,500	Value: 5.00				
2006B	2,025,000	—	—	—	2.50	3.50
2006B Proof	4,500	Value: 5.00				
2007B	18,024,000	—	—	—	2.50	3.50
2007B Proof	4,000	Value: 5.00				

KM# 24a.3 FRANC
4.4000 g., Copper-Nickel, 23.1 mm. **Obv:** 23 Stars around figure **Rev:** Value and date within wreath **Edge:** Reeded **Designer:** A. Bovy

Date	Mintage	F	VF	XF	Unc	BU
2001B	3,022,000	—	—	—	3.00	5.00
2001B Proof	6,000	Value: 7.00				

Date	Mintage	F	VF	XF	Unc	BU
2002B	1,024,000	—	—	—	3.00	5.00
2002B Proof	6,000	Value: 7.00				
2003B	2,022,000	—	—	—	3.00	5.00
2003B Proof	5,500	Value: 7.00				
2004B	2,026,000	—	—	—	3.00	5.00
2004B Proof	5,000	Value: 7.00				
2005B	1,024,000	—	—	—	3.00	5.00
2005B Proof	4,500	Value: 7.00				
2006B	2,026,000	—	—	—	3.00	5.00
2006B Proof	4,000	Value: 7.00				
2007B	3,024,000	—	—	—	3.00	5.00
2007B Proof	4,000	Value: 7.00				

KM# 21a.3 2 FRANCS
8.8000 g., Copper-Nickel, 27.4 mm. **Obv:** 23 Stars around figure **Rev:** Value within wreath **Edge:** Reeded **Designer:** A. Bovy

Date	Mintage	F	VF	XF	Unc	BU
2001B	4,022,000	—	—	—	4.00	7.00
2001B Proof	6,000	Value: 10.00				
2002B	1,024,000	—	—	—	4.50	7.50
2002B Proof	6,000	Value: 10.00				
2003B	1,022,000	—	—	—	4.50	7.50
2003B Proof	5,500	Value: 10.00				
2004B	1,026,000	—	—	—	4.50	7.50
2004B Proof	5,000	Value: 10.00				
2005B	2,024,000	—	—	—	4.00	7.00
2005B Proof	4,500	Value: 10.00				
2006B	7,026,000	—	—	—	4.50	7.50
2006B Proof	4,000	Value: 10.00				
2007B	16,024,000	—	—	—	4.50	7.50
2007B Proof	4,000	Value: 10.00				

KM# 40a.4 5 FRANCS
13.2000 g., Copper-Nickel, 31.3 mm. **Obv:** William Tell right **Rev:** Shield flanked by sprigs **Edge:** DOMINUS PROVIDEBIT and 13 stars raised **Designer:** Paul Burkhard

Date	Mintage	F	VF	XF	Unc	BU
2001B	1,022,000	—	—	—	6.50	9.50
2001B Proof	6,000	Value: 15.00				
2002B	1,024,000	—	—	—	6.50	9.50
2002B Proof	6,000	Value: 15.00				
2003B	1,022,000	—	—	—	6.50	9.50
2003B Proof	5,500	Value: 15.00				
2004B	526,000	—	—	—	7.50	11.00
2004B Proof	5,000	Value: 15.00				
2005B	524,000	—	—	—	7.50	11.00
2005B Proof	4,500	Value: 15.00				
2006B	526,000	—	—	—	7.50	11.00
2006B Proof	4,000	Value: 15.00				
2007B	524,000	—	—	—	7.50	11.00
2007B Proof	4,000	Value: 15.00				

COMMEMORATIVE COINAGE

KM# 92 5 FRANCS
15.0000 g., Bi-Metallic Gold center in Copper-Nickel ring, 33 mm. **Subject:** Zurcher Sechselauten **Obv:** Value within circle **Rev:** Burning strawman within circle **Edge:** Reeded **Designer:** John Grüniger

Date	Mintage	F	VF	XF	Unc	BU
2001B	170,000	—	—	—	8.00	12.00
2001B Proof	20,000	Value: 24.00				

KM# 98 5 FRANCS
15.0000 g., Bi-Metallic Gold center in Copper-Nickel ring, 33 mm. **Subject:** Escalade 1602-2002 **Obv:** Value within circle **Rev:** Swirling ladders design within circle **Edge:** Reeded **Note:** Weight can vary 14.8-15 g.

Date	Mintage	F	VF	XF	Unc	BU
2002B	130,000	—	—	—	8.00	12.00
2002B Proof	15,000	Value: 24.00				

KM# 103 5 FRANCS
15.0000 g., Bi-Metallic Gold center in Copper-Nickel ring, 33 mm. **Subject:** Chalandamarz **Obv:** Value within circular inscription and designed wreath **Rev:** Boys shaking bells within 3/4 designed wreath **Edge:** Reeded **Designer:** Gian Vonzun

Date	Mintage	F	VF	XF	Unc	BU
2003B	96,000	—	—	—	8.00	12.00
2003B Proof	12,000	Value: 24.00				

KM# 107 10 FRANCS
15.0000 g., Bi-Metallic Copper-Nickel center in Aluminum-Bronze ring, 33 mm. **Obv:** Value **Rev:** Matterhorn Mountain **Edge:** Segmented reeding **Designer:** Stephan Bundi

Date	Mintage	F	VF	XF	Unc	BU
2004B	94,976	—	—	—	—	20.00
2004B Proof	12,168	Value: 36.00				

KM# 111 10 FRANCS
15.0000 g., Bi-Metallic Copper-Nickel center in Aluminum-Bronze ring, 33 mm. **Obv:** Value **Rev:** Jungfrau mountain **Edge:** Segmented reeding **Designer:** Stephan Bundi

Date	Mintage	F	VF	XF	Unc	BU
2005B	77,791	—	—	—	—	17.00
2005B Proof	10,495	Value: 30.00				

KM# 114 10 FRANCS
15.0000 g., Bi-Metallic Copper-Nickel center in Aluminum-Bronze ring, 33 mm. **Obv:** Value **Rev:** Piz Bernina mountain **Edge:** Segmented reeding **Designer:** Stephan Bundi

Date	Mintage	F	VF	XF	Unc	BU
2006B	Est. 96,000	—	—	—	—	15.00
2006B Proof	Est. 12,000	Value: 25.00				

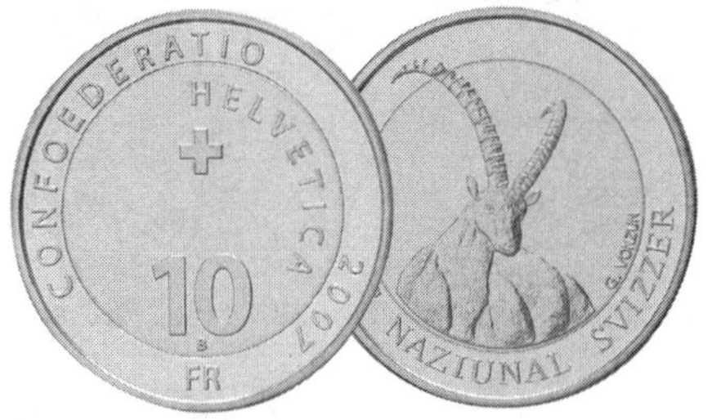

KM# 118 10 FRANCS
14.4800 g., Bi-Metallic Copper-Nickel center in Aluminum-Bronze ring, 32.94 mm. **Subject:** Swiss National Park **Obv:** Value **Rev:** Ibex **Edge:** Segmented reeding

Date	Mintage	F	VF	XF	Unc	BU
2007B	96,000	—	—	—	10.00	15.00
2007B Proof	12,000	Value: 30.00				

KM# 126 10 FRANCS
15.0000 g., Bi-Metallic Copper-Nickel center in Aluminum-Bronze ring, 33 mm. **Obv:** Small national arms **Obv. Legend:** CONFEDERATIO - HELVETICA **Rev:** Golden Eagle alighting **Rev. Legend:** PARK NATIONAL SUISSE **Rev. Designer:** Niklaus Heeb **Edge:** Segmented reeding

Date	Mintage	F	VF	XF	Unc	BU
2008B	95,000	—	—	—	10.00	12.00
2008B Proof	12,000	Value: 30.00				

KM# 93 20 FRANCS
20.0000 g., 0.9250 Silver 0.5948 oz. ASW, 32.6 mm. **Subject:** Mustair Cloister **Obv:** Church floor plan **Rev:** Cloister of Müstair **Edge:** "DOMINUS PROVIDEBIT" and 13 stars **Designer:** Hans-Peter von Ah

Date	Mintage	F	VF	XF	Unc	BU
2001B	50,076	—	—	—	25.00	30.00
2001B Proof	8,767	Value: 55.00				

KM# 94 20 FRANCS
20.0000 g., 0.8350 Silver 0.5369 oz. ASW, 32.6 mm. **Subject:** Johanna Spyri **Obv:** Value within handwritten background **Rev:** Bust facing **Designer:** Silvia Goeschke

Date	Mintage	F	VF	XF	Unc	BU
2001B	60,364	—	—	—	22.00	28.00
2001B Proof	6,799	Value: 50.00				

KM# 99 20 FRANCS
20.0000 g., 0.8350 Silver 0.5369 oz. ASW, 33 mm. **Obv:** St. Gall and bear cub **Rev:** St. Gall Cloister **Edge:** Lettered **Designer:** Hans-Peter von Ah

Date	Mintage	F	VF	XF	Unc	BU
2002B	35,895	—	—	—	22.00	28.00
2002B Proof	6,250	Value: 50.00				

KM# 100 20 FRANCS
20.0000 g., 0.8350 Silver 0.5369 oz. ASW, 33 mm. **Subject:** REGA **Obv:** Value, inscription and cross above rotating propeller **Rev:** Rescue helicopter in flight **Edge:** Lettered **Designer:** Raphael Schenker

Date	Mintage	F	VF	XF	Unc	BU
2002B	37,314	—	—	—	22.00	28.00
2002B Proof	6,453	Value: 50.00				

KM# 101 20 FRANCS
20.0000 g., 0.8350 Silver 0.5369 oz. ASW, 33 mm. **Subject:** Expo '02 **Obv:** Value and date within circle **Rev:** Child at water's edge within beaded circle **Edge:** Lettered **Designer:** Hervé Graumann

Date	Mintage	F	VF	XF	Unc	BU
2002B	51,899	—	—	—	22.00	28.00
2002B Proof	7,691	Value: 50.00				

KM# 104 20 FRANCS
19.9700 g., 0.8350 Silver 0.5361 oz. ASW, 32.5 mm. **Subject:** St. Moritz Ski Championships **Obv:** Value in snow storm **Rev:** Skier in snow storm **Edge:** Lettered, 13 stars **Edge Lettering:** DOMINUS PROVIDEBIT **Designer:** Claude Kuhn

Date	Mintage	F	VF	XF	Unc	BU
2003B	39,411	—	—	—	22.00	28.00
2003B Proof	6,471	Value: 50.00				

KM# 106 20 FRANCS
20.0000 g., 0.8350 Silver 0.5369 oz. ASW, 33 mm. **Subject:** Bern, Old Town **Obv:** Stylized clock tower and buildings **Rev:** Stylized aerial view of Berner Altstadt **Edge:** Lettered **Edge Lettering:** DOMINUS PROVIDEBIT **Designer:** Franz Fedier

Date	Mintage	F	VF	XF	Unc	BU
2003B	38,644	—	—	—	22.00	28.00
2003B Proof	5,909	Value: 50.00				

KM# 108 20 FRANCS
20.0000 g., 0.8350 Silver 0.5369 oz. ASW, 33 mm. **Obv:** Value **Rev:** The Three Castles of Bellinzona **Edge:** Lettered with 13 stars **Edge Lettering:** DOMINUS PROVIDEBIT **Designer:** Marco Prati

Date	Mintage	F	VF	XF	Unc	BU
2004B	29,697	—	—	—	22.00	28.00
2004B Proof	5,190	Value: 55.00				

KM# 109 20 FRANCS
20.0000 g., 0.8350 Silver 0.5369 oz. ASW, 33 mm. **Obv:** Value **Rev:** Chillon Castle and reflection **Edge:** Lettered with 13 stars **Edge Lettering:** DOMINUS PROVIDEBIT **Designer:** Jean-Benoît Lévy

Date	Mintage	F	VF	XF	Unc	BU
2004B	35,133	—	—	—	22.00	28.00
2004B Proof	5,670	Value: 55.00				

KM# 121 20 FRANCS
20.0000 g., 0.8350 Silver 0.5369 oz. ASW, 33 mm. **Subject:** FIFA Centennial **Obv:** Flower in center **Rev:** Soccer ball with value at left

Date	Mintage	F	VF	XF	Unc	BU
2004B Proof only	14,041	Value: 60.00				

KM# 122 20 FRANCS
20.0000 g., 0.8350 Silver 0.5369 oz. ASW, 33 mm. **Subject:** Chapel Bridge Lucerne **Obv:** Value **Rev:** View of Chapel Bridge **Edge:** Lettered **Edge Lettering:** DOMINUS PROVIDEBIT

Date	Mintage	F	VF	XF	Unc	BU
2005B	44,359	—	—	—	22.00	28.00
2005B Proof	5,998	Value: 50.00				

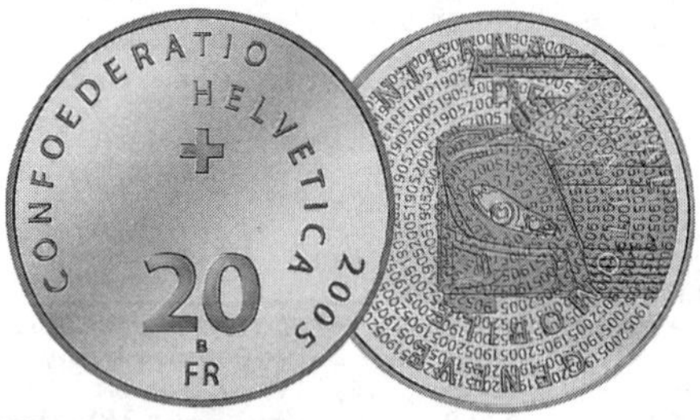

KM# 112 20 FRANCS
20.0000 g., 0.8350 Silver 0.5369 oz. ASW, 33 mm. **Subject:** Geneva Motor Show **Obv:** Value **Rev:** Partial view of prototype car **Edge:** Lettered **Edge Lettering:** "DOMINUS PROVIDEBIT" **Designer:** Roger Pfund

Date	Mintage	F	VF	XF	Unc	BU
2005B	44,100	—	—	—	22.00	28.00
2005B Proof	6,000	Value: 55.00				

KM# 115 20 FRANCS
20.0000 g., 0.8350 Silver 0.5369 oz. ASW, 33 mm. **Obv:** Value **Rev:** 1906 Post Bus **Edge Lettering:** DOMINUS PROVIDEBIT **Designer:** Raphael Schenker

Date	Mintage	F	VF	XF	Unc	BU
2006B	64,915	—	—	—	22.00	28.00
2006B Proof	7,998	Value: 55.00				

KM# 117 20 FRANCS

20.0000 g., 0.8350 Silver 0.5369 oz. ASW, 33 mm. **Obv:** Value and legend **Rev:** Swiss Parliament Building **Edge Lettering:** ***DOMINUS PROVIDEBIT ********** **Designer:** Benjamin Pfäffli

Date	Mintage	F	VF	XF	Unc	BU
2006B	64,994	—	—	—	22.00	28.00
2006B Proof	8,000	Value: 50.00				

KM# 119 20 FRANCS

20.0000 g., 0.8350 Silver 0.5369 oz. ASW, 33 mm. **Subject:** National Bank Centennial **Obv:** Value **Rev:** Partial face **Edge Lettering:** DOMINUS PROVIDEBIT

Date	Mintage	F	VF	XF	Unc	BU
2007B	Est. 50,000	—	—	—	17.50	25.00
2007B Proof	Est. 12,000	Value: 45.00				

KM# 124 20 FRANCS

20.0000 g., 0.8350 Silver 0.5369 oz. ASW, 33 mm. **Series:** Famous buildings **Subject:** Munot castle of Schaffhausen **Obv. Legend:** CONFEDERATIO - HELVETICA **Rev:** Two views of castle **Rev. Legend:** MUNOT

Date	Mintage	F	VF	XF	Unc	BU
2007B	50,000	—	—	—	22.50	25.00
2007B Proof	7,000	Value: 50.00				

KM# 127 20 FRANCS

20.0000 g., 0.8350 Silver 0.5369 oz. ASW, 33 mm. **Subject:** 100th Anniversary Hockey **Obv:** Small national arms **Obv. Legend:** CONFEDERATIO - HELVETICA **Rev:** Two players, one about to swing at puck **Rev. Legend:** ICE HOCKEY 1908-2008 **Rev. Designer:** Roland Hirter

Date	Mintage	F	VF	XF	Unc	BU
2008B	50,000	—	—	—	22.00	25.00
2008B Proof	7,000	Value: 50.00				

KM# 95 50 FRANCS

11.2900 g., 0.9000 Gold 0.3267 oz. AGW, 25 mm. **Obv:** Landscape and value **Rev:** Heidi and goat running **Edge:** Lettered **Designer:** Albrecht Schnider

Date	Mintage	F	VF	XF	Unc	BU
2001B Proof	3,967	Value: 375				

KM# 102 50 FRANCS

11.2900 g., 0.9000 Gold 0.3267 oz. AGW, 25 mm. **Subject:** Expo '02 **Obv:** Value **Rev:** Aerial view of 3 lakes landscape **Edge:** Lettered **Designer:** Max Matter

Date	Mintage	F	VF	XF	Unc	BU
2002B Proof	4,856	Value: 350				

KM# 105 50 FRANCS

11.2900 g., 0.9000 Gold 0.3267 oz. AGW, 25 mm. **Obv:** Skier and value **Rev:** St. Moritz city view **Edge:** Lettered **Designer:** Andreas His

Date	Mintage	F	VF	XF	Unc	BU
2003B Proof	4,000	Value: 350				

KM# 123 50 FRANCS

11.2900 g., 0.9000 Gold 0.3267 oz. AGW, 25 mm. **Subject:** FIFA Centennial **Obv:** FIFA depicting Wilhelm Tell **Rev:** Soccer ball on left value on right **Designer:** Joaquin Jimenez

Date	Mintage	F	VF	XF	Unc	BU
2004B Proof	10,000	Value: 385				

KM# 110 50 FRANCS

11.2900 g., 0.9000 Gold 0.3267 oz. AGW, 25 mm. **Obv:** Value **Rev:** Mountain **Edge:** Lettered with 13 stars **Edge Lettering:** DOMINUS PROVIDEBIT **Designer:** Stephan Bundi

Date	Mintage	F	VF	XF	Unc	BU
2004B Proof	7,000	Value: 385				

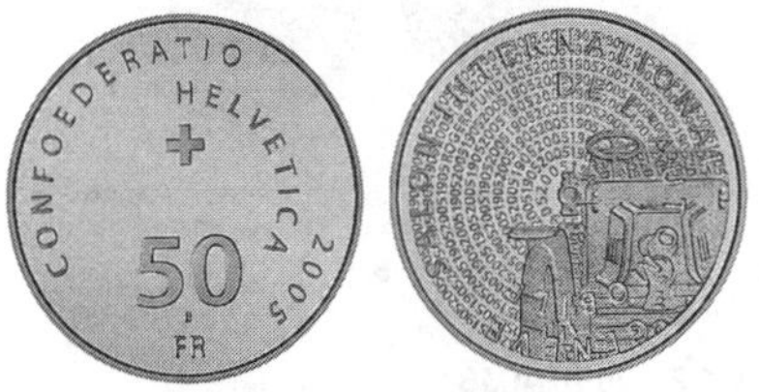

KM# 113 50 FRANCS

11.2900 g., 0.9000 Gold 0.3267 oz. AGW, 25 mm. **Subject:** Geneva Motor Show **Obv:** Value **Rev:** Partial view of an antique car **Edge:** Lettered **Edge Lettering:** DOMINUS PROVIDEBIT **Designer:** Roger Pfund

Date	Mintage	F	VF	XF	Unc	BU
2005B Proof	6,000	Value: 350				

KM# 116 50 FRANCS

11.2900 g., 0.9000 Gold 0.3267 oz. AGW, 25 mm. **Obv:** Value **Rev:** Swiss Guardsman **Edge Lettering:** "Dominus Providebit" **Designer:** Rudolf Mirer

Date	Mintage	F	VF	XF	Unc	BU
2006B Proof	6,000	Value: 385				

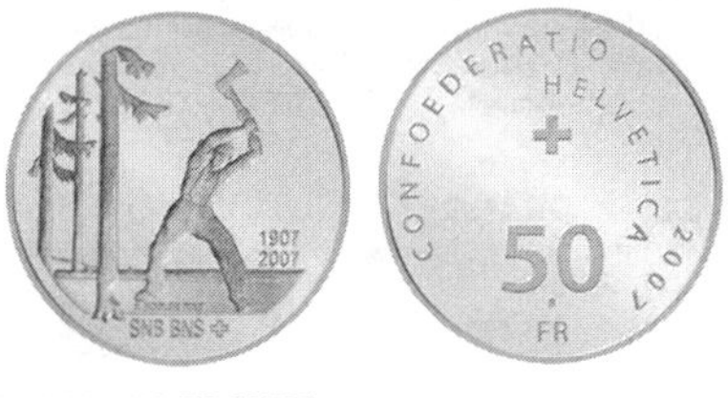

KM# 120 50 FRANCS

11.2900 g., 0.9000 Gold 0.3267 oz. AGW, 25 mm. **Subject:** National Bank Centennial **Obv:** Value **Rev:** Wood cutter **Edge Lettering:** DOMINUS PROVIDEBIT

Date	Mintage	F	VF	XF	Unc	BU
2007B Proof	6,000	Value: 350				

KM# 125 50 FRANCS

11.2900 g., 0.9000 Gold 0.3267 oz. AGW, 25 mm. **Subject:** 100th Anniversary SNB **Obv. Legend:** CONFEDERATIO - HELVETICA **Rev:** "Lumberjack" from painting by Ferdinand Hodler **Rev. Inscription:** SNB BNS +

Date	Mintage	F	VF	XF	Unc	BU
2007B Proof	6,000	Value: 350				

ESSAIS

KM#	Date	Mintage	Identification	Mkt Val
E12	2000	—	20 Francs. Silver. KM#97	240
E13	2001	—	20 Francs. Silver. KM#93	245
E14	2002	700	5 Francs. Bi-Metallic. KM#98 Escalade	160
E15	2003	700	5 Francs. Bi-Metallic. KM#103 Chalandamarz	170
E16	2004	700	10 Francs. Bi-Metallic. KM#107.	260
E19	2005	500	20 Francs. Silver. 20.0000 g. 33 mm. Motor Show. KM#112.	260
E20	2006	500	20 Francs. Silver. 20.0000 g. 33 mm. Parliament Building. KM#117.	245
E21	2007	—	20 Francs. Silver. 20.0000 g. 33 mm. KM#119. Munot	250

MINT SETS

KM#	Date	Mintage	Identification	Issue Price	Mkt Val
MS35	2001 (9)	21,532	KM#21a.3, 23a.3, 24a.3, 26c, 27, 29a, 40a.4, 46, 92 Zurich Sechselauten	—	30.00
MS36	2002 (9)	17,920	KM#21a.3, 23a.3, 24a.3, 26c, 27, 29a, 40a.4, 46, 98 Escalade	—	35.00
MS37	2002 (9)	2,000	KM#21a.3, 23a.3, 24a.3, 26c, 27, 29a, 40a.4, 46, 98 Includes a medal and different cover (intended as a birth year set for 2002 from the mint)	—	190
MS38	2003 (9)	17,200	KM#21a.3, 23a.3, 24a.3, 26c, 27, 29a, 40a.4, 46, 103 Chalandamarz	—	35.00
MS39	2004 (9)	16,000	KM#21a.3, 23a.3, 24a.3, 26c, 27, 29a, 40a.4, 46, 107 Matterhorn	—	60.00
MS40	2005 (9)	16,000	KM#21a.3, 23a.3, 24a.3, 26c, 27, 29a, 40a.4, 46, 111 Jung Frau	—	40.00
MS41	2006 (9)	16,000	KM#21a.3, 23a.3, 24a.3, 26c, 27, 29a, 40a.4, 46, 114 Piz Berhina	—	160
MS42	2007 (8)	—	KM#21a.3, 23a.3, 24a.3, 26c, 27, 29a, 40a.4, 118 (IBEX)	—	35.00

PROOF SETS

KM#	Date	Mintage	Identification	Issue Price	Mkt Val
PS30	2001 (9)	5,184	KM#21a.3, 23a.3, 24a.3, 26c, 27, 29a, 40a.4, 46, 92 Zurich Sechselauten	—	67.50
PS31	2002 (9)	4,518	KM#21a.3, 23a.3, 24a.3, 26c, 27, 29a, 40a.4, 46, 98 Escalade	—	72.50
PS32	2003 (9)	4,520	KM#21a.3, 23a.3, 24a.3, 26c, 27, 29a, 40a.4, 46, 103 Chatandamarz	—	72.50
PS33	2004 (9)	4,168	KM#21a.3, 23a.3, 24a.3, 26c, 27, 29a, 40a.4, 46, 107 Matterhorn	68.00	85.00
PS34	2005 (9)	4,497	KM#21a.3, 23a.3, 24a.3, 26c, 27, 29a, 40a.4, 46, 111 Jung Frau	68.00	72.50
PS35	2006 (9)	4,000	KM#21a.3, 23a.3, 24a.3, 26c, 27, 29a, 40a.4, 46, 114 Piz Berhina	68.00	275
PS36	2007 (7)	4,000	KM#21a.3, 23a.3, 24a.3, 26c, 27, 29a, 40a.4, plus National Park	68.00	77.50

SYRIA

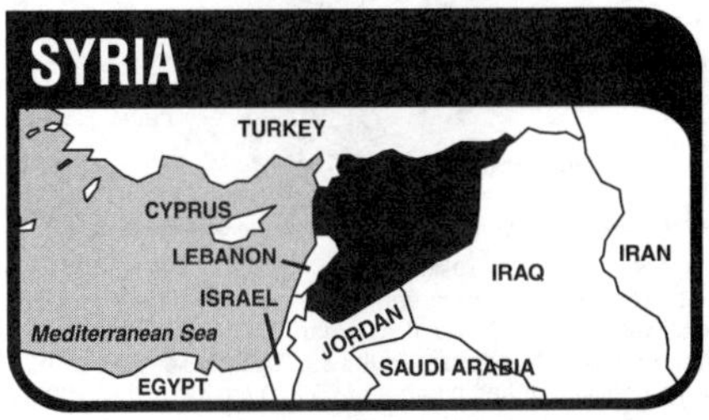

The Syrian Arab Republic, located in the Near East at the eastern end of the Mediterranean Sea, has an area of 71,498 sq. mi. (185,180 sq. km.) and a population of *12 million. Capital: Greater Damascus. Agriculture and animal breeding are the chief industries. Cotton, crude oil and livestock are exported.

TITLES

الجمهورية السورية

al-Jumhuriya(t) al-Suriya(t)

الجمهورية لعربية السورية

al-Jumhuriya(t) al-Arabiya(t) as-Suriya(t)

SYRIAN ARAB REPUBLIC

STANDARD COINAGE

KM# 129 5 POUNDS

7.5300 g., Nickel-Clad Steel, 24.5 mm. **Obv:** National arms within design and beaded border **Rev:** Old fort and latent image above value within design and beaded border **Edge:** Reeded and lettered **Edge Lettering:** "CENTRAL BANK 5 SYP"

Date	Mintage	F	VF	XF	Unc	BU
AH1424-2003	—	—	—	—	1.00	1.50

KM# 130 10 POUNDS
9.5300 g., Copper-Nickel-Zinc, 27.4 mm. **Obv:** National arms within beaded border **Rev:** Ancient ruins with latent image within beaded border **Edge:** Reeded and lettered **Edge Lettering:** "10 SYRIAN POUNDS"

Date	Mintage	F	VF	XF	Unc	BU
AH1424-2003	—	—	—	—	2.00	3.00

KM# 131 25 POUNDS
8.4000 g., Bi-Metallic Copper-Nickel in Nickel-Brass ring, 25 mm. **Obv:** National arms within beaded border **Rev:** Building and latent image within beaded border **Edge:** Reeded and lettered **Edge Lettering:** "CENTRAL BANK OF SYRIA 25"

Date	Mintage	F	VF	XF	Unc	BU
AH1424-2003	—	—	—	—	4.50	6.00

TAJIKISTAN

The Republic of Tajikistan (Tadjiquistan), was formed from those regions of Bukhara and Turkestan where the population consisted mainly of Tajiks. It is bordered in the north and west by Uzbekistan and Kyrgyzstan, in the east by China and in the south by Afghanistan. It has an area of 55,240 sq. miles (143,100 sq. km.) and a population of 5.95 million. It includes 2 provinces of Khudzand and Khatlon together with the Gorno-Badakhshan Autonomous Region with a population of 5,092,603. Capital: Dushanbe. Tajikistan was admitted as a constituent republic of the Soviet Union on Dec. 5, 1929. In August 1990 the Tajik Supreme Soviet adopted a declaration of republican sovereignty, and in Dec. 1991 the republic became a member of the CIS.

After demonstrations and fighting, the Communist government was replaced by a Revolutionary Coalition Council on May 7, 1992. Following further demonstrations President Nabiev was ousted on Sept. 7, 1992. Civil war broke out, and the government resigned on Nov. 10, 1992. On Nov. 30, 1992 it was announced that a CIS peacekeeping force would be sent to Tajikistan. A state of emergency was imposed in Jan. 1993. A ceasefire was signed in 1996 and a peace agreement signed in June 1997.

MONETARY SYSTEM
100 Drams = 1 Somoni

REPUBLIC

DECIMAL COINAGE

KM# 2.1 5 DRAMS
2.0500 g., Brass Clad Steel, 16.5 mm. **Obv:** Crown within 1/2 star border **Rev:** Value within design **Edge:** Plain

Date	Mintage	F	VF	XF	Unc	BU
2001(sp)	—	—	—	—	0.50	0.75
2006(sp)	—	—	—	—	0.50	0.75

KM# 2.2 5 DRAMS
Brass Clad Steel, 16.5 mm. **Obv:** Crown with 1/2 star border **Rev:** Large value within design

Date	Mintage	F	VF	XF	Unc	BU
2006(sp)	—	—	—	—	.75	1.25

KM# 3.1 10 DRAMS
2.4700 g., Brass Clad Steel, 17.5 mm. **Obv:** Crown within 1/2 star border **Rev:** Value within design **Edge:** Plain

Date	Mintage	F	VF	XF	Unc	BU
2001(sp)	—	—	—	—	0.75	1.00
2006(sp)	—	—	—	—	0.75	1.00

KM# 3.2 10 DRAMS
Brass Clad Steel, 17.5 mm. **Obv:** Crown within 1/2 star border **Rev:** Large value within design

Date	Mintage	F	VF	XF	Unc	BU
2006(sp)	—	—	—	—	1.00	1.50

KM# 4.1 20 DRAMS
2.7300 g., Brass Clad Steel, 18.5 mm. **Obv:** Crown within 1/2 star border **Rev:** Value within design **Edge:** Plain

Date	Mintage	F	VF	XF	Unc	BU
2001(sp)	—	—	—	—	1.00	1.25
2006(sp)	—	—	—	—	1.00	1.25

KM# 4.2 20 DRAMS
Brass Clad Steel, 18.5 mm. **Obv:** Crown within 1/2 star border **Rev:** Large value within design

Date	Mintage	F	VF	XF	Unc	BU
2006(sp)	2	—	—	—	1.50	2.00

KM# 5.1 25 DRAMS
2.8000 g., Brass, 19.1 mm. **Obv:** Crown within 1/2 star border **Rev:** Value within design **Edge:** Plain

Date	Mintage	F	VF	XF	Unc	BU
2001(sp)	—	—	—	—	1.50	1.75
2006(sp)	—	—	—	—	1.50	1.75

KM# 5.2 25 DRAMS
Brass, 19.1 mm. **Obv:** Crown within 1/2 star border **Rev:** Large value within design

Date	Mintage	F	VF	XF	Unc	BU
2006(sp)	—	—	—	—	1.75	2.50

KM# 6.1 50 DRAMS
3.5500 g., Brass, 21 mm. **Obv:** Crown within 1/2 star border **Rev:** Value within design **Edge:** Plain

Date	Mintage	F	VF	XF	Unc	BU
2001(sp)	—	—	—	—	1.75	2.00

KM# 6.2 50 DRAMS
Brass, 21 mm. **Obv:** Crown within 1/2 star border **Rev:** Large value within design

Date	Mintage	F	VF	XF	Unc	BU
2001(sp)	—	—	—	—	2.00	3.00

KM# 7 SOMONI
5.1500 g., Copper-Nickel-Zinc, 23.9 mm. **Obv:** King's bust 1/2 right **Rev:** Value **Edge:** Reeded and plain sections

Date	Mintage	F	VF	XF	Unc	BU
2001(sp)	—	—	—	—	3.50	5.00

KM# 12 SOMONI
5.2100 g., Copper-Nickel-Zinc, 24 mm. **Subject:** Year of Aryan Civilization **Obv:** National arms above value **Rev:** Ancient archer in war chariot **Edge:** Segmented reeding

Date	Mintage	F	VF	XF	Unc	BU
2006(sp)	100,000	—	—	—	—	4.00

KM# 12a SOMONI
20.0000 g., 0.9250 Silver 0.5948 oz. ASW, 24 mm. **Subject:** Year of Aryan Civilization **Obv:** National arms above value **Rev:** Ancient archer in war chariot **Edge:** Segmented reeding

Date	Mintage	F	VF	XF	Unc	BU
2006(sp) Proof	1,500	Value: 50.00				

KM# 13 SOMONI
5.2100 g., Copper-Nickel-Zinc, 24 mm. **Subject:** Year of Aryan Civilization **Obv:** National arms above value **Rev:** Two busts left **Edge:** Segmented reeding

Date	Mintage	F	VF	XF	Unc	BU
2006(sp)	100,000	—	—	—	—	4.00

KM# 13a SOMONI
20.0000 g., 0.9250 Silver 0.5948 oz. ASW, 24 mm. **Subject:** Year of Aryan Civilization **Obv:** National arms above value **Rev:** Two busts left **Edge:** Segmented reeding

Date	Mintage	F	VF	XF	Unc	BU
2006 Proof	1,500	Value: 50.00				

KM# 16 SOMONI
5.2400 g., Copper-Nickel-Zinc, 23.95 mm. **Subject:** 800th Anniversary Birth of Jaloliddini Rumi **Obv:** Small arms above value in cartouche **Rev:** 1/2 length figure facing **Edge:** Segmented reeding

Date	Mintage	F	VF	XF	Unc	BU
2007	—	—	—	—	3.00	4.00

KM# 8 3 SOMONI
6.3200 g., Copper-Nickel-Zinc, 25.5 mm. **Obv:** National arms **Rev:** Crown above value within design **Edge:** Lettered

Date	Mintage	F	VF	XF	Unc	BU
2001(sp)	—	—	—	—	5.00	7.00

KM# 10 3 SOMONI
Bi-Metallic, 25.5 mm. **Subject:** 80th Year - Dushanbe City **Obv:** Value below arms within circle **Rev:** Statue in arch within circle

Date	Mintage	F	VF	XF	Unc	BU
2004(sp)	—	—	—	—	6.50	9.00

KM# 10a 3 SOMONI
6.9800 g., 0.9250 Silver 0.2076 oz. ASW, 25.5 mm. **Subject:** 80th Anniversary of Republic **Obv:** Value below arms within circle **Rev:** Statue in arch within circle

Date	Mintage	F	VF	XF	Unc	BU
2004 Proof	1,000	Value: 55.00				

KM# 14 3 SOMONI
6.3000 g., Bi-Metallic Copper-Nickel center in Brass ring, 25.5 mm. **Subject:** 2700th Anniversary of Kulyab **Obv:** National arms above value **Rev:** Kulyab city arms **Edge:** Lettered

Date	Mintage	F	VF	XF	Unc	BU
2006(sp)	100,000	—	—	—	6.00	7.50

KM# 14a 3 SOMONI

0.9250 Silver **Subject:** 2700th Anniversary of Kulyab **Obv:** National arms above value **Rev:** Kulyab city arms

Date	Mintage	F	VF	XF	Unc	BU
2006 Proof	—	Value: 55.00				

KM# 9 5 SOMONI

7.1000 g., Copper-Nickel-Zinc, 26.4 mm. **Obv:** Turbaned head right **Rev:** Crown above value within design **Edge:** Reeded and plain sections with a star

Date	Mintage	F	VF	XF	Unc	BU
2001(sp)	—	—	—	—	7.50	9.00

KM# 11 5 SOMONI

6.9400 g., Bi-Metallic Copper-Nickel center in Brass ring, 26.5 mm. **Subject:** 10th Anniversary - Constitution **Obv:** Arms above value within circle **Rev:** Flag and book within circle **Edge:** Lettered

Date	Mintage	F	VF	XF	Unc	BU
2004(sp)	—	—	—	—	7.50	10.00

KM# 11a 5 SOMONI

8.5500 g., 0.9250 Silver 0.2543 oz. ASW, 26.5 mm. **Subject:** 10th Anniversary - Constitution **Obv:** Arms above value within circle **Rev:** Flag and book within circle

Date	Mintage	F	VF	XF	Unc	BU
2004 Proof	2,000	Value: 50.00				

KM# 15 5 SOMONI

7.0000 g., Bi-Metallic Copper-Nickel center in Brass ring, 26.5 mm. **Subject:** 15th Anniversary of Independence **Obv:** National arms above value **Rev:** Government building **Edge:** Lettered

Date	Mintage	F	VF	XF	Unc	BU
2006(sp)	100,000	—	—	—	7.50	10.00

TANZANIA

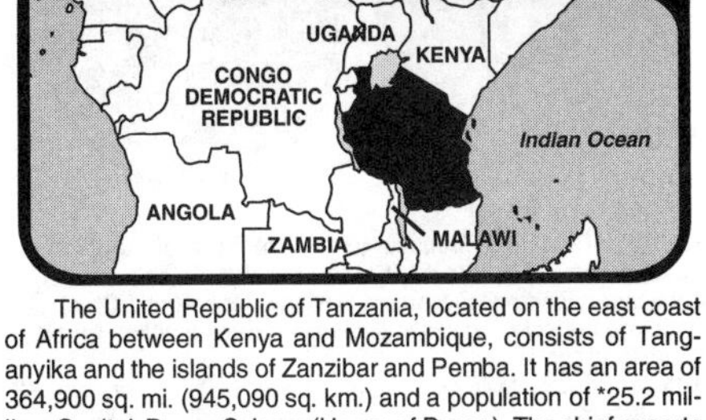

The United Republic of Tanzania, located on the east coast of Africa between Kenya and Mozambique, consists of Tanganyika and the islands of Zanzibar and Pemba. It has an area of 364,900 sq. mi. (945,090 sq. km.) and a population of *25.2 million. Capital: Dar es Salaam (Haven of Peace). The chief exports are cotton, coffee, diamonds, sisal, cloves, petroleum products, and cashew nuts.

Tanzania is a member of the Commonwealth of Nations. The President is Chief of State.

REPUBLIC

STANDARD COINAGE

100 Senti = 1 Shilingi

KM# 56 500 SHILLINGS

31.4600 g., 0.9250 Silver 0.9356 oz. ASW, 38.6 mm. **Obv:** Arms with supporters above value **Rev:** African dhow **Edge:** Reeded

Date	Mintage	F	VF	XF	Unc	BU
2001 Proof	—	Value: 40.00				

THAILAND

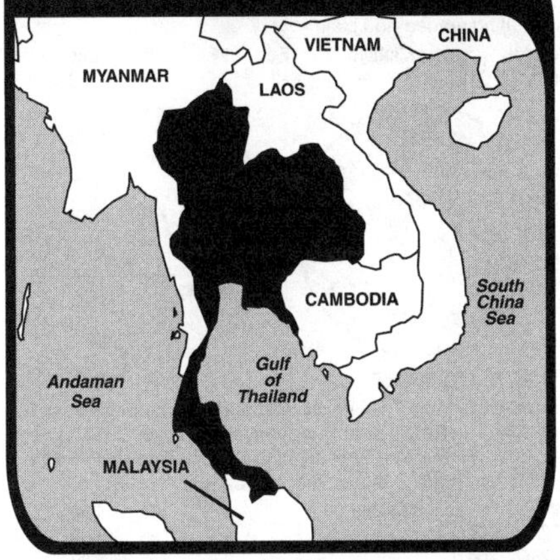

The Kingdom of Thailand (formerly Siam), a constitutional monarchy located in the center of mainland Southeast Asia between Burma and Laos, has an area of 198,457 mi. (514,000 sq. km.) and a population of *55.5 million. Capital: Bangkok. The economy is based on agriculture and mining. Rubber, rice, teakwood, tin and tungsten are exported.

The history of The Kingdom of Siam, the only country in south and Southeast Asia that was never colonized by an European power, dates from the 6th century A.D. when Thai people started to migrate into the area a process that accelerated with the Mongol invasion of China in the 13th century. After 400 years of sporadic warfare with the neighboring Burmese, King Taskin won the last battle in 1767. He founded a new capital, Dhonburi, on the west bank of the Chao Praya River. King Rama I moved the capital to Bangkok in 1782, thus initiating the so-called Bangkok Period of Siamese coinage characterized by Pot Duang money (bullet coins) stamped with regal symbols.

The Portuguese, who were followed by the Dutch, British and French, introduced the Thai to the Western world. Rama III of the present ruling dynasty negotiated a treaty of friendship and commerce with Britain in 1826, and in 1896 the independence of the kingdom was guaranteed by an Anglo-French accord.

In 1909 Siam ceded to Great Britain its suzerain rights over the dependencies of Kedah, Kelantan, Trengganu and Perlis, Malay states situated in southern Siam just north of British Malaya, which eliminated any British jurisdiction in Siam proper.

The absolute monarchy was changed into a constitutional monarchy in 1932.

On Dec. 8, 1941, after five hours of fighting, Thailand agreed to permit Japanese troops passage through the country to invade Northern British Malaysia. This eventually led to increased Japanese intervention and finally occupation of the country. On Jan. 25, 1942, Thailand declared war on Great Britain and the United States. A free Thai guerilla movement was soon organized to counteract the Japanese. In July 1943 Japan transferred the four northern Malay States back to Thailand. These were returned to Great Britain after peace treaties were signed in 1946.

RULERS

Rama V (Phra Maha Chulalongkorn), 1868-1910
Rama VI (Phra Maha Vajiravudh), 1910-1925
Rama VII (Phra Maha Prajadhipok), 1925-1935
Rama VIII (Phra Maha Ananda Mahidol), 1935-1946
Rama IX (Phra Maha Bhumifhol Adulyadej), 1946-

MONETARY SYSTEM

Old currency system

2 Solos = 1 Att
2 Att = 1 Sio (Pai)
2 Sio = 1 Sik
2 Sik = 1 Fuang
2 Fuang = 1 Salung (not Sal'ung)
4 Salung = 1 Baht
4 Baht = 1 Tamlung
20 Tamlung = 1 Chang

UNITS OF OLD THAI CURRENCY

Chang -	ชั่ง	Sik -	ซีก
Tamlung -	ตำลึง	Sio (Pai) -	เสี้ยว
Baht -	บาท	Att -	อัฐ
Salung -	สลึง	Solos -	โสฬส
Fuang -	เฟื้อง		

MINT MARKS

H-Heaton Birmingham

DATING

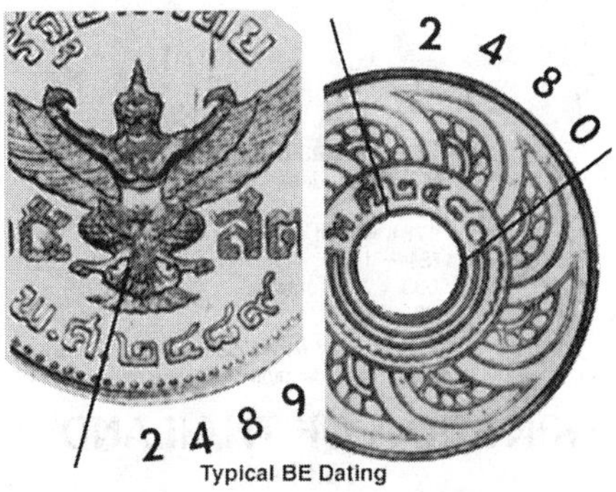

Typical BE Dating

Typical CS Dating

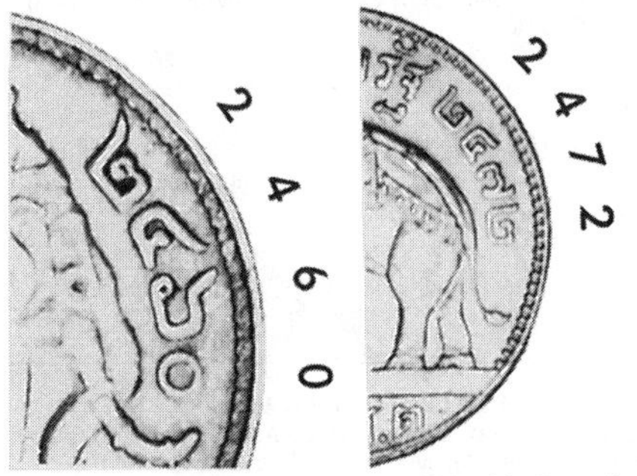

NOTE: Sometimes the era designator *BE* or *CS* will actually appear on the coin itself.

Denomination

2-1/2 (Satang)

RS Dating

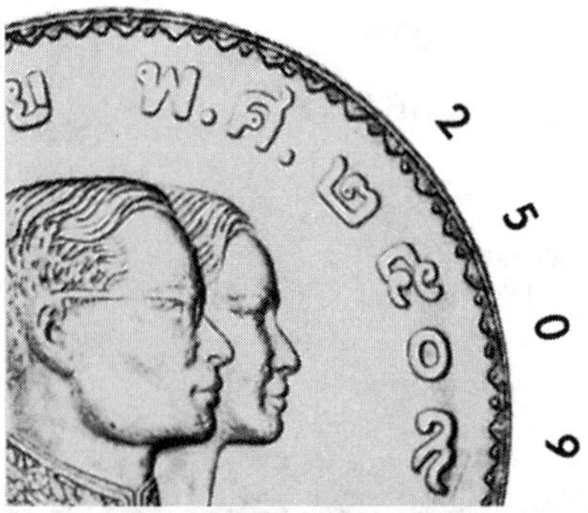

DATE CONVERSION TABLES

B.E. date - 543 = A.D. date
Ex: 2516 - 543 = 1973
R.S. date + 1781 = A.D. date
Ex: 127 + 1781 = 1908
C.S. date + 638 = A.D. date
Ex 1238 + 638 = 1876

Primary denominations used were 1 Baht, 1/4 and 1/8 Baht up to the reign of Rama IV. Other denominations are much scarcer.

KINGDOM OF THAILAND

1939-

DECIMAL COINAGE

25 Satang = 1 Salung; 100 Satang = 1 Baht

Y# 187 25 SATANG = 1/4 BAHT

1.9000 g., Aluminum-Bronze, 15.93 mm. **Ruler:** Bhumipol Adulyadej (Rama IX) **Obv:** Head left **Rev:** Steepled building **Edge:** Reeded

Date	Mintage	F	VF	XF	Unc	BU
BE2545 (2002)	—	—	—	—	0.10	—
BE2547 (2004)	—	—	—	—	0.10	—
BE2549 (2006)	—	—	—	—	0.10	—

Y# 203 50 SATANG = 1/2 BAHT

2.4000 g., Brass **Ruler:** Bhumipol Adulyadej (Rama IX) **Obv:** Head left **Rev:** Steepled building divides value

Date	Mintage	F	VF	XF	Unc	BU
BE2544 (2001)	—	—	—	—	0.10	—
BE2545 (2002)	—	—	—	—	0.10	—
BE2547 (2004)	—	—	—	—	0.10	—

Y# 183 BAHT

3.4500 g., Copper-Nickel, 20 mm. **Ruler:** Bhumipol Adulyadej (Rama IX) **Obv:** Head left **Rev:** Palace **Edge:** Reeded **Note:** Varieties exist.

Date	Mintage	F	VF	XF	Unc	BU
BE2544 (2001)	—	—	—	—	0.10	—
BE2545 (2002)	—	—	—	—	0.10	—
BE2546 (2003)	—	—	—	—	0.10	—
BE2547 (2004)	—	—	—	—	0.10	—
BE2548 (2005)	—	—	—	—	0.10	—
BE2549 (2006)	—	—	—	—	0.10	—

Y# 219 5 BAHT

7.4600 g., Copper-Nickel Clad Copper, 24 mm. **Ruler:** Bhumipol Adulyadej (Rama IX) **Obv:** Head left **Rev:** Penjahwat **Edge:** Coarse reeding **Note:** Circulation coinage.

Date	Mintage	F	VF	XF	Unc	BU
BE2549 (2006)	—	—	—	—	0.50	—

Y# 373 10 BAHT

8.5000 g., Bi-Metallic Brass center in Copper-Nickel ring, 26 mm. **Ruler:** Bhumipol Adulyadej (Rama IX) **Subject:** Department of Lands Centennial February 17 2444-2544 **Obv:** Conjoined busts facing divides circle **Rev:** Department seal within circle **Edge:** Alternating reeded and plain

Date	Mintage	F	VF	XF	Unc	BU
BE2544(2001)	—	—	—	—	2.50	—

Y# 227 10 BAHT

8.5400 g., Bi-Metallic Aluminum-bronze center in Stainless steel ring, 26 mm. **Ruler:** Bhumipol Adulyadej (Rama IX) **Obv:** Head left within circle **Rev:** Temple of the Dawn within circle **Edge:** Segmented reeding **Note:** Varieties exist.

Date	Mintage	F	VF	XF	Unc	BU
BE2544 (2001)	—	—	—	—	3.00	—
BE2545 (2002)	—	—	—	—	3.00	—
BE2546 (2003)	—	—	—	—	3.00	—
BE2547 (2004)	—	—	—	—	3.00	—
BE2548 (2005)	—	—	—	—	3.00	—
BE2549 (2006)	—	—	—	—	3.00	—

Y# 381 10 BAHT

8.5500 g., Bi-Metallic Brass center in Copper-Nickel ring, 26 mm. **Ruler:** Bhumipol Adulyadej (Rama IX) **Subject:** Centennial of Irrigation Department June 13 **Obv:** Conjoined busts facing divides circle **Rev:** Department logo **Edge:** Alternating reeded and plain

Date	Mintage	F	VF	XF	Unc	BU
BE2545(2002)	—	—	—	—	2.00	—

Y# 382 10 BAHT

8.5500 g., Bi-Metallic Brass center in Copper-Nickel ring, 26 mm. **Ruler:** Bhumipol Adulyadej (Rama IX) **Subject:** Department of Internal Trade 60th Anniversary May 5 **Obv:** Head left **Rev:** Department logo **Edge:** Alternating reeded and plain

Date	Mintage	F	VF	XF	Unc	BU
BE2545(2002)	—	—	—	—	2.00	—

Y# 383 10 BAHT

8.5500 g., Bi-Metallic Brass center in Copper-Nickel ring, 26 mm. **Ruler:** Bhumipol Adulyadej (Rama IX) **Subject:** State Highway Department 90th Anniversary April 1 **Obv:** Conjoined busts facing divides circle **Rev:** Department logo **Edge:** Alternating reeded and plain

Date	Mintage	F	VF	XF	Unc	BU
BE2545(2002)	—	—	—	—	2.00	—

Y# 384 10 BAHT

8.5500 g., Bi-Metallic Brass center in Copper-Nickel ring, 26 mm. **Ruler:** Bhumipol Adulyadej (Rama IX) **Subject:** Vajira Hospital 90th Anniversary January 2 **Obv:** Conjoined busts facing divides circle **Rev:** Hospital logo **Edge:** Alternating reeded and plain

Date	Mintage	F	VF	XF	Unc	BU
BE2545(2002)	—	—	—	—	2.00	—

Y# 385 10 BAHT

8.5500 g., Bi-Metallic Brass center in Copper-Nickel ring, 26 mm. **Ruler:** Bhumipol Adulyadej (Rama IX) **Subject:** 20th World Scouting Jamboree **Obv:** Rama IX wearing a scouting uniform **Rev:** Jamboree logo **Edge:** Alternating reeded and plain

Date	Mintage	F	VF	XF	Unc	BU
BE2545(2002)	—	—	—	—	2.00	—

Y# 387 10 BAHT

8.5500 g., Bi-Metallic Brass center in Copper-Nickel ring, 26 mm. **Ruler:** Bhumipol Adulyadej (Rama IX) **Subject:** King's 75th Birthday December 5 **Obv:** Head left **Rev:** Royal crown in radiant oval **Edge:** Alternating reeded and plain

Date	Mintage	F	VF	XF	Unc	BU
BE2545(2002)	—	—	—	—	2.00	—

Y# 400 10 BAHT

8.5500 g., Bi-Metallic Brass center in Copper-Nickel ring, 26 mm. **Ruler:** Bhumipol Adulyadej (Rama IX) **Obv:** Head left **Rev:** APEC logo **Edge:** Segmented reeding

Date	Mintage	F	VF	XF	Unc	BU
BE2546-2003	—	—	—	—	3.00	—

Y# 405 10 BAHT

8.5400 g., Bi-Metallic Brass center in Copper-Nickel ring, 26 mm. **Ruler:** Bhumipol Adulyadej (Rama IX) **Subject:** "CITES COP" **Obv:** Bust 3/4 left within circle **Rev:** "CITES" logo **Edge:** Segmented reeding

Date	Mintage	F	VF	XF	Unc	BU
ND(2003)	—	—	—	—	2.00	—

Y# 409 10 BAHT

Bi-Metallic **Ruler:** Bhumipol Adulyadej (Rama IX) **Subject:** 150th Anniversary of King Rama V

Date	Mintage	F	VF	XF	Unc	BU
BE2546(2003)	—	—	—	—	2.50	—

Y# 391 10 BAHT

8.5000 g., Bi-Metallic Brass center in Copper-Nickel ring, 26 mm. **Ruler:** Bhumipol Adulyadej (Rama IX) **Subject:** Inspector General's Department Centennial May 6 **Obv:** Head left within circle **Rev:** Department seal within circle and design **Edge:** Alternating reeded and plain

Date	Mintage	F	VF	XF	Unc	BU
BE2546(2003)	—	—	—	—	1.75	—

Y# 392 10 BAHT

8.5000 g., Bi-Metallic Brass center in Copper-Nickel ring, 26 mm. **Ruler:** Bhumipol Adulyadej (Rama IX) **Subject:** 80th Birthday of Princess May 6 **Obv:** Bust 1/4 right **Rev:** Crowned emblem and value **Edge:** Alternating reeded and plain **Note:** This is the king's sister.

Date	Mintage	F	VF	XF	Unc	BU
BE2546(2003)	—	—	—	—	1.75	—

Y# 396 10 BAHT

8.5500 g., Bi-Metallic Brass center in Copper-Nickel ring, 26 mm. **Ruler:** Bhumipol Adulyadej (Rama IX) **Subject:** 90th Anniversary of the Government Savings Bank April 1 **Obv:** Uniformed bust facing within circle **Rev:** Bank emblem **Edge:** Alternating reeded and plain

Date	Mintage	F	VF	XF	Unc	BU
BE2546(2003)	—	—	—	—	2.00	—

Y# 410 10 BAHT
8.4500 g., Bi-Metallic Brass center in Copper-Nickel ring, 25.9 mm. **Obv:** King in uniform **Rev:** Thammasat University arms **Edge:** Segmented reeding **Note:** 70th Anniversary of Thammasat University

Date	Mintage	F	VF	XF	Unc	BU
BE2547(2004)	—	—	—	—	2.50	—

Y# 411 10 BAHT
Bi-Metallic **Ruler:** Bhumipol Adulyadej (Rama IX) **Subject:** 70th Anniversary Royal Institute

Date	Mintage	F	VF	XF	Unc	BU
BE2547(2004)	—	—	—	—	2.50	—

Y# 412 10 BAHT
Bi-Metallic **Ruler:** Bhumipol Adulyadej (Rama IX) **Subject:** 72nd Anniversary of Queen's Birthday

Date	Mintage	F	VF	XF	Unc	BU
BE2547(2004)	—	—	—	—	2.50	—

Y# 413 10 BAHT
Bi-Metallic **Ruler:** Bhumipol Adulyadej (Rama IX) **Subject:** World Conservation Congress

Date	Mintage	F	VF	XF	Unc	BU
BE2547(2004)	—	—	—	—	2.50	—

Y# 414 10 BAHT
Bi-Metallic **Ruler:** Bhumipol Adulyadej (Rama IX) **Subject:** Anti Drugs

Date	Mintage	F	VF	XF	Unc	BU
BE2547(2004)	—	—	—	—	2.50	—

Y# 415 10 BAHT
Bi-Metallic **Ruler:** Bhumipol Adulyadej (Rama IX) **Subject:** Bicentennial of King Rama IV

Date	Mintage	F	VF	XF	Unc	BU
BE2547(2004)	—	—	—	—	2.50	—

Y# 416 10 BAHT
Bi-Metallic **Ruler:** Bhumipol Adulyadej (Rama IX) **Subject:** 100th Anniversary of Army Transportation

Date	Mintage	F	VF	XF	Unc	BU
BE2548(2005)	—	—	—	—	2.50	—

Y# 417 10 BAHT
Bi-Metallic **Ruler:** Bhumipol Adulyadej (Rama IX) **Obv:** Baby head

Date	Mintage	F	VF	XF	Unc	BU
BE2548(2005)	—	—	—	—	2.50	—

Y# 402 10 BAHT
8.4400 g., Bi-Metallic Brass center in Copper-Nickel ring, 26 mm. **Ruler:** Bhumipol Adulyadej (Rama IX) **Obv:** Bust 1/4 left within circle **Rev:** Treasury Department seal within circle **Edge:** Segmented reeding

Date	Mintage	F	VF	XF	Unc	BU
BE2548(2005)	—	—	—	—	2.50	—

Y# 406 10 BAHT
8.4400 g., Bi-Metallic Brass center in Copper-Nickel ring, 26 mm. **Ruler:** Bhumipol Adulyadej (Rama IX) **Subject:** 60th Anniversary of Reign **Obv:** Bust 1/4 left within circle **Rev:** Royal Crown on display **Edge:** Segmented reeding

Date	Mintage	F	VF	XF	Unc	BU
BE2549 (2006)	—	—	—	—	2.50	—

Y# 418 10 BAHT
Bi-Metallic **Ruler:** Bhumipol Adulyadej (Rama IX) **Subject:** 25th Asia-Pacific Scout Jamboree

Date	Mintage	F	VF	XF	Unc	BU
BE2549 (2006)	—	—	—	—	2.50	—

Y# 424 10 BAHT
8.4300 g., Bi-Metallic Brass center in Copper-Nickel ring, 25.98 mm. **Ruler:** Bhumipol Adulyadej (Rama IX) **Subject:** 150th Birthday of Prince Jaturon Ratsamee **Obv:** Bust of Prince facing 3/4 right **Rev:** Radiant badge **Edge:** Segmented reeding

Date	Mintage	F	VF	XF	Unc	BU
BE2549(2006)	—	—	—	—	2.50	—

Y# 425 10 BAHT
8.4300 g., Bi-Metallic Brass center in Copper-Nickel ring, 25.98 mm. **Ruler:** Bhumipol Adulyadej (Rama IX) **Subject:** Centenary of Royal Mounted Army **Obv:** Conjoined king's busts left **Rev:** Royal crown above emblem **Edge:** Segmented reeding

Date	Mintage	F	VF	XF	Unc	BU
BE2550(2007)	—	—	—	—	2.50	—

Y# 426 10 BAHT
8.4300 g., Bi-Metallic Brass center in Copper-Nickel ring, 25.98 mm. **Ruler:** Bhumipol Adulyadej (Rama IX) **Subject:** Centenary of 1st Thai Commercial Bank **Obv:** Conjoined king's busts left **Rev:** Garuda Bird **Edge:** Segmented reeding

Date	Mintage	F	VF	XF	Unc	BU
BE2550(2007)	—	—	—	—	2.50	—

Y# 374 20 BAHT
15.1000 g., Copper-Nickel, 32 mm. **Ruler:** Bhumipol Adulyadej (Rama IX) **Subject:** Chulalongkorn University 84th Anniversary March 26 **Obv:** Three conjoined busts right **Rev:** University emblem divides value **Edge:** Reeded

Date	Mintage	F	VF	XF	Unc	BU
BE2544(2001)	—	—	—	—	3.50	—
BE2544(2001) Proof	—	Value: 17.50				

Y# 375 20 BAHT
15.1000 g., Copper-Nickel **Ruler:** Bhumipol Adulyadej (Rama IX) **Subject:** Civil Service Comission 72nd Anniversary April 1 **Obv:** Conjoined busts left **Rev:** Civil service emblem divides value **Edge:** Reeded

Date	Mintage	F	VF	XF	Unc	BU
BE2544(2001)	—	—	—	—	3.50	—
BE2544(2001) Proof	—	Value: 17.50				

Y# 393 20 BAHT
5.0000 g., Copper-Nickel, 32 mm. **Ruler:** Bhumipol Adulyadej (Rama IX) **Subject:** 80th Birthday of Princess May 6 (King's sister) **Obv:** Bust 1/4 right **Rev:** Crowned emblem and value **Edge:** Reeded

Date	Mintage	F	VF	XF	Unc	BU
BE2546(2003)	—	—	—	—	3.50	—
BE2546(2003) Proof	—	Value: 17.50				

Y# 419 20 BAHT
Copper-Nickel, 31.9 mm. **Ruler:** Bhumipol Adulyadej (Rama IX) **Subject:** 50th Anniversary of Audit Department of Cooperatives

Date	Mintage	F	VF	XF	Unc	BU
BE2545(2002)	—	—	—	—	3.50	—

Y# 386 20 BAHT
15.0000 g., Copper Nickel, 32 mm. **Ruler:** Bhumipol Adulyadej (Rama IX) **Subject:** Centennial of Thai Banknotes 2445-2545 **Obv:** Conjoined busts left **Rev:** Coat of arms in center of seal **Edge:** Reeded

Date	Mintage	F	VF	XF	Unc	BU
BE2545(2002)	—	—	—	—	3.50	—
BE2545(2002) Proof	—	Value: 17.50				

Y# 388 20 BAHT
15.0000 g., Copper-Nickel, 32 mm. **Ruler:** Bhumipol Adulyadej (Rama IX) **Subject:** King's 75th Birthday December 5 **Obv:** Head left **Rev:** Royal crown in radiant oval **Edge:** Reeded

Date	Mintage	F	VF	XF	Unc	BU
BE2545(2002)	—	—	—	—	3.50	—
BE2545(2002) Proof	—	Value: 17.50				

Y# 397 20 BAHT
15.0000 g., Copper-Nickel, 32 mm. **Ruler:** Bhumipol Adulyadej (Rama IX) **Subject:** Centennial of the National Police April 19 **Obv:** Conjoined busts left **Rev:** National Police emblem above banner **Edge:** Reeded

Date	Mintage	F	VF	XF	Unc	BU
BE2545(2002)	—	—	—	—	3.50	—

Y# 398 20 BAHT
15.0000 g., Copper-Nickel, 32 mm. **Ruler:** Bhumipol Adulyadej (Rama IX) **Subject:** 50th Birthday of the Crown Prince July 28 **Obv:** Bust facing **Rev:** Crowned monogram **Edge:** Reeded

Date	Mintage	F	VF	XF	Unc	BU
BE2545(2002)	—	—	—	—	3.50	—

Y# 420 20 BAHT
Copper-Nickel, 31.9 mm. **Ruler:** Bhumipol Adulyadej (Rama IX) **Subject:** 150th Anniversary Rama V

Date	Mintage	F	VF	XF	Unc	BU
BE2546(2003)	—	—	—	—	3.50	—

Y# 421 20 BAHT
Copper-Nickel, 31.9 mm. **Ruler:** Bhumipol Adulyadej (Rama IX) **Obv:** King Rama IV

Date	Mintage	F	VF	XF	Unc	BU
BE2547(2004)	—	—	—	—	3.50	—

Y# 422 20 BAHT
Copper-Nickel, 31.9 mm. **Ruler:** Bhumipol Adulyadej (Rama IX) **Subject:** 72nd Anniversary of Queen's Birthday

Date	Mintage	F	VF	XF	Unc	BU
BE2547(2004)	—	—	—	—	3.50	—

Y# 423 20 BAHT
Copper-Nickel, 31.9 mm. **Ruler:** Bhumipol Adulyadej (Rama IX) **Subject:** 50th Birthday of Princess Sirinahorn

Date	Mintage	F	VF	XF	Unc	BU
BE0215(2005)	—	—	—	—	3.50	—

Y# 403 20 BAHT
15.0200 g., Copper-Nickel, 32 mm. **Ruler:** Bhumipol Adulyadej (Rama IX) **Obv:** Bust 1/4 left **Rev:** Treasury Department seal **Edge:** Reeded

Date	Mintage	F	VF	XF	Unc	BU
BE2548(2005)	—	—	—	—	4.00	—

Y# 407 20 BAHT
15.0200 g., Copper Nickel, 32 mm. **Ruler:** Bhumipol Adulyadej (Rama IX) **Subject:** 60th Anniversary of Reign **Obv:** Head left **Rev:** Royal Crown on display **Edge:** Reeded

Date	Mintage	F	VF	XF	Unc	BU
BE2549 (2006)	—	—	—	—	—	4.00
BE2549 (2006) Proof	—	Value: 18.50				

Y# 404 50 BAHT
21.0000 g., Copper-Nickel, 36 mm. **Ruler:** Bhumipol Adulyadej (Rama IX) **Subject:** Air Force 50th Anniversary May 7 **Obv:** Uniformed bust facing **Rev:** Crowned wings within 3/4 wreath **Edge:** Reeded

Date	Mintage	F	VF	XF	Unc	BU
2546 (2003)	—	—	—	—	12.50	—

Y# 389 600 BAHT
22.1500 g., 0.9250 Silver 0.6587 oz. ASW, 35 mm. **Ruler:** Bhumipol Adulyadej (Rama IX) **Subject:** King's 75th Birthday **Obv:** King's portrait **Rev:** Royal crown in radiant oval **Edge:** Reeded

Date	Mintage	F	VF	XF	Unc	BU
BE2545(2002)	—	—	—	—	25.00	—
BE2545(2002) Proof	—	Value: 45.00				

Y# 394 600 BAHT
22.1500 g., 0.9250 Silver 0.6587 oz. ASW, 35 mm. **Ruler:** Bhumipol Adulyadej (Rama IX) **Subject:** 80th Birthday of Princess **Obv:** Bust half right **Rev:** Crowned emblem and value **Edge:** Reeded

Date	Mintage	F	VF	XF	Unc	BU
BE2546(2003)	—	—	—	—	35.00	—
BE2546(2003) Proof	—	Value: 75.00				

Y# 401 600 BAHT
22.1500 g., 0.9250 Silver 0.6587 oz. ASW, 35 mm. **Ruler:** Bhumipol Adulyadej (Rama IX) **Subject:** Queen's Birthday **Obv:** Crowned monogram **Rev:** Crowned bust 1/4 left **Edge:** Reeded

Date	Mintage	F	VF	XF	Unc	BU
BE2547(2004) Proof	—	Value: 45.00				

Y# 408 600 BAHT
22.1500 g., 0.9250 Silver 0.6587 oz. ASW, 35 mm. **Ruler:** Bhumipol Adulyadej (Rama IX) **Subject:** 60th Anniversary of Reign **Obv:** Rama IX **Rev:** Royal Crown on display **Edge:** Reeded

Date	Mintage	F	VF	XF	Unc	BU
BE2549 (2006)	—	—	—	—	35.00	—
BE2549 (2006) Proof	—	Value: 75.00				

Y# 390 7500 BAHT
15.0000 g., 0.9000 Gold 0.4340 oz. AGW, 26 mm. **Ruler:** Bhumipol Adulyadej (Rama IX) **Subject:** King's 75th Birthday **Obv:** King's portrait **Rev:** Royal crown in radiant oval **Edge:** Reeded

Date	Mintage	F	VF	XF	Unc	BU
BE2545(2002)	—	—	—	—	450	475
BE2545(2002) Proof	—	Value: 550				

Y# 395 9000 BAHT
15.0000 g., 0.9000 Gold 0.4340 oz. AGW, 26 mm. **Ruler:** Bhumipol Adulyadej (Rama IX) **Subject:** 80th Birthday of Princess **Obv:** Bust half right **Rev:** Crowned emblem and value **Edge:** Reeded

Date	Mintage	F	VF	XF	Unc	BU
BE2546 (2003)	—	—	—	—	450	475
BE2546 (2003) Proof	—	Value: 700				

TOGO

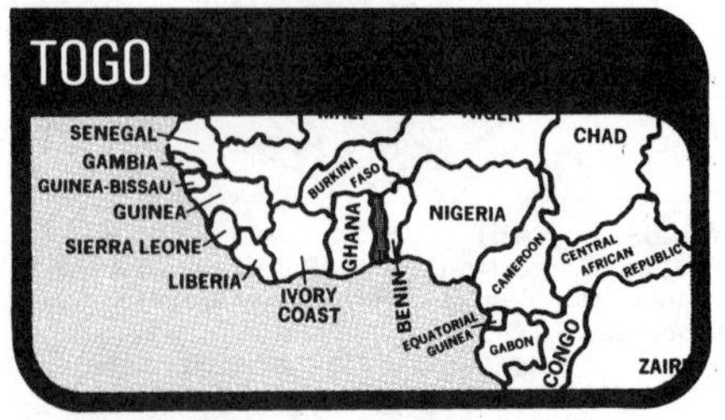

The Republic of Togo (formerly part of German Togoland), situated on the Gulf of Guinea in West Africa between Ghana and Dahomey, has an area of 21,622 sq. mi. (56,790 sq. km.) and a population of *3.4 million. Capital: Lome. Agriculture and herding, the production of dyewoods, and the mining of phosphates and iron ore are the chief industries. Copra, phosphates and coffee are exported.

MINT MARK
(a) - Paris, privy marks only

MONETARY SYSTEM
100 Centimes = 1 Franc

REPUBLIC

STANDARD COINAGE

100 Centimes = 1 Franc

KM# 43 250 FRANCS
5.0000 g., 0.9990 Silver 0.1606 oz. ASW **Subject:** German President Horst Kohler **Obv:** National arms **Obv. Legend:** REPUBLIQUE TOGOLAISE **Rev:** Gilt figure

Date	Mintage	F	VF	XF	Unc	BU
2004 Proof	—	Value: 15.00				

KM# 29 500 FRANCS
7.0500 g., 0.9990 Silver 0.2264 oz. ASW, 30 mm. **Obv:** National arms above value **Rev:** Multicolor tiger **Edge:** Plain

Date	Mintage	F	VF	XF	Unc	BU
2001 Proof	—	Value: 50.00				

KM# 41 500 FRANCS
10.0000 g., 0.9990 Silver 0.3212 oz. ASW **Subject:** XVIII World Football Championship - Germany 2006 **Obv:** National arms **Obv. Legend:** REPUBLIQUE TOGOLAISE **Rev:** Two players, map of Germany in background

Date	Mintage	F	VF	XF	Unc	BU
2001 Proof	—	Value: 22.50				

KM# 44 500 FRANCS
7.0000 g., 0.9990 Silver 0.2248 oz. ASW **Subject:** German Chancellor Helmut Schmidt **Obv:** National arms **Obv. Legend:** REPUBLIQUE TOGOLAISE **Rev:** Gilt figue

Date	Mintage	F	VF	XF	Unc	BU
ND(2004) Proof	—	Value: 22.50				

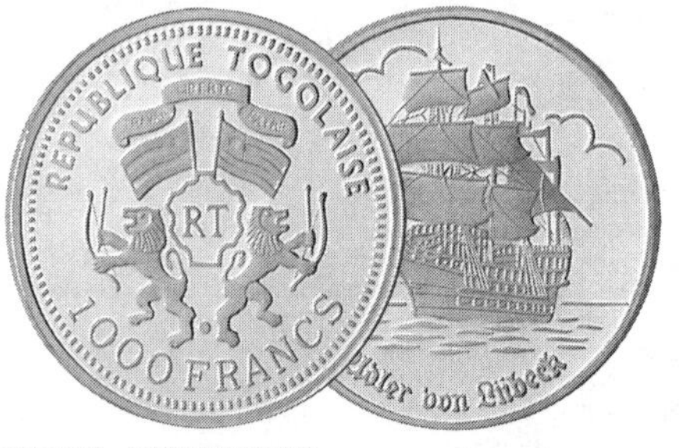

KM# 17 1000 FRANCS
14.9500 g., 0.9990 Silver 0.4802 oz. ASW, 35 mm. **Obv:** National arms **Obv. Legend:** REPUBLIQUE TOGOLAISE **Rev:** German sailing ship **Rev. Legend:** Adler von Lübeck **Edge:** Plain

Date	Mintage	F	VF	XF	Unc	BU
2001 Proof	—	Value: 50.00				

KM# 35 1000 FRANCS
14.7000 g., 0.9990 Silver 0.4721 oz. ASW, 36 mm. **Subject:** World Cup Soccer - Bern 1954 **Obv:** National arms **Rev:** Bust facing and tower **Edge:** Plain

Date	Mintage	F	VF	XF	Unc	BU
2001 Proof	—	Value: 40.00				

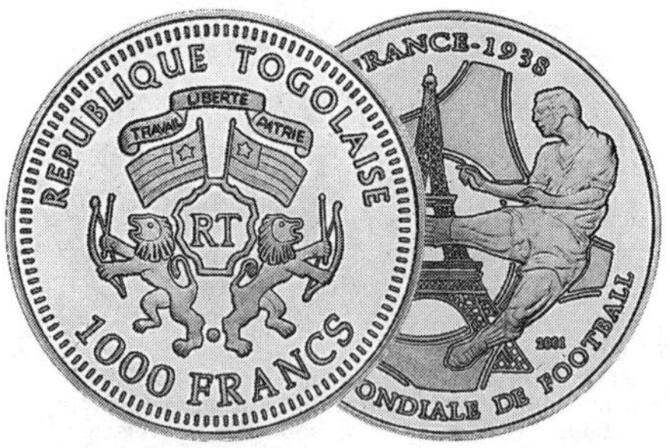

KM# 36 1000 FRANCS
19.9100 g., 0.9990 Silver 0.6395 oz. ASW, 38.1 mm. **Subject:** World Cup Soccer - France 1938 **Obv:** National arms **Rev:** Eiffel Tower behind soccer player kicking ball **Edge:** Reeded

Date	Mintage	F	VF	XF	Unc	BU
2001 Proof	—	Value: 40.00				

KM# 40 1000 FRANCS
14.9700 g., Silver, 35 mm. **Obv:** National arms **Obv. Legend:** REPUBLIQUE TOGOLAISE **Rev:** Imperial German sailing ship **Rev. Legend:** "PREUSSEN" **Edge:** Plain

Date	Mintage	F	VF	XF	Unc	BU
2001 Proof	—	Value: 40.00				

KM# 37 1000 FRANCS
19.9700 g., 0.9990 Silver 0.6414 oz. ASW, 40 mm. **Subject:** World Cup Soccer - USA 1994 **Obv:** National arms **Obv. Legend:** REPUBLIQUE TOGOLAISE **Rev:** Soccer player kicking ball **Rev. Legend:** COUPE MONDIALE DE FOOTBALL **Edge:** Reeded

Date	Mintage	F	VF	XF	Unc	BU
2002 Proof	—	Value: 40.00				

KM# 34 1000 FRANCS
30.9200 g., 0.9990 Silver 0.9931 oz. ASW, 39 mm. **Obv:** Bust with headdress left within circle **Rev:** Gold plated baboon within circle **Edge:** Reeded **Note:** Date in Chinese numerals.

Date	Mintage	F	VF	XF	Unc	BU
2004 Proof	—	Value: 50.00				

KM# 39 1000 FRANCS

62.2400 g., 0.9999 Silver 2.0008 oz. ASW, 50 mm. **Subject:** Year of the Monkey **Obv:** Gold plated world globe **Rev:** Gold plated center with radiant holographic monkey within circle **Edge:** Reeded and lettered sections **Edge Lettering:** PAN ASIA BANK TAIWAN in English and Chinese **Note:** Date in Chinese numerals.

Date	Mintage	F	VF	XF	Unc	BU
2004 Proof	—	Value: 90.00				

KM# 38 1000 FRANCS

30.7300 g., 0.9990 Silver 0.9870 oz. ASW, 39 mm. **Subject:** Year of the Monkey **Obv:** Head with headdress 1/4 right within circle **Rev:** Gold plated monkey within circle **Edge:** Reeded **Note:** Note: Date in Chinese numerals.

Date	Mintage	F	VF	XF	Unc	BU
2004 Proof	—	Value: 50.00				

KM# 24 1000 FRANCS

31.1035 g., 0.9990 Silver 0.9990 oz. ASW, 40 mm. **Obv:** National arms **Obv. Legend:** REPUBLIQUE TOGOLAISE **Rev:** Convex statue of Princess Kyninska of Sparta horseback left **Rev. Legend:** SPORTS - ANTIQUES **Edge:** Plain

Date	Mintage	F	VF	XF	Unc	BU
2004	2,500	—	—	—	—	55.00

KM# 25 1000 FRANCS

31.1035 g., 0.9990 Silver 0.9990 oz. ASW, 40 mm. **Obv:** National arms **Obv. Legend:** REPUBLIQUE TOGOLAISE **Rev:** Concave statue of Princess Kyninska of Sparta horseback right **Rev. Legend:** SPORTS - ANTIQUES **Edge:** Plain

Date	Mintage	F	VF	XF	Unc	BU
2004	2,500	—	—	—	—	55.00

KM# 26 1000 FRANCS

1.2440 g., 0.9999 Gold 0.0400 oz. AGW, 13.92 mm. **Obv:** National arms **Obv. Legend:** REPUBLIQUE TOGOLAISE **Rev:** Convex statue of Nike **Edge:** Plain

Date	Mintage	F	VF	XF	Unc	BU
2004 Proof	5,000	Value: 60.00				

KM# 27 1000 FRANCS

1.2440 g., 0.9999 Gold 0.0400 oz. AGW, 13.92 mm. **Obv:** National arms **Obv. Legend:** REPUBLIQUE TOGOLAISE **Rev:** Concave statue of Nike **Edge:** Plain

Date	Mintage	F	VF	XF	Unc	BU
2004 Proof	5,000	Value: 60.00				

KM# 45 1000 FRANCS

Silver **Subject:** 170th Anniversary German Railroad, Nürnberg - Fürth **Obv:** National arms **Obv. Legend:** REPUBLIQUE TOGOLAISE **Rev:** Early steam locomotive "Adler"

Date	Mintage	F	VF	XF	Unc	BU
2005 Proof	—	Value: 45.00				

KM# 46 1000 FRANCS

1.2400 g., 0.9999 Gold 0.0399 oz. AGW **Subject:** 250th Anniversary Birth of Wolfgang Amadeus Mozart **Obv:** National arms **Obv. Legend:** REPUBLIQUE TOGOLAISE

Date	Mintage	F	VF	XF	Unc	BU
2006 Proof	—	Value: 75.00				

KM# 42 2000 FRANCS

62.2000 g., 0.9990 Silver 1.9977 oz. ASW **Series:** Lunar **Subject:** Year of the Monkey **Obv:** World map **Obv. Legend:** REPUBLIQUE TOGOLAISE **Rev:** Monkey

Date	Mintage	F	VF	XF	Unc	BU
2004 Proof	—	Value: 125				

ESSAIS

KM#	Date	Mintage	Identification	Mkt Val
E17	ND(2003)	2	150000 Cfa Francs-100 Africa. Bi-Metallic. President and map. Elephant head on map.	250

TOKELAU ISLANDS

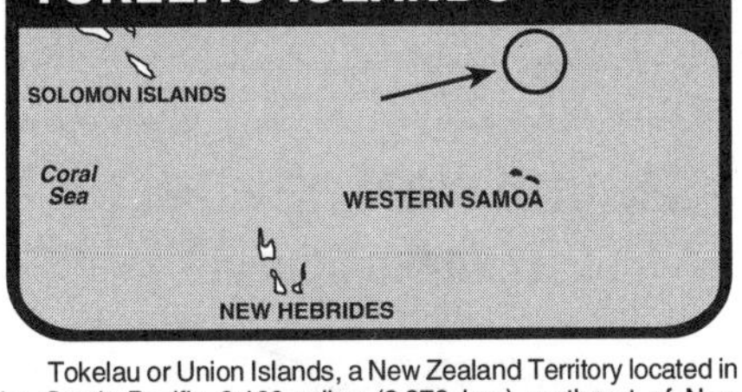

Tokelau or Union Islands, a New Zealand Territory located in the South Pacific 2,100 miles (3,379 km.) northeast of New Zealand and 300 miles (483 km.) north of Samoa, has an area of 4 sq. mi. (10 sq. km.) and a population of *2,000. Geographically, the group consists of four atolls - Atafu, Nukunono, Fakaofo and Swains – but the last belongs to American Samoa (and the United States claims the other three). The people are of Polynesian origin; Samoan is the official language. The New Zealand Minister for Foreign Affairs governs the islands; councils of family elders handle local government at the village level. The chief settlement is Fenuafala, on Fakaofo. It is connected by wireless technology with the offices of the New Zealand Administrative Center, located at Apia, Western Samoa. Subsistence farming and the production of copra for export are the main occupations. Revenue is also derived from the sale of postage stamps and, since 1978, coins.

Tokelau Islands issued its first coin in 1978, a "$1 Tahi Tala," Tokelauan for "One Dollar."

RULER

British

MINT MARK

PM - Pobjoy

NEW ZEALAND TERRITORY

STANDARD COINAGE

KM# 30 5 TALA

31.1000 g., 0.9990 Silver 0.9988 oz. ASW, 40 mm. **Series:** Save the Whales **Obv:** Crowned head right **Obv. Legend:** TOKELAU **Obv. Designer:** Raphael Maklouf **Rev:** Fin Whale on mother of pearl insert **Edge:** Plain

Date	Mintage	F	VF	XF	Unc	BU
2002 Proof	2,000	Value: 55.00				

KM# 32 5 TALA

31.1000 g., 0.9990 Silver 0.9988 oz. ASW, 40 mm. **Ruler:** Elizabeth II **Obv:** Elizabeth II **Rev:** Capt. Smith and ship General Jackson **Edge:** Reeded

Date	Mintage	F	VF	XF	Unc	BU
2003 Proof	—	Value: 35.00				

KM# 33 5 LIMA TALA

28.6500 g., Silver, 38.60 mm. **Ruler:** Elizabeth II **Obv:** Crowned head right **Obv. Legend:** TOKELAU **Rev:** Sailing ship **Rev. Legend:** >> CUTTY SARK << 1869 **Edge:** Reeded

Date	Mintage	F	VF	XF	Unc	BU
2005 Proof	—	Value: 45.00				

TONGA

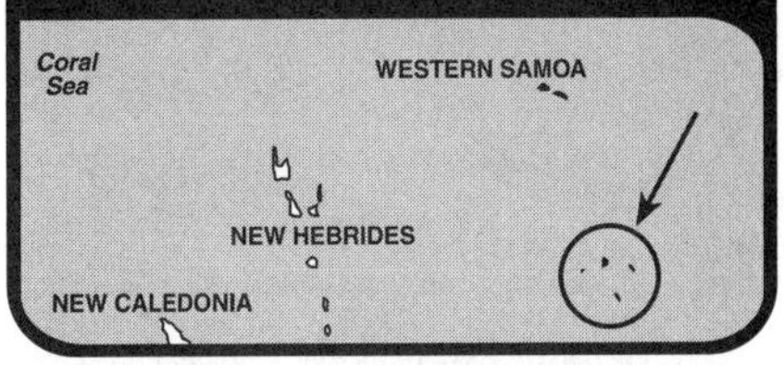

The Kingdom of Tonga (or Friendly Islands) is an archipelago situated in the southern Pacific Ocean south of Western Samoa and east of Fiji comprised of 150 islands. Tonga has an area of 270 sq. mi. (748 sq. km.) and a population of *100,000. Capital: Nuku'alofa. Primarily agricultural, the kingdom exports bananas and copra.

The monarchy is a member of the Commonwealth of Nations. King Siosa Tupou V is Head of State and Government.

RULER

King Taufa'ahau IV, 1965-2006

King Siosa Tupou V, 2006-

KINGDOM

DECIMAL COINAGE

100 Senti = 1 Pa'anga; 100 Pa'anga = 1 Hau

KM# 66a SENITI

Copper Plated Steel, 17.5 mm. **Ruler:** King Taufa'ahau Tupou IV **Series:** World Food Day **Obv:** Ear of corn **Obv. Legend:** TONGA **Rev:** Vanilla plant **Rev. Legend:** FAKALAHI ME'AKAI **Edge:** Plain

Date	Mintage	F	VF	XF	Unc	BU
2002	—	—	—	0.10	0.35	0.75
2003	—	—	—	0.10	0.35	0.75
2004	—	—	—	0.10	0.35	0.75

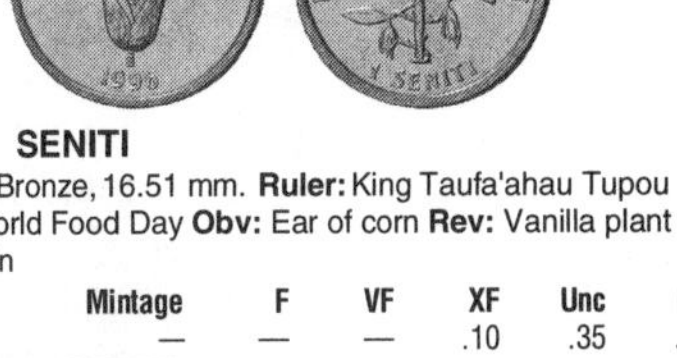

KM# 66 SENITI

1.8000 g., Bronze, 16.51 mm. **Ruler:** King Taufa'ahau Tupou IV **Series:** World Food Day **Obv:** Ear of corn **Rev:** Vanilla plant **Edge:** Plain

Date	Mintage	F	VF	XF	Unc	BU
2005	—	—	—	.10	.35	.75

KM# 67a 2 SENITI

Copper Plated Steel, 21 mm. **Ruler:** King Taufa'ahau Tupou IV **Series:** World Food Day **Obv:** Taro plants **Obv. Legend:** TONGA **Rev:** Paper doll cutouts form design in center circle of sprays **Rev. Legend:** PLANNED FAMILIES • FOOD FOR ALL

Date	Mintage	F	VF	XF	Unc	BU
2002	—	—	—	0.15	0.65	1.25
2003	—	—	—	0.15	0.65	1.25
2004	—	—	—	0.15	0.65	1.25

KM# 68a 5 SENITI
2.7900 g., Nickel Plated Steel, 19.39 mm. **Ruler:** King Taufa'ahau Tupou IV **Series:** World Food Day **Obv:** Hen with chicks **Obv. Legend:** TONGA **Rev:** Coconuts **Rev. Legend:** FAKALAHI ME'AKAI **Edge:** Reeded

Date	Mintage	F	VF	XF	Unc	BU
2002	—	—	—	0.25	0.75	1.35
2003	—	—	—	0.25	0.75	1.35
2004	—	—	—	0.25	0.75	1.35
2005	—	—	—	0.25	0.75	1.35

KM# 68 5 SENITI
2.8000 g., Copper-Nickel, 19.5 mm. **Ruler:** King Taufa'ahau Tupou IV **Series:** World Food Day **Obv:** Hen with chicks **Rev:** Coconuts above sprig **Edge:** Reeded

Date	Mintage	F	VF	XF	Unc	BU
2005	—	—	.10	.25	.75	1.25

KM# 69a 10 SENITI
Nickel Plated Steel, 23.5 mm. **Ruler:** King Taufa'ahau Tupou IV **Series:** World Food Day **Obv:** Uniformed bust facing **Obv. Legend:** F•A•O - TONGA **Rev:** Banana tree **Rev. Legend:** FAKALAHI ME'AKAI

Date	Mintage	F	VF	XF	Unc	BU
2002	—	—	—	0.30	1.00	1.75
2003	—	—	—	0.30	1.00	1.75
2004	—	—	—	0.30	1.00	1.75

KM# 70 20 SENITI
11.3000 g., Copper-Nickel, 28.5 mm. **Ruler:** King Taufa'ahau Tupou IV **Series:** World Food Day **Obv:** Uniformed bust facing **Obv. Legend:** TONGA **Rev:** Yams **Rev. Legend:** FAKALAHI ME'AKAI **Edge:** Reeded

Date	Mintage	F	VF	XF	Unc	BU
2003	—	—	0.25	0.50	1.25	2.00
2004	—	—	0.25	0.50	1.25	2.00

KM# 71 50 SENITI
14.6000 g., Copper-Nickel, 32.5 mm. **Ruler:** King Taufa'ahau Tupou IV **Series:** World Food Day **Obv:** Uniformed bust facing **Obv. Legend:** TONGA **Rev:** Tomatoe plants **Rev. Legend:** FAKALAHI ME'AKAI **Edge:** Plain **Shape:** 12-sided

Date	Mintage	F	VF	XF	Unc	BU
2002	—	—	0.45	0.75	1.50	2.50
2003	—	—	0.45	0.75	1.50	2.50
2004	—	—	0.45	0.75	1.50	2.50

KM# 178 PA'ANGA
31.1000 g., 0.9990 Silver 0.9988 oz. ASW, 40 mm. **Ruler:** King Taufa'ahau Tupou IV **Series:** Save the Whales **Obv:** Crown within wreath above national arms within circle **Obv. Legend:** KINGDOM OF TONGA **Rev:** Right Whale on mother of pearl insert **Edge:** Plain

Date	Mintage	F	VF	XF	Unc	BU
2002 Proof	2,000	Value: 60.00				

KM# 179 2 PA'ANGA
Silver **Ruler:** King Taufa'ahau Tupou IV **Subject:** King's 85th Birthday **Obv:** National arms

Date	Mintage	F	VF	XF	Unc	BU
2003 Proof	—	Value: 100				

TRANSNISTRIA

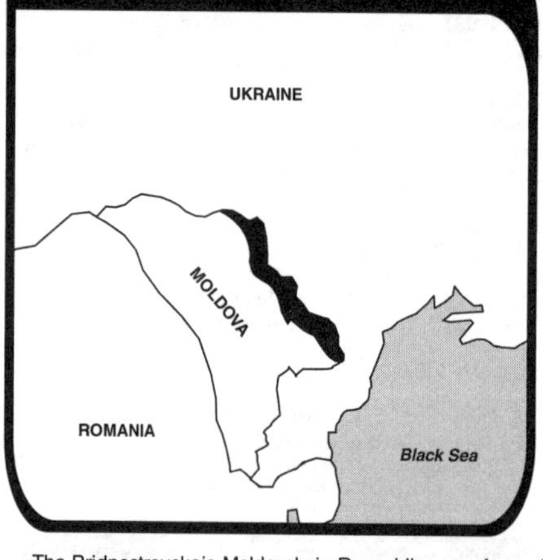

The Pridnestrovskaia Moldavskaia Respublica was formed in 1990, even before the separation of Moldavia from Russia. It has an area of 11,544 sq. mi. (29,900 sq. km.) and a population of 555,000. Capital: Tiraspol.

Transnistria (or Transdniestra) has a president, parliament, army and police forces, but as yet it is lacking international recognition.

MOLDAVIAN REPUBLIC

STANDARD COINAGE

1 Rublei = 100 Kopeek

KM# 2 5 KOPEEK
0.7000 g., Aluminum, 17.9 mm. **Obv:** State arms **Obv. Legend:** ПРИДНЕСТРОВСКАЯ МОЛДАВСКАЯ РЕСПУБЛИКА **Rev:** Value flanked by wheat stalks **Edge:** Plain

Date	Mintage	F	VF	XF	Unc	BU
	—	—	—	—	0.50	0.65

KM# 3 10 KOPEEK
1.0000 g., Aluminum, 20 mm. **Obv:** State arms **Obv. Legend:** ПРИДНЕСТРОВСКАЯ МОЛДАВСКАЯ РЕСПУБЛИКА **Rev:** Value flanked by wheat stalks **Edge:** Plain

Date	Mintage	F	VF	XF	Unc	BU
2005	—	—	—	—	0.75	0.90

KM# 5 25 KOPEEK
2.1500 g., Brass, 17 mm. **Obv:** National arms **Rev:** Value flanked by wheat stalks **Edge:** Plain

Date	Mintage	F	VF	XF	Unc	BU
2002	—	—	—	—	1.00	1.20
2005	—	—	—	—	1.00	1.20

KM# 4 50 KOPEEK
2.7500 g., Brass, 19 mm. **Obv:** State arms **Obv. Legend:** ПРИДНЕСТРОВСКАЯ МОЛДАВСКАЯ РЕСПУБЛИКА **Rev:** Value within wreath **Edge:** Plain

Date	Mintage	F	VF	XF	Unc	BU
2005	—	—	—	—	1.25	1.50

KM# 7 100 RUBLEI
14.1600 g., 0.9250 Silver-Billon 0.4211 oz., 32 mm. **Subject:** City of Tiraspol **Obv:** National arms **Rev:** Statue and buildings **Edge:** Plain

Date	Mintage	F	VF	XF	Unc	BU
2002 Proof	—	Value: 50.00				

KM# 8 100 RUBLEI
14.1600 g., 0.9250 Silver 0.4211 oz. ASW, 32 mm. **Subject:** City of Tiraspol **Obv:** National arms **Rev:** Cameo above fortress **Edge:** Plain

Date	Mintage	F	VF	XF	Unc	BU
2002 Proof	—	Value: 50.00				

KM# 9 100 RUBLEI
14.1600 g., 0.9250 Silver 0.4211 oz. ASW, 32 mm. **Subject:** K. K. Gedroets **Obv:** National arms **Rev:** Bust facing flanked by sprigs, beaker and book **Edge:** Plain

Date	Mintage	F	VF	XF	Unc	BU
2002 Proof	500	Value: 50.00				

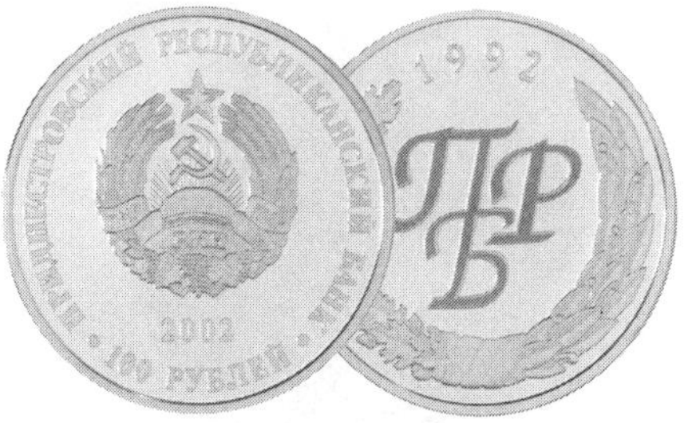

KM# 10 100 RUBLEI
14.0400 g., 0.9250 Silver 0.4175 oz. ASW, 32 mm. **Subject:** 10th Anniversary - Trans-Dniester Republican Bank **Obv:** National arms **Rev:** Colorized monogram within 3/4 wreath with "1992" at top **Edge:** Plain

Date	Mintage	F	VF	XF	Unc	BU
2002 Proof	500	Value: 50.00				

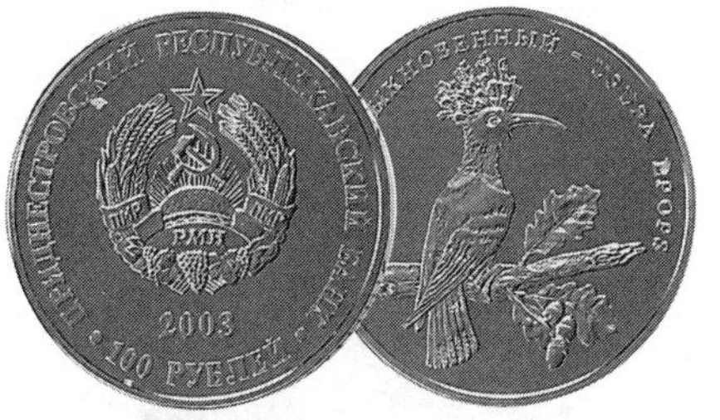

KM# 11 100 RUBLEI
14.1400 g., 0.9250 Silver 0.4205 oz. ASW, 32 mm. **Obv:** National arms **Rev:** Hoopoe (Upupa Epops) bird on branch **Edge:** Plain

Date	Mintage	F	VF	XF	Unc	BU
2003 Proof	500	Value: 50.00				

KM# 12 100 RUBLEI
14.1400 g., 0.9250 Silver 0.4205 oz. ASW, 32 mm. **Obv:** National arms **Rev:** Shield flanked by sprigs **Edge:** Plain

Date	Mintage	F	VF	XF	Unc	BU
2003 Proof	500	Value: 50.00				

KM# 13 100 RUBLEI
14.1400 g., 0.9250 Silver 0.4205 oz. ASW, 32 mm. **Subject:** 80th Anniversary of Nationhood **Obv:** National arms **Rev:** Map and multicolor flag **Edge:** Plain

Date	Mintage	F	VF	XF	Unc	BU
2004 Proof	500	Value: 50.00				

KM# 14 100 RUBLEI
14.1400 g., 0.9250 Silver 0.4205 oz. ASW, 32 mm. **Obv:** National arms **Rev:** Doe and fawn flanked by trees **Edge:** Plain

Date	Mintage	F	VF	XF	Unc	BU
2004 Proof	1,000	Value: 45.00				

KM# 15 100 RUBLEI
14.1400 g., 0.9250 Silver 0.4205 oz. ASW, 32 mm. **Obv:** National arms **Rev:** Eurasian Griffon bird on rock **Edge:** Plain

Date	Mintage	F	VF	XF	Unc	BU
2005 Proof	1,000	Value: 45.00				

TRINIDAD & TOBAGO

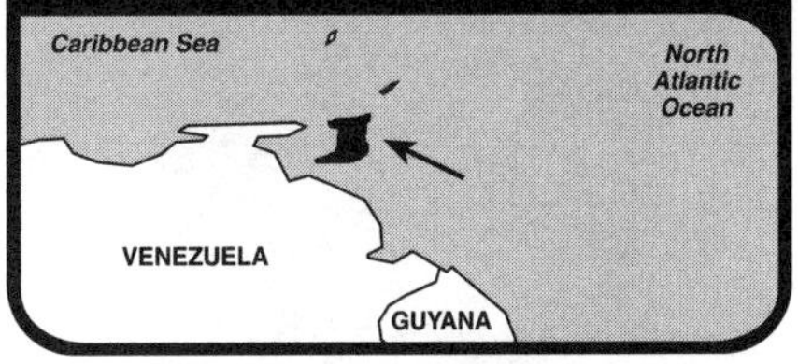

The Republic of Trinidad and Tobago is situated 7 miles (11 km.) off the coast of Venezuela, has an area of 1,981 sq. mi. (5,130 sq. km.) and a population of *1.2 million. Capital: Port-of-Spain. The island of Trinidad contains the world's largest natural asphalt bog. Birds of Paradise live on little Tobago, the only place outside of their native New Guinea where they can be found in a wild state. Petroleum and petroleum products are the mainstay of the economy. Petroleum products, crude oil and sugar are exported.

Trinidad and Tobago is a member of the Commonwealth of Nations. The President is Chief of State. The Prime Minister is Head of Government.

MONETARY SYSTEM
100 Cents = 1 Dollar

REPUBLIC

STANDARD COINAGE

KM# 29 CENT
1.9500 g., Bronze, 17.76 mm. **Obv:** National arms **Rev:** Hummingbird and value **Edge:** Plain

Date	Mintage	F	VF	XF	Unc	BU
2001	—	—	—	0.20	0.35	1.00
2002	—	—	—	0.20	0.35	1.00
2005	—	—	—	0.20	0.35	1.00

KM# 30 5 CENTS
3.3100 g., Bronze, 21.2 mm. **Obv:** National arms **Rev:** Bird of paradise and value **Edge:** Plain

Date	Mintage	F	VF	XF	Unc	BU
2001	—	—	—	0.10	0.25	1.00
2002	—	—	—	0.10	0.25	1.00
2003	—	—	—	0.10	0.25	1.00
2005	—	—	—	0.10	0.25	1.00

KM# 31 10 CENTS
1.4000 g., Copper-Nickel, 16.2 mm. **Obv:** National arms **Rev:** Hibiscus and value **Edge:** Reeded

Date	Mintage	F	VF	XF	Unc	BU
2001	—	—	—	0.20	0.50	1.00
2002	—	—	—	0.20	0.50	1.00
2003	—	—	—	0.20	0.50	1.00
2004	—	—	—	0.20	0.50	1.00
2005	—	—	—	0.20	0.50	1.00
2006	—	—	—	0.20	0.50	1.00

KM# 32 25 CENTS
3.5700 g., Copper-Nickel, 20 mm. **Obv:** National arms **Rev:** Chaconia and value **Edge:** Reeded

Date	Mintage	F	VF	XF	Unc	BU
2001	—	—	—	0.15	0.40	0.80
2002	—	—	—	0.15	0.40	0.80
2003	—	—	—	0.15	0.40	0.80
2004	—	—	—	0.15	0.40	0.80
2005	—	—	—	0.15	0.40	0.80
2006	—	—	—	0.15	0.40	0.80
2007	—	—	—	0.15	0.40	0.80

TRISTAN DA CUNHA

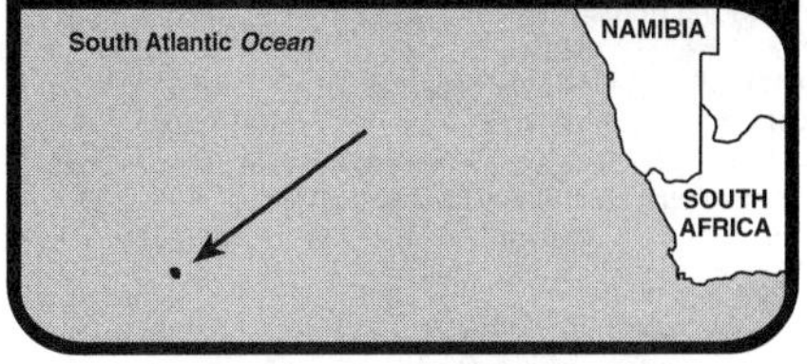

Tristan da Cunha is the principal island and group name of a small cluster of volcanic islands located in the South Atlantic midway between the Cape of Good Hope and South America, and 1,500 miles (2,414 km.) south-southwest of the British colony of St. Helena. The other islands are inaccessible, Gough, and the three Nightingale Islands. The group, which comprises a dependency of St. Helena, has a total area of 40 sq. mi. (104 sq. km.) and a population of less than 300. There is a village of 60 houses called Edinburgh. Potatoes are the staple subsistence crop.

MONETARY SYSTEM
Sterling until 1961
25 Pence = 1 Crown
100 Pence = 1 Pound

ST. HELENA DEPENDENCY

STANDARD COINAGE

KM# 13a 50 PENCE
28.2800 g., 0.9250 Silver 0.8410 oz. ASW, 38.6 mm. **Subject:** Centennial of Queen Victoria's Death **Obv:** Crowned bust right **Rev:** Crown and veil on half length female facing left within oval circle **Edge:** Reeded

Date	Mintage	F	VF	XF	Unc	BU
2001 Proof	10,000	Value: 50.00				

KM# 13b 50 PENCE
47.5400 g., 0.9166 Gold 1.4009 oz. AGW, 38.6 mm. **Subject:** Centennial of Queen Victoria's Death **Obv:** Crowned bust right **Rev:** Crown and veil on half length female facing left within oval circle **Edge:** Reeded

Date	Mintage	F	VF	XF	Unc	BU
2001 Proof	100	Value: 1,400				

KM# 12 50 PENCE
29.1000 g., Copper-Nickel, 38.6 mm. **Subject:** Queen Elizabeth's 75th Birthday **Obv:** Crowned bust right **Obv. Designer:** Raphael Maklouf **Rev:** Crowned bust facing **Edge:** Reeded

Date	Mintage	F	VF	XF	Unc	BU
2001	—	—	—	—	7.00	8.00

KM# 12a 50 PENCE
28.2800 g., 0.9250 Silver 0.8410 oz. ASW, 38.6 mm. **Subject:** Queen's 75th Birthday **Obv:** Crowned bust right **Rev:** Crowned bust facing **Edge:** Reeded

Date	Mintage	F	VF	XF	Unc	BU
2001 Proof	10,000	Value: 40.00				

KM# 12b 50 PENCE
47.5400 g., 0.9166 Gold 1.4009 oz. AGW, 38.6 mm. **Obv:** Crowned bust right **Rev:** Crowned bust facing

Date	Mintage	F	VF	XF	Unc	BU
2001 Proof	75	Value: 1,450				

KM# 13 50 PENCE
29.6000 g., Copper-Nickel, 38.7 mm. **Subject:** Centennial of Queen Victoria's Death **Obv:** Crowned bust right **Obv. Designer:** Raphael Maklouf **Rev:** Crown and veil on half length female facing left within oval circle **Edge:** Reeded

Date	Mintage	F	VF	XF	Unc	BU
2001	—	—	—	—	8.00	10.00

KM# 14 CROWN
24.1200 g., 0.9250 Silver 0.7173 oz. ASW, 38.5 mm. **Obv:** Crowned bust right **Rev:** Pope John Paul II **Edge:** Reeded

Date	Mintage	F	VF	XF	Unc	BU
2005	—	—	—	—	25.00	27.50
2005 Proof	—	Value: 30.00				

KM# 15 CROWN
25.0000 g., Copper-Nickel, 38.83 mm. **Ruler:** Elizabeth II **Series:** Privateering ships of the South Atlantic **Obv:** Crowned bust right **Obv. Legend:** ELIZABETH II — TRISTAN DA CUNHA **Rev:** Sailing ship "Tybalt" **Edge:** Reeded

Date	Mintage	F	VF	XF	Unc	BU
2006	—	—	—	—	8.00	—

KM# 16 CROWN
25.0000 g., Copper-Nickel, 38.83 mm. **Ruler:** Elizabeth II **Series:** Privateering ships of the South Atlantic **Obv:** Crowned bust right **Obv. Legend:** ELIZABETH II — TRISTAN DA CUNHA **Rev:** Sailing ship "Syren" **Edge:** Reeded

Date	Mintage	F	VF	XF	Unc	BU
2006	—	—	—	—	8.00	—

KM# 17 CROWN
25.0000 g., Copper-Nickel, 38.83 mm. **Ruler:** Elizabeth II **Series:** Privateering ships of the South Atlantic **Obv:** Crowned bust right **Obv. Legend:** ELIZABETH II — TRISTAN DA CUNHA **Rev:** Sailing ship "Pride of Baltimore" **Edge:** Reeded

Date	Mintage	F	VF	XF	Unc	BU
2006	—	—	—	—	8.00	—

KM# 18 CROWN
25.0000 g., Copper-Nickel, 38.83 mm. **Ruler:** Elizabeth II **Series:** Privateering ships of the South Atlantic **Obv:** Crowned bust right **Obv. Legend:** ELIZABETH II — TRISTAN DA CUNHA **Rev:** Sailing ship "Hornet" **Edge:** Reeded

Date	Mintage	F	VF	XF	Unc	BU
2006	—	—	—	—	8.00	—

KM# 19 CROWN
25.0000 g., Copper-Nickel, 38.83 mm. **Ruler:** Elizabeth II **Series:** Privateering ships of the South Atlantic **Obv:** Crowned bust right **Obv. Legend:** ELIZABETH II — TRISTAN DA CUNHA **Rev:** Sailing ship "Griffen" **Edge:** Reeded

Date	Mintage	F	VF	XF	Unc	BU
2006	—	—	—	—	8.00	—

KM# 20 CROWN
25.0000 g., Copper-Nickel, 38.83 mm. **Ruler:** Elizabeth II **Series:** Privateering ships of the South Atlantic **Obv:** Crowned bust right **Obv. Legend:** ELIZABETH II — TRISTAN DA CUNHA **Rev:** Sailing ship "Enterprise" **Edge:** Reeded

Date	Mintage	F	VF	XF	Unc	BU
2006	—	—	—	—	6.00	—

KM# 21 CROWN
25.0000 g., Copper-Nickel, 38.83 mm. **Ruler:** Elizabeth II **Series:** Privateering ships of the South Atlantic **Obv:** Crowned bust right **Obv. Legend:** ELIZABETH II — TRISTAN DA CUNHA **Rev:** Sailing ship "Columbus" **Edge:** Reeded

Date	Mintage	F	VF	XF	Unc	BU
2006	—	—	—	—	8.00	—

KM# 22 CROWN
25.0000 g., Copper-Nickel, 38.83 mm. **Ruler:** Elizabeth II **Series:** Privateering ships of the South Atlantic **Obv:** Crowned bust right **Obv. Legend:** ELIZABETH II — TRISTAN DA CUNHA **Rev:** Sailing ship "Chausseur" **Edge:** Reeded

Date	Mintage	F	VF	XF	Unc	BU
2006	—	—	—	—	8.00	—

KM# 23 CROWN
25.0000 g., Copper-Nickel, 38.83 mm. **Ruler:** Elizabeth II **Series:** Privateering ships of the South Atlantic **Obv:** Crowned bust right **Obv. Legend:** ELIZABETH II — TRISTAN DA CUNHA **Rev:** Sailing ship "Cabot" **Edge:** Reeded

Date	Mintage	F	VF	XF	Unc	BU
2006	—	—	—	—	8.00	—

KM# 24 CROWN
25.0000 g., Copper-Nickel, 38.83 mm. **Ruler:** Elizabeth II **Series:** Privateering ships of the South Atlantic **Obv:** Crowned bust right **Obv. Legend:** ELIZABETH II — TRISTAN DA CUNHA **Rev:** Sailing ship "Black Prince" **Edge:** Reeded

Date	Mintage	F	VF	XF	Unc	BU
2006	—	—	—	—	8.00	—

KM# 25 CROWN
25.0000 g., Copper-Nickel, 38.83 mm. **Ruler:** Elizabeth II **Series:** Privateering ships of the South Atlantic **Obv:** Crowned bust right **Obv. Legend:** ELIZABETH II — TRISTAN DA CUNHA **Rev:** Sailing ship "Argus" **Edge:** Reeded

Date	Mintage	F	VF	XF	Unc	BU
2006	—	—	—	—	8.00	—

KM# 26 CROWN
25.0000 g., Copper-Nickel, 38.83 mm. **Ruler:** Elizabeth II **Series:** Privateering ships of the South Atlantic **Obv:** Crowned bust right **Obv. Legend:** ELIZABETH II — TRISTAN DA CUNHA **Rev:** Sailing ship "True Blooded Yankee" **Edge:** Reeded

Date	Mintage	F	VF	XF	Unc	BU
2006	—	—	—	—	8.00	—

PIEFORTS

KM#	Date	Mintage	Identification	Mkt Val
P1	2001	500	50 Pence. 0.9250 Silver. 56.5400 g. 38.6 mm.	100
P2	2001	500	50 Pence. 0.9250 Silver. 56.5600 g. 38.6 mm. Reeded edge. Proof KM-13a.	100

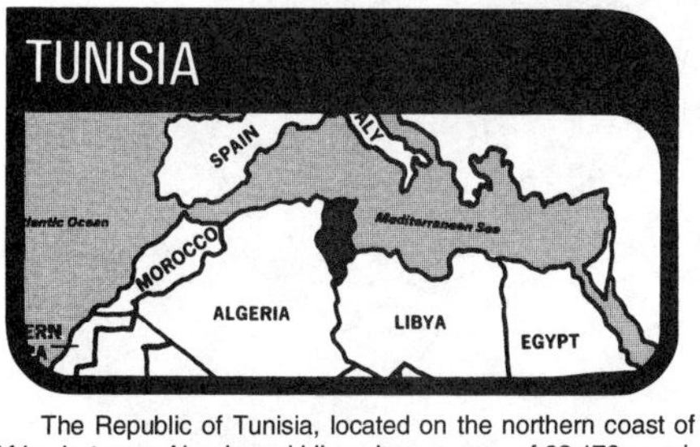

The Republic of Tunisia, located on the northern coast of Africa between Algeria and Libya, has an area of 63,170sq. mi. (163,610 sq. km.) and a population of *7.9 million. Capital: Tunis. Agriculture is the backbone of the economy. Crude oil, phosphates, olive oil, and wine are exported.

TITLES

المملكة التونسية

al-Mamlaka al-Tunisiya

الجمهورية التونسية

al-Jumhuriya al-Tunisiya

al-Amala al-Tunisiya
(Tunisian Protectorate)

REPUBLIC

DECIMAL COINAGE

1000 Millim = 1 Dinar

KM# 348 5 MILLIM
1.4900 g., Aluminum, 24 mm. **Obv:** Oak tree and dates **Rev:** Value within sprigs

Date	Mintage	F	VF	XF	Unc	BU
AH1426-2005	—	—	—	—	0.50	—

KM# 306 10 MILLIM
3.5000 g., Brass, 19 mm. **Obv:** Inscription and dates within inner circle of design **Rev:** Value in center of design **Edge:** Reeded

Date	Mintage	F	VF	XF	Unc	BU
AH1426-2005	—	—	0.15	0.25	0.50	—

KM# 307 20 MILLIM
4.5000 g., Brass, 22 mm. **Obv:** Inscription and dates within center circle of design **Rev:** Value within center of design

Date	Mintage	F	VF	XF	Unc	BU
AH1426-2005	—	—	0.30	0.50	0.80	—
AH1428-2007	—	—	0.30	0.50	0.80	—

KM# 308 50 MILLIM
6.0000 g., Brass, 25 mm. **Obv:** Inscription and dates within center circle of design **Rev:** Value in center of design

Date	Mintage	F	VF	XF	Unc	BU
AH1428-2007	—	—	0.65	0.85	1.25	—

KM# 309 100 MILLIM
7.5000 g., Brass, 27 mm. **Obv:** Inscription and dates within center circle of design **Rev:** Value in center of design

Date	Mintage	F	VF	XF	Unc	BU
AH1426-2005	—	—	1.25	1.50	2.00	—

KM# 346 1/2 DINAR
Copper-Nickel **Obv:** Shield within circle **Rev:** 2 Hands with fruit and wheat sprig **Note:** Rim varieties exist.

Date	Mintage	F	VF	XF	Unc	BU
AH1426-2005	—	—	1.00	2.50	4.50	—
AH1428-2007	—	—	1.00	2.50	4.50	—

KM# 347 DINAR
Copper-Nickel **Series:** F.A.O. **Obv:** Shield within circle **Rev:** Female half figure right

Date	Mintage	F	VF	XF	Unc	BU
AH1428-2007	—	—	2.00	4.00	7.50	—

KM# 350 5 DINARS
10.0000 g., Bi-Metallic Copper-Nickel center in Brass ring, 29 mm. **Obv:** National arms **Rev:** Former president Habib Bourguiba **Edge:** Six reeded and six plain sections **Shape:** 12-sided

Date	Mintage	F	VF	XF	Unc	BU
AH1423-2002	—	—	—	—	6.50	8.00

KM# 352 100 DINARS
38.0000 g., 0.9000 Gold 1.0995 oz. AGW, 40 mm. **Subject:** United Nations **Obv:** National arms above value **Rev:** UN logo on stylized hand **Edge:** Reeded

Date	Mintage	F	VF	XF	Unc	BU
AH1424-2003 Proof	—	Value: 1,150				

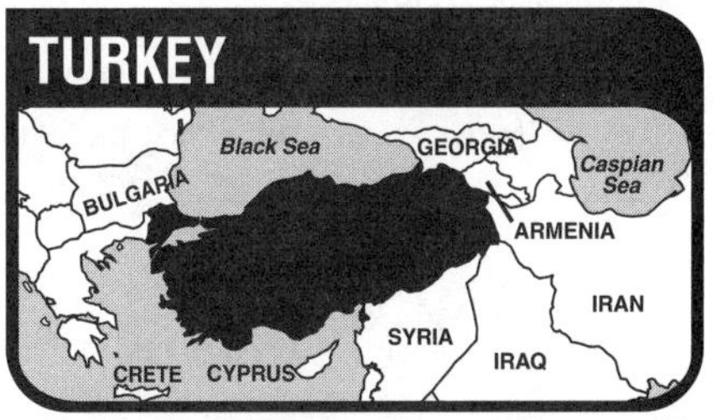

The Republic of Turkey, a parliamentary democracy of the Near East located partially in Europe and partially in Asia between the Black and the Mediterranean Seas, has an area of 301,382 sq. mi. (780,580 sq. km.) and a population of *55.4 million. Capital: Ankara. Turkey exports cotton, hazelnuts, and tobacco, and enjoys a virtual monopoly in meerschaum.

RULER
Republic, AH1341/AD1923-

Mint mark
"d" for darphane (meaning mint) is used on coins for overseas market.

REPUBLIC

DECIMAL COINAGE

Western numerals and Latin alphabet

40 Para = 1 Kurus; 100 Kurus = 1 Lira

Mintage figures of the 1930s and early 1940s may not be exact. It is suspected that in some cases, figures for a particular year may include quantities struck with the previous year's date.

KM# 1104 25000 LIRA (25 Bin Lira)
2.7000 g., Copper-Zinc, 17 mm. **Obv:** Head left **Rev:** Value **Edge:** Plain

Date	Mintage	F	VF	XF	Unc	BU
2001	—	—	—	—	2.00	—
2002	—	—	—	—	2.00	—
2003	—	—	—	—	2.00	—

KM# 1105 50000 LIRA (50 Bin Lira)
3.2000 g., Copper-Nickel-Zinc, 17.75 mm. **Obv:** Head left within circle **Rev:** Value **Edge:** Plain

Date	Mintage	F	VF	XF	Unc	BU
2001	—	—	—	—	0.50	—
2002	—	—	—	—	0.50	—
2003	—	—	—	—	0.50	—
2004	—	—	—	—	0.50	—

KM# 1106 100000 LIRA (100 Bin Lira)
4.6000 g., Copper-Nickel-Zinc, 21 mm. **Obv:** Head with hat right within circle **Rev:** Value **Edge:** Plain

Date	Mintage	F	VF	XF	Unc	BU
2001	—	—	—	—	0.75	—
2002	—	—	—	—	0.75	—
2003	—	—	—	—	0.75	—
2004	—	—	—	—	0.75	—

KM# 1137 250000 LIRA
6.4200 g., Copper-Nickel-Zinc, 23.4 mm. **Obv:** Bust facing within circle **Rev:** Value **Edge Lettering:** "T.C." six times dividing reeded sections

Date	Mintage	F	VF	XF	Unc	BU
2002	—	—	—	—	1.00	—
2003	—	—	—	—	1.00	—
2004	—	—	—	—	1.00	—

KM# 1161 500000 LIRA
4.6000 g., Copper-Nickel, 21 mm. **Obv:** Value and date within sprigs **Rev:** One sheep **Edge:** Plain

Date	Mintage	F	VF	XF	Unc	BU
2002	—	—	—	—	2.50	—

KM# 1162 750000 LIRA
6.4000 g., Copper-Nickel, 23.5 mm. **Obv:** Value and date within sprigs **Rev:** Angora Ram **Edge:** Plain

Date	Mintage	F	VF	XF	Unc	BU
2002	—	—	—	—	3.50	—

KM# 1163 1000000 LIRA
12.0000 g., Copper-Nickel, 31.9 mm. **Obv:** Value and date within sprigs **Rev:** Turbaned bust 1/4 left divides dates **Edge:** Reeded

Date	Mintage	F	VF	XF	Unc	BU
2002	—	—	—	—	5.00	—

KM# 1170 1000000 LIRA
31.4200 g., 0.9250 Silver 0.9344 oz. ASW, 38.6 mm. **Subject:** Mevlana Celaleddin-I Rumi **Obv:** Value and date in wreath **Rev:** Turbaned bust **Edge:** Reeded

Date	Mintage	F	VF	XF	Unc	BU
2002 Proof	—	Value: 30.00				

KM# 1139 1000000 LIRA
11.8700 g., Bi-Metallic Brass center in Copper-Nickel ring, 32.1 mm. **Subject:** Foundation of the Mint **Obv:** Building and value within circle **Rev:** Legend and date inscription **Edge:** Plain **Note:** This coin type is produced by a machine outside the money museum at the Istanbul Mint. Visitors pay 1 mio lira, press a button and strike a coin with the actual date of their visit. Many other dates exist in unknown and unregistered quantities.

Date	Mintage	F	VF	XF	Unc	BU
06 Mayis 2002	—	—	—	—	5.00	—
10 Mayis 2002	—	—	—	—	5.00	—
28 Kasim 2002	—	—	—	—	5.00	—
9 Kasim 2002	—	—	—	—	5.00	—
19 Kasim 2002	—	—	—	—	5.00	—
2 December 2003	—	—	—	—	5.00	—
4 December 2003	—	—	—	—	5.00	—
5 December 2003	—	—	—	—	5.00	—
7 December 2003	—	—	—	—	5.00	—
13 Jan 2003	—	—	—	—	5.00	—
17 Jan 2003	—	—	—	—	5.00	—
18 Jan 2003	—	—	—	—	5.00	—

KM# 1107 3000000 LIRA
31.4700 g., 0.9250 Silver 0.9359 oz. ASW, 38.6 mm. **Series:** Olympics **Obv:** Value and date within wreath **Rev:** Long jumper and logo **Edge:** Reeded

Date	Mintage	F	VF	XF	Unc	BU
2002 Proof	—	Value: 32.50				

KM# 1110 5000000 LIRA
67.0000 g., Bronze, 50 mm. **Subject:** Children's Day **Obv:** Legend and inscription **Rev:** Dancing children **Edge:** Plain

Date	Mintage	F	VF	XF	Unc	BU
2001 Matte	1,583	—	—	—	25.00	—

KM# 1142 7500000 LIRA
31.2500 g., 0.9250 Silver 0.9293 oz. ASW, 38.5 mm. **Subject:** Cahit Arf, Turkish mathematician (1910-1997) **Obv:** Mathematical formula within circle **Rev:** 1/2-length figure facing **Edge:** Reeded

Date	Mintage	F	VF	XF	Unc	BU
2001 Proof	—	Value: 30.00				

KM# 1143 7500000 LIRA
31.2500 g., 0.9250 Silver 0.9293 oz. ASW, 38.5 mm. **Obv:** Ornamented circle design **Rev:** 1/2-length bust facing **Edge:** Reeded

Date	Mintage	F	VF	XF	Unc	BU
2001 Proof	—	Value: 30.00				

KM# 1144 7500000 LIRA
31.2500 g., 0.9250 Silver 0.9293 oz. ASW, 38.5 mm. **Subject:** Koca Yusuf Baspehlivan **Obv:** Two figures wrestling **Rev:** Portrait on circular background **Edge:** Reeded

Date	Mintage	F	VF	XF	Unc	BU
2001 Proof	—	Value: 30.00				

KM# 1120 7500000 LIRA
15.4000 g., 0.9250 Silver 0.4580 oz. ASW **Subject:** Bird Series - Saz Horozu **Obv:** Value and date within sprigs **Rev:** Purple swamphen on ground **Edge:** Plain **Shape:** 4-sided **Note:** 28.1 x 28.1mm

Date	Mintage	F	VF	XF	Unc	BU
2001 Proof	—	Value: 27.50				

KM# 1121 7500000 LIRA
15.4000 g., 0.9250 Silver 0.4580 oz. ASW **Subject:** Bird Series - Toy **Obv:** Value and date within sprigs **Rev:** Greater Bustard on ground **Edge:** Plain **Shape:** 4-sided **Note:** 28.1 x 28.1mm

Date	Mintage	F	VF	XF	Unc	BU
2001 Proof	—	Value: 27.50				

KM# 1122 7500000 LIRA
15.4000 g., 0.9250 Silver 0.4580 oz. ASW **Subject:** Bird Series - Yaz Ordegi **Obv:** Value and date within sprigs **Rev:** White-headed Duck on ground **Edge:** Plain **Shape:** 4-sided **Note:** 28.1 x 28.1mm

Date	Mintage	F	VF	XF	Unc	BU
2001 Proof	—	Value: 27.50				

KM# 1123 7500000 LIRA
15.4000 g., 0.9250 Silver 0.4580 oz. ASW **Subject:** Bird Series - Dikkuyruk **Obv:** Value and date within sprigs **Rev:** Marbled teal on water **Edge:** Plain **Shape:** 4-sided **Note:** 28.1 x 28.1mm

Date	Mintage	F	VF	XF	Unc	BU
2001 Proof	—	Value: 27.50				

KM# 1124 7500000 LIRA
15.4000 g., 0.9250 Silver 0.4580 oz. ASW **Subject:** Bird Series - Yesil Arikusu **Obv:** Value and date within sprigs **Rev:** Bee-eater on branch **Edge:** Plain **Shape:** 4-sided **Note:** 28.1 x 28.1mm

Date	Mintage	F	VF	XF	Unc	BU
2001 Proof	—	Value: 27.50				

KM# 1125 7500000 LIRA
15.4000 g., 0.9250 Silver 0.4580 oz. ASW **Subject:** Bird Series - Kucuk Karabatak **Obv:** Value and date within sprigs **Rev:** Three pygmy cormorants **Edge:** Plain **Shape:** 4-sided **Note:** 28.1 x 28.1mm

Date	Mintage	F	VF	XF	Unc	BU
2001 Proof	—	Value: 27.50				

KM# 1126 7500000 LIRA
15.4000 g., 0.9250 Silver 0.4580 oz. ASW **Subject:** Bird Series - Kizil Akbaba **Obv:** Value and date within sprigs **Rev:** Eurasian griffon **Edge:** Plain **Shape:** 4-sided **Note:** 28.1 x 28.1mm

Date	Mintage	F	VF	XF	Unc	BU
2001 Proof	—	Value: 27.50				

KM# 1127 7500000 LIRA
15.4000 g., 0.9250 Silver 0.4580 oz. ASW **Subject:** Bird Series - Sah Kartal **Obv:** Value and date within sprigs **Rev:** Eagles **Edge:** Plain **Shape:** 4-sided **Note:** 28.1 x 28.1mm

Date	Mintage	F	VF	XF	Unc	BU
2001 Proof	—	Value: 27.50				

KM# 1128 7500000 LIRA
15.4000 g., 0.9250 Silver 0.4580 oz. ASW **Subject:** Bird Series - Ala Sigireik **Obv:** Value and date within sprigs **Rev:** Rosy starling on ground **Edge:** Plain **Shape:** 4-sided **Note:** 28.1 x 28.1mm

Date	Mintage	F	VF	XF	Unc	BU
2001 Proof	—	Value: 25.00				

KM# 1129 7500000 LIRA
15.4000 g., 0.9250 Silver 0.4580 oz. ASW **Subject:** Bird Series - Izmir Yalicapkini **Obv:** Value and date within sprigs **Rev:** White-throated kingfisher on stump **Edge:** Plain **Shape:** 4-sided **Note:** 28.1 x 28.1mm

Date	Mintage	F	VF	XF	Unc	BU
2001 Proof	—	Value: 25.00				

KM# 1130 7500000 LIRA
15.4000 g., 0.9250 Silver 0.4580 oz. ASW **Subject:** Bird Series - Turac **Obv:** Value and date within sprigs **Rev:** Black francolin birds on the ground **Edge:** Plain **Shape:** 4-sided **Note:** 28.1 x 28.1mm

Date	Mintage	F	VF	XF	Unc	BU
2001 Proof	—	Value: 25.00				

KM# 1131 7500000 LIRA
15.4000 g., 0.9250 Silver 0.4580 oz. ASW **Subject:** Bird Series - Kelaynak **Obv:** Value and date within sprigs **Rev:** Two Bald Ibis birds on ground **Edge:** Plain **Shape:** 4-sided **Note:** 28.1 x 28.1mm

Date	Mintage	F	VF	XF	Unc	BU
2001 Proof	—	Value: 25.00				

KM# 1132 7500000 LIRA
15.4000 g., 0.9250 Silver 0.4580 oz. ASW, 28.1x28.1 mm. **Subject:** Bird Series - Sakalli Akbaba **Obv:** Value and date within sprigs **Rev:** Bearded vulture **Edge:** Plain **Shape:** 4-sided **Note:** 28.1 x 28.1mm

Date	Mintage	F	VF	XF	Unc	BU
2001 Proof	—	Value: 25.00				

KM# 1133 7500000 LIRA
15.4000 g., 0.9250 Silver 0.4580 oz. ASW **Subject:** Bird Series - Tepeli Pelikan **Obv:** Value and date within sprigs **Rev:** Dalmatian pelican on rock **Edge:** Plain **Shape:** Square **Note:** 28.1 x 28.1mm

Date	Mintage	F	VF	XF	Unc	BU
2001 Proof	—	Value: 22.50				

KM# 1134 7500000 LIRA
15.4000 g., 0.9250 Silver 0.4580 oz. ASW **Subject:** Bird Series - Ishakkusu **Obv:** Value and date within sprigs **Rev:** European scops owl on branch **Edge:** Plain **Shape:** 4-sided **Note:** 28.1 x 28.1mm

Date	Mintage	F	VF	XF	Unc	BU
2001 Proof	—	Value: 22.50				

KM# 1117 7500000 LIRA
31.4700 g., 0.9250 Silver 0.9359 oz. ASW **Subject:** Iznik Tabak **Obv:** Two peacocks within circle **Rev:** Iznik Tabak (Nicean pottery) 1570; Circle of flowers at center

Date	Mintage	F	VF	XF	Unc	BU
2001 Proof	1,349	Value: 30.00				

KM# 1135 7500000 LIRA
31.0300 g., 0.9250 Silver 0.9228 oz. ASW, 38.5 mm. **Subject:** Mevlana Celaleddin-i Rumi **Obv:** Dancer within circle **Rev:** Turbaned bust 3/4 right above dates **Edge:** Reeded

Date	Mintage	F	VF	XF	Unc	BU
2001 Proof	—	Value: 30.00				

KM# 1145 7500000 LIRA
15.6100 g., 0.9250 Silver 0.4642 oz. ASW, 27.9 x 38.6 mm. **Series:** Flowers **Obv:** Value and date within sprigs **Rev:** Paeonia turcica **Edge:** Reeded **Shape:** Oval

Date	Mintage	F	VF	XF	Unc	BU
2002 Proof	—	Value: 17.50				

KM# 1146 7500000 LIRA
15.6100 g., 0.9250 Silver 0.4642 oz. ASW, 27.9 x 38.6 mm. **Series:** Flowers **Obv:** Value and date within sprigs **Rev:** Orchis anatolica **Edge:** Reeded **Shape:** Oval

Date	Mintage	F	VF	XF	Unc	BU
2002 Proof	—	Value: 17.50				

KM# 1147 7500000 LIRA
15.6100 g., 0.9250 Silver 0.4642 oz. ASW, 27.9 x 38.6 mm. **Series:** Flowers **Obv:** Value and date within sprigs **Rev:** Iris pamphylica **Edge:** Reeded **Shape:** Oval

Date	Mintage	F	VF	XF	Unc	BU
2002 Proof	—	Value: 17.50				

KM# 1148 7500000 LIRA
15.6100 g., 0.9250 Silver 0.4642 oz. ASW, 27.9 x 38.6 mm. **Series:** Flowers **Obv:** Value and date within sprigs **Rev:** Gladiolus anatolicus **Edge:** Reeded **Shape:** Oval

Date	Mintage	F	VF	XF	Unc	BU
2002 Proof	—	Value: 17.50				

KM# 1149 7500000 LIRA
15.6100 g., 0.9250 Silver 0.4642 oz. ASW, 27.9 x 38.6 mm. **Series:** Flowers **Obv:** Value and date within sprigs **Rev:** Crocus sativus **Edge:** Reeded **Shape:** Oval

Date	Mintage	F	VF	XF	Unc	BU
2002 Proof	—	Value: 17.50				

KM# 1150 7500000 LIRA
15.6100 g., 0.9250 Silver 0.4642 oz. ASW, 27.9 x 38.6 mm. **Series:** Flowers **Obv:** Value and date within sprigs **Rev:** Campanula betulifolia **Edge:** Reeded **Shape:** Oval

Date	Mintage	F	VF	XF	Unc	BU
2002 Proof	—	Value: 17.50				

KM# 1151 7500000 LIRA
15.6100 g., 0.9250 Silver 0.4642 oz. ASW, 27.9 x 38.6 mm. **Series:** Flowers **Obv:** Value and date within sprigs **Rev:** Centaurea tchihatcheffii **Edge:** Reeded **Shape:** Oval

Date	Mintage	F	VF	XF	Unc	BU
2002 Proof	—	Value: 17.50				

KM# 1152 7500000 LIRA
15.6100 g., 0.9250 Silver 0.4642 oz. ASW, 27.9 x 38.6 mm. **Series:** Flowers **Obv:** Value and date within sprigs **Rev:** Tchihatchewia isatidea **Edge:** Reeded **Shape:** Oval

Date	Mintage	F	VF	XF	Unc	BU
2002 Proof	—	Value: 17.50				

KM# 1153 7500000 LIRA
15.6100 g., 0.9250 Silver 0.4642 oz. ASW, 27.9 x 38.6 mm. **Series:** Flowers **Obv:** Value and date within sprigs **Rev:** Linum anatolicum **Edge:** Reeded **Shape:** Oval

Date	Mintage	F	VF	XF	Unc	BU
2002 Proof	—	Value: 17.50				

KM# 1154 7500000 LIRA
15.6100 g., 0.9250 Silver 0.4642 oz. ASW, 27.9 x 38.6 mm. **Series:** Flowers **Obv:** Value and date within sprigs **Rev:** Cyclamen trochopteranthum **Edge:** Reeded **Shape:** Oval

Date	Mintage	F	VF	XF	Unc	BU
2002 Proof	—	Value: 17.50				

KM# 1155 7500000 LIRA
15.6100 g., 0.9250 Silver 0.4642 oz. ASW, 27.9 x 38.6 mm. **Series:** Flowers **Obv:** Value and date within sprigs **Rev:** Tulipa orphanidea **Edge:** Reeded **Shape:** Oval

Date	Mintage	F	VF	XF	Unc	BU
2002 Proof	—	Value: 17.50				

KM# 1156 7500000 LIRA
15.6100 g., 0.9250 Silver 0.4642 oz. ASW, 27.9 x 38.6 mm. **Obv:** Value and date within sprigs **Rev:** Stenbergia candida **Edge:** Reeded **Shape:** Oval

Date	Mintage	F	VF	XF	Unc	BU
2002 Proof	—	Value: 17.50				

KM# 1157 7500000 LIRA
15.6100 g., 0.9250 Silver 0.4642 oz. ASW, 27.9 x 38.6 mm. **Series:** Flowers **Obv:** Value and date within sprigs **Rev:** Arum maculatum **Edge:** Reeded **Shape:** Oval

Date	Mintage	F	VF	XF	Unc	BU
2002 Proof	—	Value: 17.50				

KM# 1118 10000000 LIRA
31.4700 g., 0.9250 Silver 0.9359 oz. ASW, 38.6 mm. **Subject:** Divrigi Ulu Camii **Obv:** Artwork within circle **Rev:** Ornate door at the Divrigi ulu Camii (Divrigi Great Mosque) built 1228 in Sivas Province **Edge:** Reeded

Date	Mintage	F	VF	XF	Unc	BU
2001 Matte	15,000	—	—	—	30.00	—

KM# 1159 10000000 LIRA
31.4200 g., 0.9250 Silver 0.9344 oz. ASW, 38.6 mm. **Subject:** Bogazici'nde Yalilar **Obv:** Value and date within sprigs **Rev:** Waterfront buildings **Edge:** Reeded

Date	Mintage	F	VF	XF	Unc	BU
2001 Proof	—	Value: 30.00				

KM# 1160 10000000 LIRA
31.4200 g., 0.9250 Silver 0.9344 oz. ASW, 38.6 mm. **Obv:** Turkish mint symbol within circle **Rev:** Mosque within surrounding buildings **Edge:** Reeded

Date	Mintage	F	VF	XF	Unc	BU
2002 Proof	—	Value: 30.00				

KM# 1140 10000000 LIRA
31.4600 g., 0.9250 Silver 0.9356 oz. ASW, 38.6 mm. **Subject:** 75th Anniversary of TRT (Türkiye Radyo Televizyon) **Obv:** Large mint mark and design within circle **Rev:** Radio microphone **Edge:** Reeded

Date	Mintage	F	VF	XF	Unc	BU
2002 Proof	—	Value: 30.00				

REFORM DECIMAL COINAGE

2005 - 100,000 Old Lira = 1 New Lira

KM# 1164 NEW KURUS
2.7200 g., Brass, 17 mm. **Obv:** Head left within circle **Rev:** Value **Edge:** Plain

Date	Mintage	F	VF	XF	Unc	BU
2005	—	—	—	—	0.15	—
2006	—	—	—	—	0.15	—
2007	Est. 3,000	—	—	—	—	—

KM# 1165 5 NEW KURUS
2.9500 g., Copper-Nickel, 17.1 mm. **Obv:** Head left within circle **Rev:** Value **Edge:** Plain

Date	Mintage	F	VF	XF	Unc	BU
2005	—	—	—	—	0.25	—
2006	—	—	—	—	0.25	—

KM# 1166 10 NEW KURUS
3.8300 g., Copper-Nickel, 19.4 mm. **Obv:** Head with hat right within circle **Rev:** Value **Edge:** Plain

Date	Mintage	F	VF	XF	Unc	BU
2005	—	—	—	—	0.50	—
2006	—	—	—	—	0.50	—
2007	—	—	—	—	0.50	—

KM# 1167 25 NEW KURUS
5.3000 g., Copper-Nickel, 21.5 mm. **Obv:** Head facing within circle **Rev:** Value **Edge:** Reeded

Date	Mintage	F	VF	XF	Unc	BU
2005	—	—	—	—	0.50	—
2006	—	—	—	—	1.00	—
2007	—	—	—	—	0.60	—

KM# 1168 50 NEW KURUS
7.0000 g., **Ring Composition:** Brass **Center Composition:** Copper-Nickel, 23.8 mm. **Obv:** Head right within circle **Rev:** Value within circle **Edge:** Reeded

Date	Mintage	F	VF	XF	Unc	BU
2005	—	—	—	—	2.00	—
2006	—	—	—	—	2.00	—
2007	—	—	—	—	1.00	—

KM# 1169 NEW LIRA
8.5000 g., Bi-Metallic Brass center in Copper-Nickel ring, 26 mm. **Obv:** Head 1/4 left within circle **Rev:** Value within circle **Edge:** Segmented Reeding **Note:** Varieties of weights and other details exist.

Date	Mintage	F	VF	XF	Unc	BU
2005	—	—	—	—	2.50	—
2006	—	—	—	—	2.50	—
2007	—	—	—	—	2.50	—
2008	—	—	—	—	2.50	—

KM# 1171 5 NEW LIRA
12.0000 g., Bi-Metallic Brass center in Copper-Nickel ring, 32 mm. **Subject:** 23rd Universiade in red holder **Obv:** Stylized bird within circle **Rev:** Logo within circle

Date	Mintage	F	VF	XF	Unc	BU
ND (2005)	10,000	—	—	—	12.50	—

KM# 1172 5 NEW LIRA
12.0000 g., Bi-Metallic Copper-Nickel center in Brass ring, 32 mm. **Subject:** 23rd Universiade in blue holder **Obv:** Stylized bird within circle **Rev:** Logo within circle

Date	Mintage	F	VF	XF	Unc	BU
ND (2005)	10,000	—	—	—	12.50	—

KM# 1173 20 NEW LIRA
31.3600 g., 0.9250 Silver 0.9326 oz. ASW, 38.6 mm. **Obv:** Value within sprigs and circle **Rev:** Aegean Carpet **Edge:** Reeded

Date	Mintage	F	VF	XF	Unc	BU
2005 Proof	5,000	Value: 30.00				

KM# 1174 20 NEW LIRA
31.4300 g., 0.9250 Silver 0.9347 oz. ASW, 38.6 mm. **Obv:** Value within sprigs and circle **Rev:** Mostar Bridge **Edge:** Reeded

Date	Mintage	F	VF	XF	Unc	BU
2005 Proof	5,000	Value: 50.00				

KM# 1175 20 NEW LIRA
23.4500 g., 0.9250 Silver 0.6974 oz. ASW, 38.6 mm. **Obv:** Value within sprigs and circle **Rev:** Angora Goat **Edge:** Reeded

Date	Mintage	F	VF	XF	Unc	BU
2005 Proof	5,000	Value: 60.00				

KM# 1176 20 NEW LIRA
23.4600 g., 0.9250 Silver 0.6977 oz. ASW, 38.6 mm. **Obv:** Value within sprigs and circle **Rev:** Long-eared Desert Hedgehog **Edge:** Reeded

Date	Mintage	F	VF	XF	Unc	BU
2005 Proof	5,000	Value: 60.00				

KM# 1177 20 NEW LIRA
23.4100 g., 0.9250 Silver 0.6962 oz. ASW, 38.6 mm. **Obv:** Value within sprigs and circle **Rev:** Anatolian Mouflon **Edge:** Reeded

Date	Mintage	F	VF	XF	Unc	BU
2005 Proof	5,000	Value: 60.00				

KM# 1178 20 NEW LIRA
23.4300 g., 0.9250 Silver 0.6968 oz. ASW, 38.6 mm. **Obv:** Value within sprigs and circle **Rev:** Striped Hyena **Edge:** Reeded

Date	Mintage	F	VF	XF	Unc	BU
2005 Proof	5,000	Value: 60.00				

KM# 1179 20 NEW LIRA
23.4300 g., 0.9250 Silver 0.6968 oz. ASW, 38.6 mm. **Obv:** Value within sprigs and circle **Rev:** Hazel Dormouse **Edge:** Reeded

Date	Mintage	F	VF	XF	Unc	BU
2005 Proof	5,000	Value: 60.00				

KM# 1180.1 20 NEW LIRA
23.5000 g., 0.9250 Silver 0.6988 oz. ASW, 38.6 mm. **Obv:** Value within sprigs and circle **Rev:** Angora Cat with plain eyes **Edge:** Reeded

Date	Mintage	F	VF	XF	Unc	BU
2005 Proof	5,000	Value: 60.00				

KM# 1180.2 20 NEW LIRA
23.5000 g., 0.9250 Silver 0.6988 oz. ASW, 38.6 mm. **Obv:** Value within sprigs and circle **Rev:** Cat with mismatched colored eyes **Edge:** Reeded

Date	Mintage	F	VF	XF	Unc	BU
2005 Proof	—	Value: 65.00				

KM# 1181 20 NEW LIRA
23.3700 g., 0.9990 Silver 0.7506 oz. ASW, 38.6 mm. **Obv:** Value within sprigs and circle **Rev:** Anatolian Leopard **Edge:** Reeded

Date	Mintage	F	VF	XF	Unc	BU
2005 Proof	5,000	Value: 60.00				

KM# 1182 20 NEW LIRA
23.2500 g., 0.9250 Silver 0.6914 oz. ASW, 38.6 mm. **Obv:** Value within sprigs and circle **Rev:** Turkish Kangal Dog **Edge:** Reeded

Date	Mintage	F	VF	XF	Unc	BU
2005 Proof	—	Value: 60.00				

KM# 1183 20 NEW LIRA
23.4600 g., 0.9250 Silver 0.6977 oz. ASW, 38.6 mm. **Obv:** Value within sprigs and circle **Rev:** Five-toed Jerboa **Edge:** Reeded

Date	Mintage	F	VF	XF	Unc	BU
2005 Proof	5,000	Value: 60.00				

KM# 1184 20 NEW LIRA
23.2600 g., 0.9250 Silver 0.6917 oz. ASW, 38.6 mm. **Obv:** Value within sprigs and circle **Rev:** Brown Bear **Edge:** Reeded

Date	Mintage	F	VF	XF	Unc	BU
2005 Proof	5,000	Value: 60.00				

KM# 1185 20 NEW LIRA
23.5300 g., 0.9250 Silver 0.6997 oz. ASW, 38.6 mm. **Obv:** Value within sprigs and circle **Rev:** Desert Monitor **Edge:** Reeded

Date	Mintage	F	VF	XF	Unc	BU
2005 Proof	5,000	Value: 60.00				

TURKS & CAICOS ISLANDS

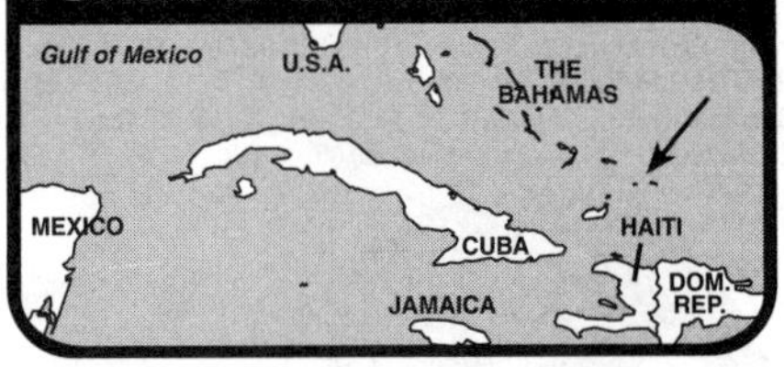

The Colony of the Turks and Caicos Islands, a British colony situated in the West Indies at the eastern end of the Bahama Islands, has an area of 166 sq. mi. (430 sq.km.) and a population of *10,000. Capital: Cockburn Town, on Grand Turk. The principal industry of the colony is the production of salt, which is gathered by raking. Salt, crayfish, and conch shells are exported.

RULER
British

MONETARY SYSTEM
1 Crown = 1 Dollar U.S.A.

BRITISH COLONY

STANDARD COINAGE

KM# 233 5 CROWNS
26.4300 g., Copper-Nickel, 39.2 mm. **Ruler:** Elizabeth II **Subject:** Royal Navy Submarines **Obv:** Head with tiara right **Obv. Designer:** Ian Rank-Broadley **Rev:** Old and modern submarines **Edge:** Reeded

Date	Mintage	F	VF	XF	Unc	BU
2001	—	—	—	6.00	10.00	12.00

KM# 236 20 CROWNS
31.2000 g., 0.9990 Silver 1.0021 oz. ASW, 38.9 mm. **Obv:** Crowned head right **Obv. Designer:** Ian Rank-Broadley **Rev:** Bust right facing divides dates **Edge:** Reeded

Date	Mintage	F	VF	XF	Unc	BU
2001 Proof	—	Value: 40.00				

KM# 245 20 CROWNS
31.1600 g., 0.9990 Silver 1.0008 oz. ASW, 39 mm. **Obv:** Crowned head right **Rev:** Richard II (1377-1399) **Edge:** Reeded

Date	Mintage	F	VF	XF	Unc	BU
2002 Proof	—	Value: 40.00				

KM# 246 20 CROWNS
Hafnium, 38.6 mm. **Ruler:** Elizabeth II **Subject:** H.M. Queen Elizabeth, The Queen Mother **Obv:** Crowned head right **Rev:** Crowned bust right within circle **Edge:** Reeded

Date	Mintage	F	VF	XF	Unc	BU
2002	—	Value: 125.00				

TUVALU

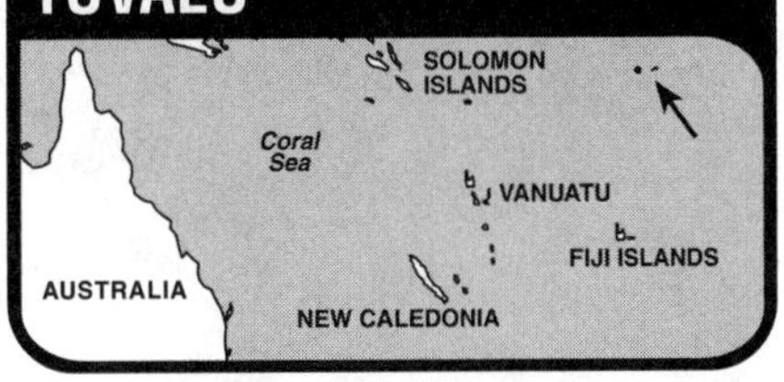

Tuvalu (formerly the Ellice or Lagoon Islands of the Gilbert and Ellice Islands), located in the South Pacific north of the Fiji Islands, has an area of 10 sq. mi. (26 sq.km.) and a population of *9,000. Capital: Funafuti. The independent state includes the islands of Nanumanga, Nanumea, Nui, Niutao, Viatupa, Funafuti, Nukufetau, Nukulailai and Nurakita. The latter four islands were claimed by the United States until relinquished by the Feb. 7, 1979, Treaty of Friendship signed by the United States and Tuvalu. The principal industries are copra production and phosphate mining.

Tuvalu is a member of the Commonwealth of Nations. Elizabeth II is Head of State as Queen of Tuvalu.

RULER
British, until 1978

MONETARY SYSTEM
100 Cents = 1 Dollar

CONSTITUTIONAL MONARCHY WITHIN THE COMMONWEALTH

STANDARD COINAGE

KM# 40 DOLLAR
20.0000 g., Brass, 38.7 mm. **Ruler:** Elizabeth II **Subject:** Dinosaurs **Obv:** Crowned head right **Obv. Designer:** Raphael Maklouf **Rev:** Giganotosaurus **Edge:** Reeded **Note:** See KM#49.

Date	Mintage	F	VF	XF	Unc	BU
2002	50,000	—	—	—	12.00	15.00

KM# 41 DOLLAR
20.0000 g., Brass, 38.7 mm. **Ruler:** Elizabeth II **Subject:** Dinosaurs **Obv:** Crowned head right **Rev:** Dromaeosaurus **Edge:** Reeded **Note:** See KM#50.

Date	Mintage	F	VF	XF	Unc	BU
2002	50,000	—	—	—	12.00	15.00

KM# 42 DOLLAR
20.0000 g., Brass, 38.7 mm. **Ruler:** Elizabeth II **Subject:** Dinosaurs **Obv:** Crowned head right **Rev:** Seismosaurus **Edge:** Reeded **Note:** See KM#52.

Date	Mintage	F	VF	XF	Unc	BU
2002	50,000	—	—	—	12.00	15.00

KM# 43 DOLLAR
20.0000 g., Brass, 38.7 mm. **Ruler:** Elizabeth II **Subject:** Dinosaurs **Obv:** Crowned head right **Rev:** Stegosaurus **Edge:** Reeded **Note:** See KM#51.

Date	Mintage	F	VF	XF	Unc	BU
2002	50,000	—	—	—	12.00	15.00

KM# 49 5 DOLLARS

62.5000 g., 0.9990 Silver 2.0073 oz. ASW, 49.9 mm. **Subject:** Dinosaurs **Obv:** Crowned head right **Rev:** Giganotosaurus **Edge:** Reeded

Date	Mintage	F	VF	XF	Unc	BU
2002 Proof	1,000	Value: 75.00				

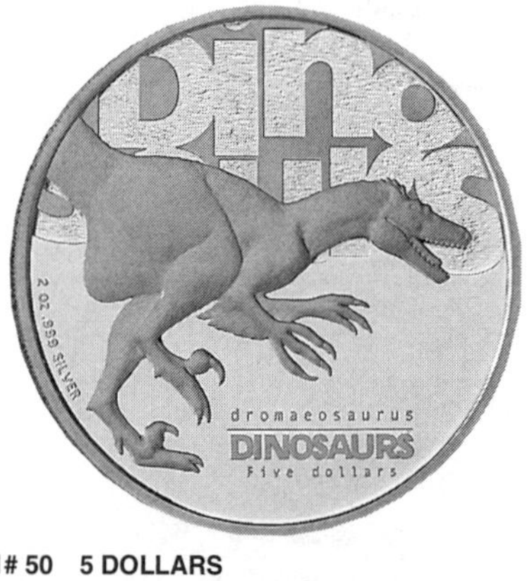

KM# 50 5 DOLLARS

62.5000 g., 0.9990 Silver 2.0073 oz. ASW, 49.9 mm. **Subject:** Dinosaurs **Obv:** Crowned head right **Rev:** Dromaeosaurus **Edge:** Reeded

Date	Mintage	F	VF	XF	Unc	BU
2002 Proof	1,000	Value: 75.00				

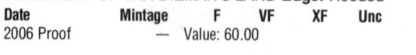

KM# 51 5 DOLLARS

62.5000 g., 0.9990 Silver 2.0073 oz. ASW, 49.9 mm. **Subject:** Dinosaurs **Obv:** Crowned head right **Rev:** Stegosaurus **Edge:** Reeded

Date	Mintage	F	VF	XF	Unc	BU
2002 Proof	1,000	Value: 75.00				

KM# 52 5 DOLLARS

62.5000 g., 0.9990 Silver 2.0073 oz. ASW, 49.9 mm. **Subject:** Dinosaurs **Obv:** Crowned head right **Rev:** Seismosaurus **Edge:** Reeded

Date	Mintage	F	VF	XF	Unc	BU
2002 Proof	1,000	Value: 75.00				

KM# 53 DOLLAR

Silver **Obv:** Crowned head right **Rev:** 1955 Mercedes Benz 300 SL Gullwing

Date	Mintage	F	VF	XF	Unc	BU
2006 Proof	—	Value: 40.00				

KM# 54 DOLLAR

Silver **Obv:** Crowned head right **Rev:** 1963 Jaguar E-Type colorized

Date	Mintage	F	VF	XF	Unc	BU
2006 Proof	—	Value: 40.00				

KM# 55 DOLLAR

Silver **Obv:** Crowned head right **Rev:** 1969 Datsun 240Z

Date	Mintage	F	VF	XF	Unc	BU
2006	—	—	—	—	40.00	—

KM# 58 DOLLAR

31.3100 g., 0.9990 Silver And Enamel 1.0056 oz., 40.51 mm. **Ruler:** Elizabeth II **Subject:** 400th Anniversary of First European Sighting of Australia **Obv:** Crowned bust right **Obv. Legend:** QUEEN ELIZABETH II **Rev:** Bust of Captain James Cook at left, his ship; "H.M.S. Endeavor" within ship's wheel **Rev. Inscription:** 1770 DISCOVERY - EASTERN AUSTRALIA **Edge:** Reeded

Date	Mintage	F	VF	XF	Unc	BU
2006 Proof	—	Value: 60.00				

KM# 59 DOLLAR

31.3100 g., 0.9990 Silver And Enamel 1.0056 oz., 40.51 mm. **Ruler:** Elizabeth II **Subject:** 400th Anniversary of First European Sighting of Australia **Obv:** Crowned bust right **Obv. Legend:** QUEEN ELIZABETH II **Rev:** Bust of Abel Jansoon Tasman at left, his Dutch ship within ship's wheel **Rev. Legend:** 1642 DISCOVERY OF VAN DIEMAN'S LAND **Edge:** Reeded

Date	Mintage	F	VF	XF	Unc	BU
2006 Proof	—	Value: 60.00				

KM# 60 DOLLAR

Silver And Enamel, 40.51 mm. **Ruler:** Elizabeth II **Subject:** 400th Anniversary of First European Sighting of Australia **Obv:** Crowned bust right **Obv. Legend:** QUEEN ELIZABETH II **Rev:** Bust of William Dampier at right, his ship within ship's wheel **Rev. Legend:** 1688 BRITISH DISCOVERY OF AUSTRALIA **Edge:** Reeded

Date	Mintage	F	VF	XF	Unc	BU
2006 Proof	—	Value: 60.00				

KM# 61 DOLLAR

31.3100 g., 0.9990 Silver And Enamel 1.0056 oz., 40.51 mm. **Ruler:** Elizabeth II **Subject:** 400th Anniversary of First European Sighting of Australia **Obv:** Crowned bust right **Obv. Legend:** QUEEN ELIZABETH II **Rev:** Dutch ship"Duyfken" within ship's wheel **Rev. Legend:** 1606 FIRST EUROPEAN DISCOVERY AUSTRALIA **Edge:** Reeded

Date	Mintage	F	VF	XF	Unc	BU
2006 Proof	—	Value: 60.00				

KM# 62 DOLLAR

31.1035 g., 0.9990 Silver 0.9990 oz. ASW, 40.51 mm. **Ruler:** Elizabeth II **Obv:** Crowned bust right **Obv. Legend:** ELIZABETH II **Rev:** Multicolor Great White Shark **Edge:** Reeded

Date	Mintage	F	VF	XF	Unc	BU
2007 Proof	5,000	Value: 85.00				

KM# 63 DOLLAR

0.9990 Silver, 40 mm. **Ruler:** Elizabeth II **Series:** Fighting Ships of WW II **Obv:** Crowned bust right **Obv. Legend:** QUEEN ELIZABETH II - TUVALU **Obv. Designer:** Raphael Maklouf **Rev:** USSR Sevastopol, multicolor water

Date	Mintage	F	VF	XF	Unc	BU
2007 Proof	1,500	Value: 60.00				

KM# 64 DOLLAR

0.9990 Silver, 40 mm. **Ruler:** Elizabeth II **Series:** Fighting Ships of WW II **Obv:** Crowned bust right **Obv. Legend:** QUEEN ELIZABETH II - TUVALU **Obv. Designer:** Raphael Maklouf **Rev:** HMS Hood, multicolor water and smoke

Date	Mintage	F	VF	XF	Unc	BU
2007 Proof	1,500	Value: 60.00				

KM# 65 DOLLAR

0.9990 Silver, 40 mm. **Ruler:** Elizabeth II **Series:** Fighting Ships of WW II **Obv:** Crowned bust right **Obv. Legend:** QUEEN

ELIZABETH II - TUVALU **Obv. Designer:** Raphael Maklouf **Rev:** Bismarck, multicolor water and gun flashes

Date	Mintage	F	VF	XF	Unc	BU
2007 Proof	1,500	Value: 60.00				

KM# 66 DOLLAR

0.9990 Silver, 40 mm. **Ruler:** Elizabeth II **Series:** Fighting Ships of WW II **Obv. Legend:** QUEEN ELIZABETH II - TUVALU **Obv. Designer:** Raphael Maklouf **Rev:** IJN Yamato, multicolor water and rising sun

Date	Mintage	F	VF	XF	Unc	BU
2007 Proof	1,500	Value: 60.00				

KM# 67 DOLLAR

0.9990 Silver, 40 mm. **Ruler:** Elizabeth II **Series:** Fighting Ships of WW II **Obv:** Crowned bust right **Obv. Legend:** QUEEN ELIZABETH II - TUVALU **Obv. Designer:** Raphael Maklouf **Rev:** USS Missouri

Date	Mintage	F	VF	XF	Unc	BU
2007 Proof	1,500	Value: 60.00				

KM# 68 DOLLAR

31.1030 g., 0.9990 Silver 0.9989 oz. ASW, 40 mm. **Ruler:** Elizabeth II **Obv:** Crowned bust right **Obv. Legend:** QUEEN ELIZABETH II - TUVALU **Rev:** Red-back Spider, multicolor

Date	Mintage	F	VF	XF	Unc	BU
2006 Proof	5,000	Value: 60.00				

KM# 69 100 DOLLARS

Gold **Ruler:** Elizabeth II **Obv:** Crowned head right **Rev:** Red 1963 Corvette Sting Ray

Date	Mintage	F	VF	XF	Unc	BU
2006 Proof	250	Value: 1,450				

UGANDA

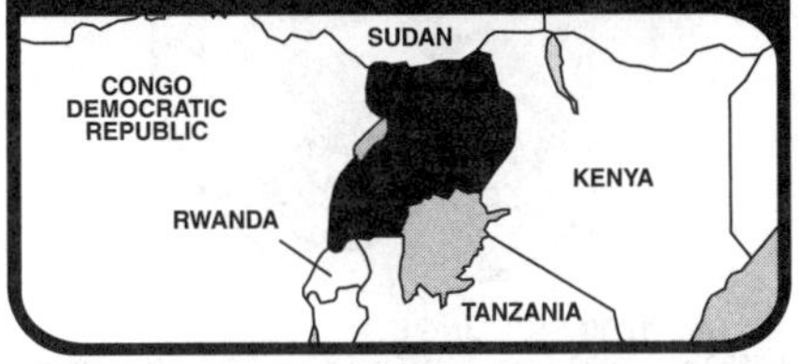

The Republic of Uganda, a former British protectorate located astride the equator in east-central Africa, has an area of 91,134 sq. mi. (236,040 sq. km.) and a population of *17 million. Capital: Kampala. Agriculture, including livestock, is the basis of the economy; there is some mining of copper, tin, gold and lead. Coffee, cotton, copper and tea are exported.

Uganda is a member of the Commonwealth of Nations. The president is Chief of State and Head of Government.

For earlier coinage refer to East Africa.

MONETARY SYSTEM

100 Cents = 1 Shilling

REPUBLIC

STANDARD COINAGE

KM# 66 50 SHILLINGS

Nickel Plated Steel **Obv:** National arms **Rev:** Antelope head facing

Date	Mintage	F	VF	XF	Unc	BU
2003	—	—	—	—	1.00	1.25

KM# 67 100 SHILLINGS

7.0000 g., Copper-Nickel, 26.9 mm. **Obv:** National arms **Rev:** African bull **Edge:** Reeded

Date	Mintage	F	VF	XF	Unc	BU
2003	—	—	—	—	1.50	1.75

KM# 129 100 SHILLINGS

3.5000 g., Stainless Steel, 24 mm. **Obv:** National arms **Rev:** Monkey with elf-like ears **Edge:** Plain

Date	Mintage	F	VF	XF	Unc	BU
2004	—	—	—	—	1.50	—

KM# 135 100 SHILLINGS

Steel, 23 mm. **Subject:** Animals of the Chinese New Year **Rev:** Ox

Date	Mintage	F	VF	XF	Unc	BU
2004	—	—	—	—	0.75	—

KM# 136 100 SHILLINGS

Steel, 23 mm. **Subject:** Animals of the Chinese New Year **Rev:** Goat

Date	Mintage	F	VF	XF	Unc	BU
2004	—	—	—	—	0.75	—

KM# 137 100 SHILLINGS

Steel, 23 mm. **Subject:** Animals of the Chinese New Year **Rev:** Horse

Date	Mintage	F	VF	XF	Unc	BU
2004	—	—	—	—	0.75	—

KM# 138 100 SHILLINGS

Steel, 23 mm. **Subject:** Animals of the Chinese New Year **Rev:** Dragon

Date	Mintage	F	VF	XF	Unc	BU
2004	—	—	—	—	0.75	—

KM# 139 100 SHILLINGS

Steel, 23 mm. **Subject:** Animals of the Chinese New Year **Rev:** Dog

Date	Mintage	F	VF	XF	Unc	BU
2004	—	—	—	—	0.75	—

KM# 140 100 SHILLINGS

Steel, 23 mm. **Subject:** Animals of the Chinese New Year **Rev:** Tiger

Date	Mintage	F	VF	XF	Unc	BU
2004	—	—	—	—	0.75	—

KM# 141 100 SHILLINGS

Steel, 23 mm. **Subject:** Animals of the Chinese New Year **Rev:** Snake

Date	Mintage	F	VF	XF	Unc	BU
2004	—	—	—	—	0.75	—

KM# 142 100 SHILLINGS

Steel, 23 mm. **Subject:** Animals of the Chinese New Year **Rev:** Rooster

Date	Mintage	F	VF	XF	Unc	BU
2004	—	—	—	—	0.75	—

KM# 143 100 SHILLINGS

Steel, 23 mm. **Subject:** Animals of the Chinese New Year **Rev:** Rabbit

Date	Mintage	F	VF	XF	Unc	BU
2004	—	—	—	—	0.75	—

KM# 144 100 SHILLINGS

Steel, 23 mm. **Subject:** Animals of the Chinese New Year **Rev:** Rat

Date	Mintage	F	VF	XF	Unc	BU
2004	—	—	—	—	0.75	—

KM# 145 100 SHILLINGS

Steel, 23 mm. **Subject:** Animals of the Chinese New Year **Rev:** Pig

Date	Mintage	F	VF	XF	Unc	BU
2004	—	—	—	—	0.75	—

KM# 130 100 SHILLINGS

Steel, 23 mm. **Rev:** Type I of five different monkeys

Date	Mintage	F	VF	XF	Unc	BU
2004	—	—	—	—	1.50	—

KM# 131 100 SHILLINGS

Steel, 23 mm. **Rev:** Type II of five different monkeys

Date	Mintage	F	VF	XF	Unc	BU
2004	—	—	—	—	1.50	—

KM# 132 100 SHILLINGS

Steel, 23 mm. **Rev:** Type III of five different monkeys

Date	Mintage	F	VF	XF	Unc	BU
2004	—	—	—	—	1.50	—

KM# 133 100 SHILLINGS

Steel, 23 mm. **Rev:** Type IV of five different monkys

Date	Mintage	F	VF	XF	Unc	BU
2004	—	—	—	—	1.50	—

KM# 134 100 SHILLINGS

Steel, 23 mm. **Rev:** Type V of five different monkeys

Date	Mintage	F	VF	XF	Unc	BU
2004	—	—	—	—	1.50	—

KM# 188 100 SHILLINGS

Copper-Nickel **Series:** Zodiac **Obv:** Rat **Obv. Legend:** BANK OF UGANDA

Date	Mintage	F	VF	XF	Unc	BU
2004	—	—	—	—	1.50	—

KM# 189 100 SHILLINGS

Copper-Nickel **Series:** Zodiac **Obv:** Ox **Obv. Legend:** BANK OF UGANDA

Date	Mintage	F	VF	XF	Unc	BU
2004	—	—	—	—	1.50	—

KM# 190 100 SHILLINGS

Copper-Nickel **Series:** Zodiac **Obv:** Tiger

Date	Mintage	F	VF	XF	Unc	BU
2004	—	—	—	—	1.50	—

KM# 191 100 SHILLINGS

Copper-Nickel **Series:** Zodiac **Obv:** Rabbit **Obv. Legend:** BANK OF UGANDA

Date	Mintage	F	VF	XF	Unc	BU
2004	—	—	—	—	1.50	—

KM# 192 100 SHILLINGS

Copper-Nickel **Series:** Zodiac **Obv:** Dragon **Obv. Legend:** BANK OF UGANDA

Date	Mintage	F	VF	XF	Unc	BU
2004	—	—	—	—	1.50	—

KM# 193 100 SHILLINGS

Copper-Nickel **Series:** Zodiac **Obv:** Snake **Obv. Legend:** BANK OF UGANDA

Date	Mintage	F	VF	XF	Unc	BU
2004	—	—	—	—	1.50	—

KM# 194 100 SHILLINGS

Copper-Nickel **Series:** Zodiac **Obv:** Horse **Obv. Legend:** BANK OF UGANDA

Date	Mintage	F	VF	XF	Unc	BU
2004	—	—	—	—	1.50	—

KM# 195 100 SHILLINGS

Copper-Nickel **Series:** Zodiac **Obv:** Sheep **Obv. Legend:** BANK OF UGANDA

Date	Mintage	F	VF	XF	Unc	BU
2004	—	—	—	—	1.50	—

KM# 196 100 SHILLINGS

Copper-Nickel **Series:** Zodiac **Obv:** Monkey **Obv. Legend:** BANK OF UGANDA

Date	Mintage	F	VF	XF	Unc	BU
2004	—	—	—	—	1.50	—

KM# 197 100 SHILLINGS

Copper-Nickel **Series:** Zodiac **Obv:** Rooster **Obv. Legend:** BANK OF UGANDA

Date	Mintage	F	VF	XF	Unc	BU
2004	—	—	—	—	1.50	—

KM# 198 100 SHILLINGS

Copper-Nickel **Series:** Zodiac **Obv:** Dog **Obv. Legend:** BANK OF UGANDA

Date	Mintage	F	VF	XF	Unc	BU
2004	—	—	—	—	1.50	—

KM# 199 100 SHILLINGS

Copper-Nickel **Series:** Zodiac **Obv:** Boar **Obv. Legend:** BANK OF UGANDA

Date	Mintage	F	VF	XF	Unc	BU
2004	—	—	—	—	1.50	—

KM# 200 100 SHILLINGS

Copper-Nickel **Series:** Zodiac **Subject:** Year of the Monkey **Obv. Legend:** BANK OF UGANDA

Date	Mintage	F	VF	XF	Unc	BU
2004	—	—	—	—	2.00	—

KM# 201 100 SHILLINGS

Copper-Nickel **Series:** Zodiac **Subject:** Year of the Monkey **Obv. Legend:** BANK OF UGANDA

Date	Mintage	F	VF	XF	Unc	BU
2004	—	—	—	—	2.00	—

KM# 202 100 SHILLINGS

Copper-Nickel **Series:** Zodiac **Subject:** Year of the Monkey **Obv. Legend:** BANK OF UGANDA

Date	Mintage	F	VF	XF	Unc	BU
2004	—	—	—	—	2.00	—

KM# 203 100 SHILLINGS

Copper-Nickel **Series:** Zodiac **Subject:** Year of the Monkey **Obv. Legend:** BANK OF UGANDA

Date	Mintage	F	VF	XF	Unc	BU
2004	—	—	—	—	2.00	—

KM# 204 100 SHILLINGS

Copper-Nickel **Series:** Zodiac **Subject:** Year of the Monkey **Obv. Legend:** BANK OF UGANDA

Date	Mintage	F	VF	XF	Unc	BU
2004	—	—	—	—	2.00	—

KM# 68 200 SHILLINGS

8.0500 g., Copper-Nickel, 24.9 mm. **Obv:** National arms **Rev:** Cichlid fish above value and date **Edge:** Plain

Date	Mintage	F	VF	XF	Unc	BU
2003	—	—	—	—	2.00	2.25

KM# 69 500 SHILLINGS

9.0000 g., Aluminum-Brass, 23.5 mm. **Obv:** National arms **Rev:** East African crowned crane head left **Edge:** Reeded

Date	Mintage	F	VF	XF	Unc	BU
2003	—	—	—	—	2.50	3.00

KM# 77 1000 SHILLINGS
19.8400 g., Copper-Nickel, 38.6 mm. **Subject:** Colourful Big Five of Africa **Obv:** Arms with supporters **Rev:** Multicolor rhinocerous within stamp design in front of outlined African map **Edge:** Reeded

Date	Mintage	F	VF	XF	Unc	BU
2001 Proof	—	Value: 25.00				

KM# 78 1000 SHILLINGS
19.8400 g., Copper-Nickel, 38.6 mm. **Subject:** Colourful Big Five of Africa **Obv:** Arms with supporters **Rev:** Multicolor lion within stamp design in front of outlined African map **Edge:** Reeded

Date	Mintage	F	VF	XF	Unc	BU
2001 Proof	—	Value: 25.00				

KM# 79 1000 SHILLINGS
19.8400 g., Copper-Nickel, 38.6 mm. **Subject:** Coulourful Big Five of Africa **Obv:** Arms with supporters **Rev:** Multicolor water buffalo within stamp design in front of outlined African map **Edge:** Reeded

Date	Mintage	F	VF	XF	Unc	BU
2001 Proof	—	Value: 25.00				

KM# 80 1000 SHILLINGS
19.8400 g., Copper-Nickel, 38.6 mm. **Subject:** Colourful Big Five of Africa **Obv:** Arms with supporters **Rev:** Multicolor leopard within stamp design in front of outlined map **Edge:** Reeded

Date	Mintage	F	VF	XF	Unc	BU
2001 Proof	—	Value: 25.00				

KM# 81 1000 SHILLINGS
19.8400 g., Copper-Nickel, 38.6 mm. **Subject:** Colourful Big Five of Africa **Obv:** Arms with supporters **Rev:** Multicolor elephant within stamp design in front of outlined map **Edge:** Reeded

Date	Mintage	F	VF	XF	Unc	BU
2001 Proof	—	Value: 25.00				

KM# 173 1000 SHILLINGS
Silver **Subject:** XVII World Football Championship Games - Korea and Japan **Obv. Legend:** BANK OF UGANDA **Rev:** Football - gilt

Date	Mintage	F	VF	XF	Unc	BU
2001 Proof	—	Value: 30.00				

KM# 82 1000 SHILLINGS
24.8300 g., 0.9990 Silver 0.7975 oz. ASW, 38.6 mm. **Subject:** World of Football **Obv:** Arms with supporters **Rev:** Soccer ball globe **Edge:** Reeded

Date	Mintage	F	VF	XF	Unc	BU
2002 Proof	—	Value: 30.00				

KM# 83 1000 SHILLINGS
24.8300 g., 0.9990 Silver 0.7975 oz. ASW, 38.6 mm. **Subject:** World of Football **Obv:** Arms with supporters **Rev:** Soccer ball in net **Edge:** Reeded

Date	Mintage	F	VF	XF	Unc	BU
2002 Proof	—	Value: 30.00				

KM# 84 1000 SHILLINGS
24.8300 g., 0.9990 Silver 0.7975 oz. ASW, 38.6 mm. **Subject:** World of Football **Obv:** Arms with supporters **Rev:** Goalie catching ball, red kicker insert at right **Edge:** Reeded

Date	Mintage	F	VF	XF	Unc	BU
2002 Proof	—	Value: 30.00				

KM# 85 1000 SHILLINGS
24.8300 g., 0.9990 Silver 0.7975 oz. ASW, 38.6 mm. **Subject:** World of Football **Obv:** Arms with supporters **Rev:** Two players going after the ball, red runner insert at left **Edge:** Reeded

Date	Mintage	F	VF	XF	Unc	BU
2002 Proof	—	Value: 30.00				

KM# 86 1000 SHILLINGS
24.8300 g., 0.9990 Silver 0.7975 oz. ASW, 38.6 mm. **Subject:** World of Football **Obv:** Arms with supporters **Rev:** Player kicking ball, blue kicker insert at right **Edge:** Reeded

Date	Mintage	F	VF	XF	Unc	BU
2002 Proof	—	Value: 30.00				

KM# 101 1000 SHILLINGS
29.4400 g., Silver Plated Bronze (Specific gravity 8.8675), 38.5 mm. **Subject:** Gorillas **Obv:** Arms with supporters **Rev:** Seated gorilla **Edge:** Reeded

Date	Mintage	F	VF	XF	Unc	BU
2002 Proof	—	Value: 15.00				

KM# 102 1000 SHILLINGS
29.4400 g., Silver Plated Bronze (Specific gravity 8.8675), 38.5 mm. **Subject:** Gorillas **Obv:** Arms with supporters **Rev:** Gorilla eating **Edge:** Reeded

Date	Mintage	F	VF	XF	Unc	BU
2002 Proof	—	Value: 15.00				

KM# 103 1000 SHILLINGS
29.4400 g., Silver Plated Bronze (Specific gravity 8.8675), 38.5 mm. **Subject:** Gorillas **Obv:** Arms with supporters **Rev:** Gorilla on all fours **Edge:** Reeded

Date	Mintage	F	VF	XF	Unc	BU
2002 Proof	—	Value: 15.00				

KM# 104 1000 SHILLINGS
29.4400 g., Silver Plated Bronze (Specific gravity 8.8675), 38.5 mm. **Subject:** Gorillas **Obv:** Arms with supporters **Rev:** Gorilla female with infant **Edge:** Reeded

Date	Mintage	F	VF	XF	Unc	BU
2002 Proof	—	Value: 15.00				

KM# 106 1000 SHILLINGS
29.1600 g., Silver Plated Bronze (Specific gravity 8.8096), 38.6 mm. **Subject:** Marine Life **Obv:** Arms with supporters **Rev:** Multicolor sea horses **Edge:** Reeded

Date	Mintage	F	VF	XF	Unc	BU
2002 Proof	—	Value: 15.00				

KM# 107 1000 SHILLINGS
29.1600 g., Silver Plated Bronze (Specific gravity 8.8096), 38.6 mm. **Subject:** Marine Life **Obv:** Arms with supporters **Rev:** Multicolor Hammerhead sharks **Edge:** Reeded

Date	Mintage	F	VF	XF	Unc	BU
2002 Proof	—	Value: 12.50				

KM# 108 1000 SHILLINGS
29.1600 g., Silver Plated Bronze (Specific gravity 8.8096), 38.6 mm. **Subject:** Marine Life **Obv:** Arms with supporters **Rev:** Multicolor Stingray **Edge:** Reeded

Date	Mintage	F	VF	XF	Unc	BU
2002 Proof	—	Value: 12.50				

KM# 109 1000 SHILLINGS
29.1600 g., Silver Plated Bronze (Specific gravity 8.8096), 38.6 mm. **Subject:** Marine Life **Obv:** Arms with supporters **Rev:** Multicolor Seal **Edge:** Reeded

Date	Mintage	F	VF	XF	Unc	BU
2002 Proof	—	Value: 12.50				

KM# 110 1000 SHILLINGS
29.1600 g., Silver Plated Bronze (Specific gravity 8.8096), 38.6 mm. **Subject:** Marine Life **Obv:** Arms with supporters **Rev:** Multicolor sea turtle **Edge:** Reeded

Date	Mintage	F	VF	XF	Unc	BU
2002 Proof	—	Value: 12.50				

KM# 111 1000 SHILLINGS
29.1600 g., Silver Plated Bronze (Specific gravity 8.8096), 38.6 mm. **Subject:** Marine Life **Obv:** Arms with supporters **Rev:** Multicolor dolphins **Edge:** Reeded

Date	Mintage	F	VF	XF	Unc	BU
2002 Proof	—	Value: 12.50				

KM# 112 1000 SHILLINGS
29.1600 g., Silver Plated Bronze (Specific gravity 8.8096), 38.6 mm. **Subject:** Marine Life **Obv:** Arms with supporters **Rev:** Multicolor octopus **Edge:** Reeded

Date	Mintage	F	VF	XF	Unc	BU
2002 Proof	—	Value: 12.50				

KM# 113 1000 SHILLINGS
29.1600 g., Silver Plated Bronze (Specific gravity 8.8096), 38.6 mm. **Subject:** Marine Life **Obv:** Arms with supporters **Rev:** Multicolor red fish **Edge:** Reeded

Date	Mintage	F	VF	XF	Unc	BU
2002 Proof	—	Value: 15.00				

KM# 114 1000 SHILLINGS
29.1600 g., Silver Plated Bronze (Specific gravity 8.8096), 38.6 mm. **Subject:** Marine Life **Obv:** Arms with supporters **Rev:** Multicolor black fish with white dots **Edge:** Reeded

Date	Mintage	F	VF	XF	Unc	BU
2002 Proof	—	Value: 15.00				

KM# 115 1000 SHILLINGS
29.1600 g., Silver Plated Bronze (Specific gravity 8.8096), 38.6 mm. **Subject:** Marine Life **Obv:** Arms with supporters **Rev:** Multicolor yellow and black striped fish **Edge:** Reeded

Date	Mintage	F	VF	XF	Unc	BU
2002 Proof	—	Value: 15.00				

KM# 105 1000 SHILLINGS
29.2000 g., Silver Plated Bronze (Specific gravity 9.0123), 38.6 mm. **Subject:** Pope John Paul II **Obv:** Arms with supporters **Rev:** Pope saying mass, design of Zambian 1000 Kwacha KM-160 **Edge:** Reeded **Note:** Muling error

Date	Mintage	F	VF	XF	Unc	BU
2003 Proof	—	Value: 300				

KM# 216 1000 SHILLINGS
Bronze **Subject:** Christmas **Obv. Legend:** BANK OF UGANDA **Rev:** Peace on Earth

Date	Mintage	F	VF	XF	Unc	BU
2004	500	—	—	—	—	40.00

KM# 121 2000 SHILLINGS
25.0000 g., 0.9250 Silver 0.7435 oz. ASW, 38.6 mm. **Subject:** Queen Elizabeth's 75th Birthday **Obv:** Arms with supporters above crowned head right **Rev:** Queen accepting flowers from children **Edge:** Reeded

Date	Mintage	F	VF	XF	Unc	BU
2001 Proof	2,000	Value: 35.00				

KM# 75 2000 SHILLINGS
49.9000 g., 0.9990 Silver 1.6027 oz. ASW, 50 mm. **Subject:** Illusion: "Spirit of the Mountain" **Obv:** Crowned head right divides date above arms with supporters **Rev:** Landscape and tree that looks like a male portrait **Edge:** Reeded

Date	Mintage	F	VF	XF	Unc	BU
2001 Proof	—	Value: 50.00				

KM# 100 2000 SHILLINGS
31.4000 g., 0.9990 Silver 1.0085 oz. ASW, 38.8 mm. **Obv:** Crowned head right divides date above arms with supporters **Rev:** Bust of Henry M. Stanley facing **Edge:** Reeded

Date	Mintage	F	VF	XF	Unc	BU
2002	—	—	—	—	22.50	30.00

KM# 175 2000 SHILLINGS
15.5500 g., 0.9990 Silver 0.4994 oz. ASW **Series:** Famous Places in China **Subject:** Yugan Garden - Shanghai **Obv:** Two dragons **Obv. Legend:** BANK OF UGANDA

Date	Mintage	F	VF	XF	Unc	BU
2003 Proof	3,000	Value: 35.00				

KM# 187 2000 SHILLINGS
4.0000 g., 0.9999 Gold 0.1286 oz. AGW **Series:** Guanyin **Subject:** Fulun **Obv:** Lotus blossom **Obv. Legend:** BANK OF UGANDA

Date	Mintage	F	VF	XF	Unc	BU
2003 Proof	—	Value: 200				

KM# 205 2000 SHILLINGS
Silver **Subject:** XXVIII Summer Olympics - Athens 2004 **Obv. Legend:** BANK OF UGANDA **Rev:** Sprinter

Date	Mintage	F	VF	XF	Unc	BU
2003 Proof	500	Value: 60.00				

KM# 176 2000 SHILLINGS
15.5500 g., 0.9990 Silver 0.4994 oz. ASW **Series:** Famous Places in China **Subject:** Tiger Hill Pagoda - Jiangsu **Obv:** Two dragons **Obv. Legend:** BANK OF UGANDA

Date	Mintage	F	VF	XF	Unc	BU
2003 Proof	3,000	Value: 35.00				

KM# 177 2000 SHILLINGS
15.5500 g., 0.9990 Silver 0.4994 oz. ASW **Series:** Famous Places in China **Subject:** Mount Huangshan - Anhwei **Obv:** Two dragons **Obv. Legend:** BANK OF UGANDA

Date	Mintage	F	VF	XF	Unc	BU
2003 Proof	3,000	Value: 35.00				

KM# 178 2000 SHILLINGS
15.5500 g., 0.9990 Silver 0.4994 oz. ASW **Series:** Famous Places in China **Subject:** Zhangjiajie - Hunan **Obv:** Two dragons **Obv. Legend:** BANK OF UGANDA

Date	Mintage	F	VF	XF	Unc	BU
2003 Proof	3,000	Value: 35.00				

KM# 179 2000 SHILLINGS
15.5500 g., 0.9990 Silver 0.4994 oz. ASW **Series:** Famous Places in China **Subject:** Stone Forest - Yunnan **Obv:** Two dragons **Obv. Legend:** BANK OF UGANDA

Date	Mintage	F	VF	XF	Unc	BU
2003 Proof	3,000	Value: 35.00				

KM# 180 2000 SHILLINGS
15.5500 g., 0.9990 Silver 0.4994 oz. ASW **Series:** Famous Places in China **Subject:** Potala Palace - Lhasa, Tibet **Obv:** Two dragons **Obv. Legend:** BANK OF UGANDA

Date	Mintage	F	VF	XF	Unc	BU
2003 Proof	3,000	Value: 35.00				

KM# 181 2000 SHILLINGS
15.5500 g., 0.9990 Silver 0.4994 oz. ASW **Series:** Famous Places inChina **Subject:** Yangtse River Gorges **Obv:** Two dragons **Obv. Legend:** BANK OF UGANDA

Date	Mintage	F	VF	XF	Unc	BU
2003 Proof	3,000	Value: 35.00				

KM# 182 2000 SHILLINGS
31.1000 g., 0.9990 Silver 0.9988 oz. ASW **Series:** Chinese symbolism **Subject:** Harmony **Obv. Legend:** BANK OF UGANDA **Rev:** Dragon and phoenix

Date	Mintage	F	VF	XF	Unc	BU
2003 Proof	3,000	Value: 60.00				

KM# 183 2000 SHILLINGS
31.1000 g., 0.9990 Silver 0.9988 oz. ASW **Series:** Chinese symbolism **Subject:** Happiness **Obv. Legend:** BANK OF UGANDA **Rev:** Unicorn

Date	Mintage	F	VF	XF	Unc	BU
2003 Proof	3,000	Value: 60.00				

KM# 184 2000 SHILLINGS
31.1000 g., 0.9990 Silver 0.9988 oz. ASW **Series:** Chinese symbolism **Subject:** Health and long life **Obv. Legend:** BANK OF UGANDA **Rev:** Two cranes

Date	Mintage	F	VF	XF	Unc	BU
2003 Proof	3,000	Value: 60.00				

KM# 185 2000 SHILLINGS
31.1000 g., 0.9990 Silver 0.9988 oz. ASW **Series:** Chinese symbolism **Subject:** Success **Obv. Legend:** BANK OF UGANDA **Rev:** Carp

Date	Mintage	F	VF	XF	Unc	BU
2003 Proof	3,000	Value: 60.00				

KM# 186 2000 SHILLINGS
31.1000 g., 0.9990 Silver 0.9988 oz. ASW **Series:** Chinese symbolism **Subject:** Wealth **Obv. Legend:** BANK OF UGANDA **Rev:** Toad

Date	Mintage	F	VF	XF	Unc	BU
2003 Proof	3,000	Value: 60.00				

KM# 206 2000 SHILLINGS
31.1000 g., 0.9990 Silver 0.9988 oz. ASW **Series:** Chinese symbolic floral New Year paintings **Obv. Legend:** BANK OF UGANDA **Rev:** Carp and Lotus blossom - multicolor

Date	Mintage	F	VF	XF	Unc	BU
2004 Proof	2,000	Value: 60.00				

KM# 207 2000 SHILLINGS
31.1000 g., 0.9990 Silver 0.9988 oz. ASW **Series:** Chinese symbolic floral New Year paintings **Obv. Legend:** BANK OF UGANDA **Rev:** Deer - multicolor

Date	Mintage	F	VF	XF	Unc	BU
2004 Proof	2,000	Value: 60.00				

KM# 208 2000 SHILLINGS
31.1000 g., 0.9990 Silver 0.9988 oz. ASW **Series:** Chinese symbolic floral New Year paintings **Subject:** Abundance **Obv. Legend:** BANK OF UGANDA **Rev:** Fruit - multicolor

Date	Mintage	F	VF	XF	Unc	BU
2004 Proof	2,000	Value: 60.00				

KM# 209 2000 SHILLINGS
31.1000 g., 0.9990 Silver 0.9988 oz. ASW **Series:** Chinese symbolic floral New Year paintings **Subject:** Peace and prosperity **Obv. Legend:** BANK OF UGANDA **Rev:** Multicolor

Date	Mintage	F	VF	XF	Unc	BU
2004 Proof	2,000	Value: 60.00				

KM# 210 2000 SHILLINGS
31.1000 g., 0.9990 Silver 0.9988 oz. ASW **Series:** Chinese symbolic floral New Year paintings **Subject:** Happiness **Obv. Legend:** BANK OF UGANDA **Rev:** Multicolor

Date	Mintage	F	VF	XF	Unc	BU
2004 Proof	2,000	Value: 60.00				

KM# 211 2000 SHILLINGS
31.1000 g., 0.9990 Silver 0.9988 oz. ASW **Series:** Chinese Dieties **Subject:** Happiness **Obv. Legend:** BANK OF UGANDA **Rev:** Fú - multicolor

Date	Mintage	F	VF	XF	Unc	BU
2004 Proof	2,000	Value: 60.00				

KM# 212 2000 SHILLINGS
31.1000 g., 0.9990 Silver 0.9988 oz. ASW **Series:** Chinese Deities **Subject:** Prosperity **Obv. Legend:** BANK OF UGANDA **Rev:** Lù - multicolor

Date	Mintage	F	VF	XF	Unc	BU
2004 Proof	2,000	Value: 60.00				

KM# 213 2000 SHILLINGS
31.1000 g., 0.9990 Silver 0.9988 oz. ASW **Series:** Chinese Dieties **Subject:** Health and Long Life **Obv. Legend:** BANK OF UGANDA **Rev:** Shòu - multicolor

Date	Mintage	F	VF	XF	Unc	BU
2004 Proof	2,000	Value: 60.00				

KM# 217 2000 SHILLINGS
31.1000 g., 0.9990 Silver 0.9988 oz. ASW **Obv:** Lotus blossom **Obv. Legend:** BANK OF UGANDA **Rev:** Guanyin - multicolor

Date	Mintage	F	VF	XF	Unc	BU
2005 Proof	2,000	Value: 75.00				

KM# 221 2000 SHILLINGS
Silver Plated Bronze **Series:** XIX World Football Championship - South Africa 2010 **Obv:** National arms **Obv. Legend:** BANK OF UGANDA **Rev:** Player about to kick

Date	Mintage	F	VF	XF	Unc	BU
2005 Proof	10,000	Value: 15.00				

KM# 222 2000 SHILLINGS
Silver Plated Bronze **Series:** XIX World Football Championship - South Afrika 2010 **Obv:** National arms **Obv. Legend:** BANK OF UGANDA **Rev:** Ball in net

Date	Mintage	F	VF	XF	Unc	BU
2005 Proof	10,000	Value: 15.00				

KM# 223 2000 SHILLINGS
Silver Plated Bronze **Series:** XIX World Football Championship - South Afrika 2010 **Obv:** National arms **Obv. Legend:** BANK OF UGANDA **Rev:** Player, map of Afrika

Date	Mintage	F	VF	XF	Unc	BU
2005 Proof	10,000	Value: 15.00				

KM# 224 2000 SHILLINGS
Silver Plated Bronze **Series:** XIX World Football Championship - South Afrika 2010 **Obv:** National arms **Obv. Legend:** BANK OF UGANDA **Rev:** Goalkeeper with ball

Date	Mintage	F	VF	XF	Unc	BU
2005 Proof	10,000	Value: 15.00				

KM# 225 2000 SHILLINGS
Silver Plated Bronze **Series:** XIX World Football Championship - South Afrika 2010 **Obv:** National arms **Obv. Legend:** BANK OF UGANDA **Rev:** Player and ball

Date	Mintage	F	VF	XF	Unc	BU
2005 Proof	10,000	Value: 15.00				

KM# 226 2000 SHILLINGS
40.0000 g., Gilt Bronze **Series:** Zodiac **Subject:** Year of the Dog **Obv:** Two dragons **Obv. Legend:** BANK OF UGANDA **Rev:** Three dogs - multicolor

Date	Mintage	F	VF	XF	Unc	BU
2006 Proof	—	Value: 45.00				

KM# 227 2000 SHILLINGS
40.0000 g., Gilt Bronze **Series:** Zodiac **Subject:** Year of the Dog **Obv:** Archaic Chinese characters **Obv. Legend:** BANK OF UGANDA **Rev:** Two dogs - multicolor

Date	Mintage	F	VF	XF	Unc	BU
2006 Proof	—	Value: 45.00				

KM# 227a 2000 SHILLINGS
31.1000 g., 0.9990 Silver 0.9988 oz. ASW **Series:** Zodiac **Subject:** Year of the Dog **Obv:** Archaic Chinese characters **Obv. Legend:** BANK OF UGANDA **Rev:** Two dogs - multicolor

Date	Mintage	F	VF	XF	Unc	BU
2006 Proof	3,000	Value: 75.00				

KM# 234 2000 SHILLINGS
31.1000 g., 0.9990 Silver 0.9988 oz. ASW **Series:** Zodiac **Subject:** Year of the Dog **Obv. Legend:** BANK OF UGANDA **Rev:** Tibet Terrier with pup surrounded by 10 symbols

Date	Mintage	F	VF	XF	Unc	BU
2006 Proof	—	Value: 75.00				

KM# 172 5000 SHILLINGS
4.0000 g., 0.9999 Gold 0.1286 oz. AGW **Series:** Guanyin **Subject:** Chilian **Obv:** Lotus blossom **Obv. Legend:** BANK OF UGANDA

Date	Mintage	F	VF	XF	Unc	BU
2001 Proof	—	Value: 200				

KM# 174 5000 SHILLINGS
4.0000 g., 0.9999 Gold 0.1286 oz. AGW **Series:** Guanyin **Subject:** Fuyu **Obv:** Lotus blossom **Obv. Legend:** BANK OF UGANDA

Date	Mintage	F	VF	XF	Unc	BU
2002 Proof	—	Value: 200				

KM# 87 5000 SHILLINGS
33.7300 g., 0.8500 Silver 0.9217 oz. ASW, 38.65 mm. **Subject:** "The Big Five" **Obv:** Arms with supporters **Rev:** Rhinoceros **Edge:** Reeded

Date	Mintage	F	VF	XF	Unc	BU
2002 Proof	—	Value: 50.00				

KM# 88 5000 SHILLINGS
33.7300 g., 0.8500 Silver 0.9217 oz. ASW, 38.65 mm. **Subject:** "The Big Five" **Obv:** Arms with supporters **Rev:** Lion **Edge:** Reeded

Date	Mintage	F	VF	XF	Unc	BU
2002 Proof	—	Value: 50.00				

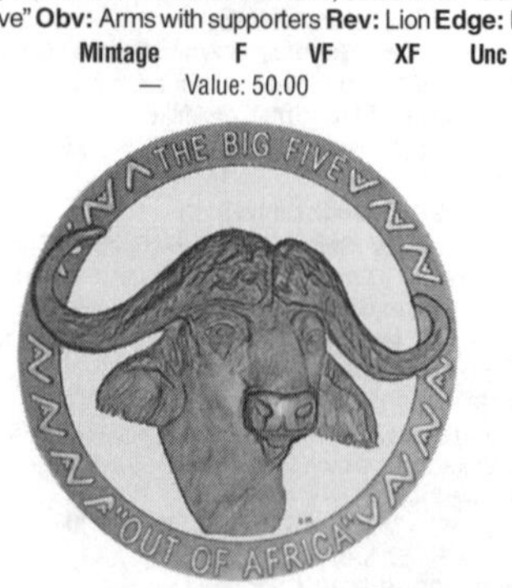

KM# 89 5000 SHILLINGS
33.7300 g., 0.8500 Silver 0.9217 oz. ASW, 38.65 mm. **Subject:** "The Big Five" **Obv:** Arms with supporters **Rev:** Cape Buffalo **Edge:** Reeded

Date	Mintage	F	VF	XF	Unc	BU
2002 Proof	—	Value: 50.00				

KM# 90 5000 SHILLINGS
33.7300 g., 0.8500 Silver 0.9217 oz. ASW, 38.65 mm. **Subject:** "The Big Five" **Obv:** Arms with supporters **Rev:** Leopard **Edge:** Reeded

Date	Mintage	F	VF	XF	Unc	BU
2002 Proof	—	Value: 50.00				

KM# 91 5000 SHILLINGS
33.7300 g., 0.8500 Silver 0.9217 oz. ASW, 38.65 mm. **Subject:** "The Big Five" **Obv:** Arms with supporters **Rev:** Elephant **Edge:** Reeded

Date	Mintage	F	VF	XF	Unc	BU
2002 Proof	—	Value: 50.00				

KM# 96 5000 SHILLINGS
31.1035 g., 0.9990 Silver 0.9990 oz. ASW, 40.6 mm. **Subject:** Matthew Flinders **Obv:** Arms with supporters below crowned head right dividing date **Rev:** Multicolor bust half left at right with ship and harbor scene at left **Edge:** Plain **Shape:** Continent of Australia

Date	Mintage	F	VF	XF	Unc	BU
2002 Proof	2,500	Value: 47.50				

KM# 97 5000 SHILLINGS
31.1035 g., 0.9990 Silver 0.9990 oz. ASW, 40.6 mm. **Subject:** Matthew Flinders - H. M. S. Investigator **Obv:** Crowned head right divides date above arms with supporters **Rev:** Multicolor cameo at upper right of ship **Edge:** Plain **Shape:** Continent of Australia

Date	Mintage	F	VF	XF	Unc	BU
2002 Proof	2,500	Value: 47.50				

KM# 98 5000 SHILLINGS
31.1035 g., 0.9990 Silver 0.9990 oz. ASW, 40.6 mm. **Subject:** Matthew Flinders - Meeting at Encounter Bay **Obv:** Crowned head right divides date above arms with supporters **Rev:** Date and inscription divides multicolor busts facing **Edge:** Plain **Shape:** Continent of Australia

Date	Mintage	F	VF	XF	Unc	BU
2002 Proof	2,500	Value: 47.50				

KM# 99 5000 SHILLINGS
31.1035 g., 0.9990 Silver 0.9990 oz. ASW, 40.6 mm. **Subject:** Matthew Flinders - First Circumnavigation of Terra Australia - 1802 **Rev:** Multicolor bust right on Australian map showing his route around Australia **Edge:** Plain **Shape:** Continent of Australia

Date	Mintage	F	VF	XF	Unc	BU
2002 Proof	2,500	Value: 47.50				

KM# 214 5000 SHILLINGS
4.0000 g., 0.9999 Gold 0.1286 oz. AGW **Series:** Guanyin **Subject:** Shile **Obv:** Lotus blossom **Obv. Legend:** BANK OF UGANDA

Date	Mintage	F	VF	XF	Unc	BU
2004 Proof	—	Value: 200				

KM# 220 5000 SHILLINGS
4.0000 g., 0.9999 Gold 0.1286 oz. AGW **Series:** Guanyin **Subject:** Songjing **Obv:** Lotus blossom **Obv. Legend:** BANK OF UGANDA

Date	Mintage	F	VF	XF	Unc	BU
2005 Proof	—	Value: 200				

KM# 228 6000 SHILLINGS
4.0000 g., 0.9999 Gold 0.1286 oz. AGW **Series:** Zodiac **Subject:** Year of the Dog **Obv:** Archaic Chinese characters **Obv. Legend:** BANK OF UGANDA **Rev:** Yorkshire Terrier and "Fú" - Happiness

Date	Mintage	F	VF	XF	Unc	BU
2006 Proof	14,000	Value: 225				

KM# 229 6000 SHILLINGS
4.0000 g., 0.9999 Gold 0.1286 oz. AGW **Series:** Zodiac **Subject:** Year of the Dog **Obv:** Archaic Chinese characters **Obv. Legend:** BANK OF UGANDA **Rev:** Yorkshire Terrier and "Lù" - Prosperity

Date	Mintage	F	VF	XF	Unc	BU
2006 Proof	14,000	Value: 225				

KM# 230 6000 SHILLINGS
4.0000 g., 0.9999 Gold 0.1286 oz. AGW **Series:** Zodiac **Subject:** Year of the Dog **Obv:** Archaic Chinese characters **Obv. Legend:** BANK OF UGANDA **Rev:** Yorkshire Terrier and "Shòu" - Health and Long Life

Date	Mintage	F	VF	XF	Unc	BU
2006 Proof	14,000	Value: 225				

KM# 235 6000 SHILLINGS
3.1100 g., 0.9999 Gold 0.1000 oz. AGW **Series:** Zodiac **Subject:** Year of the Dog **Obv. Legend:** BANK OF UGANDA **Rev:** Tibet Terrier with pup surrounded by 10 symbols

Date	Mintage	F	VF	XF	Unc	BU
2006 Proof	—	Value: 150				

KM# 231 8000 SHILLINGS
8.0000 g., 0.9999 Gold 0.2572 oz. AGW **Series:** Zodiac **Subject:** Year of the Dog **Obv:** Archaic Chinese characters **Obv. Legend:** BANK OF UGANDA **Rev:** Yorkshire Terrier and "Fú" - Happiness

Date	Mintage	F	VF	XF	Unc	BU
2006 Proof	1,000	Value: 375				

KM# 232 8000 SHILLINGS
8.0000 g., 0.9999 Gold 0.2572 oz. AGW **Series:** Zodiac **Subject:** Year of the Dog **Obv:** Archaic Chinese characters **Obv. Legend:** BANK OF UGANDA **Rev:** Yorkshire Terrier and "Lù" - Prosperity

Date	Mintage	F	VF	XF	Unc	BU
2006 Proof	1,000	Value: 375				

KM# 215 10000 SHILLINGS
10.0000 g., 0.9999 Gold 0.3215 oz. AGW **Obv:** Lotus blossom **Obv. Legend:** BANK OF UGANDA **Rev:** Buddha

Date	Mintage	F	VF	XF	Unc	BU
2004 Proof	3,000	Value: 425				

KM# 76 12000 SHILLINGS
6.2207 g., 0.9999 Gold 0.2000 oz. AGW, 22 mm. **Subject:** Illusion: "Spirit of the Mountain" **Obv:** Crowned head right divides date above arms with supporters **Rev:** Landscape and tree that looks like a male portrait **Edge:** Reeded

Date	Mintage	F	VF	XF	Unc	BU
2001 Proof	—	Value: 220				

KM# 236 20000 SHILLINGS
15.5500 g., 0.9999 Gold 0.4999 oz. AGW **Series:** Zodiac **Subject:** Year of the Dog **Obv. Legend:** BANK OF UGANDA **Rev:** Tibet Terrier with pup surrounded by 10 symbols

Date	Mintage	F	VF	XF	Unc	BU
2006 Proof	—	Value: 650				

UKRAINE

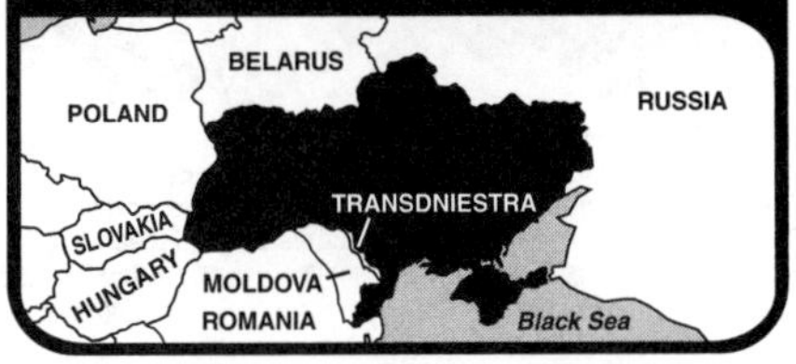

Ukraine (formerly the Ukrainian Soviet Socialist Republic) is bordered by Russia to the east, Russia and Belarus to the north, Poland, Slovakia and Hungary to the west, Romania and Moldova to the southwest and in the south by the Black Sea and the Sea of Azov. It has an area of 233,088 sq. mi. (603,700 sq. km.) and a population of 51.9 million. Capital: Kyiv (Kiev). Coal, grain, vegetables and heavy industrial machinery are major exports.

Ukraine is a charter member of the United Nations and has inherited the third largest nuclear arsenal in the world.

MONETARY SYSTEM
(1) Kopiyka
(2) Kopiyky КОПІЙКИ
(5 and up) Kopiyok КОПІЙОК
100 Kopiyok = 1 Hrynia ГРИВЕНЬ
100,000 Karbovanetsiv = 1 Hryni or Hryven)

REPUBLIC

REFORM COINAGE

September 2, 1996

100,000 Karbovanets = 1 Hryvnia; 100 Kopiyok = 1 Hryvnia; The Kopiyok has replaced the Karbovanet

KM# 6 KOPIYKA
1.5300 g., Stainless Steel, 15.96 mm. **Obv:** National arms **Rev:** Value within wreath **Edge:** Plain

Date	Mintage	F	VF	XF	Unc	BU
2001	—	—	—	0.35	0.75	—
2002	—	—	—	0.35	0.75	—
2003	—	—	—	0.35	0.75	—
2004	—	—	—	0.35	0.75	—
2005	—	—	—	0.35	0.75	—
2006	—	—	—	0.35	0.75	—
2007	—	—	—	0.35	0.75	—

KM# 4b 2 KOPIYKY
1.8000 g., Stainless Steel, 17.3 mm. **Obv:** National arms **Rev:** Value in wreath **Edge:** Plain

Date	Mintage	F	VF	XF	Unc	BU
2001	—	—	0.20	0.50	1.00	—
2002	—	—	0.20	0.50	1.00	—
2004	—	—	0.20	0.50	1.00	—
2005	—	—	0.20	0.50	1.00	—
2006	—	—	0.20	0.50	1.00	—
2007	—	—	0.20	0.50	1.00	—

KM# 7 5 KOPIYOK
4.3000 g., Stainless Steel, 23.91 mm. **Obv:** National arms **Rev:** Value within wreath **Edge:** Reeded

Date	Mintage	F	VF	XF	Unc	BU
2001	—	—	0.50	3.00	6.00	—
2003	—	—	—	0.50	1.00	—
2004	—	—	—	0.50	1.00	—
2005	—	—	—	0.50	1.00	—
2006	—	—	—	0.50	1.00	—
2007	—	—	—	0.50	1.00	—

KM# 1.1b 10 KOPIYOK
1.7000 g., Aluminum-Bronze, 16.24 mm. **Obv:** National arms **Rev:** Value within wreath

Date	Mintage	F	VF	XF	Unc	BU
2001	—	—	2.00	5.00	6.00	—
2002	—	—	0.60	1.25	2.50	—
2003	—	—	0.50	1.00	2.25	—
2004	—	—	0.50	1.00	2.25	—
2005	—	—	0.50	1.00	2.25	—
2006	—	—	0.50	1.00	2.25	—
2007	—	—	0.50	1.00	2.25	—

KM# 2.1b 25 KOPIYOK
Aluminum-Bronze

Date	Mintage	F	VF	XF	Unc	BU
2001	—	—	0.80	3.00	6.00	—
2006	—	—	0.80	3.00	6.00	—
2007	—	—	0.80	3.00	6.00	—

KM# 3.3b 50 KOPIYOK
Aluminum-Bronze

Date	Mintage	F	VF	XF	Unc	BU
2001	—	—	1.00	2.00	4.00	—
2006	—	—	1.00	2.00	4.00	—
2007	—	—	1.00	2.00	4.00	—

KM# 8b HRYVNIA
6.9000 g., Aluminum-Bronze

Date	Mintage	F	VF	XF	Unc	BU
2001	—	—	—	2.50	4.50	—
2002	—	—	—	3.50	6.50	—
2003	—	—	—	2.50	4.50	—

KM# 208 HRYVNIA
6.8000 g., Aluminum-Bronze, 26 mm. **Subject:** 60th Anniversary - Victory over the Nazis **Obv:** National arms above value **Rev:** Uniform lapel with Soviet military medals group **Edge:** Lettered **Edge Lettering:** Date and denomination

Date	Mintage	F	VF	XF	Unc	BU
2004	5,000,000	—	—	—	4.00	—

KM# 209 HRYVNIA
6.7400 g., Aluminum-Bronze, 26 mm. **Obv:** National arms above value **Rev:** Half length figure of Volodymyr the Great facing holding church model building and staff **Edge:** Lettered **Edge Lettering:** Date and denomination

Date	Mintage	F	VF	XF	Unc	BU
2004	10,000,000	—	—	—	3.50	—
2005	—	—	—	—	3.00	—
2006	—	—	—	—	3.00	—

KM# 228 HRYVNIA
6.8000 g., Aluminum-Bronze, 26 mm. **Subject:** WW II Victory 60th Anniversary **Obv:** Value **Rev:** Soldiers in a "V" of search lights **Edge:** Reeded

Date	Mintage	F	VF	XF	Unc	BU
2005	5,000,000	—	—	—	4.00	—

KM# 8a HRYVNIA
7.1000 g., Brass, 26 mm. **Obv:** National arms **Rev:** Value, sprigs and designs **Note:** Prev. KM#8.

Date	Mintage	F	VF	XF	Unc	BU
2006	—	—	—	2.50	4.50	—

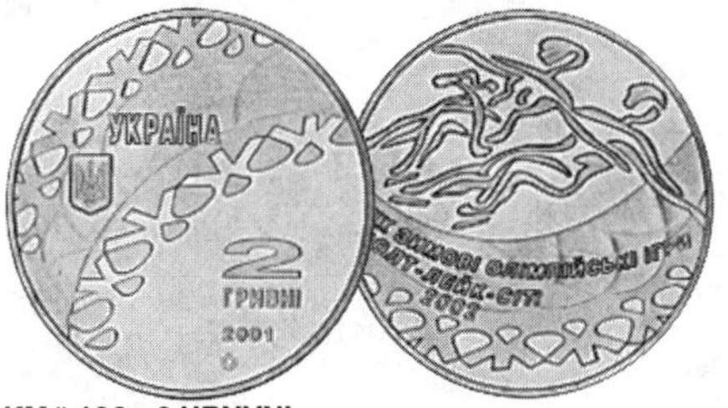

KM# 106 2 HRYVNI
12.8000 g., Copper-Nickel-Zinc, 31 mm. **Series:** Olympics - Salt Lake City, 2002 **Obv:** National arms, value and designs **Rev:** Stylized ice dancing couple **Edge:** Reeded

Date	Mintage	F	VF	XF	Unc	BU
2001	30,000	—	—	—	12.00	—

KM# 133 2 HRYVNI
12.8000 g., Copper-Nickel-Zinc, 31 mm. **Subject:** Kindness to Children **Obv:** National arms above value flanked by sprigs and doves **Rev:** Two children frolicking under fountain of knowledge **Edge:** Reeded

Date	Mintage	F	VF	XF	Unc	BU
2001	100,000	—	—	—	6.00	—

KM# 134 2 HRYVNI
12.8000 g., Copper-Nickel-Zinc, 31 mm. **Subject:** 5th Anniversary of Constitution **Obv:** National arms above value flanked by sprigs **Rev:** Building above book flanked by sprigs **Edge:** Reeded

Date	Mintage	F	VF	XF	Unc	BU
2001	30,000	—	—	—	16.00	—

KM# 111 2 HRYVNI
12.8000 g., Copper-Nickel-Zinc, 31 mm. **Series:** Flora and Fauna **Obv:** National arms and date divides wreath, value within **Rev:** Lynx and offspring **Edge:** Reeded

Date	Mintage	F	VF	XF	Unc	BU
2001	30,000	—	—	—	22.00	—

KM# 136 2 HRYVNI
12.8000 g., Copper-Nickel-Zinc, 31 mm. **Subject:** Mykolaiv Zoo **Obv:** Man running alongside large cat **Rev:** Twelve animals **Edge:** Reeded

Date	Mintage	F	VF	XF	Unc	BU
2001	30,000	—	—	—	30.00	—

KM# 137 2 HRYVNI
12.8000 g., Copper-Nickel-Zinc, 31 mm. **Subject:** Mykhailo Ostrohradskiy (Mathematician) **Obv:** National arms divides date and value divided by wavy line graph **Rev:** Head 1/4 left **Edge:** Reeded

Date	Mintage	F	VF	XF	Unc	BU
2001	30,000	—	—	—	10.00	—

KM# 138 2 HRYVNI
12.8000 g., Copper-Nickel-Zinc, 31 mm. **Subject:** Larix Polonica **Obv:** Value within wreath **Rev:** Pine branch with cone **Edge:** Reeded

Date	Mintage	F	VF	XF	Unc	BU
2001	30,000	—	—	—	18.50	—

KM# 139 2 HRYVNI
12.8000 g., Copper-Nickel-Zinc, 31 mm. **Subject:** Volodymyr Dal **Obv:** Books **Rev:** Head right **Edge:** Reeded

Date	Mintage	F	VF	XF	Unc	BU
2001	30,000	—	—	—	10.00	—

KM# 147 2 HRYVNI
12.8000 g., Copper-Nickel-Zinc, 31 mm. **Series:** Olympics - Salt lake City, 2002 **Obv:** National arms and value on ice design **Rev:** Stylized hockey player **Edge:** Reeded

Date	Mintage	F	VF	XF	Unc	BU
2001	30,000	—	—	—	12.00	—

KM# 149 2 HRYVNI
12.8000 g., Copper-Nickel-Zinc, 31 mm. **Subject:** Mykhailo Drahomanov (Historian, Politician, etc.) **Obv:** National arms and value **Rev:** Bust right **Edge:** Reeded

Date	Mintage	F	VF	XF	Unc	BU
2001	30,000	—	—	—	10.00	—

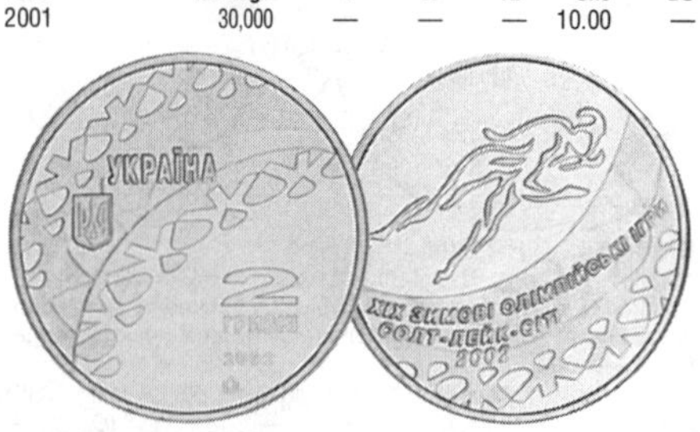

KM# 150 2 HRYVNI
12.8000 g., Copper-Nickel-Zinc, 31 mm. **Series:** Olympics - Salt lake City, 2002 **Obv:** National arms and value on ice design **Rev:** Speed skater **Edge:** Reeded

Date	Mintage	F	VF	XF	Unc	BU
2002	30,000	—	—	—	10.00	—

KM# 155 2 HRYVNI
12.8000 g., Copper-Nickel-Zinc, 31 mm. **Series:** Flora and Fauna **Obv:** National arms and date divides wreath, value within **Rev:** Eurasian Eagle Owl **Edge:** Reeded

Date	Mintage	F	VF	XF	Unc	BU
2002	30,000	—	—	—	30.00	—

KM# 156 2 HRYVNI
12.8000 g., Copper-Nickel-Zinc, 31 mm. **Subject:** Olympics - Athens, 2004 **Obv:** Two ancient figures above value **Rev:** Swimmer **Edge:** Reeded

Date	Mintage	F	VF	XF	Unc	BU
2002 Prooflike	30,000	—	—	—	10.00	—

KM# 166 2 HRYVNI
12.8000 g., Copper-Nickel-Zinc, 31 mm. **Subject:** Leonid Glibov, writer (1827-1893) **Obv:** National arms and value within scroll and wreath **Rev:** 1/2-length bust right **Edge:** Reeded

Date	Mintage	F	VF	XF	Unc	BU
2002	30,000	—	—	—	10.00	—

KM# 154 2 HRYVNI
12.8000 g., Copper-Nickel-Zinc, 31 mm. **Subject:** Mykola Lysenko (composer) **Obv:** Musical score and value **Rev:** Head 1/4 right **Edge:** Reeded

Date	Mintage	F	VF	XF	Unc	BU
2002	30,000	—	—	—	10.00	—

KM# 167 2 HRYVNI
12.8000 g., Copper-Nickel-Zinc, 31 mm. **Series:** Flora and Fauna **Obv:** National arms and date divides wreath, value within **Rev:** European Bison **Edge:** Reeded

Date	Mintage	F	VF	XF	Unc	BU
2003	50,000	—	—	—	17.00	—

KM# 168 2 HRYVNI
12.8000 g., Copper-Nickel-Zinc, 31 mm. **Obv:** National arms and date divides wreath, value within **Rev:** Long-snouted Sea Horse **Edge:** Reeded

Date	Mintage	F	VF	XF	Unc	BU
2003	50,000	—	—	—	17.50	—

KM# 169 2 HRYVNI
12.8000 g., Copper-Nickel-Zinc, 31 mm. **Subject:** Volodymyr Vernadskyi (academic) **Obv:** National arms, value and world globe **Rev:** Head on hand looking down **Edge:** Reeded

Date	Mintage	F	VF	XF	Unc	BU
2003	30,000	—	—	—	10.00	—

KM# 170 2 HRYVNI
12.8000 g., Copper-Nickel-Zinc, 31 mm. **Subject:** Volodymyr Korolenko (writer) **Obv:** National arms above book and value **Rev:** Bearded head 1/4 right above dates **Edge:** Reeded

Date	Mintage	F	VF	XF	Unc	BU
2003	30,000	—	—	—	10.00	—

KM# 171 2 HRYVNI
12.8000 g., Copper-Nickel-Zinc, 31 mm. **Subject:** Viacheslav Chornovil (politician) **Obv:** Arms with supporters within beaded circle **Rev:** Head 1/4 left **Edge:** Reeded

Date	Mintage	F	VF	XF	Unc	BU
2003	30,000	—	—	—	12.00	—

KM# 178 2 HRYVNI
1.2400 g., 0.9999 Gold 0.0399 oz. AGW, 13.92 mm. **Obv:** National arms flanked by dates within beaded circle **Rev:** Spotted Salamander divides beaded circle **Edge:** Plain

Date	Mintage	F	VF	XF	Unc	BU
2003	10,000	—	—	—	—	150

KM# 179 2 HRYVNI
12.8000 g., Copper-Nickel-Zinc, 31 mm. **Subject:** Singer Boris Gmyrya **Obv:** Value, arms ,date and musical symbol **Rev:** Head 1/4 left and dates **Edge:** Reeded

Date	Mintage	F	VF	XF	Unc	BU
2003	30,000	—	—	—	10.00	—

KM# 180 2 HRYVNI
12.8000 g., Copper-Nickel-Zinc, 31 mm. **Subject:** 70th Anniversary National Aviation University **Obv:** World globe behind national arms, value and date **Rev:** Wright Brothers biplane **Edge:** Reeded

Date	Mintage	F	VF	XF	Unc	BU
2003	30,000	—	—	—	12.50	—

KM# 181 2 HRYVNI
12.8000 g., Copper-Nickel-Zinc, 31 mm. **Subject:** Ostap Veresay (musician) **Obv:** Musical stringed instrument and ornamental design **Rev:** Bust facing playing stringed instrument **Edge:** Reeded

Date	Mintage	F	VF	XF	Unc	BU
2003	30,000	—	—	—	10.00	—

KM# 182 2 HRYVNI
12.8000 g., Copper-Nickel-Zinc, 31 mm. **Subject:** Olympics **Obv:** Two ancient women with seedlings **Rev:** Boxer **Edge:** Reeded

Date	Mintage	F	VF	XF	Unc	BU
2003	30,000	—	—	—	10.00	—

KM# 183 2 HRYVNI
12.8000 g., Copper-Nickel-Zinc, 31 mm. **Subject:** Vasyl Sukhomlynski (teacher) **Obv:** Children, books, value and national arms **Rev:** Head 1/4 right **Edge:** Reeded

Date	Mintage	F	VF	XF	Unc	BU
2003	30,000	—	—	—	8.50	—

KM# 184 2 HRYVNI
12.8000 g., Copper-Nickel-Zinc, 31 mm. **Subject:** Andriy Malyshko (poet) **Obv:** Ornamental shawl, national arms and value **Rev:** Head 1/4 right flanked by radiant sun and tree **Edge:** Reeded

Date	Mintage	F	VF	XF	Unc	BU
2003	30,000	—	—	—	8.50	—

KM# 201 2 HRYVNI
12.8000 g., Copper-Nickel-Zinc, 31 mm. **Subject:** Azov Dolphin **Obv:** National arms and date divides wreath, value within **Rev:** Harbor Porpoises **Edge:** Reeded

Date	Mintage	F	VF	XF	Unc	BU
2004	30,000	—	—	—	15.00	—

KM# 202 2 HRYVNI
12.8000 g., Copper-Nickel-Zinc, 31 mm. **Subject:** Football World Cup - 2006 **Obv:** Soccer ball in net **Rev:** Two soccer players **Edge:** Reeded

Date	Mintage	F	VF	XF	Unc	BU
2004	50,000	—	—	—	8.00	—

KM# 203 2 HRYVNI
12.8000 g., Copper-Nickel-Zinc, 31 mm. **Subject:** Serhiy Lyfar (ballet artist) **Obv:** Stylized dancer **Rev:** Head right **Edge:** Reeded

Date	Mintage	F	VF	XF	Unc	BU
2004	30,000	—	—	—	10.00	—

KM# 210 2 HRYVNI
12.8000 g., Copper-Nickel-Zinc, 31 mm. **Subject:** 170 Years of the Kyiv National University **Obv:** National arms in center above value dividing scientific items **Rev:** University building main entrance **Edge:** Reeded

Date	Mintage	F	VF	XF	Unc	BU
2004	50,000	—	—	—	8.00	—

KM# 211 2 HRYVNI
12.8000 g., Copper-Nickel-Zinc, 31 mm. **Subject:** Oleksander Dovzhenko (movie producer, writer) **Obv:** Boy standing in small boat **Rev:** Head facing **Edge:** Reeded

Date	Mintage	F	VF	XF	Unc	BU
2004	30,000	—	—	—	10.00	—

KM# 212 2 HRYVNI
12.8000 g., Copper-Nickel-Zinc, 31 mm. **Subject:** Mykola Bazhan (poet, translator) **Obv:** Winged pens and value **Rev:** Head 1/4 left **Edge:** Reeded

Date	Mintage	F	VF	XF	Unc	BU
2004	30,000	—	—	—	10.00	—

KM# 213 2 HRYVNI
12.8000 g., Copper-Nickel-Zinc, 31 mm. **Subject:** Mykhailo Kotsubynsky (writer) **Obv:** Two reclining figures **Rev:** Head 1/4 right **Edge:** Reeded

Date	Mintage	F	VF	XF	Unc	BU
2004	30,000	—	—	—	10.00	—

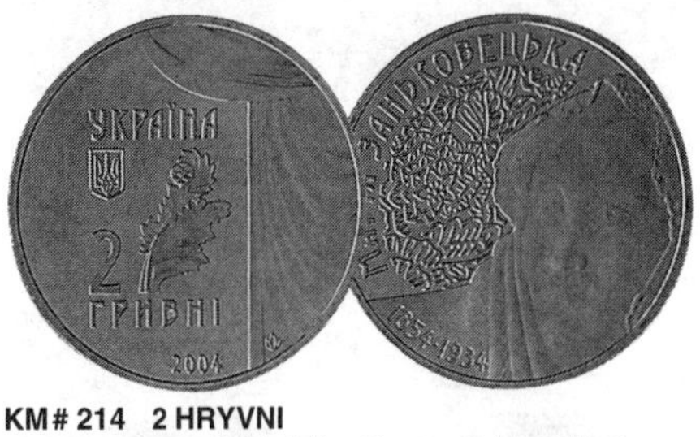

KM# 214 2 HRYVNI
12.8000 g., Copper-Nickel-Zinc, 31 mm. **Subject:** Maria Zankovetska (actress) **Obv:** National arms, value and drawn curtain **Rev:** Hooded head 1/4 left **Edge:** Reeded

Date	Mintage	F	VF	XF	Unc	BU
2004	30,000	—	—	—	10.00	—

KM# 215 2 HRYVNI
12.8000 g., Copper-Nickel-Zinc, 31 mm. **Subject:** Mykhailo Maksymovych (historian, archaeologist) **Obv:** National arms above building and value **Rev:** Bust left **Edge:** Reeded

Date	Mintage	F	VF	XF	Unc	BU
2004	30,000	—	—	—	10.00	—

KM# 216 2 HRYVNI
12.8000 g., Copper-Nickel-Zinc, 31 mm. **Subject:** Mykhailo Deregus (painter) **Obv:** National arms and value on artists palette **Rev:** Head right **Edge:** Reeded

Date	Mintage	F	VF	XF	Unc	BU
2004	30,000	—	—	—	10.00	—

KM# 217 2 HRYVNI
12.8000 g., Copper-Nickel-Zinc, 31 mm. **Subject:** Nuclear Power Engineering of Ukraine **Obv:** National arms and value in atomic design **Rev:** Nuclear reactor **Edge:** Reeded

Date	Mintage	F	VF	XF	Unc	BU
2004	30,000	—	—	—	12.50	—

KM# 227 2 HRYVNI
1.2400 g., 0.9999 Gold 0.0399 oz. AGW, 13.92 mm. **Obv:** National arms divides dates within beaded circle **Rev:** Flying White Stork divides beaded circle **Edge:** Plain

Date	Mintage	F	VF	XF	Unc	BU
2004	10,000	—	—	—	—	150

KM# 330 2 HRYVNI
12.8000 g., Copper-Nickel-Zinc, 31 mm. **Subject:** 200th Anniversary of Kharkiv University **Obv:** National arms and solar system **Rev:** University buildings and reflection **Edge:** Reeded

Date	Mintage	F	VF	XF	Unc	BU
2004	50,000	—	—	—	9.00	—

KM# 331 2 HRYVNI
12.8000 g., Copper-Nickel-Zinc, 31 mm. **Subject:** Ukraine National Academy of Law named after Yaroslav the Wise **Obv:** National arms above National Academy of Law arms and date **Rev:** Building **Edge:** Reeded

Date	Mintage	F	VF	XF	Unc	BU
2004	30,000	—	—	—	12.50	—

KM# 332 2 HRYVNI
12.8000 g., Copper-Nickel-Zinc, 31 mm. **Subject:** Yuri Fedkovych (poet, writer) **Obv:** National arms, value and man on horse **Rev:** Bust 1/4 right and dates **Edge:** Reeded

Date	Mintage	F	VF	XF	Unc	BU
2004	30,000	—	—	—	9.00	—

KM# 346 2 HRYVNI
12.8000 g., Copper-Nickel-Zinc, 31 mm. **Subject:** Boris Liatoshynsky (composer) **Obv:** Musical G Clef symbol and value below national arms **Rev:** Head 1/4 left **Edge:** Reeded

Date	Mintage	F	VF	XF	Unc	BU
2005	20,000	—	—	—	10.00	—

KM# 347 2 HRYVNI
12.8000 g., Copper-Nickel-Zinc, 31 mm. **Subject:** Volodymyr Filatov (surgeon) **Obv:** Light passing through the lens of an eye **Rev:** Head with cap facing **Edge:** Reeded

Date	Mintage	F	VF	XF	Unc	BU
2005	20,000	—	—	—	10.00	—

KM# 348 2 HRYVNI
12.8000 g., Copper-Nickel-Zinc, 31 mm. **Obv:** Books between stylized horsemen **Rev:** Ulas Samchuk **Edge:** Reeded

Date	Mintage	F	VF	XF	Unc	BU
2005	20,000	—	—	—	10.00	—

KM# 349 2 HRYVNI
12.8000 g., Copper-Nickel-Zinc, 31 mm. **Subject:** Pavlo Virsky (ballet artist) **Obv:** National arms in flower circle **Rev:** Bust right **Edge:** Reeded

Date	Mintage	F	VF	XF	Unc	BU
2005	20,000	—	—	—	10.00	—

KM# 350 2 HRYVNI
12.8000 g., Copper-Nickel-Zinc, 31 mm. **Obv:** Roses and grapes **Rev:** Poet Maksym Rylsky **Edge:** Reeded

Date	Mintage	F	VF	XF	Unc	BU
2005	20,000	—	—	—	10.00	—

KM# 351 2 HRYVNI
1.2400 g., 0.9999 Gold 0.0399 oz. AGW, 13.9 mm. **Obv:** National arms within beaded circle **Rev:** Scythian horseman depicted on golden plaque **Edge:** Plain

Date	Mintage	F	VF	XF	Unc	BU
2005	15,000	—	—	—	120	—

KM# 352 2 HRYVNI
12.8000 g., Copper-Nickel-Zinc, 31 mm. **Subject:** Serhiy Vsekhsviatsky (astronomer) **Obv:** "Solar Wind" depiction **Rev:** Head right **Edge:** Reeded

Date	Mintage	F	VF	XF	Unc	BU
2005	20,000	—	—	—	12.00	—

KM# 353 2 HRYVNI
12.8000 g., Copper-Nickel-Zinc, 31 mm. **Subject:** 50 Years of Kyivmiskbud **Obv:** National arms **Rev:** Buildings **Edge:** Reeded

Date	Mintage	F	VF	XF	Unc	BU
2005	20,000	—	—	—	12.00	—

KM# 354 2 HRYVNI
12.8000 g., Copper-Nickel-Zinc, 31 mm. **Subject:** 75 Years of Zhukovsky Aerospace University in Kharkiv **Obv:** Building divides book outline **Rev:** Airplane, computer monitor and books **Edge:** Reeded

Date	Mintage	F	VF	XF	Unc	BU
2005	30,000	—	—	—	10.00	—

KM# 356 2 HRYVNI
12.8000 g., Copper-Nickel-Zinc, 31 mm. **Subject:** Oleksander Korniychuk (writer, playright) **Obv:** Theatrical masks and feather **Rev:** Bust 1/4 right **Edge:** Reeded

Date	Mintage	F	VF	XF	Unc	BU
2005	20,000	—	—	—	12.00	—

KM# 357 2 HRYVNI
12.8000 g., Copper-Nickel-Zinc, 31 mm. **Obv:** National arms and date divides wreath, value within **Rev:** Sandy Mole Rat **Edge:** Reeded

Date	Mintage	F	VF	XF	Unc	BU
2005	60,000	—	—	—	15.00	—

KM# 359 2 HRYVNI
12.8000 g., Copper-Nickel-Zinc, 31 mm. **Obv:** National arms **Rev:** Tairov Wine Institute building and cameo **Edge:** Reeded

Date	Mintage	F	VF	XF	Unc	BU
2005	20,000	—	—	—	12.00	—

KM# 360 2 HRYVNI
12.8000 g., Copper-Nickel-Zinc, 31 mm. **Subject:** 300 Years to David Guramishvili (poet) **Obv:** Georgian and Ukrainian style ornamentation **Rev:** Head right **Edge:** Reeded

Date	Mintage	F	VF	XF	Unc	BU
2005	30,000	—	—	—	8.00	—

KM# 361 2 HRYVNI
12.8000 g., Copper-Nickel-Zinc, 31 mm. **Subject:** Dmytro Yavornytsky (historian, archaeologist, writer) **Obv:** National arms **Rev:** Bust 3/4 right **Edge:** Reeded

Date	Mintage	F	VF	XF	Unc	BU
2005	30,000	—	—	—	8.00	—

KM# 375 2 HRYVNI
12.8000 g., Copper-Nickel-Zinc, 31 mm. **Subject:** Oleksiy Alchevsky (banker) **Obv:** Steam train, factory, National arms and value **Rev:** Head with beard facing **Edge:** Reeded

Date	Mintage	F	VF	XF	Unc	BU
2005	20,000	—	—	—	10.00	—

KM# 376 2 HRYVNI
12.8000 g., Copper-Nickel-Zinc, 31 mm. **Subject:** Illia Mechnikov (biologist, Nobel prize laureate) **Obv:** Amoeba and National arms **Rev:** Bust with beard facing **Edge:** Reeded

Date	Mintage	F	VF	XF	Unc	BU
2005	20,000	—	—	—	10.00	—

KM# 377 2 HRYVNI
12.8000 g., Copper-Nickel-Zinc, 31 mm. **Subject:** Vsevolod Holubovych (politician) **Obv:** National arms **Rev:** Head 1/4 left **Edge:** Reeded

Date	Mintage	F	VF	XF	Unc	BU
2005	20,000	—	—	—	9.00	—

KM# 378 2 HRYVNI
12.8000 g., Copper-Nickel-Zinc, 31 mm. **Subject:** Volodymyr Vynnychenko (writer, politician) **Obv:** National arms **Rev:** Head facing **Edge:** Reeded

Date	Mintage	F	VF	XF	Unc	BU
2005	20,000	—	—	—	9.00	—

KM# 383 2 HRYVNI
12.8000 g., Copper-Nickel-Zinc, 31 mm. **Subject:** Kyiv National University of Economics **Obv:** National arms, value and graph **Rev:** University building **Edge:** Reeded

Date	Mintage	F	VF	XF	Unc	BU
2006	60,000	—	—	—	6.50	—

KM# 384 2 HRYVNI
12.8000 g., Copper-Nickel-Zinc, 31 mm. **Subject:** Viacheslav Prokopovych (historian, publist) **Obv:** National arms **Rev:** Bust facing **Edge:** Reeded

Date	Mintage	F	VF	XF	Unc	BU
2006	30,000	—	—	—	6.50	—

KM# 385 2 HRYVNI
12.8000 g., Copper-Nickel-Zinc, 31 mm. **Subject:** Heorhii Narbut (artist) **Obv:** Peasant couple **Rev:** Silhouette of standing figure on one leg facing right **Edge:** Reeded

Date	Mintage	F	VF	XF	Unc	BU
2006	30,000	—	—	—	8.00	—

KM# 386 2 HRYVNI
12.8000 g., Copper-Nickel-Zinc, 31 mm. **Subject:** Oleh Antonov (aircraft engineer) **Obv:** Large jet plane **Rev:** Bust 1/4 right **Edge:** Reeded

Date	Mintage	F	VF	XF	Unc	BU
2006	45,000	—	—	—	8.00	—

KM# 391 2 HRYVNI
12.8000 g., Copper-Nickel-Zinc, 31 mm. **Obv:** National arms above value in wreath **Rev:** Bush Katydid Grasshopper **Edge:** Reeded

Date	Mintage	F	VF	XF	Unc	BU
2006	60,000	—	—	—	8.00	—

KM# 398 2 HRYVNI
12.8000 g., Copper-Nickel-Zinc, 31 mm. **Subject:** Mykhailo Hrushevskyi **Obv:** National arms and value **Edge:** Reeded

Date	Mintage	F	VF	XF	Unc	BU
2006	45,000	—	—	—	6.50	—

KM# 397 2 HRYVNI
12.8000 g., Copper-Nickel-Zinc, 31 mm. **Subject:** Dmytro Lutsenko **Obv:** National arms and value **Edge:** Reeded

Date	Mintage	F	VF	XF	Unc	BU
2006	30,000	—	—	—	7.00	—

KM# 393 2 HRYVNI
12.8000 g., Copper-Nickel-Zinc, 31 mm. **Subject:** Mykola Strazhesko **Obv:** National arms and value **Edge:** Reeded

Date	Mintage	F	VF	XF	Unc	BU
2006	45,000	—	—	—	6.00	—

KM# 395 2 HRYVNI
12.8000 g., Copper-Nickel-Zinc, 31 mm. **Subject:** Mykola Vasylenko **Obv:** National arms and value

Date	Mintage	F	VF	XF	Unc	BU
2006	30,000	—	—	—	9.00	—

KM# 394 2 HRYVNI
12.8000 g., Copper-Nickel-Zinc, 31 mm. **Subject:** Volodymyr Chekhivsky **Obv:** National arms and value **Edge:** Reeded

Date	Mintage	F	VF	XF	Unc	BU
2006	30,000	—	—	—	9.00	—

KM# 396 2 HRYVNI
12.8000 g., Copper-Nickel-Zinc, 31 mm. **Subject:** Ivan Franko **Obv:** National arms and value **Edge:** Reeded

Date	Mintage	F	VF	XF	Unc	BU
2006	45,000	—	—	—	7.00	—

KM# 400 2 HRYVNI
12.8000 g., Copper-Nickel-Zinc, 31 mm. **Subject:** Mykhailo Lysenko **Obv:** National arms and value **Edge:** Reeded

Date	Mintage	F	VF	XF	Unc	BU
2006	35,000	—	—	—	6.50	—

KM# 403 2 HRYVNI
1.2400 g., 0.9999 Gold 0.0399 oz. AGW, 13.92 mm. **Subject:** Ram **Obv:** National arms **Edge:** Plain

Date	Mintage	F	VF	XF	Unc	BU
2006	10,000	—	—	—	75.00	—

KM# 404 2 HRYVNI
1.2400 g., 0.9999 Gold 0.0399 oz. AGW, 13.92 mm. **Subject:** Bull **Obv:** National arms **Edge:** Plain

Date	Mintage	F	VF	XF	Unc	BU
2006	10,000	—	—	—	75.00	—

KM# 406 2 HRYVNI
1.2400 g., 0.9999 Gold 0.0399 oz. AGW, 13.92 mm. **Subject:** The Twins **Obv:** National arms **Edge:** Plain

Date	Mintage	F	VF	XF	Unc	BU
2006	10,000	—	—	—	75.00	—

KM# 408 2 HRYVNI
1.2400 g., 0.9999 Gold 0.0399 oz. AGW, 13.92 mm. **Subject:** Hedgehog **Obv:** National arms **Edge:** Plain

Date	Mintage	F	VF	XF	Unc	BU
2006	10,000	—	—	—	75.00	—

KM# 399 2 HRYVNI
12.8000 g., Copper-Nickel-Zinc, 31 mm. **Subject:** Serhii Ostapenko **Obv:** National arms **Edge:** Reeded

Date	Mintage	F	VF	XF	Unc	BU
2006	30,000	—	—	—	6.50	—

KM# 401 2 HRYVNI
12.8000 g., Copper-Nickel-Zinc, 31 mm. **Subject:** The Economy University of Kharkiv

Date	Mintage	F	VF	XF	Unc	BU
2006	30,000	—	—	—	7.00	—

KM# 428 2 HRYVNI
12.8000 g., Copper-Nickel-Zinc, 31 mm. **Subject:** Serhii Koroljov **Obv:** National arms

Date	Mintage	F	VF	XF	Unc	BU
2007	35,000	—	—	—	7.50	—

KM# 429 2 HRYVNI
12.8000 g., Copper-Nickel-Zinc, 31 mm. **Subject:** Les Kurbas **Obv:** National arms **Edge:** Reeded

Date	Mintage	F	VF	XF	Unc	BU
2007	35,000	—	—	—	6.50	—

KM# 430 2 HRYVNI
12.8000 g., Copper-Nickel-Zinc, 31 mm. **Subject:** Olexander Liapunov **Obv:** Small national arms above geometrical depiction of celestial mechanics grafics **Rev:** Large bust facing **Edge:** Reeded

Date	Mintage	F	VF	XF	Unc	BU
2007	35,000	—	—	—	6.50	—

KM# 431 2 HRYVNI
1.2400 g., 0.9999 Gold 0.0399 oz. AGW, 13.92 mm. **Subject:** Steppe Marmot **Obv:** National arms **Edge:** Plain

Date	Mintage	F	VF	XF	Unc	BU
2007	10,000	—	—	—	80.00	—

KM# 107 5 HRYVEN
9.4000 g., Bi-Metallic Brass center in Copper-Nickel ring, 28 mm. **Subject:** New Millennium **Obv:** Spiral design within circle **Rev:** Mother and child within circle **Edge:** Segmented reeding

Date	Mintage	F	VF	XF	Unc	BU
2001	50,000	—	—	—	30.00	—

KM# 112 5 HRYVEN
16.5400 g., Copper-Nickel-Zinc, 35 mm. **Subject:** Ostrozhska Academy **Obv:** Value, old writing and printing artifacts **Rev:** Seated figures, partial building and crowned arms with supporters **Edge:** Reeded

Date	Mintage	F	VF	XF	Unc	BU
2001	30,000	—	—	—	18.00	—

KM# 129 5 HRYVEN
16.5400 g., Copper-Nickel-Zinc, 35 mm. **Subject:** 10th Anniversary - National Bank **Obv:** National arms between two arches **Rev:** Large building central entrance **Edge:** Reeded

Date	Mintage	F	VF	XF	Unc	BU
2001	50,000	—	—	—	12.50	—

KM# 132 5 HRYVEN
16.5400 g., Copper-Nickel-Zinc, 35 mm. **Subject:** 10th Anniversary - National Independence **Obv:** Arms with supporters within beaded circle **Rev:** Building on map within beaded circle **Edge:** Reeded

Date	Mintage	F	VF	XF	Unc	BU
2001	100,000	—	—	—	7.00	—

KM# 135 5 HRYVEN
16.5400 g., Copper-Nickel-Zinc, 35 mm. **Subject:** 1100th Anniversary - Poltava **Obv:** National arms above value flanked by flower sprigs **Rev:** Buildings above shield **Edge:** Reeded

Date	Mintage	F	VF	XF	Unc	BU
2001	50,000	—	—	—	12.50	—

KM# 140 5 HRYVEN
9.4000 g., Bi-Metallic Brass center in Copper-Nickel ring, 28 mm. **Subject:** 10th Anniversary of Military forces **Obv:** Crossed maces, arms and date within wreath and circle **Rev:** Circle in center of cross within wreath and circle **Edge:** Reeded and plain sections

Date	Mintage	F	VF	XF	Unc	BU
2001	30,000	—	—	—	60.00	—

KM# 148 5 HRYVEN
16.5400 g., Copper-Nickel-Zinc, 35 mm. **Subject:** 400 Years of Krolevets **Obv:** National arms above gateway and value **Rev:** Krolivets city arms flanked by designs **Edge:** Reeded

Date	Mintage	F	VF	XF	Unc	BU
2001	30,000	—	—	—	15.00	—

KM# 151 5 HRYVEN
16.5400 g., Copper-Nickel-Zinc, 35 mm. **Subject:** City of Khotyn **Obv:** Value within arch above sprigs **Rev:** Castle below crowned shield **Edge:** Reeded

Date	Mintage	F	VF	XF	Unc	BU
2002	30,000	—	—	—	15.00	—

KM# 152 5 HRYVEN
16.5400 g., Copper-Nickel-Zinc, 35 mm. **Obv:** Sun and flying geese divides beaded circle **Rev:** "AN-225 Mrija" cargo jet divide beaded circle **Edge:** Reeded

Date	Mintage	F	VF	XF	Unc	BU
2002	30,000	—	—	—	35.00	—

KM# 158 5 HRYVEN
9.4300 g., Bi-Metallic Brass center in Copper-Nickel ring, 28 mm. **Subject:** 70th Anniversary of Dnipro Hydroelectric Power Station **Obv:** Turbine within circle **Rev:** Large dam within circle **Edge:** Reeded and plain sections

Date	Mintage	F	VF	XF	Unc	BU
2002	30,000	—	—	—	30.00	—

KM# 159 5 HRYVEN
16.5400 g., Copper-Nickel-Zinc, 35 mm. **Obv:** Arms with supporters within beaded circle **Rev:** Battle scene around Batig in 1652 divides beaded circle **Edge:** Reeded

Date	Mintage	F	VF	XF	Unc	BU
2002	30,000	—	—	—	18.00	—

KM# 163 5 HRYVEN
16.5400 g., Copper-Nickel-Zinc, 35 mm. **Subject:** Christmas **Obv:** National arms in star above value flanked by designed sprigs **Rev:** Christmas pageant scene **Edge:** Reeded

Date	Mintage	F	VF	XF	Unc	BU
ND(2002)	30,000	—	—	—	55.00	—

KM# 157 5 HRYVEN
16.5400 g., Copper-Nickel, 35 mm. **Sub6.5ject:** 1100th Anniversary - City of Romny **Obv:** Sprigs divide national arms and value **Rev:** City view **Edge:** Reeded

Date	Mintage	F	VF	XF	Unc	BU
2002	30,000	—	—	—	18.00	—

KM# 200 5 HRYVEN
9.4000 g., Bi-Metallic Brass center in Copper-Nickel ring, 28 mm. **Obv:** Bandura strings over ornamental design **Rev:** Bandura divides circle and wreath **Edge:** Segmented reeding

Date	Mintage	F	VF	XF	Unc	BU
2003	30,000	—	—	—	15.00	—

KM# 172 5 HRYVEN
16.5400 g., Copper-Nickel-Zinc, 35 mm. **Subject:** Easter **Obv:** Circle of Easter eggs, national arms in center above value **Rev:** Religious celebration **Edge:** Reeded

Date	Mintage	F	VF	XF	Unc	BU
2003	50,000	—	—	—	15.00	—

KM# 173 5 HRYVEN
16.5400 g., Copper-Nickel-Zinc, 35 mm. **Subject:** Antonov AN-2 Biplane **Obv:** National arms sun face and flying geese divide beaded circle **Rev:** World's largest biplane divides beaded circle **Edge:** Reeded

Date	Mintage	F	VF	XF	Unc	BU
2003	50,000	—	—	—	15.00	—

KM# 185 5 HRYVEN
9.4000 g., Bi-Metallic Brass center in Copper-Nickel ring, 28 mm. **Subject:** 150th Anniversary of the Central Ukrainian Archives **Obv:** Value, signature and seal **Rev:** Hourglass divides books and circle **Edge:** Segmented reeding

Date	Mintage	F	VF	XF	Unc	BU
2003	30,000	—	—	—	15.00	—

KM# 186 5 HRYVEN
16.5400 g., Copper-Nickel-Zinc, 35 mm. **Subject:** 2500th Anniversary of the City of Yevpatoria **Obv:** National arms, date and value with partial sun background **Rev:** Ancient amphora and modern city view **Edge:** Reeded

Date	Mintage	F	VF	XF	Unc	BU
2003	30,000	—	—	—	15.00	—

KM# 187 5 HRYVEN
16.5400 g., Copper-Nickel-Zinc, 35 mm. **Subject:** 60th Anniversary - Liberation of Kiev **Obv:** Eternal flame monument **Rev:** Battle scene and map of the offense **Edge:** Reeded

Date	Mintage	F	VF	XF	Unc	BU
2003	30,000	—	—	—	14.00	—

KM# 204 5 HRYVEN
16.5400 g., Copper-Nickel-Zinc, 35 mm. **Subject:** 50th Anniversary - Pivdenne Space Design Office **Obv:** Satellite orbiting Earth **Rev:** Satellite above moonscape **Edge:** Reeded

Date	Mintage	F	VF	XF	Unc	BU
2004	30,000	—	—	—	13.50	—

KM# 205 5 HRYVEN
16.5400 g., Copper-Nickel-Zinc, 35 mm. **Subject:** 2500 Anniversary City of Balaklava **Obv:** National arms between two ancient ships **Rev:** Harbor view above pillar **Edge:** Reeded

Date	Mintage	F	VF	XF	Unc	BU
2004	30,000	—	—	—	11.50	—

KM# 218 5 HRYVEN
16.9400 g., 0.9250 Silver 0.5038 oz. ASW, 33 mm. **Obv:** National arms, value and solar system **Rev:** Kharkov University buildings **Edge:** Reeded

Date	Mintage	F	VF	XF	Unc	BU
2004 Proof	7,000	Value: 40.00				

KM# 219 5 HRYVEN
16.9400 g., 0.9250 Silver 0.5038 oz. ASW, 33 mm. **Obv:** National arms above value dividing scientific items **Rev:** Kiev University building main entrance **Edge:** Reeded

Date	Mintage	F	VF	XF	Unc	BU
2004 Proof	7,000	Value: 40.00				

KM# 220 5 HRYVEN
9.4300 g., Bi-Metallic BRASS center in COPPER-NICKEL ring, 28 mm. **Subject:** 50 Years of Ukraine's Membership in UNESCO **Obv:** National arms in center of sprigs and circle **Rev:** Building within sprigs and circle **Edge:** Segmented reeding

Date	Mintage	F	VF	XF	Unc	BU
2004	50,000	—	—	—	12.00	—

KM# 221 5 HRYVEN
16.5400 g., Copper-Nickel-Zinc, 35 mm. **Subject:** Ice Breaker "Captain Belousov" **Obv:** National arms on ship's wheel and anchor **Rev:** Ice breaker ship **Edge:** Reeded

Date	Mintage	F	VF	XF	Unc	BU
2004	30,000	—	—	—	10.00	—

KM# 222 5 HRYVEN
16.5400 g., Copper-Nickel-Zinc, 35 mm. **Subject:** Whit Sunday **Obv:** National arms in flower wreath above value flanked by sprigs **Rev:** Four dancing women and child **Edge:** Reeded

Date	Mintage	F	VF	XF	Unc	BU
2004	50,000	—	—	—	12.00	—

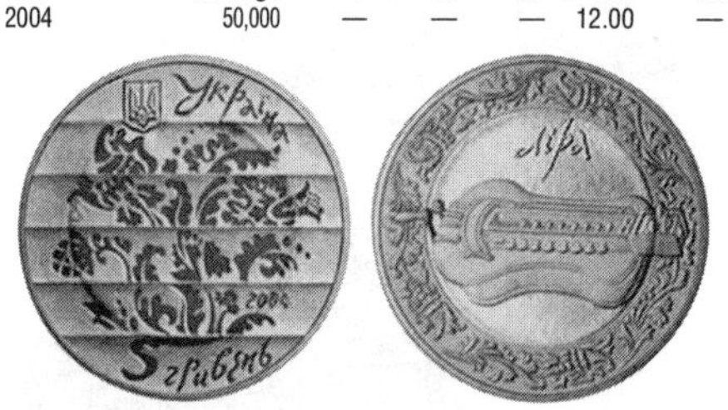

KM# 333 5 HRYVEN
9.4000 g., Bi-Metallic Brass center in Copper-Nickel ring, 28 mm. **Obv:** Horizontal lines across flowery design **Rev:** Cossack-style lyre within circle and wreath **Edge:** Segmented reeding

Date	Mintage	F	VF	XF	Unc	BU
2004	30,000	—	—	—	14.00	—

KM# 334 5 HRYVEN
16.5400 g., Copper-Nickel-Zinc, 35 mm. **Subject:** 250th Anniversary of Kirovohrad **Obv:** National arms above crossed cannons and value **Rev:** Arms with supporters above city view **Edge:** Reeded

Date	Mintage	F	VF	XF	Unc	BU
2004	30,000	—	—	—	12.00	—

KM# 335 5 HRYVEN
16.5400 g., Copper-Nickel-Zinc, 35 mm. **Subject:** 350 Years to Kharkiv **Obv:** Assumption Cathedral, value and national arms **Rev:** Kharkiv State Industrial Building complex **Edge:** Reeded

Date	Mintage	F	VF	XF	Unc	BU
2004	30,000	—	—	—	12.50	—

KM# 336 5 HRYVEN
9.4000 g., Bi-Metallic Brass center in Copper-Nickel ring, 28 mm. **Subject:** 50th Anniversary of Crimean Union With Ukraine **Obv:** National arms on wheat sheaf on map **Rev:** Crowned lion on shield flanked by pillars within rope wreath **Edge:** Segmented reeding

Date	Mintage	F	VF	XF	Unc	BU
2004	30,000	—	—	—	14.00	—

KM# 337 5 HRYVEN
16.5400 g., Copper-Nickel-Zinc, 35 mm. **Obv:** National arms on sun, flying geese divide beaded circle **Rev:** AN-140 Airliner divides beaded circle **Edge:** Reeded

Date	Mintage	F	VF	XF	Unc	BU
2004	50,000	—	—	—	12.00	—

KM# 362 5 HRYVEN
16.5400 g., Copper-Nickel-Zinc, 35 mm. **Obv:** National arms on sun with flying geese divide beaded circle **Rev:** AN-124 jet divides beaded circle **Edge:** Reeded

Date	Mintage	F	VF	XF	Unc	BU
2005	60,000	—	—	—	10.00	—

KM# 364 5 HRYVEN
16.5400 g., Copper-Nickel-Zinc, 35 mm. **Subject:** City of Korosten 1300th Anniversary **Obv:** National arms **Rev:** Ancient earring below modern building and bridge **Edge:** Reeded

Date	Mintage	F	VF	XF	Unc	BU
2005	30,000	—	—	—	10.00	—

KM# 365 5 HRYVEN
16.5400 g., Copper-Nickel-Zinc, 35 mm. **Subject:** City of Sumy 350th Anniversary **Obv:** National arms **Rev:** City view behind city arms **Edge:** Reeded

Date	Mintage	F	VF	XF	Unc	BU
2005	30,000	—	—	—	10.00	—

KM# 366 5 HRYVEN
16.5400 g., Copper-Nickel-Zinc, 35 mm. **Subject:** The Protection of the Virgin **Obv:** National arms on Cossack regalia **Rev:** Wedding scene **Edge:** Reeded

Date	Mintage	F	VF	XF	Unc	BU
2005	45,000	—	—	—	10.00	—

KM# 368 5 HRYVEN
16.5400 g., Copper-Nickel-Zinc, 35 mm. **Subject:** Sorochynsky Fair **Obv:** Busts facing each other flanked by sprigs **Rev:** Farmer with family in ox cart **Edge:** Reeded

Date	Mintage	F	VF	XF	Unc	BU
2005	60,000	—	—	—	10.00	—

KM# 379 5 HRYVEN
16.5400 g., Copper-Nickel-Zinc, 35 mm. **Subject:** 500th Anniversary - Kalmiuska Palanqua Cossack Settlement **Obv:** Cossack in ornamental frame and national arms **Rev:** Soldiers **Edge:** Reeded

Date	Mintage	F	VF	XF	Unc	BU
2005	30,000	—	—	—	10.00	—

KM# 380 5 HRYVEN
16.5400 g., Copper-Nickel-Zinc, 35 mm. **Subject:** Sviatohirsky Assumption Monastery **Obv:** Madonna and child flanked by angels **Rev:** Hillside monastery **Edge:** Reeded

Date	Mintage	F	VF	XF	Unc	BU
2005	45,000	—	—	—	10.00	—

KM# 387 5 HRYVEN
16.5400 g., Copper-Nickel-Zinc, 35 mm. **Subject:** Vernadsky Antarctic Station **Obv:** Flag and buildings **Rev:** Antarctica map within compass face **Edge:** Reeded

Date	Mintage	F	VF	XF	Unc	BU
2006	60,000	—	—	—	10.00	—

KM# 388 5 HRYVEN
16.9300 g., 0.9250 Silver 0.5035 oz. ASW, 33 mm. **Subject:** Year of the Dog **Obv:** Value on textile art **Rev:** Stylized dog **Edge:** Reeded

Date	Mintage	F	VF	XF	Unc	BU
2006 Proof	12,000	Value: 50.00				

KM# 389 5 HRYVEN
16.9300 g., 0.9250 Silver 0.5035 oz. ASW, 33 mm. **Subject:** Zodiac - Ram **Obv:** Sun face **Rev:** Ram **Edge:** Reeded

Date	Mintage	F	VF	XF	Unc	BU
2006 Proof	10,000	Value: 40.00				

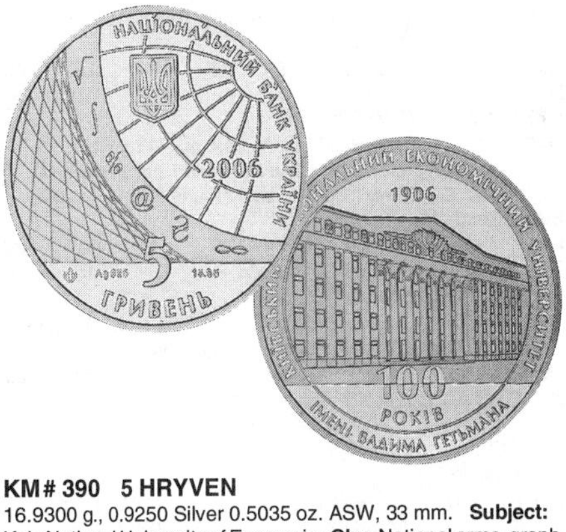

KM# 390 5 HRYVEN
16.9300 g., 0.9250 Silver 0.5035 oz. ASW, 33 mm. **Subject:** Kyiv National University of Economics **Obv:** National arms, graph above value **Rev:** University building within circle **Edge:** Reeded

Date	Mintage	F	VF	XF	Unc	BU
2006 Proof	5,000	Value: 37.50				

KM# 402 5 HRYVEN
9.4200 g., Bi-Metallic Brass center in Copper-Nickel ring, 28 mm. **Obv:** Symbolic sound of music **Rev:** Tsimbal stringed musical instrument **Edge:** Segmented reeding

Date	Mintage	F	VF	XF	Unc	BU
2006	100,000	—	—	—	10.00	—

KM# 409 5 HRYVEN
16.5400 g., Copper-Nickel-Zinc, 35 mm. **Subject:** 10 Years of the Constitution of Ukraine **Obv:** National arms **Edge:** Reeded

Date	Mintage	F	VF	XF	Unc	BU
2006	30,000	—	—	—	13.50	—

KM# 411 5 HRYVEN
16.5400 g., Copper-Nickel-Zinc, 35 mm. **Subject:** 15 Years of Ukraine Independence **Obv:** National arms **Edge:** Reeded

Date	Mintage	F	VF	XF	Unc	BU
2006	75,000	—	—	—	7.00	—

KM# 413 5 HRYVEN
16.5400 g., Copper-Nickel-Zinc, 35 mm. **Subject:** 10 Years to the Currency Reform in Ukraine **Obv:** National arms **Edge:** Reeded

Date	Mintage	F	VF	XF	Unc	BU
2006	45,000	—	—	—	8.00	—

KM# 405 5 HRYVEN
16.8200 g., 0.9250 Silver 0.5002 oz. ASW, 33 mm. **Subject:** Bull **Obv:** National arms

Date	Mintage	F	VF	XF	Unc	BU
2006 Proof	10,000	Value: 40.00				

KM# 415 5 HRYVEN
16.5400 g., Copper-Nickel-Zinc, 35 mm. **Subject:** 750 Years of the City of L'viv **Obv:** National arms **Edge:** Reeded

Date	Mintage	F	VF	XF	Unc	BU
2006	60,000	—	—	—	12.00	—

KM# 416 5 HRYVEN
16.8200 g., 0.9250 Silver 0.5002 oz. ASW, 33 mm. **Subject:** Mykhailo Hrushevskyi **Obv:** National arms

Date	Mintage	F	VF	XF	Unc	BU
2006 Proof	5,000	Value: 45.00				

KM# 417 5 HRYVEN
16.8200 g., 0.9250 Silver 0.5002 oz. ASW, 33 mm. **Subject:** Dmytro Lutsenko **Obv:** National arms

Date	Mintage	F	VF	XF	Unc	BU
2006 Proof	3,000	Value: 140				

KM# 418 5 HRYVEN
16.8200 g., 0.9250 Silver 0.5002 oz. ASW, 33 mm. **Subject:** Ivan Franko **Obv:** National arms

Date	Mintage	F	VF	XF	Unc	BU
2006 Proof	5,000	Value: 45.00				

KM# 407 5 HRYVEN
16.8200 g., 0.9250 Silver 0.5002 oz. ASW, 33 mm. **Subject:** The Twins **Obv:** National arms

Date	Mintage	F	VF	XF	Unc	BU
2006 Proof	10,000	Value: 40.00				

KM# 420 5 HRYVEN
16.5400 g., Copper-Nickel-Zinc, 35 mm. **Subject:** Epiphany **Obv:** National arms **Edge:** Reeded

Date	Mintage	F	VF	XF	Unc	BU
2006	75,000	—	—	—	10.00	—

KM# 422 5 HRYVEN
16.5400 g., Copper-Nickel-Zinc, 35 mm. **Subject:** Saint Kyryl Church **Obv:** National arms

Date	Mintage	F	VF	XF	Unc	BU
2006	45,000	—	—	—	10.00	—

KM# 432 5 HRYVEN
16.5400 g., Copper-Nickel-Zinc, 35.00 mm. **Subject:** 100th Anniversary of "Motor Sich" **Obv:** Small national arms above eagle in flight with two globes in background **Rev:** Jet engine **Edge:** Reeded

Date	Mintage	F	VF	XF	Unc	BU
2007	45,000	—	—	—	10.00	—

KM# 419 5 HRYVEN
16.8200 g., 0.9250 Silver 0.5002 oz. ASW, 33 mm. **Subject:** Year of the Pig **Obv:** National arms **Edge:** Reeded

Date	Mintage	F	VF	XF	Unc	BU
2007 Proof	15,000	Value: 40.00				

KM# 113 10 HRYVEN
33.6220 g., 0.9250 Silver 0.9999 oz. ASW, 38.61 mm. **Subject:** Ivan Mazepa (Cossack leader) **Obv:** Arms with supporters within beaded circle **Rev:** Half figure divides beaded circle flanked by palace and oval shield **Edge:** Reeded

Date	Mintage	F	VF	XF	Unc	BU
2001 Proof	5,000	Value: 125				

KM# 114 10 HRYVEN
33.6220 g., 0.9250 Silver 0.9999 oz. ASW, 38.61 mm. **Subject:** Yaroslav the Wise (Cossack leader) **Obv:** Value within grape wreath **Rev:** Mosaic head facing, half length figure facing holding scroll and dome building **Edge:** Reeded

Date	Mintage	F	VF	XF	Unc	BU
2001 Proof	3,000	Value: 1,000				

KM# 115 10 HRYVEN
33.6220 g., 0.9250 Silver 0.9999 oz. ASW, 38.61 mm. **Series:** Ukranian Flora and Fauna **Obv:** National arms and date divides wreath, value within **Rev:** Lynx with offspring **Edge:** Reeded

Date	Mintage	F	VF	XF	Unc	BU
2001 Proof	3,000	Value: 350				

KM# 130 10 HRYVEN
33.6220 g., 0.9250 Silver 0.9999 oz. ASW, 38.61 mm. **Subject:** 10th Anniversary - National Bank **Obv:** National arms and value between arches **Rev:** Large building entrance **Edge:** Reeded

Date	Mintage	F	VF	XF	Unc	BU
2001 Proof	3,000	Value: 145				

KM# 131 10 HRYVEN
33.6220 g., 0.9250 Silver 0.9999 oz. ASW, 38.61 mm. **Series:** Olympics **Obv:** National arms and value on ice **Rev:** Stylized ice dancing couple **Edge:** Reeded

Date	Mintage	F	VF	XF	Unc	BU
2001 Proof	15,000	Value: 45.00				

KM# 141 10 HRYVEN
33.6220 g., 0.9250 Silver 0.9999 oz. ASW, 38.61 mm. **Subject:** Flora and Fauna **Obv:** National arms and date divides wreath, value within **Rev:** Pine branch with cone **Edge:** Reeded

Date	Mintage	F	VF	XF	Unc	BU
2001 Proof	3,000	Value: 200				

KM# 142 10 HRYVEN
33.6220 g., 0.9250 Silver 0.9999 oz. ASW, 38.61 mm. **Subject:** Khan Palace in Bakhchisarai **Obv:** Value in arch **Rev:** Courtyard view **Edge:** Reeded

Date	Mintage	F	VF	XF	Unc	BU
2001 Proof	3,000	Value: 245				

KM# 143 10 HRYVEN
4.3110 g., 0.9000 Gold 0.1247 oz. AGW, 16 mm. **Subject:** 10 Years Independence **Obv:** National arms **Rev:** Parliament building on map **Edge:** Plain

Date	Mintage	F	VF	XF	Unc	BU
2001 Proof	3,000	Value: 700				

KM# 165 10 HRYVEN
33.6220 g., 0.9250 Silver 0.9999 oz. ASW, 38.61 mm. **Subject:** Olympics **Obv:** National arms and value on ice **Rev:** Stylized hockey player **Edge:** Reeded

Date	Mintage	F	VF	XF	Unc	BU
2001 Proof	15,000	Value: 45.00				

KM# 229 10 HRYVEN
33.6220 g., 0.9250 Silver 0.9999 oz. ASW, 38.61 mm. **Obv:** National arms and date divides wreath, value within **Rev:** Eurasian Eagle Owl on branch **Edge:** Reeded

Date	Mintage	F	VF	XF	Unc	BU
2002 Proof	3,000	Value: 450				

KM# 145 10 HRYVEN
33.6220 g., 0.9250 Silver 0.9999 oz. ASW, 38.61 mm. **Subject:** Ivan Sirko **Obv:** Arms with supporters within beaded circle **Rev:** Cossack battle scene divides beaded circle **Edge:** Reeded

Date	Mintage	F	VF	XF	Unc	BU
2002 Proof	3,000	Value: 275				

KM# 146 10 HRYVEN
33.6220 g., 0.9250 Silver 0.9999 oz. ASW, 38.61 mm. **Obv:** National arms and value on ice **Rev:** Stylized speed skater **Edge:** Reeded

Date	Mintage	F	VF	XF	Unc	BU
2002 Proof	3,000	Value: 70.00				

KM# 160 10 HRYVEN
33.9500 g., 0.9250 Silver 1.0096 oz. ASW, 38.61 mm. **Obv:** Value encircled by angels flanked by stars **Rev:** Steepled church and tower **Edge:** Reeded

Date	Mintage	F	VF	XF	Unc	BU
2002 Proof	3,000	Value: 200				

KM# 161 10 HRYVEN
33.6220 g., 0.9250 Silver 0.9999 oz. ASW, 38.61 mm. **Subject:** Grand Prince Vladimir Monomakh **Obv:** Value within jewelry design **Rev:** Bust holding book flanked by buildings and St. George **Edge:** Reeded

Date	Mintage	F	VF	XF	Unc	BU
2002 Proof	3,000	Value: 350				

KM# 162 10 HRYVEN
33.6220 g., 0.9250 Silver 0.9999 oz. ASW, 38.61 mm. **Subject:** Prince Svyatoslav **Obv:** Value in ornate design **Rev:** Armored half length figure facing **Edge:** Reeded

Date	Mintage	F	VF	XF	Unc	BU
2002 Proof	3,000	Value: 375				

KM# 164 10 HRYVEN
33.6220 g., 0.9250 Silver 0.9999 oz. ASW, 38.61 mm. **Subject:** Christmas **Obv:** National arms within star above value **Rev:** Christmas pageant scene **Edge:** Reeded

Date	Mintage	F	VF	XF	Unc	BU
ND(2002) Proof	3,000	Value: 475				

KM# 176 10 HRYVEN
33.6220 g., 0.9250 Silver 0.9999 oz. ASW, 38.61 mm. **Subject:** Olympics **Obv:** Two ancient women with seedlings **Rev:** Swimmer **Edge:** Reeded

Date	Mintage	F	VF	XF	Unc	BU
2002 Proof	15,000	Value: 47.50				

KM# 177 10 HRYVEN
33.6220 g., 0.9250 Silver 0.9999 oz. ASW, 38.61 mm. **Subject:** Hetman Pylyp Orlik 1672-1742 **Obv:** Arms with supporters within beaded circle **Rev:** Standing figure facing holding scroll flanked by other standing figures **Edge:** Reeded

Date	Mintage	F	VF	XF	Unc	BU
2002 Proof	3,000	Value: 275				

KM# 198 10 HRYVEN
33.6220 g., 0.9250 Silver 0.9999 oz. ASW, 38.61 mm. **Obv:** National arms and date divides wreath, value within **Rev:** European bison **Edge:** Reeded

Date	Mintage	F	VF	XF	Unc	BU
2003 Proof	2,000	Value: 500				

KM# 189 10 HRYVEN
33.6220 g., 0.9250 Silver 0.9999 oz. ASW, 38.61 mm. **Subject:** Olympics **Obv:** Two ancient women with seedlings **Rev:** Boxer **Edge:** Reeded

Date	Mintage	F	VF	XF	Unc	BU
2003 Proof	15,000	Value: 45.00				

KM# 190 10 HRYVEN
33.6220 g., 0.9250 Silver 0.9999 oz. ASW, 38.61 mm. **Obv:** Fancy art work and sculpture **Rev:** Livadia Palace view **Edge:** Reeded

Date	Mintage	F	VF	XF	Unc	BU
2003 Proof	3,000	Value: 185				

KM# 191 10 HRYVEN
33.6220 g., 0.9250 Silver 0.9999 oz. ASW, 38.61 mm. **Obv:** National arms on sun, flying geese divides beaded circle **Rev:** Antonov AN-2 biplane divides beaded circle **Edge:** Reeded

Date	Mintage	F	VF	XF	Unc	BU
2003 Proof	3,000	Value: 185				

KM# 192 10 HRYVEN
33.6220 g., 0.9250 Silver 0.9999 oz. ASW, 38.61 mm. **Obv:** Easter eggs around arms above value **Rev:** Easter celebration **Edge:** Reeded

Date	Mintage	F	VF	XF	Unc	BU
2003 Proof	3,000	Value: 325				

KM# 193 10 HRYVEN
33.6220 g., 0.9250 Silver 0.9999 oz. ASW, 38.61 mm. **Obv:** Angels, national arms and value **Rev:** The protection of the Virgin Mary over the Pochayiv Monastery **Edge:** Reeded

Date	Mintage	F	VF	XF	Unc	BU
2003 Proof	Est. 8,000	Value: 125				

KM# 194 10 HRYVEN
33.6220 g., 0.9250 Silver 0.9999 oz. ASW, 38.61 mm. **Obv:**

National arms and date divide wreath, value within **Rev:** Long-snouted seahorse **Edge:** Reeded

Date	Mintage	F	VF	XF	Unc	BU
2003 Proof	2,000	Value: 550				

KM# 195 10 HRYVEN
33.6220 g., 0.9250 Silver 0.9999 oz. ASW, 38.61 mm. **Subject:** Kyrylo Rozumovskyi (Cossack leader) **Obv:** Arms with supporters within beaded circle **Rev:** Half length figure 1/4 left within beaded circle **Edge:** Reeded

Date	Mintage	F	VF	XF	Unc	BU
2003 Proof	3,000	Value: 275				

KM# 196 10 HRYVEN
33.6220 g., 0.9250 Silver 0.9999 oz. ASW, 38.61 mm. **Subject:** Pavlo Polubotok (Cossack leader) **Obv:** Arms with supporters within beaded circle **Rev:** Half length figure within beaded circle **Edge:** Reeded

Date	Mintage	F	VF	XF	Unc	BU
2003 Proof	3,000	Value: 350				

KM# 197 10 HRYVEN
33.6220 g., 0.9250 Silver 0.9999 oz. ASW, 38.61 mm. **Obv:** Map, national arms and value **Rev:** Genoese Fortress in Sudak **Edge:** Reeded

Date	Mintage	F	VF	XF	Unc	BU
2003 Proof	3,000	Value: 175				

KM# 339 10 HRYVEN
33.6220 g., 0.9250 Silver 0.9999 oz. ASW, 38.61 mm. **Subject:** Ostrozhsky Family **Obv:** Our Lady of Duben and Elias Icon **Rev:** Three cameos above crowned shield **Edge:** Reeded

Date	Mintage	F	VF	XF	Unc	BU
2004 Proof	3,000	Value: 150				

KM# 340 10 HRYVEN
33.6220 g., 0.9250 Silver 0.9999 oz. ASW, 38.61 mm. **Subject:** St. Yura Cathedral **Obv:** Statue of St. George on horse killing dragon **Rev:** Cathedral **Edge:** Reeded

Date	Mintage	F	VF	XF	Unc	BU
ND (2004) Proof	8,000	Value: 65.00				

KM# 342 10 HRYVEN
33.6220 g., 0.9250 Silver 0.9999 oz. ASW, 38.61 mm. **Subject:** Defense of Sevastopol 1854-56 **Obv:** National arms and value above fortifications map **Rev:** Cannon and ships **Edge:** Reeded

Date	Mintage	F	VF	XF	Unc	BU
2004 Proof	10,000	Value: 70.00				

KM# 343 10 HRYVEN
33.6220 g., 0.9250 Silver 0.9999 oz. ASW, 38.61 mm. **Subject:** Perejaslav Cossack Rada of 1654 **Obv:** National arms above value **Rev:** Standing figures facing **Edge:** Reeded

Date	Mintage	F	VF	XF	Unc	BU
2004 Proof	8,000	Value: 90.00				

KM# 206 10 HRYVEN
33.9100 g., 0.9250 Silver 1.0084 oz. ASW, 38.61 mm. **Subject:** Azov Dolphin **Obv:** National arms and date divides wreath, value within **Rev:** Harbor Porpoises **Edge:** Reeded

Date	Mintage	F	VF	XF	Unc	BU
2004 Proof	8,000	Value: 70.00				

KM# 207 10 HRYVEN
33.9100 g., 0.9250 Silver 1.0084 oz. ASW, 38.61 mm. **Subject:** Football World Cup - 2006 **Obv:** Soccer ball in net **Rev:** Two soccer players **Edge:** Reeded

Date	Mintage	F	VF	XF	Unc	BU
2004 Proof	50,000	Value: 75.00				

KM# 223 10 HRYVEN
33.9100 g., 0.9250 Silver 1.0084 oz. ASW, 38.61 mm. **Obv:** National arms on sun, flying geese and value divides beaded circle **Rev:** AH-140 Airliner divides beaded circle **Edge:** Reeded

Date	Mintage	F	VF	XF	Unc	BU
2004 Proof	10,000	Value: 60.00				

KM# 224 10 HRYVEN
33.9100 g., 0.9250 Silver 1.0084 oz. ASW, 38.61 mm. **Subject:** Ice Breaker "Captain Belousov" **Obv:** National arms on ship's wheel and anchor **Rev:** Ice breaker ship **Edge:** Reeded

Date	Mintage	F	VF	XF	Unc	BU
2004 Proof	10,000	Value: 50.00				

KM# 225 10 HRYVEN
33.6220 g., 0.9250 Silver 0.9999 oz. ASW, 38.61 mm. **Subject:** Whit Sunday **Obv:** National arms within wreath above value flanked by sprigs **Rev:** Four women folk dancers and child **Edge:** Reeded

Date	Mintage	F	VF	XF	Unc	BU
2004 Proof	10,000	Value: 100				

KM# 358 10 HRYVEN
33.6220 g., 0.9250 Silver 0.9999 oz. ASW, 38.61 mm. **Subject:** Spalax Arenarius Reshetnik (mole) **Obv:** National arms and date divides wreath, value within **Rev:** Mole rat **Edge:** Reeded

Date	Mintage	F	VF	XF	Unc	BU
2005 Proof	8,000	Value: 60.00				

KM# 367 10 HRYVEN
33.6220 g., 0.9250 Silver 0.9999 oz. ASW, 38.61 mm. **Subject:** The Protection of the Virgin **Obv:** National arms on Cossack regalia **Rev:** Wedding scene **Edge:** Reeded

Date	Mintage	F	VF	XF	Unc	BU
2005 Proof	8,000	Value: 60.00				

KM# 370 10 HRYVEN
33.6220 g., 0.9250 Silver 0.9999 oz. ASW, 38.61 mm. **Subject:** 60 Years UN Membership **Obv:** National arms, value and olive branch **Rev:** UN logo above partial globe **Edge:** Reeded

Date	Mintage	F	VF	XF	Unc	BU
2005 Proof	5,000	Value: 50.00				

KM# 371 10 HRYVEN
33.6220 g., 0.9250 Silver 0.9999 oz. ASW, 38.61 mm. **Subject:** National Anthem **Obv:** Musical score, national arms, value and date **Rev:** Coiled legend around holographic flower **Edge:** Reeded

Date	Mintage	F	VF	XF	Unc	BU
2005 Proof	3,000	Value: 175				

KM# 372 10 HRYVEN
33.6220 g., 0.9250 Silver 0.9999 oz. ASW, 38.61 mm. **Subject:** 100 Years of Olha Kobylianska Music and Drama Theatre in Chernivtsi **Obv:** Statue **Rev:** Theater **Edge:** Reeded

Date	Mintage	F	VF	XF	Unc	BU
2005 Proof	5,000	Value: 50.00				

KM# 373 10 HRYVEN
33.6220 g., 0.9250 Silver 0.9999 oz. ASW, 38.61 mm. **Subject:** Sviatohirsky Lavra Monastery **Obv:** Madonna and child flanked by angels **Rev:** Monastery on river bank **Edge:** Reeded

Date	Mintage	F	VF	XF	Unc	BU
2005 Proof	8,000	Value: 75.00				

KM# 381 10 HRYVEN
33.8600 g., 0.9250 Silver 1.0069 oz. ASW, 38.61 mm. **Subject:**

Baturyn Hetman Capital City **Obv:** National arms within sun rays, value flanked by standing figures **Rev:** Four cameos and banner above city view **Edge:** Reeded

Date	Mintage	F	VF	XF	Unc	BU
2005 Proof	5,000	Value: 65.00				

KM# 382 10 HRYVEN
33.8600 g., 0.9250 Silver 1.0069 oz. ASW, 38.61 mm. **Subject:** Symyrenko Family **Obv:** Country name below national arms within sprigs **Rev:** Family tree **Edge:** Reeded

Date	Mintage	F	VF	XF	Unc	BU
2005 Proof	5,000	Value: 52.50				

KM# 392 10 HRYVEN
33.6220 g., 0.9250 Silver 0.9999 oz. ASW, 38.61 mm. **Obv:** National arms above value in wreath **Rev:** Grasshopper **Edge:** Reeded

Date	Mintage	F	VF	XF	Unc	BU
2006 Proof	8,000	Value: 65.00				

KM# 424 10 HRYVEN
33.6221 g., 0.9250 Silver 0.9999 oz. ASW, 38.61 mm. **Subject:** Chyhyryn **Obv:** National arms

Date	Mintage	F	VF	XF	Unc	BU
2006 Proof	5,000	Value: 65.00				

KM# 425 10 HRYVEN
33.6220 g., 0.9250 Silver 0.9999 oz. ASW, 38.61 mm. **Subject:** 10 Years of the Clearing House **Obv:** National arms

Date	Mintage	F	VF	XF	Unc	BU
2006 Proof	5,000	Value: 60.00				

KM# 410 10 HRYVEN
33.6220 g., 0.9250 Silver 0.9999 oz. ASW, 38.61 mm. **Subject:** 10 Years of the Constitution of Ukraine **Obv:** National arms

Date	Mintage	F	VF	XF	Unc	BU
2006 Proof	5,000	Value: 65.00				

KM# 421 10 HRYVEN
33.6221 g., 0.9250 Silver 0.9999 oz. ASW, 38.61 mm. **Subject:** Epiphany **Obv:** National arms

Date	Mintage	F	VF	XF	Unc	BU
2006 Proof	10,000	Value: 60.00				

KM# 423 10 HRYVEN
33.6220 g., 0.9250 Silver 0.9999 oz. ASW, 38.61 mm. **Subject:** Saint Kyryl Church **Obv:** National arms

Date	Mintage	F	VF	XF	Unc	BU
2006 Proof	8,000	Value: 60.00				

KM# 427 10 HRYVEN
33.6220 g., 0.9250 Silver 0.9999 oz. ASW, 38.61 mm. **Subject:** Twentieth Winter Olympic Games of 2006 **Obv:** National arms

Date	Mintage	F	VF	XF	Unc	BU
2006 Proof	5,000	Value: 60.00				

KM# 144 20 HRYVEN
67.2400 g., 0.9250 Silver 1.9996 oz. ASW, 50 mm. **Subject:** 10 Years Independence **Obv:** National arms **Rev:** Parliament building on map within beaded circle **Edge:** Segmented reeding

Date	Mintage	F	VF	XF	Unc	BU
2001 Proof	1,000	Value: 5,000				

KM# 174 20 HRYVEN
14.7000 g., Bi-Metallic .916 Gold center in .925 silver ring, 31 mm. **Subject:** "Kyiv Rus" Culture **Obv:** Old arms of Ukraine, Prince and a cathedral model in his hand and princess **Rev:** Old Rus earring **Edge:** Reeded and plain sections

Date	Mintage	F	VF	XF	Unc	BU
2001 Proof	2,000	Value: 540				

KM# 175 20 HRYVEN
14.7000 g., Bi-Metallic .916 Gold center in .925 Silver ring, 31 mm. **Subject:** Scythian Culture **Obv:** Warrior with a bowl in his hand and to the right, a Queen of Scythia **Rev:** Stylized horse flanked by pagasists **Edge:** Reeded and plain sections

Date	Mintage	F	VF	XF	Unc	BU
2001 Proof	2,000	Value: 550				

KM# 153 20 HRYVEN
67.2400 g., 0.9250 Silver 1.9996 oz. ASW, 50 mm. **Obv:** National arms on sun and flying geese divides beaded circle **Rev:** "AN-225 Mrija" cargo jet divides beaded circle **Edge:** Reeded and plain sections

Date	Mintage	F	VF	XF	Unc	BU
2002 Proof	2,002	Value: 1,500				

KM# 188 20 HRYVEN
67.2400 g., 0.9250 Silver 1.9996 oz. ASW, 50 mm. **Subject:** 60th Anniversary - Liberation of Kiev **Obv:** Eternal flame monument **Rev:** Map and battle scene **Edge:** Segmented reeding

Date	Mintage	F	VF	XF	Unc	BU
2003 Proof	2,000	Value: 500				

KM# 226 20 HRYVEN
62.2000 g., 0.9250 Silver 1.8497 oz. ASW, 50 mm. **Subject:** "Our Souls Do Not Die" **Obv:** National arms above value **Rev:** Bust of Taras Shevchenko facing flanked by standing figures **Edge:** Segmented reeding

Date	Mintage	F	VF	XF	Unc	BU
2004 Proof	4,000	Value: 150				

KM# 344 20 HRYVEN
67.2440 g., 0.9250 Silver 1.9997 oz. ASW, 50 mm. **Subject:** 2006 Olympic Games **Obv:** Woman holding flame and branch **Rev:** Six athletes around flame within square design **Edge:** Segmented reeding

Date	Mintage	F	VF	XF	Unc	BU
2004 Proof	5,000	Value: 110				

KM# 363 20 HRYVEN
67.2440 g., 0.9250 Silver 1.9997 oz. ASW, 50 mm. **Obv:** National arms on sun with flying geese divides beaded circle **Rev:** AN-124 jet plane divides beaded circle **Edge:** Segmented reeding

Date	Mintage	F	VF	XF	Unc	BU
2005 Proof	5,000	Value: 175				

KM# 369 20 HRYVEN
67.2440 g., 0.9250 Silver 1.9997 oz. ASW, 50 mm. **Subject:** Sorochynsky Fair **Obv:** Busts facing each other flanked by flower sprigs **Rev:** Farmer leading family in ox cart **Edge:** Segmented reeding

Date	Mintage	F	VF	XF	Unc	BU
2005 Proof	5,000	Value: 120				

KM# 374 20 HRYVEN
67.2440 g., 0.9250 Silver 1.9997 oz. ASW, 50 mm. **Subject:** 60th Anniversary of Victory in WWII **Obv:** Flying cranes divides value, date and national arms **Rev:** V-shaped searchlight beams filled with soldiers, order of the Patriotic War at bottom left **Edge:** Segmented reeding

Date	Mintage	F	VF	XF	Unc	BU
2005 Proof	5,000	Value: 110				

KM# 412 20 HRYVEN
67.2500 g., 0.9250 Silver 1.9999 oz. ASW, 50 mm. **Subject:** 15 Years of Ukraine Independency **Obv:** National arms

Date	Mintage	F	VF	XF	Unc	BU
2006 Proof	7,000	Value: 110				

KM# 426 50 HRYVEN
17.6300 g., 0.9000 Gold 0.5101 oz. AGW, 25 mm. **Subject:** Nestor - The Chronicler **Obv:** National arms

Date	Mintage	F	VF	XF	Unc	BU
2006 Proof	5,000	Value: 650				

KM# 345 100 HRYVEN
34.5594 g., 0.9000 Gold 1.0000 oz. AGW, 32 mm. **Subject:** The Golden Gate **Obv:** National arms above value between two stylized cranes **Rev:** Riders approaching castle gate **Edge:** Segmented reeding

Date	Mintage	F	VF	XF	Unc	BU
2004 Proof	2,000	Value: 2,500				

KM# 414 100 HRYVEN
1000.0000 g., 0.9990 Silver 32.117 oz. ASW, 100 mm. **Subject:** 10 Years to the Currency Reform in Ukraine **Obv:** National arms

Date	Mintage	Good	VG	F	VF	XF
2006 Proof	1,501	Value: 5,500				

KM# 199 100 HRYVNIAS
31.1000 g., 0.9000 Gold 0.8999 oz. AGW, 32 mm. **Subject:** Ancient Scythian Culture **Obv:** National arms above ornamental design and value within rope wreath **Rev:** Ancient craftsmen and jewelry **Edge:** Reeded

Date	Mintage	F	VF	XF	Unc	BU
2003 Proof	1,500	Value: 4,000				

MINT SETS

KM#	Date	Mintage	Identification	Issue Price	Mkt Val
MS2	2001 (8)	5,000	KM#1.1b, 2.1b, 3.3b, 4b, 6, 7, 8b, 129	—	40.00
MS3	2006 (8)	5,000	KM#1.1b, 2.1b, 3.3b, 4b, 6, 7, 8b, 411	—	15.00

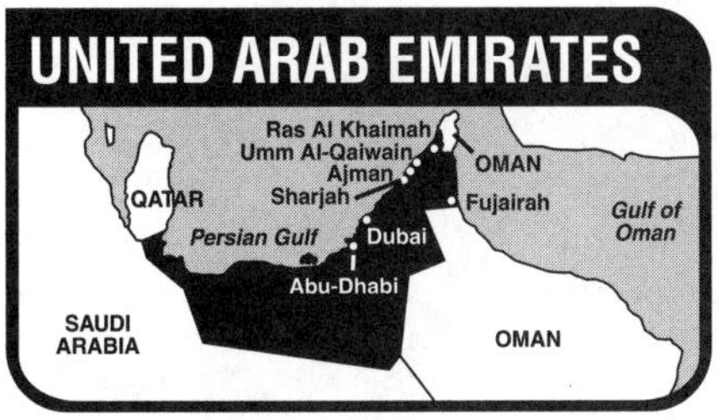

The seven United Arab Emirates (formerly known as the Trucial Sheikhdoms or States), located along the southern shore of the Persian Gulf, are comprised of the Sheikhdoms of Abu Dhabi, Dubai, al-Sharjah, Ajman, Umm al Qaiwain, Ras al-Khaimah and al-Fujairah. They have a combined area of about 32,000 sq. mi. (83,600 sq. km.) and a population of *2.1 million. Capital: Abu Zaby (Abu Dhabi). Since the oil strikes of 1958-60, the economy has centered about petroleum.

TITLES

الامارات العربية المتحدة

al-Imara(t) al-Arabiya(t) al-Muttahida(t)

UNITED EMIRATES

STANDARD COINAGE

KM# 2.2 5 FILS
Bronze **Series:** F.A.O. **Obv:** Value **Rev:** Fish above dates **Note:** Reduced size.

Date	Mintage	F	VF	XF	Unc	BU
AH1422-2001	—	—	0.10	0.15	0.30	1.00

KM# 3.2 10 FILS
Bronze **Obv:** Value **Rev:** Arab dhow above dates **Note:** Reduced size.

Date	Mintage	F	VF	XF	Unc	BU
1422 (2001)	—	—	0.20	0.35	0.80	1.20

KM# 4 25 FILS
3.5000 g., Copper-Nickel, 20 mm. **Obv:** Value **Rev:** Gazelle above dates

Date	Mintage	F	VF	XF	Unc	BU
AH1425-2005	—	—	0.20	0.40	0.75	1.00

KM# 16 50 FILS
4.3000 g., Copper-Nickel, 21 mm. **Obv:** Value **Rev:** Oil derricks above dates **Shape:** 7-sided **Note:** Reduced size.

Date	Mintage	F	VF	XF	Unc	BU
AH1425-2005	—	—	0.25	0.45	1.35	1.85

KM# 49 DIRHAM
6.3700 g., Copper-Nickel, 24 mm. **Subject:** 25th Anniversary - Armed Forces Unification **Obv:** Value **Rev:** Heraldic eagle within rope wreath **Edge:** Reeded

Date	Mintage	F	VF	XF	Unc	BU
ND (2001)	250,000	—	—	—	3.50	4.00

KM# 51 DIRHAM
6.3300 g., Copper-Nickel, 24 mm. **Subject:** 50 Years of Formal Education **Obv:** Value **Rev:** Symbolic design **Edge:** Reeded

Date	Mintage	F	VF	XF	Unc	BU
ND (2003)	—	—	—	—	3.50	4.00

KM# 52 DIRHAM
6.4000 g., Copper-Nickel, 24 mm. **Subject:** Abu Dhabi National Bank 35th Anniversary **Obv:** Value **Rev:** Towers divide dates within circle **Edge:** Reeded

Date	Mintage	F	VF	XF	Unc	BU
ND (2003)	—	—	—	—	3.50	4.00

KM# 54 DIRHAM
6.4000 g., Copper-Nickel, 24 mm. **Subject:** 40th Anniversary of Crude Oil Exports **Obv:** Value **Rev:** "ADCO" logo **Edge:** Reeded

Date	Mintage	F	VF	XF	Unc	BU
ND (2003)	—	—	—	—	3.50	4.00

KM# 73 DIRHAM
Copper-Nickel, 24 mm. **Subject:** Dubai 2003

Date	Mintage	F	VF	XF	Unc	BU
2004	—	—	—	—	3.50	4.00

KM# 74 DIRHAM
Copper-Nickel, 24 mm. **Subject:** First Gulf Bank

Date	Mintage	F	VF	XF	Unc	BU
2004	—	—	—	—	3.50	4.00

KM# 81 DIRHAM
6.3000 g., Copper-Nickel **Subject:** First National Bank - 25 Years of Excellence

Date	Mintage	F	VF	XF	Unc	BU
ND(2004)	—				3.50	4.00

KM# 6.2 DIRHAM
6.4000 g., Copper-Nickel, 24 mm. **Obv:** Value **Rev:** Jug above dates **Edge:** Reeded **Note:** Reduced size.

Date	Mintage	F	VF	XF	Unc	BU
AH1425-2005	—	—	0.35	0.65	1.85	2.25
AH1428-2007	—	—	0.35	0.65	1.85	2.25

KM# 75 DIRHAM
Copper-Nickel, 24 mm. **Subject:** Honoring the Mother of the Nation

Date	Mintage	F	VF	XF	Unc	BU
2005	—	—	—	—	3.50	4.00

KM# 77 DIRHAM
6.3000 g., Copper-Nickel, 24 mm. **Obv:** Value **Rev:** Zakum Development Co. logo **Edge:** Reeded

Date	Mintage	F	VF	XF	Unc	BU
ND(2007)	—	—	—	—	3.50	4.00

KM# 76 DIRHAM
6.3700 g., Copper-Nickel, 24 mm. **Subject:** 75th Anniversary Sharjah International Airport **Obv:** Value **Obv. Legend:** UNITED ARAB EMIRATES **Rev:** Three birds in flight under arc **Edge:** Reeded

Date	Mintage	F	VF	XF	Unc	BU
ND(2007)	—	—	—	—	3.00	4.00

KM# 78 DIRHAM
6.4000 g., Copper-Nickel, 23.95 mm. **Obv:** Value **Obv. Legend:** UNITED ARAB EMIRATES **Rev:** Large "50" with Police badge in "0" **Rev. Legend:** ABU DHABI POLICE GOLDEN JUBILEE **Edge:** Reeded

Date	Mintage	F	VF	XF	Unc	BU
ND(2007)	—	—	—	—	3.50	4.00

KM# 79 DIRHAM
6.4300 g., Copper-Nickel, 24.03 mm. **Obv:** Value **Obv. Legend:** UNITED ARAB EMIRATES **Rev:** Large "30" and logo **Rev. Legend:** 30TH ANNIVERSARY OF THE 1ST LNG SHIPMENT **Rev. Inscription:** ADGAS **Edge:** Reeded

Date	Mintage	F	VF	XF	Unc	BU
ND(2007)	—	—	—	—	3.50	4.00

KM# 47 50 DIRHAMS

40.2200 g., 0.9250 Silver 1.1961 oz. ASW, 40 mm. **Subject:** 25th Anniversary - Women's Union (1975-2000) **Obv:** Bust right **Rev:** Stylized gazelle **Edge:** Reeded

Date	Mintage	F	VF	XF	Unc	BU
ND(2001) Proof	5,000	Value: 55.00				

KM# 59 50 DIRHAMS

40.0000 g., 0.9250 Silver 1.1895 oz. ASW, 40 mm. **Subject:** 25th Anniversary - Arab Bank of Investment and Foreign Trade **Edge:** Reeded

Date	Mintage	F	VF	XF	Unc	BU
ND(2001) Proof	2,000	Value: 65.00				

KM# 60 50 DIRHAMS

40.0000 g., 0.9250 Silver 1.1895 oz. ASW, 40 mm. **Subject:** 25th Anniversary - Armed Forces Unification **Edge:** Reeded

Date	Mintage	F	VF	XF	Unc	BU
ND(2001) Proof	10,000	Value: 65.00				

KM# 61 50 DIRHAMS

40.0000 g., 0.9250 Silver 1.1895 oz. ASW, 40 mm. **Subject:** 30th Anniversary - Al-Ain National Museum **Edge:** Reeded

Date	Mintage	F	VF	XF	Unc	BU
ND(2002) Proof	5,000	Value: 65.00				

KM# 62 50 DIRHAMS

40.0000 g., 0.9250 Silver 1.1895 oz. ASW, 40 mm. **Subject:** 25th Anniversary - University of the U.A.E. **Obv:** Bust facing 7/8 right **Edge:** Reeded

Date	Mintage	F	VF	XF	Unc	BU
ND(2002) Proof	5,000	Value: 65.00				

KM# 63 50 DIRHAMS

40.0000 g., 0.9250 Silver 1.1895 oz. ASW, 40 mm. **Subject:** 25 Years - Etisalat Jubilee **Edge:** Reeded

Date	Mintage	F	VF	XF	Unc	BU
ND(2002) Proof	5,000	Value: 65.00				

KM# 64 50 DIRHAMS

40.0000 g., 0.9250 Silver 1.1895 oz. ASW, 40 mm. **Subject:** Sheikh Hamdan Bin Rashid Al Maktoum Award for Medical Sciences **Edge:** Reeded

Date	Mintage	F	VF	XF	Unc	BU
ND(2002) Proof	2,000	Value: 65.00				

KM# 65 50 DIRHAMS

40.0000 g., 0.9250 Silver 1.1895 oz. ASW, 40 mm. **Subject:** Al Ahmadia School Foundation Committee **Obv:** Bust facing slightly left **Rev:** Building **Edge:** Reeded

Date	Mintage	F	VF	XF	Unc	BU
ND(2002) Proof	5,000	Value: 60.00				

KM# 67 50 DIRHAMS

40.0000 g., 0.9250 Silver 1.1895 oz. ASW, 40 mm. **Subject:** 20th Anniversary - Establishment of the Administrative Development Institute **Edge:** Reeded

Date	Mintage	F	VF	XF	Unc	BU
ND(2002) Proof	2,000	Value: 65.00				

KM# 68 50 DIRHAMS

40.0000 g., 0.9250 Silver 1.1895 oz. ASW, 40 mm. **Subject:** 30th Anniversary - U.A.E. Central Bank **Edge:** Reeded

Date	Mintage	F	VF	XF	Unc	BU
ND(2003) Proof	5,000	Value: 60.00				

KM# 69 50 DIRHAMS

40.0000 g., 0.9250 Silver 1.1895 oz. ASW, 40 mm. **Subject:** 58th Annual Meeting of the World Bank Group and the Int'l Money Fund **Obv:** Colored dots **Edge:** Reeded

Date	Mintage	F	VF	XF	Unc	BU
ND(2003) Proof	10,000	Value: 50.00				

KM# 50 50 DIRHAMS

40.0000 g., 0.9250 Silver 1.1895 oz. ASW, 40 mm. **Obv:** Value **Rev:** FIFA 2003 World Youth Soccer Championship **Edge:** Reeded

Date	Mintage	F	VF	XF	Unc	BU
ND(2003) Proof	—	Value: 65.00				

KM# 66 50 DIRHAMS

40.0000 g., 0.9250 Silver 1.1895 oz. ASW, 40 mm. **Subject:** Quality Certification for the Ministry of Finance and Industry **Edge:** Reeded

Date	Mintage	F	VF	XF	Unc	BU
ND(2003) Proof	3,000	Value: 65.00				

KM# 70 50 DIRHAMS

40.0000 g., 0.9250 Silver 1.1895 oz. ASW, 40 mm. **Subject:** 40th Anniversary - First Oil Export from Abu Dhabi Onshore Oil Fields (ADCO) **Edge:** Reeded

Date	Mintage	F	VF	XF	Unc	BU
ND(2004) Proof	—	Value: 65.00				

KM# 71 50 DIRHAMS

40.0000 g., 0.9250 Silver 1.1895 oz. ASW, 40 mm. **Subject:** 25th Anniversary - Sharjah City for Humanitarian Services (SCHS) **Edge:** Reeded

Date	Mintage	F	VF	XF	Unc	BU
ND(2005) Proof	—	Value: 65.00				

KM# 80 50 DIRHAMS

40.1400 g., Silver, 39.96 mm. **Subject:** Sharjah - Cultural Capital **Obv:** Large value at center **Obv. Legend:** UNITED ARAB EMIRATES **Rev:** Large flame like logo **Edge:** Reeded

Date	Mintage	F	VF	XF	Unc	BU
ND(2006) Proof	—	Value: 75.00				

KM# 82 50 DIRHAMS

40.0000 g., Silver, 40 mm. **Subject:** 25th Anniversary Emirates Banks Association **Obv:** Value **Obv. Legend:** UNITED ARAB EMIRATES **Rev:** Logo **Edge:** Reeded

Date	Mintage	F	VF	XF	Unc	BU
ND(2007) Proof	—	Value: 75.00				

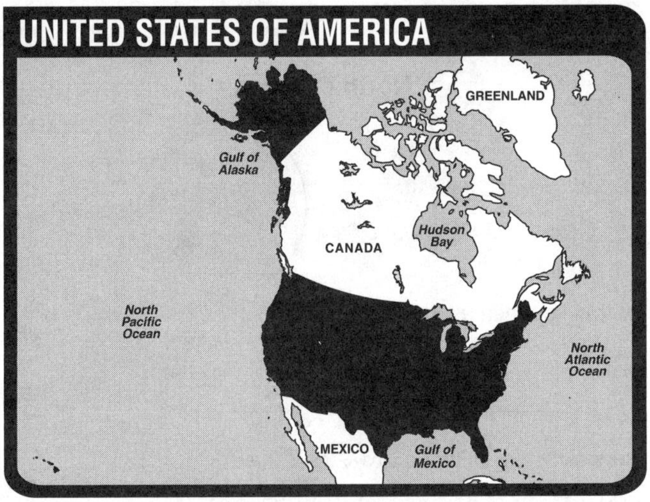

CIRCULATION COINAGE

CENT

Lincoln Cent

Lincoln Memorial

KM# 201b COPPER PLATED ZINC 19 mm. **Notes:** MS60 prices are for brown coins and MS65 prices are for coins that are at least 90% original red. The 1983 "doubled die reverse" shows doubling of "United States of America." The 1984 "doubled die" shows doubling of Lincoln's ear on the obverse.

Date	Mintage	XF-40	MS-65	Prf-65
2001	4,959,600,000	—	4.00	—
2001D	5,374,990,000	—	4.00	—
2001S	(3,099,096)	—	—	4.00
2002	3,260,800,000	—	4.00	—
2002D	4,028,055,000	—	4.00	—
2002S	(3,157,739)	—	—	4.00
2003	3,300,000,000	—	3.50	—
2003D	3,548,000,000	—	3.50	—
2003S	(3,116,590)	—	—	4.00
2004	3,379,600,000	—	3.50	—
2004D	3,456,400,000	—	3.50	—
2004S	2,992,069	—	—	4.00
2005	3,935,600,000	—	3.50	—
2005D	3,764,450,000	—	3.50	—
2005S	3,273,000	—	—	4.00
2006	4,290,000,000	—	2.00	—
2006D	3,944,000,000	—	2.50	—
2006S	2,923,105	—	—	4.00
2007	—	—	1.50	—
2007D	—	—	1.50	—
2007S	—	—	—	4.00

5 CENTS

Jefferson Nickel

Pre-war design resumed

KM# A192 COPPER-NICKEL 19.53 mm. 5.0000 g. **Designer:** Felix Schlag **Notes:** KM#192 design and composition resumed. The 1979-S and 1981-S Type II proofs have clearer mint marks than the Type I proofs of those years.

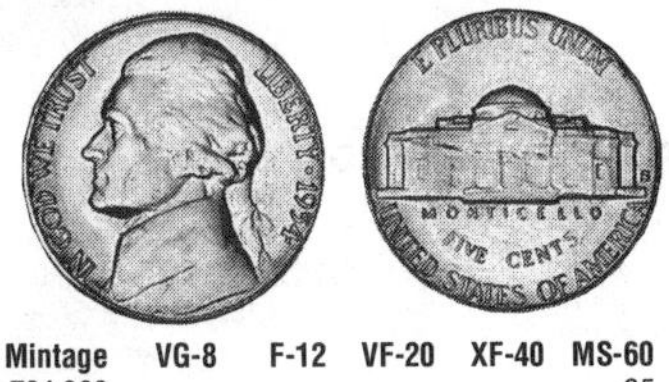

Date	Mintage	VG-8	F-12	VF-20	XF-40	MS-60	MS-65	-65FS	Prf-65
2001P	675,704,000	—	—	—	—	.25	.50	20.00	—
2001D	627,680,000	—	—	—	—	.25	.50	20.00	—
2001S	(3,099,096)	—	—	—	—	—	—	—	2.00
2002P	539,280,000	—	—	—	—	.25	.50	—	—
2002D	691,200,000	—	—	—	—	.25	.50	—	—
2002S	(3,157,739)	—	—	—	—	—	—	—	2.00
2003P	441,840,000	—	—	—	—	.25	.50	—	—

Date	Mintage	VG-8	F-12	VF-20	XF-40	MS-60	MS-65	-65FS	Prf-65
2003D	383,040,000	—	—	—	—	.25	.50	—	—
2003S	(3,116,590)	—	—	—	—	—	—	—	2.00

Jefferson - Peace Reverse

Jefferson era peace medal design: two clasped hands, pipe and hatchet

KM# 360 COPPER NICKEL 21.2 mm. 5.0000 g. **Obv. Designer:** Felix Schlag **Rev. Designer:** Norman E. Nemeth

Date	Mintage	MS-65	Prf-65	Date	Mintage	MS-65	Prf-65
2004P	361,440,000	1.00	—	2004S	—	—	13.00
2004D	372,000,000	1.00	—				

Jefferson - Keelboat Reverse

Lewis and Clark's Keelboat

KM# 361 COPPER NICKEL 21.2 mm. 5.0000 g. **Obv. Designer:** Felix Schlag **Rev. Designer:** Al Maletsky

Date	Mintage	MS-65	Prf-65	Date	Mintage	MS-65	Prf-65
2004P	366,720,000	1.00	—	2004S	—	—	13.00
2004D	344,880,000	1.00	—				

Jefferson large profile - Bison Reverse

KM# 368 COPPER NICKEL 21.2 mm. 5.0000 g. **Obv. Designer:** Joe Fitzgerald and Don Everhart II **Rev. Designer:** Jamie Franki and Norman E. Nemeth

Date	Mintage	MS-65	Prf-65	Date	Mintage	MS-65	Prf-65
2005P	448,320,000	1.00	—	2005S	—	—	7.50
2005D	487,680,000	1.00	—				

Jefferson - Pacific Coastline

KM# 369 COPPER NICKEL 21.2 mm. 5.0000 g. **Obv. Designer:** Joe Fitzgerald and Don Everhart **Rev. Designer:** Joe Fitzgerald and Donna Weaver

Date	Mintage	MS-65	Prf-65	Date	Mintage	MS-65	Prf-65
2005P	394,080,000	1.00	—	2005S	—	—	6.50
2005D	411,120,000	1.00	—				

Jefferson large facing portrait - Enhanced Monticello Reverse

KM# 381 COPPER-NICKEL 0 oz. 21 mm. 5.0000 g. **Obv. Designer:** Jamie N. Franki and Donna Weaver **Rev. Designer:** Felix Schlag and John Mercanti

Date	Mintage	MS-65	Prf-65
2006P	693,120,000	1.00	—
2006D	809,280,000	1.00	—
2006S	—	—	4.00
2007P	—	.50	—
2007D	—	.50	—
2007S	—	—	4.00

DIME

Roosevelt Dime

KM# 195a COPPER-NICKEL CLAD COPPER 17.9 mm. 2.2700 g. **Designer:** John R. Sinnock **Notes:** The 1979-S and 1981-S Type II proofs have clearer mint marks than the Type I proofs of those years. On the 1982 no-mint-mark variety, the mint mark was inadvertently left off.

Mint mark
1968-present

1982 No mint mark

Date	Mintage	MS-65	Prf-65	Date	Mintage	MS-65	Prf-65
2001P	1,369,590,000	1.00	—	2004S	(1,804,396)	—	4.75
2001D	1,412,800,000	1.00	—	2005P	1,412,000,000	1.00	—
2001S	(2,249,496)	—	1.00	2005D	1,423,500,000	1.00	—
2002P	1,187,500,000	1.00	—	2005S	—	—	2.25
2002D	1,379,500,000	1.00	—	2006P	1,381,000,000	1.00	—
2002S	(2,268,913)	—	2.00	2006D	1,447,000,000	1.00	—
2003P	1,085,500,000	1.00	—	2006S	—	—	2.25
2003D	986,500,000	1.00	—	2007P	—	1.00	—
2003S	(2,076,165)	—	2.00	2007D	—	1.00	—
2004P	1,328,000,000	1.00	—	2007S	—	—	2.25
2004D	1,159,500,000	1.00	—				

Roosevelt Dime

KM# A195 SILVER 0 oz. ASW.

Date	Mintage	Prf-65	Date	Mintage	Prf-65
2001S	(849,600)	5.00	2005S	—	3.50
2002S	(888,826)	5.00	2006S	—	3.50
2003S	(1,090,425)	4.00	2007S	—	3.50
2004S	—	4.50			

QUARTER

50 State Quarters

Kentucky

KM# 322 COPPER-NICKEL CLAD COPPER

Date	Mintage	MS-63	MS-65	Prf-65
2001P	353,000,000	1.20	7.00	—
2001D	370,564,000	1.00	8.00	—
2001S	(3,009,800)	—	—	11.00

KM# 322a 0.9000 **SILVER** 0.1808 oz. ASW. 6.2500 g.

Date	Mintage	MS-63	MS-65	Prf-65
2001S	(849,500)	—	—	21.00

New York

KM# 318 COPPER-NICKEL CLAD COPPER

Date	Mintage	MS-63	MS-65	Prf-65
2001P	655,400,000	1.00	8.50	—
2001D	619,640,000	1.00	8.50	—
2001S	(3,009,800)	—	—	11.00

KM# 318a 0.9000 **SILVER** 0.1808 oz. ASW. 6.2500 g.

Date	Mintage	MS-63	MS-65	Prf-65
2001S	(849,600)	—	—	24.00

North Carolina

KM# 319 COPPER-NICKEL CLAD COPPER

Date	Mintage	MS-63	MS-65	Prf-65
2001P	627,600,000	1.00	7.50	—
2001D	427,876,000	1.00	8.50	—
2001S	(3,009,800)	—	—	11.00

KM# 319a 0.9000 **SILVER** 0.1808 oz. ASW. 6.2500 g.

Date	Mintage	MS-63	MS-65	Prf-65
2001S	(849,600)	—	—	22.00

Rhode Island

KM# 320 COPPER-NICKEL CLAD COPPER 0 oz. 5.6000 g.

Date	Mintage	MS-63	MS-65	Prf-65
2001P	423,000,000	1.00	6.50	—
2001D	447,100,000	1.00	8.00	—
2001S	(3,009,800)	—	—	11.00

KM# 320a 0.9000 **SILVER** 0.1808 oz. ASW. 6.2500 g.

Date	Mintage	MS-63	MS-65	Prf-65
2001S	(849,600)	—	—	19.00

Vermont

KM# 321 COPPER-NICKEL CLAD COPPER

Date	Mintage	MS-63	MS-65	Prf-65
2001P	423,400,000	1.20	7.00	—
2001D	459,404,000	1.00	7.00	—
2001S	(3,009,800)	—	—	11.00

KM# 321a 0.9000 **SILVER** 0.1808 oz. ASW. 6.2500 g.

Date	Mintage	MS-63	MS-65	Prf-65
2001S	(849,600)	—	—	19.00

Indiana

KM# 334 COPPER-NICKEL CLAD COPPER 5.6700 g.

Date	Mintage	MS-63	MS-65	Prf-65
2002P	362,600,000	1.00	6.00	—
2002D	327,200,000	1.00	6.50	—
2002S	(3,084,185)	—	—	4.00

KM# 334a 0.9000 **SILVER** 0.1808 oz. ASW. 6.2500 g.

Date	Mintage	MS-63	MS-65	Prf-65
2002S	(892,229)	—	—	9.00

Louisiana

KM# 333 COPPER-NICKEL CLAD COPPER

Date	Mintage	MS-63	MS-65	Prf-65
2002P	362,000,000	1.00	6.50	—
2002D	402,204,000	1.00	7.00	—
2002S	(3,084,185)	—	—	4.00

KM# 333a 0.9000 **SILVER** 0.1808 oz. ASW. 6.2500 g.

Date	Mintage	MS-63	MS-65	Prf-65
2002S	(892,229)	—	—	9.00

Mississippi

KM# 335 COPPER-NICKEL CLAD COPPER 5.6700 g.

Date	Mintage	MS-63	MS-65	Prf-65
2002P	290,000,000	1.00	5.00	—
2002D	289,600,000	1.00	6.00	—
2002S	(3,084,185)	—	—	4.00

KM# 335a 0.9000 **SILVER** 0.1808 oz. ASW. 6.2500 g.

Date	Mintage	MS-63	MS-65	Prf-65
2002S	(892,229)	—	—	9.00

Ohio

KM# 332 COPPER-NICKEL CLAD COPPER

Date	Mintage	MS-63	MS-65	Prf-65
2002P	217,200,000	1.00	6.50	—
2002D	414,832,000	1.00	7.00	—
2002S	(3,084,185)	—	—	4.00

KM# 332a 0.9000 **SILVER** 0.1808 oz. ASW. 6.2500 g.

Date	Mintage	MS-63	MS-65	Prf-65
2002S	(892,229)	—	—	9.00

Tennessee

KM# 331 COPPER-NICKEL CLAD COPPER

Date	Mintage	MS-63	MS-65	Prf-65
2002P	361,600,000	1.40	6.50	—
2002D	286,468,000	1.40	7.00	—
2002S	(3,084,185)	—	—	4.00

KM# 331a 0.9000 **SILVER** 0.1808 oz. ASW. 6.2500 g.

Date	Mintage	MS-63	MS-65	Prf-65
2002S	(892,229)	—	—	9.00

Alabama

KM# 344 COPPER-NICKEL CLAD COPPER 5.6700 g.

Date	Mintage	MS-63	MS-65	Prf-65
2003P	225,000,000	1.00	7.00	—
2003D	232,400,000	1.00	7.00	—
2003S	(3,270,603)	—	—	3.50

KM# 344a 0.9000 **SILVER** 0.1808 oz. ASW. 6.2500 g.

Date	Mintage	MS-63	MS-65	Prf-65
2003S	—	—	—	5.25

Arkansas

KM# 347 COPPER-NICKEL CLAD COPPER

Date	Mintage	MS-63	MS-65	Prf-65
2003P	228,000,000	1.00	7.00	—
2003D	229,800,000	1.00	7.00	—
2003S	(3,270,603)	—	—	3.50

KM# 347a 0.9000 **SILVER** 0.1808 oz. ASW. 6.2500 g.

Date	Mintage	MS-63	MS-65	Prf-65
2003S	—	—	—	5.25

Illinois

KM# 343 COPPER-NICKEL CLAD COPPER 5.6700 g.

Date	Mintage	MS-63	MS-65	Prf-65
2003P	225,800,000	1.10	7.00	—
2003D	237,400,000	1.10	6.00	—
2003S	(3,270,603)	—	—	3.50

KM# 343a 0.9000 **SILVER** 0.1808 oz. ASW. 6.2500 g.

Date	Mintage	MS-63	MS-65	Prf-65
2003S	—	—	—	5.25

Maine

KM# 345 COPPER-NICKEL CLAD COPPER

Date	Mintage	MS-63	MS-65	Prf-65
2003P	217,400,000	1.00	6.50	—
2003D	213,400,000	1.00	8.00	—
2003S	(3,270,603)	—	—	3.50

KM# 345a 0.9000 **SILVER** 0.1808 oz. ASW. 6.2500 g.

Date	Mintage	MS-63	MS-65	Prf-65
2003S	—	—	—	5.25

Missouri

KM# 346 COPPER-NICKEL CLAD COPPER

Date	Mintage	MS-63	MS-65	Prf-65
2003P	225,000,000	1.00	7.00	—
2003D	228,200,000	1.00	7.00	—
2003S	(3,270,603)	—	—	3.50

KM# 346a 0.9000 **SILVER** 0.1808 oz. ASW. 6.2500 g.

Date	Mintage	MS-63	MS-65	Prf-65
2003S	—	—	—	5.25

Florida

KM# 356 COPPER-NICKEL CLAD COPPER 5.6700 g.

Date	Mintage	MS-63	MS-65	Prf-65
2004P	240,200,000	.75	6.50	—
2004D	241,600,000	.75	7.00	—
2004S	—	—	—	5.00

KM# 356a 0.9000 **SILVER** 0.1808 oz. ASW. 6.2500 g.

Date	Mintage	MS-63	MS-65	Prf-65
2004S	—	—	—	6.00

Iowa

KM# 358 COPPER-NICKEL CLAD COPPER 5.6700 g.

Date	Mintage	MS-63	MS-65	Prf-65
2004P	213,800,000	.75	6.50	—
2004D	251,800,000	.75	7.00	—
2004S	—	—	—	5.00

KM# 358a 0.9000 **SILVER** 0.1808 oz. ASW. 6.2500 g.

Date	Mintage	MS-63	MS-65	Prf-65
2004S	—	—	—	6.00

Michigan

KM# 355 COPPER-NICKEL CLAD COPPER 5.6700 g.

Date	Mintage	MS-63	MS-65	Prf-65
2004P	233,800,000	.75	6.50	—
2004D	225,800,000	.75	6.50	—
2004S	—	—	—	5.00

KM# 355a 0.9000 **SILVER** 0.1808 oz. ASW. 6.2500 g.

Date	Mintage	MS-63	MS-65	Prf-65
2004S	—	—	—	6.00

Texas

KM# 357 COPPER-NICKEL CLAD COPPER 5.6700 g.

Date	Mintage	MS-63	MS-65	Prf-65
2004P	278,800,000	.75	7.00	—
2004D	263,000,000	.75	7.00	—
2004S	—	—	—	5.00

KM# 357a 0.9000 **SILVER** 0.1808 oz. ASW. 6.2500 g.

Date	Mintage	MS-63	MS-65	Prf-65
2004S	—	—	—	6.00

Wisconsin

KM# 359 COPPER-NICKEL CLAD COPPER 5.6700 g.

Date	Mintage	MS-63	MS-65	Prf-65
2004P	226,400,000	1.00	8.00	—
2004D	226,800,000	1.00	10.00	—
2004D Extra Leaf Low	Est. 9,000	300	600	—
2004D Extra Leaf High	Est. 3,000	400	900	—
2004S	—	—	—	5.00

KM# 359a 0.9000 **SILVER** 0.1808 oz. ASW. 6.2500 g.

Date	Mintage	MS-63	MS-65	Prf-65
2004S	—	—	—	6.00

California

KM# 370 COPPER-NICKEL CLAD COPPER 5.7000 g.

Date	Mintage	MS-63	MS-65	Prf-65
2005P	257,200,000	.75	5.00	—
2005P Satin Finish	Inc. above	3.50	6.00	—
2005D	263,200,000	.75	5.00	—
2005D Satin Finish	Inc. above	3.50	6.00	—
2005S	—	—	—	3.00

KM# 370a 0.9000 **SILVER** 0.1808 oz. ASW. 6.2500 g.

Date	Mintage	MS-63	MS-65	Prf-65
2005S	—	—	—	5.50

Kansas

KM# 373 COPPER-NICKEL CLAD COPPER 0 oz.

Date	Mintage	MS-63	MS-65	Prf-65
2005P	263,400,000	.75	5.00	—
2005P Satin Finish	Inc. above	3.50	6.00	—
2005D	300,000,000	.75	5.00	—
2005D Satin Finish	Inc. above	3.50	6.00	—
2005S	—	—	—	3.00

KM# 373a 0.9000 **SILVER** 0.1808 oz. ASW. 6.2500 g.

Date	Mintage	MS-63	MS-65	Prf-65
2005S	—	—	—	5.50

Minnesota

KM# 371 COPPER-NICKEL CLAD COPPER 5.7000 g.

Date	Mintage	MS-63	MS-65	Prf-65
2005P	226,400,000	.75	5.00	—
2005P Satin Finish	Inc. above	3.50	6.00	—
2005D	226,800,000	.75	5.00	—
2005D Satin Finish	Inc. above	3.50	6.00	—
2005S	—	—	—	3.00

KM# 371a 0.9000 **SILVER** 0.1808 oz. ASW. 6.2500 g.

Date	Mintage	MS-63	MS-65	Prf-65
2005S	—	—	—	5.50

Oregon

KM# 372 COPPER-NICKEL CLAD COPPER 5.6700 g.

Date	Mintage	MS-63	MS-65	Prf-65
2005P	316,200,000	.75	5.00	—
2005P Satin Finish	Inc. above	3.50	6.00	—
2005D	404,000,000	.75	5.00	—
2005D Satin Finish	Inc. above	3.50	6.00	—

Date	Mintage	MS-63	MS-65	Prf-65
2005S	—	—	—	3.00

KM# 372a 0.9000 **SILVER** 0.1808 oz. ASW. 6.2500 g.

Date	Mintage	MS-63	MS-65	Prf-65
2005S	—	—	—	5.50

West Virginia

KM# 374 **COPPER-NICKEL CLAD COPPER** 5.6700 g.

Date	Mintage	MS-63	MS-65	Prf-65
2005P	365,400,000	.75	5.00	—
2005P Satin Finish	Inc. above	3.50	6.00	—
2005D	356,200,000	.75	5.00	—
2005D Satin Finish	Inc. above	3.50	6.00	—
2005S	—	—	—	3.00

KM# 374a 0.9000 **SILVER** 0.1808 oz. ASW. 6.2500 g.

Date	Mintage	MS-63	MS-65	Prf-65
2005S	—	—	—	5.50

Colorado

KM# 384 **COPPER-NICKEL CLAD COPPER** 24 mm. 5.6400 g.

Date	Mintage	MS-63	MS-65	Prf-65
2006P	274,800,000	.75	5.00	—
2006P Satin Finish	Inc. above	3.00	5.00	—
2006D	294,200,000	.75	5.00	—
2006D Satin Finish	Inc. above	3.00	5.00	—
2006S	—	—	—	5.00

KM# 384a 0.9000 **SILVER** 0.1808 oz. ASW. 6.2500 g.

Date	Mintage	MS-63	MS-65	Prf-65
2006S	—	—	—	5.75

Nebraska

KM# 383 **COPPER-NICKEL CLAD COPPER** 24.16 mm. 5.7300 g.

Date	Mintage	MS-63	MS-65	Prf-65
2006P	318,000,000	.75	6.00	—
2006P Satin Finish	Inc. above	3.00	5.00	—
2006D	273,000,000	.75	6.00	—
2006D Satin Finish	Inc. above	3.00	5.00	—
2006S	—	—	—	5.00

KM# 383a 0.9000 **SILVER** 0.1808 oz. ASW. 6.2500 g.

Date	Mintage	MS-63	MS-65	Prf-65
2006S	—	—	—	5.75

Nevada

KM# 382 **COPPER-NICKEL CLAD COPPER** 24.21 mm. 5.6800 g.

Date	Mintage	MS-63	MS-65	Prf-65
2006P	277,000,000	.75	6.00	—
2006P Satin Finish	Inc. above	3.00	5.00	—
2006D	312,800,000	.75	6.00	—
2006D Satin Finish	Inc. above	3.00	5.00	—
2006S	—	—	—	5.00

KM# 382a 0.9000 **SILVER** 0.1808 oz. ASW. 6.2500 g.

Date	Mintage	MS-63	MS-65	Prf-65
2006S	—	—	—	5.75

North Dakota

KM# 385 **COPPER-NICKEL CLAD COPPER** 24.23 mm. 5.6100 g.

Date	Mintage	MS-63	MS-65	Prf-65
2006P	305,800,000	.75	5.00	—
2006P Satin Finish	Inc. above	3.00	5.00	—
2006D	359,000,000	.75	5.00	—
2006D Satin Finish	Inc. above	3.00	5.00	—
2006S	—	—	—	5.00

KM# 385a 0.9000 **SILVER** 0.1808 oz. ASW. 6.2500 g.

Date	Mintage	MS-63	MS-65	Prf-65
2006S	—	—	—	5.75

South Dakota

KM# 386 **COPPER-NICKEL CLAD COPPER** 24.18 mm. 5.6400 g.

Date	Mintage	MS-63	MS-65	Prf-65
2006P	245,000,000	.75	5.00	—
2006P Satin Finish	Inc. above	3.00	5.00	—
2006D	265,800,000	.75	5.00	—
2006D Satin Finish	Inc. above	3.00	5.00	—
2006S	—	—	—	5.00

KM# 386a 0.9000 **SILVER** 0.1808 oz. ASW. 6.2500 g.

Date	Mintage	MS-63	MS-65	Prf-65
2006S	—	—	—	5.75

Idaho

KM# 398 **COPPER-NICKEL CLAD COPPER**

Date	Mintage	MS-63	MS-65	Prf-65
2007P	294,600,000	.75	8.00	—
2007D	286,800,000	.75	8.00	—
2007S	—	—	—	4.00

KM# 398a 0.9000 **SILVER** 0.1808 oz. ASW. 6.2500 g.

Date	Mintage	MS-63	MS-65	Prf-65
2007S	Inc. above	—	—	6.50

Montana

KM# 396 **COPPER-NICKEL CLAD COPPER**

Date	Mintage	MS-63	MS-65	Prf-65
2007P	257,000,000	.75	8.00	—
2007D	256,240,000	.75	5.00	—
2007S	—	—	—	4.00

KM# 396a 0.9000 **SILVER** 0.1808 oz. ASW. 6.2500 g.

Date	Mintage	MS-63	MS-65	Prf-65
2007S	Inc. above	—	—	6.50

Utah

KM# 400 COPPER-NICKEL CLAD COPPER

Date	Mintage	MS-63	MS-65	Prf-65
2007P	—	.75	8.00	—
2007D	—	.75	8.00	—
2007S	—	—	—	4.00

KM# 400a 0.9000 **SILVER** 0.1808 oz. ASW. 6.2500 g.

Date	Mintage	MS-63	MS-65	Prf-65
2007S	Inc. above	—	—	6.50

Washington

KM# 397 COPPER-NICKEL CLAD COPPER

Date	Mintage	MS-63	MS-65	Prf-65
2007P	265,200,000	.75	8.00	—
2007D	280,000,000	.75	8.00	—
2007S	—	—	—	4.00

KM# 397a 0.9000 **SILVER** 0.1808 oz. ASW. 6.2500 g.

Date	Mintage	MS-63	MS-65	Prf-65
2007S	Inc. above	—	—	6.50

Wyoming

KM# 399 COPPER-NICKEL CLAD COPPER

Date	Mintage	MS-63	MS-65	Prf-65
2007P	—	.75	8.00	—
2007D	—	.75	8.00	—
2007S	—	—	—	4.00

KM# 399a 0.9000 **SILVER** 0.1808 oz. ASW. 6.2500 g.

Date	Mintage	MS-63	MS-65	Prf-65
2007S	Inc. above	—	—	6.50

Alaska

KM# 424 COPPER-NICKEL CLAD COPPER

Date	Mintage	MS-63	MS-65	Prf-65
2008P	—	.75	8.00	—
2008D	—	.75	8.00	—
2008S	—	—	—	4.00

KM# 424a 0.9000 **SILVER** 0.1808 oz. ASW. 6.2500 g.

Date	Mintage	MS-63	MS-65	Prf-65
2008S	—	—	—	6.50

Arizona

KM# 423 COPPER-NICKEL CLAD COPPER

Date	Mintage	MS-63	MS-65	Prf-65
2008P	—	.75	8.00	—
2008D	—	.75	8.00	—
2008S	—	—	—	4.00

KM# 423a 0.9000 **SILVER** 0.1808 oz. ASW. 6.2500 g.

Date	Mintage	MS-63	MS-65	Prf-65
2008S	—	—	—	6.50

Hawaii

KM# 425 COPPER-NICKEL CLAD COPPER

Date	Mintage	MS-63	MS-65	Prf-65
2008P	—	.75	8.00	—
2008D	—	.75	8.00	—
2008S	—	—	—	4.50

KM# 425a 0.9000 **SILVER** 0.1808 oz. ASW. 6.2500 g.

Date	Mintage	MS-63	MS-65	Prf-65
2008S	—	—	—	6.50

New Mexico

KM# 422 COPPER-NICKEL CLAD COPPER

Date	Mintage	MS-63	MS-65	Prf-65
2008P	—	.75	8.00	—
2008D	—	.75	8.00	—
2008S	—	—	—	4.00

KM# 422a 0.9000 **SILVER** 0.1808 oz. ASW. 6.2500 g.

Date	Mintage	MS-63	MS-65	Prf-65
2008S	—	—	—	6.50

Oklahoma

KM# 421 COPPER-NICKEL CLAD COPPER

Date	Mintage	MS-63	MS-65	Prf-65
2008P	—	.75	8.00	—
2008D	—	.75	8.00	—
2008S	—	—	—	4.00

KM# 421a 0.9000 **SILVER** 0.1808 oz. ASW. 6.2500 g.

Date	Mintage	MS-63	MS-65	Prf-65
2008S	—	—	—	6.50

HALF DOLLAR

Kennedy Half Dollar

Regular design resumed

KM# A202b COPPER-NICKEL CLAD COPPER 30.6 mm. 11.3400 g. **Notes:** KM#202b design and composition resumed. The 1979-S and 1981-S Type II proofs have clearer mint marks than the Type I proofs of those years.

Date	Mintage	MS-65	Prf-65	Date	Mintage	MS-65	Prf-65
2001P	21,200,000	9.00	—	2005D	3,500,000	9.00	—
2001D	19,504,000	9.00	—	2005D Satin finish	1,160,000	10.00	—
2001S	(2,235,000)	—	10.00	2005S	2,275,000	—	7.00
2002P	3,100,000	10.00	—	2006P	2,400,000	12.00	—
2002D	2,500,000	10.00	—	2006P Satin finish	847,361	12.00	—
2002S	(2,268,913)	—	8.00	2006D	2,000,000	20.00	—
2003P	2,500,000	14.00	—	2006D Satin finish	847,361	14.00	—
2003D	2,500,000	14.00	—	2006S	1,934,965	—	10.00
2003S	2,076,165	—	6.00	2007P	—	7.00	—
2004P	2,900,000	14.00	—	2007P Satin finish	—	—	—
2004D	2,900,000	14.00	—	2007D	—	7.00	—
2004S	1,789,488	—	13.00	2007D Satin finish	—	—	—
2005P	3,800,000	9.00	—	2007S	—	—	10.00
2005P Satin finish	1,160,000	8.00	—				

KM# B202b SILVER

Date	Mintage	Prf-65	Date	Mintage	Prf-65
2001S	(849,600)	20.00	2005S	1,069,679	9.00
2002S	(888,816)	14.00	2006S	988,140	11.00
2003S	(1,040,425)	14.50	2007S	—	12.00
2004S	1,175,935	14.00			

DOLLAR

Sacagawea Dollar

Sacagawea bust right, with baby on back Eagle in flight left

KM# 310 COPPER-ZINC-MANGANESE-NICKEL CLAD COPPER 26.4 mm. 8.0700 g.

Date	Mintage	MS-63	Prf-65	Date	Mintage	MS-63	Prf-65
2001P	62,468,000	2.00	—	2005S	—	—	22.50
2001D	70,909,500	2.00	—	2006P	4,900,000	2.50	—
2001S	(3,084,600)	—	100.00	2006D	2,800,000	5.00	—
2002P	3,865,610	2.00	—	2006S	—	—	22.50
2002D	3,732,000	2.00	—	2007P	—	2.50	—
2002S	(3,157,739)	—	28.50	2007D	—	2.50	—
2003P	3,090,000	3.00	—	2007S	—	—	22.50
2003D	3,090,000	3.00	—				
2003S	(3,116,590)	—	20.00				
2004P	2,660,000	2.50	—				
2004D	2,660,000	2.50	—				
2004S	—	—	22.50				
2005P	2,520,000	2.50	—				
2005D	2,520,000	2.50	—				

Presidents

George Washington

KM# 401 COPPER-ZINC-MANGANESE-NICKEL CLAD COPPER 26.4 mm. 8.0700 g. **Notes:** Date and mint mark incuse on edge.

Date	Mintage	MS-63	MS-65	Prf-65
2007P	176,680,000	2.00	—	—
ND (2007) Plain edge error	Inc. above	75.00	—	—
2007D	163,680,000	2.00	—	—
2007S	—	—	—	—

James Madison

KM# 404 COPPER-ZINC-MANGANESE-NICKEL CLAD COPPER 26.4 mm. 8.0700 g. **Notes:** Date and mint mark incuse on edge.

Date	Mintage	MS-63	MS-65	Prf-65
2007P	—	2.00	3.00	—
2007D	—	2.00	3.00	—
2007S	—	—	—	—

John Adams

KM# 402 COPPER-ZINC-MANGANESE-NICKEL CLAD COPPER 26.4 mm. 8.0700 g. **Notes:** Date and mint mark incuse on edge.

Date	Mintage	MS-63	MS-65	Prf-65
2007P	112,420,000	2.00	5.00	—
2007P Double edge lettering	Inc. above	250	—	—
2007D	102,810,000	2.00	5.00	—
2007S	—	—	—	8.00

Thomas Jefferson

KM# 403 COPPER-ZINC-MANGANESE-NICKEL CLAD COPPER 26.4 mm. 8.0700 g. **Notes:** Date and mint mark incuse on edge.

Date	Mintage	MS-63	MS-65	Prf-65
2007P	—	2.00	3.00	—
2007D	—	2.00	3.00	—
2007S	—	—	—	—

Andrew Jackson

KM# 428 COPPER-ZINC-MANGANESE-NICKEL CLAD COPPER 8.0700 g.

Date	Mintage	MS-63	MS-65	Prf-65
2008P	—	—	—	—
2008D	—	—	—	—
2008S	—	—	—	—

James Monroe

KM# 426 COPPER-ZINC-MANGANESE-NICKEL CLAD COPPER 8.0700 g.

Date	Mintage	MS-63	MS-65	Prf-65
2008P	—	2.00	3.00	—
2008D	—	2.00	3.00	—
2008S	—	—	—	—

John Quincy Adams

KM# 427 COPPER-ZINC-MANGANESE-NICKEL CLAD COPPER 8.0700 g.

Date	Mintage	MS-63	MS-65	Prf-65
2008P	—	2.00	5.00	—
2008D	—	2.00	5.00	—
2008S	—	—	—	8.00

Martin van Buren

KM# 429 COPPER-ZINC-MANGANESE-NICKEL CLAD COPPER 8.0700 g.

Date	Mintage	MS-63	MS-65	Prf-65
2008P	—	2.00	5.00	—
2008D	—	2.00	5.00	—
2008S	—	—	—	8.00

COMMEMORATIVE COINAGE 2001-PRESENT

All commemorative silver dollar coins of 1982-present have the following specifications: diameter - 38.1 millimeters; weight - 26.7300 grams; composition - 0.9000 silver, 0.7736 ounces actual silver weight. All commemorative $5 coins of 1982-present have the following specificiations: diameter - 21.6 millimeters; weight - 8.3590 grams; composition: 0.9000 gold, 0.242 ounces actual gold weight.

Note: In 1982, after a hiatus of nearly 20 years, coinage of commemorative half dollars resumed. Those designated with a 'W' were struck at the West Point Mint. Some issues were struck in copper-nickel. Those struck in silver have the same size, weight and composition as the prior commemorative half-dollar series.

HALF DOLLAR

U. S. CAPITOL VISITOR CENTER. KM# 323 Copper-Nickel Clad Copper 11.3400 g. **Obv. Designer:** Dean McMullen **Rev. Designer:** Alex Shagin and Marcel Jovine

Date	Mintage	Proof	MS-65	Prf-65
2001P	99,157	—	13.50	—
2001P	—	(77,962)	—	17.50

FIRST FLIGHT CENTENNIAL. KM# 348 Copper-Nickel Clad Copper 11.3400 g. **Obv. Designer:** John Mercanti **Rev. Designer:** Donna Weaver

Date	Mintage	Proof	MS-65	Prf-65
2003P	57,726	—	15.50	—
2003P	—	(111,569)	—	15.50

AMERICAN BALD EAGLE. KM# 438 Copper-Nickel Clad Copper 30.6 mm. 11.3400 g. **Obverse:** Two eaglets in nest with egg

Date	Mintage	Proof	MS-65	Prf-65
2008	Est. 750,000	—	—	—

DOLLAR

AMERICAN INDIAN - BISON. KM# 325 Designer: James E. Fraser.

Date	Mintage	Proof	MS-65	Prf-65
2001D	197,131	—	260	—
2001P	—	(272,869)	—	290

CAPITOL VISITOR CENTER. KM# 324 Obv. Designer: Marika Somogyi **Rev. Designer:** John Mercanti

Date	Mintage	Proof	MS-65	Prf-65
2001P	66,636	—	35.00	—
2001P	—	(143,793)	—	45.00

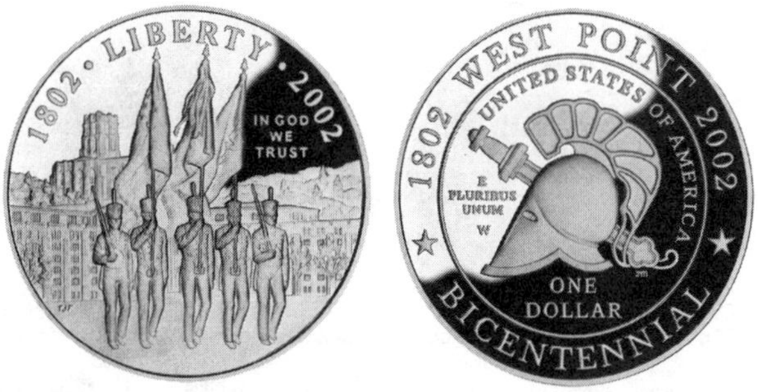

WEST POINT MILITARY ACADEMY BICENTENNIAL. KM# 338 Obv. Designer: T. James Ferrell **Rev. Designer:** John Mercanti

Date	Mintage	Proof	MS-65	Prf-65
2002W	103,201	—	20.50	—
2002W	—	(288,293)	—	19.50

WINTER OLYMPICS - SALT LAKE CITY. KM# 336 Obv. Designer: John Mercanti **Rev. Designer:** Donna Weaver

Date	Mintage	Proof	MS-65	Prf-65
2002P	35,388	—	35.00	—
2002P	—	(142,873)	—	42.00

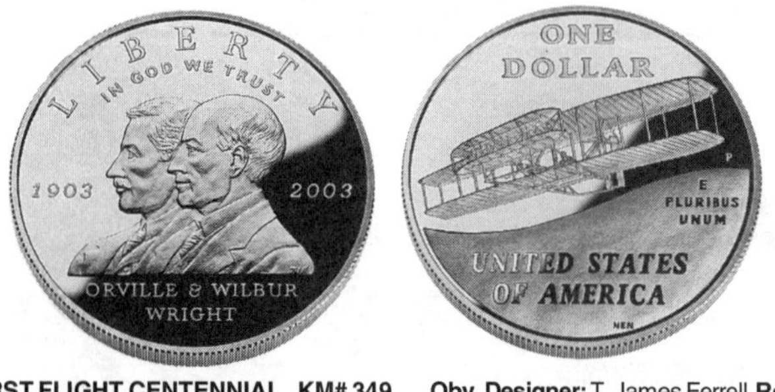

FIRST FLIGHT CENTENNIAL. KM# 349 Obv. Designer: T. James Ferrell **Rev. Designer:** Norman E. Nemeth **Obverse:** Orville and Wilbur Wright **Reverse:** Wright Brothers airplane

Date	Mintage	Proof	MS-65	Prf-65
2003P	53,761	—	37.00	—
2003P	—	(193,086)	—	32.00

125TH ANNIVERSARY OF EDISON'S ELECTRIC LIGHT. KM# 362 Obv. Designer: Donna Weaver **Rev. Designer:** John Mercanti

Date	Mintage	Proof	MS-65	Prf-65
2004P	68,031	—	40.00	—
2004P	—	(213,409)	—	41.00

LEWIS AND CLARK CORPS OF DISCOVERY BICENTENNIAL. KM# 363

Date	Mintage	Proof	MS-65	Prf-65
2004P	90,323	—	35.00	—
2004P	—	(288,492)	—	33.00

CHIEF JUSTICE JOHN MARSHALL, 250TH BIRTH ANNIVERSARY. KM# 375 Obv. Designer: John Mercanti **Rev. Designer:** Donna Weaver

Date	Mintage	Proof	MS-65	Prf-65
2005P	48,953	—	37.50	—
2005P	—	(141,993)	—	40.00

U.S. MARINE CORPS, 230TH ANNIVERSARY. KM# 376

Date	Mintage	Proof	MS-65	Prf-65
2005P	130,000	—	47.00	—
2005P	—	(370,000)	—	54.00

BENJAMIN FRANKLIN, 300TH ANNIVERSARY OF BIRTH. KM# 387 Obv. Designer: Norman E. Nemeth **Obverse:** Youthful Franklin flying kite **Reverse:** Revolutionary era "Join or Die" snake cartoon illustration

Date	Mintage	Proof	MS-65	Prf-65
2006P	58,000	—	53.00	—
2006P	—	(142,000)	—	57.00

BENJAMIN FRANKLIN, 300TH ANNIVERSARY OF BIRTH. KM# 388 Obverse: Bust 3/4 right, signature in oval below **Reverse:** Continental Dollar of 1776 in center

Date	Mintage	Proof	MS-65	Prf-65
2006P	58,000	—	52.00	—
2006P	—	(142,000)	—	54.00

SAN FRANCISCO MINT MUSEUM. KM# 394 Obverse: 3/4 view of building **Reverse:** Reverse of 1880s Morgan silver dollar

Date	Mintage	Proof	MS-65	Prf-65
2006S	—	—	50.00	—
2006S	—	—	—	46.00

CENTRAL HIGH SCHOOL DESEGREGATION. KM# 418 Obverse: Childrens feet walking left with adult feet in military boots **Reverse:** Little Rock's Central High School

Date	Mintage	Proof	MS-65	Prf-65
2007P	—	—	50.00	—
2007P	—	—	—	50.00

JAMESTOWN - 400TH ANNIVERSARY. KM# 405 Obverse: Two settlers and Native American **Reverse:** Three ships

Date	Mintage	Proof	MS-65	Prf-65
2007P	—	—	50.00	—
2007P	—	—	—	56.00

AMERICAN BALD EAGLE. KM# 439 Obverse: Ealge with flight, mountain in background at right **Reverse:** Great Seal of the United States

Date	Mintage	Proof	MS-65	Prf-65
2008P	Est.500,000	—	50.00	—

$5 (HALF EAGLE)

CAPITOL VISITOR CENTER. KM# 326 Designer: Elizabeth Jones.

Date	Mintage	Proof	MS-65	Prf-65
2001W	6,761	—	2,150	—
2001W	—	(27,652)	—	465

2002 SALT LAKE CITY WINTER OLYMPICS. KM# 337 Designer: Donna Weaver.

Date	Mintage	Proof	MS-65	Prf-65
2002W	10,585	—	555	—
2002W	—	(32,877)	—	510

SAN FRANCISCO MINT MUSEUM. KM# 395 Obverse: Frontal view of entrance **Reverse:** Eagle as on 1860's $5. Gold.

Date	Mintage	Proof	MS-65	Prf-65
2006	—	—	—	—

JAMESTOWN - 400TH ANNIVERSARY. KM# 406 Obverse: Settler and Native American **Reverse:** Jamestown Memorial Church ruins

Date	Mintage	Proof	MS-65	Prf-65
2007W	—	—	285	—
2007W	—	—	—	275

AMERICAN BALD EAGLE. KM# 440 Obverse: Two eagles on branch **Reverse:** Eagle with shield

Date	Mintage	Proof	MS-65	Prf-65
2008W	Est. 100,000	—	—	—

$10 (EAGLE)

FIRST FLIGHT CENTENNIAL. KM# 350 0.9000 Gold 0.4837 oz. AGW. 16.7180g. **Designer:** Donna Weaver

Date	Mintage	Proof	MS-65	Prf-65
2003P	10,129	—	625	—
2003P	—	(21,846)	—	560

AMERICAN EAGLE BULLION COINS

SILVER DOLLAR

KM# 273 0.9993 **SILVER** 0.9992 oz. ASW. 40.6mm. 31.1010 g. **Obv. Designer:** Adolph A. Weinman **Rev. Designer:** John Mercanti

Date	Mintage	Unc	Prf.
2001	9,001,711	21.20	—
2001W	746,154	—	34.00
2002	10,539,026	21.20	—
2002W	(647,342)	—	35.00
2003	8,495,008	21.20	—
2003W	747,831	—	34.00
2004	8,882,754	21.20	—
2004W	(783,219)	—	37.00
2005	8,891,025	21.20	—
2005W	823,000	—	34.00
2006	10,676,522	21.20	—
2006W	—	—	40.00
2006P Reverse Proof	250,000	—	300
2006W Burnished Unc.	470,000	105	—
2007	9,028,036	21.20	—
2007W	—	—	35.00
2007	—	—	35.00
2008	—	21.70	—
2008W	—	—	35.00

GOLD $5

KM# 216 0.9167 **GOLD** 0.1000 oz. AGW. 16.5mm. 3.3930 g. **Obv. Designer:** Augustus Saint-Gaudens **Rev. Designer:** Miley Busiek

Date	Mintage	Unc	Prf.
2001	269,147	111	—
2001W	(37,547)	—	123
2002	230,027	111	—
2002W	(40,864)	—	123
2003	245,029	111	—
2003W	(40,634)	—	123
2004	250,016	111	—
2004W	(35,481)	—	123
2005	300,043	110	—
2005W	48,455	—	123
2006	285,006	112	—
2006W	—	—	120
2006W Burnished Unc.	—	120	—
2007	190,010	100.00	—
2007W	—	—	138
2008	—	100.00	—
2008W	—	—	138

GOLD $10

KM# 217 0.9167 **GOLD** 0.2500 oz. AGW. 22mm. 8.4830 g. **Obv. Designer:** Augustus Saint-Gaudens **Rev. Designer:** Miley Busiek

Date	Mintage	Unc	Prf.
2001	71,280	266	—
2001W	(25,630)	—	283
2002	62,027	266	—
2002W	(29,242)	—	283
2003	74,029	266	—
2003W	(31,000)	—	283
2004	72,014	266	—
2004W	(29,127)	—	283
2005	72,015	266	—
2005W	34,637	—	283
2006	60,004	266	—
2006W	—	—	283
2006W Burnished Unc.	—	335	—
2007	34,004	266	—
2007W	—	—	291
2008	—	266	—
2008W	—	—	283

GOLD $25

KM# 218 0.9167 **GOLD** 0.5000 oz. AGW. 27mm. 16.9660 g. **Obv. Designer:** Augustus Saint-Gaudens **Rev. Designer:** Miley Busiek

Date	Mintage	Unc	Prf.
2001	48,047	509	—
2001W	(23,261)	—	475
2002	70,027	509	—
2002W	(26,646)	—	543
2003	79,029	509	—
2003W	(29,000)	—	543
2004	98,040	509	—
2004W	(27,731)	—	543
2005	80,023	509	—
2005W	33,598	—	543
2006	66,005	512	—
2006W	—	—	450
2006W Burnished Unc.	—	700	—
2007	47,002	512	—
2007W	—	—	543
2008	—	509	—
2008W	—	—	543

GOLD $50

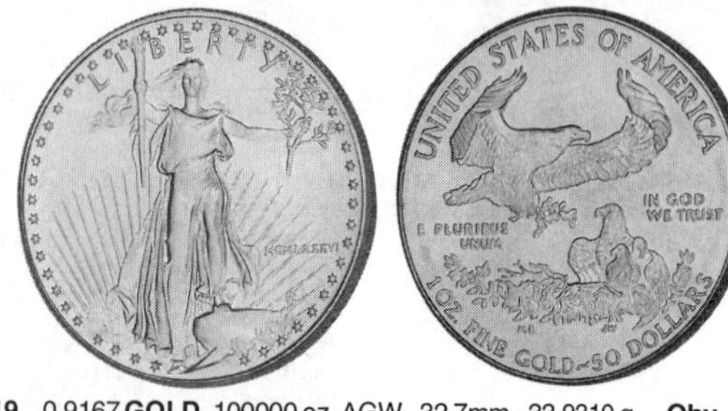

KM# 219 0.9167 **GOLD** 100000 oz. AGW. 32.7mm. 33.9310 g. **Obv. Designer:** Augustus Saint-Gaudens **Rev. Designer:** Miley Busiek

Date	Mintage	Unc	Prf.
2001	143,605	1,025	—
2001W	(24,580)	—	1,085
2002	222,029	1,025	—
2002W	(24,242)	—	1,085
2003	416,032	1,025	—
2003W	(29,000)	—	1,085
2004	417,019	1,025	—
2004W	(28,731)	—	1,085
2005	356,555	1,025	—
2005W	34,695	—	1,085
2006	237,510	1,025	—
2006W	—	—	1,085
2006W Reverse Proof	(10,000)	—	4,350
2007	140,016	1,025	—
2007W	—	—	1,085
2008	—	1,025	—
2008W	—	—	1,085

PLATINUM $10

KM# 327 0.9995 **PLATINUM** 0.0999 oz. 3.1100 g. **Obv. Designer:** John Mercanti

Date	Mintage	Unc	Prf.
2001W	(12,193)	—	247

KM# 283 0.9995 **PLATINUM** 0.0999 oz. 3.1100 g. **Obv. Designer:** John Mercanti **Rev. Designer:** Thomas D. Rogers Sr

Date	Mintage	Unc	Prf.
2001	52,017	235	—
2002	23,005	235	—
2003	22,007	235	—
2004	15,010	240	—
2005	14,013	240	—
2006	11,001	235	—
2007	13,003	240	—
2008	—	240	—

KM# 339 0.9995 **PLATINUM** 0.0999 oz. 3.1100 g. **Obv. Designer:** John Mercanti

Date	Mintage	Unc	Prf.
2002W	(12,365)	—	247

KM# 351 0.9995 **PLATINUM** 0.0999 oz. 3.1100 g. **Obv. Designer:** John Mercanti **Rev. Designer:** Al Maletsky

Date	Mintage	Unc	Prf.
2003W	(8,161)	—	300

KM# 364 0.9995 **PLATINUM** 0.0999 oz. 3.1100 g. **Obv. Designer:** John Mercanti

Date	Mintage	Unc	Prf.
2004W	(6,846)	—	900

KM# 377 0.9995 **PLATINUM** 0.0999 oz. 3.1100 g. **Obv. Designer:** John Mercanti **Rev. Designer:** Donna Weaver

Date	Mintage	Unc	Prf.
2005W	8,000	—	410

KM# 389 0.9995 **PLATINUM** 0.0999 oz. 17mm. 3.1100 g.

Date	Mintage	Unc	Prf.
2006W	—	—	225

KM# 414 0.9995 **PLATINUM** 0.0999 oz. 3.1100 g.

Date	Mintage	Unc	Prf.
2007W	—	—	245

KM# 434 0.9995 **PLATINUM** 0.0999 oz. 3.1100 g.

Date	Mintage	Unc	Prf.
2008W	—	—	245

PLATINUM $25

KM# 284 0.9995 **PLATINUM** 0.2502 oz. 7.7857 g. **Obv. Designer:** John Mercanti **Rev. Designer:** Thomas D. Rogers Sr

Date	Mintage	Unc	Prf.
2001	21,815	578	—
2002	27,405	578	—
2003	25,207	578	—
2004	18,010	578	—
2005	12,013	578	—
2006	12,001	583	—
2006W Burnished Unc.	—	1,300	—
2007	8,402	578	—
2007W Burnished Unc.	—	1,100	—
2008	—	578	—

KM# 328 0.9995 **PLATINUM** 0.2502 oz. 7.7857 g. **Obv. Designer:** John Mercanti

Date	Mintage	Unc	Prf.
2001W	(8,858)	—	603

KM# 340 0.9995 **PLATINUM** 0.2502 oz. 7.7857 g. **Obv. Designer:** John Mercanti

Date	Mintage	Unc	Prf.
2002W	(9,282)	—	603

KM# 352 0.9995 **PLATINUM** 0.2502 oz. 7.7857 g. **Obv. Designer:** John Mercanti **Rev. Designer:** Al Maletsky

Date	Mintage	Unc	Prf.
2003W	(6,045)	—	603

KM# 365 0.9995 **PLATINUM** 0.2502 oz. 7.7857 g. **Obv. Designer:** John Mercanti

Date	Mintage	Unc	Prf.
2004W	(5,035)	—	1,750

KM# 378 0.9995 **PLATINUM** 0.2502 oz. 7.7857 g. **Obv. Designer:** John Mercanti **Rev. Designer:** Donna Weaver

Date	Mintage	Unc	Prf.
2005W	6,424	—	870

KM# 390 0.9995 **PLATINUM** 0.2502 oz. 22mm. 7.7857 g.

Date	Mintage	Unc	Prf.
2006W	—	—	603

KM# 415 0.9995 **PLATINUM** 0.2502 oz. 7.7857 g.

Date	Mintage	Unc	Prf.
2007W	—	—	603

KM# 435 0.9995 **PLATINUM** 0.2502 oz. 7.7857 g.

Date	Mintage	Unc	Prf.
2008W	—	—	603

PLATINUM $50

KM# 285 0.9995 **PLATINUM** 0.4997 oz. 15.5520 g. **Obv. Designer:** John Mercanti **Rev. Designer:** Thomas D. Rogers Sr

Date	Mintage	Unc	Prf.
2001	12,815	1,106	—
2002	24,005	1,106	—
2003	17,409	1,106	—
2004	98,040	1,106	—
2005	9,013	1,106	—
2006	9,602	1,106	—
2006W Burnished Unc.	—	1,650	—
2007	—	1,106	—
2007W Burnished Unc.	—	1,500	—
2008	—	1,106	—

KM# 329 0.9995 **PLATINUM** 0.4997 oz. 15.5520 g. **Obv. Designer:** John Mercanti

Date	Mintage	Unc	Prf.
2001W	(8,268)	—	1,166

KM# 341 0.9995 **PLATINUM** 0.4997 oz. 15.5520 g. **Obv. Designer:** John Mercanti

Date	Mintage	Unc	Prf.
2002W	(8,772)	—	1,166

KM# 353 0.9995 **PLATINUM** 0.4997 oz. 15.5520 g. **Obv. Designer:** John Mercanti **Rev. Designer:** Al Maletsky

Date	Mintage	Unc	Prf.
2003W	(6,181)	—	1,166

KM# 366 0.9995 **PLATINUM** 0.4997 oz. 15.5520 g. **Obv. Designer:** John Mercanti

Date	Mintage	Unc	Prf.
2004W	(4,886)	—	2,750

KM# 379 0.9995 **PLATINUM** 0.4997 oz. 15.5520 g. **Obv. Designer:** John Mercanti **Rev. Designer:** Donna Weaver

Date	Mintage	Unc	Prf.
2005W	5,720	—	1,675

KM# 391 0.9995 **PLATINUM** 0.4997 oz. 27mm. 15.5520 g.

Date	Mintage	Unc	Prf.
2006W	—	—	1,166

KM# 416 0.9995 **PLATINUM** 0.4997 oz. 15.5520 g.

Date	Mintage	Unc	Prf.
2007W	—	—	1,166

KM# 436 0.9995 **PLATINUM** 0.4997 oz. 15.5520 g.

Date	Mintage	Unc	Prf.
2008W	—	—	1,166

PLATINUM $100

KM# 286 0.9995 **PLATINUM** 0.9995 oz. 31.1050 g. **Obv. Designer:** John Mercanti **Rev. Designer:** Thomas D. Rogers Sr

Date	Mintage	Unc	Prf.
2001	14,070	2,192	—
2002	11,502	2,192	—
2003	8,007	2,192	—
2004	7,009	2,192	—
2005	6,310	2,192	—
2006	6,000	2,192	—
2006W Burnished Unc.	—	2,550	—
2007	—	2,192	—
2007W Burnished Unc.	—	2,450	—
2008	—	2,192	—

KM# 330 0.9995 **PLATINUM** 0.9995 oz. 31.1050 g. **Obv. Designer:** John Mercanti

Date	Mintage	Unc	Prf.
2001W	(8,990)	—	2,307

KM# 342 0.9995 **PLATINUM** 0.9995 oz. 31.1050 g. **Obv. Designer:** John Mercanti

Date	Mintage	Unc	Prf.
2002W	(9,834)	—	2,307

KM# 354 0.9995 **PLATINUM** 0.9995 oz. 31.1050 g. **Obv. Designer:** John Mercanti **Rev. Designer:** Al Maletsky

Date	Mintage	Unc	Prf.
2003W	(6,991)	—	2,192

KM# 367 0.9995 **PLATINUM** 0.9995 oz. 31.1050 g. **Obv. Designer:** John Mercanti **Rev. Designer:** Donna Weaver

Date	Mintage	Unc	Prf.
2004W	(5,833)	—	3,500

KM# 380 0.9995 **PLATINUM** 0.9995 oz. 31.1050 g. **Obv. Designer:** John Mercanti **Rev. Designer:** Donna Weaver

Date	Mintage	Unc	Prf.
2005W	6,700	—	2,600

KM# 392 0.9995 **PLATINUM** 0.9995 oz. 33mm. 31.1050 g.

Date	Mintage	Unc	Prf.
2006W	—	—	2,307

KM# 417 0.9995 **PLATINUM** 0.9995 oz. 31.1050 g.

Date	Mintage	Unc	Prf.
2007W	—	—	2,307

KM# 437 0.9995 **PLATINUM** 0.9995 oz. 31.1050 g.

Date	Mintage	Unc	Prf.
2008W	—	—	2,307

MINT SETS

Mint, or uncirculated, sets contain one uncirculated coin of each denomination from each mint produced for circulation that year. Values listed here are only for those sets sold by the U.S. Mint. Sets were not offered in years not listed.

Date	Sets Sold	Issue Price	Value
2001	1,066,900	14.95	18.00
2002	1,139,388	14.95	15.50
2003	1,002,555	14.95	18.50
2004	844,484	16.95	58.00
2005	—	16.95	10.75
2006	—	16.95	16.50
2007	—	—	22.95

MODERN COMMEMORATIVE COIN SETS

Capitol Visitor Center

Date	Price
2001 3 coin set: proof half, silver dollar, gold $5; KM323, 324, 326.	445

American Buffalo

Date	Price
2001 2 coin set: 90% silver unc. & proof $1.; KM325.	460
2001 coin & currency set 90% unc. dollar & replicas of 1899 $5 silver cert.; KM325.	240

Winter Olympics - Salt Lake City

Date	Price
2002 2 coin set: proof 90% silver dollar KM336 & $5.00 Gold KM337.	420
2002 4 coin set: 90% silver unc. & proof $1, KM336 & unc. & proof gold $5, KM337.	940

First Flight Centennial

Date	Price
2003 3 coin set: proof gold ten dollar KM350, proof silver dollar KM349 & proof clad half dollar KM348.	575

Lewis and Clark Bicentennial

Date	Price
2004 Coin and pouch set.	100.00
2004 coin and currency set: Uncirculated silver dollar, two 2005 nickels, replica 1901 $10 Bison note, silver plated peace medal, three stamps & two booklets.	85.00
2004 Westward Journey Nickel series coin and medal set: Proof Sacagawea dollar, two 2005 proof nickels and silver plated peace medal.	35.00

Thomas Alva Edison

Date	Price
2004 Uncirculated silver dollar and light bulb.	60.00

U.S. Marine Corps.

Date	Price
2005 American Legacy: Proof Marine Corps dollar, Proof John Marshall dollar and 10 piece proof set.	180
2005 Uncirculated silver dollar and stamp set.	75.00

Chief Justice John Marshall

Date	Price
2005 Coin and Chronicles set: Uncirculated silver dollar, booklet and BEP intaglio portrait.	60.00
2005 American Legacy: Proof Marine Corps dollar, Proof John Marshall dollar and 10 piece proof set.	180

Benjamin Franklin Tercentennary

Date	Price
2006 Coin and Chronicles set: Uncirculated "Scientist" silver dollar, four stamps, Poor Richards Almanac and intaglio print.	65.00

PROOF SETS

Proof coins are produced through a special process involving specially selected, highly polished planchets and dies. They usually receive two strikings from the coin press at increased pressure. The result is a coin with mirrorlike surfaces and, in recent years, a cameo effect on its raised design surfaces. Proof sets have been sold off and on by the U.S. Mint since 1858.

Date	Sets Sold	Issue Price	Value
2001S 10 piece	2,249,498	19.95	98.00
2001S 5 quarter set	774,800	13.95	52.00
2001S Silver	849,600	31.95	148
2002S 10 piece	2,319,766	19.95	32.00
2002S 5 quarter set	764,419	13.95	19.00
2002S Silver	892,229	31.95	61.00
2003 X#207, 208, 209.2	—	44.00	28.75
2003S 10 piece	2,175,684	19.95	22.00
2003S 5 quarter set	1,225,507	13.95	13.50
2003S Silver	1,142,858	31.95	29.50
2004S 11 piece	1,804,396	22.95	36.00
2004S 5 quarter set	987,960	15.95	18.00
2004S Silver 11 piece	1,187,673	37.95	32.00
2004S Silver 5 quarter set	594,137	23.95	21.00
2005S Silver 5 quarter set	—	23.95	20.00
2005S American Legacy	—	—	98.00
2005S American Legacy	—	—	125
2005S 11 piece	—	22.95	16.00
2005S 5 quarter set	—	15.95	12.50
2005S Silver 11 piece	—	37.95	32.00
2006S Silver 10 piece	—	37.95	32.00
2006S Silver 5 quarter set	—	23.95	22.00
2006S 10 piece clad	—	22.95	25.00
2006S 5 quarter set	—	15.95	13.00
2007S 5 quarter set	—	13.95	15.50
2007S Silver 5 quarter set	—	22.95	25.50
2007S 14 piece clad	—	—	44.00
2007S Silver 14 piece	—	—	55.00

UNCIRCULATED ROLLS

Listings are for rolls containing uncirculated coins. Large date and small date varieties for 1960 and 1970 apply to the one cent coins.

Date	Cents	Nickels	Dimes	Quarters	Halves
2001P	2.00	5.50	8.00	—	16.00
2001D	2.00	7.00	7.50	—	14.00
2002P	2.00	4.50	7.50	—	28.00
2002D	2.00	4.50	7.50	—	29.00
2003P	2.00	8.50	7.50	—	26.00
2003D	2.00	4.00	7.50	—	26.00
2004P Peace Medal Nickel	2.00	11.50	7.50	—	36.50
2004D Peace Medal Nickel	—	10.00	—	—	36.50
2004P Keelboat Nickel	2.00	4.25	7.50	—	—
2004D Keelboat Nickel	—	3.75	—	—	—
2005P Bison Nickel	2.00	4.00	7.50	—	23.50
2005D Bison Nickel	—	3.75	—	—	23.50
2005P Ocean in view Nickel	2.00	3.75	7.50	—	—
2005D Ocean in view Nickel	—	3.75	—	—	—
2006P	1.50	3.75	9.00	—	30.00
2006D	1.50	3.75	9.00	—	30.00
2007P	1.50	4.00	8.00	—	25.00
2007D	1.50	4.00	8.00	—	25.00

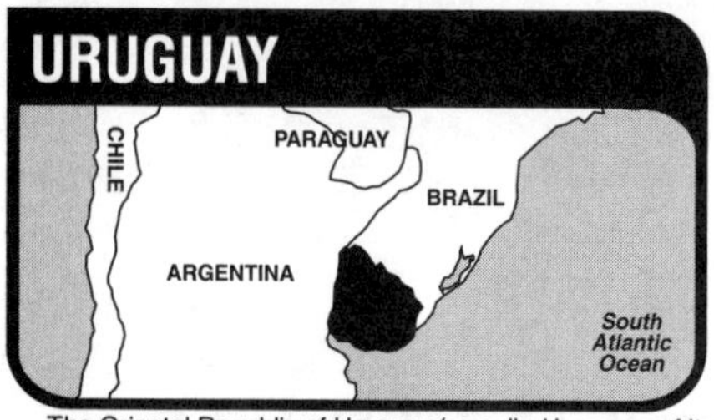

The Oriental Republic of Uruguay (so called because of its location on the east bank of the Uruguay River) is situated on the Atlantic coast of South America between Argentina and Brazil. This South American country has an area of 68,536 sq. mi. (176,220 sq. km.) and a population of *3 million. Capital: Montevideo. Uruguay's chief economic asset is the rich, rolling grassy plains. Meat, wool, hides and skins are exported.

MINT MARKS

A - Paris, Berlin, Vienna
(a) Paris, privy marks only
D - Lyon (France)
H - Birmingham
Mx, Mo - Mexico City
(p) - Poissy, France
So - Santiago (Small O above S)
(u) – Utrecht

REPUBLIC

REFORM COINAGE

March 1993

1,000 Nuevos Pesos = 1 Uruguayan Peso; 100 Centesimos = 1 Uruguayan Peso (UYP)

KM# 106 50 CENTESIMOS

2.9400 g., Stainless Steel, 20.97 mm. **Obv:** Bust of Artigas right **Obv. Legend:** REPUBLICA ORIENTAL DEL URUGUAY **Rev:** Value, date and sprig **Edge:** Plain **Note:** Coin rotation.

Date	Mintage	F	VF	XF	Unc	BU
2002	—	—	—	0.35	0.75	1.00
2005	—	—	—	0.35	0.75	1.00

KM# 103.2 UN PESO URUGUAYO

3.5000 g., Aluminum-Bronze, 19.95 mm. **Obv:** Bust of Artigas right **Obv. Legend:** REPUBLICA ORIENTAL DEL URUGUAY **Rev:** Value and date **Edge:** Plain **Note:** Medal rotation; left point of bust shoulder points at "P" in Republic.

Date	Mintage	F	VF	XF	Unc	BU
2005So	—	—	—	—	0.50	0.75

KM# 104.2 2 PESOS URUGUAYOS

4.4900 g., Aluminum-Bronze, 23.0 mm. **Obv:** Bust of Artigas right **Obv. Legend:** REPUBLICA ORIENTAL DEL URUGUAY **Rev:** Value and date **Edge:** Plain **Note:** Medal rotation. Left point of bust shoulder points at "P" in "Republic".

Date	Mintage	F	VF	XF	Unc	BU
2007So	—	—	—	0.75	1.50	2.00

KM# 120.1 5 PESOS URUGUAYOS

6.2400 g., Aluminum-Bronze, 26 mm. **Obv:** Bust of Antigas right **Obv. Legend:** REPUBLICA ORIENTAL DEL URUGUAY **Rev:** Value **Edge:** Plain **Note:** Left point of bust shoulder points at "U" in "Republic".

Date	Mintage	F	VF	XF	Unc	BU
2003	—	—	—	—	2.50	3.00

KM# 120.2 5 PESOS URUGUAYOS

6.3000 g., Aluminum-Bronze, 26 mm. **Obv:** Bust of Antigas right **Obv. Legend:** REPUBLICA ORIENTAL DEL URUGUAY • **Rev:** Value, date **Note:** Left point of bust shoulder points at "P" in "Republic".

Date	Mintage	F	VF	XF	Unc	BU
2005So	—	—	—	—	2.50	3.00

KM# 122 1000 PESOS URUGUAYOS

26.9500 g., 0.9000 Silver 0.7798 oz. ASW, 40 mm. **Subject:** XVIII World Championship Football - Germany 2006 **Obv:** National arms **Obv. Legend:** REPUBLICA ORIENTAL DEL URUGUAY **Rev:** Soccer player and value **Edge:** Reeded

Date	Mintage	F	VF	XF	Unc	BU
2003 Proof	50,000	Value: 50.00				

KM# 123 1000 PESOS URUGUAYOS

27.0400 g., 0.9000 Silver 0.7824 oz. ASW, 40 mm. **Subject:** XVIII World Championship Football - Germany 2006 **Obv:** National arms above date **Obv. Legend:** REPUBLICA ORIENTAL DEL URUGUAY **Rev:** Stylized soccer player and value **Edge:** Reeded

Date	Mintage	F	VF	XF	Unc	BU
2004 Proof	50,000	Value: 50.00				

KM# 125 1000 PESOS URUGUAYOS

27.0000 g., Silver **Subject:** 100th Anniversary FIFA - 1930 Championship **Obv:** Football before net **Obv. Legend:** REPUBLICA ORIENTAL DEL URUGUAY **Rev:** Sun of national flag

Date	Mintage	F	VF	XF	Unc	BU
2004 Proof	—	Value: 45.00				

KM# 124 1000 PESOS URUGUAYOS

27.0400 g., 0.9000 Silver 0.7824 oz. ASW, 40 mm. **Subject:** XVIII World Championship Football - Germany 2006 **Obv:** National arms above date **Obv. Legend:** REPUBLICA ORIENTAL DEL URUGUAY **Rev:** FIFA trophy **Edge:** Reeded

Date	Mintage	F	VF	XF	Unc	BU
2005 Proof	—	Value: 50.00				

KM# 126 5000 PESOS URUGUAYOS

Gold **Subject:** 100th Anniversary FIFA - 1930 Championship **Obv:** Football **Obv. Legend:** REPUBLICA ORIENTAL DEL URUGUAY **Rev:** Tower of Homage in Montevideo

Date	Mintage	F	VF	XF	Unc	BU
2004 Proof	—	Value: 325				

KM# 127 5000 PESOS URUGUAYOS

7.7800 g., 0.9999 Gold 0.2501 oz. AGW **Subject:** XVIII World Championship Football - Germany 2006 **Obv:** National arms **Obv. Legend:** REPUBLICA ORIENTAL DEL URUGUAY **Rev:** Stylized player and value

Date	Mintage	F	VF	XF	Unc	BU
2004 Proof	25,000	Value: 325				

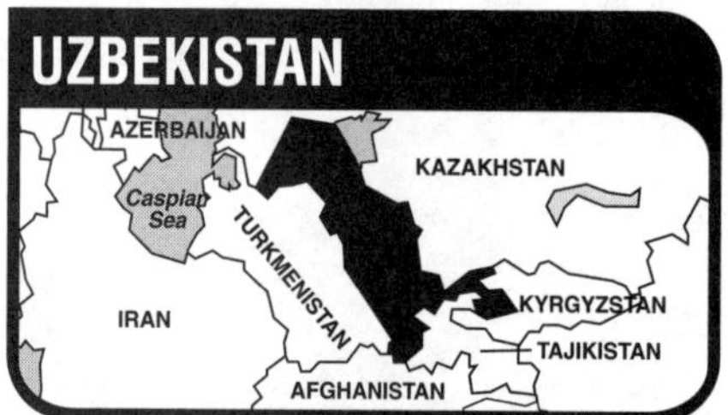

The Republic of Uzbekistan (formerly the Uzbek S.S.R.), is bordered on the north by Kazakhstan, to the east by Kirghizia and Tajikistan, on the south by Afghanistan and on the west by Turkmenistan. The republic is comprised of the regions of Andizhan, Bukhara, Dzhizak, Ferghana, Kashkadar, Khorezm (Khiva), Namangan, Navoi, Samarkand, Surkhan-Darya, Syr-Darya, Tashkent and the Karakalpak Autonomous Republic. It has an area of 172,741 sq. mi. (447,400 sq. km.) and a population of 20.3 million. Capital: Tashkent. Crude oil, natural gas, coal, copper, and gold deposits make up the chief resources, while intensive farming, based on artificial irrigation, provides an abundance of cotton.

MONETARY SYSTEM

100 Tiyin = 1 Som

REPUBLIC

STANDARD COINAGE

KM# 13 5 SOM

3.3500 g., Brass Plated Steel, 21.2 mm. **Obv:** National arms **Rev:** Value and map **Edge:** Plain

Date	Mintage	F	VF	XF	Unc	BU
2001	—	—	—	—	1.35	1.75

Note: 2 reverse map varieties known

KM# 14 10 SOM

2.7100 g., Nickel-Clad Steel, 19.75 mm. **Obv:** National arms **Rev:** Value and map **Edge:** Plain

Date	Mintage	F	VF	XF	Unc	BU
2001	—	—	—	—	2.00	2.50

Note: 2 reverse map varieties exist

KM# 15 50 SOM

8.0000 g., Nickel-Clad Steel, 26.2 mm. **Obv:** National arms **Rev:** Value and map **Edge:** Plain and reeded sections

Date	Mintage	F	VF	XF	Unc	BU
2001	—	—	—	—	3.50	4.00

KM# 16 50 SOM

7.9000 g., Nickel-Clad Steel, 26.3 mm. **Subject:** 2700th Anniversary of Shahrisabz Town **Obv:** National arms **Rev:** Statue and ruins above value **Edge:** Reeded and plain sections

Date	Mintage	F	VF	XF	Unc	BU
2002	—	—	—	—	3.75	4.50

KM# 18 100 SOM

Bronze **Subject:** 500th Anniversary Death of 'Aliser Navoi **Obv:** National arms **Obv. Legend:** O'ZBEKISTON MARKAZIY BANKI **Rev:** 'Aliser Navoi

Date	Mintage	F	VF	XF	Unc	BU
2001	—	—	—	10.00	15.00	18.00

KM# 19 100 SOM

31.1000 g., 0.9990 Silver 0.9988 oz. ASW **Obv:** National arms **Obv. Legend:** O'ZBEKISTON MARKAZIY BANKI **Rev:** Parliament building in Toskent

Date	Mintage	F	VF	XF	Unc	BU
2001 Proof	1,000	Value: 90.00				

KM# 20 100 SOM

31.1000 g., 0.9990 Silver 0.9988 oz. ASW **Obv:** National arms **Obv. Legend:** O'ZBEKISTON MARKAZIY BANKI **Rev:** Amir-Timur Museum

Date	Mintage	F	VF	XF	Unc	BU
2001 Proof	1,000	Value: 90.00				

KM# 21 100 SOM

31.1000 g., 0.9990 Silver 0.9988 oz. ASW **Obv:** National Arms **Obv. Legend:** O'BEKISTON MARKAZY BANKI **Rev:** Toskent town hall

Date	Mintage	F	VF	XF	Unc	BU
2001 Proof	1,000	Value: 90.00				

KM# 22 100 SOM

31.1000 g., 0.9990 Silver 0.9988 oz. ASW **Obv:** National arms **Obv. Legend:** O'ZBEKISTON MARKAZIY BANKI **Rev:** World

Date	Mintage	F	VF	XF	Unc	BU
2001 Proof	1,000	Value: 90.00				

KM# 23 100 SOM

31.1000 g., 0.9990 Silver 0.9988 oz. ASW **Obv:** National arms **Obv. Legend:** O'ZBEKISTON MARKAZIY BANKI **Rev:** Football player

Date	Mintage	F	VF	XF	Unc	BU
2001 Proof	1,000	Value: 90.00				

KM# 24 100 SOM

31.1000 g., 0.9990 Silver 0.9988 oz. ASW **Obv:** National arms **Obv. Legend:** O'BEKISTON MARKAZIY BANKI **Rev:** Track runner

Date	Mintage	F	VF	XF	Unc	BU
2001 Proof	1,000	Value: 90.00				

KM# 25 100 SOM

31.1000 g., 0.9990 Silver 0.9988 oz. ASW **Obv:** National arms **Obv. Legend:** O'ZBEKISTON MARKAZIY BANKI **Rev:** Judo expert

Date	Mintage	F	VF	XF	Unc	BU
2001 Proof	1,000	Value: 90.00				

KM# 26 100 SOM

31.1000 g., 0.9990 Silver 0.9988 oz. ASW **Obv:** National arms **Obv. Legend:** O'ZBEKISTON MARKAZIY BANKI **Rev:** Tennis player

Date	Mintage	F	VF	XF	Unc	BU
2001 Proof	1,000	Value: 90.00				

KM# 27 100 SOM

31.1000 g., 0.9990 Silver 0.9988 oz. ASW **Obv:** National arms **Obv. Legend:** O'ZBEKISTON MARKAZIY BANKI **Rev:** Lenk monument in Timur

Date	Mintage	F	VF	XF	Unc	BU
2001 Proof	1,000	Value: 90.00				

KM# 28 100 SOM

31.1000 g., 0.9990 Silver 0.9988 oz. ASW **Obv:** National arms **Obv. Legend:** O'ZBEKISTON MARKAZIY BANKI **Rev:** Aliser Navoi monument

Date	Mintage	F	VF	XF	Unc	BU
2001 Proof	1,000	Value: 90.00				

KM# 29 100 SOM
31.1000 g., 0.9990 Silver 0.9988 oz. ASW **Obv:** National arms **Obv. Legend:** O'ZBEKISTON MARKAZIY BANKI **Rev:** Registan in Samarkand

Date	Mintage	F	VF	XF	Unc	BU
2001 Proof	1,000	Value: 90.00				

KM# 30 100 SOM
31.1000 g., 0.9990 Silver 0.9988 oz. ASW **Obv:** National arms **Obv. Legend:** O'BEKISTON MARKAZIY BANKI **Rev:** Bell tower in Toskent

Date	Mintage	F	VF	XF	Unc	BU
2001 Proof	1,000	Value: 90.00				

KM# 17 100 SOM
7.9200 g., Nickel Plated Steel, 26.95 mm. **Subject:** 10th Annniversary State Currency **Obv:** National arms **Obv. Legend:** O'ZBEKISTON MARKAZIV BANKI **Rev:** Sun rays over outlined map and value **Rev. Legend:** O'BEKISTON MILLIY VALYUTASIGA **Edge:** Lettered

Date	Mintage	F	VF	XF	Unc	BU
2004	—	—	—	17.50	27.50	—

VANUATU

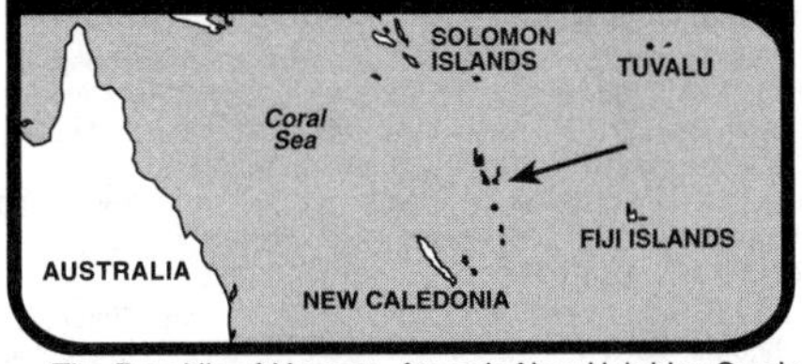

The Republic of Vanuatu, formerly New Hebrides Condominium, a group of islands located in the South Pacific 500 miles (800 km.) west of Fiji, were under the joint sovereignty of Great Britain and France. The islands have an area of 5,700 sq. mi. (14,760 sq. km.) and a population of 165,000, mainly Melanesians of mixed blood. Capital: Port-Vila. The volcanic and coral islands, while malarial land subject to frequent earthquakes, are extremely fertile, and produce copra, coffee, tropical fruits and timber for export.

The New Hebrides were discovered by Portuguese navigator Pedro de Quiros (sailing under orders by the King of Spain) in 1606, visited by French explorer Bougainville in 1768, and named by British navigator Capt. James Cook in 1774. Ships of all nations converged on the islands to trade for sandalwood, prompting France and Britain to relinquish their individual claims and declare the islands a neutral zone in 1878. The New Hebrides were placed under the control of a mixed Anglo-French commission of naval officers during the native uprisings of 1887, and established as a condominium under the joint sovereignty of France and Great Britain in 1906.

Vanuatu became an independent republic within the Commonwealth in July 1980. A president is Head of State and the Prime Minister is Head of Government.

MINT MARK
(a) - Paris, privy marks only

MONETARY SYSTEM
Francs until 1983
Vatu to Present

REPUBLIC

STANDARD COINAGE

KM# 38 50 VATU
28.3200 g., Silver, 38.60 mm. **Obv:** National arms **Obv. Legend:** RIPABLIK / VANUATU **Rev:** Early sailing ship center - left, stylized compass at right **Rev. Legend:** HISTORY OF SEAFARING / PEDRO FERNANDEZ DE QUIRÓS **Edge:** Reeded

Date	Mintage	F	VF	XF	Unc	BU
2005 Proof	—	Value: 45.00				

KM# 41 50 VATU
25.0000 g., 0.9000 Silver 0.7234 oz. ASW **Series:** Protection of Marine Life **Obv:** National arms **Rev:** Tiger Shark - multicolor

Date	Mintage	F	VF	XF	Unc	BU
2005 Proof	—	Value: 75.00				

KM# 42 50 VATU
25.0000 g., 0.9000 Silver 0.7234 oz. ASW **Series:** Protection of Marine Life **Obv:** National arms **Rev:** Sea Turtle - multicolor

Date	Mintage	F	VF	XF	Unc	BU
2006 Proof	—	Value: 75.00				

KM# 43 50 VATU
25.0000 g., 0.9000 Silver 0.7234 oz. ASW **Series:** Protection of Marine Life **Obv:** National arms **Rev:** Sea Horse - multicolor

Date	Mintage	F	VF	XF	Unc	BU
2006 Proof	—	Value: 75.00				

VATICAN CITY

The State of the Vatican City, a papal state on the right bank of the Tiber River within the boundaries of Rome, has an area of 0.17 sq. mi. (0.44 sq. km.) and a population of *775. Capital: Vatican City.

Today the Pope exercises supreme legislative, executive and judicial power within the Vatican City, and the State of the Vatican City is recognized by many nations as an independent sovereign state under the temporal jurisdiction of the Pope, even to the extent of ambassadorial exchange. The Pope is of course, the head of the Roman Catholic Church.

PONTIFFS
John Paul II, 1978-2005
Sede Vacante, April 2 - 19, 2005
Benedict XVI, 2005-

MINT MARK
Commencing 1981
R – Rome

MONETARY SYSTEM
100 Centesimi = 1 Lira (thru 2002)
100 Euro Cent = 1 Euro

DATING
Most Vatican coins indicate the regnal year of the pope preceded by the word *Anno* (or an abbreviation), even if the *anno domini* date is omitted.

CITY STATE

DECIMAL COINAGE

100 Centesimi = 1 Lira

KM# 331 10 LIRE
1.6000 g., Aluminum, 23.2 mm. **Ruler:** John Paul II **Obv:** Bust left **Rev:** Papal arms **Edge:** Plain **Designer:** Laura Cretella

Date	Mintage	F	VF	XF	Unc	BU
2001/XXIII	—	—	0.50	0.75	3.00	—

KM# 332 20 LIRE
3.5700 g., Brass, 21.2 mm. **Ruler:** John Paul II **Obv:** Bust left **Rev:** Papal arms **Edge:** Plain **Designer:** Laura Cretella

Date	Mintage	F	VF	XF	Unc	BU
2001/XXIII	—	—	0.50	0.75	3.00	—

KM# 333 50 LIRE
4.5000 g., Copper-Nickel, 19.2 mm. **Ruler:** John Paul II **Obv:** Pius XII bust left **Rev:** Papal arms **Edge:** Plain **Designer:** Laura Cretella

Date	Mintage	F	VF	XF	Unc	BU
2001/XXIII	—	—	0.50	0.75	3.00	—

KM# 334 100 LIRE
4.5000 g., Copper-Nickel, 22 mm. **Ruler:** John Paul II **Obv:** Bust left **Rev:** Papal arms within circle **Edge:** Reeded and plain sections **Designer:** Laura Cretella

Date	Mintage	F	VF	XF	Unc	BU
2001/XXIII	—	—	0.50	1.00	2.50	—

KM# 335 200 LIRE
5.0000 g., Brass, 22 mm. **Ruler:** John Paul II **Obv:** Bust right **Rev:** Papal arms within circle **Edge:** Reeded **Designer:** Laura Cretella

Date	Mintage	F	VF	XF	Unc	BU
2001/XXIII	—	—	0.50	1.00	2.25	—

KM# 336 500 LIRE
6.7700 g., Bi-Metallic Aluminum-Bronze center in Stainless steel ring, 25.7 mm. **Ruler:** John Paul II **Obv:** Head left **Rev:** Papal arms within circle **Edge:** Reeded and plain sections **Designer:** Laura Cretella

Date	Mintage	F	VF	XF	Unc	BU
2001/XXIII	—	—	—	3.50	7.00	—

KM# 338 1000 LIRE
14.6000 g., 0.8350 Silver 0.3919 oz. ASW, 31.4 mm. **Ruler:** John Paul II **Subject:** Peace **Obv:** Stylized dove in front of globe **Rev:** Crowned shield **Edge Lettering:** +++ TOTVSTVVS +++ MMI

Date	Mintage	F	VF	XF	Unc	BU
2001/XXIII	—	—	—	15.00	25.00	—

KM# 337 1000 LIRE
8.8500 g., Copper-Nickel, 26.9 mm. **Ruler:** John Paul II **Obv:** Bust right **Rev:** Crowned shield **Edge:** Reeded and plain sections **Designer:** Laura Cretella

Date	Mintage	F	VF	XF	Unc	BU
2001/XIV	—	—	—	5.50	7.00	—

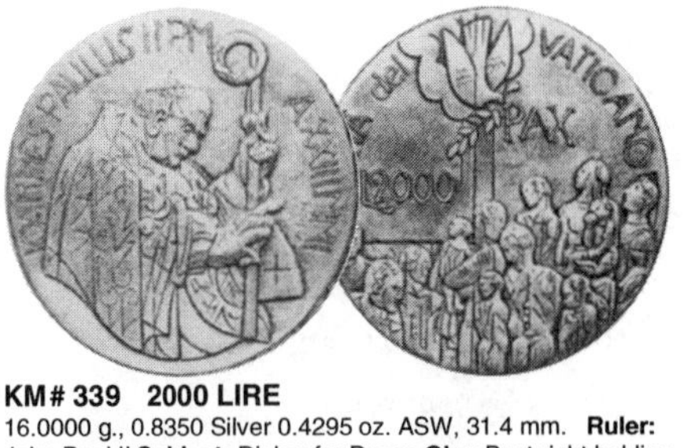

KM# 339 2000 LIRE
16.0000 g., 0.8350 Silver 0.4295 oz. ASW, 31.4 mm. **Ruler:** John Paul II **Subject:** Dialog for Peace **Obv:** Bust right holding croizer **Rev:** Dove above crowd **Edge:** Reeded **Designer:** Floriano Bodini

Date	Mintage	F	VF	XF	Unc	BU
2001/XXIII	16,000	—	—	25.00	35.00	—
2001/XXIII Proof	8,000	Value: 40.00				

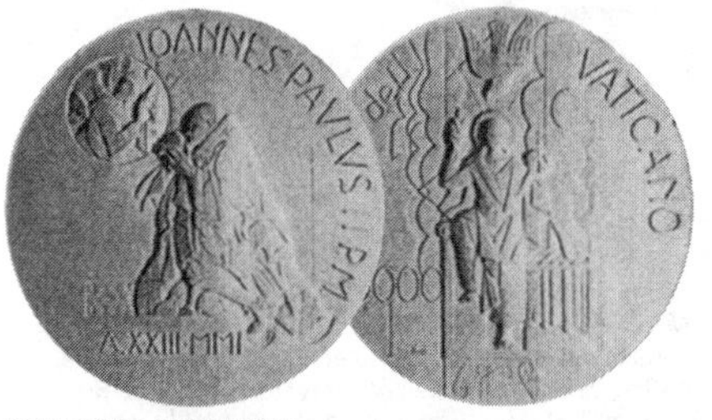

KM# 340 5000 LIRE
18.0000 g., 0.8350 Silver 0.4832 oz. ASW, 32 mm. **Ruler:** John Paul II **Subject:** Easter **Obv:** Kneeling Pope praying **Rev:** Standing figure flanked by clouds below dove **Edge:** Reeded and plain sections **Designer:** Floriano Bodini

Date	Mintage	F	VF	XF	Unc	BU
2001/XXIII Proof	16,000	Value: 30.00				

KM# 390 50000 LIRE

7.5000 g., 0.9170 Gold 0.2211 oz. AGW, 23 mm. **Ruler:** John Paul II **Subject:** Religeous symbols **Obv:** Bust right **Rev:** Cross

Date	Mintage	F	VF	XF	Unc	BU
2001//XXIIIR Proof	6,000	Value: 300				

KM# 391 100000 LIRE

15.0000 g., 0.9170 Gold 0.4422 oz. AGW, 28.00 mm. **Ruler:** John Paul II **Subject:** Religious symbols **Obv:** Bust right **Rev:** Chi rho with Alpha and Omega letters

Date	Mintage	F	VF	XF	Unc	BU
2001//XXIIIR Proof	6,000	Value: 600				

EURO COINAGE

John Paul II

KM# 341 EURO CENT

2.2700 g., Copper Plated Steel, 16.2 mm. **Ruler:** John Paul II **Obv:** Bust 1/4 left **Obv. Designer:** Guido Veroi **Rev:** Value and globe **Rev. Designer:** Luc Luyex **Edge:** Plain

Date	Mintage	F	VF	XF	Unc	BU
2002R	80,000	—	—	—	115	—
2002R Proof	9,000	Value: 175				
2003R	65,000	—	—	—	55.00	—
2003R Proof	13,000	Value: 145				
2004R	65,000	—	—	—	25.00	—
2004R Proof	13,000	Value: 145				
2005R	85,000	—	—	—	25.00	—
2005R Proof	16,000	Value: 140				

KM# 342 2 EURO CENT

3.0300 g., Copper Plated Steel, 18.7 mm. **Ruler:** John Paul II **Obv:** Bust 1/4 left **Obv. Designer:** Guido Veroi **Rev:** Value and globe **Edge:** Grooved

Date	Mintage	F	VF	XF	Unc	BU
2002R	80,000	—	—	—	115	—
2002R Proof	9,000	Value: 175				
2003R	65,000	—	—	—	55.00	—
2003R Proof	13,000	Value: 145				
2004R	65,000	—	—	—	25.00	—
2004R Proof	13,000	Value: 145				
2005R	85,000	—	—	—	25.00	—
2005R Proof	16,000	Value: 140				

KM# 343 5 EURO CENT

3.8600 g., Copper Plated Steel, 21.2 mm. **Ruler:** John Paul II **Obv:** Bust 1/4 left **Obv. Designer:** Guido Veroi **Rev:** Value and globe **Edge:** Plain

Date	Mintage	F	VF	XF	Unc	BU
2002R	80,000	—	—	—	115	—
2002R Proof	9,000	Value: 175				
2003R	65,000	—	—	—	55.00	—
2003R Proof	13,000	Value: 145				
2004R	65,000	—	—	—	28.00	—
2004R Proof	13,000	Value: 145				
2005R	85,000	—	—	—	28.00	—
2005R Proof	16,000	Value: 140				

KM# 344 10 EURO CENT

4.0700 g., Brass, 19.7 mm. **Ruler:** John Paul II **Obv:** Bust 1/4 left **Obv. Designer:** Guido Veroi **Rev. Designer:** Luc Luycx **Edge:** Reeded

Date	Mintage	F	VF	XF	Unc	BU
2002R	80,000	—	—	—	115	—
2002R Proof	9,000	Value: 175				
2003R	65,000	—	—	—	55.00	—
2003R Proof	13,000	Value: 145				
2004R	65,000	—	—	—	35.00	—
2004R Proof	13,000	Value: 145				
2005R	85,000	—	—	—	35.00	—
2005R Proof	16,000	Value: 140				

KM# 345 20 EURO CENT

5.7300 g., Brass, 22.1 mm. **Ruler:** John Paul II **Obv:** Bust 1/4 left **Obv. Designer:** Guido Veroi **Rev:** Map and value **Rev. Designer:** Luc Luycx **Edge:** Notched

Date	Mintage	F	VF	XF	Unc	BU
2002R	80,000	—	—	—	115	—
2002R Proof	9,000	Value: 175				
2003R	65,000	—	—	—	55.00	—
2003R Proof	13,000	Value: 145				
2004R	65,000	—	—	—	38.00	—
2004R Proof	13,000	Value: 145				
2005R	85,000	—	—	—	38.00	—
2005R Proof	16,000	Value: 140				

KM# 346 50 EURO CENT

7.8100 g., Brass, 24.2 mm. **Ruler:** John Paul II **Obv:** Bust 1/4 left **Obv. Designer:** Guido Veroi **Rev:** Map and value **Rev. Designer:** Luc Luycx **Edge:** Reeded

Date	Mintage	F	VF	XF	Unc	BU
2002R	80,000	—	—	—	115	—
2002R Proof	9,000	Value: 175				
2003R	65,000	—	—	—	55.00	—
2003R Proof	13,000	Value: 145				
2004R	65,000	—	—	—	42.00	—
2004R Proof	13,000	Value: 145				
2005R	85,000	—	—	—	42.00	—
2005R Proof	16,000	Value: 140				

KM# 347 EURO

7.5000 g., Bi-Metallic Copper-Nickel center in Brass ring, 23.2 mm. **Ruler:** John Paul II **Obv:** Bust 1/4 left **Obv. Designer:** Guido Veroi **Rev:** Value and map **Rev. Designer:** Luc Luycx **Edge:** Reeded and plain sections

Date	Mintage	F	VF	XF	Unc	BU
2002R	80,000	—	—	—	100	—
2002R Proof	9,000	Value: 185				
2003R	65,000	—	—	—	75.00	—
2003R Proof	13,000	Value: 145				
2004R	65,000	—	—	—	60.00	—
2004R Proof	13,000	Value: 145				
2005R	85,000	—	—	—	60.00	—
2005R Proof	16,000	Value: 140				

KM# 348 2 EURO

8.5200 g., Bi-Metallic Brass center in Copper-Nickel ring, 25.7 mm. **Ruler:** John Paul II **Obv:** Bust 1/4 left **Obv. Designer:** Guido Veroi **Rev:** Value and map **Rev. Designer:** Luc Luycx **Edge:** Reeded **Edge Lettering:** 2's and stars

Date	Mintage	F	VF	XF	Unc	BU
2002R	80,000	—	—	—	165	—
2002R Proof	9,000	Value: 215				
2003R	65,000	—	—	—	100	—
2003R Proof	13,000	Value: 185				
2004R	65,000	—	—	—	80.00	—
2004R Proof	13,000	Value: 185				
2005R	85,000	—	—	—	80.00	—
2005R Proof	16,000	Value: 180				

KM# 358 2 EURO

8.5000 g., Bi-Metallic Brass center in Copper-Nickel ring, 25.75 mm. **Ruler:** John Paul II **Subject:** 75th Anniversary of the Founding of the Vatican City State **Obv:** St. Peter's Square within city walls, dates 1929-2004 **Rev:** Value and map **Edge:** Reeding over 2's and stars **Designer:** Luciana de Simoni

Date	Mintage	F	VF	XF	Unc	BU
2004R	85,000	—	—	—	25.00	—

KM# 349 5 EURO

18.0000 g., 0.8350 Silver 0.4832 oz. ASW, 32 mm. **Ruler:** John Paul II **Subject:** 24th Anniversary of Reign **Obv:** Bust 1/4 left **Rev:** Allegorical female and bridge **Edge:** Lettered **Edge Lettering:** +++ TOTUS TUUS +++ MMII

Date	Mintage	F	VF	XF	Unc	BU
2002R Proof	10,000	Value: 125				

KM# 354 5 EURO

18.0000 g., 0.9250 Silver 0.5353 oz. ASW, 34 mm. **Ruler:** John Paul II **Subject:** Year of the Rosary **Obv:** Pope praying the rosary **Rev:** "Our Lady of Pompei" presenting rosaries to Saints Dominic and Catherine **Edge:** Reeded **Designer:** Roberto Mauri

Date	Mintage	F	VF	XF	Unc	BU
2003R Proof	10,000	—	—	—	65.00	—

KM# 359 5 EURO

18.0000 g., 0.9250 Silver 0.5353 oz. ASW, 32 mm. **Ruler:** John Paul II **Subject:** 150th Anniversary of the Proclamation of the Dogma of the Immaculate Conception **Obv:** Virgin Mary **Rev:** Two Papal coat of arms **Edge:** Reeded and plain sections **Designer:** Claudia Momoni

Date	Mintage	F	VF	XF	Unc	BU
2004R	13,000	—	—	—	60.00	—

KM# 350 10 EURO

22.0000 g., 0.8350 Silver 0.5906 oz. ASW, 34 mm. **Ruler:** John Paul II **Subject:** 24th Anniversary of Reign **Obv:** Pope holding crucifix **Rev:** Risen Christ (Message of peace) **Edge:** Reeded **Designer:** Floriano Bodini

Date	Mintage	F	VF	XF	Unc	BU
2002R Proof	10,000	Value: 80.00				

KM# 355 10 EURO

22.0000 g., 0.9250 Silver 0.6542 oz. ASW, 34 mm. **Ruler:** John Paul II **Subject:** 25th Anniversary of Reign **Obv:** Pope praying **Rev:** St. Peter receiving the keys of Earth and Heaven **Edge:** Reeded **Designer:** Amalia Mistichelli

Date	Mintage	F	VF	XF	Unc	BU
2003R Proof	10,000	Value: 80.00				

KM# 360 10 EURO

22.0000 g., 0.9250 Silver 0.6542 oz. ASW, 34 mm. **Ruler:** John Paul II **Obv:** Pope praying for peace **Rev:** Tree of Life rooted in virtues **Edge:** Reeded and plain sections **Designer:** Maria Carmela Colaneri

Date	Mintage	F	VF	XF	Unc	BU
2004R	13,000	—	—	—	90.00	—

KM# 361 20 EURO

6.0000 g., 0.9170 Gold 0.1769 oz. AGW **Ruler:** John Paul II **Subject:** Roots of Faith **Rev:** Noah's Ark **Designer:** Floriano Bodini

Date	Mintage	F	VF	XF	Unc	BU
2002	2,800	Value: 1,100				

KM# 351 20 EURO

6.0000 g., 0.9166 Gold 0.1768 oz. AGW, 21 mm. **Ruler:** John Paul II **Rev:** Moses being found in floating basket **Edge:** Reeded **Designer:** Floriano Bodini

Date	Mintage	F	VF	XF	Unc	BU
2003R Proof	2,800	Value: 1,100				

KM# 363 20 EURO

6.0000 g., 0.9170 Gold 0.1769 oz. AGW, 21 mm. **Ruler:** John Paul II **Rev:** David slaying Goliath **Designer:** Floriano Bodini

Date	Mintage	F	VF	XF	Unc	BU
2004/XXVIIR Proof	3,050	Value: 1,000				

KM# 362 50 EURO

15.0000 g., 0.9170 Gold 0.4422 oz. AGW **Ruler:** John Paul II **Subject:** Roots of Faith **Rev:** Sacrifice of Abraham **Designer:** Floriano Bodini

Date	Mintage	F	VF	XF	Unc	BU
2002 Proof	2,800	Value: 1,950				

KM# 352 50 EURO

15.0000 g., 0.9166 Gold 0.4420 oz. AGW, 28 mm. **Ruler:** John Paul II **Rev:** Moses receiving the Ten Commandments **Edge:** Reeded **Designer:** Floriano Bodini

Date	Mintage	F	VF	XF	Unc	BU
2003R Proof	2,800	Value: 1,950				

KM# 364 50 EURO

15.0000 g., 0.9170 Gold 0.4422 oz. AGW **Ruler:** John Paul II **Rev:** Judgement of Solomon **Designer:** Floriano Bodini

Date	Mintage	F	VF	XF	Unc	BU
2004/XXVIIR Proof	3,050	Value: 1,850				

EURO COINAGE

Sede Vacante

KM# 365 EURO CENT

2.2700 g., Copper Plated Steel **Ruler:** Sede Vacante **Obv:** Arms of Cardinal Jorge Arturo Medina Estevez **Obv. Designer:** Daniela Longo **Rev:** Value and globe **Rev. Designer:** Luc Luycx

Date	Mintage	F	VF	XF	Unc	BU
MMV (2005)R	60,000	—	—	—	40.00	45.00

KM# 366 2 EURO CENT

3.0300 g., Copper Plated Steel **Ruler:** Sede Vacante **Obv:** Arms of Cardinal Jorge Arturo Medina Estevez **Obv. Designer:** Daniela Longo **Rev:** Value and globe **Rev. Designer:** Luc Luycx

Date	Mintage	F	VF	XF	Unc	BU
MMV (2005)R	60,000	—	—	—	37.00	42.00

KM# 367 5 EURO CENT

3.8600 g., Copper Plated Steel **Ruler:** Sede Vacante **Obv:** Arms of Cardinal Jorge Arturo Medina Estevez **Obv. Designer:** Daniela Longo **Rev:** Value and globe **Rev. Designer:** Luc Luycx

Date	Mintage	F	VF	XF	Unc	BU
MMV (2005)R	60,000	—	—	—	42.00	45.00

KM# 368 10 EURO CENT

4.0700 g., Brass **Ruler:** Sede Vacante **Obv:** Arms of Cardinal Jorge Arturo Medina Estevez **Obv. Designer:** Daniela Longo **Rev:** Map and value **Rev. Designer:** Luc Luycx

Date	Mintage	F	VF	XF	Unc	BU
MMV (2005)R	60,000	—	—	—	45.00	48.00

KM# 369 20 EURO CENT

Brass **Ruler:** Sede Vacante **Obv:** Arms of Cardinal Jorge Arturo Medina Estevez **Obv. Designer:** Daniela Longo **Rev:** Map and value **Rev. Designer:** Luc Luycx

Date	Mintage	F	VF	XF	Unc	BU
MMV (2005)R	60,000	—	—	—	47.00	50.00

KM# 370 50 EURO CENT

7.8100 g., Brass **Ruler:** Sede Vacante **Obv:** Arms of Cardinal Jorge Arturo Medina Estevez **Obv. Designer:** Daniela Longo **Rev:** Map and value **Rev. Designer:** Luc Luycx

Date	Mintage	F	VF	XF	Unc	BU
MMV (2005)R	60,000	—	—	—	50.00	55.00

KM# 371 EURO

7.5000 g., Bi-Metallic **Ruler:** Sede Vacante **Obv:** Arms of Cardinal Jorge Arturo Medina Estevez **Obv. Designer:** Daniela Longo **Rev:** Value and map **Rev. Designer:** Luc Luycx

Date	Mintage	F	VF	XF	Unc	BU
MMV (2005)R	60,000	—	—	—	65.00	70.00

KM# 372 2 EURO

8.5200 g., Bi-Metallic **Ruler:** Sede Vacante **Obv:** Arms of Cardinal Jorge Arturo Medina Estevez **Obv. Designer:** Daniela Longo **Rev:** Map and value **Rev. Designer:** Luc Luycx

Date	Mintage	F	VF	XF	Unc	BU
MMV (2005)R	60,000	—	—	—	70.00	75.00

KM# 373 5 EURO

18.0000 g., 0.9250 Silver 0.5353 oz. ASW, 32 mm. **Ruler:** Sede Vacante **Obv:** Dove within square **Rev:** Arms of Cardinal Jorge Arturo Medina Estevez **Edge:** Reeded **Designer:** Daniela Longo

Date	Mintage	F	VF	XF	Unc	BU
MMV (2005)R Proof	13,440	Value: 200				

EURO COINAGE

Benedict XVI

KM# 375 EURO CENT

2.2900 g., Copper-Plated-Steel, 16.24 mm. **Ruler:** Benedict XVI **Obv:** Pope's bust facing 3/4 right **Obv. Legend:** CITTA' DEL VATICANO **Rev:** Value and globe **Edge:** Plain

Date	Mintage	F	VF	XF	Unc	BU
2006R	85,000	—	—	—	12.00	16.00
2006R Proof	16,000	Value: 28.00				
2007R	—	—	—	—	15.00	20.00
2007R Proof	16,000	Value: 25.00				

KM# 376 2 EURO CENT

3.0300 g., Copper-Plated-Steel, 18.73 mm. **Ruler:** Benedict XVI **Obv:** Pope's bust facing 3/4 right **Obv. Legend:** CITTA' DEL VATICANO **Rev:** Value and globe **Edge:** Plain

Date	Mintage	F	VF	XF	Unc	BU
2006R	85,000	—	—	—	15.00	18.00
2006R Proof	16,000	Value: 30.00				
2007R	—	—	—	—	18.00	22.00
2007R Proof	16,000	Value: 28.00				

KM# 377 5 EURO CENT

3.9600 g., Copper-Plated-Steel, 21.21 mm. **Ruler:** Benedict XVI **Obv:** Pope's bust facing 3/4 right **Obv. Legend:** CITTA' DEL VATICANO **Rev:** Value and globe **Edge:** Plain

Date	Mintage	F	VF	XF	Unc	BU
2006R	85,000	—	—	—	17.00	20.00
2006R Proof	16,000	Value: 32.50				
2007R	—	—	—	—	20.00	24.00
2007R Proof	16,000	Value: 30.00				

KM# 378 10 EURO CENT

4.0800 g., Brass, 19.73 mm. **Ruler:** Benedict XVI **Obv:** Pope's bust facing 3/4 right **Obv. Legend:** CITTA' DEL VATICANO **Rev:** Map and value **Edge:** Coarse reeding

Date	Mintage	F	VF	XF	Unc	BU
2006R	85,000	—	—	—	18.00	22.00
2006R Proof	16,000	Value: 35.00				
2007R	—	—	—	—	22.50	25.00
2007R Proof	16,000	Value: 32.00				

KM# 385 10 EURO CENT

4.0700 g., Brass **Ruler:** Benedict XVI **Obv:** Arms of Cardinal Jorge Arturo Medina Estevez **Obv. Designer:** Daniela Longo **Rev:** Relief map of Western Europe, stars, lines and value **Rev. Designer:** Luc Luycx

Date	Mintage	F	VF	XF	Unc	BU
MMVII (2007)R	—	—	—	—	35.00	—

KM# 379 20 EURO CENT

5.7200 g., Brass, 22.23 mm. **Ruler:** Benedict XVI **Obv:** Pope's bust facing 3/4 right **Obv. Legend:** CITTA' DEL VATICANO **Rev:** Map and value **Edge:** Plain with seven indents

Date	Mintage	F	VF	XF	Unc	BU
2006R	85,000	—	—	—	20.00	25.00
2006R Proof	16,000	Value: 40.00				
2007R	—	—	—	—	25.00	27.50
2007R Proof	16,000	Value: 38.00				

KM# 386 20 EURO CENT

Brass **Ruler:** Benedict XVI **Obv. Designer:** Daniela Longo **Rev:** Relief map of Western Europe, stars, lines and value **Rev. Designer:** Luc Luycx

Date	Mintage	F	VF	XF	Unc	BU
MMVII (2008)R	—	—	—	—	25.00	27.50

KM# 380 50 EURO CENT

7.8200 g., Brass, 24.23 mm. **Ruler:** Benedict XVI **Obv:** Pope's bust facing 3/4 right **Obv. Legend:** CITTA' DEL VATICANO **Rev:** Map and value **Edge:** Coarse reeding

Date	Mintage	F	VF	XF	Unc	BU
2006R	85,000	—	—	—	25.00	30.00
2006R Proof	16,000	Value: 50.00				
2007R	—	—	—	—	28.00	32.50
2007R Proof	16,000	Value: 48.00				

KM# 387 50 EURO CENT

7.8100 g., Brass **Ruler:** Benedict XVI **Rev:** Relief map of Western Europe, stars, lines and value **Rev. Designer:** Luc Luycx

Date	Mintage	F	VF	XF	Unc	BU
MMVIII (2008)R	—	—	—	—	28.00	32.50

KM# 381 EURO

7.4700 g., Bi-Metallic Copper-Nickel center in brass ring., 23.23 mm. **Ruler:** Benedict XVI **Obv:** Pope's bust facing 3/4 right **Obv. Legend:** CITTA' - DEL VATICANO **Rev:** Value and map **Edge:** Segmented smooth and reeded

Date	Mintage	F	VF	XF	Unc	BU
2006R	85,000	—	—	—	28.00	32.00
2006R Proof	16,000	Value: 55.00				
2007R	—	—	—	—	32.50	40.00
2007R Proof	16,000	Value: 52.00				

KM# 388 EURO

7.5000 g., Bi-Metallic **Ruler:** Benedict XVI **Rev:** Relief map of Western Europe, stars, lines and value **Rev. Designer:** Luc Luycx

Date	Mintage	F	VF	XF	Unc	BU
MMVIII (2008)R	—	—	—	—	32.50	40.00

KM# 374 2 EURO

Bi-Metallic **Ruler:** Benedict XVI **Subject:** World Youth Day **Obv:** Cologne Cathedral **Rev:** Value and Euro map

Date	Mintage	F	VF	XF	Unc	BU
2005R	—	—	—	—	90.00	—

KM# 382 2 EURO

8.5200 g., Bi-Metallic Brass center in Copper-Nickel ring., 25.69 mm. **Ruler:** Benedict XVI **Obv:** Pope's bust facing 3/4 right **Obv. Legend:** CITTA' - DEL VATICANO **Rev:** Value and map **Edge:** Reeded with stars and alternating 2's

Date	Mintage	F	VF	XF	Unc	BU
2006R	85,000	—	—	—	32.00	40.00
2006R Proof	16,000	Value: 65.00				
2007R	—	—	—	—	35.00	45.00
2007R Proof	16,000	Value: 62.00				

KM# 389 2 EURO

8.5200 g., Bi-Metallic **Ruler:** Benedict XVI **Rev:** Relief map of Western Europe, stars, lines and value **Rev. Designer:** Luc Luycx

Date	Mintage	F	VF	XF	Unc	BU
MMVII (2007)R	—	—	—	—	35.00	45.00

KM# 383 5 EURO

18.0000 g., 0.9250 Silver 0.5353 oz. ASW **Ruler:** Benedict XVI **Subject:** Life reborn **Obv:** Bust left **Rev:** Children playing among branches of an olive tree

Date	Mintage	F	VF	XF	Unc	BU
2005R Proof	13,000	Value: 100				

KM# 384 10 EURO

22.0000 g., 0.9250 Silver 0.6542 oz. ASW **Ruler:** Benedict XVI **Subject:** Disciples of Emanaus **Obv:** Bust left **Rev:** Three men seated at table

Date	Mintage	F	VF	XF	Unc	BU
2006R Proof	13,000	Value: 215				

MINT SETS

KM#	Date	Mintage	Identification	Issue Price	Mkt Val
MS107	2001 (8)	26,000	KM#331-338	21.25	200
MS108	2002 (8)	65,000	KM#341-348	12.00	975
MS109	2003 (8)	65,000	KM#341-348	15.00	500
MS110	2004 (8)	85,000	KM#341-348	16.50	335
MS111	2005 (8)	85,000	KM#341-348.	32.50	335
MS112	MMV (2005) (8)	60,000	KM#365-372 Sede Vacante	—	425
MS113	2006 (8)	—	KM#375-382	—	200
MS114	2007 (8)	—	KM#375-382	—	220

PROOF SETS

KM#	Date	Mintage	Identification	Issue Price	Mkt Val
PS13	2001 (2)	—	KM#390, 391	—	900
PS15	2002 (8)	9,000	KM#341-348	75.00	1,450
PS16	2003 (8)	13,000	KM#341-348	78.00	1,200
PS17	2004 (8)	13,000	KM#341-348	—	1,200
PS18	2005 (8)	16,000	KM#341-348, plus silver medal.	150	1,175
PS19	2006 (8)	—	KM#375-382 plus silver medal	—	375
PS20	2007 (8)	16,000	KM#375-382 plus silver medal	—	315

VENEZUELA

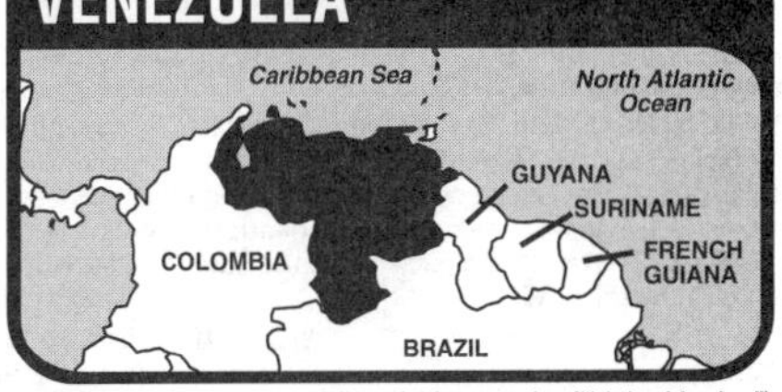

The Bolivarian Republic of Venezuela ("Little Venice"), located on the northern coast of South America between Colombia and Guyana, has an area of 352,145 sq. mi.(912,050 sq. km.) and a population of 20 million. Capital: Caracas. Petroleum and mining provide a significant portion of Venezuela's exports. Coffee, grown on 60,000 plantations, is the chief crop. Metalurgy, refining, oil, iron and steel production are the main employment industries.

GOVERNMENT

Republic, 1823-present

MINT MARKS

A - Paris
(a) - Paris, privy marks only
(aa) - Altena
(b) - Berlin
(bb) - Brussels
(cc) – Canada
(c) - Caracas
(d) - Denver

H, Heaton - Heaton, Birmingham
(l) - London
(m) - Madrid
(mm) - Mexico
(o) - Ontario
(p) - Philadelphia
(s) - San Francisco
(sc) - Schwerte - Vereinigte Deutsche Nickelwerke
(w) - Werdohl - Vereinigte Deutsche Metalwerke

ENGRAVER'S INITIALS
W. W. – William Wyon

REPUBLICA BOLIVARIANA DE VENEZUELA

REFORM COINAGE

2000-

100 Centimos = 1 Bolivar "Fuerte"

Y# 87 CENTIMO
Copper **Obv:** National arms **Obv. Legend:** REPÚBLICA BOLÍVARIANA DE VENEZUELA **Rev:** Eight stars at left, large value at right

Date	Mintage	F	VF	XF	Unc	BU
2007	—	—	—	—	—	0.25

Y# 88 5 CENTIMOS
Copper **Obv:** National arms **Obv. Legend:** REPÚBLICA BOLÍVARIANA DE VENEZUELA **Rev:** Eight stars at left, large value at right

Date	Mintage	F	VF	XF	Unc	BU
2007(c)	—	—	—	—	—	0.50

Y# 89 10 CENTIMOS
Nickel **Obv:** National arms **Obv. Legend:** REPÚBLICA BOLÍVARIANA DE VENEZUELA **Rev:** Eight stars at left, large value at right

Date	Mintage	F	VF	XF	Unc	BU
2007(c)	—	—	—	—	—	0.75

Y# 90 12-1/2 CENTIMOS
Nickel, 23 mm. **Obv:** National arms **Obv. Legend:** REPÚBLICA BOLÍVARIANA DE VENEZUELA **Rev:** Large value, eight stars below in sprays **Edge:** Plain

Date	Mintage	F	VF	XF	Unc	BU
2007(c)	—	—	—	—	—	1.50

Y# 91 25 CENTIMOS
Nickel **Obv:** National arms **Obv. Legend:** REPÚBLICA BOLÍVARIANA DE VENEZUELA **Rev:** Eight stars at left, large value at center right

Date	Mintage	F	VF	XF	Unc	BU
2007(c)	—	—	—	—	—	2.00

Y# 92 50 CENTIMOS
Nickel **Obv:** National arms **Obv. Legend:** REPÚBLICA BOLÍVARIANA DE VENEZUELA **Rev:** Eight stars at left, large value at center right

Date	Mintage	F	VF	XF	Unc	BU
2007(c)	—	—	—	—	—	3.00

Y# 93 BOLIVAR
Bi-Metallic Nickel center in Aluminum-Bronze ring **Obv:** Eight stars at left of national arms, large value at right **Obv. Legend:** REPÚBLICA BOLÍVARIANA DE VENEZUELA **Rev:** Head of Bolívar left **Rev. Designer:** Albert Barre

Date	Mintage	F	VF	XF	Unc	BU
2007(c)	—	—	—	—	—	5.00

Y# 80 10 BOLIVARES
2.3300 g., Nickel Clad Steel, 17 mm. **Obv:** National arms left of denomination **Obv. Legend:** REPÚBLICA BOLÍVARIANA DE VENEZUELA **Rev:** Head of Bolívar left with new mint mark at left, 7-sided outline surrounds **Rev. Legend:** BOLÍVAR - LIBERTADOR **Rev. Designer:** Albert Barre **Edge:** Reeded **Note:** Struck at Maracay Mint.

Date	Mintage	F	VF	XF	Unc	BU
2001(c)	—	—	—	—	0.25	0.50
2002(c)	—	—	—	—	0.25	0.50

Note: May have slight design modifications to obverse

Y# 80a 10 BOLIVARES
1.7390 g., Aluminum-Zinc, 17 mm. **Obv:** National arms and value **Obv. Legend:** REPÚBLICA BOLÍVARIANA DE VENEZUELA **Rev:** Head of Bolívar left **Rev. Legend:** BOLÍVAR - LIBERTADOR **Rev. Designer:** Albert Barre **Edge:** Reeded

Date	Mintage	F	VF	XF	Unc	BU
2001(c)	—	—	—	—	0.50	0.75
2002(c)	—	—	—	—	0.50	0.75

Note: May have slight design modifications to obverse

Y# 81 20 BOLIVARES
4.3200 g., Nickel Clad Steel, 20 mm. **Obv:** National arms left of denomination **Obv. Legend:** REPÚUBLICA BOLÍVARIANA DE VENEZUELA **Rev:** Head of Bolivar left, with new mint mark at left, 7-sided outline surrounds **Rev. Legend:** BOLÍVAR - LIBERTADOR **Rev. Designer:** Albert Barre **Edge:** Plain **Note:** Struck at Maracay Mint.

Date	Mintage	F	VF	XF	Unc	BU
2001(c)	—	—	—	—	0.25	0.50
2002(c)	—	—	—	—	0.25	0.50

Note: May have slight design modifications to obverse

Y# 81a 20 BOLIVARES
3.2650 g., Aluminum-Zinc, 20 mm. **Obv:** National arms and value **Obv. Legend:** REP?BLICA BOL?VARIANA DE VENEZUELA **Rev:** Head of Bol?var left **Rev. Legend:** BOL?VAR - LIBERTADOR **Rev. Designer:** Albert Barre **Edge:** Plain

Date	Mintage	F	VF	XF	Unc	BU
2001(c)	—	—	—	—	0.65	1.00
2002(c)	—	—	—	—	0.65	1.00

Note: May have slight design modifications to obverse

Date	Mintage	F	VF	XF	Unc	BU
2004(c)	—	—	—	—	0.65	1.00

Note: May have obverse design modifications

Y# 82 50 BOLIVARES
6.6500 g., Nickel Clad Steel, 23 mm. **Obv:** National arms left of denomination **Rev:** Head of Bolivar left with new mint mark at left, 7-sided outline surrounds **Rev. Designer:** Albert Barre **Edge:** Reeded **Note:** Dates 2001 and 2004 may have slight design modifications to the obverse

Date	Mintage	F	VF	XF	Unc	BU
2001(c)	—	—	—	—	0.30	—
2004(c)	—	—	—	—	0.30	0.80

Y# 83 100 BOLIVARES
6.8200 g., Nickel Clad Steel, 25 mm. **Obv:** National arms and value **Obv. Legend:** REPÚBUBLICA BOLÍVARIANA DE VENEZUELA **Rev:** Head of Bolívar left **Rev. Legend:** BOLÍVAR - LIBERTADO **Rev. Designer:** Albert Barre **Edge:** Plain **Note:** Dates 2002 and 2004 may have slight design modifications to the obverse.

Date	Mintage	F	VF	XF	Unc	BU
2001(c)	—	—	—	0.60	1.25	1.50
2002(c)	—	—	—	0.60	1.25	1.50
2004(c)	—	—	—	0.60	1.25	1.50

Y# 85 1000 BOLIVARES
8.4000 g., Bi-Metallic Copper-Nickel center in Brass ring, 24 mm. **Obv:** National arms and value in center **Obv. Legend:** REPÚBLICA BOLÍVARIANA DE VENEZUELA **Rev:** Head of Bolívar left **Rev. Legend:** BOLÍVAR - LIBERTADOR **Rev. Designer:** Albert Barre **Edge Lettering:** "BCV 1000" four times

Date	Mintage	F	VF	XF	Unc	BU
2005(c)	9,000,000	—	—	—	1.00	2.00

VIET NAM

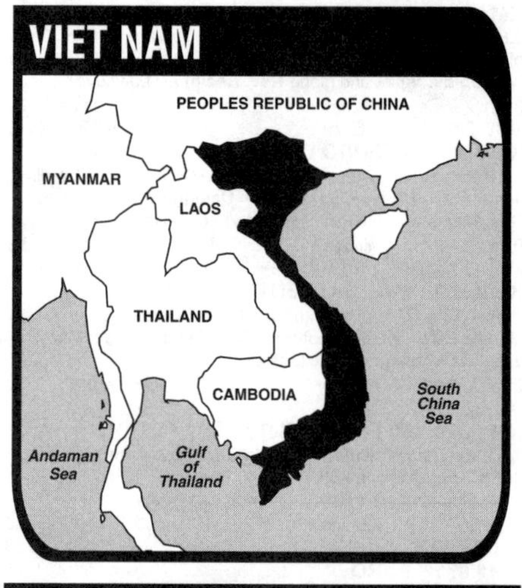

SOCIALIST REPUBLIC

The Socialist Republic of Viet Nam, located in Southeast Asia west of the South China Sea, has an area of 127,300 sq. mi. (329,560 sq. km.) and a population of *66.8 million. Capital: Hanoi. Agricultural products, coal, and mineral ores are exported.

The activities of Communists in South Viet Nam led to the second Indochina war which came to a brief halt in 1973 (when a cease-fire was arranged and U.S. forces withdrew), but it didn't end until April 30, 1975 when South Viet Nam surrendered unconditionally. The two Viet Nams were reunited as the Socialist Republic of Viet Nam on July 2, 1976.

NOTE: For earlier coinage refer to French Indo-China or Tonkin.

SOCIALIST REPUBLIC

STANDARD COINAGE

KM# 71 200 DONG
3.1000 g., Nickel Clad Steel, 20.75 mm. **Obv:** National emblem **Rev:** Denomination

Date	Mintage	F	VF	XF	Unc	BU
2003	125,000,000	0.10	0.15	0.25	0.35	0.50

KM# 74 500 DONG
4.5000 g., Nickel-Clad Steel, 21.86 mm. **Obv:** National emblem **Rev:** Denomination **Edge:** Segmented reeding

Date	Mintage	F	VF	XF	Unc	BU
2003	175,000,000	0.15	0.20	0.35	0.50	1.00

KM# 72 1000 DONG
3.7000 g., Brass Plated Steel, 19.75 mm. **Obv:** National emblem **Rev:** Bat De Pagoda in Hanoi **Edge:** Reeded

Date	Mintage	F	VF	XF	Unc	BU
2003	250,000,000	0.20	0.35	0.50	0.75	1.50

KM# 75 2000 DONG
5.0000 g., Brass Plated Steel, 23.92 mm. **Obv:** National emblem **Rev:** Highland Stilt House in Tay Nguyen above value **Edge:** Segmented reeding

Date	Mintage	F	VF	XF	Unc	BU
2003	—	—	—	—	2.25	2.75

KM# 64 5000 DONG
1.2441 g., 0.9999 Gold 0.0400 oz. AGW, 13.92 mm. **Subject:** Year of the Snake **Obv:** State emblem **Rev:** Sea snake **Edge:** Reeded

Date	Mintage	F	VF	XF	Unc	BU
2001	—	—	—	—	60.00	75.00

KM# 67 5000 DONG
1.2441 g., 0.9999 Gold 0.0400 oz. AGW, 13.9 mm. **Subject:** Year of the Horse **Obv:** State emblem **Rev:** Horse **Edge:** Reeded

Date	Mintage	F	VF	XF	Unc	BU
2002	28,000	—	—	—	50.00	65.00

KM# 73 5000 DONG
7.6000 g., Brass, 25 mm. **Obv:** National emblem **Rev:** Chua Mot Cot Pagoda in Hanoi

Date	Mintage	F	VF	XF	Unc	BU
2003	500,000,000	0.50	0.75	1.00	1.25	2.50

KM# 57 10000 DONG
20.0000 g., 0.9250 Silver 0.5948 oz. ASW, 38.7 mm. **Subject:** Year of the Snake **Obv:** State emblem above value **Obv. Legend:** "CONG HOA XA HOI CHU NGHIA VIET NAM" **Rev:** Sea snake **Rev. Legend:** "...VIET NAM" **Edge:** Reeded

Date	Mintage	F	VF	XF	Unc	BU
2001(S) Proof	3,500	Value: 50.00				

KM# 58 10000 DONG
20.0000 g., 0.9250 Silver 0.5948 oz. ASW **Subject:** Year of the Snake **Obv:** State emblem above value **Obv. Legend:** "CONG HOA XA HOI CHU NGHIA VIET NAM" **Rev:** Bamboo viper **Rev. Legend:** "...VIET NAM"

Date	Mintage	F	VF	XF	Unc	BU
2001(S) Proof	3,500	Value: 50.00				

KM# 59 10000 DONG
20.0000 g., 0.9250 Silver 0.5948 oz. ASW **Subject:** Year of the Snake **Obv:** State emblem above value **Obv. Legend:** "CONG HOA XA HOI CHU NGHIA VIET NAM" **Rev:** Multicolor holographic, cobra in center **Rev. Legend:** "...VIET NAM"

Date	Mintage	F	VF	XF	Unc	BU
2001(S) Proof	3,500	Value: 40.00				

KM# 61 10000 DONG
20.0000 g., 0.9990 Silver 0.6423 oz. ASW, 38.7 mm. **Subject:** Year of the Horse **Obv:** State emblem **Rev:** Horse with octagonal latent image **Edge:** Reeded

Date	Mintage	F	VF	XF	Unc	BU
2001 Proof	3,800	Value: 40.00				

Note: In proof set only

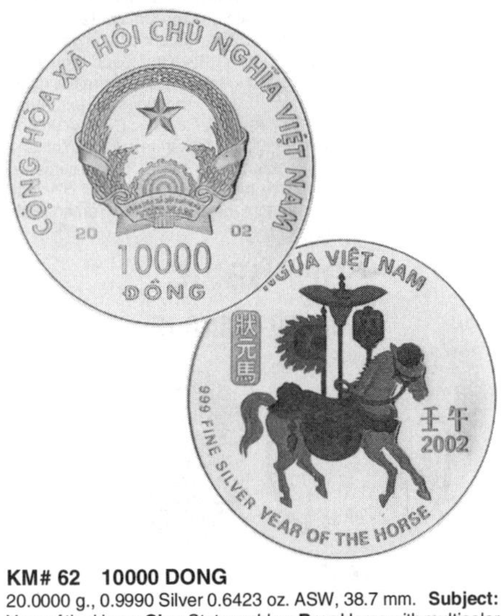

KM# 62 10000 DONG
20.0000 g., 0.9990 Silver 0.6423 oz. ASW, 38.7 mm. **Subject:** Year of the Horse **Obv:** State emblem **Rev:** Horse with multicolor accouterments **Edge:** Reeded

Date	Mintage	F	VF	XF	Unc	BU
2001 Proof	3,800	Value: 40.00				

Note: In proof set only

KM# 63 10000 DONG
20.0000 g., 0.9990 Silver 0.6423 oz. ASW, 38.7 mm. **Subject:** Year of the Horse **Obv:** State emblem **Rev:** Multicolor holographic horse in center **Edge:** Reeded

Date	Mintage	F	VF	XF	Unc	BU
2001 Proof	3,800	Value: 37.50				

Note: In proof set only

KM# 76 10000 DONG
20.0000 g., 0.9990 Silver 0.6423 oz. ASW, 38.7 mm. **Obv:** State emblem **Rev:** Multicolored Grey-shanked Douc Langur monkey **Edge:** Reeded

Date	Mintage	F	VF	XF	Unc	BU
2004 Proof	6,200	Value: 40.00				

KM# 65 20000 DONG
7.7759 g., 0.9999 Gold 0.2500 oz. AGW, 22 mm. **Subject:** Year of the Snake **Obv:** State emblem **Rev:** Sea snake **Edge:** Reeded

Date	Mintage	F	VF	XF	Unc	BU
2001(S) Proof	—	Value: 250				

Note: Issued in a replica Faberge egg

KM# 68 20000 DONG
7.7759 g., 0.9999 Gold 0.2500 oz. AGW, 22 mm. **Subject:** Year of the Horse **Obv:** State emblem **Rev:** Horse **Edge:** Reeded

Date	Mintage	F	VF	XF	Unc	BU
2002 Proof	1,800	Value: 285				

KM# 66 50000 DONG
15.5518 g., 0.9999 Gold 0.4999 oz. AGW, 27 mm. **Subject:** Year of the Snake **Obv:** State emblem **Rev:** Multicolor holographic King Cobra **Edge:** Reeded

Date	Mintage	F	VF	XF	Unc	BU
2001(S) Proof	3,200	Value: 550				

KM# 69 50000 DONG
15.5518 g., 0.9999 Gold 0.4999 oz. AGW, 27 mm. **Subject:** Year of the Horse **Obv:** State emblem **Rev:** Multicolor holographic horse **Edge:** Reeded

Date	Mintage	F	VF	XF	Unc	BU
2002 Proof	3,800	Value: 525				

PROOF SETS

KM#	Date	Mintage	Identification	Issue Price	Mkt Val
PS4	2001(S) (3)	3,500	KM#57-59	120	140
PS5	2001(S) (2)	—	KM#59, 66	—	560
PS6	2001(S) (2)	—	KM#65-66	—	770
PS7	2002 (3)	3,800	KM#61-63	—	115

WEST AFRICAN STATES

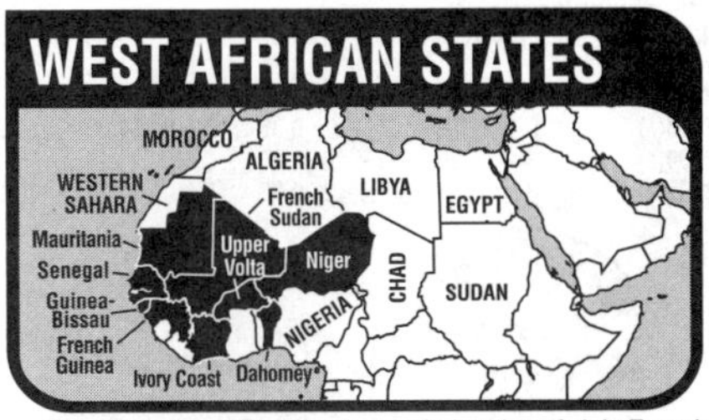

The West African States, a former federation of eight French colonial territories on the northwest coast of Africa, has an area of 1,831,079 sq. mi. (4,742,495 sq. km.) and a population of about 17 million. Capital: Dakar. The constituent territories were Mauritania, Senegal, Dahomey, French Sudan, Ivory Coast, Upper Volta, Niger and French Guinea.

MINT MARK
(a)- Paris, privy marks only

MONETARY SYSTEM
100 Centimes = 1 Franc

FEDERATION

STANDARD COINAGE

KM# 8 FRANC
1.6000 g., Steel **Obv:** Taku - Ashanti gold weight **Rev:** Value and date **Designer:** R. Joly

Date	Mintage	F	VF	XF	Unc	BU
2001(a)	—	—	—	0.10	0.35	0.60
2002(a)	—	—	—	0.10	0.35	0.60

KM# 2a 5 FRANCS
3.0000 g., Aluminum-Nickel-Bronze, 20 mm. **Obv:** Taku - Ashanti gold weight divides value value **Rev:** Gazelle head facing

Date	Mintage	F	VF	XF	Unc	BU
2001(a)	—	—	0.10	0.20	0.40	0.60
2002(a)	—	—	0.10	0.20	0.40	0.60
2003(a)	—	—	0.10	0.20	0.40	0.60
2004(a)	—	—	0.10	0.20	0.40	0.60
2005(a)	—	—	0.10	0.20	0.40	0.60

KM# 10 10 FRANCS
4.0400 g., Brass, 23.4 mm. **Series:** F.A.O. **Obv:** Taku - Ashanti gold weight divides value **Rev:** People getting water **Designer:** R. Joly

Date	Mintage	F	VF	XF	Unc	BU
2002(a)	—	—	0.25	0.50	1.25	1.50
2003(a)	—	—	0.25	0.50	1.25	1.50
2004(a)	—	—	0.25	0.50	1.00	1.50
2005(a)	—	—	0.25	0.50	1.00	1.50

KM# 9 25 FRANCS
7.9500 g., Aluminum-Bronze, 27 mm. **Series:** F.A.O. **Obv:** Taku - Ashanti gold weight divides value **Rev:** Figure filling tube

Date	Mintage	F	VF	XF	Unc	BU
2001(a)	—	—	0.25	0.75	1.75	2.00
2002(a)	—	—	0.25	0.75	1.75	2.00
2003(a)	—	—	0.25	0.75	1.75	2.00
2004(a)	—	—	0.25	0.75	1.50	2.00
2005(a)	—	—	0.25	0.75	1.50	2.00

KM# 6 50 FRANCS
5.0900 g., Copper-Nickel, 22 mm. **Series:** F.A.O. **Obv:** Taku - Ashanti gold weight **Rev:** Value within mixed beans, grains and nuts **Designer:** R. Joly

Date	Mintage	F	VF	XF	Unc	BU
2001(a)	—	—	0.35	0.50	1.25	1.50
2002(a)	—	—	0.35	0.50	1.25	1.50
2003(a)	—	—	0.35	0.50	1.25	1.50
2004(a)	—	—	0.35	0.50	1.25	1.50
2005(a)	—	—	0.35	0.50	1.25	1.50

KM# 4 100 FRANCS
7.0700 g., Nickel, 26 mm. **Obv:** Taku - Ashanti gold weight **Rev:** Value within flowers **Designer:** R. Joly

Date	Mintage	F	VF	XF	Unc	BU
2001(a)	—	—	0.60	0.85	2.25	2.75
2002(a)	—	—	0.60	0.85	2.25	2.75
2003(a)	—	—	0.60	0.85	2.25	2.75
2004(a)	—	—	0.60	0.75	2.00	2.75
2005(a)	—	—	0.60	0.75	2.00	2.75

KM# 14 200 FRANCS
6.9000 g., Bi-Metallic Brass center in Copper-Nickel ring, 24.4 mm. **Obv:** Taku - Ashanti gold weight **Rev:** Agricultural produce and value **Edge:** Segmented reeding **Designer:** Raymond Joly

Date	Mintage	F	VF	XF	Unc	BU
2003	—	—	1.00	1.60	4.00	6.00
2004(a)	—	—	1.00	1.60	4.00	6.00
2005(a)	—	—	1.00	1.60	4.00	6.00

KM# 15 500 FRANCS
10.6000 g., Bi-Metallic Copper-Nickel center in Brass ring, 27.9 mm. **Obv:** Taku - Ashanti gold weight **Rev:** Agricultural produce and value **Edge:** Segmented reeding **Designer:** Raymond Joly

Date	Mintage	F	VF	XF	Unc	BU
2003	—	—	2.25	4.00	10.00	12.00
2004(a)	—	—	2.25	4.00	10.00	12.00
2005(a)	—	—	2.25	4.00	10.00	12.00

KM# 16 1000 FRANCS
22.2000 g., 0.9000 Silver 0.6423 oz. ASW **Obv:** Taku - Ashanti gold weight **Rev:** Agricultural produce above sprays surrounded by names of member countries

Date	Mintage	F	VF	XF	Unc	BU
2002(a) Proof	500	Value: 90.00				

YEMEN REPUBLIC

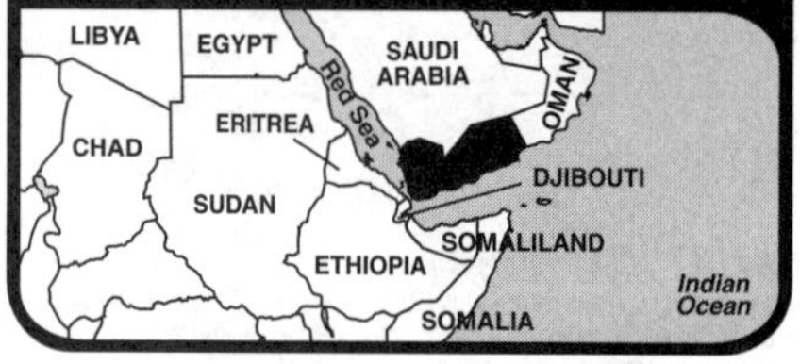

The Republic of Yemen, formerly Yemen Arab Republic and Peoples Democratic Republic of Yemen, is located on the southern coast of the Arabian Peninsula. It has an area of 205,020 sq. mi. (531,000 sq. km.) and a population of 12 million. Capital: San'a. The port of Aden is the main commercial center and the area's most valuable natural resource. Recent oil and gas finds and a developing petroleum industry have improved their economic prospects. Agriculture and local handicrafts are the main industries. Cotton, fish, coffee, rock salt and hides are exported.

On May 22, 1990, the Yemen Arab Republic (North Yemen) and Peoples Democratic Republic of Yemen (South Yemen) merged into a unified Republic of Yemen. Disagreements between the two former governments simmered until civil war erupted in 1994, with the northern forces of the old Yemen Arab Republic eventually prevailing.

REPUBLIC

MILLED COINAGE

KM# 26 5 RIYALS
4.5000 g., Stainless Steel, 22.85 mm. **Obv:** Denomination within circle **Rev:** Building **Shape:** 21-sided

Date	Mintage	F	VF	XF	Unc	BU
AH1421-2001	—	—	—	—	1.75	2.25
AH1425-2004	—	—	—	—	1.75	2.25

KM# 27 10 RIYALS
6.0500 g., Stainless Steel, 26 mm. **Obv:** Denomination within circle **Rev:** Bridge at Shaharah

Date	Mintage	F	VF	XF	Unc	BU
AH1424-2003	—	—	—	—	2.75	3.50

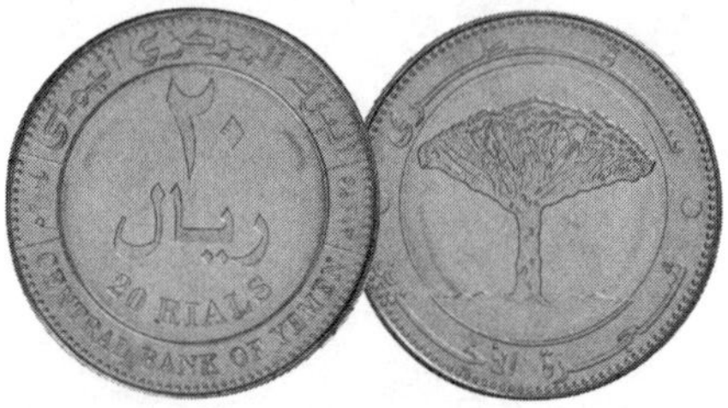

KM# 29 20 RIALS
7.1000 g., Bi-Metallic Brass plated Steel center in Stainless Steel ring, 29.85 mm. **Obv:** Value within circle **Rev:** Tree within circle **Edge:** Reeded

Date	Mintage	F	VF	XF	Unc	BU
AH1425-2004	—	—	—	—	4.00	5.00

KM# 30 500 RIALS
21.2500 g., Copper-Nickel-Zinc, 35.2 mm. **Subject:** City of San'a **Obv:** Value **Rev:** City gate below artwork **Edge:** Reeded

Date	Mintage	F	VF	XF	Unc	BU
AH1425-2004	—	—	—	—	30.00	35.00

KM# 31 1000 RIALS
73.3000 g., Pewter Antique silver finish, 60.3 mm. **Subject:** City of San'a **Obv:** Value **Rev:** City gate below artwork **Edge:** Plain
Note: Illustration reduced.

Date	Mintage	F	VF	XF	Unc	BU
AH1425-2004	—	—	—	—	45.00	50.00

The Federal Republic of Yugoslavia, formerly the Socialist Federal Republic of Yugoslavia, a Balkan country located on the east shore of the Adriatic Sea, has an area of 39,450 sq. mi. (102,173 sq. km.) and a population of 10.5 million. Capital: Belgrade. The chief industries are agriculture, mining, manufacturing and tourism. Machinery, nonferrous metals, meat and fabrics are exported.

The name Yugoslavia appears on the coinage in letters of the Cyrillic alphabet alone until formation of the Federated Peoples Republic of Yugoslavia in 1953, after which both the Cyrillic and Latin alphabets are employed. From 1965, the coin denomination appears in the 4 different languages of the federated republics in letters of both the Cyrillic and Latin alphabets.

DENOMINATIONS

Para ПАРА
Dinar, ДИНАР, Dinara ДИНАРА
Dinari ДИНАРИ, Dinarjev

RULERS

Petar I, 1918-1921
Alexander I, 1921-1934
Petar II, 1934-1945

MINT MARKS

(a) - Paris, privy marks only
(b) - Brussels
(k) - КОВНИЦА,...А.Д. = Kovnica, A.D. (Akcionarno Drustvo) Belgrade
(l) - London
(p) - Poissy (thunderbolt)
(v) – Vienna

MONETARY SYSTEM

100 Para = 1 Dinar

FEDERAL REPUBLIC

STANDARD COINAGE

KM# 180 DINAR
4.4000 g., Copper-Zinc-Nickel, 20 mm. **Obv:** National arms within circle **Rev:** Building **Edge:** Reeded

Date	Mintage	F	VF	XF	Unc	BU
2002	60,780,000	—	—	—	0.25	0.45

KM# 181 2 DINARA
5.2000 g., Copper-Nickel-Zinc, 21.9 mm. **Obv:** National arms within circle **Rev:** Church **Edge:** Reeded

Date	Mintage	F	VF	XF	Unc	BU
2002	71,053,000	—	—	—	0.25	0.45

KM# 182 5 DINARA
6.3000 g., Copper-Nickel-Zinc, 24 mm. **Obv:** National arms **Rev:** Domed building, denomination and date at left **Edge:** Reeded

Date	Mintage	F	VF	XF	Unc	BU
2002	30,966,000	—	—	—	1.25	1.50

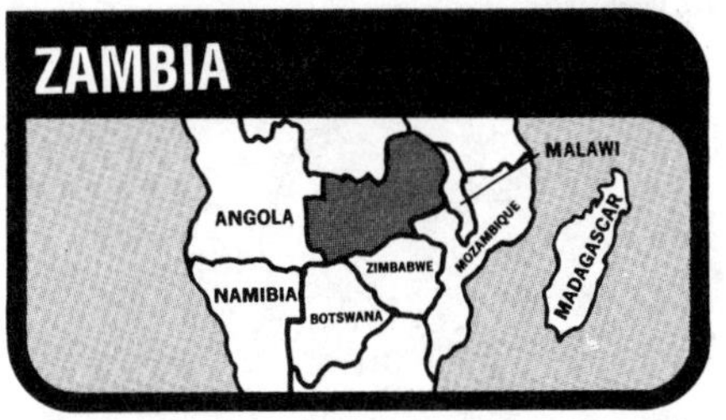

The Republic of Zambia (formerly Northern Rhodesia), a landlocked country in south-central Africa, has an area of 290,586 sq. mi. (752,610 sq. km.) and a population of*7.9 million. Capital: Lusaka. The economy of Zambia is based principally on copper, of which Zambia is the world's third largest producer. Copper, zinc, lead, cobalt and tobacco are exported. Zambia is a member of the Commonwealth of Nations. The President is the Head of State and the Head of Government.

REPUBLIC

DECIMAL COINAGE

100 Ngwee = 1 Kwacha

KM# 156 500 KWACHA
15.0000 g., 0.9990 Silver 0.4818 oz. ASW, 34.2 mm. **Subject:** Football World Champion - 1954 Germany **Obv:** Crowned head right within circle above arms with supporters and value **Rev:** Soccer game scene in front of Berlin Wall **Edge:** Plain

Date	Mintage	F	VF	XF	Unc	BU
2001 Proof	—	Value: 35.00				

KM# 174 500 KWACHA
15.0000 g., 0.9990 Silver 0.4818 oz. ASW, 34.2 mm. **Subject:** 1972 Munich Olympics **Obv:** Crowned head right above arms with supporters **Rev:** Torch runner in stadium **Edge:** Reeded

Date	Mintage	F	VF	XF	Unc	BU
2002 Proof	—	Value: 25.00				

KM# 87 1000 KWACHA
28.9100 g., Copper-Nickel, 38 mm. **Series:** Patrons of the Ocean **Obv:** Arms with supporters above crowned head right within circle **Rev:** Sea turtle **Edge:** Reeded

Date	Mintage	F	VF	XF	Unc	BU
2001 Proof	—	Value: 15.00				

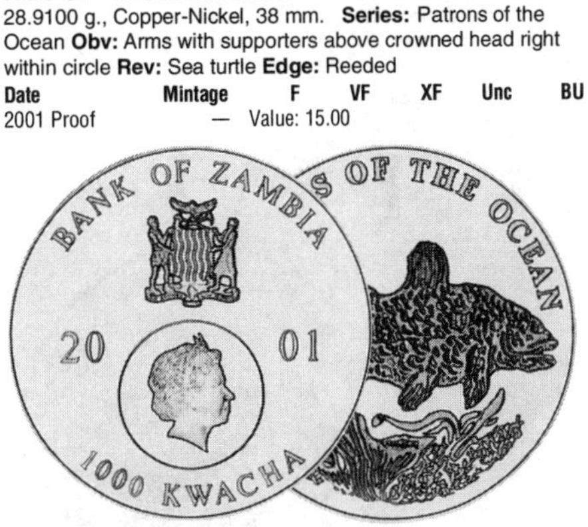

KM# 88 1000 KWACHA
28.9100 g., Copper-Nickel **Series:** Patrons of the Ocean **Obv:** Arms with supporters above crowned head right within circle **Rev:** Coelacanth

Date	Mintage	F	VF	XF	Unc	BU
2001 Proof	—	Value: 15.00				

KM# 89 1000 KWACHA
28.9100 g., Copper-Nickel **Series:** Patrons of the Ocean **Obv:** Arms with supporters above crowned head right within circle **Rev:** Sea horse and fish

Date	Mintage	F	VF	XF	Unc	BU
2001 Proof	—	Value: 15.00				

KM# 90 1000 KWACHA
28.9100 g., Copper-Nickel **Series:** Patrons of the Ocean **Obv:** Arms with supporters above crowned head right within circle **Rev:** Two dolphins

Date	Mintage	F	VF	XF	Unc	BU
2001 Proof	—	Value: 15.00				

KM# 159 1000 KWACHA
31.2200 g., 0.9990 Silver 1.0027 oz. ASW, 38.6 mm. **Obv:** Crowned head right divides date above arms with supporters **Rev:** Bust 1/4 left **Edge:** Reeded

Date	Mintage	F	VF	XF	Unc	BU
2002	—	—	—	—	35.00	37.50

KM# 74 1000 KWACHA

29.0000 g., Copper-Nickel, 40 mm. **Obv:** Crowned head right above arms with supporters divides date **Rev:** Dated calendar within circular design **Shape:** 7-sided

Date	Mintage	F	VF	XF	Unc	BU
2002 Proof-like	—	—	—	—	—	12.50
2003 Proof-like	—	—	—	—	—	12.50
2004 Proof-like	—	—	—	—	—	12.50

KM# 167 1000 KWACHA

25.0000 g., Copper-Nickel, 38.6 mm. **Subject:** 50th Anniversary of Elizabeth II's Coronation **Obv:** Crowned head right above arms with supporters **Rev:** Crown on pillow above crossed scepters **Edge:** Reeded

Date	Mintage	F	VF	XF	Unc	BU
ND(2003)	—	—	—	—	8.00	9.00

KM# 169 1000 KWACHA

25.0000 g., Copper-Nickel, 38.6 mm. **Obv:** Crowned head right above arms with supporters **Rev:** Prince William on jet ski **Edge:** Reeded

Date	Mintage	F	VF	XF	Unc	BU
2003	—	—	—	—	8.00	9.00

KM# 171 1000 KWACHA

25.0000 g., Copper-Nickel, 38.6 mm. **Obv:** Crowned head right above arms with supporters **Rev:** Crowned bust facing **Edge:** Reeded

Date	Mintage	F	VF	XF	Unc	BU
ND(2003)	—	—	—	—	8.00	9.00

KM# 172 1000 KWACHA

25.0000 g., 0.9250 Silver 0.7435 oz. ASW, 38.6 mm. **Obv:** Crowned head right above arms with supporters **Rev:** Crowned bust facing **Edge:** Reeded

Date	Mintage	F	VF	XF	Unc	BU
ND(2003) Proof	5,000	Value: 45.00				

KM# 160 1000 KWACHA

29.3000 g., Silver Plated Bronze (Specific gravity 9.099), 38.6 mm. **Subject:** Pope John Paul II **Obv:** National arms **Rev:** Pope saying mass **Edge:** Reeded **Note:** Specific gravity 9.099

Date	Mintage	F	VF	XF	Unc	BU
2003 Proof	—	Value: 20.00				

KM# 118 2000 KWACHA

31.1035 g., 0.9990 Silver 0.9990 oz. ASW, 38.6 mm. **Subject:** Centennial of the Anglo-Japanese Alliance **Obv:** Queen Elizabeth **Rev:** Fantasy Japanese coin design **Edge:** Reeded

Date	Mintage	F	VF	XF	Unc	BU
2002	500	—	—	—	65.00	70.00

KM# 166 4000 KWACHA

25.0000 g., 0.9250 Silver 0.7435 oz. ASW, 38.6 mm. **Subject:** Queen Elizabeth's 75th Birthday **Obv:** Crowned head right above arms with supporters **Rev:** Bust with hat facing **Edge:** Reeded

Date	Mintage	F	VF	XF	Unc	BU
2001 Proof	2,000	Value: 35.00				

KM# 85 4000 KWACHA

25.1000 g., 0.9250 Silver 0.7464 oz. ASW, 37.9 mm. **Series:** Wildlife Protection **Obv:** Crowned head right below arms **Rev:** Lion head hologram **Edge:** Reeded **Note:** Lighter weight and smaller diameter than official specifications

Date	Mintage	F	VF	XF	Unc	BU
2001 Proof	—	Value: 60.00				

KM# 110 4000 KWACHA

20.0000 g., 0.9990 Silver 0.6423 oz. ASW, 37.9 mm. **Series:** Patrons of the Ocean **Obv:** Crowned head right within circle below arms with supporters **Rev:** Sea turtle **Edge:** Reeded

Date	Mintage	F	VF	XF	Unc	BU
2001 Proof	—	Value: 45.00				

KM# 111 4000 KWACHA

20.0000 g., 0.9990 Silver 0.6423 oz. ASW **Series:** Patrons of the Ocean **Obv:** Crowned head right divides date below arms with supporters **Rev:** Coelacanth fish

Date	Mintage	F	VF	XF	Unc	BU
2001 Proof	—	Value: 50.00				

KM# 112 4000 KWACHA

20.0000 g., 0.9990 Silver 0.6423 oz. ASW **Series:** Patrons of the Ocean **Obv:** Crowned head right divides date below arms with supporters **Rev:** Sea horse and fish

Date	Mintage	F	VF	XF	Unc	BU
2001 Proof	—	Value: 48.00				

KM# 113 4000 KWACHA

20.0000 g., 0.9990 Silver 0.6423 oz. ASW **Series:** Patrons of the Ocean **Obv:** Crowned head right divides date below arms with supporters **Rev:** Two dolphins

Date	Mintage	F	VF	XF	Unc	BU
2001 Proof	—	Value: 50.00				

KM# 114 4000 KWACHA

50.0000 g., 0.9990 Silver 1.6059 oz. ASW **Subject:** Illusion **Obv:** Arms with supporters below crowned head right **Rev:** Cat within window **Edge:** Plain **Note:** 50x50mm

Date	Mintage	F	VF	XF	Unc	BU
2001 Proof	5,000	Value: 55.00				

KM# 175 4000 KWACHA

23.0000 g., 0.9990 Silver 0.7387 oz. ASW, 40 mm. **Obv:** Head with tiara right divides date above arms **Rev:** Dated calendar **Shape:** Seven-sided

Date	Mintage	F	VF	XF	Unc	BU
2002 Prooflike	—	—	—	—	—	50.00
2003 Prooflike	15,000	—	—	—	—	50.00
2004 Prooflike	5,000	—	—	—	—	50.00

KM# 168 4000 KWACHA

25.0000 g., 0.9250 Silver 0.7435 oz. ASW, 38.6 mm. **Subject:** 50th Anniversary of Elizabeth II's Coronation **Obv:** Crowned head right above arms with supporters **Rev:** Crown on pillow above crossed scepters **Edge:** Reeded

Date	Mintage	F	VF	XF	Unc	BU
ND(2003) Proof	5,000	Value: 45.00				

KM# 170 4000 KWACHA

25.0000 g., 0.9250 Silver 0.7435 oz. ASW, 38.6 mm. **Obv:** Crowned head right above arms with supporters **Rev:** Prince William on jet ski **Edge:** Reeded

Date	Mintage	F	VF	XF	Unc	BU
2003 Proof	5,000	Value: 45.00				

KM# 117 5000 KWACHA

31.3000 g., 0.9990 Silver 1.0053 oz. ASW, 38.6 mm. **Subject:** African Wildlife **Obv:** Arms with supporters **Rev:** Elephant mother and calf grazing on grass **Edge:** Reeded

Date	Mintage	F	VF	XF	Unc	BU
2001 Matte	—	—	—	—	28.00	—
2001 Proof	—	Value: 45.00				

KM# 142 5000 KWACHA

28.6400 g., 0.9990 Silver 0.9198 oz. ASW, 38.5 mm. **Subject:** African Wildlife **Obv:** Queen Elizabeth's portrait above national arms and denomination **Rev:** Adult and juvenile elephants **Edge:** Reeded

Date	Mintage	F	VF	XF	Unc	BU
2002 Matte	—	Value: 40.00				
2002 Proof	—	Value: 32.00				

KM# 143 5000 KWACHA

28.8600 g., 0.9990 Silver 0.9269 oz. ASW, 38.5 mm. **Subject:** African Wildlife **Obv:** Arms with supporters **Rev:** Elephant **Edge:** Reeded

Date	Mintage	F	VF	XF	Unc	BU
2002 Matte	—	—	—	—	40.00	—

KM# 165 5000 KWACHA

31.1000 g., 0.9990 Silver 0.9988 oz. ASW, 38.5 mm. **Obv:** Crowned bust right divides date **Rev:** Two African elephants **Edge:** Reeded

Date	Mintage	F	VF	XF	Unc	BU
2003 Matte	—	—	—	—	35.00	—
2003 Proof	—	Value: 30.00				

KM# 94 40000 KWACHA

31.1035 g., 0.9999 Gold 0.9999 oz. AGW, 37.9 mm. **Series:** Wildlife Protection **Obv:** Arms with supporters above crowned head right **Rev:** Holographic lion head **Edge:** Reeded

Date	Mintage	F	VF	XF	Unc	BU
2001 Proof	—	Value: 975				

KM# 153.1 40000 KWACHA

47.5400 g., 0.9166 Gold 1.4009 oz. AGW, 39 mm. **Subject:** Queen Victoria **Obv:** Crowned head right within ornate frame divides date above arms with supporters **Rev:** Crowned head with veil facing left **Edge:** Reeded

Date	Mintage	F	VF	XF	Unc	BU
2001 Proof	1	—	—	—	—	—

Note: Medallic die alignment

KM# 153.2 40000 KWACHA

47.5400 g., 0.9166 Gold 1.4009 oz. AGW, 39 mm. **Subject:** Queen Victoria **Obv:** Crowned head right within ornate frame divides date above arms with supporters **Rev:** Crowned head with veil facing left **Edge:** Reeded

Date	Mintage	F	VF	XF	Unc	BU
2001 Matte	1	—	—	—	—	—

Note: Coin die alignment

KM# 154.1 40000 KWACHA

47.5400 g., 0.9166 Gold 1.4009 oz. AGW, 39 mm. **Subject:** Edward VII **Obv:** Crowned head right within ornate frame divides date above arms with supporters **Rev:** Crowned bust right **Edge:** Reeded

Date	Mintage	F	VF	XF	Unc	BU
2001 Proof	1	—	—	—	—	—

Note: Medallic die rotation

KM# 154.2 40000 KWACHA

47.5400 g., 0.9166 Gold 1.4009 oz. AGW, 39 mm. **Subject:** Edward VII **Obv:** Crowned head right within ornate frame divides date above arms with supporters **Rev:** Crowned bust right **Edge:** Reeded

Date	Mintage	F	VF	XF	Unc	BU
2001 Matte	1	—	—	—	—	—

Note: Coin die alignment

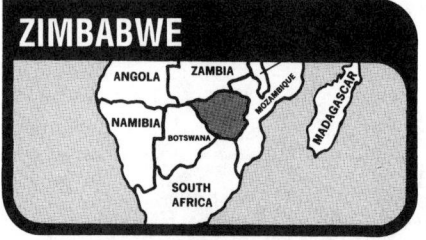

ZIMBABWE

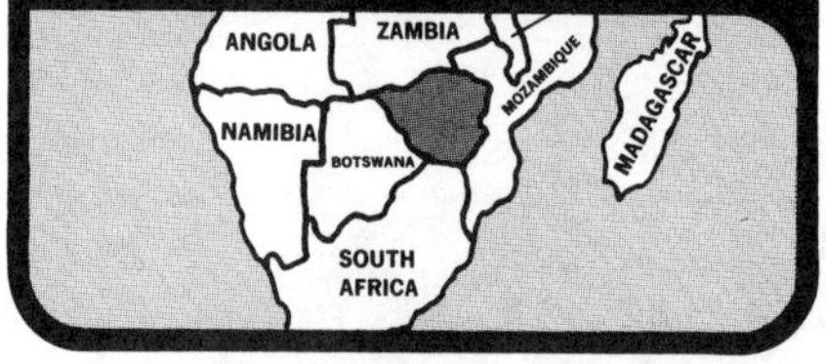

The Republic of Zimbabwe (formerly the Republic of Rhodesia or Southern Rhodesia), located in the east-central part of southern Africa, has an area of 150,804 sq. mi. (390,580 sq. km.) and a population of *10.1 million. Capital: Harare (formerly Salisbury). The economy is based on agriculture and mining. Tobacco, sugar, asbestos, copper, chrome, ore and coal are exported.

On April 18, 1980 pursuant to an act of the British Parliament, the colony of Southern Rhodesia became independent as the Republic of Zimbabwe, a member of the British Commonwealth of Nations, until recently suspended.

MONETARY SYSTEM

100 Cents = 1 Dollar

MINT

Harare

REPUBLIC

DECIMAL COINAGE

KM# 3a 10 CENTS

Nickel-Plated Steel, 20 mm. **Obv:** National emblem **Rev:** Baobab tree, value **Edge:** Plain **Mint:** Harare **Designer:** Jeff Huntly

Date	Mintage	F	VF	XF	Unc	BU
2001	—	—	0.15	0.30	0.75	1.00
2002	—	—	0.15	0.30	0.75	1.00
2003	—	—	0.15	0.30	0.45	1.00

KM# 4a 20 CENTS

Nickel-Plated Steel, 23 mm. **Obv:** National emblem **Rev:** Birchenough Bridge over the Sabi River, value below **Edge:** Plain **Mint:** Harare **Designer:** Jeff Huntly

Date	Mintage	F	VF	XF	Unc	BU
2001	—	—	0.20	0.40	1.25	1.50
2002	—	—	0.20	0.40	1.25	1.50
2003	—	—	0.20	0.40	1.25	1.50

KM# 5a 50 CENTS

Nickel-Plated Steel, 26 mm. **Obv:** National emblem **Rev:** Radiant sun rising, symbolic of independence, value **Edge:** Plain **Mint:** Harare **Designer:** Jeff Huntly

Date	Mintage	F	VF	XF	Unc	BU
2001	—	—	0.40	1.00	1.75	2.00
2002	—	—	0.40	1.00	1.75	2.00
2003	—	—	0.40	1.00	1.75	2.00

KM# 6a DOLLAR

Nickel-Plated Steel, 29 mm. **Obv:** National emblem **Rev:** Zimbabwe ruins amongst trees, value **Edge:** Reeded **Mint:** Harare **Designer:** Jeff Huntly

Date	Mintage	F	VF	XF	Unc	BU
2001	—	—	1.00	1.50	3.00	3.50
2002	—	—	1.00	1.50	3.00	3.50
2003	—	—	1.00	1.50	3.00	3.50

KM# 12a 2 DOLLARS

Brass-Plated Steel, 24.5 mm. **Obv:** National emblem **Rev:** Pangolin below value **Edge:** Reeded **Mint:** Harare

Date	Mintage	F	VF	XF	Unc	BU
2001	—	—	1.25	2.25	5.00	6.00
2002	—	—	1.25	2.25	5.00	6.00
2003	—	—	1.25	2.25	5.00	6.00

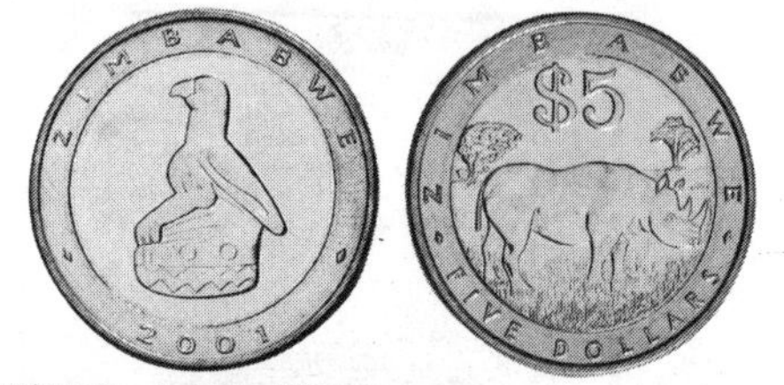

KM# 13 5 DOLLARS

9.0500 g., Bi-Metallic Nickel-plated-Steel center in Brass ring, 27.4 mm. **Obv:** Bird on nest within circle **Rev:** Rhinoceros within circle **Edge:** Reeded **Mint:** Harare

Date	Mintage	F	VF	XF	Unc	BU
2001	—	—	—	—	7.50	8.50
2002	—	—	—	—	7.50	8.50
2003	—	—	—	—	7.50	8.50

Premium Edition
The National Bank of Rwanda presents:
AFRICAN ELEPHANT
2007
SIYONALI Y'U RWANDA
1000 IGIHUMBI
➤ The first silver coin with gold and precious cut diamonds!
➤ 3 ounces of pure silver – world limited edition!
FIRST EDITION – DIAMOND COIN* - RWANDA
* The animals´ visible eyes are each filled with a 0.01 carat diamond.
Republic of Rwanda / 1000 Frw. / Silver 999/1000 / Gold (24 carat) / 93.30 grams / Diamonds: 0.01 carat / Proof 500 copies / BU 1500 copies

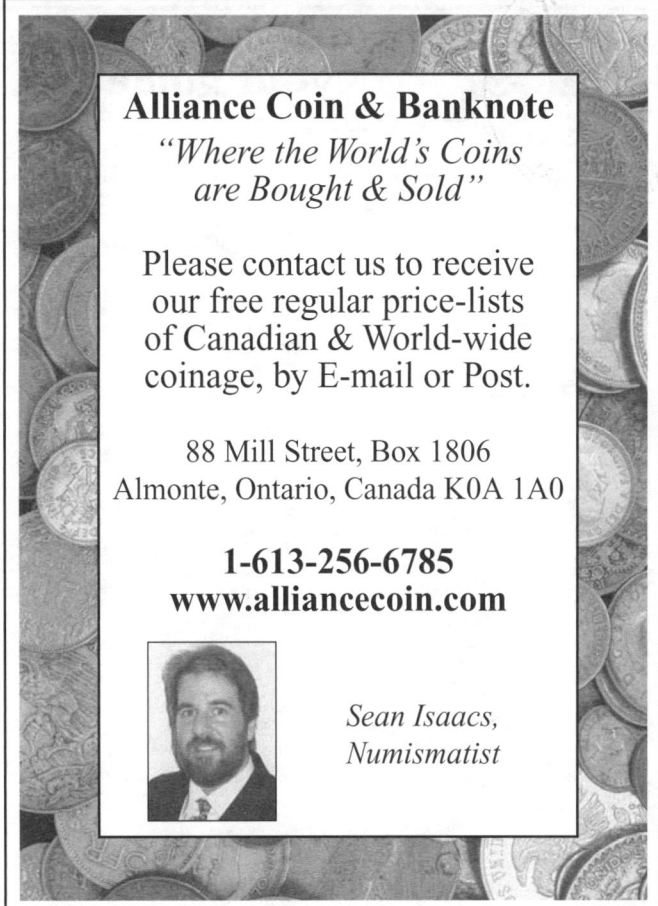